DEVELOPMENTAL PSYCHOPATHOLOGY

DEVELOPMENTAL PSYCHOPATHOLOGY

SECOND EDITION

Volume One: Theory and Method

Editors

DANTE CICCHETTI

and

DONALD J. COHEN

WILEY

John Wiley & Sons, Inc.

Published by John Wiley & Sons, Inc., Hoboken, New Jersey.
Published simultaneously in Canada.

For general information on our other products and services please contact our Customer Care Department within the United States at (800) 762-2974, outside the United States at (317) 572-3993 or fax (317) 572-4002.

Wiley also publishes its books in a variety of electronic formats. Some content that appears in print may not be available in electronic books. For more information about Wiley products, visit our web site at www.wiley.com.

Library of Congress Cataloging-in-Publication Data:

Developmental psychopathology / editors, Dante Cicchetti & Donald Cohen.—
2nd ed.
   p.   cm.
ISBN-13: 978-0-471-23736-5, ISBN-10: 0-471-23736-1 (v. 1 : cloth)
ISBN-13: 978-0-471-23737-2, ISBN-10: 0-471-23737-X (v. 2 : cloth)
ISBN-13: 978-0-471-23738-9, ISBN-10: 0-471-23738-8 (v. 3 : cloth)
ISBN-13: 978-0-471-23735-8, ISBN-10: 0-471-23735-3 (set)
[etc.]
  1. Mental illness—Etiology. 2. Developmental psychology. 3. Mental
illness—Risk factors. 4. Adjustment (Psychology). I. Cicchetti, Dante.
II. Cohen, Donald J.
  RC454.4.D483 2006
  616.89—dc22

Printed in the United States of America.

10 9 8 7 6 5 4 3 2 1

These volumes are dedicated to
Marianne Gerschel.

Contents

Preface to Developmental Psychopathology, *Second Edition*

It has been over a decade since the first two volumes of *Developmental Psychopathology* were published. These volumes were extremely well received: They have been highly cited in the literature and they have served as a valuable resource for researchers and practitioners alike. The expansion of the second edition of *Developmental Psychopathology* from two to three volumes speaks to the continued growth of the field, as well as to the ascendance of theory and research in the area of neuroscience informed by a developmental perspective.

There can be no doubt that the discipline of developmental psychopathology has grown significantly in a relatively short period of time. The more than 30 years that have elapsed since the initiation of the schizophrenia high-risk projects (Garmezy & Streitman, 1974) have been marked by significant contributions to the field. Noteworthy among these are the publication of Achenbach's (1974) first text, Rutter and Garmezy's (1983) chapter in the *Handbook of Child Psychology,* and the continued growth of the journal *Development and Psychopathology,* including the Millennium Special Issue entitled *Reflecting on the Past and Planning for the Future of Developmental Psychopathology* (Cicchetti & Sroufe, 2000). A not insignificant contributor to this rapid growth can be found in the very definitional parameters of the discipline. Theorists and researchers in the field of developmental psychopathology use a lifespan framework to elucidate the many factors that can contribute to the development of mental disorders in individuals at high risk, as well as those operative in individuals who have already manifested psychological disturbances or who have averted such disorders despite their high risk status. In essence, a developmental psychopathology perspective provides a broad, integrative framework within which the contributions of diverse disciplines can be incorporated and enhanced (Cicchetti & Sroufe, 2000). Thus, rather than having to develop new theories and methods, those

working within a developmental psychopathology framework can build on and extend previously established traditions. The ability to incorporate knowledge from diverse disciplines and to encourage interdisciplinary research will expedite growth within the field of developmental psychopathology.

As with the previous edition, the current volumes were not organized exclusively around thematic psychiatric disorders. Rather, authors were encouraged to explore developmentally relevant theories, methods of assessment, and domains of functioning. Although many chapters do address specific psychiatric disorders, it is the processes that contribute to the emergence of psychopathology that are emphasized rather than the psychiatric disorders per se.

Volume I, *Theory and Method* presents various approaches to understanding developmental influences on risk and maladaptation. As previously, the volume begins with an explication of the discipline of developmental psychopathology. Within this chapter, a number of significant advances within the field are noted, including the increased attention to processes and mechanisms, the use of multiple levels of analysis, the rise of developmental neuroscience, and the evolution of translational research paradigms. Chapters address a range of topics, including approaches to diagnoses of disorders, developmental epidemiology, diverse theoretical perspectives, various contextual issues, and new frontiers in statistical techniques for developmental phenomena. The volume concludes with a chapter on prevention and intervention.

Volume II, *Developmental Neuroscience,* was added to acknowledge the significant growth in this area since the publication of the first edition of this *Handbook.* Given the seminal historical role that neuroscience played in the emergence of developmental psychopathology (Cicchetti, 1990; Cicchetti & Posner, 2005), it is only fitting that developmental neuroscience has both informed and been informed by developmental psychopathology theorizing.

Neural plasticity, brain imaging, behavioral and molecular genetics, stress and neurobiology, immunology, and environmental influences on brain development are covered in this volume.

Volume III, *Risk, Disorder, and Adaptation* presents various perspectives on contributors to disorder. For example, chapters address the role of social support, family processes, and early experience on adaptation and maladaptation. Other chapters address specific disorders, including mental retardation, language disorders, autism, disorders of attention, obsessive-compulsive disorders, Tourette's syndrome, social anxiety, schizophrenia, antisocial disorders, substance abuse, and dissociative disorders. A number of chapters on resilience despite adversity also are included. The volume concludes with a chapter on stigma and mental illness.

All authors were asked to conclude their chapters with discussions of future research directions and needs. Thus, these volumes serve not only to highlight current knowledge in the field of developmental psychopathology, but also to suggest avenues to pursue for progress to continue. In particular, it is increasingly important to incorporate multiple-levels-of-analysis approaches when investigating maladaptation, psychopathology, and resilience (Cicchetti & Blender, 2004; Cicchetti & Dawson, 2002). The examination of multiple systems, domains, and ecological levels in the same individuals over developmental time will yield a more complete depiction of individual patterns of adaptation and maladapation. Moreover, such methods are likely to be extremely valuable in elucidating how interventions may affect brain-behavior relations (see, e.g., Caspi et al., 2002, 2003; Cicchetti & Posner, 2005; Fishbein, 2000; Goldapple et al., 2004; Kandel, 1979, 1998, 1999). Such endeavors could result in significant progress toward understanding psychopathology, highlighting efficacious interventions, and ultimately decreasing the burden of mental illness (Cicchetti & Toth, in press).

I now turn to more personal considerations. Although Donald Cohen is no longer with us, he worked closely with me as we developed our plans for the second edition of *Developmental Psychopathology*. Given our collaboration on the first edition of the volumes and our discussions leading up to the publication of these volumes, I thought it only fitting that he be listed as my coauthor. I believe in my heart that Donald would be pleased to have his name affiliated with these volumes and when I shared this plan with his wife, Phyllis, she gave her enthusiastic endorsement. However, I hasten to add that, unfortunately, Donald's illness and untimely death precluded his active involvement in editing the chapters in these volumes. Thus, despite our many

conversations as the plan for these volumes unfolded, I alone am responsible for the final editing of all chapters.

In closing, I want to dedicate these volumes to my dear friend, Marianne Gerschel. Marianne is a true visionary and she has contributed significantly to my work in the area of developmental psychopathology. Without her belief in the value of this field, my efforts and accomplishments would have been greatly compromised.

Finally, as I write this preface, I am ending a significant era in my life. After more than two decades as the director of Mt. Hope Family Center, I am leaving Rochester and to accept a position at the Institute of Child Development, University of Minnesota. There I will be the director of an interdisciplinary center that will emphasize a multiple-levels-of-analysis approach to research and intervention in developmental psychopathology.

This transition is difficult, as Mt. Hope Family Center and my colleagues there have contributed greatly to the growth and development of the field of developmental psychopathology. It is reassuring to know that Mt. Hope Family Center will continue to build upon a solid foundation under the capable directorship of my long-time collaborator and friend, Sheree L. Toth. Although I welcome the new opportunities and challenges that await me, I cannot help being a bit sad to leave. My spirits are buoyed by the knowledge that my work at Mt. Hope Family Center will continue and by my excitement at returning to my roots at the Institute of Child Development where I will have both University and community support to use the field of developmental psychopathology to extend my vision for helping disenfranchised individuals and families throughout the nation and the world.

DANTE CICCHETTI, PhD

Rochester, NY
July 2005

REFERENCES

Achenbach, T. M. (1974). *Developmental psychopathology.* New York: Ronald Press.

Caspi, A., McClay, J., Moffitt, T., Mill, J., Martin, J., Craig, I. W., et al. (2002). Role of genotype in the cycle of violence in maltreated children. *Science, 297,* 851–854.

Caspi, A., Sugden, K., Moffitt, T. E., Taylor, A., Craig, I. W., Harrington, H. L., et al. (2003). Influence of life stress on depression: Moderation by a polymorphism in the 5-HTT gene. *Science, 301,* 386–389.

Cicchetti, D. (1990). A historical perspective on the discipline of developmental psychopathology. In J. Rolf, A. Masten, D. Cicchetti, K. Nuechterlein, & S. Weintraub (Eds.), *Risk and protective factors in the development of psychopathology* (pp. 2–28). New York: Cambridge University Press.

Cicchetti, D., & Blender, J. A. (2004). A multiple-levels-of-analysis approach to the study of developmental processes in maltreated children. *Proceedings of the National Academy of Sciences, 101*(50), 17325–17326.

Cicchetti, D., & Dawson, G. (Eds.). (2002). Multiple levels of analysis. *Development and Psychopathology, 14*(3), 417–666.

Cicchetti, D., & Posner, M. I. (Eds.). (2005). Integrating cognitive and affective neuroscience and developmental psychopathology. *Development and Psychopathology, 17*(3).

Cicchetti, D., & Sroufe, L. A. (Eds.). (2000). Reflecting on the past and planning for the future of developmental psychopathology. *Development and Psychopathology, 12*(3), 255–550.

Cicchetti, D., & Toth, S. L. (in press). A developmental psychopathology perspective on preventive interventions with high-risk children and families. In A. Renninger & I. Sigel (Eds.), *Handbook of child psychology (6th ed.).* Hoboken, NJ: Wiley.

Fishbein, D. (2000). The importance of neurobiological research to the prevention of psychopathology. *Prevention Science, 1,* 89–106.

Garmezy, N., & Streitman, S. (1974). Children at risk: Conceptual models and research methods. *Schizophrenia Bulletin, 9,* 55–125.

Goldapple, K., Segal, Z., Garson, C., Lau, M., Bieling, P., Kennedy, S., et al. (2004). Modulation of cortical-limbic pathways in major depression. *Archives of General Psychiatry, 61*(1), 34–41.

Kandel, E. R. (1979). Psychotherapy and the single synapse. *New England Journal of Medicine, 301,* 1028–1037.

Kandel, E. R. (1998). A new intellectual framework for psychiatry. *American Journal of Psychiatry, 155,* 475–469.

Kandel, E. R. (1999). Biology and the future of psychoanalysis: A new intellectual framework for psychiatry revisited. *American Journal of Psychiatry, 156,* 505–524.

Rutter, M., & Garmezy, N. (1983). Developmental psychopathology. In E. M. Hetherington (Ed.), *Handbook of child psychology* (4th ed., Vol. 4, pp. 774–911). New York: Wiley.

Contributors

Thomas M. Achenbach, PhD
University of Vermont
Burlington, Vermont

Adrian Angold, MRCPsych
Duke University Medical Center
Durham, North Carolina

Theodore P. Beauchaine, PhD
University of Washington
Seattle, Washington

Lars R. Bergman, PhD
Stockholm University
Stockholm, Sweden

Jacquelyn Buckley, PhD
Johns Hopkins Bloomberg School of Public Health
Baltimore, Maryland

Allison A. Buskirk, MA
University of Maryland
College Park, Maryland

Alice S. Carter, PhD
University of Massachusetts, Boston
Boston, Massachusetts

Elaine Cassidy, PhD
Robert Wood Johnson Foundation
Princeton, New Jersey

Jude Cassidy, PhD
University of Maryland
College Park, Maryland

Nicole Charles, MSEd
Germantown Academy
Ft. Washington, Pennsylvania

Dante Cicchetti, PhD
Mt. Hope Family Center
University of Rochester
Rochester, New York
and
Institute of Child Development
University of Minnestota
Minneapolis, Minnesota

E. Jane Costello, PhD
Duke University Medical Center
Durham, North Carolina

Carolyn Pape Cowan, PhD
University of California, Berkeley
Berkeley, California

Philip A. Cowan, PhD
University of California, Berkeley
Berkeley, California

Nicki R. Crick, PhD
Institute of Child Development
University of Minnesota
Minneapolis, Minnesota

Edward L. Deci, PhD
University of Rochester
Rochester, New York

Sapana Donde, MPhil
George Washington University
Washington, DC

Stephen A. Erath, MS
Pennsylvania State University
Philadelphia, Pennsylvania

Sarah E. Fine, PhD
Brown University
Providence, Rhode Island

Peter Fonagy, PhD, FBA
University College London
London, England

George Gergely, PhD, DSc
Hungarian Academy of Sciences
Budapest, Hungary

Tyhesha N. Goss, MAT
University of Pennsylvania
Philadelphia, Pennsylvania

Gilbert Gottlieb, PhD
University of North Carolina, Chapel Hill
Chapel Hill, North Carolina

Isabela Granic, PhD
The Hospital for Sick Children
Toronto, Ontario, Canada

Wendy S. Grolnick, PhD
Clark University
Worcester, Massachusetts

Vinay Harpalani, PhD
University of Pennsylvania
Philadelphia, Pennsylvania

Susan Harter, PhD
University of Denver
Denver, Colorado

Jonathan Hill, PhD
University of Liverpool
Liverpool, England

Kimberly Hoagwood, PhD
Columbia University
New York, New York

Tom Hollenstein, PhD
Queens University
Kingston, Ontario, Canada

Nicholas S. Ialongo, PhD
John Hopkins Bloomberg School of Public Health
Baltimore, Maryland

Carroll E. Izard, PhD
University of Delaware
Newark, Delaware

Cleopatra Y. Jacobs, MA
University of Pennsylvania
Philadelphia, Pennsylvania

Peter S. Jensen, MD
Columbia University
New York, New York

Janna Jilnina, MEd, MA
Harvard University
Cambridge, Massachusetts

Roger Kobak, PhD
University of Delaware
Newark, Delaware

Jennifer G. La Guardia, PhD
Waterloo University
Waterloo, Ontario, Canada

Karlen Lyons-Ruth, PhD
Harvard Medical School
Cambridge, Massachusetts

David Magnusson, PhD
Stockholm University
Stockholm, Sweden

Susan E. Marakovitz, PhD
University of Massachusetts, Boston
Boston, Massachusetts

Penny Marsh, MA
University of Washington
Seattle, Washington

Allison J. Mostow, PhD
Johns Hopkins University School of Medicine
Baltimore, Maryland

Peter Mundy, PhD
University of Miami
Coral Gables, Florida

Michèle Muñoz-Miller, BA
University of Pennsylvania
Philadelphia, Pennsylvania

Jenae M. Niederhiser, PhD
George Washington University Medical Center
Washington, DC

Gil G. Noam, EdD
Harvard Graduate School of Education
Cambridge, Massachusetts

Jeffrey G. Parker, PhD
Penn State University
University Park, Pennsylvania

Hanno Petras, PhD
Johns Hopkins Bloomberg School of Public Health
Baltimore, Maryland

Robert C. Pianta, PhD
University of Virginia
Charlottesville, Virginia

Andrew Pickles, PhD
University of Manchester
Manchester, England

Leslie A. Rescorla, PhD
Bryn Mawr College
Bryn Mawr, Pennsylvania

Fred A. Rogosch, PhD
Mt. Hope Family Center
University of Rochester
Rochester, New York

Kenneth H. Rubin, PhD
University of Maryland
College Park, Maryland

Richard M. Ryan, PhD
University of Rochester
Rochester, New York

Felicisima C. Serafica, PhD
Ohio State University
Columbus, Ohio

Elizabeth A. Shirtcliff, PhD
University of Wisconsin
Madison, Wisconsin

Marian Sigman, PhD
University of California, Los Angeles
Los Angeles, California

Sara S. Sparrow, PhD
Yale University
New Haven, Connecticut

Margaret Beale Spencer, PhD
University of Pennsylvania
Philadelphia, Pennsylvania

Mary Target, PhD
University College London
London, England

Sheree L. Toth, PhD
Mt. Hope Family Center
University of Rochester
Rochester, New York

Christopher J. Trentacosta, MA
University of Delaware
Newark, Delaware

Luis A. Vargas, PhD
University of New Mexico
Albuquerque, New Mexico

Alexander von Eye, PhD
University of Michigan
Ann Arbor, Michigan

Michael T. Willoughby, PhD
University of North Carolina, Chapel Hill
Chapel Hill, North Carolina

Shaunqula Wilson, BS
University of Pennsylvania
Philadelphia, Pennsylvania

Julie C. Wojslawowicz, PhD
University of Maryland
College Park, Maryland

Kathleen E. Woods, MA
Institute of Child Development
University of Minnesota
Minneapolis, Minnesota

Copeland H. Young, BA
Harvard University
Cambridge, Massachusetts

Eric A. Youngstrom, PhD
Case Western Reserve University
Cleveland, Ohio

Carolyn Zahn-Waxler, PhD
University of Wisconsin
Madison, Wisconsin

Lauren Zitner, BA
New York State Psychiatric Institute
New York, New York

Yair Ziv, PhD
Westat
Rockville, Maryland

CHAPTER 1

Development and Psychopathology

DANTE CICCHETTI

In this chapter, we discuss the principles inherent to a developmental psychopathology perspective. We want to underscore that, if taken in isolation, many aspects of a developmental approach to psychopathology can be found in other fields that focus on the study of individuals with high-risk conditions and mental disorders. Nonetheless, the incorporation and integration of previously discrete concepts serve to set developmental psychopathology apart from other disciplines. In particular, a focus on the interplay between normality and pathology, the growing acceptance of the importance of a multiple-levels-of-analysis and multidomain approach, and an emphasis on the utilization of a developmental framework for comprehending adaptation and maladaptation across the life course are among those elements that are central to a developmental psychopathology approach. Whereas traditional viewpoints conceptualize maladaptation and disorder as inherent to the individual, the developmental psychopathology framework places them in the dynamic relationship between the individual and the internal and external contexts (Cicchetti, 1987; Sameroff, 2000). Rather than competing with existing theories and facts, the developmental psychopathology perspective provides a broad, integrative framework within which the contributions of separate disciplines can be finally realized in the larger context of understanding individual development and functioning. It is our conviction that the principles of developmental psychopathology

provide a much-needed conceptual scaffolding for facilitating this multidisciplinary integration.

To begin, we describe principles that have guided the field of developmental psychopathology. We then examine the historical origins of the field. We next explicate the definitional parameters of the discipline and discuss issues that are integral to research conducted within a developmental psychopathology framework. We conclude by describing some important future directions for prevention, research on interventions, and research on developmental psychopathology.

WHAT IS DEVELOPMENTAL PSYCHOPATHOLOGY?

Developmental psychopathology is an evolving scientific discipline whose predominant focus is elucidating the interplay among the biological, psychological, and social-contextual aspects of normal and abnormal development across the life span (Cicchetti, 1993; Cicchetti & Toth, 1998; Rutter & Sroufe, 2000; Sameroff, 2000). In their seminal article, Sroufe and Rutter (1984, p. 18) proposed that developmental psychopathology could be defined as *"the study of the origins and course of individual patterns of behavioral maladaptation,* whatever the age of onset, whatever the causes, whatever the transformations in behavioral manifestation, and however complex the course of the developmental pattern may be." Relatedly, the Institute of Medicine (1989) produced a report, entitled *Research on Children and Adolescents with Mental, Behavioral, and Developmental Disorders,* written from the integrative perspective of developmental psychopathology and highly influential in the development of the *National Plan for Research on Child and Adolescent Mental Disorders* (National Advisory Mental Health Council, 1990; see also Jensen et al., 1993). In its report, the Institute stated that a developmental psychopathology approach should take into account "the emerging behavioral repertoire, cognitive and language functions, social and emotional processes, and changes occurring in anatomical structures and physiological processes of the brain" (p. 14).

Given the intimate relation between the study of normality and psychopathology, theoreticians and researchers who predominantly focus on normal processes also espouse similar perspectives about the nature of development. For example, Cairns (1990, p. 42) conceptualized the study of normal development as necessitating a holistic, synthetic science: "Maturational, experiential, and cultural contributions are inseparably coalesced in ontogeny. Hence, developmental studies should be multilevel, concerned with ontogenetic integration, and employ person-oriented as well as variable-oriented analyses."

In a related vein, Gottlieb (1991, p. 7; see also Gottlieb, Wahlsten, & Lickliter, 1998) depicted individual normal development as characterized by

> an increase of complexity of organization (i.e., the emergence of new structural and functional properties and competencies) at all levels of analysis (e.g., molecular, subcellular, cellular, organismic) as a consequence of horizontal and vertical coactions among the organisms' parts, including organism-environment coactions.

For Gottlieb (1992), horizontal coactions take place at the same level of analysis (e.g., gene-gene, cell-cell, person-person, environment-environment), whereas vertical coactions occur at a different level of analysis (e.g., cell-tissue, organism-environment, behavioral activity-nervous system) and are reciprocal. As such, vertical coactions are capable of influencing developmental organization from either lower-to-higher or higher-to-lower levels of the developing system (Gottlieb, 1992). Thus, epigenesis is viewed as probabilistic rather than predetermined, with the bidirectional nature of genetic, neural, behavioral, and environmental influence over the course of individual development capturing the essence of Gottlieb's conception of probabilistic

epigenesis. In an earlier period, the influential psychiatrist Adolf Meyer proffered a psychobiological orientation to normality and psychopathology that bore striking similarity to Gottlieb's more contemporary position. For Meyer (1950, 1957; see also Rutter, 1988), the psychobiological approach depicted humans as integrated organisms such that their thoughts and emotions could affect their functioning all the way down to the cellular and biochemical level, and conversely, that occurrences at these lower biological levels could influence thinking and feeling.

In one of the initial statements concerning the goals of developmental psychopathology, Cicchetti (1990, p. 20) remarked, "Developmental psychopathology should bridge fields of study, span the life cycle, and aid in the discovery of important new truths about the processes underlying adaptation and maladaptation, as well as the best means of preventing or ameliorating psychopathology." Cicchetti further commented, "This discipline should contribute greatly to reducing the dualisms that exist between the clinical study of and research into childhood and adult disorders, between the behavioral and biological sciences, between developmental psychology and psychopathology, and between basic and applied science" (p. 20).

Theorists and researchers in the field of developmental psychopathology aim to bring together, within a life span framework, the many contributions to the study of individuals at high risk for developing mental disorders and those who have already manifested such disorders. Developmental psychopathologists do not espouse or adhere to a particular theory that could account for all developmental phenomena (Cicchetti & Sroufe, 2000; Rutter & Sroufe, 2000). Rather, they seek to integrate knowledge across scientific disciplines at multiple levels of analysis and within and between developmental domains (Cicchetti & Blender, 2004; Cicchetti & Dawson, 2002; Cicchetti & Posner, in press; see also Cacioppo, Bernston, Sheridan, & McClintock, 2000, and Kosslyn et al., 2002).

Developmental psychopathologists strive to engage in a comprehensive evaluation of biological, psychological, social, and cultural processes and to ascertain how the interaction among these multiple levels of analysis may influence individual differences, the continuity or discontinuity of adaptive or maladaptive behavioral patterns, and the pathways by which normal and pathological developmental outcomes may be achieved (Cicchetti & Dawson, 2002; Cicchetti & Sroufe, 2000). In practice, this entails comprehension of and appreciation for the developmental transformations and reorganizations that occur over time; an analysis of the risk and protective factors and mechanisms operating within and outside the individual and his or her environment over the course of development; the investigation of how emergent functions, competencies, and developmental tasks modify the expression of a disorder or lead to new symptoms and difficulties; and the recognition that a particular stressor or set of stressful circumstances may eventuate in different biological and psychological difficulties, depending on when in the developmental period the stress occurs (Cicchetti & Aber, 1986; Cicchetti & Cannon, 1999; Cicchetti & Walker, 2001, 2003; Gunnar, Morison, Chisholm, & Shchuder, 2001; Institute of Medicine, 1989; Rutter, 1988; Sanchez, Ladd, & Plotsky, 2001). Moreover, various difficulties will constitute different meanings for an individual depending on cultural considerations (Garcia Coll, Akerman, & Cicchetti, 2000), as well as an individual's experiential history and current level of psychological and biological organization and functioning. The integration of the experience, in turn, will affect the adaptation or maladaptation that ensues.

Developmental psychopathologists stress that disordered individuals may move between pathological and nonpathological forms of functioning. In addition, even in the midst of psychopathology, individuals may display adaptive and maladaptive processes so that it becomes possible to delimit the presence, nature, and boundaries of the underlying psychopathology. Furthermore, developmental psychopathology is a perspective that is especially applicable to the investigation of transitional points in development across the life span (Rutter, 1990; Schulenberg, Sameroff, & Cicchetti, 2004). Development extends throughout the entire course of life, and adaptive and maladaptive processes emerge over the life span. From infancy through senescence, each period of life has its own developmental agenda and contributes in a unique manner to the past, present, and future organization of individual development. Rutter has conjectured that key life turning points may be times when the presence of protective mechanisms could help individuals redirect themselves from a risk trajectory onto a more adaptive developmental pathway (Elder, 1974; Quinton & Rutter, 1988). Likewise, Toth and Cicchetti (1999) have suggested that these periods of developmental transition may also be times when individuals are most amenable to profiting from therapeutic interventions.

With respect to the emergence of psychopathology, all periods of life are consequential in that the developmental process may undergo a pernicious turn toward mental disorder at any phase (Cicchetti & Cannon, 1999; Cicchetti & Walker, 2003; Moffitt, 1993; Post, Weiss, & Leverich, 1994; Rutter, 1996; Zigler & Glick, 1986). Many mental disorders have several distinct phases (Rutter & Sroufe, 2000). The factors that are associated with the onset of a disorder may be very different from those that are associated with the cessation of a disorder or with its repeated occurrence (Courchesne, Townsend, & Chase, 1995; Post et al., 1996). In contrast to the often dichotomous world of mental disorder/nondisorder depicted in psychiatry, a developmental psychopathology perspective recognizes that normality often fades into abnormality, that adaptive and maladaptive may take on differing definitions depending on whether one's time referent is immediate circumstances or long-term development, and that processes within the individual can be characterized as having shades or degrees of psychopathology.

Since the field of developmental psychopathology has emerged as a new science that is the product of an integration of various disciplines, the efforts of which had been previously distinct and separate (Cicchetti, 1984b, 1990), it has contributed to dramatic knowledge gains in the multiple biological and psychological domains of child and adult development (Cicchetti & Cohen, 1995a, 1995b; Cicchetti & Sroufe, 2000; Rutter & Sroufe, 2000). Notably, there has been an emphasis on increasingly specific process-level models of normal and abnormal development, an acknowledgment that multiple pathways exist to the same outcome and that the effects of one component's value may vary in different systems, and an intensification of interest in biological and genetic factors, as well as in social and contextual factors related to the development of maladaptation and psychopathology (Caspi et al., 2002, 2003; Cicchetti & Aber, 1998; Cicchetti & Cannon, 1999; Cicchetti & Posner, in press; Cicchetti & Rogosch, 1996; Cicchetti & Tucker, 1994; Cummings, Davies, & Campbell, 2000; Gottesman & Hanson, 2005; Plomin & McGuffin, 2003; Plomin & Rutter, 1998; Rutter et al., 1997; Sameroff, 2000).

Although process-oriented research continues to be underrepresented in the field, there are a number of notable exceptions. Moreover, there is increasing recognition of the dynamic interplay of influences over developmental time. Perhaps the most dramatic example of this is the work on experience-dependent brain development (Black, Jones, Nelson, & Greenough, 1998; Greenough, Black, & Wallace, 1987). The viewpoint is now widely shared that neurobiological development and experience are mutually influencing (Cicchetti & Tucker, 1994; Eisenberg, 1995; Nelson & Bloom, 1997). Brain development impacts behavior, of course; however, the development of the brain itself is impacted by experience. Specifically, it has been demonstrated that social and psychological experiences can modify gene expression and brain structure, functioning, and organization. Alterations in gene expression influenced by social and psychological experiences produce changes in patterns of neuronal and synaptic connections (E. R. Kandel, 1998, 1999). These changes not only contribute to the biological bases of individuality, but also play a prominent role in initiating and maintaining the behavioral anomalies that are induced by social and psychological experiences.

Although not in the vocabulary of psychopathologists until the past several decades, concepts of pathways to psychopathology are now prominent in the field (Cicchetti, 1990; Cicchetti & Rogosch, 1996; Sroufe, 1989), having been in use in biology (Mayr, 1964; von Bertalanffy, 1968). It is now common knowledge that subgroups of individuals manifesting similar problems arrived at them from different beginnings (known as equifinality) and that the same risk factors may be associated with different outcomes (known as multifinality). This understanding has proven to be critical, not only because it has the potential to bring about important refinements in the diagnostic classification of mental disorders, but also because it calls attention to the importance of continuing to conduct process-oriented investigations (cf. Bergman & Magnusson, 1997; von Eye & Bergman, 2003). Investigators have shifted the emphasis of their questions from, for example, "What is the antecedent of conduct disorder?" to "What are the factors that initiate and maintain individuals on pathways probabilistically associated with Conduct Disorder and related outcomes?" and "What differentiates those progressing to Antisocial Personality Disorder from those progressing to depression and those being free from maladaptation or a handicapping condition?" As researchers increasingly conceptualize and design their investigations at the outset with the differential pathway concepts of equifinality and multifinality as a foundation, we will come progressively closer to achieving the unique goals of the discipline of developmental psychopathology—to explain the development of individual patterns of adaptation and maladaptation (Cairns, Cairns, Xie, Leung, & Heane, 1998; Cicchetti & Rogosch, 1996; Sroufe & Rutter, 1984).

Likewise, as we have drawn the distinction between factors that initiate pathways and factors that maintain or deflect individuals from pathways, there is a growing recognition of the role of the developing person as a processor of experience. The environment does not simply create an individual's experience; rather, individuals also actively create their experiences and their own environments in a changing world (Cummings et al., 2000; Scarr & McCartney, 1983). Individuals select, integrate, and actively affect their own development and the environment in a dynamic fashion (Bergman & Magnusson, 1997;

Cicchetti & Tucker, 1994; Rutter et al., 1997; Wachs & Plomin, 1991).

The principle of contextualism conceptualizes developmental processes as the ongoing interaction between an active, changing individual and a continuously unfolding, dynamic context (Cicchetti & Aber, 1998; Cummings et al., 2000). Thus, maladaptation and psychopathology are considered to be products of the transaction among an individual's intraorganismic characteristics, adaptational history, and the current context (Boyce et al., 1998; Sroufe, 1997). Moreover, we now know that social contexts exert effects not only on psychological processes, but also on biological structures, functions, and processes (Boyce et al., 1998; Cicchetti, 2002; Cicchetti & Tucker, 1994; Eisenberg, 1995; Nelson & Bloom, 1997).

There also has been a veritable explosion in our knowledge of developmental neurobiology, that area of neuroscience that focuses on factors regulating the development of neurons, neuronal circuitry, and complex neuronal organization systems, including the brain (Ciaranello et al., 1995). In addition, advances in the field of molecular genetics (see Lander & Weinberg, 2000; Lewin, 2004) have contributed to the understanding of neurological disease, allowing scientists for the first time to understand the genetic basis of certain disorders without requiring foreknowledge of the underlying biochemical abnormalities. These accomplishments have helped to engender renewed excitement for the potential contributing role that the field of molecular genetics can play in comprehending the development of psychopathology (Caspi et al., 2002, 2003; Cicchetti & Blender, 2004; Kaufman et al., 2004; Plomin & McGuffin, 2003; Plomin & Rutter, 1998; Rutter & Plomin, 1997; Waldman, 2003).

Developmental psychopathologists have begun to recognize that the milieu in which an individual develops is likely to profoundly influence the course of epigenesis (Boyce et al., 1998; Cicchetti & Aber, 1998; Garcia Coll et al., 2000; Garcia Coll & Vasquez Garcia, 1996; Hoagwood & Jensen, 1997; Richters & Cicchetti, 1993). The dynamic interplay of risk and protective processes may have differential impact depending on the cultural norms, practices, values, and beliefs. Cultures may be characterized on a continuum ranging from sociocentric (emphasizing community, family, and interconnectedness) to individualistic (emphasizing individuality, autonomy, and personal achievement; Garcia Coll et al., 2000; Shweder, 1991). The ideal self correspondingly varies with respect to the degree to which the self is defined in terms of relatedness to others versus in terms of autonomy and achievement. As such, cultural groups will differ in their socialization goals for desired outcomes for well-functioning members of the culture. Norms for appropriate and inappropriate behavior will have different thresholds, and discipline strategies will vary in accord with what behaviors are regarded as desirable or unacceptable.

For example, Canino and Guarnaccia (1997) noted that psychiatric epidemiological studies have shown that Puerto Rican adolescents exhibit lower rates of Conduct Disorder and substance abuse than adolescents in mainland United States; this difference may be attributable to greater monitoring and supervision of teenagers in the culture, consistent with a more sociocentric emphasis and a more authoritarian parenting orientation, fostering deference to adults and social institutions. Conversely, the high rate of teen pregnancies among Puerto Rican youth (Garcia Coll & Vazquez Garcia, 1996) may suggest that these girls assume more adult-like responsibilities earlier in their lives, thereby decreasing the likelihood of their involvement in conduct disordered and substance-abusing behaviors.

To provide a further illustration of how an individual's cultural milieu may influence the developmental course, Luthar and McMahon (1996) discovered that inner-city youth whose peer relationships were aggressive nonetheless were popular with their peers. Thus, in addition to the more typical pathway to peer popularity (i.e., prosocial behaviors, academic success), Luthar and McMahon identified a less typical pathway characterized by disruptive and aggressive behaviors and poor academic functioning. They hypothesized that within the crime-, violence-, and poverty-laden disenfranchised communities where these youth reside, aggressive behaviors that are viewed as deviant by the mainstream may be associated with prestige and high status among particular socioeconomic groups (cf. Richters & Cicchetti, 1993).

Moreover, risk and protective processes and the manner in which they transact may vary depending on priorities of the culture. Consequently, the individual's response to an event, as well as the reactions of other members of the culture, will influence the salience of the event and how it is responded to. Culture also may influence the mode of symptom expression. Cultural values, beliefs, and practices may tend to suppress manifestation of distress in one domain (e.g., socioemotional), while tolerating the expression in another domain (e.g., physical; Weisz, Weiss, Alicke, & Klotz, 1987). For example, Serafica (1997) noted a tendency for physical manifestations of distress to be tolerated among Asian American families, as compared with less acceptance of psychological expression.

Immersion in the mainstream culture by immigrating adolescents from other cultures is likely to generate signif-

icant difficulties in adaptation, particularly if the values of the home culture are in conflict with those in the mainstream culture (Canino & Guarnaccia, 1997). Acculturation pressures may generate stress for youths as they bridge two cultural worlds. Similarly, individuals from existing subcultures nested within the broader American culture may experience conflicts when the meaning they attribute to behaviors and events is at odds with the mainstream cultural prescriptions. Thus, culture must be incorporated into how developmental psychopathologists conceptualize causal processes influencing the developmental course and how adaptation and psychopathology are defined (Flores, Cicchetti, & Rogosch, 2005; Garcia Coll et al., 2000; Hoagwood & Jensen, 1997).

HISTORICAL ROOTS OF DEVELOPMENTAL PSYCHOPATHOLOGY

The field of developmental psychopathology first came into ascendance during the 1970s, predominantly through being highlighted as an important perspective by researchers conducting prospective longitudinal studies of children at risk for becoming schizophrenic (Watt, Anthony, Wynne, & Rolf, 1984). Also instrumental in the field's emergence were epidemiological investigations of families exhibiting discord, disharmony, and disruption but where there was no parental mental disorder (Rutter & Quinton, 1984) and studies of the links between cumulative risk factors and developmental outcome (Sameroff, Seifer, Barocas, Zax, & Greenspan, 1987). Likewise, research on the causes, correlates, and consequences of secure and insecure attachment (Ainsworth, Blehar, Waters, & Wall, 1978; Sroufe, 1983; Sroufe, Carlson, Levy, & Egeland, 1999), investigations of children with a variety of handicapping conditions (Cicchetti & Pogge-Hesse, 1982; Cicchetti & Sroufe, 1976, 1978; N. O'Connor & Hermelin, 1978), and studies in life span developmental psychology (Baltes, Reese, & Lipsitt, 1980) were influential in furthering interest in developmental psychopathology.

It was not until the last several decades of the twentieth century that the discipline of developmental psychopathology began to exert a major impact on the manner in which researchers studied children and adults with high-risk conditions and mental disorders (see, e.g., Cicchetti, 1984a; Cicchetti & Richters, 1997; Rutter, 1986; Rutter & Garmezy, 1983; Sroufe & Rutter, 1984; Zigler & Glick, 1986). Conceptualizations of the nature of mental disorder, etiological models of risk and psychopathology, the scientific questions that were posed, and the design and data analytic strategies were reexamined, challenged, and cast in a new light by developmental psychopathologists (Cicchetti & Hinshaw, 2003; Cicchetti & Richters, 1997; Granic & Hollenstein, 2003; Richters, 1997; Richters & Cicchetti, 1993; Rutter & Sroufe, 2000; Sroufe, 1989; Wakefield, 1992, 1997).

The field of developmental psychopathology owes its emergence and coalescence to a number of historically based endeavors in a variety of disciplines, including embryology, genetics, the neurosciences, philosophy, sociology, and clinical, developmental, and experimental psychology (see Cicchetti, 1990, for an elaboration). As is the case in tracing the pathways to discovery in clinical medicine, the influences of these diverse disciplines on the field of developmental psychopathology illustrate the manner in which advances in our knowledge of developmental processes and within particular scientific domains mutually inform each other. Notably, a number of the major theoretical systematizers in these diverse scientific fields depicted psychopathology as a distortion or exaggeration of the normal condition and reasoned that the study of normal biological, psychological, and social processes could be more clearly understood through the investigation of pathological phenomena (Cicchetti & Cohen, 1995c).

A basic theme appears in the writings of these earlier thinkers: Because all psychopathology can be conceived as a distortion, disturbance, or degeneration of normal functioning, it follows that, if one wishes to understand pathology more fully, then one must understand the normal functioning against which psychopathology is compared (Cicchetti, 1984b). Not only is knowledge of normal biological, psychological, and social processes very helpful for understanding, preventing, and treating psychopathology (Cicchetti & Hinshaw, 2002; Cicchetti & Toth, 1992; Toth & Cicchetti, 1999), but also the deviations from and distortions of normal development that are seen in pathological processes indicate in exciting ways how normal development may be better investigated and understood (Baron-Cohen, Tager-Flusberg, & Cohen, 1993; Cicchetti, 2003; Freud, 1965; Sroufe, 1990). Similarly, information obtained from investigating psychopathology can augment the comprehension of normal development (Cicchetti, 1984b, 1993, 2003; Rutter, 1986; Rutter & Garmezy, 1983; Sroufe, 1990; Weiss, 1969).

Since the nineteenth century, research in embryology has provided a rich empirical foundation for the emergence of organismic theories of development that possess great significance for comprehending the emergence and course of adaptive and maladaptive functioning (see, e.g., Cairns, 1983; Fishbein, 1976; Sameroff, 1983; Waddington, 1957; Weiss, 1969). From the research programs of such major embryologists as Hans Spemann (1938; Kuo, 1939, 1967), the principles of differentiation in development, a dynamically active organism and of a hierarchically integrated system that were later used in the investigation of the processes contributing to abnormal development within the neurosciences, psychology, and experimental psychopathology were derived (Cicchetti, 1990). Within the field of neurology, Santiago Ramon y Cajal (1893, 1937) utilized embryos to study the developing nervous system; he demonstrated that nerve cells possess terminal structures that contact with other nerve cells but do not fuse with them (i.e., that the nerve fibers are contiguous rather than continuous), thereby providing additional empirical support for the existence of a hierarchically integrated nervous system.

One of the most dominant ideas that contributed to the blossoming of the developmental perspective was Herbert Spencer's (1862/1900) "developmental hypothesis," in which ontogenesis was depicted as a uniform process that was governed by universal laws and principles (see also J. A. Glick, 1992; Kaplan, 1967). Throughout the ensuing period, the maturation of developmental psychology as a discipline has exerted a profound effect on the field of developmental psychopathology. The advances made in our knowledge of basic neurobiological, perceptual, cognitive, linguistic, representational, social, social-cognitive, emotional, and motivational domains have provided a firm empirical basis against which developmental psychopathologists could discover new truths about the processes underlying adaptation and maladaptation, as well as the best means of preventing and treating psychopathology (Cicchetti & Toth, 1998). Moreover, the influences of clinical psychology, psychiatry, and developmental psychopathology can be seen increasingly in the research ideas of developmental psychologists (Parke, 2004).

Writing in the late 1970s, Eisenberg (1977) urged his psychiatric colleagues to adopt a developmental framework, presenting it as a helpful unifying perspective that would enable clinical investigators to frame the difficulties they encounter in investigating and treating psychopathology. Eisenberg believed that the concept of development could serve as "the crucial link between genetic determinants and environmental variables, between . . . psychology and sociology, [and between] . . . 'physiogenic and psychogenic' causes" (p. 225). Moreover, he proposed that the term *development* be used in a broad sense and that it include "not only the roots of behavior in prior maturation as well as the residual of earlier stimulation, both internal and external, but also the modulations of that behavior by the social fields of the experienced present" (p. 225).

As developmental psychology has evolved toward becoming an ever more applied area of specialization (Shonkoff, 2000), field placements, research opportunities in diverse settings, and exposure to a range of cultural, racial, and ethnic groups are becoming more commonplace in doctoral training programs. Moreover, the growing recognition of the need to integrate developmental psychology with other scientific fields has contributed to the influx of training opportunities in settings as diverse as day care centers, family court, detention centers, mental health clinics, early intervention programs, and schools (Zigler, 1998).

An outgrowth of the attention to applied and policy-relevant issues that has obvious connections with a developmental psychopathology perspective is that scientists have developed an appreciation for the diversity of patterns of individual and family development that exist across cultures and settings (Cicchetti & Aber, 1998; Crick & Zahn-Waxler, 2003; Davies & Cicchetti, 2004; Garcia Coll et al., 1996, 2000; Swanson et al., 2003). Diversity based on ethnicity, gender, race, culture, handicap, and psychopathology was long ignored by researchers in mainstream academic developmental psychology. Now that we are accruing more knowledge about diversity in development, we are learning that the same rules of normal ontogenesis do not necessarily exist for, or apply to, all children and families (see, e.g., Baldwin, Baldwin, & Cole, 1990; Davies & Cicchetti, 2004; Garcia Coll et al., 1996; Karmiloff-Smith, 1998; Rutter & Sroufe, 2000). Without a sophisticated understanding of the range of diversity in normal development, we would be severely hampered in our attempts to elucidate the pathways to adaptation and maladaptation in high-risk and disordered individuals of varying backgrounds. Thus, developmental psychology has been integral to fostering the emergence of developmental psychopathology.

There also have been a number of landmark publications that have given great momentum to the developmental perspective on psychopathology. Included among these are Anna Freud's (1965) *Normality and Pathology in Childhood,* Santostefano and Baker's (1972) and Kohlberg, LaCrosse, and Rick's chapters in the *Manual of Child Psychopathology* (Wolman, 1972), Garmezy's (1974a, 1974b) articles on high-risk research in the *Schizophrenia Bulletin,* and Achenbach's (1974) textbook, *Developmental Psychopathology.* In addition, Santostefano's (1979) book, *A Biodevelopmental Approach to Clinical Child Psychology,* Rutter's (1980) volume, *Scientific Foundations of Developmental Psychiatry,* Rutter and Garmezy's (1983) chapter in the *Handbook of Child Psychology,* and the special issue on developmental psychopathology, considered by many to

mark the modern-day emergence of the field, published in *Child Development,* the premiere journal on normal development (Cicchetti, 1984a), all played a major role in advancing the developmental psychopathology perspective. Over the past several decades, a symposium series on developmental psychopathology was initiated (Cicchetti, 1989), a journal devoted to theory and research on developmental psychopathology, *Development and Psychopathology,* published its inaugural issue in 1989, and numerous special issues have been devoted to topics in developmental psychopathology. Finally, the publication of the first edition of the present volumes (Cicchetti & Cohen, 1995a, 1995b) and the inclusion of a chapter on developmental psychopathology in each of the past two editions of the *Handbook of Child Psychology* (Cicchetti & Toth, 1998, in press) attest to the significant growth of the discipline.

DEFINITIONAL PARAMETERS OF DEVELOPMENTAL PSYCHOPATHOLOGY

Multiple theoretical perspectives and diverse research strategies and findings have contributed to the emergence of the field of developmental psychopathology. A wide range of content areas, scientific disciplines, and methodologies have been germane (Cicchetti & Hinshaw, 2003; Cicchetti & Richters, 1997). Risk factors and protective factors have been established at multiple levels of analysis and in multiple domains. Various researchers have convincingly demonstrated that risks may be genetic, biochemical, physiological, cognitive, affective, experiential, intrafamilial, socioeconomic, social, or cultural (Caspi et al., 2002, 2003; Cicchetti & Aber, 1986; Cicchetti & Blender, 2004; Cicchetti & Sroufe, 2000). Contributions to the field of developmental psychopathology have come from many areas of the social and biological sciences.

It cannot even be stated a priori that a particular piece of research is or is not relevant to a developmental psychopathology perspective. An investigation of a single age group—even adults, for example—may be useful for resolving a perplexing methodological conundrum or revealing a new approach that brings about a series of critical new developmental studies. Likewise, some longitudinal studies of infants, children, adolescents, and adults may be so poorly conceived that they shed little light on development or psychopathology. In essence, we eschew an orthodoxy that states that some types of studies are part of the domains of developmental psychopathology, whereas others are not. Thus, we believe that a "big tent," multidisciplinary approach to the investigation of the relation between normality and psychopathology offers the most promise for advancing our knowledge of normal and abnormal developmental processes.

At the same time, a core identity for the field can be defined, manifest in a set of issues and perspectives, that makes it possible to set research directions. Central, of course, is the emphasis given to discovering processes of development, with the goal of comprehending the emergence, progressive unfolding, and transformation of patterns of adaptation and maladaptation over time. Based on this perspective, it is possible to evaluate our current understanding of psychopathology in general, as well as more particular problems of functioning. Although it is hazardous to say a particular study is or is not an example of developmental psychopathology (because one must consider the longer, more programmatic view of the research), it is possible to look at work in the field in terms of progress toward a developmental understanding. We can ask, for example, how evolved is our developmental understanding of child maltreatment, conduct problems, depression, Bipolar Disorder, or Schizophrenia. We can examine work with regard to promoting such a developmental understanding, and we can suggest the kinds of studies needed to move us toward an understanding of developmental processes.

Developmental psychopathology refers not simply to the search for the indicators or predictors of later disturbance, though these are of interest, but also to the description of the interactive processes that lead to the emergence and guide the course of disturbed behavior. In trying to understand why individuals react as they do, some researchers will emphasize one set of initiating and maintaining conditions, whereas others will argue that such factors must be examined in developmental studies, not simply be taken as givens. Increasingly, interdisciplinary multiple-levels-of-analysis investigations must assume ascendance in the field of developmental psychopathology.

CONCEPTUAL ISSUES AND PRINCIPLES

To elaborate more completely on the definitional parameters that undergird the field of developmental psychopathology, we now turn to an in-depth explication of its major conceptual issues and principles. Our delimitation of the principles is not presented in any presumed order of importance, nor is it meant to be an all-inclusive list.

Risk and Protective Factors

It is instructive to consider the role of risk factor research in answering etiological questions about the emergence of psychopathology. Depending on the stage of research, an association between a factor or characteristic and a psychopathological outcome will indicate increasing levels of specificity regarding the degree to which the factor suggests or constitutes causal processes contributing to a psychopathological outcome (Kazdin, Kraemer, Kessler, Kupfer, & Offord, 1997; Kraemer et al., 1997; Kraemer, Stice, Kazdin, Offord, & Kupfer, 2001). Establishing that a putative risk factor operates at the same point in time as a psychopathological outcome allows for the putative risk factor to be regarded as a correlate of the disorder. Because of the concurrent assessment of the putative risk and the outcome, it is not possible to determine if the putative risk contributed to the negative outcome or whether the negative outcome led to the putative risk factor. For example, determining that a substance-abusing adolescent has friends who also abuse drugs tells the researcher only that drug abuse and drug-abusing friends are correlated. It is not possible to differentiate whether drug use is a consequence of associating with drug-using peers or whether individuals who use drugs seek out peers who also use drugs. Similarly, if depression and substance abuse are assessed as co-occurring at a single point in time, then it is not possible to ascertain whether depression contributes to substance abuse or whether substance abuse contributes to depression.

To establish a construct as a risk factor for negative outcome, it is necessary to determine that the putative risk was present prior to the emergence of the negative outcome. Thus, a risk factor allows for prediction of a later outcome. Knowing that a child exhibits a disruptive behavior disorder or that a child's parent is an alcoholic allows one to predict that there is greater risk for the child to subsequently exhibit drug use problems. The risk factor implies greater potential; it is probabilistic risk, and not all individuals who exhibit the risk factor will develop the negative outcome (see, e.g., Cicchetti & Rizley, 1981; Kraemer et al., 2001; Luthar, Cicchetti, & Becker, 2000; Zubin & Spring, 1977).

Although the determination of risk factor status due to temporal precedence is an advance over knowledge of a variable as a correlate, knowing that a construct serves as a risk factor does not establish that the construct operates to cause the negative outcome. The next phase of research necessary to move toward an etiological understanding of maladaptive psychopathological outcomes is to differentiate between risk indicators and risk mechanisms (T. G. O'Connor & Rutter, 1996). Risk mechanisms specify the processes through which risk factors operate to generate an outcome. Kraemer and colleagues (1997) strove to further define risk factors as either markers or causal risk factors. *Markers* are risk factors that are not causally involved in determining outcomes. Markers are either *fixed* (factors that cannot be changed, such as sex or premature birth) or *variable* (features that spontaneously change, such as age, or that may be modified, such as through intervention). If changing a variable marker results in change in the potential for a negative outcome, then the variable marker is implicated as a *causal risk factor.*

Despite the fact that markers are not involved in causing a negative outcome, they are valuable in terms of elucidating potential processes that do have causal impact on outcomes. A marker may contribute to delineating a third factor that contributes directly to both the marker and the negative outcome. Discovering causal factors that contribute to the marker may result in identifying causal risk factors that operate to produce the psychopathological outcome. Markers thus have a spurious relation to outcomes yet may be valuable in clarifying causal mechanisms. For example, if dropping out of school is related to subsequent increases in drug use, then dropping out of school would be implicated as a risk factor for drug use. If an intervention were applied to decrease dropping out of school and no differential impact on drug use was obtained, then the association between school dropout and increased drug use would be spurious, and dropping out of school would be regarded as a variable marker. Some other factor contributing to both school dropout and drug use may be implicated. For example, Conduct Disorder could potentially be a third variable that contributes to both school dropout and drug use, thereby accounting for the spurious relation between school dropout and increased drug use.

In contrast, if an intervention to reduce school dropout decreases subsequent drug use, then dropping out of school would be implicated as a causal risk factor for drug use. The research process thus would have moved further to identifying a cause of drug use. Nevertheless, the identification of a causal risk factor does not imply that the cause of a negative outcome has been ascertained. The causal mechanism (or one of them) remains to be identified. However, school dropout would be involved in some way with the causal mechanism. A delineation of other casual risk factors could provide direction for the causal source through determining the ways multiple causal risk factors are interrelated. In so doing, a common element may be ascertained that may carry more explanatory power as the causative risk mechanism. Thus, it is necessary for research to proceed in stages to progressively isolate risk mechanisms from myriad correlates, risk factors, markers, and causal risk factors.

Mental disorders are likely to be caused by multiple processes rather than singular causes (Cicchetti & Sroufe, 2000; Institute of Medicine, 1994). Thus, the identification of a causal risk factor will contribute to elucidating only one aspect of a more complex matrix of causes. Within individuals, there are likely to be multiple component processes rather than unitary causes that contribute to psychopathological outcomes (Cicchetti & Blender, 2004). Moreover, different individuals are likely to develop the same mental disorder through different constellations of processes. Thus, attention to identification of multiple risk mechanisms is important. Within individuals, single risk processes may not have sufficient power to eventuate in a mental disorder on their own. However, their impact might become more potent as they are combined with additional sources of risk. Collectively, multiple risk processes may operate additively, amassing greater potential that psychopathology will ensue. Additionally, risk processes may coact synergistically with an exponential rather than additive impact on increasing the potential for maladaptive or psychopathological outcomes (cf. Rutter, 1990). Risk factors tend to co-occur rather than occur in isolation (Rutter, 1990; Sameroff et al., 1987). Some risk factors may contribute to the development of other problems that, in turn, become risk factors for other mental disorders as development proceeds.

The operation of risk processes must further be considered in the context of protective factors that the developing individual also may experience. Protective processes function to promote competent development and reduce the negative impact of risk processes (Luthar et al., 2000). Thus, protective factors may counterbalance the impact of risk processes, thereby decreasing the likelihood that the risk process will eventuate in maladaptive or psychopathological outcomes (Cicchetti & Aber, 1986; Luthar et al., 2000). For example, the impact on later substance use of neurodevelopmental anomalies that are consequences of maternal drug abuse may be reduced for children placed in adoptive homes in which structure, active engagement, warmth, and closeness are provided. These protective processes may dilute the potential of the neurodevelopmental anomaly to contribute to a substance abuse outcome. Alternatively, protective factors may operate in an interactive manner: The protective factor may reduce a negative outcome within a high-risk group but have limited impact within a low-risk group. For example, in considering parental alcoholism as a risk factor for adolescent substance abuse, high parental monitoring may be particularly valuable in reducing adolescent substance use in families without an alcoholic parent. In contrast, in families without an alcoholic parent, the degree of parental monitoring may be unrelated (or less strongly related) to adolescent substance use. Thus, as a protective factor, parental monitoring would be particularly important in reducing negative outcomes only within the group in which the risk processes associated with parental alcoholism have the potential to operate. Consequently, understanding the etiologic role of risk processes on substance abuse outcomes must occur within a wider framework that also incorporates investigation of processes that may protect the individual from negative outcomes through counterbalancing or diluting the impact of risk factors.

It is essential to realize that risk factors do not function in a static manner. Rather, over the course of development, there is an ongoing dynamic progression among the various risk processes involved in shaping the developmental course of the individual and contributing to maladaptive and psychopathological outcomes. Cicchetti (1999; Cicchetti & Lynch, 1993; Cicchetti & Toth, 1998) has drawn attention to the importance of conceptualizing risk and protective factors in an ecological-transactional developmental model. At each level of the ecology, risk and protective factors may operate in tandem, transacting with features of the individual (i.e., the current organization of biological, emotional, cognitive, representational, and interpersonal development). Not only do external factors influence the development of the individual, but also the individual exerts influence on the external levels of the ecology, including family members, peers, and the school environment. Patterns of influence are thus mutual, as development proceeds with ongoing transactions between the individual and the external world.

Additionally, transactions occur among the different internal domains for the individual (i.e., biological, cognitive, affective, representational, and interpersonal). Not only do biological processes (e.g., genetic predispositions, neurodevelopmental anomalies) influence domains of psychological functioning, but also psychological experience, in turn, influences biological structure and function (Cicchetti & Tucker, 1994; Eisenberg, 1995). The quality of the transactions of mutual influence within the individual and between the individual and the external world shapes the character of individual development, and different developmental pathways ensue. Most important, the dynamic balance of risk and protective processes that operate over the course of development structures the developmental pathways in which individuals engage, with a progression of high risk and few protective resources engendering greater vulnerability and incompetence in the individual, contrasting with relative competence attained among individuals who experience fewer risks and numerous protective, growth-enhancing resources. Accordingly,

understanding the roots of vulnerability to mental disorder requires moving beyond features of the current context when these problems emerge to articulating the course of development that individuals have experienced and how risk and protective processes have structured the organization of the individual.

Contextual Influences

Developmental psychopathologists have been cognizant of the importance of contextual influences in defining what constitutes abnormality. Clearly, no behavior or pattern of adaptation can be viewed as pathological except in particular contexts (Cicchetti & Schneider-Rosen, 1986; Luthar & McMahon, 1996; Richters & Cicchetti, 1993; Werner & Kaplan, 1963). Further, chronological age and developmental stage or level of biological and psychological organization are important defining features of context for clinicians and researchers interested in chronicling the development of mental disorders.

Although there is a growing awareness that contextual factors play an important role in defining phenomena as psychopathological (Jensen & Hoagwood, 1997; Richters & Cicchetti, 1993; Wakefield, 1992), there are vast differences in how the contexts for human development are conceptualized. Bronfenbrenner's (1979) articulation of nested levels in the ecology of human development marked a great stride forward to conceptualizing contexts. The macro-, exo-, meso-, and microsystems delimited by Bronfenbrenner clearly and powerfully alert the developmental psychopathologist to important and vastly different sources of contextual influence on individual development.

Situational and interpersonal influences operate at the microsystem level in Bronfenbrenner's (1979) schema and have been the traditional focus of psychological study. However, it has thus far proven to be far more difficult to conceptualize specific macro-, exo-, and mesosystem influences on development. Part of the difficulty in pinpointing the effects of these more distal contexts is that documenting their impact on individual development requires cross-fertilization with the disciplines that study these macro phenomena: anthropology, demography, sociology, economics, and epidemiology. Parental workplace, school transitions, violent communities, persistent poverty, and unsupportive stress-laden ecologies are all examples of contexts that exert influence on the development of psychopathology in children and adults (Brooks-Gunn, Duncan, & Aber, 1997; Cicchetti & Toth, 1997; Eccles, Lord, & Roeser, 1996; Luthar, 1999; Lynch & Cicchetti, 1998; Richters & Martinez, 1993). Consequently, societal-, community-, and institutional-level influences on individual development are now beginning to be examined in systematic, rigorous, empirical fashion. Now that the field of developmental psychopathology has begun to incorporate a multiple-levels-of-analysis perspective (Cicchetti & Blender, 2004; Cicchetti & Dawson, 2002), it will become more common for scientists investigating contextual aspects of problem behaviors and mental disorders to include assessments of higher levels of contexts into their research armamentaria (Boyce et al., 1998; Cicchetti & Aber, 1998).

The Mutual Interplay between Normality and Psychopathology

A focus on the boundary between normal and abnormal development is central to a developmental psychopathology perspective. Such a viewpoint emphasizes not only how knowledge from the study of normal development can inform the study of high-risk conditions and mental disorders, but also how the investigation of risk and pathology can enhance our comprehension of normal development (Cicchetti, 1984b, 1990; Sroufe, 1990).

Before the field of developmental psychopathology could emerge as a distinct discipline, the science of normal development needed to mature, and a broader basis of firm results had to be acquired. As dramatic gains in developmental neurobiology, neuroimaging, and molecular genetics have occurred, in concert with an increased comprehension of hormonal, emotional, social, social-cognitive, and representational processes, we now possess a much stronger ability to utilize knowledge of normative development as a yardstick against which to measure psychopathology.

The central focus of developmental psychopathology involves the elucidation of developmental processes and how they function, as indicated and elaborated by the examinations of extremes in the distribution (i.e., individuals with psychopathology). Developmental psychopathologists also direct attention toward variations in the continuum between the mean and the extremes. These variations may represent individuals who are currently not divergent enough to be considered disordered but who may progress to further extremes as development continues. Such individuals may be vulnerable to developing future disordered outcomes, or developmental deviations may, for some individuals, reflect either the earliest signs of an emerging dysfunction or an already existing dysfunction that is partially compensated for by other processes within or outside the individual.

Because of the interrelations between the investigation of normal and abnormal development, developmental psy-

chopathologists must be cognizant of normal pathways of development within a given cultural context (Garcia Coll et al., 1996), uncover deviations from these pathways, articulate the developmental transformations that occur as individuals progress through these deviant developmental courses, and identify the processes and mechanisms that may divert an individual from a particular pathway and onto a more or less adaptive course (Cicchetti & Aber, 1986; Cicchetti & Rogosch, 1996; Sroufe, 1989).

Developmental psychopathologists have long argued that one gains valuable information about an organism's normal functioning through studying its abnormal condition. Relatedly, developmental psychopathologists have asserted that theories of normal development can be affirmed, challenged, and augmented by incorporating knowledge about atypical development. As Werner (1948, p. 23) has stated, "A whole series of mental diseases are important to developmental psychology in that they represent the regression, the dissolution, of the higher mental processes, or inhibitions of the genetically advanced levels." Furthermore, Werner believed that because

> psychopathology will shed light on the genetic data of other developmental fields . . . the results of psychopathology . . . become valuable in many ways for the general picture of mental development, just as psychopathology is itself enriched and its methods facilitated by the adoption of the genetic approach. (p. 33–34)

Despite the fact that developmental psychopathologists emphasize the mutual interplay between normal and atypical development, most contemporary theory and research have focused on the contributions that normal development can make to advancing our knowledge of psychopathological processes. There has been significantly less recognition that the investigation of high-risk conditions and mental disorders can augment our comprehension of normal developmental processes; however, this is beginning to change (see, e.g., Cicchetti, 1996, 2003).

Understanding how psychopathological conditions evolve and how aberrations of component developmental systems that exist among disordered individuals eventuate may be informative for elucidating critical components of development that are not typically evident (Chomsky, 1968; Cicchetti, 2003; Lenneberg, 1967; T. G. O'Connor, 2003). Often, the examination of a system in its smoothly operating normal or healthy state does not afford us the opportunity to comprehend the interrelations among its component subsystems. In usual circumstances, the integration of component developmental systems may be so well established that it is difficult to determine how normal functioning is dependent on this confluence. When there is a clear aberration or deficit in a component system within a disordered population, examination of how that atypicality relates to the organization of other component systems can reveal information regarding the interdependency of components not readily apparent under normal conditions (Cicchetti & Sroufe, 1978). Thus, the interest of developmental psychopathologists in the convergences and divergences between normality and psychopathology can be mutually beneficial for understanding development across the range of variation (Cicchetti & Cohen, 1995c; Sroufe, 1990). As M. Glick (1997, p. 242) has explicated: "Just as normative developmental principles have been instrumental for elucidating many facets of psychopathology, findings from . . . research with disordered adults and with children and adolescents having special needs have enhanced understanding of normal processes."

"Experiments of nature" are "naturally arising conditions in which there is a possibility of separating otherwise confounding processes or opportunities to examine processes that for ethical or practical reasons would not have been possible" (T. G. O'Connor, 2003, p. 837). Because they enable us to isolate the components of the integrated system, investigation of these natural experiments sheds light on the normal structure of the system. If we choose to ignore or bypass the investigation of these experiments of nature, we are likely to construct theories that will eventually be contradicted by critical discoveries in research on psychopathology (Lenneberg, 1967). The utilization of diversity of natural experiments is critical because, when extrapolating from nonnormal populations with the goal of informing developmental theory, it is important that a range of populations and conditions be considered. To make generalizations beyond the risk process or mental disorder investigated, it is necessary to examine an entire spectrum of disordered modifications.

Historically, experiments of nature have been utilized in a variety of disciplines to contribute to the normal understanding of the phenomena under investigation (Cicchetti, 1990; for work in basic medicine, see, e.g., McQuarrie, 1944). As Good and Zak (1956) noted, one value of incorporating experiments of nature into our research armamentaria is that these natural experiments enable observations and discoveries that would be extremely difficult, if not impossible, to duplicate in the laboratory setting. Theoreticians and researchers in a number of fields, including genetics, embryology, neurology, neuropsychology, psychiatry, and clinical and developmental psychology, have examined experiments of nature to elucidate theory and research

in their respective disciplines (Goldstein, 1939; Inhelder, 1943/1968; Jackson, 1884/1958; Lenneberg, 1967; Luria, 1966/1980; Meyer, 1934, 1957; Shakow, 1967; B. Tizard Hodges, 1978; J. Tizard & Tizard, 1971; Weiss, 1939, 1961). Research in immunobiology likewise has a long history of utilizing experiments of nature to elucidate basic mechanisms in the functioning of the immune system (Good, 1991; Good & Zak, 1956; Sanna & Burton, 2000; Smith, 2000). Moreover, in recent decades, Rutter (1994, 2000; Rutter, Pickles, Murray, & Eaves, 2001) has eloquently articulated ways in which natural experiments are useful for the testing of causal hypotheses on the causes and courses of psychopathology.

The examination of individuals with high-risk conditions and mental disorders can provide a natural entrée into the study of system organization, disorganization, and reorganization that is otherwise not possible due to the constraints associated with research involving human participants. Through investigating a variety of high-risk and mentally disordered conditions, it is possible to gain significant insight into processes of development not generally achieved through sole reliance on investigations of relatively homogeneous nondisordered populations. Research conducted with atypical populations also can elucidate the behavioral and biological consequences of alternative pathways of development, provide important information about the range and variability of individual response to challenge and adversity, and help to specify the limits of behavioral and biological plasticity (Baron-Cohen, 1995; Cicchetti, Rogosch, Maughan, Toth, & Bruce, 2003; Damasio, Grabowski, Frank, Galaburda, & Damasio, 1994; Fries & Pollak, 2004; Gunnar et al., 2001). Finally, findings proffered by experiments of nature also hold considerable promise for informing prevention and intervention strategies (Cicchetti & Hinshaw, 2002).

DEVELOPMENTAL PATHWAYS

Since its inception as an emergent interdisciplinary science, diversity in process and outcome has been conceived as among the hallmarks of the developmental psychopathology perspective. As Sroufe (1990, p. 335) has asserted, "One of the principal tasks of developmental psychopathology is to define families of developmental pathways, some of which are associated with psychopathology with high probability, others with low probability." Even before a mental disorder emerges, certain pathways signify adaptational failures that probabilistically forebode subsequent psychopathology (Sroufe, 1990). Thus, developmental psychopathologists have articulated the expectation that there are multiple contributors to adaptive and maladaptive outcomes in any individual, that these factors and their relative contributions vary among individuals, and that there are myriad pathways to any particular manifestation of adaptive and disordered behavior (Cicchetti, 1993; Robins, 1966; Robins & Rutter, 1990; Sroufe & Jacobvitz, 1989). In addition, it is believed that there is heterogeneity among individuals who develop a specific disorder with respect to the features of their disturbance, as well as among individuals who evidence maladaptation but do not develop a disorder. In accord with this view, the principles of equifinality and multifinality derived from general systems theory (von Bertalanffy, 1968) are germane.

Equifinality refers to the observation that in any open system (cf. Mayr, 1964, 1988), a diversity of pathways, including chance events or what biologists refer to as nonlinear epigenesis, may lead to the same outcome. Stated differently, in an open system (i.e., one where there is maintenance in change, dynamic order in processes, organization, and self-regulation), the same end state may be reached from a variety of different initial conditions and through different processes. This is referred to as equifinality, an organismic process that possesses significant implications for biological and psychological regulatory systems and for behavioral and biological plasticity (Cicchetti & Tucker, 1994; Curtis & Cicchetti, 2003). In contrast, in a closed system, the end state is inextricably linked to and determined by the initial conditions. If either of the conditions change or the processes are modified, then the end state also will be modified (von Bertalanffy, 1968).

Initial descriptions of equifinality emanated from work in embryology. For example, the development of a normal organism was shown to occur from a whole ovum, a divided ovum, or two fused ova. Further, it was demonstrated that different initial sizes and different courses of growth can eventuate in the same ultimate size of an organism (von Bertalanffy, 1968; Waddington, 1957). Within the discipline of developmental psychopathology, equifinality has been invoked to explain why a variety of developmental pathways may eventuate in a given outcome, rather than expecting a singular primary pathway to the adaptive or maladaptive outcome.

The principle of multifinality (Wilden, 1980) suggests that any one component may function differently depending on the organization of the system in which it operates. Multifinality states that the effect on functioning of any one component's value may vary in different systems. Actual effects will depend on the conditions set by the values of additional components with which it is structurally linked. Consequently, the pathology or health of a system

must be identified in terms of how adequately its essential functions are maintained. Stated differently, a particular adverse event should not necessarily be seen as leading to the same psychopathological or nonpsychopathological outcome in every individual. Likewise, individuals may begin on the same major pathway and, as a function of their subsequent "choices," exhibit very different patterns of adaptation or maladaptation (Cicchetti & Tucker, 1994; Rutter, 1989; Sroufe, 1989; Sroufe, Egeland, & Kreutzer, 1990).

A pathways approach builds on knowledge gained from variable-oriented studies; however, attention is shifted to exploring the common and the uncommon outcomes, as well as alternative routes by which outcomes are achieved by different individuals (cf. Cicchetti & Schneider-Rosen, 1986). Thus, what might be considered error variance at the group level must be critically examined for understanding diversity in process and outcome. The emphasis on person-centered observation highlights the transition from a focus on variables to a focus on individuals, and this transition is essential for demonstrating equifinality and multifinality in the developmental course. The examination of patterns of commonality within relatively homogeneous subgroups of individuals and concomitant similarity in profiles of contributory processes becomes an important data analytic strategy. Moreover, the need to examine the totality of attributes, psychopathological conditions, and risk and protective processes in the context of each other rather than in isolation is seen as crucial for understanding the course of development taken by individuals. For example, the presence of a childhood depressive disorder has different developmental implications depending on whether it occurs alone or in conjunction with Conduct Disorder. Similarly, the nature of alcoholism varies considerably depending on differences in the life course of antisociality. Thus, this orientation highlights the importance of an organizational view of development (cf. Cicchetti, 1993; Cicchetti & Sroufe, 1978; Sroufe et al., 1990; Waters & Sroufe, 1983). The meaning of any one attribute, process, or psychopathological condition needs to be considered in light of the complex matrix of individual characteristics, experiences, and social-contextual influences involved, the timing of events and experiences, and the developmental history of the individual.

This attention to diversity in origins, processes, and outcomes in understanding developmental pathways does not suggest that prediction is futile as a result of the many potential individual patterns of adaptation (Sroufe, 1989). There are constraints on how much diversity is possible, and not all outcomes are equally likely (Cicchetti & Tucker, 1994; Sroufe et al., 1990). Nonetheless, the appreciation of equifinality and multifinality in development encourages theorists and researchers to entertain more complex and varied approaches to how they conceptualize and investigate development and psychopathology. Researchers should increasingly strive to demonstrate the multiplicity of processes and outcomes that may be articulated at the individual, person-oriented level within existing longitudinal data sets. Ultimately, future endeavors must conceptualize and design research at the outset with these differential pathways concepts as a foundation. Is so doing, progress toward achieving the unique goals of developmental psychopathology to explain the development of individual patterns of adaptation and maladaptation will be realized (cf. Sroufe & Rutter, 1984).

Multiple Levels of Analysis

Over the course of the past several decades, it has been increasingly acknowledged that the investigation of developmental processes, both normal and abnormal, is an inherently interdisciplinary enterprise (Pellmar & Eisenberg, 2000). Scientists must utilize different levels and methods of analysis depending on the questions being addressed in their research. Although some problems are best handled with the methods and concepts of a single discipline, other issues require interdisciplinary integration. In fact, history reveals that disciplines themselves often evolve from interdisciplinary efforts. For example, neuroscience developed as scientists working in a number of different fields began to work in concert to solve some of the common scientific mysteries that existed about the nervous system (Cowan, Harter, & Kandel, 2000). As knowledge flourishes and as new questions are posed that must be addressed, additional fields continue to be integrated into the dynamic discipline of neuroscience.

Since its inception, developmental psychopathology has been conceived as an interdisciplinary science (Cicchetti, 1990; Cicchetti & Toth, 1991). A number of influential theoretical perspectives, including the organizational perspective (Cicchetti & Schneider-Rosen, 1986; Cicchetti & Sroufe, 1978; Sroufe, 1979, 1997) and Gottlieb's notions of probabilistic epigenesis (Gottlieb, 1991; Gottlieb & Halpern, 2002), have long advocated the importance of multidomain, interdisciplinary research.

Nonetheless, most of what is known about the correlates, causes, pathways, and sequelae of mental disorders has been gleaned from investigations that focused on relatively narrow domains of variables. It is apparent from the questions addressed by developmental psychopathologists that progress toward a process-level understanding of mental

disorders will require research designs and strategies that call for the simultaneous assessment of multiple domains of variables both within and outside of the developing person (Cicchetti & Dawson, 2002). Similarly, research in the area of resilience must follow these interdisciplinary multiple-levels-of-analysis perspectives (Cicchetti & Blender, 2004; Curtis & Cicchetti, 2003). In some instances, reference to variables measured in other domains is essential to clarify the role(s) of variables of interest for other questions; it is necessary to consider variables from other domains as competing explanations for postulated causal paths. To understand psychopathology fully, all levels of analysis must be examined and integrated. Each level both informs and constrains all other levels of analysis. Moreover, the influence of levels on one another is almost always bidirectional (Cicchetti & Cannon, 1999; Cicchetti & Tucker, 1994).

Because different levels of analysis constrain other levels, as scientists learn more about multiple levels of analysis, researchers conducting their work at each level will need to develop theories that are consistent across all levels. When disciplines function in isolation, they run the risk of creating theories that ultimately will be incorrect because vital information from other disciplines has either been ignored or is unknown. Just as is the case in systems neuroscience, it is critical that there be an integrative framework that incorporates all levels of analysis about complex systems in the development of psychopathology.

One of the major challenges confronting scientific progress involves establishing communication systems among disciplines. For example, despite tremendous technological advances in neuroimaging and molecular genetics, great knowledge gaps remain between scientists who possess competence with the technologies and methods of brain imaging and genetics and those who are comfortable with the complex issues inherent in the investigation of development and psychopathology. Consequently, the field has not yet made optimal use of the advances in technology that have taken place (Posner, Rothbart, Farah, & Bruer, 2001).

RESILIENCE

As stated previously, developmental psychopathologists are as interested in individuals at high risk for the development of pathology who do not manifest it over time as they are in individuals who develop an actual mental disorder (Cicchetti, 1993; Cicchetti & Garmezy, 1993; Cicchetti & Toth, 1991; Luthar, 2003; Luthar et al., 2000; Masten, 1989, 2001; Masten, Best, & Garmezy, 1990; Rutter, 1990; Sroufe & Rutter, 1984). Relatedly, developmental psychopathologists also are committed to understanding pathways to competent adaptation despite exposure to conditions of adversity (Cicchetti & Rogosch, 1997; Egeland, Carlson, & Sroufe, 1993; Flores et al., 2005; Kim-Cohen, Moffitt, Caspi, & Taylor, 2004; Masten, 2001; Masten et al., 2004). In addition, developmental psychopathologists emphasize the need to understand the functioning of individuals who, after having diverged onto deviant developmental pathways, resume normal functioning and achieve adequate adaptation (Cicchetti & Rogosch, 1997; Masten et al., 1990).

Resilience has been operationalized as the individual's capacity for adapting successfully and functioning competently despite experiencing chronic adversity or following exposure to prolonged or severe trauma (Luthar et al., 2000; Masten et al., 1990). The roots of work on resilience can be traced back to prior research in diverse areas, including investigations of individuals with Schizophrenia and their offspring, studies of the effects of persistent poverty, and work on coping with acute and chronic stressors (Cicchetti & Garmezy, 1993). By uncovering the mechanisms and processes that lead to competent adaptation despite the presence of adversity, developmental psychopathologists have helped to enhance the understanding of both normal development and psychopathology. We concur with Rutter (1990, p. 210) that resilience does not exist statically in the "psychological chemistry of the moment." It is a dynamic process, and genetic, biological, and psychological processes exert a vital role in how individuals fare when they are exposed to adversity (Curtis & Cicchetti, 2003; Kim-Cohen et al., 2004).

Within this perspective, it is important that resilient functioning not be conceptualized as a static or traitlike condition, but as being in dynamic transaction with intra- and extraorganismic forces (Cicchetti, Rogosch, Lynch, & Holt, 1993; Egeland et al., 1993). Research on the processes leading to resilient outcomes offers great promise as an avenue for facilitating the development of prevention and intervention strategies (Cicchetti & Toth, 1992; Toth & Cicchetti, 1999). Through the examination of the proximal and distal processes and mechanisms that contribute to positive adaptation in situations that more typically eventuate in maladaptation, researchers and clinicians will be better prepared to devise ways of promoting competent outcomes in high-risk populations (Luthar & Cicchetti, 2000).

TRANSLATIONAL RESEARCH

In recent years, the National Institute of Mental Health (NIMH) has become greatly interested in fostering and supporting translational research in the behavioral and so-

cial sciences (Cicchetti & Toth, 2000, in press b). As funding decisions at the NIMH increasingly become tied to reducing the burden of mental illness and to the real-world application of research findings, investigators will need to devise and implement policy-relevant investigations. In a report of the National Advisory Mental Health Council on Behavioral Sciences (2000) entitled *Translating Behavioral Science into Action,* strategies for enhancing contributions of behavioral science to society more broadly are proposed. The report of the workgroup concludes, "At present too few researchers are attempting to bridge across basic, clinical, and services research, and not enough are working with colleagues in related allied disciplines to move research advances out of the laboratory and into clinical care, service delivery, and policymaking" (p. v). In this report, "translational research is defined as research designed to address how basic behavioral processes inform the diagnosis, prevention, treatment, and delivery of services for mental illness, and, conversely, how knowledge of mental illness increases our understanding of basic behavioral processes" (p. iii). This formulation of translational research is in direct accord with two of the key tenets of a developmental psychopathology perspective, namely, the reciprocal interplay between basic and applied research and between normal and atypical development (Cicchetti & Toth, 1991, in press a).

The parameters of developmental psychopathology lend themselves to fostering translational research that has implications for society, policymakers, and individuals with mental disorders and their families. The very subject matter of the field, which encompasses risk and resilience, prevention and intervention, the elucidation of precipitants of mental illness, the mediating and moderating processes that contribute to or mitigate against the emergence and maintenance of psychopathology, a multiple-levels-of-analysis approach, and the incorporation of principles of normal development into the conduct of empirical investigations, necessitates thinking clearly about the implications of the work and devising strategies that will remedy the problems being studied.

PREVENTION AND INTERVENTION

Now that we have examined some illustrative principles of a developmental psychopathology perspective and their relevance to investigating adaptation and psychopathology, we next discuss how the developmental psychopathology framework can similarly assist in the development and provision of prevention and intervention to individuals who are at high risk for or who have developed psychopathology.

Theory and research on basic developmental processes can and should inform prevention and intervention efforts to a greater extent than is the current norm. Clinical research on treatment and preventive strategies can provide unprecedented and essential insights translatable to the making of further theoretical advances (Cicchetti & Hinshaw, 2002; Cicchetti & Toth, 1999; Kellam & Rebok, 1992; Koretz, 1991).

For example, if the developmental course is altered as a result of the implementation of a randomized preventive intervention trial and the risk for negative outcomes is reduced, then prevention research has contributed to specifying the processes that are involved in the emergence of maladaptive developmental outcomes and psychopathology (Cicchetti & Rogosch, 1996; Coie et al., 1993; Hinshaw, 2002; Kellam & Rebok, 1992). Accordingly, preventive intervention research can be conceptualized as true experiments in modifying the course of development, thereby providing insights into the etiology and pathogenesis of disordered outcomes. The time has come to conduct randomized prevention trials that not only assess behavioral changes, but also ascertain whether abnormal neurobiological structures, functions, and organizations are modifiable or are refractory to intervention. There is growing evidence that successful intervention modifies not only maladaptive behavior, but also the cellular and physiological correlates of behavior (D. B. Kandel, 1998; E. R. Kandel 1979, 1999).

Prevention research is based on theoretical models of how risk conditions are related to adverse outcomes. As such, it posits processes that link the risk condition to the negative outcome (Institute of Medicine, 1994; Munoz, Mrazek, & Haggerty, 1996; Reiss & Price, 1996). Intervention efficacy may be enhanced by knowledge of developmental norms, appreciation of how a developmental level may vary within the same age group, sensitivity to the changing meaning that problems and disorders have at different developmental levels, attention to the effects of developmental transitions and reorganizations, and an understanding of the factors that are essential to incorporate into the design and implementation of preventive interventions (Cicchetti & Rogosch, 1999; Cicchetti & Toth, 1999; Coie et al., 1993; Institute of Medicine, 1994; Munoz et al., 1996; Noam, 1992; Reiss & Price, 1996; Toth & Cicchetti, 1999).

Inquiries regarding developmental theory and findings on basic developmental processes are all too often quite removed from both clinical practice and clinical research (Cicchetti & Toth, 1998; Kazdin, 1999). Despite rhetoric directed to the principle that developmental theory should inform active clinical intervention with children and ado-

lescents—and the converse contention that treatment research should inform relevant theory—the gap between these two endeavors is still broad. Indeed, in many ways, those who perform basic developmental research and promote developmental theory appear to constitute a different culture from those who pursue related prevention and intervention efforts. At the extremes, clinically oriented investigators and practitioners perceive basic academic developmental science as overly concerned with central tendencies and universal, developmental norms, to the exclusion of the rich variability and nonnormative behavior patterns that they confront on a daily basis. Conversely, theorists and academic scientists appear to construe much of the clinical endeavor as atheoretical and ungrounded in core scientific principles and theories (Cicchetti & Toth, 1991, 1998).

This state of affairs is particularly distressing given the advances that are being made in a host of basic behavioral and biomedical sciences and the urgent clinical needs of large numbers of children, adolescents, and families afflicted by mental and developmental disorders (U.S. Department of Health and Human Services, 1999). Because of the field's still nascent ideas as to the underlying mechanisms of most forms of psychopathology, the need for direct application of basic research advances to enhance clinical efforts can only be described as essential. Yet, despite the increasing call for translational research that can bridge basic and applied efforts, the barriers that exist regarding the application of such basic research advances to clinically relevant work are real (Institute of Medicine, 2000). It is essential that so-called basic investigators receive updated information about fundamental processes that are relevant to clinical disorders.

Another means of closing the schisms that exist between academic researchers and clinicians is to undertake interdisciplinary, collaborative preventive interventions that take into account multiple levels of influence, spanning genes to neighborhoods and individuals to social groups (Cicchetti & Dawson, 2002). Indeed, integrative, multidisciplinary efforts that bridge these different cultures can capitalize on unprecedented opportunities for fostering a mutual perspective. As stated earlier, a central tenet of developmental psychopathology is that the understanding of atypical development can inform the understanding of normal development, and vice versa, as long as consideration is given to contextual variables and developmental principles in the explanation of how development can go awry (Cicchetti & Cohen, 1995a, 1995b). We extend this assertion through our contention that methodologically rigorous prevention and intervention science can provide a unique lens through which to discern the processes responsible for the development, maintenance, and alteration of both typical and atypical functional patterns (Cicchetti & Toth, 1992; Hinshaw, 2002; Kellam & Rebok, 1992).

There are several reasons prevention and intervention efforts can play an essential role in bridging the world of research and clinical work and in fostering theoretical advances. First, investigations of clinical populations may inform understanding of processes responsible for healthy and atypical development, but again, only so long as careful attention is directed to the underlying mechanisms responsible for pathological outcomes (Hinshaw, 2002). Second, and crucially, whereas much of the work in the field is, of necessity, naturalistic and correlational in nature, given ethical constraints on randomly assigning developing persons to key environmental or psychobiological conditions, the gold standard for clinical intervention and prevention research is the randomized clinical trial. The experimental nature of such investigations provides an unprecedented opportunity to make causal inferences in the field (Cook & Campbell, 1979; Kraemer, Wilson, Fairburn, & Agras, 2002). Although the types of independent variables manipulated in clinical or prevention trials may be several steps removed from crucial, underlying etiologic factors, given that such trials are primarily concerned with the practical, clinical goals of alleviating suffering and promoting competence rather than isolating primary causal variables, careful research design and assiduous measurement of ancillary, process variables through which intervention effects may occur can shed unexpected light on theory-driven mechanisms underlying healthy and pathological development (Hinshaw, 2002; Kraemer et al., 2002).

Finally, as research on the contributors to resilient functioning has evolved, several scientists have suggested, based on knowledge of the extant empirical literature, how to develop preventive interventions aimed at promoting competent adaptation in a variety of high-risk groups (see, e.g., Cowen, 1991, 1994; Luthar & Cicchetti, 2000; Yoshikawa, 1994). A number of recommendations for competence-promoting interventions have been made, including the following: (1) They must be firmly grounded in theory and research; (2) efforts should be directed not only toward reducing maladaptation and psychopathology but also at promoting competence; (3) programs must capitalize on the particular resources and strengths of individual children in specific populations; (4) there should be a focus on vulnerability and protective processes that operate across multiple levels of influence; and (5) they should be guided by a strong developmental-contextual theoretical perspective (Luthar & Cicchetti, 2000). In addition, prevention and intervention should be designed to elucidate the mediators and moderators of resilient outcomes and recovery to adaptive functions.

CONCLUSION

In a relatively brief period, developmental psychopathologists have contributed significantly to our understanding of risk, disorder, and adaptation across the life course. Much of the momentum of developmental psychopathology has stemmed from an openness to preexisting knowledge in combination with a willingness to question established beliefs, thereby continuing to promote disciplinary growth. The integration of concepts and methods derived from areas of endeavor that are too often isolated from each other has resulted in knowledge advances that might have been missed in the absence of cross-disciplinary dialogue.

Numerous challenges lie ahead, and we must have the courage to continue to critically examine the implicit as well as the explicit conceptual and scientific assumptions that exist in the field of developmental psychopathology to sustain our momentum and to foster new advances (Cicchetti & Richters, 1997). Future investigations must strive to attain enhanced fidelity between the elegance and complexity of the theoretical models and definitional parameters inherent to a developmental psychopathology perspective and the design, measurement, and data analytic strategies employed in our investigations (Granic & Hollenstein, 2003; Richters, 1997). Moreover, we believe that the continuation and elaboration of the mutually enriching interchanges that have occurred within and across disciplines interested in normal and abnormal development will enhance not only the science of developmental psychopathology, but also the benefits to be derived for society as a whole.

The impressive array of findings in the more recent psychological developmental literature mentioned earlier, in concert with the concomitant progress made in the neurosciences, genetics, and related disciplines, has led to increasing acknowledgment of the need to conduct collaborative, multidisciplinary, multidomain studies on normal, high-risk, and psychopathological populations. It has now become more widely accepted that research into pathological conditions must proceed hand-in-hand with so-called basic research into human functioning. As progress in ontogenetic approaches to various subdisciplines of developmental psychopathology continues, the common theoretical and empirical threads running through this work will coalesce to establish a foundation on which an increasingly sophisticated developmental psychopathology discipline can grow. The power embodied by cross-disciplinary collaborations that utilize multiple-levels-of-analysis methodologies promises to significantly strengthen our capacity to decrease the burden of mental illness for society.

REFERENCES

Achenbach, T. M. (1974). *Developmental psychopathology.* New York: Ronald Press.

Ainsworth, M. D. S., Blehar, M. C., Waters, E., & Wall, S. (1978). *Patterns of attachment: A psychological study of the Strange Situation.* Hillsdale, NJ: Erlbaum.

Baldwin, A., Baldwin, C., & Cole, R. (1990). Stress-resistant families and stress-resistant children. In J. Rolf, A. Masten, D. Cicchetti, K. Nuechterlein, & S. Weintraub (Eds.), *Risk and protective factors in the development of psychopathology* (pp. 257–280). New York: Cambridge University Press.

Baltes, P. B., Reese, H. W., & Lipsitt, L. P. (1980). Life-span developmental psychology. *Annual Review of Psychology, 32,* 65–110.

Baron-Cohen, S. (1995). *Mindblindness.* Cambridge, MA: MIT Press.

Baron-Cohen, S., Tager-Flusberg, H., & Cohen, D. J. (Eds.). (1993). *Understanding other minds: Perspectives from developmental cognitive neuroscience.* New York: Oxford University Press.

Bergman, L. R., & Magnusson, D. (1997). A person-oriented approach in research on developmental psychopathology. *Development and Psychopathology, 9,* 291–319.

Black, J., Jones, T. A., Nelson, C. A., & Greenough, W. T. (1998). Neuronal plasticity and the developing brain. In N. E. Alessi, J. T. Coyle, S. I. Harrison, & S. Eth (Eds.), *Handbook of child and adolescent psychiatry* (pp. 31–53). New York: Wiley.

Boyce, W. T., Frank, E., Jensen, P. S., Kessler, R. C., Nelson, C. A., Steinberg, L., et al. (1998). Social context in developmental psychopathology: Recommendations for future research from the MacArthur Network on Psychopathology and Development. *Development and Psychopathology, 10,* 143–164.

Bronfenbrenner, U. (1979). *The ecology of human development: Experiments by nature and design.* Cambridge, MA: Harvard University Press.

Brooks-Gunn, J., Duncan, G. J., & Aber, J. L. (Eds.). (1997). *Neighborhood poverty: Context and consequences for children* (Vol. 1). New York: Russell Sage Foundation.

Cacioppo, J. T., Bernston, G. G., Sheridan, J. F., & McClintock, M. K. (2000). Multilevel integrative analysis of human behavior: Social neuroscience and the complementing nature of social and biological approaches. *Psychological Bulletin, 126,* 829–843.

Cairns, R. B. (1983). The emergence of developmental psychology. In P. Mussen (Ed.), *Handbook of child psychology* (Vol. 1, pp. 41–102). New York: Wiley.

Cairns, R. B. (1990). Developmental epistemology and self-knowledge: Towards a reinterpretation of self-esteem. In G. Greenberg & E. Tobach (Eds.), *Theories of the evolution of knowing: The T. C. Schneirla conference series* (Vol. 4, pp. 69–86). Hillsdale, NJ: Erlbaum.

Cairns, R. B., Cairns, B., Xie, H., Leung, M. C., & Heane, S. (1998). Paths across generations: Academic competence and aggressive behaviors in young mothers and their children. *Developmental Psychology, 34,* 1162–1174.

Cajal, S. R. Y. (1893). New findings about the histological structure of the central nervous system. *Archives for Anatomy and Physiology,* 319–428.

Cajal, S. R. Y. (1937). *Recollections of my life.* Philadelphia: American Philosophical Society.

Canino, G., & Guarnaccia, P. (1997). Methodological challenges in the assessment of Hispanic children and adolescents. *Applied Developmental Science, 1,* 124–134.

Caspi, A., McClay, J., Moffitt, T., Mill, J., Martin, J., Craig, I. W., et al. (2002). Role of genotype in the cycle of violence in maltreated children. *Science, 297,* 851–854.

Caspi, A., Sugden, K., Moffitt, T. E., Taylor, A., Craig, I. W., Harrington, H. L., et al. (2003). Influence of life stress on depression: Moderation by a polymorphism in the 5-HTT gene. *Science, 301,* 386–389.

Chomsky, N. (1968). *Language and mind.* New York: Harcourt Brace.

Ciaranello, R., Aimi, J., Dean, R. S., Morilak, D., Porteus, M. H., & Cicchetti, D. (1995). Fundamentals of molecular neurobiology. In D. Cicchetti & D. J. Cohen (Eds.), *Developmental psychopathology: Theory and method* (Vol. 1, pp. 109–160). New York: Wiley.

Cicchetti, D. (Ed.). (1984a). *Developmental psychopathology.* Chicago: University of Chicago Press.

Cicchetti, D. (1984b). The emergence of developmental psychopathology. *Child Development, 55,* 1–7.

Cicchetti, D. (1987). Developmental psychopathology in infancy: Illustration from the study of maltreated youngsters. *Journal of Consulting and Clinical Psychology, 55,* 837–845.

Cicchetti, D. (Ed.). (1989). *Rochester Symposium on Developmental Psychopathology: The emergence of a discipline* (Vol. 1). Hillsdale, NJ: Erlbaum.

Cicchetti, D. (1990). A historical perspective on the discipline of developmental psychopathology. In J. Rolf, A. Masten, D. Cicchetti, K. Nuechterlein, & S. Weintraub (Eds.), *Risk and protective factors in the development of psychopathology* (pp. 2–28). New York: Cambridge University Press.

Cicchetti, D. (1993). Developmental psychopathology: Reactions, reflections, projections. *Developmental Review, 13,* 471–502.

Cicchetti, D. (1996). Child maltreatment: Implications for developmental theory. *Human Development, 39,* 18–39.

Cicchetti, D. (1999). A developmental psychopathology perspective on drug abuse. In M. D. Glantz & C. R. Hartel (Eds.), *Drug abuse: Origins and interventions* (pp. 97–118). Washington, DC: American Psychological Association.

Cicchetti, D. (2002). How a child builds a brain: Insights from normality and psychopathology. In W. W. Hartup & R. A. Weinberg (Eds.), *Minnesota Symposia on Child Psychology: Vol. 32. Child psychology in retrospect and prospect* (pp. 23–71). Mawah, NJ: Erlbaum.

Cicchetti, D. (2003). Experiments of nature: Contributions to developmental theory. *Development and Psychopathology, 15*(4), 833–1106.

Cicchetti, D., & Aber, J. L. (1986). Early precursors to later depression: An organizational perspective. In L. Lipsitt & C. Rovee-Collier (Eds.), *Advances in infancy* (Vol. 4, pp. 87–137). Norwood, NJ: Ablex.

Cicchetti, D., & Aber, J. L. (Eds.). (1998). Contextualism and developmental psychopathology [Special issue]. *Development and Psychopathology, 10*(2), 137–426.

Cicchetti, D., & Blender, J. A. (2004). A multiple-levels-of-analysis approach to the study of developmental processes in maltreated children. *Proceedings of the National Academy of Sciences, 101*(50), 17325–17326.

Cicchetti, D., & Cannon, T. D. (1999). Neurodevelopmental processes in the ontogenesis and epigenesis of psychopathology. *Development and Psychopathology, 11,* 375–393.

Cicchetti, D., & Cohen, D. J. (Eds.). (1995a). *Developmental psychopathology: Risk, disorder, and adaptation* (Vol. 2). Hoboken, NJ: Wiley.

Cicchetti, D., & Cohen, D. J. (Eds.). (1995b). *Developmental psychopathology: Theory and method* (Vol. 1). Hoboken, NJ: Wiley.

Cicchetti, D., & Cohen, D. J. (Eds.). (1995c). Perspectives on developmental psychopathology. In Ð. Cicchetti & D. J. Cohen (Eds.), *Developmental psychopathology: Theory and method* (Vol. 1, pp. 3–20). Hoboken, NJ: Wiley.

Cicchetti, D., & Dawson, G. (Eds.). (2002). Multiple levels of analysis [Special issue]. *Development and Psychopathology, 14*(3), 417–666.

Cicchetti, D., & Garmezy, N. (Eds.). (1993). Milestones in the development of resilience. *Development and Psychopathology, 5*(4), 497–774.

Cicchetti, D., & Hinshaw, S. P. (Eds.). (2002). Prevention and intervention science: Contributions to developmental theory [Special issue]. *Development and Psychopathology, 14*(4), 667–981.

Cicchetti, D., & Hinshaw, S. P. (Eds.). (2003). Conceptual, methodological, and statistical issues in developmental psychopathology: A special issue in honor of Paul E. Meehl [Special issue]. *Development and Psychopathology, 15*(3), 497–832.

Cicchetti, D., & Lynch, M. (1993). Toward an ecological/transactional model of community violence and child maltreatment: Consequences for children's development. *Psychiatry, 56,* 96–118.

Cicchetti, D., & Pogge-Hesse, P. (1982). Possible contributions of the study of organically retarded persons to developmental theory. In E. Zigler & D. Balla (Eds.), *Mental retardation: The developmental difference controversy* (pp. 277–318). Hillsdale, NJ: Erlbaum.

Cicchetti, D., & Posner, M. I. (in press). Cognitive and affective neuroscience and developmental psychopathology. *Development and Psychopathology, 17*(3).

Cicchetti, D., & Richters, J. E. (Eds.). (1997). Conceptual and scientific underpinnings of research in developmental psychopathology. *Development and Psychopathology, 9*(2), 189–471.

Cicchetti, D., & Rizley, R. (1981). Developmental perspectives on the etiology, intergenerational transmission, and sequelae of child maltreatment. *New Directions for Child Development, 11,* 32–59.

Cicchetti, D., & Rogosch, F. A. (1996). Equifinality and multifinality in developmental psychopathology. *Development and Psychopathology, 8,* 597–600.

Cicchetti, D., & Rogosch, F. A. (1997). The role of self-organization in the promotion of resilience in maltreated children. *Development and Psychopathology, 9,* 799–817.

Cicchetti, D., & Rogosch, F. A. (1999). Psychopathology as risk for adolescent substance use disorders: A developmental psychopathology perspective. *Journal of Clinical Child Psychology, 28,* 355–365.

Cicchetti, D., Rogosch, F. A., Lynch, M., & Holt, K. (1993). Resilience in maltreated children: Processes leading to adaptive outcome. *Development and Psychopathology, 5,* 629–647.

Cicchetti, D., Rogosch, F. A., Maughan, A., Toth, S. L., & Bruce, J. (2003). False belief understanding in maltreated children. *Development and Psychopathology, 15,* 1067–1091.

Cicchetti, D., & Schneider-Rosen, K. (1986). An organizational approach to childhood depression. In M. Rutter, C. Izard, & P. Read (Eds.), *Depression in young people: Clinical and developmental perspectives* (pp. 71–134). New York: Guilford Press.

Cicchetti, D., & Sroufe, L. A. (1976). The relationship between affective and cognitive development in Down's syndrome infants. *Child Development, 47,* 920–929.

Cicchetti, D., & Sroufe, L. A. (1978). An organizational view of affect: Illustration from the study of Down's syndrome infants. In M. Lewis & L. Rosenblum (Eds.), *The development of affect* (pp. 309–350). New York: Plenum Press.

Cicchetti, D., & Sroufe, L. A. (Eds.). (2000). Reflecting on the past and planning for the future of developmental psychopathology [Special issue]. *Development and Psychopathology, 12*(3), 255–550.

Cicchetti, D., & Toth, S. L. (1991). The making of a developmental psychopathologist. In J. Cantor, C. Spiker, & L. Lipsitt (Eds.), *Child behavior and development: Training for diversity* (pp. 34–72). Norwood, NJ: Ablex.

Cicchetti, D., & Toth, S. L. (1992). The role of developmental theory in prevention and intervention. *Development and Psychopathology, 4,* 489–493.

Cicchetti, D., & Toth, S. L. (1997). Transactional ecological systems in developmental psychopathology. In S. S. Luthar, J. Burack, D. Cicchetti, & J. Weisz (Eds.), *Developmental psychopathology: Perspectives on adjustment, risk, and disorder* (pp. 317–349). New York: Cambridge University Press.

Cicchetti, D., & Toth, S. L. (1998). Perspectives on research and practice in developmental psychopathology. In W. Damon (Ed.), *Handbook of child psychology* (5th ed., Vol. 4, pp. 479–583). New York: Wiley.

Cicchetti, D., & Toth, S. L. (Eds.). (1999). *Rochester Symposium on Developmental Psychopathology: Developmental approaches to prevention and intervention* (Vol. 9). Rochester, NY: University of Rochester Press.

Cicchetti, D., & Toth, S. L. (Eds.). (2000). Social policy implications of research in developmental psychopathology [Special issue]. *Development and Psychopathology, 12*(4), 551–885.

Cicchetti, D., & Toth, S. L. (in press a). A developmental psychopathology perspective on preventive interventions with high risk children and families. In A. Renninger and I. Sigel (Eds.), *Handbook of Child Psychology* (6th Ed.). Hoboken, NJ: Wiley.

Cicchetti, D., & Toth, S. L. (in press b). Translational research and developmental psychopathology [Special issue]. *Development and Psychopathology, 18*(3).

Cicchetti, D., & Tucker, D. (1994). Development and self-regulatory structures of the mind. *Development and Psychopathology, 6,* 533–549.

Cicchetti, D., & Walker, E. F. (Eds.). (2001). Stress and development: Biological and psychological consequences [Special issue]. *Development and Psychopathology, 13*(3), 413–753.

Cicchetti, D., & Walker, E. F. (Eds.). (2003). *Neurodevelopmental mechanisms in psychopathology.* New York: Cambridge University Press.

Coie, J. D., Watt, N. F., West, S. G., Hawkins, D., Asarnow, J. R., Markman, H. J., et al. (1993). The science of prevention: A conceptual framework and some directions for a national research program. *American Psychologist, 48,* 1013–1022.

Cook, T. D., & Campbell, D. C. (1979). *Quasi-experimentation: Design and analysis issues for field settings.* Boston: Houghton Mifflin.

Courchesne, E., Townsend, J., & Chase, C. (1995). Neurodevelopmental principles guide research on developmental psychopathologies. In D. Cicchetti & D. J. Cohen (Eds.), *Developmental psychopathology: Theory and methods* (Vol. 1, pp. 195–226). Hoboken, NJ: Wiley.

Cowan, W. M., Harter, D. H., & Kandel, E. R. (2000). The emergence of modern neuroscience: Some implications for neurology and psychiatry. *Annual Review of Neuroscience, 23,* 323–391.

Cowen, E. L. (1991). In pursuit of wellness. *American Psychologist, 46,* 404–408.

Cowen, E. L. (1994). The enhancement of psychological wellness. *American Journal of Community Psychology, 22,* 149–179.

Crick, N. R., & Zahn-Waxler, C. (2003). The development of psychopathology in females and males: Current progress and future challenges. *Development and Psychopathology, 15*(3), 719–742.

Cummings, E. M., Davies, P. T., & Campbell, S. B. (2000). *Developmental psychopathology and family process: Theory, research, and clinical implications.* Notre Dame, IN: University of Notre Dame Press.

Curtis, W. J., & Cicchetti, D. (2003). Moving research on resilience into the 21st century: Theoretical and methodological considerations in examining the biological contributors to resilience. *Development and Psychopathology, 15,* 773–810.

Damasio, H., Grabowski, T., Frank, R., Galaburda, A., & Damasio, A. (1994). The return of Phineas Gage: Clues about the brain from the skull of a famous patient. *Science, 264,* 1102–1105.

Davies, P. T., & Cicchetti, D. (Eds.). (2004). Family systems and developmental psychopathology [Special issue]. *Development and Psychopathology, 16*(3), 477–797.

Eccles, J. S., Lord, S., & Roeser, R. W. (1996). Round holes, square pegs, rocky roads, and sore feet: A discussion of stage-environment fit theory applied to families and school. In D. Cicchetti & S. L. Toth (Eds.), *Rochester Symposium on Developmental Psychopathology: Adolescence—Opportunities and challenges* (Vol. 7, pp. 47–92). Rochester, NY: University of Rochester Press.

Egeland, B., Carlson, E. A., & Sroufe, L. A. (1993). Resilience as process. *Development and Psychopathology, 5,* 517–528.

Eisenberg, L. (1977). Development as a unifying concept in psychiatry. *British Journal of Psychiatry, 131,* 225–237.

Eisenberg, L. (1995). The social construction of the human brain. *American Journal of Psychiatry, 152,* 1563–1575.

Elder, G. H. (1974). *Children of the great depression.* Chicago: University of Chicago Press.

Fishbein, H. (1976). *Evolution, development, and children's learning.* Pacific Palisades, CA: Goodyear.

Flores, E., Cicchetti, D., & Rogosch, F. A. (2005). Predictors of resilience in maltreated and nonmaltreated Latino children. *Developmental Psychology, 41,* 338–351.

Freud, A. (1965). *Normality and pathology in childhood: Assessments of development.* New York: International Universities Press.

Fries, A., & Pollak, S. D. (2004). Emotion understanding in postinstitutionalized Eastern European children. *Development and Psychopathology, 16*(2), 355–369.

Garcia Coll, C. T., Akerman, A., & Cicchetti, D. (2000). Cultural influences on developmental processes and outcomes: Implications for the study of development and psychopathology. *Development and Psychopathology, 12,* 333–356.

Garcia Coll, C. T., Crnic, K., Lamberty, G., Wasik, B., Jenkins, R., Garcia, H., et al. (1996). An integrative model for the study of developmental competencies in minority children. *Child Development, 67,* 1891–1914.

Garcia Coll, C. T., & Vasquez Garcia, H. A. (1996). Definitions of competence during adolescence: Lessons from Puerto Rican adolescent mothers. In D. Cicchetti & S. L. Toth (Eds.), *Rochester Symposium on Developmental Psychopathology: Adolescence—Opportunities and challenges* (Vol. 7, pp. 283–308). Rochester, NY: University of Rochester Press.

Garmezy, N. (1974a). Children at risk: Conceptual models and research methods. *Schizophrenia Bulletin, 9,* 55–125.

Garmezy, N. (1974b). Children at risk: The search for the antecedents of Schizophrenia. *Schizophrenia Bulletin, 8,* 14–90.

Glick, J. A. (1992). Werner's relevance for contemporary developmental psychology. *Developmental Psychology, 28*(4), 558–565.

Glick, M. (1997). The developmental approach to adult psychopathology. In S. S. Luthar, J. A. Burack, D. Cicchetti, & J. R. Weisz (Eds.), *Developmental psychopathology: Perspectives on adjustment, risk, and disorder* (pp. 227–247). New Haven, CT: Yale University Press.

Goldstein, K. (1939). *The organism.* New York: American Book Company.

Good, R. A. (1991). Experiments of nature in the development of modern immunology. *Immunology Today, 12,* 283–286.

Good, R. A., & Zak, S. J. (1956). Disturbances in gamma globulin synthesis as "experiments of-nature." *Pediatrics, 18,* 109–149.

Gottesman, I. I., & Hanson, D. R. (2005). Human development: Biological and genetic processes. *Annual Review of Psychology, 56,* 263–286.

Gottlieb, G. (1991). Experiential canalization of behavioral development: Theory. *Developmental Psychology, 27,* 4–13.

Gottlieb, G. (1992). *Individual development and evolution: The genesis of novel behavior.* New York: Oxford University Press.

Gottlieb, G., & Halpern, C. T. (2002). A relational view of causality in normal and abnormal development. *Development and Psychopathology, 14*(3), 421–436.

Gottlieb, G., Wahlsten, D., & Lickliter, R. (1998). The significance of biology for human development: A developmental psychobiological systems view. In R. Lerner (Ed.), *Handbook of child psychology: Vol. 1. Theoretical models of human development* (pp. 233–273). New York: Wiley.

Granic, I., & Hollenstein, T. (2003). Dynamic systems methods for models of developmental psychopathology. *Development and Psychopathology, 15,* 641–670.

Greenough, W., Black, J., & Wallace, C. (1987). Experience and brain development. *Child Development, 58,* 539–559.

Gunnar, M. R., Morison, S. J., Chisholm, K., & Shchuder, M. (2001). Salivary cortisol levels in children adopted from Romanian orphanages. *Development and Psychopathology, 13,* 611–628.

Hinshaw, S. P. (2002). Prevention/intervention trials and developmental theory: Commentary on the Fast Track Special Section. *Journal of Abnormal Child Psychology, 30,* 53–59.

Hoagwood, K., & Jensen, P. S. (1997). Developmental psychopathology and the notion of culture: Introduction to the special section on "The fusion of cultural horizons: Cultural influences on the assessment of psychopathology in children and adolescents." *Applied Developmental Science, 1,* 108–112.

Inhelder, B. (1943/1968). *The diagnosis of reasoning in the mentally retarded.* New York: John Day.

Institute of Medicine. (1989). *Research on children and adolescents with mental, behavioral, and developmental disorders.* Washington, DC: National Academy Press.

Institute of Medicine. (1994). *Research on children and adolescents with mental, behavioral, and developmental disorders.* Washington, DC: National Academy Press.

Institute of Medicine. (2000). *Bridging disciplines in the brain, behavioral, and clinical sciences.* Washington, DC: National Academy Press.

Jackson, J. H. (1884/1958). Evolution and dissolution of the nervous system. In J. Taylor (Ed.), *The selected writings of John Hughlings Jackson* (Vol. 2, pp. 45–75). New York: Basic Books.

Jensen, P. S., & Hoagwood, K. (1997). The book of names: DSM-IV in context. *Development and Psychopathology, 2,* 231–249.

Jensen, P. S., Koretz, D., Locke, B. Z., Schneider, S., Radke-Yarrow, M., Richters, J. E., et al. (1993). Child and adolescent psychopathology research: Problems and prospects for the 1990s. *Journal of Abnormal Child Psychology, 21*(5), 551–580.

Kandel, E. R. (1979). Psychotherapy and the single synapse. *New England Journal of Medicine, 301,* 1028–1037.

Kandel, E. R. (1998). A new intellectual framework for psychiatry. *American Journal of Psychiatry, 155,* 475–469.

Kandel, E. R. (1999). Biology and the future of psychoanalysis: A new intellectual framework for psychiatry revisited. *American Journal of Psychiatry, 156,* 505–524.

Kaplan, B. (1967). Meditations on genesis. *Human Development, 10,* 65–87.

Karmiloff-Smith, A. (1998). Development itself is the key to understanding developmental disorders. *Trends and Cognitive Science, 2*(10), 389–398.

Kaufman, J., Yang, B., Douglas-Palumberi, H., Houshyar, S., Lipschitz, D., Krystal, J., et al. (2004). Social supports and serotonin transporter gene moderate depression in maltreated children. *Proceedings of the National Academy of Sciences of the United States of America, 101*(49), 17316–17321.

Kazdin, A. E. (1999). Current (lack of) theory in child and adolescent therapy research. *Journal of Clinical Child Psychology, 28,* 533–543.

Kazdin, A. E., Kraemer, H., Kessler, R., Kupfer, D., & Offord, D. (1997). Contributions of risk-factor research to developmental psychopathology. *Clinical Psychology Review, 17,* 375–406.

Kellam, S. G., & Rebok, G. W. (1992). Building developmental and etiological theory through epidemiologically based preventive intervention trials. In J. McCord & R. E. Tremblay (Eds.), *Preventing antisocial behavior: Interventions from birth through adolescence* (pp. 162–195). New York: Guilford Press.

Kim-Cohen, J., Moffitt, T. E., Caspi, A., & Taylor, A. (2004). Genetic and environmental processes in young children's resilience and vulnerability to socioeconomic deprivation. *Child Development, 75*(3), 651–668.

Koretz, D. (1991). Prevention-centered science in mental health. *American Journal of Community Psychology, 19,* 453–458.

Kosslyn, S. M., Cacioppo, J. T., Davidson, R. J., Hugdahl, K., Lovallo, W. R., Spiegal, D., et al. (2002). Bridging psychology and biology: The analysis of individuals in groups. *American Psychologist, 57,* 341–351.

Kraemer, H. C., Kazdin, A. E., Offord, D. R., Kessler, R. C., Jensen, P. S., & Kupfer, D. J. (1997). Coming to terms with the terms of risk. *Archives of General Psychiatry, 54,* 337–343.

Kraemer, H. C., Stice, E., Kazdin, A., Offord, D., & Kupfer, D. (2001). How do risk factors work together? Mediators, moderators, and independent, overlapping, and proxy risk factors. *American Journal of Psychiatry, 158,* 848–856.

Kraemer, H. C., Wilson, G. T., Fairburn, C. G., & Agras, W. S. (2002). Mediators and moderators of treatment effects in randomized clinical trials. *Archives of General Psychiatry, 59,* 877–884.

Kuo, Z. Y. (1939). Studies in the physiology of the embryonic nervous system: IV. Development of acetylcholine in the chick embryo. *Journal of Neurophysiology, 2,* 488–493.

Kuo, Z. Y. (1967). *The dynamics of behavior development.* New York: Random House.

Lander, E. S., & Weinberg, R. A. (2000). Genomics: Journey to the center of biology. *Science, 287,* 1777–1782.

Lenneberg, E. (1967). *Biological foundations of language.* New York: Wiley.

Lewin, B. (2004). *Genes VIII.* Upper Saddle River, NJ: Pearson Education.

Luria, A. R. (1980). *Higher cortical functions in man.* New York: Basic Books. (Original work published 1966)

Luthar, S. S. (1999). *Poverty and children's adjustment.* Thousand Oaks, CA: Sage.

Luthar, S. S. (Ed.). (2003). *Resilience and vulnerability: Adaptation in the context of childhood adversities.* New York: Cambridge University Press.

Luthar, S. S., & Cicchetti, D. (2000). The construct of resilience: Implications for intervention and social policy. *Development and Psychopathology, 12,* 857–885.

Luthar, S. S., Cicchetti, D., & Becker, B. (2000). The construct of resilience: A critical evaluation and guidelines for future work. *Child Development, 71,* 543–562.

Luthar, S. S., & McMahon, T. (1996). Peer reputation among inner city adolescents: Structure and correlates. *Journal of Research on Adolescence, 6,* 581–603.

Lynch, M., & Cicchetti, D. (1998). An ecological-transactional analysis of children and contexts: The longitudinal interplay among child maltreatment, community violence, and children's symptomatology. *Development and Psychopathology, 10,* 235–257.

Masten, A. S. (1989). Resilience in development: Implications of the study of successful adaptation for developmental psychopathology. In D. Cicchetti (Ed.), *Rochester Symposium on Developmental Psychopathology: The emergence of a discipline* (Vol. 1, pp. 261–294). Hillsdale, NJ: Erlbaum.

Masten, A. S. (2001). Ordinary magic: Resilience processes in development. *American Psychologist, 56*(3), 227–238.

Masten, A. S., Best, K., & Garmezy, N. (1990). Resilience and development: Contributions from the study of children who overcome adversity. *Development and Psychopathology, 2,* 425–444.

Masten, A. S., Burt, K. B., Roisman, G. I., Obradovic, J., Long, J. D., & Tellegen, A. (2004). Resources and resilience in the transition to adulthood: Continuity and change. *Development and Psychopathology, 16*(4), 1071–1096.

Mayr, E. (1964). The evolution of living systems. *Proceedings of the National Academy of Sciences, 51,* 934–941.

Mayr, E. (1988). *Toward a new philosophy of biology.* Cambridge, MA: Harvard University Press.

McQuarrie, I. (1944). *The experiments of nature and other essays.* Lawrence: University of Kansas Press.

Meyer, A. (1934). The psychobiological point of view. In M. Bentley & E. Cowdry (Eds.), *The problem of mental disorder* (pp. 51–70). New York: McGraw-Hill.

Meyer, A. (1950). Anatomical lessons from prefrontal leucotomy: A report based on the investigation of 122 brains. *International Congress of Psychiatry, 3,* 107–146.

Meyer, A. (1957). *Psychobiology: A science of man.* Springfield, IL: Charles C. Thomas.

Moffitt, T. E. (1993). Adolescence-limited and life-course-persistent anti-social behavior: A developmental taxonomy. *Psychological Review, 100,* 674–701.

Munoz, R. F., Mrazek, P. J., & Haggerty, R. J. (1996). Institute of Medicine report on prevention of mental disorders. *American Psychologist, 51,* 1116–1122.

National Advisory Mental Health Council. (1990). *National plan for research on child and adolescent mental disorders* (No. 90-1683). Rockville, MD: U.S. Department of Health and Human Services.

National Advisory Mental Health Council on Behavioral Science. (2000). *Translating behavioral science into action: Report of the National Advisory Mental Health Counsel's behavioral science workgroup* (No. 00-4699). Bethesda, MD: National Institutes of Mental Health.

Nelson, C. A., & Bloom, F. E. (1997). Child development and neuroscience. *Child Development, 68,* 970–987.

Noam, G. (1992). Development as the aim of clinical intervention. *Development and Psychopathology, 4,* 679–696.

O'Connor, N., & Hermelin, B. (1978). *Seeing and hearing and space and time.* London: Academic Press.

O'Connor, T. G. (2003). Natural experiments to study the effect of early experience: Progress and limitations. *Development and Psychopathology, 15*(4), 837–852.

O'Connor, T. G., & Rutter, M. (1996). Risk mechanisms in development: Some conceptual and methodological considerations. *Developmental Psychology, 32,* 787–795.

Parke, R. D. (2004). The society for research in child development at 70: Progress and promise. *Child Development, 75*(1), 1–24.

Pellmar, T. C., & Eisenberg, L. (Eds.). (2000). *Bridging disciplines in the brain, behavioral, and clinical sciences.* Washington, DC: National Academy Press.

Plomin, R., & McGuffin, P. (2003). Psychopathology in the postgenomic era. *Annual Review of Psychology, 54,* 205–228.

Plomin, R., & Rutter, M. (1998). Child development, molecular genetics, and what to do with genes once they are found. *Child Development, 69,* 1223–1242.

Posner, M. I., Rothbart, M. K., Farah, M., & Bruer, J. (2001). The developing human brain [Special issue]. *Developmental Science, 4,* 253–287.

Post, R., Weiss, S. R. B., & Leverich, G. S. (1994). Recurrent affective disorder: Roots in developmental neurobiology and illness progression based on changes in gene expression. *Development and Psychopathology, 6,* 781–814.

Post, R., Weiss, S. R. B., Leverich, G. S., George, M., Frye, M., & Ketter, T. (1996). Developmental neurobiology of cyclic affective illness: Implications for early therapeutic interventions. *Development and Psychopathology, 8,* 273–305.

Quinton, D., & Rutter, M. (1988). *Parenting and breakdown: The making and breaking of intergenerational links.* Aldershot, England: Avebury.

Reiss, D., & Price, R. H. (1996). National research agenda for prevention research: The National Institute of Mental Health report. *American Psychologist, 51,* 1109–1115.

Richters, J. E. (1997). The Hubble hypothesis and the developmentalist's dilemma. *Development and Psychopathology, 9,* 193–229.

Richters, J. E., & Cicchetti, D. (1993). Mark Twain meets DSM-III-R: Conduct disorder, development, and the concept of harmful dysfunction. *Development and Psychopathology, 5,* 5–29.

Richters, J. E., & Martinez, P. (1993). Violent communities, family choices, and children's chances: An algorithm for improving the odds. *Development and Psychopathology, 60,* 1068–1075.

Robins, L. (1966). *Deviant children grow up.* Baltimore: Williams & Wilkins.

Robins, L., & Rutter, M. (Eds.). (1990). *Straight and devious pathways from childhood to adulthood.* New York: Cambridge University Press.

Rutter, M. (1980). Introduction. In M. Rutter (Ed.), *Scientific foundations of developmental psychiatry* (pp. 1–8). London: Heinemann Medical.

Rutter, M. (1986). The developmental psychopathology of depression: Issues and perspectives. In M. Rutter, C. Izard, & P. Read (Eds.), *Depression in children: Developmental perspectives* (pp. 3–30). New York: Guilford Press.

Rutter, M. (1988). Epidemiological approaches to developmental psychopathology. *Archives of General Psychiatry, 45,* 486–495.

Rutter, M. (1989). Age as an ambiguous variable in developmental research: Some epidemiological considerations from developmental psychopathology. *International Journal of Behavioral Development, 12,* 1–34.

Rutter, M. (1990). Psychosocial resilience and protective mechanisms. In J. Rolf, A. S. Masten, D. Cicchetti, K. Nuechterlein, & S. Weintraub

(Eds.), *Risk and protective factors in the development of psychopathology* (pp. 181–214). New York: Cambridge University Press.

Rutter, M. (1994). Beyond longitudinal data: Causes, consequences, changes, and continuity. *Journal of Consulting and Clinical Psychology, 62,* 928–940.

Rutter, M. (1996). Developmental psychopathology as an organizing research construct. In D. Magnusson (Ed.), *The lifespan development of individuals: Behavioral, neurobiological, and psychosocial perspectives* (pp. 394–413). New York: Cambridge University Press.

Rutter, M. (2000). Psychosocial influences: Critiques, findings, and research needs. *Development and Psychopathology, 12,* 375–405.

Rutter, M., Dunn, J., Plomin, R., Simonoff, E., Pickles, A., Maughan, B., et al. (1997). Integrating nature and nurture: Implications of person-environment correlations and interactions for developmental psychopathology. *Development and Psychopathology, 9,* 335–364.

Rutter, M., & Garmezy, N. (1983). Developmental psychopathology. In E. M. Hetherington (Ed.), *Handbook of child psychology* (4th ed., Vol. 4, pp. 774–911). New York: Wiley.

Rutter, M., Pickles, A., Murray, R., & Eaves, L. (2001). Testing hypotheses on specific environmental causal effects on behavior. *Psychological Bulletin, 127,* 291–324.

Rutter, M., & Plomin, R. (1997). Opportunities for psychiatry from genetic findings. *British Journal of Psychiatry, 17,* 209–219.

Rutter, M., & Quinton, D. (1984). Parental psychiatric disorder: Effects on children. *Psychological Medicine, 14,* 853–880.

Rutter, M., & Sroufe, L. A. (2000). Developmental psychopathology: Concepts and challenges. *Development and Psychopathology, 12,* 265–296.

Sameroff, A. J. (1983). Developmental systems: Contexts and evolution. In P. Mussen (Ed.), *Handbook of child psychology* (Vol. 1, pp. 237–294). New York: Wiley.

Sameroff, A. J. (2000). Developmental systems and psychopathology. *Development and Psychopathology, 12,* 297–312.

Sameroff, A. J., Seifer, R., Barocas, R., Zax, M., & Greenspan, S. (1987). Intelligence quotient scores of 4 year old children: Social-environmental risk factors. *Pediatrics, 79,* 343–350.

Sanchez, M. M., Ladd, C. O., & Plotsky, P. M. (2001). Early adverse experience as a developmental risk factor for later psychopathology: Evidence from rodent and primate models. *Development and Psychopathology, 13,* 419–450.

Sanna, P. P., & Burton, P. R. (2000). Role of antibodies in controlling viral disease: Lessons from experiments in nature and gene knockouts. *Journal of Virology, 74,* 9813–9817.

Santostefano, S. (1979). *A biodevelopmental approach to clinical child psychology.* New York: Wiley.

Santostefano, S., & Baker, H. (1972). The contribution of developmental psychology. In B. Wolman (Ed.), *Manual of child psychopathology* (pp. 1113–1153). New York: McGraw-Hill.

Scarr, S., & McCartney, K. (1983). How people make their own environments: A theory of genotype-environment effects. *Child Development, 54,* 424–435.

Schulenberg, J., Sameroff, A., & Cicchetti, D. (Eds.). (2004). The transition from adolescence to adulthood. *Development and Psychopathology, 16*(4), 799–1172.

Serafica, F. C. (1997). Psychopathology and resilience in Asian American children and adolescents. *Applied Developmental Science, 1,* 145–155.

Shakow, D. (1967). Understanding normal psychological function: Contributions from Schizophrenia. *Archives of General Psychiatry, 17,* 306–319.

Shonkoff, J. P. (2000). Science, policy, and practice: Three cultures in search of a shared mission. *Child Development, 71,* 181–187.

Shweder, R. A. (1991). *Thinking through cultures: Expeditions in cultural psychology.* Cambridge, England: Cambridge University Press.

Smith, C. I. E. (2000). Experiments of nature: Primary immune defects deciphered and defeated. *Immunological Reviews, 178,* 5–7.

Spemann, H. (1938). *Embryonic development and induction.* New Haven, CT: Yale University Press.

Spencer, H. (1862/1900). *First principles* (6th ed.). New York: Appleton.

Sroufe, L. A. (1979). The coherence of individual development: Early care, attachment, and subsequent developmental issues. *American Psychologist, 34,* 834–841.

Sroufe, L. A. (1983). Infant-caregiver attachment and patterns of adaptation in preschool: The roots of maladaptation and competence. In M. Perlmutter (Ed.), *Minnesota Symposium in Child Psychology* (Vol. 16, pp. 41–83). Hillsdale, NJ: Erlbaum.

Sroufe, L. A. (1989). Pathways to adaptation and maladaptation: Psychopathology as developmental deviation. In D. Cicchetti (Ed.), *Rochester Symposium on Developmental Psychopathology: The emergence of a discipline* (Vol. 1, pp. 13–40). Hillsdale, NJ: Erlbaum.

Sroufe, L. A. (1990). Considering normal and abnormal together: The essence of developmental psychopathology. *Development and Psychopathology, 2,* 335–347.

Sroufe, L. A. (1997). Psychopathology as an outcome of development. *Development and Psychopathology, 9,* 251–268.

Sroufe, L. A., Carlson, E. A., Levy, A. K., & Egeland, B. (1999). Implications of attachment theory for developmental psychopathology. *Development and Psychopathology, 11,* 1–13.

Sroufe, L. A., Egeland, B., & Kreutzer, T. (1990). The fate of early experience following developmental change: Longitudinal approaches to individual adaptation in childhood. *Child Development, 61,* 1363–1373.

Sroufe, L. A., & Jacobvitz, D. (1989). Diverging pathways, developmental transformations, multiple etiologies, and the problem of continuity in development. *Human Development, 32,* 196–203.

Sroufe, L. A., & Rutter, M. (1984). The domain of developmental psychopathology. *Child Development, 55,* 17–29.

Swanson, D. P., Beale-Spencer, M., Harpalani, V., Dupree, D., Noll, E., Ginzburg, S., et al. (2003). Psychosocial development in racially and ethnically diverse youth: Conceptual and methodological challenges in the 21st century. *Development and Psychopathology, 15,* 743–772.

Tizard, B., & Hodges, J. (1978). The effect of early institutional rearing on the development of eight-year-old children. *Journal of Child Psychology and Psychiatry, 19,* 99–118.

Tizard, J., & Tizard, B. (1971). The social development of two-year-old children in residential nurseries. In H. R. Schaffer (Ed.), *The origins of human social relations* (pp. 147–160). London: Academic Press.

Toth, S. L., & Cicchetti, D. (1999). Developmental psychopathology and child psychotherapy. In S. Russ & T. Ollendick (Eds.), *Handbook of psychotherapies with children and families* (pp. 15–44). New York: Plenum Press.

U.S. Department of Health and Human Services. (1999). *Mental health: A report of the surgeon general.* Rockville, MD: Author.

von Bertalanffy, L. (1968). *General system theory.* New York: Braziller.

von Eye, A., & Bergman, L. R. (2003). Research strategies in developmental psychopathology: Dimensional identity and the person-oriented approach. *Development and Psychopathology, 15,* 553–580.

Wachs, T. D., & Plomin, R. (Eds.). (1991). *Conceptualization and measurement of organism-environment interaction.* West Lafayette, IN: Purdue University Press.

Waddington, C. H. (1957). *The strategy of genes.* London: Allen & Unwin.

Wakefield, J. C. (1992). Disorder as harmful dysfunction: A conceptual critique of DSM-III-R's definition of mental disorder. *Psychological Review, 99,* 232–247.

Wakefield, J. C. (1997). When is development disordered? Developmental psychopathology and the harmful dysfunction analysis of mental disorder. *Development and Psychopathology, 9,* 269–290.

Waldman, I. D. (2003). Prospects and problems in the search for genetic influences on neurodevelopment and psychopathology: Application to childhood disruptive disorders. In D. Cicchetti & E. Walker (Eds.), *Neurodevelopmental mechanisms in psychopathology* (pp. 257–292). New York: Cambridge University Press.

Waters, E., & Sroufe, L. A. (1983). Competence as a developmental construct. *Developmental Review, 3,* 79–97.

Watt, N., Anthony, E. J., Wynne, L., & Rolf, J. (Eds.). (1984). *Children at risk for Schizophrenia: A longitudinal perspective.* New York: Cambridge University Press.

Weiss, P. A. (1939). *Principles of development: A text in experimental embryology.* New York: Henry Holt.

Weiss, P. A. (1961). Deformities as cues to understanding development of form. *Perspectives in Biology and Medicine, 4,* 133–151.

Weiss, P. A. (1969). *Principles of development.* New York: Hafner.

Weisz, J. R., Weiss, J., Alicke, B., & Klotz, M. L. (1987). Effectiveness of psychotherapy with children and adolescents: A meta-analysis for clinicians. *Journal of Consulting and Clinical Psychology, 55,* 542–549.

Werner, H. (1948). *Comparative psychology of mental development.* New York: International Universities Press.

Werner, H., & Kaplan, B. (1963). *Symbol formation.* New York: Wiley.

Wilden, A. (1980). *System and structure.* London: Tavistock.

Wolman, B. B. (Ed.). (1972). *Manual of child psychopathology.* New York: McGraw-Hill.

Yoshikawa, H. (1994). Prevention as cumulative protection: Effects of early family support and education on chronic delinquency and its risks. *Psychological Bulletin, 115*(1), 28–54.

Zigler, E. (1998). A place of value for applied and policy studies. *Child Development, 69,* 532–542.

Zigler, E., & Glick, M. (1986). *A developmental approach to adult psychopathology.* New York: Wiley.

Zubin, J., & Spring, B. (1977). Vulnerability: A new view of Schizophrenia. *Journal of Abnormal Psychology, 56,* 103–126.

CHAPTER 2

What's in a Name? Problems versus Prospects in Current Diagnostic Approaches

PETER S. JENSEN, KIMBERLY HOAGWOOD, and LAUREN ZITNER

Dramatic advances have been noted in the past 15 years in our understanding of childhood psychopathology. With the emergence of more tightly defined nosologic and diagnostic systems (e.g., *Diagnostic and Statistical Manual of Mental Disorders III, DSM-III-R,* and *DSM-IV,* American Psychiatric Association, 1980, 1987, 1994), we have seen the advent of large epidemiologic studies focused on describing risk factors and the prevalence of child psychopathology (e.g., see Costello et al., 1996; Flisher et al., 2000; Friedman, Katz-Leavy, Manderscheid, & Sondheimer, 1998; Goodman et al., 1998; Huffman, Mehlinger, & Kerivan, 2000; Shaffer et al., 1996), with most of these studies documenting overall ratings of moderate to severely impairing forms of psychopathology ranging from 3% to 22%. Although these widely diverging rates appear to cast significant doubt on how well our nosologic systems are actually working, most investigators in the field have concluded that these variations in rates are due principally to differences in methods in combining and weighting data from different sources and to variations in the level of impairment required before something should be deemed a disorder (Boyle et al., 1996; Regier et al., 1998).

Thus, the field has largely converged around similar conclusions supporting the descriptive manifestations of various forms of childhood psychopathology, as well as the importance of requirements of impairment, in order for the formal diagnosis of a mental disorder to be made. Likewise, the field has largely agreed that rates will vary as a function of the degree of impairment required for "caseness," and that these distinctions and determinations are largely set by policy and service availability considerations, rather than actual differences in children from sample to sample or any fundamental disagreements about the symptoms of psychopathology (Shaffer et al., 1996).

Longitudinal studies have also been essential, in that they have demonstrated both that many forms of psychopathology persist over childhood into adulthood, and that in many instances, psychopathology is often not stable; that is, many children with apparently severe conditions may no longer meet such criteria at later age points, just as presumably healthy children may develop significant mental health problems at later ages (Bennett et al., 1999; Bennett, Lipman, Racine, & Offord, 1998; Bennett & Offord, 2001; Loeber,

Stouthamer-Loeber, & White, 1999). These studies have been exceptionally important, because they serve as a two-edged reminder that (1) these conditions can have severe and prolonged impact many years later and hence need to be taken seriously; that is, they are not "just a stage"; and (2) the initial diagnoses of at least some forms of mental disorder or psychopathology in children and adolescents should be viewed cautiously, to the extent that children, their brains, and their larger environments can change, so that possibilities for amelioration and perhaps even "cure" should not be foreclosed.

The development of more reliable diagnostic systems and measures has also spawned a great deal of research into effective psychosocial and psychopharmacologic intervention methods for persons suffering from these conditions. Beginning in the early and mid-1990s, a host of large-scale prevention and intervention trials were begun, with many now successfully completed. Both in children and adults, these many empirical studies generated important findings about "what works" for the various mental disorders that have been studied; further, they have led to a call for implementing evidence-based practices (EBPs) in the real world (Office of the Surgeon General, 1999). This outcome, arguably, is one of the distal impacts of our embracing and implementing a more descriptive, atheoretical, and easily operationalized diagnostic system.

ALL IS NOT AS IT SEEMS: PROBLEMS BELOW THE SURFACE

Despite these advances in diagnosis and treatment, a number of particularly thorny difficulties have remained incompletely addressed, adding an air of disquietude to the otherwise seemingly certain sense of progress. For example, the current diagnostic systems often do not exactly fit many real-world patients, and patients often have symptom constellations that cross multiple diagnostic categories but rest securely in none. Many times, such persons may show evidence of substantial impairment, suggesting that they have a clear clinical need for some type of intervention, but our classificatory system somehow misses them (Angold, Costello, Farmer, Burns, & Erkanli, 1999). Other patients, perhaps the majority, who *do* meet criteria for a *DSM* disorder actually have more than one, often two or three, regardless of whether they are found in epidemiologic studies or clinical settings. Unfortunately, the many combinatory patterns of diagnostic profiles undermine the credibility and swamp the usefulness of the classification system.

Imagine if we had a system for classifying common respiratory illnesses, with over 100 of these illnesses presumably relatively common, and that most people with such illnesses usually had two or more. If we were to try to study such respiratory illnesses, studying them in pure form would omit most patients with bona fide illness, and attempting to study them in their more complex presentation would at some point surely overtax our ability to group, classify, and make sense of what we think we see. Or consider the physician who, after taking a careful history, learns of a patient's 1-week history of watery eyes, cough, loss of appetite and nausea, stomach cramping and diarrhea, general fatigue, and sore joints and muscles. The physician then examines the patient and finds a mildly elevated temperature (101 degrees), somewhat dry mucous membranes in the nose and mouth, and hyperactive bowel sounds, but no evidence of abdominal tenderness or swelling, and a mildly elevated pulse with a low normal blood pressure. Rather than assume the patient has 12 to 13 different syndromes (based on the total count of the signs and symptoms described, most physicians might make a *single diagnosis* [flu], perhaps complicated by slight dehydration, especially if this occurs during a particular time of the year). Knowing any one of the symptoms thoroughly would not be as informative as understanding the overall pattern and underlying illness process. Such a global understanding of the patterns and processes is especially important if one wishes to make meaningful predictions about the course of this constellation of symptoms, or to make sensible recommendations about what should be done (bed rest, hydration, light and nutritious meals, and time). Interestingly, the sore joints presenting without the other symptoms might be suggestive of an altogether different process (previous injury, overexercise, arthritis, or even lupus).

It is in our understanding of the underlying illness process, the overall patterning of the signs and symptoms, and the history and context of the symptoms that enables distinctions to be made between a flu syndrome and an exercise injury. But, as is the case in childhood mental health problems, what should we do if our major symptom profile descriptions and common categories result in 10 or more major groups (e.g., anxiety disorders, Obsessive Compulsive Disorder, Major Depression, Bipolar Disorder, Attention-Deficit/Hyperactivity Disorder, Conduct Disorder, Oppositional Defiant Disorder, Tourette's syndrome, Autism, other developmental disorders, and substance use disorders), any of which might commonly co-occur, generating 2^{10} (1,024) possible different patterns, particularly when issues of history, context, and contributing/exacerbating factors are generally not considered as a part of the taxonomic approach? How can we be sure that we are forming sensible clusters of symptom patterns that seem to hang together?

Concerns about our classification approaches are not limited to the child psychopathology field alone. Reservations have been raised about the overly descriptive nature of the various versions of *DSM* that do not take into account the effects of various etiologic and contextual factors readily discerned by experienced clinicians. Instead, currently observable behaviors are highlighted, and these taxonomic models of psychopathology generally do not consider the possibility that "psychopathology" in some instances may reflect the attempts of the organism to adapt to the broader environmental context. Moreover, these concepts of psychopathology assume a relatively stable deficit *within the individual* (American Psychiatric Association, 1994). Perhaps most important, these diagnostic approaches have been appropriately criticized on the grounds of both over- and underinclusiveness, the potential for misdiagnosis and misuse, and credibility (Richters & Cicchetti, 1993; Wakefield, 1992a, 1992b). Compounding all of these difficulties is the fact that revisions often have occurred before sufficient research documenting the usefulness and validity of the categories outlined in previous versions had been conducted.

The purposes of this chapter are to (1) briefly review the purposes of diagnostic and classification systems in general; (2) review the merits and constraints of the current *DSM* classification system that relies on a descriptive symptom-based approach, examining the benefits and hazards afforded by these classification and diagnostic strategies; (3) outline alternative approaches that take fuller advantage of other forms of clinical data; and (4) make recommendations for the next generation of classification systems, both in terms of the nature of these systems as well as the programs of research that will be needed to expand our knowledge of psychopathology and mental disorders.

PURPOSES OF CLASSIFICATION AND DIAGNOSIS

Why classify? And why is classification important in science? The simple answer is that classification renders induction possible. For science to occur, there must be groupings of phenomena, and these groupings must be structured in such a way as to render reliable the generalizations established in connection with observations (Pratt & Foucault, 1977). In fact, it can be argued that there can be no science without classification (Wallace, 1994). Yet, selection and construction of nosologic systems involves decisions. Such systems do not arise naturally but are imposed on nature through decisions of inclusion and exclusion. Foucault (1970) noted that taxonomies are not part of any effort to "look harder and more closely" at things but, rather, "to restrict deliberately the area of its experience"—that is, to reduce the observer's awareness by censoring out large ranges of a given object's features. The implication of this is that taxonomies are not objective legitimizations of the "true nature" or division of things, because any nosologic system presupposes certain human-made decisions and methodologies (Dupre, 1993; Sadler, Wiggins, & Schwartz, 1994).

A brief look at the history of biological classification systems offers instructive lessons in the prevailing ideas about science and its relationship to objects of study. Numerical taxonomy arose in part from the work of the French natural historian Adanson, who, in 1763, recommended that any classification of items should be based on overall similarity, developed by attention to describing the external features of the objects in question. The outward visible form was the defining aspect of any description and was thought to constitute a supraordinate connection across disparate phenomena.

In the post-Newtonian period, the basis of taxonomy changed. The idea arose that things had internal structures, not just outwardly observable characteristics, and that these structures were not visible but invisible, internalized *essences*. Drawing in part on the thinking of Aristotle and Plato, essentialism was adopted by biologists in the seventeenth and eighteenth centuries and applied to the concept of species. Species' essence became a causal mechanism that operated on any given member of a species and constituted the essence of what that species was. With the advent of Cuvier's (1835) work on comparative anatomy, living things were seen as dynamic systems, and analysis of systems required understanding of the function of each part. Cuvier referred to the idea of functional organization in terms of "archetypes" or plans, according to which the organisms were constructed. Only after Darwin did a more thoroughgoing theory of classification based on cladistics make understanding of evolutionary relationships possible (Pratt & Foucault, 1977). The concept of an archetype became isomorphic with the concept of common ancestry, and groupings according to evolutionary relationships became possible. It is interesting to note that classification systems in psychiatry have not invoked the explanatory power that evolutionary theory enables, yet it may now be possible to construct a psychiatric classification system that embodies the workings of evolution (e.g., see Jensen et al., 1997; Leckman & Mayes, 1998; Marks & Nesse, 1994; Nettle, 2004).

The transformation of taxonomies from outwardly visible descriptions, to essentialist notions of invisible structures, to evolutionary adaptive relations implies that the kinds of questions about objects being classified need modification. It is no longer appropriate to simply ask of an object, What is the natural kind to which it belongs? (an *essentialist* question). Rather, we should ask, What is the goal underlying the intent to classify the object? (Dupre, 1993; Popper, 1994).

In this context, it is instructive to note the purposes to which classification systems have been put. Feinstein (1972) noted that classification serves three principal functions: denomination (assigning a common name to a group of phenomena), qualification (enhancing the usefulness of the name or category by adding pertinent descriptive features such as characteristic signs, symptoms, age of onset), and prediction (probabilistic statements about the clinical course, outcome, response to treatment, etc.). The typical standard that has promoted the longevity of most classification systems is their *usefulness.* However, any system may have multiple purposes, and these purposes do not necessarily converge. Thus, a given classification system designed to serve scientific purposes might be purposively narrow, avoiding false positives and overinclusiveness, with the goal of determining common etiologies and an array of specific treatments. On the other hand, such a system may do a disservice to persons who are suffering from a similar symptom profile, yet who could be excluded from treatment or services if they do not fit the narrower profile more appropriate for certain research purposes. Thus, a system designed to identify persons in need of public services may be quite broad (witness the broad categories used in the Department of Education's determination of a child's eligibility for special education services), even though heterogeneous etiologies may be embedded in the descriptive profile (Eisenberg, 1995).

BENEFITS OF PSYCHIATRIC DIAGNOSIS

Increased Diagnostic Reliability

The more modern versions of the *DSM,* from *DSM-III* on, were developed principally to first solve the problem of unreliability in diagnoses. As a consequence, clearly operationalized lists of symptom criteria were developed for disorders that psychiatrists and other mental health professionals found to characterize similar clusters of patients seen in practice. Prior to that point, a number of studies had demonstrated that psychiatric diagnoses among different experts rarely achieved agreement greater than 20% to 30%. Given clinicians' difficulties in coming to agreement on the nature of the difficulties of a given patient, the re-

cent *DSM* systems (from *DSM-III* forward) were meant to offer a clean break from the theory-burdened, nonempirical diagnostic practices of the past. At the very least, these systems were meant to be reliable, with the goal that over time, scientists and classificationists would work toward more etiologically based systems. The history of knowledge development in the medical sciences has often been characterized as moving from descriptive models of understanding illnesses and syndromes to a better knowledge of underlying pathophysiology (though this level of understanding has yet to be achieved in many areas of clinical medicine; Eisenberg, 1995). According to this view, just as in other areas of medicine, a symptomatic stage of classification is a necessary precursor to the development of empirically demonstrated etiologic theories (Sadler, Wiggins, & Schwartz, 1994).

Increased Scientific Communication and Accelerated Scientific Discovery

With the goal of eventually identifying empirically based etiologic underpinnings of mental disorders, recent *DSM* developers made an explicit attempt to move beyond expert consensus that characterized earlier *DSM* versions and to rely instead on empirical documentation via extensive field trials and reanalyses of existing data sets. Particularly in *DSM-IV,* such data were used to determine the inclusion/exclusion of specific diagnostic criteria, diagnostic thresholds, and required levels of impairment (e.g., see Lahey et al., 1994). In addition, higher thresholds were established for making revisions; greater attention was paid to the needs of users in the fields of education, research, and clinical practice; and increased breadth and quality of the field's participation was sought in developing the revision by establishing multiple workgroups, each with 50 to 100 advisors and participants. Other attempts to move the *DSM* classification system forward included the abandonment of hierarchical assumptions (beginning first with *DSM-III-R*) and the explicit attempt to be atheoretical by avoiding clinical or etiologic inferences, relying instead on readily described, easily observed (or reported) behavioral, cognitive, and emotional symptoms (Frances, Pincus, Widiger, Davis, & First, 1994)—as if such an approach were atheoretical!

Nonetheless, the advent of more scientifically replicable diagnostic systems and assessment measures also led to new activities not previously seen in the children's mental health field: large-scale federally sponsored clinical trials testing various interventions with children or adolescents meeting specific diagnostic criteria. These include the National

Institute of Mental Health Multi-Modal Treatment Study of ADHD (MTA Cooperative Group, 1999), studies of the various Research Units on Pediatric Psychopharmacology (McDougle et al., 2002; Research Units on Pediatric Psychopharmacology Anxiety Study Group, 2002), the Treatment of Adolescent Depression Study Team (2004), and a bevy of industry-sponsored studies (see Pappadopulos, Guelzow, Wong, Ortega, & Jensen, 2004, for a review). Paralleling these pharmacologic studies are many studies testing the efficacy of specific forms of psychotherapy for various conditions, ranging from Major Depression (Brent et al., 1997; Clarke et al., 2002) to anxiety disorders (Silverman, Kurtines, Ginsburg, Weems, Rabian, et al., 1999), OCD (Franklin, Foa, & March, 2003), Conduct Disorder (Kazdin & Whitley, 2003), and Oppositional Defiant Disorder (Hood & Eyberg, 2003; Webster-Stratton, Reid, & Hammond, 2004).

These many empirical studies have increasingly led to a call for the need to implement EBPs, with the a priori assumption that unless proven otherwise, childhood conditions when manifest should be treated by one of the EBPs, with the concomitant implication that funding of practices that are not evidence based be withheld. Thus, one might argue that for good or ill, the distal end of this process of unification of the scientific field in favor of a particular nosology and diagnostic system has led to changes beyond scientific arenas into societal practices, including changes in policies about how taxpayer dollars are spent.

CONSTRAINTS OF CURRENT SYSTEMS

Increased Reliability, but at What Cost?

Although the recent diagnostic systems have achieved reliability when tested in formal research settings, concerns have been raised that excessive emphasis on test-retest and interrater reliability runs the risk of generating unicausal or theoretically impoverished models of psychopathology, simply because classes of information that are more important yet more difficult to operationalize and assess reliably tend to be eliminated from scientific consideration. For example, symptom-only descriptive approaches may fail to take into account the effects of various etiologic factors, experience, and developmental history on individuals' current functioning, as well as other contextual factors more readily discerned by experienced clinicians (Perry, Cooper, & Michels, 1987; Rutter & Shaffer, 1980; Vaillant, 1984). Interviewing patients for reliably reported signs and symptoms of disorders necessarily omits por-

tions of clinical reality, such as information pertaining to contextual, interactional, and/or historical factors that may have contributed to the development of the condition. Observable behaviors are highlighted, as if divorced from meaning and motivation, and inconvenient or difficult classes of information are eliminated or, at best, truncated (Trickett, 1996; Wallace, 1994). These taxonomic models of psychopathology generally do not consider the possibility that psychopathology in some instances may actually reflect the attempts of the organism to adapt to the broader environmental context. Failing to take such issues into consideration could redirect clinicians' (or society's) intervention efforts to what would be principally seen as "helping disturbed individuals" rather than addressing problematic environments.

Categorical Distinctions versus Dimensional Characteristics?

A major conceptual consideration underpinning determination of mental disorder depends on whether one considers that the underlying construct is a true category, qualitatively different from other disordered as well as normal states, or whether in fact caseness simply reflects difficulties in functioning at the extreme end of a continuum. Although most psychiatric disorders, child and adult alike, can be shown to be quantitatively different from "normal" states, such differences do not necessarily reflect qualitative differences. Large differences between two groups on a number of markers do not necessarily make them different *in kind,* any more than concluding that tall persons and short persons are qualitatively different, or that there appears to be a "tall syndrome"—weighing a lot, having long fingers, and wearing big hats. Finding both quantitative and qualitative differences among persons with and without a particular definition of mental disorder *might* constitute a partial argument in support of that particular definition of mental disorder, but two different kinds, even when such can be identified, may have the same final common pathway, in terms of the observable phenomenology, just as two cases of the same kind may have very different outcomes, making the sole use of qualitative distinctions as an indicator of mental disorder problematic (Andreasen & Glick, 1988). To return to the model of height, it is not being short or tall alone that makes someone "pathologically" tall versus normally tall. It may be other associated factors, such as the presence of a disturbance in the endocrine system or bone metabolism (Eisenberg, 1995).

If one asks whether the current *DSM* "carve[s] nature at its joints," the research literature principally answers in the negative. For example, in a study of the diagnostic criteria for depression using a sample of monozygotic and dizygotic twins, Kendler and Gardner (1998) examined the diagnostic criteria for number of symptoms, severity, and duration, finding that number of symptoms and severity (but not duration) predicted increased likelihood of subsequent episodes in the index case and the twin. However, there was no natural cut point at four symptoms: Even persons with fewer than five symptoms, as well as having less severe symptoms (below the diagnostic threshold) were at greater risk for subsequent episodes of depression, both in the index case and the twin. These findings suggested that even subthreshold depressive symptoms reveal the same underlying diathesis. In addition, no support was found for the requirement of 2 weeks' duration or some threshold of clinical severity. Thus, Major Depressive Disorder appeared to be a diagnostic convention imposed on a continuum of depressive symptoms of varying severity, impairment, and duration. Similar results have been found in the area of genetic studies of ADHD, where heritability analyses of full-syndrome versus subthreshold symptom states suggested that the condition likely reflected a continuum versus an all-or-none, present-absent psychopathological state (Levy, Hay, McStephen, Wood, & Waldman, 1997; Rasmussen et al., 2002), and analyses of the age-of-onset criterion fail to make important distinctions in course, outcome, and response to treatment (Barkley & Biederman, 1997).

At present, there is little evidence to indicate *natural* dichotomies between cases and noncases in most of our categories of child and adolescent psychopathology, perhaps with Autism and childhood-onset Schizophrenia being two exceptions. This has led many scholars to advocate *dimensional* approaches to the definition and assessment of child and adolescent psychopathology rather than *categorical* diagnostic approaches. Yet, both clinical practice and policymaking often require dichotomous decisions about the mental health of youths. Clinicians must make dichotomous decisions to treat or withhold treatment on a daily basis; researchers seek to classify the phenotypes of psychopathology to conduct genetic studies; and policymakers often engage in activities such as counting the number of youths who need mental health services but have not received them. Thus, there is a tension between the need for categorical definitions of mental disorder for many important purposes and the lack of evidence to support such dichotomous categorizations.

Conceptual Problems with Mental Disorder Construct

These recent strategies to address some of the difficulties of the *DSM* taxonomies may have been useful and appear to

have led to research advances and attempts to apply research findings to real-world practices. However, no nosologic approach, whether *DSM, International Classification of Diseases 10,* or various dimensional systems for measuring psychopathology (e.g., see Achenbach, 1993, 1995) has adequately addressed the thorny construct of "mental disorder." Frances (1994), the leader of the *DSM-IV* effort, stated that "there could not be any worse term than 'mental disorder,'" yet he noted that other terms were even more unsatisfactory. Because the *DSM*s are meant to be a "way station" en route to more valid approaches, he cautioned investigators and clinicians not to reify the diagnoses and taxonomic system. Even the term "mental disorder" implies a mind-body dichotomy that is outmoded and not embraced by most present-day basic neuroscientists and developmental neurobiologists (Black, Sirevaag, Wallace, Savin, & Greenough, 1989; Greenough & Black, 1992; Nelson & Bloom, 1997; Strumwasser, 1994). Most likely, there is no hard and fast line between so-called biological and sociocultural factors in health, normality, and disease (Eisenberg, 1995), and few (if any) of the so-called mental disorders can be conceptualized purely at a molar or individual organismic level. Thus, if one were to simplify our understanding of tuberculosis as a biologic infectious disease in some individuals but not others, such a conceptual framework might lead one to a very different set of interventions (pharmacotherapeutics) than if one were to approach the problem from a public health perspective, guided by the knowledge that many persons are exposed to the tubercle bacillus but never develop active illness, unless accompanied by socioeconomic and environmental factors such as poverty, crowding, and other, as yet unidentified factors. Thus, for many mental health problems, it takes understanding of the person *and* his or her current environment to understand the disorder or disease. This applies not only to mental disorders, but also to many other complex illnesses, such as hypertension, diabetes, heart disease, immune diseases, and cancer (Margolis, 1994).

What complicates our definition of mental disorder is that our understanding of individuals' behavioral and emotional symptoms often depends on and is constituted by the person's culture, psychosocial and biologic history, and environment. Such complexity appears to fly in the face of traditional approaches to disease and disorder classification. For example, Syndenham characterized disease this way:

> Nature, in the production of disease, is uniform and consistent; so much so, that for the same disease in different persons the symptoms are for the most part the same; and the self-same phenomena that you would observe in the sickness

of a Socrates you would observe in the sickness of a simpleton. (quoted in Wiggins & Schwartz, 1994)

This principle may be somewhat true of many aspects of diseases such as pneumococcal pneumonia; it may be less applicable to diseases of the mind and brain. For example, cultural factors play an important role in determining when a symptom is a symptom, what constitutes impairment, and which cases need treatment. Rogler (1993) noted that a fine-grained analysis of psychotic symptoms with highly structured diagnostic instruments is difficult to make without knowledge of the culture's social values and traditions.

Even when question items are appropriately translated, the language and culture may use constructs that do not map neatly onto the *DSM*. For example, Manson (1995) noted that one item from the Diagnostic Interview Schedule that combined guilt, shame, and sinfulness required three different questions in the Hopi language to avoid confounding different items and meanings. Rogler notes that the configuring of symptoms into disorders may require changes from culture to culture, yet few studies have taken these issues fully into account. By way of exception, Canino et al. (1987), in implementing an epidemiologic survey of Puerto Rico, not only conducted tests to ascertain the reliability and validity of the diagnostic instruments, but added new items as needed and changed algorithms for various disorders in Puerto Rico. As a consequence of these changes, they found 66% lower disorder rates of Obsessive-Compulsive Disorder versus the unadjusted diagnostic algorithms. In contrast, dysthymia was 60% higher (Rogler, 1993) when adjusting for cultural factors.

Kleinman (1977) noted that it is fallacious to assume that mental illness is an "entity, a thing to be discovered in pure form by stripping away the layers of cultural camouflage. . . . There can be no stripping away of layers of cultural accretion in order to isolate a culture-free entity." The differential impact of disease processes on the brain (versus other bodily organs) is due in part to the brain's high degree of evolved plasticity, malleable throughout life by virtue of learning and sculpting processes occurring at the level of individual dendritic spines, cells, synapses, and neuronal circuits (Greenough & Black, 1992; Nelson & Bloom, 1997). Culture and context structure many, if not all, aspects of mental illness: A given person's subjective experience is culturally shaped, as are the meanings he or she ascribes to symptoms, as is the phenomenon of having a mental disorder itself, and ultimately, even the classification systems by which different groups of persons are classified (or diagnosed).

Is the Disorder within the Individual?

Viewed through the lens of developmental psychopathology, one must ask whether a given disorder need be conceptualized as "within the person" or even "mental" per se. Indeed, some anthropologists have noted that the interiorized sense of self—the psychological human versus his or her society and environment—is a relatively recent phenomenon, mostly of Western and industrialized society. Western-raised ethnologists who have studied and lived in communal societies have described their own loss of the sense of the individual self in these societies (Shweder & Bourne, 1991; Wallace, 1994). With a greater focus on the larger social context, it is quite plausible to suggest that families, communities, or society at large are "dysfunctional" (e.g., Fromm, 1955). The notion of a disorder being only *in the person* belies an individualistic metaphysic: namely, that minds reside in brains, but that minds, and subsequently mental disorders, do not reside in the social world. This is an implausible and logically unsustainable tenet (Sadler & Hulgus, 1994; Shweder & Bourne, 1991; Trickett, 1996). Instead, minds, as well as all mental disorders, reside in communities, neighborhoods, and families, facts that have great significance for and guide the activities of most clinicians.

If one conceptualizes the disorder as something that does not necessarily lie inside the skin of an individual, but may in some instances reside in the transactions between the individual and the environment, an entirely different set of measurement and assessment demands are imposed on the investigator. Meaningful outcomes can no longer be captured by an exclusive focus on signs and symptoms. Instead, adaptive functioning, the nature of the surrounding environment, and the relationship between organism and environment become critical areas for assessment, perhaps even central for understanding of a given disorder. In fact, it seems plausible that understanding of individual organismic functioning may be more explanatory and more fully addressable in terms of prediction *if* the larger context is assessed. The study of simple descriptive phenomena characterizing a given individual thus gives way to a relational understanding of the processes occurring between the individual and his or her environment.

To employ two simple illustrations: The study of the ebb and flow of the tides, though interesting and describable in great detail, will remain poorly understood if one fails to appreciate the relationship between the tides and the respective positions of the earth and the moon. Similarly, young infants' social-emotional behaviors, though interesting descriptively, become more understandable when the child's affective state is understood as a function of the relationship with and proximity to the child's attachment figure. Once the functional processes and adaptive tasks that are facilitated by the child's proximity to and relationship with the caregiving parent are understood, better prediction of the child's affective state becomes possible, and new hypotheses follow from this fuller appreciation. This example illustrates the essential criterion whereby any new model can be judged: whether the new model offers increased ability to generate more accurate predictions about current and future behavior.

Thus, understanding the broad range of children's adaptive outcomes as a function of their environments is necessary to fully appreciate the terms "functioning," "functional processes," and "outcomes." Hoagwood, Jensen, Petti, and Burns (1996) have outlined a conceptual model (the SFCES model, denoting "symptoms," "functioning," "consumer-oriented," "environmental," and "systems/services") to guide the assessment of children within their environments across a range of outcomes. According to the SFCES model, symptomatic and diagnostic variables constitute an insufficient basis to characterize children's mental health outcomes. Adequate understanding becomes possible only to the extent that cognitive and social functioning; peer and family relationships; the nature of the child's school, neighborhood, and home environments; and cultural and societal contexts are also assessed and understood. Fuller understanding is realizable when these variables are characterized not just cross-sectionally but as a series of embedded, evolving, and dynamic transactions between the child, parents, family, neighborhood, school, and larger societal and cultural contexts *over time* (Boyce et al., 1998). Likewise, measurement of *processes* and reciprocal transactions between the organism and his or her environment and the potential adaptive (versus maladaptive) nature of the child's symptoms with respect to his or her environment is central to the understanding of mental disorders. Once understood, some such disorders might be better characterized as behavioral, emotional, transactional, or environmental, rather than as simply mental.

Can the *Diagnostic and Statistical Manual* (or Any Classification System) Be Atheoretical?

Sadler, Wiggins, and Schwartz (1994) have argued cogently that no diagnostic system can be truly atheoretical, because all observational statements are influenced by theoretical presuppositions. Likewise, this century's most re-

spected philosophers of science have suggested that it is impossible for any basic natural science, much less the clinical sciences, to be "value free" (Popper, 1994; Wallace, 1994). Any classificatory system is heavily influenced by the values, aims, and theories of the classifiers (Frances et al., 1994; Sadler, Wiggins, & Schwartz, 1994). The current *DSM* and other *DSM*-like approaches, by virtue of operationalizing criteria based on the presence of observable or reportable symptoms of individuals, by default imply that some kinds of clinical data are nosologically irrelevant. Consequently, Sadler and Hulgus (1994) argue that because the current *DSM* systems do not always fully account for and specify the relevance of interactional data, they fit the needs of a biologic psychiatry much better than family-interactional, sociologic, developmental, or life history models of disorder. Frances and colleagues explicitly acknowledge this limitation, noting that although *DSM-IV* "attempts" to be atheoretical, no frame of reference can be without theory, and they suggest that *DSM*'s descriptive approach could possibly be more useful within behavioral and biologic orientations. On the other hand, although *DSM-IV* does not preclude other axes that might incorporate such data, integration of these perspectives into the *DSM* system is not likely to occur in the near future, in part because of the conceptual and methodological complexities that such an expansion of the classification system would entail.

Definitional Problems with Core Clinical Constructs

Upon close inspection, many terms in the *DSM* presuppose clinical determinations based on subjective judgments and norms within a given societal context. As a result, some experts have concluded that the presence of the diagnostic criteria alone are insufficient grounds for determining "when a case is a case" (Boyle et al., 1996). Many terms that are taken for granted (e.g., disorder, disturbance, failure, dysfunction, distortion, subaverage, deficit) are heavily value laden, subject to varying interpretations and idiosyncratic clinical practices. Further, the clinical norms on which such terms are based are subject to shifting values and changing societal inputs over time (Margolis, 1994). Remarkably, even core clinical constructs, such as "clinically significant impairment," are tautological (Fulford, 1994); that is, "clinically significant impairment" is the type of impairment that an experienced clinician recognizes and feels is severe enough to warrant treatment! Unless logically disentangled and recognized for what they are, such tautologies can masquerade as, or even interfere with, the accumulation of knowledge.

Even when one determines the presence or absence of symptoms using the most rigorous methods, such as face-to-face diagnostic interviews, variations in mental disorder definitions are marked, based on ancillary determinations that are not necessarily part of the *DSM* criteria. And these variations affect mental health service need and use. For example, Angold et al. (1999) examined the impact of various definitions of *impairment* on rates of serious emotional disturbance, after first requiring that all children considered met all *DSM* symptomatic criteria. Using five different definitions of impairment in their study, Angold and colleagues compared children with neither impairment nor a diagnosis, those with no full-blown disorder but with impairment, those with disorder but no impairment, and those with both disorder and impairment. Even among those who met both symptom and more stringent impairment criteria, only 59% reported "need for services," and fewer still (19%) of those meeting diagnostic criteria with levels of impairment as specified within the *DSM* criteria reported any need for services. Even with the most stringent impairment criteria, 66% of those with a defined serious emotional disturbance were not being served.

ALTERNATIVE APPROACHES

Given these problems, many authors have explored alternative approaches to conceptualizing mental health and illness. We describe some of the leading candidates below.

Harmful Dysfunction

Wakefield (1992a, 1992b) has noted that the philosophical underpinnings of the *DSM*'s accounts of disorder are structurally flawed and has argued that other accounts, such as "harmful dysfunction," better describe a valid, conceptually sound construct of disorder that has the dual requirements of some sort of biologic dysfunction and cultural and contextual appraisal (see Kirk & Hsieh, 2004; Wakefield, Pottick, & Kirk, 2002) of impairment ("harm") to warrant the determination of "true" mental disorder status. Both components (harm *and* dysfunction) must be addressed to identify a mental disorder. This approach appears promising, but it is still problematic to the extent that, for most mental disorders, it has not been possible to identify a biologic dysfunction within individuals, even in those with severely impairing conditions where evidence for genetic factors is indisputable (e.g., Autism). In addition, the defi-

nition suffers from the tautological definition of dysfunction as a "biologic system not behaving as it was designed to do" (from an evolutionary perspective), and such definitions invoke anachronistic notions of some hard and fast lines between so-called biologic and sociocultural factors (Nelson & Bloom, 1997; Wallace, 1994).

The similarity between Wakefield's concept of an "internal mechanism gone awry" and the pre-Darwinian (Cuvier, 1835) notion of the function of parts is notable. The same problems that applied to those earlier conceptualizations of classification may apply here. Nonetheless, in the same way that a more complete theory of classification became possible after the theory of evolution was enunciated, a dysfunction of a natural process cannot be understood outside of the context (the "ancestral environment of evolutionary adaptedness") within which the process evolved. Thus, some presumed biologic dysfunctions are more readily conceptualized as the displacement of an organism from its original ecological niche, but these niches may be unknown to us at present (for additional discussion, see Bjorklund & Pellegrini, 2000; Jensen et al., 1997).

Empirical Taxonomic Approaches

One solution has been to dispense with the current diagnostic classification systems, such as *DSM-IV*, adopting instead an "empirical" taxonomic approach, such as one of the various rating systems that has utilized statistical methods to derive "factors" from the many possible observed or reported behaviors and symptoms, with the notion that the symptoms will converge into meaningful patterns or profiles that hang together statistically. Although this approach can be a useful initial tool for descriptive purposes, as a full-fledged classification tool it falls far short on a number of fronts. For example, such methods do not yet have a satisfactory way to obtain information from all possible informant sources and to reconcile that information when inevitable discrepancies arise. Whose report is to be trusted?

Consider a given youth, where rating scale information from parents, teachers, and the youth herself indicates no recent symptoms of depression or suicidal ideation, but the youth's best friend confides to the school counselor that the youth is storing up *more* pills to "really end it all" this coming weekend. When confronted by the school counselor with the best friend's information, the youth admits to feelings of hopelessness and "no way out," to an earlier attempt that left her nauseated 2 weeks earlier, and to the presence of a now likely fatal cache of pills stored in her school locker. How meaningful could a classification system be if based on methods that do not have means to incorporate such information and consider and reconcile discrepancies in order to obtain a more valid picture of the youth's feelings and behaviors? Or to consider additional complicating factors, such as the teen's desperation over the sexual abuse she is experiencing at the hands of an older brother, versus another teen who experiences the same wish to end it all, but without any identifiable precipitating circumstances other than a family history of teenage-onset depression in the mother and maternal grandmother.

Regardless of whether one uses a *DSM-IV* approach or an empirically derived taxonomic approach (e.g., see Achenbach, 1995), a more in-depth understanding of the possible circumstances surrounding each of these two instances of depression would remain obscure to either approach. Most certainly, effective service interventions would differ between these two examples. Actual service methods might overlap between the two cases (e.g., psychotherapy, medication) but still not be totally synonymous, because the former example would require a quite different approach to intervening with the family.

Definition of Disorder by Impairment Status

The most common cutoff applied to determine mental disorder caseness is the construct of impairment, such that in order to be a true case of disorder, one must suffer from some degree of impairment. This is an interesting distinction, and one not necessarily applied equally to other supposed disorders. Hypertension for many persons involves no apparent impairment, at least in the present tense, and treatment in asymptomatic persons is only employed because of the statistical likelihood of future impairment (disability or death) as a result of the untreated condition. In fact, the treatment itself is likely to result in side effects that could be reasonably construed as impairments.

Even accepting the need for impairment, the problem of determining the precise cutoff for the degree of impairment is inescapable. A number of strategies have been employed to minimize the numbers of false positives and false negatives (Hsiao, Bartko, & Potter, 1989; Lahey et al., 1994; Piacentini, Cohen, & Cohen, 1992), but such strategies must still rely on some other criterion against which the determination of a false positive or negative is made. How much impairment, and as judged by whom? Although the requirement of impairment seems a comfortable position at first glance, close inspection reveals that the many definitions of impairment can yield dramatically different rates of disorder (Angold et al., 1999).

In part, the current requirement for impairment as embodied in the *DSM-IV* stems from the fact that for mental disorders among both adults and children, we have no sure knowledge of the *underlying disease processes*. Just as with hypertension or with the presence of an asymptomatic malignant tumor, although neither result in current impairment, both are known to have certain consequences if left untreated, hence medical necessity is generally taken for granted. From a symptomatic perspective, these might be viewed as analogues to mental disorders' subthreshold conditions. For example, once we have obtained reliable markers for the likelihood of future onsets of Autism or Schizophrenia, prevention and early intervention strategies become possible. Eisenberg (1995) has noted that as science progresses, so do our assumptions of what constitutes mental disorder. Over 100 years ago, knowledge of hemoglobinopathies such as thallasemia was limited to the overt description of the clinical phenomenology of symptoms and affected bodily organs. After decades of research, precise knowledge of the point mutations in the molecular structure of the hemoglobin molecule underlying these conditions is now available, and persons totally asymptomatic can be identified and are considered cases from the perspective of prevention, early intervention, and genetic counseling. With time, better knowledge of the basic neural, psychological, and social processes underlying the mental disorders should allow us to worry less about what should be a case and more about the health merits, the appropriate services, and the ethical issues involved in intervening with an illness process that is reasonably well understood.

Pragmatic Approaches

To avoid the conceptual problems noted earlier and to answer the question, When is a case a case? we suggest that the first question that must be addressed is, A case for what purpose? For example, Sonuga-Barke (1998) notes that to distinguish between various definitions of disorder, one must clarify whether one wishes to define mental disorder for purposes of the clinical utility of such a definition (the pragmatic view) or the construct validity (the ontologic view). Although the ultimate goal of classification is *usefulness* (Frances, 1998), as Eisenberg (1995) has noted, there are many "usefulnesses." What works for researchers to define some presumably homogeneous entity (i.e., the attempt to "carve nature at its joints") may not work well for clinicians and policymakers, who often wish to know, Who needs care?

One potential route out of such an impasse has been described by Zarin and Earls (1993), who have recommended that methods of decision analysis be applied to such issues. They note that the essential components of diagnostic decision making—choice of external validator, choice of discriminator, and choice of cutoff scores—might be implemented very differently, depending on whether the clinician's or investigator's objectives are to (1) determine which children need psychiatric care and where overall assessments of disability are most relevant; (2) determine what clinicians do in real-world practice, that is, services research, which often varies from the ideal world of academic practice; or (3) determine which children are valid cases of a specific disorder for purposes of research into etiology, genetic factors, treatment response, and likelihood of persistence/recurrence. Thus, Caseness for what purpose? is the relevant question, and it must be appreciated that any cutoff or discriminator will result in some false negatives and false positives. The choice of cutoffs will often depend on the relative costs of false negatives versus false positives, vis-à-vis the clinical or research objectives.

Rather than reifying mental disorder as simple symptom counts that cross some relatively arbitrary threshold, Rogler (1993) suggests that, within given cultures, a quick decision with substantial face validity can be accomplished for many purposes to avoid attributing symptom, case, or impairment status to conditions or situations that actually reflect some form of goal-directed, culturally situated behavior. Although this is eminently sensible, we are unaware of any systematic testing of such approaches to determine if they can be reliably done, and whether multiple, culturally informed raters would agree among themselves with such face valid decisions. This recommendation hearkens back to the etiological diagnostic formulations of previous DSMs, yet such an approach, if cautiously implemented, even in Anglo-American cultures, may help avoid according mental disorder status to some conditions that many would regard instead as adaptive responses (e.g., certain forms of Conduct Disorder; Richters & Cicchetti, 1993). Such an approach may also avert criticism that our diagnostic approaches too often ignore the obvious (Jensen & Hoagwood, 1997).

In an important sense, expert clinicians' judgments concerning symptom, impairment, and mental disorder status that make use of all available data over time constitute a not easily replaced "LEAD" ("longitudinal," "expert," and making use of "all data") (Spitzer, 1983), if not gold standard. Yet, such judgments, too, are situated in culture and time, reflecting in part both scientific findings and cultural

norms (Eisenberg, 1995). As culture changes or science advances, these determinations do as well. To this extent, the judgment of what constitutes a case (in terms of medical necessity or need for treatment) can never be fully satisfied by statistical approaches or complex equations and must instead take into account societal values, willingness to pay, determination of what constitutes a "problem in living" versus a disorder (such as the boundaries between transient sadness and Major Depressive Disorder), as well as the assembled experiences and norms of the families seeking care for their children and the mental health care providers within that cultural context. Without some metric that has been carefully calibrated to take into account these dimensions, any determination of mental disorder (apart from scientifically established qualitative differences in underlying disease processes) must remain more or less arbitrary.

CONCLUSION AND FUTURE PERSPECTIVES: NEED FOR A NEW PARADIGM

An overarching concern relates to the fact that in the area of child psychopathology, most well-documented risk factors appear to be common to most disorders; that is, the presence of any risk factor rarely has been found to be specific for any given disorder (Sameroff, Seifer, Barocas, Zax, & Greenspan, 1987; Werry, Reeves, & Elkind, 1987). Furthermore, as a general rule, treatments are not diagnosis specific but are symptom and context specific. These facts, coupled with what we know about the malleability of the early organism and the sensitivity of the brain to early environmental influences, suggest that we should work to move beyond static or descriptive models for understanding childhood psychopathology, such as embodied in our DSM classification approaches.

Developmental Psychopathology Models

In contrast to the behavioral, quasi-descriptive models of psychopathology, theorists with a developmental perspective working with infants, children, adolescents, and adults are usually keenly interested in the processes whereby behavior unfolds and in understanding how any particular form of psychopathology is molded by environmental input. Developmental approaches to psychopathology begin from the premise that it is essential to understand the complex historical pathways of an evolving organism that is attempting to master the tasks and demands imposed by the environment, as these environmental inputs and individual responses simultaneously shape new organismic capacities. From this perspective, the descriptive state of psychopathology or dysfunction presumed intrinsic to an individual is no more salient than the nature of the transactions of the individual with the environment and the extent to which these transactions enhance or broaden the individual's behavioral repertoire for future environmental transactions and task mastery. Viewed from a developmental psychopathology perspective, understanding the processes of adaptation over time within a continuously unfolding, ever-changing context is essential.

Developmental approaches to psychopathology often seek to examine dysfunction not as a state of *being* of the individual, but as an epigenetic pattern of transactions of the organism with the environment. Some pathologic patterns (though potentially adaptive in the immediacy) can lead to increasing oscillations in the child's (or adult's) performance of age-appropriate social and cognitive tasks, may eventually lead to increased difficulties that generalize beyond the immediate domain or sphere of functioning, and may increase the likelihood of emerging disabilities/impairments in other areas of function. Although even this developmental approach also runs the risk of becoming a tautology, this perspective suggests that impairment or loss of capacity in performing age-appropriate, cultural- and context-specific tasks might constitute an additional, useful criterion to establish the presence of psychopathology. Of course, an age-referenced measure of impairment alone constitutes an insufficient criterion for psychopathology, because it ignores the person's family and current history, pattern of experiences, and current circumstances. Yet, this criterion can be seen as increasingly salient when the loss of capacity can be demonstrated to be relatively enduring and/or permanent, and potentially can lead to other disabilities or incapacities across other contexts, as the increasing demands of the environment, the exigencies of the developing organism, and the relative incapacities collide.

Of note, the measurement demands required to assess a dynamic relational system do not conform a priori to either dimensional or categorical approaches to assessment of psychopathology. In fact, a significant limitation to both of these approaches as typically employed is that they presuppose that that which is being assessed lies within the given individual. The categorical and dimensional approaches each have advantages and disadvantages as well as a generous number of adherents (Cantwell, 1996), but a unilateral focus on either approach to the exclusion of careful assessments of the transactions over time between individuals and their environments will fail to capture the context-rich processes that are needed for an integrative understanding of the phenomenon.

Thus, taking a step back, we suggest that questions of an *essentialist nature,* such as, What is *the* core cause of this behavior problem? or What is the "true" prevalence of this disorder? are inappropriate for a system that cannot classify behaviors into essential categories. If this is not or cannot be the goal, then it is appropriate to ask, What question does the classification system answer? What is the purpose of classifying? Within the scientific framework that we advocate, we suggest instead that studies of a given behavior (or disorder) should begin from the operational assumptions that there will likely be significant individual differences in the manifestations of these behaviors, that they will be derived from many different etiologies, and that they will express themselves quite differently in different contexts and transactions with the environment (Cicchetti, 1987). As a further step in reconciling some of the difficulties in our current diagnostic approaches, we suggest that there is a need for a more avowedly open, self-critical, developmental stance toward our diagnostic entities. Greater awareness in the research and clinical communities is essential to avoid the reification of psychiatric labels and to enact a more etiologically based process and context-elaborated nosology.

Need for a Typology and Theory of Contexts

Although we are critical of the limitations of the current diagnostic systems, these criticisms should not imply the need to return to past systems based on unsubstantiated or untestable theories. Instead, careful description and operationalization of *all* relevant phenomena are needed. These include individual symptomatic, functional, family-interactional, past history of services or treatments and response to them, contextual and longitudinal-historical phenomena. These processes, if captured fully, can yield an informative database able to characterize disordered processes and functions. As others have argued (Boyce et al., 1998; Sadler & Hulgus, 1994; Trickett, 1996), a major limitation of the characterization of persons in contexts has been the absence of a typology and adequate theory of context. The *DSM-IV* Axis IV (level of stressors within the past year) is a modest beginning, but a broader and more rigorous approach to assessment and toward a contextual nosologic system is needed. Sadler and Hulgus (1994) suggest that a nosology of context could provide the structural form for patients' unique historical and environmental backgrounds and offer a methodology to combine diagnostic and contextual information for individual subjects. Such a typology could expand our search for disorders and psychopathology to environmental and historical contexts for a given individual and ensure that clinically salient life events are incorporated into treatment planning. Nosologic practices would thereby better reflect salient psychosocial factors along with person-based psychological and biological factors to understand individuals' outcomes. Sadler and Hulgus (1994) suggest three levels for the development of a contextual nosologic system: (1) syndromes of personal history (e.g., early parental death, incest); (2) syndromes of the interpersonal environment (e.g., victimization, divorce, death of spouse); and (3) syndromes of the extrapersonal environment (e.g., media influence, catastrophe, homelessness, loss of employment). Of note, more explicit operationalizations of such criteria are now emerging (e.g., see Dausch, Miklowitz, & Richards, 1996; Group for the Advancement of Psychiatry, 1996), but they are still very much at the beginning.

Other authors have suggested that more attention be paid to the culture-specific presentations of individual symptoms as a function of the individual's larger social environment (Trickett, 1996). For example, Alarcon (1995) describes the development of recommendations in the *DSM-IV* that included cultural statements in the introduction, cultural considerations for each diagnosis, and so on. These recommendations are a first step, but they are a modest step indeed, given the strong evidence for culture-bound syndromes and the misapplication of diagnosis to different cultural and ethnic communities. As Alarcon notes, less favorable diagnoses are frequently applied to poor ethnic communities, and any diagnostic system (including the *DSM-IV*) runs the risk of becoming a vehicle of an ethnocentric view of mental disorder. Such problems can partly be addressed by developing an international item pool to permit alternative classification of cases using mutually compatible instruments and translations of concepts, but these recommendations still fall short of careful specification and description of ordered and disordered processes (as in the theory and measurement of attachment).

Rogler (1993) notes the need for careful examination and attention to symptoms and their characterization at three levels: (1) the assessment of symptoms and their meanings, (2) the patterning of symptoms and their disorders, and (3) the interpersonal context of the diagnostic interview process itself. Thus, symptoms may be part of one cultural context but may not qualify as symptoms per se in another setting (e.g., devoutly religious persons hearing the voices of recently deceased relatives). Maximum diagnostic error is likely to occur when a category developed in one culture is applied to another. Thus, the construct of Conduct Disorder, though potentially useful in a clinically referred population for both treatment and research, may be quite problematic when used to characterize children in the community from another cultural or ethnic background (Richters & Cicchetti, 1993). Moreover, studies suggest that even though the criteria for conditions such as Conduct Disorder do not fully take context into account, clinicians consider these factors nonetheless when presented vignettes that differ by social context and asked to judge whether the described youth does or does not have a mental disorder (Kirk & Hsieh, 2004).

Application of Multiple Methods and Conceptual Frameworks

Another way to address the difficulties with the current diagnostic and nosologic systems is to approach the problem with multiple conceptual frameworks and methodologies. For example, Maton (1993) advocates the use of linked ethnographic and empirical methodologies, and Weisner (1996) argues that ethnographic methods are the most important approach to understanding individual functioning. Although ethnographic approaches have their own limitations (including subjectivity, potential unreliability, sampling bias, and replicability), problems with quantitative methods include the lack of validity of the construct and its measurement derived from one person or setting and applied to another, where important constructs and patterns of a given cultural setting are ignored. Ideally, quantitative and qualitative approaches must be linked and used together. Both constitute critical tools in understanding disordered processes and mental illness (Shinn, 1990; Trickett, 1996; Weisner, 1996).

Through a systematic application of methodologies that capture interactional processes and that reflect the variety of different perspectives about psychopathology, we believe it will be possible to elucidate a common underlying developmental or pathogenic process. In this way, it should be possible to improve understanding of what criteria validate mental illness, in much the same way that an internist applies understanding about an internal pathophysiologic characteristic (e.g., elevated blood pressure) to define a latent illness state, even though the person is currently asymptomatic. Thus, Kleinman (1988) has suggested that the validity of psychiatric diagnoses should involve a conceptual and iterative tacking back and forth between the psychiatric diagnostic system and its rules of classification, alternative taxonomies, clinical experience, the patient's interpretation, and the cultural and historical contexts in which the diagnostic system, words, languages, and meaning are situated. In other words, in the absence of firm biologic demarcations, a diagnosis is an interpretation, and its ultimate validity must be indexed by reference to the cultural norms, values, and languages of a particular society, as well as the environmental demands and constraints of a person's particular contexts.

Given the fluidity of language, meaning, and contexts in human society, as a general rule diagnostic systems and assessment approaches should be understood as more or less arbitrarily and temporarily constructed systems to further scientific investigations (Popper, 1994; Wiggins & Schwartz, 1994). The use of current systems to inform reimbursement procedures and decisions about who should receive care may operate at odds with one another. Under some conditions, different systems may be needed for different settings and purposes.

As a note of caution, Jablensky (1994) points out that all classificatory efforts to date based on primary essences (e.g., disordered process, etiology, genetic pattern course, or response to treatment) have not fared well, compared to more eclectic approaches, which have generated a fair amount of innovative research and have found useful and practical applications.

Closing Comments

Studies of language, meaning, and the history of science indicate that the reasons for the construction of any classification system determine the kinds of questions that may be asked of the items within it. Language is a system of signs, and the language of classification systems *constructs* (rather than discovers) meaning. Such constructions set parameters on the kinds of questions that can legitimately be asked of the categories into which "normal" and "abnormal" behaviors are divided. Studies of language suggest that the meaning of language is not fixed but changes as its production and use changes. Likewise, the changing positions of psychiatric diagnoses within prevailing social notions of what constitutes disease and mental illness suggest that socially specific events can produce fluctuations in diagnostic categories, as language, its meaning, and use change over time.

Given what we know about early plasticity and children's responsiveness to environmental modifications and the counterintuitive and atheoretical nature of current nosologic systems, alternative (and better) ways to understand these phenomena of childhood behavioral and emotional disturbances are needed, as opposed to the simplistic notion that disorders reside within persons. Many of our mental disorders might be reconceptualized to reflect interactions between brain and environment and the consolidation of these interactions over time (Garruto, Little, & Weitz, 2004). Thus, psychiatric disorders are the result of not just environmental factors, nor of biologic factors exclusively. Rather, disorders are the result of the progressive development of the brain as it unfolds within the constraints of the genomic map and the particular environmental circumstances and context of a given organism in a particular history. Such an approach, if supported by robust measures and analytic methods, is more likely to lead to a closer approximation of the underlying developmental processes, as well as provide opportunities for timely service, treatment, and preventive interventions.

REFERENCES

Achenbach, T. M. (1993). *Manual for the Child Behavior Checklist and revised Child Behavior Profile.* Burlington, VT: University Associates in Psychiatry.

Achenbach, T. M. (1995). Empirically based assessment and taxonomy: Applications to clinical research. *Psychological Assessment, 7*(3), 261–274.

Alarcon, R. D. (1995). Culture and psychiatric diagnosis: Impact on DSM-IV and ICD-10. *Psychiatric Clinics of North America, 18*(3), 449–465.

American Psychiatric Association. (1980). *Diagnostic and statistical manual of mental disorders* (3rd ed.). Washington, DC: Author.

American Psychiatric Association. (1987). *Diagnostic and statistical manual of mental disorders* (3rd ed. revised). Washington, DC: Author.

American Psychiatric Association. (1994). *Diagnostic and statistical manual of mental disorders* (4th ed.). Washington, DC: Author.

Andreasen, N. C., & Glick, I. D. (1988). Bipolar affective disorder and creativity: Implications and clinical management. *Comprehensive Psychiatry, 29*(3), 207–217.

Angold, A., Costello, E., Farmer, E. M. Z., Burns, B. J., & Erkanli, A. (1999). Impaired but undiagnosed. *Journal of the American Academy of Child and Adolescent Psychiatry, 38*(2), 129–137.

Barkley, R. A., & Biederman, J. (1997). Toward a broader definition of the age-of-onset criterion for attention-deficit-hyperactivity-disorder. *Journal of the American Academy of Child and Adolescent Psychiatry, 36*(9), 1204–1210.

Bennett, K. J., Lipman, E. L., Brown, S., Racine, Y., Boyle, M. H., & Offord, D. R. (1999). Predicting conduct problems: Can high-risk children be identified in kindergarten and grade 1? *Journal of Consulting and Clinical Psychology, 67*(4), 470–480.

Bennett, K. J., Lipman, E. L., Racine, Y., & Offord, D. R. (1998). Do measures of externalising behaviour in normal populations predict later outcome? Implications for targeted interventions to prevent conduct disorder. *Journal of Child Psychology and Psychiatry, 39*(8), 1059–1070.

Bennett, K. J., & Offord, D. R. (2001). Screening for conduct problems: Does the predictive accuracy of conduct disorder symptoms improve with age? *Journal of the American Academy of Child and Adolescent Psychiatry, 40*(12), 1418–1425.

Bjorklund, D. F., & Pellegrini, A. D. (2000). Child development and evolutionary psychology. Child Development, 71(6), 1687–1708.

Black, J. E., Sirevaag, A. M., Wallace, C. S., Savin, M. H., & Greenough, W. T. (1989). Effects of complex experience on somatic growth and organ development in rats. Developmental Psychobiology, 22(7), 727–752.

Boyce, W. T., Frank, E., Jensen, P. S., Kessler, R. C., Nelson, C. A., & Steinberg, L. (1998). Social context in developmental psychopathology: Recommendations for future research from the MacArthur network on psychopathology and development. *Development and Psychopathology, 10*(2), 143–164.

Boyle, M. H., Offord, D. R., Racine, Y., Szatmari, P., Fleming, J. E., & Sanford, M. (1996). Identifying thresholds for classifying childhood psychiatric disorder: Issues and prospects. *Journal of the American Academy of Child and Adolescent Psychiatry, 35*(11), 1440–1448.

Brent, D. A., Holder, D., Kolko, D., Birmaher, B., Baugher, M., Roth, C., et al. (1997). A clinical psychotherapy trial for adolescent depression comparing cognitive, family, and supportive therapy. *Archives of General Psychiatry, 54*(9), 877–885.

Canino, G. J., Bird, H. R., Shrout, P. E., Rubio-Stipec, M., Bravo, M., Martinez, R., et al. (1987). The prevalence of specific psychiatric disorders in Puerto Rico. *Archives of General Psychiatry, 44*(8), 727–735.

Cantwell, D. P. (1996). Classification of child and adolescent psychopathology. *Journal of Child Psychology and Psychiatry and Allied Disciplines, 37*(1), 3–12.

Cicchetti, D. (1987). Developmental psychopathology in infancy: Illustration from the study of maltreated youngsters. *Journal of Consulting and Clinical Psychology, 55*(6), 837–845.

Clarke, G. N., Hornbrook, M., Lynch, F., Polen, M., Gale, J., O'Connor, E., et al. (2002). Group cognitive-behavioral treatment for depressed adolescent offspring of depressed parents in a health maintenance organization. *Journal of the American Academy of Child and Adolescent Psychiatry, 41*(3), 305–313.

Costello, E. J., Angold, A., Burns, B. J., Erkanli, A., Stangl, D. K., & Tweed, D. L. (1996). The Great Smoky Mountains Study of Youth: Functional impairment and serious emotional disturbance. *Archives of General Psychiatry, 53*(12), 1137–1143.

Cuvier, L. (1835). *Leçons d'anatomie comparée* (2nd ed.). Paris: Crochard.

Dausch, B. M., Miklowitz, D. J., & Richards, J. A. (1996). Global Assessment of Relational Functioning scale (GARF): Pt. II. Reliability and validity in a sample of families of bipolar patients. *Family Process, 35*(2), 175–189.

Dupre, J. (1993). *The disorder of things: Metaphysical foundations of the disunity of science.* Cambridge, MA: Harvard University Press.

Eisenberg, L. (1995). *Doing away with the illusion of homogeneity: Medical progress through disease identification.* Unpublished manuscript, Johns Hopkins Hospital, Baltimore, MD.

Feinstein, A. R. (1972). Clinical biostatistics. 13. On homogeneity, taxonomy, and nosography. *Clinical Pharmacology and Therapeutics, 13*(1), 114–129.

Flisher, A. J., Kramer, R. A., Hoven, C. W., King, R. A., Bird, H. R., Davies, M., et al. (2000). Risk behavior in a community sample of children and adolescents. *Journal of the American Academy of Child and Adolescent Psychiatry, 39*(7), 881–887.

Foucault, M. (1970). *The order of things* (English ed.). London: Tavistock.

Frances, A. J. (1994). Preface. In J. Z. Sadler, O. P. Wiggins, & M. A. Schwartz (Eds.), *Philosophical perspectives on psychiatric diagnostic classification* (pp. i–iv). Baltimore: Johns Hopkins University Press.

Frances, A. J. (1998). Problems in defining clinical significance in epidemiological studies. *Archives of General Psychiatry, 55*(2), 119.

Frances, A. J., Pincus, H. A., Widiger, T. A., Davis, W. W., & First, M. B. (1994). DSM-IV: Work in progress. In J. E. Mezzich & M. R. Jorge (Eds.), *Psychiatric epidemiology: Assessment concepts and methods* (pp. 116–135). Baltimore: Johns Hopkins University Press.

Franklin, M., Foa, E., & March, J. S. (2003). The pediatric obsessive-compulsive disorder treatment study: Rationale, design, and methods. *Journal of Child and Adolescent Psychopharmacology, 13*(Suppl. 1), S39–S51.

Friedman, R. M., Katz-Leavy, J. W., Manderscheid, R. W., & Sondheimer, D. L. (1998). Prevalence of serious emotional disturbance in children and adolescents: An update. In R. W. Manderscheid & M. A. Sonnenschein (Eds.), *Mental health, United States, 1998* (pp. 110–112). Washington, DC: U.S. Government Printing Office.

Fromm, E. (1955). *The sane society.* Oxford: Rinehart.

Fulford, K. W. M. (1994). Closet logics: Hidden conceptual elements in the DSM and ICD classification of mental disorders. In J. Z. Sadler, O. P. Wiggins, & M. A. Schwartz (Eds.), *Philosophical perspectives on psychiatric diagnostic classification* (pp. 211–232). Baltimore: Johns Hopkins University Press.

Garruto, R. M., Little, M. A., & Weitz, C. A. (2004). Environmental stress and adaptational responses: Consequences for human health outcomes. *Collegium Antropologicum, 28*(2), 509–540.

Goodman, S. H., Hoven, C. W., Narrow, W. E., Cohen, P., Fielding, B., Alegria, M., et al. (1998). Measurement of risk for mental disorders and competence in a psychiatric epidemiologic community survey: The National Institute of Mental Health Methods for the Epidemiology of Child and Adolescent Mental Disorders (MECA) study. *Social Psychiatry and Psychiatric Epidemiology, 33*(4), 162–173.

Greenough, W. T., & Black, J. E. (1992). Induction of brain structure by experience: Substrates for cognitive development. In M. R. Gunnar & C. A. Nelson (Eds.), *Developmental behavioral neuroscience* (pp. 155–200). Hillsdale, NJ: Erlbaum.

Group for the Advancement of Psychiatry Committee on the Family. (1996). Global Assessment of Relational Functioning scale (GARF): I. Background and rationale. *Family Process, 35*(2), 155–172.

Hoagwood, K., Jensen, P. S., Petti, T., & Burns, B. J. (1996). Outcomes of mental health care for children and adolescents: I. A comprehensive conceptual model. *Journal of the American Academy of Child and Adolescent Psychiatry, 35*(8), 1055–1063.

Hood, K. K., & Eyberg, S. M. (2003). Outcomes of parent-child interaction therapy: Mothers' reports of maintenance three to six years after treatment. *Journal of Clinical Child and Adolescent Psychology, 32*(3), 419–429.

Hsiao, J. K., Bartko, J. J., & Potter, W. Z. (1989). Diagnosing diagnoses: Receiver operating characteristic methods and psychiatry. *Archives of General Psychiatry, 46*(7), 664–667.

Huffman, L. C., Mehlinger, S. L., & Kerivan, A. S. (2000). Risk factors for academic and behavioral problems at the beginning of school. In *Off to a good start: Research on the risk factors for early school problems and selected federal policies affecting children's social and emotional development and their readiness for school.* Chapel Hill: University of North Carolina, FPG Child Development Center.

Jablensky, A. (1994). Methodologic issues in psychiatric classification. In J. E. Mezzich, M. R. Jorge, & I. M. Salloum (Eds.), *Psychiatric epidemiology: Assessment concepts and methods* (pp. 69–80). Baltimore: Johns Hopkins University Press.

Jensen, P. S. (1995). Discussion: Scales versus categories? Never play against a stacked deck. *Journal of the American Academy of Child and Adolescent Psychiatry, 34*(4), 485–487.

Jensen, P. S., & Hoagwood, K. (1997). The book of names: DSM-IV in context. *Development and Psychopathology, 9*(2), 231–249.

Jensen, P. S., Mrazek, D., Knapp, P. K., Steinberg, L., Pfeffer, C., Schowalter, J., et al. (1997). Evolution and revolution in child psychiatry: ADHD as a disorder of adaptation. *Journal of the American Academy of Child and Adolescent Psychiatry, 36*(12), 1672–1681.

Kazdin, A. E., & Whitley, M. K. (2003). Treatment of parental stress to enhance therapeutic change among children referred for aggressive and antisocial behavior. *Journal of Consulting and Clinical Psychology, 71*(3), 504–515.

Kendler, K. S., & Gardner, C. O., Jr. (1998). Boundaries of major depression: An evaluation of DSM-IV criteria. *American Journal of Psychiatry, 155*(2), 172–177.

Kirk, S. A., & Hsieh, D. K. (2004). Diagnostic consistency in assessing conduct disorder: An experiment on the effect of social context. *American Journal of Orthopsychiatry, 74*(1), 43–55.

Kleinman, A. M. (1977). Depression, somatization and the "new cross-cultural psychiatry." *Social Science and Medicine, 11*(1), 3–10.

Kleinman, A. M. (1988). *Rethinking psychiatry: From cultural category to personal experience.* New York: Free Press.

Lahey, B. B., Applegate, B., McBurnett, K., Biederman, J., Greenhill, L., Hynd, G. W., et al. (1994). DSM-IV field trials for attention deficit hyperactivity disorder in children and adolescents. *American Journal of Psychiatry, 151*(11), 1673–1685.

Leckman, J. F., & Mayes, L. C. (1998). Understanding developmental psychopathology: How useful are evolutionary accounts? *Journal of the American Academy of Child and Adolescent Psychiatry, 37*(10), 1011–1021.

Levy, F., Hay, D. A., McStephen, M., Wood, C., & Waldman, I. (1997). Attention-deficit hyperactivity disorder: A category or a continuum? Genetic analysis of a large-scale twin study. *Journal of the American Academy of Child and Adolescent Psychiatry, 36*(6), 737–744.

Loeber, R., Stouthamer-Loeber, M., & White, H. R. (1999). Developmental aspects of delinquency and internalizing problems and their association with persistent juvenile substance use between ages 7 and 18. *Journal of Clinical Child Psychology, 28*(3), 322–332.

Manson, S. M. (1995). Culture and major depression: Current challenges in the diagnosis of mood disorders. *Psychiatric Clinics of North America, 18*(3), 487–501.

Margolis, J. (1994). Taxonomic puzzles. In J. Z. Sadler, O. P. Wiggins, & M. A. Schwartz (Eds.), *Philosophical perspectives on psychiatric diagnostic classification: Johns Hopkins series in psychiatry and neuroscience* (pp. 104–128). Baltimore: Johns Hopkins University Press.

Marks, I. M., & Nesse, R. M. (1994). Fear and fitness: An evolutionary analysis of anxiety disorders. *Ethology and Sociobiology, 15*(5/6), 247–261.

Maton, K. I. (1993). A bridge between cultures: Linked ethnographic-empirical methodology for culture anchored research. *American Journal of Community Psychology, 21*(6), 747–773.

McDougle, C. J., Scahill, L., McCracken, J. T., Aman, M. G., Tierney, E., Arnold, L. E., et al. (2002). Research Units on Pediatric Psychopharmacology (RUPP) Autism Network: Background and rationale for an initial controlled study of risperidone. *Child and Adolescent Psychiatric Clinics of North America, 9*(1), 201–224.

MTA Cooperative Group. (1999). A 14-month randomized clinical trial of treatment strategies for attention-deficit/hyperactivity disorder: Multimodal treatment study of children with ADHD. *Archives of General Psychiatry, 56*(12), 1073–1086.

Nelson, C. A., & Bloom, F. E. (1997). Child development and neuroscience. *Child Development, 68*(5), 970–987.

Nettle, D. (2004). Evolutionary origins of depression: A review and reformulation. *Journal of Affective Disorders, 81*(2), 91–102.

Office of the Surgeon General. (1999). *Mental health: A report of the Surgeon General.* Washington, DC: U.S. Government Printing Office.

Pappadopulos, E. A., Guelzow, T. B., Wong, C., Ortega, M., & Jensen, P. S. (2004). A review of the growing evidence base for pediatric psychopharmacology. *Child and Adolescent Psychiatric Clinics of North America, 13*(4), 817–855.

Perry, S., Cooper, A. M., & Michels, R. (1987). The psychodynamic formulation: Its purpose, structure, and clinical application. *American Journal of Psychiatry, 144*(5), 543–550.

Piacentini, J. C., Cohen, P., & Cohen, J. (1992). Combining discrepant diagnostic information from multiple sources: Are complex algorithms better than simple ones? *Journal of Abnormal Child Psychology, 20*(1), 51–63.

Popper, K. R. (1994). The myth of the framework. In *Defense of science and rationality* (p. 6). New York: Routledge.

Pratt, V., & Foucault, M. (1977). Foucault and the history of classification theory. *Studies in History and Philosophy of Science, 8*(2), 163–171.

Rasmussen, E. R., Neuman, R. J., Heath, A. C., Levy, F., Hay, D. A., & Todd, R. D. (2002). Replication of the latent class structure of attention-deficit/hyperactivity disorder (ADHD) subtypes in a sample of Australian twins. *Journal of Child Psychology and Psychiatry and Allied Disciplines, 43*(8), 1018–1028.

Regier, D. A., Kaelber, C. T., Rae, D. S., Farmer, M. E., Knauper, B., Kessler, R. C., et al. (1998). Limitations of diagnostic criteria and assessment instruments for mental disorders: Implications for research and policy. *Archives of General Psychiatry, 55*(2), 109–115.

Research Unit on Pediatric Psychopharmacology Anxiety Study Group. (2001). Fluvoxamine for the treatment of anxiety disorders in children and adolescents. *New England Journal of Medicine, 344*(17), 1279–1285.

Richters, J. E., & Cicchetti, D. (1993). Mark Twain meets DSM-III-R: Conduct disorder, development, and the concept of harmful dysfunction. *Development and Psychopathology, 5*(1/2), 5–29.

Rogler, L. H. (1993). Culturally sensitizing psychiatric diagnosis. A framework for research. *Journal of Nervous and Mental Diseases, 181*(7), 401–408.

Rutter, M., & Shaffer, D. (1980). DSM-III: A step forward or back in terms of the classification of child psychiatric disorders? *Journal of the American Academy of Child Psychiatry, 19*(3), 371–394.

Sadler, J. Z., & Hulgus, Y. F. (1994). Enriching the psychosocial context of a multiaxial nosology. In J. Z. Sadler, O. P. Wiggins, & M. A. Schwartz (Eds.), *Philosophical perspectives on psychiatric diagnostic classification* (pp. 261–278). Baltimore: Johns Hopkins University Press.

Sadler, J. Z., Wiggins, O. P., & Schwartz, M. A. (1994). Introduction. In J. Z. Sadler, O. P. Wiggins, & M. A. Schwartz (Eds.), *Philosophical perspectives on psychiatric diagnostic classification* (pp. 1–13). Baltimore: Johns Hopkins University Press.

Sameroff, A. J., Seifer, R., Barocas, R., Zax, M., & Greenspan, S. (1987). Intelligence quotient scores of 4-year-old children: Social-environmental risk factors. *Pediatrics, 79*(3), 343–350.

Shaffer, D., Fisher, P., Dulcan, M. K., Davies, M., Piacentini, J. P., Schwab-Stone, M. E., et al. (1996). The Nimh Diagnostic Interview

Schedule for Children version 2.3 (DISC-2.3): Description, acceptability, prevalence rates, and performance in the MECA study. *Journal of the American Academy of Child and Adolescent Psychiatry, 35*(7), 865–877.

Shinn, M. (1990). Mixing and matching: Levels of conceptualization, measurement, and statistical analysis in community research. In P. Tolan, C. Keys, F. Chertok, & J. Leonard (Eds.), *Researching community psychology: Issues of theory and methods* (pp. 111–126). Washington, DC: American Psychological Association.

Shweder, R. A., & Bourne, E. J. (1991). Does the concept of person vary cross-culturally? In R. A. Shweder (Ed.), *Thinking through cultures: Expeditions in cultural psychology* (pp. 113–155). Cambridge, MA: Harvard University Press.

Silverman, W. K., Kurtines, W. M., Ginsburg, G. S., Weems, C. F., Rabian, B., & Serafini, L. T. (1999). Contingency management, self-control, and education support in the treatment of childhood phobic disorders: A randomized clinical trial. *Journal of Consulting and Clinical Psychology, 67*(5), 675–687.

Sonuga-Barke, E. J. (1998). Categorical models of childhood disorder: A conceptual and empirical analysis. *Journal of Child Psychology and Psychiatry and Allied Disciplines, 39*(1), 115–133.

Spitzer, R. L. (1983). Psychiatric diagnosis: Are clinicians still necessary? *Comprehensive Psychiatry, 24*(5), 399–411.

Strumwasser, F. (1994). The relations between neuroscience and human behavioral science. *Journal of the Experimental Analysis of Behavior, 61*(2), 307–317.

Treatment for Adolescents with Depression Study Team. (2004). Fluoxetine, cognitive-behavioral therapy, and their combination for adolescents with depression: Treatment for Adolescents with Depression Study (TADS) randomized controlled trial. *Journal of the American Medical Association, 292*(7), 807–820.

Trickett, E. J. (1996). A future for community psychology: The contexts of diversity and the diversity of contexts. *American Journal of Community Psychology, 24*(2), 209–234.

Vaillant, G. E. (1984). A debate on DSM-III: The disadvantages of DSM-III outweigh its advantages. *American Journal of Psychiatry, 141*(4), 542–545.

Wakefield, J. C. (1992a). The concept of mental disorder. On the boundary between biological facts and social values. *American Psychologist, 47*(3), 373–388.

Wakefield, J. C. (1992b). Disorder as harmful dysfunction: A conceptual critique of DSM-III-R's definition of mental disorder. *Psychological Review, 99*(2), 232–247.

Wakefield, J. C., Pottick, K. J., & Kirk, S. A. (2002). Should the DSM-IV diagnostic criteria for conduct disorder consider social context? *American Journal of Psychiatry, 159*(3), 380–386.

Wallace, E. R. I. V. (1994). Psychiatry and its nosology: A historico-philosophical overview. In J. Z. Sadler, O. P. Wiggins, & M. A. Schwartz (Eds.), *Philosophical perspectives on psychiatric diagnostic classification* (pp. 16–86). Baltimore: Johns Hopkins University Press.

Webster-Stratton, C., Reid, M. J., & Hammond, M. (2004). Treating children with early-onset conduct problems: Intervention outcomes for parent, child, and teacher training. *Journal of Clinical Child and Adolescent Psychology, 33*(1), 105–124.

Weisner, T. S. (1996). Why ethnography should be the most important method in the study of human development. In R. Jessor, A. Colby, & R. A. Shweder (Eds.), *Ethnography and human development: Context and meaning in social inquiry* (pp. 305–324). Chicago: University of Chicago Press.

Werry, J. S., Reeves, J. C., & Elkind, G. S. (1987). Attention deficit, conduct, oppositional, and anxiety disorders in children: Pt. I. A review of research on differentiating characteristics. *Journal of the American Academy of Child and Adolescent Psychiatry, 26*(2), 133–143.

Wiggins, O. P., & Schwartz, M. A. (1994). The limits of psychiatric knowledge and the problem of classification. In J. Z. Sadler, O. P. Wiggins, & M. A. Schwartz (Eds.), *Philosophical perspectives on psychiatric diagnostic classification: Johns Hopkins series in psychiatry and neuroscience* (pp. 89–103). Baltimore: Johns Hopkins University Press.

Zarin, D. A., & Earls, F. (1993). Diagnostic decision making in psychiatry. *American Journal of Psychiatry, 150*(2), 197–206.

CHAPTER 3

Developmental Epidemiology

E. JANE COSTELLO and ADRIAN ANGOLD

In this chapter, we discuss developmental psychopathology from the viewpoint of epidemiology, "the study of health and illness in human populations" (Kleinbaum, Kupper, & Morgenstern, 1982, p. 2). After a brief introduction to some of the basic concepts of the epidemiological method, we discuss what modern epidemiology is and does, what questions it addresses, some of the key methods it uses, and how these methods can be applied to the special problems of developmental psychopathology. We present a short history of how child psychiatric epidemiology has grown into developmental epidemiology, illustrating how these changes reflect society's changing concerns about the mental health of children. In the final section, we describe some of the

ways developmental epidemiology is branching out and taking on the concerns and methods of related areas: life course and intergenerational epidemiology; transnational epidemiology; genetic epidemiology; the study of burden of disease, including the economic costs of psychiatric illness; and the use of epidemiologic designs to test hypotheses about the causes of psychiatric disorders.

By the end of the chapter, we hope to have made the case that (1) the goal of epidemiological research is disease prevention; (2) understanding the development of a disease and intervening to prevent and control it are equally important aspects of epidemiological research; (3) understanding the development of a disease may point to different kinds of intervention at different stages in the developmental process; and (4) understanding individual development is a critical part of understanding and intervening in the disease process, because both risk for and expression of disorder change over the life course.

The work reported here was supported in part with grants from the National Institute of Mental Health (P30-MH57761, R01-MH063970, R01-MH01002, K02-MH01167), the National Institute on Drug Abuse (R01-DA011301, R01-DA016977), and the William T. Grant Foundation.

WHAT IS EPIDEMIOLOGY?

Epidemiology is the study of patterns of disease in human populations (Kleinbaum et al., 1982). Patterns, or nonrandom distributions, of disease occur in both time and space. The task of epidemiology is to understand observed patterns of pathology along these two dimensions and to use this understanding as a basis for prevention and treatment. For example, a pattern has been observed linking exposure to environmental lead in infancy with the development of behavioral and learning problems in later years (Needleman & Bellinger, 1991). The causal relationship appears to be sufficiently strong to justify primary preventive measures to remove lead from gas and domestic paint to protect those children who might otherwise be vulnerable to such exposures.

Epidemiology, "an exact and basic science of social medicine and public health" (Earls, 1979, p. 256), emerged as an influential branch of medicine in the nineteenth century. Like the rest of medicine, it is an action-oriented discipline, whose purpose is intervention to control disease. Epidemiology has both similarities to and differences from clinical medicine. Scientific knowledge about the cause and course of disease is one of the tools that both share. Epidemiology reflects clinical medicine also in using two methods of attack: a tactical method, concerned with the practical and administrative problems of disease control at the day-to-day level, and a strategic method, concerned with finding out what causes disease so that new weapons of control and cure can be engineered (Earls, 1980; Susser, 1973). Thus, epidemiologists can be found, in their tactical or public health role, reporting on the prevalence of AIDS and advising on how to control its spread, while, at the same time, as part of a wide strategic plan to control the disease, they are carrying out multicenter clinical research trials of new vaccines and treatments.

Epidemiology is also like clinical medicine in its understanding of the concept of disease in broad terms. In this chapter, we adopt the definition of disease as a pathological process, which may have biological, psychological, and social dimensions (Kleinbaum et al., 1982; Susser, 1973). Disease in this sense includes, but is by no means limited to, identified syndromes of known etiology. The unifying theme is that, at some point, a decision is made that a pathological process is present in an individual, who is then regarded as a "case." The thorny problems of case identification in child and adolescent psychopathology are discussed later in this chapter.

Epidemiology *diverges* from clinical medicine to the extent that it concentrates on understanding and controlling disease processes in the context of the population at risk, whereas the primary focus of clinical medicine is the individual patient. This does not mean that epidemiology is not concerned with the individual; on the contrary, it is very much concerned with understanding the individual's illness and the causes of that illness. The difference lies in the frame of reference. Put crudely, clinical medicine asks What is wrong with this person and how should I treat him or her? Epidemiology asks What is wrong with this person and what is it about him or her that has resulted in this illness? Why is this child depressed, but not her brother? If her mother is also depressed, is the child's depression a cause, a consequence, or an unrelated, chance co-occurrence? Such questions immediately set the individual child within a frame of reference of other children, or other family members, or other people of the same sex or race or social class. As we shall discuss later, this approach to understanding pathology has important effects on the way information is collected, the kind of information collected, the methods used to analyze it, and the conclusions that can be drawn from it.

As the study of patterns of disease distribution in time and space, epidemiology thus encompasses a great deal more than simply counting how many people have smallpox or AIDS. "Epidemiology counts" (Freedman, 1984, p. 931), but it does far more than that. The methods developed to count cases are useful for many purposes, for example, to estimate the need for and probable cost of mental health services, or to monitor the effect of a new treatment. However, these methods provide only one part of the information needed to understand the course, causes, and prevention of disease. Figure 3.1 (Kleinbaum et al., 1982) shows how the study of disease patterns in time and space informs both public health and scientific epidemiology (Susser, 1973).

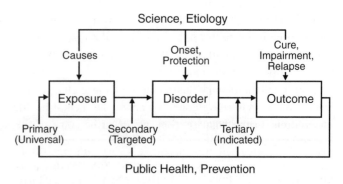

Figure 3.1   Model of the relationship between scientific and public health epidemiology.

Scientific Epidemiology

From the strategic or scientific point of view, the issues at each level have to do with identifying the stages by which a disease progresses through its natural course, generating and testing hypotheses about causal pathways, and inventing and testing methods for prevention to be implemented by the tactical, public health arm of the health care professions. The success or failure of attempts to prevent a disorder can then provide important information about the causes of the problem. The course of disease can be divided into three stages: (1) exposure, dealing with causes; (2) disorder, dealing with the manifestation of a disease in clinical signs and symptoms; and (3) outcome, examining what leads to different outcomes for different patients. These three stages invite different kinds of preventive intervention: (1) primary, or universal, prevention tries to reduce the risk of exposure to agents promoting the disease; (2) secondary, or targeted, prevention is directed at saving those who have been exposed from developing the disease; and (3) tertiary, or indicated, prevention focuses on reducing the damage caused in those who actually become ill. Tertiary prevention encompasses both reducing the residual damage from an illness and, where necessary, protecting the rest of society from harm, either through infection or from a sick person's dangerous behavior.

Although this approach to disease prevention was first articulated at a time when acute, infectious diseases such as cholera and smallpox were the chief preoccupation of epidemiology, it applies with minor modifications to chronic or episodic diseases, such as heart disease and cancer, which are the main causes of mortality in industrialized countries today. Applied to psychopathology, it also provides a model for exploring the development of psychiatric disorders (Rutter, 1990).

Public Health Epidemiology

At the tactical level, public health and primary care workers are often involved in what has been called "shoe-leather epidemiology" (Kleinbaum et al., 1982, p. 25). This might take the form of tracing the pathways by which a cluster of suicides spreads through a high school, or isolating the source of a neurotoxic element in the water supply, or teaching lifestyle changes to cardiac patients to reduce the risk of stress-related disease. The aim is to identify key points in the development and transmission of a disease at which intervention can act to reduce the prevalence of the disease or the harm caused by it. Such interventions may be directed at preventing exposure to the causes of the disorder, at preventing the onset of the disorder in those who are vulnerable to it, or at minimizing death rates or residual impairment in those who survive. Taking depression as an example, primary prevention might include antibullying programs in schools; secondary prevention might be directed at the children of depressed parents, who are known to be a high-risk group (Clark et al., 2002); and tertiary or indicated prevention might examine the ability of adequate treatment to prevent relapse.

There is a great deal of interchange between the public health aspects and the scientific aspects of epidemiology, and also between different levels of investigative and preventive effort. At each of these levels, both strategic and tactical efforts are needed. Indeed, the real-world nature of epidemiology means that the answers to many scientific questions, such as the paths of disease transmission, have at some stage to be tested by regarding a preventive intervention as a scientific experiment. The classic example is the story of how John Snow (1855), by having the handle removed from the Broad Street water pump during the 1853 cholera epidemic in London, tested his hypothesis that (1) cholera was caused by an invisible, self-reproducing agent living in water; (2) the agent flourished in water heavily contaminated with sewage; and (3) therefore, if a community drawing its water from a contaminated supply was forced (by his action in disabling the pump) to use water from a different water company, drawn from a purer source, the rate of disease would fall.

CHARACTERISTICS OF RESEARCH IN PSYCHIATRIC EPIDEMIOLOGY

Epidemiology, as this brief introduction demonstrates, is less a body of substantive knowledge than it is a way of looking at problems. The great historical victories over infectious diseases and the recent achievements in helping to reduce mortality and morbidity from chronic illnesses such as cardiovascular disease (Dawber, 1980) came as a result of looking at clinical problems in a new way. Here we introduce the basic requirements for studying the epidemiology of any disorder (Kleinbaum et al., 1982) and discuss their implications for developmental psychopathology.

Epidemiologic research presupposes the ability to (1) measure disease frequency in the population of interest; (2) make valid generalizations from samples to populations; that is, to avoid sampling or ascertainment bias; and (3) measure the impact of risk factors on disease without confusion among multiple competing risks; that is, to avoid confounding among risk factors. We discuss each of these challenges in turn.

Measuring the Frequency of Disease

The question of how many people exposed to a risk factor for a disease actually become sick, how many avoid disease, and how many die or recover is central to epidemiological research. The most frequently used measures involve the concept of a rate, "an instantaneous potential for change in one quantity per unit change in another quantity" (Kleinbaum et al., 1982, p. 3). Timing is implicit in the idea of a rate. Epidemiology deals most often with incidence rates, which measure the extent to which new cases of a disorder appear in the previously healthy population over a specified period of time, and prevalence rates, which measure all the cases, whether new or previously existing, observed during a specified period. Usually, the epidemiologist is concerned with relative rates of disease onset in two or more groups of people who differ on exposure to a risk or preventive factor. For example, in a Swedish study, the prevalence of drunkenness in adolescence among girls who reached menarche earlier than the norm for the population was found to be high, relative to the rate found in girls of the same age whose menarche occurred within the normal age range (Stattin & Magnusson, 1990). Relative rates thus become the metric for answering questions about a possible causal role played by putative risk factors in the onset of disorder. In this example, Stattin and Magnusson found that, at age 14, 75% of girls who had reached menarche before age 11 had been drunk at least once, compared with only 29% of girls who reached menarche after age 13. Furthermore, the rate of frequent drunkenness remained higher across adolescence for early than for later maturing girls. This led to speculations about the mechanism by which early puberty could put girls at risk (Moffitt, Caspi, Belsky, & Silva, 1992).

Defining a "Case"

In any context where decisions have to be made leading to action to prevent or treat illness, categories have to be created. Making a diagnosis means putting an individual into a category: "Has Disorder X" or "Does not have Disorder X." Even if the goal is to eliminate a risk factor that potentially affects everyone in the community, such as environmental pollutants or unsafe automobiles, it is still necessary to define categories of affected and nonaffected individuals to measure the effectiveness of a primary prevention or to calculate costs and benefits; for example, how many cases of learning disability were prevented by reducing environmen-

tal lead? How much does it cost to prevent one case of learning disability, and how much is saved by doing so?

The relationship among symptoms, diagnosis, and the concept of disease has exercised many brains (Meehl, 1992; Pickles & Angold, 2003). A diagnosis encapsulates a mixed bag of information: the number and severity of symptoms, the duration of symptomatology, the date of onset, the likelihood of exposure to a causal factor, and the level of functional impairment. All of these have implications for a decision about whether intervention is indicated. For some forms of pathology, there is little ambiguity about how the diagnosis should be made; either it is fairly self-evident, like a broken bone, or the rules have been sanctified by use, like the stages of cervical cancer, or there is a clearly identifiable pathogen that acts as a marker for the disease, as in tuberculosis. Few types of psychopathology can invoke any one of these as a decision rule for diagnosis. There are no reliable pathognomic markers; the boundaries between one disorder and another, or between normality and disorder, are generally ill-defined (Pickles & Angold, 2003), as Kendell (1976) demonstrated in his classic exploration of the boundaries of depression. Classification systems arise and pass away, while older classifications may still retain some of their sway. To confuse matters further, psychiatry often makes use of familiar language in its diagnostic terminology (e.g., "depression," "anxiety"), not necessarily in the vernacular meaning of the term. In his review of childhood depression, for example, Angold (1988) identified eight different ways the term "depression" is used in the description of psychopathology:

- As the low end of normal mood fluctuations
- As a description of psychic pain felt in response to some unpleasant situation
- As a trait
- As an individual symptom
- As a syndrome
- As a disorder
- As a disease
- As a cause of handicap or disability

The implications for treatment are likely to differ, depending on which definition is being used.

Taxonomy, Instrumentation, and Mechanisms

In identifying cases of a disorder, it is important to distinguish between the problems that can be solved by a well-designed diagnostic instrument and those that have to be solved at the level of the taxonomic system that defines what a case is (Meehl, 1992; Wing, Bebbington, & Robins,

1981). For example, L. N. Robins (1989) presented evidence that some *DSM* disorders are consistently diagnosed more validly (using several criteria of validity) than others, using both clinical and epidemiological methods. This, Robins believed, suggests that "part of the source of invalidity lies in the diagnostic grammar of the systems whose criteria standardized interviews evaluate" (p. 57). She used the phrase "diagnostic grammar" because, she argued, "[diagnosis] is much like a language. The criteria include elements that have special relations to each other like parts of speech—symptoms (nouns?); severity (adjectives?); clustering (verbs?); age of onset, frequency, and duration (adverbs?)" (p. 61). If the grammar is wrong, the sentence will not make sense, however clearly it is articulated. Much of the process of developing a good diagnostic grammar is carried out through careful clinical work. Epidemiology, however, can contribute in several ways. It provides feedback about the relationship between symptom patterns seen in clinical and community samples, which can throw light on possible biases affecting the results (see later discussion). It can also provide information about the prevalence of different disorders in the community and their patterns of distribution by age, sex, and so on. This information can then influence clinicians' expectations about the relative likelihood that a given patient has one disorder rather than another. In practice, it is well-known that physicians make diagnostic judgments on the basis of very few items of information (Cantwell, 1988; Meehl, 1954). Good prevalence information can be a very important part of the clinician's database.

Psychiatric epidemiologists have long been active collaborators with clinicians in the work carried out around the world to improve psychiatric taxonomies (L. N. Robins, 1985, 1989). However, the task facing epidemiology is even more difficult than that facing clinical psychiatry. The clinician can assume a certain level of suffering in a patient who has come seeking help; the problem is to figure out exactly where the suffering lies. Epidemiologists, working most of the time in the community, have to identify cases among people most of whom are not seeking treatment. They have to convince themselves and others that the criteria they use are valid: that a clinician would identify this person as a "case" of a given disorder whether or not the individual came seeking treatment.

For child psychiatry, this problem of case definition is even more complex. Children rarely refer themselves for treatment, even when severely symptomatic. Thus, the rule of thumb that equates illness with seeking treatment is even less accurate for children than it is for adults. Refer-

ral for treatment may have more to do with characteristics of a child's mother, teacher, or pediatrician than with the child's own behavior or feelings (E. J. Costello & Janiszewski, 1990; Dulcan et al., 1990; Shepherd, Oppenheim, & Mitchell, 1971).

A third aspect of case identification is the discovery of mechanisms that underlie the development of psychiatric disorders. These mechanisms exist at many different levels, from genes to brain structure and functioning. Despite much exciting progress in identifying mechanisms (discussed later), none is yet ready for use in everyday clinical or epidemiologic diagnosis. Child psychiatry is still largely dependent for case identification on asking verbal questions.

Using Question-and-Answer Methods to Identify Cases

Psychiatry confronts two problems that make it particularly difficult to develop reliable and accurate measures of symptoms and diagnoses using question-and-answer methods. One is that there are no "gold standard" measures that can be used to evaluate the accuracy of a test: a postmortem or an MRI will not tell us whether a child really had Separation Anxiety Disorder. The second problem is with the standard procedure for assessing the reliability of a question-and-answer measure: the test-retest reliability procedure, which uses two interviewers to interview the same subject on two different occasions about the same period of time. Whereas one can take someone's temperature repeatedly without appreciably altering body temperature, interviewing someone at length about emotionally sensitive topics can hardly be done without affecting how the individual thinks or feels about these issues. The first interview is thus likely to affect how the subject responds to the second interview. For example, in a test-retest study in which children were interviewed twice, we found that boys who, at the first interview, admitted that they told a lot of lies, were much more likely than other boys to deny, at the second interview, other kinds of deviant behavior to which they had previously admitted (Angold & Costello, 1995). However, a lot is now known about how to improve accuracy in child psychiatric interviewing, and current methods are remarkably reliable (Shaffer, Lucas, & Richters, 1999).

Classifying Cases in the Clinic and the Community

The problem of equating cases found in community studies with referred cases has been addressed in several ways in child psychiatric epidemiology. First, diagnostic instruments have been developed that meticulously translate clinical diagnostic criteria into methods for identifying the same symptoms in nonreferred cases (Angold & Costello, 2000; Angold, Cox, Prendergast, Rutter, & Simonoff, 1992; Chambers et al., 1985; A. J. Costello, Edelbrock, Kalas, Kessler, & Klaric, 1982; Herjanic & Campbell, 1977; Hodges, McKnew, Cytryn, Stern, & Kline, 1982; Shaffer, Fisher, Lucas, Dulcan, & Schwab-Stone, 2000).

Second, most measures for community use now include, or are used with, measures of functional impairment, so that the relationship between symptoms and a child's ability to carry out the normal tasks of daily life can become the subject of empirical review. At the same time, current attempts to classify psychiatric disorders into a coherent taxonomy have adopted a multiaxial system by which a clinician is encouraged to describe the patient from several points of view, of which psychiatric diagnosis is only one (American Psychiatric Association, 1994; Rutter et al., 1969; Rutter, Shaffer, & Sturge, 1979). Several current epidemiological assessment instruments adopt the same multiaxial approach (Angold & Costello, 2000; Shaffer et al., 2000).

Third, the psychometric studies that are carried out as part of the process of instrument development include studies of referred and nonreferred samples and interviews using both clinicians and trained lay interviewers. Instruments can then be revised so that "caseness" has the same meaning wherever or by whomever a child is recruited or assessed.

Developmental Issues in Case Identification

One reason establishing rates of disorder is even more of a problem for child psychiatric epidemiology is that there is a need to reconcile a nondevelopmental psychiatric taxonomy, such as the *DSM* system, with the realities of child development. The *DSM* system sticks closely to an implicit medical model, according to which a disease, although it has a developmental course along the lines sketched earlier, is defined as a disease by virtue of the fact that every case has roughly the same etiology, pathogenesis, risk factors, presentation, course, and treatment response. Measles is measles is measles. For example, the diagnostic criteria for *DSM-IV* Major Depressive Episode are described as being similar in their essential features in children, adolescents, and adults (American Psychiatric Association, 1994); the only differences specified are additions to two of the symptoms: "(1) depressed mood. In children and adolescents, can be irritable mood" and "(3) significant weight loss or weight gain. . . . In children, consider failure to make expected weight gains" (p. 327). A section on age-specific features of depression (p. 220) discusses symptoms or forms of comorbidity with other disorders that may occur with different frequency at different ages, but no reference is made to any aspect of children's cognitive, social, and bodily development that might influence a child's ability to experience or respond to different symptoms. Neither the similarities nor the differences specified by the *DSM* have a firm basis in developmental data about the manifestation of depression at different stages of life (Angold & Worthman, 1993; Cicchetti & Schneider-Rosen, 1984, 1986; E. J. Costello et al., 2002; Digdon & Gotlib, 1985).

In summary, epidemiology shares with clinical psychiatry a concern for and involvement in the problems of case identification. These problems occur at two levels: the level of defining the characteristics of a disorder and the level of developing methods for identifying those who have the disorder so defined. Arguments about the reliability and validity of psychiatric assessment have frequently confused these two levels, as L. N. Robins (1985, 1989) has so clearly demonstrated. Only when we can clearly describe the causal pathway for each disorder, from exposure through onset to outcome, as in Figure 3.1, will we be in a position to be satisfied with the validity of our taxonomy and the reliability of our diagnostic tools.

Ascertainment Bias in Case Identification

Once researchers are able accurately to identify cases of the disorder of interest, the next concern is to ensure that the sample of cases that they recruit for research purposes accurately represents the distribution of cases in the community. The reason this is so important is the need for the relationship between the disorder and its putative risk factors to be the same in the sample as in the general population. It is the nature of epidemiological research that questions of causality can rarely be answered by laboratory studies in which all but the key variable are carefully controlled or randomly varied. It is not feasible to test the causal role of poverty, for example, by randomly assigning newborns to be raised in high- and low-income households, or the role of maternal temperament by the sort of cross-fostering studies that are considered ethical with other primates (Suomi, 1991). One way to compensate is to pay very careful attention to the characteristics of the population from which the study samples are drawn, that is, not only to the numerator of a rate of disease (the number of cases within a given period) but also to the denominator of the rate (the population at risk). Only when we know that the sample selected for study accurately mirrors the population from which it is drawn (or when we know exactly what the biases are and how to control for them) can we specify exactly to whom our causal analyses apply.

This necessity usually rules out samples of convenience and mandates very careful thought about the choice of population for a study. For example, if the question has to do with the causal role played by the peer group in adolescent delinquency, and the sample consists of young people recruited from 10th-grade classrooms, neither the denominator nor the numerator can, by definition, include persons who have dropped out of school. Thus, the conclusions about causal processes that can be drawn from such a study are limited to those relevant to 10th graders who attend school, not to the age group in general. Because dropping out of school and delinquency are known to be associated, the selection of a school-based sampling frame results in a sample that may be biased in important ways.

The problem of ascertainment bias is even more acute when clinic-based samples are used. There are many reasons people get into treatment, and reasons they do not, and these may mislead the researcher trying to understand risk factors for disease. For example, Berkson (1946, p. 50) used Mayo Clinic records to show that among people with two illnesses, "each disease is itself aggravated in its symptoms and more likely to be noted by the patient . . . [the] effect would be to increase relatively the representation of multiple diagnoses in the hospital and in general to increase the discrepancy between hospital and parent population." This led to a spurious belief that cholecystic disease was causally related to diabetes, when in fact, in the general population the association between the two diseases was zero.

Berkson (1946) argued from these analyses that it is more cost-efficient to carry out representative community studies earlier rather than later in the process of studying comorbidity and etiology because bias-free studies have to be done at some point in any case. Meehl (1992, p. 124) is another writer who has pointed out that "millions of dollars of tax money have been wasted" performing studies in clinical settings where the biases inherent in case selection mean that the studies cannot answer the questions about causal association that they are designed to address.

The danger of ascertainment bias is one reason many epidemiological studies use samples that are carefully selected to be representative of the general population. The disease of interest may be quite rare in the community, which often means that the case-identification stage of such studies is expensive; large numbers of people must be surveyed to identify a relatively small number of cases. With child psychiatric disorders, the issue is compounded because reports from different informants—parents, children, teachers, peers—may identify very different children

as cases (Achenbach, McConaughy, & Howell, 1987; Rutter, Tizard, & Whitmore, 1970). Depending on the question being studied, it may be necessary to interview three or more people to establish whether a child is or is not a case according to the study criteria. The risk factors for a disorder identified by one informant may also be quite different from the risk factors for the disorder as identified by another informant. For example, in a study of children with symptoms of hyperactivity, inattention, and impulsivity (E. J. Costello, Loeber, & Stouthamer-Loeber, 1991), 61% of children identified as hyperactive by both parents and teachers were boys; however, boys made up 77% of children identified as hyperactive by teachers alone, but only 38% of children identified by mothers alone.

For the researcher interested in developmental influences on the expression of psychopathology, the situation becomes even more complex. For example, Figure 3.2 shows the rate of separation anxiety symptoms reported by children between the ages of 7 and 16 and by parents about their children. The parents' report data showed low rates of symptoms and a modest effect of the child's age on the rate of symptoms. The rate of symptoms reported by the children, in contrast, fell sevenfold as the age of the child increased. If the purpose of the study had been to select a sample of cases of Separation Anxiety Disorder, the bias caused by relying exclusively on one informant or the other would have varied depending on the age of the children surveyed.

Controlling Bias in Estimating the Influence of Risk Factors

The third set of threats to the validity of a causal link has to do with competing risk factors or confounders. In most

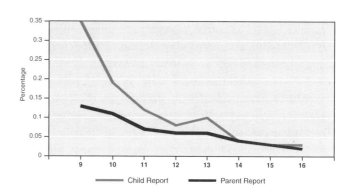

Figure 3.2 Mean separation anxiety symptoms by age and source of information. Data from the Great Smoky Mountains Study.

etiological studies, more than one risk factor is involved. The problem is to figure out the relative importance of various risk factors so that decisions about intervention can be focused where they will be most effective. It is useful to distinguish between two distinct characteristics of factors that influence the probability of disease: confounding and effect modification (Miettinen, 1974).

Confounding distorts the impact of a risk factor on the risk of disease because of the presence of some extraneous variable. A factor may act as a confounder in one study but not in another. Consider, for example, two groups at high and low levels of genetic risk for a disease that is also affected by poverty. If everyone in one group was at high genetic risk, a "real" relationship between poverty and disease might be obscured in that community; almost everyone who was poor would also be at genetic risk, so it would not be possible to say which factor was causing the disorder. In the second community, where not all the poor were at high genetic risk and not all the group at high genetic risk were poor, it would be possible to look separately at the rates of disorder in four groups (poor nonaffected, rich nonaffected, poor affected, rich affected) and figure the risk associated with poverty.

Effect modification, or synergy, refers to the different impact of a risk factor at different levels of another variable (Rothman, 1976). This relationship is not specific to any particular study; it is a "real" relationship among two or more risk factors. For example, if both the gene for phenylketonuria (PKU) and a diet high in phenylalanine are necessary for PKU to occur, rates of the disorder will vary in different communities depending on how many people inherit the gene and how many eat a high-phenylalanine diet. The relationship between gene and diet remains constant across sites, but diet will act as an effect modifier, controlling the expression of the gene. Another example is the relationship among peak height velocity (PHV, the "growth spurt" of early adolescence), change of school, and depressive symptoms. The period of PHV may be a time when youngsters are particularly vulnerable to symptoms of depression (Simmons & Blyth, 1987), particularly when they have to deal with stressful events. It happens that, in the American school system, most children move from middle school to high school between eighth and ninth grades. This coincides with the time when many girls, but few boys, are at PHV. School change could thus be acting as an effect modifier, increasing the risk of depression in girls but not in boys.

Clinical as well as epidemiologic research has to deal with confounders and effect modifiers. Lively debates are in progress about whether and how to derive causal infer-

ences from observational studies with many potential confounders (Dehejia & Wahba, 1999; Kaufman & Cooper, 1999; J. Robins, 1997; J. Robins, Greenland, & Hu, 1999; J. Robins, Hernan, & Brumback, 2000; Vineis & Porta, 1996; Weinberg & Umbach, 2000; Winship & Morgan, 1999). Sometimes it is possible to narrow down the list of potential causes using careful study design. When standard experimental designs are inappropriate or infeasible, quasi-experimental methods may be found that reduce the risk that cases and noncases differ not only on the putative risk factor, but in lots of other ways as well (Shadish, Cook, & Campbell, 2002). For example, in our study of all 9-, 11-, and 13-year-old American Indian children living on a federal reservation, it happened that after we had assessed the children for 4 years, a casino was opened that gave every enrolled tribal member a sizable income supplement. After another 4 years, we looked at children's psychiatric symptoms before and after the "intervention." We found that children whose families moved out of poverty had reduced Conduct Disorder symptoms, but that the intervention had little effect on depression, anxiety, or Attention-Deficit/Hyperactivity Disorder (ADHD; E. J. Costello, Compton, Keeler, & Angold, 2003). Because every man, woman, and child on the reservation received the income supplement, there was no possibility that the effect of an increased income could be confounded with the sort of qualities (hard work, thrift, etc.) that could cause both an income increase and a reduction in behavioral symptoms.

The other set of methods to deal with competing risk factors is statistical. Epidemiologists have always been careful to make it clear that nonexperimental studies can show associational but not causal relationships between risk factors and outcomes. Recently, however, they are coming closer to claiming the ability to talk about "causal associations" (J. Robins, 1997; J. Robins et al., 2000). Some have gone so far as to claim that properly designed observational studies can produce results that are superior to those based on experimental designs, because they often have a level of ecological validity that experimental studies lack (Benson & Hartz, 2000; Concato, Shah, & Horwitz, 2000; Winship & Morgan, 1999).

The idea that some effect modifiers could operate as protective factors has been widely discussed (Garmezy, 1988; Loeber, Farrington, Stouthamer-Loeber, Moffitt, & Caspi, 1998; Stouthamer-Loeber et al., 1993). As Rutter (1985) has pointed out, there are logical problems in identifying something as a protective factor, except in the presence of a risk or vulnerability; the concept of protection implies the presence of risk. However, in terms of Figure 3.1, it is reasonable to talk about protection from risk factors for a disease, as well as protection from risk of disease, given exposure. For example, decent sewage systems protect the whole community from exposure to the cholera vibrio, and good nutrition might help to protect an individual exposed to the infection from actually developing the disease.

Measuring the Impact of Risk and Protective Factors

One implication of this discussion of risk factors is that it is possible to rank risk (and protective) factors in terms of their relative importance to the rate of an observed disorder, and thus to make decisions about the most cost-efficient preventive strategies. There are several ways to calculate the importance of a factor's contribution to the prevalence of a disease. Two of these are risk ratio or relative risk and excess or attributable risk. Relative risk is a ratio comparing two risks of disease, often, the risk of a disease in a group exposed to a risk factor compared with the risk in a nonexposed group (e.g., the risk of depression in children of divorced parents compared with the risk to children in intact families). Attributable risk is an estimate of the extra cases of disease (above the rate in the nonexposed population) attributable to exposure to a particular risk factor. Attributable risk is a function of two factors: the relative risk in groups exposed and not exposed to the risk factor and the frequency of the risk factor in the population. Thus, even if the relative risk associated with a risk factor is high, the attributable risk, and thus the decrease in incidence of the disease if that risk factor were removed, may be low if the proportion of people in the population exposed to that risk factor is low. For example, there might be a high relative risk for lung cancer associated with exposure to a chemical used only in one particular industry, but the attributable risk would be low if only a few people worked in that industry and were exposed to that chemical. From a public health viewpoint, a greater reduction in the number of cases of lung cancer might be achieved by removing a risk factor with a lower relative risk but to which more people are exposed, for example, asbestos or cigarette smoke (Lilienfeld & Lilienfeld, 1980; Rothman, 1976). Measures of relative risk are particularly important for the scientific aspect of epidemiology, because they are a way of estimating the causal impact of risk factors. Measures of attributable risk are of particular interest from the practical point of view, because they can generate an estimate of the impact of a risk or protective factor in real or proportional terms.

This discussion of causality begs an underlying question: whether it makes any sense to think about human behavioral development in terms of continuity and causes. Some developmental psychologists have argued that predic-

tion is not only difficult but is unnecessary for the study of psychopathology (Lewis, 1990). Epidemiology has not adopted this approach; on the contrary, it has put its money on its ability to control disease through the prediction of causal pathways, and historically this has been an immensely successful bet. The interesting question is whether it is an approach that will prove to be as effective in the area of developmental psychopathology as it has been for infectious diseases.

Summary

In this section, we have discussed three functions of epidemiology: (1) to measure disease frequency and risk exposure; (2) to make valid generalizations from samples to populations; and (3) to control bias in relating risk factors to disease. The next question is whether, and how, the methods and ideas that have evolved over the past century, primarily to tackle infectious diseases, can be adapted to a moving target like developmental psychopathology.

WHAT IS DEVELOPMENTAL EPIDEMIOLOGY?

Epidemiology is inherently a developmental discipline, as shown in Figure 3.1, in the sense that it is concerned with the development of disease and how to intervene in that process. However, we talk about developmental epidemiology as a special variety of epidemiology when we are dealing with child psychopathology. The reason is that in this case, we have to take account of another developmental model: the model that describes the development of the individual. From this point of view, developmental epidemiology can be seen as concerned with the interaction between two developmental processes: of the organism (the child) and of the disease. The importance of understanding this interaction was pointed out by Anna Freud (1965; see Cicchetti, 1990a; Rutter, 1988), but her view of what develops was somewhat different from the view of both developmental psychology and developmental psychopathology today. In this chapter, our use of the concept of development, which follows that of developmental psychology and biology, will be familiar to developmentalists but may carry different implications for child psychiatrists and pediatricians trained to use the term development either in the context of psychodynamic theories of personality (Dare, 1985) or to refer to specific, mainly physical or cognitive, stages of development (American Psychiatric Association, 1994). For clarification, we offer a brief review of what we understand by development.

The Concept of Development

Earlier in this chapter, we discussed epidemiology as a scientific method of understanding the development of disease (see Figure 3.1). This approach shows marked similarities with the way the word development is applied to biological organisms (Hay & Angold, 1993). As Nagel (1957, p. 15) defined it:

> The concept of development involves two essential components: the notion of a system possessing a definite structure and a definite set of preexisting capacities; and the notion of a sequential set of changes in the system, yielding relatively permanent but novel increments not only in its structure but in its modes of operation.

The process of disease progression has much in common with development: It is "programmed" by the nature of the transformation of the organism that begins the process, and in general it follows a reasonably regular course, although with wide variations in its rate. Furthermore, there is hierarchical integration as diseases develop. Each stage in the progress of a given disease builds on the previous stages, and many of the manifestations of earlier stages are "integrated" into later symptomatology.

This has much in common with the idea of *epigenesis,* as developed by Gottlieb (1991, p. 7):

> Individual development is characterized by an increase of complexity of organization (i.e., the emergence of new structural and functional properties and competencies) at all levels of analysis (molecular, subcellular, cellular, organismic) as a consequence of horizontal and vertical coactions among the organisms' parts, including organism-environment coactions. Horizontal coactions are those that occur at the same level (gene-gene . . . organism-organism), whereas vertical coactions occur at different levels (. . . cell-tissue . . . behavioral activity-nervous system) and are reciprocal, meaning that they can influence each other in either direction, from lower to higher or from higher to lower levels of the developing system.

For example, the genome controls cell structure, but environmentally induced cytoplasmic changes are capable of switching genes on and off (Ho, 1984; Jollos, 1934); neural differentiation in the mammalian visual cortex is dramatically affected by sensory experience (Black & Greenough, 1986); and neuroendocrine mechanisms are powerfully influenced by sociocultural factors (Mineka, Gunnar, & Champoux, 1986; Worthman, 1987; Worthman & Konner, 1987). Recent longitudinal epidemiologic studies showed that a functional polymorphism in the gene encoding the neurotransmitter-metabolizing enzyme monoamine oxidase

A (MAOA) moderated the effect of early maltreatment, so that maltreated children, if they owned the allele conferring high levels of MAOA expression, were less likely to develop antisocial problems in adolescence (Caspi et al., 2002; Foley et al., 2004). Thus, the concept of development used here (1) presupposes change and novelty, (2) underscores the importance of timing in behavioral establishment and organization, (3) emphasizes multiple determination, and (4) leads us not to expect invariant relationships between causes and outcomes across the span of development (Cacioppo & Tassinary, 1991; Cairns, 1991).

Behavior is seen as resulting from the dynamic interaction of multiple interdependent systems in both the individual and the environment. As summarized by Eisenberg (1977, p. 220), "The process of development is the crucial link between genetic determinants and environmental variables, between individual psychology and sociology." It is characteristic of such systems that they consist of feedback and feed-forward loops of varying complexity. Organism and environment are mutually constraining, however, with the result that developmental pathways show relatively high levels of canalization (Angoff, 1988; Cairns, Gariepy, & Hood, 1990; Gottlieb, 1991; Greenough, 1991; McGue, 1989; Plomin, DeFries, & Loehlin, 1977; Scarr & McCartney, 1983). For example, consider the well-established path to substance abuse (Kandel & Davies, 1982):

Beer or wine → Cigarettes or hard liquor
→ Marijuana → Other illicit drugs

It is characteristic of this pathway that the number of individuals at each level becomes smaller, but that those at the higher levels continue to show behaviors characteristic of the earlier stages. Having described such a pathway, the task is to understand the process by which it is established and to invent preventive strategies appropriate to the various stages of the developmental pathway. Such strategies must be appropriate to the developmental stage of both the individual at risk and the disorder.

Research based on this view of development has been going on for several decades, as these volumes attest, but has taken some time to influence child psychiatric epidemiology (Angold & Costello, 1991; Broidy et al., 2003; Brook, Cohen, & Jaeger, 1998; Buka & Lipsitt, 1994; E. J. Costello & Angold, 1993; Jaffee et al., 2002; Rutter, 1988). Conversely, until recently, developmental psychopathology has paid less attention to some of the key concerns of epidemiology—in particular, the importance of representative samples and controls for confounding—but this is beginning to change.

Implications of a Developmental Approach to Child Psychiatric Epidemiology

Child psychiatry, in its current manifestation in the United States, has modeled its nosology and its concepts of health and disease on adult psychiatry, using the same nomenclature and static assumptions about causality, risk factors, course, and outcome. But children are not scaled-down adults, and this approach causes serious problems for the epidemiologist concerned with explaining patterns of disease distribution in the community. Why, for example, do rates of depressive disorders, which are low in prepubertal children of both sexes, continue low in postpubertal boys but rise very sharply in postpubertal girls (Angold, Costello, & Worthman, 1999; Angold, Worthman, & Costello, 2003)? Is the increase causally associated with age, or with pubertal status, or with something else entirely? To understand these phenomena, it seems reasonable to postulate that children are organisms developing at a different rate from adults, organisms in whom developmental changes dramatically alter both the ways they can manifest their genetic endowment and the nature of their interactions with their surroundings. Here we consider the implications of some basic principles of developmental theory for the epidemiology of child psychiatric disorders.

Implication 1: Development Implies Change

This may seem to be an obvious statement, but child psychiatric epidemiology has not always taken the idea of change very seriously. This is partly the result of the current systems for the classification of diseases, which are essentially nondevelopmental. Most disorders have definitions that take no account of age or developmental level, sometimes in spite of overwhelming evidence that age-dependent changes are a central feature of the phenomenology of the disorders involved. Conduct Disorder is a good example. Loeber and colleagues (Loeber, Keenan, & Zhang, 1997) identified three different developmental pathways involving antisocial behavior. If a cross-sectional, snapshot view was taken of behavior at any point in time, children who pursued any of these three pathways shared many characteristics. Longitudinal studies, however, revealed different patterns. Children who followed the authority conflict path tended to show conduct problems early in life, to have trouble at school because of hyperactivity and learning difficulties as well as conduct problems, to explore a wide range of different deviant behaviors, and to remain deviant well into adulthood. Some of the same behaviors could be found in other children at any given time, but a second group of these followed a different, covert pathway, with a higher remission rate.

These children tended to have started showing deviant behavior later in childhood than the first group and to have had fewer problems at school or with peers. Longitudinal studies also suggested the existence of a third group who, like the first, were aggressively deviant in adolescence, but who showed little or no early Conduct Disorder. The evidence for these different developmental patterns has been pieced together from a multitude of different studies, using both clinical and population samples, and is much stronger for boys than for girls (Loeber & Baicker-McKee, 1990). The *DSM-IV*, in contrast, ignores strong evidence that Conduct Disorder in children is a precursor of Antisocial Personality Disorder in adults (L. N. Robins & Price, 1991; L. N. Robins & Wish, 1977), to the extent of coding Conduct Disorder on Axis I (Clinical Disorders) and adult Antisocial Personality Disorder on Axis II (Personality Disorders and Mental Retardation).

Questions about development and change can be addressed using methods developed to identify developmental trajectories (Land & Nagin, 1996; Nagin & Tremblay, 2001a). These methods have been used, for example, to show that there are important differences between children who show persistent, rather than time-limited, conduct problems (Foster, Nagin, Hagan, Costello, & Angold, 2005; Maughan, Pickles, Rowe, Costello, & Angold, 2000; Nagin & Tremblay, 2001b) or obesity (Mustillo et al., 2003).

Implication 2: Development Is Goal-Directed

If we accept what Mayr (1982) called the biological "metaphor" or "heuristic" of development, then we accept a teleonomic, goal-directed explanation as part of that metaphor. In Mayr's words:

> A physiological process or a behavior that owes its goal-directedness to the operation of a program can be designated as teleonomic. . . . All the processes of individual development (ontogeny) as well as all seemingly goal-directed behaviors of individuals fall in this category, and are characterized by two components: they are guided by a program, and they depend on the existence of some endpoint or goal which is foreseen in the program regulating the behavior. . . . Each particular program is the result of natural selection and is constantly adjusted by the selective value of the achieved endpoint. (p. 48)

Teleonomic activities are distinguished by Mayr from other types of teleological processes—most important, for our purposes, from those performed by adapted systems (e.g., the cardiovascular or respiratory systems) that "owe their adaptedness to a past selectionist process" (p. 49; see also Hay & Angold, 1993).

TABLE 3.1   Salient Development Issues

Age (Years)	Issues
0–1	Biological regulation; harmonious dyadic interaction; formation of an effective attachment relationship.
1–2.5	Exploration, experimentation, and mastery of the object world (caregiver as secure base); individualization and autonomy; responding to external control of impulses.
3–5	Flexible self-control; self-reliance; initiative; identification and gender concept; establishing effective peer contacts (empathy).
6–12	Social understanding (equity, fairness); gender constancy; same-sex chumships; sense of "industry" (competence); school adjustment.
13+	Formal operations (flexible perspective taking; "as if" thinking); loyal friendships (same sex): beginning heterosexual relationships; emancipation; identity.

From "The Domain of Developmental Psychopathology," by L. A. Sroufe and M. Rutter, 1984, *Child Development, 55*, p. 22.

A teleonomic approach has particular advantages for developmental epidemiology, given its concern with disease elimination and service provision. It enables us to conceive of disease states in terms of inability to achieve one or more of the goals of development, and it points preventive efforts in the direction of those situations in which a particular process or task seems to be particularly salient at a certain phase of life. For example, Sroufe and Rutter (1984, p. 22) have outlined "a series of developmental issues . . . based on the collective experience of numerous developmentalists . . . cutting across affective, cognitive, and social domains" (reproduced in Table 3.1).

Table 3.1 has two major implications for epidemiology. First, it implies that if we want to prevent, for example, Conduct Disorder, we need to define the goal of orderly conduct and the various systems (affect, cognition, impulse, and muscular control) that are most involved with regulating conduct at different developmental stages. This means that we need research to address such questions as the following: Do children who have achieved the goal of forming secure attachments around 1 year of age find behavioral control at age 5 easier than insecurely attached children (Greenberg, Speltz, & DeKlyen, 1993; Lyons-Ruth, 1996)? Intervention designs can be used to test a hierarchical, causal relationship among the various stages (see Cicchetti, 1990b; Cicchetti & Toth, 1992, for a more detailed discussion of this point).

A second, linked implication is that pathology that looks very different at different stages may be causally linked; for example, the "anxious attachment" of a 1-year-old may be causally linked to the emotional lability and superficial friendliness of the same child at age 5, and to an inability to form lasting intimate relationships as an adult. If this were the case, then, from a public health point of view, efforts to support secure attachments in infants would be justified, not just by the manifest anxiety of some 1-year-olds, but by the chance of preventing the social disruption caused by those same children as adolescents and adults.

Implication 3: The Goal of Development Is Normality

Normality is a state not requiring intervention: We would argue the value for developmental epidemiological research of taking the position that the goal of development is normality. That is, among the multiple outcomes of any developmental process there exists a wide range that are not likely to cause a child any serious problems in moving to the next developmental phase or task; any of these outcomes should be defined as normal. Normality and pathology in an epidemiological context can thus be defined in terms of decision making: Is some sort of intervention indicated?

In this respect, epidemiology moves along a different track from much of developmental psychopathology. The latter has tended to adopt the viewpoint of developmental psychology, that many phenomena of interest are best measured on some sort of continuous scale, representing a hypothesized underlying distribution of symptoms or capacities in the population. This makes sense for disciplines whose aim is to map out the pathways by which children's thoughts, feelings, and actions change over time under different internal and external controls (Pickles & Angold, 2003). The specific concern of epidemiology, however, functioning as it does at the interface between scientific understanding and public health, is with those patterns of thought, feeling, and action about which "something must be done" at a given stage for the sake of the child's present or future well-being, or in response to pressures from families, schools, or society in general. Thus, we define a developmental abnormality from an epidemiological point of view as "a state in which intervention is indicated," and normality as "a state in which intervention is not indicated." These definitions do not necessarily require that an intervention be available or effective, only that pathology has a social meaning as well as a medical and a developmental one, and that a corollary of defining a syndrome as pathological is that one would intervene if it were feasible. In this, public health and clinical medicine are alike.

This view of normality and abnormality requires us to take into account not only the symptom or behavior, but also the developmental stage at which it occurs, in deciding whether to devote major efforts to prevention. Taking an example from externalizing behaviors, Loeber and Le Blanc

(1990) pulled together evidence from many studies to argue that behavior that is not highly predictive of later Conduct Disorder in most children at a certain stage may be highly predictive in a specific child if (1) it first occurs earlier than in "normal" children; (2) it occurs with greater frequency than in "normal" children; and (3) it forms part of a "larger-than-normal" or more diversified symptom cluster. These developmental abnormalities frequently go together (Cohen, 1990; Farrington, 1983; Tolan, 1987). This implies that, for example, boys younger than 12 who commit minor acts of theft, vandalism, and substance abuse should be treated as showing a serious problem for which intervention is needed, whereas boys who first commit such acts after age 12 should not be treated so seriously. This is based on evidence that children who begin such acts early are likely to show a much higher rate of delinquency in their late teens than those who begin later (Fréchette & Le Blanc, 1987; Tolan, 1987) and to continue showing delinquent behavior for a longer period of time (Le Blanc & Fréchette, 1989).

Thus, the concept of goal-directed changes toward developmentally appropriate, normal behavior provides a framework within which to study patterns of pathology in time and space and links the study of human development to the study of disease under the heading of developmental epidemiology.

FROM CHILD PSYCHIATRIC EPIDEMIOLOGY TO DEVELOPMENTAL EPIDEMIOLOGY: A BRIEF HISTORY

In this section, we trace the history of developmental epidemiology from the earliest days of child psychiatry to the present.

The Origins of Child Psychiatric Epidemiology

Work on the epidemiology of child and adolescent psychiatric disorders was first undertaken in the late nineteenth century to answer the most pressing question that faced the emerging discipline of child psychiatry: how to classify and care for children with severe disabilities, many of whom were likely to be a public expense for much of their lives. In this context, the main concerns were to identify the nature of the deficits shown by severely impaired children and to find out how many of such children there were.

In the nineteenth century, the disease concept of psychiatric illness replaced the earlier view of psychiatric illness as "moral insanity" (Prichard, 1837).

Mental disease was regarded as a "thing" residing within the affected individual; cases could therefore be counted in the same way as in the epidemiology of physical disease. At the same time, reforms in the administration of psychiatric services (e.g., the assumption by the state of responsibility for mental hospitals) increased the need for statistics and paved the way for epidemiological studies. (Jablensky, 1986, p. 274)

There appear to have been few children in mental hospitals or asylums in the nineteenth century (von Gontard, 1988), but an analogous problem arose here, too: how to identify children who could never be expected to become self-sufficient adults and for whom long-term care, probably at public expense, would be needed (Grob, 1985).

Distinguishing Psychiatric Disorder from Severe Mental Retardation

An important and basic distinction to be made by the end of the nineteenth century was one between "imbeciles" and "lunatics." As universal education spread across Europe and the United States in the second half of the century, children who could not handle the demands of the educational system became a visible and troubling group. In their historical overview of child psychiatry, Chess and Habibi (1978) pointed out that the distinction between, and division of responsibility for, "idiots" and "lunatics" was far from clear until the twentieth century; in 1876, all the charter members of the American Association on Mental Deficiency were psychiatrists, and the child guidance movement in the United States began at the University of Pennsylvania in a clinic set up by Witmer in 1894 primarily to care for the feebleminded. Gradually, over the course of the nineteenth century, specific groups of children were described, and causes for their disabilities were identified. John Langdon Down (1867), a psychiatrist and superintendent of a large asylum for idiots, described Down syndrome, and William Ireland (1877), superintendent of the Scottish National Institution for Imbecile Children, developed a classification into such categories as epileptic, microcephalic, and inflammatory idiocy, demonstrating that the same phenomenon of idiocy could result from many different causes. Mental retardation slowly became recognized as a problem to be treated separately from behavioral and emotional problems. Children with severe developmental deficits began to be seen as lying on a continuum of disability with children who were struggling to survive the new compulsory education system, rather than as simply part of the general class of severely dysfunctional children (although, of course, some children might have both intellectual and psychiatric problems). For example, special classes for the "feebleminded" were mandated in England by the Elementary Education Act (Defective and Epileptic Children) of 1899. Throughout the industrialized world, as the right of all children to education was acknowledged, the care of the mentally retarded largely moved out of the sphere of psychiatry, unless emotional or behavioral problems were also severe. Causal theories focused on genetics, perinatal insults, and early environmental adversity; treatment centered on pinpointing precise deficits and maximizing children's potential, rather than "curing" them, as the pioneers in the treatment of idiocy had hoped to do (von Gontard, 1988).

Distinguishing among Psychiatric Disorders

From the same period, descriptions can be found of children whose cognitive development was normal but who showed serious emotional or behavioral problems. In 1835, the physician James Prichard (1786–1848) wrote that "idiotism and imbecility are observed in childhood, but insanity, properly so termed, is rare before the age of puberty" (1837, p. 127). Following Pinel, the French psychiatrist who had first described "madness without delirium," Prichard distinguished "moral insanity" from, on the one hand, "mania, or raving madness . . . in which the mind is totally deranged" (p. 16), and which he attributed to physical causes such as convulsions, and, on the other hand, imbecility or mental retardation. He thus used "moral" in its eighteenth-century sense of pertaining to personality or character. Henry Maudsley (1879), writing 30 years later, used the term in its nineteenth-century sense, referring to ethics and norms. He distinguished between instinctive insanity, which was "an aberration and exaggeration of instincts and passions," and moral insanity, which was a defect of the moral qualities along a dimension of "viciousness to those extreme manifestations which pass far beyond what anyone would call wickedness" (p. 289). In the process, he broadened the realm of child psychiatry to include problems of conduct previously seen to be the responsibility of religion and the law. Maudsley preferred to use the term "affective" (where Prichard used "moral") "as being a more general term and expressing more truly the fundamental condition of nerve-element, which shows itself in affections of the mode of feeling generally, not of the special mode of moral feeling only" (p. 280).

When writing about etiology rather than classification, however, Prichard and Maudsley followed the French tradition in distinguishing between moral and physical causes of mental disorder, using moral in the sense of what came to be called exogenous causes. Prichard (1837), quoting Georget, listed among moral causes of insanity domestic grief, disappointment in love, political events, fanaticism, jealousy, poverty or reversal of fortune, reading romances, and excessive study. Mental retardation was seen as stemming exclusively from physical causes: either convulsions of some type in the early years, or some defect transmitted from the parent. This defect might itself be inherited, or it might be "traceable to parental intemperance and excess" (p. 44; see Maudsley, 1879).

The dominant causal theory of psychopathology in the second half of the nineteenth century was genetic: Heredity and degeneration caused disease, which started with scarcely perceptible signs in early childhood but took a progressive and irreversible course and would probably be transmitted to future generations if the affected individual were permitted to breed. Even when the proximal cause of insanity was a moral one, "the different forms of insanity that occur in young children . . . are almost always traceable to nervous disease in the preceding generation" (Maudsley, 1879, p. 68).

Psychiatrists in the nineteenth century thus had a developmental causal theory about psychopathology, but it was a narrow form of developmental theory: The development of the disease was progressive and irreversible, tied to the development of the child only in that it manifested itself differently as the child grew, but impervious to other influences, such as treatment or learning. "All one could do was to prevent the most extreme manifestations by strict punishment and to protect those not affected" (von Gontard, 1988, p. 579). The most effective defense for society was to prevent the procreation of the insane, and eugenics and lifelong segregation in asylums were seen as more effective intervention strategies than attempting treatment or cure. Although a continuum of severity was documented in child psychiatric disorders, as it was in mental retardation, the continuum was interpreted quite differently. It took the form of a continuum of degeneration caused by the disease within the individual across time, rather than a distribution of severity that would remain fairly constant across individuals over time, as was the case for mental retardation. Thus, the prognosis, even for children who presented with mild symptoms, was believed to be gloomy.

Psychoanalytic Theory and Developmental Psychopathology

One of the strengths of the psychoanalytic approach to psychopathology, as its theory and treatment methods developed around the turn of the twentieth century, was that it rejected the therapeutic pessimism of much contemporary child psychiatry. Although Sigmund Freud himself accepted that individuals had innate or constitutional characteristics, he developed what his daughter, Anna Freud (1965, p. 520), described as an:

> etiological formula of a sliding scale of internal and external influences: that there are people whose sexual constitution would not have led them into a neurosis if they had not had [certain] experiences, and these experiences would not have had a traumatic effect on them if their libido had been otherwise disposed. (See S. Freud, 1916–1917, p. 347.)

Children whose libido "disposed" them to pathology could be saved by the right environment, or therapy, or both. Thus, although even mild symptoms could be ominous, the course was not inevitable.

Psychoanalytic theory was fundamentally developmental at a time when the term had no place in mainline child psychiatry; as an example, the entries under the heading "Development" in the index of Anna Freud's *Normality and Pathology in Childhood* (1965) take up two columns, whereas there is not a single entry under that heading in two of the classics of mid-twentieth-century American child psychiatry (Chess & Habibi, 1978; Kanner, 1945, 1972). Psychoanalytic theory was also developmental in the multiple senses discussed in this chapter and throughout this volume: It emphasized the multiple determination of outcomes, the transformation and hierarchical integration of behavior, and the emergence of novelty. In the words of Anna Freud (1965, pp. 166–167):

> As we abandon thinking in terms of specific causes of dissociality, we become able to think increasingly in terms of successful or unsuccessful transformations of the self-indulgent and asocial trends and attitudes which normally are part of the original nature of the child. This helps to construct developmental lines which lead to pathological results, although these are more complex, less well defined, and contain a wider range of possibilities than the lines of normal development.

This approach held sway over child psychiatry for almost a century, despite a lack of empirical evidence supporting its interpretation of the etiology of mental disorders (Grunbaum, 1977). In the past 2 decades, Freudian developmental psychopathology, with its emphasis on etiology, has largely been replaced, particularly in the United States, by a more phenomenological approach whose goal has been to follow the example of medicine, which looks for diseases that have a standard etiology and set of manifestations, and of some

branches of psychology, which seek to pin down concepts like intelligence in forms that are deliberately designed to transcend differences that are a function of developmental factors (Cairns & Cairns, 1991). However, although the content of psychodynamic theory has not stood up to empirical research, the form of the theory, with its emphasis on how the development of the child and of the disease are intertwined, retains considerable attraction as a model for developmental psychopathology and epidemiology.

Distinguishing Normal from Abnormal

In contrast to the earlier concentration on severe disorder, work began in the 1940s to differentiate between what Lapouse and Monk (1958) called "deviations from the usual pattern" from behavior that could be seen (at least in hindsight) to be part of the picture of normal development:

> One of the great psychiatric dilemmas of our time is the decision as to what is normal and what is abnormal in human behavior. Lacking specific tests to make the distinction, the diagnostician has recourse mainly to his clinical judgment which rests on his training, experience, perceptiveness, and theoretical persuasion. In child psychiatry, Leo Kanner pointed out that recorded symptoms "are of necessity those of selected groups and not of the total population of children"; and, he continued, "This selectiveness, in the absence of 'normal controls' has often resulted in a tendency to attribute to single behavior items an exaggerated 'seriousness' with regard to their intrinsic psychopathologic significance. The seriousness becomes attached to the signal regardless of what it announces and who announces it. The high annoyance threshold of many fond and fondly resourceful parents keeps away from clinics and out of reach of statistics a multitude of early breath holders, nail biters, nose pickers and casual masturbators who, largely because of this kind of parental attitude, develop into reasonably happy and well-adjusted adults." (Lapouse & Monk, 1958, p. 1136, quoting Kanner, 1945)

By 1970 a number of older general population studies (Cullen & Boundy, 1966; Cummings, 1944; Griffiths, 1952; Haggerty, 1925; Lapouse, 1966; Lapouse & Monk, 1958, 1964; Long, 1941; McFie, 1934; Olson, 1930; Wickman, 1928; Young-Masten, 1938; Yourman, 1932) had reported prevalences of individual problem behaviors reported by parents and teachers of older children and adolescents. One of the achievements of these early child psychiatric epidemiologists was to document just how common individual "abnormal" behaviors are in the general population of children. For example, in their survey of a random sample of 6- to 12-year-olds in Buffalo, New York, Lapouse and Monk (1958) found that 43% of children were reported by their mother to have seven or more fears or worries, 49% to be overactive, and 48% to lose their tempers twice a week or more. Similarly, Shepherd et al. (1971) found that, on their scale of 25 "deviant" behaviors, only 40% of a population sample of elementary school children in Buckinghamshire, England, was not deviant. However, only 2.6% of the children were deviant in seven or more areas. Some of these studies (e.g., Cummings, 1944; Griffiths, 1952; Macfarlane, Allen, & Honzik, 1954) also illustrate a point that seems often to have been forgotten until recently (Loeber & Stouthamer-Loeber, 1997; Tremblay et al., 1999): that some conduct problems now associated with *DSM-IV* Conduct Disorder, such as lying and some forms of aggression, actually have their peak prevalence before age 5 rather than during adolescence.

Measuring Child and Adolescent Psychopathology

The problem with the approach to measuring the prevalence of child psychopathology used in these two studies was illuminated by a review of prevalence studies commissioned for President Carter's Commission on Mental Illness (M. S. Gould, Wunsch-Hitzig, & Dohrenwend, 1980). Prevalence estimates of childhood psychopathology varied widely, depending on whether parents or teachers were surveyed (at that time, children were rarely asked about their own problems). Estimates of the prevalence of "maladjustment" varied widely even when they were based on data from the same informant group: from 6.6% to 22% according to teachers, and from 10.9% to 37% according to mothers. It is difficult either to plan service delivery systems or to examine causal factors if the rate of the disorder itself is so imprecise.

The questionnaires used in the 1950s and 1960s had three other disadvantages for epidemiological research: (1) They were not designed to distinguish clearly among different syndromes or diagnostic clusters of symptoms; (2) they did not take developmental changes into account; and (3) they did not, as a rule, differentiate symptoms of a disorder from any impairment in functioning that might accompany those symptoms but not be a part of the syndrome itself. For example, failing to perform at age-appropriate levels in school could be a symptom of general mental retardation, a specific learning difficulty, or attentional problems associated with ADHD or depression, or it could result from repeated absence from school because of acute separation anxiety or a chronic physical illness. General maladjustment scales did not make it easy to study the relationship between symptoms and impaired functioning in a way that might illuminate causal relationships.

Epidemiologists and clinical researchers have tackled this problem in several different ways in recent decades. The goal of all these approaches is to elicit information that will identify children with psychiatric syndromes or disorders, but the methods differ substantially. Some have developed survey-type questionnaires consisting of questions designed to mirror the symptoms described in a psychiatric taxonomy such as the *DSM* or *ICD*. Others, wanting to capture more of the detailed information about symptom severity, duration, age at onset, and associated impairment that is needed, together with symptom reports, to make a diagnosis or devise a treatment plan, have developed structured psychiatric interviews (Shaffer et al., 1999). The goal (Angold, 2002) has been to mirror as closely as possible the diagnostic skill of experienced child psychiatrists, while overcoming the twin problems that clinicians are notoriously unreliable (Zubin, 1978) and are usually too expensive to be used in large or longitudinal community studies. Here we discuss one or two issues about the use of questionnaires that have implications for developmental epidemiology; the area is covered in detail elsewhere (Angold, 2002; Shaffer et al., 1999).

Questionnaires for Assessing Child Psychopathology

There are hundreds of questionnaires designed for the child, teacher, or parent to complete, covering psychopathology in general or specific syndromes. We discuss just one set of these as examples of the strengths and weaknesses of this approach for developmental epidemiology. Achenbach and his colleagues set out to develop a set of interrelated symptom questionnaires (now called the Achenbach System of Empirically Based Assessment: ASEBA; Achenbach & Rescorla, 2000, 2001, 2003) whose items were selected using a mixture of clinical and epidemiologic methods. The original set of behavioral and emotional problems was compiled from clinical sources, but the process of reducing the list to the number finally selected was based on studies using general population samples. The first of the questionnaires, the Child Behavior Checklist (CBCL; Achenbach & Edelbrock, 1983), was designed for use by parents whose children were 4 through 16. Items endorsed by fewer than 5% or more than 95% of parents were rejected, and language was simplified to be understandable by anyone with a fourth grade education. Achenbach and Edelbrock carried out extensive factor-analytic studies of how items clustered together in children of different age groups and genders. Many of the syndromes identified in this way showed clear links to the standard diagnostic labels used in psychiatry (Verhulst, van der Ende, Ferdinand, & Kasius, 1997). This is not surprising, as the original set of items was submitted by clinicians familiar with how children's symptoms tend to present. However, the CBCL proved to have much higher test-retest reliability than clinicians did and was quick to administer and score.

The work of Achenbach and his colleagues has provided some powerful tools for developmental epidemiology, both practically and conceptually. First, the extensive data collection and careful standardization on large samples set high standards for instrument development. Second, the team developed a closely integrated set of scales associated with the original CBCL, covering infancy to adulthood and available in versions for parent, teacher, and self-report. Third, the list of emotional and behavioral problems is set in the context of questions about the child's social competencies and school performance; basic sociodemographic information also is collected. Fourth, a lot of work has gone into language and layout, and the 4-page questionnaires collect a great deal of information in a brief time (about 20 minutes). As a result of these virtues, the instruments are very widely used for both clinical and epidemiological purposes. They have been translated into many languages, encouraging cross-cultural studies of the generalizability of the identified symptoms and syndromes and their correlates (e.g., van Eldik, Treffers, Veerman, & Verhulst, 2004; Verhulst, Achenbach, Althaus, & Akkerhuis, 1988; Weisz, 1989).

The many virtues of the questionnaire approach adopted by Achenbach and colleagues make it all the more important to recognize its limitations (Achenbach, 1985). First, the strategy of omitting rarely endorsed symptoms means that this method cannot be used to describe some of the most severe and disabling problems, for example, those seen in autistic children. Second, it is important to note that the questionnaire method is predicated on the assumption that the respondent knows the child well enough to be able to make ratings on items like "Feels too guilty" or "Lying or cheating." A checklist is thus a very well-designed form for recording information about a child that the respondent already knows, but the data that it provides can only be as good as the respondent's knowledge of the child in question. Third, this method produces a series of scale scores for each child, standardized relative to a population sample matched for age, sex, and social class. These scores cannot be used to answer such public health questions as "How many children need treatment?," unless certain decision rules are applied to them. A "clinical cut point" has been identified for the global behavioral problem score of the ASEBA checklists, based on a comparison of the scores of children referred for mental health services during the previous year with the scores of nonreferred children (Achen-

bach, 1991). However, as we discuss later, there is reliable evidence from national data and community surveys that fewer than 5% of children are receiving mental health treatment at any time, despite similarly strong evidence that three to five times as many have a psychiatric problem that entails significantly impaired functioning. Receipt of services is a poor criterion for defining need for services (Burns et al., 1995; E. J. Costello, Burns, Angold, & Leaf, 1993; E. J. Costello, Pescosolido, Angold, & Burns, 1998). It is also worth emphasizing that scale scores are standardized to identify a priori a certain percentage of the population as being in the clinical range. Thus, they cannot be used to provide prevalence estimates.

Interviews for Identifying Psychiatric Disorders in Children and Adolescents

The checklist approach does not provide the detailed information about symptom severity, duration, age at onset, and associated impairment that is needed, together with symptom reports, to make a diagnosis or devise a treatment plan. Alternative approaches are needed, ones more closely related to the process of clinical decision making. Beginning with the work of Michael Rutter in the 1960s, a large number of structured psychiatric interviews have been developed. They have much in common. All structured interviews aim to:

- Structure information coverage, so that all interviewers will have collected all relevant information (both confirmatory and disconfirmatory) from all subjects.
- Define how relevant information is to be collected.
- Structure the process by which relevant information is combined to produce a final diagnosis.

Interviews vary widely in how they go about these tasks. However, a general distinction can be made between Interviewer-based (or investigator-based) interviews, respondent-based interviews, and best estimate interviews.

Interviewer-Based Interviews. These are interviews that require the interviewer to make an informed decision based on what the respondent says. Interviewers are expected to question until they can decide whether a symptom meeting the definitions provided by the interview (or known to them from their training) is present or absent. This group of interviews includes the Anxiety Disorders Interview Schedule (Silverman & Rabian, 1995), the Child and Adolescent Psychiatric Assessment (CAPA; Angold & Costello, 2000), the Child Assessment Schedule (Hodges,

1993; Hodges et al., 1982), the paper-and-pencil (not the computerized) versions of the Diagnostic Interview Schedule for Children and Adolescents (DICA; Reich, 2000) and its close relative the Missouri Assessment of Genetics Interview for Children, the Interview Schedule for Children and Adolescents (Sherrill & Kovacs, 2000), various versions of the Kiddie Schedule for Affective Disorders and Schizophrenia (K-SADS; Ambrosini, 2000), and the Pictorial Instrument for Children and Adolescents (Ernst, Cookus, & Moravec, 2000).

Three of these interviewer-based interviews (the K-SADS-P IVR, the DICA, and the CAPA) provide extensive sets of definitions of symptoms and/or detailed guidance on the conduct of the interview. Such glossaries are particularly important when an interviewer-based interview is to be used by nonclinician interviewers because they provide detailed guidance as to what the interviewer is supposed to be looking for in making symptom ratings. Nonclinician interviewers have been shown to be able to make such "clinical" judgments with high reliability when they have received adequate training with such glossaries (Angold & Costello, 1995).

Respondent-Based Interviews.   In other psychiatric interviews, it is the respondent who makes the final decision about whether a symptom is present, typically by answering yes or no to each question. The interviewer makes no such decisions, but simply reads the questions. Because the decision as to the presence or absence of psychopathology lies with the respondent in such interviews, we refer to them as respondent-based. The Diagnostic Interview Schedule for Children (DISC; Shaffer et al., 2000), the computer-assisted version of the DICA (Reich, 2000), and the Dominic-R (Valla, Bergeron, & Smolla, 2000) are the three representatives of this approach.

A variant on these two approaches to interviewing is taken in the Development and Well-Being Assessment (Goodman, Ford, Richards, Gatward, & Meltzer, 2000), which is widely used around the world. Here the interviewer uses a respondent-based approach first, then supplements the information by asking additional questions. The responses to these are integrated with the structured responses by an experienced clinician, who formulates the diagnosis.

The distinction between interviewer- and respondent-based interviews is not hard and fast in actual practice, because there has been considerable cross-fertilization between these approaches. For instance, CAPA, which has its roots in the interviewer-based tradition, includes a subset of questions that are to be asked verbatim of all subjects, as in a respondent-based interview, but then allows further questioning for clarification. On the other hand, the DICA, which had previously been a respondent-based interview, now requires interviewers to question much more flexibly, and is currently an interviewer-based instrument (Reich, 2000). Although the distinction between interviewer- and respondent-based interviews provides a useful rough-and-ready typology, it is really better to consider interviews as lying at various locations along three dimensions: (1) degree of specification of questions, (2) degree of definition of symptom concepts, and (3) degree of flexibility in questioning permitted to the interviewers (Angold, 2002).

Summary

In this section, our goal has been to see where developmental epidemiology came from and how it got to be where it is today. The problems that had to be formulated and solved were of two kinds: how to conceive of the nature of childhood psychopathology and how to measure it. Progress in the past century has been extraordinary in both areas. However, as we discuss later, this progress has brought developmental epidemiology to a point where radically new concepts, and new methods, are now needed. Before we get there, however, we look at how epidemiologists in other areas of medicine have thought about developmental questions, and give some examples from psychiatry.

EPIDEMIOLOGY AS A DEVELOPMENTAL METHOD

Much of this section is inspired by Breslow and Day's (1980, 1987) two-volume *Statistical Methods in Cancer Research*. As those authors point out:

> Most chronic diseases are the result of a process extending over decades, and many of the events occurring in this period play a substantial role. (1987, p. 2)

In the study of physical growth, of mental and hormonal development, and in the process of aging, the essential feature is that changes over time are followed at the individual level. Longitudinal surveillance and recording of these events is therefore a natural mode of study to obtain a complete picture of disease causation.

Many psychiatric disorders fall into the category of chronic diseases, and the methods developed by cancer and cardiovascular epidemiologists to explore causal relationships in such diseases can, we believe, provide at least a useful starting place for thinking about psychiatric disorders.

Chronic disease epidemiologists view the diseases they study as having inherent developmental processes of their own—processes that obey certain laws and follow certain stages even as they destroy the individual in whom they develop (Hay & Angold, 1993). Developmental epidemiology asks what happens when developmental processes embodied in pathogenesis collide with the process of human development.

Risk, Exposure, and the Meaning of Time

Many questions can be answered only by methods that take into account temporal characteristics of risk factors, including their onset and the "dose," or level of exposure, over time. Age at first exposure, time since first exposure, duration of exposure, and intensity of exposure are all interrelated aspects of timing that may have different implications for causality and thus for prevention. The kinds of questions we are thinking of include the following:

- Does physical abuse by parental figures cause psychiatric disorders in children? Is a single blow a sufficient cause, or does abuse have to go on for a period of time, or happen at a certain level of severity, before it constitutes a risk factor? Are children of different ages or developmental stages differentially vulnerable to physical abuse as a risk factor? What risks are associated with removing children of different ages from home because of physical abuse?

- Why are depressive disorders rare in both prepubertal girls and boys, but much more common in postpubertal girls? What causes the observed sex difference to develop? Is it associated with hormonal, morphological, or social changes occurring around puberty? Why is earlier-than-average maturation apparently a positive event for boys but a negative one, associated with increased risk of behavioral and school problems, for girls?

A risk factor may have a different impact on the risk of disease, depending on when it first occurs, how long it is present, and the level of intensity at which it occurs. For example, insulation workers exposed to asbestos had a cumulative risk of dying of mesothelioma over a 20-year period (controlling for other causes of death) that was the same irrespective of age at first exposure (Peto, Seidman, & Selikoff, 1982). Here, *length of exposure* was the critical aspect of risk. In contrast, the risk of breast cancer following irradiation appears to be highest in girls exposed at ages 0 through 9, falling with age until there is little excess

risk for breast cancer associated with exposure to radiation after age 40 (Howe, 1982). Cases of breast cancer attributable to irradiation begin to occur some 10 years after exposure and continue thereafter at a roughly constant level, suggesting that the absolute excess risk increases with time since exposure. Thus, *timing of exposure* is the critical aspect of the risk exposure.

However, different sorts of radiation can have different durations as risk factors for cancer; for example, bone sarcomas occurring after exposure to the radioisotope 224Ra, which has a half-life of 3.6 days, cluster in a period of 5 to 10 years following first exposure, whereas bone sarcomas following exposure to 226Ra, which has a half-life of 1,600 years, occur at a constant rate beginning 5 years after first exposure (Mays & Spiess, 1984). In the latter case, exposure to the decay products of the radioisotope continues at virtually constant levels after absorption of the radium.

A longitudinal study of British male doctors' smoking provides an example of dose-related risk: The annual death rate per 100,000 men, between 1951 and 1971, standardized for age, was 1,317 for nonsmokers, 1,518 for those currently smoking 1 to 14 cigarettes a day, 1,829 for those currently smoking 15 to 24 a day, and 2,452 for those smoking over 24 a day (Doll & Peto, 1976). This was true inspective of age, and risk fell quite rapidly in those who gave up smoking (Breslow & Day, 1987). In this case, *amount of exposure* was the critical factor.

Examples from Developmental Psychopathology

These examples illustrate the importance for developmental epidemiology of thinking about different aspects of development: age at first exposure, time since first exposure, duration of exposure, intensity of exposure. Here we present some examples of how child psychiatric researchers have used ingenious designs to tease out the same issues.

The importance of *age at first exposure* has been studied most intensively of all the aspects of risk over time in child psychopathology because of the theoretical importance attached to early experiences in the Freudian and other psychodynamic models of development. For example, researchers investigating the role of attachment in children's development have concentrated on the very early months and years of life as the crucial period during which the inability to form one or more such relationships may have damaging effects that last into childhood and perhaps even into adulthood (Sroufe, 1988). The critical date of onset of risk appears to occur after 6 months, but the duration of the risk period is not yet clear. (Hay, 1985; Hay, Pawlby, Angold, Harold, & Sharp, 2003) has presented evidence that maternal depression, which presumably interferes with mothers' ability to form normal relationships with their infants, affects motor development if it occurs during the 1st year of life, and language development but not motor development if it occurs during the 2nd year of life. This is a case where age at first exposure appears to interact with the developmental processes most salient at a particular age. In another example of the importance of timing, Rutter (1985) has pointed out that once children have achieved urinary continence at around age 2, there is a period of risk for relapse into incontinence that appears to coincide with starting school. Once this period of risk is over, the chance of developing enuresis is very slight. In this case, age at exposure is clearly the critical developmental risk factor because no parallel increase in functional enuresis occurs at later times of stress, such as moving to middle or high school, and there is no delay between the stress and the symptoms.

Timing of exposure has rarely been treated separately in studies of child psychopathology. G. W. Brown and Harris (1978), in their work on the social origins of depression, argued that women who lost their mother in the 1st decade of life were more vulnerable as adults to depressive episodes in the face of severe life events. However, theirs was a retrospective study that did not address the question of whether these women were also at greater risk of depressive episodes during later childhood and adolescence. It is not clear whether the crucial factor was the length of time since exposure to the risk factor of mother's death, or the age of the child at the time of exposure, or some combination of the two.

Timing of puberty has emerged as an important aspect of risk in relation to both depression and behavioral problems. In a longitudinal study that measured not only age at menarche but also morphological development, Tanner staging (Marshall & Tanner, 1969), and levels of gonadal and steroidal hormones, it was clear that it was high levels of estrogen and testosterone, not timing of puberty, that predicted adolescent depression (Angold et al., 1999). On the other hand, there are many studies showing that girls who are early in developing the morphological signs of puberty, indexed by Tanner stage or menarche, are at risk for behavioral problems if they have unsupportive families (Ge, Brody, Conger, & Murry, 2002; Ge, Conger, & Elder, 1996; Magnusson, Stattin, & Allen, 1985; Moffitt et al., 1992).

Duration of exposure to poverty was examined by Offord and colleagues (1992) in their repeated surveys of a representative sample of children in Ontario. They showed that children whose families were living below the poverty

level at two measurement points were at increased risk of behavioral disorders, compared with children whose families were below the poverty level on one occasion only, or never. In a longitudinal study from Dunedin, New Zealand, Moffitt (1990) found that children identified at age 13 as both delinquent and hyperactive had experienced significantly more family adversity (poverty, poor maternal education and mental health), consistently from the age of 7, than children who were only delinquent or only hyperactive at age 13:

> The most striking increase in the antisocial behavior of ADD+delinquent boys [diagnosed at age 13] occurred between the ages of 5 and 7, when they attained a mean antisocial rating that was not reached by other delinquent boys until 6 years later. School entry and reading failure coincided temporally with this exacerbation of antisocial behavior. These data suggest that the problem behavior of this group, despite being generally persistent, is responsive to experience. The data also reveal a key point of vulnerability that could be a target for intervention: reading readiness. (p. 906)

Another example comes from the Great Smoky Mountains Study. Children who had been assessed over an 8-year period were classified into four groups on the basis of their body-mass index (a ratio of weight to height) at each assessment: no obesity (72.8%), childhood-only obesity (5.1%), adolescent-only obesity (7.5%), and chronic obesity (14.8%). Only the chronically obese group was at increased risk of psychiatric disorder (Mustillo et al., 2003). This is an example of duration of exposure as the key risk characteristic. It is also an example of the impact of intensity of exposure, because no effects were found of overweight that fell below the threshold of obesity.

Intensity of exposure to lead (Needleman & Bellinger, 1991) provides an example of a definite dose-response relationship. Another aspect of intensity is the number of different risk factors to which a child is exposed (Seifer, Sameroff, Baldwin, & Baldwin, 1989). Rutter (1985) and others have pointed out that children exposed to one risk factor are at increased risk of exposure to others (e.g., no father in the home and poverty), and that the dose-response relationship to an increasing number of different risk factors is not a simple linear one. Most children appear to be able to cope with a single adverse circumstance, but rates of psychopathology rise sharply in children exposed to several adverse circumstances or events (Seifer et al., 1989).

These examples show that it is possible to design studies that at least begin to allow us to tease out the respective roles played by time since first exposure, age or developmental stage at first exposure, duration of exposure, and intensity of exposure. Multistage models of risk, which have been developed to address the complexities of causality in chronic disease, are one way of putting the pieces together. Several such models have been proposed, particularly in the context of carcinogenesis (Peto, 1984), and have been reviewed in terms of developmental psychopathology by Pickles (1993). Statistical techniques for exploring causality in such multistage models have made great strides recently (J. Robins, 1997). The challenge is to incorporate all the various aspects of risk into a single model and distinguish the ones that carry the tune from those that are just noise.

CONCLUSIONS AND FUTURE DIRECTIONS: DEVELOPMENTAL EPIDEMIOLOGY

We have described how child psychiatric epidemiology has developed over the past 50 years as a collaborative activity of basic, clinical, and public health scientists working together to understand the magnitude of the problem of child mental illness and to identify key risk factors. Many of the fundamental problems of conceptualization and measurement have been solved, or at least reduced to manageable proportions.

Up to this point, the role of epidemiology has been mainly a descriptive one, addressing the basic questions How many? Who? Where? When? We are now in the position of being at least as capable of answering these questions reliably and accurately in child psychiatry as are chronic disease epidemiologists in other areas of medicine.

However, child psychiatry is changing, and epidemiology will change as well. The goal is now to understand how risk exposure and vulnerability change over the life course, and how the requirements of "normal" development at each developmental stage shape the types of psychopathology that emerge if these requirements are not met. The term "developmental epidemiology," first coined by Kellam in the 1970s (Kellam, Ensminger, & Turner, 1977), is useful to describe what epidemiology is doing these days.

In this concluding section, we describe some rapidly growing research areas that will contribute to the next generation of studies to the shift from child psychiatric epidemiology to developmental epidemiology. The different approaches overlap in many areas, but we discuss the future under seven headings: longitudinal research, genetic epidemiology, life course epidemiology, intergenerational epidemiology, prevention science, studies of burden and cost, and surveillance studies.

Longitudinal Research

Longitudinal research is almost the sine qua non for testing developmental hypotheses about causes and risks. Although there have been many longitudinal developmental studies, some of them beginning at birth (or even before), longitudinal studies of psychiatric disorders had to await the development of appropriate technology, specifically, data collection methods that validly and reliably translated the psychiatric taxonomy into instruments that could be used repeatedly with the same subjects (see earlier discussion).

Table 3.2 lists some current studies with data that can be used to address issues in developmental epidemiology. The criteria used for selecting these studies were that they had (1) a representative population-based sample, (2) data collection beginning in childhood and continuing at least into adolescence, (3) at least two waves of assessment on the same subjects, and (4) data that could be used to make *DSM* or *ICD* diagnoses on all subjects in at least one data wave. (Several other studies have done psychiatric assessments on a subset of participants to evaluate their use of questionnaire measures elsewhere in the study. These do not provide a very solid basis for estimating prevalence or diagnostic continuity and so are omitted from this list.)

An example of how longitudinal studies can be used to address developmental questions can be found in a recent paper on the Great Smoky Mountains Study (E. J. Costello, Mustillo, Erkanli, Keeler, & Angold, 2003). Annual interviews with 1,420 young people over a period from age 9 through 16 provided data to address such questions as the following: Does the prevalence of different disorders increase or decrease with age? Do children with a disorder continue to have the same disorder (homotypic continuity) or a different disorder (heterotypic continuity)?

Longitudinal analyses showed that, although the average annual prevalence of psychiatric disorder was around 13%, over the period of the study more than one child in three (36.7%) had one or more disorders. Some disorders (ADHD, separation anxiety, functional enuresis) dominated the picture in childhood but had almost disappeared by age 16. Depression and drug abuse were predominantly disorders of adolescence. Anxiety disorders in general had a U-shaped distribution, falling to their lowest point at age 12. Although wave-to-wave continuity was not very high, over the course of the study there was a high degree of homotypic continuity (see Table 3.3 on p. 63). The increased likelihood of an episode of a disorder following an earlier episode was statistically significant for every diagnosis except specific phobia.

TABLE 3.2 Summary of Ongoing Longitudinal Epidemiologic Studies of Child and Adolescent Psychiatric Disorders

Key References	Study	Location	Number of Subjects	Race/Ethnicity	Year of Birth	Age at Start of Study	Interview, Informants, and Taxonomy	Time Frame of Interview
Krueger, Caspi, Moffitt, & Silva (1998)	Dunedin Longitudinal Study	Dunedin, New Zealand	1,037	White	1972–1973	Birth	DIS[a] at 18 (C)[b]; *DSM-III-R*[c]	Past 12 months
Fergusson & Horwood (2001)	Christchurch Health and Development Study	Christchurch, New Zealand	1,265	White	1977	Birth	DIS (C); *DSM-III-R, DSM-IV*[d]	Past 12 months
Cohen, Cohen, & Brook (1993)	New York State Study	New York State	975	White	1965–1974	1–10	DISC[e] (C, P); *DSM-III-R*	Past 6 months
Reinherz, Giaconia, Hauf, Wasserman, & Paradis (2000)	Boston Study	Boston	763	White	1971	6	DIS at age 18 (C); *DSM-III-R*	Past 12 months
Ford, Goodman, & Meltzer (2003)	British National Survey	England, Scotland, Wales	10,438	93% White	1984–1994	5–15	DAWBA[f] (C, P); *DSM-IV*	Current
Wittchen, Nelson, & Lachner (1998)	Early Developmental Stages of Psychopathology	Munich, Germany	3,021	White	1980–1983	14–24	CIDI[g] (C); *DSM-IV*	Past 12 months
Angold et al. (2002)	Caring for Children in the Community	North Carolina	920	60% African American; 38% White; 2% other	1976–1986	9–17	CAPA[h] (C, P); *DSM-IV*	Past 3 months
Simonoff et al. (1997)	Virginia Twin Study of Adolescent Behavioral Development	Virginia	2,762	White	1974–1983	8–16	CAPA (C, P); *DSM-III-R*	Past 3 months
E. J. Costello, Mustillo, et al. (2003)	Great Smoky Mountains Study	North Carolina	1,420	70% White; 25% American Indian; 5% African American	1980–1984	9, 11, 13	CAPA (C, P); *DSM-IV*	Past 3 months
Angold, Egger, Erkanli, & Keeler (unpublished)	Preschool Age Psychiatric Assessment	North Carolina	307	54% African American; 35% White; 11% other	1996–1999	2–5	PAPA[i] (P); *DSM-IV*	Past 3 months

Notes:
[a] Diagnostic Interview Schedule (L. N. Robins, Helzer, Cottler, & Goldring, 1989).
[b] C = Child report; P = Parent report.
[c] *Diagnostic and Statistical Manual of Mental Disorders*, third edition, revised (American Psychiatric Association, 1987).
[d] *Diagnostic and Statistical Manual of Mental Disorders*, fourth edition (American Psychiatric Association, 1994).
[e] Diagnostic Interview Schedule for Children (Shaffer et al., 1996).
[f] Development and Well-Being Assessment (Goodman, Ford, Richards, et al., 2000).
[g] Composite International Diagnostic Interview (Andrews & Peters, 1998).
[h] Child and Adolescent Psychiatric Assessment (Angold et al., 1995).
[i] Preschool-Age Psychiatric Assessment (Egger, Ascher, & Angold, 1999).

TABLE 3.3 Homotypic and Heterotypic Continuity, with and without Controls for Comorbidity

Predicting To	Past Depression	Past Anxiety	Past Conduct Disorder	Past Oppositional Defiant Disorder	Past ADHD	Past Substance Abuse
Depression	7.0 (3.1, 15.9)[c]	3.0 (1.7, 5.4)[c]				
Controlling for comorbidity	4.2 (2.1, 8.3)[c]	2.7 (1.8, 5.2)[b]				
Anxiety	5.7 (2.2, 14.5)[c]	2.4 (1.6, 3.7)[c]				
Controlling for comorbidity	2.8 (1.2, 6.5)[a]	2.0 (1.2, 3.4)[a]				
Conduct Disorder			11.2 (5.9, 21.1)[c]			
Controlling for comorbidity			10.3 (4.3, 24.7)[c]			
Oppositional Defiant Disorder				3.7 (2.2, 6.2)[c]	2.0 (1.1, 3.8)[a]	
Controlling for comorbidity				4.7 (2.7, 8.1)[c]	2.1 (1.1, 4.2)[a]	
ADHD			2.2 (1.0, 4.5)[a]		10.7 (5.2, 22.3)[c]	
Controlling for comorbidity			1.8 (0.9, 3.9)		9.6 (4.4, 21.2)[c]	
Substance abuse		2.0 (1.2, 3.5)[a]	2.7 (1.2, 6.5)[a]			21.3 (6.3, 72.5)[c]
Controlling for comorbidity		2.0 (1.1, 3.7)[a]	1.7 (0.6, 4.7)			25.7 (7.8, 85.4)[c]

Note: [a]$p < .05$; [b]$p < .01$; [c]$p < .001$; NS = Not significant.

Adapted from "Prevalence and Development of Psychiatric Disorders in Childhood and Adolescence," by E. J. Costello, S. Mustillo, A. Erkanli, G. Keeler, and A. Angold, 2003, *Archives of General Psychiatry, 60,* pp. 837–844.

In contrast, there was relatively little prediction from one disorder to another (heterotypic continuity), and it was almost entirely restricted to girls. Anxiety predicted depression, and depression predicted anxiety. Anxiety and Conduct Disorder predicted substance abuse, and there was some movement among the disruptive behavior disorders, perhaps suggesting that the *DSM* taxonomy fits boys better than it does girls.

There are now several research groups that have used their longitudinal data to look at continuities and discontinuities in mental illness from childhood into adolescence and beyond. Some of the longitudinal studies have followed their subjects into adulthood (Caspi, Moffitt, Newman, & Silva, 1996; Cohen, 1996; Fergusson & Woodward, 2000; Reinherz, Giaconia, Hauf, Wasserman, & Silverman, 1999; Rohde, Lewinsohn, Kahler, Seeley, & Brown, 2001). These

are beginning to show indications of continuity between temperamental characteristics in early childhood and the onset of psychiatric disorders in late adolescence and young adulthood (Caspi et al., 1996; Cohen, 1996). Two examples come from the Dunedin study, a birth cohort of around 1,000 children from New Zealand who have been evaluated every 2 years since birth.

The first set of analyses (Jaffee et al., 2002) started from hints in the literature that juvenile-onset Major Depressive Disorder (MDD) may be etiologically distinct from adult-onset MDD. In these analyses, early childhood risk factors covered the period from birth to age 9 years. Diagnoses of MDD were made according to *DSM* criteria at three points prior to adulthood (ages 11, 13, and 15 years) and three points during adulthood (ages 18, 21, and 26 years). Four groups were defined: individuals first diagnosed as having

MDD in childhood, but not in adulthood ($n = 21$); individuals first diagnosed as having MDD in adulthood ($n = 314$); individuals first diagnosed in childhood whose depression recurred in adulthood by age 26 years ($n = 34$); and never-depressed individuals ($n = 629$). The two juvenile-onset groups had similar high-risk profiles on the childhood measures. Compared with the adult-depressed group, the juvenile-onset groups experienced more perinatal insults and motor skills deficits, more caretaker instability, criminality, and psychopathology in their family of origin, and more behavioral and socioemotional problems. The adult-onset group's risk profile was similar to that of the never-depressed group with the exception of elevated childhood sexual abuse. These analyses made it clear that the distinction between juvenile- versus adult-onset MDD is important for understanding heterogeneity in depression.

A second example from the same study revisited the theory that there are two types of adolescent delinquency, childhood-onset and adolescence-limited, that their manifestations in adolescence are indistinguishable, but that their consequences for persistence into adulthood are different (Moffitt, 1993). At the 26-year follow-up (Moffitt, Caspi, Harrington, & Milne, 2002), the childhood-onset delinquents were the most elevated on psychopathic personality traits, mental health problems, substance dependence, numbers of children, financial problems, work problems, and drug-related and violent crime, including violence against women and children. The adolescent-onset delinquents were less extreme at 26 years but showed elevated impulsive personality traits, mental health problems, substance dependence, financial problems, and property offenses. A third group of men who had been aggressive as children but not very delinquent as adolescents emerged as low-level chronic offenders who were anxious, depressed, and socially isolated and had financial and work problems.

These two examples serve to show how, as developmental epidemiology grows up, it can contribute to developmental psychopathology and also shine new light on some of the accepted verities of adult psychiatry.

A next step in the use of descriptive longitudinal studies for developmental epidemiology needs to be to combine them in programs of joint analyses or meta-analysis. For example, the National Institute on Drug Abuse recently funded a consortium of eight groups with longitudinal data to pool their thinking about the psychiatric precursors of adolescent drug use and abuse. This group is developing new methods for the meta-analysis of longitudinal data sets that could be used in the future to look at many other areas of developmental psychopathology. More standardized diagnostic methods make this sort of collaboration feasible.

A second goal for the future must be to work out ways of releasing data from these studies for public access so that future researchers can take advantage of these incredibly valuable resources. There are many issues to be worked out, not the least of them the protection of participants' privacy and the rights of the scientists who labored for so many years to collect the data. But these are soluble problems, and the benefits of bringing fresh minds to bear on issues in developmental epidemiology are likely to be tremendous.

Genetic Epidemiology

There have been two revolutions in genetic epidemiology in the past 2 decades that will have a tremendous impact on developmental psychopathology in the next decade.

Psychiatric Behavioral Genetics

The first revolution occurred when the methods of psychiatric epidemiology were applied to behavioral genetics. Psychiatric interviews like those described earlier were used in studies with genetically informative designs, such as twin, adoption, family, and migrant studies. For the first time, researchers explored not only the genetics of scalar characteristics, such as intelligence, but also of categorical disorders such as depression, measured in ways that approximate clinical diagnosis. Furthermore, behavioral geneticists began to take seriously issues of sampling, so that they could talk about the contribution of genes to disease in the population as a whole, rather than in highly selected families or groups. There have also been some longitudinal studies looking at how genes can have different effects at different developmental stages (Eaves & Silberg, 2003; Jacobson, Prescott, & Kendler, 2002; Lesch, 2002).

An important example of this approach is the work emerging from the Virginia Twin Study of Adolescent Behavioral Development (VTSABD), a population-based sample of twin pairs followed through adolescence into adulthood. One set of analyses investigated the role of genetic and environmental factors in the association between depressive symptoms and symptoms of Overanxious Disorder (OAD), simple phobias, and separation anxiety in 8- to 13-year-old and 14- to 17-year-old girls (Silberg, Rutter, & Eaves, 2001). There were distinct patterns underlying the association between depression and the different anxiety syndromes during the course of development. First, specific genetic influences on depression after age 14 reflected liability to symptoms of earlier OAD and simple phobias. Second, aspects of the shared environment that influenced symptoms of depression before age 14 contributed to symptoms of separation anxiety and simple phobias later in adolescence. Third, the shared environmental influence on depression in older girls also affected liability to symptoms of concurrent OAD and persistent separation anxiety. These results suggest that depression before and after age 14 may be etiologically distinct syndromes. Earlier symptoms of OAD and, to a lesser extent, phobic symptoms reflect the same genetic risk, and separation anxiety symptoms both before and after age 14 reflect the same environmental risk that influence liability to depressive symptoms expressed in middle to late adolescence.

Molecular Genetics

The second genetic revolution occurred when it became feasible to apply the methods of molecular genetics to epidemiologic samples. This development opens up the opportunity to use not only twin or adoption studies but a wide range of samples to test theories about candidate genes for specific symptoms. Even more exciting is the new opportunity to use the treasure-house of data from longitudinal studies to test for gene-environment interactions. Such studies can answer questions about which genes interact with which environmental factors, at what developmental stage. Two examples provide first glimpses of what is likely to be one of the most fruitful areas of developmental epidemiology in the next decade.

Investigators studied the male children from the Dunedin longitudinal study sample (Caspi et al., 2002) from birth to adulthood to determine why some children who are maltreated grow up to develop antisocial behavior, whereas others do not. A functional polymorphism in the gene encoding the neurotransmitter-metabolizing enzyme monoamine oxidase A (MAOA) was found to moderate the effect of maltreatment. Maltreated children with a genotype conferring high levels of MAOA expression were less likely to develop antisocial problems. These findings provide epidemiological evidence that genotypes can moderate children's sensitivity to environmental insults. The finding has since been replicated in the VTSABD (Foley et al., 2004).

In other analyses, the Dunedin team investigated why stressful experiences lead to depression in some people but not in others (Caspi et al., 2003). A functional polymorphism in the promoter region of the serotonin transporter (5-HTT) gene was found to moderate the influence of stressful life events on depression. Individuals with one or two copies of the short allele of the 5-HTT promoter polymorphism exhibited more depressive symptoms, diagnosable depression, and suicidality in relation to stressful life events than individuals homozygous for the long allele. Again, an individual's response to environmental insults is moderated by his or her genetic makeup. This finding has recently been replicated (Kendler, Kuhn, & Prescott, 2004).

Geneticists have for generations been telling us that genes express themselves only in an environment, and that the key questions have to do with the relationships between the two over time. Developmental epidemiology and genetic epidemiology are already merging, and the process will continue in the next decade.

In the future, no epidemiologic study will fail to collect biomaterial for DNA and to ask participants to consent to the collection of biomaterial for DNA. In the immediate future, existing studies are going back and obtaining blood or cheek scrapes, or asking participants to consent to a new use of already collected biodata. Collaboration between molecular geneticists and epidemiologists with longitudinal data on representative samples offers an amazing opportunity for progress in understanding the biological and social origins of disease.

Life Course Epidemiology

Life course epidemiology is the study of long-term effects on chronic disease risk of physical and social exposures during gestation, childhood, adolescence, young adulthood, and later adult life. It includes studies of the biological, behavioral, and psychosocial pathways that operate across an individual's life course, as well as across generations, to influence the development of chronic diseases (Ben-Shlomo & Kuh, 2002; Kuh & Ben-Shlomo, 1997).

Psychiatric disorders are increasingly showing themselves to be chronic diseases. For example, across childhood and adolescence, for every psychiatric disorder except specific phobias, the likelihood of an episode has been shown to be significantly higher in youth with a history of the same disorder than in those with no previous history (E. J. Costello, Mustillo, et al., 2003). As data accumulate from prospective studies, it is becoming clear that the onset of most adult psychiatric disorders lies much further back in childhood than had been suspected from adult studies relying on retrospective recall of onset (Kim-Cohen et al., 2003).

In many ways, life course and developmental epidemiology mirror one another. Life course epidemiology, however, has taken on a special concern with the "embodiment" of social phenomena into the biological (Krieger, 2001), encapsulated in the concept of "health inequalities." This concern arose historically from work showing that mortality from many diseases is spread unequally across the population (Wilkinson, 1994) and that these differences in risk can be linked to social inequalities that often go back to infancy or even to the parental generation (e.g., Barker, 1998; Davey Smith, Gunnell, & Ben-Shlomo, 2000; Leon, 2000). This body of work has had enormous significance for international thinking about social policy and is having a direct effect on the allocation of public resources in some countries.

Developmental epidemiology needs to take on board the social, economic, and political implications of the fact that children are born with different levels of risk for psychiatric disorder, that their family's socioeconomic status is part of the predictive equation, and that community-level interventions (E. J. Costello, Compton, et al., 2003), as well as individual treatment can influence how well individuals are able to function. Future studies will include health disparities (in the broad sense of medical and psychiatric health) as part of their remit.

Intergenerational Epidemiology

A life course approach to developmental epidemiology is not limited to individuals in a single generation, but can intertwine biological and social transmission of risk across generations, recognizing that geographic and secular characteristics may be unique to that cohort of individuals (Cairns, Elder, & Costello, 1996; Stein, Susser, Saenger, & Marolla, 1975).

Experiences of the previous generation can operate at many different levels of generality. They may be specific to the mother-child dyad (e.g., the effect of drug use during pregnancy) or may affect everyone living in a certain neighborhood (e.g., poverty or exposure to an environmental toxin). All mothers and children may be affected by a particular event, such as a period of famine or disease, or children may be affected by their mother's developmental stage (e.g., children of teen mothers or elderly mothers).

Models for intergenerational research have recently developed (Cairns et al., 1996; Friedman & Haywood, 1994; Rossi, 1989), and statistical methods have become more tractable (Muthen & Muthen, 2000; L. N. Robins, 1992; Zeger & Liang, 1992). Undertaking transgenerational studies requires a level of commitment from both researchers and funding agencies that is hard to sustain over the necessary length of time, especially in the United States with its 5-year funding cycles. Many American researchers have looked abroad to find countries that have nurtured such studies and governments that understand their importance (e.g., Chasiotis, Scheffer, Restemeier, & Keller, 1998; Granger et al., 1998; Krueger et al., 1998). However, we can hope that as policymakers become more aware of the overlapping pattern of risk factors among chronic diseases and the risks associated with very early exposures, they will come to understand the immense returns from investment in multigenerational research.

Prevention Science

The strongest test of a developmental theory about causes of disease is an intervention that manipulates a core etiological factor and tests the outcome. Prevention science is the discipline that has arisen to put this principle into practice. Its strongest growth has been in the area of AIDS prevention, but it has also been an important force in developmental psychopathology, with its own academic societies and research journals.

Prevention science uses theory about the causes of disease to generate interventions, which when tested provide information not only about the effectiveness of the intervention, but also about the etiology of the disease (Dodge, 2001). The famous Broad Street pump intervention described earlier (Snow, 1855) is a classic example of prevention science: If dirty water caused cholera, then removing access to dirty water should both prevent new cases and support the etiologic hypothesis.

As described earlier, epidemiology traditionally divides prevention into thee categories, depending on the mean level of risk in the population of concern. Primary prevention programs like clean water, car seat belts, and parental leave programs are examples of primary or universal prevention. The scientific questions at this level have to do with what is prevented downstream by universal programs upstream. For example, the "Just Say No" drug abstinence program was introduced as a primary prevention for all children in school, designed to stop drug use before it began. Unfortunately, the developmental science behind it was inadequate, and the results were null if not negative (Lynam et al., 1999). In another careful study of a primary prevention program for school-age children, Stattin and colleagues (Mahoney & Stattin, 2000) evaluated the youth recreation centers that are a ubiquitous feature of Swedish towns. Usually, these are places where young people can hang out, with very little adult supervision or structured activity. Participation in activities with low structure was associated with high levels of antisocial behavior for boys and girls, whereas participation in highly structured leisure activities was linked to low levels of antisocial behavior. Despite several studies, however, community leaders still strongly support these recreation centers: an example of how long it takes for research to influence policy.

On the other hand, primary prevention with both children (Kellam, Koretz, & Moscicki, 1999) and families (E. J. Costello, Compton, et al., 2003) can be effective and suggest etiologic pathways that could be explored in further research. But prevention science has done relatively little in the way of *primary* prevention for mental health problems. It is highly likely that primary prevention programs that improve early nutrition or provide more family leave have effects on the development of psychopathology, but they have not been treated as scientific tests of theory, and so we do not know.

Secondary, or high-risk, intervention programs are much more likely to be subjected to scientifically informative testing, and this is where the bulk of prevention science has been done. There is a large number of interventions based on high-risk children, schools, and communities, and many of them have survived the trial by fire of National Institutes of Health review committees and are both theory-driven and scientifically sound. This is not the place to review this literature; the main issue for developmental epidemiology is that such studies should be epidemiologically sound. This means that it should be clear how far their results can be generalized. Does an intervention to reduce bullying (Olweus, 1993) work with girls as well as boys? In which age groups? In which ethnic groups? What can we learn about what drives bullying?

A good example of a secondary intervention that yields insights for developmental epidemiology is the "Fast Track" program for aggressive children in grade school. This was based on clearly articulated theory about cognitive difficulties that could interact with environmental risk to produce aggressive behavior in socially ambiguous situations (Dodge, Pettit, & Bates, 1994). Hostile attributional bias was indeed found to be a partial mediator of the effect of the intervention on reductions in aggressive behavior.

Tertiary interventions have hardly been explored in the context of tests of developmental theory. Once children have developed clinically defined psychiatric disorders, interventions focus on clinical treatment rather than tertiary prevention, although pediatricians (Kendrick, 1999), psychologists (Williams, Holmbeck, & Greenley, 2002), and psychiatrists (Pols et al., 1996) are beginning to talk about the need for a focus on tertiary prevention. Given the early onset of most psychiatric disorders, this is clearly a vitally important area for future work.

Within this broad framework there is a wide variety of intervention strategies, some of which may take developmental issues into account. A good example is suicide prevention, which was comprehensively reviewed by Gould and colleagues (M. Gould, Greenberg, Velting, & Shaffer, 2003). Among the primary prevention efforts they discuss are gun control programs at the national and local level and schoolwide suicide awareness curricula. Secondary preven-

tion efforts have included skills training programs for youth, whether identified through screening or self-referred, screening programs to try to identify children with suicidal ideas, training for gatekeepers such as primary care pediatricians, peer counseling programs, crisis centers, and hot lines. Other approaches include training the media on how to report suicide so as to minimize "copy cat" behavior, and postsuicide counseling in schools and among the friends of youth who have killed themselves. Tertiary care programs focus on following up suicide attempters in an effort to reduce repeat episodes. Research on the effectiveness of all these strategies is patchy, and some continue to be used despite doubts about their developmental appropriateness and effectiveness (M. Gould et al., 2003). However, suicide is one of the few areas in child and adolescent mental health in which one can see the skeleton of an integrated prevention strategy beginning to emerge.

It sometimes feels as though progress in implementing prevention programs in the mental health area has been glacially slow, and public policy often impervious to evidence. But prevention scientists are determined people, and they are building a powerful set of weapons in the form of statistical methods, meta-analytic studies, and cost-benefit analyses that will help them to get their message across in the next decade.

Burden of Illness and Costs and Effectiveness of Interventions

As we described earlier, epidemiology (the study of where, when, why, and to whom diseases occur) has a dual role: to increase our understanding of what causes an illness (scientific epidemiology) and to help institute policies to prevent or control it (public health epidemiology). Implementing policies to prevent or control disease costs money. Before allocating resources to any disease, policymakers need to know how big the problem is, what interventions are available, how useful they are, and how much they cost. So epidemiology has historically been concerned with estimating the burden of disease and the cost and effectiveness of interventions (E. J. Costello & Angold, 2000).

Developmental epidemiology has a new role to play in this area, for all the reasons discussed in the section on life course epidemiology. It is becoming increasingly clear that we cannot afford to wait to intervene until, for example, a child develops Conduct Disorder. Treatment at that stage is expensive, labor-intensive (Henggeler, Melton, Brondino, Scherer, & Hanley, 1997), and of modest effectiveness (Lipsey & Wilson, 1998). It is imperative that we apply what is known about early predictors to develop interventions that can be used earlier in the development of the disorder. This is an enormous research program and is addressed elsewhere in these volumes.

The role of the developmental epidemiologist is often that of record keeper: to measure the burden of disease (World Health Organization, 1996), the need for (E. J. Costello et al., 1993; Rice, Woolston, Stewart, Kerker, & Horwitz, 2002), cost of, and barriers to services (Flisher et al., 1997; Leslie, Rosenheck, & Horwitz, 2001; Owens et al., 2002) at different developmental stages, and the changes in disease incidence as new interventions are introduced (C. H. Brown, Berndt, Brinales, Zong, & Bhagwat, 2000; Ialongo et al., 1993; Kellam, Rebok, Mayer, Ialongo, & Kalodner, 1994).

None of these activities is new to epidemiology in general, but they have been a long time coming to the area of child psychiatric disorders. The next decade will see a significant expansion of cost, cost-benefit, and cost-effectiveness studies, either as new studies or as additions to ongoing ones.

Mental Health Surveillance

Tracking the prevalence (ongoing cases) and incidence (new cases) of diseases over time is a basic task of epidemiology, but one that has hardly begun in the area of child psychopathology. We rely on agencies of the Centers for Disease Control and Prevention (CDC) to tell us how many cases of SARS there were last year in the United States, and whether the incidence of AIDS is increasing or decreasing. But it would be no use to ask CDC the same questions about prepubertal depression or early-onset Schizophrenia; no one there is responsible for these disorders, although their social cost may well be as high (Murray & Lopez, 1996). One exception to this is the area of drug use and abuse, on which annual surveys of the school-age population have been available since 1975 from the University of Michigan's Institute for Social Research. Thirty years of data can be tracked to show the rise and fall in use of different drugs. Another exception is the CDC's Youth Risk Behavior Surveillance System, an anonymous population survey set up in 1990:

> to monitor priority health risk behaviors that contribute markedly to the leading causes of death, disability, and social problems among youth and adults in the United States. These behaviors, often established during childhood and early adolescence, include tobacco use, unhealthy dietary behaviors, inadequate physical activity, alcohol and other drug use, sexual behaviors that contribute to unintended pregnancy and sexually transmitted diseases, including HIV infection, [and]

behaviors that contribute to unintentional injuries and violence. (Kann, 2001)

These data can be used to show, for example, a small but steady decline in the proportion of children who had their first alcoholic drink before age 13, from 32.7% in 1991 to 27.8% in 2003. On the other hand, the proportion making a suicidal attempt serious enough to need medical attention has increased from 1.7% in 1991 to 2.9% in 2003.

Because the data come from different (anonymous) samples each year, they cannot be used to track an individual's progression. They do, however, provide hints of what legal or cultural changes might be doing to the development of risk behaviors across adolescence.

Clearly, a major task for developmental epidemiology in the next decade will be to help CDC to shoulder the task of charting national rates of child and adolescent psychiatric disorders over time, as it has done for national rates of other serious conditions. However, with the exception of these brief anonymous surveys and some work on Autism, little has yet been done. One reason for this is that problems of assessment have made it possible to argue that child psychiatric disorders cannot be measured with sufficient reliability and validity to justify such activities. This is no longer the case. Given the limitations of reliance on verbal report of symptoms, measurement of psychiatric symptoms and syndromes is as reliable as in many other areas of medicine, and there are measures available at many different levels of detail, from brief questionnaires to detailed clinical assessments.

Work is currently in progress to integrate brief psychiatric measures into national surveys such as the National Health Interview Survey (NHIS) and the National Health and Nutrition Examination Survey (NHANES-IV). NHANES has recently been using some modules of the DISC and the DISC Predictive Screener, and the NHIS is using a short questionnaire, the Strengths and Difficulties Questionnaire (Goodman, Ford, Simmons, Gatward, & Meltzer, 2000), that is also used in several other countries. This will make international comparisons feasible. More work is needed to evaluate the validity of these measures across the age range and to assess their usefulness as a measure of the burden of child mental illness in the community. It is clear, however, that in the next decade it will be possible to stop treating assessment issues as research problems to be funded by federal research agencies and move them over to being issues to be dealt with by surveillance and monitoring agencies such as CDC. This will have many advantages. First, it will make it possible to treat psychiatric disorders as on a par with other medical conditions. Second, it will produce national data sets, such as those produced by NHIS, that can be used to look at the sorts of questions raised by life course epidemiology: what environmental, political, and social conditions breed psychiatric disorders, and how societies should address these problems. Third, it will relieve the National Institute of Mental Health scientific research budget of the responsibility for basic prevalence studies and free up research dollars for questions on the scientific side of epidemiology, questions about causes and consequences.

This chapter has covered a lot of ground: from the first stirrings of understanding about childhood psychiatric disorders to the possibility of using molecular genetics to identify gene-environment interactions that can generate psychiatric disorder. There are fuzzy boundaries between developmental epidemiology and developmental psychopathology, life course epidemiology, genetic epidemiology, services research, and several other areas. It will be important to keep these boundaries pervious, to share a common language where possible, and to learn and use one another's methods.

REFERENCES

Achenbach, T. M. (1985). *Assessment and taxonomy of child and adolescent psychopathology.* Beverly Hills, CA: Sage.

Achenbach, T. M. (1991). *Manual for the Child Behavior Checklist 4-18 and 1991 profile.* Burlington: University of Vermont, Department of Psychiatry.

Achenbach, T. M., & Edelbrock, C. (1983). *Manual for the Child Behavior Checklist and Child Behavior Profile.* Burlington: University of Vermont.

Achenbach, T. M., McConaughy, S. H., & Howell, C. T. (1987). Child/adolescent behavioral and emotional problems: Implications of cross-informant correlations for situational specificity. *Psychological Bulletin, 101,* 213–232.

Achenbach, T. M., & Rescorla, L. A. (2000). *Manual for the ASEBA preschool forms and profiles: An integrated system of multi-informant assessment.* Burlington: University of Vermont, Department of Psychiatry.

Achenbach, T. M., & Rescorla, L. A. (2001). *Manual for the ASEBA school-age forms and profiles.* Burlington: University of Vermont, Research Center for Children, Youth, and Families.

Achenbach, T. M., & Rescorla, L. A. (2003). *Manual for the ASEBA adult forms and profiles.* Burlington: University of Vermont, Research Center for Children, Youth, and Families.

Ambrosini, P. J. (2000). Historical development and present status of the Schedule for Affective Disorders and Schizophrenia for school-age children (K-SADS). *Journal of the American Academy of Child and Adolescent Psychiatry, 39,* 49–58.

American Psychiatric Association. (1994). *Diagnostic and statistical manual of mental disorders* (4th ed.). Washington, DC: Author.

Angoff, W. H. (1988). The nature-nurture debate, aptitudes, and group differences. *American Psychologist, 43,* 713–720.

Angold, A. (1988). Childhood and adolescent depression: II. Research in clinical populations. *British Journal of Psychiatry, 153,* 476–492.

Angold, A. (2002). Diagnostic interviews with parents and children. In M. Rutter & E. Taylor (Eds.), *Child and adolescent psychiatry: Modern approaches* (pp. 32–51). Oxford: Blackwell Scientific Publications.

Angold, A., & Costello, E. J. (1991). Developing a developmental epidemiology. In D. Cicchetti & S. Toth (Eds.), *Rochester Symposium on Developmental Psychology* (Vol. 3, pp. 75–96). Hillsdale, NJ: Erlbaum.

Angold, A., & Costello, E. J. (1995). A test-retest reliability study of child-reported psychiatric symptoms and diagnoses using the Child and Adolescent Psychiatric Assessment (CAPA-C). *Psychological Medicine, 25,* 755–762.

Angold, A., & Costello, E. J. (2000). The Child and Adolescent Psychiatric Assessment (CAPA). *Journal of the American Academy of Child and Adolescent Psychiatry, 39,* 39–48.

Angold, A., Costello, E. J., & Worthman, C. M. (1999). Pubertal changes in hormone levels and depression in girls. *Psychological Medicine, 29,* 1043–1053.

Angold, A., Cox, A., Prendergast, M., Rutter, M., & Simonoff, E. (1992). *The Child and Adolescent Psychiatric Assessment (CAPA): Version 3.0.* Unpublished interview schedule, Duke University Medical Center, Developmental Epidemiology Program.

Angold, A., Egger, H. L., Erkanli, A., & Keeler, G. (unpublished). *Prevalence and comorbidity of psychiatric disorders in preschoolers attending a large pediatric service.*

Angold, A., Erkanli, A., Farmer, E. M. Z., Fairbank, J. A., Burns, B. J., Keeler, G., et al. (2002). Psychiatric disorder, impairment, and service use in rural African American and White youth. *Archives of General Psychiatry, 59,* 893–901.

Angold, A., & Worthman, C. M. (1993). Puberty onset of gender differences in rates of depression: A developmental, epidemiologic and neuroendocrine perspective. *Journal of Affective Disorders, 29,* 145–158.

Angold, A., Worthman, C. M., & Costello, E. J. (2003). Puberty and depression. In C. Hayward (Ed.), *Gender differences at puberty* (pp. 137–164). New York: Cambridge University Press.

Barker, D. J. (1998). *Mothers, babies, and health in later life.* Edinburgh, Scotland: Churchill Livingstone.

Ben-Shlomo, Y., & Kuh, D. (2002). A life course approach to chronic disease epidemiology: Conceptual models, empirical challenges and interdisciplinary perspectives. *International Journal of Epidemiology, 31,* 285–293.

Benson, K., & Hartz, A. (2000). A comparison of observational studies and randomized, controlled trials. *New England Journal of Medicine, 342,* 1878–1886.

Berkson, J. (1946). Limitations of the application of fourfold table analysis to hospital data. *Biometrics Bulletin, 2,* 47–52.

Black, J. E., & Greenough, W. T. (1986). Induction of pattern in neural structure by experience: Implications for cognitive development. In M. E. Lamb, A. Brown, & B. Rogoff (Eds.), *Advances in developmental psychology* (Vol. 4, pp. 1–50). Hillsdale, NJ: Erlbaum.

Breslow, N. E., & Day, N. E. (1980). *Statistical methods in cancer research: Vol. I. The analysis of case control studies.* Lyon, France: WHO International Agency for Research on Cancer.

Breslow, N. E., & Day, N. E. (1987). *Statistical methods in cancer research: Vol. II. The design and analysis of cohort studies.* Lyon, France: WHO International Agency for Research on Cancer.

Broidy, L., Nagin, D., Tremblay, R., Bates, J., Brame, B., Dodge, K. A., et al. (2003). Developmental trajectories of childhood disruptive behaviors and adolescent delinquency: A six-site, cross-national study. *Developmental Psychology, 39,* 222–245.

Brook, J. S., Cohen, P., & Jaeger, L. (1998). Developmental variations in factors related to initial and increased levels of adolescent drug involvement. *Journal of Genetic Psychology, 159,* 179–194.

Brown, C. H., Berndt, D., Brinales, J., Zong, X., & Bhagwat, D. (2000). Evaluating the evidence of effectiveness for preventive interventions: Using a registry system to influence policy through science. *Addictive Behaviors, 25,* 955–964.

Brown, G. W., & Harris, T. O. (1978). *The social origins of depression: A study of psychiatric disorder in women.* New York: Free Press.

Buka, S. L., & Lipsitt, L. (1994). Toward a developmental epidemiology. In S. Friedman & H. Haywood (Eds.), *Developmental follow-up: Concepts, domains, and methods* (pp. 331–350). San Diego: Academic Press.

Burns, B. J., Costello, E. J., Angold, A., Tweed, D., Stangl, D., Farmer, E. M. Z., et al. (1995). Children's mental health service use across service sectors. *Health Affairs, 14,* 147–159.

Cacioppo, J. T., & Tassinary, L. G. (1991). Inferring psychological significance from physiological signals. *American Psychologist, 45,* 16–26.

Cairns, R. B. (1991). Multiple metaphors for a singular idea. *Developmental Psychopathology, 27,* 23–26.

Cairns, R. B., & Cairns, B. D. (1991). Social cognition and social networks: A developmental perspective. In D. J. Pepler & K. H. Rubin (Eds.), *The development and treatment of childhood aggression* (pp. 249–278). Hillsdale, NJ: Erlbaum.

Cairns, R. B., Elder, G. H., & Costello, E. J. (1996). *Developmental science.* New York: Cambridge University Press.

Cairns, R. B., Gariépy, J. L., & Hood, K. E. (1990). Development, microevolution, and social behavior. *Psychological Review, 97,* 49–65.

Cantwell, D. P. (1988). DSM-III studies. In M. Rutter, A. H. Tuma, & I. S. Lann (Eds.), *Assessment and diagnosis in child psychopathology* (pp. 3–36). New York: Guilford Press.

Caspi, A., McClay, J., Moffitt, T. E., Mill, J., Martin, J., Craig, I. W., et al. (2002). Role of genotype in the cycle of violence in maltreated children. *Science, 297,* 851–854.

Caspi, A., Moffitt, T. E., Newman, D. L., & Silva, P. A. (1996). Behavioral observations at age 3 years predict adult psychiatric disorders: Longitudinal evidence from a birth cohort. *Archives of General Psychiatry, 53,* 1033–1039.

Caspi, A., Sugden, K., Moffitt, T., Taylor, A., Craig, I., Harrington, H., et al. (2003). Influence of life stress on depression: Moderation by a polymorphism in the 5-HTT gene. *Science, 301,* 386–389.

Chambers, W. J., Puig-Antich, J., Hirsch, M., Paez, P., Ambrosini, P. J., Tabrizi, M. A., et al. (1985). The assessment of affective disorders in children and adolescents by semistructured interview: Test-retest reliability of the Schedule for Affective Disorders and Schizophrenia for School-age Children, present episode version. *Archives of General Psychiatry, 42,* 696–702.

Chasiotis, A., Scheffer, D., Restemeier, R., & Keller, H. (1998). Intergenerational context discontinuity affects the onset of puberty: A comparison of parent-child dyads in West and East Germany. *Human Nature, 9,* 321–339.

Chess, S., & Habibi, M. (1978). *Principles and practice of child psychiatry.* New York: Plenum Press.

Cicchetti, D. (1990a). An historical perspective on the discipline of developmental psychopathology. In J. Rolf, A. Masten, D. Cicchetti, K. Neuchterlein, & S. Weintraub (Eds.), *Risk and protective factors in the development of psychopathology* (pp. 1–28). New York: Cambridge University Press.

Cicchetti, D. (1990b). Perspectives on the interface between normal and atypical development. *Developmental Psychopathology, 2,* 329–333.

Cicchetti, D., & Schneider-Rosen, K. (1984). Toward a developmental model of the depressive disorders. *New Directions for Child Development, 26,* 5–27.

Cicchetti, D., & Schneider-Rosen, K. (1986). An organizational approach to childhood depression. In M. Rutter, C. E. Izard, & P. B. Read (Eds.), *Depression in young people: Developmental and clinical perspectives* (pp. 71–134). New York: Guilford Press.

Cicchetti, D., & Toth, S. L. (1992). The role of developmental theory in prevention and intervention. *Developmental Psychopathology, 4,* 489–493.

Clark, M. S., Sexton, T. J., McClain, M., Root, D., Kohen, R., & Neumaier, J. F. (2002). Overexpression of 5-HT1B receptor in dorsal raphe nucleus using herpes simplex virus gene transfer increases anxiety behavior after inescapable stress. *Journal of Neuroscience, 22,* 4550–4562.

Cohen, J. (1990). Things I have learned (so far). *American Psychologist, 45,* 1304–1312.

Cohen, J. (1996). Childhood risks for young adult symptoms of personality disorder: Method and substance. *Multivariate Behavioral Research, 21,* 121–148.

Cohen, P., Cohen, J., & Brook, J. (1993). An epidemiological study of disorders in late childhood and adolescence: 2. Persistence of disorders. *Journal of Child Psychology and Psychiatry, 34,* 869–877.

Concato, J., Shah, N., & Horwitz, R. (2000). Randomized, controlled trials, observational studies, and the hierarchy of research designs. *New England Journal of Medicine, 342,* 1887–1982.

Costello, A. J., Edelbrock, C., Kalas, R., Kessler, M. D., & Klaric, S. H. (1982). *The National Institute of Mental Health Diagnostic Interview Schedule for Children (DISC).* Rockville, MD: National Institute of Mental Health.

Costello, E. J., & Angold, A. (1993). Toward a developmental epidemiology of the disruptive behavior disorders. *Development and Psychopathology, 5,* 91–101.

Costello, E. J., & Angold, A. (2000). Developmental psychopathology and public health: Past, present, and future. *Development and Psychopathology, 12,* 599–618.

Costello, E. J., Burns, B. J., Angold, A., & Leaf, P. J. (1993). How can epidemiology improve mental health services for children and adolescents? *Journal of the American Academy of Child and Adolescent Psychiatry, 32,* 1106–1113.

Costello, E. J., Compton, S. N., Keeler, G., & Angold, A. (2003). Relationships between poverty and psychopathology: A natural experiment. *Journal of the American Medical Association, 290,* 2023–2029.

Costello, E. J., & Janiszewski, S. (1990). Who gets treated? Factors associated with referral in children with psychiatric disorders. *Acta Psychiatrica Scandinavica, 81,* 523–529.

Costello, E. J., Loeber, R., & Stouthamer-Loeber, M. (1991). Pervasive and situational hyperactivity—Confounding effect of informant: A research note. *Journal of Child Psychology and Psychiatry, 32,* 367–376.

Costello, E. J., Mustillo, S., Erkanli, A., Keeler, G., & Angold, A. (2003). Prevalence and development of psychiatric disorders in childhood and adolescence. *Archives of General Psychiatry, 60,* 837–844.

Costello, E. J., Pescosolido, B. A., Angold, A., & Burns, B. J. (1998). A family network-based model of access to child mental health services. In J. Morrissey (Ed.), *Research in community mental health* (pp. 165–190). Greenwich, CT: JAI.

Costello, E. J., Pine, D. S., Hammen, C., March, J. S., Plotsky, P. M., Weissman, M. M., et al. (2002). Development and natural history of mood disorders. *Biological Psychiatry, 52,* 529–542.

Cullen, K. J., & Boundy, C. A. P. (1966). The prevalence of behavior disorders in the children of 1,000 Western Australian families. *Medical Journal of Australia, 2,* 805–808.

Cummings, J. D. (1944). The incidence of emotional symptoms in school children. *British Journal of Educational Psychology, 14,* 151–161.

Dare, C. (1985). Psychoanalytic theories of development. In M. Rutter & L. Hersov (Eds.), *Child and adolescent psychiatry: Modern approaches* (pp. 204–215). Oxford: Blackwell Scientific Publications.

Davey Smith, G., Gunnell, D., & Ben-Shlomo, Y. (2000). Life-course approaches to socio-economic differentials in cause specific adult mortality. In D. Leon & G. Walt (Eds.), *Poverty, inequality and health: An international perspective* (pp. 88–124). Oxford: Oxford University Press.

Dawber, T. R. (1980). *The Framingham Study: The epidemiology of coronary heart disease.* Cambridge, MA: Harvard University Press.

Dehejia, R. H., & Wahba, S. (1999). Causal effects in nonexperimental studies: Reevaluating the evaluation of training programs. *Journal of the American Statistical Association, 94,* 1053–1062.

Digdon, N., & Gotlib, I. H. (1985). Developmental considerations in the study of childhood depression. *Developmental Review, 5,* 162–199.

Dodge, K. (2001). The science of youth violence prevention: Progressing from developmental epidemiology to efficacy to effectiveness to public policy. *American Journal of Preventive Medicine, 20,* 63–70.

Dodge, K. A., Pettit, G. S., & Bates, J. E. (1994). Socialization mediators of the relation between socioeconomic status and child conduct problems. *Child Development, 65,* 649–665.

Doll, R., & Peto, R. (1976). Mortality in relation to smoking: 20 years' observations on male British doctors. *British Medical Journal, 2,* 1525–1536.

Down, J. (1867). Observations on an ethnic classification of idiots. *Journal of Mental Science, 13,* 121–123.

Dulcan, M. K., Costello, E. J., Costello, A. J., Edelbrock, C., Brent, D., & Janiszewski, S. (1990). The pediatrician as gatekeeper to mental health care for children: Do parents' concerns open the gate? *Journal of the American Academy of Child and Adolescent Psychiatry, 29,* 453–458.

Earls, F. (1979). Epidemiology and child psychiatry: Historical and conceptual development. *Comprehensive Psychiatry, 20,* 256–269.

Earls, F. (1980). Prevalence of behavior problems in 3-year-old children: A cross-national replication. *Archives of General Psychiatry, 37,* 1153–1157.

Eaves, L. J., & Silberg, J. L. (2003). Modulation of gene expression by genetic and environmental heterogeneity in the timing of a developmental milestone. *Behavior Genetics, 33,* 1–6.

Eisenberg, L. (1977). Development as a unifying concept in psychiatry. *British Journal of Psychiatry, 131,* 225–237.

Ernst, M., Cookus, B. A., & Moravec, B. C. (2000). Pictorial Instrument for Children and Adolescents (PICA-III-R). *Journal of the American Academy of Child and Adolescent Psychiatry, 39,* 94–99.

Farrington, D. P. (1983). Offending from 10 to 25 years of age. In K. T. VanDusen & S. A. Mednick (Eds.), *Prospective studies of crime and delinquency* (pp. 17–37). Boston: Kluwer-Nijhoff.

Fergusson, D., & Horwood, L. (2001). The Christchurch health and development study: Review of findings on child and adolescent mental health. *Australian and New Zealand Journal of Psychiatry, 35,* 287–296.

Fergusson, D., & Woodward, L. (2000). Educational, psychosocial, and sexual outcomes of girls with conduct problems in early adolescence. *Journal of Child Psychology and Psychiatry and Allied Disciplines, 41,* 779–792.

Flisher, A. J., Kramer, R. A., Grosser, R. C., Alegria, M., Bird, H. R., Bourdon, K. H., et al. (1997). Correlates of unmet need for mental health services by children and adolescents. *Psychological Medicine, 27,* 1145–1154.

Foley, D. L., Eaves, L. J., Wormley, B., Silberg, J. L., Maes, H. H., Kuhn, J., et al. (2004). Childhood adversity, monoamine oxidase A genotype, and risk for conduct disorder. *Archives of General Psychiatry, 61,* 738–744.

Ford, T., Goodman, R., & Meltzer, H. (2003). The British child and adolescent mental health survey 1999: The prevalence of DSM-IV disorders. *Journal of the American Academy of Child and Adolescent Psychiatry, 42,* 1203–1211.

Foster, H., Nagin, D. S., Hagan, J., Costello, E. J., & Angold, A. (2005). *A life course dynamics perspective on poverty and family structure as stress histories and child conduct disorder.* Unpublished manuscript. Available from Dr. Foster at hfoster@neo.tamu.edu.

Fréchette, M., & Le Blanc, M. (1987). *Délinquences et délinquants.* Chicoutimi, Québec: Gaetan Morin.

Freedman, D. X. (1984). Psychiatric epidemiology counts. *Archives of General Psychiatry, 41,* 931–933.

Freud, A. (1965). *Normality and pathology in childhood.* New York: International Universities Press.

Freud, S. (1953–1974). Complete introductory lectures on psychoanalysis 1916–1917 (J. Strachey, Trans.). In J. Strachey, A. Strachey, & A. Tyson (Eds.), *Standard edition of the complete psychological works of Sigmund Freud* (Vol. 15). London: Hogarth Press.

Friedman, S., & Haywood, H. (1994). *Developmental followup: Concepts, domains, and methods.* San Diego: Academic Press.

Garmezy, N. (1988). Longitudinal strategies, causal reasoning and risk research: A commentary. In M. Rutter (Ed.), *Studies of psychosocial risk* (pp. 29–44). Cambridge, England: Cambridge University Press.

Ge, X., Brody, G., Conger, R., & Murry, V. (2002). Contextual amplification of pubertal transition effects on deviant peer affiliation and externalizing among African American children. *Developmental Psychology, 38,* 42–54.

Ge, X., Conger, R. D., & Elder, G. H. (1996). Coming of age too early: Pubertal influences on girls' vulnerability to psychological distress. *Child Development, 67,* 3386–3400.

Goodman, R., Ford, R., Simmons, H., Gatward, R., & Meltzer, H. (2000). Using the Strength and Difficulties Questionnaire (SDQ) to screen for child psychiatric disorders in a community sample. *British Journal of Psychiatry, 177,* 534–539.

Goodman, R., Ford, T., Richards, H., Gatward, R., & Meltzer, H. (2000). The development and well-being assessment: Description and initial validation of an integrated assessment of child and adolescent psychopathology. *Journal of Child Psychology and Psychiatry, 41,* 645–656.

Gottlieb, G. (1991). Experiential canalization of behavioral development: Theory. *Developmental Psychopathology, 27,* 4–13.

Gould, M., Greenberg, T., Velting, D., & Shaffer, D. (2003). Youth suicide risk and preventive interventions: A review of the past 10 years. *Journal of the American Academy of Child and Adolescent Psychiatry, 42,* 386–405.

Gould, M. S., Wunsch-Hitzig, R., & Dohrenwend, B. P. (1980). Formulation of hypotheses about the prevalence, treatment, and prognostic significance of psychiatric disorders in children in the United States. In B. P. Dohrenwend (Ed.), *Mental illness in the United States: Epidemiological estimates* (pp. 9–44). New York: Praeger.

Granger, D. A., Serbin, L. A., Schwartzman, A., Lehoux, P., Cooperman, J., & Ikeda, S. (1998). Children's salivary cortisol, internalizing behaviour problems, and family environment: Results from the Concordia Longitudinal Risk Project. *International Journal of Behavioral Development, 22,* 707–728.

Greenberg, M. T., Speltz, M. T., & DeKlyen, M. (1993). The role of attachment in the early development of disruptive behavior problems. *Development and Psychopathology, 5,* 191–213.

Greenough, W. T. (1991). Experience as a component of normal development: Evolutionary considerations. *Developmental Psychopathology, 27,* 14–17.

Griffiths, W. (1952). *Behavior difficulties of children as perceived and judged by parents, teachers, and children themselves.* Minneapolis: University of Minnesota Press.

Grob, G. N. (1985). The origins of American psychiatric epidemiology. *American Journal of Public Health, 75,* 229–236.

Grunbaum, A. (1977). Is pychoanalysis a psuedoscience? Karl Popper versus Sigmund Freud. *Zeitschrift fur Philosophische Forschung, 31,* 333–353.

Haggerty, M. E. (1925). The incidence of undesirable behavior in public school children. *Journal of Educational Research, 12,* 102–122.

Hay, D. F. (1985). Learning to form relationships in infancy: Parallel attainments with parents and peers. *Developmental Review, 5,* 122–161.

Hay, D. F., & Angold, A. (1993). Introduction: Precursors and causes in development and pathogenesis. In D. F. Hay & A. Angold (Eds.), *Precursors and causes in development and psychopathology* (pp. 1–21). Chichester, England: Wiley.

Hay, D. F., Pawlby, S., Angold, A., Harold, G., & Sharp, D. (2003). Pathways to violence in the children of mothers who were depressed postpartum. *Developmental Psychology, 39,* 1083–1094.

Henggeler, S. W., Melton, G. B., Brondino, M. J., Scherer, D. G., & Hanley, J. R. (1997). Multisystemic therapy with violent and chronic juvenile offenders and their families: The role of treatment fidelity in successful dissemination. *Journal of Consulting and Clinical Psychology, 65,* 821–833.

Herjanic, B., & Campbell, W. (1977). Differentiating psychiatrically disturbed children on the basis of a structured interview. *Journal of Abnormal Child Psychology, 5,* 127–134.

Ho, M. W. (1984). Environment and heredity in development and evolution. In M. W. Ho & P. T. Saunders (Eds.), *Beyond neo-Darwinism: An introduction to the new evolutionary paradigm* (pp. 267–289). San Diego: Academic Press.

Hodges, K. (1993). Structured interviews for assessing children. *Journal of Child Psychology and Psychiatry, 34*(1), 49–68.

Hodges, K., McKnew, D., Cytryn, L., Stern, L., & Kline, J. (1982). The Child Assessment Schedule (CAS) diagnostic interview: A report on reliability and validity. *Journal of the American Academy of Child Psychiatry, 21,* 468–473.

Howe, G. R. (1982). Epidemiology of radiogenic breast cancer. In J. D. Boice & J. J. R. Fraumeni (Eds.), *Radiation carcinogenesis: Epidemiology and biological significance* (pp. 119–129). New York: Raven Press.

Ialongo, N. S., Horn, W. F., Pascoe, J. M., Greenberg, G., Packard, T., Lopez, M., et al. (1993). The effects of a multimodal intervention with attention-deficit hyperactivity disorder children: A 9-month follow-up. *Journal of the American Academy of Child and Adolescent Psychiatry, 32,* 182–189.

Ireland, W. W. (1877). *On idiocy and imbecility.* London: Churchill.

Jablensky, A. (1986). Epidemiological surveys of mental health of geographically defined populations in Europe. In M. M. Weissman, J. K. Myers, & C. E. Ross (Eds.), *Community surveys of psychiatric disorders* (pp. 257–313). New Brunswick, NJ: Rutgers University Press.

Jacobson, K. C., Prescott, C. A., & Kendler, K. S. (2002). Sex differences in the genetic and environmental influences on the development of antisocial behavior. *Development and Psychopathology, 14,* 395–416.

Jaffee, S. R., Moffitt, T. E., Caspi, A., Fombonne, E., Poulton, R., & Martin, J. (2002). Differences in early childhood risk factors for juvenile-onset and adult-onset depression. *Archives of General Psychiatry, 59,* 215–222.

Jollos, V. (1934). Inherited changes produced by heat treatment in Drosophila melanogaster. *Genetics, 16,* 476–494.

Kandel, D. B., & Davies, M. (1982). Epidemiology of depressive mood in adolescents: An empirical study. *Archives of General Psychiatry, 39,* 1205–1212.

Kann, L. (2001). The youth risk behavior surveillance system: Measuring health-risk behaviors. *American Journal of Health Behavior, 25,* 272–277.

Kanner, L. (1945). *Child psychiatry.* Springfield, IL: Charles C. Thomas.

Kanner, L. (1972). *Child psychiatry* (4th ed.). Springfield, IL: Charles C. Thomas.

Kaufman, J. S., & Cooper, R. S. (1999). Seeking causal explanations in social epidemiology. *American Journal of Epidemiology, 150,* 113–128.

Kellam, S. G., Ensminger, M. E., & Turner, R. J. (1977). Family structure and the mental health of children. *Archives of General Psychiatry, 34,* 1012–1022.

Kellam, S. G., Koretz, D., & Moscicki, E. (1999). Core elements of developmental epidemiologically based prevention research. *American Journal of Community Psychology, 27,* 463–482.

Kellam, S. G., Rebok, G. W., Mayer, L. S., Ialongo, N., & Kalodner, C. R. (1994). Depressive symptoms over first grade and their response to a developmental epidemiologically based preventive trial aimed at improving achievement. *Development and Psychopathology, 6,* 463–481.

Kendell, R. E. (1976). The classification of depressions: A review of contemporary confusion. *British Journal of Psychiatry, 129,* 15–28.

Kendler, K. S., Kuhn, J., & Prescott, C. A. (2004). The interrelationship of neuroticism, sex, and stressful life events in the prediction of episodes of major depression. *American Journal of Psychiatry, 161,* 631–636.

Kendrick, T. (1999). Primary care options to prevent mental illness. *Annals of Medicine, 31,* 359–363.

Kim-Cohen, J., Caspi, A., Moffitt, T., Harrington, H., Milne, B., & Poulton, R. (2003). Prior juvenile diagnoses in adults with mental disorder: Developmental follow-back of a prospective-longitudinal cohort. *Archives of General Psychiatry, 60,* 709–717.

Kleinbaum, D. G., Kupper, L. L., & Morgenstern, H. (1982). *Epidemiologic research: Principles and quantitative methods.* New York: Van Nostrand Reinhold.

Krieger, N. (2001). Theories for social epidemiology in the 21st century: An ecosocial perspective. *International Journal of Epidemiology, 30,* 668–677.

Krueger, R., Caspi, A., Moffitt, T., & Silva, P. (1998). The structure and stability of common mental disorders (DSM-III-R): A longitudinal epidemiological study. *Journal of Abnormal Psychology, 107,* 216–227.

Kuh, D. L., & Ben-Shlomo, Y. (1997). *A life course approach to chronic disease epidemiology.* Oxford: Oxford University Press.

Land, K. C., & Nagin, D. S. (1996). Micro-models of criminal careers: A synthesis of the criminal careers and life course approaches via semiparametric mixed Poisson regression models, with empirical applications. *Journal of Quantitative Criminology, 12,* 163–191.

Lapouse, R. (1966). The epidemiology of behavior disorders in children. *American Journal of Dysfunctional Children, 111,* 594–599.

Lapouse, R. L., & Monk, M. A. (1958). An epidemiologic study of behavior characteristics in children. *American Journal of Public Health, 48,* 1134–1144.

Lapouse, R., & Monk, M. A. (1964). Behavior deviations in a representative sample of children: Variation by sex, age, race, social class and family size. *American Journal of Orthopsychiatry, 34,* 436–447.

Le Blanc, M., & Fréchette, M. (1989). *Male criminal activity from childhood through youth: Multilevel and developmental perspectives.* New York: Springer-Verlag.

Leon, D. A. (2000). Common threads: Underlying components of inequalities in mortality between and within countries. In D. Leon & G. Walt (Eds.), *Poverty, inequality and health: An international perspective* (pp. 58–87). Oxford: Oxford University Press.

Lesch, K. P. (2002). *Neuroticism and serotonin: A developmental genetic perspective.* Washington, DC: American Psychological Association.

Leslie, D. L., Rosenheck, R. A., & Horwitz, S. M. (2001). Patterns of mental health utilization and costs among children in a privately insured population. *Health Services Research, 36,* 113–127.

Lewis, M. (1990). Challenges to the study of developmental psychopathology. In M. Lewis & S. M. Miller (Eds.), *Handbook of developmental psychopathology* (pp. 29–40). New York: Plenum Press.

Lilienfeld, A. M., & Lilienfeld, D. E. (1980). *Foundations of epidemiology* (2nd ed.). New York: Oxford University Press.

Lipsey, M. W., & Wilson, D. B. (1998). Effective intervention for serious juvenile offenders: A synthesis of research. In R. Loeber & D. P. Farrington (Eds.), *Serious and violent juvenile offenders* (pp. 313–345). Thousand Oaks, CA: Sage.

Loeber, R., & Baicker-McKee, C. (1990). *The changing manifestations of disruptive/antisocial behavior from childhood to early adulthood: Evolution or tautology?* Unpublished manuscript, University of Pittsburgh, PA.

Loeber, R., Farrington, D. P., Stouthamer-Loeber, M., Moffitt, T. E., & Caspi, A. (1998). The development of male offending: Key findings from the first decade of the Pittsburgh Youth Study. *Studies on Crime and Crime Prevention, 7,* 141–171.

Loeber, R., Keenan, K., & Zhang, Q. (1997). Boys' experimentation and persistence in developmental pathways toward serious delinquency. *Journal of Child and Family Studies, 6,* 321–357.

Loeber, R., & Le Blanc, M. (1990). Toward a developmental criminology. In M. Tonry & N. Morris (Eds.), *Crime and justice: An annual review.* Chicago: University of Chicago Press.

Loeber, R., & Stouthamer-Loeber, M. (1997). The development of juvenile aggression and violence: Some common misconceptions and controversies. *American Psychologist, 53,* 242–259.

Long, A. (1941). Parents' reports of undesirable behavior in children. *Child Development, 12,* 43–62.

Lynam, D. R., Milich, R., Zimmerman, R., Novak, S. P., Logan, T. K., Martin, C., et al. (1999). Project DARE: No effects at 10-year follow-up. *Journal of Consulting and Clinical Psychology, 67,* 590–593.

Lyons-Ruth, K. (1996). Attachment relationship among children with aggressive behavior problems: The role of disorganized early attachment patterns. *Journal of Consulting and Clinical Psychology, 64,* 64–73.

Macfarlane, J. W., Allen, L., & Honzik, M. P. (1954). *University of California publications in child development.* Berkeley: University of California Press.

Magnusson, D., Stattin, H., & Allen, V. L. (1985). Biological maturation and social development: A longitudinal study of some adjustment processes from mid-adolescence to adulthood. *Journal of Youth and Adolescence, 14,* 267–283.

Mahoney, J. L., & Stattin, H. (2000). Leisure activities and adolescent antisocial behavior: The role of structure and social context. *Journal of Adolescence, 23,* 113–127.

Marshall, W. A., & Tanner, J. M. (1969). Variations in pattern of pubertal changes in girls. *Archives of Disease in Childhood, 44,* 291–303.

Maudsley, H. (1879). *The pathology of mind* (3rd ed.). London: Macmillan.

Maughan, B., Pickles, A., Rowe, R., Costello, E. J., & Angold, A. (2000). Developmental trajectories of aggressive and non-aggressive conduct problems. *Journal of Quantitative Criminology, 16,* 199–221.

Mayr, R. (1982). *The growth of biological thought: Diversity, evolution and intelligence.* Cambridge, MA: Harvard University Press.

Mays, C. W., & Spiess, H. (1984). Bone sarcomas in patients given radium-224. In J. D. Boice & J. J. F. Fraumeni (Eds.), *Radiation carcinogenesis: Epidemiology and biological significance* (pp. 241–252). New York: Raven Press.

McFie, B. S. (1934). Behavior and personality difficulties in school children. *British Journal of Educational Psychology, 4,* 34.

McGue, M. (1989). Nature-nurture and intelligence. *Nature, 340,* 507–508.

Meehl, P. E. (1954). *Clinical versus statistical prediction: A theoretical analysis and review of the evidence.* Minneapolis: University of Minnesota Press.

Meehl, P. E. (1992). Factors and taxa, traits and types, differences in degree and differences in kind. *Journal of Personality, 60,* 117–174.

Miettinen, O. S. (1974). Confounding and effect modification. *American Journal of Epidemiology, 100,* 350–353.

Mineka, S., Gunnar, M., & Champoux, M. (1986). Control and early socioemotional development: Infant rhesus monkeys reared in controllable versus uncontrollable environments. *Child Development, 57,* 1241–1256.

Moffitt, T. E. (1990). Juvenile delinquency and attention deficit disorder: Boys' developmental trajectories from age 3 to age 15. *Child Development, 61,* 893–910.

Moffitt, T. E. (1993). Adolescence-limited and life-course-persistent antisocial behavior: A developmental taxonomy. *Psychological Review, 100,* 674–701.

Moffitt, T. E., Caspi, A., Belsky, J., & Silva, P. A. (1992). Childhood experience and the onset of menarche: A test of a sociobiological model. *Child Development, 63,* 47–58.

Moffitt, T. E., Caspi, A., Harrington, H., & Milne, B. J. (2002). Males on the life-course persistent and adolescence-limited antisocial pathways: Follow-up at age 26. *Development and Psychopathology, 14,* 179–207.

Murray, C. J. L., & Lopez, A. D. (1996). *The global burden of disease.* Geneva, Switzerland: World Health Organization.

Mustillo, S., Worthman, C., Erkanli, A., Keeler, G., Angold, A., & Costello, E. J. (2003). Obesity and psychiatric disorder: Developmental trajectories. *Pediatrics, 111,* 851–859.

Muthen, B., & Muthen, L. K. (2000). Integrating person-centered and variable-centered analyses: Growth mixture modeling with latent trajectory classes. *Alcoholism: Clinical and Experimental Research, 24,* 882–891.

Nagel, E. (1957). Determinism and development. In D. B. Harris (Eds.), *The concept of development* (pp. 15–26). Minneapolis: University of Minnesota Press.

Nagin, D. S., & Tremblay, R. E. (2001a). Analyzing developmental trajectories of distinct but related behaviors: A group-based method. *Psychological Methods, 6,* 18–34.

Nagin, D. S., & Tremblay, R. E. (2001b). Parental and early childhood predictors of persistent physical aggression in boys from kindergarten to high school. *Archives of General Psychiatry, 58,* 389–394.

Needleman, H. L., & Bellinger, D. (1991). The health effects of low level exposure to lead. *Annual Review of Public Health, 12,* 111–140.

Offord, D. R., Boyle, M. H., Racine, Y. A., Fleming, J. E., Cadman, D. T., Blum, H. M., et al. (1992). Outcome, prognosis, and risk in a longitudinal follow-up study. *Journal of the American Academy of Child and Adolescent Psychiatry, 31,* 916–923.

Olson, W. C. (1930). *Problem tendencies in children.* Minneapolis: University of Minnesota Press.

Olweus, D. (1987, Fall). Schoolyard bullying: Grounds for intervention. *School Safety,* 4–11.

Olweus, D. (1993). *Bullying at school: What we know and what we can do.* Malden, MA: Blackwell Publishers.

Owens, P. L., Hoagwood, K., Horwitz, S. M., Leaf, P. J., Poduska, J. M., Kellam, S. G., et al. (2002). Barriers to children's mental health services. *Journal of the American Academy of Child and Adolescent Psychiatry, 41,* 731–738.

Peto, J. (1984). Early- and late-stage carcinogenesis in mouse skin and in man. In M. Börzsönyi, N. E. Day, K. Lapis, & H. Yamasaki (Eds.), *Models, mechanisms and etiology of tumour promotion* (IARC Scientific Publications No. 56, pp. 359–371). Lyon, France: International Agency for Research on Cancer.

Peto, J., Seidman, H., & Selikoff, I. J. (1982). Mesothelioma mortality in asbestos workers: Implications for models of carcinogenesis and risk assessment. *British Journal of Cancer, 45,* 124–135.

Pickles, A. (1993). Stages, precursors and causes in development. In D. F. Hay & A. Angold (Eds.), *Precursors and causes in development and psychopathology* (pp. 23–49). Chichester, England: Wiley.

Pickles, A., & Angold, A. (2003). Natural categories or fundamental dimensions: On carving nature at the joints and the rearticulation of psychopathology. *Development and Psychopathology, 15,* 529–551.

Plomin, R., DeFries, J. C., & Loehlin, J. C. (1977). Genotype: Environment interaction and correlation in the analysis of human behavior. *Psychological Bulletin, 84,* 309–322.

Pols, R. G., Sellman, D., Jurd, S., Baigent, M., Waddy, N., Sacks, T., et al. (1996). What is the psychiatrist's role in drugs and alcohol? *Australian and New Zealand Journal of Psychiatry, 30,* 540–548.

Prichard, J. C. (1837). *A treatise on insanity and other disorders affecting the mind.* Philadelphia: Haswell, Barrington and Haswell.

Reich, W. (2000). Diagnostic Interview for Children and Adolescents (DICA). *Journal of the American Academy of Child and Adolescent Psychiatry,* 59–66.

Reinherz, H. Z., Giaconia, R. M., Hauf, A. M., Wasserman, M. S., & Paradis, A. D. (2000). General and specific childhood risk factors for depression and drug disorders by early adulthood. *Journal of the American Academy of Child and Adolescent Psychiatry, 39,* 223–231.

Reinherz, H. Z., Giaconia, R. M., Hauf, A. M., Wasserman, M. S., & Silverman, A. B. (1999). Major depression in the transition to adulthood: Risks and impairments. *Journal of Abnormal Psychology, 108,* 500–510.

Rice, B. J., Woolston, J., Stewart, E., Kerker, B. D., & Horwitz, S. M. (2002). Differences in younger, middle, and older children admitted to child psychiatric inpatient services. *Child Psychiatry and Human Development, 32,* 241–261.

Robins, J. (1997). Causal inference from complex longitudinal data. In M. Berkane (Ed.), *Latent variable modeling and applications to causality: Lecture notes in statistics* (pp. 69–117). New York: Springer Verlag.

Robins, J., Greenland, S., & Hu, F. (1999). Rejoinder comments on "Estimation of the causal effect of a time-varying exposure on the marginal mean of a repeated binary outcome." *Journal of the American Statistical Association, 94,* 708–712.

Robins, J., Hernan, M., & Brumback, B. (2000). Marginal structural models and causal inference in epidemiology. *Epidemiology, 11,* 550–560.

Robins, L. N. (1985). Epidemiology: Reflections on testing the validity of psychiatric interviews. *Archives of General Psychiatry, 42,* 918–924.

Robins, L. N. (1989). Diagnostic grammar and assessment: Translating criteria into questions. *Psychological Medicine, 19,* 57–68.

Robins, L. N. (1992). Longitudinal methods in the study of normal and pathological development. *Fortschr Neurol Psychiatry,* 627–684.

Robins, L. N., & Price, R. K. (1991). Adult disorders predicted by childhood conduct problems: Results from the NIMH Epidemiologic Catchment Area Project. *Psychiatry, 54,* 113–132.

Robins, L. N., & Wish, E. (1977). Childhood deviance as a developmental process: A study of 223 urban Black men from birth to 18. *Social Forces, 56,* 448–473.

Rohde, P., Lewinsohn, P. M., Kahler, C. W., Seeley, J. R., & Brown, R. A. (2001). Natural course of alcohol use disorders from adolescence to young adulthood. *Journal of the American Academy of Child and Adolescent Psychiatry, 40,* 83–90.

Rossi, A. S. (1989). A life-course approach to gender, aging, and intergenerational relations. In K. W. Schaie & C. Schoder (Eds.), *Social structure and aging* (pp. 207–236). Hillsdale, NJ: Erlbaum.

Rothman, K. J. (1976). Reviews and commentary: Causes. *American Journal of Epidemiology, 104,* 587–592.

Rutter, M. (1985). Resilience in the face of adversity: Protective factors and resistance to psychiatric disorder. *British Journal of Psychiatry, 147,* 598–611.

Rutter, M. (1988). Epidemiological approaches to developmental psychopathology. *Archives of General Psychiatry, 45,* 486–495.

Rutter, M. (1990). Changing patterns of psychiatric disorders during adolescence. In J. Bancroft & J. M. Reinisch (Eds.), *Adolescence and puberty* (pp. 124–145). New York: Oxford University Press.

Rutter, M., Lebovici, S., Eisenberg, L., Sneznevskij, A. V., Sadoun, R., Brooke, E., et al. (1969). A tri-axial classification of mental disorders in childhood: An international study. *Journal of Child Psychology and Psychiatry, 10,* 41–61.

Rutter, M., Shaffer, D., & Sturge, C. (1979). *A guide to a multi-axial classification scheme for psychiatric disorders in childhood and adolescence.* London: Frowde.

Rutter, M., Tizard, J., & Whitmore, K. (1970). *Education, health, and behaviour.* London: Longman.

Scarr, S., & McCartney, K. (1983). How people make their own environments: A theory of genotype-environment effects. *Child Development, 54,* 424–435.

Seifer, R., Sameroff, A. J., Baldwin, C. P., & Baldwin, A. (1989, April). *Risk and protective factors between 4 and 13 years of age.* Paper presented at the annual meeting of the Society for Research in Child Development, San Francisco.

Shadish, W., Cook, T., & Campbell, D. (2002). *Experimental and quasi-experimental designs for generalized causal inference.* Boston: Houghton Mifflin.

Shaffer, D., Fisher, P., Lucas, C. P., Dulcan, M. K., & Schwab-Stone, M. E. (2000). NIMH Diagnostic Interview Schedule for Children version IV (NIMH DISC-IV): Description, differences from previous versions, and reliability of some common diagnoses. *Journal of the American Academy of Child and Adolescent Psychiatry, 39,* 28–38.

Shaffer, D., Lucas, C. P., & Richters, J. E. (1999). *Diagnostic assessment in child and adolescent psychopathology.* New York: Guilford Press.

Shepherd, M., Oppenheim, B., & Mitchell, S. (1971). *Childhood behavior and mental health.* London: University of London Press.

Sherrill, J. T., & Kovacs, M. (2000). Interview Schedule for Children and Adolescents (ISCA). *Journal of the American Academy of Child and Adolescent Psychiatry, 39,* 67–75.

Silberg, J., Rutter, M., & Eaves, L. (2001). Genetic and environmental influences on the temporal association between earlier anxiety and later depression in girls. *Biological Psychiatry, 49,* 1040–1049.

Silverman, W. K., & Rabian, B. (1995). Test-retest reliability of the DSM-III-R childhood anxiety disorders symptoms using the Anxiety Disorders Interview Schedule for Children. *Journal of Anxiety Disorders, 9,* 139–150.

Simonoff, E., Pickles, A., Meyer, J. M., Silberg, J. L., Maes, H. H., Loeber, R., et al. (1997). The Virginia Twin Study of adolescent behavioral development: Influences of age, sex and impairment on rates of disorder. *Archives of General Psychiatry, 54,* 801–808.

Simmons, R. G., & Blyth, D. A. (1987). *Moving into adolescence: The impact of pubertal change and school context.* Hawthorne, NY: Aldine de Gruyter.

Snow, J. (1855). *On the mode of communication of cholera* (2nd ed.). London: Churchill.

Sroufe, L. A. (1988). The role of infant-caregiver attachment in development. In J. Belsky & T. Nezworski (Eds.), *Clinical implications of attachment* (pp. 18–38). Hillsdale, NJ: Erlbaum.

Sroufe, L. A., & Rutter, M. (1984). The domain of developmental psychopathology. *Child Development, 55,* 17–29.

Stattin, H., & Magnusson, D. (1990). *Paths through life: Vol. 2. Pubertal maturation in female development.* Hillsdale, NJ: Erlbaum.

Stein, Z., Susser, M., Saenger, G., & Marolla, F. (1975). *Famine and human development: The Dutch hunger winter of 1944–1945.* New York: Oxford University Press.

Stouthamer-Loeber, M., Loeber, R., Farrington, D., Zhang, Q., Van Kammen, W. B., & Maguin, E. (1993). The double edge of protective and risk factors for delinquency: Interrelations and developmental patterns. *Development and Psychopathology, 5,* 683–701.

Suomi, S. J. (1991). Adolescent depression and depressive symptoms: Insights from longitudinal studies with rhesus monkeys. *Journal of Youth and Adolescence, 20,* 273–287.

Susser, M. (1973). *Causal thinking in the health sciences: Concepts and strategies in epidemiology.* New York: Oxford University Press.

Tolan, P. H. (1987). Implications of age of onset for delinquency risk. *Journal of Abnormal Child Psychology, 15,* 47–65.

Tremblay, R. E., Japel, C., Perusse, D., Boivin, M., Zoccolillo, M., Montplaisir, J., et al. (1999). The search for the age of "onset" of physical aggression: Rousseau and Bandura revisited. *Criminal Behavior and Mental Health, 9,* 24–39.

Valla, J.-P., Bergeron, L., & Smolla, N. (2000). The Dominic-R: A pictorial interview for 6- to 11-year-old children. *Journal of the American Academy of Child and Adolescent Psychiatry, 39,* 85–93.

van Eldik, T., Treffers, P. D., Veerman, J. W., & Verhulst, F. C. (2004). Mental health problems of deaf Dutch children as indicated by parents' responses to the Child Behavior Checklist. *American Annals of the Deaf, 148,* 390–395.

Verhulst, F. C., Achenbach, T. M., Althaus, M., & Akkerhuis, G. W. (1988). A comparison of syndromes derived from the Child Behavior Checklist for American and Dutch girls aged 6–11 and 12–16. *Journal of Child Psychology and Psychiatry, 29,* 879–895.

Verhulst, F. C., van der Ende, J., Ferdinand, R. F., & Kasius, M. C. (1997). The prevalence of DSM-III-R diagnoses in a national sample of Dutch adolescents. *Archives of General Psychiatry, 54,* 329–336.

Vineis, P., & Porta, M. (1996). Causal thinking, biomarkers, and mechanisms of carcinogenesis. *Journal of Clinical Epidemiology, 49,* 951–956.

von Gontard, A. (1988). The development of child psychiatry in 19th century Britain. *Journal of Child Psychology and Psychiatry, 29,* 569–588.

Weinberg, C. R., & Umbach, D. M. (2000). Choosing a retrospective design to assess joint genetic and environmental contributions to risk. *American Journal of Epidemiology, 152,* 197–203.

Weisz, J. R. (1989). Culture and the development of child psychopathology: Lessons from Thailand. In D. V. Cicchetti (Ed.), *Rochester Symposium on Developmental Psychopathology* (Vol. I). New York: Cambridge University Press.

Wickman, E. K. (1928). *Children's behavior and teachers' attitudes.* New York: The Commonwealth Fund.

Wilkinson, R. G. (1994). Inequalities and health. *Lancet, 343,* 538.

Williams, P. G., Holmbeck, G. N., & Greenley, R. N. (2002). Adolescent health psychology. *Journal of Consulting and Clinical Psychology, 70,* 828–842.

Wing, J. K., Bebbington, P., & Robins, L. N. (1981). *What is a case?* London: Grant McIntyre.

Winship, C., & Morgan, S. L. (1999). The estimation of causal effects from observational data. *Annual Review of Sociology, 25,* 659–707.

Wittchen, H.-U., Nelson, C. B., & Lachner, G. (1998). Prevalence of mental disorders and psychosocial impairments in adolescents and young adults. *Psychological Medicine, 28,* 109–126.

World Health Organization. (1996). *The global burden of disease.* Geneva, Switzerland: World Health Organization.

Worthman, C. M. (1987). Interactions of physical maturation and cultural practice in ontogeny: Kikuyu adolescents. *Cultural Anthropology, 2,* 29–38.

Worthman, C. M., & Konner, M. J. (1987). Testosterone levels change with subsistence hunting effort in Kung San men. *Clinical Chemistry, 36,* 1769–1773.

Young-Masten, I. (1938). Behavior problems of elementary school children: A descriptive and comparative study. *Genetic Psychology Monographs, 20,* 123–180.

Yourman, J. (1932). Children identified by their teachers as problems. *Journal of Educational Sociology, 5,* 334–343.

Zeger, S. L., & Liang, K. Y. (1992). An overview of methods for the analysis of longitudinal data. *Statistics in Medicine, 11,* 1825–1839.

Zubin, J. (1978). Research in clinical diagnosis. In B. B. Wolman (Ed.), *Clinical diagnosis of mental disorders* (pp. 3–14). New York: Plenum.

CHAPTER 4

The Origins and Development of Psychopathology in Females and Males

CAROLYN ZAHN-WAXLER, NICKI R. CRICK, ELIZABETH A. SHIRTCLIFF, and KATHLEEN E. WOODS

At birth and throughout development, males and females differ in obvious and subtle ways. Shaped by evolution and sculpted by culture, these differences have become deeply ingrained. Early in civilization sex roles were clearly differentiated. Males hunted and fended off foes, while females bore and reared the offspring; both were essential to the success of subsequent generations. These roles became increasingly diversified, modified by socialization, and (except for childbearing) shared over the course of time. Our evolutionary heritage, however, is a reminder of the different biologically based functions for which males and females were prepared. This has influenced to a considerable degree their different roles and status in cultures and societies, as well as their different interests, skills, affective styles, and personality traits. The entrenchment of these sex

differences over time has created different patterns of costs and benefits, as well as different strengths and vulnerabilities. These differences are also reflected in (1) the types of disorders and problems males and females develop, (2) the ways their difficulties are manifested and managed, and (3) how external events impinge on and are interpreted by them. Not only may males and females differ on strengths and vulnerabilities, but also the same quality or trait may have both positive and negative adaptational features.

Research on gender and the development of psychopathology is recent in origin and has focused on three primary issues. The first issue has captured the most attention and involves evaluation of sex differences in the prevalence of psychopathology during different periods of development. The second issue is more complex and focuses on similarities and differences in the antecedents, development, correlates, and consequences of psychopathology in males and females from childhood to adolescence and beyond. This type of research emphasizes identification of developmental trajectories toward psychopathology and includes attention to sex differences in contributory factors and in the outcomes that accrue. The third issue involves sex differences in how problems are expressed.

Prevalence rates for almost all psychiatric disorders and psychological problems reflect a sex-based imbalance (American Psychiatric Association, 2000). Males are over-represented in some disorders, for example, Autism and Attention-Deficit/Hyperactivity (ADHD), Conduct, and Antisocial Personality Disorders. Females are overrepresented in other disorders, for example, anxiety, mood (except for bipolar illness), eating, and Borderline Personality Disorder. Forms of self-injury differ; males are more accident-prone and likely to commit suicide, whereas females more often attempt suicide and engage in body mutilation. Males are more often victims of physical violence, and females are more often victims of relational aggression as well as sexual abuse and physical violence in partner relationships. Even where prevalence rates are the same, there are other differences; for example, males show earlier onset of Schizophrenia than females, and there are differences in symptom expression. Biological and genetic factors can contribute to sex differences in the emergence and developmental course of problems. Boys and girls also experience different socialization, interpersonal relationships, adverse events, and cultural norms that can create different adaptive and maladaptive patterns.

This brief description of differences between the problems of females and males just begins to scratch the surface of a still largely unexplored territory. There are sex differences at all levels of problems (clinical, subclinical, and normative problems), as well as in correlated affective, behavioral, and cognitive styles. Normative variations may inform different manifestations of more serious problems in terms of their antecedents, correlates, and consequences. Conversely, knowledge of contributions to more severe disorders can inform processes associated with more normative patterns of development. A developmental psychopathology perspective is uniquely suited to explore gender-related questions across a continuum of severity of symptoms. Problems more characteristic of males or females are closely tied to different time periods, as the problems of males typically emerge early in development.

Rutter, Caspi, and Moffitt (2003) make the point that sex differences in mental disorders fall into two main groups. There are the early-onset neuropsychiatric disorders, such

as Autism, developmental language disorders, ADHD, Conduct Disorder, and dyslexia, that show a marked male preponderance. Then there are the adolescent-onset emotional disorders, such as depressive/mood disorders, anxiety disorders, and eating disorders, which show a marked female preponderance. Anxiety disorders and antisocial disorders do not fit as neatly into this classification of childhood- versus adolescent-onset. Although anxiety problems peak in adolescence, particularly in girls, anxiety is more common in girls than boys even at an early age. And although the early-onset form of antisocial disorders is associated with neurodevelopmental impairment and more common in males, antisocial disorders also peak again in adolescence.

Because the etiologies of early- versus late-onset disorders may be different, developmental stage becomes a starting point for examining possible causes for different problems in males and females. At the same time, it is necessary to move beyond this dichotomy to consider the (1) early onset of problems in girls, (2) late onset of problems in boys, (3) presence of early signs of problems in both boys and girls that go unnoticed until more pronounced symptoms emerge later in development, and (4) factors that contribute to individual differences *within* groups of boys and girls. We focus in this chapter on childhood and adolescence, but we also consider the implications of developmental processes for some problems first seen in early adulthood but that may have earlier origins. We do not assume that there have to be differential rates of problems for the sex of the child to matter. Rates of a given disorder could be similar for males and females, but they could differ in their manifestations, causes, or patterns of interaction with other etiologic and predictive variables. The study of sex differences in psychopathology at different stages of development requires appreciation of similarities as well as differences between males and females. Increasingly, investigators have come to realize that rather than simply being a nuisance variable, sex differences can provide a means to study causal mechanisms and unravel the complex etiologies that characterize different forms of emotional and behavioral problems (e.g., Crick & Zahn-Waxler, 2003; Rutter et al., 2003).

For a long time, problems commonly were studied in only one sex (more often males). When both males and females were studied in the same research design, results were based on analyses of the total sample. Thus, there was not a comprehensive empirical literature from which to develop hypotheses or generalizations about sex, gender, and the development of psychopathology. This has started to change, as investigators have had to confront and explain those pesky but intriguing differences that often emerge when separate analyses are conducted for males and females. A confluence of factors makes the time ripe for significant headway in theory and research. Following recognition that physical health problems often differ in the two sexes, public funding of mental health research now mandates inclusion of both females and males in research designs. New and improved technologies and methodologies for studying both biological and psychosocial processes have also contributed to a more substantial database. This makes it possible to begin to characterize the variety of ways in which females and males differ on average. Clinicians and scientists now focus more intensively on problems that have been underinvestigated in one sex because they occurred less frequently, for example, aggression, antisocial behavior, and violence in girls (Bell, Foster, & Mash, 2005; Putallaz & Bierman, 2004) and depression in boys (e.g., Gjerde & Block, 1996; Pollack, 1998).

The terms sex and gender have been used in various ways and often are used synonymously (Maccoby, 2004). Typically, *sex* refers to the biological differences between males and females. The term *gender* was introduced to distinguish sociocultural forces from biological processes, but this distinction has proved difficult to maintain. Historically, the study of sex differences focused on how and why average differences in personality, cognition, emotions, ability, problems, and/or biological and genetic factors between the sexes might arise. In most cases, sex differences in some quality or behavior occur with overlapping distributions, sometimes with highly sex-differentiated "tails" of the distribution. Most disorders and symptoms have both overlapping distributions and clearly sex-differentiated tails.

In many cases, this focus on differences between two groups of individuals (i.e., males and females) has ignored the large within-sex variance. Some have argued that this can exaggerate, reinforce, and even create sex differences in the minds of others. Although there are problems with accurate estimation of differences in rates, it is now clear that the differences are not simply artifactual but do actually exist (Hartung & Widiger, 1998). But less attention has been paid to the enormous within-sex variability, for example, in antisocial patterns in girls and depression in boys. By focusing on within-subject variability, simultaneously for males and females, we will come closer to understanding etiologic factors that operate both similarly and differently for the two sexes.

The term gender is also used to describe power relations in social structures throughout cultures (Stewart & McDermott, 2004). According to this viewpoint, absent other cues and definitions, maleness signals authority, status, competence, social power, and influence, and femaleness signals lack of authority, low status, incompetence, and little power and influence. Gender also signals more positive as-

sociations with femaleness (e.g., compassion, nurturance) and more negative ones with maleness (e.g., psychopathy, violence). Power relations may play some role in different rates and etiologies of symptoms in males and females.

Rutter et al. (2003) recently argued for the appropriateness of using the terms gender and sex interchangeably in discussions of their role(s) in psychopathology. Maintaining the distinction, they argue, creates an artificial dichotomy suggesting that biological and environmental processes are distinct and fully separable, both conceptually and in terms of measurement and evaluation of causal mechanisms. In this chapter, we use the term sex to characterize findings where research subjects have been classified as male or female. Otherwise, we use sex and gender interchangeably to avoid the different causal implications.

Most of the empirical efforts have focused on biological *or* environmental factors that distinguish between males and females in their relative rates of disturbance, with little emphasis on how these factors interact to influence developmental outcomes. At one end of the continuum, some disorders, such as Autism, result primarily from genetic, neurological, and other more biologically driven factors. At the other end, environmental factors play a major role (e.g., maltreatment). However, even here, biological predispositions cannot be dismissed, just as environmental factors could alter the expression and severity of autistic behaviors. Between these two extremes is a wide range of other emotional and behavioral problems and disorders where both biological factors and environmental processes are likely implicated. To a greater or lesser degree, then, the emergence, progression, and remission of psychiatric and psychological problems will reflect complex interactions of biological and environmental factors, and these factors will not be fully separable. This again highlights the need for a developmental psychopathology perspective and the use of stress-diathesis models to examine the best approximations possible of endogenous and exogenous processes. It will be important to determine the roles of these different sets of factors and the ways they combine and interact for different types of disorders and problems. Some processes may cut across types of disorders; others may be specific to particular disorders.

Mechanisms that could explain sex differences include a number of possibilities: Boys and girls may (1) be exposed to different environmental risk and protective factors, (2) be exposed to different levels of the same environmental risk and protective factors, (3) have different biological processes or mechanisms of gene expression (such that these influences may be differentially amplified or diminished for one sex or the other), (4) require different thresholds of biological or genetic risk for serious problems to develop, and (5) differentially experience interactions of these environmental and biological/genetic influences. Also, certain biological and environmental processes are expected to operate similarly for males and females.

In short, any number of possibilities may apply, depending on varying constellations of factors. This highlights the need to avoid premature conclusions about similar or different operative processes for the two sexes based on a limited number of studies. Both scientific parsimony and cultural ideologies of equality tend to favor explanations that view the nature and causes of problems in males and females as similar. However, research designs often have not been adequate to address the question of similar versus different causes (e.g., only one sex is studied; samples are not large enough to conduct analyses separately for females and males; constructs are not adequately measured). In our view, this has interfered with identifying potential factors that might lead to differential processes and patterns of psychopathology.

In this chapter, we consider a range of conceptual, methodological, statistical, and substantive issues in the study of sex differences in the development of psychopathology. We review salient issues in the context of specific disorders/problems and also examine crosscutting themes. This includes discussion of comorbidity of problems, which is quite common and differs for males and females. We also consider underlying processes across disorders that may create differential risk; for example, the notion of the extreme male brain has been used to explain the increased likelihood of multiple male-preponderant disorders. To our knowledge, no one has proposed the counterpart of the extreme female brain that may be associated with increased likelihood of multiple female-preponderant disorders; we consider this possibility as well. At the same time, we believe it is important not to reduce the issue of sex differences to one of male versus female disorders, given the enormous overlap for both normative and pathological processes. It is essential to avoid developing sex stereotypes of the problems males and females face. We attempt to provide a balanced perspective that takes these issues into account, considering both similarities between the sexes as well as differences that have begun to emerge.

We begin with a discussion of biological and genetic sex differences that may contribute to different patterns of resilience and vulnerability in females and males. This literature is based primarily on research with animals and adult humans. We then provide a descriptive summary review of the principal domains in which girls and boys differ, normatively, in infancy, childhood, and adolescence, as well as

differ in the environments they experience. Many of the themes that emerge here resurface in subsequent sections on specific disorders and problems as we discuss biological and environmental processes implicated in rates, trajectories, and outcomes for boys and girls. We consider problems in four areas: (1) pervasive developmental (Autism and childhood Schizophrenia), (2) externalizing (ADHD, Oppositional-Defiant Disorder, Conduct Disorder, and substance use), (3) internalizing (depression, anxiety, eating), and (4) personality. We highlight what is known about the prevalence, nature, etiology, and theories of each disorder in males and females. Because there is considerable variation on what is known, the sections vary in length and organization. Last, we discuss problems, progress, and future directions for theory and research on sex differences in psychopathology.

BIOLOGICAL SEX DIFFERENCES

Sexual dimorphisms of behavior are often assumed to be derived from sexual dimorphisms of the brain and body. Evolutionary explanations for sexual dimorphisms also implicate biological underpinnings of behavior to explain sex differences in behavior. Understanding sex differences in biological mechanisms is twofold. A wealth of literature documents robust sex differences in biological systems. Animal studies also demonstrate sex differences in neural circuitry and neurotransmitter systems. These studies highlight the importance of understanding masculinization, the process of becoming more male-like (e.g., development of testes, penis, and scrotum; induction of male traits) and defeminization, the process of removing female-like traits (e.g., regression of female internal ducts; R. J. Nelson, 2000). Parallel studies in humans are now beginning to accumulate evidence for the male and female brain. Apart from obvious physical differences between males and females, however, discovering the implications of biological sexual dimorphisms for normative and risk behavior is an important next step toward understanding sex differences. Here we review biological mechanisms that may contribute to sex differences in psychopathology, including genes, hormones, neurotransmitters, brain development, and pharmacokinetics.

Genetic Contributions

At the most basic level, males and females differ in their genetic makeup. The Institute of Medicine (2001) report appropriately titled the first two chapters "Every Cell Has a Sex" and "Sex Begins in the Womb," thereby emphasizing the developmental significance of genetic contributions to sex dimorphisms. In addition to the observation that females have two X chromosomes and males have one X and one Y chromosome, which contains the SRY gene that will later cause the bipotential gonad to differentiate as a testes, females and males differ genetically in other less obvious ways. These include complete and incomplete X inactivation, enzymatic and hormonal interactions, nonrandom allele distributions, and sex selection. Each of these processes may contribute to different pathways of development in males and females beginning when the ovum and sperm fuse.

Within each cell in a female, one X chromosome is inactivated (Latham, 1996). On a cell-by-cell basis, a maternal or paternal X chromosome will be expressed. X inactivation renders females less susceptible to X-linked mutations (e.g., color blindness) and potentially may contribute to their reduced susceptibility to male-dominated psychopathology that tends to begin early in childhood (reviewed later). Further, the process of X inactivation is not complete, so females are exposed to 10% to 15% greater quantity of X-derived proteins (Disteche, 1995). Recent magnetic resonance imaging (MRI) studies show that X inactivation and incomplete inactivation patterns contribute to sex differences in brain areas related to emotion and mood (J. N. Giedd, personal communication, August 19, 2004 by telephone).

Within each cell in a male, one Y chromosome is expressed. The Y chromosome codes for few genes (only eight in mice), but among these few is the SRY gene. The SRY gene has received much attention because it codes for testes differentiation and the eventual cascade resulting in testosterone secretion from the developing male gonads. Appreciating the fact that the Y chromosome codes for more than testes differentiation will lead to a greater understanding of Y chromosome functions not directly linked to SRY and testosterone (Arnold, Rissman, & De Vries, 2003). A provocative line of research aimed at isolating the direct effects of the SRY gene versus other Y chromosome effects in the brain and on behavior revealed that sex accounted for more of the variation in the brain and behavior of mice than the complement of the SRY gene (in genetic XX or XY mice). This suggests that masculinization and defeminization in the brain are due to hormonally mediated genetic effects (i.e., SRY-specific effects), as well as other Y-linked sources of sexual differentiation (De Vries et al., 2002). Further, genetic differences between males and females lead to enzymatic and hormonal sex differences (reviewed extensively in Migeon & Wisniewski, 1998). Some genetic differences are derived from the X

and Y chromosomes, but many genes, enzymes, and hormones become dimorphic by interacting with X- or Y-linked biomarkers. For example, at least seven enzymatic steps are necessary for converting cholesterol to testosterone and dihydrotestosterone (DHT); these enzymes are not located on the Y chromosome (MacLaughlin & Donahoe, 2004). Nevertheless, the end point of this process becomes fundamentally different in the male and female (Migeon & Wisniewski, 1998, 2003). Testosterone, in turn, regulates gene expression differently in the male and female and is more heritable in the male than in the female (Hong et al., 2001). Genetic differences between males and females may also exist if allele determinism is nonrandom or if genetic expression of an allele interacts with promoters on the X chromosome. This would result in males and females having different patterns of gene expression derived distantly from their XX or XY complement.

Although chromosomal endowment is arguably the furthest domain from which social processes influence sexually dimorphic mechanisms, nevertheless social factors can influence gene expression, leading to gene-environment correlations and interactions, and Grant (1996, 1998) has proposed a theoretical model in which social processes influence sexual determination (i.e., likelihood of conceiving males or females). Thus, dominant women with high testosterone are more likely to conceive sons, particularly when times are tough, and thereby parent the gender that they are most suited to raise. If the physiological mechanism for Grant's hypothesis is supported, then this idea is a good example of the negligible value of rigidly distinguishing between biological and social forces that influence sex and gender (Rutter et al., 2003). It is also an intriguing example of a biosocial interaction in which genetic and biological forces may be exacerbated by social phenomena. In sum, gender differences may be due to chromosomal differences arising from (1) chromosomal dissimilarities related to inactivation, (2) biological processes related to other chromosomes or hormonal factors that interact with the X and Y chromosomes, or (3) enzymatic differences resulting from other chromosomes.

Neuroendocrine Contributions

Hormones are powerful regulating factors that influence gene expression. W. C. Young, Goy, and Phoenix (1964) first presented the *organizational-activational hypothesis,* based largely on rodent and primate models, which postulates that following some genetic signal, androgenic hormones directly cause the masculinization and defeminization of brain mechanisms of behavior during a critical period early in development. Masculinization occurs on a continuum as a function of the amount of hormone present in utero. These masculinizing hormones exert an effect on behavior independent of circulating hormones. After a period of relative quiescence (e.g., the juvenile period), these circuits that were organized by androgens are later activated (Hutchison, 1997). Many researchers still consider (implicitly or explicitly) gonadal steroids to instantiate sexual differentiation of the human body, brain, and behavior (Arnold et al., 2003).

Based on the timing and duration of effects, neuroendocrine influences on the brain and behavior are divided into organizational effects, processes initiated and terminated in utero, and activational effects, processes initiated after the termination of the juvenile period. Activational effects must be further differentiated into developmental opportunities at puberty, concurrent effects in late adolescence or adulthood, cyclical activation, and disorganizational effects (McEwen, 1992). The study of sex differences in hormones must necessarily consider the developmental stage at which effects begin, when they are observed and measured, how long effects last, and other biosocial forces expected to influence pathways of development (Udry, 2000). Before reviewing sex differences in hormone effects, however, a note of caution is warranted. Many studies that assess the organizational-activational hypothesis are based on animal models of behavior. Animal models are informative but are more simple than the human condition. Research in humans is often limited to correlational studies conducted at opportunistic developmental stages (Udry, Morris, & Kovenock, 1995) or on experiments of nature, that is, intersex individuals (see reviews by Migeon & Wisniewski, 1998, 2003). Experiments of nature provide powerful evidence for both the diversity of neuroendocrine effects on sex differences and the intense environmental factors that play critical roles. Overemphasizing either biological or environmental contributions to the organization of sex differences has had drastically bleak effects on the quality of life of intersex individuals (see Bradley, Oliver, Chernick, & Zucker, 1998, and M. Diamond & Sigmundson, 1997, for an ongoing debate). Recent historical events should remind us all that disentangling neuroendocrine contributions to sex differences must necessarily acknowledge the complexity of these effects (Colapinto, 2000; http://slate.msn.com/id/2101678).

Studies on intersex individuals have provided support for the organizational-activational hypothesis but have also added much additional complexity to human sexual differentiation (Migeon & Wisniewski, 1998, 2003). A full review

of the neuroendocrinology of experiments of nature is beyond the scope of the current review. Nevertheless, two brief examples are described to illustrate the limitations of the view that gonadal steroids are simple mediators of sexual dimorphisms. Genetic mutations in the gene coding for the testosterone receptor cause genetic XY individuals to be unable to respond to testosterone (when the mutation is complete rather than mosaic), and these individuals, by and large, have female sexual identity. On the other hand, the adrenal gland of congenital adrenal hyperplasia individuals makes androgens instead of corticoids. Consequently, these individuals are prenatally exposed to heightened androgen levels and experience some physical, neural, and behavioral masculinization, although, by and large, they retain female sexual identity. A complex picture emerges, then, in which the addition of testosterone does not lead to masculine gender identity, but the subtraction of testosterone leads to feminine gender identity. This simplistic supposition is meant to demonstrate that the central tenets of the organizational-activational hypothesis may remain unchallenged, but human development imparts complexities for biological processes that contribute to the development of masculine and feminine sexual identity (see M. Diamond & Yates, 2004, and MacLaughlin & Donahoe, 2004, for reviews).

Organizational effects of hormones begin after the testes differentiate in utero, and the testes begin to secrete testosterone and Müllerian inhibiting hormone. Testosterone directly causes the masculine internal structures to differentiate and, through its conversion to DHT, indirectly causes the masculine external genitals to differentiate. Müllerian inhibiting hormone causes the internal female structures to regress. Testosterone also indirectly causes brain structures to be masculinized through its conversion to estrogen. Testosterone, more easily than estrogen, readily crosses the blood-brain barrier; testosterone is then converted to estrogen in the brain by the enzyme aromatase. Most evidence indicates that estrogen is responsible for defeminizing and testosterone is responsible for masculinizing brain structures (Hutchison, 1997). In humans, the default is female, which means that female sex will develop prenatally in the absence of a signal from the testes. Without the SRY gene, the bipotential gonad will develop into an ovary; without DHT, the external genitals will proceed to develop into labia and clitoris; and the internal female structures will proceed to develop in the absence of Müllerian inhibiting hormone (see Collaer & Hines, 1995, and Hines & Collaer, 1993, for reviews).

Beginning in early infancy and nearly complete by 2 years of age, there is a period of relative quiescent hormonal activity. *Activational effects* begin when hormone levels rise during adrenarche and gonadarche. Circuitry originally organized by gonadal steroids become operational again at this hormonal signal, although the precise trigger of this developmental stage remains unknown (Grumbach, 2002). This process begins earlier in girls than boys. Although sex differences at the hypothalamic level appear negligible, the end point of the gonadotropin-releasing hormone (GnRH) pulse generator is different in males and females: (1) Hormone release is cyclical in females but not in males; (2) target organs differ in girls and boys (i.e., ovaries and testes); (3) the source organ of androgens in males is the testes, and in females it is predominantly the adrenal gland; (4) hormone levels of androgens and estrogens differ in boys and girls (Grumbach, 2002); and (5) the measurement of steroids is different in boys and girls (Granger, Shirtcliff, Booth, Kivlighan, & Schwartz, 2004).

Although animal models reveal robust sex differences in the activational role of gonadal steroids, effects in humans appear more subtle (see McEwen, 2001, 2002; McEwen & Alves, 1999). In one of the strongest tests of activational effects of gonadal steroids, Finkelstein and colleagues (Finkelstein et al., 1997, 1998; Liben et al., 2002; Schwab et al., 2001; Susman et al., 1998) conducted a randomized, double-blind, crossover placebo-controlled trial on adolescents with delayed puberty. Males were injected with testosterone and females were injected with estrogen in increasing dosages meant to mimic natural puberty. Effects of testosterone and estrogen on behavior problems, aggression, mood, sexual behavior, spatial ability, and cognition were surprisingly sparse. Despite the fact that gonadal steroids conspicuously rise at the time that sex differences emerge in a broad range of behaviors, direct causal links have yet to be found in humans, but are likely to be permissively related to sex differences (Grumbach, 2002). Studies on concurrent activational effects of steroid hormones reveal small yet robust sex differences in hormone-behavior relationships (Steiner, Dunn, & Born, 2003). Emotion regulation, mood, and psychopathology appear to have a small yet robust relationship with testosterone and estrogen, respectively (Alexander & Peterson, 2004; Booth, Johnson, & Granger, 1999; McEwen & Alves, 1999). These associations must be understood in the context of critical windows of opportunity, changing biological paradigms, and complex interactions with other biological systems (see Rubinow & Schmidt, 1996, for a review). Indeed, interactions with other systems have provided some of the most interesting neuroendocrine data to date.

In addition to sex differences in gonadal steroids, other hormones also show consistent sex differences, and the moderating role of gonadal steroids can change the func-

tional role of other hormones differently in boys and girls. For example, the hypothalamic-pituitary-adrenal (HPA) axis interacts extensively with gonadal steroids (Viau, 2002), with testosterone suppressing and estrogen enhancing activity of the HPA axis (Rhodes & Rubin, 1999). This may render females more responsive to the long-term consequences of stress. Estrogen and progesterone exert a protective effect for females' stress response, but at the same time, these hormones also dampen negative feedback mechanisms of cortisol on earlier stages of the HPA axis. Consequently, the ability of females to recover from stress may be delayed compared to their male counterparts (E. A. Young, 1998). Similarly, Taylor and colleagues (2000) have proposed that the female response to stress is fundamentally different from that of males in that oxytocin and endogenous opioids are central to the tend-and-befriend response to stress in females, whereas vasopressin is implicated more in males (Insel & Fernald, 2004; Rhodes & Rubin, 1999). Further, estrogen heightens the tend-and-befriend stress response, and testosterone dampens it. Consequently, this pathway is more easily accessed in females than males (Taylor, Lewis, et al., 2002).

Finally, social moderators of the stress response such as social support behave differently in females than males (Kirschbaum, Klauer, Filipp, & Hellhammer, 1995; Taylor, Dickerson, & Klein, 2002). The HPA and HPG (hypothalamic-pituitary-gonadal) axes, and the social moderation of these interactions, may also behave differently in boys and girls at puberty (Hayward & Sanborn, 2002) and in utero (Reznikov, Nosenko, & Tarasenko, 1999). Maternal stress prevents the development of sexual dimorphism in the brain; administration of hydrocortisone exerted parallel effects, suggesting that early in development the gonadal and adrenal steroids are mutually dependent (Reznikov et al., 1999). The role of gonadal steroids as causes and consequences of sex dimorphisms is complex; it changes with development, is modified by other systems, and appears cyclical (McEwen, 2001; McEwen & Alves, 1999). It is the rule, rather than the exception, that gonadal steroid changes result from earlier biological interactions. These steroids in turn change higher processes through positive or negative feedback mechanisms (Hutchison, 1997).

There are challenges to understanding biological contributions to sex differences in psychopathology due to the limited critical window for the timing of sexual differentiation. Without that information, understanding the mechanisms behind further sexual differentiation later in development is confounded by earlier processes and concurrent change (Institute of Medicine, 2001; Rutter et al.,

2003). The *organizational-activational hypothesis,* at face value, posits that gonadal steroids are central to sexual dimorphisms of the brain and behavior. Consequently, hormonal manipulations should uncover mechanisms behind sexual dimorphisms. When gonadal steroids are not implicated, as is often the case in practical settings, it is unclear whether this is due to inaccurate hormonal measurement or timing, to complex biological interactions, or because other factors account for the dimorphism. It is disconcerting that when gonadal steroids are not key statistical mediators, researchers interpret this to be de facto proof of social and cultural forces. Rather than elucidating dimorphic mechanisms, this view has contributed to a poor understanding of complex biological and biosocial mechanisms of sexual dimorphism and, in turn, their respective malleability. A developmental science perspective is a useful framework for refining our current level of understanding by emphasizing multiple levels of analysis, biosocial and bio-bio interactions, the importance of time and timing, and the critical appreciation of context (Cairns, Elder, & Costello, 1996).

Neurotransmitter Levels and Activity

There are sex differences in neurotransmitter levels and function. Patterns of sex differences in neurotransmitters change across development, providing further support for the idea that sex differences are derived more from differences in the pattern of biological expression, timing, and duration of biological changes than from differences in levels and expression of a hormone or neurotransmitter. Diverse consequences of castration, for instance, point to the complex regulatory role of gonadal steroids in the development of brain circuits and neurotransmitter function (Rubinow & Schmidt, 1996; Sumner & Fink, 1998). This section emphasizes developmental effects in its review of sex differences in neurotransmitters, including gamma-aminobutyric acid (GABA), glutamate, acetylcholine, dopamine, and serotonin (5HT).

GABA is an inhibitory neurotransmitter with implications for psychopathology treatment and intervention (see reviews by Krystal et al., 2002; Petty, 1995). GABA has receptors located nearly everywhere in the brain but notably in sexually dimorphic brain areas (McCarthy, Auger, & Perrot-Sinal, 2002). GABA has extensive connections in the hippocampus, thalamus, and hypothalamus and thereby is regulated by and helps to regulate the HPG axis (McCarthy et al., 2002). Early in fetal development, GABA is actually excitatory (Owens & Kriegstein, 2002), and it is during this window of excitation that GABA is centrally involved in sexual dimorphisms of the developing brain. According to McCarthy and colleagues (2002; McCarthy, Davis, & Mong, 1997), gonadal steroids increase excitatory functions of GABA. Increased neuronal excitability during this sensitive period, in turn, cause permanent cytoarchitectural differences in the male brain, predominantly at the level of synaptogenesis and apoptosis more so than cell migration. These positive steroid-GABA feedback loops are notable in the hypothalamus, bed nucleus of the stria terminalis, and medial amygdala. Because male brains have heightened exposure to testosterone and, through aromatization, to estrogen, they are exposed to higher levels of GABAnergic neuronal excitation, which permanently masculinize the brain. Thus, GABA, in conjunction with gonadal steroids, is directly implicated in sexual dimorphisms of the developing brain.

Around the same developmental window (Sims & Robinson, 1999), sex steroids up-regulate glutamate. Glutamate is an excitatory neurotransmitter, which has been implicated in forms of psychopathology such as Schizophrenia, Posttraumatic Stress Disorder (PTSD), and Anxiety Disorders (Bergink, van Megen, & Westenberg, 2004; Chambers et al., 1999; Goff & Coyle, 2001; Schiffer, 2002) and is a key component of Sapolsky's (1990) model of neurotoxicity and mechanisms of neuron death. Sex steroids modulate neurotransmission of glutamate, which leads to increased excitation, particularly in males and the limbic system. Glutamate is central to the regulation of sex steroids by GnRH in the hypothalamus such that testosterone and estrogen regulate release of glutamate from the hypothalamus, and glutamate causes the release of GnRH and the activation of the HPG axis. Glutamate's role is distinct from GABA by remaining excitatory in both males and females (Grumbach, 2002), but the male brain is exposed to more neuronal excitation as a result of both GABA and glutamate (McCarthy et al., 1997).

Acetylcholine is an extremely diverse neurotransmitter integrally involved in cognition, notably attentional processes, learning, and memory (Berger-Sweeney, 2003). Acetylcholine has a multifarious sex difference in that the cholinergic system is more sensitive in females, but the system is larger in males. Differences in the timing of the development of the cholinergic system may help explain sexual dimorphisms in acetylcholine-mediated processes (Berger-Sweeney, 2003). Rhodes and Rubin (1999) postulate that, compared to males, females show more functional sex differences in acetylcholine. Females have higher levels of acetylcholine and more cholinergic uptake and activity, and their cholinergic system is more sensitive to blockade and stimulation. Compared to females, males show more dimorphism, or structural sex advantages: Brain areas with cholinergic projections are bigger in males than females, and they have more cholinergic receptors. Thus, males and females may achieve equivalent cholinergic activity through diverse means (i.e., equifinality). Sex differences in acetylcholine may account for sex differences in psychopathology if females and males prove to have different propensities for disequilibrium in the cholinergic system (Rhodes & Rubin, 1999). One way males and females may achieve functional sex differences in acetylcholine is through interactions with estrogen (McEwen, 2001; McEwen & Alves, 1999) or other gonadal steroids (Rubinow & Schmidt, 1996).

Dopamine has obvious links to reward, sexual behavior, and psychopathology (Diehl & Gershon, 1992; Hietala & Syvalahti, 1996; Schultz, 2001). In addition, dopamine has extensive connections with sex hormones, including testosterone, estrogen, and progesterone (Di Paolo, 1994), and dopamine activity is altered by castration (Quinones-Jenab et al., 2001). Dopamine is centrally related to appetitive social interactions in the model of the social brain proposed by Insel and Fernald (2004). Briefly, Insel (2003) suggests that the dopaminergic neural circuitry for reward is also responsible for establishing active maternal motivation. Through interactions with oxytocin during a critical window when maternal behavior is established and in sexually dimorphic brain areas rich with estrogen receptors, dopamine helps females become "addicted to love" (Insel, 2003). Formation of partner preference in males, through activation of vasopressin rather than oxytocin, is also postulated to be derived from social information connecting to dopaminergic reward circuitry (Insel & Fernald, 2004). Human functional magnetic resonance imaging (fMRI) studies also show reward circuitry being activated in response to maternal and romantic love (Bartels & Zeki, 2000, 2004). Dopamine is thus postulated to have functional sex differences that relate closely to the appetitive cues of sex, maternal, paternal, and social cues.

Insel (Insel & Winslow, 1998) also identifies 5HT as a neural substrate of social and affiliative behavior. Sex differences in this model are instantiated as estrogen, oxytocin, and dopamine activity in the female (reviewed earlier) but testosterone, vasopressin, and 5HT activity in the male. Although Insel's model does not further explicitly address sex differences, Taylor et al. (2000) postulate that females are more invested in social recognition and use this regulation system when experiencing stress more than males, although the underlying circuitry operates in both males and females (Geary & Flinn, 2002). Sex differences in 5HT are complicated by the diverse functions of 5HT receptor type, number, and distribution in addition to dynamic interactions with sex hormones. Much attention

has focused on the 2A receptor subtype because it is distributed in brain areas related to emotion and mood (Bagdy, 1998). Females are less responsive to 5HT than are males; 5HT receptors are down-regulated in females; there is more receptor binding in males. On the other hand, females have higher baseline 5HT levels, more serotonergic fibers in sexually dimorphic areas of the brain, a more potent response to antidepressants than males, and are more sensitive to the anxiolytic effects of 5HT agonists (see Zhang, Ma, Barker, & Rubinow, 1999). In humans, positron emission tomography studies show that there is more 5HT 2A binding in men than women in frontal and cingulated cortices, brain areas related to mood disturbance, and postmortem studies of depressed men and women reveal higher levels of 5HIAA in females (Biver et al., 1996). Serotonin interacts extensively with both estrogen and testosterone. Estrogen exerts a regulatory role over 5HT 2A receptor activity, whereas testosterone is coupled more closely with 5HT 1A receptor activity. Castration increases 5HT 1A receptor activity in mood-related brain areas, and administration of testosterone reverses these changes (Zhang et al., 1999). Conversely, estrogen primarily regulates 5HT 2A receptor activities in brain areas related to mood and cognition (Fink & Sumner, 1996). Testosterone administration likewise changes 5HT 2A receptor function, but this appears to be mediated by its conversion to estrogen in aromatase-rich brain areas (Fink, Sumner, McQueen, Wilson, & Rosie, 1998; Sumner & Fink, 1998). An additional sex difference in 5HT exists in that sex hormones regulate 5HT differently in males and females (McEwen, 2001; McEwen & Alves, 1999), suggesting that serotonergic activity in males and females differs at multiple levels of analysis.

In sum, the literature on sex differences in neurotransmitter levels and function emphasizes diverse functions in various neurotransmitters. Sex differences in one component are often balanced by opposing sex differences in another. This literature thereby emphasizes equifinality, the process of achieving the same end through different means (discussed more later). This review has de-emphasized the specific neural circuitry involved with each neurotransmitter, though clearly, neurotransmitters function differently across structures.

Brain Structure and Function

A wealth of animal research has been devoted to understanding the nature of sex differences in neural structure and function. This literature highlights interactions of gonadal steroids with neural circuitry related to sexual function, including Phoenix and Goy's original work (1967), and behaviors with clear sex differences, such as spatial abilities, aggression, and male bird song (Collaer & Hines, 1995; Ruble & Martin, 1998). Often, the organizing effects of genetic and environmental forces are also acknowledged. More attention has been paid recently to human sex differences in neural structures with the advent of structural and functional brain imaging, notably sex differences in developmental trajectories (Giedd, 2001).

Sex differences in human brain circuits are conspicuously scarce. In adults, males have greater cerebrum, cerebral white matter, and ventricular matter, whereas females have greater total cortex volume (Goldstein et al., 2001). The developing male brain is about 10% larger than the female brain. After correcting for brain volume differences, females have a relatively larger caudate, and males have a larger globus pallidus (Giedd, 1997; Giedd, Castellanos, Rajapakse, Vaituzis, & Rapoport, 1997). When overall brain size is controlled, women are sometimes found to have a relatively larger corpus callosum than men (for reviews and different interpretations, see Bishop & Wallsten, 1997; Holloway, Anderson, Defendini, & Harper, 1993). Although the functional significance of this potential difference is unknown, it has been suggested that the relatively larger corpus callosum of women allows the language centers of the left and right hemispheres to communicate with each other. Consistent sex differences in the corpus callosum in children and adolescents have not been noted (Giedd et al., 1996, 1999).

Nonetheless, sex differences in developmental trajectories are intriguing. Interpreting sex differences in the size of brain structures is complicated by the fact that both larger and smaller structures may indicate enhanced function. Larger structures may confer greater protection from neuronal loss or environmental insult; smaller structures may reflect enhanced neuronal pruning with more mature, differentiated brain areas. Giedd and colleagues (Giedd, 1997; Giedd et al., 1997) have shown that the lateral ventricles increased in size in males notably after age 11, but showed more gradual increased size in females. Amygdala volume increased more for males than females, but hippocampal volume increased more in females than males. Many of the dimorphic brain areas are related to mood, emotion, and emotion regulation. For instance, the curve of development of the frontal cortex, caudate, and temporal lobes in girls is considerably faster than in boys, by as much as 20 months. Sex differences in the development of some brain areas, such as the prefrontal cortex, are largely

mediated by age-related changes rather than pubertal transition. Problems in emotion regulation may arise when physical development is not synchronized with brain development or when development in one system is not synchronized with another. For example, frontal lobe development is independent of Tanner stage, but current models show that the development of the limbic system follows the pubertal developmental trajectory. Dahl's (2004) model posits that problems in emotion regulation arise when development of the limbic system, related to the pubertal transition, advances emotion and mood difficulties before the inhibitory and regulatory role of the prefrontal cortex is fully matured. Similarly, Ge and colleagues (Ge, Conger, & Elder, 1996, 2001) suggest that early-maturing girls are at risk for problems because their social and cognitive development is not as advanced as their physical form.

Functional MRI has made it possible to more directly assess sex differences in the neural processing of emotion. For example, McClure and colleagues (2004) found that adult men and women subjectively viewed angry faces similarly, yet women showed greater orbitofrontal and amygdala activation when processing these unambiguously threatening faces. Although this pattern of sex differences was not yet consolidated by adolescence in this study (McClure et al., 2004), another fMRI study found that, compared to adolescent males, adolescent females exhibit greater prefrontal and amygdala activation while viewing fearful faces (Killgore & Yurgelun-Todd, 2001). These studies demonstrate the potential for fMRI to shed light on sexual dimorphisms in affective circuitry and neural processing.

Biological sex differences in brain areas may be derived from genetic, hormonal, or environmental forces. The study of sex differences derived from environmental forces, such as environmental toxins or interactions with stress or challenge, is still in its infancy. Evidence for genetic forces comes from a recent study by Giedd and colleagues (2005) on males with Klinefelter's syndrome, a 46-XXY chromosomal complement. The presence of the Y chromosome makes 46-XXY individuals unequivocally male, but they differ in various behavioral and physical ways from normal males because of enhanced exposure to X proteins that fail to inactivate. The total cerebral volume, frontal and temporal gray matter, caudate nucleus, parietal white matter, and cerebellum were found to be smaller in 46-XXY male brains compared to their XY counterparts. Preliminary evidence also shows that monozygotic (MZ) twin male brains are more similar than MZ twin female brains, and this may be in part because, compared to twin males, identical twin females are less similar to each other because X inactivation is not complete. Thus, the complement of XY and XX chromosomes can directly affect brain structure and, perhaps, function.

Finally, sex differences in brain areas may also be derived from hormonal influences in utero, at puberty, or concurrently (reviewed earlier). Sex differences in adults were evident specifically in brain areas dense in sex steroid receptors, suggesting a possible organizational role for sex steroids (Goldstein et al., 2001). Much of animal research on sex differences has pursued neuroendocrine mediation of brain volume because brain areas that show sex dimorphisms often have robust patterns of hormone receptors and are often changed by castration and/or hormone replacement. For instance, castration reduces neurotransmitter and brain structure in the cortex, hippocampus, amygdala, hypothalamus, and brain stem. McEwen (1992, 2002) has presented thorough reviews of the relative diversity of functions that hormones have in specific brain areas. This work also emphasizes the complexity of neuroendocrine interactions with neurotransmitters across different brain structures.

In sum, provocative research has begun to highlight small, robust sex dimorphisms in developing brain circuitry. These sex differences are hypothesized to be derived from genetic, hormonal, and environmental forces, though research that distinguishes among these possibilities is scarce. Studies that assess functional sex differences in brain circuitry are of utmost importance for biobehavioral research on psychopathology.

Pharmacokinetics and Pharmacodynamics

The Institute of Medicine (2001) has emphasized how little is currently known about sex differences in pharmacokinetics and, especially, pharmacodynamics. Several different, sometimes conflicting, forces influence how quickly and efficiently males and females metabolize and respond to drugs. For example, an intriguing pattern of gender differences in antidepressant prescription, use, efficacy, and pattern of side effects highlights that the causes and consequences of sex differences in pharmacokinetics and pharmacodynamics will have broad implications for how effectively males and females respond to drugs (see Yonkers, Kando, Cole, & Blumenthal, 1992, for a review). Females are more likely to have atypical depression and consequently are likely to be prescribed tricyclic antidepressants, whereas males are more likely to be prescribed selective serotonin reuptake inhibitors. The response to antidepressants in females will be influenced by their hormonal milieu, and thus will change from day to day (Meibohm, Beierle, & Derendorf, 2002). This is because estrogen is itself an antidepressant. Selective serotonin reuptake inhibitors are more effective on days when estrogen levels are high, and women using contraception tend to maintain higher blood antidepressant levels (Yonkers et al., 1992). Slower clearance of antidepressants in females will lead to longer duration of drug effects, but this may practically result in more drug side effects in women than men. Thus, changing and dynamic forces influence sex differences in pharmacokinetics and -dynamics. This section reviews sex differences in bioavailability, distribution, metabolism, and excretion, which can influence how males and females respond to drugs.

Bioavailability refers to the rate and extent of absorption of a drug. Sex differences in many aspects of bioavailability appear negligible, but gastric emptying time is slower in females due primarily to sex hormone interactions (Gandhi, Aweeka, Greenblatt, & Blaschke, 2004). This suggests that females maintain higher bioavailability during some phases of the menstrual cycle (Anthony & Berg, 2002a, 2002b). Sex differences in distribution are often mediated by sex differences in body composition. Females have lower body weight, more fat distribution, smaller organ size and blood flow, and fewer binding proteins depending on the hormonal milieu (Gandhi et al., 2004; Meibohm et al., 2002). Thus, females will, on average, have greater drug distribution. Drug metabolism is primarily influenced by enzymatic sex differences, which will favor males or females depending on the enzymatic interaction. These differences are often subtle and drug-specific and may also vary across the menstrual cycle and with contraception use (Gandhi et al., 2004). Sex differences in excretion favor males in that renal clearance is faster in individuals with higher weight and thus will be, on average, faster in males. However, even after correcting for body weight, males have faster filtration than females (Gandhi et al., 2004; Meibohm et al., 2002). Sex differences in pharmacodynamics are promising avenues for future research (Institute of Medicine, 2001). One consistent sex difference in pharmacodynamics is that females are more susceptible to drug side effects, even when males and females achieve similar levels of the drug in the blood (Gandhi et al., 2004; Meibohm et al., 2002). In sum, through opposing sex differences in pharmacokinetics, males and females may achieve similar drug effects. Some differences are derived from differences in body weight. Others are derived from different susceptibilities of males and females to side effects and pharmacodynamic interactions.

A consistent theme in this review is that sex differences in a specific biological system, area, or mechanism are often countered by an opposing difference in another system, area, or mechanism. Actions of testosterone frequently mirror estrogen. Maternal behavior under the control of oxytocin parallels vasopressin and pair bonding in males. The male advantage of the globus pallidus opposes the female advantage of the caudate, making the basal ganglia roughly similar in size in males and females. Enzymes involved in drug metabolism may favor males or females. Thus, through different biological means, both sexes may achieve similar functional abilities. This observation should not minimize the importance of biological sex differences, but rather highlights the importance of understanding biological subtleties. Because males and females function differently, they have relative strengths and vulnerabilities that may be affected differently when these biological systems are stressed. Geary and Flinn (2002) emphasize this by pointing out that both the tend-and-befriend and fight-or-flight response to stress operate in males and females, but to different degrees. Thus, a similar environmental challenge may exert very different biological force on men and women when each gender activates its primary default system. Because the underlying circuitry is more or less labile in men and women, understanding the biological contributions of sex will not be realized until sex differences in the social environment are also carefully scrutinized. The process of equifinality gives way to multifinality when social and environmental forces take effect (Cicchetti & Walker, 2001).

TYPICAL SEX DIFFERENCES IN CHILDHOOD AND ADOLESCENCE

The development of male and female children shares many common features. From the standpoint of physical development, embryos begin as relatively undifferentiated cellular structures that multiply and differentiate to form the brain, organs, and limbs. At birth, infants already possess largely rudimentary abilities in physical, cognitive, perceptual, social, and emotional functioning that develop throughout childhood and adolescence. Children develop language, motor coordination and physical capacities, thought, emotional expression and control, and interpersonal skills that become expressed in social interactions with familiar and unfamiliar others. Both boys and girls negotiate the developmental tasks of self-regulation (of motor behavior, cognitive activity, emotion), communication (through language and action), and social interaction (e.g., with caregivers, peers; Bell et al., 2005).

As children grow older, they play increasingly active roles in engagements with their environments. One major developmental task of childhood is to become an independent adult, establishing the physical, cognitive, social, and emotional attributes needed to begin to function autonomously in the world at large. Another major developmental task is to become an interdependent adult, establishing corresponding attributes needed to function in relationships with others. Many aspects of these developmental tasks are similar for girls and boys; from an evolutionary perspective, they have also developed different qualities or abilities associated with their later roles in producing and rearing the next generation of children.

Given differences in the biological capabilities and normative roles of adult men and women, the development of boys and girls would be expected to diverge in specific abilities that provide the foundations for these functions (Bell et al., 2005). Children's engagement in gender stereotypical activities consonant with these sex roles are seen in a wide variety of settings, in terms of their free play, chores, interests, activities, and preferences (Ruble & Martin, 1998). These sex-typed differences begin in the first years of life and continue throughout childhood and adolescence. They are undoubtedly linked in complex ways to sex differences in biology, cognition, social and emotional styles, temperament, and socialization experiences.

Biological and Physical Development

Biologically, boys begin with a developmental disadvantage compared to girls. In utero and throughout infancy, boys have lower survival rates, poorer immune function, and slower biological development than girls, with evidence suggesting that prenatal exposure to testosterone accounts for this relative disadvantage (Geary, 1998, 2002; Keenan & Shaw, 1997). High levels of circulating hormones in males also may be associated with slow maturation of parts of the temporal cortex relative to females (McClure, 2000). The faster development of girls has been implicated as a protective factor against mild genetic anomalies and learning disabilities. Boys show more early-onset disorders associated with neurodevelopmental impairment. From a biological standpoint, young girls appear better prepared for the developmental tasks of the early years of life. By school age, boys are about 1 year behind girls in physical maturity (Eme, 1992). There also are possible neurological differences that include, for example, hemispheric lateralization, where there is a right hemisphere advantage for females for processing emotional cues such as facial expressions (McClure, 2000). Beginning in infancy, there is also evidence of a developmental advantage for the left hemisphere for females for processing verbal stimuli (see Heller, 1993). Although girls may be favored in terms of some biological processes, others may create risk, perhaps for different types of problems.

Biological and hormonal factors have been implicated in boys' and girls' early expression of sex-typed behaviors. For example, hormonal factors have been proposed to account for boys' lower levels of interest in infants and orientation toward people compared with girls (Maccoby, 1998), differences that are already present in the first months of life (Geary, 2002). Toy and play preferences vary as a function of prenatal exposure to hormones, with androgen exposure in girls related to a preference for boy playmates, rough-and-tumble play, and sex-typed boy toys (Ruble & Martin, 1998). By puberty, the advantages of rapid development of females relative to males disappear and may even be detrimental (Hayward, 2003). During puberty, there are dramatic increases in testosterone for boys and estradiol for girls. Hormonal changes associated with puberty (especially early puberty), in females in particular, have been associated with more problems, such as depression. Differences between boys' and girls' physical abilities also increase during puberty (Geary, 2002). Thus, biological development in infancy and childhood favors girls over boys, but this advantage diminishes and sometimes reverses in adolescence and adulthood.

Cognition and Language

When sex differences in language are present, they favor girls (Keenan & Shaw, 1997; Maccoby, 1998; Ruble & Martin, 1998). Boys have more reading problems and other learning disabilities. Young girls have larger vocabularies than boys and show relative advances in using language to label and describe objects, events, and personal experience and preferences. Girls initiate verbal interchanges more often than boys and are more responsive to the verbal communications of others. Although there is little evidence of sex differences in overall cognitive functioning or IQ, girls and boys differ in the ways they attend to and process information (Geary, 1998, 2002). For example, boys and girls remember similar amounts, but different types, of spatial information when engaged in exploratory play; boys remember routes, whereas girls remember landmarks. Even in infancy, boys are more likely to attend to physical aspects of their environments (e.g., lights, sounds), whereas girls tend to attend to the consequences of environmental objects or events (e.g., attending to others' responses). Throughout the school-age years, girls are likely

to show greater academic achievement. But by adolescence, they begin to decline in certain domains relative to boys, particularly in areas having to do with math and science (Ruble & Martin, 1998). Boys excel in spatial skills, particularly mental rotation, more often than girls. The extent to which these differences reflect inherent qualities or socialization is not clear (Jacobs & Eccles, 1992; Jussim & Eccles, 1992).

Emotions and Temperament

A number of sex differences in temperament have been seen in neonates (see review by Weinberg, Tronick, Cohn, & Olson, 1999). Male newborns are less responsive to social and auditory stimuli and less able to maintain eye contact than female newborns. Male newborns also have greater difficulty maintaining affective regulation; they display more irritability, crying, facial grimacing, lability of emotional states, and rapid buildup of arousal. During infancy and toddler years, there is some evidence that males exhibit more irritability and anger, and girls more fearfulness (Ruble & Martin, 1998). From very early on girls smile more than boys. By the 2nd year of life, girls are more empathic and prosocial (Zahn-Waxler, Robinson, & Emde, 1992). Two-year-old girls show more affective discomfort and remorse after transgression (Cummings, Hollenbeck, Iannotti, Radke-Yarrow, & Zahn-Waxler, 1986; Kochanska, DeVet, Goldman, Murray, & Putnam, 1994), and their anger is more likely to be linked to feelings of guilt and shame (Zahn-Waxler & Robinson, 1995). Preschool girls are better at affective perspective-taking than boys, showing greater understanding of others' problems (Denham, McKinley, Couchard, & Holt, 1990). These differences continue throughout childhood and adolescence.

Young girls are more able than boys to control negative emotions under conditions of disappointment (P. M. Cole, 1986; Saarni, 1984). This may reflect their heightened awareness of others' affective states and sensitivity to the impact of their negative feelings on others. This greater social awareness and sensitivity in girls develops early and is seen at all ages (see review by Brody, 1985; McClure, 2000). By preschool and beyond, boys are more physically active and show more frustration, anger, and dysregulation of emotion than girls (Zahn-Waxler, Schmitz, Fulker, Robinson, & Emde, 1996). Girls use more emotional strategies and ruminate about problems more, in contrast to boys, who use more distraction and aggressive strategies (Nolen-Hoeksema & Girgus, 1994; Zeman & Shipman, 1998). Girls tend to ruminate specifically over things they have done wrong and report more guilt about inconsiderate behavior than do boys (Bybee, 1998). Boys also are more likely than girls to dissemble sadness (Zeman & Shipman, 1997) as they start to hide these kinds of negative emotions over the course of time. By adolescence, girls report more (and more intense) sadness, shame, and guilt, whereas boys tend to deny these emotions. As girls and boys mature, girls continue to inhibit negative affect and show positive, prosocial emotions relative to boys (Maccoby, 1998, 2002; Zahn-Waxler, 2000), whereas boys continue to show more anger and dysregulated emotion. Girls also become increasingly concerned about reading other people for signs of approval and disapproval.

A recent meta-analytic study of temperament (Else-Quest, Hyde, & Goldsmith, in press) found higher levels of effortful control in girls than boys. This included intentional attention shifting, inhibitory control or the ability to control inappropriate behaviors, and perceptual sensitivity or the ability to perceive low-intensity environmental stimuli. Perceptual sensitivity may reflect girls' greater awareness of environmental change. In contrast, boys showed higher levels of some features of surgency. That is, boys were rated higher on activity, high-intensity pleasure, and impulsivity but did not differ from girls on shyness or sociability. A third dimension of temperament, negative affectivity, did not yield sex differences (except for a small effect of greater fearfulness in girls). Negative affectivity consists of anger, frustration, emotional intensity, difficulty, and fear.

Social Development

From very early ages, boys' play themes emphasize action, characterized by attention to objects (e.g., tools, inanimate mechanical objects, constructing), action (e.g., rough-and-tumble play, action hero play), and personal achievement and power. In contrast, girls engage in play with relationship and family themes and incorporate objects into relationship-oriented fantasy (Geary, 2002; Maccoby, 2002; Nicolopoulou, 1997). By preschool and middle childhood, children are much more likely to play with same-sex than opposite-sex peers, likely because of shared interests and play styles (Maccoby, 1998). Boys engage in more public play in large groups and in higher levels of physical aggression than girls (Coie & Dodge, 1998; Maccoby, 1990). Boys tend to issue direct commands and establish dominance physically.

Aggression has been typically defined as behaviors that are intended to hurt or harm others. For many years, research focused on physical aggression (i.e., hitting, pushing, punching, kicking, biting, and attacking the property

of others), which is much more common in boys than girls (for reviews, see Coie & Dodge, 1998; Maccoby & Jacklin, 1974; Ruble & Martin, 1998). Boys also typically show more direct forms of verbal aggression than girls, by teasing and insulting others. As noted by Maccoby (2004, p. 9), "Simply put, it has been quite clearly established that males are the more confrontational sex." This sex difference begins in the preschool years, is most pronounced between the ages of 3 and 7, and continues throughout development (Coie & Dodge, 1998). As boys make progress in impulse control they are less likely to anger quickly and hit others. Also, as they become more muscular and able to inflict serious bodily harm, physical fighting becomes more aversive and less frequent. This drop-off begins earlier for girls (Maccoby, 2004) and is probably linked to their earlier facility with language and impulse control. These sex differences are also present in 5- to 7-year-old children's mental representations of physical aggression (Zahn-Waxler et al., 2005).

Recently, more attention has been paid to forms of aggression that inflict harm through threats or damage to relationships. It has been suggested that the claim for greater male aggression is based on too narrow a definition that focuses primarily on the physical and in-your-face verbal aspects. Individuals can also hurt others by ignoring them, excluding them from desired social activities, gossiping about them, and alienating their friends. These often more subtle forms of aggression have been studied under the rubric of relational aggression, indirect aggression, or social aggression (Cairns, Cairns, Neckerman, Ferguson, & Gariepy, 1989; Crick, 1997; Crick & Grotpeter, 1995; Galen & Underwood, 1997; Lagerspetz, Bjorkqvist, & Peltonen, 1988; Underwood, 2003). Most of what is known about these forms of aggression comes from the literature on relational aggression, which involves acts such as threatening to end a friendship or using "the silent treatment" to control or punish a peer (Crick & Grotpeter, 1995). Although some mixed findings have been obtained showing either no sex differences or boys being higher on relational aggression (e.g., David & Kistner, 2000; C. H. Hart, Nelson, Robinson, Olson, & McNeilly-Choque, 1998; NICHD Early Child Care Research Network, 2004; Tomada & Schneider, 1997), the majority of studies have demonstrated that girls are more relationally aggressive than boys (Crick & Zahn-Waxler, 2003), particularly when observational techniques have been used to assess aggression (Ostrov & Keating, 2004; Ostrov, Woods, Jansen, Casas, & Crick, 2004).

Girls and boys differ on other important qualities of their social lives (Eisenberg & Fabes, 1998; Maccoby,

1990). Girls spend more time indoors, interact in smaller groups, have one or two best friends, and engage in more turn-taking and prosocial behavior than boys. Girls attempt to influence each other with compliments, requests for advice, or imitation. These differences affect the interactions of girls with boys. Preschool girls have difficulty influencing boys, although boys do not have difficulty influencing girls (Serbin, Sprafkin, Elman, & Doyle, 1982). Thus, the spheres of influence for girls and boys differ, and girls may have less impact than boys in group settings. Girls' focus on relationships continues throughout childhood and adolescence (Maccoby, 2002; Crick & Zahn-Waxler, 2003). Their social interactions are more likely than boys' to be characterized by cooperation and harmony and themes of relationships and family. This more cooperative, polite, and other-focused interaction style may disadvantage females in mixed-sex groups.

Subjective Well-Being and Self-Esteem

Males tend to experience higher levels of well-being than females. Several meta-analyses and reviews of studies conducted since 1984 have found significant but small effects sizes indicating higher self-esteem in males than females, particularly beginning in adolescence (Harter, 1993; Ruble & Martin, 1998). Some research indicates that self-esteem decreases in females but not in males during adolescence, and that it may actually become enhanced during this period for males (Block & Robins, 1993). During adolescence, girls have more appearance and weight concerns that are part of low self-esteem, whereas boys report more positive aspects of the self, such as self-confidence and success expectations (Ruble & Martin, 1998).

Sex Roles and Sex-Role Stereotypes

The sex differences described are consistent with sex-role stereotypes. These differences often are not large in magnitude and are likely to characterize subsets of males and females who may often fall at the tail ends of the distributions. These individuals, however, contribute to the formation and maintenance of stereotypes and also may be overrepresented in disorders associated with male or female qualities. Adult measures of feminine sex-role traits typically include items that reflect a caring orientation (e.g., "compassionate," "understanding," "sensitive to others' needs") and an immature, submissive style (e.g., "childlike," "gullible," "soft-spoken"; Bem, 1978). Traits associated with masculine sex role mainly reflect qualities of competence and achievement (e.g., "assertive," "athletic,"

"a leader," "self-reliant," "forceful"). Masculine items for children's stereotypes include "active," "careless," and "aggressive," and feminine items include "gentle," "polite," and "sad" (Alfieri, Ruble, & Higgins, 1996). Sex stereotypes begin early. By preschool, boys and girls view anger as a male trait and sadness as a female trait (Karbon, Fabes, Carlo, & Martin, 1992). These children also believe that males lack the capacity to feel sad.

Girls characterized by the feminine ideal or stereotype are described as dependent, relationship-driven, emotional, helpless, passive, and self-sacrificing (Aube, Fichman, Saltaris, & Koestner, 2000; B. I. Hart & Thompson, 1996; Hill & Lynch, 1983; Wichstrom, 1999). These patterns are consistent with internalizing symptoms. Boys characterized by the masculine ideal are described as independent, self-driven, rational, active, and self-enhancing. On the face of it, the male qualities are more positive than the female qualities. However, extremes of more masculine behaviors also pose risk. Even in normative samples, males score higher than females on autistic features and psychopathic traits (Baron-Cohen, 2002; Hamburger, Lilienfeld, & Hogben, 1996).

The studies we have reviewed on sex differences and sex stereotypes were based mainly on normative samples, in the sense that psychopathology was not a focus. However, it seems clear that many, if not most, of the differences identified are potentially relevant to the nature of psychiatric and psychological problems in males and females. Most studies of sex differences in the domains reviewed do not screen for symptoms. So it is entirely possible that some of the sex differences thought to be normative may, in fact, also reflect individuals at the extremes who are already troubled or who have propensities toward problems that may become more full blown in certain contexts.

Next we summarize aspects of socialization that may affect developmental outcomes for males and females. Here, too, much of the research is based on unscreened and presumed (but not demonstrated) normative samples.

DIFFERENTIAL TREATMENT

All cultures create abundant and redundant opportunities for social learning, development, and change in children. In addition to parents as socialization figures, there are siblings, other relatives, peers, teachers, institutions, subcultures, and society as a whole. Initially, influence centers in the family. But soon, most children enter nursery school, day care, and then elementary school, where they experience additional environmental influences. Messages about societal expectations for appropriate male and female behavior also reach children early in life, through television, books, and movies. We focus here primarily on the parent-child relationship because this is where research on sex differences has centered, noting also the importance of these other areas for understanding differences in adaptive and maladaptive development.

General Features of Socialization

Socialization has been conceptualized and measured at both microscopic and macroscopic levels, with many gradations in between. Parental cognitions reflected in expectations, attitudes, and attributions about different behaviors in girls and boys may create biases and diatheses toward gender-differentiated patterns. For example, parental preferences for male over female infants (Cowan, Cowan, & Kerig, 1993) suggests a higher regard for males that, in turn, may be reflected in better self-concept in boys than girls later in development. General discipline and control practices also may differ (e.g., authoritarian, authoritative, and permissive styles; physical control versus psychological control), as may more specific techniques and practices (e.g., monitoring, love withdrawal, spanking). Parenting has been conceptualized as well in terms of the affective relationship with the child (e.g., nurturant versus rejecting) and quality of attachment (e.g., secure, insecure, disorganized). Forms of child maltreatment (physical abuse, sexual abuse, neglect) can be construed as global negative environmental factors. Parental psychopathology (e.g., depression, Schizophrenia) creates atypical environmental contexts. Another factor concerns the quality of the relationship between the parents. Marital discord and anger are risk factors, as are single parenthood, poverty, and violent neighborhoods.

These aspects of socialization are environmental processes; that is, they reflect constellations of affective, behavioral, and cognitive stimuli that impinge on the child, both directly and indirectly. At the same time, many are embedded in parental characteristics that reflect dispositions and are partly determined by genetic factors. For example, parental depression can create a palpable climate of chronic distress and despair. Depression is also a disorder that is heritable to some degree. Moreover, these conditions can interact with child dispositions that also have some biological bases. It is possible that there are both similarities and differences in how these parent-associated environmental influences affect the development of boys and girls.

Next we consider some of the ways that (presumed) normative parenting processes can inform us about sex differences in children and adolescents. Other, more global, often negative aspects of the environment (e.g., parental psychopathology, parental conflict, maltreatment) are reviewed in subsequent sections relevant to psychopathology.

Socialization of Sex Differences

Parents treat boys and girls differently in terms of the behaviors mothers and fathers model, the kinds of training and instruction they use, the opportunities and resources they provide, and the ways they monitor and manage their children's activities (Leaper, 2002). These differences are implicated in the development of male and female sex roles and may also be relevant to the quality of interpersonal functioning. Studies often find bidirectional influences, beginning in infancy. For example, mothers are more likely to respond contingently to emotional displays from infant sons than daughters. This may reflect, in part, higher levels of negativity and difficulty regulating emotions in sons; mothers may be making an extra effort to calm and regulate their sons. As another example, mothers talk more to young daughters than sons, partly because the verbal skills of daughters are more advanced. In both instances, the mothers respond differently to boys and girls with respect to their emotions and language in ways that become habitual and possibly influential patterns of communication. Leaper has suggested that if negative emotionality is more prevalent among infant and toddler boys than girls, parents may distance themselves from sons in ways that encourage more independent problem solving. Conversely, girls' more advanced verbal skills may elicit more active involvement from parents in ways that lead to more interdependent social learning.

The quality of the attachment relationship predicts different patterns of adjustment for preschool boys and girls (Turner, 1991). Compared with securely attached children, insecurely attached preschool boys were more aggressive and disruptive, whereas insecurely attached preschool girls were more dependent and showed more positive expressive behavior. Parents are more likely to foster autonomy in their sons than daughters; they also show more physical affection to daughters than sons, in ways that are likely to foster interpersonal closeness (Leaper, 2002). Another way emotional closeness may be encouraged is through discussions of emotional experiences. Several studies indicate that parents discuss more emotional experiences and use more frequent and varied emotional words with their daughters than sons (Leaper, 2002). The emotions discussed also differ depending on the sex of the child, with sadness discussed more often with girls and anger more often with boys. Anger is a self-assertive emotion, consistent with the traditional masculine role. Sadness is more passive and inner-directed, consistent with the feminine sex role. With boys, parents more often emphasize the causes and consequences of emotions; with girls, they emphasize the experience itself (Cervantes & Callanan, 1998; Fivush, 1989). Parents also expect young girls to have more intropunitive negative emotions (sadness, guilt, fear) and boys to have more extrapunitive negative emotions (anger; Brody & Hall, 1993). Although most research is correlational in design, there are some longitudinal studies indicating that parenting predicts later outcomes in children's social and emotional development (Chaplin, Cole, & Zahn-Waxler, 2005; Leaper, 2002). Chaplin et al. found that fathers, in particular, engaged in sex-stereotyped treatment, responding more to girls' submissive emotions and more to boys' disharmonious emotions. Moreover, parental attention to submissive emotions at preschool age predicted submissive emotions 2 years later.

Parents encourage gender-typed play in many different ways. Of particular interest is how parents handle physical play. Parents may actually discourage physical play in their daughters relative to sons (Fagot, 1978). Parents may contribute to sex differences in activity levels, fathers in particular, by engaging sons in stimulating, physical play, hence amplifying existing sex differences in activity levels. At the most simple level, the sex-typed toys given to boys and girls assure that most of their childhood play will involve enacting and practicing the different roles and activities they will assume as men and women. Mother-daughter dyads are especially likely to engage in sociodramatic play that involves domestic roles and collaborative activities. This could create preferences and skills for feminine-stereotyped affiliative activities (Leaper, 2002). Conversely, fathers' play with sons is more likely to be task-oriented (e.g., putting together a train set) or sports-oriented. Later in childhood and in adolescence, there is evidence for gender intensification as additional social influences are brought to bear on boys and girls going through dramatic biological changes (see review by Leaper, 2002).

It has been said that girls are more often socialized in ways that interfere with self-actualization, that is, to be dependent, compliant, and unassertive (Kavanagh & Hops, 1994). From a young age, girls are perceived as being more fragile and dependent and are therefore more protected and socialized to be dependent on interpersonal relationships (Gurian, 1987; Hill & Lynch, 1983). It might also be said that males are often socialized in a way that interferes with

their development of interpersonal relationships. In combination, a number of observational studies of young children provide support for these ideas. Preschool girls asked to explain why they succeed or fail on performance tasks express more self-derogation, whereas boys give more self-enhancing explanations (Burgner & Hewstone, 1993). This may reflect different parental socialization practices around achievement issues. In a study by Alessandri and Lewis (1993), 3-year-old girls achieved as much as boys but received more negative evaluations and less praise and attention from their middle-class parents for similar accomplishments. Shyness and dependency are treated more positively in females than males, which may help to confirm females' anxiety and uncertainty (Simpson & Stevenson-Hinde, 1985).

Mothers more often show disapproval by frowning when their infant daughters display anger, but support the expression of anger in male infants with looks of empathic concern (Malatesta & Haviland, 1982). Mothers more often accept anger and retaliation as an appropriate response to another's anger in their 2- to 3-year-old sons, but encourage their daughters to resolve anger by reestablishing the damaged relationship (Fivush, 1989, 1991). Mothers of 2-year-olds require their girls more than boys to relinquish toys to guests (Ross, Tesla, Kenyon, & Lollis, 1990). This may contribute to daughters feeling less entitled and ultimately being less likely to try to keep things that they want. Parents of 3-year-olds are more likely to override and negate the verbal assertions of their daughters than those of their sons (Kerig, Cowan, & Cowan, 1993). Mothers of 2-year-olds more often reason with their daughters than sons, pointing out the harmful consequences for others of their aggression (Smetana, 1989). Mothers appear to show greater authenticity in their expressions of anger toward preschool daughters than sons (P. M. Cole, Teti, & Zahn-Waxler, 2003).

Summary reviews of the child-rearing literature indicate some other ways in which parents treat their boys and girls differently. Parents are reported to discourage exploration of the physical environment more often in girls than boys (Siegal, 1987). Parents use more power-assertive discipline and physical punishment with boys than girls (Lytton & Romney, 1991). Discouragement of exploration by girls also limits their opportunities to deviate and heightens exposure to the socializing influences of the family environment. The power-oriented approaches more often used with boys have sometimes been equated with harsher treatment of boys. However, parents may be harder on girls in other ways, including greater pressure to *anticipate* the consequences of their negative acts, rather than, as with boys, reacting after consequences have occurred. This capacity to anticipate (cognitively and affectively), and then refrain from doing harm, is central to the internalization of responsibility and the development of conscience.

Cumulatively, the socialization research indicates that parents are more restrictive and demanding of mature interpersonal behavior in girls, but are more tolerant of anger, assertiveness, misbehavior, and mistakes in boys. In the extreme, this could encourage or exacerbate different problems in boys and girls over the course of development. Also worth noting is that most of the research on parenting is actually research on mothering. Some studies show that fathers make independent contributions to the socialization of their offspring (e.g., Denham et al., 2000), Several studies indicate that fathers engage in more differential treatment of their sons and daughters than mothers do (Siegal, 1987), indicating that fathers may play an important role in the adaptive and maladaptive development of their children.

PERVASIVE DEVELOPMENTAL DISORDERS

Autism, Pervasive Developmental Disorders (or Autism Spectrum Disorders, PDD) is a family of disorders characterized by deficits in three domains, resulting in social impairment, communication abnormalities, and stereotyped behaviors (American Psychiatric Association, 2000). Autism usually is diagnosed by age 3, but parents frequently report concerns as early as the 1st year of life. Autism is distinguished from other PDD primarily by the age at which symptoms begin, symptom severity, and mental impairment. Other PDD or Autism Spectrum Disorders include Childhood Disintegration Disorder (where normal development is followed by the emergence of autistic symptoms), Asperger's Disorder (where language is preserved), Rett's Disorder (which primarily affects females and is linked to a genetic abnormality), and childhood Schizophrenia. The distinct categorization of Asperger's is of some debate (Volkmar, Lord, Bailey, Schultz, & Klin, 2004). Autism and Schizophrenia are considered in greater detail next.

Autism

The prevalence of Autism was reported as 2 to 5 cases per 10,000 in the *DSM-IV* (American Psychiatric Association, 2000), with rates showing an increase over the past few decades (Volkmar, Szatmari, & Sparrow, 1993). The sex difference in Autism and PDD is quite pronounced. Estimates of the ratio of males to females range from 2:1 to 16:1 (Koenig & Tsatsanis, 2005), although general consensus is that the ratio lies between 4:1 and 7:1 (Rutter et al., 2003; Volkmar et al., 2004). If some aspects of Autism look different in girls, those girls may not be diagnosed equally with males of similar functioning (Koenig & Tsatsanis, 2005). Estimating the sex ratio of Autism is also complicated by the fact that the ratios change as a function of IQ (Volkmar et al., 1993). At low IQs, the sex ratio is 2:1 or 3:1, but at higher IQs, substantially more males than females are affected, with some sex ratio estimates as high as 27:1. Exploration of the etiology of Autism has frequently considered sex differences to be central (Bailey, Phillips, & Rutter, 1996). Biological explanations emphasize genetic, hormonal, and neurocircuitry differences, and social-cognitive explanations emphasize theory of mind, social recognition, and social-emotional sensitivity.

Autism may be comorbid with Schizophrenia later in life (American Psychiatric Association, 2000). It is also frequently comorbid with mental retardation (about 75% of cases). In adolescence, Autism is sometimes comorbid with Obsessive-Compulsive Disorder (OCD), and autistic adolescent girls may respond to pharmacological treatment of OCD better than boys (Koenig & Tsatsanis, 2005). Comorbidity with depression and anxiety is also noted in adolescents (American Psychiatric Association, 2000), particularly higher-functioning adolescents and autistic females. This may result, in part, from being socially ostracized due to atypical social functioning in autistic individuals (Koenig & Tsatsanis, 2005).

Genetic/Biological Explanations

Autism appears largely genetic in origin. Concordance for MZ twins is very high, yielding heritability estimates of approximately 91% to 93% (Bailey et al., 1995). Subsets of Autism Spectrum Disorders, such as Rett's Disorder, are caused by genetic anomalies (Volkmar et al., 2004). Individuals with genetic disorders such as Turner's syndrome, where females are born with one X chromosome, frequently display autistic symptoms (Skuse et al., 1997). These girls are more likely to express autistic symptoms when the X chromosome is maternal rather than paternal. Skuse (1999, 2000) has postulated that genetic imprinting of the X chromosome can explain the heritability of Autism and other PDD. Briefly, the X chromosome in male offspring is necessarily of maternal origin, whereas females have both a maternal and a paternal X. The paternal

X is hypothesized to have a protective locus against Autism, which the maternal X lacks. As noted earlier, normal males are lower than females on social skills and emotion regulation. Genetic risk, combined with the absence of the protective paternal X (and more limited social-emotional capacities), more often places males below the autistic threshold.

Genetic imprinting may also be implicated in sexual dimorphisms of the HPG axis (Lopez, Merchenthaler, Liposits, & Negro-Vilar, 1996). Hormones are thought to play a role, with pre- and postnatal testosterone exposure increasing risk for Autism (Koenig & Tsatsanis, 2005). Individuals with Autism have high testosterone levels and show early signs of puberty (Baron-Cohen, 2002). Another model suggests that oxytocin (lower in males than females) and vasopressin (higher in males than females) are involved in the pathogenesis of Autism (Insel, O'Brien, & Leckman, 1999), although there is no animal model of Autism and human studies have not yet been done. Nevertheless, sex differences in gonadal steroids, oxytocin, and vasopressin are in the direction predicted by the sex ratio in Autism.

Genetic and hormonal factors that play a role in Autism may help lead to differences in neural circuitry and function. The brain is enlarged in autistic individuals, especially toddlers, with particular structural abnormalities in the medial temporal lobe, cerebellum, fusiform face area, and amygdala (Volkmar et al., 2004). Functional MRI studies also show hypoarousal in social brain areas. Interestingly, individuals with Williams syndrome, a neurogenetic disorder characterized by augmented emotion and face processing, show nearly opposite patterns of brain structure (Reiss et al., 2004). It is notable that many of the areas affected in Autism are linked directly with processing social and emotional information, functions clearly impaired in Autism.

The Extreme Male Brain Theory of Autism

Baron-Cohen (2002; Baron-Cohen, Richler, Bisarya, Gurunathan, & Wheelwright, 2003) postulated that Autism is the extreme form of the male brain. Sex differences in Autism reflect the extreme ends of the sex dimorphism in functions of empathizing and systematizing. Other models similarly postulate that sex differences in Autism reflect the underlying sex dimorphisms in social and communication abilities (see Koenig & Tsatsanis, 2005; Volkmar et al., 2004).

Although both systematizing and empathizing are present in both sexes, males do show relatively more systematizing and interest in inanimate objects, and females show more interest in the interpersonal, social realm. Frequent interests and behaviors that occur among children with Autism and Asperger's syndrome (e.g., attention to detail, collecting, interest in mathematics, mechanical knowledge, scientific and technical information) are presumed to represent an extreme on the systematizing dimension of the male brain and a relative absence of empathizing (e.g., perspective taking, empathy, eye contact, communication; Baron-Cohen et al., 2003; Baron-Cohen & Wheelwright, 2004). Although biological explanations are likely, for example, differences in protective hormonal or genetic complements (Insel et al., 1999; Koenig & Tsatsanis, 2005; Skuse, 2000) or in brain structure, function, and circuitry, the evidence is based mainly on outward expressions of extremes in normative sex differences. Boys are at higher risk for Autism, but the social ramifications may be particularly challenging for girls, who may be more ostracized for displaying autistic symptoms because it is atypical for their sex (Koenig & Tsatsanis, 2005). This may lead to heightened comorbidity with anxiety and depression, especially as girls reach adolescence.

Schizophrenia

Schizophrenia has been divided into two classes of symptoms. Positive symptoms reflect an exaggeration of normal functions, such as disorganized speech, delusions, and hallucinations; negative symptoms reflect a blunting of normal functions, such as flat affect, alogia, and avolition (American Psychiatric Association, 2000). Lifetime prevalence of Schizophrenia lies between 0.5% and 1.0% of the total population, with roughly equal proportions of males and females; however, this equality is complicated by sampling biases. Males more often undergo involuntary treatment and females more often undergo voluntary treatment (Walker & Lewine, 1993).

Compared to females, males have an earlier age of onset by 5 to 6 years (Nasser, Walders, & Jenkins, 2002); are more likely to have an insidious onset (Alaghband-Rad, Hamburger, Giedd, Frazier, & Rapoport, 1997); and have a more chronic course and respond less well to drug treatments (American Psychiatric Association, 2000; Gruzelier, 1994). The common symptoms in males and females complicate the generalization that males have more severe symptoms. Whereas females score higher than males on the unreality syndrome, males are more likely to express negative symptoms and to have hemispheric imbalances related to the active and withdrawn syndromes (Gruzelier, 1994). Another complication is that the severity of Schizophrenia symptoms may interact with age (Seeman, 2002). In young cohorts, males often appear more impaired. This may be due in part to females having a longer duration of high functioning because they benefit from the networks and premorbid competence established before symptom onset.

Genetic/Biological Explanations

Schizophrenia is highly genetic, with stable heritability estimates over 80% (Cannon, Kaprio, Lonnqvist, Huttunen, & Koskenvuo, 1998), and there do not appear to be sex differences in heritability estimates. Sex hormones have been implicated as potential mechanisms behind sex differences in the expression of Schizophrenia. Sex hormones exert protective effects against Schizophrenia, so females' later age of onset may be derived from high-circulating estrogens in adolescent females. Females are also protected from Schizophrenia symptoms while pregnant, but then are at high postpartum risk. The absorption, metabolism, and clearance of neuroleptic medications vary across the menstrual cycle. Near- and postmenopausal drops in sex steroids may explain the poor functioning evident in midlife and older schizophrenic females (Seeman, 2002). Schizophrenic males are more likely than schizophrenic females to have a history of childhood brain injury. Obstetric complications may also influence the etiology of Schizophrenia, including childhood-onset Schizophrenia in males more than females (Alaghband-Rad et al., 1997; Walker, Walder, Lewine, & Loewy, 2002).

Developmental Precursors

Other sex differences in the etiology and expression of Schizophrenia have been observed. For example, Walker and colleagues (Walker, Grimes, Davis, & Smith, 1993) used home videos to explore whether affect in childhood in individuals who later developed Schizophrenia was different from their unaffected siblings'. They found that preschizophrenic females expressed less joy throughout infancy and adolescence; this finding in males was not as consistent. In a comprehensive review, Walker and colleagues (2002) conclude that there are clear sex differences in premorbid childhood behavior, with males being more noncompliant, inappropriate, abrasive, moody, and disagreeable and females being overly inhibited, sensitive, conforming, withdrawn, and anhedonic. These differences in premorbid behaviors were evident in infancy and increased throughout childhood and adolescence. This is another example of extremes of normative sex differences observed in childhood and adolescence.

The aforementioned sex differences may reflect early signs of different trade-offs for schizophrenic males and females. While adult females with Schizophrenia may be more likely than male schizophrenics to be married, have

children, and attain a higher education, they are also more likely to report marital stress, strained family relationships, and deteriorating social and financial networks (Nasser et al., 2002). Research on sex differences in the etiology of Schizophrenia has been hampered by the original conceptualization of Schizophrenia as a genderless disease (Nasser et al., 2002), because the male:female ratio was often equal. Establishing sex differences in prevalence may be one step toward understanding sex differences in psychopathology (Rutter et al., 2003), yet the Schizophrenia literature illustrates why it is not always a necessary condition. Beneath equal prevalence rates may lie different developmental courses and biopsychosocial risk profiles for males and females (i.e., equifinality).

EXTERNALIZING DISORDERS AND PROBLEMS

Externalizing disorders and problems are reflected in patterns of disturbance that are directed outward and are disruptive to others. In this section we consider Attention-Deficit Hyperactivity disorder, Conduct Disorder, Oppositional Defiant disorder, and related subclinical problems. Substance use is also included given its strong associations with antisocial, disruptive patterns. This decision is somewhat arbitrary given the substantial comorbidity of substance use with anxiety and depression as well.

Attention-Deficit/Hyperactivity Disorder

Two key dimensions, inattention/disorganization and hyperactivity/impulsivity, characterize the symptoms of ADHD. Symptoms must be elevated relative to age-mates, begin in early childhood (prior to age 7), persist over time, and be displayed in a variety of clinically relevant contexts (American Psychiatric Association, 2000). Most of the research has been conducted with males (for a review, see Barkley, 1998).

Estimates of the prevalence of ADHD indicate that boys are three times more likely than girls to be diagnosed with the disorder (American Psychiatric Association, 2000). This estimate comes from research with community samples. Studies targeting clinical samples indicate an even greater preponderance of ADHD among boys (Gaub & Carlson, 1997). Estimates based on clinical samples may be biased by the significantly larger number of boys than girls referred for treatment prior to adolescence. Studies of adolescents and adults have shown that the gender gap in ADHD narrows with age (e.g., P. Cohen et al., 1993).

For many years, diagnostic criteria emphasized the hyperactive aspects of this disorder to the neglect of features that involve inattention. Even though formal diagnostic criteria currently give equal emphasis to both features, the more overt feature of hyperactivity may overshadow the attention problems that are more likely to characterize girls. The *DSM* specification that symptoms must have their onset prior to age 7 also may contribute to the underdetection of ADHD in girls, particularly those who have attention problems as opposed to hyperactivity (Barkley & Biederman, 1997; Nadeau, Littman, & Quinn, 1999).

ADHD is accompanied by many associated impairments in cognition, language, family relations, peer relations, and emotion regulation. In community or nonreferred samples, girls with ADHD appear less impaired than boys in many of these ways. In clinic samples, however, either boys and girls do not differ or girls sometimes show greater impairment, suggesting that it is only the most severely afflicted girls who are referred (Hinshaw & Blachman, 2005). With respect to comorbidity, boys with ADHD appear to have higher rates of other disruptive disorders than girls. A recent meta-analysis found higher rates of internalizing disorders in girls than boys with ADHD (Gershon, 2002). Longitudinal studies into adolescence and adulthood are needed to examine a possible increase in comorbidity for girls, as their rates of internalizing disorders begin to increase markedly relative to boys. Although boys and girls with ADHD do not differ on learning disabilities, girls show lower intelligence, particularly in clinic samples (Gaub & Carlson, 1997; Gershon, 2002). There also may be higher rates of comorbid substance disorders with ADHD in girls than boys (Biederman et al., 2002; Disney, Elkins, McGue, & Iacono, 1999).

Genetic/Biological Explanations

Most of what is known about the etiology of ADHD comes from research conducted with male children and adolescents. It is one of the most heritable psychiatric disorders, with estimates ranging form .7 to .8 (see Tannock, 1998) and heritability levels comparable for males and females (Rhee, Waldman, Hay, & Levy, 1999). Although familial loading is comparable for the two sexes in some studies, there are hints of greater familial loading of ADHD in biological relatives of females than males (Hinshaw & Blachman, 2005). ADHD is linked to maternal substance use, low birthweight, and other biological factors in both males and females (Hinshaw & Blachman, 2005).

Boys and girls with ADHD show similar levels of deficits in executive functions, for example, in response or-

ganization, planning, and shift setting (Gaub & Carlson, 1997; Gershon, 2002). In terms of neural deficits, measured by structural MRI, Castellanos et al. (2001) found that although both boys and girls with ADHD had smaller total cerebral volumes (around 4%) and were similar on most other measures (Castellanos et al., 2002), some other differences between ADHD and control groups were not as pronounced for girls as for boys. An EEG study (Clarke, Barry, McCarthy, & Selikowitz, 2001) found that group differences between ADHD and control girls were not as large as those between comparable groups of boys.

Environmental Explanations

Environmental factors, including parenting styles, are not thought to cause ADHD, but socialization processes may interact with biological predispositions to influence severity, impairment, and comorbidity (Biederman et al., 1995; Hinshaw, 1999). Hinshaw and Blachman (2005) consider different family processes implicated in the prediction of functioning of boys and girls with ADHD in another setting; specifically, transactional processes may be subtler in nature and mediated through the internal distress (depression) in the mother. Future studies of the role of sex/gender in the etiology, prevalence, and developmental course of this disorder are needed. In particular, well-designed prospective studies of both representative and clinical samples with sufficient power to detect gender effects (main effects and interactions) are an important next step.

Conduct Disorder and Problems

Conduct Disorder (CD) consists of an ongoing pattern of behavior that violates the rights of others or age-appropriate societal norms (American Psychiatric Association, 2000). Diagnostic criteria require demonstration of disruptive behaviors in at least three of the following four areas: aggression to people and animals, destruction of property, deceitfulness or theft, and serious violations of rules or status violations (American Psychiatric Association, 2000). Antisocial behavior also has been studied under the rubric of externalizing problems, which include aggressive and delinquent behaviors (Achenbach, 1991a, 1991b). In this section, we draw both from the literature on CD and from studies of externalizing problems.

Prevalence rates for CD range from less than 1% to greater than 10% in the general population, with substantially higher prevalence rates typically found in males (American Psychiatric Association, 2000; Maughan, Rowe, Messer, Goodman, & Meltzer, 2004). Estimates based on epidemiological samples in the United Kingdom and the United States range from 2 to 4 boys to each girl, averaged across wide age groups (Moffitt, Caspi, Rutter, & Silva, 2001). This is consistent with males' higher levels of serious criminal behavior, physical violence, and other forms of brutality. Similar sex differences are obtained for other kinds of assessments of antisocial behaviors (Foster, 2005). Although the prevalence rate is substantially lower for girls than boys, it is still a problem for girls, and rates have been increasing in recent years (Putallaz & Bierman, 2004). Physical aggression and CD show continuity over long periods of time (Coie & Dodge, 1998), with prediction sometimes lower for females than males (Zoccolillo, Pickles, Quinton, & Rutter, 1992). Girls show more disparate negative outcomes (Moffitt et al., 2001; Pajer, 1998).

CD is comorbid with other externalizing (e.g., ADHD, substance-related disorders), internalizing (e.g., anxiety, depression), and learning disorders (American Psychiatric Association, 2000; Hinshaw & Anderson, 1996). Compared with boys with CD, girls with CD are at higher risk of developing comorbid internalizing conditions such as anxiety, depression, and somatization (Loeber & Keenan, 1994; Robins, 1986; Zoccolillo, 1993). There are unique implications for females and the next generation. These girls are more likely to become sexually active at a young age, choose antisocial partners, become teenage mothers, and raise children with CD (Serbin et al., 1998). Thus, the same risk factor (i.e., CD) may be predictive of later pathways for females and males in terms of the manner in which their disruptive behavior is manifested across development (multifinality).

Because so much of the work on the etiology, course, and manifestation of CD has focused on males, some have questioned the applicability to females (e.g., Zoccolillo, 1993), particularly given their low levels of physical aggression and crime. Some have proposed sex differences in type of symptoms (Côté, Tremblay, Nagin, Zoccolillo, & Vitaro, 2002) and number of risk factors necessary for CD to occur (e.g., McCabe, Rogers, Yeh, & Hough, 2004). Highly aggressive adolescent females and males do differ in forms of antisocial behavior. Whereas males showed more physical aggression, females showed more status violations and conflicts with authority (Maughan, Pickles, Rowe, Costello, & Angold, 2000). Zoccolillo has suggested that because the base rates of correlates such as aggression and crime are so much lower in females than males, females with CD should be compared to other females who do not have the diagnosis, rather than being compared to males. In his view, more accurate identification of CD in

females may be facilitated both by including symptoms more relevant to female forms of antisocial behavior and by lowering the threshold for problem behavior shown by females. There are a number of important reasons not to create different thresholds for diagnosis of CD in males and females (Moffitt et al., 2001; Zahn-Waxler, 1993). At the same time, there are reasons to support the idea of other criteria that may more accurately capture female forms of acting out.

Developmental Models and Pathways

There is growing consensus on developmental models of CD behavior that include dual pathways (Moffitt, 1993; Patterson, Capaldi, & Bank, 1991). An important contemporary issue concerns whether the same developmental models apply to males and females. This debate is currently reflected in the question of whether childhood-onset and adolescent-onset subtypes (American Psychiatric Association, 2000) apply to both sexes. For males, the two subtypes are distinguishable in terms of their etiology and developmental course. Childhood-onset type is diagnosed in children who meet criteria for CD prior to the age of 10. These children are at increased risk for a severe and persistent course of the disorder, with antisocial behavior that escalates in adolescence and continues into adulthood, sometimes in the form of Antisocial Personality Disorder and related patterns of psychopathy (Cale & Lilienfeld, 2002). Early-onset CD is linked to cognitive and neurological deficits, comorbid ADHD, poor parenting, parental antisocial behavior, and other features of family dysfunction (Moffitt, 1993). Aguilar and colleagues (Aguilar, Sroufe, Egeland, & Carlson, 2000) have stressed the importance of psychosocial factors (e.g., child maltreatment, single-parent home, high levels of life stress) in predicting the onset of life-course-persistent antisocial behaviors.

The extremely low rates of early-onset CD in girls in several early studies, including the epidemiological research of Moffitt et al. (2001), where only six girls were identified (less than 0.6% of their community-based sample), have led to questions about how applicable a child-onset type of CD is to females. In a high-risk sample (McCabe et al., 2004), child-onset, as well as adolescent-onset, trajectories emerged among both females and males with CD. Although child-onset type was more frequent among males, half of the females with the disorder had a childhood onset, suggesting that child-onset type is not rare for them. A similar conclusion was reached in another study that includes high-risk samples from four American communities where five times as many early-onset girls were identified as in the Moffitt et al. research (Conduct Problems Prevention Research Group, 1999, 2002).

Youth with adolescent-onset CD are more likely to stop offending by young adulthood, and the nature of their offenses is often less serious than that of life-course-persistent youth (Moffitt, 1993). Silverthorn and Frick (1999) propose a different developmental course for females. They describe a single "delayed-onset trajectory" for antisocial girls, who are thought to share many of the same risk factors as childhood-onset boys. Moffitt and Caspi (2001), in contrast, propose that both early-onset and adolescent-onset types similarly apply to males and females. However, the ratios of males to females for the two subtypes differ; males predominate for early onset of conduct problems, but this disparity lessens substantially for adolescent-onset problems.

Other epidemiological work has examined differences in prevalence rates associated with age and sex of the child (e.g., P. Cohen et al., 1993; Lahey et al., 2000; Maughan et al., 2004). This work also indicates the need to consider the interaction of both gender and age to understand the development and course of CD. Prevalence rates for males tend to increase quite steadily into adolescence. Rates for females tend to remain quite low until early adolescence, but then grow closer to those of males and continue to increase, all the while remaining lower than rates in males (Maughan et al., 2004). In a sample that ranged in age from 10 to 20 years, P. Cohen et al. again found an overall greater prevalence in males than females across age groups. However, for males, the rates showed a linear decrease from age 10 to age 20, whereas for females, the rates were curvilinear, with CD peaking at age 16 and then dropping back down.

The Role of Physical Aggression in Conduct Problems

Early and persistent physical aggression has been linked concurrently and longitudinally to a variety of negative outcomes, including later externalizing problems and delinquency (see review by the NICHD Early Child Care Research Network, 2004). A recent examination of physical aggression from 2 years to third grade yielded five aggression trajectories, three of which were characterized by at least moderate physical aggression at some point during this time. This study is notable in that it included more than 1,100 children from 10 locations across the United States. Of the two highest aggression groups, one was characterized by moderate physical aggression that remained elevated (another had shown a decline), and the other showed high and stable physical aggression. The higher trajectory groups also showed more problems of other kinds by third

grade, including observed and teacher-reported externalizing problems. Physical aggression tended to remain more stable in the context of family adversity. It was possible to distinguish between normative age-related aggressive behavior and problematic behavior that emerged in early childhood. The large sample size theoretically made it possible to study how developmental processes and risk factors would interact with sex of the child. Although no interactions were detected, just as in the Moffitt et al. (2001) study, the number of girls who show serious physical aggression (i.e., the high and stable group) was too small (*n* = 8) to make meaningful comparisons of boys and girls at the extreme. Even when physical aggression was expressed by girls it was at quite low levels.

Physical aggression is often strongly comorbid with relational aggression, and both are also related to other significant social problems (Crick, 1996; Crick & Grotpeter, 1995; for a review, see Coie & Dodge, 1998) and personality pathology (Crick, Murray-Close, & Woods, in press; Werner & Crick, 1999). Several studies have shown that relational aggression provides unique information about other forms of psychopathology above and beyond physical aggression primarily for girls (e.g., Crick, 1996).

Genetic/Biological Explanations

Twin studies indicate a genetic contribution to conduct problems for both sexes, though the estimates of relative contributions of genetics versus shared environment vary, as does the magnitude of sex differences in heritability (Foster, 2005; Jacobson, Prescott, & Kendler, 2002). The consistent sex differences in overt aggression in animals and humans have led to many studies of the role of hormones that differentiate males and females, particularly testosterone. Testosterone has often (but not invariably) been linked with aggressive and dominant behavior in males, but research with females has been limited, precluding parallel conclusions (Susman & Pajer, 2004). Estrogen (estradiol) may be linked to more dominant and antisocial behavior in girls. It may have direct effects on the brain that influence impulsive or nonreflective behavior. Or the effects may be indirect in terms of early pubertal timing, which is associated with more behavior problems in girls. Adrenal androgens have been linked to aggressive behavior in girls, and this relationship appears to parallel the relationships between testosterone and antisocial behavior in boys (Susman & Pajer, 2004).

Less is known about sexual differentiation of the brain relevant to antisocial behavior compared to differentiation of the reproductive system. Some brain areas that may possibly be relevant to antisocial behavior have been identified, including the prefrontal cortex, caudate nucleus, limbic system, and other brain areas (Segovia et al., 1999; Susman & Pajer, 2004). Low levels of the neurotransmitter serotonin (5HT) have been associated with aggressive and violent behavior and Antisocial Personality Disorder (see Susman & Pajer, 2004). Although many more studies have been conducted with males than females, there is a growing body of literature with females indicating similar patterns. Notably, although females overall have higher serotonin levels than males, depressed individuals are also known to have low serotonin levels. Of the psychiatric disorders, depression is the one that is most likely to co-occur with CD, especially during adolescence, when rates of depression increase, particularly in girls. Hence, the etiologic links between serotonin, types of problems, and gender are undoubtedly complex and important to parse in future research. With respect to comorbidity, there is also the question of temporal ordering of conduct problems and depression. In the Dunedin Longitudinal Study (Moffitt et al., 2001), depression typically emerged *after* the onset of CD in girls.

Low cortisol levels and low heart rate are indicators of low autonomic nervous system (ANS) arousal. Though there are exceptions, several studies of male children, adolescents, and adults have found that antisocial behavior is linked to low cortisol levels, low heart rate, and low heart rate variability (Lahey, Hart, Pliszka, Applegate, & McBurnett, 1993; Susman & Pajer, 2004). More recent studies of antisocial girls have confirmed this pattern for cortisol (e.g., Fishbein, Dax, Lozovsky, & Jaffe, 1992; Pajer, Gardner, Kirillova, & Vanyukov, 2001; Susman, Dorn, Inoff-Germain, Nottelmann, & Chrousos, 1997). Moreover, girls with low cortisol showed poor executive function, lack of empathy, impulsivity, and aggression (Pajer et al., 2001). Notably, several of these characteristics are more often found in males than females in normative samples. Although many developmental studies do not find sex differences in cortisol levels, sometimes lower levels are seen in boys than girls (Essex, Klein, Cho, & Kalin, 2002), and more frequently the HPA axis is modulated differently in boys and girls. Explanations for low cortisol in antisocial individuals have included dysfunctions of the stress system such as the need for stimulation in low-arousal individuals and/or adaptation to an aversive environment whereby the system has become habituated or canalized due to early high levels of stress (Susman & Pajer, 2004). Low cardiac activity has been linked to antisocial, aggressive behavior in male children, adolescents, and adults, reflecting reduced noradrenergic functioning and a fearless, stimulus-seeking temperament. Boys show lower heart rate than girls. Little is known about the implications of low cardiac activity for girls, indicating the need for further research.

Environmental Explanations

A number of environmental factors have been implicated in the development of antisocial behavior in both boys and girls (Zahn-Waxler & Polanichka, 2004). Examples include lack of parental warmth, poor supervision, and either overly harsh or overly permissive discipline styles. Parental depression and marital conflict have also been linked to disruptive behavior patterns in offspring. Most studies are not longitudinal, and there are few that consider outcomes separately for males and females. Studies do exist, however that show interactions of etiologic factors with sex of child in ways that affect developmental outcomes. McFadyen-Ketchum, Bates, Dodge, and Pettit (1996) found that mothers' coercive behavior and lack of affection predicted increases in boys' physically aggressive and disruptive behavior from kindergarten to third grade. In contrast, these same maternal behaviors predicted *decreases* in the same behaviors of girls. Similarly, mothers' anger directed toward their preschool children predicted continued conduct problems in elementary school for sons but decreased problems for daughters (P. M. Cole et al., 2003). Research also indicates the importance of paternal discipline and practices in the differential prediction over time of aggression in boys and girls (Crick, 2003).

Other research suggests that the environment can differentially influence boys' and girls' externalizing problems (see Zahn-Waxler & Polanichka, 2004). In a longitudinal study of youth at three time points (Davies & Windle, 1997), family discord played a greater role in the development of conduct problems in girls than in boys. In another longitudinal study (Windle, 1992), stressful life events and low family support predicted problem behaviors for adolescent girls but not boys. Sixth-grade girls also appear to be more sensitive than boys to positive parenting in ways that reduce their antisocial behavior (Griffin, Botvin, Scheier, Diaz, & Miller, 2000).

Although onset of delinquent behaviors can spur later criminal involvement for both boys and girls but in different ways (Tolan & Thomas, 1995), the contribution was small once psychosocial factors were considered. For boys, criminal involvement was best explained by their participation in deviant peer groups. For girls, family factors, school achievement, and acceptance were more important in determining the extent of delinquent patterns. In two large-scale, longitudinal studies (Eron, 1992), males and females responded differently to child-rearing practices in ways linked to different levels of aggression and differential prediction of aggression over time. Loeber and Stouthamer-Loeber (1986) identified a number of studies that found antisocial girls to be more sensitive to disruptions in the social environment, particularly at home. Because attachment to the home environment is especially strong for girls, stressors and disruptions can substantially affect girls' functioning. Because girls spend more time at home and are monitored more closely by their parents, they may be less susceptible to negative neighborhood influences (Kroneman, Loeber, & Hipwell, 2004).

Adolescent antisocial girls and female criminals may come from family backgrounds that are more dysfunctional than those of antisocial boys (Cloninger & Guze, 1970; Henggeler, Edwards, & Borduin, 1987). For example, mother-adolescent dyads and parents in families of female delinquents had higher rates of conflict than their counterparts in families of male delinquents. Moreover, fathers of female delinquents were more neurotic than the fathers of male delinquents. Parental psychopathology is more common for females than males with conduct problems, and maternal contributions to the perpetuation of deviance in female delinquents have been described (Lewis et al., 1991). Female delinquents more often come from violent, abusive homes than do males (Lewis et al., 1991). Often, they become enmeshed in violent relationships with men, perpetuating family traditions of violence and showing child abuse and neglect. Highly aggressive girls experience more family adversity than males (Maughan et al., 2000). Conduct problems are found in both females and males with a childhood history of sexual abuse (Kendall-Tackett, Williams, & Finkerlhor, 1993).

Biosocial Explanations

Evidence of biosocial interactions was identified in an all-male sample of adolescents (Rowe, Maughan, Worthman, Costello, & Angold, 2004). Testosterone was related to CD symptoms in boys with deviant peers and to leadership in boys with nondeviant peers. Similarly, work has shown an interaction between pubertal timing and school context on delinquency in girls, whereby early-maturing girls in mixed-sex school settings who were exposed to older peers were at the greatest risk (Caspi, Lynam, Moffitt, & Silva, 1993). Early maturers from an all-girls' school, in contrast, were more protected because they had little exposure to the reinforcements and opportunities for delinquency that older peers provide. It remains to be determined whether similar interactions are present for the opposite sex in each of these studies.

Although both biological and environmental processes may influence the etiology and course of antisocial behavior similarly in females and males, there are also many examples of different processes. The issue is further complicated by the fact that biological and environmental processes are continually interactive and not fully separable. This makes it difficult to study the development, progression, and remission of antisocial behaviors in ways that are meaningful for both females and males. However, evidence continues to accumulate requiring that we pay much closer attention to these issues in our theories and research designs.

Oppositional Defiant Disorder

The essential feature of Oppositional Defiant Disorder (ODD) is a recurrent and persistent pattern of negativistic, defiant, disobedient, and hostile behavior toward authority figures (American Psychiatric Association, 2000). Symptoms of ODD include short temper, purposely annoying others, blaming others for mistakes, oppositional behavior, and noncompliance.

Prevalence rates for ODD range from 2% to 16% across studies. Some studies have shown no sex differences (e.g., Lahey et al., 2000; Lumley, McNeil, Herschell, & Bahl, 2002); however, when differences have been found, males tend to show a higher prevalence (e.g., Carlson, Tamm, & Gaub, 1997; Maughan et al., 2004). Compared to CD, the sex differences are quite small and often nonexistent. This is consistent with the idea that ODD is a less serious form of CD that is expressed to a great extent within the family context, where other interpersonal dynamics may make it easier for girls to express oppositional behavior.

Biological and Environmental Contributions

Whereas much research has been devoted to biological, psychosocial, and child-specific characteristics related to the etiology of CD (for reviews, see Earls, 1994; Frick & Loney, 1999; Hinshaw & Anderson, 1996), there is little research on ODD. Recently, researchers have begun to examine similarities and differences in the etiology and course of ODD based on the sex of the child. Webster-Stratton (1996) has examined sex differences in oppositional behavior problems in 4- to 7-year-olds in three areas of risk factors: child-specific variables (e.g., difficult temperament, high rate of disruptive behavior), parenting variables (e.g., discipline strategies), and other family variables (e.g., parental discord, parental psychopathology). Boys and girls with an ODD diagnosis were actually quite similar in ratings assessing risk factors in each of these three areas. Only a few sex differences were found: Boys were more physically aggressive with parents, and mothers used more physically negative parenting behaviors with boys than girls. Similarly, in another early childhood sample, Nixon (2002) found relatively few differences between boys and girls diagnosed with ODD in risk factors in the areas of child characteristics, parenting behavior, mother-father relationship, and family risk factors. However, in mother-child interactions, mothers criticized boys more often and boys were less compliant than girls.

Even less is known about sex similarities and differences in the etiology of ODD in middle childhood and adolescence. An increase in prevalence of symptoms among both boys and girls during adolescence may reflect greater strivings toward independence and autonomy that become increasingly common at this time. Much of the research on development and outcomes of ODD in males and females makes use of cross-sectional designs, which do not permit conclusions about changes in individuals in the course of the disorder (Lahey et al., 2000).

Oppositional Defiant Disorder as a Pathway to Conduct Disorder

Although ODD is seen as a milder form of disruptive behavior than CD, it can be a precursor to CD. Hinshaw and Anderson (1996) report that despite the evidence of a pattern in which ODD precedes CD, the majority of these youngsters do not appear to progress to the more severe constellation of antisocial behaviors. Moreover, the progression from less serious oppositional and defiant behaviors to more serious aggression, stealing, and major rule violations may be a form of heterotypic continuity of antisocial functioning (Hinshaw & Anderson, 1996). Research is needed to examine whether developmental patterns differ for males and females, or whether the progression from ODD to CD is more characteristic of boys than girls. A sex difference would be anticipated based on the developmental differences in CD. If so, it will be important to learn more about biological and socialization factors that would help to explain the more frequent progression to more serious antisocial behavior in boys than girls who initially showed similar levels of disruptive behaviors.

When children display symptoms of ODD, the behaviors are not only disturbing to adults in positions of authority (e.g., parents and teachers), but also are aversive to peers, which could contribute to further maladjustment. Carlson et al. (1997) found that children (grades K–5) with ODD diagnoses were ignored more often than control children.

Additionally, girls with ODD diagnoses had more social problems than boys with ODD diagnoses. Other girls may find the oppositional, antisocial behaviors associated with ODD in girls especially disturbing, as they may damage friendship formation and other aspects of peer relations (Webster-Stratton, 1996).

In future work, it will be important to examine whether there are sex differences in how ODD is manifested. There are some suggestions of differences, but this work is still in its early stages. It will also be necessary to keep in mind the influence of setting and reporter in assessments of children's symptoms of ODD. Webster-Stratton (1996) found differences in mothers' and fathers' reports of the same child's symptoms: Fathers reported more internalizing symptoms among girls than boys, whereas mothers reported more externalizing symptoms among boys than girls. Fathers and mothers may have different expectations of their child's behavior based on gender socialization. Teacher reports did not correlate with mother or father reports, thus suggesting some "setting-specificity." This fits with the fact that much of the oppositional behavior that is part of this disorder occurs in the family setting and is directed toward parents.

Substance Use

Substance use disorders include substance abuse, which involves problematic use that results in negative occupational or interpersonal consequences, and substance dependence, which involves problematic use that leads to withdrawal symptoms when use is discontinued (American Psychiatric Association, 2000). Because drug abuse traditionally was considered to be primarily a problem in males, females were rarely studied (Lynch, Roth, & Carroll, 2002). Recent research on drug use/abuse in females indicates numerous sex differences in biological response, correlates and causes, and long-term effects and consequences. Research with children and adolescents has focused mainly on subclinical substance use, as opposed to substance use disorder or substance dependence, because these clinical disorders are rare among youth of this age (Chassin & Ritter, 2001). Still, it is a major problem and is also often associated with other serious problems in adolescents, most notably conduct problems and antisocial personality.

Developmental Course

Substance use typically begins during the early adolescent years (Chassin & Ritter, 2001), although it can occur in the elementary years for some children (R. Y. Cohen,

Brownell, & Felix, 1990). Age of onset and frequency of substance use are of particular interest because they are relatively strong predictors of substance use progression (Kandel, Yamaguchi, & Chen, 1992). Studies and theories of substance use in childhood and adolescence have focused primarily on boys (Andrews, 2005). Findings from recent studies highlight some important differences (Andrews, 2005). Boys begin to use substances at a younger age than girls (e.g., Johnson, Arria, Borges, Ialongo, & Anthony, 1995). However, prospective research shows that girls' involvement in substances increases at a faster rate than boys during late childhood and early adolescence (Andrews & Tildesley, 2003; R. Y. Cohen et al., 1990). Some studies have shown that by sixth, seventh, and eighth grades, girls' use of cigarettes, alcohol, and marijuana exceeds that of boys, and girls may become dependent more quickly (Andrews, 2005; Andrews, Tildesley, Duncan, Hops, & Severson, in press). Substance use among 12th graders in the United States has declined since 1975 (Johnston, O'Malley, & Bachman, 2002), but the decrease is larger for boys than girls, leading to few discrepancies in current prevalence rates.

Biological/Genetic Explanations

The psychobiology of smoking suggests that nicotine has antidepressant properties, and chemicals in cigarettes function as MAO inhibitors. Girls often find it more difficult than boys to stop using substances, are more likely to relapse, and sometimes are less responsive to treatment interventions (Latimer, Newcomb, Winters, & Stinchfield, 2000; Lewinsohn, Hops, Roberts, Seeley, & Andrews, 1993). Females are more vulnerable than males to depression and hence may be more likely to relapse to reduce negative affect. Avoidance of weight gain may also be a contributory factor, as females strive for the lean body that is part of the sociocultural image of a desirable body type. Weight concerns predict initiation of smoking among adolescent girls but not boys (French, Perry, Leon, & Fulkerson, 1994).

Biological models of substance use have focused primarily on heritability and genetic influence (e.g., Crabbe, 2002; McGue, 1994; Prescott, Aggen, & Kendler, 1999; Russell, 1990). Some studies suggest that this association is stronger for males than for females (e.g., Jang, Livesley, & Vernon, 1997), and alcoholism characterized by early onset, violence, and criminality is mainly limited to males (Cloninger, 1987). However, other studies have shown stronger genetic influence for females and shared environmental influences for males (e.g., Prescott et al., 1999). Several investigators have suggested reward-deficiency

pathways of addiction (e.g., through dopaminergic, opiodergic, serotonergic, and cholinergic receptors) that are common across substances and could have a genetic link (Koob & Le Moal, 2001; Robinson & Berridge, 2000, 2001). Research on biological factors has also targeted early pubertal development as a potential contributor to substance use. Girls who reach puberty earlier than their peers are more likely to use substances such as marijuana and alcohol (e.g., Petersen, Graber, & Sullivan, 1990; Stattin & Magnusson, 1990). Their social experiences with older peers (particularly older boys) may create risk for substance use (Magnusson, Stattin, & Allen, 1985).

The deviance-proneness (Sher, 1991; Zucker, 1994) or problem behavior (Jessor, 1987) model posits that substance abuse is the result of temperamental and personality characteristics associated with externalizing and antisocial behavior patterns. Aggressive behavior, in fact, is one of the most robust, and most widely studied, childhood and adolescent predictors of adolescent and adult substance use, abuse, and disorder (for reviews, see Andrews, 2005; Chassin & Ritter, 2001; Hawkins, Catalano, & Miller, 1992; White & Hansell, 1996; Zucker, Fitzgerald, & Moses, 1995). Antisocial Personality Disorder, which is one of the most frequent *DSM* diagnoses in alcohol and drug abusers, is much more common in males than females. Thus, the deviance-proneness/problem behavior theory may apply more to substance use in boys than girls. Because past research on the deviance proneness model and substance use/abuse has been restricted to aggressive behaviors more typical of boys (Chassin & Ritter, 2001), it hasn't been adequately studied for girls and the forms of aggression more typical for them, such as relational aggression (Chassin & Ritter, 2001).

The negative affect model of the development of substance use is based on the premise that substances are used as self-medication to alleviate negative emotion and reduce emotional stress (Cooper, Frone, Russell, & Mudar, 1995; Sher, 1991; Zucker, 1994). Cross-sectional evidence provides support for the hypothesized link between alleviation of negative feelings and substance use in adolescent samples. For example, adolescent depression is associated with concurrent adolescent drug use, heavy alcohol use, and nicotine dependence (Deykin, Buka, & Zeena, 1992; Fergusson, Lynskey, & Horwood, 1996; Rohde, Lewinsohn, & Seeley, 1996). However, findings from prospective studies have been mixed, with some studies demonstrating links between negative affectivity and future substance use/abuse (e.g., Caspi, Moffitt, Newman, & Silva, 1996; Henry et al., 1993) and others not (e.g., Chassin, Curran, Hussong, & Colder, 1996; Chassin, Pillow, Curran, Molina,

& Barrera, 1993). The negative affect model may be more applicable for girls than for boys (e.g., Andrews, 2005; Chassin, Pitts, & DeLucia, 1999; Rohde et al., 1996). Further research is needed to test this proposition and also to determine whether the deviance-prone model is more applicable to boys.

Past research on negative emotionality has focused on features such as general emotional distress, depressive symptoms, anger, and anxiety (Chassin & Ritter, 2001; Collins & Shirley, 2001). Other aspects of negative affect such as guilt and shame may also be predictive of substance use. These emotions typically are linked to strong feelings of inadequacy and regret that, in some instances, generalize to negative evaluations of the entire self (Tangney, Wagner, Hill-Barlow, Marschall, & Gramzow, 1996). When this happens, some individuals may turn to substance use to alleviate these uncomfortable feelings. Because girls are more likely than boys to experience these negative self-conscious emotions (Zahn-Waxler, 2000), they may be more often susceptible to these processes. Because substances act on the reward system, negative emotions may be replaced temporarily by pleasurable feelings. It would also be useful to separate anger from other negative emotions to determine whether deviance-proneness and negative affect models become more strongly gender-based when anger and hostility are considered separately.

Environmental Explanations

In addition to different types and levels of negative emotions in boys and girls, aspects of their social relationships may influence self-medication. Because girls are more likely to invest in and derive psychologically relevant information about the self and others from interpersonal relationships (Cross & Madson, 1997; Geary, 1998; Leadbeater, Blatt, & Quinlan, 1995; Maccoby, 1990), they may more often experience heightened distress when they encounter interpersonal problems and relational ties are threatened, particularly with friends and romantic partners (Crick & Zahn-Waxler, 2003). For boys, other types of failure experiences may lead to self-medication.

In summary, research on the role of gender in substance use problems provides some evidence for gender-specific pathways and effects of substance use among youth. It will be important to consider the role of parents' substance use, not only in terms of direct effects but also in terms of parental practices and parent-child interactions, for example, their different relationships with sons and daughters (Andrews, 2005). There is also a literature on the role of peer socialization in substance use/abuse that could inform future research on how these environmental processes may differentially affect boys and girls' substance use and abuse.

INTERNALIZING DISORDERS AND PROBLEMS

Internalizing disorders and problems are reflected in patterns of disturbance that are directed inward and are highly distressing to the individuals afflicted. In this section, we consider mood disorders, anxiety disorders, eating disorders, and related subclinical problems. We also provide a conceptual analysis of the role that early anxiety may play in the later development of depression.

Mood Disorders

The essential feature of Major Depression and Dysthymia is either depressed mood or loss of interest or pleasure in nearly all activities. In children and adolescents, the mood may be irritable rather than sad. Additional symptoms include vegetative signs (e.g., changes in appetite or weight), cognitive signs (e.g., difficulty thinking and concentrating), and emotional signs (e.g., feelings of worthlessness or guilt). Most of the developmental literature is on unipolar depression and dysthymia. Bipolar Disorder is not considered here, as research with children and adolescents is more recent, with little known about sex differences.

Beginning in adolescence, females are two to three times more likely than males to experience unipolar depressive disorders, as seen in both community-based and clinically referred samples (Kessler, McGonagle, Swartz, Blazer, & Nelson, 1993; Nolen-Hoeksema, 1990; Weissman & Klerman, 1977; Weissman, Leaf, Bruce, & Florio, 1988). It is also present whether depression is diagnosed as a disorder or measured along a continuum of symptom severity. In this section, we consider both clinical and subclinical levels of depression.

The rates of depression are low in childhood and comparable for boys and girls (with boys sometimes showing slightly higher rates; Anderson, Williams, McGee, & Silva, 1987; Kashani & Carlson, 1987; Kashani, Holcomb, & Orvaschel, 1986; Poznanski & Mokros, 1994). Prevalence rates increase dramatically during puberty, particularly in girls. Lifetime prevalence of Major Depression in adolescent females is between 20.8% and 31.6% (Kessler et al., 1993; Lewinsohn et al., 1993; Lewinsohn, Rohde, & Seeley, 1998), and the prevalence of subclinical depression is as high as 59% (Roberts, Andrews, Lewinson, & Hops, 1990). Lewinsohn, Rohde, et al. estimate that 35% of girls will have had at least one episode of Major Depression by age

19. For boys, rates remain the same or increase to a lesser extent (Anderson et al., 1987; Angold & Rutter, 1992).

Studies based both on diagnostic interviews and standardized self-reports indicate that this change in rates begins around age 13 to 15 (Angold, Costello, & Worthman, 1998; Ge, Lorenz, Conger, Elder, & Simons, 1994; Petersen, Sargiani, & Kennedy, 1991; Wichstrom, 1999). There is a 4% to 23% increase in diagnosed depression in adolescents between the ages of 15 and 18 (Hankin, Abramson, Moffitt, Silva, & McGee, 1998). After puberty, the lifetime prevalence in females is twice that of males (Lewinsohn et al., 1993). Comorbidity of depressive and anxiety disorders is much more common in girls than boys (Lewinsohn, Rohde, & Seeley, 1995); moreover, depression that is comorbid with more than one anxiety disorder is virtually exclusive to females (Lewinsohn, Zinbarg, Seeley, Lewinsohn, & Sack, 1997). Female gender and presence of a coexisting anxiety disorder are also related to severity of initial depression (McCauley et al., 1993). Co-occurrence of symptoms is even higher when subclinical levels are considered. Although depression and anxiety can be clearly differentiated at biological, cognitive, behavioral, and affective levels, the extent to which they overlap and co-occur suggests that the combination represents a unique but common form of depression, particularly in females.

Females show a different constellation of depressive symptoms than males, notably, more anxiety, more somatic symptoms, hypersomnia, weight gain, increased appetite, fatigue, psychomotor retardation, and body image disturbance (see review by Zahn-Waxler, Race, & Duggal, 2005). Increased appetite and weight gain seem to be the most distinct symptoms in women and adolescent girls. Higher rates of crying, sadness, and negative self-concept have been noted for school-age and adolescent girls.

In research by Gjerde (1995) and Gjerde and Block (1996), dysphoric males often expressed their unhappiness directly and without hesitation, by acting on the world in an aggressive, hostile manner. Dysphoric symptoms in female adolescents, in contrast, were characterized by introspection, absence of open hostility, and a mostly hidden preoccupation with self. As early as age 7, boys who later showed Dysthymia were aggressive, self-aggrandizing, and undercontrolled, whereas dysthymic girls were intropunitive, oversocialized, overcontrolled, anxious, and introspective (Block, Gjerde, & Block, 1991). Young girls who later became depressed also had close relationships. The sadness and anxiety in depressed girls and hostility in depressed boys can be seen as exaggerations of normative sex differences. These studies focus on subclinical depression. Fur-

ther studies of males and females with clinical depression are needed to determine whether their symptomatology shows a similar pattern. Other research suggests that young depressed boys show a pattern of acting out (Kovacs, 1996).

Genetic/Biological Explanations

Some studies report similar heritability estimates for depressive disorders in males and females; several others find differences (e.g., Bierut et al., 1999; Jacobson & Rowe, 1999; Kendler, Gardner, Neale, & Prescott, 2001; Tambs, Harris, & Magnus, 1995). Kendler, Garnder, et al. suggest that in genetic linkage studies, the impact of some loci on risk for Major Depression will vary in men and women. Genetics are also involved in the etiology of depression through their effect on sensitivity to environmental events. Silberg, Rutter, Neale, and Eaves (2001) found that genetics had a larger effect on the development of depression in adolescent girls who had experienced a negative event in the previous year than on those who did not. Kendler and colleagues (Kendler, 1998; Kendler et al., 1995) found that persons at greater genetic risk were twice as likely to develop Major Depression in response to severe stress than those at lower genetic risk. Genetic risk also altered sensitivity to the environment for women only (Kendler et al., 1995). At puberty, girls' negative life events and stability of depression over time are more genetically mediated than for boys (Silberg et al., 1999).

Biological processes have been studied in terms of hormones that increase during puberty, timing of puberty, physical bodily changes, and interactions of body change and weight gain. Angold and colleagues (Angold, Costello, Erklani, & Worthman, 1999; Angold et al., 1998) have examined the influence of hormones and body development on depression. Angold et al. (1998) found that pubertal development (measured by Tanner stages), but not age, accounted for increased rates of depression. Boys showed higher rates of depression than girls before reaching Tanner stage III (the midpoint of puberty, when body changes become apparent but before menarche). Girls showed much higher rates of depression than boys at and after Tanner stage III (Angold et al., 1998). Angold et al. (1999) then examined hormones associated with pubertal development and reproduction. Testosterone and estradiol were more strongly related to depression than Tanner stages. A positive association between estradiol and later depressive affect has been shown even after the course of a year (Paikoff, Brooks-Gunn, & Warren, 1991).

This link between estradiol and depressive affect may seem counterintuitive because estradiol is thought to enhance mood, has antidepressant properties, and increases the efficacy of antidepressants (McEwen, 2002). However, variability and changes in estradiol levels also vary as a function of pubertal development, with peaking diurnal variability near the time of menarche (Angold et al., 1999). Given that heightened levels and variability frequently co-occur (i.e., the law of initial values), it is possible that adolescent girls at risk for depression have high levels and, more important, the most variable estradiol levels. It would be valuable in future research on hormones and depression to study these processes during adrenarchy in middle childhood and also to examine the possibly protective function of oxytocin given its role in caregiving and relaxation (Cyranowski, Frank, Young, & Shear, 2000; Frank & Young, 2000).

Early puberty in girls (but not boys) is associated with more depression. Young girls may have not yet acquired coping skills to deal with the pressures and stresses of early physical maturation. Angold et al. (1998) and others did not find an effect of pubertal timing on depression, but several others have found such associations. Girls who reach puberty earlier are more likely to have or to develop depressive symptoms than those who reach puberty on time (e.g., Brooks-Gunn & Warren, 1989; Ge et al., 1996; Graber, Lewinsohn, Seeley, & Brooks-Gunn, 1997; Hayward et al., 1997; Paikoff et al., 1991; Stice, Presnell, & Bearman, 2001). Stice et al. also show that high body mass, body dissatisfaction, and dieting partially mediate the link between early puberty and depression. As early puberty is also linked with antisocial patterns in girls, it is clearly a time of high risk. Early puberty results from a complex mix of biological, social, and contextual factors. Genes, as well as environmental influence like nutrition, exercise, and weight, play a role. Depression in mothers may induce early puberty in daughters (Ellis & Garber, 2000), as well as the presence of unrelated adult male father figures (also see Moffitt, Caspi, Belsky, & Silva, 1992). Animal studies suggest that chemicals known as pheromones produced by unrelated adult males accelerate female pubertal development. Although the vermonasal organ is vestigial in humans, a similar process may occur for these girls.

Associations between HPA axis functioning and psychopathology may differ for males and females. In adolescents who were normal, depressed, or depressed with comorbid externalizing problems (Klimes-Dougan, Hastings, Granger, Usher, & Zahn-Waxler, 2001), females with depressive symptoms showed a flattened diurnal rhythm. The other groups, in contrast, showed the typical diurnal pattern of high early morning cortisol levels and a marked decline over the course of the day. Depressed girls also showed a more gradual decline in cortisol following discussion of a conflict. In a longitudinal study of younger children (Smider et al., 2002), girls showed higher cortisol levels than boys at age 4.5 years. For girls only, high cortisol predicted more depression and anxiety a year and a half later. Girls' greater physiological reactivity may reflect early proneness to later internalizing symptoms. In a study of stress responses in adults (Stroud, Salovey, & Epel, 2002), women showed greater cortisol reactions to social rejection challenges, and men showed greater cortisol responses to achievement challenges. Social rejection has been linked to depression.

Environmental Explanations

Parental depression (most often studied in mothers) creates substantial risk for depression in offspring (Beardslee, Versage, & Gladstone, 1998; Davies & Windle, 1997; Downey & Coyne, 1990; Garber, Keiley, & Martin, 2002; Goodman & Gotlib, 1999; Hammen, Burge, Burney, & Adrian, 1990; Hops, 1996). Offspring are at greater risk for depression if both parents are depressed (Birmaher et al., 1996; McCauley, Pavlidis, & Kendell, 2001). The lifetime risk of depression for children with a depressed parent has been estimated at 45% (Hammen et al., 1990). Because depression is heritable, it is commonly assumed that children of depressed parents are at increased risk due to genetic similarity. However, the experiences of these children can differ markedly as well.

Depressed parents are, on average, less reciprocal, attuned, and engaged in interactions with their children as early as infancy. In addition to the sadness that marks depression, depressed parents express a greater range and less control of other negative emotions such as anxiety, guilt, irritability, and hostility than controls. Children exposed to a depressed parent's despair and lack of pleasure in daily activities can come to experience these emotions through contagion and imitation. Depressed parents often model helpless, passive styles of coping. They tend to use discipline methods that are either ineffectual, coercive, or guilt-inducing (Beardslee et al., 1998; Cummings, DeArth-Pendley, Du Rocher Schudlich, & Smith, 2001; Downey & Coyne, 1990; Gelfand & Teti, 1990; Goodman & Gotlib, 1999; Zahn-Waxler, 2000). These conditions would be expected to affect both boys and girls, yet differences are also likely.

In infancy, males may be more vulnerable than females to the socioemotional effects of maternal depression, particularly in situations that involve interactional stress or challenge (Weinberg, Olson, Beeghly, & Tronick, 2005). Prior studies had suggested that male infants, in general, show greater difficulty than female infants maintaining affective regulation in mother-infant interactions. Typically, this heightens mothers' responsiveness to boys' affective and behavioral displays and helps to maintain greater coordination or synchrony in mother-male than mother-female interactions (Weinberg et al., 1999). However, depressed mothers would be expected to have difficulty maintaining this coordination, hence setting the stage for environmental adversity more likely to be experienced by male than female infants.

In childhood and adolescence, girls of depressed mothers are more susceptible to the influences of maternal depression than are boys with respect to internalizing problems (Boyle & Pickles, 1997; Conger et al., 1993; Cummings et al., 2001; Hops, 1996; Sheeber, Davis, & Hops, 2002). Moreover, the effects of maternal depression on adolescent girls' depression become stronger as girls mature. Longitudinal studies indicate long-term effects of maternal depression on later development of depression in daughters but not sons (Davies & Windle, 1997; Duggal, Carlson, Sroufe, & Egeland, 2001; Fergusson, Horwood, & Lynsky, 1995). In one study, depressive symptoms increased over time in adolescent daughters, but not sons, who provided comfort and suppressed their own aggression (B. Davis, Sheeber, Hops, & Tildesley, 2000). Adolescent girls provide more support to depressed mothers than do sons. They also express more sadness, worry, and withdrawal than sons, as well as responsibility for the mother's depression (Klimes-Dougan & Bolger, 1998). Daughters may be susceptible to their mother's unhappiness because they spend more time with her and have stronger emotional ties than sons (Gurian, 1987). Mothers' modeling of depressive behavior also may be particularly salient to girls and linked to sex roles.

Parental conflict and divorce play a role in children's depression. Depression of a parent can itself lead to marital conflict, and vice versa, and frequently they co-occur (Beardslee et al., 1998; Conger et al., 1993; Cummings et al., 2001; Davies & Windle, 1997; Downey & Coyne, 1990). Marital discord and divorce lead to both internalizing problems (depression, anxiety), for which females generally are at higher risk, and externalizing problems (aggression, antisocial behavior), for which males generally are at higher risk. Parental divorce can influence the development of depression in adolescents through increased family conflicts, financial difficulties, unavailability of parents, less parental warmth and involvement,

and changes in the family (Aseltine, 1996). When exposed to family conflict and discord, adolescent girls are more likely than boys to develop depression and related problems (Aseltine, 1996; Crawford, Cohen, Midlarsky, & Brook, 2001; Dadds, Atkinson, Turner, Blums, & Lendich, 1999; Formoso, Gonzales, & Aiken, 2000; Garnefski, 2000; Vuchinich, Emery, & Cassidy, 1988).

Girls show more interpersonal concern and involvement in family problems (especially involving mothers), which contributes to girls' higher rates of depressed mood than boys (Gore, Aseltine, & Colten, 1993). Davies and Lindsay (2004) have recently reported a similar pattern. For girls only, elevated levels of communion partly accounted for their greater reactivity to conflict between parents and likelihood of internalizing problems. Communion (i.e., interpersonal connectedness and concern) was based on items from a sex-role inventory, such as "I care what happens to others"; "When someone's feelings have been hurt, I try to make him/her feel better." Even prior to adolescence, girls show more fear, emotional distress, and feelings of blame and responsibility than boys (Davies & Lindsay, 2004). Aube et al. (2000) found that unassertive girls who also felt overly responsible for others were more depressed than boys.

Effects of maternal depression and family discord on gender-linked symptoms are also seen very early in development (Essex, Klein, Cho, & Kraemer, 2003; Zahn-Waxler, Iannotti, Cummings, & Denham, 1990). Essex et al. found that boys exposed to maternal depression in infancy had a preponderance of internalizing problems relative to externalizing problems, but if subsequently exposed to marital conflict, the mix toward externalizing problems increased to match levels of clinic-referred children. For girls, the preponderance of internalizing problems increased to match levels of clinic-referred children when initial exposure to marital conflict occurred in the toddler/preschool period. Overall, girls showed more depression and anxiety than boys, which is not often found in community samples of young children. This may reflect differences in instruments, as the Health Behavior Questionnaire items used by Essex et al. are similar to *DSM* symptoms and are not weighted by sex of child. Instruments like the Child Behavior Checklist, in contrast, require that girls endorse more symptoms than boys to achieve the same standardized score.

Less support from one's family, particularly one's mother, is related to more depression and difficulty among adolescents (Aseltine, Gore, & Colten, 1994; Barrerra & Garrison-Jones, 1992; T. Field, Diego, & Sanders, 2001;

Ge et al., 1994; McFarlane, Bellissimo, & Norman, 1995). The impact of familial support and relationships with parents can be particularly great for girls. In one study, conflict with the mother that was associated with submissive coping was related to concurrent depression and predicted increases in these symptoms 1 year later for adolescent daughters but not sons (Powers & Welsh, 1999). Although adolescents who view their parents as very caring are unlikely to develop depression, girls with overprotective fathers show more symptoms (Avison & McAlpine, 1992). Parental overprotection may create a diminished sense of mastery that can lead to depression. The difficulties girls face balancing their need for family support and intimacy with their need for increased autonomy in adolescence may contribute to their higher rates of depression than boys (McGrath, Keita, & Strickland, 1990).

Life Events and Quality of Relationships

Some researchers report that girls and boys are similarly exposed and vulnerable to the effects of stressful life events (Avison & McAlpine, 1992; Gore et al., 1992; Kendler, Thornton, & Prescott, 2001). Others indicate that girls do report more negative events, or that they may experience the same events as more negative than boys (Goodyer, 2001; Gore et al., 1992). Girls tend to show different patterns in the relationship between life events and depression than boys, particularly after puberty (Ge et al., 1994; Silberg et al., 1999). Females are more likely than males to experience or be affected by the stresses of others in addition to their parents, which also would create vulnerability to depression. The timing of major life events also plays a role in the etiology of depression. Adolescents going through multiple life changes simultaneously are at greater risk (Petersen et al., 1991). This is especially true for girls, who are more likely than boys to experience puberty as they make the transition to different, larger, more challenging schools (Simmons, Burgeson, & Carlton-Ford, 1987).

Because girls are more invested than boys in interpersonal relationships with friends and romantic partners (Leadbeater, Kuperminc, Blatt, & Herzog, 1999; Simmons & Blyth, 1987), they are more likely to become depressed when relationships are disrupted or changed, as often happens at adolescence (Cyranowski et al., 2000; Leadbeater et al., 1999). Heightened interpersonal focus and reliance on others are inversely related to agency and instrumentality, which can protect against depression (Allgood-Merten, Lewinsohn, & Hops, 1990; Nolen-Hoeksema & Girgus, 1994). Girls show fewer of these instrumental traits than do boys. Also, popularity is negatively linked to depression in

girls but not boys (Oldenberg & Kerns, 1997). Interpersonal vulnerability may lead to helplessness, fear of abandonment, and a heightened need for intimacy (Leadbeater et al., 1999), creating a cycle and escalation of personal distress.

Distinctions have been made between dependent life events and independent life events. Dependent events are those in which the person contributes to the event through his or her own actions (e.g., breaking up with someone, getting a bad grade). Independent events are not influenced by the person experiencing the event (e.g., death of a relative, a natural disaster). Both types of events can contribute to depression (Kendler, Karkowski, & Prescott, 1999; Williamson, Birmaher, Anderson, Al-Shabbout, & Ryan, 1995). Dependent interpersonal events are closely tied to depression for adolescent girls (Rudolph, 2002). In a longitudinal study of adolescents (Ge et al., 1994), changes in uncontrollable events also predicted increases in girls' but not boys' depression. Moreover, symptom changes were related to change in stressful events only for girls.

Gender-Based Theories of Depression

Cumulatively, these findings on sex differences in correlates and predictors of depression point to the need for gender-based theories. One of the first serious attempts to understand depression in adolescent girls can be found in the gender-intensification hypothesis (Hill & Lynch, 1983). In this view, cultural reinforcement of the feminine ideal or stereotype promotes behaviors that are dependent, relationship-driven, emotional, helpless, passive, and self-sacrificing. These behaviors are hypothesized to create risk for depression. Before puberty, gender roles are more fluid and girls are not expected to adhere to them. At puberty, however, expectations change, and many girls place more emphasis on conforming to the sex roles set out by their culture (Allgood-Merten et al., 1990; Aube et al., 2000; B. I. Hart & Thompson, 1996; Huselid & Cooper, 1994; Wichstrom, 1999). One aspect of conformity concerns lack of self-expression and self-assertion. Harter and colleagues (Harter, Waters, Whitesell, & Kastilic, 1998) found that the "loss of voice" and low self-worth in adolescence, more common to females than males and implicated in depression, is restricted to a subset of girls who endorse a feminine orientation. Loss of voice refers to the display of false self-behavior, including suppression of opinions. Negative views of the self are thought to contribute to the development of depression in girls (Allgood-Merten et al., 1990; Avison & McAlpine, 1992; Block & Gjerde, 1990; Gjerde & Block, 1996; Lewinsohn, Gotlib, Lewinsohn, Seeley, & Allen, 1998). The self-conscious emotions of guilt and shame also are part of this process. They are linked to depression and are more common in females than males (Zahn-Waxler, Cole, & Barrett, 1991).

Several recent theories have been advanced to explain high rates of depression in adolescent females (Cyranowski et al., 2000; Hankin & Abramson, 2001; Nolen-Hoeksema & Girgus, 1994). Although no current framework can provide a full etiological account of depression in females, these models represent important first efforts to integrate multiple factors that interact to increase girls' risk for depression. Cyranowski et al. proposed that female gender socialization and increased levels of hormones such as oxytocin (which is associated with reproduction and caregiving) at puberty can intensify the need for affiliation in girls. This, in turn, can contribute to a difficult adolescent transition and a depressogenic diathesis. Gender intensification would result from such vulnerabilities as insecure attachments to parents, an anxious or inhibited temperament, and low instrumental coping skills. These factors interact with stressful life events, particularly in the interpersonal domain. More specifically, Cyranowski et al. hypothesize that the increase in interpersonal stressors related to friendship roles and dating during adolescence interacts with girls' increased need for affiliation, making girls more vulnerable to depression following negative interpersonal events.

Hankin and Abramson (2001) proposed a cognitive vulnerability-stress model in which preexisting vulnerabilities (resulting from genetics, personality, and environmental adversity) contribute to cognitive vulnerabilities and the likelihood of experiencing negative events. Over time, repetitions of events, emotions, and attributions that are negative lead to greater depression. This model helps explain the greater depression in girls because girls report more negative affect (neuroticism), experience more negative events such as sexual abuse, and show more cognitive vulnerability in the form of rumination and negative inferential style than boys.

Nolen-Hoeksema and Girgus (1994) advanced three hypotheses: (1) The causes of depression are the same for girls and boys, but become more prevalent for girls in adolescence; (2) there are different causes for depression in girls and boys, and the causes for girls become more prevalent in early adolescence; and (3) girls are more likely than boys to carry risk factors for depression even before early adolescence, but the risk factors lead to depression only in the face of challenges that increase in early adolescence. They looked at risk factors in personality, biology, and social challenges and concluded that model 3 would most likely provide the greatest explanatory power. Although

longitudinal research is needed for definitive conclusions, good candidates for risk factors more common in girls than boys in childhood included low instrumentality, low dominance and aggression, and a tendency to dwell on problems (i.e., ruminative coping, which can increase and prolong negative mood). When such factors combine in adolescence with biological and social challenges faced by girls, depression may ensue. Given multiple causes of adolescent depression, it is unlikely that one model will be sufficient.

We have emphasized explanations for the preponderance of female depression in the adolescent period. Some risk factors may be the same for males and females, and some obviously differ in both biological terms and social consequences, for example, early puberty. More information is needed about sex differences in the expression of depression and risk factors that may be more salient for males.

Following a review of anxiety disorders, we extend gender-based models of depression downward in age to consider developmental precursors. We focus on the confluence of anxiety, rumination, socialization, social sensitivity, and stress reactivity in childhood.

Anxiety Disorders

There are a number of different anxiety disorders experienced by children and adolescents: Panic, Agoraphobia, Specific Phobia, Social Phobia, Posttraumatic Stress, Separation, and Generalized Anxiety. All are characterized by fears and/or anxieties, but they may differ in their form of expression or context depending on the disorder.

Prevalence rates for anxiety disorders have been estimated to be greater than 10% in a large number of epidemiological studies, with some surveys indicating up to 20% of children and adolescents (see Albano & Krain, 2005). An individual anxiety disorder may occur alone, but more often than not they are comorbid with each other and with depression. Anxiety disorders are higher for females than males, beginning in childhood. Girls have more fears and worries than boys and experience them more intensively (Gullone & King, 1993; Ollendick, Yang, Dong, Xia, & Lin, 1995; W. K. Silverman, LaGreca, & Wasserstein, 1995; Spence, 1998). These sex differences in fear and anxiety are present in the 1st years of life at clinical levels (A. S. Carter, Briggs-Gowan, Jones, & Little, 2003) and continue through adolescence (King, Gullone, Tonge, & Ollendick, 1993). Girls develop anxiety disorders faster than boys. By 6 years of age, twice as many girls have developed an anxiety disorder (Lewinsohn, Gotlib, et al., 1998). Given the high comorbidity and common internalizing nature of anxiety and mood disorders, particularly in girls, there are many parallels in developmental course, antecedents, correlates, and consequences of the two types of disorders. For both males and females, anxiety or depressive disorders during adolescence confer a strong risk for recurrences in early adulthood (Pine, Cohen, Gurley, Brook, & Ma, 1998).

Several epidemiological studies also indicate that anxiety disorders are more common in girls than in boys and these differences become more pronounced during adolescence and continue through adulthood (e.g., Anderson et al., 1987; Kashani & Orvaschel, 1990; Kessler et al., 1993; Lewinsohn, Gotlib, et al., 1998; McGee, Feehan, Williams, & Anderson, 1992). The description that follows draws from a comprehensive review of sex differences in different types of anxiety disorders in children and adolescents by Albano and Krain (2005). In general, girls with anxiety disorders tend to experience somatic complaints at a higher rate than boys. Female adolescents present with more compulsions, more symptoms overall, and greater impairment than male adolescents with Obsessive-Compulsive Disorder (Berg et al., 1989; Maggini et al., 2001; Valleni-Basile et al., 1994). Panic Disorder is more common among female than male adolescents (Kearney & Allan, 1995), and this sex difference continues into adulthood. Panic attacks in females are associated with advanced pubertal development (Hayward, Killen, Hammer, & Litt, 1992; Morris & March, 2004). There are also sex differences in the presentation of social anxiety symptoms (Weinstock, 1999). Studies of children with phobic disorders consistently find a higher prevalence among females in community and clinical samples (Ollendick, King, & Frary, 1989; Strauss & Last, 1993). Adolescent girls and women are at higher risk for the development of PTSD than are boys and men (Breslau, Davis, Andreski, & Peterson, 1991; Hanna & Grant, 1997; Kessler et al., 1994), but apparently only when PTSD is comorbid with other disorders, such as depression (Kilpatrick et al., 2003). Subclinical social anxiety is common in children and adolescents, especially for girls. Girls report higher levels of social anxiety than boys, particularly the social evaluative aspect (Crick & Ladd, 1993; LaGreca & Stone, 1993; Vernberg, Abwender, Ewell, & Beery, 1992).

Genetic/Biological Explanations

There is substantial evidence for familial transmission of anxiety disorders. Although the extent of genetic versus environmental influences is still debated (see Feigon, Waldman, Levy, & Hay, 2001; Rose & Ditto, 1983; Silove, Manicavasagar, O'Connell, & Morris-Yates, 1995; Wood, McLeod, Sigman, Hwang, & Chu, 2003), heritable factors

play a role (Crowe, Noyes, & Persico, 1987; Kendler, Heath, Martin, & Eaves, 1986; Noyes, Clarkson, Crowe, Yates, & McChesney, 1987). In behavior genetics research on anxiety at 7 years of age, both physiological and social anxiety symptoms showed heritability (Warren, Schmitz, & Emde, 1999). Lichtenstein and Annas (2000) have reported sex differences in heritability of types of irrational fears in 8- to 9-year-old twins. Similarly, Kendler, Jacobson, Myers, and Prescott (2002) found sex-specific genetic risk factors for agoraphobia, social, situational, and blood-injury phobias. The authors note the limited power of twin studies, even with large sample sizes, to resolve sex-specific genetic effects.

Disinhibited behavior patterns reflect daring and fearlessness, which are more common in boys than girls. Effortful control, which requires restraint and the ability to inhibit oneself, is more characteristic of girls than boys (Else-Quest et al., in press). Inhibited temperament in young children is associated with the later development of anxiety and anxiety disorders. Sex differences in behavioral inhibition are not always apparent early in life, but developmental trajectories appear to differ (Kagan, 2001). Behavioral inhibition (high reactivity in infancy and fearfulness at 2 years) predicted anxiety at 7.5 years of age more strongly in girls than boys. For girls, but not boys, early behavioral inhibition predicted later sympathetic activation of the cardiovascular system when confronted with an aversive stimulus (white noise).

Neurobiological mechanisms are implicated in the development of anxiety disorders, but there is little research on possible sex differences. This is puzzling given the sex differences seen early on in life, with girls more anxious and fearful than boys, and the physiological symptoms that often accompany anxiety (shortness of breath, palpitations or racing heart, shakiness, dizziness, flushes/chills, sweating, and headaches). This physiological reactivity is manifested both in central nervous system and autonomic nervous system activity. The fact that males more often show patterns of low autonomic arousal than females suggests the need to consider these factors in relation to (sex differences in) anxiety, as well as to examine differences in brain structure, function, and activity that may play mediating and moderating roles.

The startle reflex is a psychophysiological measure of reactivity that may be a vulnerability marker for anxiety. An early predisposition to react fearfully may reflect enhanced susceptibility. Behavioral inhibition has been linked both to anxiety disorders and risk for anxiety disorders by having a parent with an anxiety disorder (see Grillon, Dierker, & Merikangas, 1998). Grillon et al. found that startle not only discriminated between children at low and high risk, but did so in different ways for high-risk males and females. For high-risk females, overall startle levels were elevated compared to other groups, suggesting generalization of fear to the entire experimental context. In contrast, high-risk males showed greater magnitude of startle potentiation during aversive anticipation, a more context-specific response. Sex differences in the brain structures of these high-risk groups may underlie affective responses to explicit (i.e., threat signal) and contextual (i.e., experiment room) threatening stimuli. The amygdala is implicated in startle response to explicit and contextual cues, whereas the bed nucleus of the stria terminalis is involved in response to contextual cues (M. Davis, Campeau, Kim, & Falls, 1995).

Another promising approach for understanding neural structures implicated in anxiety involves the use of fMRI. McClure et al. (2004) compared adolescent and adult males' and females' responses to threat. Adult women activated orbitofrontal cortex and amygdala selectively to unambiguous threat cues, and adult men and adolescents of both sexes showed a less discriminating pattern of activation. Sex differences in neural responses to threat may not be fully apparent until adulthood; a more definitive answer awaits further research with larger sample sizes and at different stages of development. This work is consistent with other studies showing heightened reactivity to threat by females, for example, greater accuracy in identifying anger and hostility, increases in skin conductance, and startle potentiation to threatening scenes.

There is also some evidence that males and females differentially engage brain structures associated with processing of emotional stimuli (orbitofrontal cortex, amygdala, and anterior cingulate gyrus; see McClure et al., 2004). Various hormonal changes affecting neurotransmitter and other systems that interact with hormones released in response to stress also may modulate anxiety in females (Goodyer, Herbert, Tamplin, & Altham, 2000; Rubinow & Schmidt, 1996; Slap, Khalid, Paikoff, Brooks-Gunn, & Warren, 1994; Susman, Nottelmann, & Inoff-Germain, 1987). Early puberty is associated with greater anxiety in females only. The mechanisms accounting for associations between pubertal timing, hormonal activity, and anxiety are not yet understood (Hayward & Sanborn, 2002).

Environmental Explanations

Initially, the parent-child relationship provides a primary interpersonal context where boys and girls can learn to become fearful (Gerull & Rapee, 2002). As children mature,

they are exposed to a wider range of behavioral models and contexts that include teachers and peers. Thus, there are further occasions to observe models that vary in how children cope with challenging and novel situations, as well as in the anxiety and fear they show. Socialization research intended to explain normative sex differences may also be relevant to more extreme variations. Boys are allowed and encouraged to explore their physical environments, which creates opportunities to master the unfamiliar and to feel comfortable or safe in a variety of contexts. In contrast, girls' exploration is often curtailed. Agoraphobic individuals are at ease only when they are close to home, finding it difficult or impossible to traverse certain distances.

A number of socialization experiences may contribute to heightened anxiety in girls. Fearfulness is accepted and sometimes encouraged in girls, but is less tolerated in boys. Parents are more tolerant, however, of anger, assertion, and misbehavior in boys. Society and culture reinforce these messages. One would expect that these processes would leave girls feeling more insecure, fearful, and anxious, whereas boys would be more likely to gain confidence and certainty in their actions. Research is needed to examine these different socialization processes in high-risk environments. This would help to determine when socialization processes are unrelated to psychopathology and when they help to shape sex differences in internalizing problems.

In addition to the family environment (Ginsburg, Siqueland, Masia-Warner, & Hedtke, 2004), peer relationships may play a critical role in shaping sex differences in pathological anxiety states (LaGreca & Lopez, 1998). Peer victimization has a greater effect on anxiety levels of girls than boys (Crick & Bigbee, 1998; Grills & Ollendick, 2002). Girls not only report more anxiety than boys, but being victimized leads to more negative opinions of themselves, which, in turn, makes them vulnerable to increased anxiety. Boys may more often externalize victimization experiences and view their peers rather than themselves in negative terms. Blaming others may protect against the development of anxiety but create risk for externalizing problems.

Several factors more common to girls than boys are associated with risk for anxiety as well as depression; these include more major life events, higher self-consciousness, lower self-esteem, and more emotional reliance (Lewinsohn, Gotlib, et al., 1998). Girls also report higher social competence and more social support from friends, which can be viewed as a trade-off that confers advantage in social relationships but that has an emotional cost (Rudolph & Conley, 2005). That is, interpersonal sensitivity is linked with social skills but also with emotional distress. This may be reflected at the physiological level as well. Recently, Shirtcliff, Booth, and Granger (2004) showed that several aspects of social competence were associated with trait cortisol across a 2-year period in girls only. There was an interaction with social anxiety, specifically fear of negative evaluation, such that socially competent girls who were also fearful had high trait cortisol. Also consistent with the depression literature, sex differences in anxiety in adolescence result from differences in interpersonal stress and emotional reactions to stress (see Rudolph, 2002, for a review) and perceptions of negative interpersonal events as stressful (Wagner & Compas, 1990). Because females place greater value on close relationships than do males, they are also more affected by separation and loss, becoming anxious and depressed (Goodyer & Altham, 1991). In prospective epidemiological research, prediction of Generalized Anxiety Disorder in adults from stressful life events in adolescence was seen only for females, suggesting enduring negative effects (Pine, Cohen, Johnson, & Brook, 2002).

One common explanation for sex differences in anxiety (as in depression) is that of sex-role orientation. Feminine sex role in adults (both males and females) is related to increased self-report of fears, whereas masculine sex role is related to less fear (Carey, Dusek, & Spector, 1988; Dillon, Wolf, & Katz, 1985; Ginsburg & Silverman, 2000; Tucker & Bond, 1997). Essex and colleagues (2005) have identified two pathways to later internalizing problems. One pathway began with children who were temperamentally inhibited and prone to sadness as preschoolers, and socially inhibited in the face of new social and academic challenges as they transitioned into school. The other pathway was defined by girls who expressed more prosocial behaviors as they made the school transition. Anxiety and depression in third grade thus may be partly the product of biological sex and socially constrained roles. The connections between prosociality and anxiety/depression speak to possible adverse consequences of a strong interpersonal orientation as childhood precursors to later internalizing problems. In another study, prosocial themes in 7-year-olds' representations of conflict and distress (more common in girls than boys) predicted greater anxiety in girls but not boys in early adolescence (Zahn-Waxler et al., 2005).

Links between Anxiety and Depression: A Developmental Perspective

Most of the work reviewed to this point has focused on explanations for sex differences in depression and anxiety that appear in adolescence (see Zahn-Waxler, 2000), with

limited attention to childhood precursors. We know that externalizing problems emerge early in life, are more common in boys than girls, and show substantial continuity across time. Not only are girls much less likely than boys to engage in disruptive, antisocial, physically aggressive behavior during childhood, but when they do aggress they are more likely also to be depressed and anxious. This "gender paradox of comorbidities" (Loeber & Keenan, 1994) suggests that even "poorly behaved" girls experience greater internal pressures, constraints, and distress than boys with similar problems. Comorbidity of anxiety and depression is more common in girls than boys, whether or not externalizing problems also are present. Exploration of early and middle childhood may provide insights about why internalizing problems more often emerge later in development than externalizing problems. Comorbidity patterns in childhood may provide clues not only about sex differences in depression, but also why girls vary among themselves.

Childhood Antecedents of Depression

A decade has passed since the seminal paper by Nolen-Hoeksema and Girgus (1994) on different models for explaining sex differences in depression that appear to first emerge in adolescence. Since that time evidence has continued to accrue for model 3, the developmental model. It posits that vulnerability factors more common to girls than boys may be present in childhood, but lead to depression only in the face of challenges that increase in adolescence. Several of the risk factors for girls and protective factors for boys appear to reflect either extreme expressions of normative sex differences in early child characteristics and socialization experiences or normative differences that occur in the context of particularly challenging environments. A body of literature on childhood antecedents of adolescent and adult depression has begun to emerge (Block & Gjerde, 1990; Block et al., 1991; Gurian, 1987; Keenan & Hipwell, 2005; McCauley et al., 2001; Nolen-Hoeksema & Girgus, 1994; Zahn-Waxler, 2000; Zahn-Waxler et al., 1991). In our analysis, we emphasize early anxiety as a precursor to later depression. Anxiety shows stability over time in childhood (e.g., Ialongo, Edelsohn, Werthamer-Larsson, Crockett, & Kellam, 1995). The female preponderance in Major Depression may be secondary to a sex difference in specific anxiety disorders. The fact that Generalized Anxiety Disorder and Panic Disorder often precede depressive episodes in early adolescence suggests that early anxiety may lead to later depression, especially in girls (Parker & Hadzi-Pavlovic, 2004; also see Hankin & Abramson, 2001).

Several longitudinal studies now suggest that anxiety is often an integral feature of depression and that it precedes depression developmentally, and hence may be a prodromal sign of depression. Anxiety disorders in childhood and adolescence often precede and predict later depressive disorders. In one retrospective study of children with comorbid anxiety and depression, two-thirds became anxious before they became depressed (Kovacs, Gatsonis, Paulauskas, & Richards, 1989). Several prospective longitudinal studies have found that anxiety temporally precedes depression in children, adolescents, and even young adults (e.g., Breslau, Schultz, & Peterson, 1995; D. A. Cole, Peeke, Martin, Truglio, & Seroczynski, 1998; Lewinsohn, Gotlib, & Seeley, 1995). Prepubertal-onset anxiety disorder precedes recurrent Major Depression across generations in high-risk families (Warner, Weissman, Mufson, & Wickramaratne, 1999). In one study, inhibited 3-year-olds were unassertive and depressed at 21 years (Caspi, 2000). In another study, inhibited temperament in toddlers predicted generalized social anxiety in adolescence for girls only (C. E. Schwartz, Snidman, & Kagan, 1999).

Rumination in childhood can help to explain developmental associations between early anxiety and later depression. Although research has focused on ruminative responses *to* depression beginning in adolescence, rumination is likely to be present *before* depression develops. Rumination involves worry, perseveration, and even obsession (at times) about one's inner state and may begin in childhood as anxiety and worry develop. Rumination can magnify problems, overwhelm the child, and eventually create depression. It may also maintain or exacerbate depression by augmenting accessibility and recall of negative events (Bower, 1981).

A Biosocial Analysis of Childhood Precursors of Adolescent Depression

Because anxiety involves biological dysregulation of limbic, vegetative, and autonomic systems, the heightened, sustained arousal can eventually tax these systems, causing the organism to withdraw from environmental stimulation and shut down—in short, to become depressed. Not all depression is preceded by anxiety, and anxiety does not always lead to depression. But the pathway from anxiety to depression occurs with sufficient regularity to postulate that anxiety often plays an etiologic role. Because females are more likely than males to develop depression and to have earlier (and also comorbid) anxiety, girls would be expected to experience a developmental pathway from anxiety to depression more often than boys.

The abrupt appearance of depressive symptoms in adolescents and adults, without clear external triggers, is sometimes taken as evidence both for discontinuity of depression in development and for the primacy of biological processes. However, this depression may result from earlier stress and trauma. Post and colleagues (Meyersburg & Post, 1979; Post et al., 1996) proposed a crucial role for stressful or traumatic life events in precipitating initial depressive episodes in genetically predisposed persons. Initial episodes lead to future episodes that over time occur in closer proximity and eventually without environmental precipitants. This model was derived from work on the "kindling" of seizure disorders, in which seizures become more spontaneously generated over the years. Based on this work, F. K. Goodwin and Jamison (1990) argued that depression appearing "out of the blue" in young adults may have origins in early environmental trauma that helps create biological vulnerability. Repeated exposure to psychological stress over time may sensitize children so that later on, even brief exposures to similar stressors (or even thoughts and images in the absence of apparent stress that serve as reminders) could induce depression.

Dienstbier (1984) has proposed that different temperaments might lead to different emotion-attributional styles and levels of guilt. Proneness to emotional tension should result in intense discomfort and distress following transgression or stressful events. When distress is internal, the child is more likely to experience the links between tension and transgression and come to experience anticipatory anxiety. Temperamentally anxious children may develop "affective maps" or "somatic markers" of their experiences where threat- or stress-related information becomes particularly salient (Damasio, Tranel, & Damasio, 1991; Derryberry & Reed, 1994). This physiological reactivity may facilitate the early, rapid development of mechanisms related to conscience, such as guilt and restraint from wrongdoing, as well as feelings of responsibility in emotionally challenging encounters that do not involve transgression.

We propose that young girls not only are more likely than boys to experience anxiety, but also to interpret their environments in ways that create depressive cognitions. Because of their strong interpersonal orientation, girls are often in close physical proximity to caregivers. This can influence how the family climate is represented in conscious and unconscious memory, the scripts girls develop about early family life, and the accessibility of these memories. The literature on emotion language provides clues about how negative emotions and cognitions become fused as young girls are drawn into a communication process that is depressogenic in nature (see review by Zahn-Waxler, 2000). Parents (mainly mothers) talk more about internalizing emotions (sadness, fear), providing greater detail and elaboration, with daughters than sons. Distressed and depressed parents talk more about these negative emotions than do well mothers (Zahn-Waxler, 2000). Young girls in these families will often be in a position to internalize emotional negative scripts that can be readily accessed.

Greater access to negative affect-based memories about family life or other social relationships (e.g., with teachers, friends, and classmates) that are unhappy and conflictual may provide material for a nascent form of ruminative coping and negative cognitions that may contribute to later depression. Because this process is likely to occur more often with young daughters than sons, girls may come to dwell more on negative events where they have little or no control. Through a complex set of processes socialization is thought to prime these memories and affective, physiological arousal (anxiety) to ingrain them into memory. There are many ways in which early negative emotions, behaviors, and cognitions could combine and lead to later depression, particularly for girls. We consider one prototypic model: the development of a depressogenic style in a young girl of a depressed parent who comes to feel guilty and responsible for the parent's problems. Other adverse environmental conditions could have a similar effect. Boys would not necessarily be immune to these processes, given similar temperaments and experiences.

During the preschool years, children can easily become overinvolved in parental conflict and distress. For example, they try to get fighting parents to make up or to help or cheer up a depressed mother (Cummings, Zahn-Waxler, & Radke-Yarrow, 1981; Radke-Yarrow, Zahn-Waxler, Richardson, Susman, & Martinez, 1994). They also develop *scripts* of overinvolvement in others' distress that include themes of empathy and guilt (Zahn-Waxler, Kochanska, Krupnick, & McKnew, 1990). These patterns are more common in girls than boys. Thus, girls of depressed mothers tend to become overinvolved in another's distress. They also show unassertive, submissive ways of coping with conflict (Hay, Zahn-Waxler, Cummings, & Iannotti, 1992), whereas boys do not.

These patterns of participation in parental conflict and distress, in conjunction with high levels of anxiety and internalized distress, create a possible pathway to depression. In attributional theories, adult depression is characterized by overwhelming feelings of both helplessness and responsibility. A young child with an emotionally distressed caregiver fundamentally cannot help the parent, and consequently this may lead to feelings of helplessness and failure. The belief, however, that they can create change would be intermittently reinforced by their occasional successful efforts to assume responsibility. These children also become part of a large climate of despair by their close proximity to parental distress, with contagion of mood a likely outcome. Thus, young children, more often girls, could experience depression-like symptoms of helplessness and responsibility early and repeatedly due to empathic overinvolvement. These girls could come to feel that life requires more from them than they can give, leading to defeatism and despair. Although family stress negatively impacts the mental health of both girls and boys, having a strong caring orientation or involvement in family processes in the context of parental psychopathology and discord is seen as particularly harmful to girls (Gore et al., 1993).

In summary, the literature on young children suggests that most of the risk factors that create disproportionate risk for depression in adolescent girls are set in place much earlier and that childhood anxiety may provide a pathway to later depression.

Eating Disorders

Few psychiatric disorders are as clearly sex-linked as are Anorexia Nervosa (AN) and Bulimia Nervosa (BN; American Psychiatric Association, 2000). AN is marked by self-starvation; BN involves a syndrome of binging and purging. A review of epidemiological studies of AN suggests that it occurs in eight or more women for every one man, and the difference for BN may be larger (Pawluck & Gorey, 1998). The criteria for diagnosing these disorders are quite restrictive, and many females who experience substantial eating problems do not qualify for a clinical diagnosis. Studies that focus on less severe eating problems, such as weight and shape dissatisfaction or dieting, consistently involve many more females than males, beginning in elementary school. Although it appears in all American ethnic groups (Smolak & Levine, 2001), AN is found in lower rates in African American girls, which may be related to more flexible ideal body images. At least among girls, poor body image predicts the development of eating disorders (Attie & Brooks-Gunn, 1989; Stice & Bearman, 2001).

Several community-based studies have examined the prevalence of eating disorders (see Garvin & Striegel-Moore, 2001, for a review), but only one included men and examined only AN because BN had not yet been officially recognized. Relatively little research has been done on preadolescents, adolescents, ethnic minority groups, and males (Garvin & Striegel-Moore, 2001). More epidemiological data are needed to make definitive statements about the prevalence of eating disorders. Current estimates are that AN occurs in less than 1% of postpubertal American women (Garvin & Striegel-Moore, 2001). BN is considerably more common, with a lifetime prevalence rate of 3% (Garvin & Striegel-Moore, 2001). Among adolescents, the rates are probably lower, with 0.5% to 1.0% meeting criteria for AN and 1% for BN (Thompson & Smolak, 2001). Many more females suffer from subthreshold disorders. The rate for subthreshold and full-syndrome eating disorders may be as high as 10% among adolescents (Agras, 2001).

The vast majority of research concerning eating disorders has been done with females. Hence, the diagnostic criteria have been developed based largely on females' symptoms and do not reflect a lack of sensitivity to them. However, some of the criteria may be arbitrary in ways that lead to underdetection of the problem in children (e.g., inclusion of amenorrhea as a diagnostic criterion for AN). Of the disorders that are comorbid with AN and BN, depression is most frequent. Depression and eating problems co-occur at subclinical levels starting before age 14 (Graber & Brooks-Gunn, 2001). Depression and eating problems may be causally related. For example, Stice and Bearman (2001) reported that negative body image and disturbed eating predict the development of depression in adolescence.

Girls are more likely than boys to report disturbed eating attitudes and behaviors (A. Field, Camargo, Taylor, Berkey, Robert, & Colditz, 2001). They more often think they are overweight when they are not and more often engage in binge eating. Girls' eating problems increase with age, whereas boys do not, and may be related to the increasing pressure with age for girls to be thin. Both boys and girls agree that weight plays a larger role in determining attractiveness for teenage girls than for boys (Jones, 2001). Puberty can also be seen as a time that takes girls away from their thin ideal body shape, whereas boys move closer to the male body ideal of greater size and muscularity.

Genetic/Biological Explanations

Some studies have shown fairly substantial rates of MZ twins' concordance for AN and BN (e.g., Bulik, Sullivan, Wade, & Kendler, 2000). Recent data suggest a genetic linkage signal for AN on chromosome 1 and for BN on chromosome 10p (Bulik et al., 2003; Devlin et al., 2002). Genetics are implicated in obesity, which is a risk factor for eating disorders (Meyer & Stunkard, 1993) and in this way may indirectly affect the development of eating disorders.

Information about biological factors is quite limited. Prospective studies that would include biological assays prior to the emergence of an eating disorder are not feasible given the low rates of occurrence and the high cost of the tests. Serotonin and dopamine levels have been implicated in the etiology of eating disorders (Kaye & Strober, 1999), and pharmacological studies provide some support as well. However, this literature is based on comparisons of neurotransmitter and hormonal levels of recovered anorexics and bulimics to normal females. It is not known how long it takes to recover; moreover, these disorders may permanently alter brain chemistry. In one prospective study, negative emotionality during the preschool years predicted a drive for thinness in adolescence (Martin et al., 2000).

Eating disorders are more common in girls who reach puberty early than those who are on time or late maturers. Girls gain as much as 40 pounds during puberty and begin to have a normative higher percentage of body fat compared to males. It is not surprising that girls become dissatisfied with their body, particularly when they mature early. What is less clear is why a relatively small proportion go on to engage in health- and life-threatening activities. It will be important to learn more about the interaction of biological and psychological forces. For example, Smolak, Levine, and Gralen (1993) reported that girls who went through puberty early and began dating early scored higher on a measure of disturbed eating later in adolescence, compared to girls who experienced *either* early puberty *or* early dating *or* neither stressor.

Environmental Explanations

Parents' comments have been shown to affect children's body esteem, beginning in elementary school (see review by Smolak, 2005). Daughters appear to be more affected than sons, even when parents do not respond differentially to them (D. Schwartz, Phares, Tantleff-Dunn, & Thompson, 1999; Smolak, Levine, & Schermer, 1999). Adolescents whose fathers were worried about the child's body shape were more likely to be constant dieters a year later (A. Field et al., 2001). Some (e.g., Smolak et al., 1999) but not all (e.g., Attie & Brooks-Gunn, 1989) researchers find that maternal modeling of body image and eating problems is related to daughters' eating problems.

Body objectification theory (Fredrickson & Roberts, 1997) is relevant to the heightened risk of females to develop eating disorders. Sex differences in body image are proposed to result from differences in how men and women's bodies are treated by society. Women's bodies are much more likely to be looked at, evaluated, and treated as objects. Females learn that males' opinions about their appearance are important to their well-being. Already by third grade about 75% of girls have experienced sexual harassment (Murnen & Smolak, 2000). By middle school, this becomes normative for girls, and the threat of date rape begins (Bryant, 1993; J. Silverman, Raj, Mucci, & Hathaway, 2001). Also at this time, girls try to reduce such threats (e.g., by avoiding events or not speaking in class). At the same time girls are learning that their body poses a risk, they are also learning that being attractive may help them succeed socially and professionally.

Fredrickson and Roberts (1997) propose that girls gradually internalize that objectifying gaze and self-monitor their attractiveness, including whether they are thin enough. This leads to the normalization of body dissatisfaction among adolescent girls and women. Both experimental and longitudinal data indicate that one of the best predictors of eating problems is internalization of the thin ideal (Thompson & Stice, 2001). There are several reasons girls become susceptible to cultural pressures. These include stronger investment in social relationships, exposure to more consistent pressures from multiple socialization agents, and greater likelihood of living in a culture of thinness than boys (see review by Smolak, 2005). Girls are more likely than boys to be influenced by messages about body image from peers, parents, and media, yet there are signs that images of the ideal male body are becoming more unrealistic (Pope, Olivardia, Gruber, & Borowiecki, 1999). It will be important to learn whether boys increasingly experience these pressures and, in turn, their risk for eating disorders. Perfectionism is thought to play a role in the development and maintenance of eating disorders (Abramson, Bardone-Cone, Vohs, Joiner, & Heatherton, 2005; Shafran & Mansell, 2001). It would be important to study perfectionism in females and males, as well as emotions relevant to the pursuit of perfection and the failure to achieve it, namely, guilt and shame (Jambekar, Masheb, & Grilo, 2003).

PERSONALITY TRAITS, DISORDERS, AND PROBLEMS

This section briefly explores questions about the developmental antecedents of personality disorders and the role of personality in other disorders. Unlike other sections, there is little in the way of theory or data—only some important developmental questions that merit further consideration. Personality disorders involve an enduring, stable pattern of cognitions, emotions, and behavior that

are considered atypical for one's culture and that result in marked reductions in functioning for the individual (American Psychiatric Association, 2000). Traditionally, clinicians and other mental health professionals have viewed personality as lacking in cohesiveness and durability prior to the age of 18, which has contributed to a nondevelopmental emphasis and a lack of empirical data on the etiology and course of these disorders (Bleiberg, 2001; Geiger & Crick, 2001; Kernberg, Weiner, & Bardenstein, 2000; Paris, 2003). This is puzzling given the preponderance of literature on stability of temperament, which is viewed as an early expression of personality. Moreover, personality has been posited to begin forming early in life, substrates of which may be present at birth (Hartup & van Lieshout, 1995). Diagnosis of Antisocial Personality Disorder requires a developmental history of conduct problems; developmental precursors have not been posited for other personality disorders for the reasons noted. Research is needed on early variations in personality that may represent different vulnerabilities for males and females for the development of different personality disorders.

There are sex differences in the prevalence of a number of personality disorders (American Psychiatric Association, 2000). Some are more typical of men (e.g., Antisocial Personality Disorder, Narcissistic Personality Disorder) and others more typical of women (e.g., Borderline Personality Disorder, Histrionic Personality Disorder; American Psychiatric Association, 2000; J. D. Carter, Joyce, Mulder, Sullivan, & Luty, 1999; for a review, see Paris, 2003). Because boys are far more likely than girls to be diagnosed with CD they are also at later greater risk for Antisocial Personality Disorder. Results from one prospective community study have also shown impulsive disorders like CD and ODD are also precursors to Narcissistic Personality Disorder (Kasen et al., 2001). Parental maltreatment can be a precursor of Borderline Personality Disorder and other disorders as well (Paris, 2001). Notably, the sex differences in the types of personality disorders mirror extremes of normative differences seen even in childhood and adolescence, that is, extreme antisocial behavior and inflated self-esteem in males versus relationship problems, emotionality, and dependency in females.

Geiger and Crick (2001) have proposed a developmental psychopathology model of factors that indicate risk for personality pathology during childhood and adolescence. In this model, it is posited that childhood features associated with atypical personality development may be identified in terms of difficulties negotiating developmentally appropriate, normative tasks that have relevance for particular disorders. Based on a content analysis of *DSM* criteria for diagnosis of personality disorders, features of pathology were identified as relevant to the nature of particular aspects of personality disorders, as well as to maladaptive development during childhood. An example is a childhood tendency to view the world in a hostile, paranoid manner (Crick & Dodge, 1994). Paranoid ideation may indicate a type of compromised social cognitive competence indicative of Borderline, Paranoid, or Schizotypal Personality Disorders.

The childhood tendency to view the world in a hostile, paranoid manner is elicited in different contexts for boys and girls that may influence the nature of their ideation and the later form of their personality problems. These and other features identified by Geiger and Crick (2001) may provide fruitful avenues for exploring differential pathways toward (and away from) different personality disorders for boys versus girls. Additional theoretical models, as well as empirical tests of these models, are needed before the role of development and sex in personality pathology development can be determined. Research on Axis II disorders utilizing longitudinal designs, targeting equal numbers of boys and girls, and using large community samples in addition to clinical samples would help to increase existing knowledge of personality pathology.

The personality trait of neuroticism has been implicated in depressive disorders and sex differences in depression. Although causal connections are difficult to establish, recent research has suggested that neuroticism is a better predictor of depression in adult females than males, with females scoring higher than males on both of these dimensions (R. D. Goodwin & Gotlib, 2004). Notably, women also scored higher than men on agreeableness, extraversion, and conscientiousness, and men scored higher on openness to experience, dimensions that also correspond to childhood sex differences discussed earlier, for example, compliance and responsibility in girls and exploration in boys. From a developmental perspective, early anxiety, inhibition, and fearfulness may be temperamental qualities that are forerunners of neuroticism, suggesting a causal rather than correlational role of neuroticism in depression.

Neuroticism typically is defined in terms of negative affectivity, which includes the combination of extrapunitive (e.g., anger, hostility) and intropunitive (e.g., sadness, fear/anxiety, guilt) negative emotions. In the adult literature, these have been shown to be viable constructs at both their combined and individual levels (Watson & Clark, 1992). Neuroticism technically includes anger/hostility as well as the emotions more directly related to internalizing problems, but it is possible that anger/hostility plays a lesser role. It would be useful to examine the predictive power of neuroticism for depression, with and without the externalizing component. Unlike adults, where women score higher on neuroticism, young boys and girls do not differ on the temperament trait of negative affectivity (Else-Quest et al., in press), a concept similar to neuroticism. A breakdown of negative affectivity into extrapunitive and intropunitive emotions at different stages of development and an analysis of continuities over time for both males and females would help to clarify the nature of precursors of neuroticism.

FUTURE DIRECTIONS

This overview of research on the development of psychopathology makes it abundantly clear that there are sex differences in types, rates, antecedents, correlates, trajectories, comorbidities, and consequences of problems in females and males. Although there are important similarities, it is essential to appreciate the differences in order to advance scientific knowledge and to develop more effective treatments. Evidence continues to accrue indicating the need for developmental models that allow for different parameters for males and females when genetic and environmental factors implicated in psychopathology are studied (Jacobson & Rowe, 1999). The long history of ignoring the possibility of gender-specific or gender-relevant models for the sake of parsimonious causal explanations has led to a sometimes oversimplified and fragmented understanding of the etiology of sex differences in psychiatric and psychological problems. Parenthetically, we have treated sex as a dichotomous variable in this review, consistent with how research participants were classified in the studies reviewed. The study of homosexuals and transgendered individuals regarding the issues addressed will be important in future research.

Conceptual Considerations

The construct of inhibition has emerged in this review not only as a symptom, but also as both a risk and protective factor for different forms of psychopathology in females and males. Bjorklund and Kipp (1996) proposed that cognitive inhibition mechanisms evolved from the need to control social and emotional responses in small groups of hominids for the purposes of cooperation and group cohesion. Moreover, the pressures to inhibit certain potentially inappropriate social and emotional responses were thought to be greater on female than male hominids, resulting in enhanced inhibition abilities for females in a range of contexts. The motivation for inhibition stemmed from females' roles in bearing and rearing children and the need for greater parental investment than males, roles that continue to this day. Bjorklund and Kipp's reexamination of their own data and review of other research provided support for this point of view. Although sex differences may not be present for behavioral inhibition in children as a temperamental trait, there is substantial evidence that females are better able to inhibit and control their impulses, behaviors, and emotions than males, beginning early in life.

We have seen that inhibition also plays a role in several forms of internalizing psychopathology more common to females than males. Disinhibition, in contrast, is common to several forms of externalizing psychopathology and neurodevelopmental psychiatric problems seen more often in males. Inhibition had and still has adaptive value, but it carries risk for problems in functioning, particularly for females. That is, it may result in conscientious, responsible behavior under optimal conditions, and it may stifle normal development when other risk factors are present. The same is true of disinhibition, which is often problematic but under certain conditions creates openness to experience and opportunities for growth. It will be important to identify etiologic factors that distinguish adaptive and maladaptive functioning.

It will also be valuable to learn more about the development of the neural bases of inhibition, which are localized in functional areas of the neocortex, more specifically, the prefrontal cortex, which receives projections from the mediodorsal nucleus of the thalamus.

There are sex differences in maturation of the neocortex, with girls maturing faster (and thus able to inhibit a prepotent response earlier) than boys (A. Diamond, 1990). Most of the research on brain maturation has emphasized the deleterious consequences of delayed maturation for certain types of disorders more common to males. However, there may be risks associated with early maturation for other types of problems and disorders more common to females when coupled with other risk factors, some of which may not be obvious. For example, high intelligence is associated with depression, particularly in girls (Gjerde, 2005), who may better understand the implications of societal constraints. In conjunction with neural inhibitory processes, a pathway to anxiety and depression can be hypothesized. Early resilience may disguise problems such as

anxiety, and early vulnerabilities to depression may take a subtler, less recognizable form.

Delayed neural maturation due in part to high levels of circulating testosterone that hypermasculinize the brain early in development has been associated with the extreme male brain (Baron-Cohen, 2002). This is thought to increase the probability of certain kinds of problems associated with behavioral, motor, social, and emotional disinhibition, for example, sexual attacks and compulsions, physical violence and brutality, tics, and problems in social communication and understanding emotions. The extreme male brain theory has the advantage of grouping apparently disparate psychiatric and psychological problems in a single unifying framework. What it does not do, however, is explain why a given hypermasculinized individual is more likely to develop one type of problem (e.g., Autism) than another (e.g., Conduct Disorder). The theory is based mainly on observable differences that have yet to be examined in relation to genetic, neural, and hormonal patterns for both males and females and for different kinds of problems.

Another issue to be addressed is whether or not there is an extreme female brain, and if so, what are the distinguishing characteristics. Baron-Cohen (2002) suggests that there is, but that it is not relevant to psychopathology. The prototypic person would be highly empathic but deficient in object-related skills (e.g., classification, systemization, and spatial skills). Such a person would be good at organizing and making sense of the social world. In this view, because one can function in society even without scientific skills, such individuals would not be at risk.

What the extreme brain theory fails to consider, however, are the adverse consequences of a hyperdeveloped capacity for empathy (more common to females) similar to the adverse consequences of a hyperdeveloped capacity for systematizing (more common to males). Whereas the extreme of systematizing is viewed as maladaptive in Baron-Cohen's system, the extreme of empathizing is not, for the reasons just noted. Empathizing is defined broadly by Baron-Cohen (2002) to include the capacity to (1) share and take turns; (2) refrain from rough-and-tumble play, physical aggression, and violence; (3) show concern for another's distress; (4) infer others' thoughts and intentions; (5) decode facial and vocal expressions; (6) value interpersonal relationships; (7) engage in indirect or relational aggression, which requires better mind-reading skills than physical aggression; (8) use speech that is cooperative, reciprocal, and collaborative; (9) talk about emotions; (10) engage in sensitive parenting practices; and (11) prefer face and eye contact. Our literature review has revealed

links between some of these qualities (more common to females) and internalizing problems (also more common to
females). A necessary expansion of the theory would include the extreme female brain as a risk factor for internalizing or inhibitory disorders, in contrast to externalizing
and other forms of disinhibitory disorders and problems.

Earlier we discussed how sex-role stereotypes or exaggerations of feminine and masculine qualities are reflected
in the different types of problems that males and females
tend to develop. Baron-Cohen's addition of the systematizing dimension (at the extreme) provides an example of a
framework for understanding types of male-dominated disorders like Autism and Asperger's syndrome, where there
is often an intense interest in the world of objects, often to
the exclusion of people. High-functioning individuals with
these developmental disorders are sometimes highly gifted
in areas like mathematics and physics. The origins of the
idea of the extreme male brain derive from the conceptual
work of Geschwind and Galaburda (1985), who discussed
the role of an asymmetrical nervous system that included
anomalous cerebral dominance and emphasized the role of
testosterone in the intrauterine environment. They viewed
these conditions as responsible not only for a range of developmental disorders but also for special talents more
common to males than females. It is important to raise
questions about such theories and to make certain that they
are not used to justify stereotypes and prejudices about sex
differences. At the same time, it is important to recognize
that there may be some underlying biological bases for
both assets and liabilities that are more common to one sex
than the other.

Because the extreme male brain is broadly defined, including both the ability to systematize and lack of empathy and covering a wide range of disorders, one would
anticipate different biological and environmental factors
would be implicated. One important next step in research
will be to determine whether there are different patterns
of brain structure, function, and circuitry (and other biological and environmental processes) that underlie the different types of problems characterized by the extreme
male brain and the extreme female brain. This framework
could provide a starting point for examining how similar
qualities of individuals can be adaptive or maladaptive,
convey protection or risk, reflect resilience or vulnerability, and signal the fact that there are trade-offs or costs
and benefits to be weighed.

Most of the relevant brain imaging work has been conducted with animals and adults. Few studies have compared females and males with a sufficient sample size, and
even fewer are based on a developmental perspective. Some

EEG studies demonstrate different patterns of asymmetry
for males and females at risk for depression (Miller et al.,
2002; Tomarken, Dichter, Garber, & Simien, 2004). It
would be fruitful now to follow-up such research on sex
differences in brain imaging studies. Research with children and adolescents is needed to examine the evolution of
possible sex differences in brain structure, function, and
circuitry over time and how they interact with experience,
symptomatology, and self-evaluation. One challenge will
be to develop rigorous and realistic stimulus conditions for
developmental paradigms.

R. J. Nelson (2004) has emphasized the importance of
diminished self-esteem in the development of internalizing
problems and how these may stem from interactions between brain structures devoted to social-cognitive appraisals and those involved in regulating affective
responding. Based on neuroimaging research (e.g., Fossati
et al., 2003) on the substrates that underlie self-referential
thinking, that is, a network of activations in the medial and
dorsolateral prefrontal cortex that relate to thinking about
oneself, Nelson proposes ways that this self-reflective region may be co-activated with regions that organize affective responding in anxious individuals. The combined
network of such neural activity may ultimately result in enduring low self-evaluation. Heller (1993) similarly has proposed that the higher rate of depression in females may be
affected by certain coping strategies such as rumination
that produce certain cognitions to influence the neurophysiological mechanisms underlying mood, in part, by activating certain regions of the brain. Because adolescence is
likely to be a sensitive period for neurobiological organization relevant to self-concept (E. E. Nelson, Leibenluft,
McClure, & Pine, in press), this is an ideal time to examine
neural mechanisms underlying the ruminative and depressogenic cognitions, more common to girls, that are linked
to anxiety and depression.

The Role of Emotions in the Development of Psychopathology

Relatively little research has been devoted to the issue of
the role of emotions in the development of psychopathology. Emotions and psychopathology are sometimes viewed
as redundant constructs, but this is far from true. Sometimes emotions are linked in obvious ways to psychiatric
diagnosis or psychological classification; at other times
they are not. For example, mood disorders may or may not
involve the expression of sadness. Depression may involve
an excess of other negative emotions (e.g., guilt, anxiety,
anger, irritability); it may involve a lack of positive affect

(anhedonia) or a surfeit of positive affect in depressed individuals as they try to please others and mask negative feelings. Given the sex differences in many of these emotions, the study of the evolution of these emotions in their pathological forms and their associations with different kinds of problems will be important for understanding their etiologic significance. The picture becomes even more complex when one considers that (1) there are undoubtedly different subtypes of depression linked to different emotional patterns and ways these subtypes are expressed; (2) similar issues exist with respect to most other kinds of emotional and behavioral problems; and (3) co-occurring emotions will differ in relation to different patterns of comorbidity of psychiatric disorders and psychological problems. In addition to types of emotions, there is the question of the modulation, dysregulation, intensity, and suppression of emotions and how dysfunctional patterns may develop into different forms and manifestations of psychopathology in girls and boys.

Whereas many disorders and problems of childhood and adolescence are no longer present in adulthood, the opposite is not true. It is now widely believed that many or most adult problems originate earlier in life. This is why a developmental perspective is so important in trying to examine prospectively the early processes that come into play to influence later psychopathology (i.e., equifinality). The role of early emotions in the development of psychopathology is underexplored. One approach from a discrete emotions perspective would be to study processes by which particular emotions or combinations of emotions that underlie particular forms of problems become stylized, entrenched, possibly automatic ways of responding over time (Malatesta & Wilson, 1988). What factors contribute to the types of emotions seen more often in girls or boys, and what determines when they reflect too much of a good thing (bearing in mind that all emotions serve adaptive functions)? Another approach is to examine undifferentiated negative affectivity early in development to determine, for example, why the same constellation of negative emotions differentially predicts externalizing problems for boys and internalizing problems for girls (Rothbart, Ahadi, & Hershey, 1994). It may be that total undifferentiated negative affectivity scores are similar, but that boys show a preponderance of anger and hostility and girls show relatively more sadness, anxiety, and guilt.

Emotion dysregulation is a risk factor for child psychopathology beginning early in development (see Keenan, 2000). Given the increasing evidence for the early emergence of some forms of psychopathology, as well as precursor patterns, this would be a valuable future research direction for understanding the etiology of sex differences in psychopathology. We have not discussed the diagnosis of psychiatric disorders in the 1st years of life because this work is more recent in origin and has not yet focused on sex differences (DelCarmen-Wiggins & Carter, 2004). It is to be hoped that this will change as more research is conducted.

Examination of emotions in boys and girls from high- and low-risk environments, in conjunction with assessment of socialization of emotions, is another important next step in this research area. Progress has been made in the development of instruments and observational paradigms to assess socialization of emotion (Chaplin et al., 2005; Eisenberg, Cumberland, & Spinrad, 1998; Klimes-Dougan et al., 2005; O'Neal & Malatesta-Magai, 2001) in ways that capture subtle but potentially powerful processes that help to shape the types of emotions that are acceptable or unacceptable for boys or girls to express. Although most of this research has focused on childhood, recent work indicates its relevance to understanding sex differences in psychopathology in adolescence and for exploring risk by gender interactions (Klimes-Dougan et al., 2005).

Methodological and Analytic Considerations

Many of the normative sex differences reviewed also were prominently present in the sections on psychopathology. Some have argued that if similar differences in problems are seen at both normal and clinical levels, this has no particular bearing on the etiology of sex differences in psychopathology. That is, the sex differences observed at clinical levels are just a reflection of base rate differences; to be etiologically informative, interactions must be demonstrated whereby the differences become exaggerated at clinical levels. Clearly, interactions provide essential information, but even in their absence much can be learned. For example, if girls show 2 to 3 times as many depressive symptoms as boys (or boys show 2 to 3 times as many conduct symptoms) within the normal range, these same ratios at the clinical level reflect a qualitative as well as a quantitative difference as suffering and dysfunction become evident.

Sex differences in base rates of symptoms also have implications for how symptoms are treated in different classification systems. In psychiatric systems, the number of symptoms required to be diagnosed with a disorder is absolute, so that males and females are treated equally in this regard. As we noted earlier, Zoccolillo (1993) recommended that fewer symptoms be required to reach criteria for conduct problems for females than males, given their lower base rates for certain forms of antisocial behavior, such as physical violence. A number of arguments have been made against doing so. In several psychological systems, cutoffs are different for males and females, depending on the base rates of these problems in females and males in the general population. Thus, for example, use of standardized scores from such instruments as the Achenbach Child Behavior Checklist or the Revised Social Anxiety Scale for Children to identify risk groups for study will result in risk groups in which males have higher levels of externalizing problems and lower levels of internalizing problems than females at the onset. These differences in different classification systems raise the question of what it means to equate males and females on problems and how the data should be treated for research purposes.

This is part of a larger issue of what it means to control for sex in statistical analysis, where creating equal conditions through statistical control can end up playing a large role in determining the nature of the generalizations from our data sets. When studying sex differences in psychopathology, it is important to distinguish between methodological and statistical assumptions of equality. Our studies should be designed to compare and, when appropriate, equate males and females. This involves designing studies that (1) include both males and females, (2) include enough males and females to have the statistical power to detect/reject an interaction with gender, and (3) use observational scoring systems that are not gender-specific and that query behaviors seen in both sexes (e.g., physical, verbal, and relational aggression).

Statistically, our analytical strategies should discover the level of analysis at which sex differences emerge. Four distinct levels of sex differences are possible. First, boys and girls could differ in the measurement validity of a construct. For example, the measurement of salivary testosterone is more valid in boys than girls (Shirtcliff, Granger, & Likos, 2002). Second, boys and girls could have different latent factor structures so that constructs are weighted toward different items across the sexes. For example, attention problems may load with externalizing behavior problems in boys, but not girls (Granger et al., 2003). Third, sex differences in levels or prevalence of psychopathology or a risk/protective factor for psychopathology may be evident (Rutter et al., 2003). Fourth, risk and protective pathways for emerging symptoms may differ for girls and boys. This highlights the need for studies to be conceptually, methodologically, and statistically designed to examine sex differences a priori, not just dealt with as post hoc irritants.

The primary focus on one sex or the other in many past investigations has had adverse consequences for under-

standing the role of gender in the development of psychopathology. It will be more difficult in some areas than others to rectify these imbalances, particularly where disparities in prevalence rates are so large, for example, Autism and eating disorders. However, for both externalizing and internalizing problems, the disparities are often not so pronounced. The problem is perhaps more serious for research on externalizing problems, where in many studies girls were excluded from samples altogether. When girls have been included they have constituted a minority of the target groups of interest (e.g., children with ADHD; physically aggressive children), and the results obtained have been relevant primarily for boys. Although the same is sometimes true for internalizing problems, it has been an issue less often because greater efforts have been made to include as many boys in the samples as girls. In efforts to rectify problems of the past, sometimes only girls with externalizing problems are studied. This is at once laudatory and problematic because historical, contextual changes may have occurred in the interim and because only indirect comparisons of male and female samples can be made.

Research by Angold and colleagues (1996) provide an interesting example of the importance of including both males and females in the same research designs. They reported a phenomenon they called "disappearing depression," wherein an all-male sample showed a fall in depressive symptoms between 8 and 11 years of age. This led to the proposal that, in contrast to girls, early puberty for males might be protective, and that differing psychological and social stressors for girls and boys also could play a role. However, in a subsequent study, they found the same fall in symptoms from 8 to 11 years in girls, illustrating both the difficulties posed by making inferences based on one sex and the value of follow-up research with the other sex. In another example, Tomarken and Davidson (1994) found that defensiveness was characterized by relative left frontal brain activation in an all-female sample. In a subsequent study (Kline, Allen, & Schwartz, 1998), this pattern was replicated for females, but males showed an opposite pattern.

In many studies, sex main effects have been considered to the exclusion of the interactions of sex with other salient factors. Although sex differences are interesting and important in their own right, a developmental psychopathology approach also requires exploration of the moderating role of sex. When interactions are considered, that is, to assess whether a given etiologic factor predicts problems exclusively or more strongly for one sex, traditional statistical procedures (e.g., ANOVA, hierarchical linear regression) pose limitations, as main effects are evaluated prior to interaction effects. This and other factors restrict the statistical power for testing interactions hypothesized to be significant for understanding the role of gender in the development of psychopathology. Frequently, this will lead to the appearance of null results that researchers accept as de facto proof of sex similarities and consequently collapse across the sexes in subsequent analyses. This may mask possible small but important effects. Also, although statistical techniques do provide ways to examine nonlinear relations, the majority of hypotheses and models tested are based on assumptions of linearity. Many of the gender-related factors and processes relevant to adaptation and maladaptation have been seen to operate differently depending on level and context; for example, physical aggression may be essential under some circumstances, and empathy has been described as at the center of what it means to be fully human. Both, however, have been linked to different forms of psychopathology when expressed in the extreme, and associations may be nonlinear as a particular attribute becomes increasingly maladaptive.

Analytic problems can contribute to deterministic understanding of biological predispositions, a simplistic understanding of psychosocial forces, and an ignorance of the complex and reciprocal relationship between biological and psychosocial forces. Interactive effects with other complex biopsychosocial moderators are overlooked (e.g., time, timing, context, and critical developmental windows), which does little to clarify the interactional nature of the etiology of sex differences in psychopathology. Researchers need to consider the level at which sex differences are expected and to entertain the possibility, even when sex differences are null, that similarities between the sexes should not be confused with equality between the sexes. Although equifinality may render males and females similar at one developmental stage, they can diverge along different developmental trajectories of risk and resilience (i.e., multifinality).

New approaches are needed to more adequately account for and statistically evaluate those effects that are most salient for advancing knowledge of the moderating role of sex in the development of psychopathology. Ascertainment of the relative strength of sex differences in associations between factors relevant to adjustment difficulties for boys versus girls is central to future research and theory development. Several statistical experts (e.g., Jessor, Van Den Bos, Vanderryn, Costa, & Turbin, 1995; McCall, 1991; McClelland & Judd, 1993) have emphasized the difficulties inherent in detecting moderators in field research and that even interactions that are weak or modest in magnitude are noteworthy. Because existing statistical approaches are not effective for identifying moderator effects, which are important in research on gender, new approaches are needed. That interactions have emerged in the literature on both biological and psychosocial processes, despite these problems, attests to the importance of identifying different processes that may be present but undetectable through present conventional approaches.

It is recommended that data be presented separately for males and females even when interactions are not found, so that trends in individual studies may eventually be represented in meta-analytic reviews. This could be done for main effects as well. Hoffman (1977) provides a compelling example of a largely unnoticed effect until several samples were combined. In studies of newborns' reflexive cries in response to other newborns, girls were more responsive than boys. Reflexive crying is viewed as a primitive precursor of empathy, the quality described as deficient in the extreme male brain. It may reflect a hard-wired response that, consistent with Baron-Cohen's theory, differentiates male and female infants to a certain degree.

Prospective longitudinal approaches, which include equal samples of females and males, are needed to better clarify gender-related differences in etiologies and in trajectories. Growth curve modeling techniques may help to examine male and female trajectories over time as well as what factors track with changes in levels of symptoms. In examining correlates that track with level of symptoms among males and females, for any given disorder where prevalence rates differ, it will be important to test how well other correlates besides those commonly associated with the sex with greater prevalence rates track with problems for the other sex.

Research on gender and psychopathology will be advanced by recognition of the needs (1) for better and more diverse methods and paradigms, (2) for information at all levels of analysis (e.g., genetic, biological, psychosocial, environmental, societal) to better understand the etiology of emotional and behavioral problems of females and males, and (3) to resist premature conclusions about processes being similar *or* different for the two sexes, as both are likely to be true under certain circumstances. This is no longer an era of grand theories but one of necessarily more circumscribed theories that focus on particular structures, functions, and activity within different parts of the brain and body and different ways the organism engages with the external world and is influenced by it. The interactions of these internal and external worlds are sometimes explored, but not frequently, and rarely from a developmental perspective. By starting with samples of males and females equated (as far as possible) on clinical problems and finding later sex differences (e.g., in prevalence, antecedents, comorbidities, and/or developmental trajectories), more stringent tests of (similar and different) mechanisms become possible.

Epidemiological studies with representative samples are important for establishing prevalence rates of problems (Rutter et al., 2003), yet we need also to understand how mechanisms may differ by gender, even in the absence of differences in sex ratio. Work with clinical samples is also needed, despite sample biases that sometimes may be present, for understanding of biases can lead to understanding of processes. Moreover, sample bias can be minimized in research that identifies separate groups of participants with normal, subclinical, or clinical levels of problems, who are not already receiving treatment, to be studied in the same research design. In this way it becomes possible to consider whether etiologic factors operate in similar or different ways, depending on the severity of problems. This is important because many of the generalizations about sex differences and interactions regarding either internalizing or externalizing problems are derived from psychological studies of subclinical levels of problems and have not directly assessed psychiatric symptoms.

Conclusions

Ultimately, the goals of research on gender and psychopathology are to minimize the problems and enhance the well-being of both boys and girls as they make developmental transitions to become independent *and* interdependent members of society. We have not addressed treatment because it is beyond the scope of this review. Because efficacy of interventions is rarely examined in relation to gender (Davies & Lindsay, 2004), relatively little is known about processes that contribute to possible differential effectiveness. We do know that pharmacological interventions may be more or less efficacious across the sexes, and side effects of drugs may interfere with treatment in females more than males (Yonkers & Brawnman-Mintzer, 2002). One can view psychotherapeutic treatments as socialization and learning experiences that allow the person to become more functional. There is some evidence that girls, particularly adolescent girls, are more responsive than boys to a range of psychotherapeutic treatments (Weisz, Weiss, Han, Granger, & Morton, 1995). Intervention research may provide clues about processes about dif-

ferential effectiveness and how treatments might be tailored as a function of gender.

It has been over 30 years since Maccoby and Jacklin (1974) published their seminal book on the psychology of sex differences. They concluded then that boys and girls were more similar than different, with one exception, that being a greater propensity for physical aggression and violence in boys. A multitude of studies have confirmed this difference since then, yet other notable and robust sex differences have been identified and there has been a dramatic expansion of interest and knowledge about these other differences. We have considered the implications of these other differences, as well as of physical aggression, for adaptive and maladaptive functioning of males and females. Thirty years from now there will be similar limitations to the generalizations drawn here, based as they are on information available at the time. Much of the research still focuses on sex differences per se, with less emphasis on within-sex variability. This leads to a focus on prototypic male and female patterns and how exaggerations (and/or combinations with certain risk factors) may reflect problems rather than normative differences. However, failure to conform to "sex-appropriate" behaviors by showing behaviors more common to the opposite sex also can have heightened adverse consequences, as we have seen, for example, for girls with Autism, ADHD, and conduct problems. Similarly, boys who show feminine interests and characteristics are at risk. Thus, the issues are far more complex, as future research will demonstrate. The most interesting questions have yet to be addressed.

Much of the work we considered was not explicitly formulated to examine biosocial interactions (Moffitt, Caspi, & Rutter, 2005), or even bio-bio or social-social interactions with respect to gender. Yet both the animal and human literature point to the fact that genetic and biological contributions to adaptation and psychopathology are often strongly dependent on environmental processes; moreover, environments alter biological structures and functions. As Wallen (1996, p. 364) puts it, "Nature needs nurture" in order to understand behavioral sex differences. Environmental and socialization processes are especially difficult to measure in large-scale prediction studies and hence may not fare well in making their roles known. Because mental health problems are often the result of a stress-diathesis process that includes both biological and environmental factors, equivalently valid and reliable assessment is necessary to understand the different directions of movement toward psychopathology of males and females. Moffitt et al. indicate that a major task for future research will be to develop more adequate environmental measures to test crucial gene-environment interactions, especially given the advances in genotyping, brain imaging, and other biologically based measures. Continued pursuit of questions about the etiology of similarities and differences in males and females from a developmental psychopathology perspective can help to advance our understanding of their mental health problems and to alleviate their suffering.

ACKNOWLEDGMENTS

The authors wish to thank Jong-hyo Park, PhD, for her meticulous literature review for several sections of this chapter and her diligent editorial work. The senior author would also like to thank the National Institute of Mental Health Intramural Research Program for support in the preparation of this chapter.

REFERENCES

Abramson, L. Y., Bardone-Cone, A. M., Vohs, K. D., Joiner, T. E., Jr., & Heatherton, T. F. (2005). The paradox of perfectionism and bulimia: Toward a resolution. In L. B. Alloy & J. H. Riskind (Eds.), *Cognitive vulnerability to bulimia* (pp. 329–364). Hillsdale, NJ: Erlbaum.

Achenbach, T. M. (1991a). *Manual for the Child Behavior Checklist/4–18 and 1991 profile.* Burlington: University of Vermont, Department of Psychiatry.

Achenbach, T. M. (1991b). *Manual for the Youth Self-Report and 1991 profile.* Burlington: University of Vermont, Department of Psychiatry.

Agras, W. S. (2001). The consequences and costs of the eating disorders. *Psychiatric Clinics of North America, 24,* 371–379.

Aguilar, B., Sroufe, L. A., Egeland, B., & Carlson, E. (2000). Distinguishing the early-onset/persistent and adolescence-onset antisocial behavior types: From birth to 16 years. *Development and Psychopathology, 12,* 109–132.

Alaghband-Rad, J., Hamburger, S. D., Giedd, J. N., Frazier, J. A., & Rapoport, J. L. (1997). Childhood-onset Schizophrenia: Biological markers in relation to clinical characteristics. *American Journal of Psychiatry, 154,* 64–68.

Albano, A. M., & Krain, A. (2005). Anxiety disorders in girls. In D. J. Bells, S. L. Foster, & E. J. Mash (Eds.), *Behavioral and emotional problems in girls* (pp. 79–116). New York: Kluwer Academic/Plenum.

Alessandri, S. M., & Lewis, M. (1993). Parental evaluation and its relation to shame and pride in young children. *Sex Roles, 29,* 335–343.

Alexander, G. M., & Peterson, B. S. (2004). Testing the prenatal hormone hypothesis of tic-related disorders: Gender identity and gender role behavior. *Development and Psychopathology, 16,* 407–420.

Alfieri, T., Ruble, D. N., & Higgins, E. T. (1996). Gender stereotypes during adolescence: Developmental changes and the transition to junior high school. *Developmental Psychology, 32,* 1129–1137.

Allgood-Merten, B., Lewinsohn, P. M., & Hops, H. (1990). Sex differences and adolescent depression. *Journal of Abnormal Psychology, 99,* 55–63.

American Psychiatric Association. (2000). *Diagnostic and statistical manual of mental disorders* (4th ed., text rev.). Washington, DC: Author.

Anderson, J. C., Williams, S., McGee, R., & Silva, P. A. (1987). DSM-III disorders in preadolescent children: Prevalence in a large sample from the general population. *Archives of General Psychiatry, 44,* 69–76.

Andrews, J. A. (2005). Substance abuse in girls. In D. J. Bell, S. L. Foster, & E. J. Mash (Eds.), *Behavioral and emotional problems in girls* (pp. 181–209). New York: Kluwer Academic/Plenum.

Andrews, J. A., & Tildesley, E. A. (2003, April). *Intentions and use of alcohol, tobacco, marijuana, and inhalants among 1st through 8th graders.* Paper presented at the biennial meeting of the Society for Research in Child Development, Tampa, FL.

Andrews, J. A., Tildesley, E. A., Duncan, S., Hops, H., & Severson, H. H. (in press). Elementary children's behaviors and attitudes regarding substance use. *Journal of Clinical Child Psychology.*

Angold, A., Costello, E. J., Erkanli, A., & Worthman, C. (1999). Pubertal changes in hormone levels and depression in girls. *Psychological Medicine, 29,* 1043–1053.

Angold, A., Costello, E. J., & Worthman, C. M. (1998). Puberty and depression: The roles of age, pubertal status and pubertal timing. *Psychological Medicine, 28,* 51–61.

Angold, A., Erkanli, A., Loeber, R., Costello, E. J., Van Kammen, W., & Stouthamer-Loeber, M. (1996). Disappearing depression in a population sample of boys. *Journal of Emotional and Behavioral Disorders, 4,* 95–104.

Angold, A., & Rutter, M. (1992). Effects of age and pubertal status on depression in a large clinical sample. *Development and Psychopathology, 4,* 5–28.

Anthony, M., & Berg, M. J. (2002a). Biologic and molecular mechanisms for sex differences in pharmacokinetics, pharmacodynamics, and pharmacogenetics: Part I. *Journal of Women's Health and Gender-Based Medicine, 11,* 601–615.

Anthony, M., & Berg, M. J. (2002b). Biologic and molecular mechanisms for sex differences in pharmacokinetics, pharmacodynamics, and pharmacogenetics: Part II. *Journal of Women's Health and Gender-Based Medicine, 11,* 617–629.

Arnold, A. P., Rissman, E. F., & De Vries, G. J. (2003). Two perspectives on the origin of sex differences in the brain. *Annals of the New York Academy of Sciences, 1007,* 176–188.

Aseltine, R. H. (1996). Pathways linking parental divorce with adolescent depression. *Journal of Health and Social Behavior, 37,* 133–148.

Aseltine, R. H., Gore, S., & Colten, M. E. (1994). Depression and the social developmental context of adolescence. *Journal of Personality and Social Psychology, 67,* 252–263.

Attie, I., & Brooks-Gunn, J. (1989). Development of eating problems in adolescent girls: A longitudinal study. *Developmental Psychology, 25,* 70–79.

Aube, J., Fichman, L., Saltaris, C., & Koestner, R. (2000). Gender differences in adolescent depressive symptomatology: Towards an integrated social-developmental model. *Journal of Social and Clinical Psychology, 19,* 297–313.

Avison, W. R., & McAlpine, D. D. (1992). Gender differences in symptoms of depression among adolescents. *Journal of Health and Social Behavior, 33,* 77–96.

Bagdy, G. (1998). Serotonin, anxiety, and stress hormones: Focus on 5-HT receptor subtypes, species and gender differences. *Annals of the New York Academy of Sciences, 851,* 357–363.

Bailey, A., Le Couteur, A., Gottesman, I., Bolton, P., Simonoff, E., Yuzda, E., et al. (1995). Autism as a strongly genetic disorder: Evidence from a British twin study. *Psychological Medicine, 25,* 63–77.

Bailey, A., Phillips, W., & Rutter, M. (1996). Autism: Towards an integration of clinical, genetic, neuropsychological, and neurobiological perspectives. *Journal of Child Psychology and Psychiatry, 37,* 89–126.

Barkley, R. A. (1998). *Attention deficit hyperactivity disorder: A handbook for diagnosis and treatment* (2nd ed.). New York: Guilford Press.

Barkley, R. A., & Biederman, J. (1997). Toward a broader definition of the age-of-onset criterion for attention-deficit-hyperactivity disorder. *Journal of the American Academy of Child and Adolescent Psychiatry, 36,* 1204–1210.

Baron-Cohen, S. (2002). The extreme male brain theory of Autism. *Trends in Cognitive Sciences, 6,* 248–254.

Baron-Cohen, S., Richler, J., Bisarya, D., Gurunathan, N., & Wheelwright, S. (2003). The systemizing quotient: An investigation of adults with Asperger syndrome or high-functioning Autism, and normal sex differences. *Philosophical Transactions of the Royal Society of London. Series B, Biological Sciences, 358,* 361–374.

Baron-Cohen, S., & Wheelwright, S. (2004). The empathy quotient: An investigation of adults with Asperger syndrome or high functioning Autism, and normal sex differences. *Journal of Autism and Developmental Disorders, 34,* 163–175.

Barrera, M., & Garrison-Jones, C. (1992). Family and peer social support as specific correlates of adolescent depressive symptoms. *Journal of Abnormal Child Psychology, 20,* 1–16.

Bartels, A., & Zeki, S. (2000). The neural basis of romantic love. *NeuroReport, 11,* 3829–3834.

Bartels, A., & Zeki, S. (2004). The neural correlates of maternal and romantic love. *Neuroimage, 21,* 1155–1166.

Beardslee, W. R., Versage, E., & Gladstone, T. (1998). Children of affectively ill parents: A review of the past ten years. *Journal of the American Academy of Child and Adolescent Psychiatry, 37,* 1134–1141.

Bell, D. J., Foster, S. L., & Mash, E. J. (2005). *Behavioral and emotional problems in girls.* New York: Kluwer Academic/Plenum, Clinical Child Psychology Series.

Bem, S. L. (1978). *Bem Sex Role Inventory manual.* Palo Alto, CA: Mind Garden.

Berg, C. Z., Rapoport, J. L., Whitaker, A., Davies, M., Leonard, H., Swedo, S. E., et al. (1989). Childhood obsessive compulsive disorder: A two-year prospective follow-up of a community sample. *Journal of the American Academy of Child and Adolescent Psychiatry, 28,* 528–533.

Berger-Sweeney, J. (2003). The cholinergic basal forebrain system during development and its influence on cognitive processes: Important questions and potential answers. *Neuroscience and Biobehavioral Reviews, 27,* 401–411.

Bergink, V., van Megen, H. J., & Westenberg, H. G. (2004). Glutamate and anxiety. *European Neuropsychopharmacology, 14,* 175–183.

Biederman, J., Mick, E., Faraone, S. V., Braaten, E., Doyle, A., Spencer, T., et al. (2002). Influence of gender on attention deficit hyperactivity disorder in children referred to a psychiatric clinic. *American Journal of Psychiatry, 159,* 36–42.

Biederman, J., Milberger, S., Faraone, S. V., Kiely, K., Guite, J., Mick, E., et al. (1995). Family-environment risk factors for attention deficit hyperactivity disorder: A test of Rutter's indicators of adversity. *Archives of General Psychiatry, 52,* 464–470.

Bierut, L. J., Heath, A. C., Bucholz, K. K., Dinwiddie, S. H., Statham, D. J., Dunne, M. P., et al. (1999). Major depressive disorder in a community-based twin sample: Are there different genetic and environmental contributions for men and women? *Archives of General Psychiatry, 56,* 557–563.

Birmaher, B., Ryan, N. D., Williamson, D. E., Brent, D. A., Kaufman, J., Dahl, R. E., et al. (1996). Childhood and adolescent depression: A review of the past 10 years, part I. *Journal of the American Academy of Child and Adolescent Psychiatry, 35,* 1427–1439.

Bishop, K. M., & Wahlsten, D. (1997). Sex differences in the human corpus callosum: Myth or reality? *Neuroscience and Biobehavioral Reviews, 21,* 581–601.

Biver, F., Lotstra, F., Monclus, M., Wikler, D., Damhaut, P., Mendlewicz, J., et al. (1996). Sex difference in 5HT2 receptor in the living human brain. *Neuroscience Letters, 204,* 25–28.

Bjorklund, D. F., & Kipp, K. (1996). Parental investment theory and gender differences in the evolution of inhibition mechanisms. *Psychological Bulletin, 120,* 163–188.

Bleiberg, E. (2001). *Treating personality disorders in children and adolescents: A relational approach.* New York: Guilford Press.

Block, J. H., & Gjerde, P. F. (1990). Depressive symptoms in late adolescence: A longitudinal perspective on personality antecedents. In J. E. Rolf, A. S. Masten, D. Cicchetti, K. H. Nuechterlein, & S. Weintraub (Eds.), *Risk and protective factors in the development of psychopathology* (pp. 334–360). New York: Cambridge University Press.

Block, J. H., Gjerde, P. F., & Block, J. H. (1991). Personality antecedents of depressive tendencies in 18-year-olds: A prospective study. *Journal of Personality and Social Psychology, 60,* 726–738.

Block, J. H., & Robins, R. W. (1993). A longitudinal study of consistency and change in self-esteem from early adolescence to early adulthood. *Child Development, 64,* 901–923.

Booth, A., Johnson, D. R., & Granger, D. A. (1999). Testosterone and men's depression: The role of social behavior. *Journal of Health and Social Behavior, 40,* 130–140.

Bower, G. (1981). Mood and memory. *American Psychologist, 36,* 129–148.

Boyle, M. H., & Pickles, A. (1997). Maternal depressive symptoms and ratings of emotional disorder symptoms in children and adolescents. *Journal of Child Psychology and Psychiatry, 38,* 981–992.

Bradley, S. J., Oliver, G. D., Chernick, A. B., & Zucker, K. J. (1998). Experiment of nurture: Ablatio penis at 2 months, sex reassignment at 7 months, and a psychosexual follow-up in young adulthood. *Pediatrics, 102,* 9.

Breslau, N., Davis, G. C., Andreski, P., & Peterson, E. (1991). Traumatic events and posttraumatic stress disorder in an urban population of young adults. *Archives of General Psychiatry, 48,* 216–222.

Breslau, N., Schultz, L., & Peterson, E. (1995). Sex differences in depression: A role for preexisting anxiety. *Psychiatry Research, 58,* 1–12.

Brody, L. R. (1985). Gender differences in emotional development: A review of theories and research. *Journal of Personality, 53,* 102–149.

Brody, L. R., & Hall, J. A. (1993). Gender and emotion. In M. Lewis & J. Haviland (Eds.), *Handbook of emotions* (pp. 447–460). New York: Guilford Press.

Brooks-Gunn, J., & Warren, M. P. (1989). Biological and social contributions to negative affect in young adolescent girls. *Child Development, 60,* 40–55.

Bryant, A. (1993). Hostile hallways: The AAUW survey on sexual harassment in America's schools. *Journal of School Health, 63,* 355–357.

Bulik, C., Devlin, B., Bacanu, S., Thornton, L., Klump, K., Fichter, M., et al. (2003). Significant linkage on chromosome 10p in families with bulimia nervosa. *American Journal of Human Genetics, 72,* 200–207.

Bulik, C., Sullivan, P., Wade, T., & Kendler, K. (2000). Twin studies of eating disorders: A review. *International Journal of Eating Disorders, 27,* 1–20.

Burgner, D., & Hewstone, M. (1993). Young children's causal attributions for success and failure: "Self-enhancing" boys and "self-derogating" girls. *British Journal of Developmental Psychology, 11,* 125–129.

Bybee, J. (1998). The emergence of gender differences in guilt during adolescence. In J. Bybee (Ed.), *Guilt and children* (pp. 113–125). San Diego: Academic Press.

Cairns, R. B., Cairns, B. D., Neckerman, H. J., Ferguson, L. I., & Gariepy, J. L. (1989). Growth and aggression: 1. Childhood to early adolescence. *Developmental Psychology, 25,* 320–330.

Cairns, R. B., Elder, G. H., & Costello, E. J. (1996). *Developmental science.* New York: Cambridge University Press.

Cale, E. M., & Lilienfeld, S. O. (2002). Sex differences in psychopathy and antisocial personality disorder: A review and integration. *Clinical Psychology Review, 22,* 1179–1207.

Cannon, T. D., Kaprio, J., Lonnqvist, J., Huttunen, M., & Koskenvuo, M. (1998). The genetic epidemiology of Schizophrenia in a Finnish twin cohort: A population-based modeling study. *Archives of General Psychiatry, 55,* 67–74.

Carey, M. P., Dusek, J. B., & Spector, I. P. (1988). Sex roles, gender, and fears: A brief report. *Phobia Practice and Research Journal, 1,* 114–120.

Carlson, C. L., Tamm, L., & Gaub, M. (1997). Gender differences in children with ADHD, ODD and co-occurring ADHD/ODD identified in a school population. *Journal of the American Academy of Child and Adolescent Psychiatry, 36,* 1706–1714.

Carter, A. S., Briggs-Gowan, M. J., Jones, S. M., & Little, T. D. (2003). The Infant-Toddler Social and Emotional Assessment (ITSEA): Factor structure, reliability, and validity. *Journal of Abnormal Child Psychology, 31,* 495–514.

Carter, J. D., Joyce, P. R., Mulder, R. T., Sullivan, P. F., & Luty, S. E. (1999). Gender differences in the frequency of personality disorders in depressed outpatients. *Journal of Personality Disorders, 13,* 67–74.

Caspi, A. (2000). The child is the father of the man: Personality continuities from childhood to adulthood. *Journal of Personality and Social Psychology, 78,* 158–172.

Caspi, A., Lynam, D., Moffitt, T. E., & Silva, P. A. (1993). Unraveling girls' delinquency: Biological, dispositional, and contextual contributions to adolescent misbehavior. *Developmental Psychology, 29,* 19–30.

Caspi, A., Moffitt, T., Newman, D., & Silva, P. (1996). Behavioral observations at age 3 predict adult psychiatric disorders. *Archives of General Psychiatry, 53,* 1033–1039.

Castellanos, F. X., Giedd, J. N., Berquin, P. C., Walter, J. N., Sharp, W., Tran, T., et al. (2001). Quantitative brain magnetic resonance imaging in girls with attention-deficit/hyperactivity disorder. *Archives of General Psychiatry, 58,* 289–295.

Castellanos, F. X., Lee, P. P., Sharp, W., Jeffries, N. O., Greenstein, D. K., Clasen, L. S., et al. (2002). Developmental trajectories of brain volume abnormalities in children and adolescents with attention-deficit/hyperactivity disorder. *Journal of the American Medical Association, 288,* 1740–1748.

Cervantes, C. A., & Callanan, M. A. (1998). Labels and explanations in mother-child emotion talk: Age and gender differentiation. *Developmental Psychology, 34,* 88–98.

Chambers, R. A., Bremmer, J., Moghaddam, B., Southwick, S. M., Charney, D. S., & Krystal, J. H. (1999). Glutamate and post-traumatic stress disorder: Toward a psychobiology of dissociation. *Seminar on Clinical Neuropsychiatry, 4*(4), 274–281.

Chaplin, T. M., Cole, P. M., & Zahn-Waxler, C. (2005). Parental socialization of emotion expression: Gender differences and relations to child adjustment. *Emotion, 5,* 80–88.

Chassin, L., Curran, C., Hussong, A., & Colder, C. (1996). The relation of parent alcoholism to adolescent substance use: A longitudinal follow-up study. *Journal of Abnormal Psychology, 105,* 70–80.

Chassin, L., Pillow, D., Curran, P., Molina, B., & Barrera, M. (1993). The relation of parental alcoholism to adolescent substance use: A test of three mediating mechanisms. *Journal of Abnormal Psychology, 102,* 3–19.

Chassin, L., Pitts, S., & DeLucia, C. (1999). A longitudinal study of children of alcoholics: Predicting young adult substance use disorders, anxiety, and depression. *Journal of Abnormal Psychology, 108,* 106–119.

Chassin, L., & Ritter, J. (2001). Vulnerability to substance use disorders in childhood and adolescence. In R. E. Ingram & J. M. Price (Eds.), *Vulnerability to psychopathology: Risks across the lifespan* (pp. 107–134). New York: Guilford Press.

Cicchetti, D., & Walker, E. F. (2001). Stress and development: Biological and psychological consequences. *Development and Psychopathology, 13,* 413–418.

Clarke, A. R., Barry, R. J., McCarthy, R., & Selikowitz, M. (2001). Age and sex effect in the EEG: Difference in the two subtypes of attention-deficit/hyperactivity disorder. *Clinical Neurophysiology, 112,* 815–826.

Cloninger, C. R. (1987). Neurogenetic adaptive mechanisms in alcoholism. *Science, 236,* 410–416.

Cloninger, C. R., & Guze, S. B. (1970). Female criminals: Their personal, familial, and social backgrounds. *Archives of General Psychiatry, 23,* 554–558.

Cohen, P., Cohen, J., Kasen, S., Velez, C. N., Hartmark, C., Johnson, J., et al. (1993). An epidemiological study of disorders in late childhood and adolescence: I. Age- and gender-specific prevalence. *Journal of Child Psychology and Psychiatry, 34,* 851–867.

Cohen, R. Y., Brownell, K. D., & Felix, M. R. J. (1990). Age and sex differences in health habits and beliefs of school children. *Health Psychology, 9,* 208–224.

Coie, J. D., & Dodge, K. A. (1998). The development of aggression and antisocial behavior. In W. Damon (Series Ed.) & N. Eisenberg (Vol. Ed.), *Handbook of child psychology: Vol. 3. Social, emotional, and personality development* (5th ed., pp. 779–861). New York: Wiley.

Colapinto, J. (2000). *As nature made him: The boy who was raised as a girl.* New York: HarperCollins.

Cole, D. A., Peeke, L. G., Martin, J. M., Truglio, R., & Seroczynski, A. D. (1998). A longitudinal look at the relation between depression and anxiety in children and adolescents. *Journal of Consulting and Clinical Psychology, 66,* 451–460.

Cole, P. M. (1986). Children's spontaneous control of facial expression. *Child Development, 57,* 1309–1321.

Cole, P. M., Teti, L. O., & Zahn-Waxler, C. (2003). Mutual emotion regulation and the stability of conduct problems between preschool and early school age. *Development and Psychopathology, 15,* 1–18.

Collaer, M. L., & Hines, M. (1995). Human behavioral sex differences: A role for gonadal hormones during early development? *Psychological Bulletin, 118,* 55–107.

Collins, R. L., & Shirley, M. C. (2001). Vulnerability to substance use disorders in adulthood. In R. Ingram & J. M. Price (Eds.), *Vulnerability to psychopathology: Risk across the lifespan* (pp. 135–164). New York: Guilford Press.

Conduct Problems Prevention Research Group. (1999). Initial impact of the Fast Track prevention trial for conduct problems: I. The high-risk sample. *Journal of Consulting and Clinical Psychology, 67,* 631–647.

Conduct Problems Prevention Research Group. (2002). Evaluation of the first 3 years of the Fast Track prevention trial with children at high risk for adolescent conduct problems. *Journal of Abnormal Child Psychology, 30,* 19–35.

Conger, R. D., Conger, K. J., Elder, G. H., Lorenz, F. O., Simons, R. L., & Whitbeck, L. B. (1993). Family economic stress and adjustment of early adolescent girls. *Developmental Psychology, 29,* 206–219.

Cooper, M. L., Frone, M. R., Russell, M., & Mudar, P. (1995). Drinking to regulate positive and negative emotions: A motivational model of alcohol use. *Journal of Personality and Social Psychology, 69,* 990–1005.

Côté, S., Tremblay, R. E., Nagin, D. S., Zoccolillo, M., & Vitaro, F. (2002). Childhood behavioral profiles leading to adolescent conduct disorder: Risk trajectories for boys and girls. *Journal of the American Academy of Child and Adolescent Psychiatry, 41,* 1086–1094.

Cowan, P. A., Cowan, C. P., & Kerig, P. K. (1993). Mothers, fathers, sons, and daughters: Gender differences in family formation and parenting style. In P. A. Cowan & D. Field (Eds.), *Family, self, and society: Toward a new agenda for family research* (pp. 165–195). Hillsdale, NJ: Erlbaum.

Crabbe, J. C. (2002). Genetic contributions to addiction. *Annual Review of Psychology, 53,* 435–462.

Crawford, T. N., Cohen, P., Midlarsky, E., & Brook, J. S. (2001). Internalizing symptoms in adolescents: Gender differences in vulnerability to parental distress and discord. *Journal of Research on Adolescence, 11,* 95–118.

Crick, N. R. (1996). The role of relational aggression, overt aggression, and prosocial behavior in the prediction of children's future social adjustment. *Child Development, 67,* 2317–2327.

Crick, N. R. (1997). Relational and overt aggression in preschool. *Developmental Psychology, 33,* 579–588.

Crick, N. R. (2003). A gender-balanced approach to the study of childhood aggression and reciprocal family influences. In A. C. Crouter & A. Booth (Eds.), *Children's influence on family dynamics: The neglected side of family relationships* (pp. 229–235). Mahwah, NJ: Erlbaum.

Crick, N. R., & Bigbee, M. A. (1998). Relational and overt forms of peer victimization: A multi-informant approach. *Journal of Consulting and Clinical Psychology, 66,* 337–347.

Crick, N. R., & Dodge, K. A. (1994). A review and reformulation of social information-processing mechanisms in children's social adjustment. *Psychological Bulletin, 115,* 74–101.

Crick, N. R., & Grotpeter, J. K. (1995). Relational aggression, gender, and social-psychological adjustment. *Child Development, 66,* 710–722.

Crick, N. R., & Ladd, G. W. (1993). Children's perceptions of their peer experiences: Attributions, loneliness, social anxiety, and social avoidance. *Developmental Psychology, 29,* 244–254.

Crick, N. R., Murray-Close, D., & Woods, K. (in press). Borderline personality features in childhood: A short-term longitudinal study. *Development and Psychopathology.*

Crick, N. R., & Zahn-Waxler, C. (2003). The development of psychopathology in females and males: Current progress and future challenges. *Development and Psychopathology, 15,* 719–742.

Cross, S. E., & Madson, L. (1997). Models of the self: Self construals and gender. *Psychological Bulletin, 122,* 5–37.

Crowe, R. R., Noyes, R., & Persico, A. M. (1987). Pro-opiomelanocortin (POMC) gene excluded as a cause of panic disorder in a large family. *Journal of Affective Disorders, 12,* 23–27.

Cummings, E. M., DeArth-Pendley, G., Du Rocher Schudlich, T., & Smith, D. A. (2001). Parental Depression and family functioning: Toward a process-oriented model of children's adjustment. In S. R. H. Beach (Ed.), *Marital and famly process in depression: A scientific foundation for clinical practice* (pp. 89–110). Washington, DC: American Psychological Association.

Cummings, E. M., Hollenbeck, B., Iannotti, R. J., Radke-Yarrow, M., & Zahn-Waxler, C. (1986). Early organization of altruism and aggression: Developmental patterns and individual differences. In C. Zahn-Waxler, E. M. Cummings, & R. J. Iannotti (Eds.), *Altruism and aggression: Biological and social origins* (pp. 165–188). New York: Cambridge University Press.

Cummings, E. M., Zahn-Waxler, C., & Radke-Yarrow, M. (1981). Young children's responses to expressions of anger and affection by others in the family. *Child Development, 52,* 1274–1282.

Cyranowski, J. M., Frank, E., Young, E., & Shear, M. K. (2000). Adolescent onset of the gender difference in lifetime rates of major depression. *Archives of General Psychiatry, 57,* 21–27.

Dadds, M. R., Atkinson, E., Turner, C., Blums, G. J., & Lendich, B. (1999). Family conflict and child adjustment: Evidence for a cognitive-contextual model of intergenerational transmission. *Journal of Family Psychology, 13,* 194–208.

Dahl, R. E. (2004). Adolescent brain development: A period of vulnerabilities and opportunities [Keynote address]. *Annals of the New York Academy of Science, 1021,* 1–22.

Damasio, A. R., Tranel, D., & Damasio, H. (1991). Somatic markers and the guidance of behavior: Theory and preliminary testing. In H. S. Levin, H. M. Eisenberg, & A. L. Benton (Eds.), *Frontal lobe function and dysfunction* (pp. 217–229). New York: Oxford University Press.

David, C. F., & Kistner, J. A. (2000). Do positive self-perceptions have a "dark side"? Examination of the link between perceptual bias and aggression. *Journal of Abnormal Child Psychology, 28,* 327–337.

Davies, P. T., & Lindsay, L. L. (2004). Interparental conflict and adolescent adjustment: Why does gender moderate early adolescent vulnerability? *Journal of Family Psychology, 18,* 160–170.

Davies, P. T., & Windle, M. (1997). Gender-specific pathways between maternal depressive symptoms, family discord, and adolescent adjustment. *Developmental Psychology, 33,* 657–668.

Davis, B., Sheeber, L., Hops, H., & Tildesley, E. (2000). Adolescent responses to depressive parental behaviors in problem-solving interactions: Implications for depressive symptoms. *Journal of Abnormal Child Psychology, 5,* 451–465.

Davis, M., Campeau, S., Kim, M., & Falls, W. A. (1995). Neural systems of emotion: The amygdala's role in fear and anxiety. In J. L. McGaugh & N. M. Weinberger (Eds.), *Brain and memory: Modulation and mediation of neuroplasticity* (pp. 3–40). London: Oxford University Press.

DelCarmen-Wiggins, R., & Carter, A. (2004). *Handbook of infant, toddler, and preschool mental health assessment.* New York: Oxford University Press.

Denham, S. A., McKinley, M., Couchard, E. A., & Holt, R. (1990). Emotional and behavioral predictors of preschool peer ratings. *Child Development, 61,* 1145–1152.

Denham, S. A., Workman, E., Cole, P. M., Weissbrod, C., Kendziora, K. T., & Zahn-Waxler, C. (2000). Prediction of externalizing behavior problems from early to middle childhood: The role of parental socialization and emotion expression. *Development and Psychopathology, 12,* 23–45.

Derryberry, D., & Reed, M. A. (1994). Temperament and the self-organization of personality. *Development and Psychopathology, 6,* 653–676.

Devlin, B., Bacnau, S., Klump, K., Bulik, C., Fichter, M., Halmi, K., et al. (2002). Linkage analysis of anorexia nervosa incorporating behavioral covariates. *Human Molecular Genetics, 11,* 689–696.

De Vries, G. J., Rissman, E. F., Simerly, R. B., Yang, L. Y., Scordalakes, E. M., Auger, C. J., et al. (2002). A model system for study of sex chromosome effects on sexually dimorphic neural and behavioral traits. *Journal of Neuroscience, 22,* 9005–9014.

Deykin, E. Y., Buka, S. L., & Zeena, Z. H. (1992). Depressive illness among chemically dependent adolescents. *American Journal of Psychiatry, 149,* 1341–1347.

Diamond, A. (1990). Rate of maturation of the hippocampus and the developmental progression of children's performance on the delayed non-matching to sample and visual paired comparison tasks. *Annals of the New York Academy of Sciences, 608,* 394–433.

Diamond, M., & Sigmundson, H. K. (1997). Sex reassignment at birth: Long-term review and clinical implications. *Archives of Pediatrics and Adolescent Medicine, 151,* 298–304.

Diamond, M., & Yates, A. (2004). *Sex and gender* (Vol. 13). Philadelphia: Saunders.

Diehl, D. J., & Gershon, S. (1992). The role of dopamine in mood disorders. *Comprehensive Psychiatry, 33,* 115–120.

Dienstbier, R. A. (1984). The role of emotion in moral socialization. In C. Izard, J. Kagan, & R. Zajonc (Eds.), *Emotions, cognition and behavior* (pp. 484–514). New York: Cambridge University Press.

Dillon, K. M., Wolf, E., & Katz, H. (1985). Sex roles, gender, and fear. *Journal of Psychology, 119,* 355–359.

Di Paolo, T. (1994). Modulation of brain dopamine transmission by sex steroids. *Reviews in the Neurosciences, 5,* 27–41.

Disney, E. R., Elkins, I. J., McGue, M., & Iacono, W. G. (1999). Effects of ADHD, conduct disorder, and gender on substance use and abuse in adolescence. *American Journal of Psychiatry, 156,* 1515–1521.

Disteche, C. M. (1995). Escape from X inactivation in human and mouse. *Trends in Genetics, 11,* 17–22.

Downey, G., & Coyne, J. C. (1990). Children of depressed parents: An integrative review. *Psychological Bulletin, 108,* 50–76.

Duggal, S., Carlson, E. A., Sroufe, L. A., & Egeland, B. (2001). Depressive symptomatology in childhood and adolescence. *Development and Psychopathology, 13,* 143–164.

Earls, F. (1994). Oppositional-defiant and conduct disorders. In M. Rutter, E. Taylor, & L. Hersov (Eds.), *Child and adolescent psychiatry* (3rd ed., pp. 308–329). Oxford: Blackwell Scientific Publications.

Eisenberg, N., Cumberland, A., & Spinrad, T. L. (1998). Parental socialization of emotion. *Psychological Inquiry, 9,* 241–273.

Eisenberg, N., & Fabes, R. A. (1998). Prosocial development. In W. Damon (Series Ed.) & N. Eisenberg (Vol. Ed.), *Handbook of child psychology* (5th ed., Vol. 3, pp. 701–778). New York: Wiley.

Ellis, B. J., & Garber, J. (2000). Psychosocial antecedents of variations in girls' pubertal timing: Maternal depression, stepfather presence, and marital and family stress. *Child Development, 71,* 485–501.

Else-Quest, N., Hyde, J., & Goldsmith, H. H. (in press). Gender differences in temperament: A meta-analysis. *Psychological Bulletin.*

Eme, R. F. (1992). Selective female affliction in the developmental disorders of childhood: A literature review. *Journal of Clinical Child Psychology, 21,* 354–364.

Eron, L. D. (1992). Gender differences in violence: Biology and/or socialization. In K. Bjorkqvist & P. Niemela (Eds.), *Of mice and women: Aspects of female aggression* (pp. 89–97). San Diego: Academic Press.

Essex, M. J., Klein, M. H., Cho, E., & Kalin, N. H. (2002). Maternal stress beginning in infancy may sensitize children to later stress exposure: Effects on cortisol and behavior. *Biological Psychiatry, 52,* 776–784.

Essex, M. J., Klein, M. H., Cho, E., & Kraemer, H. C. (2003). Exposure to maternal depression and marital conflict: Gender differences in children's later mental health symptoms. *Journal of the American Academy of Child and Adolescent Psychiatry, 42,* 728–737.

Essex, M. J., Kraemer, H. C., Armstrong, J. M., Boyce, W. T., Goldsmith, H. H., Klein, M. H., et al. (2005). *Exploring risk factors for the emergence of children's mental health problems.* Unpublished manuscript. Available from mjessex@wisc.edu.

Fagot, B. I. (1978). The influence of sex of child on parental reactions to toddler children. *Child Development, 49,* 459–465.

Feigon, S. A., Waldman, I. D., Levy, F., & Hay, A. D. (2001). Genetic and environmental influences on separation anxiety disorder symptoms and their moderation by age and sex. *Behavior Genetics, 31,* 403–411.

Fergusson, D. M., Horwood, L. J., & Lynsky, M. T. (1995). Maternal depressive symptoms and depressive symptoms in adolescents. *Journal of Child Psychology and Psychiatry and Allied Disciplines, 36,* 1161–1178.

Fergusson, D., Lynskey, M., & Horwood, L. (1996). Comorbidity between depressive disorders and nicotine dependence in a cohort of 16 year olds. *Archives of General Psychiatry, 53,* 1043–1047.

Field, A., Camargo, C., Taylor, C., Berkey, C., Robert, S., & Colditz, G. (2001). Peer, parent, and media influences on the development of weight concerns and frequent dieting among preadolescent girls and boys. *Pediatrics, 107,* 54–60.

Field, T., Diego, M., & Sanders, C. (2001). Adolescent depression and risk factors. *Adolescence, 36,* 491–498.

Fink, G., & Sumner, B. E. (1996). Oestrogen and mental state. *Nature, 383,* 306.

Fink, G., Sumner, B. E., McQueen, J. K., Wilson, H., & Rosie, R. (1998). Sex steroid control of mood, mental state and memory. *Clinical and Experimental Pharmacology and Physiology, 25,* 764–775.

Finkelstein, J. W., Susman, E. J., Chinchilli, V. M., D'Arcangelo, M. R., Kunselman, S. J., Schwab, J., et al. (1998). Effects of estrogen or testosterone on self-reported sexual responses and behaviors in hypogonadal adolescents. *Journal of Clinical Endocrinology and Metabolism, 83,* 2281–2285.

Finkelstein, J. W., Susman, E. J., Chinchilli, V. M., Kunselman, S. J., D'Arcangelo, M. R., Schwab, J., et al. (1997). Estrogen or testosterone increases self-reported aggressive behaviors in hypogonadal adolescents. *Journal of Clinical Endocrinology and Metabolism, 82,* 2433–2438.

Fishbein, D. H., Dax, E. M., Lozovsky, D. B., & Jaffe, J. H. (1992). Neuroendocrine responses to a glucose challenge in substance users with high and low levels of aggression, impulsivity, and antisocial personality. *Neuropsychobiology, 25,* 106–114.

Fivush, R. (1989). Exploring sex differences in the emotional content of mother-child conversations about the past. *Sex Roles, 20,* 675–691.

Fivush, R. (1991). Gender and emotion in mother-child conversations about the past. *Journal of Narrative and Life History, 1,* 325–341.

Formoso, D., Gonzales, N. A., & Aiken, L. S. (2000). Family conflict and children's internalizing and externalizing behavior: Protective factors. *American Journal of Community Psychology, 28,* 175–199.

Fossati, P., Hevenor, S. J., Graham, S. J., Grady, C., Keightley, M. L., Craik, F., et al. (2003). In search of the emotional self: An fMRI study using positive and negative emotional words. *American Journal of Psychiatry, 160,* 1938–1945.

Foster, S. L. (2005). Aggression and antisocial behavior. In D. J. Bell, S. L. Foster, & E. J. Mash (Eds.), *Behavioral and emotional problems in girls* (pp. 149–180). New York: Kluwer Academic/Plenum.

Frank, E., & Young, E. (2000). Pubertal changes and adolescent challenges: Why do rates of depression rise precipitously for girls between ages 10 and 15 years? In E. Frank (Ed.), *Gender and its effects on psychopathology* (pp. 85–102). Washington, DC: American Psychiatric Press.

Fredrickson, B. L., & Roberts, T.-A. (1997). Objectification theory: Toward understanding women's lived experiences and mental health risks. *Psychology of Women Quarterly, 21,* 173–206.

French, S. A., Perry, C. L., Leon, G. R., & Fulkerson, J. A. (1994). Weight concerns, dieting behavior, and smoking initiation among adolescents: A prospective study. *American Journal of Public Health, 84,* 1818–1820.

Frick, P. J., & Loney, B. R. (1999). Outcomes of children and adolescents with oppositional defiant disorder and conduct disorder. In H. C.

Quay & A. E. Hogan (Eds.), *Handbook of disruptive behavior disorders* (pp. 507–524). New York: Kluwer Academic/Plenum.

Galen, B. R., & Underwood, M. K. (1997). A developmental investigation of social aggression among children. *Developmental Psychology, 33,* 589–600.

Gandhi, M., Aweeka, F., Greenblatt, R. M., & Blaschke, T. F. (2004). Sex differences in pharmacokinetics and pharmacodynamics. *Annual Review of Pharmacology and Toxicology, 44,* 499–523.

Garber, J., Keiley, M., & Martin, N. C. (2002). Developmental trajectories of adolescents' depressive symptoms: Predictors of change. *Journal of Consulting and Clinical Psychology, 70,* 79–95.

Garnefski, N. (2000). Age differences in depressive symptoms, antisocial behavior, and negative perceptions of family, school, and peers among adolescents. *Journal of the American Academy of Child and Adolescent Psychiatry, 39,* 1175–1181.

Garvin, V., & Striegel-Moore, R. (2001). Health services research for eating disorders in the Unites States: A status report and a call to action. In R. Striegel-Moore & L. Smolak (Eds.), *Eating disorders: Innovative directions in research and practice* (pp. 135–152). Washington, DC: American Psychological Association.

Gaub, M., & Carlson, C. L. (1997). Gender differences in ADHD: A meta-analysis and critical review. *Journal of the American Academy of Child and Adolescent Psychiatry, 36,* 1036–1045.

Ge, X., Conger, R. D., & Elder, G. H., Jr. (1996). Coming of age too early: Pubertal influences on girls' vulnerability to psychological distress. *Child Development, 67,* 3386–3400.

Ge, X., Conger, R. D., & Elder, G. H., Jr. (2001). Pubertal transition, stressful life events, and the emergence of gender differences in adolescent depressive symptoms. *Developmental Psychology, 37,* 404–417.

Ge, X., Lorenz, F. O., Conger, R. D., Elder, G. H., & Simons, R. L. (1994). Trajectories of stressful life events and depressive symptoms during adolescence. *Developmental Psychology, 30,* 467–483.

Geary, D. C. (1998). *Male, female: The evolution of human sex differences.* Washington, DC: American Psychology Association.

Geary, D. C. (2002). Sexual selection and human life history. In R. V. Kail (Ed.), *Advances in child development and behavior* (Vol. 30, pp. 41–100). San Diego: Academic Press.

Geary, D. C., & Flinn, M. V. (2002). Sex differences in behavioral and hormonal response to social threat: Commentary on Taylor et al. (2000). *Psychological Review, 109,* 743–751.

Geiger, T. C., & Crick, N. R. (2001). A developmental psychopathology perspective on vulnerability to personality disorders. In R. Ingram & J. M. Price (Eds.), *Vulnerability to psychopathology: Risk across the lifespan* (pp. 57–102). New York: Guilford Press.

Gelfand, D. M., & Teti, D. M. (1990). The effects of maternal depression on children. *Clinical Psychology Review, 10,* 329–353.

Gershon, J. (2002). A meta-analytic review of gender differences in ADHD. *Journal of Attention Disorders, 5,* 143–154.

Gerull, F. C., & Rapee, R. M. (2002). Mother knows best: Effects of maternal modeling on the acquisition of fear and avoidance behaviour in toddlers. *Behavior Research and Therapy, 40,* 279–287.

Geschwind, N., & Galaburda, A. M. (1985). Cerebral lateralization: Biological mechanisms, associations, and pathology: I. A hypothesis and a program for research. *Archives of Neurology, 42,* 428–459.

Giedd, J. N. (1997). Normal development. *Child and Adolescent Psychiatric Clinics of North America, 6,* 265.

Giedd, J. N. (2001). Neuroimaging of pediatric neuropsychiatric disorders: Is a picture really worth a thousand words? *Archives of General Psychiatry, 58,* 443–444.

Giedd, J. N. (August 19, 2004). Personal communication (by phone).

Giedd, J. N., Blumenthal, J., Jeffries, N. O., Rajapakse, J. C., Vaituzis, A. C., Liu, H., et al. (1999). Development of the human corpus callosum during childhood and adolescence: A longitudinal MRI study. *Progress in Neuropsychopharmacology and Biological Psychiatry, 23,* 571–588.

Giedd, J. N., Castellanos, F. X., Rajapakse, J. C., Vaituzis, A. C., & Rapoport, J. L. (1997). Sexual dimorphism of the developing human brain. *Progress in Neuropsychopharmacology and Biological Psychiatry, 21,* 1185–1201.

Giedd, J. N., Clasen, L. S., Wallace, G. L., Molloy, E. A., Blumenthal, J., Nelson, J. E., et al. (2005). XXY (Klinefelter syndrome): A pediatric quantitative magnetic resonance imaging study. Unpublished manuscript. Available from jgiedd@helix.nih.gov.

Giedd, J. N., Rumsey, J. M., Castellanos, F. X., Rajapakse, J. C., Kaysen, D., Vaituzis, A. C., et al. (1996). A quantitative MRI study of the corpus callosum in children and adolescents. *Developmental Brain Research, 91,* 274–280.

Ginsburg, G. S., & Silverman, W. K. (2000). Gender role orientation and fearfulness in children with anxiety disorders. *Journal of Anxiety Disorders, 14,* 57–67.

Ginsburg, G. S., Siqueland, L., Masia-Werner, C., & Hedtke, K. A. (2004). Anxiety disorders in children: Family matters. *Cognitive and Behavioral Practice, 11,* 28–43.

Gjerde, P. F. (1995). Alternative pathways to chronic depressive symptoms in young adults: Gender differences in developmental trajectories. *Child Development, 66,* 1277–1300.

Gjerde, P. F. (2005). *Preschool personality characteristics predict vulnerability to depression in young adults.* Poster presented at the biennial meeting of the Society for Research in Child Development, Tampa, FL.

Gjerde, P. F., & Block, J. (1996). A developmental perspective on depressive symptoms in adolescence: Gender differences in autocentric-allocentric modes of impulse regulation. In D. Cicchetti & S. Toth (Eds.), *Adolescence: Opportunities and challenges* (Vol. 7, pp. 167–196). Rochester, NY: University of Rochester Press.

Goff, D. C., & Coyle, J. T. (2001). The emerging role of glutamate in the pathophysiology and treatment of Schizophrenia. *American Journal of Psychiatry, 158,* 1367–1377.

Goldstein, J. M., Seidman, L. J., Horton, N. J., Makris, N., Kennedy, D. N., Caviness, V. S., et al. (2001). Normal sexual dimorphism of the adult human brain assessed by in vivo magnetic resonance imaging. *Cerebral Cortex, 11,* 490–497.

Goodman, S. H., & Gotlib, I. H. (1999). Risk for psychopathology in the children of depressed mothers: A developmental model for understanding mechanisms of transition. *Psychological Review, 106,* 458–490.

Goodwin, F. K., & Jamison, K. J. (1990). *Manic-depressive illness.* London: Oxford University Press.

Goodwin, R. D., & Gotlib, I. H. (2004). Gender differences in depression: The role of personality factors. *Psychiatry Research, 126,* 135–142.

Goodyer, I. M. (2001). Life events: Their nature and effects. In I. M. Goodyer (Ed.), *The depressed child and adolescent* (2nd ed., pp. 204–232). New York: Cambridge University Press.

Goodyer, I. M., & Altham, P. M. E. (1991). Lifetime exit events and recent social and family adversities in anxious and depressed school-age children and adolescents: I. *Journal of Affective Disorders, 21,* 219–228.

Goodyer, I. M., Herbert, J., Tamplin, A., & Altham, P. M. E. (2000). Recent life events, cortisol, dehydroepiandrosterone and the onset of major depression in high-risk adolescents. *British Journal of Psychiatry, 177,* 499–504.

Gore, S., Aseltine, R. H., & Colten, M. E. (1992). Social structure, life stress, and depressive symptoms in a high school-aged population. *Journal of Health and Social Behavior, 33,* 97–113.

Gore, S., Aseltine, R. H., & Colten, M. E. (1993). Gender, social-relational involvement, and depression. *Journal of Research on Adolescence, 3,* 101–125.

Graber, J., & Brooks-Gunn, J. (2001). Co-occurring eating and depressive problems: An 8-year study of adolescent girls. *International Journal of Eating Disorders, 30,* 37–47.

Graber, J. A., Lewinsohn, P. M., Seeley, J. R., & Brooks-Gunn, J. (1997). Is psychopathology associated with the timing of pubertal development? *Journal of the American Academy of Child and Adolescent Psychiatry, 36,* 1768–1776.

Granger, D. A., Shirtcliff, E. A., Booth, A., Kivlighan, K. T., & Schwartz, E. B. (2004). The "trouble" with salivary testosterone. *Psychoneuroendocrinology, 29,* 1229–1240.

Granger, D. A., Shirtcliff, E. A., Zahn-Waxler, C., Usher, B., Klimes-Dougan, B., & Hasting, P. (2003). Salivary testosterone diurnal variation and psychopathology in adolescent males and females: Individual differences and developmental effects. *Development and Psychopathology, 15,* 431–449.

Grant, V. J. (1996). Sex determination and the maternal dominance hypothesis. *Human Reproduction, 11,* 2371–2375.

Grant, V. J. (1998). *Maternal personality, evolution and the sex ratio.* New York: Routledge.

Griffin, K. W., Botvin, G. J., Scheier, L. M., Diaz, T., & Miller, N. L. (2000). Parenting practices as predictors of substance use, delinquency, and aggression among urban minority youth: Moderating effects of family structure and gender. *Psychology of Addictive Behaviors, 14,* 174–184.

Grillon, C., Dierker, L., & Merikangas, K. R. (1998). Fear-potentiated startle in adolescent offspring of parent with anxiety disorders. *Biological Psychiatry, 44,* 990–997.

Grills, A. E., & Ollendick, T. H. (2002). Peer victimization, global self-worth, and anxiety in middle school children. *Journal of Clinical Child and Adolescent Psychology, 31,* 59–68.

Grumbach, M. M. (2002). The neuroendocrinology of human puberty revisited. *Hormone Research, 57*(Suppl. 2), 2–14.

Gruzelier, J. H. (1994). Syndromes of Schizophrenia and schizotypy, hemispheric imbalance and sex differences: Implications for developmental psychopathology. *International Journal of Psychophysiology, 18,* 167–178.

Gullone, E., & King, N. J. (1993). The fears of youth in the 1990s: Contemporary normative data. *Journal of Genetic Psychology, 154,* 137–153.

Gurian, A. (1987). Depression in young girls: Early sorrows and depressive disorders. In R. Formanek & A. Gurian (Eds.), *Women and depression: A lifespan perspective* (Springer series: Focus on women, Vol. 11, pp. 57–83). New York: Springer.

Hamburger, M. E., Lilienfeld, S. O., & Hogben, M. (1996). Psychopathy, gender, and gender roles: Implications for antisocial and histrionic personality disorders. *Journal of Personality Disorders, 10,* 41–55.

Hammen, C., Burge, D., Burney, E., & Adrian, C. (1990). Longitudinal study of diagnoses in children of women with unipolar and bipolar affective disorder. *Archives of General Psychiatry, 47,* 1112–1117.

Hankin, B. L., & Abramson, L. Y. (2001). Development of gender differences in depression: An elaborated cognitive vulnerability-transactional stress theory. *Psychological Bulletin, 127,* 773–796.

Hankin, B. L., Abramson, L. Y., Moffitt, T. E., Silva, P. A., & McGee, R. (1998). Development of depression from preadolescence to young adulthood: Emerging gender differences in a 10-year longitudinal study. *Journal of Abnormal Psychology, 107,* 128–140.

Hanna, E. Z., & Grant, B. F. (1997). Gender differences in DSM-IV alcohol use disorders and major depression as distributed in the general population: Clinical implications. *Comprehensive Psychiatry, 38,* 202–212.

Hart, B. I., & Thompson, J. M. (1996). Gender role characteristics and depressive symptomatology among adolescents. *Journal of Early Adolescence, 16,* 407–426.

Hart, C. H., Nelson, D. A., Robinson, C. C., Olson, S. F., & McNeilly-Choque, M. K. (1998). Overt and relational aggression in Russian nursery school-age children: Parenting style and marital linkages. *Developmental Psychology, 34,* 687–697.

Harter, S. (1993). Vision of self: Beyond the me in the mirror. In R. Dienstbier (Ed.), *Nebraska Symposium on Motivation: Vol. 40. Developmental perspectives on motivation* (pp. 99–144). Lincoln: University of Nebraska Press.

Harter, S., Waters, P. L., Whitesell, N. R., & Kastilic, D. (1998). Level of voice among high-school females and males: Relational context, support, and gender orientation. *Developmental Psychology, 34,* 892–901.

Hartung, C. M., & Widiger, T. A. (1998). Gender differences in the diagnosis of mental disorders: Conclusions and controversies of the DSM-IV. *Psychological Bulletin, 123,* 260–278.

Hartup, W. W., & van Lieshout, C. F. M. (1995). Personality development in social context. *Annual Review of Psychology, 46,* 655–687.

Hawkins, J. D., Catalano, R. F., & Miller, J. Y. (1992). Risk and protective factors for alcohol and other drug problems in adolescence and early adulthood: Implications for substance abuse prevention. *Psychological Bulletin, 112,* 64–105.

Hay, D. F., Zahn-Waxler, C., Cummings, E. M., & Iannotti, R. J. (1992). Young children's views about conflict with peers: A comparison of the daughters and sons of depressed and well women. *Journal of Child Psychology and Psychiatry, 33,* 669–683.

Hayward, C. (2003). *Gender differences at puberty.* New York: Cambridge University Press.

Hayward, C., Killen, J. D., Hammer, L., & Litt, I. F. (1992). Pubertal stage and panic attack history in sixth- and seventh-grade girls. *American Journal of Psychiatry, 149,* 1239–1243.

Hayward, C., Killen, J. D., Wilson, D. M., Hammer, L. D., Litt, I. F., Kraemer, H. C., et al. (1997). Psychiatric risk associated with early puberty in adolescent girls. *Journal of the American Academy of Child and Adolescent Psychiatry, 36,* 255–262.

Hayward, C., & Sanborn, K. (2002). Puberty and the emergence of gender differences in psychopathology. *Journal of Adolescent Health, 30,* 49–58.

Heller, W. (1993). Gender differences in depression: Perspectives from neuropsychology. *Journal of Affective Disorders, 29,* 129–143.

Henggeler, S. W., Edwards, J., & Borduin, C. M. (1987). The family relations of female juvenile delinquents. *Journal of Abnormal Child Psychology, 15,* 199–209.

Henry, B., Feehan, M., McGee, R., Stanton, W., Moffitt, T., & Silva, P. (1993). The importance of conduct problems and depressive symptoms in predicting adolescent substance use. *Journal of Abnormal Child Psychology, 21,* 469–480.

Hietala, J., & Syvalahti, E. (1996). Dopamine in Schizophrenia. *Annals of Medicine, 28,* 557–561.

Hill, J. P., & Lynch, M. E. (1983). The intensification of gender-related role expectations during early adolescence. In J. Brooks-Gunn & A. Petersen (Eds.), *Girls at puberty: Biological and psychosocial perspectives* (pp. 201–228). New York: Plenum Press.

Hines, M., & Collaer, M. L. (1993). Gonadal hormones and sexual differentiation of human behavior: Developments from research on endocrine syndromes and studies of brain structure. *Annual Review of Sex Research, 4,* 1–48.

Hinshaw, S. P. (1999). Psychosocial intervention for childhood ADHD: Etiologic and developmental themes, comorbidity, and integration with pharmacotherapy. In D. Cicchetti & S. L. Toth (Eds.), *Rochester Symposium on Developmental Psychopathology: Vol. 9. Developmental approaches to prevention and intervention* (pp. 221–270). Rochester, NY: University of Rochester Press.

Hinshaw, S. P., & Anderson, C. A. (1996). Conduct and oppositional defiant disorders. In E. J. Mash & R. A. Barkley (Eds.), *Child psychopathology* (pp. 113–149). New York: Guilford Press.

Hinshaw, S. P., & Blachman, D. R. (2005). Attention deficit/hyperactivity disorder in girls. In D. J. Bell, S. L. Foster, & E. J. Mash (Eds.), *Behavioral and emotional problems in girls* (pp. 117–180). New York: Kluwer Academic/Plenum.

Hoffman, M. L. (1977). Sex differences in empathy and related behaviors. *Psychological Bulletin, 84,* 712–722.

Holloway, R. L., Anderson, P. J., Defendini, R., & Harper, C. (1993). Sexual dimorphism of the human corpus callosum from three independent samples: Relative size of the corpus callosum. *American Journal of Physical Anthropology, 92,* 481–498.

Hong, Y., Gagnon, J., Rice, T., Perusse, L., Leon, A. S., Skinner, J. S., et al. (2001). Familial resemblance for free androgens and androgen glucuronides in sedentary Black and White individuals: The HERITAGE Family Study—Health, risk, factors, exercise training and genetics. *Journal of Endocrinology, 170,* 485–492.

Hops, H. (1996). Intergenerational transmission of depressive symptoms: Gender and developmental considerations. In C. Mundt & M. J. Goldstein (Eds.), *Interpersonal factors in the origin and course of affective disorders* (pp. 113–129). London: Gaskell/Royal College of Psychiatrists.

Huselid, R. F., & Cooper, M. L. (1994). Gender roles as mediators of sex differences in expressions of pathology. *Journal of Abnormal Psychology, 103,* 595–603.

Hutchison, J. B. (1997). Gender-specific steroid metabolism in neural differentiation. *Cellular and Molecular Neurobiology, 17,* 603–626.

Ialongo, N., Edelsohn, G., Werthamer-Larsson, L., Crockett, L., & Kellam, S. (1995). The significance of self-reported anxious symptoms in first grade children: Prediction to anxious symptoms and adaptive functioning in fifth grade. *Journal of Child Psychology and Psychiatry and Allied Disciplines, 36,* 427–437.

Insel, T. R. (2003). Is social attachment an addictive disorder? *Physiology and Behavior, 79,* 351–357.

Insel, T. R., & Fernald, R. D. (2004). How the brain processes social information: Searching for the social brain. *Annual Review of Neuroscience, 27,* 697–722.

Insel, T. R., O'Brien, D. J., & Leckman, J. F. (1999). Oxytocin, vasopressin, and Autism: Is there a connection? *Biological Psychiatry, 45,* 145–157.

Insel, T. R., & Winslow, J. T. (1998). Serotonin and neuropeptides in affiliative behaviors. *Biological Psychiatry, 44,* 207–219.

Institute of Medicine. (2001). *Exploring the biological contributions to human health: Does sex matter?* Washington, DC: National Academy Press.

Jacobs, J. E., & Eccles, J. S. (1992). The impact of mothers' gender-role stereotype beliefs on mothers' and children's ability perceptions. *Journal of Personality and Social Psychology, 63,* 932–944.

Jacobson, K. C., Prescott, C. A., & Kendler, K. S. (2002). Sex differences in genetic and environmental influences on development of antisocial behavior. *Development and Psychopathology, 14,* 395–416.

Jacobson, K. C., & Rowe, D. C. (1999). Genetic and environmental influences on the relationships between family connectedness, school connectedness, and adolescent depressed mood: Sex differences. *Developmental Psychology, 35,* 926–939.

Jambekar, S. A., Masheb, R. M., & Grilo, C. M. (2003). Gender differences in shame in patients with binge-eating disorder. *Obesity Research, 11,* 571–577.

Jang, K. L., Livesley, J. W., & Vernon, P. A. (1997). Gender-specific etiological differences in alcohol and drug problems: A behavioral genetic analysis. *Addictions, 92,* 1265–1276.

Jessor, R. (1987). Problem behavior theory, psychosocial development, and adolescent problem drinking. *British Journal of Addiction, 82,* 331–342.

Jessor, R., Van Den Bos, J., Vanderryn, J., Costa, F. M., & Turbin, M. S. (1995). Protective factors in adolescent problem behavior: Moderator effects and developmental change. *Developmental Psychology, 31,* 923–933.

Johnson, E. O., Arria, A. M., Borges, G., Ialongo, N., & Anthony, J. C. (1995). The growth of conduct problem behaviors from middle childhood to early adolescence: Sex differences and the suspected influence of early alcohol use. *Journal of Studies on Alcohol, 56,* 661–671.

Johnston, L. D., O'Malley, P., & Bachman, J. G. (2002). *Monitoring the Future national survey results on drug use, 1975–2001.* Rockville, MD: U.S. Department of Health and Human Services.

Jones, D. C. (2001). Social comparison and body image: Attractiveness comparisons to models and peers among adolescent girls and boys. *Sex Roles, 45,* 645–664.

Jussim, L., & Eccles, J. S. (1992). Teacher expectations: II. Construction and reflection of student achievement. *Journal of Personality and Social Psychology, 63,* 947–961.

Kagan, J. (2001). Temperamental contributions to affective and behavioral profiles in childhood. In S. G. Hofmann & P. M. DiBartolo (Eds.), *From social anxiety to social phobia: Multiple perspectives* (pp. 216–234). Needham Heights, MA: Allyn & Bacon.

Kandel, D. B., Yamaguchi, K., & Chen, K. (1992). Stages of progression in drug involvement from adolescence to adulthood: Further evidence for the gateway theory. *Journal of Studies on Alcohol, 53,* 447–457.

Karbon, M., Fabes, R. A., Carlo, G., & Martin, C. L. (1992). Preschoolers' beliefs about sex and age differences in emotionality. *Sex Roles, 27,* 377–390.

Kasen, S., Cohen, P., Skodol, A. E., Johnson, J. G., Smailes, E., & Brook, J. S. (2001). Childhood depression and adult personality disorder: Alternative pathways of continuity. *Archives of General Psychiatry, 58,* 231–236.

Kashani, J. H., & Carlson, G. A. (1987). Seriously depressed preschoolers. *American Journal of Psychiatry, 144,* 348–350.

Kashani, J. H., Holcomb, W. R., & Orvaschel, H. (1986). Depression and depressive symptoms in preschool children from the general population. *American Journal of Psychiatry, 143,* 1138–1143.

Kashani, J. H., & Orvaschel, H. (1990). A community study of anxiety in children and adolescents. *American Journal of Psychiatry, 147,* 313–318.

Kavanagh, K., & Hops, H. (1994). Good girls? Bad boys? Gender and development as contexts for diagnosis. In T. H. Ollendick & R. J. Prinz (Eds.), *Advances in clinical child psychology* (Vol. 16, pp. 45–79). New York: Plenum Press.

Kaye, W., & Strober, M. (1999). Neurobiology of eating disorders. In D. Charney, E. Nestler, & W. Bunney (Eds.), *Neurobiological foundations of mental illness* (pp. 891–906). New York: Oxford University Press.

Kearney, C. A., & Allan, W. D. (1995). Panic disorder with or without agoraphobia. In A. R. Eisen, C. A. Kearney, & C. E. Schaefer (Eds.), *Clinical handbook of anxiety disorders in children and adolescents* (pp. 251–281). Northvale, NJ: Aronson.

Keenan, K. (2000). Emotion dysregulation as a risk factor for child psychopathology. *Clinical Psychology: Science and Practice, 7,* 418–434.

Keenan, K., & Hipwell, A. E. (2005). Preadolescent clues to understanding depression in girls. *Clinical Child and Family Psychology Review, 8,* 89–105.

Keenan, K., & Shaw, D. (1997). Developmental and social influences on young girls' early problem behavior. *Psychological Bulletin, 121,* 95–113.

Kendall-Tackett, K. A., Williams, L. M., & Finkerlhor, D. (1993). Impact of sexual abuse on children: A review and synthesis of recent empirical studies. *Psychological Bulletin, 113,* 164–180.

Kendler, K. S. (1998). Major depression and the environment: A psychiatric genetic perspective. *Pharmacopsychiatry, 31,* 5–9.

Kendler, K. S., Gardner, C. O., Neale, M. C., & Prescott, C. A. (2001). Genetic risk factors for major depression in men and women: Similar or different heritabilities and same or partly distinct genes? *Psychological Medicine, 31,* 605–616.

Kendler, K. S., Heath, A., Martin, N. G., & Eaves, L. J. (1986). Symptoms of anxiety and depression in a volunteer twin population: The etiologic role of genetic and environmental factors. *Archives of General Psychiatry, 43,* 213–221.

Kendler, K. S., Jacobson, K. C., Myers, J., & Prescott, C. A. (2002). Sex differences in genetic and environmental risk factors for irrational fears and phobias. *Psychological Medicine, 32,* 209–217.

Kendler, K. S., Karkowski, L. M., & Prescott, C. A. (1999). Causal relationship between stressful life events and the onset of major depression. *American Journal of Psychiatry, 156,* 837–848.

Kendler, K. S., Kessler, R. C., Walters, E. E., MacLean, C., Neale, M. C., Heath, A. C., et al. (1995). Stressful life events, genetic liability, and onset of an episode of major depression. *American Journal of Psychiatry, 152,* 833–842.

Kendler, K. S., Thornton, L. M., & Prescott, C. A. (2001). Gender differences in the rates of exposure to stressful life events and sensitivity to their depressogenic effects. *American Journal of Psychiatry, 158,* 587–593.

Kerig, P. K., Cowan, P. A., & Cowan, C. P. (1993). Marital quality and gender differences in parent-child interaction. *Developmental Psychology, 29,* 931–939.

Kernberg, P. F., Weiner, A. S., & Bardenstein, K. K. (2000). *Personality disorders in children and adolescents.* New York: Basic Books.

Kessler, R. C., McGonagle, K. A., Swartz, M., Blazer, D. G., & Nelson, C. B. (1993). Sex and depression in the National Comorbidity Survey I: Lifetime prevalence, chronicity and recurrence. *Journal of Affective Disorders, 29,* 85–96.

Kessler, R. C., McGonagle, K. A., Zhao, S., Nelson, C. B., Hughes, M., Eshleman, S., et al. (1994). Lifetime and 12-month prevalence of DSM-III-R psychiatric disorders in the United States: Results from the National Comorbidity Study. *Archives of General Psychiatry, 51,* 8–19.

Killgore, W. D., & Yurgelun-Todd, D. A. (2001). Sex differences in amygdala activation during the perception of facial affect. *NeuroReport, 12,* 2543–2547.

Kilpatrick, D. G., Ruggiero, K. J., Acierno, R., Saunders, B. E., Resnick, H. S., & Best, C. L. (2003). Violence and risk of PTSD, major depression, substance abuse/dependence, and comorbidity: Results from the National Survey of Adolescents. *Journal of Consulting and Clinical Psychology, 71,* 692–700.

King, N. J., Gullone, E., Tonge, B. J., & Ollendick, T. H. (1993). Self-reports of panic attacks and manifest anxiety in adolescents. *Behaviour Research and Therapy, 31,* 111–116.

Kirschbaum, C., Klauer, T., Filipp, S. H., & Hellhammer, D. H. (1995). Sex-specific effects of social support on cortisol and subjective responses to acute psychological stress. *Psychosomatic Medicine, 57,* 23–31.

Klimes-Dougan, B., & Bolger, A. K. (1998). Coping with maternal depressed affect and depression: Adolescent children of depressed and well mothers. *Journal of Youth and Adolescence, 27,* 1–15.

Klimes-Dougan, B., Brand, A. E., Zahn-Waxler, C., Usher, B., Hastings, P. D., Kendziora, K., et al. (2005). *Parental emotion socialization in adolescence: Sex, age, and risk differences.* Manuscript submitted for publication. Available from klimes@umn.edu.

Klimes-Dougan, B., Hastings, P. D., Granger, D. A., Usher, B. A., & Zahn-Waxler, C. (2001). Adrenocortical activity in at-risk and normally developing adolescents: Individual differences in salivary cortisol basal levels, diurnal variation, and responses to social challenges. *Development and Psychopathology, 13,* 695–719.

Kline, J. P., Allen, J. B., & Schwartz, G. E. (1998). Is left frontal brain activation in defensiveness gender specific? *Journal of Abnormal Psychology, 107,* 149–153.

Kochanska, G., DeVet, K., Goldman, M., Murray, K., & Putman, S. P. (1994). Maternal reports of conscience development and temperament in young children. *Child Development, 65,* 852–868.

Koenig, K., & Tsatsanis, K. D. (2005). Pervasive developmental disorders in girls. In D. J. Bell, S. L. Foster, & E. J. Mash (Eds.), *Behavioral and emotional problems in girls* (pp. 211–237). New York: Kluwer Academic/Plenum.

Koob, G. F., & Le Moal, M. (2001). Drug addiction, dysregulation of reward, and allostasis. *Neuropsychophamacology, 24,* 97–129.

Kovacs, M. (1996). Presentation and course of major depressive disorder during childhood and later years of the life span. *Journal of the American Academy of Child and Adolescent Psychiatry, 35,* 705–715.

Kovacs, M., Gatsonis, C., Paulauskas, S. L., & Richards, C. (1989). Depressive disorders in childhood: IV. A longitudinal study of comorbidity with and risk for anxiety disorders. *Archives of General Psychiatry, 46,* 776–782.

Kroneman, L., Loeber, R., & Hipwell, A. E. (2004). Is neighborhood context differently related to externalizing problems and delinquency for girls compared with boys? *Clinical Child and Family Psychology Review, 7,* 109–122.

Krystal, J. H., Sanacora, G., Blumberg, H., Anand, A., Charney, D. S., Marek, G., et al. (2002). Glutamate and GABA systems as targets for novel antidepressant and mood-stabilizing treatments. *Molecular Psychiatry, 7,* S71–S80.

Lagerspetz, K. M. J., Bjorkqvist, K., & Peltonen, T. (1988). Is indirect aggression typical of females? Gender differences in aggressiveness in 11–12-year-old children. *Aggressive Behavior, 14,* 303–315.

LaGreca, A. M., & Lopez, N. (1998). Social anxiety among adolescents: Linkages with peer relations and friendships. *Journal of Abnormal Child Psychology, 26,* 83–94.

LaGreca, A. M., & Stone, W. L. (1993). Social Anxiety Scale for Children-Revised: Factor structure and concurrent validity. *Journal of Clinical Child Psychology, 22,* 17–27.

Lahey, B. B., Hart, E. L., Pliszka, S., Applegate, B., & McBurnett, K. (1993). Neurophysiological correlates of conduct disorder: A rationale and a review of research. *Journal of Clinical Child Psychology, 22,* 141–153.

Lahey, B. B., Schwab-Stone, M., Goodman, S. H., Waldman, I. D., Canino, G., Rathouz, P. J., et al. (2000). Age and gender differences in oppositional behavior and conduct problems: A cross-sectional household study of middle childhood and adolescence. *Journal of Abnormal Psychology, 109,* 488–503.

Latham, K. E. (1996). X chromosome imprinting and inactivation in the early mammalian embryo. *Trends in Genetics, 12,* 134–138.

Latimer, W. W., Newcomb, M., Winters, K. C., & Stinchfield, R. D. (2000). Adolescent substance abuse treatment outcome: The role of substance abuse problem severity, psychosocial and treatment factors. *Journal of Consulting and Clinical Psychology, 68,* 684–696.

Leadbeater, B. J., Blatt, S. J., & Quinlan, D. M. (1995). Gender-linked vulnerabilities to depressive symptoms, stress, and problem behaviors in adolescents. *Journal of Research on Adolescence, 5,* 1–29.

Leadbeater, B. J., Kuperminc, G. P., Blatt, S. J., & Hertzog, C. (1999). A multivariate model of gender differences in adolescents' internalizing and externalizing problems. *Developmental Psychology, 35,* 1268–1282.

Leaper, C. (2002). Parenting girls and boys. In M. H. Bornstein (Ed.), *Handbook of parenting: Vol. 1. Children and parenting* (2nd ed., pp. 189–225). Mahwah, NJ: Erlbaum.

Lewinsohn, P. M., Gotlib, I. H., Lewinsohn, M., Seeley, J. R., & Allen, N. B. (1998). Gender differences in anxiety disorders and anxiety symptoms in adolescents. *Journal of Abnormal Psychology, 107,* 109–117.

Lewinsohn, P. M., Gotlib, I. H., & Seeley, J. R. (1995). Adolescent psychopathology: IV. Specificity of psychosocial risk factors for depression and substance abuse in older adolescents. *Journal of the American Academy of Child and Adolescent Psychiatry, 34,* 1221–1229.

Lewinsohn, P. M., Hops, H., Roberts, R. E., Seeley, J. R., & Andrews, J. A. (1993). Adolescent psychopathology I: Prevalence and incidence of depression and other DSM-III-R disorders in high school students. *Journal of Abnormal Psychology, 102,* 133–144.

Lewinsohn, P. M., Rohde, P., & Seeley, J. R. (1995). Adolescent psychopathology: III. The clinical consequences of comorbidity. *Journal of the American Academy of Child and Adolescent Psychiatry, 34,* 510–519.

Lewinsohn, P. M., Rohde, P., & Seeley, J. R. (1998). Major depressive disorder in older adolescents: Prevalence, risk factors, and clinical implications. *Clinical Psychology Review, 18,* 765–794.

Lewinsohn, P. M., Zinbarg, R., Seeley, J. R., Lewinsohn, M., & Sack, W. H. (1997). Lifetime comorbidity among anxiety disorders and between anxiety disorders and other mental disorders in adolescents. *Journal of Anxiety Disorders, 11,* 377–394.

Lewis, D. O., Yeager, C. A., Cobham-Portorreal, C. S., Klein, N., Showalter, C., & Anthony, A. (1991). A follow-up of female delinquents: Maternal contributions to the perpetuation of deviance. *Journal of the American Academy of Child and Adolescent Psychiatry, 30,* 197–201.

Liben, L. S., Susman, E. J., Finkelstein, J. W., Chinchilli, V. M., Kunselman, S., Schwab, J., et al. (2002). The effects of sex steroids on spatial performance: A review and an experimental clinical investigation. *Developmental Psychology, 38,* 236–253.

Lichtenstein, P., & Annas, P. (2000). Heritability and prevalence of specific fears and phobias in childhood. *Journal of Child Psychology and Psychiatry, 41,* 927–937.

Loeber, R., & Keenan, K. (1994). The interaction between conduct disorder and its comorbid conditions: Effects of age and gender. *Clinical Psychology Review, 14,* 497–523.

Loeber, R., & Stouthamer-Loeber, M. (1986). Family factors as correlates and predictors of juvenile conduct problems and delinquency. In M. Tonry & N. Morris (Eds.), *Crime and justice: An annual review of research* (pp. 29–149). Chicago: University of Chicago Press.

Lopez, F. J., Merchenthaler, I., Liposits, Z., & Negro-Vilar, A. (1996). Steroid imprinting and modulation of sexual dimorphism in the luteinizing hormone-releasing hormone neuronal system. *Cellular and Molecular Neurobiology, 16,* 129–141.

Lumley, V. A., McNeil, C. B., Herschell, A. D., & Bahl, A. B. (2002). An examination of gender differences among young children with disruptive behavior disorders. *Child Study Journal, 32,* 89–100.

Lynch, W. J., Roth, M. E., & Carroll, M. E. (2002). Biological basis of sex differences in drug abuse: Preclinical and clinical studies. *Psychopharmacology, 164,* 121–137.

Lytton, H., & Romney, D. (1991). Parents' differential socialization of boys and girls: A meta-analysis. *Psychological Bulletin, 109,* 287–296.

Maccoby, E. E. (1990). Gender and relationships: A developmental account. *American Psychologist, 45,* 513–520.

Maccoby, E. E. (1998). *The two sexes: Growing up apart, coming together.* Cambridge, MA: Harvard University Press.

Maccoby, E. E. (2002). Gender and group process: A developmental perspective. *Current Directions in Psychological Science, 11,* 54–58.

Maccoby, E. E. (2004). Aggression in the context of gender development. In M. Putallaz & K. L. Bierman (Eds.), *Aggression, antisocial behavior, and violence among girls* (pp. 3–22). New York: Guilford Press.

Maccoby, E. E., & Jacklin, C. N. (1974). *The psychology of sex differences.* Stanford: Stanford University Press.

MacLaughlin, D. T., & Donahoe, P. K. (2004). Sex determination and differentiation. *New England Journal of Medicine, 350,* 367–378.

Maggini, C., Ampollini, P., Gariboldi, S., Cella, P. L., Pelizza, L., & Marchesi, C. (2001). The Parma high school epidemiological survey: Obsessive-compulsive symptoms. *Acta Psychiatrica Scandinavica, 103,* 441–446.

Magnusson, D., Stattin, H., & Allen, V. L. (1985). Biological maturation and social development: A longitudinal study of some adjustment processes from mid-adolescence to adulthood. *Journal of Youth and Adolescence, 14,* 267–283.

Malatesta, C. Z., & Haviland, J. (1982). Learning display rules: The socialization of emotion expression in infancy. *Child Development, 53,* 991–1003.

Malatesta, C. Z., & Wilson, A. (1988). Emotion cognition interaction in personality development: A discrete emotions, functionalist analysis. *British Journal of Social Psychology, 27,* 91–112.

Martin, G., Wertheim, E., Prior, M., Smart, D., Sanson, A., & Oberklaid, F. (2000). A longitudinal study of the role of childhood temperament in the later development of eating concerns. *International Journal of Eating Disorders, 27,* 150–163.

Maughan, B., Pickles, A., Rowe, R., Costello, E. J., & Angold, A. (2000). Developmental trajectories of aggressive and non-aggressive conduct problems. *Journal of Quantitative Criminology, 16,* 199–221.

Maughan, B., Rowe, R., Messer, J., Goodman, R., & Meltzer, H. (2004). Conduct disorder and oppositional defiant disorder in a national sample: Developmental epidemiology. *Journal of Child Psychology and Psychiatry, 45,* 609–621.

McCabe, K. M., Rodgers, C., Yeh, M., & Hough, R. (2004). Gender differences in childhood onset conduct disorder. *Development and Psychopathology, 16,* 179–192.

McCall, R. B. (1991). So many interactions, so little evidence why. In T. D. Wachs, & R. Plomin (Eds.), *Conceptualization and measurement of organism-environment interactions* (pp. 142–161). Washington, DC: U.S. American Psychological Association.

McCarthy, M. M., Auger, A. P., & Perrot-Sinal, T. S. (2002). Getting excited about GABA and sex differences in the brain. *Trends in Neurosciences, 25,* 307–312.

McCarthy, M. M., Davis, A. M., & Mong, J. A. (1997). Excitatory neurotransmission and sexual differentiation of the brain. *Brain Research Bulletin, 44,* 487–495.

McCauley, E., Myers, K., Mitchell, J., Calderon, R., Schloredt, K., & Treder, R. (1993). Depression in young people: Initial presentation and clinical course. *Journal of the American Academy of Child and Adolescent Psychiatry, 32,* 714–722.

McCauley, E., Pavlidis, K., & Kendall, K. (2001). Developmental precursors of depression: The child and the social environment. In I. M. Goodyer (Ed.), *The depressed child and adolescent* (2nd ed., pp. 46–78). New York: Cambridge University Press.

McClelland, G. H., & Judd, C. M. (1993). Statistical difficulties of detecting interactions and moderator effects. *Psychological Bulletin, 114,* 376–390.

McClure, E. B. (2000). A meta-analytic review of sex differences in facial expression processing and their development in infants, children and adolescents. *Psychological Bulletin, 126,* 424–453.

McClure, E. B., Monk, C. S., Nelson, E. E., Zarahn, E., Leibenluft, E., Bilder, R. M., et al. (2004). A developmental examination of gender differences in brain engagement during evaluation of threat. *Biological Psychiatry, 55,* 1047–1055.

McEwen, B. S. (1992). Steroid hormones: Effect on brain development and function. *Hormone Research, 37,* S1–S10.

McEwen, B. S. (2001). Estrogens effects on the brain: Multiple sites and molecular mechanisms [Invited review]. *Journal of Applied Physiology, 91,* 2785–2801.

McEwen, B. S. (2002). Estrogen actions throughout the brain. *Recent Progress in Hormone Research, 57,* 357–384.

McEwen, B. S., & Alves, S. E. (1999). Estrogen actions in the central nervous system. *Endocrine Reviews, 20,* 279–307.

McFadyen-Ketchum, S. A., Bates, J. E., Dodge, K. A., & Pettit, Y. S. (1996). Pattern of change in early childhood aggressive-disruptive behavior: Gender differences in predictions from early coercive and affectionate mother-child interactions. *Child Development, 67,* 2417–2433.

McFarlane, A. H., Bellissimo, A., & Norman, G. R. (1995). The role of family and peers in social self-efficacy: Links to depression in adolescence. *American Journal of Orthopsychiatry, 65,* 402–410.

McGee, R., Feehan, M., Williams, S., & Anderson, J. (1992). DSM-III disorders from age 11 to age 15 years. *Journal of the American Academy of Child and Adolescent Psychiatry, 31,* 50–59.

McGrath, E., Keita, G. P., & Strickland, B. R. (1990). *Women and depression: Risk factors and treatment issues: Final report of the American Psychological Association's National Task Force on Women and Depression.* Washington, DC: American Psychological Association.

McGue, M. (1994). Genes, environment, and the etiology of alcoholism. In R. Zucker, G. Boyd, & J. Howard (Eds.), *The development of alcohol problems: Exploring the psychosocial matrix of risk* (NIAAA Research Monograph 26, pp. 1–40). Washington, DC: U.S. Government Printing Office.

Meibohm, B., Beierle, I., & Derendorf, H. (2002). How important are gender differences in pharmacokinetics? *Clinical Pharmacokinetics, 41,* 329–342.

Meyer, J., & Stunkard, A. (1993). Genetics and human obesity. In A. Stunkard & T. Wadden (Eds.), *Obesity: Theory and therapy* (2nd ed., pp. 137–150). New York: Raven Press.

Meyersberg, H. A., & Post, R. M. (1979). A holistic developmental view of neural and psychological processes. *British Journal of Psychiatry, 135,* 139–155.

Migeon, C. J., & Wisniewski, A. B. (1998). Sexual differentiation: From genes to gender. *Hormone Research, 50,* 245–251.

Migeon, C. J., & Wisniewski, A. B. (2003). Human sex differentiation and its abnormalities. *Best Practice and Research Clinical Obstetrics and Gynaecology, 17,* 1–18.

Miller, A., Fox, N. A., Cohn, J. F., Forbes, E. E., Sherrill, J. T., & Kovacs, M. (2002). Regional patterns of brain activity in adults with a history of childhood-onset depression: Gender differences and clinical variability. *American Journal of Psychiatry, 159,* 934–940.

Moffitt, T. E. (1993). Adolescence-limited and life-course-persistent antisocial behavior: A developmental taxonomy. *Psychological Review, 100,* 674–701.

Moffitt, T. E., & Caspi, A. (2001). Childhood predictors differentiate life-course persistent and adolescent-limited antisocial pathways among males and females. *Development and Psychopathology, 13,* 355–375.

Moffitt, T. E., Caspi, A., Belsky, J., & Silva, P. A. (1992). Childhood experience and the onset of menarche: A test of a sociobiological model. *Child Development, 63,* 47–58.

Moffitt, T. E., Caspi, A., & Rutter, M. (2005). Strategy for investigating interactions between measured genes and measured environments. *Archives of General Psychiatry, 62,* 473–481.

Moffitt, T. E., Caspi, A., Rutter, M., & Silva, P. A. (2001). *Sex differences in antisocial behavior.* New York: Cambridge University Press.

Morris, T. L., & March, J. S. (2004). *Anxiety disorders in children and adolescents* (2nd ed.). New York: Guilford Press.

Murnen, S., & Smolak, L. (2000). The experience of sexual harassment among grade-school students: Early socialization of female subordination? *Sex Roles, 43,* 1–17.

Nadeau, K., Littman, E. B., & Quinn, P. O. (1999). *Understanding girls with ADHD.* Silver Spring, MD: Advantage Books.

Nasser, E. H., Walders, N., & Jenkins, J. H. (2002). The experience of Schizophrenia: What's gender got to do with it? A critical review of the current status of research on Schizophrenia. *Schizophrenia Bulletin, 28,* 351–362.

Nelson, E. E., Leibenluft, E., McClure, E. B., & Pine, D. S. (in press). The social re-orientation of adolescence: A neuroscience perspective on the process and its relation to psychopathology. *Psychological Medicine, 35,* 163–174.

Nelson, R. J. (2000). *An introduction to behavioral endocrinology.* New York: Sinaur.

Neslon, R. J. (November 22, 2004). Personal communication by telephone.

NICHD Early Child Care Research Network. (2004). Trajectories of physical aggression from toddlerhood to middle childhood. *Monographs of the Society for Research in Child Development, 69*(4, Serial No. 278).

Nicolopoulou, A. (1997). Worldmaking and identity formation in children's narrative play-acting. In B. D. Cox & C. Lightfoot (Eds.), *Sociogenetic perspectives on internalization* (pp. 157–187). Mahwah, NJ: Erlbaum.

Nixon, R. D. V. (2002). Child and family variables associated with behavior problems in preschoolers: The role of child gender. *Child and Family Behavior Therapy, 24,* 1–19.

Nolen-Hoeksema, S. (1990). *Sex differences in depression.* Palo Alto, CA: Stanford University Press.

Nolen-Hoeksema, S., & Girgus, J. S. (1994). The emergence of gender differences in depression during adolescence. *Psychological Bulletin, 115,* 424–443.

Noyes, R., Clarkson, C., Crowe, R. R., Yates, W. R., & McChesney, C. M. (1987). A family study of generalized anxiety disorder. *American Journal of Psychiatry, 144,* 1019–1024.

Oldenburg, C. M., & Kerns, K. A. (1997). Association between peer relationships and depressive symptoms: Testing moderator effects of gender and age. *Journal of Early Adolescence, 17,* 319–337.

Ollendick, T. H., King, N. J., & Frary, R. B. (1989). Fears in children and adolescents: Reliability and generalizability across gender, age, and nationality. *Behavior Research and Therapy, 27,* 19–26.

Ollendick, T. H., Yang, B., Dong, Q., Xia, Y., & Lin, L. (1995). Perceptions of fear in other children and adolescents: The role of gender and friendship status. *Journal of Abnormal Child Psychology, 23,* 439–452.

O'Neal, C., & Malatesta-Magai, C. (2001, August). Emotion socialization and regulation: The emotions as a child measure. In C. O'Neal (Chair), *Multiple approaches to emotion socialization: Methodology and emotional development.* Paper presented at the annual meeting of the American Psychological Association, San Francisco.

Ostrov, J. M., & Keating, C. F. (2004). Gender differences in preschool aggression during free play and structured interactions: An observational study. *Social Development, 13,* 255–277.

Ostrov, J. M., Woods, K. E., Jansen, E. A., Casas, J. F., & Crick, N. R. (2004). An observational study of delivered and received aggression, gender, and social-psychological adjustment in preschool: "This white crayon doesn't work . . ." *Early Childhood Research Quarterly, 19,* 355–371.

Owens, D. F., & Kriegstein, A. R. (2002). Is there more to GABA than synaptic inhibition? *Nature Reviews Neuroscience, 3,* 715–727.

Paikoff, R. L., Brooks-Gunn, J., & Warren, M. P. (1991). Effects of girls' hormonal status on depressive and aggressive symptoms over the course of one year. *Journal of Youth and Adolescence, 20,* 191–215.

Pajer, K. (1998). What happens to "bad" girls? A review of the adult outcomes of antisocial adolescent girls. *American Journal of Psychiatry, 155,* 862–870.

Pajer, K., Gardner, W., Kirillova, G. P., & Vanyukov, M. M. (2001). Sex differences in cortisol level and neurobehavioral disinhibition in children of substance abusers. *Journal of Child and Adolescent Substance Abuse, 10,* 65–76.

Paris, J. (2001). Psychosocial adversity. In W. J. Liversley, *Handbook of personality disorders: Theory, research, and treatment* (pp. 231–241). New York: Guilford Press.

Paris, J. (2003). *Personality disorders over time: Precursors, course, and outcome.* Washington, DC: American Psychiatric Publishing.

Parker, G., & Hadzi-Pavlovic, D. (2004). Is the female preponderance in major depression secondary to a gender difference in specific anxiety disorders? *Psychological Medicine, 34,* 461–470.

Patterson, G. R., Capaldi, D., & Bank, L. (1991). An early starter model for predicting delinquency. In D. J. Pepler & K. H. Rubin (Eds.), *Development and treatment of childhood aggression* (pp. 139–168). Hillsdale, NJ: Erlbaum.

Pawluck, D. E., & Gorey, K. M. (1998). Secular trends in the incidence of anorexia nervosa: Integrative review of population-based studies. *International Journal of Eating Disorders, 23,* 347–352.

Petersen, A. C., Graber, J. A., & Sullivan, P. (1990, March). *Pubertal timing and adjustment in adolescence: Variations in effects.* Paper presented at the third biennial meeting of the Society for Research in Adolescence, Atlanta, GA.

Petersen, A. C., Sarigiani, P. A., & Kennedy, R. E. (1991). Adolescent depression: Why more girls? *Journal of Youth and Adolescence, 20,* 247–271.

Petty, F. (1995). GABA and mood disorders: A brief review and hypothesis. *Journal of Affect Disorders, 34,* 275–281.

Phoenix, C., Goy, R., & Young, W. (1967). Sexual behavior: General aspects. In L. Martini & W. Ganong (Eds.), *Neuroendocrinology* (Vol. 2). New York: Academic Press.

Pine, D. S., Cohen, P., Gurley, D., Brook, J., & Ma, Y. (1998). The risk for early-adulthood anxiety and depressive disorders in adolescents with anxiety and depressive disorders. *Archives of General Psychiatry, 55,* 56–64.

Pine, D. S., Cohen, P., Johnson, J. G., & Brook, J. S. (2002). Adolescent life events as predictors of adult depression. *Journal of Affective Disorders, 68,* 49–57.

Pollack, W. S. (1998). *Real boys: Rescuing our sons from the myths of boyhood.* New York: Random House.

Pope, H., Olivardia, R., Gruber, A., & Borowiecki, J. (1999). Evolving ideals of male body image as seen through action toys. *International Journal of Eating Disorders, 26,* 65–72.

Post, R. M., Weiss, S. R. B., Leverich, G. S., George, M. S., Frye, M., & Ketter, T. A. (1996). Developmental psychobiology of cyclic affective illness: Implications for early therapeutic intervention. *Development and Psychopathology, 8,* 273–305.

Powers, S. I., & Welsh, D. P. (1999). Mother-daughter interactions and adolescent girls' depression. In M. Cox & J. Brooks-Gunn (Eds.), *Conflict and closeness: The formation, functioning, and stability of families* (pp. 243–281). Mahwah, NJ: Erlbaum.

Poznanski, E. O., & Mokros, H. B. (1994). Phenomenology and epidemiology of mood disorders in children and adolescents. In W. M. Reynolds & H. F. Johnston (Eds.), *Handbook of depression in children and adolescents: Issues in clinical child psychology* (pp. 19–39). New York: Plenum Press.

Prescott, C. A., Aggen, S. H., & Kendler, K. S. (1999). Sex differences in the sources of genetic liability to alcohol abuse and dependence in a population-based sample of U.S. twins. *Alcoholism, Clinical, and Experimental Research, 23,* 1136–1144.

Putallaz, M., & Bierman, K. L. (2004). *Aggression, antisocial behavior, and violence among girls: A developmental perspective.* New York: Guilford Press.

Quinones-Jenab, V., Perrotti, L. I., Fabian, S. J., Chin, J., Russo, S. J., & Jenab, S. (2001). Endocrinological basis of sex differences in cocaine-induced behavioral responses. *Annals of the New York Academy of Sciences, 937,* 140–171.

Radke-Yarrow, M., Zahn-Waxler, C., Richardson, D. T., Susman, A., & Martinez, P. (1994). Caring behavior in children of clinically depressed and well mothers. *Child Development, 65,* 1405–1414.

Reiss, A. L., Eckert, M. A., Rose, F. E., Karchemskiy, A., Kessler, S., Chang, M., et al. (2004). An experiment of nature: Brain anatomy parallels cognition and behavior in Williams syndrome. *Journal of Neuroscience, 24,* 5009–5015.

Reznikov, A. G., Nosenko, N. D., & Tarasenko, L. V. (1999). Prenatal stress and glucocorticoid effects on the developing gender-related brain. *Journal of Steroid Biochemistry and Molecular Biology, 69,* 109–115.

Rhee, S. H., Waldman, I. D., Hay, D. A., & Levy, F. (1999). Sex differences in genetic and environmental influences on DSM-III-R attention-deficit/hyperactivity disorder. *Journal of Abnormal Psychology, 108,* 24–41.

Rhodes, M. E., & Rubin, R. T. (1999). Functional sex differences ("sexual diergism") of central nervous system cholinergic systems, vasopressin, and hypothalamic-pituitary-adrenal axis activity in mammals: A selective review. *Brain Research Reviews, 30,* 135–152.

Roberts, R. W., Andrews, J. A., Lewinsohn, P. M., & Hops, H. (1990). Assessment of depression in adolescents using the Center for Epidemiologic Studies Depression Scale. *Psychological Assessment, 2,* 122–128.

Robins, L. N. (1986). The consequences of conduct disorder in girls. In D. Olweus, J. Block, & M. Radke-Yarrow (Eds.), *Development of antisocial and prosocial behavior* (pp. 385–414). Orlando, FL: Academic Press.

Robinson, T. E., & Berridge, K. C. (2000). The psychology and neurobiology of addiction: An incentive-sensitization view. *Addiction, 95,* S91–S117.

Robinson, T. E., & Berridge, K. C. (2001). Incentive-sensitization and addiction. *Addiction, 96,* 103–114.

Rohde, P., Lewinsohn, P. M., & Seeley, J. R. (1996). Psychiatric comorbidity with problematic alcohol use in high school adolescents. *Journal of the American Academy of Child and Adolescent Psychiatry, 35,* 101–109.

Rose, R. J., & Ditto, W. B. (1983). A developmental-genetic analysis of common fears from early adolescence to early adulthood. *Child Development, 54,* 361–368.

Ross, H., Tesla, C., Kenyon, B., & Lollis, S. (1990). Maternal intervention in toddler peer conflict: The socialization of principles of justice. *Developmental Psychology, 26,* 994–1003.

Rothbart, M. K., Ahadi, S. A., & Hershey, K. L. (1994). Temperament and social behavior in childhood. *Merrill-Palmer Quarterly, 40,* 21–39.

Rowe, R., Maughan, B., Worthman, C. M., Costello, E. J., & Angold, A. (2004). Testosterone, antisocial behavior, and social dominance in boys: Pubertal development and biosocial interaction. *Biological Psychiatry, 55,* 546–552.

Rubinow, D. R., & Schmidt, P. J. (1996). Androgens, brain, and behavior. *American Journal of Psychiatry, 153,* 974–984.

Ruble, D., & Martin, C. (1998). Gender development. In W. Damon & N. Eisenberg (Eds.), *Handbook of child psychology: Social, emotional and personality development* (5th ed., Vol. 3, pp. 993–1016). New York: Wiley.

Rudolph, K. D. (2002). Gender differences in emotional responses to interpersonal stress during adolescence. *Journal of Adolescent Health, 30S,* 3–13.

Rudolph, K. D., & Conley, C. S. (2005). The socioemotional costs and benefits of social-evaluative concerns: Do girls care too much? *Journal of Personality, 73,* 115–137.

Russell, M. (1990). Prevalence of alcoholism among children of alcoholics. In M. Windle & J. S. Searles (Eds.), *Children of alcoholics: Critical perspectives* (pp. 9–38). New York: Guilford Press.

Rutter, M., Caspi, A., & Moffitt, T. E. (2003). Using sex differences in psychopathology to study causal mechanisms: Unifying issues and research strategies. *Journal of Child Psychology and Psychiatry, 44,* 1092–1115.

Saarni, C. (1984). An observational study of children's attempts to monitor their expressive behavior. *Child Development, 55,* 1504–1513.

Sapolsky, R. M. (1990). Glucocorticoids, hippocampal damage and the glutamatergic synapse. *Progress in Brain Research, 86,* 13–23.

Schiffer, H. H. (2002). Glutamate receptor genes: Susceptibility factors in Schizophrenia and depressive disorders? *Molecular Neurobiology, 25,* 191–212.

Schultz, W. (2001). Reward signaling by dopamine neurons. *Neuroscientist, 7,* 293–302.

Schwab, J., Kulin, H. E., Susman, E. J., Finkelstein, J. W., Chinchilli, V. M., Kunselman, S. J., et al. (2001). The role of sex hormone replacement therapy on self-perceived competence in adolescents with delayed puberty. *Child Development, 72,* 1439–1450.

Schwartz, C. E., Snidman, N., & Kagan, J. (1999). Adolescent social anxiety as an outcome of inhibited temperament in childhood. *Journal of the American Academy of Child and Adolescent Psychiatry, 38,* 1008–1015.

Schwartz, D., Phares, V., Tantleff-Dunn, S., & Thompson, J. (1999). Body image, psychological functioning, and parental feedback regarding physical appearance. *International Journal of Eating Disorders, 25,* 339–343.

Seeman, M. V. (2002). The role of sex hormones in psychopathology: Focus on Schizophrenia. *Primary Care, 29,* 171–182, viii.

Segovia, S., Guillamon, A., del Cerro, M. C., Ortega, E., Perez-Laso, C., Rodriguez-Zafra, M., et al. (1999). The development of brain sex differences: A multisignaling process. *Behavioral Brain Research, 105,* 69–80.

Serbin, L. A., Cooperman, J. M., Peters, P. L., Lehoux, P. M., Stack, D. M., & Schwartzman, A. E. (1998). Intergenerational transfer of psychosocial risk in women with childhood histories of aggression, withdrawal, or aggression and withdrawal. *Developmental Psychology, 34,* 1246–1262.

Serbin, L. A., Sprafkin, C., Elman, M., & Doyle, A. (1982). The early development of sex-differentiated patterns of social influence. *Canadian Journal of Behavioral Science, 14,* 350–363.

Shafran, R., & Mansell, W. (2001). Perfectionism and psychopathology: A review of research and treatment. *Clinical Psychology Review, 21,* 879–906.

Sheeber, L., Davis, B., & Hops, H. (2002). Gender-specific vulnerability to depression in children of depressed mothers. In S. H. Goodman & I. H. Gotlib (Eds.), *Children of depressed parents: Mechanisms of risk and implications for treatment* (pp. 253–274). Washington, DC: American Psychological Association.

Sher, K. J. (1991). *Children of alcoholics: A critical appraisal of theory and research.* Chicago: University of Chicago Press.

Shirtcliff, E. A., Booth, A., & Granger, D. A. (2004, October). *Social anxiety moderates the relationship between trait cortisol levels and social competence in girls.* Poster presented at the Society for Research in Psychopathology, St. Louis, MO.

Shirtcliff, E. A., Granger, D. A., & Likos, A. (2002). Gender differences in the validity of testosterone measured in saliva by immunoassay. *Hormones and Behavior, 42,* 62–69.

Siegal, M. (1987). Are sons and daughters treated more differently by fathers than mothers? *Developmental Review, 7,* 183–209.

Silberg, J., Pickles, A., Rutter, M., Hewitt, J., Simonoff, E., Maes, H., et al. (1999). The influence of genetic factors and life stress on depression among adolescent girls. *Archives of General Psychiatry, 56,* 225–232.

Silberg, J., Rutter, M., Neale, M., & Eaves, L. (2001). Genetic moderation of environmental risk for depression and anxiety in adolescent girls. *British Journal of Psychiatry, 179,* 116–121.

Silove, D., Manicavasagar, V., O'Connell, D., & Morris-Yates, A. (1995). Genetic factors in early separation anxiety: Implications for the genesis of adult anxiety disorders. *Acta Psychiatrica Scandinavia, 92,* 17–24.

Silverman, J., Raj, A., Mucci, L., & Hathaway, J. (2001). Dating violence against adolescent girls and associated substance use, unhealthy weight control, sexual risk behavior, pregnancy, and suicidality. *Journal of the American Medical Association, 28,* 572–579.

Silverman, W. K., LaGreca, A., & Wasserstein, S. (1995). What do children worry about? Worries and their relation to anxiety. *Child Development, 66,* 671–686.

Silverthorn, P., & Frick, P. J. (1999). Developmental pathways to antisocial behavior: The delayed-onset pathway in girls. *Development and Psychopathology, 11,* 101–126.

Simmons, R. G., & Blyth, D. A. (1987). *Moving into adolescence: The impact of pubertal change and school context.* New York: Aldine de Gruyter.

Simmons, R. G., Burgeson, R., & Carlton-Ford, S. (1987). The impact of cumulative change in early adolescence. *Child Development, 58,* 1220–1234.

Simpson, A. E., & Stevenson-Hinde, J. (1985). Temperamental characteristics of three-to-four-year-old boys and girls and child-family interactions. *Journal of Child Psychology and Psychiatry, 26,* 43–53.

Sims, K. D., & Robinson, M. B. (1999). Expression patterns and regulation of glutamate transporters in the developing and adult nervous system. *Critical Reviews in Neurobiology, 13,* 169–197.

Skuse, D. H. (1999). Genomic imprinting of the X chromosome: A novel mechanism for the evolution of sexual dimorphism. *Journal of Laboratory and Clinical Medicine, 133,* 23–32.

Skuse, D. H. (2000). Imprinting, the X-chromosome, and the male brain: Explaining sex differences in the liability to Autism. *Pediatric Research, 47,* 9–16.

Skuse, D. H., James, R. S., Bishop, D. V., Coppin, B., Dalton, P., Aamodt-Leeper, G., et al. (1997). Evidence from Turner's syndrome of an imprinted X-linked locus affecting cognitive function. *Nature, 387,* 705–708.

Slap, G. G., Khalid, N., Paikoff, R. L., Brooks-Gunn, J., & Warren, M. P. (1994). Evolving self-image, age, pubertal manifestations, and pubertal hormones: Preliminary findings in young adolescent girls. *Journal of Adolescent Health, 15,* 327–335.

Smetana, J. G. (1989). Toddlers' social interactions in the context of moral and conventional transgressions in the home. *Developmental Psychology, 25,* 499–509.

Smider, N. A., Essex, M. J., Kalin, N. H., Buss, K. A., Klein, M. H., Davidson, R. J., et al. (2002). Salivary cortisol as a predictor of socioemotional adjustment during kindergarten: A prospective study. *Child Development, 73,* 75–92.

Smolak, L. (2005). Eating disorders. In D. J. Bell, S. L. Foster, & E. J. Mash (Eds.), *Behavioral and emotional problems in girls* (pp. 463–487). New York: Kluwer Academic/Plenum.

Smolak, L., & Levine, M. P. (2001). Body image in children. In J. K. Thompson & L. Smolak (Eds.), *Body image, eating disorders, and obesity in youth: Assessment, prevention and treatment* (pp. 41–66). Washington, DC: American Psychological Association.

Smolak, L., Levine, M. P., & Gralen, S. (1993). The impact of puberty and dating on eating problems among middle school girls. *Journal of Youth and Adolescence, 22,* 355–368.

Smolak, L., Levine, M. P., & Schermer, F. (1999). Parental input and weight concerns among elementary school children. *International Journal of Eating Disorders, 25,* 263–271.

Spence, S. H. (1998). A measure of anxiety symptoms among children. *Behaviour Research and Therapy, 36,* 545–566.

Stattin, H., & Magnusson, D. (1990). *Pubertal maturation in female development.* Hillsdale, NJ: Erlbaum.

Steiner, M., Dunn, E., & Born, L. (2003). Hormones and mood: From menarche to menopause and beyond. *Journal of Affect Disorders, 74,* 67–83.

Stewart, A. J., & McDermott, C. (2004). Gender in psychology. *Annual Review of Psychology, 55,* 519–544.

Stice, E., & Bearman, S. (2001). Body image and eating disturbances prospectively predict increases in depressive symptoms in adolescent girls: A growth curve analysis. *Developmental Psychology, 37,* 597–607.

Stice, E., Presnell, K., & Bearman, S. K. (2001). Relation of early menarche to depression, eating disorders, substance abuse, and co-morbid psychopathology among adolescent girls. *Developmental Psychology, 37,* 608–619.

Strauss, C. C., & Last, C. G. (1993). Social and simple phobias in children. *Journal of Anxiety Disorders, 7,* 141–152.

Stroud, L. R., Salovey, P., & Epel, E. S. (2002). Sex differences in stress responses: Social rejection versus achievement stress. *Biological Psychiatry, 52,* 318–327.

Sumner, B. E., & Fink, G. (1998). Testosterone as well as estrogen increases serotonin 2A receptor mRNA and binding site densities in the male rat brain. *Molecular Brain Research, 59,* 205–214.

Susman, E. J., Dorn, L. D., Inoff-Germain, G., Nottelmann, E. D., & Chrousos, G. P. (1997). Cortisol reactivity, distress behavior, and behavioral and psychological problems in young adolescents: A longitudinal perspective. *Journal of Research on Adolescence, 7,* 81–105.

Susman, E. J., Finkelstein, J. W., Chinchilli, V. M., Schwab, J., Liben, L. S., D'Arcangelo, M. R., et al. (1998). The effect of sex hormone replacement therapy on behavior problems and moods in adolescents with delayed puberty. *Journal of Pediatrics, 133,* 521–525.

Susman, E. J., Nottelmann, E. D., & Inoff-Germain, G. (1987). Hormonal influences on aspects of psychological development during adolescence. *Journal of Adolescent Health Care, 8,* 492–504.

Susman, E. J., & Pajer, K. (2004). Biology-behavior integration and antisocial behavior in girls. In M. Putallaz & K. L. Bierman (Eds.), *Aggression, antisocial behavior, and violence among girls* (pp. 23–47). New York: Guilford Press.

Tambs, K., Harris, J. R., & Magnus, P. (1995). Sex-specific causal factors and effects of common environment for symptoms of anxiety and depression in twins. *Behavior Genetics, 25,* 33–44.

Tangney, J. P., Wagner, P. E., Hill-Barlow, D., Marschall, D. E., & Gramzow, R. (1996). Relation of shame and guilt to constructive and destructive responses to anger across the lifespan. *Journal of Personality and Social Psychology, 70,* 797–809.

Tannock, R. (1998). Attention deficit hyperactivity disorder: Advances in cognitive, neurobiological, and genetic research. *Journal of Child Psychology and Psychiatry, 39,* 65–99.

Taylor, S. E., Dickerson, S. S., & Klein, L. C. (2002). Toward a biology of social support. In C. R. Snyder & S. J. Lopez (Eds.), *Handbook of positive psychology* (pp. 556–569). New York: Oxford University Press.

Taylor, S., Klein, L. C., Lewis, B. P., Gruenewald, T. L., Gurung, R. A. R., & Updegraff, J. A. (2000). Biobehavioral response to stress in females: Tend and befriend, not fight-or-flight. *Psychological Review, 107,* 411–429.

Taylor, S. E., Lewis, B. P., Gruenewald, T. L., Gurung, R. A. R., Updegraff, J. A., & Klein, L. C. (2002). Sex differences in biobehavioral responses to threat: Reply to Geary and Flinn (2002). *Psychological Review, 109,* 751–753.

Thompson, J. K., & Smolak, L. (2001). Body image, eating disorders, and obesity in youth: The future is now. In J. K. Thompson & L. Smolak (Eds.), *Body image, eating disorders, and obesity in youth: Assessment, prevention and treatment* (pp. 1–18). Washington, DC: American Psychological Association.

Thompson, J. K., & Stice, E. (2001). Thin-ideal internalization: Mounting evidence for a new risk factor for body image disturbance and eating pathology. *Current Directions in Psychological Science, 10,* 181–183.

Tolan, P. H., & Thomas, P. (1995). The implications of age of onset for delinquency risk: II. Longitudinal data. *Journal of Abnormal Child Psychology, 23,* 157–181.

Tomada, G., & Schneider, B. H. (1997). Relational aggression, gender, and peer acceptance: Invariance across culture, stability over time, and concordance among informants. *Developmental Psychology, 33,* 601–609.

Tomarken, A. J., & Davidson, R. J. (1994). Frontal brain activation in repressors and nonrepressors. *Journal of Abnormal Psychology, 103,* 339–349.

Tomarken, A. J., Dichter, G. S., Garber, J., & Simien, C. (2004). Resting frontal brain activity: Linkage to maternal depression and socioeconomic status among adolescents. *Biological Psychology, 67,* 77–102.

Tucker, M., & Bond, N. W. (1997). The roles of gender, sex role, and disgust in fear of animals. *Personality and Individual Differences, 22,* 135–138.

Turner, P. J. (1991). Relations between attachment, gender, and behavior with peers in preschool. *Child Development, 62*, 1475–1488.

Udry, J. R. (2000). Biological limits of gender construction. *American Sociological Review, 65*, 443–457.

Udry, J. R., Morris, N., & Kovenock, J. (1995). Androgen effects on women's gendered behavior. *Journal of Biosocial Science, 27*, 359–369.

Underwood, M. K. (2003). *Social aggression among girls.* New York: Guilford Press.

Valleni-Basile, L. A., Garrison, C. Z., Jackson, K. L., Waller, J. L., Mckeown, R. E., Addy, C. L., et al. (1994). Frequency of obsessive-compulsive disorder in a community sample of young adolescents. *Journal of the American Academy of Child and Adolescent Psychiatry, 33*, 782–791.

Vernberg, E. M., Abwender, D. A., Ewell, K. K., & Beery, S. H. (1992). Social anxiety and peer relationships in early adolescence: A prospective analysis. *Journal of Clinical Child Psychology, 21*, 189–196.

Viau, V. (2002). Functional cross-talk between the hypothalamic-pituitary-gonadal and -adrenal axes. *Journal of Neuroendocrinology, 14*, 506–513.

Volkmar, F. R., Lord, C., Bailey, A., Schultz, R. T., & Klin, A. (2004). Autism and pervasive developmental disorders. *Journal of Child Psychology and Psychiatry, 45*, 135–170.

Volkmar, F. R., Szatmari, P., & Sparrow, S. S. (1993). Sex differences in pervasive developmental disorders. *Journal of Autism and Developmental Disorders, 23*, 579–591.

Vuchinich, S., Emery, R., & Cassidy, J. (1988). Family members as third parties in dyadic family conflict: Strategies, alliances and outcomes. *Child Development, 59*, 1293–1302.

Wagner, B. M., & Compas, B. E. (1990). Gender, instrumentality, and expressivity: Moderators of the relation between stress and psychological symptoms during adolescence. *American Journal of Community Psychology, 18*, 383–406.

Walker, E. F., Grimes, K. E., Davis, D. M., & Smith, A. J. (1993). Childhood precursors of Schizophrenia: Facial expressions of emotion. *American Journal of Psychiatry, 150*, 1654–1660.

Walker, E. F., & Lewine, R. R. (1993). Sampling biases in studies of gender and Schizophrenia. *Schizophrenia Bulletin, 19*, 1–7; discussion 9–14.

Walker, E. F., Walder, D. J., Lewis, R. R., & Loewy, R. (2002). Sex differences in the origins and premorbid development of Schizophrenia. In F. Lewis-Hall & T. S. Williams (Eds.), *Psychiatric illness in women: Emerging treatments and research* (pp. 193–214). Washington, DC: American Psychiatric Publishing.

Wallen, K. (1996). Nature needs nurture: The interaction of hormonal and social influences on the development of behavioral sex differences in rhesus monkeys. *Hormones and Behavior, 30*, 364–378.

Warner, V., Weissman, M. M., Mufson, L., & Wickramaratne, P. J. (1999). Grandparents, parents and grandchildren at high risk for depression: A three-generation study. *Journal of the American Academy of Child and Adolescent Psychiatry, 38*, 289–296.

Warren, S. L., Schmitz, S., & Emde, R. N. (1999). Behavioral genetic analyses of self-reported anxiety at 7 years of age. *Journal of the American Academy of Child and Adolescent Psychiatry, 38*, 1403–1408.

Watson, D., & Clark, L. A. (1992). Affects separable and inseparable: On the hierarchical arrangement of the negative affects. *Journal of Personality and Social Psychology, 62*, 489–505.

Webster-Stratton, C. (1996). Early-onset conduct problems: Does gender make a difference? *Journal of Consulting and Clinical Psychology, 64*, 540–551.

Weinberg, M. K., Olson, K. L., Beeghly, M., & Tronick, E. Z. (2005). *Making up is hard to do especially for mothers with high levels of depressive symptoms and their infant sons.* Manuscript submitted for publication. Available from Weinberg@al.tch.harvard.edu.

Weinberg, M. K., Tronick, E. Z., Cohn, J. F., & Olson, K. L. (1999). Gender differences in emotional expressivity and self-regulation during early infancy. *Developmental Psychology, 35*, 175–188.

Weinstock, L. S. (1999). Gender differences in the presentation and management of social anxiety disorder. *Journal of Clinical Psychiatry, 60*, 9–13.

Weissman, M. M., & Klerman, G. L. (1977). Sex differences and the epidemiology of depression. *Archives of General Psychiatry, 34*, 98–111.

Weissman, M. M., Leaf, P. J., Bruce, M. L., & Florio, L. (1988). The epidemiology of dysthymia in five communities: Rates, risks, comorbidity, and treatment. *American Journal of Psychiatry, 145*, 815–819.

Weisz, J. R., Weiss, B., Han, S. S., Granger, D. A., & Morton, T. (1995). Effects of psychotherapy with children and adolescents revisited: A meta-analysis of treatment outcome studies. *Psychological Bulletin, 117*, 450–468.

Werner, N. E., & Crick, N. R. (1999). Relational aggression and social-psychological adjustment in a college sample. *Journal of Abnormal Psychology, 108*, 615–623.

White, H. R., & Hansell, S. (1996). The moderating effects of gender and hostility on the alcohol-aggression relationship. *Journal of Research in Crime and Delinquency, 33*, 451–472.

Wichstrom, L. (1999). The emergence of gender differences in depressed mood during adolescence: The role of intensified gender socialization. *Developmental Psychology, 35*, 232–245.

Williamson, D. E., Birmaher, B., Anderson, B. P., Al-Shabbout, M., & Ryan, N. D. (1995). Stressful life events in depressed adolescents: The role of dependent events during the depressive episode. *Journal of the American Academy of Child and Adolescent Psychiatry, 34*, 591–598.

Windle, M. (1992). A longitudinal study of stress buffering for adolescent problem behaviors. *Developmental Psychology, 28*, 522–530.

Wood, J. J., McLeod, B. D., Sigman, M., Hwang, W., & Chu, B. C. (2003). Parenting and childhood anxiety: Theory, empirical findings, and future directions. *Journal of Child Psychology and Psychiatry, 44*, 134–151.

Yonkers, K. A., & Brawnman-Mintzer, O. (2002). The pharmacologic treatment of depression: Is gender a critical factor? *Journal of Clinical Psychiatry, 63*, 610–615.

Yonkers, K. A., Kando, J. C., Cole, J. O., & Blumenthal, S. (1992). Gender differences in pharmacokinetics and pharmacodynamics of psychotropic medication. *American Journal of Psychiatry, 149*, 587–595.

Young, E. A. (1998). Sex differences and the HPA axis: Implications for psychiatric disease. *Journal of Gender Specific Medicine, 1*, 21–27.

Young, W. C., Goy, R. W., & Phoenix, C. H. (1964). Hormones and sexual behavior. *Science, 143*, 212–218.

Zahn-Waxler, C. (1993). Warriors and worriers: Gender and psychopathology. *Development and Psychopathology, 5*, 79–89.

Zahn-Waxler, C. (2000). The development of empathy, guilt, and internalization of distress: Implications for gender differences in internalizing and externalizing problems. In R. Davidson (Ed.), *Anxiety, depression, and emotion* (pp. 222–265). New York: Oxford University Press.

Zahn-Waxler, C., Cole, P. M., & Barrett, K. C. (1991). Guilt and empathy: Sex differences and implications for the development of depression. In K. Dodge & J. Garber (Eds.), *Emotional regulation and dysregulation* (pp. 243–272). New York: Cambridge University Press.

Zahn-Waxler, C., Iannotti, R. J., Cummings, E. M., & Denham, S. (1990). Antecedents of problem behaviors in children of depressed mothers. *Development and Psychopathology, 2*, 271–291.

Zahn-Waxler, C., Kochanska, G., Krupnick, J., & McKnew, D. (1990). Patterns of guilt in children of depressed and well mothers. *Developmental Psychology, 26,* 51–59.

Zahn-Waxler, C., Park, J., Usher, B., Belouad, F., Cole, P., & Gruber, R. (2005). *Young children's representations of conflict and distress: A longitudinal study of boys and girls with disruptive behavior problems.* Unpublished manuscript.

Zahn-Waxler, C., & Polanichka, N. (2004). All things interpersonal: Socialization and female aggression. In M. Putallaz & K. Bierman (Eds.), *Aggression, antisocial behavior and violence among girls: A developmental perspective* (pp. 48–68). New York: Guilford Press.

Zahn-Waxler, C., Race, E., & Duggal, S. (2005). Mood disorders and symptoms in girls. In D. J. Bell, S. L. Foster, & E. J. Mash (Eds.), *Handbook of behavioral and emotional problems in girls* (pp. 25–77). New York: Kluwer Academic/Plenum.

Zahn-Waxler, C., & Robinson, J. (1995). Empathy and guilt: Early origins of feelings of responsibility. In K. Fisher & J. Tangney (Eds.), *Self-conscious emotions: Shame, guilt, embarrassment, and pride* (pp. 143–173). New York: Guilford Press.

Zahn-Waxler, C., Robinson, J., & Emde, R. N. (1992). The development of empathy in twins. *Developmental Psychology, 28,* 1038–1047.

Zahn-Waxler, C., Schmitz, S., Fulker, D., Robinson, J., & Emde, R. (1996). Behavior problems in 5-year-old monozygotic twins: Genetic and environmental influences, patterns of regulation, and internalization of control. *Development and Psychopathology, 8,* 103–122.

Zeman, J., & Shipman, K. (1997). Social-contextual influences on expectancies for managing anger and sadness: The transition from middle childhood to adolescence. *Developmental Psychology, 33,* 917–924.

Zeman, J., & Shipman, K. (1998). Influence of social context on children's affect regulation: A functionalist perspective. *Journal of Nonverbal Behavior, 22,* 141–165.

Zhang, L., Ma, W., Barker, J. L., & Rubinow, D. R. (1999). Sex differences in expression of serotonin receptors (subtypes 1A and 2A) in rat brain: A possible role of testosterone. *Neuroscience, 94,* 251–259.

Zoccolillo, M. (1993). Gender and the development of conduct disorder. *Development and Psychopathology, 5,* 65–78.

Zoccolillo, M., Pickles, A., Quinton, D., & Rutter, M. (1992). The outcome of childhood conduct disorder: Implications for defining adult personality disorder and conduct disorder. *Psychological Medicine, 22,* 971–986.

Zucker, R. A. (1994). Pathways to alcohol problems and alcoholism: A developmental account of the evidence for multiple alcoholisms and for contextual contributions to risk. In R. Zucker, G. Boyd, & J. Howard (Eds.), *The development of alcohol problems: Exploring a biopsychosocial matrix of risk* (pp. 255–289). Rockville, MD: National Institute on Alcohol Abuse and Alcoholism.

Zucker, R. A., Fitzgerald, H. E., & Moses, H. D. (1995). Emergence of alcohol problems and the several alcoholisms: A developmental perspective on etiologic theory and life course trajectory. In D. Cicchetti & D. J. Cohen (Eds.), *Developmental psychopathology: Risk, disorder, and adaptation* (pp. 677–711). Oxford: Wiley.

CHAPTER 5

Developmental Issues in Assessment, Taxonomy, and Diagnosis of Psychopathology: Life Span and Multicultural Perspectives

THOMAS M. ACHENBACH and LESLIE A. RESCORLA

In revising this chapter for the second edition of *Developmental Psychopathology,* we address numerous advances in knowledge and methods related to developmental issues in assessment, taxonomy, and diagnosis of psychopathology. The previous version of the chapter outlined applications of developmental perspectives to adult psychopathology as an important future direction. Since then, new research has addressed developmental issues in assessment, taxonomy, and diagnosis of adult psychopathology. Consequently, this chapter now takes account of psychopathology across the life span.

Another innovation is the inclusion of multicultural perspectives. Forced and voluntary migrations of millions of people to unfamiliar cultures raise many new challenges for mental health, educational, social, and correctional systems. At the same time, a growing body of research is revealing fascinating multicultural similarities and differences in psychopathology assessed by the same standardized procedures. This work provides a basis for applying what is now known about assessment, taxonomy, and diagnosis to culturally diverse groups. It also provides a foundation for the additional efforts that are needed. To set the stage for considering assessment, taxonomy, and diagnosis, we first outline the life span and multicultural perspectives that are now so important. Thereafter, we address the developmental and psychopathology components of developmental psychopathology, the nature of assessment, taxonomy, and diagnosis, relevant methodologies, life span and multicultural applications, the benefits of quantification, and future directions.

LIFE SPAN PERSPECTIVES

Developmental approaches to the study of psychopathology originated with efforts to advance our understanding of maladaptive functioning between birth and maturity (Achenbach, 1974, 1982; Cicchetti, 1984; Rutter & Garmezy, 1983). It is now clearly recognized that behavioral and emotional problems in the young need to be understood in relation to developmental sequences, norms, and processes. However, it is also becoming clear that developmental approaches are needed to understand psychopathology at older ages. In many countries, challenges posed by the growing legions of elderly people are raising awareness of the need to cope with developmental changes in functioning during the last decades of life. Developmental perspectives can also illuminate adaptive and maladaptive functioning in the early and middle adult years when many changes occur in social roles, relationships, responsibilities, careers, self-concepts, and biological characteristics, including health. Although developmental issues in assessment, taxonomy, and diagnosis have received more attention with respect to children and adolescents than adults, life span perspectives argue for expanding our horizons to include developmental issues pertaining to adults as well.

A particularly important issue concerns the need to obtain multisource data for purposes of assessment, taxonomy, and diagnosis. It is now widely accepted that no single source can serve as a gold standard for assessing child and adolescent functioning. Instead, because agreement among informants is typically low to moderate (Achenbach, McConaughy, & Howell, 1987), assessment of children should include data from multiple informants. The data must then be systematically compared and integrated to identify both the consistencies and variations among reports of an individual's functioning.

In the assessment of elders whose mental competence may be questionable, it is common to obtain information from other informants, such as a spouse or grown child. In the assessment of younger adults, by contrast, data are typically obtained solely from the adults who are being assessed, mainly via interviews, tests, and questionnaires. Yet, meta-analyses of cross-informant correlations for assessment of adult psychopathology have revealed only modest agreement between self-reports and reports by others (Achenbach, Krukowski, Dumenci, & Ivanova, 2005). A major challenge for improving assessment, taxonomy, and diagnosis of adult psychopathology is therefore to apply to adults the principles and methods for integrating multi-informant data that have been developed for children and adolescents. Other lessons learned from the developmental study of child and adolescent psychopathology can also be applied throughout adulthood.

MULTICULTURAL PERSPECTIVES

Mental health professionals are increasingly expected to help people from diverse cultural backgrounds. In some cases, the need to cope with cultural diversity arises from influxes of foreign refugees and immigrants. In other cases, the need to cope with cultural diversity arises from migrations within a country. And in still other cases, the need to cope with cultural diversity arises from greater awareness of cultural differences among people who have long coexisted in a particular area.

Cultural diversity raises a variety of challenges for mental health professionals. Perhaps the most obvious is differences in language. Because mental health professionals may not be fluent in the languages of all the groups to be served, interpreters may be needed. Even when language is not a barrier, however, cultural differences related to ethnicity, religion, place of origin, and socioeconomic status (SES) may affect communications between mental health professionals and the people they serve.

For assessment, taxonomy, and diagnosis of psychopathology, a fundamental multicultural issue is whether the same procedures can be used to assess people from different cultures. This issue raises questions such as the following:

- Can mental health professionals readily use the same procedures to assess the problems and adaptive functioning of people from different cultures?
- Do people from different cultures accept the same assessment procedures as effective ways of communicating information?
- What can we learn from comparisons of assessment data obtained from people of different cultures?
- Can mental health professionals learn to distinguish characteristics that are specific to individuals from stereotypical characteristics of particular cultural groups?

To answer these questions, systematic research is needed to compare the results of standardized assessment procedures applied to representative samples of people from different cultures. As detailed later, a growing body of research is available to answer these questions for diverse cultures. Such research can also help us distinguish between aspects of psychopathology that are relatively consistent versus those that are more variable across cultures. Throughout this chapter, we highlight the importance of comparing findings for people who differ in culture and developmental level, as they are assessed from different perspectives, to identify important consistencies and differences in levels and patterns of psychopathology.

DEVELOPMENTAL PSYCHOPATHOLOGY

Developmental approaches to the study of psychopathology have become increasingly influential over the past 3 decades. These approaches have greatly advanced our understanding of maladaptive functioning in childhood and adolescence. Developmental approaches to psychopathology have also helped to shape training and practice. However, much remains to be done to integrate the study, prevention, and treatment of psychopathology with the study of development across the life span.

Assessment, taxonomy, and diagnosis are central foci around which developmental approaches to psychopathology can be organized. As a preface to considering assessment, taxonomy, and diagnosis, it is first important to introduce what we mean by *development* and *psychopathology*. We use both of these concepts broadly, with a minimum of theoretical assumptions. Although particular theories of development and psychopathology may help us understand particular phenomena, the utility of these concepts would be diminished by limiting their meanings to the tenets of particular theories.

The Developmental Component

We use *developmental* to encompass processes, changes, sequences, and characteristics that are typically associated with age. Chronological age (CA) is the most obvious developmental yardstick, but it may serve as a proxy for many other developmental parameters. For some purposes, it may be preferable to use other developmental parameters that do not necessarily correlate highly with CA. Mental age and other indexes of cognitive developmental level, for example, would not correlate highly with CA in samples that included children with mental retardation, whose cognitive levels would be below their CAs, or very bright children, whose cognitive levels would be above their CAs. Biological parameters are also important developmental indexes. Nevertheless, even when a parameter other than CA provides a more precise index of developmental variables, CA remains an important common denominator because of CA-related differences in biological maturity and social status. Our use of the term developmental is intended to stimulate new ideas rather than to mold thinking according to the dictates of any single concept of development.

In addition to identifying characteristics that are associated with particular developmental parameters, a developmental perspective focuses on adaptation. By identifying adaptive and maladaptive processes, we can shed light on the origins of favorable versus unfavorable outcomes. This, in turn, provides a basis for inferring causal factors in psychopathology and for interventions to prevent or treat psychopathology by enhancing factors that lead to favorable outcomes.

Developmental Theories

Some of the most influential theories of human psychological functioning have been developmental. Psychoanalytic theory, for example, interprets adult psychopathology in terms of childhood precursors involving psychosexual stages, fixations, and regressions (S. Freud, 1940). Piaget's (1983) theory portrays adult cognitive functioning as an outgrowth of stage-like advances and reorganizations. Learning theories attribute deviant behavior to the environmental contingencies experienced throughout the individual's lifetime (e.g., Bandura, 1977). Theories about infants' attachment to their caregivers have been used to explain later interpersonal functioning in terms of persisting attachment representations (e.g., Cassidy & Shaver, 1999). Genetic theories hypothesize sequences of biological determinants that start at conception and continue through the eventual emergence of psychopathology (Rutter, 1991).

Because different theories can help us understand different aspects of development and psychopathology, the developmental study of psychopathology should not be restricted to the tenets of any single theory.

It may seem obvious that an organism's behavior at a particular point is in many respects an outgrowth of its previous history. It is much less obvious how and to what extent the organism's previous history determines successful adaptation versus pathological maladaptation at particular points. The diverse theories attest to the range of possible ways to view development and to the multitude of variables that may be associated with differences in developmental periods and levels. Although it is not feasible for us to take account of all variables posited by all theories of development, the different theories provide rich arrays of clues and concepts for guiding the developmental study of psychopathology.

Developmental Considerations in Assessment, Taxonomy, and Diagnosis

Knowledge of development should guide assessment, taxonomy, and diagnosis of psychopathology. For example, knowledge of cognitive development would argue against using interviews that require children to judge their own behavioral and emotional problems before they are cognitively capable of making and communicating such judgments. Although this may seem obvious, Breton et al. (1995) found that even normal 9- to 11-year-olds failed to understand many questions on the Diagnostic Interview Schedule for Children (DISC; Shaffer, 1992), which is widely used to make psychiatric diagnoses. Knowledge of development is thus needed to tailor assessment methods to the specific capabilities of those who are being assessed. Assessment should also be designed to detect possible developmental differences that have not previously been identified.

In designing assessment procedures to take account of developmental differences, it is important to be sensitive to developmental variations in the *content* and *patterning* of the relevant phenomena, as well as to parameters that can be measured in a uniform fashion across broad age spans. For example, height, weight, and IQ are expressed in numbers for people of all ages. Yet, the physical and cognitive configurations underlying these numbers change markedly across the life span. Thus, children who weigh 40 pounds at age 5 and 120 pounds at age 15 have not merely grown three times as large; their body proportions have changed, pubertal development has occurred, and their adolescent appearance causes people to treat them differently.

Analogously, the cognitive processes and specific responses that yield an IQ of 100 at age 5 are very different from those that yield an IQ of 100 at age 15. By the same token, psychopathological conditions that bear the same diagnostic label at different ages, such as Attention-Deficit/Hyperactivity Disorder (ADHD), may be phenotypically quite different at ages 5, 15, and 30, may involve different underlying processes, and may have different consequences for the individual's adaptation. We should therefore be aware that when diagnostic terms such as ADHD are applied to people of different ages, they may not actually represent encapsulated disorders that are the same at all ages.

We must also remember that certain behaviors may be considered normal during one developmental period but deviant at earlier or later developmental periods. For example, high levels of motor activity that are normal for preschoolers would be considered deviant in adolescents. Conversely, degrees of sexual interest that are normal for adolescents would be considered deviant for preschoolers.

Developmental Methodology

Developmental approaches contribute methodology that is essential for comparing functioning at different ages and for linking variables assessed at one age with those assessed at other ages. Longitudinal research is a hallmark of developmental methodology and is essential for determining relations between variables assessed at different ages. Certain classic longitudinal studies have had major impacts on views of relations between childhood characteristics and broad aspects of later functioning (e.g., Bayley, 1968; Kagan & Moss, 1962). Others have revealed developmental relations between childhood characteristics and adult psychopathology (e.g., Hofstra, van der Ende, & Verhulst, 2002a, 2002b; Krueger, Caspi, Moffit, & Silva, 1998).

Despite their importance, real-time longitudinal studies are costly, seldom use broadly representative samples, and take many years to yield results. More practical methods for obtaining longitudinal data have therefore been sought. These include follow-up (or catch-up) studies, in which people assessed at one age are sought for reassessment at a later point in time, and follow-back studies, which seek to obtain records of the earlier history of people for whom outcomes are known. Follow-up and follow-back studies are usually quicker and more economical than real-time longitudinal studies. Follow-up and follow-back designs may also be used to select individuals who have particular risk or outcome characteristics that would be difficult to study with real-time longitudinal designs because of obstacles to repeatedly assessing large enough samples of such individuals.

Examples of influential follow-up studies of childhood disorders include Robins's (1966) study of adults who had been assessed at a child guidance clinic many years earlier and a long-term follow-up of autistic children by Kanner, Rodriquez, and Ashenden (1972). Follow-back studies that started with known adult outcomes include comparisons of the early school records of people who differed in adult psychiatric diagnoses (Lewine, Watt, Prentky, & Fryer, 1980).

Because longitudinal research is essential for linking early characteristics with later outcomes, it is important to consider strategies for applying longitudinal methodology. In later sections, we present research designs that are especially useful for illuminating the developmental course of psychopathology.

The Psychopathology Component

We use the term *psychopathology* broadly to encompass persistent behavior, thoughts, and emotions that are likely to impede the accomplishment of developmental tasks necessary for long-term adaptation. For children, the important developmental tasks include at least the following: regulation of biological functions relevant to eating, sleeping, elimination, and energy expenditure; maintenance of close relationships with family and peers; acquisition of academic and social skills; preparation for adult occupational and social roles; and formation of a stable sense of personal identity. For adults, important developmental tasks include achievement of mature occupational and social roles; establishment of close relationships with other adults; responsible citizenship; and, for those who have children, responsible parenthood and creation of loving, healthy home environments. For older adults, important developmental tasks include constructive coping with the aging process; changing or giving up occupational roles; facing the loss of friends and loved ones, as well as one's own demise; maintaining a sense of independence; and preserving close attachments without becoming burdensome.

A key aim of this chapter is to advance our ways of thinking about psychopathology. Because psychopathology can be conceptualized in different ways for different purposes, it is important to consider the relative utility of various models for assessment, taxonomy, and diagnosis.

Nosologically Based Models

Nosological models for psychopathology originated in the nineteenth century with efforts to bring psychopathology out of the realm of demonology and into the realm of phys-ical medicine. An important thrust of these efforts was to model the classification of mental disorders on classifications of diseases, which are called *nosologies*.

Contemporary psychiatric nosologies stem largely from Emil Kraepelin's (1883) efforts to construct descriptive categories of major adult disorders for which, Kraepelin hoped, different physical causes would eventually be found. Kraepelin's nosology included diagnostic categories such as Schizophrenia (originally called dementia praecox, that is, premature or early dementia) and manic-depressive (bipolar) disorder, which have remained cornerstones of psychiatric nosologies ever since. Kraepelin's nosology was intended to be "descriptive" in the sense of being based on observations of patients. For adult disorders characterized by extreme forms of behavioral, emotional, and cognitive deviance, such as Schizophrenia and bipolar disorders, Kraepelin's descriptive approach established diagnostic categories that still survive. Furthermore, some disorders that were initially described in terms of both mental and physical abnormalities were eventually found to have specific physical causes. An example is general paresis, which involves mental and physical deterioration that by the late nineteenth century was found to be caused by syphilitic infection. Another example is Down syndrome, which Langdon Down (1866) described in terms of mental retardation and physical abnormalities, although it was only in 1959 that the cause was found to be a chromosomal abnormality (Lejeune, Gautier, & Turpin, 1959).

Efforts to describe disorders clinically and then to find physical etiologies have thus yielded some notable successes. Early success in discovering the etiology of paresis helped to establish the physical disease model for psychiatric nosology. Alternatively, success in pinpointing the etiology of Down syndrome had to wait for nearly a century of advances in genetic research.

Kraepelinian diagnostic categories have long molded clinical practice, theory, training, and funding for research and services. In the United States, versions of Kraepelinian nosology have been embodied in successive editions of the American Psychiatric Association's (1952, 1968, 1980, 1987, 1994) *Diagnostic and Statistical Manual of Mental Disorders* (*DSM-I, DSM-II, DSM-III, DSM-III-R, DSM-IV*). At the international level, the *International Classification of Diseases* (ninth edition, *ICD-9;* tenth edition, *ICD-10;* World Health Organization, 1978, 1992) has also embodied versions of Kraepelinian nosology.

The "Top-Down" Strategy.   In applying current versions of nosologically based models, experts formulate

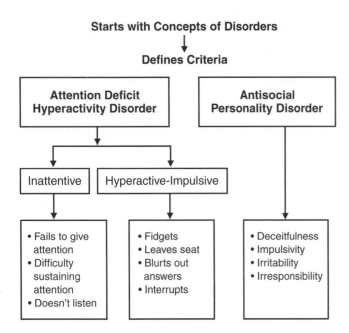

Figure 5.1   The "top-down" approach to assessment and taxonomy of psychopathology. Copyright by T. M. Achenbach. Reproduced by permission.

diagnostic categories and then choose criteria with which to define the categories. In effect, the experts start at the top with categories and then work down to the criteria, as illustrated in Figure 5.1. The diagnostic criteria for some disorders state that symptoms and impairment must be present in more than one context. However, the nosologically based paradigm does not provide specific assessment operations for obtaining and coordinating data from multiple sources. Instead, for each case, the diagnostician decides what data to obtain, what assessment methods and sources to use, and how to combine data into yes-or-no decisions about each symptom. The diagnostic data may thus differ greatly from case to case, but the same fixed decision rules are used to make diagnoses for both genders and all ages.

Empirically Based Models

For disorders having no known physical cause, an alternative to nosologically based models is to use statistical procedures to identify problems that tend to co-occur in large samples of people. Sets of statistically co-occurring problems are known as *syndromes*. (The original Greek meaning of "syndrome" was "the act of running together"; Gove, 1971, p. 2320.) The empirical identification of syndromes does not imply any assumptions about the cause of the syndromes. Some syndromes may ultimately be found to have physical causes, and others may be found to have experiential causes or combinations of physical and experiential causes.

Efforts to develop empirically based models for child psychopathology began during the 1940s and 1950s in reaction to the lack of diagnostic categories for childhood disorders (e.g., Hewitt & Jenkins, 1946; Himmelweit, cited in Eysenck, 1953). The advent of powerful computers in the 1960s facilitated factor analysis of large pools of problem items scored for large samples of children (Achenbach, 1966; Miller, 1967; Quay, 1964). The syndromes identified by factor analysis are scored by summing the scores for the problem items that compose a syndrome. Because the empirically based approach uses statistical analyses to aggregate problems that are then scored in terms of syndromes, it is also known as the *dimensional, quantitative,* or *multivariate* approach.

The "Bottom-Up" Strategy.   The empirically based approach can be described as working from the bottom up, because it starts with quantitative scores for many specific problems obtained for many individuals from informants who see them under diverse conditions. The item scores are then analyzed statistically to identify syndromes of problems that tend to occur together, as illustrated in Figure 5.2. A score for each syndrome scale is computed by summing the scores of the items that compose the scale. Norms for the syndrome scales are then constructed from data obtained for large representative samples of people.

Variations on the Bottom-Up Strategy.   In addition to empirically derived syndrome scales, numerous scales have been constructed according to criteria other than empirically identified associations among problems, even though factor analysis may have been employed as well. As an example, the Behavior Assessment System for Children was developed from an initial set of constructs chosen by Reynolds and Kamphaus (1992). Collections of items were

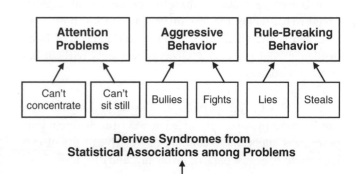

Figure 5.2   The "bottom-up" approach to assessment and taxonomy of psychopathology. Copyright by T. M. Achenbach. Reproduced by permission.

written to conform to definitions of the constructs. An item was assigned to a scale if it was "clearly linked in terms of content to the construct underlying its scale" (p. 72). Although factor analyses were performed, items were moved or deleted from the obtained factors on the basis of "reasonableness of content for the hypothesized scale dimension"; "consistency of item placement across age levels and . . . between parent and teacher respondents"; "the need for each scale to have a sufficient number of discriminating items to be reliable"; and "clinical judgment" (pp. 72–73). As an example of clinical judgment, Reynolds and Kamphaus stated that "The rating scale item 'Says "I want to die" or "I wish I were dead"' was retained on the Depression scale despite low loadings because of its clear relevance" (p. 73). Also, "Several pairs of final scales initially were part of a single scale. Examples include Depression/Withdrawal and Hyperactivity-Attention Problems" (p. 80).

Theoretically Based Models

There has been abundant theorizing about the nature of particular disorders and also about the nature of psychopathology in general. Nineteenth-century nosological efforts were initially based on the theory that all mental disorders are caused by brain diseases (Griesinger, 1845/1867). Kraepelin's (1883) initial aim was to describe differences among disorders for which different physical causes were expected to be found. However, by the 1915 version of his nosology, Kraepelin included disorders thought to be of psychological origin. He also included personality disorders, which he viewed as occupying a border region between illness and eccentricity. Although subsequent psychiatric nosologies have continued to be modeled on nosologies of physical diseases, they have not been dictated by any single etiological theory.

The Psychoanalytic Model.   Historically, the most influential general theory of psychopathology has been psychoanalysis. Sigmund Freud (1917/1963) proposed theoretical explanations for the development of particular disorders such as obsessive-compulsive versus hysterical neurosis. With respect to childhood disorders, Anna Freud (1965) proposed a Developmental Profile for assessing individual children in terms of developmental sequences hypothesized by analytic theory. The Developmental Profile includes diagnostic categories specified in terms such as the following: "There is permanent drive regression to fixation points which leads to conflicts of a neurotic type" (p. 147). Little has been published on how children are to be distinguished with respect to the assessment criteria or

diagnostic categories of the Developmental Profile. Instead, most publications illustrate how a Developmental Profile might be completed for a particular child (e.g., Yorke, 1980).

The Group for the Advancement of Psychiatry Classification.   Another theoretically based model for childhood disorders was proposed by the Group for the Advancement of Psychiatry (GAP; 1966). The GAP classification was described as being designed to operationally define disorders with a minimum of inference (p. 209). Although the GAP classification provided far more categories than Anna Freud's Developmental Profile, many of its categories required extensive psychodynamic inferences, and no assessment operations were actually specified for determining whether a child met the criteria for particular categories. As an example, the GAP category of Psychoneurotic Disorders was defined as:

> disorders based on unconscious conflicts over the handling of sexual and aggressive impulses which, though removed from awareness by the mechanism of repression, remain active and unresolved. . . . The anxiety, acting as a danger signal to the ego, ordinarily sets into operation certain defense mechanisms, in addition to repression, and leads to the formation of psychological symptoms which symbolically deal with the conflict, thus achieving a partial though unhealthy solution. (pp. 229–230)

A FRAMEWORK FOR THE DEVELOPMENTAL STUDY OF PSYCHOPATHOLOGY

To advance the developmental study of psychopathology, it is helpful to have a clear framework of issues to be addressed. Because no single research study can simultaneously address all the issues, programmatic research to improve the assessment, taxonomy, and diagnosis of psychopathology is needed to resolve these issues.

Developmental Differences

We previously stressed the importance of developmental parameters in all research on psychopathology. To obtain an accurate picture of psychopathology, it is essential to gear assessment procedures to the developmental level of the participants, to determine what features are associated with clinical deviance at each level, and to construct taxonomies that reflect features characterizing each developmental level. The features that discriminate between forms of deviance are apt to change with development. It is therefore important for assessment and taxonomy to take account of developmental changes occurring in individuals, so that the same individuals can be studied longitudinally. Both the differences and the links between developmental levels should be rigorously tested.

Sources of Data

Stemming largely from nosological models, clinical interviews have long been the main sources of data for assessing adult psychopathology. Beginning in the 1970s, structured diagnostic interviews were developed to obtain yes-or-no decisions about whether adult patients met specific research diagnostic criteria (RDC) for major mental disorders, such as Schizophrenia and manic-depressive psychoses (e.g., Overall & Hollister, 1979). The structured interviews included the Schedule for Affective Disorders and Schizophrenia (SADS; Endicott & Spitzer, 1978) and the Diagnostic Interview Schedule (DIS; Robins, Helzer, Croughan, & Ratcliff, 1981).

The explicit criteria and decision rules embodied in various versions of RDC laid the foundations for *DSM-III* (American Psychiatric Association, 1980). Departing from the narrative-inferential format of *DSM-I* and *DSM-II* (American Psychiatric Association, 1952, 1968), *DSM-III* defined disorders in terms of lists of symptoms and other criteria, such as age of onset and duration of the symptoms. When using *DSM-III* and its successors, *DSM-III-R* and *DSM-IV* (American Psychiatric Association, 1987, 1994), the diagnostician is to make a yes-or-no decision about whether a patient meets each of the criteria required for a particular disorder. If the patient is deemed to meet all the requisite criteria, the patient is diagnosed as having the disorder. Diagnostic criteria and decision rules have thus become far more explicit than those provided by *DSM-I* and *DSM-II*. However, neither *DSM-III* nor its successors have specified assessment operations for determining whether the diagnostic criteria are met, except for specifying that an IQ score of 70 or lower is required for diagnosing mental retardation. As one approach to operationalizing *DSM* diagnostic criteria, the structured interviews that had been developed in the 1970s to make RDC diagnoses were subsequently revised to conform to *DSM-III* (e.g., Robins, Helzer, Ratcliff, & Seyfried, 1982; Spitzer, 1983).

Multi-Informant Data for Children

Some of the structured diagnostic interviews for adults were modified for diagnosing children. Examples include the Kiddie-SADS (Ambrosini, 2000; Puig-Antich & Chambers, 1978), which is a child version of the SADS (Endicott & Spitzer, 1978), and the Diagnostic Interview Schedule for Children (DISC; Costello, Edelbrock, Dulcan, Kalas, & Klaric, 1984; Shaffer et al., 1996), which is a child version of the DIS (Robins et al., 1982). Because it was recognized that children may not be able to provide full accounts of their own psychopathology, versions of the structured child interviews were also developed to obtain diagnostic information from the children's parents (e.g., DISC-P; Costello et al., 1984; Shaffer et al., 1996).

Unfortunately, the parallel structured diagnostic interviews for children and their parents did not solve problems arising from children's inability to give full accounts of their own psychopathology. Numerous studies have found little agreement between *DSM* diagnoses made from DISC interviews with children (including adolescents) and those made from interviews with their parents (e.g., Costello et al., 1984; Shaffer et al., 1996; Verhulst, van der Ende, Ferdinand, & Kasius, 1997). Furthermore, little agreement has been found between diagnoses obtained from structured child and parent interviews and clinicians' diagnoses based on other data (e.g., Costello et al., 1984; A. L. Jensen & Weisz, 2002; Lewczyk, Garland, Hurlburt, Gearity, & Hough, 2003; Rettew, Achenbach, Doyle, Ivanova, & Dumenci, 2005).

Perhaps we should not be surprised by the poor agreement between diagnoses made from structured interviews of children and their parents, or between these interviews and diagnoses made by clinicians who use other data. When asked to give yes-or-no answers to questions about psychopathology, children and their parents are apt to draw on different perceptions and memories of the children's functioning; to be differently motivated to report, distort, or withhold information; to understand questions differently; and to be differently affected by interviewers and the interview situation. Clinicians are also apt to differ from children and parents with respect to their information about the children, their memories of the information, how they combine pieces of information, and how they generate responses to questions about diagnoses.

Meta-analyses of many studies have yielded a mean r of .60 between reports of children's problems by people who play similar roles with respect to the children, such as pairs of parents, pairs of teachers, pairs of mental health workers, and pairs of observers (Achenbach et al., 1987). Between pairs of informants who play different roles with respect to the children, such as parents versus teachers and parents versus mental health workers, the mean r was .28. And between children's self-reports and reports by other people, the mean r was .22. These modest cross-informant rs indicate that diagnoses of children are likely to vary with the source of the data and that no one informant can substitute for all others.

Multi-Informant Data for Adults

Although the need for multi-informant data to assess child psychopathology is now widely recognized, assessment of adult psychopathology still relies mainly on interviews with the adults themselves. Yet, research shows that diagnoses based only on interviews with the adults in question are not likely to agree with diagnoses based on other sources of data. For example, studies of agreement between adults' self-reports of problems and reports by people who know the adults have yielded average correlations in the .20s to .40s (Achenbach et al., 2005; Klonsky, Oltmanns, & Turkheimer, 2002; Meyer, 2002; Meyer et al., 2001). In reviewing numerous studies of diagnoses of adult psychopathology, Meyer et al. concluded, "There was meager correspondence between diagnoses derived from a single clinician using (clinical interviews) and the diagnoses derived from the multimethod evaluations . . . after correcting for agreements due to chance, about 70% of the interview-based diagnoses were in error" (p. 151). Furthermore, even when the same adults were interviewed twice, once by trained lay interviewers using the DIS and once by psychiatrists using the Schedules for Clinical Assessment in Neuropsychiatry, agreement between the two interviews was extremely low, as exemplified by a kappa = .20 for Major Depressive Disorder (Eaton, Neufeld, Chen, & Cai, 2000).

For elderly adults whose mental competence is in question, it is common to obtain data from people who know the elders, such as spouses, grown children, and caregivers. The need to obtain information from others argues for routine use of parallel assessment instruments that have been developed to obtain and systematically compare assessment data from multiple informants regarding the functioning of elderly people (Achenbach, Newhouse, & Rescorla, 2004).

In adopting life span perspectives on psychopathology, we should apply lessons already learned about needs and methods for cross-informant assessment of children to assessment of adults and the elderly. The aspects of functioning to be assessed, the sources of data, and the assessment instruments must, of course, be geared to the developmental levels of the people who are being assessed.

Epidemiological Aspects

Many studies of development and psychopathology employ samples chosen for convenience rather than for representa-

tiveness with respect to important populations. This is understandable in light of the need to find people who are willing and able to participate in a particular study. However, convenience samples are often biased by selective factors that make them unrepresentative of populations. As a result, the distributions of variables and the findings in such samples cannot necessarily be generalized to other people.

If our knowledge of psychopathology is derived mainly from people who are conveniently available, we may be misled by problems that are of low frequency, do not actually distinguish normal from deviant individuals, or have different meanings among people who are not included in the convenience samples.

As an example, both the early psychoanalytic and behavioral literatures used children's fears of animals to model theories of the etiology and treatment of psychopathology. In a famous and influential case study, Sigmund Freud (1909/1953) devoted a 145-page article to illustrating the psychodynamics of Little Hans's horse phobia. In the behavioral tradition, Watson and Rayner (1920) experimentally conditioned Little Albert to fear a white rat, and Jones (1924) used Watson's principles to treat 2-year-old Peter's fear of a white rabbit.

Both the psychodynamic and behavioral traditions thus made children's fears paradigmatic for the subsequent literature on psychopathology. Yet, epidemiological studies have shown that fears of specific animals, situations, or places (other than school) are not actually much more common among children considered to be clinically deviant than among representative samples of nonreferred children (Achenbach, Howell, Quay, & Conners, 1991; Achenbach & Rescorla, 2001). Epidemiological research has also shown that specific fears are reported for *fewer* clinically referred than nonreferred adults (Achenbach & Rescorla, 2003).

Other epidemiological findings have indicated that some problems employed as criteria for nosological categories are not reported more often for clinically referred than nonreferred children. "Always on the go," for example, was a criterial symptom for the *DSM-III* category of Attention Deficit Disorder and is also a criterial symptom for the *DSM-IV* category of ADHD (American Psychiatric Association, 1980, 1994). Yet, this item was endorsed more often for a nationally representative sample of *nonreferred* children than for demographically matched *referred* children (Achenbach et al., 1991). Other nosological criteria have likewise been chosen without epidemiological evidence that they actually discriminate between clinical and nonclinical populations.

Diagnoses of behavioral and emotional disorders seldom depend on a single deviant characteristic. Instead, most disorders involve problems that many people manifest in some degree at some time in their lives. To identify people as being clinically deviant, we therefore need to know the distribution of particular problems among people considered to be relatively normal, as well as among those who are considered deviant enough to need professional help. Because many selective factors affect referral to a particular setting, we also need data on people who are seen in different settings. And we need to know the outcomes of particular problems in both referred and nonreferred populations. This requires that epidemiological samples be reassessed longitudinally to determine which problems have relatively good versus poor outcomes when treated versus untreated and what other variables predict outcomes. Such research is important not only to determine what problems distinguish people who need help from those who do not, but also to identify risk and protective factors on which preventive and therapeutic efforts can be based.

Multivariate Aspects

Because so many different kinds and degrees of problems may evoke concern, it is important to standardize the recording and analysis of problems. The difficulty of assessing and aggregating multiple problems in large samples argues for using multivariate approaches to aggregating and analyzing standardized data. Each score for an individual problem obtained from self-reports, informants' reports, observations, or tests is subject to sampling and measurement error. However, by using multivariate statistical methods, we can aggregate scores on numerous problems from multiple sources to identify patterns that characterize groups of people. This is analogous to computed tomography (CT) scanning, where numerous low-grade X-ray pictures are integrated by computer to produce high-grade images. Once we identify patterns of problems, we can use them to group people for research on the etiology, course, prognosis, and effectiveness of treatment for each pattern. Those multivariate patterns that are found to be reliable and to validly discriminate between people who differ in other important ways can then serve taxonomic functions, as detailed in later sections.

Operational Definitions

Operational definitions of variables provide basic tools for scientific research. Although scientific thought and theory also involve abstractions that are not operationalized, empirical tests of scientific ideas typically involve variables that are specified in terms of assessment operations. The results of the assessment operations provide the empirical content of the science.

Discussions of psychopathology are replete with terms that are used as if their meaning were self-evident. Terms (and their abbreviations) such as Conduct Disorder (CD), Oppositional Defiant Disorder (ODD), Antisocial Personality Disorder (APD), and ADHD are common examples from the *DSM* nosology. Terms such as Emotionally Disturbed (ED) and Learning Disabled (LD) are used with similar aplomb in special education circles, reflecting the influence of Public Law 94-142 (PL 94-142), the Education of the Handicapped Act (1977, 1981), which specifies eligibility for special education services (reauthorized as PL 101-476, Individuals with Disabilities Act, 1990; PL 105-17, 1997).

The need for operational definitions has been acknowledged in efforts to improve nosologies. In their diagnostic classification of childhood disorders, GAP (1966, p. 209), for example, "attempted to set forth operational definitions of clinical categories." *DSM-III* and its successors have also been heralded as providing operational definitions (e.g., Rapoport & Ismond, 1996, p. 13). However, neither the GAP classification nor the *DSM* has defined behavioral and emotional disorders according to specific assessment operations. But what about the *DSM*'s lists of explicitly stated criteria that are required for particular diagnoses? These criteria do not constitute operational definitions, because no operations are specified for determining whether a person manifests each criterial feature. Nor are operations specified for combining assessment data from multiple sources. This lack of truly operational definitions for disorders may be one reason reliability and cross-informant agreement are low for GAP and *DSM* diagnoses (e.g., Beitchman, Dielman, Landis, Benson, & Kemp, 1978; Freeman, 1971; A. L. Jensen & Weisz, 2002; Lewczyk et al., 2003; Shaffer, Fisher, Lucas, Dulcan, & Schwab-Stone, 2000).

Categories such as those specified by the *DSM* and PL 101-476 serve important administrative functions, such as providing guidelines for reimbursement of services. However, these categories were not derived from empirical findings on distinctions among disorders in actual samples of troubled people. The categories should therefore not be mistaken for "types" of people or "types" of disorders. Although people may indeed have the kinds of problems highlighted by administrative categories, people do not necessarily come packaged according to these categories. That is, we should not assume that people are intrinsically ADHD, CD, ODD, APD, ED, or LD. Unless we empirically test (1) the associations among features that are used to define the categories and (2) the power of the features to discriminate between normal and troubled people, we cannot know how best to distinguish among kinds of disorders. To improve our ability to distinguish between normal and clinically deviant people, as well as among patterns of clinical deviance, we need programmatic research that yields more robust groupings than most administrative categories have provided. Such research is needed to advance our overall understanding of psychopathology as well.

THE ROLES OF ASSESSMENT AND TAXONOMY IN THE DEVELOPMENTAL STUDY OF PSYCHOPATHOLOGY

To improve our ways of distinguishing the normal from the deviant and one kind of deviance from another, it is helpful to distinguish between two related tasks. One task is to *assess individual cases* to identify their distinguishing features. The second task is to *construct taxonomies* for grouping cases according to their distinguishing features. These tasks are essential steps in identifying the target disorders to be studied in each developmental period. They also form the basis for diagnostic decisions about individual cases. To improve diagnostic decision making, we need reliable and valid procedures for identifying the distinguishing features of individual cases, for grouping cases according to their distinguishing features, and for effectively integrating all the relevant data into optimal decisions. To clarify the different tasks, we first address assessment and taxonomy as scientific endeavors that can be better understood if we avoid the multiple meanings of the term "diagnosis," which we address later.

Although diagnosis is an essential part of clinical services, scientific efforts are needed to improve both diagnosis and its links to services. The following sections therefore focus on the scientific process, which "proceeds in endless cycles of observation and measurement, hypothesis testing, and the development of theory, a process dependent on a valid system of classification or taxonomy" (McClellan & Werry, 2000, p. 19).

Assessment

Assessment refers to gathering data with which to identify the distinguishing features of individual cases. Every case can be distinguished from other cases in many ways. Effective assessment requires selecting optimal features for the kinds of decisions to be made. To know what features are likely to be optimal, we need data from representative sam-

ples of cases for which the distributions, validity, and utility of various features have been tested.

Psychometric principles provide guidance for determining the methodological adequacy of assessment data. As applied to the assessment of behavioral/emotional problems, these principles can be summarized as follows:

- Assessment should employ standardized procedures.
- Multiple items should be used to sample each aspect of functioning.
- Items should be aggregated to provide quantitative scores for each aspect of functioning.
- Scores should be normed to indicate how an individual compares with relevant reference groups.
- To be developmentally sensitive, the normative reference groups should be formed according to age levels or other indexes of development.
- To be considered psychometrically sound, assessment procedures must be reliable and valid, although the types of reliability and validity vary with the type of procedure.

In addition to these principles, psychometric theory prescribes specific standards for constructing sound assessment procedures. Psychometric theory does not, however, tell us *which* of the many features of individual cases should be assessed. Instead, we should select features that are found to discriminate between people whose behavioral/emotional problems differ with respect to etiology, course, prognosis, and/or the most appropriate intervention. To determine which features specifically discriminate between people according to these variables, research is needed to test the discriminative power of various features. Rather than attempting to test every possible feature one by one, it is preferable to identify sets of features that tend to co-occur. Because assessment of each feature is subject to unique sources of variance, scores for sets of covarying features are likely to be more reliable than scores for individual features. Furthermore, sets of covarying features are likely to be more useful than individual features for generating and testing hypotheses, as well as for managing individual cases. The task of aggregating covarying features into sets with which to identify similar cases is the task of taxonomy, to which we now turn.

Taxonomy

It is helpful to distinguish between classification in general and taxonomy in particular. *Classification* refers to any systematic ordering of phenomena into classes, groups, or types. Many classifications are constructed merely for the convenience of users. Administrative classifications, for example, are designed to meet particular organizational needs. The people who design such classifications may start with knowledge of the organization's needs and the ways prospective users of a classification customarily view the phenomena to be classified. They then attempt to mesh the users' classificatory behavior with the needs that the classification is to meet.

As an example, health insurers construct their own classifications of disorders to specify reimbursements for mental health services. A key question is whether a particular classification scheme enables the insurer's actuaries to compute costs accurately enough for the insurer to charge rates that are competitive but high enough to be profitable after covering all costs. For third-party payers that are not funded by premiums based on costs, such as Medicaid, the problem is complicated by unpredictable changes in the size and nature of the covered population, variations in the mental health services obtained, providers' techniques for coping with low reimbursement rates, and the vicissitudes of government funding. Considering the variety of factors that affect third-party payers' classification schemes, it is no wonder that so many classifications have been devised for reimbursement of mental health services.

In contrast to the broad concept of classification, *taxonomy* refers to a subset of classifications that are intended to reflect intrinsic differences between cases assigned to different classes. Taxonomies of plants and animals, for example, are based on features that are intended to capture important differences among species. Various features can be chosen to distinguish among groups of plants and animals, such as physical characteristics, interbreeding, and hypothesized evolutionary relations. Although the concept of species is so familiar as to seem self-evident, species is not an intrinsic property of living things. Instead, species is a taxonomic construct that is imposed on subsets of features, such as having four legs or laying eggs. Certain features are selected from all the features that might be used to distinguish among individual plants and animals (Levin, 1979). Taxonomic constructs such as species reflect distinctions based on scientifically identified intrinsic characteristics of groups of individuals, rather than reflecting distinctions that are not based on intrinsic differences among groups of individuals.

Are Behavioral and Emotional Disorders "Natural Kinds"?

Zachar (2000) has distinguished between taxonomies that consist of *natural kinds* and those that consist of *practical kinds*. He defined a natural kind as "an entity that is regular (nonrandom) and internally consistent from one instance to the next" (p. 167). Examples include naturally occurring elements such as gold. By contrast, practical kinds "are stable patterns that can be identified with varying levels of reliability and validity" (p. 167).

Zachar (2000) argues that psychopathology is better viewed in terms of practical kinds than natural kinds. Although some may believe that taxonomies of psychopathology should identify natural kinds, both the empirically based approach and the version of the nosologically based approach embodied in *DSM* focus on practical kinds. In other words, they both define taxa in terms of sets of features no one of which is both necessary and sufficient to classify an individual's problems as belonging to a particular taxon. Both approaches are thus *polythetic* in the sense of specifying sets of features from which various subsets of the features can qualify an individual for a taxon.

Constructing Taxonomies of Behavioral and Emotional Problems

In constructing taxonomies of behavioral and emotional problems, we should be aware that the problems can be aggregated according to different taxonomic principles. Certain taxonomic principles may be useful for one stage of knowledge or for one stage of development but not for other stages of knowledge or development. Furthermore, different taxonomic principles may be useful for different kinds of disorders or for different purposes at the same stage of knowledge or for the same developmental stage. Cognitive measures, for example, may be useful for grouping people according to educability, whereas measures of behavior problems may be useful for grouping the same people for management purposes.

We also need to be aware that the features chosen to characterize cases represent abstractions with which to link cases that are expected to be similar in other important ways. When we abstract a subset of features from the many features that could be identified, we form a hypothetical construct of the case—a conceptual abstraction intended to capture the important aspects of the case. If our notion of the individual case and our grouping of cases according to certain shared features both involve hypothetical constructs, how should we match our construct of the individual case to the constructs of a taxonomy? Answers to this question must take account of both the methodological possibilities for assessing individual cases and the mental processes involved in matching the features of the individual case to the features used to define taxonomic groupings of cases.

Prototypes as Taxonomic Models

Classification systems have traditionally defined categories in terms of criteria that are "singly necessary and jointly sufficient" for classifying individual cases (Cantor, Smith, French, & Mezzich, 1980, p. 182). That is, a case was assigned to a particular category if, and only if, it met all the criteria for that category. Conversely, all cases that met the criteria for a particular category were ipso facto assigned to that category.

Cognitive research indicates that people's mental use of categories does not conform to the classical model whereby cases are categorized according to features that are both necessary and sufficient. As illustrated by familiar categories such as furniture, for example, the objects that people categorize together do not all share the same defining features (Rosch & Mervis, 1975). Instead, certain objects classified as furniture, such as tables and chairs, have little similarity to other objects that are also classified as furniture, such as lamps and rugs.

Objects that have the most features of a category are considered to be the most typical of the category and are more quickly and reliably categorized than are objects that have fewer of the category's features (Smith & Medin, 1981). For example, a sparrow is more prototypical of birds than an ostrich is. Furthermore, objects that have features of multiple categories are especially difficult to categorize reliably. As an example, a tomato is difficult to categorize as a fruit or a vegetable, because it has features of both categories.

Instead of being rigidly defined by criterial features that must all be present in all members of a category, mental representations of categories consist of sets of imperfectly correlated features known as *prototypes* (Rosch, 1978). Consequently, people judge category membership according to the degree of overlap between the features of a case and the set of prototypical features that define a category. In other words, people judge cases having many features of a prototype to be very typical of the category represented by that prototype. They judge cases that have few features of a prototype to be less typical of that category. Cases that manifest features of more than one prototype are judged to lie on the border between the categories represented by those prototypes.

According to the prototype view, people make quantitative judgments of the resemblance between particular cases and particular categories. That is, the degree of resemblance between a case and a category is judged according to the number of prototypical features that the case shares with the category. Furthermore, if each prototypical feature of a case and of a category can be scored in terms of the intensity or certainty with which the feature is manifested, then the case's resemblance to the category can be quantified in terms of the sum or other aggregation of scores on all the prototypical features.

If the human minds that must use taxonomies actually conceptualize categories in terms of quantifiable prototypes, why not use quantifiable prototypes in taxonomies of psychopathology? The possibilities for doing this are presented after we consider conventional diagnostic thinking.

DIAGNOSIS

The term *diagnosis* conveys an aura of clinical authority, implying that it reveals an essential truth about what is really wrong with a patient. Yet, the term has multiple meanings that sow confusion when we move from research tasks conceptualized in terms of assessment and taxonomy to clinical practice conceptualized in terms of diagnoses. To clarify relations between the research tasks and clinical practice, it is helpful to distinguish among the different meanings of diagnosis discussed next.

Diagnostic Processes

Diagnostic processes involve gathering the data needed for diagnostic decisions. Such processes are analogous to what we earlier defined as assessment. However, because diagnosis implies gathering data to determine which disease a person has, diagnostic processes connote a narrower range of possibilities than the more neutral term assessment.

Formal Diagnoses

Formal diagnoses involve assigning cases to the categories of a diagnostic classification. Accordingly, a leading psychiatric diagnostician, Samuel Guze (1978, p. 53), defined diagnosis as "the medical term for classification." This is the sense in which the categories of the *DSM,* GAP, and *ICD* nosologies are diagnoses. When a clinician states that a person meets the *DSM* criteria for Conduct Disorder or Antisocial Personality Disorder, for example, the clinician is making a formal diagnosis.

Diagnostic Formulations

Diagnostic formulations are efforts to elucidate multiple aspects of an individual's condition. When a clinician interprets a person's problems in terms of physical vulnerabilities, developmental history, family dynamics, stress, and rejection by peers, for example, the clinician makes a diagnostic formulation. A diagnostic formulation should weave all the findings of the diagnostic process into a comprehensive picture of the case. The diagnostic formulation thus provides a broader basis for developing treatment plans than a formal diagnosis does. Yet, it is by means of the formal diagnosis that the individual case is linked to others like it.

The formal diagnosis helps the clinician apply existing knowledge about a class of cases to a diagnostic formulation for a new case. For knowledge about a class of cases to be accurately applied to a new case, reliable procedures are needed for gathering data, integrating data into a diagnosis, and selecting the appropriate formal diagnosis. Furthermore, the system from which the formal diagnosis is selected must be reliable, must be valid with respect to important correlates of its diagnostic categories, and must encompass cases like the one being diagnosed. In short, the credibility of diagnosis depends on the same methodological standards as assessment and taxonomy do. Diagnosis thus involves gathering data to identify the distinguishing features of individual cases and grouping cases according to their distinguishing features, just as assessment and taxonomy do. Whichever terminology is used, the value of such procedures ultimately depends on whether they help people.

Comorbidity Issues

Since the introduction of explicit diagnostic criteria by *DSM-III* (American Psychiatric Association, 1980), many people have been found to meet the criteria for more than one disorder (e.g., Costello et al., 1984; Livingston, Dykman, & Ackerman, 1990; Weinstein, Noam, Grimes, Stone, & Schwab-Stone, 1990). Termed *comorbidity,* the tendency for people to meet criteria for multiple disorders has a variety of implications. The apparent co-occurrence of two disorders could mean, for example, that one disorder results from the other, or that the same risk factors lead to both disorders, or that the two disorders are not really separate but are manifestations of the same underlying condition (Achenbach, 1991a; Caron & Rutter, 1991).

Most *DSM* and *ICD* categories are not based on evidence for the independent existence of a separate disorder for each category. Nor do the *DSM* and *ICD* specify assessment operations for reliably discriminating between disorders. When assessment procedures have been designed to operationalize *DSM* criteria for disorders, high rates of comorbidity have often been found. For example, two studies have shown that 96% of boys who met *DSM* criteria for CD also met criteria for ODD (Faraone, Biederman, Keenan, & Tsuang, 1991; Walker et al., 1991). In addition, the *DSM-III-R* field trials found that 84% of clinic-referred children who met criteria for CD also met criteria for ODD (Spitzer, Davies, & Barkley, 1990). Because the *DSM* criteria for these disorders have not been proven to distinguish between separate entities, the very high rates of overlap between diagnoses suggest that the diagnostic criteria may be interdependent.

Unidirectional versus Bidirectional Comorbidity

The specific rates of comorbidity reported in many studies may be misleading, because they reflect computation of the overlap between diagnoses in only one direction. That is, they reflect the percentage of individuals having diagnosis A who also have diagnosis B. If diagnoses A and B have different prevalence rates in a sample, this unidirectional computation yields a different rate of comorbidity than would be obtained by computing the percentage of individuals having disorder B who also have disorder A. For example, suppose that 50 children in a sample of 100 obtain a diagnosis of CD (diagnosis A) and that 48 of these 50 obtain a diagnosis of ODD (diagnosis B). The unidirectional comorbidity of ODD (diagnosis B) among children who have CD (diagnosis A) is 48/50 = 96%. However, if 80 of the children have ODD, and 48 of these have CD, the unidirectional comorbidity of CD among children who have ODD is 48/80 = 60%. By recomputing published comorbidity rates bidirectionally (i.e., as the mean of the comorbidities of A to B and B to A), McConaughy and Achenbach (1994) obtained quite different rates from those based on the unidirectional comorbidities. When comorbidity is conceptualized in terms of the co-occurrence of two categorically defined disorders, it is thus important to consider the bidirectional rates of comorbidity between the disorders.

Berkson's Bias

Apparent comorbidity among disorders may also be misleading in other ways, as detailed elsewhere (Achenbach, 1991a; Caron & Rutter, 1991). Suppose, for example, that individuals manifesting a particular disorder have *X* probability of referral. Suppose, too, that individuals manifesting another disorder have *Y* probability of referral. Even if the disorders do not tend to co-occur in the population as a whole, people who have both disorders have $X + Y - XY$ probability of referral. This is obviously higher than individuals who have only X or Y probability of referral. If we study only referred people, then we may conclude that the two disorders tend to occur together. Yet, if we study the entire population (including nonreferred people), we might find that the two disorders have no more than chance co-occurrence, because individuals having any one disorder without the other are much more common in the nonreferred portion of the population than in the referred portion.

Known as *Berkson's bias* (Berkson, 1946), the tendency of apparent comorbidity to be inflated by referral biases is one of many artifactual ways that findings of co-occurrence between even independently verifiable disorders can arise. The different effects of referral biases on different problems has been demonstrated by comparing comorbidities obtained among empirically based syndromes in demographically similar referred and nonreferred samples (McConaughy & Achenbach, 1994).

Implications of Comorbidity

If two disorders are operationally defined according to mutually independent assessment procedures, and if the two disorders are demonstrated to occur together with greater than chance frequency in unbiased samples of the general population, then the comorbidity of these particular disorders may be quite informative. However, if diagnoses are not based on operational definitions of empirically separable disorders, then findings of comorbidity may merely reflect a lack of clear boundaries between diagnostic categories or an inability of diagnosticians to validly distinguish between disorders that do not really co-occur with more than chance frequency.

Rather than taking findings of comorbidity at face value as reflecting the co-occurrence of two distinct disorders, we should therefore examine the diagnostic system itself for possible artifactual sources of apparent comorbidity. The high rate of overlap found between diagnoses of ODD and CD (Faraone at al., 1991; Spitzer, Davies, & Burkley, 1990; Walker et al., 1991), for example, invites scrutiny of the diagnostic system to determine whether ODD and CD truly represent separate disorders. The arbitrariness of the distinctions between the diagnostic categories of ODD and CD is highlighted by the major changes they underwent from *DSM-III* to *DSM-III-R,* with further changes in *DSM-IV. DSM-III* (American Psychiatric Association, 1980) listed five criteria for ODD, of which only two needed to be met for the diagnosis. *DSM-III-R* (American Psychiatric

Association, 1987), by contrast, listed nine criteria, of which five were needed for the diagnosis. *DSM-IV* lists eight criteria, of which four are needed for the diagnosis. Furthermore, the *DSM* criteria for diagnoses of CD also underwent major changes from *DSM-III* to *DSM-III-R,* with further changes in *DSM-IV. DSM-III* provided four distinct categories, plus a residual category of Atypical CD. *DSM-III-R,* by contrast, provided only one set of explicit criteria for CD, although once the prescribed number of criteria were met, the disorder could be categorized as "group type," "solitary aggressive type," or "undifferentiated type," according to the diagnostician's judgment. *DSM-IV* has dispensed with these types in favor of "childhood-onset type" versus "adolescent-onset type."

Classification systems should incorporate changes based on new knowledge. However, the *DSM-III-R* and *DSM-IV* revisions were not derived from empirical tests of the co-occurrence of particular features or of whether the criteria for ODD and CD actually discriminated between distinctly different disorders in representative samples of children. Furthermore, no provision was made for calibrating diagnoses made from one edition of the *DSM* with those made from previous editions. It should not be surprising, therefore, that very different distributions of ODD and CD were obtained when applying *DSM-III* versus *DSM-III-R* to the same children, and that many children met criteria for both ODD and CD (Lahey et al., 1990). *DSM-IV* diagnostic criteria yield still different distributions of these diagnoses.

DSM-III-R and *DSM-IV* specify that the diagnosis of ODD is not to be made if the criteria for CD are met. Does this mean that ODD is a mild version of CD, a developmentally early version, or a by-product? Or does it mean that the two disorders are intrinsically related in some other way? Similar questions arise from overlaps among other diagnostic categories that are not derived from actual data on relations among problems. Based on a detailed examination of these and other issues, Lilienfeld, Waldman, and Israel (1994, p. 71) cautioned that the application of the term comorbidity to psychopathology "encourages the premature reification of diagnostic entities" that have not actually been validated.

LONGITUDINAL DESIGNS FOR THE DEVELOPMENTAL STUDY OF PSYCHOPATHOLOGY

Many kinds of research designs can contribute to the developmental study of psychopathology. However, longitudinal designs, in which the same people are assessed at two or more points in their development, provide the most direct tests of relations between developmental parameters and patterns of problems. In the following sections, we illustrate some variations on traditional longitudinal designs that may be especially useful for developmental research related to assessment, taxonomy, and diagnosis.

Accelerated Longitudinal Designs

The ability of traditional longitudinal designs to shed light on psychopathology has been limited by the difficulty of maintaining participant samples, research teams, and funding over long periods. In addition, most longitudinal studies have been handicapped by their failure to compare different birth cohorts and by their use of different assessment procedures at different ages. The latter limitations affect real-time, follow-up, and follow-back studies alike.

Life span developmental psychologists have emphasized the need to take account of differences related to birth cohorts and times of measurement, as well as differences related to age (e.g., Baltes, 1987). Unfortunately, it is difficult to include cohort and time-of-measurement comparisons in traditional longitudinal research designs.

One way to improve longitudinal research on psychopathology is to assess multiple birth cohorts by the same methods over several uniform intervals. Such designs have been variously called "convergence" (Bell, 1953, 1954), "longitudinal-sequential" (Schaie, 1965), "mixed-longitudinal" (van't Hoff, Roede, & Kowalski, 1991), and "cohort-sequential" (Baltes, Cornelius, & Nesselroade, 1979). Because several birth cohorts are assessed in the same way over the same period, the longitudinal findings for each cohort can be compared with the findings for each other cohort. We can thus determine whether changes with age are similar in all cohorts or whether the changes differ among cohorts or times of measurement.

An additional strength of cohort-sequential designs is that they can potentially reveal developmental sequences over a longer period of time than the real time spanned by the study. For this reason, they are also called *accelerated longitudinal designs*. How can we perform this magic of accelerating longitudinal research? The logic is as follows:

- At Time 1, individuals from several adjoining birth cohorts are assessed in a uniform fashion. For example, in June 2007, a test is administered to cohorts of children who are 6, 7, 8, or 9 years old (designated as Cohorts 6, 7, 8, and 9).

- At Times 2, 3, and 4, the same test is readministered to the same children. In our example, the test is readministered in 2008, 2009, and 2010 to Cohorts 6, 7, 8, and 9, who will be 9 to 12 years old at the final administration in 2010.

- Individuals from one cohort are matched to individuals in another cohort. In our example, children from Cohort 6 are matched to children in Cohort 7 with respect to demographic variables and test scores obtained at ages 7 and 8. That is, a particular Cohort 6 middle-SES boy named Chris is matched to a particular Cohort 7 middle-SES boy named Scott whose test scores at ages 7 and 8 were similar to the scores obtained by Chris at ages 7 and 8.

- The accuracy of predicting scores obtained by individuals in one cohort from earlier scores obtained by matched individuals in another cohort is then tested. In our example, we compute the correlation between scores obtained at age 6 by Cohort 6 children and scores obtained at age 9 by their matched counterparts from Cohort 7. For purposes of comparison, we then compute the correlation between the scores obtained at age 6 by the Cohort 6 children and their own scores at age 9. Suppose the correlation between age 6 and 9 scores within Cohort 6 is significant. Suppose also that the between-cohort correlation from scores obtained at age 6 by Cohort 6 children to the age 9 scores obtained by their matched Cohort 7 counterparts is of the same magnitude as the correlation from age 6 to age 9 within Cohort 6. These findings would indicate that the score obtained at age 6 by a Cohort 6 child, such as Chris, can be used to predict the score obtained at age 9 by a Cohort 7 child, such as Scott, with as much accuracy as prediction of Scott's age 9 score from his own age 6 score.

- If the findings outlined in the step above are replicated for the other combinations of cohorts in the study, it may become possible to create matched sets of individuals across the four cohorts to predict scores obtained by Cohort 9 at age 12 from scores obtained by Cohort 6 at age 6. An accelerated longitudinal study that requires 3 years of real time (2008–2010) could thus yield results spanning 6 years of development (ages 6 to 12).

Although developmental psychologists have long discussed the cohort-sequential concept, its applications were limited mainly to identifying cohort and time-of-measurement effects in personality and cognitive tests (e.g., Nesselroade & Baltes, 1974; Schaie, Labouvie, & Buech, 1973).

The need for uniform assessment of multiple birth cohorts over several years might seem to make accelerated longitudinal studies of psychopathology prohibitive. On the other hand, accelerated longitudinal studies can be far more cost-effective than traditional longitudinal studies that require as many years to collect data as the developmental period spanned. But would the magic of predicting from early assessments of psychopathology in one cohort to later assessments in another cohort actually work? The answer depends on the specific assessment procedures, participant samples, and developmental periods spanned. The magic has, in fact, worked very well in accelerated longitudinal studies of psychopathology, as illustrated in the following section.

Accelerated Longitudinal Analyses of Aggressive versus Delinquent Behavior

The nosological category of CD has typically included both aggressive and nonaggressive conduct problems. As an example, the *DSM-IV* criteria for CD include 15 kinds of behavior, such as "aggression to people and animals," "destruction of property," "deceitfulness or theft," and "serious violations of rules" (American Psychiatric Association, 2000, pp. 98–99). Because only three kinds of behavior are required for CD, some children may be diagnosed as having CD solely on the basis of three very aggressive behaviors, whereas others may be diagnosed as having CD solely on the basis of three nonaggressive behaviors.

In contrast to the single diagnostic category provided by *DSM* for different kinds of conduct problems, factor analyses of diverse samples of problem behaviors have typically shown that aggressive and nonaggressive conduct problems tend to load on different factors (e.g., Achenbach, Conners, Quay, Verhulst, & Howell, 1989; Quay, 1993). Aggressive conduct problems may certainly be comorbid with nonaggressive conduct problems in many individuals, just as other kinds of problems may be comorbid. However, because the *DSM*'s nosological model classifies children in the single category of CD whether they manifest only aggressive conduct problems, only nonaggressive conduct problems, or both, it is fair to ask whether the CD category may obscure potentially important differences in patterns of conduct problems.

One way to test for differences between these patterns is to compare their developmental courses. Accelerated longitudinal analyses have been used to do this over ages 4 to 18 years in a randomly selected sample of Dutch children (Stanger, Achenbach, & Verhulst, 1997). The children were assessed with the Child Behavior Checklist (CBCL; Achenbach, 1991b) completed by their parents

five times at 2-year intervals. At each assessment, the parents rated their child on diverse behavioral and emotional problem items. Factor analyses of the problem items produced eight syndromes that included a syndrome designated as *Aggressive Behavior* and one designated as *Delinquent Behavior* (subsequently designated as *Rule-Breaking Behavior;* Achenbach & Rescorla, 2001), which comprised nonaggressive conduct problems such as lying, stealing, running away from home, truancy, and hanging around others who get in trouble.

To compare the developmental courses of the Aggressive and Delinquent syndromes, Stanger et al. (1997) applied an accelerated longitudinal strategy as follows:

- They used CBCL Aggressive and Delinquent syndrome scores for seven birth cohorts of children who were 4, 5, 6, 7, 8, 9, or 10 years old at Time 1. The children were 12, 13, 14, 15, 16, 17, or 18 years old, respectively, at Time 5, which was 8 years later.

- They matched each child in each of the youngest six birth cohorts to a child in the cohort that was 2 years older. (Cohorts differing by 2 years of age were matched to take account of the 2-year intervals between assessments.)

- The matched "partners" were of the same gender and similar SES, and they obtained similar standard scores on the Aggressive and Delinquent syndromes at the two earliest ages at which both members of the pair had been assessed, that is, at Time 1 and Time 2. In other words, Stanger et al. paired children who differed by 2 years of age, who were of the same gender, and who were similar with respect to SES, Aggressive syndrome scores, and Delinquent syndrome scores at two assessment points 2 years apart.

- Separately for the Aggressive and Delinquent syndromes, Stanger et al. then computed Pearson correlations (*r*) between children's scores from Time 1 to Time 2, Time 3, Time 4, and Time 5. These *r*s reflected the stability of the rank ordering of the children's own scores on a particular syndrome over periods of 2, 4, 6, and 8 years (i.e., the within-cohort stability of scores).

- Stanger et al. also computed analogous *r*s between the syndrome scores obtained at Time 1 by children in the younger cohorts and the syndrome scores obtained by those children's matched partners in the 2-years-older cohorts at Times 2, 3, 4, and 5. These *r*s thus reflected the stability of the rank ordering of scores when *r*s were computed between one cohort of children at Time 1 and those children's matched partners in another cohort at

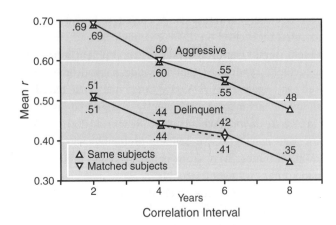

Figure 5.3 Within-cohort (same subjects) predictive correlations over intervals of 2 to 8 years and between-cohort (matched subjects) predictive correlations over 6 years for Dutch children. Each predictive correlation for the Aggressive Behavior syndrome was significantly greater than for the corresponding Delinquent Behavior syndrome at $p < .001$. *Source:* From Stanger et al., 1997, p. 54. "Accelerated Longitudinal Comparison of Aggressive versus Delinquent Syndromes," by C. Stanger, T. M. Achenbach, and F. C. Verhulst, 1997, *Development and Psychopathology, 9,* p. 54. Reprinted with permission of Cambridge University Press.

Times 2, 3, 4, and 5 (i.e., the between-cohort stability of scores).

Separately for the Aggressive and Delinquent syndromes, Figure 5.3 displays the mean within-cohort and between-cohort *r*s obtained over intervals of 2, 4, and 6 years, plus the within-cohort *r*s over 8 years for the seven cohorts of children. The within-cohort *r*s extended 2 years beyond the ages that were included in the between-cohort *r*s.

Figure 5.3 reveals two important findings:

1. Averaged across the seven birth cohorts, the mean between-cohort *r*s were as large as the within-cohort *r*s for both the Aggressive syndrome and the Delinquent syndrome over 2-year and 4-year periods and for the Aggressive syndrome over 6-year periods. The only exception was a mean between-cohort *r* that was only .01 lower than the mean within-cohort *r* over 6 years for the Delinquent syndrome, a trivial difference that was not statistically significant. Thus, later scores for the Aggressive and Delinquent syndromes were predicted as well from the early scores of children's matched partners from a different cohort as from the children's own early scores. This indicated that accelerated longitudinal analyses worked for the Aggressive and Delinquent syndromes.

2. At all data points for both the within-cohort and between-cohort *r*s, children's rank orders on the Ag-

gressive syndrome were more stable than on the Delinquent syndrome. The greater stability of Aggressive than Delinquent syndrome scores was shown by within-cohort and between-cohort *r*s that were .21 higher ($p < .001$ computed by *z* transformation) for the Aggressive syndrome than for the Delinquent syndrome, averaged over all intervals.

To compare the developmental trajectories for the Aggressive and Delinquent syndromes, Stanger et al. averaged scores obtained by children in each cohort at each age for which the cohort was assessed. Separately for each gender, Figure 5.4 displays the mean Aggressive and Delinquent raw scores at ages 4 to 18 (because the seven cohorts were

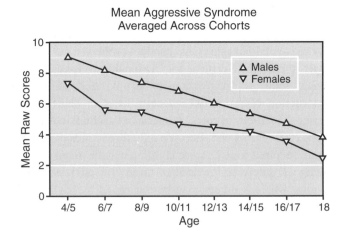

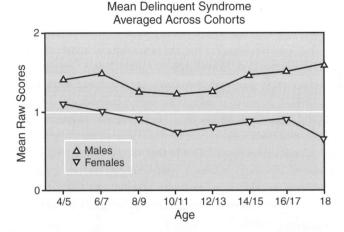

Figure 5.4 Mean Aggressive Behavior and Delinquent Behavior syndrome scores averaged across seven birth cohorts of Dutch children, separately for males and females. *Source:* From Stanger et al., 1997, p. 54. "Accelerated Longitudinal Comparison of Aggressive versus Delinquent Syndromes," by C. Stanger, T. M. Achenbach, and F. C. Verhulst, 1997, *Development and Psychopathology, 9,* p. 51. Reprinted with permission of Cambridge University Press.

initially assessed at different ages, data were averaged for pairs of adjoining years, for example, ages 4/5, up to age 18, when data were obtained for only one cohort). Looking at Figure 5.4, you can see that Aggressive syndrome scores declined steadily from ages 4/5 to 18. By contrast, Delinquent syndrome scores showed more complex relations to age, with increases at ages 12/13 for both genders. Girls' Delinquent syndrome scores then declined at age 18, although the data were based on only one cohort at that age.

The Stanger et al. data thus show more linear developmental trends, as well as greater developmental stability in individual differences, for Aggressive syndrome scores than Delinquent syndrome scores. Although Aggressive and Delinquent syndrome scores were significantly associated with each other (rs ranged from .53 at ages 4/5 to .63 at age 18), the findings revealed important differences in the developmental courses of aggressive and nonaggressive conduct problems.

Based on the findings of strong between-cohort predictive relations, predictions could potentially be made from Time 1 scores obtained by one cohort to Time 4 scores obtained by its matched cohort when 8 years older. For example, Time 1 scores obtained at age 4 by the Cohort 4 children could be used to predict Time 4 scores obtained at age 12 by their matched counterparts in Cohort 6. A study spanning 6 years of real time could thus be used to test predictive relations over 8 years of development. Furthermore, tests of predictive relations can be extended to 12 years by matching individuals from successive cohorts to provide predictive correlations between age 4 scores obtained by Cohort 4 members at Time 1 with age 16 scores obtained by Cohort 10 members at Time 4. (To take account of developmental changes in mean scores, the scores need to be standardized within each cohort at each time of assessment.) The potential power of accelerated longitudinal designs greatly increases the attractiveness of short-term longitudinal studies, which are usually far more feasible than long-term studies.

Accelerated longitudinal designs are among the many potential methodological contributions of developmental approaches to psychopathology. They illustrate both the complexity and the promise of developmental perspectives for advancing the study of psychopathology. Cohort and time-of-measurement effects, as well as intraindividual developmental sequences, highlight the need for complex multivariate conceptualizations. The complexity should not deter efforts to cope with the challenges of interrelations between development and psychopathology, however, because powerful research tools are available for coping with such challenges.

Path Designs

Path designs use regression statistics to test predictive pathways between variables assessed at developmentally early points and variables assessed for the same people at developmentally later points. Unlike accelerated longitudinal designs, path designs cannot test relations between variables over developmental periods that are longer than the real-time periods spanned by those developmental periods. However, path designs can test the degree to which multiple variables assessed at different early points in development individually and collectively contribute to the prediction of a particular outcome variable assessed at a later point in development. They can also test the indirect effects of independent variables that predict variables that, in turn, predict the outcome variables of interest.

Various statistical techniques are available for conducting path analyses (Bollen, 1989; Meehl & Waller, 2002). However, without going into the details of the various statistical techniques, we can illustrate some ways in which path designs can contribute to developmental research on the assessment and taxonomy of psychopathology.

Six-Year Predictive Pathways for Aggressive versus Delinquent Behavior

As reported in our illustration of accelerated longitudinal designs, factor analyses have yielded syndromes designated as Aggressive Behavior and Delinquent Behavior (also called Rule-Breaking Behavior). Both within-cohort and between-cohort correlations showed significantly greater developmental stability for scores on the Aggressive syndrome than the Delinquent syndrome among Dutch children (Stanger et al., 1997). Another way to evaluate the developmental course of syndromes is via path designs. This has been done in a national probability sample of American children who were assessed three times over a period of 6 years (Achenbach, Howell, McConaughy, & Stanger, 1995a). Eight empirically based syndromes and numerous family variables were assessed at each of the three points, using methodology similar to that of the Dutch study on which the accelerated longitudinal analyses were based. In addition, at the second and third assessments, information was obtained about potentially important life events that had occurred since the preceding assessment, such as stressful experiences.

Figure 5.5 shows the pathways for Time 1 and Time 2 variables that significantly predicted Time 3 scores on the Aggressive and Delinquent syndromes. The Time 3 syndrome scores were computed by combining parents' ratings

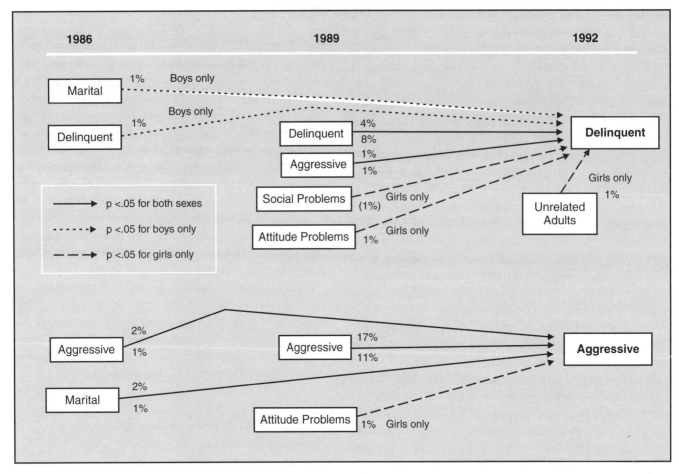

Figure 5.5   Predictive pathways to scores for Aggressive Behavior and Delinquent Behavior syndrome scores in an American national sample. *Source:* From "Six-Year Predictors of Problems in a National Sample of Children and Youth: I. Cross-Informant Syndromes," by T. M. Achenbach, C. T. Howell, S. H. McConaughy, and C. Stanger, 1995a, *Journal of the American Academy of Child and Adolescent Psychiatry, 34,* p. 343.

on the CBCL, teachers' ratings on the Teacher's Report Form (TRF; Achenbach, 1991b), and adolescents' self-ratings on the Youth Self-Report (YSR; Achenbach, 1991b). The Time 1 syndrome scores were computed from parents' ratings on the ACQ Behavior Checklist (Achenbach et al., 1991), whereas the Time 2 syndrome scores were computed from parents' ratings on the CBCL.

The numerals on the predictive paths in Figure 5.5 indicate the effect sizes (ES) in terms of the percentage of variance in the Time 3 syndrome scores that was uniquely accounted for by each of the significant predictors, with the effects of the other predictors partialed out. Each ES for boys is printed above the solid and dotted lines, and each ES for girls is printed below the solid and dashed lines (solid lines = effects that were significant for both genders; dotted lines = effects that were significant only for boys; dashed lines = effects that were significant only for girls). For example, if you look under the Time 2 head-

ing for the Delinquent syndrome in the top portion of Figure 5.5, you can see that the topmost ES was 4% for the prediction of Time 3 Delinquent syndrome scores from Time 2 Delinquent syndrome scores for boys. Beneath the 4% ES for boys, you can see that the corresponding ES for girls was 8%. For both genders, there were also 1% ES for prediction of Time 3 Delinquent syndrome scores from Time 2 Aggressive syndrome scores. For girls only, there were 1% ES for prediction of Time 3 Delinquent scores from Time 2 Social Problems syndrome scores (low Time 2 Social Problems scores predicted high Time 3 Delinquent scores) and Attention Problems syndrome scores. There was an additional 1% ES for the number of unrelated adults living in the girls' homes between Time 2 and Time 3.

Looking under the Time 1 heading in Figure 5.5, you can see that, for boys, the following two predictors directly accounted for 1% of variance in Time 3 Delinquent scores: the

Time 1 marital status of the boys' parents (Time 3 Delinquent scores were higher if parents were single, separated, or divorced than if they were married or widowed), and the Time 1 Delinquent scores.

In summary, for both genders, more variance in Time 3 Delinquent scores was accounted for by earlier scores on the Delinquent syndrome than by any other variable. However, significant variance was also accounted for by other variables, including scores on the Aggressive, Social Problems, and Attention Problems syndromes, parents' marital status at Time 1, and the number of unrelated adults living in the home between Time 2 and Time 3.

If you look now at the lower portion of Figure 5.5, you can see that Time 2 Aggressive syndrome scores accounted for 17% of the variance in Time 3 Aggressive syndrome scores for boys and 11% for girls. Time 1 Aggressive syndrome scores accounted for an additional 2% of the variance in Time 3 Aggressive syndrome scores for boys and 1% for girls. The only other significant predictors were parents' Time 1 marital status (2% ES for boys; 1% ES for girls) and Time 2 Attention Problems syndrome scores (1% ES for girls only).

By comparing the predictive paths found for Time 3 Delinquent versus Aggressive syndrome scores, you can see that the ES from earlier versions of the same syndrome were smaller for the Delinquent than the Aggressive syndrome: The ES for the Time 1 and Time 2 Delinquent syndromes summed to 5% for boys and 8% for girls, whereas the ES for the Time 1 and Time 2 Aggressive syndrome summed to 19% for boys and 12% for girls. In addition, more numerous other predictors were found for the Delinquent syndrome than the Aggressive syndrome. The other predictors included the Time 2 Aggressive syndrome scores for both genders, Time 2 Social Problems syndrome scores as negative predictors for girls, and the number of unrelated adults in the home between Times 2 and 3 as positive predictors for girls.

Although path designs differ markedly from accelerated longitudinal designs, findings from our examples of these different designs in the Netherlands and the United States suggest the following conclusions about the taxonomic properties of the Aggressive versus Delinquent syndromes:

- Early scores on each syndrome are significant predictors of later scores on the same syndrome, indicating developmental stability in the degree to which individuals manifest each kind of problem.
- The developmental stability of the Aggressive syndrome is greater than the developmental stability of the Delinquent syndrome in terms of the degree to which individ-

uals' rank orders remain consistent over substantial periods of development.
- The course of the Delinquent syndrome in relation to age, gender, and other kinds of problems is more variable than the course of the Aggressive syndrome.
- Overall, the findings suggest that the Aggressive syndrome is more trait-like than the Delinquent syndrome in that individuals maintain more consistent rank orders in relation to peers of the same age and gender, and later Aggressive syndrome scores are predicted more exclusively by scores on the same syndrome than is true for the Delinquent syndrome.

Path Analysis via Structural Equation Modeling

Path analysis can also make use of structural equation modeling (SEM) of hypothesized latent variables that are measured in terms of multiple manifest variables. The researcher specifies a model that includes relations between both the latent and the manifest variables. Mediator variables are often specified as being affected by developmentally early variables but, in turn, as affecting developmentally later variables. As an example, path analyses were used to test predictors of the latent variable of adult aggression from a variety of measures obtained when the adults were children, 15 years earlier (Huesmann, Moise-Titus, Podolski, & Eron, 2003). The latent variable of adult aggression was derived by SEM from 11 manifest variables, including Minnesota Multiphasic Personality Inventory scores, plus self-ratings and informant ratings of various kinds of direct and indirect aggression. Childhood measures of peer-nominated aggression and violent television viewing were found to be significant direct predictors of adult aggression. In addition, as a direct predictor of peer-nominated aggression and violent television viewing, low school achievement was an indirect predictor of adult aggression. Although the results indicated that viewing violent television can increase aggression over long periods, both the preference for viewing violent television and the continuity of aggression from childhood to adulthood may also reflect individual differences in achievement and in the trait-like aspects of aggression indicated by the accelerated longitudinal and path analyses that we described previously.

Growth Curve Designs

Both accelerated longitudinal and path designs examine changes over time in groups based on mean scores for each group. In contrast, growth curve designs permit investigation of changes in individuals as well as changes in groups over time (Rogosa, Brandt, & Zimowski, 1982). Latent growth curve analysis uses longitudinal data for each individual to model a growth trajectory for that individual. In addition, an average growth trajectory for all individuals is obtained. Each individual growth curve and the group function are described by a set of parameters. For linear functions, these parameters are the intercept and the slope of the line. When growth is not monotonic, quadratic, or cubic, functions may be fit to the data, resulting in parameters for these terms as well. The intercept of the function often represents the initial status of the individual on the dependent measure (i.e., at the first data collection point). The slope represents change in the dependent measure per unit of time over the time period from the first data collection point to the last. The variance estimates for intercept and slope indicate the degree to which individuals in the sample manifest differences in these parameters.

Researchers have developed many statistical procedures to analyze growth in individuals over time. Such procedures include *individual growth curve analysis* (Rogosa et al., 1982), *random effects modeling* (Laird & Ware, 1982), and *hierarchical linear modeling* (HLM; Raudenbush & Bryk, 2002). As HLM is one of the most widely used of these techniques, our summary focuses on this set of procedures.

Hierarchical Linear Modeling Procedures for Examining Growth over Time

HLM is called a hierarchical model because it describes the data in terms of at least two stages or levels. For growth curve analysis, HLM uses Level 1 to specify a within-subject model for each individual in the sample, based on data collected at different points in time. For example, ordinary least squares (OLS) regression could generate a growth trajectory for each person based on that person's score on the CBCL Aggressive syndrome scale at four time points, such as at ages 9, 12, 15, and 18. If the best fit to the data points is a straight line, then Person A's growth over time will be described by Person A's intercept (score at Time 1, or age 9) and A's slope (rate of change in score per year starting at age 9 and ending at age 18). Because no fitted line perfectly captures all data points, each function also contains an error term. In its simplest form, each person's growth over time is represented by Equation 1.

$$\text{Equation 1: } Y_t = a + bX + E$$

where Y_t = The dependent measure of the Aggressive syndrome score at Time "t"

  a = Person A's score at age 9 (the initial data point)

X = The number of time units between the initial time point and time "t" (e.g., age 12 = +3)

E represents random error or residual deviation from the predicted score for each individual

In HLM, the Level 2 or between-subjects model predicts the values of each individual's parameters. Thus, the parameters of the Level 1 model are the outcome measures of the Level 2 model. The first step in this analysis is to determine the total amount of variation in the intercept and slope parameters. When individuals have very different initial scores on the dependent measure and they show very different rates of change in the dependent measure over time, then variance in both the intercept and the slope will be high. Variance in the intercept will be minimal when all individuals start at the same point, whereas variance in the slope will be minimal when all individuals decrease (or increase) in the dependent measure at the same rate over time. HLM uses a chi-square procedure to determine if the variances in the intercept and slope are significantly different from zero. If one of these parameters is not significantly different from zero, then the model is constrained or fixed so that individuals are not allowed to have their own values on this parameter in subsequent analyses.

In typical HLM analyses, the first Level 2 model has no predictors. This is called an *unconditional* model, because no additional factors, such as gender, SES, diagnosis, referral status, or life experiences, are used to predict individual growth. In this basic unconditional Level 2 model, the individual parameters from Level 1 (*a* and *b*) are predicted only by the "population" mean (derived from the data) and random deviation. The basic unconditional model at Level 2 appears in Equations 2a and 2b:

$$\text{Equation 2a: } a = \beta_{00} + \text{Random deviation}$$
$$\text{Equation 2b: } b = \beta_{10} + \text{Random deviation}$$

Thus, the unconditional model states that the best estimate of an individual's slope or intercept is the population parameter plus some random deviation or error.

At the next stage in the analysis, HLM contrasts this unconditional model with a *conditional* model in which some additional factor is entered as a predictor to explain individual differences in either intercept or slope. For example, one might predict that clinically referred children would have higher Aggressive syndrome scores than nonreferred children (reflected in a higher intercept value). One might also predict that children being treated for aggressive behavior problems might show more improvement over time than children receiving no treatment (steeper negative slope). To test these predictions, the predictor of referral status or "group" is added to the Level 2 model. Because group in this example is a dichotomous variable, it would be coded using a dummy variable such as 0 = Nonreferred and 1 = Referred. Equations 3a and 3b depict the conditional model:

Equation 3a: $a = \beta_{00} + \beta_{01}$ (group) + Random deviation
Equation 3b: $b = \beta_{10} + \beta_{11}$ (group) + Random deviation

According to these equations, the individual differences in intercept and slope parameters at Level 1 are determined both by the population values for these parameters and by the child's status as nonreferred or referred (plus random deviation).

HLM next determines whether the conditional model with predictors is a significant improvement over the unconditional model with no predictors. Essentially, HLM determines the percentage of total variance explained when predictors are added to the model relative to the total variance in the parameters with no predictors. It also tests the significance of each predictor using t tests.

Application of Hierarchical Linear Modeling to Developmental Psychopathology

For purposes of explication, we have presented HLM in its simplest form. However, HLM permits analyses that are much more complex. Multiple predictors can be entered at Level 2, and their main effects and interactions can be examined. For example, not only referral status but also gender and SES might be associated with both initial status and change over time in Aggressive syndrome scores. Additionally, some studies might necessitate a 3-level model. For example, a study might compare Aggressive syndrome scores over time in individuals (Level 1) as a function of gender, SES, and referral status (Level 2) in three different countries, such as the United States, the Netherlands, and Korea (Level 3).

Growth curve analysis has become very widely used in developmental research. Because it preserves information about individual trajectories over time and permits examination of multiple predictors of those trajectories, it is very useful for answering major questions in developmental psychopathology. Furthermore, HLM can handle missing data in ways that traditional analysis of variance (ANOVA) and analysis of covariance (ANCOVA) procedures cannot. In a repeated measures ANOVA design, participants who have missing data at one data point may be eliminated from the analysis or may have scores imputed to them. In HLM, however, individuals can remain in the analysis even if they

have some missing data. That is, intercepts and slopes can be calculated for all individuals as long as they have scores for most of the data points (e.g., three out of the four).

Hierarchical Linear Modeling Analyses of Externalizing Problems

Galambos, Barker, and Almeida (2003) used HLM to examine parent and peer influences on the trajectories of externalizing and internalizing problems across five time points from grade 6 to grade 9. Their Time 1 sample consisted of 109 Canadian boys and girls, but attrition reduced the sample to 75 at Time 5. HLM retained all participants in the analysis but gave more weight in the parameter estimation procedure to children with complete data across the five time points.

For illustrative purposes, we will describe Galambos et al.'s (2003) use of HLM to analyze externalizing problems, which were measured by a 24-item self-report questionnaire. At each time point, the children used ratings from 1 (never) to 5 (almost every day) for how many times in the past month they had engaged in behaviors such as disobeying their parents, using drugs, damaging property, or being suspended from school. They also reported on whether they associated with deviant peers. Mothers' and fathers' self-reports on a parenting questionnaire at Time 1 were averaged to yield scores for support (warmth), behavioral control (limit setting), and psychological control (disapproval).

When main effects for all measures were analyzed using HLM, associating with deviant peers was the only measure significantly affecting the Time 1 status score (intercept) on externalizing problems. Behavioral control was the only measure significantly associated with the rate of change (slope) in externalizing problems over time. Children whose parents exerted more behavioral control showed smaller increases in externalizing problems over time than their peers.

In the second model, all four main effects plus the interactions between deviant peers and the three parenting measures were analyzed using HLM. The same two main effects were significant (deviant peers for the intercept and behavioral control for the slope). The interaction between deviant peers and behavioral control also had a significant effect on the slope of externalizing problems. Follow-up analyses tested slopes in the four groups produced by a median split on both deviant peers and behavioral control. Only the group who scored above the median on deviant peers and above the median on behavioral control had a slower increase in externalizing problems over time. As the authors concluded, children who had more deviant peers had higher externalizing problems scores at Time 1, and there was a general trend for all children to increase in externalizing problems over time. However, only children whose parents exerted more behavioral control in the face of greater association with deviant peers showed reduced increases in externalizing problems over time. When additional HLM analyses included gender as a covariate, the same basic results were obtained. Interestingly, boys demonstrated higher Time 1 scores (higher intercept) than girls, but girls showed faster increases (higher slope) in externalizing problems from grades 6 to 9 than boys.

LIFE SPAN APPLICATIONS

To apply developmental approaches to psychopathology across the life span, we should consider lessons learned from research on children. Changes in the prevalence, patterning, and possibilities for assessing problems do not end at maturity. Although the changes may be slower and less conspicuously associated with biological development than during childhood, adult psychopathology may be no more independent of developmental changes than is child psychopathology. However, to test the developmental course of psychopathology, its correlates, and its outcomes, we need assessment procedures and taxonomic constructs that can take account of both the changes and the continuities in psychopathology from childhood to adulthood and old age. Furthermore, it would be desirable to quantify adult assessment and taxonomy in ways that lend themselves to powerful developmental research designs, such as accelerated longitudinal, path, and growth curve designs.

The value of measures that can track continuities and changes over significant periods of adulthood has been demonstrated in studies of cognitive functioning. As an example, latent growth models were applied to 11 cognitive measures for 550 Swedish adults who were initially tested at age 44 to 88 and were then retested at intervals of 3 and 6 years thereafter (Finkel, Reynolds, McArdle, Gatz, & Pedersen, 2003). The results revealed different trajectories for different kinds of abilities, including stability into old age for crystallized ability, linear declines in other abilities, and significant acceleration in linear declines after age 65 for measures that depended on speed. Significant individual variations in growth curves were found for some of the measures.

Similar growth curve analyses can be applied to scores measuring psychopathology in adults, such as those derived from the Achenbach System of Empirically Based Assessment (ASEBA) forms for adults: the Adult Self-Report and Adult Behavior Checklist for Ages 18 to 59 and the Older Adult Self-Report and Older Adult Behavior Checklist for Ages 60 to 90+ (Achenbach et al., 2004; Achenbach & Rescorla, 2003). Some problem scales are common to both adult age groups. Examples include the empirically based Anxious/Depressed, Somatic Complaints, and Thought Problems syndrome scales and the DSM-oriented Depressive Problems, Anxiety Problems, Somatic Problems, and Antisocial Personality Problems scales. One syndrome scale, named Intrusive, is specific to ages 18 to 59. Other scales are specific to ages 60 to 90+, such as the Irritable/Disinhibited, Memory/Cognition Problems, Worries, and Functional Impairment syndrome scales. Some syndrome scales for ages 18 to 59 have counterpart scales on the CBCL, TRF, and YSR, which are the ASEBA forms for ages 6 to 18. These syndrome scales include Attention Problems, Aggressive Behavior, and Rule-Breaking Behavior.

Longitudinal research has shown that high problem scores on the adult Intrusive syndrome, as well as on the adult Aggressive Behavior syndrome, are strongly predicted by high scores on the child/adolescent Aggressive syndrome (Achenbach, Howell, McConaughy, & Stanger, 1995c). These findings indicate that some aggressive children and adolescents are socially intrusive as adults, whereas others remain more overtly aggressive. The same research shows that high child and adolescent scores on the Attention Problems syndrome predict high scores on the adult version of this syndrome. However, the adult version is characterized less by overactivity and more by irresponsibility than the child/adolescent version.

Because parallel self-report and other-report forms are available for ages 11 to 90+, developmental analyses of adult psychopathology can be compared for self-reports, reports by others, and aggregations of multisource data. In addition, because many of the empirically based and nosologically based scales for adults and older adults are similar to those for children and adolescents, ASEBA forms are well suited to both long-term longitudinal studies and to multigeneration family studies. Multigeneration family studies are particularly useful in behavior genetics research designed to identify genetic effects, environmental effects, and their interactions in parents and their children.

MULTICULTURAL APPLICATIONS

To avoid incorrectly assuming that findings in a single culture reflect universals, it is important to apply the same standardized assessment procedures for psychopathology to people from a variety of cultures. If the assessment procedures are found to function similarly in different cultures, they offer the potential for testing the course and correlates of psychopathology across the different cultures. Findings that are similar in different cultures can be assumed to have greater generality than findings that are obtained in only a single culture. An additional advantage of assessment procedures that function similarly in different cultures is that they foster multicultural collaborations, which can greatly extend the reach of developmental research on psychopathology.

Multicultural Consistencies and Differences

As an example of multicultural research, Crijnen, Achenbach, and Verhulst (1997, 1999) and Verhulst et al. (2003) compared the performance of empirically based instruments completed by parents of representative samples of children in 12 cultures and self-report instruments completed by representative samples of youths in 7 cultures, respectively. The cultures were Australia, Belgium, China, Germany, Greece, Israel, Jamaica, the Netherlands, Puerto Rico, Sweden, Thailand, Turkey, and the United States. Completion rates in all cultures were at least 80% for parents' reports and at least 78% for youths' self-reports. The mean total problems scores were quite similar across most cultures, as were gender differences in problem scores. Youths reported more problems than parents in all cultures. Using the approach pioneered by Crijnen et al. and Verhulst et al., we have since analyzed data for more than 60,000 children assessed in 30 cultures to obtain a more extensive picture of the similarities and differences between reported problems (Achenbach & Rescorla, 2006; Rescorla et al., 2005).

Although these multicultural studies indicated some notable cross-cultural differences in scores for certain syndromes, Pearson rs between mean problem item scores for every combination of cultures were large, according to Cohen's (1988) criteria. (Pearson rs were computed by first obtaining the mean score for each problem item within each culture and then computing the r between the mean scores on all the items for Culture A versus Culture B, and then Culture A versus Culture C, and so on for all pairs of cultures.) The mean of the cross-cultural correlations ranged from .74 to .78 among all pairings of the cultures for which parents' ratings were analyzed, .74 among all the cultures for which teachers' ratings were analyzed, and .75 among all pairings of the cultures for which youths' self-ratings

were analyzed. These substantial rs indicated that the same problems tended to receive relatively high, medium, or low scores across the cultures. For cultures from which cross-informant rs were available (e.g., rs between parent and teacher ratings), no culture's cross-informant r differed significantly from the mean of the rs for the available cultures (Verhulst & Achenbach, 1995). These findings indicate that the empirically based instruments performed similarly in diverse cultures.

Another aspect of multicultural research involves demonstrating whether the same syndromes of problems are found in different cultures. The 8-syndrome model derived from U.S. CBCL, TRF, and YSR data has been tested against data from many other cultures. In one study, the U.S. syndromes were closely replicated in data from the Netherlands (deGroot, Koot, & Verhulst, 1994). In another study, confirmatory factor analysis (CFA) of the eight CBCL syndromes in data from a large Turkish sample indicated excellent fit (Dumenci, Erol, Achenbach, & Simsek, 2004). When applying CFA to data from 30 very diverse cultures, Ivanova et al. (2005) found that the configural invariance of the 8-syndrome model was well supported in all cultures.

In the Netherlands and the United States, the empirically based instruments have been used in parallel longitudinal studies of large, representative samples of children and adolescents. Predictive correlations from initial scores on empirically based syndromes to subsequent scores and to various signs of disturbance over 6 years were very similar in the Dutch and American samples (Achenbach, Howell, McConaughy, & Stanger, 1995a, 1995b, 1995c, 1998; Verhulst & van der Ende, 1992a, 1992b). Furthermore, a 14-year follow-up of the Dutch sample showed that adult *DSM* diagnoses and signs of disturbance were significantly predicted by initial scores on the empirically based instruments (Hofstra, van der Ende, & Verhulst, 2001, 2002a, 2002b). The multicultural comparisons of empirically based instruments thus show that they can be used in similar ways across diverse cultures with fairly similar results.

Direct comparisons have been made for a few adult disorders in representative samples assessed in different cultures with the same nosologically based instruments. For example, Helzer et al. (1990) reported age-standardized lifetime prevalence rates of alcohol abuse and dependence for epidemiological samples from St. Louis, Edmonton, Puerto Rico, Taiwan, and Korea. Completion rates ranged from 67% in Taiwan to 91% in Puerto Rico. Although no direct statistical comparisons were made between cultures, some differences were quite large, with alcohol dependence ranging from 2.9% of metropolitan Taiwanese men to 20.4% of Korean men. For participants who were diagnosed as having alcohol dependence, there was considerable similarity in the rank ordering of the frequency of the criterial symptoms, with Spearman correlations ranging from .66 between Edmonton and Korea to .94 between St. Louis and both Edmonton and Korea.

Prevalence rates for more diverse diagnostic categories have been reported in a study of 14 countries (WHO World Mental Health Survey Consortium, 2004). Although versions of the Composite International Diagnostic Interview (CIDI) were used in all countries, disorders thought to have "low relevance" (p. 2587) were omitted in some countries, and difficulties in implementing the initial surveys resulted in large amounts of missing data in some countries. In addition, completion rates were under 80% for 13 of the 14 countries, with the completion rate being only 45.9% in France and from 50.6% to 57.8% in four other countries. The variations in the CIDI and the modest completion rates may have contributed to the great variation found for prevalence rates, which ranged from 4.3% in Shanghai to 26.4% in the United States for any disorder identified by the CIDI. When tabulated within the broad categories of anxiety, mood, impulse control, and substance use/dependence disorder, the prevalence rates also showed great variation among the 14 countries. For example, the prevalence rates for mood disorders ranged from 2.4% in Shanghai to 18.2% in the United States.

Although we found no studies that directly compared prevalence rates of DISC-based *DSM* diagnoses of child disorders in different cultures, studies using similar versions of the DISC with general population samples in single cultures have reported substantial differences in prevalence rates for *DSM-III-R* diagnoses (Breton et al., 1999; Shaffer et al., 1996; Steinhausen, Metzke, Meier, & Kannenberg, 1997, 1998; Verhulst et al., 1997). These studies all made *DSM-III-R* diagnoses from the DISC, but methodological differences in the ways they obtained and combined data from parent and self-reports and in their yes/no decision rules for making diagnoses may have contributed more to the apparent differences in prevalence rates than did cultural factors. As detailed by Achenbach and Rescorla (2006), nosological research on cross-cultural consistencies and differences requires operationalizing nosological constructs via assessment procedures that uniformly and effectively take account of informant variations in large representative samples drawn from different cultures.

ADVANCING ASSESSMENT, TAXONOMY, AND DIAGNOSIS

To set the stage for considering how assessment, taxonomy, and diagnosis can be advanced, Figure 5.6 illustrates the dynamic and continuous relations between them.

To be accurate, diagnosis requires ways of conceptualizing the phenomena that are to be diagnosed. Taxonomies provide structures for conceptualizing psychopathology in terms of similarities and differences that can then provide targets for diagnosis. Taxonomic structures for behavioral and emotional problems are commonly conceptualized in terms of syndromes. The value of particular syndromes depends on the degree to which they are found to have important correlates, such as differences in etiology, prognosis without intervention, responsiveness to particular interventions, and long-term developmental pathways. To develop reliable, valid, and useful taxonomies, we need reliable and valid assessment of diverse samples of people. After a taxonomy has been derived from assessment data, the taxonomy can be used to guide assessment of new cases to determine which taxa the cases resemble.

In Figure 5.6, "diagnosis" includes *diagnostic processes, formal diagnoses,* and *diagnostic formulations.* To avoid confusion about diagnosis, it is important to keep in mind these three different aspects of diagnosis. Assessment and taxonomy are important contributors to all three. Diagnostic

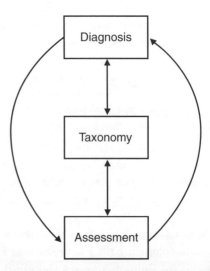

Figure 5.6   Relations between assessment, taxonomy, and diagnosis. As explained in text, "diagnosis" includes *diagnostic processes* (gathering data), *formal diagnoses* (classifying cases and disorders), and *diagnostic formulations* (integrating all relevant data for each case). Copyright by T. M. Achenbach. Reproduced by permission.

processes clearly include assessment operations that should be guided by a taxonomy of syndromes. Formal diagnoses involve identification of the taxa that are most relevant to each case. And diagnostic formulations integrate information specific to the case with the type of information on which taxonomic decisions and formal diagnoses are based.

Challenges to Be Met

DSM-III (American Psychiatric Association, 1980) was an important milestone in advancing the nosological approach toward more explicit and testable criteria for psychopathology. Since 1980, *DSM-III* and its successors have generated a tremendous amount of research, as well as major changes in clinical training and practice. An especially important research goal has been to improve the diagnosis of *DSM*-defined disorders via structured interviews. Accordingly, enormous resources have been invested in revising and testing structured interviews as ways of operationalizing the *DSM-III, DSM-III-R,* and *DSM-IV* criteria for childhood disorders (e.g., Costello et al., 1984; Lahey et al., 1996; Shaffer et al., 1996). Substantial resources have also been invested in operationalizing *DSM* criteria for adult disorders via structured interviews (e.g., Regier et al., 1998).

Efforts to diagnose *DSM*-defined disorders via structured interviews have molded research, training, and practice according to the *DSM*'s diagnostic model, which requires yes-or-no decisions about each criterial feature of each diagnostic category. Diagnostic interviews, such as the DISC for children and DIS for adults, are viewed as quasi gold standards for assessing psychopathology. However, studies of structured diagnostic interviews have revealed certain challenges to assessment, taxonomy, and diagnosis of psychopathology. We first summarize these challenges at the level of specific methodological issues. We then consider possibilities for advancing assessment, taxonomy, and diagnosis to improve understanding, prevention, and treatment of psychopathology.

Challenges Revealed by Studies of Structured Diagnostic Interviews

The challenges can be summarized as follows:

1. *Test-retest attenuation:* Fewer symptoms are typically reported at second interviews than at initial interviews, causing declines in the number of diagnoses over even very short periods such as a week (e.g., Edelbrock, Costello, Dulcan, Kalas, & Conover, 1985; Helzer, Spitznagel, & McEvoy, 1987; P. Jensen et al., 1995; R. E. Roberts, Solovitz, Chen, & Casat, 1996).

2. *Low to moderate cross-informant agreement:* People report different symptoms about themselves than others report for them, causing disagreements between diagnoses based on self-reports versus informant reports (e.g., Achenbach et al., 1987, 2005; Klonsky et al., 2002; Meyer, 2002; Meyer et al., 2001).

3. *Diagnoses made from structured interviews show mediocre agreement with clinical diagnoses:* Even when designed to operationalize the *DSM* criteria, structured interviews such as the DISC and DIS often produce different *DSM* diagnoses than do clinical assessments (e.g., Costello et al., 1984; Eaton et al., 2000; A. L. Jensen & Weisz, 2002; Lewczyk et al., 2003; Rettew et al., 2005).

4. *High rates of comorbidity:* Rates of comorbidity between some diagnoses are so high as to raise questions about whether the diagnoses actually represent different disorders (e.g., Faraone et al., 1991; Walker et al., 1991; Wilens et al., 2002).

5. *Great variations in prevalence rates of* DSM *diagnoses made from structured interviews in epidemiological surveys:* Despite operationalization of *DSM* criteria via structured interviews, prevalence rates show much greater variation than would be expected from sampling differences (e.g., Achenbach & Rescorla, 2006; Breton et al., 1999; Shaffer et al., 1996; Verhulst et al., 1997).

The challenges raised by studies of structured diagnostic interviews expose fundamental problems that cut across assessment, taxonomy, and diagnosis. These problems need to be addressed in efforts to improve understanding, prevention, and treatment of psychopathology. Some of the problems revealed by studies of structured interviews may characterize other assessment procedures as well. For example, test-retest attenuation, low to moderate cross-informant agreement, and high rates of covariation (i.e., comorbidity) among different kinds of problems are found in most procedures for obtaining information about people's problems (e.g., Achenbach & Rescorla, 2001, 2003; Krueger, 2002; Krueger & Piasecki, 2002). Agreement between most assessment procedures and *DSM* clinical diagnoses also tends to be low, although this may be most troubling for procedures that are explicitly designed to correspond to *DSM* diagnoses (e.g., DuPaul, Power, Anastopoulos, & Reid, 1998; Gadow et al., 2002). If assessment procedures are not specifically designed to correspond to *DSM* diagnoses, their modest agreement with *DSM* clinical diagnoses is less surprising than if they are designed to correspond to *DSM* diagnoses.

Although some of the challenges faced by structured interviews are quite general, the problems are exacerbated by the *DSM* requirement to make diagnoses according to fixed rules for the criteria that must be met. For example, a decline in the number of symptoms endorsed from one occasion to another may reflect the general phenomenon of test-retest attenuation. However, according to *DSM*'s fixed rules for the number of symptoms required for each diagnosis, a reduction of even one symptom can change diagnostic decisions from yes to no for *DSM* diagnoses. Similarly, disagreements between informants' reports of even a single symptom can cause major differences in diagnoses made on the basis of self-reports versus reports by various other informants. In addition, the great sensitivity of *DSM* diagnoses to the precise definition, number, duration, and co-occurrence of reported symptoms may contribute to the great variations in prevalence rates found in different epidemiological studies. For example, R. E. Roberts, Attkisson, and Rosenblatt (1998) found prevalence rates ranging from 1% to 50% among epidemiological studies of diagnoses of child and adolescent disorders. Assessment procedures that have uniformly operationalized a particular set of taxonomic constructs have yielded more consistent epidemiological findings than structured interviews that have attempted to operationalize *DSM* diagnostic criteria but that have varied considerably in how they obtained judgments of whether each criterion was met (e.g., Crijnen et al., 1997, 1999; Rescorla et al., 2005; Verhulst et al., 2003).

Other Types of Challenges

Assessment, taxonomy, and diagnosis also face challenges raised by the need to identify and combine optimal sources and kinds of assessment data for taxonomy and diagnosis; the need to take account of variations related to age, gender, and sources of data; and the need to distinguish between cultural differences and individual differences. Table 5.1 summarizes these challenges. Progress in meeting the various challenges requires systematic research that can bridge the gaps between nosological and empirically based approaches to provide assessment procedures, taxonomic constructs, and diagnostic targets that can be used by both approaches.

QUANTITATIVE AIDS TO MEETING THE CHALLENGES

DSM-III, DSM-III-R, and *DSM-IV* have brought significant advances in making diagnostic criteria more explicit. However, the *DSM*'s diagnostic criteria and categories are based on the assumption that each diagnostic category represents a separate disorder. This assumption is indeed tenable for disorders for which specific pathogens or other physical abnormalities have been identified. For example, diagnostic categories for infectious diseases such as tuberculosis, diphtheria, and AIDS can be confidently defined in terms of pathogens that are necessary (though not always sufficient) for the disorder to occur. Diagnostic categories for cancer can be defined in terms of specific kinds and locations of tissue pathology, even if specific pathogens have not been identified.

Some forms of psychopathology may eventually be found to involve physical pathogens and/or other physical abnormalities. However, until physical abnormalities are validated, it may be premature to require yes/no decisions for diagnoses of behavioral and emotional problems. Because even physical abnormalities may not all be identifiable in terms of yes/no dichotomies, the search for physical abnormalities may also be more productive if diagnostic criteria and categories are quantified. Even if the current *DSM-IV* diagnostic categories are to be retained in *DSM-V,* they could benefit from quantification by allowing each criterial feature to be scored quantitatively and by aggregating the scored features into a total score for each diagnosis.

If retention of the categorical diagnostic format is desired, cut points can nevertheless be established on distributions of quantitative scores. Rather than being established a priori by committees of experts, the cut points can be based on scores that discriminate efficiently between representative samples of people who are judged to be relatively normal (i.e., "healthy" samples) versus people who are judged to need mental health services. To take account of age, gender, and informant differences, cut points can be established on the basis of separate distributions obtained for people of

TABLE 5.1   Challenges to Be Met for Advancing Assessment, Taxonomy, and Diagnosis

1. *Test-retest attenuation:* The decline in problems reported from initial interviews to subsequent interviews.
2. *Low to moderate cross-informant agreement:* Different informants tend to report different problems.
3. *Limited agreement between diagnoses made from structured interviews and clinical diagnoses.*
4. *High rates of comorbidity:* Comorbidity between some diagnoses is so high as to raise questions about whether the diagnoses represent different disorders.
5. *Great variations in prevalence rates of DSM diagnoses made from structured interviews in epidemiological surveys.*
6. *The need to integrate multisource data.*
7. *The need to take account of differences related to age, gender, and sources of data.*
8. *The need to distinguish individual differences from cultural differences.*

each gender within particular age ranges, according to assessment data obtained from different kinds of informants. To avoid transferring the disadvantages of purely categorical diagnoses to diagnoses based on scores, the cut points should be based on findings of variations related to age, gender, and type of informant. In addition, levels of deviance can be identified to distinguish between people who have extreme degrees of the problems encompassed by a diagnostic category versus people who have less extreme degrees of the problems versus people who are in the normal range. Even if cut points are imposed on distributions of scores, the continuous scores should be retained to provide more precise measures of problems than are provided by categorization. Quantitative diagnostic scores also have advantages for measuring change over time, such as by comparing scores before, during, and after treatment and by comparing scores at different points in development.

Advantages of Quantification for Research

Quantification of the criterial features of diagnostic categories and of the diagnostic categories themselves offers a variety of advantages for most kinds of research on psychopathology.

Preserving Information

One advantage is that quantification of features typically preserves more information about the features than yes/no categorization does. This is especially true when neither the boundaries of each feature nor of the diagnostic categories are well validated. In such cases, imposition of unvalidated boundaries and categorical assessment procedures may cause cases to be misclassified. Even if certain disorders are ultimately found to have categorical boundaries, the inevitability of measurement error will prevent assessment procedures from infallibly distinguishing between individuals whose problems fall within those boundaries and individuals whose problems are not entirely congruent with the categorical boundaries.

Avoiding Forced Choices

Quantified assessment procedures avoid forced choices because they capture the degree to which individuals' problems approximate particular diagnostic categories and because quantification can take account of measurement error. By indicating the degree to which individuals' problems resemble each relevant diagnostic category, quantified assessment can help to prevent the premature closure risked by placing individuals in diagnostic categories that may be wrong.

Increasing Precision

A further advantage of quantification is that it can improve research by increasing the precision of data obtained about each characteristic of each individual. It can also improve research by making possible the use of more varied and powerful analytic tools than are available for categorical data. These analytic tools are especially useful for the following research areas that are increasingly important for advancing assessment, taxonomy, and diagnosis: identification of patterns of psychopathology and their correlates; life span developmental analyses of adaptive and maladaptive functioning; behavior genetics; epidemiology; efficacy, effectiveness, and outcomes of different kinds of interventions; pharmacokinetics of medications; biochemical correlates of behavioral and emotional problems; and multicultural applications.

Advantages of Quantification for Conceptualizing Psychopathology

In addition to the advantages it offers for research, quantification can also improve our ways of thinking about psychopathology, as outlined in the following sections.

Quantitative Aspects of Prototypes

In earlier sections, we outlined prototypes as models for taxonomy. Insofar as people mentally represent categories in terms of prototypes (sets of correlated features), people's representations of even categorical taxonomic constructs involve quantification. That is, a prototype for a category encompasses multiple features that are not perfectly correlated with each other. On the other hand, individuals who manifest many features of a prototype are more easily assigned to the category represented by that prototype than individuals who manifest fewer features of the prototype. Individuals who manifest multiple features of more than one prototype may be especially hard to classify by a single category. If such individuals have enough problems to need mental health services, then their problems can be described in terms of scores on multiple prototypes. According to *DSM*'s rules, individuals who manifest enough prototypical features of two categories to qualify for both categories are assumed to have the disorders represented by both categories; that is, they have comorbid disorders. (Although *DSM* has some preemptive rules, such as CD taking precedence over ODD when criteria for both disorders are met, these rules are often suspended in research and practice.)

If diagnostic categories are quantified in terms of the number of their prototypical features, the categories would correspond more closely to people's mental representations in terms of prototypes. In other words, because people use the number of features corresponding to their mental prototypes as a basis for classifying individuals and because the reliability and confidence with which individuals are classified depend on the number of prototypical features manifested, diagnostic categories may be used more effectively if they take advantage of the quantification that is inherent in mental classification processes. Because psychopathology often includes features of multiple diagnostic categories, quantification of each category would allow users of the categories to think about borderline cases and comorbidity explicitly in terms of the scores obtained for each diagnostic category. Borderline cases, for example, could be operationally defined in terms of scores that are high enough to be somewhat above the normal range but not so high as to be clearly clinically deviant. Furthermore, manifestations of features of multiple categories could be explicitly documented in terms of profiles of scores for all the relevant categories without implying that each elevated score indicated a separate (or comorbid) disorder.

Conceptualizing Cross-Informant Variations

Quantification of diagnostic categories can also facilitate conceptualization of cross-informant variations in assessment data. By allowing for variations in the degree to which particular problems are manifested, quantified taxonomic categories can help us use both the differences and the similarities in reports by different sources for determining the overall level of individuals' problems and how consistently they are manifested. For example, if all sources report high levels of hyperactivity for a child, this would provide consistent evidence for a disorder that involves hyperactivity, such as the Hyperactive-Impulsive type of ADHD. On the other hand, suppose that hyperactivity is reported by certain informants but not others. A purely categorical system forces us to choose among different informants' reports to make a yes/no decision about whether the individual is hyperactive. However, quantified categories enable us to integrate scores obtained from the different informants into the scores for each relevant category. This can be done by averaging scores, using weighted means of scores, matching profile patterns from different informants to profile types, and matching scores from different informants to latent classes or latent profiles.

In summary, the quantitative aspects of mental prototypes provide a natural basis for conceptualizing psycho-pathology in terms of quantified categories. Quantified categories can mitigate difficulties in making diagnostic decisions about individuals who need help but whose problems are too diverse to meet criteria for a single diagnostic category, as well as individuals who meet criteria for multiple diagnostic categories. Quantified categories also facilitate thinking about individuals who have significant problems that correspond to a particular diagnostic category but that do not quite reach the threshold required for a categorical diagnosis. In addition, when different sources report different problems for an individual, profiles of quantified categories scored from each source can be used to document similarities and differences in how the individual is perceived.

Advantages of Quantification for Mental Health Services

For mental health services, a fundamental advantage of quantification is that decisions about who needs services and what kind of services they need can be based on consideration of clients' profiles of adaptive and maladaptive functioning rather than on whether they meet categorical criteria for a particular diagnostic category. Excessive reliance on diagnostic categories as a basis for treatment decisions may exclude clients who need help but do not fit the categories. On the other hand, if clients meet criteria for a diagnostic category, then it may be too readily assumed that they are deviant even if they are adapting well. Furthermore, excessive reliance on diagnostic categories may cause treatment to focus more narrowly on the categories than is warranted either by the client's needs or by the ability of categorically based treatments to ameliorate broad spectra of problems. This may be especially true when a mental health service specializes in a particular diagnostic category such as depression, anxiety, or ADHD. Because the diagnostic procedures, treatment modalities, and clinicians in such services tend to focus on the target category, clients and their problems may be viewed primarily in terms of that category. Assessment of multiple quantified categories can reveal the degree to which individuals' problems really are or are not concentrated in a particular diagnostic category.

EFFORTS TO QUANTIFY DIAGNOSTIC CATEGORIES

The following sections outline some efforts to confer the benefits of quantification on *DSM* diagnostic categories.

Rating Scales for *Diagnostic and Statistical Manual* Categories

One approach to quantifying diagnostic categories has been to reproduce the symptom criteria for individual *DSM* categories in rating scale formats.

ADHD Rating Scale IV

DuPaul et al. (1998) constructed the ADHD Rating Scale IV, which consists of the *DSM-IV* symptom criteria for the Inattentive and Hyperactive-Impulsive types of ADHD. Parents and teachers rate each symptom as 0 = never or rarely, 1 = sometimes, 2 = often, or 3 = very often. The symptom scores are then summed to provide scale scores for Inattention, Hyperactivity-Impulsivity, and Total ADHD. DuPaul et al. reported that categorical diagnoses of ADHD correlated between .08 and .44 with scores on the scales of the ADHD Rating Scale IV completed by parents and teachers. However, the authors also reported correlations of .76 to .88 between teachers' ratings on the ADHD Rating Scale IV and the corresponding quantitative scales of the Conners Teacher Rating Scale 39 (C-TRS; Conners, 1997).

Youth's Inventory 4

In an effort to quantify a broader range of *DSM* diagnostic categories, Gadow and Sprafkin (1998, 1999) developed rating scales consisting of symptoms from multiple *DSM-IV* categories. As an example, the Youth's Inventory 4 (YI-4; Gadow & Sprafkin, 1999) is a self-rating form consisting of *DSM-IV* symptoms that youths are to rate 0, 1, 2, or 3 according to gradations like those of the ADHD Rating Scale IV. Symptom severity scores are obtained by summing the numerical ratings on each scale. Versions of a companion rating form, the Adolescent Symptom Inventory 4 (ASI-4; Gadow & Sprafkin, 1998), are designed to obtain parent and teacher ratings of many of the same *DSM* symptoms.

Using a sample of 11- to 18-year-olds whose parents requested an outpatient evaluation at a university clinic, Gadow et al. (2002) tested associations between symptom severity scores on the *DSM* scales of the YI-4 and *DSM* diagnoses in the youths' clinic charts. Gadow et al. bundled diagnoses into the following five groups: ADHD, ODD, CD, depressive disorders, and anxiety disorders. Because most youths received more than one *DSM* diagnosis, many youths were included in multiple diagnostic groups. Gadow et al. then identified the YI-4 *DSM* scales whose symptom severity scores had the highest point-biserial rs with the diagnoses. The highest rs ranged from .06 for the YI-4 ODD scale with *DSM* diagnoses of ODD to .38 for the Major Depressive Disorder scale with *DSM* diagnoses of depressive disorders, with mean $r = .25$ (computed by Fisher's z transformation).

Although the authors did not report associations between diagnoses and parent or teacher ratings, the Pearson rs between the YI-4 and parents' ASI-4 ratings on corresponding *DSM* scales ranged from .05 to .50. All correlations between the YI-4 and teachers' ASI-4 ratings on the corresponding *DSM* scales were extremely low ($r < .18$). However, the YI-4 scales yielded many rs in the .60s and .70s with the youths' self-ratings on non*DSM*-based scales scored quantitatively from the Children's Depression Inventory (Kovacs, 1992), the Multidimensional Anxiety Scale for Children (March, 1997), and the YSR (Achenbach, 1991b). Thus, although YI-4 *DSM* symptom severity scores did not yield much agreement with *DSM* clinical diagnoses nor with parent or teacher ratings, self-ratings on the YI-4 *DSM* symptom scales were strongly associated with self-ratings on other quantitative measures of problems.

Findings for the ADHD Rating Scale IV and the YI-4 thus suggest that parent, teacher, and self-ratings of actual *DSM* symptom items do not necessarily agree well with *DSM* diagnoses that are based on the same items. The impediments to agreement between the *DSM* scales and *DSM* diagnoses might include the diagnosticians' use of multiple sources of data, plus their use of additional criteria such as the duration of symptoms.

DSM-Oriented Scales

Another approach to quantifying *DSM* diagnostic categories is to start with items that are of proven value for obtaining ratings by the relevant informants and then selecting those items that are very consistent with *DSM* diagnostic categories, whether or not the items have exact counterparts among the *DSM* symptom items. Because each *DSM* diagnostic category in effect represents a diagnostic construct, experts' understanding of the diagnostic constructs may provide a good basis for selecting items that are appropriately rated by informants but that may not be literally the same as the *DSM* symptom criteria. However, because experts' judgments may vary with such characteristics as their professional training, the settings in which they work, the types of clients they see, and their cultural backgrounds, it is important to identify items on which judgments by diverse experts converge.

To make use of judgments by experts who varied greatly with respect to their training, work settings, clients, and cultures, Achenbach, Dumenci, and Rescorla (2001) invited 22 psychiatrists and psychologists from 16 cultures around the world to rate problem items for their consistency with

DSM diagnostic categories for child and adolescent disorders. The experts had all published on psychopathology and had a mean of 19.1 years of experience since their first doctorate. Five had both MD and PhD degrees. The experts were given the *DSM* criteria for nine categories of disorders that are defined largely in terms of behavioral and emotional problems. They then rated each problem item as 0 = not consistent, 1 = somewhat consistent, or 2 = very consistent with each *DSM* category. Because the objective was to obtain the experts' judgments of the diagnostic constructs represented by the *DSM* categories, they could rate problem items as being very consistent with a category even if the items did not have precise counterparts among the *DSM* symptom criteria.

Items that were rated as very consistent with a *DSM* category by a substantial majority of the experts (at least 64%) were assigned to a scale for that category. The scales are designated as "*DSM*-oriented" because they capture what is common to diverse experts' understanding of the diagnostic constructs underlying *DSM* categories, rather than being verbatim statements of the *DSM* criteria. Enough items met criteria to form *DSM*-oriented scales that were designated as follows: Affective Problems (including Dysthymia and Major Depression); Anxiety Problems (including Generalized Anxiety Disorder, Separation Anxiety Disorder, and Specific Phobia); Somatic Problems (including Somatization and Somatoform Disorders); ADHD Problems (including Hyperactive-Impulsive and Inattentive types); Oppositional Defiant Problems; and Conduct Problems.

To enable users to judge the degree of deviance indicated by scores on the *DSM*-oriented scales, normative data were obtained for a national probability sample of 6- to 18-year-olds who had not received mental health services in the preceding 12 months (i.e., a "healthy sample" in epidemiological terms). Scores on the *DSM*-oriented scales are displayed on profiles in relation to norms for each gender according to particular age ranges, separately for parent ratings on the CBCL, teacher ratings on the TRF, and self-ratings on the YSR (Achenbach & Rescorla, 2001).

Relations to Diagnostic and Statistical Manual *Diagnoses*

Point-biserial *r*s have been reported between *DSM-IV* clinical diagnoses and the *DSM*-oriented scales in a university outpatient clinic sample (Achenbach & Rescorla, 2001, p. 130). Like the diagnoses reported by Gadow et al. (2002) for youths who completed the YI-4, the diagnoses were obtained from clinical records and were based on multiple sources of data. However, unlike the ages 11 to 18 spanned by the Gadow et al. data for self-ratings on the YI-4, the

data for the *DSM*-oriented scales spanned ages 6 to 18 and were obtained from parents' ratings on the CBCL/6–18. For the same groupings of diagnoses as were reported by Gadow et al., the correlations between *DSM* clinical diagnoses and the corresponding *DSM*-oriented scales ranged from .34 for CD to .60 for ADHD, with mean *r* = .45 (computed by Fisher's *z* transformation).

As another way of assessing *DSM* diagnoses, clinicians administered the *DSM-IV* Checklist (Hudziak, 1998) to family members who were involved in the clinical evaluation of the children. The *DSM-IV* Checklist consists of questions corresponding to each of the criterial symptoms for each diagnostic category. Although the questions are quoted from the *DSM-IV* symptom criteria, clinical interviewers are free to rephrase the questions for the benefit of the interviewees. The score for each diagnostic category is the sum of symptoms judged to be present. For the same diagnostic groupings as used by Gadow et al., the Pearson *r*s with the corresponding *DSM*-oriented scales ranged from .43 for Anxiety Disorders to .80 for ADHD, with mean *r* = .63 (computed by Fisher's *z* transformation). Recall that the *DSM*-oriented scales do not consist of items reproduced verbatim from the *DSM* symptom criteria. Nevertheless, their mean *r* of .45 with *DSM* clinical diagnoses and .63 with scores for *DSM* diagnoses on the clinician-administered *DSM-IV* Checklist were significantly higher ($p < .05$) than the mean *r* of .25 between *DSM* clinical diagnoses and the YI-4 scales that did consist of verbatim *DSM* symptom criteria. This suggests that quantification of *DSM* diagnostic constructs may not be most effectively done by obtaining informants' responses to the verbatim *DSM* symptom criteria.

Bridging Gaps between Nosologically and Empirically Based Constructs

The top-down and bottom-up strategies that characterize nosologically and empirically based constructs, respectively, are arguably the most common approaches to taxonomy of psychopathology. Each makes use of existing knowledge and concepts in different ways. Both may help to advance assessment, taxonomy, and diagnosis, especially if the potential strengths of both can be combined. One way to combine their strengths is to use a common set of assessment procedures for nosologically and empirically based constructs. Such a combination is exemplified by the *DSM*-oriented scales that are scored from the same pool of items from which empirically based syndromes are scored (Achenbach et al., 2004; Achenbach & Rescorla, 2001, 2003). For children, adults, and the elderly, scores for both types of scales are displayed on profiles in relation to age-, gender-, and informant-specific norms derived from the same national probability samples. The two types of scales have similar psychometric properties, and there are medium to strong associations between some scales of the two types (Achenbach, Bernstein, & Dumenci, 2005; Achenbach, Dumenci, & Rescorla, 2003b). The ability to score both types of scales from the same items that can be rated by the people being assessed and by informants in about 15 minutes makes it easy to compare and contrast nosologically and empirically based findings in many research and clinical contexts for many purposes.

Longitudinal Research Designs

In previous sections, we presented accelerated longitudinal, path, and growth curve designs as examples of research designs that may be especially useful for developmental research related to assessment, taxonomy, and diagnosis. Some longitudinal studies, such as the Dunedin project (Feehan, McGee, Williams, & Nada-Raja, 1995; Newman et al., 1996), have reported *DSM* diagnoses for the same participants at different ages. However, application of powerful longitudinal designs to nosological constructs has been limited by the difficulty of operationalizing nosological constructs via structured diagnostic interviews that need to be repeated on large representative samples of participants over long periods. Additionally, major changes in diagnostic criteria from one edition of the *DSM* to another make it hard to link diagnoses based on the different editions. Finally, although longitudinal growth models can utilize categorical variables such as diagnoses, these categorical variables do not capture as much information about individual differences between people as quantitative scales do.

DSM-oriented scales that can be scored quantitatively from the same brief assessment instruments as empirically based scales provide new opportunities for doing research on nosologically based constructs and for directly comparing the results with those for empirically based constructs. Scores on quantitative *DSM*-oriented scales based on ratings from multiple informants can readily serve as indicators for latent variable analyses. Latent variables estimated from such indicators can then serve as predictors, moderators, mediators, and outcomes in path and/or growth curve analyses. It is thus possible to use accelerated longitudinal, path, and growth curve designs to track relations between developmentally early and later measures of nosologically based constructs to test their developmental stability and the degree to which they predict various outcomes.

Genetic and Other Biological Research

Quantified phenotypic measures of nosological constructs make it possible to test complex quantitative models for genetic and environmental effects on psychopathology. Because these measures can be economically obtained for very large samples of twins and other genetically informative samples, they yield much more powerful genetic analyses than do structured diagnostic interviews, which would be financially prohibitive for such large samples (e.g., Boomsma et al., 2001).

In addition to genetic research, studies of other biological variables can be strengthened by using quantitative measures of nosological constructs. For example, several studies have found significant correlations between the empirically based Aggressive Behavior syndrome and a variety of biochemical measures (e.g., Birmaher et al., 1990; Gabel, Stadler, Bjorn, Shindledecker, & Bowden, 1993; Hanna, Yuwiler, & Coates, 1995; Scerbo & Kolko, 1994). Quantitative scales for measuring nosologically based constructs can provide more powerful and differentiated tests of associations between biochemical variables and diagnostic constructs.

Research on Secular Trends in Psychopathology

It has been widely noted that the previously rare diagnoses of Pervasive Developmental Disorders (PDD), including Autism and Asperger's Disorder, are becoming more common (e.g., Chakrabarti & Fombonne, 2001). Reviews of a variety of documents have also led to the conclusion that adolescent conduct disorders, substance abuse, depression, and suicide have increased (Rutter & Smith, 1995). Secular (i.e., long-term) changes in rates of psychopathology are apt to be very important, because they may provide clues about etiological factors and protective factors. Secular changes in rates of psychopathology may also argue for new efforts at prevention and treatment. Unfortunately, changing rates of diagnoses may reflect changing diagnostic criteria, diagnostic categories, and even the willingness of mental health workers to make certain diagnoses. As an example, Autism was previously blamed on unconscious parental attitudes (e.g., Wolman, 1970, p. vii), which meant that it was a very undesirable diagnosis. In recent years, Autism has come to be regarded as a developmental disability for which intensive services are now provided. Even documentation of suicide may reflect cultural changes, as there is evidence that suicides by young people were previously underreported on death certificates (Males, 1991).

To measure changes in the behavioral and emotional problems on which diagnoses are based, it is necessary to assess representative samples of the population with the same standardized procedures at different points in time. Problem rates can then be compared to measure changes, whether or not there have been changes in diagnostic criteria, categories, or willingness to make certain diagnoses. As an example, studies in the United States and the Netherlands have used the same standardized procedures to obtain CBCL and TRF ratings of representative samples of children at intervals as long as 23 years (Achenbach, Dumenci, & Rescorla, 2002, 2003a; Verhulst, van der Ende, & Rietbergen, 1997). Completion rates ranged from 82% to 93% in the American samples and 82% to 85% in the Dutch samples. In the American samples, empirically based syndromes and *DSM*-oriented scales showed similar patterns of small but significant increases in problem scores in the 1980s, followed by decreases in problem scores in the 1990s. From 1983 to 1993, the Dutch samples showed little change. A new Dutch sample is being assessed in 2005 (to be updated when data are available).

A study in the United Kingdom compared parents' reports of problems for 15- and 16-year-olds in cohorts that were assessed in 1974, 1986, and 1999 (Collishaw, Maughan, Goodman, & Pickles, 2004). The assessment instruments differed somewhat among the three studies, and only 11 problem items were similar enough for comparison across the three cohorts. Significant increases in conduct problems were found from the 1974 to the 1986 and 1999 cohorts. Emotional problems and hyperactivity were significantly higher in the 1999 than in the 1974 or 1986 cohorts. Although it is certainly possible that secular trends differ among countries, it is difficult to draw firm conclusions from the U.K. data because of differences in the assessment instruments and because the completion rates were evidently only 62% in 1974 and 45% in 1986 (Collishaw et al., 2004, p. 1353). The 1999 completion rate was evidently not reported, but samples with high completion rates often include larger proportions of people with problems than do samples with low completion rates.

The findings suggest that there has not been a general worsening of children's problems over the past 2 decades in the United States or the Netherlands. Because these studies did not assess children younger than 7 years and did not include many of the symptoms used to define PDD, they may not have been able to detect increases in problems that underlie the increasing rates of PDD diagnoses. However, because the CBCL for ages 1.5 to 5 (CBCL/1.5–5) and the Caregiver-Teacher Report Form for ages 1.5 to 5 (C-TRF) include a *DSM*-oriented Pervasive Developmental Problems scale, it would be feasible to administer the CBCL/1.5–5 and C-TRF to parents, preschool teachers,

TABLE 5.2 Potential Advantages of Quantifying Criterial Features and Taxonomic Constructs

1. Avoids yes/no forced choices about the presence of features and diagnosis of disorders.
2. Allows cut points on distributions of scores that can reflect age, gender, informant, clinical status, and other differences.
3. Provides more precise measurement of psychopathology than categorization does.
4. Allows use of more powerful analytic tools than categorization does for research on patterns of psychopathology, developmental trajectories, behavior genetics, epidemiology, effects of interventions, pharmacokinetics, biochemical variables, and cross-cultural variations.
5. Corresponds to mental representations of taxa in terms of prototypes.
6. Quantified covariation between problems avoids dilemmas of comorbidity between categorical disorders.
7. Facilitates aggregation of multisource data in taxonomic constructs.
8. Provides more precise basis for decisions about treatment and evaluations of progress and outcomes.
9. Facilitates targeting of specific problems in relevant contexts.
10. Measures specific problems independently of criteria for diagnoses.

and day care providers at intervals of a few years to see whether PDD problems are increasing. If scores on the PDD scale do not increase but the prevalence of PDD diagnoses continues to increase, this would suggest that increases in the diagnoses are not accounted for by increases in PDD problems. Such a finding might mean that diagnosticians have become more sensitive to PDD problems or have become more willing to make PDD diagnoses for other reasons. Table 5.2 summarizes potential advantages of quantifying criterial features and taxonomic constructs.

FUTURE DIRECTIONS

Important advances are being made in the developmental study of psychopathology, but much remains to be done. In this section, we outline some future directions for advancing assessment, taxonomy, and diagnosis. Although they are by no means the only important directions, they are particularly important for extending the developmental study of psychopathology to adults, to the elderly, and to more diverse cultures.

Life Span Directions

There are many studies of child/adolescent psychopathology and adult psychopathology. Research on psychopathology among the elderly is also growing rapidly. However, there is far less research on the developmental course of psychopathology from childhood into adulthood and from adulthood into old age. Several factors may be to blame for the paucity of research that bridges major developmental periods. One factor is that clinicians and researchers tend to specialize in work with children and adolescents, or adults, or the elderly, rather than spanning these different periods. A second factor is that concepts of psychopathology tend to be formulated separately for children and adolescents, for adults, and for the elderly. And a third factor is that assessment, taxonomy, and diagnosis tend to be segmented according to these major periods of life.

To fully understand both adaptive and maladaptive functioning within each period of life, as well as the continuities and discontinuities between periods, we need assessment procedures that provide continuity across broad age spans. Much of the research on prediction of adult psychopathology from childhood variables has used very different measures of child and adult problems. Because certain behaviors that are considered deviant in childhood would not be deviant for adults and vice versa, assessment must be tailored to the developmental level of the people to be assessed. However, methodologically similar measures that include content that is similar for people of different ages, as well as developmentally specific content, are likely to provide better pictures of continuities and discontinuities between developmental periods than are measures that differ with respect to both methodology and content. Our section on "Life Span Applications" illustrated some ways in which similar standardized methodology has been applied to the assessment of psychopathology across major periods of life. However, far more needs to be done to systematically compare and contrast findings for different periods of life and to bridge the gaps between them with longitudinal research. Use of similar standardized methods to assess people as they grow older makes it possible to apply accelerated longitudinal designs, which can yield developmental findings more quickly and cost-effectively than traditional longitudinal designs. For clinical as well as research purposes, similar standardized methods can also be used to assess different generations within families, such as parents and their children, to identify cross-generational similarities and differences.

Multicultural Directions

Globalization has many facets. Although economic globalization may be the most publicized facet, cultural globalization is also important. Cultural globalization stems partly from increasing access to a common set of media for information and entertainment. It also stems from mass movements of immigrants and refugees from their indigenous cultures to very different cultures. Host cultures are often unprepared to provide mental health and related services to the newcomers. In addition to language barriers, challenges arise from differences in attitudes toward mental health services, as well as from cultural differences in what is deemed to be normal versus abnormal. Other challenges arise when mental health professionals from developed cultures seek to help people in less-developed cultures (Achenbach, Rescorla, & Ivanova, 2005).

Both to build a more comprehensive science of developmental psychopathology and to apply that science to helping more people, it is important to use assessment instruments and data that extend across multiple cultures. Our section on "Multicultural Research" reviewed multicultural findings for psychopathology in children and adults, using both bottom-up and top-down assessment procedures. However, the multicultural studies published to date have mainly assessed psychopathology in terms of syndromes and diagnostic categories developed in Western cultures.

To advance multicultural understanding and applications of the science of developmental psychopathology, it is important to take account of possible cultural variations in the patterning of psychopathology, as well as in the prevalence of particular problems. In the empirically based, bottom-up approach, data from many cultures can be included in the statistical derivation of syndromes. After a multicultural syndrome model has been constructed, data from individual cultures can be tested for goodness of fit to the multicultural model. Although the multicultural model may embody syndrome structures that reflect what is common to the patterning of problems across the different cultures, individual cultures may also be found to differ in certain particulars. For example, data from culture A may not fit the multicultural syndrome model as well as data from cultures B, C, and D. Further testing of the data from culture A may reveal a syndrome that is not found in the multicultural syndrome model. Conversely, other cultures may be found to lack one or more syndromes that are in the multicultural syndrome model.

The process of deriving a multicultural syndrome model and then testing data from individual cultures against the multicultural model can reveal both similarities and differences between the patterns of problems in different cultures. Distributions of scores obtained on the multicultural syndromes by representative samples of people from different cultures can be compared to identify cross-cultural similarities and differences in problem scores on each syndrome.

Because the diagnostic categories of the top-down, nosologically based approach are formulated by panels of mental health experts, one way to take account of multicultural factors is to include experts from many cultures. However, because many cultures lack indigenously trained experts, the available experts may largely share the Western diagnostic concepts and assumptions that are embodied in current nosologies. It may therefore be worth developing ways that data from multiple cultures can be more directly incorporated into the diagnostic categories of the nosological approach, such as by quantifying diagnostic data from different cultures, as outlined next.

Quantification of Diagnostic Criteria

Nosological approaches typically require categorical yes/no judgments of each criterial feature of each diagnostic category. These approaches also require yes/no decisions as to whether an individual meets the overall criteria for a diagnosis. However, the categorical, yes/no format is not necessarily an immutable part of the nosological approach. In fact, the Nomenclature Planning Work Group for *DSM-V* concluded that it will be "important that consideration be given to advantages and disadvantages of basing part or all of *DSM-V* on dimensions rather than categories" (Rounsaville et al., 2002, p. 12).

A dimensional approach, whereby symptoms are summed to obtain a score for a diagnosis, is often viewed as the main quantitative alternative to the categorical approach. However, summing the number of symptoms is only one of many ways to reap the benefits of quantification for increasing precision and statistical power. For example, allowing diagnosticians to rate symptoms and other diagnostic criteria on 3-step scales rather than requiring yes/no forced choices could make the diagnostic process easier, more reliable, and better differentiated. Categorical cut points could still be retained for deciding whether an individual meets criteria for a diagnosis by specifying diagnostic thresholds in terms of the sum of 3-step ratings rather than the number of symptoms. Further benefits of quantification could be obtained by providing age-, gender-, and culture-specific norms for the distributions of scores within each diagnostic category. For categories in which the distributions of scores differed significantly by age, gender, and/or culture, diagnostic thresholds could be chosen to mark a similar degree of deviance for each group, if desired. Quantification could also be used to combine data from multiple sources as a basis for making diagnostic decisions.

As an alternative to dimensional approaches, person-centered quantification could be used to identify categories of individuals who have similar patterns of problems. Methods for using quantitative diagnostic data to identify types or categories of individuals include latent profile analysis, cluster analysis, and latent class analysis. A particularly important use of quantification for individual patterns is known as *patient-focused analysis*. This involves repeated measurement of individuals' scores during and after interventions to detect statistically reliable changes in magnitudes and/or slope parameters (e.g., Lambert, Hansen, & Finch, 2001). In short, even elementary quantification, such as rating diagnostic criteria on 3-step scales, could enable the nosological approach to capitalize on the many benefits of quantification that have long been utilized by other approaches to assessment and taxonomy.

Use of Norms to Evaluate Interventions

Numerous studies have been designed to improve prevention and treatment of psychopathology (e.g., Kazdin, 2000, 2003; Kazdin & Weisz, 2003; C. Roberts, Kane, Thomson, Bishop, & Hart, 2003). However, when prevention and treatment are targeted on diagnoses that are assumed to reflect enduring characteristics of the individuals who meet diagnostic criteria, as implied by diagnoses such as ADHD and personality disorders, it is difficult to evaluate the effects of the interventions because the diagnoses are not expected to change. Whether or not particular forms of psychopathology actually involve such enduring conditions, accurate evaluation of intervention effects requires measurement of change from clinical deviance toward the normal range of functioning. To determine whether interventions do produce statistically significant improvements, controlled studies are needed in which norms are used to measure the degree to which participants' preintervention scores move from being clinically deviant to being more typical of scores obtained by representative normative samples of peers (Achenbach, 2001; Kendall, Marrs-Garcia, Nath, & Sheldrick, 1999; Sheldrick, Kendall, & Heimberg, 2001). Because successful adaptation requires not only an absence of problems but also the presence of positive competencies, the effects of interventions should be evaluated in relation to norms for competencies as well as for problems.

Use of Multisource Data

Low levels of agreement between clinical diagnoses and diagnostic interviews, as well as the modest correlations between reports by different informants for both adult and child psychopathology, indicate that no single source of data is likely to suffice for comprehensive assessment of psychopathology. Although assessment of children usually includes data from multiple informants, multi-informant data are also needed for adults. Even when multi-informant data are obtained, challenges remain with respect to documenting specific similarities and differences between reports by different informants. As an example of ways to compare reports by multiple informants, we have developed computer software that displays data from multiple informants in terms of side-by-side comparisons of item scores and histograms of scale scores (Achenbach et al., 2004; Achenbach & Rescorla, 2001, 2003). The software also displays the degree of agreement between informants in terms of Q correlations and compares the Q correlations obtained for each case with those obtained for large samples of informants. However, much more research is needed on how best to integrate data from different sources as a basis for decisions about diagnoses, interventions, and outcomes.

SUMMARY

Numerous advances are occurring in knowledge and methods related to developmental issues in assessment, taxonomy, and diagnosis of psychopathology. In this chapter, we defined *psychopathology* as persistent behavior, thoughts, and emotions that are likely to interfere with developmental tasks necessary for long-term adaptation. The major themes of our chapter are summarized next.

First, it has become clear that developmental approaches are needed to understand psychopathology across the life span. This means that we need assessment procedures, taxonomic constructs, and diagnoses geared to the problems characteristic of each developmental period. At the same time, to track developmental sequences and outcomes, continuity is needed between assessment procedures from one developmental period to another.

Second, the developmental study of child and adolescent psychopathology has prompted recognition of the importance of multisource data for adults as well as children. Research has indicated that correlations between adults' self-reports and reports by other informants are as low as those found for children and adolescents.

Third, multicultural perspectives are essential. By applying the same standardized multi-informant assessment procedures in different cultures, we can identify similarities and differences in rates of reported problems to learn whether the same assessment procedures, taxonomic constructs, and diagnoses are applicable in different cultures. Procedures that are found to perform similarly in different cultures can be used to test the course and correlates of psychopathology across the different cultures.

We described developmental methodology that is applicable to the study of psychopathology across the life span. Real-time longitudinal, accelerated longitudinal, path, and growth curve designs are especially useful.

We contrasted nosologically based models of psychopathology that employ a *top-down* strategy (whereby experts formulate diagnostic categories and then choose criteria for the categories) with empirically based models that employ a *bottom-up* strategy (whereby problems scored for large samples of people are analyzed statistically to derive syndromes of co-occurring problems). We explained that *assessment* refers to gathering data to identify the distinguishing features of individual cases, whereas *taxonomy* refers to grouping cases according to their distinguishing features. Prototypes, which represent categories quantitatively in terms of sets of imperfectly correlated features, provide taxonomic models that mesh well with human information processing. We also discussed three different meanings of the term *diagnosis,* that is, *diagnostic processes, formal diagnoses,* and *diagnostic formulations.* In this context, we suggested that the high rates of comorbidity found for *DSM* diagnoses raise questions about whether each diagnostic category truly represents a separate disorder.

To advance assessment, taxonomy, and diagnosis, we need to meet the following challenges: test-retest attenuation, that is, the tendency for more problems to be reported at initial than subsequent assessments; limited cross-informant agreement; limited agreement between clinical diagnoses and diagnoses made from structured diagnostic interviews; high rates of comorbidity; great variations in prevalence rates of *DSM* diagnoses made from structured interviews; the need to integrate multisource data; the need to take account of differences related to age, gender, and data sources; and the need to distinguish individual differences from cultural differences. We suggested that quantification of nosologically based constructs could address many of these challenges. Quantification can also make nosologically based constructs more suitable for powerful longitudinal research designs, genetic and other biological research, and research on secular trends in psychopathology.

We then outlined future directions that we feel would advance the study of developmental psychopathology.

REFERENCES

Achenbach, T. M. (1966). The classification of children's psychiatric symptoms: A factor-analytic study. *Psychological Monographs, 80*(No. 615).

Achenbach, T. M. (1974). *Developmental psychopathology.* New York: Ronald Press.

Achenbach, T. M. (1982). *Developmental psychopathology.* (2nd ed.). New York: Wiley.

Achenbach, T. M. (1991a). "Comorbidity" in child and adolescent psychiatry: Categorical and quantitative perspectives. *Journal of Child and Adolescent Psychopharmacology, 1,* 271–278.

Achenbach, T. M. (1991b). *Integrative guide for the 1991 CBCL/4–18, YSR, and TRF profiles.* Burlington: University of Vermont, Department of Psychiatry.

Achenbach, T. M. (2001). What are norms and why do we need valid ones? *Clinical Psychology: Science and Practice, 8,* 446–450.

Achenbach, T. M., Bernstein, A., & Dumenci, L. (2005). *DSM*-oriented scales and statistically based syndromes for ages 18 to 59: Linking taxonomic paradigms to facilitate multitaxonomic approaches. *Journal of Personality Assessment, 84,* 47–61.

Achenbach, T. M., Conners, C. K., Quay, H. C., Verhulst, F. C., & Howell, C. T. (1989). Replication of empirically derived syndromes as a basis for taxonomy of child/adolescent psychopathology. *Journal of Abnormal Child Psychology, 17,* 299–323.

Achenbach, T. M., Dumenci, L., & Rescorla, L. A. (2001). *Ratings of relations between DSM-IV diagnostic categories and items of the CBCL/6–18, TRF, and YSR.* Burlington: University of Vermont, Research Center for Children, Youth, and Families. Available from www.ASEBA.org.

Achenbach, T. M., Dumenci, L., & Rescorla, L. A. (2002). Ten-year comparisons of problems and competencies for national samples of youth: Self, parent, and teacher reports. *Journal of Emotional and Behavioral Disorders, 10,* 194–203.

Achenbach, T. M., Dumenci, L., & Rescorla, L. A. (2003a). Are American children's problems still getting worse? A 23-year comparison. *Journal of Abnormal Child Psychology, 31,* 1–11.

Achenbach, T. M., Dumenci, L., & Rescorla, L. A. (2003b). DSM-oriented and empirically based approaches to constructing scales from the same item pools. *Journal of Clinical Child and Adolescent Psychology, 32,* 328–340.

Achenbach, T. M., Howell, C. T., McConaughy, S. H., & Stanger, C. (1995a). Six-year predictors of problems in a national sample of children and youth: I. Cross-informant syndromes. *Journal of the American Academy of Child and Adolescent Psychiatry, 34,* 336–347.

Achenbach, T. M., Howell, C. T., McConaughy, S. H., & Stanger, C. (1995b). Six-year predictors of problems in a national sample of children and youth: II. Signs of disturbance. *Journal of the American Academy of Child and Adolescent Psychiatry, 34,* 488–498.

Achenbach, T. M., Howell, C. T., McConaughy, S. H., & Stanger, C. (1995c). Six-year predictors of problems in a national sample: III. Transitions to young adult syndromes. *Journal of the American Academy of Child and Adolescent Psychiatry, 34,* 658–669.

Achenbach, T. M., Howell, C. T., McConaughy, S. H., & Stanger, C. (1998). Six-year predictors of problems in a national sample: IV. Young adult signs of disturbance. *Journal of the American Academy of Child and Adolescent Psychiatry, 37,* 718–727.

Achenbach, T. M., Howell, C. T., Quay, H. C., & Conners, C. K. (1991). National survey of problems and competencies among 4- to 16-year-olds: Parents' reports for normative and clinical samples. *Monographs of the Society for Research in Child Development, 56*(Serial No. 225).

Achenbach, T. M., Krukowski, R. A., Dumenci, L., & Ivanova, M. Y. (2005). Assessment of adult psychopathology: Meta-analyses and implications of cross-informant correlations. *Psychological Bulletin, 131,* 361–382.

Achenbach, T. M., McConaughy, S. H., & Howell, C. T. (1987). Child/adolescent behavioral and emotional problems: Implications of cross-informant correlations for situational specificity. *Psychological Bulletin, 101,* 213–232.

Achenbach, T. M., Newhouse, P. A., & Rescorla, L. A. (2004). *Manual for the ASEBA Older Adult forms and profiles.* Burlington: University of Vermont, Research Center for Children, Youth, and Families.

Achenbach, T. M., & Rescorla, L. A. (2001). *Manual for the ASEBA School-Age forms and profiles.* Burlington: University of Vermont, Research Center for Children, Youth, and Families.

Achenbach, T. M., & Rescorla, L. A. (2003). *Manual for the ASEBA Adult forms and profiles.* Burlington: University of Vermont, Research Center for Children, Youth, and Families.

Achenbach, T. M., & Rescorla, L. A. (2006). Multicultural aspects of child and adolescent psychopathology: Empirically based and diagnostic perspectives. New York: Guilford Press.

Achenbach, T. M., Rescorla, L. A., & Ivanova, M. (2005). International cross-cultural consistencies and variations in child and adolescent psychopathology. In C. R. Reynolds & C. L. Frisby (Eds.), *Comprehensive handbook of multicultural school psychology.* Hoboken, NJ: Wiley.

Ambrosini, P. J. (2000). Historical development and present status of the Schedule for Affective Disorders and Schizophrenia for School-Age Children (K-SADS). *Journal of the American Academy of Child and Adolescent Psychiatry, 39,* 49–58.

American Psychiatric Association. (1952). *Diagnostic and statistical manual of mental disorders.* Washington, DC: Author.

American Psychiatric Association. (1968). *Diagnostic and statistical manual of mental disorders* (2nd ed.). Washington, DC: Author.

American Psychiatric Association. (1980). *Diagnostic and statistical manual of mental disorders* (3rd ed.). Washington, DC: Author.

American Psychiatric Association. (1987). *Diagnostic and statistical manual of mental disorders* (3rd ed., rev.). Washington, DC: Author.

American Psychiatric Association. (1994). *Diagnostic and statistical manual of mental disorders* (4th ed.). Washington, DC: Author.

American Psychiatric Association. (2000). *Diagnostic and statistical manual of mental disorders* (4th ed., text rev.). Washington, DC: Author.

Baltes, P. B. (1987). Theoretical propositions of life-span developmental psychology: On the dynamics between growth and decline. *Developmental Psychology, 23,* 611–626.

Baltes, P. B., Cornelius, S. W., & Nesselroade, J. R. (1979). Cohort effects in developmental psychology. In J. R. Nesselroade & P. B. Baltes (Eds.), *Longitudinal research in the study of behavior and development* (pp. 61–87). New York: Academic Press.

Bandura, A. (1977). *Social learning theory.* Englewood Cliffs, NJ: Prentice-Hall.

Bayley, N. (1968). Behavioral correlates of mental growth: Birth to thirty-six years. *American Psychologist, 23,* 1–17.

Beitchman, J. H., Dielman, T. E., Landis, J. R., Benson, R. M., & Kemp, P. L. (1978). Reliability of the Group for the Advancement of Psychiatry diagnostic categories in child psychiatry. *Archives of General Psychiatry, 35,* 1461–1466.

Bell, R. Q. (1953). Convergence: An accelerated longitudinal approach. *Child Development, 24,* 145–152.

Bell, R. Q. (1954). An experimental test of the accelerated longitudinal approach. *Child Development, 25,* 281–286.

Berkson, J. (1946). Limitations of the application of fourfold table analysis to hospital data. *Biometrics Bulletin, 2,* 47–53.

Birmaher, B., Stanley, M., Greenhill, L., Twomey, J., Gavrilescu, A., & Rabinovich, H. (1990). Platelet imipramine binding in children and adolescents with impulsive behavior. *Journal of the American Academy of Child and Adolescent Psychiatry, 29,* 914–918.

Bollen, K. A. (1989). *Structural equations with latent variables.* New York: Wiley.

Boomsma, D. I., van Beijsterveldt, T., van Baal, C., Stroet, T., Polderman, T., Groot, A., et al. (2001, July). *Genetic analysis of DSM-IV oriented scales in 3-year-old Dutch twins.* Paper presented at Behavior Genetics Association, Boulder, CO.

Breton, J. J., Bergeron, L., Valla, J.-P., Berthiaume, C., Gaudet, N., Lambert, J., et al. (1999). Quebec child mental health survey: Prevalence of DSM-III-R mental health disorders. *Journal of Child Psychology and Psychiatry, 40,* 375–384.

Breton, J. J., Bergeron, L., Valla, J. P., Lepine, S., Houde, L., & Gaudet, N. (1995). Do children aged 9 through 11 years understand the DISC Version 2.5 questions? *Journal of the American Academy of Child and Adolescent Psychiatry, 34,* 946–954.

Cantor, N., Smith, E. E., French, R. D. S., & Mezzich, J. (1980). Psychiatric diagnosis as prototype categorization. *Journal of Abnormal Psychology, 89,* 181–193.

Caron, C., & Rutter, M. (1991). Comorbidity in child psychopathology: Concepts, issues and research strategies. *Journal of Child Psychology and Psychiatry, 32,* 1063–1080.

Cassidy, J., & Shaver, P. R. (Eds.). (1999). *Handbook of attachment: Theory, research, and clinical applications.* New York: Guilford Press.

Chakrabarti, S., & Fombonne, E. (2001). Pervasive developmental disorders in preschool children. *Journal of the American Medical Association, 285,* 3093–3099.

Cicchetti, D. (1984). The emergence of developmental psychopathology. *Child Development, 55,* 1–7.

Cohen, J. (1988). *Statistical power analysis for the behavioral sciences* (2nd ed.). New York: Academic Press.

Collishaw, S., Maughan, B., Goodman, R., & Pickles A. (2004). Time trends in adolescent mental health. *Journal of Child Psychology and Psychiatry, 45,* 1350–1362.

Conners, C. K. (1997). *Conners' Teacher Rating Scale-Revised.* North Tonawanda, NY: Multi-Health Systems.

Costello, A. J., Edelbrock, C., Dulcan, M. K., Kalas, R., & Klaric, S. H. (1984). *Report on the Diagnostic Interview Schedule for Children (DISC).* Pittsburgh, PA: University of Pittsburgh, Department of Psychiatry.

Crijnen, A. A. M., Achenbach, T. M., & Verhulst, F. C. (1997). Comparisons of problems reported by parents of children in 12 cultures: Total problems, externalizing, and internalizing. *Journal of the American Academy of Child and Adolescent Psychiatry, 36,* 1269–1277.

Crijnen, A. A. M., Achenbach, T. M., & Verhulst, F. C. (1999). Comparisons of problems reported by parents of children in twelve cultures: The CBCL/4–18 syndrome constructs. *American Journal of Psychiatry, 156,* 569–574.

deGroot, A., Koot, H. M., & Verhulst, F. C. (1994). Cross-cultural generalizability of the CBCL cross-informant syndromes. *Psychological Assessment, 6,* 225–230.

Down, J. L. H. (1866). Observations on an ethnic classification of idiots. London Hospital Reports, 3, 259–262.

Dumenci, L., Erol, N., Achenbach, T. M., & Simsek, Z. (2004). Measurement structure of the Turkish translation of the Child Behavior Checklist using confirmatory factor analytic approaches to validation of syndromal constructs. *Journal of Abnormal Child Psychology, 32,* 335–340.

DuPaul, G. J., Power, T. J., Anastopoulos, A. D., & Reid, R. (1998). *ADHD Rating Scale-IV: Checklists, norms, and clinical interpretation.* New York: Guilford Press.

Eaton, W. W., Neufeld, K., Chen, L.-S., & Cai, G. (2000). A comparison of self-report and clinical diagnostic interviews for depression. *Archives of General Psychiatry, 57,* 217–222.

Edelbrock, C., Costello, A. J., Dulcan, M. K., Kalas, R., & Conover, N. C. (1985). Age differences in the reliability of the psychiatric interview of the child. *Child Development, 56,* 265–275.

Education of the Handicapped Act. (1977). Public Law 94–142 Federal Register, 42, p. 42478. Amended in Federal Register. (1981), 46, p. 3866.

Endicott, J., & Spitzer, R. L. (1978). A diagnostic interview. *Archives of General Psychiatry, 35,* 837–844.

Eysenck, H. J. (1953). *The structure of human personality.* London: Methuen.

Faraone, S. V., Biederman, J., Keenan, K., & Tsuang, M. T. (1991). Separation of DSM-III attention deficit disorder and conduct disorder: Evidence from a family-genetic study of American child psychiatric patients. *Psychological Medicine, 21,* 109–121.

Feehan, M., McGee, R., Williams, S. M., & Nada-Raja, S. (1995). Models of adolescent psychopathology: Childhood risk and the transition to adulthood. *Journal of the American Academy of Child and Adolescent Psychiatry, 34,* 670–680.

Finkel, D., Reynolds, C. A., McArdle, J. J., Gatz, M., & Pedersen, N. L. (2003). Latent growth curve analyses of accelerating decline in cognitive abilities in late adulthood. *Developmental Psychology, 39,* 535–550.

Freeman, M. (1971). A reliability study of psychiatric diagnosis in childhood and adolescence. *Journal of Child Psychology and Psychiatry, 12,* 43–54.

Freud, A. (1965). *Normality and pathology in childhood.* New York: International Universities Press.

Freud, S. (1940). Outline of psychoanalysis. In J. Strachey (Ed. & Trans.), *The standard edition of the complete psychological works of Sigmund Freud* (Vol. 23, pp. 141–205). London: Hogarth Press.

Freud, S. (1953). Analysis of a phobia in a five-year-old boy. In J. Strachey (Ed. & Trans.), *Standard edition of the complete works of Sigmund Freud* (Vol. 7, pp. 3–149). London: Hogarth Press. (Original work published 1909)

Freud, S. (1963). Introductory lectures on psychoanalysis: Part III. General theory of neuroses. In J. Strachey (Ed. & Trans.), *Standard edition of the complete psychological works of Sigmund Freud* (Vol. 16, pp. 243–463). London: Hogarth Press. (Original work published 1917)

Gabel, S., Stadler, J., Bjorn, J., Shindledecker, R., & Bowden, C. (1993). Dopamine-beta-hydroxylase in behaviorally disturbed youth: Relationship between teacher and parent ratings. *Biological Psychiatry, 34,* 434–442.

Gadow, K. D., & Sprafkin, J. (1998). *Adolescent Symptom Inventory 4 norms manual.* Stony Brook, NY: Checkmate Plus.

Gadow, K. D., & Sprafkin, J. (1999). *Youth's Inventory 4 manual.* Stony Brook, NY: Checkmate Plus.

Gadow, K. D., Sprafkin, J., Carlson, G. A., Schneider, J., Nolan, E. E., Mattison, R. E., et al. (2002). A DSM-IV referenced, adolescent self-report rating scale. *Journal of the American Academy of Child and Adolescent Psychiatry, 41,* 671–679.

Galambos, N. L., Barker, E. T., & Almeida, D. M. (2003). Parents do matter: Trajectories of change in externalizing and internalizing problems in early adolescence. *Child Development, 74,* 578–594.

Gove, P. (Ed.). (1971). *Webster's third new international dictionary of the English language.* Springfield, MA: Merriam.

Griesinger, W. (1867). *Mental pathology and therapeutics* [Die Pathologie und Therapie der psychischen Krankheiten] (C. L. Robertson &

J. Rutherford, Trans.). London: New Sydenham Society. (Original work published 1845)

Group for the Advancement of Psychiatry. (1966). *Psychopathological disorders in childhood: Theoretical considerations and a proposed classification.* GAP Report No. 62. Washington, DC: Author.

Guze, S. (1978). Validating criteria for psychiatric diagnosis: The Washington University approach. In M. S. Akiskal & W. L. Webb (Eds.), *Psychiatric diagnosis: Exploration of biological predictors* (pp. 49–59). New York: Spectrum.

Hanna, G. L., Yuwiler, A., & Coates, J. K. (1995). Whole blood serotonin and disruptive behaviors in juvenile obsessive-compulsive disorder. *Journal of the American Academy of Child and Adolescent Psychiatry, 34,* 28–35.

Helzer, J. E., Canino, G. J., Yeh, E.-K., Bland, R. C., Lee, C. K., Hwu, H.-G., et al. (1990). Alcoholism: North America and Asia. *Archives of General Psychiatry, 47,* 313–319.

Helzer, J. E., Spitznagel, E. L., & McEvoy, L. (1987). The predictive validity of lay DIS diagnoses in the general population: A comparison with physician examiners. *Archives of General Psychiatry, 44,* 1069–1077.

Hewitt, L. E., & Jenkins, R. L. (1946). *Fundamental patterns of maladjustment: The dynamics of their origin.* Springfield: State of Illinois.

Hofstra, M. B., van der Ende, J., & Verhulst, F. C. (2001). Adolescents' self-reported problems as predictors of psychopathology in adulthood: 10-year follow-up study. *British Journal of Psychiatry, 179,* 203–209.

Hofstra, M. B., van der Ende, J., & Verhulst, F. C. (2002a). Child and adolescent problems predict DSM-IV disorders in adulthood: A 14-year follow-up of a Dutch epidemiological sample. *Journal of the American Academy of Child and Adolescent Psychiatry, 41,* 182–189.

Hofstra, M. B., van der Ende, J., & Verhulst, F. C. (2002b). Pathways of self-reported problem behaviors from adolescence into adulthood. *American Journal of Psychiatry, 159,* 401–407.

Hudziak, J. J. (1998). *DSM-IV Checklist for Childhood Disorders.* Burlington: University of Vermont, Research Center for Children, Youth, and Families.

Huesmann, L. R., Moise-Titus, J., Podolski, C.-L., & Eron, L. D. (2003). Longitudinal relations between children's exposure to TV violence and their aggressive and violent behavior in young adulthood: 1977–1992. *Developmental Psychology, 39,* 201–221.

Individuals with Disabilities Education Act. (1990, 1997). Public Law 101-476. 20 U.S. C. 1401 et seq. (Reauthorized July 1997). Public Law 105-17. 20 U.S. C. 1400 et seq.

Ivanova, M. Y., Achenbach, T. M., Dumenci, L., Rescorla, L. A., Almqvist, F., Bilenberg, N., et al. (2005). *Testing the configural invariance of the Child Behavior Checklist syndromes in 29 cultures.* Manuscript submitted for publication.

Jensen, A. L., & Weisz, J. R. (2002). Assessing match and mismatch between practitioner-generated and standardized interview-generated diagnoses for clinic-referred children and adolescents. *Journal of Consulting and Clinical Psychology, 70,* 158–168.

Jensen, P., Roper, M., Fisher, P., Piacentini, J., Canino, G., Richters, J., et al. (1995). Test-retest reliability of the Diagnostic Interview Schedule for Children (DISC 2.1): Parent, child, and combined algorithms. *Archives of General Psychiatry, 52,* 61–71.

Jones, M. C. (1924). A laboratory study of fear: The case of Peter. *Pedagogical Seminary, 31,* 308–315.

Kagan, J., & Moss, H. A. (1962). *Birth to maturity.* New York: Wiley.

Kanner, L., Rodriquez, A., & Ashenden, B. (1972). How far can autistic children go in matters of social adaptation? *Journal of Autism and Childhood Schizophrenia, 2,* 9–33.

Kazdin, A. E. (2000). *Psychotherapy for children and adolescents: Directions for research and practice.* New York: Oxford University Press.

Kazdin, A. E. (2003). *Research design in clinical psychology* (4th ed.). Needham Heights, MA: Allyn & Bacon.

Kazdin, A. E., & Weisz, J. R. (Eds.). (2003). *Evidence-based psychotherapies for children and adolescents.* New York: Guilford Press.

Kendall, P. C., Marrs-Garcia, A., Nath, S. R., & Sheldrick, R. C. (1999). Normative comparisons for the evaluation of clinical significance. *Journal of Consulting and Clinical Psychology, 67,* 285–299.

Klonsky, E. D., Oltmanns, T. F., & Turkheimer, E. (2002). Informant-reports of personality disorder: Relation to self-reports and future research directions. *Clinical Psychology: Science and Practice, 9,* 300–311.

Kovacs, M. (1992). *Children's Depression Inventory manual.* North Tonawanda, NY: Multi-Health Systems.

Kraepelin, E. (1883, 1915). *Compendium der psychiatrie.* Leipzig: Abel.

Krueger, R. F. (2002). Psychometric perspectives on comorbidity. In J. E. Helzer & J. J. Hudziak (Eds.), *Defining psychopathology in the 21st century* (pp. 41–54). Washington, DC: American Psychiatric Press.

Krueger, R. F., Caspi, A., Moffitt, T. E., & Silva, P. A. (1998). The structure and stability of common mental disorders (DSM-III-R): A longitudinal-epidemiological study. *Journal of Abnormal Psychology, 107,* 216–227.

Krueger, R. F., & Piasecki, T. M. (2002). Toward a dimensional and psychometrically-informed approach to conceptualizing psychopathology. *Behaviour Research and Therapy, 40,* 485–499.

Lahey, B. B., Flagg, E. W., Bird, H. R., Schwab-Stone, M. E., Canino, G., Dulcan, M. K., et al. (1996). The NIMH Methods for the Epidemiology of Child and Adolescent Mental Disorders (MECA) study: Background and methodology. *Journal of the American Academy of Child and Adolescent Psychiatry, 35,* 855–864.

Lahey, B. B., Loeber, R., Stouthamer-Loeber, M., Christ, M. A. G., Green, S., Russo, M. F., et al. (1990). Comparison of DSM-III and DSM-III-R diagnoses for prepubertal children: Changes in prevalence and validity. *Journal of the American Academy of Child and Adolescent Psychiatry, 29,* 620–626.

Laird, N. M., & Ware, H. (1982). Random-effects models for longitudinal data. *Biometrics, 38,* 963–974.

Lambert, M. J., Hansen, N. B., & Finch, A. E. (2001). Patient-focused research: Using patient outcome data to enhance treatment effects. *Journal of Consulting and Clinical Psychology, 69,* 159–172.

Lejeune, J., Gautier, M., & Turpin, R. A. (1959). Mongolisme: Une maladie chromosomique (trisomy). *Bulletin de l'Académie Nationale de Médicine, Paris, 143,* 256–265.

Levin, D. A. (1979). The nature of plant species. *Science, 204,* 381–384.

Lewczyk, C. M., Garland, A. F., Hurlburt, M. S., Gearity, J., & Hough, R. L. (2003). Comparing DISC-IV and clinician diagnoses among youths receiving public mental health services. *Journal of the American Academy of Child and Adolescent Psychiatry, 42,* 349–356.

Lewine, R. R. J., Watt, N. F., Prentky, R. A., & Fryer, J. H. (1980). Childhood social competence in functionally disordered psychiatric patients and in normals. *Journal of Abnormal Psychology, 89,* 132–138.

Lilienfeld, S. O., Waldman, I. D., & Israel, A. C. (1994). A critical examination of the use of the term and concept of comorbidity in psychopathology research. *Clinical Psychology: Science and Practice, 1,* 71–83.

Livingston, R. L., Dykman, R. A., & Ackerman, P. T. (1990). The frequency and significance of additional self-reported psychiatric diagnoses in children with attention deficit disorder. *Journal of Abnormal Child Psychology, 18,* 465–478.

Males, M. (1991). Teen suicide and changing cause-of-death certification, 1953–1987. *Suicide and Life Threatening Behavior, 21,* 245–259.

March, J. (1997). *MASC: Multidimensional Anxiety Scale for Children.* North Tonawanda, NY: Multi-Health Systems.

McClellan, J. M., & Werry, J. S. (Eds.). (2000). Research psychiatric diagnostic interviews for children and adolescents. *Journal of the American Academy of Child and Adolescent Psychiatry, 39,* 19–27.

McConaughy, S. H., & Achenbach, T. M. (1994). Comorbidity of empirically based syndromes in matched general population and clinical samples. *Journal of Child Psychology and Psychiatry, 35,* 1141–1157.

Meehl, P. E., & Waller, N. G. (2002). The path analysis controversy: A new statistical approach to strong appraisal of verisimilitude. *Psychological Methods, 3,* 283–300.

Meyer, G. J. (2002). Implications of information gathering methods for a refined taxonomy of psychopathology. In L. E. Beutler & M. L. Malik (Eds.), *Rethinking the DSM* (pp. 69–105). Washington, DC: American Psychological Association.

Meyer, G. J., Finn, S. E., Eyde, L. D., Kay, G. G., Moreland, K. L., Dies, R. R., et al. (2001). Psychological testing and psychological assessment. *American Psychologist, 56,* 128–165.

Miller, L. C. (1967). Louisville Behavior Checklist for males, 6–12 years of age. *Psychological Reports, 21,* 885–896.

Nesselroade, J. R., & Baltes, P. B. (1974). Adolescent personality development and historical change: 1970–1972. *Monographs of the Society for Research in Child Development, 39*(Serial No. 154).

Newman, D. L., Moffitt, T. E., Caspi, A., Magdol, L., Silva, P., & Stanton, W. R. (1996). Psychiatric disorder in a birth cohort of young adults: Prevalence, comorbidity, clinical significance, and new case incidence from ages 11 to 21. *Journal of Consulting and Clinical Psychology, 64,* 552–562.

Overall, J. E., & Hollister, L. E. (1979). Comparative evaluation of research diagnostic criteria for Schizophrenia. *Archives of General Psychiatry, 36,* 1198–1205.

Piaget, J. (1983). Piaget's theory. In P. H. Mussen (Series Ed.) & W. Kessen (Vol. Ed.), *Handbook of child psychology: Vol. 1. History, theory, and methods* (4th ed.). New York: Wiley.

Puig-Antich, J., & Chambers, W. (1978). *The Schedule for Affective Disorders and Schizophrenia for School-Aged Children (Kiddie-SADS).* New York: New York State Psychiatric Institute.

Quay, H. C. (1964). Personality dimensions in delinquent males as inferred from the factor analysis of behavior ratings. *Journal of Research in Crime and Delinquency, 1,* 33–37.

Quay, H. C. (1993). The psychobiology of undersocialized aggressive conduct disorder: A theoretical perspective. *Development and Psychopathology, 5,* 165–180.

Rapoport, J. L., & Ismond, D. R. (1996). *DSM-IV training guide for diagnosis of childhood disorders.* New York: Brunner/Mazel.

Raudenbush, S. W., & Bryk, A. S. (2002). *Hierarchical linear models: Applications and data-analysis methods.* Newbury Park, CA: Sage.

Regier, D. A., Kaelber, C. T., Rae, D. S., Farmer, M. E., Knauper, B., Kessler, R. C., et al. (1998). Limitations of diagnostic criteria and assessment instruments for mental disorders. *Archives of General Psychiatry, 55,* 109–115.

Rescorla, L. A., Achenbach, T. M., Ivanova, M. Y., Dumenci, L., Almqvist, F., Bilenberg, N., et al. (2005). *Problems reported by parents of children ages 6 to 16 in 30 cultures.* Manuscript submitted for publication.

Rettew, D. C., Achenbach, T. M., Doyle, A. C., Ivanova, M. Y., & Dumenci, L. (2005). *Meta-analyses of agreement between standardized diagnostic interviews and clinical diagnoses.* Manuscript submitted for publication.

Reynolds, C. R., & Kamphaus, R. W. (1992). *Behavior Assessment System for Children Teacher Rating Scales.* Circle Pines, MN: American Guidance Service.

Roberts, C., Kane, R., Thomson, H., Bishop, B., & Hart, B. (2003). The prevention of depressive symptoms in rural school children: A randomized controlled trial. *Journal of Consulting and Clinical Psychology, 71,* 622–628.

Roberts, R. E., Attkisson, C., & Rosenblatt, A. (1998). Prevalence of psychopathology among children and adolescents. *American Journal of Psychiatry, 155,* 715–725.

Roberts, R. E., Solovitz, B. L., Chen, Y.-W., & Casat, C. (1996). Retest stability of DSM-III-R diagnoses among adolescents using the Diagnostic Interview Schedule for Children (DISC-2.1C). *Journal of Abnormal Child Psychology, 24,* 349–362.

Robins, L. N. (1966). *Deviant children grown up.* Baltimore: Williams and Wilkens.

Robins, L. N., Helzer, J. E., Croughan, J., & Ratcliff, K. S. (1981). National Institute of Mental Health Diagnostic Interview Schedule: Its history, characteristics, and validity. *Archives of General Psychiatry, 38,* 381–389.

Robins, L. N., Helzer, J. E., Ratcliff, K. S., & Seyfried, W. (1982). Validity of the Diagnostic Interview Schedule, Version II: DSM-III diagnoses. *Psychological Medicine, 12,* 855–870.

Rogosa, D., Brandt, D., & Zimowski, M. (1982). A growth curve approach to the measurement of change. *Psychological Bulletin, 92,* 726–748.

Rosch, E. (1978). Principles of categorization. In E. Rosch & B. B. Lloyd (Eds.), *Cognition and categorization* (pp. 27–48). Hillsdale, NJ: Erlbaum.

Rosch, E., & Mervis, C. B. (1975). Family resemblances: Studies in the internal structure of categories. *Cognitive Psychology, 7,* 573–605.

Rounsaville, B. J., Alarcon, R. D., Andrews, G., Jackson, J. S., Kendell, R. E., & Kendler, K. (2002). Basic nomenclature issues for DSM-V. In D. J. Kupfer, M. B. First, & D. E. Regier (Eds.), *A research agenda for DSM-V* (pp. 1–29). Washington, DC: American Psychiatric Association.

Rutter, M. (1991). Nature, nurture, and psychopathology: A new look at an old topic. *Development and Psychopathology, 3,* 125–136.

Rutter, M., & Garmezy, N. (1983). Developmental psychopathology. In P. Mussen (Ed.), *Handbook of child psychology* (4th ed., Vol. 4, pp. 775–911). New York: Wiley.

Rutter, M., & Smith, D. J. (Eds.). (1995). *Psychosocial disorders in young people: Time trends and their causes.* Chichester, England: Wiley.

Scerbo, A. S., & Kolko, D. (1994). Salivary testosterone and cortisol in disruptive children: Relationship to aggressive, hyperactive, and internalizing behaviors. *Journal of the American Academy of Child and Adolescent Psychiatry, 33,* 1174–1184.

Schaie, K. W. (1965). A general model for the study of developmental problems. *Psychological Bulletin, 64,* 92–107.

Schaie, K. W., Labouvie, G. V., & Buech, B. V. (1973). Generational and cohort-specific differences in adult cognitive functioning: A fourteen-year study of independent samples. *Developmental Psychology, 9,* 151–166.

Shaffer, D. (1992). *Diagnostic Interview Schedule for Children, version 2.3.* New York: Columbia University, Division of Child Psychiatry.

Shaffer, D., Fisher, P., Dulcan, M. K., Davies, M., Piacentini, J., Schwab-Stone, M. E., et al. (1996). The NIMH Diagnostic Interview Schedule for Children version 2.3. (DISC-2.3): Description, acceptability, prevalence rates, and performance in the MECA study. *Journal of the American Academy of Child and Adolescent Psychiatry, 35,* 865–877.

Shaffer, D., Fisher, P., Lucas, C. P., Dulcan, M. K., & Schwab-Stone, M. E. (2000). NIMH Diagnostic Interview Schedule for Children version IV (NIMH DISC-IV): Description, differences from previous versions, and reliability of some common diagnoses. *Journal of the American Academy of Child and Adolescent Psychiatry, 39,* 28–38.

Sheldrick, R. C., Kendall, P. C., & Heimberg, R. G. (2001). The clinical significance of treatments: A comparison of three treatments for conduct disordered children. *Clinical Psychology: Science and Practice, 8,* 418–430.

Smith, E. E., & Medin, D. L. (1981). *Categories and concepts.* Cambridge, MA: Harvard University Press.

Spitzer, R. L. (1983). Psychiatric diagnosis: Are clinicians still necessary? *Comprehensive Psychiatry, 24,* 399–411.

Spitzer, R. L., Davies, M., & Barkley, R. A. (1990). The DSM-III-R field trial of disruptive behavior disorders. *Journal of the American Academy of Child and Adolescent Psychiatry, 29,* 690–697.

Stanger, C., Achenbach, T. M., & Verhulst, F. C. (1997). Accelerated longitudinal comparison of aggressive versus delinquent syndromes. *Development and Psychopathology, 9,* 43–58.

Steinhausen, H. C., Metzke, C. W., Meier, M., & Kannenberg, R. (1997). Behavioral and emotional problems reported by parents for ages 6 to 17 in a Swiss epidemiological study. *European Child and Adolescent Psychiatry, 6,* 136–141.

Steinhausen, H. C., Metzke, C. W., Meier, M., & Kannenberg, R. (1998). Prevalence of child and adolescent psychiatric disorders: The Zurich Epidemiological Study. *Acta Psychiatrica Scandinavica, 98,* 262–271.

van't Hoff, M. A., Roede, M. J., & Kowalski, C. (1991). A mixed longitudinal data analysis model. *Human Biology, 49,* 165–179.

Verhulst, F. C., & Achenbach, T. M. (1995). Empirically based assessment and taxonomy of psychopathology: Cross-cultural applications. *European Child and Adolescent Psychiatry, 4,* 61–76.

Verhulst, F. C., Achenbach, T. M., van der Ende, J., Erol, N., Lambert, M. C., Leung, P. W. L., et al. (2003). Comparisons of problems reported by youths from seven countries. *American Journal of Psychiatry, 160,* 1479–1485.

Verhulst, F. C., & van der Ende, J. (1992a). Six-year developmental course of internalizing and externalizing problem behaviors. *Journal of the American Academy of Child and Adolescent Psychiatry, 31,* 924–931.

Verhulst, F. C., & van der Ende, J. (1992b). Six-year stability of parent-reported problem behavior in an epidemiological sample. *Journal of Abnormal Child Psychology, 20,* 595–610.

Verhulst, F. C., van der Ende, J., Ferdinand, R. F., & Kasius, M. C. (1997). The prevalence of DSM-III-R diagnoses in a national sample of Dutch adolescents. *Archives of General Psychiatry, 54,* 329–336.

Verhulst, F. C., van der Ende, J. R. A., & Rietbergen, A. (1997). Ten-year time trends of psychopathology in Dutch children and adolescents: No evidence for strong trends. *Acta Psychiatrica Scandinavica, 96,* 7–13.

Walker, J. L., Lahey, B. B., Russo, M. F., Frick, P. J., Christ, M. A. G., McBurnett, K., et al. (1991). Anxiety, inhibition, and conduct disorder in children: I. Relations to social impairment. *Journal of the American Academy of Child and Adolescent Psychiatry, 30,* 187–191.

Watson, J. B., & Rayner, R. (1920). Conditioned emotional reactions. *Journal of Experimental Psychology, 3,* 1–14.

Weinstein, S. R., Noam, G. G., Grimes, K., Stone, K., & Schwab-Stone, M. (1990). Convergence of DSM-III diagnoses and self-reported symptoms in child and adolescent inpatients. *Journal of the American Academy of Child and Adolescent Psychiatry, 29,* 627–634.

WHO World Mental Health Survey Consortium. (2004). Prevalence, severity, and unmet need for treatment of mental disorders in the World Health Organization world mental health surveys. *Journal of the American Medical Association, 291,* 2581–2590.

Wilens, T. E., Biederman, J., Brown, S., Tanguay, S., Monuteaux, M. C., Blake, C., et al. (2002). Psychiatric comorbidity and functioning in clinically referred preschool children and school-age youths with ADHD. *Journal of the American Academy of Child and Adolescent Psychiatry, 41,* 262–268.

Wolman, B. B. (1970). *Children without childhood.* New York: Grune & Stratton.

World Health Organization. (1978). *Mental disorders: Glossary and guide to their classification in accordance with the ninth revision of the International Classification of Diseases* (9th ed.). Geneva, Switzerland: World Health Organization.

World Health Organization. (1992). *Mental disorders: Glossary and guide to their classification in accordance with the tenth revision of the International Classification of Diseases* (10th ed.). Geneva, Switzerland: World Health Organization.

Yorke, C. (1980). The contributions of the Diagnostic Profile and the assessment of developmental lines to child psychiatry. *Psychiatric Clinics of North America, 3,* 593–603.

Zachar, P. (2000). Psychiatric disorders are not natural kinds. *Philosophy, Psychiatry, Psychology, 7,* 167–182.

CHAPTER 6

Comprehensive Psychological Assessment: A Developmental Psychopathology Approach for Clinical and Applied Research

ALICE S. CARTER, SUSAN E. MARAKOVITZ, and SARA S. SPARROW

In this chapter, we present a model of Comprehensive Psychological Assessment that has been developed to inform the assessment process in both clinical and research settings and has been influenced by the core tenets of developmental psychopathology. Comprehensive Psychological Assessment draws on the tenets of developmental psychopathology at each stage in the assessment process, from developing and honing the question or questions to be addressed, identifying the components of the model that will be actively employed, choosing appropriate instrumentation, interpreting qualitative and quantitative information derived, and ultimately, when appropriate, making and implementing recommendations for prevention, intervention, and public policy. The Comprehensive Psychological Assessment model applies throughout the life span, but in this chapter we illustrate the components and application of the model for children and adolescents.

Researchers and clinicians are accustomed to using hypotheses and referral questions as catalysts for initiating the assessment process. Following the refinement of hypotheses and questions, the next step is to identify the relevant domains of functioning that need to be evaluated. Within the realm of clinical applications and research focused on developmental psychopathology, it is extremely rare that only one domain of functioning (e.g., expressive language ability) is a sufficient target of evaluation. Because relative strengths and weaknesses in a single domain may or may not be isolated, investigators and clinicians generally recognize the importance of capturing patterns of functioning across multiple developmental domains. For example, without knowledge of a child's general mental level or intellectual functioning, the meaning of below-average performance in one or more additional domains is ambiguous and potentially misleading. More specifically, a below-average score on a measure of receptive language that is administered as a proxy for cognitive functioning could capture low intellectual functioning. However, it could also represent a specific language delay or disorder, a visual attention problem, or a broader pattern of developmental deviance such as that seen in Autism. Ultimately, patterns of strengths and weaknesses across domains have important implications for understanding developmental trajectories, diagnostic complexities, and contextual influences.

The research or clinical question in combination with pertinent empirical literatures drives the selection of domains that will be the focus of any specific assessment application. Once relevant domains are identified, the careful selection of measures and choice of methods takes place. To capture the most coherent and accurate characterization of the intricacies of an individual's functioning, a currently accepted standard is to utilize a multimethod, multi-informant approach (Johnston & Murray, 2003). In research applications, shared variance attributable to different informants and methods can be modeled statistically using methods such as structural equation modeling (Kline, 1998), and shared variance that is attributable to nested contexts (e.g., family, classroom, school) can be modeled using hierarchical linear modeling (Raudenbush, Bryk, Cheong, & Congdon, 2000). At present, there are newly emerging but few empirical guidelines that clinicians can use for systematically integrating information that spans not only multiple domains of functioning but also multiple informants and methods (Kraemer et al., 2003). Thus, in clinical settings, when informants present differing views about either the child's functioning or features of the child's ecology, the evaluator must predominantly rely on clinical judgment and intuition in the next phase of the assessment process: interpretation of obtained findings. In both research and clinical applications, interpretation of assessment findings can be aided by striving to form conceptualizations and impressions that are grounded in the tenets of developmental psychopathology.

Developmental psychopathology is inherently interdisciplinary in scope and encourages cross-fertilization of epistemologies and methodologies. Cicchetti and Sroufe (2000, p. 256) elegantly state that what is central to the discipline of developmental psychopathology is

> to engage in comprehensive evaluation of biological, psychological, social and cultural processes and to ascertain how these multiple levels of analysis may influence individual differences, the continuity and discontinuity of adaptive and maladaptive patterns and the pathways by which the same developmental outcomes may be achieved. (p. 256)

The Comprehensive Psychological Assessment model is designed to press researchers and clinicians to move toward conducting assessments with a grasp of the multiple domains that compose the individual's functioning as well as the relevant ecologies that transact with the individual's functioning over time. Moreover, we continue to advocate for understanding and recognizing the separate and interwoven relations between current resources and adaptive functioning. Adopting this approach presents both challenges and responsibilities, as clinicians and researchers must embrace multiple complexities simultaneously but still be able to generate meaningful conclusions.

Consistent with one of the thrusts in developmental psychopathology, a major task for clinicians and researchers is to distinguish between adaptive and maladaptive presentations. This can be done only with attention to developmental considerations and an understanding of broader contextual influences. While it is necessary to make use of knowledge about what is normative in each domain at each age or stage, it is not sufficient. The selection of relevant domains and instruments should also be informed by knowledge of both normative and atypical developmental processes relevant to the question or hypothesis posed. This is central when the question or hypothesis to be addressed clearly involves specific diagnoses, developmental disabilities, and categories of psychopathology. More often in clinical settings than in research endeavors, the initial question is too limited and understanding of both typical and atypical developmental processes allows for the expansion or reformulation of the question to one that is more appropriate. For example, if asked to evaluate a preschool child described as phobic of vacuum cleaners, the evaluator would need to appreciate the intensity, frequency, and quality of developmentally normative fears as well as the pathological manifestations of fears in this age group. Although fear of vacuum cleaners may be within normal developmental expectations, the evaluator should draw on knowledge of other psychopathological conditions to determine whether the form and intensity of the behavior is normal or pathological and whether concomitant behaviors exist that would provide evidence of psychopathology (e.g., extreme withdrawal, ritualistic behaviors, necessity for sameness, problems in peer relations).

Across domains of functioning, finding the boundary between normative, at-risk or subclinical, and clinical categories can be challenging, particularly when individual functioning is understood within the multiple contexts that may be influencing current competencies. The developmental psychopathology perspective not only highlights boundaries between normative and psychopathological presentations but also calls attention to the heterogeneous nature of specific disorders and the multiple ways an individual can manifest a particular disorder. Further heterogeneity and complexity emerges because comorbidity in psychopathological conditions occurs with high frequency (Costello, Mustillo, Erkanli, Keeler, & Angold, 2003). Even if the referral question appears quite narrow (e.g., Does this individual have a learning disability?), a comprehensive assessment strategy addresses multiple aspects of the individual's current development and the manner in which the answer to this specific question may be influencing broader aspects of functioning (e.g., Is the learning disability influencing self-esteem and/or peer relationships?).

In addition to attending to salient domains and interdependence between domains, developmental psychopathology is concerned with the interplay among the individual's neurobiology and genetics, domains of functioning, and ecological contexts. There is recognition that interplay among domains and levels can take many forms, including those that are additive, interactive, mediational, nonlinear, and transactional functions, and that there are bidirectional influences between the individual and the environment (Boyce et al., 1998; Cicchetti, 1990; Cicchetti & Blender, 2004). Research methods are increasingly available to elucidate the nature of the interplay between child and ecological factors (e.g., Sameroff & MacKenzie, 2003). In clinical applications, the Comprehensive Psychological Assessment model serves to compel the evaluator to move beyond a simple description of measured strengths and weaknesses. A more thorough consideration of the manner in which interplay of strengths and weaknesses in specific cognitive, language, sensorimotor, and social-emotional areas may interact with multiple contextual demands to better explain the individual's functioning would minimally entail reflecting on the forms of interplay that might be most explanatory for a particular child or adolescent as well as possible bidirectional and/or transactional influences.

Finally, although evaluators often have only a single snapshot or cross-sectional view of the individual's functioning, developmental psychopathologists advocate for an overarching concern with trajectories and pathways (i.e., continuities and discontinuities). Thus, even when a clinical assessment or research study occurs at a particular point in time, concern with multifinality (i.e., the same risk factors may result in different presentations) and equifinality (i.e., different risk factors may result in the same presentation) is valuable and highlights the importance of obtaining a complete developmental history. A relevant example would be the evaluation of a child who presented with reading difficulties. Longitudinal research has revealed associations between early language impairment, difficulties with letter identification, deficiencies in phonological awareness, and underdeveloped expressive vo-

cabulary among children who are at risk for reading problems or who are reading disabled (cf. McCardle, Scarborough, & Catts, 2001). Also, research findings indicate that reading difficulties run in families (Plomin, 2001). Knowledge of these risk factors would shape the information that a skilled evaluator obtained in the process of taking developmental and family history. In addition, informed by developmental psychopathology, the evaluator might also recognize how risk and protective factors interact and, in essence, that neglecting to ask appropriate and specific questions as part of taking a developmental and family history could negatively impact the child's developmental trajectory. With the reading disability example, failure to diagnose and remediate a reading disability in the early grades can lead to a widening academic achievement gap and more pronounced problems later in elementary school that require a much more intensive intervention program (Lyon, 1996). Indeed, failure to intervene early may place constraints on later academic achievements.

In summary, the tenets of developmental psychopathology guide each phase of the comprehensive assessment process. One could argue that employing a comprehensive assessment process that focuses on multiple domains of individual and contextual functioning is inherently consistent with the tenets of developmental psychopathology. However, it is not adequate to assess multiple domains or contextual levels. The developmental psychopathology lends a three-dimensional perspective of breadth, by examining multiple individual and contextual domains; depth, by orienting the evaluator to stage-salient domains and contextual influences that require greater focus as well as examining these domains with respect to both adaptive and maladaptive features; and time, by recognizing continuities and discontinuities in developmental processes. Finally, the three-dimensional form that emerges from this union of breadth, depth, and time is not structurally uniform at any given point in time as the interplay of domains and contextual influences may vary across development. The Comprehensive Psychological Assessment approach has the potential to enrich the evaluator's perspective on the uniqueness of each child and to promote respect for and valuing of family members, school personnel, and others in the child's nested ecological systems, as they are recognized as playing a significant role in optimizing the child's developmental progress. Moreover, fully embracing this process makes it difficult for the evaluator to maintain a detached stance in part because the evaluator becomes part of the child's nested ecological system and grasps the extent to which the evaluation process is both influenced by and influences the child's current and future functioning.

In addition to building on the tenets of developmental psychopathology, the model of Comprehensive Psychological Assessment presented in this chapter is rooted in earlier work in the study of individual differences in both Europe and the United States. In particular, the assessment field owes much to nineteenth-century scientists who sought to understand mental retardation through the measurement of individuals (Bellack & Hersen, 1980). In 1892, Galton's publication of *Classification of Men According to Their Natural Gifts* provided the foundation for the modern study of individual psychology. Some 35 years later, Alfred Binet developed the first widely accepted test of intelligence used for screening schoolchildren (Binet & Simon, 1905). Binet undertook this task at the request of the French government to provide information for program planning and placement of children who were mentally retarded. Shortly thereafter, in 1910, Goddard, director of the Psychology Laboratory at Vineland Training School in New Jersey, translated Binet's scale into English, a development that launched the large-scale use of individual intelligence testing in the United States. Consistent with our position that assessment of a single domain of functioning is rarely adequate, it is of interest that the diagnosis of mental retardation now requires assessment of multiple domains of functioning. To meet criteria for a diagnosis, an individual must achieve standard scores in both intellectual functioning and adaptive behavior that are at least 2 standard deviations below the population mean (American Association on Mental Retardation, 2002; Battaglia & Carey, 2003).

In presenting the Comprehensive Psychological Assessment model, we do not intend to review the large library of currently available assessment instruments or to instruct the reader in the administration of these instruments. Rather, our aim is to advance the reader's understanding of critical conceptual and theoretical issues that shape the development and implementation of the Comprehensive Psychological Assessment model as well as to challenge clinicians and researchers to become, quoting Kaufman (1994), "intelligent testers." We advocate employing a comprehensive, developmentally sensitive conceptual framework even when pragmatic considerations restrict the range and number of assessment tools that can be employed.

MODEL OF COMPREHENSIVE PSYCHOLOGICAL ASSESSMENT

Deriving partly from a developmental psychopathology framework and partly from our knowledge of the history and practice of assessment, we have chosen to emphasize that a comprehensive approach to assessment is critical. The investigation of an individual's functioning should be multidimensional, multilevel, and dynamic in nature. *Multidimensional* evaluation is necessary because an individual can rarely be understood through a single score in one domain or subtest or through a global summary score that averages performance across domains (Kaufman & Lichtenberger, 1999). There are myriad major domains of functioning that should be kept in mind as possible targets for assessment. Some of the major domains that psychologists generally consider central to understanding an individual's functioning are cognition, language, academic achievement, motor coordination, and social-emotional development. We also incorporate intraindividual levels and methods of analysis reflecting cellular, genetic, and neurobiological domains (Cicchetti & Blender, 2004; Cicchetti & Dawson, 2002) in our definition of multidimensional. Although various domains of functioning have historically been discussed as if they are independent, interdependence across domains is in fact the norm. Further, skill acquisition and/or deficit in one domain often influences functioning in other domains. *Multilevel* refers to viewing individuals within multiple, nested contexts (Bronfenbrenner, 1986). Nested contexts can be conceptualized in various ways (Bronfenbrenner, 1977; Cicchetti, Toth, & Maughan, 2000) but generally move from those that are proximal to the individual, such as the family, to those that are more distal, such as institutions, community, and culture. Finally, for an assessment to better illuminate critical issues and processes, we suggest that consideration be given to the *dynamic* interplay that occurs among domains within the individual and across levels within the environment as well as between the individual and salient contexts.

Multidimensional Components

One aspect of our model is that assessment needs to be *multidimensional* in nature. Multidimensional assessment rests on first understanding the contribution of the biological substrate of the individual.

Biological Substrate

The biological substrate is always present and inextricably intertwined with observed functioning. New approaches and methods from a variety of disciplines, including molecular and quantitative genetics, radiology, psychoneuroimmunology, physics, and medicine are available for assessing biological contributions to individual functioning. Some of the newer methods that are now being utilized are evaluation of the individual's genome (i.e., allelic variation and cytogenetic abnormalities), structural and functional neuroimaging, and assays designed to measure hypothalamic-pituitary-adrenal (HPA) axis functioning (i.e., salivary and blood cortisol). These advances are facilitating our understanding of transactions between biological and psychological processes. Research findings have started to illuminate the manner in which biology can moderate the impact of stressful life events (e.g., maltreatment; see Cicchetti & Blender, 2004), how traumatic events may dysregulate biological processes (e.g., HPA axis functioning following environmental deprivation associated with Romanian orphanages; Gunnar, Morison, Chisholm, & Schuder, 2001), and that early disruption in brain development can have cascading influences on subsequent development (e.g., Autism and face perception; Schultz, 2005). Currently, these exciting findings have limited bearing on clinical assessments. However, recent molecular genetic and metabolic findings have influenced routine clinical practice. Increasingly, evaluators will refer for genetic, neurological, and metabolic workups when individuals present with dysmorphic features, family history of mental retardation, or growth abnormalities (Battaglia & Carey, 2003). Indeed, an increasing number of individuals who present with developmental delay or mental retardation are now identified as having genetic syndromes and cytogenetic abnormalities.

In conducting a comprehensive assessment, it behooves the evaluator to be familiar with the research and clinical literatures describing individuals with known genetic or neurological abnormalities. Many of these disorders are associated with specific patterns of functioning. For example, children with Fragile X syndrome are reported to have relative weaknesses in tasks requiring sequencing and attention and relative strengths in simultaneous and verbal tasks (Dykens, Hodapp, & Leckman, 1987). Thus, when evaluating a child or adolescent who has a known genetic or neurological abnormality, areas of functioning that have previously been associated with a particular disorder might receive more attention in the evaluation. Moreover, as the field appears to be on the cusp of genetic and neuroimaging breakthroughs regarding genes involved in brain development and cognitive functions (e.g., phonological decoding), neurobiological findings may increasingly guide both assessment and intervention efforts (e.g., Chapman, Raskind, Thomson, Berninger, & Wijsman, 2003; Grigorenko et al., 1997).

It is also important to recognize that knowledge regarding neurobiological functioning provides necessary but insufficient information to fully understand an individual's functioning across developmental domains. For example, knowing that a person has a specific genetic abnormality such as Down syndrome does not provide sufficient information to make predictions about cognitive, academic, or adaptive functioning and does not inform decisions regarding educational and vocational placements. Heterogeneity in the range of functioning across developmental domains has been demonstrated repeatedly in studies of individuals with documented or suspected genetic and neurological abnormalities. Although genetic conditions and neurological difficulties place some constraints on the range of possible outcomes these individuals may achieve, learning or other nonbiologic influences are often more crucial to the individual's current and future functioning.

Current Resources and Functional Adjustment

There are innumerable ways to divide observed functioning. When choosing relevant domains of assessment, there is a tension between selecting a larger number of categories that provide an elaborated view of the child or adolescent (i.e., splitters) and the need to reduce the number of domains to facilitate an efficient, timely evaluation (i.e., lumpers). We consider several primary domains to be of central importance in capturing an overall view of a child's or adolescent's functioning. Consistent with our previous presentation of the Comprehensive Psychological Assessment model (Sparrow, Carter, Racusin, & Morris, 1995), the domains we highlight are cognition, language, social-emotional, sensorimotor, academic achievement, adaptive behavior, and school functioning. These specific domains were chosen for three reasons. First, it is in these areas that the available assessment instruments have attained the greatest scientific rigor and are most likely to provide reliable and valid results. Second, in our clinical experience, a profile of strengths and weaknesses in these aspects of development is most crucial for making determinations regarding intervention strategies and treatment. Third, many of these domains are essential for diagnostic purposes (e.g., cognition and adaptive functioning for a diagnosis of Mental Retardation or cognition and academic functioning for a diagnosis of Learning Disability).

Furthermore, these domains are especially amenable to an assessment approach geared toward distinguishing between the individual's current resources and the adaptive integration of these resources into a functioning whole, which we refer to in our model as *functional adjustment*.

Current resources refer to competencies, skills, and endowments as well as cognitive, social-emotional, and behavioral styles. A developmental perspective enables us to expand the idea of current resources to incorporate not only fully attained competencies or skills but also those that are emerging or are evident only under specific conditions of support or scaffolding. Individuals vary in the degree to which they are able to apply their resources to problems encountered in day-to-day situations. Thus, we differentiate between an individual's capabilities (i.e., resources) and an individual's functional adjustment, or ability to integrate those resources in day-to-day life. Sternberg and colleagues (Sternberg, Wagner, Williams, & Horvath, 1995) have made a similar point in highlighting the importance of assessing practical intelligence in addition to those aspects of intelligence that are captured by traditional IQ assessment instruments. Although it is not possible to evaluate resources and adjustment independently, different assessment approaches place relatively greater emphasis on either individual capacities or adaptive integration.

Our emphasis on functional adjustment outcomes as a means of capturing integrative functioning through psychological assessment differs from other psychological assessment models that typically focus primarily on resources. One means of measuring functional adjustment is through assessment of adaptive behavior, a term that has been equated with daily performance of personal and social sufficiency. A second way to assess functional adjustment is to evaluate how the child or adolescent performs in important everyday contexts such as school. A third way to assess functional adjustment is by making use of measures of impairment that have more typically been part of psychiatric evaluations (Bird et al., 1996; Bird et al., 1990; Canino, Costello, & Angold, 1999). Too often, the emphasis of an assessment is on the individual's capacities or resources without due attention to how these capacities influence behavior in the contexts that compose an individual's "real world."

To illustrate this distinction between current resources and functional adjustment, let us consider the manner in which psychopathological conditions such as Major Depression or Attention-Deficit/Hyperactivity Disorder (ADHD) may contribute to discordance between current resources and functional adjustment. Given the episodic nature of depression, a child may have a typical developmental trajectory prior to onset of the disorder, with consistent competencies across each of the primary domains we include as current resources (i.e., cognition, language, sensorimotor, academic achievement, and social-emotional). However, with the onset of the depressive episode, there may be a significant decline in the child's ability to perform age-expected tasks of daily living and to be sufficiently motivated to engage in social and academic activities. In this instance, although there may be subtle declines in some aspects of current resources (e.g., performance on timed tasks and tasks involving visuospatial performance), the deterioration in interpersonal relations and school performance (e.g., participating actively in the classroom, completing assignments) is likely to be more dramatic because of the affective and motivational aspects of depression. ADHD presents a different developmental pattern due to the early onset and the nonepisodic nature of the disorder. In the evaluation setting, it would not be unusual for the clinician to obtain a clear picture of the child's or adolescent's current resources. In part, this characterization could be derived because the evaluation setting differs dramatically from most school settings in terms of the presence of a high degree of structure, one-on-one interaction, and limited distractions. However, for an individual who carries a diagnosis of ADHD, there is often a discrepancy between the measured current resources and application of these resources in school, with peers, and in the home (i.e., functional adjustment).

The distinction between current resources and functional adjustment is grounded in developmental psychopathology because there is recognition that the child's overall adaptation in day-to-day settings (i.e., functional adjustment) reflects not only current resources but the interaction of those resources with available contextual supports and affordances. Thus, the current resources are inherently focused on what the individual brings to the child-environment transaction, whereas functional adjustment reflects an integration of what the child and environment bring to the transaction. Further, by broadening the scope of assessment beyond the evaluation setting to include the child's functioning in natural or everyday settings, the evaluator is more likely to learn about risk and protective factors that may exist in the child and environmental contexts. Specifically, research has shown that children who do not yet evidence diagnosable psychopathology but who do evidence impairment (i.e., one form of measuring functional adjustment) are at higher risk for developing a psychiatric disorder (Bird et al., 1996). Although clinicians and researchers most often use functional adjustment measures to capture negative deviations from age-expected behavior, it is our hope that new measures of functional adjustment will be developed that also allow for characterizing optimal functioning, in part because it is possible that optimal functioning serves as a protective factor in children's development.

Domains Associated with Current Resources: Cognition and Social-Emotional Exemplars

The five primary target domains of assessment in current resources that we emphasize in our model are cognition, language, sensorimotor, social-emotional, and academic achievement; the two functional adjustment domains are school functioning and adaptive behavior. When conducting a Comprehensive Psychological Assessment, it is critical to understand the following aspects of each domain of functioning: (1) the theories that inform major constructs within the domain; (2) how the domain is defined with respect to component parts; (3) developmental characteristics of the component parts, including normative expectations and stage-salient features; and (4) how these component parts can be measured using existing instrumentation at different points in the life span. Because a thorough examination of each of these domains is beyond the scope of this chapter, we present overviews of the cognitive, social-emotional, and academic achievement domains as exemplars of current resources as well as an overview of adaptive behavior to represent functional adjustment.

Cognition. Cognition refers to processes whereby individuals acquire knowledge from the environment. There are numerous views of the nature and development of cognition as well as variation in the number and type of mental processes identified as central to cognition. Across multiple approaches to cognition, including Piagetian, neuropsychological, information processing, and contextual (Flavell, Miller, & Miller, 2002), it is generally recognized that cognition involves both basic and higher-level processes such as attention, perception, memory, reasoning, problem solving, and abstract thinking as well as executive functions such as planning, choosing strategies, and enacting strategies. Although there is overlap between the components and processes associated with cognition and theories of intelligence, it must be clearly stated that we do not consider the term cognition to be a synonym for Intellectual Quotient (IQ) or intelligence. Definitions of IQ generally include the following elements: basic mental processes such as attention and perception, higher-order thinking such as problem solving and reasoning, and adaptation to the environment (Sattler, 2001). However, in practice, IQ represents a summary score on a standardized "intelligence" test that is derived from a combination of scales. These scales measure

some aspects of cognition but are also influenced by functioning in other noncognitive domains, such as fine motor coordination.

Cognition is a broader term that subsumes both functions assessed by traditional standardized IQ tests and other functions that are not included on standardized IQ tests (e.g., learning strategies). In our model of Comprehensive Psychological Assessment, we favor characterizing an individual's cognitive abilities in a manner that draws from cognitive science, neuropsychology, and neuroscience rather than exclusively from a more traditional stance based on theories and notions of intelligence. We have adopted this approach because empirical investigations in these disciplines are advancing our understanding of specific aspects of cognition, such as problem solving, verbal and visual-spatial processing, attention, memory, and executive functions, as well as patterns of strengths and weaknesses that may confer risk or be associated with learning, developmental, and psychiatric disorders. Additionally, there are standardized measures that have been developed to assess each of these components in ways that are more comprehensive than what is obtained from IQ testing alone. Finally, by making use of multiple but overlapping measures of cognitive functioning, the clinician or researcher can look for consistencies and inconsistencies in the pattern of findings and generate more robust interpretations. The Cross-Battery approach (Flanagan & Ortiz, 2001; McGrew & Flanagan, 1998) is a formalized system for performing cognitive assessments in this manner.

Despite the pitfalls of relying solely on intelligence tests to capture an individual's cognitive functioning, it is still necessary to use these tests. It is encouraging that in recent years several of the major intelligence tests (i.e., KABC-II: Kaufman & Kaufman, 2004; SB5: Roid, 2003; WPPSI-III: Wechsler, 2002; WISC-IV: Wechsler, 2003) have undergone substantial revision. Some positive trends in the construction of these tests are evident, such as expanding the number of factors used to characterize intelligence and incorporating tasks that purport to access more novel problem solving and thereby also provide information about future learning potential (e.g., KAIT: Kaufman & Kaufman, 1993; KABC-II: Kaufman & Kaufman, 2004). Because IQ measures are derived from multiple subtests and are therefore multifactorial and complex, an analysis of the underlying contributing components in the test is required for adequate interpretation and is often more informative than reporting a global IQ score. We advocate interpreting cognitive tests that comprise multiple subtests or scales using profile analysis of relative, statistically and/or clinically significant strengths and weaknesses within IQ tests. Controversy regarding this practice continues, with advocates for (e.g., Carroll, 2000; Davison & Kuang, 2000) and against (Watkins, 2000) profile analysis. While advocating for the use of profile analysis, we recognize that care must be taken to avoid overinterpretation of observed discrepancies that may reflect systematic or nonsystematic error variance. This is done best when discrepancies are interpreted in the context of other data about the child or adolescent (Davison & Kuang, 2000).

In the cognitive domain, initial characterization of the individual's functioning may be derived from the information generated from intelligence tests. However, we also suggest that assessment of cognitive abilities and problem-solving style at minimum requires consideration and possibly examination of attention, perception, memory, and executive functions. The extent to which these basic and higher-order mental processes are examined will be determined by the questions or hypotheses at hand. Regardless of whether it becomes necessary to directly evaluate the child's or adolescent's skills in these areas, it is important for researchers and clinicians to have an understanding of these cognitive subcomponents.

Attention is a process that involves orienting, selecting, and sustaining focus on relevant information in the environment and ignoring competing, irrelevant information (Mirsky, Anthony, & Duncan, 1991; Posner & Petersen, 1990; Rothbart, Posner, & Hershey, 1995). Thus, a child or adolescent must demonstrate the capacity to sustain attention by maintaining his or her focus on the important dimensions of the task presented without being distracted or pulled off-task by unimportant dimensions. To accomplish this focus, the child or adolescent must simultaneously ignore a wide range of environmental happenings and details, including both external and internal stimuli. Attention is considered to be a limiting front-end feature of the perceptual process that controls the amount and quality of the information available for higher-order cognitive processes (Rothbart et al., 1995). The development of the attention system is undergoing particularly rapid and qualitative changes during the early childhood years. As children advance from infancy to early childhood, there is increased efficiency in terms of making use of orienting and selecting strategies as well as enhanced ability to sustain attention and ignore distracters (Ruff & Lawson, 1990; Ruff & Rothbart, 1996). Ultimately, attention is a critical prerequisite for the successful performance of more complex cognitive processes.

Perception is considered to be another step in the processing of sensory/attentional information. Across modalities, perception involves detection, discrimination, and localization (Sparrow & Davis, 2000). Information that is perceived through sensory systems is then transformed into higher-order codes for use by the various higher-order cognitive subsystems. Although there are multiple sensory systems, the process of transforming information from the visual and auditory systems into higher-order codes has been extensively investigated (Kolb & Whishaw, 2002; Lezak, 1995; Temple, 1997). In turn, this perceptual material informs higher-order cognition such as representation, categorization, and formation of early concepts.

Memory is another aspect of cognition that should be examined as part of a comprehensive assessment. Memory is considered to be the set of processes that temporarily holds new information while it is being utilized or processed for other purposes (short-term memory) or more permanently holds learned information for future reference and use (long-term memory). It is also useful to distinguish between declarative memories or facts accessible to conscious recall (i.e., knowing that) and procedural memories or automatic operations and skills (i.e., knowing how; Kolb & Whishaw, 2002). Some models of memory (Atkinson & Shriffin, 1968) emphasize that information is momentarily entered into the sensory register and then transferred to short-term memory that has limited capacity. For material to reach long-term memory, strategies such as rehearsal need to be applied to the information in immediate short-term memory. Recently, there have been efforts to draw on current models of memory (Baddeley, 1992; Cabeza & Nyberg, 2003; Engle, Tuholski, & Laughlin, 1999; Squire & Schacter, 2002) to refine specific measures of memory (e.g., WRAML-II; Sheslow & Adams, 2003) as well as those measures that are incorporated into standardized tests of intelligence (e.g., SB5; Roid, 2003; WISC-IV; Wechsler, 2003) and of phonological processing (e.g., CTOPP; Wagner, Torgesen, & Rashotte, 1999).

Another critical aspect of cognition is the executive functions. The term executive functions has a number of definitions (cf. Zelazo, Carter, Reznick, & Frye, 1997) but includes those control and regulatory processes that (1) integrate information perceived in the external world and transform perception into higher-order symbols, (2) compare incoming information to what is stored in memory, and (3) combine the incoming perceptions with information about the person's internal physiological state and biological drives. In addition, the executive system guides the determination of appropriate behavioral responses to a given situation by (1) deciding on appropriate goals, (2) developing plans to meet those goals, and (3) organizing the required behavioral programs to carry them out. Executive functioning is probably the most complex aspect of the cognitive module because a variety of higher-order cognitive functions are required to select, plan, organize, and implement a behavioral response appropriate to a constantly changing world. Because of this complexity and the degree to which these skills are interwoven with other aspects of cognition, our understanding of and ability to assess this set of abilities in children and adolescents has evolved gradually. However, in the past decade, ongoing clinical interest and empirical investigations have enabled the development of promising standardized measures (e.g., D-KEFS: Delis, Kaplan, & Kramer, 2001; BRIEF-Preschool Version: Gioia, Espy, & Isquith, 2003; BRIEF: Gioia, Isquith, Guy, & Kenworthy, 2000; NEPSY: Korkman, Kirk, & Kemp, 1998). When cognition is assessed in a more comprehensive manner such that multiple measures of the various subcomponents of the cognitive system are employed, the researcher or clinician has the subsequent challenging task of interpreting and integrating both qualitative and quantitative findings. To the extent that standard measures were available for use and consistencies emerged in support of a meaningful pattern of strengths and weaknesses, this approach can illuminate the cognitive contributions that are operating for the individual.

Nevertheless, making use of profile analysis not only within but also across instruments is controversial. Different assessment instruments have unique psychometric properties and the normative groups used may be quite dissimilar with respect to factors such as age bands of comparison, representativeness of the normative sample, and construct validity. Although tests also vary with respect to reliability, it is possible to incorporate the reliability of different assessment instruments when making profile comparisons. Still, we suggest that in the hands of a skilled clinician, research specialist, or practitioner-scientist, the process of combining findings from sufficient but independent sources of measurement and subjecting the data to profile analysis has added and will continue to add materially to our understanding of the *differential* patterns of cognitive functioning that distinguish among clients with *similar* overall levels of cognitive functioning.

Social-Emotional Functioning. Comprehensive understanding of an individual's functioning also necessitates characterizing social-emotional competencies, vulnerabilities, and deficits as well as social-emotional and behavioral problems, symptoms, and disorders. Traditional approaches to assessing social-emotional functioning have focused on identifying whether an individual is exhibiting prominent deviations from social-emotional expectations, such as wor-

rying to excess, showing a lack of pleasure and/or heightened feelings of sadness, exhibiting patterns of relating that are atypical and/or lack stability, and interpreting situations in a distorted fashion. Making determinations about the presence of such extreme or deviant behaviors and their duration, intensity, and quality is critical in terms of accurately identifying disorder for the purposes of diagnosis and, ultimately, treatment. However, guided by a developmental psychopathology framework, the assessment of social-emotional functioning is recognized as a more encompassing endeavor for several reasons. First, the emphasis expands to allow for delineating not only social-emotional deficits but also competencies, subthreshold manifestations of symptoms, and risk factors. Second, deficits, risks, and competencies are understood in a developmental context, meaning that the child's developmental stage and negotiation of salient age-appropriate tasks are considered. Third, distinctions are made as to whether social-emotional development is following a normative trajectory, occurring in a gradual but typical manner resulting in underdeveloped or immature functioning, or whether there are atypical or deviant features that indicate a developmental trajectory consistent with a marked disability (e.g., Autism, Schizophrenia).

In many respects, traditional approaches to the assessment of social-emotional functioning have been limited by an overemphasis on diagnostic considerations as well as a historical reliance on projective measures. Although making diagnostic determinations and characterizing an individual's understanding of ambiguous stimuli can be informative for understanding the individual's current functioning and making intervention recommendations, we argue that assessment in this domain should be more securely rooted in our understanding of social, emotional and behavioral development as well as the extent to which these realms are inherently intertwined. To do so, it is incumbent on researchers and clinicians to develop a clear, coherent, and contemporary framework for social-emotional functioning.

Because the current body of research on social and emotional development is vast, it has been challenging to identify core facets of this domain that can be evaluated in a reliable and valid fashion. Nevertheless, theories and studies of social-emotional development do provide some guidelines about such core facets. Studies of the emotional component of the social-emotional domain have focused on the following types of processes: (1) emotional milestones (e.g., recognizing and labeling facial expressions, understanding of emotions); (2) intensity, frequency, and quality of emotional reactivity and expressiveness; and (3) emotion regulation/coping. Studies of the social component of the social-emotional domain have focused on (1) the acquisition of discrete relational skills, such as joint attention and specific social skills (e.g., sharing); (2) interpersonal relationship processes, including interpersonal styles, behaviors such as direct and relational aggression, and knowledge about friendships; and (3) peer group processes (e.g., teasing, classification of popular, peer-rejected, and peer-neglected children). Furthermore, it is useful to delineate the meaning of social and emotional competence. Denham and colleagues (2003) have posited that emotional competence is composed of emotional expressiveness, emotion knowledge, and emotion regulation. Rose-Krasnor (1997) posits a multilayered framework that rests on the theoretical concept of effectiveness in interaction, offers a second tier that delineates the contributions of context as well as self and other perspectives, and rests on basic skills and motivations. Cole and colleagues (Cole, Martin, & Dennis, 2004) focus on both normative and psychopathological processes inherent in emotion regulation.

At this point in time, these facets may serve to organize the evaluation of a child's or adolescent's social-emotional functioning but cannot necessarily be measured in a reliable and valid manner because few appropriate standardized normed assessment tools of this nature have been developed. Our current knowledge of age-expected performance of specific competencies and the range and variation of social and emotional functioning among children and adolescents is extremely limited. Large-scale representative studies (i.e., epidemiological research) as well as development and norming of new or existing clinical measures are needed. Indeed, the few normed clinical instruments that are available focus almost exclusively on symptoms of social-emotional and behavioral disorders with increasing, albeit restricted, attention to competencies. These assessment instruments fall into the broad categories of behavior rating scales (e.g., Child Behavior Checklist [CBCL]: Achenbach, 2001; Achenbach & Rescorla, 2000, 2001; ITSEA: Briggs-Gowan & Carter, 1998; Carter, Briggs-Gowan, Jones, & Little, 2003; BASC: Reynolds & Kamphaus, 1992) and structured and semistructured diagnostic interviews (e.g., CAPA: Angold, Cox, Prendergast, Rutter, & Simonoff, 1987; DISC IV; Shaffer, Fisher, Lucas, Dulcan, & Schwab-Stone, 2000; PAPA: Egger & Angold, 2004). Information about a child's or adolescent's social-emotional functioning can also be obtained from adult caregivers such as parents and teachers, from the child, and/or from clinical observation in the evaluation context and in more naturalistic environments such as at home or at school. One promising avenue in the

evaluation of social-emotional functioning is the development of structured observational diagnostic tools (e.g., ADOS: Lord et al., 2000; DB-DOS: Wakschlag et al., 2002, in press) that can be used in conjunction with checklists and interviews. To date, these instruments are quite specialized in the sense that they are most relevant when the evaluator has targeted a particular diagnostic category and when evaluating young children or individuals with limited capacities to verbally express or reflect on their own social and emotional functioning and behaviors.

Empirical advances in understanding other aspects of adaptive and maladaptive social-emotional processes have been slow to affect clinical assessment, although some influences are evident. The influences may gradually take root when clinicians adopt new terms and concepts and/or when newly standardized measures that have drawn directly from current research become available. For example, increased understanding of the temperament dimension of behavioral inhibition and its relation to the emergence of anxiety disorders (Biederman et al., 2001; Hayward, Killen, Kraemer, & Taylor, 1998; Rosenbaum et al., 2000; Schwartz, Snidman, & Kagan, 1999) has facilitated the willingness of psychologists and other mental health professionals to consider that a young child may be having difficulties due to early emerging anxiety and has informed the development of measures such as the Infant-Toddler Social and Emotional Assessment (ITSEA) that includes both a General Anxiety Scale and an Inhibition to Novelty Scale within the Internalizing Domain (Carter et al., 2003).

We view the continuum of social-emotional adjustment as ranging from optimal functioning to clinical disorder. Between these two fuzzy categories are gradations with diffuse boundaries. The continuum includes age-adequate/average, temperamental variation that may place a child at risk for later psychopathology, and subthreshold/subclinical. Given the current state of knowledge and limited availability of standardized assessment instruments, judgments regarding where on the continuum children and adolescents fall is largely a matter of clinical judgment. Standardized assessment tools are still predominantly restricted to problem and competence checklists and measures of adaptive functioning (that may serve as a proxy for impairment). Other forms of assessment such as structured and semistructured diagnostic interviews that have adequate reliability and validity and can contribute critical information to a clinical evaluation are too rarely administered because of time constraints and training issues. To enhance understanding of the social-emotional continuum and the boundaries between categories along the continuum, studies that utilize epidemiological sampling techniques and/or national standardization sampling frameworks are needed.

Academic Achievement.   Almost all achievement assessment is focused on evaluating an individual's current skills and factual knowledge. Skill development is the primary focus in the early school years, with most achievement assessment focused on basic reading decoding and comprehension, spelling, writing, and arithmetic skills. As children progress into the later primary grades and through high school, assessment of skill development is still important, but the assessment must be broadened to include an evaluation of specific areas of knowledge (e.g., science, social studies, history). When a child or adolescent experiences difficulties in basic academic skill areas, it can be useful to administer more specialized tests that examine the component skills required to achieve in a basic academic skill area. Due to recent policy interest in reading as a gateway to broader academic achievement as well as studies of the genetics of reading disabilities that emphasize component processes, a number of tests are available that provide more specialized assessments of the elements that support reading ability (e.g., identification of letter-sound relationships, phonological awareness, phonemic segmentation and blending). The Comprehensive Test of Phonological Processing (CTOPP; Wagner et al., 1999) is one example of an assessment tool that addresses phonological processing that may underlie risk for reading disabilities. These more specialized measures of reading disability highlight he heterogeneity of reading disabilities and emphasize the varied developmental pathways that can result in a reading disability (cf. McCardle et al., 2001). Standardized, normed instruments to address mathematical skills and writing have not reached a similar level of sophistication. However, there are measures available that break down the component skills required to achieve in the areas of mathematics and written expression. For example, the KeyMath (Connolly, 1998) distinguishes among basic concepts (e.g., numeration, geometry), operations, (e.g., addition, division), and applications (e.g., measurement, estimation).

Academic achievement represents the outcome of very specific areas of formal learning. Typically, achievement assessment is focused on academic-related abilities gained in formal learning environments such as school. These assessments almost always represent the implementation of what a child or adolescent has acquired from educational opportunities and are therefore affected by cultural, environmental, and curricular exposure. Here we are limiting academic achievement to the individual's learned capacities rather than the degree to which these abilities are employed in everyday settings.

Domains Associated with Functional Adjustment: Adaptive Behavior Exemplar

The goal of determining how the domains of development affect a child's or adolescent's everyday life (e.g., school performance, peer relationships) is inherent in any assessment, yet the examination of an individual's performance of age-appropriate tasks in everyday settings such as school and home is often neglected. The two domains that have received more attention with respect to day-to-day performance and whether performance meets culturally imposed age expectations are academic functioning in the classroom and adaptive behavior across settings. We highlight adaptive behavior in this chapter as there are well-standardized, norm-referenced measures developed for this domain.

Adaptive Behavior.   Adaptive behavior primarily has been considered an important domain for the classification of mental retardation (Sattler, 2001). However, in our clinical and empirical work with children and adolescents who vary widely in terms of cognitive level and psychopathology, we have become convinced of the contribution that adaptive behavior offers to comprehensive assessment of all populations, not only those suspected of functioning in the mentally retarded range. We have found adaptive behavior particularly useful for describing decrements in day-to-day functioning associated with learning disabilities and psychiatric conditions.

Adaptive behaviors are typically thought of as sets of concrete behaviors that reflect personal and social sufficiency in day-to-day life at home, in school, and in the community (Sparrow, Balla, & Cicchetti, 1984). In discussing the multifactorial structure of adaptive behavior, Schalock (1999) offers the following components: (1) gross and fine motor or physical skills; (2) independent daily living skills such as dressing, bathing, cooking; (3) cognitive, communication, and academic skills such as reading, writing, managing a checkbook; and (4) social competence skills requiring establishing and maintaining friendships as well as social reasoning and comprehension. These categories mirror the domains that are assessed by the Vineland Adaptive Behavior Scales (Sparrow et al., 1984), including the following domains: communication, daily living skills, socialization, and motor skills.

Acquiring information concerning adaptive behavior skills provides a window into the individual's ability to integrate current resources across developmental domains in the contexts of daily life. Mastery of stage-specific tasks will be manifest in the practical negotiation of the everyday integration of domains such as cognition, language, social-emotional functioning, and academic achievement. Deficiencies in communication, socialization, and daily living skills often appear as a function of cognitive delay or an emotional disturbance. It is important to note that there is not a one-to-one correspondence between cognitive and adaptive functioning, although stronger associations will be observed for individuals at the lower end of the cognitive continuum. Also, a child's or adolescent's linguistic and cognitive level will place some constraints on his or her adaptive behavior skill level. Psychiatric symptoms such as social withdrawal, oppositionality, depression, and anxiety can interfere with a child's or adolescent's ability to perform routine behaviors (e.g., making a bed, interacting with friends in social settings, bathing, crossing a street independently). Determining if a deficit in adaptive behavior is the result of a social-emotional disturbance, is associated with cognitive limitations, or reflects both social-emotional and cognitive contributions is important in making appropriate intervention recommendations. At the same time, it is essential to recognize that adaptive behavior is modifiable and that teaching an individual how to behave in an age-adequate manner is likely to exert reciprocal influences on other developmental domains. Distinguishing skill deficits from motivational deficits is central to appropriate intervention planning. It is also important to be aware that some children will have very low adaptive functioning because they are not expected to engage in age-appropriate adaptive behaviors, particularly in the domain of daily living skills (e.g., making their bed, assisting with chores). Knowledge of the most central tasks of development, coupled with an adaptive behavior profile, provides a vehicle for evaluating the individual's practical integration of competencies across developmental domains.

Thus, whereas development in cognition, language, social-emotional, and motor domains drives the acquisition of adaptive behaviors, adaptive behavior in this model is largely thought of as the end result of how well a child or adolescent integrates these domains in everyday life. For this reason, adaptive behavior may provide a vehicle for measuring a very challenging area within the social-emotional domain, childhood impairment, which is also referred to as disability, psychosocial or functional impairment, or limitations (Pickles et al., 2001; Simeonsson et al.,

2003). To the extent that a decrement in adaptive behavior can be quantified using existing interview and checklist assessments of adaptive behavior, it may be possible to also quantify disability or impairment associated with psychiatric disorder in childhood and adolescence.

Multilevel, Contextual Components. The Comprehensive Psychological Assessment approach not only considers individual functioning from a multidimensional perspective but also places the individual in multiple, nested contexts (Bronfenbrenner, 1986). These contexts can be conceptualized in various ways (Bronfenbrenner, 1977; Cicchetti et al., 2000) but generally move from those that are proximal to the individual, such as the family and peers, to those that are more distal, such as institutions, community, and culture. It is important for clinicians and researchers to be aware of the major spheres of contextual influences, such as the family, peers, institutional settings (i.e., day care, school, afterschool), and culture. As well, they should be developmentally informed, able to detect features of specific contexts that might promote or hinder development at particular ages and/or stages. Theorists and researchers in the field of developmental psychopathology have made strides toward establishing a better understanding of the nested ecologies that transact with individual functioning to affect development. At the more proximal levels of family and peers, methods exist for systematically examining parent-child interactions, parenting styles, quality of parent-child relationships, direct as well as indirect family processes, peer interactions, friendships, social status, and peer group processes. At the institutional level, the settings that have received the most empirical attention are day care, Head Start, school, and afterschool programming. Measures that have been developed to assess these settings focus on qualifications of the adults who are interacting with children (e.g., educational background, certifications); adult-child ratios; environmental characteristics, including safety features; developmental appropriateness of materials available to children; and qualities of caregiver-child relationships and interactions (Friedman & Amadeo, 1999; Rutter & Maughan, 2002). Gathering information about the quality of out-of-home environments that involve nonparental relationships and how these may transact with family processes is necessary to our understanding of how to ensure that typically developing children have access to quality environments that foster competencies and that children who are at risk or manifesting problems have access to appropriate interventions implemented in the same or similar settings.

Another contextual level that we are now recognizing, defining, and measuring in more sophisticated and meaningful ways is community. Innovative work has been conducted to quantify multiple aspects of community, including social cohesion (e.g., Silk, Sessa, Sheffield Morris, Steinberg, & Avenevoli, 2004), community violence exposure (e.g., Gorman-Smith & Tolan, 1998), and neighborhood characteristics as distinct from family-level poverty. This work has capitalized on advances in demography, applying aggregated census data to individual families in specific block codes as well as innovative observational and qualitative ethnographic methods that permit careful characterization of subtle qualities of neighborhood experience (e.g., Leventhal & Brooks-Gunn, 2003).

Bringing multilevel contextual considerations to bear in the assessment process can easily become unwieldy for the researcher or clinician. Further, when there is risk at one level of the broader ecology, there is an increased likelihood of risk across multiple levels of the broader ecology (Sameroff, Seifer, & McDonough, 2004). Consideration should be given to the manner in which risk factors may exert influence on child functioning, including both direct and/or indirect mechanisms. Recent studies highlight that more distal influences are often mediated by proximal influences in the family (Rutter, 2005). Further, it is now clear that individual factors can moderate the impact of contextual influences such as stressful life events or cumulative risk. Examples include moderation of stressful life events by genetic endowment (Caspi, Sugden, & Moffit, 2003; Rutter, 2005) and moderation of cumulative risk by security of attachment (Belsky & Fearon, 2002) in the prediction of psychological adjustment. Although individual factors may improve probabilistic outcomes through moderation, it is important not to revert to blaming the victims of sledgehammer environmental conditions that fail to meet acceptable human standards, such as exposure to neighborhood violence and wartime conditions.

Contextual Levels: Family and Culture as Exemplars

In this section, we discuss family and cultural levels within the multilevel contextual system as examples of the manner in which relevant aspects of levels can be identified and relevant developmental processes considered as they relate to assessment.

Family. Understanding the family context is a complex undertaking because there are numerous family features and factors that are relevant to understanding the individual's functioning. From a systems perspective, families are "complex structures comprised of interdependent groups of individuals. Members of a family system devise strategies for meeting the needs of individual family members and the group as a whole" (Carter & Murdock, 2001, pp. 8–9). This definition points to the necessity of first characterizing a family in terms of features, such as who is considered a member, how many members make up the group, and the gender and age of each family member. In the process of obtaining this information, the clinician will also start to identify the "family form." As Carter and Murdock point out, the nature and organization of families has changed substantially since the 1960s. Although myths persist that the family is synonymous with a heterosexual, two-parent household, the reality is that there has been an increase in both single-parent households and gay and lesbian single-parent and two-parent households (Black, Gates, Sanders, & Taylor, 2000; U.S. Census Bureau, 2000), as well as increasing recognition of the role that close relatives such as aunts, uncles, and grandparents may play in caretaking and child rearing (Dressler, 1985; Wilson & Tolson, 1990).

Descriptive features of the family context are a reasonable starting point for shaping a conceptualization about the influence the family may have on a child or adolescent, yet care should be taken to gather additional information that sheds light on what factors contributed to the current family form. For example, a child may be living in a family headed by a two-parent household that has been stable in terms of membership but stressful due to parent conflict. Alternatively, the two-parent household might be a second marriage that is amicable and in which socioeconomic status has improved. In the first example, the potential positive influences of family stability and two-parent heads of household may be overshadowed by the more concerning, chronic exposure to intense anger expression and verbal hostility during parent conflicts (Cummings & Davies, 1994, 2002). In the second scenario, concerns about the effects on a child being raised by a stepparent might be less informative than knowing that in this reconstituted family the child is deriving benefits from an improvement in socioeconomic status and an affectively positive family climate.

Quality of relationships within the family are central to multiple domains of children's functioning. From a family life cycle perspective, parent-child interactions are highly salient in early childhood and continue to play a role in child social competence through adolescence (Weinfeld, Ogawa, & Egeland, 2002). However, different dimensions of parenting appear to be more or less important depending on the domain of child functioning and the age or stage of the child's development. Broader characteristics of family climate, including communication styles, affective tone and expressiveness, warmth, cohesion, and adaptability, can also be assessed with both questionnaire and observational methods and have been shown to influence cognitive and social-emotional outcomes for children.

Central dimensions of family that are routinely assessed in the developmental psychopathology literature include observations of parent-child interactions as well as parent reports of parenting stress and marital satisfaction and parent and child reports of parenting styles, communication, and overall family functioning. From the assessment perspective, it is important to recognize that associations with most dimensions of family and child functioning assessed have been found in normative, psychopathological, and developmental disability populations. At the same time, unique issues need to be addressed at different points in the family life cycle and when families are facing unique life transitions or events (e.g., the recent diagnosis of a child with a disability or chronic health condition). Specialized assessments have been developed and are often needed for understanding how individuals within families adapt to specific life stressors and transitions (Reaction to Diagnosis Interview: Pianta & Marvin, 1992) and the kinds of accommodations they employ. Many brief checklists are available that address family functioning in clinical evaluations. However, in most cases, the family brings an identified child as the target of an evaluation and will be surprised if asked to respond to questions about broader family functioning. Administering family questionnaires to the parents, child, and/or siblings requires the evaluator to convey to the family the importance of understanding proximal contextual factors in the child's adaptation. Unfortunately, most clinical training does not encourage the use of family measures as a part of a child clinical or neuropsychological evaluation. Indeed, one of the few situations in which the clinician is compelled to address family relationships is in the unfortunate circumstance of maltreatment or neglect.

Culture. As societies around the globe become increasingly diverse, researchers and clinicians must increase their competence with respect to understanding variations in culture, the role of culture in both typical and atypical developmental patterns, and the need to integrate the cultural context of the evaluation into the comprehensive assessment approach. With respect to our Comprehensive Psychological Assessment model, knowing about a child's or adolescent's cultural background may inform the selection of tests to assess relevant domains, the manner in which the evaluator approaches the child and family about

their current concerns, and the interpretation of behavioral observations and quantitative test findings. Adopting the view that for each of us, whether we are assuming the role of clinician or researcher, acquiring cultural competence is a self-work in progress is particularly critical given the influence of immigration on demography and the fact that the manner in which culture is defined and understood in institutions such as the field of psychology has changed significantly in recent history (see Garcia Coll, Akerman, & Cicchetti, 2000) and will continue to change.

One general definition of culture refers to shared values, beliefs, and practices that are transmitted across generations within a group (cf. Pinderhughes, 1989). It is important to distinguish culture from race and ethnicity and to recognize that the most recent population genetics findings support that there are no discrete boundaries between racial groups (Rosenberg et al., 2002). Although it is possible to identify small group differences between populations, most of the variability across all humans comes from within-population differences (Rosenberg et al., 2002). Indeed, race may be best defined as a social construct employed within social relationships for classifying and distinguishing among individuals according to physical characteristics (Suyemoto & Dimas, 2003). Ethnicity refers to a particular kind of culture that is usually associated with a common geographic region or national origin (Pinderhughes, 1989). Understanding the role of culture in development is becoming more complex in part because families are increasingly multiethnic, multicultural, and multiracial. There are also wide variations in acculturation patterns within and across ethnic, cultural, and racial groupings. For example, the number of multiethnic children has steadily increased over the past 30 years (U.S. Census Bureau, 2000). Moreover, consistent with our view of nested ecological contexts as applied in the Comprehensive Psychological Assessment model, it is critical to recognize that culture is not a static entity but is dynamic and responsive to the settings and conditions to which the family must adapt (Christensen, Emde, & Fleming, 2004). Thus, family rituals, day-to-day routines, and religious and household practices through which culture is maintained and transmitted across generations are influenced by factors such as immigration patterns, economic conditions, and exposure to other cultural groups.

Scholars who study cultural influences on development advocate that cultural beliefs, values, and practices be a central focus of assessments of children (Betancourt & Lopez, 1993; Christensen et al., 2004; Garcia Coll & Magnuson, 2000). This presumes that researchers and clinicians acquire training in culturally competent assessment practice. In addition to openness to and celebration of diversity, researchers and clinicians must engage in a process of self-awareness to avoid biases that could lead to over- or underpathologizing the child or family practices and beliefs. Because cultural differences can exacerbate an already complex power dynamic between the assessor and the assessed, cultural proficiency is central to gathering reliable and valid information. For an extensive iscussion of cultural competence, see the American Psychological Association's (2002) *Guidelines on Multicultural Education, Training, Research, Practice, and Organizational Change for Psychologists* (http://www.apa.org/pi/multiculturalguidelines). Also, Christensen et al. (2004) offer some excellent suggestions for integrating awareness of family culture when conducting a young child assessment. Specifically, they recommend talking with families about the following: (1) perceptions of the child's difficulties or distress, (2) how the child's behavior is viewed relative to other child behavior in their cultural group, (3) cultural explanations for the child's difficulties or distress, and (4) parental experiences with and preferences for treatment.

Issues of culture are often directly relevant to the appropriateness of a particular instrument for a given individual or target group. A potentially complicated issue that is related to culture is that of assessing multilingual individuals. It is not sufficient to employ a measure that has been translated into the target population's or client's native language because the translation may not be appropriate for the population under study or the family seeking treatment. Although translation and back-translation have traditionally been held as a standard, it is not a sufficient practice because there is no guarantee that the psychometric properties of the instrument will remain stable across cultural, racial, or ethnic groups. Whether an instrument has been translated into a new language or is going to be used with a cultural, ethnic, or racial group on which it was not normed, evaluating cultural appropriateness is often facilitated through the use of focus groups and/or pilot testing in the target population. This strategy can provide feedback on content validity, particularly with respect to going beyond the quantitative data that inform whether measures evidence similar scale structure across groups and whether patterns of expected associations with both related and unrelated constructs (i.e., convergent and discriminant validity) are observed. Indeed, when evaluating cultural bias, it is insufficient and often misleading to review item content. Although documenting that a test or scale evidences comparable scale structure and internal consistency is useful, the evaluating bias requires determining whether or not a test functions in the same manner across groups (e.g., has the same sensitivity and specificity; Sattler, 2001). In addition, because it is rare to obtain appropriate within-ethnic group reliability and validity data, investigators who are working with minority populations are encouraged to report internal consistency statistics when presenting findings. It is not appropriate to assume that the internal consistency or factor structure obtained in a dominant culture population will be comparable when a scale is employed with ethnic/racial minority groups.

McCain and colleagues (McCain, Kelley, & Fishbein, 1999) conducted a study with the Toddler Behavior Screening Inventory (TBSI) that highlights the importance of attending to possible response differences across ethnic/racial groups. Specifically, they examined patterns of responding on the TBSI comparing Black/African American and White parents with respect to both ratings of mean frequencies of problem behaviors and level of concern. Of interest, although there were no differences in the frequencies of problem behaviors, Black/African American parents were more likely to be concerned about their children's problem behaviors. This finding indicates that Black/African American families were using a lower threshold for concern.

At this point in time, very few psychological tests, scales, or interview assessments have been examined for cultural, racial, or ethnic appropriateness for even the largest racial/ethnic groups in the United States. This is particularly challenging for the clinician, who must struggle to make meaning from an individual profile. Researchers and test developers should be encouraged not only to increase diversity within samples (i.e., matching regional demographic characteristics) but to gather adequately large samples to permit cross-group validation.

Interplay within and across Multiple Domains and Contexts

The following example illuminates the challenges of integrating information across domains of functioning and contextual levels. A Latina girl is referred based on a concern that she has significant attentional and hyperactivity problems. During a developmental interview, the examiner learns that there have been several significant recent stressors in the family (e.g., death of a grandparent who was a caretaker, move secondary to mother's promotion) and a chronic childhood illness (asthma). In addition, the child is reported to show symptoms of hyperactivity at home but not in school and is observed to be quite active and inattentive during the evaluation. Upon formal assessment, the child has an unremarkable cognitive and academic profile with average scores in all domains assessed. In contrast, based on both parent and teacher reports, her social and adaptive skills appear to be below average. The parents report that difficulties in these areas of functioning represent a change. In her previous school and community, which were more culturally diverse, she had many friends and was engaged in many activities.

This scenario highlights the complexities of children's lives in our modern society. Children struggle with loss, family and community transitions, and the need to situate one's ethnic/racial identity within relationships across multiple contextual levels. Moreover, a child's or adolescent's profile of strengths and weaknesses across developmental domains transacts with contextual risk and protective factors to shape developmental trajectories.

In this clinical scenario, the question of attentional difficulties and impulsivity might best be addressed through a formulation that takes into account both individual and ecological factors. Given the occurrence of significant recent life stressors, the lack of neurocognitive indicators of attentional deficits such as a relative weakness in executive functions or working memory and the lack of pervasiveness in symptom presentation across contexts or time, a prudent approach might entail the following: (1) Identify the psychopathological risks, such as ADHD and/or anxiety; (2) adopt an intervention approach that first addresses the individual and contextual risks; and (3) promote follow-up that will allow for further clarification of the diagnostic picture. Steps might be taken to help the child cope with the recent transitions and aid in the development of new friendships. Following a period of transition and, ideally, social reengagement, the evaluator might examine whether the attentional and impulsivity problems persist in the home or have generalized to other settings. By examining multiple levels of the child's ecology (e.g., recent family stressors, community transitions, and threats to cultural identity), it is possible to develop a more comprehensive understanding of the child's current presentation and to develop an intervention approach that recognizes the complexities of the child's day-to-day life situation.

This example highlights some aspects of interplay across both domains and contexts. There are several features of the interplay within and among domains and contexts that often arise when conducting assessments of children and adolescents. Directly relevant to interplay at the multidimensional level of the Comprehensive Psychological Assessment model is that despite the desire of test developers to create pure measures of particular constructs, this ideal is rarely, if ever, realized. Because a problem or strength in one domain may influence observed performance on a test purported to assess a separate domain, it is very important

to understand the different skills that specific tests require and to look across tests to determine the child's or adolescent's profile of abilities. Related to this measurement problem is the reality that a deficit, delay, or diagnosis in one domain of functioning places children at higher risk in other domains of functioning, independent of assessment method. For example, children with specific language disorders, reading disabilities, and cognitive impairments are all at higher risk for a mental health disturbance (Beitchman, Wilson, & Johnson, 2001; Benasich, Curtiss, & Tallal, 1993). Reciprocally, children who have sought treatment for psychiatric disorders evidence increased rates of learning and language difficulties (Jenkins, Bax, & Hart, 1980). For some children, a primary language problem may lead to social withdrawal, and social withdrawal diminishes opportunities for acquiring and enhancing social skills; thus, a negative feedback cycle can be set into motion. The evaluator's awareness of commonly occurring problems across domains influences decisions regarding the identification of appropriate domains of assessment.

Interplay across nested contexts is similar to interplay across observed domains with respect to impact on individual functioning. Just as risk in one domain places children at risk in other domains of functioning, risks at one contextual level are likely to co-occur with risks at other contextual levels. Given the complexity of assessing contextual factors and the high likelihood of co-occurrence of risk factors across different levels of the child's or adolescent's environment, many researchers advocate the use of cumulative risk models and measures (e.g., Sameroff et al., 2004). In these cumulative risk factor models, demographic risk factors such as poverty status, single-parent household, low maternal education, unemployment, and child sex are included along with family factors such as insensitive and/or harsh parenting style, marital discord, and exposure to domestic violence and community factors such as exposure to violence and lack of neighborhood social cohesion. Interplay across nested contexts and domains can take myriad forms. In clinical settings, we cannot reliably determine whether influences at the domain and contextual levels are additive, moderating, mediating, or transactional. However, consideration of conceptual and statistical models can aid in understanding reciprocal influences between the individual's functioning and the contexts of his or her daily life. It can be particularly helpful to consider these models when integrating information about previous functioning or when reevaluating a child or adolescent. Recognizing the reality constraints in the child's and family's ecology should moderate the recommendations that are offered to families. For example, it is within the role of the clinical evaluator to help a family understand the systems that may aid the child's developmental progress and to assist parents in advocating for the child within these systems.

TEST CONSTRUCTION AND SCALING ISSUES

A developmentally informed comprehensive perspective on psychological assessment can be achieved only with a basic understanding of psychometric and methodological issues. We begin our discussion of these issues with a focus on standardization, reliability, and validity. Although these concepts are frequently given only passing attention in clinical practice and research, conceptual issues such as item scaling and a test's factor structure are critical considerations for assessing the development of an individual or group. This section briefly reviews some of the influences of psychometric issues on measures that try to describe developmental processes.

Item Selection

One psychometric issue in test construction that will influence a test's sensitivity to developmental change is item selection, often discussed under the rubric of content validity. The seemingly simple act of developing or choosing a specific item (or a specific behavior, if using a behavioral approach to assessment) for a specific measure depends on our understanding of the normal progression and unfolding of abilities as well as the appropriateness of particular items for describing phenomenology at specific ages and stages of development. Items are typically chosen and retained on tests based on their content, structure, and statistical characteristics. An item's content represents a sample of the measured domain or function; its structure represents the item's format. For example, if one were developing a vocabulary measure, content could be varied by changing the words included in the item, and structure, by changing the response required by the individual (e.g., seeing if the child touches the object that is named, asking for a definition of the word, requesting that the child or adolescent point to a picture within an array of pictures that best represents the word, asking the child or adolescent to use the word in a sentence). Critical developmental considerations are involved in decisions regarding content. For instance, the population of words that can be used across development changes significantly, from few if any during early infancy, to thousands, if not hundreds of thousands, during adolescence and adulthood. To best represent and assess an individual's vocabulary, an understanding of the

normal developmental progression of language abilities is necessary. In addition, developmental considerations are inherent in choosing the structure for an item. Younger children have been shown to have a more extensive receptive vocabulary than expressive (or written) vocabulary. Within the expressive domain, an item requiring a young child to label an object or picture of a familiar object would yield a very different view of vocabulary than an item requiring a verbal definition or use in a sentence. This language example, like examples that could have been drawn from multiple domains, has obvious developmental implications. Once an item pool is selected that varies in both content and structure, sophisticated statistical item-scaling methods can be employed to determine the difficulty level of items and to assign developmentally appropriate ordering of scale items (e.g., Rasch scaling method; Woodcock & Dahl, 1971).

Some theoretical statistical models are conceptually useful for guiding the construction of developmentally appropriate items and measures. For example, based on its underlying assumptions (i.e., item parameter invariance across groups), item response or latent trait theory suggests that a general measure can be developed with scaling that can be compared across subjects of greatly differing abilities. In addition, this model suggests that one can use completely different groups of items for different groups of participants and still compare their results. Given these assumptions, one could choose different sets of developmentally appropriate items for groups of participants who are at very different developmental stages, develop measures from each set of items, and still be able to compare the actual scores obtained across the groups or within a group across time. Although this item development model is considered to be very strong in theory, there are few actual examples of its use outside of the achievement or adaptive behavior domains. Even within the achievement area, the use of sets of anchor or calibration items has been required to help this model work. This strategy has significant advantages given recent developments in longitudinal modeling of trajectories (Sayer & Cumsille, 2001).

The statistical properties of each item within a particular measure also have to be considered in the developmental context. One of the most difficult measurement problems in assessing developmental functions occurs when a distribution of scores is nonnormal, especially when there is a positive or negative skew. Most often, nonnormal distribution of scores occurs with those items that fall at either end of the continuum of difficulty. When a large portion of the chosen items is either too easy or too difficult for a specific developmental level, there will be little variability in performance on those items. Items that are too easy will result in many individuals obtaining the highest scores possible on the measure (ceiling effect), and items that are too difficult will result in a majority of individuals obtaining very low scores (floor effect). This problem is easily illustrated if one considers what would happen if a majority of the items on a reading test were at the fifth-grade reading level and it was given either to a group of first-graders (floor effect) or 12th graders (ceiling effect). In either situation, it is not possible to accurately scale or measure an individual's true abilities because they fall within the tail end of either distribution. It is also extremely difficult to examine change, over time, in individuals who are already scoring at the ceiling of a measure, or who may be limited to scoring at the floor end of a measure. Such developmentally insensitive measures also severely limit one's ability to compare relations between constructs. In part, this is due to the statistical restrictions in variance that ceiling and floor effects cause. Restriction in variance (i.e., all respondents obtaining approximately the same score) will always limit the amount of covariance possible between measures (i.e., the ability of scores on one measure to predict scores on another measure, or on the same measure at a future point in time).

Standardization

The traditional standardization approach is often developmental, in that norms are developed to compare individuals to their age-based peer group. In many ways, the concept of norms is central to a developmental perspective for assessment. Although traditionally a norm is considered to represent the average test performance of a standardization sample, it is very easy to consider a norm as representing the average, median, or modal performance of a particular developmental level or stage. In a majority of the tests available, the most typical way to operationalize development has been based on chronological age, partly because of ease of use. A developmental level or stage, though, may be defined based on an individual's ability to perform a particular cognitive task (i.e., object permanence). Regardless of the dimension chosen as an index of developmental level, and in order to obtain a norm for reference purposes, a decision on where to partition the dimension has to be made. For example, with respect to the Vinelad Adaptive Behavior Scales, when developing special population norms for Autism, a decision was made to divide individuals who were mute from those who had any expressive language (Carter et al., 1998).

Normative data also have to be considered within the cultural, historical, and societal frameworks in which they are developed. There has been considerable discussion regarding the concept of cohort effects in developmental research. In some domains, the historical events of the nation (i.e., the Great Depression, World War II) or of a local community (i.e., tsunami, casinos) may have very strong effects on an individual's developmental progression in a number of domains. Norms developed in such situations may not be adequate representations for a different cohort that has not had similar environmental/historical/cultural experiences. For this reason, periodic restandardization of measures is very important.

Reliability

There are many different types of reliability estimates that are critical to consider in a developmentally informed manner in the Comprehensive Psychological Assessment model. One of the first reliability coefficients typically evaluated when reviewing a particular test or scale is test-retest reliability. The test-retest reliability coefficient is a direct examination of change over a short period in development. Typically, one would test a group of participants at one point in time and then again 2 weeks to 2 months later. In a developmental framework, even the shorter time frame of 2 weeks may be a time period in which the features of development being assessed undergo change. For example, a 2-week test-retest period for a measure designed to assess the first few months of infancy may be too long, as 2 weeks in a 1-month-old infant's lifetime represents a large portion of the infant's life and a period of rapid change in abilities. In contrast, a 2-week period in the life of a 15-year-old constitutes a smaller percentage of development and may represent a period in which little change is occurring. This issue is somewhat similar to the problem of comparing age- or grade-equivalent scores, as the likelihood of high concordance across age and grade standard scores varies based on whether a child is young for grade (e.g., has skipped a grade), old for grade (e.g., started kindergarten at age 7), or in the expected grade for age. Specifically, there may be a range of 4 years within a given classroom, with children between the ages of 7 and 10 years all in the third grade. Grade equivalents take into consideration that the older third-graders have not been exposed to academic material beyond the third-grade level, and therefore it is unlikely that they will have mastered this material. Thus, if academic achievement is comparable for the 7- and 10-year-old third-graders, they will achieve comparable scores using norms based on grade. In contrast, standard scores will be quite different if norms based on age are utilized, with the 7-year-old appearing much more competent than the 10-year-old. Given that a test-retest reliability coefficient is designed to assess the consistency of a measure and is dependent on the stability of the assessed behavior, one has to consider that it may also include some variance caused by true individual changes that occur during certain periods of development.

The reliability of measurement is also important for comparing scores across different measures. When comparing the scores from two different measures, a statistically significant difference is based on the standard error of the difference scores, which is calculated using the reliability coefficients of each measure. The lower the reliability, the greater the score difference required before one is secure in deciding that there is a significant discrepancy. Individuals at different developmental levels may require larger or smaller score differences because of differences in the reliability of the measures used at different levels. Given that younger children may also have a more limited range of scores on such a scale, especially when one considers their limited raw score performances, it may be psychometrically less common for them to exhibit such a magnitude of differences between the measures. Large standard errors of measurement, reflecting low reliability coefficients, are of particular concern if there are floor or ceiling effects limiting the variability of individual performance on the measures involved. This is most likely to occur at the lowest and highest ages for which a measure is designed to assess. However, it is unlikely that large standard errors of measurement can be obtained when there are floor or ceiling effects because range restriction in the scores obtained will artificially inflate the reliability coefficients. When reliability coefficients are inflated due to limited variance, the standard error of the differences is artificially decreased, and interpretations may be wrongly made regarding differences between measures when this might not be the case.

Validity

The construct validity of a measure also may be affected by developmental processes. Although many measures are analyzed by using factor analytic methods to confirm their underlying traits or constructs, very few are analyzed within a developmental framework. When developing a measure that is designed for longitudinal use, it is extremely valuable to test whether the latent structure of the measure is comparable across developmental periods or ages (e.g., Carter et al., 2003). Such an analytic plan is also

required to describe the changing patterns of the traits or constructs over development. Rather than making an assumption that a particular measure has the same structure, or even measures the same traits/constructs over development, it is necessary to formally evaluate these properties.

In addition to a measure's construct validity, there are developmental considerations regarding its predictive validity. Most measures are more predictive over shorter time periods than over longer periods, but there may be exceptions (e.g., sleeper effects). Measures that have inadequate validity with respect to psychometric criteria will artificially limit our understanding of both the underlying dimensions and the processes of change that are occurring and/or lead to mistaken conclusions about functioning at one time point and over time. Therefore, such basic psychometric considerations are central to any strong developmental model for assessment.

Sensitivity-Specificity

Although a test or measure may be a reliable and valid measure of an underlying construct or behavior, there is still an issue of how useful it might be for a given diagnostic or classification purpose (e.g., meets criteria for Oppositional Defiant Disorder, is peer-rejected, has a learning disability). Of most concern within this realm is the problem of misclassification and its impact on the person being classified. The measures of sensitivity (proportion of a sample found to fall within a diagnostic category) and specificity (proportion of a sample not falling within a diagnostic category) help to determine how well any test can be used for a specific diagnostic purpose. In addition, the measures of predictive value of a positive result and predictive value of a negative result provide information regarding how useful a particular test is for a specific population being classified. These latter concepts have significant applicability in evaluating a specific test for use with various populations during different developmental periods. One should not expect any one test to have stable sensitivity and specificity for a particular diagnostic decision across the developmental spectrum. For example, there are many specific diagnostic conditions (e.g., dementia, depression, speech disorders) that might have different base rates at different ages. If we have a test that has very good sensitivity and specificity (e.g., 80% to 90%) at one developmental level, and try to use it with another developmental group that has a different base rate of the disorder, then the sensitivity and specificity could change significantly and the test may not be adequate for the purpose at hand, even though its reliability and psychometric properties remain strong and stable.

METHODS

In approaching specific assessment strategies, whether for clinical or research applications, a common starting point is to review available tests or instruments. As noted earlier, we advocate an alternative approach, which is to begin by determining the domains and constructs within domains most relevant to the questions being asked. Once domains and constructs are determined, it is important to select the methods that will be most informative. The methods may include standardized tests, which represent the most structured of available procedures, but other available methods should also be considered. In isolation, standardized tests are rarely sufficient to answer the questions that researchers and clinicians attempt to answer. For example, even when evaluating intelligence, the obtained scores on a particular IQ test can be interpreted only in the context of observational and situational data (e.g., compliance, attention, motivation). The Cross-Battery approach (Flanagan & Ortiz, 2001; McGrew & Flanagan, 1998) offers an excellent guide for identifying unique and shared abilities across cognitive subtests of multiple instruments. To the extent that a multitrait, multi-informant, multimethod matrix can be developed to address the questions of interest, multiple sources of method error variance can be examined and a clearer understanding of the constructs under consideration will emerge (Campbell & Fiske, 1959).

For heuristic purposes, we have chosen to discuss reporting sources and specific types of tools for gathering information that are particularly relevant to a Comprehensive Psychological Assessment approach and that demonstrate how the use of multiple methods enriches the validity and generalizability of the outcome.

Reporting Source

The routine evaluation of individuals in isolation is artificial and provides only a partial picture of current functioning. Typically, multiple sources of information can be obtained about multiple domains of functioning as well as contextual factors. For children and adolescents, examples include contacting teachers and caregivers to obtain additional information in the domains of academic, cognitive, social-emotional, and adaptive functioning as well as reviewing school records for academic achievement. For adults, examples include interviewing spouses and family members to obtain relevant information in the domains of personality and social and adaptive functioning as well as medical chart review as an adjunct to a neuropsychological evaluation. Because multiple informants often provide conflicting information, their inclusion often complicates data integration. However, conflicting data are often informative and contribute an added dimension to the assessment, especially in terms of understanding the systems in which the individual functions. As informants may have access to different samples of behavior in multiple settings, conflicting information may reflect true variability in current functioning. On the other hand, conflicting information may be a function of observer or interviewer biases. When the informant will be involved in implementing recommendations, having some knowledge of any potential biases may be extremely useful. It should also be acknowledged that in some situations, the use of other informants is the only way to obtain information about a relevant domain, either because the behaviors of interest have such a low base rate of occurrence and are unlikely to occur in the testing situation or because the individual is unable to provide the information (e.g., coma, psychosis, dementia, severe retardation, infancy). When considering the inclusion of multiple informants, care must be taken to protect the individual's confidentiality. Informed consent must be secured from the individual or legal guardian prior to obtaining information from outside sources.

Interviews, Rating Scales, and Questionnaires

In the past, interviews were more commonly employed in clinical assessments, and rating scales and questionnaires more commonly employed in research applications. However, as more questionnaires and rating scales become available with appropriate normative information, and as clinical interview methods are standardized, the versatility of these methods increases. For each method, the adequacy of the sample on which normative data are based should be evaluated carefully along a number of dimensions: sample size, representativeness of age, sex, socioeconomic status, ethnicity, and size of community. For example, when evaluating an individual to rule out a diagnosis of mental retardation, both intelligence and adaptive behavior must be assessed with instruments that have been normed on a large sample that is representative of the total population. However, it may also be important to determine how a mentally retarded individual is functioning relative to other individuals with the same diagnosis. Therefore, the existence of additional norms, including a representative sample of individuals who are mentally retarded, might influence the selection of a specific instrument for this purpose.

A central concern when employing interviews, rating scales, or questionnaires is the potential bias of the informant, typically discussed in terms of response styles. For example, an informant may attempt to present in a socially conventional manner or in a negative light to gain access to treatment or services. Some scales have incorporated social desirability indices or veracity scales which can detect such response biases and provide correction formulas (e.g., MMPI-2: Graham, 1991). A second concern is the reliability of the instrument. For both rating scales and interviews, the more structured the format, the easier it is to obtain adequate test-retest and interrater reliability coefficients. Similarly, the lower the inference level required to make ratings (either for the informant or the interviewer), the greater the probability that adequate reliability can be obtained.

Observational Methods

Consistent with interview, rating scale, and questionnaire data, observational methods vary along a continuum of structure and the level of inference required to evaluate the constructs of interest. In addition, observational data add the dimension of time, and decisions must be made regarding the time frame of the analysis (e.g., continuous versus time or event sampling). The unit of analysis in terms of a microanalytic or macroanalytic focus must also be considered. Such decisions will be driven by the constructs under study. When conducting evaluations, we continually make observations that guide our subsequent behavior and decision-making processes. Research employing observational methods in areas such as interpersonal processes and play have made significant contributions to our knowledge base. However, few structured observational methods have been developed and standardized sufficiently to permit their use in clinical applications. As previously mentioned, one exception is the Autism Diagnostic Observational Schedule (ADOS; Lord et al., 2000). The ADOS is a semi-structured, interactive observational tool designed to assess social and communicative functioning in individuals who may have an Autism spectrum disorder. The assessment involves a variety of social occasions and "presses" designed to elicit behaviors relevant to a diagnosis of Autism. A standardized diagnostic algorithm can be computed, composed of a subset of rated social and communicative behaviors, and consistent with Autism criteria in the *Diagnostic and Statistical Manual of Mental Disorders IV* (American Psychiatric Association, 1994) and the *Inter-*

national Classification of Diseases 10 (World Health Organization, 1992). The use of presses to elicit behaviors that might not be commonly observed in an evaluation session is one of the innovative aspects of the ADOS. Recently, Wakschlag et al. (2002, in press), using the ADOS as a model, developed an observational tool to aid in the diagnosis of preschoolers with disruptive behavior disorders. The child is observed in three contexts that vary the degree of external regulatory support that is afforded, including interactions with the examiner and with a parent. Both problem behaviors and competencies are coded using a coding scheme that attends not only to the frequency of behaviors salient for a diagnosis of disruptive behavior but also for the quality of these behaviors.

Projective Methods

Freud introduced the term "projection" in 1894 and explained it as a strategy for assigning attributions (Exner, 1991). Since the introduction of projective techniques in the United States in the 1930s, their use has been highly controversial. The basic assumption underlying the use of projective techniques is that an individual's responses to an ambiguous stimulus or set of stimuli reveal something about the way he or she perceives, interprets, and organizes the information presented (Maloney & Ward, 1976). A further assumption is that these perceptions, interpretations, and organizational strategies inform the examiner about personality, unconscious processes, psychopathology, and reality testing. A primary feature of all projective techniques is that they involve a relatively unstructured demand or task. Typically, the examinee is not aware of how the test will be interpreted. Controversy has centered on issues of reliability and validity and has led to attempts to standardize administration, scoring, and interpretation by developing methods of quantifying ratings of responses. Over the years, many systems have been proposed for one of the most widely used projective techniques, the Rorschach Inkblot task. For example, systems have been developed by Beck (1944), Klopfer & Donaldson (1962), and Rappaport, Gill, and Schaffer (1968). Exner has built on previous methods to develop a comprehensive system for the Rorschach Inkblot task that includes normative data. Other currently employed projective methods include sentence completion tasks, figure drawings, and storytelling tasks.

Despite the controversy, projective techniques continue to be employed as a primary means of assessing and understanding personality and emotional development in school-age children and adults. Play interview techniques are also employed with preschool-age children, making use of the same set of projective assumptions to assess social-emotional functioning. The McArthur Network Collaborative Study of children's use of narratives, directed by Robert Emde, built on sentence completion tasks and play interviews to develop the MacArthur Story Stem Battery (Emde, Wolf, & Oppenheim, 2003). This task involves the presentation of structured story stems that are organized around relevant themes (e.g., attachment, separation, misbehavior) accompanied by toy props. This kind of methodology presents an opportunity for developing a quantifiable normed projective instrument for use with preschoolers.

IMPLEMENTING THE MODEL: HYPOTHESIS-DRIVEN ASSESSMENT

The terms comprehensive and developmental, emphasized throughout this chapter, must remain salient at each phase of implementation. To recapitulate, by *comprehensive,* we refer to obtaining data about the individual's functioning across a broad range of domains (i.e., cognition, language, social-emotional and personality, adaptive behavior, and academic/occupational achievement). The assessment should address not only functioning within domains, but also reciprocal influences between domains. By *developmental,* we refer to the notion that an individual's functioning in these domains can be understood only in the context of normative expectations for performance during a given developmental period (Cicchetti, 1984).

Goals of the Assessment

Assessment is aimed at painting a comprehensive picture of an individual's functioning within and across domains as it relates to the level of development. This model of Comprehensive Psychological Assessment is applicable to the evaluation of individuals and groups for research or for clinical purposes. In each case, one must establish (1) the goals of the assessment; (2) the relevant domains of assessment; (3) appropriate instruments; (4) the relations among selected instruments; (5) contextual factors that influence performance on these instruments; (6) a synthesis and interpretation of the obtained information, which provides a parsimonious understanding of the individual's current functioning; and (7) communication of this understanding of the individual's functioning to relevant levels of the developmental system, along with recommendations for any indicated interventions. When the model is implemented, these component parts are not necessarily discrete or sequential. Rather, the examiner engages in an ongoing inter-active feedback loop among all of these component parts at each phase of the evaluation.

Because of the multifactorial characteristics of any single measure, it is critical to use multiple measures and to have a good understanding of unique and shared abilities (i.e., latent constructs) that will contribute to the score obtained on a specific instrument. At the individual level, the use of multiple measures permits an analysis of patterns of convergence and divergence across instruments. Once measurement error is minimized, it is possible to determine patterns of relative strengths and weaknesses across multiple domains of development. Thus, the use of multiple instruments heightens one's confidence in a given finding because the error contribution from a single measurement source is minimized. At the nomothetic level, cluster and factor analytic approaches have been employed to identify patterns of functioning across relevant developmental domains that can lead to the successful classification of discrete subtypes or groups of individuals. An example of employment of this approach can be seen in clinical research that seeks to identify specific subtypes of learning disabilities (Fletcher, 1985; Morris, Blashfield, & Satz, 1986; Rourke, 1985).

Hypothesis-Driven Assessment Approach

In clinical situations, we endorse utilizing a strategy of hypothesis-driven assessment. Hypothesis-driven assessment refers to a process in which each step in the evaluation is guided by hypotheses generated from currently available information. A dynamic process is involved: The available information changes throughout the course of the assessment. A comparison between this approach and a standard comprehensive battery is analogous to the distinction between theory-driven research and shotgun research. The hypothesis-driven approach has a higher probability of hitting the relevant target in terms of obtaining information that is truly explanatory in the individual case. Kaufman (1983, 1994; Flanagan & Kaufman, 2004) has written widely about this approach to assessment. His major focus has been on intelligence and the most widely used tests of intelligence. In this model, we advocate the application of this approach across the spectrum of assessed domains. At points in the life span when developmental changes may play a larger role, it is critical to apply a developmentally informed perspective to hypothesis generation, instrument selection, and inferences derived from observational and quantitative data.

When presented with the task of selecting the initial goals of the assessment and choosing the domains that will be emphasized, the first piece of information that is available is typically the referral question. Based on the referral question, initial hypotheses are generated. These initial hypotheses guide the identification of relevant domains to assess, which in turn guide the selection of available instruments. Ideally, each domain of assessment relevant to the referral question will be addressed in a preliminary way in the first session with the individual. Based on the preliminary data, the next step of the assessment is designed. The preliminary data may support or disconfirm the initial hypotheses or may suggest additional hypotheses meriting further exploration. This approach is in marked contrast to administering a standard, lengthy battery to all individuals. A practical implication of this approach is that multiple assessment sessions over time are preferred to one or two extended sessions.

The use of multiple sessions provides an opportunity to score and evaluate information, refine hypotheses, and customize selection of instruments to elucidate strengths and weaknesses of the individual being evaluated. Intersession variability has often been considered a component of unexplained or error variance from a test-and-measurement perspective. However, when dealing with an individual case, this variability may be quite informative. Understanding the immediate assessment situation as a context that can exert influence on the individual's functioning can be quite informative. The immediate evaluation setting refers to situational factors in the testing, such as the physical environment of the testing room, the gender and/or race of the examiner, interpersonal style and/or comfort level of the examiner, order and number of tasks presented, the child's or adolescent's physical health, and the child's or adolescent's understanding of the purpose of the testing. The examiner should be attentive to the child's or adolescent's unique responses and interpretations of the testing experience and their impact on the examiner's behaviors. Thus, the use of multiple sessions often provides a more reliable and accurate estimate of the individual's behavior. This is especially important when evaluating children, whose behavior is likely to change and be more variable over time.

Appropriate and Inappropriate Referral and Research Questions

To implement this approach to assessment successfully, referral questions should be specific and should be based on information about the individual in multiple settings of the developmental system. Specific questions facilitate the generation of preliminary hypotheses to be pursued during the assessment. This is true for research studies that inves-

tigate groups of individuals and make clinical evaluations of individuals. For example, a global request regarding an individual's IQ score when there is a nonstated concern about language functioning may interfere with the selection of the most appropriate instruments for evaluating intelligence and language in this individual, because different IQ tests vary in their emphasis on verbal functioning in the determination of global intelligence. Similarly, when conducting research, it is important to determine the specific construct being measured and the interaction of the construct with the dependent variables under study. For example, if the interest is in evaluating children diagnosed with ADHD and non-ADHD children on listening vocabulary, the selection of a cognitive test must take into consideration how much the instrument is influenced by the attentional behavior associated with the diagnosis of ADHD. Thus, if an instrument is selected and used in isolation (e.g., a test of listening vocabulary such as the Peabody Picture Vocabulary Test, Revised: Dunn & Dunn, 1981), it is critical to recognize all the known influences that may contribute to the obtained scores. Attentional difficulties may well compromise performance on this task, such that presumed group differences in listening vocabulary are more parsimoniously explained in terms of differences in attentional ability.

Steps to Interpretation

The steps to interpretation that we describe assume that multiple measures have been employed to evaluate multiple domains of functioning. The initial phase of interpretation involves a systematic analysis of each of the individual measures administered. Because many of the measures comprise multiple subtests, this process involves identifying the unique and shared abilities assessed within the subtests that compose each of the individual tests administered. Consistent with the approach described by Kaufman (1990) for the Wechsler scales and by Sparrow et al. (1984) for the Vineland Adaptive Behavior Scales, we advocate beginning the analysis of individual tests by analyzing the most global and psychometrically robust level (e.g., Full-Scale IQ [FSIQ] or Adaptive Behavior Composite). In this first step, it is essential to recognize the contribution of the variability in the subtests or subdomains underlying the global scores (e.g., statistically and/or clinically significant Verbal IQ [VIQ] and Performance IQ [PIQ] discrepancies, or communication, socialization, daily living skills, and/or motor discrepancies).

Often, a global score may misrepresent an individual's functioning because of the variability of the component scores. Subsequently, we proceed from the most molar (i.e., global score) to the next most robust level of analysis, proceeding systematically to the most molecular level of analysis (i.e., an individual item within a particular subtest). To guide this exploration and prevent interpretations of differences that may be a function of chance, it is critical to use available psychometric data. For example, prior to interpreting a profile of strengths and weaknesses based on a pattern of subtest scores, one must account for the fact that there are differences in the reliabilities of each of the subtests that compose various scales. This is accomplished by determining whether observed subtest scatter is meaningful. In both research and clinical settings, the evaluator must address both statistical and clinical significance. The latter case involves the clinician's examining the normative data to determine whether a particular degree of variability is markedly unusual. A common fallacy in test interpretation is that statistical significance is viewed as clinically meaningful, even when 40% of the population may evidence a statistically significant level of variability.

A further caution at the level of individual test analysis is to employ developmental knowledge to inform the interpretation of particular patterns of subtest variability. Specifically, one must be sensitive to the fact that individual subtests on a given instrument may purportedly reflect the *same* underlying abilities at *different* developmental levels but be assessed with tasks that, at least on the surface, appear quite distinct. This type of discontinuity arises on the Stanford Binet Intelligence Scales, fifth edition (SB5; Roid, 2003) when assessing verbal reasoning. At Verbal Level 2, the child is asked to describe the cause and effect of events depicted in pictures, whereas at Verbal 3 the child must sort plastic chips with pictures on them into meaningful categories. Alternatively, individual subtests may assess *different* underlying abilities at different developmental levels but make use of tasks that on the surface appear similar. For example, on the Vocabulary subtests of the Weschler Preschool and Primary Scale of Intelligence, third edition (WPPSI-III; Wechsler, 2002) and the Weschler Intelligence Scale for Children, fourth edition (WISC-IV; Wechsler, 2003), the child initially names pictures, and then must make a shift to generating definitions, a qualitative change in task demands.

Employing a Comprehensive Psychological Assessment approach increases the level of interpretive complexity, in part because of a lack of empirical guidelines for synthesizing information across different tests. Thus, when there is variability in the information obtained across two or more tests, there are no empirical data to guide the deter-

mination of whether the variability is statistically or clinically meaningful. The interpreter must rely on his or her knowledge of the specific task demands of and latent abilities assessed by the different tests. This knowledge must be complemented by a grasp of the contextual influences present when each of the tasks was administered. To help clarify discrepant information about a specific ability, it is often valuable to administer additional measures that illuminate the specific ability with greater precision.

The increase in journals dedicated to research on measurement and assessment should provide an additional source of guidance on interpreting test information. For example, studies employing comprehensive assessment approaches with large numbers of subjects provide important information about patterns of functioning evidenced by individuals with specific disorders, such as learning disabilities or neurological dysfunction (see Kaufman, 1994). Contextual factors to be considered in evaluating performance on multiple measures include not only influences evident in the testing situation, but also available background information and a profile of the individual's functioning within the developmental systems levels. For example, when evaluating an individual with suspected depression, it is critical to consider the salient developmental challenges in which the individual is engaged (e.g., peer relations and individuation in adolescence), developmentally appropriate modes of expression (e.g., capacities for affective expression, attention, behavioral control), and domains of functioning known to influence the onset and maintenance of depression (e.g., social support, life events).

Once a parsimonious understanding of the individual's functioning across the relevant domains is achieved and appropriate recommendations are determined, it is critical to communicate this information to the pertinent individuals in the applicable levels of the individual's developmental system. Often, an exquisite evaluation is conducted, resulting in interpretations and recommendations that offer great potential for assistance to the individual, but the results are communicated inadequately or in a manner that interferes with the implementation of the recommendations. Even when the individual receiving the recommendation agrees with the evaluator, failure to implement recommendations may occur because the recipient fails to understand the findings on which the recommendations are based. When an understanding of the relation of the findings to the recommendations is achieved, the intervenors can generalize the bases of the recommendations to new situations. A second difficulty emerges when the individual receiving the recommendations understands the findings and agrees with the recommendations, but does not have the skills or knowledge to communicate the findings to the appropriate agents within the developmental systems levels in which the individual assessed will require intervention. Thus, it is incumbent on the evaluator to take the time to make certain that the pertinent individuals in the developmental systems levels understand the findings and the relation of the findings to the recommendations. In addition, more often than not, recipients of the information will require guidelines and support to ensure implementation of the recommendations they accept.

RECENT ADVANCES AND DIRECTIONS FOR FUTURE RESEARCH

Many of the directions for future research offered in the first edition of this volume a decade ago (Sparrow et al., 1995) are still relevant. It is our hope that by highlighting areas in which there have been advances that can be applied to the Comprehensive Psychological Assessment model as well as areas in which there is current momentum, we can generate directions for future research that have the potential for being realized in the next decade. In many respects, the assessment process is one that theorists, empiricists, and practitioners require to pursue individual and joint agendas aimed at understanding individual functioning within multilevel contexts throughout the course of development, as well as the identification of processes involved in normative and psychopathological development. The shared need for well-articulated assessment models, developmentally sensitive instrumentation, and rigorous approaches to the interpretation of findings should provide the impetus for future innovations.

In our Comprehensive Psychological Assessment model, we discuss the importance of understanding the interplay among multiple domains within the individual and multiple contextual levels as well as transactions between the individual and contextual levels. There have been many advances that facilitate the goal of understanding these complex systems: (1) refined characterization of specific domains of individual functioning and ecological levels that have led to improved instrumentation, (2) new statistical methods that allow for more sophisticated understanding of the psychometric properties of instruments and their applicability in different subpopulations, and (3) new integrative approaches to standardization that allow improved interpretation of findings across instruments and domains.

Researchers and clinicians have contributed to increasingly sophisticated conceptualizations of multiple domains of individual functioning such as cognition, language, academic skills, and socioemotional functioning as well as levels of the ecological system such as families and peers, institutions, communities, and culture. There has been a corresponding expansion of innovative methods for evaluating both individual functioning and multilevel, nested contexts. In terms of individual functioning, we have highlighted the advances made in areas such as cognition and acquisition of academic skills. For example, there are new standardized, norm-referenced measures available to assess attention and executive functions (e.g., D-KEFS: Delis et al., 2001; BRIEF-Preschool Version: Gioia et al., 2003; BRIEF: Gioia et al., 2000; NEPSY: Korkman et al., 1998) and underlying reading abilities (e.g., CTOPP: Wagner et al., 1999). Another area that has seen dramatic instrument development is the domain of social-emotional development and psychopathology focused on young children (Carter, Briggs-Gowan, & Davis, 2004; DelCarmen-Wiggins & Carter, 2004). Consistent with measures available for older children, the majority of new instruments involve problem/competence checklists and diagnostic interviews. However, other innovations are also evident in those structured observational systems that have been developed for use with specific populations (ADOS: Lord et al., 2000; DB-DOS: Wakschlag et al., 2002, in press).

With respect to nested ecologies, researchers have continued to systematically measure parent-child interactions and peer relationships. Newer developments have also arisen to meet the need to better characterize the quality of out-of-home environments such as day care, Head Start, and schools as well as the quality of caregiver-child relationships. Assessment of neighborhoods has also become possible with integration of observational, ethnographic, demographic, and self-report instruments (Leventhal & Brooks-Gunn, 2003). These measures are still predominantly being used for research purposes. However, as research increasingly incorporates hypotheses about the role of contextual levels on individual functioning and needs to make use of such measures, it is likely that additional progress in measurement development will be fostered, perhaps even with new applications fitting for clinical use.

Although these developments are encouraging, there are other arenas in which less progress has been made. In particular, in our previous chapter (Sparrow et al., 1995), we urged that enhanced conceptualization, methods, and measurement of cognition and adaptive functioning at the low end of the spectrum were needed. Because of the limited number of appropriate items at the low end of many assessment instruments, floor effects limit our ability to generate a meaningful profile of strengths and weaknesses. These issues continue to be relevant at this point in time, and the paucity of sensitive, developmentally appropriate measures leads to circumscribed understanding of these individuals, their ecologies, and how best to address the needs of these individuals across the life span.

Statistical methods that inform developmentally sensitive psychometric analysis (e.g., Rasch scaling) as well as methods of multigroup modeling to examine structural invariance, or the comparability of factor structure, across age and cultural groups are currently in use to improve the development and limits of a wide range of instruments (Little, 1997). To the extent that investigators test for structural invariance across age groups it becomes possible to model development over time with greater confidence that the same latent constructs are being assessed at different time/age points. There has been concurrent progress in statistical methods that can be applied to understanding developmental trajectories (Collins & Sayer, 2001). Although expensive, we hope that in the next decade publishing companies might consider longitudinal norming of standardized measures so that empirical findings regarding stability and errors of measurement can inform our understanding of continuity and discontinuity at both the group and individual levels. At present, when an individual is assessed at multiple points in time, it is complicated to determine when scores reflect true developmental change in either a positive or negative direction and when, in contrast to reflecting true developmental change, an apparent change over time is actually a function of retest or practice effects or falls within the measurement error of the instrument.

Another development in the psychometric arena is the increasing number of test instruments that are being normed concurrently with instruments that assess a different domain of functioning. Recent examples are the conorming of the Wechsler Intelligence Scale for Children, third edition (WISC-III) and Wechsler Individual Achievement Test, second edition (WIAT-II) and of the Kaufman Assessment Battery for Children, second edition (KABC-II) with the Vineland Adaptive Behavior Scales, second edition (Vineland-II). We hope that this is a persistent trend because interpreting relative strengths and weaknesses across domains and characterizing profiles of functioning across domains is greatly facilitated by the use of a shared normative sample. That is, with conorming, one has greater confidence that a standard score of 100 on test A is comparable to a standard score of 100 on test B.

Related to the issue of conorming is improving the ability to engage in profile analysis; there have been recent efforts to develop new methods for aggregating data from multiple informants and methods that go beyond shared variance approaches and take into consideration the value of different measures for obtaining information about children in different contexts (Kraemer et al., 2003).

CONCLUSION

There is much to be enthusiastic about in the field of assessment and measurement, with the development of new measures that have stronger conceptual and psychometric properties, sophisticated statistical methods, and empirically informed approaches for integrating data across methods, informants, and time. Most researchers and clinicians have an implicit approach to assessment that guides their work, but there are few arenas in which explicit examination of the underpinnings and process of assessment approaches are examined. We have found that the process of articulating a working model or conceptual framework for Comprehensive Psychological Assessment facilitates a more systematic approach to measurement selection, data collection, and interpretation in both clinical and research settings. Just as the tenets of developmental psychopathology have influenced the Comprehensive Psychological Assessment model presented in this chapter, it is likely that advances in the field of assessment will contribute to a richer understanding of developmental psychopathology. Ultimately, pursuit of a multidimensional, multilevel, and dynamic perspective on individual functioning should result in increased knowledge about development in normative and psychopathological populations as well as enhance the success of intervention efforts that promote mental health and well-being.

REFERENCES

Achenbach, T. M. (2001). *Child Behavior Checklist for ages 6–18 (CBCL/6–18)*. Burlington: University of Vermont, Research Center for Children, Youth, and Families.

Achenbach, T. M., & Rescorla, L. (2000). *Child Behavior Checklist for ages 1½–5 (CBCL/1½ to 5)*. Burlington: University of Vermont, Research Center for Children, Youth, and Families.

American Association on Mental Retardation. (2002). *Mental retardation: Definition, classification, and system of supports* (10th ed.). Washington, DC: Author.

American Psychiatric Association. (1994). *Diagnostic and statistical manual of mental disorders* (4th ed.). Washington, DC: Author.

American Psychological Association. (2002). *Guidelines on multicultural education, training, research, practice, and organizational change for psychologists*. Washington, DC: Author.

Angold, A., Cox, A., Prendergast, M., Rutter, M., & Simonoff, E. (1987). *The Child and Adolescent Psychiatric Assessment (CAPA)*. London: MRC Child Psychiatry Unit, Institute of Psychiatry.

Atkinson, R. C., & Shiffrin, R. M. (1968). Human memory: A proposed system and its control processes. In K. W. Spence & J. T. Spence (Eds.), *The psychology of learning and motivation* (Vol. 2, pp. 88–195). Oxford: Academic Press.

Baddeley, A. (1992). Working memory. *Science, 255,* 556–559.

Battaglia, A., & Carey, J. C. (2003). Diagnostic evaluation of developmental delay/mental retardation: An overview. *American Journal of Medical Genetics: Pt. C. Seminars in Medical Genetics, 117*(1), 3–14.

Beck, S. J. (1944). *Rorschach's test: Vol. I. Basic processes*. Oxford: Grune & Stratton.

Beitchman, J. H., Wilson, B., & Johnson, C. J. (2001). Fourteen year follow-up of speech/language-impaired and control children: Psychiatric outcome. *Journal of the American Academy of Child and Adolescent Psychiatry, 40*(1), 75–82.

Bellack, A. S., & Hersen, M. (1980). *Introduction to clinical psychology*. New York: Grune & Stratton.

Belsky, J., & Fearon, R. M. P. (2002). Infant-mother attachment security, contextual risk, and early development: A moderational analysis. *Development and Psychopathology, 14*(2), 293–310.

Benasich, A. A., Curtiss, S., & Tallal, P. (1993). Language, learning and behavioral disturbances in childhood: A longitudinal perspective. *Journal of the American Academy of Child and Adolescent Psychiatry, 32*(3), 585–594.

Betancourt, H., & Lopez, S. R. (1993). The study of culture, ethnicity, and race in American psychology. *American Psychologist, 48*(6), 629–637.

Biederman, J., Hirshfeld, D. R., Rosenbaum, J. F., Herot, C., Friedman, D., Snidman, N., et al. (2001). Further evidence of the association between behavioral inhibition and social anxiety in children. *American Journal of Psychiatry, 158*(1), 49–57.

Binet, A., & Simon, J. (1905). Methodes nouvelles pour le diagnostic du niveau-intellectuel des anormaux. *L'Annee Psychologique, 11,* 191–244.

Bird, H. R., Andrews, H., Schwab-Stone, M., Goodman, S., Dulcan, M., Richters, J., et al. (1996). Global measures of impairment for epidemiologic and clinical use with children and adolescents. *International Journal of Methods in Psychiatric Research, 6,* 295–307.

Bird, H. R., Yager, T. J., Stagheeza, B., Gould, M. S., Canino, G., & Rubio-Stipec, M. (1990). Impairment in the epidemiological measurement of childhood psychopathology in the community. *Journal of the American Academy of Child and Adolescent Psychiatry, 29,* 796–803.

Black, D., Gates, G., Sanders, S., & Taylor, L. (2000). Demographics of the gay and lesbian population in the United States: Evidence from available systematic data sources. *Demography, 37*(2), 139–154.

Boyce, W. T., Frank, E., Jensen, P. S., Kessler, R. C., Nelson, C. A., Steinberg, L., et al. (1998). Social context in developmental psychopathology: Recommendations for future research from the MacArthur Network on Psychopathology and Development. *Development and Psychopathology, 10,* 143–164.

Briggs-Gowan, M. J., & Carter, A. S. (1998). Preliminary acceptability and psychometrics of the Infant-Toddler Social and Emotional Assessment (ITSEA): A new adult-report questionnaire. *Infant Mental Health Journal, 19*(4), 422–445.

Bronfenbrenner, U. (1977). Toward an experimental ecology of human development. *American Psychologist, 32*(7), 513–531.

Bronfenbrenner, U. (1986). Ecology of the family as a context for human development: Research perspectives. *Developmental Psychology, 22*(6), 723–742.

Cabeza, R., & Nyberg, L. (2003). Special issue on functional neuroimaging of memory. *Neuropsychologist, 41,* 241–244.

Campbell, D. T., & Fiske, D. W. (1959). Convergent and discriminant validations by the multitrait-multimethod matrix. *Psychological Bulletin, 56,* 81–105.

Canino, G., Costello, E. J., & Angold, A. (1999). Assessing functional impairment for child mental health services research: A review of measures. *Journal of Mental Health Services, 1,* 93–108.

Carroll, J. B. (2000). Commentary on profile analysis. *School Psychology Quarterly, 15*(4), 449–456.

Carter, A. S., Briggs-Gowan, M. J., & Davis, N. (2004). Assessment of young children's social-emotional development and psychopathology: Recent advances and recommendations for practice. *Journal of Child Psychology and Psychiatry, 45*(1), 109–134.

Carter, A. S., Briggs-Gowan, M. J., Jones, S. M., & Little, T. D. (2003). The Infant-Toddler Social and Emotional Assessment (ITSEA): Factor structure, reliability, and validity. *Journal of Abnormal Child Psychology, 31*(5), 495–514.

Carter, A. S., & Murdock, K. K. (2001). The family as a context of psychological functioning. In E. L. Grigorenko & R. J. Sternberg (Eds.), *Family environment and intellectual functioning: A life-span perspective* (pp. 1–22). Mahwah, NJ: Erlbaum.

Carter, A. S., Volkmar, F. R., Sparrow, S. S., Wang, J. J., Lord, C., Dawson, G., et al. (1998). The Vineland Adaptive Behavior Scales: Supplementary norms for individuals with Autism. *Journal of Autism and Developmental Disorders, 28*(4), 287–302.

Caspi, A., Sugden, K., & Moffitt, T. E. (2003). Influence of life stress on depression: Moderation by a polymorphism in the 5-HTT gene. *Science, 301,* 386–389.

Chapman, N. H., Raskind, W. H., Thomson, J. B., Berninger, V. W., & Wijsman, E. M. (2003). Segregation analysis of phenotypic components of learning disabilities: Vol. II. Phonological decoding. *American Journal of Medical Genetics: Pt. B. Neuropsychiatric Genetics, 121*(1), 60–70.

Christensen, M., Emde, R. N., & Fleming, C. (2004). Cultural perspectives for assessing infants and young children. In R. DelCarmen-Wiggins & A. S. Carter (Eds.), *Handbook of infant, toddler, and preschool mental health assessment* (pp. 7–23). New York: Oxford University Press.

Cicchetti, D. (1984). The emergence of developmental psychopathology. *Child Development, 55*(1), 1–7.

Cicchetti, D. (1990). A historical perspective on the discipline of developmental psychopathology. In J. E. Rolf, A. S. Masten, D. Cicchetti, K. H. Nuchterlein, & S. Weintraub (Eds.), *Risk and protective factors in the development of psychopathology* (pp. 2–28). New York: Cambridge University Press.

Cicchetti, D., & Blender, J. A. (2004). A multiple-levels-of-analysis approach to the study of developmental processes in maltreated children. *PNAS, 101*(50), 17325–17326.

Cicchetti, D., & Dawson, G. (2002). Multiple levels of analysis [Special issue: Multiple levels of analysis, Editorial]. *Development and Psychopathology, 14*(3), 417–420.

Cicchetti, D., & Sroufe, L. A. (2000). The past as prologue to the future: The times they've been a-changin'. *Development and Psychopathology, 12*(3), 255–264.

Cicchetti, D., Toth, S. L., & Maughan, A. (2000). An ecological-transactional model of child maltreatment. In A. J. Sameroff, M. Lewis, & S. M. Miller (Eds.), *Handbook of developmental psychopathology* (2nd ed., pp. 689–722). Dordrecht, The Netherlands: Kluwer Academic.

Cole, P. M., Martin, S. E., & Dennis, T. A. (2004). Emotional regulation as a scientific construct: Methodological challenges and directions for child development research. *Child Development, 75*(2), 317–333.

Collins, L., & Sayer, A. G. (Eds.). (2001). *New methods for the analysis of change*. Washington, DC: American Psychological Association.

Connolly, A. J. (1988). *KeyMath-Revised: A diagnostic inventory of essential mathematics.* Circle Pines, MN: American Guidance Service.

Costello, J., Mustillo, S., Erkanli, A., Keeler, G., & Angold, A. (2003). Prevalence and development of psychiatric disorders in childhood and adolescence. *Archives of General Psychiatry, 60*(8), 837–844.

Cummings, E. M., & Davies, P. T. (1994). *Children and marital conflict: The impact of family dispute and resolution.* New York: Guilford Press.

Cummings, E. M., & Davies, P. T. (2002). Effects of marital conflict on children: Recent advances and emerging themes in process-oriented research. *Journal of Child Psychology and Psychiatry and Allied Disciplines, 43*(1), 31–63.

Davison, M. L., & Kuang, H. (2000). Profile patterns: Research and professional interpretation. *School Psychology Quarterly, 15*(4), 457–464.

DelCarmen-Wiggins, R., & Carter, A. (Eds.). (2004). *Handbook of infant, toddler, and preschool mental health assessment.* New York: Oxford University Press.

Delis, D. C., Kaplan, E., & Kramer, J. H. (2001). *Delis-Kaplan Executive Function System.* San Antonio, TX: Psychological Corporation.

Denham, S. A., Blair, K. A., DeMulder, E., Levitas, J., Sawyer, K., Auerbach-Major, S., et al. (2003). Preschool emotional competence: Pathway to social competence? *Child Development, 74*(1), 238–256.

Dressler, W. W. (1985). Extended family relationships, social support, and mental health in a southern Black community. *Journal of Health and Social Behavior, 26*(1), 39–48.

Dunn, L. M., & Dunn, L. M. (1981). *Peabody Picture Vocabulary Test-Revised.* Circle Pines, MN: American Guidance Service.

Dykens, E. M., Hodapp, R. M., & Leckman, J. F. (1987). Strengths and weaknesses in the intellectual functioning of males with fragile X syndrome. *American Journal of Mental Deficiency, 92*(2), 234–236.

Egger, H. L., & Angold, A. (2004). The Preschool Age Psychiatric Assessment (PAPA): A structured parent interview for diagnosing psychiatric disorders in preschool children. In R. DelCarmen-Wiggins & A. S. Carter (Eds.), *Handbook of infant, toddler, and preschool mental health assessment* (pp. 223–243). New York: Oxford University Press.

Emde, R. N., Wolf, D. P., & Oppenheim, D. (2003). *Revealing the inner worlds of young children: The MacArthur Story Stem Battery and Parent-Child Narratives.* New York: Oxford University Press.

Engle, R. W., Tuholski, S. W., & Laughlin, J. E. (1999). Working memory, short-term memory, and general fluid intelligence: A latent-variable approach. *Journal of Experimental Psychology, 128*(3), 309–331.

Exner, J. E., Jr. (1991). *The Rorschach: A comprehensive system: Vol. 2. Interpretation* (2nd ed.). Oxford: Wiley.

Flanagan, D. P., & Kaufman, A. S. (2004). *Essentials of WISC-IV assessment.* Hoboken, NJ: Wiley.

Flanagan, D. P., & Ortiz, S. O. (2001). *Essentials of cross-battery assessment.* New York: Wiley.

Flavell, J. H., Miller, P. H., & Miller, S. A. (2002). *Cognitive development* (4th ed.). Englewood Cliffs, NJ: Prentice-Hall.

Fletcher, J. M. (1985). External validation of learning disability typologies. In B. P. Rourke (Ed.), *Neuropsychology of learning disabilities: Essentials of subtype analysis* (pp. 187–211). New York: Guilford Press.

Friedman, S. L., & Amadeo, J. (1999). The child-care environment: Conceptualizations, assessments, and issues. In S. L. Friedman & T. D. Wachs (Eds.), *Measuring environment across the life span: Emerging methods and concepts* (pp. 127–165). Washington, DC: American Psychological Association.

Galton, F. (1892). Classification of men according to their natural gifts. In F. Galton (Ed.), *Hereditary genius: An inquiry into its laws and consequences* (pp. 12–32). New York: Macmillan.

Garcia Coll, C., Akerman, A., & Cicchetti, D. (2000). Cultural influences on developmental processes and outcomes: Implications for the study of development and psychopathology. *Development and Psychopathology, 12*(3), 333–356.

Garcia Coll, C., & Magnuson, K. (2000). Cultural differences as sources of developmental vulnerabilities and resources. In J. P. Shonkoff & S. J. Meisels (Eds.), *Handbook of early childhood intervention* (2nd ed., pp. 94–114). New York: Cambridge University Press.

Gioia, G. A., Espy, K. A., & Isquith, P. K. (2003). *Behavior Rating Inventory of Executive Function: Professional manual.* Lutz, FL: Psychological Assessment Resources.

Gioia, G. A., Isquith, P. K., Guy, S. C., & Kenworthy, L. (2000). *Behavior Rating Inventory of Executive Function: Professional manual.* Odessa, FL: Psychological Assessment Resources.

Gorman-Smith, D., & Tolan, P. (1998). The role of exposure to community violence and developmental problems among inner-city youth. *Development and Psychopathology, 10*(1), 101–116.

Graham, J. R. (1991). *MMPI-2: Assessing personality and psychopathology.* New York: Oxford University Press.

Grigorenko, E. L., Wood, F. B., Meyer, M. S., Hart, L. A., Speed, W. C., Shuster, A., et al. (1997). Susceptibility loci for distinct components of developmental dyslexia on chromosomes 6 and 15. *American Journal of Human Genetics, 60*(1), 27–39.

Gunnar, M. R., Morison, S. J., Chisholm, K., & Schuder, M. (2001). Salivary cortisol levels in children adopted from Romanian orphanages. *Development and Psychopathology, 13*(3), 611–628.

Hayward, C., Killen, J. D., Kraemer, H. C., & Taylor, C. B. (1998). Linking self-reported childhood behavioral inhibition to adolescent social phobia. *Journal of the American Academy of Child and Adolescent Psychiatry, 37,* 1308–1316.

Jenkins, S., Bax, M., & Hart, H. (1980). Behaviour problems in pre-school children. *Journal of Child Psychology and Psychiatry, 21*(1), 5–17.

Johnston, C., & Murray, C. (2003). Incremental validity in the psychological assessment of children and adolescents. *Psychological Assessment, 15*(4), 496–507.

Kaufman, A. S. (1983). Intelligence: Old concepts, new perspective. In G. W. Hynd (Ed.), *The school psychologist: An introduction* (pp. 95–117). Syracuse, NY: Syracuse University Press.

Kaufman, A. S. (1990). *Assessing adolescent and adult intelligence.* Needham Heights, MA: Allyn & Bacon.

Kaufman, A. S. (1994). *Intelligent testing with the WISC-III.* Oxford: Wiley.

Kaufman, A. S., & Kaufman, N. L. (1993). *Kaufman Adolescent and Adult Intelligence Test (KAIT).* Circle Pines, MN: American Guidance Service.

Kaufman, A. S., & Kaufman, N. L. (2004). *Kaufman Assessment Battery for Children (KABC-II)* (2nd ed.). Circle Pines, MN: American Guidance Service.

Kaufman, A. S., & Lichtenberger, E. O. (1999). *Essentials of WAIS-III assessment.* New York: Wiley.

Kline, R. B. (1998). *Principles and practices of structural equation modeling.* New York: Guilford Press.

Klopfer, B., & Donaldson, H. H. (1962). *The Rorschach technique: An introductory manual.* New York: Harcourt, Brace.

Kolb, B., & Whishaw, I. Q. (2002). *Fundamentals of human neuropsychology* (5th ed.). New York: Worth/Freeman.

Korkman, M., Kirk, U., & Kemp, S. (1998). *NEPSY: A developmental neuropsychological assessment.* San Antonio, TX: Psychological Corporation.

Kraemer, H. C., Measelle, J. R., Ablow, J. C., Essex, M. J., Boyce, W. T., & Kupfer, D. J. (2003). A new approach to integrating data from multiple informants in psychiatric assessment and research: Mixing and matching contexts and perspectives. *American Journal of Psychiatry, 160*(9), 1566–1577.

Leventhal, T., & Brooks-Gunn, J. (2003). Children and youth in neighborhood contexts. *Current Directions in Psychological Science, 12*(1), 27–31.

Lezak, M. D. (1995). *Neuropsychological assessment* (3rd ed.). London: Oxford University Press.

Little, T. D. (1997). Mean and covariance structures (MCAS) analyses of cross-cultural data: Practical and theoretical issues. *Multivariate Behavioral Research, 32,* 53–76.

Lord, C., Risi, S., Lambrecht, L., Cook, E. H., Jr., Leventhal, B. L., DiLavore, P. C., et al. (2000). The Autism Diagnostic Observation Schedule–Generic: A standard measure of social and communication deficits associated with the spectrum of Autism. *Journal of Autism and Developmental Disorders, 30*(3), 205–223.

Lyon, R. (1996). Learning disabilities. *The Future of Children: Special Education for Students with Learning Disabilities, 6*(1), 54–76.

Maloney, M. P., & Ward, M. P. (1976). *Psychological assessment: A conceptual approach.* Oxford: Oxford University Press.

McCain, A. P., Kelley, M. L., & Fishbein, J. (1999). Behavioral screening in well-child care: Validation of the Toddler Behavior Screening Inventory [Special issue: Pediatric mental health services in primary care settings]. *Journal of Pediatric Psychology, 24*(5), 415–422.

McCardle, P., Scarborough, H. S., & Catts, H. W. (2001). Predicting, explaining, and preventing children's reading difficulties. *Learning Disabilities Research and Practice, 16*(4), 230–239.

McGrew, K. S., & Flanagan, D. P. (1998). *The intelligence test desk reference (ITDR): Gf-Gc cross-battery assessment.* Needham Heights, MA: Allyn & Bacon.

Mirsky, A. F., Anthony, B. J., & Duncan, C. C. (1991). Analysis of the elements of attention: A neuropsychological approach. *Neuropsychology Review, 2*(2), 109–145.

Morris, R., Blashfield, R., & Satz, P. (1986). Developmental classification of reading-disabled children. *Journal of Clinical and Experimental Neuropsychology, 8*(4), 371–392.

Pianta, R. C., & Marvin, R. S. (1992). *Manual for classification of the reaction to diagnosis of interview.* Unpublished manual, University of Virginia, Charlottsville.

Pickles, A., Rowe, R., Simonoff, E., Foley, D., Rutter, M., & Silberg, J. (2001). Child psychiatric symptoms and psychosocial impairment: Relationship and prognostic significance. *British Journal of Psychiatry, 179*(3), 230–235.

Pinderhughes, E. (1989). *Understanding race, ethnicity, and power: The key to efficacy in clinical practice.* New York: Free Press.

Plomin, R. (2001). Genetic factors contributing to learning and language delays and disabilities. *Child and Adolescent Psychiatric Clinics of North America, 10*(2), 259–277.

Posner, M. I., & Petersen, S. E. (1990). The attention system of the human brain. *Annual Review of Neuroscience, 13,* 25–42.

Rappaport, D., Gill, M. M., & Schaffer, R. (1968). *Diagnostic psychological testing.* New York: International Universities Press.

Raudenbush, S., Bryk, A., Cheong, Y. F., & Congdon, R. (2000). *HLM5: Hierarchical linear and nonlinear modeling.* Lincolnwood, IL: Scientific Software International.

Reynolds, C., & Kamphaus, R. (1992). *BASC.* Circle Pines, MN: American Guidance Service.

Roid, G. H. (2003). *Stanford-Binet intelligence scales* (5th ed.). Itasca, IL: Riverside.

Rose-Krasnor, L. (1997). The nature of social competence: A theoretical review. *Social Development, 6*(1), 111–135.

Rosenbaum, J. E., Biederman, J., Hirshfeld-Becker, D. R., Kagan, J., Snidman, N., Friedman, D., et al. (2000). A controlled study of behavioral inhibition in children of parents with panic disorder and depression. *American Journal of Psychiatry, 157,* 2002–2020.

Rosenberg, N. A., Pritchard, J. K., Weber, J. L., Cann, H. M., Kidd, K. K., Zhivotovsky, L. A., et al. (2002, December 20). Genetic structure of human populations. *Science, 298,* 2381–2385.

Rothbart, M. K., Posner, M. I., & Hershey, K. L. (1995). Temperament, attention, and developmental psychopathology. In D. Cicchetti & D. J. Cohen (Eds.), *Developmental psychopathology: Vol. 1. Theory and methods* (pp. 315–340). Oxford: Wiley.

Rourke, B. P. (Ed.). (1985). *Neuropsychology of learning disabilities: Essentials of subtype analysis.* New York: Guilford Press.

Ruff, H. A., & Lawson, K. R. (1990). Development of sustained, focused attention in young children during free play. *Developmental Psychology, 26*(1), 85–93.

Ruff, H. A., & Rothbart, M. K. (1996). *Attention in early development: Themes and variations.* New York: Oxford University Press.

Rutter, M. (2005). Environmentally mediated risks for psychopathology: Research strategies and findings. *Journal of the American Academy of Child and Adolescent Psychiatry, 44*(1), 3–18.

Rutter, M., & Maughan, B. (2002). School effectiveness findings: 1979–2002. *Journal of School Psychology, 40,* 451–475.

Sameroff, A., & MacKenzie, M. J. (2003). Research strategies for capturing transactional models of development: The limits of the possible. *Development and Psychopathology, 15*(3), 613–640.

Sameroff, A., Seifer, R., & McDonough, S. C. (2004). Contextual contributors to the assessment of infant mental health. In R. DelCarmen-Wiggins & A. S. Carter (Eds.), *Handbook of infant, toddler, and preschool mental health assessment* (pp. 61–76). New York: Oxford University Press.

Sattler, J. M. (2001). *Assessment of children: Cognitive applications* (4th ed.). La Mesa, CA: Jerome Sattler.

Sayer, A. G., & Cumsille, P. E. (2001). Second-order latent growth models. In L. Collins & A. G. Sayer (Eds.), *New methods for the analysis of change* (pp. 179–200). Washington, DC: American Psychological Association.

Schalock, R. L. (1999). *Adaptive behavior and its measurements.* Washington, DC: American Association on Mental Retardation.

Schultz, R. T. (2005). Developmental deficits in social perception in Autism: The role of the amygdala and fusiform face area. *International Journal of Developmental Neuroscience, 23*(2/3), 125–141.

Schwartz, C. E., Snidman, N., & Kagan, J. (1999). Adolescent social anxiety as an outcome of inhibited temperament in childhood. *Journal of the American Academy of Child and Adolescent Psychiatry, 38*(8), 1008–1015.

Shaffer, D., Fisher, P., Lucas, C. P., Dulcan, M. K., & Schwab-Stone, M. E. (2000). NIMH Diagnostic Interview Schedule for Children Version IV (NIMH DISC-IV): Description, differences from previous versions, and reliability of some common diagnoses. *Journal of the American Academy of Child and Adolescent Psychiatry, 39,* 28–38.

Sheslow, D., & Adams, W. (2003). *Wide range assessment of memory and learning* (2nd ed.). Wilmington, DE: Wide Range.

Silk, J. S., Sessa, F. M., Sheffield Morris, A., Steinberg, L., & Avenevoli, S. (2004). Neighborhood cohesion as a buffer against hostile maternal parenting. *Journal of Family Psychology, 18*(1), 135–146.

Simeonsson, R. J., Leonardi, M., Lollar, D., Bjorck-Akesson, E., Hollenweger, J., & Martinuzzi, A. (2003). Applying the International

Classification of Functioning, Disability and Health (ICF) to measure childhood disability. *Disability and Rehabilitation: An International Multidisciplinary Journal, 25*(11/12), 602–610.

Sparrow, S. S., Balla, D. A., & Cicchetti, D. (1984). *The Vineland Adaptive Behavior Scales: Survey form.* Circle Pines, MN: American Guidance Service.

Sparrow, S. S., Carter, A. S., Racusin, G., & Morris, R. (1995). Comprehensive psychological assessment through the lifespan: A developmental approach. In D. Cicchetti & D. J. Cohen (Eds.), *Handbook of developmental psychopathology: Theory and methods* (pp. 81–105). New York: Wiley.

Sparrow, S. S., Cicchetti, D. V., & Balla, D. A. (2005). *Vineland Adaptive Behavior Scales* (2nd ed.). Circle Pines, MN: American Guidance Service.

Sparrow, S. S., & Davis, S. M. (2000). Recent advances in the assessment of intelligence and cognition. *Journal of Child Psychology and Psychiatry and Allied Disciplines, 41*(1), 117–131.

Squire, L. R., & Schacter, D. L. (2002). *Neuropsychology of memory* (3rd ed.). New York: Guilford Press.

Sternberg, R. J., Wagner, R. K., Williams, W. M., & Horvath, J. A. (1995). Testing common sense. *American Psychologist, 50*(11), 912–927.

Suyemoto, K. L., & Dimas, J. M. (2003). To be included in the multicultural discussion: Check one box only. In J. S. Mio & G. Y. Iwamasa (Eds.), *Culturally diverse mental health: The challenges of research and resistance* (pp. 55–81). New York: Brunner-Routledge.

Temple, C. (1997). *Developmental cognitive neuropsychology.* East Essex, England: Psychology Press.

The Psychological Corporation. (2001). *Wechsler Individual Achievement Test—Second Edition.* San Antonio, TX: Author.

U.S. Census Bureau. (2000). *Census Bureau projects doubling of nation's population by 2001.* Available from U.S. Department of Commerce News at http://www.census.gov/Press Release/www/2000/cb00-05.html.

Wagner, R. K., Torgesen, J. K., & Rashotte, C. A. (1999). *Comprehensive test of phonological processing.* Austin, TX: ProEd.

Wakschlag, L., Leventhal, B., Briggs-Gowan, M., Danis, B., Keenan, K., Hill, C., et al. (in press). Defining the "disruptive" in preschool behavior: What diagnostic observation can teach us. *Clinical Child and Family Psychology Review.*

Wakschlag, L., Leventhal, B., Danis, B., Keenan, K., Egger, H., & Carter, A. (2002). *The Disruptive Behavior Diagnostic Observation Schedule (DB-DOS), Version 1.1.* Unpublished manuscript, University of Chicago.

Watkins, M. W. (2000). Cognitive profile analysis: A shared professional myth. *School Psychology Quarterly, 15*(4), 465–479.

Wechsler, D. (1991). *Wechsler Intelligence Scale for Children* (3rd ed.). San Antonio, TX: Psychological Corporation.

Wechsler, D. (2002). *Wechsler Preschool and Primary Scale of Intelligence* (3rd ed.). San Antonio, TX: Psychological Corporation.

Wechsler, D. (2003). *Wechsler Intelligence Scale for Children* (4th ed.). San Antonio, TX: Psychological Corporation.

Weinfeld, N. S., Ogawa, J. R., & Egeland, B. (2002). Predictability of observed mother-child interaction from preschool to middle childhood in a high-risk sample. *Child Development, 73*(2), 528–543.

Wilson, M. N., & Tolson, T. F. (1990). Familial support in the Black community. *Journal of Clinical Child Psychology, 19*(4), 347–355.

Woodcock, R., & Dahl, M. (1971). *A common scale for the measurement of person ability and test item* (AGS Paper No. 10). Circle Pines, MN: American Guidance Service.

World Health Organization. (1992). *ICD-10: The ICD-10 classification of mental and behavioural disorders: Clinical descriptions and diagnostic guidelines.* Geneva, Switzerland: Author.

Zelazo, P. D., Carter, A., Reznick, J., & Frye, D. (1997). Early development of executive function: A problem-solving framework. *Review of General Psychology, 1*(2), 198–226.

CHAPTER 7

Developmental Pathways

ANDREW PICKLES and JONATHAN HILL

PATHWAYS AS A FRAMEWORK FOR DEVELOPMENTAL PROCESSES

It is a feature of an evolving language, that groups—we scientists among them—take an everyday word, preferably one with exploitable connotations, and subvert its meaning to serve a rather different purpose. For scientists, this achieves certain short-term gains. First, what is thought to be a new concept can be introduced by the use of familiar words, helping in the process of getting the idea understood and accepted. Second, the words are rarely casually chosen, but instead have some meaning in everyday language

that shares something with their new intended use. Analogy has long been recognized as an important means by which new scientific theory becomes accepted (Feyerabend, 1975). In understanding something new, it helps to think in terms of something that we think we already understand. Explicit analogy is, however, surprisingly rare. Explicit analogy is often too stark, the shortcomings too self-evident, and the possible similarities and differences too numerous. Instead, we pick these everyday words and use them metaphorically. Metaphors achieve our immediate aim of giving an impression of the concept we are trying to communicate, but seem to do this without raising critical thought. However, in the longer run, such lack of criticism and resulting imprecision can allow quite different and inconsistent understandings to coexist.

The use of the term "pathway" to describe aspects of development from childhood to adulthood has been one such all too alluring metaphor. It conjures up images of pathways through a landscape of life's trials and tribulations, and implies, without actually saying so, that what we are about as scientists shares much with a distinguished literary tradition. We are like Dickens, except he lacked our theoretical and statistical insight and expertise! However, as we should expect, pathway has been seldom defined, and indeed it is used in several rather different ways. In this chapter, the different meanings of the term are reviewed and illustrated with examples, before going on to a more detailed consideration of the application of a pathways perspective in developmental psychopathology.

We start with a review of the possible features implied by the terms path and pathway and their translation into the understanding of development and psychopathology.

A PATHWAY AS PROTOTYPE OR IDEAL TYPE

The concept of a pathway has proved widely useful in the biological sciences, specifically in relation to development and psychopathology. In common with other terms that allow individuals to be classified, pathways can be proposed as either prototypes or ideal types. Both are selective of the features of reality that are given emphasis; both recognize fuzziness, and both attempt to overcome this vagueness by defining attributes in a clear and precise way. Moreover, both confront individual variability by recognizing individuals who more or less conform to the type. However, ideal types are a thought construct that postulates connections that provide a conceptual unity. Ideal types are concerned with empirical analysis to discover new or better ways of conceptualizing patients and their disorders. By contrast, a prototype consists of a list of attributes and is more concerned with explicating the meaning of a word as used. In this chapter, we are concerned almost exclusively with pathways as an ideal type. Whether developmental pathways are proposed as empirically identifiable constructs or as thought constructs only is less clear.

ELABORATING THE METAPHOR

The developmental pathway is a remarkably productive metaphor. However, its status is not yet clear. It is undoubt-

edly already a useful summary term in the field of development and psychopathology, and findings are often reported in terms of pathways. However, it is not clear whether the concept has yet claimed a place in shaping research questions. The answer in most cases is probably no because it is uncommon for researchers to report that their study questions and designs were shaped by a consideration of the various possibilities generated from a consideration of pathways. Also, generally, developmental pathways are described in terms of a small subset of the large number of questions and ideas that they evoke, suggesting that they have not been employed to push the boundaries of current knowledge.

In this section, we outline the scope of the concept when applied to development; we then provide two illustrations of the principles, before going on to a more detailed consideration.

At its simplest, the idea of the pathway suggests a route that is traveled over time, in which there are constraints over the directions the traveler can take, and there is an ordered sequence of events or experiences; hence, the outcome is to a significant degree predictable. The metaphor opens out, and becomes highly productive, if we envisage a traveler (walker) taking one of a number of possible pathways over a changing terrain, for example, encompassing relatively easy walking before climbing up steep mountainous paths. If developmental pathways resemble such physical paths, we can make predictions, such as that there will be phases of the journey where the path taken by an individual is highly predictable but punctuated by points at which choices are made among different paths. Paths may run in parallel, diverge, and converge; points on a path are both destinations or outcomes and starting points for further development; different paths may arrive at the same destination; the physical characteristics of a path may change considerably, as it crosses different terrains, while remaining the same path. The pathway metaphor also provokes ideas regarding mechanisms in development. For example, there are multiple ways in which decisions regarding which path to take can be made. They can be based on an overview of the ultimate aim or destination of the journey, perhaps using a map, or they may be determined by more immediate factors, such as whether the visible path looks easy or difficult. A path may be chosen because it is desirable, or because it is the only one remaining after others have been rejected, for example, because they seem too risky. Decisions at any one point are also often influenced by the cumulative effects of the journey on the traveler. The weary walker is likely to choose the easier path! Furthermore, the choice of path may be the result of the joint effects of such different mechanisms and may vary as the path is traversed. It may be possible by observing the pathways taken by large numbers of people to identify subgroups who make predictable choices. In other words, under some conditions, use of pathways may provide an indication of a taxonomy of travelers! This is by no means an exhaustive overview of the ways the metaphor of pathways may inform questions in development and psychopathology.

ILLUSTRATIONS

By way of illustration, we present two diagrams that represent the use of pathways in developmental psychopathology. The first (Figure 7.1) is drawn from our own work that examines the impact of childhood sexual abuse on the risk of subsequent adult depression (Hill et al., 2001). The second (Figure 7.2) represents the results of a path analysis of the development of Conduct Disorder symptoms in boys (based

on Morrell & Murray, 2003). We briefly consider each in turn, returning to them later for further consideration.

Figure 7.1 shows how a sequence of experiences in childhood and adulthood is associated with adult depression. From a common starting point (level of risk), the different experiences and choices are used to define paths, the slope of each path reflecting the degree of change in risk of depression its choice results in, and its thickness reflecting how frequently that path is taken by the women of this general population sample. There is no selective display of paths, although those paths that are very rarely taken could be omitted. This diagram clearly emphasizes bifurcation, multiplicity of routes, and distinguishes the size of the effect from the relative frequency of different pathways.

Figure 7.2 is a traditional path diagram commonly associated with the reporting of results from analysis using structural equation modeling (SEM) or an equivalent set of path analysis regressions. From the outset, we are clearly

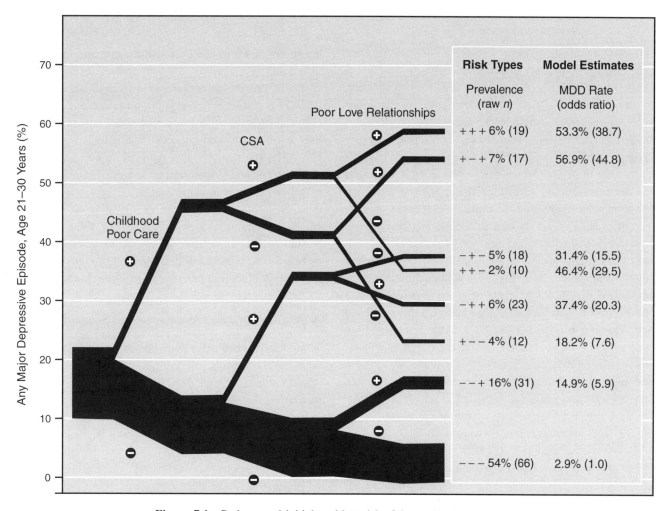

Figure 7.1   Pathways with high and low risk of depression in adulthood.

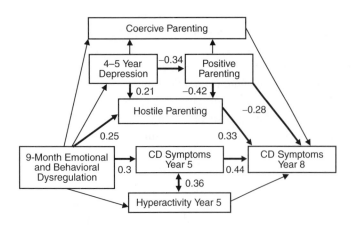

Figure 7.2   Path analysis of development of conduct disorder symptoms in boys. Adapted from "Parenting and the Development of Conduct Disorder and Hyperactive Symptoms in Childhood: A Prospective Longitudinal Study from 2 Months to 8 Years," by J. Morrell and L. Murray, 2003, *Journal of Child Psychology and Psychiatry, 44,* pp. 489–508.

dealing with something quite different. The variables are being considered as continuous and not discrete, and how a path is interpreted in such a diagram depends to a substantial extent on the configuration of other paths, in particular on the connecting paths that have been excluded. Whether a path is included or not commonly rests on a priori theory, the empirical fit of the overall SEM and on the statistical significance of or improvement in fit on adding a particular path. In this diagram, paths significant at the $p < .05$ are shown in bold. When several paths converge on an outcome, it is not explicit, indeed it is no longer true, that a given individual reaches that outcome by means of one path only. Thus, there are three main paths to high conduct symptoms at age 8, and a child with earlier conduct symptoms and exposed to low levels of positive parenting and high levels of hostile parenting may be on all three paths at once. The magnitude of a path is usually described by a standardized path coefficient. What the diagram emphasizes is the relative importance of variables, which is a combination of the magnitude of the effect of that variable and the variability of that variable in the sample; in particular, it emphasizes sequences of important variables by which effects are transmitted forward in time.

Thus, it is clear that although both representations draw on and illustrate developmental pathways, they do so in quite different ways. Before we can assess their relative advantages, we need to explore in more detail the features and implications of supposing a developmental pathway.

FEATURES OF DEVELOPMENTAL PATHWAYS

There are numerous aspects of the metaphor that require interpretation as features of developmental pathways.

Pathways as Deterministic

"A developmental perspective implies that changes in social behavior are related to age in an orderly way" (Patterson, 1993). However, most of us believe development involves rather more than that. Rutter and Rutter (1993) add to this that "change . . . is carried forward in some way that has implications for a person's pattern or level of functioning at some later time." Development thus involves both change over time that follows a pattern common to all, but also interindividual differences and the mechanisms by which such individual differences persist and evolve. The notion of pathways plays an important role in emphasizing both of these aspects of development. Indeed, the restriction in the direction of travel and movement implied by a pathway strongly presupposes persistence. However, it does not necessarily imply persistence of, say, symptoms, but rather, lawful sequences that may involve symptomatic discontinuity.

There are major influences on development, such as whether a child has a Y chromosome, that act as a persistent determinant with respect to some outcomes, such as hormonal status and physical characteristics. However, generally, the concept of a pathway in development is of more use in understanding the nature of continuities that entail some, or even considerable, uncertainties. Then the concept refers to sequences in which a set of circumstances, processes, or behaviors at one time, when contrasted with an alternative set of circumstances, processes, or behaviors, is associated at some later time with an increased likelihood of one outcome rather than another.

A Pathway Implies a Developmental Sequence

That B is reached after A is intrinsic to the concept of a pathway. The strong interpretation when applied to development might be that A has to occur before B can take place, and that A cannot follow B. The pathway concept requires that time passes after A is left and before B is reached. In particular, developmentally it may be the amount of time that passes that is crucial or age-related developmental stages that are the key.

In practice, these ideas are valuable but rarely amenable to such precise application. Certainly, age-related milestones, such as the appearance of attachment behaviors in response to threat at 6 to 9 months, are characteristic of processes in normal development, and the development of particular areas of competence *may* be necessary for others. For example, the ability to solve false belief tasks, taken to provide evidence of the development of a theory of mind, probably precedes and is clearly relevant to social competences that involve taking another's perspective. However, the concept of developmental milestones implies a functional unity that may not be present. In this case, there does not appear to be a general perspective-taking capacity that emerges fully formed. Rather, the same children show different capabilities in different contexts, and different perspective-taking competences appear at different ages (J. Dunn, 1996). The capacity to solve formal tests of theory of mind, such as false belief tests, might be expected to precede the ability to deceive in social interactions, supporting a pathway concept. However, children who fail false belief tests show deception in social interactions in some contexts (Newton, 1994).

In spite of these complexities, there are clearly developmental progressions in the range and sophistication of children's capacities to manage competing demands or rights within social interactions, and these are highly relevant to the development of psychopathology. For example, physical aggression reported by parents appears toward the end of the 1st year of life and increases until around 2 years of age and then declines (Tremblay et al., 1999). This decline is probably in part related to the development of alternative methods of solving social conflict. J. Dunn, Slomkowski, Donelan-McCall, and Herrera (1995) found that at age 33 months, children were less able when angry or distressed than at other times to sustain their reasoning powers, but by 47 months, when assessed with siblings, they were more capable of using reasoned argument when they were angry. Even if it could be shown that a failure to develop the capacity to use reason during conflict predicted persistence of aggression, or predicted its increase, it would fall short of the requirement that A has to precede B. However, it would support the role of an age-related normal developmental milestone as a protective factor against persistent aggression.

Developmental Pathways as Prediction

The metaphor of the pathway indicates that we know where it goes, what influences the traveler, and how the traveler is influenced. In other words, it implies simultaneously prediction and explanation. However, developmental investigations of psychopathology may fail to provide these, at least at the outset. This is particularly the case where a

pathway is thought of as an orderly sequence of behaviors or symptoms over time. For example, a range of taxonomies of antisocial pathways during childhood have been advanced (Loeber, 1991; Moffitt, 1993; D. F. Nagin & Tremblay, 1999), and several recent studies have sought to refine them (e.g., D. F. Nagin & Tremblay, 2001). This has been done without proposing mechanisms. Nevertheless, the ultimate aim of refining descriptive taxonomies of pathways is to provide an improved characterization of the classes of individuals against which to set the investigation of mechanism.

In straightforward taxonomies, symptoms seen at one time are predictive of the same or analogous symptoms at a later time. However, pathways may be composed of orderly change in intensity or type of symptoms, for example, with age (D. F. Nagin & Tremblay, 2001) or type of symptom. That orderly change may result in an evolution in symptoms that extend into other domains than those of the early symptoms. In criminology, among adolescents this is often viewed as an accumulation process as individuals extend their repertoire of types of crime. This leads to the idea that the variety of crimes rather than the frequency of crimes should be used to measure progress along a criminal pathway. However, if we extend the time frame, both starting earlier and following further into adulthood, then we see some symptoms that become less prominent while others are acquired that could be regarded as drawn from a rather different domain. Moffitt (1994, p. 12) describes such potential heterotypic continuity in the sequence "biting and hitting at age 4, shoplifting and truancy at 10, selling drugs and stealing cars at 16, robbery and rape at 22, and fraud and child abuse at 30." We are able to characterize some of the distinctive features of those on different pathways, and from these features hypothesize about the potential mechanisms that form the link in the pathway. In this case, Moffitt and colleagues (Moffitt, 1993; Moffitt, Caspi, Dickson, Silva, & Stanton, 1996) suggest that the underlying mechanisms include neuropsychological dysfunction, impaired linguistic skills, impulsivity, and a hostile stance toward others.

Pathways as Distinct

A direct translation of the idea of a pathway refers to an individual who is following one route, and by definition cannot be following others. This applies clearly to circumstances where a person is either in or not in some state, or to binary choices. For example, a child is either in school or out of school, and a girl is either pregnant or not pregnant. These states are therefore candidates for markers or choice points on a pathway.

However, an individual's circumstances or characteristics are multifaceted. For example, the same child can be depressed and good at schoolwork. One pathway may be envisaged in which childhood depression is a factor that links earlier to later development, and academic performance may be a factor that links a different set of early developmental features to later ones. Here, then, a pathway is conceived of as a sequence of parallel processes, symptoms, or events, several of which may apply to any one person. In the same way, there are numerous metabolic pathways that may be in different states within the same individual. This fundamental distinction between pathways that are mutually exclusive and differentiate individuals, and ones that refer to sequences of processes or qualities, may in many respects become blurred. For example, teenage pregnancy may matter in development because of its association with loss of education, work opportunities, or social support. Each of these may have the predominant role in relation to subsequent developments, and each of these varies both among those teenagers who are pregnant and those who are not. We might therefore conclude that what matters is a particular aspect of functioning rather than an event that either does or does not happen, in which case, the concept of the pathway shifts from one that entails individuals to one that entails sequences of processes. This allows for such possibilities that a pathway may be pathological for some but not for others, a possibility clearly falling within the capacity of the physical pathway metaphor where fitter and more experienced individuals may choose a route that would be for others too strenuous. Conversely, taking the example of childhood depression and academic performance, each of these may be thought of as contributing to two pathways of succeeding processes, or to the generation of four groups representing four discrete person-based pathways.

Continuity Punctuated by Change

Developmental approaches almost always look to early childhood as the shaper of all that follows, that most of what we observe is a maturational unfolding. However, the concept of a pathway draws our attention to the possibility that different influences may operate at different times, or the same influence may operate differently at different times, and that discrete events may have long-term consequences. Changes, reflected in clear breaks with the past, often referred to as turning points, are natural elements of a pathways model.

In developmental neurobiology, pathways have a role both as a microlevel literal description and as a macrolevel metaphor at the level of the development of the whole organism. A macrolevel normal developmental pathway requires that the early growth of neuronal pathways in the brain and their subsequent trimming occur appropriately. This involves both a propitious set of genes and exposure to the right environmental stimuli at the right time. Failure to acquire experience and skills during the period when neuronal trimming relevant to that brain capacity is occurring can be permanently disabling. This was vividly demonstrated by Hubel and Wiesel's experiments into the effects on the development of the visual cortex of cats and monkeys of the timing of visual stimulus. Animals reared with one eye sutured closed had no vision in that eye and had shrinkage of the lateral geniculate body serving that eye, diminution in the number of connections to the visual cortex, and in the cortex a shift in the number of connections from the deprived to the nondeprived eye (Hubel, Wiesel, & LeVay, 1976). Crucially, this effect was seen only if the visual deprivation occurred in the first 3 months. After that, even prolonged deprivation had no discernable effect. The general principle suggested by these experiments is that neuronal connections can be modulated by environmental influences during a critical period of postnatal development. Hubel and Wiesel speculated that other aspects of brain functioning, such as language, complex perceptual tasks, learning, memory, and personality, may have different programs of development that are similarly sensitive to specific environmental inputs at some points, but not at others. Such sensitivity of the nervous system to the effects of experience may represent the fundamental mechanism by which the organism adapts to its environment during the period of growth and development.

Studies of the effects of early postnatal disruptions of the mother-infant relationship in rodents and nonhuman primates have amply supported this view. In rodents, early separation from mother leads to persistent alterations in neuroendocrine functioning (Sanchez, Ladd, & Plotsky, 2001). Furthermore, these alterations are accompanied by behavioral changes. Huot, Thrivikraman, Meaney, and Plotsky (2001) found that in rats, early postnatal separation was associated with later preference for alcohol (ethanol). This effect was mediated via altered corticosteroid responses to stress. The mechanisms are complex and are likely to involve gene expression and altered density of neurons in structures such as the hippocampus (Huot, Plotsky, Lenox, & McNamara, 2002). Two points are particularly relevant to the concept of pathways. First, postnatal maternal separation has different effects on subsequent neuroendocrine function, depending on its timing. Second, although the effects of maternal separation are long-lasting and mediated via genetic mechanisms, subsequent experiences can influence some aspects of the outcome. Rats exposed to postnatal separation and subsequently provided with environmental enrichment showed reversal of the hypothalamic-pituitary-adrenal (HPA) and behavioral responses to stress, but not of the expression of corticotrophin-releasing factor (CRF) mRNA (Francis, Diorio, Plotsky, & Meaney, 2002).

Extensive work into Old World rhesus monkeys has revealed the profound effects of early disruption of the mother-infant relationship. Mothers exposed to unpredictable foraging regimes become less responsive to their offspring, who develop insecure patterns of attachment (Rosenblum & Andrews, 1994). Over time, they become less socially competent, more fearful, are hyperresponsive to stressful stimuli, and show persistent alterations of corticotrophin-releasing factor, somatostatin and biogenic amines in the cerebrospinal fluid (Coplan et al., 1998). Widespread and persistent effects on behaviors and neuroendocrine functioning following separation of rhesus monkeys from their mothers have also been demonstrated.

Bolton, Park, Higgins, Griffiths, and Pickles (2002) found that among children with tuberous sclerosis, almost all those with temporal lobe epilepsy with onset before 15 months later met diagnostic criteria for Autism, whereas this was rare among other children with tuberous sclerosis, even those with temporal lobe epilepsy, provided onset was later. These researchers speculated that the epilepsy disrupted selective brain development during the period when children would normally be acquiring metarepresentational and theory of mind skills.

Particular events may also have long-term consequences if they open or close opportunities. Occasionally, these are quite formal and explicit, such as the substantial employment restrictions placed on ex-offenders in many U.S. states (Dale, 1976). This represents an extreme element of the potentially more pervasive problem of labeling. Loeber and Leblanc (1990) argued that labeling theory is the only truly developmental criminological theory. Primary deviance may arise for a multitude of specific reasons, but once enacted, secondary deviance follows as an adaptive response to societal reaction to this primary deviance. The original causes recede into the past, to be replaced by contemporaneous societal disapprobation, degradation, and isolation. Link (Link, Cullen, Struening, Shrout, & Dohrenwend, 1989) argues that in the mental health context, the negative consequences occur through their impact on self-image, expectations of rejection, and withdrawal,

leaving the individual poorly equipped to deal with life's vicissitudes. Secondary deviance thus becomes likely. The emphasis is incremental, consistent with a stepping-stone perspective and of a pathway that constrains possibilities for positive change.

Pathway Networks and Equifinality

Almost any geographical map shows a network of paths. Our discussion up till now has largely presupposed that different paths diverge. Although that may be almost a logical necessity when considering one-step links from a single origin, this is by no means the case for the longer journey. Pathways offering the opportunity to rejoin a nondeviant pathway may be frequent. Turning points, mentioned earlier, represent clear examples. Thus, Rutter and colleagues (Pickles & Rutter, 1991; Quinton, Pickles, Maughan, & Rutter, 1993) found evidence for positive school experience and the gaining of a nondeviant supportive partner as paths that could enable some to be diverted from the pathway leading from childhood Conduct Disorder to poor adult social functioning. In fact, the main pathway appeared dominant, with rather few individuals either finding or choosing these turning-point paths. Nonetheless, for those who did, the effects appeared substantial, these paths seeming to take them back to something close to the nondeviant pathway, at least in the short run. The extent of continuity from child conduct problems is still subject to considerable debate (Zoccolillo, 1993), but typical figures would suggest that because so few were diverted along these particular paths, other unidentified diversionary paths or turning points and processes must exist.

While pathway divergence may be expected close to the origin, so, too, it is natural to expect a multiplicity of pathways converging on a destination. The concept of equifinality, that there may be different ways of reaching the same end state, has received considerable attention (Cicchetti & Rogosch, 1996). For example, it seems likely that there are many developmental determinants of Major Depression in adult life, and that some of these act additively to increase risk, and others are relevant to subgroups, suggesting distinct pathways (Kendler, Gardner, & Prescott, 2002). It is well established that the role of social adversity in precipitating episodes of Major Depression in adults depends on the number of previous episodes the individual has experienced. Life events have a decreasing role with increasing numbers of episodes (Kendler, Thornton, & Gardner, 2000). However, in the presence of high genetic risk, life events are not strongly associated even with early episodes of depression (Kendler, Thornton, & Gardner,

2001). Thus, in relation to any given episode of Major Depression, there may be one pathway in individuals at low genetic risk that entails life events combined with other sources of vulnerability, possibly related to childhood experiences (Brown & Harris, 1978; Harris, Brown, & Bifulco, 1990), and another pathway in which these factors play a part but in which mechanisms associated with previous episodes of depression are prominent. And there may be a yet quite different pathway to Major Depression in individuals at high genetic risk.

Similarly, there may be different pathways from childhood adversities to depression, depending on the nature of the adversities. Associations between poor parental care (reflected in neglect, lack of supervision, or institutional care) and adult depression and between child sexual abuse (CSA) and adult depression have been identified in numerous studies of referred and general population samples (Fergusson & Mullen, 1999; Kendler et al., 2002; Nelson et al., 2002). Recent studies of the relationship between age of onset of depression and early childhood experiences suggest different pathways. On the basis of six waves of data collection up to age 26 in a representative birth cohort in New Zealand, juvenile-onset (before age 17) was found to differ from later, adult-onset depression in several key respects (Jaffee et al., 2002). Juvenile-onset depression was associated with an increased family history of antisocial behaviors and with indices of family instability such as loss of a parent through death, separation, or divorce, but not with CSA. The juvenile-onset group had also shown more evidence of other mental health problems in childhood and adolescence, such as conduct problems and hyperactivity, and were more likely to have been assessed as having poorer motor skills and greater temperamental inhibition. By contrast, those with adult-onset depression, compared with individuals with no history of depression, had an increased rate of CSA and residence changes, but not any of the other indices of family instability. Hill, Pickles, Byatt, and Rollinson (2004) found similar differences in a general population sample of women age 25 to 35 assessing childhood risks and psychopathology retrospectively. Juvenile-onset depression was associated with multiple indices of early childhood psychopathology and with poor parental care. It was also associated with poor social functioning in childhood, teenage pregnancy, and poor social functioning in adult life. Women with adult-onset depression had functioned well as children and had experienced few adversities. The juvenile- and adult-onset groups differed markedly in their histories of CSA. Juvenile-onset depression was associated with a history of sexual abuse involving intercourse, but adult-onset depression was associated with contact CSA without intercourse. Hill et al.

hypothesized that the juvenile-onset pathway involves early interactions and transactions between symptomatic behaviors, impaired functioning, and multiple adversities, including possible post-traumatic symptoms associated with severe CSA. By contrast, well-functioning children without multiple adversities, and indeed often with supportive families, who experience CSA that does not involve intercourse use a coping strategy that enables them to maintain good functioning in childhood, but this may confer vulnerability in adult life, perhaps when involved in adult sexual relationships.

It may be that the question of whether different pathways arrive at the same point depends on the way that point is defined. Phenotypes in psychopathology are generally, rather crudely, characterized by symptoms rather than by mechanisms. In most cases, therefore, we do not know whether pathways converge to one common mechanism underpinning psychopathology, or there are different mechanisms underpinning the same symptomatic appearance. It is possible, for example, to envisage convergence to a final common cognitive mechanism for depression, one not involving life events and another that does. In the first, there is an interplay between self-devaluative cognitions and normal low mood, leading to a downward spiral and hence to depression (Teasdale, 1988), without the involvement of life events. In the second, life events interact with self-devaluative cognitions, leading to a similar downward spiral (Lewinsohn, Joiner, & Rohde, 2001). Equally, the same symptom complex may arise from different physiological or psychological mechanisms, in which case it might be argued there is not true convergence of pathways. For example, Major Depression is associated with altered reactivity of the HPA axis and reduced hippocampal volumes, but there are indications that this is the case only following a history of child maltreatment (Heim, Newport, Bonsall, Miller, & Nemeroff, 2001; Vythilingam et al., 2002). This might indicate that abnormalities of the HPA are implicated in depression that is associated with child maltreatment, but not in depression that has other origins. In that case, although different pathways appear to converge on the same condition, there is no convergence to a common mechanism.

Mechanisms May Vary Over Time along a Developmental Pathway

The pathways metaphor has the potential to free up our thinking in relation to mechanisms in development. It includes, for example, the ideas that different mechanisms may operate at different points in a pathway. We apply this thinking to a consideration of antisocial pathways.

Overall, it is likely that the life-course-persistent pathway for antisocial children represents, to a substantial degree, the unfolding, in an orderly sequence, of the consequences of a vulnerability arising from a mixture of cognitive and temperamental risks (Hill, 2002; Moffitt et al., 1996). Furthermore, many of the well-established correlations of life-course-persistent antisocial behavior problems with environmental adversities, such as harsh parenting, probably reflect shared genetic influences rather than purely environmental contributions to the pathway. However, even where there is substantial stability over time arising from individual psychopathology, a variety of processes act simultaneously and cumulatively and may influence or participate in pathways. Family, school, peer, and neighborhood environments are commonly relatively stable and therefore tend to exert relatively consistent influences over time. The child is in constant interaction with those around him or her and at each stage and in each social realm may be significantly creating the environment (evocative interactions) and selecting environments (proactive interactions; Caspi & Moffitt, 1995; Plomin & Bergman, 1991). Maladaptive behaviors can therefore be maintained by interactional styles by progressive accumulation of their own consequences and by evoking maintaining responses from others.

Equally, there are numerous points in development where the direction of the pathway may be altered. For example, the temperamental vulnerability for some forms of antisocial behaviors is thought to consist of a tendency to show intense irritability in response to everyday demands, such as diaper changes. This in turn may affect parents' behaviors so they avoid situations that result in distress or attempt to quickly dampen the distress, with the consequence that neither the parent nor the child develops effective ways of managing negative emotions (Keenan & Shaw, 2003). If this is correct, then steps in the pathway include an effect of the child's behavior to increase ineffective parental responses to intense negative emotions *and* an effect of this parenting on the child's subsequent capacity to deal with negative emotions, for example, with peers. Once antisocial behavior problems have become established, parenting style may cease to have an effect, or different aspects of parenting may become more relevant.

Nature of Pathway Risk May Change with Development

The risk mechanism associated with a pathway link need not remain constant as progress is made along a pathway link. Family breakdown may present psychological stresses in the short run, but for women and children can present longer-term financial hardship. In other cases, some aspect of a pathway may offer short-term advantages that become a risk in the longer run. School dropout can bring short-term financial benefit through early access to employment, relative economic disadvantage impacting only later on when lack of qualifications impedes career advancement. It has also been argued that pathways that bring early stress can also bring longer-term benefits. Economic and educational investment rely on this premise, but more specifically, psychological examples may exist, so-called steeling in which exposure to stress results in increased subsequent resilience in the face of risks for psychopathology being an example (Rutter & Rutter, 1993). The proposed mechanism for steeling effects whereby successful navigation of challenging experiences results in increased competence and self-esteem is intuitively appealing and of wide interest, but few persuasive examples exist from observational studies.

Pathways Need Not Be Universal—Mechanisms May Vary across Different Pathways

Depending on the features used to define a pathway, the experience of and risks and possible benefits from a pathway need not be the same for all individuals. This is perhaps most obvious where the environment presented by the pathway interacts with the biological characteristics of different individuals. Sex differences are often striking, particularly in relation to antisocial behavior, and various explanations have been proposed to explain the gross differences, from measurement artifact (Zoccolillo, 1993) to different thresholds on a continuous trait model (Cloninger & Gottesman, 1987; Eme & Kavanagh, 1995). However, differences in the patterns of development have also been reported. For example, very few girls show early-onset antisocial behaviour problems, and most adolescent-onset girls have poor adult outcomes. Silverthorn and Frick (1999) argue that there is thus only one developmental trajectory for antisocial girls; it is similar to the early-onset trajectory for boys in terms of the severity of risk factors but delayed due to the higher threshold for girls associated with strong socialization during elementary school, hormonal differences, different social pressures/cognitive impacts associated with puberty, and greater peer pressure. Moffitt, Caspi, Rutter, and Silva (2001, chaps. 12, 13) examined a range of childhood risk factors and personality traits for evidence of the higher thresholds suggested for Conduct Disorder in girls. They concluded that in the Dunedin sample, girls who met criteria for Conduct Disorder "do not pass a higher threshold that requires a stronger aetiological press" (p. 158) and that previous evidence to the contrary was either based on possibly selective officially identified cases of Conduct Disorder or empirically weak studies. Evidence for sex-differentiated patterns of outcome did find support: boys with more work, substance use, and legal problems, and girls with more relationship, depression, suicide, and health problems. Developmental differences in childhood have, however, been identified by Rowe et al. (2002), who find early oppositional behavior indexing a pathway with quite different outcomes for boys and girls; for boys, it links to Conduct Disorder, whereas for girls, the pathway links to depression.

The effects of biological differences within sexes are now increasingly evident. Rowe, Maughan, Worthman, Costello, and Angold (2004) find evidence for the effects of deviant peers, a frequently cited route into antisocial behavior, being much increased for boys with high testosterone. Interactions with biological differences indexed by genotype have now also been reported, such that childhood adversity results in increased antisocial behavior for specific MAOA genotypes (Caspi et al., 2002).

More familiar interaction effects among behavioral measures can also be found. Coie, Terry, Zakriski, and Lochman (1995) followed a Black inner-city U.S. sample from third grade (age 8) with assessments at 6th, 8th, and 10th grades. Among adolescent boys, self-reported externalizing problems were not predicted by either aggression or rejection, assessed using peer nomination in grade 3. However, the combination of aggression and rejection was associated (as evidenced in a significant interaction term) with increasing levels of externalizing behaviors across the three follow-up assessment points. In girls, the results were more complex, in that only aggression predicted self-reported externalizing problems, and only rejection was associated with parental reports of such problems in adolescence. The findings for males were consistent with the hypothesis that children who both are antisocial and have peer difficulties have a more pervasive disorder that may make them more vulnerable to development of the broad antisocial personality profile in adult life (Coie et al., 1995; Quay, 1993).

Identifying subgroups or subpathways may be crucial to identifying mechanisms. This was illustrated in successive reports from the Montreal Longitudinal Study of 909 male children (Tremblay, Masse, Vitaro, & Dobkin, 1995; Vitaro, Tremblay, Kerr, Pagani, & Bukowski, 1997), attempting to determine whether deviant peers contribute to a pathway leading from earlier to later childhood antisocial behaviors. In one view, having deviant peers is part of the wider set of social difficulties of antisocial children. In

that case, any links between having deviant peers at one time and being antisocial at a later time, which might have indicated that deviant peers add to the risk by reinforcing deviance, are in fact explained by the extent of the child's earlier antisocial behaviors. This was supported by analyses of the whole sample using SEM (Tremblay et al., 1995) and is consistent with other findings from general population longitudinal studies (Woodward & Fergusson, 1999). In the alternative view, there is a contribution from deviant peers to the risk for antisocial behaviors, and the Montreal data provided evidence in favor of this possibility in one subgroup but not in others. Vitaro et al. created four categories of boys based on assessments at ages 11 and 12 (highly conforming, moderately conforming, moderately disruptive, and highly disruptive) and four groups of friends' behaviors (nonaggressive, average, aggressive, no friends). After controlling for levels of antisocial behaviors at age 11, having aggressive friends at age 11 was associated with increased delinquency at age 13, but *only* in the moderately disruptive group. Thus, both highly disruptive and conforming boys appeared to be on pathways that had already become consolidated and not susceptible to the effects of peers' behaviors, but the direction of the moderately disruptive group was still open to peer influences.

Elements on a Pathway Vary in Their Explanatory Potential

Pathways described solely in terms of symptomatic or behavioral continuities do not examine hypotheses regarding mechanisms. However, pathways can be readily constructed in which elements have explanatory potential. Studies conducted into physical abuse, social information processing in children, and aggression provide good examples. Dodge (1993) hypothesized that children who are prone to aggression focus on threatening aspects of others' actions, interpret hostile intent in the neutral actions of others, and are more likely to select and to favor aggressive solutions to social challenges (Crick & Dodge, 1994; Pettit, Poloha, & Mize, 2001), and that these information-processing biases are the result of repeated exposure to physical maltreatment. Dodge, Pettit, Bates, and Valente (1995) tested this model in a sample of 507 children recruited from kindergarten. Physical abuse documented in kindergarten was strongly associated with conduct problems in grades 3 and 4. Encoding errors, hostile attributions, accessing and favoring aggressive responses were each associated with conduct problems in grades 3 or 4 and with having experienced physical abuse. Using structural equation models, encoding errors and accessing aggressive responses mediated the link between physical abuse and conduct problems, but hostile attributions and positive evaluation of aggressive responses did not. There was also a direct association of physical abuse with conduct problems not mediated via the information-processing variables. Thus, there was partial evidence for a pathway involving information-processing biases, but also for one or more other pathways operating via other mechanisms.

The Effects of Symptoms and Behaviors on Pathways and Dynamic Relationships with Mechanisms

It is common for symptoms, whether thought of dimensionally or categorically, to be considered only as outcomes of preceding processes. However, the pathways concept envisages them also as possible influences on subsequent functioning. This is well illustrated in the case of depression in adolescence. Continuities between adolescent depression and episodes in adult life are well established (Harrington, Fudge, Rutter, Pickles, & Hill, 1990) and may represent a disorder that starts in adolescence and recurs through adult life. However, it is probable that episodes of depression themselves alter the risk of later episodes through social or cognitive mechanisms. Increased negative life events and excessive emotional reliance on others, both associated with risk for further depression, were found in adolescents in a general population sample after they had recovered from an episode of Major Depression (Rhode, Lewinsohn, & Seeley, 1994). Episodes of depression may also alter the likelihood of further episodes through an increase in cognitive vulnerability. According to Teasdale (1988), episodes of depression increase the strength of association between mood and dysfunctional cognitive processing. Cognitive risk for recurrence arises from the ease with which these patterns of processing become reestablished, following recovery, in the face of mild negative affect. In support of this hypothesis, Lewinsohn, Allen, Seeley, and Gotlib (1999) found an increased association between low mood and dysfunctional thinking styles following adolescent depression, and this in turn predicted recurrence.

The pathway analogy suggests that the path choices available at any location are the same regardless of the path taken by an individual to reach that location. This feature is often referred to technically as a Markov, first-order auto-regressive, or memory-less property, the last referring to how future progress depends on the current state (location) but not on the past. This is a very strong assumption, but one that is testable. Moreover, elaborations of the pathway analogy that take into account how travelers bring with them the experience of previous routes and use this infor-

mation in choosing their next path allow this assumption to be relaxed.

Pathways through Contexts

A wealth of theory and empirical findings is available explaining associations at individual and aggregate levels, but work integrating these is much scarcer. Leventhal and Brooks-Gunn (2000) provide a review of neighborhood effects and extend the ideas of Sampson, Raudenbush, and Earls (1997) to an integrated developmental model. With respect to antisocial behavior, several studies (e.g., Loeber & Wikstrom, 1993; Sampson & Groves, 1989; Sampson, Raudenbush, & Earls, 1997) point to the apparent importance of parental monitoring and discipline, peers and neighborhood population instability, and social efficacy. However, in general, the research findings are too scant to draw any firm conclusions about potential pathways. Thus, for example, Kerr and Stattin (2000) argue that most published measures and effects of parental monitoring reflect adolescents' own willingness to disclose to parents and that parents themselves have little independent effect.

SOME LIMITATIONS OF THE PATHWAYS CONCEPT

It is evident from the preceding discussion that the concept of pathways can provide a valuable means of structuring questions and hypotheses regarding development and psychopathology. However, there are issues to be addressed in development that are not opened up by the pathways metaphor. One concerns causality in development. The pathways analogy provides an excellent framework for what might be termed the Humean account of causality in terms of whether B follows A, and whether A is necessary or sufficient for B (Hume, 1777/1902). Given the multiple potential causal factors and outcomes in development, sorting this out is a major and essential task. However, when we try to take more from the metaphor, we could be misled into a rather simplistic model of development as essentially channeled and open to switches of direction at key points. Generally, the causal models that we have considered so far do not suffer from such limitations, largely because causal accounts that are not necessary consequences of the pathways framework have been imported. Thus, for example, various social cognitive hypotheses have been introduced into the causal explanation of the origins or maintenance of antisocial behaviors in children, and these can be expressed within the pathways paradigm but are not necessarily illuminated by it. The models that inform these hypotheses are ones concerning attributional processes, perspective taking, and affect recognition in social contexts.

The general point is that the developing individual, in childhood and adult life, is an active participant, in interaction with the environment, and that, except at pathway junctions, this is not the image conjured up by the idea of a pathway. Furthermore, individuals reach particular points on developmental pathways with competences or vulnerabilities that have been shaped by constitutional factors and by experience. For example, the contrast between an effect of deviant peers on moderately, but not highly aggressive, boys (Vitaro et al., 1997) can be expressed in terms of two different pathways. However, the key question is, What do boys in the moderately aggressive group bring to their interactions with peers that the highly aggressive do not, and what influences their responses? Differences in information processing, executive function, autonomic responses, and quality of relating with the peers are all candidates (Hill, 2002).

There is a risk, also, that the pathways metaphor may place too much emphasis on discrete events or stages. Clearly, the Humean analysis requires that event A and outcome B can be identified, and that is, in general, how developmental studies are conducted. However, often these analyses are, at best, illuminating snapshots of an evolving process and, at worst, simply artifacts of the timing of measurements. This is well illustrated by J. Dunn's (1996) discussion of the relationship between children's social experiences and their subsequent abilities to solve theory of mind tasks. Experiences of pretend play and participation in disputes and conversations about the social world have all been found to be associated with subsequent ability to solve theory of mind tasks. However, as Dunn points out, children's capacities for perspective taking are likely to influence their participation in these social interactions and in turn, their participation to enhance perspective taking. It may not be possible to carry out studies that capture events over the time frame of such mutual influences. Within a pathways model, one might distinguish, for example, between a path where such mutual interactions take place, and one where they do not, but the causal processes within the pathway, and especially their temporal relations, require other models.

The issue of the time course of causal influences in development is also not readily envisaged in a pathways framework. The questions center on the time over which an influence has to operate before it makes a difference, and on the durability of such influences. For some influences, such as early exposure to adverse parenting in nonhuman primates, timing rather than duration appears to be

crucial and, we have argued, is well encompassed by the concept of a pathway. Similarly, discrete traumatic events may have long-term consequences (Bolton et al., 2002; Hill et al., 2000), and these also are usefully interpreted within the pathways analysis. However, the pathways model does not obviously suggest that, depending on the nature of the causal factor, different periods of exposure may be necessary before one or the other pathway is joined. For example, close relationships in childhood and in adult life are associated with better functioning in the presence of risks, such as other adverse relationships or institutional care (Rutter, Quinton, & Hill, 1990), and therefore can be thought of as leading to a switch from a higher- to a lower-risk pathway. However, we have no idea how long a good relationship has to last before it becomes protective, and indeed how many answers there are to that question. It may be that for some purposes, such as solving practical problems, a good relationship takes immediate effect, and that for others, such as engendering attachment security or reducing proneness to depressogenic cognitions, it may take longer.

Similar considerations apply to the durability of protective factors. Some effects we may expect to endure only as long as the relationship, and others to last several years after a relationship has ended. Studies that are able to titrate duration of exposure to impact on development are rare. However, naturally occurring variations in the time infants and young children spent in Romanian orphanages before adoption have provided an opportunity to examine the issue (Kreppner et al., 2001; Rutter, Pickles, Eaves, & Murray, 2001). Rates of atypical attachment behaviors, inattention, and overactivity and of quasi-autistic features were found in the adoptees, and the levels were associated with how long they had been in an institution before adoption. Many of these abnormalities attenuated over time, suggesting that the impact of institutional rearing, to a certain extent, falls away.

The pathways metaphor is also limited in its implied conceptualization of the landscape. Development entails much more than a progression over time, even one that is described as occurring in interaction with the environment. The child functions in a social and educational milieu that is also developing, in that peer competences are increasing, as are adult expectations. This means that ways of functioning that served well at one point in development may not be effective subsequently. For example, the difficulty for a child who has not progressed with his peers in developing the capacity to hold on to a line of reasoning in an argument (J. Dunn et al., 1995) is not only that he has not acquired the skill, but he has to find a way of being socially effective with peers who have. They are likely to be more effective negotiators and also to earn the approval of adults whose age-related expectations have changed. The experiences of social ineffectiveness and criticism from adults are, in turn, likely to increase the likelihood that he will use aggressive "solutions" in social interactions.

Finally, unlike the case of the great majority of travelers, who set out with the intention of reaching some chosen destination and among whom some may even plan their route with a map, we attribute very little foresight to those on developmental pathways. Causal processes in science are assumed to work from the past and current to the future, and explanations involving intentions and expectations test the limits of this restriction.

CAUSAL AND FORMAL MODELS

The frequent use of SEM as the analysis environment in which to operationalize developmental pathways both illustrates the strong connections between notions of causal pathway and of developmental pathway but has restricted the more general exploration of their interrelationship.

Causal Pathways

The literature on developmental pathways often takes for granted the causal status of suggested pathways. There are at least two ways in which the causal analysis literature is helpful: methods of analysis and formal representation. Different methods of analysis, and the evidence that each method offers as to the nature of a causal link, are discussed in the next section. We consider here the formal representation of causes, many of which involve quite explicit use of paths.

In their overview of causal modeling methods, Greenland and Brumback (2002) identify graphical models (e.g., Robins, 2001), potential-outcome (counterfactual) models (e.g., Rothman & Greenland, 1998), sufficient-component cause models (Rothman, 1976), and structural equation models (Pearl, 2000) as the distinct and largely complementary alternatives. We cannot provide a complete overview of each; instead, and in a most uneven fashion, we point to particular aspects that seem to have special relevance to developmental pathways. Consideration of potential-outcome (counterfactual) models we defer to the next section.

Graphical Models

Graphical models look very much like SEM path diagrams, but without the boxes, circles, and arrows for errors. They are also nonparametric and thus in themselves not estimation tools. Their primary use is in identifying the conditions under which independence and conditional independence apply (Greenland, Pearl, & Robins, 1999). They are thus very useful in showing what analysis or experimental design does or does not lead to the estimation of effects of one path uncontaminated by the effects of another. As an example, consider Figure 7.3.

If we were interested in the direct path from X to Y, we might think that examining the relationship between X and Y in a sample selected to be homogeneous for Z would allow us to do this, as we would have eliminated variation in Z and thus controlled for the indirect path from X to Y via Z. Graphical modeling theory tells us that such an approach is flawed, because selection on the basis of Z induces correlation between X and U where none existed before, with the result that the simple relationship of X and Y in the sample selected for a specific value of Z is confounded by uncontrolled variation in U (Robins & Greenland, 1992). We should therefore be wary of examining relationships from childhood to adulthood in a group selected for some adolescent outcome.

Structural Equation Modeling Path Diagrams

From its name alone, path analysis would seem to be a highly relevant tool for examining developmental pathways. Path analysis, first systematically developed by Sewall Wright (1921), exploits linearity assumptions to allow the covariance between two variables on a path diagram to be decomposed into contributions arising from each legitimate path that connects them, with simple rules for determining the legitimate paths (Heise, 1975; Wright, 1934). Implicit in these diagrams is the fact that

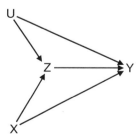

Figure 7.3 Confounding of the causal relationship of X to Y by Z.

we are modeling these sets of variables as a set of simultaneous equations. These would now be commonly estimated in software for SEM.

If, to the traditional diagram, a residual variance is added to each variable in the form of a double-headed arrow running both from and to that variable, then the path-tracing rules for legitimate paths can be reduced to (1) trace backward from a variable, (2) change direction at a two-headed arrow, then (3) trace forward. These rules allow us to identify how the value of a later variable can be influenced by an earlier variable either by a direct path or by an indirect path via another variable. Multiplication of the (standardized) coefficients along each chain gives the expected (standardized) covariance for that path, and these may be summed to give the total, direct and indirect expected covariances (or effects).

But do they correspond to paths that embody the features we have described for a developmental pathway? What have these analyses and diagrams got to do with pathways of the kind that we have been considering? Clearly, when applied to cross-sectional data, the idea that these paths could describe developmental pathways is not justified. Nonetheless, what about applications to longitudinal data? It is clear that many authors using these methods with developmental data treat these paths as synonymous with developmental pathways. In fact, their equivalence is very far from clear. In SEM-related path diagrams, whereas we commonly speak as though different paths relate to different individuals, in fact they relate to the characteristics of individuals. Individuals with high scores on multiple risk dimensions have their outcome scores multiply elevated—it is as if they pass down several paths at the same time. Moreover, the complete path diagram is being presented as a description of the population process, and there is little elucidation of individual differences in that process. All individuals share common path coefficients and seem to differ only in the residual errors and disturbances.

If we consider the simplest of cases of a single pathway from X to Y as represented in the simple regression Y = a + bX + e, the model allows for two alternative pathways to a high value of Y. If we assume that b is positive, then the first is that from X, for which a high value of X is required. The second is through the disturbance term e, which summarizes all the other pathways not being explicitly considered. Clearly, for a given value of Y, the bigger the residual e, the more likely is the individual to have followed one of these other pathways. Thus, models either in which these variances and disturbances were given more substance or that allowed for interindividual differences in path coefficients might be preferred. Random coefficient models offer one

possibility; later, we examine one particular example of these, namely, growth curve models.

Path models can provide considerable insight into the mechanism by which variation in one variable gives rise to variation in some later variable, especially where variables that play a theoretically critical intermediate role are included. One aspect of SEM path representation that has become very widely used is the distinction and decomposition into direct and indirect effects; of particular interest is where it can be shown that there are no effects of the first variable on the last variable once the effects of the intervening variables have been accounted for. If the effects are mediated by the intervening variables and there are no residual direct effects, this is interpreted as strong evidence for their being a causal pathway. Thus, a mediating variable, usually synonymous with an intervening, intermediate, or contingent variable, "is a variable that occurs on a causal pathway from an independent to a dependent variable. It causes variation in the dependent variable and itself is caused to vary by the independent variable" (Last, 1995, p. 87). Tests for such mediation have been formulated within the SEM framework and are described later. In psychiatry, biometrical genetics, and social medicine, the estimation of direct and indirect effects has been largely synonymous with the use of path analysis and path diagrams.

There has been substantial argument for the shortcomings of path and SEM analysis from those associated with the interactionist perspective, who find such variable-based analyses unsatisfactory, preferring instead individual-based analysis of the kinds to be discussed later (von Eye & Bergman, 2003). This is related to one of the major limitations of SEM path models, namely, their inability to represent interactions. In fact, this is not a strict limitation, multiple group methods and a number of more recent methods enabling these to be considered (Schumacker & Marcoulides, 1998). Nonetheless, few substantive applications have pursued them.

Multifactorial Causation and the Sufficient-Component Cause Model

A variety of conditions have to be met before, during, or after a causal event for the effects of a cause to occur. Sometimes these conditions are not of interest; we simply assume that they are met. Such assumptions often more or less explicitly restrict the scope of the circumstances under which the cause may have an effect. However, other conditions, or the same conditions when viewed from a different

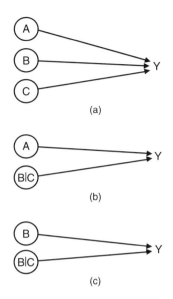

Figure 7.4 Component cause models (a) top, (b) middle, (c) bottom. Adapted from "Causes," by K. J. Rothman, 1976, *American Journal of Epidemiology, 104,* pp. 587–592.

theoretical perspective or different point of interest, cannot be treated in this way. Instead, the presence of a condition is seen as an integral part of a more complicated causal process where the condition becomes better considered as another cause. With multiple causes, a more developed terminology is necessary.

Rothman (1976; Rothman & Greenland, 1998) has suggested that we need to consider component causes. The idea of component causes is helpful for a variety of reasons. First, they can be classified as being necessary or sufficient. If the occurrence of just one of the component causes is enough for the effects to be observed, this cause is sufficient. If all other causes may be present and yet no effect is observed unless one particular cause is also present, then this particular cause is a necessary cause.

This simple decomposition has all sorts of implications as to what we might expect to observe in our data. Figure 7.4a shows three causes—A, B, and C—influencing a single outcome Y. These causes are each sufficient: Only one needs to be present before the outcome can occur. Typically, one of these paths, say A, is a composite path representing all the other ways the outcome could occur in the absence of paths B and C. This allows us to focus on elucidating the causal mechanism relating to B and C without its being necessary (we hope) to explain every other possible way the outcome could have come about. The apparent need to explain everything about an outcome is not an uncommon stumbling block for novice researchers, and a residual composite pathway helps avoid this. It also means that we focus on the effects of B and/or

C in elevating the rate of the outcome over and above some background or base rate that would be occurring as a result of the ever-present generic path A.

To make the discussion less abstract, we consider a hypothetical case in which B is exposure to familial discord, C is deviant peer group, and the outcome Y is delinquency. Formalizing the consideration of outcome rates, the causal model suggests that in the absence of B and C, outcomes can occur only through path A, and that over some period of observation, the outcome might be observed in a proportion p_A of children. For children also exposed to and thus at risk of B, outcome occurrences will be observed for a proportion p_A, through path A, and a proportion p_B, through path B. Similarly for children exposed to C. Both B and C are sufficient; that is, exposure to either parental discord or a deviant peer group raises the rate of subsequent delinquency. For children exposed to both B and C, some will succumb through path A, some through path B, and some through path C. If these rates are individually comparatively small and having a deviant peer group is not associated with familial discord, then comparatively few children are exposed to both risk factors and few individuals progress down both the B and C causal paths jointly. This means that the rate of the delinquency outcome expected for children exposed to both B and C will be the simple additive sum of the proportions arising through each possible path, that is, $p_A + p_B + p_C$.

In more complicated examples it becomes necessary to separate pathways from the risk factors. Figure 7.4b shows a rather different circumstance in which both B and C are necessary to pathway 2 in order that the outcome rate is elevated over that of the base or background rate through pathway 1. Because the rate is not increased if either B or C is absent, then B and C are not sufficient causes. When they occur together they form a sufficient cause, and a sufficient cause corresponds to a pathway. This describes a circumstance of total synergy between B and C, each risk factor potentiating the effect of the other.

Figure 7.4c shows the case where B is necessary and sufficient to pathway 2, but is necessary but not sufficient to pathway 3. C is also necessary but not sufficient to pathway 3. Here the presence of C only partially potentiates the risk posed by B. Partial synergy of this kind implies that B is a component of more than one sufficient cause (pathway).

Figure 7.4a, in which the outcome rate is given by the simple sum of $p_A + p_B + p_C$, the cause-specific rates, provides a benchmark against which we can test for synergy. Table 7.1 shows the expected outcome rates in the presence and absence of B and C, the two risk factors of interest, for the complete and partial synergy models of Figures 7.4b and 7.4c.

TABLE 7.1   Expected Outcome Rates Corresponding to the Additive Models of Figure 7.4

	Figure		
	7.4a	7.4b	7.4c
P_A	A	A	A
P_{AB}	A + B	A	A + B
P_{AC}	A + C	A	A
P_{ABC}	A + B + C	A + BC	A + B + BC

An empirical test of whether there is synergy between B and C will therefore be to compare the relative fit (of expected to observed rates or frequencies) of Figures 7.4b and 7.4c with that of Figure 7.4a.

This simple classification and thought experiment delivers some straightforward expectations and criteria for describing aspects of processes. It is therefore rather surprising to realize that it is almost entirely inconsistent with the way that we have been trained and most of us actually analyze our research studies! The argument suggests that our null expectation should be that the combined effect on an outcome rate of specific component causes will be additive in their individual effects on the outcome rate. However, for perfectly sound statistical (and some good epidemiological) reasons, we have been taught that we should not combine effects additively on the rate scale but should do this on the logistic (log-odds) scale, or the log scale to which the logistic scale closely approximates when the base outcome rate is low. Table 7.2 shows the expected rates under a model that is additive on the log scale, that is, equivalent to those from a logistic regression with additive effects for two specific risk factors B and C for a study where the outcome rate is low.

What we see is that the rate expected when B alone is present is exp(b) × the base rate. More critical, the effect when both B and C are present is not additive in their individual effects. Instead, it is multiplicative. Under the Rothman additive model, if the base rate was 1%, and each component cause resulted in further rates of 1%, then the rate expected when either B or C was present would be 2%, and when both risk factors B and C were present it would be 3%. Under the main effects logistic model, the corresponding rates would be 1%, 2%, 2%, and when both risk factors are present it would be 4%.

There are several implications. First, in the case of relatively rare outcomes and risk factors, substantial positive synergy is implied by logistic models with just main effects. Synergy is not at all synonymous with the need for a significant interaction term. Second, although our psychological theory may tend to emphasize the possibility of positive potentiation of one risk factor by another, in practice we may be more likely to find we need negative interactions in logistic regression analyses as a means of bringing the model more closely into line with the null expectations of the often plausible additive component cause model. Third, it should be emphasized that the foregoing is not a criticism of logistic regression, a form of analysis that remains a most elegant tool. But it does explain previous academic argument as to whether there were, or were not, synergistic effects, for example, the fierce debate between Brown (Brown, Harris, & Copeland, 1977), who proposed vulnerability factors for depression using an additive model, and Tennant and Bebbington (1978), who argued against their existence based on the absence of interaction in the logistic framework. The consensus among epidemiologists (e.g., Blot & Day, 1979) is that synergy does not require or equate to an interaction in a logistic regression. Moreover, this does undermine the perhaps simpleminded, but ever so appealing, interpretation that the inclusion of a risk factor as a main effect in a logistic regression represents the inclusion of an alternative pathway. It might be an approximation to it, but in fact, it more closely represents a rather different elaboration of the pathway model, to which we now turn.

Stages, Steps, and Intervening States

As yet, we have not attempted to examine the means by which Rothman's sufficient causes might take their effect. As a consequence of some unspecified mechanism, the risk factors open a channel through which maldevelopment can occur. There is no differentiation of the process along that channel, and the outcome was observed as being the result of what looked like a single-stage process. However, a substantial body of psychological theory has regarded development as progression through a series of stages (e.g., Deanna, 1976, regarding Kohlberg's stages of moral development) that provide an opportunity for identifying developmental changes in etiology: One set of risk and protective factors may influence progress to an intermediate outcome, and another set may be

TABLE 7.2   Expected Outcome Rates for Figure 7.4a with Multiplicative Effects

P_A	exp(A)		= Base rate
P_{AB}	exp(A + B)	= exp(A) × exp(B)	= Base rate × exp(B)
P_{AC}	exp(A + C)	= exp(A) × exp(C)	= Base rate × exp(C)
P_{ABC}	exp(A + B + C)	= exp(A) × exp(B) × exp(C)	= Base rate × exp(B) × exp(C)

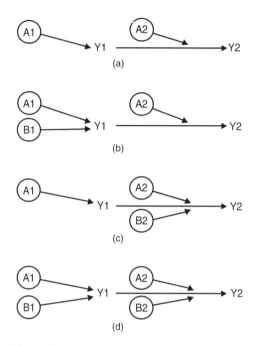

Figure 7.5 Multistep component cause model.

important in the progression from intermediate to final outcome. The supposition of a stage in fact provides a model with a remarkable range of capacities that were first elaborated for cancer development but that Pickles (1993) described more fully in the context of psychopathology.

As we did with the single-stage models, we now consider some risk factor scenarios for a two-stage process with intermediate outcome Y1 and final outcome of interest Y2.

In Figure 7.5a, background factors alone act to generate both intermediate and final outcomes. In Figures 7.5b through 7.5d, within each stage the presence of the additional risk factors, each representing a sufficient and necessary component cause with respect to their immediate outcome, acts as before in an additive fashion. However, at the second stage (and any postulated later stages), the background and risk factors cannot act on everybody; they can act only on those that have experienced the intermediate outcome Y1. Achieving the intermediate outcome is a prerequisite either to being exposed to the second-stage risk factors or to their having any effect. The result is that, unlike when combining effects within a stage, combining effects across stages is multiplicative: The larger the stage-one effect, the larger will be the number at risk to the second-stage risk factors. With background factors alone, the rate in Figure 7.5a is $p_{A1} \times p_{A2} = A1 \times A2$, whereas in Figure 7.5b it is $(A1 + b) \times A2$, in Figure 7.5c it is $A1 \times (A2 + c)$, and in Figure 7.5d with both risk factors present it is $(A1 + b) \times (A2 + c)$. With background rates of 1% and additive within-stage component-cause effects of

1%, the expected rates corresponding to Figures 7.5a through 7.5d are 0.1%, 0.2%, 0.2%, and 0.4%.

Thus, how the effects of risk and protective factors combine to increase or decrease the rate of the final outcome will depend on the transitions they impact, additive effects being expected if the factors operate on the same stage transition or multiplicative effects if they act on different stages in the sequence. A main effects logistic model is therefore rather more consistent with the idea of risk factors acting on different steps on a single but extended pathway, than it is with multiple distinct paths.

Of course, we typically do not know whether there are intermediate outcomes. Just as in cancer research we might postulate intermediate stages in cell development prior to the final stage of uncontrolled replication of malignant cells, so in psychopathology we might postulate a variety of intermediate cognitive, behavioral, or social states or circumstances en route to our final focal outcome. As we have seen, a logistic model with main effects implies a level of positive synergy between risk factors. Synergy has often been conceptualized as some form of "chemistry of the moment"—the immediate coincidence of risk factors being necessary for it to occur. By contrast, postulating an intermediate stage, together with risk factors that act on different stage transitions, provides all that is necessary for such apparent synergy. Moreover, this synergy is one in which the exposure to each of the apparently synergistic risk factors could be separated by years. We would argue that this is much the more likely way synergy occurs in psychosocial development than through chemistry of the moment. A final elaboration of the argument is that the finding of partial synergy might suggest that one risk factor may operate on both stage transitions, whereas the other operates on only one.

Staged pathways also have implications for timing. Where the intermediate stages are not observed, the effects on the final outcome of risk factors for early stages may not be observed for some considerable time, and the outcome rate may seem to lag variation in risk factor exposure: The risk factor can be removed, and yet new cases continue to appear for years. Risk factors for later stages are likely to show their effects more immediately.

ISSUES IN THE INVESTIGATION OF DEVELOPMENTAL PATHWAYS

Here we consider factors in the design and measurement of studies that allow them to be informative about the nature and existence of developmental pathways.

Longitudinal Studies Are Not Necessarily Developmental

Longitudinal research and developmental research are far from synonymous. The former refers to the method of collecting and analyzing data on individuals or populations measured over time. However, as several authors have commented (Sampson & Laub, 1997), it is a sad irony that much of the research using this method in fact is no more than a glorified cross-sectional study, and often without the researchers being aware of it. Thus, for example, many researchers use forms of random effects models that mechanically pool between-subject (cross-sectional) and within-subject (change) information, effectively confounding the precious information on change (which was the whole justification for the study) with the cross-sectional information (which we all know is suspect). Also, as Sampson and Laub point out, much longitudinal research labors under an inheritance of static theory, be that sociological or, more commonly in our case, adult psychiatric typologies.

Prospective and Retrospective Methods in Pathways Research

Prospective study is rightly seen as the benchmark, with strengths that are contrasted with the disadvantages of retrospective investigations. It is commonly asserted that retrospective reporting, typically referring back to childhood from adult life, is unreliable and is not able to provide accurate information on the temporal sequences that are essential for delineating pathways. Adults without psychopathology are prone to underreport childhood difficulties (Maughan & Rutter, 1997), not necessarily as a result of state-dependent memory, but as a consequence of the lack of mental or verbal rehearsal of events that those with poorer outcomes may have undertaken (Hardt & Rutter, 2004). Spuriously strong associations may result from shared method variance—the general tendency for reports from the same source to be correlated.

However, the time scale for the prospective investigation of pathways to adult disorders will necessarily be long, meaning that a program of research will take several generations. Furthermore, a major advantage of retrospective study is that the final steps in a pathway can be explored quite precisely, whereas the earlier ones are necessarily examined in broader outline. In the pathways metaphor, if the outcome is analogous to reaching a summit, the climber has an immediate appreciation of the final steps and a panoramic view of the pathway, one that is hazy on the details.

The validity of retrospective reports is supported where they yield findings similar to those from prospective study. We described earlier multiple differences in the early childhood antecedents of juvenile- and adult-onset depression found both in the prospective Dunedin Multidisciplinary Health and Development Study (Jaffee et al., 2002) and in the retrospective Wirral Woman's Health Survey (Hill et al., 2004). They were consistent in suggesting that there may be different pathways to adult depression, depending on age of onset, implicating different childhood vulnerabilities and adversities. The prospective study is likely to have yielded the more reliable and accurately timed assessments of childhood experiences and psychopathology, but the similarity of the findings between the retrospective and prospective studies suggests that the panoramic view afforded retrospectively was reasonably accurate.

Discrete Combinatorial Pathways, Log-Linear Models, Clusters, Types and Antitypes

Although much of the evidence for pathways has not been based on any attempt to formalize how the concept of a pathway could be operationalized, there is much to be gained by doing this. When speaking of analysis, we immediately confront a substantial fissure in statistical thinking and research experience and understanding: that between dimensional and categorical approaches. Though we should be striving to bridge this fissure (Pickles & Angold, 2003), it nonetheless is easier to organize our discussion separately.

Our first pathways diagram of Figure 7.1 shows the estimated population distribution over a sequence of dimensions. The first considers the overall average rate of depression, then that rate split by quality of parental care in childhood, then that rate split by the joint distribution of parental care and childhood sexual abuse, and eventually by the full joint distribution that includes quality of adult love relationships. That full joint frequency distribution could be analyzed in a variety of ways: as a series of logistic regressions (Hill et al., 2001), as a log-linear model, or as a cluster analysis. Within each of these there are various extensions that are perhaps particularly appropriate to the analysis of developmental pathways.

The sequence of logistic regressions, focusing on each bifurcation in sequence, clearly appeals to a perspective of chains of effects, consistent with the search for potential turning points. Although not necessary, in practice there is a tendency to assume that previous experience largely has its effects through main effects, even through the main effects of the immediately prior variable only.

This lack of memory effect implies that future development depends only on the current state, not on how it was arrived at. This Markovian property might be entirely consistent with many pathway models but may not be entirely appropriate to development. The calculation of the extent to which early stage effects are transmitted to the eventual outcome is described in Winship and Mare (1983). The method represents an elaboration of path modeling in the case of binary variables where the simultaneous equations take the probit form, and where effects of each variable may arise from two sources: the effect of the observed binary value and the effect of the latent continuous (conditionally normal) variable that may underlie the observed binary variable. This second effect arises where the binary variable reflects an underlying propensity that has been measured subject to error in categorical form. Both effects may be of interest; for example, psychiatrists might want to distinguish the effects of an actual episode of depression from the effects of a predisposition for depression, the latter reflecting genetics, among other things. Pickles and Rutter (1991) work through the path model calculus in tracing the effects of a turning-point event. Their illustration makes clear that although the concept of a chain of effects has theoretical appeal, if the effects are transmitted by the binary event occurrence only, then unless the links in the chain follow near deterministically, effects are not transmitted far along the chain before their effects fade out.

The variables that form the sequence can be characteristics of the individuals or can be features of their context or environment. That combination of individual and contextual features, with no analytical priority being given to one or the other, is a critical feature of what has become known as the "person-oriented approach." Proponents of this approach argue for distinctive methods of analysis (Bergman, Magnusson, & El-Khouri, 2003; Magnusson & Bergman, 1990). One of these, though it predates the approach, is a form of log-linear/multidimensional contingency table modeling known as configural frequency analysis. Von Eye (1990; von Eye, Spiel, & Wood, 1996) provide a modern presentation of the approach. The basic approach consists of fitting a main effects-only model, which assumes independence among the marginal variables of the table, and then comparing the expected frequencies with those observed. Attention is focused on so-called types, combinations of variable values or cells with a much greater frequency than expected. With longitudinal developmental data, such types may represent the common developmental pathways. Antitypes, reflecting pathways less frequently taken than expected, may also be found but are typically of

less interest. The method elaborates statistical testing in the context of there being many potential types and commonly sparse data.

A second method used in the person-oriented approach is to identify a typology of developmental histories based on a variation of cluster analysis. The primary distinctive feature is the preliminary removal of aberrant outlier histories (Bergman, 1988, 1998), which, once dropped, allow for the recovery of much simpler and clearer cluster structures.

However derived, the typology of developmental histories identified is expected to provide insight in its own right and, by assigning individuals to types, can be used to consider the ways they also contrast with respect to other variables.

Discrete Combinatorial Pathways: Removing a Pathway and Attributable Fractions

For both practical and conceptual reasons, it would be very desirable to estimate what the impact would be of removing a component causal pathway. Of course, observing someone with depression does not reveal the pathway that was responsible, as even those exposed to CSA may develop depression by a mechanism not involving CSA. Among cases exposed to a particular risk, the attributable fraction of cases of depression produced by a particular risk exposure is estimated as

$$AF_e = \frac{(RR-1)}{RR}$$

where RR is the causal risk ratio (or odds ratio, if the outcome is not too common). If we wanted to estimate the fraction of all cases, say among the CSA-exposed and -unexposed, that would not have occurred if there had been no CSA exposure, the population attributable fraction AF_p, this will depend on the proportion p of the population that are exposed:

$$AF_p = \frac{p(RR-1)}{[p(RR-1)+1]}$$

Applied to the Wirral Women's Health Study, these expressions yield estimates of RR of 4.29, $AF_e = 0.77$, and with 18.6% CSA-exposed, $AF_p = 0.38$. Can we interpret this as implying that if we were able to remove exposure to CSA the rate of depression would be reduced by 38%? Not necessarily.

First, those exposed to CSA may have elevated rates of exposure to other risk factors. We know that in the population, those exposed to CSA also have unusually high levels of childhood neglect, and removing their CSA exposure cannot automatically be expected to reduce their exposure to neglect. Some interventions might do that, but not all. We therefore need to adjust for the confounding effects of neglect. Walter (1976) shows how we can compose an adjusted AF_p as a weighted sum of the AF_p's in strata k, k = 1, K of the confounding factors, that is, $\Sigma w_k AF_{p(k)}$. Among the not-neglected stratum, the impact of CSA was very substantial, with an RR of 6.55 and $AF_{p(not\ neglected)}$ of 0.42. Among the neglected stratum, the impact of CSA was much more modest, generating an RR of 1.35 and an $AF_{p(neglected)}$ of 0.13. With neglect stratum population proportions of $w_{not\ neglected} = 0.71$ and $w_{neglected} = 0.29$, the adjusted population attributable fraction is 0.34. This corresponds to the estimated impact of lowering each of the two CSA-exposed arms in Figure 7.1 (one for the neglected and one for the not-neglected) to their corresponding neglect-similar but CSA-unexposed arms. Although adjustment for a second or even third confounder would be possible, for any adjusted population attributable fraction in a nonrandomized study there will always remain other possibly unmeasured confounders that could be included.

Second, an assumption has been made that removing the exposure has no other effects on the disposition and effects of other risks. Many policies designed to reduce CSA could be expected to reduce neglect as well, leading to larger reductions than expected, or might give rise to unintended breakup of family relationships, leading to smaller reductions than expected.

Thus, the practicality and seemingly simple interpretability of population attributable fractions as estimating the impact of closing off a pathway to some outcome should not be allowed to curtail critical thought.

Turning Points

The concept of a turning point can be seen as an elaboration of the idea of a pathway. It presupposes that there are forces at work that result in a substantial degree of predictability in the continuity of negative states or trajectories, but that there exist classes of event or experience that can perturb this. Turning points hold considerable intuitive appeal. They are the stuff of both much great literature and popular biography and autobiography and form the subject matter of much appealing qualitative research. However, for a more critical evaluation, turning points must satisfy a number of requirements.

The first is that it must be possible to gather data where the circumstances for a possible turning, the preconditioning event, have occurred and yet no turning event took place. This is the exact opposite of its popular and qualitative use that is entirely selective, identifying turning events and then asking subjects to nominate a temporally associated circumstance to which the turning event might be attributed. That approach can never disprove the causal role of any nominated preconditioning event.

But to gather data on preconditioning events regardless of whether they triggered a turning-point event or not requires a style of data collection that is much more closed. The set of potential preconditioning events must be known in advance such that it can be collected for those both with and without a turning-point event. Formally, it does not require a complete time diary of these preconditioning event occurrences, but almost so. Event histories are commonly analyzed using survival analysis methods, and here the conceptual logic behind the partial likelihood derivation of the Cox proportional hazards survival model is instructive (Cox, 1972). In this context, a Cox model would focus exclusively on the times at which turning-point events occurred and would consider the circumstances at that time of those who turned and compare them with the circumstances of those who could have turned but did not.

A second requirement is that the change brought about must have an impact that is not short-lived, but one that sets in train processes that sustain and support progress along the new path for an extended period. Thus, the event itself can involve a radical dislocation with the past, such as the move to a distant neighborhood that disrupted delinquency careers (West, 1982), but need not be so immediately life-transforming. The constructive role that a supportive partner can play (Quinton et al., 1993) is likely to owe more to the ongoing benefit in managing life's difficulties and opportunities than to a sudden charge of self-esteem (see also "Some Limitations of the Pathway Concept"). Nonetheless, the mechanism by which the precondition gives rise to the turning point should at the very least be theoretically elaborated and preferably empirically pursued and confirmed. However, as emphasized elsewhere in this chapter, the belief that effects can be transmitted across time through a sequence of steps, transitions, or links in a chain is not readily tenable unless there are some traits or persistent risk factors that are common to the operation of each step, inducing some correlation.

A third requirement is to properly consider the mechanisms that lead up to the occurrence of the preconditioning circumstances. This is necessary to characterize how different are those who experience the preconditioning event from those who do not.

A final important consideration is that turning points are often culturally specific. For example, one of the ways that negative turning points may have their effect is through "lost opportunities." This may occur where access is restricted to a specific age at entry, as in many educational settings. Gaining or failing to gain access to some tier of education has therefore often been seen as a potential turning point. Recent changes in many countries to allow access across an extended age span may remove or modify such effects.

Mediation, Direct, and Indirect Effects

We have seen that one of the features expected of many conceptualizations of developmental pathways is the Markovian property. In the progression from A to C, if passage is mediated by B, then, having taken account of B, there are no direct effects of previous history. Illustrated in Figure 7.6, this technique matches with our intuitive notion of pathway in that the removal of the direct path from the causal exposure X to outcome Y leaves just the single pathway via Z. If $Pr(Y|Z, X) = Pr(Y|Z)$, then X is considered as having no direct effect on Y; its effects are mediated or are indirect through Z.

Baron and Kenny (1986) and Judd and Kenny (1981) describe four steps in investigating such mediation in SEM path diagrams: (1) Show that X is correlated with Y; (2) show that X is correlated with Z; (3) show that Z is correlated with Y; and (4) show that the effect (partial correlation) of X on Y controlling for Z is zero. In the regression framework, we would be comparing the regression of Y on X (model 1) and the regression of Y on X and Z (model 2). The estimated coefficients identify component pathways (see next section), and background effects due to possibly numerous other component causes are summarized within the error terms of the regressions. As commonly used, a

significant coefficient for X in model 1, but a nonsignificant coefficient in model 2, is taken as evidence of mediation. Without further evidence, such a result could arise from Z being a confounder rather than a mediator, the association between X and Z implied as causal in the diagram in fact being merely correlational. Some difficulties in the use of this decomposition are discussed by Cole and Hernan (1998).

Where the focus is on estimating the direct effects of Z, the problem can also be viewed as one where the simple association of Z and Y is not an estimate of the causal effect of Z because individuals have been selectively assigned to or chosen nonrandomly their Z status. Adjustment for observed factors such as X that are correlated with Z can be made by use of the propensity score (Rosenbaum, 2002). Though not necessary, the theoretical arguments for the propensity score are typically based on the idea of counterfactuals—the outcome individuals would have experienced had they been exposed to a level of risk factor different to that which they did in fact, that is, had taken a path other than the one they did. For binary developmental state or exposure Z, the propensity score is the probability of Z as a function of the selection variables X, typically estimated as the predicted values obtained from a logistic regression with Z as outcome and X as predictors. Then matching, stratification, and covarying this estimated propensity in estimating the effect of Z on Y all provide a potentially valid means of estimating the causal association.

An interesting fourth approach, used in what Robins (Robins, Hernan, & Brumback, 2002) refers to as marginal structural modeling, is to use the propensity score as the basis of the calculation of weights. In the case where Z is binary, individuals with Z = 1 receive the weight 1/propensity score, and those with Z = 0 receive the weight 1/(1 − propensity score). In a sample weighted in this way, X and Z are uncorrelated, allowing the simple association between Z and Y to be interpreted causally.

Natural Experiments and Instrumental Variables

We reviewed earlier the compelling evidence that early adverse experiences in rodents and nonhuman primates have long-term behavioral and neuroendocrine consequences. The key features of these studies that make them relatively straightforward to interpret are that the depriving conditions were specified and manipulated experimentally and so were not correlated with any preexisting qualities of the parental animals, and that an adequate subsequent rearing environment could be guaranteed. Analogous experimental manipulation of the experiences of children is clearly out

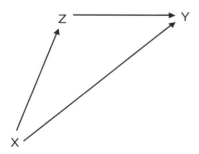

Figure 7.6   Direct and indirect effects.

of the question, and so alternative methods for attempting to identify whether there are early points of divergence have to be identified.

The majority of children grow up in families where there are strong continuities of relationships and parenting (e.g., Pianta, Sroufe, & Egeland, 1989), making the task of disentangling early and late effects more difficult. In the previous section, various adjustments for the possible measured confounding effects X on the estimation of the causal path Z→Y were presented. However, typically we can never be sure that there might not also exist unmeasured confounding variables, such as U in Figure 7.7. Their presence would prevent us from interpreting the association Z→Y as causal. The instrumental variable (IV) approach is capable of overcoming this limitation. This approach relies on there being a variable R, the instrumental variable, which is correlated with Z but that is known to have no effect on Y except through Z, that is, is entirely mediated through Z.

Then, in the simplest case of Z and Y being continuous, if in the regression of Y on Z we replace Z by the predicted value of Z obtained from the regression of Z on R, then the estimated effect is the causal effect of Z unconfounded by the unmeasured, even unmeasurable, effects of U.

The IV approach is clearly powerful, but finding suitable variables R is rarely possible in entirely observational studies. Many social experiments make use of the approach in so-called encouragement designs, in which a random subgroup are encouraged to participate in some program Z, the encouragement being designed to be sufficient to increase the proportion participating but not sufficient to in itself materially influence the outcome. Such a design and method of analysis is clearly suited to the evaluation of educational programs that may be cast in a developmental framework. In observational studies, instrumental variables are often identified either by the use of very strong

theory, rarely as convincing to readers as it seems to be to authors, or by imaginative use of auxiliary data and of natural experiments. Administrative systems provide one common source. State intervention in child care has provided a number of opportunities for such investigation. Hodges and Tizard (1989) followed into adolescence a group of children who had experienced institutional care up to at least age 2, some of whom were then adopted and others returned to their families of origin, and compared them with adolescents who had not been exposed to institutional care. The family experiences of the adopted children were more advantageous in numerous respects than those returned to their own families, and this was reflected in their superior educational and behavioral performance. However, compared to the adolescents with no history of institutional care, the adopted children were overfriendly with strangers, they had more peer difficulties, and they were less likely to have formed close friendships. This suggests a long-term effect of institutional privation, not modified by later, potentially protective experiences. Rutter et al. (2001) provide other examples of natural experimental research opportunities.

Measurement Error in the Analysis of Developmental Pathways

Developmental models often focus on a single domain, analyzing repeated measures of some nominally comparable ability. This gives us the opportunity to examine critically a particular form of the direct and indirect effects decomposition. When we sketch out a model of development in which we have several pathways leading to some common node or developmental state, both our mental models and the pathway diagram immediately impose the Markovian assumption, suggesting that development beyond that node is independent of which pathway was followed in reaching that node. The alternative, less parsimonious model would require either additional paths from earlier periods of development or that the node for current developmental level be somehow disaggregated into a finer set of levels that are distinguished by developmental history (a higher-order Markov approach used with discrete variables).

Path Models and Latent Variable Model

The major advantage of the SEM approach is its ability, when applied to studies with suitable measurement designs, to tackle the problem of measurement error. Measurement error is ubiquitous and its impact often poorly understood.

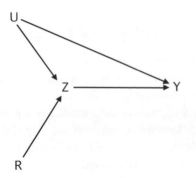

Figure 7.7 Controlling for unobserved confounder U by the use of an instrumental variable R.

TABLE 7.3   Summary Statistics from Longitudinal Cognitive Ability Study

	Age			
	6	7	9	11
Mean	18.03	25.82	35.26	46.59
Standard deviation	6.37	7.32	7.80	10.39
Correlation matrix				
Age 7	.809			
9	.806	.850		
11	.765	.831	.867	

Source: "A Longitudinal Investigation of the Intellectual Differentiation Hypothesis," by R. T. Osbourne and D. E. Suddick, 1972, *Journal of Genetic Psychology, 110,* pp. 83–89.

This issue is well illustrated using the data of Osbourne and Suddick (1972) on the development of cognitive ability. This considers continuity between the ages of 6, 7, 9, and 11 years in a continuous measure of children's general ability. Summary statistics for data on 204 children are shown in Table 7.3.

As described in G. Dunn, Everitt, and Pickles (1993), a plausible starting model is the first-order autoregressive model shown in Figure 7.8 in which, in considering ability at one age, having taken into account ability at the previous measurement, there should be no association with any earlier measure. A feature of such a model is that an early measure may influence a later measure but only through an intermediate measure. The model consists of 3 regressions (Y2 on Y1, Y3 on Y2, and Y4 on Y3), but in addition to estimating the coefficients with standardized regression coefficients (.809, .850, and .867, respectively), SEM software also estimates a goodness-of-fit. In this case, a very poor fit is obtained, reflected in a chi-square of 61.82 with 3 degrees of freedom (10 observed summary statistics −7 parameters: the variances for F1, E2, E3, and E4 and the 3 regression coefficients b1, b2, and b3). This poor fit immediately tells us something is wrong. For many researchers, their instinct is to conclude that additional relationships must exist, for example, from Y1 to Y3 and Y2 to Y4.

Those additional relationships correspond to "sleeper effects," that there is some part of a measure at one time that seems to have no effect on the immediately next measure but yet can influence the subsequent measure. There are circumstances where such effects are plausible (e.g., where the tests given have varying content and two tests far apart have a more similar content, say, being more mathematical). However, in general, more biologically based sleeper effects are frequently considered implausible. How can we improve the model fit without adding these sleeper effects?

One way is to take the issue of measurement error seriously. In the classical measurement error model, the observed measurement is related to a "true score" F and an additive measurement error E of constant variance, that is:

$$Y_i = F_i + E_i$$

The true score F is an example of a latent variable or factor, and in this simple case, one that involves no factor loading and is also therefore a simple random effect. Usually, replicate measurements are necessary to identify and estimate the measurement error separately from the true score. However, a structural equation model of the four measurements, graphically shown in Figure 7.9, can be fitted with constraints, enabling measurement error and true score variances to be identified with only single measurements per occasion. Imposing constraints such that the measurement error variance remains the same over the four occasions achieves identification of the model and involves only one more parameter than the previous model (3 regression coefficients between the factors and variances for F1, D2, D3, D4 and the single common measurement error variance for the Es). Allowing for measurement results in a huge

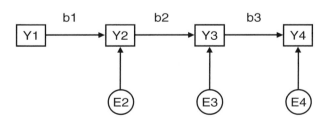

Figure 7.8 Model with autoregression between observed cognitive scores.

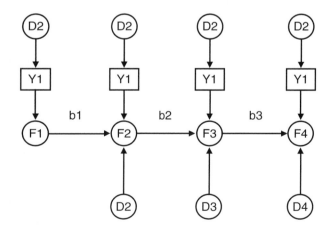

Figure 7.9 Model with autoregression between latent "true-score" cognitive measures.

improvement in model fit, giving a well-fitting model with 2df goodness-of-fit chi-square of 1.43. Clearly, this model has no need of additional sleeper effects—it already fits so well. How has this come about?

In the model with regression among observed variables, measurement error in the predicting variable results in the estimated regression coefficient being attenuated, estimated as being smaller than it should have been in the absence of measurement error. This underestimation results in the predicted association among the most temporally distant variables, given by the product of the standardized regression coefficients b1 × b2 × b3, being even more underestimated (a 10% underestimation in each coefficient resulting in a $1 - 0.9 \times 0.9 \times 0.9 = 27\%$ underestimation of their product). Allowing for measurement error corrects each regression coefficient and removes this gross underestimation of the model predicted long-term association.

There are important implications from this very modest example. The first is that although measurement error in a covariate X1 may result in systematic underestimation of its relationship with some response, it can also give rise to overestimation of the effects of some other covariate, X2, with which X1 is correlated. There are numerous reports that current health is not only associated with contemporaneous risk factors, but also independently with the same risk factors measured in childhood. Is this because the risk has its effect through an accumulation of risk exposure, or is it an artifact of measurement error in the contemporaneous measurements and that these contemporaneous measures tend to be correlated with childhood measures? This latter possibility is rarely explored.

Misclassification, Comorbidity, and Nonspecific Continuity

A common concern in psychiatry is the lack of specificity both of risk factors and in risk factor effects. Risk factors commonly raise risk for a wide variety of outcomes, and we find correspondingly high levels of comorbidity. Similarly, for many disorders, a current diagnosis raises rates for numerous future ones. Such poor specificity provides evidence against simple and distinct developmental pathways. However, just as measurement error hid the simple continuity model for ability, so classification errors in diagnosis could be masking much greater degrees of specificity.

In contrast to the numerous structural equation analyses of continuous measures, there are a meager number that have examined developmental pathways through discrete states that have accounted for misclassification, and probably none in a thoroughgoing fashion. The conceptual framework for such models is latent transition modeling, in which the switching among states can be only indirectly observed. Pickles and Rutter (1991) considered a latent class transition model for the development of adult antisocial behavior from childhood. The model suggested that misclassification error substantially increased the apparent amount of change, that is, exaggerated levels of resolved childhood conduct problems and new-onset adult antisocial behavior. Accounting for that error suggested much higher rates of continuity. However, the association of this much-reduced level of change with putative turning-point events became all the more striking.

Growth Curve, Trajectory, and Mixture Models

Growth curve and trajectory models represent developmental processes with some pathway-like properties but that allow effects of history beyond the current state to influence likely future development. These models can be considered forms of multilevel, random effects or latent variable/SEM models (Raudenbush, 2001; Rogosa & Willett, 1985). In these models, an individual's path for the development of some feature is typically characterized by a baseline intercept and some slope for trend over time. Values of the intercept and slope vary from individual to individual but together form some bivariate random effect/latent variable distribution. In addition, allowance is made for occasion- and individual-specific disturbance, frequently thought to be made up largely of measurement error. With suitable repeated measure data, these individual intercepts and slopes can be estimated, allowing individual developmental trajectories to be calculated. Figure 7.10 shows a plot of such trajectories for the development of language for children with Autism, Pervasive Developmental Disorder, Not Otherwise Specified (PDD-NOS), and developmental delay (Taylor, Pickering, Lord, & Pickles, 1998).

Empirically, they can be considered as nothing more than a model-based smoothing of the raw observed language scores, but they are nonetheless useful for that. The top right plot shows clearly that the groups differ substantially on average. However, the remaining plots show that within each group there is substantial variation among individuals, with the result that there is substantial overlap among groups. This cautions us not to overstate the distinctiveness of the developmental pathways of each group.

A modification of the approach can also be used to identify homogeneity rather than heterogeneity. Instead of allowing individual trajectories to vary continuously with respect to intercept and slope, they can be restricted to a finite set of alternatives. This allows the estimation of a set

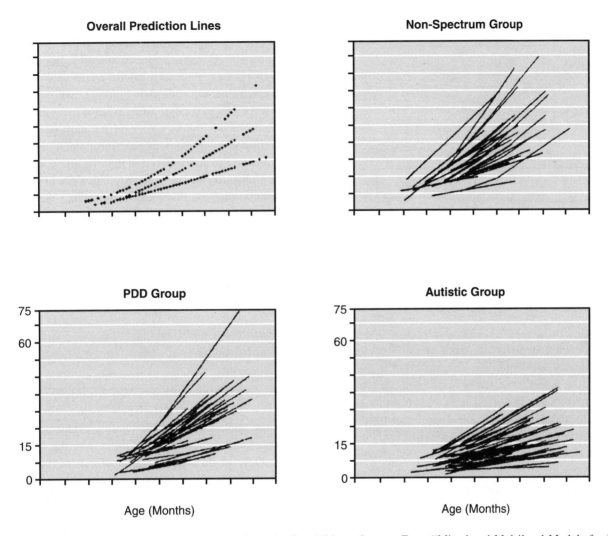

Figure 7.10 Estimated individual growth trajectories for children. *Source:* From "Mixed and Multilevel Models for Longitudinal Data: Growth Curve Analysis of Language Development" (pp. 127–144), by A. Taylor, K. Pickering, C. Lord, and A. Pickles, in *Recent Advances in the Statistical Analysis of Medical Data,* B. Everitt & G. Dunn (Eds.), 1998, London: Arnold.

of discrete developmental pathways with individuals having a higher or lower probability of belonging to each pathway. This kind of approach has been much used in criminology (e.g., D. F. Nagin & Tremblay, 2001).

From the perspective of SEM, these models can be seen as a restricted version of mixture covariance analysis (Muthen, 2001). In this approach, the underlying pattern of association among a set of continuous (latent) variables can themselves vary according to class, where class itself is a discrete latent variable. In an analysis of the development of drinking behavior using data from age 18 from the National Longitudinal Study of Youth and illustrated in Figure 7.11, Muthen and Muthen (2000) finds evidence for a normative pattern of development for 77% of the sample, where drinking rises from age 18 to a broad peak repre-

senting heavy drinking about once every 2 months until age 25, followed by a slow decline. A second class of 10% show rapid and continuous increase to the end of the period of study at age 30. A third class of 14% are already drinking heavily more than 3 times a month by age 18, but show continuous decline.

Moderator Effects

A moderator or effect modifier gives rise "to variation in the magnitude of a measure of exposure effect across levels of another variable" (Last, 1995, p. 254). This is most clear when Z changes the relationship between X and Y without directly influencing the level or probability of exposure to X. It suggests that Z somehow defines different

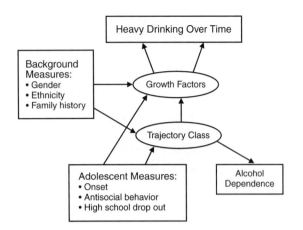

Figure 7.11 Mixture growth curve model of drinking behavior and dependence. *Source:* Adapted from "Second Generation SEM Growth Analysis" (pp. 291–322), by B. Muthen in L. M. Collins and A. Sayer (Eds.), 2001, *New Methods for the Analysis of Change,* Washington, DC: American Psychological Association.

subpopulations in which different causal chains operate. Terms like resiliency, susceptibility, and buffering factors may correspond to moderators. Early harsh, punitive, and hostile home environment predicted later victimization by peers, but only for children who had a low number of friendships; friendships acts as a moderating variable (where does this come from?). In this example, the moderation may be achieved contemporaneously, but where the impact of some risk experience can be carried forward in time through altered cognition or behavior, then moderation of the effects of that risk may occur at some point more distant in time.

Testing for moderation consists of testing for an interaction effect of risk and moderator on outcome, although, as we have described, care should be taken as to whether the appropriate null model is one of additive or multiplicative main effects (Tennant & Bebbington, 1978). For a pure moderator, we would also want to confirm the absence of any effect of the moderator in the absence of the risk exposure. Thus, in Brown's (Brown & Harris, 1977) social causation models of depression, vulnerability factors, such as caring for multiple children under age 5, must not be associated with depression in the absence of the provoking agent of life events.

In latent variable modeling, moderation can be approached using multiple group analysis, where different paths may be allowed in moderator negative and moderator positive groups, or by the use of random coefficient models.

Developmental Pathways and Genes

The potential importance of genetics in the development of psychopathology is reflected in a burgeoning research ef-

fort into the identification of important genes and in estimating genetic contributions to variation in psychopathological outcomes. However, we often think about the effects of genes in a remarkably primitive fashion. We may have progressed from deterministic thinking, that the presence or absence of a particular allele at some locus may result in an unavoidable outcome, but for the most part, this has been replaced by a nebulous long-term stable propensity that gives rise to an expectation that the allele will increase the probability of the outcome. This fails to tackle the fundamental problem that must be overcome, one inadvertently perpetuated by the additive decompositions so fondly estimated by twin researchers, that of pitting nature *versus* nurture. The models that we entertain with respect to psychosocial variables are frequently complex and dynamic—they are developmental models. How do we integrate genetics into these models?

Genetic Contingency and Gene-Environment Interaction

Our discussion of causes made it clear that we often had to specify certain conditions or maintained hypotheses before we could expect to observe the effects of that cause. Exactly the same applies with genes and can provide one route to treatment. Thus, remove phenylalanine from the dietary environment and we do not observe the effects of the PKU gene on mental retardation. Improve childhood social environments and we may not see the effects of the MAOA gene on adult antisocial behavior.

Exactly where a genetically influenced pathway leads may be culturally mediated. Genes appear to be the major factor influencing variation in age of puberty. However, whether this leads to increased rates of incomplete education as a result of early-maturing girls associating with and leaving school at the same time as an older peer group appears to be culturally moderated. Traditional (less modern) societies may impose social controls that preclude such mixed-age association. More modern societies may allow forms of dating among young children, making association with older children unnecessary. The pathway from early puberty genes to incomplete education may operate only in the transition stage between traditional and modern societies. Of course, these same genes may now be associated with some new pathway to some other outcome.

Developmental Variation in the Importance of Genes

In the example just given, although genetic expression is environmentally contingent, the genetic vulnerability is perceived as time-invariant. However as we noted earlier, animal studies have shown how gene expression can alter substantially in development, and often is under environmental control (Fish et al., 2004). Studies of human subjects suggest that the effects of different genes may follow different developmental timetables. Findings reported by the Specific Language Impairment Consortium (2002) from a genome screen for specific language impairment strongly suggested two genes associated with language impairment. However, these two genes were linked to quite distinct measures of language. One of these was a standard measure of expressive language in middle childhood; the other was linked to a measure of nonword repetition. This latter measure is thought to reflect a child's ability to learn a new word from a single hearing. This is an ability that would clearly be helpful, indeed perhaps the rate-limiting skill for the rapid expansion of vocabulary during the early stages of speech development. However, by middle childhood, all children have heard most of the words they need for everyday speech many, many times (hence the need to test this ability by the use of novel nonwords). Thus, this ability may no longer be the limiting factor in the use of language in middle childhood. Instead, perhaps some syntax-related skill limits language complexity, and it is this to which the second gene may be associated. This would be consistent with the genes having their effects on two distinct pathways to specific language impairment, one with early onset but with a substantial amount of subsequent resolution (as it does not constrain eventual vocabulary acquisition), whereas the other results in divergent development at a point where language structure is becoming more complex. Currently, this interpretation is little more than a hypothetical example, because we lack the necessary longitudinal data to be convincing, and more recent multivariate analysis questions the apparent specificity of early reports.

Gene-Environment Correlations

Plomin and Bergman (1991) elaborated how many apparent effects of the familial environment may in fact be the consequences of correlated and unmeasured genetic effects. This can arise in three ways: (1) passively, as where the child-rearing environment is influenced by parental genes that are inevitably correlated with child genes; (2) actively, as where children genetically predisposed to antisocial behavior may find themselves in unsupervised environments as a consequence of truanting; and (3) evocatively, as where children genetically predisposed to hostility can evoke negative reactions from their caregivers. Study designs able to account for such confounding effects of genes in examining environmental influences on development are

in principle little different from the more general problem of confounders already described, but they inevitably tend to exploit the natural experiment of mating and different kinds of sibship that arise.

FUTURE DIRECTIONS AND CONCLUSIONS

We have reviewed the conceptualization and the previous and current use of the developmental pathway term. But, how is it and its use likely to be developed in the future?

Future Directions

In some respects, the metaphor of developmental pathways has already been remarkably productive in the investigation of psychopathology. However, its full potential may not yet have been realized. It is commonly used as an innocuous summary term that allows researchers to convey the general area in which they are working. It becomes a tool with a more specific purpose when it is used to pose questions that might not otherwise be addressed, such as whether an outcome at one point in development is also a starting point for, and influence on, subsequent processes. However, it is uncommon for it to be employed to set up highly specific predictions, of the form "pathway theory would predict x, rather than y." For example, if there are multiple possible pathways, some more advantageous than others for long-term outcomes, and with genuine choice points, it follows that we should be able to identify phases in development around which future directions hinge. That means there should be other phases that are less pivotal. We reviewed earlier some of the evidence that this is indeed the case in the interplay among experience, neurobiology, and behavior. However, we have little idea how general this principle is over development. If it were more generally applicable, fascinating and important questions regarding mechanisms could be generated. A key issue would be, What are the mechanisms whereby at one time there is substantial instability and openness to external influences, and at other times considerable stability and an imperviousness to experience? In the case of the developing visual system or HPA regulation, it is plausible to suppose that there may be substantial periods over which gene expression is stable and impervious to environmental influences, punctuated by shorter critical phases of instability and sensitivity to the environment.

When we press the model in relation to psychosocial processes, it begins to set up interesting questions. The transition from adolescence to adult life appears to represent a key phase over which there are branching points involving peer group, employment, and choice of romantic partner that have consequences that tend to be stable. The metaphor of the pathway suggests ways in which mechanisms might be conceptualized. Decisions at the branching point of a pathway may be made on the basis of the visible attractiveness of one pathway over another, making it desirable, for example, because the path has an exciting view, or because of features of the other paths that make them undesirable. Often, however, the immediate characteristics of the alternative pathways are less relevant than information about where the path leads. These considerations may be in competition; for example, one path is steep and difficult but leads to a fine restaurant, and the other is easy and pleasant but leads to a burger bar.

This suggests a program of work into the interplay between short- and long-term considerations in relation to, for example, education and relationships, in normal development starting in early adolescence, and into ways this is altered by individual differences, for example, in affect regulation. The pathway model would predict that normal development over adolescence is characterized by an increased use of long-term considerations in day-to-day behaviors, as a phase of pathway divergence approaches. It would also predict that, given the major negative implications of going down adverse pathways, the deployment of these longer-term considerations is generally not readily undermined by short-term considerations or emotional factors. Parents and peers may have a crucial role in ensuring the use of long-term considerations where there is a risk of this being undermined. An understanding of the normal or prevailing case could then inform the study of less advantageous or deviant pathways. For example, in relation to early adolescence, if the prediction is correct that the young person's behaviors are still determined mainly by short-term considerations, then if the young person has opportunities for sexual experiences, he or she will be vulnerable to making decisions about them that do not have a long-term perspective. This vulnerability will be further increased where parents and peers are not available to counter the use of short-term considerations. Later in adolescence, in some individuals the behaviors may still be dominated by features of the immediate landscape, or the use of long-term considerations may be readily undermined by emotional processes, such as strong attachment or sexual needs.

Used in this way, the pathway framework has the potential to bring particular questions into focus for study using a wide range of methods, including those that cur-

rently do not have a strong developmental emphasis. For example, theories of depression, discussed earlier, propose that vulnerable individuals have a heightened propensity to generate self-devaluative beliefs during periods of normal low mood. Techniques of study include eliciting beliefs during low mood induction, or simply by asking subjects about their thoughts during a recent time when they felt low. Experimental approaches informed by the pathway considerations reviewed here might similarly elicit cognitions about relationships with an emphasis on immediate and long-term considerations under varying conditions of affective challenge.

Another distinctive element of future research is likely to be the formulation of pathways that involve a much more complete elaboration across the various levels of explanation from neurobiology to cognitive psychology and on to psychosocial experience. We are beginning to see glimpses of the elements of such integrated pathways, most notably in the recent findings of gene-environment interaction (Caspi et al., 2003). However, each such pathway is likely to involve a very considerable research effort and will of necessity involve constructive interdisciplinary collaboration of a kind that is often fraught with difficulties. The elucidation of each will be exciting, but progress will be slow.

The pathways perspective also has implications for the way we conceive of outcomes in the evaluation of treatments. Ultimately, the goal of treatment is to reduce symptoms and impairment; however, this takes on a new complexion when considered in the context of developmental pathways. We reviewed earlier ways in which episodes of depression may influence pathways via effects on social functioning and cognitive processes. We do not, however, know whether treatment for depression also increases the likelihood of following a more advantageous pathway, nor whether treatments differ in this respect. Studies of differential treatment effects have been conducted. For example, Hollon et al. (2005) found that relapse rates in the year following cognitive therapy for depression were substantially lower than following medication. Follow-up informed by pathway considerations would also examine social, biological, and cognitive variables thought to influence risks for subsequent depression and other forms of psychopathology. In adolescence, improving the way choices with long-term implications are made, in the areas of education/work, peer group, and romantic partners, could have a greater impact on subsequent risk for psychopathology than treatments that bring about immediate symptomatic or functional changes.

Finally, the clinical implications of findings and concepts from pathways research are considerable. Overall, the effect would be to draw attention in assessment to multiple aspects of functioning over considerable periods of time, instead of the more narrow focus on recent symptoms. More specifically, identifying key features of pathways to current psychopathology would provide the focus for treatment and suggest criteria for judging effectiveness. These may be quite distinct from symptomatic improvement. For example, substantial reduction in overall level of deviant behaviors with some antisocial adolescents may not be realistic, but promoting educational or vocational activities that have the potential to open new opportunities in the longer term may be crucial to their subsequent pathways. Therapeutically, the emphasis on a subset of difficulties with long-term implications, rather than on all of the young person's (often substantial) problems, also can lead to more modest and achievable treatment goals. Treatment strategies could also target ways of reducing the likelihood of behaviors that put a young person on a deviant pathway and increasing the chances of creating stable advantageous pathways. These might focus on cognitions associated with these behaviors and on processes that favor decisions associated with beneficial pathways, and on ways these may be undermined, for example, by attachment or sexual needs.

Conclusions

The use of the pathway metaphor has helped get the concept of developmental pathways into the common scientific vocabulary. Indeed, it is fair to say that the metaphor has dominated conceptualization, there being no widely shared definitions of the general concept of a developmental pathway that offer greater precision than the metaphor itself. Nonetheless, we have seen that a full and almost literal consideration of the metaphor reveals a quite remarkable number of detailed features, be they implications, qualities, constraints, or possibilities, that a developmental pathway should or could possess. It is in these last words where the major weakness of the concept is seen, in that there seems to be no identifiable set of features that are necessary for some longitudinal sequence of states, levels, and events to be referred to as a developmental pathway. We have seen examples of the use of the concept that in detail seem to share almost nothing. This finding mirrors how we use metaphors in our everyday language: to point to the presence of some feature rather than its absence.

But what a useful idea it remains! Indeed, one could argue that our mistake is that we have not pressed the idea to its limits. The richness of the metaphor provides us with a long list of thought experiments and hypotheses that need

to be addressed. Sometimes addressing these may be decisive in determining whether a pathway exists or not, such as determining whether A always precedes B which always precedes C. More often, however, addressing these will be informative about how the pathway is being conceived, which aspects of the metaphor are being highlighted as applying in this case, and thus sharpening our specific definition. If the developmental pathway concept is in its general form too unrestrictive, then in any specific case we must be clearer about which features apply and which do not.

We have also seen that even when we have identified the specific features that do apply to a specific case, the mechanisms that result in these features are the familiar mechanisms of biological and psychosocial development more generally. Developmental pathways add no new mechanisms. Instead, they provide a framework within which the action of several possibly fragmented processes can be combined, the mechanisms for each process being imported from elsewhere.

Can developmental pathways serve a useful, purely descriptive role, one in which it is intended that no causal attribution be made? Our instinct here is to say no. We illustrated examples, such as the growth curve models for language development, that are at one level little more than the smoothing of raw data, where description is clearly prominent. However, this was perhaps the example that drew least from the concept of a developmental pathway. In general, in defining developmental pathways researchers believe they are indicating causally important relationships. Thus, developmental pathways ought to have some consistent mapping to causal pathways and associated methods of analysis. It was clear that often the various formal, heuristic, and statistical causal pathway models each had something to contribute to our understanding, elaboration of prediction, and method of study of developmental pathways. But that is not to say that they were equivalent. Indeed, there is often a danger that one statistical representation of a pathway may be uncritically and inappropriately imposed on developmental data where another representation would be better suited.

The concept of a developmental pathway has been used in ways that have little in common and may even be mutually inconsistent, and has been haphazardly related to any causal model framework. Although in each case, further clarity and detailed elaboration should be sought, removing scope for confusion by restricting the concept to one particular formalization is probably not our recommendation. The major strength of the concept of a developmental pathway is as a device to stimulate the imagination and to provide a framework for synthesis and integration. This we believe it does very well.

REFERENCES

Baron, R. M., & Kenny, D. A. (1986). The moderator-mediator variable distinction in social psychological research: Conceptual, strategic and statistical considerations. *Journal of Personality and Social Psychology, 51,* 1173–1182.

Bergman, L. R. (1988). You can't classify all of the people all of the time. *Multivariate Behavioral Research, 23,* 425–441.

Bergman, L. R. (1998). A pattern-oriented approach to studying individual development: Snapshots and processes. In R. D. Cairns, L. R. Bergman, & J. Kagan (Eds.), *Methods and models for studying the individual* (pp. 83–121). Thousand Oaks, CA: Sage.

Bergman, L. R., Magnusson, D., & El-Khouri, B. M. (2003). *Studying individual development in an interindividual context: A person-oriented approach.* London: Erlbaum.

Blot, W. J., & Day, N. E. (1979). Synergism and interaction: Are they equivalent? *American Journal of Epidemiology, 110,* 99–100.

Bolton, P., Park, R., Higgins, N., Griffiths, P., & Pickles, A. (2002). Neuro-epileptic determinants of Autism spectrum disorders in tuberous sclerosis. *Brain, 125,* 1247–1255.

Brown, G. W., & Harris, T. O. (1978). *Social origins of depression.* London: Tavistock.

Brown, G. W., Harris, T. O., & Copeland, J. R. (1977). Depression and loss. *British Journal of Psychiatry, 130,* 1–18.

Caspi, A., McCaly, J., Moffitt, T., Mill, J., Martin, J., Craig, I., et al. (2002). Role of genotype in the cycle of violence in maltreated children. *Science, 297,* 851–854.

Caspi, A., & Moffitt, T. (1995). The continuity of maladaptive behaviour: From description to understanding in the study of antisocial behaviour. In D. Cicchetti & D. Cohen (Eds.), *Developmental psychopathology* (Vol. 2, pp. 472–511). New York: Wiley.

Caspi, A., Sugden, K., Moffitt, T. E., Taylor, A., Craig, I., Harrington, H., et al. (2003). Influence of life-stress on depression: Moderation by a polymorphism in the 5-HTT gene. *Science, 301,* 386–389.

Cicchetti, D., & Rogosch, F. A. (1996). Equifinality and multifinality in developmental psychopathology. *Development and Psychopathology, 8,* 597–600.

Cloninger, C. R., & Gottesman, I. I. (1987). Genetic and environmental factors in antisocial behavior disorder. In S. A. Mednick, T. E. Moffitt, & S. A. Stack (Eds.), *The causes of crime* (pp. 92–109). Cambridge, England: Cambridge University Press.

Coie, J., Terry, R., Zakriski, A., & Lochman, J. (1995). Early adolescent social influences on delinquent behaviour. In J. McCord (Ed.), *Coercion and punishment in long-term perspectives* (pp. 229–244). New York: Cambridge University Press.

Cole, S. R., & Hernan, M. A. (2002). Fallability in estimating direct effects. *International Journal of Epidemiology, 31,* 163–165.

Coplan, J. D., Trost, R. C., Owens, M. J., Cooper, T. B., Gorman, J. M., Nemeroff, C. B., et al. (1998). Cerebrospinal fluid concentrations of somatostatin and biogenic amines in grown primates reared by mothers exposed to manipulated foraging conditions. *Archives of General Psychiatry, 55,* 473–477.

Cox, D. R. (1972). Regression models and life-tables. *Journal of the Royal Statistical Society of London. Series B, Biological Sciences, 24,* 406–424.

Crick, N. R., & Dodge, K. A. (1994). A review and reformulation of social-processing mechanisms in children's social adjustment. *Psychological Bulletin, 115,* 74–101.

Dale, M. (1976). Barriers to the rehabilitation of ex-offenders. *Crime and Delinquency, 22,* 322–337.

Deanna, K. (1976). Short-term longitudinal evidence for the sequentiality of Kohlberg's early stages of moral development. *Developmental Psychology, 12,* 162–166.

Dodge, K. A. (1993). Social cognitive mechanisms in the development of conduct disorder and depression. *Annual Review of Psychology, 44,* 559–584.

Dodge, K. A., Pettit, G. S., Bates, J. E., & Valente, E. (1995). Social information: Processing patterns partially mediate the effect of early physical abuse on later conduct problems. *Journal of Abnormal Psychology, 104,* 632–643.

Dunn, G., Everitt, B., & Pickles, A. (1993). *Modelling covariances and latent variables using EQS.* London: Chapman & Hall.

Dunn, J. (1996). Children's relationships: Bridging the divide between cognitive and social development [Emmanuel Miller Lecture, 1995]. *Journal of Child Psychology and Psychiatry, 37,* 507–518.

Dunn, J., Slomkowski, C. M., Donelan-McCall, N., & Herrera, C. (1995). Conflict understanding and relationships: Developments and differences in the preschool years. *Early Education and Development, 6,* 303–316.

Eme, R. F., & Kavanagh, L. (1995). Sex differences in conduct disorder. *Journal of Clinical Child Psychology, 24,* 406–426.

Fergusson, D. M., & Mullen, P. E. (1999). *Childhood sexual abuse: An evidence based perspective.* Thousand Oaks, CA: Sage.

Feyerabend, P. (1975). *Against method.* London: Verso.

Fish, E. W., Shahrokh, D., Bagot, R., Caldji, C., Bredy, T., Szyf, M., et al. (2004). Epigenetic programming of stress responses through variations in maternal care. *Annals of the New York Academy of Sciences, 1036,* 167–180.

Francis, D. D., Diorio, J., Plotsky, P. M., & Meaney, M. J. (2002). Environmental enrichment reverses the effects of maternal separation on stress reactivity. *Journal of Neurosciences, 22,* 7840–7843.

Greenland, S., & Brumback, B. (2002). An overview of relations among causal modelling methods. *International Journal of Epidemiology, 31,* 1030–1037.

Greenland, S., Pearl, J., & Robins, J. M. (1999). Causal diagrams for epidemiologic research. *Epidemiology, 10*(1), 37–48.

Hardt, J., & Rutter, M. (2004). Validity of adult retrospective reports of adverse childhood experiences: Review of the evidence. *Journal of Child Psychology and Psychiatry, 45,* 260–274.

Harrington, R., Fudge, H., Rutter, M., Pickles, A., & Hill, J. (1990). Adult outcome of childhood and adolescent depression: Psychiatric status. *Archives of General Psychiatry, 47,* 465–473.

Harris, T., Brown, G. W., & Bifulco, A. (1990). Loss of parent in childhood and adult psychiatric disorder: A tentative overall model. *Development and Psychopathology, 2*(3), 311–327.

Heim, C., Newport, D. J., Bonsall, R., Miller, A. H., & Nemeroff, C. B. (2001). Altered pituitary-adrenal axis responses to provocative challenge tests in adult survivors of childhood abuse. *American Journal of Psychiatry, 158*(4), 575–581.

Heise, D. R. (1975). *Causal analysis.* New York: Wiley-Interscience.

Hill, J. (2002). Biological, psychological and social processes in the conduct disorders. *Journal of Child Psychology and Psychiatry, Annual Research Review, 43,* 133–164.

Hill, J., Davis, R., Byatt, M., Burnside, E., Rollinson, L., & Fear, S. (2000). Child sexual abuse and affective symptoms in women: A general population study. *Psychological Medicine, 30,* 1283–1291.

Hill, J., Pickles, A., Burnside, E., Byatt, M., Rollinson, L., Davis, R. et al. (2001). Sexual abuse, poor parental care and adult depression: Evidence for different mechanisms. *British Journal of Psychiatry, 179,* 104–109.

Hill, J., Pickles, A., Byatt, M., & Rollinson, L. (2004). Juvenile versus adult onset depression: Multiple differences imply different pathways. *Psychological Medicine, 34,* 1483–1493.

Hodges, J., & Tizard, B. (1989). Social and family relationships of ex-institutional adolescents. *Journal of Child Psychology and Psychiatry, 30,* 77–97.

Hollon, S. D., Derubeis, R. J., Shelton, R. C., Amsterdam, J. D., Salomon, R. M., O'reardon, J. P., et al. (2005). Prevention of relapse following cognitive therapy vs medications in moderate to severe depression. *Archives of General Psychiatry, 62*(4), 417–422.

Hubel, D. H., Wiesel, T. N., & LeVay, S. (1976). Functional architecture of area 17 in normal and monocularly deprived macaque monkeys. *Cold Spring Harbor Symposia on Quantitative Biology, 40,* 581–589.

Hume, D. (1902). *An enquiry concerning human understanding* (L. A. Selby-Bigge, Ed. & Trans., 2nd ed.). Oxford: Oxford University Press. (Original work published 1777)

Huot, R. L., Plotsky, P. M., Lenox, R. H., & McNamara, R. K. (2002). Neonatal maternal separation reduces hippocampal mossy fibre density in adult Long Evans rats. *Brain Research, 950,* 52–63.

Huot, R. L., Thrivikraman, K. V., Meaney, M. J., & Plotsky, P. M. (2001). Development of adult ethanol preference and anxiety as a consequence of neonatal maternal separation in Long Evans rats and reversal with antidepressant treatment. *Psychopharmacology, 158,* 366–373.

Jaffee, S. R., Moffitt, T. E., Caspi, A., Fombonne, E., Poulton, R., & Martin, J. (2002). Differences in early childhood risk factors for juvenile-onset and adult-onset depression. *Archives of General Psychiatry, 59,* 215–222.

Judd, C. M., & Kenny, D. A. (1981). Process analysis: Estimating mediation in treatment evaluations. *Evaluation Review, 5,* 602–619.

Keenan, K., & Shaw, D. S. (2003). Starting at the beginning: Exploring the etiology of antisocial behavior in the first years of life. In B. B. Lahey, T. E. Moffitt, & A. Caspi (Eds.), *Causes of conduct disorder and juvenile delinquency* (pp. 153–181). New York: Guilford Press.

Kendler, K. S., Gardner, C. O., & Prescott, C. A. (2002). Toward a comprehensive developmental model for major depression in women. *American Journal of Psychiatry, 159,* 1133–1145.

Kendler, K. S., Thornton, L. M., & Gardner, C. O. (2000). Stressful life events and previous episodes in the etiology of major depression in women: An evaluation of the "kindling" hypothesis. *American Journal of Psychiatry, 157,* 1243–1251.

Kendler, K. S., Thornton, L. M., & Gardner, C. O. (2001). Genetic risk, number of previous episodes, and stressful life events in predicting onset of major depression. *American Journal of Psychiatry, 158*(4), 582–586.

Kerr, M., & Stattin, H. (2000). What parents know, how they know it, and several forms of adolescent adjustment: Further support for a reinterpretation of monitoring. *Developmental Psychology, 36,* 366–380.

Kreppner, J. M., O'Connor, T. G., Rutter, M., Beckett, C., Castle, J., Croft, C., et al. (2001). Can innattention/hyperactivity be an institutional deprivation syndrome? *Journal of Abnormal Child Psychology, 29,* 513–528.

Last, J. M. (1995). *A dictionary of epidemiology.* New York: Oxford University Press.

Leventhal, T., & Brooks-Gunn, J. (2000). The neighborhoods they live in: The effects of neighborhood residence on child and adolescent outcomes. *Psychological Bulletin, 126,* 309–337.

Lewinsohn, P., Allen, N. B., Seeley, J. R., & Gotlib, I. H. (1999). First onset versus recurrence of depression: Differential processes of psychosocial risk. *Journal of Abnormal Psychology, 108,* 483–489.

Lewinsohn, P. M., Joiner, T. E., Jr., & Rohde, P. (2001). Evaluation of cognitive diathesis-stress models in predicting major depressive disorder in adolescents. *Journal of Abnormal Psychology, 110,* 203–215.

Link, B., Cullen, F., Struening, E., Shrout, P., & Dohrenwend, B. (1989). A modified labeling approach to mental disorders: An empirical assessment. *American Sociological Review, 50,* 400–423.

Loeber, R. (1991). Natural histories of conduct problems, delinquency and associated substance abuse: Evidence from developmental progressions. *Advances in Clinical Psychology, 11,* 73–124.

Loeber, R., & Leblanc, M. (1990). Toward a developmental criminology. In M. Tonry & N. Morris (Eds.), *Crime and justice* (Vol. 12, pp. 375–437). Chicago: University of Chicago Press.

Loeber, R., & Wikstrom, P. (1993). Individual pathways to crime in different types of neighbourhood. In D. Farrington, R. Sampson, & P.-O. Wikstrom (Eds.), *Integrating individual and ecological perspectives* (pp. 169–204). Stockholm, Sweden: Liber-Verlag.

Magnusson, D., & Bergman, L. R. (1990). A pattern approach to the study of pathways from childhood to adulthood. In L. N. Robins & M. Rutter (Eds.), *Straight and devious pathways from childhood to adulthood* (pp. 101–115). Cambridge, England: Cambridge University Press.

Maughan, B., & Rutter, M. (1997). Retrospective reporting of childhood adversity: Issues in assessing long-term recall. *Journal of Personality Disorders, 11,* 19–33.

Moffitt, T. E. (1993). Adolescence-limited and life-course persistent antisocial behavior: A developmental taxonomy. *Psychological Review, 100,* 674–701.

Moffitt, T. E. (1994). Natural histories of delinquency. In E. Weiterkamp & H. J. Kerner (Eds.), *Cross-national longitudinal research on human development and criminal behaviour* (pp. 3–61). Dordrecht, The Netherlands: Kluwer Academic Press.

Moffitt, T. E., Caspi, A., Dickson, N., Silva, P., & Stanton, W. (1996). Childhood-onset versus adolescent-onset antisocial conduct problems in males: Natural history from ages 3 to 18 years. *Development and Psychopathology, 8,* 399–424.

Moffitt, T. E., Caspi, A., Rutter, M., & Silva, P. (2001). *Sex differences in anti-social behaviour.* Cambridge, England: Cambridge University Press.

Morrell, J., & Murray, L. (2003). Parenting and the development of conduct disorder and hyperactive symptoms in childhood: A prospective longitudinal study from 2 months to 8 years. *Journal of Child Psychology and Psychiatry, 44,* 489–508.

Muthen, B. (2001). Second generation structural equation modeling with a combination of categorical and continuous latent variables: New opportunities for latent class/latent growth modelling. In L. M. Collins & A. Sayer (Eds.), *New methods for the analysis of change* (pp. 291–322). Washington, DC: American Psychological Association.

Muthen, B., & Muthen, L. (2000). Integrating person-centred and variable-centred analyses: Growth mixture modelling with latent trajectory classes. *Alcoholism: Clinical and Experimental Research, 24,* 882–891.

Nagin, D. F., & Tremblay, R. E. (1999). Trajectories of boys' physical aggression, opposition, and hyperactivity on the path to physically violent and non-violent juvenile delinquency. *Child Development, 70,* 1181–1196.

Nagin, D. F., & Tremblay, R. E. (2001). Parental and early childhood predictors of persistent physical aggression in boys from kindergarden to high school. *Archives of General Psychiatry, 58,* 389–394.

Nagin, D. S., Pagani, L., Tremblay, R. E., & Vitaro, F. (2003). Life course turning points: The effect of grade retention on physical aggression. *Development and Psychopathology, 15,* 343–361.

Nelson, E. C., Heath, A. C., Madden, P. A., Cooper, M. L., Dinwiddie, S. H., Bucholz, K. K., et al. (2002). Association between self-reported childhood sexual abuse and adverse psychosocial outcomes: Results from a twin study. *Archives of General Psychiatry, 59*(2), 139–145.

Newton, P. E. (1994). *Preschool prevarication: An investigation of the cognitive prerequisites for deception.* Unpublished doctoral dissertation, University of Portsmouth, NH.

Osbourne, R. T., & Suddick, D. E. (1972). A longitudinal investigation of the intellectual differentiation hypothesis. *Journal of Genetic Psychology, 110,* 83–89.

Patterson, G. R. (1993). Orderly change in a stable world: The antisocial trait as a chimera. *Journal of Consulting and Clinical Psychology, 61,* 911–919.

Pearl, J. (2000). *Causality: Models, reasoning, and inference.* Cambridge, England: Cambridge University Press.

Pettit, G. S., Poloha, J. A., & Mize, J. (2001). Perceptual and attributional processes in aggression and conduct problems. In J. Hill & B. Maughan (Eds.), *Conduct disorders in childhood and adolescence* (pp. 292–319). New York: Cambridge University Press.

Pianta, R. C., Sroufe, L. A., & Egeland, B. (1989). Continuity and discontinuity in maternal sensitivity at 6, 24, and 42 months in a high risk sample. *Child Development, 60*(2), 481–487.

Pickles, A. (1993). Stages, precursors and causes in development. In D. F. Hay & A. Angold (Eds.), *Precursors and causes in development and psychopathology* (pp. 23–49). Chichester, England: Wiley.

Pickles, A., & Angold, A. (2003). Natural categories or fundamental dimensions: On carving nature at the joints and the re-articulation of psychopathology. *Development and Psychopathology, 15,* 529–551.

Pickles, A., & Rutter, M. (1991). Statistical and conceptual models of "turning points" in developmental processes. In D. Magnusson, L. Bergman, G. Rudinger, & B. Torestad (Eds.), *Problems and methods in longitudinal research* (pp. 133–195). Cambridge, England: Cambridge University Press.

Plomin, R., & Bergman, C. S. (1991). The nature of nurture: Genetic influences on "environmental" measures. *Behavioral and Brain Sciences, 10,* 1–15.

Quay, H. C. (1993). The psychobiology of undersocialized aggressive conduct disorder: A theoretical perspective. *Development and Psychopathology, 5,* 165–180.

Quinton, D., Pickles, A., Maughan, B., & Rutter, M. (1993). Partners, peers and pathways: Assortative pairing and continuities in conduct disorder. *Development and Psychopathology, 5,* 763–783.

Raudenbush, S. W. (2001). Towards a coherent framework for comparing trajectories of individual change. In L. M. Collins & A. G. Sayer (Eds.), *New methods for the analysis of change* (pp. 135–158). New York: Sage.

Robins, J. M. (2001). Data, design, and background knowledge in etiologic inference. *Epidemiology, 10,* 37–48.

Robins, J. M., & Greenland, S. (1992). Identifiability and exchangeability for direct and indirect effects. *Epidemiology, 3,* 143–155.

Robins, J. M., Hernan, M. A., & Brumback, B. (2002). Marginal structural models and causal inference in epidemiology. *Epidemiology, 11,* 550–560.

Rogosa, D., & Willett, J. B. (1985). Understanding correlates of change by modelling individual differences in growth. *Psychometrika, 50,* 203–228.

Rohde, P., Lewinsohn, P. M., & Seeley, J. R. (1994). Are adolescents changed by an episode of major depression? *Journal of the American Academy of Child and Adolescent Psychiatry, 33,* 1289–1298.

Rosenbaum, P. R. (2002). *Observational studies* (2nd ed.). New York: Springer-Verlag.

Rosenblum, L. A., & Andrews, M. W. (1994). Influences of environmental demand on maternal behaviour and infant development. *Acta Paediatrica, 397*(Suppl.), 57–63.

Rothman, K. J. (1976). Causes. *American Journal of Epidemiology, 104,* 587–592.

Rothman, K. J., & Greenland, S. (1998). *Modern epidemiology* (2nd ed.). Philadelphia: Lippincott.

Rowe, R., Maughan, B., Pickles, A., Costello, E. J., & Angold, A. (2002). The relationship between DSM-IV oppositional defiant disorder and conduct disorder: Findings from the Great Smoky Mountains Study. *Journal of Child Psychology and Psychiatry, 43,* 365–374.

Rowe, R., Maughan, B., Worthman, C., Costello, E. J., & Angold, A. (2004). Testosterone, antisocial behavior and social dominance in boys: Pubertal development and biosocial interaction. *Biological Psychiatry, 55,* 546–552.

Rutter, M., Pickles, A., Eaves, L., & Murray, R. (2001). Testing hypotheses on environmental risk mechanisms. *Psychological Bulletin, 127,* 291–324.

Rutter, M., Quinton, D., & Hill, J. (1990). Adult outcome of institution-reared children: Males and females compared. In L. Robins & M. Rutter (Ed.), *Straight and devious pathways from childhood to adulthood* (pp. 135–157). New York: Cambridge University Press.

Rutter, M., & Rutter, M. (1993). *Developing minds: Challenge and continuity across the lifespan.* New York: Basic Books.

Sampson, R. J. (1993). Family and community-level influences on crime: A contextual theory and strategies for research testing. In D. Farrington, R. Sampson, & P.-O. Wikstrom (Eds.), *Integrating individual and ecological perspectives* (pp. 153–168). Stockholm, Sweden: Liber-Verlag.

Sampson, R. J., & Groves, W. (1989). Community structure and crime: Testing social-disorganization theory. *American Journal of Sociology, 94,* 774–802.

Sampson, R. J., & Laub, J. H. (1997). A life-course theory of cumulative disadvantage and the stability of delinquency. In T. P. Thornberry (Ed.), *Developmental theories of crime and delinquency* (pp. 133–161). New Brunswick, NJ: Transaction.

Sampson, R. J., Raudenbush, S. W., & Earls, F. (1997). Neighborhoods and violent crime: A multilevel study of collective efficacy. *Science, 277,* 918–924.

Sanchez, M. M., Ladd, C. O., & Plotsky, P. M. (2001). Early adverse experience and psychopathology. *Development and Psychopathology, 13,* 419–450.

Schumacker, R. E., & Marcoulides, G. A. (1998). *Interaction and nonlinear effects in structural equation modeling.* Mahwah, NJ: Erlbaum.

Silverthorn, P., & Frick, P. J. (1999). Developmental pathways to antisocial behavior: The delayed-onset pathway in girls. *Development and Psychopathology, 11,* 101–126.

Specific Language Impairment Consortium. (2002). A genome-wide scan identifies two novel loci involved in specific language impairment. *American Journal of Human Genetics, 70,* 384–398.

Taylor, A., Pickering, K., Lord, C., & Pickles, A. (1998). Mixed and multilevel models for longitudinal data: Growth curve analysis of language development. In B. Everitt & G. Dunn (Eds.), *Recent advances in the statistical analysis of medical data* (pp. 127–144). London: Arnold.

Teasdale, J. D. (1988). Cognitive vulnerability to persistent depression. *Cognition and Emotion, 2,* 247–274.

Tennant, C., & Bebbington, P. (1978). The social causation of depression: A critique of the work of Brown and colleagues. *Psychological Medicine, 8,* 565–575.

Tremblay, R. E., Japel, C., Perusse, D., Boivin, M., Zoccolillo, M., Montplaisir, J., et al. (1999). The search for the age of "onset" of physical aggression: Rousseau and Bandura revisited. *Criminal Behaviour and Mental Health, 9,* 24–39.

Tremblay, R. E., Masse, L. C., Vitaro, F., & Dobkin, P. L. (1995). The impact of friends' deviant behaviour on early onset of delinquency: Longitudinal data from six to thirteen years of age. *Development and Psychopathology, 7,* 649–668.

Vitaro, F., Tremblay, R. E., Kerr, M., Pagani, L., & Bukowski, W. M. (1997). Disruptiveness, friends' characteristics, and delinquency in early adolescence: A test of two competing models of development. *Child Development, 68,* 676–689.

von Eye, A. (1990). *Introduction to configural frequency analysis: The search for types and antitypes in cross-classifications.* Cambridge, England: Cambridge University Press.

von Eye, A., & Bergman, L. R. (2003). Research strategies in developmental psychopathology: Dimensional identity and the person-oriented approach. *Development and Psychopathology, 15,* 553–580.

von Eye, A., Spiel, C., & Wood, P. (1996). *Configural frequency analysis in applied psychological research.* London: Sage.

Vythilingam, M., Heim, C., Newport, J., Miller, A. H., Anderson, E., Bronen, R., et al. (2002). Childhood trauma associated with smaller hippocampal volume in women with major depression. *American Journal of Psychiatry, 159,* 2072–2079.

Walter, S. D. (1976). The estimation and interpretation of attributable risk in health research. *Biometrics, 32,* 829–849.

West, D. J. (1982). *Delinquency: Its roots, careers and prospects.* London: Heinemann.

Winship, C., & Mare, R. D. (1983). Structural equations and path analysis for discrete data. *American Journal of Sociology, 89,* 54–110.

Woodward, L. J., & Fergusson, D. M. (1999). Childhood peer relationships problems and psychosocial adjustment in late adolescence. *Journal of Abnormal Child Psychology, 27,* 87–104.

Wright, S. (1921). Correlation and causation. *Journal of Agricultural Research, 20,* 557–585.

Wright, S. (1934). On the method of path coefficients. *Annals of Mathematical Statistics, 5,* 161–215.

Zoccolillo, M. (1993). Gender and the development of conduct disorder. *Development and Psychopathology, 5,* 65–78.

CHAPTER 8

Emotions and Developmental Psychopathology

CARROLL E. IZARD, ERIC A. YOUNGSTROM, SARAH E. FINE, ALLISON J. MOSTOW, and CHRISTOPHER J. TRENTACOSTA

A full understanding of the processes that lead to normal development and psychopathology requires a multifaceted approach that cuts across several specialties and disciplines. These disciplines range from molecular biology and neurophysiology to social psychology and behavioral ecology. The scope of research in these domains includes study of neural, perceptual, cognitive, social, and overt behavioral (action) processes. The conceptual integration of the rapidly emerging contributions from these fields of investigation present one of the greatest challenges in the biological and psychological sciences. Understanding the forces within the individual and in individual-environment trans-

action that drive the processes of self-organization within and across neural, perceptual-cognitive, and action systems adds another aspect to the challenge (Cicchetti & Tucker, 1994; Izard, Ackerman, Schoff, & Fine, 2000; Levinson, 1999; M. Lewis & Granic, 2000). In this chapter, we assume that the motivational processes associated with emotions are major players in self-organization within and across systems, in self-regulation, and in determining the adaptiveness of developmental trajectories. We take this position while remaining aware that a broad construct like self-regulation, often used in explaining the roots of psychopathology, requires research in attentional/cognitive regulation and emotion regulation, as well as regulation at the neurobiological level (Calkins & Fox, 2002; Posner & Rothbart, 2000).

Many facets of normal development and functioning depend on the emotions and the brain and behavioral systems associated with them. For example, the social functions of emotions underlie attachment behavior and interpersonal relations (Panksepp, 2001), and the neural substrates of emotions play a pivotal role in memory and the motivational control of attention and cognitive processes (Cicchetti & Tucker, 1994; Tucker, 2001). Emotions serve a wide variety of functions that are critical to survival and adaptation, and they play a key role in goal-directed behavior (Campos, Mumme, Kermoian, & Campos, 1994; Darwin, 1872/1998; Izard, 1977; Lazarus, 1991). Thus, dysfunction in any of the emotion systems (e.g., interest, joy, sadness, anger, fear, shame, guilt) may contribute to the development of psychopathology.

The tendency of each basic emotion to motivate a particular type of cognition and action may be considered its executive function. Even in human suffering and psychopathology, emotions retain their executive function or inherent capacity to motivate adaptive cognition and action (Izard & Ackerman, 2000). Yet, person and contextual factors can alter this capacity and prevent its realization. Differences between emotion processes in normal and abnormal development relate primarily to the coordination of the components of emotion and to the connections among the emotion, cognitive, and action systems (Izard, 1979; Izard et al., 2000; Keltner & Kring, 1998; Kring & Bachorowski, 1999). Lack of coordination among emotion components (e.g., emotion arousal and feelings without emotion expression in Schizophrenia; Kring & Neale, 1996) and maladaptive intersystem connections (e.g., anger and shame linked to aggression and violence in delinquent youth; Baumeister, Smart, & Boden, 1996) help explain psychopathological processes and the role of emotions as causes and consequences of psychopathology. Poor intersystem connections tend to vitiate the inherently adaptive functions of emotions (Ackerman, Abe, & Izard, 1998).

Normative developmental tasks include laying the groundwork for coordinating emotion arousal, emotion motivation, and nonverbal and verbal emotion expression in the context of personality and social functioning (Abe & Izard, 1999a; Izard et al., 2000). Utilization of coordinated emotion system responding in adaptive behavior depends on the development of connections between the emotion, cognitive, and action systems (Ackerman et al., 1998; Izard, 2002). Without coordination among emotion components and effective intersystem connections, qualitative differ-

ences between normal and psychopathological development will occur in affective-cognitive structures or emotion-cognition relations and in emotion-thought-action patterns.

Coordination and regulation of the elements of an emotion system does not mean that all its components (neurobiological processes, subjective feeling, and expression) and the factors that contribute to its activation always follow a typical or set course (Ellsworth, 1994). Effective coordination of emotion processes sometimes depends on the intensity of the stimulus or emotion-eliciting situation and the way the executive functions of emotions play out in person-environment interactions. Sometimes the coordination of emotion system components depends, at least in part, on the executive functions of the cognitive systems. For example, it might prove quite adaptive to suppress the *expression* of anger *feelings* in response to provocative remarks by a person in authority or the expression of joy at that person's social blunder. This sort of interaction between executive functions in cognition and emotion processes depends on adaptive connections between the emotions and cognitive systems.

APPROACHES TO THE STUDY OF EMOTIONS AND PSYCHOPATHOLOGY

Two recent papers on the topic of emotions and psychopathology describe quite different approaches to this broad topic. They also testify to the rapidly growing body of literature concerned with the role of emotions in abnormal development and behavior.

An Approach Emphasizing the Social Functions of Emotion

In the first of these papers, the authors examined five categories of psychopathology in terms of the social functions of emotions (Keltner & Kring, 1998). The authors, along with a number of other theorists (e.g., Averill, 1992; Campos, Campos, & Barrett, 1989), assume that emotions represent adaptations to problems in forming and maintaining relationships. For example, emotion expressions elicit responses from others and play a part in coordinating aspects of social interactions, and emotion experiences gauge the significance of events and responses in social contexts. The authors maintain that emotions provide a wealth of information relevant to interpersonal interactions, conflict resolution, and social adjustment (cf. Forgas, 2002). Their perspective on emotions strongly suggests that disturbances in emotion experience or expression impact relationships negatively and contribute to various forms of psychopathology. They argue that deficits in approach-related emotion systems or motivation for social contact contributes to depression, diminished emotion expressivity to the uncoordinated social interactions in schizophrenic individuals, heightened fear and diminished positive emotion to Social Phobia, and deficient emotion regulation to Borderline Personality Disorder (Keltner & Kring, 1998). Although some of these perturbations in emotion processes may affect an individual in a number of ways, researchers have placed emphasis on the problems created by deficits or limitations in the social functions of emotions.

In this chapter, we also examine the role of the social functions of emotions in psychopathology, but we place equal emphasis on intrapersonal functions of emotions, their role in motivating and organizing the thought and action involved in individual adjustment and personality development and functioning (Izard, 1993; Levinson, 1999). We consider emotion thresholds and the related construct of trait emotionality as examples of emotion-related personality factors or individual differences that may contribute to either normal or abnormal development, to resiliency or psychopathology (Fredrickson, 2000; Izard, 2002; Rothbart, Ahadi, & Evans, 2000).

A Dimensional Approach

In the second of these papers on emotions and psychopathology, the authors (Kring & Bachorowski, 1999) adopted a perspective that views emotions and their functions in terms of the two broad dimensions of approach and withdrawal, theory rooted in neuropsychological research (Davidson, 1992; Davidson & Tomarken, 1989; Gray, 1979, 1982, 1995). They suggest that the functions of emotions in persons with psychopathology remain comparable to these functions in normal individuals. Problems arise, in part, when deficits occur in any one of the components in emotion processes: "perception, experience, intensity, or display" (Kring & Bachorowski, 1999, p. 577). Disturbance in any one of these components can impair a person's "ability to achieve one or more emotion functions in an adaptive fashion" (p. 577).

Kring and Bachorowski (1999) discussed the relations of depression, anxiety disorders, psychopathy, and Schizophrenia to various disturbances in emotion processing and, in particular, to the hypothesized behavior activation and behavioral inhibition systems (Gray, 1978, 1995) and the conceptually similar approach and withdrawal motivation systems (Davidson, 1994). They review a substantial body of literature that suggests relations between various forms of psychopathology and these hypothesized systems. De-

pression relates to deficits in the approach motivation system (Depue, Krauss, & Spoont, 1987), anxiety disorders to disturbances in the withdrawal motivation system (Barlow, 1988; Gray, 1978), psychopathy to dysfunction in both the approach/behavioral activation system (strong) and withdrawal/inhibition system (weak), and Schizophrenia to problems in both the activation/approach systems and the inhibition/withdrawal systems (Fowles, 1994). Kring and Bachorowski note that a number of pathological conditions cannot be explained in terms of dysfunction in a single motivation system, a single dimension of emotionality, or a single component of emotion processes. For example, depression may include a combination of high negative affect and low positive affect, Schizophrenia a diminished emotion expression and possibly diminished emotion experience as well (Earnst & Kring, 1999), and psychopathy a discordance between emotion experience and its verbal articulation (Cleckley, 1941) as well as disjunction between components of the emotion process.

These reviews document the complex and highly significant role of emotions in psychopathology. Yet, they also leave room for additional approaches to understanding emotions as both causes and consequences of abnormal development. Keltner and Kring (1998) focused on the social functions of emotions. Much work remains in examining the role of emotion traits or emotionality as assessed in temperament and personality (Rothbart et al., 2000). Kring and Bachorowski (1999) organized their review in a framework of affective dimensions, and they leave open a number of issues relating to discrete emotions. Each of the two papers examined a half-dozen categories of psychopathology, all of them largely in relation to research on adults. The authors of these reviews were not always able to find unique emotion characteristics or emotion-related cognitive or behavioral correlates for each diagnostic category. This apparent lack of disorder-specific emotion features may reflect the underlying dimensional nature of psychopathology, the fuzzy boundaries between the criteria that attempt to separate categories of psychological disorders. It may also reflect the need for further study of emotion processes in abnormal behavior. In any case, insofar as we are unable to relate aspects of emotion system functioning or malfunctioning to particular mental health problems, we leave a challenge for future research and analysis.

The Present Approach to Understanding the Role of Emotions in Psychopathology

In this chapter, we review the emotional aspects of psychological disorders and attempt to find new links between emotion processes and psychopathology. We align emotion systems functioning and nosological categories in ways not emphasized in previous reviews of the relations of emotions to psychopathology. First, we consider systematically both the individual and social functions of emotions. We recognize that these two types of functions do not constitute orthogonal sets of emotion characteristics. However, some functions of particular discrete emotions apparently have more direct influence on personality or individual functioning than on social functioning (e.g., individual- or self-oriented shame motivation toward self-improvement; Tomkins, 1963). Moreover, consideration of individual differences in emotion thresholds or trait emotionality should help in discussing the related constructs of temperament and personality as factors in the development of psychopathology (Schultz, Izard, & Bear, 2004). Such discussions would complement explanations of psychopathology based on emotion processes that are more strongly influenced by contextual factors. Although some of the effects of an emotion threshold on an individual's adjustment or adaptation may appear in both social and nonsocial contexts, emotion thresholds that help determine characteristic mood and levels of positive and negative emotionality clearly relate to normal and abnormal personality functioning (Izard, Libero, Putnam, & Haynes, 1993; cf. Watson & Clark, 1992).

Yet, one could reasonably speculate that an abnormally high threshold for the emotion of interest-excitement might tend to preclude or greatly diminish sustained constructive endeavors or exciting activities of any sort, including social interactions. Such a lack of engagement in the environment characterizes those suffering an episode of Major Depression (Cicchetti & Toth, 1995). The behavior of depressive patients suggests that they also have an abnormally high threshold for enjoyment-joy. The consequent lack of joy experiences reduces feelings of self-confidence and self-worth and tends to diminish social interactions (Izard, 1977; Marshall & Izard, 1972). Higher levels of the emotions of interest and joy are associated with higher levels of extroversion or sociability (Izard et al., 1993). Thus, the effects on personality functioning stemming from this pattern of thresholds for positive emotions could have a strong impact on social functioning.

Second, we see if attention to the functions of discrete emotions (Frijda, 1986, 1994; Izard, 1989; Izard & Ackerman, 2000; Plutchik, 1980; Tomkins, 1962, 1963) can add to our understanding of psychopathology in terms of different but related sets of broad affective dimensions: positive and negative emotionality (Watson & Clark, 1992), behavioral activation and inhibition systems (Gray, 1995), and

approach and avoidance motivation systems (Davidson, 1992). We also review evidence relating specific emotions and patterns of emotions to psychopathology. In pursuing the discrete emotions approach to understanding the development of psychopathology, we consider three overlapping facets of emotion processes: the organizational and motivational functions of discrete emotions, their developmental functions, and their effects on personality and social functioning.

Finally, we discuss several topics relating discrete emotions theory and research to psychopathology that researchers have not dealt with or emphasized in previous reviews. Here, we briefly define these topics; later, we use them to guide our discussion of several types of psychological disorders.

The Developmental Functions of Emotions

Clearly, certain emotions are more prominent in one period of development than another, and these stage-salient emotions serve adaptive functions (see Abe & Izard, 1999a, and Izard, 1991, for reviews). For example, healthy young infants stimulate growth-inducing social interaction and gain social support by smiling readily and frequently and at virtually anyone who enters their perceptual field. On the other hand, if stage-salient emotions become dysregulated, either under- or overregulated, they become dysadaptive and can lead to psychopathology. For example, high-intensity and frequent expressions of anger and sadness in toddlerhood relates significantly to the trait of neuroticism at age 3.5 years (Abe & Izard, 1999b).

Emotion-Cognition Relations

In recent years, neuroscience has greatly increased our understanding of both the modular and interactive output of the brain systems underlying the emotions and various types of cognitive processes (Bechara, Damasio, Tranel, & Damasio, 1997; Damasio, 1994, 1998, 1999; Davidson, 1992; LeDoux, 1996; LeDoux, Romanski, & Xagoraris, 1989). For example, the evidence indicates that brain systems can generate and sustain emotional behavior in the absence of any cognition other than perceptual discrimination (LeDoux, Sakaguchi, & Reis, 1984). Yet, critica questions about some of the basic processes remain unanswered: What is the significance of modular and relatively independent functioning of the emotion systems? Are there individual differences in modularity, perhaps in children at risk for Autism or Schizophrenia, that suggest the need for more attention to the development of emotion-cognition relations (Simons, Fitzgibbons, & Fiorito, 1993)? What is the nature of the perceptual, cognitive, or information-processing bias that characterizes aggressive children, psychopathic youth, and adults with anxiety disorders (Crick & Dodge, 1994; McNally, 1996; Schultz, Izard, & Ackerman, 2000)? Does such a bias signal dysfunction in brain systems concerned mainly with perception, cognition, and information processing associated with rational decision making? Does it represent a deficit in emotion systems and emotion information processing (Schultz et al., 2000)? Or does it signal problems in both emotion systems and cognitive processes, as well as in emotion socialization?

The development of emotion-cognition relations can be studied using "experiments in nature" (see Cicchetti, 2002). Such studies can be found in the research on children with Down syndrome, autistic people, and children who have experienced maltreatment. Both children with Down syndrome and children who experienced maltreatment use fewer words to express internal states, including words referring to emotion in self and other. The ability to express verbally one's own and others' feelings is considered a hallmark of early emotional development and a predictor of later social competence (Denham, 1998; Izard, 2002). In normally developing children, internal state language correlated with play behaviors, but this relation did not hold for the children with Down syndrome (Beeghly & Cicchetti, 1997). These findings suggest that intersystem connections emerge between cognitive-language abilities and socioemotional regulatory behaviors for normally developing children. These connections may be delayed and diminished for children with Down syndrome. Similarly, Autism may be characterized by a dissociation between emotion and cognition, whereby cognitive "systemizing" dominates and empathetic processing is less prominent (Baron-Cohen, 2003). This dissociation is particularly evident in brain imaging of people with Autism during an emotion recognition task. Brain regions involved in cognitive processing (i.e., temporal lobes) show increased activation, whereas emotion-processing regions (i.e., amygdala) show decreased activation (Baron-Cohen et al., 1999).

These experiments in nature suggest that the emergence of intersystem connections between emotion and cognition is a hallmark of normal emotional development. When these connections fail to develop, problem behaviors are likely to emerge, even for children without developmental disorders. The link between poor intersystem connections and emerging psychopathology is particularly relevant for children raised in abusive and impoverished environments. Children who experience abuse show abnormal emotion-processing patterns and sensitivity to anger that may prove adaptive in the home environment but is maladaptive in other contexts (e.g., peer interactions at school; Pollak, Cicchetti, Klor-

man, & Brumaghim, 1997). The delayed development of internal state language may further compound maltreated children's problems as frequent experience of negative emotion and sensitivity to anger cues do not cohere with the cognitive ability to communicate these experiences verbally (Beeghly & Cicchetti, 1997).

Emotions, Culture, and Socialization Processes

We expect cultural factors and socialization to affect the way that emotions influence the development of psychopathology and the emergence and meaning of symptoms. Appraisals that lead to emotions, attitudes toward emotions, emotion labels, emotion concepts, and emotion expressions vary across cultures (Izard, 1971; Markus & Kitayama, 1991; Matsumoto, 1990), and these differences may cause variations in the relations between emotions and psychopathology. A certain set of symptoms leads Chinese psychiatrists to diagnose a patient as psychasthenic, whereas a very similar set of symptoms and underlying biochemical changes lead American psychiatrists to diagnose the patient as depressive. Although in the biomedical framework these are interchangeable diagnoses, a highly persuasive set of arguments based on cultural psychology suggests that psychasthenic patients in China have different affective-cognitive structures and suffer in significantly different ways from depressives in the United States (Shweder, 1988). Within cultures, variations in socialization practices result in individual differences in children's ability to express and regulate emotions, and socialization involving extreme forms of parent-child interactions like abuse or maltreatment may impede emotional development, alter neurobiological stress-response systems, and increase the likelihood of psychopathology (Cicchetti, 1990, 2002; Cicchetti & Rogosch, 2001a, 2001b; Shipman & Zeman, 2001).

Expressing Emotion

As early as infancy, individuals begin to develop a characteristic style of expressing emotions, and the frequency of expression of various discrete emotions tends to remain stable over time (Hyson & Izard, 1985; Izard, Hembree, & Huebner, 1987). Expression styles in toddlerhood predict expectable personality characteristics, including neuroticism, at age 3.5 years (Abe & Izard, 1999b). In later development, some aspects of emotion expression relate to many forms of psychopathology. We see attenuated or discordant expression in people at risk for Schizophrenia (Simons et al., 1993), prolonged expression of negative emotions (particularly sadness and anger) in depression (Blumberg & Izard, 1986), dampened or developmentally delayed expression in Down Syndrome Disorder (Cicchetti & Sroufe, 1976; Emde, Katz, & Thorpe, 1978), inappropriate or incongruous expression in Autism (Sigman & Capps, 1997), and deceptive expression in psychopathy (Cleckley, 1941; Patrick, 1994). Furthermore, expressions of particular emotions in certain conditions characterize aggressive rejected children (Hubbard, 2001) and delinquent youth (Keltner, Moffitt, & Stouthamer-Loeber, 1995) and may reveal the type of abuse that leads to a Posttraumatic Stress Disorder (Bonanno et al., 2002).

Emotion Patterns

Provocative situations, whether real or imagined, typically elicit a pattern of discrete emotions, and different patterns of emotions characterize some psychological disorders. Patterns of emotions are particularly evident in anxiety and depression (Izard, 1972; Izard & Youngstrom, 1996). Understanding such patterns of emotions and the implications of co-occurring emotions for emotion regulation and emotion motivation should help in understanding and treating emotions-related problems (Izard, 2002) and in discerning the roots of some forms of psychopathology.

Emotion Knowledge: Its Role in Emotion Communication, Empathy, and Adaptive and Maladaptive Behavior

Emotion communication plays a key role in social interactions and the development of the attachment bond and other relationships (Ainsworth, Blehar, Waters, & Wall, 1978; Bowlby, 1969, 1973; Hobson, 1995). Before children acquire language, emotion communication depends on facial, vocal, and postural cues in expressive behavior (Izard et al., 1995; Zivin, 1986). Soon after the beginning of language acquisition, children use words to label and talk about their own and others' feelings (Bretherton & Beeghley-Smith, 1982), and the verbal component of emotion communication grows steadily in early childhood (Dunn, Bretherton, & Munn, 1987; Izard, 1971).

Both before and after language acquisition, effective emotion communication depends on the ability of the participants to detect and respond in a meaningful fashion to each other's emotion signals. After language acquisition, both accurate emotion perception and emotion labeling become critical in emotion communication and essential to empathic responding and prosocial behavior. These emotion-related skills form the foundation for emotion knowledge (Izard, 2001) and the construct of emotional intelligence (Mayer & Salovey, 1997). Deficits in emotion knowledge are associated with low socioemotional and academic competence (Denham, 1998; Izard et al., 2001)

and with internalizing behavior (Fine, Izard, Mostow, Trentacosta, & Ackerman, 2003).

Emotion Regulation and Dysregulation

Researchers view emotion regulation and attention regulation as the critical components of self-regulation, the key to adaptive psychological and neurobiological functioning (Calkins & Fox, 2002; Posner & Rothbart, 2000). Current theory and research indicate that the study of each of these three broad interrelated constructs requires a multilevel approach that considers processes at the neural, emotional, and cognitive levels (Cicchetti & Dawson, 2002).

A large body of literature attests to the significance of emotion regulation for adaptive behavior and the role of emotion dysregulation in maladaptive behavior and psychopathology (Cicchetti & Rogosch, 2001a; Eisenberg et al., 1995; for a review, see Eisenberg, 2000; Eisenberg, Fabes, & Losoya, 1997). Trauma, in the form of socioemotional deprivation, significant negative life events, or child maltreatment, often leads to emotion dysregulation and psychopathology (Cicchetti & Lynch, 1995; Cicchetti & Rogosch, 2001b). Inability to regulate emotions may preclude empathic or prosocial responding (Eisenberg et al., 1996), a condition that may characterize a number of psychological disorders.

EMOTION REGULATION AND DYSREGULATION AND PSYCHOPATHOLOGY

Emotion regulation is central to normal development, and poor emotion regulation or dysregulation is a key factor in the development of psychopathology. The prominent role of emotion regulation and dysregulation in normal and abnormal behavior may become clearer when we consider the number and complexity of the relevant systems or components that contribute to the management of emotions.

Several widely cited and quite useful definitions and treatments of emotion regulation explain it largely in terms of a combination of cognitive, behavioral, and social processes (Folkman & Lazarus, 1990; Kopp, 1989; Thompson, 1994; Thompson & Calkins, 1996). A researcher's emphasis on one or more of these three types of regulatory processes depends on his or her definition of emotion. For example, when researchers define emotions as cognition-dependent phenomena, they focus on processes involved in the deployment of attention, reinterpretation of the eliciting event, and actions that change the meaning of the person-environment relationship

(Folkman & Lazarus, 1990). For the most part, approaches to emotion regulation that focus on cognitive, behavioral, and social processes have addressed issues relating to socioemotional competence and adaptive behavior. They usually do not deal specifically with the role of emotion regulation in psychopathology.

A few researchers concerned with emotion regulation have recognized that it entails a multiplicity of systems and domains of functioning (Cicchetti & Tucker, 1994; Izard & Kobak, 1991). They suggest that the key components of emotion regulation include neurobiological systems, traits of emotionality/temperament/personality (e.g., emotion thresholds), cognitive processes, interpersonal relationships, and intersystem interactions and connections. They recognize different types of regulatory processes. Some of the processes of emotion regulation proceed more or less automatically and preconsciously (e.g., changes in brain and neural systems that influence emotion activation thresholds and responses to stress). Other processes of emotion regulation, like those dependent on executive functions of emotions and cognition, occur in consciousness or can be accessed reflectively.

Executive functions of emotions consist of their inherently motivational and goal-oriented qualities, which may include action tendencies. All of these characteristics of emotion and the way they play out in person-environment transactions affect emotion regulation. Executive functions of cognition as it relates to emotions consist of attentional control and consequent appraisal and attributional processes that activate a particular emotion and decision-making processes relating to coping strategies (Posner & Rothbart, 2000). These processes help determine the initial emotion response to a given event or situation and monitor the appropriateness of the emotion for a particular context. Hence they have direct implications for emotion regulation.

The factors governing emotion regulation are an interrelated set of modular systems. Each has some separate functions, and each may have a significant influence on the other. We review these regulatory systems briefly here and note some of the ways they relate to psychopathology.

Neurobiological Processes in Emotion Regulation and Psychopathology

Virtually any neurobiological system may affect emotion regulation. We examine three that play critical roles: the prefrontal cortex (PFC), particularly as it relates to other regulatory systems; the hypothalamus-pituitary-adrenal (HPA) system; and the vagal (Xth cranial) nerve complex

(VC) of the autonomic nervous system (ANS). All three of these systems are influenced by fundamental mechanisms of self-regulation mediated by the neurochemically specific pathways (e.g., norepinephrine, dopamine, acetylcholine, serotonin) that project from the brain stem (Cicchetti & Tucker, 1994). All three of the systems, as modulated by fundamental neurochemical processes, appear to have the capacity to influence the threshold and intensity of emotion arousal.

Much of the research on the regulatory functions of the PFC, the HPA system, and the VC has focused on the broad construct of stress and responses to stress. (An exception is the recent conception of the VC as the neural basis of the social engagement system; Porges, 2001.) Although stress undoubtedly involves negative emotions, the extant research rarely makes it possible to identify stress-response processes related to a particular emotion or pattern of specific emotions. Even when researchers can specify whether the emotions involved are approach or avoidant in nature, they still may not find it possible to identify discrete emotions (Davidson, 1998). Nevertheless, studies that attempt to relate the functioning of these major regulatory systems to dysadaptive behavior and psychopathology have implications for the regulation and dysregulation of discrete emotions.

Emotion Activation and Regulation: The Prefrontal Cortex and Amygdala

The PFC is central to adaptive functioning, and understanding of its functions seems necessary to advance the science of psychopathology. The PFC plays a critical role in processing emotion information and regulating emotional responding and in the executive functions of cognition (Damasio, 1994; LeDoux, 1996; Posner & Rothbart, 2000). It is also involved in the regulation of the VC and the HPA systems. Effects of damage to the PFC highlight its role in the executive functions of cognition. Researchers compared the performance of patients with lesions in the ventromedial area of the PFC with normal controls on a task involving risk-related decisions (Bechara et al., 1997). The investigators measured the behavioral effects of participants' decisions as they proceeded through the task and also recorded their emotional (skin conductance) responses. The patients with damage to the ventromedial PFC did not respond emotionally to task activities, and thus nonconscious internal emotion signals failed to protect them from risky decisions. In contrast, the normal patients showed conditioned emotional responding to high-risk activities, and internal emotion signals enabled them to perform adaptively on the task.

Recent reviews (Herman & Cullinan, 1997; Sullivan & Gratton, 2002) of studies of the neurocircuitry of stress (interpretable as negative emotion) make it clear that the PFC exerts control over the highly interactive HPA and VC systems. Thus, the PFC, through its connections to the HPA and VC, influences neurophysiological responses to stress and threat (Herman & Cullinan, 1997), as well as to positively toned social stimuli (Porges, 2001). The PFC projects directly to the hypothalamus, which initiates activity in the HPA system and the release of glucocorticoids that facilitate adaptive responses to stress. (The HPA system regulation is also strongly influenced by the hippocampus; Herman & Cullinan, 1997.) The PFC's control over the generative aspects of these neural systems for responding to affective stimuli shows that it is intricately involved in emotion regulation. The PFC and its relations to the HPA system and the VC definitely have implications for a number of psychopathological conditions (Sullivan & Gratton, 2002).

Although the neocortex is normally involved in emotion information processing, emotion regulation, and emotional responding, emotions can occur without benefit of the regulatory functions of the PFC. This is probably particularly so when the individual perceives dangerous stimuli that can elicit an adaptive response after only minimal processing. Using animal models, LeDoux (1996) and his colleagues (LeDoux, Sakaguchi, Iwata, & Reis, 1986; LeDoux et al., 1984) and Davis and his colleagues (Campeau & Davis, 1995) have demonstrated that fear conditioning can occur through a subcortical route. Fear behavior can emerge without input to or output from the relevant region of the neocortex and thus without benefit of accompanying higher-order cognition and its influence on coping strategies. In this subcortical activation process, emotion occurs rapidly, automatically, and unconsciously and therefore makes immediate and distinct demands on regulatory systems.

LeDoux (1996) has described the thalamo-amygdala circuit for information processing and emotion activation as the "low road" to emotion. When emotion responses are learned through this pathway, they tend to make indelible memories that resist extinction (LeDoux et al., 1989). Other studies have shown that repeated stimulation (kindling) of the amygdala lowers the threshold for the activation of emotion and increases the likelihood of increasing its intensity and duration and creating chronic anxiety (Rosen & Schulkin, 1997). Researchers have also observed kindling-like processes in depressive patients, suggesting experienced-based lowered emotion thresholds (Cicchetti & Toth, 1995). Repeated stimulation or kindling of the amygdala and possibly other limbic structures changes emotion thresholds, suggesting that the neural substrates of emotions may have their own emotion regulatory functions that can be adversely affected by the social and physical environment (Cicchetti & Tucker, 1994; Rosen & Schulkin, 1997).

Research from multiple laboratories indicates that the amygdala is an effective mediator of emotion activation, and findings from research on emotion activation with animal models may generalize to human beings (Rosen & Schulkin, 1997). Evidence for such generalization came from a study in which investigators compared neurological patients who had bilateral damage to the amygdala and patients who had bilateral damage to the hippocampus, a structure critical to memory and to emotion-cognition interactions (Bechara et al., 1995). In an auditory conditioning experiment, the brain-damaged patients and a normal control group were shown a sequence of colored cards in which the green one (conditioned stimulus) was followed by a blast of a nearby ship's horn (unconditioned stimulus). Emotional response was measured in terms of the skin conductance response (SCR). The patients with bilateral damage to the amygdala did not show an elevated SCR, but they remembered the colors of the cards and other declarative information about the experiment. The patients with bilateral damage to the hippocampus showed an elevated SCR (emotional response), but they did not remember declarative information about the experiment. The control patients showed both an elevated SCR and good memory for the details of the experiment. Current evidence suggests that the amygdala may play a role in evaluating the significance of emotion-related stimuli regardless of their valence (Davidson, Pizzagalli, Nitschke, & Putnam, 2002).

It does not take trauma or injury to change brain structures and functions (Greenough, Black, & Wallace, 1987; Rosen & Schulkin, 1997). Negative life events and a number of factors in harsh environments may produce experience-based changes in brain and neural processes and thereby contribute to under- or overregulation of emotions and consequent psychopathology. In contrast, frequent positive emotion experiences contribute to the development of empathy, moral reasoning, and other aspects of adaptive behavior (Kochanska & Murray, 2000).

In summary, the PFC normally exercises considerable control over emotion and responses to activating stimuli. In the intact individual, both the PFC and the amygdala participate in the information processing that leads to emotion and coping responses. Emotional learning and responding without benefit of PFC serve immediate survival functions but have serious limitations for long-term adaptation. The

PFC is central among the neocortical structures that provide the neural substrates for the executive functions of cognition that govern the conception, planning, and performance of coping strategies.

The Vagal Nerve Complex

The VC is that part of the parasympathetic branch of the ANS that modulates activity of the visceral organs. Of particular importance to the self-regulation of emotion and behavioral adaptation, the tonic firing of the vagus nerve slows the cardiac and respiratory systems and influences the voluntary regulation of the muscles of facial and vocal expression of emotion. Although high basal vagal tone relates to adaptive attentional, cognitive, and behavioral functioning (Porter, Porges, & Marshall, 1988), the ability to both enhance and suppress vagal tone may prove adaptive in responding to different forms of stress or challenge (Porges, Doussard-Roosevelt, Portales, & Greenspan, 1996). The VC has been conceived as the neural underpinning of the social engagement system and as a system that may be changed by early experience (Porges, 2001).

A rapidly increasing number of studies have shown that the parasympathetic nervous system (PNS) and its control by the vagus (Xth cranial) nerve figures significantly in emotion regulation. In particular, research supports the hypothesis that vagal control of the heart and especially heart rate variability (indexed in terms of vagal tone) has direct relations to emotion regulation and coping ability (Porges, 2001). The relations between vagal tone, emotion regulation, and adaptation suggest that dysfunction in the PNS or VC may play a prominent role in the development of psychopathology.

Baseline vagal tone relates to both soothability and behavioral reactivity. It also tends to be associated with ability to focus attention and self-soothe, evidence of its role in emotion regulation (Porges, 1992). Infants with low basal vagal tone and an inability to suppress vagal activity have more behavior problems during the preschool years (Porges et al., 1996). Parental emotion coaching may influence basal vagal tone, which in turn predicts various behavioral outcomes, including child health and peer relations (Gottman, Katz, & Hooven, 1996). Vagal tone, like other indexes of emotion regulation, increases with age (Izard, Porges, et al., 1991).

The Hypothalamus-Pituitary-Adrenal System

Researchers identify the HPA system as a critical neurobiological system for responding to and coping with stress (De Kloet & McEwen, 1976; Sapolsky, Krey, & McEwen, 1986). The HPA system appears to have an especially important role in responding to processive stress or stressful events or conditions that require interpretation by the PFC or other higher brain structures (Herman & Cullinan, 1997).

Stress activates the HPA and the release of cortisol and other glutocorticoids by the adrenal gland. These neurobiological changes prepare the individual for defense and coping. However, person traits and person-environment transactions, particularly experience in difficult or harsh conditions, may lead to hypersecretion of glucocorticoids. Hypersecretion can lead to illness and psychopathology, including hypertension, affective disorders, and Posttraumatic Stress Disorders (Herman & Cullinan, 1997). The HPA system can be modified by early experience, and resultant changes in its structures and functions figure in the development of psychopathology (Gunnar & Donzella, 2002; Suomi, 1991).

Since the early work of Kagan and his colleagues (Kagan, Reznick, & Snidman, 1987), a growing number of researchers have shown important relations between the HPA system, emotion regulation, and adaptation. In general, this research shows that higher average cortisol levels are associated with internalizing and withdrawal behavior (and probably underlying emotion responses including shyness or fearfulness; Kagan, 1998). Lower average cortisol levels were associated with both positive and negative approach behaviors (e.g., Smider et al., 2002). However, in clinic-referred school-age boys, low cortisol levels (averaged across two time points taken 2 years apart) were associated with early onset and persistence of aggression (McBurnett, Lahey, Rathouz, & Loeber, 2000; cf. Cicchetti & Rogosch, 2001b).

Neurobiological Regulatory Systems, Brain Asymmetry, and Psychopathology

The interrelations among the PFC, HPA, and VC make it difficult to specify their separate roles in causal processes that contribute to psychopathology. Moreover, psychopathology that has precipitating factors in the environment or in person-environment transactions may, in turn, have adverse effects on the functioning of neurobiological systems (Greenough et al., 1987). Another factor in the relations of these systems to psychopathology apparently derives from brain hemisphere asymmetry (Davidson, 1994; Davidson, Marshall, Tomarken, & Henriques, 2000). Some individuals exhibit functional asymmetries, and a right hemisphere bias appears to have quite different implications for adaptation than does a left hemisphere bias.

A recent review (Sullivan & Gratton, 2002) revealed a number of relations between differential functioning of the brain hemispheres, neurobiological systems, and psychopathology. Left-biased PFC activity is associated with positive emotion and approach behavior. Right lesions to the PFC suppress stress-induced HPA activity and corticosterone responses and result in anxiety. Excessive right PFC activity appears to be a trait-like characteristic of highly anxious people, who may become predisposed to a number of stress-related psychopathologies that relate to chronic high levels of glucocorticoids. Right bias predisposes people to shyness, withdrawal, and defensive behavior. Withdrawal behavior, depression, and anxiety are also associated with increased HPA activity, chronic elevations in basal cortisol, and deficient feedback regulation. However, depression appears to be related to left-sided PFC hypofunction (at least for women; A. L. Miller et al., 2002) and anxiety to right-sided PFC hyperfunction. Anticipation of an anxiety-provoking stimulus causes people with Social Phobia to show highly elevated right-sided anterior cortical activation. Functional deficits in right-sided PFA-striatal circuitry is related to Attention-Deficit/Hyperactivity Disorder (ADHD) symptomatology, and persistent symptoms of ADHD prevent normal cortisol release in response to stressful conditions. Maturational deficits in PFC may predispose individuals to Schizophrenia, which is characterized by cerebral asymmetry and severe blunting of HPA activity and cortisol release.

Individual and Social Processes in Emotion Regulation and Psychopathology

A number of personality and interpersonal processes contribute to emotion regulation. Some of these have received too little attention in basic research.

Emotion System Functioning

Founders of the disciplines of biology and psychology called attention to the dynamic relations among emotions and the power of one emotion to influence another (Darwin, 1872/1998; James, 1890/1965). Tomkins (1962, 1963) greatly extended and elaborated this principle and described emotion-emotion dynamics in psychopathology, for example, the shame-fear bind in paranoid Schizophrenia and the sad-mad pattern in prolonged distress or depression (Tomkins, 1963). More recent empirical studies have confirmed the foresight of these early thinkers and demonstrated, for example, that anger is about as prominent as sadness in depressed children (Blumberg & Izard, 1986) and adults (Marshall & Izard, 1972). One can surmise that in these potentially pathological patterns of emotions, one emotion attenuates or amplifies the effects of another, as when shame leads to anger and violence (Baumeister et al.,

1996; H. Lewis, 1971; Tangney, Wagner, Barlow, Marschall, & Gramzow, 1996). One could interpret cognitive and cognitive-behavioral therapy techniques, such as distraction and restructuring, as devices to elicit a new emotion to attenuate or eliminate an undesirable one.

Emotion-Cognition Relations in Emotion Regulation and Psychopathology

Since the early phase of the emotion revolution in psychological science, researchers have acknowledged the significance of emotion-cognition relations for adaptation (Cicchetti & Schneider-Rosen, 1984; Izard, 1978; Izard, Kagan, & Zajonc, 1984). Imagery, distraction, and cognitive restructuring or reinterpretation for managing attentional and cognitive processes are widely used as emotion regulation techniques in everyday life as well as in various approaches to psychotherapy (e.g., Beck, 1976). As shown in later sections of this chapter, missing, ineffective, or dysfunctional connections between emotion and cognition characterize certain psychological disorders.

Research attests to the importance of the early development of emotional understanding and the significance of emotion knowledge for emotion regulation and coping strategies (Cutting & Dunn, 1999; Izard et al., 2001; see Denham, 1998, and Harris, 1999, for reviews). Emotion perception and emotion labeling, which form the foundation for emotion knowledge (Izard, 2001) and the construct of emotional intelligence (Salovey & Mayer, 1990), are subject to environmental influences that create perceptual-cognitive biases in information processing (Barth & Bastiani, 1997; cf. Crick & Dodge, 1994). These biases can put the individual at risk for aggressive behavior and become symptoms of other forms of psychopathology (Fine, Trentacosta, Izard, Mostow, & Campbell, 2004; Schultz et al., 2000).

Interpersonal Relations, Emotion Regulation, and Psychopathology

Relations between emotions and the prototypical social relationship, infant-mother attachment, run deep and strong (Ainsworth et al., 1978; Bowlby, 1980; Izard, Haynes, Chisholm, & Baak, 1991). Some theorists have explicitly recognized interpersonal relationships as a highly significant contributor to emotion regulation (Izard & Kobak, 1991). Disruptions of the attachment relationship elicit strong expressions of the discrete emotions of anger (protest) and sadness (despair, call for help) in 13-month-old infants (Shiller, Izard, & Hembree, 1986). Disruptions in attachment appear to place children at risk for psychopathology (Kobak, Little, Race, & Acosta, 2001). Strong emotion responses to attachment disruptions, separation, or loss of a loved one continue throughout the life span (Izard & Ackerman, 1997).

Causal Processes in Psychopathology

The high degree of specialization that characterizes today's science makes it difficult to gain perspective on causal processes. Today's highly specialized scientists may tend to see the roots of a problem as lying solely or primarily in their domain of expertise. We often make claims such as this one: The data suggest that cortisol activity may add to our understanding of behavioral development (Smider et al., 2002). An approach conscious of the interdependence of highly interactive neurobiological and psychological systems might word the claim more like this: "Within the context of the current set of predictors, variable X accounts for unique variance in outcome Y."

Selective perception of variables in a particular domain as dominant or unique predictors may serve to advance knowledge, particularly within specialties, but it may fail to keep the complexity of the broad picture clearly in mind. Our review in this chapter undoubtedly reflects our selective perception of the significance of the individual and social functions of emotions, especially in relation to cognition and behavioral coping strategies, in normal and abnormal development. Nevertheless, we consider the contributions from research on neurobiological systems and social relationships as they relate to discrete emotions, the emotions system, and the development of psychopathology. The extent to which researchers have considered multilevel causal processes in the development of a particular type of psychopathology varies across psychological disorders and the specific diagnostic categories.

EMOTIONS AND THE DEVELOPMENT OF PSYCHOPATHOLOGY IN INFANCY AND EARLY CHILDHOOD

In this section, we discuss the role of emotions in the development of psychopathology in very young children. Perhaps at no other stage of life are the intrapersonal and social functions of emotions so inextricably linked as in infancy and early childhood. In this early stage of development, the primary context in which emotional development takes place is the relationship between the child and the primary caregiver on which its life depends. Within this relationship, emotion patterns and affective-cognitive structures

begin to self-organize, the brain's emotion centers develop and are shaped by the affective displays of the caregiver and caregiving experiences, and the ability to regulate the expressive components of emotion experience emerges. However, the infant is not merely an empty vessel to be filled with whatever affective experience the caregiver provides, but is an active agent, bringing to the table tendencies and thresholds for emotion perception, expression, and regulation. These evolutionarily and genetically determined qualities in the infant exert significant influence on the caregiver and result in reciprocal cycles of emotion patterns for both participants in the relationship (e.g., Gianino & Tronick, 1992; Tronick & Weinberg, 1997). The consequences of these early patterns of dyadic interaction between caregiver and child reverberate throughout the child's life, sowing the seeds for both normal and abnormal developmental trajectories (M. Lewis, Feiring, & Rosenthal, 2000).

Child maltreatment is perhaps the most damaging circumstance in caregiver-child relationships and has the potential to derail normal development of intersystem connections between the cognitive and emotions systems, perception of emotions in the self and others, and neurobiological mechanisms that regulate emotion experience and expression (Cicchetti & Lynch, 1995). However, maltreatment often co-occurs with several other factors that can also hamper emotional development, including maternal psychopathology, poverty, intrauterine drug exposure, and an environment that may expose the child to violence and multiple caregiver changes (Morrison, Frank, Holland, & Kates, 1999). This cluster of factors can coalesce to create a pressure cooker of stress in which the infant emotion systems are developing and self-organizing, and it is during the first 3 years of life when maltreatment and its cofactors can have the most destructive effects (Mrazek, 1993).

As we have become more aware of the importance of early emotional development for later adaptive functioning and the vulnerability of infants and toddlers to adverse environments, so also have we become more attentive to patterns of maladaptive emotion expression and regulation in the first few years of life. However, the field of detection and diagnosis of early childhood psychopathology is itself still in its infancy. Researchers and practitioners have developed and are in the process of refining and determining empirical support for a system of diagnostic classification for mental disorders in children up to 3 years old (DC: 0 to 3, *Diagnostic Classification of Mental Health and Developmental Disorders of Infancy and Early Childhood,* Zero to Three, 1994; Cesari et al., 2003; Emde & Wise, 2003; Guédeney et al.,

2003; Stafford, Zeanah, & Scheeringa, 2003). The DC: 0 to 3 system describes some of the early symptoms of derailed emotional development in an attempt to go beyond simply downward-scaling adult disorders described in the *Diagnostic and Statistical Manual of Mental Disorders IV*. This system focuses on developmentally salient aspects of affective experience, regulation, and behaviors and emphasizes the context and role of the caregiver-child relationship in the emergence of early problems. We refer to this classification system in our discussion of the role of emotions in the development of early disorders.

Developmental Functions of Emotions in Infancy and the Caregiver-Child Relationship

The infant emerges into the world prepared to detect and respond to emotions from adults who are essential for its survival. Newborns show a preference for the human face above other visual stimuli and exhibit the ability to detect and respond to facial signals and engage in nonverbal communication. They stick out their tongue and open their mouth in response to adult expressions (Meltzoff & Moore, 1983). These behaviors suggest that infants have a predisposition to attend and respond to facial expressions in the primary caregiver. During this first stage of life, emotions provide an essential survival function, as the infant engages adults with expressions of joy, enlists the aid of caregivers with expressions of sadness or fear, and explores its environment when motivated by the emotion of interest. When these evolutionarily influenced emotions do not achieve the intended (or adaptive) caregiver response over time, as in the case of an infant whose mother is depressed or for a child whose caregiver is abusive or neglectful, these modular emotion systems can become dysregulated, producing rippling changes in the child's threshold for and organization of emotion experience and expression, neurobiological regulation of emotion, and perception of emotions in others and self.

Beyond basic survival functions, emotions in both the infant and the caregiver play an essential role in the formation of an attachment bond during the 1st year of life, the very context in which children first experience emotional reciprocity and regulation. Negative emotion expression in both mothers and infants are significant predictors of attachment security (Izard, Haynes, et al., 1991). Maternal depression is also predictive of insecure attachment in infants (Martins & Gaffan, 2000). S. B. Campbell et al. (2004) found that maternal depression interacted with maternal sensitivity to predict preschoolers' attachment security, such that depressed mothers with low sensitivity were more likely to have insecurely attached preschoolers than were depressed mothers who were highly sensitive to their children.

Attachment security is predictive of consistency in use of emotion regulation strategies, emotion dysregulation, and both internalizing and externalizing behaviors in later childhood (M. L. Diener, Mangelsdorf, McHale, & Frosch, 2002; Gilliom, Shaw, Beck, Schonberg, & Lukon, 2002; Vondra, Shaw, Swearingen, Cohen, & Owens, 2001). Disorganized attachment, which may be due in part to interactions that provoke fear in the infant as a result of the caregiver's behaviors and therefore confusion as the infant seeks to regulate its experience of fear by seeking proximity to the adult that triggered the emotion, has been linked with both aggressive behavior in childhood and development of psychopathology in later life (van Ijzendoorn, Schuengel, & Bakermans-Kranenburg, 1999). Some have suggested that these resultant aggressive behaviors may themselves be maladaptive attempts at emotion regulation (van der Kolk & Fisler, 1994). From these findings it is clear that normal emotional development in early childhood is not only determined by the inborn characteristics and developmentally salient emotions of the child but is also greatly influenced by the emotional behaviors, expressions, and perceptions of the caregiver.

Early Development of Intersystem Connections

As the emotions systems develop and self-organize, connections form between cognitions and emotions and between different discrete emotions. These connections are initiated and solidified as a result of early experiences such as affect perception of emotions in others and emotional responses to situations. Developmental theory suggests that internalized early representations of caregivers provide fundamental organizing information for children's emotion responses to others and point to the role of maladaptive intersystem connections in the development of psychopathology early in life. Children who have been maltreated by their caregivers form negative relational schemas that mediate the relation between maltreatment and rejection in late childhood peer relationships (Shields, Ryan, & Cicchetti, 2001). In these situations in which the caregiver may exhibit angry, abusive behaviors, affective-cognitive structures may form that link representations of interpersonal relationships with the emotions of anger, fear, or sadness. Emotion patterns may also form, yoking fear at the caregivers' behavior to anger and subsequent aggressive behaviors.

Maladaptive intersystem connections may result in later emotion perception errors. For example, physically abused children tend to perceive anger when it is not present (Pollak, Cicchetti, Hornung, & Reed, 2000), which has been found to predict aggression (Fine et al., 2004). Neglected children tend to have difficulty discriminating and identifying emotion expressions (Fries & Pollak, 2004; Pollak et al., 2000). Although connections between certain actions or expressions and the emotion systems may result in more rapid evaluation and perception of emotion and promote mobilization of a response that promotes self-preservation (M. M. Bradley & Lang, 1999; Pollak & Sinha, 2002), outside of the maltreatment context they may place the child at a disadvantage. These connections may serve an essential survival function for a vulnerable child in a threatening environment, but automatic triggering of negative emotions in peer relationships may result in inappropriate social behaviors.

Emotions systems may also interconnect with memories of certain events, and in the case of trauma can result in the emergence of disproportionate emotion responses to certain environments or other stimuli. Upon the introduction of a traumatic stimulus, the child may experience overwhelming fear or terror, while the brain reacts through a complex and cascading series of intracellular reactions that stimulate the HPA system and release neurohormones that prepare the body to respond to the threat (Kaufman & Charney, 2001). However, these immediate biological and experiential components of emotion responses are not the terminal consequence of trauma. Instead, they may represent the initial events in a series of self-organizing intersystem connections that play a role in the development and maintenance of longer-term symptoms of Traumatic Stress Disorder (Zero to Three, 1994).

Once the traumatic event or circumstances have ended and the child is in a safe environment, there is a possibility that the trauma has had such an intense impact on the emotions systems that it is prominently imprinted in the child's catalogue of experience. Therefore, one of the symptoms that typifies Traumatic Stress Disorder is some reexperiencing of the traumatic incident(s) through compulsive and repetitive play, distress at reminders of the trauma, or dissociative behaviors (see Streeck-Fischer & van der Kolk, 2000, for a review). These symptoms clearly involve memories of the traumatic and stressful circumstances linked with intense and overwhelming emotions, including terror and despair. An example of reexperience of a trauma is a toddler who was exposed to conditions of chronic deprivation and, after having lived in a safe and nurturing foster home for several months, continued to gorge food to the point of choking and compulsively grabbed food from others' plates during meals. Although the toddler's foster care environment presented no real threat, she continued to experience the fear and distress of impending starvation at each meal. In this example, the situation involving food triggers a cognitive-affective-behavior structure in which the memory of deprivation has formed a link with the fear emotion system. Once triggered, the emotion of fear leads to a behavior (i.e., gorging) previously associated with survival but that is inappropriate to the current situation.

The emotions systems also play a role in several aspects of memory function, such as the content, accuracy, intensity, and accessibility of memories (Pollak, Cicchetti, & Klorman, 1998; Post, Leverich, Xing, & Weiss, 2001). Post and colleagues likened the intrusive memories or reexperiencing a traumatic event to "affective seizures," analogous to the motor seizures that typify the neurological disorder of epilepsy. Similar to the kindling model of epilepsy, repeated experiencing of the traumatic memory may eventually lead to spontaneous, untriggered reexperiencing and intense emotion which, if left untreated, has an ever-increasing negative impact on individual functioning. In the aftermath of chronic maltreatment or deprivation, the developing brain may be more vulnerable to formation of abnormal emotion-memory connections and low thresholds for activation of both the reexperience of the trauma and accompanying flooding of negative emotions such as fear or sadness. These affective-cognitive structures and the thresholds for their activation may solidify and crystallize in the absence of early intervention, resulting in increased risk for the development of affective and behavioral disorders, as well as hampered formation of additional attachment relationships throughout childhood, adolescence, and adulthood (Post et al., 2001).

Emotion Expression in Caregiver-Infant Relationships

Expressions of emotions from both infants and caregivers provide essential communication signals that influence responding and impact the infant's emotional development (Izard et al., 1995). Thus, emotion expressions from both partners play a key role in the emergence and experience of psychopathology in infancy and early childhood. In typical emotional development, infants rely on expressions of their caregivers to provide information important to survival. Infants quickly learn to reference their caregivers' expressions and vocal tone when introduced to novel stimuli (Moses, Baldwin, Rosicky, & Tidball, 2001) and match caregivers' expressions with their own (Termine & Izard, 1988). When caregivers are experiencing depression and exhibiting frequent expressions of sadness and constriction of affective expression in general, infants also show early signs of derailed emotional development, exhibiting angry and sad facial expressions earlier and more frequently than infants of nondepressed mothers (Jones, Field, Fox, Lundy, & Davalos, 1997).

Although negative emotion expression from the caregiver does not necessarily represent a maladaptive pattern of interaction (see Halberstadt & Eaton, 2002, for a review), hostility expressed about the child in conversation has been associated with increased risk for verbal abuse (Calam, Bolton, Barrowclough, & Roberts, 2002). Economically disadvantaged children of mothers who show high levels of negative emotion expression were less accurate in their understanding of anger cues and anger-related terms (Raver & Spagnola, 2002). Parental expressions of anger during direct interactions with their young children predict later behavioral difficulties (Denham et al., 2000). In some cases, parental anger displays or expressions of fear due to past trauma engender fear and conflict that disorganizes the attachment bond (van Ijzendoorn et al., 1999). Thus, frequent and intense caregiver expression of negative emotions impact very young children's ability to perceive emotions in others and regulate their own emotion experiences.

Frequency of negative emotion expressions in infancy is also predictive of early problems and difficult temperament in toddlerhood (Abe & Izard, 1999b), which may promote a reciprocal cycle of negative emotions and punitive responses from the caregiver that continues throughout childhood (Eisenberg et al., 1999). However, expressions of negative emotions themselves are not inherently maladaptive. Infants use negative emotion expression to signal the need for assistance and comfort from a caregiver, and the negative emotion of anger provides motivation to remove a frustrating barrier to mastery of tasks or acquisition of a desired object (Abe & Izard, 1999a). Emotion expression becomes maladaptive when it interferes with normal developmental functioning. In extreme cases, young children's experience of sadness or fear becomes so overwhelming that it constitutes a primary affective disorder (Zero to Three, 1994). In adults, disorders such as depression and anxiety are typified not only by displays of negative emotion but also by cognitions such as thoughts of hopelessness or of undesirable events that might take place (American Psychiatric Association, 1994). In very young children, these disorders have been primarily characterized either by

intense, prolonged negative emotion expression or very constricted expression of emotions and are often associated with, but not specific to, a primary caregiving relationship (Zero to Three, 1994).

Regulation of Emotion Systems in Infancy and Early Childhood

One of the most important developmental tasks in early childhood is the formation of strategies for successful regulation of negative emotions. Children who become derailed in their development of adaptive modulation of emotion may become so severely dysregulated that they are unable to pursue developmentally salient activities. As described by the DC: 0 to 3 system, the diagnosis of a primary regulatory disorder suggests an overarching deficit in the regulatory systems, including emotion regulation, that results in unusual patterns of behavior characterized by either undercontrolled or overcontrolled expression of emotion as well as other behavioral responses to the environment (Zero to Three, 1994). Although direct empirical links have not yet been established, it may be that children who have been maltreated are more likely to experience primary regulatory disorders, as maltreated preschoolers are much more likely to exhibit either undercontrolled or overcontrolled dysregulated emotion patterns than are nonmaltreated preschoolers (Maughan & Cicchetti, 2002).

In normal development, caregivers provide a close relationship with the infant that affects the actual formation of brain structures that influence social responding, feelings of well-being, and emotion regulation (see Kraemer, 1992, for a review). Synchrony in maternal-infant displays of affect, a situation in which the mother modulates her own affect to "follow the child's lead" with respect to facial expressions and behaviors, is predictive of self-regulation in toddlerhood, particularly for infants with difficult temperament (Feldman, Greenbaum, & Yirmiya, 1999). Consistent maternal emotion responsiveness in early childhood, characterized by frequent displays of positive emotions, influences the development of adaptive social interactions and emotion regulation in young children (Landry, Smith, Swank, Assel, & Vellet, 2001). This type of consistent responsiveness requires adaptive emotion regulation on the part of the caregiver that allows her to modulate her own inner emotion experience depending on the affective needs of the child. When the caregiver is experiencing severe dysregulation in her own emotion systems, whether because of depression or some other psychopathology, the infant is placed at risk for abnormal or nonoptimal emotional development and insecure attachment (Ashman, Dawson, Panagiotides, Yamada, & Wilkinson, 2002; Hipwell, Goossens, Melhuish, & Kumar, 2000). For example, prolonged stress, such as that experienced by the child of a depressed mother, has long-term implications for hormone levels and electrical activity in the brain, which are in turn related to the development of affective disorders (Ashman et al., 2002; Dawson et al., 1999). The impact of emotional stress has been detected as early as infancy, when patterns of increased right frontal brain activity have been identified in children as young as 1 month of age who have depressed mothers (Jones et al., 1997).

Child maltreatment also has negative implications for the development of adequate emotion regulation. Children who have experienced maltreatment show abnormal neurobiological patterns, such as elevations in morning salivary cortisol levels, which have also been linked with children's processing and regulation of emotion (Cicchetti & Rogosch, 2001a, 2001b). Maltreatment also directly relates to deficits in children's ability to regulate their emotional experiences (Maughan & Cicchetti, 2002), and emotional dysregulation mediates the maltreatment-externalizing relation (Shields & Cicchetti, 2001). However, some research suggests that parental socialization of emotion expression further mediates the relation between maltreatment and child emotion dysregulation, such that maltreated children who have fewer expectations of support for their displays of emotion have more difficulty generating adaptive ways of coping with and regulating anger (Shipman & Zeman, 2001).

Maltreating caregivers' response to their children's emotion displays is clearly an important mechanism through which children learn to internally regulate their affective experience and points to potential deficits in the caregiver's own emotion-processing abilities that predict regulation difficulties in the child. Caregivers who abuse or neglect their young children show less emotion perspective-taking and less understanding of their children's emotion displays (Shipman & Zeman, 2001). Although results are mixed, there is some evidence that maltreating caregivers make more errors in their perception of facial expressions of emotion and may show a tendency to perceive negative emotions and hostile intent in the affective signals of their children (Balge & Milner, 2000; Milner, 1993; cf. Camras et al., 1988).

When caregivers misperceive their children's emotion displays or are unable to cope with negative displays of emotion from children, they may respond punitively in these situations rather than supporting or coaching the child to successfully and adaptively regulate intense nega-

tive emotion. Some parents may have difficulty regulating their own responses to child negative emotion and experience increased distress in these situations. Parental distress in response to children's negative emotion adversely affects their ability to help externally regulate child emotion in ways that help lower the intensity of the child's experience and outward display and is negatively related to children's ability to understand emotions (Fabes, Leonard, Kupanoff, & Martin, 2001). Punitive responses to children's negative emotion displays are negatively related to children's ability to regulate intense negative emotions (Eisenberg et al., 1999). Reciprocal cycles of dysregulation between parents and children suggest a model of intergenerational transmission of nonoptimal emotion experiences that derail emotional development and lead to the emergence of psychopathology.

EMOTIONS AND DEPRESSION

Depression is in many respects a prototypical disturbance of emotion. Mood disturbance is the defining feature of unipolar and bipolar depressive disorders. Considerable research has examined the role of emotion in depressive disorders, including attention to the subjective emotional experience of individuals suffering from depression, emotion regulation, emotion recognition and mood-congruent memory, emotion expression, and the neurophysiological substrates of emotional contributions to depression. After an overview of the neurobiology of depression, this section focuses on dimensional models of emotion and depression and then on the role of discrete emotions in depression.

Overview of Neurobiology of Emotions in Depression

Studies at the cognitive and behavioral levels indicate that the affective symptomatology of depression includes loss of interest and enjoyment, increased sadness, shame, and guilt, and the tendency for prolonged sadness to elicit inner-directed anger (Blumberg & Izard, 1985; Marshall & Izard, 1972; also see H. Lewis, 1971; Tomkins, 1963). Thresholds for the activation of these emotion systems undoubtedly have determinants in both biogenetic and environmental processes. Infants' capacities to perceive the world as affectionate and friendly or indifferent and hostile emerge from brain systems that subserve the positive emotions of interest and joy and the negative emotions of sadness, shame, guilt, and anger (cf. Panksepp, 2001). Neuroscientists have begun to map the neural circuitry of these emotions and trace their development. They have long recognized that the development of such brain systems depends in large part on environment and early experience (Greenough et al., 1987). Scientists have not yet determined whether biogenetic substrates or environmental factors have primacy in causal processes (Davidson et al., 2002). The evidence does suggest that the interplay of biological and social factors is critical in the development of depression.

Drawing largely on the work of Damasio (1994), Davidson and his colleagues (Davidson, 2000; Davidson et al., 2002), and A. L. Miller et al. (2002), we identify the several brain systems or neural circuitries involved in the activation and regulation of the emotions in depression and indicate how they may contribute to the disorder. Researchers have identified relevant systems in the prefrontal cortices (PFC), anterior cingulate cortex (ACC), hippocampus, and amygdala.

The Prefrontal Cortex

As noted earlier, the PFC plays a highly significant role in emotion, higher-order cognition, and emotion-cognition relations (Bechara et al., 1997; Damasio, 1994). The role of the PFC in depression may be explained by the fact that it houses the representational processes involved in goals and goal-directed coping strategies (E. K. Miller & Cohen, 2001). Lesions in the ventromedial PFC reduce or eliminate the emotion arousal that normally guides decision-making processes in risky situations (Bechara et al., 1997; Damasio, 1994). Resulting maladaptive choices and subsequent losses and problems can contribute to sadness and the patterns of emotions in depression. Researchers have also linked vulnerability to negative mood states and depression to left hemisphere PFC hypoactivation and right hemisphere PFC hyperactivation (Davidson et al., 2002). In EEG studies, several investigators have reported the neurological symptoms of reduced left relative to right PFC activation. Yet, this pattern of apparently asymmetrical functioning in the left and right brain hemispheres does not always appear in depression (Davidson et al., 2002), and it may vary with the sex and psychiatric history of the individual (A. L. Miller et al., 2002). Some evidence suggests that variability in PFC activation may itself constitute a symptom of depression (Debener et al., 2000).

Anterior Cingulate Cortex

The ACC is a crucial region of the brain for the interaction of emotion, attention, and working memory (Damasio, 1994). Research indicates that the ACC has functionally distinct regions for emotion processes (rostral and ventral areas) and cognitive processes (dorsal areas). Consistent

with the assumption that the ACC plays a critical role in the neurophysiological processes in emotion regulation, its emotion area has extensive connections to the PFC, amygdala, hypothalamus, and brainstem (Devinsky, Morrell, & Vogt, 1995). Damage to the ACC (and possibly adjoining PFC areas) creates a condition of "suspended animation" characterized by absence of expressive behavior in face and body, as well as inability to reason and an apparent lack of emotion feelings (Damasio, 1994, p. 71).

The symptoms of neurological patients with damage to the ACC may bear some similarity to those found in extreme forms of depression, where a seemingly total lack of the positive emotions of interest and enjoyment leads to drastically maladaptive disengagement with the social and physical environment (Marshall & Izard, 1972). Several investigators have indeed observed decreased ACC activation in Major Depression. The decreased activation appears in the dorsal region, which may relate to effortful control (see Davidson et al., 2002, for a review). Researchers have related developmental increases in effortful control to maturation of the ACC, as well as the PFC and its associated executive functions. They have identified effortful control as a temperament factor that plays a critical role in the development of emotion regulation, self-control, and adaptive behavior (Posner & Rothbart, 2000). Although a number of behavioral neuroscientists have speculated about cross-talk among these brain areas, understanding the functional relations between the emotion and cognitive areas of the ACC, between them and the PFC, and the implications of these interactions for adaptive behavior and psychopathological conditions such as depression remains a challenge for future research.

The Hippocampus

The hippocampus participates in important aspects of cognition, and its integrity is critical to the creation of memories of new facts (Damasio, 1994). It subserves contextual, spatial, declarative, and episodic learning and memory (see Davidson et al., 2002, for a review). Apparently due to their inability to form and retain memories of provocative events, neurological patients with damage to the hippocampus often experience emotions without conscious awareness of the cause or activating event (Damasio, 1999). An inability to remember the facts or circumstances that cause an emotion might make its regulation more difficult and its duration longer, conditions that characterize Major Depression. Although hippocampal dysfunction may relate to depression and other forms of psychopathology, hippocampal activity occurs with positive as well as negative emotion arousal (see Davidson et al., 2002, for a review). Its role in emotion and depression may stem from its unequivocal effects on learning and memory, both of which are prominent mediators of emotion activation. Individuals suffering either depression or anxiety disorders show a deficiency in their ability to experience and express emotion appropriate to the context, a context regulation problem that results in context-inappropriate expressions of feelings (Davidson, Jackson, & Kalin, 2000).

Major Depression is associated with decreased hippocampal volume as well as hippocampal dysfunction that may result in decreased inhibitory regulation of the HPA system. These conditions, however, also characterize other forms of psychopathology (e.g., Posttraumatic Stress Disorder and Borderline Personality Disorder). Moreover, these findings come from correlational studies and do not identify cause-effect relations (Davidson et al., 2002). Some evidence suggests that in females, the decrease in hippocampal volume is associated with lifetime duration of depression and is thus a symptom rather than a cause (Sheline, 2000). In any case, substantial evidence supports the correlation.

The Amygdala

The literature reveals three findings relating the functioning of the amygdala to depression (Davidson et al., 2002). As in the case of the hippocampus, the data show correlations, not cause, and some inconsistencies across studies. The first of these findings, more often supported than not, shows a relation between increased volume in the amygdala, particularly left amygdalar volume, and depression. Second, some investigators have found increased blood flow or glucose metabolism in the amygdala of depressed patients. Third, several studies have shown a positive correlation between trait-like negative emotionality and Manic Depressive Disorder. Consistent with this finding is the observation that relief from depression mediated by antidepressant drugs is accompanied by a decrease in amygdalar activation.

Status of the Neurobiology of Depression

Neurobiological research has revealed a number of promising leads regarding the causes and effects of depression. Current evidence reveals that some brain and neural systems (e.g., the prefrontal and anterior cingulate cortices, hippocampus, and amygdala) are more involved in depression than others. The findings are consistent with the conceptual framework of this chapter and underscore the necessity of a multifaceted, multilevel, cross-disciplinary approach to the study of depression, as well as other forms of psychopathology.

Dimensional Models of Emotion in Depression

Several different models of emotion and motivation have been productively applied to depression. We focus on four: (1) motivational models concentrating on behavior activation and behavioral inhibition; (2) approach and withdrawal models of emotion; (3) the two-dimensional, positive and negative affect models of emotion, which have been elaborated into the tripartite model of depression and anxiety, and (4) three-dimensional models of emotion space that include a dimension of dominance or perceived control. As will be seen, there is considerable overlap among these models, offering opportunities for integration.

Motivational Systems Model: Behavioral Activation and Inhibition

Depressive disorders offered a prototype for the development of biological models of psychopathology focusing on motivational systems (Depue & Iacono, 1989; Fowles, 1994; Gray & McNaughton, 1996). These motivational models have since been generalized to other major forms of psychopathology (Beauchaine, 2001; Beauchaine, Katkin, Strassberg, & Snarr, 2001; Depue, 1996; Fowles, 1994; Johnson & Roberts, 1995; Quay, 1993, 1997).

Gray (Gray & McNaughton, 1996) has developed an influential model of biological motivational systems. Rooted in neurophysiology, Gray's model hypothesizes that three distinct motivational systems impel much of our behavior. Although these systems served adaptive functions over the course of evolutionary history, it is possible for these systems to lead to maladaptive expressions, either due to extreme individual differences or because of the transaction between the organism and specific environmental demands. Thus, these systems undergird both normal functioning and pathological processes.

The three systems in Gray's model include the Behavioral Activation System (BAS), Behavioral Inhibition System (BIS), and the Fight or Flight System (FFS). The FFS has received much less attention than the other motivational systems; most discussions of Gray's model concentrate on the BAS and BIS exclusively (Matthews & Gilliland, 1999). However, it is worth bearing in mind that Gray posited a third dimension. The FFS may prove helpful in reconciling Gray's model with other theories and observations described later (e.g., White & Depue, 1999).

The BAS motivates approach behaviors, including social engagement and positive valance emotion experiences such as happiness. The BAS may also be associated with subjective feelings of confidence, pleasure, drive to obtain a goal, and anger. BAS also appears linked to reward dominance and sensation seeking (Zuckerman, Joireman, Kraft, & Kuhlman, 1999), constructs that emphasize an individual's willingness to seek out hedonic stimulation. At a neurophysiological level, the BAS involves primarily dopaminergic pathways (Carver & White, 1994; Gray & McNaughton, 1996).

The BIS motivates withdrawal behaviors, including social avoidance and harm avoidance. In neurophysiological terms, the BIS appears to involve serotonergic or norepinephrine pathways. The BIS is oriented toward cues of harm or punishment, and it inhibits ongoing behavior in the presence of novel stimuli or signals of nonreward (extinction) or punishment. The BIS and BAS are thought to be distinct but antagonistic systems, analogous to the brake and gas pedals in a car (Mash & Wolfe, 1999).

Investigations examining the relationship of BAS and BIS to emotion experiences or personality traits have mapped out a logical set of associations. High levels of BAS are associated with higher trait extraversion, sensation seeking, and agreeableness. High BAS also appears to be associated with increased self-report of positive emotions such as happiness, joviality, and excitement. Conversely, BIS appears most strongly associated with trait neuroticism and negative affect. BIS shows strong correlations with measures of anxiety and shyness (Matthews & Gilliland, 1999).

Depression Involving High Behavioral Inhibition System, Low Behavioral Activation System. In Gray's model, unipolar depression is a condition involving a combination of pathological elevations of BIS and low levels of BAS. At the symptomatic level, the high activation of the BIS would be associated with increased negative affect, increased shyness, and increased tension and somatic complaints, such as psychomotor agitation. The markedly low level of BAS would be associated with a sense of anhedonia (i.e., "loss of interest in activities that used to be pleasurable"; American Psychiatric Association, 2001, p. 349), and a lack of motivation to engage in social interaction or other reward-oriented activity. The antithesis of depression, in BIS/BAS terms, would be Conduct Disorder: Various theoreticians have formulated Conduct Disorder as representing the combination of low BIS (resulting in disinhibition and decreased salience of punishment) with high BAS (leading to high reward dominance and the pursuit of short-term goals without concern for the long-term consequences; Fowles, 1994; Hare, 1999; Quay, 1993).

Depue has developed a very similar model of depression, although he uses slightly different terms, referring to the approach/positive emotion system as the Behavioral Fa-

cilitation System (BFS) instead of BAS (Depue & Iacono, 1989). Depue more recently has been focusing on three personality "superfactors" that include emotional and neurobehavioral substrates: positive affectivity, which primarily involves dopaminergic pathways (Depue & Collins, 1999; Depue & Lenzenweger, 2001; Depue, Luciana, Arbisi, Collins, & Leon, 1994); constraint, principally linked to serotonergic (5HT) functioning; and negative emotionality, also principally linked to serotonergic (5HT) functioning (Depue, 1996). Like Gray, Depue conceptualizes unipolar depression as involving hypoactivation of the BFS/BAS and hyperactivation of the BIS or negative emotionality system (Depue & Iacono, 1989; Depue & Lenzenweger, 2001).

Mania as Behavioral Activation System Dysregulation. Bipolar Disorder, or manic depression, is characterized by the occurrence of depressive as well as hypomanic or manic episodes (American Psychiatric Association, 2001). The emotional and behavioral presentation of a depressive episode in Bipolar Disorder is largely indistinguishable from a unipolar depressive episode. In both cases, the depressive episode is likely to involve high levels of negative affect (i.e., high BIS) as well as low levels of behavioral activation or facilitation.

Hypomanic and manic episodes are defined by the same symptoms in the current psychiatric classification symptoms. Hypomania involves either less severe symptom expression or shorter duration. Both hypomania and mania can involve elated or expansive mood, irritability, grandiosity or inflated self-esteem, decreased need for sleep, pressured speech, racing thoughts or flight of ideas, distractibility, increased goal-directed activity (socially, academically, or sexually), or excessive involvement in pleasurable activities that have a high potential for painful consequences. With the exception of irritability, these symptoms map fairly neatly onto a putative behavioral activation system (e.g., BAS/BFS). Irritability might appear to be an exception if it is conceptualized as involving putatively negative emotions. However, the discrete emotion of anger is distinct from other negative valance emotions in several important respects, discussed later. Also, the irritability in mania seems most likely to manifest when people or circumstances impinge on the manic individual's pursuit of goal-directed behaviors.

Thus, hypomania and mania can be conceptualized as manifestations of dysregulation in the BAS. There is mounting evidence consistent with this formulation. Self-report measures of depressive symptomatology are positively correlated with reports of BIS and negatively correlated with

BAS. High self-reported levels of BAS/BFS are also markers for physiological differences in cortisol levels, dopaminergic activity, and lifetime history or future risk for the development of Bipolar Disorder (Depue & Collins, 1999; Depue, Krauss, Spoont, & Arbisi, 1989; Depue et al., 1994; Klein & Depue, 1984; Klein, Depue, & Slater, 1985, 1986; Klein, Lewinsohn, & Seeley, 1996; Lewinsohn, Seeley, Buckley, & Klein, 2002).

Current models of Bipolar Disorder focus on dysregulation of both the BIS and BAS (Depue & Iacono, 1989; Depue & Zald, 1993; Johnson & Roberts, 1995). Low levels of BAS would lead to anhedonic depressive features. Moderate levels of BAS characterize "euthymic" behavior, or functioning within the normal limits of individuals without Bipolar Disorder. High levels of BAS activation could create hypomania, which generally feels subjectively pleasant and often involves extreme productivity, perhaps artistically as well as in the pursuit of other activities (Jamison, 1993; Lozano & Johnson, 2001). Extreme elevations of BAS result in the incapacitating aspects of mania, including disinhibited and impulsive behaviors that often lead to law-breaking and arrest (Hirschfeld et al., 2000; Pliszka, Sherman, Barrow, & Irick, 2000) as well as the more disorganized and psychotic presentations leading to emergency psychiatric hospitalization. High levels of BIS appear more associated with trait neuroticism (Lozano & Johnson, 2001), the negative affect symptoms associated with a depressive episode (Depue & Iacono, 1989), and potentially with the high rate of anxious symptoms observed in conjunction with Bipolar Disorder (Kessler, 1994).

Because BIS and BAS are thought to be independent systems and not polar opposites, it should be possible to experience states that involve varying degrees of activation of both systems. Although it was originally thought that Bipolar Disorder typically involved distinct episodes of mania and depression, often separated by periods of relatively euthymic functioning, data increasingly suggest that manic and depressive episodes can occur independently or simultaneously. Mania and depression appear to involve distinct risk factors or triggers (Alloy, Abramson, & Francis, 1999; Johnson, Meyer, Winett, & Small, 2000; Johnson & Miller, 1997; Johnson & Roberts, 1995; Johnson et al., in press). Additionally, mania and depression respond to different pharmacological agents: Lithium and anticonvulsants such as divalproex appear to have more pronounced antimanic properties, whereas compounds such as lamictal and selective serotonin reuptake inhibitors appear to have antidepressive qualities (Calabrese et al., 2000; Findling, Feeny, Stansbrey, DelPorto-Bedoya, & Demeter, 2002; Keck & McElroy, 2003).

The clinical phenomenon of "mixed states" also supports the theory that depression and mania might involve two separate systems that could potentially be dysregulated at the same time. Mixed episodes are periods during which an individual simultaneously experiences symptoms of both mania and depression. These have been recognized clinically since Kraepelin's initial formulation of the syndrome of manic depression. In the BIS/BAS framework, mixed states represent the unfortunate confluence of high levels of activation of both BIS and BAS. Mixed states are described as being subjectively terrible experiences, "black manias" that are intensely unpleasant (Jamison, 1993, 1995). Actuarial statistics bear out a higher association between mixed states and suicide attempts or arrests for violent behavior (Goodwin & Jamison, 1990; Pliszka et al., 2000).

The BIS/BAS framework generates an interesting prediction, which, to our knowledge, has yet to be tested. If mixed states represent high activation of both BIS and BAS, then the depressive symptoms expressed during a mixed state should not include those symptoms that would be associated with low BAS activation. Instead, mixed states should primarily reflect the depressive symptoms that would be linked to high BIS activation. Specifically, a BIS/BAS model of mixed states would predict that mixed episodes tend to involve higher levels of anxiety, excessive guilt, psychomotor agitation, and sleep disturbance (especially early morning awakening)—all features of high BIS activation. Conversely, mixed episodes should involve relatively few symptoms of anhedonia, lack of energy, or psychomotor retardation. These would all be features of low BAS activation and thus incompatible with the high BAS activation involved in a manic state. A corollary of the BIS/BAS model of Bipolar Disorder would be that individuals might experience times with high BIS activation but normal BAS activation. These periods should be characterized by the high BIS features of depression without the associated low BAS features. As we will see below, a high BIS combined with moderate BAS activation pattern is characteristic of anxiety disorders, and Generalized Anxiety Disorder (GAD) in particular. Thus, it is intriguing to consider the frequency with which Bipolar Disorder is reported to be comorbid with anxiety disorders (and GAD in particular; Kessler, 1994; Kessler, Rubinow, Holmes, Abelson, & Zhao, 1997). The finding that individuals dealing with Bipolar Disorder report high lifetime rates of GAD is consistent with the BIS/BAS model of independent motivational systems. Because relatives of bipolar probands are not at higher risk of GAD, and because GAD and Bipolar Disorder appear to have no shared genetic variance (Zuckerman, 1999), it seems plausible that what appears to be comorbid GAD in cases with Bipolar Disorder may actually be a high BIS and moderate BAS manifestation of the bipolar syndrome.

Neurophysiology and Approach/Withdrawal Systems

A largely independent line of scientific inquiry into the neurophysiological underpinnings of emotion has generated a two-dimensional model of approach versus withdrawal systems. The withdrawal system implicates negative emotions, such as shyness, fear, and sadness. The approach system clearly involves positive valance emotions such as happiness, enjoyment, and excitement; for a while, this system was equated with positive affect. However, anger appears to be an approach emotion, in spite of the fact that anger tends to be classified as a negative emotion in analyses of self-report (Tellegen, Watson, & Clark, 1999; Watson, 2000b; Watson & Tellegen, 1985; cf. Mehrabian, 1995b; Russell & Mehrabian, 1977; Youngstrom, Frazier, & Butt, 2003).

Withdrawal emotions appear associated with increased right hemispheric cortical activation, particularly of the right prefrontal cortical region. Conversely, approach emotions are associated with increased left hemispheric activation. Most individuals show greater resting activation of the left hemisphere than the right hemisphere. This pattern of activation suggests that people would generally report experiencing higher state levels of positive emotions than negative emotions. This hypothesis has been borne out by studies of subjective well-being (E. Diener & Diener, 1996) as well as state emotion (Watson, 2000b).

Individuals with depression show higher levels of right hemispheric activation as well as decreased left hemispheric activation, yielding a higher ratio of right:left activation than found in nondepressed individuals (Davidson, 1998, 2000; Tomarken & Keener, 1998). A more detailed discussion of the specific neurophysiological pathways occurs in a later section. For present purposes, it is important to note the congruence between the approach/withdrawal model and the BAS/BIS model. The withdrawal system of emotions corresponds closely with the characterization of the BIS: Both involve most of the negative valance emotions, both involve sensitivity to cues of threat, and both are associated with increased sympathetic autonomous activation. Similarly, the approach system of emotions aligns with the BAS system described by Gray and others. The inclusion of anger as an approach emotion, which initially seemed problematic when approach was being equated with positive emotionality, actually now appears consonant with observations of irritability and aggression in mania (Woz-

niak & Biederman, 1997; Wozniak et al., 1995). Along the same lines, some evidence suggests that anger can be associated with dopaminergic activation, consistent with a BAS or an approach model of emotion.

The approach/withdrawal model has illuminated understanding of the physiological underpinnings of emotion and also provided a physiological marker associated with depression. The right:left activation ratio appears to be both a state and trait marker for depression. Individuals who have recovered from a depressive episode tend to still have higher right:left ratios of cortical activation, suggesting a trait-like component that persists beyond the depressive episode. At present, it is unclear whether this ratio represents a preexisting diathesis for depression, or whether it is a reorganization of neural activation patterns that persists after the episode (a "scar" or kindling hypothesis; Post et al., 2001). However, depressive episodes entail even more marked right:left ratios of activation, and the activation asymmetry changes in response to interventions for depression as well as modalities such as meditation. For now, this body of work provides strong corroboration of the role of emotional systems in depression, possibly as a vulnerability factor, definitely as a state marker, and probably as a risk factor for relapse.

Positive Affect, Negative Affect, and Depression

The most prominent models of emotion structure in contemporary personality and social psychology focus on two major dimensions of emotion. These have been labeled *positive affect* and *negative affect* (Tellegen et al., 1999; Watson, Clark, & Harkness, 1994; Watson, Wiese, Vaidya, & Tellegen, 1999), *valence and arousal* (Lang, 1995; Russell, 1980), or *energy and tension* (Thayer, 1967, 2001). Statistically, these models are equivalent, resulting from rotations of a two-dimensional factor structure (Barrett & Russell, 1999). For the purposes of this review, we use the terms positive affect (PA) and negative affect (NA) for two reasons: In factor analyses of self-report data, the simplest structure usually corresponds to a PA-NA model, and the PA-NA terminology has been more commonly used in discussions of emotion and psychopathology (S. J. Bradley, 2000; Keltner & Kring, 1998; Kring & Bachorowski, 1999).

Two major conceptual advances pertaining to depression have developed through the application of the PA-NA model of emotion. One is the idea that trait NA, or an individual's predisposition to experience negative emotions with more frequency and intensity, increases the risk for the development of many kinds of psychopathology, including depression (S. J. Bradley, 2000; Watson & Clark, 1984; Zuckerman, 1999). High trait NA is likely to be the confluence of genetic factors as well as learning history (Loehlin, 1992). Individual differences in emotion activation thresholds have important consequences in terms of interpersonal interaction (Keltner et al., 1995) and cognitive associations (Izard, 1991). Through the formation of "affective-cognitive structures," emotions shape the building blocks of personality (Izard, 1993; Izard et al., 1993). Trait NA is strongly correlated with the personality factor of neuroticism or emotional instability, which also is correlated with most forms of psychopathology (Krueger, Caspi, Moffitt, Silva, & McGee, 1996), and with anxiety and mood disorders in particular (Krueger, 1999a). Conceptually, NA plays a central role in psychopathology. To the extent that pathology causes subjective distress, it by definition involves increases in state NA (Wakefield, 1997). High trait NA represents an individual difference in an adaptive emotional system that can, given the right environmental circumstances, support the development of what could be diagnosed as a psychiatric disorder.

The second major contribution of PA-NA models to the understanding of depression focuses on the differentiation of depression from anxiety. Depression and anxiety frequently co-occur. In diagnostic interviews, individuals meeting criteria for a mood disorder are very likely to also meet criteria for an anxiety disorder, and vice versa, especially when considering lifetime histories of functioning. Similarly, individuals reporting high scores on traditional measures of depressive symptoms are also likely to report high scores on instruments intended to measure anxiety (Clark & Watson, 1991). In fact, the correlation between measures of depression and anxiety often falls in the $r = .70$ to $.80$ range. This is high enough to raise concerns about whether these instruments truly are measuring distinct constructs (i.e., it challenges their discriminant validity; D. T. Campbell & Fiske, 1959). By the same token, there are questions about whether anxiety and depression truly represent distinct diagnostic entities. In addition to the challenge posed by the high rate of comorbidity, behavioral genetic studies have indicated that GAD and depression share both a common genetic component and a common factor of "individual-specific" or "unique environmental" experiences (Kendler et al., 1995). Based on this and other evidence, it has been argued that GAD may be a prodromal version of Major Depression (Mineka, Watson, & Clark, 1998).

Careful examination of the existing measures of anxiety and depression through the lens of the PA-NA emotion model generated the observation that most instruments were capturing NA in general, but without adequately measuring other emotion or symptom patterns that might help differentiate anxiety and depression (Clark & Watson, 1991). This conceptual analysis led to the formulation of the tripartite model of depression and anxiety. According to this model, both anxiety and depression include high levels of NA as a core feature. Thus, measures that primarily tap NA will not be able to distinguish between the two syndromes. According to the tripartite model, what is unique to depression is a pronounced low level of PA. This pattern corresponds to the anhedonia and loss of interest in pleasurable activity and the lack of energy characterizing depressive states (Thayer, 1996). Anxiety disorders, on the other hand, do not involve diminutions of PA and may actually involve slight increases in some positive emotions such as interest-excitement (Izard & Youngstrom, 1996). Conversely, the tripartite model posits that anxiety disorders are marked by high levels of fear and physiological hyperarousal that are not implicated in depressive episodes (Watson, Clark, et al., 1995). Thus, the tripartite model makes the prediction that anxiety and depression should be distinguishable via profiles of emotion. The emotional pattern for depression would be low PA, high NA, and moderate fear and physiological hyperarousal (i.e., "within normal limits"). Anxiety disorders were posited to result in moderate PA, high NA, and high fear or physiological hyperarousal. By extension, the tripartite model also implies that truly comorbid anxiety and depression should involve the defining features of both anxiety and depression; in other words, comorbid anxiety and depression would include low PA and high fear/physiological hyperarousal at the same time, in addition to the shared component of elevated NA.

The tripartite model has been tested by multiple research groups using data from both multiple age groups and populations. These include college students (Burns & Eidelson, 1998; Joiner, 1996; Joiner et al., 1999; Watson, Clark, et al., 1995; Watson, Weber, et al., 1995), adults in the community (Krueger, 1999b; Watson, Clark, et al., 1995) or Air Force (Joiner et al., 1999), patient samples (Brown, Chorpita, & Barlow, 1998; Burns & Eidelson, 1998; Joiner et al., 1999; Krueger, 1999b; Watson, Clark, et al., 1995; Watson, Weber, et al., 1995), and school-age children in the community (Chorpita, 2002; Lonigan, Hooe, David, & Kistner, 1999), outpatient (Chorpita, Albano, & Barlow, 1998), and inpatient settings (Joiner, Catanzaro, & Laurent, 1996; Joiner & Lonigan, 2000). These studies have been remarkably consistent in terms of supporting the tripartite model's formulation of depression as involving low PA and high NA. Findings have been more complicated with regard to anxiety and fear or physiological hyperarousal. Fear and physiological hyperarousal show the strongest relations to Panic Disorder (Brown et al.,

1998). GAD appears principally to correlate with high NA and not so much higher fear or physiological hyperarousal (Chorpita et al., 1998). This linkage of GAD with high NA actually is consistent with the high rates of psychiatric comorbidity and the shared genetic and environmental components between GAD and depression (which also implicates high levels of NA). Interestingly, simple phobias and Obsessive-Compulsive Disorder, both of which appear to have distinct genetic factors from GAD and Panic Disorder (Kendler et al., 1995), do not show strong associations with fear or physiological hyperarousal.

The tripartite model has clear implications for assessment. Tools that concentrate on the distinct emotional features of depression versus anxiety should do a better job of discriminating these conditions (e.g., the Mood and Anxiety Symptoms Questionnaire, which was developed specifically with the tripartite model in mind; Watson, Clark, et al., 1995). Such improvements in instrumentation would not only increase the accuracy of differential diagnosis, but they also will provide clearer definitions of phenotypes for the investigation of risk factors and treatment response. The tripartite model underscores the centrality of low positive affect, or anhedonia, as perhaps being the defining component of depression. If sadness and happiness are polar opposites, as suggested by some emotions researchers (Russell & Carroll, 1999), then the two core symptoms of depression in the *DSM* nosology, sadness and loss of interest in pleasurable activity, might actually be manifestations of the same emotional construct of low PA.

Three-Dimensional Models

Although most researchers currently ascribe to two-dimensional models of emotion, there are data suggesting that emotion space possesses a third dimension (Mehrabian, 1995b, 1996; Russell & Mehrabian, 1977; Youngstrom et al., 2003). This dimension has typically been labeled "dominance," and it appears to relate to the degree of perceived control that the organism has over the emotion-eliciting situation. The dominance dimension separates fear (low dominance) and anger (high dominance; Mehrabian, 1996; Youngstrom et al., 2003), addressing one of the more problematic conflations of a two-dimensional model (e.g., Lavoie, Miller, Conway, & Fleet, 2001). The dominance dimension also separates confidence and pride from awe, suggesting that dominance is not simply a subfactor of hostility splintering from negative affect.

Although research here is much sparser, there is evidence to suggest that a dominance dimension is also implicated in depression. Specifically, lower levels of dominance are associated with higher scores on measures of

depressive symptoms (Mehrabian, 1995a, 1997). In a three-dimensional framework, anxiety and depression share the negative/unpleasant valence and low dominance (i.e., submissiveness, in Mehrabian's terminology) with anxiety disorders, including more arousal/activation (Mehrabian, 1997). The inclusion of a dominance dimension in models of depression is thought-provoking given recent attention to the role of submissiveness in the genesis of depressive disorders (Allan & Gilbert, 1997; Gilbert & Allan, 1998; Gilbert, Allan, Brough, Melley, & Miles, 2002; Gilbert, Allan, & Trent, 1995). Plutchik (1993) has speculated that depression would be associated with downward shifts in emotional dominance, and therefore decreases in perceived control of affectively salient cues would be linked to increases in depression. Dominance thus could provide a framework for integrating helplessness/hopelessness models of depression into an emotion model of psychopathology (Abramson, Metalsky, & Alloy, 1989; Seligman & Peterson, 1986).

Discrete Emotion Models

In contrast to the dimensional models discussed earlier, discrete emotion models emphasize the unique properties of distinct emotion systems. Discrete emotion models provide an opportunity for more textured analyses of behavior and neurophysiological underpinnings. At the same time, discrete emotion models entail considerably more complexity than two- or three-dimensional models of emotions, and it is important to determine that the increased complexity provides sufficient improvement in models of psychopathology to justify the adoption of less parsimonious models.

Current formulations of discrete emotions models emphasize that emotions and cognitions are reciprocally influential. Biological, temperamental differences in the emotion systems may be amplified or attenuated by environmental experiences, learning, and cognition. Izard (1977) has described "affective-cognitive structures," patterns of spreading activation in neural networks that represent the amalgam of emotional and cognitive experiences. For example, there is an innate neural system responsible for the emotion of fear. Although all humans have the anatomical structures necessary for the experience of fear, individuals differ in their tendency to respond to environmental stimuli with fear. These differences are further shaped by learning history. Two children might witness the same car accident, yet one might respond with more severe and persistent anxiety due to a preexisting difference in temperament. In some situations, the environment and the emotional predisposition will combine to produce a new tendency to respond differently to subsequent environmental stimuli.

In discrete emotions models, psychopathology represents the confluence of biological differences in emotion activation (forming a diathesis, or predisposition), coupled with environmental experiences and learned responses that generate stress. By dint of individual learning history, affective-cognitive structures can become quite complicated and idiosyncratic. In this regard, each individual's personal story and constellation of emotions and memories is unique. At the same time, certain discrete emotions are likely to be centrally involved in different forms of pathology. Fear is intrinsically linked to Panic Disorder, and disgust to simple phobias of spiders, snakes, and blood. Anger is more implicated in pathological expressions of aggression than would be sadness.

Patterns of Emotions in Depression

Discrete emotions models of psychopathology conceptualize disorders as involving constellations of emotions, or "emotion profiles." Some of the emotions are prototypically involved in the disorder, and others may only become attached to the affective-cognitive structure in a subset of cases. The "profiles of emotion" approach has been applied to both depression and anxiety disorders. The emotion profile involved in depression always involves high levels of sadness and diminution of happiness, joy, and pleasure. This has been found with self-report of discrete emotions in children (Blumberg & Izard, 1985, 1986) as well as adults (Clark, Watson, & Mineka, 1994). In addition, the profile of discrete emotions involved in depression often involves high levels of guilt, shyness, shame, and self-directed hostility. To some extent, elevations of these emotions reflect the involvement of general negative affect, as predicted and documented in the discussion of the tripartite model of depression and anxiety. Similarly, the hallmark features of high sadness and low happiness are consonant with the low PA or anhedonic component of depression.

However, a discrete emotions approach can inform models of depression beyond simply recapitulating a dimensional model such as the tripartite formulation. For example, a discrete emotions approach emphasizes the unique contribution of guilt to depression. Although there are a variety of discrete emotions that show strong factor loadings on NA (i.e., they involve high levels of activation and a negative valence), guilt shows a stronger relation to depression than do most other of the negative emotions. Indeed, excessive guilt is one of the diagnostic features of Major Depression according to the official psychiatric classification system (American Psychiatric Association,

2001). On the other hand, anger expressed outward appears to be less commonly associated with depression, and contempt toward others also appears to play a diminished role in depression. These are theoretically interesting inasmuch as they are exceptions to a simplistic "depression involves increases in negative affect" model. They also are consistent with models that make the approach/withdrawal distinction: Depression involves an increase in withdrawal-related emotions (shyness, sadness, guilt) and a decrease in approach-related emotions (e.g., happiness, affection, and anger).

Discrete emotions also help to cleave disorders into distinct entities. Anxiety and depression show distinct profiles, for example. Although both anxiety and depression involve substantial activation of negative emotions, depression is characterized by marked sadness and a lack of positive affect, whereas anxiety is signified by higher elevations of fear and variable amounts of positive affect (Izard & Youngstrom, 1996). In many cases, the heightened arousal of anxiety may be difficult to differentiate from anxiety, and part of cognitive therapy often involves reframing or relabeling diffuse arousal as excitement rather than fear (cf. Schachter & Singer, 1962). Further discrete emotions distinctions are discussed later.

At the same time, discrete emotions models also elaborate some of the commonalities between depression and anxiety. Both clearly involve high levels of trait inhibition (Kagan, 1994, 1997; Kagan, Snidman, Zentner, & Peterson, 1999), which also has been conceptualized as trait shyness (M. Lewis, 1995). Over the life span, inhibition and shyness are likely to be associated with trait neuroticism (Costa & McCrae, 1995; McCrae & Costa, 1986), which itself is a major associated feature of anxiety, depression, and psychopathology in general (S. J. Bradley, 2000; Zuckerman, 1999).

Profiles of Emotion and Manic Depression

Currently, there are no data to support a distinction between the emotion profiles of a unipolar depressive episode versus a depressed episode in the course of a bipolar illness. However, the emotion profile of a manic episode is clearly distinct. Hypomania and mania both involve high levels of interest-excitement and enjoyment. Indeed, "elated mood" is one of the cardinal features of manic episodes in children (Geller & Luby, 1997) as well as adults (Goodwin & Jamison, 1990). The grandiose component of the hypomanic or manic mood episode also entails feelings of self-assurance, confidence, pride, and potentially contempt and arrogance.

Most of these discrete emotions could be assimilated into a two-dimensional model of emotion and psychopathology. In a PA/NA model, mania would be described as involving extreme levels of PA activation. If one accepts the congruence of PA with Thayer's (2001) dimension of energy and with Gray's BAS, then the increased energy, excitement, and enthusiasm associated with hypomania and mania are also consonant with a two-dimensional model.

However, another prominent feature of mania is frequent irritability or rage. Irritable mood is one of the diagnostic symptoms of a manic episode, although *DSM-IV* stipulates that if mood is predominantly irritable instead of elated, then four other symptoms of mania must be present (instead of three; American Psychiatric Association, 2001). Irritability and rages are arguably the most prominent and impairing symptoms in juvenile presentations of Bipolar Disorder (Biederman, 1998; Carlson, 2002; Papolos, 1999). The centrality of irritability and anger to mania is a challenge to the PA-NA model of psychopathology, inasmuch as anger, hostility, and irritation are all classified as negative emotions, whereas mania otherwise appears to involve hyperactivation of the PA system.

The association of both anger and positive emotions with mania is less problematic for other dimensional models. In the BIS/BAS framework, both positive affect and instrumental or predatory aggression can be expressions of high BAS activation. Anger and irritability also are likely emotional responses to efforts to thwart or redirect the pursuit of goal-directed behaviors in a manic episode. Similarly, anger appears to involve increased left hemispheric cortical activation, consistent with its being an approach emotion in the approach/withdrawal framework articulated by Davidson and colleagues (Davidson, 1994, 2000; Henriques & Davidson, 1997; Tomarken & Keener, 1998). In a three-dimensional (PA, NA, dominance) emotion model, anger, irritability, grandiosity, and self-assurance are all high-dominance emotions, providing a theoretical context for the co-occurrence of these emotions in mania. Discrete emotions models also have no difficulty accommodating the distinct constellation of emotions that can be associated with mania, making a discrete emotions approach preferable to a simple two-dimensional model.

Differentiation of Discrete Emotions from Dimensional Models

Discrete emotions models of psychopathology have the potential to accommodate more textured descriptions of disorders than do dimensional models. Anger, for example, does not pose any special challenges to incorporation in a discrete

emotions model, because each emotion is posited to possess unique motivational properties (Izard, 1972). As discussed, the distinction between anger and fear is obscured by the valence-activation or PA-NA model of emotions.

Another potential distinction developed in the context of discrete emotion models is the differentiation of anger turned inward ("anger in" in Spielberger's, 1999, nomenclature, or "inner-directed hostility" in Izard's, 1972, formulation) versus anger overtly expressed toward another person or object ("anger out" for Spielberger; Spielberger, 1999; Spielberger, Reheiser, & Sydeman, 1995). Whereas anger out is a better predictor of verbal and physical aggression, anger in and inner-directed hostility are associated with depression (Blumberg & Izard, 1986; Izard, 1972; Izard & Youngstrom, 1996). Dimensional models can describe different forms of aggression, but they do not readily accommodate different forms of anger. For example, the Gray motivational model can describe three distinct motivational mechanisms for aggression: (1) defensive aggression in response to an imminent threat to oneself or extremely close others (motivated by the FFS); (2) predatory or instrumental aggression (motivated by the BAS); and (3) impulsive aggression (motivated by deficits in the BIS). However, it is not clear that all of these different forms would be associated with anger, nor do these descriptions of aggression capture the anger in versus anger out distinction.

A third, related issue that may be better resolved by a discrete emotions approach than a two-dimensional model of emotions has to do with emotion distinctions revolving around "perceived controllability" and dominance. Situational cues that activate the FFS could lead to either fear and flight or anger and defensive aggression. The difference between fear and anger in response to a threat will depend on the perception of controllability: Is the threat one that can be defeated or escaped? If it is judged (preconsciously) to be unbeatable, then the FFS will activate a fear response. Conversely, if the threat is vincible (or alternatively, inescapable), then the FFS will elicit the anger emotional system to motivate defensive aggression.

A fourth issue that is more adequately explained by discrete emotions than a dimensional approach pertains to the phenomenological characterization of anxiety disorders and their differences from depression as well as each other. PA and NA are not adequate to fully portray the differences between depression and anxiety, as recognized even in early formulations of the tripartite model (discussed earlier). Instead, a third dimension was invoked to more fully characterize anxiety disorders. This third dimension was initially conceptualized as physiological hyperarousal, but subsequent studies that included discrete emotion measures demonstrated that fear was the discrete emotion most prominently associated with the physiological symptoms that were uniquely elevated in anxiety as opposed to depression. Further research on the anxiety disorders currently suggests that generalized anxiety disorder is the *DSM-IV* condition most closely associated with elevated NA (and also with higher trait neuroticism or BIS), whereas Panic Disorder is the condition most strongly linked to elevations in fear and physiological hyperarousal.

Simple phobias and Obsessive-Compulsive Disorder (OCD) also provide interesting examples illustrating the value of a discrete emotions approach. Although both phobias and OCD are considered anxiety disorders, the most pronounced emotional experience associated with many simple phobias, and with the contamination-oriented forms of OCD, is disgust. Phobias pertaining to snakes, spiders, and blood all involve an elicitation of disgust that is more marked than the fear or anxiety reported when people confront relevant stimuli (Davey, 1994a, 1994b; Davey, Buckland, Tantow, & Dallos, 1998; Davey, Forster, & Mayhew, 1993; Davey, McDonald et al., 1998). Similarly, disgust is the most elevated emotion in a profile of negative emotions activated in individuals suffering from OCD when imagining the object of their compulsions (Watson, 2000a). Thus, discrete emotions may prove useful in differentiating depression—which will include sadness and hypoactivation of positive emotions such as interest-excitement and happiness—from various anxiety disorders that may primarily involve elevations of NA generally (i.e., GAD), fear (i.e., Panic Disorder), or disgust (simple phobias, some OCD).

EXTERNALIZING BEHAVIOR PROBLEMS

Externalizing (or disruptive behavior) disorders include ADHD, Conduct Disorder (CD), and Oppositional Defiant Disorder (ODD), which are diagnosed in childhood and adolescence, and Antisocial Personality Disorder (APD), which is diagnosed in adulthood. Whenever possible, we discuss emotion processes as they relate directly to these disorders. Because little research examines emotion processes in populations meeting specific diagnostic criteria, most of this review focuses on emotion processes as they relate to the behaviors or personality traits that underlie these disorders. For example, disruptive behavior disorders are often characterized by aggression, hyperactivity,

impulsivity, and criminal behavior. In addition, these disorders are often associated with personality traits such as psychopathy and sensation seeking.

Each behavior or personality process associated with disruptive behavior disorders is likely to relate to somewhat different emotion processes. For example, the conception of impulsive aggression differs from current conceptualizations of psychopathic behavior. These constructs likely refer to differences in emotion regulation and associated structural and neurochemical impairments (Davidson, Putnam, & Larson, 2000). Even within a particular behavior, inconsistencies may exist. For instance, much research distinguishes between reactive and proactive aggression (e.g., Dodge & Coie, 1987), and their emotional correlates may differ. Reactive aggression is characterized by problems with anger expression and regulation, whereas proactive aggression appears to be motivated by negative approach emotions or callous and unemotional traits (Frick & Morris 2004; Loeber & Coie, 2001). Whenever appropriate, we highlight discrepant emotional correlates of disruptive behavior disorders and externalizing behavior problems.

The Developmental Functions of Emotions in Externalizing Behavior Problems

Abe and Izard's (1999b) review of the developmental functions of emotions and Lemerise and Dodge's (2000) discussion of the development of anger and hostility provide useful frameworks for considering how and when disruptions in emotional development foster the emergence and maintenance of externalizing problem behaviors. In infancy, anger expression, which can later become maladaptive, dysregulated, and prominent in many externalizing problem behaviors, fosters the development of autonomy and serves other adaptive functions in responding to discomfort and restraint (Abe & Izard, 1999b). Furthermore, interactions between infants and their caregivers provide the infants with their first opportunities to properly regulate emotions such as anger. Also, the emotional expressions that infants observe in adults provide the infants with their earliest source of information about the way emotional exchanges occur in the environment. Therefore, it is not surprising that beginning in early toddlerhood, children exposed to frequent angry maternal responses and interadult conflict are more likely to engage in noncompliant behavior (Crockenberg, 1985; Cummings, Iannotti, & Zahn-Waxler, 1985).

Beginning with the rapid increase in anger expression between infant and caregiver that coincides with the emergence of locomotion (Campos, Kermoian, & Zumbahlen, 1992), angry and oppositional behaviors continue to increase throughout the 2nd year of life. During toddlerhood and the preschool years, children begin to acquire the capacity to use self-conscious emotions, particularly shame and guilt, which depend on at least a rudimentary awareness of self. The motivation inherent in these emotions and the associated capacity to respond empathically help children regulate anger and aggression (Abe & Izard, 1999b). Supporting the importance of self-conscious emotions and empathy for anger regulation, research conducted in childhood and adulthood shows that abundant shame, deficient shame-free guilt, and reduced empathy predict destructive responses to anger and psychopathic behavior (Barry et al., 2000; Tangney et al., 1996). It is likely that a maladaptive balance between shame and guilt and the reduced capacity for empathy begin to emerge by the preschool years.

By the end of the preschool years, angry and aggressive behaviors become less common, and those children who exhibit consistent negative emotionality are more likely to continue to display aggressive behavior (Eisenberg et al., 1996). As children enter elementary school, they begin to increasingly show the capacity for self-evaluative emotions, make self-comparisons, and engage in social perspective taking (Abe & Izard, 1999b). In light of these abilities, which hinge on engagement in the social world, the peer context becomes particularly important for gauging the development of inappropriate externalizing problem behaviors through middle and late childhood. Lemerise and Dodge (2000) noted that display rules become particularly salient during this period for peer situations involving anger. Not surprisingly, children who are not accepted by their peers tend to have difficulty managing their anger and, as a result, are more likely to make retaliatory responses (Bryant, 1992; Hubbard & Coie, 1994).

In adolescence, conflicting emotions and emotion patterns become more prominent, and adolescents with a more poorly developed sense of self and understanding of the complexity of personal relationships exhibit less positive emotion and more anger (Abe & Izard, 1999b; Hauser & Safyer, 1994). It is likely that consistent anger-driven peer difficulties, deficient empathy, and maladaptive patterns of self-conscious emotions emerging in childhood would contribute to a shallower personal and interpersonal understanding during adolescence. As a result, children with these difficulties are most likely to persist with retaliatory, aggressive behaviors and begin to exhibit the delinquent behavior associated with CD emerging in childhood, continu-

ing in adolescence, and possibly culminating with APD and more severe criminal behavior in adulthood.

Emotion-Cognition Relations and Externalizing Problem Behaviors

Two social cognitive models are particularly relevant to the discussion of emotions in externalizing behaviors: Crick and Dodge's (1994) reformulated social information processing (SIP) model and Baumeister et al.'s (1996) theory of self-esteem, emotion, and aggression and violence.

Crick and Dodge (1994) asserted that difficulties at any one of the six stages of their SIP model lead to maladaptive behaviors, and deficient processing at each step has a circular and reciprocal influence on the other steps. Their model receives much of its support from studies showing that children with "hostile attributional biases" (the tendency to attribute hostile intent to ambiguous peer situations in hypothetical vignettes, and the second step in the SIP model) tend to engage in more aggressive behaviors (Dodge, Price, Bachorowski, & Newman, 1990). The SIP model is now the dominant social cognitive model to describe the development of childhood aggressive behavior, although Crick and Dodge's reformulation of the model included little discussion of the role of emotion.

Lemerise and Arsenio (2000) sought to incorporate emotion processes into the SIP model. Their integrated emotional and social information-processing model added emotion processes such as emotion recognition, empathic responding, and the use of display rules to the reformulated SIP model. In support of the Lemerise and Arsenio model, recent evidence shows that emotion perception biases predict aggressive behavior in children and social information processes mediate the relation between emotion knowledge and aggressive behavior (Dodge, Laird, Lochman, & Zelli, 2002; Fine et al., 2004; Schultz et al., 2000). These findings suggest that basic emotion cue recognition and resulting perceptual biases are appropriately placed in the first step of the SIP model (Lemerise & Arsenio, 2000). Furthermore, children's emotionality may influence emotional aspects of social information processing. In a recent study, children's characteristic emotionality predicted their emotion perception patterns, and emotion perception partially mediated the relation between emotionality and aggression (Schultz et al., 2004).

Baumeister et al. (1996) asserted that, contrary to conventional wisdom, high self-esteem (not low self-esteem) in adolescents with a brittle ego is associated with interpersonal violence and aggression. They argued that high self-esteem combined with situations of threat to a vulnerable ego bring about aggressive reactions through the mediating role of emotion. When criticized, people who have largely inaccurate and inflated views of themselves face an important choice. They must either reevaluate and change their self-appraisal or enter a shame-induced spiral to anger and, ultimately, aggression and violence. To support their theoretical assertions, Baumeister and colleagues cited empirical evidence of relations between unstable but high self-esteem and angry responses. They also cited evidence linking shame, anger, and aggressive responding (Tangney et al., 1996). Although the entire model has not yet been empirically tested, it is a noteworthy social cognitive model because it incorporates a self-conscious emotion (shame) into its conceptualization of aggression and violence. Therefore, this model fits well with the assertion that an important developmental milestone, the development of self-conscious emotions, may occur in a maladaptive manner and in certain circumstances lead to maladaptive patterns of externalizing behavior, including violence.

Emotion, Culture, Socialization Practices, and Externalizing Problem Behaviors

The vast majority of empirical research on the relations between emotion socialization and problem behaviors has focused on the family context, in particular, parental socialization of emotion. Eisenberg, Cumberland, and Spinrad (1998) provided a detailed discussion of parental socialization of emotion and a descriptive model where parenting practices predict specific emotion-related practices, which in turn predict aspects of children's emotional competence and later behavioral outcomes. Much research supports aspects of the model presented by Eisenberg and her colleagues. Specifically, family expression of positive emotions is associated with low levels of child aggression, and family expression of negative emotions is associated with increased levels of child aggression (Halberstadt, Crisp, & Eaton, 1999). More specifically, children exposed to conflict and anger between their parents are more likely to develop aggressive behaviors (Cummings, 1994). In recent research conducted by Eisenberg and her colleagues (Eisenberg, Gershoff, et al., 2001; Eisenberg, Losoya, et al., 2001), low levels of parental warmth as well as low maternal positive expressivity and high maternal negative expressivity predicted externalizing problem behaviors through their effects on children's ability to regulate attention and emotion.

Although extensive research has examined parental socialization practices, little research has examined cultural variation related to socialization of emotion or the impact that the peer group may have on socialization of emotion. The small body of research that does exist suggests that there is some degree of cultural variation regarding the extent to which children are encouraged to express emotion. Specifically, a cross-cultural study showed that children in the United States were encouraged to express their emotions with more frequency than children in Japan, and the U.S. children also exhibited higher levels of aggression (Zahn-Waxler, Friedman, Cole, Mizuta, & Hiruma, 1996). Although not yet examined empirically, it is possible that different emotion socialization practices across cultures may explain part of the difference in levels of aggression and violent behavior among cultures.

Emotion Expression and Externalizing Problem Behaviors

Not surprisingly, the expression of anger is related to externalizing problem behaviors in numerous studies of children and adolescents (Cole, Zahn-Waxler, & Smith, 1994; Jenkins & Oatley, 1996; Keltner et al., 1995). However, the relation between anger and aggressive behavior is more consistent for boys and for children showing more reactive aggression than proactive aggression. In one study, preschool girls with externalizing problem behaviors tended to respond with less anger when placed in a disappointing situation (Cole et al., 1994). In another study, angry nonverbal behaviors in response to a laboratory-based game predicted reactive aggression but not proactive aggression (Hubbard et al., 2002). However, facial expressions of anger did not differentiate between reactive and proactive aggression.

Increased or decreased expressions of emotions other than anger also relate to externalizing problem behaviors. Adolescent boys with externalizing problem behaviors showed decreased facial expression of embarrassment (Keltner et al., 1995). Also, as previously mentioned, increased shame expression and reduced feelings of guilt are associated with anger-fueled destructive aggression (Tangney et al., 1996). Finally, reduced expression of guilt as well as an absence of empathy and the presence of emotions that are shallow and constricted were shown to relate to psychopathic behaviors in a sample of children (Barry et al., 2000).

Emotion Patterns in Externalizing Problem Behaviors

The previous section shows that other emotions besides anger relate to externalizing problem behaviors (Berkowitz, 1990), yet few studies have examined how these patterns of emotions lead to these behaviors. Tangney and colleagues (Tangney et al., 1996; Tangney, Wagner, Fletcher, & Gramzow, 1992) provide preliminary evidence for the links between shame, shame-free guilt, anger, and destructive aggression. Shame-proneness was shown to predict anger, and shame-free guilt was generally inversely related to anger. More specifically, proneness to shame predicted responses to anger that were destructive and aggressive and resulted in negative consequences. Guilt, on the other hand, generally related to more constructive responses to anger, including taking corrective action and initiating discussion. These studies succeed in linking difficulties with self-conscious emotions and difficulties managing anger presumed to arise early in development with externalizing problem behaviors. Future research is needed to more specifically examine this pattern of shame, guilt, and anger as it emerges across childhood and as it relates to Baumeister and colleagues' (1996) social cognitive model of aggression and violence.

Emotion Knowledge in Externalizing Problem Behaviors

Although some community studies offer contradictory evidence (e.g., Izard et al., 2001), most studies of children with externalizing problem behaviors show deficient emotion knowledge and understanding of self and others (Arsenio, Cooperman, & Lover, 2000). Casey and Schlosser (1994) found that boys with externalizing disorders showed poor understanding of their own emotions when receiving praise from a peer. The boys with externalizing problems said that they expressed more positive emotion during the peer praise situation, but they had actually expressed more hostile emotion (anger, contempt, and disgust) than boys without diagnosed externalizing disorders.

Children with externalizing behavior problems also show poor understanding of other children's emotions. Children with ADHD or CD performed poorer than children without an externalizing disorder on a nonverbal emotion-processing task providing vocal and facial cues of emotion (Cadesky, Mota, & Schachar, 2000). However, children with comorbid ADHD and CD did not perform worse than children without an externalizing disorder. In another set of studies, a specific subset of children with externalizing problems, those presenting with "psychopathic tendencies," showed deficits in the recognition of fear or sadness in facial expressions and vocalizations (Blair, Budhani, Colledge, & Scott, in press; Blair, Colledge, Murray, & Mitchell, 2001; Stevens, Charman, & Blair, 2001).

Other studies show that children with externalizing problem behaviors may have a specific emotion perception bias which often leads them to interpret nonanger cues as expressions of anger. In studies of economically disadvantaged Head Start children, children who provided more anger responses to items where the correct answer was another emotion tended to show more aggressive behavior later in childhood (Fine et al., 2004; Schultz et al., 2000). Similar results were found in samples of middle-class elementary school children (Schultz, 2000; Trentacosta, Izard, Mostow, & Fine, 2001) and in children with CD (but not ADHD; Cadesky et al., 2000). Biased processing of nonanger emotion cues as anger cues may sometimes result from physical abuse that occurs early in childhood (Pollak et al., 2000).

Emotion Regulation and Externalizing Problem Behaviors

Deficits in emotion regulation, the ability to modulate an internal feeling and the related physiological process, are central to the development of externalizing problem behaviors. In a community sample of children, Eisenberg et al. (2000) showed that both the attentional (attention shifting and focusing) and behavioral (impulse control and behavioral inhibition) components of emotion regulation predict externalizing behavior problems 2 years later. As another example, children with ADHD combined type (but not inattentive type) exhibited emotion regulation deficits relative to comparison children without ADHD when completing a frustrating task (Maedgen & Carlson, 2000). Furthermore, children with ADHD were less able to manage their emotion expressions than comparison children even when given explicit instructions to mask their expression of emotion (Walcott & Landau, 2004). Other research suggests that emotion dysregulation mediates the relation between family and environmental factors, including maltreatment, harsh parenting, and violent victimization, and later aggressive behavior (Chang, Schwartz, Dodge, & McBride-Chang, 2003; Schwartz & Proctor, 2000; Shields & Cicchetti, 1997).

A related area of research focuses specifically on anger regulation and suggests that dysregulation of anger is predictive of externalizing problem behaviors. At age 3, boys who focused on the desired object during a frustration task showed increased anger (Gilliom et al., 2002). At age 6, boys who had engaged in this poor anger regulation technique were more likely to have externalizing behavior problems. On the other hand, boys who engaged in effective anger regulation strategies, including distraction and passive waiting, showed fewer externalizing behavior problems 3 years later (Gilliom et al., 2002).

Recently, neuroscience research has increased our understanding of possible brain structures and circuits involved in emotion regulation. Davidson, Putnam, et al. (2000) specify a circuit most likely involved in impulsive aggression. Central to this circuit is the orbital frontal cortex (OFC) and the amygdala. The OFC relates to processes involved in reversal learning (altering an emotional response to a stimulus that received previous conditioning). The OFC and other structures in the prefrontal cortex provide inhibitory pathways to the amygdala. Therefore, impulsive aggression may result from impaired emotion regulation and, more specifically, disturbance in the OFC, amygdala, and related structures. As evidence, impulsive criminals show decreased PFC blood flow, and individuals with OFC lesions show increased impulsive aggression (Davidson, Putnam, et al., 2000).

The same emotion regulation circuit may not apply to psychopathic behavior and instrumental aggression (Blair, 2004). As evidence, "predatory" criminals did not show decreased lateral PFC metabolism (Davidson, Putman, et al., 2000). Therefore, it is important to examine differences in brain functioning for psychopathic individuals. A recent study found that criminal psychopaths showed less emotion-related activity in the cingulate cortex as well as the amygdala (Kiehl et al., 2001). However, they showed greater activation than controls in areas of the frontal cortex. The results support the notion that psychopaths use more cognitive processing for emotional stimuli than nonpsychopathic individuals (Kiehl et al., 2001). These preliminary findings need to be replicated and extended to understand emotion regulation circuitry uniquely associated with psychopathic behavior.

AUTISM

Autism is a disorder marked by impaired social and emotional interactions (American Psychiatric Association, 1994). In 1943, Kanner first described autistic children as having "come into the world with innate inabilities to form the usual, biologically provided affective contact with people" (p. 250). Although much has been learned about Autism since Kanner's original description, many theorists still focus on impairments in interpersonal relationships when conceptualizing autistic children's core deficits (see Waterhouse & Fein, 1997, for a review) and when developing interventions for children with Autism (e.g., Bauminger,

2002). Similar to Kanner's original conceptualization of autistic children as lacking "affective contact," some theorists still believe that deficits in the emotion system are central features of Autism, contributing significantly to autistic children's impaired social interactions. For example, Hobson (1993) proposes that children with Autism show severe abnormalities in innate emotion-related competencies necessary for interpersonal relationships, such as expressing, perceiving, and coordinating emotions with others; responding to others' negative emotions; and showing appropriate awareness of self and others. Because autistic children have a greatly diminished capacity for "intersubjective engagement," they fail to develop an understanding of others' mental states or of their social world in general (Hobson, 1993).

However, other Autism theorists focus on the primary significance of other factors, such as problems with attention (e.g., Courchesne et al., 1994) or executive function skills (e.g., Ozonoff, 1995) when explaining autistic children's social impairments. Regardless of the particular theoretical view, evidence strongly suggests that at least some emotion processes are affected in Autism. This section, devoted to the role of emotions in Autism, aims to describe differences in autistic children's emotion systems and elaborate the connections between emotion system deficits and impairments in social functioning.

Developmental Differences

Consistent with the idea that emotions are particularly influential in the formation and maintenance of social relationships (Izard, 1991; Keltner & Kring, 1998), differences in the emotion systems of autistic children exert a negative influence on their social functioning and contribute significantly to the impaired social interactions that characterize Autism. Little is known about the development of discrete emotions in Autism. However, beginning early in the autistic child's life, aspects of social development are abnormal. These developmental differences influence social interactions and emotional development as well.

One such developmental difference between individuals with Autism and typically developing children is the lack of joint attention behaviors observed in infants and children with Autism (e.g., Osterling & Dawson, 1994). Typically developing children engage in joint attention behaviors, such as looking at or pointing toward their caregiver when playing with toys, to focus their caregiver's attention on an event or object. Such behaviors allow the child and caregiver to share play experiences. Furthermore, when a caregiver attempts to involve a child though pointing and gazing, typically developing children tend to turn their attention toward the caregiver. Autistic children, however, rarely look to their caregivers when playing with toys, and they appear unable to follow others' pointing gestures or gazes (Sigman & Capps, 1997).

Because autistic children do not demonstrate joint attention behaviors, they are deprived of the opportunities of closeness and connection that such behaviors are intended to provide. Sharing play experiences provides rich opportunities for mothers and children to experience positive emotions together. According to differential emotions theory, sharing positive emotion is an important developmental task that functions to strengthen social bonds and build strong interpersonal relationships (Izard, 2002). Furthermore, empirical evidence suggests that early mother-child interactions involving shared positive emotions predict later positive socialization in typically developing children (Kochanska, Forman, & Coy, 1999). Autistic children's failure to experience positive emotion sharing through joint attention behaviors likely has far-reaching implications for their emotional development.

Also different among children with Autism is their failure to demonstrate social referencing behaviors. Unlike typically developing children who turn to their caregivers' faces when situations are ambiguous, children with Autism rarely look toward others' faces for information. This lack of social referencing behavior may indicate that children with Autism are not interested or able to read others' emotion expressions (Sigman & Capps, 1997). Autistic children's failure to show social referencing behavior limits the information available to them during ambiguous situations. More important, it also prevents them from learning about their world through others' emotional responses and deprives them from opportunities to share meaning with their caregivers (Sigman & Capps, 1997).

Language development is significantly impaired in children with Autism (see Lord & Paul, 1997, for a review). In typically developing children, language emerges from and utilizes preverbal forms of social communications, such as joint attention and social referencing behavior. Severely impaired in these basic skills, autistic children have communication difficulties throughout their lives (Sigman & Capps, 1997). Children with Autism seem especially impaired in pragmatics, the ability to use language in a socially functional manner (e.g., Baltaxa, 1977). Furthermore, children with Autism may have difficulty correctly using language relating to social relationships. For example, Hobson (1993) describes an individual with Autism who was unable to comprehend the meaning of the simple word "friend."

Delayed and atypical language skills may serve to hinder autistic children's emotional development. Because of their difficulty engaging in typical social discourse, children with Autism are at least partially deprived of the normative social conversations crucial for learning and communicating information, including emotion information. Failure to engage in emotion-related conversations furthers the autistic child's difficulty perceiving, interpreting, and utilizing emotion information.

Emotion-Cognition Connections

In addition to deficits in the emotion system, children with Autism also tend to show differences in their cognitive functioning. In fact, whereas some theorists conceptualize problems with emotions as the core psychological deficit in children with Autism, others believe that autistic children's primary impairment lies in social cognition or information processing (see Sigman & Capps, 1997, for a review). For example, researchers have focused on cognitive problems such as deficits in executive functions (e.g., Ozonoff, 1995), lack of a theory of mind (e.g., Baron-Cohen, 1995), and lack of central coherence in processing information (e.g., Frith, 1989) when describing the core deficits that characterize Autism.

Some theorists have hypothesized that the primary deficit in Autism is not merely emotional or cognitive, but instead derives from deficits in both the emotion and the cognitive systems (e.g., Sigman & Capps, 1997; Sigman, Dissanayuke, Arbelle, & Ruskin, 1997). Specifically, Sigman and her colleagues speculate that autistic children's primary deficit is their lack of an integrated system of emotion and cognition. Empirical evidence also supports the theory that in autistic children, deficiencies in the emotion and cognitive systems are not independent (e.g., Buitelaar & van der Wees, 1997). Autistic children's deficits in both the emotion and cognitive systems can be conceived of as impairments in the development of adaptive emotion-cognition connections (Izard, 2002).

Typically developing children rapidly form connections between emotions and cognitions, beginning early in life (Izard, 1971). As children share affective experiences with others and learn to understand their social environment, these emotion-cognition connections enable them to act adaptively in their environment. Beginning in infancy, children with Autism are much less likely to share emotional experiences with others. Because of these missed opportunities, children with Autism gain less of an understanding of themselves, others, their relationships, and their societies (Sigman & Capps, 1997). In sum, children with

Autism miss out on valuable experiences that are fundamental to the development of healthy emotion-cognition connections. Without the emotion-cognition connections necessary for understanding and navigating one's social world, children with Autism have extreme difficulty.

Emotion Expression

Children with Autism were initially thought to exhibit affective "flatness" or "unresponsiveness" (e.g., Bettelheim, 1967). Although it is commonly recognized that autistic children do suffer from affective disturbances, theorists currently believe that these disturbances are not characterized by flatness. A number of empirical studies shed light on the actual differences in emotion expression in autistic children. One such study investigating parental perceptions of children's emotion expressions found that when compared to normal children, older, nonretarded autistic children expressed more negative emotions and fewer positive emotions (Capps, Kasari, Yirmiya, & Sigman, 1993). Specifically, parents reported that autistic children more frequently displayed sadness, fear, anger, shame, and guilt than typical children, and they less frequently displayed joy. Furthermore, according to parent perceptions, younger autistic children displayed more sadness and fear, as well as less joy and interest, than typically developing children (Capps et al., 1993).

In a similar vein, Yirmiya, Kasari, Sigman, and Mundy (1989) found that although young autistic children displayed positive emotions when interacting with parents and adults, they also expressed negative emotions more frequently than mentally retarded and typically developing children. Furthermore, more frequently than comparison children, autistic children displayed facial "blends," with part of their face expressing a negative emotion and part expressing a positive emotion. It is possible that autistic children display these facial blends when they find social situations confusing (Sigman & Capps, 1997).

Snow, Hertzig, and Shapiro (1987) compared autistic preschoolers to developmentally delayed preschoolers on a live interaction task with mothers, preschool teachers, and a child psychiatrist. Whereas the previously described studies found that parents described autistic children as expressing more negative emotions, the videotaped interaction paradigm revealed only fewer positive expressed emotions among autistic children. Negative affect, which was rarely expressed in either group, did not differ in frequency between the autistic and the developmentally delayed preschoolers. However, autistic children displayed positive emotions under different conditions than their de-

velopmentally delayed counterparts, such as when playing alone (Snow et al., 1987).

Interesting findings emerge from a pair of studies comparing autistic children to those with Down syndrome (Bieberich & Morgan, 1998, 2004). In the initial study comparing the emotion expressions of these two groups during a semistructured play situation with their mothers, children with Autism showed more negative affect and less positive affect than children with Down syndrome (Bieberich & Morgan, 1998). Although the authors found no differences in negative affect when the same groups were compared 2 years later, differences in positive affect remained. Specifically, children with Autism less frequently engaged in positive affect sharing (e.g., smiling, making eye contact, and actively engaging mother in play) than did children with Down syndrome (Bieberich & Morgan, 2004).

In contrast to the studies finding differences in frequency of positive or negative emotion expression, another study comparing facial expressions of autistic preschoolers to typical preschoolers found that both groups expressed both positive and negative emotions at similar rates (McGee, Feldman, & Chernin, 1991). For the majority of the time, both groups displayed neutral facial expressions. However, autistic children often expressed happiness, sadness, and anger at times incongruent to the specific situation. Similar to the study by Snow et al. (1987), whereas typical children showed happiness during peer or teacher interactions, autistic children expressed happiness when playing alone (McGee et al., 1991).

Although evidence conflicts as to the specific differences in autistic children's expressed positive or negative emotions, studies tend to agree that they do not show flat or unresponsive affect. Children with Autism do express emotions, though these emotions somehow differ from typically developing children, as well as other groups of mentally retarded children. Whether these differences reflect the amount of expressed emotion, the specific emotions activated, or the situations where they are expressed, they likely contribute to the impairments in social interactions characteristic of children with Autism.

Emotion Knowledge

The ability to perceive and interpret others' emotions are core facets of the broad construct of emotion knowledge (Izard, 1971, 1993). Studies suggest that autistic children may be at least somewhat limited in these competencies. However, the extent of these limitations is not well understood. The work of Hobson and colleagues suggests that autistic children tend to have specific impairments in emotion knowledge skills. One such study showed that children with Autism had difficulty matching facial expressions with corresponding vocal expressions and bodily gestures typical of discrete emotions (Hobson, 1986). However, they were able to complete similar yet emotion-unrelated tasks, suggesting that their difficulty was specifically in coordinating emotion-related information.

In another early study by Weeks and Hobson (1987), children were instructed to match photographs of faces. Whereas nonautistic children tended to use emotion expressions to sort these photographs, children with Autism tended to group the photographs based on the type of hat worn in the picture (Weeks & Hobson, 1987). Furthermore, when the autistic children were asked specifically to match the photographs by emotion expression, many were not able to do so. Children with Autism may not only be less likely to utilize emotion information, they may also be unable to discriminate and perceive emotion cues (Sigman & Capps, 1997).

A study by Bolte and Poustka (2003) also supports the view that individuals with Autism have an impaired ability to recognize emotions. This study compared the performance of three groups, those with Autism, those with Schizophrenia, and an unaffected group, on a computer-based facial emotion recognition task. Individuals with Autism showed poorer performance on this task than the unaffected and schizophrenic groups. In addition, when examining the emotion recognition abilities of the autistic group's parents and siblings, performance was poorer in relatives from families with multiple autistic children than in families with only one autistic child. The authors conclude that deficits in detecting emotion facial cues are part of the endophenotype of Autism (Bolte & Poustka, 2003). Endophenotypes can be defined as "stable, heritable, quantifiable, endogenous characteristics that identify genetic risk" (Conklin & Iacono, 2003).

An additional study investigating emotion perception skills utilized a nontraditional procedure to further examine emotion recognition abilities of autistic children and adolescents (Celani, Battacchi, & Arcidiancono, 1999). This study included three groups of participants all matched on verbal mental age: individuals with Autism, individuals with Down syndrome, and a typically developing group. To assure that autistic individuals did not use "perceptual, piecemeal processing strategies" and instead used "holistic processing" when perceiving facial expressions, pictures of faces expressing happiness and sadness were presented for only 750 msec. After each face was presented, three additional faces were presented, and partici-

pants were asked to choose the photograph of the person with the same expression as was presented previously. On this "delayed-matching task," individuals with Autism performed worse than the groups of nonautistic individuals (Celani et al., 1999).

This study also investigated autistic individuals' tendencies to evaluate a face as pleasant based on whether it expressed happiness or a neutral expression. Whereas nonautistic groups preferred facial expressions of happiness, autistic individuals showed no preference for happy faces. These tasks suggest that individuals with Autism were less able to perceive and interpret the happy and sad faces than nonautistic individuals. The authors point out that although autistic individuals' ability to recognize emotions is not completely absent, the way they process emotion information may be qualitatively different from that of nonautistic individuals (Celani et al., 1999).

It is important to note that several studies have not found emotion perception deficits in autistic individuals, especially when groups are matched on verbal measures of mental age (e.g., Ozonoff, Pennington, & Rogers, 1990). However, given the aforementioned evidence, it is likely that autistic children do have at least some difficulty perceiving emotion cues in others. These limitations in emotion knowledge skills probably contribute significantly to their impaired social interactions. For example, if children have difficulty interpreting emotion information during a peer interaction, they may respond to peers inappropriately. Such inappropriate responses may lead to additional social mishaps and impoverished peer relationships.

Emotion theorists have long believed that emotion knowledge is a prerequisite for effective emotion communication. One cannot articulate or discuss emotion information, a component of healthy social interactions, without understanding emotion cues. Therefore, it is important to examine whether autistic children's impairments in emotion knowledge also extend to specific difficulties with emotion communication. Although children with Autism show extreme socially related language impairments in general, it is useful to determine whether children with Autism are capable of communicating emotion information when specifically asked to do so.

Studies suggest that children with Autism are able to provide appropriate responses when asked to describe situations eliciting basic emotions, such as joy and sadness. However, when conceptualizing and describing "self-conscious" emotions such as pride and shame, which require an understanding of social norms and moral behavior (M. Lewis, 1993), these children appear to have more difficulty (e.g., Capps, Yirmiya, & Sigman, 1992).

In one study, nonretarded autistic children and typically developing children provided similar responses when describing situations evoking the simple emotion of happiness. However, in contrast to typically developing children, children with Autism never referred to birthday parties (Capps et al., 1992). Children with Autism also generally provided appropriate responses when describing experiences of sadness. However, interesting differences emerged when comparing autistic children's and typically developing children's responses to times they felt embarrassed and proud. When describing events evoking both embarrassment and pride, children with Autism required more prompts from the examiners and more time to respond. In contrast to the typically developing children, who provided different experiences for happiness and pride, one quarter of the autistic children described the same situation for both of these positive emotion experiences (Capps et al., 1992).

Furthermore, autistic children frequently described external, uncontrollable events and made fewer references to an audience when describing embarrassing situations. Failure to refer to an audience when recounting embarrassing events may stem from early deficits in joint attention and emotion-sharing behaviors, suggesting that autistic children may experience and develop emotions differently (Capps et al., 1992). Similarly, a more recent study by Hillier and Allinson (2002) found differences in high-functioning autistic children's understanding of embarrassment. In this study, children with high-functioning Autism had more difficulty distinguishing nonembarrassing from embarrassing scenarios compared to typically developing children. They also had more difficulty providing appropriate justifications for certain embarrassing situations (Hillier & Allinson, 2002).

In a similar vein, recent research also suggests that high-functioning children with Autism have a "less coherent" understanding of jealousy than typically developing children (Bauminger, 2004). Although the autistic children in this study expressed jealousy in similar situations as typically developing children, their jealousy-related behaviors were different, as was their understanding of the emotion itself. The author discusses the findings in terms of the gap between high-functioning autistic children's intact capacity to experience a socially mediated emotion and their impoverished ability to comprehend it (Bauminger, 2004).

In sum, children with Autism appear relatively competent in their ability to interpret and describe their own emotions. However, they show differences compared to typically developing children, especially when emotions are complex and socially mediated. During actual social situations, when multiple social and emotion cues must be perceived and interpreted rapidly, it is likely that autistic children's differences in emotion understanding and emotion communication will lead to significant difficulties in social interactions (Capps et al., 1992).

Empathy

Because children with Autism have at least some difficulty with emotion perception and emotion communication, one may assume that they are less able than typically developing children to empathize with others' distress. Theory and research tends to corroborate this assumption. In explaining the autistic person's limited capacity to show empathy, Baron-Cohen (2002) theorizes that individuals with Autism have an extreme version of the male brain. Inherent in the male brain is the drive to "systemize," which refers to understanding the rules directing the behavior of a system, as well as predicting and controlling a system's behavior. This drive to systemize is in contrast to the female's drive to "empathize" (Baron-Cohen, 2002). Using the Empathy Quotient, a self-report questionnaire, Baron-Cohen and Wheelwright (2004) demonstrated that adult males score lower in empathy than adult females, and individuals with high-functioning Autism or Asperger's syndrome have an "empathy deficit" when compared to controls.

Empirical studies of autistic children also suggest decreased empathic responding. One study used a three-component model of empathy conceptualized by Feshbach (1982) to compare high-functioning autistic children and normal children (Yirmiya, Sigman, Kasari, & Mundy, 1992). The three components of empathy investigated were recognition and discrimination of others' affective states, affective perspective-taking ability, and emotional response (Feshbach, 1982). Typically developing children performed significantly better on all three components of empathy than autistic children, suggesting that empathizing with others is more difficult for children with Autism (Yirmiya et al., 1992).

In other studies, experimenters have created situations in which children's parents have feigned distress (e.g., feeling ill, accidentally hurting themselves with a toy hammer), and children's empathic responses have then been evaluated (Sigman, Kasari, Kwon, & Yirmiya, 1992). In these contrived situations, typically developing children and mentally retarded children looked at the distressed parent, appeared concerned and upset, and offered comfort. In contrast, children with Autism tended to ignore their parents' distress, failing to make eye contact with them or offer comfort and support (Sigman et al., 1992). Such behaviors suggest that compared to mentally retarded or typically developing children, children with Autism are less interested in or less responsive to others' emotional responses (Sigman, 1998).

Autistic children's lack of responsiveness cannot be explained by being unaware of or overly aroused by another's distress (Corona, Dissanayuke, Arbelle, Wellington, & Sigman, 1998). Whatever the reason for autistic children's lack of interest or responsiveness to others' emotions, it has significant implications for their emotional development. Without the interest or ability to interpret another's emotional response and evaluate it as similar to or different from one's own, it seems unlikely that children with Autism will grow to appreciate others' emotional experiences or learn more deeply about their own feelings (Sigman & Capps, 1997). Children with Autism do not appear able to, or interested in, using others' experiences as opportunities to further understand emotions.

Another study evaluated autistic children's responses to the distress of an unfamiliar adult and also to a loud, unexpected, ambiguous sound (Bacon, Fein, Morris, Waterhouse, & Allen, 1998). Results showed that low-functioning but not high-functioning autistic children were much less likely than children in the control groups to look at the distressed adults when the adults banged their hands, knees, or elbows on the table or wall, exclaiming "Ouch." Furthermore, both low-functioning and high-functioning autistic children failed to orient toward the adult in the room when they heard the ambiguous sound. Whereas children in control groups turned toward the adult for information, neither autistic group demonstrated this social referencing behavior. This lack of social referencing behavior suggests that children with Autism, whether high- or low-functioning, may simply not find others' emotion expressions interesting or informative (Bacon et al., 1998).

It seems likely that impoverished emotion knowledge, in addition to a diminished interest in gathering emotion information from others, may contribute to autistic children's difficulties communicating about emotions, empathizing, and responding appropriately to others' distress. One can assume that these difficulties hinder autistic children's ability to comprehend and navigate their social world. Furthermore, the reduced capacity to understand and express empathy prevents the autistic child from the positive social and emotional experiences inherent in providing comfort to others in need.

Neurobiological Processes in Emotion Regulation in Autism

In attempting to further understand the core deficits in Autism, researchers have tried to identify biological systems affected in individuals with the disorder. Much research focuses on brain systems underlying the emotional and social impairments present in Autism. In 1990, a network of brain regions connected to social cognition and emotion was proposed by Brothers. One such neural structure involved in responding to social and emotional information is the amygdala (Brothers, 1990), part of the limbic system. Because the limbic system (including the amygdala) has long been known to play a role in emotion, the emotional and social impairments present in individuals with Autism may reflect underlying dysfunction in this system.

Studies using various techniques to investigate the role of the amygdala in Autism provide convincing evidence that the amygdala is at least one of the neural regions that shows abnormal functioning in individuals with Autism (see Baron-Cohen et al., 2000, for a review). For example, studies have shown that nonhuman primates with lesions on the amygdala show changes in their social behavior similar to those seen in autistic individuals. These social behavior changes include social isolation, failure to initiate social transactions, and inappropriate responses to social gestures (e.g., Emery et al., 1998; Kling & Brothers, 1992). Furthermore, lesions to the entire amygdala caused a syndrome in monkeys called Kluver-Bucy syndrome (Aggleton & Passingham, 1981), a syndrome considered by some to be an animal model of Autism.

Additional studies using fMRI provide compelling evidence that the amygdala plays a role in perceiving social and emotion information and is impaired in individuals with Autism (Baron-Cohen et al., 1999). Adults with and without Autism Spectrum Disorders were asked to look at photographs of people's eyes and determine their thoughts or feelings. In contrast to control subjects, who demonstrated activation of the amygdala when processing information about emotions and mental states, subjects with Autism Spectrum Disorders did not show this amygdala activation (Baron-Cohen et al., 1999).

In another study, subjects with and without amygdala damage were given an emotion recognition task requiring them to interpret emotions from a picture of a full face and a picture of the eye region alone (Adolphs, Baron-Cohen, & Tranel, 2002). Subjects with unilateral and bilateral amygdala damage performed similar to controls when interpreting basic emotions. However, they performed significantly worse than controls when attempting to interpret more "social emotions" (e.g., guilt, arrogance, admiration) from both the whole face and the eye region. These findings suggest that the amygdala is implicated in interpreting certain emotions related to social interactions, thereby supporting the theory of dysfunction in the amygdala among individuals with Autism (Adolphs et al., 2002). Furthermore, MRI scans of adolescents and adults with and without Autism showed that individuals with Autism had reduced volumes in the amygdala and hippocampus, possibly signifying that connections between limbic structures and other brain structures are underdeveloped (Aylward et al., 1999).

In further examining neural correlates, researchers compared fMRI results of children and adolescents with high-functioning Autism Spectrum Disorders with typically developing controls when matching and labeling emotion facial expressions (Wang, Dapretto, Hariri, Sigman, & Bookheimer, 2004). When matching emotion expressions, children in the Autism spectrum group showed more activity in the precuneus and less activity in the fusiform gyrus, an area commonly known for face identification, than typically developing children. Additionally, typically developing children showed more activation in the amygdala during the emotion-matching task, requiring more perceptual demands and therefore less conscious processing, than during the more cognitive verbal labeling task. In contrast, children with Autism Spectrum Disorders showed no difference in amygdala activation between the two tasks, suggesting differences in their neural networks when automatically processing emotion facial expressions (Wang et al., 2004). These findings support the hypothesis of abnormal amygdala functioning in autistic children and provide insight into additional brain regions implicated in Autism. Taken together, lesion and neuroimaging studies contribute evidence for neural correlates of Autism, including amygdala-related differences. However, research has been inconsistent, and further investigation is needed (Sweeten, Posey, Shekhar, & McDougle, 2002).

Current research also points to vagal pathways as playing a role in both normal social behavior and in the impaired social behavior present in Autism. The polyvagal theory distinguishes between primitive vertebrates, which have only an unmyelinated vagus, and mammals, which have both unmyelinated and myelinated vagal pathways (e.g., Porges, 2002). According to this theory, these pathways serve different functions and drive three different behavioral strategies: social engagement, mobilization, and immobilization. Unique to mammals, the Social Engagement System depends on myelinated vagal motor fibers and includes neural structures related to emotional and social behaviors. This system can also involve a calm state. The Social Engagement System includes brain structures that control various muscles, such as facial muscles responsible for emotion expressions and middle ear muscles responsible for hearing human voices. These muscles enable mammals to observe social stimuli and actively engage in the social environment (Porges, 2002).

The polyvagal theory has clinical applications that have been employed in preliminary studies to address the social deficits in children with Autism. Specifically, an intervention has been designed that involves stimulating the "neural regulation of the Social Engagement System" (Porges, 2002, p. 10). The model on which the intervention was based assumes that children with Autism have a Social Engagement System that is intact both neuroanatomically and neurophysiologically. However, they have functional deficits in this system, including dysfunctional regulation of the somatomotor component (e.g., impaired facial expressions) and the autonomic component (e.g., difficulty maintaining calm states). Through stimulating the neural regulation of autistic children's brainstems, social behavior should improve, as the system will begin functioning properly (Porges, 2002).

This intervention has used acoustic stimulation as the method of improving neural regulation, specifically, stimulating the middle ear muscles. Middle ear muscles are important in hearing human voices, but they cannot effectively filter out environmental sounds when neural tone is low. Regulation of these middle ear muscles relates neuroanatomically to regulating muscles that control facial expressions, as well as those controlling vocal intonation. Receiving the "acoustic stimulation" did, in fact, increase autistic children's social engagement behaviors. Specifically, autistic children receiving the acoustic stimulation showed decreased sensitivity to sounds and increased sharing behaviors (Porges, 2002). In addition, parents of these children were less intrusive after the intervention (Porges, 2003).

Continued research into the specific emotional and social impairments that characterize Autism, as well as the neural structures that may contribute to them, should further our understanding of an extremely complex developmental disability. Increased understanding of the development of children with Autism will continue enabling theorists to translate theory into research-based interventions that aim to promote healthy emotional and social development for children and families facing the challenges inherent in this syndrome.

CONCLUSION

The flourishing of research on emotions over the past 2 decades has significantly affected virtually all areas of behavioral science, including developmental risk and psychopathology. Increasing knowledge of the experience-dependent nature of neurobiological development in the emotion systems has put the nature-nurture argument about causal processes in psychological disorders in a new perspective. Most scientists now recognize the interdependence of biogenetic and experiential factors in normal and abnormal development. Both genes and experience contribute to the development of a hardy personality characterized by positive emotionality, optimism, and socioemotional competence. Both types of factors influence the processes involved in developing a psychopathological condition characterized by negative emotionality, pessimistic or biased appraisal processes, and maladaptive behavior.

Emotion science can serve as a model for the increasingly popular multidimensional approach to research in psychopathology. Virtually all definitions of emotion acknowledge that it involves neural, psychomotor, and experiential components and that emotion typically exists in intimate interaction with perception and cognition. Thus, emotion is by definition a complex construct that requires cross-disciplinary, multilevel, and multidimensional investigations. The evidence reviewed in this chapter suggests that the same holds for any psychopathological condition.

Although we could examine only a limited set of disorders, we showed that emotions figure prominently in conditions ranging from infant stress disorders to internalizing and externalizing problems and Autism. In our analysis of depression, we found that various models hinge on concepts of emotionality and that each model may offer leads for further research.

Throughout the chapter we recognized both the intrapersonal and interpersonal functions of emotions. Though little research has specifically concerned this distinction in emotion functions, we propose that intrapersonal functions serve important roles in one's sense of well-being, whereas interpersonal functions relate to sociality and adaptive social behavior. We suggest that these two types of processes may figure differentially in various disorders, and yet, we recognize an element of arbitrariness in distinguishing between them. We doubt that all the functions of emotions fall into categories with hard boundaries.

Although we considered multiple approaches, the writing of this chapter was guided in part by differential emotions theory and a discrete emotions approach to the study of psychopathology. Wherever possible we identified the role of specific emotions in particular disorders. At the same time, we emphasized the need to examine self-organizing patterns of emotions, a notion that may relate more closely to dimensional approaches to the study of emotion and psychopathology.

Finally, our discussion of emotions and psychopathology assumes some modularity and relative independence among emotion, cognitive, and behavioral systems involved in developmental processes. We see the study of the development of connections between these systems as paramount in advancing our knowledge of the field of psychopathology. Progress in our understanding of experience-dependent brain and neurobiological development has changed our conception of intersystem connections from one defined largely in terms of behavioral output to one that includes particular populations of synapses and neurons. We have also become more aware of the possibility that sensitive periods in early development may optimize the formation of certain adaptive connections between the emotions and other systems and that a harsh environment during these periods may increase the likelihood of serious psychopathology.

FUTURE DIRECTIONS

Undoubtedly, many of the exciting advances in the area of emotions and psychopathology will come from interdisciplinary or cross-specialty collaborative teams. All noteworthy theories of emotion recognize the critical role of research on emotion-related behavioral, cognitive, and neural systems.

We see emotion-perception, emotion-cognition, and emotion-cognition-action interfaces as hot topics for future research in both normal and abnormal development. These areas have already claimed the attention of interdisciplinary researchers. For example, they have pointed to cortical midline structures as junctures where interaction of perception, emotion feeling, and cognition mediate the development of emotion knowledge and self-reflective consciousness (Northoff & Bermpohl, 2004). These researchers, like other interdisciplinary investigators, necessarily build on the work of specialists that provided much of the content of this chapter.

Study of the various perception-emotion-cognition-action interfaces promises to increase our understanding of normal and abnormal development of emotion knowledge and emotion regulation. We propose that such intersystem research will also improve our perspective on the development of relations among emotion vocabulary, emotion knowledge, and emotion regulation, and clarify the critical role of the first two in the growth of the third. Understanding the development of these key aspects of emotion competence should help in developing effective preventive interventions. In turn, evaluations of emotion-centered prevention programs can lead to refinements in emotion theory (Cicchetti & Hinshaw, 2002; Izard, Fine, Mostow, Trentacosta, & Campbell, 2002). Next, we detail potential advancements in basic research for particular developmental problems and suggest ways that evaluations of prevention and treatment programs for well-defined problems can enhance emotion theory.

Internalizing Behavior Problems and Psychopathology

Previous research indicates that emotion knowledge predicts internalizing problems across childhood (Fine et al., 2003), yet few programs specifically address understanding of emotion in treatment protocols (for an exception, see Kendall, Aschenbrand, & Hudson, 2003). Basic research should further investigate whether poor emotion knowledge predicts internalizing psychopathology generally or is specific to some internalizing problems but not others. Then specific prevention programs and treatments could incorporate modules on emotion knowledge. Outcome research could assess whether emotion knowledge improves with treatment and whether increases in emotion knowledge are necessary for reductions in internalizing problems, as emotion theory would suggest.

Additionally, more basic research is needed on developmental changes in emotion thresholds in children with internalizing psychopathology. For example, children at risk for depression may have a low threshold for experiencing sadness, and children at risk for Panic Disorder may have a low threshold for experiencing fear. Studies of emotion thresholds may help to explain the development of these affective disorders across childhood and adolescence. Also, the role of anger in internalizing problems is understudied. Anger has been related to depression (see Blumberg & Izard, 1986), and irritability can be a feature of Bipolar Disorder. However, it is still unclear how much the propensity to experience anger places children at risk for these disorders and how much anger is involved in other internalizing disorders (i.e., anxiety disorders). It would also be helpful to examine the presence of unique patterns of emo-

tions in the mixed states that characterize the bipolar mood disorders in children.

As interventions for internalizing problems are refined, we can begin to examine whether emotion regulation is an important part of the process of prevention and treatment of internalizing psychopathology. Specifically, do children need to experience and learn how to manage emotion during the intervention in order to reduce their internalizing psychopathology? The theory behind our prevention program for Head Start children (see Izard, Trentacosta, King, & Mostow, 2004) suggests that emotion regulation mediates behavioral outcomes, but only additional intervention effectiveness studies with follow-up assessments can answer that question and inform emotion theory.

Externalizing Behavior Problems and Psychopathology

Future basic research on emotions and externalizing problems must continue to distinguish emotional correlates of forms of aggression and inform the prevention and treatment of these problems. Some of these problems involve the development of the self-conscious emotions involved in moral development. Both guilt and empathy, and probably shame as well, are absent or underdeveloped in children with strong psychopathic tendencies. Frick (2004) and others found that children with psychopathic tendencies have callous or "unemotional" traits. Because the preschool years are a sensitive period for the developmental of self-conscious emotions and empathic behavior and for fostering the development of emotion competence, emotion-centered prevention and intervention programs may prove most beneficial in early childhood. Basic research, particularly with children at risk due to poverty, maltreatment, and other psychologically threatening conditions, should also be extended. For example, to understand what it means to have unemotional traits, brain imaging studies could examine whether children with these traits process emotional information in ways different from other children. The tendency to favor cognitive processing over emotional processing has been shown in psychopathic adults (Blair, 2003).

Evaluations of programs to prevent aggression, violence, and other externalizing problems can also inform research and theory on the role of emotions in the development of externalizing psychopathology. For example, many programs designed to reduce childhood aggression include anger regulation techniques. If the theoretical distinction between reactive (anger-motivated) aggression and proactive (non-anger-motivated) aggression proves valid, then programs that focus primarily on anger regulation should reduce reactive but not proactive aggression. On the other hand, programs that focus on empathy training may reduce children's proactive aggression but not their reactive aggression.

Autism and Other Developmental Disorders

One avenue for refining our understanding of emotion-related functioning in children with Autism may be to explore similarities and differences in the emotion competence of children with high-functioning Autism and those with Asperger's syndrome. Researchers could investigate whether children with high-functioning Autism and those with Asperger's syndrome (matched on intelligence) perform differently on emotion perception tasks. Given the previously established links between children's verbal ability and emotion knowledge (e.g., Izard et al., 2001), one may expect children with Asperger's syndrome to perform better in these domains. Such an investigation would add to the growing body of literature attempting to differentiate these two disorders (see Howlin, 2003, for a review).

Carefully conducted evaluations of prevention and treatment programs for children with Autism Spectrum Disorders would enable us to systematically explore the relation between emotion knowledge and peer relations that have been established in nonautistic populations (see Mostow, Izard, Fine, & Trentacosta, 2002). Intervention outcomes for existing programs targeting emotion functioning in autistic populations are emerging in the literature. For example, Bauminger (2002) evaluated a comprehensive cognitive-behavioral intervention targeting "social-emotional understanding and social interaction." The intervention found improvements in multiple areas of social functioning and some increased emotion understanding. Because explaining specific causes for positive outcomes can be complicated, future research should implement theoretically coherent emotion-based interventions and carefully evaluate them with matched control groups. With this methodology, we would have the opportunity to explore possible changes in emotion skills and subsequent improvements in social behavior and peer relations in children with Autism. Such a study could empirically test the hypothesis that even in autistic children, improved emotion knowledge and emotion regulation can translate into positive social outcomes.

REFERENCES

Abe, J. A., & Izard, C. E. (1999a). The developmental functions of emotions: An analysis in terms of differential emotions theory. *Cognition and Emotion, 13,* 523–549.

Abe, J. A., & Izard, C. E. (1999b). A longitudinal study of emotion expression and personality relations in early development. *Journal of Personality and Social Psychology, 77,* 566–577.

Abramson, L. Y., Metalsky, G. I., & Alloy, L. B. (1989). Hopelessness depression: A theory-based subtype of depression. *Psychological Review, 96,* 358–372.

Ackerman, B. P., Abe, J. A., & Izard, C. E. (1998). Differential emotions theory and emotional development: Mindful of modularity. In M. Mascolo & S. Griffin (Eds.), *What develops in emotional development? Emotions, personality, and psychotherapy* (pp. 85–106). New York: Plenum Press.

Adolphs, R., Baron-Cohen, S., & Tranel, D. (2002). Impaired recognition of social emotions following amygdala damage. *Journal of Cognitive Neuroscience, 14,* 1264–1274.

Aggleton, J. P., & Passingham, R. E. (1981). Syndrome produced by lesions of the amygdala in monkeys (Macaca mulatta). *Journal of Comparative and Physiological Psychology, 95,* 961–977.

Ainsworth, M. D., Blehar, M. P., Waters, E., & Wall, S. (Eds.). (1978). *Patterns of attachment: A psychological study of the Strange Situation.* Hillsdale, NJ: Erlbaum.

Allan, S., & Gilbert, P. (1997). Submissive behaviour and psychopathology. *British Journal of Clinical Psychology, 36*(Pt 4), 467–488.

Alloy, L. B., Abramson, L. Y., & Francis, E. L. (1999). Do negative cognitive styles confer vulnerability to depression? *Current Directions in Psychological Science, 8,* 128–132.

American Psychiatric Association. (1994). *Diagnostic and statistical manual of mental disorders* (4th ed.). Washington, DC: Author.

American Psychiatric Association. (2001). *Diagnostic and statistical manual of mental disorders* (4th ed., rev.). Washington, DC.

Arsenio, W. F., Cooperman, S., & Lover, A. (2000). Affective predictors of preschoolers' aggression and peer acceptance: Direct and indirect effects. *Developmental Psychology, 36,* 438–448.

Ashman, S. B., Dawson, G., Panagiotides, H., Yamada, E., & Wilkinson, C. W. (2002). Stress hormone levels of children of depressed mothers. *Development and Psychopathology, 14,* 333–349.

Averill, J. R. (1992). The structural bases of emotional behavior: A metatheoretical analysis. In M. S. Clark (Ed.), *Emotion: Review of personality and social psychology* (pp. 1–24). Thousand Oaks, CA: Sage.

Aylward, E. H., Minshew, N. J., Goldstein, G., Honeycutt, N. A., Augustine, A. M., Yates, K. O., et al. (1999). MRI volumes of amygdala and hippocampus in non-mentally retarded autistic adolescents and adults. *Neurology, 53,* 2145–2150.

Bacon, A. L., Fein, D., Morris, R., Waterhouse, L., & Allen, D. (1998). The responses of autistic children to the distress of others. *Journal of Autism and Developmental Disorders, 28,* 129–142.

Balge, K. A., & Milner, J. S. (2000). Emotion recognition ability in mothers at high and low risk for child physical abuse. *Child Abuse and Neglect, 24,* 1289–1298.

Baltaxa, C. A. M. (1977). Pragmatic deficits in the language of autistic adolescents. *Journal of Pediatric Psychology, 2,* 176–180.

Barlow, D. H. (1988). *Anxiety and its disorders: The nature and treatment of anxiety and panic.* New York: Guilford Press.

Baron-Cohen, S. (1995). *Mindblindness.* Cambridge, MA: MIT Press.

Baron-Cohen, S. (2002). The extreme male brain theory of Autism. *Trends in Cognitive Sciences, 6,* 248–254.

Baron-Cohen, S. (2003). *The essential difference: The truth about the male and female brain.* New York: Basic Books.

Baron-Cohen, S., Ring, H. A., Bullmore, E. T., Wheelwright, S., Ashwin, C., & Williams, S. C. R. (2000). The amygdala theory of Autism. *Neuroscience and Biobehavioral Reviews, 24,* 355–364.

Baron-Cohen, S., Ring, H., Wheelwright, S., Bullmore, E., Brammer, M., Simmons, A., et al. (1999). Social intelligence in the normal and autistic brain: An fMRI study. *European Journal of Neuroscience, 11,* 1891–1898.

Baron-Cohen, S., & Wheelwright, S. (2004). The empathy quotient: An investigation of adults with Asperger syndrome or high functioning Autism, and normal sex differences. *Journal of Autism and Developmental Disorders, 34,* 163–175.

Barrett, L. F., & Russell, J. A. (1999). The structure of current affect: Controversies and emerging consensus. *Current Directions in Psychological Science, 8,* 10–14.

Barry, C. T., Frick, P. J., DeShazo, T. M., McCoy, M. G., Ellis, M., & Loney, B. R. (2000). The importance of callous-unemotional traits for extending the concept of psychopathy to children. *Journal of Abnormal Psychology, 109,* 335–340.

Barth, J. M., & Bastiani, A. (1997). A longitudinal study of emotion recognition and preschool children's social behavior. *Merrill-Palmer Quarterly, 43,* 107–128.

Baumeister, R. F., Smart, L., & Boden, J. M. (1996). Relation of threatened egotism to violence and aggression: The dark side of high self-esteem. *Psychological Review, 103,* 5–33.

Bauminger, N. (2002). The facilitation of social-emotional understanding and social interaction in high-functioning children with Autism: Intervention outcomes. *Journal of Autism and Developmental Disorders, 32,* 283–298.

Bauminger, N. (2004). The expression and understanding of jealousy in children with Autism. *Development and Psychopathology, 16,* 157–177.

Beauchaine, T. P. (2001). Vagal tone, development, and Gray's motivational theory: Toward an integrated model of autonomic nervous system functioning in psychopathology. *Development and Psychopathology, 13,* 183–214.

Beauchaine, T. P., Katkin, E. S., Strassberg, Z., & Snarr, J. (2001). Disinhibitory psychopathology in male adolescents: Discriminating conduct disorder from attention-deficit/hyperactivity disorder through concurrent assessment of multiple autonomic states. *Journal of Abnormal Psychology, 110,* 610–624.

Bechara, A., Damasio, H., Tranel, D., & Damasio, A. R. (1997). Deciding advantageously before knowing the advantageous strategy. *Science, 275,* 1293–1294.

Bechara, A., Tranel, D., Damasio, H., Adolphs, R., Rockland, C., & Damasio, A. R. (1995). Double dissociation of conditioning and declarative knowledge relative to the amygdala and hippocampus in humans. *Science, 269,* 1115–1118.

Beck, A. T. (1976). *Cognitive therapy and the emotional disorders.* Madison, CT: International Universities Press.

Beeghly, M., & Cicchetti, D. (1997). Talking about self and other: Emergence of an internal state lexicon in young children with Down syndrome. *Development and Psychopathology, 9,* 729–748.

Berkowitz, L. (1990). On the formation and regulation of anger and aggression: A cognitive-neoassociationistic analysis. *American Psychologist, 45,* 494–503.

Bettelheim, B. (1967). *The empty fortress: Infantile Autism and the birth of self.* New York: Free Press.

Bieberich, A. A., & Morgan, S. B. (1998). Brief report: Affective expression in children with Autism or Down syndrome. *Journal of Autism and Developmental Disorders, 28,* 333–338.

Bieberich, A. A., & Morgan, S. B. (2004). Self-regulation and affective expression during play in children with Autism or Down syndrome: A short-term longitudinal study. *Journal of Autism and Developmental Disorders, 342,* 439–448.

Biederman, J. (1998). Resolved: Mania is mistaken for ADHD in prepubertal children. *Journal of the American Academy of Child and Adolescent Psychiatry, 37,* 1091–1093.

Blair, R. J. R. (2003). A neurocognitive model of the psychopathic individual. In M. A. Ron & T. W. Robbins (Eds.), *Disorders of brain and mind* (Vol. 2, pp. 400–418). Cambridge, UK: Cambridge University Press.

Blair, R. J. R. (2004). The roles of orbital frontal cortex in the modulation of antisocial behavior. *Brain and Cognition, 55,* 198–208.

Blair, R. J. R., Budhani, S., Colledge, E., & Scott, S. (in press). Deafness to fear in boys with psychopathic tendencies. *Journal of Child Psychology and Psychiatry.*

Blair, R. J. R., Colledge, E., Murray, L., & Mitchell, D. G. (2001). A selective impairment in the processing of sad and fearful expressions in children with psychopathic tendencies. *Journal of Abnormal Child Psychology, 29,* 491–498.

Blumberg, S. H., & Izard, C. E. (1985). Affective and cognitive characteristics of depression in 10- and 11-year-old children. *Journal of Personality and Social Psychology, 49,* 194–202.

Blumberg, S. H., & Izard, C. E. (1986). Discriminating patterns of emotions in 10- and 11-year-old children's anxiety and depression. *Journal of Personality and Social Psychology, 51,* 852–857.

Bolte, S., & Poustka, F. (2003). The recognition of facial affect in autistic and schizophrenic subjects and their first-degree relatives. *Psychological Medicine, 33,* 907–915.

Bonanno, G. A., Keltner, D., Noll, J. G., Putnam, F. W., Trickett, P. K., LeJeune, J., et al. (2002). When the face reveals what words do not: Facial expressions of emotion, smiling, and the willingness to disclose childhood sexual abuse. *Journal of Personality and Social Psychology, 83,* 94–110.

Bowlby, J. (1969). *Attachment and loss: Vol. I. Attachment.* New York: Basic Books.

Bowlby, J. (1973). *Attachment and loss: Vol. II. Separation: Anxiety and anger.* New York: Basic Books.

Bowlby, J. (1980). *Attachment and loss* (Vol. III). New York: Basic Books.

Bradley, M. M., & Lang, P. J. (1999). Fearfulness and affective evaluations of pictures. *Motivation and Emotion, 23,* 1–13.

Bradley, S. J. (2000). *Affect regulation and the development of psychopathology.* New York: Guilford Press.

Bretherton, I., & Beeghly-Smith, M. (1982). Talking about internal states: The acquisition of an explicit theory of mind. *Developmental Psychology, 18,* 906–921.

Brothers, L. A. (1990). The social brain. A project for integrating primate behavior and neurophysiology in a new domain. *Concepts in Neuroscience, 1,* 27–51.

Brown, T. A., Chorpita, B. F., & Barlow, D. H. (1998). Structural relationships among dimensions of the *DSM-IV* anxiety and mood disorders and dimensions of negative affect, positive affect, and autonomic arousal. *Journal of Abnormal Psychology, 107,* 179–192.

Bryant, B. K. (1992). Conflict resolution strategies in relation to children's peer relations. *Journal of Applied Developmental Psychology, 13,* 35–50.

Buitelaar, J. K., & van der Wees, M. (1997). Are deficits in the decoding of affective cues and in mentalizing abilities independent? *Journal of Autism and Developmental Disorders, 27,* 539–557.

Burns, D. D., & Eidelson, R. J. (1998). Why are depression and anxiety correlated? A test of the tripartite model. *Journal of Consulting and Clinical Psychology, 66,* 461–473.

Cadesky, E. B., Mota, V. L., & Schachar, R. J. (2000). Beyond words: How do children with ADHD and/or conduct problems process nonverbal information about affect? *Journal of the American Academy of Child and Adolescent Psychiatry, 39,* 1160–1172.

Calabrese, J. R., Suppes, T., Bowden, C. L., Sachs, G. S., Swann, A. C., McElroy, S. L., et al. (2000). A double-blind, placebo-controlled, prophylaxis study of lamotrigine in rapid-cycling bipolar disorder: Lamictal 614 Study Group. *Journal of Clinical Psychiatry, 61,* 841–850.

Calam, R., Bolton, C., Barrowclough, C., & Roberts, J. (2002). Maternal expressed emotion and clinician ratings of emotional maltreatment potential. *Child Abuse and Neglect, 26,* 1101–1106.

Calkins, S., & Fox, N. (2002). Self-regulatory processes in early personality development: A multilevel approach to the study of childhood social withdrawal and aggression. *Development and Psychopathology, 14,* 477–498.

Campbell, D. T., & Fiske, D. W. (1959). Convergent and discriminant validation by multitrait-multimethod matrix. *Psychological Bulletin, 56,* 81–105.

Campbell, S. B., Brownell, C. A., Hungerford, A., Spieker, S. J., Mohan, R., & Blessing, J. S. (2004). The course of maternal depressive symptoms and maternal sensitivity as predictors of attachment security at 36 months. *Development and Psychopathology, 16,* 231–252.

Campeau, S., & Davis, M. (1995). Involvement of subcortical and cortical afferents to the lateral nucleus of the amygdala in fear conditioning measured with fear-potentiated startle in rats trained concurrently with auditory and visual conditioned stimuli. *Journal of Neuroscience, 15,* 2312–2327.

Campos, J. J., Campos, R. G., & Barrett, K. C. (1989). Emergent themes in the study of emotional development and emotion regulation. *Developmental Psychology, 25,* 394–402.

Campos, J. J., Kermoian, R., & Zumbahlen, M. R. (1992). Socioemotional transformations in the family system following infant crawling onset. In N. Eisenberg & R. A. Fabes (Eds.), *Emotion and its regulation in early development: New directions for child development, No. 55: The Jossey-Bass education series* (pp. 25–40). San Francisco: Jossey-Bass/Pfeiffer.

Campos, J. J., Mumme, D. L., Kermoian, R., & Campos, R. G. (1994). A functionalist perspective on the nature of emotion. *Monographs for the Society for Research in Child Development, 59*(1, Serial No. 240).

Camras, L. A., Ribordy, S., Hill, J., Martino, S., Spaccarrelli, S., & Stefani, R. (1988). Recognition and posing of emotional expressions by abused children and their mothers. *Developmental Psychology, 24,* 776–781.

Capps, L., Kasari, C., Yirmiya, N., & Sigman, M. (1993). Parental perception of emotional expressiveness in children with Autism. *Journal of Consulting and Clinical Psychology, 61,* 475–484.

Capps, L., Yirmiya, N., & Sigman, M. (1992). Understanding of simple and complex emotions in non-retarded children with Autism. *Journal of Child Psychology and Psychiatry and Allied Disciplines, 33,* 1169–1182.

Carlson, G. A. (2002). Bipolar disorder in children and adolescents: A critical review. In D. Shaffer & B. Waslick (Eds.), *The many faces of depression in children and adolescents* (Vol. 21, pp. 105–128). Washington, DC: APPI Press.

Carver, C. S., & White, T. L. (1994). Behavioral inhibition, behavioral activation, and affective responses to impending reward and punishment: The BIS/BAS scales. *Journal of Personality and Social Psychology, 67,* 319–333.

Casey, R. J., & Schlosser, S. (1994). Emotional responses to peer praise in children with and without a diagnosed externalizing disorder. *Merrill-Palmer Quarterly, 40,* 60–81.

Celani, G., Battacchi, M. W., & Arcidiancono, L. (1999). The understanding of the emotional meaning of facial expressions in people with Autism. *Journal of Autism and Developmental Disorders, 29,* 57–66.

Cesari, A., Maestro, S., Cavallaro, C., Chilosi, A., Pecini, C., Pfanner, L., et al. (2003). Diagnostic boundaries between regulatory and multisystem developmental disorders: A clinical study. *Infant Mental Health Journal, 24,* 365–377.

Chang, L., Schwartz, D., Dodge, K. A., & McBride-Chang, C. (2003). Harsh parenting in relation to child emotion regulation and aggression. *Journal of Family Psychology, 17,* 598–606.

Chorpita, B. F. (2002). The tripartite model and dimensions of anxiety and depression: An examination of structure in a large school sample. *Journal of Abnormal Child Psychology, 30,* 177–190.

Chorpita, B. F., Albano, A. M., & Barlow, D. H. (1998). The structure of negative emotions in a clinical sample of children and adolescents. *Journal of Abnormal Psychology, 107,* 74–85.

Cicchetti, D. (1990). The organization and coherence of socioemotional, cognitive, and representational development: Illustrations through a developmental psychopathology perspective of Down syndrome and child maltreatment. In R. Thompson (Ed.), *Nebraska Symposium on Motivation* (Vol. 36, pp. 259–366). Lincoln: University of Nebraska Press.

Cicchetti, D. (2002). The impact of social experience on neurobiological systems: Illustration from a constructivist view of child maltreatment. *Cognitive Development, 17,* 1407–1428.

Cicchetti, D., & Dawson, G. (2002). Editorial: Multiple levels of analysis. *Development and Psychopathology, 14,* 417–420.

Cicchetti, D., & Hinshaw, S. P. (2002). Editorial: Prevention and intervention science: Contributions to developmental theory. *Development and Psychopathology, 14,* 667–671.

Cicchetti, D., & Lynch, M. (1995). Failures in the expectable environment and their impact on individual development: The case of child maltreatment. In D. Cicchetti & D. J. Cohen (Eds.), *Developmental psychology: Risk, disorder, and adaptation* (Vol. 2, pp. 32–71). New York: Wiley.

Cicchetti, D., & Rogosch, F. A. (2001a). Diverse patterns of neuroendocrine activity in maltreated children. *Development and Psychopathology, 13,* 677–693.

Cicchetti, D., & Rogosch, F. A. (2001b). The impact of child maltreatment and psychopathology on neuroendocrine functioning. *Development and Psychopathology, 13,* 783–804.

Cicchetti, D., & Schneider-Rosen, K. (1984). Theoretical and empirical considerations in the investigation of the relationship between affect and cognition in atypical populations of infants. In C. E. Izard, J. Kagan, & R. Zajonc (Eds.), *Emotions, cognition and behavior* (pp. 366–406). New York: Cambridge University Press.

Cicchetti, D., & Sroufe, L. A. (1976). The relationship between affective and cognitive development in Down's syndrome infants. *Child Development, 47,* 920–929.

Cicchetti, D., & Toth, S. L. (1995). Developmental psychopathology and disorders of affect. In D. Cicchetti & D. J. Cohen (Eds.), *Developmental psychopathology* (pp. 369–420). New York: Wiley.

Cicchetti, D., & Tucker, D. (1994). Development and self-regulatory structures of the mind [Special issue: Neural plasticity, sensitive periods, and psychopathology]. *Development and Psychopathology, 6,* 533–549.

Clark, L. A., & Watson, D. (1991). Tripartite model of anxiety and depression: Psychometric evidence and taxonomic implications. *Journal of Abnormal Psychology, 100,* 316–336.

Clark, L. A., Watson, D., & Mineka, S. (1994). Temperament, personality, and the mood and anxiety disorders [Special issue: Personality and psychopathology]. *Journal of Abnormal Psychology, 103,* 103–116.

Cleckley, H. (1941). *The mask of sanity.* St. Louis, MO: Mosby.

Cole, P. M., Zahn-Waxler, C., & Smith, D. K. (1994). Expressive control during a disappointment: Variations related to preschoolers' behavior problems. *Developmental Psychology, 30,* 835–846.

Conklin, H. M., & Iacono, W. G. (2003). At issue: Assessment of Schizophrenia: Getting closer to the cause. *Schizophrenia Bulletin, 29,* 405–411.

Corona, R., Dissanayuke, C., Arbelle, S., Wellington, P., & Sigman, M. (1998). Is affect aversive to young children with Autism? Behavioral and cardiac responses to experimenter distress. *Child Development, 69,* 1494–1502.

Costa, P. T., & McCrae, R. R. (1995). Domains and facets: Hierarchical personality assessment using the Revised NEO Personality Inventory. *Journal of Personality Assessment, 64,* 21–50.

Courchesne, E., Townsend, J. P., Akshoomoff, N. A., Yeung-Courchesne, R., Press, G. A., Murakami, J. W., et al. (1994). A new finding: Impairment in shifting attention in autistic and cerebellar patients. In S. H. Broman & J. Grafman (Eds.), *Atypical cognitive deficits in developmental disorders: Implications for brain function* (pp. 101–137). Hillsdale, NJ: Erlbaum.

Crick, N. R., & Dodge, K. A. (1994). A review and reformulation of social information processing mechanisms in children's social adjustment. *Psychological Bulletin, 115,* 74–101.

Crockenberg, S. (1985). Toddlers' reactions to maternal anger. *Merrill-Palmer Quarterly, 31,* 361–373.

Cummings, E. M. (1994). Marital conflict and children's functioning. *Social Development, 3,* 16–36.

Cummings, E. M., Iannotti, R. J., & Zahn-Waxler, C. (1985). Influence of conflict between adults on the emotions and aggression of young children. *Developmental Psychology, 21,* 495–507.

Cutting, A. L., & Dunn, J. (1999). Theory of mind, emotion understanding, language, and family background: Individual differences and interrelations. *Child Development, 70,* 853–865.

Damasio, A. R. (1994). *Descartes' error: Emotion, reason, and the human brain.* New York: Putnam.

Damasio, A. R. (1998). Emotion in the perspective of an integrated nervous system. *Brain Research Reviews, 26,* 83–86.

Damasio, A. R. (1999). *The feeling of what happens: Body and emotion in the making of consciousness.* New York: Harcourt Brace.

Darwin, C. (1872/1998). *The expression of the emotions in man and animals.* New York: Oxford University Press.

Davey, G. C. L. (1994a). The "disgusting" spider: The role of disease and illness in the perpetuation of fear of spiders. *Society & Animals, 2,* 17–25.

Davey, G. C. L. (1994b). Self-reported fears to common indigenous animals in an adult UK population: The role of disgust sensitivity. *British Journal of Psychology, 85,* 541–554.

Davey, G. C. L., Buckland, G., Tantow, B., & Dallos, R. (1998). Disgust and eating disorders. *European Eating Disorders Review, 6,* 201–211.

Davey, G. C. L., Forster, L., & Mayhew, G. (1993). Familial resemblances in disgust sensitivity and animal phobias. *Behaviour Research and Therapy, 31,* 41–50.

Davey, G. C. L., McDonald, A. S., Hirisave, U., Prabhu, G. G., Iwawaki, S., Jim, C. I., et al. (1998). A cross-cultural study of animal fears. *Behaviour Research and Therapy, 36,* 735–750.

Davidson, R. J. (1992). Prolegomenon to the structure of emotion: Gleanings from neuropsychology. *Cognition and Emotion, 6,* 245–268.

Davidson, R. J. (1994). Asymmetric brain function, affective style, and psychopathology: The role of early experience and plasticity [Special

issue: Neural plasticity, sensitive periods, and psychopathology]. *Development and Psychopathology, 6,* 741–758.

Davidson, R. J. (1998). Affective style and affective disorders: Perspectives from affective neuroscience. *Cognition and Emotion, 12,* 307–330.

Davidson, R. J. (2000). Affective style, psychopathology, and resilience: Brain mechanisms and plasticity. *American Psychologist, 55,* 1196–1214.

Davidson, R. J., Jackson, D. C., & Kalin, N. H. (2000). Emotion, plasticity, context and regulation: Perspectives from affective neuroscience. *Psychological Bulletin, 126,* 890–906.

Davidson, R. J., Marshall, J. R., Tomarken, A. J., & Henriques, J. B. (2000). While a phobic waits: Regional brain electrical and autonomic activity in social phobics during anticipation of public speaking. *Biological Psychiatry, 47,* 85–95.

Davidson, R. J., Pizzagalli, D., Nitschke, J. B., & Putnam, K. M. (2002). Depression: Perspectives from affective neuroscience. *Annual Review of Psychology, 53,* 545–574.

Davidson, R. J., Putnam, K. M., & Larson, C. L. (2000). Dysfunction in the neural circuitry of emotion regulation: A possible prelude to violence. *Science, 289,* 591–594.

Davidson, R. J., & Tomarken, A. J. (1989). Laterality and emotion: An electrophysiological approach. In F. Boller & J. Grafman (Eds.), *Handbook of neuropsychology* (pp. 419–441). Amsterdam: Elsevier.

Dawson, G., Frey, K., Self, J., Panagiotides, H., Hessl, D., Yamada, E., et al. (1999). Frontal brain electrical activity in infants of depressed and nondepressed mothers: Relation to variations in infant behavior. *Development and Psychopathology, 11,* 589–605.

Debener, S., Beauducel, A., Nessler, D., Brocke, B., Heilemann, H., & Kayser, J. (2000). Is resting anterior EEG alpha asymmetry a trait marker for depression? Findings for healthy adults and clinically depressed patients. *Neuropsychobiology, 41,* 31–37.

De Kloet, E. R., & McEwen, B. S. (1976). Differences between cytosol receptor complexes with corticosterone and dexamethasome in hippocampal tissue from rat brain. *Biochimica et Biophysica Acta, 421,* 124–132.

Denham, S. A. (1998). Emotional development in young children. New York: Guilford Press.

Denham, S. A., Workman, E., Cole, P. M., Weissbrod, C., Kendziora, K. T., & Zahn-Waxler, C. (2000). Prediction of externalizing behavior problems from early to middle childhood: The role of parental socialization and emotion expression. *Development and Psychopathology, 12,* 23–45.

Depue, R. A. (1996). A neurobiological framework for the structure of personality and emotion: Implications for personality disorders. In J. F. Clarkin & M. F. Lenzenweger (Eds.), *Major theories of personality disorder* (pp. 347–390). New York: Guilford Press.

Depue, R. A., & Collins, P. F. (1999). Neurobiology of the structure of personality: Dopamine, facilitation of incentive motivation, and extraversion. *Behavioral and Brain Sciences, 22,* 491–569.

Depue, R. A., & Iacono, W. G. (1989). Neurobehavioral aspects of affective disorders. *Annual Review of Psychology, 40,* 457–492.

Depue, R. A., Krauss, S. P., & Spoont, M. R. (1987). A two dimensional threshold model of seasonal bipolar affective disorder. In D. Magnusson & A. Ohman (Eds.), *Psychopathology: An interactional perspective* (pp. 95–123). New York: Academic Press.

Depue, R. A., Krauss, S., Spoont, M. R., & Arbisi, P. (1989). General behavior inventory identification of unipolar and bipolar affective conditions in a nonclinical university population. *Journal of Abnormal Psychology, 98,* 117–126.

Depue, R. A., & Lenzenweger, M. F. (2001). A neurobehavioral dimensional model. In W. J. Livesley (Ed.), *Handbook of personality disor-*

ders: Theory, research, and treatment (pp. 136–176). New York: Guilford Press.

Depue, R. A., Luciana, M., Arbisi, P., Collins, P., & Leon, A. (1994). Dopamine and the structure of personality: Relation of agonist-induced dopamine activity to positive emotionality. *Journal of Personality and Social Psychology, 67,* 485–498.

Depue, R. A., & Zald, D. H. (1993). Biological and environmental processes in nonpsychotic psychopathology: A neurobehavioral perspective. In C. G. Costello (Ed.), *Basic issues in psychopathology* (pp. 127–237). New York: Guilford Press.

Devinsky, O., Morrell, M. J., & Vogt, B. A. (1995). Contributions of anterior cingulate cortex to behaviour. *Brain Research, 118,* 279–306.

Diener, E., & Diener, C. (1996). Most people are happy. *Psychological Science, 7,* 181–185.

Diener, M. L., Mangelsdorf, S. C., McHale, J. L., & Frosch, C. A. (2002). Infants' behavioral strategies for emotion regulation with fathers and mothers: Associations with emotional expressions and attachment quality. *Infancy, 3,* 153–174.

Dodge, K. A., & Coie, J. D. (1987). Social-information-processing factors in reactive and proactive aggression in children's peer groups. *Journal of Personality and Social Psychology, 53,* 1146–1158.

Dodge, K. A., Laird, R., Lochman, J. E., & Zelli, A. (2002). Multidimensional latent-construct analysis of children's social information processing patterns: Correlations with aggressive behavior problems. *Psychological Assessment, 14,* 60–73.

Dodge, K. A., Price, J. M., Bachorowski, J., & Newman, J. P. (1990). Hostile attribution biases in severely aggressive adolescents. *Journal of Abnormal Psychology, 99,* 385–392.

Dunn, J., Bretherton, I., & Munn, P. (1987). Conversations about feeling states between mothers and their young children. *Developmental Psychology, 23* 132–139.

Earnst, K. S., & Kring, A. M. (1999). Emotional responding in deficit and non-deficit Schizophrenia. *Psychiatry Research, 88,* 191–207.

Eisenberg, N. (2000). Emotion, regulation, and moral development. *Annual Review of Psychology, 51,* 665–697.

Eisenberg, N., Cumberland, A., & Spinrad, T. L. (1998). Parental socialization of emotion. *Psychological Inquiry, 9,* 241–273.

Eisenberg, N., Fabes, R., & Losoya, S. (1997). Emotional responding: Regulation, social correlates, and socialization. In P. Salovey & D. Sluyter (Eds.), *Emotional development and emotional intelligence: Educational implications* (pp. 129–167). New York: Basic Books.

Eisenberg, N., Fabes, R. A., Murphy, B., Karbon, M., Smith, M., & Maszk, P. (1996). The relations of children's dispositional empathy-related responding to their emotionality, regulation, and social functioning. *Developmental Psychology, 32,* 195–209.

Eisenberg, N., Fabes, R. A., Murphy, B., Maszk, P., Smith, M., & Karbon, M. (1995). The role of emotionality and regulation in children's social functioning: A longitudinal study. *Child Development, 66,* 183–201.

Eisenberg, N., Fabes, R. A., Shepard, S. A., Guthrie, I. K., Murphy, B. C., & Reiser, M. (1999). Parental reactions for children's negative emotions: Longitudinal relations to quality of children's social functioning. *Child Development, 70,* 513–534.

Eisenberg, N., Gershoff, E. T., Fabes, R. A., Shepard, S. A., Cumberland, A. J., Losoya, S. H., et al. (2001). Mothers' emotional expressivity and children's behavior problems and social competence: Mediation through children's regulation. *Developmental Psychology, 37,* 475–490.

Eisenberg, N., Guthrie, I. K., Fabes, R., Shepard, S., Losoya, S., Murphy, B., et al. (2000). Prediction of elementary school children's externalizing problem behaviors from attentional and behavioral regulation and negative emotionality. *Child Development, 71,* 1367–1382.

Eisenberg, N., Losoya, S., Fabes, R. A., Guthrie, I. K., Reiser, M., Murphy, B., et al. (2001). Parental socialization of children's dysregulated expression of emotion and externalizing problems. *Journal of Family Psychology, 15,* 183–205.

Ellsworth, P. C. (1994). William James and emotion: Is a century of fame worth a century of misunderstanding? *Psychological Review, 101,* 222–229.

Emde, R. N., Katz, E. L., & Thorpe, J. K. (1978). Emotional expression in infancy: Early deviations in Down's syndrome. In M. Lewis & L. Rosenblum (Eds.), *The development of affect* (pp. 351–360). New York: Plenum Press.

Emde, R. N., & Wise, B. K. (2003). The cup is half full: Initial clinical trials of DC: 0–3 and a recommendation for revision. *Infant Mental Health Journal, 24,* 437–446.

Emery, N. J., Machado, C. J., Capitanio, J. P., Mendoza, S. P., Mason, W. A., & Amaral, D. G. (1998). The role of the amygdala in rhesus monkeys (Macaca mulatta). *Journal of Comparative Psychology, 111,* 1–8.

Fabes, R. A., Leonard, S. A., Kupanoff, K., & Martin, C. (2001). Parental coping with children's negative emotions: Relations with children's emotional and social responding. *Child Development, 72,* 907–920.

Feldman, R., Greenbaum, C. W., & Yirmiya, N. (1999). Mother-infant affect synchrony as an antecedent of the emergence of self-control. *Developmental Psychology, 35,* 223–231.

Feshbach, N. (1982). Sex differences in empathy and social behavior in children. In N. Eisenberg (Ed.), *The development of prosocial behavior* (pp. 315–338). New York: Cambridge University Press.

Findling, R. L., Feeny, N. C., Stansbrey, R. J., DelPorto-Bedoya, D., & Demeter, C. (2002). Somatic treatment for depressive illnesses in children and adolescents. *Child and Adolescent Psychiatric Clinics of North America, 11,* 555–578.

Fine, S. E., Izard, C. E., Mostow, A. J., Trentacosta, C. J., & Ackerman, B. P. (2003). First grade emotion knowledge as a predictor of fifth grade self-reported internalizing behaviors in children from economically disadvantaged families. *Development and Psychopathology, 15,* 331–342.

Fine, S. E., Trentacosta, C. J., Izard, C. E., Mostow, A. J., & Campbell, J. L. (2004). Anger perception bias, caregivers' use of physical discipline, and aggression in children at risk. *Social Development, 13,* 213–228.

Folkman, S., & Lazarus, R. S. (1990). Coping and emotion. In N. L. Stein & B. Leventhal (Eds.), *Psychological and biological approaches to emotion* (pp. 313–332). Hillsdale, NJ: Erlbaum.

Forgas, J. P. (2002). Feeling and doing: Affective influences on interpersonal behavior. *Psychological Inquiry, 13,* 1–28.

Fowles, D. C. (1994). A motivational theory of psychopathology. In W. D. Spaulding (Ed.), *Integrative views of motivation, cognition, and emotion* (Vol. 41, pp. 181–238). Lincoln: University of Nebraska Press.

Fredrickson, B. L. (2000). *Cultivating positive emotions to optimize health and well-being.* Available from http://journals.apa.org/prevention/volume3/pre0030001c.html.

Frick, P. J. (2004). Developmental pathways to conduct disorder: Implications for serving youth who show severe aggressive and antisocial behavior. *Psychology in the Schools: Special Differentiation of Emotional Disturbance and Social Maladjustment, 41,* 823–834.

Frick, P. J., & Morris, A. S. (2004). Temperament and developmental pathways to conduct problems. *Journal of Clinical Child and Adolescent Psychology, 33,* 54–68.

Fries, A. B. W., & Pollak, S. D. (2004). Emotion understanding in postinstitutionalized Eastern European children. *Development and Psychopathology, 16,* 355–369.

Frijda, N. H. (1986). *The emotions.* New York: Cambridge University Press.

Frijda, N. H. (1994). Emotions are functional, most of the time. In P. Ekman & R. J. Davidson (Eds.), *The nature of emotion: Fundamental questions* (pp. 112–122). New York: Oxford University Press.

Frith, U. (1989). *Autism: Explaining the enigma.* London: Basil Blackwell.

Geller, B., & Luby, J. (1997). Child and adolescent bipolar disorder: A review of the past 10 years. *Journal of the American Academy of Child and Adolescent Psychiatry, 36,* 1168–1176.

Gianino, A., & Tronick, E. Z. (1988). The mutual regulation model: The infant's self and interactive regulation and coping and defensive capacities. In T. M. Field & P. M. McCabe (Eds.), *Stress and coping across development* (pp. 47–68). Hillsdale, NJ: Erlbaum.

Gilbert, P., & Allan, S. (1998). The role of defeat and entrapment (arrested flight) in depression: An exploration of an evolutionary view. *Psychological Medicine, 28,* 585–598.

Gilbert, P., Allan, S., Brough, S., Melley, S., & Miles, J. N. (2002). Relationship of anhedonia and anxiety to social rank, defeat and entrapment. *Journal of Affective Disorders, 71,* 141–151.

Gilbert, P., Allan, S., & Trent, D. R. (1995). Involuntary subordination or dependency as key dimensions of depressive vulnerability? *Journal of Clinical Psychology, 51,* 740–752.

Gilliom, M., Shaw, D. S., Beck, J. E., Schonberg, M. A., & Lukon, J. L. (2002). Anger regulation in disadvantaged preschool boys: Strategies, antecedents, and the development of self-control. *Developmental Psychology, 38,* 222–235.

Goodwin, F. K., & Jamison, K. R. (1990). *Manic-depressive illness.* New York: Oxford University Press.

Gottman, J. M., Katz, L., & Hooven, C. (1996). Parental meta-emotion philosophy and the emotional life of families: Theoretical models and preliminary data. *Journal of Family Psychology, 10,* 243–268.

Gray, J. A. (1978). The neuropsychology of anxiety. *British Journal of Psychology, 69,* 417–434.

Gray, J. A. (1979). A neuropsychological theory of anxiety. In C. E. Izard (Ed.), *Emotions in personality and psychopathology* (pp. 126–142). New York: Plenum Press.

Gray, J. A. (1982). *The neuropsychology of anxiety.* London: Oxford University Press.

Gray, J. A. (1995). A model of the limbic system and basal ganglia: Applications to anxiety and Schizophrenia. In M. S. Gazzaniga (Ed.), *The cognitive neurosciences* (pp. 1165–1176). Cambridge, MA: MIT Press.

Gray, J. A., & McNaughton, N. (1996). The neuropsychology of anxiety: Reprise. In D. A. Hope (Ed.), *Perspectives in anxiety, panic and fear* (Vol. 43, pp. 61–134). Lincoln: University of Nebraska Press.

Greenough, W. T., Black, J. E., & Wallace, C. S. (1987). Experience and brain development. *Child Development, 58,* 539–559.

Guédeney, N., Guédeney, A., Rabouam, C., Mintz, A., Danon, G., Huet, M. M., et al. (2003). The Zero-to-Three diagnostic classification: A contribution to the validation of this classification from a sample of 85 under-threes. *Infant Mental Health Journal, 24,* 313–336.

Gunnar, M. R., & Donzella, B. (2002). Social regulation of the cortisol levels in early human development. *Psychoneuroendocrinology, 27,* 199–220.

Halberstadt, A. G., Crisp, V. W., & Eaton, K. L. (1999). Family expressiveness: A retrospective and new directions for research. In P. Philippot, R. S. Feldman, & E. Coats (Eds.), *The social context of nonverbal behavior* (pp. 25–46). New York: Cambridge University Press.

Halberstadt, A. G., & Eaton, K. L. (2002). A meta-analysis of family expressiveness and children's emotion expressiveness and understanding. *Marriage and Family Review, 34,* 35–62.

Hare, R. D. (1999). Psychopathy as a risk factor for violence. *Psychiatric Quarterly, 70,* 181–197.

Harris, P. (1999). Individual differences in understanding emotion: The role of attachment status and psychological discourse. *Attachment and Human Development, 1,* 307–324.

Hauser, S. T., & Safyer, A. W. (1994). Ego development and adolescent emotions. *Journal of Research on Adolescence, 4,* 487–502.

Henriques, J. B., & Davidson, R. J. (1997). Brain electrical asymmetries during cognitive task performance in depressed and nondepressed subjects. *Biological Psychiatry, 42,* 1039–1050.

Herman, J. P., & Cullinan, W. E. (1997). Neurocircuitry of stress: Central control of the hypothalamo-pituitary-adrenocortical axis. *Trends in Neurosciences, 20,* 78–84.

Hillier, A., & Allinson, L. (2002). Beyond expectations: Autism, understanding embarrassment, and the relationship with theory of mind. *Autism, 6,* 299–314.

Hipwell, A. E., Goossens, F. A., Melhuish, E. C., & Kumar, R. (2000). Severe maternal psychopathology and infant-mother attachment. *Development and Psychopathology, 12,* 157–175.

Hirschfeld, R. M. A., Williams, J. B. W., Spitzer, R. L., Calabrese, J. R., Flynn, L., Keck, P. E. J., et al. (2000). Development and validation of a screening instrument for bipolar spectrum disorder: The Mood Disorder Questionnaire. *American Journal of Psychiatry, 157,* 1873–1875.

Hobson, R. P. (1986). The autistic child's appraisal of expressions of emotion: A further study. *Journal of Child Psychology and Psychiatry and Allied Disciplines, 27,* 671–680.

Hobson, R. P. (1993). *Autism and the development of mind.* Hove, England: Erlbaum.

Hobson, R. P. (1995). Apprehending attitudes and actions: Separable abilities in early development? *Development and Psychopathology, 7,* 171–182.

Howlin, P. (2003). Outcome in high-functioning adults with Autism with and without early language delays: Implications for the differentiation between Autism and Asperger syndrome. *Journal of Autism and Developmental Disorders, 33,* 3–13.

Hubbard, J. A. (2001). Emotion expression processes in children's peer interaction: The role of peer rejection, aggression, and gender. *Child Development, 72,* 1426–1438.

Hubbard, J. A., & Coie, J. D. (1994). Emotional correlates of social competence in children's peer relations. *Merrill-Palmer Quarterly, 40,* 1–20.

Hubbard, J. A., Smithmyer, C. M., Ramsden, S. R., Parker, E. H., Flanagan, K. D., Dearing, K. F., et al. (2002). Observational, physiological, and self-report measures of children's anger: Relations to reactive versus proactive aggression. *Child Development, 73,* 1101–1118.

Hyson, M. C., & Izard, C. E. (1985). Continuities and changes in emotion expressions during brief separation of 13 and 18 months. *Developmental Psychology, 21,* 1165–1170.

Izard, C. E. (1971). *The face of emotion.* New York: Appleton-Century-Crofts.

Izard, C. E. (1972). *Patterns of emotions: A new analysis of anxiety and depression.* New York: Academic Press.

Izard, C. E. (1977). *Human emotions.* New York: Plenum Press.

Izard, C. E. (1978). On the ontogenesis of emotions and emotion-cognition relationships in infancy. In M. Lewis & L. A. Rosenblum (Eds.), *The development of affect* (pp. 389–413). New York: Plenum Press.

Izard, C. E. (1979). Emotions in personality and psychopathology: An introduction. In C. E. Izard (Ed.), *Emotions in personality and psychopathology* (pp. 1–8). New York: Plenum Press.

Izard, C. E. (1989). The structure and functions of emotions: Implications for cognition, motivation, and personality. In I. S. Cohen (Eds.), *The G. Stanley Hall lecture series* (pp. 35–73). Washington, DC: American Psychological Association.

Izard, C. E. (1991). *The psychology of emotions.* New York: Plenum Press.

Izard, C. E. (1993). Four systems of emotion activation: Cognitive and noncognitive processes. *Psychological Review, 100,* 68–90.

Izard, C. E. (2001). Emotional intelligence or adaptive emotions? *Emotion, 1,* 249–257.

Izard, C. E. (2002). Translating emotion theory and research into preventive interventions. *Psychological Bulletin, 128,* 796–824.

Izard, C. E., & Ackerman, B. P. (1997). Emotions and self-concepts across the life span. In K. W. Schaie & M. P. Lawton (Eds.), *Annual review of gerontology and geriatrics: Focus on emotion and adult development* (Vol. 17, pp. 1–26). New York: Springer.

Izard, C. E., & Ackerman, B. P. (2000). Motivational, organizational, and regulatory functions of discrete emotions. In M. Lewis & J. Haviland-Jones (Eds.), *Handbook of emotions* (2nd ed., pp. 253–322). New York: Guilford Press.

Izard, C. E., Ackerman, B. P., Schoff, K. M., & Fine, S. E. (2000). Self-organization of discrete emotions, emotion patterns, and emotion-cognition relations. In M. D. Lewis & I. Granic (Eds.), *Emotion, development, and self-organization* (pp. 15–36). Cambridge, UK: Cambridge University Press.

Izard, C. E., Fantauzzo, C. A., Castle, J. M., Haynes, O. M., Rayias, M. F., & Putnam, P. H. (1995). The ontogeny and significance of infants' facial expressions in the first nine months of life. *Developmental Psychology, 31,* 997–1013.

Izard, C. E., Fine, S. E., Mostow, A. J., Trentacosta, C. J., & Campbell, J. (2002). Emotion processes in normal and abnormal development and preventive intervention. *Development and Psychopathology, 14,* 761–787.

Izard, C. E., Fine, S. E., Schultz, D., Mostow, A. J., Ackerman, B. P., & Youngstrom, E. A. (2001). Emotion knowledge as a predictor of social behavior and academic competence in children at risk. *Psychological Science, 12,* 18–23.

Izard, C. E., Haynes, O. M., Chisholm, G., & Baak, K. (1991). Emotional determinants of infant-mother attachment. *Child Development, 62,* 906–917.

Izard, C. E., Hembree, E. A., & Huebner, R. R. (1987). Infants' emotion expressions to acute pain: Developmental change and stability of individual differences. *Developmental Psychology, 23,* 105–113.

Izard, C. E., Kagan, J., & Zajonc, R. (Eds.). (1984). *Emotions, cognition, and behavior.* New York: Cambridge University Press.

Izard, C. E., & Kobak, R. R. (1991). Emotions system functioning and emotion regulation. In J. Garber & K. A. Dodge (Eds.), *The development of emotion regulation and dysregulation* (pp. 303–321). New York: Cambridge University Press.

Izard, C. E., Libero, D. Z., Putnam, P., & Haynes, O. M. (1993). Stability of emotion experiences and their relation to traits of personality. *Journal of Personality and Social Psychology, 64,* 847–860.

Izard, C. E., Porges, S. W., Simons, R. F., Haynes, O. M., Hyde, C., Parisi, M., et al. (1991). Infant cardiac activity: Developmental changes and relations with attachment. *Developmental Psychology, 27,* 432–443.

Izard, C. E., Trentacosta, C. J., King, K. A., & Mostow, A. J. (2004). An emotion-based prevention program for Head Start children. *Early Education and Development, 15,* 407–422.

Izard, C. E., & Youngstrom, E. A. (1996). The activation and regulation of fear and anxiety. In B. Brown (Ed.), *Perspectives on anxiety, panic, and fear* (Vol. 43, pp. 1–57). Lincoln: University of Nebraska Press.

James, W. (1890/1965). *The principles of emotion.* New York: Dover.

Jamison, K. R. (1993). *Touched with fire: Manic-depressive illness and the artistic temperament.* New York: Free Press.

Jamison, K. R. (1995). *An unquiet mind: A memoir of moods and madness.* New York: Vintage Books.

Jenkins, J. M., & Oatley, K. (1996). Emotional episodes and emotionality through the life span. In C. Magai & S. H. McFadden (Eds.), *Handbook of emotion, adult development, and aging* (pp. 421–441). New York: Academic Press.

Johnson, S. L., Meyer, B., Winett, C., & Small, J. (2000). Social support and self-esteem predict changes in bipolar depression but not mania. *Journal of Affective Disorders, 58,* 79–86.

Johnson, S. L., & Miller, I. (1997). Negative life events and time to recovery from episodes of bipolar disorder. *Journal of Abnormal Psychology, 106,* 449–457.

Johnson, S. L., & Roberts, J. E. (1995). Life events and bipolar disorder: Implications from biological theories. *Psychological Bulletin, 117,* 434–449.

Johnson, S. L., Sandrow, D., Meyer, B., Winters, R., Miller, I., Solomon, D., et al. (in press). Increases in manic symptoms after life events following goal-attainment. *Journal of Abnormal Psychology.*

Joiner, T. E., Jr. (1996). A confirmatory factor-analytic investigation of the tripartite model of depression and anxiety in college students. *Cognitive Therapy and Research, 20,* 521–539.

Joiner, T. E., Jr., Catanzaro, S. J., & Laurent, J. (1996). Tripartite structure of positive and negative affect, depression, and anxiety in child and adolescent psychiatric inpatients. *Journal of Abnormal Psychology, 105,* 401–409.

Joiner, T. E., Jr., & Lonigan, C. J. (2000). Tripartite model of depression and anxiety in youth psychiatric inpatients: Relations with diagnostic status and future symptoms. *Journal of Clinical Child Psychology, 29,* 372–382.

Joiner, T. E., Jr., Steer, R. A., Beck, A. T., Schmidt, N. B., Rudd, M. D., & Catanzaro, S. J. (1999). Physiological hyperarousal: Construct validity of a central aspect of the tripartite model of depression and anxiety. *Journal of Abnormal Psychology, 108,* 290–298.

Jones, N. A., Field, T., Fox, N. A., Lundy, B., & Davalos, M. (1997). EEG activation in 1-month-old infants of depressed mothers. *Development and Psychopathology, 9,* 491–505.

Kagan, J. (1994). *Galen's prophecy: Temperament in human nature.* New York: Basic Books.

Kagan, J. (1997). Temperament and the reactions to unfamiliarity. *Child Development, 68,* 139–143.

Kagan, J. (1998). Biology and the child. In W. Damon & N. Eisenberg (Eds.), *Handbook of child psychology: Vol. 3. Social, emotional, and personality development* (pp. 177–235). New York: Wiley.

Kagan, J., Reznick, J. S., & Snidman, N. (1987). The physiology and psychology of behavioral inhibition in children. *Child Development, 58,* 1459–1473.

Kagan, J., Snidman, N., Zentner, M., & Peterson, E. (1999). Infant temperament and anxious symptoms in school age children. *Development and Psychopathology, 11,* 209–224.

Kanner, L. (1943). Autistic disturbances of affective contact. *Nervous Child, 2* 217–250.

Kaufman, J., & Charney, D. (2001). Effects of early stress on brain structure and function: Implications for understanding the relationship between child maltreatment and depression. *Development and Psychopathology, 13,* 451–471.

Keck, P. E., & McElroy, S. L. (2003). Redefining mood stabilization. *Journal of Affective Disorders, 73,* 163–169.

Keltner, D., & Kring, A. M. (1998). Emotion, social function, and psychopathology. *Review of General Psychology, 2,* 320–342.

Keltner, D., Moffitt, T. E., & Stouthamer-Loeber, M. (1995). Facial expressions of emotion and psychopathology in adolescent boys. *Journal of Abnormal Psychology, 104,* 644–652.

Kendall, P. C., Aschenbrand, S. G., & Hudson, J. L. (2003). Child-focused treatment of anxiety. In A. Kazdin & J. Weisz (Eds.), *Evidence-based psychotherapies for children and adolescents* (pp. 81–100). New York: Guilford Press.

Kendler, K. S., Walters, E. E., Neale, M. C., Kessler, R. C., Heath, A. C., & Eaves, L. J. (1995). The structure of the genetic and environmental risk factors for six major psychiatric disorders in women: Phobia, generalized anxiety disorder, panic disorder, bulimia, major depression, and alcoholism. *Archives of General Psychiatry, 52,* 374–383.

Kessler, R. C. (1994). The National Comorbidity Survey of the United States. *International Review of Psychiatry, 6,* 365–376.

Kessler, R. C., Rubinow, D. R., Holmes, C., Abelson, J. M., & Zhao, S. (1997). The epidemiology of DSM-III-R bipolar I disorder in a general population survey. *Psychological Medicine, 27,* 1079–1089.

Kiehl, K. A., Smith, A. M., Hare, R. D., Mendrek, A., Forster, B. B., Brink, J., et al. (2001). Limbic abnormalities in affective processing by criminal psychopaths as revealed by functional magnetic resonance imaging. *Biological Psychiatry, 50,* 677–684.

Klein, D. N., & Depue, R. A. (1984). Continued impairment in persons at risk for bipolar affective disorder: Results of a 19-month follow-up study. *Journal of Abnormal Psychology, 93,* 345–347.

Klein, D. N., Depue, R. A., & Slater, J. F. (1985). Cyclothymia in the adolescent offspring of parents with bipolar affective disorder. *Journal of Abnormal Psychology, 94,* 115–127.

Klein, D. N., Depue, R. A., & Slater, J. F. (1986). Inventory identification of cyclothymia: IX. Validation in offspring of bipolar I patients. *Archives of General Psychiatry, 43,* 441–445.

Klein, D. N., Lewinsohn, P. M., & Seeley, J. R. (1996). Hypomanic personality traits in a community sample of adolescents. *Journal of Affective Disorders, 38,* 135–143.

Kling A., & Brothers, L. (1992). The amygdala and social behavior. In J. P. Aggleton (Ed.), *The amygdala* (pp. 353–378). New York: Wiley.

Kobak, R., Little, M., Race, E., & Acosta, M. C. (2001). Attachment disruptions in seriously emotionally disturbed children: Implications for treatment [Special issue: Attachment in mental health institutions]. *Attachment and Human Development, 3,* 243–258.

Kochanska, G., Forman, D. R., & Coy, K. C. (1999). Implications of the mother-child relationship in infancy for socialization in the second year of life. *Infant Behavior and Development, 22,* 249–265.

Kochanska, G., & Murray, K. (2000). Mother-child mutually responsive orientation and conscience development: From toddler to early school age. *Child Development, 71,* 417–431.

Kopp, C. B. (1989). Regulation of distress and negative emotions: A developmental view. *Developmental Psychology, 25,* 343–354.

Kraemer, G. W. (1992). A psychobiological theory of attachment. *Behavioral and Brain Sciences, 15,* 493–541.

Kring, A. M., & Bachorowski, J. A. (1999). Emotions and psychopathology. *Cognition and Emotion, 13,* 575–599.

Kring, A. M., & Neale, J. M. (1996). Do schizophrenics show a disjunctive relationship among expressive, experiential, and psychophysiological components of emotion? *Journal of Abnormal Psychology, 102,* 249–257.

Krueger, R. F. (1999a). Personality traits in late adolescence predict mental disorders in early adulthood: A prospective-epidemiological study. *Journal of Personality, 67,* 39–65.

Krueger, R. F. (1999b). The structure of common mental disorders. *Archives of General Psychiatry, 56,* 921–926.

Krueger, R. F., Caspi, A., Moffitt, T. E., Silva, F., & McGee, R. (1996). Personality traits are differentially linked to mental disorders: A multitrait-multidiagnosis study of an adolescent birth cohort. *Journal of Abnormal Psychology, 105,* 299–312.

Landry, S. H., Smith, K. E., Swank, P. R., Assel, M. A., & Vellet, S. (2001). Does early responsive parenting have a special importance for children's development or is consistency across early childhood necessary? *Developmental Psychology, 37,* 387–403.

Lang, P. J. (1995). The emotion probe: Studies of motivation and attention. *American Psychologist, 50,* 372–385.

Lavoie, K. L., Miller, S. B., Conway, M., & Fleet, R. P. (2001). Anger, negative emotions, and cardiovascular reactivity during interpersonal conflict in women. *Journal of Psychosomatic Research, 51,* 503–512.

Lazarus, R. S. (1991). *Emotion and adaptation.* New York: Oxford University Press.

LeDoux, J. E. (1996). *The emotional brain: The mysterious underpinnings of emotional life.* New York: Simon & Schuster.

LeDoux, J. E., Romanski, L., & Xagoraris, A. (1989). Indelibility of subcortical emotional memories. *Journal of Cognitive Neuroscience, 1,* 238–243.

LeDoux, J. E., Sakaguchi, A., Iwata, J., & Reis, D. J. (1986). Interruption of projections from the medial geniculate body to an archneostriatal field disrupts the classical conditioning of emotional responses to acoustic stimuli in the rat. *Neuroscience, 17,* 615–627.

LeDoux, J. E., Sakaguchi, A., & Reis, D. J. (1984). Subcortical efferent projections of the medial geniculate nucleus mediate emotional responses conditioned by acoustic stimuli. *Journal of Neuroscience, 4,* 683–698.

Lemerise, E. A., & Arsenio, W. F. (2000). An integrated model of emotion processes and cognition in social information processing. *Child Development, 71,* 107–118.

Lemerise, E. A., & Dodge, K. A. (2000). The development of anger and hostile interactions. In M. Lewis & J. M. Haviland-Jones (Eds.), *Handbook of emotions* (pp. 594–606). New York: Guilford Press.

Levinson, K. L. (1999). *The development of internalizing symptoms in economically disadvantaged children: Effects of caregiver emotionality, family instability, child gender, and temperament.* Newark: University of Delaware, Department of Psychology.

Lewinsohn, P. M., Seeley, J. R., Buckley, M. E., & Klein, D. N. (2002). Bipolar disorder in adolescence and young adulthood. *Child and Adolescent Psychiatric Clinics of North America, 11,* 461–476.

Lewis, H. (1971). *Shame and guilt in neurosis.* New York: International Universities Press.

Lewis, M. (1993). Self-conscious emotions: Embarrassment, pride, shame, and guilt. In M. Lewis & J. M. Haviland (Eds.), *Handbook of emotions* (pp. 563–573). New York: Guilford Press.

Lewis, M. (1995). *Shame: The exposed self.* New York: Free Press.

Lewis, M., Feiring, C., & Rosenthal, S. (2000). Attachment over time. *Child Development, 71,* 707–720.

Lewis, M., & Granic, I. (Eds.). (2000). *Emotion, development, and self-organization.* New York: Cambridge University Press.

Loeber, R., & Coie, J. D. (2001). Continuities and discontinuities of development, with particular emphasis on emotional and cognitive components of disruptive behaviour. In J. Hill & B. Maughan (Eds.),

Conduct disorders in childhood and adolescence: Cambridge child and adolescent psychiatry (pp. 379–407). New York: Cambridge University Press.

Loehlin, J. C. (1992). *Genes and environment in personality development* (Vol. 2). Thousand Oaks, CA: Sage.

Lonigan, C. J., Hooe, E. S., David, C. F., & Kistner, J. A. (1999). Positive and negative affectivity in children: Confirmatory factor analysis of a two-factor model and its relation to symptoms of anxiety and depression. *Journal of Consulting and Clinical Psychology, 67,* 374–386.

Lord, C., & Paul, R. (1997). Language and communication in Autism. In D. J. Cohen & F. R. Volkmar (Eds.), *Handbook of Autism and pervasive developmental disorders* (2nd ed., pp. 195–225). New York: Wiley.

Lozano, B. E., & Johnson, S. L. (2001). Can personality traits predict increases in manic and depressive symptoms? *Journal of Affective Disorders, 63,* 103–111.

Maedgen, J. W., & Carlson, C. L. (2000). Social functioning and emotional regulation in the attention deficit hyperactivity disorder subtypes. *Journal of Clinical Child Psychology, 29,* 30–42.

Markus, H. R., & Kitayama, S. (1991). Culture and the self: Implications for cognition, emotion, and motivation. *Psychological Review, 98,* 224–253.

Marshall, A. G., & Izard, C. E. (1972). Depression as a pattern of emotions and feelings: Factor-analytic investigations. In C. E. Izard (Ed.), *Patterns of emotions: A new analysis of anxiety and depression* (pp. 237–254). New York: Academic Press.

Martins, C., & Gaffan, E. A. (2000). Effects of early maternal depression on patterns of infant-mother attachment: A meta-analytic investigation. *Journal of Child Psychology and Psychiatry, 41,* 737–746.

Mash, E. J., & Wolfe, D. A. (1999). *Abnormal child psychology.* New York: Brooks/Cole Wadsworth.

Matsumoto, D. (1990). Cultural similarities and differences in display rules. *Motivation and Emotion, 14,* 195–214.

Matthews, G., & Gilliland, K. (1999). The personality theories of H. J. Eysenck and J. A. Gray: A comparative review. *Personality and Individual Differences, 26,* 583–626.

Maughan, A., & Cicchetti, D. (2002). Impact of child maltreatment and interadult violence on children's emotional regulation abilities and socioemotional adjustment. *Child Development, 73,* 1525–1542.

Mayer, J. D., & Salovey, P. (1997). What is emotional intelligence? In P. S. D. Sluyter (Ed.), *Emotional development and emotional intelligence: Implications for educators* (pp. 3–31). New York: Basic Books.

McBurnett, K., Lahey, B. B., Rathouz, P. J., & Loeber, R. (2000). Low salivary cortisol and persistent aggression in boys referred for disruptive behavior. *Archives of General Psychiatry, 57,* 38–43.

McCrae, R. R., & Costa, P. T. (1986). Clinical assessment can benefit from recent advances in personality psychology. *American Psychologist, 41,* 1001–1003.

McGee, G. G., Feldman, R. S., & Chernin, L. (1991). A comparison of emotional facial displays by children with Autism and typical preschoolers. *Journal of Early Intervention, 15,* 237–245.

McNally, R. J. (1996). Cognitive bias in the anxiety disorders. In D. A. Hope (Ed.), *Nebraska Symposium on Motivation: Vol. 43. Perspectives on anxiety, panic, and fear* (pp. 211–250). Lincoln: University of Nebraska Press.

Mehrabian, A. (1995a). Distinguishing depression and trait anxiety in terms of basic dimensions of temperament. *Imagination, Cognition and Personality, 15,* 133–143.

Mehrabian, A. (1995b). Framework for a comprehensive description and measurement of emotional states. *Genetic, Social, and General Psychology Monographs, 121,* 339–361.

Mehrabian, A. (1996). Pleasure-arousal-dominance: A general framework for describing and measuring individual differences in temperament. *Current Psychology: Developmental, Learning, Personality, Social, 14,* 261–292.

Mehrabian, A. (1997). Comparison of the PAD and PANAS as models for describing emotions and for differentiating anxiety from depression. *Journal of Psychopathology and Behavioral Assessment, 19,* 331–357.

Meltzoff, A. N., & Moore, M. K. (1983). Newborn infants imitate adult facial gestures. *Child Development, 54,* 702–709.

Miller, A. L., Fox, N. A., Cohn, J. F., Forbes, E. E., Sherrill, J. T., & Kovacs, M. (2002). Regional patterns of brain activity in adults with a history of childhood-onset depression: Gender differences and clinical variability. *American Journal of Psychiatry, 159,* 934–940.

Miller, E. K., & Cohen, J. D. (2001). An integrative theory of prefontal cortex function. *Annual Review of Neuroscience, 24,* 167–202.

Milner, J. S. (1993). Social information processing and physical child abuse. *Clinical Psychology Review, 13,* 275–294.

Mineka, S., Watson, D., & Clark, L. A. (1998). Comorbidity of anxiety and unipolar mood disorders. *Annual Review of Psychology, 49,* 377–412.

Morrison, J., Frank, S., Holland, C., & Kates, W. (1999). Emotional development and disorders in young children in the child welfare system. In J. Silver, B. Amster, & T. Haecker (Eds.), *Young children and foster care: A guide for professionals* (pp. 33–64). Baltimore: Paul H. Brookes.

Moses, L. J., Baldwin, D. A., Rosicky, J. G., & Tidball, G. (2001). Evidence for referential understanding in the emotions domain at twelve and eighteen months. *Child Development, 72,* 718–735.

Mostow, A. J., Izard, C. E., Fine, S. E., & Trentacosta, C. J. (2002). Modeling the emotional, cognitive, and behavioral predictors of peer acceptance. *Child Development, 73,* 1775–1787.

Mrazek, P. J. (1993). Maltreatment and infant development. In C. H. Zeanah Jr. (Ed.), *Handbook of infant mental health* (pp. 159–170). New York: Guilford Press.

Northoff, G., & Bermpohl, F. (2004). Cortical midline structures and the self. *Trends in Cognitive Sciences, 8,* 102–107.

Osterling, J., & Dawson, G. (1994). Early recognition of children with Autism: A study of first birthday home videotapes. *Journal of Autism and Developmental Disorders, 24,* 247–257.

Ozonoff, S. (1995). Executive functions in Autism. In E. Schopler & G. B. Mesibov (Eds.), *Learning and cognition in Autism* (pp. 199–219). New York: Plenum Press.

Ozonoff, S., Pennington, B. F., & Rogers, S. J. (1990). Are there emotion perception deficits in young autistic children? *Journal of Child Psychology and Psychiatry and Allied Disciplines, 31,* 343–361.

Panksepp, J. (2001). The long-term psychobiological consequences of infant emotions: Prescriptions for the twenty-first century. *Infant Mental Health Journal, 22,* 132–173.

Papolos, D. F. (1999). *The bipolar child: The definitive and reassuring guide to childhood's most misunderstood disorder.* New York: Broadway Books.

Patrick, C. J. (1994). Emotion and psychopathy: Startling new insights. *Psychophysiology, 31,* 319–330.

Pliszka, S. R., Sherman, J. O., Barrow, M. V., & Irick, S. (2000). Affective disorder in juvenile offenders: A preliminary study. *American Journal of Psychiatry, 157,* 130–132.

Plutchik, R. (1980). A general psychoevolutionary theory of emotion. In R. Plutchik & H. Kellerman (Eds.), *Emotion: Theory, research, and experience* (pp. 3–33). New York: Academic Press.

Plutchik, R. (1993). Emotions and their vicissitudes: Emotions and psychopathology. In M. Lewis & J. M. Haviland (Eds.), *Handbook of emotions* (pp. 53–66). New York: Guilford Press.

Pollak, S. D., Cicchetti, D., Hornung, K., & Reed, A. (2000). Recognizing emotions in faces: Developmental effects of child abuse and neglect. *Developmental Psychology, 36,* 679–688.

Pollak, S. D., Cicchetti, D., & Klorman, R. (1998). Stress, memory, and emotion: Developmental considerations from the study of child maltreatment. *Development and Psychopathology, 10,* 811–828.

Pollak, S. D., Cicchetti, D., Klorman, R., & Brumaghim, J. T. (1997). Cognitive brain event-related potentials and emotion processing in maltreated children. *Child Development, 68,* 773–787.

Pollak, S. D., & Sinha, P. (2002). Effects of early experience on children's recognition of facial displays of emotion. *Developmental Psychology, 38,* 784–791.

Porges, S. W. (1992). Autonomic regulation and attention. In B. A. Campbell & H. Hayne (Eds.), *Attention and information processing in infants and adults: Perspectives from human and animal research* (pp. 201–223). Hillsdale, NJ: Erlbaum.

Porges, S. W. (2001). The polyvagal theory: Phylogenetic substrates of a social nervous system. *International Journal of Psychophysiology, 42,* 123–146.

Porges, S. W. (2002). Polyvagal theory: Three neural circuits regulate behavioral reactivity. *Psychological Science Agenda, 15,* 9–11.

Porges, S. W. (2003). Polyvagal theory: Phylogenetic contributions to social behavior. *Physiology and Behavior, 79,* 503–513.

Porges, S. W., Doussard-Roosevelt, J. A., Portales, A. L., & Greenspan, S. I. (1996). Infant regulation of the vagal "brake" predicts child behavior problems: A psychobiological model of social behavior. *Developmental Psychobiology, 29,* 697–712.

Porter, F. L., Porges, S. W., & Marshall, R. E. (1988). Newborn pain cries and vagal tone: Parallel changes in response to circumcision. *Child Development, 59,* 495–505.

Posner, M., & Rothbart, M. (2000). Developing mechanisms of self-regulation. *Development and Psychopathology, 12,* 427–441.

Post, R. M., Leverich, G. S., Xing, G., & Weiss, S. R. B. (2001). Developmental vulnerabilities to the onset and course of bipolar disorder. *Development and Psychopathology, 13,* 581–598.

Quay, H. C. (1993). The psychobiology of undersocialized aggressive conduct disorder: A theoretical perspective [Special issue: Toward a developmental perspective on conduct disorder]. *Development and Psychopathology, 5,* 165–180.

Quay, H. C. (1997). Inhibition and attention deficit hyperactivity disorder. *Journal of Abnormal Child Psychology, 25,* 7–13.

Raver, C. C., & Spagnola, M. (2002). "When my mommy was angry, I was speechless": Children's perceptions of maternal emotional expressiveness within the context of economic hardship. *Marriage and Family Review, 34,* 63–88.

Rosen, J. B., & Schulkin, J. (1997). From normal fear to pathological anxiety. *Psychological Review, 105,* 325–350.

Rothbart, M., Ahadi, S., & Evans, D. (2000). Temperament and personality: Origins and outcomes. *Journal of Personality and Social Psychology, 78,* 122–135.

Russell, J. A. (1980). A circumplex model of affect. *Journal of Personality and Social Psychology, 39,* 1161–1178.

Russell, J. A., & Carroll, J. M. (1999). On the bipolarity of positive and negative affect. *Psychological Bulletin, 125,* 3–30.

Russell, J. A., & Mehrabian, A. (1977). Evidence for a three-factor theory of emotions. *Journal of Research in Personality, 11,* 273–294.

Salovey, P., & Mayer, J. D. (1990). Emotional intelligence. *Imagination, Cognition and Personality, 9,* 185–211.

Sapolsky, R. M., Krey, L. C., & McEwen, B. S. (1986). The neuroendocrinology of stress and aging: The glucocorticoid cascade hypothesis. *Endocrinology Review, 7,* 284–301.

Schachter, S., & Singer, S. (1962). Cognitive, social, and physiological determinants of emotional state. *Psychological Review, 69,* 379–399.

Schultz, D. (2000). *Emotion attributions, behavioral functioning, and sociometric status.* Unpublished doctoral dissertation. University of Delaware, Newark.

Schultz, D., Izard, C. E., & Ackerman, B. P. (2000). Children's anger attributional bias: Relations to family environment and social adjustment. *Social Development, 9,* 284–301.

Schultz, D., Izard, C. E., & Bear, G. G. (2004). Emotionality, emotion information processing, and aggression. *Development and Psychopathology, 16,* 371–387.

Schwartz, D., & Proctor, L. J. (2000). Community violence exposure and children's social adjustment in the school peer group: The mediating roles of emotion regulation and social cognition. *Journal of Consulting and Clinical Psychology, 68,* 670–683.

Seligman, M. E. P., & Peterson, C. (1986). A learned helplessness perspective on childhood depression: Theory and research. In M. Rutter, C. E. Izard, & P. B. Read (Eds.), *Depression in young people: Developmental and clinical perspectives* (pp. 223–250). New York: Guilford Press.

Sheline, Y. I. (2000). 3D MRI studies of neuroanatomic changes in unipolar major depression: The role of stress and medical comorbidity. *Biological Psychiatry, 48,* 791–800.

Shields, A., & Cicchetti, D. (1997). Emotion regulation among school-age children: The development and validation of a new criterion Q-sort scale. *Developmental Psychology, 33,* 906–916.

Shields, A., & Cicchetti, D. (2001). Parental maltreatment and emotion dysregulation as risk factors for bullying and victimization in middle childhood. *Journal of Clinical Child Psychology, 30,* 349–363.

Shields, A., Ryan, R. M., & Cicchetti, D. (2001). Narrative representations of caregivers and emotion dysregulation as predictors of maltreated children's rejection by peers. *Developmental Psychology, 37,* 321–337.

Shiller, V. M., Izard, C. E., & Hembree, E. A. (1986). Patterns of emotion expression during separation in the Strange Situation procedure. *Developmental Psychology, 22,* 378–382.

Shipman, K. L., & Zeman, J. (2001). Socialization of children's emotion regulation in mother-child dyads: A developmental psychopathology perspective. *Development and Psychopathology, 13,* 317–336.

Shweder, R. A. (1988). Suffering in style. *Culture, Medicine, and Psychiatry, 12,* 479–497.

Sigman, M. (1998). The Emanuel Miller Memorial Lecture 1997: Change and continuity in the development of children with Autism. *Journal of Child Psychology and Psychiatry, 39,* 817–827.

Sigman, M., & Capps, L. (1997). *Children with Autism: A developmental perspective.* Cambridge, MA: Harvard University Press.

Sigman, M., Dissanayuke, C., Arbelle, S., & Ruskin, E. (1997). Cognition and emotion in children and adolescents with Autism. In D. J. Cohen & F. R. Volkmar (Eds.), *Handbook of Autism and pervasive developmental disorders* (2nd ed., pp. 901–919). New York: Wiley.

Sigman, M., Kasari, C., Kwon, J., & Yirmiya, N. (1992). Responses to the negative emotions of others by autistic, mentally retarded, and normal children. *Child Development, 63,* 796–807.

Simons, R. F., Fitzgibbons, L., & Fiorito, E. (1993). Emotion-processing in anhedonia. In N. Birbaumer & A. Ohman (Eds.), *The organization of emotion* (pp. 288–306). Toronto: Hogrefe-Huber.

Smider, N. A., Essex, M. J., Kalin, N. H., Buss, K. A., Klein, M. H., Davidson, R. J., et al. (2002). Salivary cortisol as a predictor of socioemotional adjustment during kindergarten: A prospective study. *Child Development, 73*, 75–92.

Snow, M. E., Hertzig, M. E., & Shapiro, T. (1987). Expression of emotion in young autistic children. *Journal of the American Academy of Child and Adolescent Psychiatry, 26*, 836–838.

Spielberger, C. D. (1999). *State-Trait Anger Expression Inventory, revised research edition 2*. Odessa, FL: Psychological Assessment Resources.

Spielberger, C. D., Reheiser, E. C., & Sydeman, S. J. (1995). Measuring the experience, expression, and control of anger. In H. Kassinove (Ed.), *Anger disorders: Definition, diagnosis, and treatment* (pp. 49–67). Washington, DC: Taylor & Francis.

Stafford, B., Zeanah, C. H., & Scheeringa, M. (2003). Exploring psychopathology in early childhood: PTSD and attachment disorders in DC: 0–3 and *DSM-IV. Infant Mental Health Journal, 24*, 398–409.

Stevens, D., Charman, T., & Blair, R. J. R. (2001). Recognition of emotion in facial expressions and vocal tones in children with psychopathic tendencies. *Journal of Genetic Psychology, 162*, 201–211.

Streeck-Fischer, A., & van der Kolk, B. A. (2000). Down will come baby, cradle and all: Diagnostic and therapeutic implications of chronic trauma on child development. *Australian and New Zealand Journal of Psychiatry, 34*, 903–918.

Sullivan, R. M., & Gratton, A. (2002). Prefrontal cortical regulation of hypothalamic-pituitary-adrenal function in the rat and implications for psychopathology: Side matters. *Psychoneuroendocrinology, 27*, 99–114.

Suomi, S. J. (1991). Uptight and laid-back monkeys: Individual differences in the response to social challenges. In S. E. Brauth, W. S. Hall, & R. J. Dooling (Eds.), *Plasticity of development* (pp. 27–56). Cambridge, MA: MIT Press.

Sweeten, T. L., Posey, D. J., Shekhar, A., & McDougle, C. J. (2002). The amygdala and related structures in the pathophysiology of Autism. *Pharmacology, Biochemistry, and Behavior, 71*, 449–455.

Tangney, J. P., Wagner, P. E., Barlow, D. H., Marschall, D. E., & Gramzow, R. (1996). Relation of shame and guilt to constructive versus destructive responses to anger across the lifespan. *Journal of Personality and Social Psychology, 70*, 797–809.

Tangney, J. P., Wagner, P., Fletcher, C., & Gramzow, R. (1992). Shamed into anger? The relation of shame and guilt to anger and self-reported aggression. *Journal of Personality and Social Psychology, 62*, 669–675.

Tellegen, A., Watson, D., & Clark, L. A. (1999). On the dimensional and hierarchical structure of affect. *Psychological Science, 10*, 297–303.

Termine, N. T., & Izard, C. E. (1988). Infants' responses to their mothers' expressions of joy and sadness. *Developmental Psychology, 24*, 223–229.

Thayer, R. E. (1967). Measurement of activation through self-report. *Psychological Reports, 20*, 663–678.

Thayer, R. E. (1996). *The origin of everyday moods: Managing energy, tension, and stress*. New York: Oxford University Press.

Thayer, R. E. (2001). *Calm energy: How people regulate mood with food and exercise*. New York: Oxford University Press.

Thompson, R. A. (1994). Emotion regulation: A theme in search of definition. *Monographs of the Society for Research in Child Development, 59*, 25–52, 250–283.

Thompson, R. A., & Calkins, S. D. (1996). The double-edged sword: Emotional regulation for children at risk. *Development and Psychopathology, 8*, 163–182.

Tomarken, A. J., & Keener, A. D. (1998). Frontal brain asymmetry and depression: A self-regulatory perspective. *Cognition and Emotion, 12*, 387–420.

Tomkins, S. S. (1962). *Affect, imagery, consciousness: Vol. I. The positive affects*. New York: Springer.

Tomkins, S. S. (1963). *Affect, imagery, consciousness: Vol. II. The negative affects*. New York: Springer.

Trentacosta, C. J., Izard, C. E., Mostow, A. J., & Fine, S. E. (2001). *Anger attribution bias and an emotion-centered preventive intervention*. Unpublished manuscript. University of Delaware: Newark, DE.

Tronick, E. Z., & Weinberg, M. K. (1997). Depressed mothers and infants: Failure to form dyadic states of consciousness. In P. Cooper & L. Murray (Eds.), *Postpartum depression and child development* (pp. 54–81). New York: Guilford Press.

Tucker, D. M. (2001). Motivated anatomy: A core-and-shell model of corticolimbic architecture. In G. Gainotti (Ed.), *Handbook of neuropsychology* (2nd ed., Vol. 5, pp. 125–160). New York: Elsevier Science.

van der Kolk, B. A., & Fisler, R. E. (1994). Childhood abuse and neglect and loss of self-regulation. *Bulletin of the Menninger Clinic, 58*, 145–168.

van Ijzendoorn, M. J., Schuengel, C., & Bakermans-Kranenburg, M. J. (1999). Disorganized attachment in early childhood: Meta-analysis of precursors, concomitants, and sequelae. *Development and Psychopathology, 11*, 225–249.

Vondra, J. I., Shaw, D. S., Swearingen, L., Cohen, M., & Owens, E. B. (2001). Attachment stability and emotional and behavioral regulation from infancy to school age. *Development and Psychopathology, 13*, 13–33.

Wakefield, J. C. (1997). When is development disordered? Developmental psychopathology and the harmful dysfunction analysis of mental disorder. *Development and Psychopathology, 9*, 269–290.

Walcott, C. M., & Landau, S. (2004). The relation between disinhibition and emotion regulation in boys with attention deficit hyperactivity disorder. *Journal of Clinical Child and Adolescent Psychology, 33*, 772–782.

Wang, A. T., Dapretto, M., Hariri, A. R., Sigman, M., & Bookheimer, S. Y. (2004). Neural correlates of facial affect processing in children and adolescents with Autism spectrum disorder. *Journal of the American Academy of Child and Adolescent Psychiatry, 43*, 481–490.

Waterhouse, L., & Fein, D. (1997). Perspectives on social impairment. In D. J. Cohen & F. R. Volkmar (Eds.), *Handbook of Autism and pervasive developmental disorders* (2nd ed., pp. 901–919). New York: Wiley.

Watson, D. (2000a). Affect and psychopathology. In D. Watson (Ed.), *Mood and temperament* (pp. 235–261). New York: Guilford Press.

Watson, D. (Ed.). (2000b). *Mood and temperament*. New York: Guilford Press.

Watson, D., & Clark, L. A. (1984). Negative affectivity: The disposition to experience aversive emotional states. *Psychological Bulletin, 96*, 465–490.

Watson, D., & Clark, L. A. (1992). Affects separable and inseparable: On the arrangement of the negative affects. *Journal of Personality and Social Psychology, 62*, 489–505.

Watson, D., Clark, L. A., & Harkness, A. R. (1994). Structures of personality and their relevance to psychopathology [Special issue: Personality and psychopathology]. *Journal of Abnormal Psychology, 103*, 18–31.

Watson, D., Clark, L. A., Weber, K., Assenheimer, J. S., Strauss, M. E., & McCormick, R. A. (1995). Testing a tripartite model: II. Exploring the symptom structure of anxiety and depression in student, adult, and patient samples. *Journal of Abnormal Psychology, 104*, 15–25.

Watson, D., & Tellegen, A. (1985). Toward a consensual structure of mood. *Psychological Bulletin, 98,* 219–235.

Watson, D., Weber, K., Assenheimer, J. S., Clark, L. A., Strauss, M. E., & McCormick, R. A. (1995). Testing a tripartite model: I. Evaluating the convergent and discriminant validity of anxiety and depression symptom scales. *Journal of Abnormal Psychology, 104,* 3–14.

Watson, D., Wiese, D., Vaidya, J., & Tellegen, A. (1999). The two general activation systems of affect: Structural findings, evolutionary considerations, and psychobiological evidence. *Journal of Personality and Social Psychology, 76,* 820–838.

Weeks, S. J., & Hobson, R. P. (1987). The salience of facial expression for autistic children. *Journal of Child Psychology and Psychiatry and Allied Disciplines, 28,* 137–151.

White, T. L., & Depue, R. A. (1999). Differential association of traits of fear and anxiety with norepinephrine- and dark-induced pupil reactivity. *Journal of Personality and Social Psychology, 77,* 863–877.

Wozniak, J., & Biederman, J. (1997). Childhood mania: Insights into diagnostic and treatment issues. *Journal of the Association for Academic Minority Physicians, 8,* 78–84.

Wozniak, J., Biederman, J., Kiely, K., Ablon, J. S., Faraone, S., Mundy, E., et al. (1995). Mania-like symptoms suggestive of childhood-onset bipolar disorder in clinically referred children. *Journal of the American Academy of Child and Adolescent Psychiatry, 34,* 867–876.

Yirmiya, N., Kasari, C., Sigman, M., & Mundy, P. (1989). Facial expressions of affect in autistic, mentally retarded and normal children. *Journal of Child Psychology and Psychiatry and Allied Disciplines, 30,* 725–735.

Yirmiya, N., Sigman, M., Kasari, C., & Mundy, P. (1992). Empathy and cognition in high-functioning children with Autism. *Child Development, 63,* 150–160.

Youngstrom, E. A., Frazier, T. W., & Butt, Z. A. (2003). *The ugly emotions: Evidence for a third emotional dimension of dominance.* Manuscript submitted for publication

Zahn-Waxler, C., Friedman, R. J., Cole, P. M., Mizuta, I., & Hiruma, N. (1996). Japanese and United States preschool children's responses to conflict and distress. *Child Development, 67,* 2462–2477.

Zero to Three. (1994). *Diagnostic classification of mental health and developmental disorders of infancy and early childhood.* Washington, DC: Author.

Zivin, G. (1986). Processes of expressive behavior development. *Merrill-Palmer Quarterly, 32,* 103–140.

Zuckerman, M. (1999). *Vulnerability to psychopathology: A biosocial model.* Washington, DC: American Psychological Association.

Zuckerman, M., Joireman, J., Kraft, M., & Kuhlman, D. M. (1999). Where do motivational and emotional traits fit within three factor models of personality? *Personality and Individual Differences, 26,* 487–504.

CHAPTER 9

Joint Attention, Social Competence, and Developmental Psychopathology

PETER MUNDY and MARIAN SIGMAN

Starting as early as 3 to 6 months of age, infants begin to develop the remarkable capacity to coordinate their attention with a social partner in relation to some third object or event (D'Entremont, Hains, & Muir, 1997; Morales, Mundy, & Rojas, 1998; Scaife & Bruner, 1975). Bruner and Sherwood (1983) referred to this as joint attention skill development. In the 1st years of life, this involves the social integration of overt aspects of visual attention, as when a toddler shows a toy to a parent. Theoretically, though, this capacity is elaborated with development and comes to involve the social coordination of covert aspects of attention, such as when social partners coordinate attention to psychological phenomena, such as ideas, intentions, and emotions. Joint attention plays a role in many aspects of human social interaction, including when a 6-year-old child sits in class on the first day of first grade and tries to follow the attention and ideas of his teacher, or when a 16-year-old

child sits in the basement of her home in Moscow exchanging jokes with her friends, or when a 46-year-old father exchanges eye contact with his 14-year-old son to share his pleasure in witnessing beautiful waves breaking off the north shore of Kauai. Indeed, processes involved in joint attention contribute to social interactions, social learning, and social cognition across the life span (Baldwin, 1995; Mundy, 2003; Tomasello, 1995).

Theory and research on this domain have most frequently focused on the relations of joint attention to language development and social cognition in young children (e.g., Bruner, 1975; Carpenter, Nagell, & Tomasello, 1998). This perspective has been productive and has provided new insights into the nature of early atypical, as well as typical, development (e.g., Baldwin, 1995; Carpenter et al., 1998; Corkum & Moore, 1998; Morales et al., 1998; Mundy & Neal, 2001; Sigman & Ruskin, 1999; Ulvund & Smith, 1996; Yoder & Warren, 2002). However, what may be less well recognized is that, in addition to social cognition, joint attention development also reflects a developmental integration of social executive

The preparation of this chapter was supported by a grant from NICHD to the first author (RO1 HD38052).

and social motivation processes (e.g., Mundy, 1995, 2003; Mundy, Sigman, & Kasari, 1993; Sigman, 1998). Moreover, this integration of early executive, motivation, and social-cognitive processes suggests that infant joint attention may be fundamental to the development of social competence in childhood, as well as developmental psychopathology (e.g., Goldsmith & Rogoff, 1997; Mundy & Willoughby, 1996, 1998; Sheinkopf, Mundy, Claussen, & Willoughby, 2004).

Over the past 2 decades the importance of comprehending the foundations of social competence has become increasingly clear to clinical and developmental science. Social competence contributes to a wide array of adaptive outcomes among children, from school readiness and academic success (Blair, 2002; Raver, 2002) to risk and resilience in the face of vulnerability for developmental psychopathology (Masten & Coatsworth, 1998). Social competence, though, is a complex construct. Definitions typically emphasize a capacity for a prosocial behavior style that involves numerous processes, including (1) the ability to regulate attention and emotional reactivity in the dynamic flow of social interaction; (2) the ability to self-monitor, correct errors, and integrate the behavior of self with others in positive goal-related activity; and (3) the tendency to express agreeableness, interest in others, and positive emotions with peers and adults (Eisenberg et al., 1997; Masten & Coatsworth, 1998; Rothbart & Bates, 1998).

One approach to the study of social competence has been to define and measure processes in infancy that presumably contribute to the foundation for the subsequent mature expression of facility with social interaction and exchange. In this regard, research has most frequently concentrated on attachment and related patterns of early parent-child interactions, as well as investigations of temperament to understand the development of emotional and self-regulatory processes that emerge in the first few years of life (e.g., Calkins & Fox, 2002; Fox, Henderson, Rubin, Calkins, & Schmidt, 2001; Kochanska, Murray, & Coy, 2000; Masten & Coatsworth, 1998; Rothbart, Posner, & Rosicky, 1994). These avenues of research have provided powerful insights into the nature and development of social competence (Masten & Coatsworth, 1998). However, the complexity of this domain is such that additional lines of inquiry are required to fully understand the factors involved in socially competent behavior. In this regard, we suggest that measures of infant joint attention skills development provide information about early social communicative, social emotion, and social-neurodevelopment that are indispensable to a veridical understanding of human social competencies.

Several different forms of joint attention typically develop in the 3- to 18-month period of infancy (Bates, Camaioni, & Volterra, 1976; Carpenter et al., 1998; Seibert, Hogan, & Mundy, 1982). One form involves the infant's ability to follow the direction of gaze, head turn, and/or pointing gesture of another person (Scaife & Bruner, 1975). This behavior may be referred to as the "responding to joint attention" skill (RJA; Mundy et al., 2003; Seibert et al., 1982). Another type of skill involves the infant's use of eye contact and/or deictic gestures (e.g., a pointing or showing) to spontaneously initiate coordinated attention with a social partner. This type of protodeclarative act (Bates et al., 1976) may be referred to as the "initiating joint attention" skill (IJA; Mundy et al., 2003; Seibert et al., 1982). These behaviors, especially IJA, appear to serve social functions. That is, the goal and reinforcement of these behaviors seem to revolve around the sharing of experience with others and the positive valence such early social sharing has for young children (Bates et al., 1976; Mundy, 1995; Rheingold, Hay, & West, 1976). Alternatively, social attention coordination may also be used for less social but more instrumental purposes (Bates et al., 1976). For example, infants and young children may use eye contact and gestures to initiate attention coordination with another person to elicit aid in obtaining an object or event. This may be referred to as a protoimperative act (Bates et al., 1976) or "initiating behavior regulation/requests" (IBR; Mundy et al., 2003). This chapter focuses on these three types of behaviors, which are illustrated in Figure 9.1.

There are at least five distinct but overlapping strands of theory that forge connections between joint attention and the subsequent development of social competence (Mundy & Willoughby, 1996, 1998; Sheinkopf et al., 2004). Perhaps the most obvious notion is that joint attention is related to language development (e.g., Baldwin, 1995) and language development is related to social competence (e.g., Baker & Cantwell, 1987; Beitchman, Hood, & Inglis, 1990). Therefore, joint attention may be related to the development of social competence in children as an epiphenomenon of its relations to language development. However, longitudinal research suggests that, even after controlling for variance associated with differences in language development, infant joint attention predicts differences in the development of preschool to school-age social competencies in samples of typically developing children, as well as "at risk" and developmentally disordered children (Acra, Mundy, Claussen, Scott, & Bono, 2003; Lord, Floody, Anderson, & Pickles, 2003; Sheinkopf et al., 2004; Sigman & Ruskin, 1999; Vaughan et al., 2004). Clearly, other avenues of connection between joint attention and social outcomes

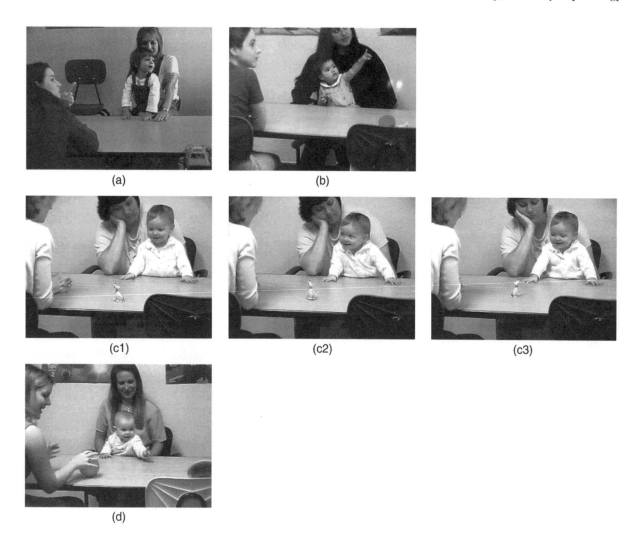

Figure 9.1   Illustrations of (a) responding to joint attention-RJA; (b) initiating joint attention-IJA, "pointing:' (c) IJA, "alternating gaze"; and (d) initiating behavior regulating/resuests-IBR, "pointing" from the Early Social Communication Scales. *Sources:* From "Assessing Interactional Competencies: The Early Social Communication Scales," by J. M. Seibert, A. E. Hogan, and P. C. Mundy, 1982, *Infant Mental Health Journal, 3,* pp. 244–245; and *A Manual for the Abridged Early Social Communication Scales (ESCS),* by P. Mundy et al., 2003, available from the University of Miami Psychology Department, Coral Gables, FL, at pmundy@miami.edu.

need to be considered. Therefore, after reviewing the longitudinal data on this issue, research and theory connected to four complementary and related models of the links between infant joint attention and social competence are examined. These models of joint attention development are (1) the caregiver/scaffolding model (e.g., Bakeman & Adamson, 1984; Bruner, 1975; Siller & Sigman, 2002; Tomasello & Farrar, 1986), (2) the social-cognitive model (e.g., Baron-Cohen, 1995; Bretherton, 1991; Bruner, 1975; Tomasello, 1995), (3) the social motivation model (e.g., Dawson, Munson, et al., 2002; Hobson, 1993; Mundy, 1995; Trevarthen & Aitken, 2001), and (4) the neurodevelopmental executive function model (e.g., Dawson, Munson,

et al., 2002; Griffith, Pennington, Wehner, & Rogers, 1999; Mundy, Card, & Fox, 2000; Vaughan & Mundy, in press).

This chapter examines the nature and validity of these models. Prior to arriving at this appraisal, a more concrete sense of our view of the fundamental linkage between infant joint attention and social competence may be better appreciated if one considers the following assertion. Joint attention measures provide an index of individual differences in processes associated with the capacity of infants (and ultimately children) to pay attention to what others attend to and to share experiences in social interactions (see Figure 9.1). As noted earlier, we assume that the capacity to pay attention to what others attend to is essential to adaptive participation in social interactions, not just in infancy but *throughout the life span.* Indeed, it is difficult to think of infants and children effectively participating in social learning opportunities with caregivers, peers, or teachers without sufficient mastery of this capacity. Reciprocally, a disturbance in the tendency to attend to what others attend to may make important contributions to several forms of childhood psychopathology, such as Attention-Deficit/Hyperactivity Disorder (ADHD) and other externalizing disorders, as well as the Pervasive Developmental Disorders, including Autism. We believe that measures of joint attention provide a singularly important but relatively unrecognized window onto executive, motivational, cognitive, and environmental processes that early on contribute to stable differences in the development of social attention management and social competence throughout the life span. The primary goal of this chapter is to stimulate further thought and research on this assertion.

To this end, we must speak to the potential *incremental validity* of measures of infant joint attention in the study of social competence. Other measures of infant development have been both theoretically and empirically related to the development of social competence in childhood. As previously noted, these involve but are not limited to measures of infant attention management and related self-regulatory processes, attachment, empathy, and dimensions of temperament (e.g., Blair, 2002; Kochanska et al., 2000; Masten & Coatsworth, 1998; Rothbart & Bates, 1998). It makes little sense to champion the unique and vital contribution of joint attention research if measures of this domain simply provide an alternative route of access to processes that are well measured by more commonly used research paradigms. In this regard, we believe it is important to note that the ecological context of joint attention assessment is quite different from that of other attention management and self-regulatory measures in infancy. The latter often involve the observation of the behavioral activation or inhibition of children *in response* to externally imposed social task demands (e.g., Kochanska, Coy, & Murray, 2001) or to a social challenge, as in the Strange Situation attachment assessment paradigm (Ainsworth, Bell, & Stayton, 1972). However, mature social competence presumably involves the appropriate initiation of positive social behaviors, as well as appropriate responses *to* the social behaviors and demands of other people. Examining only behavior *responses* to task demands or social challenges may give an incomplete picture of processes involved in the development of social competence. Infant joint attention measures provide an important complement in this regard because they involve observations of the tendency of infants to

spontaneously initiate social attention bids in the context of semistructured interactions with others, as well as observations of the ability to respond to the social bids of a social partner (see Figure 9.1; Mundy et al., 2003). This facet of measurement may allow research on infant joint attention to provide a more complete picture of the potentially different motivation, self-regulatory, and social-cognitive processes involved in initiating and responding to social behaviors (Mundy, 1995, 2003; Mundy et al., 1993, 2000).

It is also important to recognize that measures of joint attention may be conducted in the context of either caregiver-infant interactions (Bakeman & Adamson, 1984) or infant-tester interactions (Seibert et al., 1982). By comparing responses and patterns of correlations across data from both paradigms it is possible to better understand which aspects of social competence in infants are specific to interactions with their caregivers versus more general features of their social presentation that are expressed with strangers as well as familiar caregivers. Thus, it is possible to examine the generalizability of social processes associated with infant joint attention. This, as we will see, may be especially critical when examining the degree to which joint attention and attachment processes reflect unique or overlapping processes associated with the development of social competence in young children.

DEVELOPMENTAL PSYCHOPATHOLOGY AND JOINT ATTENTION

It is also an aim of this chapter to illustrate one of the distinguishing principles that guides research within a developmental psychopathology perspective. The developmental examination of maladaptive and psychopathological behaviors can elucidate disorders and is also integral to understanding the processes that are essential to human nature (Cicchetti, 1984, 1990; Rutter, 1986). This is very much the case with respect to understanding the fundamental importance of joint attention to human nature. Much of the theory described in this chapter initially grew out of our clinical research on Autism (e.g., Mundy & Sigman, 1989; Sigman & Capps, 1997; Sigman & Mundy, 1989).

Autism is a neurodevelopmental syndrome (Dawson, Webb, et al., 2002) personified by a robust disturbance of social competence with syndrome-specific deficits in joint attention skill development (Mundy & Sigman, 1989; Mundy, Sigman, Ungerer, & Sherman, 1986; Sigman, 1998). Attempts to better understand the connection between joint attention disturbance and impaired social competencies in children affected by Autism led to observations that young children's tendencies to initiate joint attention (IJA) bids involved emotional processes as well as cognitive processes (Kasari, Sigman, Mundy, & Yirmiya, 1990; Mundy, Kasari, & Sigman, 1992). It also led to research demonstrating that individual differences in IJA were related to parents' perception of the social relatedness of their children with Autism, as well as parent reports of relatedness among children with typical development (Mundy, Sigman, & Kasari, 1994). These findings stimulated our initial theory on the points of continuity between infant joint attention and childhood social competence (Mundy & Willoughby, 1996, 1998), as well as a series of unique empirical observations on the continuity between joint attention and preschool or childhood social development that is described in this chapter (Acra et al., 2003; Sheinkopf et al., 2004; Sigman & Ruskin, 1999; Vaughan et al., 2003).

The presumptive biological nature of Autism also kindled efforts to understand the neurodevelopment of joint attention (Dawson, Munson, et al., 2002; Griffith et al., 1999; Hendersen, Yoder, Yale, & McDuffie, 2002; McEvoy, Rogers, & Pennington, 1993; Mundy et al., 2000). This, in turn, contributed to theory linking joint attention to frontal executive systems involved in self-monitoring (Mundy, 2003; Nichols, Fox, & Mundy, 2005), social motivations, and affective expressivity (Mundy, 1995; Venezia, Messinger, Thorp, & Mundy, 2004), or those systems involved in mediating sensitivity to the reinforcement value of social interactions (Dawson, Munson, et al., 2002; Mundy, 1995; Nichols et al., 2005) and self-regulation (Morales, Mundy, Crowson, Neal, & Delgado, 2005). The possible commonality between joint attention and these potentially frontally mediated processes provides a new and essential component to theory on the links between infant joint attention, social competence, and developmental psychopathology. Moreover, these observations, stemming from the initial study of Autism, open up new vistas on the nature of the neural systems and functions that may support the fundamental human capacity for experience sharing and cultural cognition (Mundy, 2005). The discussion of this new neuropsychological perspective on joint attention development takes center stage in one of the final sections of this chapter. In the concluding section, we further elaborate on this developmental psychopathology perspective by discussing how joint attention research and theory, stemming initially from considerations most relevant to Autism, may be brought to bear on other topics in child psychopathology, such as ADHD and risk and resilience associated with maltreatment.

Each of the topics introduced in the preceding sections of this chapter is discussed in more detail following an overview of the nature and measurement of infant joint attention development.

JOINT ATTENTION: THEORY AND MEASUREMENT

The construct of joint attention has been a focus for research and theory for some time. In their attempt to understand symbolic development, Werner and Kaplan (1963) described one aspect of the environment that stimulated representational and symbolic development in infancy as the "primordial sharing" situation, in which an infant and social partner were aware of their common perceptions of the same object. Harriet Rheingold and her colleagues (1976) marveled at the change in social facilities that occurred as children increased their bids to share the experience of objects in the later part of the 2nd year. The work of these scholars, as well as several others, alerted many in the community of developmental scientists to the essential role that the emergent capacity for joint attention may play in early development. However, at least with regard to our own circumscribed efforts, the related but independent work of Jerome Bruner and Elizabeth Bates and their colleagues spurred much of our research and theory on this aspect of early development. Bruner (1975) suggested that any complete theory of language development, including modular theories (Chomsky, 1965), must recognize that infants become adept at social attention coordination and related social communication skills prior to the emergence of spoken words. In Bruner's view, these skills reflected the emergence of a general, non-linguistic cognitive platform that contributed to subsequent language development. This perspective was based on numerous empirical observations, including research that indicated that some infants as young as 6 months could follow the direction of gaze, head turn, and pointing gesture of a social partner (Scaife & Bruner, 1975). The later observation was rather unexpected because the prevailing notion at the time was that infants were egocentric and could not adopt the perspective of others until after the 2nd year of life (Piaget, 1952). Nevertheless, it is a replicable observation (Morales et al., 1998), with some recent studies suggesting that the incipient appearance of this skill may occur as early as 3 to 4 months (e.g., D'Entremont et al., 1997). Scaife and Bruner's paradigm for measuring gaze following became the template for one measure of infant joint attention, referred to herein as "responding to joint attention" (RJA, Seibert et al., 1982; see Figure 9.1a).

Concurrent with Bruner's contributions, Bates and her colleagues (Bates, Benigni, Bretherton, Camaioni, &

Volterra, 1979) borrowed from the study of linguistic pragmatics to develop a functional taxonomy of the different types of intentional, social communication bids that infants display. Bates et al. distinguished between behaviors infants used to initiate episodes of joint attention for declarative purposes (protodeclaratives) and behaviors used for instrumental or imperative purposes (protoimperatives). The implicit goal of declaratives is to share the experience of an object or event with a social partner, and the motivation or reinforcement of the behavior is thought to stem in large part from the visual regard or emotional response of the social partner to the child (Bates et al., 1976; Mundy, 1995). The prototypic behavior here is showing a toy to a partner; pointing and alternating eye contact may also be used for this protodeclarative function (see Figures 9.1b and 9.1c).

Instead of the social motivation to share experiences with others, protoimperatives are used to elicit assistance from a social partner in obtaining an object or an event. Here the reinforcement appears to be obtaining the object or event rather than the social regard or emotional response of the partner. Hence, the motivation and reinforcement for the development of this type of behavior is regarded as less social. The use of eye contact, reaching, and pointing to elicit aid in obtaining an object that is beyond the infant's grasp exemplify this type of behavior (see Figure 9.1d). The terminology used by Seibert et al. (1982) to refer to the former as "initiating joint attention" skills (IJA) and the latter as "initiating behavior regulation/requesting" skills (IBR) is used in this chapter. Most of the research and theory covered in this chapter pertains to RJA, IJA, and IBR.

Concurrent with the contributions of Bruner, Bates, and others, theory was emerging on an intrinsic motivation system for human relatedness and communication. Trevarthen and Hubley (1978) proposed a human motivational system basic to episodes of intersubjectivity or shared awareness with others. This motivation system guides goal-directed social behaviors from early infancy and is expressed in terms of two developmental stages involving "primary" and "secondary" intersubjectivity. Primary intersubjectivity occurs early on (0 to 6 months) and reflects an infant motivational system that promotes the tendency to use and respond to eye contact, facial affect, vocal behavior, and body posture in interactions with caregivers. This primarily dyadic interactive phase of social development provides the information and experience that, in combination with cognitive maturation, allows infants to begin to develop representations of self and other as having both distinct and shared affective experience. That is, they become capable of "secondary intersubjectivity," or a conscious awareness of both self and other sharing an experience (Tomasello, 1995; Trevarthen & Hubley, 1978). The emergence of secondary intersubjectivity is thought to occur between 6 and 18 months and the experience of secondary intersubjectivity has positive reinforcement value for the child. Therefore, it also contributes to ongoing motivation for social interactions (Tronick, 1998).

In social interactions in the 9- to 18-month period, the capacity for secondary intersubjectivity increasingly supports infants' abilities to engage in intentional social communication with others, as evidenced by the more frequent and systematic use of eye contact, conventional gestures, and signal-repair strategies (Rheingold et al., 1976; Tomasello, 1995; Trevarthen & Aitken, 2001). Intentional participation in communication implicitly suggests that infants are aware that social partners have the mental capacity to receive and interpret communicative signals. Hence, the notion of secondary intersubjectivity has become central to much of the theory and research that emphasizes that infant joint attention skills reflect the incipient development of social cognition or knowledge about other people (e.g., Bretherton, 1991; Carpenter et al., 1998; Moore, 1996; Tomasello, 1995). This social-cognitive perspective on intersubjectivity and joint attention has become the prominent model for theory and research on this domain (e.g., Carpenter et al., 1998). Indeed, it may be so prominent that other important processes involved in this domain have received less attention than they warrant. The work of several research groups (Adamson & MacArthur, 1995; Kasari et al., 1990; Trevarthen & Aitken 2001; Tronick, 1998) reminds us that a consideration of motivational processes may be necessary to a veridical understanding of the role of joint attention in social development. Moreover, in addition to social cognition and motivation, there has been relatively little recognition of the possibility that joint attention development may also reflect the interplay of attention/self-regulation processes with social-cognitive and social-motivation processes (Dawson, Munson et al., 2002; Mundy et al., 2000). The result has been a lack of an integrated multiprocess approach to theory and research on joint attention. This may have reflected the nature of the goals, questions, and levels of measurement researchers have chosen to emphasize in their research.

Measurement Issues and the Self-Organizing Hypothesis

One principal goal of developmental research on joint attention has been to define the ages at which specific types of social attention coordination skills first emerge (e.g.,

Bakeman & Adamson, 1984; Butterworth & Jarrett, 1991; Carpenter et al., 1998; Corkum & Moore, 1998). Related to this approach has been the goal of better defining when social cognition truly emerges in infancy (Tomasello, 1995). Consequently, experimental and longitudinal research has often emphasized the analysis of age group differences and the use of categorical or ordinal measurement. In particular, researchers have utilized criterion-related mastery of one or another type of joint attention skill to separate children into groups: (1) those who appear capable of a specific aspects of joint attention and social cognition at a particular age and (2) those who do not appear capable of a specific skill at a specific age. For example, Carpenter et al. used criterion scores to rate the age of onset of joint attention skills in a sample of 24 infants in their seminal study of joint attention skills development. This is a viable and useful approach. It enabled these researchers to examine processes that were related to age-related shifts in joint attention development. However, all paradigms have strengths and weaknesses, and one weakness of this approach is that it fosters a discontinuous view of joint attention development. Criterion-referenced measures may encourage the view that joint attention skills are either present or absent in young children.

Within an age group, though, infants often display a significant range of individual differences on any measure of joint attention development (e.g., Carpenter et al., 1998; Corkum & Moore, 1998; Morales et al., 1998; Mundy & Gomes, 1998; Scaife & Bruner, 1975). For example, at 6 months of age infants display a range of RJA abilities (Morales et al., 1998). These skills may not be consolidated in a majority of infants at this time, so the *average* age of mastery of RJA may be after about 8 or 9 months (Corkum & Moore, 1998). Nevertheless, evidence of the development of this skill is clear in *some* infants at an earlier age. So, is the correct estimate for age of onset of this skill when some infants first display RJA (perhaps 6 months) or when most infants display this skill (perhaps 9 months)? Equally, if not more, important is the observation that after the onset of a joint skill for *most* children, such as pointing to share attention, infants display significant individual differences with regard to how frequently or consistently they use this skill in social interactions (e.g., Henderson et al., 2002; Mundy et al., 2000).

Some may argue that these individual differences reflect measurement error. However, several studies now indicate that observations of these individual differences carry meaningful information about early social development. Individual differences in the frequency and consistency of joint attention behaviors, especially IJA and RJA,

display significant levels of longitudinal stability or test-retest reliability in the 9- to 18-month period (Block et al., 2003; Mundy et al., 2000; Mundy & Gomes, 1998; Sheinkopf et al., 2004). The stability in IJA is even evident across different interactive partners (i.e., infant-tester versus infant-caregiver paradigms) in the 9- to 12-month period (Vaughan et al., 2003). As was noted earlier, individual differences in infants' expression of IJA, RJA, and even IBR also appear to be meaningfully related to later preschool cognitive and behavioral outcomes (e.g., Carpenter et al., 1998; Sheinkopf et al., 2004; Sigman & Ruskin, 1999; Ulvund & Smith, 1996). Hence it seems unlikely that individual differences in infant joint attention simply reflect measurement error.

Relatively little research has focused on examining the nature and meaning of individual differences in early joint attention. Indeed, the degree to which individual differences are considered to be an essential topic varies with the level of measurement employed in research. For example, when using dichotomous age-of-onset measures, Carpenter et al. (1998, p. 110) may have been quite correct in stating that

> whereas such things as attention following . . . are very likely prerequisites of word learning and, therefore, should be related to the ability to acquire words, there is no reason to suspect that the age of emergence of these skills for a given infant should be related in a systematic way to the number of words an infant acquires.

However, a shift from a categorical (present or absent) level of measurement to the interval or ratio level of measurement involved in measuring the frequencies of joint attention behaviors displayed by infants (e.g., Mundy & Gomes, 1998) lends itself to a rather different perspective. Indeed, there may be fundamental reasons for the expectations that individual differences on measures of the frequency or consistency of use of joint attention bids should be related to the rate of lexical development, as well as other aspects of development in young children. This in part is because, beyond the measurement of social-cognitive maturational status, joint attention measures may also provide indices of critical features of the social interactive style of young children that play a *self-organizing* role in their development (Baldwin, 1995; Mundy & Neal, 2001).

Much of early learning takes place in unstructured or incidental social learning situations, and theory suggests that joint attention skills assist infants in organizing social information processing in these situations (Baldwin, 1995). In language learning, for example, much of early lexical acquisition takes place in unstructured or incidental social learning situations where parents provide learning opportunities by referring to a new object or event, but infants need to discriminate among a number of potential referents in the environment to focus on the correct object/event in order to acquire the appropriate new word-object/event association. The correct discrimination among potential referents allows infants to avoid possible referential mapping errors (Baldwin, 1995). To improve the chance of correct discriminations infants utilize the direction of gaze of the parent (i.e., use RJA skill) to limit the number of potential stimuli to attend to and increase the likelihood of a correct word-learning experience (Baldwin, 1995). Similarly, when infants initiate bids for joint attention, the responsive caregiver may follow the child's line of regard and take advantage of the child's focus of attention to provide a new word in a context that maximizes the opportunity to learn (cf. Tomasello, 1995).

Beyond learning language, the self-organizing function of joint attention may also play an important role in social development. Theoretically, joint attention involves an integration of information about self-experience of an object or event with information about how others experience the same object or event. Therefore, the more frequently infants engage in joint attention, the more comparative social information they have for building richer representations of self and other (Mundy et al., 1993). Moreover, the more they engage in joint attention, the more practiced they become in the types of social attention management that is necessary for facile participation in social interactions. Finally, it is also the case that the positive affective component of initiating joint attention bids (see Figure 9.1) may contribute to a positive sense of relatedness between caregiver and infant. Therefore, some aspects of joint attention may serve to elicit positive nurturance from primary or secondary caregivers, which contributes to a decrease in developmental vulnerability among some at-risk groups of children (Mundy & Willoughby, 1996, 1998). Unfortunately, it may also be the case that a robust attenuation of joint attention leads to a severe impoverishment of self-organized social information processing that impairs typical early social behavior development, and even social neurodevelopment (Mundy & Crowson, 1997; Mundy & Neal, 2001). Hence, joint attention may be regarded as an early developing *self-organizing facility* that serves to elicit and/or organize social information input in a manner that optimizes early social learning and social development (e.g., Baldwin, 1995; Bruner, 1975; Mundy & Neal, 2001; Mundy & Willoughby, 1998). This hypothesis is consistent with the broader, long-standing notion that infants and chil-

dren may make substantial contributions to their own development (e.g., Bell, 1979; Sameroff, 2000; Scarr, 1992).

Several corollaries follow from this aspect of theory on joint attention development. If joint attention reflects a self-organizing facility in early development, then the more consistent or frequent use of joint attention skills may lead to more and clearer social learning opportunities for infants. Therefore, reliable or stable individual differences in the frequency of joint attention skill utilization by infants and children may be expected to relate not only to lexical development, but to a host of other developmental outcomes as well (Mundy & Gomes, 1998; Mundy & Willoughby, 1996, 1998). For example, it would seem at least plausible that the frequency or especially the consistency with which 5-year-olds use joint attention-related skills could contribute to their success in negotiating the new demands of teacher-related didactic social information flow in the classroom or the novel peer-related social information flow on the playground. It may well be that the 5-year-old who can consistently follow the attention of teachers and peers has an easier time adapting to the academic and social demands of kindergarten than does the 5-year-old who is less facile with this aspect of joint attention.

Second, this aspect of theory suggests it may be very important to understand the factors that contribute to individual differences in the frequency of joint attention during development. In this regard, it is possible that differences in frequency of use of joint attention may reflect differences in the consistency with which children utilize social cognition in social interactions. However, to the best of our knowledge, current theory on social cognition does not describe either the mechanisms or the phenomenology of the processes that would contribute to individual differences in joint attention utilization among children. Alternatively, research and theory on the social motivation processes derived from experience or temperamental factors, as well as the contribution of attention regulation and self-regulation for joint attention has been formulated in part based on attempts to understand individual differences in this domain of development, may contribute to differences in the tendency of infants and children to employ their joint attention skills (e.g., Morales et al., 2005; Sheinkopf et al., 2004; Vaughan et al., 2003). Thus, simply by moving from a level of measurement associated with questions about age of onset to questions about individual or clinical group differences, new and important perspectives on infant joint attention development may be revealed.

This chapter focuses on studies that employed the latter types of measures to examine individual differences in infant joint attention development. Support for the self-organizing hypothesis of joint attention development is presented later in the chapter (e.g., Bono, Daley, & Sigman, 2004; Crowson, 2001), and the factors that give rise to individual differences in infants' frequency of use of different types of joint attention skills are considered.

MEASUREMENT ISSUES: CAREGIVER VERSUS TESTER-INFANT INTERACTION PARADIGMS

Another interesting measurement issue in joint attention research concerns the context of assessment. It was previously noted that joint attention might be assessed in an infant-caregiver interaction paradigm (Bakeman & Adamson, 1984; Tomasello & Farrar, 1986) or in the context of an infant-tester paradigm (Bates et al., 1979; Seibert et al., 1982; Wetherby & Prutting, 1984). The infant-caregiver interaction paradigm emphasizes dyadic measures of the duration or frequency of interactive episodes where both the caregiver and child are focused on the same object or event during a period of free play. These periods of infant-caregiver shared attention may be referred to as *episodes of joint engagement*. Hypothetically, because of the familiarity of the interactive partner, this paradigm may provide data on the optimal capacity of the infant to participate in joint attention or episodes of joint engagement. Indeed, in the period of development between 9 and 24 months, significant differences have been observed in the tendency for infant-caregiver dyads to engage in episodes of joint engagement (e.g., Carpenter et al., 1998; Thorp, 2005). However, because the level of measurement involves observations of the dyad (i.e., the behavior of both partners in semistructured interactions), it is often difficult to tease apart the contribution of infants and caregivers in understanding the causal influences that contribute to developmental differences in joint engagement.

Alternatively, in the infant-tester paradigm, the influence of the social partner on the infant may be reduced by training testers to use responsive but standardized patterns of interactive behaviors. For example, in the Early Social Communication Scales (ESCS; Mundy et al., 2003; Seibert et al., 1982), tester behavior is yoked to the infant's behavior. That is, during the assessment, the tester maintains neutral affect as much as possible and minimizes movements and verbalizations until the infant's direct communicative bids to the tester. Upon observing a bid from the infant, the tester responds warmly and enthusiastically, but briefly, and then returns to a neutral interactive and affective state. By minimizing movement, verbal behavior, and

affect until the infant bids, this paradigm presumably yields a clearer picture of differences in the infant's tendency to spontaneously initiate joint attention bids. However, it is possible that the novelty of interactions with the testers may attenuate social communicative behavior for some infants relative to their behavior in interactions with a caregiver. This concern is mitigated to some degree by the observation that infants in the 2nd year tend to display as many affective communicative signals to strangers as they do to their mother (Jones & Tarja, 1989).

Although both paradigms have been used for over 2 decades, little is known about the relations of data derived from infant-tester paradigms and infant-caregiver joint attention paradigms. Recently, however, significant but modest correlations were observed between the tendency to display IJA on the ESCS and infants' tendency to alternate eye contact between a caregiver and a common referent in episodes of joint engagement (Vaughan et al., 2003). There is also some evidence that differences among infants in the frequency and types of joint attention behaviors displayed on the ESCS predict subsequent dyadic measures of frequency or duration of episodes of joint engagement (Crowson, 2001; Markus-Meyer, Mundy, Morales, Delgado, & Yale, 2000). Furthermore, the tendency of infants to initiate joint attention on the ESCS has been observed to correlate with parent report of social behaviors in typical and at-risk infants (Acra et al., 2003: Mundy et al., 1994; Vaughan et al., 2004).

These data suggest that young children may display significant consistency in the degree to which they initiate and participate in joint attention with strangers and caregivers. The operative word here, though, is "suggests," as far too little work has been done on this vital issue to yield firm conclusions at this time. Nevertheless, recent research provides support for the reliability and validity of the type of infant-tester measures of joint attention that are the focus of discussion in this chapter. With this background in mind, let us begin a more detailed consideration of the role of joint attention in research on developmental psychopathology and social competence. Our own work in this regard began with research that attempted to better define the nature of the social impairments of Autism.

JOINT ATTENTION, AUTISM, AND DEVELOPMENTAL PSYCHOPATHOLOGY

Autism is a biologically based disorder that may be more prevalent than once thought, occurring at a rate of 3 to

6:1,000 (Dawson, Osterling, Rinaldi, Carver, & McPartland, 2001; Fombonne, 2003). It is characterized by impaired social and communication development (Bailey, Philips, & Rutter, 1996; Kanner, 1943). However, prior to the 1980s, very little empirical work had been undertaken to define the nature of the social impairments that were characteristic of these children (Howlin, 1978; Mundy & Sigman, 1989; Sigman, Ungerer, Mundy, & Sherman, 1987). This paucity of information contributed to what was initially a poorly developed diagnostic system for Autism. Indeed, 20 years ago there was only one descriptive item for the social deficits of Autism in the *Diagnostic and Statistical Manual of Mental Disorders III,* "a pervasive lack of responsiveness to others" (American Psychiatric Association, 1980), and this remained the sole criterion of the social impairments of this syndrome until late in the 1980s (e.g., American Psychiatric Association, 1987). This descriptor was too broad to provide diagnostic precision. Moreover, it appeared to be inaccurate, as research indicated that many children with Autism responded to structured social learning environments, reacted when imitated by others, and displayed attachment behaviors (Mundy & Sigman, 1989; Sigman & Capps, 1997; Sigman & Ungerer, 1984). The overly broad and inaccurate nature of this criterion likely contributed substantially to an underestimation of the prevalence of Autism (see Wing & Potter, 2002, for a related discussion). Indeed, it was only with the publication of the most recent nosology (e.g., American Psychiatric Association, 1994) that we have had sufficiently well-articulated diagnostic criteria to begin to provide a clear and comprehensive description of the social impairments of Autism.

Rather than displaying a "pervasive lack of responsiveness to others," it has become clear that people with Autism display a *pattern of strengths and weaknesses* in the acquisition of social and communication skills, and this pattern changes with development (Mundy & Sigman, 1989). In part, this pattern of strengths and weaknesses in social communication is exemplified by a robust failure to adequately develop RJA and IJA skills. Alternatively, children with Autism are less impaired in IBR skills to communicate their instrumental needs (Curcio, 1978; Loveland & Landry, 1986; Mundy et al., 1986; Sigman, Mundy, Ungerer, & Sherman, 1986; Wetherby & Prutting, 1984).

Joint attention disturbance in Autism may be central to what Kanner (1943) described as the children's inability to relate themselves in the ordinary way to people and situations. In particular, it seemed possible to us that an absence of the shared affective acknowledgment of objects or events

that is integral to IJA behavior in infancy (see Figure 9.1) contributed to a sense of "a lack of relatedness" that clinicians often used in making the diagnosis of Autism with young children (Mundy & Sigman, 1989). Subsequently, the notion that joint attention disturbance is central to the pathology of Autism has become incorporated into many diagnostic and screening instruments (Baron-Cohen et al., 1996; Charman, 1998; Lord et al., 1999; Stone, Coonrod, & Ousley, 2000). Indeed, research on joint attention served to identify and provide an operational definition of the social symptom criteria used in the fourth edition of the *Diagnostic and Statistical Manual,* such as "a lack of spontaneous seeking to share enjoyment, interests, or achievements with other people (e.g., by a lack of showing, bringing or pointing out objects of interest)" (American Psychiatric Association, 2000, p. 75).

Numerous detailed reviews of the research on joint attention and Autism are available (e.g., Charman, 1998; Leekam, Lopez, & Moore, 2000; Mundy & Burnette, in press; Sigman & Kasari, 1995), so we do not repeat these efforts here. In brief, though, observations suggest that joint attention disturbance may be manifest in children with Autism at least as early as between 12 and 18 months of age (e.g., Osterling, Dawson, & Munson, 2002; Swettenham et al., 1998). Although early on in life children with Autism display important deficits in both IJA and RJA skills, the impairment in RJA appears to remit to a significant degree with development (Leekam et al., 2000; Mundy et al., 1994). The impairment in IJA, however, remains robust even in older children (Baron-Cohen, 1995; Sigman & Ruskin, 1999). IJA deficits are related to cognitive and language outcomes in children with Autism (Mundy et al., 1991; Sigman & Ruskin, 1999), as well as parent reports of social symptom intensity (Mundy et al., 1994) and long-term social behavioral outcomes among children with Autism (Lord et al., 2003; Sigman & Ruskin, 1999). In addition, they also appear to be related to the tendency of children with Autism to express and share positive affect with others (Kasari et al., 1990). Interestingly, though, neither IJA nor RJA disturbance seems to be related to attachment in these children (Capps, Sigman, & Mundy, 1994), and many children with Autism do not exhibit evidence of disturbance relative to developmental control samples on measures of attachment (Sigman & Mundy, 1989). These observations were among the first to suggest that joint attention and attachment may reflect distinct developmental domains.

Although IJA may reflect a more robust locus of social impairment in Autism, this is not to say that delays in RJA development are not important. Recent research suggests that RJA development may be critical to early intervention responsiveness in young children with Autism. Bono et al. (2004) followed the development of 29 children with Autism between approximately 4 and 5 years of age. Data on the amount of time children were in structured interventions per week were collected, as were data on joint attention using the ESCS. Data from standardized language assessments were also gathered. The results revealed that across this 1-year period, both IJA and RJA were significantly related to language gains. Surprisingly, though, amount of intervention was only weakly related to language gain across the 1-year interval. However, a significant conditional intervention effect was observed such that positive effects for intervention intensity on language were observed for children with better-developed RJA skills. Thus, the relative frequency or consistency of joint attention behaviors displayed by children with Autism may be a marker of individual differences in intervention responsively among these children. Such a possibility was anticipated by theory on the role of joint attention impairment as both a symptom of Autism and as part of the etiology of the developmental disorder of Autism (Mundy & Crowson, 1997). The findings of Bono et al., 2004 are also quite consistent with the hypothetical self-organizing function of joint attention, at least among children with Autism.

INFANT JOINT ATTENTION AND CHILDHOOD SOCIAL COMPETENCE: LONGITUDINAL STUDIES

Observations that joint attention impairments are integral to the social developmental disturbance of Autism are important for several reasons. They provide much needed information about the nature of this disorder that has contributed to improvements in the diagnosis and treatment of individuals and families affected by it (Mundy & Thorp, in press). Theoretically, these observations also support the hypothesis that infant joint attention reflects aspects of early development that are fundamental to the development of subsequent social competence in children. If this is true, then longitudinal research should reveal evidence of significant lines of continuity between infant joint attention and later measures of childhood social competence. Moreover, evidence of such links should be observable not only in samples of children with Autism but in other samples of children as well, including children with typical development; recent research suggests that this is the case. First,

we provide a more detailed synopsis of the longitudinal research on Autism cited in earlier sections of this chapter, then we consider research on at-risk and typically developing groups of infants.

In one of the first longitudinal studies to address this issue, Sigman and Ruskin (1999) followed a sample of 51 children with Autism for 6 to 8 years. At the beginning of this study, the children were 3 to 6 years old. They were assessed with the ESCS and other social-emotional measures, such as an index of empathy. Standardized cognitive and language data were also collected at the inception of this study. A variety of outcome data were collected, including measures of the frequency of initiations of play by the children with Autism with peers as an index of individual differences in social engagement. An important observation in this study was that IJA behavior in the children with Autism (as well as in a control sample) was a significant predictor of individual differences in social engagement 6 to 8 years later, even after considering covariance with language and cognitive development. Alternatively, RJA behavior was related to language but not to social outcomes in these children. In a related study, Travis, Sigman, and Ruskin (2001) also observed that measures of both IJA and empathy make significant concurrent contributions to the explanation of variance in the level of peer engagement and prosocial behavior in a structured task among higher-functioning 8- to 15-year-old children with Autism.

Similar to the data from Sigman and Ruskin (1999), longitudinal observations have recently been reported by Cathy Lord and her colleagues (2003). These researchers followed 95 children with Autism from 2 to 9 years of age. The intellectual and language levels of the children were assessed at the beginning of this study. Their social status was assessed with parent report on the Autism Diagnostic Interview (ADI) and with direct observations on the Autism Diagnostic Observation Schedule (ADOS). The ADI and the ADOS provide measures of IJA and RJA, in addition to composite social, communication, and repetitive behavior symptom domain scores. The IJA and RJA measures obtained from the ADOS are similar but not identical to those derived from the ESCS.

In their outcome assessments at age 9, Lord et al. (2003) used teachers' reported observations on the Penn Interactive Peer Play Scale (PIPPS; Fantuzzo et al., 1995) to assess social engagement and competence in the children with Autism. The PIPPS yields three factors: a prosocial Interaction measure, an avoidant Disconnection measure, and an externalizing Disruption measure that are combined into a total social engagement score. The results of the study indicated that neither ADI nor ADOS domain scores predicted social interaction outcome scores in this sample. However, ADOS IJA item scores predicted PIPPS total social engagement scores above and beyond variance associated with Verbal IQ. Thus, two studies using related but different methods have indicated that IJA measures significantly predict individual differences in the long-term social outcomes of children with Autism (Lord et al., 2003; Sigman & Ruskin, 1999).

As noted, it is not clear whether the observations of Sigman and Ruskin (1999) and Lord et al. (2003) reflect a general developmental phenomenon associated with joint attention or one that pertains only to the development of children with Autism. A recent study by Sheinkopf et al. (2004) begins to address this issue. These authors reported data from a longitudinal study of 30 infants with in utero cocaine exposure. Joint attention skills (i.e., IJA, RJA, and IBR) were assessed with the ESCS at 12, 15, and 18 months, and composite (average) measures of these domains were computed. These children were participants in a preschool intervention program at the University of Miami (the Linda Ray Intervention Center; LRIC); therefore, it was possible to gather social outcome data from preschool teacher reports of peer-related classroom behavior at 36 months. These reports were gathered using the Adaptive Social Behavior Inventory (ASBI; Hogan, Scott, & Bauer, 1992), the PIPPS (Fantuzzo et al., 1995), and selected subscales from the Child Behavior Checklist/2–3 (CBCL; Achenbach, 1992). There was considerable covariance among the data from these convergent methods. Therefore, the data from these measures were combined to yield reliable teacher report indices of three dimensions of problematic and adaptive behavior: (1) A *Disruptive Behavior* score was derived by standardizing and calculating the mean of CBCL Aggression, ASBI Disrupt, and PIPPS Disruption scales; (2) a *Withdrawn Behavior* score was derived by standardizing and calculating the mean of CBCL Anxiety, CBCL Withdrawn, and PIPPS Disconnection; and (3) a *Positive Social Behavior* score was derived by standardizing and calculating the mean of ASBI Comply, ASBI Express, and PIPPS Interaction.

The results indicated that IJA, RJA, and IBR each made significant contributions to the prediction of Disruptive Behavior. IJA and RJA were negatively associated with teacher reports of more disruptive behavior, and IBR positively related to this dimension (Sheinkopf et al., 2004). The results also indicated that RJA was negatively associated with teacher reports of Withdrawn Behavior but positively associated with Positive Social Behavior. Thus, processes associated with IJA appeared to be associated

with decreased risk for externalizing disturbance in this sample. Processes associated with RJA were also associated with decreased risk for externalizing and internalizing disturbances and an increased likelihood of displaying what preschool teachers regarded as prosocial behaviors. Alternatively, it may have been that higher rates of IBR reflect an impulsive and object reward-driven style of behavior in this at-risk sample of young children that was associated with risk for externalizing disturbance. Finally, it is important to note that variance associated with cognition and language did not appear to mediate the associations between joint attention measures and social behavior outcomes in this study (Sheinkopf et al., 2004).

The Sheinkopf et al. (2004) study is perhaps the first to document continuity between joint attention development and childhood social development in groups of children other than those affected by Autism. However, it was not clear if the 36-month assessment in this study was too early to provide an optimal index of stable individual differences in the social outcomes of at-risk children. Preliminary results of a longer-term follow-up of LRIC children have been reported (Acra et al., 2003). In this study, outcome data were collected on 42 children at 6 to 7 years of age in first grade. Cognitive and language outcomes were measured with the Differential Abilities Scales (Elliot, 1990) and the Woodcock Language Proficiency Battery-Revised (WLPB-R; Woodcock, 1991). Social outcomes were examined with both teacher and parent report on the Social Skills Rating Scales (SSRS; Gresham & Elliot, 1990) and the Behavior Assessment System for Children (BASC; Reynolds & Kamphaus, 1992). The results indicated that joint attention measures were correlated with social outcomes as measured by both parent and teacher report data. Therefore, parent and teacher report data were combined into composite measures including a measure of Social Competence (parent and teacher SSRS Social Skills summary scores, BASC Adaptability summary scores, and BASC Social Skills summary scores) and a measure of Hyperactivity and Attention Problems (parent and teacher SSRS Hyperactivity scores, BASC Hyperactivity scores, and BASC Attention Problems scores).

Consistent with data reported by Sheinkopf et al. (2004), the zero-order correlations observed by Acra et al. (2003) revealed that 18-month IJA measures were positively related to first grade Social Competence but negatively associated with Hyperactivity and Attention Problems. Unlike the data from Sheinkopf et al., though, RJA was significantly associated with language development but not with social development in this study. Moreover, IBR displayed the same pattern of correlations as did

IJA. That is, IBR displayed a significant positive association with Social Competence and a significant negative association with Hyperactivity and Attention Problems. Not surprising, though, cognition, language, and especially reading ability were also significantly correlated with Social Competence and Hyperactivity and Attention Problems. Multiple regression analyses revealed that 18-month IJA, but not IBR, made a significant contribution to both first grade Social Competence and Hyperactivity and Attention problems, after variance associated with this aspect of development (e.g., reading ability) was considered. Thus, infant IJA was observed to be the most consistent longitudinal correlate of social behavior outcomes in a high-risk sample (Acra et al., 2003; Sheinkopf et al., 2004), just as it was in samples of children with Autism (Lord et al., 2003; Sigman & Ruskin, 1999). However, it was still not clear from these findings whether the nature of associations between infant joint attention and social outcomes was sufficiently robust to be observed in samples with typical development, or whether these associations were limited to samples with atypical development.

Data relevant to this issue have been presented in a study by Vaughan et al. (2004), who examined the development of 41 typically developing infants from 12 to 30 months of age. At 12 months, ESCS data were collected on joint attention development. At 15 months, parent report data on dimensions of temperament that were expected to relate to executive and affective processes associated with joint attention and social outcomes were also assessed (e.g., Inhibitory Control, Attention Shifting, and Social Fear). A standardized cognitive and language assessment was administered at 24 months. Finally, at 30 months, social outcome was assessed with parent report data on the Infant-Toddler Social Emotional Assessment (ITSEA; Carter & Briggs-Gowan, 2000), which provided scaled scores for Externalizing Behavior, Social Competence, Internalizing Behavior, and Dysregulation.

Consistent with Sheinkopf et al. (2004), the results of this study indicated that both 12-month IJA and RJA were significantly and negatively related to ITSEA parent report measures of Externalizing. More frequent infant IJA bids and consistent RJA trial performance at 12 months were associated with parent ratings indicative of children who displayed less evidence of difficulty with impulsivity, defiance, high activity, and aggression at 30 months. Vaughan et al. (2004) also observed that IJA was negatively correlated with Internalizing behaviors but was positively and significantly correlated with a measure of Social Competence at 30 months. The latter provides parent reports concerning compliance, attention regulation, emotional awareness, and prosocial behaviors. Twelve-month IJA was significantly and positively associated with an index of cognitive development (Bayley Mental Index) at 24 months, consistent with previous reports of a link between infant IJA and childhood intellectual development (Ulvund & Smith, 1996). However, this association did not mediate the relation between IJA and social outcomes. Furthermore, 24-month parent ratings of temperament (e.g., Attention Regulation and Inhibitory Control) were significantly associated with 30-month ratings of social outcome on the ITSEA. However, neither IJA nor RJA was related to these 24-month temperament measures. Indeed, IJA, RJA, and Inhibitory Control had unique and significant paths of association with Externalizing. IJA and Inhibitory Control also displayed unique and significant associations with 30-month Social Competence.

Thus, the results of the Vaughn et al. (2004) study were similar to those of the Sheinkopf et al. (2004) study in that IJA and RJA were both related to social outcomes in the 2nd to 3rd year of life. Longer-term longitudinal studies of social outcomes in school-age children, though, suggest that IJA may have greater or more consistent predictive validity (Acra et al., 2003; Lord et al., 2003: Sigman & Ruskin, 1999). This pattern of data suggests that IJA and RJA may tap into distinct but overlapping constellations of processes that lead to differences in their predictive validity for social competence in childhood.

In the following sections, the nature of common and distinct processes that may serve to link infant joint attention with the development of social competence in childhood is considered in more detail.

UNDERSTANDING THE LINKS BETWEEN JOINT ATTENTION AND CHILDHOOD SOCIAL COMPETENCE

Several longitudinal studies provide some support for the contention that individual differences in infant joint attention are important and related to subsequent aspects of social competence and behavior disturbance in children. What processes, though, contribute to this important development link? One obvious possibility is that joint attention is associated with language development (e.g., Baldwin, 1995), and individual differences in language are associated with differences in social competence (Beitchman et al., 1990). This possibility, though, is mitigated to some extent by the observation that joint attention measures are related to social outcomes in children even after controlling for variance in performance on standardized language and cognitive measures (Acra et al., 2003; Sheinkopf et al., 2004; Sigman & Ruskin, 1999; Vaughan et al., 2004). This issue has by no means been definitively addressed. Nevertheless, these observations suggest the need to look beyond language to identify other factors that may be involved. Indeed, as previously noted, there are at least four conceptual models that are useful in organizing research and theory: (1) the caregiving/scaffolding model, (2) the social-cognitive model, (3) the social motivation model, and (4) the neurodevelopmental executive model.

The caregiving/scaffolding model proposes that adult or caregiver contributions are essential to providing the types of organized and responsive social interactions that allow infants to develop joint attention skills (e.g., Bruner, 1983; Goldsmith & Rogoff, 1997) and to subsequently develop social competence in childhood (Masten & Coatsworth, 1998). Therefore, continuity in caregiver behavior may contribute to the connections between infant joint attention and later social competence. In the social cognition model, the development or maturation of the capacity to understand others' thoughts, intentions, and feelings is thought to be crucial to joint attention development (e.g., Bretherton, 1991; Tomasello, 1995), and that social cognition is also essential for subsequent social competence (Dunn, 1995). The social motivation model suggests that joint attention skills reflect sensitivity to the reward value of sharing with others (e.g., Dawson, Munson, et al., 2002; Mundy, 1995; Trevarthen & Aitken, 2001), and, because these motivational factors also play a role in the development of social competence, motivation processes contribute to the developmental linkage between these domains. Finally, the neurode-velopmental executive model is related to both the social-cognitive and social-motivation models. It holds that joint attention development may involve frontal and temporal cortical and subcortical attention control, emotion regulation, and even "social executive" functions that also contribute to social development and social competence. In particular, the social executive capacity to engage in integrated self and other behavior monitoring may be a component of joint attention, social cognition, and social competence (U. Frith & Frith, 2001; Mundy, 2003; Vaughan & Mundy, in press).

A more detailed analysis of each of these models is provided in the following sections of this chapter. We recognize, though, that these models do not necessarily represent mutually exclusive perspectives. Rather, they offer an organizational heuristic for describing what we know, and *don't know,* about the links between infant joint attention and social competence. Unfortunately, what we

don't know currently significantly exceeds what we do know about joint attention. What we do know (or at least suspect) is that each of these models contains more than a grain of truth about the nature of joint attention development. It will be in the recognition of their complementary nature, and their synthesis, that progress will be made in delineating how we become capable of finding common ground with the thoughts, feelings, and points of views of other people.

The Caregiving/Scaffolding Model

In his formulation of joint attention development, Bruner (1983) emphasized that early parent-infant interactions often occur within common "formats" or "routines" during which infants and caregiver are focused on the same object or event. These "joint engagement" episodes form a rich interactive context that may contribute to joint attention development in infants (Bakeman & Adamson, 1984). One hypothesis is that, during joint engagement episodes, caregivers "scaffold" the abilities of their infants well before their infants are capable of demonstrating independent joint attention ability (Bruner, 1983; Danis, Bourdais, & Ruel, 2000; Kaye, 1982). Scaffolding refers to a process by which a capable partner modifies a task according to the emerging abilities of the child, or the child's "zone of proximal development," so that the child may successfully complete the task and, in repetitions of this supported practice, come to develop the self-management capacity necessary to the independent expression of skills involved in successful task performance (Vygotsky, 1978). One method of scaffolding in joint engagement is evident when caregivers follow the focus of attention of their infant. Caregivers then can capitalize on the focus of interest of the child to provide new information about the shared focus of attention (e.g., an object or event label). Caregivers may also interact with the child around the shared focus of attention, such as when they make eye contact while imitating the infant's actions on the toy or affective reactions to the toy. Theoretically, this social interactive enrichment around an object that the infants are already motivated to explore stimulates their awareness of social attention coordination, which contributes to joint attention development.

There is ample evidence for the role of caregivers in scaffolding the joint attention abilities of their infants (e.g., S. Landry, Smith, Miller-Loncar, & Swank, 1997; Legerstee, Varghese, & van Beek, 2002; Raver & Leadbeater, 1995; Roach, Barratt, Miller, & Leavitt, 1998). In a seminal longitudinal study, Bakeman and Adamson (1984) examined infants' development of joint engagement with their mother and with peers from the ages of 6 to 18 months. They investigated "active" joint engagement, where infants appear to acknowledge social attention sharing by looking back and forth between their caregiver and the object or event that is the common focus for the dyad. They also coded "passive" joint engagement, wherein infants do not look to caregivers, but both interactive partners share a common focus. The results indicated that both passive and active attention sharing in joint engagement were significantly more likely to occur when infants played with mothers than with peers. These results suggested that caregiver behavior played an important role in the ability of the child to participate in joint engagement.

Research on the effect of following the attention of infant and language development is also consistent with the scaffolding model and suggests that the interactive strategy adopted by the parent can facilitate or interfere with language learning. In particular, caregiver language that follows the infant's current focus of attention appears to be important for language acquisition. Reporting on data from a sample of 10 infants between the ages of 14 and 23 months (mean age = 17.4), Tomasello and Farrar (1986) found that words referring to objects, which were already a focus of the infant's attention, were comprehended better than words heard while the examiner was trying to switch the child's attention. There were no statistical differences in regard to the effect on word production, which the adults attributed to shyness with strangers. Dunham, Dunham, and Curwin (1993) corroborated these findings in a series of controlled studies with twenty-eight 18-month-old infants. These findings also have been substantiated in investigations of unstructured mother-infant play interactions (e.g., Akhtar, Dunham, & Dunham, 1991; Laakso, Poikkeus, Eklund, & Lyytines, 1999). In their longitudinal study of 24 mother-infant dyads, Carpenter et al. (1998) found predictive relations between 12- and 15-month maternal utterances that "followed in" to the infant's focus of attention and word comprehension as measured by the MacArthur Communicative Development Inventory (MCDI) at those same age points, as well as a predictive relation between 12-month maternal language following and 15-month MCDI language production.

Theoretically, if caregiver responsivity and scaffolding have an effect on infant joint attention development, and related caregiver behaviors are also associated with subsequent development of social competence in childhood, then it may well be that stable individual differences in caregiving contribute to a link between infant joint attention and

childhood social development. Surprisingly little research directly addressing this important possibility is currently available. Nevertheless, several studies indirectly bear on this hypothesis.

Research indicates that there are stable individual differences in terms of the degree to which caregivers and infants spend time in joint engagement interactions. In their longitudinal study of 24 infants from 9 to 15 months, Carpenter et al. (1998) found some evidence for both stability and continuity of maternal utterances that followed in to the child's focus of attention. Masur and Turner (2001) also found evidence for both stability and continuity for global ratings of maternal responsiveness in 20 mothers when their infants were 10, 13, 17, and 21 months. However, neither group of researchers controlled for infant behavior when assessing stability coefficients. This may be critical because infant maturation may also contribute to the tendency of dyads to engage in joint engagement. Indeed, in our own research, parent report of language ability as early as at 9 and 12 months predicted differences in the growth of the average duration of joint engagement episodes between 9 and 18 months in a large sample of typically developing infants (Thorp, 2005).

Other research has examined the links between caregiver behavior in joint engagement and joint attention development in Autism (Siller & Sigman, 2002). This study indicated that caregivers of children with Autism followed in to the attention focus of their children as much as did caregivers of children with developmental delay and caregivers of typically developing children matched on language capacities. Perhaps even more important, caregivers of children with Autism who showed higher levels of responsive "following in" behavior during joint engagement interactions had children who developed better joint attention and language ability over a period of years than children of less responsive caregivers. These findings suggest a developmental link between parental sensitivity and the child's subsequent development of joint attention skills in children with Autism. This may be an extremely important observation that has considerable applied value. For example, recall that IJA disturbance is a fundamental feature of Autism and reflects a lack of a tendency among children with Autism to spontaneously share their interest in objects and events with others. What constitutes the most effective approach to this fundamental feature of Autism? In some types of intervention with Autism, the therapist tries to direct the attention of the child to a task and to shape the behavior, through operant "discrete trial" training, to achieve some performance goal, such as providing an object label on command (Lovaas, 1987). However, increasingly, interventionists recognize that, if the spontaneous generation of shared experience is an important goal for intervention, then it may be important to begin with the interests of the child. The rationale here is that, if a child does not first demonstrate an interest in an object, it is unlikely that an intervention procedure will be able to teach the child to share his or her interest with others. So several interventions now train parents and professional to follow the attention or interest of the child and to scaffold that unilateral interest toward social sharing. This requires a very different social-emotional orientation for the therapist (or parent) than is typically described in stricter behavioral intervention orientations. Nevertheless, evidence is beginning to emerge that this shared-attention scaffolding approach may be a very important component to effective intervention with young children with Autism (Greenspan & Wieder, 2000; Gutstein & Sheely, 2002).

Outside of research on Autism, several studies have suggested that general measures of caregiver social behavior and responsiveness are related to joint attention development. Wachs and Chan (1986) observed that a more positive social home environment was related to the development of IJA skills (protodeclaratives), but not to IBR skill development (protoimperatives). Flanagan, Coppa, Riggs, and Alario (1994) reported that less responsive caregiving among teenage mothers was associated with better IBR development, and enhanced caregiver responsiveness was associated with better IJA development in their infants. Goldsmith and Rogoff (1997) carried out a seminal study in which they observed that dyads involving caregivers with depression were significantly less likely to enter into episodes of joint engagement than were dyads with caregivers who were not affected by depression. These studies used different methods and samples but consistently indicated that factors associated with the social responsiveness and the emotional quality of caregiving may impact joint attention development. These results are quite consistent with the scaffolding model. However, more research is needed to directly examine the degree to which specific types of scaffolding behaviors in caregivers may affect the development of joint attention in typically developing infants across the first and 2nd year of life.

Research on the connection of joint attention development with caregiver social behavior and responsiveness leads to another important possibility. If the development of joint attention is related to qualitative aspects of caregiving, then perhaps joint attention is significantly influenced by the attachment quality of infant-caregiver dyads. If so,

such a relation would be very important to consider in understanding the links between joint attention and outcomes. Several studies have provided data relevant to this issue. For example, previously reviewed studies indicate that a robust disturbance of joint attention (especially IJA) is characteristic of children with Autism. However, other research indicates that children with Autism display attachment behaviors that are quite similar to those exhibited by developmentally delayed control children (Sigman & Mundy, 1989; Sigman & Ungerer, 1984). This suggests that there is a dissociation between attachment and joint attention developmental processes in children with Autism. This view was supported by a study by Capps et al. (1994), which reported that, although IBR was a significant correlate of differences in attachment behavior in a sample of children with Autism, IJA behavior was not associated with attachment.

Does this mean that attachment and joint attention development are not strongly associated in other samples of children? An authoritative answer to this question is not yet at hand. However, it is noteworthy that relatively clear evidence of an association between attachment and joint attention has been revealed only in studies that have included observations of disorganized attachment. The latter refers to an atypical pattern of behavior that may be associated with poor if not abusive caregiving environments. Schölmerich, Lamb, Leyendecker, and Fracasso (1997) observed that, in a low-socioeconomic status sample, disorganized attachment status, but not avoidant or anxious-ambivalent attachment status, was related to the degree to which caregivers and infants entered into joint engagement episodes in social interactions. Claussen, Mundy, Malik, and Willoughby (2002) also did not observe an effect for secure versus insecure groups, but did observe an effect for disorganized attachment on joint attention development as measured on the ESCS.

In the Claussen et al. (2002) study, groups of infants at risk for cognitive and behavioral disturbance associated within utero cocaine exposure with either secure, insecure, or disorganized attachment status were compared on the ESCS at 12 and 18 months of age. The results revealed no effect of attachment on RJA but an attenuation of IBR and IJA development in the disorganized group. IBR development was lower for the disorganized group, but increased from 12 to 18 months. However, IJA bids actually decreased from 12 to 18 months in the toddlers from disorganized attachment dyads. One interpretation of these results is that less than optimal caregiving associated with disorganized attachment may lead to a general attenuation of the tendency of the toddler to initiate communicative bids, but also a *reduction* over the 12- to 18-month period in the social motivation for secondary intersubjectivity, as measured by the development of IJA bids.

A similar set of observations has been provided in a study of children adopted from institutional orphanages in Asia at an adoption clinic at the University of Minnesota (Kroupina, Kuefner, Iverson, & Johnson, 2003). Infants entered these institutions shortly after birth, but many of these orphanages had few attendants. Therefore, although they provided for the physical needs of the children, they often provided minimal social-emotional nurturance. As children were adopted, they were brought to this country at different ages and after different lengths of stay in these institutions. They were administered the ESCS as part of a broader developmental assessment at the university clinic. The results revealed that age of adoption or length of stay in the orphanage did not have an effect on RJA or IBR development, both of which exhibited monotonic age-related increases. However, the age-related development of IJA was U-shaped such that, after about 14 months of living in the orphanages, the IJA development of the infants displayed a significant and systematic age-related decline. This profile of declining IJA skill is very similar to the pattern observed by Claussen et al. (2002) in their study of infants with substantial biosocial risk and disorganized attachment status. These data raise the possibility that there may be sensitive periods in which appropriate social stimulation or social reinforcement is needed to promote adequate development of joint attention in the 2nd year of life.

In another dissertation at the University of Miami, Block (2005) examined the association between attachment and joint attention in samples of typically developing infants from infant-caregiver dyads with secure or insecure, but not disorganized, attachment. This study observed little evidence of an association of secure or insecure attachment assessed with the Strange Situation paradigm at 18 months and infant-tester joint attention measures of development on the ESCS in the 2nd year of life. However, 12-month infants from dyads with secure and anxious-ambivalent attachment ratings exhibited more IJA bids to their mothers, who were seated in the testing room during the ESCS, than was the case for infants from avoidant dyads. These observations raise the possibility that attachment may be related to the specific expression of joint attention within the caregiver-infant dyad, but not necessarily to the general capacity of infants to engage in joint attention with other people, such as a tester in the ESCS. Interestingly, Block (2005) also observed a conditional effect such that infant IJA behavior was more strongly associated with 24-month cognitive/

language outcomes in children who displayed higher rates of behaviors associated with insecure rather than secure attachment in the strange situation. This observation is consistent with the relative vulnerability hypothesis of joint attention development (Mundy & Willoughby, 1996, 1998). This hypothesis acknowledges that caregiving may play a role in joint attention development. However, it stipulates that joint attention also reflects constitutional social motivation and executive functions (see subsequent sections), and these may serve to facilitate the capacity of infants to relate to others and self-organize positive social interactions. To the degree this is true, joint attention skills may serve to mitigate the developmental risk that ensues for some forms of less than optimal caregiving.

Additional evidence consistent with the self-organizing, vulnerability hypothesis has been presented by Crowson (2001). This study examined the relations between joint attention and 24-month outcome in 15-month-olds from either secure ($n = 22$) or insecure ($n = 21$) infant-caregiver attachment dyads. Twenty-four-month outcome in this study was measured in terms of performance on standardized measures of cognitive and language development, as well as with a measure of the tendency of toddlers and caregivers to engage in joint engagement in a 12-minute social interaction paradigm (Bakeman & Adamson, 1984; Tomasello & Farrar, 1986). Crowson found that RJA was related to cognitive and language outcomes in both groups. However, the relations of IJA to outcomes appeared to be conditional on attachment security. In the secure attachment group, 15-month IJA was not related to outcome. However, the tendency of caregivers to follow in on the line of regard of their infants to establish joint attention at 24 months was related to individual differences in language development, replicating earlier observations by Tomasello and Farrar. However, this maternal behavior was not related to language development in the insecure group, and the group difference in the size of this correlation was significant even though there was no difference in caregiver following in behavior across the groups.

Alternatively, in the insecure group, the tendency of infants to display IJA behaviors at 15 months (e.g., showing) with a tester was related to infants' tendencies to initiate joint attention in interaction with caregivers at 24 months, and both of these behavior tendencies were associated with language development in this group. These observations were interpreted to suggest that infants' ability to self-organize social information flow had relatively little impact in the context of the more optimal social learning environment that is presumably provided by responsive caregivers in secure dyads. However, in insecure dyads, infants had more of the "responsibility" to create optimal social learning opportunities with their less responsive caregivers. In these dyads, IJA skills served to enable infants to engage their caregivers and self-organize social interactions in such a way as to optimize their development and to decrease the developmental risk incurred by the less sensitive caregiving that is associated with insecure attachment status. These are provocative results, but they need to be replicated before strong conclusions may be drawn.

What can be concluded from this research is that the social environment created by the caregivers may contribute substantially to joint attention development and its relations to outcomes. Direct observations of scaffolding as measured in joint engagement interactions likely provides one of the best means for evaluating the effect of caregiving on joint attention. Alternatively, measures of attachment may have a less direct and perhaps even non-linear relation to infant joint attention development. However, we know all too little about caregiver-child interactions in joint attention development. More work of this kind is needed, and it may have ramifications for both basic and clinically relevant research issues on joint attention development.

There are also good reasons to believe that the perspective of the caregiving model alone does not provide a complete picture of the links between infant joint attention development and social outcomes in children. For example, caregiving factors have been related to the development of IJA (e.g., Claussen et al., 2002; Wachs & Chen, 1986) but not so clearly to RJA (e.g., Claussen et al., 2002; Crowson, 2001; Kroupina et al., 2003). However, there is at least as much evidence that RJA is connected with the development of social competence in childhood as there is evidence of a link with IJA (Sheinkopf et al., 2004; Sigman & Ruskin, 1999; Vaughan et al., 2004). Thus, to understand the different pattern of relations of IJA and RJA with social outcomes, it may be important to consider factors beyond caregiver scaffolding. In this regard, it is interesting to consider whether the social-cognitive model enhances our understanding of the processes that may underpin the developmental links between infant joint attention and childhood social competence.

The Social Cognition Model

Recall that part of the foundation for the social-cognitive model emanates from Bruner's (1975) proposal that, before language acquisition, infants develop the ability to intentionally share information with social partners (i.e.,

communicate) through nonverbal means, such as pointing and showing gestures and eye contact. Bruner and Sherwood (1983) used the term "joint attention" to refer to a subset of these skills and suggested that they reflected a general preverbal cognitive platform that was essential to language development. The notion that preverbal infants *intentionally* share information with others was subsequently elaborated to suggest that joint attention specifically reflects social-cognitive development in infancy (Bretherton, 1991). As previously noted, the logic here is that if infants use gestures and eye contact to intentionally communicate with others, then they must have some awareness not only of the social signal value of their behaviors, but also that others have powers of perception and intention that may be affected by the infant's behavior. Thus, theory has come to suggest that early prelinguistic communication skills, especially joint attention development, reflects the emergence of social cognition or infants' "understanding" that others have intentions (Baron-Cohen, 1995; Leslie & Happé, 1989; Tomasello, 1995). Indeed, if one observes 15-month-olds alternating their gaze to share their pleasure in an object, or pointing to show, or pointing to obtain an object (see Figures 9.1c, 9.1b, and 9.1d, respectively), it is difficult to escape the interpretation that these infants are possessed of some degree of understanding that others have emotions and intentions that may be shared and/or directed (Bretherton, 1991).

Of course, the development of social-cognitive awareness is not completed in infancy. Indeed, many researchers suggest that a basic "theory of mind," or the ability to attribute independent mental states to others, does not mature and become clearly evident until about 4 years of age (Wellman, Cross, & Watson, 2001). This ability may be indexed with performance on a false belief task in which children are asked to predict the behavior of another person based on the child's understanding of the beliefs of the other person. False beliefs that are not consonant with the perceptual information available to the child are used so the child cannot solve the problem through his or her own knowledge. Instead, the children must think about the other person's knowledge to solve the problem (see Wellman et al., 2001).

Even after the emergence of this skill in many children by 4 years, significant individual differences have been observed, with some children displaying less understanding of the intentions, feelings, and mental states of others relative to their peers (Astington, 2001; Cutting & Dunn, 2002). Furthermore, critical to the social-cognitive model, several studies now indicate that differences on theory of mind measures of social cognition in young children is related to both positive (prosocial) and negative (behavior problem) indices of social competence in preschool (Capage & Watson, 2001; Jenkins & Astington, 2000) and school-age (Dunn, 1995; Dunn, Cutting, & Fischer, 2002) children.

Social cognition, though, may also be associated with factors that may inhibit social competence in some contexts. So, for example, Cutting and Dunn (2002) have reported that better-developed social-cognitive skills in 5-year-olds may be associated with enhanced sensitivity to teacher criticism in the 1st year of school. It is also important to recognize that numerous studies suggest that performance on theory of mind measures is significantly correlated with language development (e.g., Peterson, 2004; Ruffman, Slade, Rowlandson, Rumsey, & Garnham, 2003). Therefore, differences in language development may account for part of the relation between social cognition and social competence.

These last two caveats notwithstanding, research and theory on joint attention and social cognition lead to the logical expectation that, (1) if joint attention is an early manifestation of social cognition, and (2) if social cognition is related to later social competence in children, (3) then social cognition may mediate part or all of the relations between social competence and social outcomes observed in recent longitudinal research. This set of assertions rests on the key assumption that infant joint attention behaviors primarily reflect social-cognitive development. Although this assumption has intuitive appeal, the nature of the connection between joint attention and social cognition may be less clear and probably more complex than suggested by the rather simple formulation offered here.

There is surprisingly little direct evidence of a connection between joint attention and social cognition. Indeed, we are aware of only one study that has provided data on this issue. Charman et al. (2000) followed a sample of 13 typically developing infants from 20 to 44 months of age as part of a study on the early identification of Autism. At 20 months, an alternating gaze measure was employed (Figure 9.1c), which involved children spontaneously initiating eye contact with a tester or parent when presented with an interesting toy spectacle. After controlling for differences in IQ and language development, the 20-month IJA alternating gaze measure was a significant predictor of 44-month social-cognitive ability measured on a false belief paradigm.

There are, however, at least two important indirect lines of research that provide data consistent with a connection between infant joint attention and social cognition. One of these involves the observation that children with Autism

display relatively robust disturbances not only in the development of joint attention skills but also in theory of mind task performance. The co-occurrence of these forms of impairment in Autism has suggested that these domains may share a common cognitive foundation (e.g., Leslie & Happé, 1989). Another line of research involves more recent observations from neurophysiological and neuroimaging research (e.g., U. Frith & Frith, 2001; Mundy et al., 2000). This literature indicates that infant joint attention and later performance on theory of mind measures may have common cortical dorsal-medial, orbitofrontal, and temporal cortical activation correlates (Mundy, 2003). Thus, the literature also suggests that joint attention and theory of mind performance share common process foundations. The nature of these common processes, though, is not completely clear at this time and may involve executive as well as social-cognitive processes (see the section on the "Neurodevelopment Executive Model").

Another type of research that is useful in evaluating the connections between joint attention and social cognition involves examining the age of onset of the social-cognitive component of joint attention. Some have argued that true joint attention does not occur until the infant is capable of the simultaneous awareness of self and other contemplating a common object (Tomasello, 1995). This integrated awareness of the perception of self and other is not thought to occur until some time in the 2nd year. However, more recent research and theory suggests that social cognition may only gradually become part of joint attention after several months of practice with social attention (Brooks & Meltzoff, 2002; Moore, 1996). Indeed, the rudiments of joint attention, especially RJA, may emerge between 3 and 6 months of life (D'Entremont et al., 1997; Hood, Willen, & Driver, 1998; Morales et al., 1998; Scaife & Bruner, 1975) and well before theory suggests that social-cognitive processes affect or organize behavior (Mundy & Sigman, 1989; Tomasello, 1995). Indeed, recent empirical efforts indicate that infants display RJA skills in the 1st year of life, but a clear association between this behavior and social cognition does not emerge until the 2nd year of life (Brooks & Meltzoff, 2002; Woodward, 2003).

One way to conceptualize these recent data on joint attention is to think of social cognition as an emergent function that develops, in part, as a consequence of infants' practice with joint attention and joint engagement with others (Mundy & Neal, 2001; Mundy et al., 1993). In this regard, we find it useful to think of joint attention development in terms of two phases: a "learning to" phase and a "learning from" phase (Vaughan & Mundy, in press). In the

1st year of development, several basic processes contribute to the capacity of infants to engage in IJA and RJA behaviors. Theoretically, the basic processes that support this "learning to" phase of joint attention development include but are not limited to operant learning (Corkum & Moore, 1998), intersensory integration (Flom & Pick, 2003), motivation for social engagement (Mundy, 1995; Trevarthen & Aitken, 2001), executive attention-regulation processes (Mundy et al., 2000), and imitation (Meltzoff & Moore, 1997; Pomares, Mundy, Vaughan, Block, & Delgado, 2003). With practice, the numerous processes involved in social attention coordination become integrated and routinized, enabling infants to gradually move from the "learning to" phase to the "learning from" phase of joint attention development. In the "learning to" phase of skill acquisition, more neurocognitive resources are utilized than when the skill become routinized (e.g., Wu, Kansaku, & Mark, 2004). Thus, in the "learning from" phase more resources become available to engage in integrative cognitive activities in the context of joint attention interactions with others. That is, practice with the attention management necessary for joint attention combines with neurodevelopmental maturation of cognitive representational and memory resources (Case, 1987) to make it increasingly likely that infants have the capacity to not only engage in joint attention but also process and compare proprioceptive information about their own experience of an object or event with exteroceptive information about their social partners' experience of the same object or event during a joint attention episode (Mundy et al., 1993).

This comparative process, in the context of social interactions about a common referent, provides the infant with seminal information about the behavioral confluence of self and other that contributes to the development of an awareness that others have thoughts or feelings that are similar to (or different from) the infant's (Bruner, 1975; Werner & Kaplan, 1963). Indeed, there may be specific neural systems and social executive functions that facilitate self-other information comparison and integration that allows infants to simulate others' experience based on their own experience, and this simulation gives rise to social cognition (U. Frith & Frith, 2001; Mundy, 2003; Stich & Nichols, 1992; see "Neurodevelopment Executive Model" section for more details). Thus, this theoretical perspective suggests that joint attention may be viewed as a contributing *cause* of social-cognitive development as much as or more than being a *consequence* of social-cognitive development. From this perspective, joint attention may be reasonably viewed as a special form of infant social engagement that contributes to self-constructivist aspects of cognitive

development (Piaget, 1952) that are especially important for subsequent social competence (Mundy, 2003; Mundy & Crowson, 1997; Mundy & Neal, 2001). Theoretically, the constructivist characteristic of the "learning from" phase provides another example of the self-organizing functions of infant joint attention skill development. That is, the more frequently infants engage in episodes of joint attention with others, the more opportunities they have to expand their understanding of similarities and differences in the responses of self and other to external objects and events. It is also very likely that because IJA frequently occurs in the context of sharing positive experiences with others (Mundy et al., 1992), frequent IJA bids may well provide a medium for developing a positive sense of relatedness to others in infancy that has benefits for social development (for discussion, see Mundy & Willoughby, 1996, 1998). The reader may recognize the commonality between this model ascribed to joint attention development and current theory on the importance of imitation for the early development of self-other understanding (Meltzoff & Decety, 2003). Indeed, current research and theory on joint attention and imitation provide important convergent information on social cognition, even though we still know far to little about how these domains relate or interact in development. However, recall that joint attention involves the measures of both self-initiated acts and responsive acts while imitation measures focus on the latter. This is an important distinction. Awareness of one's own intentional behaviors may provide a foundation that is necessary to perceiving and understanding the intentions of others (Mundy, 2003, 2005) and voluntary self-initiated actions may be critical to the development of representations of intentionality in the self (Lau, Rogers, Haggard, & Passingham, 2004). Hence, self-initiated joint attention acts, in interactions with social partners, may provide an distinct building block of social-cognitive development that is not available through interactions involving imitation or responding to the joint attention behavior of others (Mundy et al., 1993).

The foregoing analysis suggests that the social-cognitive model accounts for some part of the linkage between joint attention and social competence in childhood but does not provide a complete account of the factors that link these domains in development. Other basic processes, more fully described in the next sections on social motivation and neurodevelopment, may need to be considered to understand the connections among joint attention, social cognition, and social competence.

It is also the case that there are empirical observations that do not fit neatly with the current versions of the social-cognitive model. As was the case with the caregiver/scaffolding model, we are not aware of a variant of the social-cognitive perspective that makes explicit process differentiations regarding different types of joint attention behaviors. Therefore, the social-cognitive model does not currently provide a ready explanation of why different forms of joint attention behaviors in infancy (IJA, RJA, and IBR) appear to display different patterns of connections with social and behavioral outcomes (Shienkopf et al., 2004; Sigman & Ruskin, 1999; Vaughan et al., 2004). Second, infants in recent longitudinal studies (e.g., Sheinkopf et al., 2004; Vaughan et al., 2004) displayed a range of joint attention skills did not reflect the presence or absence of skill but rather reflected a range of differences from "some" use of joint attention bids to the "frequent" use of joint attention. One challenge for the social-cognitive model is to describe the meaning of this level of individual difference in terms of social-cognitive processes. Third, although joint attention bids may ultimately come to reflect social-cognitive processes, social cognition may not be a primary factor in early joint attention development (Brooks & Meltzoff, 2002; Woodward, 2003). Thus, the social-cognitive model may be less applicable to research on the connections between developmental outcomes and joint attention measured in the early, 3- to 12-month "learning to" phase of development (e.g., Morales et al., 2005; Vaughan et al., 2004). For example, recall that in their study, Vaughan et al. observed that IJA and RJA at 12 months were negatively correlated with parent report of behavior disturbance at 30 months on the Externalizing scale of the ITSEA (Carter & Briggs-Gowan, 2000). The Externalizing domain has 24 items reflecting Defiance (12 items), Activity/Impulsivity (6 items), and Peer Aggression (6 items). In discussing her findings, Vaughan noted that there were few if any items on this scale that appeared to tap social cognition. Hence, there was little content on this scale to suggest that social cognition played a role in the associations between joint attention and this aspect of social outcome in this study. Instead, Vaughan et al. noted that previous research indicated that IJA and RJA had been associated with inhibition and impulse control (Griffith et al., 1999). IJA has also been associated with positive emotional expressivity as early as 9 to 12 months (Mundy et al., 1992; Vaughan et al., 2003) and that RJA at 6 months predicts self-regulatory behavior in a delay of gratification paradigm at 24 months of age (e.g., Morale et al., 2005). Therefore, at least part of the associations of IJA and RJA with the Externalizing that were observed in the Vaughan et al. study may have been carried by these processes. This observation suggests that, in addition to social cognition, it may be important to consider other processes that may con-

tribute to continuity between joint attention and social competence. One essential dimension in this regard may be social-emotional and related motivation process.

The Social Motivation Model

Researchers ask at least two related but distinct questions about the behaviors displayed by infants in Figure 9.1: How are infants able to share attention and experience with others? and Why do infants share attention and experiences with others? The second question leads to reflection on the motivation factors and processes that contribute to the human tendency to share experience with others. For example, consider the following vignette. You attend an event that you are sure you will enjoy (a play, a concert, a sporting event, etc.) and a friend accompanies you to the event. During the event, there is the strong likelihood that several things will happen: (1) You will see/experience something that is rewarding for you, yet (2) you will turn away from the rewarding event (momentarily disengage) to make eye contact with your friend, and (3) in conjunction with the latter, you will experience a sense of relatedness with your friend and possibly a heightened sense of enjoyment regarding the shared experience of the event. In that moment you and your friend are likely engaged in joint attention, much like the infant in Figure 9.1c. Why do we engage in this behavior even when viewing the event by ourselves would be pleasurable? Does the sharing of experience with others hold some positive reward value that motivates people to engage in acts of joint attention throughout the life span? Does this motivation system assist in bootstrapping the development of joint attention and its critical early self-organizing functions in human social development?

Some would respond with an unequivocal yes to the last two questions and go on to suggest that human beings have an innate motivation for sharing experiences or engaging in intersubjectivity. Several groups of developmental scientists have argued that there is an intrinsic preference to orient to social stimuli and faces (Bard, Platzman, Lester, & Suomi, 1992; Valenza, Simion, Cassia, & Umilta, 1996) and that motivation to engage with caregivers in interactions involving the facial and vocal expression of positive affect contributes an organizing fulcrum around which much of early social and cognitive development revolves (Hobson, 2002; Stern, 1985; Trevarthen, 1979; Trevarthen & Aitken, 2001). With this unfortunately long sentence we have stated a basic tenet of the motivation model.

Recall that between birth and 6 months of age, caregiver-infant dyads increasingly engage in social communication motivation interactions that involve face-to-face sharing of nonverbal emotional information, or what has been referred to as primary intersubjectivity (Trevarthen, 1979). Theoretically, the tendency of infants to engage in these interactions is mediated, in part, by an intrinsic neural motivation system. Research suggests that this motivation system may involve temporal, orbitofrontal, and dorsal-frontal brain systems serving the perception of social stimuli (e.g., facial affect), the association of stimuli with positive reward value, and the association of self-initiated social attention behavior with positive rewards (Amador, Schlag-Rey, & Schlag, 2000; Eisenberger, Lieberman, & Williams, in press; Mundy, 2003; Trevarthen & Aitken, 2001; Wantanabe, 1996). Specific neuropeptide-neurotransmitter systems may also be involved that contribute to either a general endogenous reward system involved in learning (Holroyd & Coles, 2002) or a specific system involved in mediating the sensitivity of individuals to the reward value of social stimuli (Panksepp, 1979). Moreover, individual differences in early intrinsic social communication motivation may be associated with a general reward and motivation modulation system that affects the tendency of individuals to display a trait-like tendency to move toward positively rewarding stimuli (behavioral activation) and to avoid threatening or stressful stimuli (behavior inhibition; Gray, 1982). There is some evidence that this behavioral activation and inhibition system is associated with asymmetry in frontal activity (e.g., Sutton & Davidson, 1997) and that the influence of this asymmetric frontal motivation system may be observed in infants in the 1st year of life (Fox & Davidson, 1987, 1988). Some have even suggested that the motivation processes associated with frontal asymmetry may be specifically related to joint attention development and its impairment in Autism (Mundy, 1995).

Other research and theory suggest that, rather than relying solely on an intrinsic biological motivation process, such interactive behaviors as joint attention bids may take on social reward value through processes associated with external operant learning and reinforcement (Corkum & Moore, 1998). Consonant with this, much of the literature on the caregiver/scaffolding model at least implicitly suggests that environmental factors (caregiving) influence children's motivation to engage in social communication and joint attention, at least with selected social partners. Thus, the degree to which the social reward value of interactions reflects intrinsic versus learned processes is a central and as yet unresolved point of debate regarding this model.

In either case, though, a major assumption of this model is that systems of motivation processes serve to organize early behavior and to prioritize social orienting, social in-

teractions, and social information processing in infancy (Dawson, Meltzoff, Osterling, Rinaldi, & Brown, 1998; Mundy & Neal, 2001; Trevarthen & Aitken, 2001). This prioritization assures a sufficient input of social information to the infant to allow the next step of the development of a more elaborate capacity for sharing of experience with others vis-à-vis some third object, as in secondary intersubjectivity (Trevarthen & Aitken, 2001) or joint attention (Bruner & Sherwood, 1983; Tomasello, 1995). The strength of this motivation system, though, is likely to vary from individual to individual because of either inherent biological differences in sensitivity to social reward or learned differences in the reward value of social stimuli (Dawson, Munson et al., 2002; Mundy, 1995; Mundy & Willoughby, 1998). The resulting variability in social motivation significantly contributes to differences among infants in the tendency to engage in different types of joint attention skills. A corollary here is the hypothesis that when the motivation to engage in episodes of joint attention and intersubjectivity chronically slips below a critical threshold, because of either endogenous or exogenous processes, the risk for psychopathology increases (Mundy, 1995; Mundy & Willoughby, 1996; Stern, 1985; Trevarthen & Aitken, 2001).

What sort of empirical verification is there for this model? Well, if joint attention and sharing of experience with others has positive reward value for infants, it may then be reasonable to expect that affect, especially positive affect, should be associated with joint attention development. Indeed, Adamson and Bakeman (1985) have observed that from late in the 1st year through the 2nd year, the exchange of positive affect increasingly becomes a characteristic of infant-caregiver joint attention interactions. Subsequent research has attempted to clarify the degree to which affect is a common component of different types of joint attention skills. Kasari and her colleagues (1990) examined this issue in an investigation of the nature of joint attention deficits in Autism.

Recall that children with Autism displayed more robust deficits in IJA than RJA or IBR types of behavior. Kasari et al. (1990) hypothesized that the relative severity of IJA deficits may reflect the type of biologically based impairment of affective relatedness to others that Kanner (1943) suggested was a core feature of this disorder. Therefore, to examine the role of affect in autistic joint attention disturbance, Kasari and her colleagues integrated ESCS ratings of joint attention with systematic ratings of facial affect. Several important observations were noted in this study. First, infants in the typical control sample conveyed positive affect significantly more often to social partners in the context of IJA bids compared to IBR or RJA behaviors. Alternatively, children with Down syndrome and children with Autism did not display differences in affect across IJA and IBR measures, but for different reasons. The Down syndrome children displayed high but equal rates of positive affect across both IJA and IBR bids; the children with Autism displayed low but equal rates of positive affect in IJA and IBR. Infants' expression of positive affect was not a major component of RJA for any group.

These results suggested that the sharing of positive affective experiences with others is a major component of IJA behavior in typical development, and that an attenuation of positive affect in social interactions may be an important component of IJA deficits in children with Autism (Kasari et al., 1990). To examine this issue further, we reexamined the association of affect and joint attention in an independent and larger sample of typically developing infants. This study again revealed that approximately 60% of all IJA bids displayed by toddlers on the ESCS in the 2nd year involved the conveyance of positive affect, but less than 30% of IBR and RJA bids involved the sharing of positive affect (Mundy et al., 1992). These data were interpreted to suggest that IJA in the 2nd year might provide an operational definition of the development of secondary intersubjectivity. That is, IJA, at least as measured on the ESCS, provides a measure that is sensitive to motivation and cognitive factors involved in the tendency of infants to initiate communicative bids to spontaneously share their positive affective experience of object or events with a social partner (see Figure 9.1c).

The argument for a motivation component in IJA rests, in part, on the assumption that some form of internal motivation is necessary to initiate a social behavior to spontaneously convey or share affect in IJA with the social partner. Alternatively, it is possible that the positive affect in IJA is a reactive rather than an intentional sharing of positive affective experience with others. That is, when engaged in triadic attention deployment, infants may smile in response to looking at the face of a social partner rather than as a conveyance of their own preexisting affective state. This type of reactive affective display would be more ambiguous with regard to the possible role of endogenous motivation processes. However, our recent data indicate that, between 8 and 10 months, there is a developmental shift in the association of affect with IJA (Venezia et al., 2004). Prior to 10 months, when typically developing infants engage in an alternating gaze IJA bid (Figure 9.1c), they tend to display affect reactively. That is, they tend to display affect after they look at the face of their social partner. This may be part of "learning to" display af-

fect in IJA development. After 10 months, though, infants tend to smile first at the object or event that has caught their interest and then convey their ongoing affective reaction to an object or event with an IJA bid. One interpretation of these results is that, after about 10 months, many infants begin to display a pattern of behavior that is consistent with the possibility that they are motivated and intend to initiate sharing affect with others as part of an IJA bid (Venezia et al., 2004).

The current state of the argument for the role of motivation in joint attention development may be conjectural, but it also has considerable face validity (see Figure 9.1c). This unintended pun notwithstanding, the data on the facial emotional component of IJA are at least consistent with the hypothesis that this type of joint attention behavior may reflect a prosocial motivation to share affective experience with others. Of course, if this is true, then joint attention, or at least IJA development, may be related to aspects of temperament, such as emotional reactivity. Data from two recent studies are consistent with this possibility. Vaughan et al. (2003) observed that 9-month infant-tester IJA on the ESCS was significantly related to parent reports of "low pleasure" or a heightened tendency to express positive affect on the Infant Behavior Questionnaire (Rothbart, 1981). Parents' ratings of fearful responsiveness to novelty was later associated with IJA at 12 months. Neither IBR nor RJA displayed significant relations with indices of emotional reactivity (Vaughan et al., 2003).

Thus, current research suggests that some forms of joint attention, such as IJA, may reflect the tendency of infants to engage others in the spontaneous sharing of affective experience of objects or events. Alternatively, other measures of joint attention, such as RJA, do not as clearly involve affective sharing. This distinction may contribute to the different and unique paths of association observed between RJA, IJA, and social outcomes in children (Sheinkopf et al., 2004; Vaughan et al., 2004). However, as noted earlier, still other processes (e.g., self-regulatory processes) may also be involved in the connections between measures of infant joint attention skills and social competence. The breadth and nature of these additional processes are beginning to be revealed in research on the neurodevelopmental executive model of joint attention.

The Neurodevelopment Executive Model

The emergence of the neurodevelopmental executive model of joint attention has been stimulated in no small part by the need to better understand the nature of joint attention disturbance in Autism. It was previously noted that Autism is a biologically based disorder (Dawson et al., 2001) and that a cardinal symptom of this syndrome is a robust early disturbance of joint attention development (Mundy & Sigman, 1989; Mundy et al., 1986). Remember, however, that with development, there is evidence of dissociation in the course of joint attention impairments. In the 1st years of life, children with Autism display a clear deficit in RJA skills. Nevertheless, they begin to display basic gaze following by 2 years of age (Charwarska, Klin, & Volkmar, 2003), and problems in RJA appear to remit to an adaptively significant degree among many older children with Autism and those with higher mental ages (Leekam et al., 2000; Mundy et al., 1994; Sigman & Ruskin, 1999). Alternatively, IJA-related deficits appear to remain a profound source of disturbance throughout childhood with Autism (Leslie & Happé, 1989; Lord et al., 2001; Mundy et al., 1994; Sigman & Ruskin, 1999), although some children with Autism display improvement even in this area (Kasari, Freeman, & Paparella, 2001).

This literature on joint attention disturbances in Autism has numerous implications. First, examining the neural substrates of an early emerging cardinal symptom, such as joint attention impairment, may be essential to understanding the neurodevelopmental etiology of this disorder. Second, the research on dissociation in the development of IJA and RJA impairments in Autism suggests that it is possible that these two forms of joint attention reflect different constellations of neurodevelopmental processes. Numerous studies have now been reported that bear on this possibility.

Caplan and colleagues (1993) provided what may have been the first data on this issue. This research team studied the behavioral outcome of 13 infants who underwent hemispherectomies in an attempt to treat their intractable seizure disorders. The ESCS was used to assess the post-surgical development of joint attention and related behaviors among these children. Positron emission tomography (PET) data were gathered prior to surgical intervention. PET data indicated that metabolic activity in the dorsal-frontal cortex, especially the left frontal cortex, predicted the development of IJA skill in this sample. However, the PET data did not predict the development of the capacity to respond to the joint attention bids or to initiate requesting bids. Moreover, metabolic activity recorded from other brain regions (e.g., ventral-orbitofrontal, temporal, parietal, and occipital cortices) was not significantly associated with the development of joint attention or other social communication skills in this study. Thus, dorsal-frontal activity appeared to be specifically related to the development of the tendency to spontaneously initiate social attention coordination with others to share experience.

A post hoc explanation of this frontal connection to IJA was offered in a later paper based on the social motivation model (Mundy, 1995). By about 10 months of age, a frontal and left-lateralized system emerges that plays a role in the executive and emotional processes associated with approach tendencies involved in positive social affiliative behaviors (e.g., Fox, 1991). Mundy suggested that IJA impairment in Autism might reflect a disturbance in the emergence of this left frontal social-approach system. Based on earlier work (Panksepp, 1979), the specific hypothesis was that pathology in Autism involved the early onset of a disturbance in frontal neurotransmitter mediated sensitivity to the reward value of social stimuli. This attenuated social reward sensitivity hypothetically creates an affective social motivation imbalance that results in a robust decrease in the tendency to direct attention to social stimuli. This, in turn, leads to a dramatic reduction in the tendency of infants with Autism to initiate joint attention bids and a related reduction in social information input to the child that results in a marginalization of subsequent social-cognitive and social-behavior development (Dawson et al., 1998; Mundy, 1995; Mundy & Crowson, 1997; Mundy & Neal, 2001).

To begin to test aspects of this model, a study was conducted at the University of Maryland in collaboration with the research team of Nathan Fox (Mundy et al., 2000). This study examined the hypothesis that EEG activity in a left-lateralized, frontal-cortical system would be a significant correlate of IJA among infants with typical development. Baseline EEG and ESCS joint attention data were collected on 32 infants at 14 to 18 months of age. The results indicated that individual differences in 18-month IJA were predicted by a complex pattern of 14-month EEG activity in the 4Hz to 6Hz band that included indices of left medial-frontal EEG activation, as well as indices of right central deactivation, left occipital activation, and right occipital deactivation. Although the location of the generators of the EEG data could not be definitively determined in this study, the frontal correlates of IJA reflected activity from electrodes at F3 and C3 of the 10/20-placement system (Jasper, 1958). These electrodes were positioned above a point of confluence of Brodmann's areas 6, 8, and 9 of the medial-frontal cortex of the left hemisphere (Martin, 1996). This area includes aspects of the frontal eye fields and supplementary motor cortex, commonly observed to be involved in attention control (Posner & Petersen, 1990). Moreover, theory on the anterior attention network (Posner & Petersen, 1990) suggested that, in addition to medial frontal cortical activity, data from these electrodes may have reflected activity in the anterior cingulate (Brodmann's area 24), a subcortical structure contiguous with the ventral surface of Brodmann's cortical areas 6, 8, 9 (Martin, 1996). Alternatively, neither RJA nor IBR measures were associated with a similar pattern of EEG activity (Mundy et al., 2000). However, RJA at 18 months was predicted by EEG indices of left parietal activation and right parietal deactivation at 14 months.

These data suggested that at least two neural systems might be involved in joint attention development: a temporal and parietal system for RJA and a dorsal-medial cortical system for IJA. Other research provides support for this dual process model and also offers hypotheses about the nature of the process that may be involved in these two systems (for recent reviews, see Mundy, 2003; Vaughan & Mundy, in press). This additional research is reviewed in the next sections, beginning with information on the connections between RJA-related behaviors and parietal and temporal systems.

RESPONDING TO JOINT ATTENTION AND THE PARIETAL-TEMPORAL PROCESS

RJA is a complex behavior. On the ESCS, it involves the ability of the child to attend to and process information provided by another person and then to disengage attention as well as reorient to correctly follow the direction of gaze, head and body posture, and pointing gesture of a social partner. Much of the work related to RJA focuses on mapping the cortical systems that are engaged in processing the direction of gaze of a social partner.

Wicker, Michel, Henaff, and Decety (2002) observed that neural groups in the posterior superior temporal sulcus (STS) were activated in response to faces with direct or horizontally averted eye gaze, but not to faces with downward eye gaze. However, Wicker et al. did not observe differences between direct and averted eye gaze conditions. Alternatively, Puce, Allison, Bentin, Gore, and McCarthy (1998) reported that videos of face stimuli with gaze moving horizontally from forward to averted gaze elicited greater posterior STS activation compared to faces with static forward gaze. Face matching on the basis of direction of gaze also elicited activation of neurons in the left posterior STS, and identity-based face matching elicited bilateral activation from the fusiform and inferior occipital gyri (Hoffman & Haxby, 2000). Similarly, George, Driver, and Dolan (2001) reported that direct gaze stimuli elicited more fusiform activation than averted gaze stimuli. Kingstone, Friesen, and Gazzaniga (2000) have also reported data on gaze following in two split-brain patients that was

consistent with the notion that parietal as well as temporal subsystems specialized for face processing and processing of information relevant to spatial orientation combine to support the development of gaze following. Finally, Hooker (2002) used whole-brain fMRI to compare neural activity in response to (1) horizontal eye movement stimuli that provide directional information about where a visual stimulus would appear, or (2) arrow stimuli that provided equivalent directional information, or (3) eye movements that did not provide directional information. Hooker observed more activity in the STS in the first condition compared to either of the other conditions. Alternatively, Hooker reported more activity in the fusiform gyrus and prefrontal cortex in the eye motion control condition (condition 3) compared to the other conditions. Similarly, Kingstone, Tipper, Ristic, and Ngan (2004) also compared the response of shifts in attention elicited by direction of gaze (eye stimuli) versus a direction indicator (arrow stimuli) and observed that the neural systems that subserved the respective orienting were not equivalent. The STS was clearly engaged when the stimuli were eyes versus arrows. These data are consistent with the notion that the STS may develop a specialization for processing gaze-related, social-spatial orientation information.

The results of these human imaging studies are consistent with earlier reports from comparative research that provide experimental evidence of temporal (i.e., STS) and parietal involvement in gaze following (Emery, 2000). In two studies, presurgical monkeys demonstrated a clear ability to discriminate face stimuli on the basis of direction of gaze (Cambell, Heywood, Cowey, Regard, & Landis, 1990; Heyward & Cowey, 1992). After resection of the STS, however, the gaze discrimination abilities of the monkeys fell to chance. Eacott, Heywood, Gross, and Cowey (1993) compared two groups of monkeys, those with and without STS surgically induced lesions, on a task requiring discriminating between pairs of eyes directed straight ahead or averted 5 or more degrees. The results indicated that the nonlesion monkeys were capable of discriminating targets involving horizontal eye gaze shifts of greater than 5 degrees, but the STS lesion animals were not.

Few studies, though, have reported a significant connection between RJA or gaze following and activity in the frontal cortices. Calder et al. (2002) suggested that perhaps task difficulty needed to be considered in this regard. Most studies have examined passive gaze following on tasks that did not require the perception or inference of intentions on the basis of eye gaze. These authors suggested that more complex presentations of sequences of gaze stimuli may elicit inferential social-cognitive processing and evidence of more dorsal contributions to the neural substrate of gaze following. To this end, Calder et al. used PET to examine the neural responses of 9 female volunteers to a relatively complex sequence of faces with gaze averted left or right, gaze direct, and gaze down orientations. Hypothetically, this procedure elicited interpretation of the nature of meaning of the gaze direction (i.e., the intentionality of gaze direction). In this paradigm, evidence of activation in the dorsal-medial-frontal cortex (BA 8, 9), the anterior cingulate (BA 32), and the STS was observed in response to horizontal gaze aversion. This study, unlike most others, employed a sample of women rather than men. Therefore, it is unclear whether an unrecognized gender effect may have also played a role in these observations. Nevertheless, the degree to which research participants attempt to process the "meaning" of gaze rather than simply direction of gaze may elicit a frontal component associated with RJA-related behaviors.

Another line of connection to the STS-parietal systems has been described by Meltzoff and Decety (2003). These authors provided an important research review that indicates neural activity associated with imitation clusters in the STS and parietal lobes, as well as the dorsal-cortical supplementary motor areas (BA 8, 9). In particular, they note that there may be an abundance of "mirror" neurons in STS and parietal lobes. Mirror neurons are motor neurons that activate both when an individual performs a particular action and when an individual observes the same action performed by another person (Rizzolatti & Arbib, 1998). These neurons may be integral to imitation. Thus, the proposed location of some of the neural mediators of imitation may overlap with the systems that are thought to mediate the development of gaze following and RJA. Indeed, from a task analytic point of view, this makes a great deal of sense. Gaze following and RJA basically involve copying the eye movements and/or head turns of a social partner. Indeed, RJA development has been observed to display a significant path of association with imitation development in a longitudinal study of typically developing infants (Pomares et al., 2003). However, there were no observations of significant associations between the development of IJA and imitation. This is not too surprising, as IJA behaviors are self-generated and do not appear to involve a discernable social copying component. Thus, it may be useful in future research to better understand the degree to which imitation and gaze following/RJA, but perhaps not IJA, reflect common biobehavioral processes in early development. Indeed, the importance of this issue has long been recognized in research on Autism because this syndrome involves deficits in imitation as well as joint attention skill development (e.g., Rogers & Pennington, 1991).

In addition to the specifically social information-processing functions of the STS and parietal cortices, this system also mediates more general, basic attention functions. For example, this system is also associated with the posterior attention network, which by 2 to 4 months of age contributes to the capacity to disengage from a focal central stimulus and reorient to a new aspect of the environment (Posner & Dehaene, 1994; Rothbart et al., 1994). The capacity to disengage may also be fundamental to RJA-related behaviors (Mundy et al., 2000). This is because, in their development, infants must learn to disengage from a preferred social stimulus (e.g., face of caregiver) to follow gaze and reorient to some new, shared focus of attention (see Figure 9.1). It is important to recognize the potential contribution of this basic function of the posterior attention system to the development of RJA for two reasons. One reason has been outlined by the recent work of R. Landry and Bryson (2004) that reports that 3- to 7-year-old children with Autism are impaired in their ability to disengage visual attention from an attractive central stimulus in order to reorient to peripheral targets. R. Landry and Bryson suggest that this type of impairment may contribute to social disturbances in Autism. We would agree and further suggest that it will be important to determine empirically if disengagement impairment as measured on a nonsocial task, such as described by R. Landry and Bryson, is related to the disturbances of joint attention development in Autism. Equally important will be to determine if variance associated with a nonsocial disengagement task fully explains or mediates the relation observed between RJA and outcomes in Autism such as intervention responsiveness (e.g., Bono et al., in press). Our guess is that nonsocial disengagement tasks will help us to understand some of the components of the processing impairment intrinsic to joint disturbance in Autism. However, because joint attention measurement is specific to the expression of attention management in social interactions, and social attention management likely involves many component processes not indexed by nonsocial attention measures, it seems unlikely that nonsocial measures will fully explain the significance of joint attention impairment in Autism. This, of course, is merely an opinion that we hope will either be corrected or supported by future research.

Another reason that understanding the role of disengagement in RJA may be important relates to the role of attention management in self-regulation. Rothbart et al. (1994) suggested that the capacity to disengage attention from a stimulus might be critical to the developing capacity of infants to modulate arousal in interactions with people and objects. For example, infants may disengage and briefly turn away from caregivers to modulate negative or positive affective arousal that occurs in response to processing information in social interactions. Thus, attention management may contribute to self-regulation processes that enable children to participate in social interaction more adaptively and for longer periods of time (Rothbart et al., 1994). This link between disengagement and self-regulation may help to explain part of the connection between RJA and the subsequent development of social competencies. For example, Morales et al. (2005) recently reported that RJA measured in the context of infant-caregiver interactions at 6 months predicts the tendency of toddlers to use disengagement strategies to self-regulate in a delay of gratification paradigm. Infants with better RJA skills at 6 months tended to look away from the desired object more frequently in the delay of gratification task. Thus, theory and research on disengagement of attention may assist us to better understand the RJA impairments in Autism as well as the connections between infant RJA and social outcomes. Much more work is needed on this intriguing possibility.

INITIATING JOINT ATTENTION AND FRONTAL PROCESSES

The study of the neural correlates of social initiations like IJA is a bit more difficult than the study of responsive behaviors such as RJA. This is because it is more complicated to establish a paradigm that is compelling enough to encourage children to spontaneously initiate valid social bids while also allowing for sufficient experimental control to gather imaging or electrophysiological data. Therefore, relatively few studies have been conducted on the neural correlates of IJA or its analogues. Previously, we noted that Caplan et al. (1993) and Mundy et al. (2000) provided PET and EEG data, respectively, that suggested that IJA may be related to frontal activity, specifically left dorsal-medial-frontal activity (Brodmann's areas 6, 8, 9). A more recent EEG study conducted by Henderson et al. (2002) has provided a seminal replication and extension of these earlier observations.

Henderson et al. (2002) used the ESCS in a study of the degree to which baseline EEG at 14 months predicted 18-month joint attention development in 27 typically developing infants. However, compared to Mundy et al. (2000), they used a higher-density array of 64 electrodes to improve the spatial resolution of their data. Moreover, because the total ESCS scores for measures of IJA and other domains used in Mundy et al. were composites of several behaviors, the Henderson team reasoned that the exact nature of the associations with EEG activity were unclear in that earlier study. Therefore, Henderson et al. compared the EEG correlates of only two types of behaviors: self-initiated pointing to share attention with respect to an active mechanical toy (IJA pointing) and self-initiated pointing to elicit aid in obtaining an out-of-reach object (IBR pointing). In the ESCS, the former involves pointing to an active mechanical toy that is within easy reach, and the latter involves pointing to an inactive toy that is out of reach.

Henderson et al. (2002) found no significant correlations between any of the 14-month EEG data and IBR pointing at 18 months. However, in the 3Hz to 6Hz band, IJA pointing at 18 months was significantly predicted by 14-month EEG data, indicative of greater brain activity over the medial frontal cortex. These correlations involved electrodes that were placed above cortical regions corresponding to Brodmann's areas 6, 8, and 9. Henderson et al. also analyzed data from the 6Hz to 9Hz bands, which revealed 15 significant correlations between 14-month EEG data and 18-month IJA pointing. Again, higher bilateral activity corresponding to the previously identified medial-frontal sites was a strong predictor of IJA pointing at 18 months. In addition, though, IJA pointing at 18 months was also predicted by activity in this bandwidth from the orbitofrontal, temporal, and dorsolateral-frontal cortical regions.

The bilateral nature of the Henderson et al. (2002) findings suggested that Mundy's (1995) social motivation model's focus on only left frontal contributions to IJA processes may, at best, be incomplete. Indeed, these bilateral data are consistent with data from Vaughan et al. (2003) that suggest that IJA may be associated not only with positive affect and motivation tendencies associated with relative left frontal activation but also with negative affect and motivation tendencies that have been associated with relative right frontal activation. Nevertheless, the Henderson et al. study again indicated that IJA development might reflect dorsal-frontal cortical functions (Mundy et al., 2000). However, it also suggested that IJA might be affected by a broader cortical system that also may involve ventral "social brain" and dorsolateral functions that have been identified as contributing to IJA in other studies (Dawson, Munson, et al., 2002; Griffith et al., 1999). There was, however, little evidence for parietal involvement in IJA in this study.

The study of Henderson et al. (2002) also provided information about the social specificity of the link between IJA and dorsal-cortical brain activity. Remember that the specific dorsal-medial-frontal cortical areas involved in IJA corresponded to aspects of both the frontal eye fields and supplementary motor cortex associated with the control of saccadic eye movement and motor planning (BA 6, 8; Martin, 1996). Therefore, these associations could simply reflect the motor control of the eye movements and/or gestural behaviors that are intrinsic to joint attention behaviors. However, the simple elegance of the Henderson et al. study controls for this possible interpretation. The gross motor topography of IJA pointing and IBR pointing is virtually identical on the ESCS. Therefore, a neuromotor explanation of the different cortical correlates of IJA and IBR appears unlikely. Instead, because IJA pointing and IBR pointing appear to serve different social communicative functions, it is reasonable to assume that the difference in EEG correlates of these infant behaviors also reflects differences in the neurodevelopmental substrates of these social communicative functions.

The data from Henderson et al. (2002) suggest that IJA behaviors reflect a complex system of brain activity that includes not only the dorsal-medial cortex but also activity associated with the dorsolateral, orbitofrontal, and temporal cortex. Several neuropsychological studies have provided data consistent with this more complex systems view of IJA. In a study of the possible functions that contribute to joint attention deficits in Autism, IJA as well as RJA performance was observed to be associated with a spatial reversal task, which comparative research indicates involves dorsolateral mediation of response inhibition, planning, and memory (Griffith et al., 1999; McEvoy et al., 1993). Spatial reversal tasks involve searching for hidden objects and flexibly inhibiting reach and altering search strategies throughout the task. Hence, these data suggest that frontal mediation of inhibitory planning and memory may not necessarily be a specific component of IJA but may be a general frontal component of both types of joint attention skills. However, although they displayed joint attention deficits, the children with Autism in this study did not display deficits on the spatial reversal task. Thus, these results suggested that functions associated with spatial reversal impairment were related to joint attention development but not so clearly related to joint attention impairments in Autism.

Another important neuropsychological study has been provided by Dawson, Munson, et al. (2002), who examined the degree to which joint attention in Autism was correlated with neuropsychological measures associated with an orbitofrontal brain system, rather than a dorsolateral-frontal system. This study was based on the hypothesis that an IJA disturbance in Autism involves an impairment of the reward sensitivity that is mediated by an orbitofrontal and temporal circuit (Dawson, Munson, et al., 2002). To assess this dimension, the authors presented children with a delay-not match to sample task (DNMS). This is another type of object search task, but it is designed, in part, to measure children's sensitivity to reinforcement. Specifically, it measures the capacity of the child to adopt a search strategy that involves ignoring a visual sign that has previously been associated with finding the hidden object (e.g., an "M&M's" reward) in order to look in a hiding place associated with a novel sign. Performance on this task has previously been associated with orbitofrontal activity in comparative research. For comparative purposes, Dawson, Munson, et al. also presented children with an A-not-B reversal task previously associated with dorsolateral activity. The results indicated that joint attention in both children with Autism and typical controls was associated with the DNMS task, but not the A-not-B task. Thus, consistent with findings from Henderson et al. (2002), this study provided evidence of a more ventral-frontal contribution to joint attention. Dawson, Munson, et al., however, used a composite measure of IJA and RJA in their study. Therefore, it was difficult to determine if this more ventral component was associated specifically with IJA.

This issue has been addressed in a new study by Nichols et al. (2005). They worked with 39 typically developing infants and examined the relations of DNMS task performance with measures of IJA and RJA in the 14- to 18-month period. However, because previous research had implicated the contribution of the dorsal-medial cortex to IJA, the authors also examined data from a behavioral task that hypothetically may be related to activity in this brain region. The dorsal-medial cortex appears to play a fundamental role in self-monitoring and self-awareness (Buch, Luu, & Posner, 2000; Craik et al., 1999; C. Frith & Frith, 1999; U. Frith & Frith, 2001; Johnson et al., 2002; Stuphorn, Taylor, & Schall, 2000). For example, recent research indicates that the dorsal-medial-frontal cortex plays a role in encoding and recalling words and actions that involve self-reference awareness, but not necessarily those that do not involve self-reference (Craik et al., 1999; Johnson et al., 2002). Nichols et al. used a measure of infant self-recognition as a means for accessing this domain of behavior. They hypothesized that if the data from Henderson et al. (2002) were correct, then it was likely that variance in both an orbital-frontal-related behavior (DNMS) and a putative dorsal-medial-related behavior (self-recognition) would make unique contributions to the explanation of variance in IJA development.

Consistent with this hypothesis, both task performance on the DNMS and the self-recognition measures made significant contributions to a multiple regression for 18-month IJA. However, these measures did not contribute to the explanation of 18-month RJA data. Hence, consistent with the findings of Henderson et al. (2002), the data indicated that measures associated with both orbitofrontal and dorsal-medial-frontal systems were related to IJA development. The contribution of these systems to RJA is less clear. The integrated functioning of these two brain systems may be critical not only for IJA development, but for later-developing aspects of social engagement and social competence as well. A better appreciation of how these systems, especially the dorsal-medial-frontal system, may contribute to social competence may be gleaned from the recent literature on the anterior attention system (Posner & Petersen, 1990; Rothbart et al., 1994).

ON THE NATURE OF DORSAL-MEDIAL CORTICAL FUNCTIONS

The anterior attention system is associated with functions of the dorsal-medial-frontal cortex (BA 8, 9) and the anterior cingulate (BA 24). This anterior network may become more active after the posterior parietal system and is thought to make numerous contributions to the planning, self-initiation, and self-monitoring of goal-directed behaviors, including visual orienting (Rothbart et al., 1994). One important process here is the anterior attention system's contribution to the capacity to share attention across dual tasks or foci of attention (Birrell & Brown, 2000; Rushworth, Hadland, Paus, & Siplia, 2002; Stuss, Shallice, Alexander, & Picton, 1995). Thus, the anterior attention system may play a role in infants' ability to maintain representations of self, a social partner, and an interesting object spectacle, while flexibly switching attention among these foci in IJA behaviors (Mundy et al., 2000; see Figure 9.1, c1–c3). This attention-switching facility of the anterior system plays a critical role in the supervisory attention system (SAS; Norman & Shallice, 1986), which functions to guide attention deployment and behavior, *depending on the motivational context of the task* (e.g., Amador et al., 2000; Buch et al., 2000).

Ultimately, the anterior system comes to participate in monitoring and representing the self, as well as switching attention between internal proprioceptive (self-information) and exteroceptive information about external events (Faw, 2003). For example, two research groups have reported that self-referenced memory processes preferentially activate the dorsal-medial-frontal cortical component of this anterior system (Craik et al., 1999; Johnson et al., 2002). Other research on self-monitoring indicates that, in EEG studies, when people make an erroneous saccadic response in an attention deployment task, there is a negative deflection in the stimulus and response-locked event-related potentials (ERP), called the error-related negativity, or ERN (Buch et al., 2000; Luu, Flaisch, & Tucker, 2000). Source location suggests that the ERN emanates from an area of the dorsal-medial-frontal cortex (DMFC) proximal to the anterior cingulate (AC) cortex (Luu et al., 2000). Observations of the ERN suggest that not only are there specific cell groups within the DMFC/AC that are active in initiating a behavioral act, such as orienting to a stimulus, but there are also distinct cell groups involved in processing the positive or negative outcome of the response behavior (i.e., accuracy and reward information; Amador et al., 2000; Holroyd & Coles, 2002). Thus, like the orbitofrontal cortex, the dorsal-medial-frontal cortex appears to play a role in the appraisal of the valence of stimuli, in the generation or modulation of emotional responses to stimuli, and in mediating the subjective experience of emotion and reward in social behavior (e.g., Hornak et al., 2003; Lane, Fink, Chua, & Dolan, 1997; Ochsner, Bunge, Gross, & Gabireli, 2002; Teasdale et al., 1999). Indeed, specific lesions of the orbital-frontal cortex or dorsal-medial-frontal cortex (BA 9 and anterior cingulate) appear to be associated with deficits in voice and face expression recognition, social behavior, and appraisal of subjective emotional states (Hornak et al., 2003).

Finally, with respect to directing attention to external and internal events, Frith and Frith (C. Frith & Frith, 1999; U. Frith & Frith, 2001) have argued that the DMFC/AC integrates proprioceptive self-information (e.g., emotions or intentions) with exteroceptive perceptions processed by the STS about the goal-directed behaviors and emotions of others. This integrative activity may be facilitated by the abundance of connections between the DMFC/AC and the STS (Morecraft, Guela, & Mesulam, 1993). Indeed, cell groups in and around BA 8, 9 may be especially well connected to the STS (Ban, Shiwa, & Kawamura, 1991). We have described this putative facility for integrating proprioceptive self-information with exteroceptive social perceptions as a social executive function (SEF) of the dorsal-medial-frontal cortex and anterior cingulate system (Mundy, 2003). Hypothetically, this SEF utilizes the DMFC/AC facility to split attention among multiple representations in working memory to compare and integrate the actions of self and others. This integration gives rise to the capacity to infer the intentions of others by matching them with representations of self-initiated actions or intentions (Stich & Nichols, 1992) and recent research suggests that the representation of self-intention is mediated by circuits within the DMFC that include the supplementary motor cortex (Lau et al., 2003). Once this integration begins to occur in the DMFC/AC, a fully functional, adaptive human social-cognitive system emerges with experience (C. Frith & Frith, 1999; U. Frith & Frith, 2001). Indeed, there is considerable evidence that DMFC/AC activity is associated with attributing intentionality and performance on theory of mind measures in adults (Brunet, Sarfati, Hardy-Bayle, & Decety, 2000; Castelli, Happé, Frith, & Frith, 2000; Fletcher et al., 1995; Gallagher et al., 2000; Goel, Grafman, Sadato, & Hallett, 1995; Schultz, Romanski, & Tsatsanis, 2000). Of course, this version of the neurodevelopment model asserts that the social-cognitive facility is an emergent property of the DMFC/AC system. That is, earlier DMFC/AC behaviors, such as joint attention, contribute to the emergence of social cognition as much as or to a greater degree than social cognition contributes to the development of joint attention.

CONCLUSIONS AND FUTURE DIRECTIONS: JOINT ATTENTION AND RESEARCH ON ATTENTION-DEFICIT/HYPERACTIVITY DISORDER AND MALTREATMENT

The literature and ideas discussed in this chapter have revolved around several main themes. First, the study of joint attention does not fall only within the purview of those interested in language development or social cognition, but also has relevance for those interested in more general aspects of social competence associated with the development of social motivation, self-regulation, and executive processes. Second, research is beginning to suggest that observation of joint attention skills may provide unique information about early *social* neuropsychological processes that contribute to the development of social competence (e.g., social executive attention management, self-other monitoring). Third, joint attention may be a vehicle or platform for social constructivist process in early development. Finally, joint attention provides an operationalization and means of measuring individual differences in the tendency of young children to engage in episodes of intersubjectivity with others. Intersubjective process is a pivotal component of several theories of early interpersonal development and the pathological sequelae of disturbances in this domain

(e.g., Fonagy, 2003; Stern, 1985; Tronick, 1998). Therefore, developmental and neuropsychological theory suggests that, beyond its prominent application in research on Autism, measures of joint attention skill development in young children may have important applications to broader aspects of theory and research in developmental psychopathology. An important future direction for research on joint attention is to examine these potential applications.

To support these assertions, we have reviewed a recent set of longitudinal studies that provide evidence of significant predictive associations between individual differences in infant joint attention skill development and observations of social competence and behavior disturbance in toddlers and children. We have also suggested that no one model currently provides a full and veridical explanation of the links between joint attention and competent versus impaired social development in childhood. Rather, joint attention is a complex and fundamental skill. Individual differences in development within this domain are affected by differences in caregiving, but also reflect variability in the neurodevelopment of executive, motivation, and social-cognitive functions. Indeed, joint attention skill development may be considered a nexus around which much of early social neurobehavioral development revolves (Mundy, 1995).

Of course, the question comes to mind, If joint attention is such an important "nexus" in early development, why hasn't it become a more prominent focus for research on early processes involved in developmental psychopathology? Historically, there may have been several issues and misconstruals concerning joint attention that have held back research and theory development in this regard. For example, for some, the identification and examination of age-related changes in the emergence of different types of skills is the primary goal of developmental research on joint attention. Clearly, this is an essential goal of developmental research. Nevertheless, the focus on age-related change might have obfuscated an equally important developmental phenomenon. Children in all age and developmental groups (i.e., typical or atypical) that we have examined display significant individual differences in the development of joint attention skills. Why do such striking differences in the development of such a fundamental social skill domain arise, and what meaning do they have for the social outcomes of children?

The resolution of these questions constitutes another essential goal of basic and applied research on joint attention development. The task of addressing this goal has recently been facilitated by the observation that individual differences in infant joint attention development may be reliably and validly assessed beginning at about 6 months of age and with increasing precision through 18 to 36 months of age (e.g., Adamson, Bakeman, & Deckner, 2004; Mundy et al., 2000; Sheinkopf et al., 2004). Indeed, thanks in part to research on Autism, numerous video-based observational methods have now been developed to assess joint attention and related social communication competencies in young children (e.g., Adamson et al., 2004; Lord et al., 1999; Mundy et al., 2003; Stone et al., 2000; Wetherby, Allen, Cleary, Kublin, & Goldstein, 2002). Moreover, to increase the efficiency of these measures, research groups have developed parent report measures of joint attention and related skills (Baron-Cohen et al., 1996; Robins, Fein, Barton, & Green, 2001; Wetherby et al., 2002) as well as live scoring systems for some of the structured observation-based research instruments (Thorp & Mundy, 2004). Hence, a wealth of measures now exist that may be put to better use in understanding the role of individual differences in joint attention skill acquisition in typical and atypical social-emotional development. Indeed, a useful goal of one component of future research in this arena will be to determine if a combination of extant measures, such as parent report and live observation methods, may provide greater precision, reliability, and validity in the assessment of this fundamental domain of development.

Research on joint attention and social competence may have also been hampered by the misconception that the study of joint attention is applicable only to the more extreme forms of social developmental psychopathology, such as Autism. To be sure, research on joint attention has been instrumental in opening new perspectives on the neurobehavioral development, diagnosis, and treatment of children with Autism (e.g., Kasari et al., 2001; Mundy, 2003; Mundy & Crowson, 1997; Mundy & Sigman, 1989; Whalen & Schreibman, 2003). The observation that joint attention impairment is associated with the deep-seated social and behavioral impairments of Autism, however, also gives reason to suspect that lesser impairments of joint attention skills may play a role in other aspects of developmental psychopathology. We hope this chapter has provided the reader with a more detailed appreciation of this possibility. For example, the content and emerging neuropsychological validity of joint attention measures suggest that they provide a unique paradigm for the assessment of social attention management abilities in young children. As such, it is plausible to suggest that the measurement of joint attention skills may be instrumental in the early identification of children at risk for attention-related disorders and associated externalizing behavior disturbance (e.g., ADHD). Indeed, the recent observations that better joint attention development at 18 months was negatively associated with first grade parent and teacher ratings of hyperactivity and attention problems in children with in utero cocaine exposure provide intriguing support for this hypothesis (Acra et al., 2003). One potentially significant area of future research may be to follow up on the distinct possibility that joint attention reflects individual differences in the development of social attention regulation that ultimately are related to the expression of childhood ADHD and related externalizing forms of developmental psychopathology.

Another issue that may have hampered the realization of the utility of joint attention measures in developmental psychopathology is the confusion regarding the nature of the overlap of joint attention with other domains of inquiry. For example, after reading the section on the social motivation model in this chapter, it may be reasonable to suggest that, in some sense, "joint attention is just another term for intersubjectivity." This is true in part, and recognizing the connections between joint attention and intersubjectivity may be of some benefit to the science of developmental psychopathology.

Theory on intersubjectivity plays a major role in several contemporary formulations of developmental psychopathology. To translate this theory to research, though, requires operational measures with adequate psychometric properties. Although some relevant measures exist, research on intersubjective processes in developmental psychopathology could undoubtedly benefit from additional empirical paradigms and perspectives. Joint attention assessments provide one additional paradigm in this regard that offers highly reliable infant/toddler measures of the tendency to engage in intersubjectivity with either caregivers or unfamiliar social partners. We have tried to emphasize here, and elsewhere (e.g., Mundy et al., 1992; Mundy & Hogan, 1994), that these measures provide a useful means of examining theory about how impairments in the capacity for intersubjectivity in young children may develop and how these may relate to subsequent typical or atypical social-emotional development.

To reiterate the logic of this proposition, we believe that (1) if measures of joint attention, especially measures of IJA, provide a meaningful index of the tendency of infants to engage in positive episodes of intersubjectivity with others (e.g., Mundy et al., 1992; Mundy & Hogan, 1994); and (2) the capacity to engage in positive episodes of intersubjectivity may be a critical aspect of self- and social-emotional development that ultimately affects the ability of children to establish an adaptive level of relatedness with peers, teachers, and other caregivers (e.g., Cicchetti & Toth, 1995; Stern, 1985; Trevarthen & Aitken, 2001; Tronick, 1998); then (3) infant and toddler measures of joint attention may be useful in developmental psychopathological research on early risk and resilience to disturbances in interpersonal relatedness and intersubjectivity (Mundy & Willoughby, 1996, 1998).

This logic suggests that research on joint attention may well have applications to numerous avenues of research on developmental psychopathology. For example, it may be useful to utilize measures of joint attention to identify disturbances of interpersonal processes related to the cross-generation transmission of risk for affective disorders (Goldsmith & Rogoff, 1997). It is also likely that joint attention theory and research will play a fundamental role in the future study of developmental pathological processes incurred in the context of maltreatment or neglectful caregiving. Disturbances in multiple developmental processes related to self-regulation, a sense of relatedness to others, social motivation, and social-cognitive processes may be foremost among the negative sequelae of abusive and neglectful caregiving (e.g., Cicchetti, 1996; Fonagy, 2003). We would argue that measures of joint attention reflect these multiple processes across development in infancy. Therefore, these measures may provide a complement to methods currently in use that will contribute to a better understanding of the interactive self-organizing and neurobehavioral processes that are involved in translating poor caregiving into chronic self-related pathology in some individuals.

Indeed, research is beginning to provide support for this conjecture. For example, work by Kroupina et al. (2003) suggests that caregiver neglect may have little impact on joint attention development in the 1st year of life. However, if neglect continues past 14 months, a specific deleterious effect may be observed on IJA development, but not necessarily RJA or IBR. Similarly, in some of our own research, Claussen et al. (2002) has reported that disorganized attachment, an extreme form of insecure attachment that has been associated with poor, inconsistent, and even punitive caregiving, is associated with a decline in IJA development between 12 and 18 months in children with in utero cocaine exposure. These studies suggest that there may be a sensitive period in IJA development relative to effects of extremes of impoverished caregiving. If so, understanding the nature of this sensitive period effect may be illuminating with regard to early developmental psychopathological process. Interestingly, Cicchetti, Rogosch, Maughan, Toth, and Bruce (2003) have also recently reported that maltreatment has a deleterious effect on theory of mind development and

that this effect may be especially pronounced for maltreatment that occurs in toddlerhood rather than early infancy or childhood. The apparent similarity of the sensitive periods of maltreatment effects observed for joint attention (Claussen et al., 2002; Kroupina et al., 2003) and ToM development (Cicchetti et al., 2003) is both remarkable and intriguing. At a minimum, the similarity across these studies may provide additional evidence for commonalities in processes that underpin joint attention and ToM development. More important, though, the combination of these findings suggests that the examination of both joint attention and ToM development in future longitudinal studies may be especially revealing with regard to the effects of maltreatment on critical social-cognitive, social-executive, and social-motivation processes in children.

In this regard, we would argue that factors that lead to a significant attenuation of IJA development may lead to an imbalance in social-emotional, self-organizing functions that may have a pernicious effect on the psychological and emotional development of children. This hypothesis is based on a constructivist view of development (Cicchetti, 2002; Cicchetti & Tucker, 1994; Piaget, 1952) and its relevance for understanding the role of joint attention in social development. Accordingly, behavior control, as well as the knowledge about self and other, necessary to adaptive social behavior is gained through an active process in which the individual continually structures and restructures experience and meaning through self-initiated behavioral/cognitive/emotional activity in social interactions. Piaget developed the notion that early cognitive development derived in large part from the actions infants took on objects in their world. Indeed, a major component of cognitive development was described in terms of the redescription of overt action (sensorimotor schemes) to covert mental representations of action (the semiotic function) in the first 2 years of life. For the most part, Piaget's formulations focused on the development of knowledge about objects, and unfortunately did not speak as clearly to social-cognitive or social-emotional development. Nevertheless, as we noted, it may be that the infant's capacity to initiate actions in social interaction, such as initiating joint attention bids, and to note both self-experience and social reactions to self-initiated action (e.g., integrative self-other monitoring), constitutes a major early constructivist process that facilitates typical social-emotional and social-cognitive development. With regard to the latter it may be that the early exercise and monitoring of self-initiated joint attention bids is critical to developing representations of self-intentions (Lau et al., 2004) that provide a critical comparative foundation for interpreting the intentions of others (Mundy,

2003, in press). An attenuation of the tendency to initiate joint attention bids, therefore, may not only be a marker of a negative effect of past pathological process, but also a marker of an ongoing disturbance in social constructivist developmental processes that contributes to subsequent layers of psychopathology over time and age (for discussion of this transactional perspective applied to Autism, see Mundy & Crowson, 1997; Mundy & Neal, 2001).

We would also suggest that recent theory and research on the frontal and temporal-parietal processes associated with joint attention (e.g., Henderson et al., 2002; Mundy, 2003; Vaughan & Mundy, in press) may contribute to research and theory on the neurodevelopmental effects of maltreatment (Cicchetti, 2002). If an outcome of maltreatment in some children is an attenuation of IJA and we can examine the neural correlates of IJA associated with social executive functions such as integrative self-other monitoring, then we may be able to better understand the neuropsychological sequelae of maltreatment. For example, if maltreatment is associated with IJA impairment but not the social attention management that is involved in RJA (Claussen et al., 2002; Kroupina et al., 2003), it might be informative to undertake a sequence of imaging studies to determine if maltreatment is specifically associated with changes in frontal, self-system processes associated with IJA development, but spares aspects of social information (e.g., processing and following of eye gaze) and attention regulation processes associated with temporal functions.

The conceptual overlap of joint attention with the literature on temperament, caregiving, attachment, and social cognition may have also limited the recognition of the independent contributions that the study of joint attention may make to the field of developmental psychopathology. Some researchers may view joint attention simply as a by-product of these other domains of development. Therefore, connections between joint attention and social competence or psychopathology could be nothing more than an epiphenomenon of these more basic facets of social and emotional development. Examining this possibility is extremely important, and much more research will be needed before a firm verdict can be reached on this complex issue. However, research to date suggests that caregiver behavior alone may not completely explain all the relations between joint attention and developmental outcomes. For example, caregiver behaviors may not have as much impact on RJA as on IJA (e.g., Claussen et al., 2002), but both types of joint attention have been related to social outcomes (Sheinkopf et al., 2004). Moreover, although complex connections exist between joint attention, temperament, attachment, and social cognition, the evidence available to date suggests that

the relations between joint attention and social-emotional outcomes in children cannot be reduced simply to mediation by these other domains of development (Sheinkopf et al., 2004; Vaughan et al., 2004).

Recall that the incremental validity for joint attention measures in this regard may, in part, reflect the nature of their assessment. Joint attention measures, such as the ESCS, provide multiple indices of the capacity of children to initiate and respond to social bids in the context of interactions with familiar or unfamiliar partners. Although other infant measures of emotional expressivity, motivation, executive attention management, and social cognition are available, the interactive context of joint attention measures lends them an ecological validity that suggests that they may at least complement other measures currently used to examine early social-emotional development. However, in addition to their ecological validity, the content of joint attention measures also likely makes contributions to their incremental validity.

To explore this issue a bit further, consider one contemporary theory linking attachment to social developmental outcomes in children and adults. In a brilliant integration of nativist (i.e., genetic) and social (i.e., attachment) models of development, Peter Fonagy (2003) has suggested that a primary adaptive function of attachment is to contribute to a mental mechanism that facilitates the understanding of internal states in self and others. With apologies for the oversimplification, Fonagy suggests that attachment process contributes to typical and atypical personality development by moderating constitutional neurodevelopmental processes involved in social-cognitive development. According to Fonagy, the social-cognitive mental mechanism that arises from the interaction of neurodevelopmental genotype and social, caregiving variation associated with attachment overlaps with theory of mind social cognition, but more clearly involves the capacity for social affective as well as social epistemological representations. Thus, Fonagy's Interpersonal Interpretive Mechanism (IIM) is a warmer version of the relatively coolly cognitive ToM module that many social-cognitive theorists have described. Fonagy (2003, p. 15) describes the IIM as follows:

We conceive of IIM as the collection of neurocognitive mechanisms that are naturally selected to evolve under the influence of early social interactions predominantly with the attachment figure and that serve to mediate the impact of the quality of early relationships into adult personality functions.

So what are these neurocognitive mechanisms, or better yet, how do we measure them? Of course, we would suggest that observation of joint attention skills provides one essential approach to the early measurement of "the neurocognitive mechanisms" in Fonagy's model. Theoretically, joint attention skills reflect neurodevelopmental constructivist processes that have evolved to yield the early foundation for the development of the capacity for interpersonal interpretation (e.g., Mundy, 1995; Tomasello, 1995). This early foundation involves the social executive capacity for integrative self-other monitoring and the development of social cognition through the simulation of other minds (C. Frith & Frith, 1999; U. Frith & Frith, 2001; Mundy, 2003; Mundy et al., 1993). This social executive capacity may develop, to some extent, under the influence of early social interactions with the attachment figure. If so, research and theory on joint attention may provide a rich empirical and theoretical framework for the more detailed study of how caregiver influence and attachment process contribute to the development of IIM. Of interest, though, there was little if any overt recognition of the relevance of the literature on joint attention for examining the IIM developmental model incorporated into Fonagy's seminal formulation. This illustrates the current Zeitgeist, which does not yet clearly recognize the potential utility of joint attention measurement for theory and research on early typical and atypical interpersonal development.

It may also be instructive to take current models of interpersonal development, which emphasize caregiver effects, and turn them around to examine development from alternative perspectives. For example, Fonagy (2003) suggests that attachment may moderate the neurocognitive development of interpersonal interpretation. If this is true, is the converse also possible? Can the neurocognitive development of interpersonal functions, such as infant joint attention, moderate the effects of attachment?

Although it is a truly unfortunate condition, Autism has the benefit of teaching us many lessons about human nature. One lesson is that differences in joint attention development and the related capacities for interpersonal interpretation and engagement may reflect differences in constitutional (genetically constrained) neurobiological developmental processes. This observation raises intriguing possibilities for future research and theory. Consider for the moment the notion that a genotype does not describe a definitive phenotypic expression of behavior. Rather, the genotype sets upper and lower limits, or a "reaction range," for the expression of a behavioral phenotype (Waddington, 1962). Thus, children may vary on the range of effect that the environment has on their development of these skills. Accordingly, children with a low set point for the reaction range of their joint attention skill development may be es-

pecially at risk with respect to the potential detrimental effects of poor caregiving. Poor caregiving in these children may inhibit development to such an extent that joint attention skill acquisition falls below some critical level, leading to a clinically significant disturbance of self-constructivist behavior in social development. Alternatively, other children may have a higher constitutional reaction range for joint attention development. Among these children, poor caregiving may diminish their joint attention tendencies to some degree. However, their reaction range is such that even lower outcomes in these children are well above the criterion levels needed for adaptive self-constructivist social development. Therefore, these children may have sufficient reservoirs of the interpersonal capacity for joint attention that they can exercise in the context of alternative caregivers (e.g., other parent, relatives, or community adults such as preschool teachers). Thus, these children maintain sufficient positive social self-constructivist tendencies in interactions with alternative caregivers and other social partners (e.g., peers) to compensate for less than optimal primary caregiver attachment.

We previously described this model in terms of the "vulnerability hypothesis" of joint attention development (Mundy & Willoughby, 1996, 1998). That is, children at risk for developmental psychopathology because of environmental circumstance (e.g., poor caregiving, teratogen exposure) may display attenuated joint attention development as a group. However, within any at-risk group of infants and toddlers, individual differences in joint attention will be apparent, and the better development of infant joint attention will be a significant marker of constitutional neurodevelopmental factors associated with lower vulnerability to environmental pathogenic process within the group. The recent work of Sheinkopf et al. (2004) provided the first test of this hypothesis and demonstrated that individuals in an at-risk sample of cocaine-exposed infants who displayed better IJA and RJA skills at 12, 15, and 18 months received better teacher ratings of social behavior outcomes at 36 months of age. Unpublished work by Crowson (2001) and Block (2005) also suggests that better joint attention skill development, particularly IJA development, may moderate some of the negative effects of insecure attachment on early development in young children. Still, many more studies of this ilk will be needed before the significance of joint attention for developmental psychopathology, as well as typical development, may be fully appreciated. We look forward to the next generation of research on this issue and trust that it will yield fascinating and useful new perspectives on joint attention and typical and atypical interpersonal development.

ACKNOWLEDGMENTS

We would like to thank Danielle Thorp for her contributions to the section of this chapter on caregiver scaffolding. We would also like to dedicate this chapter to the memory of Elizabeth Bates, whose seminal thinking continues to enrich research and theory on joint attention, as well as numerous other areas of developmental science.

REFERENCES

Achenbach, T. M. (1992). *Child Behavior Checklist, 2–3 manual.* Burlington, VT: University Medical Education Associates.

Acra, C. F., Mundy, P., Claussen, A., Scott, K., & Bono, K. (2003, April). *Infant joint attention and social outcomes in 6 to 7 year-old at risk children.* Paper presented at the symposium of the Society for Research in Child Development, Tampa, FL.

Adamson, L., & Bakeman, R. (1985). Affect and attention: Infants observed with mothers and peers. *Child Development, 56,* 582–593.

Adamson, L., Bakeman, R., & Deckner, D. (2004). The development of symbol infused joint engagement. *Child Development, 75,* 1171–1187.

Adamson, L., & MacArthur, D. (1995). Joint attention, affect and culture. In C. Moore & P. Dunham (Eds.), *Joint attention: Its origins and role in development* (pp. 205–221). Hillsdale, NJ: Erlbaum.

Ainsworth, M., Bell, S., & Stayton, D. (1972). Individual differences in the development of some attachment behaviors. *Merrill-Palmer Quarterly, 18,* 123–143.

Akhtar, N., Dunham, F., & Dunham, P. (1991). Directive interactions and early language development: The role of joint attention focus. *Journal of Child Language, 18,* 41–49.

Amador, N., Schlag-Rey, M., & Schlag, J. (2000). Reward predicting and reward detecting neuronal activity in the primate supplementary eye field. *Journal of Neurophyisology, 84,* 2166–2170.

American Psychiatric Association. (1980). *Diagnostic and statistical manual of mental disorders* (3rd ed.). Washington, DC: Author.

American Psychiatric Association. (1987). *Diagnostic and statistical manual of mental disorders* (3rd ed., rev.). Washington, DC: Author.

American Psychiatric Association. (1994). *Diagnostic and statistical manual of mental disorders* (4th ed.). Washington, DC: Author.

American Psychiatric Association. (2000). *Diagnostic and statistical manual of mental disorders* (4th ed., text rev.). Washington, DC: Author.

Astington, W. (2001). The future of theory of mind research: Understanding motivational states, the role of language and real world consequences. *Child Development, 72,* 685–687.

Bailey, A., Philips, W., & Rutter, M. (1996). Autism: Towards an integration of clinical, genetic, neuropsychological, and neurobiological perspectives. *Journal of Child Psychology and Psychiatry, 37,* 89–126.

Bakeman, R., & Adamson, L. (1984). Coordinating attention to people and objects in mother-infant and peer-infant interaction. *Child Development, 55,* 1278–1289.

Baker, L., & Cantwell, D. (1987). Factors associated with the development of psychiatric illness in children with early speech/language problems. *Journal of Autism and Developmental Disabilities, 17,* 499–510.

Baldwin, D. A. (1995). Understanding the link between joint attention and language. In C. Moore & P. J. Dunham (Eds.), *Joint attention: Its origins and role in development* (pp. 131–158). Hillsdale, NJ: Erlbaum.

Ban, T., Shiwa, T., & Kawamura, K. (1991). Cortico-cortical projections from the prefrontal cortex to the superior temporal sulcal area (STS) in the monkey studied by means of HRP method. *Archives of Italian Biology, 129,* 259–272.

Bard, K., Platzman, K., Lester, B., & Suomi, S. (1992). Orientation to social and nonsocial stimuli in neonatal chimpanzees and humans. *Infant Behavior and Development, 15,* 43–56.

Baron-Cohen, S. (1995). *Mindblindness.* Cambridge, MA: MIT Press.

Baron-Cohen, S., Cox, A., Baird, G., Swettenham, J., Nightingale, N., Morgan, K., et al. (1996). Psychological markers in the detection of Autism in infancy in a large population. *British Journal of Psychiatry, 168,* 158–163.

Bates, E., Benigni, L., Bretherton, I., Camaioni, L., & Volterra, V. (1979). *The emergence of symbols: Cognition and communication in infancy.* New York: Academic Press.

Bates, E., Camaioni, L., & Volterra, V. (1976). Sensorimotor performatives. In E. Bates (Ed.), *Language and context: The acquisition of performatives* (pp. 49–71). New York: Academic Press.

Beitchman, J., Hood, J., & Inglis, A. (1990). Psychiatric risk in children with speech and language disorders. *Journal of Abnormal Child Psychology, 18,* 283–296.

Bell, R. (1979). Parent, child and reciprocal influences. *American Psychologist, 34,* 821–826.

Birrell, J., & Brown, V. (2000). Medial-frontal cortex mediates perceptual attention set shifting in the rat. *Journal of Neuroscience, 20,* 4320–4324.

Blair, C. (2002). School readiness: Integrating cognition and emotion in a neurobiological conceptualization of children's functioning at school entry. *American Psychologist, 57,* 111–127.

Block, J. (2005). *Infant joint attention, attachment and cognitive/language outcomes in 24 month-old preschool children.* Unpublished doctoral dissertation, University of Miami, Coral Gables, FL.

Block, J., Mundy, P., Pomares, Y., Vaughan, A., Delgado, C., & Gomes, Y. (2003, April). *Different developmental profiles of joint attention skills from 9 to 18 months.* Poster session presented at the Society for Research in Child Development, Tampa, FL.

Bono, M., Daley, T., & Sigman, M. (2004). Relations among joint attention, amount of intervention, and language gain in early Autism. *Journal of Autism and Developmental Disorders, 34,* 495–505.

Bretherton, I. (1991). Intentional communication and the development of an understanding of mind. In D. Frye & C. Moore (Eds.), *Children's theories of mind: Mental states and social understanding* (pp. 49–75). Hillsdale, NJ: Erlbaum.

Brooks, R., & Meltzoff, A. (2002). The importance of eyes: How infants interpret adult looking behavior. *Developmental Psychology, 38,* 958–966.

Bruner, J. (1975). From communication to language: A psychological perspective. *Cognition, 3,* 255–287.

Bruner, J. (1983). *Child's talk: Learning to use language.* New York: Norton.

Bruner, J., & Sherwood, V. (1983). Thought, language, and interaction in infancy. In J. Call, E. Galenson, & R. Tyson (Eds.), *Frontiers of infant psychiatry* (pp. 38–55). New York: Basic Books.

Brunet, E., Sarfati, Y., Hardy-Bayle, M. C., & Decety, J. (2000). A PET investigation of the attribution of intentions with a nonverbal task. *Neuroimage, 11,* 157–166.

Buch, G., Luu, P., & Posner, M. (2000). Cognitive and emotional influences in the anterior cingulate cortex. *Trends in Cognitive Science, 4,* 214–222.

Butterworth, G., & Jarrett, N. (1991). What minds have in common is space: Spatial mechanisms in serving joint visual attention in infancy. *British Journal of Developmental Psychology, 9,* 55–72.

Calder, A., Lawrence, A., Keane, J., Scott, S., Owen, A., Christoffels, I., et al. (2002). Reading the mind from eye gaze. *Neuropsychologia, 40,* 1129–1138.

Calkins, S., & Fox, N. (2002). Self-regulatory processes in early personality development: A multilevel approach to the study of childhood social withdrawal and aggression. *Development and Psychopathology, 14,* 477–498.

Cambell, R., Heywood, C., Cowey, A., Regard, M., & Landis, T. (1990). Sensitivity to eye gaze in prosopagnosic patients and monkeys with superior temporal sulcus ablation. *Neuropsychologia, 28,* 1123–1142.

Capage, L., & Watson, A. (2001). Individual differences in theory of mind, aggressive behavior and social skills in young children. *Early Education and Development, 12,* 613–628.

Caplan, R., Chugani, H., Messa, C., Guthrie, D., Sigman, M., Traversay, J., et al. (1993). Hemispherectomy for early onset intractable seizures: Presurgical cerebral glucose metabolism and postsurgical nonverbal communication patterns. *Developmental Medicine and Child Neurology, 35,* 582–592.

Capps, L., Sigman, M., & Mundy, P. (1994). Attachment security in children with Autism. *Developmental Psychopathology, 6,* 29–261.

Carpenter, M., Nagell, K., & Tomasello, M. (1998). Social cognition, joint attention, and communicative competence from 9 to 15 months of age. *Monographs of the Society for Research in Child Development, 63*(4, Serial No. 255).

Carter, A., & Briggs-Gowan, M. (2000). *Infant toddler social and emotional assessment.* New Haven, CT: Yale University, Early Development Project.

Case, R. (1987). The structure and process of intellectual development. *International Journal of Psychology, 22,* 571–607.

Castelli, F., Happé, F., Frith, U., & Frith, C. (2000). Movement and mind: A functional imaging study of perception and interpretation of complex intentional movement patterns. *Neuroimage, 12,* 314–325.

Charman, T. (1998). Specifying the nature and course of the joint attention impairment in Autism in the preschool years: Implications for diagnosis and intervention. *Autism: The International Journal of Research and Practice, 2,* 61–79.

Charman, T., Baron-Cohen, S., Swettenham, J., Baird, G., Cox, A., & Drew, A. (2000). Testing joint attention, imitation, and play: Infant precursors to language and theory of mind. *Cognitive Development, 15,* 481–498.

Charwarska, K., Klin, A., & Volkmar, F. (2003). Automatic attention cuing through eye movement in 2-year-old children with Autism. *Child Development, 74,* 1108–1123.

Chomsky, N. (1965). *Aspects of the theory of syntax.* Oxford: MIT Press.

Cicchetti, D. (1984). The emergence of developmental psychopathology. *Child Development, 55,* 1–7.

Cicchetti, D. (1990). Perspectives on the interface between normal and atypical development. *Development and Psychopathology, 2,* 329–333.

Cicchetti, D. (1996). Child maltreatment: Implications for developmental theory. *Human Development, 39,* 18–39.

Cicchetti, D. (2002). The impact of social experience on neurobiological systems: An illustration from a constuctivist view of child maltreatment. *Cognitive Development, 17,* 1407–1428.

Cicchetti, D., Rogosch, F., Maughan, A., Toth, S., & Bruce, J. (2003). False belief understanding in maltreated children. *Development and Psychopathology, 15,* 1067–1092.

Cicchetti, D., & Toth, S. L. (1995). A developmental psychopathology perspective on child abuse and neglect. *Journal of the American Academy of Child and Adolescent Psychiatry, 34,* 541–565.

Cicchetti, D., & Tucker, D. (1994). Development and self-regulatory structures of the mind. *Development and Psychopathology, 6,* 533–549.

Claussen, A. H., Mundy, P. C., Malik, S. A., & Willoughby, J. C. (2002). Joint attention and disorganized attachment status in infants at risk. *Development and Psychopathology, 14,* 279–291.

Corkum, V., & Moore, C. (1998). The origins of joint visual attention in infants. *Developmental Psychology, 34,* 28–38.

Craik, F., Moroz, T., Moscovich, M., Stuss, D., Winocur, G., Tulving, E., et al. (1999). In search of the self: A positron emission tomography study. *Psychological Science, 10,* 26–34.

Crowson, M. M. (2001). Attachment quality and infant joint attention skills: Predictors of mother-toddler interactions. *Dissertation Abstracts International: Science and Engineering, 62,* 2515.

Curcio, F. (1978). Sensorimotor functioning and communication in mute autistic children. *Journal of Autism and Childhood Schizophrenia, 8,* 281–292.

Cutting, A. L., & Dunn, J. (2002). The cost of understanding other people: Social cognition predicts young children's sensitivity to criticism. *Journal of Child Psychology and Psychiatry and Allied Disciplines, 43,* 849–860.

Danis, A., Bourdais, C., & Ruel, J. (2000). The co-construction of joint action between mothers and 2–4 month old infants. *Infant and Child Development, 9,* 181–198.

Dawson, G., Meltzoff, A., Osterling, J., Rinaldi, J., & Brown, E. (1998). Children with Autism fail to orient to naturally-occurring social stimuli. *Journal of Autism and Developmental Disorder, 28,* 479–485.

Dawson, G., Munson, J., Estes, A., Osterling, J., McPartland, J., Toth, K., et al. (2002). Neurocognitive function and joint attention ability in young children with Autism spectrum disorder versus developmental delay. *Child Development, 73,* 345–358.

Dawson, G., Osterling, J., Rinaldi, J., Carver, L., & McPartland, J. (2001). Brief report: Recognition memory and stimulus-reward associations: Indirect support for the role of the ventromedial prefrontal dysfunction in Autism. *Journal of Autism and Developmental Disorders, 31,* 337–341.

Dawson, G., Webb, S., Schellenberg, G., Dager, S., Friedman, S., Aylward, E., et al. (2002). Defining the broader phenotype of Autism: Genetic, brain and behavioral perspectives. *Development and Psychopathology, 14,* 581–611.

D'Entremont, B., Hains, S., & Muir, D. (1997). A demonstration of gaze following in 3- to 6-month-olds. *Infant Behavior and Development, 20,* 569–572.

Dunham, P., Dunham, F., & Curwin, A. (1993). Optimal social structures and adaptive infant development. In P. Dunham & C. Moore (Eds.), *Joint attention: Its origins and role in development* (pp. 159–188). Hillsdale, NJ: Erlbaum.

Dunn, J. (1995). Children as psychologists: The later correlates of individual differences in understanding of emotions and other minds. *Cognition and Emotion, 9,* 187–201.

Dunn, J., Cutting, A., & Fischer, N. (2002). Old friends, new friends: Predictions of children's perspective on their friends at school. *Child Development, 73,* 621–635.

Eacott, M., Heywood, C., Gross, C., & Cowey, A. (1993). Visual discrimination impairments following lesions of the superior temporal sulcas are not specific for facial stimuli. *Neuropsychologia, 31,* 609–619.

Elliott, C. D. (1990). *Differential ability scales.* San Antonio, TX: Harcourt Brace.

Eisenberg, N., Guthrie, I., Fabes, R., Reiser, M., Murphy, B. C., Holgren, R., et al. (1997). The relations of regulation and emotionality to resiliency and competent social functioning in elementary school children. *Child Development, 68,* 295–311.

Eisenberger, N., Lieberman, M., & Williams, K. (in press). Does rejection hurt? An fMRI study of social exclusion. *Science.*

Emery, N. (2000). The eyes have it: The neuroethology, function and evolution of social gaze. *Neuroscience and Biobehavioral Reviews, 24,* 581–604.

Fantuzzo, J., Sutton-Smith, B., Coolahan, K. C., Manz, P. H., Canning, S., & Debnam, D. (1995). Assessment of preschool play interaction behaviors in young low-income children: Penn Interactive Peer Play Scale. *Early Childhood Research Quarterly, 10,* 105–120.

Faw, B. (2003). Prefrontal executive committee fro perception, working memory, attention, long-term memory, motor control and thinking: A tutorial review. *Consciousness and Cognition, 12,* 83–139.

Flanagan, P., Coppa, D., Riggs, S., & Alario, A. (1994). Communicative behavior of infants of teen mothers. *Journal of Adolescent Health, 15,* 169–175.

Fletcher, P., Happé, F., Frith, U., Baker, S., Dloan, R., Frackowiak, R., et al. (1995). Other minds in the brain: A functional imaging study of "theory of mind" in story comprehension. *Cognition, 57,* 109–128.

Flom, R., & Pick, A. (2003). Verbal encouragement and joint attention in 18-month-old infants. *Infant Behavior and Development, 26,* 121–134.

Fombonne, E. (2003). The prevalence of Autism. *Journal of the American Medical Association, 289,* 87–79.

Fonagy, P. (2003). The development of psychopathology from infancy to adulthood: The mysterious unfolding of a disturbance in time. *Infant Mental Health, 24,* 212–239.

Fox, N. (1991). It's not left, it's right: Electroencephalograph asymmetry and the development of emotion. *American Psychologist, 46,* 863–872.

Fox, N., & Davidson, R. (1987). EEG asymmetry in ten month old infants in response to approach of a stranger and maternal separation. *Developmental Psychology, 23,* 233–240.

Fox, N., & Davidson, R. (1988). Patterns of brain electrical activity during facial signs of emotion in 10-month-old infants. *Developmental Psychology, 24,* 230–236.

Fox, N., Henderson, H., Rubin, S., Calkins, S., & Schmidt, L. (2001). Continuity and discontinuity of behavioral inhibition and exuberance: Physiological and behavioral influences across the first four years of life. *Child Development, 72,* 1–21.

Frith, C., & Frith, U. (1999). Interacting minds: A biological basis. *Science, 286,* 1692–1695.

Frith, U., & Frith, C. (2001). The biological basis of social interaction. *Current Directions in Psychologic Science, 10,* 151–155.

Gallagher, H., Happé, F., Brunswick, P., Fletcher, P., Frith, U., & Frith, C. (2000). Reading the mind in cartoons and stories: An fMRI study of "theory of mind" in verbal and nonverbal tasks. *Neuropsychologia, 38,* 11–21.

George, N., Driver, J., & Dolan, R. (2001). Seen gaze direction modulates fusiform activity and its coupling with other brain areas during face processing. *Neuroimage, 13,* 1102–1112.

Goel, V., Grafman, J., Sadato, N., & Hallett, M. (1995). Modeling other minds. *NeuroReport, 6,* 1741–1746.

Goldsmith, D., & Rogoff, B. (1997). Mothers' and toddlers' coordinated joint focus of attention: Variations with maternal dysphoric symptoms. *Developmental Psychology, 33,* 113–119.

Gray, J. A. (1982). *The neuropsychology of anxiety: An enquiry into the functions of the septo-hippocampal system.* New York: Oxford University Press.

Greenspan, S., & Wieder, S. (2000). A developmental approacho difficulties in relating and communication in Autism spectrum disorders and related syndromes. In A. Wetherby & B. Prizant (Eds.), *Autism spectrum disorders: A transactional developmental perspective* (Communication and language intervention series, Vol. 9, pp. 279–306). Baltimore: Paul H. Brookes.

Gresham, F. M., & Elliott, S. N. (1990). *Social Skills Rating System.* Circle Pines, MN: American Guidance Service.

Griffith, E., Pennington, B., Wehner, E., & Rogers, S. (1999). Executive functions in young children with Autism. *Child Development, 70,* 817–832.

Gutstein, S., & Sheely, R. (2002). *Relationship development intervention with young children: Social and emotional development activities for Asperger Syndrome, Autism, PDD and NLD.* Philadelphia, PA: Jessica Kingsley.

Henderson, L., Yoder, P., Yale, M., & McDuffie, A. (2002). Getting the point: Electrophysiological correlates of protodeclarative pointing. *International Journal of Developmental Neuroscience, 20,* 449–458.

Heyward, C., & Cowey, A. (1992). The role of the "face cell" area in the discrimination and recognition of faces by monkeys. *Philosophical Transactions of the Royal Society of London, 335,* 31–38.

Hobson, P. (1993). *Autism and the development of mind.* Hillsdale, NJ: Erlbaum.

Hobson, P. (2002). *The cradle of thought: Exploring the origins of thinking.* London: Pan Macmillan.

Hoffman, E., & Haxby, J. (2000). Distinct representation of eye gaze and identity in the distributed human neural system for face perception. *Nature Neuroscience, 3,* 80–84.

Hogan, A. E., Scott, K. G., & Bauer, C. R. (1992). The Adaptive Social Behavior Inventory (ASBI): A new assessment of social competence in high-risk three-year-olds. *Journal of Psychoeducational Assessment, 10,* 230–239.

Holroyd, C., & Coles, M. (2002). The neural basis of human error processing: Reinforcement learning, dopamine and the error related negativity. *Psychological Review, 109,* 679–709.

Hood, B., Willen, J., & Driver, J. (1998). Adult's eyes trigger shifts of visual attention in human infants. *Psychological Science, 9,* 131–134.

Hooker, C. (2002). The neurocognitive basis of gaze perception: A model of social signal processing. *Dissertation Abstracts International: Science and Engineering, 63,* 2058.

Hornak, J., Braham, E., Rolls, R., Morris, J., O'Doherty, P., Bullock, P., et al. (2003). Changes in emotion after circumscribed surgical lesions of the orbitofrontal and cingulate cortices. *Brain, 126,* 1691–1712.

Howlin, P. (1978). The assessment of social behavior. In M. Rutter & E. Schopler (Eds.), *Autism: A reappraisal of concept and treatment* (pp. 63–69). New York: Plenum.

Jasper, H. (1958). The 1020 international electrode system. *EEG and Clinical Neurophysiology, 10,* 371–375.

Johnson, S., Baxter, L., Wilder, L., Pipe, J., Heiserman, J., & Prigatano, G. (2002). Neural correlates of self-reflection. *Brain, 125,* 1808–1814.

Jones, S., & Tarja, R. (1989). Smile production in older infants: The importance of a social recipient for the facial signal. *Child Development, 60,* 811–818.

Kanner, L. (1943). Autistic disturbances of affective contact. *Nervous Child, 2,* 217–250.

Kasari, C., Freeman, S., & Paparella, T. (2001). Early intervention in Autism: Joint attention and symbolic play. In L. M. Glidden (Ed.), *International review of research in mental retardation: Autism* (Vol. 23, pp. 207–237). San Diego: Academic Press.

Kasari, C., Sigman, M., Mundy, P., & Yirmiya, N. (1990). Affective sharing in the context of joint attention interactions of normal, autistic, and mentally retarded children. *Journal of Autism and Developmental Disorders, 20,* 87–100.

Kaye, K. (1982). *The mental and social life of babies: How parents create persons.* Chicago: University of Chicago Press.

Kingstone, A., Friesen, C. K., & Gazzaniga, M. (2000). Reflexive joint attention depends on lateralized cortical functions. *Psychological Science, 11,* 159–166.

Kingstone, A., Tipper, C., Ristic, J., & Ngan, E. (2004). The eyes have it! An fMRI investigation. *Brain and Cognition, 55,* 269–271.

Kochanska, G., Coy, K., & Murray, K. (2001). The development of self-regulation in the first four years of life. *Child Development, 72,* 1091–1111.

Kochanska, G., Murray, K., & Coy, K. C. (2000). Inhibitory control as a contributor to conscience in childhood: From toddler to early school age. *Child Development, 68,* 263–277.

Kroupina, M., Kuefner, D., Iverson, S., & Johnson, D. (2003, April). *Joint attention skills of post-institutionalized children.* Poster presented at the Society for Research in Child Development, Tampa, FL.

Laasko, M., Poikkeus, A., Eklund, K., & Lyytines, P. (1999). Social interaction behaviors and symbolic play competencies as predictors of language development and their associations with maternal directing strategies. *Infant Behavior and Development, 22,* 541–556.

Landry, R., & Bryson, S. (2004). Impaired disengagement of attention in young children with Autism. *Journal of Child Psychology and Psychiatry, 45,* 1115–1122.

Landry, S., Smith, K., Miller-Loncar, C., & Swank, P. (1997). Responsiveness and initiative: Two aspects of social competence. *Infant Behavior and Development, 20,* 259–262.

Lane, R., Fink, G., Chua, P., & Dolan, R. (1997). Neural activation during selective attention to subjective emotional responses. *NeuroReport, 8,* 3969–3972.

Lau, H., Rogers, R., Haggard, P., & Passingham, R. E. (2004). Attention to intention. *Science, 303,* 1208–1209.

Leekam, S., Lopez, B., & Moore, C. (2000). Attention and joint attention in preschool children with Autism. *Developmental Psychology, 36,* 261–273.

Legerstee, M., Varghese, J., & van Beek, Y. (2002). Effects of maintaining and redirecting infant attention on the production of referential communication in infants with and without Down syndrome. *Infant Behavior and Development, 20,* 71–82.

Leslie, A. (1987). Pretense and representation: The origins of "theory of mind." *Psychological Review, 94,* 412–426.

Leslie, A., & Happé, F. (1989). Autism and ostensive communication: The relevance of metarepresentation. *Development and Psychopathology, 1,* 205–212.

Lord, C., Floody, H., Anderson, D., & Pickles, A. (2003, April). *Social engagement in very young children with Autism: Differences across contexts.* Paper presented at the Society for Research in Child Development, Tampa, FL.

Lord, C., Risi, S., Lambrecht, L., Cook, E., Leventhal, B., DiLavore, P., et al. (1999). The Autism Diagnostic Observations Schedule-Generic: A standard measure of social and communication deficits associated with Autism spectrum disorder. *Journal of Autism and Developmental Disorders, 30,* 205–223.

Lovaas, I. (1987). Behavioral treatment and normal education and intellectual functioning in young autistic children. *Journal of Consulting and Clinical Psychology, 55,* 3–9.

Loveland, K., & Landry, S. (1986). Joint attention and language in Autism and developmental language delay. *Journal of Autism and Developmental Disorders, 16,* 335–349.

Luu, P., Flaisch, T., & Tucker, D. (2000). Medial-frontal cortex in action monitoring. *Journal of Neuroscience, 20,* 464–469.

Markus-Meyer, J., Mundy, P., Morales, M., Delgado, C., & Yale, M. (2000). Individual differences in infant skills as predictors of child-caregiver joint attention and language. *Social Development, 9,* 302–315.

Martin, J. (1996). *Neuroanatomy: Text and atlas* (2nd ed.). New York: McGraw-Hill.

Masten, A., & Coatsworth, D. (1998). The development of competence in favorable and unfavorable environments: Lessons form research on successful children. *American Psychologist, 53,* 205–220.

Masur, E., & Turner, M. (2001). Stability and consistency in mothers' and infants' interactive styles. *Merrill-Palmer Quarterly, 47,* 100–120.

McEvoy, R., Rogers, S., & Pennington, R. (1993). Executive function and social communication deficits in young autistic children. *Journal of Child Psychology and Psychiatry, 34,* 563–578.

Meltzoff, A., & Decety, J. (2003). What imitation tells us about social cognition: A rapprochement between developmental psychology and cognitive neuroscience. *Philosophical Transactions of the Royal Society of London, 358,* 491–500.

Meltzoff, A., & Moore, M. (1997). Explaining facial imitation: A theoretical model. *Early Development and Parenting, 6,* 179–192.

Moore, C. (1996). Theories of mind in infancy. *British Journal of Developmental Psychology, 14,* 19–40.

Morales, M., Mundy, P., Crowson, M., Neal, R., & Delgado, C. (2005). Individual differences in infant attention skills, joint attention, and emotion regulation behavior. *International Journal of Behavioral Development, 29,* 259–263.

Morales, M., Mundy, P., & Rojas, J. (1998). Following the direction of gaze and language development in 6-month-olds. *Infant Behavior and Development, 21,* 373–377.

Morecraft, R., Guela, C., & Mesulam, M. (1993). Architecture of connectivity within the cingulo-frontal-parietal neurocognitive network for directed attention. *Archives of Neurology, 50,* 279–283.

Mundy, P. (1995). Joint attention and social-emotional approach behavior in children with Autism. *Development and Psychopathology, 7,* 63–82.

Mundy, P. (2003). The neural basis of social impairments in Autism: The role of the dorsal medial-frontal cortex and anterior cingulate system. *Journal of Child Psychology and Psychiatry, 44,* 793–809.

Mundy, P. (in press). Motivation, self-regulation and the neurodevelopment of intention sharing. *Brain and Behavior Sciences.*

Mundy, P., & Burnette, C. (in press). Joint attention and neurodevelopmental models of Autism. In F. Volkmar, A. Klin, & R. Paul (Eds.), *Handbook of Autism and pervasive developmental disorders* (3rd ed.). Hoboken, NJ: Wiley.

Mundy, P., Card, J., & Fox, N. (2000). EEG correlates of the development of infant joint attention skills. *Developmental Psychobiology, 36,* 325–338.

Mundy, P., & Crowson, M. (1997). Joint attention and early communication: Implications for intervention with Autism. *Journal of Autism and Developmental Disorders, 6,* 653–676.

Mundy, P., Delgado, C., Block, J., Venezia, M., Hogan, A., & Seibert, J. (2003). *A manual for the abridged Early Social Communication Scales (ESCS).* (Available from the University of Miami Psychology Department, Coral Gables, FL, at pmundy@miami.edu)

Mundy, P., & Gomes, A. (1998). Individual differences in joint attention skills in the second year. *Infant Behavior and Development, 21,* 469–482.

Mundy, P., & Hogan, A. (1994). Joint attention, intersubjectivity and autistic psychopathology. In D. Cicchetti & S. Toth (Eds.), *Rochester Symposium on Developmental Psychopathology: Disorder and dysfunction of the self* (pp. 1–31). Rochester, NY: University of Rochester Press.

Mundy, P., Kasari, C., & Sigman, M. (1992). Joint attention, affective sharing, and intersubjectivity. *Infant Behavior and Development, 15,* 377–381.

Mundy, P., & Neal, R. (2001). Neural plasticity, joint attention and a transactional social-orienting model of Autism. *International Review of Mental Retardation, 23,* 139–168.

Mundy, P., & Sigman, M. (1989). Specifying the nature of the social impairment in Autism. In G. Dawson (Ed.), *Autism: New perspectives on diagnosis, nature, and treatment* (pp. 3–21). New York: Guilford Press.

Mundy, P., Sigman, M., & Kasari, C. (1993). The theory of mind and joint attention deficits in Autism. In S. Baron-Cohen, H. Tager-Flusberg, & D. Cohen (Eds.), *Understanding other minds: Perspectives from Autism* (pp. 181–203). Oxford: Oxford University Press.

Mundy, P., Sigman, M., & Kasari, C. (1994). Joint attention, developmental level, and symptom presentation in young children with Autism. *Development and Psychopathology, 6,* 389–401.

Mundy, P., Sigman, M., Ungerer, J., & Sherman, T. (1986). Defining the social deficits of Autism: The contribution of nonverbal communication measures. *Journal of Child Psychology and Psychiatry, 27,* 657–669.

Mundy, P., & Thorp, D. (in press). The neural basis of early joint attention behavior. In T. Charman & W. Stone (Eds.), *Early social-communication in Autism spectrum disorders.* New York: Guilford Press.

Mundy, P., & Willoughby, J. (1996). Nonverbal communication, joint attention, and early socio-emotional development. In M. Lewis & M. Sullivan (Eds.), *Emotional development in atypical children* (pp. 65–87). New York: Wiley.

Mundy, P., & Willoughby, J. (1998). Nonverbal communication, affect, and social-emotional development. In A. M. Wetherby, S. F. Warren, & J. Reichle (Eds.), *Transitions in prelinguistic communication* (Vol. 7, pp. 111–133). Baltimore: Paul H. Brookes.

Nichols, K., Fox, N., & Mundy, P. (2005). Joint attention, self-recognition and neurocognitive functioning. *Infancy, 7,* 35–51.

Norman, D., & Shallice, T. (1986). Attention to action: Willed and automatic control of behavior. In R. Davidson, G. Schwartz, & D. Shapiro (Eds.), *Consciousness and self-regulation* (pp. 1–18). New York: Plenum Press.

Ochsner, K., Bunge, S., Gross, J., & Gabireli, J. (2002). Rethinking feelings: An fMRI study of the cognitive regulation of emotion. *Journal of Cognitive Neuroscience, 14,* 1215–1229.

Osterling, J., Dawson, G., & Munson, J. (2002). Early recognition of 1-year-old infants with Autism spectrum disorder versus mental retardation. *Development and Psychopathology, 14,* 239–251.

Panksepp, J. (1979). A neurochemical theory of Autism. *Trends in Neurosciences, 2,* 174–177.

Peterson, C. (2004). Theory of mind development in oral deaf children with cochlear implants or conventional hearing. *Journal of Child Psychology and Psychiatry, 45,* 1096–1106.

Piaget, J. (1952). *The origins of intelligence in children.* New York: Norton.

Pomares, Y., Mundy, P., Vaughan, A., Block, J., & Delgado, C. (2003, April). *On the relations between infant joint attention, imitation and language.* Poster presented at the Society for Research in Child Development, Tampa, FL.

Posner, M., & Dehaene, S. (1994). Attentional networks. *Trends in Neuroscience, 17,* 75–79.

Posner, M., & Petersen, S. (1990). The attention system of the human brain. *Annual Review of Neuroscience, 13,* 25–42.

Puce, A., Allison, T., Bentin, S., Gore, J., & McCarthy, G. (1998). Temporal cortex activation in humans viewing eye and mouth movements. *Journal of Neuroscience, 18,* 2188–2199.

Raver, C. (2002). Emotions matter: Making the case for the role of young children's emotional development for early school readiness. *SRCD Social Policy Report 16,* 3.

Raver, C., & Leadbeater, B. J. (1995). Factors influencing joint attention between socioeconomically disadvantaged adolescent mothers and their infants. In C. Moore & P. J. Dunham (Eds.), *Joint attention: Its origins and role in development* (pp. 251–272). Hillsdale, NJ: Erlbaum.

Reynolds, C., & Kamphaus, R. (1992). *Behavior Assessment System for Children: manual.* Circle Pines, MN: American Guidance Services.

Rheingold, H. L., Hay, D. F., & West, M. J. (1976). Sharing in the second year of life. *Child Development, 47,* 1148–1158.

Rizzolatti, G., & Arbib, M. (1998). Language within our grasp. *Trends in Neuroscience, 21,* 188–194.

Roach, M., Barratt, S., Miller, J., & Leavitt, L. (1998). The structure of mother-child play: Young children with Down syndrome and typically developing children. *Developmental Psychology, 23,* 241–248.

Robins, D., Fein, D., Barton, M., & Green, J. (2001). The Modified Checklist for Autism in toddlers: An initial study investigating the early detection of Autism and pervasive developmental disorders. *Journal of Autism and Developmental Disorders, 31,* 131–144.

Rogers, S., & Pennington, B. (1991). A theoretical approach to the deficits in infantile Autism. *Developmental Psychopathology, 6,* 635–652.

Rothbart, M. (1981). Measurement of temperament in infancy. *Child Development, 52,* 569–578.

Rothbart, M., & Bates, J. (1998). Temperament. In W. Damon & N. Eisenberg (Eds.), *Handbook of child psychology: Vol. 3. Social, emotional and personality development* (5th ed., pp. 105–176). New York: Wiley.

Rothbart, M., Posner, M., & Rosicky, J. (1994). Orienting in normal and pathological development. *Development and Psychopathology, 6,* 635–652.

Ruffman, T., Slade, L., Rowlandson, K., Rumsey, C., & Garnham, A. (2003). How language relates to belief, desire and emotion understanding. *Cognitive Development, 18,* 139–158.

Rushworth, M., Hadland, K., Paus, T., & Siplia, P. (2002). Role of the human medial frontal cortex in task switching: A combined fMRI and TMS study. *Journal of Neurophysiology, 87,* 2577–2592.

Rutter, M. (1986). Child Psychiatry: Looking 30 years ahead. *Journal of Child Psychology and Psychiatry, 27,* 803–840.

Sameroff, A. J. (2000). Developmental systems and psychopathology. *Development and Psychopathology, 12,* 297–312.

Scaife, M., & Bruner, J. (1975). The capacity for joint visual attention in the infant. *Nature, 253,* 265–266.

Scarr, S. (1992). Developmental theories for the 1990's: Development and individual differences. *Child Development, 63,* 1–19.

Schölmerich, A., Lamb, M. E., Leyendecker, B., & Fracasso, M. P. (1997). Mother-infant teaching interactions and attachment security in Euro-American and Central-American immigrant families. *Infant Behavior and Development, 20*(2), 165–174.

Schultz, R., Romanski, L., & Tsatsanis, K. (2000). Neurofunctional models of autistic disorder and Asperger syndrome: Clues from neuroimaging. In A. Klin, F. Volkmar, & S. Sparrow (Eds.), *Asperger syndrome* (pp. 172–209). New York: Guilford Press.

Seibert, J. M., Hogan, A. E., & Mundy, P. C. (1982). Assessing interactional competencies: The Early Social Communication Scales. *Infant Mental Health Journal, 3,* 244–245.

Sheinkopf, S., Mundy, P., Claussen, A., & Willoughby, J. (2004). Infant joint attention skill and preschool behavioral outcomes in at-risk children. *Development and Psychopathology, 16,* 273–291.

Sigman, M. (1998). The Emanuel Miller Memorial Lecture 1997: Change and continuity in the development of children with Autism. *Journal of Child Psychology and Psychiatry, 39,* 817–827.

Sigman, M., & Capps, L. (1997). *Children with Autism: A developmental perspective.* Cambridge, MA: Harvard University Press.

Sigman, M., & Kasari, C. (1995). Joint attention across context in normal and autistic children. In P. Dunham & C. Moore (Eds.), *Joint attention: Its origins and role in development* (pp. 189–203). Hillsdale, NJ: Erlbaum.

Sigman, M., & Mundy, P. (1989). Social attachments in autistic children. *Journal of the American Academy of Child and Adolescent Psychiatry, 28,* 74–81.

Sigman, M., Mundy, P., Sherman. T., & Ungerer, J. (1986). Social interactions of autistic, mentally retarded, and normal children and their caregivers. *Journal of Child Psychology and Psychiatry, 27,* 647–656.

Sigman, M., & Ruskin, E. (1999). Continuity and change in the social competence of children with Autism, Down syndrome, and developmental delay. *Monographs of the Society for Research in Child Development, 64*(Serial No. 256), 1–108.

Sigman, M., & Ungerer, J. (1984). Attachment behaviors in autistic children. *Journal of Autism and Related Disabilities, 14,* 231–244.

Sigman, M., Ungerer, J., Mundy, P., & Sherman, T. (1987). Cognition in autistic children. In D. J. Cohen & A. M. Donnellan (Eds.), *Handbook of Autism and atypical development* (pp. 103–120). New York: Wiley.

Siller, M., & Sigman, M. (2002). The behaviors of parents of children with Autism predict the subsequent development of their children's communication. *Journal of Autism and Developmental Disorders, 22,* 77–89.

Stern, D. (1985). *The interpersonal world of the infant.* New York: Basic Books.

Stich, S., & Nichols, S. (1992). Folk psychology: Simulation versus tacit theory. *Mind and Language, 7,* 29–65.

Stone, W., Coonrod, E., & Ousley, O. (2000). Brief report: Screening Tool for Autism in Two-years-olds (STAT): Development and preliminary data. *Journal of Autism and Developmental Disorders, 30,* 607–612.

Stuphorn, V., Taylor, T., & Schall, J. (2000). Performance monitoring by the supplementary eye field. *Nature, 408,* 857–860.

Stuss, D., Shallice, T., Alexander, M., & Picton, T. (1995). A multidimensional approach to anterior attention functions. In J. Grafman, K. Holyoak, & F. Boller (Eds.), *Structure and function of the human prefrontal cortex: Annals of the New York Academy of Science* (Vol. 769, pp. 191–211). New York: New York Academy of Sciences.

Sutton, S., & Davidson, R. (1997). Prefrontal brain asymmetry: A biological substrate of the behavioral approach and inhibition systems. *Psychological Science, 8,* 204–210.

Swettenham, J., Baron-Cohen, S., Charman, T., Cox, A., Baird, G., Drew, A., et al. (1998). The frequency and distribution of spontaneous attention shifts between social and nonsocial stimuli in autistic, typically developing, and nonautistic developmentally delayed infants. *Journal of Child Psychology and Psychiatry, 39,* 747–753.

Teasdale, J., Howard, R., Cox, S., Ha, Y., Brammer, M., Williams, S., et al. (1999). Functional MRI of the cognitive generation of affect. *American Journal of Psychiatry, 156,* 209–215.

Thorp, D. (2005). *Joint engagement and language development: The contributions of the mother and child.* Unpublished PhD dissertation, Department of Psychology, University of Miami, Coral Gables.

Thorp, D., & Mundy, P. (2004). *Observation and parent report measures of social-communication skills in young children with Autism.* Manuscript submitted for publication.

Tomasello, M. (1995). Joint attention as social cognition. In C. Moore & P. Dunham (Eds.), *Joint attention: Its origins and role in development* (pp. 103–130). Hillsdale, NJ: Erlbaum.

Tomasello, M., & Farrar, M. J. (1986). Joint attention and early language. *Child Development, 57,* 1454–1463.

Travis, L., Sigman, M., & Rushkin, E. (2001). Links between social understanding and social behavior in verbally able children with Autism. *Journal of Autism and Developmental Disorders, 31,* 119–130.

Trevarthen, C. (1979). Communication and cooperation in early infancy: A description of primary intersubjectivity. In M. Bullowa (Ed.), *Before speech: The beginning of interpersonal communication* (pp. 49–66). Cambridge, England: Cambridge University Press.

Trevarthen, C., & Aitken, K. (2001). Infant intersubjectivity: Research, theory and clinical applications. *Journal of Child Psychology and Psychiatry, 42,* 3–48.

Trevarthen, C., & Hubley, P. (1978). Secondary intersubjectivity: Confidence, confiding and acts of meaning in the first year. In A. Lock (Ed.), *Action, gesture, and symbols: The emergence of language* (pp. 183–229). London: Academic Press.

Tronick, E. (1998). Dyadically expanded states of consciousness and the process of therapeutic change. *Infant Mental Health Journal, 19,* 290–299.

Ulvund, S., & Smith, L. (1996). The predictive validity of nonverbal communication skills in infants with perinatal hazards. *Infant Behavior and Development, 19,* 441–449.

Valenza, E., Simion, F., Cassia, V., & Umilta, C. (1996). Face preference at birth. *Journal of Experimental Psychology: Human Perception and Performance, 22,* 892–903.

Vaughan, A., & Mundy, P. (in press). Neural systems and the development of gaze following and related joint attention skills. In R. Flom, K. Lee, & D. Muir (Eds.), *The ontogeny of gaze processing in infants and children.* Mahwah, NJ: Erlbaum.

Vaughan, A., Mundy, P., Acra, F., Block, J., Gomez, Y., Delgado, C., et al. (2004). *Contributions of joint attention and temperament to social competence, dysregulation, externalizing and internalizing behavior in normally developing children.* Manuscript submitted for publication.

Vaughan, A., Mundy, P., Block, J., Burnette, C., Delgado, C., & Gomez, Y. (2003). Child, caregiver and temperament contributions to infant joint attention. *Infancy, 4,* 603–616.

Venezia, M., Messinger, D., Thorp, D., & Mundy, P. (2004). The development of anticipatory smiling. *Infancy, 6,* 397–406.

Vygotsky, L. (1978). *Mind in society: The development of higher psychological processes.* Cambridge, MA: Harvard University Press.

Wachs, T., & Chan, A. (1986). Specificity of environmental action, as seen in environmental correlates of infants' communication performance. *Child Development, 57,* 1464–1474.

Waddington, C. H. (1962). *New patterns in genetics and development.* New York: Columbia University Press.

Wantanabe, M. (1996). Reward expectancy in primate frontal neurons. *Nature, 382,* 629–632.

Wellman, H., Cross, P., & Watson, J. (2001). Meta-analysis of theory of mind development: The truth about false belief. *Child Development, 72,* 695–684.

Werner, H., & Kaplan, B. (1963). *Symbol formation.* Oxford: Wiley.

Wetherby, A., Allen, L., Cleary, J., Kublin, K., & Goldstein, H. (2002). Validity and reliability of the Communication and Symbolic Behavior Scales developmental profile with very young children. *Journal of Speech, Language and Hearing Research, 45,* 1202–1218.

Wetherby, A. M., & Prutting, C. A. (1984). Profiles of communicative and cognitive-social abilities in autistic children. *Journal of Speech and Hearing Research, 27,* 364–377.

Whalen, C., & Schreibman, L. (2003). Joint attention training for children with Autism using behavior modification procedures. *Journal of Child Psychology and Psychiatry, 44,* 456–468.

Wicker, B., Michel, F., Henaff, M., & Decety, J. (2002). Brain regions involved in the perception of gaze. *Neuroimage, 8,* 221–227.

Wing, L., & Potter, D. (2002). The epidemiology of autistic spectrum disorders: Is the prevalence rising? *Mental Retardation and Developmental Disabilities, 8,* 151–161.

Woodcock, R. (1991). *Woodcock Language Proficiency Battery-Revised.* Allen, TX: Measurement/Learning/Consultants.

Woodward, A. (2003). Infants' developing understanding of the link between looker and object. *Developmental Science, 6,* 297–311.

Yoder, P., & Warren, S. (2002). The effects of prelinguistic milieu teaching and parent responsivity education on dyads involving children with intellectual disabilities. *Journal of Speech-Language and Hearing, 45,* 1158–1174.

CHAPTER 10

Attachment, Stress, and Psychopathology: A Developmental Pathways Model

ROGER KOBAK, JUDE CASSIDY, KARLEN LYONS-RUTH, and YAIR ZIV

John Bowlby's (1969/1982, 1973, 1980) attachment theory provided an innovative and compelling account of the parent-child relationship and its influence on personality development. In contrast to psychoanalytic models that stressed instinctual drives and intrapsychic conflict, Bowlby provided a framework for understanding how children's early experiences in close relationships shape expectancies about the self and others and lead to strategies for maintaining access to an attachment figure. These aspects of personality are activated in situations of danger, challenge, or threat and provide the individual with strategies for managing and coping with stress. More extreme stress is generally thought to lead to more intense activa-

tion of the attachment system. In this sense, the child's emerging confidence in the availability of an attachment figure is thought to play a major role in shaping the stress regulatory aspects of personality. Ainsworth's pioneering study of a nonclinical sample of Baltimore infants and their mothers provided an empirical foundation for Bowlby's theory of personality development (Ainsworth, Blehar, Waters, & Wall, 1978).

Beginning in the 1980s, researchers began to explore the relation between individual differences in attachment and psychopathology in more severely disturbed populations of parents and children. Early studies tended to view infant attachment insecurity as a risk factor for the subsequent emergence of psychopathology. These studies resulted in two key advances: First, researchers identified atypical forms of infant attachment, and second, the studies illustrated the need to understand attachment risk within the broader context of developmental models of psychopathology. During the past decade, spurred by the development of new attachment measures, researchers have begun to consider how insecure and atypical attachment organization in preschool, childhood, adolescence, and adulthood creates risk for psychopathology. The move to life span measures of attachment and the use of these measures as risk factors for psychopathology have further highlighted the need for a more comprehensive theoretical framework to guide construct validation and hypothesis testing.

Bowlby's (1973, 1988) concept of developmental pathways provides an important conceptual model for understanding the relation between attachment and psychopathology. Developmental pathways can be used as a general metaphor for tracking individual differences across development periods and for accounting for both normal and atypical developmental outcomes (Cicchetti, 1993; Rutter & Sroufe, 2000). A central task for the field of developmental psychopathology is to identify pathways that lead to psychopathology. Cicchetti and Rogosch (1996) have further elaborated the potential complexity of the pathways concept with the concepts of *equifinality* and *multifinality.* Equifinality suggests that there are multiple pathways to a particular disorder at a particular developmental period. For instance, adolescent Conduct Disorder may be distinguished between early- and late-onset versions based on different pathways leading to the disorder. Similarly, the concept of multifinality suggests that no single factor determines a subsequent pathway, but rather, the effect of a risk factor on a subsequent disorder will depend on both its timing and its relation to other risk factors.

We begin our review with a summary of Bowlby's thinking about attachment and developmental pathways. The developmental pathways model places attachment-related aspects of personality into a much broader theoretical framework that includes multiple levels of analysis and the continuing influence of the caregiving environment. In this levels of analysis approach, an individual's attachment organization continues to interact with and mutually influence the caregiving environment. This dynamic transaction shapes an individual's developmental trajectory from infancy through adulthood. Whereas responsive caregiving and secure attachment tend to maintain an individual on a more optimal trajectory, nonresponsive/disrupted care and insecure attachment move the individual toward less adap-

tive functioning. Moreover, Bowlby viewed the caregiving environment as influenced by contextual factors, including the larger family, community, and cultural contexts. In his view, an individual's pathway toward psychopathology is the product of processes operating at multiple levels of analysis.

After reviewing the theory of attachment and developmental pathways, we discuss research on attachment and psychopathology as framed by three levels of analysis: (1) attachment organization, (2) caregiving quality, and (3) caregiving context. In this multilevel model, risk for psychopathology may occur at the individual, relationship, or contextual levels, and at each of these levels the degree of risk may vary. We begin our review at the individual level of attachment organization and consider how attachment insecurity and disorganization create risk for psychopathology. Although the majority of studies have assessed attachment insecurity in infancy, new measures of attachment organization at later developmental periods have been tested as later risk factors. Next, we review studies that examine risk for psychopathology at the level of caregiving quality. These risk factors range from insensitive care (Ainsworth et al., 1978), to frightened or frightening behaviors (Main & Hesse, 1990), to attachment disruptions and abusive parenting. Finally, we consider risk for psychopathology at the level of the caregiving context. Contextual risk factors include family violence, poverty, and parental psychopathology, all of which may work to decrease caregiving quality and increase attachment risk.

In the next part of the chapter, we describe different approaches to modeling the ongoing transactions among attachment, caregiving quality, and contextual risk. Although many of the early studies of attachment and psychopathology used relatively simple main effects models that viewed attachment insecurity as a risk factor for psychopathology, later studies have moved toward more complex models. Additive risk models took into account multiple factors in addition to attachment insecurity and have evolved toward more sophisticated models of transactional processes such as mediation, diathesis-stress, and early experience. Mediation models hold promise for helping investigators to distinguish attachment from nonattachment risk for psychopathology. Diathesis-stress models suggest that attachment insecurity is most likely to result in psychopathology under conditions of high stress. This model elaborates on the view of attachment as a stress regulatory system and suggests that symptoms are most likely to emerge when attachment-related coping breaks down.

Finally, early experience models require longitudinal designs and test the claim that early experience makes a unique and lasting contribution to later adaptation and psychopathology (Sroufe, Carlson, Levy, & Egeland, 1999). In the last part of our chapter, we use the developmental pathways model in conjunction with consideration of levels of analysis to point to important areas for further research.

ATTACHMENT AS A STRESS REGULATORY SYSTEM: A BEHAVIORAL SYSTEMS APPROACH

The cornerstone of Bowlby's theory of attachment was the notion, borrowed from ethology, of a "behavioral system." A behavioral system is a species-specific system of behaviors that leads to certain predictable outcomes at least one of which contributes to the individual's reproductive fitness. The concept of the behavioral system involves inherent motivation to maintain a set goal; there is no need to view component behaviors as the by-product of any more fundamental processes or "drive." In the first volume of his attachment trilogy, Bowlby (1969/1982) proposed a theory of human personality and relationships that drew on the ethological and evolutionary thinking of the time. Bowlby's behavioral control systems model of personality focused on four major behavioral systems: attachment, caregiving, fear, and exploration. At the level of personality organization, the dynamic relationship among these behavioral systems can be thought of as a predisposition or strategy for managing and coping with stress.

Bowlby conceived of attachment as a control system that continually monitors the availability of an attachment figure. The attachment system becomes most active under two conditions related to activation of the fear system, perceived threats to an attachment figure's availability and perceived danger in the environment, and one condition involving the exploratory system: perceived challenge in situations involving exploration and novelty. Activation of the attachment system typically results in behaviors designed to reestablish contact with the attachment figure or to restore confidence in the attachment figure's availability. Bowlby (1969/1982) proposed that the level of attachment activation varies as a function of perceived threat or challenge.

The child's appraisal of danger, challenge, or threat to an attachment figure's availability changes dramatically with development. Whereas in infancy physical separations in strange environments are appraised as threats to the caregiver's availability, in later developmental periods physical separations are rarely perceived as a threat to availability due to the child's increased representational, communicative, and planning capability. In later developmental periods, unplanned disruptions of the relationship or verbal threats of rejection or abandonment are more likely to be perceived as threats to the caregiver's availability (see Kobak, Cassidy, & Ziv, 2004). Developmental changes also alter appraisals of danger and challenge. Moreover, the individual's growing competency and mastery of the environment continually changes the types of tasks that are likely to be perceived as challenging, and appraisals of danger are increasingly shaped by cultural information and associative learning.

Bowlby's view of personality organization is based on a dynamic conception of how the attachment behavioral system interacts with other behavioral systems, such as exploration, fear, and caregiving. The fear and attachment systems function in a synchronous manner. When an individual perceives clues to danger in the environment, not only is the fear system and a fight/flight response activated, but the attachment system is simultaneously activated and the individual copes with danger by seeking protection from a caregiving figure. Threats to the availability of an attachment figure also serve to activate the fear system. Thus, fear increases activation of the attachment system, and the individual copes with fear by regaining access to protection or safety offered by an attachment figure. In this sense, attachment can be understood as a biologically evolved coping strategy for managing fear and distress. The exploratory system has an antithetical relation to the attachment and fear systems. The emergency responses associated with high activation of fear and attachment take precedence over exploration. However, when access to an attachment figure is assured, exploration can take precedence over safety-related concerns.

The dynamic interplay among the attachment, fear, and exploratory systems leads to two very important hypotheses about how attachment influences adaptation. On the one hand, the attachment system serves a major protective and coping function when the individual is faced with situations of danger (referred to as the "safe haven" function of the attachment relationship). Second, confidence in the caregiver's availability is thought to enhance the child's ability to explore in novel or challenging situations (the "secure base" function).

Consideration of the secure base and safe haven functions provides general guidelines for understanding how secure attachment promotes successful coping with stress and exploration of the environment. Both functions of attachment suggest that attachment processes are most important in contexts involving danger and challenge. Whereas situations of challenge are likely to activate the attachment system at fairly low levels, situations of danger are likely to activate attachment at fairly high levels. Although individual differences in attachment may be observed in subtle ways in contexts involving challenge or exploration, they are most likely to be evident in contexts involving danger or threat.

Attachment Organization as an Aspect of Personality: Implications for Stress Regulatory Strategies

During the past decade, researchers have drawn increased attention to the stress regulatory function of attachment (Fearon & Belsky, 2004), and a growing body of research on the behavioral and psychophysiological correlates of individual differences in attachment security highlights the importance of the stress regulatory function of attachment (Burgess, Marshall, Rubin, & Fox, 2003; Hertsgaard, Gunnar, Erickson, & Nachmias, 1995; Spangler & Grossman, 1993; Stevenson-Hinde & Marshall, 1999). In fact, Ainsworth and colleagues' (1978) Strange Situation procedure, the central assessment tool of individual differences in infant attachment security, uses multiple contextual cues (i.e., an unfamiliar environment, an unfamiliar adult, and physical separation) to elicit high levels of infant distress and corresponding activation of the attachment system. Based on her understanding of the interplay among the attachment, exploration, and fear behavioral systems, Ainsworth identified three major attachment patterns: secure, avoidant, and resistant. She identified these patterns by observing how infants used their caregivers to manage separation distress. Infants judged secure are able to utilize their caregiver as a resource in managing stress. They signal distress directly, seek contact or interaction with the caregiver, and derive comfort from the interaction.

In contrast, the avoidant pattern of behavior is marked by less obvious signals of distress and attempts to reduce the activation of the attachment system through diversionary activities, such as ignoring the caregiver or focusing on objects without obvious interest or engagement. As a result, the caregiver is not utilized as a resource for coping with distress and the attachment system is deactivated through diversionary strategies. The resistant pattern is also marked by ineffective use of the caregiver for coping with distress. These children openly display distress signals and may seek contact with the caregiver, but contact is not effective in reducing distress. As a result, these chil-

dren appear to be characterized by a chronic activation of the attachment system that simultaneously reduces or inhibits exploratory activity. Both of the anxious strategies, avoidant and resistant, are marked by the lack of coordination between the attachment, fear, and exploratory systems. Avoidant infants are likely to seem less fearful and minimize attachment behaviors, and resistant infants are likely to seem distressed and maximize their attachment behaviors (Main, 1990).

These consistently observed patterns of behavior under the stressful conditions created by Ainsworth's Strange Situation procedure illustrate differing organizations for how children coordinate the attachment system with the fear and exploratory behavioral systems (Sroufe & Waters, 1977). Drawing on Bowlby's concept of internal working models, Ainsworth and her colleagues (1978) suggested that attachment patterns were organized by infants' expectations or forecasts of the availability and responsiveness of their caregivers. Much of Ainsworth's observational work was designed to show that the expectations that guided the infant's behavior in the Strange Situation were derived from the quality of actual interactions that the child had with his or her caregiver. Her finding that sensitive caregiving during the first 12 months predicted a secure attachment pattern in the Strange Situation supported Bowlby's contention that the child's attachment organization is shaped by experiences with caregivers. Further support linking attachment organization in the Strange Situation to sensitive caregiving has come from a number of subsequent studies (see Belsky, 1999; DeWolff & van IJzendoorn, 1997, for reviews).

The child's expectations (or "internal working model") of a caregiver's availability and responsiveness form the core of attachment-related features of the child's personality. This attachment organization is likely to be particularly important in guiding the child's behavior in stressful situations and will influence the degree to which the child is able to effectively manage stress. If the child is secure or confident in the caregiver's availability, he or she can maintain a lower level of attachment activation and corresponding increased ability to attend to and explore the environment (Bowlby, 1973, 1979). Confident expectations also allow the child to effectively communicate his or her needs and use the caregiver as a source of comfort when distressed (Kobak & Duemmler, 1994).

These relatively primitive models and their associated behavioral strategies for managing distress that are observed in the Strange Situation become more sophisticated and elaborated with development. As the child matures, the confident expectations that guide secure behavior in the Strange Situation become more refined and integrated with expectancies that the child has developed in other attachment relationships. Most important, expectations about the caregiver's likely behavior create the context within which the child develops an emerging sense of self. The child's sense of efficacy in managing distress or challenging situations, along with his or her view of the self as worthy of support, become central mechanisms through which the attachment organization is carried forward to new relationships and contexts beyond the immediate family (Bowlby, 1973; Bretherton & Munholland, 1999).

Attachment and Developmental Pathways

In considering developmental pathways, Bowlby (1979, p. 104) wrote:

> In the picture of personality functioning that emerges there are two main sets of influences. The first concerns the presence or absence, partial or total, of a trustworthy figure willing and able to provide the kind of secure base required at each phase of the life cycle. These constitute the external, or environmental influences. The second set concerns the relative ability or inability of an individual, first, to recognize when another person is both trustworthy and willing to provide a base and, second when recognized, to collaborate with that person in such a way that a mutually rewarding relationship is initiated and maintained. These constitute the internal, or organismic influences. Throughout the life cycle the two sets of influences interact in complex and circular ways.

Continuity and Change

Drawing on Waddington's (1957) epigenetic model of development, Bowlby conceived of the individual's attachment organization as part of a continuing interaction with the caregiving environment. This transaction shapes an individual's pathway, with some individuals moving along adaptive pathways and others branching in less optimal directions. In the last chapter of the second volume of the attachment trilogy, Bowlby (1973) formalized a model of the complex and changing relations between personality and the caregiving environment. This model posits that attachment processes operate at multiple levels. At the *individual* level, attachment organization provides a set of expectancies and regulatory strategies that becomes increasingly stable with development. At the environmental level, the availability and responsiveness of the caregiver play a continuing role in providing support and influencing expecta-

tions for self and others. At a third level, both the child and the caregiver are influenced by the wider family context. The context can support or reduce the caregiver's responsiveness and ability to protect the child from danger in the environment.

Although both attachment organization and the caregiving environment channel an individual along a particular pathway and thus tend to account for continuity in development, both are subject to change. Caregiving quality may change with stressors or supports in the family environment and subsequently influence the child's confidence in the caregiver and the child's attachment security. Change in the caregiving environment may move the child's pathways in either more positive or more negative directions. In this sense, a pathways model requires ongoing assessment of the child's attachment organization, the quality of care, and the wider family context. Further change in attachment organization should be "lawful" or predicted by changes in caregiving quality or the family context.

Environmental Sensitivity

A final aspect of Bowlby's model has often been overlooked. Bowlby posited that attachment organization was most sensitive to the caregiving environment early in development and gradually became more stable and resistant to change. This environmental sensitivity hypothesis suggests that an individual's pathway is likely to be more strongly influenced by caregiving quality early in development. Whereas in early development, attachment organization is very sensitive to the caregiving environment, by adolescence and adulthood, attachment organization has become a more stable factor and plays a larger role in maintaining an individual on his or her developmental pathway. Each of these core premises of a pathways models—levels of analysis, continuity and change, and early environmental sensitivity—provides important guidance to modeling the pathways that lead to psychopathology.

Attachment Organization as a Source of Continuity

Much attachment research has emphasized the extent to which infant attachment organization creates continuity in a child's developmental pathway (Main, Kaplan, & Cassidy, 1985; Waters, Merrick, Treboux, Crowell, & Albersheim, 2000). Such continuity between infancy and later developmental periods is consistent with Bowlby's notion of *homeorhesis,* or the self-sustaining nature of personality. Attachment organization may contribute to continuity in a child's developmental trajectory in several ways. First, continuity may be maintained by the expectations that the child carries forward to new situations. The expectancies for self and others and stress regulatory strategies that the child develops within the attachment relationship are thought to generalize beyond the relationship to influence adaptation in peer and school environments (Sroufe, 1983; Sroufe, Schork, Motti, Lawroski, & LaFreniere, 1985). Early attachment organization may also play an important role in shaping the child's behavior in later developing periods and eliciting reactions form others that tend to confirm and perpetuate the child's expectancies.

A second way in which attachment organization may serve to maintain a developmental pathway is through influence on the caregiver-child relationship. The strategies for regulating attachment that the child develops in infancy may influence how the caregiver engages the child in subsequent developmental periods. For instance, avoidant attachment has been viewed as a strategy designed to minimize conflict with a potentially rejecting caregiver (Main & Weston, 1981). However, by not signaling distress, the child may elicit caregiver behavior that confirms the child's expectancies that the caregiver will not respond. Further, isolation or dysfunctional anger that may accompany an insecure strategy may result in behavior that further elicits rejections by the caregiver.

Lawful Discontinuity in Attachment Organization

Despite theoretical and empirical support for the contribution of attachment organization to continuity in a child's developmental trajectory, there is substantial evidence that attachment organization remains open to change. This is particularly true of early developmental periods when attachment organization is subject to substantial change and instability. During the infant period, change is evident over the relatively short period of 6 months. In the Minnesota longitudinal study, 62% of children remained stable in attachment security between 12 and 18 months, and 28% changed. Some of the change in attachment organization was accounted for by caregiving variables. For instance, the move from secure to insecure was associated with caregivers who experienced less joy in feeding their infants (Egeland & Farber, 1984) and the move from insecure to secure occurred when mothers reported lower levels of negative life events (Vaughn, Egeland, Sroufe, & Waters, 1979). Over longer periods change in attachment organization become more likely.

The evidence for lawful discontinuities in attachment security (Belsky, Fish, & Isabella, 1991) is consistent with Bowlby's view of attachment. His pathways model stressed that attachment organization remains sensitive to the care-

giving environment throughout the years of immaturity, and the working models that form the core of attachment organization need to be continuously updated and revised to promote successful adaptation to the environment.

The Environmental Responsiveness of Attachment Organization

According to Bowlby, internal aspects of personality continuously interact with the caregiving environment. While the child's attachment organization can influence the caregiver, the caregiver continues to influence the child. As a result, the working models that form the core of the child's attachment organization are open to updating and revision to accommodate new information. This process of updating and revising models includes incorporating developmental changes in the child-caregiver relationship that allow more complex and sophisticated coordination of activities (Thompson, 1999). Updating may also accommodate changes in the quality of care available to the child. Thus, a child with secure attachment in infancy may encounter a major disruption of a relationship with a caregiver during the preschool period. Alternatively, a child with insecure attachment may find that a parent becomes more available, or may form a relationship with a new caregiver who is trustworthy and who behaves in ways that are inconsistent with previous models. To accommodate these developmental and relational changes, the child must revise and update his or her working models and related strategies.

The capacity for updating and revising models changes substantially with development. Bowlby (1973, p. 367) posited that attachment organization would have "a fair degree of sensitivity to the environment, especially to family environment, during the early years of life, but a sensitivity that diminishes throughout childhood and is already very limited by the end of adolescence." This environmental sensitivity hypothesis suggests that the child's early experience with caregivers has a unique and important role in shaping attachment organization, and that this influence gradually decreases with development.

Two hypotheses follow from the concept of environmental sensitivity. First, attachment organization should be less stable during early developmental periods and become more stable in later developmental periods. Further, to the extent that there is continuity in attachment organization in infancy and early childhood, much of this continuity is likely to be attributable to stability in the caregiving environment.

Second, the relative contributions that attachment organization and the caregiving environment make to an individual's pathway will change across development (see Fraley & Brumbaugh, 2004). During the early years, measures of the caregiving environment should account for relatively more variance in developmental outcomes; during later years, attachment-related aspects of the child's personality should become more important as the contribution of the caregiving environment gradually diminishes. Further, to the extent that there is continuity in attachment organization in infancy and early childhood, much of this continuity is likely to be attributable to stability in the caregiving environment.

Empirical tests of the environmental sensitivity hypotheses depend on longitudinal designs and simultaneous measurement of both attachment organization and the caregiving environment. Most of the initial longitudinal studies have tended to focus assessment on attachment organization without strong measurement of the caregiving environment. Further, the more extensive focus on attachment organization raises a number of questions about measurement error and the validation of the measures in the post-infancy period (Weinfield, Sroufe, Egeland, & Carlson, 1999). Although longitudinal studies that measure individual differences in attachment security across developmental periods are limited, there is some evidence that measures of attachment security become more stable at later developmental periods.

Early studies of relatively small middle-class samples suggested fairly high rates of stability in Strange Situation classifications between 12 and 18 months (Waters, 1978). However, as researchers began to study larger and more diverse samples, estimates for 12- to 18-month stability were substantially reduced (Barnett, Ganiban, & Cicchetti, 1999; Egeland & Erickson, 1987; Egeland & Farber, 1984; Lyons-Ruth, Repacholi, McLeod, & Silva, 1991; Thompson, Lamb, & Estes, 1982; Vondra, Hommerding, & Shaw, 1999). More recent studies examining attachment over 12- to 24-month periods and using preschool classification of attachment organization suggest modest stability in attachment organization between the infant and toddler periods (National Institute of Child Health and Human Development [NICHD] Early Child Care Research Network, 2001; Seifer et al., 2004; Vondra, Shaw, Swearingen, Cohen, & Owens, 2001). Lower rates of stability would tend to support the environmental sensitivity hypothesis, particularly in circumstances where the quality of the care was subject to change. However, studies that assess both attachment organization and the quality of caregiving over time are needed to adequately address this question.

The environmental sensitivity hypothesis predicts relatively greater stability in attachment organization at later developmental periods. Tests of this hypothesis have been hindered by the lack of standard measures for assessing attachment organization in childhood and early adolescence (Greenberg, 1999; Thompson & Raikes, 2003). However, by middle adolescence through adulthood, Main and Goldwyn's (1998) classification of states of mind with respect to attachment in the Adult Attachment Interview (AAI) has been widely accepted as a measure of attachment-related aspects of personality. To date, two studies have examined stability of the AAI over 2 years. These studies cover the same time frame as the infant to toddler studies. They also provide an important point of comparison with the infant and toddler studies in terms of Bowlby's concept of decreasing environmental sensitivity. In one study of newly-weds from low-risk environments, 85% maintained the same secure/insecure AAI classification across 2 years (Crowell, Treboux, & Waters, 2002). In another study, substantial stability over 2 years again emerged in a sample of moderately at-risk adolescents (Allen, Boykin McElhaney, Kuperminc, & Jodl, in press).

In summary, the comparison of studies examining stability of attachment organization during different developmental periods lends support to Bowlby's notion that attachment-related aspects of personality become more stable and less sensitive to the caregiving environment by late adolescence and adulthood. However, even in these later developmental periods, there is evidence that attachment organization remains open to accommodating changes in the caregiving environment.

The Caregiving Environment and Developmental Pathways

Describing the caregiving environment, Bowlby (1979, p. 133) wrote:

> The behavior of parents, and of anyone else in a care-giving role, is complementary to attachment behavior. The roles of the caregiver are first to be available and responsive as and when wanted and, second, to intervene judiciously should the child or older person who is being cared for be heading for trouble.

The evidence for lawful discontinuity and early environmental sensitivity supports Bowlby's developmental pathways model and the continuing role of the caregiving environment in maintaining a child on a developmental trajectory. Bowlby (1969/1982) postulated that the caregiver's behavior toward the child is organized by a caregiving behavioral control system whose set goal is protection of the child and ensuring the child's reproductive fitness. George and Solomon (1999) have noted that this aspect of attachment theory has not received a great deal of attention from attachment researchers. In his developmental pathways model, Bowlby clearly emphasized the ongoing importance of the caregiving environment in shaping developmental trajectories.

In spite of the theoretical importance that Bowlby assigned to the caregiving environment, it has received relatively little attention from researchers who study attachment beyond infancy. One of the problems in studying caregiving beyond infancy is that the boundaries are poorly defined between what constitutes "available and responsive care" and what deals with other aspects of caregiving in the extensive literature on parenting. For instance, although establishing clear rules and expectations for the preschooler is widely accepted as a part of optimal or authoritative parenting, many may view this as separate and independent of attachment-related caregiving. Yet, much of optimal parenting behavior may be incorporated in what Bowlby viewed as available and responsive care in the fourth stage of the attachment relationship, the "goal-corrected partnership" (see Kobak & Duemmler, 1994, for a discussion). Yet, despite the ambiguities in defining the boundaries between parenting in general and attachment-related caregiving, attachment theory provides several useful guidelines for conceptualizing the caregiving environment.

The *quality of care* that is available to the child represents the most proximal aspect of the caregiving environment. Bowlby (1979, p. 104) conceived of the quality of care in terms of the "presence or absence, partial, or total, of a trustworthy figure willing and able to provide the kind of secure base required at each phase of the life cycle." The quality of care has been most extensively investigated during infancy. In this period, Ainsworth developed measures of caregiver sensitivity that captured important aspects of Bowlby's notion of available and responsive caregiving, particularly at times when the child's attachment system is active. Attachment researchers have relied extensively on Ainsworth's measures of caregiver sensitivity to assess the quality of the caregiving environment. These measures have been effective at distinguishing between infants judged secure and insecure in the Strange Situation (for a review, see Belsky, 1999; DeWolff & van IJzendoorn, 1997).

The surrounding family or *caregiving context* represents a more distal component of the caregiving environment. Caregiving context may either directly influence attachment processes affecting the child's attachment organization or may indirectly influence the quality of care that is available to the child. A variety of factors have been considered as possible contextual influences on the child's attachment security. These factors fall into three broad categories: (1) personality and psychological health of the caregiver (see Belsky, 1999, for a review), (2) marital or adult attachment relationships (Owen & Cox, 1997), and (3) stress associated with poverty (including educational attainment, income-to-needs ratio, minority status, and stressful life events; van IJzendoorn, Schuengel, & Bakermans-Kranenburg, 1999).

The AAI has introduced an additional element into consideration of the caregiving environment. By providing a measure of the caregiver's attachment organization, new questions can be considered about how the caregiver's attachment may mediate or moderate the effects of caregiving quality and caregiving context on the child. A "free to evaluate" or secure state of mind in the AAI has been linked to infant attachment organization, and it may also play an important role in enhancing supportive family relationships and buffering the child from contextual stressors.

Summary

Bowlby's developmental pathways model specifies three major levels of analysis: *attachment organization* at the individual level, *quality of care* at the relationship level, and *caregiving context* at the family level. A fully specified developmental pathways model requires assessment of each of these levels at each developmental period. To successfully test the model, researchers need to assess attachment organization, caregiving quality of care, and contextual supports and challenges experienced by both the child and the caregiver. Not only is assessment of current functioning at each level of analysis required, but a complete pathways model also requires assessment of prior functioning at each level. Only by following an individual across developmental periods is it possible to adequately map continuity and discontinuity in an individual's developmental pathway.

DEVELOPMENTAL PATHWAYS TO PSYCHOPATHOLOGY: A REVIEW OF RESEARCH

The developmental pathways model can be used to consider a wide range of developmental outcomes. For instance, Bowlby was particularly interested in pathways that would lead to the development of a "healthy self-reliant person." An essential ingredient of a self-reliant personality is "a capacity to rely trustingly on others when occasion demands and to know on whom it is appropriate to rely" (1973, p. 359). Empirical support for this model comes from studies linking attachment and caregiving quality to broad domains of socioemotional competence (Belsky & Cassidy, 1994).

Psychopathology represents a complex developmental outcome. Whereas secure attachment organization can be seen as a protective factor or one that reduces the likelihood of pathways leading to psychopathology, insecure attachment has been viewed as a risk factor or one that increases the likelihood of disorder. The pathways model places attachment risk within a larger context of multiple risk factors that operate at multiple levels and that transact with each other in ways that may increase or decrease the likelihood of psychopathology. A multilevel approach that assesses *attachment organization, caregiving quality,* and *caregiving context* creates an opportunity to more fully understand how attachment related risk contributes to the development of psychopathology.

A first step toward a more comprehensive model of attachment and psychopathology requires identification of risk at each level of analysis in each developmental period. The degree of risk may vary along several dimensions, including the severity of particular risk factors, persistence or risk factors over time, and the accumulation of numbers of stressors. In reviewing studies of attachment and psychopathology, we attempt to identify a continuum of risk at each level of analysis. Current findings can inform future studies of attachment and psychopathology and lead to greater specificity about the conditions under which developmental pathways lead to psychopathology.

Our review begins with attachment-related personality structure as a risk factor for psychopathology. This level of analysis has received by far the most research attention. In reviewing attachment assessments in infancy, preschool, adolescence, and adulthood, we identify a continuum of personality risk for psychopathology. We pursue a similar strategy as we consider risk for psychopathology at the levels of caregiving quality and caregiving context.

ATTACHMENT ORGANIZATION AND PSYCHOPATHOLOGY: A CONTINUUM OF INDIVIDUAL RISK

A guiding hypothesis in most studies of attachment and psychopathology is that insecure attachment organization increases risk for disorder. Initial tests of this hypothesis often relied on low-risk samples of convenience, and for the most part, these studies provided minimal support

for the hypothesis (Greenberg, 1999; Sroufe, 1988). In several samples, children with insecure attachments did not develop psychopathology, and secure attachment patterns did not reduce risk for the emergence of symptoms (Bates, Maslin, & Frankel, 1985). However, as attachment researchers began to study samples at greater risk for psychopathology as a result of poverty, parental psychopathology, or clinical status, more support for attachment insecurity as a risk factor emerged. These samples with higher rates of psychopathology also led investigators to expand Ainsworth's classification of infant attachment patterns to include atypical behaviors (Crittenden, 1985; Lyons-Ruth, Connell, Zoll, & Stahl, 1987; Main & Solomon, 1990; Radke-Yarrow, Cummings, Kuczynski, & Chapman, 1985) and patterns of atypical behavior in the newer measures of attachment organization in older children and adults (Cassidy, Marvin, & MacArthur Working Group on Attachment, 1992; Crittenden, 1992, 1994; Main & Goldwyn, 1998).

Measurement of attachment organization is a critical problem for researchers. Studies of attachment in infancy have used Ainsworth's Strange Situation (Ainsworth et al., 1978) as a standard and validated measure of early attachment organization. By contrast, measures of attachment organization in preschool and childhood are not as well validated or standardized. For instance, in the preschool period, researchers have relied on behavioral observations using either the MacArthur or Crittenden Preschool Systems or the Attachment Q-Sort (Waters & Deane, 1985). Childhood studies have used both narrative (Verschueren & Marcoen, 1999) and reunion procedures to assess attachment (Main & Cassidy, 1988). Adolescent and adult studies have used the AAI (Allen & Land, 1999; Hesse, 1999) or a variety of self-report measures. Further validation of these newer measures remains an important topic for further research.

Despite the difference in measurement strategies, most systems have continued to assess patterns of atypical attachment behavior. The discovery of disorganized/disoriented behavior in the Strange Situation (Main & Hesse, 1990; Main & Solomon, 1990) has led to a new generation of studies that have examined this behavior as an additional potential risk for subsequent psychopathology. Atypical patterns of attachment have also been identified in the Main and Cassidy (1988) procedure with children who had been disorganized as infants showing controlling/punitive or controlling/caregiving patterns with their mother. Finally, in the AAI, a variety of atypical discourse patterns have been identified (e.g., the Unresolved Loss and Trauma classification, the Preoccupied with Trauma subclassification, and the Insecure/Cannot Classify classification). Lyons-Ruth, Yellin, Melnick, and Atwood (2003) have recently added to these atypical AAI patterns with ratings of hostile/helpless aspects of discourse. These atypical patterns have been most prevalent in high-risk or clinical samples and suggest that individuals with atypical attachment organization may be at increased risk for psychopathology.

Infant Attachment and Psychopathology

Many of the early studies of attachment and psychopathology relied on normal middle class samples that generally are exposed to less caregiving or contextual risk than clinical or low income samples. Later studies of high risk or clinical samples better illustrate the transactions between attachment, caregiving and contextual risk, and the role of developmental pathways to psychopathology.

Low-Risk Samples

A summary of studies of infant attachment and psychopathology can be found in the first section of Table 10.1. Studies that relied primarily on normal samples of convenience generally do not have any indicators of contextual risk and are considered to be low-risk samples. These low-risk studies generally produced mixed results. Whereas Bates and his colleagues (1985) found no relation between anxious attachment measured at 13 months and externalizing symptoms at age 3, Fagot and Kavanagh (1990) reported that avoidant attachment was associated with a broad composite measure of problem behaviors assessed at four different time points when children were between 24 and 48 months of age. In another study, both avoidant and resistant attachment were associated with externalizing symptoms at age 6, though prediction of symptoms was enhanced by maternal reports of life stress (Lewis, Feiring, McGuffog, & Jaskir, 1984).

Greenberg (1999) has noted that low-risk samples put investigators at a disadvantage in detecting a relation between attachment and psychopathology. First, low base rates of psychopathology make it more difficult to detect statistically significant effects and increase the threat of Type II errors. A further limitation of the early low-risk studies is that they were conducted before it was possible to separate out the children with disorganized attachment. An additional limitation of some of the low-risk studies is that the absence of caregiving and contextual risk may serve as unspecified third variables that buffer children from risk associated with insecure attachments. As a result, the findings

from these low-risk studies have limited value in explaining the relations between attachment and psychopathology.

High-Risk Samples: Behavior Problems and Global Psychopathology

In contrast to low-risk samples, high-risk samples are at increased risk for psychopathology as a result of low socioeconomic status (SES) or parental adjustment problems. Low SES is thought to increase risk by increasing children's exposure to stressors associated with poverty, including financial strain, residential mobility, violence, single-parent status, and lower levels of maternal education. A variety of parenting adjustment factors, including depressive symptoms, lower levels of social support, teen parenting, and substance abuse, also covary with poverty. These factors have all been identified as main effects for child psychopathology, especially externalizing symptoms.

Most studies of infant attachment using high-risk samples have focused on disruptive, aggressive, and externalizing symptoms as outcomes. The Minnesota Parent-Child Project represents the first major longitudinal investigation of infant attachment and psychopathology in a high-risk sample (see Sroufe, Egeland, Carlson, & Collins, 2005). These investigators were the first to report that avoidant infant attachment increased children's risk for behavior problems and for teacher-reported hostility, isolation, and lack of compliance at age 4 (Erickson, Sroufe, & Egeland, 1985). Avoidant infant attachment continued to predict behavior problems in elementary school, with the effects being strongest for boys and aggressive behaviors (Renken, Egeland, Marvinney, Mangelsdorf, & Sroufe, 1989). In that study, assessment of contextual risk using measures of maternal life stress and relationship support during infancy and early childhood substantially improved the prediction of middle school behavior problems.

In a further follow-up on the Minnesota sample, Aguilar, Sroufe, Egeland, and Carlson (2000) used attachment and early caregiving variables to investigate Moffitt's (e.g., 1990, 1993) theory regarding early- versus late-onset adolescent antisocial behavior. The early-onset persistent group was distinguished by indices of socioemotional history, including the presence of avoidant attachment at 12 and 18 months. Although avoidant attachment contributed to identifying early onset of adolescent antisocial behavior, this group was distinguished by a broad array of psychosocial risk during infancy and early childhood, including physical abuse, caregiver unavailability, and life stress.

A growing number of studies suggest that disorganized infant attachment may be an important risk factor for later

TABLE 10.1   Attachment and Psychopathology in Infancy, Preschool, Childhood, Adolescence, and Adulthood

Study	Outcome Symptoms	Sample and Study Characteristics	Risk Factors		
			Attachment	Caregiving	Context
Infant Attachment and Psychopathology					
Fagot & Kavanagh (1990)	Problem Behavior (24, 27, 30, and 48 months)	Longitudinal (N = 109)	Avoidant (Strange Situation at 18 months)	None	None
Lewis et al. (1984)	Externalizing at age 6 for boys	Longitudinal (N = 113)	Insecure (Strange Situation at 12 months)	None	Life stress
Bates et al. (1985)	Externalizing at age 3	Longitudinal (N = 120)	Insecure (Strange Situation at 13 months)	Insensitivity	Infant temperament Irritability
Belsky & Fearon (2002a)	Problem behaviors at 3 years	NICHD sample Longitudinal (N = 1015)	Insecure attachment (Strange Situation at 15 months)	None	Cumulative risk factors
Fearon & Belsky (2004)	Attentional performance (54 months)	NICHD sample Longitudinal (N = 918)	Insecure, disorganized (Strange Situation at 15 months)	None	Cumulative risk factors
Goldberg et al. (1995)	Internalizing and externalizing at age 4	Longitudinal (N = 145)	Avoidant (Strange Situation at 12–18 months)	None	Medical risk: Cystic fibrosis or congenital heart defects
Belsky & Fearon (2002b)	Problem behaviors (36 months)	NICHD sample Longitudinal (N = 1,015)	Insecure (Strange Situation at 15 months)	Sensitivity (24 months)	None
Shaw & Vondra (1995)	Behavior problems at age 3	Longitudinal (N = 100)	Insecure (Strange Situation at 12 and 18 months)	Maternal parenting practices	Low SES
Shaw et al. (1996)	Disruptive behavior at age 5	Longitudinal (N = 100)	Disorganized (Strange Situation at 12 months)	None	Maternal aggression, difficult temperament, low SES
Shaw et al. (1997)	Internalizing (36 months)	Longitudinal (N = 86)	Disorganized (Strange Situation 12 months)	Parenting conflicts	Parenting stress, negative life events, low SES
Munson et al. (2001)	Externalizing problems at age 9	Longitudinal (N = 101)	Avoidant and disorganized (Strange Situation at 12–18 months)	None	Teen mothers, maternal depressive symptoms
Ogawa et al. (1997)	Dissociation at age 17	Longitudinal (N = 168)	Avoidant and disorganized (Strange Situation at 12 months)		Low SES, chronicity and severity of trauma exposure
Warren et al. (1997)	Anxiety disorder at age 17, K-SADS	Longitudinal (N = 172)	Ambivalent (Strange Situation at 12 months)	None	Low SES, maternal anxiety
Renken et al. (1989)	Internalizing and externalizing in middle childhood	Longitudinal (N = 191)	Insecure (Strange Situation at 18 months)	Inadequate or hostile parenting	Low SES, chaotic or stressful life events
Aguilar et al. (2000)	Early onset adolescent antisocial behavior	Longitudinal (N = 180)	Avoidant attachment (12 and 18 months)	Inadequate care (6, 24, 36, and 4months) Low SES, maternal depression, stressful life events	Low SES, maternal depression, stressful life event

(continued)

TABLE 10.1   *Continued*

Study	Outcome Symptoms	Sample and Study Characteristics	Risk Factors		
			Attachment	Caregiving	Context
Infant Attachment and Psychopathology					
Sroufe et al. (1999)	K-SADS global psychopathology at age 17½	Longitudinal (N = 120)	Avoidant and disorganized attachment (12 and 18 months)	Family interaction age 13	Low SES, peer relationship problems
Lyons-Ruth et al. (1993)	Peer aggression at age 5	Longitudinal (N = 62)	Disorganized (Strange Situation at 18 months)	Mother infant interaction	Maternal depression, low infant IQ, low SES
Lyons-Ruth et al. (1989)	Problem behavior and anxiety in preschool	Longitudinal (N = 64)	Insecure, disorganized (Strange Situation at 12 months)	None	Depressed mothers, low SES
Carlson (1998)	Child Behavior Problems, dissociation in adolescence	Longitudinal (N = 157)	Disorganized (Strange Situation at 12 months)	24- and 42-month caregiving quality	Low SES
Preschool Attachment and Psychopathology					
Fagot & Pears (1996)	Problem behavior at age 7	Longitudinal (N = 96)	Coercive (Strange Situation at 18 months) (Preschool Assessment; Crittenden, 1992 measured at 30 months)	None	None
DeVito & Hopkins (2001)	Conduct disorder at age 4	Cross-sectional (N = 60)	Coercive (Preschool Assessment; Crittenden, 1992)	Permissive parenting	Marital dissatisfaction
Vondra et al. (2001)	Externalizing and internalizing at age 3.5	Longitudinal (N = 223)	Strange Situation (12 and 18) Crittenden (24) Atypical provide best predictor Strange Situation did not add predictive value	None	Low SES
Seifer et al. (2004)	Externalizing and total problems	Cross-sectional (N = 720)	Disorganized MacArthur Preschool System 36 months	None	Prenatal cocaine exposure, parental self-esteem
Turner (1991)	Disruptive behavior at age 4	Cross-sectional (N = 40)	Insecure (separation-reunion episode)	None	None
Greenberg et al. (1991)	Oppositional Defiant Disorder at preschool	Cross-sectional (N = 50)	Disorganized/controlling (separation reunion episode)	None	Clinically referred (boys only)
Greenberg et al. (2001)	Oppositional Defiant Disorder	Boys only, longitudinal (N = 80 clinic 80 matched)	Insecure MacArthur Preschool System	Poor parenting practices	Adverse family ecology
Childhood Attachment and Psychopathology					
Cohn (1990)	Problem behavior at age 6	Cross-sectional (N = 89)	Insecure (reunion episodes with mother after separation at age 6)	None	None
Solomon et al. (1995)	Conduct problems at age 5–8	Cross-sectional (N = 69)	Disorganized/controlling (separation-reunion episode)	None	None

TABLE 10.1 *Continued*

Study	Outcome Symptoms	Sample and Study Characteristics	Risk Factors		
			Attachment	Caregiving	Context

Childhood Attachment and Psychopathology

Study	Outcome Symptoms	Sample and Study Characteristics	Attachment	Caregiving	Context
Moss et al. (1996)	Externalizing behavior at preschool and the early school years	Longitudinal (*N* = 77)	Disorganized/controlling and ambivalent (separation-reunion episode at age 5–7)	None	None
Moss et al. (2004)	Externalizing and internalizing at age 7	Longitudinal (*N* = 242)	Control/punitive Control/caregiving	Mother-child interaction	Loss, family climate, poor marital satisfaction
Verschueren & Marcoen (1999)	Internalizing and externalizing at age 5	Cross-sectional (*N* = 80)	Insecure with both mother and father (attachment story completion task)	None	None
Easterbrooks et al. (1993)	Internalizing and externalizing behavior at age 7	Cross-sectional (*N* = 45)	Insecure (separation-reunion episode)	None	None
Graham & Easterbrooks (2000)	Depression at age 8	Cross-sectional (*N* = 85)	Insecure (separation-reunion episode)	None	Maternal depression, low SES

Adolescent Attachment and Psychopathology

Study	Outcome Symptoms	Sample and Study Characteristics	Attachment	Caregiving	Context
Nakashi-Eisikovits et al. (2002)	Maladaptive personality disorders in adolescence	Clinically referred Cross-sectional (*N* = 294)	Disorganized (clinician-reported attachment questionnaire)	None	None
Allen et al. (1996)	Antisocial personality disorder at age 14	Upper-middle class adolescents Longitudinal (*N* = 142)	Derogation and lack of resolution of trauma (AAI at age 25)	None	Psychiatric inpatients
Brown & Wright (2003)	Internalizing problems in adolescence	Clinically referred sample Cross-sectional	Ambivalent (separation anxiety test)	None	None
Kobak, Sudler, & Gamble (1991)	Depressive symptoms ages 14–18	Elevated depressive symptoms Longitudinal (*N* = 48)	Insecurity Preoccupation AAI	Observed dysfunctional anger	Negative life events
Muris & Meesters (2002)	Anxiety disorder in adolescence	Cross-sectional (*N* = 280)	Insecure (attachment style questionnaire)	None	Behavioral inhibition
Marsh et al. (2003)	Internalizing and risky behavior in adolescence	Public school students Cross-sectional (*N* = 123)	Preoccupied attachment (AAI Q-set)	Maternal dependence	Academic risk factors and school suspension

Adult Attachment and Psychopathology

Study	Outcome Symptoms	Sample and Study Characteristics	Attachment	Caregiving	Context
Allen et al. (1998)	PTSD, anxiety disorders, mood disorders, depression or dysthymia, eating disorders	Women only Cross-sectional (*N* = 166)	Enmeshed (Adult Attachment Scale, self-report)	None	Psychiatric inpatients
Allen et al. (1998)	PTSD, dissociative disorders, personality disorders	Women only Cross-sectional (*N* = 166)	Avoidant (Adult Attachment Scale, self-report)	None	Psychiatric inpatients
Cassidy (1995)	Generalized anxiety disorder	Cross-sectional (*N* = 128)	Greater anger and vulnerability on the inventory of Adult Attachment	None	None

(continued)

345

TABLE 10.1   *Continued*

Study	Outcome Symptoms	Sample and Study Characteristics	Risk Factors		
			Attachment	Caregiving	Context
Adult Attachment and Psychopathology					
Cole-Detke & Kobak (1996)	Depression, eating disorder	College women only Cross-sectional (N = 61)	Preoccupied, Dismissing (AAI Q-set)	None	None
Fonagy et al. (1996)	Affective disorders, substance abuse, eating disorder, borderline personality disorder, Antisocial personality disorder	Cross-sectional (N = 167)	Unresolved (AAI)	None	Inpatients
Mickelson et al. (1997)	Mood disorder, anxiety disorder, PTSD	National comorbidity survey Cross-sectional (N = 8,098)	Insecure (Attachment Style questionnaire)	Parental over protectiveness	Parental divorce, childhood interpersonal trauma, parental psychopathology
Muller et al. (2001)	Self-reported psychopathology symptoms	Cross sectional (N = 66)	Negative view of self (Attachment Style Questionnaire)	None	Childhood maltreatment
Patrick et al. (1994)	Dysthymia, borderline personality disorder	Women only Cross-sectional (N = 24)	Dismissing, preoccupied (AAI)	None	Inpatients
Rosenstein & Horowitz (1996)	Late adolescent depression, antisocial personality disorder	Cross-sectional (N = 60)	Preoccupied, dismissing (AAI)	None	Inpatients
Tyrrell & Dozier (1997)	MDD, bipolar, schizoaffective, Schizophrenia	Cross-sectional (N = 54)	Unresolved, dismissing (AAI)	None	Inpatients
Van Emmichoven et al. (2003)	Selective attention and information processing	Outpatients Cross-sectional (N = 84)	Insecure attachment (AAI)	None	Anxiety disorder

symptom outcomes. In contrast to the avoidant and resistant forms of insecure attachment, infant disorganized attachment behavior does not show the comprehensible strategic organization characterizing other patterns of attachment behavior. Thus, the term *disorganized* refers to the apparent lack of a consistent strategy for organizing responses to the need for comfort and security when under stress (Main & Solomon, 1986). The particular combinations of disorganized behaviors observed in infancy tend to be idiosyncratic and diverse but include apprehensive, helpless, or depressed behaviors, unexpected alternations of approach and avoidance toward the attachment figure, and other conflict behaviors, such as prolonged freezing or stilling or slowed "underwater" movements (see Main & Solomon, 1990, for a full description). The notion that these disorganized attachment behaviors reflect the lack of an effective attachment strategy for regaining a sense of security in the face of

stress has gained support from recent studies relating attachment disorganization to elevated cortisol secretion after exposure to brief stressors (Hertsgaard et al., 1995; Spangler & Grossmann, 1993).

As the studies in Table 10.1 indicate, disorganized infant attachment is often associated with later psychopathology. For instance, Lyons-Ruth, Alpern, and Repacholi (1993) studied 62 low-income families to examine the relation between infant attachment at 18 months and teacher ratings of child behavior problems at 5 years of age. Infant disorganization was the strongest single predictor of deviant levels of hostile behavior toward peers in the classroom, with 71% of hostile preschoolers classified as disorganized in their infant attachment relationships. Maternal psychosocial problems independently predicted hostile aggression in preschool and combined additively with infant attachment security. In a follow-up study when the children were age 7,

83% of children identified by teachers as highly externalizing were both disorganized in infancy and below the national mean in mental development scores at 18 months, compared with 13% of nonexternalizing children (Lyons-Ruth, Easterbrooks, & Cibelli, 1997).

Further support for a relation between infant disorganization and later aggression emerged from a study that followed children into middle childhood. Munson and colleagues (Munson, McMahon, & Spieker, 2001) followed a sample of 101 children who were born to teenage mothers and measured externalizing symptoms at multiple time points from preschool to third grade. Both avoidant and disorganized attachment along with maternal depressive ymptoms were associated with higher levels of child externalizing problems at age 9. In another study, Shaw, Owens, Vondra, and Keenan (1996) examined disorganized attachment at 12 months, maternal personality, and child-rearing disagreements during the second year as predictors of disruptive behavior at age 5. They found that these early risk factors were as predictive of disruptive behavior at age 5 as was child aggression assessed at age 3 years.

Infant disorganized attachment has also been related to adolescent global psychopathology. In the Minnesota study, infant disorganization predicted psychopathology as assessed with the Kiddie Schedule for Affective Disorders and Schizophrenia (K-SADS) interview when participants were age 17 (Sroufe et al., 1999). Avoidant infant attachment made a further independent contribution to late adolescent psychopathology, as did measures of later experience, including parent-teen interaction at age 13 (boundary dissolution and support for teen autonomy) and problems in peer relationships.

High-Risk Samples: Internalizing and Dissociative Symptoms

Several studies have investigated infant attachment as a predictor of internalizing outcomes. Warren, Huston, Egeland, and Sroufe (1997) reported that adolescents who had been classified as resistant as infants were at increased risk for anxiety disorders (assessed in the K-SADS) at age 17. This effect was significant even after maternal anxiety and infant temperament were controlled in multiple regression analyses. In contrast, when infant anxious resistan attachment was used to predict all other types of psychopathology, no significant results emerged. Disorganized attachment was not assessed as a predictor in that study. In another study, Shaw and his colleagues (Shaw, Keenan, Vondra, Delliquadri, & Giovannelli, 1997) used a broad risk model to identify factors that increased teacher ratings of preschool internalizing prob-

lems. They found that infant attachment disorganization increased risk for internalizing, as did negative life events, parenting hassles, and child-rearing disagreements. In contrast, Lyons-Ruth et al. (1997) found that internalizing symptoms at age 7 were related to avoidance rather than disorganization.

Dissociative symptoms have also been linked to infant attachment patterns, particularly to disorganized attachment. These symptoms are thought to result from a failure to integrate different states and views of self. The failure to maintain a coherent self-organization that results in dissociative symptoms may parallel the breakdown in organized attachment strategies that results in disorganized infant behavior. Ogawa, Sroufe, Weinfield, Carlson, and Egeland (1997) investigated whether trauma, sense of self, quality of early mother-child relationship, temperament, and intelligence were related to dissociative symptoms measured at four time points across 19 years. Assessed at age 19 by the Dissociative Experiences Scale (Bernstein & Putnam, 1986) and at earlier points by teacher reports of dissociative symptoms, both the avoidant and disorganized patterns of attachment were strong predictors of dissociation at nonclinical levels. However, only disorganized attachment predicted clinical levels of dissociation. In addition, maternal emotional unavailability during the first 2 years of life was a robust predictor of clinical levels of dissociation. Surprisingly, in the most comprehensive analysis, childhood trauma predicted only teacher-reported symptoms that were concurrent with abuse in middle childhood but did not predict dissociative symptoms at age 19. Carlson (1998) further explored the antecedents and consequences of attachment disorganization to test the link between infant disorganization and later issociative symptoms. She found that attachment disorganization was significantly correlated with environmental antecedents (e.g., maternal relationship and risk status, caregiving quality, and infant history of maltreatment), but not with infant temperament or maternal health history. In addition, infant disorganization was correlated with teens' reports of dissociative symptoms 18 years later.

In summary, the inclusion of the disorganized classification and the extension of attachment studies to high-risk samples have generally led to more consistent results linking infant attachment to subsequent psychopathology. The available studies point to several general conclusions. First, both infant avoidant and disorganized forms of insecure attachment can be understood as increasing the likelihood that a child will develop some form of psychopathology. The findings support the notion that avoidant and disorganized attachment are risk factors for a wide range of symptoms or general disorder. Although there is some support for specific links between avoidant attachment and subsequent externalizing disorders as well as between resistant attachment and subsequent internalizing disorders, these findings are in need of replication.

Preschool Attachment and Psychopathology

During the past decade, preschool measures of attachment organization have made it possible to extend attachment research beyond infancy. Many of the initial studies have tended to focus on questions of the concurrent and predictive validity of preschool measures as well as the degree of continuity between infant and preschool attachment. Two observational systems, the MacArthur Preschool System (Cassidy et al., 1992) and the Preschool Assessment (Crittenden, 1994), rely on relatively brief separations from the caregiver to activate the attachment system. These two systems arrive at classifications of attachment organization in different ways. In one investigation of the relation between the two systems, results suggested good agreement at the level of insecurity/security and poor agreement when specific types of insecurity were compared (Solomon & George, 1999). The Attachment Q-Sort is also used to assess attachment with preschool children; raters can be either a parent or an observer.

Evidence of a link between preschool attachment and problem behavior came from a study that examined 96 children in the Strange Situation at 18 months and in Crittenden's Preschool System at 30 months (Fagot & Pears, 1996). Although there was substantial instability between the Strange Situation and Preschool classifications, much of the instability was consistent with Crittenden's predictions of developmental reorganization of the child's capacities. Concurrent observations of both parenting and child behavior at 30 months indicated that both parenting and child behaviors differed by attachment classification and predicted children's performance on achievement tests and teacher reports of problem behavior at age 7. Similarly, DeVito and Hopkins (2001) found concurrent associations between preschool attachment and disruptive behavior. Children who were classified as coercively attached (similar to resistant) scored significantly higher on the measure of disruptive behavior than either the defended (similar to avoidant) or secure children.

In a low-income sample of 223 children, Vondra and her colleagues (2001) used the Strange Situation at 12 and 18 months and Crittenden's Preschool System at 24 months. Observers coded child behavior and emotion regulation in a stressful parent-child teaching task during laboratory visits. Comparison of the Strange Situation and the Preschool Assessment classifications suggested modest stability. Preschool classifications also showed

good concurrent associations with indices of child regulation and predicted maternal reports of children's externalizing and internalizing behavior problems at age 3.5 years. The three atypical or disorganized classifications provided the best prediction of negative child outcomes.

Together, these studies lend support to a connection between preschool attachment and behavior problems. However, the cross-sectional findings leave open the possibility that coercive attachment patterns and disruptive or problem behavior are identified by similar behaviors. The two longitudinal studies that demonstrate the ability of the Preschool Assessment to account for later psychopathology provide more compelling evidence for the predictive validity of the preschool system.

The second widely used preschool assessment, the MacArthur Preschool System, has been used in both short-term longitudinal and cross-sectional studies. Seifer and his colleagues (2004) examined the attachment status of 732 children exposed in utero to cocaine, opiates, and other substances. Attachment was assessed at 18 months with the Strange Situation and 36 months with the MacArthur system. Attachment status at 18 months was associated with child temperament and caregiver-child interaction; at 36 months, attachment was associated with child temperament, child behavior problems, and caregivers' parenting self-esteem. The stability of attachment security between the two assessments was marginally above chance expectations.

Although cross-sectional studies support attachment insecurity as a risk factor for disruptive problem behaviors, only one study has examined preschool attachment risk in clinically diagnosed children. Speltz, Greenberg, and DeKlyen (1990) studied 80 clinic-referred preschool boys who were diagnosed with Oppositional Defiant Disorder (ODD) compared with a case-matched group of 80 nonproblem boys. Over half of the boys with ODD diagnoses (54%) exhibited an insecure attachment strategy during reunion, as opposed to 18% of comparison group boys. All insecure patterns were overrepresented in the clinic group. Clinic boys were also more likely than comparison boys to engage in provocative behavior when separated from their mother. The attachment classification, however, provided little concurrent prediction of problem severity or the course of the disorder in the 2 years following clinic referral.

In a follow-up to the Speltz study, Greenberg, Speltz, DeKlyen, and Jones (2001) further examined the correlates of early disruptive behavior problems, including vulnerable child characteristics, poor parenting practices, insecure attachment, and adverse family ecology. Results indicated that the combination of these factors provided relatively high sensitivity and specificity, clearly differentiating referred from comparison boys. A dramatic increase in clinic status occurred when three or more factors were present, and specific combinations of factors were differentially predictive of conduct problems. However, no correlates were found to be either necessary or sufficient for clinic status.

School-Age Attachment and Psychopathology

Measurement of attachment organization in the school-age period has included both laboratory-based reunion procedures (Cassidy, 1988; Main & Cassidy, 1988) and representational measures based on narrative and story completion (Verschueren & Marcoen, 1999). The Main and Cassidy reunion procedure provides insights into how infant disorganization may be transformed during the school-age period. In addition to classifying the major attachment strategies of secure, avoidant, and ambivalent, the new system also identified several atypical patterns: controlling-punitive, controlling-caregiving, and behaviorally disorganized or insecure-other (Cassidy et al., 1992; see also Main & Cassidy, 1988). By 6 years of age, the majority of children who had been classified as disorganized infants shifted their attachment behavior into a controlling role-reversed pattern (Main & Cassidy, 1988; Wartner, Grossmann, Fremmer-Bombik, & Suess, 1994). Main and Cassidy viewed the strategy shift as an attempt by the child to resolve the paradox presented by a frightened/frightening caregiver.

Cross-sectional studies have generally identified early childhood attachment insecurity as a risk factor for aggressive or problem behaviors. Cohn (1990) found that insecurely attached first-grade boys were less well liked by peers and teachers and were perceived as more aggressive and as having more behavior problems than were their secure counterparts. Easterbrooks, Davidson, and Chazan (1993) examined the school-age attachment classifications and found that both environmental risk and insecure attachment were associated with poorer behavioral adaptation among 7-year-olds. In a larger and more representative sample of children between the ages of 7 and 9, Graham and Easterbrooks (2000) found that both attachment security and socioeconomic risk were significantly related to children's depressive symptoms. In this sample, secure attachment buffered children at socioeconomic risk for depressive symptoms.

School-age disorganized attachment has also been identified as a risk factor for psychopathology. Solomon, George, and De Jong (1995) found that 5- to 8-year-old children classified as controlling differed from other children both in their symbolic representations and behavior problems. These children demonstrated doll play characterized by themes of

catastrophe and helplessness or by inhibition of play. Moss, Parent, Gosselin, Rousseau, and St-Laurent (1996) further explored the association between school-age disorganized/controlling status and problem behaviors and found that the disorganized and controlling children were more likely to have higher teacher ratings of problem behaviors.

In a more recent study, Moss, Cyr, and Dubois-Comtois (2004) examined the correlates of attachment in a sample of 242 children, including 37 classified as disorganized. Stressful life events were measured at ages 5 to 7, along with mother-child interactive quality, parenting stress, marital satisfaction, and teacher-reported behavior problems. All three disorganized subgroups had poorer mother-child interactive patterns and more difficult family climates than secure or insecure-organized children. Analyses of the disorganized subgroups suggested that the controlling/punitive group had higher maternal reports of child-related stress, whereas the children in the controlling/caregiving group was more likely to have experienced the loss of a close family member. In comparison with secure children, controlling/punitive children had higher externalizing scores, and controlling/caregiving children had higher internalizing scores.

An important aspect of childhood involves moving toward a more integrated model of self and others. This is likely to require that children begin to integrate or generalize from their experiences in multiple attachment relationships. Verschueren and Marcoen (1999) used a story completion measure of child-mother and child-father attachment to consider how different relationships influence children's representation of self and their behavioral manifestations of self-esteem. The predictive power of child-mother and child-father attachments differed according to the domain of child functioning. The child's view of self was better predicted by the quality of the child-mother attachment representation, and the child's anxious/withdrawn behavioral problems were better predicted by the quality of the child-father attachment representation. These findings illustrate the need to broaden the scope of attachment assessment to include secondary attachment figures and the role that anxious attachment to fathers may play as a risk factor for psychopathology.

Adolescent and Adult Attachment and Psychopathology

Most studies of adolescent and adult attachment organization have relied on the AAI to identify attachment organization or "states of mind" with respect to attachment (George, Kaplan, & Main, 1996; Hesse, 1999; Main & Goldwyn, 1998). The AAI classifications generally parallel the three major classifications identified at earlier developmental periods. Subjects who value attachment and provide a coherent description of experiences with attachment figures are judged autonomous (or secure) with respect to attachment. Subjects who devalue or divert attention from attachment topics are judged dismissing (or avoidant) of attachment issue. Subjects who are passively or angrily engaged in discussing attachment are judged preoccupied (or ambivalent). The formal characteristics of participants classified as unresolved with respect to loss or trauma parallel the descriptions of disorganized behavior in infancy. Participants are classified as unresolved if they show a momentary lapse in monitoring of reasoning or discourse during the interview. This lapse is viewed as a momentary loss of an organized strategy for directing attention to interview topics and is usually assigned along with a classification for one of the three organized discourse strategies.

The AAI was initially developed to understand how caregivers' states of mind might predict infants' attachment security (Hesse, 1999). Despite a large effect size found between caregivers' states of mind and their infants' attachment organization (van IJzendoorn et al., 1995), much remains to be understood about how adults' states of mind influence caregiving quality and child attachment. In adolescent and adult studies, the concurrent validity of the AAI depends on its ability to account for observed behavior with caregivers at times when the attachment system is activated. Adolescent AAIs have shown theoretically predicted relationships with parent-teen interaction, with secure adolescents achieving more balanced assertiveness, less anger, and more support during conflict discussions (Kobak, Cole, Ferenz-Gillies, Fleming, & Gamble, 1993), as well as higher levels of autonomy and relatedness (Allen, Moore, & Kuperminc, 1997) and age-appropriate secure base behavior (J. P. Allen & Land, 1999). More recently, Roisman and his colleagues (Roisman, Padrón, Sroufe, & Egeland, 2002) found that the quality of parent-teen interactions at age 13 predicts a secure state of mind at age 19. The AAI has also demonstrated strong stability over 2-year periods in both late adolescence (Allen et al., in press) and adulthood (Crowell et al., 2002).

Studies of adolescents' AAIs and psychopathology have been limited to samples that are at slightly elevated risk by virtue of poor school performance (Marsh, McFarland, Allen, Boykin McElhaney, & Land, 2003) or increased depressive symptoms (Kobak, Sudler, & Gamble, 1991). In the Marsh study, preoccupied teens were prone to more risky or problem behaviors when their mother was coded as high on autonomy during a parent-teen problem-solving discussion. In contrast, preoccupied teens with a mother who was low in autonomy were more vulnerable to

internalizing symptoms. These findings illustrate a transactional process, with parental behavior acting as a stressor in interaction with teen's attachment organization. Kobak and colleagues also found an association between adolescents' preoccupied states of mind and depressive symptoms.

A substantial association between severe adolescent psychopathology and AAI state of mind also emerged from a 10-year longitudinal study. Allen, Hauser, and Borman-Spurrell (1996) compared 66 adults who had been psychiatrically hospitalized at age 14 to 76 adults who had not been hospitalized. When interviewed at age 25, virtually all of the previously hospitalized adolescents displayed insecure attachment organizations, in contrast to a more typical mixture of security and insecurity in the comparison group. Unresolved trauma in the AAI accounted for much of this insecurity, and insecurity in adult attachment organization at age 25 was also linked to self-reported criminal behavior and use of hard drugs in young adulthood.

A number of investigators have conducted cross-sectional studies of adult AAI status and psychopathology (see Dozier, Stovall, & Albus, 1999, for a review). In one study of 82 inpatients and 85 case-matched controls, Fonagy and colleagues (1996) found some indications that, compared with the controls, psychiatric patients were more likely to be classified as preoccupied and unresolved with respect to loss or abuse. Anxiety disorders were associated with unresolved status, and Borderline Personality Disorder (BPD) was linked to experience of the lack of resolution of severe trauma. A similar association between unresolved trauma and borderline personality emerged from a study of 24 adult female patients with BPD or Dysthymia (Patrick, Hobson, Castle, Howard, & Maughan, 1994). These studies generally suggest that insecure states of mind are associated with psychopathology, but they leave open the question of direction of effects and for the most part have not measured caregiving in the patient's family of origin or contextual risk. Nor have they included assessments of the caregiving or attachment relationships formed with their own children.

A Continuum of Personality Risk for Psychopathology

Although attachment organization has been assessed at each phase of the life span, the majority of longitudinal studies have examined the effect of infant attachment organization on pathways to subsequent disorder. Studies of childhood, adolescent, and adult attachment organization have had to address questions of the validity of attachment measures and often have been limited to cross-sectional designs. A major area for future research will involve further validation of postinfancy attachment measures and inclusion of these measures in longitudinal designs of high-risk samples.

Despite these limitations, the studies suggest a continuum of attachment risk for psychopathology. Not surprisingly, secure attachment generally serves as a protective factor. There is also support for the two major insecure patterns of deactivating (avoidant/dismissing) and hyperactivating (resistant/preoccupied) as risk factors for psychopathology. Deactivating attachment generally has been associated with increased risk for behavior and externalizing problems in preschool and childhood; hyperactivating attachment often has been associated with increased risk for anxiety disorders and internalizing symptoms, particularly during adolescence and adulthood. Atypical attachment patterns tend to represent increased risk for psychopathology across developmental periods. Infant disorganization, childhood controlling/punitive and controlling/caregiving, and unresolved status with respect to loss or trauma in the AAI have produced the most consistent association with more severe forms of psychopathology that include dissociative symptoms, borderline personality, or psychiatric hospitalization. There is some evidence that these atypical patterns may be further differentiated between controlling/punitive versus controlling/caregiving behaviors and between lack of resolution of loss versus lack of resolution of trauma in the AAI.

CAREGIVING AND PSYCHOPATHOLOGY: A CONTINUUM OF RELATIONAL RISK

> The behavior of parents, and of anyone else in a caregiving role, is complementary to attachment behavior. The roles of the caregiver are, first, to be available and responsive as and when wanted and, second, to intervene judiciously should the child or older person who is being cared for be heading for trouble. (Bowlby, 1979, p. 133)

Despite the theoretical importance that Bowlby (1973, 1979) assigned to caregiving in understanding attachment processes, and despite Ainsworth's (Ainsworth et al., 1978) pioneering studies of caregiver sensitivity during infancy, attachment researchers have devoted relatively little effort to assessing a caregiver's availability and responsiveness beyond the infancy period. Yet, in the studies that have assessed the quality of care beyond infancy, this factor often enhances predictions made by attachment or makes an independent contribution to predicting psychopathology. Bowlby's notion that available and responsive care continues to be a critical factor beyond infancy can be further developed by considering studies of (1) caregiving quality in childhood and adolescence, (2) atypical caregiv-

ing behaviors, and (3) attachment-related traumas or the breakdown in the protective function of the caregiving environment. From a theoretical perspective, these three aspects of the caregiving environment constitute a continuum of caregiving risk for psychopathology.

Insensitive Caregiving and Risk for Psychopathology

Not only did Bowlby propose that caregiver sensitivity is an antecedent of infant attachment security (and there is substantial evidence that this is the case; DeWolff & van IJzendoorn, 1997), but Bowlby's pathways model also suggests that caregiving quality continues to be a primary factor in a child's trajectory and that insensitive care can contribute not only to the child's attachment security but also to psychopathology. This point is illustrated by Belsky and Fearon's (2002a) study in which attachment security assessed at 15 months and caregiving sensitivity assessed at 24 months were used to predict a range of developmental outcomes that included problem behaviors at 36 months. A comparison of secure children who later received insensitive care with insecure children who later received sensitive care indicated that in the case of all outcomes, insecurely attached children who subsequently experienced highly sensitive mothering significantly outperformed secure children who subsequently experienced insensitive mothering. These results highlight the importance of postinfancy quality of care in shaping children's developmental trajectories.

The studies reviewed in Table 10.1 lend further support to the continued importance of the caregiving environment in influencing developmental outcomes. For instance, Shaw and Vondra (1995) found that parenting practices were a unique predictor of problem behavior at 36 months. In the longitudinal Minnesota sample, postinfancy quality of care (at 24, 36, and 42 months) was an important predictor of psychopathology. Inadequate parenting in early childhood contributed to internalizing and externalizing symptoms in middle childhood (Renken, Egeland, Marvinney, Mangelsdorf, & Sroufe, 1989), to early onset of adolescent antisocial behavior (Aguilar et al., 2000), and to dissociative symptoms in childhood and adolescence (Carlson, 1998). Preschool assessments of permissive parenting and poor parenting practices have also been linked to ODD in the preschool period (Greenberg et al., 2001).

Relatively few attachment studies have assessed caregiving quality in the middle childhood period. However, adolescent attachment researchers have found that observational measures of dysfunctional anger and of maternal autonomy during parent-teen conflict discussion may moderate the effect of attachment security on risk behaviors and internalizing symptoms (Kobak et al., 1991; Marsh et al., 2003). The continued importance of measuring the caregiving relationship in adolescence is also illustrated by the contribution that observations of parent-child interaction (particularly boundary dissolution) at age 13 made to accounting for global psychopathology at age 17½ (Sroufe et al., 1999).

Deviant Caregiving and Psychopathology

The measures of caregiving quality used in many attachment studies often derive from observations of largely nonclinical low-risk samples. Thus, although dysfunctional anger, insensitivity, or maternal autonomy may all increase risk for psychopathology, many children experience these forms of care and do not develop symptoms. In many respects, these nonoptimal forms of caregiving parallel the insecure attachment patterns that may create only limited risk for the development of symptoms. As attachment researchers have considered caregiving in more extreme or clinical samples, more deviant forms of caregiving have been identified.

For instance, Main and Hesse (1990) suggested that frightening (threatening, frightened, or dissociated) parental behavior explains why infants develop disorganized attachment relationships. Schuengel, Bakermans-Kranenburg, and van IJzendoorn (1999) tested this hypothesis by coding frightened or frightening maternal behavior with infants during two 2-hour home visits. These behaviors were associated with marginally higher rates of infant disorganization in the Strange Situation. Mothers' unresolved status in the AAI further differentiated infant outcomes. Secure mothers with unresolved loss displayed less frightening behavior than other mothers, and unresolved loss in secure mothers did not predict disorganized attachment of their infants. Frightening behavior predicted infant disorganized attachment irrespective of maternal security.

Lyons-Ruth, Bronfman, and Parsons (1999) expanded the range of atypical maternal behavior by developing the Atypical Maternal Behavior Instrument for Assessment and Classification (AMBIANCE). This instrument assesses a broader range of types of disrupted affective communication between mother and infant. Disrupted affective communication was indexed by the frequency of maternal, negative-intrusive, role-confused, withdrawing, disoriented, and contradictory behaviors in response to infant cues, as well as by the frightened/frightening behaviors included on the Main and Hesse (1992) coding inventory. Lyons-Ruth and her colleagues found that, as predicted, the frequency of atypical caregiving behaviors was significantly related to the infant's display of disor-

ganized attachment. These atypical maternal behaviors, which were coded in the Strange Situation assessment, demonstrated cross-situational stability in that they were significantly related to similar behaviors observed in an unstructured home observation. In addition, higher levels of atypical maternal behavior in the Strange Situation were associated with increased infant distress at home. Neither infant gender nor cumulative demographic risk were significantly related to maternal atypical behavior.

The more surprising finding, however, was that there were substantial differences in maternal behavior *within* the group of disorganized infants, with mothers of disorganized/insecure infants displaying significantly more atypical behaviors than mothers of disorganized/secure infants. In particular, mothers of disorganized/insecure infants displayed significantly higher rates of both role confusion and negative-intrusive behavior than mothers of disorganized/secure infants. In contrast, mothers of disorganized/secure infants exhibited significantly higher rates of withdrawal than mothers of disorganized/insecure infants (Lyons-Ruth et al., 1999). However, only the mothers of disorganized/insecure infants differed significantly from mothers of organized infants in their overall rates of atypical behavior. Subsequent analyses also indicated that disrupted maternal communication was related both to maternal hostile-helpless state of mind and to lack of resolution of loss or trauma in the AAI (Lyons-Ruth et al., in press).

Goldberg, Benoit, Blokland, and Madigan (2003) coded atypical maternal behavior in 197 mother-infant pairs using the AMBIANCE codes in a free-play assessment. Both maternal unresolved status in the AAI and infant disorganized attachment were systematically related to atypical maternal behavior. These relations between disorganized maternal and child attachment and disrupted communication were subsequently replicated in a sample of adolescent mothers (Madigan, Pederson, & Moran, 2003). These data provide preliminary empirical validation for the AMBIANCE and suggest that measures of deviant caregiving may be useful in better understanding children's trajectories toward psychopathology. Further assessment of atypical types of caregiving behavior at later developmental periods could make a substantial contribution to understanding risk for psychopathology.

Attachment-Related Trauma and Psychopathology

In addition to extreme deviations in the daily quality of care experienced by children, children may be exposed to another class of events that shake their confidence in their caregiver's availability and expose them to traumatic levels of stress. These traumatic events may be added to deviant caregiving to further expand the continuum of caregiving risk for psychopathology. Attachment-related trauma results from serious threats to the individual's well-being or survival combined with the child's appraisal of loss, rejection, or abandonment by an attachment figure (Kobak et al., 2004). Because children's survival is often dependent on their parents' availability and protection, it is not uncommon for appraised threats of rejection, abandonment, and loss to be simultaneously perceived as a threat to survival. By adulthood, threats to the availability of an attachment figure do not necessarily signal threats to survival; as a result, many adult traumas may be the product of compound fear situations in which a threat to the self is combined with a perceived threat of loss or abandonment by an attachment figure. Kobak and colleagues identified four major types of attachment-related trauma: (1) attachment disruptions, (2) physical or sexual abuse by a parent, (3) loss of an attachment figure through death, and (4) attachment injuries. These types of attachment-related trauma may influence an individual's ability to maintain organized coping and could substantially increase risk for the emergence of psychopathology.

Attachment disruptions were a major topic in both Bowlby's (1951) and Ainsworth's (1962) seminal articles on the effects of maternal deprivation. Attachment disruptions can be understood as an extreme form of separation that differ from normal daily separations by being more prolonged or involving little planning or communication with the attachment figure. The way the child appraises and evaluates the disruption will be influenced both by developmental level and by experience. Infants and young children may be particularly vulnerable to negative effects of prolonged separation, as they lack the ability to form joint plans or represent the attachment figure during the absence. Older children are more capable of managing long separation from parents as long as these separations are accompanied by planning and continued communication. The attachment-related impact of a disruption is also influenced by the child's own appraisal. For instance, a child whose parents threaten to abandon or send the child away (Bowlby, 1973) may be more likely to appraise physical separation as an abandonment or rejection. Similarly, when divorce or marital separations are accompanied by high levels of conflict or disagreements about child rearing, the child will be more likely to appraise marital separations as an abandonment (Grych & Fincham, 1993).

Kobak, Little, Race, and Acosta (2001) examined the effects of attachment disruptions on psychopathology and functioning among a group of 9- to 11-year-old boys who had been classified as severely emotionally disturbed and a matched comparison group. Disruptions were classified on a 4-point scale ranging from maintaining a continuous relationship, to complete abandonment or loss of the attachment figure. Boys who had been placed in severely emotionally disturbed classrooms had much higher rates of attachment disruptions with their biological mothers. Across the entire sample, higher levels of attachment disruptions were associated with higher teacher ratings of dissociative symptoms and higher scores for dependency on ratings of the teacher-student relationship. The most extreme forms of disruption have been investigated in the case of young children who have been institutionalized (Chisholm, Carter, Ames, & Morison, 1995; Marcovitch et al., 1997; O'Connor, Marvin, Rutter, Olrick, & Britner, 2003).

Physical or sexual assault by an attachment figure is likely to expose the victim to feeling intensely frightened and helpless. When the perpetrator of abuse is also an attachment figure the child faces an inescapable dilemma. As Main and Hesse (1990) have pointed out, abuse creates a unique attachment-related trauma in which the child's source of safety and protection simultaneously becomes a source of alarm. Abuse creates a further problem for the child insofar as it is frequently a chronic aspect of the parent-child relationship, and the child is thus faced with an ongoing trauma. Egeland, Yates, Appleyard, and van Dulmen (2002) examined the effects of early childhood maltreatment on antisocial behavior in adolescence in a longitudinal study of 140 high-risk children and their families. The alienation from supportive social relationships that followed abuse helped to explain the relation between early maltreatment and later antisocial behavior. The link with antisocial behavior was accounted for primarily by physical abuse in early childhood, not emotional neglect.

The loss of an attachment figure through death may or may not be a frightening experience (Bonanno & Kaltman, 1999). Fear is more likely if the loss is sudden, making it impossible to prepare for the absence of the attachment figure. Fear usually accompanies the threat of loss rather than actual loss. Thus, initial news of events involving perceived danger to the life of the attachment figure can produce extreme fear even if they do not necessarily result in the death of the attachment figure. Although the threat of loss is ultimately an appraisal process that is likely to differ across individuals (Bowlby, 1980), several contextual factors are likely to make the threat of loss particularly traumatic. There is evidence that violent death is more likely to produce intense fear and difficulties following the loss in comparison with losses that occur through natural causes (Zisook, Chentsova-Dutton, & Schuchter, 1998). Bowlby

(1973) emphasized that exposure to violence or suicide threats could be particularly frightening to children.

Drawing on her clinical work with distressed couples, Johnson (2002; Johnson, Makinen, & Millikin, 2001) suggested a fourth type of attachment-related trauma. She described compound fear situations in which an adult, when faced with a life-threatening situation, feels abandoned by his or her attachment figure. According to Johnson attachment injuries are "wounds arising from abandonment by a present attachment figure in a situation of urgent need." (Johnson, 2002, p. 15). These events are traumatic in that they elicit intense fear associated with isolation and abandonment. In addition, these events fundamentally shake the adult's confidence in the partner's availability and responsiveness. If attachment injuries can occur in the context of adult attachment relationships, similar events may have a profound influence on parent-child attachments. If the attachment figure ignores, dismisses, or denies distressing events, the child may feel abandoned and isolated at a time of urgent need. Diamond and Stern (2003) have identified these moments as the basis of potential impasses in treatment of adolescent children and their parents.

A Continuum of Caregiving Risk for Psychopathology

The continuum of caregiving risk in many ways parallels the continuum of attachment risk. Whereas insensitive caregiving has been associated with insecure attachment, more extreme forms of deviant caregiving behavior such as frightened or frightening parenting or disrupted affective communication have been associated with disorganized attachment. Although researchers have had some success in identifying nonoptimal patterns of caregiving in parent-teen dyads that are associated with teens' attachment insecurity in the AAI (Allen & Land, 1999), much less research is available on more deviant types of caregiving behavior at later periods of development. The codes for frightened or frightening behavior (Main & Hesse, 1992) or disrupted affective communication (Lyons-Ruth et al., 1999) need to be extended to later developmental periods.

Observations of caregiving behavior at later periods have identified several types of atypical behavior related to boundary dissolution that have been developed (Fish, Belsky, & Youngblade, 1991; Sroufe, Jacobvitz, Mangelsdorf, DeAngelo, & Ward, 1985). The form that deviant caregiving will take is likely to change with development. In infancy, atypical caregiving may be readily apparent from the parent's unusual and contradictory affective communication with the infant. However, in later developmental periods, the child may have developed strategies for coping with atypical parental behaviors, including extreme avoidance and disengagement, that make it more difficult to observe deviant caregiving behavior. As a result, the child's strategies for coping with deviant care may need to be assessed as part of a continuing relational pattern or a relational diathesis for psychopathology (Lyons-Ruth & Jacobvitz, 1999).

In addition to the more microanalytic measures of caregiving provided by observational coding systems, measures of attachment-related trauma could make an important contribution to measuring the caregiving risk that may substantially increase risk for psychopathology across the life span. Children at all ages remain vulnerable to more extreme forms of attachment-related trauma. A central contribution of attachment research in infancy and early childhood has been the identification of traumatic experience in early periods of development. Work on the sequelae of early trauma needs to be supplemented by assessments of later attachment-related traumas that may seriously deflect children toward psychopathology.

CONTEXTUAL STRESSORS AND SUPPORTS: A CONTINUUM OF CONTEXTUAL RISK

The surrounding family or *caregiving context* represents a more distal component of the caregiving environment than quality of care. A variety of factors have been considered possible contextual influences on child attachment and psychopathology. These factors fall into three broad categories: (1) stress and poverty (including educational attainment, income-to-needs ratio, minority status, and stressful life events), (2) personality and psychological health of the caregiver (see Belsky, 1999, for a review), and (3) marital or adult attachment relationships (Owen & Cox, 1997).

The caregiver's state of mind assessed in the AAI has introduced an additional element into consideration of the caregiving environment and its effect on developmental pathways leading to psychopathology. By providing a measure of the caregiver's attachment organization, new questions can be considered about how the caregiver's attachment may mediate or moderate the effects of caregiving quality and caregiving context on the child. A secure or a free-to-evaluate state of mind in the AAI has been linked to infant attachment organization, and it may also play an important role in enhancing supportive family relationships and helping the parent to cope with contextual stressors.

Poverty, Caregivers' Psychological Health, and Cumulative Risk

The studies in Table 10.1 linking attachment insecurity to symptom outcomes have extensively relied on low-income samples. Many of these contextual risk factors are related to poverty and include financial strain, residential mobility, neighborhood risk, teen parenting, single-parent status, and increased levels of negative life events. Factors associated with poverty may increase risk for psychopathology in several ways. First, many of the factors associated with poverty, such as financial strain, neighborhood violence, unemployment, and residential mobility, are likely to increase both caregiver's and child's stress exposure. When combined with limited educational and employment opportunities, stress may become both chronic and cumulative and reduce the caregiver's and child's capacity to successfully cope. Second, additional factors related to caregivers' personality and mental health status, such as caregiver depression, substance abuse, and antisocial behavior, may further reduce the caregiver's ability to manage the stressors associated with poverty.

When poverty cofactors and caregiver adjustment difficulties are combined into cumulative risk indices, these factors often account for substantial variance in psychopathology outcomes in both children and adults (Aguilar et al., 2000; Shaw et al., 1996). These stressors operate cumulatively in the development of antisocial behavior and are often associated with low SES (Ackerman, Izard, Schoff, Youngstrom, & Kogos, 1999; Bolger, Patterson, Thompson, & Kupersmidt 1995). The cumulative risk model provides a way of identifying a continuum of risk as the number of risk factors increases for an individual or family.

Contextual risk factors and cumulative risk models have formed a critical third level of analysis in most of the studies of attachment and psychopathology. In many of these studies, contextual risk factors produce main effects on symptoms that are independent of attachment or caregiving risk. Contextual risk has also provided a context for identifying more extreme disorders in both attachment and caregiving. Risk factors have generally increased the likelihood of children moving from organized attachment strategies to less coherent strategies (Egeland & Sroufe, 1981; Lyons-Ruth et al., 1991; Spieker & Booth, 1988; Vaughn et al., 1979). Risk factors have also played an important role in accounting for instability of attachment classification from 12 to 18 months (Barnett et al., 1999; Egeland & Erickson, 1987; Egeland & Farber, 1984; Thompson et al., 1982; Vondra et al., 1999).

Although cumulative risk has formed an important background for investigations of attachment and psychopathology, a central question concerns whether attachment theory can contribute to conceptualizing how contextual risk operates to produce child psychopathology. That is, to what extent can an attachment model differentiate the types of contextual risk factors that are most likely to influence attachment organization, caregiving quality, and symptom outcomes? Attachment theory can identify several types of attachment-related contextual risks. These include insecure adult attachment relationships, attachment-related family-of-origin experiences, representations of attachment that influence caregiver personality, and parenting stressors.

Insecure or Violent Adult Attachment Relationships

The relationships that the caregiver has with other adults may serve either to protect the caregiver from contextual stressors or increase the caregiver's vulnerability. Insecure adult attachments may create risk to children in a number of ways. Most obviously, if a caregiver is insecure in an adult relationship, that anxiety may preoccupy him or her and reduce the quality of available and responsive care to the child. The insecurity of adult relationships may conform to a general continuum, ranging from insecure but stable relationships to violent relationships. A substantial literature suggests that exposure to partner violence has a negative impact on children's development (see Grych & Fincham, 1990, for review). Correlational data indicate that exposure to interparental violence in childhood is associated with prospective indices of child behavior problems (Grych, Jouriles, Swank, McDonald, & Norwood, 2000). Several studies have found that exposure to partner violence has a particularly strong impact on infants and preschoolers (Fantuzzo, Boruch, Beriama, & Atkins, 1997).

Family of Origin and Caregiver States of Mind

The resources that a caregiver brings to managing contextual stressors may vary both with the quality of support available in adult relationships and with the internal personality resources that the caregiver uses to cope. The AAI has made a major contribution to assessing attachment-related aspects of the caregiver's personality. By assessing attachment-related aspects of the caregiver's personality, the AAI makes it possible to consider how adult attachment security may moderate the effects of cumulative stress on the quality of care and child psychopathology. Main and

Goldwyn (1998) have identified two forms of secure individuals with the AAI: those who coherently depict a continuous history of secure relationships with parents (continuous secure) and those who probably had not been securely attached in childhood yet who currently value attachment and provide a coherent description of past experiences (earned secure). Lichtenstein, Belsky, and Crnic (1998) examined whether earned secure individuals would be similar to continuous secure individuals in their ability to provide available and responsive care to their children under conditions of high stress. Results indicated that insecure states of mind were associated with poor-quality parenting, whereas the earned and continuous secures both provided higher quality of parenting in conditions of high stress. Additional links between unresolved or hostile-helpless states of mind and atypical caregiving behavior were reviewed earlier in relation to caregiving risk.

Insecure states of mind in the AAI may also increase contextual risk if they contribute to the caregiver's risk for psychopathology and adjustment difficulties. Although the studies of the AAI and psychopathology are almost entirely limited to cross-sectional designs (see Dozier et al., 1999, for a review), they do suggest that adult insecurity is associated with increased parental psychopathology.

Parenting Stressors and Caregiver Burden

Attachment theory may also contribute to understanding caregiving context by directing attention to the aspects of the parent-child relationship that create stress for the caregiver. These stresses may include conflictual parent-child relationships, as well as the burden imposed by having to manage a child who is having difficulties with successfully adapting in school and peer contexts. Another aspect of parenting stress is related to the number of children. It is likely that the caregiver's level of stress may increase substantially with the number of children in the family, particularly when children are experiencing major adjustment difficulties or psychopathology. These types of stressors may substantially reduce available and responsive care and may in some cases increase the risk for hostile parenting or abuse.

A Continuum of Contextual Risk for Psychopathology

Caregiving context may be broadly conceived as both the distal factors that influence daily family life, the more proximal interpersonal processes that influence the caregiver-child relationship, and the caregiver's personality or internal

resources for coping with stress and maintaining close relationship. Contextual stressors may be roughly categorized into attachment- and non-attachment-related categories. Non-attachment-related stressors tend to include the more distal poverty cofactors, including financial hardship, residential instability, low level of caregiver education, teen parenthood, and neighborhood-related risk. These might be considered a more distal set of variables that create a context for caregiving and attachment. More proximal attachment-related stressors are created by insecurity or threats to the availability of the caregiver's attachment figures. These stressors often involve conflict and lack of security in the caregiver's close relationships with his or her family of origin, with other adults, and with children. These attachment-related stressors include insecure, conflicted, or violent adult attachment relationships, insecure or unresolved caregiver states of mind with respect to family of origin, and high levels of parental burden created by child difficulties and large numbers of children. In each of these categories, a continuum of risk can be identified. Studies of contextual risk might benefit by creating separate continua for attachment- and non-attachment-related contextual risk in calculating cumulative risk indices.

Contextual stressors can directly and indirectly transact with children's developmental pathways. First, distal stressors such as poverty that operate at the contextual level may *directly* influence the child's personality and adaptation by limiting educational opportunities in the home and school, creating more neighborhood difficulties, and increasing the likelihood of peer difficulties. Second, contextual level stressors may influence the child *indirectly* by their effect on the child's caregiver. If the caregiver can successfully manage the stresses associated with poverty in a way that maintains the caregiver's availability and responsiveness to the child, the child may be protected from the negative effects of contextual stressors. Risk to the child is increased when more distal sources of contextual risk are compounded with the caregiver's interpersonal stressors.

MODELING TRANSACTIONAL PROCESSES IN DEVELOPMENTAL PATHWAYS LEADING TO PSYCHOPATHOLOGY

An attachment model of developmental pathways posits ongoing bidirectional transactions among personality, caregiving, and contextual risk. Risk at one level transacts with risk at other levels. As risk becomes more extreme at any one level, the probability of psychopathology increases. Risk in one period of development may increase the probability of poor adaptation at a later period. A comprehensive theoretical model of contextual, caregiving, and attachment risk poses several major challenges for researchers. First, an adequate test of the model requires assessment at each level of analysis across developmental periods. Second, the ongoing transactions among contextual, caregiving, and attachment levels across developmental periods are complex and difficult to model. During the past 20 years, research on attachment and psychopathology has evolved to address increasingly sophisticated models of pathways leading to psychopathology. Beginning with relatively simplistic main effects models of infant attachment insecurity as a predictor of psychopathology, attachment researchers have moved to more complex multilevel models of risk that come closer to capturing the complexity of Bowlby's theory. Much of this evolution was fostered by a generation of studies of high-risk samples and an understanding of contextual variables that influence both caregiving and attachment. The development of the AAI has also offered new opportunities to consider how adult attachment organization moderates the effects of contextual risk on caregiving quality and child outcomes.

Main Effects Models

The relation between attachment insecurity and psychopathology remains a central issue in developmental pathways models. However, this view of attachment as a main effect for psychopathology has changed. A newer view of attachment insecurity focuses on the conditions in which attachment insecurity is a risk factor for psychopathology. Our review of the literature suggests that conditions of caregiving or contextual risk greatly increase the effect of attachment insecurity as a risk factor for psychopathology.

Atypical attachment and caregiving behaviors may produce reliable main effects for psychopathology. These more extreme forms of attachment disorder include disorganized attachment behaviors in infancy, child controlling attachment behaviors in childhood, and adolescent and adult unresolved states of mind with respect to loss and trauma. These new classifications introduce a range of more severe forms of attachment insecurity that may produce larger effects as simple predictors or correlates of psychopathology (see Figure 10.1). In addition, the development of reliable and valid measures of atypical attachment organization for older children and adults may offer more stable and reliable measures of attachment-related deviations at older ages. Such deviations are likely to be more stable and more similar to personality traits and potentially more predictive of psychopathology. The many cross-

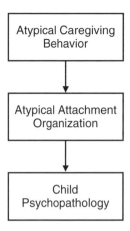

Figure 10.1 Main effects model of attachment and caregiving risk for psychopathology.

sectional studies of adult AAIs and psychopathology (Dozier et al., 1999) suggest that this measure may have more potential for discovering simple main effects. However, once again, many of these cross-sectional findings were discovered in clinical or high-risk samples, leaving open the question of direction of effects.

Cumulative Risk Models

The study of high-risk samples also helped attachment researchers to add contextual and caregiving risk to the earlier studies that focused exclusively on attachment risk. In assessing contextual risk, attachment researchers could draw from other risk studies that had primarily focused on contextual variables. These studies suggested that single risk factors rarely produced significant effects on symptom outcomes. However, the accumulation of multiple risk factors produced much more consistent negative effects on children's development outcomes (Liaw & Brooks-Gunn, 1994; Rutter, 1979; Sameroff, Seifer, Baldwin, & Baldwin, 1993). Cumulative risk indices have also been assessed by adding the various risk factors associated with low SES status, such as low income, residential instability, neighborhood risk, and low level of caregiver education (Ackerman et al., 1999). Using cumulative risk as a general index of contextual stressors provides a way of measuring risk at the contextual level. A number of attachment researchers have also developed measures of caregiving risk (Lyons-Ruth et al., 1993; Seifer et al., 2004; Shaw & Vondra, 1995). The Minnesota longitudinal study increased the reliability of measures of the caregiving environment by aggregating ratings of caregiving quality across multiple observations of caregivers and children in the first 4 years of life (Weinfield et al., 1999).

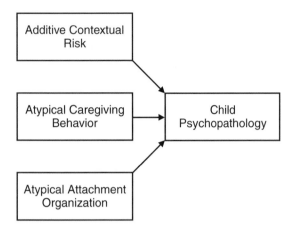

Figure 10.2   Additive model of contextual, caregiving, and attachment risk for psychopathology.

By measuring risk at multiple levels of analysis, more comprehensive models of psychopathology can be tested. Additive models were an initial step in this direction by including contextual, caregiving, and attachment risk as multiple independent predictors of later psychopathology (see Figure 10.2). Studies that adopted this approach often found that each of the levels of risk added unique variance to symptom outcomes (Kobak et al., 1991; Lyons-Ruth et al., 1993, 1997). For instance, Shaw and Vondra (1995) found that both parenting conflicts and caregivers' exposure to stressful events added to infant disorganized attachment in predicting children's internalizing problems at 36 months. Other tests of the additive model have found that the prediction of psychopathology is enhanced when contextual and caregiver risk are added to infant attachment measures (Carlson, 1998; Sroufe et al., 1999).

Mediational Models

Assessing the multiple levels of contextual, caregiving, and attachment risk also makes it possible for attachment researchers to consider how the effects of risk at one level of analysis might be mediated through its effect on risk at another level of analysis. There are several possible mediational models of attachment processes (see Figure 10.3). The most widely tested model views quality of care as a mediator between the caregiver's state of mind in the AAI and the infant's attachment organization (van IJzendoorn, 1995). Although there is some evidence that caregiver sensitivity mediates some but not all of the relation between the caregiver's attachment state of mind and infant attachment, the transmission gap suggests that there may be other processes linking caregiver state of mind to infant attach-

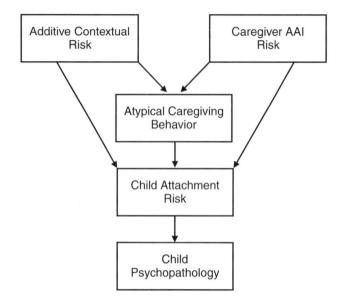

Figure 10.3   Mediational model of attachment-related risk for psychopathology.

ment. For instance, if an insecure caregiver state of mind increases risk for contextual stressors, such as depressive symptoms or relationship instability, contextual stressors might mediate some of the association between the caregiver's state of mind and the child's attachment security.

There are a number of other mediation models relevant to attachment. These include (1) the child's attachment risk mediating the relation between caregiving risk and psychopathology, (2) the child's attachment risk mediating the link between contextual risk and psychopathology, and (3) the parent's AAI risk mediating between contextual risk and psychopathology. For instance, investigators have found that negative and coercive parenting elicits coercive cycles of parent-child interaction that are often associated with child externalizing problems (Patterson, DeBaryshe, & Ramsey, 1989). Attachment may be relevant to these processes insofar as parent-child coercive cycles increase attachment insecurity or disorganization and subsequent externalizing behavior. Attachment risk may also mediate between contextual risk and psychopathology. For instance, cumulative contextual stressors have often produced main effects for externalizing problems (Conger et al., 2002). An attachment model would test the extent to which attachment risk mediated this relationship.

To date, there have been relatively few tests of mediational models of attachment processes. However, developmental psychopathology studies have documented significant relations between different levels of analysis (e.g., the link between contextual and caregiving risk). For example, a number of studies suggest that contextual risk can increase caregiving risk to the child by reducing the quality of care available to the child. Stress for the parent reduces his or her availability to the child and increases the likelihood of harsh or abusive parenting (McLoyd, 1990). Pianta, Egeland, and Sroufe (1990) examined maternal sensitivity from 6 and 24 months to 42 months. Decreased maternal sensitivity was predicted by stressful environmental and child characteristics for both boys and girls. If maternal insensitivity increases the child's risk for psychopathology, caregiving risk could be tested as a possible mediator.

A growing number of attachment studies indicate that contextual risk can increase the child's risk for an insecure or disorganized attachment. For example, contextual factors such as poor family support, chronic drug use, foster care placement, family violence, conflictual relationships with parents, parental depression, paranoia, antisocial behavior, and sexual exploitation increase the child's risk for insecure attachment (Das Eiden, Peterson, & Coleman, 1999; Lyons-Ruth, Lyubchik, Wolfe, & Bronfman, 2002; Seifer & Schiller, 1995; van IJzendoorn, 1995; van IJzendoorn & Bakermans-Kranenburg, 1996). Finally, an extensive literature suggests that caregiving insensitivity increases risk for insecure attachment (i.e., insecurity; see Belsky, 1999, for reviews) and that frightened, frightening, or atypical maternal behavior accounts for significant variance in disorganized attachment (Goldberg et al., 2003; Lyons-Ruth et al., 1999; Madigan et al., in press; Schuengel et al., 1999).

Although there is empirical support for parts of each of the mediation models, showing links between one level of analysis and the next does not provide a full test of mediation. These models would need to include symptom outcomes and show that the effect of one level of analysis on symptom outcomes is fully mediated through a second level of analysis.

Diathesis Stress Models

Attachment theory suggests that secure attachment organization promotes resilient coping with stress, and insecure attachment organization generally results in less adaptive coping. The notion that insecure attachment is most likely to increase risk for psychopathology under high-stress conditions is consistent with a diathesis stress model of attachment and psychopathology (see Figure 10.4). At a theoretical level, it has been suggested that symptoms are most likely to emerge when organized coping strategies breakdown (Kobak, Ferenz-Gillies, Everhart, & Seabrook, 1994;

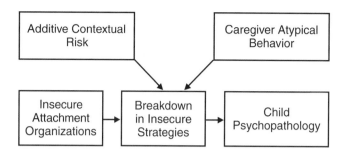

Figure 10.4 Diathesis stress model of attachment-related risk for psychopathology.

Kobak & Shaver, 1987). This breakdown in organized coping is most likely under high or chronic stress conditions. By considering a continuum of contextual risk (i.e., varying levels of stress or "allostatic load"; McEwen, 1998), we can test the notion that psychopathology is most likely when individuals with insecure attachment face high levels of stress.

Not only may the child's insecure attachment organization serve as a diathesis for psychopathology, but theoretically, the caregiver's insecure state of mind in the AAI could also serve as a diathesis for caregiver psychopathology or breakdowns in the caregiving system. By providing a measure of adult attachment security, the AAI makes it possible to test the notion that insecure attachment is a diathesis for psychopathology that is most evident under conditions of stress in both children and their caregivers. By considering both child and caregiver attachment insecurity as a diathesis for psychopathology, several types of diathesis stress models can be tested. Examples of these include (1) contextual/interpersonal stressors x child attachment organization = child symptoms, (2) contextual/interpersonal stressors x caregiver states of mind = caregiver psychopathology, and (3) parent-child conflict x child attachment organization = child psychopathology.

A critical question for a diathesis stress model of attachment and psychopathology is identifying and measuring the sources of stress encountered by the child and caregiver. Belsky and Fearon (2002b) drew on cumulative risk models to index stressors to which children were exposed in the NICHD study. They used a cumulative risk model to measure the social context of the 946 children from 1 to 36 months. Attachment security at 15 months was tested as a moderator of the association between contextual risk and problem behaviors at age 3 years. The effect of attachment insecurity varied as a function of contextual risk. Insecure-avoidant infants who were exposed to high levels of contextual risk proved most vulnerable to developing problem behaviors. These findings highlight the importance of moving away from simple main effects models linking attachment insecurity to psychopathology. In this large sample, avoidant attachment increased risk for problem behaviors only when infants experienced high levels of cumulative risk.

Another way to evaluate diathesis stress models is to use laboratory tasks that allow observation of behavior under varying levels of stress or challenge (Kobak & Duemmler, 1994). Marsh and colleagues (2003) tested a diathesis stress model of attachment and psychopathology based on a conflict discussion between mothers and teens. They found that teens' preoccupied attachment was associated with differential symptom outcomes depending on the degree to which mothers asserted autonomous opinions during the interaction. Low displays of maternal autonomy resulted in preoccupied teens having more internalizing symptoms, and high displays resulted in preoccupied teens having more risk behaviors. The nature of the stresses that teens with high- and low-autonomous mothers experience needs further investigation, but presumably extremes in maternal behavior increase the child's stress in the parent-teen conflict discussion. These stresses, when combined with an insecure attachment strategy, result in increased psychopathology.

Early Experience Models

A central question for a developmental pathways model is the extent to which early experiences with attachment security, caregiving quality, and contextual stressors continue to exert an influence on the child's adaptation beyond the child's current attachment security and caregiving environment. This question becomes important in light of the discontinuity demonstrated in developmental pathways. Longitudinal studies have demonstrated that children's adaptation can dramatically change from infancy and early childhood to later developmental periods (Roisman et al., 2002; Sroufe, Egeland, & Kreutzer, 1990). Whereas some children with insecure relationship histories move toward more adaptive functioning in childhood and adolescence, other children with secure histories may encounter substantial adversity that results in problem behavior. The early experience hypothesis suggests that early relationship history should continue to account for significant variance in later adaptation beyond that accounted for by contemporaneous assessments of the child's environment (see Figure 10.5). Although there are a number of longitudinal studies that include infant attachment, relatively few studies control for concurrent functioning when using early experience to account for later outcomes.

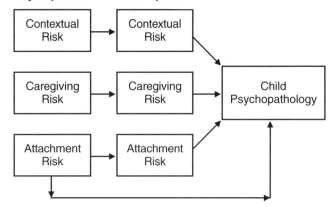

Early Experience   Later Experience

Figure 10.5   Early experience model of attachment-related risk for psychopathology.

Tests of the early experience hypothesis require high standards of measurement across developmental periods. The Minnesota study has established a standard in this respect; as a result, the initial tests of the early experience hypothesis come primarily from this study. Sroufe et al. (1990) divided 190 high-risk children into two groups. One group showed positive adaptation in the infant/toddler period followed by poor preschool adaptation, and the other group showed consistently poor adaptation in both the early and later periods. The two groups were then compared in elementary school. Children who showed positive adaptation in the infant/toddler period showed greater rebound in the elementary school years, despite poor functioning in the preschool period.

Yates, Dodds, Sroufe, and Egeland (2003) provided a further test of the early experience hypothesis with respect to how caregiving context may influence child psychopathology. Partner violence toward mothers was measured from multiple interviews when the children were in the preschool period (age 18 to 64 months) and again during the early elementary school years. Later exposure to partner violence was entered to account for later teen psychopathology at age 16. In addition, other variables, including abuse history and stressful life events, were controlled. Yet, even with later exposure to partner violence controlled, preschool partner violence accounted for externalizing adolescent symptoms in the case of boys and internalizing adolescent symptoms in the case of girls.

SUMMARY AND FUTURE DIRECTIONS

Over the past 2 decades, there have been substantial advances in research examining attachment and psychopathology. The early attachment and psychopathology studies often tested relatively simple models of infant attachment insecurity predicting psychopathology in low-risk samples. During the past 15 years, the extension of attachment research to high-risk samples has led to several important advances. First, investigators have tended to view attachment-related risk in the context of other risk factors. This has led to more powerful models of the development of psychopathology and a better understanding of the role that attachment plays in the emergence of symptoms. Second, the study of high-risk samples has led to an expansion of classifications to include atypical attachment behaviors that may be more closely linked with psychopathology. Furthermore, more recent studies have been based on larger sample sizes that allow investigators to test more complex models of developmental pathways, including early experience and diathesis-stress models.

Each of these advances has moved attachment research closer to testing the transactions between attachment and caregiving that formed the core of Bowlby's developmental pathways model. Yet, there are several major challenges to further advances in the field. These include developing measures of attachment organization across the life span, assessing not only caregiving quality but also the role that adult internal models of attachment play in the caregiver's personality and ability to manage stress, and examining how more distal contextual risk factors may influence more proximal stress exposure for both the child and the caregiver. Each of these challenges suggests important directions for future research.

Measuring Attachment Organization

Attachment organization is a complex construct that is difficult to measure. It not only consists of core expectations about the availability and responsiveness of attachment figures, but also comes to form the basis for expectations about the self, including a sense of self-worth and self-efficacy. In addition, these core expectations, or internal working models, are thought to guide strategies for regulating attachment behavior, particularly in contexts involving distress or challenge. Ainsworth's Strange Situation has become the gold standard for measuring attachment organization in infancy and as a result has been extensively used in studies of development and psychopathology.

Two approaches have been taken to validating attachment measures in the preschool and childhood period. One approach is to assume continuity between infant attachment and subsequent measures of attachment. This approach assumes that later measures should correlate with the infant measures. The relative lack of stability in attachment organization even between 12 and 18 months in the Strange Situation makes this a questionable approach. As we have seen, Bowlby viewed early attachment organization as sensitive to the caregiving environment and thus as subject to change during this period. A second approach is to expect that an attachment organization be validated against measures of attachment behavior in the natural environment (Weinfield et al., 1999). Although home observations are an invaluable source of information about caregiver sensitivity in infancy, the opportunity to observer attachment behavior in the natural environment decreases with age as the child's growing capacities make the readily observable instances of reliance on the caregiver much less frequent.

Attachment research could benefit from more traditional approaches to construct validation. These approaches begin with the use of strategies to reduce measurement error. The use of single assessments of attachment security has inherent limits. Multiple methods and multiple measures are one of the most effective ways of reducing measurement error. Even the Strange Situation assessment in infancy has been shown to have systematic sources of error (e.g., David & Lyons-Ruth, 2005) and can benefit from multiple assessments. In the Minnesota study, measurement of attachment security was substantially improved by aggregating Strange Situation assessments at 12 and 18 months (Weinfield et al., 1999). In preschool and childhood, measures of attachment organization could make much more extensive use of multiple measures. Models of self and other, as well as the assessment of attachment strategies, need to be better operationalized. For example, the notion of self/other expectancies could be rated by observing behavior in situations designed to activate the attachment system, and as the child grows older, by other methods, including self-report and narrative methods such as story completion measures.

The AAI has proved useful in assessing teens' attachment organization, and the three organized attachment categories have been validated with concurrent measures of the observed quality of communication during parent-teen conflict discussions (Allen & Land, 1999; Kobak et al., 1993). The unresolved category remains to be similarly validated in this age range. An important point in all these studies is that measurement error can be reduced both by repeated measures and by the use of multiple methods. In sum, future research on attachment organization needs to move away from single measures of the attachment construct.

As attachment researchers develop and validate measures of attachment organization, more description is needed of atypical attachment patterns and behaviors. The identification of controlling attachment strategies in childhood (Main & Cassidy, 1988) and hostile-helpless states of mind in adulthood (Lyons-Ruth et al., in press) demonstrates the value of extending description to capture aspects of attachment that deviate from more typical forms of insecurity. Moreover, the factors that influence attachment organization at later periods of development need further consideration. Not only are multiple caregivers likely to have an influence and contribute to a child's attachment organization, but experiences with peers become increasingly important, particularly with the development of adolescent romantic relationships (Furman, Simon, Shaffer, & Bouchey, 2002).

Understanding the Caregiver

Attachment researchers have often spent more time studying children and their attachment organization than they have spent studying the children's caregivers. As a result, the caregiving side of the attachment relationship is less well understood. The lack of research on caregiving is surprising in light of the degree of importance that the caregiving environment plays in Bowlby's pathways model. Caregiving behavior is organized by a caregiving behavioral system whose biological function is to provide protection and support for the developing child (George & Solomon, 1999). The caregiving system normally engages the parent in ongoing monitoring of the child's needs and accounts for the parent's investment in the child's success in ultimately reproducing and caring for the next generation. The caregiving system promotes a sensitivity to the child's signals that complements the child's need to experience the parent as available and responsive. A caregiver's success in achieving the goals of protection and nurturance of the child can be a source of pride, and child difficulties that signal a failure to achieve these goals can be a source of guilt and lead to a sense of failure.

Because the infant's sense of security depends not on adult-perceived physical safety but on the child's experience of caregiver responsiveness, success in caregiving depends on the caregiver's ability to attend to, interpret, and respond to the child's needs and signals (Ainsworth et al., 1978). Ainsworth's measures of sensitivity provided a basis for assessing caregiving quality in infancy. However, devel-

opmental changes in the child require new measures of caregiving quality at later developmental periods. Laboratory interaction paradigms may be particularly useful in assessing caregiving quality in later developmental periods (see Allen & Land, 1999; Crowell, Treboux, Gao, et al., 2002; Kobak et al., 1993). Observational paradigms have been widely used by researchers using descriptive dimensions of caregiving quality, such as support validation, negative comments, and support for autonomy, and many of these dimensions may be useful to attachment researchers. Future studies need to consider whether there are aspects of optimal parenting that are clearly more important to a child's attachment security.

A critical area for future research centers on the factors that facilitate or hinder the caregiver's ability to provide available and responsive care to the child. Two major types of factors are relevant to caregiving. On the one hand, there are the contextual stressors and supports that have been identified in the pathways model. On the other hand, there are individual differences in the internal resources that caregivers bring to the parent-child relationship. The development of the AAI has provided a valuable tool for better understanding individual differences in caregivers' internal resources and coping capacities. Further, the links that have been identified between insecure states of mind and adult psychopathology (Dozier et al., 1999) suggest that states of mind may have profound influence on adult functioning and potentially reduce the caregiver's availability and responsiveness to the child.

Caregivers' states of mind in the AAI may also have an important influence on how the caregiver manages the contextual stressors and supports that shape children's developmental trajectories. For instance, a secure state of mind may promote the development of supportive adult relationships and support more effective coping with the stressors associated with poverty. To the extent that the caregiver develops supportive adult relationships and effectively manages stressors, he or she is likely to maintain the capacity to remain available to the child. As a result, the child's risk for experiencing deviant care and the associated risk for psychopathology is substantially reduced. Alternatively, a caregiver whose state of mind is characterized by lack of resolution of trauma may be at increased risk for insecure adult attachments that are a source of stress rather than support. Further, when faced with cumulative levels of high stress, this caregiver's strategies may be vulnerable to breaking down and to the emergence of symptoms. Overwhelmed by contextual stressors and the symptoms of his or her own psychopathology, the caregiver is likely to have much more difficulty maintaining available and responsive care to the child. Further, these stressors may lead to an abdication of the caregiving role or basic violations of caregiving boundaries (Fish et al., 1991; Sroufe, Jacobvitz, et al., 1985), which may substantially increase the child's risk for atypical attachment and psychopathology. The transactions among caregiver states of mind, contextual supports and stressors, and caregiving quality are a promising but largely unexplored area for attachment research (Kobak & Mandelbaum, 2003).

Identifying and Measuring Stressors in the Caregiving Environment

Both attachment research and studies examining risk have consistently found that accumulating risk factors substantially elevate children's risk for psychopathology. However, the mechanisms that link cumulative risk to caregiving and attachment are poorly understood. We have suggested that stress models represent an important way of linking contextual risk to caregiving and attachment. From the standpoint of attachment theory, stress normally activates the attachment system, and seeking proximity and support from a caregiver is a primary mechanism for coping with stress. Further, the experience of high levels of stress may hinder the caregiver's capacity to provide available and responsive care. Thus, we have proposed a diathesis-stress model of attachment and psychopathology. This model posits that insecure and atypical attachment strategies are particularly vulnerable to breaking down under conditions of high stress and leaves the individual at increased risk for maladaptive responses and symptomatic behavior under conditions of high stress.

Although diathesis-stress models are a theoretically compelling approach to understanding the links among contextual risk, attachment, and psychopathology, the degree to which contextual risk factors are experienced as stressful by caregivers and children is in need of further investigation. At least three levels of contextual stress may be distinguished: (1) distal factors that influence the family environment, such as poverty and poverty cofactors (e.g., residential mobility, low educational attainment); (2) more proximal factors, such as caregiver personality and psychopathology; and (3) relationship processes. Relational factors have two aspects. Well-functioning relationships can serve as a stress buffer and support; alternatively, conflicted relationships can serve as a major source of stress exposure.

In assessing relational stressors it is important to distinguish caregiver stressors from child stressors. If the caregiver has the personality resources to cope with stress,

caregiving quality may be maintained and the child may be protected from stressors. The effect of stress on the attachment relationship may also be bidirectional. When the child experiences high levels of stress in the neighborhood, school, or peer contexts, these may impact the child and create challenges and stress for the caregiver. By categorizing distal and relational stressors, new questions can be addressed that might increase the specificity of cumulative risk models. Some stressors may have more impact on the child than others, and the degree to which caregiving is affected by stress could vary substantially.

Finally, it is important to use multiple methods for assessing stress. Whereas many of the early studies relied on caregiver reports of major disruptive events, later studies moved toward smaller and more frequently occurring sources of stress. Stress may be measured at multiple levels, ranging from individual child and caregiver physiology, to daily interpersonal stressors, to environmental stressors associated with poverty, to major disruptive life events such as loss and trauma.

Testing Models of Transactional Processes

Bowlby's developmental pathways model has several implications for the design of studies of attachment and psychopathology. First, the most effective studies will include multiple levels of assessment. These assessments should include measures of attachment-related constructs at the individual level, of caregiving quality at the relationship level, and of distal and proximal stressors at the contextual level. Second, for prediction of psychopathology, it is important to assess the degree to which cumulative risk factors increase both the child's and the caregiver's exposure to stress. Third, longitudinal data are required to understand the dynamic relations among attachment-related aspects of personality, caregiving quality, and contextual risk. Although few existing studies comprehensively assess attachment, caregiving, and contextual risk, many of the more recent attachment studies that we have reviewed indicate that psychopathology is better understood when more than one level of assessment is incorporated in the study design.

Studies that follow the guidelines of a developmental pathways model will offer new opportunities to understand transactional processes that contribute to psychopathology. Three types of models appear to offer the most promise for hypothesis testing. Diathesis-stress models provide a specific hypothesis for how attachment organization and contextual stressors transact to produce psychopathology. More specifically, risk is increased when children with more extreme forms of insecure attachment organization encounter high levels of stressors. Diathesis-stress models can be tested at the level of both the child's and the caregiver's attachment organization. In the case of caregivers, unresolved or hostile-helpless states of mind are thought to form a diathesis for deviant caregiving that should become most evident when caregivers encounter high levels of stress. A similar diathesis-stress hypothesis could also be tested for the emergence of caregiver psychopathology.

Mediation models may provide a way of distinguishing between attachment- and non-attachment-related risk for psychopathology. A large number of factors may increase risk for psychopathology, and many of these factors may elevate risk independent of attachment or caregiving processes. By testing the extent to which contextual or other risk factors are mediated through caregiving quality or attachment organization, more accurate estimates of the relative contribution of attachment processes to the emergence of psychopathology become possible.

Finally, longitudinal designs that incorporate multiple levels of assessment will provide a critical test of the early experience hypothesis. The most rigorous test of this hypothesis requires that assessment of attachment, caregiving, or contextual risk *early* in development accounts for variance in later outcomes above the variance accounted for by contemporaneous assessments of attachment, caregiving, and contextual risk. These longitudinal studies are the most demanding in terms of requiring multiple levels of measurement across developmental periods. It is these models, however, that most closely approximate a test of Bowlby's developmental pathways model.

Levels of Analysis and Attachment-Based Intervention

A common focus of most attachment interventions is to increase the child's sense of confidence in the availability and responsiveness of the caregiver (Levy & Orlans, 2003). However, the techniques of attachment interventions change dramatically with the developmental stage of the child. During infancy and early childhood, interventions must necessarily work at the caregiving level to improve the quality of care available to the child. As the caregiver increases his or her capacity to understand the child, accurately read his or her signals, and respond appropriately, the child is likely to gain confidence in the caregiver's availability and establish a foundation for increased self-confidence. A variety of techniques have been adopted to increase the caregiver's empathy and responsiveness to the child (Dozier,

Higley, Albus, & Nutter, 2002). These include providing parents with video-based feedback, increasing parents' capacity to observe, reflect, and verbalize their attributions about the child, and exploring the relevance of the parent's own caregiving history as it influences interactions with the child (Marvin, Cooper, Hoffman, & Powell, 2002).

As the child matures, interventions often maintain a dual focus on both the child's attachment and the caregiver's level of analysis. By middle childhood, the child's capacity for verbal communication and perspective taking transform the attachment relationship into a cooperative partnership (Bowlby, 1969/1982; Kobak & Duemmler, 1994). As a result, interventions may focus on both the child's and the caregiver's attributions and attachment strategies for maintaining the relationship. If successful, such interventions would contribute to reducing dysfunctional anger, increasing perspective taking, and reassuring the child of the availability and responsiveness of the caregiver. This focus on the attachment aspect of the relationship may be combined with other parenting interventions that focus more on the management and containment of disruptive child behavior (Cavell, 2000).

Both the caregiver's and the child's ability to engage in and benefit from intervention can be strongly influenced by the factors operating at the contextual level. Family-of-origin experiences and caregiver's state of mind with respect to attachment are both likely to influence the caregiver's style of forming a relationship with a therapist and the nature of the therapeutic relationship (Dozier, Lomax, Tyrell, & Lee, 2001). Contextual stressors associated with poverty limit caregivers' ability to utilize treatment and may be a common pathway through which contextual risk factors influence parenting behavior, perceptions of the child, and child behavior problems. Attachment-based interventions may improve a caregiver's ability to manage stress in multiple ways. First, interventions that reduce problematic child behavior may also reduce parental stressors. Second, attachment-based interventions may highlight the importance of using other adults as sources of support. Third, the ability of a caregiver or child to form a supportive relationship with the therapist may provide an important way of managing stress and benefiting from intervention.

REFERENCES

Ackerman, B. P., Izard, C. E., Schoff, K., Youngstrom, E. A., & Kogos, J. (1999). Contextual risk, caregiver emotionality, and the problem behaviors of six- and seven-year-old children from economically disadvantaged families. *Child Development, 70,* 1415–1427.

Aguilar, B., Sroufe, L. A., Egeland, B., & Carlson, E. (2000). Distinguishing the early-onset/persistent and adolescence-onset antisocial behavior types: From birth to 16 years. *Development and Psychopathology, 12,* 109–132.

Ainsworth, M. D. (1962). The effects of maternal deprivation: A review of findings and controversy in the context of research strategy. In *Deprivation of maternal care: A reassessment of its effects* [Public Health Papers No. 14]. Geneva, Switzerland: World Health Organization.

Ainsworth, M. D., Blehar, M., Waters, E., & Wall, S. (1978). *Patterns of attachment: A psychological study of the strange situation.* Hillsdale, NJ: Erlbaum.

Allen, J. P., Boykin McElhaney, K., Kuperminc, G. P., & Jodl, K. M. (in press). Stability and change in attachment security across adolescence. *Child Development.*

Allen, J. P., Hauser, S. T., & Borman-Spurrell, E. (1996). Attachment theory as a framework for understanding sequelae of severe adolescent psychopathology: An 11-year follow-up study. *Journal of Consulting and Clinical Psychology, 64,* 254–263.

Allen, J. P., & Land, D. (1999). Attachment in adolescence. In J. Cassidy & P. R. Shaver (Eds.), *Handbook of attachment: Theory, research, and clinical applications* (pp. 319–335). New York: Guilford Press.

Allen, J. P., Moore, C. M., & Kuperminc, G. P. (1997). Developmental approaches to understanding adolescent deviance. In S. S. Luthar, J. A. Burack, D. Cicchetti, & J. R. Weisz (Eds.), *Developmental psychopathology: Perspectives on adjustment, risk, and disorder* (pp. 548–567). New York: Cambridge University Press.

Barnett, D., Ganiban, J., & Cicchetti, D. (1999). Maltreatment, negative expressivity, and the development of Type D attachments from 12 to 24 months of age. *Monographs of the Society for Research in Child Development, 64,* 97–118.

Bates, J. E., Maslin, C. A., & Frankel, K. A. (1985). Attachment security, mother-child interaction, and temperament as predictors of behavior-problem ratings at age three years. *Monographs of the Society for Research in Child Development, 50,* 167–193.

Belsky, J. (1999). Interactional and contextual determinants of attachment security. In J. Cassidy & P. R. Shaver (Eds.), *Handbook of attachment: Theory, research, and clinical applications* (pp. 249–264). New York: Guilford Press.

Belsky, J., & Cassidy, J. (1994). Attachment: Theory and evidence. In M. Rutter & D. F. Hay (Eds.), *Development through life: A handbook for clinicians* (pp. 373–402). Oxford, England: Blackwell.

Belsky, J., & Fearon, R. M. P. (2002a). Early attachment security, subsequent maternal sensitivity, and later child development: Does continuity in development depend upon continuity of caregiving? *Attachment & Human Development, 4,* 361–387.

Belsky, J., & Fearon, R. M. P. (2002b). Infant-mother attachment security, contextual risk, and early development: A moderational analysis. *Development and Psychopathology, 14,* 293–310.

Belsky, J., Fish, M., & Isabella, R. A. (1991). Continuity and discontinuity in infant negative and positive emotionality: Family antecedents and attachment consequences. *Developmental Psychology, 27,* 421–431.

Bernstein, E. M., & Putnam, F. (1986). Development, reliability, and validity of a dissociation scale. *Journal of Nervous and Mental Disease, 174,* 727–735.

Bolger, K. E., Patterson, C. J., Thompson, W. W., & Kupersmidt, J. B. (1995). Psychosocial adjustment among children experiencing persistent and intermittent family economic hardship. *Child Development, 66,* 1107–1129.

Bonanno, G. A., & Kaltman, S. (1999). Toward an integrative perspective on bereavement. *Psychological Bulletin, 125,* 760–776.

Bowlby, J. (1951). Maternal care and mental health. *Bulletin of the World Health Organization, 3,* 355–533.

Bowlby, J. (1969/1982). *Attachment and loss: Vol. 1. Attachment.* New York: Basic Books.

Bowlby, J. (1973). *Attachment and loss: Vol. 2. Separation.* New York: Basic Books.

Bowlby, J. (1979). *The making and breaking of affectional bonds.* London: Tavistock.

Bowlby, J. (1980). *Attachment and loss: Vol. 3. Loss.* New York: Basic Books.

Bowlby, J. (1988). *A secure base: Parent-child attachment and healthy human development.* London: Routledge.

Bretherton, I., & Munholland, K. A. (1999). Internal working models in attachment relationships: A construct revisited. In J. Cassidy & P. R. Shaver (Eds.), *Handbook of attachment: Theory, research, and clinical applications* (pp. 89–111). New York: Guilford Press.

Brown, L. S., & Wright, J. (2003). The relationship between attachment strategies and psychopathology in adolescence. *Psychology and Psychotherapy: Theory, Research and Practice, 76,* 351–367.

Burgess, K. B., Marshall, P. J., Rubin, K. H., & Fox, N. A. (2003). Infant attachment and temperament as predictors of subsequent externalizing problems and cardiac physiology. *Journal of Child Psychology and Psychiatry, 44,* 819–831.

Carlson, E. A. (1998). A prospective longitudinal study of attachment disorganization/disorientation. *Child Development, 69,* 1107–1128.

Cassidy, J. (1988). Child-mother attachment and the self in six-year-olds. *Child Development, 59,* 121–134.

Cassidy, J., & Marvin, R. S., with the MacArthur Working Group on Attachment. (1992). *Attachment organization in three and four years olds: Procedures and coding manual.* Unpublished manuscript, University of Virginia.

Cavell, T. A. (2000). *Working with parents of aggressive children: A practitioner's guide.* Washington, DC: American Psychological Association.

Chisholm, K., Carter, M. C., Ames, E. W., & Morison, S. J. (1995). Attachment security and indiscriminately friendly behavior in children adopted from Romanian orphanages. *Development and Psychopathology, 7,* 283–294.

Cicchetti, D. (1993). Developmental psychopathology: Reactions, reflections, projections. *Developmental Review, 13,* 471–502.

Cicchetti, D., & Rogosch, F. A. (1996). Equifinality and multifinality in developmental psychopathology. *Development and Psychopathology, 8,* 597–600.

Cohn, D. A. (1990). Child-mother attachment of six-year-olds and social competence at school. *Child Development, 61,* 152–162.

Cole-Detke, H., & Kobak, R. (1996). Attachment processes in eating disorder and depression. *Journal of Consulting and Clinical Psychology, 64,* 282–290.

Conger, R. D., Wallace, L. E., Sun, Y., Simons, R. L., McLoyd, V. C., & Brody, G. H. (2002). Economic pressure in African American families: A replication and extension of the family stress model. *Developmental Psychology, 38,* 179–193.

Crittenden, P. M. (1985). Maltreated infants: Vulnerability and resilience. *Journal of Child Psychology and Psychiatry, 26*(1), 85–96.

Crittenden, P. M. (1992). Quality of attachment in the preschool years. *Development and Psychopathology, 4,* 209–241.

Crittenden, P. M. (1994). *Preschool assessment of attachment* (2nd ed.). Unpublished manuscript, family relations Institute, Miami, FL.

Crowell, J., Treboux, D., Gao, Y., Fyffe, C., Pan, H., & Waters, E. (2002). Assessing secure base behavior in adulthood: Development of a measure, links to adult attachment representations, and relations to couples' communication and reports of relationships. *Developmental Psychology, 38,* 679–693.

Crowell, J. A., Treboux, D., & Waters, E. (2002). Stability of attachment representations: The transition to marriage. *Developmental Psychology, 38,* 467–479.

Das Eiden, R., Peterson, M., & Coleman, T. (1999). Maternal cocaine use and the caregiving environment during early childhood. *Psychology of Addictive Behaviors, 13,* 293–302.

David, D., Lyons-Ruth, K. (2005). Differential Attachment Responses of Male and Female Infants to Frightening Maternal Behavior: Tend or Befriend vs Fight or Flight? *Infant Mental Health Journal, 26*(1), 1–18.

DeVito, C., & Hopkins, J. (2001). Attachment, parenting, and marital dissatisfaction as predictors of disruptive behavior in preschoolers. *Development and Psychopathology, 13,* 215–231.

DeWolff, M., & van IJzendoorn, M. H. (1997). Sensitivity and attachment: A meta-analysis on parental antecedents of infant attachment. *Child Development, 68,* 571–591.

Diamond, G., & Stern, R. (2003). Attachment based family therapy for depressed adolescents. In S. Johnson & V. Whiffen (Eds.), *Attachment processes in couple and family therapy* (pp. 191–212). New York: Guilford Press.

Dozier, M., Higley, E., Albus, K., & Nutter, A. (2002). Intervening with foster infants' caregivers: Targeting three critical needs. *Infant Mental Health Journal, 23,* 541–554.

Dozier, M., Lomax, L., Tyrell, C., & Lee, S. (2001). The challenge of treatment for clients with dismissing states of mind. *Attachment and Human Development, 3,* 62–76.

Dozier, M., Stovall, K. C., & Albus, K. E. (1999). Attachment and psychopathology in adulthood. In J. Cassidy & P. R. Shaver (Eds.), *Handbook of attachment: Theory, research, and clinical applications* (pp. 497–519). New York: Guilford Press.

Easterbrooks, M. A., Davidson, C. E., & Chazan, R. (1993). Psychosocial risk, attachment, and behavior problems among school-aged children. *Development and Psychopathology, 5,* 389–402.

Egeland, B., & Erickson, M. (1987). A developmental view of the psychological consequences of maltreatment. *School Psychology Review, 16,* 156–168.

Egeland, B., & Farber, E. A. (1984). Infant-mother attachment: Factors related to its development and changes over time. *Child Development, 55,* 753–771.

Egeland, B., & Sroufe, L. A. (1981). Attachment and early maltreatment. *Child Development, 52,* 44–52.

Egeland, B., Yates, T., Appleyard, K., & van Dulmen, M. (2002). The long-term consequences of maltreatment in the early years: A developmental pathway model to antisocial behavior. *Children's Services: Social Policy, Research, & Practice, 5,* 249–260.

Erickson, M. F., Sroufe, L. A., & Egeland, B. (1985). The relationship between quality of attachment and behavior problems in preschool in a high-risk sample. *Monographs of the Society for Research in Child Development, 50,* 147–166.

Fagot, B. I., & Kavanagh, K. (1990). The prediction of antisocial behavior from avoidant attachment classification. *Child Development, 61,* 864–873.

Fagot, B. I., & Pears, K. C. (1996). Changes in attachment during the third year: Consequences and predictions. *Development and Psychopathology, 8,* 325–344.

Fantuzzo, J., Boruch, R., Beriama, A., & Atkins, M. (1997). Domestic violence and children: Prevalence and risk in five major U.S. cities. *Journal of the American Academy of Child and Adolescent Psychiatry, 36,* 116–122.

Fearon, P. R. M., & Belsky, J. (2004). Attachment and attention: Protection in relation to gender and cumulative social-contextual adversity. *Child Development, 75,* 1677–1693.

Fish, M., Belsky, J., & Youngblade, L. (1991). Developmental antecedents and measurement of intergenerational boundary violation in a nonclinic sample. *Journal of Family Psychology, 4,* 278–297.

Fonagy, P., Leigh, T., Steele, M., Steele, H., Kennedy, R., Mattoon, G., et al. (1996). The relation of attachment status, psychiatric classification, and response to psychotherapy. *Journal of Consulting and Clinical Psychology, 64,* 22–31.

Fraley, C., & Brumbaugh, C. (2004). A dynamical systems approach to conceptualizing and studying stability and change in attachment security. In S. W. Rholes & J. A. Simpson (Eds.), *Adult attachment: Theory, research, and clinical implications* (pp. 86–132). New York: Guilford Press.

Furman, W., Simon, V., Shaffer, L., & Bouchey, H. (2002). Adolescents' working models and styles for relationships with parents, friends, and romantic partners. *Child Development, 73,* 241–255.

George, C., Kaplan, N., & Main, M. (1996). *Adult attachment interview protocol* (3rd ed.). Unpublished manuscript, University of California at Berkeley.

George, C., & Solomon, J. (1999). Attachment and caregiving: The caregiving behavioral system. In J. Cassidy & P. R. Shaver (Eds.), *Handbook of attachment: Theory, research, and clinical applications* (pp. 649–670). New York: Guilford Press.

Goldberg, S., Benoit, D., Blokland, K., & Madigan, S. (2003). Atypical maternal behavior, maternal representations, and infant disorganized attachment. *Development and Psychopathology, 15,* 239–257.

Goldberg, S., Gotowiec, A., & Simmons, R. J. (1995). Infant-mother attachment and behavior problems in healthy and chronically ill preschoolers. *Development and Psychopathology, 7,* 267–282.

Graham, C. A., & Easterbrooks, M. A. (2000). School-aged children's vulnerability to depressive symptomatology: The role of attachment security, maternal depressive symptomatology, and economic risk. *Development and Psychopathology, 12,* 201–213.

Greenberg, M. T. (1999). Attachment and psychopathology in childhood. In J. Cassidy & P. R. Shaver (Eds.), *Handbook of attachment: Theory, research, and clinical applications* (pp. 469–496). New York: Guilford Press.

Greenberg, M. T., Speltz, M. L., DeKlyen, M., & Endriga, M. C. (1991). Attachment security in preschoolers with and without externalizing behavior problems: A replication. *Development and Psychopathology, 3,* 413–430.

Greenberg, M. T., Speltz, M. L., DeKlyen, M., & Jones, K. (2001). Correlates of clinic referral for early conduct problems: Variable- and person-oriented approaches. *Development and Psychopathology, 13,* 255–276.

Grych, J. H., & Fincham, F. D. (1990). Marital conflict and children's adjustment: A cognitive-contextual framework. *Psychological Bulletin, 108,* 267–290.

Grych, J. H., & Fincham, F. D. (1993). Children's appraisals of marital conflict: Initial investigations of the cognitive-contextual framework. *Child Development, 64,* 215–230.

Grych, J. H., Jouriles, E. N., Swank, P. R., McDonald, R., & Norwood, W. D. (2000). Patterns of adjustment among children of battered women. *Journal of Consulting and Clinical Psychology, 68,* 84–94.

Hertsgaard, L., Gunnar, M., Erickson, M. F., & Nachmias, M. (1995). Adrenocortical responses to the Strange Situation in infants with disorganized/disoriented attachment relationships. *Child Development, 66,* 1100–1106.

Hesse, E. (1999). The adult attachment interview: Historical and current perspectives. In J. Cassidy & P. R. Shaver (Eds.), *Handbook of attachment: Theory, research, and clinical applications* (pp. 395–433). New York: Guilford Press.

Johnson, S. M. (2002). *Emotionally focused couple therapy with trauma survivors: Strengthening attachment bonds.* New York: Guilford Press.

Johnson, S. M., Makinen, J. A., & Millikin, J. W. (2001). Attachment injuries in couple relationships: A new perspective on impasses in couples therapy. *Journal of Marital and Family Therapy, 27,* 145–155.

Kobak, R., Cassidy, J., & Ziv, Y. (2004). Attachment related trauma and posttraumatic stress disorder: Implications for adult adaptation. In S. W. Rholes & J. A. Simpson (Eds.), *Adult attachment: Theory, research, and clinical implications* (pp. 388–407). New York: Guilford Press.

Kobak, R., Cole, H. E., Ferenz-Gillies, R., Fleming, W. S., & Gamble, W. (1993). Attachment and emotion regulation during mother-teen problem-solving: A control theory analysis. *Child Development, 64,* 231–245.

Kobak, R., & Duemmler, S. (1994). Attachment and conversation: Toward a discourse analysis of adolescent and adult security. In K. Bartholomew & D. Perlman (Eds.), *Advances in personal relationships: Vol. 5. Attachment processes in adulthood* (pp. 121–149). London: Jessica Kingsley.

Kobak, R., Ferenz-Gillies, R., Everhart, E., & Seabrook, L. (1994). Maternal attachment strategies and emotion regulation with adolescent offspring. *Journal of Research on Adolescence, 4,* 553–566.

Kobak, R., Little, M., Race, E., & Acosta, M. C. (2001). Attachment disruptions in seriously emotionally disturbed children: Implications for treatment. *Attachment & Human Development, 3,* 243–258.

Kobak, R., & Mandelbaum, T. (2003). Caring for the caregiver: An attachment approach to assessment and treatment of child problems. In S. Johnson & V. Whiffen (Eds.), *Attachment processes in couple and family therapy* (pp. 144–164). New York: Guilford Press.

Kobak, R., & Shaver, P. (1987, June). *Strategies for maintaining felt security: A theoretical analysis of continuity and change in styles of social adaptation.* Paper presented at the Conference in honor of John Bowlby's 80th Birthday, London, England.

Kobak, R., Sudler, N., & Gamble, W. (1991). Attachment and depressive symptoms during adolescence: A developmental pathways analysis. *Developmental Psychopathology, 3,* 461–474.

Levy, T., & Orlans, M. (2003). Creating and repairing attachment in biological, foster, and adoptive families. In S. Johnson & V. Whiffen (Eds.), *Attachment processes in couple and family therapy* (pp. 165–190). New York: Guilford Press.

Lewis, M., Feiring, C., McGuffog, C., & Jaskir, J. (1984). Predicting psychopathology in six-year-olds from early social relations. *Child Development, 55,* 123–136.

Liaw, F., & Brooks-Gunn, J. (1994). Cumulative familial risks and low-birthweight children's cognitive and behavioral development. *Journal of Clinical Child Psychology, 23,* 360–372.

Lichtenstein, J., Belsky, J., & Crnic, K. (1998). Earned security, daily stress, and parenting: A comparison of five alternative models. *Development and Psychopathology, 10,* 21–38.

Lyons-Ruth, K., Alpern, L., & Repacholi, B. (1993). Disorganized infant attachment classification and maternal psychosocial problems as predictors of hostile-aggressive behavior in the preschool classroom. *Child Development, 64,* 572–585.

Lyons-Ruth, K., Bronfman, E., & Parsons, E. (1999). Maternal frightened, frightening, or atypical behavior and disorganized infant attachment patterns. *Monographs of the Society for Research in Child Development, 64,* 67–96.

Lyons-Ruth, K., Connell, D. B., Zoll, D., & Stahl, J. (1987). Infants at social risk: Relations among infant maltreatment, maternal behavior, and infant attachment behavior. *Developmental Psychology, 23,* 223–232.

Lyons-Ruth, K., Easterbrooks, M. A., & Cibelli, C. D. (1997). Infant attachment strategies, infant mental lag, and maternal depressive symptoms: Predictors of internalizing and externalizing problems at age 7. *Developmental Psychology, 33*(4), 681–692.

Lyons-Ruth, K., & Jacobvitz, D. (1999). Attachment disorganization: Unresolved loss, relational violence, and lapses in behavioral and attentional strategies. In J. Cassidy & P. R. Shaver (Eds.), *Handbook of attachment: Theory, research, and clinical applications* (pp. 520–554). New York: Guilford Press.

Lyons-Ruth, K., Lyubchik, A., Wolfe, R., & Bronfman, E. (2002). Parental depression and child attachment: Hostile and helpless profiles of parent and child behavior among families at risk. In S. H. Goodman & I. H. Gotlib (Eds.), *Children of depressed parents: Mechanisms of risk and implications for treatment* (pp. 89–120). Washington, DC: American Psychological Association.

Lyons-Ruth, K., Repacholi, B., McLeod, S., & Silva, E. (1991). Disorganized attachment behavior in infancy: Short-term stability, maternal and infant correlates, and risk-related subtypes. *Development and Psychopathology, 3,* 377–396.

Lyons-Ruth, K., Yellin, C., Melnick, S., & Atwood, G. (2003). Childhood experiences of trauma and loss have different relations to maternal unresolved and hostile-helpless states of mind on the AAI. *Attachment & Human Development, 5,* 330–352.

Lyons-Ruth, K., Zoll, D., Connell, D., & Grunebaum, H. U. (1989). Family deviance and family disruption in childhood: Associations with maternal behavior and infant maltreatment during the first two years of life. *Development and Psychopathology, 1,* 219–236.

Madigan, S., Pederson, D., & Moran, G. (2003, April). *Bridging the gap between unresolved states of mind and disorganized attachment relationships: Links to atypical maternal behavior.* Poster presented at the biennial meeting of the Society for Research in Child Development, Tampa, FL.

Main, M. (1990). Cross-cultural studies of attachment organization: Recent studies, changing methodologies, and the concept of conditional strategies. *Human Development, 33,* 48–61.

Main, M., & Cassidy, J. (1988). Categories of response to reunion with the parent at age 6: Predictable from infant attachment classifications and stable over a 1-month period. *Developmental Psychology, 24,* 415–426.

Main, M., & Goldwyn, R. (1998). *Adult attachment rating and classification systems.* Unpublished manuscript, University of California at Berkeley.

Main, M., & Hesse, E. (1990). Parents' unresolved traumatic experiences are related to infant disorganized attachment status: Is frightened and/or frightening parental behavior the linking mechanism? In M. T. Greenberg, D. Cicchetti, & E. M. Cummings (Eds.), *Attachment in the preschool years: Theory, research, and intervention* (pp. 161–182). Chicago: University of Chicago Press.

Main, M., & Hesse, E. (1992). *Frightening, frightened, dissociated, or disorganized behavior on the part of the parent: A coding system for parent-infant interactions.* Unpublished manuscript, University of California at Berkeley.

Main, M., Kaplan, N., & Cassidy, J. (1985). Security in infancy, childhood, and adulthood: A move to the level of representation. *Monographs of the Society for Research in Child Development, 50,* 66–104.

Main, M., & Solomon, J. (1986). Discovery of an insecure-disorganized/disoriented attachment pattern. In T. B. Brazelton & M. W. Yogman (Eds.), *Affective development in infancy* (pp. 95–124). Westport, CT: Ablex Publishing.

Main, M., & Solomon, J. (1990). Procedures for identifying infants as disorganized/disoriented during the Ainsworth Strange Situation. In M. T. Greenberg, D. Cicchetti, & E. M. Cummings (Eds.), *Attachment in the preschool years: Theory, research, and intervention* (pp. 121–160). Chicago: University of Chicago Press.

Main, M., & Weston, D. R. (1981). The quality of the toddler's relationship to mother and to father: Related to conflict behavior and the readiness to establish new relationships. *Child Development, 52,* 932–940.

Marcovitch, S., Goldberg, S., Gold, A., Washington, J., Krekewich, K., & Handley-Derry, M. (1997). Determinants of behavioral problems in Romanian children adopted in Ontario. *International Journal of Behavioral Development, 20,* 17–31.

Marsh, P., McFarland, F. C., Allen, J. P., Boykin McElhaney, K., & Land, D. (2003). Attachment, autonomy, and multifinality in adolescent internalizing and risky behavioral symptoms. *Development and Psychopathology, 15,* 451–467.

Marvin, R. S., Cooper, G., Hoffman, K., & Powell, B. (2002). The circle of security project: Attachment-based intervention with caregiver-preschool child dyads. *Attachment and Human Development, 4,* 107–124.

McEwen, B. S. (1998). Protective and damaging effects of stress mediators. *New England Journal of Medicine, 228,* 171–179.

McLoyd, V. C. (1990). The impact of economic hardship on Black families and children: Psychological distress, parenting, and socioemotional development. *Child Development, 61,* 311–346.

Mickelson, K. D., Kessler, R. C., & Shaver, P. R. (1997). Adult attachment in a nationally representative sample. *Journal of Personality and Social Psychology, 73,* 1092–1106.

Moffitt, T. E. (1990). Juvenile delinquency and Attention Deficit Disorder: Boys' developmental trajectories from age 3 to age 15. *Child Development, 61,* 893–910.

Moffitt, T. E. (1993). Adolescence-limited and life-course-persistent antisocial behavior: A developmental taxonomy. *Psychological Review, 100,* 674–701.

Moss, E., Cyr, C., & Dubois-Comtois, K. (2004). Attachment at Early School Age and Developmental Risk: Examining Family Contexts and Behavior Problems of Controlling-Caregiving, Controlling-Punitive, and Behaviorally Disorganized Children. *Developmental Psychology, 40,* 519–532.

Moss, E., Parent, S., Gosselin, C., Rousseau, D., & St-Laurent, D. (1996). Attachment and teacher-reported behavior problems during the preschool and early school-age period. *Development and Psychopathology, 8,* 511–525.

Muller, R. T., LeMieux, K., & Sicoli, L. A. (2001). Attachment and psychopathology among formerly maltreated adults. *Journal of Family Violence, 16,* 151–169.

Munson, J. A., McMahon, R. J., & Spieker, S. J. (2001). Structure and variability in the developmental trajectory of children's externalizing problems: Impact of infant attachment, maternal depressive symptomatology, and child sex. *Development and Psychopathology, 13,* 277–296.

Muris, P., & Meesters, C. (2002). Attachment, behavioral inhibition, and anxiety disorders symptoms in normal adolescents. *Journal of Psychopathology and Behavioral Assessment, 24,* 97–106.

Nakashi-Eisikovits, O., Dutra, L., & Westen, D. (2002). Relationship between attachment patterns and personality pathology in adolescents. *Journal of the American Academy of Child and Adolescent Psychiatry, 41,* 1111–1123.

National Institute of Child Health and Human Development Early Child Care Research Network. (2001). Child-care and family predictors of preschool attachment and stability from infancy. *Developmental Psychology, 37,* 847–862.

O'Conner, T. G., Marvin, R. S., Rutter, M., Olrick, J. T., & Britner, P. A. (2003). Child-parent attachment following early institutional deprivation. *Development and Psychopathology, 15,* 19–38.

Ogawa, J. R., Sroufe, L. A., Weinfield, N. S., Carlson, E. A., & Egeland, B. (1997). Development and the fragmented self: Longitudinal study of dissociative symptomatology in a nonclinical sample. *Development and Psychopathology, 9,* 855–879.

Owen, M. T., & Cox, M. J. (1997). Marital conflict and the development of infant-parent attachment relationships. *Journal of Family Psychology, 11,* 152–164.

Patrick, M., Hobson, R. P., Castle, D., Howard, R., & Maughan, B. (1994). Personality disorder and the mental representation of early social experience. *Development and Psychopathology, 6,* 375–388.

Patterson, G., DeBaryshe, B., Ramsey, E. (1989). A developmental perspective on antisocial behavior. *American Psychologist, 45,* 329–335.

Pianta, R. C., Egeland, B., & Sroufe, L. A. (1990). Maternal stress and children's development: Prediction of school outcomes and identification of protective factors. In J. E. Rolf, A. S. Masten, D. Cicchetti, K. H. Nuechterlein, & S. Weintraub (Eds.), *Risk and protective factors in the development of psychopathology* (pp. 215–235). New York: Cambridge University Press.

Radke-Yarrow, M., Cummings, E. M., Kuczynski, L., & Chapman, M. (1985). Patterns of attachment in two- and three-year-olds in normal families and families with parental depression. *Child Development, 56,* 884–893.

Renken, B., Egeland, B., Marvinney, D., Mangelsdorf, S., & Sroufe, L. A. (1989). Early childhood antecedents of aggression and passive-withdrawal in early elementary school. *Journal of Personality, 57,* 257–281.

Roisman, G. I., Padrón, E., Sroufe, L. A., & Egeland, B. (2002). Earned-secure attachment status in retrospect and prospect. *Child Development, 73,* 1204–1219.

Rosenstein, D. S., & Horowitz, H. A. (1996). Adolescent attachment and psychopathology. *Journal of Consulting and Clinical Psychology, 64,* 244–253.

Rutter, M. (1979). Maternal deprivation, 1972–1978: New findings, new concepts, new approaches. *Child Development, 50,* 283–305.

Rutter, M., & Sroufe, L. A. (2000). Developmental psychopathology: Concepts and challenges. *Development and Psychopathology, 12,* 265–296.

Sameroff, A. J., Seifer, R., Baldwin, A., & Baldwin, C. (1993). Stability of intelligence from preschool to adolescence: The influence of social and family risk factors. *Child Development, 64,* 80–97.

Schuengel, C., Bakermans-Kranenburg, M. J., & van IJzendoorn, M. H. (1999). Frightening maternal behavior linking unresolved loss and disorganized infant attachment. *Journal of Consulting and Clinical Psychology, 67,* 54–63.

Seifer, R., LaGasse, L. L., Lester, B., Bauer, C. R., Shankaran, S., Bada, H. S., et al. (2004). Attachment status in children prenatally exposed to cocaine and other substances. *Child Development, 75,* 850–868.

Seifer, R., & Schiller, M. (1995). The role of parenting sensitivity, infant temperament, and dyadic interaction in attachment theory and assessment. *Monographs of the Society for Research in Child Development, 60,* 146–174.

Shaw, D. S., Keenan, K., Vondra, J. I., Delliquadri, E., & Giovannelli, J. (1997). Antecedents of preschool children's internalizing problems: A longitudinal study of low-income families. *Journal of the American Academy of Child and Adolescent Psychiatry, 36*(12), 1760–1767.

Shaw, D. S., Owens, E. B., Vondra, J. I., & Keenan, K. (1996). Early risk factors and pathways in the development of early disruptive behavior problems. *Development and Psychopathology, 8,* 679–699.

Shaw, D. S., & Vondra, J. I. (1995). Infant attachment security and maternal predictors of early behavior problems: A longitudinal study of low-income families. *Journal of Abnormal Child Psychology, 23,* 335–357.

Solomon, J., & George, C. (1999). The measurement of attachment security in infancy and childhood. In J. Cassidy & P. R. Shaver (Eds.), *Handbook of attachment: Theory, research, and clinical applications* (pp. 287–318). New York: Guilford Press.

Solomon, J., George, C., & De Jong, A. (1995). Children classified as controlling at age six: Evidence of disorganized representational strategies and aggression at home and at school. *Development and Psychopathology, 7,* 447–463.

Spangler, G., & Grossmann, K. E. (1993). Biobehavioral organization in securely and insecurely attached infants. *Child Development, 64,* 1439–1450.

Speltz, M. L., Greenberg, M. T., & DeKlyen, M. (1990). Attachment in preschoolers with disruptive behavior: A comparison of clinic-referred and nonproblem children. *Development and Psychopathology, 2,* 31–46.

Spieker, S. J., & Booth, C. L. (1988). Maternal antecedents of attachment security. In J. Belsky & T. Nezworski (Eds.), *Clinical implications of attachment* (pp. 95–135). Hillsdale, NJ: Erlbaum.

Sroufe, L. A. (1983). Infant-caregiver attachment and patterns of adaptation in preschool: The roots of maladaptation and competence. In M. Perlmutter (Ed.), *Minnesota Symposia on Child Psychology: Vol. 16. Development and policy concerning children with special needs* (pp. 41–83). Hillsdale, NJ: Erlbaum.

Sroufe, L. A. (1988). The role of infant-caregiver attachment in development. In J. Belsky & T. Nezworski (Eds.), *Clinical implications of attachment* (pp. 18–38). Hillsdale, NJ: Erlbaum.

Sroufe, L. A., Carlson, E. A., Levy, A. K., & Egeland, B. (1999). Implications of attachment theory for developmental psychopathology. *Development and Psychopathology, 11,* 1–13.

Sroufe, L. A., Egeland, B., Carlson, E., & Collins, A. (2005). *The development of the person: The Minnesota study of risk and adaptation from birth to adulthood.* New York: Guilford Press.

Sroufe, L. A., Egeland, B., & Kreutzer, T. (1990). The fate of early experience following developmental change: Longitudinal approaches to individual adaptation in childhood. *Child Development, 61,* 1363–1373.

Sroufe, L. A., Jacobvitz, D., Mangelsdorf, S., DeAngelo, E., & Ward, M. J. (1985). Generational boundary dissolution between mothers and their preschool children. A relationship systems approach. *Child Development, 56,* 317–325.

Sroufe, L. A., Schork, E., Motti, F., Lawroski, N., & LaFreniere, P. (1985). The role of affect in social competence. In C. Izard & J. Kagan (Eds.), *Emotions, cognition, and behavior* (pp. 289–319). New York: Cambridge University Press.

Sroufe, L. A., & Waters, E. (1977). Heart rate as a convergent measure in clinical and developmental research. *Merrill-Palmer Quarterly, 23,* 3–27.

Stevenson-Hinde, J., & Marshall, P. J. (1999). Behavioral inhibition, heart period, and respiratory sinus arrhythmia: An attachment perspective. *Child Development, 70,* 805–816.

Thompson, R. A. (1999). Early attachment and later development. In J. Cassidy & P. Shaver (Eds.), *Handbook of attachment: Theory, research, and clinical applications* (pp. 265–286). New York: Guilford Press.

Thompson, R. A., Lamb, M. E., & Estes, D. (1982). Stability of infant-mother attachment and its relationship to changing life circumstances in an unselected middle-class sample. *Child Development, 53,* 144–148.

Thompson, R. A., & Raikes, H. A. (2003). Toward the next quarter-century: Conceptual and methodological challenges for attachment theory. *Development and Psychopathology, 15,* 691–718.

Turner, P. J. (1991). Relations between attachment, gender, and behavior with peers in preschool. *Child Development, 62,* 1475–1488.

Van Emmichoven, I. A. Z., van Ijzendoorn, M. H., De Ruiter, C., & Brosschot, J. F. (2003). Selective processing of threatening information: Effects of attachment representation and anxiety disorder on attention and memory. *Development and Psychopathology, 15,* 219–237.

van IJzendoorn, M. (1995). Adult attachment representations, parental responsiveness, and infant attachment: A meta-analysis on the predictive validity of the Adult Attachment Interview. *Psychological Bulletin, 117,* 387–403.

van IJzendoorn, M. H., & Bakermans-Kranenburg, M. J. (1996). Attachment representations in mothers, fathers, adolescents, and clinical groups: A meta-analytic search for normative data. *Journal of Consulting and Clinical Psychology, 64,* 8–21.

van IJzendoorn, M. H., Schuengel, C., & Bakermans-Kranenburg, M. J. (1999). Disorganized attachment in early childhood: Meta-analysis of precursors, concomitants, and sequelae. *Development and Psychopathology, 11,* 225–249.

Vaughn, B. E., Egeland, B. R., Sroufe, L. A., & Waters, E. (1979). Individual differences in infant-mother attachment at twelve and eighteen months: Stability and change in families under stress. *Child Development, 50,* 971–975.

Verschueren, K., & Marcoen, A. (1999). Representation of self and socioemotional competence in kindergartners: Differential and combined effects of attachment to mother and father. *Child Development, 70,* 183–201.

Vondra, J. I., Hommerding, K. D., & Shaw, D. S. (1999). Stability and change in infant attachment style in a low-income sample. *Monographs of the Society for Research in Child Development, 64,* 119–144.

Vondra, J. I., Shaw, D. S., Swearingen, L., Cohen, M., & Owens, E. B. (2001). Attachment stability and emotional and behavioral regulation from infancy to preschool age. *Development and Psychopathology, 13,* 13–33.

Waddington, C. (1957). *The strategy of genes.* Cambridge, MA: Harvard University Press.

Warren, S. L., Huston, L., Egeland, B., & Sroufe, L. A. (1997). Child and adolescent anxiety disorders and early attachment. *Journal of the American Academy of Child and Adolescent Psychiatry, 36,* 637–644.

Wartner, U. G., Grossmann, K., Fremmer-Bombik, E., & Suess, G. (1994). Attachment patterns at age six in south Germany: Predictability from infancy and implications for preschool behavior. *Child Development, 65,* 1014–1027.

Waters, E. (1978). The reliability and stability of individual differences in infant-mother attachment. *Child Development, 49,* 483–494.

Waters, E., & Deane, K. E. (1985). Defining and assessing individual differences in attachment relationships: Q-methodology and the organization of behavior in infancy and early childhood. *Monographs of the Society for Research in Child Development, 50,* 41–65.

Waters, E., Merrick, S., Treboux, D., Crowell, J., & Albersheim, L. (2000). Attachment security in infancy and early adulthood: A twenty-year longitudinal study. *Child Development, 71,* 684–689.

Weinfield, N. S., Sroufe, L. A., Egeland, B., & Carlson, E. A. (1999). The nature of individual differences in infant-caregiver attachment. In J. Cassidy & P. R. Shaver (Eds.), *Handbook of attachment: Theory, research, and clinical applications* (pp. 68–88). New York: Guilford Press.

Yates, T. M., Dodds, M. F., Sroufe, L. A., & Egeland, B. (2003). Exposure to partner violence and child behavior problems: A prospective study controlling for child physical abuse and neglect, child cognitive ability, socioeconomic status, and life stress. *Development and Psychopathology, 15,* 199–218.

Zisook, S., Chentsova-Dutton, Y., & Shuchter, S. R. (1998). PTSD following bereavement. *Annals of Clinical Psychiatry, 10,* 157–163.

CHAPTER 11

Self-Processes and Developmental Psychopathology

SUSAN HARTER

The field of developmental psychopathology has undergone ontogenetic change in the past 2 decades, making numerous contributions (Cicchetti, 1993; Sroufe & Rutter, 1984). It has provided a unique perspective on both mental health and mental illness. It has challenged the very definition of psychopathology (see Cicchetti & Cohen, 1995; Sameroff, 2000). It has set the stage for the conceptualization of both risk and resilience for various disorders across the life span (see Cicchetti, 2004; Luthar & Cicchetti, 2000; Rutter & Sroufe, 2000) toward the goal of defining efforts at prevention, intervention, and treatment.

Critical to this endeavor has been a sensitivity to individual development over time, addressing why certain individuals' pathological conditions remain stable, whereas others are amenable to change. Moreover, as Sameroff (2000) cogently argues, the same symptoms may be caused by quite different processes at different developmental periods. In addition, for certain individuals suffering emotional, psychological, and behavioral disorders in childhood, there is little evidence of continuity into adulthood, whereas for others, symptoms persist. Understanding precisely why these differences exist represents a major challenge to the field.

Genetic studies have played a major role in enhancing our understanding of various pathologies (see review in Pennington, 2002). However, there has been a growing appreciation for the fact that the genetic throw of the dice is but one contributor to the various forms of psychopathol-

ogy. There has also been commendable attention to the fact that there is often no singular cause for a particular disorder; rather, there can be multiple pathways. For example, Cicchetti and Rogosch (1996, 2001) have argued that with regard to child maltreatment, there are multiple dimensions leading to subtypes of maltreatment symptomatology that involve a variety of neurological and psychological developmental processes. In our work, to take another example, we have examined the multiple pathways to depression among adolescents (Harter, 1999; from a methodological perspective, longitudinal studies have been critical in unraveling many of these issues; see Cicchetti, 2004).

Wearing my hat as a developmentalist, I am concerned, however, that the "development" in developmental psychopathology has not been given sufficient attention in terms of the contribution of development to our understanding of various forms of pathology. Development seems to be defined merely as time or age, leading to the importance of longitudinal research in this field. However, *age,* as a developmental predictor, has also been criticized as insufficient, as a crude marker for ontogenetic change (see Rutter & Sroufe, 2000). And well it should be, given the vast individual differences in normal and pathological development at any age. Historically, individual differences at any age level have been the bane of the developmentalist's existence. Moreover, our traditional developmental icons, Freud, Erikson, and Piaget, have fallen from theoretical grace because they did not sufficiently heed the warning that individual differences were damaging to their grand stage models.

Research funded by the W. T. Grant Foundation.

In our sophisticated efforts to right some of these theoretical wrongs, in our attempts to devise minitheories of a construct or a disorder, have we thrown out the developing baby with the bathwater? Have we turned our conceptual backs on the many developmental sequences that have been documented? Have we not respected the fact that contemporary investigators are quick to acknowledge that there are individual differences in the age at which developmental milestones are achieved? Therein lies the intrigue for those of us who continue to document interesting and compelling developmental sequences, while at the same time highlighting individual differences in the timing and manifestation of the particular behaviors that define any given normative developmental sequence. Might a basic appreciation for normative developmental sequences provide a backdrop for our understanding of deviations from those norms and thereby enhance our knowledge of the forms that pathology may take at different developmental levels?

I agree that an undue emphasis on the universals of developmental progressions (Rutter & Sroufe, 2000) may not be the beacon of light that illuminates our vision of developmental psychopathology, particularly if we adopt the very global developmental stage models of Freud, Erikson, and Piaget. Yet respect for the more circumscribed normative developmental sequences that have emerged in recent years, complemented by an acknowledgment of individual differences at any age, can provide insights into the causes of deviations from these normative paths. Moreover, it can prevent us from overinterpreting what are normative developmental "anomalies" (e.g., all-or-none thinking in the young child) as pathological.

In this chapter, therefore, I intend to put a little more "development" into our thinking about developmental psychopathology, particularly with regard to the *self-system*. Specifically, I focus on normative developmental changes in self-understanding and processes of self-evaluation across three periods of childhood (early, middle, and late childhood) and three periods of adolescence (early, middle, and late adolescence). For each of these six developmental periods, I first describe the normative developmental features of self-description and self-evaluation, drawing heavily on material presented in an earlier volume on the construction of the self (Harter, 1999). For each period, features include the salient content of the self, the structure or organization of self-constructs, the valence and accuracy of self-representations, the nature of social comparisons in forming self-judgments, and sensitivity to others as sources of information that may be relevant to self-representations.

Second, I describe the *normative developmental liabilities* that mark the emergence of each period or stage. The very fabric of development involves advances to new stages that may bring with them normative liabilities that should *not* be interpreted as pathological, liabilities that will dissipate as even more advanced developments and skills are acquired. There are numerous examples of where movement to a new stage of cognitive development leads to liabilities, given that the individual lacks "cognitive control" (see Fischer, 1980) over emerging new skills. Given that the self is not only a cognitive construction but a *social* construction (see Harter, 1999), crafted in the crucible of interactions with significant others, normative developmental manifestations of the self will necessarily be affected by socialization by parents and peers, to name the two key influences.

Third, I indicate how, at each developmental period, more serious forms of *psychopathology* may emerge given that self-development can be seriously derailed due to cognitive-developmental and socialization influences. These are to be distinguished from normative developmental liabilities in their severity and the extent to which they compromise the functioning of the child or adolescent at each period.

In addressing these three developmental components of the self-system, namely, normative developmental influences, liabilities associated with movement to a new developmental level, and more serious forms of psychopathology at each level, two causal factors, cognitive and social factors, are the primary focus on this chapter. I leave complex genetic interpretations in the hands of the many talented colleagues who have contributed to this subdomain of developmental psychology. However, where relevant, I touch generally on how genetic factors may indirectly affect self-representations and self-evaluations.

THE I-SELF AND THE ME-SELF

In addressing these themes, I occasionally draw on a distinction in the literature between the I-self and the Me-self. The majority of scholars who have devoted thoughtful attention to the self have come to a similar conclusion: Two distinct but intimately intertwined aspects of self can be meaningfully identified, self as subject (the I-self) and self as object (the Me-self). William James (1890, p. 197) introduced this distinction, defining the I-self as the actor or knower, whereas the Me-self is the object of one's knowledge, "an empirical aggregate of things objectively known." James also identified particular features or components of both the I-self and the Me-self. Components of the I-self included (1) self-awareness, an appreciation for one's internal states, needs, thoughts, and emotions; (2) self-agency, the sense of the authorship of one's thoughts and actions; (3) self-continuity, the sense that one remains the same person over time; and (4) self-coherence, a stable sense of the self as a single, coherent, bounded entity. Components of the Me-self included the "material me," the "social me," and the "spiritual me," which in contemporary models translates into new domains of the self-concept as well as global self-esteem.

The distinction between the I-self and the Me-self has proved amazingly viable and appears as a recurrent theme in most theoretical treatments of the self. Others embellished on James's formulation and have employed somewhat different terminology, but the essence of the distinction has been retained. Dickstein (1977), for example, contrasted the "dynamic" self that possesses a sense of personal agency and control to the self as the object of one's knowledge and evaluation. Lewis and Brooks-Gunn (1979) initially defined this duality as the existential self and the categorical self. The task of the developing I-self, the self as subject, is to develop the realization that it is "existential" in that it exists as separate from others. The Me-self, namely, self as object, is referred to as "categorical" in that the developing child must construct categories by which to define himself or herself (e.g., age and gender labels). Wylie (1979, 1989) has summarized the essence of the distinctions that have been drawn by numerous theorists. The I-self is the active observer, whereas the Me-self is the observed, the product of the observing process when attention is focused on the self.

More recently, Lewis (1991, 1994) has adopted new terminology. He now refers to the I-self as the "machinery of the self," which represents basic biological, perceptual, and cognitive processes. Lewis describes the Me-self as the "idea of me," allowing the child to form representations of the self.

Actual cognitive representations of the self begin to emerge in rudimentary form in the second half of the 2nd year. Both the machinery of the self and the idea of me can undergo considerable change over the course of childhood and adolescence.

Until the past decade, major empirical attention had been devoted to the Me-self, to the study of the self as an object of one's knowledge and evaluation, as evidenced by the myriad studies on self-concept and self-esteem (see Harter, 1983; Wylie, 1979, 1989). More recently, the I-self, which James himself regarded as an elusive if not incorrigible con-struct, has become more prominent in accounts of self-development. As we will come to appreciate in this chapter, both the structure and content of the Me-self at any given developmental level necessarily depend on the particular I-self capabilities, namely, those cognitive processes that define the knower. Thus, the cognitive-developmental changes in I-self processes will directly influence the nature of the self-theory that the child is constructing.

It should be noted that most scholars conceptualize the self as a theory that must be cognitively constructed. Those theorists in the tradition of adult personality and social psychology have suggested that the self theory should possess the characteristics of any formal theory, defined as a hypothetico-deductive system. Such a personal epistemology should, therefore, meet those criteria by which any good theory is evaluated, namely, the degree to which it is parsimonious, empirically valid, internally consistent, coherently organized, testable, and useful. From a developmental perspective, however, the self theories created by children cannot meet these criteria, given numerous cognitive limitations that have been identified in Piagetian (Piaget, 1960) and neo-Piagetian formulations (e.g., Case, 1992; Fischer, 1980); that is, the I-self in its role as constructor of the Me-self does not, in childhood, possess the capacities to create a hierarchically organized system of postulates that are internally consistent, coherently organized, testable, or empirically valid. In fact, it is not until late adolescence, if not early adulthood, that the abilities to construct a self-portrait meeting the criteria of a good formal theory potentially emerge. Therefore, in our developmental analysis of the self as a cognitive construction, it will be essential to examine how the changing characteristics of the I-self processes that define each developmental stage directly impact the Me-self, that is, the self-theory that is being constructed.

DEVELOPMENTAL DIFFERENCES IN SELF-REPRESENTATIONS DURING CHILDHOOD

In the following sections, the nature of self-representations and self-evaluations, at each of three periods of childhood—very early childhood, early to middle childhood, and middle to late childhood—are examined (see Table 11.1 for summary of cardinal features). For each period, there is a prototypical self-descriptive cameo (taken from Harter, 1999) that reflects the cardinal features of the content and structure of the self at that developmental level. Discussion fo-

TABLE 11.1   Normative Developmental Changes in Self-Representations during Childhood

Age Period	Salient Content	Structure/ Organization	Valence/ Accuracy	Nature of Comparisons	Sensitivity to Others
Very early childhood	Concrete, observable characteristics; simple taxonomic attributes in the form of abilities, activities, possessions, preferences	Isolated representations; lack of coherence, coordination; all-or-none thinking	Unrealistically positive; inability to distinguish real from ideal selves	No direct comparisons	Anticipation of adult reactions (praise, criticism); rudimentary appreciation of whether one is meeting others' external standards
Early to middle childhood	Elaborated taxonomic attributes; focus on specific competencies	Rudimentary links between representations; links typically opposites; all-or-none thinking	Typically positive inaccuracies persist	Temporal comparisons with self when younger; comparisons with age-mates to determine fairness	Recognition that others are evaluating the self; initial introjection of others' opinions; others' standards becoming self-guides in regulation of behavior
Middle to late childhood	Trait labels that focus on abilities and interpersonal characteristics; comparative assessments with peers; global evaluation of worth	Higher-order generalizations subsume several behaviors; ability to integrate opposing attributes	Both positive and negative evaluations; greater accuracy	Social comparison for purpose of self-evaluation	Internalization of others' opinions and standards, which come to function as self-guides

cuses on an appreciation for these normative developmental changes that are critical as a backdrop against which one can judge whether a child's self-representations are age-appropriate. Against this backdrop, I examine the normative developmental liabilities for the construction of the self at this period. Finally, I examine what cognitive and social factors at each period will lead to distortions in self-development, deviations that can be considered more pathological in nature.

Very Early Childhood

Consistent with the theme of this chapter, we first address the very earliest verbal manifestations of the self. A cameo of normative self-descriptions will be followed by an analysis of the primary features at this age level, approximately 3 to 5. Normative *liabilities* are then discussed. Finally, pathological forms of self-development that go beyond normative liabilities are described.

Verbal Cameo of Normative Self-Representations and Self-Evaluations

I'm 3 years old and I live in a big house with my mother and father and my brother, Jason, and my sister, Lisa. I have blue eyes and a kitty that is orange and a television in my own room. I know all of my ABCs, listen: A, B, C, D, E, F, G, H, J, L, K, O, P, Q, R, X, Y, Z. I can run real fast. I like pizza and I have a nice teacher at preschool. I can count up to 100, want to hear me? I love my dog Skipper. I can climb to the top of the

jungle gym, I'm not scared! I'm never scared! I'm always happy. I have brown hair and I go to preschool. I'm really strong. I can lift this chair, watch me!

Such descriptions will typically be observed in 3- to 4-year-olds. Noteworthy in this descriptive cameo is the nature of the attributes selected to portray the self. Theory and evidence (see Fischer, 1980; Fischer & Canfield, 1986; S. Griffin, 1992; Harter, 1996, 1998; Higgins, 1991; Watson, 1990) indicate that the young child can construct only very concrete cognitive representations of observable features of the self (e.g., "I know my ABCs"; "I can count"; "I live in a big house"). Damon and Hart (1988) label these categorical identifications, reflecting the fact that the young child understands the self only as separate, taxonomic attributes that may be physical (e.g., "I have blue eyes"), active (e.g., "I can run real fast"; "I can climb to the top"), social (e.g., "I have a brother, Jason, and a sister, Lisa"), or psychological (e.g., "I'm always happy"). It is noteworthy that particular skills are touted (running, climbing) rather than generalizations about abilities, such as being athletic or good at sports. Moreover, often these behavioral descriptions will spill over into actual demonstrations of abilities ("I'm really strong. I can lift this chair, watch me!"), suggesting that these emerging self-representations are still very directly tied to behavior. From a cognitive-developmental perspective, they do not represent higher-order conceptual categories through which the self is defined. In addition to concrete descriptions of behaviors, the young child defines the self in terms of preferences (e.g., "I like pizza"; "I love my dog Skipper") as well as possessions ("I have a kitty that is orange and a television in my own room"). Thus, as Rosenberg (1979) cogently observes, the young child acts as a demographer or radical behaviorist in that his or her self-descriptions are limited to characteristics that are potentially observable by others.

From the standpoint of organization, the self-representations of this period are highly differentiated or isolated from one another; that is, the young child is incapable of integrating these compartmentalized representations of self, and thus self-descriptive accounts appear quite disjointed. This lack of coherence is a general cognitive characteristic that pervades the young child's thinking across a variety of domains (Fischer, 1980). As Piaget (1960) himself observed, young children's thinking is transductive, in that they reason from particular to particular, in no logical order.

Neo-Piagetians have elaborated on these processes. For example, Case (1992) refers to this level as "interrelational," in that young children can forge rudimentary links in the form of discrete event-sequence structures that are defined in terms of physical dimensions, behavioral events, or habitual activities. However, they cannot coordinate two such structures (see also S. Griffin, 1992), in part because of working memory constraints that prevent young children from holding several features in mind simultaneously. Fischer's (1980) formulation is very similar. He labels these initial structures "single representations." Such structures are highly differentiated from one another, as the cognitive limitations at this stage render the child incapable of integrating single representations into a coherent self-portrait.

Moreover, self-evaluations during this period are likely to be unrealistically positive (e.g., "I know all of my ABCs" [which he or she doesn't!]) because young children have difficulty distinguishing between their desired and their actual competence, a confusion initially observed by both S. Freud (1952) and Piaget (1932). Thus, young children cannot yet formulate an ideal self-concept that is differentiated from a real self-concept. Rather, their descriptions represent a litany of talents that may transcend reality (Harter & Pike, 1984). For contemporary cognitive-developmentalists, such overstated virtuosity stems from another cognitive limitation of this period: the inability of young children to bring social comparison information to bear meaningfully on their perceived competencies (Frey & Ruble, 1990). The ability to use social comparison toward the goal of self-evaluation requires that the child be

able to relate one concept (his or her own performance) to another (someone else's performance), a skill that is not sufficiently developed in the young child. Thus, self-descriptions typically represent an overestimation of personal abilities. It is important to appreciate, however, that these apparent distortions are normative in that they reflect cognitive limitations rather than conscious efforts to deceive the listener.

Another manifestation of the self-structure of very young children is their inability to acknowledge that they can possess attributes of opposing valence, for example, good and bad, or nice and mean (Fischer, Hand, Watson, Van Parys, & Tucker, 1984). This all-or-none thinking can be observed in the cameo, in that all of the attributes appear to be positive. Young children's self-representations may also include emotion descriptors (e.g., "I'm always happy"). However, children at this age do not acknowledge that they can experience both positive and negative emotions, particularly at the same time. The majority will deny that they have negative emotions (e.g., "I'm never scared!") as salient features of their descriptive self-portrait. Other procedures reveal that they do have rudimentary concepts of such single negative emotions as mad, sad, and scared (see Bretherton & Beeghly, 1982; Dunn, 1988; Harter & Whitesell, 1989). However, a growing body of evidence now reveals that young children are incapable of appreciating the fact that they can experience seemingly opposing emotional reactions simultaneously (Carroll & Steward, 1984; Donaldson & Westerman, 1986; Gnepp, McKee, & Domanic, 1987; Harris, 1983; Harter & Buddin, 1987; Reissland, 1985; Selman, 1980). For Fischer and colleagues (e.g., Fischer & Ayoub, 1994), this dichotomous thinking represents the natural fractionation of the mind. Such "affecting splitting," as they term it, constitutes a normative form of dissociation that is the hallmark of very young children's thinking about both self and other.

It is important to appreciate the normative nature of this all-or-none thinking in understanding young children's reactions to everyday life events, particularly as they apply to the experience of negative affects. For example, one of our young interview participants described a situation in which he was being punished by his mother: "When I'm all bad my mother gets all mad, and when she's all mad, she gets a lot bigger!" In situations where the child is consumed with anger toward a parent or sibling, he or she may staunchly deny any feelings of affection or love (e.g., claiming only "I hate you!"). With regard to issues of loss, the young child may be pervasively sad over the death of a loved one, totally unable to acknowledge the positive emotions that were undoubtedly also felt for the individual. Thus, at this particular developmental period, one would not want to conclude that such all-or-none reactions are abnormal or have clinical implications.

Cognitive limitations of this period extend to the inability of young children to create a concept of their overall worth as a person, namely, a representation of their global self-esteem or self-worth (Harter, 1990b). Such a self-representation requires a higher-order integration of domain-specific attributes that have first been differentiated. Young children do begin to describe themselves in terms of concrete cognitive abilities, physical abilities, how they behave, how they look, and friendships they have formed (Harter, 1990b). However, these domains are not clearly differentiated from one another, as revealed through factor-analytic procedures (Harter, 1998; Harter & Pike, 1984).

Behaviorally Presented Self-Esteem in Young Children. The fact that young children cannot cognitively or verbally formulate a general concept of their worth as a person does not mean they lack the experience of self-esteem. Rather, our findings (see Haltiwanger, 1989; Harter, 1990b, 1999) reveal that young children manifest self-esteem in their behavior. In examining the construct of behaviorally presented self-esteem, we first invoked the aid of nursery school and kindergarten teachers who had considerable experience with young children. We found that early childhood educators frequently make reference to children's self-esteem and that this is a very meaningful concept that distinguishes children from one another.

As a first step, we conducted open-ended interviews with about 20 teachers to generate an item pool from which we would eventually select those that best discriminate between high and low self-worth children. Teachers were asked to describe those behaviors that characterize the high self-esteem child, those that characterize the low self-esteem child, and those they felt did not allow them to discriminate between the two groups. Teachers had definite opinions about behaviors that were both relevant and irrelevant to this construct.

From these interviews we culled 84 behavioral descriptors, phrases that represent behaviors ranging from those that teachers felt did discriminate between high and low self-esteem children to those they felt were not relevant. We next employed a Q-sort procedure in which we asked a separate group of teachers to sort these 84 items into those that were most descriptive of the high self-esteem child at one end of the distribution, those that were most like the low self-esteem child at the other end, and those that were

neither like nor unlike the high or low self-esteem child in the middle. Thus, teachers performed a single sort based on their view of the prototype of both the high and low self-esteem child. Reliability analyses indicated very substantial agreement among teachers.

Behaviors That Discriminate between High and Low Self-Esteem Children. There were two primary categories of items that defined the high self-esteem child:

1. *Active displays of confidence, curiosity, initiative, and independence:* Examples include: trusts his or her own ideas, approaches challenge with confidence, initiates activities confidently, takes initiative, sets goals independently, is curious, explores and questions, is eager to try doing new things. Two other behaviors seemed to convey the more general manifestation of these attributes: describes self in positive terms and shows pride in his or her work.

2. *Adaptive reaction to change or stress:* Examples include: able to adjust to changes, comfortable with transitions, tolerates frustration and perseveres, able to handle criticism and teasing.

Similar categories describing the low self-esteem child representing the converse of these two sets of items emerged:

1. *Failure to display confidence, curiosity, initiative, independence:* Examples include: doesn't trust his or her own ideas, lacks confidence to initiate, lacks confidence to approach challenge, is not curious, does not explore, hangs back, watches only, withdraws and sits apart, describes self in negative terms, does not show pride in his or her work.

2. *Difficulty in reacting to change or stress:* Examples include: gives up easily when frustrated, reacts to stress with immature behavior, reacts inappropriately to accidents.

This content analysis is particularly illuminating given what it reveals about the nature of self-esteem as seen through the collective eyes of experienced teachers. They suggest two primary dimensions, one active and one reactive. The active dimension represents a style of approach rather than the display of skills per se. That is, the high self-esteem child manifests confidence in the world; the low self-esteem child avoids challenge, novelty, and exploration of the world. The reactive dimension involves the response of the child to change, frustration, or stress. The high self-esteem child reacts more adaptively, whereas the low self-esteem child reacts with immature, inappropriate, or avoidant behaviors.

Of particular interest are the categories of behaviors that do *not* seem to discriminate between high and low self-esteem children according to teachers. Most noteworthy, if not striking, was the fact that *competence* per se is not a correlate of overall self-esteem in young children. It would appear that confidence, as a behavioral style, is not synonymous with competence, at least at this age level. This is illuminating because it suggests that the origins of a sense of confidence during early childhood do not necessarily reside in the display of skills, more objectively defined. During later childhood, the link between confidence in the self and one's level of competence apparently becomes stronger. This developmental pattern will include parental support, sensitivity, and contingent responsiveness, in general, as well as specific support for exploration, mastery, and curiosity that will promote a sense of confidence. As will become apparent in the antecedents of self-esteem that emerge in middle childhood, competence will become a much more critical factor. We would argue, in bridging these two developmental periods, that socialization practices that reward displays of confidence will lead the child to engage in behaviors that allow him or her to develop skills and competencies that will subsequently become a defining predictor of self-esteem.

Additional Functions of the Socializing Environment.   In addition to the effect of parenting on behavioral manifestations of self-esteem, Higgins (1991), building on the efforts of Case (1985), Fischer (1980), and Selman (1980), focuses on how self-development during this period involves the interaction between the young child's cognitive capacities and the role of socializing agents. He provides evidence for the contention that at Case's stage of interrelational development and Fischer's stage of single representations, very young children can place themselves in the same category as the parent who shares their gender, which forms an initial basis for identification with that parent. Thus, the young boy can evaluate his overt behavior with regard to the question "Am I doing what Daddy is doing?" Attempts to match that behavior, in turn, will have implications for which attributes become incorporated into the young child's self-definition. Thus, these processes represent one way that socializing agents impact the self.

Higgins (1991) observes that at the interrelational stage, young children can also form structures allowing them to detect the fact that their behavior evokes a reaction in others, notably parents, which in turn causes psychological re-

actions in the self. These experiences shape the self to the extent that the young child chooses to engage in behaviors designed to please the parents. Stipek, Recchia, and McClintic (1992), in a laboratory study, have provided empirical evidence for this observation, demonstrating that slightly before the age of 2, children begin to anticipate adult reactions, seeking positive responses to their successes and attempting to avoid negative responses to failure. At this age, they also find that young children show a rudimentary appreciation for adult standards, for example, by turning away from adults and hunching their shoulders in the face of failures (see also Kagan, 1984, who reports similar distress reactions). For Mascolo and Fischer (1995), such reactions constitute rudimentary forms of shame. Shame at this period, like self-esteem, can only be *behaviorally* manifest. Children do not understand the concept at a verbal level (see Harter, 1999). Moreover, although young children are beginning to recognize that their behavior has an impact on others, their perspective-taking skills are extremely limited (see Harter, 1999; Selman, 1980). Thus, they are unable to incorporate others' opinions of the self into a realistic self-evaluation that can be verbalized.

The Role of Narrative in the Co-Construction of the Self.   Another arena in which socialization agents in general and parental figures in particular impact children's self-development involves the role of narratives in promoting the young child's autobiographical memory, or a rudimentary story of the self. The infantile amnesia that one observes before the age of approximately 2 can be overcome only by learning from adults how to formulate their own memories as *narratives*. Initially, parents recount to the child stories about his or her past and present experiences. With increasing age and language facility, children come to take on a more active role in that parent and child co-construct the memory of a shared experience (Eisenberg, 1985; Hudson, 1990a, 1990b; Nelson, 1986, 1990, 1993; Rogoff, 1990; Snow, 1990). However for the young child, such narratives are still highly scaffolded by the parents, who reinforce aspects of experience that they feel are important to codify and remember (Fivush, Gray, & Fromhoff, 1987; Fivush & Hudson, 1990; Nelson, 1989). Through these interactions, an autobiographical account of the self is created. Of further interest are findings demonstrating individual differences in maternal styles of narrative construction (see Bretherton, 1993; Nelson, 1990, 1993). For example, Tessler (1991) has distinguished between an elaborative style (where mothers present an embellished narrative) and a pragmatic style (focusing more on useful information). Elaborative mothers were more effective in establishing and eliciting memories with their young children.

For most developmental memory researchers, language is the critical acquisition allowing one to establish a personal narrative and to overcome infantile amnesia (Fivush & Hamond, 1990; Hudson, 1990a; Nelson, 1990; Pillemer & White, 1989). The mastery of language in general and of personal pronouns in particular enables young children to think and talk about the I-self and to expand their categorical knowledge of the Me-self (Bates, 1990; P. J. Miller, Potts, Fung, Hoogstra, & Mintz, 1990). Moreover, representations of the self in language are further facilitated by acquisition of the past tense, which occurs toward the second half of the 3rd year.

Howe (2003) and Howe and Courage (1993) argue, however, that the emergence of language is not sufficient to explain the demise of infantile amnesia and the emergence of an ability to create autobiographical memories. They note that self-knowledge is also required; that is, an appreciation for the self as an independent entity with actions, attributes, affects, and thoughts that are distinct from those of others is required for the development of autobiographical memory. Without the clear recognition of an independent I-self and Me-self, there can be no referent around which personally experienced events can be organized. Thus, for Howe and Courage, the emergence of the infant's sense of self is the cornerstone in the development of autobiographical memory that further shapes and solidifies one's self-definition.

Linguistic interactions with parents also impact the developing child's representation of self in semantic memory (Bowlby, 1969; Nelson, 1989, 1993; Snow, 1990). As Bowlby first noted, early semantic memory is conferred by caregivers. Parents convey considerable descriptive and evaluative information about the child, including labels to distinguish one from others (e.g., "You're a big boy"), evaluative descriptors of the self (e.g., "You are so smart"; "You're a good girl"), as well as rules and standards and the extent to which the child has met parental expectations (e.g., "Big boys don't cry"). Consistent with Cooley's (1902) model of the looking-glass self, children incorporate these labels and evaluations into their self-definition in the form of general trait knowledge (represented in semantic memory). Thus, the linguistic construction of the self is a highly interpersonal process, with caregivers making a major contribution to its representation in both autobiographical and semantic memory.

More recently, experts on infant memory development have suggested additional processes that may account for childhood amnesia (see Hayne, 2004). Reviewing numerous studies of infant memory, Hayne concludes that there are three developmental processes that may add to our understanding of the infant's failure to retain autobiographical content. First, the large corpus of research first reveals that the *speed* with which infants encode information increases as a function of age. Second, the *retention* interval dramatically increases as a function of age during infancy. Third, the *flexibility* of memory retrieval improves during infancy, meaning that memories are not as bound by specific contextual or proximal cues, where changes in such cues can disrupt or preclude memory retrieval. Older infants have been found to gradually utilize more or different retrieval cues, allowing them to access memories in a wider range of situations. These newer explanations are not incompatible with earlier theories of the function of language and self-development but provide additional explanations for the phenomenon of infantile amnesia.

Normative Liabilities for Self-Development during Very Early Childhood

Clearly, infantile amnesia, given its several sources, including the lack of the development of the I-self and the Me-self around which memories can be organized, precludes a conscious sense of self for the infant and toddler. However, once very young children are able to verbally describe the self, their self-representations are limited to reflecting concrete descriptions of behaviors, abilities, emotions, possessions, and preferences that are potentially observable by others. These attributes are also highly differentiated or isolated from one another, leading to rather disjointed accounts, because at this age, young children lack the ability to integrate such characteristics. For some, this lack of a logical self-theory may be cause for concern, if not consternation. However, these features are normative in that the I-self processes, namely, the cognitive structures available at this developmental period, preclude a more logical rendering of the Me-self.

Self-representations are also likely to be unrealistically *positive* for several reasons. First, young children lack the cognitive ability to engage in social comparison for the purpose of self-evaluation. From a cognitive-developmental perspective, this skill, like many of the abilities that are unavailable to the preoperational child, as Piaget (1960) revealed, requires that one be able to hold two dimensions in mind simultaneously in order to compare them. Conservation tasks represent a prototype. Here, we apply this analysis to the inability to hold in mind an evaluation of one's own attributes while simultaneously thinking about another's attributes, and then comparing them. This is beyond the abilities of the very young child.

Second, and for similar reasons, very young children are unable to distinguish between their *actual* self-attributes and their *ideal* self-attributes. This requires discriminating between the two, holding each in mind simultaneously, and comparing the two judgments, a cognitive ability that the very young child lacks. As a result, self-evaluations are unrealistically positive because the fusion of the two favors the ideal or desirable self-concept. Were one dealing with older children, one might interpret such a tendency to reflect socially desirable responding as the conscious distortion of one's self-evaluation to be favorable. Cognitive-developmental interpretations lead to a different conclusion: that the very young child's positive evaluations reflect cognitive limitations rather than a conscious attempt to deceive.

Third, young children lack the perspective ability to understand and therefore incorporate the perceived opinions of significant others toward the self (Harter, 1999; Selman, 1980). As will become evident in the discussion of middle childhood, the ability to appreciate others' evaluations of the self become powerful determinants of one's own sense of worth as a person emerges in middle childhood. At that developmental juncture, children typically believe and therefore incorporate the views of those socializing agents whose opinions they value, such as significant others who are nurturant and powerful (Harter, 1999). These processes are described later, in the context of Cooley's (1902) formulation of the looking-glass self that our own research has demonstrated to be alive and well, as an explanation for the antecedents of one's level of self-esteem beginning in middle childhood.

Cognitive limitations also lead to young children's inability to acknowledge that they can possess both positive and negative self-attributes. That is, the all-or-none, black-and-white thinking that is characteristic of the preoperational child extends to his or her conceptualizations of self. One must be one or the other. To the extent that the majority of socializing agents are relatively benevolent and supportive, the psychological scale will tip toward positive self-attributes. Thus, the young child will bask in the glow of overall virtuosity (albeit unrealistic).

The inability to possess a verbalizable concept of one's self-esteem can also be explained in terms of the cognitive limitations of this period. As will be documented, the subsequent ability to compare one's actual self-attributes with one's ideal self-attributes will become an important determinant of one's level of self-esteem. Perspective-taking abilities will also become critical given that the internal-

ization of the opinions of significant others becomes a powerful predictor of one's overall sense of personal worth. It was noted that *behavioral* manifestations of self-esteem do emerge during early childhood. However, it is an interesting empirical question as to whether the level of self-esteem so displayed parallels or predicts the concept of one's self-esteem that will emerge in middle childhood.

The description of the normative liabilities that impact conceptions and manifestations of the self during early childhood follows from normative cognitive limitations. One may question, however, the extent to which these actually reflect *psychological* liabilities. That is, many of the cognitive limitations of this period may serve as *protective* factors, to the extent that the very young child maintains very positive, albeit potentially unrealistic, perceptions of self. Positive self-views may serve as motivating factors, as emotional buffers, contributing to the young child's development. They may propel the child toward growth-building mastery attempts, instill a sense of confidence, and lead the child to rebuff perceptions of inadequacy, all of which may foster positive future development. From an evolutionary perspective, such liabilities may well represent very critical strengths for this developmental level. This issue will be revisited as we move up the ontogenetic ladder of representations and evaluations of the self.

Pathological Self-Processes and Outcomes in Early Childhood

A critical goal of this chapter is to distinguish between normative liabilities in the formation of the self and more pathological processes and outcomes at each developmental level. In very early childhood, what could serve to seriously derail normative self-development, leading to outcomes that would seriously compromise a very young child's psychological development? Typically, the causes of pathology involve an interaction between the child's level of cognitive development and chronic negative treatment at the hands of caregivers.

The Effects of Abuse.   It should first be noted that it is not uncommon for children who experience severe and chronic sexual abuse to have also been subjected to other types of maltreatment, including verbal, physical, and emotional abuse (see Cicchetti, 2004; Harter, 1999; Rossman & Rosenberg, 1998). The normative penchant for very young children to engage in all-or-none thinking (e.g., all good versus all bad) will lead abused children, who have a rudimentary sense of parental attitudes toward the self, to view the Me-self as *all bad*. As noted earlier, the more typical pattern for children who are socialized by benevolent, supportive parents is to view the self as all good. Abuse, as well as severe neglect (Bowlby, 1969) can, in turn, lead to early forms of depression, in which the very young child eventually becomes listless, unconnected to caregivers, and eventually emotionally numb.

Abuse or maltreatment can also affect I-self functions, for example, self-awareness, one of the basic functions of the I-self as originally described by James (1892). Briere (1992) points to a feature of abusive relationships that interferes with the victim's lack of awareness of self. The fact that the child must direct sustained attention to external threats draws energy and focus away from the developmental task of self-awareness. Thus, the hypervigilance to others' reactions, what Briere (1989) terms "other directedness," interferes with the ability to attend to one's own needs, thoughts, and desires.

Research findings support these contentions. Cicchetti (1989) and colleagues (Cicchetti, Beeghly, Carlson, & Toth, 1990) found that maltreated children (ages 30 to 36 months) report less internal-state language, particularly negative internal feeling and physiological reactions, than do their nonmaltreated, securely attached counterparts (see also Beeghly & Cicchetti, 1994). Similar findings have been reported by Beeghly, Carlson, and Cicchetti (1986). Coster, Gersten, Beeghly, and Cicchetti (1989) have reported that maltreated toddlers use less descriptive speech, particularly about their own feelings and actions. Gralinsky, Feshbach, Powell, and Derrington (1993) have observed that older maltreated children report fewer descriptions of inner states and feelings than children with no known history of abuse. Thus, there is a growing body of evidence that the defensive processes that are mobilized by maltreated children interfere with one of the primary tasks of the I-self, namely, awareness of inner thoughts and feelings. Moreover, lack of self-awareness should also interfere with the ability to develop autobiographical memory.

Many attachment theorists contribute to our understanding of how maltreatment in early childhood can adversely influence self-development. There is considerable consensus that the vast majority of maltreated children form insecure attachments with their primary caregivers (Cicchetti et al., 1990; Crittenden & Ainsworth, 1989; Erickson, Egeland, & Pianta, 1989; Schneider-Rosen, Braunwald, Carlson, & Cicchetti, 1985; Westen, 1993). More recent findings have revealed that maltreated infants are more likely to develop disorganized-disoriented Type D attachment relationships (Barnett, Ganiban, & Cicchetti, 1999; Carlson, Cicchetti, & Barnett, 1989). Thus, the effects of early sexual and/or physical abuse, coupled with other forms of parental insensitivity, disrupt the attachment

bond, which in turn interferes with the development of positive working models of self and others. The foundation of attachment theory rests on the premise that if the caregiver has fairly consistently responded to the infant's needs and signals and has respected the infant's need for independent exploration of the environment, the child will develop an internal working model of the self as valued, competent, and self-reliant. Conversely, if the parent is insensitive to the infant's needs and signals, is inconsistent, and rejecting of the infant's bid for comfort and exploration, the child will develop an internal working model of the self as unworthy, ineffective, and incompetent (Ainsworth, 1979; Bowlby, 1973; Bretherton, 1991, 1993; Crittenden & Ainsworth, 1989; Sroufe & Fleeson, 1986). Clearly, the parental practices that have been associated with child abuse represent precisely the kind of treatment that would lead children to develop insecure attachments, as well as a concept of the self as unlovable and lacking in competence.

One critical function of parenting is to assist the child in creating a narrative of the self, the beginnings of one's life story, as it were, an autobiographical account that includes the perceptions of self and other (see Hudson, 1990a, 1990b; Nelson, 1986; Snow, 1990). Initially, these narratives are highly scaffolded by parents, who reinforce aspects of experience that they feel are important to codify and to remember or to forget (Fivush & Hudson, 1990; Hudson, 1990a; Nelson, 1986, 1990, 1993; Rogoff, 1990; Snow, 1990). More recent findings have revealed that the narratives of maltreated children contain more negative self-representations and more negative maternal representations compared to narratives of nonmaltreated children (Toth, Cicchetti, Macfie, & Emde, 1997; Toth, Cicchetti, Macfie, Maughan, & Vanmeenen, 2000). Moreover, such narratives show less coherence; that is, the self that is represented is less coherent or more fragmented (Crittenden, 1994; Macfie, Cicchetti, & Toth, 2001). These findings reveal greater signs of dissociative symptoms that reflect disruptions in the integration of memories and perceptions about the self. Thus, maltreatment at the hands of caregivers severely disrupts normative self-development that in turn leads to associated pathological symptoms, where it has been found that conflictual themes in young children's narratives predict externalizing problems in particular. Moreover, severe and chronic abuse has been associated with disorders such as Borderline Personality Disorder, where symptoms emerge later in development during adulthood (Putnum, 1993; Westen, 1993).

Language and False-Self Behavior. Language clearly promotes heightened levels of relatedness and allows for the creation of a personal narrative. Stern (1985), however, alerts us to the liabilities of language. He argues that language can drive a wedge between two simultaneous forms of interpersonal experience, as it is lived and as it is verbally represented. The very capacity for objectifying the self through verbal representations allows one to transcend, and therefore potentially distort, one's immediate experience and to create a fantasized construction of the self. As noted in the previous section, there is the potential for incorporating the biases of caregivers' perspectives on the self because initially, adults dictate the content of narratives incorporated in autobiographical memory (Bowlby, 1980; Bretherton, 1987; Crittenden, 1994; Pipp, 1990). Children may receive subtle signals that certain episodes should not be retold or are best "forgotten" (Dunn, Brown, & Beardsall, 1991). Bretherton describes another manifestation, "defensive exclusion," in which negative information about the self or other is not incorporated because it is too psychologically threatening (see also Cassidy & Kobak, 1988). Wolf (1990) describes several mechanisms, such as deceit and fantasy, whereby the young child, as author of the self, can select, edit, or change the "facts" in the service of personal goals, hopes, or wishes (see also Dunn, 1988).

Such distortions may well contribute to the formation of a self that is perceived as inauthentic if one accepts the falsified version of experience. Winnicott's (1958) observations alert us to the fact that intrusive or overinvolved mothers, in their desire to comply with maternal demands and expectations, lead infants to present a false outer self that does not represent their own inner experiences. Moreover, such parents may reject the infant's "felt self," approving only of the falsely presented self (Crittenden, 1994). As Stern (1985) notes, the display of a false self incurs the risk of alienating oneself from those inner experiences that represent one's true self (see also Main & Solomon, 1990). Thus, linguistic abilities not only allow one to share experiences with others, but also to withhold them.

The Impoverished Self.   As noted in the discussion of normative development during early childhood, an important function of parenting is to scaffold the child's construction of autobiographical memory in the form of a narrative of one's nascent life story. However, clinicians observe that maltreatment and neglect sow the seeds for children, beginning in early to middle childhood, to develop what we have come to call an "impoverished self," which has its roots in the early socialization practices of caregivers who fail to assist the child in the co-construction of a

positive, rich, and coherent self-narrative. In this regard, research (Tessler, 1991) has revealed individual differences among mothers: Some help to construct an embellished narrative, whereas others encourage a more restricted narrative that focuses on useful information, leading to fewer autobiographical memories. Clinical observations reveal that there is another group of parents who, because of their own dysfunction (e.g., depression) and parental inadequacies, do little to nothing in the way of co-constructing with the child a self-narrative. The seeds of an impoverished self, therefore, begin in early childhood and continue into middle childhood and beyond, if such children do not receive therapeutic intervention.

When these children come to the attention of family therapists, they lack a vocabulary to define the self, in that there is little in the way of autobiographical memory and descriptive or evaluative concepts about the self. An impoverished self represents one form of pathology, as the individual has few personal referents or self-concepts around which to organize present experiences. As a result, the behavior of such children will often appear to be disorganized. Moreover, to the extent that a richly defined self promotes motivational functions in terms of guides to regulate behavior and to set future goals, such children may appear aimless, with no clear pursuits. A clinical colleague of mine, Donna Marold (personal communication, August 1998), has astutely observed that these children do not have dreams for the future, whereas most children do have future aspirations. For example, the prototypical child in early to mid childhood indicates that he or she is going to be on a team someday. Marold notes, however, that the families of children with an impoverished self typically do not create or construct the type of narratives that provide a basis for autobiographical memory and a sense of self. Nor do such parents provide the type of personal labels or feedback that would lead to the development of semantic memory for self-attributes. Often, these are parents who do not take photographs of the children or the family, nor do they post the child's artwork or school papers on the refrigerator door. Marold has also observed that such parents do not have special rituals, such as cooking the child's favorite food or reading (and rereading) cherished bedtime stories.

What type of therapeutic interventions might be applicable in such cases, and how can they be guided by developmental theory and research? Therapists (myself included) have learned through trial and error that, with older children, one cannot simply try to instill, teach, or scaffold the self-structures appropriate for their age level, namely, trait labels that represent generalizations that integrate behavioral or taxonomic self-attributes. With such children, there are few attributes to build on. Thus, one must begin at the beginning, using techniques that help the child create the missing narratives, the autobiographical memory, the self-labels. Marold has successfully employed a number of very basic techniques to achieve this goal, techniques that necessarily enlist the aid of parents. She suggests that the parent and child create a scrapbook in which whatever materials that might be available (the scant photograph, perhaps the school picture; a child's drawing; anything that may make a memory more salient) are collected and talked about. Where such materials are not available, Marold suggests cutting pictures out of magazines that represent the child's favorite possessions, activities, preferences—the very features that define the young child's sense of self. If there have been no routines that help to solidify the child's sense of self, Marold recommends that parents be counseled to establish routines, for example, establishing some family rituals (e.g., Friday night pizza) around a child's favorite food. Obviously, these techniques require collaboration with the parents and depend on their ability to recreate their child's past experiences, something that not all parents are equipped to do. In this regard, the therapist can serve as an important role model. From the standpoint of our developmental analysis, an impoverished self requires this type of support in early childhood.

Early to Middle Childhood

The verbal cameo of typical self-descriptions at the next stage of development, early to middle childhood, reveal both advances over the previous stage, as well as limitations, primarily due to cognitive-developmental level. After describing normative features, liabilities are addressed and contrasted to pathological features that may develop given child-rearing practices that compromise the self.

Verbal Cameo of Normative Self-Representations and Self-Evaluations

I have a lot of friends, in my neighborhood, at school, and at my church. I'm good at schoolwork, I know my words, and letters, and my numbers. I can run fast, and I can climb high, a lot higher than I could when I was little, and I can run faster, too. I can also throw a ball real far, I'm going to be on some kind of team when I am older. I can do lots of stuff real good. Lots! If you are good at things you can't be bad at things, at least not at the same time. I know some other kids who are bad at things but not me! (Well, maybe sometime later I could be just a very little bad, but not very often.) My

parents are real proud of me when I do good at things. It makes me really happy and excited when they watch me!

Such self-descriptions are typical of children ages 5 to 7. Some of the features of the previous stage persist: Self-representations are still typically very positive, and the child continues to overestimate his or her virtuosity. References to various competencies, for example, social skills, cognitive abilities, and athletic talents, are common self-descriptors. With regard to the advances of this age period, children begin to display a rudimentary ability to intercoordinate concepts that were previously compartmentalized (Case, 1985; Fischer, 1980). For example, they can form a category or representational set that combines a number of their competencies (e.g., good at running, jumping, schoolwork; having friends in the neighborhood, at school, and at church). However, all-or-none thinking persists. In Case's model and its application to the self (S. Griffin, 1992), this stage is labeled "unidimensional" thinking. At this age, such black-and-white thinking is supported by another new cognitive process: the child's ability to link or relate representational sets to one another, to "map" representations onto one another, to use Fischer's terminology. Of particular interest to self-development is one type of representational mapping that is extremely common in the thinking of young children: a link in the form of opposites. For example, in the domain of physical concepts, young children can oppose up and down, tall and short, thin and wide or fat, although they cannot yet meaningfully coordinate these representations.

Opposites can also be observed within the realm of the descriptions of self and others, where the child's ability to oppose good to bad is especially relevant. As observed earlier, the child develops a rudimentary concept of the self as good at a number of skills. Given that good is defined as the opposite of bad, this cognitive construction typically precludes the young child from being bad, at least at the same time. Thus, the oppositional mapping takes the necessary form of "I'm good and therefore I can't be bad." However, other people may be perceived as bad at these skills, as the cameo description reveals ("I know some other kids who are bad at things but not me!"). Children at this age may acknowledge that they could be bad at some earlier or later time ("Well, maybe sometime later I could be just a very little bad, but not very often"). However, the structure of such mappings typically leads the child to overdifferentiate favorable and unfavorable attributes, as demonstrated by findings revealing young children's inability to integrate attributes such as nice and mean (Fischer et al., 1984) or smart and dumb (Harter, 1986a). Moreover, the mapping structure leads to the persistence of self-descriptions laden with virtuosity.

These principles also apply to children's understanding of their emotions, in that they cannot integrate emotions of opposing valance such as happy and sad (Harter & Buddin, 1987). There is an advance over the previous period, as children come to appreciate the fact that they can have two emotions of the same valence (e.g., "It makes me really happy and excited when [my parents] watch me"); that is, they can develop representational sets for feelings of the same valence, but there are separate emotion categories, one for positive emotions (happy, excited, proud) and one for negative emotions (sad, mad, scared). However, children at this stage cannot yet integrate the sets of positive and negative emotions, sets that are viewed as conceptual opposites and therefore incompatible. The inability to acknowledge that one can possess both favorable and unfavorable attributes, or that one can experience both positive and negative emotions, represents a cognitive liability that is a hallmark of this period of development. Unlike the previous period, now, due to greater cognitive and linguistic abilities, the child is able to verbally express his or her staunch conviction that one cannot possess both positive and negative characteristics at the same time. As one 5-year-old vehemently put it, "Nope, there is no way you could be smart and dumb at the same time. You only have one mind!"

The Role of the Socializing Environment. In addition to cognitive-developmental features affecting self-development, socializing agents also have an impact in interaction with cognitive acquisitions. Thus, children acquire an increasing cognitive appreciation for the perspective of others, which influences self-development. The relational processes of this level allow the child to realize that socializing agents have a particular viewpoint (not merely a reaction) toward them and their behavior (Higgins, 1991). As Selman (1980) observes, the improved perspective-taking skills at this age permit children to realize that others are actively evaluating the self (although children have not yet internalized these evaluations sufficiently to make independent judgments about their attributes). Nevertheless, as Higgins argues, the viewpoints of others begin to function as *self-guides* as the child comes to further identify with what he or she perceives socializing agents expect of the self. These self-guides function to aid the child in the regulation of his or her behavior.

One can recognize in these observations mechanisms similar to those identified by Bandura (1991) in his theory of the development of self-regulation. Early in development, children's behavior is more externally controlled by reinforcement, punishment, direct instruction, and modeling. Gradually, children come to anticipate the reactions of others and to internalize the rules of behavior set forth by significant others. As these become more internalized, personal standards, the child's behavior comes more under the control of evaluative self-reactions (self-approval, self-sanctions), aiding in self-regulation and the selection of those behaviors that promote positive self-evaluation. The contribution of cognitive-developmental theory is to identify more clearly those cognitive structures making such developmental acquisitions possible. Moreover, the structures underlying such a shift represent rudimentary processes required for the incorporation of the evaluative opinions of significant others leading to self-evaluations. However, at this age level, cognitive-developmental limitations preclude the internalization of others' standards and opinions toward the self. Internalization, in which the child comes personally to "own" these standards and opinions, awaits further developmental advances.

As Higgins (1991) and Selman (1980), among others (see also Gesell & Ilg, 1946), have pointed out, although children at this age do become aware that others are critically evaluating their attributes, they lack the type of self-awareness that would allow them to be critical of their own behavior. In I-self/Me-self terminology, the child's I-self is aware that significant others are making judgments about the Me-self, yet the I-self cannot directly turn the evaluative beacon on the Me-self. These processes will emerge only when the child becomes capable of internalizing the evaluative judgments of others for the purpose of self-evaluation. As a result, children at this age period will show little interest in scrutinizing the self. As Anna Freud (1965) observed, young children do not naturally take themselves as the object of their own observation. They are much more likely to direct their inquisitiveness toward the outside world of events rather than the inner world of intrapsychic experiences.

With regard to other forms of interaction between cognitive-developmental level and the socializing environment, there are certain advances in the ability to utilize social comparison information, although there are also limitations. Frey and Ruble (1985, 1990) and Suls and Sanders (1982) provide evidence that at this stage, children first focus on temporal comparisons (how I am performing now, compared to when I was younger) and age norms, rather than individual difference comparisons with age-mates. As our prototypical subject tells us, "I can climb a lot higher than when I was little and I can run faster, too." Suls and Sanders observe that such temporal comparisons are particularly gratifying to young children given the rapid skill development at this age level. As a result, such comparisons contribute to the highly positive self-evaluations that typically persist at this age level. Evidence (reviewed in Ruble & Frey, 1991) now reveals that younger children do engage in certain forms of social comparison; however, it is directed toward different goals than for older children. For example, young children use such information to determine if they have received their fair share of rewards, rather than for purposes of self-evaluation. Moreover, findings reveal that young children show an interest in others' performance to obtain information about the task demands that can facilitate their understanding of mastery goals and improve their learning (Frey & Ruble, 1985; Ruble & Dweck, 1995). However, they do not yet utilize such information to assess their competence, in large part due to the cognitive limitations of this period; thus, their evaluations continue to be unrealistic.

Normative Liabilities for Self-Development between Early to Middle Childhood

Many of the features of the previous stage persist, in that self-representations are typically very positive, and the child continues to overestimate his or her abilities. Moreover, the child at this period still lacks the ability to develop an overall concept of his or her worth as a person. With regard to advances, children do begin to display a rudimentary ability to intercoordinate self-concepts that were previously compartmentalized; for example, they can construct a representational set that combines a number of their competencies (e.g., good at running, jumping, schoolwork). However, all-or-none thinking persists due to a new cognitive process in which different valence attributes are verbally conceptualized as opposites (e.g., good versus bad, nice versus mean). Typically, this all-or-none structure leads to self-attributes that are all positive, and these beliefs are even more intractable than in the previous period given cognitive and linguistic advances that bring such beliefs into consciousness to the extent that the socializing environment supports such positivity.

Rudimentary processes allow the child to appreciate the fact that others are evaluating the self, although cognitive-developmental limitations preclude the child from internalizing these evaluations. Advances include the ability to make temporal comparisons to one's past performance. Given the rapid skill development during these years, such comparisons contribute to the highly positive self-evaluations that typically persist at this age level. The failure to use social comparison information for the purpose of self-evaluation, however, contributes to the persistence of unrealistically favorable self-attributes. As noted in describing the previous period, children at this stage are not consciously distorting their self-perceptions. Rather, they have not yet acquired the cognitive skills to develop more realistic self-perceptions.

Pathological Processes and Outcomes during Early to Middle Childhood

The potentials for pathological self-development that were identified for very early childhood exist for this subsequent period of development, particularly if the caregiving of socializing agents remains consistently negative. However, the effects may be amplified given that cognitive and linguistic acquisitions make such effects more evident, and given that the child is more able, with linguistic and cognitive advances, to better verbalize negative self-evaluations. In the case of chronic and severe abuse, the major coping strategy is *dissociation,* in which the individual attempts to cognitively split off the traumatic event from consciousness, to detach the self from the traumatic event (Herman, 1992; Putman, 1993; Terr, 1991). When such abuse occurs at this period of childhood, it conspires with the natural or normative penchant for cognitive dissociation, splitting, or fragmentation (Fischer & Ayoub, 1994). Moreover, the very construction of cognitive structures that consciously lead the child of this age to think in terms of opposites (one must be all good or all bad) leads to a painful awareness of that one must be *all bad,* that the self is totally flawed. This, in turn, can lead to compromising symptoms of depression.

Briere (1992), based on clinical cases, provides a complementary analysis of the sequential "logic" that governs the abused child's attempt to make meaning of his or her experiences. Given maltreatment at the hands of a parent or family member, the child first surmises, "Either I am bad or my parents are bad." However, the assumption of young children that parents or adult authority figures are always right leads to the conclusion that parental maltreatment must be due to the fact that they themselves were bad, that the act was their fault, and that therefore they deserve to be punished. When children are repeatedly assaulted, they come to conclude that they must be "very bad," contributing to the sense of fundamental badness at their core.

From a cognitive-developmental perspective, the young child who is abused will readily blame the self (Herman, 1992; Piaget, 1932; Watson & Fischer, 1993; Westen, 1993); that is, given young children's natural egocentrism, they will take responsibility for events they did not cause or cannot control. Moreover, as Piaget demonstrated, young children focus on the deed (e.g., the abusive act) rather than on the intention (e.g., the motives of the perpetrator). As Herman points out, the child must construct some version of reality that justifies continued abuse and therefore inevitably concludes that his or her innate badness is the cause.

From an attachment theory perspective, the processes outlined in the preceding section will continue to negatively impact the self-development of children, to the extent that caregiving practices such as lack of sensitivity, neglect, noncontingent responsiveness, and other forms of maltreatment leading to insecure attachment styles continue. The impact of these practices may be amplified to the extent that the child can now *verbalize* his or her sense of inadequacy and lack of lovability. These now become etched in the child's conscious realization and expression of a negative sense of self. These should readily translate into experiences of profound sadness and lack of energy, symptoms of depression at this age level. Although no research to our knowledge has yet to examine our behaviorally presented self-esteem construct in depressed children, it can be predicted that there would be strong relationships between depression and behaviorally manifested low self-esteem at this age level.

The preceding section on very early childhood described the rudimentary antecedents of the impoverished self that reside in the fact that caregivers do not adequately support the child's construction of an autobiographical narrative of the sense of self. The effects of such lack of scaffolding should become more evident as children move into middle childhood and should be able to verbally express their autobiographical sense of self, a narrative of their past life story, with implications for the future. However, the failure to express dreams for the future, to positively describe one's capabilities, to express pride in one's accomplishments all reflect pathological distortions of self-development. These symptoms should represent serious red flags that require clinical intervention.

Middle to Late Childhood

There are dramatic differences between the emerging self-representations during middle to late childhood, ages 8 to 11, and those of the earlier childhood stages. The verbal cameo will illustrate these changes, followed by an analysis of why self-descriptions normatively change. As with any developmental advances, there are also accompanying lia-

bilities. A discussion of these liabilities is followed by how more extreme or pathological forms of self-development may be manifested.

Verbal Cameo of Normative Self-Representations and Self-Evaluations

I'm in fourth grade this year, and I'm pretty popular, at least with the girls. That's because I'm nice to people and helpful and can keep secrets. Mostly I am nice to my friends, although if I get in a bad mood I sometimes say something that can be a little mean. I try to control my temper, but when I don't, I'm ashamed of myself. I'm usually happy when I'm with my friends, but I get sad if there is no one to do things with. At school, I'm feeling pretty smart in certain subjects like language arts and social studies. I got As in these subjects on my last report card and was really proud of myself. But I'm feeling pretty dumb in math and science, especially when I see how well a lot of the other kids are doing. Even though I'm not doing well in those subjects, I still like myself as a person, because math and science just aren't that important to me. How I look and how popular I am are more important. I also like myself because I know my parents like me and so do other kids. That helps you like yourself.

Such self-descriptions are typically observed in children ages 8 to 11. In contrast to the more concrete self-representations of younger children, older children are much more likely to describe the self in such terms as "popular," "nice," "helpful," "mean," "smart," and "dumb." Children moving into late childhood continue to describe themselves in terms of their competencies (e.g., smart, dumb). However, self-attributes become increasingly interpersonal as relations with others, particularly peers, become an increasingly salient dimension of the self (see also Damon & Hart, 1988; Rosenberg, 1979).

From the standpoint of those emerging cognitive-developmental (I-self) processes, these attributes represent traits in the form of higher-order generalizations or concepts, based on the integration of more specific behavioral features of the self (see Fischer, 1980; Siegler, 1991). Thus, in the preceding cameo, the higher-order generalization that she is "smart" is based on the integration of scholastic success in both language arts and social studies. That she also feels "dumb" represents a higher-order construction based on her math and science performance. "Popular" also combines several behaviors, namely, being nice, being helpful, and keeping secrets.

The preceding developmental analysis focused primarily on advances in the ability to conceptualize self-attributes. However, the processes that emerge during this age period can also be applied to emotion concepts. Thus, the child develops a representational system in which positive emotions (e.g., "I'm usually happy when I'm with my friends") are integrated with negative emotional representations (e.g., "I get sad if there is no one to do things with"), as a growing number of empirical studies reveal (Carroll & Steward, 1984; Donaldson & Westerman, 1986; Fischer, Shaver, & Carnochan, 1990; Gnepp et al., 1987; Harris, 1983; Harris, Olthof, & Meerum-Terwogt, 1981; Harter, 1986b; Harter & Buddin, 1987; Reissland, 1985; Selman, 1980).

This represents a major conceptual advance over the previous two age periods, during which young children deny that they can have emotions of opposing valences. Our own developmental findings (see Harter & Buddin, 1987) reveal that at this age, the simultaneous experience of positive and negative emotions can initially be brought to bear only on different targets. As one child subject observed, "I was sitting in school feeling worried about all of the responsibilities of a new pet but I was happy that I had gotten straight As on my report card." In Fischerian (Fischer, 1980) terms, the child at this level demonstrates a "shift of focus," directing the positive feeling to a positive target or event and then shifting to the experience of a negative feeling that is attached to a negative event. In middle childhood, the concept that the very same target can simultaneously provoke both a positive and a negative emotion is not yet cognitively accessible. However, by late childhood, positive and negative emotions can be brought to bear on one target given the emergence of representational systems that better allow the child to integrate emotion concepts that were previously differentiated. Sample responses from our empirical documentation of this progression (Harter & Buddin, 1987) were as follows: "I was happy that I got a present but mad that it wasn't what I wanted"; "If a stranger offered you some candy, you would be eager for the candy but worried about whether it was okay."

Social Processes. A more balanced view of self, in which positive as well as negative attributes of the self are acknowledged, is also fostered by social comparison. As our prototypical subject reports, "I'm feeling pretty dumb in math and science, especially when I see how well a lot of the other kids are doing." A number of studies conducted in the 1970s and early 1980s presented evidence revealing that it is not until middle childhood that the child can apply comparative assessments with peers in the service of self-evaluation. From a cognitive-developmental perspective, the ability to use social comparison information toward the goal of self-evaluation requires that the child have the ability to relate one concept to another si-

multaneously, an ability not sufficiently developed at younger ages. In addition to the contribution of advances in cognitive development (see also Moretti & Higgins, 1990), age stratification in school stimulates greater attention to individual differences between age-mates (Higgins & Bargh, 1987; Mack, 1983). More recent findings reveal that the primary motive for children in this age period to utilize social comparison is for personal competence assessment.

The ability to utilize social comparison information for the purpose of self-evaluation is founded on cognitive-developmental advances, namely, the ability to simultaneously compare representations of self and others. However, it is also supported by the socializing environment. For example, evidence reveals that as children move up the academic ladder, teachers make increasing use of social comparison information (J. P. Eccles & Midgley, 1989; J. S. Eccles, Midgley, & Adler, 1984) and that students are well aware of these educational practices (Harter, 1996). Moreover, parents may contribute to the increasing salience of social comparison, to the extent that they make comparative assessments of how their child is performing relative to siblings, friends, or classmates.

A Developmental Acquisition Sequence of the Understanding of Pride and Shame. In the cameo self-description, the child not only describes the self in terms of basic emotions such as happy and sad, but also makes reference to self-affects or self-conscious emotions such as pride and shame ("I got As in [language arts and social studies] on my last report card and was really proud of myself"; "I try to control my temper, but when I don't, I'm ashamed of myself"). It is not until this age level that self-affects appear in the child's repertoire of self-representations.

Cooley's (1902) formulation spoke to this issue in that the development of the self includes not only the internalization of the opinions of significant others but the incorporation of their affective reactions to the self, specifically, pride and shame, leading ultimately to the ability to feel proud of oneself as well as ashamed of oneself. Moreover, Cooley set the stage for a developmental analysis of how these emotions might emerge. Although pride and shame could clearly be experienced by adults in the absence of others, Cooley noted that "the thing that moves us to pride and shame is not the merely mechanical reflection of ourselves, but an imputed sentiment, the imagined effect of this reflection upon another's mind" (p. 153). Cooley was clear that this sentiment is social in nature, based on social custom and opinion, although it becomes somewhat removed from these sources through an implied internalization process. Cooley writes that the adult is

> not immediately dependent upon what others think; he has worked over his reflected self in his mind until it is a steadfast portion of his thought, an idea and conviction apart, in some measure, from its external origin. Hence this sentiment requires time for its development and flourishes in mature age rather than in the open and growing period of youth. (p. 199)

Cooley's views on the internalization of others' opinions about the self paved the way for a more developmental perspective on how the attitudes of others are incorporated into the self.

In our own work (Harter, 1999), we have provided documentation for a 4-stage developmental sequence governing the development of the conceptual *understanding* of pride and shame. Younger children may manifest or display the emotions of pride and shame through facial expressions and bodily posture (see review by Stipek, 1995). However, it is not until middle to late childhood that they can verbalize the capacity to be proud or ashamed *of oneself* and that such self-affects become part of their self-definition. In particular, we were interested in the substages that appeared to be precursors of the child's emerging ability to appreciate the fact that one could be proud or ashamed of the self in the absence of any observation by others.

Focusing on the socialization component of both pride and shame, we devised a procedure that would be sensitive to the role of the observing parent; that is, we sought to determine whether parents were required to "support" the reported experience of pride and shame (Harter, 1999). Toward this end, we designed two sets of vignettes. To assess shame, we constructed a pictorial vignette with several frames and a brief story line to accompany the pictures. The story concerned a situation in which the parents have forbidden the child to take any money from a very large jar of coins in the parents' bedroom. However, the child transgresses and takes a few coins. There are two separate story sequences. In one sequence, no one observes the act, and no one ever finds out (an outcome we attempted to ensure by describing the money jar as very large, whereas the child took only a few coins). In the second sequence, the parent catches the child in the act. The primary dependent measures included the subject's description of the emotions that the story child would feel in the first sequence (where the act is not detected) and a description of the emotions that both child and parent would

feel in the second situation (where the parent catches the child in the act).

To assess an understanding of pride, we selected a gymnastic feat as the demonstration of competence. In the first sequence, the child goes to the playground on a Saturday when no one else is there and tries out a flip on the bars, one that he or she has been working on at school. The child attempts this maneuver, which he or she has never been able to perform successfully before, and does it really well. In the first sequence, the child leaves the bars knowing that he or she was the only one at the playground and thus no one else observed the flip. The child is then asked what feeling he or she would have at that time. In the second pride sequence, the parent accompanies the child to the playground and observes the child successfully performing the flip for the first time. The child is asked how he or she would feel, as well as how the observing parent would feel having watched the child doing the flip. In all conditions, pictorial aids in the form of photographs of facial expressions of a series of emotions by a child, for the first sequence, and by a child and a parent, for the second sequence, are presented to the children to facilitate their identification of relevant affects.

The results for both pride and shame revealed a highly age-related, parallel, 4-stage sequence that is interpretable within our socialization framework. Moreover, the stages that emerged are consistent with Selman's (1980) developmental model of self-awareness, in which children gradually begin to observe and critically evaluate the self. At our first level, ages 4 to 5, there is no mention of either pride or shame on the part of the story child or the parent in either sequence, whether the child is observed or not observed. Participants give very clear responses about their potential emotional reactions to these situations, reactions that are quite telling. In the transgression situation where the story child is not observed by the parents, participants report that the child character (with whom they are encouraged to identify) would feel scared or worried about the possibility of detection. When caught by the parent, he or she feels extremely scared or worried about the likelihood of punishment. However, there is no acknowledgment of pride or shame.

In the pride sequences of stories, these youngest subjects report that they would feel happy, glad, and excited in the situation where their gymnastic feat is not observed by the parent. In the story where the parent witnesses their performance, they report that both they and the parent would feel happy, glad, and excited; that is, there is no mention of pride, on the part of either the parent or the story child. Thus, children at this first level are aware that their parents have reactions to their behavior. However, consistent with Selman's (1980) first level of self-awareness and with Higgins's (1991) analysis, the child is not yet aware that others are evaluating the self, nor can the I-self critically evaluate or affectively react to the Me-self.

Our second level at ages 5 to 6 represents a very interesting transition period. Children now demonstrate their first use of the terms "ashamed" and "proud." However, their usage is restricted to reactions of the parents. Thus, the parental response to the child's transgression is to be ashamed of the child. However, the child does not yet acknowledge that he or she is ashamed of the self. Rather, the child is still scared or worried about the parents' reaction. Similarly, in the case of the gymnastic feat, the subjects describe how the parent is proud of the child. However, the child is not yet proud of the self; rather, he or she is excited, happy, glad.

This level parallels Selman's (1980) second stage of self-awareness and is consistent with Higgins's (1991) analysis; that is, the child's I-self is aware that others are observing and evaluating and affectively reacting to his or her Me-self ("I observe you evaluating and being proud or ashamed of me"). This second level, therefore, provides the necessary building blocks for the emergence of the looking-glass self (Cooley, 1902), in which one comes to internalize the attitudes, opinions, and affective sentiments of significant others toward the self; that is, children must first be sensitive to the fact that they are being evaluated in order to direct their attention to the specific content of others' approval, criticism, and emotional reactions.

At our third level, children between the ages of 6 and 7 acknowledge that shame and pride can be directed by the self, toward the self. Thus, in the situation where the act has been observed, not only will parents be ashamed or proud of the child, but children report that they, too, will feel ashamed or proud of themselves, seemingly in response to the parental reaction. However, what also places children at this level is the fact that they do not report any feelings of shame or pride in the story sequence specifying the absence of parental observation. This seems to be another critical transitional level in our socialization sequence: The act must be observed in the case of both a transgression (in order to experience shame) and the demonstration of competence (in order to experience pride). In the absence of parental observation, no such potential self-affects are acknowledged. This level parallels Selman's (1980) third stage of self-awareness, when the child begins to incorpo-

rate the observations of others into his or her own self-perceptions, such that he or she can directly evaluate the self. Thus, the I-self can now adopt an attitude toward the Me-self that parallels the attitude of significant others, although these self-attitudes and self-affects must still be scaffolded by others.

The hallmark of the fourth level, beginning at ages 7 to 8, is that in the absence of parental observation, children spontaneously acknowledge that the story children will feel ashamed of themselves or proud of themselves. (It should be noted that the stories in which the child was not observed were always presented first, so that any response of shame or pride on the part of the child was not simply a generalization from the sequence in which he or she was observed.) Therefore, at this level, children appear to have internalized the standards by which shame and pride can be experienced in the absence of direct parental observation. Interestingly, the large majority of children at this level do not merely report the emotions of shame and pride, but specifically indicate "I would feel ashamed (or proud) of myself." Thus, they appear to be at the stage where these emotions do function as self-affects in the sense that one is truly ashamed or proud of the self. This final level in our sequence is consistent with Selman's (1980) fourth stage, in which the I-self can now observe and critically evaluate the Me-self in the absence of the direct presence or reactions of significant others.

In summary, this sequence not only reveals the gradual nature of the normative developmental emergence of self-affects, but also suggests that the critical, underlying processes involve parental socialization. Thus, we have inferred that children must first experience others as models who are proud or ashamed of them in order to internalize these functions themselves. Even when they first develop the ability to acknowledge that they are proud or ashamed of themselves, children still need the scaffolding of parental surveillance or observation. The final stage in the internalization process occurs when these self-affects are experienced in the absence of observations by others, when the I-self can be directly ashamed of the Me-self, when one is all by oneself.

Possible Genetic Influences on Self-Esteem. The discussion thus far has focused on psychological mechanisms that account for a child's level of self-esteem, describing the contribution of cognitive-developmental and social determinants. For many years, these have been the prevailing theories. Recently, neurological and genetic models have come to the fore. The 1990s were declared the

Decade of the Brain, and it became obvious that our splintered subfields needed to be integrated if we were truly to understand development and human behavior. How might such a genetic perspective be applied to differences in levels of self-esteem in children? I am not a geneticist, nor have I done such work. However, other investigators present findings that suggest (statistical) heritability of self-esteem. The empirical findings cannot be disputed (see McGuire et al., 1999; Neiss, Sedikides, & Stevenson, 2002).

Does this mean that there is a "self-esteem" gene? I think not. Might there be heritability? Yes. What might be a thoughtful explanation? We know a great deal about heritability from many compelling studies of intelligence, temperament, athleticism, and creativity, to name but a few characteristics. There are also considerable data demonstrating the heritability of conditions such as various learning disabilities, Autism, and Attention-Deficit/Hyperactivity Disorder (ADHD; see Pennington, 2002). These studies can be linked to the issue of the heritability of self-esteem. That is, if the genetic throw of the dice causes a child to be intellectually competent, athletically competent, or attractive by current societal standards, and if parents, peers, and others reward those characteristics and also reinforce their importance, then according to James (1890, 1892) and our own findings, this child is on the path to high self-esteem. If children are genetically blessed with a sociable temperament and are rewarded for their sociability by parents, teachers, and peers, then, from a looking-glass self perspective, they will receive positive feedback that will enhance their self-esteem. Thus, I see the constructs that I have identified to be mediators of self-esteem, impacted by genetics. But I do not think it is reasonable to conclude that there is a direct connection between genes and self-esteem.

Normative Liabilities for Self-Development during Middle to Late Childhood

A cardinal thesis of this chapter is that cognitive advances, that is, movement to new cognitive-developmental levels, paradoxically bring about normative liabilities for the self-system, as implied in the discussion of normative self-descriptions. In this section, the liabilities are highlighted. The ability to be able to construct a global perception of one's worth as a person represents a major developmental acquisition, a milestone, in terms of a shift from mere domain-specific self-perceptions to an integrated sense of one's overall self-esteem. However, other cognitive-developmental acquisitions can serve to lower the valence of this global perception of self, leading to lowered self-

esteem. Findings clearly reveal (see Harter, 1999) that beginning in middle childhood, self-perceptions become more negative, normatively, compared to the very positive self-perceptions of the majority of young children. As noted earlier, the emergence of three cognitive skills are noteworthy in this regard: (1) the ability to use social comparison for the purpose of self-evaluation, (2) the ability to differentiate real from ideal self-perceptions, and (3) increases in social perspective-taking skills.

The ability to employ social comparison for the purpose of self-evaluation (see Maccoby, 1980; Moretti & Higgins, 1990; Ruble & Frey, 1991) leads many, with the exception of the most competent or adequate in any given domain, to fall short in their self-evaluations. If one therefore judges oneself deficient compared to others in domains that are deemed important to the self (typically defined by the importance hierarchies of significance to others), then global self-esteem will be eroded. Thus, the very ability and penchant, supported by the culture (e.g., family, peers, schools, the media), to compare oneself with others makes one vulnerable in valued domains (e.g., appearance, popularity, scholastic competence, athletic performance, and behavioral conduct).

A second newfound cognitive ability to emerge in middle to late childhood involves the capacity to make the distinction between one's real and one's ideal self. From a Jamesian perspective, this skill involves the ability to distinguish between one's actual competencies or adequacies and those to which one aspires, namely, those that one deems important. The cognitive realization that one is not meeting one's expectations (an ability that young children do not possess) will necessarily lower one's overall level of self-esteem, as James's (1890) formulation accurately predicts. Moreover, findings (see Glick & Zigler, 1985; Leahy & Shirk, 1985; Oosterwegel & Oppenheimer, 1993) reveal that the real-ideal discrepancy tends to increase with development. Two causes of such an increase can be identified. First, as noted earlier, social comparison processes lead older children to lower the valence of their self-perceptions, viewing themselves less positively. Second, given increasing perspective-taking skills, children are becoming increasingly cognizant of the standards and ideals that socializing agents hold for their behavior. Moreover, parents, teachers, and peers may normatively raise the bar in terms of their expectations, leading to higher self-ideals in an attempt to please significant others.

Increased perspective-taking skills can also *directly* impact self-perceptions, leading them to be more realistic. Protected by limitations in the ability to divine what others truly think of the self, younger children can maintain very positive self-perceptions. The developing ability to more accurately assess the opinions that others hold about one's characteristics, coupled with increasing concern about the importance of the views of others toward the self, normatively lead many older children to realistically lower their self-evaluations.

We can ask whether these processes that lead to more realistic self-evaluations in fact represent liabilities. Many have argued (see review in Harter, 1999) that realistic self-evaluations are more adaptive beginning in middle to late childhood. Thus, the initial liabilities, in terms of psychological blows to one's self-image, may be temporary as the child seeks to realistically readjust his or her self-perceptions and pursue more adaptive paths of development that are consistent with his or her actual attributes.

Pathological Self-Processes and Outcomes in Middle to Late Childhood

Pathological outcomes will typically result from an interaction between a child's cognitive-developmental level and the behavior of socializing agents, where parental figures are the most immediate influences. During middle to late childhood, when children add to their repertoire of domain-specific self-evaluations the more global concept of self-esteem, both types of self-representations are vulnerable to the influence of caregivers. As described in the sections on normative processes, benevolent socializing agents readily provide the nurturance, approval, and support that is mirrored in self-evaluations that are positive. Approval, in the form of the reflected appraisals of others, is, therefore, internalized as acceptance of self. However, in the search for their image in the social mirror, children may well gaze through a glass darkly. Caregivers lacking in responsiveness, nurturance, encouragement, and approval, as well as socializing agents who are rejecting, punitive, or neglectful, will cause their children to develop tarnished images of self. Attachment theorists echo this theme (see Bretherton, 1991; Sroufe, 1990). They observe that children who experience parents as emotionally available, loving, and supportive of their mastery efforts will construct a working model of the self as lovable and competent. In contrast, children who experience attachment figures as rejecting or emotionally unavailable and nonsupportive will construct a working model of the self as unlovable, incompetent, and generally unworthy.

In the extreme, children subjected to severe and chronic abuse create images of the self that are despicable (Briere, 1992; Fischer & Ayoub, 1994; Herman, 1992; McCann &

Pearlman, 1992; Terr, 1990; van der Kolk, 1987; Westen, 1993; Wolfe, 1989). More than constructing negative self-perceptions, they view the self as fundamentally flawed. Often, excessively high and unrealistic parental standards that are unattainable contribute to these negative views of self. Thus, the Me-self, both at the level of domain-specific self-perceptions and one's sense of global self-esteem, may be irrevocably damaged.

A central tenet of neo-Piagetian models is that movement to a new stage of development can be fostered by socializing agents or, alternatively, can be delayed if such environmental support is not forthcoming. One can imagine scenarios in which there would be little environmental support for the integration of positive and negative attributes or positive and negative emotions. For example, in situations where children are chronically and severely abused, family members typically reinforce negative evaluations of the child that are then incorporated into the self-portrait (Briere, 1992; Fischer & Ayoub, 1994; Harter, 1998; Herman, 1992; Terr, 1990; Westen, 1993). As a result, there may be little scaffolding for the kind of self-structure that would allow the child to develop as well as integrate both positive and negative self-evaluations. Moreover, negative self-evaluations that become automatized (Siegler, 1991) will be even more resistant to change.

Thus, to the extent that there is little or no support for the normative integration of positive and negative attributes, children will not advance cognitively. If the majority of feedback from socializing agents is negative, then children in this age range (8 to 12) may remain at the previous level of all-or-none thinking, viewing their behavior as overwhelmingly negative.

A considerable body of research (see review in Harter, 1999) reveals that there is a very robust relationship between negative self-perceptions, including low self-esteem, and depression. Depressive symptoms include lack of energy, profound sadness in the form of depressed affect, and hopelessness. Depression, in turn, is highly predictive of suicidal ideation and suicidal behavior. Thus, caregiving practices resulting in very negative perceptions of the self put children at risk for serious forms of depressive pathology.

Moreover, not only do the evaluations of significant others result in representations of self, but they provoke powerful self-affects in the form of pride and shame (see Harter, 1999). Thus, children who receive praise and support for their efforts will develop a sense of pride in their accomplishments. However, children who are chronically criticized for their performance will develop a sense of shame that can be psychologically crippling. At this level of development, the child has internalized shame as a self-affect, carrying the burden of being ashamed of the self.

For children who have experienced severe and chronic abuse, these processes are exacerbated and extend to guilt and shame. Closely linked to abuse victims' perceptions of low self-esteem, self-blame, and a sense of inner badness are emotional reactions of guilt and shame (see Briere, 1992; Herman, 1992; Kendall-Tackett, Williams, & Finkelhor, 1993; McCann & Pearlman, 1992; Terr, 1990; Westen, 1993; Wolfe, 1989). Normatively, such self-affects are intimately related to evaluative self-perceptions, both of which result from the internalization of the opinions of significant others (Cooley, 1902; Harter, 1998). Thus, the blame, stigmatization, condemnation, and ostracism that parents, family, and society express toward the abuse victim not only are incorporated into attributions of self-blame but also result in powerful negative affects directed toward the self. The sexual abuse victim is made to feel humiliated for his or her role in shameful acts. Guilt and shame are also fueled by the perception that one's badness led to the abuse, rather than the abuse being the cause of one's negative self-views.

In addition to the incorporation of the opinions of significant others, children come to internalize the standards and values of those who are important to them, including the values of the larger society. Perceptions of one's physical attractiveness, in relation to the importance that is attached to meeting cultural standards of appearance, contribute heavily to one's overall sense of worth as a person (see Harter, 1993, 1999). Those who feel they have attained the requisite physical attributes will experience relatively high levels of self-esteem. Conversely, those who feel that they fall short of the punishing standards of appearance that represent the cultural ideal will suffer from low self-esteem and depression. A related liability can be observed in the eating-disordered behavior of females in particular, many of whom display symptoms (e.g., associated with anorexia) that are life-threatening (Harter, 1999). Our own recent findings (Kiang & Harter, 2004) provide support for a model in which endorsement of the societal standards of appearance leads to low self-esteem, which in turn predicts both depression and eating-disordered behavior. Finally, genetic factors that may lead to physical characteristics that do not meet cultural standards of attractiveness will also contribute to this pattern and may be particularly resistant to change.

DEVELOPMENTAL DIFFERENCES IN SELF-REPRESENTATIONS DURING ADOLESCENCE

The period of adolescence represents a dramatic developmental transition, given pubertal and related physical changes, cognitive-developmental advances, and changing social expectations. With regard to cognitive-developmental acquisitions, adolescents develop the ability to think abstractly (Case, 1985; Fischer, 1980; Flavell, 1985; Harter, 1983; Higgins, 1991). From a Piagetian (Piaget, 1960) perspective, the capacity to form abstractions emerges with the stage of formal operations in early adolescence. These newfound acquisitions, according to Piaget, should equip the adolescent with the hypothetico-deductive skills to create a formal theory. This observation is critical to the topic of self-development, given the claims of many (e.g., Epstein, 1973, 1981, 1991; Greenwald, 1980; Kelly, 1955; Markus, 1980; Sarbin, 1962) that the self is a personal epistemology, a cognitive construction; that is, a theory that should possess the characteristics of any formal theory. Therefore, a self-theory should meet those criteria by which any good theory is evaluated, criteria that include the degree to which it is parsimonious, empirically valid, internally consistent, coherently organized, testable, and useful. From a Piagetian perspective, entry into the period of formal operations should make the construction of such a theory possible, be it a theory about elements in the world or a theory about the self.

However, as will become apparent, self-representations during early and middle adolescence fall far short of these criteria. The self-structure of these periods is not coherently organized, nor are the postulates of the self-portrait internally consistent. Moreover, many self-attributes fail to be subjected to tests of empirical validity; as a result, they can be extremely unrealistic. Nor are self-representations particularly parsimonious. Thus, the Piagetian framework fails to provide an adequate explanation for the dramatic developmental changes in the self-structure that can be observed across the substages of adolescence. Rather, as in our analysis of how self-representations change during childhood, a neo-Piagetian approach is needed to understand how changes in cognitive-developmental I-self processes result in very different Me-self organization and content at each of three age levels: early adolescence, middle adolescence, and late adolescence.

Early Adolescence

As in our examination of self-development during childhood, for each age level we first describe the normative de-

TABLE 11.2 Normative Developmental Changes in Self-Representations during Adolescence

Age Period	Salient Content	Structure/ Organization	Valence/ Accuracy	Nature of Comparisons	Sensitivity to Others
Early adolescence	Social skills, attributes that influence interactions with others or one's social appeal; differentiation of attributes according to roles	Intercoordination of trait labels into single abstractions; abstractions compartmentalized; all-or-none thinking; opposites; don't detect, integrate opposing abstractions	Positive attributes at one point in time; negative attributes at another lead to inaccurate overgeneralizations	Social comparison continues although less overt	Compartmentalized attention to internalization of different standards and opinions of those in different relational contexts
Middle adolescence	Further differentiation of attributes associated with different roles and relational contexts	Initial links between single abstractions, often opposing attributes; cognitive conflict caused by seemingly contradictory characteristics; concern over which reflect one's true self	Simultaneous recognition of positive and negative attributes; instability, leading to confusion and inaccuracies	Comparisons with significant others in different relational contexts; personal fable	Awareness that the differing standards and opinions of others represent conflicting self-guides, leading to confusion over self-evaluation and vacillation with regard to behavior; imaginary audience
Late adolescence	Normalization of different role-related attributes; attributes reflecting personal beliefs, values, and moral standards; interest in future selves	Higher-order abstractions that meaningfully integrate single abstractions and resolve inconsistencies, conflict	More balanced, stable view of positive and negative attributes; greater accuracy; acceptance of limitations	Social comparison diminishes as comparisons with one's own ideals increase	Selection among alternative self-guides; construction of one's own self-standards that govern personal choices; creation of one's own ideals toward which the self aspires

velopmental changes in self-representations and self-evaluations (see Table 11.2). Second, the normative liabilities of each age period are be explored. Third, the implications for pathological self-development at each age are discussed. We begin with early adolescence and a prototypical cameo.

Verbal Cameo of Normative Self-Representations and Self-Evaluations

I'm an extrovert with my friends: I'm talkative, pretty rowdy, and funny. I'm fairly good-looking, if I do say so. All in all, around people I know pretty well I'm awesome, at least I think my friends think I am. I'm usually cheerful when I'm with my friends, happy and excited to be doing things with them. I like myself a lot when I'm around my friends. With my parents, I'm more likely to be depressed. I feel sad as well as mad and also hopeless about ever pleasing them. They think I spend too much time at the mall with my friends, and that I don't do enough to help out at home. They tell me I'm lazy and not very responsible, and it's hard not to believe them. I get real sarcastic when they get on my case. It makes me dislike myself as a person. At school, I'm pretty intelligent. I know that because I'm smart when it comes to how I do in classes, I'm curious about learning new things, and I'm also creative when it comes to solving problems. My teacher says so. I get better grades than most, but I don't brag about it because that's not cool. I can be a real introvert around people I don't know well. I'm shy, uncomfortable, and nervous. Some-

times I act really dumb and say things that are just plain stupid. Then I worry about what they must think of me, probably that I'm a total dork. I just hate myself when that happens.

With regard to the content of the self-portraits of young adolescents, interpersonal attributes and social skills that influence interactions with others or one's social appeal are typically quite salient, as findings by Damon and Hart (1988) reveal. Thus, our prototypical young adolescent admits to being talkative, rowdy, funny, good-looking, and downright awesome. Presumably, these characteristics enhance one's acceptance by peers. In addition to social attributes, self-representations also focus on competencies such as one's scholastic abilities (e.g., "I'm intelligent") and affects (e.g., "I'm cheerful" and "I'm depressed").

From a developmental perspective, there is considerable evidence that during adolescence the self becomes increasingly differentiated (see Harter, 1998). There is a proliferation of selves that vary as a function of social context. These include self with father, mother, close friends, romantic partners, and peers, as well as the self in the role of student, on the job, and as an athlete (Gecas, 1972; N. Griffin, Chassin, & Young, 1981; Hart, 1988; Harter, Bresnick, Bouchey, & Whitesell, 1997; Harter & Monsour, 1992; Smoller & Youniss, 1985). For example, as the cameo reveals, the adolescent may be cheerful and rowdy with friends, depressed and sarcastic with parents, intelligent, curious, and creative as a student, and shy and uncomfortable around people he or she does not know. A critical developmental task, therefore, is the construction of multiple selves that will undoubtedly vary across different roles and relationships, as James (1892) observed over 100 years ago.

In keeping with the major themes of this chapter, both cognitive and social processes contribute to this proliferation of selves. Cognitive-developmental advances described earlier promote greater differentiation (see Fischer, 1980; Fischer & Canfield, 1986; Harter, 1990b; Harter & Monsour, 1992; Keating, 1990). Moreover, these advances conspire with socialization pressures to develop different selves in different relational contexts (see Erikson, 1968; Grotevant & Cooper, 1986; Hill & Holmbeck, 1986; Rosenberg, 1986). For example, bids for autonomy from parents make it important to define oneself differently with peers in contrast to parents (see also Steinberg & Silverberg, 1986; White, Speisman, & Costos, 1983). Rosenberg points to another component of the differentiation process in observing that as one moves through adolescence, one is more likely to be treated differently by those in different relational contexts. In studies from our own laboratory (see Harter et al., 1997; Harter & Monsour, 1992), we have found that the percentage of overlap in self-attributes generated for different social contexts ranges from 25% to 30% among seventh and eighth graders and decreases during adolescence, to a low of approximately 10% among older teenagers.

Many (although not all) of the self-descriptions to emerge in early adolescence represent abstractions about the self, based on the newfound cognitive ability to integrate trait labels into higher-order self-concepts (see Case, 1985; Fischer, 1980; Flavell, 1985; Harter, 1983; Higgins, 1991). For example, as the prototypical cameo reveals, one can construct an abstraction of the self as "intelligent" by combining such traits as smart, curious, and creative. Alternatively, one may create an abstraction that the self is a "dork" given situations where one feels dumb and "just plain stupid." Similarly, an adolescent could construct abstractions that he or she is an "extrovert" (integrating the traits of rowdy, talkative, and funny) as well as that he or she is also an "introvert" in certain situations (when one is shy, uncomfortable, and nervous). With regard to emotion concepts, one can be depressed in some contexts (combining sad, mad, and hopeless) and cheerful in others (combining happy and excited). Thus, abstractions represent more cognitively complex concepts about the self in which various trait labels can now be appropriately integrated into even higher-order generalizations.

Although the ability to construct such abstractions reflects a cognitive advance, these representations are highly compartmentalized; that is, they are quite distinct from one another (Case, 1985; Fischer, 1980; Higgins, 1991). For Fischer, these "single abstractions" are overdifferentiated, and therefore the young adolescent can think about each of them only as isolated self-attributes. According to Fischer, structures that were observed in childhood reappear at the abstract level. Thus, just as single representations were compartmentalized during early childhood, Fischer argues that when the adolescent first moves to the level of abstract thought, he or she lacks the ability to integrate the many single abstractions that are constructed to define the self in different relational contexts. As a result, adolescents will engage in all-or-none thinking at an abstract level. For Fischer, movement to a qualitatively new level of thought brings with it lack of "cognitive control"; as a result, adolescents at the level of single abstractions can think only about isolated self-attributes. Thus, contrary to earlier models of mind (Piaget, 1960), in which formal operations usher in newfound cognitive-developmental abilities that should allow one to create an integrated theory of self, fragmentation of self-representations during early adolescence is more the rule than the exception (Fischer & Ayoub, 1994; Harter & Monsour, 1992).

Another manifestation of the compartmentalization of these abstract attributes can be observed in the tendency of the young adolescent to be unconcerned about the fact that across different roles, certain postulates appear inconsistent, as the prototypical self-description implies. (In contrast, at middle adolescence, there is considerable concern.) During early adolescence, the inability to integrate seemingly contradictory characteristics of the self (intelligent versus airhead, extrovert versus introvert, depressed versus cheerful) has the psychological advantage of sparing the adolescent conflict over opposing attributes in his or her self-theory (Harter & Monsour, 1992). Moreover, as Higgins (1991) observes, the increased differentiation functions as a cognitive buffer, reducing the possibility that negative attributes in one sphere may spread or generalize to other spheres (see also Linville, 1987; Simmons & Blyth, 1987). Thus, although the construction of multiple selves sets the stage for attributes to be contradictory, most young adolescents do not identify potential contradictions or experience conflict, given the compartmentalized structure of their abstract self-representations.

Evidence for these claims comes from our own research (see Harter et al., 1997; Harter & Monsour, 1992), in which we asked adolescents at three developmental levels—early adolescence (seventh grade grade), middle adolescence (ninth grade), and late adolescence (11th grade)—to generate self-attributes across several roles and then indicate whether any of these attributes represented opposites (e.g., cheerful versus depressed, rowdy versus calm, studious versus lazy, at ease versus self-conscious). After identifying any such opposites, they were asked whether any such pairs caused them conflict; that is, were they perceived as clashing in their personality? Across studies, the specific roles have varied. They have included self with a group of friends, with a close friend, with parents (mother versus father), in romantic relationships, in the classroom, and on the job. Across a number of converging indices (e.g., number of opposites, number of conflicts, percentage of opposites in conflict), the findings revealed that attributes identified as contradictory and experienced as conflicting were infrequent among young adolescents.

An examination of the protocols of young adolescents reveals that there are potential opposites that go undetected. Examples not identified as opposites by young adolescents (but that appeared contradictory to our research team) included being talkative as well as shy in romantic relationships, being uptight with family but carefree with friends, being both caring and insensitive with friends, being a good student as well as troublemaker in school, being self-conscious in romantic relationships but easygoing with friends, being lazy as a student but hardworking on the job. These observations bolster the interpretation, from Fischer's (1980) theory, that young adolescents do not yet have the cognitive ability to simultaneously compare these attributes to one another, and therefore they tend not to detect, or be concerned about, self-representations that are potential opposites. As one young adolescent put it, when confronted with the fact that he had indicated that he was both caring and rude, "Well, you are caring with your friends and rude to people who don't treat you nicely. There's no problem. I guess I just think about one thing about myself at a time and don't think about the other until the next day." When another young adolescent was asked why opposite attributes did not bother her, she succinctly exclaimed, "That's a stupid question. I don't fight with myself!" As will become apparent, this pattern changes dramatically during middle adolescence.

The differentiation of role-related selves beginning in early adolescence can also be observed in the tendency to report differing levels of self-esteem across relational contexts. In the prototypical description, the young adolescent reports that with friends, "I like myself a lot"; however, with parents, I "dislike myself as a person." Around "people I don't know well, I just hate myself."

In addition, although the concept of self-esteem has heretofore been reserved for perceptions of global self-esteem, we have introduced the construct of relational self-esteem (Harter, Waters, & Whitesell, 1998). Beginning in the middle school years, adolescents discriminate their level of perceived self-esteem, how much they like themselves as a person, across relational contexts. We have examined these perceptions across a number of such contexts, including self-esteem with parents, with teachers, with male classmates, and with female classmates. Factor analyses reveal clear patterns with high loadings on the designated factors (i.e., each relational context) and negligible cross-loadings. We have also examined the discrepancy between individuals' highest and lowest relational self-esteem scores. While a minority of adolescents (approximately one-fourth) were found to report little variation in self-esteem across contexts, the vast majority (the remaining three-fourths) report that their self-esteem did vary significantly as a function of the relational context. In the extreme, one female participant reported the lowest possible self-esteem score with parents and the highest possible self-esteem score with female classmates.

In addition to documenting such variability, our goal has been to identify potential causes of these individual differences. In addressing one determinant, we adopted Cooley's (1902) looking-glass self perspective, in which the opinions of significant others are incorporated into one's sense of personal worth. Building on our previous empirical efforts (see Harter, 1990b), we hypothesized that context-specific support, in the form of validation for who one is as a person, should be highly related to self-esteem in the corresponding context. The findings corroborated the more specific prediction that support within a given relationship was more highly associated with relational self-esteem in that relationship, compared to self-esteem in the other three contexts (Harter et al., 1998). Thus, the pattern of results suggests a refinement of the looking-glass self formulation, in that support in the form of validation from particular significant others will have its strongest impact on how one evaluates one's sense of worth in the context of those particular others.

These findings highlight the fact that with the proliferation of multiple selves across roles, adolescents become very sensitive to the potentially different opinions and standards of the significant others in each context. As the cameo description reveals, the adolescent reports high self-esteem around friends who think he or she is "awesome," lower self-esteem around parents who think he or she is "lazy" and "irresponsible," and the lowest level of self-esteem around strangers, who "probably [think] that I'm a total dork." As Rosenberg (1986) observes, adolescents demonstrate a heightened concern with the reflected appraisals of others. He notes that other people's differing views of the self (e.g., the respect of the peer group counterposed to the critical stance of parents) will inevitably lead to variability in the self-concept across contexts.

In addition to their sensitivity to feedback from others, young adolescents continue to make use of social comparison information. However, with increasing age, children shift from more conspicuous to more subtle forms of social comparison as they become more aware of the negative social consequences of overt comparisons; for example, they may be accused of boasting about their superior performance (Pomeranz, Ruble, Frey, & Greulich, 1995). As the prototypical young adolescent describes in the cameo, "I get better grades than most, but I don't brag about it because that's not cool."

Normative Liabilities for Self-Development during Early Adolescence

As with the entry into any new developmental level, there are liabilities associated with these emerging self-processes. For example, although abstractions are developmentally advanced cognitive structures, they are removed from concrete, observable behaviors and therefore are more susceptible to distortion. The adolescent's self-concept, therefore, becomes more difficult to verify and is often less realistic. As Rosenberg (1986, p. 129) observes, when the self comes to be viewed as a collection of abstractions, uncertainties are introduced, as there are "few objective and unambiguous facts about one's sensitivity, creativity, morality, dependability, and so on." Moreover, the necessary skills to apply hypothetico-deductive thinking to the postulates of one's self-system are not yet in place. Although the young adolescent may have multiple hypotheses about the self, he or she does not yet possess the ability to correctly deduce which are true, leading to distortions in self-perceptions.

The all-or-none thinking of this period, in the form of overgeneralizations that the young adolescent cannot cognitively control, also contributes to unrealistic self-representations; at one point in time, one may feel totally intelligent or awesome, whereas at another point in time, one may feel like a dork. Thus, the adolescent sense of self will vacillate, given the inability to cognitively control one's self-representations. In describing this "barometric self" during adolescence, Rosenberg (1986) points to a different set of causes. He cites considerable literature reveal-

ing that adolescents experience an increased concern with what their peers think of them, findings that are relevant to Cooley's (1902) looking-glass self model. This heavy dependence on the perceptions of other's opinions tends to set the stage for volatility in one's assessment of the self. However, there is inevitable ambiguity about others' attitudes toward the self, as one can never have direct access to the mind of another. Thus, attributions about others' thought processes may change from one time period to another. The second reason for fluctuating self-evaluations inheres in the fact that different significant others have different opinions of the self, depending on the situation or moment in time. Third, adolescents' concern with what others think of them leads to efforts at impression management, provoking variations in the self across relational contexts. Finally, at times, adolescents are treated as more adult-like (e.g., on a job), whereas at other times, they are treated as more child-like (e.g., with parents at home). Thus, the self fluctuates in tandem.

Our own findings on the emergence of how self-esteem varies as a function of one's relationships (what we have termed "relational self-esteem") is consistent with Rosenberg's (1986) analysis (Harter, 1999). The young adolescent is not yet troubled by what could be viewed as inconsistent self-representations because he or she cannot simultaneously evaluate them as contradictory. However, there are liabilities associated with this inability. The compartmentalization of abstractions about the self precludes the construction of an integrated portrait of self. The fact that different significant others may hold differing opinions about the self makes it difficult to develop the sense that the self is coherent. With movement into middle adolescence, abstract self-descriptors become far less isolated or compartmentalized. However, as will be demonstrated, the emerging structures that follow bring with them new liabilities.

Finally, there are domain-specific normative liabilities that are associated with educational transitions. Young adolescents all shift from an elementary school to either a middle school or a junior high school that typically draws from several elementary feeder schools. Thus, they must now move into a group of peers, many of whom they have previously not known (typically two-thirds to three-fourths of the peer group will be new). Given the young adolescent's heightened concern with how others view the self, an important source of global self-esteem, there may be understandable shifts in global self-esteem if individuals perceive that their social acceptance is higher or lower than when they were in elementary school.

J. P. Eccles and colleagues (1989) have also pointed to different emphases within the educational system during the transition to middle school or junior high school that have implications for perceptions of one's scholastic competence. They note that there is considerably more emphasis on social comparison (public posting of grades, ability grouping; teachers, in their feedback to classes, verbally acknowledging the personal results of competitive activities). These educational practices represent a mismatch given the adolescent's needs. At a time when young adolescents are painfully self-conscious, the school system heightens the salience of social comparison in conjunction with publicizing each student's performance. In addition to the greater emphasis on social comparison, the standards for performance shift from *effort* to *ability,* according to J. P. Eccles and colleagues. They note that in elementary school, there is more emphasis on effort, that is, "Try harder and you can do better." In middle and junior high schools, however, poorer performance is attributed to lack of scholastic ability, leading the young adolescent to feel that he or she does not have the aptitude to succeed, that he or she lacks intelligence. For those not performing well, these practices can lead to declines in self-perceptions of academic ability, shifts that will be exacerbated in contexts of high public feedback and greater social comparison.

Pathological Self-Processes and Outcomes during Early Adolescence

Beginning in early adolescence, there is a heightened concern with how others view the self, a normative process that has implications for salience of those determinants of self-esteem that have been articulated in Cooley's (1902) looking-glass self formulation. If significant others provide support for who one is as a person, for those attributes that one feels truly define the self, then one will experience the self as authentic. However, the construction of a self that is too highly dependent on the internalization of the opinions of others can, under some circumstances, lead to the creation of a false self that does not mirror one's authentic experience. In our own research (Harter, 1999), we have found that it is not until early adolescence that the concept of acting as a false self becomes very salient in the consciousness of young teenagers. The detection of hypocrisy, not only in others but in oneself, emerges as a critical filter in evaluating others as well as oneself.

Our own findings (Harter, Marold, Whitesell, & Cobbs, 1996) reveal that unhealthy levels of false-self behavior are particularly likely to emerge if caregivers make their approval contingent on the young adolescent's living up to unrealistic standards of behavior based on unattainable standards dictated by parents. We have labeled this phenomenon "conditional support," although from interviews we have learned that this is a misnomer, in that adolescents do not perceive parental responses in the face of such demands as "supportive." Rather, conditionality reflects the psychological hoops through which young adolescents must jump in order to please the parents, given the parental agenda. Adolescents who experience such a conditional atmosphere are faced with the option of adopting a socially implanted self. That is, they must learn to suppress what they feel are true self-attributes in an attempt to garner the needed approval from parental caretakers. Here, the terminology purposely switches from "caregiver" to "caretaker" in a metaphorical effort to convey the fact that such socialization practices "take away" from the care of who one is as a person, from true-self development. Our findings reveal that those experiencing high levels of conditionality from parents will express hopelessness about their ability to please the parents that then translates into high levels of false-self behavior in an attempt to garner some level of needed parental support. Of particular relevance is that high levels of false-self behavior are directly related to low levels of self-esteem. As our overall model has revealed (Harter, 1999), low levels of self-esteem are highly correlated with self-reported depressive symptomatology that can, for some adolescents, lead to suicidal thoughts and actions.

Chronic and severe abuse puts one at even more extreme risk for suppressing one's true self and displaying various forms of inauthentic or false-self behavior. Such a process has its origins in childhood, in the very forms of parenting that constitute psychological abuse. As described earlier, parenting practices that lack attunement to the child's needs, fail in empathy, don't provide validation, threaten harm, coerce, and enforce compliance all cause the true self to go underground (Bleiberg, 1984; Stern, 1985; Winnicott, 1958, 1965) and lead to what Sullivan (1953) labeled "not me" experiences.

Moreover, as described in the sections on childhood, the ability to express oneself verbally allows one to falsify what is shared with others. In the maltreated child, secrecy pacts around sexually abusive interactions further provoke the child defensively to exclude such episodic memories from awareness (see also Bretherton, 1993). Thus, sexual and physical abuse cause the child to split off experiences, either consciously or unconsciously, relegating them to a private or inaccessible part of the self. The very disavowal,

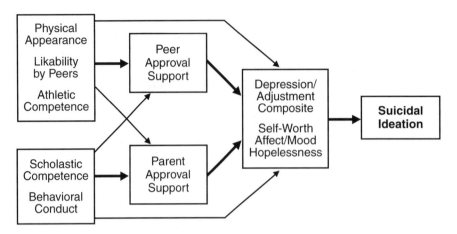

Figure 11.1   Our model of predictors and correlations of the depression/adjustment composite.

repression, or dissociation of one's experiences, coupled with psychogenic amnesia and numbing as defensive reactions to abuse, set the stage for loss of one's true self.

Herman (1992) introduces other dynamics that represent barriers to authenticity among victims of abuse. She notes that the malignant sense of inner badness is often camouflaged by the abused child's persistent attempts to be good. In adopting different roles designed to please the parent, to be the perfect child, one comes to experience one's behavior as false or inauthentic (see also A. Miller, 1990). Thus, one develops a socially acceptable false self that conforms to the demands and desires of others in an attempt to obtain their approval (see Harter et al., 1996). If one's true self, corroded with inner badness, were to be revealed, it would be met with scorn and contempt. Therefore, it must be concealed at all costs. Although these dynamics begin in childhood, during adolescence there is much more conscious awareness of these dynamics and a realization that one is being false or phony. Based on our own findings (Harter, 1999), young adolescents acknowledge that lack of parental validation and support, coupled with conditionality in which approval is contingent on meeting very high and often unrealistic standards, lead to a constellation of negative outcomes. These include high levels of false-self behavior, lack of knowledge about one's true self, depression, low self-esteem, and hopelessness. These dynamics would appear to be even more exaggerated among victims of abuse, compromising their sense of authenticity.

Our overall model of the determinants, correlates, and consequences of self-esteem (see Figure 11.1) becomes increasingly relevant at early adolescence and beyond, where there is strong empirical support across numerous studies (see review in Harter, 1999). Findings reveal that lack of both parental support and peer support can lead to patho-

logical levels of low self-worth, depressed affect, and hopelessness, which in turn may provoke suicidal ideation if not suicidal behaviors.

Our own findings (see Harter, 1999) reveal that whereas peer support increases in the predictability of global self-esteem between late childhood and early adolescence, the impact of parental support does *not* decline. Previous textbook portrayals of adolescence imply that parental influence declines as one moves into adolescence. However, nothing is further from the truth when one examines the impact of parental support, including conditionality, on self-processes, such as false-self behavior, global self-esteem, and the related correlates of depressed affect, hopelessness, and suicidal ideation.

That said, the peer culture does come to loom large in adolescence. Peer support and approval, or its absence, is a powerful predictor of what we have labeled the depression/adjustment composite that includes self-esteem, self-worth, and affect/mood along a continuum of depressed to cheerful, hopeless to hopeful, that has empirically been demonstrated to predict suicidal thinking. Lack of peer approval appears to be more directly linked to perceived inadequacies in the domains of physical appearance, likability by peers, and athletic competence.

Peer Rejection, Humiliation, and Implications for the High-Profile School Shootings.   Recently, we have become more focused on the role of peer *rejection,* not merely the lack of peer approval. Our initial interest in this construct came from an analysis of the emerging profiles of the 11 high-profile cases in which White, middle-class older male children and adolescents, from small cities or suburbs, have gone on shooting sprees killing peers and, in a few cases, school officials who were random targets rather than specifically identified individuals. In the analysis of media reports, it became evident that all of these male youth killers had a history of peer rejection and *humiliation.* As a psychologist who for many years has contributed to (and kept up with) the literature on emotional development in children and adolescents, I was astounded to learn that we have no empirical literature on humiliation. There is ample literature on shame, guilt, and embarrassment, but nothing specifically about humiliation. Yet, we can all appreciate the fact, be it from our own experience or the experience of our children, that humiliation is a daily event in most schools and in the lives of many children. Of course, for the school shooters, extreme feelings of chronic humiliation by peers due to excessive teasing, taunting, and physical insults eventually led them to psychologically "snap," leading to random deaths and, in the case of the Columbine teens, to suicide.

An examination of the media accounts of the school shooters made it obvious that many of the determinants in our model could be found in the lives of these adolescents (see Harter, Low, & Whitesell, 2003). As a result, we examined a revised model in which we added angry aggression and violent ideation to the model. We examined this model in a normative sample of middle school students. Using path-analytic techniques, we demonstrated that the data fit the model exceedingly well. That is, the antecedents in the model, perceived inadequacies in the domains of competence and inadequacy, predicted humiliating rejection from peers and parents alike. These determinants, in turn, predicted low self-esteem, depressed affect, angry affect, and hopelessness, all of which predicted *both* suicidal ideation and violent ideation. Consistent with the clinical literature on the comorbidity of internalizing and externalizing symptoms, we found a correlation of $r = .55$ between suicidal ideation and violent ideation toward others. Thus, the determinants in our model, if negative, put adolescents at pathological risk for endangering their own, as well as others', lives.

We have also pursued more directly the emotion of humiliation and its role in contributing to violent ideation. In the Harter, Low, et al. study (2003), we wrote vignettes that simulated some of the types of humiliating events that were experienced by the school shooters. We then asked middle school students what other emotions (e.g., anger, depression) and behaviors they might experience along a continuum from do nothing to acting violently toward the perpetrators as well as toward anyone (given the randomness of the actual school shooting events). The vignettes were designed to be humiliating, and the majority of students reported that they would be humiliated. We also iden-

tified a group of violent ideators (in the minority) and compared them to those who did not report that they would think about violent revenge. We then sought to determine what distinguished the two groups, and found that those entertaining violent thoughts expressed higher levels of anger and depression. In addition, the violent ideators reported higher levels of negative determinants in the model, for example, more peer rejection, less parental support, lower self-concept scores (in terms of appearance, peer likability), lower self-worth, and greater hopelessness. Thus, certain factors in histories of violent ideators propel them to thoughts of seriously harming others as well as themselves, pathological outcomes that may require clinical interventions given that they may be putting themselves and others at serious risk.

In a subsequent study, we sought to more specifically investigate the factors that lead humiliation to result in violent ideation and suicidal ideation, given the paucity of work on the emotion of humiliation. Our findings revealed that the role of an *audience who mocks the victim* is a particularly critical determinant. Prototypical reactions include revenge, wanting to hide, and attempts to minimize the humiliation (Harter, Kiang, Whitesell, & Anderson, 2003). We are currently pursuing this prototypical approach to humiliation.

Is There a Dark Side to High Self-Esteem? Our own modeling efforts, as reported, reveal that it is *low* self-esteem that is consistently related to suicidal and violent thinking. These findings are consistent with the broader literature (see Harter, 1999) revealing that high self-esteem is a psychological commodity associated with positive adjustment and mental health outcomes. Low self-esteem, in contrast, has been viewed as a liability and has been associated with poor adjustment (e.g., depression, anxiety, conduct problems, teen pregnancy). However, currently there is controversy over whether there may also be a dark side to high self-esteem.

So what is the controversy? One group of theorists (Baumeister, Smart, & Boden, 1996) have argued that there is a subset of individuals with high but fragile self-esteem who are often aggressive in response to perceived ego threats. Baumeister et al. contend that individuals who report high self-esteem in combination with high narcissism, low empathy, and sensitivity to rejection will, in the face of threats to the ego, exhibit violent tendencies.

We (Harter & McCarley, 2004) believe that Baumeister et al.'s (1996) composite of predictors has some merit, with the exception of the role of self-esteem. Specifically, we predicted that high narcissism, low empathy, and sensitivity to rejection coupled with *low* self-esteem (not high self-esteem) would lead young adolescents, in the face of threats to the ego, to violent ideation. To assess violent ideation, participants read humiliating scenarios that represented threats to the ego and were then asked to rate how they would typically respond in such a situation, ranging from doing nothing to seriously harming the perpetrator. Self-esteem was measured by our Global Self-Worth Scale (Harter, 1985). Narcissism, empathy, and sensitivity to rejection were assessed by adaptations of previously developed measures, all of which were found to be reliable (alphas ranging from .76 to .87). Regression analyses revealed that high narcissism and low empathy significantly predicted violent ideation. However, in contrast to Baumeister et al.'s claims, higher self-esteem was associated with lower levels of violent ideation. Further, when self-reported conduct (positive to negative) and the frequency of experiencing humiliating events were included in the model, they both explained a substantial proportion of the variance in violent ideation. In addition to regression analyses, identification of two extreme groups, those high and low on violent ideation, differed significantly with violent ideators reporting higher narcissism, lower empathy, and greater sensitivity to rejection, as Baumeister et al. would predict, but reported *lower* self-esteem that is not consistent with their formulation. In a subsequent study, we added fluctuating self-esteem, conduct, and the frequency of humiliating rejection. These increased the predictability of violence ideation, both in regression analyses and in comparisons of violent and nonviolent ideators. Violent ideators reported more fluctuations in self-esteem, greater conduct problems, and a greater frequency of having established humiliating events that were ego-threatening. Thus, our understanding of the precursors of violent thoughts is enhanced given that lack of empathy and narcissism are clear predictors, although high self-esteem is not. In fact, self-esteem and narcissism correlated −.01, revealing that these are different constructs both conceptually, given how scales define the two constructs, and empirically. Narcissism entails a sense of entitlement, superiority, and exhibitionism, whereas high self-esteem is defined as liking and respecting who one is as a person. Clearly, there is a need to distinguish between these two concepts conceptually, methodologically, and empirically.

Finally, in this study (Harter & McCarley, 2004) we uncovered an interesting finding that is cause for concern. In the high-profile cases of the school shooters, the vast majority had not been in any major trouble with the law and had *not* come to the attention of teachers or school personnel as potential troublemakers. In fact, teachers, school officials, and students were astounded that these boys committed such violent acts. Debriefing efforts of the surviving students and families at Columbine, conducted by University of Denver clinicians and some in private practice, revealed that students and their families were realistically fearful that they would not be able to detect who, in the future, might commit such acts because there were few warning signs that the shooters were capable of such behavior. These concerns are real, given findings from Harter and McCarley (2004). In this study, we asked teachers to rate student conduct (getting in trouble, potential for violent thinking). Among the subgroup of violent ideators who had rated their own conduct as quite negative, teachers misrated one-third of the group, giving them very positive scores on conduct. This is concerning with regard to the difficulty in assessing certain students as being at risk. Although such violent ideators may not be at risk for violent *action* (given the low percentage of such acts in most schools), violent ideation represents a different kind of pathological risk factor to the extent that it interferes with attention to and concentration on scholastic endeavors, with socially appropriate behaviors that would promote positive peer interactions and so on. The very presence of this subgroup of violent ideators suggests that they represent a type of student with intrapsychic dynamics that are different from those students with histories of conduct problems, delinquency, and acting-out patterns, all of whom readily come to the attention of teachers, school officials, and students. Those not showing these patterns are of concern in terms of their identification. One of our goals is to devise a short form of our instruments that will allow schools to identify those who may have escaped the attention of school personnel but are nevertheless at pathological risk. Many of these processes begin in early adolescence (and even late childhood) but continue into middle and later adolescence, as the range of ages of the actual school shooters reveals, continuing the presence of risk factors.

Pathological Eating-Disordered Behavior. Our model identifies one self-concept domain that robustly affects global self-esteem across ages and cultures, namely, perceived physical appearance or attractiveness. In reviewing the inextricable link between perceived appearance and self-esteem, between the outer self and the inner self (see Harter, 1999), it became very apparent that this link is profoundly impacted by cultural standards of appearance for each gender. That cultures tout physical attractiveness as the measure of one's worth as a person has been amply demonstrated in contemporary society, as well as historically (Hatfield & Sprecher, 1986). The empirical findings (reviewed in Harter, 1999) reveal that correlations range from the 40s to the 80s. Moreover, investigators have revealed that these relationships are not merely statistical but are very much embedded in the consciousness of individuals who are aware of this link. In our own work (Kiang & Harter, 2004), we have found strong support for a model in which awareness of current cultural values (e.g., being attractive will lead to higher self-esteem, meeting standards of appearance will make people more popular, people who are overweight are discriminated against) are highly endorsed. However, there is variability in these scores. Such awareness predicts perceptions of one's own appearance, which in turn predicts level of self-esteem and eating-disordered perceptions and behaviors. Specifically, those endorsing these cultural values or links report more negative views of their appearance, lower self-esteem, more psychological correlates of eating disorders, and more eating-disordered behaviors.

This particular study was conducted with college students. However, the seeds of such a model are sown in early adolescence (if not earlier) as teenagers of both genders are well aware of the prevailing norms for desirable appearance. For adult females in the 2000s, one must be tall, very thin, weigh very little (around 110 to 115), have ample breasts, and, of course, have a pretty face and hair, an unattainable combination for more than 90% of the female population. (Recent statistics from a September, 2004 National Public Radio [NPR] report indicated that the average American woman is 5′4″ and weighs 140.) Standards have been exceedingly punishing for females for decades. What is new within the past 2 decades is the fact that the bar has been raised for males in our society. No longer is appeal to be judged by status, wealth, position, and power but by physical standards of attractiveness as well. Muscular build (strong abs and biceps), good physique, and attractive hair (on head as well as face) have all come to define the new ideals for men (see Harter, 1999).

These standards are not lost on our young adolescents. In fact, children succumb to the same discouragement as adults about not being able to emulate the models, singers, and movie stars in the limelight. The importance of meeting these standards becomes particularly salient during early adolescence, as teenagers face inevitable pubertal changes that signal their impending adulthood. Thus, they look to the adult standards as the physical markers for what defines attractiveness, appeal, and social acceptability, all of which determine one's self-esteem.

The genetic throw of the dice leads some young adolescent males and females to fare better than others in the appearance wars. For example, early-maturing girls are at a distinct disadvantage given the current emphasis on thinness and height because on average they are heavier and shorter compared to later-maturing girls. The pattern is just the opposite for adolescent males; earlier-maturing males tend to be taller and more muscular, which gives them a physical edge. Thus, beginning in earnest during early adolescent, evaluations of one's appearance take on critical implications for one's global self-esteem. Those not meeting the gold standard are at serious risk for pathological forms of depression and possibly suicide as well as eating disorders that can be life-threatening. Although this preoccupation initially becomes quite salient in early adolescence, it continues throughout the life span.

Middle Adolescence

Unlike more classic treatments of development in which adolescence is treated as one stage, more recent theory and empirical research (see Harter, 1999) reveals that with regard to self-processes there are three definable substages during the teenage years. The period of middle adolescence is markedly different, in terms of representations of the self, from the preceding stage of early adolescence as well as the stage that follows in late adolescence and early adulthood. It is a fascinating stage in that while there are cognitive advances, these also represent psychological minefields. The normative features of self-development necessarily overlaps with a discussion of the liabilities at this age level. However, these are contrasted to more pathological processes that may emerge in middle adolescence.

Verbal Cameo of Normative Self-Representations and Self-Evaluations

What am I like as a person? You're probably not going to understand. I'm complicated! With my really close friends, I am very tolerant. I mean, I'm understanding and caring. With a group of friends, I'm rowdier. I'm also usually friendly and cheerful, but I can get pretty obnoxious and intolerant if I don't like how they're acting. I'd like to be friendly and tolerant all of the time, that's the kind of person I want to be, and I'm disappointed in myself when I'm not. At school, I'm serious, even studious every now and then, but on the other hand, I'm a goof-off too, because if you're too studious, you won't be popular. So I go back and forth, which means I don't do all that well in terms of my grades. But that causes problems at home, where I'm pretty anxious when I'm around my parents. They expect me to get all As, and get pretty annoyed with me when report cards come out. I care what they think about me, and so then I get down on myself, but it's not fair! I mean, I worry about how I probably should get better grades, but I'd be mortified in the eyes of my friends if I did too well.

So, I'm usually pretty stressed-out at home, and can even get very sarcastic, especially when my parents get on my case. But I really don't understand how I can switch so fast from being cheerful with my friends, then coming home and feeling anxious, and then getting frustrated and sarcastic with my parents. Which one is the real me? I have the same question when I'm around boys. Sometimes, I feel phony. Say I think some guy might be interested in asking me out. I try to act different, like Britney Spears, I'll be a real extrovert, fun-loving and even flirtatious, and think I am really good-looking. It's important to be good-looking like the models and movie stars. That's what makes you popular. I know in my heart of hearts that I can never look like her, so why do I even try? It makes me hate myself and feel depressed. Plus, when I try to look and act like her, then everybody, I mean *everybody* else is looking at me like they think I am totally weird! They don't act like they think I'm attractive, so I end up thinking I look terrible. I just hate myself when that happens! Because it gets worse! Then I get self-conscious and embarrassed and become radically introverted, and I don't know who I really am! Am I just acting like an extrovert, am I just trying to impress them, when really I'm an introvert? But I don't really care what they think, anyway. I mean, I don't want to care, that is. I just want to know what my close friends think. I can be my true self with my close friends. I can't be my real self with my parents. They don't understand me. What do they know about what it's like to be a teenager? They treat me like I'm still a kid. At least at school, people treat you more like you're an adult. That gets confusing, though. I mean, which am I? When you're 15, are you still a kid or an adult? I have a part-time job and the people there treat me like an adult. I want them to approve of me, so I'm very responsible at work, which makes me feel good about myself there. But then I go out with my friends and I get pretty crazy and irresponsible. So, which am I, responsible or irresponsible? How can the same person be both? If my parents knew how immature I act sometimes, they would ground me forever, particularly my father. I'm real distant with him. I'm pretty close to my mother, though. But it's hard being distant with one parent and close to the other, especially if we are all together, like talking at dinner. Even though I am close to my mother, I'm still pretty secretive about some things, particularly the things about myself that confuse me. So I think a lot about who is the real me, and sometimes I try to figure it out when I write in my diary, but I can't resolve it. There are days when I wish I could just become immune to myself!

Self-descriptions are likely to increase in length during this period, as adolescents become increasingly introspective as well as morbidly preoccupied with what others think of them (Broughton, 1978; Elkind, 1967; Erikson, 1959, 1968; Harter, 1990a; Lapsley & Rice, 1988; Rosenberg, 1979). The unreflective self-acceptance of earlier periods of development vanishes, and, as Rosenberg observes, what were formerly unquestioned self-truths now become problematic self-hypotheses. The tortuous search for the self involves a concern with what or who I am (Broughton, 1978), a task made more difficult given the multiple Me's that crowd the self-landscape. There is typically a further proliferation of selves as adolescents come to make finer differentiations; in the cameo, the adolescent describes a self with really close friends (e.g., tolerant) versus with a group of friends (e.g., intolerant) and a self with mother (e.g., close) versus father (e.g., distant). The acquisition of new roles, for example, self at a job, may also require the construction of new context-specific attributes (e.g., responsible).

Moreover, additional cognitive I-self processes emerge that give the self-portrait a very new look (Case, 1985; Fischer, 1980). Whereas, in the previous stage, single abstractions were isolated from one another, during middle adolescence one acquires the ability to make comparisons between single abstractions, that is, between attributes within the same role-related self or across role-related selves. Fischer labels these new structures "abstract mappings"; the adolescent can now "map" constructs about the self onto one another, directly comparing them. Mappings thus force the individual to compare and contrast different attributes. It should be noted that abstract mappings have features in common with the "representational" mappings of childhood, in that the cognitive links that are initially forged often take the form of opposites. During adolescence, these opposites can take the form of seemingly contradictory abstractions about the self (e.g., tolerant versus intolerant, extrovert versus introvert, responsible versus irresponsible, good-looking versus unattractive, as in the cameo).

However, the abstract mapping structure has limitations as a means of relating two concepts to one another, in that the individual cannot yet truly integrate such self-representations in a manner that would resolve apparent contradictions. Therefore, at the level of abstract mappings, the awareness of these opposites causes considerable intrapsychic conflict, confusion, and distress (Fischer et al., 1984; Harter & Monsour, 1992; Higgins, 1991) given the inability to coordinate these seemingly contradictory self-attributes. For example, our prototypical adolescent agonizes over whether she is an extrovert or an introvert ("Am I just acting like an extrovert, am I just trying to impress them, when really I'm an introvert?"; "So which am I, responsible or irresponsible? How can the same person be both?"). Such cognitive-developmental limitations contribute to the emergence of what James (1892) identified as the "conflict of the different Me's."

In addition to such confusion, these seeming contradictions lead to very unstable self-representations, which is also cause for concern (e.g., "I don't really understand how I can switch so fast from being cheerful with my friends, then coming home and feeling anxious, and then getting frustrated and sarcastic with my parents. Which one is the real me?"). The creation of multiple selves, coupled with the emerging ability to detect potential contradictions between self-attributes displayed in different roles, naturally ushers in concern over which attributes define the true self. However, from a normative perspective, the adolescent at this level is not equipped with the cognitive skills to solve fully the dilemma (e.g., "So I think a lot about who is the real me, and sometimes try to figure it out when I write in my diary, but I can't resolve it").

As introduced in the section on early adolescence, our own research has been directed toward an examination of the extent to which adolescents at three developmental levels both identify opposing self-attributes and report that they are experienced as conflictual (Harter et al., 1997; Harter & Monsour, 1992). Across several studies, we have determined that young adolescents infrequently detect opposites within their self-portrait. However, it was predicted, according to the analysis presented earlier, that there would be a dramatic rise in the detection of opposing self-attributes as well as an acknowledgment that such apparent contradictions lead to conflict within the self-system. Our most recent procedure for examining these issues is illustrated in the protocol presented in Figure 11.2. Adolescents are first asked to generate six attributes for each role, writing them on the lines associated with each interpersonal context. These contexts have varied from study to study; however, in the sample protocol, we asked them to generate attributes for six roles: self with mother, with father, with a romantic interest, with their best friend, with a group of friends, and in their role as student in the classroom. As in our original procedure (Harter & Monsour, 1992), respondents were then asked to identify any pairs of attributes they perceived to reflect opposites, by connecting them with lines. Next, they indicated whether any of these opposites were experienced as clashing or in conflict with each other, by putting arrowheads on the lines connecting those pairs of opposites.

Across three different studies (see Harter et al., 1997), we have found that the number of opposing self-attribute pairs, as well as the number of opposites in conflict, increases between early and middle adolescence. This pattern of findings supports the hypothesis that the abstract

Figure 11.2   Prototypical self-portrait of a 15-year-old girl.

mapping structures that emerge in middle adolescence allow one to detect, but not to meaningfully integrate, these apparent contradictions. Thus, they lead to the phenomenological experience of intrapsychic conflict. We have asked teenagers to verbally elaborate on the opposites and conflicts that they reported on our task. As one 14-year-old put it, "I really think I am a happy person and I want to be that way with everyone, not just my friends; but I get depressed with my family, and it really bugs me because that's not what I want to be like." Another 15-year-old, in describing a conflict between self-attributes within the realm of romantic relationships, exclaimed, "I hate the fact that I get so nervous! I wish I wasn't so inhibited. The real me is talkative. I just want to be natural, but I can't." Another 15-year-old girl explained, "I really think of myself as friendly and open to people, but the way the other girls act, they force me to become an introvert, even though I know I'm not." In exasperation, one ninth grader observed of the self-portrait she had constructed, "It's not right, it should all fit together into one piece!" These comments suggest that at this age level, there is a need for coherence; there is a desire to bring self-attributes into harmony with one another. Yet, in midadolescence, the cognitive abilities to create such a self-portrait are not yet in place.

An examination of the protocol in Figure 11.2 illustrates the fact that adolescents can identify two types of opposing attributes, those occurring within a given role (e.g., frustrated and withdrawn in the classroom) and those occurring across relational contexts (e.g., close with mother but distant with father; rowdy with a group of friends but quiet with one's best friend). We became curious about whether there were more opposing attributes and associated conflict within particular roles (e.g., rowdy versus withdrawn with friends). Among those social psychologists who have focused on the adult self, it has been argued that consistency within a particular relationship is critical; therefore, perceived violations of this consistency ethic, where one displays opposing attributes within a role, should be particularly discomforting to the individual (Gergen, 1968; Vallacher, 1980). According to these theorists, the adoption of different behaviors in different roles should be less problematic or conflictual for adults, because they represent appropriate adaptation to different relational contexts rather than inconsistency.

From a developmental perspective, we did not expect these processes to be in place during adolescence. Adolescents are actively concerned with creating, defining, and differentiating role-related selves, and thus there is relatively little overlap in the self-attributes associated with different roles. Moreover, opposing attributes across relational contexts become more marked or salient in midadolescence, when teenagers develop the cognitive ability to detect seeming contradictions. The very salience of these opposites leads to a greater focus on contradictions across roles rather than within roles. Perceived conflict caused by opposing attributes should also be greater across roles, particularly with the onset of midadolescence, when teenagers can begin to compare characteristics across such roles but cannot integrate these salient and seemingly contradictory self-attributes. As can be seen in Figure 11.3, the number

of opposites identified at midadolescence and beyond is far greater for attributes identified across roles than within each role, confirming our expectation. The pattern was obtained for opposites in conflict.

Figure 11.3 also reveals that for across-role opposites, at every age level, females detect more contradictory attributes than do males. These findings replicate two other studies in which similar gender differences were obtained (see Harter et al., 1997). Moreover, in one study in which we asked subjects to indicate how upset they were over conflicting attributes, the pattern revealed that females become more upset over conflicting attributes across early, middle, and late adolescence, whereas males become less upset. Elsewhere, we have offered a general interpretation of this pattern, drawing on those frameworks that emphasize the greater importance of relationships for females than males (Chodorow, 1989; Eichenbaum & Orbach, 1993; Gilligan, 1982; Jordan, 1991; J. B. Miller, 1986; Rubin, 1985). These theorists posit that the socialization of girls involves far more embeddedness within the family, as well as more concern with connectedness to others. Boys, in contrast, forge a path of independence and autonomy in which the logic of moral and social decisions takes precedence over affective responses to significant others.

In extrapolating from these observations, we have suggested that in an effort to maintain the multiple relationships that girls are developing during adolescence, and to create harmony among these necessarily differentiated roles, opposing attributes within the self become particularly salient as well as problematic. Boys, in contrast, can move more facilely among their different roles and multiple selves to the extent that such roles are logically viewed as more independent of one another. However, these general observations require further refinement, including an empirical examination of precisely which facets of the relational worlds of adolescent females and males are specifically relevant to gender differences in opposing attributes displayed across different contexts.

Closer examination of the gender effects reveals that it is a subset of female adolescents who report more opposites and greater conflict compared to males. We have determined that adolescent females who endorse a feminine gender orientation (eschewing masculine traits) may be particularly vulnerable to the experience of opposing attributes and associated conflict. Feminine adolescent females, compared to females who endorse an androgynous orientation, report more conflict, particularly in roles that involve teachers, classmates, and male friends (in contrast to roles involving parents and female friends). Several hy-

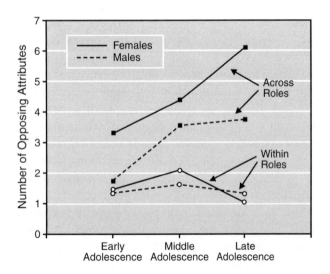

Figure 11.3 Gender differences in the number of opposing attributes identified across roles.

potheses would be worth pursuing in this regard. Is it that feminine girls report more contradictions in those public contexts where they feel they may be acting inappropriately by violating feminine stereotypes of behavior? Given that femininity as assessed by sex-role inventories is largely defined by caring, sensitivity, and attentiveness to the needs and feelings of others, might female adolescents who adopt this orientation be more preoccupied with relationships, making opposing attributes and accompanying conflict more salient? Moreover, might it be more important for feminine girls to be consistent across relationships, a stance that may be difficult to sustain to the extent that significant others in different roles are encouraging or reinforcing different characteristics? These are all new directions in which attention to gender issues should proceed.

The challenges posed by the need to create different selves are also exacerbated for ethnic minority youth in this country, who must bridge "multiple worlds," as Cooper and her colleagues point out (Cooper, Jackson, Azmitia, Lopez, & Dunbar, 1995). Minority youth must move between multiple contexts, some of which may be with members of their own ethnic group, including family and friends, and some of which may be populated by the majority culture, including teachers, classmates, and other peers who may not share the values of their family of origin. Rather than assume that all ethnic minority youth will react similarly to the need to cope with such multiple worlds, these investigators have highlighted several different patterns of adjustment. Some youth are able to move facilely across the borders of their multiple worlds, in large part because the values of the family, teachers, and peers are relatively similar. Others, for whom there is less congruence in values across contexts, adopt a bicultural stance, adapting to the world of family as well as to that of the larger community. Others find the transition across these psychological borders more difficult, and some find it totally unmanageable. Particularly interesting is the role that certain parents play in helping adolescents navigate these transitions, leading to more successful adaptations for some than others.

As observed earlier, adolescents during this period become extremely preoccupied with the opinions and expectations of significant others in different roles. As our prototypical respondent indicates, "I care what my parents think about me"; "I want to know what my close friends think"; "I don't care what [everybody else] thinks. I mean, I don't want to care, that is"; "I want [adults at work] to approve of me"; that is, adolescents gaze intently into the social mirror for information about what standards and

attributes to internalize. However, as the number of roles proliferate, leading to messages from different significant others that are potentially contradictory, adolescents may become confused or distressed about just which characteristics to adopt. We see this in the cameo self-description with regard to scholastic performance, in that the adolescent feels she "should get better grades" to please her parents but confesses that "I'd be mortified in the eyes of my friends if I did too well." As Higgins (1991) observes, in their attempt to incorporate the standards and opinions of others, adolescents at this level develop conflicting "self-guides" across different relational contexts as they attempt to meet the incompatible expectations of parents and peers. He reports evidence indicating that such discrepancies have been found to produce confusion, uncertainty, and indecision with regard to self-evaluation and self-regulation, consistent with our own findings. Moreover, as Rosenberg (1986) notes, the serious efforts at perspective taking that emerge at this stage make one aware that no human being can have direct access to another's mind, leading to inevitable ambiguity about others' attitudes toward oneself, producing yet another source of doubt and confusion.

The potential for displaying differing levels of self-esteem across relational contexts is also exacerbated during this period, to the extent that significant others are providing different levels of validation for who one is as a person (see also Rosenberg, 1986). For example, the cameo self-description reveals that the adolescent gets down on herself for not getting the grades her parents expect. She hates herself when she feels peers think she is weird, but she feels good about herself on the job, where supervisors give her more positive feedback. Our own evidence has revealed that not only does self-esteem become differentiated by context beginning in early adolescence, but it becomes further differentiated in middle to late adolescence. For example, individuals come to develop different levels of self-esteem with their mother and their father (Harter, 1999), levels that in turn are directly related to their perceptions of approval from each parent.

Normative Liabilities during Middle Adolescence

Midadolescence brings with it a preoccupation with what significant others think of the self, a task that is made more challenging given the proliferation of roles that demand the creation of multiple selves. The addition of new role-related selves can be observed in the fact that adolescents make finer discriminations, for example, self with a close friend versus self with a group of friends, and self with mother versus self with father. Moreover, there is relatively little overlap in the personal attributes that define the self in each role. The proliferation of multiple selves ushers in the potential for such attributes to be viewed as contradictory. Moreover, the emergence of new cognitive processes such as abstract mappings forces the adolescent to compare and contrast different attributes, exacerbating the likelihood that contradictions will be detected. Mapping, in the form of identification of opposites, is problematic, as the individual cannot yet truly integrate such self-representations in a manner that would resolve the contradictions. Thus, the adolescent is likely to experience conflict, confusion, and distress. Opposites and associated conflict are particularly likely to occur for attributes in different roles, rather than in the same role. Females are particularly likely to display these negative outcomes. Opposing self-attributes also lead to unstable self-representations, in addition to concern over which characteristics represent one's true self.

With regard to the impact of the socializing environment, adolescents gaze intently into the social mirror for information about what standards and attributes to internalize. However, contradictory messages from different significant others can lead to confusion about just what characteristics to adopt. Differential support, in the form of approval or validation, will also lead to differing levels of self-worth across relational contexts. The contradictory feedback that adolescents may receive from different sources will, therefore, lead to volatility in self-esteem across interpersonal contexts.

Contradictory standards and feedback can also contribute to a lowering of global self-esteem between early and midadolescence (see findings reviewed by Harter, 1990a), to the extent that one cannot meet the expectations of everyone in each relational context. Given that the adolescent does not meet the standards of others, he or she is likely to experience less approval, which in turn will lead to lower global self-esteem. Moreover, the abstract mapping structure, coupled with the penchant for introspection, may also contribute to lowered self-esteem because it facilitates the comparison of one's ideal and real self-concepts. Such a focus can lead to a heightened awareness of the discrepancy between how one perceives the self to be in reality (e.g., "I can get pretty obnoxious and intolerant") and how one would ideally like to be (e.g., "I'd like to be friendly and tolerant all of the time. That's the kind of person I want to be, and I'm disappointed in myself when I'm not"). The realm of physical appearance is particularly critical. This adolescent wants to look like Britney Spears and knows she doesn't, and this sets up another painful discrepancy between how she would like to look and how she

actually does. In reality, she does not value her appearance, falling far short of the cultural standards for beauty.

Cognitive-developmental advances during midadolescence also represent limitations that can lead to distortions in the interpretation of the opinions of significant others. As observed earlier, with new cognitive capacities comes difficulty in controlling and applying them effectively. For example, teenagers have difficulty differentiating their own mental preoccupations from what others are thinking, leading to a form of adolescent egocentrism that Elkind (1967) has labeled the "imaginary audience." Adolescents falsely assume that others are as preoccupied with their behavior and appearance as they themselves are. As our prototypical respondent exclaims, "Everybody, I mean everybody else is looking at me like they think I am totally weird!" With regard to lack of cognitive control, this phenomenon represents overgeneralization (or failure to differentiate) as adolescents project their own concerns onto others.

Interestingly, the inability to control and to effectively apply new cognitive structures can result not only in a lack of differentiation between self and other, as in the imaginary audience phenomenon, but also in excessive or unrealistic differentiation. The latter penchant can be observed in another form of adolescent egocentrism that Elkind (1967) has identified as the "personal fable." In creating narratives that come to define the self, the adolescent asserts that his or her thoughts and feelings are uniquely experienced. No one else can possibly understand or experience the ecstasy of his or her rapture or the intensity of his or her despair. Adults, particularly parents, are likely to be singled out in this regard. As the prototypical adolescent exclaims, "My parents don't understand me. What do they know about what it's like to be a teenager?" Her initial comment to the interviewer when asked to describe what she was like ("You're probably not going to understand") also reflects this type of overdifferentiation between self and other.

The liabilities of this period, therefore, are legion with regard to potential conflict and confusion over contradictory attributes and messages, concern over which characteristics define the true self, distortions in the perception of self versus others, and a preoccupation with discrepancies between the real and ideal self-concepts that can lead to lowered self-esteem. Some of these processes would appear to be problematic for particular subgroups of adolescents, for example, females who adopt a feminine gender orientation and ethnic minority youth who are challenged by the need to create selves that bridge "multiple worlds," for example, with one's own ethnic group and groups within the mainstream majority culture.

An appreciation for the ramifications of these normative processes is critical in interpreting the unpredictable behaviors, shifting self-evaluations, and mood swings that are observed in many adolescents during this age period. Such displays are less likely to be viewed as intentional or pathological and more likely to meet with empathy and understanding to the extent that normative cognitive-developmental changes can be invoked as in part responsible. For many parents, as well as other adults working closely with teenagers, these seemingly inexplicable reactions often lead to perplexity, exasperation, and anger, provoking power struggles and altercations that strain the adolescent-adult relationship. The realization that this is a normative part of development that should not persist forever may provide temporary comfort to adults who feel beleaguered and ineffectual in dealing with adolescents of this age. Indeed, it gives a more charitable rendering to this period of development.

Much of the preceding discussion has focused on normative liabilities based on the *cognitive-developmental* changes in the *structure* of adolescent thought at this period. However, there are also normative liabilities that can stem from the *content* of the adolescent self-portrait. Our prototypical female adolescent aspires to look like Britney Spears, given the importance of physical appearance that increases during adolescence. However, like the majority of adolescents, she cannot meet the punishing standards put forth by the media that define today's ideals for beauty (Harter, 1999). The demand that one be excessively thin, tall, and long-legged, with ample breasts and a pretty face is an ideal that the vast majority of females in this culture cannot attain (Kilbourne, 1994). Applying a Jamesian (James, 1892) perspective, the discrepancy between the extreme importance attached to appearance and perceptions of inadequacy in one's appearance can set the stage for lowered self-esteem for females. The problem is exacerbated for females whose pubertal development does not favor the cultural ideal of beauty (Harter, 1999). With the onset of puberty, girls put on body fat and hips become wider, each of which violates the norms of thinness, one criterion for physical attractiveness. Males are more favored because puberty brings about physical changes more in keeping with the contemporary norms of male attractiveness. Males become taller and more muscular, attributes that are valued by society. Many of these normative liabilities interact, in that there can be conflict and confusion over one's self-attributes, for example, vacillations in whether one feels attractive or unattractive. However, as we shall see in the next section, taken to the extreme, in some individuals these can lead to more pathological processes and outcomes.

Pathological Self-Processes and Outcomes in Middle Adolescence

With regard to a focus on meeting cultural standards of appearance, females are much more likely to suffer from processes that move into the realm of pathology. From the perspective of our own model of the causes and correlates of self-esteem, an intense preoccupation with attempts to meet the impossible standards of beauty, coupled with very negative perceptions of one's body image, can lead to extremely low self-esteem, depression, and, in the extreme, eating-disordered behaviors. We have documented the links between the high importance attached to physical appearance and negative perceptions of one's body image, leading to extremely negative reports of self-esteem and depression, among those in midadolescence. In the subsequent section on later adolescence and emerging adulthood, we provide further documentation about how these processes can lead to pathological eating-disordered behaviors.

Numerous findings (reviewed in Harter, 1999; see also Nolen-Hoeksema & Girgus, 1994) reveal that dramatic gender differences in depression emerge in middle adolescence. The discrepancy between impossible ideals of appearance and one's perception of one's own body image contributes to very low self-esteem for some, particularly those who are overweight, that in turn leads to profound depression that can require clinical intervention.

The potential for such internalizing symptoms looms large for girls during middle adolescence. The potential for the escalation of violence, as in the case of the high-profile cases of school shootings by White, middle-class adolescents, is also apparent. Intense rejection by peers, at a time when self-consciousness and the need for approval are so salient, sets the stage for violent ideation that can turn to action. The fragile and vacillating self-structures of this particular period can, in the face of such humiliation, lead to lack of control, both over cognitions about the self (Harter, 1999) and behaviors that these cognitions may drive. Given the lack of cognitive control (Fischer, 1980), the adolescent during this period may act more impulsively on his or her thoughts. Recent work on the adolescent brain supports the view that the frontal cortex is not yet completely developed, leading to gaps in executive functions that could serve to curb such impulsive, violent intentions and behaviors.

While the fragmented self is a normative liability of this period of middle adolescence, a history of severe and chronic physical and sexual abuse may lead to pathological outcomes. The effects of abuse on the self-system are legion (see review in Harter, 1999). From a developmental perspective, a history of abuse can lead to dissociative symptoms that serve to further fragment the fragile multiple selves in the process of psychological construction (see also Putnum, 1993; Westen, 1993). As a result, there is no core self at the helm, and there is little communication between multiple selves that become "alters," compromising the ability to develop an integrated self. As a result, there is the risk for dissociative identity disorders that represent severe pathological conditions that may require years of treatment.

Late Adolescence

Our final period, late adolescence that may extend into early adulthood, is critical to characterize because many of the conflicts and confusions of the preceding period of middle adolescence decline, normatively. The verbal cameo and subsequent analysis illustrate these changes. There are fewer liabilities with the ensuing developmental advances. However, the shift to higher levels of abstraction bring new challenges in terms of self-definition. These are described, as well as pathological implications for teenagers emerging into young adulthood.

Verbal Cameo of Normative Self-Representations and Self-Evaluations

I'm a pretty conscientious person, particularly when it comes to things like doing my homework. It's important to me because I plan to go to college next year. Eventually I want to go to law school, so developing good study habits and getting top grades are both essential. (My parents don't want me to become a lawyer; they'd rather I go into teaching, but law is what I want to pursue.) Every now and then I get a little lackadaisical and don't complete an assignment as thoroughly or thoughtfully as I could, particularly if our high school has a big football or basketball game that I want to go to with my friends. But that's normal, I mean, you can't just be a total grind. You'd be pretty boring if you were. You have to be flexible. I've also become more religious as I have gotten older, not that I am a saint or anything. Religion gives me a sense of purpose, in the larger scheme of things, and it provides me with personal guidelines for the kind of adult I'd like to be. For example, I'd like to be an ethical person who treats other people fairly. That's the kind of lawyer I'd like to be, too. I don't always live up to that standard; that is, sometimes I do something that doesn't feel that ethical. When that

happens, I get a little depressed because I don't like myself as a person. But I tell myself that it's natural to make mistakes, so I don't really question the fact that deep down inside, the real me is a moral person. Basically, I like who I am, so I don't stay depressed for long. Usually, I am pretty upbeat and optimistic. I guess you could say that I'm a moody person. I'm not as popular as a lot of other kids. You have to look a certain way, have the right body image, wear the right clothes, to be accepted. At our school, it's the jocks who are looked up to. I've never been very athletic, but you can't be good at everything, let's face it. Being athletic isn't that high on my own list of what is important, even though it is for a lot of kids in our school. I try to think that, anyway. But I don't really care what they think anymore, at least I try to convince myself that I don't. I try to believe that what I think is what counts. After all, I have to live with myself as a person and to respect that person, which I do now, more than a few years ago. I'm pretty much being the kind of person I want to be. I'm doing well at things that are important to me, like getting good grades. That's what is probably most important to me right now. Having a lot of friends isn't that important to me. I wouldn't say I was unpopular, though. While I am basically an introvert, especially on a date when I get pretty self-conscious, in the right social situation, like watching a ball game with my friends, I can be pretty extroverted. You have to be adaptive around other people. It would be weird to be the same kind of person on a date and with my friends at a football game! For example, when our team has a winning season and goes to the playoffs, everyone in the whole school is proud; what the team does reflects on all of us. On a date, the feelings are much more intimate, just between you and the other person. As much as I enjoy my high school friends and activities, I'm looking forward to leaving home and going to college, where I can be more independent, although I'm a little ambivalent. I love my parents, and really want to stay connected to them, plus, what they think about me is still important to how I feel about myself as a person. So leaving home will be bittersweet. But sometimes it's hard to be mature around them, particularly around my mom. I feel a lot more grown-up around my dad; he treats me more like an adult. I like that part of me because it feels more like my true self. My mom wants me to grow up, but another part of her wants me to remain "her little baby." I'll probably always be somewhat dependent on my parents. How can you escape it? But I'm also looking forward to being on my own.

With regard to the content of the self-representations that begin to emerge in late adolescence and early adulthood, typically, many of the attributes reflect personal beliefs, values, and moral standards that have become internalized or, alternatively, constructed from one's own experiences (see findings by Damon & Hart, 1988). These characteristics are exemplified in the prototypical cameo, as the adolescent expresses the personal desire to go to college, which requires good grades and discipline in the form of study habits. Although classmates tout athletics as the route to popularity, there is less concern at this age with what others think ("I don't really care what they think anymore, at least I try to convince myself that I don't"). In addition, there is a focus on one's future selves, for example, not only becoming a lawyer, but also an ethical lawyer, as a personal goal. Noteworthy in this narrative is the absence of an explicit reference to the potential origins of these goals, for example, parental encouragement or expectations that one pursue such a career. Moreover, this adolescent's career choice does not conform to the parents' occupational goals for their child.

The failure to acknowledge the socialization influences that might have led to these choices does not necessarily indicate that significant others such as peers and parents had no impact. In fact, findings (see Steinberg, 1990) reveal that the attitudes of adolescents and their parents are quite congruent when it comes to occupational, political, and religious decisions and convictions. Rather, the fact that the impact of significant others is not acknowledged suggests that older adolescents and young adults have come to "own" various values as personal choices rather than attribute them to the sources from which they may have been derived (Damon & Hart, 1988). In Higgins's (1991) terminology, older adolescents have gone through a process in which they have actively selected among alternative self-guides and are no longer merely buffeted about by the expectations of significant others; that is, self-guides become increasingly internalized and less tied to their social origins. Moreover, there is a greater sense of direction as the older adolescent comes to envisage future or "possible" selves (Markus & Nurius, 1996) that function as ideals toward which one aspires.

Another feature of the self-portrait of the older adolescent can be contrasted with the period before; now, many potentially contradictory attributes are no longer described as characteristics in opposition to one another. Thus, being conscientious as a student does not appear to conflict with one's lackadaisical attitude toward schoolwork: "That's normal, I mean, you can't just be a total grind. You'd be pretty boring if you were. You have to be flexible." Similarly, one's perception of the self as ethical does not conflict with the acknowledgment that one also has engaged in some unethical behaviors ("It's natural to make mistakes"). Nor does introversion conflict with extroverted behaviors: "You have to be adaptive around other people. It would be weird to be the same kind of person on a date and with my friends at a football game!"

There are cognitive acquisitions that allow the older adolescent to overcome some of the liabilities of the previous period, when potentially opposing attributes were viewed as contradictory and as a cause of internal conflict. The general cognitive advances during this period involve the construction of higher-order abstractions that involve the meaningful intercoordination of single abstractions (see Case, 1985; Fischer, 1980; Fischer & Canfield, 1986). For example, the fact that one is both introverted and extroverted can be integrated through the construction of a higher-order abstraction that defines the self as "adaptive." The observation that one is both depressed and cheerful or optimistic can be integrated under the personal rubric of "moody." Similarly, being "flexible" can allow one to coordinate conscientiousness with the tendency to be lackadaisical. The higher-order concept of "ambivalence" integrates the desire to be independent yet still remain connected to parents. Moreover, "bittersweet" reflects a higher-order abstraction combining both excitement over going to college with sadness over leaving one's parents. Such higher-order abstractions provide self-labels that bring meaning and therefore legitimacy to what formerly appeared to be troublesome contradictions within the self.

Neo-Piagetians such as Case (1985) and Fischer (1980) observe that developmental acquisitions at these higher levels typically require greater scaffolding by the social environment in the form of support, experiences, instruction, and so on in order for individuals to function at their optimal level. If these new skills are fostered, they will help the adolescent to integrate opposing attributes in a manner that does not produce conflict or distress. Thus, efforts to assist the adolescent in realizing that it is normal to display seemingly contradictory traits, and perhaps quite appropriate, may alleviate perceptions of conflict. Moreover, helping teenagers to provide higher-order labels that integrate opposing attributes (e.g., flexible, adaptive, moody, inconsistent) may avert some of the distress that was salient during middle adolescence. These suggestions derive from the observations of Fischer, Case, and others to the effect that these cognitive solutions will not necessarily emerge automatically with development. Nor will the potential benefits derived from movement to late adolescence and early adulthood necessarily accrue; that is, the levels described in this chapter represent a normative sequence of development. However, the age levels are somewhat arbitrary in that certain individuals may not attain a given level at the designated age period. Development may be delayed or even arrested if there is not sufficient support for the transition to a new level of conceptualization, particularly for the higher stages.

The assertion that the changing cognitive structures emerge—ideally—in late adolescence to early adulthood will allow for a potential reduction in the number of contradictory attributes identified in one's self-portrait, as well as diminished conflict, has found partial support in our own findings. For example, in one study (Harter & Monsour, 1992) in which adolescents described their attributes in four roles—with parents, with friends, with romantic others, and as a student—there was a dramatic rise in the number of opposites and conflicts identified at midadolescence, followed by a slight decline among older adolescents. Evidence that older adolescents become better able to consolidate or integrate seeming contradictions within the self-theory come from the comments they made in response to a follow-up interview. As one older adolescent explained, "Sometimes I am really happy, and sometimes I get depressed. I'm just a moody person." Another commented, "I can be talkative, and I can be quiet. I'm flexible, plus they complement each other. It's good to be both ways."

The tendency to *normalize* or find value in seeming inconsistency can also be observed in the comments of older adolescents, for example, "You wouldn't be the same person on a date as you are with your parents, and you shouldn't be. That would be weird." Another asserted, "It wouldn't be normal to act the same way with everyone. You act one way with your friends and a different way with your parents. That's the way it should be." Others made similar comments, for example, "It's good to be able to be different with different people in your life. You'd be pretty strange and also pretty boring if you weren't"; "You can be outgoing with friends and then shy on a date because you are just different with different people; you can't always be the same person and probably shouldn't be"; "There are situations where you are a good listener and others where you are talkative. It's good to be both." Thus, older adolescents come to the conclusion that it is desirable to be different across relational contexts, and in so doing, they would appear to be cultivating the stance that social psychologists (see Gergen, 1968; Mischel, 1973; Vallacher, 1980) identify as more the rule than the exception for adults.

The Role of the Socializing Environment

Recent evidence (see Harter et al., 1997) indicates that the ability to resolve potentially contradictory attributes may be more difficult for some role-pair combinations than for others, particularly for females. For example, as Figure 11.3 reveals, when all role pairs are combined, there is no decline in the number of opposing attributes identified

across roles. In fact, for older adolescent females, there is actually a further increase. The fact that six roles were included in the study generating the data in Figure 11.3 (compared to only four in the original Harter & Monsour, 1992, study) may have been partly responsible, as the inclusion of additional roles increased the probability that opposing attributes might be detected; that is, there were 15 possible role pairs that might contain contradictions, compared to only six role pairs in the original study. In increasing the number of roles, we also separated the reports of self-attributes with mother and with father (whereas in the earlier study, we merely inquired about self with parents).

The separation of self-attributes with each parent potentially enhances the likelihood that characteristics with each may contradict attributes in roles with peers. Examples generated by adolescent respondents in mid- to late adolescence included being short-tempered with mother versus a good listener in romantic relationships; respectful with father versus assertive with friends; and distant from father but attentive with a romantic interest. Adolescent bids for autonomy from parents (Cooper, Grotevant, & Condon, 1983; Hill & Holmbeck, 1986; Steinberg, 1990), coupled with the increasing importance of the peer group (Brown, 1990; Savin-Williams & Berndt, 1990), would lead to the expectation that attributes expressed with mother and father might well differ from those displayed with peers (namely, friends and romantic partners), leading to a greater potential for contradictions.

However, the separation of self with mother and self with father also creates the potential for attributes with mother to be in opposition to attributes with father. The potential for attributes with each parent to appear contradictory can be observed in the cameo, where the prototypical older adolescent feels much more mature with father than with mother. Moreover, such conflicts begin to be observed in midadolescence, where the prototypical teenager indicated that she was "close" with her mother but "distant" with her father, a difference that became problematic if they were all together, such as talking at dinner.

When the findings in Figure 11.3 are broken down by relationship pairs, opposing attributes and associated conflicts were most frequent for the combination of self with mother versus self with father, beginning in midadolescence and increasing in late adolescence, a pattern that we have since replicated in a subsequent study. Examples include being close with mother versus distant with father; stubborn with mother versus respectful with father; open with mother but not with father; at ease with mother but defensive with father; and hostile with mother but cheerful with father. Moreover, such opposites between self with mother versus self with father, as well as associated conflict, increased dramatically for older girls in particular.

The fact that older female adolescents reported increasing contradiction, whereas male adolescents did not, suggests that cognitive-developmental explanations are incomplete. The separation of attributes with mother and with father, in particular, would appear to make it more difficult for certain adolescents to cognitively resolve or normalize the contradictions that are provoked by these roles, contradictions produced by the opposing attributes with mother versus father, as well as those attributes with each parent that contradict the characteristics that one displays with peers. Contradictions between self with parents and self with peers is more understandable, given developmental bids for autonomy. But why should adolescents (particularly adolescent females) report increasingly different characteristics with mother and father?

Here, we can only speculate. Family therapists observe that children and adolescents typically develop different relationships with each parent, which in turn may cause the salient attributes in each relationship to vary considerably. Contributing to these dynamics is the fact that each parent may have a different set of expectations about those characteristics that he or she values and therefore attempts to foster. First, the adolescent may become caught in a struggle between two parents who are encouraging and reinforcing different facets of his or her personality, provoking opposing attributes and resulting conflict. Second, both of these roles, self with mother and self with father, occur within the same general context, the family, whereas other multiple roles are not as likely to be called on simultaneously. These particular conditions may exacerbate the contradictions and conflicts that adolescents experience in their respective roles with mother versus father. These family dynamics appear to be relevant to the increase in across-role opposing attributes for female adolescents in particular, who may be more likely to be sensitive to the fact that they are behaving differently with mother versus father. As observed in the previous section on the period of midadolescence, females display more concern over relationship issues, which may make opposing attributes more salient. Adolescent females may also feel that to remain connected to both mother and father, it is important to be consistent across these relationships, a task that can be problematic for the reasons cited earlier.

Although the gender literature suggests that connectedness is more critical to females than to males (Chodorow, 1989; Eichenbaum & Orbach, 1993; Gilligan, 1982; Gilli-

gan, Lyons, & Hanmer, 1989; Jordan, 1991; J. B. Miller, 1986; Rubin, 1985), the adolescent literature reveals that it is important for teenagers of both genders to remain connected to parents in the process of individuation and the establishment of autonomy (Cooper et al., 1983; Hill & Holmbeck, 1986; Steinberg, 1990). As our prototypical subject reveals, although it is important to go to college where he or she can be more independent, it is also important to stay connected to parents.

Contextual factors such as the family, therefore, will conspire with cognitive development to impact the extent to which opposites and conflicts are experienced. Another example of the role of context can be observed in cross-cultural research by Kennedy (1994). Kennedy adapted our procedure in comparing the self-understanding of American and Korean youth. He finds that there are different age-related peaks in conflict among adolescents in the two cultures. Korean youth report increased conflict between opposing attributes in 10th and 12th grades, findings that he interprets in terms of the demands of the school context at those particular grade levels. In Korea, 10th grade is the 1st year of high school, and the new students are required to be deferential to the juniors and seniors, a relationship that many 10th-graders find oppressive. Kennedy argues that these demands exert a strain on the self-system and destabilize students' sense of self as they struggle to find a niche in the peer hierarchy of high school. During 12th grade, there are different demands, for example, intense preparation for the college entrance exams. This pressure leads to challenges in balancing the demands of academics, peer relationships, and family commitments, resulting in greater conflict.

Future research should attend to such contextual factors and attempt to assess the underlying processes more directly. To return to our own findings in this regard, it would be of interest to determine whether the conflict between self-attributes with mother versus father is more intense if the adolescent is living in a two-parent family where both mother and father are in the same household, or if the parents are divorced and living apart. One hypothesis is that living under the same roof with both parents makes it difficult to avoid conflict if different attributes in each relationship are demanded simultaneously. Alternatively, conflict may be exacerbated in the situation of divorce to the extent that in an acrimonious separation, each parent intensifies his or her differential expectations for the attributes they want the adolescent to display as part of a power struggle in which the adolescent becomes a pawn. Such processes would be intriguing to investigate.

Finally, with regard to developmental changes in the self, evidence from longitudinal studies reveals that self-esteem or global self-worth improves in later adolescence (see Engel, 1959; O'Malley & Bachman, 1983; Rosenberg, 1986; Simmons, Rosenberg, & Rosenberg, 1973). Several interpretations of these gains have been suggested (see Harter, 1990b; McCarthy & Hoge, 1982). Reductions in the discrepancy between one's ideal self and one's real self, between one's aspirations and one's successes, according to James's (1892) formulation, may be in part responsible. As the prototypical adolescent indicates, he or she has more self-respect now compared to a few years ago and observes, "I'm pretty much being the kind of person I want to be. I'm doing well at things that are important to me like getting good grades and being ethical." Gains in personal autonomy and freedom of choice may also play a role, in that the older adolescent may have more opportunity to select performance domains in which he or she is successful. Such freedom may also provide one with more opportunity to select those support groups that will provide the positive regard necessary to promote or enhance self-esteem, consistent with the looking-glass self formulation. Increased role-taking ability may also lead older teenagers to behave in more socially acceptable ways that enhance the evaluation of the self by others, such that the favorable attitudes of others toward the self are internalized as positive self-worth.

These others include parents. Although it has been common in treatments of adolescent development to suggest that the influence of peers increases, whereas the impact of parental opinion declines, findings do not support the latter contention. As our cameo subject indicates, "What my parents think about me is still important to how I feel about myself as a person." Our own findings reveal that the correlation between classmate approval and global self-esteem does increase during childhood and adolescence; however, the correlation between parental approval and global self-esteem, which is high in childhood, does not decline during adolescence (Harter, 1990b). The latter correlation does decline, however, during the college years among students who are away from home.

More specific evaluations of self-esteem continue to vary by relationship context (Harter et al., 1998) throughout the high school years as adolescents make finer distinctions (e.g., between their self-esteem with mother and with father). However, we did not anticipate the fact that for the vast majority of individuals, self-esteem in one particular relational domain is much more highly related to global self-esteem than is relational self-esteem in all other con-

texts. The specific domain occupying this position varies from adolescent to adolescent. For example, with our prototypical adolescent, self as student in the academic domain is most important ("Getting good grades is what is most important to me now"), and his or her self-esteem in that particular context is higher than in other domains. Thus, focusing on that particular context would appear to be very adaptive in that it should promote more positive feelings of global self-esteem.

Normative Liabilities during Late Adolescence

Many of the limitations of the preceding period of midadolescence would appear to be overcome as a result of changes during late adolescence. Attributes reflecting personal beliefs, values, and standards become more internalized, and the older adolescent would appear to have more opportunity to meet these standards, thereby leading to enhanced self-esteem. The focus on future selves also gives the older adolescent a sense of direction. A critical cognitive advance can be observed in the ability to construct higher-order abstractions that involve the meaningful integration of single abstractions that represent potential contradictions in the self-portrait (e.g., depressed and cheerful do not conflict because they are both part of being moody). The older adolescent can also resolve potentially contradictory attributes by asserting that he or she is flexible or adaptive, thereby subsuming apparent inconsistencies under more generalized abstractions about the self. Moreover, older adolescents are more likely to normalize potential contradictions, asserting that it is desirable to be different across relational contexts and that it would be weird or strange to be the same with different people.

Nevertheless, conflict between role-related attributes does not totally abate in later adolescence. Conflict will be more likely to occur if the new skills that allow for an integration of seeming contradictions are not fostered by the socializing environment. Furthermore, opposing attributes across particular role combinations, notably self with mother versus self with father, continue to be problematic in late adolescence, especially for girls. To the extent that one's mother and father elicit or reinforce opposing attributes, cognitive solutions for integrating seeming contradictions would appear to be more difficult to invoke.

Last, although the internalization of standards and opinions that the adolescent comes to own as personal choices and attitudes toward the self represents a developmental advance, there are liabilities associated with this process. As Rosenberg (1986) observes, the shift in the locus of self-knowledge from an external to an internal source can introduce uncertainty. As long as major truths about the self derive from omniscient and omnipotent adults, there is little doubt about their veracity. However, when the locus of self-knowledge shifts inward and adolescents must rely on their own autonomous judgment and insight to reach conclusions about the self, then the sense of certainty can be compromised.

Pathological Self-Processes and Outcomes in Late Adolescence/Early Adulthood

Many of the pathological processes that have been described in the earlier periods of adolescence can be observed in late adolescence, albeit in a somewhat different form due to developmental advances. Preoccupation with impossible cultural standards of attractiveness looms even larger as the older adolescent anticipates emerging adulthood, making it even more critical to attain these standards to be socially acceptable and successful in the new adult world order (Harter, 1999). For females, failure to meet these standards can lead to more pathological processes, which may include eating disorders.

For example, in one study conducted in our laboratory by Danis (see Harter, 1999), two eating-disordered groups of women college students were identified, those with symptoms of anorexia and those with symptoms of bulimia. These two groups were compared to a control sample who did not display such symptoms. Both the anorexic and the bulimic group reported significantly higher scores on the importance of appearance, toward the very top of the 4-point scale, compared to the normative sample. They each reported extremely low scores with regard to their evaluation of their physical appearance, creating a large discrepancy, namely, importance scores vastly higher than perceived appearance scores. This discrepancy clearly predicted very low self-esteem scores for the two eating-disordered groups compared to the normal sample. These low self-esteem scores, in turn, were highly predictive of extremely high levels of self-reported depression.

Of particular interest were the findings that although both eating-disordered groups reported this negative constellation of symptoms, those in the bulimic group were more at risk given the lowest ratings of perceived physical appearance, self-esteem, and depression. Danis interpreted this difference between the two eating-disordered groups in terms of perceptions of control. She argued that those with symptoms of anorexia were objectively thinner, leading them to possibly feel more successful in terms of their weight control. The bulimics, who by definition binge and purge, were interpreted to be less in control; moreover,

on average, this group was heavier. That said, those with anorexia are more at risk for malnourishment that can affect bone development, brain development, and body development in general, and in the extreme, they are at risk for death. Those with bulimic symptoms are also at risk for a variety of physical symptoms, including damage to the mouth and esophagus and other compromising physical growth symptoms. Of course, there are also numerous psychological symptoms, including disruptions within the family, compromised academic achievement, and impaired social functioning.

In another study on this same topic (Kiang & Harter, 2004), we developed an instrument to assess the extent to which young college-age women bought into cultural messages about the link between meeting cultural standards of attractiveness and outcomes such as popularity, approval, love, and economic and job success. The findings revealed that those who strongly endorsed these links reported markedly lower self-esteem, depression, and eating-disordered symptoms. Young adults at this period are *less* likely to report the vacillations that are observed during middle adolescence, marking their perceptions of negativity as more stable because they have become entrenched in these views as a core belief system.

Male adolescents are clearly at continued risk for violence, particularly the type of violence that emanates from peer rejection and humiliation. Chronic rejection and humiliation are likely culprits for violent ideation (Harter, in press) and for violent action, as in the case of the school shooters. Unlike the impulsive acts of the school shooters in middle adolescence, the acts of Eric Harris and Dylan Kleibold from Columbine, who were older teens, were far more *planful*. For over a year, they had developed their strategies, some of which were revealed in Harris's written manifesto. Although this is speculative, in examining the media accounts of the 11 high-profile school shooting cases, it would appear that the dynamics may be different from what we normally consider to be delinquent, conduct-disordered behavior that had come to the attention of teachers, school officials, school psychologists, peers, and parents. In most of these cases, there were few warning signs with regard to the male shooters having been in trouble with the law, having been identified as troublemakers in the school, having clinical diagnoses, or being placed in special classes for students with a penchant for acting out. As noted earlier (Harter & McCarley, 2004), we found that 33% of those reporting to us that they had serious thoughts of harming others who humiliated them went undetected by their classroom teachers who were given parallel rating forms. Thus, there is a need to discriminate the form of violence that has recently emerged from previous acts that have been committed by known delinquents and conduct-disordered youth who have come to the attention of school and mental health professionals and who commit different types of crimes, for example, drive-by shootings to target one individual versus the random shooting of as many classmates as possible. The dynamics appear to be different and deserve our attention.

The construction of multiple selves, though a normative process, can also have pathological implications. It was pointed out in the section on middle adolescence that the effects of abuse can lead to dissociative symptoms that prevent one's multiple selves from being integrated. In the severest cases, this can lead to Dissociative Identity Disorder (what used to be termed Multiple Personality Disorder). Abuse has also been found to impact the valence (positive or negative) of those attributes judged to be one's core self (versus more peripheral attributes). Normatively, we have found that when asked to rate the attributes across multiple relational contexts with regard to whether they are central core characteristics or more peripheral, less important attributes that define the self, normative samples of older adolescents will define their most important attributes as *positive* and assign their more negative characteristics to the periphery of the self, that is, as less important attributes (Harter & Monsour, 1992). This self-protective strategy has been defined normatively as "ben-effectance" by Greenwald (1980), or seeing one's positive attributes as central to the self and one's negative attributes as more peripheral.

Our colleagues Fischer and Ayoub (1994) employed our multiple selves procedure with an inpatient sample of seriously abused older adolescent girls, finding just the opposite pattern. Compared to a normative sample, the abused patients identified *negative* attributes as their core self, relegating what few positive characteristics they could identify as peripheral. Herein we can detect another deleterious effect of abuse on self-processes leading to potential pathological outcomes; these require clinical intervention that we would hope can restore a more positive balance of self-perceptions.

CONCLUSIONS AND FUTURE DIRECTIONS

At the outset, I set forth a framework in which I first applauded the many efforts of those in the field who have tried to give dignity and depth to the field of developmental psychopathology, who have attempted to carve out a distinct subdiscipline that clearly warrants our attention. Much has been learned about the developmental trajectories of particular disorders in childhood and adolescence, focusing on individual differences and multiple pathways to a given disorder. This has yielded a vast array of findings that are not only interesting for their scientific merit but have greatly aided clinicians in their treatment of the various pathologies of childhood and adolescence.

In my reading of this literature, a subset of publications in the larger field of clinical psychology, it seems that often there has been a top-down approach in which diagnostic criteria initially established for adults have been applied to children and adolescents, with some modifications for the age of the individual. Yet the approach, including in the forthcoming *DSM-V,* still involves lists and categories of symptoms specifying criteria (e.g., numbers of symptoms in each category) to arrive at a diagnosis. With the exception of certain age-related criteria, there has been little emphasis on process models of pathology or an appreciation for what we know about normative sequences of development as a backdrop for our understanding of psychopathology.

Basic empirical research on the various disorders of childhood and adolescence has devoted more attention to the processes and dynamics underlying given disorders. Clearly, much of the exciting longitudinal work addresses development in an important sense, namely, how these disorders unfold over time. To what extent can we predict an individual's future with regard to the course of a given form of psychopathology? These are critical endeavors contributing to our understanding of disordered behaviors.

That said, however, as I suggested in the introduction, we could put more "development" into the discipline of developmental psychopathology. The fields of developmental psychology and clinical psychology have for too long been segregated. Elsewhere I have commented on the fact that there has been too much segregation between the fields of traditional social psychology, as applied to adults, and developmental psychology. Often, top-down models of adult social psychological phenomena are glibly applied to children, employing the same paradigms and models as well as watered-down versions of instruments that primarily attend to vocabulary level, not changes that might be sensitive to the developmental level of the child or adolescent.

What would it mean to put more "development" into developmental psychopathology? At one level, the direction that the field has taken in the past 2 decades may seem to have made this task increasingly difficult. We have engaged in theoretical homicide. We have shot down our early heroes: Piaget, Freud, Vygotsky, Werner, and Erikson. We have been critical of their grand formulations, the omnibus theories that we now view as too vague and imprecise; we have struggled with the distinction between scope and precision, seemingly opting for the latter. Now we scramble to create minitheories of our own pet constructs for our own given age level or population, minitheories that will pepper the publication landscape of our ever-so-fragmented proliferation of journals that speak primarily to our specialty. Where are the developmental compasses, be they theoretical, methodological, or empirical, that could guide us in understanding psychopathological conditions that are very real in the lives of children and adolescents?

There may be a middle ground where we can adopt the developmental spirit of our forefathers who illuminated fascinating developmental sequences, albeit somewhat broad, vague, imprecise, cumbersome, and therefore not so amenable to rigorous documentation. By that I mean that we can take a particular construct of interest, narrowing our scope but addressing precision in terms of identifying the developmental sequence and the underlying processes that govern the unfolding of that construct.

My goal for this chapter was to adopt such an approach and to apply it to the self-system. We know that there are disorders that involve the self. Might not an initial understanding of the normative developmental progression of self-understanding aid us in thinking about such disorders? Yet we need to go far beyond the documentation of such normative sequences. Thus, I have attempted to take an expanded approach, first identifying three periods of childhood and three periods of adolescence where we can identify clear changes with regard to self-development. Within each of these six periods, I have identified three levels of analysis: normative-developmental descriptions of how self-processes change; and normative liabilities that I have argued are just that, bumps in the psychological road that will be leveled out, developmentally graded, as it were, through the help of naturally occurring neurological development but even more strongly by the attentive and thoughtful scaffolding of socializing agents in the lives of children and adolescents. With regard to the latter, there are those who have emphasize the importance of such scaffolding (Fischer, Rogoff, and others) who are making powerful contributions to our understanding of development. Finally, I made the distinction between normative liabilities and more severe pathological self processes.

We could adopt such an approach in domains other than the self that are relevant to developmental psychopathology, for example, aggression, school violence, ADHD, depression, emotionality, abuse and trauma, Autism, and neurological conditions. Obviously, some of this work has been conducted by individual investigators, and very effectively. However, we lack such an approach as an overarching model for how to understand developmental psychopathology. Moreover, we do not employ such a model in most of our training programs for graduate students. A truly developmental perspective would force us to think differently about how and why symptoms in a family of disorders may differ or, conversely, appear to be similar over time.

I would modestly suggest that perhaps the most valuable contribution of the framework that I have attempted to articulate is the distinction between normative developmental liabilities and truly pathological processes. An understanding of this distinction could be invaluable for clinicians, giving them guidance about how not to overpathologize. Moreover, such an understanding could greatly enhance our ability to comfort concerned parents of children and adolescents who may come to our clinics, by emphasizing that certain behaviors that appear pathological are normal manifestations of development, albeit sometimes painful perturbations for the child and family alike. Moreover, we can offer comfort to the distressed child or adolescent client, emphasizing that many of these normative liabilities are just that, normal, common experiences that are shared with others their age. Obviously, we also need to be clear on the distinction between such normative liabilities and truly pathological processes that require a different set of clinical interventions. It is hoped that this type of approach could bring developmental researchers and clinicians committed to an understanding of developmental psychopathology closer together, for the good of each of us, the clients and families we serve as well as the field at large.

REFERENCES

Ainsworth, M. (1979). Infant-mother attachment. *American Psychologist, 34,* 932–937.

Bandura, A. (1991). Self-regulation of motivation through anticipatory and regulatory mechanisms. In R. A. Dienstbier (Ed.), *Nebraska Symposium on Motivation: Vol. 26. Perspectives on motivation* (pp. 99–125). Lincoln: University of Nebraska Press.

Barnett, D., Ganiban, J., & Cicchetti, D. (1999). Maltreatment, negative expressivity, and the development of type D attachments from 12 to 24 months of age. *Monographs of the Society for Research in Child Development, 64*(3 Serial No. 258), 97–118.

Bates, E. (1990). Language about me and you: Pronominal reference and the emerging concept of self. In Cicchetti & M. Beeghly (Eds.), *The self in transition: Infancy to childhood* (pp. 1–15). Chicago: University of Chicago Press.

Baumeister, R. F., Smart, L., & Boden, J. M. (1999). Relation of threatened egotism to violence and aggression: The dark side of high self-esteem. *Psychological Review, 103,* 5–33.

Beeghly, M., Carlson, V., & Cicchetti, D. (1986, April). *Child maltreatment and the self: The emergence of internal state language in low SES 30-month-olds.* Paper presented at the International Conference on Infant Studies, Beverly Hills, CA.

Beeghly, M., & Cicchetti, D. (1994). Child maltreatment, attachment, and the self-system: Emergence of an internal state lexicon at high social risk. *Development and Psychopathology, 6,* 5–30.

Bleiberg, E. (1984). Narcissistic disorders in children. *Bulletin of the Menninger Clinic, 48,* 501–517.

Bowlby, J. (1969). *Attachment and loss: Vol. 1. Attachment.* New York: Basic Books.

Bowlby, J. (1973). *Attachment and loss: Vol. 2. Separation: Anxiety and anger.* New York: Basic Books.

Bowlby, J. (1980). *Attachment and loss: Vol. 3. Loss, sadness, and depression.* New York: Basic Books.

Bretherton, I. (1987). New perspectives on attachment relations: Security, communication, and internal working models. In J. D. Osofsky (Ed.), *Handbook of infant development* (2nd ed., pp. 1061–1101). New York: Wiley.

Bretherton, I. (1991). Pouring new wine into old bottles: The social self as internal working model. In M. R. Gunnar & L. A. Sroufe (Eds.), *Minnesota Symposia on Child Development: Vol. 23. Self processes and development* (pp. 1–41). Hillsdale, NJ: Erlbaum.

Bretherton, I. (1993). From dialogue to internal working models: The co-construction of self in relationships. In C. A. Nelson (Ed.), *Minnesota Symposia on Child Psychology: Vol. 26. Memory and affect* (pp. 237–363). Hillsdale, NJ: Erlbaum.

Bretherton, I., & Beeghly, M. (1982). Talking about internal states: The acquisition of an explicit theory of mind. *Developmental Psychology, 18,* 906–921.

Briere, J. (1989). *Therapy for adults molested as children.* New York: Springer.

Briere, J. (1992). *Child abuse trauma: Theory and treatment of the lasting effects.* Newbury Park, CA: Sage.

Broughton, J. (1978). The development of the concepts of self, mind, reality, and knowledge. In W. Damon (Ed.), *Social cognition* (pp. 75–100). San Francisco: Jossey-Bass.

Brown, B. B. (1990). Peer groups and peer cultures. In S. S. Feldman & G. Elliot (Eds.), *At the threshold: The developing adolescent* (pp. 171–196). Cambridge, MA: Harvard University Press.

Carlson, V., Cicchetti, D., & Barnett, D. (1989). Disorganized/disoriented attachment relationships in maltreated infants. *Developmental Psychology, 25,* 525–531.

Carroll, J. J., & Steward, M. S. (1984). The role of cognitive development in children's understandings of their own feelings. *Child Development, 55,* 1486–1492.

Case, R. (1985). *Intellectual development: Birth to adulthood.* New York: Academic Press.

Case, R. (1992). *The mind's staircase.* Hillsdale, NJ: Erlbaum.

Cassidy, J., & Kobak, R. R. (1988). Avoidance and its relationship to other defensive processes. In J. Belsky & T. Nezworski (Eds.), *Clinical implications of attachment* (pp. 300–326). Hillsdale, NJ: Erlbaum.

Chodorow, N. (1989). *Feminism and psychoanalytic theory.* New Haven, CT: Yale University Press.

Cicchetti, D. (1989). How research on child maltreatment has informed the study of child development: Perspectives from developmental psychology. In D. Cicchetti & V. Carlson (Eds.), *Child maltreatment: Theory and research on the causes and consequences of child abuse and neglect* (pp. 309–350). New York: Cambridge University Press.

Cicchetti, D. (1993). Developmental psychopathology: Reactions, reflections, and projections. *Developmental Review, 13,* 471–502.

Cicchetti, D. (2004). An odyssey of discovery: Lessons learned through three decades of research on child maltreatment. *American Psychologist, 59,* 728–741.

Cicchetti, D., Beeghly, M., Carlson, V., & Toth, S. L. (1990). The emergence of the self in atypical populations. In D. Cicchetti & M. Beeghly (Eds.), *The self in transition: Infancy to childhood* (pp. 309–340). Chicago: University of Chicago Press.

Cicchetti, D., & Cohen, D. J. (1995). Perspectives in developmental psychopathology. In D. Cicchetti & D. J. Cohen (Eds.), *Developmental psychopathology: Theory and methods* (Vol. 1, pp. 3–22). New York: Wiley.

Cicchetti, D., & Rogosch, F. A. (1996). Equifinality and multifinality in developmental psychopathology. *Development and Psychopathology, 8,* 597–600.

Cicchetti, D., & Rogosch, F. A. (2001). Diverse patterns of neuroendocrine activity in maltreated children. *Development and Psychopathology, 13,* 677–694.

Cooley, C. H. (1902). *Human nature and the social order.* New York: Charles Scribner & Sons.

Cooper, C. R., Grotevant, H. D., & Condon, S. M. (1983). Individuality and connectedness both foster adolescent identity formation and role taking skills. In H. D. Grotevant & C. R. Cooper (Eds.), *Adolescent development in the family: New directions for child development* (pp. 43–59). San Francisco: Jossey-Bass.

Cooper, C. R., Jackson, J. F., Azmitia, M., Lopez, E., & Dunbar, N. (1995). Bridging students' multiple worlds: African American and Latino youth in academic outreach programs. In R. F. Marcias & R. G. Garcia-Ramos (Eds.), *Changing schools, changing students: An anthology of research on language minorities* (pp. 211–234). Santa Barbara: University of California Linguistic Minority Research Institute.

Coster, W. J., Gersten, M. S., Beeghly, M., & Cicchetti, D. (1989). Communicative functioning in maltreated toddlers. *Developmental Psychology, 25,* 1020–1029.

Crittenden, P. M. (1994). Peering into the black box: An exploratory treatise on the development of self in young children. In D. Cicchetti & S. L. Toth (Eds.), *Rochester Symposium on Developmental Psychopathology: Vol. 5. Disorders and dysfunctions of the self* (pp. 79–148). Rochester, NY: University of Rochester Press.

Crittenden, P. M., & Ainsworth, M. D. S. (1989). Child maltreatment and attachment theory. In D. Cicchetti & V. Carlson (Eds.), *Theory and research on the causes and consequences of child abuse and neglect* (pp. 432–463). New York: Cambridge University Press.

Damon, W., & Hart, D. (1988). *Self-understanding in childhood and adolescence.* New York: Cambridge University Press.

Dickstein, E. (1977). Self and self-esteem: Theoretical foundations and their implications for research. *Human Development, 20,* 129–140.

Donaldson, S. K., & Westerman, M. A. (1986). Development of children's understandings of ambivalence and causal theories of emotion. *Developmental Psychology, 22,* 655–662.

Dunn, J. (1988). *The beginnings of social understanding.* Cambridge, MA: Harvard University Press.

Dunn, J., Brown, J., & Beardsall, L. (1991). Family talk about feeling states and children's later understanding of others' emotions. *Developmental Psychology, 27,* 445–448.

Eccles, J. P., & Midgley, C. (1989). State/environment fit: Developmentally appropriate classrooms for early adolescents. In R. Ames & C. Ames (Eds.), *Research on motivation in education* (Vol. 3, pp. 139–181). New York: Academic Press.

Eccles, J. S., Midgley, C., & Adler, T. (1984). Grade-related changes in the school environment: Effects on achievement motivation. In

J. G. Nicholls (Ed.), *The development of achievement motivation* (pp. 282–231). Greenwich, CT: JSI Press.

Eichenbaum, L., & Orbach, S. (1993). *Understanding women: A feminist psychoanalytic approach*. New York: Basic Books.

Eisenberg, A. (1985). Learning to describe past experiences in conversation. *Discourse Processes, 8,* 177–204.

Elkind, D. (1967). Egocentrism in adolescence. *Child Development, 38,* 1025–1034.

Engel, M. (1959). The stability of the self-concept in adolescence. *Journal of Abnormal and Social Psychology, 58,* 211–217.

Epstein, S. (1973). The self-concept revisited or a theory of a theory. *American Psychologist, 28,* 405–416.

Epstein, S. (1981). The unity principle versus the reality and pleasure principles or the tale of the scorpion and the frog. In M. D. Lynch, A. A. Norem-Hebeisen, & K. Gergen (Eds.), *Self-concept: Advances in theory and research* (pp. 82–110). Cambridge, MA: Ballinger.

Epstein, S. (1991). Cognitive-experiential self theory: Implications for developmental psychology. In M. R. Gunnar & L. A. Sroufe (Eds.), *Minnesota Symposium on Child Development: Vol. 23. Self-processes and development* (pp. 111–137). Hillsdale, NJ: Erlbaum.

Erickson, M. F., Egeland, B., & Pianta, R. (1989). The effects of maltreatment on the development of young children. In Cicchetti & V. Carlson (Eds.), *Child maltreatment: Theory and research on the causes and consequences of child abuse and neglect* (pp. 647–684). New York: Cambridge University Press.

Erikson, E. H. (1959). Identity and the life cycle. *Psychological Issues, 1,* 18–164.

Erikson, E. H. (1968). *Identity, youth, and crisis.* New York: Norton.

Fischer, K. W. (1980). A theory of cognitive development: The control and construction of hierarchies of skills. *Psychological Review, 87,* 477–531.

Fischer, K. W., & Ayoub, C. (1994). Affective splitting and dissociation in normal and maltreated children: Developmental pathways for self in relationships. In D. Cicchetti & S. Toth (Eds.), *Rochester Symposium on Developmental Psychopathology: Vol. 5. Disorders and dysfunctions of the self* (pp. 149–222). Rochester, NY: University of Rochester Press.

Fischer, K. W., & Canfield, R. (1986). The ambiguity of stage and structure in behavior: Person and environment in the development of psychological structure. In I. Levin (Ed.), *Stage and structure: Reopening the debate* (pp. 246–267). New York: Plenum Press.

Fischer, K. W., Hand, H. H., Watson, M. W., Van Parys, M., & Tucker, J. (1984). Putting the child into socialization: The development of social categories in preschool children. In L. Katz (Ed.), *Current topics in early childhood education* (Vol. 5, pp. 27–72). Norwood, NJ: Ablex.

Fischer, K. W., Shaver, P., & Carnochan, P. (1990). How emotions develop and how they organize development. *Cognition and Emotion, 4,* 81–127.

Fivush, R., Gray, J. T., & Fromhoff, F. A. (1987). Two-year-olds talk about the past. *Cognitive Development, 2,* 393–409.

Fivush, R., & Hamond, N. R. (1990). Autobiographical memory across the preschool years: Toward reconceptualizing childhood amnesia. In R. Fivush & J. A. Hudson (Eds.), *Knowing and remembering in young children* (pp. 223–248). New York: Cambridge University Press.

Fivush, R., & Hudson, J. A. (Eds.). (1990). *Knowing and remembering in young children.* New York: Cambridge University Press.

Flavell, J. H. (1985). *Cognitive development* (2nd ed.). Englewood Cliffs, NJ: Prentice-Hall.

Freud, A. (1965). *Normality and pathology in childhood.* New York: International Universities Press.

Freud, S. (1952). *A general introduction to psychoanalysis.* New York: Washington Square Press.

Frey, K. S., & Ruble, D. N. (1985). What children say when the teacher is not around: Conflicting goals in social comparison and performance assessment in the classroom. *Journal of Personality and Social Psychology, 48,* 550–562.

Frey, K. S., & Ruble, D. N. (1990). Strategies for comparative evaluation: Maintaining a sense of competence across the life span. In R. J. Sternberg & J. Kolligian Jr. (Eds.), *Competence considered* (pp. 167–189). New Haven, CT: Yale University Press.

Gecas, V. (1972). Parental behavior and contextual variations in adolescent self-esteem. *Sociometry, 36,* 332–345.

Gergen, K. J. (1968). Personal consistency and the presentation of self. In C. Gordon & J. Gergen (Eds.), *The self in social interaction* (pp. 299–308). New York: Wiley.

Gesell, A., & Ilg, F. (1946). *The child from five to ten.* New York: Harper & Row.

Gilligan, C. (1982). *In a different voice: Psychological theory and women's development.* Cambridge, MA: Harvard University Press.

Gilligan, C., Lyons, N., & Hanmer, T. J. (1989). *Making connections.* Cambridge, MA: Harvard University Press.

Glick, M., & Zigler, E. (1985). Self-image: A cognitive-developmental approach. In R. Leahy (Ed.), *The development of the self* (pp. 1–54). New York: Academy Press.

Gnepp, J., McKee, E., & Domanic, J. A. (1987). Children's use of situational information to infer emotion: Understanding emotionally equivocal situations. *Developmental Psychology, 23,* 114–123.

Gralinsky, J., Fesbach, N. D., Powell, C., & Derrington, T. (1993, April). *Self-understanding: Meaning and measurement of maltreated children's sense of self.* Paper presented at the meeting of the Society for Research in Child Development, New Orleans, LA.

Greenwald, A. G. (1980). The totalitarian ego: Fabrication and revision of personal history. *American Psychologist, 7,* 603–618.

Griffin, N., Chassin, L., & Young, R. D. (1981). Measurement of global self-concept versus multiple role specific self-concepts in adolescents. *Adolescence, 49–56.*

Griffin, S. (1992). Structural analysis of the development of their inner world: A neo-structured analysis of the development of intrapersonal intelligence. In R. Case (Ed.), *The mind's staircase* (pp. 189–206). Hillsdale, NJ: Erlbaum.

Grotevant, H. D., & Cooper, C. R. (1986). Individuation in family relationships. *Human Development, 29,* 83–100.

Haltiwanger, J. (1989, April). *Behavioral referents of presented self-esteem in young children.* Paper presented at the meeting of the Society for Research in Child Development, Kansas City, MO.

Harris, P. L. (1983). What children know about the situations that provoke emotion. In M. Lewis & C. Saarni (Eds.), *The socialization of affect* (pp. 162–185). New York: Plenum Press.

Harris, P. L., Olthof, T., & Meerum-Terwogt, M. (1981). Children's knowledge of emotion. *Journal of Experimental Child Psychology, 36,* 490–509.

Hart, D. (1988). The adolescent self-concept in social context. In D. K. Lapsley & F. C. Power (Eds.), *Self, ego, and identity* (pp. 71–90). New York: Springer-Verlag.

Harter, S. (1983). Developmental perspectives on the self-system. In P. Mussen & E. M. Hetherington (Eds.), *Handbook of child psychology: Vol. 4. Socialization, personality, and social development* (4th ed., pp. 275–385). New York: Wiley.

Harter, S. (1985). *The Self-Perception Profile for Children.* Unpublished manual, University of Denver, Denver, CO.

Harter, S. (1986a). Cognitive-developmental processes in the integration of concepts about emotions and the self. *Social Cognition, 4,* 119–151.

Harter, S. (1986b). Processes underlying the construction, maintenance, and enhancement of the self-concept in children. In J. Suls & A. G. Greenwald (Eds.), *Psychological perspectives on the self* (Vol. 3, pp. 137–181). Hillsdale, NJ: Erlbaum.

Harter, S. (1990a). Adolescent self and identity development. In S. S. Feldman & G. R. Elliot (Eds.), *At the threshold: The developing adolescent* (pp. 352–387). Cambridge, MA: Harvard University Press.

Harter, S. (1990b). Causes, correlates and the functional role of global self-worth: A life-span perspective. In R. Sternberg & J. Kolligian Jr. (Eds.), *Competence considered* (pp. 67–98). New Haven, CT: Yale University Press.

Harter, S. (1993). Causes and consequences of low self-esteem in children and adolescents. In R. Baumeister (Ed.), *Self-esteem: The puzzle of low self-regard* (pp. 87–116). New York: Plenum.

Harter, S. (1996). Teacher and classmate influences on scholastic motivation, self-esteem, and choice. In K. Wentzel & J. Juvonen (Eds.), *Social motivation: Understanding children's school adjustment* (pp. 11–42). Cambridge, England: Cambridge University Press.

Harter, S. (1998). The development of self-representations. In W. Damon (Series Ed.) & N. Eisenberg (Vol. Ed.), *Handbook of child psychology: Vol. 3. Social emotional, and personality development* (5th ed., pp. 553–617). New York: Wiley.

Harter, S. (1999). *The construction of the self.* New York: Guilford Press.

Harter, S. (in press). Symbolic interactionism revisited: Potential liabilities for the self constructed in the crucible of interpersonal relationships. *Merrill-Palmer Quarterly.*

Harter, S., Bresnick, S., Bouchey, H. A., & Whitesell, N. R. (1997). The development of multiple role-related selves during adolescence. *Development and Psychopathology, 9,* 835–854.

Harter, S., & Buddin, B. J. (1987). Children's understanding of the simultaneity of two emotions: A five-stage developmental acquisition sequence. *Developmental Psychology, 23,* 388–399.

Harter, S., Kiang, L., Whitesell, N. R., & Anderson, A. V. (2003, April). *A prototype approach to the emotion of humiliation in college students.* Poster presented at the Society for Research in Child Development Convention, in Tampa, FL.

Harter, S., Low, S., & Whitesell, N. R. (2003). What have we learned from Columbine: The impact of the self-system on suicidal and violent ideation among adolescents. *Journal of Youth Violence, 2,* 3–26.

Harter, S., Marold, D. B., Whitesell, N. R., & Cobbs, G. (1996). A model of the effects of parent and peer support on adolescent false self behavior. *Child Development, 55,* 1969–1982.

Harter, S., & McCarley, K. (2004, April). *Is there a dark side to high self-esteem leading to adolescent violence?* Poster presented at the American Psychological Association Convention, Honolulu.

Harter, S., & Monsour, A. (1992). Developmental analysis of conflict caused by opposing attributes in the adolescent self-portrait. *Developmental Psychology, 28,* 251–260.

Harter, S., & Pike, R. (1984). The pictorial scale of perceived competence and social acceptance for young children. *Child Development, 55,* 1969–1982.

Harter, S., Waters, P., & Whitesell, N. R. (1998). Relational self-worth: Differences in perceived worth of a person across interpersonal contexts. *Child Development, 69,* 756–766.

Harter, S., & Whitesell, N. R. (1989). Developmental changes in children's understanding of single, multiple and blended emotion concepts. In C. Saarni & P. L. Harris (Eds.), *Children's understanding of*

emotion (pp. 81–116). Cambridge, England: Cambridge University Press.

Hatfield, E., & Sprecher, S. (1986). *Mirror, mirror . . . The importance of appearance in everyday life.* New York: State University of New York Press.

Hayne, H. (2004). Infant memory development: Implications for childhood amnesia. *Developmental Review, 24,* 33–73.

Herman, J. (1992). *Trauma and recovery.* New York: Basic Books.

Higgins, E. T. (1991). Development of self-regulatory and self-evaluative processes: Costs, benefits, and tradeoffs. In M. R. Gunnar & L. A. Sroufe (Eds.), *Minnesota Symposia on Child Development: Vol. 23. Self processes and development* (pp. 125–166). Hillsdale, NJ: Erlbaum.

Higgins, E. T., & Bargh, J. A. (1987). Social cognition and social perception. *Annual Review of Psychology, 38,* 369–425.

Hill, J. P., & Holmbeck, G. N. (1986). Attachment and autonomy during adolescence. In G. J. Whitehurst (Ed.), *Annals of child development* (Vol. 3, pp. 145–189). Greenwich, CT: JAI Press.

Howe, M. L. (2003). Memories from the cradle. *Current Directions in Psychological Science, 12,* 62–65.

Howe, M. L., & Courage, M. L. (1993). On resolving the enigma of infantile amnesia. *Psychological Bulletin, 113,* 305–326.

Hudson, J. A. (1990a). Constructive processes in children's autobiographical memory. *Developmental Psychology, 26,* 180–187.

Hudson, J. A. (1990b). The emergence of autobiographical memory in mother-child conversation. In R. Fivush & J. A. Hudson (Eds.), *Knowing and remembering in young children* (pp. 166–196). New York: Cambridge University Press.

James, W. (1890). *Principles of psychology.* Chicago: Encyclopedia Britannica.

James, W. (1892). *Psychology: The briefer course.* New York: Henry Holt.

Jordan, J. V. (1991). The relational self: A new perspective for understanding women's development. In J. Strauss & G. Goethals (Eds.), *The self: Interdisciplinary approaches* (pp. 136–149). New York: Springer-Verlag.

Kagan, J. (1984). *The nature of the child.* New York: Basic Books.

Keating, D. P. (1990). Adolescent thinking. In S. S. Feldman & G. Elliot (Eds.), *At the threshold: The developing adolescent* (pp. 54–90). Cambridge, MA: Harvard University Press.

Kelly, G. A. (1955). *The psychology of personal constructs.* New York: Norton.

Kendall-Tackett, K. A., Williams, L. M., & Finkelhor, D. (1993). Impact of sexual abuse on children: A review and synthesis of recent empirical studies. *Psychological Bulletin, 113,* 164–180.

Kennedy, B. (1994). *The development of self-understanding in adolescence.* Unpublished doctoral dissertation, Harvard University, Cambridge, MA.

Kiang, L., & Harter, S. (2004). *Social-cultural values of appearance and attachment processes: An integrated model of eating disorder symptomatology.* Unpublished manuscript, University of Denver.

Kilbourne, J. (1994). Still killing us softly: Advertising and the obsession with thinness. In P. Fallon, M. Katzman, & S. Wooley (Eds.), *Feminist perspectives on eating disorders* (pp. 395–418). New York: Guilford Press.

Lapsley, D. K., & Rice, K. (1988). The "new look" at the imaginary audience and personal fable: Toward a general model of adolescent ego development. In D. K. Lapsley & F. C. Power (Eds.), *Self, ego, and identity: Integrative approaches* (pp. 109–129). New York: Springer-Verlag.

Leahy, R. L., & Shirk, S. R. (1985). Social cognition and the development of the self. In R. L. Leahy (Ed.), *The development of the self* (pp. 123–150). New York: Academic Press.

Lewis, M. (1991). Ways of knowing: Objective self awareness or consciousness. *Developmental Review, 11,* 231–243.

Lewis, M. (1994). Myself and me. In S. T. Parker, R. W. Mitchell, & M. L. Boccia (Eds.), *Self-awareness in animals and humans: Developmental perspectives* (pp. 20–34). New York: Cambridge University Press.

Lewis, M., & Brooks-Gunn, J. (1979). *Social cognition and the acquisition of self.* New York: Plenum Press.

Linville, P. W. (1987). Self-complexity as a cognitive buffer against stress-related illness and depression. *Journal of Personality and Social Psychology, 52,* 663–676.

Luthar, S. S., & Cicchetti, D. (2000). The construct of resilience: Implications for intervention and social policy. *Development and Psychopathology, 71,* 543–562.

Maccoby, E. (1980). *Social development.* New York: Wiley.

Macfie, J., Cicchetti, D., & Toth, S. (2001). The development of dissociation in maltreated preschool-aged children. *Development and Psychopathology, 13,* 233–254.

Mack, J. E. (1983). Self-esteem and its development: An overview. In J. E. Mack & S. L. Ablong (Eds.), *The development and sustaining of self-esteem* (pp. 1–44). New York: International Universities Press.

Main, M., & Solomon, J. (1990). Procedures for identifying infants as disorganized/disoriented during the Ainsworth Strange Situation. In M. Greenberg, D. Cicchetti, & M. Cummings (Eds.), *Attachment during the preschool years: Theory, research, and intervention* (pp. 121–160). Chicago: University of Chicago Press.

Markus, H. (1980). The self in thought and memory. In D. M. Wegner & R. R. Vallacher (Eds.), *The self in social psychology* (pp. 42–69). New York: Oxford University Press.

Markus, H., & Nurius, P. (1996). Possible selves. *American Psychologist, 41,* 954–969.

Mascolo, M. F., & Fischer, K. W. (1995). Developmental transformations in appraisals for pride, shame, and guilt. In J. P. Tangney & K. W. Fischer (Eds.), *Self-conscious emotions: The psychology of shame, guilt, embarrassment, and pride* (pp. 64–113). New York: Guilford Press.

McCann, I. L., & Pearlman, L. A. (1992). *Psychological trauma and the adult survivor* (pp. 211–259). New York: Brunner/Mazel.

McCarthy, J., & Hoge, D. (1982). Analysis of age effects in longitudinal studies of adolescent self-esteem. *Developmental Psychology, 18,* 372–379.

McGuire, S., Manke, B., Saudino, K. J., Reiss, D., Hetherington, E. M., & Plomin, R. (1999). Perceived competence and self-worth during adolescence: A longitudinal behavioral genetic study. *Child Development, 70,* 1283–1296.

Miller, A. (1990). *Thou shalt not be aware.* New York: Meridan.

Miller, J. B. (1986). *Toward a new psychology of women* (2nd ed.). Boston: Beacon Press.

Miller, P. J., Potts, R., Fung, H., Hoogstra, L., & Mintz, J. (1990). Narrative practices and the social construction of self in childhood. *American Ethnologist, 17,* 292–311.

Mischel, W. (1973). Toward a cognitive social learning reconceptualization of personality. *Psychological Review, 80,* 252–283.

Moretti, M. M., & Higgins, E. T. (1990). The development of self-esteem vulnerabilities: Social and cognitive factors in developmental psychopathology. In R. J. Sternberg & J. Kolligian Jr. (Eds.), *Competence considered* (pp. 286–314). New Haven, CT: Yale University Press.

Neiss, M. B., Sedikides, C., & Stevenson, J. (2002). Self-esteem: A behavioural genetic perspective. *European Journal of Personality, 16,* 351–367.

Nelson, K. (1986). *Event knowledge: Structure and function in development.* Hillsdale, NJ: Erlbaum.

Nelson, K. (Ed.). (1989). *Narratives from the crib.* Cambridge, MA: Harvard University Press.

Nelson, K. (1990). Remembering, forgetting, and childhood amnesia. In R. Fivush & J. A. Hudson (Eds.), *Knowing and remembering in young children* (pp. 301–316). New York: Cambridge University Press.

Nelson, K. (1993). Events, narratives, memory: What develops. In C. A. Nelson (Ed.), *Minnesota Symposia on Child Psychology: Vol. 26. Memory and affect* (pp. 1–24). Hillsdale, NJ: Erlbaum.

Nolen-Hoeksema, S., & Girgus, J. S. (1994). The emergence of gender differences in depression during adolescence. *Psychological Bulletin, 115,* 424–443.

O'Malley, P., & Bachman, J. (1983). Self-esteem: Change and stability between 13 and 23. *Developmental Psychology, 19,* 257–268.

Oosterwegel, A., & Oppenheimer, L. (1993). Development of the self-system: How children perceive their own and others' ideas about themselves. *Journal of Applied Developmental Psychology, 14,* 443–460.

Pennington, B. F. (2002). *The development of psychopathology.* New York: Guilford Press.

Piaget, J. (1932). *The moral judgment of the child.* New York: Harcourt, Brace & World.

Piaget, J. (1960). *The psychology of intelligence.* Patterson, NJ: Littlefield-Adams.

Pillemer, D. B., & White, S. H. (1989). Childhood events recalled by children and adults. In H. W. Reese (Ed.), *Advances in child development and behavior* (Vol. 21, pp. 297–340). San Diego: Academic Press.

Pipp, S. (1990). Sensorimotor and representational internal representational working models of self, other, and relationship: Mechanisms of connection and separation. In D. Cicchetti & M. Beeghly (Eds.), *The self in transition: Infancy to childhood* (pp. 243–264). Chicago: University of Chicago Press.

Pomeranz, E. V., Ruble, D. N., Frey, K. S., & Greulich, F. (1995). Meeting goals and confronting conflict: Children's changing perceptions of social comparison. *Child Development, 66,* 723–738.

Putnam, F. W. (1993). Dissociation and disturbances of the self. In D. Cicchetti & S. Toth (Eds.), *Rochester Symposium on Developmental Psychopathology: Vol. 5. Disorders and dysfunctions of the self* (pp. 251–266). Rochester, NY: University of Rochester Press.

Reissland, N. (1985). The development of concepts of simultaneity in children's understanding of emotions. *Journal of Child Psychology and Psychiatry, 26,* 811–824.

Rogoff, B. (1990). *Apprenticeship in thinking.* New York: Oxford University Press.

Rosenberg, M. (1979). *Conceiving the self.* New York: Basic Books.

Rosenberg, M. (1986). Self-concept from middle childhood through adolescence. In J. Suls & A. G. Greenwald (Eds.), *Psychological perspective on the self* (Vol. 3, pp. 107–135). Hillsdale, NJ: Erlbaum.

Rossman, B. B., & Rosenberg, M. S. (Eds.). (1998). *Multiple victimization of children.* New York: Haworth Press.

Rubin, L. (1985). *Just friends: The role of friendship in our lives.* New York: Harper.

Ruble, D. N., & Dweck, C. (1995). Self-conceptions, person conception, and development. In N. Eisenberg (Ed.), *Review of personality and social psychology: The interface* (Vol. 15, pp. 109–139). Thousand Oaks, CA: Sage.

Ruble, D. N., & Frey, K. S. (1991). Changing patterns of comparative behavior as skills are acquired: A functional model of self-evaluation. In J. Suls & T. A. Wills (Eds.), *Social comparison: Contemporary theory and research* (pp. 70–112). Hillsdale, NJ: Erlbaum.

Rutter, M., & Sroufe, L. A. (2000). Developmental psychopathology: Concepts and challenges. *Development and Psychopathology, 12,* 265–296.

Sameroff, A. (2000). Development systems and psychopathology. *Development and Psychopathology, 12,* 297–312.

Sarbin, T. R. (1962). A preface to a psychological analysis of the self. *Psychological Review, 59,* 11–22.

Savin-Williams, R. C., & Berndt, T. J. (1990). Friend and peer relations. In S. S. Feldman & G. Elliot (Eds.), *At the threshold: The developing adolescent* (pp. 277–307). Cambridge, MA: Harvard University Press.

Schneider-Rosen, K., Braunwald, K. G., Carlson, V., & Cicchetti, D. (1985). Current perspectives in attachment theory: Illustration from the study of maltreated infants. In I. Bretherton & E. Waters (Eds.), *Growing points in attachment theory and research: Monographs of the Society for Research in Child Development* (Vol. 50, pp. 104–210). Chicago: University of Chicago Press.

Selman, R. L. (1980). *The growth of interpersonal understanding.* New York: Academic Press.

Siegler, R. S. (1991). *Children's thinking* (2nd ed.). Englewood Cliffs, NJ: Prentice-Hall.

Simmons, R. G., & Blyth, D. A. (1987). *Moving into adolescence: The impact of pubertal change and school context.* New York: Aldine de Gruyter.

Simmons, R. G., Rosenberg, F., & Rosenberg, M. (1973). Disturbances in the self-images at adolescence. *American Sociological Review, 38,* 553–568.

Smollar, J., & Youniss, J. (1985). Adolescent self-concept development. In R. L. Leahy (Ed.), *The development of self* (pp. 247–266). New York: Academic Press.

Snow, K. (1990). Building memories: The ontogeny of autobiography. In D. Cicchetti & M. Beeghly (Eds.), *The self in transition: Infancy to childhood* (pp. 213–242). Chicago: University of Chicago Press.

Sroufe, L. A. (1990). An organizational perspective on the self. In D. Cicchetti & M. Beeghly (Eds.), *The self in transition: Infancy to childhood* (pp. 281–308). Chicago: University of Chicago Press.

Sroufe, L. A., & Fleeson, J. (1986). Attachment and the construction of relationships. In W. Hartup & Z. Rubin (Eds.), *Relationships and development* (pp. 51–71). New York: Cambridge University Press.

Sroufe, L. A., & Rutter, M. (1984). The domain of developmental psychopathology. *Child Development, 55,* 17–29.

Steinberg, L. (1990). Interdependency in the family: Autonomy, conflict, autonomy in the parent-adolescent relationship. In S. Feldman & G. Elliot (Eds.), *At the threshold: The developing adolescent* (pp. 255–276). Cambridge, MA: Harvard University Press.

Steinberg, L., & Silverberg, S. B. (1986). The vicissitudes of autonomy in adolescence. *Child Development, 57,* 841–851.

Stern, D. (1985). *The interpersonal world of the infant.* New York: Basic Books.

Stipek, D. (1995). The development of pride and shame in toddlers. In J. P. Tangney & K. W. Fischer (Eds.), *Self-conscious emotions: The psychology of shame, embarrassment, and pride* (pp. 237–252). New York: Guilford Press.

Stipek, D., Recchia, S., & McClintic, S. (1992). Self-evaluation in young children: *Monographs of the Society for Research in Child Development, 57,* 1–84.

Sullivan, H. S. (1953). *The interpersonal theory of psychiatry.* New York: Norton.

Suls, J., & Sanders, G. (1982). Self-evaluation via social comparison: A developmental analysis. In L. Wheeler (Ed.), *Review of personality and social psychology* (Vol. 3, pp. 67–89). Beverly Hills, CA: Sage.

Terr, L. (1990). *Too scared to cry.* New York: Basic Books.

Terr, L. (1991). Childhood traumas: An outline and overview. *American Journal of Psychiatry, 148,* 10–20.

Tessler, M. (1991). *Making memories together: The influence of mother-child joint encoding on the development of autobiographical memory style.* Unpublished doctoral dissertation, City University of New York Graduate Center, New York.

Toth, S. L., Cicchetti, D., Macfie, J., & Emde, R. N. (1997). Representations of self and other in the narrative of neglected, physically abused, and sexually abused preschoolers. *Development and Psychopathology, 9,* 781–796.

Toth, S. L., Cicchetti, D., Macfie, J., Maughan, A., & Vanmeenen, K. (2000). Narrative representations of caregivers and self in male preschoolers. *Attachment and Human Development, 2,* 271–305.

Vallacher, R. R. (1980). An introduction to self-theory. In D. M. Wegner & R. R. Vallacher (Eds.), *The self in social psychology* (pp. 3–30). New York: Oxford University Press.

van der Kolk, B. A. (1987). *Psychological trauma.* Washington, DC: American Psychiatric Press.

Watson, M. (1990). Aspects of self development as reflected in children's role playing. In D. Cicchetti & M. Beeghly (Eds.), *The self in transition: Infancy to childhood* (pp. 281–307). Chicago: University of Chicago Press.

Watson, M., & Fischer, K. (1993). Structural change in children's understanding of family roles and divorce. In R. R. Cocking & K. A. Renninger (Eds.), *The development and meaning of psychological distance* (pp. 123–144). Hillsdale, NJ: Erlbaum.

Westen, D. (1993). The impact of sexual abuse on self structure. In D. Cicchetti & S. Toth (Eds.), *Rochester Symposium on Developmental Psychopathology: Vol. 5. Disorders and dysfunctions of the self* (pp. 223–250). Rochester, NY: University of Rochester Press.

White, K., Speisman, J., & Costos, D. (1983). Young adults and their parents: Individuation to mutuality. In H. D. Grotevant & C. R. Cooper (Eds.), *New directions for child development: Adolescent development in the family* (pp. 61–76). San Francisco: Jossey-Bass.

Winnicott, D. W. (1958). *From pediatrics to psychoanalysis.* London: Hogarth Press.

Winnicott, D. W. (1965). *The maturational processes and the facilitating environment.* New York: International Universities Press.

Wolf, D. P. (1990). Being of several minds: Voices and version of the self in early childhood. In D. Cicchetti & M. Beeghly (Eds.), *The self in transition: Infancy to childhood* (pp. 183–212). Chicago: University of Chicago Press.

Wolfe, D. (1989). *Child abuse.* Newbury Park, CA: Sage.

Wylie, R. C. (1979). *The self concept: Theory and research on selected topics* (Vol. 2). Lincoln: University of Nebraska Press.

Wylie, R. C. (1989). *Measures of self-concept.* Lincoln: University of Nebraska Press.

CHAPTER 12

Peer Relationships, Child Development, and Adjustment: A Developmental Psychopathology Perspective

JEFFREY G. PARKER, KENNETH H. RUBIN, STEPHEN A. ERATH, JULIE C. WOJSLAWOWICZ, and ALLISON A. BUSKIRK

It is a measure of the persuasiveness of the cumulative body of research on children's peer relationships that it has become trite to claim that peer experiences significantly shape development and the development of psychopathology. Few contemporary psychologists—and few laypersons, for that matter—doubt that children come to know themselves at least partly from how they are treated by peers; that relationships with peers provide rich opportunities for learning cooperation, gaining support, or developing interpersonal skills; or that persistent difficulties in getting along with childhood peers are likely to portend difficulties with others later in life and, in the extreme, clinically significant behavioral and affective disorders.

This has not always been the case. When we introduced this chapter a decade ago, we noted its timeliness by observing that it coincided with what appeared to be a nascent and important shift away from "regarded variations in children's experiences with peers as derivative of broader achievements or failings of personality development and without developmental consequences of their own" (Parker, Rubin, Price, & DeRosier, 1995, p. 96).

Even as the developmental significance of peer experiences has become less disputable, understanding the roots and consequences of peer experiences has grown more complex and arguably less tractable. To begin with, it is more difficult now than a decade ago to understand which children are experiencing difficulties with their peer relationships. The past decade has witnessed unprecedented advances in the development and refinement of methods for studying adjustment with peers (e.g., see Bukowski & Cillessen, 1998), so much so that space considerations now prevent us from treating assessment issues as comprehensively as we did a decade ago. If advances in assessments have made unprecedented progress, why is it so much harder today than a decade ago to represent children's peer difficulties?

The paradox lies in the growing appreciation for the great diversity of ways in which success or failure with peers may be played out in life and represented in assessments. A decade ago, the effort to conceptualize and assess individual differences in children's adjustment with peers was dominated by a focus on sociometric status in school classrooms and grades. A watershed in interest in peer group acceptance and rejection may have been reached in the early 1990s beginning with the publication of a landmark volume edited by Asher and Coie (1990), but research on this construct remains a dominate focus today (e.g., Cillessen & Bukowski, 2000; Furman, 1996).

Today, evidence has slowly mounted to suggest that gauging adjustment with peers is not as simple as understanding the degree to which individuals are accepted or rejected by significant peer groups. Instead, steady progress has been made, especially recently, in understanding that other dimensions of adjustment also exist and carry weight. For example, researchers have suggested that being well liked or popular in a peer group may be something altogether distinct from being perceived by other children as popular (Lease, Kennedy, & Axelrod, 2002; Lease, Musgrove, & Axelrod, 2002). Some children are perceived by peers to be popular, although more objective assessments indicate that they are not. When compared to children who are well liked by others, children perceived to be popular appear to have some personal characteristics that are more usually associated with rejection (Buskirk, Rubin, Burgess, Booth-LaForce, & Rose-Krasnor, 2004; LaFontana & Cillessen, 1999; Parkhurst & Hopmeyer, 1998). Another element of complication derives from recent research on friendship. Friendship and acceptance are connected in important ways (e.g., George & Hartmann, 1996; Newcomb, Bukowski, & Bagwell, 1999; Sabongui, Bukowski, & Newcomb, 1998). However, friendships appear to play different functions in children's development than does group acceptance; moreover, group acceptance neither guarantees nor precludes successful friendship experiences (Asher, Parker, & Walker, 1996; Bigelow, Tesson, & Lewko, 1996; Brendgen, Little, & Krappmann, 2000; Hoza, Molina, Bukowski, & Sippola,

1995; Ladd, Kochenderfer, & Coleman, 1997; Parker, Saxon, Asher, & Kovacs, 1999). Yet another element of complication is the recent discovery that children develop enemies somewhat independently of their group standing and success with friends (Abecassis, 2003; Parker & Gamm, 2003). We have only a beginning understanding of the developmental significance of such mutual antipathies, but we can conclude safely at this early stage that the presence of these relationships challenges our understanding of social competence and what it means to be successful with agemates (Hodges & Card, 2003).

An additional challenge stems from recent recognition that many ostensibly positive peer experiences may also encourage maladjustment. For example, decades of research have documented the social difficulties of aggressive children, but new evidence suggests that, in specific circumstances, individuals who are "mean" can be attractive to others (Farmer, Estell, Bishop, O'Neil, & Cairns, 2003; Hawley, 2005; Rodkin, Farmer, Pearl, & Van Acker, 2000). Conversely, while appropriately celebrated for their positive influence on children's satisfaction and development, recent evidence suggests that friendships can also be a source of tension, and friends can deeply disappoint their partners. Children often value their friends because they provide opportunities for emotional support and self-disclosure, and researchers have typically assumed that self-disclosure in friendship indicates healthy functioning. However, some friendships are characterized by aggressive behavior (e.g., Crick & Nelson, 2002; Poulin & Boivin, 2000) and other recent evidence suggests that children who discuss deviance in their disclosures with friends are at increased risk for deviance themselves (e.g., Brendgen, Vitaro, & Bukowski, 2000; Dishion, Andrews, & Crosby, 1995; Dishion, Spracklen, Andrews, & Patterson, 1996; Keenan, Loeber, Zhang, Stouthamer-Loeber, & Van Kammen, 1995; Poulin, Dishion, & Haas, 1999; Urberg, Degirmencioglu, & Pilgrim, 1997) and discussions of personal problems among friends that become preoccupying can increase rather than decrease children's risk of internalizing disorders (Rose, 2002). Likewise, having multiple friends is usually and rightly considered a positive sign of adjustment with peers. Yet, in specific friendships, feelings of jealousy can arise in one member if their friend's interest in, or activities with, an outsider highlights their own shortcomings in important areas or is perceived as an infringement on the quality or sovereignty of the relationship. There is evidence that feelings of jealousy, an emotional experience born from closeness, can damage children's intrapersonal adjustment and result in negative behavior

(Parker, Low, Walker, & Gamm, 2005). Romantic relationships, too, can be characterized by intense conflict and feelings of insecurity, exploitation, and sadness (Joyner & Udry, 2000; Richards, Crowe, Larson, & Swarr, 1998). The double-edged nature of these bonds, as it were, make it more risky now than a decade ago to make assumptions about the protective factors associated with various positive indicators of adjustment with peers or the risks associated with markers that appeared uniformly negative.

Finally, a discernable and natural progression has taken place in the balance of simple descriptive versus process-oriented studies in this area. This is perhaps most readily apparent in the evolution of research on children's rejection by the peer group. When closing our chapter a decade ago, we lamented that insufficient attention had been paid to the processes underlying sociometric classification and categorization in the study of peer rejection. Instead, researchers appeared content to conduct study after study comparing rejected children to other children on variable after variable. We noted (Parker et al., 1995, p. 144): "Few data exist, for example, on the frequency with which peer rejected children are excluded from playground games, experience teasing and taunts, or are otherwise victimized by other children." Our concern at the time was that sociometric status researchers were elevating the traditional categories of popular, rejected, neglected, and controversial to social address variables (Bronfenbrenner & Crouter, 1983) and might be losing sight of whether and how they were grounded in the day-to-day experiences of children. Without such an understanding, little progress seemed possible in understanding the processes by which sociometric status groups arise and how they influence individuals, dyads, and groups.

The circumstances today are different. Although the classification and comparison of children of differing sociometric status remains an important field of inquiry, many of these same investigators have begun to study bullied and victimized children (see Juvonen & Graham, 2001; Ladd & Burgess, 1999; Rodkin & Hodges, 2003). Peer rejection and peer victimization are distinct constructs but overlap in important ways. However, by formulating their questions in terms of a specific type of interpersonal process (peer victimization and bullying), this newer tradition requires a smaller leap from description to process. However, as Bronfenbrenner and Crouter (1983) also pointed out, process-oriented accounts of social experience seldom provide the same satisfying generalizations about individuals that social address models appear to. Instead, they demand close attention to the moderating effects of person- and context-level variables. Thus, as our understanding of

peer victimization has grown, it has become apparent that the developmental significance of this experience is not simple (Boulton, Trueman, Chau, Whitehand, & Amatya, 1999; Graham & Juvonen, 2001; Hanish & Guerra, 2004; Hodges, Boivin, Vitaro, & Bukowski, 1999; Juvonen & Graham, 2001; Kochenderfer & Ladd, 1997; Olweus, 1993; Salmivalli, Huttunen, & Lagerspetz, 1997; Salmivalli & Voeten, 2004). Whether and in what way victimization affects children appears to depend on the context in which it occurs. For example, is the child a member of a numerically larger subgroup or perhaps a member of a minority ethnic group? Is aggression otherwise normative for the group in which victimization occurred? Is the perpetrator a dominant or submissive individual in terms of status in the relevant peer group? What are children's attributions for why a particular aggressive act occurs? Is the victimized child also a perpetrator at other times? What are the child's social resources (e.g., Does the child have friends?)? Is the perpetrator or the victim socially skilled? What about the self-esteem and gender of the perpetrator or victim? Was the abuse of a physical, verbal, direct, or indirect nature? Our task has become complicated indeed.

ORGANIZATION OF THE CHAPTER

Normative developmental trends in children's peer experiences provide a foundation for understanding peer relationships from a developmental psychopathology perspective. Thus, in the first section, we trace peer experiences and relationships from their building blocks in infancy and early childhood through their advances in adolescence when increasingly stable and intimate friendships are formed and romantic relationships take shape.

Following this, we discuss the major theoretical frameworks that have guided thinking and research on the importance and impact of peer relationships. The study of children's adjustment with peers sits at the juncture of a number of different scientific frameworks, but is the central focus of none. As such, we review how several theoretical perspectives have been insightful and provocative in particular respects. As will be apparent, in some formulations, peer experiences are suggested to contribute to development in ways that are unique from children's experiences with adults; in others, peer experiences offer an important countervailing influence to the influence of adults; in still others, peer experiences and adult influences are seen to share many similarities. Further, in some cases, the implications of unsuccessful adjustment with peers are drawn out explicitly, though in others they are only implied.

In the next section, we illustrate some of the many dimensions along which children's peer experiences may differ. This discussion emphasizes that even within the broad domains of friendship and peer acceptance, the potential for individual differences in peer experiences are numerous.

In the following sections, we tackle the implications of problematic peer relationships. The possibility that children with problematic peer relationships are at increased risk for later adjustment difficulties has attracted clinicians, epidemiologists, and others to the study of peer adjustment in the hopes of improving the early identification and prevention of adolescent and adult mental health disturbances. Studies in this area form an important interface between the sciences of developmental psychology, child clinical psychology, and developmental psychopathology. Our review turns initially to the question of the interface of peer relationship difficulties and psychological disorders. Next, relying heavily on the principles of developmental psychopathology, we take a longitudinal perspective and discuss developmental pathways and transactional models to illuminate the links between early peer problems and maladjustment later in life.

Following this, we review research pertaining to reciprocal influences between children and their peers to support a model of the processes underlying peer maladjustment. This model specifies the reciprocal roles of child social cognition and behavior and peer appraisals and responses in the unfolding of peer adjustment or maladjustment, with attention to the emerging understanding of emotion in this process.

Finally, we use child social anxiety to illustrate how the principles of developmental psychopathology may guide our understanding of peer maladjustment and end our chapter with some discussion of directions for future research.

DEVELOPMENTAL TRENDS IN CHILDREN'S PEER INTERACTION AND RELATIONSHIPS

As with any class of complex behavior, understanding children's behavior with peers requires an appreciation of the child's developmental status and the dynamic organization of the behavior over time (Cairns, 1979; Cicchetti, 1990). Although the argument that one must consider development when considering the meaning of behavior for actors and recipients seems obvious, in fact, the study of social development has been decidedly nondevelopmental for most of

its history (Cairns, 1979; Sroufe & Jacobvitz, 1989). Moreover, an understanding of the major mileposts and transformations in peer experiences that occur with age is necessary to recognize and understand individual patterns of adaptation and maladaptation with peers (Cicchetti, 1993; Selman & Schultz, 1990; Sroufe & Rutter, 1984). Deviations, delays, or distortions in the development of peer relationships derive their meaning only through consideration of the timing, nature, and course of peer experiences in the average or expectable instance.

In this section, we examine children's peer experiences and relationships from infancy through adolescence. Our concern is with the general developmental changes in the quantity, quality, and context of children's peer contacts and relationships. These normative patterns then provide a framework for considering the role of peer experiences in development and the considerable variation existing among individual children in the success of their adjustment with peers.

Infancy and Early Childhood

Infants have obvious motor, cognitive, and verbal limitations that restrict their capabilities for, and interest in, peer interaction in the first 3 to 4 months of life. However, smiling, vocalizing, and reaching toward peers appears toward the end of the first half year of life and infants begin to coordinate their interactions with other children shortly thereafter (D. F. Hay, Pederson, & Nash, 1982; Vandell, Wilson, & Buchanan, 1980). These initial exchanges are short, two-turn reciprocal chains, typically involving an infant exhibiting a social behavior, such as pointing or vocalizing toward another baby, and the other baby's responding in kind. Agonistic acts and object-centered activities are rare at this age. Interestingly, even at these early ages, considerable variability in interactive behavior is evident; some infants repeatedly direct social acts toward other children, whereas other infants do so very rarely (National Institute of Child Health and Human Development-Early Child Care Research Network, 2001).

Growing Reciprocities

The social exchanges of older infants and toddlers are more predictable, complex, coordinated, and lengthier (Dishion, Andrews, & Crosby, 1995; Eckerman, 1993; Eckerman & Didow, 1996; Eckerman & Peterman, 2001; Ross, 1982). Around the time of the first birthday, children become capable of shared activity with peers (Howes, 1996). Initially, these activities center primarily on objects (Mueller & Brenner, 1977). Divisive struggles over objects are common, but so, too, are more integrative exchanges, such as imitation of other infants' behaviors toward objects, particularly as children reach the age of 20 to 24 months. An age-mate makes an ideal model of what to do with objects, and toddlers' imitations of one another and other exchanges around objects mark the emergence of the earliest forms of cooperative and coordinated activity (Eckerman & Peterman, 2001).

The object-centeredness of children's peer interchanges declines from the beginning to the end of the 2nd year of life (Mueller & Brenner, 1977). Mueller and Silverman (1989) suggest that this signals a subtle but significant transformation in peer relationships in that it marks a transition from a focus on activities to a focus on the social relationship itself.

The period from 16 or 18 months to about 3 years is marked by social interaction that is increasing socially oriented and more truly complementary and coordinated (e.g., Eckerman & Peterman, 2001; Ross, 1982). The consolidation of locomotion and, especially, the emergence of the ability to communicate meaning through language, play significant roles in this transformation (e.g., Dunn, 1988; Howes, 1992). It is during this period that lighthearted and playful games can first be identified in toddlers' interactive exchanges (Ross, 1982). Eckerman and Peterman (2001) outline a developmental progression of toddlers' cooperative and coordinated action over this period. In their model, at around 16 months of age, toddlers participate in ritualized coordinated action, usually with familiar and older peers. From 20 to 24 months, nonritualized coordinated action with peers emerges, primarily through nonverbal imitative acts. Nonverbal imitative activity during this period promotes shared understanding of social interaction, which sets the stage for verbal means of achieving coordinated action. Finally, from 28 to 32 months, toddlers integrate verbal and nonverbal means of achieving coordinated action.

Fantasy Play

Social pretend play permits young children to successfully work through fears and other emotional issues (Parker & Gottman, 1989; Rubin, Fein, & Vandenberg, 1983; Sawyer, 1997). In addition, even very young children use pretend play to establish and maintain social relationships with peers (Eckerman, 1996; Gottman, 1983). Howes (1992) describes the gradually unfolding sequence that takes place over the span from 16 months to 3 years in the growth of children's skills at communicating meaning in the context of social pretense. At the beginning of this period, chil-

dren's play and games have a complementary and reciprocal structure (e.g., run-chase). Thus, their play is built on familiar and well-learned scripts or routines, permitting the children to play cooperatively with little need to communicate meaning. Social pretense at this point consists of little more than one child's imitation of the isolated pretense acts of another.

As language and symbolic capacity matures, however, social pretense undergoes regular, sequential changes. From 16 to 20 months, children's pretense becomes more abstract and distant from their actions. Children will not only match or imitate the pretend acts of other children but also attempt to recruit the partner to join their pretend play. These efforts are not routinely successful, but it is clear that children are beginning to understand that nonliteral meanings can be shared by partners.

From 21 to 24 months, children engage in similar pretend actions in the context of broader joint activity. Attempts to recruit others into pretense are more frequent and more successful. Although children organize materials for sociodramatic play, there is little or no joint organization of the pretend play itself. Scripted joint play emerges from 25 to 30 months, and the assignment of social roles in play (e.g., doctor, mother, father, police officer) emerges shortly thereafter, from 31 to 36 months. At this point, children understand that nonliteral meaning can be shared and they can communicate these meanings effectively during pretense with partners.

Early Friendships

The formation of specific friendships begins to be observed during the period from 18 to 36 months (Schneider, 2000). These friendships are indexed by mutual interaction preference, shared affect, scripted regularities in play, and differentially sophisticated play between peers (see Howes, 1996). Indeed, the percentage of children at these ages without friends is very small, at least among children in child care settings (Howes, 1983, 1988).

Because toddlers' concepts of a friend and friendship are limited (Selman, 1980), it is sometimes assumed that these early friendships are of marginal importance to children of this age. However, children with friends acquire social skills as a result of their participation in these relationships, especially if these relationships are maintained over time (Howes, 1996). Howes and Phillipsen (1998) reported that the complexity of children's social play during the toddler years predicted increased prosocial behavior and decreased social withdrawal during the preschool years, as well as decreased social withdrawal and aggression at 9 years of age. Moreover, toddlers regularly and spontaneously discuss their friendship interactions with their parents at home, suggesting the salience of these relationships to even very young children (Krawczyk, 1985). Howes and Phillipsen (1992) found that 80% of friendships among toddlers who remained in the same child care setting lasted for 3 years. Nevertheless, friendships at this age are less stable than friendships formed after 3 years of age (see Schneider, 2000).

Mileposts of the Preschool Years

Peer interaction after the 3rd year and over the course of the remaining years preceding formal schooling continues to change in frequency and quality (Dunn, 1993). Children direct increasing amounts of attention to peers, and spend increasing amounts of time with peers, especially if they are enrolled in child care settings (Hartup, 1983; Schindler, Moely, & Frank, 1987).

Conflict

As might be expected from the increased contact and interest, conflict between age-mates increases in frequency and intensity over this period (D. Chen, Fein, & Tam, 2001; Vaughn, Vollenwieder, Bost, Azria-Evans, & Snider, 2003). In comparison to older children, preschoolers' conflicts are more likely to involve struggles over objects (Killen, 1991). Object struggles are not strictly pragmatic disputes, however, and probably involve disputes over moral issues and elements of social control as well (see D. F. Hay & Ross, 1982; Killen, 1991). For example, disputes over objects may arise from the demands on children to protect their interactive space (Corsaro, 1985). According to Corsaro, preschoolers' social interaction is especially fragile, in that intrusions by other peers can lead interactive episodes to terminate quickly without formal marking or opportunity for negotiation. Realization of this fact leads children to resists others' attempts to join in play, sometimes through claims and counterclaims of friendship. Regardless of its source, conflict exchanges during the preschool years may provide important opportunities for social-cognitive development and learning to manage conflict (Shantz & Hartup, 1992; Vaughn et al., 2003). Indeed, Vaughn et al. found that about one-third of preschool children with high observed social competence were also high on observational ratings of both dominance and prosocial behavior.

Overall, however, the proportion of conflict or aggressive interactions to friendly interaction declines across the preschool period as increasing language, self-regulation, and social-cognitive capacities allow children to resolve conflicts of interest in more prosocial ways (Coie & Dodge,

1998; Hartup, Laursen, Stewart, & Eastenson, 1988; D. F. Hay, Castle, & Davies, 2000). Conversely, prosocial behavior (e.g., helping, sharing, empathy) increases from the toddler years to the early preschool years (e.g., Eisenberg & Fabes, 1998; D. F. Hay, Castle, Davies, Demetriou, & Stimson, 1999) and is linked with peer acceptance during this period (e.g., Bierman & Erath, in press).

Play

Children's play also increases in social complexity during the preschool period; the most notable changes occur with respect to sociodramatic play, which increases notably over this period (Goncu, Patt, & Kouba, 2002; Rubin et al., 1983; Sawyer, 1997). Howes, Matheson, and Wu (1992) explored the role of complex social pretend play, which consisted not only of pretend play with defined roles (i.e., social pretend play), but also of meta-communication about pretend play (e.g., explicitly assigning roles, proposing a play script, prompting the other child). Complex social pretend play began to emerge around 36 months and increased through 60 months.

The skills of communicating meaning in social pretense are largely mastered by 3 years of age; thus, preschoolers' spontaneous social pretense is more likely to serve broader developmental functions (Howes & Phillipsen, 1998). Spontaneous fantasy play is especially critical to the establishment and maintenance of friendships in preschool (see Corsaro, 1985; Gottman & Parkhurst, 1980; Howes, 1992; Parker & Gottman, 1989). In addition, it provides preschool children with a vehicle for working through major concerns and fears (see Corsaro, 1985; Howes, 1992; Kramer & Gottman, 1992; Parker & Gottman, 1989). Not surprisingly, then, spontaneous pretend play during the preschool ages, especially between best friends, is more frequent and elaborate than at any other point in development (e.g., Corsaro, 1985; Forbes, Katz, & Paul, 1986; Howes, 1992).

Gender Differentiation

Normative gender differences in peer interaction also begin to emerge during the preschool years. Around the age of 3, children begin to show a strong preference for interacting with same-sex peers (Fabes, Martin, & Hanish, 2003; Maccoby, 1998; Powlishta, Serbin, & Moller, 1993). Although play is the primary form of social interaction for both sexes during early childhood (Maccoby, 1998), the type of play typical among groups of boys and girls shows distinctive features. For example, beginning in preschool, boys more often choose to interact with peers in larger groups that emphasize competition, hero and rescue themes, and rough-

and-tumble play, whereas girls more often play in smaller groups and emphasize conversation, cooperation, and relationship themes (Benenson, Apostoleris, & Parnass, 1997; Maccoby, 1998). Boys also display higher levels of activity, aggression, and positive emotionality, whereas girls engage in more frequent play in the proximity of adults (Fabes et al., 2003; Martin & Fabes, 2001). Interestingly, sex-differentiated play appears to be amplified by exposure to same-sex peers during the preschool years (Martin & Fabes, 2001), perhaps because both boys and girls make more positive overtures and responses to same-sex peers and to play behavior consistent with the preferences of their own sex (Fagot, 1985; Maccoby, 1998).

Developments in Later Childhood

The period of middle to late childhood, covering roughly the period from 6 years to 11 or 12 years, is characterized by a great deal of change and growth in interpersonal skills and in the context and quality of children's peer relationships.

Diversity and Differentiation

Positive peer experiences and friendships in preschool contribute to a smoother and more positive transition to formal schooling (Ladd, Kochenderfer, & Coleman, 1996). However, entry into formal schooling in turn greatly transforms peer experiences by increasing the size of the sphere of children's peer contacts. In addition, children's involvement in extracurricular and other forms of youth sports during middle childhood provides opportunities to develop friendships and affiliations outside of school. In fact, descriptive research suggests that the possibility of positive peer experiences is an important motive that attracts youth to organized sports activities (see M. R. Weiss & Smith, 1999; M. R. Weiss, Smith, & Theeboom, 1996).

However, in addition to an increase in the number of available peers, children entering middle and later childhood are likely to encounter unprecedented variability in the ascribed (e.g., sex, race, ethnicity) characteristics and personalities of their peers, especially in school contexts. These differences contribute to discernible hierarchies of power and popularity (McHale, Dariotis, & Kauh, 2003), to salient similarities among playmates or friends (e.g., Kupersmidt, DeRosier, & Patterson, 1995; Newcomb et al., 1999), and to groups that are rigidly segregated along various lines (e.g., Abrams, Rutland, & Cameron, 2003; Horn, 2003).

Sex segregation is the most noticeable. The earlier trend toward a sex-segregated friendship group intensifies during this period, such that peer interactions and close friendships occur almost exclusively with same-sex peers during middle childhood (D. M. Kovacs, Parker, & Hoffman, 1996; Sroufe, Bennett, Englund, & Urban, 1993). Indeed, at this age children who buck this imperative and have friendships primarily with members of the opposite sex tend to be children who are less well-liked by peers, less socially skilled, and more aggressive than children who form primarily same-sex friendships (D. M. Kovacs et al., 1996).

However, sex is not the only social category that divides children's groups beginning in early childhood. Children's recognition of race and ethnic differences also begins in the preschool period (e.g., Aboud, 1988). Preschoolers' sorting and labeling of others based on race or ethnicity is neither as accurate nor as comprehensive as it will become in middle childhood, however. Further, it is largely not until the middle childhood years that children begin to hold negative views about the categories to which they do not belong (Killen, Lee-Kim, McGlothlin, Stangor, 2002; Powlishta, Serbin, Doyle, & White, 1994). The rapidity with which children recognize and use social categories leaves an impression of a broad, qualitative, and domain-general developmental change in reasoning. However, recent research suggests that this is an oversimplification (Killen & Stangor, 2001; Killen, Stangor, Horn, & Sechrist, 2004). Children who are prejudiced in one domain (e.g., toward the opposite sex) are not necessarily prejudiced in other domains (e.g., toward another race) and evidence suggests that the recognition, use, and abuse of social categories develops from a complex interplay of environmental support, attitudes toward others, and a growing self-understanding (Liben & Bigler, 2002; Powlishta et al., 1994). Moreover, after a period of initial intensification, prejudicial attitudes decline across later childhood (Powlishta et al., 1994). Further, children show important developmental changes in their judgments of in-group and out-group members from age 5 years to 16 years (Abrams et al., 2003). In particular, with age, children attend not solely to a target individual's social category or group membership status, but also to the extent to which his or her personal characteristics conform versus deviate from those typical of the category. For example, children of all ages show bias in favor of in-group members over out-group members. With age, however, children become sensitive to differences among members within (versus between) groups—in both their in-groups and out-groups (Killen, Lee-Kim, et al., 2002). Among older children, then, typical in- and out-group biases can be erased or even reversed in the right circumstances. For example, older children during this period, but not younger children, show evidence of sensitivity to so-called "black sheep" (Abrams et al., 2003). That is, with older children, members of out-groups who are not especially prototypical of the groups may be preferred over members of the in-group who are deviant from the in group norms.

Play

Whereas preschoolers' play involves a great deal of spontaneous and unstructured fantasy and pretense, this type of play declines steadily across middle childhood, to the point of being almost entirely absent by the end of this period (Baumeister & Senders, 1989; Rubin et al., 1983). Simple roughhousing, or rough-and-tumble play, also declines with age, although it does not disappear entirely, at least among boys (Boulton, 1996; Pellegrini, 2002; Pellegrini & Smith, 1998). Instead, the cooperative play of elementary school-age children increasingly involves adult-organized activities (e.g., playing sports) or games with formal (e.g., dodgeball, kickball, board games) or informal (e.g., tag, king-of-the-mountain, hide-and-seek) rules. A common aspect of these activities, and one which sets them apart from earlier peer activities, is that they involve increasingly greater divisions of labor, differentiation of roles and status, teamwork, and leadership (Rubin et al., 1983).

Aggression, Conflict, and Gossip

As noted, the preschool years appear to be critical years for learning to regulate aggression (Tremblay et al., 2005). Accordingly, most children who show elevated levels of physical aggression in preschool or kindergarten typically show important reductions of those behaviors as they enter the period of middle childhood and formal schooling. Children who do not display this expected decrease in aggression appear to be at increased risk for antisocial and aggressive behavior later throughout this period and even into adolescence and adulthood (e.g., NICHD Early Child Care Research Network, 2004; Tremblay et al., 2005). It is highly unusual, in fact, to identify aggressive children in middle childhood who do not have a history of aggressiveness extending backward to the preschool years (Brody et al., 2003). In addition, along with a general decline there is a change in the nature of aggression from preschool to later childhood such that verbal aggression (insults, derogation, threats) gradually replaces direct physical aggression over this period (Bierman, 2004; Underwood, 2003). Further, relative to early childhood, aggressive behavior in middle childhood is less instrumental (directed toward possessing objects or occupying specific space) and more specifically hostile toward others. Social-cognitive advances during middle childhood allow children to recognize the hostile

nature of some aggressive acts, which in turn may instigate increased retaliatory aggression (Coie & Dodge, 1998). Social-cognitive developments during middle childhood may also contribute to increased indirect or relational aggression, which involves attempts to harm others through relationship processes such as gossip and exclusion (Crick & Grotpeter, 1995; Underwood, 2003). Children who continue to exhibit high levels of verbal or physical aggression during the middle childhood years face a high risk of peer rejection (Bierman, 2004).

Gossip, especially humorous gossip, increases in salience and frequency among friends at this time (Parker & Gottman, 1989). Like those of adults, the spontaneous conversations of preadolescents ordinarily contain many references to the personal qualities, behaviors, and affairs of others (Eder & Enke, 1991; Gottman & Mettetal, 1986; Parker, Teasley, Meissner, & McClellan, 1994). In everyday usage, the term *gossip* may be mistakenly used in a restricted way to apply only to derisive comments made about outside others (Fine & Rosnow, 1977). Gossip technically encompasses all evaluative comments or conversations about third parties. Hence, admiring as well as pejorative statements made by children about others represent gossip (Fine & Rosnow, 1978; Gottman & Mettetal, 1986; Parker et al., 1994). A shared property of all gossip, however, is that the target or targets of discussion are not present, and thereby are not directly party to the conversation (Eder & Enke, 1991). This behind-the-back quality lends gossip some of its most distinctive and important interpersonal features, and distinguishes it from other significant forms of evaluative talk, such as self-disclosure or public ridicule.

As a form of speech, gossip has attracted intermittent scholarly attention over the years for its presumed roles in children's groups, relationships, and individual development (e.g., Eder & Enke, 1991; Gottman & Mettetal, 1986; Suls, 1977). In groups, for example, gossip may increase cohesion by clarifying and enforcing behavioral norms. Further, differential access to gossip among members has been shown to correlate with group social standing and acceptance (Parker & Seal, 1996). In relationships, participating in gossip about others may bring partners' understanding of social events and norms into closer agreement, contributing to a sense of similarity (Gottman, 1983). Observational studies suggest that children find gossip with their friends highly entertaining and use gossip as a basis for building solidarity against others through self-disclosure (Gottman, 1983; Gottman & Mettetal, 1986; Parker & Gottman, 1989; Rysman, 1977). Finally, for individuals, gossip is a form of self-expression. By gossiping about others, individuals may enhance their self-understanding through social comparison, and discrediting others publicly may help children project and maintain a positive self-image in areas of private concern (Fine, 1981; Fine & Rosnow, 1978; Suls, 1977).

At the beginning of middle childhood, children appear to possess a healthy skepticism of gossip, at least in the absence of clear evidence attesting to the veracity of the gossipers' claims (Kuttler, Parker, & LaGreca, 2002). With age, however, this skepticism appears to wane somewhat, even in the face of evidence that the gossiper may harbor ulterior motives (Kuttler et al., 2002). Ironically, then, even as they appreciate the potential unreliability of rumors, older children express less skepticism surrounding this information than do younger children. Perhaps older children are less concerned than younger children with the accuracy of the content of gossip than with using gossip to reaffirm group membership, reveal peer group attitudes, and manipulate others' inclusion in or exclusion from the group (Eder & Enke, 1991).

Prosocial Behavior

Reliable age trends have not been observed across middle childhood in children's general disposition to behave in a cooperative, helpful, or generous way toward peers. Many researchers note that prosocial behavior toward peers generally increases with age over this period (see Fabes et al., 1999, for a review). Others, however, note that older children may actually help and share less than preschoolers (e.g., Radke-Yarrow, Zahn Waxler, & Chapman, 1983). Increased concerns with self-interest, fairness, autonomy, relationship obligations and other factors may enter into older children's decisions regarding sharing and helping (Bigelow et al., 1996). Thus, a better description of the pattern of growth and maturation in this connection is one of increasing complexity, flexibility, and responsiveness to situational, intrapersonal, and interpersonal exigencies (Bigelow et al., 1996). The development of prosocial intentions and behavior over this age span does not appear to reflect a single unfolding skill. Rather it appears to reflect a complex confluence of developmental changes.

Friendships

Middle childhood spans a period of considerable transformation in children's understanding of friendship. These changes have been charted by Selman (e.g., 1980; Selman & Schultz, 1990), among others (e.g., Berndt & Perry, 1986, 1990; Bigelow et al., 1996; Damon, 1977; Youniss, 1980). Selman's framework is perhaps the best articulated, although interested readers are encouraged to consult the notable work of Bigelow et al. as well. According to Sel-

man, prior to middle childhood, children's understanding of friendship is little more than the concept of momentary playmate. Chief among the constraints in preschoolers' thinking about friendship are difficulties they have in distinguishing their own perspectives from those of others, and in appreciating the distinction between the psychological versus manifest basis for people's behavior.

As they move into middle childhood, children's discussion of friendship and friendship issues begins to indicate a maturing appreciation that feelings and intentions, not just manifest actions, keep friends together or drive them apart. Children also begin to appreciate that others' thoughts and feelings concerning social events may differ from their own. Even in the face of this advance in perspective-taking, however, children of this age for a time remain unilaterally concerned with their own, not their partner's, subjective experiences in the relationship. This unilateral perspective subsides eventually, however, and children begin to express an understanding that both parties in a relationship must coordinate and adjust their needs and actions to one another in mutually satisfying ways. But their understanding of friendship does not include an expectation that friendships can weather specific arguments or negative events. By the close of middle childhood, however, most children understand that friendship is an affective bond with continuity over time, space, and events.

Changes in children's understanding of friendship are accompanied by changes in the patterns and nature of children's involvement in friendships across middle childhood (Denton & Zarbatany, 1996; Hartup & Stevens, 1997; Newcomb & Bagwell, 1995). The number of selections of close friends that children make has been reported to increase with age up to about 11 years of age, after which it begins to decline (see Epstein, 1986). Moreover, friendship choices are more stable and more likely to be reciprocated in middle childhood than at earlier ages, although it is not clear that either the reciprocity or stability of friendships increases across the period of middle childhood itself (Schneider, 2000). Studies in which elementary school-age children have been asked to describe their expectations in friendships also indicate that children draw sharper distinctions between the supportiveness of friends and nonfriends with age (Berndt & Perry, 1986; Bigelow et al., 1996). Moreover, children's descriptions of their friendships indicate that loyalty, self-disclosure, and trust increase with age (e.g., see Berndt & Hanna, 1995; Buhrmester & Prager, 1995; Newcomb & Bagwell, 1995 for reviews).

Many authors (e.g., Golombok & Fivush, 1994; Maccoby, 1990) have suggested that same-sex friendships among females in middle childhood are closer than those among males and some authors are, as a result, dismissive of the importance of friendships to males (e.g., Benenson & Christakos, 2003). Developmental studies have documented numerous gender differences in children's friendships (see Golombok & Fivush, 1994; Maccoby, 1990, for reviews). Some studies suggest, for example, girls tend to self-disclose and provide greater emotional support to friends than do boys (Berndt & Perry, 1986, 1990; Buhmester & Furman, 1987; Buhrmester & Prager, 1995; Rose & Asher, 2000; Rubin, Dwyer, et al., 2004; Zarbatany, McDougall, & Hymel, 2000). Girls also report more intimacy in their friendships than do boys (e.g., Buhrmester & Prager, 1995; Parker & Asher, 1993; Prager, 1995; Rubin, Dwyer, et al., 2004) and spend more time thinking about their friends when their friends are not around (Richards et al., 1998). However, reliable differences in the longevity of boys and girls friendships have not been consistently observed (e.g., Parker & Seal, 1996) and boys and girls spend equal amounts of time with friends (Richards et al., 1998). Also, sex differences in friendship intimacy do not always emerge, sometimes are in the reverse direction, and, when significant, are not large (Berndt & Hanna, 1995). These and other lines of reasoning lead some to suggest that sex differences in friendship may be exaggerated at the expense of recognizing the many similarities in closeness, importance, loyalty, and enjoyment that exist across male and female same-sex friendships (e.g., Bigelow et al., 1996; Lansford & Parker, 1996). Further, echoing concerns of others (e.g., Gottman, 1983; Lansford & Parker, 1996; Prager, 1995), Hartup and Stevens (1997) note that closeness and intimacy in studies of friendship at this age are commonly defined in a feminizing manner (i.e., emphasis on exclusivity, self-disclosure, communal motives). This operationalization may dismiss agentic behaviors that may also underlie closeness and could provide a more balanced vision of closeness among males.

Cliques and Groups

Stable, polydyadic social groups, or cliques, also emerge in middle childhood and generally increase with age, at least through early adolescence (Cairns, Xie, & Leung, 1998; Henrich, Kuperminc, Sack, Blatt, & Leadbeater, 2000). Cliques are voluntary and friendship-based groups, and stand in contrast to the activity or work groups to which children can be assigned by circumstance or by adults. Cliques generally range in size from 3 to 10 members, and are almost always same sex (Brown & Klute, 2003). The

prevalence of cliques has generally not been investigated among children younger than 10 or 11 years of age. By 11 years of age, however, children report that most of their peer interaction takes place in the context of the clique, and nearly all children report being a member of a clique (X. Chen, Chang, & He, 2003; Kindermann, McCollom, & Gibson, 1995). Cliques appear to function, in part, as sources of definition and support for identity development during the preadolescent and adolescent years (Brown & Klute, 2003; Newman & Newman, 2001).

Vulnerabilities

We have so far highlighted the many advances in positive social interaction and relationships that mark middle childhood. But peer involvement at this age also has a less adaptive side in the appearance of more or less novel intra- and interpersonal attitudes and behaviors that are distressing, problematic, or difficult.

First, because group leaders invite some individuals and exclude others, the rise of cliques in middle childhood contributes to intergroup biases and exacerbates preadolescents' insecurity about their social position and acceptance (Adler & Adler, 1995). As a result, children of this age expend a good deal of their energy, thought, and conversation with friends buttressing their social status and guarding against rejection (Eder, 1985; Fine, 1987; Parker & Gottman, 1989). Children's desire to gain acceptance and avoid rejection is consistent with broader human motives of belonging (see Baumeister & Leary, 1995). Thus, the heightened concern with acceptance that children of this age display is understandable and may have adaptive elements. However, in certain vulnerable children, typical concern with acceptance is replaced by an excessive sensitivity to rejection (Downey, Lebolt, Rincon, & Freitas, 1998). Children with excessive sensitivity to rejection by peers readily perceive intentional rejection in minor or imagined insensitivities and disappointments and overreact in ways that compromise their group standing and social relationships. By contributing to interpersonal difficulties, sensitivity to rejection may contribute in turn to increases in internalizing and externalizing problems in these vulnerable individuals.

Second, vagaries in the reliability of social acceptance also appear to contribute to heightened self-consciousness and declines in self-esteem toward the end of this period and the start of adolescence, especially among girls (e.g., Eccles et al., 1993). In particular, perceptions of one's physical appearance grow especially central to broader self-esteem (Harter, 1999) and increasingly coupled to expectations of popularity and attractiveness to the opposite sex (Eccles, Barber, Jozefowicz, Malenchuk, & Vida, 1999). This confluence of factors, in turn, appear to increasingly compromise the self-esteem of those individuals who are not or do not feel sufficiently attractive. The self-esteem of early maturing girls during this period may also be compromised by sexual harassment by boys (Craig, Pepler, Connolly, & Henderson, 2001; Murnen & Smolak, 2000).

Third, despite a broad decline in aggression over the middle to late childhood, the risk of being bullied, appears to move in the opposite developmental direction (e.g., Espelage, Bosworth, & Simon, 2000; Espelage, Holt, & Henkel, 2003; Kochenderfer-Ladd, 2003; Kochenderfer-Ladd & Wardrop, 2001; Snyder et al., 2003). Bullying is characterized by the chronic victimization of a specifically selected target who is generally disadvantaged with respect to the balance of power (see Juvonen & Graham, 2001; Olweus, 1978, 1993). Unlike most acts of broader aggression, bullying often involves the cooperation of several more powerful individuals to victimize a less powerful one (Salmivalli, 2001). For the most part, reliable data on bullying among school-age children has only recently become available. The majority of epidemiologically oriented studies have been conducted in Europe and Australia. These studies have documented considerable variability in the prevalence of bullying, ranging from 15% to 20% in some countries to a high of 70% in others (King, Wold, Tudor-Smith, & Harel, 1996). Bullying behaviors among U.S. youth are less well understood. Recently, however, Nansel et al. (2001) conducted an analysis of data from a representative sample of 15,686 students in grades 6 through 10 in U.S. public and private schools who answered questions about bullying in the context of a World Health Organization's health behavior survey (1992). Approximately 30% of youth reported significant involvement in bullying as a bully (13%), victim (10.6%), or both (6.3%), rates in line with those reported by studies with smaller and less representative samples (see Juvonen & Graham, 2001). Bullying appeared to peak during grades 6 through 8, and declined thereafter. Bullying was more prevalent among boys than girls and the forms of bullying varied somewhat with sex. Both males and females reported that the most common form of bullying involved verbal belittling over looks or speech. Males reported being hit, slapped, or pushed more frequently than did females. Females more frequently reported being bullied through rumors and being the target of sexual comments. Taunting others about their religion or race was uncommon. Finally, consistent with other research (see Juvonen & Graham, 2001), being victimized by peers through bullying was associated with a sweeping range of psychosocial difficulties, including school difficulties, problem behavior, and loneliness.

Fourth, the rise in cliques and other nested arrangements of friendships present children in later childhood with novel interpersonal quandaries and sources of stress. Specifically, most children in middle childhood have several friends and are aware that their specific friends like or have friendships with other, outside children (Epstein & Karweit, 1983; George & Hartmann, 1996; Parker & Seal, 1996). Children's social adjustment may be facilitated by having many friends (Newcomb et al., 1999) or when one's friends are well connected socially (Sabongui et al., 1998). However, social life is also more complex in these circumstances. For example, the presence of outsiders may preempt opportunities for frank discussion between friends and coordination of social activities may be more complicated in groups larger than two (Benenson, Maiese, et al., 2002; Benenson, Nicholson, Waite, Roy, & Simpson, 2001; Lansford & Parker, 1999). In addition, outsiders will be sources of tension and conflict for friends if partners are squeezed between their loyalty to their friend and the obligations to others (Asher et al., 1996; Selman, 1980). Even when such dilemmas can be avoided, the time and emotional commitments that partners make to outside peers may still create problems for friends in the middle years. In particular, if young adolescents perceive outsiders as threatening the quality, uniqueness, or survival of their friendships, feelings of jealousy can arise and pose challenges to the partner, the perceived interloper, and the encompassing peer group (Parker, Low, Walker, & Gamm, 2005). Indeed, recent research suggests that jealousy over friends accounts for a good deal of the aggression and victimization in peer groups that occurs at this age and that individuals with low self-esteem are particularly vulnerable to this experience (Parker et al., 2005).

Finally, emerging evidence suggests that, along with enormous growth in positive peer relationships, later childhood also marks the period of growth in mutual antipathies, or so-called enemy relationships (see Hodges & Card, 2003). Very little is known about the prevalence of mutual antipathies among children and adolescents or when, precisely, these relationships emerge. Although some estimates indicate that these types of relationships are rare (e.g., Abecassis, 2003; Abecassis, Hartup, Haselager, Scholte, & Van Lieshout, 2002), evidence from several recent studies suggests that they may be quite commonplace, affecting from one to two out of every three children (Parker & Gamm, 2003; Rodkin, Pearl, Farmer, & Van Acker, 2003). Enemy relations between two children tend to be short-lived relationships and children who are not well accepted generally or who have negative behavioral profiles tend to be involved more often in enemy relationships. However, enemy relationships are also quite personal. Parker and Gamm (2003), for example, examined how enemies viewed one another and compared partners' perceptions to how these children were viewed by the larger peer group. Not surprisingly, children viewed their enemies negatively. However, children seemed to have uniquely negative perceptions of their enemies, views not necessarily shared by the wider group. Although these perceptions might be due to cognitive bias, other evidence suggested that they reflected a uniquely negative interaction history between the individuals who disliked one another. Children were especially likely to view their enemies as jealous and possessive over friends, even when those individuals did not have a reputation for jealousy more widely. Finally, the importance of enemy relationships for adjustment is indicated by evidence that children who are more involved in enemy relationships experience greater loneliness and dissatisfaction, even after controlling for their adjustment with friends and broader acceptance or rejection in the peer group (Parker & Gamm, 2003).

Developments in Adolescence

Many developments in peer relationships during adolescence continue trends begun in middle childhood, others reverse earlier trends, or otherwise represent developmental discontinuities. For example, the trend in middle childhood toward spending increasingly substantial amounts of time with peers continues in adolescence. This fact is readily apparent to anyone familiar with adolescents, but the results of formal assessments can be quite startling. For example, Csikszentmihalyi and Larson (1984) had adolescents indicate their activities, moods, and companions at random intervals across a 1-week period. They calculated that during a typical week, even discounting time spent in classroom instruction, high school students spend almost a third (29%) of their waking hours with peers. This is an amount more than double the amount spent with parents and other adults (13%). Moreover, adolescent peer interaction takes place with less adult guidance and control than peer interaction in middle childhood. Adolescents feel an especially strong imperative to be out with peers on the weekend, and high school teens who are alone

on Friday or Saturday nights may be extremely lonely (Larson & Richards, 1998).

Friendship Advances

Adolescents have been reported to have fewer friends on average than children in middle childhood (Epstein, 1986). Nonetheless, same-sex friends account for an increasingly larger proportion of adolescents' perceived primary social network, and friends equal or surpass parents as sources of support and advice to adolescents in many significant domains (see Van Lieshout, Cillessen, & Haselager, 1999). In a review of developmental trends in friendship selection, Epstein (1986) concluded that the stability of adolescent friendships is generally low, but increases with age. Subsequent research by Berndt and his colleagues (Berndt, Hawkins, & Hoyle, 1986; Berndt & Hoyle, 1985), however, indicates that most adolescent friendships are stable over the school year, and any developmental trend toward increasing stability is slight. School transitions, such as at entry to middle school, junior high school, and high school can disrupt the maintenance of friendships (Berndt, 1999; Berndt, Hawkins, & Jiao, 1999; Hardy, Bukowski, & Sippola, 2002; Wargo Aikins, Bierman, & Parker, 2005). As with transitions at younger ages, youth who have the skills to form friendships prior to a major adolescent transition, such as to junior high, are more likely to be able to develop positive relationships the next year than youth whose friendship skills are less well developed. In turn, youth with high-quality friendships, marked by greater intimacy, openness, and warmth, are more likely to maintain these relationships over the transition (Wargo Aikins et al., 2005).

One hallmark of friendship in adolescence is an increased emphasis on intimacy and self-disclosure (Van Lieshout et al., 1999; Zarbatany et al., 2000). Interviews and self-report assessments with adolescents consistently indicate that adolescents report greater levels of intimacy in their friendships than do younger children (Furman & Buhrmester, 1985; Sharabany, Gershoni, & Hofman, 1981; Youniss & Smoller, 1985). Further, observations of adolescent friends indicate that intimate self-disclosure becomes a salient feature of friendship interaction at this age (Gottman & Metettal, 1986; Parker & Gottman, 1989). Parker and Gottman (1989) speculated that salience of self-disclosure in friendship at this age is proportionate to the role it plays in assisting adolescents' efforts to understand themselves and their own and others' significant relationships. These authors noted that self-disclosure is sometimes apparent in the interactions of younger friends. However, in adolescent friendships, unlike at earlier ages, self-disclosure prompts lengthy and sometimes emotionally laden, psychological discussions about the nature of the personal problems and possible avenues to their resolution.

Adolescence also heralds a final and key advance in the individual's abstract understanding of friendship (Selman & Schultz, 1990). Preadolescents understand a great deal about the reciprocal operations and obligations of friendship, about the potential of friendships to withstand conflict, and about the psychological motives that motivate friends' behavior. But preadolescents' understanding of issues such as trust and jealousy in friendship is very narrowly tied to their perceptions of loyalty and friendship exclusivity. In particular, preadolescents tend to view friendships in overly exclusive terms. They regard relationships with third parties as inimical to the basic nature of friendship commitment. The significant change at adolescence, however, is that individuals begin to accept the other's need to establish relationships with others and to grow through such experiences. In particular, adolescents recognize an obligation to grant friends a certain degree of autonomy and independence. Thus, their discussions of friendship and friendship issues display more concern with how the relationship helps the partners enhance their respective self-identities and jealousy over friends declines across adolescence (Parker et al., 2005).

Cliques and Crowds

As in middle childhood, cliques are readily observed in adolescence, and membership in cliques is related to adolescents' psychological well-being and ability to cope with stress (Hansell, 1981). Brown (1990) argued that structural features of the transition to high school may account for some portion of the attraction of early adolescents to cliques, and the tendency for cliques to become increasingly heterosexual with age. Brown noted that the size of high schools and the fact that students are no longer assigned to self-contained classrooms mean that children of this age must confront a large and constantly shifting array of peers, many of whom are strangers. "Securing one's place in a clique prevents a student from having to confront this sea of unfamiliar faces alone. Including members of the opposite sex in one's circle of friends ensures participation in the heterosexually oriented series of school-sponsored social activities (mixers, proms)" (p. 181).

Whether attraction to cliques declines into late adolescence is not clear, however. In sociometric analyses of the clique structure of a large school, Shrum and Cheek (1987) found a sharp decline from 11 to 18 years of age in the proportion of students who were definitely clique members,

and a corresponding increase with age in the proportion of children who had ties to many cliques or children whose primary ties were to other children who existed at the margins of one or more cliques. This pattern would appear to fit with data suggesting that both the importance of belonging to a group and the extent of intergroup antagonism decline steadily across the high school years (see McLellan & Pugh, 1999). However, not all studies are supportive of such a trend (see Cairns et al., 1998). Age related changes must also be considered in relation to context. Montemayor and Von Komen (1985) found few age-related changes across the teen years in size of in-school groups. However, out-of-school group size increased as children grew older.

Whereas cliques represent small groups of individuals linked by friendship selections, the concept of peer subcultures, or crowds (Brown, 1990; Brown & Klute, 2003), is a more encompassing organizational framework for segmenting adolescent peer social life. A *crowd* is a reputation-based collective of similarly stereotyped individuals who may or may not spend much time together (Brown, 1990; Brown & Klute, 2003). Crowds are defined by the primary attitudes or activities their members share. Thus, crowd affiliation is assigned through the consensus of peer group, not selected by the adolescents themselves. Brown (1990) lists the following as common crowd labels among high school students: jocks, brains, loners, rogues, druggies, populars, and nerds (see also Strouse, 1999). Crowds place important restrictions on children's social contacts and relationships with peers (Brown, 1989; Eder, 1985), channeling adolescents toward certain friendships and away from others (Brown & Klute, 2003). For example, cliques are generally formed within (versus across) crowds, and adolescents report that most of their close friends come from their crowd (Brown & Klute, 2003). Crowd labels may also constrain children's ability to change their lifestyle or explore new identities (Kinney, 1999). For their part, however, many adolescents identify with the crowds to which they are assigned (Pugh & Hart, 1999) and are mindful of the social stimulus value of certain crowd memberships (e.g., deviant crowds) and actively use crowd affiliations to manage their public social identity (Kinney, 1999). Also, considerable mobility is present in crowd membership across the high school years (Strouse, 1999).

Crowd membership is an especially salient feature of social life to adolescents, and children's perceptions of crowds change in important ways with age. For example, the prototypicality and exhaustiveness of crowd labels wax and wane with development. O'Brien and Bierman (1987) reported a general shift from 13 to 16 years in the basis by which students identify and describe the crowds and other significant groups in their school. Whereas preadolescents and young adolescents focus on group members' specific behavioral proclivities, older adolescents focus on members' dispositional characteristics and values. Brown and Clasen (1986) found that, when students were asked to name the major crowds in their school, the proportion of responses that fell into typical crowd categories rose from 80% in 6th grade to 95% in 9th grade, and then fell steadily through 12th grade. The average number of crowds named increased across development, from just under 8 at 11 years to over 10 by 18 years. Adolescence also marks the appearance of crowd types (e.g., druggies, brains, punkers) that are rarely mentioned by younger children. Finally, the percentage of students who are able to correctly identify their peer-rated crowd membership increases with age (Brown & Klute, 2003).

Romantic Relationships

Romantic relationships flourish during the adolescent years, evolving from shorter-term "experiments" to longer-term alliances based on personal and relational values (Collins, 2003; Collins, Henninghausen, Schmit, & Sroufe, 1997). Reports of dating involvement among adolescents increase from 25% at age 12 to 75% at age 18 (Carver, Joyner, & Udry, 2003). The duration of romantic relationships also increases during the adolescent years, with 35% of 14- to 15-year-olds and 55% of those 16 or older reporting relationships that lasted for 11 months or more (Carver et al., 2003).

Brown (1999) outlined the progression of adolescent romantic relationships from a developmental-contextual perspective. According to Brown's model, the evolution of adolescent romantic involvement is highly sensitive to the peer context and corresponds with the course of individual identity development. During the initiation phase, concern with the quality of romantic relationships is overridden by attempts to establish a sense of efficacy as a participant in the emerging romantic culture. Adolescents realize that their romantic relationships are closely tied to their social image during the status phase, and thus their selection of romantic partners is increasingly driven by peer perception. During the affection phase, romantic relationships become more personal and less susceptible to the influence of the peer group. Adolescents in the affection phase experience heightened emotional intensity in their romantic relationships as they seek greater intimacy with their partners. Finally, pragmatic concerns about the possibility of long-term commitment supplement the emotional intensity of the affection phase during the bonding phase.

Although romantic relationships seem to appear out of the blue during the preadolescent and adolescent years, important connections between early peer experiences and adolescent romantic relationships exist (e.g., Connolly, Craig, Goldberg, & Pepler, 2004; Connolly & Goldberg, 1999; Shulman, Levy-Shiff, Kedem, & Alon, 1997). For instance, experiences of intimacy with friends and discussions about romantic involvement among friends shape adolescent romantic expectations and readiness. Peer groups also establish norms and provide guidance and support for romantic relationships, and the progression from single-sex to heterosexual peer groups during the preadolescent and adolescent years creates access to potential romantic partners. In turn, adolescent romantic relationships impact existing same-sex peer relationships and friendships. Indeed, romantic relationships promote intimate self-disclosure and elicit support among friends (Connolly & Goldberg, 1999).

Vulnerabilities

Peer experiences play an essential role in adolescents' identity development. Through their involvement in friendships and group activities, adolescents are exposed to norms and values that differ from those in their homes. Discussions with peers and friends, in particular, assist adolescents with understanding themselves and their values (Parker & Gottman, 1989). Friends in adolescence probably have no greater intrinsic influence over one another than at earlier ages (Berndt, 1999). Nonetheless, there exists concern that adolescents' involvement in peer groups contributes to a sharp and unhealthy increase in conformity and decline in autonomy. Concern has particularly been expressed that adolescents promote risk taking and other compromising behaviors in one another (e.g., Fisher & Bauman, 1988; Urberg, Cheng, & Shyu, 1991).

Evidence does support the idea that adolescents are less behaviorally autonomous of their friends than they were at younger ages and less autonomous of friends than of their parents (Fuligni, Eccles, Barber, & Clements, 2001). Further, time use data collected in a North American sample suggest that alcohol and drug use, especially on weekends, are inseparable from companionship with friends for a substantial proportion of adolescents and that partying with groups of friends on Friday and Saturday nights is a peak time for high risk behavior (Larson & Richards, 1998). Additionally, a large number of studies document similarity among members of friendship groups in behaviors such as a delinquency, substance use, and early or unsafe sexual intercourse (e.g., Dishion, Capaldi, Spracklen, & Li, 1995; Keenan et al., 1995; Poulin et al., 1999). These studies have been interpreted as evidence of peer pressure toward deviant behavior in adolescence.

Berndt (1999) cautions that similarities in deviant behavior in friendship dyads or groups partly reflect selection influences, such that individuals with deviant or aggressive tendencies tend to seek out and prefer one another. Moreover, as Berndt notes, friends have a stronger influence over one another's positive or neutral behaviors than antisocial behavior and for the most part adolescents do not anticipate that their friends will react negatively if they resist friends' invitations to engage in deviant activities. Nonetheless, convincing work by Dishion and his colleagues (Dishion et al., 1995, 1996) supports the view that social processes in friendship groups are associated with an escalation of problem behavior in vulnerable adolescents. Specifically, observations of friendship dyads indicate that relationships composed of antisocial teens respond more positively to and reinforce conversation related to rule breaking and deviant behavior than do dyads of nondeviant teens. In turn, involvement in these so-called deviancy training conversations with friends at younger ages is associated with an increase likelihood of escalating deviant behavior and rule breaking in dyad members over ensuing years (see also Keenen et al., 1995).

Apart from the brief occasions during school hours when they are involved in unstructured time with friends, adolescents generally report negative moods during weekdays at school (Csikszentmihalyi & Larson, 1984). In contrast to younger ages, time with peers on weekend evenings emerges as the emotional high point of the adolescent week. These changes in the emotional rhythms of the week are consistent with unprecedented interest and priority that adolescents ascribe to relationships with friends and romantic partners. Not all individual adolescents are able or willing to devote unprecedented time to peer activities on weekends, however, and adolescents who fall short of their own or others' expectations for social involvement may experience unprecedented and acutely negative emotions and loneliness. In their study of time use and mood during this period, for example, Larson and Richards (1998) noted that, while being alone is not generally more aversive to adolescents than to younger children, being alone on a Friday or Saturday night specifically is. Adolescents see Friday and Saturday nights as a time of the week when the most exciting peer group events happen and being alone during this time is especially painful.

Finally, although participation in dating and other forms of romantic involvement with peers of the opposite sex is a significant and welcomed developmental milepost for most heterosexual adolescents (Collins et al., 1997; Collins & Sroufe, 1999), the emergence of this new form of relating in adolescence is neither sudden nor smooth (e.g., Davila, Steinberg, Kachadourian, Cobb, & Fincham, 2004). Instead, as noted, participation in dating and romantic relationships occurs gradually in the context of networks of same-sex friendships (Brown, 1999; Connolly & Goldberg, 1999). The addition of dating partners to an existing network of friends is fraught with social challenges, and in specific friendships, the onset of dating can create a complex social triangle of potential tension (Clark-Lempers, Lempers, & Ho, 1991; Larson & Richards, 1991). As individuals begin spending more time engaged in activities with their dating partners, their time available for activities with existing friends may diminish noticeably. As a result, existing friends, especially those who have not yet begun dating themselves, may regard themselves as neglected and feel lonely (Roth & Parker, 2001). Even where established levels of contact are maintained, existing friends may resent the perceived encroachment into previously sovereign aspects of their partner's life (e.g., serving in the role of confidant). For their part, dating individuals, notwithstanding their excitement over their romantic involvements, may perceive themselves as less similar to their friends than previously or experience guilt over their neglect of existing friends. In the extreme, dating individuals may come to see their friends' frustration and impatience with them as unfair, misdirected, and motivated by petty envy (Roth & Parker, 2001).

Comment

Progress in peer relationships is not a simple unfolding developmental sequence, but, rather, a complex braiding of developmental changes across many levels of description, including the intrapersonal (changes in social understanding and concerns), the interpersonal (changes in the frequency or forms of specific behaviors), the dyadic (changes in qualities of friendships or patterns of involvement in friendships), and the group (changes in configurations of and involvement in cliques and crowds). What is more, development must be described as interlocking across levels. For example, we discussed developmental changes in how children view their behavior, their friendships, and the salient peer groups in their schools. And friendship experiences change children's expectations of friends; but changing friendship expectations lead children to change friends or to take existing friendships in new directions.

In addition, the history of the study of social development has been one of allegiance to dispositional rather than situational explanations of developmental change (Higgins

& Parsons, 1983). In other words, it has been common to assume that the impetus for major developmental change rests in facets of individual development (cognitive growth, physical maturation, etc.) rather than in the regularities of the organizational features of the social-cultural matrix within which the individual is embedded. Our review makes the limitations of this assumption apparent. Organizational features of the environment help to define the timetable for many developments in peer relationships. Were status hierarchies not such a salient structural feature of social life in middle childhood, it is doubtful that children of this age would express as much concern over this issue, and that gossip would play as central a role in their conversations as it does (Parker & Gottman, 1989). Likewise, as Brown (1990) noted, somewhat facetiously, that for too long the tendency has been to regard adolescents' interest in and allegiance to cliques and crowds as a collective expression of a biologically timed herding instinct, rather than recognize that the depersonalized and complex routine of high school can operate to increase young teenagers' motivations for this form of involvement with peers. Without attention to the social-cultural matrix underlying development, our understanding of many of the major mileposts in the development of peer relationships would be hopelessly handicapped.

PEER INTERACTION IN DEVELOPMENT AND SOCIALIZATION

The role of peer interaction in development and socialization has been discussed in many contexts and from a diverse range of theoretical perspectives. No single framework has emerged for organizing this eclectic array of theoretical and other lines of argument, any more than a single framework exists for describing the influence of mothers, fathers, siblings, grandparents, teachers, schools, communities, and the like on development. Indeed, different authors and traditions have tended to emphasize different aspects of the process and outcome of peer interaction and relationships. However, several broad perspectives seem especially important to recognize, both for their influence on scholarship in this area and for their contrasting views of the significance of children's peer experiences.

Perspectives from Personality Theory

The study of personality, with its emphasis on how and why one individual differs from another, would seem to be a natural venue for discussion of the role of peer in social-

ization and, indeed, children's peer experiences have surfaced from time to time as an important socialization context in several grand theories of personality development.

Psychoanalytic and Neo-Psychoanalytic Views

Childhood peer experiences do not figure prominently in most psychoanalytically inspired grand theories of personality development. Sigmund Freud, Erikson, Fromm, Mahler, Horney, Adler, and Jung, for example, devoted only tangential attention to children's friendships and peer experiences. Instead, these theorists focused primarily on the contributions of parents to children's healthy self-perceptions and behavioral functioning and tended to dismiss the importance of peer relationships or downplay their significance. Whereas the individual who begins life with adequate relationships with parents is assumed to succeed in peer relationships, the peer experiences themselves are not seen as central to adaptive or maladaptive personality development (Adelson & Doehrman, 1980; Grunebaum & Solomon, 1987; Youniss & Smoller, 1985).

An exception to this general trend is the attention devoted in the psychoanalytic framework to peer experiences at adolescence. Psychoanalytic authors have supposed that adolescents are drawn to friendships and peer groups in reaction to intrapsychic turmoil (see Blos, 1979; Douvan & Adelson, 1966; A. Freud, 1952). As articulated principally in the work of Anna Freud (1952) and Blos (1962), hormonal changes at puberty repotentiate sexual and aggressive drives to such an extent that children's earlier, hastily constructed defenses against Oedipal feelings are seriously compromised and threatened. As refuge from these reawakened drives, children seek the companionship of peers at this time (Douvan & Adelson, 1966).

Blos (1979), in particular, has suggested that changes at adolescence precipitate a second individuation process (the first, described by Mahler, 1952, occurring in very early childhood) or severing of parental identifications and internalizations. According to Blos, adolescents must shed their family dependencies and loosen their infantile object ties to parents to become members of the adult world. Within Blos's widely accepted framework, attachment to peers and identification with peer groups can play an important role in this process for several reasons:

- Because peers can serve as important sounding boards without arousing anxiety or guilt, adolescents can use discussions with peers to resolve internal conflicts.
- The peer group respects competencies, allowing the adolescent to develop an identity based on personal skills, especially athletic and social ones.

- The peer group provides practical and personal guidance in social situations, especially in heterosexual relationships and behavior.
- The peer group provides honest and critical evaluative feedback about the individual's behavior and personality attributes.

In Blos's view, because adolescents cannot find sexual gratification in the family, and in order to sever family dependencies, they turn to the peer group for support and security. Other psychoanalytic authors are less sanguine about the shift in dependency to peers at adolescence, though no less convinced of its necessity. Douvan and Adelson (1966) worried that in an attempt to free themselves from the control and restrictions of parents, adolescents may fall prey to the tyranny of a peer group, which requires conformity in return for security.

Whatever their specific merits, the claims of theorists such as Douvan, Adelson, Anna Freud, and Blos rest in an important way on assumptions about adolescents' intrapsychic turmoil and emotional lability. These assumptions have been difficult to substantiate, and, indeed, have been challenged in many instances or in specific ways (e.g., Csikszentmihalyi & Larson, 1984; Eccles et al., 1993; Offer, Ostrov, & Howard, 1981). That adolescence heralds a dramatic increase in children's interest in and attachment to peers seems undeniable, as we have discussed.

Sullivan's Psychiatry of Interpersonal Relationships

The psychiatrist Sullivan's (1953) views on children's and adolescents' peer relationships and friendships are similar in some ways, and sharply contrasting in others, to those of classic psychoanalysts, and have received a great deal of recent attention (e.g., Bigelow et al., 1999). Sullivan's formal theory of personality development is fraught with fanciful and arcane constructs, but his observations on the growth of human social motives and relationships have proved surprisingly trenchant. Like Sigmund Freud, Sullivan accepted that underlying biological drives motivate much of human behavior. In contrast to Sigmund Freud, however, Sullivan assumed that anxiety is unavoidable, always has an interpersonal context, interferes with need fulfillment, and leads individuals to construct elaborate security operations to minimize the experience. An important construct in Sullivan's theory is that of personifications, or mental representations of self and others based upon one's accumulated experiences interacting in personal relationships. Sullivan's construct of personifications is quite close to

Bowlby's (1982) better-known hypothesized internal working models, and may have influenced Bowlby's views (Bretherton, 1991).

Sullivan also described the emergence of five basic social needs across the period from infancy to adolescence: tenderness, co-participation in playful activity, acceptance by others, interpersonal intimacy, and sexual contact. According to Sullivan, these needs were fulfilled by specific individuals—parents, peers, same-sex best friends, and opposite-sex partners—in both a sequential and cumulative fashion. Of interest, the period of late childhood or the juvenile era (ages 6 to 9 years) is marked by the increase in the need for acceptance by peers and the development of compeer relationships founded along lines of egalitarian exchange. Somewhat later, during the period of preadolescence (ages 9 to 12 years), children's needs shift from a more general need for group approval to a need for a close, intimate tie to a specific other same-sex peer, or chum. *Chumships* are true intimate relationships, prototypical of later love and other collaborative relationships; chumships revolve around the expression of consensual validation of one another's viewpoints and self.

In addition to offering a general age/stage descriptive framework, Sullivan speculated on the many positive and negative interpersonal and intrapersonal consequences of peer experiences for children. For example, he considered the development of skills for cooperation and compromise, then competition and perspective-taking, empathy, and altruism to emerge from peer experiences in the juvenile and preadolescent eras, respectively. He also emphasized the role of peer experiences in constructing and correcting children's perceptions of self through consensual validation. And, along lines similar to the concept of a developmental deviation in developmental psychopathology, Sullivan offered speculations about malevolent transformations that might accompany developmental arrests of one form or another at specific periods of childhood. Children showing forms of developmental arrest included the malevolent child, the isolated child, the disparaging child, and the ostracized child.

Sullivan had a particularly deep interest in, and concern with, the affective consequences of peer experiences for children. For example, he offered many speculations as to the motivational origins of loneliness, its relation to estrangement in peer relationships, and its role in development and psychopathology. Sullivan defined loneliness as "the exceedingly unpleasant and driving experience connected with the inadequate discharge of the need for human intimacy, for interpersonal intimacy" (p. 290). He felt that intimacy and loneliness defined reciprocal sides of the same developmental-motivational coin, the need for inter-personal integration. According to Sullivan, loneliness "so terrible that it practically baffles recall" (p. 261) ordinar-ily was not experienced until after preadolescence, al-though precursors of loneliness could be found throughout development. In preadolescence, the potential of the loneli-ness experience becomes "really intimidating" (p. 261). At this age, loneliness arises out of "the need for intimate ex-change with a fellow being, whom we may identify as a chum, a friend, or a loved one—that is, the need for the most intimate type of exchange with respects to satisfac-tion and security" (p. 261). In Sullivan's view, loneliness rather than anxiety was the motivational force behind most significant distortions of development.

Finally, Sullivan also stressed the therapeutic potential of peer experiences. He believed that the supportive atmo-sphere of childhood friendships could wholly or partially ameliorate certain developmental arrests resulting from earlier disturbances in relationships with parents and peers. Buhrmester and Furman (1986, p. 50) note in this connection: "It is difficult to overestimate the importance Sullivan gave to the therapeutic potential of chumships. In fact, his innovative treatment for Schizophrenia involved a form of milieu therapy in which the aim was to recreate preadolescent chumships."

Research generally supports Sullivan's claim that inti-macy becomes salient during preadolescence, primarily within the context of same-sex friendships and his predic-tion regarding the role of close friendships in loneliness, the development of social perspective-taking skills, and prosocial orientations (e.g., see Hartup & Stevens, 1997). Children's perceptions of their competence with peers also become more central to their self-definition and self-esteem in preadolescence (Harter, 1999) as Sullivan predicted. Sullivan's provocative thesis about the thera-peutic potential of friendships seems to have received less attention than other aspects of his theory, unfortu-nately. Nevertheless, the work of Selman and his col-leagues (e.g., Selman & Schultz, 1990), though only partly motivated by Sullivan's views, is worth citing in this connection. In Selman's pair therapy, two young adoles-cents with socioemotional and interpersonal difficulties are paired, along with a therapist, for long-term therapy. The dyad is encouraged to play together and the partners are asked to reflect on their interaction together and their relationship. The aim is to achieve a restructuring of the children's immature interpersonal functioning and understanding, improving their individual and joint capacities for engaging in productive interaction with each other and other children. Thus, a legacy of Sulli-van's theory can be identified in recent, productive clini-cal interventions.

Havighurst's Developmental Task Approach

Havighurst (1953) drew early attention to the significance of adjustment with peers for children's well-being and personality development. He argued that adaptation to peers can be viewed as one of many important "tasks" in development. According to Havighurst (1953, p. 2), devel-opmental tasks are "those things a person is to learn if he is to be judged and to judge himself to be a reasonably happy and successful person." They are tasks in the sense that "successful achievement . . . leads to [an individual's] happiness and success with later tasks, while failure leads to unhappiness in the individual, disapproval by the society, and difficulty with later tasks" (p. 2). They are developmental in the sense that each has a period of as-cendance and is subject to arrest. Each "arises at or about a certain period in the life of the individual" (p. 2) and "if the task is not achieved at the proper time it will not be achieved well, and failure in this task will cause partial or complete failure in the achievement of other tasks yet to come" (p. 3).

According to Havighurst (1953), developmental tasks have multiple origins. Some tasks, such as learning to walk, arise mainly from physical maturation. Tasks arising from physical maturation are more universal than other tasks. Other tasks, such as learning to read, arise primarily from cultural pressure. Such tasks are culturally or subculturally relative. The expectations, values, and aspirations of the in-dividual represent the third source of developmental tasks. Like cultural tasks, these vary with the historical cultural context of the individual.

Havighurst (1953) placed considerable emphasis on peer relationships as a task of childhood. Getting along with peers, Havighurst felt, was important in its own right, as well as for its role in helping children attain other tasks in middle childhood, including (1) the development of social skills, a rational conscience, and a scale of values; (2) the learning of appropriate social attitudes; and (3) the achieve-ment of personal independence. He suggested that getting along with peers was a primary task in middle childhood; but he recognized that this challenge was, in a very real sense, a lifelong one. Indeed, he anticipated considerable continuity in adaptation over development, speculating: "The nine or ten year old already shows what he will be like, socially, at fifty" (p. 31). In this way, Havighurst antici-pated the contemporary interest in the long-term adjustment of children with peer relationships difficulties (see Rubin, Bukowski, & Parker, 1998 for a review).

Ultimately, Havighurst's concept of developmental tasks had limited influence on human development research. However, this concept is represented in most of its essential elements, including its focus on the significance of peer relationships, in contemporary organizational or adaptational accounts of development (Sroufe, 1995). Organizational theorists, however, disagree with Havighurst's characterization of development as a series of unfolding tasks that need to be accomplished and then decrease in importance. Instead, organizational theorists stress that most developmental tasks, upon emergence, remain critical to the child's continual adaptation.

Developmental Constructivist Approaches

Besides contributing to a view of children as actively engaged in efforts to interpret, organize, and use information from the environment, developmental constructivists such as Piaget (1932) and Vygotsky (1978) have stressed how structural features of interpersonal relationships influence the development of knowledge, language, social problem-solving skills, and moral behavior. An important distinction in this framework involves the differential affordances of adult-child and child-child interpersonal exchanges, a distinction that Hartup (1989, p. 120) characterized as the distinction between horizontal versus vertical relationships:

> [Children's vertical attachments are] attachments to individuals who have greater knowledge and social power than they do. These relationships, most commonly involving children and adults, encompass a wide variety of interactions among which complementary exchanges are especially salient. For example, adult actions toward children consist mainly of nurturance and controlling behaviors, whereas children's actions toward adults consist mainly of submission and appeals for succorance (Youniss, 1980). [Children's horizontal attachments are] relationships with individuals who have the same amount of social power as themselves. Ordinarily, these relationships involve other children and are marked by reciprocity and egalitarian expectations.

The concept of the differential socialization opportunities in horizontal (peer) versus vertical (adult) interpersonal contexts has been especially influential in the domains of cognitive and moral development.

Cognitive Development

Constructivist approaches to cognitive development have been reviewed in a number of connections recently (e.g., Azmitia, Lippman, & Ittel, 1999; Hogan & Tudge, 1999; Rogoff, 1997). These reviews generally conclude

that under specific circumstances, including many that occur frequently and spontaneously in the course of peer interaction, conversation with other children can promote children's perspective-taking skills, problem solving, language skills, academic achievement, scientific and logical reasoning, and a host of other important cognitive and social-cognitive accomplishments.

Piaget's (1932) influential proposal was that peers promote the advancement of one another's cognitive development through attempts to resolve discrepancies deriving from the differences in their perspectives on a problem. As children interact with other children, they become aware of the contradictions between their own view of a problem and that of their partner. This conflict provokes disequilibrium that can propel children to newer and higher levels of reasoning. Importantly, in Piaget's view it was not so much the simple exposure to the new or better problem-solving strategies of the partner, as the opportunity to confront one's own thinking that was critical; unless children appreciated the inefficiency of their old cognitive strategies they were unlikely to abandon them. According to Piaget, this type of real conceptual advance was not likely to happen in discussion with adults or others with greater status, because children were likely to unilaterally accept the conclusions of higher status individuals.

Whereas Piaget emphasized the contribution of symmetric relationships (i.e., friends, children of similar social and cognitive status), Vygotsky (1978) emphasized the contribution of asymmetric (i.e., parent-child, sibling-child, expert child-novice child) relationships to cognitive development. Thus, Vygotsky also saw peers as important to cognitive development, though by comparison to Piaget, less uniquely so.

The ideas of Piaget and Vygotsky have been explored in a great many experimental and other studies (see Gauvain, 2001). A review of this work suggests:

- In line with both Piaget's and Vygotsky's assertions, children working together can solve problems that neither child is capable of solving alone. Further, children working with other children show real cognitive advances from pre- to posttesting and these advances are stable and in most circumstances generalize to other problems.

- It is important that the partners bring conflicting perspectives to the problem; when two children share an understanding of the problem, little cognitive advance is noted.

- In line especially with Vygotsky's thinking, children also make cognitive gains when they work with partners who have a superior understanding of a problem (though this is not a prerequisite for advancement).

- Children with less advanced partners sometimes show a regression in their thinking about a task. Thus, peer collaboration is not always uniformly facilitative or even neutral. An important interactional constraint seems to be children's certainty of the correctness of their own thinking. When children are more certain of the correctness of their thinking, or the task permits children to be more certain, they are more likely to influence their partners.

- Certain types of conflicts are more likely to promote growth than others. Especially critical are "transactive" discussions—discussions that involve noticing and resolving contradictions in one's partner's logic rather than one's own logic.

- Collaborations with friends may foster greater developmental change than collaborations with nonfriends, at least when the task is a complex one requiring metacommunication skills. Friends seem more inclined to take the important steps of anticipating their partner's confusions and spontaneously justifying and elaborating their own thinking and rationales.

Overall, it appears that the research literature generally supports many of the theoretical assertions of Piaget and Vygotsky regarding the importance of peers in children's cognitive development, even as it suggests some qualifications.

Moral Development

Disputes over objects, distributions of resources, personal norms, customs and rules, respecting others, loyalty, and personal rights are all common features of peer interaction. So, too, are acts of cooperation, forgiveness, kindness, concern, respect, and altruism. In view of the ubiquity of such events, it should not be terribly surprising that peer relationships are an important context for moral development and socialization.

Psychoanalytic and social learning socialization theories have traditionally viewed moral development as children's internalization of adults' skills, knowledge, and conventions. Peer experiences generally have not figured prominently in these formulations, although social learning theorists have recognized the importance of peers as social models and reinforcers of prosocial and antisocial behavior.

Developmental constructivists such as Piaget (1932) and Kohlberg (1969) present a contrasting view. On this view, peer interaction is uniquely suited to the promotion of higher moral reasoning (and presumably behavior). Indeed, Piaget was dismissive of the ability of parents to affect any

real, meaningful change in children's development in this area. In *The Moral Judgment of the Child*, Piaget (1932) suggested that parent-child relationships were a poor context for moral development because they are marked by unilateral authority or constraint. Although children obey their parents, they do so unreflectively. As a result, the moral issues behind rules parents establish are shrouded from and necessarily mysterious to children. With peers, on the other hand, the child is aware that both participants have equal knowledge and authority. When a conflict of interest arises, the child is led to recognize that others have perspectives that differ from his or her own. Because neither of these perspectives have special authority, both children's views have an equal claim to validity, and children are motivated to use discussion, debate, negotiation, and compromise to integrate their conflicting views. The morality of peer interaction is a morality of reciprocity and mutual respect.

As might be imagined, Piaget's hypotheses about the special significance of peer interaction in moral socialization are difficult to evaluate; disentangling the contribution of peer experiences from others' influences on moral judgment is an exceedingly challenging task. However, a number of studies, reviewed by Schlaefli, Rest, and Thoma (1985) and Walker (1986), indicate that peer debate can, in fact, encourage higher levels of moral reasoning in children. In one of the best known of these studies, Damon and Killen (1982) videotaped 5- to 9-year old children in triads during discussion of a distributive justice problem. Pre- and posttests established that the children who participated in these discussions were more likely to advance in their moral reasoning than were children who discussed a similar justice problem with an adult or children who were merely exposed to the pre- and posttests. Similarly, Arbuthnot (1975) found that dyads who debated moral dilemmas toward consensus showed more change in moral reasoning than dyads who passively heard arguments about the dilemmas or who performed extraneous tasks.

These studies and others further suggest, in line with Piaget's thinking, that a crucial impetus to developmental change in the context of peer discussion is the process of transactive discussion. Transactive exchanges are exchanges in which each discussant performs mental operations on the reasoning of his or her partner (e.g., critiques, refinements, extensions, paraphrases of the partner's ideas). Children have been found to employ more transactive statements in the discussions of moral issues with peers than their discussions with mothers (Kruger & Tomasello, 1986), and the use of transactive statements has been found to be an important condition for moral developmental change through peer interaction (e.g., Damon & Killen, 1982).

Cognitive-Social Learning Perspectives

Writers influenced by cognitive-social learning theory have emphasized the ways in which peers extend, elaborate, and alter children's social skills, behavioral tendencies, and self-attributions. According to social learning theory, children generate internal rules linking social behaviors to consequences (praise, criticism, rebuke, rejection) and guide their behavior according to these rules. In part, these rules are learned through direct experience of peer punishment and reinforcement; very simply, children tend to repeat behaviors their peers approve of, and they learn to inhibit actions that peers discourage. In addition, much learning is presumably also vicarious; that is, children learn through observation of other children's behavior and the consequences that other children receive for performing various behaviors. Observation of peers introduces children to new modes of behavior and to the situational and other exigencies governing their performance.

Increasingly, social learning theorists have also stressed that much behavior is controlled by self-generated consequences, concerns, and expectations as well as external forces. Children set standards of achievement for themselves, and self-administer reinforcement when those standards are met and punishment when they are not. The intensity of children's self-reinforcement or self-punishment is governed by many features, but one important factor is social comparison to peers, or the child's assessment of how well his or her behavior compares to that of other children. Bandura (1989) proposed that when children wish to estimate their competence at an activity they tend to compare their performance to that of their peers, especially children who are similar or slightly higher in ability than themselves.

Social learning theory has also emphasized the role of social comparison, and hence peers, in the development of attitudes of personal agency or self-efficacy (Bandura, 1989). Children's beliefs about their abilities, characteristics, and vulnerabilities guide their behavior by determining what actions they attempt and how much effort and persistence they invest in these.

Within the social learning framework, peers influence the developing child according to the same laws of social learning that apply to other socialization agents, including parents, teachers, and television. However, owing to the special features and challenges of membership in peer groups, the content of what children learn from their peers is assumed to be very different in many instances from what they learn from adults. For instance, many authors note that peer experiences have powerful emotional concomitants, suggesting that children develop important emotion regulation competencies in this context (Calkins, Gill, Johnson, & Smith, 1999; Eisenberg, 2002; Eisenberg et al., 2001; Saarni, 1998, 1999; von Salisch, 2000). Observations of preschoolers, for example, suggest that friendship interaction has the implicit goal of maximizing the level of children's enjoyment during play (Parker & Gottman, 1989). For this to occur, friends must be successful in coordinating their behavior; this, in turn, necessitates that children learn skills for inhibiting action and maintaining organized behavior and attention in the face of arousal, excitement, and frustration. Other authors (e.g., Fine, 1981; Hartup, 1983) have noted the especially strong influence of peers on the amount of specific information about sex learned in early adolescence.

Particular progress has been made in the application of cognitive-social learning concepts to the study of the development of aggressive (see for example McCord, 1995; Moffitt, 1993; Nagin & Tremblay, 1999; Poulin & Boivin, 2000; Schwartz, Dodge, Pettit, & Bates, 2000; Tremblay, Mâsse, Vitaro, & Dobkin, 1995; Vernberg, Jacobs, & Hershberger, 1999; Vitaro, Brendgen, & Tremblay, 2000) and prosocial (Masters & Furman, 1981; Ollendick & Schmidt, 1987) tendencies, and to the development of sex-typed behavior (Huston & Alvarez, 1990; Moller, Hymel, & Rubin, 1992). In the last instance, for example, a great deal of research suggests preschool children reward sex-appropriate and punish sex-inappropriate behavior and toy choices (e.g., Eisenberg, Tryon, & Cameron, 1984; Moller et al., 1992). In addition to such direct influences, many authors have noted that the de facto gender segregation of children's play groups during most of childhood and adolescence suggests that boys and girls inhabit almost entirely separate worlds in childhood, with important implications for their social learning (e.g., Zarbatany, Hartmann, & Rankin, 1990). Indeed, it has been suggested that one consequence of growing up in separate worlds is that as children learn a style of interaction that works well with same-sex peers, they become progressively less effective with opposite-sex peers (Leaper, 1994; Maccoby, 1990).

Finally, social learning perspectives have played an important role in understanding how marital distress and conflict in the home may be linked to poor social outcomes in children, including friendship difficulties and child behaviors related to peer rejection (e.g., Du Rocher Schudlich, Shamir, & Cummings, 2004, for reviews). From a cognitive-social learning perspective, marital distress and conflict is thought to exert its negative impact on children's social adjustment indirectly, through the spillover of negative affect and behavior from the marital dyad to the parent-child dyad (Erel & Burman, 1995). Marital conflict and dissatisfaction predict negative attitudes about child rearing as well as insensitive, inconsistent, and harsh treatment of children (Wilson & Gottman, 2002). If children model these behaviors with peers, they are likely to experience rejection. Additionally spousal conflict and hostility can affect children directly by contributing to self-blame and expectations of threat (Grych & Fincham, 1990) and emotional insecurity (Davies, Harold, Goeke-Morey, & Cummings, 2002), and by providing them with models of coercive interpersonal behavior (Webster-Stratton & Hammond, 1999). Indeed, destructive and aggressive marital conflict has been linked with immediate child emotional distress and aggressive behavior; furthermore, children's negative emotional reactivity and aggressive behavior in the home and lab have been linked to internalizing and externalizing problems (Cummings, Goeke-Morey, & Papp, 2003, 2004).

Social Psychology

Because much of the core of the discipline of social psychology is dedicated to understanding the behaviors and attitudes of individuals in their groups and relationships, it might be supposed that the study of children's peer group and friendship experiences represents a rich and long-standing interface between that discipline and the discipline of developmental psychology. In fact, less deliberate cross-fertilization has occurred between these disciplines than might be supposed and appropriate (Durkin, 1995). There are signs that this is changing. For example, there have been several attempts recently to explore the developmental roots of relationship phenomena that are better understood by social psychologists focusing on adult relationships. Examples include research on children's forgiveness (e.g., Enright, Gassin, & Wu, 1992; Enright & the Human Development Study Group, 1991), sensitivity to rejection (Downey & Feldman, 1996), understanding of exclusion and black-sheep individuals who deviate from group norms (Abrams et al., 2003; Killen, Lee-Jim, et al., 2002), and jealousy (Parker et al., 2005). However, the primary exception remains the study of the features and processes of social support in childhood and adolescent friendships.

Interest in social support and its relation to mental health, physical health, and responses to stress has a long-and-storied history in social psychology. Indeed, a large body of empirical work in this tradition indicates that receiving social support, or feeling confident that support will be available when one needs it, helps adults cope more effectively with stressful events and appears to have short-term and long-term benefits for health and psychological well-being (see Cunningham & Barbee, 2000; Pierce, Lakey, Sarason, & Sarason, 1997). Adults commonly name their spouses as the person most likely to provide support during times of need (e.g., Dakof & Taylor, 1990). However, most adults also include friends as a primary source of support (Fehr, 2000). Interestingly, an individual's subjective belief that support is available is generally a better predictor of major outcomes, such as mental and physical health, than are assessments of objective support, such as indices of the size of a person's interpersonal network (see Cunningham & Barbee, 2000). Some investigators have also argued that adults' general perceptions of the availability of social support provide better buffering effects against risk than do the actual specific supportive behaviors provided by partners. The objective aspects of social support networks are affected by social skills that contribute to the development and maintenance of a broad, dense, and reliable network. However, the perception of and satisfaction with social support appears to be influenced by individuals' personality factors, such as attachment style, emotional stability, and extraversion (Von Dras & Siegler, 1997).

Drawing upon this literature, several authors have offered taxonomies of the supportive dimensions of childhood friendships (e.g., Asher et al., 1996). Although these formulations differ in specific ways, there appears to be a broad consensus concerning the dimensions that make up friendship support and the overall significance of these dimensions to children's adjustment and development (see Furman, 1996; Rose & Asher, 2000). In all, at least five major features of friendships and categories of social support have been discussed with some regularity.

A first important supportive feature of children's friendships is self-esteem enhancement and self-evaluation; that is, friendships help children develop and maintain an image of themselves as competent, attractive, and worthwhile. Because friends compliment one another, express care and concern over one another's problems, and boast to others about one another's' accomplishments, friendships are thought to play an especially important role in children's self-esteem and self-image. The self-esteem enhancing and self-validating properties of friendships have been hypothesized to be especially important when children are going through normative changes such as school transitions or puberty or undergoing stress (Sandler, Miller, Short, & Wolchik, 1989), but they are undoubtedly important at other times as well. Moreover, friendships may represent significant contexts for social comparison and hence personal understanding (Berndt, 1999).

A second important function of friendship is the provision of emotional security in novel or threatening situations. Even the simple presence of a friend may boost children's reassurance and confidence. This can have important implications for whether children are willing to explore new environments, try new behaviors, or take the kind of small and large risks often associated with growth.

Third, friendships are important nonfamilial contexts for intimacy and affection. The expression of caring, concern, and affection for one's partner have been rightly identified as important, perhaps even defining, characteristics of children's friendships. As they get older, children increasingly emphasize intimacy, self-disclosure, openness, and affection as components of friendship, both in their general beliefs about friendships and in their descriptions of their actual friendships (see Newcomb, Bukowski, & Bagwell, 1999).

Fourth, friends provide informational or instrumental assistance to one another. Like adults, children count on their friends' physical assistance with difficult or time-consuming tasks and look to their friends to provide constructive criticism, counsel, and information.

Finally, friends provide one another with companionship and stimulation. As Asher et al. (1996) note, the companionship aspects of childhood friendship provide some of the most enduring and romantic images of childhood friendship. Friends of all ages emphasize the enjoyment they derive from one another and from the activities they undertake jointly, although the nature of friendship companionship changes developmentally, of course. Successful and stimulating shared experiences contribute to a sense of shared history, joint fate, and a perception of investment in the relationship.

To date, the number of studies of children focusing on friendship support, stress, and adjustment is limited. The question of whether friendship support in childhood can offer the same strong-stress buffering role that is so celebrated in adulthood has not therefore been fully answered. The available evidence, however, supports the conclusion that friendship support among children functions similarly to that among adults insofar as it contributes to children's ability to cope with life stressors of many types (see Belle, 1989; Compas, 1987; Dubow, Tisak, Causey, Hryshko, & Ried, 1991; Kramer & Gottman, 1992; Wentzel, McNamara-Barry, & Caldwell, 2004). How and under what circumstances supportive friendships are beneficial in helping children and adolescents weather stress is less clear. In an insightful analysis of this problem, Berndt (1989) offers the following hypotheses and conclusions, however:

- Friendships do not buffer children from stress if the friendships themselves do not survive the stressor. In other words, evidence for an inoculating effect of positive friendships is weak. Children with better friendships do not endure stressful events better than children with less adequate friendships if the stressful event separates children from their friends. School transitions and family relocations are good examples of stressful events that increase the mortality of friendships (e.g., Wargo Aikins et al., 2005). Further, the loss of important friendships under these circumstances is, in all likelihood, itself a stressful event for children.

- Supportive friendships have the greatest influence on children's adjustment when they offer the specific type of support needed to deal with a particular stressor. For example, "when a child needs help with homework, a friend who answers questions about the assignment . . . may render more effective support than a friend who simply tries to make the child feel better about his or her abilities" (Berndt, 1989, p. 318). Indeed, support that does not match the stressor may under some circumstances be less productive than no support at all.

- Finally, the child must access or take advantage of the support that is available to him or her under the stressful circumstances. In many instances, this must be an active, purposeful process. As Asher et al. (1996) note, to do so effectively, children must recognize that a problem exists, and understand the seriousness of the problem, the problem details, and the specific emotions associated with the problem. And they must ensure that their affection and advice is perceived and received as selflessly motivated and genuine.

Likewise, recent research by Rose (2002) also sounds a cautionary note. She argues that while opportunities for self-disclosure and interpersonal support within friendships have generally positive benefits for members, in some instances these discussions dominate friends' conversation and interaction together, a process labeled *co-rumination*.

Co-ruminating friends endlessly discuss and revisit problems, speculate on solutions and hypothetical outcomes, and focus on negative feelings. Rose's (2002) data indicate that, while friends, especially boys, who co-ruminate may become closer, they may also place themselves at risk for internalizing difficulties including depression.

Cooley, Mead, and the Symbolic Interaction View

The idea that children's experiences with peers contribute to the development of their self-concepts seems an especially attractive one. This proposal is at the heart of symbolic interaction theories, and, as Bukowski and Hoza (1989) noted, can in fact, be traced back to the earliest days of American psychology. One of the first authors to emphasize this point was Cooley (1902), whose ideas were later extended by Mead (1934; see Corsaro, 1985). Mead, like Cooley before him, suggested that children experience themselves indirectly through the responses of other members of their significant peer groups. Mead suggested that the ability to reflect on the self developed gradually over the early years of life, first through imitation of peers (and adults) and later primarily as a function of peer play and games. Mead argued that participation in rule-governed games and activities with peers led children to understand and coordinate the perspectives of others in relation to the self. Thus, perspective-taking experiences resulted in an understanding of the generalized other or the organized perspective of the social group. This development, in turn, led to the emergence of an organized sense of self. Therefore, to Mead, peer interaction was essential for the development, not only of perspective-taking skills, but also for the development of self-system.

Authors influenced by this perspective have emphasized the contributions of peer relationships to specific social skills and, particularly, to children's self-presentational or impression management skills for positioning oneself effectively and adaptively in social situations (e.g., Denzin, 1977; Fine, 1981, 1987). Fine (1981), for example, has argued that childhood peer relationships, especially friendships, are important arenas for testing the bounds of acceptable behavior and developing poise under stress. He noted that within the bounds of friendship, inadequate displays will typically be ignored or corrected without loss of face. In this connection, Grunebaum and Solomon (1987) observed that:

> Much childhood play takes the form of deliberately perpetuating a loss of poise. Children everywhere play pranks, induce dizziness, trip one another, disarrange clothing, kid or

tease one another. In peer relations these tests of social poise help prepare the child for the maintenance of identity and self control later in life. (p. 480)

Interpretive Approaches to Peer Culture and Child Socialization

Interpretive writers have been highly critical of psychoanalytic, social learning, and other conceptualizations of socialization that describe socialization as the private and unilateral internalization of adult skills and knowledge (see Corsaro & Miller, 1992; Corsaro & Rizzo, 1988; Rizzo, 1989). In common with symbolic interaction and developmental constructivist authors, they stress children's proclivity to interpret, organize, and exploit information from the environment and thereby shape their own socialization experiences and outcomes. However, the interpretive approach extends the constructivist one by stressing that the "environment" itself is a social construction—a world of habitual interactive routines and shared understandings that permit children to participate further in social activity. In development, "children enter into a social system and, by interacting and negotiating with others, establish understandings that become fundamental social knowledge on which they continually build" (Corsaro & Rizzo, 1988, p. 880).

Interaction with peers plays an indispensable role in this process: By interacting with playmates in organized play groups and schools, children produce the first in a series of peer cultures in which childhood knowledge and practices are gradually transformed into the knowledge and skills necessary to participate in the adult world (Corsaro & Rizzo, 1988).

An especially valuable aspect of the interpretive approach to children's peer interaction is the stress placed on documenting the socially shared and culturally relevant meaning behind many of the recurrent and predictable interaction routines that make up much of the day-to-day social life of children with their peers. Corsaro (1985), for example, has described the shared concerns underlying the common spontaneous themes in preschooler's social fantasy play. More generally, interpretive authors have emphasized how children are frequently exposed to social knowledge in adult-child interaction they do not fully grasp. Such ambiguities will often go unresolved in that context because the orderly nature of adult-child interaction does not demand their resolution. However, these uncertainties may be readdressed later in the interaction routines that make up peer culture. Contrariwise, children also seem to appropriate certain elements of the adult culture to deal with practical problems in the peer culture. In such reciprocal fashion, children produce and reproduce their culture through their socialization experiences in the peer group.

Ethological and Evolutionary Insights

The application of ethological and evolutionary principles and methods to understanding children's peer experiences has waxed and waned over the decades. Excellent early historical examples include work by Blurton-Jones (1972b), Konner (1975), Rosenblum, Coe, and Bromley (1975), Savin-Williams (1979), and Suomi and Harlow (1975), among others. Ethologists Robert Cairns (1979) and Robert Hinde (1979), in particular, deserve singular credit for their efforts to bring broader attention to insights from evolution, social ethology, and developmental psychobiology to the hearth of the growing science of children's peer experiences. Work in this tradition declined over the ensuing decades, although evidence exists that this trend is reversing (e.g., Hawley, 2002, 2003). Complete treatment of the insights into peer experiences left by these perspectives are beyond the scope of this chapter and have been summarized by others to some degree (e.g., Rubin, Hastings, et al., 1998). A few footprints of this perspective bear mentioning however.

Animal Studies of Peer Deprivation

Because experiments involving social deprivation are possible with nonhuman primates, comparative social ethology has provided compelling, albeit isolated, illustrations of the necessity of experiences with age-mates for adequate adjustment. A series of classic studies by Harlow, Suomi, and associates (see Suomi, 1979; Suomi & Harlow, 1975), for example, established that rhesus monkeys reared with adequate adult but impoverished peer contact displayed inappropriate social, sexual, and aggressive behavior. Moreover, the longer such monkeys were denied the opportunity to interact with peers, the more glaring their social inadequacies. For obvious reasons there are no parallel studies with humans, but a study by Hollos and Cowan (1973) of children with extensive contact with their parents but grow up virtually without age-mates on isolated farms in Norway suggested that, compared to controls, social role-taking skills are impaired but tasks involving nonsocial logical cognitive operations are not. In other words, the problems that the peer isolated children displayed were specifically social.

Descriptive Studies of Child Behavior

A commitment to providing a detailed descriptive account of the behavioral repertoire of a species is a common

focus to all ethological work (Blurton-Jones, 1972b; Cairns, 1979; Strayer & Strayer, 1976). Over the years, then, ethologically inspired work has provided almost an encyclopedia wealth of data on children's behavior with age-mates. Much of this work was largely atheoretical. Early, classic examples include studies of sociability and social participation (Parten, 1932; Thomas, Loomis, & Arrington, 1933), assertiveness (Dawe, 1934), sympathetic and altruistic behaviors (Murphy, 1937), and aggression (Goodenough, 1931). Representative of this tradition is early work by Blurton-Jones (1972a). Blurton-Jones (1972a) observed the 25 oldest and youngest members of preschool group for over 2 hours each in 5 minute blocks using a rich taxonomy of codes built up over time and from experience. The detail apparent in Blurton-Jones's (1972a) codes are instructive. His codes included: get red face, cry, pucker, take, fixate, low frown, take-tug-grab, hit, jump, run, slap laugh, smile, watch, give, to name only a few. Factor analyses reveal at least three broad classes of purposeful behavior with peers; play versus work, aggression, and general social behavior. More detailed analysis of the associations among these behaviors produced further interesting observations. For example, toy use played an important role in precipitating aggression in the youngest children and therefore children who were not strongly attracted to toys were involved in fewer conflicts with their peers than other children.

Most contemporary efforts, however, have drawn more directly upon a priori theoretical premises based in ethological or evolutionary principles. An example is recent interest in rough-and-tumble play, or play fighting (e.g., Boulton, 1996; Pellegrini, 2003). Although rough-and-tumble play is a form of aggression, its playful tenor signals that the aggressive intent of the behavior should be discounted. Work by Pellegrini (2003), however, suggests a more complicated picture. Pellegrini reasoned that play fighting among males helps establish and preserve the broader social order, whereas male-female play fighting represents early sexual interest and courtship rituals. Consistent with this hypothesis, male-male play fighting preceded male-female play fighting during the transition to 6th grade. Moreover, careful observation of boys' rough-and-tumble play indicated that boys' and girls' understanding of this behavior depends on their experience with it. Whereas, while boys with less experience with play fighting tend to discount its hostile intent, boys with more experience better appreciate that the surface structure of play fighting can mask underlying subtle efforts at dominance and intimidation. Girls with greater direct experience with rough-and-tumble play, however, were more likely to see it as playful than their counterparts with no experience with this form of behavior.

Ethological Insights into Social Organization

The application of ethological principles to understanding social organization has a long history and continues to yield productive findings. As an example, building on early ethological work on social dominance, Hawley (e.g., Hawley, 1999) reinterpreted and reintroduced the concept of social dominance and made a case for its relevance for the development of personality and social functioning. Her evolutionary approach led her to focus first on the *function* of behavior (competition) over the *structure* of behavior. Consequently, she views structurally distinct behaviors (e.g., prosociality and coercion) to be functionally similar (i.e., resource control strategies); resources can be won via cooperation and forging friendly alliances or aggression. This perspective challenges us to view prosociality and antisociality to be two sides of the same coin rather than opposite ends of a single dimension.

In her studies, Hawley and colleagues have demonstrated the social and adjustment implications of resource control attempts and strategy employment. Relative social dominance ranking, for example, impacts play patterns and, thus, who attends to, defers to, or imitates who as early as the toddler years (Hawley & Little, 1999). Dominant children thus not only profit from material rewards but also their competitive competence wins social prestige not enjoyed by subordinate children. According to Hawley, the social esteem of superior competitors is not a quirk of early childhood, but is maintained over the life span. Her work with adolescents has shown that the most effective resource controllers continue to be admired (and liked) by the peer group, even though they are highly aggressive. These so-called bistrategic individuals employ both prosocial and coercive strategies in ways that (1) make them extremely effective at goal attainment, (2) earn them a reputation for aggression (both overt and relational), and (3) reveal they are at the same time highly socially skilled (Hawley, 2003; Hawley, Little, & Pasupathi, 2002). In contrast to these aggressive powerholders, noncontrollers (those who make no resource control attempts) appear to be the most at risk. Even though they are very low on aggression, they are rejected and victimized by their peers, and experience the highest levels of ill-being (Hawley et al., 2002).

Insights from Attachment Theory

As Furman (1999, p. 135) has noted, "Human beings are predisposed to affiliate with known others. We are social animals, and have been throughout the course of evolution. Natural groups are characteristic of all humans (Foley, 1987)." Bowlby's attachment theory was formulated to account for human infants' attraction to and dependence on others and to specify how early experiences with significant others, particularly adult caregivers, are carried forward in development (Ainsworth, Blehar, Waters, & Wall, 1978; Bowlby, 1982; Bretherton, 1990; Sroufe, 1983). As expressed by Sroufe and Fleeson (1986, p. 52), one of the basic premises of attachment theory is that "The young child seeks and explores new relationships within the framework of expectations for self and others that emerges from the primary relationship." In most instances, infants' most significant earliest relationship is that with their mothers. Thus, according to the theory, the early mother-child relationship lays the groundwork for the children's understanding of and participation in subsequent familial and extra-familial relationships. Because the quality of infants' attachments with their mothers varies, children's later social outlook and success with peers is expected to vary as well.

In the case of children with secure attachment histories, an internalized or working model of relationships is built up; that is, comprised of the belief that the parent is available and responsive to one's need for protection, nurturance, and physical care. In a reciprocal fashion, the child with a secure attachment history is also expected to come to regard him- or herself as competent and worthy of parental love and nurturance. In particular, attachment theory predicts at least three specific, salutary influences on children's internal working models and ultimate success with peers. First, a secure attachment relationship with the primary caregiver promotes positive social expectations. Children are disposed to engage other children, and expect peer interaction to be rewarding. Second, their experience with a responsive and empathic caregiver builds the rudiments of a social understanding of reciprocity. Finally, through a history of responsive care and support for autonomy within the relationship, the child develops a sense of self-worth and efficacy. This internal outlook is thought to be important to promoting curiosity, enthusiasm, and positive affect, characteristics that other children find attractive.

Alternatively, when parental insensitivity contributes to the development of an insecure primary attachment, children are thought to develop an internal working model of relationships that stress their unpredictable nature, and images of themselves as unworthy and ineffectual. According to Bowlby an attachment relationship that provides neither comfort nor support is likely to arouse anxiety and anger. This may lead to the insecure child's behaving in the peer group "by shrinking from it or doing battle with it" (Bowlby, 1973, p. 208). Children who "shrink" anxiously away from peers preclude themselves from the positive outcomes associated with exploration and peer play. Children who do battle with their peers likely engage in inappropriate exploration and play, thereby leading to rejection and isolation by the peer group.

Attachment theory, then, suggests a number of hypothesis concerning aspects of the quality of children's attachment with caregivers and children's later relationships, including those with peers and romantic partners (e.g., Furman, Simon, Shaffer, & Bouchey, 2002; Kerns, Contreras, & Neal-Barnett, 2000). And indeed, recent research generally supports many of these predictions. A number of studies, for example, have examined the general social orientation and specific social skills of young children with secure and insecure attachment histories. For example, evidence suggests that infants with secure attachment histories are later more popular and socially competent in the peer group during preschool and elementary school than their insecurely attached counterparts (Allen, Moore, Kuperminc, & Bell, 1998; Booth, Rubin, Rose-Krasnor, & Burgess, 2004; Clark & Ladd, 2000; Kerns, Cole, & Andrews, 1998; Schneider, Atkinson, & Tardif, 2001; Simon, Paternite, & Shore, 2001; Sroufe, 1995). Furthermore, there appears to be a contemporaneous association between the security of parent-child attachment, social competence, and peer popularity (Allen et al., 1998; Booth, Rose-Krasnor, McKinnon, & Rubin, 1994; Granot & Mayseless, 2001; Kerns, Klepac, & Cole, 1996). Likewise, research also suggests an association between children's attachment histories and qualities of their contemporaneous and later best friendships and romantic partners (Booth et al., 2004; Freitag, Belsky, Grossmann, Grossmann, & Scheurer-Englisch, 1996; Furman et al., 2002; Hodges, Finnegan, & Perry, 1999; Lieberman, Doyle, & Markiewicz, 1999; Rubin, Dwyer, et al., 2004).

Dimensions of Individual Differences in Adjustment to Peers

Peer social experiences differ in an almost bewildering array of ways across individual children. Elsewhere (Parker et al., 1995; Rubin, Parker, & Bukowski, 1998) we have argued that most attempts to conceptualize variability in children experiences fall into either efforts to repre-

sent children's friendship success, on the one hand, and group acceptance versus rejection, on the other. Although a comprehensive treatment of this issue is beyond the scope of this chapter (see Bierman, 2004; Rose & Asher, 2000; Rubin et al., 1998), a brief overview of the conceptual underpinnings and assessment options in these areas is warranted.

It is important at the outset to acknowledge the distinction between not getting along with peers and displaying troublesome behavior such as aggressiveness toward peers and social withdrawal. Behavioral assessment is one of the oldest traditions of differential child psychology (see, for example, pioneering studies of character by Buhler, 1931; Hartshorne & May, 1929), but behavioral assessments are only indirect assessments of difficulties with peers. As Parker and Asher (1987) proposed a number of years ago, this issue should be understood as the issue of whether measures of *what* the child is like with peers can substitute for measures of *whether* the child is liked by peers. In general, they cannot. Whether peers like a child is manifestly a question about that child's adjustment with peers. Although issues arise about how best to address this question, its status as a question about adjustment with peers is unassailable. Alternatively, whether what a child is like—or how the child behaves—measures adjustment with peers depends partly on the focus of the assessment. Some dimensions of behavioral differences, of course, are irrelevant or presumably only very indirectly indicative of success or failure with peers. Behavior directed toward adults or that is very academically oriented may fall in this category. By contrast, it is difficult to argue that behaviors such as aggressiveness and social withdrawal are not signs of social failure with peers. Even so, the relation between what a child is like and whether a child is liked is an imperfect one, and the task of deciding which behaviors, if any, should be taken as signs of adjustment or maladjustment with peers is a thorny one.

Additionally, a distinction needs to be made between the objective circumstances of children's experiences with peers and children's subjective appraisals, such as their social outlook, motivational orientation to social participation, and attitudes and affect surrounding groups and relationships (Bierman, 2004). Children with objective peer difficulties experience subjective distress over their circumstances. However, children's views of their social success can be widely disparate from their objective circumstances (see Bierman, 2004). Targeting children on the basis of their interpersonal outlook is an important and potentially profitable pursuit in its own right, but should not be confused with the task of identifying children with objective peer difficulties.

Friendship

Friendship is a subjective relationship and an inherently dyadic construct. Children perceive their friendship partners in particularized rather than role-related ways. They stress the uniqueness of the relationship and reject efforts to treat particular friendship partners as interchangeable with others. Researchers and other observers may note commonalities in personalities or behavioral tendencies across the friendships of a focal child, but the focal child is likely to be impressed by the distinctions and diversity among his or her individual partners and relationships.

These subjective and reciprocal properties are challenges to understanding and require special caution in assessment. For example, to gauge children's group acceptance, other children's affection for the target must be obtained by polling pertinent group members. Conclusions will be misleading if the number of polled members is too small or not representative. But they are not negatively affected by the inadvertent or unavoidable omission of an isolated and particular group member's opinion. Moreover, the focal child need not participate in this assessment. In the assessment of friendship, however, the focal child's perceptions of his or her circle of friends *must* be sought and aligned with independent evidence of reciprocity of affection obtained directly or indirectly from each of these implicated individuals (Asher et al., 1996). Moreover, evidence of reciprocity of affection alone is usually insufficient to presume or substantiate claims of friendship. Children may enjoy each other's company in school but never spend time together outside of school or in other ways have experiences together that lead them to think of each other as friends. Indeed, sometimes children have only limited direct contact with other children they report liking. For example, children can admire another child from a distance, can be grateful to someone who is only an acquaintance, or have affection for someone whose leadership facilitates the group's functioning (Parker et al., 1999). Yet, friendship generally implies that the individuals involved in the relationship not only like or admire one another, but have labeled their relationship a friendship, have some shared history together, are committed to one another, and are comfortable being perceived as a pair of friends by others. Normally, friendship cannot be presumed unless children have been expressly asked whether the relationship in question is a friendship.

There are many diverse, yet nonredundant ways of representing dimensions of differences in friendship experiences among individuals. These include distinctions among individuals in the size and organization of their friendship networks and distinctions among individuals in types of relationship properties that are typical of their friendships.

Friendship Network Size, Density, and Durability

Differences among individuals in friendship network size can be easily and reliably quantified by several techniques (see Bukowski & Cillessen, 1998; Parker et al., 1995). In early childhood, it is common to ask parents or teachers to identify how many friends a child has and perhaps who those partners are (e.g., Gottman, 1983; Howes, 1988). Typically, researchers do not give these informants specific criteria by which the presence of a friendship should be determined. Instead, it is often simply assumed that these informants share the researcher's definition of friendship, which may or may not always be the case. With older children, researchers rely primarily on reciprocal sociometric nomination procedures to assess children's involvement in friendships. Typically, children are presented with a roster or a set of pictures of their same-sex classmates (or some other functionally similar group) and asked to circle or otherwise indicate which members are their best or close friends. The pattern of choices is then examined to identify children who nominate one another. Less often, investigators have used reciprocated high ratings as an index of friendship, either alone or in conjunction with friendship nominations (e.g., Berndt & Hoyle, 1985; Bukowski, Hoza, & Newcomb, 1994). Both procedures are consistent with the requirement that friendship needs reciprocity and is predicated upon affection concerns rather than instrumental issues. When nomination measures explicitly refer to friendship (e.g., "Who are your three best friends?"), they further assure the nominations that surface do so specifically because children have recognized friendship relationships with these individuals (versus some other reason for mutual liking).

Many personal and behavioral traits of children have been reported to be correlated with the size of children's friendship networks (see Parker et al., 1999). Thus, it would appear that the differences children show in the size of their social networks are not haphazard or accidental; instead, size differences appear to reflect differences in individual children's social competence, or, in the very least, differences across children in their preferred manner of relating to others. In most instances, it is the subgroup of children who are friendless that appears to be responsible for these associations (Parker et al., 1999). It is less clear that children's personal dispositions are the primary determinant of whether children have only a few versus many friends.

A related issue is whether children accrue emotional benefits from participation in many versus only a few friendships. As Parker et al. (1999) point out, it seems unlikely that having one friend would provide children with all of their relationship needs. On the one hand, a child may derive companionship from one friendship and derive intimacy from another friendship. Thus, additional friends should help children meet their interpersonal needs more completely, thereby reducing their loneliness. On the other hand, large friendship networks increase not only the opportunities for social support but also the responsibilities and work necessary to maintain one's relationships (Rook, 1988). Furthermore, large friendship networks may increase opportunities for conflict, jealousy, and rivalry among members of the network. Very limited research exists on this point. Parker and Seal (1996) examined this issue in connection with children's feelings of loneliness. In a study of the evolution of children's social relationships over the course of a month-long summer camp, Parker and Seal assessed the reciprocal friendships of 215 8- to 10-year-old children at several time points. At every point of assessment in the study, children with more friends were less lonely than children with fewer friends. However, when children who were chronically friendless were removed from these analyses, number of friends was not significantly related to children's feelings of loneliness. These results suggest that the ability to predict loneliness from number of friends is largely a function of the distinction between children without friends and children with one or more friends and do not support the commonsense notion that more friends is always better.

In addition to size, children's friendship networks can vary in terms of how close the members are with one another. In dense networks, all of a child's friends are also friends with each other. In less dense networks, particular friendships tend to be isolated from other friendship pairs. To date, research in this area has rarely used network density as an individual-difference variable. Nonetheless, some existing research (e.g., Benenson, 1994; Parker & Seal, 1996) demonstrates that individual children do tend to show reliable differences in the density of their friendship networks. The psychological significance of network density is still an open question, however. Intuitively, a relatively connected, or dense, social network may reduce children's vulnerability to loneliness by fostering a greater sense of community, a greater sense of belonging, and a stronger feeling of security than

a less dense one that pulls children in different, and perhaps competing, directions. Of course, just the opposite may also be the case. It is possible that density contributes to loneliness by heightening the tensions, rivalries, and jealousy of network members. To date, density has been investigated so infrequently that firm conclusions are lacking (Parker et al., 1999).

Finally, some children's friendships tend to be short-lived, whereas other children are clearly capable of sustaining friendships over even very long periods of time. Instability in a network may be reflected in its size, at least when viewed over time. Children's network size can grow over time as new friends are added. Conversely, children who have made many friends may find themselves friendless at some future point if they have difficulty keeping these relationships and difficulty forming new friendships. Accordingly, the trajectory of children's friendship network size over time can augment information that is available through a one-time measurement of size alone (Parker & Seal, 1996).

Friendship Quality

Considering the wide variations in individual characteristics that children bring with them to their friendships, it is reasonable to expect that not all friendships will be alike. Such differences are likely to be related to children's subsequent adjustment, and thus investigators have sought to develop procedures for reliably and validly assessing them. The most common approach involves assessing the features of children's friendships through children's own reports (see Furman, 1996). Assessments of this type are usually conducted with questionnaires or interview procedures, and are predicated on the belief that a child's impression of a relationship is the best index of the quality of this relationship for the child (Furman, 1996).

Although less frequent than self-reports, observational techniques can also be used to study children's relationships with friends. Part of the reluctance of researchers to use observational approaches may stem from the formidable task of isolating the contributions of individual members to the observed patterns of dyadic interaction (Hinde & Stevenson-Hinde, 1976, 1987). This is a very real concern, but some promising observational methods for describing inter-dyad variation have appeared (e.g., Dunn, Cutting, & Fisher, 2002; Lansford & Parker, 1999; Simpkins & Parke, 2002; Youngblade, Park, & Belsky, 1993). Presumably, any interpersonal behavior between friends may be amenable to observational assessments. Researchers have generally been interested in dimensions of behavior that relate to the putative functions of friendship (e.g., provision of companionship, level of intimate disclosure, degree of helpful advice) or address the affective properties of the relationship (e.g., the affective bonds between friends). Children's conflict and disagreement with friends have also been of interest.

Acceptance versus Rejection in the Peer Group

Children who are liked by most members of a particular group enjoy acceptance in that group. Most children in the group have come to feel that there are many more things to like than dislike about these individuals, and this favorable perception is the prevalent attitude among the members of the group as a whole (Parker et al., 1999). Conversely, when a group rejects children, a consensus has formed among members that a particular child is undesirable, unsuitable, or uninteresting. For their part, children seek affiliation with and develop allegiances to both formal and informal peer groups because inclusion in a group provides a sense of belonging and permits avenues to self-expression and identity development that are not and cannot be cultivated in the context of even the most successful dyadic friendships (Newman & Newman, 2001).

Parker et al. (1999), among others (see Bigelow et al., 1996; Bukowski & Hoza, 1989; Rubin, Bukowski, & Parker, 1998), have stressed the importance of distinguishing friendship success from broader group acceptance. Many members of the group may hold a very positive attitude toward a particular child, but not all may consider that child a friend. Children may enjoy each other's company in school but never spend time together outside of school or in other ways have experiences together that lead them to think of each other as friends. Indeed, sometimes children have only limited direct contact with other children they report liking. For example, children can admire another child from a distance, can be grateful to someone who is only an acquaintance, or may look up to someone for their leadership and facilitation of the group's functioning. Thus, the dimension of group liking/disliking, or group acceptance/rejection specifies the *relation* of a child to a group of peers, but not the child's *relationships* with specific others. Nonetheless, children are no less keenly concerned with status of their relation to significant peer groups than they are with the state of their close friendships.

A wide variety of techniques is available for conceptualizing and assessing children's group acceptance versus rejection status, but far and away the most common procedure involves sociometric assessment to obtain group members' ratings or nominations of liked and disliked others (see Bierman, 2004; Cillessen & Bukowski, 2000; Parker et al., 1995). Sociometric assessments of group acceptance date at least as far back as Moreno (1934), who pioneered the technique of asking children to nominate liked and disliked other individuals and used the tallies from these surveys to graph sociograms that readily depicted the interpersonal structure of a groups as well as which individuals were popular and which were marginalized or rejected. Moreno's (1934) interest in group dynamics and structure did not leave the same lasting legacy as his interest in the identification of popular and unpopular individuals (but see Bukowski & Cillessen, 1998). Today, Moreno's legacy is most apparent in contemporary assessments of *sociometric status classification* particularly the version formulated and validated by Coie, Dodge, and Coppotelli (1983).

In this procedure, children in a specified group, usually a classroom, are asked to name the 3 to 5 other members they like most and like least. Based on this polling, tallies of the number of positive and negative nominations each member of the group received from all other members are obtained and combined in specific ways to categorized individuals in one of several mutually exclusive and exhaustive status categories. Broadly: Children who receive many "like" and few "dislike" nominations are labeled popular, those who receive many "like" and many "dislike" nominations are controversial. The other categories are rejected (liked by few and disliked by many), neglected (liked by few and disliked by few), and average (often, but not always, all the remaining unclassified children). Recent improvements on this approach, among other things, include efforts to enhance the classification strength of the specific categories (DeRosier & Thomas, 2003).

An alternative sociometric procedure, the *roster-and-rating* rating scale technique (Singleton & Asher, 1977), requires children to rate each of their classmates on a Likert-type scale, according to how much they like or would like to play with the child. Scale points usually range from *Not at all* (1) at the low end to "very much" or "*A lot*" (5) at the high end. By averaging the ratings that a specific child receives from his or her classmates, the researcher obtains a direct summary measure of the child's acceptance in the group. Researchers also often standardize these ratings within sex and classroom to correct for biases that may exist when children are asked to rate opposite sex classmates and to facilitate the aggregation of data across classrooms (see Bukowski, Sippola, Hoza, & Newcomb, 2000). Sociometric rating assessments offer an especially attractive alternative to nomination-based procedures with children in middle school or junior high, where it is impractical or inappropriate to define a referent group (such as circumscribed classroom) on which to base social preference and impact scores (e.g., Parker et al., 2005).

Experience with sociometric assessments of acceptance and rejection has led to the conclusion that peer group status is relatively stable over time (e.g., Cillessen, Bukowski, & Haselager, 2000; Hardy et al., 2000; Newcomb & Bukowski, 1984). For example, regardless of the particular sociometric classification system employed, popular children tend to remain popular, whereas rejected children remain rejected (e.g., Brendgen, Vitaro, Bukowski, Doyle, & Markiewicz, 2001). It has been demonstrated consistently that the neglect and controversial categories are the least stable (DeRosier & Thomas, 2003). When changes do occur it is usually from popular to average and vice-versa or from neglected to average. Rarely do popular children become rejected, and even more rarely do rejected children become popular. What is more, the available evidence supports the assertion that an individual's sociometric status classification is not only stable over time in existing groups, but consistent from one group setting to another (see Bierman, 2004).

Stability in group acceptance and rejection is important as it supports researchers' assumptions about why individual children receive the group status they do; namely, that group acceptance or rejection status reflects the social skills and other characteristics of the individual child rather than whimsical or idiosyncratic aspects of the groups in which they find themselves. Nonetheless, progress has been made recently in understanding context, reputation, and other group factors that dictate which children are rejected versus accepted in groups (e.g., Abrams et al., 2003) and it is a mistake to underestimate the role that group level factors play in status emergence and maintenance. Relatedly, researchers have sometimes asked children to nominate peers they *believe* to be popular or rejected in the group. This procedure, then, taps the peer group's *perception* of who is accepted and rejected not their actual acceptance or rejection status. Available evidence cautions against confusing these constructs. Sociometrically and peer-perceived popular individuals are almost wholly distinct groups of individuals (Buskirk et al., 2004; LaFontana & Cillessen, 1999; Parkhurst & Hopmeyer, 1998). Children perceived as popular often are not uniformly positively regarded, and might best be described as controversial (Buskirk et al., 2004; Parkhurst & Hopmeyer, 1998; see also LaFontana & Cillessen, 1999).

DIFFICULTIES WITH PEERS: SHORT- AND LONG-TERM CLINICAL SIGNIFICANCE

Given the many roles that group acceptance and friendship experiences are thought to play in development, it is not surprising that questions of whether and how children's development and well-being are compromised by persistent difficulties with peers. Questions concerning the contributions of peer interaction and friendships to development and those involving the consequences of rejection by peers or other forms of negative peer experiences are obviously related. The better we understand the roles peer experiences play in development the more prescience we can have regarding which children are likely to be at risk for broader adjustment difficulties and which areas of adjustment are likely to be compromised in these children. In actuality, however, studies of the functions of peer experiences in development and studies of the short- and long-term risks associated with peer difficulties have not often been closely connected. Instead, as a rule, clinical child psychologists and psychiatrists are vastly more familiar with the literature on parent-child relationships than the literature on child-peer relationships. Nonetheless, it is probably the case that skilled clinicians are familiar with and, at least intuitively, attentive to disturbances of childhood peer relationships owing to the close connections between difficulties with peers and clinical disorders and subclinical disturbances that bring children to the attention of clinicians. Whether they translate this awareness of peer issues into part of the actual treatment plan would be important to ascertain.

In this section, we consider evidence bearing on the clinical significance of poor peer relationships and children's adjustment. Our treatment here is necessarily brief however and interested readers are directed to our earlier version of this chapter (Parker et al., 1995) as well as a review by Deater-Decker (2001) for fuller treatments.

Rates of Clinical Referral for Disturbances in Peer Relationships

Estimates of the rates of psychiatric or other referrals specifically for disturbances in peer relationships are difficult to come by. These unknown rates are partly due to the fact that peer problems often accompany other identified problems (e.g., ADHD, disruptive behavior and conduct disorders, anxiety, depression). Nevertheless, the available evidence suggests that poor peer relationships are common reasons for referrals to child specialists. Achenbach and Edelbrock (1981) reported that 30% to 75% of children (depending on age) referred to child guidance clinics are reported by their mothers to experience peer difficulties (e.g., poor social skills, aggression). Peer difficulties are roughly twice as common among clinic children as among nonreferred children. Similarly, Hutton (1985) examined the records of 215 students referred to school psychologists by teachers in five different school districts. The most common reason for referral for both boys and girls was poor peer relationships. Poor peer relationships were cited as the basis of referral in 26.5% of the children. Moreover, problems of peer adjustment were implied (but not explicit) in other reasons for referral. For example, fighting and shy/withdrawn made up an additional 13.8% and 14.4% of the reasons for referral, respectively.

In an interesting analysis of this issue, Janes, Hesselbrock, and Schechtman (1980) divided a sample of 298 boys and 98 girls seen at a child guidance clinic over a period of years into those with and without poor peer relationships according to assessments obtained from teachers. Because of the way the assessments were conducted, Janes et al. could examine the role that poor peer relationships played in prompting the original clinic referral. Although children having difficulty getting along with peers were sometimes referred to the clinic for this reason, they were more likely to be referred for poor school achievement and behavioral problems at home and school. In other words, difficulties with peers were not likely to prompt a clinic referral unless they were accompanied by other behavior that was (presumably) more worrisome, bothersome, and disruptive to teachers/classrooms and parents. Indeed, only one in eight children identified by teachers as having difficulties with peers was seen at the clinic primarily for that reason. Janes et al.'s findings suggest that clinic referrals may grossly underestimate the prevalence of difficulties with peers unless those difficulties are combined with other difficulties that pose more problems for teachers and parents. Unless peer relationship disturbance comes to be labeled as a separate disorder with its own diagnostic category, these problems will continue to be perceived and conceptualized as secondary in nature.

Comorbidity and Co-Occurrence with Childhood Psychiatric Disorders

Disturbances in peer relationships have traditionally played little formal role in differential diagnosis and psychiatric classification. Notably, there is no formal diagnostic category for disturbed peer relationships in childhood in either the American Psychiatric Association's multiaxial diagnostic taxonomy (*Diagnostic and Statistical Manual, fourth edi-*

tion [DSM-IV], American Psychiatric Association, 1994) or the *Manual of the International Statistical Classification of Diseases* (World Health Organization, 1992).

However, as the *DSM* has been revised, peer relationships gained importance in diagnosing individuals with disorders. For example, in the *DSM-IV,* Axis IV has been restructured so that the clinician records the presence of stress in separate specific classes of stressors rather than giving a global estimate of stress across all possible stressors. Thus, in *DSM-IV,* stressors for social relationships outside the family (e.g., loss of a friend or inadequate social support) are explicitly considered in the diagnostic taxonomy. Peer relationships continue to play a role in specific disorders in a similar manner to that of *DSM-III-R.* However, it is interesting to note that the Pervasive Developmental Disorders have been expanded to include three new classifications of disorders where a primary symptom is the child's inability to engage in appropriate social interaction (i.e., Rett's Disorder, Asperger's Disorder, and Childhood Disintegrative Disorder; see *DSM-IV*). Of particular interest is Asperger's Disorder for which chronic, severe impairment in social interaction, communication, and behavior (without the language, cognitive, and self-help skill delays seen in Autism) are the essential diagnostic features.

Problems of peer adjustment also appear prominently in the makeup of most dimensions of maladjustment arising from the behavioral assessment approach. Some measures contain subscales or content, which attends to the child's success or failure in the interpersonal realm. For example, the Child Behavior Checklist (CBCL; Achenbach & Edelbrock, 1986) identifies two broad dimensions of child functioning—internalizing problems (inhibition, shy-anxious behavior) and externalizing problems (acting out, aggressive behavior)—as well as several more specific (i.e., narrow) dimensions of functioning (e.g., anxiousness, schizoid behavior, sleep disturbances, aggressiveness). Peer relationship problems are reflected in several of the items (e.g., "poor peer relations," "bad friends") that make up both the broad-band and narrow-band subscales of this measure. The New York Teacher Rating Scale (NYTRS; Miller et al., 1995), which assesses oppositional defiant disorder and conduct disorder, includes a peer relations subscale. This subscale includes items such as "helpful to others" and "has at least one good friend." A high score on this subscale reflects better functioning. The Autism Diagnostic Interview-Revised (ADI-R; Lord, Rutter, & LeCouteur, 1994), the Children's Depression Inventory (CDI; M. Kovacs, 1981), Reynolds Adolescent Depression Scale (RADS; Reynolds, 1986), and Anxiety Disorders Interview

Schedule for *DSM-IV*-Child Version (ADIS-IV-C; Silverman & Nelles, 1988) all contain content that assesses interpersonal relationships.

The Peer Relationships of Children with Psychiatric Disorders

Though peer problems clearly play a role in the diagnosis of psychiatric disorders, the peer relationships of children with specific psychiatric disorders have received substantially less interest compared to normal and distressed, but subclinical, populations of children. Therefore, relatively little is known about the type and quality of peer interactions and the impact of those interactions on the emergence and maintenance of psychiatric/psychological disorders. Prospective studies of psychiatric disorders with low prevalence rates are difficult to achieve and costly, particularly in light of the fact that sociometric assessments are the most common and most defensible methodologies for assessing adjustment with peers, and these techniques require large numbers of informants (e.g., most peers within the same grade at school)—clearly a method that is impractical for clinical settings. The use of clinical samples is more feasible, but because the disorder has emerged, this research is limited in its ability to assess premorbid developmental trends. With this in mind, several specific psychiatric disorders of childhood and adolescence are discussed next in relation to their association with peer relationship problems.

Attention Deficit/Hyperactivity Disorder

The diagnosis for Attention Deficit/Hyperactivity Disorder (ADHD) does not include problematic peer relationships as an essential symptom; however, some researchers have argued that interpersonal difficulties should serve as a defining characteristic (Landau & Moore, 1991; Whalen & Henker, 1991). Almost half of ADHD children have significant peer relationship problems (Guevremont & Dumas, 1994). Children with ADHD display large social skills deficits, often seen as intrusive, loud, annoying, and generally aversive by their peers (see Landau & Moore, 1991). In addition, there is evidence that the social reasoning of ADHD children may be more negative. For example, Whalen and Henker (1991) compared 25 ADHD and 14 normal boys ages 6 to 12 and found that the ADHD boys saw their peers in a more negative way, identifying more undesirable behaviors in peers than did the non-ADHD boys. Overall, ADHD children have been found to be more likely to experience disturbed peer relationships and rejection by peers (Landau & Moore, 1991).

A further complicating factor is the high degree of comorbidity of ADHD with other psychiatric diagnoses, particularly the other Disruptive Behavior Disorders (i.e., Conduct Disorder and Oppositional and Defiant Disorder; August, Ostrander, & Bloomquist, 1992; Barkley, Anastopoulos, Guevremont, & Fletcher, 1991) and Learning Disorders (LD; Flicek, 1992). This comorbidity may additionally contribute to peer disturbances. For example, in a study of 249 2nd through 6th graders, Flicek (1992) found that children with both ADHD and LD were most likely to be rejected and displayed the most disturbed social behavior compared to all other children.

Children with ADHD are frequently treated with stimulant medication, particularly methylphenidate (Ritalin). Results indicate that treatment with Ritalin improves the social interactions, through decreasing aversive behavior, and enhances the social status of children with ADHD (Whalen & Henker, 1991).

Conduct Disorder

As with ADHD, children with Conduct Disorder (CD) tend to have very problematic peer relationships and to be highly disliked or rejected by their peers (e.g., Hinshaw & Lee, 2003). However, unlike ADHD, the primary peer difficulty in CD tends to be aggression. Rather than being simply intrusive, irritating, and overbearing to peers, CD children tend to bully and otherwise aggress toward peers, to intimidate and victimize peers, and to violate the rights of peers (e.g., steal, lie, or destroy property).

It is hypothesized that CD children experience early maladaptive patterns of reinforcement for aggressive behavior as well as exposure to hostile role models, resulting in a hostile, self-defensive view of the world; so that, in the end, aggression becomes the response of choice to deal with interpersonal situations (Dishion & Kavanagh, 2003). Aggression can be a very effective tool for achieving goals and for controlling the behavior of others, but it also increases the likelihood that others will reciprocate the aggression. This pattern develops into a self-perpetuating negative cycle between the child and the social context whereby both the child's aggressive behavior and his or her self-defensive view of the world are continually reinforced and maintained (Coie & Dodge, 1998).

In longitudinal studies, peer rejection in early and middle childhood predicts conduct problems in late childhood and adolescence (Coie, Terry, Lenox, Lochman, & Hyman, 1995; Kraatz-Keiley, Bates, Dodge, & Pettit, 2000; Miller-Johnson, Coie, Maumary-Gremaud, Bierman, & Conduct Problems Prevention Research Group, 2002), and there is some evidence that peer rejection may play a causal role in the development of CD (Patterson, Capaldi, & Bank, 1991). When aggressive children are rejected from the broader peer group, they tend to associate with other aggressive and rejected peers (Espelage et al., 2000, 2003; Gest, Farmer, Carins, & Xie, 2003; Kiesner, Poulin, & Nicotra, 2003; Xie, Cairns, & Cairns, 1999). Involvement in a deviant peer group exposes them further to deviant models and restricts their opportunities to interact with nondeviant peers. Furthermore, deviant peers may reinforce delinquent acts through their positive responses to deviant behavior (Bagwell & Coie, 2004; Dishion, Eddy, Haas, Li, & Spracklen, 1997; Dishion et al., 1996; Dishion, McCord, & Poulin, 1999). Involvement in deviant peer groups has been found to be predictive of adolescent substance use, disruptive behavior, and delinquency (Dishion, Capaldi, & Yoerger, 1999; Dishion & Owen, 2002; Keenan et al., 1995) as well as early school dropout (Cairns, Cairns, & Neckerman, 1989). Thus, peer rejection may set in motion an escalating cycle toward conduct disorder.

In *DSM-IV* (1994), there are two subtypes of CD: Childhood Onset Type (i.e., before age 10) and Adolescent Onset Type (i.e., between ages 10 and 18). Children with Childhood Onset CD experience more disturbed peer relationships and are more likely to have persistent CD throughout adolescence and develop Antisocial Personality Disorder in adulthood (*DSM-IV*, 1994; Hinshaw, Lahey, & Hart, 1993; Hinshaw & Lee, 2003). In contrast, children with Adolescent Onset CD tend to display less aggressive behavior and to have more normative peer relationships (*DSM-IV*, 1994; Hinshaw et al., 1993).

Pervasive Developmental Disorders: Autism, Rett's, Childhood Disintegrative, and Aspergers

Unlike the previous two disorders, the primary symptom related to peer relationships for the Pervasive Developmental Disorders (PDD) is social functioning impairment (Barnhill, 2001). Autism and Asperger's Syndrome are, in large part, defined by the child's inability to engage in age appropriate social interactions (*DSM-IV*, 1994). Rett's and Child Disintegrative Disorder include a loss of social engagement and social skills from a previously normal developmental level and are associated with severe or profound mental retardation. Children with Autism and Asperger's Syndrome prefer solitary activities and have great difficulty forming and maintaining friendships. They may be completely unresponsive to and detached from social relationships, interacting with others in a nonemotional, instrumental way. In addition, their social sensitivity or

awareness of the thoughts and feelings of others may be severely limited.

Asperger's children are aloof and have aggressive tendencies (Barnhill, 2001). Research has suggested that the reason children with Asperger's Syndrome act aggressively is that they have trouble interpreting social intentions, encoding conflicts and cues, and choosing problem-solving strategies (Carothers & Taylor, 2004).

Children with Autism (but not Asperger's Syndrome) also have language (delay or absent), communication (e.g., difficulty initiating a conversation), and cognitive impairments (e.g., approximately 75% of children with Autism also have Mental Retardation; *DSM-IV*, 1994). Their language is often repetitive, stereotyped, and idiosyncratic. Research indicates that when children with Autism avoid social interaction, this avoidance predicts subsequent peer avoidance and language use (Ingersoll, Schreibman, & Stahmer, 2001).

Recent research has addressed the peer interactions of children with Autism. For example, they tend to make fewer social initiations even when compared with peers who have other developmental disabilities (Sigman & Ruskin, 1999). Very few children with Autism have friendships with same-age peers (Orsmond, Krauss, & Seltzer, 2004). Those who do have friends report a lower quality of companionship in those friendships (Bauminger & Kasari, 2000).

Anxiety Disorders

Anxiety disorders are among the most common psychological disorders of childhood and adolescence (Albano, Chorpita, & Barlow, 2003; Beidel, 1991). Children who are anxious tend to remain anxious through adolescence and adulthood, even though they may no longer meet the diagnostic criteria for an anxiety disorder (Ialongo, Edelsohn, Werthamer-Larsson, Crockett, & Kellam, 1995; Last, Perrin, Hersen, & Kazdin, 1992). Although several anxiety disorders are associated with impaired peer relationships, developmental models of social anxiety, in particular, have implicated limited social interaction and poor peer relationships (Rubin & Burgess, 2001). For example, young children with certain temperamental vulnerabilities, such as behavioral inhibition, experience psychological and physiological discomfort in social situations, which may place them at risk for the development of social anxiety. Withdrawal from social interaction during early childhood limits important socialization opportunities, and thereby may impede the development of social skills. Social skill deficits may then elicit negative peer reactions, which, in turn, perpetuate further social withdrawal and increase social anxiety (Rubin & Burgess, 2001; Rubin, Burgess, Kennedy, & Stewart, 2003). This cycle may be sustained and strengthened if anxiety decreases as a result of social avoidance because such negative reinforcement increases the likelihood of subsequent avoidance and withdrawal (Rubin, Burgess, & Coplan, 2002).

The majority of shy, withdrawn, and anxious children report having mutual friendships (Schneider, 1999; Wojslawowicz, Rubin, Burgess, Rose-Krasnor, & Booth, in press). However, the friendships of these children are relatively lacking in fun, intimacy, helpfulness and guidance, and validation and caring (Rubin, Wojslawowicz, Burgess, Rose-Krasnor, & Booth, 2004; Wojslawowicz et al., in press). Other studies indicate that social anxiety is associated with peer rejection (Inderbitzen et al., 1997) and peer victimization (Craig, 1998; Vernberg, Abwender, Ewell, & Beery, 1992). Several other anxiety disorders and multidimensional measures of anxiety have also been linked with peer problems (e.g., Grills & Ollendick, 2002).

Depression

Although deficiencies in social relationships are not required for the diagnosis of depression, current conceptualizations of the etiology and maintenance of depressive symptoms emphasize the role of social skills and dysfunctional interpersonal behavior (e.g., Joiner, Coyne, & Blalock, 1999). Children lacking in social support are believed to be at an increased risk for depression (Windle, 1992). The absence of involvement in friendship undermines self-esteem and deprives children of important pleasurable experiences, contributing to the development of depressive symptomology. Because friends also may be important in buffering children against stress, the presence of close satisfying relationships with friends could be expected to protect children from depressive affect in connection with stress (Windle, 1992). Peer relationships have been found to protect adolescents against depressive symptoms more than parental relationships (I. Hay & Ashman, 2003).

The available literature is generally supportive of a link between depression and difficulties with peers (e.g., Craig, 1998; DiFilippo & Overholser, 2000; Hammen & Rudolph, 2003; Kistner, Balthazor, Risi, & Burton, 1999; Prinstein, Boergers, Spirito, Little, & Grapentine, 2000; Vernberg, 1990). In an interesting study of this issue, Vernberg, for example, found that among young adolescents, less closeness with a best friend, infrequent contact with friends, and more experiences of victimization by peers contributed to increases over time in depressive affect. Likewise, in a 5-year longitudinal study of young boys, Cillessen, Van Lieshout, and Haselager (1992) found the experience of peer rejection led to higher levels of loneliness, which in turn increased the risk for developing depression. In their meta-analysis, Hawker and Boulton (2000) also reported links between peer victimization and several internalizing problems, including depression, anxiety, loneliness, and poor self-esteem. Depressed children tend to perceive their own status more negatively than their peers do (Cole, Martin, Peeke, Serocyznski, & Hoffman, 1998), view themselves as less accepted by their peers (Brendgen, Vitaro, Turgeon, & Poulin, 2002), and report a lower friendship quality with their best friends (Brendgen et al., 2000) compared with nondepressed children.

On the other hand, there is also support for the view that depressive affect contributes to problems with peer relationships (Joiner et al., 1999), possibly because peers make unflattering generalizations about other children's behavioral characteristics in the face of evidence of depressive affect (Peterson, Mullins, & Ridley-Johnson, 1985). A number of other factors provide further explanation for depressed children/adolescents' problematic peer relationships, including depressed children's difficulty handling conflict with peers, more emotional dysregulation during stressful peer interactions, and depressed youths' tendency to seek excessive reassurance from peers (Hammen & Rudolph, 2003).

Less evidence is available concerning the protective role of friendships in relation to depression. Based on their review of the literature, Peterson et al. (1993) concluded that good peer relationships in early adolescence do not appear to provide a protective influence; later in adolescence, close peer relationships do appear to be protective, particularly when parent relationships are impaired in some way (Peterson, Sarigiani, & Kennedy, 1991). However, depressed children with high-quality friendships may also be at risk. Recent research indicates that close friends who spent excessive amounts of time ruminating over problems (called co-rumination) are at risk for greater internalizing symptoms like depression (Rose, 2002). Girls reported more co-rumination than did boys. These findings may help explain why girls report higher levels of depressive symptoms.

Eating Disorders

The *DSM-IV* identifies Anorexia Nervosa, Bulimia Nervosa, and eating disorder not otherwise specified (EDNOS) as eating disorders. Few young children meet the *DSM* guidelines for diagnosis of an eating disorder, but many children present subclinical variations of them

(Bryant-Waugh & Lask, 1995). Children who participate in activities in which weight is a main focal point (i.e., ballet, wrestling, gymnastics) may be especially prone to developing eating disorders (Garner, Rosen, & Barry, 1998).

Recent work focusing on how children and adolescents develop disturbances in their body image and eating-related concerns has found that peers may play an important role. Oliver and Thelen (1996) examined eating concerns in children in 3rd through 5th grade. They found that children's perceptions of peer influence were associated with their eating and body image concerns. Girls were more likely than boys to believe that being thin would increase their likeability among peers, although both boys and girls viewed appearance as being related to their peer acceptance. Phares, Steinberg, and Thompson (2004) also found that girls were more concerned with eating and body image than boys. In their sample of elementary school children, they found that both boys and girls who expressed higher levels of dissatisfaction with their bodies also reported higher levels of depressive symptoms and lower levels of self-worth. Futhermore, they found that girls were more active in attempts to become or remain thin.

Loneliness and Subjective Distress

As noted, Sullivan (1953) attached considerable significance to loneliness as a motivational force in development and adjustment. At the same time, Sullivan was pessimistic about the promise of measuring loneliness with any precision:

> Now loneliness is possibly most distinguished, among the experiences of human beings, by the toneless quality of the things said about it. . . . I, in common apparently with all denizens of the English-speaking world, feel inadequate to communicate a really clear impression of the experience of loneliness in its quintessential force. (pp. 260–261)

His own pessimism notwithstanding, research does suggest that loneliness is tractable to scientific study and supports Sullivan's claims about the circumstances that give rise to loneliness and its significance as a motivational force in development (see Rotenberg & Hymel, 1999). Of particular interest, research supports an association between difficulties with peers and children's feelings of loneliness. Most research, to date, has focused on loneliness and children's group acceptance. Problematic group acceptance appears robustly associated with loneliness. This is true whether acceptance is measured with a sociometric rating-scale measure (e.g., Parker & Asher,

1993; Parker & Seal, 1996; Quay, 1992; Renshaw & Brown, 1993) or with sociometric nominations that classify children into different sociometric status groups. In the latter case, the evidence shows that rejected sociometric status is associated with greater feelings of loneliness and social dissatisfaction in early adolescence (Boivin & Hymel, 1997; Boivin, Hymel, & Bukowski, 1995; Boivin, Poulin, & Vitaro, 1994; Crick & Ladd, 1993; Parkhurst & Asher, 1992; Sanderson & Siegal, 1995; Sletta, Valas, Skaalvik, & Sobstad, 1996), during middle childhood (e.g., Crick & Ladd, 1993), and during early childhood (Cassidy & Asher, 1992). Neglected sociometric status has not been found to be associated with risk for loneliness. Furthermore, this pattern has been found not only in school contexts (the context that characterizes virtually all research conducted in this area) but in a summer camp context as well (Parker & Seal, 1996). In addition, this relation has now been obtained in several countries (e.g., Australia, Canada, the Netherlands, Norway, and the United States). Also, loneliness does not appear to be an experience that unpopular children can easily shed by changing their activities or social settings. Asher et al. (1996) queried children about their loneliness in a variety of school contexts (i.e., the classroom, physical education, lunchroom, and recess on the playground); Regardless of the activity context they were asked to consider, rejected children reported greater levels of loneliness than better accepted children. Finally, Cillessen, van Ijzendoorn, Van Lieshout, and Hartup (1992) reported that the links between the experience of peer rejection and levels of loneliness hold up longitudinally, and may be implicated in the development of depression. Importantly, it has been found that rejected/withdrawn children report more loneliness and social detachment than popular children or children who are rejected but aggressive (e.g., Gazelle & Ladd, 2003). These relations have been reported throughout childhood and early adolescence (e.g., Crick & Ladd, 1993; Parkhurst & Asher, 1992). Further, one can find a consistent link between peer victimization and loneliness (Boulton & Underwood, 1992; Kochenderfer & Ladd, 1996). Indeed, abusive peer interactions have been found to be antecedent to children's loneliness rather than a concomitant or consequence (Kochenderfer & Ladd, 1996).

Focusing on friendship indices rather than sociometric status, Parker and Asher (1993) reported that elementary school-age children without friends are lonelier than other children. Interestingly, this relation between loneliness and having a friend held for children at all levels of group acceptance, suggesting that popularity and involvement in friendships contribute additively rather than interactively to feelings of loneliness (see also Nangle, Erdley, Newman, Mason, & Carpenter, 2003). Parker and Asher also examined the relation between loneliness and six qualitative features of children's closest friendships—levels of companionship, conflict, conflict resolution, intimate disclosure, help and guidance, and personal validation. Loneliness was found to be strongly, albeit redundantly, associated with each of these six aspects of friendships. Once again, these effects were independent of the contributions of peer acceptance. For young children as well, the evidence thus far indicates that the quantity (large friendship network) and quality of friendships decrease feelings of loneliness and subjective distress due to the supportive provisions offered by this peer relationship (Burgess et al., 2005).

Poor Childhood Peer Relationships and Later Adult Adjustment

Interest in the implications of problematic relationships with peers for children's long-term behavioral and psychological adjustment dates to the earliest days of research on children's peer relationships. Indeed, the premise that children with relationship problems are at risk for later life difficulties is one of the most widely shared professional and popular beliefs about development and psychopathology and has played an important role in motivating research on children's adjustment with peers. In this section, we offer a brief overview of the basis for this conclusion. Readers interested in a more complete treatment are referred to our earlier version of this chapter (Parker et al., 1995), and reviews by Bierman (2004), Hawker and Bolton (2000), Rubin, Hastings, Chen, Stewart, and McNichol (1998), Nangle and Erdley (2001), Schneider (2000), and Deater-Decker (2001). Further, while the existence of such long-term linkages has enjoyed almost universal acceptance, opinions diverge surrounding the causal basis of this presumed association (e.g., Vernberg, 1990). We return to this question in the following section.

In general, available data do provide compelling evidence of a link between problematic peer experiences in childhood and children's risk for subsequent mental health difficulties (e.g., Booth et al., 1994; Brendgon et al., 2001; Burks, Dodge, & Price, 1995; Cairns et al., 1989; Coie, Lochman, Terry, & Hyman, 1992; Coie et al., 1992; DeRosier, Kupersmidt, & Patterson, 1994; Kochendorfer-Ladd & Waldrop, 2001; Kupersmidt & Coie, 1990; Ladd & Burgess, 2001; Ladd & Troop-Gordon, 2003; Olweus,

1993). This conclusion rests in part on numerous studies that document differences in the peer relationship histories of disordered versus nondisordered adults. Illustrative of this approach and general finding is a series of pioneering studies by Roff published in the late 1950s and early 1960s (Roff, 1957, 1960, 1961, 1963). Roff searched military service records to locate servicemen who, in middle childhood, had been referred to one of two guidance clinics in Minnesota and who later showed problematic military adjustment in the form of either a diagnosis by military psychiatrists as neurotic (Roff, 1957, 1960) or psychotic (Roff, 1961) or received a dishonorable discharge for antisocial conduct (Roff, 1963). The child clinic records of these servicemen were then reviewed for evidence of earlier difficulties with peers (e.g., dislike by the general peer group, inability to keep friends, and being regarded as odd, peculiar, or queer by other children) and compared with those of former clinic patients who had exemplary later military service records. Results indicated a strong association between disorder and poor childhood peer relationships. Specifically, about half of all neurotic servicemen had shown poor peer adjustment when seen at the clinic in childhood compared to only one in eight normal servicemen. Similarly, about two-thirds of the psychotics, but only one-fourth of the normals, had shown poor peer adjustment. Finally, twice as many of the servicemen dismissed for antisocial conduct had shown poor peer adjustment as control servicemen (54% versus 24%, respectively). In short, depending on the psychiatric or behavioral disorder, disordered servicemen were anywhere from 2 to 4 times as likely as nondisordered servicemen to have had a history of poor peer relationships.

Roff's findings are consistent with those of other researchers employing this type of case-control or follow-back design in which child guidance clinic files or other archival data are reviewed for groups of adults who are know to be psychiatrically disordered versus nondisordered. Moreover, this pattern is not limited to adults with serious psychiatric disorders, but is also characteristic of juvenile delinquents, dropouts, and high school students who do poorly academically and socially. Further, this finding is relatively unaffected by changes in methods of collecting childhood peer data because it occurs in studies that use retrospective interviews, studies that abstract guidance clinic records, and studies that use school records. Childhood peer adjustment variables under some circumstances may even distinguish disordered from nondisordered adults when many other intellectual and demographic variables do not (e.g., Cowen et al., 1973).

Despite the consistency of their conclusions, as a group the results of these studies have raised concern owing to their reliance on follow-back designs. Case-control or follow-back studies are useful for suggesting connections between adult symptoms and childhood behavior, but cannot provide data interpretable in terms of predictive risk. That is, case-control approaches do not address whether children with a certain level of type of acceptance, when compared with others with higher or more adaptive types of acceptance, have an increased likelihood of experiencing later maladjustment. Such probabilistic prediction is possible only from cohort prospective studies that first identify samples of peer adjusted and nonadjusted children and then follow these children over time to determine the proportion in each of these two groups who subsequently develop disorder. This reduces the possibility of overestimating the importance of a particular childhood characteristic (such as peer rejection) in the etiology of a subsequent disorder.

Follow-up studies are expensive, inflexible, and may require decades to complete. Moreover, to ensure that a sufficiently large number of individuals later develop some specific disorder, peer adjustment data must ideally be gathered on a large number of individuals in childhood. For these and other reasons, there are fewer prospective than case-control studies linking early peer adjustment to later outcomes. Like their counterparts, however, these studies provide compelling evidence of a link between problematic peer experiences in childhood and children's risk for subsequent mental health difficulties (e.g., Ladd & Burgess, 2001; Ollendick, Weist, Borden, & Greene, 1992; Woodward & Fergusson, 1999). Research indicates, for example, that peer relationship problems, especially peer rejection, are associated with increased rates of internalizing symptoms, such as anxiety and depressive symptoms (e.g., Coie et al., 1995; Gazelle & Ladd, 2003; Kraatz-Keiley et al., 2000). Links have also been found between early peer relationship difficulties and various forms of externalizing difficulties, including involvement in juvenile and adult criminal behavior. For example, Woodward and Fergusson (1999) found that children (age 9) with peer relationship problems were at increased risk for later criminal behavior, substance abuse, and suicidal behavior by age 18, although they were not at increased risk for depression or anxiety disorders.

As another example, Ollendick et al. (1992) identified sociometrically rejected, neglected, popular, controversial, and average status in a large sample ($n = 600$) of 9-year-old children and followed them for 5 years, documenting the incidence of subsequent academic, delinquent, behavioral, and psychological disturbance. Ollendick et al.'s findings strongly supported the risk status of rejected children. At 5-year follow-up, rejected children were perceived by their peers as less likable and more aggressive than popular children. Rejected children were also perceived by their teachers as having more conduct problems, aggression, motor excesses, and attention problems than their popular counterparts. Moreover, rejected children reported a more external locus of control and higher levels of conduct disturbance and substance abuse, performed less well academically, failed more grades, and were more likely to drop out of school and to commit delinquent offenses than the popular children. Clearly, rejected children were at risk when compared with popular children. Furthermore, rejected children differed from average children on most of these same measures, including failed grades, dropping out of school, and commission of delinquent offenses. Thus, it cannot be said that they differed only from a very well accepted group; rather, they also differed from the average child in the class. A similar pattern was evident for controversial children. Controversial children differed from popular and average children on most of the academic, behavioral, and social measures. In fact, they were similar to rejected children on most measures. For example, a similar number of controversial children (27.3%) as rejected children (33.3%) failed at least one grade and the children in the two groups committed similar numbers of delinquent offenses. Neglected children did not differ from average children on any measure and differed from popular children only on the locus of control and peer evaluation measures.

Overall, the pattern of findings from studies using both follow-back and prospective designs are consistent with the conclusion that early difficulties with peers place children at risk for subsequent, sometimes serious, disorders. This finding emerges not only from studies employing clinic samples, but also from studies of school samples as well. Further, peer difficulties have been implicated in risk for a wide range of significant outcomes, including general mental health problems, externalizing and internalizing symptoms, juvenile and adult criminality, substance abuse, school difficulties and dropping out, and severe psychopathology. We turn next to the presumed causal basis of this association.

Understanding the Link between Poor Peer Relationships and Later Adjustment Problems

Our review indicates considerable support for a link between early difficulty with peers and maladjustment later in life. How can this link be understood?

Simple Incidental and Causal Explanations

Previously, we (Parker et al., 1995) offered a characterization and critique of two alternative interpretations of the link between poor peer relationships and later personal adjustment. Both positions represent attempts to understand the links over time between deviant behaviors and problems relating to peers, with subsequent academic, behavioral, and psychiatric disturbances. The interpretations differ, however, in the extent to which they view problems in adjustment to peers as tangentially or centrally (i.e., causally) involved in the etiology of the later difficulties.

The first, or incidental, interpretation makes no assumption that problems with peers cause the interpersonal and intrapersonal difficulties they later predict. Instead, an association between these variables exists because behavioral precursors and subclinical symptoms of later disorders and deviancies perturbed peer relationships early on. As we have seen, there is considerable comorbidity between mental health disturbances and maladjustment with peers in childhood, and children respond negatively to the flat affect and social withdrawal that characterizes depressed children, for example. Disturbances in peer relationships may make particularly good red flags for later disorder, but there is no assumption that poor peer relationships make any independent contribution to later maladjustment and no reason to suspect that children who are rejected by peers for reasons other than underlying disorder will have later maladjustment.

A schematic representation of the extreme incidental view of peer disturbances and later maladjusted outcomes is shown in Figure 12.1. The model presupposes an underlying disposition to later psychopathology. This disposition may be constitutional (e.g., a biological diathesis) or derive from early environmental influences (e.g., poor early parenting or maltreatment resulting in insecure attachment) or some process of coacting constitutional and environmental factors—

its origins need not concern us here. The important feature is that this pathogenic process unfolds over time, resulting eventually in disordered outcome. The child's peer relationships are disrupted along the way (upward arrows) by the negative behavioral manifestations of the underlying pathogenic process. One might suppose that, because of reputation or other factors, these disruptions make it less likely for children to establish satisfactory peer relationships over time. However, the important influence is the underlying pathogenic process that disrupts behavior, and the peer disruptions themselves are epiphenomenal to the later maladjustment.

The alternative extreme position attributes later disturbance directly to the experience of earlier disruptions in peer relationships. Owing much to the developmental task framework, this causal position holds that many later disturbances can be traced to children's failure to establish effective and positive relationships with peers in childhood and adolescence. Because they are deprived of the important socialization experiences that positive peer interaction affords, and because they lack important sources of social support, children with peer difficulties experience more stress, have less mature and flexible social and cognitive skills, have less well-developed moral reasoning and less commitment to conventional behavior, are less socialized generally, and have more idiosyncratic patterns of thought and behavior. These factors leave them less capable of meeting social responsibilities and expectations; less able to form subsequent, satisfactory interpersonal relationships; and more vulnerable to stress and breakdown.

A schematic representation of the extreme causal position appears in Figure 12.2. Again, some hypothetical representative time points appear along the X-axis, and the relations among problems with peers, behavioral problems, and later maladjusted outcome are shown. In this instance, maladjustment is shown as the result of the cumulative

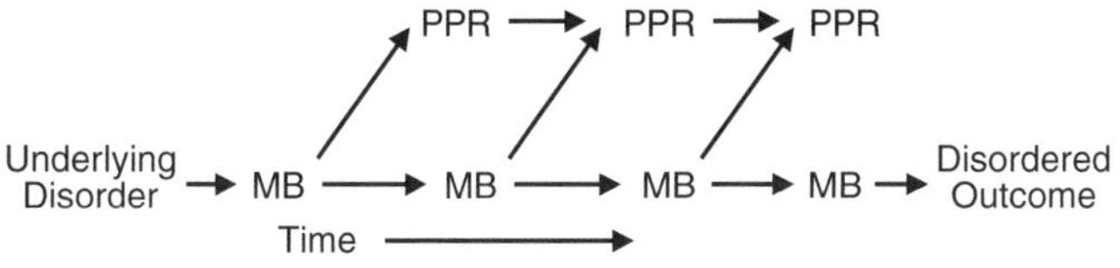

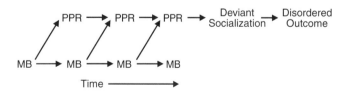

Figure 12.1   Simple incidental model of the link between peer relationship problems and later disorder. *Notes:* PPR = Problems in peer relationships; MB = Maladaptive behavior toward peers. Adapted from "Peer Relations and Later Personal Adjustment: Are Low-Accepted Children at Risk?" by J. G. Parker and S. R. Asher, 1987, *Psychological Bulletin, 102,* pp. 357–389.

Figure 12.2   Simple causal model of the link between peer relationships problems and later disorder. *Notes:* MB = Maladaptive behavior toward peers; PPR = Problems in peer relationships. Adapted from "Peer Relations and Later Personal Adjustment: Are Low-Accepted Children at Risk?" by J. G. Parker and S. R. Asher, 1987, *Psychological Bulletin, 102,* pp. 357–389.

experience of peer ostracism and failure rather than as the unfolding of an underlying pathogenic process. Note that the process of disruption begins with signs of maladaptive behavior with peers. The model is silent on the issue of the origins of this maladaptive behavior, although it is not incompatible with the argument that unspecified constitutional and early experiential factors contribute to original behavioral problems that, in turn, contribute to the development of problems with peers. Otherwise, like the incidental model, the causal model assumes that problematic behavior influences and maintains problems with peers at all ages (upward arrows) and has its own momentum (horizontal arrows).

Few studies have directly pitted causal and incidental explanations in the prediction of later maladjustment, and, indeed, because of the complexity of each explanation, it seems unlikely that any single study could do so effectively. An important prerequisite for accepting a causal model is evidence that poor peer relationships have a significant, negative impact on later maladjustment beyond the influence of child characteristics, such as behavioral style. In recent years, covariance multivariate models and cross-lagged stability models have been exploited to examine this issue, and indeed this work indicates that peer rejection contributes uniquely to multiple forms of later adjustment problems, including internalizing and externalizing symptomatology and declines in academic performance (Ladd & Burgess, 2001; Miller-Johnson, Coie, Maumary-Gremaud, Bierman, & Conduct Problems Prevention Research, 2002; Miller-Johnson, Coie, Maumary-Gremaud, Lochman, & Terry, 1999; Wentzel, 2003). Insofar as these findings suggest that peer problems are not simply a marker of a pathogenic process, a strictly incidental explanation for these linkages seems inadequate.

Interactional and Transactional Interpretations

Incidental and causal views are caricatures and not likely to be steadfastly held by many actual authors. Even so, these models have exerted an influence on how researchers conduct and interpret longitudinal research on the long-term sequelae of early problems (see Parker & Asher, 1987). Importantly, neither view is likely to prove satisfactory to explain the link between problems with peers and later adjustment. As Parker and Asher (p. 379) observed:

> The extreme incidental model seemingly denies the very real possibility that the experience of peer rejection, especially prolonged peer rejection, leads a child to view the world and him- or herself negatively.... Ongoing rejection by peers must negatively affect many aspects of the child's social, aca-

demic, affective, and moral development.... Alternatively, an extreme causal view ignores the fact that factors that antedate poor interpersonal relationships continue to play a role in subsequent outcomes. It seems likely that factors that contribute to poor peer adjustment also continue to shape the course and nature of subsequent adjustment.

More generally, students of developmental models will recognize the incidental and causal views above as specific instances of main effects models emphasizing the contributions of the child or environment, respectively (Sameroff & MacKenzie, 2003). According to the incidental model, information concerning the child's constitutional nature is sufficient to accurately predict later outcomes. Likewise, the causal model implies that, while characteristics of the child, such as aggressive or withdrawn behavioral styles, may contribute initially to peer rejection, subsequent peer interactions and socialization processes are responsible for later maladjustment. Missing from both models is any appreciable attention to (1) how characteristics of the child might condition the impact of ostracism by peers and (2) how rejection by peers contributes to what is characteristic of the child.

In other areas of psychology, interactional models have proven useful for understanding the conditional impact of environmental events on development (Sameroff & MacKenzie, 2003; Wachs, 1992). The diathesis-stress model is an example of an interactional model that is frequently drawn on in the study of developmental psychopathology (Garmezy, 1974). In this view, every child has a particular genotypic profile that defines its constitutional vulnerability to disorder. However, this genotypic vulnerability has to be activated by an environmental stressor in order for the disorder to be manifested. The impact of a particular stressor is not invariant across individuals. Rather, whether a stressor produces maladjustment depends on the child's particular constitutional make-up. A low level of stress may produce disorder for children whose genotypic vulnerability is high, but not for other children. Similarly, an extremely stressful event may produce disorder in almost all children, except those with a very low level of vulnerability. Thus, an interactional model, such as the diathesis-stress model, states that developmental outcomes can be predicted only when the interaction between child and environmental influences are taken into account.

As we noted earlier, in the study of peer relationships, very little longitudinal work has examined whether the combination of child characteristics, such as behavioral or social-cognitive style, and peer rejection places children at differential risk for later maladjustment. Several lines of research suggest, however, that there are considerable differences in the behavioral and social-cognitive profiles of low-accepted children and that considering both child and social influences may greatly enhance the predictability of disorder, both in general and of specific types (e.g., Bierman, Smoot, & Aumiller, 1993; Kupersmidt & Coie, 1990). For example, in a classic study of 95 6- to 12-year-old boys, Bierman and colleagues found that peer-rejected children who also displayed excessive aggressive behavior were most likely to exhibit severe conduct problems, whereas children who were rejected but not aggressive were most likely to exhibit passivity.

Although an interactional interpretation addresses the need for a more conditional understanding of the impact of poor peer relationships on later adjustment, it falls short of being a comprehensive model of this process, one which allows for feedback among the causes of problems with peers, the consequences of poor peer relationships, and the course of later maladjustment. In other words, we are lacking a transactional model (Sameroff & MacKenzie, 2003) of the link between difficulties with peers and later adjustment. Transactional models have been extremely helpful for conceptualizing and understanding a variety of phenomena in other areas, including Schizophrenia (Barocas & Sameroff, 1982), community violence, child maltreatment (Cicchetti & Lynch, 1993), externalizing problem behavior (Ladd & Burgess, 1999), the effects of deviant friends on delinquency and aggression (Keenan, Shaw, & Delliquadri, 1998; Kraatz-Keiley et al, 2000); and parent-child relationships (Sroufe, 1995). The basic tenets of transactional models have been cogently described by Sameroff (1995; Sameroff & MacKenzie, 2003). Within transactional systems, development is viewed as a dynamic process wherein characteristics of the child and characteristics of the environment undergo continual change through processes of mutual influence over time. The influence of any element of the

system is complex, and always bidirectional. The organism (child) in a transactional model is actively involved in attempts to organize and alter his or her environment. Changes in the environment as a result of a child's actions, on the other hand, subsequently function to produce changes in the child:

> The child is in a perpetual state of active reorganization and cannot properly be regarded as maintaining inborn characteristics as static qualities. In this view, the constants in development are not some set of traits, but rather the processes by which these traits are maintained in the transactions between organism and environment. (Sameroff, 1975, p. 281)

From a transactional perspective, the development of psychopathology is neither a product of the child nor of the environment, but rather the result of child-environmental transactions that reinforce and sustain maladaptive patterns over time.

Figure 12.3 presents one possible way of representing the link between poor peer relationships in childhood and later disordered outcomes as a transactional developmental process. As in the earlier models, Figure 12.3 begins with the assumption that biogenetic and early experiential factors combine to contribute to a behavioral style that is maladaptive to forming friendships and interacting successfully in a peer group. The specific nature of this predisposing process is left unspecific and need not concern us here. It is also explicit in Figure 12.3 that these early experiences influence not only the child's initial maladaptive behavior toward peers (MB_1 in the model) but also the child's self-perceptions and social outlook, social motivation, and social attributions ($NSOC_1$ in the model). These self-other cognitive processes, in turn, also contribute to initial behavior toward peers. Importantly, as with the other two models, children's behavior toward peers is suggested to

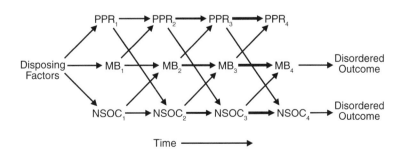

Figure 12.3 A transactional model of the link between peer relationships problems and later disorder. Note: PPR = Problems in peer relationships; MB = Maladaptive behavior toward peers; NSOC = Negative self- and other-cognitions.

contribute (upward arrows) to initial difficulties forming friendships and peer rejection (PPR$_1$ in the model).

At this point the model departs notably from the other two models. Whereas the incidental and causal models attribute the development of disorder from this point to either processes in place in the child or stable processes set off by the environmental rejection, the transactional model in Figure 12.3 posits the operation of a dynamic pattern of continuous and reciprocal influence of children's behavior toward peers, problems in peer relationships, and children's negative self- and other cognitions. Thus, peer rejection negatively influences children's perceptions of self and others. This, in turn, influences them to behave in further maladaptive ways toward peers, which, in turn, negatively influences peers' attitudes and behavior toward them, and so on, in a spiraling fashion. One iteration of this spiraling cycle of cognition-behavior-rejection-cognition is represented by the pathway NSOC$_1$ › MB$_2$ › PPR$_3$ › NSOC$_4$, and this feature of the hypothesized model is discussed at greater length in the next section. The end point of this model indicates two, rather than one, sets of disordered outcomes. This duplication is deliberate, and intended to emphasize that most disorders have cognitive/affective as well as behavioral/symptom referents.

Several specific elements of the model require further mention. First, a path from each point of difficulty with peers to each successive point of difficulty with peers is articulated, and these paths are indicated with increasing thickness. This convention is adopted to recognize that, once in place, reputational and other factors contribute momentum to peer rejection, adding coherence to the process over time (LaFontana & Cillessen, 1999, 2002).

A similar convention is adapted from each point of behavior toward peers to each subsequent point of behavior toward peers (see Figure 12.3). This pattern is included as a means to represent the increasing canalization of behavior that results from the transactional operation of this cycle over time (Sameroff, 1987). Likewise the increasingly thick pathways from each point of self- and other-cognition to each subsequent point of self- and other-cognition is intended to recognize that these internal processes are somewhat self-perpetuating and have their own coherence over time, as we will discuss.

The elements in the model in Figure 12.3 have discrete subscripts at each hypothetical time point. This convention is adopted to highlight an important point about the transactional model: Even as they retain a certain lawful coherence over time, the elements of this model can be expected to change over time as a function of their participation in the recursive cycles of influence (Sameroff, 1987). For example, initially active and aggressive children may, upon experience of peer rejection, appear sullen, withdrawn, and avoidant of peers later (Rubin, Burgess, & Coplan, 2002). As another example, children who behave unskillfully with peers may experience peer-group rejection initially, but not necessarily problems forming one or two same-sex friendships (Parker & Asher, 1993). Friendship problems may follow later, and, still later, problems relating to cross-sex others and romantic partners (Coie, 1990). Presumably, system-exogenous factors, such as how opportunities for cross-sex interaction are structured in the broader culture, partly dictate the specific nature of each element at a given time point. The broader point intended by the subscripts in Figure 12.3 is that the elements in the model should not be expected to stay constant—or even show homotypic similarity—over time (see Sroufe, 1995).

Transactional-like explanatory models have been increasingly invoked within the literature on children's peer relationships (Coie, 1990; Crick & Dodge, 1994). One illustration is the discussion by Rubin, Hastings, et al. (1998; Rubin & Burgess, 2002). Noting that a broad distinction is often drawn between internalizing and externalizing disordered outcomes, Rubin and colleagues describe the transactional pathways leading to these disparate eventual outcomes, and the complicity of peer rejection in these processes. Rubin et al. note that the distinction between externalizing and internalizing disordered outcomes parallels in certain respects the distinction between two types of at-risk infants: infants with difficult temperaments (negatively emotional, difficult to sooth, fussy, overactive) and inhibited infants with low thresholds for stimulation and arousal. Rubin et al. argue that this correspondence was not coincidental, and describe two hypothetical transactional pathways that might respectively link difficult temperament to later externalizing disorders and early inhibition to later internalizing disorder. Both pathways start with the assumption that when children with problematic temperaments are born into early risky caretaking environments (e.g., poverty, poor-parenting skills), the result is often a disruption in early parent-child attachment. In the instance of an infant with a difficult/fussy temperament, the result is often the creation of an avoidant-insecure attachment and a pattern of subsequent parenting that is authoritarian, hostile, and shows little concern for developing social competence. As a result, as preschoolers, these children behave more aggressively than other children, and hold less positive and trusting attitudes toward their peers. In this latter regard, we see the beginnings of social information processing deficits and biases. Because peers reject these children, their cognitions and feelings toward peers become even more hostile, and their behavior toward peers becomes even more aggressive. Teachers label these children as problematic, and the parents of these children respond by becoming even more controlling and autocratic. Alternatively, some parents begin to view their children's problems as being dispositionally based; the result is a parental mindset that "there is little I can do to alter my child's aggressiveness." Parental hopelessness, permissiveness, or neglect may follow (Rubin & Burgess, 2002). Powerful reputation biases in the peer group are also set in motion, which make it even less likely for these children to be accepted by peers (LaFontana & Cillessen, 1999, 2002). Over time, this reciprocal cycle of peer rejection-negative cognitions and emotions-aggressive behavior-hostile parenting-peer rejection leads to the full exclusion and isolation of these children from the peer group. Indeed, by the end of elementary school, these initially aggressive children may even begin displaying higher-than-normal rates of social isolation as a reaction to the group exclusion. Rubin et al. suggest that the eventual prognosis for children who follow this pathway is the development of externalizing disorders (e.g., delinquency).

The pathway for children with initially inhibited temperaments is very different, however (Rubin, Burgess, & Coplan, 2002). When early caretaking circumstances exacerbate these children's difficulties, they will be prone to show difficulties characteristic of resistant-insecure attachment. They will be reluctant to explore their environment, will have less well-developed social and cognitive skills, and will show anxious, inhibited behavior with peers and high rates of nonsocial play as preschoolers. Even in early childhood, these children's social overtures to peers may be ignored or refused. The upshot of this early, in vivo, rejection is an exacerbation of social anxiety and withdrawal. Rubin et al. suggest that, for a variety of reasons, the parents of these children may react to their children's social difficulties by viewing them as vulnerable and in need of overprotection, thereby exacerbating their children's sense of insecurity (Rubin & Burgess, 2002). Rubin et al. suggest that, initially, during early childhood, researchers may not find a link with sociometric rejection; however, the transactional process between negative peer response and negative self-regard has already been set into place. Eventually, these socially wary children are viewed by peers as easy marks for teasing and victimization. As they move into elementary school, the children recognize the solidity of social failure and develop even more negative self-perceptions. Eventually, too, peers regard these children as socially awkward, atypical, and not worthy of social contact. As their rejection

by peers increases, Rubin et al. predict that these children react by becoming depressed and lonely, and eventually by showing internalizing disorders and difficulties relating to others as young adults. Importantly, Rubin and colleagues also note that the two trajectories involve children being involved in friendships that serve to exacerbate their difficulties. In the case of the first trajectory described above, the aggressive child finds himself or herself in the company of friends with whom deviancy training occurs. In the case of the latter trajectory, the anxious withdrawn child finds himself or herself in the company of friends with whom co-rumination occurs.

Transactional models such as the ones offered by Rubin and colleagues present formidable research challenges. Children's peer relationships, behavior, social-cognition, and adjustment are not expected to remain constant over time, and patterns of change over time must be used to predict subsequent changes and organism states. Progress in this area has been helped by the development of statistical techniques (e.g., structural equation modeling, growth curve analyses, survival analyses) for examining bidirectional and reciprocal influences in multivariate longitudinal data sets, but the number of investigations incorporating these techniques is still very limited.

In summary, investigators have offered simple main effects, interactional, and transactional explanations for why research has shown a link between early difficulties with peers and later maladjustment. Main effects explanations differ in the extent to which they view early difficulties with peers as involved in the etiology of the later disorders, with the incidental and causal being two extreme models. Such simple linear models seem insufficient explanations on the whole, however. Interaction models recognize that any attempt to specify how difficulties with peers affect later adjustment must consider aspects of the child, such as his or her preferred behavioral style and internal attributions and understandings. Interaction models, however, are still static characterizations. Recently, dynamic, transactional models have begun to influence how authors conceptualize and analyze the link between early peer difficulties and later adjustment. These transactional models offer many advantages over other explanations because they recognize that the child and the peer group form a dynamic, interacting system that changes over time. A significant element of this system includes the mechanisms of reciprocal influence among the child's cognitions of the self and others, the child's behavior toward peers, and the peer group's collective appraisal of and behavior toward the child. This element is the focus of the next section.

PROCESSES OF RECIPROCAL BEHAVIOR AND SOCIAL COGNITION IN PEER GROUP ADJUSTMENT

In the preceding discussion of transactional models, we described a hypothetical spiraling cycle of influence, wherein children and their peers form impressions and perceptions of one another that guide their behavioral responses toward each other and determine the nature of their relationships. The components of this process included the child's cognitions about him- or herself, the child's characteristic behavior toward peers, the influence of the child's behavior on the peer group's collective appraisal and acceptance of the child, and the resulting influence of these attitudes on the peer group's collective behavior toward the child. Although this reciprocal process was presented abstractly earlier, in fact a great deal is already know about many of these variables and pathways of influence. Indeed, theory and research on the mechanisms that govern adult social interaction has a long history (e.g., Kelly, 1955) and continues to flourish (e.g., Fletcher & Fincham, 1991), while several models of the mechanisms that govern the social interaction of children have also been presented (e.g., Crick & Dodge, 1994; Lemerise & Arsenio, 2000; Rubin, Hastings, et al., 1998). Also, as we have reviewed, the study of the behavioral correlates of difficulties with peers is one of the oldest traditions within the literature on children's peer relationships. Interestingly, it was the empirical evidence indicating that children who experience peer difficulties are at risk for both concurrent and later maladjustment that served as the major impetus for what is now a substantial body of research focusing on the social-cognitive and behavioral processes underlying peer difficulties.

Our purpose in this section is to flesh out this emerging general model of how children's cognitions, emotions, and behavior affect the establishment of negative reputations among peers and peer group rejection by reviewing the existing research bearing on its key components and pathways. Before beginning, it merits noting that in several respects the research in this area has followed a developmental psychopathological perspective. First, there is an implicit understanding that the study of social maladjustment is linked with the study of normal social development. One of the major tenets of developmental psychopathology is that our understanding of risk and pathology can be enhanced by knowledge about normal development. Likewise, our understanding of normal development is expanded by knowledge about deviations in development (Cicchetti, 2002). Much of the research on the social-cognitive and behavioral correlates of peer difficulties has involved identi-

fying children who are experiencing social difficulties (e.g., children who are rejected, withdrawn, or friendless), assessing their social-cognition or behavioral orientations, and then comparing their orientations to those of children who are functioning successfully within their peer groups. As a consequence, a great deal has been learned about the social-cognitive and behavioral processes underlying both successful and unsuccessful peer relationships.

Second, there is the recognition by researchers in this area that there are likely to be different pathways by which children come to experience peer difficulties. The view that the same developmental outcome may be achieved through different avenues is a position advocated by developmental psychopathologists. For example, whereas some children can become rejected because they behave aggressively and disruptively, others may become rejected because they withdraw from peers and engage in developmentally inappropriate play (Rubin, Hastings, et al., 1998).

Finally, there is the realization, as there is in developmental psychopathology, that there are multiple mechanisms and processes involved in determining a particular maladaptive outcome. Consequently, a variety of cognitive, emotional, and behavioral mechanisms and processes have been examined, including the social-cognitive and behavioral characteristics of children who are experiencing social difficulties, as well as the social-cognitive and behavioral responses of the peers with whom the child interacts.

Although the general outline of the process we wish to describe was embedded in Figure 12.3, this process is shown in a different and clearer form in Figure 12.4. The cycle shown in Figure 12.4 is one in which the processing of social cues, the regulation of emotion and emotion processing, and the social behavior of both the target child and the members of the peer group contribute to difficulties in peer relationships or peer rejection. Figure 12.4 is a representation of the conclusions of recent research and theorizing in this area, including models offered by Coie (1990), Crick and Dodge (1994), Deater-Deckard (2001), Howes (1988), Lemerise and Arsenio (2000), and Rubin and Rose-Krasnor (1992), among others. The model in Figure 12.4 is guided by several assumptions. First, it is assumed that each individual brings into the interactive context broad representations of him- or herself and his or her relationships. These representations guide children's expectations for interaction and direct them to pursue some social goals but not others. They also influence how children interpret the behavioral cues of their interactive partners and how children evaluate alternative response options.

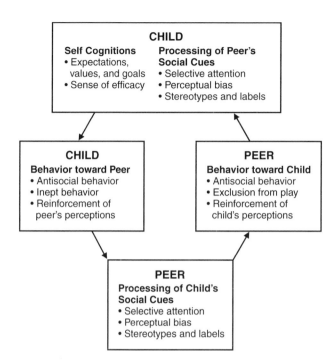

Figure 12.4 Processes of reciprocal influence in peer transactions involving children with poor adjustment with peers. Adapted from "Peers' Contribution to Children's Social Maladjustment: Description and Intervention" (pp. 341–370), by J. M. Price and K. A. Dodge, 1989, in *Peer Relations in Child Development,* T. J. Berndt & G. W. Ladd (Eds.), New York: Wiley.

Second, the model assumes that from the earliest periods of interaction, participants form specific expectations and representations of their particular partner. These representations may include the behavioral characteristics of the other, as well as emotional reactions that were experienced at the time the representation was formed. These person representations are integrated into previously existing knowledge structures, and in concert with these structures, guide each participant's behavioral responses. The valence of these person representations is extremely important. If primarily positive, then future interaction with the partner is welcomed and pursued. If, however, the valence of the behavioral and affective features of the representation of the other are primarily negative, then further interaction with that particular individual might be avoided. This process of forming person perceptions is considered to be dynamic rather than static. As long as two individuals are continuing to have contact with one another, there is the potential for the modification of existing representations and perceptions.

Finally, and consequently, the model assumes that the social outcomes of interactions (e.g., the degree to which the individuals like one another or whether they become friends) follow from the person perceptions that are formed

during the course of interaction. We turn next to some of the specific components of the model in Figure 12.4.

The Child's Self and Social Cognitions

The first component of interaction consists of the child's self, social cognitions, and emotions. When a child interacts with a peer, he or she applies a set of knowledge structures about the self, about relationships in general, and, if there has been prior experience with a particular peer, specific knowledge and memories about that peer. He or she also applies a set of specific social goals and expectations for the interaction. These goals and expectations also reflect beliefs about his or her personal and emotional efficacy in relationships in general and in the specific relationship at hand. It is hypothesized that during social interaction, these knowledge structures, emotions, and expectancies influence how the individual processes the social information available (Crick & Dodge, 1994; Deater-Deckard, 2001; Lemerise & Arsenio, 2000; Rubin & Rose-Krasnor, 1992; Saarni, 1999). In turn, the manner in which this information is processed serves to guide the child's behavior during interaction with the peer. Thus, positive views and expectations of self and relationships, along with accurate processing of information and positive emotions, should be conducive to the formation of positive and supportive relationships with peers. Conversely, negative views and expectations of self and others, along with processing biases and deficits and negative emotions, should lead to social difficulties with peers.

Self Cognitions

Children's self regard and self appraisals of their social competencies should have an important bearing on the ways they initiate and maintain social exchanges with peers (X. Chen et al., 2004; Sandstrom, Cillessen, & Eisenhower, 2003; Sandstrom & Coie, 1999). Positive self appraisals are likely to prove advantageous for the initiation of social interaction; negative self evaluations may prove disadvantageous in promoting social exchange. The dialectic between self-regard and social interaction tendencies is an area that requires serious inquiry. At present, what is known is that popular children tend to view themselves as more socially competent than their less popular age-mates, with the association between acceptance and self appraisal increasing with age (Bukowski & Hoza, 1989; Ladd & Price, 1986; Sandstrom et al., 2003; Sandstrom & Coie, 1999). Peer rejection, on the other hand, is associated with negative thoughts and feelings about the self. Unpopular or rejected children are more likely than their popular counterparts to express a less positive self-concept in the social and they are also more likely to perceive social situations as difficult (Sandstrom et al., 2003; Sandstrom & Coie, 1999). Unpopular children are more likely to report greater anxiety in social situations (Flanagan, 2005; Hymel & Franke, 1985; La Greca et al., 1988).

Although these findings suggest the general conclusion that children already experiencing difficulties with peers approach social situations feeling poorly about their social relationships and social skills, it is important to note that not all children with poor peer relationships approach social situations in this negatively disposed way. Studies of sociometrically rejected children indicate that one subset of these children, those who behave aggressively, do not report thinking poorly about their social relationships with peers (Zakriski & Coie, 1996). Rejected children who are anxious and socially reticent do, however (Hymel, Bowker, & Woody, 1993). These findings are in keeping with the results of studies concerning extremely withdrawn and extremely aggressive children; it is only the former group that reports having difficulty with their social skills and peer relationships (Boivin & Hymel, 1997; Rubin, Chen, & Hymel, 1993).

Furthermore, children who are victimized by their peers, particularly those children who self-report themselves as victimized, are more likely than their nonvictimized peers to blame themselves for their social difficulties, to report anxiety, and to indicate low feelings of overall self-worth (Graham & Juvonen, 1998).

Social Cognitions

In addition to perspectives on the self, cognitions about others and relationships are expected to be associated with, and predictive of, social difficulties with peers. Although little is known about the role of latent knowledge structures in children's social adjustment, considerable information exists on the relation between social information processing patterns of children and social outcomes (e.g., Brendgen, Bowen, Rondeau, & Vitaro, 1999; Burks, Laird, Dodge, Pettit, & Bates, 1999; Dodge, Lochman, Harnish, Bates, & Pettit, 1997; Orobio de Castro, Veerman, Koops, Bosch, & Monshouwer, 2002; Rose & Asher, 2004). To date, several theoretical models of the link between social information processing and behavior have been formulated. For example, in the social information processing model described by Rubin and Krasnor (1986), when children face an interpersonal dilemma (e.g., making new friends or acquiring an object from someone else), their thinking follows a particular

sequence. First, children may select a social goal. This entails the establishment of a representation of the desired end state of the problem-solving process. Second, they examine the task environment; this involves reading and interpreting all the relevant social cues. For example, boys and girls are likely to produce different solutions when faced with a social dilemma involving same-sex as opposed to opposite-sex peers (Rubin & Krasnor, 1983). As well, the social status, familiarity, and age of the participants in the task environment are likely to influence the child's goal and strategy selection (Krasnor & Rubin, 1983). Third, they access and select strategies; this process involves generating possible plans of action for achieving the perceived social goal, and choosing the most appropriate one for the specific situation (Burgess et al., 2005; Rabiner & Gordon, 1992; Rose & Asher, 2004). Fourth, they implement the chosen strategy. Finally, it is proposed that children evaluate the outcome of the strategy; this involves assessing the situation to determine the relative success of the chosen course of action in achieving the social goal. If the initial strategy is unsuccessful, the child may repeat it or she or he may select and enact a new strategy, or abandon the situation entirely.

In an initial attempt to understand the production of aggression in children, Dodge (1986) proposed a similar model of social information processing. This model was later revised by Crick and Dodge (1994) and then by Lemerise and Arsenio (2001), and has been applied to many different groups of children, including different types of aggressive children and nonagressive children (Crick & Dodge, 1996), children of different sociometric status (Crick & Werner, 1998), and children experiencing depression and anxiety (Bell-Dolan, Foster, & Chistopher, 1995; Garber, Keiley, & Martin, 2002; Quiggle, Garber, Panak, & Dodge, 1992), The Crick and Dodge (1994) model consists of six stages, namely, (1) the encoding of social cues; (2) the interpretation of encoded cues; (3) the clarification of social goals; (4) the accessing and generation of potential responses; (5) the evaluation and selection of responses; and (6) the enactment of the chosen response. An additional component of this model is a "database" comprised of biologically determined capabilities and cognitive structures acquired from past experiences, such as social schemas, scripts, and knowledge, which are thought to directly influence each information processing step (Crick & Dodge, 1994).

Children who have difficulties in their peer relationships demonstrate characteristic deficits or qualitative differences in thinking at various steps of these models. Several types of deficits or differences have been identified:

- Children with problems in peer relationships have difficulty discriminating a peer's social intentions. Dodge, Murphy, and Buchsbaum (1984), for example, found that popular children are better than other children at discriminating a peer's intentions, whereas rejected children are significantly worse. The importance of attending to relevant social cues is that these cues are then used to interpret another's intentions.

- Rejected children, particularly rejected children who are aggressive, are more likely than their more popular counterparts to assume malevolent intent when they are faced with negative circumstances, especially when the social cues are ambiguous (e.g., Dodge et al., 2003; see Orobio de Castro et al., 2002, for a recent review). Moreover, socially accepted (popular) children tend to attribute social successes to internal causes and expect success to continue in the future (Sobol & Earn, 1985). They also view social outcomes as more controllable than do socially unaccepted children. Alternately, children experiencing social difficulties tend to perceive their social successes as unstable and externally caused and to perceive their social failures as stable and internally caused (e.g., Dill, Vernberg, & Fonagy, 2004; Rubin & Krasnor, 1986; Wichmann, Coplan, & Daniels, 2004).

- Accepted and unaccepted children differ in their social problem-solving skills. Children who are well liked are likely to generate competent and effective solutions to interpersonal dilemmas, whereas disliked children are likely to generate incompetent or aggressive solutions (e.g., Asarnow & Callan, 1985; Ladd & Oden, 1979; Pakaslahti, Karjalainen, & Keltikangas-Jaervinen, 2002; Rubin & Daniels-Beirness, 1983), especially if they view the other's intentions as hostile (Dodge, 1980).

- Socially accepted children differ from disliked children in the manner they evaluate the probable outcomes for their behavior. In general, well-liked children are more accurate in their evaluations of the outcomes of their behavior. Disliked children, however, expect that positive outcomes will accrue if they act aggressively and that less-positive outcomes will result from nonaggressive solutions (Perry & Rasmussen, 1986). Also, compared to nonaggressive children, aggressive children are more likely to believe that an aggressive response is appropriate, and are more likely to expect positive outcomes from an aggressive response (Guerra, Huesmann, & Splinder, 2003; Huesmann & Guerra, 1997).

Complementing this research on the link between social cognition and peer difficulties is research on the relation between social information-processing and behavior. Results from research with both extreme and normal samples indicate that the manner in which children process information is related to their actual behavior, particularly when aggregated assessments of processing are conducted (e.g., Erdley & Asher, 1998; Orobio de Castro et al., 2002; Orobio de Castro, Bosch, Veerman, & Koops, 2003). Moreover, a recent study found that social information-processing mediated the association between early peer rejection and later aggressive behavior (Dodge et al., 2003). Thus, there is empirical evidence that children's social cognitions serve to guide their behavioral orientations and responses with peers.

Finally, there are experimental data supporting the link between a child's social cognitions and his social behavior and adjustment. In a novel experiment by Rabiner and Coie (1989), rejected participants were given the assignment of entering a room to initiate play with a group of peers with whom they were unacquainted. Half the boys were told that the peers liked them and wanted them to play with them. The other half was not given any kind of expectation. Consistent with evidence presented in this section, relative to the boys not given an expectation, rejected boys who expected to be liked came to be liked more by the peers. Presumably, a child's expectations of being liked led him to behave in ways that led the peers to like him.

Emotions

Recent research has demonstrated that children's emotions are associated with their peer experiences. Such research stems from the work of Saarni (1998, 1999) on emotional competence, and from a recent reformulation of Crick and Dodge's (1994) model by Lemerise and Arsenio (2000) that places emphasis on emotion processes and cognitions. Specifically, Lemerise and Arsenio argue that emotional processes should be considered at each stage of Crick and Dodge's social information processing model. For example, a child's negative emotionality or reactivity and emotion regulatory skills, in addition to the affect component of a child's representations of past experiences, should be included in the "database" that each child brings to a social situation. Also, the ways in which children encode and interpret cues may be affected by a child's mood, emotions, and arousal, and may be influenced by other peers' own affective states and emotions. For example, an offending peer with a visibly happy face may dissuade a child from assigning blame. Similarly, Lemerise and Arsenio posit that other peers' affective states and cues may influence the type (positive or negative) of goals that children choose. Furthermore, the emotional ties that children have with others might influence the ways in which children generate, evaluate, and choose a response in a social situation. Presumably, if a child has a close, intimate relationship with another, the child will process the social information positively, and choose responses that will be likely to promote maintenance of the relationship (e.g., Burgess et al., 2005).

There is some evidence that children's expressions of emotions are related to sociometric status. Compared to average-status children, Hubbard (2001) found that rejected children expressed more anger and nonverbal unhappiness. Moreover, children's emotional competence (a composite of emotional expressiveness, emotion regulation, and emotion knowledge) in 3- and 4-year-olds is concurrently and predictively associated with social competence (Denham et al., 2003). Importantly, an intervention study conducted with aggressive boys revealed that emotion regulation may influence social-information processing (Orobio de Castro et al., 2003). In this study, when aggressive boys were asked to monitor and regulate their emotions, and also to consider the emotions of the peer instigator, the children generated behavioral responses that were less aggressive in nature. The study of the influence of emotion processes on social information-processing represents an exciting new research direction that will further our understanding of social information processing, and may in turn, improve our attempts to intervene with children who experience difficulties with peers.

Child's Behavior toward Peers

The second component of the reciprocal influence model is the behavior the individual displays toward other children. Children's behavior toward other children is presumed to be driven by their self- and social cognitions. In turn, children's behavior is expected to influence the perceptions that other children develop of the child (see Figure 12.4).

A considerable body of research suggests that, although children are sometimes rejected by peers for nonbehavioral reasons such as physical stigmata, behavior plays a substantial, if not overriding, role. Many studies have documented behavioral differences between socially successful children and children experiencing difficulties in their relationships with peers (see Bierman, 2004). Much of this work is based on cross-sectional research designs utilizing existing peer groups. Such studies are open to the alternative interpretation that the behavioral differences are the result of rather than responsible for children's difficulties

with peers. Children's behavior is undoubtedly affected by being rejected by peers, however, enough research now exists to safely conclude that how children behave shapes their reception by the peer group in the first place. A set of classic longitudinal studies and studies utilizing artificial play groups, for example, show that behavioral assessments made before or during the earliest stages of acquaintanceship predict children's subsequent social acceptance (e.g., Coie & Kupersmidt, 1983; Dodge, 1983; Putallaz, 1983). More importantly, intervention studies designed to reduce children's negative behaviors or increase their repertoire of social skills have shown increases in acceptance by peers as a results of behavioral changes (see Bierman, 2004, for a recent review).

Which behaviors matter? Most research has focused on the behavioral basis of peer acceptance or rejection. Research on the behavioral correlates of sociometric standing is a several-decades-old tradition, and many lawful associations between specific behaviors and rejection by the peer group have been documented (see Rubin, Bukowski, et al., 1998, for a review). One broad class of behavior that has proven to be especially significant is aggressive behavior. Aggressive behavior has been found to correlate with rejection by peers regardless of whether peer evaluations, teacher ratings, or direct observations (Crick, Casas, & Mosher, 1997; Haselager, Cillessen, Van Lieshout, Riksen-Walraven, & Hartup, 2002; McNeilley-Choque, Hart, Robinson, Nelson, & Olsen, 1996) are used to assess children's social behavior. Furthermore, both physical and relational forms of aggression have been linked with peer rejection (Crick & Grotpeter, 1995; Underwood, 2003).

However, recent research indicates that rejection and victimization by peers may hinge, in part, on the behaviors concomitant with aggression, rather than aggression per se. Aggressive behaviors appear to place children at highest risk for peer rejection when they occur along with a broad pattern of emotionally reactive, disruptive, and unskilled behavior (Bierman, 2004). For instance, "ineffectual" and "effectual" aggressors have been distinguished on the basis of their behavior in conflict situations and on their peer experiences (Perry, Perry, & Kennedy, 1992). Ineffectual aggressors prolong and escalate conflicts, exhibit exaggerated displays of negative emotion, and eventually "lose" in conflict situations. These children are at high risk for peer rejection and victimization. In contrast, effectual aggressors behave aggressively in the service of instrumental goals and to establish dominance, and they do not prolong conflicts or exhibit heightened emotion. These children encounter little resistance from peers and are rarely victimized by peers (Perry et al., 1992). According to the results of a 2-year longitudinal study, aggressive-rejected children are more likely to experience stable elevations in aggressive behavior and peer rejection than aggressive-nonrejected and nonaggressive-rejected children (Bierman & Wargo, 1995). Importantly, research indicates that aggression may not lead to rejection if it is balanced by a set of positive qualities (e.g., social skill) that facilitate links with other children (Farmer et al., 2003).

In addition, extremely withdrawn children have been found to be more lonely and disliked and victimized by peers than are their more sociable age-mates, especially during the mid-to-late years of childhood (see Rubin, Burgess, & Coplan, 2002, for a review).

On the other hand, observational studies also suggest that children who engage in high rates of positive social behavior (e.g., conversation, smiling, prosocial sharing, and helping), who make efforts to initiate contact with others, who join ongoing play in a fluid and natural way, who cooperate, and who respect peer norms, are likely to receive more positive behavioral responses from peers and to have higher peer sociometric rating and nomination scores than other children (see Coie, 1990; Eisenberg & Fabes, 1998; Newcomb, Bukowski, & Pattee, 1993). Similarly, children who are described by their peers as helpful, supportive, cooperative, friendly, nice, calm, understanding, good at games, and good leaders are more likely to receive high sociometric ratings and many positive and few negative sociometric nominations (see Rubin, 2002). Thus, the presence of positive social skills as well as the absence of aggressive or extremely withdrawn behavior seems critical to acceptance by peers (Bierman, 2004). Bierman (2004) identified seven social skills domains that are frequently selected for social skills training on the basis of their empirical association with peer acceptance. These skill domains include social participation, emotional understanding, prosocial behavior, self-control, communication skills, fair-play skills, and social problem-solving skills.

Recent research has also emphasized the affective dimension of socially competent behavior. Halberstadt, Denham, and Dunsmore (2001) identified sending affective messages, receiving affective messages, and experiencing affect as three integrated components of affective social competence. Sending affective messages involves awareness of the need to send such a message, identification of which message to send, sending a message consistent with the demands of the situation, and managing the delivery of the affective message. Children who are more positively expressive and more adept at sending affective messages

are better liked by peers than children who are negatively expressive (Halberstadt et al., 2001). The emergence of the affective social competence model is consistent with recent conceptualizations of social competence. Eliciting positive peer responses requires not only a repertoire of appropriate behaviors, but also emotion regulation and social-cognitive skills which foster behavior that is appropriate and responsive to social and situational demands (Bierman, 2004; Sroufe, 1996).

Although the correlates of acceptance and rejection appear to be similar across age groups, Coie (1990) points out a few developmental differences that have been identified. For example, as children enter into elementary school, both athletic and academic competence becomes increasingly important determinants of social adjustment in the peer group. Children who display competence in either one or both of these domains are better liked by their peers who are less competent. In addition, with age, disruptiveness in the classroom and social withdrawal become increasingly important contributors to social rejection. Recently, Cillessen and Mayeux (2004) found that relational aggression was increasingly predictive of perceived popularity but decreasingly predictive of peer liking (i.e., sociometric popularity) from middle childhood to early adolescence; physical aggression was increasingly less disliked by peers and decreasingly predictive of perceived popularity. And, although much less is known about this issue, it appears that the behavioral correlates of peer acceptance and rejection also differ somewhat for children of different genders and from different socioeconomic circumstances (see Bierman, 2004).

Specific behaviors have also been shown to be related to the development and maintenance of friendships, although much less is known about this process (Berndt, 2002, 2004). It has been demonstrated that among children who are "hitting it off," communication becomes increasingly connected, conflicts that arise are successfully resolved, and play activities are coordinated (Gottman, 1983). As the relationship progresses, communication clarity and self-disclosure become increasingly important. Once friendships are established, cooperation and reciprocity become key elements of successful relationships (see Hartup & Stevens, 1997). Thus, the child's ability to engage in joint communication and cooperative activities with a peer as well as successfully resolve conflicts with that peer, appear to be important behavioral skills for friendships (Laursen, 1993; Laursen, Finkelstein, & Betts, 2001; Parker & Seal, 1996). On the negative side, children's behavioral orientations also have been found to contribute to the development of less desirable relationships, such as antagonistic, conflicted relationships and bully/victim relationships (Hartup & Abecassis, 2002). For example, Dodge, Price, Coie, and Christopoulos (1990) identified high-conflict, low-conflict, asymmetric (bully/victim relationships), and low-interaction dyads that developed in small play groups. Their results indicated that the rate of aggressing toward a peer was positively correlated with the rate of being the object of the peer's aggression. These aggressive exchanges contributed to the development of stable high-conflict relationships. Once developed, participants of high-conflict dyads were more aggressive toward one another and engaged in less prosocial behavior than other dyads. Not surprisingly, participants of these relationships came to dislike each other. Recent research indicates that dyadic relationship factors contribute more variance to boys' reactive aggression and hostile attributions within dyads than do actor or partner factors; furthermore, social cognitions that predict reactive aggression within dyads seem to be best explained at the dyadic level (Coie et al., 1999; Hubbard, Dodge, Cillessen, Coie, & Schwartz, 2001). That is, although general social-cognitive tendencies impact dyadic reactive aggression, social-cognitive biases that contribute to reactive aggression seem to be somewhat specific to dyadic relationships (Hubbard et al., 2001).

Obviously, a vast array of positive and negative behaviors has been linked to the development of successful and unsuccessful relationships with peers. Indeed, any attempt to catalogue the hundreds of specific behaviors that have been studied in relation to various social outcomes quickly becomes unwieldy. In an effort to impose some conceptual organization on the existing litany of behavioral correlates and to identify areas of relative neglect, Asher and Williams (1987) suggested a useful framework for considering the kinds of behaviors that should relate to adjustment with peers.

According to Asher and Williams (1987), when considering the kinds of behavior that are likely to contribute to adjustment with peers it is helpful to consider how children come to a conclusion about whether they like or dislike another child. These authors suggest that children pose a set of six metaphoric questions to themselves. The core issues for children are: (1) whether they find the partner entertaining, (2) whether they feel that they can trust the partner, (3) whether they find that the partner influences them in ways that they find acceptable, (4) whether they find that the partner facilitates rather than undermines their personal goals, (5) whether the partner makes them feel good about themselves, and (6) whether they can conclude that the partner shares their fundamental values and priorities.

Asher and Williams (1987) suggest that by considering these core issues for children, one can better understand which behaviors should and should not be expected to be related to success with peers, and why some behaviors are more robust correlates of social success than others. Behaviors that simultaneously address several core issues for children are expected to be stronger correlates of social success than behaviors that address only one concern. This argument, for example, would explain why aggression is such a strong correlate of adjustment with peers: Children who are aggressive are not fun to be around (issue A), humiliate others (issue E), are unpredictable (issue B), disrupt activities (issue D), and generate resentment (issue C). A further important element of Asher and Williams' framework is that it is the configuration of children's behavioral assets and liabilities that is most important, not the presence or absence of any single specific behavioral tendency. Thus, aggressive children who nonetheless possess skills for behaving in ways that leave others feeling good about themselves or to find them entertaining, trustworthy, persuasive, and so on, are not expected to run the same risk of peer rejection as aggressive children without these additional social skills (see Bierman, 2004). The significance of particular negative behaviors such as aggressiveness or social withdrawal, therefore, depends partly on whether child also possesses offsetting social skills. In the following section, peers' perception of the child will be explored in greater detail.

Peers' Social Cognitions

One of the basic propositions of the social interaction model is that from their initial encounter, social partners are forming representations and perceptions of one another. These cognitive processes are depicted in the third component of Figure 12.4. As is supported by the research reviewed in the previous section, children's representations and perceptions of one another are, at least in part, based on the behaviors they direct to one another. There is also evidence that children's memories and perceptions of one another are influenced by their own behavioral reputation, level of peer status, age, and liking for the peer target; situational factors (e.g., the levels of aggression within the peer group; and the peer target's gender, age, and sociometric status; Bierman, 2004; LaFontana & Cillessen, 1999, 2002).

Once children's perceptions of one another are formed, they appear to remain moderately stable over time (LaFontana & Cillessen, 1999, 2002). Thus, the impressions that are formed of a child within a particular peer group are likely to be maintained over time. One explanation for the stability of person perceptions is that the structure of social cognitive processes appears to be favorable to the maintenance of the perceptions and impressions.

To begin, there is evidence that individuals selectively attend to certain types of behavior displayed by their interactive partner, depending on their attitudes and perceptions of that particular partner. Relevant information (i.e., information that is either consistent or inconsistent with the knowledge structure) is attended to whereas irrelevant or neutral information is not. Thus, when interacting with a child, the types of behavioral displays that are likely to be attended to will be based, at least in part, on the peer's perceptions of the child. If the child is perceived to be friendly or is liked by peers, then prosocial or cooperative behavior may be a part of the peers' scheme for the child. These behaviors would be attended to. If, however, the child was perceived as aggressive or was disliked, then antisocial behaviors would be a part of the peers' schema, and as a consequence, future aggression would be likely to be attended to. In both scenarios, peers' original perceptions and representations of the child would be reinforced.

Attribution processes also appear to be oriented toward the maintenance of previously developed person perceptions. According to social information processing theorists, attributions primarily occur at an unconscious, automatic level, unless the individual behaves in an unexpected manner, is highly negative, or there is some kind of affective arousal (the peer threatens the child). These particular conditions are hypothesized to trigger explicit, conscious processing (Dodge, 1986; Rubin & Rose-Krasnor, 1992), which may lead to a modification of the original representations of the child. Thus, when interacting with a child, a peer will consciously engage in attributions only when the child is particularly negative or acts in a manner inconsistent with the peer's perceptions or schema for the child.

The automation of attributions also appears to be guided by a number of biases. Research with adults indicates that when interpreting another's behavior, individuals tend to show a bias toward confirming rather than disconfirming their existing perceptions (Fiske, 2004). Thus, unless the behaviors displayed by the partner are so highly inconsistent with developed person perceptions as to lead to conscious processing, behavioral displays are interpreted as being consistent with person perceptions (Hymel, 1986). For example, children will be more likely to attribute hostile intentions to a child they know as aggressive than to a child known to be nonaggressive. Likewise, Burgess et al. (2005) recently reported that children are *less* likely to attribute hostile intentions to a best friend than to a stranger.

Finally, Hymel (1986) found that children's explanations of a child's behavior varied as a function of both affect toward the child and the valence of the child's behavior. For liked children, positive behaviors were attributed to stable causes (e.g., traits), whereas for disliked children, negative behaviors were attributed to stable causes.

Peers' Behavior toward Child

The final component in the model of children's social interactions as depicted in Figure 12.4, is the behavioral responses directed toward the child by the peer group. Once formed, children's reputations guide other children's behavior toward them (Zeller, Vannatta, Schafer, & Noll, 2003). For example, in a classic and persuasive study, Dodge (1980) presented children with hypothetical stories about classmates with differing reputations for aggressiveness with peers. Dodge found that children were more likely to retaliate aggressively when an act was performed by a classmate with a reputation for aggressiveness, than when the same act was performed by a nonaggressive classmate.

The reputation frames that guide children's behavior toward a specific child are important, as they may entice the child who is the object of a negative reputation to behave, in turn, in ways that affirm this reputation. Indeed, research with adults indicates that when an individual expects another individual to behave in a certain way (e.g., to be friendly or unfriendly; hostile or nonhostile), his or her partner's behavior may indeed fall in line with these expectations. Thus, when an individual is led to expect unfriendly behavior from a partner, his or her behavior may indeed inspire unfriendly behavior from partners. In addition, research with adults (e.g., Fiske, 2004) indicates that individuals sometimes make inferences about other people's characteristics by referencing his or her own behavior. In a similar fashion, to the extent that children reference his or her own behavior to make inferences about another child, and their own behavior is motivated by reputation, those reputations may be strengthened. In this way, the spiraling cycle of child's cognition—child's behavior—peers' cognitions—peers' behavior is reinforced.

Illustrating the Developmental Psychopathological Approach to Peer Adjustment: The Example of Social Anxiety with Peers

In this section, we illustrate how principles of developmental psychopathology may be applied to illuminate the etiology, nature, course, and treatment of child social anxiety. Interest and research pertaining to social anxiety in children has flourished in recent years, in part, due to documentation that social anxiety places individuals at risk for problematic developmental outcomes and, in part, due to broader increased interest in the interface between emotion, cognition, and behavior. Evidence suggests, for instance, that social anxiety is linked concurrently with depressed mood, other anxiety disorders, and school maladjustment (Beidel & Turner, 1998; Morris, 2001; see Crozier & Alden, 2001, for recent reviews). In addition, social anxiety places children and adolescents at risk for social and psychological maladjustment in adulthood, including the development of other anxiety disorders, major depression, substance use disorders, and impaired occupational functioning (Beidel & Turner, 1998).

Social anxiety may be conceptualized in several alternative ways, but it is especially fruitful to view social anxiety as a form of peer maladjustment. Indeed, a growing body of research provides evidence for an association between child social anxiety and peer maladjustment. For example, cross-sectional studies with both normative and clinical child populations indicate that social anxiety is linked with self-reports of limited and low quality friendships and loneliness (Beidel & Turner, 1998; Flanagan, 2005; LaGreca & Lopez, 1998; Vernberg et al., 1992). Social anxiety has also been linked with sociometric ratings of low peer group acceptance and victimization by peers (Flanagan, 2005; Inderbitzen et al., 1997; La Greca & Stone, 1993). In addition, in retrospective accounts, socially anxious adults report fewer friends during childhood than nonanxious adults (Rapee & Heimberg, 1997) and they identify negative social experiences as contributing to the onset of social anxiety (Stemberger et al., 1995).

These associations are significant in their own right but they become of further interest as we consider the ways in which they might illustrate important principles of developmental psychopathology. For example, developmental models suggest that social anxiety emerges, in part, as a result of reciprocal transactions between individual characteristics and the social context. Rubin and colleagues have advanced a developmental model in which behavioral inhibition and social reticence in early childhood increase the risk for social skill deficits and social anxiety (e.g., Rubin, Burgess, Kennedy, et al., 2003). Rubin et al. contend that children with temperamental vulnerabilities, such as behavioral inhibition, initially experience psychological and physiological discomfort in social situations, which leads them to avoid social interaction (Rubin, Burgess, & Hast-

ings, 2002). Avoiding social interaction during early childhood limits important socialization opportunities, which in turn, impedes the normative development of social cognition and social skills in these children. These children's social skill deficits then elicit negative peer reactions which, in turn, perpetuate further social withdrawal and intensify social anxiety (e.g., Nelson, Rubin, & Fox, in press). Further, inhibited and reticent behavior may mark socially anxious children as easy targets of overt rejection and victimization by peers attempting to establish social power and dominance (Hodges, Malone, & Perry, 1997). It is easy to imagine how peer victimization would exacerbate the social avoidance and anxious affect that may have invited victimization in the first place. This apparent reciprocal cycle of characterlogic vulnerability, negative peer experiences, and problematic behavior is an excellent example of an important principle of developmental psychopathology, namely, that maladjustment is an outcome of reciprocal transactions between individuals and their social-ecological contexts (Cicchetti, 2002; Sameroff, 1995).

Likewise, an additional principle of developmental psychopathology is that normal and abnormal developmental processes are mutually informative. Rates of social anxiety increase markedly during the late childhood and early adolescent years (Beidel & Turner, 1998), with an average age of onset around 12 years (D. D. Weiss & Last, 2001). What accounts for this normative increase in this form of problematic behavior? It is possible that diagnostic or other more prosaic factors account for this developmental trend, but we find it interesting to speculate that the patterns of prevalence of social anxiety may be linked to exaggerations or distortions in normative developmental processes. Consider first that important developmental shifts take place in social cognition during the same developmental period that many children begin encountering significant difficulties with social anxiety for the first time. It is during this same period of time, for example, that children increasingly evaluate themselves in comparison to other children rather than to absolute standards (Parker et al., 1995). Likewise, developments in abstract thinking and perspective taking at this age heighten children's awareness of peer evaluation and alter their appreciation for the content and valence of peer perceptions (Crozier & Burnham, 1990). These social cognitive developments are important developmental mileposts that typically serve children well in the long run, even if they contribute to the reasonable self-consciousness that most children show at this age. But, in view of evidence that distorted and negatively biased self views are implicated in the social anxiety, it is tempting to conclude that these same normative changes also contribute to a rising tide of more problematic social anxiety when they occur within vulnerable individuals.

Along with being an era of normative changes in social and self-cognition, the period for heightened identification of social anxiety is also a period of heightened pressure for social participation with peers. As discussed earlier, it is during the period in which social anxiety becomes prevalent that children begin spending substantial amounts of time away from their families with peers. Most children initiate this re-orientation themselves and desire and welcome it. But it also is anticipated and encouraged by parents, teachers, and others, and thus does not occur entirely voluntarily. Moreover, the nature of peer participation changes developmentally at the time, becoming more complex. The task of making friends and avoiding peer rebuff may be complicated by the dynamics of the early adolescent social climate (Bukowski & Sippola, 2001). In particular, hierarchical social networks and emerging social cliques leave many children either alienated or insecure about their social position (Parker et al., 1995). Almost one-third of 11-year-olds reported losing a friend over the course of the school year (e.g., Wojslawowicz, Rubin, Burgess, Rose-Krasnor, & Booth, in press) and almost two-thirds reported being teased by peers in the previous month (Kanner, Feldman, Weinberg, & Ford, 1987). Ethnographic studies indicate that even popular children and members of cliques experience insecurities about maintaining their reputations and social statuses (Adler & Adler, 1995; Eder, 1985). If children are already vulnerable to social anxiety for other reasons, including distortions in their social cognitions, the inevitable complexity of these normative changes peer experiences may for the first time overwhelm them and make them casualties to social anxiety.

A third principle of developmental psychopathology is that heterogeneity exists across individuals in the nature, precursors, and subsequent course of psychological disorders. Anxiety disorders appear to be consistent with this model of heterogeneity (see Vasey & Dadds, 2001, for relevant reviews). Indeed, the social functioning and peer experiences of children at risk for social anxiety may be characterized by substantial heterogeneity. Thus, whereas compelling evidence links social anxiety and peer maladjustment, not all socially anxious children experience low levels of peer acceptance or suffer victimization by peers. Indeed, the findings of several studies offer evidence for variability in peer adjustment of children with social anxiety. For example, one study of elementary school children found that rejected children were no more socially anxious than average children, and that rejected and average children were more socially anxious than neglected children

(Crick & Ladd, 1993), suggesting that a significant subgroup of socially anxious children may attain average peer status despite their social concerns. Chansky and Kendall (1997) found that anxious children were just as likely to have a best friend as were controls, though they had fewer friends overall.

In addition to the available empirical evidence, there are at least two other reasons to expect heterogeneity in the peer adjustment of socially anxious children. First, socially anxious children as a group may be more motivated than others to gain acceptance and be evaluated positively by peers. The desire for acceptance and belonging in universal (Leary, 2000), but socially anxious children may elevate this desire until it becomes overbearing emotionally. Socially anxious children who are better able to manage emotion in evaluative situations may behave more adaptively than those who cannot, contributing to heterogeneity in vulnerability and outcomes. Relatedly, socially anxious children who possess better social skills, or who are somehow spared salient and humiliating victimization by peers, may weather their vulnerable years with less negative impact than those who lack the behavioral skills to bootstrap themselves out of vulnerable situations or who are somehow spared the most traumatizing forms of peer rebuff.

The concept of *equifinality* is also a point at which the literature on social anxiety may intersect with principles drawn from developmental psychopathology. Equifinality refers to the fact that diverse pathways may lead to the same ostensible outcome. Models of Conduct Disorder that emphasize differences between early- and late-starters are nice illustrations of the principle of equifinality and it is of interest to speculate as to whether parallels exist in the pathways to social anxiety. For example, some children exhibit dispositional and behavioral vulnerabilities from an early age, and thereby reach social anxiety through a long history of continuity. For other children, social anxiety may emerge after a history of positive peer relationships. The onset of social anxiety for the latter but not the former group may be more closely tied to unexpected challenges these children encountered locating a social niche and friendship network following the transition to a new school. Alternatively, some popular children may find themselves overwhelmed with the task of protecting their exalted social status. Thus, it is possible that at least two routes to social anxiety exist: one through a history of temperamental vulnerability, social skill deficits, and peer problems, and another in the absence of such negative developmental canalization. To our knowledge, different developmental models of social anxiety have not been examined empirically, despite the fact that different courses may have important implications for the stability and treatment of social anxiety.

The principle of *multifinality* suggests that similar conditions at one point in time may lead to different outcomes. Likewise, different responses to social anxiety may also predict different developmental outcomes. In early childhood, those socially wary and inhibited toddlers whose mothers (and fathers) are overprotective and intrusive are observed to be socially anxious and reticent in the peer group as preschoolers; those toddlers whose mothers (and fathers) encourage independence, provide warmth and responsivity do not appear socially fearful and reticent (e.g., Rubin, Burgess, & Hastings, 2002; Rubin, Cheah, & Fox, 2001). The adolescent and adult outcomes of children with social anxiety may be contingent upon certain responses and coping strategies that promote further decline or resilience. For example, some socially anxious children may be able to manage their negative cognitions and organize their social behavior in a way that minimizes the external visibility and negative social impact of their anxious feelings. For example, by prompting themselves to focus on the conversation rather than themselves during social interaction, some children may reduce self-focused fears of negative evaluation and display more sensitive social interaction skills. Alternatively, by asking questions, socially anxious children may simultaneously validate their partner and remove social-evaluative pressure from themselves.

Finally, the interplay between developmental research and intervention is another well-established feature of developmental psychopathology. Understanding the social functioning and coping strategies of socially impaired and nonimpaired socially anxious children may inform developmental research and intervention. For instance, the social-cognitive and social-behavioral characteristics of children who establish friendships and gain acceptance despite elevated levels of social anxiety may effectively inform intervention for socially anxious children with peer problems. That is, the social-behavioral and social-cognitive characteristics of socially anxious children without significant social impairment may be particularly suitable intervention targets.

FUTURE DIRECTIONS FOR THEORY AND RESEARCH ON CHILDREN'S PEER EXPERIENCES

Developmental psychopathologists have clearly recognized the importance of adjustment with peers in childhood, and have emphasized some of the negative consequences for children of cumulative peer rejection or friendship difficul-

ties. Even so, it can be argued that developmental psychopathologists have not taken full advantage of many of the insights of researchers who have studied children's peer relationships from outside that framework. Yet, research on children's peer relationships can in some ways be seen as paradigmatic of the developmental psychopathology approach. For example, one of the guiding propositions underlying a developmental psychopathology perspective is that individuals develop both toward increasing flexibility and increasing organization (Cicchetti, 1990; Sroufe & Rutter, 1984). This proposition aptly characterizes the pattern of development in several areas of children's peer relationships, such as the growth of children's conceptions of friendship and the developmental patterns in very young children's play. Another example is the concept of directedness, encompassing the idea that individuals selectively receive, respond to, and create experience based on past experiences and cognitive frameworks and biases. As we reviewed, much attention within the literature on children's peer relationships has been directed toward the biases and inappropriately selective social information processing of children with peer relations difficulties; we are beginning to learn how such biases contribute to individual differences in peer interaction and exacerbate the problems of certain children with budding peer relationship difficulties. As a final example, the evidence that we reviewed presented a convincing case for viewing disturbed adjustment to peers as a condition of risk. However, peer rejection has very seldom been included among the litany of illustrative risk conditions (e.g., Down's syndrome, maltreatment, failure-to-thrive, insecure attachment, depression) that are commonly cited by developmental psychopathologists (cf., Cicchetti, Lynch, Shonk, & Manly, 1992).

For their part, investigators seeking to understand children's relationships with peers have not often done so explicitly within a developmental psychopathology framework. There are signs this is changing (Cicchetti & Bukowski, 1995). For example, in 1995 a special issue of the journal *Development and Psychopathology* was devoted to exploring this interface and featured, among many other notable topics, reports on the peer experiences of children with Attention-Deficit Hyperactivity Disorder (Hinshaw & Melnick, 1995) or Autism (Lord & Maggill-Evans, 1995); the predictive outcomes of social withdrawal (Rubin, Chen, McDougall, Bowker, & McKinnon, 1995), and reports on the longitudinal stability of aggression and peer rejection (Bierman & Wargo, 1995; Burks et al., 1995; Coie et al., 1995). Another encouraging exception is emerging work on the peer experiences of maltreated children (e.g., Bolger & Patterson, 2001a, 2001b; Levendosky, Okun, & Parker,

1995; Parker & Herrera, 1996; Rogosch, Cicchetti, & Aber, 1995). Many features of maltreating families are believed to inhibit the development of competent peer relationships in abused children. A better understanding of maltreated children's peer experiences can provide developmental psychopathologists with insights into how such a profound disturbance in parent-child relationships affects the cognitive, affective, and behavioral systems of abused children. For peer relationships researchers, however, the study of maltreated children's friendships and other peer experiences can, among other things, be used as test assumptions about the role of specific skills or formative experiences in adaptive peer interaction or the development of successful friendships. Notwithstanding these encouraging exceptions, most work on children's adjustment with peers has remained somewhat disconnected from the interpretive framework and tenets of developmental psychopathology. In our view, the framework of developmental psychopathology can sharpen our understanding of some of the new and well-established findings in this area, as well as reveal directions for future work.

Accordingly, we close with several suggestions for directions for future research inspired by our reading of the state of the literature on children's peer adjustment and relationships.

Giving Context Its Due

The literature on children's and adolescents' peer adjustment remains a literature dominated by a focus on the dispositions and behavioral inclinations of individuals. For example, most of the normative developmental changes we described are assumed to have been driven by age-linked advances in individuals' language, social-cognition, and emotion regulation skills. This is the case, for example, concerning the growth children display over the early years in the complexity of their play. For the most part, cognitive, language, and affective achievements in individuals have been assumed to be responsible for the appearance of novel and more advanced forms of play with age. The bias toward dispositional explanations is not limited to normative changes however. We saw it repeatedly in the representation of individual differences, where the pervasive assumption is that differences in temperament, social cognitive and affective skills, and behavioral tendencies account for why some children are more readily rejected by peers and remains so over time.

Dispositional assumptions have contributed greatly to our understanding of the nature of developmental changes and individual variability in peer experiences. However, echoing sentiment expressed by earlier authors (e.g., Fer-

guson & Cillessen, 1993; Higgins & Parsons, 1983), our hope is that future research in this area will balance this dispositional approach with a better understanding of the organization and nature of contextual factors. As a simple start, greater attention should be devoted to documenting the contexts in which children and adolescents interact with their peers outside of school (e.g., Mahoney, Larson, & Eccles, 2005). Our understanding of children's peer experiences has been heavily shaped thus far by studies of children in school settings. Notable exceptions include efforts to understand the "subjective landscape" of adolescent activities (e.g., Kirshner, O'Donoghue, & McLaughlin, 2002; Laursen & Koplas, 1995; Morrissey & Werner-Wilson, 2005; Richards et al., 1998), the interaction opportunities afforded by different activity contexts (Benenson, Maiese, et al., 2002; Beneson, Markovits, Roy, & Denko, 2003; Beneson, Markovits, et al., 2002; Mahoney, Larson, & Eccles, 2005; Zarbatany et al., 1990), and the formal and informal sources of interpersonal support available to children in their neighborhoods (Bryant, 1985). A more complete catalogue of the settings in which children interact with peers at different points in development is essential to understanding the social challenges facing children, how peer experiences influence children, and why some children are more successful with their peers than are others.

There are other ways in which the field will benefit from fuller treatment of context, however. One of the most important would be increased understanding of the emergence, maintenance, and consequences of victimization and rejection by peers. Differences in group expectations and norms influence to a powerful extent the acceptability of specific behaviors (Boivin, Dodge, & Coie, 1995; Bukowski & Sippola, 2001; Salmivalli, 2001). For example, the general conclusion that aggression is strongly linked to group rejection masks some important contextual variability. In particular, because peer attitudes toward specific behavior are affected by group norms, some evidence suggests that aggression is less strongly linked with group rejection in group contexts where aggression is more normative (e.g., Boivin et al., 1995; Stormshak, Bierman, Bruschi, Dodge, Coie, & the Conduct Problems Prevention Research Group, 1999; Wright, Giammarino, & Parad, 1986).

Additionally, earlier we noted the self-perpetuating nature of children's reputations with peers, stressing that, once in place, group reputations tend to become self-fulfilling in that they elicit from children behavior consistent with peer expectations. Group reputations, then, are important contextual factors in behavior. Yet, to date, because the emphasis has been so heavily focused on child characteristics (e.g., social problem-solving skills, emotion regulation difficulties, attribution biases) group expectations rarely appear in our models of the determinants of behavior.

The context of behavior also includes the relationship history between individuals; The incorporation of relationship histories into models of behavior would also represent a significant advance. This type of approach is already yielding dividends, albeit to date in largely isolated corners of the literature (e.g., Parker & Herrera, 1996; Roy & Benenson, 2002). For example, the identification of aggressive children is a cornerstone of research in children's peer adjustment and a great many conceptual models have been offered as to why some children are more aggressive with peers than are others. It is widely recognized but only seldom acknowledged in these models that individuals are not indiscriminately aggressive. Instead, the social histories between any particular pair of children appears to play an important role in whether they are aggressive toward one another and relational histories account for much of the aggression that occurs within groups (Burgess et al., 2005; Coie et al., 1999; Hubbard et al., 2001). Likewise, the development of mutual animosity between specific peers appears to depend more on their specific disagreeable history together than on either individual's tendency to be disagreeable in general (Parker & Gamm, 2003). As these examples illustrate, without attention to the relational context, it may be difficult to understand individual behavior (Hinde, 1987, 1995).

Consideration of context also begs the question of culture. It is probably the case that in some cultures, the construct of popularity has little meaning; Rather than being well liked, the respect of peers may carry much of the weight in determining later outcomes. Furthermore, those who are disrespectful of adults (and peers) may be the individuals, in collectivistic cultures, who prove most shameful to their families and friends; and it may be that these disrespectful children (e.g., those who do not demonstrate "hyo" or filial piety in Asian cultures) are the ones at greatest risk for later negative outcomes (Rubin, in press). Insights into issues of this type have been occurring (e.g., Casiglia, Lo Coco, & Zappulla, 1998; X. Chen et al., 1995, 2004; Deater-Deckard & Dodge, 1997; Hamm, 2000; Khatr & Kupersmidt, 2003; Killen, Crystal, & Watanabe, 2002), but progress lags.

As a final example, we draw attention to the potential moderating role that context may play in judging the consequences of group rejection and victimization. Earlier we reviewed evidence suggesting that victimization by peers is associated with subjective distress in victims. This finding has received wide and well-deserved attention and many authors point to it as the basis for justification of intervention on behalf of victimized children. Without disputing the general conclusion, however, it is worth noting that this relation is less robust than might first appear. In particular, there is evidence that the social context of victimization plays an important role in moderating the extent to which victimization is accompanied by distress. Bellmore, Witkow, Graham, and Juvonen (2004), for example, have shown that victimization is associated with the highest levels of personal distress in classroom contexts in which the victim shares the ethnicity of many of his or her classmates. Mitigation of personal distress appears to occur in classroom contexts in which the victim is in the ethnic minority, presumably because the victim is able to dismiss the victimization by peers as racially rather than personally motivated.

Expanding the Scope of Focal Outcomes

The premise that children with relationship problems are at risk for later life difficulties is a widely shared professional and popular belief and has played an important role in motivating research on children's adjustment with peers. Evidence in support of this premise is not easy to obtain, but, as we have reviewed, it is mounting and persuasive (see also Nangle & Erdley, 2001). Even a cursory appraisal of this literature, however, reveals some narrowness, insofar as the outcomes of primary interest largely include subsequent school failure, later involvement in delinquent or adult criminal behavior, and a variety of indications of later mental illness and psychopathology. Problems in these areas are significant and are the focus of considerable public, private, and institutional concern. Thus, an effort to examine whether early negative experiences with peers can place individuals at risk for such significant disturbances is wholly appropriate and merits continuing. At the same time, we suggest that the opportunity exists for expanding the scope of the search for the later implications of earlier successful versus unsuccessful peer experiences. In particular, we suggest that the field would be well served by future research designed to uncover logical continuities in the interpersonal adjustment of individuals during the periods from childhood to emerging and later adulthood.

In many instances, this search will direct attention to outcome variables that are far more subtle than the dramatic, psychopathological outcomes so prevalent in past work. As an example, we reviewed evidence that has emerged recently suggesting that certain, vulnerable children display undue and unwarranted jealousy surrounding their best friends (Parker et al., 2005). Friendship jealousy is a source of considerable personal distress for these children and other evidence suggests that it is also at the root of a good deal of the aggression and victimization that occurs within peer groups. Jealousy, of course, is a more familiar topic in the study of adults in romantic contexts, where it is recognized as a major contributor to relationship dissatisfaction (e.g., Anderson, Eloy, Guerrero, & Spitzberg, 1995) and relationship violence (Hansen, 1991; Stets & Pirog-Good, 1987). In view of evidence that the disposition to jealousy is rooted in distorted perceptions of the self and others (see Parker et al., 2005), it would not be surprising if future research revealed that the children who display jealousy surrounding friends in middle childhood are also the individuals responsible for the bulk of the jealousy in adult romantic contexts. In addition to being of predictive and applied significance, confirmation of this longitudinal relation could also contribute to broader debates concerning the nature of the link between the friendship and romantic interpersonal contexts (e.g., Connolly, Furman, & Konarski, 2000; Furman, 1999; Furman et al., 2002; Laursen & Williams, 1997; Seiffge-Krenke, 2003). Other possible areas in which continuities seem likely include links to occupational adjustment and advancement, marital adjustment, difficulties of affect regulation, to name only a few.

Last, many, if not most of the longitudinal research on children's peer relationships has focused on negative outcomes. There has been very little work on the predictors of adaptive, functional outcomes in adolescence and adulthood.

Revisiting Competence and Incompetence

In much the same way that the search for the outcomes of negative peer experiences has focused on the dramatic, it is also the case that researchers have focused on "big-ticket" constructs in their search for the interpersonal behaviors that contribute to peer rejection and other negative peer experiences. But impulsive behavior, aggression, and social withdrawal are not the only predictors and concomitant correlates of peer rejection. More subtle contributors to peer experiences deserve attention as well. Indeed, almost all behaviors that cannot be considered normative to particular groups, contexts, and cultures, should be considered candidate behaviors for study in those contexts. An important direction for the future is to design studies that permit us to learn whether these subtler behaviors are also competencies and are as likely to predict, not only peer rejection,

but also more extensive maladaptive developmental trajectories as the "big ticket" items that have been the focus in the past (Rubin, in press).

Further Exploration of Family-to-Peers Linkages

Research concerning the family processes that contribute to adjustment in the peer group has blossomed conspicuously recently, so much so that this area of inquire should surely by counted among the handful of areas demonstrating the most significant inroads in the decade since our last review. We did not review this literature here, but comprehensive reviews are available (Ladd & Pettit, 2002; Parke & O'Neill, 1999; Rubin & Burgess, 2002). In our view, however, some unevenness in progress is evident in this area. In particular, we appear to know more about those family experiences leading to aggression, withdrawal, and peer rejection than we do about family processes that lead to social competence, peer acceptance, and the ability to form and keep qualitatively rich friendships. How children come to develop the abilities to join others in play; make friends; engage in cooperative group endeavors; mentor younger peers; demonstrate loyalty to friends; learn how, when, and to whom one should self-disclose; forgive those who have purposely or inadvertently harmed them; and so on, are topics that do not leave a lengthy trail of published developmental products. Especially lacking are process approaches to the study of parent-child linkages. Most research is organized around the outcomes of such negative parenting practices as harsh punishment, intrusiveness, over-directiveness, and over-control, and guilt induction. And almost all research on family links to peer interaction, relationship, and group endeavors is drawn from studies carried out in prototypically "western" cultures. This is certainly an area in need of attention. Once again, it behooves researchers to consider how social competencies and adaptation develops; to do so would allow strong conclusions to be drawn on how incompetencies and maladaptation become manifest.

Toward an Integrated Representation of Adjustment with Peers

At the outset, we noted that the past decade has been one of unprecedented advances in the development and refinement of methods for studying adjustment with peers. Whereas this rapid expansion has increased the range of methodological options available to researchers seeking to represent children's adjustment with peers, it has not produced an overarching framework for considering when specific measures are preferable to others or how multiple measures are related. We noted that adjustment with peers appears to have at least two primary dimensions of individual differences—success with friends and acceptance by the peer group. A wide array of measurement options are available within each of these ways of representing peer experiences. Yet, for the most part, very little is confidently known about how these broad dimensions should be integrated or how to the measurement options available within each dimension relate to one another or across dimensions.

Increased recognition of the links between friendship and group experiences appears to us to be an especially important direction for future research. Group level processes, such as those that dictate which individuals are central versus peripheral members can exert important constraints on the possibilities for friendships among members of groups. At the same time, the bonds of friendship also provide children with access to membership in selected groups (see Sabongui et al., 1998). Likewise, by serving as the broader context in which friendship experiences unfold, groups and social networks presumably shape children's experiences within friendships in significant ways. On the one hand, outsiders can have a positive influence on friendships (see Milardo & Helms-Erikson, 2000). For example, group interaction is more enjoyable in certain ways than dyadic interaction and third parties can act as mediators to resolve disputes between friends. Nonetheless, outsiders can also be significant sources of trouble for friends (Asher et al., 1996). For example, outsiders may preempt opportunities for frank discussion between friends and coordination of social activities may be more complicated and less satisfying in groups larger than two (Benenson et al., 2001; Benenson, Maiese, et al., 2002; Lansford & Parker, 1999). In addition, tension and conflict can arise between friends if participants are squeezed between their loyalty to their friend and the obligations to others (Asher et al., 1996; Selman, 1980).

To some extent, answers to how measures might be integrated should come as researchers gain more experience with data sets that include many alternative assessments and permit examination of their interrelations. But we also encourage future researchers to think conceptually concerning this issue. Hinde (1979), as one example, has encouraged researchers to consider dyadic-level assessments, such as those that identify friendships, and group-level assessments—such as those that can give rise to appraisals of acceptance or rejection—as bearing a hierarchical, and mutually influential relation to one another.

CONCLUSIONS

After initial experiences with parents and siblings, children enter into increasingly complex relationships with peers. In this chapter, we have reviewed evidence that children's experiences with other children are significant to their growth and adjustment. We have reviewed some of the ways in which peer experiences complement children's experiences with family members, particularly parents, and some of the ways in which peer experiences may be unique experiences in development.

Much of the chapter was devoted to considering the wide individual variability in children's peer experiences, which we suggested could be organized powerfully along two basic dimensions—success with friends and acceptance by the peer group. Consideration of friendship adjustment suggested both qualitative and quantitative aspects that may be linked to developmental processes and outcomes. At the acceptance level, we considered especially the child's membership in sociometrically identifiable status groups. Evidence was found for the validity of parsing children's social world into such categories; members of different sociometric groups show distinct behavioral profiles, for example. Additionally, we devoted attention to the reciprocal intrapersonal and interpersonal processes that give rise to variability in peer adjustment and to the implications of peer adjustment for short-term and long-term psychopathology. Finally, we concluded by suggesting several areas that could be prosperous areas of future research. These topics suggested themselves to us from our perspective of considering how far and in what directions the decade of research since our last review has taken us. As this discussion makes abundantly clear, there are sufficient challenges remaining in the study of children's peer experiences to keep researchers and theorists busy well beyond a further decade.

ACKNOWLEDGMENTS

We gratefully acknowledge the contributions to this chapter of our many wonderful collaborators and coauthors over the years. We are also grateful to Dante Cicchetti for this opportunity and for his instructive feedback and patience concerning the original as well as this revised version of the chapter. Finally, we are indebted to Sarah Kollat for her invaluable assistance identifying and locating pertinent literature and to Corrine Farinola for her tireless assistance tracking and typing references.

REFERENCES

Abecassis, M. (2003). I hate you just the way you are: Exploring the formation, maintenance, and needs for enemies. In E. V. E. Hodges & N. A. Card (Eds.), *Enemies and the darker side of peer relations* (pp. 5–22). San Francisco: Jossey-Bass.

Abecassis, M., Hartup, W. W., Haselager, G. J. T., Scholte, R. H. J., & Van Lieshout, C. F. M. (2002). Mutual antipathies and their significance in middle childhood and adolescence. *Child Development, 73,* 1543–1556.

Aboud, F. E. (1988). *Children and prejudice.* New York: Basil Blackwell.

Abrams, D., Rutland, A., & Cameron, L. (2003). The development of subjective group dynamics: Children's judgments of normative and deviant in-group and out-group individuals. *Child Development, 74,* 184–1856.

Achenbach, T. M., & Edelbrock, C. S. (1981). Behavioral problems and competencies reported by parents of normal and disturbed children aged four through sixteen. *Monographs of the Society for Research in Child Development, 46*(1, Serial No. 188).

Adelson, J., & Doehrman, M. J. (1980). The psychodynamic approach of adolescence. In J. Adelson (Ed.), *Handbook of adolescent psychiatry* (pp. 99–116). New York: Wiley.

Adler, P. A., & Adler, P. (1995). Dynamics of inclusion and exclusion in preadolescent cliques. *Social Psychology Quarterly, 58,* 145–162.

Ainsworth, M. D. S., Blehar, M. C., Waters, E., & Wall, S. (1978). *Patterns of Attachment.* Hillsdale, NJ: Erlbaum.

Albano, A. M., Chorpita, B. F., & Barlow, D. H. (2003). Childhood anxiety disorders. In R. A. Barkley & E. J. Mash (Eds.), *Child Psychopathology* (pp. 279–329). New York: Guilford Press.

Allen, J. D., Moore, C., Kuperminc, G., & Bell, K. (1998). Attachment and adolescent psychosocial functioning. *Child Development, 69,* 1406–1419.

American Psychiatric Association. (1994). *Diagnostic and statistical manual of mental disorders* (4th ed.). Washington, DC: Author.

Anderson, P. A., Eloy, S. V., Guerrero, L. K., & Spitzberg, B. H. (1995). Romantic jealousy and relational satisfaction: A look at the impact of jealousy experience and expression. *Communication Reports, 8*(2), 77–85.

Arbuthnot, J. (1975). Modification of moral development through role playing. *Developmental Psychology, 11,* 319–324.

Asarnow, J. R., & Callan, J. W. (1985). Boys with peer adjustment problems: Social cognitive processes. *Journal of Consulting and Clinical Psychology, 53,* 80–87.

Asher, S. R., & Coie, J. D. (1990). *Peer rejections in childhood.* New York: Cambridge University Press.

Asher, S. R., Parker, J. G., & Walker, D. L. (1996). Distinguishing friendship from acceptance: Implications for intervention and assessment. In W. M. Bukowski, A. F. Newcomb, & W. W. Hartup (Eds.), *The company they keep: Friendship during childhood and adolescence* (pp. 366–405). New York: Cambridge University Press.

Asher, S. R., & Williams, G. A. (1987). *Helping children without friends in home and school contexts.* In Children's Social Development: Information for Teachers and Parents (pp. 1–26). Urbana, IL: ERIC Clearinghouse on Elementary and Early Childhood Education.

Atlas, R., & Pepler, D. J. (1998). Observations of bullying in the classroom. *Journal of Educational Research, 92*(2), 86–99.

August, G. J., Ostrander, R., & Bloomquist, M. J. (1992). Attention deficit hyperactivity disorder: An epidemiological screening method. *American Journal of Orthopsychiatry, 62,* 387–396.

Azmitia, M., Lippman, D. N., & Ittel, A. (1999). On the relation of personal experience to early adolescents' reasoning about best friendship deterioration. *Social Development, 8,* 275–291.

Bagwell, C. L., & Coie, J. D. (2004). The best friendships of aggressive boys: Relationship quality, conflict management, and rule-breaking behavior. *Journal of Experimental Child Psychology, 88*(1), 5–24.

Bandura, A. (1989). Social cognitive theory. In R. Vasta (Ed.), *Annals of child development: Six theories of child development-Revised formulations and current issues* (Vol. 6, pp. 1–60). Greenwich, CT: JAI Press.

Barocas, R., & Sameroff, A. J. (1982). Social class, maternal psychopathology, and mediational processes in young children. *Advances in Child Behavioral Analysis and Therapy, 2,* 4–77.

Barkley, R. A., Anastopoulos, A. D., Guevremont, D. C., & Fletcher, K. E. (1991). Adolescents with ADHD: Patterns of behavioral adjustment, academic functioning, and treatment utilization. *Journal of the American Academy of Child and Adolescent Psychiatry, 30,* 752–761.

Barnhill, G. P. (2001). Social attributions and depression in adolescents with Asperger syndrome. *Focus on Autism and Other Developmental Disabilities, 16,* 46–53.

Baumeister, R. F., & Leary, M. R. (1995). The need to belong: Desire for interpersonal attachments as a fundamental human motivation. *Psychological Bulletin, 117,* 497–529.

Baumeister, R. F., & Senders, P. S. (1989). Identity development and the role of structure of children's games. *Journal of Genetic Psychology, 150,* 19–37.

Bauminger, N., & Kasari, C. (2000). Loneliness and friendship in high-functioning children with Autism. *Child Development, 71,* 447–456.

Beidel, D. C. (1991). Social phobia and overanxious disorder in school-age children. *Journal of the American Academy of Child and Adolescent Psychiatry, 30,* 545–552.

Beidel, D. C., & Turner, S. M. (1998). *Shy children, phobic adults: Nature and treatment of social phobia.* Washington, DC: American Psychological Association.

Beidel, D. C., Turner, S. M., & Morris, T. L. (1999). Psychopathology of childhood social phobia. *Journal of the American Academy of Child and Adolescent Psychiatry, 38*(6), 643–650.

Belle, D. (1989). *Children's social networks and social supports.* New York: Wiley.

Bell-Dolan, D. J., Foster, S. L., & Christopher, J. S. (1995). Girls' peer relations and internalizing problems: Are socially neglected, rejected, and withdrawn girls at risk? *Journal of Clinical Child Psychology, 24,* 463–473.

Bellmore, A. D., Witkow, M. R., Graham, S., & Juvonen, J. (2004). Beyond the Individual: The Impact of Ethnic Context and Classroom Behavioral Norms on Victims' Adjustment. *Developmental Psychology, 40*(6), 1159–1172.

Benenson, J. F. (1994). Ages four to six years: Changes in the structures of play networks of girls and boys. *Merrill-Palmer Quarterly, 40,* 478–487.

Benenson, J. F., Apostoleris, N. H., & Parnass, J. (1997). Age and sex differences in dyadic and group interaction. *Developmental Psychology, 33,* 538–543.

Benenson, J. F., & Christakos, A. (2003). The greater fragility of female's versus male's closest same-sex friendships. *Child Development, 74,* 1123–1129.

Benenson, J. F., Maiese, R., Dolensky, E., Dolensky, N., Sinclair, N., & Simpson, A. (2002). Group size regulates self-assertive versus self-deprecating responses to interpersonal competition. *Child Development, 73,* 1818–1829.

Benenson, J. F., Markovits, H., Roy, R., & Denko, P. (2003). Behavioural rules underlying learning to share: Effects of development and context. *International Journal of Behavioural Development, 27,* 116–121.

Benenson, J. F., Nicholson, C., Waite, A., Roy, R., & Simpson, A. (2001). The influence of group size on children's competitive behavior. *Child Development, 72,* 921–928.

Berndt, T. J. (1989). Obtaining support from friends in childhood and adolescence. In D. Belle (Ed.), *The social support needs of school-aged children*. New York: Wiley.

Berndt, T. J. (1996). Friendship quality affects adolescents' self-esteem and social behavior. In W. M. Bukowski, A. F. Newcomb, & W. W. Hartup (Eds.), *The company they keep: Friendship during childhood and adolescence* (pp. 346–365). New York: Cambridge University Press.

Berndt, T. J. (1999). Friends' influence on children's adjustment to school. In W. A. Collins & B. Laursen (Eds.), *Minnesota Symposia on Child Psychology: Vol. 30. Relationships as developmental contexts* (pp. 85–108). Mahwah, NJ: Erlbaum.

Berndt, T. J. (2002). Friendship quality and social development. *Current Directions in Psychological Science, 11,* 7–10.

Berndt, T. J. (2004). Children's friendships: Shifts over a half-century in perspectives on their development and their effects. *Merrill-Palmer Quarterly, 50,* 206–223.

Berndt, T. J., & Hanna, N. A. (1995). Intimacy and self-disclosure in friendships. In K. J. Rotenberg (Ed.), *Disclosure processes in children and adolescents* (pp. 57–77). New York: Cambridge University Press.

Berndt, T. J., Hawkins, J. A., & Hoyle, S. G. (1986). Changes in friendship during a school year: Effects on children's and adolescents' impressions of friendship and sharing with friends. *Child Development, 57,* 1284–1297.

Berndt, T. J., Hawkins, J. A., & Jiao, Z. (1999). Influences of friends and friendships on adjustment to junior high school. *Merrill-Palmer Quarterly, 45,* 13–41.

Berndt, T. J., & Hoyle, S. G. (1985). Stability and change in childhood and adolescent friendships. *Developmental Psychology, 21,* 1007–1015.

Berndt, T. J., & Perry, T. B. (1986). Children's perceptions of friendships as supportive relationships. *Developmental Psychology, 22,* 640–648.

Berndt, T., & Perry, T. B. (1990). Distinctive features and effects of early adolescent friendships. In R. Montemayor, G. R. Adams, & T. P. Gullotta (Eds.), *From childhood to adolescence: A transitional period?* (Vol. 2, pp. 269–287). Thousand Oaks, CA: Sage.

Bierman, K. L. (2004). *Peer rejection: Developmental processes and intervention.* New York: Guilford Press.

Bierman, K. L., & Erath, S. A. (in press). Promoting social competence in early childhood: Prevention and early intervention programs. In K. McCartney & D. Phillips (Eds.), *Handbook of early child development.* Malden, MA: Blackwell.

Bierman, K. L., Smoot, D. L., & Aumiller, K. (1993). Characteristics of aggressive-rejected, aggressive (nonrejected), and rejected (nonaggressive) boys. *Child Development, 64,* 139–151.

Bierman, K. L., & Wargo, J. B. (1995). Predicting the longitudinal course associated with aggressive-rejected, aggressive (nonrejected), and rejected (nonaggressive) status. *Development and Psychopathology, 7,* 669–682.

Bigelow, B. J., Tesson, G., & Lewko, J. H. (1996). *Learning the rules: The anatomy of children's relationships.* New York: Guilford Press.

Bigelow, B. J., Tesson, G., & Lewko, J. H. (1999). The contextual influences of sibling and dating relations on adolescents' personal relations with their close friends, dating partners, and parents: The Sullivan-Piaget-Hartup Hypothesis considered. In J. A. McLellan & M. J. V. Pugh (Eds.), *The role of peer groups in adolescent social identity: Exploring the importance of stability and change* (pp. 71–86). San Francisco: Jossey-Bass.

Blos, P. (1962). *On adolescence: A psychoanalytic interpretation.* New York: Free Press.

Blos, P. (1979). The second individuation process of adolescence. In P. Blos, *The adolescent passage: Developmental issues.* New York: International University Press.

Blurton-Jones, N. (1972a). Categories of child-child interaction. In N. Blurton-Jones (Ed.), *Ethological studies of child behavior* (pp. 65–98). New York: Cambridge University Press.

Blurton-Jones, N. (Ed.). (1972b). *Ethological studies of child behavior.* New York: Cambridge University Press.

Boivin, M., Dodge, K. A., & Coie, J. D. (1995). Individual-group behavioral similarity and peer status in experimental play groups of boys: The social misfit revisited. *Journal of Personality and Social Psychology, 69,* 269–279.

Boivin, M., & Hymel, S. (1997). Peer experiences and social self-perceptions: A sequential model. *Developmental Psychology, 33,* 135–145.

Boivin, M., Hymel, S., & Bukowski, W. M. (1995). The roles of social withdrawal, peer rejection, and victimization by peers in predicting loneliness and depressed mood in childhood. *Development and Psychopathology, 7,* 765–785.

Boivin, M., Poulin, F., & Vitaro, F. (1994). Depressed mood and peer rejection in childhood. *Development and Psychopathology, 6,* 483–498.

Bolger, K. E., & Patterson, C. J. (2001a). Developmental pathways from child maltreatment to peer rejection. *Child Development, 72*(2), 549–568.

Bolger, K. E., & Patterson, C. J. (2001b). Pathways from child maltreatment to internalizing problems: Perceptions of control as mediators and moderators. *Development and Psychopathology, 13*(4), 913–940.

Booth, C. L., Rose-Krasnor, L., McKinnon, J., & Rubin, K. H. (1994). Predicting social adjustment in middle childhood: The role of preschool attachment security and maternal style. *Social Development, 3,* 189–204.

Booth, C. L., Rubin, K. H., Rose-Krasnor, L., & Burgess, K. (2004). Attachment and friendship predictors of psychosocial functioning in middle childhood and the mediating roles of social support and self-worth. In K. Kerns & Richardson, R. A. (Eds.), *Attachment in middle childhood* (pp. 47–62). New York: Guilford Press.

Boulton, M. J. (1996). A comparison of 8- and 11-year-old girls' and boys' participation in specific types of rough-and-tumble play and aggressive fighting: Implications for functional hypotheses. *Aggressive Behavior, 22,* 271–287.

Boulton, M. J., Trueman, M., Chau, C., Whitehand, C., & Amatya, K. (1999). Concurrent and longitudinal links between friendships and peer victimization: Implications for befriending interventions. *Journal of Adolescence, 22,* 461–466.

Boulton, M. J., & Underwood, K. (1992). Bully/victim problems among middle school children. *British Journal of Educational Psychology, 62,* 73–87.

Bowlby, J. (1973). *Attachment and loss: Vol. 2. Separation, anxiety and anger.* New York: Basic Books.

Bowlby, J. (1982). *Attachment and loss: Vol. 1. Attachment.* New York: Basic Books. (Original work published 1969)

Brendgen, M., Bowen, F., Rondeau, N., & Vitaro, F. (1999). Effects of friends' characteristics on children's social cognitions. *Social Development, 8,* 41–51.

Brendgen, M., Little, T. D., & Krappmann, L. (2000). Rejected children and their friends: A shared evaluation of friendship quality? *Merrill-Palmer Quarterly, 46*(1), 45–70.

Brendgen, M., Vitaro, F., & Bukowski, W. M. (2000). Deviant friends and early adolescents' emotional and behavioral adjustment. *Journal of Research on Adolescence, 10*(2), 173–189.

Brendgen, M., Vitaro, F., Bukowski, W. M., Doyle, A. B., & Markiewicz, D. (2001). Developmental profiles of peer social preference over the course of elementary school: Associations with trajectories of externalizing and internalizing behavior. *Developmental Psychology, 37,* 308–320.

Brendgen, M., Vitaro, F., Doyle, A. B., Markiewicz, D., & Bukowski, W. M. (2002). Same-sex peer relations and romantic relationships during early adolescence: Interactive links to emotional, behavioral, and academic adjustment. *Merrill-Palmer Quarterly, 48,* 77–103.

Brendgen, M., Vitaro, F., Turgeon, L., & Poulin, F. (2002). Assessing aggressive and depressed children's social relations with classmates and friends: A matter of perspective. *Journal of Abnormal Psychology, 30,* 609–624.

Bretherton, I. (1991). The roots and growing points of attachment theory. In J. Stevenson-Hinde & C. M. Parkes (Eds.), *Attachment across the life cycle* (pp. 9–32). New York: Tavistock-Routledge.

Brody, L. M., Nagin, D. S., Tremblay, R. E., Bates, J. E., Brame, B., Dodge, K., et al. (2003). Developmental trajectories of childhood disruptive behaviors and adolescent delinquency: A six-site, cross-national study. *Developmental Psychology, 39,* 222–245.

Bronfenbrenner, U., & Crouter, A. C. (1983). The evolution of environmental models in developmental research. In P. H. Mussen (Series Ed.) & W. Kessen (Vol. Ed.), *Handbook of child psychology: Vol. 1. History, theory, and methods* (4th ed., pp. 357–414). New York: Wiley.

Brown, B. B. (1989). The role of peer groups in adolescents' adjustment to secondary school. In T. J. Berndt & G. W. Ladd (Eds.), *Peer relationships in child development* (pp. 188–216). New York: Wiley.

Brown, B. B. (1990). Peer groups and peer cultures. In S. S. Feldman & G. R. Elliott (Eds.), *At the threshold* (pp. 171–196). Cambridge, MA: Harvard University Press.

Brown, B. B. (1999). "You're going out with who?": Peer group influences on adolescent romantic relationships. In B. B. Brown & W. Furman (Eds.), *The development of romantic relationships in adolescence* (pp. 291–329). New York: Cambridge University Press.

Brown, B. B., & Clasen, D. R. (1986, March). *Developmental changes in adolescents' conceptions of peer groups.* Paper presented at the biennial meeting of the Society for Research in Adolescence, Madison, WI.

Brown, B. B., & Klute, C. (2003). Friends, cliques, and crowds. In G. R. Adams & M. D. Berzonsky (Eds.), *Blackwell handbook of adolescence* (pp. 330–348). Malden, MA: Blackwell.

Bryant, B. K. (1985). The neighborhood walk: Sources of support in middle childhood. *Monographs of the Society for Research in Child Development, 50*(3), 122.

Bryant-Waugh, R., & Lask, B. (1995). Eating disorders in children. *Journal of Child Psychology and Psychiatry, 36,* 191–202.

Buhrmester, D., & Furman, W. (1986). The changing functions of friends in childhood: A neo-Sullivan perspective. In V. J. Derlega & B. A. Winstead (Eds.), *Friendship and social interaction* (pp. 41–62). New York: Springer-Verlag.

Buhrmester, D., & Furman, W. (1987). The development of companionship and intimacy. *Child Development, 58,* 1101–1103.

Buhrmester, D., & Prager, K. (1995). In K. J. Rotenberg (Ed.), *Disclosure processes in children and adolescents* (pp. 10–56). New York: Cambridge University Press.

Bukowski, W. M., & Cillessen, A. H. (1998). *Sociometry then and now: Building on six decades of measuring children's experiences with the peer group.* San Francisco: Jossey-Bass.

Bukowski, W. M., & Hoza, B. (1989). Popularity and friendship: Issues in theory, measurement, and outcome. In T. J. Berndt & G. W. Ladd (Eds.), *Peer relations in child development* (pp. 15–45). New York: Wiley.

Bukowski, W. M., Hoza, B., & Boivin, M. (1994). Measuring friendship quality during pre- and early adolescence: The development and psychometric properties of the Friendship Qualities Scale. *Journal of Social and Personal Relationships, 11,* 471–484.

Bukowski, W. M., Hoza, B., & Newcomb, A. F. (1994). Using rating scale and nomination techniques to measure friendships and popularity. *Journal of Social and Personal Relationships, 11,* 485–488.

Bukowski, W. M., & Sippola, L. K. (2001). Groups, individuals, and victimization: A view of the peer system. In J. Juvonen & S. Graham (Eds.), *Peer harassment in school: The plight of the vulnerable and victimized* (pp. 355–377). New York: Guilford Press.

Bukowski, W. M., Sippola, L., Hoza, B., & Newcomb, A. F. (2000). Pages from a sociometric notebook: An analysis of nomination and rating scale measures of acceptance, rejection, and social preference. In A. Cillessen & W. Bukowski (Eds.), *Recent advances in the measurement of acceptance and rejection in the peer system* (pp. 11–26). San Francisco: Jossey-Bass.

Burgess, K. B., Rubin, K. H., Wojslawowicz, J. C., Rose-Krasnor, L., & Booth-LaForce, C. (2005). *Social information processing and coping styles of shy/withdrawn and aggressive children: Does friendship matter?* Manuscript under review.

Burks, V. S., Dodge, K. A., & Price, J. M. (1995). Models of internalizing outcomes of early rejection. *Development and Psychopathology, 7,* 683–696.

Burks, V. S., Laird, R. D., Dodge, K. A., Pettit, G. S., & Bates, J. E. (1999). Knowledge structures, social information processing, and children's aggressive behavior. *Social Development, 8,* 220–236.

Buskirk, A. A., Rubin, K. H., Burgess, K., Booth-LaForce, C. L., & Rose-Krasnor, L. (2004, March). *Loved, hated . . . but never ignored: Evidence for two types of popularity.* Paper presented as part of a symposium, The Many Faces of Popularity, at the biennial meeting of the Society for Research in Adolescence, Baltimore.

Cairns, R. B. (1979). *Social development: The origins and plasticity of interchanges.* San Francisco: Freeman.

Cairns, R. B., Cairns, B. D., & Neckerman, H. J. (1989). Early school dropout: Configurations and determinants. *Child Development, 60,* 1437–1452.

Cairns, R. B., Xie, H., & Leung, M. C. (1998). The popularity of friendship and the neglect of social networks: Toward a new balance. In W. M. Bukowski & A. H. Cillessen (Eds.), *Sociometry then and now: Building on six decades of measuring children's experiences with the peer group* (pp. 25–54). San Francisco: Jossey-Bass.

Calkins, S. D., Gill, K. L., Johnson, M. C., & Smith, C. L. (1999). Emotional reactivity and emotional regulation strategies as predictors of social behavior with peers during toddlerhood. *Social Development, 8*(3), 310–334.

Carothers, D. E., & Taylor, R. L. (2004). Social cognitive processing in elementary school children with Asperger syndrome. *Education and Training in Developmental Disabilities, 16,* 46–53.

Carver, K., Joyner, K., & Udry, J. R. (2003). National estimates of adolescent romantic relationships. In P. Florsheim (Ed.), *Adolescent romantic relations and sexual behavior: Theory, research, and practical implications* (pp. 23–56). Mahwah, NJ: Erlbaum.

Casiglia, A. C., Lo Coco, A., & Zappulla, C. (1998). Aspects of social reputation and peer relationships in Italian children: A cross-cultural perspective. *Developmental Psychology, 34,* 723–730.

Cassidy, J., & Asher, S. R. (1992). Loneliness and peer relations in young children. *Child Development, 63,* 350–365.

Chansky, T. E., & Kendall, P. C. (1997). Social expectations and self-perceptions in anxiety-disordered children. *Journal of Anxiety Disorders, 11,* 347–363.

Chen, D. W., Fein, G., & Tam, H. P. (2001). Peer conflicts of preschool children: Issues, resolution, incidence, and age-related patterns. *Early Education and Development, 12,* 523–544.

Chen, X., Chang, L., & He, Y. (2003). The peer group as a context: Mediating and moderating effects on the relations between academic achievement and social functioning in Chinese children. *Child Development, 74,* 710–727.

Chen, X., Rubin, K. H., & Li, B. (1995). Social and school adjustment of shy and aggressive children in China. *Development and Psychopathology, 7,* 337–349.

Chen, X., Zappulla, C., Lo Coco, A., Schneider, B., Kaspar, V., de Oliveira, A. M., et al. (2004). Self-perceptions of competence in Brazilian, Canadian, Chinese, and Italian children: Relations with social and school adjustment. *International Journal of Behavioural Development, 28,* 129–138.

Cicchetti, D. (1990). A historical perspective on the discipline of developmental psychopathology. In A. S. Masten & J. E. Rolf (Eds.), *Risk and protective factors in the development of psychopathology* (pp. 2–28). New York: Cambridge University Press.

Cicchetti, D. (1993). Developmental psychopathology: Reactions, reflections, projections. *Developmental Review, 13,* 471–502.

Cicchetti, D. (2002). How a child builds a brain: Insights from normality and psychopathology. In R. A. Weinberg & W. Hartup (Eds.), *Child psychology in retrospect and prospect: In celebration of the 75th anniversary of the Institute of Child Development* (pp. 23–71). Mahwah, NJ: Erlbaum.

Cicchetti, D., & Bukowski, W. M. (1995). Developmental processes in peer relations and psychopathology. *Development and Psychopathology, 7*(4), 587–589.

Cicchetti, D., & Lynch, M. (1993). Toward an ecological/transactional model of community violence and child maltreatment: Consequences for children's development. *Psychiatry: Interpersonal and Biological Processes, 56,* 96–118.

Cicchetti, D., Lynch, M., Shonk, S., & Manly, J. T. (1992). An organizational perspective on peer relations in maltreated children. In R. D. Parke & G. W. Ladd (Eds.), *Family-peer relationships: Modes of linkage* (pp. 345–384). Hillsdale, NJ: Erlbaum.

Cicchetti, D., & Schneider-Rosen, K. (1984). Toward a transactional model of child depression. *New Directions of Child Development, 26,* 5–27.

Cillessen, A., & Bukowski, W. (1998). *Sociometry then and now: Building on six decades of measuring children's experiences with the peer group.* San Francisco: Jossey-Bass.

Cillessen, A. H., & Bukowski, W. M. (Eds.). (2000). *Recent advances in the measurement of acceptance and rejection in the peer system.* San Francisco: Jossey-Bass.

Cillessen, A. H., Bukowski, W. M., & Haselager, G. T. (2000). Stability of sociometric categories. In A. Cillessen & W. Bukowski (Eds.), *Recent advances in the measurement of acceptance and rejection in the peer system* (pp. 75–93). San Francisco: Jossey-Bass.

Cillessen, A. H., & Mayeux, L. (2004). From censure to reinforcement: Developmental changes in the association between aggression and social status. *Child Development, 75,* 147–163.

Cillessen, A. H., van Ijzendoorn, H. W., Van Lieshout, C. F., & Hartup, W. W. (1992). Heterogeneity among peer-rejected boys: Subtypes and stabilities. *Child Development, 63,* 893–905.

Cillessen, A. H., Van Lieshout, C. F., & Haselager, G. J. (1992, August). *Children's problems caused by consistent rejection in early elementary school.* Paper presented at the Centennial Convention of the American Psychological Association, Washington, DC.

Clark, K. E., & Ladd, G. W. (2000). Connectedness and autonomy support in parent-child relationships: Links to children's socioemo-tional orientation and peer relationships. *Developmental Psychology, 36,* 485–498.

Clark-Lempers, D. S., Lempers, J. D., & Ho, C. (1991). Early, middle, and late adolescents' perceptions of their relationships with significant others. *Journal of Adolescent Research, 6,* 296–315.

Coie, J. D. (1990). Towards a theory of peer rejection. In S. R. Asher & J. D. Coie (Eds.), *Peer rejection in childhood* (pp. 365–401). Cambridge, MA: Cambridge University Press.

Coie, J. D., Cillessen, A. N., Dodge, K. A., Hubbard, J. A., Schwartz, D., Lemerise, E. A., et al. (1999). It takes two to fight: A test of relational factors and a method for assessing aggressive dyads. *Developmental Psychology, 35*(5), 1179–1188.

Coie, J. D., & Dodge, K. A. (1988). Multiple sources of data on social behavior and social status. *Child Development, 59,* 815–829.

Coie, J. D., Dodge, K. A., & Coppotelli, H. (1982). Dimensions and types of social status: A cross-age perspective. *Developmental Psychology, 18,* 557–570.

Coie, J. D., & Kupersmidt, J. (1983). A behavioral analysis of emerging social status in boys' groups. *Child Development, 54,* 1400–1416.

Coie, J. D., Lochman, J. E., Terry, R., & Hyman, C. (1992). Predicting early adolescent disorder from childhood aggression and peer rejection. *Journal of Consulting and Clinical Psychology, 60,* 783–792.

Coie, J. D., Terry, R., Lenox, K., Lochman, J., & Hyman, C. (1995). Childhood peer rejection and aggression as predictors of stable patterns of adolescent disorder. *Development and Psychopathology, 7,* 697–714.

Cole, D. A., Martin, J. M., Peeke, L. G., Seroczynski, A. D., & Hoffman, K. (1998). Are cognitive errors of underestimation predictive or reflective of depressive symptoms in children: A longitudinal study. *Journal of Abnormal Psychology, 107,* 481–496.

Collins, W. A. (2003). More than a myth: The developmental significance of romantic relationships during adolescence. *Journal of Research on Adolescence, 13,* 1–24.

Collins, W. A., Henninghausen, K. C., Schmit, D. T., & Sroufe, L. A. (1997). Developmental precursors of romantic relationships: A longitudinal analysis. In S. Shulman & W. A. Collins (Eds.), *Romantic relationships in adolescence: Developmental perspectives* (pp. 69–84). San Francisco: Jossey-Bass.

Collins, W. A., & Laursen, B. (Eds.). (1999). Friends and lovers: The role of peer relationships in adolescent romantic relationships. Relationships as developmental contexts. *Minnesota Symposia on Child Psychology* (Vol. 30, pp. 133–154). Mahwah, NJ: Erlbaum.

Collins, W. A., & Sroufe, L. A. (1999). Capacity for intimate relationships: A developmental construction. In B. B. Brown & W. Furman (Eds.), *The development of romantic relationships in adolescence* (pp. 125–147). New York: Cambridge University Press.

Compas, B. E. (1987). Coping with stress during childhood and adolescence. *Psychological Bulletin, 101,* 393–403.

Connolly, J., Craig, W., Goldberg, A., & Pepler, D. (2004). Mixed-gender groups, dating, and romantic relationships in early adolescence. *Journal of Research on Adolescence, 14,* 185–207.

Connolly, J., Furman, W., & Konarski, R. (2000). The role of peers in the emergence of heterosexual romantic relationships in adolescence. *Child Development, 71*(5), 1395–1408.

Connolly, J., & Goldberg, A. (1999). Romantic relationships in adolescence: The role of friends and peers in their emergence and development. In B. B. Brown & W. Furman (Eds.), *The development of romantic relationships in adolescence* (pp. 266–290). New York: Cambridge University Press.

Cooley, C. H. (1902). *Human nature and the social order.* New York: Scribner.

Corsaro, W. A. (1985). *Friendship and peer culture in the early years.* Norwood, NJ: Ablex.

Corsaro, W. A., & Miller, P. J. (Eds.). (1992). *Interpretative approaches to children's socialization.* San Francisco: Jossey-Bass.

Corsaro, W. A., & Rizzo, T. A. (1988). Discussione and friendship: Socialization processes in the peer culture of Italian nursery school children. *American Sociological Review, 53,* 879–894.

Cowen, E. L., Pedersen, A., Bagigian, H., Izzo, L. D., & Trost, M. A. (1973). Long-term follow-up of early detected vulnerable children. *Journal of Consulting and Clinical Psychology, 41,* 438–446.

Craig, W. M. (1998). The relationship among bullying, victimization, depression, anxiety, and aggression in elementary school children. *Personality and Individual Differences, 24,* 123–130.

Craig, W. M., Pepler, D., Connolly, J., & Henderson, K. (2001). Developmental context of peer harassment in early adolescence: The role of puberty and the peer group. In J. Juvonen & S. Graham (Eds.), *Peer harassment in school: The plight of the vulnerable and victimized* (pp. 242–261). New York: Guilford Press.

Crick, N. R., Casas, J. F., & Mosher, M. (1997). Relational and overt aggression in preschool. *Developmental Psychology, 33*(4), 579–588.

Crick, N., & Dodge, K. A. (1994). A review and reformulation of social information processing in children's social adjustment. *Psychological Bulletin, 115,* 74–101.

Crick, N. R., & Dodge, K. A. (1996). Social information-processing mechanisms on reactive and proactive aggression. *Child Development, 67,* 993–1002.

Crick, N. R., & Grotpeter, J. K. (1995). Relational aggression, gender, and social-psychological adjustment. *Child Development, 66,* 710–722.

Crick, N. R., & Ladd, G. W. (1993). Children's perceptions of their peer experiences: Attributions, loneliness, social anxiety, and social avoidance. *Development Psychology, 29,* 244–254.

Crick, N. R., & Nelson, D. A. (2002). Relational and physical victimization within friendship: Nobody told me there'd be friends like these. *Journal of Abnormal Child Psychology, 30,* 599–607.

Crick, N. R., & Werner, N. E. (1998). Response decision processes in relational and overt aggression. *Child Development, 69,* 1630–1639.

Crozier, W. R., & Alden, L. E. (2001). The social nature of social anxiety. In W. R. Crozier, & L. E. Alden (Eds.), *International handbook of social anxiety: Concepts, research and interventions relating to the self and shyness* (pp. 1–20). New York: Wiley.

Crozier, W. R., & Burnham, M. (1990). Age-related differences in children's understanding of shyness. *British Journal of Developmental Psychology, 8,* 179–185.

Csikszentmihalyi, M., & Larson, R. (1984). *Being adolescent.* New York: Basic Books.

Cummings, E. M., Goeke-Morey, M. C., & Papp, L. M. (2003). Children's responses to everyday marital conflict tactics in the home. *Child Development, 74,* 1918–1929.

Cummings, E. M., Goeke-Morey, M. C., & Papp, L. M. (2004). Everyday marital conflict and child aggression. *Journal of Abnormal Child Psychology, 32,* 191–202.

Cunningham, M. R., & Barbee, A. P. (2000). In S. S. Hendrick & C. Hendrick (Eds.), *Close relationships: A sourcebook* (pp. 273–286). Thousand Oaks, CA: Sage.

Dakof, G. A., & Taylor, S. E. (1990). Victims' perceptions of social support: What is helpful from whom? *Journal of Personality and Social Psychology, 58,* 80–89.

Damon, W. (1977). *The social world of the child.* San Francisco: Jossey-Bass.

Damon, W., & Killen, M. (1982). Peer interaction and the process of change in children's moral reasoning. *Merrill-Palmer Quarterly, 28,* 347–378.

Davies, P. T., Harold, G. T., Goeke-Morey, M. C., & Cummings, E. M. (2002). Child emotional security and interparental conflict. *Monographs of the Society for Research in Child Development, 67*(Serial No. 270).

Davila, J., Steinberg, S. J., Kachadourian, L., Cobb, R., & Fincham, F. (2004). Romantic involvement and depressive symptoms in early and late adolescence: The role of a preoccupied relational style. *Personal Relationships, 11,* 161–178.

Dawe, H. C. (1934). Analysis of two hundred quarrels of preschool children. *Child Development, 5,* 139–157.

Deater-Deckard, K. (2001). Annotation: Recent research examining the role of peer relations in the development of psychopathology. *Journal of Child Psychology and Psychiatry, 42,* 565–579.

Deater-Deckard, K., & Dodge, K. A. (1997). Externalizing behavior problems and discipline revisited: Nonlinear effects and variation by culture, context, and gender. *Psychological Inquiry, 8,* 161–175.

Denham, S. A., Blair, K. A., DeMulder, E., Levitas, J., Sawyer, K., Auerbach-Major, S., et al. (2003). Preschool emotional competence: Pathway to social competence. *Child Development, 74*(1), 238–256.

Denton, K., & Zarbatany, L. (1996). Age differences in support processes in conversations between friends. *Child Development, 67,* 1360–1373.

Denzin, N. K. (1977). *Childhood socialization.* San Francisco: Jossey-Bass.

DeRosier, M., Kupersmidt, J., & Patterson, C. (1994). Children's academic and behavioral adjustment as a function of the chronicity and proximity of peer rejection. *Child Development, 65,* 1799–1813.

DeRosier, M. E., & Thomas, J. M. (2003). Strengthening sociometric prediction: Scientific advances in the assessment of children's peer relations. *Child Development, 74,* 1379–1392.

DiFilippo, J. M., & Overholser, J. C. (2000). Suicidal ideation in adolescent psychiatric inpatients as associated with depression and attachment relationships. *Journal of Clinical Child Psychology, 29,* 155–166.

Dill, E. J., Vernberg, E. M., & Fonagy, P. (2004). Negative affect in victimized children: The roles of social withdrawal, peer rejection, and attitudes toward bullying. *Journal of Abnormal Child Psychology, 32,* 159–173.

Dishion, T. J., Andrews, D. W., & Crosby, L. (1995). Antisocial boys and their friends in early adolescence: Relationship characteristics, quality, and interactional processes. *Child Development, 66,* 139–151.

Dishion, T. J., Capaldi, D., Spracklen, K. M., & Li, F. (1995). Peer ecology of male drug use. *Development and Psychopathology, 7,* 803–824.

Dishion, T. J., Capaldi, D. M., & Yoerger, K. (1999). Middle childhood antecedents to progressions in male adolescent substance use: An ecological analysis of risk and protection. *Journal of Adolescent Research, 14*(2), 175–205.

Dishion, T. J., & Kavanagh, K. (2003). *Intervening in adolescent problem behavior: A family-centered approach.* New York: Guilford Press.

Dishion, T. J., McCord, J., & Poulin, F. (1999). When interventions harm: Peer groups and problem behavior. *American Psychologist, 54*(9), 755–764.

Dishion, T. J., & Owen, L. (2002). A longitudinal analysis of friendships and substance use: Bidirectional influence from adolescence to adulthood. *Developmental Psychology, 38*(4), 480–491.

Dishion, T. J., Spracklen, K. M., Andrews, D., & Patterson, G. (1996). Deviancy training in male adolescents friendships. *Behavior Therapy, 27*(3), 373–390.

Dodge, K. A. (1980). Social cognition and children's aggressive behavior. *Child Development, 51,* 162–170.

Dodge, K. A. (1983). Behavioral antecedents of peer social status. *Child Development, 54,* 1386–1399.

Dodge, K. A. (1986). A social information processing model of social competence in children. In M. Perlmutter (Ed.), *Minnesota Symposia on Child Psychology* (Vol. 18, pp. 77–125). Hillsdale, NJ: Erlbaum.

Dodge, K. A., Lansford, J. E., Burks, V. S., Bates, J. E., Pettit, G. S., Fontaine, R., et al. (2003). Peer rejection and social information-processing factors in the development of aggressive behavior problems in children. *Child Development, 74*(2), 374–393.

Dodge, K. A., Lochman, J. E., Harnish, J. D., Bates, J. E., & Pettit, G. S. (1997). Reactive and proactive aggression in school children and psychiatrically impaired chronically assaultive youth. *Journal of Abnormal Psychology, 106,* 37–51.

Dodge, K. A., Murphy, R. R., & Buchsbaum, K. (1984). The assessment of intention-cue detection skills in children: Implications for developmental psychopathology. *Child Development, 55,* 163–173.

Dodge, K. A., Price, J. M., Coie, J. D., & Christopoulos, C. (1990). On the development of aggressive dyadic relationships in boys' peer groups. *Human Development, 33,* 20–27.

Douvan, E., & Adelson, J. (1966). *The adolescent experience.* New York: Wiley.

Downey, G., & Feldman, S. I. (1996). Implications of rejection sensitivity for intimate relationships. *Journal of Personality and Social Psychology, 70,* 1327–1343.

Downey, G., Lebolt, A., Rincon, C., & Freitas, A. L. (1998). Rejection sensitivity and children's interpersonal difficulties. *Child Development, 69,* 1074–1091.

Dubow, E. F., Tisak, J., Causey, D., Hryshko, A., & Ried, G. (1991). A two-year longitudinal study of stressful life events, social support, and social problem-solving skills: Contributions to children's behavioral and academic adjustment. *Child Development, 62,* 583–599.

Dunn, J. (1988). *The beginnings of social understanding.* Cambridge, MA: Harvard University Press.

Dunn, J. (1993). *Young children's close relationships: Beyond attachment.* London: Sage.

Dunn, J., Cutting, A., & Fisher, N. (2002). Old friends, new friends: Predictors of children's perspective on their friends at school. *Child Development, 73,* 621–635.

Durkin, K. (1995). *Developmental social psychology: From infancy to old age.* Cambridge, MA: Blackwell.

Du Rocher Schudlich, T. D., Shamir, H., & Cummings, E. M. (2004). Marital conflict, children's representations of family relationships, and children's possessive dispositions toward peer conflict strategies. *Social Development, 13,* 171–192.

Eccles, J., Barber, B., Jozefowicz, D., Malenchuk, O., & Vida, M. (1999). Self-evaluations of competence, task values, and self-esteem. In N. G. Johnson, M. C. Roberts, & J. Worell (Eds.), *Beyond appearance: A new look at adolescent girls* (pp. 53–84). Washington, DC: American Psychological Association.

Eccles, J. S., Midgley, C., Wigfield, A., Buchanan, C. M., Rueman, D., Flanagan, C., et al. (1993). Development during adolescence: The impact of stage-environmental fit on young adolescents' experiences in schools and in families. *American Psychologist, 48,* 90–101.

Eckerman, C. O. (1993). Toddlers' achievement of coordinated action with conspecifics: A dynamic systems perspective. In E. Thelen & L. B. Smith (Eds.), *A dynamic systems approach to development: Applications* (pp. 333–357). New York: Cambridge University Press.

Eckerman, C. O. (1996). Early social-communicative development: Illustrative developmental analyses. In R. B. Cairns, G. H. Elder Jr., &

J. E. Costello (Eds.), *Developmental science* (pp. 135–167). New York: Cambridge University Press.

Eckerman, C. O., & Didow, S. M. (1996). Nonverbal imitation and toddlers' mastery of verbal means of achieving coordinated action. *Developmental Psychology, 32,* 141–152.

Eckerman, C. O., & Peterman, K. (2001). Peers and infant social/communicative development. In G. Bremner & A. Fogel (Eds.), *Blackwell handbook of infant development* (pp. 326–350). Malden, MA: Blackwell Publishers.

Eder, D. (1985). The cycle of popularity: Interpersonal relations among female adolescents. *Sociology of Education, 58,* 154–165.

Eder, D., & Enke, J. L. (1991). The structure of gossip: Opportunities and constraints on collective expression among adolescents. *American Sociological Review, 56,* 494–508.

Eisenberg, N. (2002). Emotion-related regulation and its relation to quality of social functioning. In W. W. Hartup & R. A. Weinberg (Eds.), *Child psychology in retrospect and prospect: In celebration of the 75th anniversary of the Institute of Child Development* (pp. 133–171). Mahwah, NJ: Erlbaum.

Eisenberg, N., & Fabes, R. A. (1998). Prosocial development. In W. Damon (Ed.), *Handbook of child psychology* (Vol. 3, pp. 701–778). New York: Wiley.

Eisenberg, N., Gershoff, E. T., Fabes, R. A., Shepard, S. A., Cumberland, A. J., Losoya, S. H., et al. (2001). Mothers' emotional expressivity and children's behavior problems and social competence: Mediation through children's regulation. *Developmental Psychology, 37,* 475–490.

Eisenberg, N., Tyron, K., & Cameron, E. (1984). The relation of preschoolers' peer interaction to their sex-typed toy choices. *Child Development, 55,* 1044–1050.

Enright, R. D., Gassin, E. A., & Wu, C. (1992). Forgiveness: A developmental view. *Journal of Moral Education, 21,* 99–114.

Enright, R. D., & the Human Development Study Group. (1991). The moral development of forgiveness. In W. M. Kurtines & J. L. Gewirtz (Eds.), *Handbook of moral behavior and development: Vol. 1. Theory* (pp. 123–152). Hillsdale, NJ: Erlbaum.

Epstein, J. L. (1986). Friendship selection: Developmental and environmental influences. In E. Mueller & C. Cooper (Eds.), *Process and outcome in peer relationships.* New York: Academic Press.

Epstein, J. L., & Karweit, N. (1983). *Friends in school: Patterns of influence and selection in secondary schools.* New York: Academic Press.

Erdley, C. A., & Asher, S. R. (1998). Linkages between children's beliefs about the legitimacy of aggression and their behavior. *Social Development, 7*(3), 321–339.

Erel, O., & Burman, B. (1995). Interrelatedness of marital relations and parent-child relations: A meta-analytic review. *Psychological Bulletin, 118,* 108–132.

Espelage, D. L., Bosworth, K., & Simon, T. R. (2000). Examining the social context of bullying behaviors in early adolescence. *Journal of Counseling and Development, 78,* 326–333.

Espelage, D. L., Holt, M., & Henkel, R. (2003). Examination of peer-group contextual effects on aggression during early adolescence. *Child Development, 74,* 205–220.

Fabes, R. A., Eisenberg, N., Jones, S., Smith, M., Gutherie, I., Poulin, R., et al. (1999). Regulation, emotionality, and preschoolers' socially competent peer interactions. *Child Development, 70,* 432–444.

Fabes, R. A., Martin, C. L., & Hanish, L. D. (2003). Young children's play qualities in same-, other-, and mixed-sex peer groups. *Child Development, 74,* 921–932.

Fagot, B. I. (1985). Changes in thinking about early sex role development. *Developmental Review, 5,* 83–98.

Farmer, T., Estell, D., Bishop, J., O'Neal, K., & Cairns, B. (2003). Rejected bullies or popular leaders? The social relations of aggressive subtypes of rural African American early adolescents. *Developmental Psychology, 39*(6), 992–1004.

Fehr, B. (2000). The life cycle of friendship. In S. S. Hendrick & C. Hendrick (Eds.), *Close relationships: A sourcebook* (pp. 71–84). Thousand Oaks, CA: Sage.

Ferguson, T. J., & Cillessen, A. H. N. (1993). Individual and peer group factors in the stability of social status, antisocial, and prosocial behaviors. In A. Fraczek & H. Zumkley (Eds.), *Socialization and Aggression* (pp. 115–135). New York: Springer-Verlag.

Fine, G. A. (1981). Friends, impression management, and preadolescent behavior. In S. R. Asher & J. M. Gottman (Eds.), *The development of children's friendships* (pp. 29–52). New York: Cambridge University Press.

Fine, G. A. (1987). *With the boys: Little league baseball and preadolescent culture.* Chicago: University of Chicago Press.

Fine, G. A., & Rosnow, R. L. (1978). Gossip, gossipers, gossiping. *Personality and Social Psychology Bulletin, 4,* 161–168.

Fisher, L. A., & Bauman, K. E. (1988). Influence and selection in the friend-adolescent relationship: Findings from studies of adolescent smoking and drinking. *Journal of Applied Social Psychology, 18,* 289–331.

Fiske, S. T. (2004). *Social beings: Core Motives in social psychology.* New York: Wiley.

Flanagan, K. S. (2005). *Understanding social anxiety in early adolescence: The role of peer relations.* Unpublished doctoral dissertation., University Park, PA: Pennsylvania State University.

Fletcher, G. J., & Fincham, F. D. (1991). Attribution processes in close relationships. In F. D. Fincham & G. J. Fletcher (Eds.), *Cognition in close relationships* (pp. 7–35). Hillsdale, NJ: Erlbaum.

Flicek, M. (1992). Social status of boys with both academic problems and attention-deficit hyperactivity disorder. *Journal of Abnormal Child Psychology, 20,* 353–366.

Foley, R. (1987). *Another unique species: Patterns in human evolutionary ecology.* New York: Wiley.

Forbes, D., Katz, M., & Paul, B. (1986). "Frametalk": A dramatistic analysis of children's fantasy play. In E. C. Mueller & C. R. Cooper (Eds.), *Process and outcome in peer relationships* (pp. 249–266). New York: Academic Press.

Freitag, M. K., Belsky, J., Grossmann, K., Grossmann, J. E., & Scheurer-Englisch, H. (1996). Continuity in child-parent relationships from infancy to middle childhood and relations with friendship competence. *Child Development, 67,* 1437–1454.

Freud, A. (1952). The role of bodily illness in the mental life of children. *Psychoanalytic Study of the Child, 7,* 69–81.

Fuligini, A. J., Eccles, J. S., Barber, B. L., & Clements, P. (2001). Early adolescent peer orientation and adjustment during high school. *Developmental Psychology, 37,* 28–36.

Furman, W. (1996). The measurement of friendship perceptions: Conceptual and methodological issues. In W. M. Bukowski, A. F. Newcomb, & W. W. Hartup (Eds.), *The company they keep: Friendships in childhood and adolescence* (pp. 41–65). Cambridge, MA: Cambridge University Press.

Furman, W. (1999). Friends and lovers: The role of peer relationships in adolescent romantic relationships. In W. A. Collins & B. Laursen (Eds.), *Minnesota Symposia on Child Psychology: Vol. 30. Relationships as developmental contexts* (pp. 133–154). Mahwah, NJ: Erlbaum.

Furman, W., & Buhrmester, D. (1985). Children's perceptions of the personal relationships in their social networks. *Developmental Psychology, 21,* 1016–1024.

Furman, W., Simon, V. A., Shaffer, L., & Bouchey, H. A. (2002). Adolescents' working models and styles for relationships with parents, friends, and romantic partners. *Child Development, 73,* 241–255.

Garber, J., Keiley, M. K., & Martin, N. C. (2002). Developmental trajectories of adolescents' depressive symptoms: Predictors of change. *Journal of Consulting and Clinical Psychology, 70,* 79–95.

Garmezy, N. (1974). Children at risk: The search for antecedents of Schizophrenia: Part 1. Conceptual models and research methods. *Schizophrenia Bulletin, 1,* 14–89.

Garner, D. M., Rosen, L. W., & Barry, D. (1998). Eating disorders among athletes: Research and recommendations. *Child and Adolescent Psychiatric Clinics of North America, 7,* 839–857.

Gauvain, M. (2001). *The social context of cognitive development.* New York: Guilford Press.

Gazelle, H., & Ladd, G. W. (2003). Anxious solitude and peer exclusion: A diathesis-stress model of internalizing trajectories in childhood. *Child Development, 74,* 257–278.

George, T. P., & Hartmann, D. P. (1996). Friendship networks of unpopular, average, and popular children. *Child Development, 67,* 2301–2316.

Gest, S. D., Farmer, T., Carins, B., & Xie, H. (2003). Identifying children's peer social networks in school classrooms: Links between peer reports and observed interactions. *Social Development, 12*(4), 513–529.

Golombok, S., & Fivush, R. (1994). *Gender development.* Cambridge, MA: Cambridge University Press.

Goncu, A., Patt, M. B., & Kouba, E. (2002). Understanding young children's pretend play in context. In P. K. Smith & C. H. Hart (Eds.), *Blackwell handbook of childhood social development* (pp. 418–437). Malden, MA: Blackwell.

Goodenough, F. L. (1931). *Anger in young children.* Minneapolis: University of Minnesota Press.

Gottman, J. M. (1983). How children become friends. *Monographs of the Society for Research in Child Development, 48*(3, Serial No. 201).

Gottman, J. M., & Metettal, G. (1986). Speculations about social and affective development: Friendship and acquaintanceship through adolescence. In J. M. Gottman & J. G. Parker (Eds.), *Conversation of friends: Speculations on affective development* (pp. 192–237). Cambridge, England: Cambridge University Press.

Gottman, J. M., & Parkhurst, J. T. (1980). A developmental theory of friendship and acquaintanceship processes. In W. A. Collins (Ed.), *Minnesota Symposia on Child Development: Vol. 13: Development of cognition, affect, and social relations* (pp. 197–253). Hillsdale, NJ: Erlbaum.

Graham, S., & Juvonen, J. (1998). Self-blame and peer victimization in middle school: An attributional analysis. *Developmental Psychology, 34,* 587–599.

Graham, S., & Juvonen, J. (2001). An attributional approach to peer victimization. In J. Juvonen & S. Graham (Eds.), *Peer harassment in school: The plight of the vulnerable and victimized* (pp. 49–72). New York: Guilford Press.

Granot, D., & Mayseless, O. (2001). Attachment security and adjustment to school in middle childhood. *International Journal of Behavioural Development, 25,* 530–541.

Grunebaum, H., & Solomon, L. (1987). Peer relationships, self-esteem, and the self. *International Journal of Group Psychotherapy, 37,* 475–513.

Grills, A. E., & Ollendick, T. H. (2002). Peer victimization, global self-worth, and anxiety in middle school children. *Journal of Clinical Child and Adolescent Psychology, 31,* 59–68.

Grych, J. H., & Fincham, F. D. (1990). Marital conflict and children's adjustment: A cognitive-contextual framework. *Psychological Bulletin, 108,* 267–290.

Guerra, N. G., Huesmann, L. R., & Spindler, A. (2003). Community violence exposure, social cognition, and aggression among urban elementary school children. *Child Development, 74,* 1561–1576.

Guevremont, D. C., & Dumas, M. C. (1994). Peer relationship problems and disruptive behavior disorders. *Journal of Emotional and Behavioral Disorders, 2*(3), 164–172.

Halberstadt, A. G., Denham, S. A., & Dunsmore, J. C. (2001). Affective social competence. *Social Development, 10,* 79–119.

Hamm, J. V. (2000). Do birds of a feather flock together? The variable bases for African American, Asian American, and European American adolescents' selection of similar friends. *Developmental Psychology, 36*(2), 209–219.

Hammen, C., & Rudolph, K. D. (2003). Childhood mood disorders. In R. A. Barkley & E. J. Mash (Eds.), *Child psychopathology* (2nd ed., pp. 233–278). New York: Guilford Press.

Hanish, L. D., & Guerra, N. G. (2004). Aggressive victims, passive victims, and bullies: Developmental continuity or developmental change. *Merrill-Palmer Quarterly, 50,* 17–38.

Hansell, S. (1981). Ego development and peer friendship networks. *Sociology of Education, 54,* 51–63.

Hansen, G. L. (1991). Jealousy: Its conceptualization, measurement, and integration with family stress theory. In P. Salovey (Ed.), *The psychology of jealousy and envy* (pp. 211–230). New York: Guilford Press.

Hardy, C. L., Bukowski, W. M., & Sippola, L. K. (2002). Stability and change in peer relationships during the transition to middle-level school. *Journal of Early Adolescence, 22,* 117–142.

Harter, S. (1999). *The construction of the self: A developmental perspective.* New York: Guilford Press.

Hartshorne, H., & May, M. S. (1929). *Studies in the nature of character: Vol. 1. Studies in self-control.* New York: Macmillian.

Hartup, W. W. (1983). Peer relations. In P. H. Mussen (Ed.), *Handbook of child psychology: Vol. 4. Socialization, personality, and social development* (pp. 103–196). New York: Wiley.

Hartup, W. W. (1989). Behavioral manifestations of children's friendships. In T. J. Berndt & G. W. Ladd (Eds.), *Peer relationships in child development* (pp. 46–70). New York: Wiley.

Hartup, W. W., & Abecassis, M. (2002). Friends and enemies. In P. K. Smith & C. H. Hart (Eds.), *Blackwell handbook of childhood social development* (pp. 286–306). Malden, MA: Blackwell.

Hartup, W. W., Laursen, B., Stewart, M. A., & Eastenson, A. (1988). Conflicts and the friendship relations of young children. *Child Development, 59,* 1590–1600.

Hartup, W. W., & Stevens, N. (1997). Friendships and adaptation in the life course. *Psychological Bulletin, 121,* 355–370.

Haselager, G. J. T., Cillessen, H. N., Van Lieshout, C. F. M., Riksen-Walraven, J. M. A., & Hartup, W. W. (2002). Heterogeneity among peer-rejected boys across middle childhood: Developmental pathways of social behavior. *Child Development, 73,* 446–456.

Havighurst, R. J. (1953). *Human development and education.* New York: Longmans, Green.

Hawker, D. S., & Boulton, M. J. (2000). Twenty years' research on peer victimization and psychosocial maladjustment: A meta-analytic review of cross-sectional studies. *Journal of Child Psychology and Psychiatry and Allied Disciplines, 41,* 441–455.

Hawley, P. H. (1999). The ontogenesis of social dominance: A strategy-based evolutionary perspective. *Developmental Review, 19,* 97–132.

Hawley, P. H. (2002). Social dominance and prosocial and coercive strategies of resource control in preschoolers. *International Journal of Behavioral Development, 26,* 167–176.

Hawley, P. H. (2003). Strategies of control, aggression and morality in preschoolers: An evolutionary perspective. *Journal of Experimental Child Psychology, 85*(3), 213–235.

Hawley, P. H. (2005, April). *The allure of a mean friend: Peer regard and relationship quality of aggressive high status adolescents.* Paper presented at the Biennial Meeting of the Society for Research in Adolescence, Atlanta Georgia.

Hawley, P. H., & Little, T. D. (1999). On winning some and losing some: A social relations approach to social dominance in toddlers. *Merrill-Palmer Quarterly, 45,* 185–214.

Hawley, P. H., Little, T. D., & Pasupathi, M. (2002). Winning friends and influencing peers: Strategies of peer influence in late childhood. *International Journal of Behavioral Development, 26,* 466–474.

Hay, D. F., Castle, J., & Davies, L. (2000). Toddlers' use of force against familiar peers: A precursor of serious aggression? *Child Development, 71,* 457–467.

Hay, D. F., Castle, J., Davies, L., Demetriou, H., & Stimson, C. (1999). Prosocial action in very early childhood. *Journal of Child Psychology and Psychiatry, 40,* 905–916.

Hay, D. F., Pederson, J., & Nash, A. (1982). Dyadic interaction in the first year of life. In K. H. Rubin & H. S Ross (Eds.), *Peer relationships and social skills in childhood* (pp. 11–40). New York: Springer-Verlag.

Hay, D. F., & Ross, H. (1982). The social nature of early conflict. *Child Development, 53,* 105–113.

Hay, I., & Ashman, A. F. (2003). The development of adolescents' emotional stability and general self-concept: The interplay of parents, peers, and gender. *International Journal of Disability, Development and Education, 50,* 77–91.

Henrich, C. C., Kuperminc, G. P., Sack, A., Blatt, S. J., & Leadbeater, B. J. (2000). Characteristics and homogeneity of early adolescent friendship groups: A comparison of male and female cliques and non-clique members. *Applied Developmental Science, 4,* 15–26.

Higgins, E. T., & Parsons, J. E. (1983). Social cognition and the social life of the child: Stages as subcultures. In E. T. Higgins, D. N. Ruble, & W. W. Hartup (Eds.), *Social cognition and social development* (pp. 15–62). Cambridge, England: Cambridge University Press.

Hinde, R. A. (1979). *Towards understanding relationships.* London: Academic Press.

Hinde, R. A. (1987). *Individuals, relationships and culture.* Cambridge, England: Cambridge University Press.

Hinde, R. A. (1995). A suggested structure for a science of relationships. *Personal Relationships, 2,* 1–15.

Hinshaw, S. P., Lahey, B. B., & Hart, E. L. (1993). Issues of taxonomy and comorbidity in the development of conduct disorder. *Development and Psychopathology, 5,* 31–49.

Hinshaw, S. P., & Lee, S. (2003). Conduct and oppositional defiant disorders. In R. A. Barkley & E. J. Mash (Eds.), *Child psychopathology* (2nd ed., pp. 144–198). New York: Guilford Press.

Hinshaw, S. P., & Melnick, S. M. (1995). Peer relationships in boys with attention-deficit hyperactivity disorder with and without comorbid aggression. *Development and Psychopathology, 7*(4), 627–647.

Hodges, E. V. E., Boivin, M., Vitaro, F., & Bukowski, W. M. (1999). The power of friendship: Protection against an escalating cycle of peer victimization. *Developmental Psychology, 35,* 94–101.

Hodges, E. V. E., & Card, N. A. (Eds.). (2003). *Enemies and the darker side of peer relations.* San Francisco: Jossey-Bass.

Hodges, E. V. E., Finnegan, R. A., & Perry, D. G. (1999). Skewed autonomy-relatedness in preadolescents' conceptions of their relationships with mother, father, and best friend. *Developmental Psychology, 35*(3), 737–748.

Hodges, E. V. E., Malone, M. J., & Perry, D. G. (1997). Individual risk and social risk as interacting determinants of victimization in the peer group. *Developmental Psychology, 33,* 1032–1039.

Hogan, D., & Tudge, J. (1999). Implications of Vygotsky's theory for peer learning. In A. M. O'Donnell & A. King (Eds.), *Cognitive perspectives on peer learning* (pp. 39–65). Mahwah, NJ: Erlbaum.

Hollos, M., & Cowan, P. A. (1973). Social isolation and cognitive development: Logical operations and role taking abilities in three Norwegian social settings. *Child Development, 44,* 630–641.

Horn, S. (2003). Adolescents' reasoning about exclusion from social groups. *Developmental Psychology, 39,* 11–84.

Howes, C. (1983). Patterns of friendship. *Child Development, 54,* 1041–1053.

Howes, C. (1988). Peer interaction of young children. *Monographs of the Society for Research in Child Development, 53*(Serial No. 217).

Howes, C. (1992). *The collaborative construction of pretend.* New York: SUNY Press.

Howes, C. (1996). The earliest friendships. In W. M. Bukowski, A. F. Newcomb, & W. W. Hartup (Eds.), *The company they keep: Friendship in childhood and adolescence* (pp. 66–86). Cambridge, MA: Cambridge University Press.

Howes, C., Matheson, C. C., & Wu, F. (1992). Friendships and social pretend play. In C. Howes, O. Unger, & C. C. Matheson (Eds.), *The collaborative construction of pretend.* Albany: University of New York Press.

Howes, C., & Phillipsen, L. (1992). Gender and friendship: Relationships within peer groups of young children. *Social Development, 1,* 230–242.

Howes, C., & Phillipsen, L. (1998). Continuity in children's relationships with peers. *Social Development, 7,* 340–349.

Hoza, B., Molina, B., Bukowski, W. M., & Sippola, L. K. (1995). Aggression, withdrawal and measures of popularity and friendship as predictors of internalizing and externalizing problems during early adolescence. *Development and Psychopathology, 7,* 787–802.

Hubbard, J. A. (2001). Emotion expression processes in children's peer interaction: The role of peer rejection, aggression, and gender. *Child Development, 72,* 1426–1438.

Hubbard, J. A., Dodge, K. A., Cillessen, A., Coie, J. D., & Schwartz, D. (2001). The dyadic nature of social information processing in boys' reactive and proactive aggression. *Journal of Personality and Social Psychology, 80,* 268–280.

Huesmann, L. R., & Guerra, N. G. (1997). Children's normative beliefs about aggression and aggressive behavior. *Journal of Personality and Social Psychology, 72,* 408–419.

Huston, A. C., & Alvarez, M. (1990). The socialization context of gender role development in early adolescence. In R. Motemayor, G. R. Adams, & T. P. Gullotta (Eds.), *From childhood to adolescence: A transitional period* (pp. 156–179). Newbury Park, CA: Sage.

Hutton, J. B. (1985). What reasons are given by teachers who refer problem behavior students? *Psychology in the Schools, 22,* 79–84.

Hymel, S. (1986). Interpretations of peer behavior: Affective bias in childhood and adolescence. *Child Development, 57,* 431–445.

Hymel, S., Bowker, A., & Woody, E. (1993). Aggressive versus withdrawn unpopular children: Variations in peer and self-perceptions in multiple domains. *Child Development, 64,* 879–896.

Hymel, S., & Franke, S. (1985). Children's peer relations: Assessing self-perceptions. In B. H. Schneider, K. H. Rubin, & J. E. Ledingham (Eds.), *Children's peer relationships: Issues in assessment and intervention* (pp. 75–92). New York: Springer-Verlag.

Ialongo, N., Edelsohn, G., Werthamer-Larsson, L., Crockett, L., & Kellam, S. G. (1995). The significance of self-reported anxious symptoms in first grade children: Prediction to anxious symptoms and adaptive functioning in fifth grade. *Journal of Child Psychology and Psychiatry, 36,* 427–437.

Inderbitzen, H. M., Walters, K. S., & Bukowski, A. L. (1997).The role of social anxiety in adolescent peer relations: Differences among sociometric status groups and rejected subgroups. *Journal of Clinical Child Psychology, 26*(4), 338–348.

Ingersoll, B., Schreibman, L., & Stahmer, A. (2001). Brief report: Differential treatment outcomes for children with autistic spectrum disorder based on level of peer social avoidance. *Journal of Autism and Developmental Disorders, 31,* 343–349.

Janes, C. L., Hesselbrock, V. M., & Schechtman, J. (1980). Clinic children with poor peer relations: Who refers them and why? *Child Psychiatry and Human Development, 11,* 113–125.

Joiner, T., Coyne, J., & Blalock, J. (1999). On the interpersonal nature of depression: Overview and synthesis. In J. C. Coyne & T. Joiner (Eds.), *The interactional nature of depression: Advances in interpersonal approaches* (pp. 3–19). Washington, DC: American Psychological Association.

Joyner, K., & Udry, J. R. (2000). You don't bring me anything but down: Adolescent romance and depression. *Journal of Health and Social Behavior, 41,* 369–391.

Juvonen, J., & Graham, S. (Eds.). (2001). *Peer harassment in school: The plight of the vulnerable and victimized.* New York: Guilford Press.

Kanner, A. D., Feldman, S. S., Weinburg, D. A., & Ford, M. E. (1987). Uplifts, hassles, and adaptational outcomes in early adolescents. *Journal of Early Adolescence, 7,* 371–394.

Keenan, K., Loeber, R., Zhang, Q., Stouthamer-Loeber, M., & Van Kammen, W. B. (1995). The influence of deviant peers on the development of boys' disruptive and delinquent behavior: A temporal analysis. *Development and Psychopathology, 7,* 715–726.

Keenan, K., Shaw, D., & Delliquadri, E. (1998). Evidence for the continuity of early problem behaviors: Application of a developmental model. *Journal of Abnormal Child Psychology, 26,* 441–452.

Kelly, G. A. (1955). *The psychology of personal constructs.* New York: McGraw-Hill.

Kerns, K. A., Cole, A. K., & Andrews, P. B. (1998). Attachment security, parent peer management practices, and peer relationships in preschoolers. *Merrill-Palmer Quarterly, 44,* 504–522.

Kerns, K. A., Contreras, J. M., & Neal-Barnett, A. M. (Eds.). (2000). *Family and peers: Linking two social worlds.* London: Praeger.

Kerns, K. A., Klepac, L., & Cole, A. (1996). Peer relationships and preadolescents' perceptions of security in the child-mother relationship. *Developmental Psychology, 32,* 457–456.

Khatri, P., & Kupersmidt, J. B. (2003). Aggression, peer victimization, and social relationships among Indian youth. *International Journal of Behavioral Development, 27,* 87–95.

Kiesner, J., Poulin, F., & Nicotra, E. (2003). Peer relations across contexts: Individual network homophily and network inclusion in and after school. *Child Development, 74,* 1328–1343.

Killen, M. (1991). Social and moral development in early childhood. In W. Kurtines & J. Gewirtz (Eds.), *Handbook of moral behavior and development* (pp. 115–138). Hillsdale, NJ: Erlbaum.

Killen, M., Crystal, D. S., & Watanabe, H. (2002). Japanese and American children's evaluations of peer exclusion, tolerance of differences, and prescriptions for conformity. *Child Development, 73,* 1788–1802.

Killen, M., Lee-Kim, J., McGlothlin, H., & Stangor, C. (2002). How children and adolescents evaluate gender and racial exclusion.

Monographs of the Society for Research in Child Development, 67(4, Serial No. 271).

Killen, M., & Stangor, C. (2001). Children's reasoning about social inclusion and exclusion in peer group contexts. *Child Development, 72,* 174–186.

Killen, M., Stangor, C., Horn, S., & Sechrist, G. B. (2004). Social reasoning about racial exclusion in intimate and nonintimate relationships. *Youth and Society, 35,* 293–322.

Kindermann, T. A., McCollam, T. L., & Gibson, Jr., E. (1995). Peer networks and students' classroom engagement during childhood and adolescence. In K. Wentzel & J. Juvonen (Eds.), *Social motivation: Understanding children's school adjustment* (pp. 25–49). New York: Cambridge University Press.

King, A., Wold, B., Tudor-Smith, C., & Harel, Y. (1996). The health of youth: A cross-national survey. *WHO Regional Publications* (European Series, No. 69).

Kinney, D. A. (1999). From "headbangers" to "hippies": Deliniating adolescents' active attempts to form an alternative peer culture. In J. A. McLellan & M. J. V. Pugh (Eds.), *The role of peer groups in adolescent social identity: Exploring the importance of stability and change* (pp. 21–36). San Francisco: Jossey-Bass.

Kirshner, B., O'Donoghue, J. L., & McLaughlin, M. (2002). *Youth participation: Improving institutions and communities.* San Francisco: Jossey-Bass.

Kistner, J., Balthazor, M., Risi, S., & Burton, C. (1999). Predicting dysphoria from actual and perceived acceptance in childhood. *Journal of Clinical Child Psychology, 28,* 94–104.

Kochenderfer, B. J., & Ladd, G. W. (1996). Peer victimization: Cause or consequence of school maladjustment? *Child Development, 67,* 1305–1317.

Kochenderfer, B. J., & Ladd, G. W. (1997). Victimized children's responses to peers' aggression: Behaviors associated with reduced versus continued victimization. *Development and Psychopathology, 9,* 59–73.

Kochenderfer-Ladd, B. (2003). Identification of aggressive and asocial victims and the stability of their peer victimization. *Merrill-Palmer Quarterly, 49*(4), 401–425.

Kochenderfer-Ladd B., & Wardrop, J. L. (2001). Chronicity and instability of children's peer victimization experiences as predictors of loneliness and social satisfaction trajectories. *Child Development, 72,* 134–151.

Kohlberg, L. (1969). Stage and sequence: The cognitive developmental approach to socialization. In D. A. Goslin (Ed.), *Handbook of socialization theory and research.* Chicago: Rand McNally.

Konner, M. (1975). Relations among infants and juveniles in comparative perspective. In M. Lewis & L. A. Rosenblum (Eds.), *Friendships and peer relations* (pp. 99–130). New York: Wiley.

Kovacs, M. (1981). Rating scales to assess depression in school-aged children. *International Journal of Child and Adolescent Psychiatry, 46,* 305–315.

Kovacs, D. M., Parker, J. G., & Hoffman, L. W. (1996). Behavioral, affective, and social correlates of involvement in cross-sex friendship in elementary school. *Child Development, 67,* 2269–2286.

Kraatz-Keiley, M., Bates, J. E., Dodge, K. A., & Pettit, G. S. (2000). A cross-domain growth analysis: Externalizing and internalizing behaviors during 8 years of childhood. *Journal of Abnormal Child Psychology, 28,* 161–179.

Kramer, L., & Gottman, J. M. (1992). Becoming a sibling: "With a little help from my friends." *Developmental Psychology, 28,* 685–699.

Krasnor, L., & Rubin, K. H. (1983). Preschool social problem solving: Attempts and outcomes in naturalistic interaction. *Child Development, 54,* 1545–1558.

Krawczyk, R. (1985, April). *What toddlers talk about when they talk about friends.* Paper presented at the biennial meetings of the Society for Research in Child Development. Toronto.

Kruger, A. C., & Tomasello, M. (1986). Transactive discussions with peers and adults. *Developmental Psychology, 22,* 681–685.

Kupersmidt, J. B., & Coie, J. D. (1990). Preadolescent peer status, aggression, and school adjustment as predictors of externalizing problems in adolescence. *Child Development, 61,* 1350–1362.

Kupersmidt, J. B., DeRosier, M. E., & Patterson, C. P. (1995). Similarity as the basis for children's friendships: The roles of sociometric status, aggressive and withdrawn behavior, academic achievement, and demographic characteristics. *Journal of Social and Personal Relationships, 12,* 439–452.

Kuttler, A. F., Parker, J. G., & LaGreca, A. M. (2002). Developmental and gender differences in preadolescents' judgments of the veracity of gossip. *Merrill-Palmer Quarterly, 48,* 105–132.

Ladd, G. W., & Burgess, K. B. (1999). Charting the relationship trajectories of aggressive, withdrawn, and aggressive/withdrawn children during early grade school. *Child Development, 70,* 910–929.

Ladd, G. W., & Burgess, K. B. (2001). Do relational risks and protective factors moderate the linkages between childhood aggression and early psychological and school adjustment? *Child Development, 72,* 1579–1601.

Ladd, G. W., Kochenderfer, B. J., & Coleman, C. C. (1996). Friendship quality as a predictor of young children's early school adjustment. *Child Development, 67,* 1103–1118.

Ladd, G. W., Kochenderfer, B. J., & Coleman, C. C. (1997). Classroom peer acceptance, friendship, and victimization: Distinct relational systems that contribute uniquely to children's school adjustment? *Child Development, 68,* 1181–1197.

Ladd, G. W., & Oden, S. (1979). The relationship between peer acceptance and children's ideas about helpfulness. *Child Development, 50,* 402–408.

Ladd, G. W., & Pettit, G. S. (2002). Parenting and the development of children's peer relationships. In M. H. Bornstein (Ed.), *Handbook of parenting: Vol. 5. Practical issues in parenting* (2nd ed., pp. 269–309). Mahwah, NJ: Erlbaum.

Ladd, G. W., & Price, J. M. (1986). Promoting children's cognitive and social competence: The relation between parents' perceptions of task difficulty and children's perceived and actual competence. *Child Development, 57,* 446–460.

Ladd, G. W., & Troop-Gordon, W. (2003). The role of chronic peer difficulties in the development of children's psychological adjustment problems. *Child Development, 74*(5), 1344–1367.

LaFontana, K. M., & Cillessen, A. H. N. (1999). The nature of children's stereotypes of popularity. *Social Development, 7,* 301–320.

LaFontana, K. M., & Cillessen, A. H. N. (2002). Children's perceptions of popular and unpopular peers: A multimethod assessment. *Developmental Psychology, 38,* 635–647.

LaFreniere, P., & Sroufe, L. A. (1985). Profiles of peer competence in the preschool: Interrelations between measures, influence of social ecology, and relations to attachment history. *Developmental Psychology, 21,* 56–69.

La Greca, A. M., Dandes, S. K., Wick, P., Shaw, K., & Stone, W. L. (1988). Development of the Social Anxiety Scale for Children: Reliability and concurrent validity. *Journal of Clinical Child Psychology, 17,* 84–91.

La Greca, A. M., & Lopez, N. (1998). Social anxiety among adolescents: Linkages with peer relations and friendships. *Journal of Abnormal Child Psychology, 26,* 83–94.

LaGreca, A. M., & Stone, W. (1993). Social Anxiety Scale for Children-Revised: Factor structure and concurrent validity. *Journal of Clinical Child Psychology, 22,* 17–27.

Landau, S., & Moore, L. A. (1991). Social skills deficits in children with attention deficit hyperactive disorder. *School Psychology Review, 20,* 235–251.

Lansford, J. E., & Parker, J. G. (1999). Children's interactions in triads: Behavioral profiles and effects of gender and patterns of friendships among members. *Developmental Psychology, 35,* 80–93.

Larson, R. W., & Richards, M. (1991). Daily companionship in late childhood and early adolescence: Changing developmental contexts. *Child Development, 62,* 284–300.

Larson, R. W., & Richards, M. (1998). Waiting for the weekend: Friday and Saturday nights as the emotional climax of the week. In A. C. Crouter & R. Larson (Eds.), *Temporal rhythms in adolescence: Clocks, calendars, and the coordination of daily life* (pp. 37–52). San Francisco: Jossey-Bass.

Last, C. G., Perrin, S., Hersen, M., & Kazdin, A. E. (1992). *DSM-III-R* anxiety disorders in children: Sociodemographic and clinical characteristics. *Journal of the American Academy of Child and Adolescent Psychiatry, 31,* 928–934.

Laursen, B. (1993). Conflict management among close peers. In B. Laursen (Ed.), *Close Friendships in Adolescence* (pp. 39–54). San Francisco: Jossey-Bass.

Laursen, B., Finkelstein, B. D., & Betts, N. T. (2001). A developmental meta-analysis of peer conflict resolution. *Developmental Review, 21,* 423–449.

Laursen, B., & Koplas, A. L. (1995). What's important about important conflicts? Adolescents' perceptions of daily disagreements. *Merrill-Palmer Quarterly, 41,* 536–553.

Laursen, B., & Williams, V. A. (1997). Perceptions of interdependence and closeness in family and peer relationships among adolescents with and without romantic partners. In S. Shulman & W. A. Collins (Eds.), *Romantic relationships in adolescence: Developmental perspectives—New Directions for Child Development* (No. 78, pp. 3–20). San Francisco: Jossey-Bass.

Leaper, C. (1994). Exploring the consequences of gender segregation on social relationships. In C. Leaper (Ed.), *Childhood gender segregation: Causes and consequences* (pp. 67–86). San Francisco: Jossey-Bass.

Leary, M. (2000). Affect, cognition, and the social emotions. In J. P. Forgas (Ed.), *Feeling and thinking: The role of affect in social cognition—Studies in emotion and social interaction* (2nd series, pp. 331–356). New York: Cambridge University Press.

Lease, A. M., Kennedy, C. A., & Axelrod, J. L. (2002). Children's social constructions of popularity. *Social Development, 11,* 87–109.

Lease, A. M., Musgrove, K. T., & Axelrod, J. L. (2002). Dimensions of social status in preadolescent peer groups: Likability, perceived popularity, and social dominance. *Social Development, 11,* 508–533.

Lemerise, E. A., & Arsenio, W. F. (2000). An integrated model of emotion processes and cognition in social information processing. *Child Development, 71,* 107–118.

Levendosky, A. A., Okun, A., & Parker, J. G. (1995). Depression and maltreatment as predictors of social competence and social problem-solving skills in school-age children. *Child Abuse and Neglect, 19*(10), 1183–1195.

Liben, L. S., & Bigler, R. S. (2002). The developmental course of gender differentiation: Conceptualizing, measuring, and evaluating constructs and pathways. *Monographs of the Society for Research in Child Development, 67*(2, Serial No. 269).

Lieberman, M., Doyle, A. B., & Markiewicz, D. (1999). Developmental patterns in security of attachment to mother and father in late childhood and early adolescence: Associations with peer relations. *Child Development, 70,* 202–213.

Lord, C., & Magill-Evans, J. (1995). Peer interactions of autistic children and adolescents. *Development and Psychopathology, 7*(4), 611–626.

Lord, C., Rutter, M., & LeCouteur, A. (1994). Autism Diagnostic Interview-Revised: A revised version of a diagnostic interview for caregivers of individuals with possible pervasive developmental disorders. *Journal of Autism and Developmental Disorders, 24,* 659–685.

Maccoby, E. E. (1998). *The two sexes: Growing up apart, coming together.* New York: Cambridge University Press.

Mahler, M. (1952). On child psychosis and Schizophrenia: Autistic and symbiotic infantile psychoses. *Psychoanalytic Study of the Child, 7,* 286–305.

Mahoney, J. L., Larson, R. W., & Eccles, J. S. (2005). *Organized activities as contexts of development: Extracurricular activities, after-school and community programs.* Mahwah, NJ: Erlbaum.

Martin, C. L., & Fabes, R. A. (2001). The stability and consequences of young children's same-sex peer interactions. *Developmental Psychology, 37,* 431–446.

Masters, J. C., & Furman, W. (1981). Popularity, individual friendship selection, and specific peer interaction among children. *Developmental Psychology, 17,* 344–350.

Matsumoto, D. (1997). *Culture and modern life.* Pacific Grove, CA: Brooks/Cole.

McCord, J. (1995). *Coercion and punishment in long-term perspectives.* New York: Cambridge University Press.

McHale, S. M., Dariotis, J. K., & Kauh, T. J. (2003). Social development and social relationships in middle childhood. In A. Easterbrooks & R. M. Lerner (Eds.), *Handbook of psychology: Vol. 6. Developmental psychology* (pp. 241–265). New York: Wiley.

McLellan, J. A., & Pugh, M. J. V. (1999). *The role of peer groups in adolescent social identity: Exploring the importance of stability and change.* San Francisco: Jossey-Bass.

McNeilley-Choque, M. K., Hart, C. H., Robinson, C. C., Nelson, L. J., & Olsen, S. F. (1996). Overt and relational aggression on the playground: Correspondence among different informants. *Journal of Research in Childhood Education, 11,* 47–67.

Mead, G. H. (1934). *Mind, self, and society.* Chicago: University of Chicago Press.

Milardo, R. M., & Helms-Erikson, H. (2000). Network overlap and third-party influence in close relationships. In C. Hendrick & S. Hendrick (Eds.), *Close relationships: A sourcebook* (pp. 33–45). Thousand Oaks, CA: Sage.

Miller, L. S., Klein, R. G., Piacentini, J., Abikoff, H., Shah, M. R., Samoilov, A., et al. (1995). The New York Teacher Rating Scale for disruptive and antisocial behavior. *Journal of the American Academy of Child and Adolescent Psychiatry, 34,* 359–370.

Miller-Johnson, S., Coie, J. D., Maumary-Gremaud, A., Bierman, K., & Conduct Problems Prevention Research Group. (2002). Peer rejection and aggression and early starter models of conduct disorder. *Journal of Abnormal Child Psychology, 30,* 217–230.

Miller-Johnson, S., Coie, J., Maumary-Gremaud, A., Lochman, J., & Terry, R. (1999). Relationship between childhood peer rejection and aggression and adolescent delinquency severity and type among African-American youth. *Journal of Emotional and Behavioral Disorders, 7,* 137–146.

Moffitt, T. E. (1993). Adolescence-limited and life-course-persistent antisocial behavior: A developmental taxonomy. *Psychological Review, 100,* 674–701.

Moller, L., Hymel, S., & Rubin, K. H. (1992). Sex typing in play and popularity in middle childhood. *Sex Roles, 26,* 331–353.

Montemayor, R., & Van Komen, R. (1985). The development of sex differences in friendship patterns and peer group structure during adolescence. *Journal of Early Adolescence, 5,* 285–294.

Moreno, J. L. (1934). *Who Shall Survive? A new approach to the problem of human interrelations.* Washington, DC: Nervous and Mental Disease.

Morris, T. L. (2001). Social phobia. In M. W. Vasey & M. R. Dadds (Eds.), *The developmental psychopathology of anxiety* (pp. 435–458). New York: Oxford University Press.

Morrissey, K. M., & Werner-Wilson, R. J. (2005). The relationship between out-of-school activities and positive youth development: An investigation of the influences of communities and family. *Adolescence, 40,* 67–85.

Mueller, E., & Brenner, J. (1977). The origins of social skills and interaction among playgroup toddlers. *Child Development, 48,* 854–861.

Mueller, E., & Silverman, N. (1989). Peer relations in maltreated children. In D. Cicchetti & V. Carlson (Eds.), *Child maltreatment: Theory and research on the causes and consequences of child abuse and neglect* (pp. 529–578). New York: Cambridge University Press.

Murnen, S. K., & Smolak, L. (2000). The experience of sexual harassment among grade-school students: Early socialization of female subordination? *Sex Roles, 43,* 1–17.

Murphy, L. B. (1937). *Social behavior and child psychology: An exploratory study of some roots of sympathy.* New York: Columbia University Press.

Nagin, D. S., & Tremblay, R. E. (1999). Trajectories of boys' physical aggression, opposition, and hyperactivity on the path to physically violent and nonviolent juvenile delinquency. *Child Development, 70,* 1181–1196.

Nangle, D. W., & Erdley, C. A. (Eds.). (2001). *The role of friendship in psychological adjustment.* San Francisco: Jossey-Bass.

Nangle, D. W., Erdley, C. A., Newman, J. E., Mason, C. A., & Carpenter, E. (2003). Popularity, friendship quantity, and friendship quality: Interactive influences on children's loneliness and depression. *Journal of Clinical Child and Adolescent Psychology, 32*(4), 546–555.

Nansel, T. R., Overbeck, M., Pilla, R. S., Ruan, W. J., Simon-Morton, B., & Scheidt, P. (2001). Bullying behaviors among U.S. youth: Prevalence and association with psychosocial adjustment. *Journal of the American Medical Association, 285*(16), 2094–2100.

National Institute of Child Health and Human Development (NICHD) Early Child Care Research Network. (2001). Child care and children's peer interaction at 24 and 36 months: The NICHD Study of Early Child Care. *Child Development, 72,* 1478–1500.

Nelson, L. J., Rubin, K. H., & Fox, N. A. (in press). Social and nonsocial behaviors and peer acceptance: A longitudinal model of the development of self-perceptions in children ages 4 to 7 years. *Early Education and Development.*

Newcomb, A., & Bagwell, C. (1995). Children's friendship relations: A meta-analytic review. *Psychological Bulletin, 117,* 306–347.

Newcomb, A. F., & Bukowski, W. M. (1984). A longitudinal study of the utility of social preference and social impact sociometric classification schemes. *Child Development, 55,* 1434–1447.

Newcomb, A. F., Bukowski, W. M., & Bagwell, C. L. (1999). Knowing the sounds: Friendship as a developmental context. In W. A. Collins & B. Laursen (Eds.), *Minnesota Symposia on Child Psychology: Vol. 30. Relationships as developmental contexts* (pp. 63–84). Mahwah, NJ: Erlbaum.

Newcomb, A. F., Bukowski, W. M., & Pattee, L. (1993). Children's peer relations: A meta-analyic review of popular, rejected, neglected, controversial, and average sociometric status. *Psychological Bulletin, 113,* 99–128.

Newman, B. M., & Newman, P. R. (2001). Group identity and alienation: Giving the we its due. *Journal of Youth and Adolescence, 30,* 515–538.

O'Brien, S. F., & Bierman, K. L. (1987). Conceptions and perceived influence of peer groups: Interviews with preadolescents and adolescents. *Child Development, 59,* 1360–1365.

Offer, D., Ostrov, E., & Howard, K. I. (1981). The mental health professional's concept of the normal adolescent. *Archives of General Psychiatry, 38,* 149–152.

Oliver, K. T., & Thelen, M. H. (1996). Children's perceptions of peer influence on eating outcomes. *Behavior Therapy, 27,* 25–39.

Ollendick, T. H., & Schmidt, C. R. (1987). Social learning constructs in the prediction of peer interaction. *Journal of Clinical Child Psychology, 16,* 80–87.

Ollendick, T. H., Weist, M. D., Borden, M. G., & Greene, R. W. (1992). Sociometric status and academic, behavioral, and psychological adjustment: A five-year longitudinal study. *Journal of Consulting and Clinical Psychology, 60,* 80–87.

Olweus, D. (1978). *Aggression in the schools: Bullies and whipping boys.* Oxford, England: Hemisphere.

Olweus, D. (1993). Victimization by peers: Antecedents and long-term outcomes. In K. H. Rubin & J. B. Asendorpf (Eds.), *Social withdrawal, inhibition and shyness in childhood* (pp. 315–341). Hillsdale, NJ: Erlbaum.

Orobio de Castro, B, Bosch, J. D., Veerman, J. W., & Koops, W. (2003). The effects of emotion regulation, attribution, and delay prompts on aggressive boys' social problem solving. *Cognitive Therapy and Research, 27,* 153–166.

Orobio de Castro, B., Veerman, J. W., Koops, W., Bosch, J. D., & Monshouwer, H. J. (2002). Hostile attribution of intent and aggressive behavior: A meta-analysis. *Child Development, 73*(3), 916–934.

Orsmond, G. I., Krauss, M. W., & Seltzer, M. M. (2004). Peer relationships and social and recreational activities among adolescents and adults with Autism. *Journal of Autism and Developmental Disorders, 34,* 245–256.

Pakaslahti, L., Karjalainen, A., & Keltikangas-Jaervinen, L. (2002). Relationships between adolescent prosocial problem-solving strategies, prosocial behaviour, and social acceptance. *International Journal of Behavioral Development, 26*(2), 137–144.

Parke, R. D., & O'Neil, R. (1999). Social relationships across contexts: Family-peer linkages. In W. A. Collins & B. Laursen (Eds.), *Minnesota Symposia on Child Psychology* (Vol. 30, pp. 211–239). Hillsdale, NJ: Erlbaum.

Parker, J. G., & Asher, S. R. (1987). Peer relations and later personal adjustment: Are low-accepted children at risk? *Psychological Bulletin, 102,* 357–389.

Parker, J. G., & Asher, S. R. (1993). Friendship and friendship quality in middle childhood: Links with peer group acceptance and feelings of loneliness and social dissatisfaction. *Developmental Psychology, 29,* 611–621.

Parker, J. G., & Gamm, B. K. (2003). Describing the dark side of preadolescents' peer experiences: Four questions (and data) on preadolescents' enemies. In E. V. E. Hodges & N. A. Card (Eds.), *Enemies and the darker side of peer relations* (pp. 55–72). San Francisco: Jossey-Bass.

Parker, J. G., & Gottman, J. M. (1989). Social and emotional development in a relational context: Friendship interaction from early childhood to adolescence. In T. J. Berndt & G. W. Ladd (Eds.), *Peer relations in child development* (pp. 95–131). New York: Wiley.

Parker, J. G., & Herrera, C. (1996). Interpersonal processes in friendships: A comparison of maltreated and nonmaltreated children's experiences. *Developmental Psychology, 96,* 1025–1038.

Parker, J. G., Low, C., Walker, A. R., & Gamm, B. A. (2005). Children's friendship jealousy: Assessment of individual differences and links to sex, self-esteem, aggression, and social adjustment. *Developmental Psychology, 41,* 235–250.

Parker, J. G., Rubin, K. H., Price, J., & DeRosier, M. E. (1995). Peer relationships, child development, and adjustment: A developmental psychopathology perspective. In D. Cicchetti & D. Cohen (Eds.), *Developmental Psychopathology: Vol. 2. Risk, disorder, and adaptation* (pp. 96–161). New York: Wiley.

Parker, J. G., Saxon, J., Asher, S. R., & Kovacs, D. (1999). Dimensions of children's friendship adjustment: Implications for studying loneliness. In K. J. Rotenberg & S. Hymel (Eds.), *Loneliness in childhood and adolescence.* New York: Cambridge University Press.

Parker, J. G., & Seal, J. (1996). Forming, losing, renewing, and replacing friendships: Applying temporal parameters to the assessment of children's friendship experiences. *Child Development, 67,* 2248–2268.

Parker, J. G., Teasley, S. D., Meissner, R. M., & McClellan, T. L. (1994, June). *The social construction of preadolescents' gossip: Content, gender, and interpersonal constraints.* Paper presented at the 24th Annual Symposium of the Jean Piaget Society, Chicago.

Parkhurst, J. T., & Asher, S. R. (1992). Peer rejection in middle school: Subgroup differences in behavior, loneliness, and interpersonal concerns. *Developmental Psychology, 28,* 231–241.

Parkhurst, J. T., & Hopmeyer, A. (1998). Sociometric popularity and peer-perceived popularity: Two distinct dimensions of peer status. *Journal of Early Adolescence, 18,* 125–144.

Parten, M. B. (1932). Social participation among preschool children. *Journal of Abnormal and Social Psychology, 27,* 243–269.

Pellegrini, A. D. (2002). Rough-and-tumble play from childhood through adolescence: Development and possible functions. In P. K. Smith & C. H. Hart (Eds.), *Blackwell handbook of childhood social development* (pp. 438–453). Oxford, England: Blackwell.

Pellegrini, A. D. (2003). Perceptions and functions of play and real fighting in early adolescence. *Child Development, 74,* 1522–1533.

Pellegrini, A. D., & Smith, P. K. (1998). Physical activity play: Consensus and debate. *Child Development, 69,* 609–610.

Peterson, L., Mullins, L. L., & Ridley-Johnson, R. (1985). Childhood depression: Peer reactions to depression and life stress. *Journal of Abnormal Child Psychology, 13,* 597–609.

Peterson, A. C., Sarigiani, P. A., & Kennedy, R. E. (1991). Adolescent depression: Why more girls? *Journal of Youth and Adolescence, 20,* 247–271.

Perry, D. G., Perry, L. C., & Rasmussen, P. (1986). Cognitive social learning mediators of aggression. *Child Development, 57,* 700–711.

Phares, V., Steinberg, A. R., & Thompson, J. K. (2004). Gender differences in peer and parental influences: Body image disturbance, self-worth, and psychological functioning in preadolescent children. *Journal of Youth and Adolescence, 33,* 421–429.

Piaget, J. (1932). *The moral judgment of the child.* Glencoe, IL: Free Press.

Pierce, G. R., Lakey, B., Sarason, I., & Sarason, B. (1997). *Sourcebook of social support and personality.* New York: Plenum Press.

Poulin, F., & Boivin, M. (2000). The role of proactive and reactive aggression in the formation and development of boys' friendships. *Developmental Psychology, 36,* 233–240.

Poulin, F., Dishion, T. J., & Haas, E. (1999). The peer influence paradox: Friendship quality and deviancy training within male adolescent friendships. *Merrill-Palmer Quarterly, 45,* 42–61.

Powlishta, K. K., Serbin, L. A., Doyle, A. B., & White, D. R. (1994). Gender, ethnic, and body type biases: The generality of prejudice in childhood. *Developmental Psychology, 30,* 526–536.

Powlishta, K. K., Serbin, L. A., & Moller, L. C. (1993). The stability of individual differences in gender typing: Implications for understanding gender segregation. *Sex Roles, 29,* 723–737.

Prager, K. J. (1995). *The psychology of intimacy.* New York: Guilford Press.

Price, J. M., & Dodge, K. A. (1989). Peers' contribution to children's social maladjustment: Description and intervention. In T. J. Berndt & G. W. Ladd (Eds.), *Peer relations in child development* (pp. 341–370). New York: Wiley.

Prinstein, M. J., Boergers, J., Spirito, A., Little, T. D., & Grapentine, W. L. (2000). Peer functioning, family dysfunction, and psychological symptoms in a risk factor model for adolescent inpatients' suicidal ideation severity. *Journal of Clinical Child Psychology, 29,* 392–405.

Pugh, M. J. V., & Hart, D. (1999). Identity development and peer group participation. In J. A. McLellan & M. J. V. Pugh (Eds.), *The role of peer groups in adolescent social identity: Exploring the importance of stability and change* (pp. 55–70). San Francisco: Jossey-Bass.

Putallaz, M. (1983). Predicting children's sociometric status from their behavior. *Child Development, 54,* 1417–1426.

Quiggle, N. L., Garber, J., Panak, W. F., & Dodge, K. A. (1992). Social information processing in aggressive and depressed children. *Child Development, 63,* 1305–1320.

Rabiner, D., & Coie, J. D. (1989). Effects of expectancy inductions on rejected children's acceptance by unfamiliar peers. *Developmental Psychology, 25,* 450–457.

Rabiner, D., & Gordon, L. (1992). The coordination of conflicting social goals: Differences between rejected and nonrejected boys. *Child Development, 63,* 1344–1350.

Radke-Yarrow, M., Zahn-Waxler, C., & Chapman, M. (1983). Children's prosocial dispositions and behavior. In P. H. Mussen (Ed.) & M. Hetherington (Series ed.), *Handbook of Child Psychology: Vol. 4. Socialization, personality, and social development* (pp. 469–545). New York: Wiley.

Rapee, R. M., & Heimberg, R. G. (1997). A cognitive-behavioral model of anxiety in social phobia. *Behavior Research and Therapy, 35,* 741–756.

Renshaw, P. D., & Brown, P. J. (1993). Loneliness in middle childhood: Concurrent and longitudinal predictors. *Child Development, 64,* 1271–1284.

Reynolds, W. M. (1998). A model for the screening and identification of depressed children and adolescents in school settings. *Professional School Psychology, 1,* 117–129.

Richards, M. H., Crowe, P. A., Larson, R., & Swarr, A. (1998). Developmental patterns and gender differences in the experience of peer companionship during adolescence. *Child Development, 69,* 154–163.

Rizzo, T. A. (1989). *Friendship development among children in school.* Norwood, NJ: Ablex.

Rodkin, P. C., Farmer, T. W., Pearl, R., & Van Acker, R. (2000). Heterogeneity of popular boys: Antisocial and prosocial configurations. *Developmental Psychology, 36,* 14–24.

Rodkin, P. C., & Hodges, E. V. E. (2003). Bullies and victims in the peer ecology: Four questions for psychological and school professionals. *School Psychology Review, 32,* 384–401.

Rodkin, P. C., Pearl, R., Farmer, T. W., & Van Acker, R. (2003). Enemies in the gendered societies of middle childhood: Prevalence, stability, associations with social status, and aggression. In E. V. E. Hodges & N. A. Card (Eds.), *Enemies and the darker side of peer relations* (pp. 73–88). San Francisco: Jossey-Bass.

Roff, M. (1957). *Preservices personality problems and subsequent adjustments to military service: The prediction of psychoneurotic reactions.* U.S. Air Force School of Aviation (Medical Report No. 57–136).

Roff, M. (1960). Relations between certain preservice factors and psychoneurosis during military duty. *Armed Forces Medical Journal, 11,* 152–160.

Roff, M. (1961). Childhood social interactions and young adult bad conduct. *Journal of Abnormal Social Psychology, 63,* 333–337.

Roff, M. (1963). Childhood social interactions and young adult psychosis. *Journal of Clinical Psychology, 19,* 152–157.

Rogoff, B. (1997). Evaluating development in the process of participation: Theory, methods and practice building on each other. In E. Amsel & K. A. Renninger (Eds.), *Change and development: Issues in change, method, and application* (pp. 265–285). Mahwah, NJ: Erlbaum.

Rogosch, F. A., Cicchetti, D., & Aber, J. L. (1995). The role of child maltreatment in early deviations in cognitive and affective processing abilities and later peer relationship problems. *Development and Psychopathology, 7*(4), 591–609.

Rook, S. (1988). Toward a more differentiated view of loneliness. In D. F. Hale & S. Duck (Eds.), *Handbook of personal relationships: Theory, research, and interventions* (pp. 571–589). Oxford, England: Wiley.

Rose, A. J. (2002). Co-rumination in the friendships of girls and boys. *Child Development, 73,* 1830–1843.

Rose, A. J., & Asher, S. R. (2000). Children's friendships. In S. S. Hendrick & C. Hendrick (Eds.), *Close relationships: A sourcebook* (pp. 47–57). Thousand Oaks, CA: Sage.

Rose, A. J., & Asher, S. R. (2004). Children's strategies and goals in response to help-giving and help-seeking tasks within a friendship. *Child Development, 3,* 749–763.

Rosenblum, L. A., Coe, C. L., & Bromley, L. J. (1975). Peer relations in monkeys: The influence of social structure, gender, familiarity. In M. Lewis & L. A. Rosenblum (Eds.), *Friendships and peer relations* (pp. 67–98). New York: Wiley.

Ross, H. S. (1982). The establishment of social games amongst toddlers. *Developmental Psychology, 18,* 509–518.

Rotenberg, K., & Hymel, S. (1999). *Loneliness in childhood and adolescence.* New York: Cambridge University Press.

Roth, M. A., & Parker, J. G. (2001). Affective and behavioral response to friends who neglect their friends for dating partners: Influence of gender, jealousy, and perspective. *Journal of Adolescence, 24,* 281–296.

Roy, R., & Benenson, J. F. (2002). Sex and contextual effects on children's use of interference competition. *Developmental Psychology, 38,* 306–312.

Rubin, K. H. (2002). *The friendship factor: Helping our children navigate their social world—And why it matters for their success and happiness.* New York: Viking Penguin.

Rubin, K. H. (in press). On hand-holding, spit, and the "big tickets": A commentary on research from a cultural perspective. In X. Chen, D. French, & B. Schneider (Eds.), *Peer relations in cultural context.* New York: Cambridge University Press.

Rubin, K. H., Bukowski, W., & Parker, J. G. (1998). Peer interactions, relationships, and groups. In W. Damon (Series Ed.) & N. Eisenberg (Ed.), *Handbook of child psychology: Vol. 3. Social, emotional, and personality development* (5th ed., pp. 619–700). New York: Wiley.

Rubin, K. H., & Burgess, K. B. (2001). Social withdrawal and anxiety. In M. W. Vasey & M. R. Dadds (Eds.), *The developmental psychopathology of anxiety* (pp. 407–434). New York: Oxford University Press.

Rubin, K. H., & Burgess, K. B. (2002). Parents of aggressive and withdrawn children. In M. Bornstein (Ed.), *Handbook of parenting* (2nd ed., Vol. 1, 383–418). Hillsdale, NJ: Erlbaum.

Rubin, K. H., Burgess, K. B., & Coplan, R. J. (2002). Social withdrawal and shyness. In C. H. Hart & P. K. Smith (Eds.), *Blackwell handbook of childhood social development* (pp. 330–352). Malden, MA: Blackwell.

Rubin, K. H., Burgess, K. B., & Hastings, P. D. (2002). Stability and social-behavioral consequences of toddlers' inhibited temperament and parenting. *Child Development, 73,* 483–495.

Rubin, K. H., Burgess, K. B., Kennedy, A. E., & Stewart, S. (2003). Social withdrawal in childhood. In E. Mash & R. Barkley (Eds.), *Child psychopathology* (2nd ed., pp. 372–406). New York: Guilford Press.

Rubin, K. H., Cheah, C. S. L., & Fox, N. A. (2001). Emotion regulation, parenting, and the display of social reticence in preschoolers. *Early Education and Development, 12,* 97–115.

Rubin, K. H., Chen, X., & Hymel, S. (1993). Socioemotional characteristics of withdrawn and aggressive children. *Merrill-Palmer Quarterly, 39,* 518–534.

Rubin, K. H., Chen, X., McDougall, P., Bowker, A., & McKinnon, J. (1995). The Waterloo Longitudinal Project: Predicting internalizing and externalizing problems in adolescence. *Development and Psychopathology, 7,* 751–764.

Rubin, K. H., & Daniels-Beirness, T. (1983). Concurrent and predictive correlates of sociometric status in kindergarten and grade one children. *Merrill-Palmer Quarterly, 29,* 337–351.

Rubin, K. H., Dwyer, K. M., Booth, C. L., Kim, A. H., Burgess, K. B., & Rose-Krasnor, L. (2004). Attachment, friendship, and psychosocial functioning in early adolescence *Journal of Early Adolescence, 24,* 326–356.

Rubin, K. H., Fein, G., & Vandenberg, B. (1983). Play. In P. H. Mussen (Series Ed.) & E. M. Hetherington (Vol. Ed), *Handbook of child psychology: Vol. 4. Socialization, personality and social development* (pp. 693–774). New York: Wiley.

Rubin, K. H., & Krasnor, L. R. (1983). Age and gender differences in the development of a representative social problem solving skill. *Journal of Applied Developmental Psychology, 4,* 463–475.

Rubin, K. H., & Krasnor, L. R. (1986). Social-cognitive and social behavioral perspectives on problem solving. In M. Perlmutter (Ed.), *Minnesota Symposia on Child Psychology: Vol. 18. Cognitive perspectives on children's social and behavioral development* (pp. 1–68). Hillsdale, NJ: Erlbaum.

Rubin, K. H., & Rose-Krasnor, L. (1992). Interpersonal problem solving. In V. B. Van Hasselt & M. Hersen (Eds.), *Handbook of social development* (pp. 283–323). New York: Plenum Press.

Rubin, K. H., Wojslawowicz, J. C., Burgess, K. B., Booth, C., & Rose-Krasnor, L. (2004). *The best friendships of shy/withdrawn children.* Unpublished manuscript under review, University of Maryland.

Rysman, A. (1977). How the "gossip" became a woman. *Journal of Communications, 27,* 176–180.

Saarni, C. (1998). Issues of cultural meaningfulness in emotional development. *Developmental Psychology, 34,* 647–652.

Saarni, C. (1999). *The development of emotional competence.* New York: Guilford Press.

Sabongui, A. G., Bukowski, W. M., & Newcomb, A. F. (1998). The peer ecology of popularity: The network embeddedness of a child's friend predicts the child's subsequent popularity. In W. M. Bukowski & A. H. Cillessen (Eds.), *Sociometry Then and now: Building on six decades of measuring children's experiences with the peer group* (pp. 83–92). San Francisco: Jossey-Bass.

Salmivalli, C. (2001). Group view on victimization: Empirical findings and their implications. In J. Juvonen & S. Graham (Eds.), *Peer harassment in school: The plight of the vulnerable and victimized* (pp. 398–419). New York: Guilford Press.

Salmivalli, C., Huttunen, A., & Lagerspetz, K. (1997). Peer networks and bullying in schools. *Scandinavian Journal of Psychology, 38,* 305–312.

Salmivalli, C., & Voeten, M. (2004). Connections between attitudes, group norms, and behaviour in bullying situations. *International Journal of Behavioral Development, 28,* 246–258.

Sameroff, A. J. (1995). General systems theories and developmental psychopathology. In D. Cicchetti & D. Cohen (Eds.), *Developmental Psychopathology: Vol. 1. Theory and methods* (pp. 659–695). New York: Wiley.

Sameroff, A. J. (1975). Early influences on development: Fact or fantasy. *Merrill-Palmer Quarterly, 21,* 267–294.

Sameroff, A. J. (1987). The social context of development. In N. Eisenberg (Ed.), *Contemporary topics in developmental psychology* (pp. 273–291). New York: Wiley.

Sameroff, A. J., & MacKenzie, M. J. (2003). Research strategies for capturing transactional models of development: The limits of the possible. *Development and Psychopathology, 15,* 613–640.

Sanderson, J. A., & Siegal, M. (1995). Loneliness and stable friendship in rejected and nonrejected preschoolers. *Journal of Applied Developmental Psychology, 16,* 555–567.

Sandler, E. N., Miller, P., Short, J., & Wolchik, S. A. (1989). Social support as a protective factor for children in stress. In D. Belle (Ed.), *Children's social networks and social supports* (pp. 207–307). New York: Wiley.

Sandstrom, M. J., Cillessen, A. H. N., & Eisenhower, A. (2003). Children's appraisal of peer rejection experiences: Impact on social and emotional adjustment. *Social Development, 12,* 530–550.

Sandstrom, M. J., & Coie, J. D. (1999). A developmental perspective on peer rejection: Mechanisms of stability and change. *Child Development, 70,* 955–966.

Savin-Williams, R. C. (1979). Dominance hierarchies in groups of early adolescents. *Child Development, 50,* 923–935.

Sawyer, R. K. (1997). *Pretend play as improvisation: Conversation in the preschool classroom.* Mahwah, NJ: Erlbaum.

Schindler, P. J., Moely, B. E., & Frank, A. L. (1987). Time in day care and social participation of young children. *Developmental Psychology, 23,* 255–261.

Schlaefli, A., Rest, J. R., & Thoma, S. J. (1985). Does moral education improve moral judgment? A meta-analysis of intervention studies using the Defining Issues Test. *Review of Educational Research, 55,* 319–352.

Schneider, B. H. (1999). A multimethod exploration of the friendships of children considered socially withdrawn by their school peers. *Journal of Abnormal Child Psychology, 27,* 115–123.

Schneider, B. H. (2000). *Friends and enemies: Peer relations in childhood.* London: Arnold.

Schneider, B. H., Atkinson, L., & Tardif, C. (2001). Child-parent attachment and children's peer relations: A quantitative review. *Developmental Psychology, 37*(1), 86–100.

Schwartz, D., Dodge, K. A., Pettit, G. S., & Bates, J. E. (2000). Friendship as a moderating factor in the pathway between early harsh home environment and later victimization in the peer group. *Developmental Psychology, 36*(5), 646–662.

Seiffge-Krenke, I. (2003). Testing theories of romantic development from adolescence to young adulthood: Evidence of a developmental sequence. *International Journal of Behavioral Development, 27,* 519–531.

Selman, R. L. (1980). *The growth of interpersonal understanding: Developmental and clinical analyses.* New York: Academic Press.

Selman, R, L., & Schultz, L. H. (1990). *Making a friend in youth: Developmental theory and pair therapy.* Chicago: University of Chicago Press.

Shantz, C. U., & Hartup, W. W. (1992). *Conflict in child and adolescent development.* New York: Cambridge University Press.

Sharabany, R., Gershoni, R., & Hofman, J. (1981). Girlfriend, boyfriend: Age and sex differences in intimate friendship. *Developmental Psychology, 17,* 800–808.

Shrum, W., & Cheek, N. H. (1987). Social structure during the school years: Onset of the degrouping process. *American Sociological Review, 52,* 218–223.

Shulman, S., Levy-Shiff, R., Kedem, P., & Alon, E. (1997). Intimate relationships among adolescent romantic partners and same-sex friends: Individual and systemic perspectives. In S. Shulman & W. A. Collins (Eds.), *Romantic relationships in adolescence: Developmental perspectives* (pp. 37–52). San Francisco: Jossey-Bass.

Silverman, W. K., & Nelles, W. B. (1988). The Anxiety Disorders Interview Schedule for Children. *Journal of the American Academy of Child and Adolescent Psychiatry, 27*(6), 772–778.

Simons, K. J., Paternite, C. E., & Shore, C. (2001). Patterns of parent/adolescent attachment and aggression in young adolescents. *Journal of Early Adolescence, 21,* 182–203.

Simpkins, S. D., & Parke, R. D. (2002). Do friends and nonfriends behave differently? A social relations analysis of children's behavior. *Merrill-Palmer Quarterly, 48,* 263–283.

Singleton, L. C., & Asher, S. R. (1977). Peer preferences and social interaction among third-grade children in an integrated school district. *Journal of Educational Psychology, 69,* 330–336.

Sletta, O., Valas, H., Skaalvik, E., & Sobstad, F. (1996). Peer relations, loneliness, and self-perceptions in school-aged children. *British Journal of Educational Psychology, 66,* 431–445.

Snyder, J., Brooker, M., Patrick, M. R., Snyder, A., Schrepferman, L., & Stoolmiller, M. (2003). Observed peer victimization during early elementary school: Continuity, growth, and relation to risk for child antisocial and depressive behavior. *Child Development, 74,* 1881–1898.

Sobol, M. P., & Earn, B. M. (1985). Assessment of children's attributions for social experiences: Implications for social skills training. In B. H. Schneider, K. H. Rubin, & J. E. Ledingham (Eds.), *Children's peer relations: Issues in assessment and intervention* (pp. 93–110). New York: Springer-Verlag.

Sroufe, L. A. (1983). Infant-caregiver attachment and patterns of adaptation in preschool: The roots of maladaptation. In M. Perlmutter (Ed.), *Minnesota Symposia on Child Psychology* (Vol. 16, pp. 41–83). Hillsdale, NJ: Erlbaum.

Sroufe, L. A. (1995). *Emotional development: The organization of emotional life in the early years.* Cambridge, England: Cambridge University Press.

Sroufe, L. A., Bennett, C., Englund, M., & Urban, J. (1993). The significance of gender boundaries in preadolescence: Contemporary correlates and antecedents of boundary violation and maintenance. *Child Development, 64,* 455–466.

Sroufe, L. A., & Fleeson, J. (1986). Attachment and the construction of relationships. In W. W. Hartup & Z. Rubin (Eds.), *Relationships and development* (pp. 36–54). Hillsdale, NJ: Erlbaum.

Sroufe, L. A., & Jacobvitz, D. (1989). Diverging pathways, developmental transformations, multiple etiologies, and the problem of continuity in development. *Human Development, 32,* 196–203.

Sroufe, L. A., & Rutter, M. (1984). The domain of developmental psychopathology. *Child Development, 55,* 17–29.

Stemberger, R. T., Turner, S. M., Beidel, D. C., & Calhoun, K. S. (1995). Social phobia: An analysis of possible developmental factors. *Journal of Abnormal Psychology, 104*(3), 526–531.

Stets, J. E., & Pirog-Good, M. A. (1987). Violence in dating relationships. *Social Psychology Quarterly, 50*(3), 237–246.

Stormshak, E. A., Bierman, K. L., Bruschi, C., Dodge, K. A., Coie, J. D., & the Conduct Preventions Research Group. (1999, January/February). The relation between behavior problems and peer preference in different classroom contexts. *Child Development, 70*(1), 169–182.

Strayer, F. F. (1989). Co-adaptation within the early peer group: A psychobiological study of social competence. In B. H. Schneider, G. Attili, J. Nadel, R. P. Weissberg (Eds.), *Social competence in developmental perspective* (pp. 145–174). New York: Kluwer Academic.

Strayer, F. F., & Strayer, J. (1976). An ethological analysis of social agonism and dominance relations among preschool children. *Child Development, 47,* 980–989.

Strouse, D. L. (1999). Adolescent crowd orientations: A social and temporal analysis. In J. A. McLellan & M. J. V. Pugh (Eds.), *The role of peer groups in adolescent social identity: Exploring the importance of stability and change* (pp. 37–54). San Francisco: Jossey-Bass.

Sullivan, H. S. (1953). *The interpersonal theory of psychiatry.* New York: Norton.

Suls, J. M. (1977). Gossip as social comparison. *Journal of Communication, 27,* 164–168.

Suomi, S. J., & Harlow, H. F. (1975). The role and reason of peer relationships in rhesus monkeys. In M. Lewis & L. A. Rosenblum (Eds.), *Friendship and peer relations* (pp. 153–186). New York: Wiley.

Thomas, D. S., Loomis, A. M., & Arrington, R. E. (1933). *Observational studies of social behavior.* New Haven, CT: Yale University.

Tremblay, R. E., Mâsse, L. C., Vitaro, F., & Dobkin, P. L. (1995). The impact of friends' deviant behavior on early onset of delinquency: Longitudinal data from 6 to 13 years of age. *Development and Psychopathology, 7,* 649–668.

Tremblay, R. E., Nagin, D. S., Séguin, J. R., Zoccolillo, M., Zelazo, P. D., Boivin, M., et al. (2005). Physical aggression during early childhood: Trajectories and predictors. *Canadian Child and Adolescent Psychiatry Review, 14*(1), 3–9.

Underwood, M. K. (2003). *Social aggression among girls.* New York: Guilford Press.

Urberg, K. A., Cheng, C. H., & Shyu, S. J. (1991). Grade changes in peer influence on adolescent cigarette smoking: A comparison of two measures. *Addictive Behaviors, 16,* 21–28.

Urberg, K. A., Degirmencioglu, S. M., & Pilgrim, C. (1997). Close friend and group influence on adolescent cigarette smoking and alcohol use. *Developmental Psychology, 33,* 834–844.

Vandell, D. L., Wilson, K. S., & Buchanan, N. R. (1980). Peer interaction in the first year of life: An examination of its structure, content, and sensitivity to toys. *Child Development, 51,* 481–488.

Van Lieshout, C. F. M., Cillessen, A. H., & Haselager, G. J. T. (1999). Interpersonal support and individual development. In W. A. Collins & B. Laursen (Eds.), *Minnesota Symposia on Child Psychology: Vol. 30. Relationships as developmental contexts* (pp. 37–60). Mahwah, NJ: Erlbaum.

Vasey, M. W., & Dadds, M. R. (2001). An introduction to the developmental psychopathology of anxiety. In M. W. Vasey & M. R. Dadds (Eds.), *The developmental psychopathology of anxiety* (pp. 3–26). New York: Oxford University Press.

Vaughn, B. E., Vollenweider, M., Bost, K. K., Azria-Evans, M. R., & Snider, J. B. (2003). Negative interactions and social competence for preschool children in two samples: Reconsidering the interpretation of aggressive behavior for young children. *Merrill-Palmer Quarterly, 49,* 245–278.

Vernberg, E. M. (1990). Psychological adjustment and experiences with peers during early adolescence: Reciprocal, incidental, or unidirectional relationships? *Journal of Abnormal Child Psychology, 18,* 187–198.

Vernberg, E. M., Abwender, D. A., Ewell, K. K., & Beery, S. H. (1992). Social anxiety and peer relationships in early adolescence: A prospective analysis. *Journal of Clinical Child Psychology, 21,* 189–196.

Vernberg, E. M., Jacobs, A. K., & Hershberger, S. L. (1999). Peer victimization and attitudes about violence during early adolescence. *Journal of Clinical Child Psychology, 28*(3), 386–395.

Vitaro, F., Brendgen, M., & Tremblay, R. E. (2002). Reactively and proactively aggressive children: Antecedent and subsequent characteristics. *Journal of Child Psychology and Psychiatry and Allied Disciplines, 43,* 495–506.

Von Dras, D. D., & Siegler, I. C. (1997). Stability in extraversion and aspects of social support at mid-life. *Journal of Personality and Social Psychology, 72,* 233–241.

von Salisch, M. (2000). The emotional side of sharing, emotional support, and conflict negotiation between siblings and between friends. In R. Mills & S. Duck (Eds.), *Developmental psychology of personal relationships* (pp. 49–70). Chichester, England: Wiley.

Vygotsky, L. S. (1978). *Mind in society: The development of higher psychological processes.* Cambridge, MA: Harvard University Press.

Wachs, T. D. (1992). *The nature of nurture.* Thousand Oaks, CA: Sage.

Walden, T., Lemerise, E., & Smith, M. C. (1999). Friendship and popularity in preschool classrooms. *Early Education and Development, 10,* 351–371.

Walker, L. J. (1986). Experiential and cognitive sources of moral development in adulthood. *Human Development, 28,* 133–134.

Wargo Aikins, J., Bierman, K., & Parker, J. G. (2005). Navigating the transition to junior high school: The influence of pre-transition friendship and self-system characteristics. *Social Development, 14,* 42–60.

Webster-Stratton, C., & Hammond, M. (1999). Marital conflict management skills, parenting style, and early onset conduct problems: Processes and pathways. *Journal of Child Psychology and Psychiatry, 40,* 917–927.

Weiss, D. D., & Last, C. G. (2001). Developmental variations in the prevalence and manifestation of anxiety disorders. In M. W. Vasey & M. R. Dadds (Eds.), *The developmental psychopathology of anxiety* (pp. 27–42). New York: Oxford University Press.

Weiss, M. R., & Smith, A. L. (1999). Quality of youth sport friendships: Measurement development and validation. *Journal of Sport and Exercise Psychology, 21,* 145–166.

Weiss, M. R., Smith, A. L., & Theeboom, M. (1996). "That's what friends are for": Children's and teenagers perceptions of peer relationships in the sport domain. *Journal of Sport and Exercise Psychology, 18,* 347–379.

Wentzel, K. R. (2003). Sociometric status and adjustment in middle school: A longitudinal study. *Journal of Early Adolescence, 23,* 5–28.

Wentzel, K. R., McNamara-Barry, C., & Caldwell, K. A. (2004). Friendships in middle school: Influences on motivation and school adjustment. *Journal of Educational Psychology, 96*(2), 195–203.

Whalen, C. K., & Henker, B. (1991). Therapies for hyperactive children: Comparisons, combinations, and compromises. *Journal of Consulting and Clinical Psychology, 59,* 126–137.

Wichmann, C., Coplan, R. J., & Daniels, T. (2004). The social cognitions of socially withdrawn children. *Social Development, 13,* 377–392.

Wilson, B. J., & Gottman, J. M. (2002). Marital conflict, repair, and parenting. In M. H. Bornstein (Ed.), *Handbook of parenting: Vol. 4. Social conditions and applied parenting* (2nd ed., pp. 227–258). Mahwah, NJ: Erlbaum.

Windle, M. (1992). Temperament in social support in adolescence: Interrelations with depressive symptoms and delinquent behaviors. *Journal of Youth and Adolescence, 21,* 1–21.

Wojslawowicz, J. C., Rubin, K. H., Burgess, K. B., Booth, C., & Rose-Krasnor, L. R. (in press). Behavioral characteristics associated with stable and fluid best friendship patterns in middle childhood. *Merrill-Palmer Quarterly.*

Woodward, L. J., & Fergusson, D. M. (1999). Childhood peer relationship problems and psychosocial adjustment in late adolescence. *Journal of Abnormal Psychology, 27,* 87–104.

World Health Organization. (1992). *The ICD-10 classification of mental and behavioural disorders: Clinical descriptions and diagnostic guidelines.* Geneva, Switzerland: Author.

Wright, J. C., Giammarino, M., & Parad, H. (1986). Social status in small groups: Individual group similarity and the social "misfit." *Journal of Personality and Social Psychology, 50,* 523–536.

Xie, H., Cairns, R. B., & Cairns, B. D. (1999). Social networks and configurations in inner-city schools: Aggression, popularity, and implications for students with EBD. *Journal of Emotional and Behavioral Disorders, 7,* 147–155.

Youngblade, L., Park, K., & Belsky, J. (1993). Measurement of young children's close friendship: A comparison of two independent assessment systems and their associations with attachment security. *International Journal of Behavioral Development, 16,* 563–587.

Youniss, J. (1980). *Parents and peers in social development: A Sullivan-Piaget perspective.* Chicago: University of Chicago Press.

Youniss, J., & Smoller, J. (1985). *Adolescent relations with mothers, fathers, and friends.* Chicago: University of Chicago Press.

Zakriski, A., & Coie, J. (1996). A comparison of aggressive-rejected and nonaggressive rejected children's interpretations of self-directed and other-directed rejection. *Child Development, 67,* 1048–1070.

Zarbatany, L., Hartmann, D., & Rankin, D. (1990). The psychological functions of preadolescent peer activities. *Child Development, 61,* 1067–1980.

Zarbatany, L., McDougall, P., & Hymel, S. (2000). Gender-differentiated experience in the peer culture: Links to intimacy in preadolescence. *Social Development, 9,* 62–79.

Zeller, M., Vannatta, K., Schafer, J., & Noll, R. (2003). Behavioral reputation: A cross-age perspective. *Developmental Psychology, 39,* 129–139.

CHAPTER 13

Schools, Schooling, and Developmental Psychopathology

ROBERT C. PIANTA

Understanding the nature and course of development is inextricably linked with our understanding of adaptation in school and schooling's effects on adaptation. A focus on school effects and adaptation to school has been a part of the field of developmental psychopathology since its inception (see Rutter & Maughan, 2002; Sroufe & Rutter, 1984). Within developmental psychopathology, there is little doubt that schools are settings for assessment of adaptive and maladaptive behavior patterns and sources of influence on those patterns, as is well-documented in reviews of descriptive research and intervention trials (e.g., Eccles & Gootman, 2002; Greenberg, Domitrovich, & Bumbarger, 2001; McMahon & Washburn, 2003). In the past 2 decades, with

the rise of contextualism in developmental science (Cicchetti & Aber, 1998; Lerner, 1998) and the focus on positive development in community settings (Connell, Kubisch, Schorr, & Weiss, 1995), schools have become places of even more interest to developmentalists (e.g., www.cfchildren .org). However, notwithstanding the extensive developmentally informed programs of research on schooling and its effects that have been reported in the past 10 to 15 years (e.g., Alexander & Entwisle, 1988; Eccles & Roeser, 1998; Ladd & Burgess, 1999; Morrison & Connor, 2002; C. T. Ramey et al., 2000; Stevenson & Lee, 1990), the links between developmental psychopathology and education are far from systematic or programmatic.

Deepening, extending, and more fully integrating the study of developmental psychopathology, school effects, and school adaptation is the goal of this chapter. Because the challenges to integration are fundamentally conceptual, the primary goal of the chapter is to articulate and advance a set of conceptual frameworks that can serve as tools for integrative research. Throughout, empirical work is used illustratively. In the end, the chapter points to the value for both disciplines of reconceptualizing the link between education and developmental psychopathology.

The work reported herein was supported in part by the National Center for Early Development and Learning under the Educational Research and Development Centers Program, PR/Award No. R307A60004, as administered by the Office of Educational Research and Improvement, U.S. Department of Education. It was also supported by the National Institute of Child Health and Human Development (NICHD) Study of Early Child Care (U10-HD25449) and NICHD R21-43750. The contents do not necessarily represent the positions or policies of the Office of Educational Research and Improvement, the U.S. Department of Education, or the NICHD, and endorsement by the federal government should not be assumed.

The chapter is organized into four sections. The first outlines the mutual interests of developmental psychopathologists and educators and points out theoretical and practice gains that could be the result of strategic exploitation of these interests. The second section discusses conceptual barriers to interdisciplinarity between developmental psychopathology and education and suggests an alternative, integrative perspective. The third section presents a model of schooling and the factors related to school effects and adaptation that have been identified in the literature. This section provides a map of school factors that link well to developmentally informed studies of social and behavioral outcomes. Finally, the fourth section identifies a set of integrative conclusions and future directions for further work. One way to look at the first three sections is as a discussion of three related questions: What contributions can developmental psychopathology and education make to one another? What broad conceptual principles should guide interdisciplinary integrations? What are the facets of schooling and its organization of interest to developmental psychopathology?

MUTUAL INTERESTS OF EDUCATION AND DEVELOPMENTAL PSYCHOPATHOLOGY

Across most Western societies, children are exposed to formal schooling experiences starting sometime between the ages of 4 and 7 and ending anywhere between 10 and 12 years later, longer when post-high school education is involved. Along the way, substantial developmental change routinely occurs, in part as a function of experience in school. Schools are *designed* to intentionally, formally, and strategically direct the nature and course of these changes in many areas of functioning. Schools were, and still are, conceived as a society's investment in the future; they serve to secure certain social values and provide for the future welfare of a society's citizens. In a manner that is far from trivial, schools are often viewed with the same value-laden lens as families, and just as often the same responsibility for children's and society's welfare as is attributed to families is attributed to schools. When schools are viewed as having a compensatory role in relation to family risks and liabilities (e.g., Duncan & Brooks-Gunn, 1997; Gambone, Klem, & Connell, 2002), then arguably, greater social importance is being attributed to educational settings than to the family.

From its inception, the field of developmental psychopathology has had a connection to schools, schooling, and

educational outcomes and processes. A landmark study in the field, the Isle of Wight study (Rutter, Maughan, Mortimore, Ouston, & Smith, 1979), was closely concerned with the role schools play in accounting for the differences in mental health and behavioral outcomes observed among the study participants. This interest in schooling grew into the classic *Fifteen Thousand Hours* study of secondary schools and the resultant attention to such facets of schooling as leadership, focus, organization, and teacher qualities (Rutter, 1982; Rutter et al., 1979).

Developmental psychopathology's interest in schools 25 years after *Fifteen Thousand Hours* remains strong. Rutter and Maughan (2002) conclude their recent summary of progress in research on schooling and development since that study by acknowledging a series of questions that informed their original work and that continue to press for attention. These questions involve

1. The need for hard empirical evidence on factors related to changing failing schools, including attention to contextual features (such as community attitudes), resources (intake mix), teacher recruitment, finances, and leadership;
2. Peer processes and influences within schools;
3. Characteristics of schools that matter for social, behavioral, and self-efficacy outcomes;
4. How schools foster connections to the goals of schooling and socialization;
5. How selective and nonselective school systems function to influence child outcomes;
6. How different experiences in schools affect children differently based on their pattern of strengths and limitations, and vice versa; and
7. How and why children respond so differently to the school environment.

What is notable about these questions, apart from their cogency in summarizing the state of the field in educational research, is that, as a group, they fit so harmoniously within a developmental framework or paradigm. They reflect an interest in contexts and processes, in individual differences as well as normative growth, in multiple domains of functioning, and in multilayered systems coacting across time. These are the core interests of many developmental scientists and they are here reflected in questions about experience and adaptation in school settings in ways that parallel the work already conducted, addressing analogous questions in family and child care settings. One might argue that these questions invite an extension of the *development in context* paradigm beyond its historical application to the period of infancy to preschool and into the school years.

Opportunities for Developmental Psychopathology

Recent decades of school reform (National Center for Education Statistics [NCES], 2003) illustrate the role that schooling is intended to play in American society at the outset of the twenty-first century. It is increasingly clear that schools and formal education are indeed viewed as agents of equity and access in American life, and the perceived, and realized, inability of schools to successfully function in this manner is responsible for widespread reform efforts initiated at federal, state, and local levels over the course of the past 20 years. The reform movement has crystallized the many roles schools play in addressing children's needs: Schools now strategically deliver preventive interventions to at-risk populations, have a clear role in defining and measuring adaptive functioning and pathology, and are the major provider of mental health services to children. These roles for schools provide natural links to developmental science that can be exploited in ways that advance understanding of development and support developmentally informed programming for children (e.g., Pianta, Hamre, & Stuhlman, 2003).

School Reform and Indicators of Adaptation

In almost all cases of school reform, goals germane to developmental psychopathology are explicitly stated in legislation and policy and operationalized in practice (NCES, 2003). Gambone, Klem, and Connell (2002), in their study of several integrated databases pertaining to adolescent development and young adult outcomes, identify the links between social and academic experiences for which schools are often responsible and adult functioning. In this analysis, the opportunity to engage challenging and engaging learning experiences that expand skills and competencies and to experience supportive relationships with nonparental adult figures is identified as fundamental to broad adaptational functioning in social and interpersonal relationships, employment, and emotional health and personal well-being. In nearly every community, schools are the primary nonfamilial conduit for the provision of these experiences and opportunities (NCES, 2003). It was in part due to concerns related to the attainment of broad, adult goals of economic self-sufficiency, healthy family and social relationships, and involvement in the community that attention turned to the failure of schools to produce these

outcomes and spawned the reform movement. As a consequence, in a much more formal way than 20 years ago, schools are both community resources and arbiters of metrics for success and failure, functions of interest to developmental psychopathology.

The recent No Child Left Behind Act (NCLB, 2001; NCES, 2003; http://www.ed.gov/nclb/landing.jhtml?srac =pb) is a federal initiative designed to hold schools accountable for their performance or production relative to society's needs and advances, a particular definition of accountability and outcome based on performance on standardized achievement tests. In 49 states, some form of accountability tests exist, many extending down to the third grade and most functioning to create successive skill-focused hurdles that children and youth must clear to graduate (NCES, 2003). Great debates have taken place over the use of performance on standardized achievement tests as the metric for school adaptation, with arguments against testing as the sole indicator of success resting on the need to conceptualize, value, and assess success in terms of social and interpersonal relationships, motivation and a sense of personal competence, and mental health and emotional well-being (Berliner & Biddle, 1995). To this point, in no state has a broader definition or assessment of school adaptation found its way into the accountability mechanisms (NCES, 2003). To the extent that some degree of broadening beyond academics has occurred, it is evident in the work on the Head Start National Reporting System (the accountability plan for Head Start programs), which has planned a pilot implementation of teachers' ratings of children's social functioning; the Technical Work Group affiliated with this effort is discussing direct assessment of self-regulation (Administration for Children and Families [ACF], 2003). One contribution of developmental psychopathology to education would be articulation of the ways in which social, emotional, and mental health outcomes are tied to the same long-term adult goals that schools aspire to fulfill (Eccles & Gootman, 2002; Gambone et al., 2002) and thus to provide empirical evidence for alternatives to defining school adaptation in terms of test performance.

Broad legislative initiatives aimed at improving the functioning of the child, adolescent, and adult populations as a consequence of improving schools have in turn created a set of ancillary policies that themselves have implications for developmental psychopathology. The combination of school-defined and -measured indicators of adaptive functioning, as well as schools functioning as a community's mechanism for promoting adaptive functioning in children and adults, has, at times, resulted in a system in which adaptive failure is created as a consequence of shifts in educational policy or practice (see Berliner & Biddle, 1995). Consider, for example, the current situation in Virginia and several other states, where the legal age for dropping out of school (an identified risk factor for subsequent un- or underemployment and substance use) was recently lowered, making it permissible for youth to disengage from formal schooling at age 15 instead of 16. Recent state reports indicate quite clearly that as high-stakes consequences are attached to performance on school accountability tests, an increasing number of youth (most with a history of academic failure) take advantage of this type of early dropout policy (Berliner, 2004). In this way, educational policy and accountability tests designed to increase school success conspire to exacerbate risk.

As another example of educational policies with implications for defining adaptation, every school in the country is required to screen its population of children and provide special education for those with a range of disabling conditions, including disorders related to learning and behavior. Arguments have raged for at least the past 2 decades concerning the use of various cutoff indicators and definitions to delineate and identify children with disabilities from other children struggling to perform well in school (see Ysseldyke, Algozzine, & Thurlow, 2000). Legislative and policy changes in response to these arguments create new classes of children "with" and "without" disabilities on a regular basis. These categories are an operationalization of adaptive and maladaptive functioning in the same way that systems of psychiatric nosology provide a set of descriptors for marking developmental success and failure. The educational and psychiatric nosological systems serve both scientific and service-delivery purposes. If these systems were superimposed on one another and examined in relation to an assortment of information on child functioning in school, community, and home contexts, opportunities are opened for understanding adaptive function from a range of perspectives. Typically when such efforts are conducted, a far more differentiated and contextualized vision of function is evident (Noam, Warner, & Van Dyken, 2001; Rones & Hoagwood, 2000).

Early Intervention and Prevention: The Dynamics of Community Action

Theoretical frameworks in developmental psychopathology have for some time emphasized the multilevel nature of systems that regulate developmental processes and outcome (Cicchetti & Dawson, 2002; Gottlieb & Halpern, 2002). Schooling provides developmentalists with opportunities to examine multilevel interactions given its layered

nature of community, site, classroom, teacher, and peer influences (Eccles & Roeser, 1998). Interest in promoting the functioning of the youngest children in school has in recent years been intense, again with implications for developmental psychopathology. The emergence of an entirely new service sector in schools—programs for (at-risk) 4-year-old children—has in part been the consequence of this interest (Bryant et al., 2003), stemming from developmentally oriented research showing both the critical importance of the early school years and the value of high-quality early intervention programming (e.g., see C. T. Ramey et al., 2000; C. T. Ramey & Ramey, 1998). The prekindergarten sector in public schools now serves well over a million children, mostly from low-income families and most at risk for problems in learning, behavior, and socioemotional development (Clifford, Early, & Hills, 1999). These programs are state-funded interventions for high-risk children (and sometimes their families) that have explicitly stated goals to enhance both academic and social/interpersonal success in school. Systematic, developmentally informed study of the processes by which these state prekindergarten programs and federally supported Head Start programs alter social and academic trajectories, promote resilience, and prevent problem outcomes (e.g., Bryant et al., 2003) exemplifies integration of developmental psychopathology and education that has implications for both disciplines.

For example, developmentally informed examination of the specific aspects of prekindergarten classroom experience related to growth in social and academic functioning in prekindergarten (Howes et al., in press) clearly points to the critical importance of both emotionally sensitive and intentionally instructional interactions on the part of teachers in these classrooms. These results have initiated efforts to understand the key aspects of teachers' training, knowledge, and experience that contribute to their sensitivity and intentionality, integrating developmental study with teacher education and professional development (Institute of Education Sciences [IES], 2004a; Pianta, 2003; Ready to Teach Act, H.R. 2211, 2003). Through this type of integrative inquiry, developmental psychopathology gains knowledge about the function of parameters in school settings that affect children's social and behavioral adjustment that can inform both theory and the design of interventions, while education benefits from analysis of school effects in large samples of children in which links between policy and outcome are evaluated in light of classroom processes. To the extent that standardized metrics of child functioning and classroom process are embedded in intervention programs such as those for prekindergarten at-risk children, or such as those proposed for Head Start (ACF, 2003), opportunities for further elaboration of community-school-classroom-home effects on children's adaptive functioning will emerge at the population level.

With regard to children's mental health outcomes, because they are public institutions in which nearly an entire community participates, schools frequently are the focus of efforts to promote mental health and reduce risk both at local levels and as reflected in national policy (Cowen, 1999; Rones & Hoagwood, 2000). Schools are often the locus of efforts to improve children's physical health and well-being and the single most frequently mentioned context as a site for mental health intervention (Hoagwood & Johnson, 2003; Nastasi, 1998). To quote Rones and Hoagwood, "It is now well documented that, insofar as children receive any mental health services, schools are the major providers" (p. 223). Almost a decade ago, Durlak and Wells (1997) found that 72.9% of all studies of prevention trials involving children took place in schools, with 20% of change agents being the child's teacher(s), a trend that has noticeably increased (e.g., Illinois General Assembly, SB 1951, 2003). Developmentally oriented applied psychologists are now advancing the position that developmental psychopathology and schooling become more formally linked through reforming clinical child psychology and school psychology as public health professions (Hoagwood & Johnson, 2003). Alternatively, educators have started to include developmentally informed conceptual frameworks in discussions of classroom management and teacher training initiatives that are intended to address children's behavioral and emotional needs (Evertson & Weinstein, in press). Clearly, the linkage of schooling and mental health is moving beyond add-on programs and social skills groups toward more complete integration at the conceptual and operational levels, as evinced by embedding support resources to teachers and reforms in teacher education Ready to Teach Act (H.R. 2211, 2003), as just one set of examples. In a larger, integrative conceptual frame, schooling can be viewed as a community-level action aimed at promoting mental health and can be studied as such (Rutter & Maughan, 2002).

Challenges in Moving toward Integrative Scientific and Programmatic Efforts

The ways schools function at federal, state, and community levels to deliver preventive interventions to at-risk populations, their role in defining and measuring adaptive functioning and pathology, and the very specific role they play as a major provider of mental health services are so compelling that we might conclude that prevention science, developmental psychopathology, and educational, clinical, and school psychology strategically launched integrative science and practice initiatives related to school adaptation and schooling processes. This is far from the case, and strategic integrations of these overlapping fields are the exception rather than the rule. Rones and Hoagwood (2000) note:

> The inattention in the scientific literature, even at a descriptive level, to identifying types, intensities, dose, or quality of preventive treatment services in schools is surprising . . . it is surprising that so little attention has been given to the effectiveness of school programs targeted toward prevention, reduction, or treatment of mental health problems. (p. 223)

Even less attention is paid to the ways in which daily, routine interactions between teachers and children, or among peers, function as developmental assets or risks, or the ways in which school policies and procedures shape the value of such interactions on a day-to-day basis.

Implied in this quote is the absence of conceptual, research, and programmatic linkages between the education research, policy, and practice establishments and developmental psychopathology. Particularly from the perspective of research design and conceptualization, the overlap and integration of education science and developmental psychopathology is far from realized, thereby undermining a more sophisticated understanding of developmental process and outcome and the manner in which schooling intersects with and contributes to those processes and outcomes. Pianta (2003) argues that one reason for the gap between developmental research and theory and education is that developmental scientists have rarely ventured into school settings with the goal of understanding the dynamics of schools and the way they intersect with developmental processes. Unlike child care and afterschool settings, the nature, quality, and effects of which have been well described and studied *within* developmental frameworks (e.g., National Institute of Child Health and Human Development Early Child Care Research Network [NICHD ECCRN], 2002a), school settings have not been as fully integrated in developmental research frameworks and studies. Despite the importance of contextualism in developmental science (Cicchetti & Aber, 1998; Sameroff, 2000), too often schools are treated simplistically in developmental psychopathology research. They function as locations for gathering large samples of children, as contexts in which outcomes of interest can be assessed (often cheaply), or as sites onto which intervention techniques can be grafted or applied. For their part, educational researchers and theorists have developed sophisticated understandings of schools as complex, multilevel settings, but have yet to fully integrate into that understanding an equally sophisticated understanding of human development, instead relying on outdated or oversimplified stage theories or conditioning as explanations of change and growth (see Meisels's 1999 critique of readiness definitions) or focusing exclusively on narrow conceptualizations of functioning such as is reflected in standardized test performance. The lack of full incorporation of school settings into developmental frameworks is reflected in developmental psychopathology's struggle with three challenges: (1) understanding the wide variation in implementation of standardized mental health or behavioral interventions, (2) including schooling processes in longitudinal studies, and (3) understanding how reliance on informant-based outcome assessments hold potential for misinterpretations and their reification.

Moving from Programs to Processes

Although developmental psychopathologists have arguably made great headway in identifying key ingredients of school settings that, when systematically altered, can provide preventive supports for children (Greenberg et al., 2001), it is also the case that if such efforts are to be realized in terms of reaching children in need on a widespread basis, then attention to the basic processes of schooling and the infusion of clinical trial-derived knowledge into those processes is key (Greenberg et al., 2001; Rones & Hoagwood, 2000). In the academic arena, this progression is evident in the shifting of attention over the past decade from a search for evidence-based curriculum, to a focus on processes related to implementation of curriculum, to recent calls for research on teacher training mechanisms that support high-quality implementation (IES, 2004a). This is a movement from program to process.

In conclusions drawn from their comprehensive review of school-age (and mostly school-based) prevention efforts, Greenberg et al. (2001) noted the need to focus attention on qualities of the school environment that moderate intervention effects and account for the high levels of interindividual variability in response to standardized clinical trial interventions. Understanding and ultimately harnessing factors related to program or practice *implementation* (another term for interindividual variability) is a serious chal-

lenge to developmental psychopathologists' intervention and prevention work. Large amounts of accrued evidence suggest that even the most well-described, manualized, standardized, scientifically based programs are enacted in practice in ways that vary widely from child to child and classroom to classroom (e.g., Greenberg et al., 2001). This phenomenon could be responded to as a source of error in evaluation studies, as an obstacle to delivering mental health resources to children, or as an aspect of the context into which interventions are being inserted that warrants attention in its own right. This last response is consistent with the movement from programs to processes that has occurred in some domains of academic achievement in relation to renewed attention to teacher education.

Not surprisingly, Rones and Hoagwood (2000) conclude that there is so little exploration in clinical trial research of the quality of, and factors related to, implementation, that it greatly impedes the provision of supportive services to children. They extend this position into a call for research on implementation that fully integrates mental health intervention program content into general classroom curriculum and processes. Roeser, Eccles, and Sameroff (2000, p. 466) extend the linkage between developmental studies and education even further when arguing, with respect to understanding middle school effects, that the need is for research "linking the study of adolescents' experience, motivation, and behavior in school with the study of their teachers' experience, motivation, and behavior at school." Such a perspective directly addresses the interindividual variability observed in standardized clinical trial interventions by making variation in psychological and behavioral processes of the child *and teacher* a legitimate focus of study.

The lack of an integrative, process-focused research agenda related to socioemotional adaptation in schools and school effects is in part responsible for the often-reported conclusion from reviews of intervention and prevention programs that implementation processes account for significant variation in the efficacy of such efforts (Greenberg et al., 2001; Rones & Hoagwood, 2000). Implied in the conclusions drawn by Greenberg et al., in their comprehensive review of programs for preventing mental disorders in children, is the impression that if such programs are to go to "scale," then one of the key steps will be to establish mechanisms for implementation in the natural systems in which children come into contact with developmentally salient resources—primarily schools. To some degree, developmental psychopathologists have looked at schools as settings for application of knowledge derived from basic research rather than as settings for such basic research. To the extent that this remains the case, issues such as implementation will remain a chief impediment to the contribution of developmental psychopathology to education (and children's mental health) as well as the ways knowledge of development in schools can contribute to advancing developmental psychopathology. This stance calls for developmental psychopathologists to be closely involved in the next generation of school reform, the redesign of school settings, and the training of teachers (IES, 200a; Committee for Children, 2004). Penetration and cross-fertilization of education and developmental psychopathology, although compelling, advocated widely, and discussed thoroughly, is truly in the earliest stages of formation.

Assessing School Contexts in Developmental Research

Modeling the ways school experiences can add to, mediate, and moderate established trajectories of development and can formatively shape development in newly established domains (such as in peer or romantic relationships) allows for a more "sophisticated and comprehensive" understanding of development (Cicchetti & Aber, 1998). When it comes to studies of school-age outcomes (particularly in longitudinal follow-up studies), readers can refer to almost any recent issue of a developmentally oriented journal and find reports of fairly sophisticated modeling of school-age outcomes as a function of prior experience in home contexts or history of development prior to school (e.g., Brody, Kim, Murry, & Brown, 2004; Gutman, Sameroff, & Cole, 2003; Hill, Brooks-Gunn, & Waldfogel, 2003). However, it is rare for these reports to model experiences in school. Absent information on the school context and schooling processes, it is difficult to evaluate the legacy of early experience in light of the possibility that school experience mediates or moderates the effects of prior history or concurrent experience at home. Given the information available from short-term studies of school-age children that classroom processes contribute uniquely to school-age outcomes (e.g., Brody, Dorsey, Forehand, & Armistead, 2002; Howes et al., in press; NICHD ECCRN, 2004a, 2004b), not modeling such effects could lead to overestimating the linear, direct association between early experience (or early status) and later outcome.

When school experience is modeled in longitudinal follow-up studies, particularly those with information on child outcome or experience prior to school entry, results emerge that demonstrate both the power of schooling to moderate early experience (e.g., Christian, Bachnan, & Morrison, 2001; Howes et al., in press; Morrison & Connor, 2002) and the extent to which experiences in school add to

prior history (e.g., NICHD ECCRN, 2004b). Not surprisingly, the power of early development to establish stable trajectories (Gutman et al., 2003; Hill et al., 2003) is also evident in these studies in the legacy of early experience in determining later functioning (NICHD ECCRN, 2004b).

Although not widely available a decade ago, well-standardized and validated assessments of schooling exist for a range of constructs. Standardized observational methods for assessing elementary classroom environments have been developed as a consequence of their use in several large-sample studies (e.g., Christian et al., 2001; NICHD ECCRN, 2002c). These assessments capture teacher behaviors and aspects of classroom climate related to social and academic functioning of children at both a global level and in terms of discrete behaviors and classroom conditions. Child and teacher report measures of classroom climate, school climate, teacher behavior, teacher-child relationships, and quality of peer relations and peer climate all have been developed and are used quite widely and efficiently in many research programs focused on schooling (e.g., Battistich, Solomon, Watson, & Schaps, 1997; Brody et al., 2004; Pianta et al., 2003; Roeser et al., 2000; Wentzel, 2002). Integrating these methodologies, conceptually and functionally, into programs of longitudinal research on development is another step advancing interdisciplinarity and integration.

The Determinants of Informant-Based Metrics

Informant-based assessments of behavioral and mental health outcomes are the most widely used indicators in developmental psychopathology research and clinical practice. Yet, their results can be misinterpreted because of inattention to how such ratings reveal (unexamined) combinations of child, informant, and setting characteristics (Kraemer et al., 2003). Meta-analyses as well as individual studies regularly report the association between teacher and parent report (the most commonly used informants) to be low, in the range of .25 (see Achenbach, McConaughy, & Howell, 1987; Kraemer et al., 2003). Rates of children showing elevated profiles across both school and other contexts are very low, and lower than rates showing problems in one setting only (e.g., Konold, Hamre, & Pianta, 2003). Methodological work suggests that informants in different settings are better-suited for assessment of some constructs than others, with mothers contributing less informant-related variance to assessment of internalizing behavior and teacher reports of externalizing behavior less influenced by informant factors than mother reports (Konold & Pianta, 2004; Kraemer et al., 2003).

Informant differences in the reporting of children's problem behavior are not in dispute; the issue is how they are interpreted. From a purely psychometric perspective, this lack of correspondence can be considered a function of error on the part of informants in both settings and ratings that result in imperfect estimates of a child trait. Cross-informant inconsistencies might also be interpreted in light of one informant's being accorded gold standard status with regard to a particular characteristic, either on empirical grounds (Kraemer et al., 2003) or for theoretical reasons. Or, the lack of correspondence between informants' ratings could be interpreted to reflect the contextualized nature of the behavior being rated and bring into focus how contextual and informant characteristics shape these behaviors (NICHD ECCRN, 2004b) as well as the informants' perceptions of those behaviors (Konold & Pianta, 2004). Because of the exceptionally widespread use of informant ratings in developmental psychopathology research, it is critical that these three interpretive strategies be examined more systematically (Kraemer et al., 2003) because of the potential for misinterpretation of results.

Schools are particularly well-organized to address this issue because one informant (the teacher) can provide ratings for a fairly large number of children who are under his or her supervision and with whom he or she shares no genetic relation (addressing a confound in parent-child ratings). Nested-design studies can then be conducted in which variance in judgments of problem behavior can be attributed to teacher, child, and school characteristics (e.g., Bryant et al., 2003; Hamre, Mashburn, Downer, & Pianta, 2004), and the dynamics of these associations can be modeled over time, or careful modeling of informant, situation, and trait effects can be undertaken (Kraemer et al., 2003). When these studies also assess the range of beliefs, affects, and experiences of teachers that contribute to their judgments, a more sophisticated understanding of how informant ratings reflect combinations of child, rater, and setting attributes, absent genetic confounds, would result. As implied in Roeser, Eccles, and Sameroff (1998), assessing characteristics of *teachers* that contribute to their judgments about and behavior with children is a critical missing piece of understanding school process effects, knowledge of which could transform how implementation challenges are addressed and conceptualized in school-based mental health programs (Rones & Hoagwood, 2000). Because of the prominence of informant-based rating scales in developmental psychopathology (and ultimately in clinical practice), the need to address these issues is imperative.

Summary

In sum, developmental psychopathology and education science have many points of mutual interest for strategic exploitation and exploration. For developmental psychopathologists, challenges in understanding the mechanisms of and responses to clinical trial interventions, implementing mental health programs at scale, discovery of contextual effects and moderating influences on behavioral and mental health outcomes, disaggregation of genetic confounds in analyses of contextual effects, and a more sophisticated interpretation of informant-based outcome assessments can be at least partially accomplished through integrative research designs and conceptual models that openly include school contexts in full form. For educators, research on important questions about the relative weight of schooling and the home environment, the value-added quality of schooling, or policy-related concerns about program effectiveness and development can be greatly enhanced by developmentally informed studies.

MODELS AND CONCEPTS TO GUIDE INTEGRATION AND INTERDISCIPLINARITY

The challenges facing integrative linkages between developmental psychopathology and schooling have roots in the historical, conceptual, and political forces that shape how disciplines grow up in different traditions of inquiry and institutionalization. The end result of these forces is a contemporary situation in which a variety of phenomena that ought to be of common interest and encourage common dialogue and discussion among developmentalists and educators (such as those outlined in the previous section) are often viewed through different conceptual, analytic, and theoretical lenses. As noted by Sameroff (2000), these forces coalesce to form dichotomizations that obstruct interdisciplinarity and integrative science (Towne & Hilton, 2004).

Disciplinary and mission-related dichotomies are not unique to developmental psychology and education; these barriers impede scientific progress in a variety of disciplines (Sameroff, 2000). Recent years have witnessed these dichotomies yielding to metatheoretical principles of integration and interdisciplinarity. Developmental psychopathology is one of the best examples of the use of these principles to advance integrative science, exemplified in research programs linking biological and behavioral systems such as studies of gene-environment interactions (e.g.,

McGuire et al., 1999; Waldman et al., 1998), associations between hormonal and behavioral regulation (Quas, Murowchick, Bensadoun, & Boyce, 2002; Watamura, Donzella, Alwin, & Gunnar, 2003), and neurobiological function and psychopathology (Nelson & Bloom, 1997). In contrast, developmental psychopathologists' measurement, sampling, and analysis of developmentally salient parameters (particularly contextual features) in school settings lag behind parallel efforts related to biological processes. This condition limits understanding of the nature and course of variation in emotional and behavioral disturbance (Rutter & Silberg, 2002; Sameroff, 2000) in much the same way as nature-nurture dichotomization may have constrained understanding of biobehavioral processes in development.

Systems and Development in School Settings: Two Useful Principles

General systems theory has been the primary conceptual paradigm in human development for at least the past 2 decades (see Lerner, 1998; Sameroff, 1995, 2000) and is responsible, in part, for the integration of behavioral and biological science noted earlier. Although the living systems perspective is foundational to developmental psychopathology, it has not yet penetrated educational research in anywhere near as complete a manner (for discussion of this issue, see Good & Weinstein, 1986; Pianta, 1999; Roeser et al., 2000). Dynamic, living systems models, operationalized through developmentally informed research in school settings (e.g., Lyon, 2002; Pianta, 1999; Roeser et al., 1998), are by far the exception in education science, which tends to be dominated by econometrics (Grissmer, Flanagan, Kawata, & Williamson, 2000; Rivkin, Hanushek, & Kain, 2000; Towne & Hilton, 2004), in which developmental and interactive processes are not modeled, and qualitative ethnographic approaches in which population estimates are eschewed in the pursuit of process description. One of the values of developmentally informed concepts, design, and analysis for education is a methodological and conceptual framework that integrates large-scale quantitative analysis of structure-outcome associations with attention to mechanisms and processes (e.g., NICHD ECCRN, 2002c; Towne & Hilton, 2004), an approach reflected in new funding initiatives related to school readiness interventions (Bryant et al., 2003) and clinical trial research in teachers' professional development (IES, 2004a).

Two principles of systems theory are particularly germane to bridging school effects and school adaptation with developmental psychopathology. These principles—holistic units of analysis and multilevel co-action—are evident in work on schooling focusing on relationships between teachers and children (Birch & Ladd, 1997; Hamre & Pianta, 2001; Ladd & Burgess, 1999), early intervention with high-risk preschoolers (e.g., C. T. Ramey & Ramey, 1998), school-based research and interventions with children at risk for aggressive/disruptive behavior problems (Boyle et al., 1999; Catalano et al., 2003; Greenberg et al., 2001; Ialongo et al., 1999; Walker, Stiller, Severson, Feil, & Golly, 1998), and work focusing on developmental change as a function of transitions into elementary school (Brody et al., 2002, 2004; Pianta & Cox, 1999), middle school (Roeser et al., 1998, 2000), and high school (Felner, Favazza, Shim, & Brand, 2001).

Holistic Units of Analysis

A central issue in the study of school effects and in understanding patterns of adaptation in schools is selection of the appropriate unit of analysis. Lerner (1998) emphasizes that the causes of development are *relationships* among systems and their components, not actions in isolation. With regard to schooling, a focus on relations and interactions can take two forms, one in which the goal is to understand school effects on development in a particular domain, and another for understanding patterns of adaptive and maladaptive functioning across domains.

With regard to schooling effects, a relational unit is consistent with the perspective advanced by Bronfenbrenner and Morris (1998) when they argue that the primary engine of development is proximal process—interactions that take place between the child and context(s) over extended periods of time. There are several examples of research programs that focus on relational, holistic units of analysis in schools, and the yield of these research programs for understanding the role of proximal process for both social and cognitive/achievement development has been substantial.

As one comprehensive example of a focus on relational units, Noam and Hermann's (2002) school-based prevention approach emphasizes the primary importance of a relational unit as a focus of intervention and of evaluation (Noam et al., 2001). This intervention aims to establish for each child a multifunction relationship with a "coach/mentor," based explicitly on the rationale that such relationships function as resources and resilience mechanisms in counteracting the effects of risk mechanisms. Furthermore, in their assessment of the implementation and effects of these ideas in classrooms, Noam and colleagues' work also assesses process and outcome at the relational level. Thus, the success of the intervention is not only measured in terms of academic achievement tests or problem behaviors but in terms of the child's use of the interventionist and qualities of the child's interactions with other relational and informational resources in the school. The results of this work corroborate the idea that both school adaptation and school effects can be understood, assessed, and altered through a focus on relational processes and units.

As an example of the distinction between relational and decontextualized units of analysis, Hamre and Pianta (2001) examined teachers' perceptions of their relationships with children in kindergarten and the consequences of these perceptions for understanding and predicting disciplinary infractions in the school setting. It was hypothesized that teachers' perceptions of their relationships with children provided a more accurate and context-sensitive indicator of, on the one hand, the competence of the child in the classroom setting and, on the other, the affordance value of that setting reflected in the teachers' feelings about the child. When examining prediction from teacher-child relationships, Hamre and Pianta adjusted for these same teachers' ratings of the child's disruptive problem behavior and verbal ability, both decontextualized indicators of competence. Hamre and Pianta reported that when predicting achievement as well as disciplinary infractions at school some years later, kindergarten teachers' perceptions of relational negativity, not their ratings of problem behavior or verbal IQ, were by far the strongest predictor.

In this way, conceptualization of school adaptation in context-specific, relational terms appeared to tap processes more salient for predicting future functioning (in similar settings) than did a less contextualized assessment. One might make the same argument, in the area of peer relations and social development, for the value of sociometric procedures, in the sense that indices of popularity or rejection capture relational-level functioning in a specific context (social networks) and in so doing advance understanding and prediction of function in that setting in ways that decontextualized assessment of traits or behaviors does not (Gifford-Smith & Brownell, 2003).

The gain to be had from a focus on relational processes and units is not limited solely to social processes or social problems. Understanding academic success is also improved when conceptualizing the phenomena at the relational level. For example, in the education research literature, academic growth is more successfully modeled and predicted when information is available on the qualities and quantity of the child's attention to and engagement with specific forms of instruction that map onto their prior learning history rather than simply their exposure to instruction. Thus, it is not enough to know the child is receiving a certain amount or type of instruction that predicts, for

example, growth in literacy over the first-grade year; it is the child's *engagement* in learning activities that map onto prerequisite skills (Christian et al., 2001; Morrison & Connor, 2002).

In younger children, it has been shown that the value of instructional interactions can be reflected by the ways emotions, perceptions, and motivational processes activate and shape children's help-seeking behavior (Nelson-Le Gall & Resnick, 1998; Newman, 2000). In middle schoolers, it has been amply demonstrated that achievement growth is conditioned on an assortment of motivational and emotional factors that *interact* with what is offered in the classroom (Roeser et al., 1998). More specifically, for children in which normative developmental trends lead them to value autonomy, exploration, and a sense of identity, control-oriented discipline and competitive academic values tend to produce lower levels of motivation and achievement and higher levels of problem behavior in large part because of the mismatch between context and developmental forces—a relational, interactive mechanism. Thus, instruction, or stimulation, is something more than simply demonstration, modeling, and reinforcement assessed as inputs from a teacher, but is instead a complex, socially and psychologically mediated, bidirectional process, the understanding of which can be improved through developmental science (IES, 2004a; Towne & Hilton, 2004). From a somewhat different perspective, the effective dose of schooling inputs is not accurately characterized by program-level parameters such as time allotted to instruction, curriculum, or the type of program or intervention, but is reflected in the actual engagement of the child in the ingredients of these inputs, confirmation of the importance of implementation parameters (Greenberg et al., 2001; IES, 2004a).

It is also appropriate to discuss relational or holistic units when focusing on the various domains of development that intersect with experiences in school. Particularly in educational research, motor, cognitive, social, and emotional development are often treated as independent entities on parallel paths, influenced by practice in that specific domain, such as in studies linking the amount and quality of instruction in literacy with literacy performance (Morrison & Connor, 2002). Yet, when cross-domain associations are examined, they are not infrequently detected, such as when the level and nature of instruction a child receives in school affects emotional health assessed by mothers (NICHD ECCRN, 2004b). Because educational practice is so often designed to influence domains in isolation (e.g., phonological processing, mathematics computation, on-task behavior), it is easy for education science to reinforce the notion that developmental domains are best considered as separate units of adaptation and functioning rather than facets of integrated, global patterns of adaptation to broad developmental themes (Gambone et al., 2002; Sroufe & Rutter, 1984).

Because domains of development and subsystems of behavioral competencies are interconnected in more holistic organizations, a single educational practice can trigger or stimulate multiple domains, such as when instructional practice activates motivational and cognitive processes (Roeser et al., 1998). Therefore, conceptualizing, assessing, and documenting transactional influences of educational practices across multiple domains of functioning could be a key focus of cooperation between education and developmental scientists. Cross-domain overlap is so strong that Roeser et al. emphasize the need for "cataloguing the features of academic environments that impact, either positively or negatively, on both academic and emotional outcomes simultaneously" (p. 170). Because cross-domain linkage (or asymmetry) is somewhat familiar to developmental scientists (Steinberg & Morris, 2001), this is one area in which a developmental psychopathology perspective can advance educational research. Developmental psychopathologists interested in understanding schooling in relation to mental health and socioemotional adaptation may wish to focus attention as well on how functioning in these domains varies with academic skill and instructional experiences as much as with peer relations and social systems in the school.

Multilevel Co-Action

Schools are multilevel systems, and relational processes are evident both within and across levels. For developmentalists interested in multilevel interactions and transactions (e.g., Gottlieb & Halpern, 2002; Sameroff, 1995), schools can be a rich source of evidence. For example, although there is considerable evidence that child-teacher relationships alter trajectories of development in social and academic domains (see Pianta et al., 2003, for a review), it is also the case that the nature and qualities of child-teacher interactions and relationships and their effects on development are moderated by class size (NICHD ECCRN, 2004a), teacher mood and depression (Hamre & Pianta, 2004), and the nature and organization of schools (Battistich, Watson, Solomon, Lewis, & Schaps, 1999; Felner et al., 2001).

Similarly, multilevel, multisystem interactions are evident when school and school district policies about the age/grade of transition to secondary schools interacts with school climate, procedures around accountabil-ity and discipline, and students' prior experience and attitudes and expectations to affect their performance in the new school (Eccles, Early, Fraser, Belansky, & McCarthy, 1997; Gambone et al., 2002). Multilevel co-action (Gottlieb & Halpern, 2002) is also apparent in the interaction between policies concerning age of entry to school and the nature and quality of instruction that children receive in specific domains (Morrison & Connor, 2002; Stipek, 2002). From a less process-focused perspective, multilevel interactions are evident in the class of education policy studies focused on the association between policy parameters (class size, finance, teacher credentialing) and child achievement outcomes (Grissmer et al., 2000; Rivkin et al., 2000). It is routine in investigations of these issues, often using large survey data sets, that unique variance is attributed to each of many levels—state, district, school, classroom/teacher, and peers (Rivkin et al., 2000)—although moderating and mediating proximal processes and mechanisms are not often modeled in such studies.

These two principles of general systems theory—holistic units of analysis and multilevel co-action—inform a body of work on "developmental interactionism" (Magnusson & Stattin, 1998) that focuses attention on issues of goodness of fit, relationships, mediation and moderation of effects, and related relational constructs (Boyce et al., 1998). These principles advance a more sophisticated and comprehensive (Cicchetti & Aber, 1998) picture of the dynamics and motivation of behavioral change and adaptation than do the traditional maturationist, stage theory, or behavioral conditioning paradigms typically used in education science (Good & Weinstein, 1986). These traditional theoretical paradigms stand as both obstacles to and opportunities for interdisciplinarity when developmental psychopathologists enter into and focus on education settings (Eccles, Wigfield, & Schiefele, 1998; Pianta, 1999).

Integrative, Interdisciplinary Models

The models used by investigators to approach research questions related to schooling and developmental psychopathology play a critical role in shaping findings and ultimately theory. Current conceptualizations tend to be limiting with regard to how they approach research in relation to educational practice and in terms of cross-disciplinary efforts within research programs focused on schooling and development. Moving beyond the limits imposed will require different conceptual frameworks that are more integrative and comprehensive.

Moving beyond Research/Practice Dichotomies

As noted earlier, one of the more serious conceptual impediments to a fuller realization of the mutual benefits of interdisciplinarity in education and developmental science is the tendency toward dichotomization within and across these disciplines (Sameroff, 2000). The research/practice polarity is by far the dichotomy through which developmental psychopathology and education have been most often linked and kept apart. Research/practice linkages between developmental research and education are typically centered on instruction and academic learning and only recently have focused on social interactions, peer relations, problem behavior, and psychopathology (e.g., Elias, Zins, Graczyk, & Weissberg, 2003; Evertson & Weinstein, in press; Gifford-Smith & Brownell, 2003; Greenberg et al., 2001; Hoagwood & Johnson, 2003; Weissberg & Greenberg, 1998) and are most often reflected in discussions of intervention implementation and fidelity.

The dichotomy of the research/practice framework is embodied in two of Renninger's (1998, p. 212) assumptions about schools and development:

1. If more educators (teachers, teacher educators, administrators, policymakers, parents, etc.) were knowledgeable about developmental theory and research, and had tools to think about classroom decision making that were informed by what is known about how students learn, research in developmental psychology would radically change the mainstream of educational practice.
2. If more researchers were knowledgeable about educational practice—the strengths and needs of teachers and their working about students, and invested time working with educators to consider the implications and directions of their research efforts, research could contribute more directly to practice.

From one point of view, these two assumptions advance the goal of integration and counter the dichotomization of developmental research on the one hand and educational practice on the other. Yet, at the risk of making an oversimplified interpretation, these assumptions could also lead to viewing theory and research as the province of developmental psychology and practice as isomorphic with education—what goes on in schools to change developmental outcomes.

The regular, naturalistic, instructional and social interactions among children and between children and teachers in a school setting (Pianta, 1999; Roeser et al., 1998) are no more "applied" or reflective of "practices" and therefore the province of education than are interactions between children and their mother (Sroufe, 1996) or between peers (Gifford-Smith & Brownell, 2003). In fact, viewing interactions in school settings as the proper focus of education, and the programmatic, standardized interactions that take place in intervention trials as the focus of developmental psychopathology, is one reason implementation is such a challenge to prevention/intervention research (e.g., Greenberg et al., 2001; Rones & Hoagwood, 2000). This research/practice dichotomy will continue to plague efforts to extend developmental science unless it is resolved.

That child-teacher interactions have an explicitly directed, intentional component should make them even more interesting as a focus of developmentally oriented research (IES, 2004b; Morrison & Connor, 2002; Roeser et al., 1998; Rutter & Maughan, 2002). It would seem that the agents of such interactions (e.g., teachers) would be as interesting a focus as the agents of mother-child or peer interactions (Pianta et al., 2003). As an example of work attempting to understand the parameters regulating teachers' behavior under natural conditions, Hamre and Pianta (2004) recently demonstrated that teachers' self-reported depressive symptoms predicted their harsh and withdrawn behavior toward children, and teachers' sensitive behavior was predicted by both their representations of relationships with children (Stuhlman & Pianta, 2001) and their experiences of unresolved loss (Zeller & Pianta, 2004). Further extension of this line of thinking could lead to research on the development of individuals who assume roles as educators (teachers, principals), particularly the experiential, attitudinal, and training-related mechanisms that shape their behaviors with and decisions about children over time (Rimm-Kaufman, Storm, Sawyer, Pianta, & La Paro, 2004). The science of human interaction and behavioral development, and the conceptual paradigms and methods it uses, are directly applicable to the interactions in school settings that contribute to the behavior and development of children and adults.

From a contextualist framework, schools, like families, are social and physical settings in which processes of social interaction, teaching, and engagement in activity contribute to individual (and group) patterns of growth, change, and adaptation. *Integrative* contextualism builds on the general contextualist framework (Cicchetti & Aber, 1998) by explicitly directing attention not only at features of the context but also at those aspects of developmental process that *cut across* context and give meaning to experience. When viewing schools from this perspective, overarching questions about mechanisms and processes in development can be examined using many of the same conceptual and methodological insights that have been applied (and acquired) in the study of development in other settings, such as families and child care environments.

The integrative contextualist framework depicted in Figure 13.1 is entirely consistent with the type of multilevel model of development in context that is a well-accepted feature of developmental psychopathology (Bronfenbrenner & Morris, 1998; Cicchetti & Dawson, 2002; Sameroff, 1995, 2000). In the conceptualization of developmental ecologies shown in Figure 13.1, school effects and school adaptation are fully integrated within the range of contexts that shape development, similar to what is posited in most ecological models. However, this integrative model differs from most depictions of ecological frameworks in at least one important respect. The different forms of process or activity (structural, proximal, self-regulatory, biobehavioral) that influence or form the basis of outcome trajectories are explicitly threaded through settings in such a way that process is continuous across settings rather than bounded by settings.

This emphasis on continuity of processes *across* settings, in contrast to process as *bounded within* settings, opens up ways to examine and test aspects of the general ecological-developmental model in schools as the settings of interest. For example, in generalized form, structural features of settings often operate as regulators of proximal process. In the same way that in family-focused research one might examine income or family size or parents' educational level as resource dimensions affecting parental sensitivity, in schools one might focus on per pupil expenditure, school size, or teachers' certification or experience levels as they relate directly and indirectly to child outcomes and to proximal process mechanisms such as the quality of instruction (e.g., NICHD ECCRN, 2004a). At the proximal process level, in research focused on family adaptation or family effects, child-parent relationships and interactions, parents' psychological attributes and development, sibling relationships, and peer relationships are modeled as part of the ecology. In school settings, proximal processes related to teacher-child relationships and interactions, classroom social and instructional qualities, collaborative grouping of peers, and peer sociometric status are also proximal agents of change that likely involve many of the same mechanisms as the corresponding family-based proximal processes (e.g., Gambone et al., 2002), but they have yet to be examined with this cross-validation of general principles in mind.

To elaborate, instead of positing that relational mechanisms and processes that occur between parents and children in home settings are separate or somehow different from relational processes that may be activated toward adults in child care or school settings, the model in Figure 13.1 posits that relational processes are activated and de-

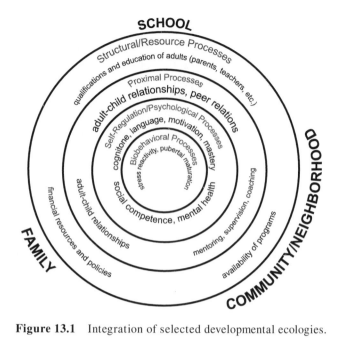

Figure 13.1   Integration of selected developmental ecologies.

velopmentally meaningful across ecologies. Adopting this perspective could lead to research on the conditions for activation, the nature, quality, and intensity of attachment experiences with adults across settings, or the developmental antecedents and consequences of various patterns of relational experience with adults in different settings (e.g., Stuhlman, 2003), that in turn could inform discussions about the relative uniqueness of experience with specific adults or the possibility of compensatory processes (O'Connor, 2003). In one such study (Stuhlman, 2003), cluster analytic approaches applied to adult-child relationship observations conducted in child care and family settings revealed that person-focused descriptions that integrated experience across child care and home settings were more robust predictors of later outcomes than setting-specific indicators modeled additively.

To continue, the processes by which self-regulation mechanisms develop and function have been widely studied in relation to family effects and patterns of adaptation in family settings. These mechanisms, involving linkages of cognitive, relational, motivational, emotional, and social processes, have been mostly examined in relation to family effects with behavioral adaptation in schools typically functioning as outcome indicators in follow-up studies. Similarly, normative biobehavioral processes related to temperament, stress reactivity, and pubertal development have received considerable attention related to developmental antecedents and sequelae in family settings. But biobehavioral development and self-regulatory processes are also relevant to understanding school adaptation and school effects (Quas et al., 2002; Watamura et al., 2003). For example, cortisol levels vary with prior experience in families (Quas et al., 2002) but also appear related to experiences during the school (or child care) day (Watamura et al., 2003) and interact with the peer network and quality of the child-teacher relationship in classroom settings (Little & Kobak, in press). In an elegant example of cross-context integration at the process level, Little and Kobak examined cortisol secretion of students as a function of the quality of their relationship with the teacher in special education classrooms for children with emotional disturbances. High levels of secretion were evident for these students, on average, indicating the stressful nature of the setting. However, the students sharing a close, emotionally supportive relationship with the teacher showed significantly lower levels of cortisol than did their classmates. In this study, adult-child relationship quality and biobehavioral regulation were examined not in family environments but in classroom settings, and results revealed mechanisms nearly identical to those revealed by research done in family settings.

Moving beyond Disciplinary Boundaries

Examples of interdisciplinarity involving developmental psychopathology and education are manifest in interagency research initiatives related to school readiness and early literacy (e.g., Lyon, 2002), teacher professional development (IES, 2004a), the recent integrative focus on positive youth development and transitions from middle childhood to high school (Eccles & Gootman, 2002; Gambone et al., 2002), research on juvenile offenders and psychopathology (Gottfredson, 2001), and research training initiatives (Towne & Hilton, 2004) that include schools and schooling as a central, not peripheral, focus.

Perhaps one of the best examples of the value of interdisciplinarity for the generation of new knowledge is the area of early literacy described in Lyon's (2002) summary of 2 decades of basic research on language development, phonological processes, cognitive and neurological mechanisms, instructional processes, and learning to read. The recent report by the National Reading Panel (NRP, 2000), in which consensus recommendations could be made concerning the value, importance, and even necessity of direct exposure of children to phonological-level information in written language, could not have been made without the focus of multiple research traditions, from a variety of disciplines, reflected in Lyon's analysis. In short, real progress on identifying basic developmental mechanisms in early literacy and the contextual conditions that activate,

stimulate, and foster growth in those mechanisms has occurred, largely as a function of efforts that crossed disciplines. Interestingly, the challenge for the next decade in literacy initiatives is how to support and ensure children's exposure to experiences at home and in schools that foster these processes, illustrating the importance of examining basic processes across multiple contexts, as in Figure 13.1. On the other hand, it continues to remain the case that even context-sensitive research, for example on delinquency (e.g., Scaramella, Conger, Spoth, & Simons, 2002), may not fully capture how schools influence peer-related experiences of at-risk youth by the way they group children or respond to individual differences.

Notable among studies that do achieve some measure of integration across several ecological levels and psychological processes is the NICHD Study of Early Child Care and Youth Development, which has followed a design strategy from inception of careful process-based assessments of key developmental settings and outcomes across multiple domains (NICHD ECCRN, 2001, 2002b, 2003). Originally designed as a careful and thorough examination of effects of child care on development, this study strategically captured structural and process dimensions of the home and child care settings to which the children were exposed in an effort to differentiate associations with developmental function and growth. As the more than 1,000 children enrolled in this prospective study moved on to school, developmentally sensitive observations of classroom settings in first, third, and fifth grades as well as child, peer, teacher, and principal report of the structural and proximal process qualities of the school environment and detailed assessments of child adjustment across multiple domains within that environment exemplified a fairly thorough integrative approach to contextualism. As ecologies of development expand as the participants move to high school, the study's focus includes experience in community activities, employment, and school and out-of-school settings as well as in families (NICHD ECCRN, 2003, 2004a).

A number of other integrative longitudinal studies have followed children from infancy into school or enrolled samples at the start of school and have included assessment of the school setting as part of their protocols (e.g., Alexander & Entwisle, 1988; Conduct Problems Prevention Research Group [CPPRG], 1999, 2002; Hill et al., 2003; Kellam, Ling, Merisca, Brown, & Ialongo, 1998; Morrison & Connor, 2002; C. T. Ramey et al., 2000; Sroufe, Carlson, Levy, & Egeland, 1999; Vitaro, Brendgen, Pagani, Tremblay, & McDuff, 1999) or at the onset of key developmental or school transitions (e.g., Eccles, Lord, & Roeser, 1996). Two very broad trends are suggested by this literature.

First, from the perspective of assessment and conceptualization, as the value of school settings is more completely assessed, particularly at the level of proximal process, a more complete picture of development in context emerges. Rather than models of linear effects of early experience, complex models emerge that describe how mechanisms of continuity and stability interact with stimulation and variation in experience (e.g., Sroufe et al., 1999; Steinberg & Morris, 2001; Vitaro et al., 1999). In these models, the school setting is an important (and underresearched) source of this variation (Morrison & Connor, 2002; Rutter & Maughan, 2002; Stevenson & Lee, 1990; Towne & Hilton, 2004; Vitaro et al., 1999). Second, when examining the broad, longitudinal patterns revealed by this work, particularly when including studies of development since birth, school effects appear fairly weak relative to home effects in early elementary school. But as the actions of peer networks, pubertal development, and increasing autonomy and selfhood emerge and interact with differentiating school contexts, the child becomes a critical active agent in determining the nature and value of school-related experience (Roeser et al., 1998; Steinberg & Morris, 2001). Learning more about how opportunity structures and assets in schools interact with self-determination remains an important goal for interdisciplinary collaborations. To accomplish such collaborations, conceptual models, research designs, and assessment protocols are needed to enable investigators to strategically sample school environments and adaptation with the same sophistication as they approach peer or family settings.

MULTILEVEL TRANSACTIONAL PROCESSES AND SCHOOL ADAPTATION

One reason for Rutter and Maughan's (2002) conclusions regarding the lack of progress in understanding school effects and school adaptation is that schools are complex—in many ways, more complex than families, or perhaps even child care settings. They involve levels of analysis that challenge conceptual and analytic models; the school setting changes year to year, month to month, day to day, and often within days; and the potential social influences (peers, teachers, other adults), instructional influences (teaching styles, curriculum, subject matter), and opportunities available to children can shift rapidly and be very hard to track and model. This complexity offers opportunity (as discussed earlier) as well as obstacles to developmental psychopathologists. In this section, attention turns to describing and mapping school settings as they intersect with development and presenting in more detail those aspects of

school settings that may be of most interest to developmental psychopathologists.

Schools: Dynamic, Multilevel Settings for Development

Eccles and Roeser (1998) apply the general ecological model to the study of development in school settings and posit nested layers related to (1) district policy and resource; (2) school-level climate, policy, and practices; (3) classroom environment, including instruction and attributes of teachers and peers; and (4) child-level factors related to motivation, ability, and socioemotional characteristics. Within these levels, Eccles and Roeser discuss the variety of specific agents that interact with one another to affect child outcomes. In particular, they attend to the dynamic interactions that take place within and across layers. Additional ideas about the study of school contexts come from Boyce et al. (1998), who present five propositions about context using a definition of context as inherently bidirectional and meaning-based. Boyce et al. emphasize the need to attend to the dynamic changes that take place in settings across time and the additive/mediated/moderated influences that features of these settings have on development. The consensus picture that emerges from these models is of school (and other settings) as dynamic, multidimensional, multilayered systems, the effects of which on development cannot be understood or modeled in simple linear, additive fashion. These broad principles are outlined next.

Schools Are Multilayered Settings

It is widely recognized that school settings reflect several layers of structural and process features that reciprocally interact to affect child outcomes and adaptation. School policies and practices are highly regulated by states (Berliner & Biddle, 1995) and in turn influence school-level structure, organization (e.g., Felner et al., 2001), and climate (Battistich et al., 1999). These more proximal processes affect and are affected by classroom-level processes such as peer networks or teacher beliefs (Brophy, 1998; Evertson & Weinstein, in press). At the same time, it is well-known through intervention research that attempts to alter classroom processes such as management or instruction are constrained by district- or school-level factors such as funding, staff resources, and even the physical facilities (Darling-Hammond, 1997; Fashola & Slavin, 1997; Felner et al., 2001). Likewise, children's achievement motivation, a child-level factor, is influenced by qualities of the classroom, such as instruction, and this association is further moderated by school-level beliefs and practices about competition, control, and support (e.g., Eccles et al., 1996, 1997; Roeser et al., 2000).

Boyce et al. (1998) discuss the difference between structural and functional aspects of contexts and identify the need to attend to interactions among structural and functional, or process, features. Although the association between structure and process has been a focus of developmentalists' research on family and child care contexts (NICHD ECCRN, 2002c), there are fewer developmentally informed studies of the associations between structural variables such as pupil-teacher ratio and process features such as instructional interactions and student engagement (Eccles & Roeser, 1998; NICHD ECCRN, 2002a, 2002b, 2002c). However, when classroom process has been observed in developmentally oriented studies, classroom interaction, student engagement, and social and academic outcomes have been shown to differ as a function of structural features such as pupil-teacher ratio (Blatchford, Goldstein, Martin, & Browne, 2002; Blatchford, Moriarty, Edmonds, & Martin, 2002; NICHD ECCRN, 2004a), but the associations are complex (discussed later).

In an elegant example of demonstrating the distinction between classroom and individual levels of experience in schools, Kellam et al. (1998) demonstrated that the positive effects of a first-grade preventive intervention on subsequent aggressive behavior in middle school was moderated by the level of overall aggressive behavior among children in the first-grade classroom. Thus, the long-term effects of this intervention on individual first graders were in part conditioned by factors at the classroom level. These illustrations from the class size and prevention literatures confirm the widespread agreement that school effects and schooling processes are best understood in studies using a multilayered systems model that emphasizes the possibilities for moderation and nested effects (Howes et al., in press).

School Settings Are Multidimensional

A central issue in studies of proximal process effects on development is the specificity of effects. To use a more familiar example, can the effects of mother-child relationships on development be attributed largely to the effects of a global dimension of mothering such as sensitivity on a broad range of outcomes, including cognitive and emotional functioning (see NICHD ECCRN, 2002a), or are there more differentiated links between specific aspects of mothering (such as emotional warmth) and specific child outcomes (such as positive mood)? The same issue is present in the study of proximal processes in child care settings, when global quality is the focus, and in schools, particu-

larly in relation to classroom climate and whether effects are best detected through global indicators or specific features of the setting (e.g., Morrison & Connor, 2002).

In a recent example of the multidimensionality of school settings, two dimensions consistently emerge from factor analysis of classroom observations: instructional support and emotional support (NICHD ECCRN, 2002c; Pianta & La Paro, 2003; Pianta, La Paro, Payne, Cox, & Bradley, 2002). More important, it has been shown that these two dimensions to some extent predict differentially children's social and academic outcomes. For example, when evaluated in the same prediction model, instructional support for learning predicts achievement outcomes to a significantly greater degree than emotional support predicts the same outcomes (Howes et al., in press). Alternatively, children's anxious behavior reported by mothers is predicted by the degree of structure and pressure in the classroom setting (NICHD ECCRN, 2004b) and higher levels of emotional support predict a very broad range of competencies, mostly social (Howes et al., in press). In fact, Morrison and Connor (2002) argue that the effects of schooling on development have to be modeled at the level of specific forms of input and resource that are matched to specific child abilities and skills. Thus, according to Morrison and Connor, it is not only necessary to conceptualize and measure the classroom setting (or school) in terms of specific aspects of the instructional or social environment, but also to gauge the effects of those experiences relative to how well they match the child's capacities and skill. In this view, school effects are predominantly in the form of interactions between specific inputs from the classroom and specific skills of the child. Morrison and Connor suggest that one reason for the lack of detected school effects in the literature (Rutter & Maughan, 2002) is that such effects have been estimated by global assessments and global conceptualizations of the potential inputs in the classroom setting rather than through designs and theories focused on specific features of settings.

School Settings Are Dynamic

A key aspect of the Boyce et al. (1998) conceptualization of contexts is their attention to the *dynamics* of how contexts change over time in the nature and quality of their effects of development. Boyce et al. emphasize that contexts broaden, deepen, differentiate, and become more specific in effects over time. *Differentiation* of the school context is seen in the increased subject matter compartmentalization of programming from elementary to middle to high school; the increasing number of teachers and other adults that interact with and are responsible for teaching children as they move through the school years; and the complex differentiation of the ways schools regulate peer interactions, interests, and competencies as children move to advanced grades in the form of interest-specific clubs, athletic programs, and leadership opportunities. As the child's experiences in school are increasingly driven by the match between the child's interests and motivations and the quality and availability of such opportunities, the effect of schooling *deepens and individualizes.* Particularly as the child becomes an increasingly active agent in seeking and drawing value from these experiences (Boyce et al., 1998), the salience of school as a setting increases. Thus, we see reports from national surveys in which high school youth describe school as a setting in which valuable relationships with adults occur, but that the nature of these relationships differs as a function of the pattern of the child's involvement in school—in one case a coach, in another a club advisor, in another a school counselor (see Gambone et al., 2002).

Pianta et al. (2003) drew a conclusion consistent with this view of the school setting as dynamic in terms of teacher-student relationships. In this review of the literature on relationships from kindergarten through 12th grade, it was apparent that through the elementary school years, the child was a far less active agent in establishing and determining the effects of relationships, with main effects of teacher-reported relationship quality the predominant form of association with child outcomes. As children entered middle school, this pattern changed considerably; the nature and quality of child-teacher relationships was far more a function of the child's (or teacher's) efforts to actively select and maintain these relationships based on mutual goals and understandings, and the effects of child-teacher relationships were increasingly evident when risk factors were active—a developmental shift from mildly promotive to more active protective influence (Rutter, 1987).

Schools Are Affected by External Demands and Macroregulations

As is also the case with the Eccles and Roeser (1998) model, Boyce et al. (1998) emphasize that contextual parameters that regulate individual development (and group behavior) also shift in response to external demands, what Sameroff (1995, 2000) would argue are macroregulations. An assortment of macroregulations regularly take place in schooling, and as has been discussed (Berliner & Biddle, 1995; NCES, 2003), the existence of such shifts in policy or practice in school settings afford developmentalists numerous opportunities to examine questions concerning transactional influences.

Aspects of schooling in which considerable macroregulation is evident are the increasing dominance of academic standards assessment (Berliner & Biddle, 1995; NCES, 2003) and discipline policies of zero tolerance for weapons and illegal substances (Noam et al., 2001). In both of these shifts, school settings have defined what is adaptive and maladaptive in relation to children's academic functioning and behavior, and a prescribed set of procedures have been put in place for schools to use in responding to children who deviate from expectations. These regulations have had profound effects on the nature of children's school experiences. In addition, policy shifts in relation to class size, student assessment, legal age for dropping out of school, retention, and requirements for experiences like summer school and tutoring have all been altered in a variety of states in response to the federal- and state-mandated attention to accountability. In nearly all these instances, policy shifts have in turn had repercussions (mostly unexamined) for process-level shifts in classrooms and schools that transform the nature of children's experiences in those settings.

For example, although 10 years ago few, if any, states (or school divisions) articulated specific performance standards for children at any grades, for the high school class of 2005 in Virginia and an assortment of other states, graduation will be determined by whether the youth passes a series of standardized tests (see Berliner & Biddle, 1995, for an extensive discussion of high-stakes testing). In New York, the Regents' examination, which was at one time a feature of college-track students' careers, is now required of all graduating seniors. The macroregulatory effects of the accountability movement has had effects on schooling experiences that extend into prekindergarten years: changes such as reductions in recess and lunch periods, increased usage of basic skills curricula and teaching methods, increased stress reported among teachers and teacher turnover, and introduction of state laws and regulations lowering the age at which children can legally drop out of school (Berliner, 2004). For the most part, these effects have been documented in the media and qualitative accounts and have received much less attention in developmental research despite the opportunity they present for studying multilayered effects of regulation on development.

One could easily recognize in these macroregulations numerous opportunities to examine variations in school experience (e.g., changes in dropout ages; shifts in the availability of unstructured time with peers in school) consistent with developmental psychopathology's interests in factors that alter the trajectory of individual and group patterns of adaptation. To the extent, for example, that unstructured time with peers is a context for negotiating and practicing positions in the social network, or the formation of cliques or crowds (Gifford-Smith & Brownell, 2003; Steinberg & Morris, 2001), elimination of such opportunities places a constraint on this developmental phenomenon. Likewise, to the extent that school is a context supporting resilience processes (Felner et al., 2001; Noam & Hermann, 2002; Noam et al., 2001; Pianta, 1999; Roeser et al., 2000), easing dropout requirements potentially undermines these processes and their effects, but such effects may also be moderated by the child's goals and skills. By reflecting the multilayered nesting of processes that regularly vary within or across school settings, developmentally informed research designs allow for evaluation of the dynamics of contextual effects that can be difficult to model in settings that are less exposed to such shifts.

Effects of School Settings Are Meaning-Based

Boyce and colleagues (1998) emphasize that attempts to model the effects of a setting on development must acknowledge the meaning of that setting for the individual child. This highly individualized conceptualization of developmental "value" for experience is consistent with the focus on relational units of analysis derived from systems theory that was discussed earlier. The implication of conditioning the value of experience in a setting on the child's developmental *needs* is that to understand, for example, the effects of schools, one must have a theory of development that posits the developmental needs of the child vis-à-vis the school setting (Connell & Wellborn, 1991). In their review of whole-school restructuring projects and their consequences for student mental health, Felner et al. (2001, p. 3) concluded that often there is a "mismatch between the conditions and practices students encounter in grades K through 12 and the developmental needs, readiness, and capacities of students."

More than a decade ago, Connell and Wellborn (1991) advanced a theory in which three basic developmental needs are posited (competence, autonomy, and relatedness) and an approach in which schools' response to those needs can be assessed through child and teacher reports. This work has been extended in numerous ways, most recently in a National Academies of Science report on youth development (Eccles & Gootman, 2002), and summarized in the Gambone et al. (2002) integration. Common across all the conceptualizations is a focus on the child's emotional and social needs for connection and relationships

(to persons, goals, and institutions or groups), a need for safety and a structured physical environment, the need for competence and meaningfully challenging opportunities for building skills, and the need for linkage and integration among settings and experiences. Connell, Aber, and Walker (1995) conceptualize these needs in terms of productivity, connectedness, and a capacity to navigate and explore.

Paralleling the articulation of developmental needs and outcomes has been a focus on what contexts do to respond to those needs and enhance positive outcomes. Again summarizing across diverse efforts, Gambone et al. (2002) identify, in addition to basic shelter and health, four mechanisms of support and opportunity: (1) supportive relationships with adults and peers, (2) opportunities for meaningful involvement and membership, (3) challenging and engaging activities and learning experiences, and (4) safety. Rarely have schools been the focus of assays of these supports and opportunities, whether in individual community settings or at state levels. Yet classroom process research has identified instructional support and emotional support as dimensions of experience related to gains in functioning for elementary school children (Howes et al., in press; NICHD ECCRN, 2004b; Pianta et al., 2002), and the literature on middle and high schools has been largely responsible for the conclusions of Gambone et al. To the extent that such assays exist at the elementary school level, observations from several thousand classrooms showing the extent of variation in instructional and social resources and the generally low level of such resources (NICHD ECCRN, 2002b, 2005), should engage the interest of many developmental psychopathologists.

Pianta (1999) advanced a theory of developmental needs and schooling that concentrates on relationships with adults and regulation of basic developmental mechanisms related to cognitive and academic performance, social and emotional development, and self-regulation that is operationalized in schools in terms of child-teacher relationships and assessed using informant report, interviews, and observations. Ladd and colleagues (Birch & Ladd, 1998; Ladd & Burgess, 1999) have also emphasized relational and social needs of children and focused on relational style as an organizing construct for understanding children's access to resources in classrooms and schools. Consistent across the Pianta and Ladd approaches is a focus on instruction and mastery support, emotional security, autonomy/relatedness, motivational needs of the child, and the value of aspects of the proximal experience of the child in school settings.

A MODEL OF TRANSACTIONAL PROCESSES IN SCHOOL SETTINGS

Drawing on the principles of the general ecological model, the elaborations of that model for school settings (Eccles & Roeser, 1998; Pianta, 1999), and the contextualist principles described by Boyce et al. (1998), Figure 13.2 depicts a model of transactional developmental processes in school settings that incorporates a multilevel view of systems and subsystems, transactional effects within and across levels of the school ecology, and an assortment of macroregulational effects related to external forces such as school and grade transitions and accountability pressures as well as influences that could be related to genetic actions (Gottlieb & Halpern, 2002). The model emphasizes cross-level interactions as well as developmental time.

In the sections that follow, three aspects of this model of schooling—structural/resource effects, proximal processes, and macroregulational aspects of schooling—are discussed in some detail using descriptions of research illustrative of the model's focus. The primary intent of this discussion is to illuminate aspects of the school setting that can be the focus of developmental psychopathology inquiry and, in so doing, provide a means of more clearly and systematically linking developmental and education science. To the extent that the science of developmental psychopathology extends to applications intended to promote positive development, knowledge of school settings is absolutely critical to the success of such endeavors. In part, knowledge of school settings helps address the research/practice dichotomy and the problem of understanding variation in implementation and fidelity (Greenberg et al., 2001; Hoagwood & Johnson, 2003; IES, 2004a).

Additionally, knowledge of school settings is critical for a more sophisticated and comprehensive theory of development (Cicchetti & Aber, 1998). For example, developmental models now typically emphasize transactional process, but precious few of these effects are uncovered in empirical studies, in part due to limits in the ways such effects occur (and therefore can be studied systematically) and the limited range of variation that often exists in experiences of children. Schools provide ways of systematically exposing very large numbers of children who vary widely on characteristics of interest (e.g., ability, prior experience) to planned variations in experience (curriculum, etc.) that in turn vary in planned (and sometimes unexpected) ways across time. Further, examining how such variation and change in experience interact with variation and change in other important regulators of development (such as pubertal timing) opens up even more territory for important examination of transactional mechanisms. Thus, school settings have embedded within them countless opportunities for studying the transactional processes that theory posits but that remain difficult to identify. Kellam and colleagues (e.g., Kellam & Rebok, 1992) have argued that systematic implementation of intervention trials in school populations as well as exploitation of school policy, practice, and organization are fundamental strategies in developmental epidemiology. Systematic implementation of prevention trials have been suggested as strategies for uncovering developmental mechanisms (Howe, Reiss, & Yuh, 2002). In short, for a theoretical and conceptual framework that emphasizes development as a product of multisystem transactional activity, school settings provide opportunities for inquiry that allow for tests of fundamental principles.

Structural Policy and Resource Effects at Building and District Levels

This discussion illustrates two school-level features, one structural and one more process-focused: class size and

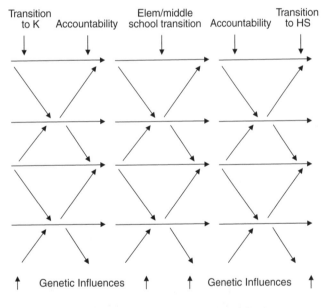

Figure 13.2 Transactional processes in school adaptation.

school climate/building organization and ethos. Although many more factors could be identified at this level (e.g., per pupil expenditures, grading and assessment practices), these will not be the focus of this discussion and readers are referred elsewhere. For example, demographic makeup of the district or building, leadership, school climate related to academic achievement and discipline, systematic student assessment, opportunities for staff training, and parent involvement (see Alexander & Entwisle, 1988; Newmann & Wehlage, 1995; Rutter et al., 1979) are also school-level features of some import. When teachers report high levels of support from school administrators and perceive these administrators to be strong leaders, children's achievement tends to be higher. Furthermore, discipline policies are a critical feature of the school environment as children transition to junior and senior high school, such that control-oriented policies (e.g., zero-tolerance policies) are related to lower levels of student motivation and achievement than are policies and practices that promote self-control, self-regulation, and cooperation (Noam et al., 2001; Roeser et al., 2000). School districts also vary in resources that affect children's outcomes, including per pupil expenditure, teacher experience, teacher salary, and teacher-pupil ratio, that are policy-relevant features of the school environment shown to relate to child outcomes (e.g., Gottfredson, 2001).

Class Size

Class size is one of the educational policy parameters receiving a lot of attention in the United States (e.g., Betts & Shkolnik, 1999; Ehrenberg, Brewer, Gamoran, & Willms, 2001; Finn & Achilles, 1999; Hanushek, 1999; Hoxby, 1998; Mosteller, 1995) and the United Kingdom (Blatchford, Goldstein, et al., 2002; Blatchford, Moriarty, et al., 2002). Evaluations of two class size initiatives concluded that lower class size was related to improved child outcomes (Finn, Gerber, Achilles, & Boyd-Zacharias, 2001; Krueger, 1999; Mosteller, 1995), with significant positive effects for lower class sizes on student achievement for nearly all grades tested, kindergarten through eithth (Finn & Achilles, 1999; Krueger, 1999; Nye, Hedges, & Konstantopoulos, 1999), and somewhat larger effects for children from disadvantaged households. The National Assessment of Educational Progress (NAEP) also shows that across districts and states, there is evidence to suggest that lower class size is associated with higher student performance (Grissmer et al., 2000). This finding is confirmed by evaluation of available data in Texas (Rivkin et al., 2000) and California (Class Size Reduction Research Consortium, 2001). Blatchford and colleagues' (Blatchford, Goldstein, et al., 2002; Blatchford, Moriarty, et al., 2002) work in En-

gland reports that lower class size is associated with improved child achievement (particularly in literacy), time on task, and enhanced teacher support for learning.

For the most part, social outcomes have not been examined in studies of class size (Ehrenberg et al., 2001), and little research links class size with observed classroom activities, practices, and processes (Blatchford, Moriarty, et al., 2002; NICHD ECCRN, 2004a; Pianta et al., 2002). In a recent comprehensive evaluation of the effects of class size on classroom process, children's social and academic outcomes in first grade, the NICHD Early Child Care Research Network presents results indicating the level of complexity and understanding that can be achieved when a developmental psychopathology model is applied to the study of educational problems and concerns. By adjusting outcome estimates for functioning prior to entry to school and a host of family, child, teacher, and school selection covariates, and having measures of ongoing process and classroom input to the child, this study examined class size and its effects on relative change in child outcomes in relation to concurrent effects on classroom processes. The results indicate differences both in child outcome and classroom process as a function of class size. Smaller *first-grade* classrooms (about 22 students or fewer) appeared more child-centered; they were marked by higher-quality teacher-child interactions, both instructionally and emotionally, and somewhat more disruptive behavior by children, but teachers in these classrooms viewed the children as competent and well-adjusted and reported feeling close to them. As classrooms added children they became more structured, with more frequent teacher-directed exchanges involving academic activities. Clearly, the size of the class did play a role in shaping children's social and academic experiences and, especially important, teachers' perceptions of children's behavior.

School Climate and Culture

School climate refers to the quality and consistency of interpersonal interactions within the school community that influence children's cognitive, social, and psychological development (Haynes, Emmons, & Ben-Avie, 1997). Climate influences children's confidence in their abilities (Cauce, Comer, & Schwartz, 1987) and teachers' efficacy beliefs (Bandura, 1994) and can shape teaching practices that affect children's motivation and self-views (MacIver, Reuman, & Main, 1995).

In middle school, children's positive perceptions of school are related to their motivation, achievement, and emotional functioning (Roeser et al., 1998, 2000). Middle school students who have higher levels of motivation and emotional well-being also believe that their schools are more developmentally appropriate in teacher-student interactions, practices, and norms (this is especially important, as many middle schools are less supportive of the developmental needs of students than are elementary schools). Teacher-student interactions that lead students to feel supported by their teachers, and smaller communities of teachers and students are also important in enhancing young adolescents' motivation and emotional well-being (Roeser et al., 1998, 2000). As a result, it appears that school climate, teacher-child interactions, and children's motivations about and attitudes toward achievement are quite interconnected during the middle school years and beyond.

Reflecting the climate of the school are mental health and associated services and reforms aimed at curriculum and school management that target proximal processes, such as child-teacher relationships and instructional quality and child outcomes (see Adelman, 1996; Battistich et al., 1997; Durlak & Wells, 1997; Haynes, 1998). Toward this end, Aber, Jones, Brown, Chaudry, and Samples (1998) report on the effects of implementing a schoolwide conflict resolution program in the New York City schools. They profiled three groups of teachers/classrooms in terms of the extent of training and implementation of the program. Teachers received different levels of standard training workshops, and their use of the program was recorded. In examining the differential effects of training levels and implementation in relation to reducing aggression, stronger effects were observed for teachers who practiced implementation with only moderate training in comparison to those who received more training but implemented less. These data suggest that the effects on children of deploying a schoolwide intervention program were conditioned not by teachers' knowledge of the program but by what teachers did to implement the program, suggesting that school-level actions operate on child outcomes principally as a function of penetration to the level of proximal processes. The evaluation design in the Aber et al. study also provides an illustration of a way to capitalize on data collected as part of routine school-based assessments to study efficacy of an intervention. The school based data collected in this study included not only child outcomes but aspects of teacher and school characteristics that helped illustrate effectiveness and reveal multilevel transactions.

One source of information about school climate comes from interventions aimed at changing climate. These interventions are often aimed at changing relationships in the school and creating a sense of community (Baker, Terry, Bridger, & Winsor, 1997; Committee for Children, 2004).

For example, the goals of the Caring Communities approach are to help children "feel psychologically safe, responsibly connected to others, practice ethical decision making and self-governance in the microcosm of the classroom" (Baker et al., 1997, p. 598). These are similar to the goals of the Comer School Development Program (Haynes, 1998), which include an emphasis on caring and sensitivity of school personnel and access to the school's resources (personal and social as well as material and instructional). The Child Development Project (e.g., Battistich et al., 1997) emphasizes students feeling emotionally supported by teachers and cultivating a school climate in which emotional resources are available and flow readily as needed. By and large, results from evaluating such projects indicate that school-level values, ethos, policies, and procedures concerning social relationships and interactions do indeed alter and shape the experiences and outcomes of children in attendance (Aber et al., 1998; Battistich et al., 1997; Haynes, 1998).

In short, school- and district-level factors clearly are to be considered in developmentally informed research on schooling. Much as has been the case in research on child care, structural aspects of settings do indeed shape proximal process and child outcomes (NICHD ECCRN, 2004a), although clearly such associations are complex and perhaps conditioned by a range of teacher and student characteristics (e.g., Finn & Achilles, 1999). Designs that more strategically examine process and outcome shifts as a function of changing educational policy and structural parameters would clearly add to our understanding in this area.

Proximal Process Effects: Classrooms, Teachers, Peers

Classroom-level variables that reflect proximal process experiences of children include engaging and appropriate instruction, opportunities for problem solving, systematic use of feedback on one's performance to guide instruction, opportunities and support for peer relations and friendships, and classroom management in which behavioral expectations are stated clearly and enforced consistently (see Evertson & Weinstein, in press), as well as relationships with teachers and peers and status within peer networks (e.g., Gifford-Smith & Brownell, 2003; Good & Brophy, 1986; Pianta, Steinberg, & Rollins, 1995). Static factors such as teacher experience, often considered a key attribute of the value of classrooms, have shown little relation to processes such as teachers' own behaviors in the classroom, children's reports of the classroom environment, or child outcomes (NICHD ECCRN, 2002b, 2004c; Stuhlman & Pianta, 2001). More specifically, Battistich et al. (1997) report that in a large sample of upper elementary school students, there were no significant associations between child-reported or teacher-reported perceptions of the school as a caring community (which included an index of teacher emotional support) and teacher age, number of years teaching, education, or ethnic status.

Classrooms

Programs of research establish that the kind of instructional and social interactions with adults that occur in classroom settings have reliable and detectable effects on children's achievement and social competence (e.g., Howes et al., in press; Meyer, Wardrop, Hastings, & Linn, 1993; Morrison & Connor, 2002; NICHD ECCRN, 2002a, 2004a; Peisner-Feinberg & Burchinal, 1997). Likewise, interactions with peers in school are also predictive of a range of social, psychological, and academic outcomes (Gifford-Smith & Brownell, 2003). Yet, despite general agreement on what constitutes positive teacher-child interactions and classroom processes, in observations of more than 1,500 classrooms (Bryant et al., 2003; NICHD ECCRN, 2002c, 2005; Pianta et al., 2002), the overwhelming conclusion to be drawn is the exceptional variability in learning experiences offered to children in the early grades (for specific results, see NICHD ECCRN, 2002c, 2005; Pianta et al., 2002). For example, in these studies, several thousand elementary classrooms were observed for at least one day, and although for the most part the typical child receives instruction in whole-group experiences, in some classrooms children are never taught in a whole group, whereas in others this is the mode of instruction all day. Similarly, although literacy instruction is the predominant activity offered to children, in a substantial number of classrooms children were offered no literacy activities at all. These carefully conducted observations of classroom process confirm the exceptionally variable nature of children's experiences (perhaps a confirmation of the importance of implementation variation in intervention studies) and the small links between this variation and typically assessed features of teachers such as education or experience. It does appear that more specific and more psychologically informative indicators, such as teachers' knowledge about subject matter, recent training in child development, or emotional indicators such as depression, play a more influential role in explaining variation in classroom process (Aber et al., 1998; CPPRG, 1999; Hamre & Pianta, 2004;

Pianta et al., 2003), although these factors are largely ignored in most research on classroom process.

Thus, we know from recent large-scale observational studies that classrooms are highly variable (e.g., NICHD ECCRN, 2002c, 2005), both in terms of the discrete activities offered to children and in terms of global qualities of the environment. For example, the degree to which classroom teachers make productive use of time or classrooms are well-managed ranges across the full spectrum of possibilities, even though kindergarten and first-grade classes appear, on average, to be positive and supportive social settings (NICHD ECCRN, 2002c; Pianta et al., 2002). How these specific features of classrooms shape child outcomes is of considerable interest, particularly in light of this high degree of variation. In analyses of contemporaneous associations between dimensions of classroom experience and social/behavioral functioning, children are rated as more attentive in classrooms that are characterized as socially and emotionally supportive (NICHD ECCRN, 2002c), and interactions with peers are less frequent in more structured classrooms in which teachers direct students' activities to a large degree (NICHD ECCRN, 2004a).

Yet, more careful analyses of the value-added quality of specific classroom features provides a more powerful base for inferences of the importance of classroom experience. One study from the NICHD ECCRN (2004b), examining social outcomes of children through the first 2 years of school, provides evidence of specific classroom effects and also the value of integrating school/classroom process fully into developmental studies. In this study, assessments of family and child care factors from birth to 54 months, achievement and social outcomes at the entry to school, and qualities of first-grade classrooms were used to predict social and behavioral functioning. In models used to predict relative change in social functioning from 54 months and kindergarten to first grade, the effects of home and child care on first-grade social functioning were accounted for largely by their associations with early social functioning (and not achievement) at preschool and kindergarten rather than unique associations with first-grade outcomes. Yet, after controlling for home and child care factors, more teacher-led structured activities in first-grade classrooms predicted mother's reports of more internalizing behavior, and classrooms rated as more emotionally supportive predicted lower levels of mother-reported internalizing behavior as well as more concurrently observed indicators of competence. Although it is not unique to see studies examining associations between child outcomes and classroom process, this study is unique for its *developmental* analysis of this issue in the context of information on prior home experiences and child outcomes prior to school entry.

Relationships between Children and Teachers

Relationships between teachers and children have been a focus of educators' concern for decades. Some experts suggest that a relationship with at least one caring adult, not necessarily a parent, is perhaps the single most important element in protecting young people who have multiple risks in their lives (e.g., Carnegie Council on Adolescent Development, 1989; Gambone et al., 2002; Resnick et al., 1997). For many children, this adult is a teacher. Particularly in adolescence, as the young person begins to exercise individuation and autonomy striving, as the parent-child relationship becomes more ambivalent or even negatively charged (Steinberg & Morris, 2001), nonfamilial relationships with adults may play an important role in supporting healthy adaptive behaviors. That this is the case is suggested by studies of younger children's relationships with their teachers (e.g., Hamre & Pianta, 2001) and by surveys of adolescents (Resnick et al., 1997), but this possibility has yet to be carefully examined in longitudinal studies. Unfortunately, there are few studies of the longitudinal effects of extrafamilial adults and even fewer studies of their developmental determinants.

In terms of specific constructs pertaining to child-teacher relationships, a number of child-reported and teacher-reported dimensions can be reliably assessed and have been cross-validated in numerous investigations. Wellborn and Connell (1987) examined variations in children's perceptions on two dimensions of relationship experience, emotional quality and psychological proximity seeking, that differentially relate (in predictable directions) to teacher's descriptions of the children as well as the children's relational histories (Lynch & Cicchetti, 1992, 1997; Toth & Cicchetti, 1996). Perceived support is a key dimension of relationships between children and teachers even at older ages. When youth were asked to identify relationships that were *emotionally* supportive—someone to count on for understanding and advice—teachers were often listed in relation to this construct. In fact, a factor associated with healthy outcomes was whether youth reported having a relationship with an adult that they identified in this way, many of whom were teachers (Resnick et al., 1997). Ryan, Stiller, and Lynch (1994) reported that the child-teacher relationship as described by children's sense of felt security was particularly salient for middle schoolers. Recently, Reddy, Rhodes, and Mulhall (2003) examined longitudinal associations between

children's reports of support from teachers and demonstrated that changes in perceived support were linked to changes in middle schoolers' depression and self-esteem.

From a teachers' perspective, features of the relationship such as a sense of closeness or conflict have been cross-validated in several studies (Birch & Ladd, 1997; Cost, Quality and Child Outcomes Study Team, 1995; Saft & Pianta, 2001), from prekindergarten through fifth grade. Conflict, or negativity, in the child-teacher relationship appears to be the factor most strongly related to child outcomes when teachers' views of the relationship are being assessed (Pianta et al., 2003). Qualities of teacher-child relationships are related to children's competencies with peers in the classroom (e.g., Birch & Ladd, 1998; Howes, 2000; Howes, Matheson, & Hamilton, 1994) and trajectories toward academic success or failure (Birch & Ladd, 1996; Hamre & Pianta, 2001; Pianta et al., 1995; van Ijzendoorn, Sagi, & Lambermon, 1992), as well as with patterns of child-mother relationships (Lynch & Cicchetti, 1992) and disruptive behavior (Hamre & Pianta, 2001).

Howes and colleagues (see Howes, 2000) have established that the quality of relationships children have with mother and form with teachers (Howes et al., 1994) plays a role in children's peer competencies, albeit relationships with teachers are stronger predictors of behavior with peers in the classroom than is the relationship with parents. Child-teacher relationships show low to moderate levels of continuity in the early grades of school, at least through second grade (Howes, Phillipsen, & Peisner-Feinberg, 2000), supporting Birch and Ladd's (1998) contention that children's relationships demonstrate a coherence across relational figures and across time. In a series of descriptive studies, changes in student adjustment from year to year were correlated in expected directions: Downward deflections are correlated with child-teacher conflict, whereas upward deflections are related to child-teacher closeness (Pianta et al., 1995).

Hamre and Pianta (2001) extended analysis of the longitudinal relations between early child-teacher relationships (in kindergarten) and child school outcomes through eighth grade. Controlling for kindergarten-entry cognitive ability and problem behavior, negativity in the child-teacher relationship reported by the child's kindergarten teacher predicted achievement test scores, disciplinary infractions, and school suspensions through eighth grade, with effects on disciplinary infractions most pronounced for children who had problems in kindergarten adjustment. The effects on eighth-grade achievement scores appeared largely mediated by effects of the kindergarten child-teacher relationship on achievement in early elementary school. This was the first study to report longitudinal findings for early child-teacher relationships extending into middle and junior high school.

The coordination of parent-child, teacher-child, and peer relationship systems has also been a focus of study. Lynch and Cicchetti (1992) have established that maltreated children, as a result of experiences with parents, are sensitized to seek certain relational experiences with teachers; they are less likely to form optimal relational patterns and to seek psychological proximity and support from teachers. Birch and Ladd (1996) studied teacher-child relationships extensively in early elementary classrooms and suggest that children have a generalized interpersonal style (moving toward, moving against, moving away) that characterizes their interactions with peers and with teachers. Those children who displayed moving against behaviors in kindergarten, such as verbal and physical aggression toward teacher and peers, were more likely to form negative relationships with teachers in first and second grade (Ladd & Burgess, 1999). Children who tended to move away from others in kindergarten were more likely to be rated as overly dependent by first-grade teachers, though there was less stability in these behaviors than in aggressive behaviors (Birch & Ladd, 1998). Observed conflict in the child-teacher relationship is related to less classroom participation and lower achievement over the first half of kindergarten (Ladd, Birch, & Buhs, 1999).

Harter (1996) discusses how relationships with teachers change from elementary to junior high school. As children move through these grades, relationships between teachers and students become less personal, more formal, more evaluative, and more competitive. These changes in available relationship support from teachers can be associated with more negative self-evaluations and attitudes toward learning because the impersonal and evaluative nature of the relational context in junior high does not match well with the children's relational needs at that age. Harter finds that this model particularly applies to students who have lower levels of intrinsic motivation. In this way, teacher-child relationships (which are typically viewed as potential resources for amelioration of risk) can actually exacerbate risk if they are either not positive or do not match the developmental needs of the child.

Consistent with this view of the ongoing needs of middle-schoolers for support from adult figures, teacher support has been found to be related to sixth-grade children's school- and class-related interests and to their pursuit of social goals (Wentzel, 1998, 2002). These self-beliefs and motiva-

tions in sixth grade in turn predicted pursuit of social goals and grades in seventh grade (Wentzel, 1998). Especially important, the support youth receive from their parents, peers, and teachers seemed to have additive, thus fairly independent, effects. Support from teachers was uniquely related to classroom functioning, and Wentzel (2002) suggests the possibility that support in teacher-child relationships may be particularly salient at transition points, such as the transition from elementary to middle school.

In contrast to what is known about parents in relation to their interactions with children, virtually nothing is known about teachers, particularly developmentally. Despite a general recognition that teacher characteristics and perceptions influence the practice of teaching, little is known about how individual teacher characteristics and perceptions impact the formation of their relationships with children. Kesner (2000) gathered data on student teachers' representations of attachment relationships with their own parents and showed that beginning teachers who viewed their relationships with their parents as secure were also those who formed relationships with students characterized as secure. In a related study, Horppu and Ikonen-Varila (2001) showed that beginning teachers' representations of attachment with their parents related to their stated motives for their work and their beliefs about a kindergarten teacher's work and goals in the classroom. Beginning teachers classified as having a secure/autonomous relationship with their parent(s) were more likely than those classified insecure to express motives that were child-centered as well as centered on goals for the self. Teachers classified as secure also described more complex conceptions of a teacher's work (involving social, emotional, and instructional components) and were more likely to view relationships with students as mutually satisfying (Horppu & Ikonen-Varila, 2001).

Finally, in an example illustrative of a focus on the determinants of relational processes, Hamre and Pianta (2004) examined depression as a predictor of caregivers' sensitivity. Analyses provided evidence of consistent and unique associations between caregivers' self-reported depression and the quality and frequency of their interactions with children. Caregivers reporting higher levels of depression were less sensitive and more withdrawn. Interestingly, the type or setting of care moderated this association, such that in family day care settings, more depressed caregivers were even more often negative in interactions, a finding attributable to the absence of other adults in the care setting. Thus, this report demonstrates that proximal process features of school-like settings that children experience (e.g., sensitivity) are associated with both structural features (such as type of care or available other adults) and psychological features of the adult in the setting (e.g., depression).

Peer Relations

Because schools are among the settings in which interactions with peers are most likely to occur, a very large proportion of naturalistic studies of peer relations take place in schools or inquire about peer relations within schools. Yet, most of these studies remain uninformed about features of the school setting that could contribute to (or be influenced by) peer relations (Gifford-Smith & Brownell, 2003). In their comprehensive review of the peer relations literature, Gifford-Smith and Brownell focus on three core aspects of peer functioning: social acceptance, friendship, and peer network status. They document the correlates of social acceptance, friendship, and peer network status in terms of associations with a range of developmental outcomes, including school dropout, delinquency, and achievement. These authors advance a perspective that notes the complex, differentiated, and interconnected linkages among these aspects of peer functioning and the ways outcome domains are differentially affected not only by standing within a particular aspect of peer functioning (such as when having a friend with shared interests is related to self-esteem or achievement motivation), but also by the linkage among aspects of peer functioning (such as is the case when low-status children who have friends are better off than low-status children without a friend).

What is striking about the Gifford-Smith and Brownell (2003) review is the extent to which the peer relations literature reflects a reliance on school settings as contexts for the assessment of peer relations (such as when gathering large samples of children's social network standing or peer nominations in classrooms and cafeterias) and that the peer contacts that give rise to social acceptance, friendship, and network status are located in schools and often regulated by school practices and policies. Thus, in a possibly profound way, what is known about peer relations is at least in part conditioned by the manner in which such relations are affected by school setting. For the most part, research focusing on the correlates of peer relations has examined associations with family characteristics and processes, other aspects of peer functioning including developmental history, and a host of outcome variables in social, personal, and achievement domains.

Surprisingly, given the extent to which peer contacts are nested in school settings, there is a lack of attention to documenting and understanding the extent to which functioning with peers is shaped by aspects of the school setting.

For example, the peer with whom a child has contact, as well as the type of contact, could vary as a function of structural elements such as classroom placement or instructional groups within the class, the size and organization of the school (Felner et al., 2001), and the availability of clubs, sports teams, and extracurricular programs offered at the school. In addition, qualities of peer relations, such as those described by Gifford-Smith and Brownell (2003), are likely to be influenced by process factors in schools such as disciplinary policies and values, the extent of emphasis on fostering positive social relationships and preventing bullying, teachers' own knowledge and skill in fostering children's successful adaptation with peers, classroom supports for social engagement and interaction, and the extent to which out-of-school time with peers is supported, fostered, and encouraged by the school and its practices. At this time, there is very little known about these connections between school settings and peer relations, despite the very large extent to which contacts among peers are embedded and distributed in school settings and processes. As at least one example of research on classroom process effects on peer relations, Hughes, Cavell, and Willson (2001) documented within classrooms that the extent and nature of teachers' interactions with a specific child are associated with the rest of the class's perceptions about that child and the likelihood of their affiliating with that child.

In addition to the ways that features of schooling may affect the nature of peer functioning, as peer relations become increasingly important in middle and high school, it could be argued that schooling processes are in turn affected by properties of peer relations either concurrently or in the past (e.g., Kellam et al., 1998). During the teenage years, adolescents spend increasing amounts of time alone with friends (Larson & Richards, 1991), and certain groups emerge, each with its own characteristics and potential for influence in schools. Crowds emerge during early adolescence as collections of peers defined by reputations and stereotypes that exert profound influence in terms of norms for their members (Gifford-Smith & Brownell, 2003). The number and types of crowds in a school can reflect the niches available for students and in turn can affect the nature and delivery of curriculum, discipline policy, and school climate in ways that shape opportunity structures (Gambone et al., 2002).

Smaller in size, cliques are groups of peers based on friendship, shared activities, and other aspects of similarity. Cliques can be input to, and output from, adolescents' need to establish a sense of identity. The strength of clique associations can be considerable, and although many teens may not be members of a clique or may participate in more than one (R. B. Cairns, Leung, Buchanan, & Cairns, 1995), adolescents' negotiation of clique membership and conflicts in membership (for one individual or between individuals) is arguably one of the primary sources of school discipline referrals and targets for classroom/school management and bullying prevention strategies (Battistich et al., 1997).

Peer groups increasingly take on an important role through high school in terms of the value they place on academic success, their role as a stimulator of cognitive and academic skills, and the shaping of perceptions, attitudes, and goals, all of which harmonize with most schools' goals (Berndt & Keefe, 1995). Youth with a history of problematic achievement and low involvement with school gravitate toward delinquent peers (B. D. Cairns & Cairns, 1994) and are likely to be most affected by shifts in dropout policies or narrowing of the opportunity structure in schools (Eccles & Gootman, 2002; Gambone et al., 2002). Although parents help establish early trajectories toward long-term educational goals, peers are the most potent influence on daily behaviors in school, time spent on homework, and a sense of school enjoyment (Steinberg & Brown, 1989).

In sum, there is ample evidence available to confirm that classrooms operate as conduits of proximal processes that play important roles in shaping children's development. Although arguably understudied in terms of inclusion in developmental designs and analysis and understanding of determinants and description of developmentally salient features, it is clear that classrooms warrant inclusion in models of key developmental settings (Bronfenbrenner & Morris, 1998).

Macroregulations: School Transitions

It was previously noted that schools are particularly interesting settings in which to examine phenomena of interest to developmentalists in part because of the manner in which large-scale regulatory actions are enacted across variations present in populations of children. Such actions allow for the examination of the ways contextual variation moderates individual characteristics, and when examined longitudinally, the subsequent response of school contexts becomes an opportunity for studying transactions.

The transitions organized into school careers are just such an opportunity. As has been demonstrated by Morrison's use of the transition into schooling and age of entry into school as a marker (Morrison & Connor, 2002), strategically capitalizing on school transitions both allows developmentalists to disentangle confounded effects (such as

age and cognitive ability or achievement, as in Morrison's research) and to examine transactions and moderation, such as is the case when children of varying achievement or social attributes are differentially exposed to certain schooling experiences (Hamre & Pianta, 2001; NICHD ECCRN, 2004b). In present-day American schooling, the opportunities for exploiting such arrangements in schools are exceptionally rich because of the focus on regular standardized assessment of children on repeated metrics and the pressure to deploy instructional resources and programming differentially as a function of performance on such metrics. Although mental health and behavioral aspects of development do not figure prominently in these discussions, developmental psychopathologists will recognize the opportunities for examining mediated and moderated linkages between achievement and behavioral/mental health outcomes.

In the discussion that follows, the transition to elementary school and the transitions to middle and high school are discussed in relation to changes in the child's experience of school and consequences for developmental outcome trajectories.

Kindergarten and the Elementary Grades

The transition to school receives much attention as a key outcome variable in educational policy and practice in large part because it is during this period that certain outcome trajectories become established (Entwisle & Alexander, 1999), which can be increasingly unresponsive to alteration as the child progresses through school. Thus, several major research effects have targeted the period of school transition for further study, particularly for children in poverty: the Head Start Transition study (S. L. Ramey & Ramey, 1992), the National Education Longitudinal Study (Meisels & Liaw, 1993), and the NICHD Study of Early Child Care (NICHD ECCRN, 2002b; see Kagan & Neuman, 1998, for a review). In considering the transition to school as a possible deflection point in development, several points are germane.

First, the ages from 4 or 5 to 7 (roughly) mark a period of change in the "developmental agenda" in many cultures (Sameroff, 1989; Sameroff & Haith, 1996; White, 1965). Entry into the culture's system of formal education and expectations of responsibility and independence within that system is one correlate of this shift. Kindergarten is a different environment from preschool or home. Goals, demands, and the nature of the classroom environment are different, as is the ecology surrounding this new environment. Kindergarten has explicit goals for literacy, numeracy, and socialization that are not formal, stated goals of preschool or home environments (Hains, Fowler, Schwartz, Kottwitz, & Rosenhoetter, 1989). The statement of these goals, their connection to a system of instruction, and the way they are tethered to success in later grades usher into kindergarten an emphasis on *formal instruction,* instruction that has the specific intent of raising the child's skill level. Such intent is not typical in preschool settings. Thus, children, teachers, and families experience the entrance into kindergarten as a qualitative shift (Belsky & MacKinnon, 1994; Bredekamp & Copple, 1997; Love, Logue, Trudeau, & Thayer, 1992; Pianta & Kraft-Sayre, 1999).

Interactions in the kindergarten classroom environment become increasingly intentional and focused on academic progress. As a result, interactions between children and teachers differ compared with those between children and their preschool teachers, or children and their parents. Gradually, these teacher-child relationships become increasingly influential to the child (Howes et al., 1994). Increased class size and child-to-teacher ratios characteristic of kindergarten change the nature of child-teacher interactions (Heaviside & Farris, 1993; NICHD ECCRN, 2004a), as does the philosophy underlying the kindergarten curriculum (Bredekamp & Copple, 1997; Kagan & Neuman, 1998; Love et al., 1992). Evidence suggests that the kindergarten experience, characterized by these new constraints, contributes to increased academic skills. Most children who enroll in kindergarten perform better than those who do not, and those exposed to more kindergarten may do better still (Dauber, Alexander, & Entwisle, 1993; Entwisle, Alexander, Cadigan, & Pallas, 1987).

The demands of kindergarten place stress on social and emotional competencies as well. Demands such as independence from adults, getting along with other children, recognition of and adherence to routine, and being alert and active for longer periods of time challenge the 5-year-old child. In preschool environments, teachers display more warmth than in kindergarten and are less demanding of the child in terms of formal routine and instruction (Love et al., 1992). Kindergarten teacher-child interactions emphasize cognitive skills over less academic activities and, as a result, demand more time for teaching new skills compared to guiding unstructured activities. Kindergarten teachers tend to group children differently to enhance autonomy; kindergarten children spend more time in large groups and less time in small groups, and kindergarten classrooms usually consist of more total children and more children per adult (NICHD ECCRN, 2002b, 2002c). In these ways, there are considerable differences between preschool and kindergarten environments. Children find this

shift somewhat challenging: The emphasis on academic skills and the demands to interact with a wide range of children are reported to be the most difficult aspects of the transition to school (Love et al., 1992).

Of special importance, it is at this point of entry into school that population-level screening mechanisms coincide with the contextual and expectation shifts noted earlier. Thus, just as children are experiencing this new environment with all its demands, schools are starting to screen for disabilities and increased attention is paid to identifying children in need of additional services (Ysseldyke et al., 2000). This confluence is largely responsible for a population-level rise in children identified as "exceptional" or "deviant" in terms of some level of documentation for eligibility for special education, mental health, behavioral, or supportive academic services (Hoagwood & Johnson, 2003; Ysseldyke et al., 2000). In this way, the transition to kindergarten offers a unique opportunity for developmental psychopathologists to examine how health and education policy and identification/eligibility mechanisms shape the psychological (e.g., teachers' beliefs) and behavioral (e.g., classroom interactions) mechanisms that may lead to diagnosis of disorder.

Although this discussion points out changes related to the major transition shift into formal schooling at kindergarten, regular grade-level shifts occur throughout elementary school that in smaller ways mirror the kindergarten transition. Increased formality and expectations and fewer opportunities for social and supportive contacts with teachers are among the most frequently acknowledged changes from grade to grade during elementary school.

Middle and High School

In most American communities, youth experience at least one major school transition, the transition into high school, and, including the shift to middle school, most often two during the years 10 to 18. The nature of these transitions is often linked to academic performance and behavioral competence in the prior grades, and the experience of the transition can be predictive of subsequent performance in those areas. Simply experiencing a school transition can be problematic; Simmons and Blyth (1987) reported that moving into a seventh- through ninth-grade junior high was associated with poorer school performance than staying in a kindergarten through eighth-grade school and that youth who transitioned into a junior high school were more at risk of school failure and (eventually) dropping out of school. This transition to junior high at seventh grade was also associated with a decline in females' self-esteem and in males' sense of being victimized than for peers in the kindergarten through eighth-grade configuration (Simmons & Blyth, 1987).

Eccles and colleagues have conducted the most extensive studies of the transitions to middle school in particular, and Eccles et al. (1996, 1997, 1998; Roeser et al., 1998, 2000) concluded that the junior high school transition contributes to declines in interest in school, intrinsic motivation, self-concept, and confidence in one's intellectual abilities, particularly for youth living in poor communities and for youth already having academic and other difficulties. Thus, transitions imposed by the organization of schooling are themselves risks or stresses on development at this age and operate in much the same way, in relation to identification and production of disorder, as does the transition to kindergarten. The challenges posed by school transitions also tend to be amplified when schools are especially big (Felner et al., 2001), creating the policy/practice response to these conditions of establishing "schools within schools" to facilitate the establishment of smaller social and instructional environments for children attending large schools (Felner et al., 2001).

Keating (1990) notes that increases in achievement slow during adolescence, but that a number of factors in school settings can promote gains, such as facilitated experiences in using cognitive skills. Yet, observational research in middle schools has shown that cognitive-processing demands are often lower than in elementary school classrooms and could account for disengagement and decreases in achievement. Students' grades may drop following the transition to middle school and to high school, and this lower performance is predictive of later dropping out. This decline in grades could be attributed to stricter grading policies in middle and high schools, but also might be attributed to some students' academic disengagement and the control ethic of most secondary schools (Wigfield, Eccles, & Pintrich, 1996). Entwisle (see Entwisle & Alexander, 1999) also found that achievement test gains are relatively small, with school quality demonstrating only small effects. She concluded that adolescents' abilities and social class standing were more potent explanatory variables for educational attainment than school quality. Other contextual factors such as those related to ethnicity, gender, family, and culture exert important influences on academic achievement.

In the view of Eccles et al. (1997), young people's perceptions of their abilities and the value they attach to academic achievement are important determinants of school achievement, even when ability and past achievement are controlled. Perceived competence also influences other motivation-related variables, such as enjoyment and interest (MacIver, Stipek, & Daniels, 1991). Such beliefs arise in part from the expectations and beliefs of parents, teachers, and other important adults.

Because risk during transition is driven by heightened complexity and developmental demands as well as the inability of schools to provide needed supports, interventions often are aimed at increasing the ability of the school to respond to children's needs by essentially reducing psychological size and complexity. Felner et al. (2001) report 40% to 50% declines in school dropout, maintenance of achievement levels, and fewer child- and teacher-reported behavioral/emotional problems for a program that creates a school within a school. Not surprisingly, teachers also reported higher job satisfaction and less burnout (see Felner et al., 2001). Common dimensions of successful secondary schools, according to Felner and colleagues, include promoting a sense of belongingness and agency, engaging families, having an integrated, quality curriculum, requiring ongoing professional development (both in curriculum content and in child development), having high expectations for students, and offering opportunities for success.

In short, transitions embedded in the organization of schools function in regular and predictable ways to transform the social and instructional environment of the setting and, consequently, children's experiences. These shifts are reflected also in the smaller, more incremental changes that take place (in American schools) when children move from grade to grade. Studies that capitalize on systematic variation in the timing and nature of how transitions are organized, as well as the variants in school transitions available in other cultures (e.g., in Norway, where classrooms remain intact for several years with the same teacher), allow for examinations of context-process-outcome links foundational to developmental theory.

Summary

Clearly, schools are as complex ecologies for development as are families or child care settings or communities. Structural features such as finances and policies related to staffing and size; process features such as classroom qualities and supports, child-teacher relationships, and peer relations; and transitional points and shifts all intersect with the trajectories of children's social and behavioral adaptation both directly and indirectly as they affect academic and cognitive functioning. The growing research literature and methodological advances in studying school effects and school adaptation afford developmental psychopathologists the conceptual and assessment tools requisite to establish the type of interdisciplinary initiatives that truly integrate schooling within developmental frameworks. As has been noted repeatedly, the complexity and organization of schools reflect a range of contextual parameters that allow developmentalists access to phenomena that would be more difficult to study in settings that are more stable or more uniform.

CONCLUSIONS, IMPLICATIONS, AND FUTURE DIRECTIONS

Nearly 2 decades ago Good and Weinstein (1986) discussed linkages between education and psychology in relation to advancing knowledge about school effects and school adaptation. They noted that the gap between psychology and education at that time seriously undermined the scientific foundation for educational policy and practice decisions. They also noted that the mechanisms and processes underlying variation in school effects were virtually unknown, foreshadowing the recent comments of Rutter and Maughan (2002). In a somewhat parallel manner, Cicchetti and Aber (1998), in their discussion of contextualism in developmental psychopathology, hoped they would not have to review the literature in another 10 years and find such a lack of attention to sophisticated analysis and measurement of contexts of development, among them schools. The cluster of recent funding initiatives that advance interdisciplinary research focused on problems of educational significance (e.g., IES, 2004a) suggests that the challenges of meaningfully integrating education science with developmental science—conceptually, procedurally, and methodologically—loom as large now as they did 20 years ago. The primary goal of this chapter has been to provide a framework for advancing scientific progress as a result of interdisciplinarity between education and developmental psychopathology, particularly for how developmental psychopathology can foster understanding of school effects on social, behavioral, and mental health outcomes and how developmental studies in educational settings can expand understanding of process and mechanisms responsible for these outcomes. Several conclusions are evident from this review that open paths for future work and initiatives; perhaps such work may diminish the frequency of calls for linkage across disciplines.

First, there is little doubt that developmental psychopathology and education, both historically and at present, share a number of mutual interests in relation to understanding and conceptualizing school effects and adaptation

in school. Going forward, school reforms provide a ready mechanism for observing the developmental consequences of major structural and policy changes and foster a setting conducive to the application and testing of prevention and intervention strategies that could reveal developmental mechanisms responsible for outcomes of interest. Schools also afford developmental psychopathologists with an assortment of available measurements, evaluations, and definitions of adaptive (and maladaptive) functioning that are windows on outcome(s) that at times parallel, supplement, or complement analogous indicators in developmental psychopathology research. Both conceptual and methodological work is needed to more fully integrate and align school-based outcome assessments with constructs of interest to developmentalists as well as for developmentalists to assist in the broadening of what is currently measured in school accountability assessments. Looking forward, it is likely that over the next decade there will be increasing dissatisfaction in the education community with the narrowness of accountability metrics and openings will emerge for cross-fertilization of this type.

Schools also provide developmental psychopathologists with strategic opportunities to test key aspects of theory. Schools offer access to variation in a wide range of proximal process variables known to influence outcome trajectories in social, behavioral, and mental health domains. To the extent that general developmental models posit processes of moderation, schools may be one of the best places to examine such possibilities given both the variation in experience and child characteristics present in schools and schooling's mandate to in fact moderate the influence of factors such as race and economic status on achievement and life success. When considering the fact that some aspects of schooling and school adaptation are assessed at the population level, systematic integration of education and developmental psychopathology allows for the study of the dynamics of context and outcome trajectories at that level. A very concrete opportunity emerging in the not too distant future will be the use of the Head Start National Reporting System as a source of information on nearly half a million children who, after Head Start, will enter the accountability system in the public schools. Linking these outcome assessments with extant data on Head Start quality and the forthcoming focus of educational policy on teacher quality (mandated by NCLB) creates intriguing opportunities for developmental epidemiologists. Furthermore, because of variation in the temporal and structural organization of schools and the predictable, regular shifts in certain organizational features of schooling present at transition periods or in relation to accountability assessment (some of which are predicated on child characteristics), schooling offers a way of examining transactional processes in development that can be difficult to model. Developmentally informed research in school settings also creates opportunities to disaggregate genetic confounds in analyses of contextual effects usually studied in families as well as for more sophisticated examination and interpretation of informant-based outcome assessments used so often in developmental psychopathology research.

Second, if the mutual interests of developmental psychopathologists and education researchers are to be exploited fruitfully, advances in the next several years will depend on careful attention to conceptual and methodological details and interdisciplinary links at multiple levels. Two very simple suggestions for fruitful and productive intersections are offered here: One focuses on what developmental psychopathology can offer to education; the second turns the arrow in the other direction.

At the conceptual level, educational research would benefit from applications of the general systems model to understanding behavior. The concepts of multilevel co-action and a focus on relational processes (teacher-child interactions and relationships, child engagement, peer interactions) are but two examples of this need, but there are many more. Educational theory and research, particularly in the areas of social development, lack updated understanding and theoretical frameworks to move beyond behaviorism as the predominant conceptual driver of policy and practice.

On the other hand, for developmental psychopathologists interested in examining school effects, a focus on specific aspects of the child's experiences as they link with specific aspects of the classroom environment is a more useful strategy than a focus on global features of the child or the setting. Current levels of attention in developmental research to conceptualizing and assessing school parameters are simply inadequate for realizing the potential benefits being discussed here. Developmental psychopathology needs to move beyond viewing schools as a locus of outcome assessments, or schools as sites for implementation of developmentally oriented interventions, or schools as sites for recruiting large samples, and instead look at schools as full partners in a program of developmental psychopathology research and training. One concrete and achievable objective going forward would be increased assessment of observed, child- or teacher-reported assessment of the school context in studies of social development, problem behavior, mental health, and peer relations. Absent these assessments, the extant literature on development in these domains is not sufficiently comprehensive or informed, given the available tools and evidence for school effects.

Third, the dichotomization of research and practice is a major conceptual and pragmatic impediment to achieving the benefits noted earlier. To some degree, one of the consequences of this dichotomy is the difficulty the field has with implementation in clinical trial research: Rather than increasing pressure for standardization of protocols, the findings on implementation suggest an alternative might be to more carefully understand the constraints present in the classroom or school context that account for variation. Although to some extent this problem can be addressed by informed individual investigators and teams of investigators representing the two disciplines and related fields supported by interdisciplinary funding mechanisms, movement on this issue is also predicated on support for the design and implementation of interdisciplinary training initiatives that involve schools as full partners and focus on education as a process of interest to developmental researchers (IES, 2004a). It would be helpful, in this regard, for developmental psychopathologists interested in school-age phenomena to spend time in schools in systematic training and observation of students and educators. Such efforts are reflected in the recent cluster of predoctoral training programs funded by the Institute for Education Sciences (2004b) that each addresses structural, process, and opportunity barriers to integration of this sort. Likewise, exposing educators and teachers-in-training to developmental psychopathology theory would advance a more sophisticated understanding of social and behavioral processes in schools that currently are among the more serious concerns of educators. Again, efforts at the legislative, policy, and training/credentialing levels that link training in the basic academic disciplines with the training of teachers are indicative of fields moving toward one another. Specific interdisciplinary initiatives resulting from these efforts might focus on the adult development of teachers: the ways their training and exposure to knowledge interacts with prior history and current experience to influence their interactions with children (IES, 2004a). Other work might focus on biobehavioral processes as they interact with schooling at multiple levels, an area that currently appears to have considerable promise. As these interdisciplinary efforts continue, particularly those devoted to graduate and undergraduate training, it will be critical for employment markets (e.g., research universities, foundations, school systems, government) to recognize the value not only of skills in one specific discipline, but also of the skills and understandings required to bridge and link conceptually and operationally.

The slow and difficult progress in understanding school effects and school adaptation, almost 30 years after *Fifteen*

Thousand Hours, is understandable given the complexity of development and the complexity of schooling. However, it is also quite clear that decades of research addressing these complexities have moved both the field of education and that of developmental psychopathology to a point at which productive integration is both possible and necessary for further advancement on these issues. It is abundantly clear that funding, legislative, and training mechanisms are now positioning these fields toward even further integration. One very productive future direction would be to capitalize on these shifts and movements through strategic support for integration at conferences, in publications, and through research-funding mechanisms, training programs, and models for practice and policy. Rutter and Maughan (2002) summarized progress in research on schooling and development since *Fifteen Thousand Hours* with a series of questions partially addressed by their original work that continues to press for attention. This could be interpreted as a sign that developmental psychopathology and education are doomed to be only distally and superficially linked. These questions are an invitation to deeper, more fundamental integration and interdisciplinarity that could not perhaps have been possible 30 years ago. The next decade, if work under way now continues to gain momentum, promises to be informative and may even result in a reformulation of the important, unanswered questions about school effects, school adaptation, and developmental psychopathology.

REFERENCES

Aber, J. L., Jones, S. M., Brown, J. L., Chaudry, N., & Samples, F. (1998). Resolving conflict creatively: Evaluating the developmental effects of a school-based violence prevention program in neighborhood and classroom context. *Development and Psychology, 10*(2), 187–213.

Achenbach, T. M., McConaughy, S. H., & Howell, C. T. (1987). Child/adolescent behavioral and emotional problems: Implications of cross-informant correlations for situational specificity. *Psychological Bulletin, 101*(2), 213–232.

Adelman, H. S. (1996). Restructuring education support services and integrating community resources: Beyond the full service school model. *School Psychology Review, 25,* 431–445.

Administration for Children and Families. (2003). *Information memorandum: Implementation of the Head Start national reporting system on child outcomes* (ACYF-IM-HS-03–07). Available from http://www.headstartinfo.org/publications/im03/im03_07.htm.

Alexander, K. L., & Entwisle, D. R. (1988). Achievement in the first 2 years of school: Patterns and processes. *Monographs of the Society for Research in Child Development, 53*(2, Serial No. 231).

Baker, J. A., Terry, T., Bridger, R., & Winsor, A. (1997). Schools as caring communities: A relational approach to school reform. *School Psychology Review, 26*(4), 586–602.

Bandura, A. (1994). *Self-efficacy: The exercise of control.* New York: Freeman.

Battistich, V., Solomon, D., Watson, M., & Schaps, E. (1997). Caring school communities. *Educational Psychologist, 32*(3), 137–151.

Battistich, V., Watson, M., Solomon, D., Lewis, C., & Schaps, E. (1999). Beyond the three R's: A broader agenda for school reform. *Elementary School Journal, 99*(5), 415–429.

Belsky, J., & MacKinnon, C. (1994). Transition to school: Developmental trajectories and school experiences. *Early Education and Development, 5*(2), 106–119.

Berliner, D. C. (2004, October). *How high stakes testing corrupts our educational measures and our educators.* Presentation for the Curry Speaker Series, sponsored by the Risk and Prevention Work Group, Curry School of Education, University of Virginia, Charlottesville.

Berliner, D. C., & Biddle, B. J. (1995). *The manufactured crisis: Myths, fraud, and the attack on America's public schools.* Redding, MA: Addison-Wesley.

Berndt, T. J., & Keefe, K. (1995). Friends' influence on adolescents' adjustment to school. *Child Development, 66,* 1312–1329.

Betts, J. R., & Shkolnik, J. L. (1999). The behavioral effects of variations in class size. *Education Evaluation and Policy Analysis, 21,* 193–213.

Birch, S. H., & Ladd, G. W. (1996). Interpersonal relationships in the school environment and children's early school adjustment. In K. Wentzel & J. Juvonen (Eds.), *Social motivation: Understanding children's school adjustment* (pp. 199–225). New York: Cambridge University Press.

Birch, S. H., & Ladd, G. W. (1997). The teacher-child relationship and children's early school adjustment. *Journal of School Psychology, 35,* 61–79.

Birch, S. H., & Ladd, G. W. (1998). Children's interpersonal behaviors and the teacher-child relationship. *Developmental Psychology, 34*(5), 934–946.

Blatchford, P., Goldstein, H., Martin, C., & Browne, W. (2002). A study of class size effects in English school reception year classes. *British Educational Research Journal, 28*(2), 171–187.

Blatchford, P., Moriarty, V., Edmonds, S., & Martin, C. (2002). Relationships between class size and teaching: A multi-method analysis of English infant schools. *American Educational Research Journal, 39*(1), 101–132.

Boyce, W. T., Frank, E., Jensen, P. S., Kessler, R. C., Nelson, C. A., Steinberg, L., et al. (1998). Social context in developmental psychopathology: Recommendations for future research from the MacArthur Network on Psychopathology and Development. *Development and Psychopathology, 10*(2), 143–164.

Boyle, M., Cunningham, C., Heale, J., Hundert, J., McDonald, J., Offord, D., et al. (1999). Helping children adjust: A tri-ministry study: I. Evaluation methodology. *Journal of Child Psychology and Psychiatry, 40*(7), 1051–1060.

Bredekamp, S., & Copple, C. (1997). *Developmentally appropriate practice in early childhood programs* (Rev. ed.). Washington, DC: National Association for the Education of Young Children.

Brody, G. H., Dorsey, S., Forehand, R., & Armistead, L. (2002). Unique and protective contributions of parenting and classroom processes to the adjustment of African American children living in single-parent families. *Child Development, 73*(1), 274–286.

Brody, G. H., Kim, S., Murry, V. M., & Brown, A. C. (2004). Protective longitudinal paths linking child competence to behavioral problems among African-American siblings. *Child Development, 75*(2), 455–467.

Bronfenbrenner, U., & Morris, P. A. (1998). The ecology of developmental processes. In W. Damon & R. M. Lerner (Eds.), *Handbook of child psychology: Vol. 1. Theoretical models of human development* (5th ed., pp. 993–1029). New York: Wiley.

Brophy, J. E. (1998). Classroom management as socializing students into clearly articulated roles. *Journal of Classroom Interaction, 33,* 1–4.

Bryant, D., Clifford, R., Saluga, G., Pianta, R., Early D., Barbarin, O., et al. (2003). *Diversity and directions in state pre-kindergarten programs.* Manuscript submitted for publication. Chapel Hill: University of North Carolina.

Cairns, B. D., & Cairns, R. B. (1994). *Lifelines and risks: Pathways of youth in our time.* Hemstead, NY: Harvester Wheatsheaf.

Cairns, R. B., Leung, M. C., Buchanan, L., & Cairns, B. D. (1995). Friendships and social networks in childhood and adolescence: Fluidity, reliability, and interrelations. *Child Development, 66,* 1330–1345.

Carnegie Council on Adolescent Development. (1989). *Turning points: Preparing American youth for the 21st century* [Report of the Task Force on Education of Young Adolescents and Carnegie Council of Adolescent Development]. New York: Carnegie Corporation.

Catalano, R. F., Mazza, J. J., Harachi, T. W., Abbott, R. D., Haggerty, K. P., & Fleming, C. B. (2003). Raising healthy children through enhancing social development in elementary school: Results after 1.5 years. *Journal of School Psychology, 41*(2), 143–164.

Cauce, A. M., Comer, J. P., & Schwartz, D. (1987). Long term effects of a systems oriented school prevention program. *American Journal of the Orthopsychiatric Association, 57,* 127–131.

Christian, K., Bachnan, H. J., & Morrison, F. J. (2001). Schooling and cognitive development. In R. J. Sternberg & E. L. Grigorenko (Eds.), *Environmental effects on cognitive abilities* (pp. 287–335). Mahwah, NJ: Erlbaum.

Cicchetti, D., & Aber, J. L. (1998). Editorial: Contextualism and developmental psychopathology. *Development and Psychopathology, 10*(2), 137–141.

Cicchetti, D., & Dawson, G. (2002). Editorial: Multiple levels of analysis. *Development and Psychopathology, 14*(3), 417–420.

Class Size Reduction Research Consortium. (2001). *Class size reduction in California: The 1998–99 evaluation findings.* San Francisco: CSR Research Consortium.

Clifford, R. M., Early, D. M., & Hills, T. W. (1999). Almost a million children in school before kindergarten: Who is responsible for early childhood services? *Young Children, 54*(5), 48–51.

Committee for Children. (2004). Research foundations for the "Second Step" program. Available from http://www.cfchildren.org.

Conduct Problems Prevention Research Group. (1999). Initial impact of the Fast Track prevention trial for conduct problems: II. Classroom effects. *Journal of Consulting and Clinical Psychology, 67*(5), 648–657.

Conduct Problems Prevention Research Group. (2002). Evaluation of the first 3 years of the Fast Track prevention trial with children at high risk for adolescent conduct problems. *Journal of Abnormal Child Psychology, 30,* 19–35.

Connell, J. P., Aber, J. L., & Walker, G. (1995). How do urban communities affect youth? Using social science research to inform the design and evaluation of comprehensive community initiatives. In J. P. Connell, A. Kubisch, L. B. Schorr, & C. Weiss (Eds.), *New approaches to evaluating community initiatives: Concepts, methods, and contexts* (pp. 93–126). Washington, DC: Aspen Institute.

Connell, J. P., Kubisch, A., Schorr, L. B., & Weiss, C. (Eds.). (1995). *New approaches to evaluating community initiatives: Concepts, methods and contexts.* Washington, DC: Aspen Institute.

Connell, J. P., & Wellborn, J. G. (1991). Competence, autonomy, and relatedness: A motivational analysis of self-system processes. In R. Gunnar & L. A. Sroufe (Eds.), *Minnesota Symposia on Child Psychology* (Vol. 23, pp. 43–77). Hillsdale, NJ: Erlbaum.

Cost, Quality and Child Outcomes Study Team. (1995). *Cost, quality and child outcomes in child care centers: Public report.* Denver: University of Colorado at Denver, Economics Department.

Cowen, E. L. (1999). In sickness and in health: Primary prevention's vows revisited. In D. Cicchetti & S. L. Toth (Eds.), *Rochester Symposium on Developmental Psychopathology: Vol. 9. Developmental approaches to prevention and intervention* (pp. 1–24). Rochester, NY: University of Rochester Press.

Darling-Hammond, L. (1997). *Doing what matters most: Investing in quality teaching.* New York: National Committee on Teaching and America's Future.

Dauber, S. L., Alexander, K. L., & Entwisle, D. R. (1993). Characteristics of retainees and early precursors of retention in grade: Who is held back? *Merrill-Palmer Quarterly, 39*(3), 326–343.

Duncan, G. J., & Brooks-Gunn, J. (Eds.). (1997). *Consequences of growing up poor.* New York: Russell Sage Foundation.

Durlak, J. A., & Wells, A. M. (1997). Primary prevention mental health programs for children and adolescents: A meta-analytic review. *American Journal of Community Psychology, 25*(2), 115–152.

Eccles, J. S., Early, D., Fraser, K., Belansky, E., & McCarthy, K. (1997). The relation of connection, regulation, and support for autonomy in the context of family, school, and peer group to successful adolescent development. *Journal of Adolescent Research, 12,* 263–286.

Eccles, J. S., & Gootman, J. A. (2002). *Community programs to promote youth development.* Washington, DC: National Academies Press.

Eccles, J. S., Lord, S., & Roeser, R. W. (1996). Round holes, square pegs, rocky roads, and sore feet: A discussion of stage-environment fir theory applied to families and school. In D. Cicchetti & S. L. Toth (Eds.), *Rochester Symposium on Developmental Psychopathology: Vol. VII. Adolescence: Opportunities and challenges* (pp. 47–92). Rochester, NY: University of Rochester Press.

Eccles, J. S., & Roeser, R. W. (1998). School and community influences on human development. In M. H. Bornstein & M. E. Lamb (Eds.), *Developmental psychology: An advanced textbook* (4th ed., pp. 503–554). Mahwah, NJ: Erlbaum.

Eccles, J. S., Wigfield, A., & Schiefele, U. (1998). Motivation to succeed. In W. Damon & N. Eisenberg (Eds.), *Handbook of child psychology: Vol. 3. Social, emotional, and personality development* (5th ed., pp. 1017–1095). New York: Wiley.

Ehrenberg, R. G., Brewer, D. J., Gamoran, A., & Willms, J. D. (2001). Class size and student achievement. *Psychological Science in the Public Interest, 2*(1), 1–30.

Elias, M., Zins, J., Graczyk, P., & Weissberg, R. (2003). Implementation, sustainability, and scaling up of social-emotional and academic innovations in public schools: Emerging models for promoting children's mental health [Special series]. *School Psychology Review, 32*(3), 303–319.

Entwisle, D. R., & Alexander, K. L. (1999). Early schooling and social stratification. In R. C. Pianta & M. J. Cox (Eds.), *The transition to kindergarten* (pp. 13–38). Baltimore: Paul H. Brookes.

Entwisle, D. R., Alexander, K. L., Cadigan, D., & Pallas, A. M. (1987). Kindergarten experience: Cognitive effects or socialization? *American Educational Research Journal, 24*(3), 337–364.

Evertson, C. M., & Weinstein, C. S. (Eds.). (in press). *The handbook of classroom management: Research, practice, and contemporary issues.* Mahwah, NJ: Erlbaum.

Fashola, O. S., & Slavin, R. E. (1997). Promising programs for elementary and middle schools: Evidence of effectiveness and replicability. *Journal of Education for Students Placed At Risk, 2,* 251–308.

Felner, R., Favazza, A., Shim, M., & Brand, S. (2001). Whole school improvement and restructuring as prevention and promotion: Lessons from project STEP and the project on high performance learning communities. *Journal of School Psychology, 39,* 177–202.

Finn, J. D., & Achilles, C. M. (1999). Tennessee's class size study: Findings, implications, misconceptions. *Educational Evaluation and Policy Analysis, 21*(2), 97–109.

Finn, J. D., Gerber, S. B., Achilles, C. M., & Boyd-Zacharias, J. (2001). The enduring effects of small classes. *Teachers College Record, 103*(2), 145–183.

Gambone, M. A., Klem, A. M., & Connell, J. P. (2002). *Finding out what matters for youth: Testing key links in a community action framework for youth development.* Philadelphia: Youth Development Strategies.

Gifford-Smith, M. E., & Brownell, C. A. (Eds.). (2003). Childhood peer relationships: Social acceptance, friendships, and peer networks [Target issue]. *Journal of School Psychology, 41*(4), 235–284.

Good, T. L., & Brophy, J. E. (1986). School effects. In M. Wittrock (Ed.), *Third handbook of research on teaching* (pp. 570–602). New York: Macmillan.

Good, T. L., & Weinstein, R. S. (1986). Schools make a difference: Evidence, criticisms, and new directions. *American Psychologist, 41*(10), 1090–1097.

Gottfredson, D. C. (2001). *Schools and delinquency.* New York: Cambridge University Press.

Gottlieb, G., & Halpern, C. T. (2002). A relational view of causality in normal and abnormal development. *Development and Psychopathology, 14*(3), 421–435.

Greenberg, M. T., Domitrovich, C., & Bumbarger, B. (2001). The prevention of mental disorders in school-aged children: Current state of the field [Special issue]. *Prevention and Treatment, 4*(1), 1–48.

Grissmer, D., Flanagan, A., Kawata, J., & Williamson, S. (2000). *Improving student achievement: What NAEP test scores tell us.* Arlington, VA: RAND.

Gutman, L. M., Sameroff, A. J., & Cole, R. (2003). Academic growth curve trajectories from 1st grade to 12th grade: Effects of multiple social risk factors and preschool child factors. *Developmental Psychology, 39*(4), 777–790.

Hains, A. H., Fowler, S. A., Schwartz, I. S., Kottwitz, E., & Rosenkoetter, S. (1989). A comparison of preschool and kindergarten teacher expectations for school readiness. *Early Childhood Research Quarterly, 4,* 75–88.

Hamre, B. K., Mashburn, A., Downer, J., & Pianta, R. (2004). *Teacher, classroom, and child factors associated with teacher ratings of preschoolers' relationships and problem behaviors.* Manuscript in preparation. Charlottesville: University of Virginia.

Hamre, B. K., & Pianta, R. C. (2001). Early teacher-child relationships and the trajectory of children's school outcomes through eighth grade. *Child Development, 72*(2), 625–638.

Hamre, B. K., & Pianta, R. C. (2004). Self-reported depression in nonfamilial caregivers: Prevalence and associations with caregiver behavior in child care settings. *Early Childhood Research Quarterly, 19*(2), 297–318.

Hanushek, E. A. (1999). Some findings from an independent investigation of the Tennessee STAR Experiment and from other investigations of class size effects. *Educational Evaluation and Policy Analysis, 21*(2), 143–168.

Harter, S. (1996). Teacher and classmate influences on scholastic motivation, self-esteem, and level of voice in adolescents. In J. Juvonen & K. Wentzel (Eds.), *Social motivation: Understanding children's school adjustment* (pp. 11–42). New York: Cambridge University Press.

Haynes, N. (1998). Creating safe and caring school communities: Comer School Development Program schools. *Journal of Negro Education, 65*(3), 308–314.

Haynes, N., Emmons, C., & Ben-Avie, M. (1997). School climate as a factor in student adjustment and achievement. *Journal of Educational and Psychological Consultation, 8*(3), 321–329.

Heaviside, S., & Farris, E. (1993). *Public school kindergarten teachers' views on children's readiness for school* (Report No. FRSS-46). Washington, DC: U.S. Department of Education, National Center for Education Statistics.

Hill, J. L., Brooks-Gunn, J., & Waldfogel, J. (2003). Sustained effects of high participation in an early intervention for low-birth-weight premature infants. *Developmental Psychology, 39*(4), 730–744.

Hoagwood, K., & Johnson, J. (2003). School psychology: A public health framework: I. From evidence-based practices to evidence-based policies. *Journal of School Psychology, 41*(1), 3–21.

Horppu, R., & Ikonen-Varila, M. (2001). Adult attachment representations, motives for working with children, and conceptions of a kindergarten teacher's work in first-year kindergarten teacher students. *Journal of Social and Personal Relationships, 18*(1), 131–148.

Howe, G., Reiss, D., & Yuh, J. (2002). Can prevention trials test theories of etiology? *Development and Psychopathology, 14*(4), 673–694.

Howes, C. (2000). Social-emotional classroom climate in child care, child-teacher relationships and children's second grade peer relations. *Social Development, 9,* 191–204.

Howes, C., Burchinal, M., Pianta, R., Bryant, D., Early, D., Clifford, R., et al. (in press). Ready to learn? Children's pre-academic achievement in pre-kindergarten programs. *Developmental Psychology.*

Howes, C., Matheson, C. C., & Hamilton, C. E. (1994). Maternal, teacher, and child care history correlates of children's relationship with peers. *Child Development, 65,* 264–273.

Howes, C., Phillipsen, L., & Peisner-Feinberg, C. (2000). The consistency and predictability of teacher-child relationships during the transition to kindergarten. *Journal of School Psychology, 38*(2), 113–132.

Hoxby, C. M. (1998). The effects of class size and composition on student achievement: New evidence from natural population variation. *National Bureau of Economics Research,* Working Paper No. 6869.

Hughes, J. N., Cavell, T. A., & Willson, V. (2001). Further support for the developmental significance of the quality of the teacher-student relationship. *Journal of School Psychology, 39*(4), 289–301.

Ialongo, N. S., Werthamer, L., Kellam, S. G., Brown, C. H., Wang, S., & & Lin, Y. (1999). Proximal impact of two first-grade preventive interventions on the early risk behaviors for later substance abuse, depression, and antisocial behavior. *American Journal of Community Psychology, 27*(5), 599–641.

Illinois General Assembly. (2003). S.B. 1951, Public Act 93-0495. Available from http://www.legis.state.il.us/legislation/publicacts/fulltext.asp?name=093-0495.

Institute of Education Sciences, U.S. Department of Education. (2004a). Teacher Quality Research: Reading and Writing Education. Available from http://www.ed.gov/programs/edresearch/applicant.html.

Institute of Education Sciences, U.S. Department of Education. (2004b). *No Child Left Behind Act.* Available from http://www.ed.gov/nclb/landing.jhtml?src=pb.

Kagan, S. L., & Neuman, M. J. (1998). Lessons from three decades of transition research. *Elementary School Journal, 98*(4), 365–381.

Keating, D. P. (1990). Adolescent thinking. In S. Feldman & G. Elliott (Eds.), *At the threshold: The developing adolescent* (pp. 54–89). Cambridge, MA: Harvard University Press.

Kellam, S. G., Ling, X., Merisca, R., Brown, C. H., & Ialongo, N. (1998). The effect of the level of aggression in the first grade classroom on the course and malleability of aggressive behavior into middle school. *Development and Psychopathology, 10*(2), 165–185.

Kellam, S. G., & Rebok, G. W. (1992). Building developmental and etiological theory through epidemiologically based preventive intervention trials. In J. McCord & R. E. Tremblay (Eds.), *Preventing antisocial behavior: Interventions from birth through adolescence* (pp. 162–195). New York: Guilford Press.

Kesner, J. E. (2000). Teacher characteristics and the quality of child-teacher relationships. *Journal of School Psychology, 38*(2), 133–150.

Konold, T. R., Hamre, B. K., & Pianta, R. C. (2003). Measuring problem behaviors in young children. *Behavioral Disorders, 28*(2), 111–123.

Konold, T. R., & Pianta, R. C. (2004). *The influence of informants on ratings of children's behavior functioning: A latent variable approach.* Manuscript submitted for publication. Charlottesville: University of Virginia.

Kraemer, H. C., Measelle, J. R., Ablow, J. C., Essex, M. J., Boyce, W. T., & Kupfer, D. J. (2003). A new approach to integrating data from multiple informants in psychiatric assessment and research: Mixing and matching contexts and perspectives. *American Journal of Psychiatry, 160*(9), 1566–1577.

Krueger, A. B. (1999). Experimental estimates of education productions. *Quarterly Journal of Economics, 114,* 497–532.

Ladd, G. W., Birch, S. H., & Buhs, E. S. (1999). Children's social and scholastic lives in kindergarten: Related spheres of influence? *Child Development, 70,* 1373–1400.

Ladd, G. W., & Burgess, K. B. (1999). Charting the relationship trajectories of aggressive, withdrawn, and aggressive/withdrawn children during early grade school. *Child Development, 70,* 910–929.

Larson, R., & Richards, M. H. (1991). Daily companionship in late childhood and early adolescence: Changing developmental contexts. *Child Development, 62,* 284–300.

Lerner, R. M. (1998). Theories of human development: Contemporary perspectives. In W. Damon & R. M. Lerner (Eds.), *Handbook of child psychology: Vol. 1. Theoretical models of human development* (5th ed., pp. 1–24). New York: Wiley.

Little, M., & Kobak, R. (in press). Emotional security with teachers and children's stress reactivity: A comparison of special education and regular classrooms. *Journal of Clinical Child and Adolescent Psychology.*

Love, J. M., Logue, M. E., Trudeau, J. V., & Thayer, K. (1992). *Transition to kindergarten in American schools* (Contract No. LC 88089001). Washington, DC: U.S. Department of Education.

Lynch, M., & Cicchetti, D. (1992). Maltreated children's reports of relatedness to their teachers. In R. C. Pianta (Ed.), *New directions in child development: Vol. 57. Relationships between children and nonparental adults* (pp. 81–108). San Francisco: Jossey-Bass.

Lynch, M., & Cicchetti, D. (1997). Children's relationships with adults and peers: An examination of elementary and junior high school students. *Journal of School Psychology, 35,* 81–100.

Lyon, G. R. (2002). Reading development, reading difficulties, and reading instruction: Educational and public health issues. *Journal of School Psychology, 40*(1), 3–6.

MacIver, D. J., Reuman, D. A., & Main, S. R. (1995). Social structuring of school: Studying what is, illuminating what could be. *Annual Review of Psychology* (46), 375–400.

MacIver, D., Stipek, D., & Daniels, D. (1991). Explaining within semester changes in student effort in junior high school and senior high school courses. *Journal of Educational Psychology, 83,* 361–371.

Magnusson, D., & Stattin, H. (1998). Person-context interaction theory. In W. Damon & R. M. Lerner (Eds.), *Handbook of child psychology: Vol. 1. Theoretical models of human development* (5th ed., pp. 685–760). New York: Wiley.

McGuire, S., Manke, B., Saudino, K. J., Reiss, D., Hetherington, E. M., & Plomin, R. (1999). Perceived competence and self-worth during adolescence: A longitudinal behavioral genetic study. *Child Development, 70,* 1283–1296.

McMahon, S. D., & Washburn, J. J. (2003). Violence prevention: An evaluation of program effects with urban African-American students. *Journal of Primary Prevention, 24,* 43–62.

Meisels, S. J. (1999). Assessing readiness. In R. C. Pianta & M. J. Cox (Eds.), *The transition to kindergarten* (pp. 39–66). Baltimore: Paul H. Brookes.

Meisels, S. J., & Liaw, F.-R. (1993). Failure in grade: Do retained students catch up? *Journal of Educational Research, 87*(2), 69–78.

Meyer, L. A., Wardrop, J. L., Hastings, C. N., & Linn, R. L. (1993). Effects of ability and settings on kindergarteners' reading performance. *Journal of Educational Research, 86*(3), 142–160.

Morrison, F. J., & Connor, C. M. (2002). Understanding schooling effects on early literacy: A working research strategy. *Journal of School Psychology, 40*(6), 493–500.

Mosteller, F. (1995). The Tennessee study of class size in the early school grades. In R. E. Behrman (Ed.), *Future of children: Vol. 5. Critical issues for children and youth* (pp. 113–127). Los Altos, CA: Center for the Future of Children, the Davis & Lucile Packard Foundation.

Nastasi, B. K. (1998). A model for mental health programming in schools and communities: Introduction to the mini-series. *School Psychology Review, 27,* 165–174.

National Center for Education Statistics. (2003). *Overview and inventory of state education reforms: 1990–2000.* Washington, DC: U.S. Department of Education, Institute of Education Sciences.

National Institute of Child Health and Human Development Early Child Care Research Network. (2001). Nonmaternal care and family factors in early development: An overview of the NICHD SECC. *Journal of Applied Developmental Psychology, 22,* 457–492.

National Institute of Child Health and Human Development Early Child Care Research Network. (2002a). Child care structure process outcome: Direct and indirect effects of child care quality on young children's development. *Psychological Science, 13,* 199–206.

National Institute of Child Health and Human Development Early Child Care Research Network. (2002b). Early child care and children's development prior to school entry: Results from the NICHD Study of Early Child Care. *American Educational Research Journal, 39,* 133–164.

National Institute of Child Health and Human Development Early Child Care Research Network. (2002c). The relation of global first grade classroom environment to structural classroom features, teacher, and student behaviors. *Elementary School Journal, 102*(5), 367–387.

National Institute of Child Health and Human Development Early Child Care Research Network. (2003). *Phase 4: Adolescence phase.* Proposal to the National Institute of Child Health and Human Development, Washington, DC.

National Institute of Child Health and Human Development Early Child Care Research Network. (2004a). Does class size in first grade relate to children's academic and social performance or observed classroom processes? *Developmental Psychology, 40*(5), 651–664.

National Institute of Child Health and Human Development Early Child Care Research Network. (2004b). Social functioning in first grade: Associations with earlier home and child care predictors and with current classroom experiences. *Child Development, 74*(6), 1639–1662.

National Institute of Child Health and Human Development Early Child Care Research Network. (2005). A day in third grade: Classroom quality, teacher, and student behaviors. *Elementary School Journal* (105), 305–323.

National Reading Panel. (2000). *Teaching children to read: An evidence-based assessment of the scientific research literature on reading and its implications for reading instruction.* Washington, DC.

Nelson, C. A., & Bloom, F. E. (1997). Child development and neuroscience. *Child Development, 68,* 970–987.

Nelson-Le Gall, S., & Resnick, L. (1998). Help seeking, achievement motivation, and the social practice of intelligence in school. In S. A.

Karabenick (Ed.), *Strategic help seeking: Implications for learning and teaching* (pp. 39–60). Hillsdale, NJ: Erlbaum.

Newman, R. S. (2000). Social influences on the development of children's adaptive help seeking: The role of parents, teachers, and peers. *Developmental Review, 20,* 350–404.

Newmann, F. M., & Wehlage, G. G. (1995). *Successful school restructuring: A report to the public and educators by the Center on Organization and Restructuring of Schools.* Madison, WI: Center on Organization and Restructuring of Schools.

Noam, G. G., & Hermann, C. A. (2002). Where education and mental health meet: Developmental prevention and early intervention in schools. *Development and Psychopathology, 14,* 861–875.

Noam, G. G., Warner, L. A., & Van Dyken, L. (2001). Beyond the rhetoric of zero tolerance: Long-term solutions for at-risk youth. *New Directions for Youth Development, 92,* 155–182.

No Child Left Behind Act. (2001). (H.R.1, 107th Congress). Available from www.ed.gov/nclb.

Nye, B., Hedges, L. V., & Konstantopoulos, S. (1999). The long-term effects of small classes: A five-year follow-up of the Tennessee class size experiment. *Education Evaluation and Policy Analysis, 21,* 127–142.

O'Connor, T. G. (2003). Natural experiments to study the effects of early experience: Progress and limitations. *Development and Psychopathology, 15*(4), 837–852.

Peisner-Feinberg, E. S., & Burchinal, M. R. (1997). Relations between preschool children's child care experiences and concurrent development: The cost, quality, and outcomes study. *Merrill-Palmer Quarterly, 43*(3), 451–477.

Pianta, R. C. (1999). *Enhancing relationships between children and teachers.* Washington, DC: American Psychological Association.

Pianta, R. C. (2003, February). *Teacher-child interactions: The implications of observational research for re-designing professional development.* Paper presentation to the Science and Ecology of Early Development (SEED), National Institute of Child Health and Human Development, Washington, DC.

Pianta, R. C., & Cox, M. J. (1999). *The transition to school.* Baltimore: Paul H. Brookes.

Pianta, R. C., Hamre, B., & Stuhlman, M. (2003). Relationships between teachers and children. In W. Reynolds & G. Miller (Eds.), *Educational psychology* (Vol. 7, pp. 199–234). Hoboken, NJ: Wiley.

Pianta, R. C., & Kraft-Sayre, M. (1999). Parents' observations about their children's transitions to kindergarten. *Young Children, 54*(3), 47–52.

Pianta, R. C., & La Paro, K. (2003). Improving early school success. *Educational Leadership, 60*(7), 24–29.

Pianta, R. C., La Paro, K. M., Payne, C., Cox, M. J., & Bradley, R. (2002). The relation of kindergarten classroom environment to teacher, family, and school characteristics and child outcomes. *Elementary School Journal, 102*(3), 225–238.

Pianta, R. C., Steinberg, M. S., & Rollins, K. B. (1995). The first two years of school: Teacher-child relationships and deflections in children's classroom adjustment. *Development and Psychopathology, 7,* 295–312.

Quas, J. A., Murowchick, E., Bensadoun, J., & Boyce, W. T. (2002). Predictors of children's cortisol activation during the transition to kindergarten. *Journal of Developmental and Behavioral Pediatrics, 23*(5), 304–313.

Ramey, C. T., Campbell, F. A., Burchinal, M., Skinner, M. L., Gardner, D. M., & Ramey, S. L. (2000). Persistent effects of early childhood education on high-risk children and their mothers. *Applied Developmental Science, 4,* 2–14.

Ramey, C. T., & Ramey, S. L. (1998). Early intervention and early experience. *American Psychologist, 53,* 109–120.

Ramey, S. L., & Ramey, C. T. (1992). *The National Head Start/Public School Early Childhood Transition Study: An overview.* Birmingham, AL: Civitan International Research Center.

Ready to Teach Act. (2003). *The Ready to Teach Act: H.R. 2211.* Available from http://edworkforce.house.gov/issues/108th/education/highereducation/2211billsummary.htm.

Reddy, R., Rhodes, J. E., & Mulhall, P. (2003). The influence of teacher support on student adjustment in the middle school years: A latent growth curve study. *Development and Psychopathology, 15*(1), 119–138.

Renninger, K. A. (1998). Developmental psychology and instruction: Issues from and for practice. In W. Damon (Series Ed.), I. E. Sigel, & K. A. Renninger (Vol. Eds.), *Handbook of child psychology: Vol. 4. Child psychology in practice* (5th ed., pp. 211–274). New York: Wiley.

Resnick, M. D., Bearman, P. S., Blum, R. W., Bauman, K., Harris, K. M., Jones, J., et al. (1997). Protecting adolescents from harm: Findings from the National Longitudinal Study of Adolescent Health. *Journal of the American Medical Association, 278,* 823–832.

Rimm-Kaufman, S., Storm, M., Sawyer, B., Pianta, R., & La Paro, K. (2004). *The teacher belief Q-sort: A measure of teachers' priorities and beliefs in relation to disciplinary practices, teaching practices, and beliefs about children.* Submitted for publication. Charlottesville: University of Virginia.

Rivkin, S. G., Hanushek, E. A., & Kain, J. F. (2000). *Teachers, schools and academic achievement.* Dallas: University of Texas at Dallas, Cecil and Ida Green Center for the Study of Science and Society.

Roeser, R. W., Eccles, J. S., & Sameroff, A. J. (1998). Academic and emotional functioning in early adolescence: Longitudinal relations, patterns, and prediction by experience in middle school. *Development and Psychopathology, 10,* 321–352.

Roeser, R. W., Eccles, J. S., & Sameroff, A. J. (2000). School as a context of early adolescents' academic and social-emotional development: A summary of research findings. *Elementary School Journal, 100,* 443–471.

Rones, M., & Hoagwood, K. (2000). School-based mental health services: A research review. *Clinical Child and Family Psychology Review, 3*(4), 223–241.

Rutter, M. (1982). The city and the child. *American Journal of Orthopsychiatry, 51*(4), 610–625.

Rutter, M. (1987). Psychosocial resilience and protective mechanisms. *American Journal of Orthopsychiatry, 57,* 316–331.

Rutter, M., & Maughan, B. (2002). School effectiveness findings, 1979–2002. *Journal of School Psychology, 40*(6), 451–475.

Rutter, M., Maughan, B., Mortimore, P., Ouston, J., & Smith, A. (1979). *Fifteen thousand hours: Secondary schools and their effects on children.* Cambridge, MA: Harvard University Press.

Rutter, M., & Silberg, J. (2002). Gene-environment interplay in relation to emotional and behavioral disturbance. *Annual Review of Psychology, 53,* 463–490.

Ryan, R. M., Stiller, J. D., & Lynch, J. H. (1994). Representations of relationships to teachers, parents, and friends as predictors of academic motivation and self-esteem. *Journal of Early Adolescence, 14*(2), 226–249.

Saft, E. W., & Pianta, R. C. (2001). Teachers' perceptions of their relationships with students: Effects of child age, gender, and ethnicity of teachers and children. *School Psychology Quarterly, 16*(2), 125–141.

Sameroff, A. J. (1989). *Commentary: General systems and the regulation of development.* Hillsdale, NJ: Erlbaum.

Sameroff, A. J. (1995). General systems theories and psychopathology. In D. Cicchetti & D. Cohen (Eds.), *Developmental psychopathology* (Vol. 1, pp. 659–695). New York: Wiley.

Sameroff, A. J. (2000). Developmental systems and psychopathology. *Development and Psychopathology, 12*(3), 297–312.

Sameroff, A. J., & Haith, M. (Eds.). (1996). *The 5 to 7 shift: The age of reason and responsibility.* Chicago: University of Chicago Press.

Scaramella, L. V., Conger, R. D., Spoth, R., & Simons, R. L. (2002). Evaluation of a social contextual model of delinquency: A cross-study replication. *Child Development, 73*(1), 175–195.

Simmons, R., & Blyth, D. (1987). *Moving into adolescence: The impact of pubertal change and school context.* New York: Aldine De Gruyter.

Sroufe, L. A. (1996). *Emotional development: The organization of emotional life in the early years.* New York: Cambridge University Press.

Sroufe, L. A., Carlson, E. A., Levy, A. K., & Egeland, B. (1999). Implications of attachment theory for developmental psychopathology. *Development and Psychopathology, 11,* 1–13.

Sroufe, L. A., & Rutter, M. (1984). The domain of developmental psychopathology. *Child Development, 55,* 17–29.

Steinberg, L., & Brown, B. (1989, March). *Beyond the classroom: Family and peer influences on high school achievement.* Invited paper presented to the Families as Educators special interest group at the annual meeting of the American Educational Research Association, San Francisco.

Steinberg, L., & Morris, A. S. (2001). Adolescent development. *Annual Review of Psychology, 52,* 83–110.

Stevenson, H. W., & Lee, S. Y. (1990). Contexts of achievement: A study of American, Chinese, and Japanese children. *Monographs of the Society for Research in Child Development, 55*(1–2, Serial No. 221).

Stipek, D. (2002). At what age should children enter kindergarten? A question for policymakers and parents. *Social Policy Report: Giving Child and Youth Development Knowledge Away, 16*(2), 3–16.

Stuhlman, M. W. (2003). *Early adult-child relationships as context for development: Patterns of relationships with mothers and caregivers and children's outcomes in first grade.* Unpublished doctoral dissertation, University of Virginia.

Stuhlman, M. W., & Pianta, R. C. (2001). Teachers' narratives about their relationships with children: Associations with behavior in classrooms. *School Psychology Review, 31*(2), 148–163.

Toth, S. L., & Cicchetti, D. (1996). The impact of relatedness with mother on school functioning. *Journal of School Psychology, 34,* 247–266.

Towne, L., & Hilton, M. (Eds.). (2004). *Implementing randomized field trials in education: Report of a workshop.* Washington, DC: Committee on Research in Education, National Research Council.

van Ijzendoorn, M. H., Sagi, A., & Lambermon, M. W. E. (1992). The multiple caretaker paradox: Some data from Holland and Israel. In R. E. Pianta (Ed.), *New directions in child development: Vol. 57. Relationships between children and non-parental adults* (pp. 5–24). San Francisco: Jossey-Bass.

Vitaro, F., Brendgen, M., Pagani, L., Tremblay, R. E., & McDuff, P. (1999). Disruptive behavior, peer association, and conduct disorder: Testing the developmental links through early intervention. *Development and Psychopathology, 11*(2), 287–304.

Waldman, I. D., Rowe, D. C., Abramowitz, A., Kozel, S. T., Mohr, J. H., Sherman, S. L., et al. (1998). Association and linkage of the dopamine transporter gene (DAT1) and attention deficit hyperactivity disorder in children. *American Journal of Human Genetics, 63,* 1767–1776.

Walker, H. M., Stiller, B., Severson, H. H., Feil, E. G., & Golly, A. (1998). First step to success: Intervening at the point of school entry to prevent antisocial behavior patterns. *Psychology in the Schools, 35,* 259–269.

Watamura, S. E., Donzella, B., Alwin, J., & Gunnar, M. R. (2003). Morning to afternoon increases in cortisol concentrations for infants and toddlers at child care: Age differences and behavioral correlates. *Child Development, 74*(4), 1006–1020.

Weissberg, R. P., & Greenberg, M. T. (1998). School and community competence-enhancement and prevention programs. In W. Damon (Ed.), *Handbook of child psychology* (5th ed., Vol. 4, pp. 877–954). New York: Wiley.

Wellborn, J. G., & Connell, J. P. (1987). *Rochester assessment package for children.* Rochester, NY: University of Rochester Press.

Wentzel, K. (1998). Social relationships and motivation in middle school: The role of parents, teachers, and peers. *Journal of Educational Psychology, 90*(2), 202–209.

Wentzel, K. (2002). Are effective teachers like good parents? Teaching styles and student adjustment in early adolescence. *Child Development, 73*(1), 287–301.

White, S. H. (1965). Evidence for a hierarchical arrangement of learning processes. *Advances in Child Behavior and Development, 2,* 187–220.

Wigfield, A., Eccles, J. S., & Pintrich, P. R. (1996). Development between the ages of 11 and 25. In D. C. Berliner & R. C. Calfee (Eds.), *Handbook of educational psychology* (pp. 148–185). New York: Macmillan.

Ysseldyke, J. E., Algozzine, B., & Thurlow, M. L. (2000). *Critical issues in special education* (3rd ed.). Boston: Houghton Mifflin.

Zeller, J., & Pianta, R. (2004). *Teachers' childhood attachments and teacher-student relationships.* Manuscript in preparation. Charlottesville: University of Virginia.

CHAPTER 14

Developmental Psychopathology from Family Systems and Family Risk Factors Perspectives: Implications for Family Research, Practice, and Policy

PHILIP A. COWAN and CAROLYN PAPE COWAN

FAMILY PROCESS PERSPECTIVES: ALTERNATIVES TO PSYCHOPATHOLOGY'S EMPHASIS ON THE INDIVIDUAL

The word "psychopathology" can be translated literally as a disease or disorder of the mind. Psychological diagnosticians tend to follow the medical model when studying or treating people with "mental illness," on the assumption that the disease or disorder is located within a person. In contrast with this individual approach, we present two related, converging perspectives on psychopathology, both of which provide a contextual analysis from the viewpoint of the family. The first, the *family systems* approach, emerged meteorically in the 1950s as an alternative conception to psychopathology's traditional focus on individuals (Goldenberg & Goldenberg, 1996). Not only did family systems theorists focus on the family relationships assumed to be involved in producing and maintaining psychopathology, but they conceptualized disorder as located in the family system. The individual diagnosed with Schizophrenia, for example, is described as the identified patient, but the pathology is located and treated in the system of relationships among mother, father, and child. The main point is not that individuals with diagnosed disorders are affected by their families, but that some family *systems* show structures and patterns of interaction that are maladaptive.

The second, *family risk factors* approach has always been a part of psychopathology, but most often as background rather than foreground. This approach attempts to identify one or two aspects of family functioning that play a central role in both the etiology and treatment of people diagnosed with disorders or experiencing high levels of psychological distress. Past and present parent-child relationships are the most frequently cited family risk factors thought to affect both normal development and psychopathology. Many theoretical perspectives suggest that patterns of positive or negative parent-child relationships tend to be repeated across generations in ways that foster adaptive functioning or psychopathology in individual family members. Mounting evidence from the past 2 decades reveals that the quality of the relationship *between* the child's parents is associated with the level of externalizing and internalizing behavior problems shown by the child. Although investigators using the family risk factors perspective occasionally examine the combined impact of two or more family risk or protective factors, their analysis is conceptu-

Preparation of this chapter was supported by a grant from NIMH to the authors: MH 31109 Enhancing family relationships: Child and teen outcomes.

alized as unidirectional: the effect *of* the family *on* individual adaptation or psychopathology in a family member.

Despite the fact that family systems and family risk factors approaches to psychopathology have not usually been differentiated from one another, we believe they are worth considering separately for three reasons. First, writings about family systems and family risk factors often appear in different books and different journals. Second, although there is some systematic research on whether family systems-oriented treatments are effective, there are very few tests of propositions derived from family systems theories because their assumptions do not match well with currently accepted models of scientific research. Thus, much of what we know about families and psychopathology from empirical studies comes from research using a family risk factors perspective. Third, the two perspectives lead to qualitatively different ideas about the etiology and locus of psychopathology and views of how family members should be involved in the structure and process of treatment.

Space precludes a detailed exploration of the applications of family systems and family risk factors perspectives to all, or even some, of the major disorders listed in the *Diagnostic and Statistical Manual of Mental Disorders IV*. We trust that it will become clear throughout the chapter that there are multiple, quite different versions of family systems theories. Our preference, in agreement with Schultz (1984), is to talk about family systems ideas as a set of lenses for looking at and thinking about the development of psychopathology from a family perspective. We see both family systems and family risk factors as contextual approaches to the understanding of psychopathology rather than as coherent, monolithic theories of how psychopathology emerges and progresses.

FAMILY STRUCTURE PERSPECTIVES: THE POLITICAL CONTEXT OF FAMILY PSYCHOPATHOLOGY

In the months leading up to the United States presidential election of 2004, the contemporary state of American families began to occupy increasing attention from political candidates and political pundits. The nature of marriage and the role of marriage and family processes in children's development became significant topics of national and local debate. Postelection discussions suggested that voters' attitudes concerning some of these issues played an important role in the outcome of the election. Despite conflicting views concerning specific "family values," neither liberals nor conservatives questioned whether families are important or play a central role in children's well-being. The question was whether some family structures or arrangements (single-parent families, cohabiting families, divorced families, gay or lesbian families) constitute risk factors for children's development, and whether other family arrangements (primarily two-parent married families) function to protect children from a variety of biopsychosocial risks. That is, over and above the notion that family processes play a central role in individual psychopathology is the idea that some families, described in terms of demographic characteristics, are less likely to support the positive development of their members.

We have deliberately chosen to begin our review of family systems and developmental psychopathology by noting some aspects of the political/policy/practice context of the discussion about the role of families in the development of psychopathology. Our point here, which we elaborate on at the end of the chapter, is that, just as perspectives on the role of the family in psychopathology make a difference to our understanding of etiology and the planning of treatment, so the social context in which family theories and treatments are developed and promulgated has profound effects on which theories of family function shape policy decisions about how scarce resources are to be allocated for the diagnosis and treatment of children and families in distress. To remain within our space limitations and provide a focused account of family systems theory, we illustrate this thesis with examples drawn primarily from the United States. We believe that the general principles we infer and some of the specific family trends we recount (e.g., changing rates of divorce, marriage, and single parenthood) apply more broadly to Western industrialized countries and cultures.

We should note that books and papers on family systems and family risk factors in developmental psychopathology are written primarily by psychologists, psychiatrists, social workers, and other mental health professionals. Writings on family structures and social policy are more likely to be produced by sociologists, demographers, and economists. Unfortunately, the literatures on these two topics rarely take cognizance of each other. One of our tasks in this chapter is to bring the two closer together.

We begin with sections that define our central concepts: developmental psychopathology, family systems, and family risk factors. After describing where family systems and family risk factor theories fit in the pantheon of theories that compete for the allegiance of researchers and clinicians, we take a brief historical look at how these theories have changed over time. Then three longer sections illustrate how family systems and family risk factors approaches

can be applied to the understanding of developmental psychopathology.

Consistent with developmental psychopathology's concern with normal development, we examine how family processes are implicated in explaining what happens when nonclinical families go through major life transitions, both expected (e.g., marriage, parenthood) and unexpected (e.g., divorce, illness). Our focus here is not only to demonstrate correlations between family relationship quality and individual developmental outcomes, but also to elucidate the mechanisms by which families have effects on their members. We then show how formulations from a family systems or family risk factor perspective can provide value-added information, both in predicting the trajectories people follow in their journeys toward or away from diagnosed disorders, and in planning interventions for those at risk or already in distress.

The application of both family systems and family risk factor models of developmental psychopathology has been governed by a fairly traditional view of the family that was current in the mid-twentieth century, when the family systems approach emerged. Toward the end of the chapter, we step back to take a brief historical look at how families have been changing over the past century. We use this perspective to raise some questions about whether a family systems or family risk factors approach to developmental psychopathology can deal adequately with the diversity and complexity of the families they are designed to understand and treat.

We conclude with a discussion of future directions in the application of a family perspective to the study of developmental psychopathology. We offer suggestions about important theoretical and research questions that constitute promising next steps in the development of the field of developmental psychopathology. In the end, we return to a discussion of the interconnection and disconnection between psychopathology research conducted from a family perspective and policy decisions about how family researchers, therapists, and families themselves will be supported.

PRINCIPLES OF DEVELOPMENTAL PSYCHOPATHOLOGY

The entire three-volume work in which this chapter appears is devoted to the definition and explication of the principles of developmental psychopathology. Here we briefly summarize the conception of the field that guides our discussion of family perspectives.

Definitions of Psychopathology

Family systems theorists and therapists do not generally devote much attention to issues in the definition of psychopathology. Different kinds of criteria are used in making the distinction between psychopathology and normal development. All of them involve a description of individuals with extreme, maladaptive deviations—from social norms and values, from the mean of a population (a continuous view of psychopathology), or from some clinically defined ideal of psychological functioning (a categorical view of psychopathology). In this chapter, we take a rather broad view, with descriptions of family systems and family risk factor approaches to phenomena ranging all the way from statistically normative levels of stress or distress to clinically diagnosed disorders.

The Prospective Study of Pathways

A family approach to developmental psychopathology is concerned with understanding mental illness and mental health in individuals by focusing on one of the primary contexts in which individuals develop. The study of developmental psychopathology involves intensive, prospective, longitudinal analyses of four major pathways or trajectories that individuals and families may follow: (1) those at high risk for mental health problems who go on to develop disorders or debilitating psychological distress, or cause great distress to others; (2) those at high risk for mental health problems who do not develop disorders, psychological distress, or severe behavior problems as we might have expected on the basis of their risk status; (3) those at low risk who do not develop disorders, psychological distress, or behavior problems, as expected; and (4) those at low risk who unexpectedly develop disorders, psychological distress, or behavior problems. In contrast with traditional approaches to the study of psychopathology, developmental psychopathology is equally interested in instances in which risk status correctly predicts or does not predict the expected outcomes. That is, the field is intensely curious about why some people develop optimally despite risk, whereas others develop problems despite conditions that typically facilitate adaptation.

Etiology: Causal Models versus Risk Models

An axiom of the study of psychopathology is that it is essential to understand the etiology of each disorder. This task has been traditionally framed as identifying causal variables, events, or conditions (A) that are associated with

a disorder (B), precede the disorder (A before B), and provide some force or action that brings the disorder into being (A → B). Furthermore, to establish causal connections, it is necessary to prove that B is not traceable to factors other than A, that there is a unique connection between cause and effect.

Providing evidence of causality in the study of families and children's development is a difficult task (P. A. Cowan, Powell, & Cowan, 1998). It is well-known that correlations alone do not provide evidence of causality, although the absence of correlations poses a serious threat to a causal claim. For example, if there is no association between the occurrence of Schizophrenia in family members and double-binding communication in the family, it is unlikely that this theory of communication-caused Schizophrenia can be supported.

Etiological formulations that attempt to establish causal explanations of disorders are based on metaphors used in pre-twentieth century medicine, which, in turn, were based on models from seventeenth-century physics. In these models, there is always a direct connection between a cause and its effect. By contrast, developmental psychopathologists have adopted risk-outcome models from the practice of public health epidemiology (Kleinbaum, Morgenstern, & Kupper, 1982), in which (1) a risk factor is an antecedent variable or condition associated with an elevated probability of a specified negative outcome in a population; (2) a protective factor is a variable or condition that reduces the probability of negative outcome despite the presence of risk; and (3) a vulnerability factor is a variable or condition that increases the probability of a negative outcome associated with a given risk.

Resilience is difficult to define. Sometimes, in cases of high risk, children and adults do exceptionally well and are described as resilient. Although resilience is sometimes conceptualized as a Teflon quality of a person, it should be interpreted more simply as a case in which risks create challenges that lead to positive outcomes.

In many cases, the predictive association between risk and outcome simply represents a correlation between the two, with no need to claim that the linkage is causal; the establishment of accurate predictors or markers is useful in identifying individuals at risk for potential problems that have a high probability of emerging in the future. In some cases, the connection can be described as a causal risk, when it can be demonstrated that a variable or condition sets a number of processes in motion that result in a given outcome. How can we determine the difference between statistical risk indicators and causal risks? The best way to establish causality is through intervention studies that use random assignment procedures to place comparable people in intervention and control groups; we describe some examples of this approach later in the chapter. Another way is to use comparison data and statistical controls in an attempt to rule out alternative possibilities, so that causal interpretations of the data become more plausible.

In developmental psychopathology, the ideal study is one that follows individuals and families forward, tracing the paths from risks to outcomes, rather than a follow-back design that begins with the diagnosis, followed by a retrospective search for antecedents. The main problem with retrospective designs in establishing causality is that, even when they show that a presumed antecedent (e.g., family conflict) is more frequent in families with a diagnosed member, they cannot reveal whether the same antecedent is associated with many disorders (multifinality) or whether there are multiple risk factors, each of which predict the same disorder (equifinalilty).

Acquisition versus Maintenance

Most theories of etiology deal with what could be called the original precipitating causes of a disorder or the factors that govern its acquisition. We want to know, for example, whether extremely harsh parenting practices that border on abuse lead to the emergence of aggressive, acting-out or shy, withdrawn, depressed behavior in a child (Cicchetti, Toth, & Maughan, 2000). Equally important for clinical practice, and a central aspect of most family system theories, is the notion that regardless of how a problematic disorder is acquired, there are causal factors or risk factors involved in how or whether it is maintained. As we will see, there is ample evidence that genetic factors are important determinants of Schizophrenia and bipolar disorders (Rutter & Sroufe, 2000) and in some cases may be considered primary factors affecting whether and how maladaptive behavior is acquired. Nevertheless, even if the acquisition process is heavily dominated by genetics, there is evidence that family interaction processes can play a key role in whether gains from hospitalization are maintained or whether patients suffer a relapse once they return home (Hooley, 2004).

Prevention: Early Intervention and Treatment

Because traditional psychopathology studies begin with people who have already been diagnosed, questions about etiology are most often raised in the context of treatment. All theories of psychopathology assume that if a disorder can be described and assessed (diagnosed), and if its etiol-

ogy can be established, it is possible to design a treatment that specifically targets the risk and causal factors known to affect the course of the disorder. By virtue of the fact that studies central to the field of developmental psychopathology are often concerned with the identification of risks long before disorders are manifested, this approach is ideally suited to the conduct of prevention science (Coie, Watt, West, & Hawkins, 1993). Once risk factors are identified, it is possible to set in motion preventive interventions that minimize risks and enhance protective factors, either to prevent a problem from occurring or to intervene early enough to reduce the severity of the problem before it becomes intractable.

FAMILY SYSTEMS APPROACHES TO PSYCHOPATHOLOGY: EARLY BEGINNINGS

The task of identifying family systems perspectives on specific diagnostic disorders is a difficult one, because most of the leading figures in the field avoided the use of diagnostic terminology in their discussions, except for some general references to the diagnoses given to the identified patient. In part, then, we must infer conceptualizations of psychopathology from the ways family therapists characterized the central problems of the families they treated.

The Founding Fathers (Mostly) of Family Systems Approaches

Around the middle of the twentieth century, groups of clinicians in different parts of the United States, beginning from different theoretical premises, challenged the notion that a focus on individual psychopathology was sufficient to provide treatment guidelines for patients who were seriously mentally ill. In different ways, each group pointed to one or two central aspects of family functioning that they believed were responsible for causing Schizophrenia or maintaining the symptoms after patients returned home from the hospital. The fact that the origins of family systems approaches began with this population in mind shaped the first generation of family systems theorists and therapists.

Nathan Ackerman, a psychoanalyst heading what later became the Ackerman Institute in New York, was an early advocate of the importance of considering family risk factors in the treatment of children (Ackerman & Sobel, 1950). Fearing rejection by colleagues, he began to hint, rather than advocate directly, that this perspective suggested that family members should be seen conjointly—all together in one room. He was finally able to argue clearly (Ackerman,

1962) that all members of a household should be in conjoint treatment whenever a child is brought in for therapy. The therapy Ackerman proposed was unlike that of many subsequent family theorists because he focused on the inner dynamics of family members that made family interaction problematic. As a result, the therapist tended to conduct individual therapies in the context of the family as a whole.

Theodore Lidz and his colleagues (Lidz, Cornelison, Fleck, & Terry, 1957) at the Yale Psychiatric Institute in New Haven objected to the prevailing tendency to blame "schizophrenogenic" mothers for their children's Schizophrenia, pointing to the fact that families of patients diagnosed with Schizophrenia were usually imbalanced in many ways, not just in the mother-child relationship. In a clinical study of families with a member diagnosed as schizophrenic, this research group found that fathers were not playing an effective parental role. Furthermore, the couple was either in a state of high unresolved conflict (marital schism) or showed patterns of avoidance of serious conflict in which one partner's ideas were accepted overtly but undermined by the other partner, and talk about the difference was forbidden (marital skew). Lidz and his group pointed to the transmission of distorted patterns across at least three generations: from grandparents to parents to grandchildren.

Around the same time, at the National Institute of Mental Health (NIMH) in Washington, DC, Lyman Wynne (Wynne, Ryckoff, Day, & Hirsch, 1958), later joined by Margaret Singer (Singer & Wynne, 1965a), also attempted to describe families with a schizophrenic member. Wynne pointed to what he called "pseudomutuality" in all of the family relationships, not just the couple relationship. Singer and Wynne showed that the thought disorder central to the diagnosis of Schizophrenia was more likely to be displayed when patients were brought together with their family to try to come to consensus on the meaning of a Rorschach (inkblot) card, but not when patients were seen alone by the researcher. That is, the disorder seemed to be located not in the functioning of the individual but in the family as a whole. In another laboratory at NIMH, Murray Bowen (1961) emphasized the fact that although maternal or parental *distance* was often blamed for triggering Schizophrenia in their offspring, families in which members had few personal boundaries and were highly *enmeshed* or *symbiotic* were overrepresented in the population of people diagnosed as schizophrenic entering treatment (he described these families as showing an "undifferentiated ego mass").

A group of clinicians at the Mental Research Institute (MRI) in Palo Alto, California, extends our portrait of the founding fathers, with one founding mother as part of that group. The members represented different disciplines, with Don Jackson from psychiatry, Virginia Satir from social work, Gregory Bateson from anthropology, and Jay Haley, John Weakland, William Fry, and, somewhat later, Paul Watzlawick from various subfields of communication. Like investigators in other parts of the country, these clinicians focused on families diagnosed with Schizophrenia and came to the view that deviant communications among family members were a central problem in families with a severely mentally ill member. One of the first widely disseminated ideas from the MRI group was the "double bind" theory of Schizophrenia, in which a family member (typically a mother) gives contradictory demands in different modalities. For example, she might say to her child "Come sit by me" but react with a shudder when the child did so. In obeying one message ("come here"), the child violated the other ("go away"). Another version of the double bind is a nonverbal message that conveys "You are not to hear what I'm telling you or see what I'm doing," with the result that after hearing or seeing what has in fact been communicated, the child has disobeyed the implicit message. What makes the double bind so binding is that other implicit messages or "family rules" prohibit the victim from leaving the field or commenting on the conflicting messages. Although it is easy to imagine that repeated, ongoing double-binding communication from one or both parents would be highly disturbing to both adults and children, the double bind hypothesis has not been empirically validated, in part because examples are often so subtle and complex that observers cannot agree about when they occur (Ringuette & Kennedy, 1966).

Bateson brought to the MRI group's writings two different models of systems theories without making a clear distinction between them. From Bertalanffy (Bertalanffy & Woodger, 1962), a philosopher and biologist who developed what he later called general system theory (Bertalanffy, 1973), Bateson drew on the central idea that systems have self-regulating properties. That is, there are internal mechanisms that operate to pull the system back when too much change has occurred, or push forward when more change is needed. Bertalanffy's model was based on living biological systems, which he described as open and always capable of moving toward new organizations. Bateson also used models and metaphors from the field of game theories (Von Neumann & Morgenstern, 1953), which assume that bargaining takes place in a zero-sum environment (if I win, you lose, and vice versa), and from cybernetics (Wiener, 1961), a field in which machine systems were designed with deviation-reducing mechanisms to bring about a return to homeostasis whenever dysregulated subsystems threatened to drive the machine out of control. These systems are not necessarily open in the same way that biological systems are. Once some change has been introduced into the system, homeostatic mechanisms operate like thermostats to bring the organization back to a prior state and are centrally important in explaining maladaptation and resistance to change. That is, within family systems theories are embedded two quite different models of self-regulation, one of which, the cybernetic example, emphasizes stability much more than change.

Why do some families continue to repeat patterns of behavior that are unproductive or destructive? Forces within the system tend to spring into action when new behavior emerges in ways that return the family to the previous homeostatic balance or set point. This formulation helps to explain why family therapists are so active compared to psychoanalytic colleagues who treat individuals. Unless the therapist disequilibrates the family with some dramatic statements, gestures, or homework assignments, the homeostatic properties of the system will frustrate the family's stated wish for change and frustrate the therapist's desire to help them change by introducing a countervailing force that resists the family's tendency to return to the tried and true.

In our view, one of the last major figures in the early origins of family systems theory is Salvador Minuchin. His initial book, *Families of the Slums,* cowritten with Montalvo, Bosman, and Schumer (1967), and his creation of the Philadelphia Child Guidance Clinic as a training center for family systems treatment helped to demonstrate that family systems principles could be applied usefully to families with a wide range of problems in a wide range of economic circumstances.

Defining Properties of Systems

Despite differences in the focus of their work, the early family systems theorists converged on a set of principles that defined the systemic approach (see Wagner & Reiss, 1995).

Wholeness

A system is composed of elements (parts) and a whole, with patterns of connections among the parts and between each part and the whole. In family systems theories, the elements are often individual family members. Each is in a relationship with each of the others, but together they constitute a family with a unique set of properties. The best-known principle describing family systems is that the whole is different from any single part and from the sum of its parts. In family terms, it is not possible to predict the behavior or level of adaptation of an individual by considering him or her in isolation; one needs to know about the context of the individual in his or her family, the pairwise relationships among the members, and how the system functions as a whole. The father and the mother may not get along with each other, and at least one of the parent-child or sibling pairs may vibrate with unresolved conflict, but we cannot conclude that this family is dysfunctional or that the child is at risk for mental illness, because from the limited information given here we do not know what happens when all the family members get together. It would make a great difference to the well-being of the children in the family whether, for example, the parents continue their escalating arguments or put aside their squabbles successfully when the child is present, or whether one parent compensates for the fact that the other parent and the child are not getting along by being exceptionally nurturant with the child.

Locus of Problems

Problems are located in the system, not in individual members. The family member brought into treatment because of highly deviant, hostile, or anxious behavior is regarded as the identified patient; other family members have designated this person as the problem, but the therapist locates the pathology in the family as a whole and helps the family to do the same.

Subsystems

Beyond the contrast between the system as a whole and the individual family members, it is necessary to be aware of how family subsystems operate. Families in which one child is allied with the mother and distant from the father, or the couple fail to work together, are quite different from families in which the couple forms a tight bond that excludes close relationships with the children.

Boundaries

Around each subsystem is an invisible enclosure called a boundary (Wagner & Reiss, 1995). One of the key defining properties of subsystems is whether the boundaries are rigid or permeable. Rigid boundaries denote subsystems that are disengaged from each other (e.g., the father has difficulty becoming included in the mother-son relationship). Families with rigid boundaries tend to promote authority and autonomy at the expense of closeness. At the other end of the adaptation continuum, boundaries can be so diffuse and permeable that subsystems become enmeshed, as, for example, when children occupy the attention of their parents so constantly that there is no separation between the life of the couple and the life of the children.

Circular Causality

We have noted that traditional scientific models and models of psychopathology describe causality in linear terms (A → B) and that it is difficult to obtain evidence in support of linear causal claims. Family systems theories make the assumption that causality is *circular*. There is mutual regulation in that change in one person in a relationship can trigger a change in the other so that changes are simultaneous (A ← B), or change can take place in a reverberating chain (A → B → C → A). If this is so, it does not always make sense to try to find out which came first, but rather to intervene to change the relationship patterns.

Structure and Process

There are two kinds of questions one can ask about families: How are they structured or organized, and how do they function? The answers help us understand how families operate to produce both stability and change in the system over time. Although the comparison is oversimplified, the same questions can be asked of a battery-operated toy that has not yet been turned on. Structural questions include, How do the parts fit together? Process questions include, What does it do once you turn on the power? Structures do not exist independently of processes. V. K. Johnson (2005, p. 256) notes that, "as dimensions of family life, family process and family structure can be thought of as two conceptually distinct lenses applied to the same set of phenomena." Structures are like static photographs or blueprints that diagram the formal relations between the parts and the whole, such as whether the parts are connected. Structural descriptions of families could include size of family; whether the parents are unmarried, married, separated, or divorced; how many members are in each subsystem; and whether communication proceeds from the top down or occurs with each person having an equal opportunity to communicate. This last sounds more like a process issue, but from this description we do not have any idea about how people talk to each other. Rather, we have simply described an aspect of structure that could be seen in a static organizational chart in a corporation.

The process aspect of a system refers to dynamic qualities that are often assessed in self-report questionnaires or interviews. A more direct way of assessing the dynamics requires videotape or other devices that allow observers to record the quality of interactions as they unfold over time. Process descriptions of families could include the quality of relationships (including closeness and distance, unresolved conflict, parenting style) and the permeability of boundaries. Although it is difficult to distinguish between structural and process levels of analysis, it can be useful to try to do so. For example, data concerning family structure (cohesion and organization) obtained in a nonclinical study of families during the preschool period contributed independently to predicting children's behavior problems in first grade, over and above observational data on the quality of marital and parent-child interaction processes (V. K. Johnson, Cowan, & Cowan, 1999).

We should note here that the concept of structure in family system theories has a different meaning from the term as sociologists use it. The similarity is that both focus on the organization of the family. Family systems theorists use structure to refer to the way family processes are arranged. Sociologists use the term to refer to different family forms described by legal bonds, living arrangements, and kinship: cohabitating, married, separated, divorced couples or single-parent families, two-parent families, and stepfamilies.

Homeostasis

We described the biological and cybernetic models that researchers at the MRI used to represent homeostatic properties of family systems. What is important about the concept of homeostasis, even when it is exemplified by a change-resisting cybernetic model, is that the system operates in self-regulating ways that can amplify or reduce the power of external stressors to affect the quality of family life.

The Novelty of the Early Family Systems Approach

Some assumptions of family systems theory are so well accepted today that it is difficult to conceive of how new they were 50 years ago, when most adult therapy was individual (although there were couples counselors and therapists) and when most children were treated in play therapy, with their parents as adjuncts to the treatment. Of course, psychoanalysts spent a great deal of time focusing on how past experiences in the family of origin operate to restrict ego and superego functioning in the present, but it would have been unthinkable (and may still be in orthodox psychoanalytic treatments) to bring the parents into the room with the child or adult patient in an effort to reconstruct the present relationship so that it functions more supportively to both generations. Child therapists in the mid-twentieth century certainly assumed that families were important, but they generally conceived of parents (mothers) as adjuncts in the treatment who could provide contextual information not available during the play therapy session or be educated about their role as a parent (A. Freud, 1965; Winnicott, 1987). Marital conflicts were often noted, and referrals for couples therapy made, but marital therapy or direct intervention in the three-generational transmission of family patterns was not included in the job description of the child therapist. The notion that child therapists may have been treating the identified patient but not intervening where the problem was located was not a part of therapeutic discourse inside or outside the consulting room then, nor is it part of therapeutic discourse in most child treatment settings today.

FAMILY RISK FACTOR APPROACHES TO PSYCHOPATHOLOGY: EARLY BEGINNINGS

In accounting for the emergence of psychopathology in a child or adult, relationship patterns from different family domains can be considered possible risk or protective factors that affect children's adaptation or maladaptation; qualities of parent-child relationships (Steinberg, 2001), couple relationships (Cummings & Davies, 1994), and intergenerational relationships (Caspi & Elder, 1988) top the list. Although genetic risk factors are usually considered in opposition to family and other environmental risk factors, as in the contrast between nature (genetics) and nurture (family; Rutter, 2002), we view the transmission of genetic materials from parents to children as an inherently family-based process, even when the transmission is accomplished through sperm donation or other artificial means. The pattern of genes transmitted and combined in the new offspring is essentially an outgrowth of family patterns associated with the two biological parents. Let us emphasize that, in contrast to the family systems emphasis on the family as the unit of analysis and the locus of pathology, the family risk factor approach assumes that one or more risk factors combine to produce psychopathology in the individual family member.

The family risk factor approach to psychopathology has both a long and a short history. One can infer a family factors approach to psychopathology from the Greek plays and myths used by Freud to illustrate his own psychodynamic views. While the Greeks placed great weight on fates, the gods, and literal deus ex machina forces that affect men's and women's behavior, the Oedipus, Electra, and Medea stories present vivid examples of how family struggles can result in destruction and madness in parents and their offspring.

Prior to the emergence of family systems theories in the 1950s and 1960s, psychodynamic theories suggested that normal development involved identification with one's parent of the same sex and internalization of his or her value

judgments as necessary; failure to complete this identification was viewed as a prime risk factor for psychopathology (S. Freud, 1905). Behavioral theories promulgated by Watson (1928) and others supported the idea that how parents reinforced and punished their children played a central role in producing either well-adjusted or maladjusted children. At midcentury, however, research on children's development was remarkably acontextual, with Gesell (Gesell, Ilg, Learned, & Ames, 1943) and Piaget (1950) paying virtually no attention to parents, and both Sigmund and Anna Freud (1965; S. Freud, 1938) focusing only on the child's internalizations, not on parental behavior, in attempts to understand children's cognitive, social, and emotional development. With the possible exception of attachment theories (Bowlby, 1961) studies of variations in parenting styles with normal children stimulated by the work of Baumrind (1971), very little systematic empirical research focused on family relationship qualities and children's adaptation. As we show, most of the growth in the family risk factors approach to developmental research occurred toward the last third of the twentieth century.

WHERE FAMILY SYSTEMS AND FAMILY RISK FACTOR THEORIES FIT IN THE PANTHEON OF PSYCHOPATHOLOGY THEORIES

How are family systems and family risk factor approaches similar to and different from the other main developmental psychopathology theories? One of us (PAC) had a professor who taught a course in theories of personality and each week covered a new theorist in class. Instead of recounting what the theorist was trying to tell us, he always began with the questions the theorist was trying to answer, demonstrating that theorists differed not so much because of fundamental disagreements in their claims, but because of differences in their questions, focus of interest, and level of analysis. The professor's approach assumed that each theory had a corner on the truth and that there are many valid perspectives on the explanation of adaptation and psychopathology.

To the extent that we can generalize about a field, the assumption that there may be many roads to Rome is not widely accepted in the study of psychopathology. It is as if students entering the field are brought to a market bazaar, with sellers hawking their wares, each saying, "Buy my bracelets and ignore the merchant in the stall next to me. The ornaments on his bracelets are colored glass but mine are precious jewels." Is the field of psychopathology really as competitive and absolute as this? Not in textbooks, where writers acknowledge in measured statements that there are many valid approaches to understanding what goes awry in development. In practice, however, many diagnosticians and therapists focus on the individual and pay relatively little attention to the individual's relationships with family, friends, and work, unless those topics are raised by the client in discussing current problems. Child therapists pay attention to the relationships between mother and child but tend to ignore both the father and the relationship between father and mother. Many biologically oriented therapists dispense drugs but spend minimal time talking with the patient, and many psychodynamically oriented therapists focus on talk and avoid prescribing drugs. Most behaviorally oriented therapists would not spend therapeutic time discussing inner defense mechanisms of parents or children, whereas nonbehavioral therapists rarely suggest systematic reinforcements or "time-out." That is, emphases in the therapist's theory of psychopathology shape the content and structure of both assessment and therapeutic practice.

In this section, we present schematic models that summarize answers to two major questions raised by researchers and clinicians who attempt to understand the role of the family in developmental psychopathology: Which domains of family life are necessary to examine when we assess families? and How do we understand both change and stability within each of these family domains?

A Six-Domain Family Risk Model

Until the 1980s, most studies of family risk factors focused on one domain of the family at a time, although some assessed that domain in multiple ways. In 1984, Belsky proposed a three-domain model that included the personal psychological resources of the parents, characteristics of the child, and contextual sources of stress and support outside the family as determinants of parenting quality leading to children's developmental outcomes. In the same year, Heinicke (1984) proposed a different three-domain model that included individual, marital, and parent-child factors in the prebirth period to predict postpartum adaptation in both mother and child. Our own five-domain model (C. P. Cowan et al., 1985) hypothesized that children's adaptation to elementary school could be predicted by a combination of information from five aspects of family life: (1) the individual personality and adaptation of mother, father, and child; (2) couple relationship quality; (3) parent-child relationship quality; (4) intergenerational family patterns; and (5) the balance of social support and life stress in family members' relationships with people

and institutions in the larger society. Because our research focused on the parents' relationships with their first child, we ignored an important sixth domain: sibling relationships (see Figure 14.1).

Recent evidence from our Schoolchildren and Their Families Project (P. A. Cowan, Cowan, & Heming, 2005) indicates that each of the first five domains assessed in the year before the oldest child enters kindergarten contributes unique variance to the prediction of the child's academic achievement and externalizing and internalizing behavior in kindergarten and first grade; taken together, these family risk measures account for substantial amounts of variance—often over 50%—in the child's adaptation to school. The design of our studies and the choice to assess multiple family domains using multimethod, multiperspective assessment tools (interviews, questionnaires, and observations of family interaction) was directly influenced by family systems theories as we described them earlier. Nevertheless, with only a few exceptions in which we examined family-level functioning (V. K. Johnson et al., 1999), our research designs are more consistent with a family risk factor model than a family systems approach because we look at predictions *from* family functioning *to* children's outcomes. As we will see, there is ample evidence from many studies in support of the hypothesis that adaptation or maladaptation within each of these domains accounts for substantial variance in child and adolescent functioning.

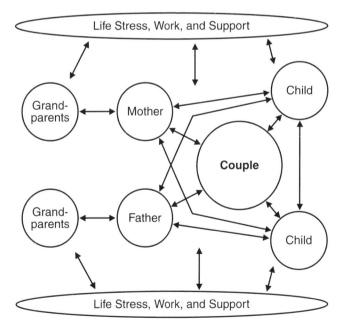

Figure 14.1 Six domains of family life involved in children's psychopathology.

A Nine-Cell Model of Alternative Explanations of Stability and Change in Each Family Domain

To understand and treat psychopathology in an identified patient, family systems theorists want us to look at the whole family, and perhaps at some of the subsystems outlined in the six-domain model. In part, their insistence on focusing on the family as a whole was stimulated by their frustration with the fact that traditional theories of psychopathology did not lead to therapies that produced change reliably (especially in patients with severe mental illness). To illustrate how family systems theories have come up with answers that are quite different from most other theories of psychopathology, we examine the following basic question: What produces stability and change in individuals, relationships, and family systems?

Why do some individuals or families show excessive resistance when situations call for change (e.g., they are unresponsive to reasonable social demands), whereas other individuals or families show excessive sensitivity to change (e.g., instantaneous reaction to the changing emotions of others)? Theoretical answers to these questions vary along two conceptual dimensions. The first dimension describes the preferred level of analysis of the theorist: Does he or she look for explanations of stability and change in biological, psychological, or social aspects of the person? The second dimension describes whether the source of change is considered to be internal, external, or interactive. Combining these dimensions yields a matrix of nine major factors affecting stability and change, each located in a different "cell" (see Figure 14.2). Each cell, then, contains a different type of theory.

Within each cell, theorists generally choose the same answer to questions about explaining normal development, explaining psychopathology, and speculating about what kind of intervention would be necessary to address problems as formulated by the theory. For example, theorists who assume that internal factors that govern change and stability shape the emergence of normal development also assume that internal conditions affect the emergence of psychopathology; not surprisingly, these theorists assume that interventions focusing on internal factors (biological functioning, defense mechanisms, cognitive schemas) should be central in whatever treatment is provided. That is, within each cell, the answers to fundamental questions about stability and change tend to come in "boxed sets."

We should state at the outset that the basic assumptions of family systems theories are consistent with social interactional theories of stability and change (cell 9). Relationships are central. Stability or change occurs as products of interactions among individuals and subsystems in the context of the family as a whole. We can now locate other competing theories with reference to this cell. We will show that the family risk factors approach appears in a number of cells, depending on the level of analysis and the theorist's reliance on external or internal theories of change. Although our descriptions highlight the differences between cells as if they represented mutually exclusive choices, we know that the theories in different cells differ in emphasis and do not represent categorically distinct approaches to developmental psychopathology.

Biological Level of Analysis

Biological factors in development can be found inside the person, in the environment, and in the interaction between the two.

Internal

In this cell, theorists assume that the path toward normal development is regulated by a system of genetic, biochemical, neurophysiological, and physical processes operating within individuals. If they malfunction, these same processes are invoked as determinants of psychological disorders such as Schizophrenia, depression, and antisocial personality. Theorists, researchers, and clinicians with a biological internal perspective often assume that biologically caused disorders will respond best, if they respond at all, to biological treatments such as the administration of psychoactive drugs. Because it is not possible to intervene at the level of genetic processes or brain functions, at least not yet, the biological internal view tends to

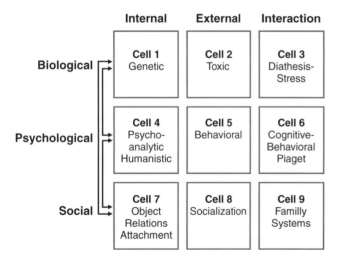

Figure 14.2   The 9-cell matrix: Alternative theories of stability and change.

emphasize stability and resistance to change and to present a somewhat pessimistic picture of the possibility of treatment. If a disorder is inherited, the message seems to be, interventions can reduce the expression of basic symptoms but nothing much can be done to change the underlying disorder. We will see that this pessimism is unwarranted on both logical and empirical grounds.

External

So pervasive that it is not always acknowledged, the physical environment plays a central role in normal development (e.g., nutrition, clean air). Malnutrition and chemically toxic conditions (e.g., lead poisoning) can also cause psychotic reactions or extreme behavior disorders (Zetin, Stasiek, Pangan, & Warren, 1988). From the biological external perspective, intervention should be directed toward the elimination of environmental deprivation or toxicity.

Interaction between Physical Environment and Biological Factors

A strictly internal view of biological factors in development is outmoded. Internal biological processes are always influenced by external biological, psychological, and social events. Genetic and neurological processes unfold within environmental niches that influence whether risk factors will be expressed in behavior. For example, even if brain scans obtained through functional magnetic resonance imaging (fMRI) show differences between groups of patients diagnosed as schizophrenic and nonschizophrenic, we do not know whether the brain (mal)function generated the schizophrenic behavior or whether biopsychosocial stressors over time led to the brain malfunction (Kandel, 2000). From the perspective of cell 3, intervention involves alterations in the biologically based functions of the individual along with shifts in the external environment. A good example of this perspective is the treatment of children with Attention-Deficit/Hyperactivity Disorder (ADHD) with a prescription of Ritalin, along with an extensive reduction of stimulation in the children's school environment (Hinshaw, 1994).

Psychological Level of Analysis

Development can be shaped by psychological forces within people, by behaviors of others directed toward them, and by the combination of internal and external psychological events.

Internal

Given a "good enough" psychosocial environment (Winnicott, 1987), forces from within unfold to produce normal development. In this cell are the humanistic theorists (Maslow, 1962; Rogers, 1961), who assume that all human beings move toward self-actualization unless they are prevented from doing so, and psychoanalysts (e.g., Erikson, 1980; S. Freud, 1938), who assume that stages of development (oral, anal) unfold on a biologically given timetable. For these theorists, psychopathology arises when natural developmental forces are disrupted (often, though not always, by parents) and the child or adult develops internal defensive armor that may temporarily reduce anxiety but impedes the exploration and risk taking necessary for developmental progress to occur. From the perspective of cell 4, intervention involves the provision of a safe holding environment in which destructive defenses can let down long enough for normal development to move forward.

External

In this cell are the familiar socialization theories (Baumrind, 1989) and behavioral theories (G. R. Patterson, 1982) that look to parenting styles or specific patterns of reinforcement by parents or other significant adults as the forces that shape normal development. According to this view, behavior that deviates from the norm, including Autism, Schizophrenia, depression, and antisocial behavior, results from conditions in which socially inappropriate rather than appropriate behavior has been reinforced.

Psychological external theories, especially the behaviorist examples, make a point of distinguishing between acquisition of behavior and its maintenance. Therapists with a traditional behavioral perspective acknowledge the importance of establishing etiology to create new prevention programs, but they focus more of their efforts on changing the physical and social environmental patterns that maintain the behavior over time than on altering the psychological makeup of the person. Their theories of change lead to clear instructions to therapists to avoid searching for the origins of current problems in early family experiences and focus instead on what is maintaining the problematic behavior now. The most popular example of psychological external theories applied to interventions are parenting classes, self-help books (Dinkmeyer & McKay, 1982; Ginott, Ginott, & Goddard, 2003; Gordon, 1980), and behavioral parent training interventions (Forgatch & DeGarmo, 1999; Webster-Stratton, Reid, & Hammond, 2001) designed to provide parents with skills to manage their children's aggressive and problematic behavior more effectively.

Interaction between Internal and Behavioral Psychological Factors

Even before family systems theories emerged in the 1950s, it was clear that both the nature of the child and the quality of parenting had to be taken into account to understand normal development and psychopathology. Parents should not get all the credit when their children turn out well or all the blame when they turn out badly. Children are agents of their own development, and the engine driving fathers' or mothers' parenting behavior is sometimes located in the child (Bell, 1968, 1988). Children's age, sex, personality, and temperament influence how mothers and fathers respond to them, just as parents' behavior influences how their children respond in return.

Piaget's (1967) theory of child development provides a good example of an interactive theory of development. As long as children's cognitive level is adequate to handle the environmental challenges they face, they can assimilate the stimulus into existing cognitive structures and respond appropriately, so that no change is necessary. When an unfamiliar stimulus or difficult problem occurs, disequilibrium follows and the child must accommodate (change his or her strategies to meet changes in environmental demands). As the child attempts to establish a new equilibrium between assimilation and accommodation, one possible outcome is cognitive reorganization at a new and higher level of intellectual functioning. Piaget's own emphasis was on interactions between the child and the physical environment, but it is clear that parents (P. A. Cowan, 1978) and peers (Piaget, 1962) also play central roles in providing external stimulation that helps to produce developmental change. Piaget himself was not much interested in psychopathology, but some of his associates (Inhelder, 1968; Schmid-Kitsikis, 1973) attempted to apply his theory to describing and understanding deviations from normal development. In general, they attempted to explain failures in developmental progression as resulting from imbalances in assimilation and accommodation (see P. A. Cowan, 1978), an internal perspective similar in form to the social interaction theories espoused by family systems theorists.

Another approach to psychological interactive models of change can be seen in cognitive-behavioral theories (Reinecke, Dattilio, & Freeman, 2003). In a traditional behavioral approach, it is assumed that manipulating the stimulus should produce a change in the response (external psychological cell). However, the child's or adult's *appraisal* of the stimulus also plays a role in his or her subsequent behavior (Lazarus & Folkman, 1984). For example, parents with high levels of conflict tend to have children who are more aggressive or depressed than children of parents with low levels of conflict, but this linkage is more likely to occur when children blame themselves for their parents' fights (Grych, Fincham, Jouriles, & McDonald, 2000).

All psychological interaction theories of change assume that there is some optimal level of fit and an optimal level of mismatch between the external forces of the environment and the internal structure and function of the child. Positive developmental progress is more likely when there is an "optimal mismatch" between the demands of the environment and the demands of the child. Vygotsky (1978) described a similar concept of "scaffolding" (Wood, Bruner, & Ross, 1976), in which parents move in at the appropriate level to help a child who is having difficulty solving a problem, and then move out once the child is on the right track.

Social Level of Analysis

At the social level of analysis, development is affected by relationships—internal representations, social transactions, and a combination of social interactions and how they are represented by the individuals involved.

Internal

It is not immediately clear what a social internal theory of stability and change should look like, because the idea that social relationships influence both normal development and psychopathology seems to be incompatible with the notion that *internal* forces are the primary determinants of both stability and change. What resolves the dilemma is the notion from both object relations (Klein, 1932; Kohut & Wolf, 1978) and attachment (Bowlby, 1988; Main, Kaplan, & Cassidy, 1985) theories that an inner symbolic representation or schema of a primary relationship, usually formed early in life and typically focused on the mother-child relationship, operates as a template that shapes expectations and behavior in the significant close relationships that one establishes over the life span. Working models characterized as secure, because they contain the assumption that a loved one will provide a secure base to protect the child from the threat of loss, facilitate normal development. Insecure working models (defined later in the chapter) lead to various forms of psychopathology (Sroufe, Duggal, Weinfield, & Carlson, 2000). Therapists adopting the social internal perspective on psychopathology attempt to change insecure working models, in part by providing a safe, secure environment in which clients can use the relationship with the therapist to gain perspective on their early relationships and develop the security needed to explore current and new intimate relationships in more productive ways (Klerman & Weissman, 1986; Mattinson & Sinclair, 1979).

External

In the psychological external cell (5), we described examples of how a parent's behavior provides reinforcement or punishment for a child's behavior. In the social external cell, we include socialization theories in which family and peer relationships (social support) and social institutions outside the nuclear family (workplace, government) affect whether individuals move toward normality or pathology in their life trajectories (Parke & Buriel, 1998). What differentiates this approach from the interactive position in the next cell (9) is that the effects are thought to be directional (acting on the person) rather than bidirectional (positing circular causality, a central tenet of the family systems approach). Theorists who emphasize social relationships and social system forces as causal risk factors that affect the development of psychopathology usually turn to social change programs in an effort to reduce or alleviate psychopathology in individuals (Sarason, 1974; Weinstein, 2002).

Interaction between Internal and External Social Factors

Family system theories represent the quintessential example of social interaction theories of stability and change. "The system" is the major unit of analysis, although subsystem balances and imbalances are important. Reciprocal interactions among individuals, and the reciprocal impact of relationships on relationships, create the conditions for normal development or psychopathology, with treatment optimally conducted with all the players in the room at the same time.

Six Domains and Nine Cells

The six-domain model describes where the investigation of psychopathology is focused, on the system as a whole or on one or more of the subsystems. The nine-cell model helps us to understand the multiple ways of conceptualizing stability and change within each domain, with corresponding theories of how adaptation or psychopathology emerges. For example, within the couple domain, it is possible to account for stability or change at a biological level (the impact of illness), a psychological level (the impact of mismatched personality styles), or a social level of analysis (the impact of dysregulated expression of negative affect). Theories can be focused on internal factors in change (attachment processes), external factors in change (cultural expectations), or the interaction between the two (what

happens when a man with an insecure model of attachment marries a woman with a secure model of attachment and is unable to fulfill the culturally stereotyped strong, silent, protector role?).

Our nine-cell classification of theories of change and stability helps us to make a more differentiated distinction between family systems and family factors approaches to developmental psychopathology. We have reserved cell 9, the social interactional cell, for family systems theories with their emphasis on normality and psychopathology as a gestalt (whole) formed by the system of reciprocally interacting relationships. Especially in the early years of family systems theories, the focus was primarily on that system and not on the individuals within it. These homeostatic theories were better able to explain why families remain stable than why they change. As we will see, because a focus on the system as a whole was not always efficacious in producing family change, some aspects of family risk factor theories have been incorporated into family treatments.

Theories that focus on the family risk factors that affect individual psychopathology appear in all of the other cells—in genetic and other biological forces (cell 1); household environment effects (cell 2); the interaction between biological and physical environment factors (cell 3); an individual's defensive system, erected to provide relief from anxieties created in the family, or an individual's appraisal of family members' behavior (cell 4); parenting behavior (cell 5); the match between parental behavior and the child's psychological organization (cell 6); working models of intimate family relationships (cell 7); and the impact of family relationships on the individual (cell 8). Each of the factors considered separately and all of the factors in combination can affect the pathways that individuals take toward or away from adaptive functioning.

In the examples of interactive theories of change presented earlier, we described interactions between external sources of stability and change *within* biological, psychological, or social levels of analysis. Physical environments have different effects on people with different genetic constitutions. Parenting behavior may be interpreted differently by children who have different interpretations of what their parents are trying to do. Family relationships may play out differently with individuals who have secure or insecure working models of relationships. It is easy to see, however, that biological processes interact with psychological and social factors to affect adaptive and maladaptive development. For example, a diathesis-stress model of psychopathology (Gottesman & Shields, 1971) suggests that genetic and other biologically based predisposing factors (the diathesis, or vulnerability) develop into full-blown psychopathology only when triggered by severe social stressors and psychological vulnerabilities.

Independence of Etiology and Treatment

Our discussion of theories located within each cell pointed to parallels among theories of normal development, psychopathology, and intervention because this is the prevailing assumption of those who apply theories of development to their intervention programs. We believe it is necessary to challenge the assumption of lockstep consistency between etiological and intervention theories on both logical and empirical grounds. The issue becomes clearer if we consider two "thought experiments." First, let us assume that variations in genetic makeup actually cause a very high proportion of the variation in level of adaptation assessed at a given point in time. It is still possible that psychological or social interventions will produce positive change in behavior. Just as height, which is highly heritable, is profoundly affected by diet, so an individual's level of psychopathology, regardless of the causal factors involved, can be changed by environmental manipulations.

Second, let us assume that instead of genes as etiological factors, variations in parents' reinforcement patterns cause a very high proportion of the variation in level of adaptation assessed at a given point in time. It is still possible that, because the patterns of interaction have been persistent and cumulative over the years, no known psychosocial intervention can produce positive change. Furthermore, well-managed drug treatments might provide conditions in which further psychosocial treatment will now be effective.

In sum, although we have followed standard practice by associating theories of etiology with theories of intervention, we emphasize that one's theory of how a disorder was caused does not necessarily dictate the most appropriate treatment approach. More specifically, if we find evidence that family risk factors play a role in causing or maintaining the disorder, this does not exclude biological or physical environment interventions as part of the treatment process. And even if we find evidence that genetic, brain, or physiological factors play a role in causing a disorder, we should be open to including family members as part of the treatment plan.

If our theory of treatment does not necessarily follow from our theory of etiology, why spend so much effort in attempts to identify the causes of a disorder? Because without a well-supported etiological or risk factor theory, it will be impossible to plan a program to prevent the occurrence of a disorder or to identify individuals and families in the early stages before the disorder reaches diagnosable levels.

CHANGES IN FAMILY SYSTEMS AND FAMILY RISK FACTOR APPROACHES TO PSYCHOPATHOLOGY OVER THE PAST 50 YEARS

Family systems theory has come a long way since its origins in the mid-twentieth century. As we look back, we see an interesting cycle in which the early family systems theories of the 1950s and 1960s had a delayed but important impact on family risk factor research in the 1970s and 1980s, which in turn began to influence a move toward integration of quite different family systems approaches to diagnosis and treatment at the end of the century.

New Family Therapy Gurus and New Schools

New charismatic family therapists joined the club created by the early founders of the field, each using the early family system theories as a starting point but offering a slightly different central idea of what was wrong and needed fixing when families came into treatment. Although all of the new leaders focused on social interaction theories of stability and change in the family system as a whole when explaining the etiology and locus of psychopathology, each emphasized the role of one or more aspects of internal psychological factors in both individual and family maladaptation. This period, in which new, competing schools of family therapy training and services were established, but in which little systematic evaluation occurred, has been characterized aptly, though perhaps too harshly, as the "battle of the brand names" (Hoffman, 1981).

One of the few second-generation family therapists to maintain a direct connection with treating mentally ill patients and their families was Carl Whitaker, who emerged as a leading figure first at Emory University in Atlanta and later in the Department of Psychiatry at the University of Wisconsin Medical School. His forte was not the construction of grand theories or the proposal of unique formulations of the central issues faced by families. His influence came through demonstrating his approach in large workshops and small, intense meetings of the movers and shakers of the family therapy world (Whitaker & Bateson, 1958). Although he focused on the systemic properties of the family, as a therapist Whitaker paid close attention to his own inner thoughts and feelings during the session and expressed them to the family. That is, he used psychodynamic notions of transference and countertransference in the therapy, primarily as a way of joining with clients at the same time that he disequilibrated them with cryptic but remarkably on-target remarks.

An offshoot of a more consistently psychodynamic family theory such as Ackerman's (1962) could be found at the Family Institute of Philadelphia led by Ivan Boszormenyi-Nagy and James Framo (1965; Framo, 1992). They developed what they called contextual family therapy, with an emphasis on adults coming to terms psychologically and in direct interaction with their parents as a way to repair distress at the individual, couple, and parent-child levels.

After leaving the Palo Alto group, Jay Haley worked with Minuchin in Philadelphia to develop structural family therapy, with a focus on the role of the therapist in changing the organization of family subsystems. Haley then started a new school of strategic therapy that focused on the family's behavioral efforts to solve problems in the here and now (Haley, 1976; Madanes, 1984). Haley delighted in a "paradoxical" approach, telling families, as they described their problems, that the problems were objectively insoluble. The central task of the therapist was to help families reframe or redefine their plight and prescribe a set of strategies that would overcome family homeostasis and facilitate change, including "prescribing the symptom," in which he would ask families to repeat a maladaptive pattern in order to bring it into the open and place it under conscious control.

One of the strongest international developments in family therapy occurred in Italy, where Mara Selvini Palazzoli, Luigi Boscolo, Guiliana Prata, and Gianfranco Cecchin became the "Milan associates" (Selvini Palazzoli, 1985; Selvini Palazzoli, Boscolo, Cecchin, & Prata, 1978). Staying close in theoretical orientation to the Palo Alto group (Bateson and colleagues), they focused on short-term intensive interventions focused on disrupting the deviant communication "games" by which severely disturbed families (with severe eating disorders, Schizophrenia) maintained a maladaptive homeostasis. Haley and the Milan associates focused on behavior but were not behaviorists, in the sense of direct teaching of communication rules, exchange of reinforcing behaviors, or consequences for unacceptable behavior.

A quite different offshoot of Bateson's ideas from the Palo Alto group was narrative therapy (M. White, 1986; M. White & Epston, 1990), which focuses on the idea that family narratives or stories are often impoverished in disturbed families; the task of the therapist, through talking, writing letters to clients, and having clients write new narratives, is to reframe and refashion these stories with new possibilities. Like many postmodern theories, narrative therapies place great emphasis on the meaning of words and the constructions that family members place on their realities, each of which has its own validity or truth.

Feminist Critiques of Family Systems Theories

In 1978, Rachel Hare-Mustin issued an opening salvo in an ongoing feminist critique of family therapy, making the point that early versions of family systems theories made highly gender-stereotyped assumptions about what constitutes pathological and nonpathological functioning in families (Walters, Carter, Papp, & Silverstein, 1988). The early masters of family therapy, almost all men, had focused their interventions on reestablishing traditional roles in chaotic families, in part by encouraging fathers to take a more active, often patriarchal role. This work virtually ignored the issues associated with the changing of women's roles stimulated by the women's movement starting in the 1960s (Chodorow, 1989; Friedan, 1963; Greer, 1980). Judging by the fact that sharply worded feminist critiques continue to appear, these issues have not yet been resolved (Almeida, 1998; Bograd, 1991; Coleman & Ganong, 2004).

In addition to the issue of roles, feminist family therapists focused on power in relationships between men and women, advocating that therapists help families to buck the cultural trends in which men hold not only the purse strings but the power to make decisions about many aspects of life inside and outside the family (Silverstein & Goodrich, 2003). The implication was that a feminist therapeutic approach would alleviate depression in women and provide examples of a better balance of gender roles for both daughters and sons. In fact, the systematic research that we are aware of suggests that less traditional divisions of labor are related to more satisfied and less symptomatic partners (Blair & Hardesty, 1994; Huppe & Cyr, 1997), but to our knowledge, there have been no direct tests of these assumptions by examining whether therapy-induced changes in the balance of power within couples are associated with more positive outcomes for the partners or their children.

Family systems theories and feminist critiques were presented and argued in the 1970s and 1980s on the basis of clinical experience, training programs in each of the family therapy schools, detailed written case materials, and sharp exchanges at national gatherings of family therapists. There was little reliance on empirical studies in the family research literature. We wonder whether the fact that family therapy training was primarily conducted in freestanding institutions that were not connected with academic or hospital research settings widened the gap between developments in the fields of family therapy and family research.

The Family Risk Factor Approach: An Expanding Focus on Family Relationships in Accounting for Psychopathology

During the 1970s and 1980s, influenced by the active ferment in family systems theories and therapies, there was a rapid rise of interest in family research, in the study of both normal development and psychopathology. Before 1960, research interest in whole families was so low that fathers were virtually invisible in research on child development. Eleven years after the publication of the first version of the *Manual of Child Psychology* (Carmichael, 1954), Nash (1965) pointed out that "father" had not been included in the index. A number of researchers, who would later become prominent, published papers on the impact of father absence (Biller, 1968; Hetherington, 1966, 1972; Mischel, 1961), but it was not until the 1980s that a body of work emerged looking at how variations in fathers when they were present were related to children's development (Bronstein & Cowan, 1988; Lamb, Pleck, Charnov, & Levine, 1987; Power & Parke, 1983). Although research interest in fathers has continued and grown (Tamis-LeMonda & Cabrera, 2002), most child psychopathology researchers continue to neglect fathers (Phares, 1992).

Just as "father absence" was the stimulus for early studies of fathers' impact on their children, so the study of how the parents' marriage affects children's development was stimulated by studies of divorce in the early 1980s (Hetherington, Cox, & Cox, 1982; Wallerstein & Kelly, 1980). Over the following 2 decades, a wealth of evidence suggested that high, unresolved couple conflict is a risk factor for most dimensions of adaptation in children (academic achievement, externalizing, internalizing; Ablow, 2005; Cummings, Davies, & Campbell, 2000; Emery, 1999).

Research on the intergenerational transmission of disorders also increased. The belief that positive or negative patterns of family interaction are repeated across generations and function as an antecedent to many different diagnoses is supported by the results of behavioral genetic studies of twins and siblings (Gottesman, 1991), epidemiological studies of family records (Mednick, Cudeck, Griffith, Talovic, & Schulsinger, 1981), and longitudinal studies of nonclinical families (Caspi & Elder, 1988). In the 1970s and early 1980s, the risk factor approach attempted to identify one or at most two family domains associated with child psychopathology. Only later, as we shall see, did these models become more inclusive as they attempted to incorporate information from all of the family domains in Figure 14.1.

A New Wave of Researcher-Clinicians

From the 1970s to the present day, some academically based researcher-therapists, influenced by family systems theory, began to focus on interventions in family subsystems, which brought new concepts and techniques to therapies focused on either parent-child or couple relationships. If we examine where the interventions were targeted, we can infer the assumptions of each approach concerning risk factors or causes of psychopathology.

Parent-Child Focus

To help parents to deal with their highly aggressive sons, Gerald Patterson (1975) began developing behavioral treatments in which parents learned techniques of reinforcement, time-out, and social learning through imitation. Presumably, parental failure to establish adequate controls was seen as the source of children's misbehavior. Seven years later, Patterson took a more systemic bidirectional approach in his theory of "coercive family processes" (G. R. Patterson, 1982). Observing mostly mothers and children in interaction, Patterson noted that when a child was aggressive and a parent responded ineffectively, the child escalated the aggression, the parent again responded ineffectively (e.g., by "nattering" instead of giving clear directions), and the child escalated again until the parent backed off, thus reinforcing high-level aggression on the part of the child. Still later, risk factor models from Patterson's group expanded to include additional measures of individual personality and functioning (G. R. Patterson & Capaldi, 1991), cognitive-behavioral conceptions, including parents' and children's interpretations of events, and the role of both sibling and peer relationships in the control of aggression.

Carolyn Webster-Stratton (1984, 1994) developed a videotape program for parents of aggressive children that presents dramatized vignettes of effective and ineffective parenting. In contrast with a more didactic teaching orientation characteristic of many behavioral interventions, Webster-Stratton's individual therapists or group leaders use the taped excerpts to elicit explorations and observations from the parents in an attempt to involve them actively in the process of adopting new strategies of discipline with their children.

A newer dimension of parent-child relationships has been investigated but not yet used in interventions. John Gottman (2001; Katz, Wilson, & Gottman, 1999) describes meta-emotion coaching as parental behavior that helps children deal with their feelings of sadness or anger. When parents are able to help their children explore their negative feelings rather than criticize them or dismiss the feelings, the children show less externalizing or internalizing behavior. What makes this construct a candidate for therapeutic trial is the suggestion from correlational studies that positive meta-emotion coaching can protect children from the vicissitudes of marital conflict in the family.

Couples Focus

Neil Jacobson, Gayla Margolin, Andrew Christensen, and Donald Baucom, separately and together, developed treatments for couples in distress (Baucom, Epstein, Rankin, & Burnett, 1996; Christensen et al., 2004; Christensen, Jacobson, & Babcock, 1995; Jacobson & Margolin, 1979). Like Patterson, they began by developing behavioral interventions based on different versions of exchange theories (one partner gives positive reinforcements in response to positive reinforcements) and on direct didactic teaching of communication strategies (e.g., using "I" statements and avoiding mind reading and blaming). Then, as Patterson had, these researcher-clinicians all moved toward more cognitive-behavioral approaches with an emphasis on how each partner *interprets* his or her own and the partner's behavior, or on such nonbehavioral concepts as the need for acceptance when partners have differences or reach impasses that cannot be resolved (Christensen & Jacobson, 2000).

Just as the early family systems theories could be divided into those with a behavioral emphasis on the transactions among family members and those with a psychodynamic emphasis on the individual in the system, the field of couples therapy encompassed both approaches to understanding trajectories of relationship health and maladaptation. Two theories of couples therapy based their assumptions on an intrapsychic view of how problems in the couple are generated, one stemming from the object relations theories of Melanie Klein (1932), the other from John Bowlby's (1982, 1989) attachment theory. Theories based on Klein's work focused more on the ways that partners who are frustrated and unsatisfied with their primary object relationship (with mother) project their unacknowledged and rejected aspects of themselves on their partner (Dicks, 1967; Mattinson & Sinclair, 1979). One partner's anger that the other is frustrating his or her needs results in either anger or depression/withdrawal. In essence, as in Bowen's family systems approach, the partners exist in a state of fusion or enmeshment in which each sees the other as an extension of himself or herself, and positive development through therapy involves a process of encouraging individuation. Object

relations theories of couple functioning were later expanded and systematized by David Scharff and Jill Scharff (D. E. Scharff & Scharff, 1991; J. S. Scharff & Bagnini, 2002).

A different intrapsychic approach to couples therapy, based on attachment theory, was developed by Clulow and his associates (Clulow, 1996; Clulow & Cudmore, 1985) at the Tavistock Marital Studies Institute in London. From this perspective, partners begin as separate individuals, and problems arise in the process of coming together. Anger or withdrawal in the couple relationship arises when individuals who are vulnerable because of insecure working models of attachment become threatened by fear of losing the relationship. One of the therapist's main tasks is to understand the working models that each partner brings to the relationship and to provide a secure base in the therapy room that partners can use as a platform to analyze and revise their distorted working models. The goal is to help each partner begin to function as a secure base for the other.

The Current Couple and Family Systems Scene: Integrations

A number of textbooks and handbooks describing couples and family therapy (Gurman & Jacobson, 2002; Gurman & Kniskern, 1981, 1991; Jacobson & Gurman, 1995) have been published over the past 2 decades. A brief comparison of later volumes with earlier ones suggests a move toward theoretical integrations. Lebow (1997) summarized the trend with an influential article in *Family Process,* noting the different meanings of "integration." Eclecticism is one alternative—the incorporation of disparate theoretical ideas and intervention techniques into family assessment and therapy. At another extreme is an integration that synthesizes disparate elements into a coherent theoretical model. Although some observers question whether this kind of integration is possible (e.g., Grunebaum, 1997), Lebow describes midlevel integrations—attempts by a theorist or therapist to give equal attention to *at least* two family domains (e.g., couple and parent-child) or levels of analysis (a subsystem and the whole family) or explanations of stability and change (biological, psychological, social or internal, external, interactive). Given the rich array of recent integrations, we are able to provide only a few examples.

Integration across Domains: Couple and Parent-Child

Behavioral interventions for parents of aggressive children have been remarkably successful (P. A. Cowan et al., 1998;

G. E. Miller & Prinz, 1990), at least in the short run. Nevertheless, when therapist-researchers looked at evidence that some children did not change whereas others improved but later reverted to baseline, several began to suspect that parenting changes were more difficult to achieve when the child's parents were engaged in high levels of conflict. Brody and Forehand (1985) added to their parenting intervention a new focus on coparenting *and* marital issues. In the Brody and Forehand study and another intervention evaluation by Dadds and his colleagues (Dadds, Sanders, Behrens, & James, 1987), a combined marital and parenting emphasis was more successful in reducing sons' problem behavior than a traditional parenting skills approach with mothers only. Webster-Stratton (1994) showed similar results in her recent work with couples whose children had behavior problems. These intervention results, as we have noted, provide evidence in support of the hypothesis that both marital and parent-child relationships play important roles in the development or maintenance of psychopathology in the child.

Integration across Domains and Levels of Analysis

By far, the majority of family theory integrations attempted to combine a focus on how psychological or biological processes of each individual play out in the transactions between partners or among family members.

Biological and Family Processes   Until relatively recently, family theorists have acknowledged but generally ignored the fact that genetic factors play some role in individual psychopathology. Plomin and his colleagues (Hetherington, Reiss, & Plomin, 1994; Plomin, 2003) have made what seems like a paradoxical claim: that behavior genetic studies can be used to make the best case for the importance of family relationship risk factors in psychopathology. To begin with, these investigators depart from the usual practice of studying only one child in each family so that they can identify the contributions of both nature and nurture to variations among siblings in behavior and adaptation. Twin studies and adoption studies have been used for some time to make the case that there is a genetic component to Schizophrenia, Bipolar Disorder, depression, and many personality traits in nonclinical populations (Gottesman, Shields, & Meehl, 1972). Somehow, the focus on finding proof of genetic risk factors obscured an obvious point: Even in twins who are genetically identical, the probability that both will be diagnosed with Schizophrenia is, at most, about 50% to 60%. This means that there must be some nongenetic factors that account for sibling differences. The contribution

of Plomin and his colleagues was to calculate a heritability index for each outcome under investigation (with perfect heritability [h] =1.0) and then to search for *two* sources to explain the remaining variance (1–h): shared environmental similarities that tend to make siblings similar (e.g., being treated similarly by parents), and nonshared environmental conditions that tend to make siblings dissimilar (e.g., being treated differently by parents). Using data from sophisticated studies of identical twins, fraternal twins, and siblings in both adoptee and nonadoptee families, these investigators interpret their results as showing that once genetic factors are accounted for, much of the remaining variation in severe psychopathology comes from nonshared family factors—conditions that make for differences between siblings. Both shared and nonshared effects are aspects of family processes that are consistent with a social external view of adaptation.

Space precludes an elaborate analysis of the nonshared approach. It has been criticized on the grounds that heritability coefficients overestimate the contribution of genetic factors to psychopathology because the estimates are specific to the population they are assessing, and that restrictions in variation within each study necessarily inflate the size of the heritability coefficient (Collins, Maccoby, Steinberg, Hetherington, & Bornstein, 2000). More recent critiques also suggest that the contributions of nonshared environments have been overestimated at the expense of shared environmental effects (Spinath, 2004). Nevertheless, in our view, Plomin and his colleagues have provided solid evidence supporting the hypothesis of an interaction of genetics and family processes in a number of *DSM* disorders (see discussion later in chapter).

Intrapersonal Cognitive Processes and Interpersonal Behavior   Consistent with the tenets of the cognitive-behavioral individual therapies growing in importance during the 1970s, some researcher-clinicians added to their analysis of couple communication patterns new ideas about how one partner's interpretation of the other's behavior could affect subsequent interactions between them. Attribution theories of couple interaction (Grych et al., 2000) pinpoint negative interpretations of the motivation behind a family member's behavior (e.g., "You did that just to frustrate me") as a risk factor for increased interpersonal conflict. In another perspective on the importance of interpretation, Christensen and Jacobson (2000) show that behavior that violates the couple relationship (e.g., adultery) is not necessarily corrosive in the long term unless one partner refuses to forgive the transgression.

Emotion Processes, Cognition, and Interpersonal Behavior In laboratory research, J. M. Gottman and Levenson (1986; Levenson & Gottman, 1983) first identified behavioral patterns (escalating negative affect) and physiological patterns (men's tendency to stonewall in verbal communication during a discussion of a marital disagreement, though their physiological arousal was high) as risk factors for couple dissatisfaction and distress. That is, both dysregulation of internal emotional arousal and dysregulation of emotional expression as partners interact are important ingredients of couple adaptation. Applying these findings to therapy (J. M. Gottman, Ryan, Carrere, & Erley, 2002), Gottman and his colleagues also emphasize the importance of each partner's aspirations and dreams and the negative consequences for relationships when one or both partners fear disappointment that their life dreams will not be realized in this relationship. Behavioral, affective, and cognitive integrations are also featured in Christensen and Jacobsen's integrative therapy (Christensen et al., 2004).

Attachment Processes and Interpersonal Behavior Emotionally focused couple therapy (EFT) was developed by Leslie Greenberg and Susan Johnson (1988) and later expanded by S. M. Johnson (2004). EFT represented a reaction to the behavioral approach. Based on observation of couples therapy tapes, these clinicians concluded that too much attention was given to cognition, problem-solving, and behavioral strategies, and not enough to emotional moments and attachment issues. Their primary hypothesis was that distress in couple relationships is caused by the fact that when differences arise, one or both partners may be vulnerable to the threat of separation and loss; one or both then react emotionally by dismissing, denying, and defending or with high levels of anger, with either alternative driving the partners further apart. Once insecurities about the relationship are aroused, Johnson argues, they are maintained by the manner in which the partners interact. Thus, explanations of psychopathology and attempts to treat couples are based on a psychological and social analysis that posits an interaction of internal and external contributions to individual distress and relationship disruption. Their retention of a behavioral communication focus in addition to the attachment focus makes their therapy quite different from the attachment-based therapy described by Clulow (1996). The attempt to integrate attachment and behavioral theories has also been a central feature of Gurman's (2002) brief integrative therapy and Christensen and Jacobson's integrative therapy (Christensen et al., 2004).

Why Integrations Are Needed

From the perspective of twenty-first-century theories of psychopathology, the need for integrations of theories explaining the development of psychopathology seems obvious. Although traditional individual and family therapies have been shown to be effective when participant are compared with those in control groups (Shadish, Ragsdale, Glaser, & Montgomery, 1995; Weisz, Weiss, Han, & Granger, 1995), it is clear that these therapies do not provide help for substantial numbers of people. On both conceptual and empirical grounds, it is easy to see that no single family domain can possibly explain how some families at similarly high levels of risk follow trajectories toward different kinds of psychopathology, and others move toward adequate or even superior levels of adaptation. Similarly, in a time when biopsychosocial models (Engel, 1980) are becoming widely accepted (Whitbourne, 2005), it does not seem reasonable to limit one's view to a single level of analysis—biological, psychological, or social—to account for the links between risks and outcomes. It seems futile to maintain either an internal or an external explanation of stability and change when there is so much evidence of protective and vulnerability effects; whether external risk factors eventuate in psychopathology depends on whether internal factors protect individuals from harm or represent vulnerabilities that make them particularly susceptible to greater distress. As Cicchetti and Dawson (2002, p. 418) wrote, "Progress toward a process-level understanding of mental disorder will require research designs and strategies that call for the simultaneous assessment of multiple domains of variables both within and outside the developing person."

Our six-domain family risk model (Figure 14.1) and the nine-cell matrix explaining stability and change (Figure 14.2) can be thought of as checklists that delineate possibilities from which integrative family theories have made choices. For example, couples therapies have begun to include individual, couple, parent-child, and three-generations perspectives on the relationship, but except for feminist family theorists, they have paid relatively little attention to stresses and supports from outside the nuclear family (see Gurman & Jacobson, 2002, for descriptions of many different approaches to couples therapy). Family therapies, especially those treating delinquent or drug-abusing adolescents, have begun to address outside-the-family issues with peers, schools, and neighborhoods (e.g., Liddle & Hogue, 2000). Conceptualizations of stability and change in family theories now regularly include internal and external psychological and social explanations, but they pay attention to biological levels of analysis primarily when psychoactive drugs are part of the treatment.

This both/and rather than either/or approach to integrations argues for the need to integrate family systems and family risk factors theories of psychopathology. Each has important limitations that the other can address. Rosenblatt (1994) provides a cogent analysis and critique of the metaphors used by family systems theorists and shows how each of the central constructs is simultaneously enlightening and limiting. For example, the assumption that families as whole systems have properties that are independent of the parts leads to the useful idea that it is normal and expectable for *systems* to resist the disequilibrium associated with change and transition. At the same time, focusing on the system ignores the fact that specific strengths and vulnerabilities of individual family members often have a marked impact on the functioning of individuals, dyads, and the system as a whole. Conversely, the family factors approach addresses the contributions of individual family members and dyads to psychopathology and adaptation, but usually fails to consider the properties of the system as a whole that protect individuals and relationships from risks in specific domains, or amplify difficulties in one domain to the point where they spill over into other domains of family life.

DEVELOPMENTAL PSYCHOPATHOLOGY IN NONCLINICAL FAMILIES

Before we examine evidence regarding family systems and family risk models of psychopathology in individuals already diagnosed by the mental health system and involved in treatment, we want to show how these models are relevant to understanding adaptation in nonclinical families. These families are not selected for studies because they are without problems, but because they have not been identified by the mental health delivery system as in need of treatment, and they have not volunteered to participate in a study because they have identified themselves or their families as in need of psychological help. Typically, they are families recruited to a study of marital relationships, parent-child relationships, normative family transitions, and the like. Nevertheless, as we know from developmental psychopathology research, some of the individuals in these families are suffering significant psychological distress, and a subset meet the criteria for one or more diagnosable disorders. Consistent with the tenets of developmental

psychopathology, we believe that research on this population is essential to the understanding of who develops psychological problems and who does not.

Family Systems Assessments of Normal Families

Several systems-level assessment approaches have been developed to allow researchers to arrive at a picture of how the family as a whole functions. Although they have all been developed by clinicians and mostly been used in the study of families with already diagnosed problems, they were all created explicitly for use with nonclinical families, and each explicitly focuses on strengths as well as weaknesses in both family structure and family process. The McMaster model of family functioning (Epstein, Ryan, Bishop, Miller, & Keitner, 2003) has led to a multimethod assessment of family problem solving, communication, family roles, affective responses and involvement, and behavioral control. Well-functioning families are able to solve problems, communicate directly and effectively, operate with a clear sense of who does what, express feelings in a context of empathy, and operate inside and outside the family in an appropriately controlled but not rigid way. The assessment includes an extensive interview of the whole family (the McMaster Structured Interview of Family Functioning; Bishop et al., 2000) and a questionnaire administered to each family member (Epstein, Baldwin, & Bishop, 1983). The assessment has been used in clinical settings in a few studies conducted in the 1970s and 1980s (see Epstein et al., 2003) and more recently by the Providence Family Study (Dickstein et al., 1998). Results demonstrate the interconnection among various levels of family assessment in families with a mentally ill parent (see discussion later in chapter).

Like the McMaster model, the Beavers systems model (Beavers & Hampson, 2003; earlier called the Beavers-Timberlawn model) uses a combination of observational ratings and self-reports to describe the family system (the Interactional Competence Scale, the Beavers Interactional Style Scales, and the Self-Report Family Inventory; Beavers & Hampson, 1990). Unlike the McMaster model, the Beavers system uses classical constructs from structural (Minuchin, 1974) and strategic (Haley, 1990) family therapy such as boundaries, power, autonomy, communication, and problem solving to classify families along two orthogonal dimensions. The first dimension places families along a competence continuum from severely dysfunctional, borderline, and midrange, through adequate, healthy, and optimal. The second dimension describes families in terms of members' tendency to turn inward toward each other or outward toward the world to get their needs met. The scales have been used successfully in evaluations of marital therapy and family therapy (Hampson & Beavers, 1996; Hampson, Prince, & Beavers, 1999). The results demonstrate a linear relationship between a family's level of competence and therapy outcomes, in which more competent families benefited more from treatment. The authors also discuss the types of therapists who were most helpful to families at the low and midranges of the scale.

Reiss and Oliveri (Reiss, 1981; Reiss & Oliveri, 1983) observed family members communicating with each other as they attempted to solve puzzle-like problems, and used both behavior and perceptions of the members to describe a "family paradigm": the orientation of the family unit to each other and to the outside world. They describe three uncorrelated dimensions: (1) Configuration refers to the ability of family members working as a group to recognize patterns; (2) coordination refers to their ability to cooperate and integrate their actions; and (3) delayed closure reflects the openness of the family to new information. Empirical evidence reveals that high scores on all of these dimensions are correlated with successful coping with physical illness and alcoholism (Reiss, Costell, Jones, & Berkman, 1980; Reiss, Gonzalez, & Kramer, 1986; Reiss & Oliveri, 1983). Speculative extensions suggest how these dimensions could be related to various categories of mental illness (Reiss & Klein, 1987).

The circumplex model of marital and family systems (Olson & Gorall, 2003) uses a single self-report instrument, the Family Adaptability and Cohesion Evaluation Scale (FACES), now in its fourth revision (FACES IV; Franklin, Streeter, & Springer, 2001). Questions cover two bipolar dimensions in which optimal functioning lies at the midpoint of a curvilinear dimension, and maladaptive functioning at each end of the curve. Relationships can range from disconnected (separateness, low closeness, low loyalty, high independence) through connected (balanced) to overly connected (too much togetherness, excessive loyalty demands, high dependency). Relationships can also range from inflexible (rigid, authoritarian, unchanging, strict discipline) through flexible, to overly flexible (constant change, lack of leadership, dramatic role shifts, erratic discipline). Olson and Gorall note that earlier versions of FACES failed to validate the curvilinear hypothesis because there were not enough items on the enmeshed and high-change ends of the continua, but that there are promising indications that FACES IV shows the expected cur ilinearity. About 10 studies find that this self-report measure correlates with observation (Kouneski, 2001). Space precludes a review of the many investigations that

have used this instrument, primarily in studies of nonclinical families.

There are other self-report measures that attempt to take a whole-system perspective on the family, including the Family Environment Scale (Moos, 1974), with dimensions of cohesion, organization, and family growth orientation, and the Family Assessment Measure (Skinner, Steinhauer, & Sitarenios, 2000; Steinhauer, Santa-Barbara, & Skinner, 1984), with both whole-family and dyadic descriptions provided by each family member. Like FACES, but with less extensive research, both of these instruments demonstrate that they differentiate between well-functioning families and families with a member who has been diagnosed with a clinical disorder.

Various authors have attempted to compare these whole-family measurement systems (e.g., Grotevant & Carlson, 1989; Hampson & Beavers, 2004), but none that we are aware of provides empirical studies of intercorrelation or differential connections with adaptive and maladaptive outcomes. The McMaster and Beavers models include both observers' and family members' perspectives, whereas the circumplex model relies on an inner view of family life from the perspective of each family member. All these models attempt to assess some level of cohesion and boundaries—whether family members turn toward each other or focus their attention outside the family—and all attempt to ascertain whether the family has a stable, flexible organization for solving problems and communicating feelings.

What remains to be worked out with these and all other measures of family functioning is that they present two different perspectives, what Reiss (1992) calls the represented and practicing family, with representations derived from family members' self-reports and descriptions of family practices derived from observers. We do not yet have very clear ideas about how well these perspectives fit together, how well they should be expected to correspond, or what the implications may be for family adaptation when family members' perceptions fail to correspond with observers' descriptions of family interaction.

Risk Factors in Family Transitions

In contrast with times of relative quiescence when family coping processes may not be as visible to outsiders, family transitions bring new challenges that call for new resources. At these times, the characteristic strengths and vulnerabilities of family members and their relationships can be seen in sharper relief (P. A. Cowan & Cowan, 2003). Even more relevant to the study of developmental psychopathology, the disequilibrium associated with making a life transition can lead either to higher levels of adaptation or to lower levels of functioning that place the individual or family further along the path toward maladaptation (McCubbin & Patterson, 1983). Our definition of transition does not include any of the innumerable small shifts in family members or in the system as a whole, but rather changes that involve a qualitative shift in each individuals' view of self and the world, social roles, and central relationships (P. A. Cowan, 1991).

The Couple's Transition to Parenthood and the First Child's Transition to School

There are two main ways to study families in transition—by following them over time and charting correlations between coping strategies and outcomes, and in experimental designs (interventions with random assignments to conditions) that evaluate whether intervention-produced skills make a difference in how transitions are managed.

Correlational Studies. Nonnormative life transitions are those triggered by suddenly occurring challenges that are either unexpected, such as earthquakes, or unexpected at a given time, such as serious illness. It is obvious that these transitions might increase the risks of disequilibrium and actual distress. By contrast, normative transitions are expectable and experienced by the majority of individuals or families in a given culture (e.g., emergence into adolescence or adulthood, entering the paid workforce, establishing an intimate relationship, cohabitation or marriage, becoming parents). Often, though not always, these transitions are actively sought and welcomed when they occur. Nevertheless, it has become clear that even when the transition brings great joy, the individual and the family is at risk for increased levels of disequilibrium and/or stress. The transition to parenthood and the child's transition to school are two cases in point in the early years of family life.

We and a number of others have described longitudinal studies that reveal the challenges faced by partners becoming parents (Belsky & Kelly, 1994; C. P. Cowan & Cowan, 2000; Cox, Paley, Payne, & Burchinal, 1999; Heinicke, 2002; Shapiro, Gottman, & Carrere, 2000). As men and women attempt to cope with the demands of caring for a small and unpredictable infant under conditions of uncertainty and sleep deprivation, they experience changes in each of the central domains of the family. They must incorporate their new identity as a parent. They take on more traditional role arrangements as couples than they expected. They each begin to forge a new relationship with their child, at the same time that they must reorganize their relationships with their parents and kin. In modern cou-

ples, both partners struggle to balance the demands of work and family responsibilities, maintain outside sources of support, and minimize outside sources of stress (C. P. Cowan & Cowan, 2000).

A review of more than 25 longitudinal studies of partners becoming parents (C. P. Cowan & Cowan, 1995) published a decade ago shows that during this period, couple conflict increases and, for the vast majority, marital satisfaction declines. A more recent overview comes to the same conclusion (Bradbury & Karney, 2004). In a second study of families whose first child was making the transition to elementary school (Cowan et al., 2005), we found that, marital satisfaction continued to decline, despite several positive changes in parents' lives during the transition-to-school period.

For couples with relatively positive relationships who become parents or see their first child off to elementary school, this decline in marital satisfaction may not prove to be problematic. As in other transitions, couples at the positive end of the distribution tend to maintain their position over time (Belsky & Pensky, 1988). Unfortunately, those with quite negative views of the relationship show a further decline over time, which may have serious consequences[1] because at the low end of the distribution, distressed marriages constitute a primary risk factor for children's adaptation (Cummings et al., 2000; Emery, 1999).

Studies of the transition to parenthood and the early child-rearing years confirm that distressed couple relationships are important to understand, but they also make it clear that a troubled marriage is only one of the family risk factors that predict children's academic, social, and emotional problems. There is now ample evidence that the other four domains in our family risk model explain significant amounts of variation in children's development. Parents' depression, mental illness, and other indicators of psychopathology place children at risk for behavior problems and other cognitive and emotional difficulties (Campbell, Cohn, & Meyers, 1995; Fendrich, Warner, & Weissman, 1990; Nolen-Hoeksema, Wolfson, Mumme, & Guskin, 1995; Sameroff, Seifer, & Zax, 1982). The behavior of each parent with the child, of course, explains substantial variance in children's adaptation (P. A. Cowan et al., 1998; Maccoby & Martin, 1983; Parke & Buriel, 1998). The intergenerational transmission of parent-child relationship quality from grandparents to parents to children is the rule rather than the exception (van Ijzendoorn, 1992). Parents'

---

[1] Later in the chapter we address whether the correlations actually represent causal influences of marital quality on children's adaptation.

work-related stress, economic stress, and other stresses from outside the nuclear family also function as risk factors for the development of psychopathology in their children (Conger, Ge, Elder, & Lorenz, 1994).

How do all of these risk factors combine to explain variations in children's adaptation? Static snapshots using multiple regression techniques suggest that family risk factors combine additively to predict children's outcomes. The more risk factors present (Sameroff, Seifer, Baldwin, & Baldwin, 1993), and the more intense the risk (Cummings & Davies, 1994), the more severe the child's problems are likely to be. In our own research (P. A. Cowan & Cowan, 2005), we used multiple regressions to analyze risk factors from each of the five family domains in our conceptual model. Results indicate that data from each domain contributed *unique* variance to the prediction of the children's achievement, externalizing problems, and internalizing problems in first grade.

Multiple regressions simply add risk predictors together but do not examine the interplay among the family factors—what we call the "dynamics" of family relationships. Structural equation models (path models) remedy this defect. In statistical terms, the connections among family domains can be direct or indirect. Depression in one or both parents may directly predict disruptions in parent-child relationships (Campbell et al., 1995; Hops, 1992). Or, it may be that depression in parents is associated with high marital conflict, and marital conflict is associated with more negative, less effective parent-child relationships (N. B. Miller, Cowan, Cowan, Hetherington, & Clingempeel, 1993).

Preventive Interventions.   There are four central justifications for considering preventive intervention programs for nonclinical couples as they make the transition to parenthood and as their first child makes the transition to school. First, with a divorce rate between 40% and 50%, it is clear that marriages are at risk. If a physical health problem had a 40% probability of occurring in a population, it would be clear that steps would have to be taken to address it. Second, risk indices in other domains of family life are also high. For example, in both our transition to parenthood and transition to school studies, with different families in each, about 33% of the men and women scored above the clinical cutoff on a widely used depression symptom scale (C. P. Cowan & Cowan, 2000). Third, we found a considerable proportion of the parents in our studies in distress as a couple, and, as we have seen, parents' marital distress is a risk factor for psychopathology in the children. Early intervention, before these problems become exacerbated, makes good sense. Fourth, if randomly assigned interventions

show effects on parent-child or marital relationship quality, investigators can draw conclusions about the causal impact of family relationships on children's adaptation.

Our randomized clinical trial of a 24-week couples group for couples becoming parents, led by a male-female team of trained mental health professionals (C. P. Cowan & Cowan, 2000), and a similar trial of a 16-week couples group for parents whose first child was entering kindergarten (C. P. Cowan, Cowan, & Heming, 2005), showed statistically significant effects. Compared with controls, parents from the couples groups showed much smaller declines in marital satisfaction in the years following the transition. The impact of the transition to parenthood group, conducted in the months surrounding the transition, lasted at least until the children were in their 1st year of elementary school (Schulz, Cowan, & Cowan, in press), almost 6 years after the intervention. Preliminary analyses show that the published positive results of the transition to school intervention from prekindergarten to first grade (C. P. Cowan et al., 2005) were also found in subsequent follow-ups at fourth grade, almost 6 years after that intervention.

An intervention for low-income mothers during the transition to parenthood by Heinicke and colleagues (Heinicke et al., 1999; Heinicke, Rineman, Ponce, & Guthrie, 2001) produced positive effects on mothers' self-reported symptoms and observed interactions with their infants. Another intervention study for expectant couples (Shapiro & Gottman, 2003) found that, compared with couples in a no-treatment control condition, couples becoming parents who participated in a 2-day psychoeducational workshop were more satisfied with their marriage; the wives reported fewer symptoms of depression and were observed to be less hostile during a couple problem-solving discussion. Two other couple-focused interventions for expectant parents are now in the process of being evaluated (John Gottman, personal communication, October, 2004; Jordan, Stanley, & Markman, 2003).

In our intervention conducted in the year before the first child entered kindergarten (C. P. Cowan et al., 2005), there were two variations: The couples groups that emphasized parenting issues resulted in a positive change in parenting but no change in marital interaction; the couples groups that emphasized marital issues resulted in a reduction in conflict between the parents during a family interaction task, as well as increases in parents' warmth and provision of structure with the child. In comparison with children whose parents were in the control condition, children whose parents participated in the couples groups emphasizing marital issues had higher tested achievement scores in kindergarten and lower levels of externalizing and peer problems in first grade. Finally, there were links between intervention-induced change and child outcomes. It appears that reductions in marital conflict and increases in effective parenting both played a causal role in children's academic and social adaptation to the early years of elementary school.

Divorce and Remarriage

Like studies of the transition to parenthood and the transition to school, examinations of the potential impact of divorce on children have been conducted using both correlational and experimental designs.

Correlational Studies. Some time ago, we were intrigued to read an early account of the changes in families following divorce by Hetherington and Camara (1984). If the reader substituted the words "transition to parenthood" for "divorce," the description would be consistent with the literature on new parents and make perfect sense. Structural equation models and regression equations describing risk factors in family dissolution and reconstitution also bear a remarkable resemblance to those obtained in studies of family formation. Parental depression following divorce is a risk factor for children (Hetherington, 1999). There is ample evidence that children fare well in families in which couples have good marriages or "good divorces" (Ahrons, 2004), but not when the relationship between their parents is full of unresolved conflict (Arendell, 1997b; Cummings & Davies, 1994; J. R. Johnston, 1994). As it does in intact families, unresolved conflict in divorced families places parent-child relationships at risk, not only in terms of relationship quality (Tein, Sandler, MacKinnon, & Wolchik, 2004), but also in terms of fathers' involvement in the daily life of the child, which tends to decrease when the parents are at war (Braver & Griffin, 2000; Carlson & McLanahan, 2002a; Coley & Chase-Lansdale, 1999). Divorce has an intergenerational aspect, in that adult children of divorce are more likely to end their own marriage (Amato, 2000). And, as it does in intact families (Conger, Elder, Lorenz, Simons, & Whitbeck, 1994; Mistry, Vandewater, Huston, & McLoyd, 2002), poverty associated with divorce, especially for women, tends to have its effects on children by disrupting family relationships, which is followed by both academic and social difficulties for the children (Hetherington & Kelly, 2002). When income level is statistically controlled, many of the associations between family structure and children's problematic outcome are reduced (Amato, 2001; Furstenberg & Teitler, 1994). That is, the negative effects of divorce come in part from the consequences associated with poverty, rather than directly from family dissolution.

Preventive Interventions. Wolchik and her colleagues (Tein et al., 2004; Wolchik et al., 2002; Wolchik, West, Westover, & Sandler, 1993) tested two versions of a preventive intervention, one for divorced mothers and one for divorced mothers and their 9- to 12-year-old daughters. Both programs provided 11 weekly sessions co-led by two master's level clinicians, who focused on improving mother-child relationship quality, teaching more effective discipline techniques, increasing fathers' access to the child, and reducing interparental conflict. Follow-ups occurred immediately and 3 months, 6 months, and 6 years after the intervention. The two programs had similar effects. An earlier evaluation at the immediate and 6-month posttests indicated that the reduction in children's externalizing behaviors was associated with reductions in the hypothesized risk variables: ineffective parental discipline and negative mother-child relationships. Neither program affected the young adolescents' internalizing.

Dilemmas in Assessing the Impact of Family Life Transitions

Interventions focused on the transition to parenthood, to school, and to divorce have a great deal to contribute to discussions of whether family processes are causally related to children's outcomes. But the question of whether the transition itself can be interpreted as causing distress in family members is difficult to answer. Several studies that compare childless couples with couples becoming parents show that couples without children also experience a decline in marital satisfaction over time (e.g., Clements & Markman, 1996; S. M. McHale & Huston, 1985; L. K. White & Booth, 1985). All of these studies began with engaged couples who were young and followed them for short periods of time. By contrast, our comparison of couples having children with a sample of couples not yet decided about having children, followed over 6 years, showed that the decline in marital satisfaction was steeper for the parents than for the couples who remained childless (Schulz et al., in press). A similar comparative study of couples with a wide range of age found the same trends (Shapiro et al., 2000). These findings do not prove that the transition to parenthood was the causal agent, because it is possible that selection factors that determined who decided to have children and who did not were operating to produce the differences.

Similar problems exist in making claims about the *impact* of divorce on children. Almost all studies of this topic have three serious flaws:

1. Until recently, investigations began only *after* the parents separated or divorced. It is reasonable to assume that there may be a selection factor in operation. Children of parents who eventually divorce have been exposed to the parents' relationship difficulty prior to the divorce (Block, Block, & Gjerde, 1989; Cherlin, Furstenberg, Chase-Lansdale, & Kiernan, 1991). It may be the cumulative effects of predivorce relationships rather than divorce itself that is responsible for difficulties that some children experience after their parents have separated.

2. Almost all studies compare children of divorced and nondivorced families, without considering the potentially detrimental impact on children of living with high-conflict parents who stay together (see earlier discussion).

3. A third design flaw, ubiquitous in current research, results from the undifferentiated research question "Does divorce hurt children—yes or no?" We agree with Amato (2000, p. 1282), who suggests a more differentiated approach: "Divorce benefits some individuals, leads others to experience temporary decrements in well-being, and forces others on a downward trajectory from which they might never recover fully. Understanding the contingencies under which divorce leads to these diverse outcomes is a priority for future research."

Family Systems and Family Transitions

Our description of the transition to parenthood, like our description of divorce, has been formulated within the framework of family risk models that provide accounts of how change in various domains of family life affect the adaptation of the children. There are very few examples of research on family transitions that adopt a family systems perspective. A welcome exception is the work of James McHale (J. P. McHale et al., 2004; J. P. McHale & Rasmussen, 1998), who explores the interconnections among individual factors (e.g., child temperament, adult symptomatology), dyadic factors (e.g., the coparenting relationship), and triadic, whole-family perspectives on the transition to parenthood and early family functioning. The whole-family measures in McHale's studies are adapted from the work of Fivaz-Depeursinge (Fivaz-Depeursinge & Corboz-Warnery, 1999), who created the Lausanne trilogue play procedure. This observation paradigm involves videotaping a mother and father together first taking turns and then working together to engage the attention of their infant, who is seated in an orthopedic car seat that the parents can swivel as they attempt to direct the infant's attention. Although some of the coding of this interaction involves a focus on individuals and dyads, combined scores represent *family* levels of coop-

eration, competition, and warmth. Some dyadic coparenting measures are derived from observation, and others are derived from discrepancies between the parents' self-reports. The research shows that parents' prenatal marital quality sets the stage for postnatal coparenting quality and the atmosphere in the family as a whole. Furthermore, high prenatal marital quality kept the parents from responding negatively when their 3-month-old babies were irritable.

Despite the relative absence of systematic studies of family transitions using a systems perspective, there have been detailed clinical descriptions of families from a systems point of view of families undergoing normative transitions such as the transition to adolescence or marriage, and by nonnormative changes resulting from illness, death of family members (e.g., Boss, 1999), and natural catastrophes (e.g., Carter & McGoldrick, 2005).

Overall similarities among systemic discussions of quite different life changes reveal that a transition in even one family member creates disequilibrium in the system as a whole. Whether families can use the period of transition as a catalyst for growth, or whether they succumb to passivity or depression, depends in part on a combination of family system competencies, the stressfulness of the transition, and the psychological, social, and financial resources of the family to meet the demands for change imposed by the transition. All of these formulations bear some resemblance to the ABC-X model initially proposed by life span sociologist Reuben Hill (1949), later expanded by Boss (Boss & Mulligan, 2003) and McCubbin (McCubbin, Thompson, Thompson, & Futrell, 1999), in which the outcome of any life stressor (X) depends on environmental demands (A), family resources (B), and appraisals of the meaning of the stressor (C).

Our conclusion is not that the family disequilibrium surrounding divorce is exactly the same as disruptions that follow when partners become parents or the first child makes the transition to school, but rather that similar risk factor models can be applied to these and other family life transitions. A great deal more research will be needed to determine the precise arrangements of the patterns of prediction, and which variables may play stronger or weaker roles in different transitions at different times.

DEVELOPMENTAL PSYCHOPATHOLOGY IN FAMILIES IN WHICH AT LEAST ONE MEMBER HAS BEEN CLINICALLY DIAGNOSED

In the previous section, we explored how multidomain family models account for variations in adaptation in nonclinical families. Here we show that similar principles apply to the explanation of clinically diagnosed psychopathology in families in which at least one of the members has received a diagnosis. Our strategy here is to focus selectively on a number of issues that illustrate current thinking about the linkage between families and psychopathology. We begin with a discussion of the pitfalls involved in validating family systems theories and then discuss the evidence for the family factors approach.

Difficulties in Validating Family Systems Theories of Psychopathology

Two kinds of evidence are cited as supportive of family systems assumptions about the etiology of various psychopathologies. First, there is considerable evidence that, as a group, families with a clinically diagnosed member differ from nonclinical families in many of the ways that family systems theorists have hypothesized (e.g., Wenar & Kerig, 2000). Second, there is also considerable evidence that treatments of families using variations of conjoint family therapy have a significant positive effect when compared with randomly selected no-treatment controls (see discussion that follows). Our task here is to explore the conclusions we can draw from these facts.

Correlational Designs

Research that compares whole-system structures or processes in families with or without a member with a specific diagnosis is a necessary first step in validating family systems theories of psychopathology. The number of studies that fit this description is not large, but the results are consistent with the theories. For example, families with a member diagnosed with Schizophrenia showed more instances of communication deviance (Singer & Wynne, 1965b) than comparable families without a member who fits that diagnostic category. Even more important for the purposes of establishing specific links between family processes and Schizophrenia is the finding that these families also produced more disordered communication responses than families whose members had other diagnoses. Another set of studies investigated the construct of expressed emotion (EE) by asking relatives of an adult hospitalized patient diagnosed with Schizophrenia or Bipolar Disorder to talk into a tape recorder for 5 minutes to describe the patient. Family members coded as high in EE make more hostile, critical, or emotionally overinvolved remarks than family members low in EE. A number of studies show that relatives of diagnosed patients are much more likely to have high EE scores than relatives of nonpatients (Bebbington & Kuipers, 1994).

Except for families with a member diagnosed with Schizophrenia or Bipolar Disorder, it is rare to find studies that show family-level differences between diagnosed and nondiagnosed families. Shaw and his colleagues (Shaw, Criss, Schonberg, & Beck, 2004) cite several studies showing that hierarchical parent-child boundaries are either too rigid or too diffuse in families of children with ADHD or general emotional difficulties, but note that previous to their own, there have been no studies that investigate the origins of hierarchical boundary differences among families. These authors assessed families at high risk by virtue of poverty when the child was a toddler and followed up with assessments at age 10. Path models revealed direct links between early parent-child relationship difficulties and later vague or enmeshed boundaries reported by the mothers. Furthermore, parental adjustment, child temperament, marital difficulties, and ecological disadvantage (low education and income, dangerous neighborhood) were all indirectly linked with inadequate boundaries, which, in turn, were related to conduct problems as reported by both the mothers and the children at age 10 and 11. Boundary disturbances have also been found to differentiate between families without a diagnosed child and families with a 6- to 10-year-old with ADHD or depression, even after controlling for the presence of maternal depression (Jacobvitz, Hazen, Curran, & Hitchens, 2004). As predicted, boys in enmeshed families more often developed ADHD, whereas girls in similar families were more likely to develop depression. Taken together, these studies begin to raise important questions about why boundary disturbances are associated with different diagnostic outcomes in different families.

This first step—establishing differences between families with and without a diagnosed member—is necessary but far from sufficient to validate family systems theories. Almost all of these studies involve single time assessments and therefore employ the logic of correlation, even when the data are presented in the form of t-tests or analysis of variance (Shaw et al., 2004, is a welcome exception). Even if, for example, the chances of deviant communication are greater in families with a member with Schizophrenia than in families without a member in this diagnostic category, we do not know whether the deviant communication causes Schizophrenia, or the diagnosed member creates conditions that lead to deviant communication, or whether both result from a direct influence of a third variable such as underlying genetic vulnerability. These objections are not easily overcome.

Intervention Designs

Although intervention designs have some advantages in determining sequences and directions of effects, they are not without problems of their own in the quest to validate family systems theories of psychopathology. It is difficult to find examples of systematic evaluations of family systems interventions, in part because investigators are often vague about what they mean by *family* treatment. Couple and family interventions are typically mixed together in research reviews and meta-analyses (Baucom, Shoham, Mueser, Daiuto, & Stickle, 1998; Shadish et al., 1995; Sprenkle, 2002). Existing examples show that, in studies using a randomized clinical trial design, conjoint family treatment produces more positive outcomes in families with members diagnosed with Schizophrenia, Conduct Disorder, or substance abuse than some form of low-dose treatment or no treatment (e.g., Diamond, Serrano, Dickey, & Sonis, 1998). A closer look suggests that, although these studies allow us to conclude that a given treatment was effective, they rarely provide direct validation for the family systems theories on which they are based. First, as we noted in the discussion of the nine-cell matrix of theories of stability and change, the demonstration that psychopathology diagnosed in a family member can be treated successfully in conjoint family therapy does not prove that family factors were the cause of the problems. What they do illustrate, and this is no small matter, is that family relationships *may* play a role in both stability and change in individual developmental pathways.

Second, what is missing from most family-based intervention studies is a demonstration not only that the treatment was effective, but also that the impact can reasonably be attributed to the *family* aspects of the treatment. This demonstration can occur by employing a research design that compares the outcomes of (1) conjoint family treatments for a given disorder with (2) treatments that use a family systems perspective, but not a conjoint treatment setting, and with (3) treatment of similar identified patients using a more traditional individually focused theoretical paradigm. We acknowledge that most therapeutic intervention studies do not compare *two* intervention groups with a control, but that is what is needed as a beginning step to examine whether the active ingredient in family systems-oriented therapy is in fact a change in the structure and process of the family system.

Some progress toward establishing family mechanisms involved in treatment can be made even without a three-group intervention design. As outlined in a special issue of *Development and Psychopathology* (Cicchetti & Hinshaw, 2002), beyond the question of whether it works, intervention designs are uniquely equipped to address the question of how to test theories of developmental psychopathology. If we can target a family process with an intervention, demonstrate using the appropriate controls that the intervention (A) produces the desired effect on the family (B),

and show that this effect is associated directly with changes in the desired outcome (C), then we have a powerful instrument for concluding that B has a causal connection with C. This would allow us to begin to confirm or disconfirm the theory on which the intervention was based.

A beginning move in the direction of identifying family mechanisms in psychopathology using intervention designs has been made in studies of EE in families with members diagnosed with Schizophrenia or Bipolar Disorder, as mentioned (Miklowitz, 2004; Pilling et al., 2002; Wahlberg & Wynne, 2001). Compared with traditional individual treatments of the patient, psychoeducational interventions with family members produce lower relapse rates after the patient leaves the hospital. Still needed in these and other intervention studies are detailed analyses of the changes in family interaction produced by these interventions and an examination of whether this change accounts for the variations in the patient outcomes.

Measurement and Statistical Issues in Correlational and Intervention Designs

Most studies of links between family functioning and psychopathology use measures and statistical analytic techniques more appropriate to the study of individuals, and occasionally dyads, than to the assessment of the family as a system.

Measurement. The source of information about the family can come from one or more family members (mother, father, child) or outside observers (family friends or researchers). The focus of that information can be on individual family members, dyads, or the system as a whole. To complicate an already complex picture, the information can be obtained in different contexts: individual interviews, dyadic interactions, the family system as a whole, or the family in the community. That is, there are 4 sources |multi| 3 foci |multi| 4 contexts, or 48 potentially different perspectives on family functioning. Only a few of these can be included in any single study. What is most seriously lacking from current research, in our view, is the examination of the family as a whole using systemic concepts to assess how the family operates.

The most well-established family system measurement systems (see earlier discussion), the McMaster model and the Beavers model, use family interviews to obtain data; this severely limits the technique to children who can talk and focus throughout a long session. A promising example of a new approach to families with infants, described briefly earlier, is the Lausanne trilogue play procedure (Fivaz-Depeursinge, 2003; Frascarolo, Favez, Carneiro, & Fivaz-Depeursinge, 2004), in which mothers and fathers interact together with their infant and the coding of this interaction yields measures of both family structure and affective process.

Statistical Techniques   Until recently, one of the chief impediments to family systems research has been statistical techniques directed toward a linear analysis of the effect of x on y, using either analysis of variance or multiple regression techniques. More recently, structural equation modeling, time series analyses, and hierarchical linear modeling allow researchers to contrast models in which there is a reciprocal effect of A on B and B on A. These techniques move us closer to testing hypotheses promulgated by family system theories 50 years ago.

What Is Needed?

In sum, despite the fact that there is considerable evidence that treatments based on family systems theories are effective, the evidence supporting family systems theories of psychopathology is at a preliminary stage. Families with a severely mentally ill member communicate differently from families without a diagnosed member, but it is not possible to tell whether the communication deviance is at the root of the disorder. The best evidence concerning the validity of family systems theories will come from follow-forward studies, with measurement that focuses on the system as a whole and demonstrates that the family-level measures contribute uniquely to our understanding variations in psychopathology and adjustment, over and above the contribution of risk factors in individual and dyadic domains. Because this kind of study is rare, and because so many studies will be needed to discover the links between measures of family-level functioning and each specific disorder we hope to understand, opportunities for research in this area will keep many investigators very busy for many decades.

Family Risk Factors and Psychopathology

In our view, the bulk of the evidence used to support the validity of family systems theories comes from family risk factor studies of the variables that each theory emphasizes as central to that approach. That is, family system theories may be located in cell 9 of our matrix (Figure 14.2), but different family theories have different emphases on specific risks, and these risks can be located in each of the remaining cells or in the interactions among them. We describe a number of examples of empirical evidence that provides support for the hypothesis that family risk factors

play an important role in the understanding of psychopathology in clinical populations.

Genetic-Family System Interactions

There is no doubt that severe psychological disorders (Schizophrenia, Bipolar Disorder, Major Depression, Antisocial Personality Disorder, and others) run in families (Gottesman et al., 1972; Meehl, 1962; Rosenthal, 1967). Given a diagnosed patient as an index, relatives are more likely to be diagnosed with that disorder than a nonindex control of the same age, sex, and general life circumstances. The central task in the field of behavioral genetics has been to disentangle the confounding due to the fact that closely related family members tend to live together, making it difficult to assess genetic effects separately from environmental effects. Earlier, we described studies of heritability that compare monozygotic twins (MZ, identical), dizygotic twins (DZ, fraternal), families with two or more nontwin children, and sometimes families with adopted at-risk children. In combination, these studies represent attempts to tease apart the contributions of genetic and family environmental risks to psychological disorders.

A related, more central question for the field of developmental psychopathology is why some individuals with family genetic vulnerabilities develop disorders and others do not. The most general answer to both of these questions originated more than 4 decades ago in a diathesis-stress model, which conceptualized genetic factors as a diathesis (vulnerability) that results in a disorder if triggered by sufficiently high levels of specific environmental stressors (Tienari, 1991; Wahlberg et al., 2004). The early work tended to describe environmental stressors in vague terms as effects not accounted for in estimates of heredity. Recent behavioral genetic studies create a more differentiated picture of the way careful consideration of genetic factors in research designs provide powerful support for the hypothesis that family risk factors play a causal role in the development of psychopathology.

Heritability-Environment Interaction.[2]   A very sophisticated Finnish Adoptive Family Study provides preliminary evidence for interaction of heredity and family environment. Tienari and his colleagues (Tienari, 1991; Wahlberg et al., 2004) identified 155 people with at least one parent diagnosed with Schizophrenia, who were adopted away, and 186 control cases, also adopted away,

---

[2] The discussion in this section has benefited from a presentation made by Avshalom Caspi to an NICHD-sponsored group considering Family Change and Variation (Los Angeles, February 2005).

whose parents had no psychotic disorder. Using Singer and Wynne's (1965a) procedure for assessing communication deviance among the adoptive parents, in combination with other diagnostic material, these researchers produced a global rating of each adoptive family's level of functioning. Early reports show that 34% of the children whose *biological* parents were not psychotic, but 62% of the children with a psychotic biological parent, were diagnosed with schizophrenic spectrum disorders when their adoptive parents were rated as disturbed in terms of psychopathology or communication deviance. By contrast, when the adoptive parents were rated as mentally healthy, 4% of the children with nonpsychotic biological parents and 3% of the children with psychotic biological parents were diagnosed with schizophrenic spectrum disorders. Given this research design that separated biological risks associated with heredity and family risks associated with the adoptive living environment, this study provides strong evidence that genetic vulnerability brought by the adoptee is more likely to result in psychopathology in the context of mental illness or disordered communication in the adoptive family environment. Conversely, adoptive parents who function well may be able to protect children from the risks associated with having a biological parent with Schizophrenia. The later results will be especially important, as the youngest adopted children have not yet reached the primary age for risk for Schizophrenia.

An important point has recently become central in behavioral genetics research: Heritability estimates hold *only for a specific population.* In a paper that helped to reframe the discussion of this topic, Turkheimer and his colleagues (Turkheimer, Haley, Waldron, D'Onofrio, & Gottesman, 2003) showed that the heritability index of IQ is almost zero at low levels of socioeconomic status, but very high in financially well-off samples, where it explains about 60% of the variance. Parental treatment that fosters similarity between siblings (shared family environment) or difference between siblings (nonshared family environment) explains little of the variation in IQ in high-income families but about 60% of the variation in low-income families. How heritable is IQ? How important is family interaction in explaining variance in IQ? The answers depend on the sociocultural context of the families we study.

Using Genetic Controls to Study Environmental Variation.   We noted that twin studies are now being used in a new way: to control for genetic influences so that the effects of family environmental variation become clear. In the Environmental Risk Longitudinal Twin Study, Caspi and Moffitt and their colleagues (Caspi et al., 2004) stud-

ied a nationally representative sample of British families with MZ and DZ twins. Mothers were asked to describe each twin for 5 minutes, as in the studies of expressed emotion described earlier. Using ratings of negativity and warmth expressed toward each 6-year-old twin in mothers' speech samples, the investigators found that within each pair (controlling for genetic factors), the twin whose mother expressed more negativity and less warmth toward him or her was rated by the classroom teacher as showing more antisocial behavior at school.

Biological Relatedness and Family Structure.   Twin studies are not the only way of studying the impact of biological and social relatedness in families. Hetherington and her colleagues (1994) examined data from the national sample from the Nonshared Environment in Adolescent Development Project (Caspi et al., 2004). Eliminating the MZ and DZ twins from a sample of families with at least two same-sex adolescent children, the researchers studied nonstepfamilies, simple stepfamilies in which all siblings were the mother's biological children and the father's stepchildren, and complex stepfamilies in which the children were combinations of his, hers, and theirs. The last two groups allowed the investigators to contrast family systems in which the children had different degrees of biological relatedness to each other and to their parents. The investigators found few differences between nonstepfamilies and simple stepfamilies in the adjustment of the children or the quality of marital and parent-child relationships. In complex stepfamilies, however, more problems were observed in the family relationships, and the adolescents showed less social responsibility and higher levels of externalizing problems. In the stepfamilies, greater caretaking and warmth was found when parents were interacting with their biological children rather than with their stepchildren. That is, genes also have an impact on the social construction of relatedness and may influence attitudes and behavior of children, parents, and others outside the nuclear family. Judgments about the importance of genetic relatedness become very important in discussions of stepfamilies, adoption, and gay and lesbian families.

Measuring   Gene-Environment   Interactions.   In studies of heritability, the impact of genetic factors on psychopathology is inferred from the differences in correlations between MZ and DZ twins. Recent methods of measuring gene functions and dysfunctions directly, rather than estimating them from family heritability, are providing more precise indicators of genetic risk. In a nationally representative sample of more than 1,000 children in Dunedin,

New Zealand, Caspi and Moffitt and their colleagues (Caspi et al., 2002) measured the neurotransmitter-metabolizing enzyme monoamine oxidase A (MAOA), located on the X (male) chromosome. Deficiencies in this gene affect neurotransmitters such as norepinephrine, serotonin, and dopamine, which have been linked with male antisocial behavior (Huang et al., 2004). Also linked with antisocial aggressive behavior is childhood maltreatment by parents (Cicchetti et al., 2000; Dodge, Pettit, & Bates, 1997). The Caspi et al. study found that when the children's MAOA activity was low (indicating deficiency), there was a very high incidence of diagnosed Conduct Disorder in adolescence and elevated levels of disposition toward violence, convictions for violent offenses, and Antisocial Personality Disorder in adulthood. Conversely, high MAOA seemed to protect children who had experienced early maltreatment from developing antisocial behaviors later on. Note that both longitudinal studies by Caspi and Moffitt are of nonclinical populations. Nevertheless, these populations included individuals with a formal *DSM-IV* diagnosis. Behavior geneticists argue that limiting studies to clinical populations reduces the sample variance in ways that can lead to biased estimates of both genetic and environmental effects on psychopathology.

Among many important implications of this research and of other studies cited in this section are two conclusions about the family as a system. First, genetic heritability is affected by the social context in which it operates and is measured. Second, genetic heritability affects the social environment through its impact on the behavior of family members by influencing their behavior in ways that have environmental impact. Although research studies have demonstrated impressively that these interactive effects occur, we do not yet have a clear idea of the mechanisms by which genetic factors affect environments and how family and other environmental factors "get under the skin" (Taylor, Repetti, & Seeman, 1997) to affect biological processes. Third, because behavior genetics analyses have been applied to a limited number of disorders in a limited number of social contexts, it is not clear how the weighting of genetic, family, and other environmental influences holds across diagnostic categories and across cultures.

Couple Relationships and Psychopathology

Both symptomatic and clinically diagnostic levels of depression co-occur with marital dissatisfaction, conflict, and distress (e.g., Whisman, Uebelacker, & Weinstock, 2004). Unhappily married couples are more likely to be depressed, and depressed individuals are more likely to exist in unhappy marriages. Although each domain influences the other, declines in marital satisfaction may play an etiological role in depression more often than vice versa (Whisman & Bruce, 1999). Some corroborating evidence comes from a review of therapy studies reporting that marital therapy is an effective treatment for depression when compared with no-treatment controls and, more important, is more effective than individual therapy with the depressed client (Teichman, 1997); the converse approach of treating depression in couples with marital problems has not been systematically evaluated. A more differentiated view of the marital quality link with depression comes from a short-term longitudinal study (Fincham, Beach, Harold, & Osborne, 1997), which suggests that for men, the causal path may lead from depression to marital dissatisfaction, whereas for women, the causal path may lead from marital dissatisfaction to depression. This is only one of many illustrations of the principle that gender affects the pathways between family risks and maladaptive outcomes.

We have noted throughout the chapter that couple relationship conflict and dissatisfaction are correlated with children's externalizing behavior in both nonclinical and clinical samples. Marital conflict is also associated with children's internalizing behavior, specifically anxiety and depression. In the Environmental Risk Longitudinal Twin Study, Jaffee and colleagues (Jaffee, Moffitt, Caspi, Taylor, & Arseneault, 2002) reported that, after controlling for genetic and nonshared parenting effects (behaviors toward siblings that enhance differences), domestic violence between parents was associated with significantly higher externalizing *and* internalizing behavior in children. Furthermore, the quality of relationships in the family had a particularly strong contribution to predicting comorbidity—children who were both aggressive and depressed. Note that in behavior genetics studies, the distinction between genetic and environmental effects is not entirely clear. In this case, genetic factors may contribute to both the parents' tendency to engage in violent behavior and to the child's vulnerability.

Parenting and Psychopathology

As examples of how parents can contribute to the onset or maintenance of children's problems, we discuss parental maltreatment, and children diagnosed with Attention-Deficit/Hyperactivity Disorders and disorders of attachment.

Parenting Behavior. Maltreatment is a serious social problem, with American rates of reported child abuse in 2002 ranging from 16 per 1,000 0- to 3-year-olds to 6 per

1,000 16- to 17-year-olds. This results in more than 2 million children who are abused in a given year, and an estimated 1,400 fatalities resulting from abuse of children by their parents and other adults in the household. It is clear that although maltreatment is manifest in the parent-child relationship, the etiological picture involves a system of by now familiar family risk factors. Building on Belsky's (1980) ecological model, Cicchetti and his colleagues argue that maltreatment involves (1) maladaptive biological and psychological resources in maltreating parents, especially depression, and drug or alcohol use; (2) unsupportive and aggressive marital relationships; (3) parent-child relationships in which the parents are more controlling, hostile, and coercive make more negative attributions about their children's behavior, and are less affectionate than nonabusing parents; (4) a history of abuse across generations (though the evidence is largely retrospective); and (5) stressors in the society outside the nuclear family, including racism, poverty, dangerous neighborhoods, unemployment, and lack of supportive social networks (for integrative summaries, see Cicchetti, 2004; Cicchetti & Lynch, 1995; Cicchetti & Toth, 2003).

A less severe but no less important form of negative interaction can be seen in the Patterson group's concept of coercive parent-child relationships. Structural equation models consistently reveal links between coercive parent-child patterns and children's and adolescents' aggression both inside and outside the family (Dishion & Patterson, 1997; G. R. Patterson, Reid, & Dishion, 1998). The model has also been tested in intervention studies demonstrating that reductions in coercive parenting are followed by decreases in adolescent aggression. Whereas coercion represents an active, intrusive parenting style, Reid, Patterson, and Snyder (2002) summarize 3 decades of research showing that parental disengagement, especially in the form of lack of monitoring of adolescents, also represents a significant risk factor for adolescent aggression. This variable is usually assessed by phoning parents in the evening and asking them if they know where their children are. We focus here on parenting, but, as in Cicchetti's ecological model of maltreatment, Capaldi and colleagues (Capaldi, Pears, Patterson, & Owen, 2003; Pears & Capaldi, 2001) present a multidomain family risk model in which parent-child relationships play a necessary but not sufficient role in explaining children's and adolescents' maladaptive behavior.

All of these studies attempting to link parenting behavior with child and adolescent outcomes are subject to the same caveats about inferring causality that we have discussed throughout the chapter. Harsh physical punishment or legally defined abuse is clearly detrimental to children and cannot

be justified, but it is not always possible to determine whether child temperament or other characteristics play some role in eliciting the parental behavior. Coercion is by definition a reciprocal construct, describing the escalating pattern created in the interaction between parent and child. Even monitoring, which clearly sounds like a parental behavior, can be an ambiguous construct; investigators point out that some adolescents spontaneously tell their parents where they are going and where they are, so that the correlations between monitoring and low aggression may reflect the quality of the relationship, not whether parents take an active, coercive part in forcing their children to reveal information concerning their whereabouts.

Parenting and Children's Attention-Deficit/Hyperactivity Disorder.[3]   A case for a bidirectional view of parenting behavior and children's characteristics can be seen very clearly in studies of children diagnosed with ADHD. There is no doubt that there are strong heritability factors in the etiology of both attention deficits and hyperactivity, but there is also evidence that the stress experienced by parents of children with these symptoms increases the probability of negative family interactions (C. Johnston & Mash, 2001). The lack of control, hyperactivity, and defiant behavior shown by these children elicit harsh or permissive reactions in parents; these parenting behaviors predict antisocial and noncompliant behavior assessed later on, even after controlling for the child's earlier ADHD behavior (Anderson, Hinshaw, & Simmel, 1994). Comparing families with a male child with and without a diagnosis of ADHD, Hinshaw and his colleagues (Hinshaw, Zupan, Simmel, Nigg, & Melnick, 1997) found that in the ADHD sample only, mothers' authoritative parenting beliefs predicted social acceptance by the boys' peers in a summer camp, even when their behavior with those peers was observed to be quite negative. To the extent that parenting beliefs were reflected in behavior, the results are consistent with the hypothesis that an authoritative parenting style can protect children with ADHD from peer rejection, but that there may be many other routes to peer acceptance for boys without ADHD.

Finally, in a variation on the genetic designs described earlier, twins with low birthweight were the focus, because low birthweight is a risk factor for ADHD (Tully, Arseneault, Caspi, Moffitt, & Morgan, 2004). Only for these initially small twins did mothers' warmth in a 5-minute

---

[3] The discussion in this section has benefited from discussion with Stephen Hinshaw.

speech sample protect children against symptoms of ADHD 6 years later. All of these findings illustrate the general principle that parenting behavior interacts with child characteristics to predict adaptive or maladaptive outcomes.

Attachment Relationships. Our emphasis here shifts from a focus on parents' behavior to the inclusion of children's inner working models and behavior in situations in which they experience a separation or threat of loss of the parent. Four ways of coping with this loss have been identified in laboratory studies of attachment (Ainsworth & Wittig, 1969; Lyons-Ruth, Alpern, & Repacholi, 1993). When a parent comes back into the lab room, his or her 12- to 18-month-old may (1) fuss but seek the parent as a secure base before continuing play (secure); (2) anxiously avoid the parent; (3) angrily attack the parent; or (4) become disorganized. Insecure attachment in the parent-child relationship has been associated with an expectable range of family risk factors, including parents' psychopathology, adolescent hospitalization (J. P. Allen, Hauser, & Borman-Spurrell, 1996), parents' insecure working models of attachment with their parents (the grandparents; Fonagy, Steele, & Steele, 1991; van Ijzendoorn & Bakermans-Kranenburg, 1997), and marital distress (Owen & Cox, 1997).

The overall classification of securely attached versus insecurely attached is relatively stable over long periods of time *in middle-class but not economically disadvantaged samples* (Vaughn, Egeland, Sroufe, & Waters, 1979). In low-income samples, changes in the child's attachment status have been related to changes in the circumstances of the parents, especially in the case of establishing or ending a romantic relationship with a partner (Egeland & Sroufe, 1981; Vondra, Hommerding, & Shaw, 1999). Infants with an early history of secure attachment are likely to show a number of positive adaptive traits in childhood and adolescence, including less anxiety and more empathy and social competence (Egeland & Carlson, 2004). By contrast, early insecure attachments represent risk factors for anxiety, depression, and low social competence.

Several investigators who take a longitudinal perspective on the links between early attachment and later psychopathology have suggested that insecure attachment is not simply an index of psychopathology or a direct cause of psychopathology (J. P. Allen et al., 1996; Cicchetti & Barnett, 1991; Davies, Cummings, & Winter, 2004; Sroufe, Carlson, Levy, & Egeland, 2003). Rather, patterns of earlier insecure attachment, in combination with difficulties in family relationships, set in motion forces that move the child in the direction of psychopathology over time if they are not counteracted by buffers in the family or other aspects of the child's environment (Egeland & Carlson, 2004). For example, maltreated children with perceptions of high positive relatedness to their mother were more depressed than nonmaltreated children, but less depressed than maltreated children who did not describe positive relatedness with their mother (Toth & Cicchetti, 1996).

Intergenerational Transmission. We have already noted that most studies of transmission, including those that employ the Adult Attachment Interview (George, Kaplan, & Main, 1985), rely on retrospective data. There are some new findings from longitudinal studies of clinical populations that use observations of parents in generation 1 (G1) as they interact with their children (G2), and then observations of G2 as adults parenting their own children. In a useful review, Serbin and Karp (2004) point out that consistency across generations is higher when the assessments of parents and children in G1-G2 occur at approximately the same age as the assessments of parents in G2 and G3 (Capaldi et al., 2003).

The fact that children tend to resemble their parents and to think (B. A. Miller, 2005) and behave (Bengtson, 1996; Luescher & Pillemer, 1998) in similar ways does not tell us a great deal about what has been transmitted or how the transmission has occurred. Five theoretical explanations of intergenerational continuity dominate the current scene. First, as we have just seen, attachment theory assumes that adults have developed working models of parent-child relationships based on experiences with key attachment figures in their family of origin, and these working models shape their expectations and reactions during interactions with their children (Bowlby, 1988). Second, some of the repetition of relationship patterns across generations is affected by genetic and other biological mechanisms (Plomin, 1994). Third, psychoanalytic formulations focus on the child's identification with the same-sex parent and the internalization of that parent's superego, both of which provide guidelines for what constitutes appropriate behavior in family relationships (Fraiberg, 1975; S. Freud, 1938). Fourth, in turn, these interactions between parent and child result in the child's creation of working models that lead to the repetition of secure or insecure attachment patterns in the next generation. Fifth, social learning theorists (Bandura, 1977; G. R. Patterson, 1975) offer a simpler explanation that does not rely on assumptions about the child's inner world: In the process of observing adults interact with others and noting which behaviors are reinforced or punished, children learn patterns of family behavior that they tend to repeat when they form their own family.

Most studies of intergenerational transmission focus on the parent-child relationship. Both family systems models and family risk models suggest that attention should be paid to three additional perspectives on continuities and discontinuities of family patterns. First, as we (P. A. Cowan, Bradburn, & Cowan, 2005) and Caspi and Elder (1988) have shown in studies of nonclinical families, children with behavior problems who are involved in conflictful relationships with their parents, and may be insecurely attached to them, are more likely to form conflictful marriages, which are followed by combative parent-child relationships, which predict problematic behavior in their children. Second, new work on family rituals provides a more system-focused perspective, suggesting that in daily rituals such as gathering together for family dinners and anniversary or religious rituals, family members in well-functioning families coconstruct stories that create family myths and preserve family values, whereas the absence of such rituals is often seen in families experiencing various forms of distress (Fiese, 1992; Pratt & Fiese, 2004). Finally, due to both genetic and environmental factors, families tend to remain in the same social class from one generation to the next, and the repetition of stressors may also contribute to continuity of adaptation across generations.

Families and Peer Groups

By referring more generally to measures of externalizing and internalizing in discussing family factors in psychopathology, and not focusing on the fact that these measures often refer to behavior with peers in schools and other social settings, we have not conveyed the central importance of the linkage between family and peer relationships. In an analysis of the data from the Oregon Social Learning Study, G. R. Patterson, Dishion, and Bank's (1984) longitudinal study of aggressive boys showed that coercive parent discipline interacted reciprocally with irritable exchanges between the target child and other family members. Furthermore, irritable exchanges within the family, especially between siblings, were described as providing "fight training" that generalized to the peer group in seventh grade and 10th grade and was associated with peer rejection, one of the major risk factors for adolescent antisocial behavior.

The question of whether fighting leads to peer rejection or rejection leads to fighting has been debated for a long time (see Parker & Asher, 1987, for the beginning of this debate). Evidence supporting the hypothesis that peer rejection may come first was found in our own longitudinal study (P. A. Cowan & Cowan, 2004). Teacher-reported peer rejection in first grade predicted antisocial behavior in fourth grade (stealing, fighting, lying), over and above earlier aggressive behavior in kindergarten. Negative interactions between the parents and between parents and children in prekindergarten and kindergarten were risk factors for peer rejection in first grade. Furthermore, based on data from the intervention with the parents as couples, we were able to show that intervention-induced positive changes in marital and parenting relationships resulted in the children's suffering less peer rejection in first grade.

Multiple Risk Models

In each of the previous sections, we saw how researchers were stretching to go beyond two domains or levels of analysis at a time and include yet another risk domain in their attempts to predict and understand psychopathology. In this section are a few studies that attempt to bring all of the domains together.

Correlational Studies. At Bradley Hospital and Brown University School of Medicine in Rhode Island, a group of researchers (Dickstein et al., 1998) is attempting to validate family systemic approaches to psychopathology by constructing measurement models that rely on multiple methods and perspectives on three levels of family interaction: marital, parent-child, and whole family. These models combine a risk factor and family systemic analysis of the family. In about 75% of their sample of 185 families, mothers had a lifetime history of mental illness. The investigators' measurement scheme followed the McMaster model of normal family functioning described earlier, which included the McMaster Structured Interview of Family Functioning, a dinnertime observation, and individual questionnaires to arrive at a family-level assessment, along with questionnaires that describe the quality of marital and parent-child relationships. Although almost all the measures were significantly intercorrelated, each also showed some independent contribution to explaining family health and maladaptation.

A unique feature of this study is that the researchers examined the correlations between family variables and groups representing a number of diagnostic categories: Major Depression, Anxiety Disorder, Bipolar Disorder, and a miscellaneous group, comparing them with no-illness controls. As expected, family-level variables, marital variables, and parent-child variables (both father-child and mother-child) all revealed some significant differences between the no-illness controls and the clinical groups, with little differentiation among diagnostic groups except for the fact that depressed mothers were the only ones to show significantly lower quality of parent-child relationships.

Consistent with the family systems assumption that the whole is not equal to the sum of the parts was the finding that the presence or absence of psychopathology in the mothers was much more strongly related to measures of whole-family functioning than to measures of marital or parent-child relationships. In other words, the functioning of the family as a whole was more disrupted than the dyadic relationships.

Multidomain Interventions In response to the difficulty of treating families with adolescents who abuse drugs, several researcher-clinicians have demonstrated the importance of considering levels of psychopathology in each family member, patterns of interactions during conjoint family treatment, and multiple settings in which families are embedded (high-crime neighborhoods, ineffective schools, drug-encouraging peer groups, inaccessible health care systems, and inconsistent juvenile justice systems). The task of the therapist is not to intervene in all of these systems, though some attempt to work with schools and peer groups, but to help the adolescent and family mobilize resources and avoid contexts that reinforce drug-abusing behavior (Liddle, 1995; Liddle et al., 2001). Applications of this approach to the treatment of already identified families have been successfully extended to preventive interventions for high-risk adolescents who are not yet clinically diagnosed (Liddle & Hogue, 2000).

A conceptually similar approach to the treatment of delinquent adolescents and abusing families, multisystemic therapy was developed by Henggeler and his colleagues (Henggeler & Borduin, 1990; Henggeler, Schoenwald, & Pickrel, 1995). Both the Liddle and Henggeler multidomain treatments were developed in a context in which studies of traditional child psychotherapy showed significant effects in studies conducted in university settings, but not when conducted in community clinic settings (Weisz, Donenberg, Han, & Weiss, 1995). Henggeler and colleagues argue that multisystemic therapies not only rise to the challenge of the level of pathology of clients in community clinics, but also fit better with the ideology of community clinics, which are more likely to use a combination of strategies, including pharmacological treatment, parent training, and school interventions, to address the problems of their clientele.

Two large-scale intervention programs developed in the 1990s also attempt to match a multidomain treatment approach to their multilevel conceptions of psychopathology. The Multimodal Treatment Study of Children with Attention-Deficit/Hyperactivity Disorders used a randomized clinical trials design to compare four 14-month treatments

of boys with ADHD: (1) a double-blind drug trial; (2) a set of behavioral treatments that included group and individual parent training, an intensive summer camp treatment, and school-based interventions; (3) a combination of the first two; and (4) treatment as usual in the community. Different analyses produced different findings, but overall, the combined drug and behavioral treatments produced more positive outcomes than either the behavioral treatments alone or the treatment as usual conditions (Owens et al., 2003). Consistent with the systematic themes we have been discussing here, both parental depression and child severity of problem were associated with less successful outcomes. In addition, reductions in parental negative discipline were responsible for positive child outcomes in this condition and only in this condition; when families were assigned to the combined behavioral treatment and drug treatment, improvements in discipline were associated with improved social skills and reduced externalizing behavior into the normal range.

Finally, a multimodal prevention program attempted to intervene early with children identified as at risk for developing conduct problems because they were already highly aggressive in kindergarten. The program combined individual social skills training with parent training programs and classroom behavioral interventions. Follow-up assessments showed that there were significant advantages for the treatment groups compared with the no-treatment groups (Conduct Problems Prevention Research Group, 1999a) and significant effects of the classroom intervention (Conduct Problems Prevention Research Group, 1999b). The success of the interventions appeared to stem from positive changes in targeted risk factors (e.g., the child's hostile attribution bias and problem-solving skills, harsh physical parenting; Bierman et al., 2002).

Tentative Conclusions about Family Risk Factors and Psychopathology

Our summary of studies makes clear that there is some support for both the family systems and family risk models of psychopathology. Many studies provided evidence that two or more of the five domains of family life we described in Figure 14.1 accounted for unique variance in a number of pathological outcomes. Other studies also provided evidence in support of the nine-cell matrix, incorporating biological, psychological, and social risk factors in some combination and paying attention to both internal and external sources of adaptation and maladaptation.

Despite these examples of how family risk domains are associated with various clinical diagnoses, there are still important gaps in our summary and in the literature itself. In this section, we have provided evidence of family factors in only a few diagnostic categories. Schizophrenia, depression, Bipolar Disorder, and aggression have been most frequently investigated, but there is some work on the more internalizing disorders—anxiety disorders, eating disorders, drug and alcohol abuse—and some on family factors in cognitive and academic competence.

An emerging concern in the literature on developmental psychopathology is that disorders are often comorbid (e.g., Davison & Neale, 1996), but we were able to find only one family study (Jaffee, Moffitt, Caspi, Taylor, & Arseneault, 2002) that investigated the links between family factors and comorbidity. Finally, although there has been increasing attention paid to the idea of pathways and trajectories in the study of developmental psychopathology, it is still not clear how family system processes or risk factors steer children and adolescents toward specific diagnostic categories—why conflict and negative interactions in marital, parent-child, and three-generational relationships lead some children in the direction of externalizing disorders, some toward internalizing, some toward both, and some toward adequate or above-adequate levels of functioning.

DEVELOPMENTAL PSYCHOPATHOLOGY IN THE CONTEXT OF CHANGING FAMILIES

In this section, we shift theoretical frames for describing families from the process and structure conceptions of psychologists, psychiatrists, social workers, nurses, and other mental health professionals to "big picture" social trends studies from the fields of sociology and demography. The historical view of family change that follows here focuses on demographic characteristics such as age, income, and ethnicity and family structure in the sense of legal definitions and living arrangements such as cohabiting, married, separated, and divorced. We present two conflicting interpretations of the meaning of the changes, one suggesting family decline over time and the other family resilience. We discuss this as a background for considering whether family system and family risk factor theories of developmental psychopathology require modification in light of the realities of family life in the twenty-first century.

Definitions

One key issue in contemporary discussions of family life is how inclusive or restrictive the definition of family should be. Current inclusive definitions center around the idea that

a family is a constellation of two or more people "related by birth, adoption, marriage, or choice . . . with socioemotional ties and enduring responsibilities, particularly in terms of one or more members' dependence on others for support and nurturance" (K. R. Allen, Fine, & Demo, 2000, p. 2). This definition encompasses couples without children, single parents with a child, and social units formed by choice, including adults who are "fictive kin," members of a two-generational commune, and gay and lesbian parents and their children. At this time in U.S. history, there are researchers and political activists who oppose the inclusion of some alternative family forms in the definition of family, particularly gay and lesbian relationships. The controversy has become part of contemporary political debates in which some argue for a definition that encompasses diverse family forms and others advocate constitutional amendments or laws that would have the effect of limiting the rights and privileges associated with family to married heterosexual parents with children. The debate is not new. Twenty-five years ago, President Carter's 1980 White House Conference on the Family ended prematurely when factional squabbles emerged about the same issues (S. L. Zimmerman, 2001, pp. 21–22).

Political disagreement about the definition of family is directly relevant to the study of developmental psychopathology. If nontraditional family arrangements are considered risk factors for children's development and adaptation, then family structure becomes an indicator of potential psychopathology. One obvious strategy to resolve the issue of defining risk factors is an examination of empirical studies on the topic, but as we show later in this section, there are profound disagreements about the interpretation of existing research results, and some data do not address these dilemmas directly.

A Century of Change in Family Life

One of the most startling demographic shifts in family life in the past century is the fact that people live longer than they used to. Men and women born in 1900 could expect to live approximately 48 years and 50 years, respectively.[4] By contrast, men and women born in the year 2000 could ex-

---

[4] Most of the trends described in this section are based on data from U.S. Census reports. We cite specific authors who have contributed specific analyses. Despite the fact that the data are drawn from the U.S. Census, we found variations in different reports of the same trends, based on the year of publication and on the base data used by different authors in calculating percentages. The figures here represent our best estimates from various sources, based on the information available in 2004.

pect to live to the age of 74 and 80, respectively. Also, family size has been reduced dramatically. The average of four children per family in 1900 has been more than cut in half by 2000. A number of notable changes in marriage have taken place in the past 50 years. The mean age of marriage has been rising (from 23 to 27 years for men and from 21 to 25 years for women). The proportion of adults never married rose from 6% of all women age 30 to 34 in 1960 to19% in 2000, and from 9% to 30% of men, with especially high rates of nonmarriage in African American communities. Of course, the most frequently cited statistic about marriage is the rising incidence of divorce, which doubled from 1900 to 1960 and doubled again by 1980, although it seems to have leveled off or even declined in the last 2 decades of the twentieth century.

Not only are children more likely to live without two parents in the home at night, but in a majority of married and cohabiting two-parent families, both parents are involved in paid work outside the home during the day. For many children, this means less adult supervision than in prior years. Changes in attitudes concerning the role of women, and economic circumstances in which real family income declined, also propelled this shift from 1950, when 12% of women worked outside the home, to the beginning of the twenty-first century, when 67% of married and single mothers of children under 5 worked outside the home at least part time.

In 1900, only 10% of teens spent some time in high school; 100 years later, only 10% fail either to complete high school or receive their GED equivalent (Sealander, 2003). The marked lengthening of school careers, the impact of child labor laws that prevent children under the age of 18 from working full time, and an emerging tendency for offspring in their 20s to live with their parents after they finish college combine to extend adolescence and delay young men's and women's transition to adulthood (Settersten, Furstenberg, & Rumbaut, 2005).

These demographic shifts are related directly to the fact that families in the United States are more diverse than they used to be (Demo, Allen, & Fine, 2000). Clearly, children and adolescents now live in a variety of family arrangements. If we focus on families with two biological parents, there are children living with parents who are married or cohabiting, others living with one parent following separation or divorce, and others still who live with one parent who is a member of a couple who never married or lived together. Some of the never-married, noncohabiting couples are in romantic relationships that could reasonably have some impact on the children; some children living with their mother have never met their father. In addition to families with two biological parents, there are stepparent families, adoptive families, and foster families. All of these categories of family structure have existed before, but over the past century the proportion of families with two married biological parents and children has contracted to approximately 25% of all families, and membership in the other categories has increased markedly.

Other demographic changes buttress our claim that the United States is increasingly a land of family diversity. In 1900, the non-White population of the country was 10% to 12% overall, and about 13% for children (Hernandez, 1996). By 1980, slightly more than 26% of Americans were children of color (8.9% Hispanic, 14.9% African American, and 2.2% other). By 1990 the figures increased again, to 12.3% Hispanic and 15.4% African American, and by 2030, it is estimated that a child of color will no longer be described as minority. Differential birth rates, foreign adoption, and immigration have all contributed to this increasingly diverse portrait of American family members.

Should We Equate Family Change with Family Decline?

Two starkly contrasting views of family change have emerged, one, an extensive body of writing characterizing the changes as evidence for "family decline" and another, more limited body of work, evaluating the same changes as evidence for "family resilience."

The Family Decline Interpretation

In the 1990s, a number of sociologists and demographers (Popenoe, 1993; Waite & Gallagher, 2000), leaders of conservative family organizations (Dobson & Bauer, 1990), and politicians (Bennet, 1992), became alarmed by the changes in family life that we have described, interpreting them as leading to the decline of the American family and, by implication, the decline of families in most Western industrialized societies. From the roughly simultaneous shifts in family size, marriage rates, divorce rates, single parenthood, and mothers of young children working outside the home, these interpreters of family trends draw conclusions about the source of increases in the incidence of marital problems and divorce and of behavior problems in children and youth. Couples and their children are not doing well, they argue, *because* of the shifts away from traditional nuclear family structures. They attribute the shifts to a motivated move away from "family values" toward adults' self-focused concern with their own development:

"Quite clearly, in this age of the me-generation, the individual rather than the family increasingly comes first" (Popenoe, 1993, p. 538).

The Family Resilience Interpretation

Another interpretation of the same historical data has sometimes been characterized as demonstrating family resilience (Amato, 2005; Demo et al., 2000; Skolnick, 1991; Stacey, 1996). The resilience interpretation holds that, although it is true that many social indicators are indicative of change in the family, the changes by and large represent flexible adaptations to changing and challenging circumstances. Men and women are wise to marry later because marriages of younger couples are more at risk. It is sensible for couples to be wary of making commitments, given what they see happening to the marriages of their parents and friends. Some argue further that given a more complex, difficult, and diverse social structure, it is something to be celebrated that so many families do relatively well.

The family resilience view argues that the negative consequences of family change have been overstated. Single parenthood does not represent the arrangement that most men and women aspire to, according to interviews with children, adolescents, and adults (Ahrons, 2004; McLanahan, 2002), but most single mothers manage to raise children who function successfully in their world. Worries about mothers working outside the home are greatly exaggerated. In general, outside of children of mothers who are employed during the child's 1st year (Baydar & Brooks-Gunn, 1991), few differences have been found between children of mothers at home and those employed outside the home (Harvey, 1999). Some of the differences that have been found are due to selection factors (Vandell & Ramanan, 1992), especially economic or marital circumstances that propel some reluctant mothers into the workforce. It has been suggested that mothers who work outside the home bring not only economic benefits, but also positive role models and examples of making successful, productive contributions in life, especially to their daughters (e.g., Moorehouse, 1993). Another argument supporting the family resilience view is that even though divorce can be difficult for all family participants, it may shield the child from ongoing conflict or violence between the parents, and many children of divorce lead successful lives over the long haul (Ahrons, 2004; Amato, 2000).

Problems with the Family Decline Interpretation

Although the fact that the demographic trends in many social indicators follow a similar time line makes the family decline interpretations seem plausible, we believe that this interpretation of the data is fundamentally flawed in a number of ways.

Traditional Families as the Gold Standard. Most interpretations of family decline hold up traditional families—two-married-parent families with fathers at work and mothers and children at home—as the standard of comparison against which historical changes in family life are to be evaluated. As we briefly described earlier, many traditional two-parent families are under considerable stress; significant proportions of parents show significant depressive symptoms and/or marital strain, and children show diagnosable problems early in their school careers. The data on family arrangements and relationship satisfaction suggest that even if risks of difficulty are higher in nontraditional families, a return to traditional arrangements would provide no guarantee that adults and children would fare much better or that family relationship quality would improve.

Most of our references to traditional families focused on heterosexual parents. There is a growing body of research focused on families with same-sex parents, primarily lesbian families. Contrary to the implicit or explicit expectations of family decline theorists that these families are less stable and less supportive of children's adaptation, the evidence suggests that children of lesbian and gay parents are not significantly different from children of heterosexual parents on a number of major indicators of adjustment and adaptation (Arendell, 1997a; Golombok & Tasker, 1994; Lamb, 1999; C. J. Patterson, 2002). Stacey and Biblarz's (2001) survey of the literature argues that findings revealing that children of lesbian and gay parents show superior adaptation have been downplayed or overlooked in these studies.

Problems of Causal Inference. There are two major difficulties in inferring that associations between family change and increases in psychopathology are causally connected. First, a common practice in the evaluation of social trends is to note that two social indicators are changing around the same period of time and to conclude that change in one *causes* change in the other. To draw such a conclusion, it would be necessary to show that these changes co-occur within the same families. That is, assuming that there is an increase in youth violence over time, researchers would have to show that this increase occurred in "nontraditional" families or families that became nontraditional in the process of separation and divorce. Even then, correlation would not establish conclusive proof of causation.

Studies of families in transition have not produced results that unequivocally support the family decline argument. For example, as we have seen, although divorce and single parenthood represent risk factors for elevated levels of behavior problems in children and adolescents, there are more exceptions to the rule than exemplars of the decline hypothesis (Hetherington & Kelly, 2002); in fact, most children of single parents fare reasonably well. By reporting only the fact that there are statistically significant differences between family types, family decline authors overstate the magnitude of the effects to make it appear that changes in the direction of nontraditional family structures account for the major proportion of social problems and psychopathology in children and youth.

Conflicting Evidence for the Conclusion of Declining Well-Being of Children and Youth.   A central implication from most of the social trends we described is that children and youth are living in less stable, less traditional families than they used to, and that, as a consequence, they are experiencing more difficulties than their age-mates in earlier times. The facts relevant to conclusions about trends for children and youth are quite difficult to come by because many of the social indicators of health, behavior, and well-being have been gathered systematically only since the 1980s. After an extensive search of the literature, we conclude that there is a very mixed picture concerning the claim that today's youth are in a state of intellectual, emotional, and moral decline.

We know that children's physical health and life expectancy have improved dramatically from 1900 to 2000. In addition, from 1939 to 1970, both African Americans and European Americans showed a marked reduction in the proportion living in poverty, with a leveling off in the subsequent 30 years (Brown et al., 1999). Public concerns about the state of American children and youth tend to focus on adolescent sexual behavior and teen pregnancy, substance abuse, and violence. There is no question that U.S. youth are more sexually active, and active at a younger age, than they were 100 years ago (Brown et al., 1999). Nevertheless, sexual risk taking defined as engaging in unprotected sex has declined since 1982. Although the proportion of unmarried teenagers having babies increased from the 1970s to the 1980s, the most recent data show that teen pregnancy has been declining since then. The declines are even more evident in some subgroups than others. For example, the overall rate of teen pregnancy dropped by approximately 20% in the 1990s, but by as much as 30% in African American teens (Ventura, Anderson, Martin, & Smith, 1998), and there are wide variations among states

in both the teen pregnancy rates and the declines in live births. The often-cited fact that teen pregnancy rates in the United States are much higher than those in other countries is mitigated somewhat by the observation that the differences are substantially reduced when race and income are statistically controlled (Kirby, 1999). In contrast with public perceptions of increasing problems (Guzman, Lippman, Moore, & O'Hare, 2003), teen violence and substance abuse also show declining trends.

What has risen considerably in the past 3 decades is the frequency of diagnosed mental illnesses in children and youth (Eberstadt, 2004). Mental health professionals are diagnosing an increasing number of children at younger ages with serious mental disorders, and many of those children are being treated with psychiatric drugs developed for adults. Diagnostic categories that have shown significant increases are ADHD (more males than females), eating disorders, and Asperger's syndrome and other autistic spectrum disorders. It is not clear whether the increases in incidence and prevalence of the disorders represent a true increase in the occurrence of psychopathology or whether the trends reflect increased attention to the mental health and illness of children and youth, increases in diagnostic skill, more efficient reporting and data collection, or media attention to these illnesses.

We are not arguing that the increases in child and youth mental illness are illusory, but rather that changes in the adaptation of young people require further systematic research before we can claim to understand the data. Whatever conclusion is ultimately drawn about historical trends, the picture is not consistent with the simple statement that the "decline" of U.S. families has been responsible for a crisis in U.S. youth.

No Proof That "Family Values" Play a Central Role in Family Change.   A central feature of the family decline interpretation has been the conclusion that changing family values are the motivating force behind changing family trends, and the subsequent argument that a shift in family values would have a salutary effect. Although there are studies indicating that, on the average, there have been shifts in some aspects of family values over the past few decades (S. L. Zimmerman, 2001), we are aware of no data relevant to the claim that men and women who have less traditional family arrangements value self more and family less, or that troubled children and youth are more likely to have parents who hold self-focused rather than family-oriented attitudes.

Those who accept the interpretation that family values are responsible for family change in the past century fail to consider the possibility that external social systems rather than internally held values may play a central role in how families are arranged. Families are embedded in the social and political structure of a society (Bronfenbrenner, 1979). Social and economic policies, and the institutions that administer them or fail to do so, have a great deal to do with the quality of family life. For example, despite a new government emphasis on promoting marriage (see later discussion), there are "marriage penalties" in the tax law, and a couple can be declared ineligible for welfare because of the combined income of the two partners. That is, there are government policies and procedures that lower the incentive for low-income couples to enter into a formal marital arrangement. Often, women work because their financial circumstances make it necessary to have two parents' incomes to provide for and protect their children adequately. Laws regulating welfare, and marriage and economic conditions, are only two of many possible external contexts that affect family behavior and family change.

Confounding of Family Diversity and Family Decline. Finally, we are concerned about an unfortunate slippage in discussions of family decline, in which the indicators of greatest concern (e.g., single parenthood, poverty) are associated with changes that have taken place with more frequency in members of minority groups, especially minority groups who are also experiencing economic hardship. It turns out, then, that policies suggested to remedy the ills of family decline (e.g., marriage promotion) are often directed at low-income minority groups, without recognition of the fact that in sheer numbers, the social indicators of concern occur more frequently in European American families and that they occur across the whole socioeconomic spectrum.

Problems with the Family Resilience Interpretation

Our conclusion from the fact that the family decline arguments are seriously flawed is not that the family resilience interpretation is the correct one. Writers advancing the family resilience view often criticize the family decline theories for focusing only on family structure (married or not, divorced or not), when it is the quality of family relationships that determines the developmental course of adaptation or psychopathology. Countering this argument, some authors point out that studies with careful statistical controls for income show reduced links between divorce or single parenthood and negative effects for children, but the associations are not eliminated completely (Cherlin, Chase-Lansdale, & McRae, 1998; Furstenberg & Kiernan, 2001). Similarly, to state that divorce has long-term effects

in "only" 20% of children risks minimizing a significant and important social problem. The fact that 40% to 50% of contemporary couples who marry will divorce indicates that there are serious difficulties in maintaining adult intimate relationships over time.

We agree with Cherlin and Furstenberg (Cherlin et al., 1998; Furstenberg & Cherlin, 1991), family sociologists who conclude that historical increases in divorce, cohabitation, and single parenthood have brought with them the potential for increased risks for children's development—by their nature or because they bring with them other potentially disruptive changes, especially poverty. We also agree with Amato (2000), a family sociologist whom we quoted earlier, who suggests that it is necessary to ask more differentiated questions about who will benefit and who will suffer when family changes and transitions occur.

A Developmental Psychopathology Perspective on Resolving the Debate

We raised the question of whether family change should be equated with family decline. Our answer is yes and no. On one hand, it would be foolhardy for researchers, clinicians, and policymakers to ignore the possibility that there are some special challenges involved in raising a child in divorced and single-parent families. On the other hand, we must recognize the fact that nontraditional family structures do not account for the vast majority of diagnosable problems in children, adolescents, and adults. Clearly, it is necessary to identify the strengths in nontraditional families that lead most of the children who live in them to meet the academic and social challenges that life imposes, just as we try to understand what is operating in traditional families when children in two-parent families succumb to diagnosable pathology.

A synthesis of the family decline and family resilience perspectives is entirely consistent with the assumptions of developmental psychopathology that we described earlier. First, it is necessary to acknowledge that some family structures are associated with higher risks for adaptation than others, while noting that (1) higher risks do not automatically mean higher levels of distress, (2) lower-risk families are not problem-free, and (3) the majority of members of families in any of the structures we have described are functioning outside the realm of what is considered psychopathology.

Second, family structure represents a static picture of the family at a point in time. Families often go through multiple transitions simultaneously or in quick succession, and it is often the disequilibration associated with the transition (e.g., moving house, drops in income, single parenthood, the birth of new children) rather than the end point (e.g., divorce) that plays a causal role in the adults' and children's adaptation (G. R. Patterson & Capaldi, 1991).

The issue, then, is not whether family decline or family resilience views of historical family change are correct. Both views have implications for our understanding of developmental psychopathology. As family decline proponents have framed the discussion, psychopathology and resilience are located in some family forms *by definition*. In a view more consistent with the principles of developmental psychopathology, we conclude that (1) U.S. families are becoming more diverse, (2) more families are moving toward nontraditional family structures, (3) some nontraditional families are having difficulties coping with the demands of raising children, and (4) a substantial number of families with more traditional family structures are having similar difficulties in personal adjustment, establishing satisfying family relationships, and coping with the challenges and demands of life outside the family.

Expanding Considerations of Family Diversity: Meeting the Challenge of Understanding Contemporary Families

How is the field of developmental psychopathology responding to the changes in family life that all observers agree have occurred? Our conclusion is that there is a fundamental gap in the research on developmental psychopathology, in which the research questions have not caught up to the realities of life in families. Despite some promising beginnings, we still know very little about differences in models of risk-protection-outcome in different populations. This is a critically important question not only for theories of developmental psychopathology, but also for the targeting of interventions directed toward reducing the family risk factors and increasing the family protective factors associated with specific problems and disorders. There is also a critical gap in the family intervention literature. Although a number of family theorists and clinicians argue that family theory and therapy practice need to pay attention to the diversity of families, and reject the idea that "one [intervention] size fits all," few if any of the creative modifications suggested to meet the needs of diverse populations have been subjected to rigorous evaluation.

Gender

We have noted that there are marked gender differences in the incidence of some types of psychopathology (e.g., depression, externalizing) and that there may be gender dif-

ferences in family risk patterns for these disorders, with depression more likely to be associated with difficulties in mother-daughter relationships and aggression more likely to be associated with difficulties in fathers' relationships with both daughters and sons (P. A. Cowan, Cowan, Ablow, Johnson, & Measelle, 2005). We have also noted that there appear to be gender differences in the way men and women deal with conflict and disagreement in their relationship as couples. The need to create more complex theoretical family models of psychopathology that take gender into account has been noted by the feminist critics of traditional family therapy (discussed earlier) and has begun to occur in family therapies (T. S. Zimmerman, 2001), but investigating differences in connections among fathers, mothers, sons, and daughters has not been a central focus of family research.

Age

Despite the fact that marriages are occurring later in life, and childbirth is extending to mothers in their early 40s and beyond, almost all of the contemporary research on couples, especially investigations that use observations of marital discussions, is based on couples between age 20 and 40. We know very little from direct observations about marriages of older couples (but see Charles & Carstensen, 2002; Levenson, Carstensen, & Gottman, 1994), except that they tend to express more positive emotion than younger couples do when they discuss a disagreement. This finding may be attributable in part to the fact that studies of older couples are more likely to include spouses with positive relationships that have withstood the test of time, but increased positivity could also come from the perspective that age brings or from a lessening of stresses associated with early careers and the rearing of young children.

Two sets of questions about age relevant to developmental psychopathology remain to be answered. First, are the models of risk factors that have been established for parents who have their first child in their 20s different from models for families in which parents are in their late 30s or mid-40s? For example, analyses of our own data (C. P. Cowan & Cowan, 2000) indicate that marital satisfaction declines more after the birth of a first child for couples in their 30s than for couples in their 20s. We know of no data that address whether the risk of decline increases for samples of 40-year-old parents of young children.

Second, older parent-adult child relationships are rarely studied (Ryff & Seltzer, 1996), and there is almost no information based on direct observation of couples or observations of parents with their adult children. Are the risk factor models that account for distress and the protective factors that reduce distress in older parent-child relationships different from models established in studies of younger couples? For example, does marital conflict and marital withdrawal in older couples have the same negative impact on their adult children that we have seen with couples with young children and adolescents? Also, outside of the assumption that children tend to become more autonomous and independent in late adolescence in Western industrialized societies (Bowen, 1978), we are not aware of family system theories suggesting that family process qualities change with the age of the participants. In other words, neither theory nor research on developmental psychopathology provide much of a *developmental* perspective on the links between family functioning and adaptation in clinical or nonclinical families. Especially given the longer life span of modern adults, it seems important to seek answers to these questions if we are to understand the emergence of psychopathology throughout the life span.

Income

We are struck by the fact that, although information and concern about low-income families exists in the form of thousands of studies and reports, there have been few systematically tested income-based interventions for this group (for an exception, see Gennetian, Knox, & Miller, 2000). Virtually all studies of couples therapy and early interventions for couples are composed of middle-class, primarily European American participants (Dion, Devaney, McConnell, Hill, & Winston, 2003). Family therapies have sometimes targeted low-income families, but almost always with a focus on minority status rather than low income (Robbins, Schwartz, & Szapocznik, 2004; Robbins et al., 2003; Szapocznik et al., 2004). We have a great deal to learn about whether and how couple and family interventions require modification in order to address the needs of families in different economic circumstances.

Ethnicity[5]

In the 1970s, a book reviewing research across all fields of psychology was entitled *Even the Rat Was White* (Guthrie,

---

[5] We do not have space here to deal with the complex issues involved in describing individuals and families in terms of ethnicity, race, culture, and minority status. We are aware that race is a social construction (Smedley & Smedley, 2005), ethnicity is unclear as a designation, and minority status is a relative term depending on the demographics of the territory being discussed. Here we use the terms "ethnic group" and "minority group" interchangeably, with the understanding that each of these terms has unresolved ambiguities.

1976). Over the past 3 decades, it has been encouraging to find a number of researchers studying families of color (e.g., Brody & Flor, 1996; Coll, Meyer, & Brillon, 1995; McLoyd, 1990; Parke & Buriel, 1998), describing mental health issues unique to each ethnic group (e.g., Serafica, 1990), and proposing necessary modifications of family therapies to create more culturally sensitive interventions that fit the beliefs and practices of ethnic minority families (e.g., McGoldrick, Giordano, & Pearce, 1996). As examples, we focus here on three major ethnic subgroupings: African American, Asian American, and Latino families. We recognize that there are many other subcultures in the United States and many other ethnic groups across the world, and that there are important variations within each of these subgroupings that we do not have the space to describe in adequate detail.

Research on Cultural Differences and Similarities. In the early years of research on minority mental health, almost all studies involved comparisons of one or more minority groups with Caucasian samples, with concepts and measures developed on middle-class Whites applied to minority participants (an "etic" approach). This research strategy led to an emphasis on differences that were interpreted as problems and deficits in the minority groups (Jones & Korchin, 1982). By contrast, most current writers have adopted an *emic* approach, which attempts to describe both strengths and vulnerabilities of individuals, families, and cultural institutions from the perspective of members of a specific group.

In reading a number of descriptions of minority families from within their own cultural perspective (e.g., McGoldrick et al., 1996), we were struck by the fact that over and above obvious uniqueness, there were a number of similarities among the accounts of different groups. Attempts to understand African American, Latino, and Asian American families typically begin with a history of the circumstances of their emigration (voluntary or forced) to the United States and, especially for Latino and Asian families, an account of differences between generations, depending on whether they immigrated as adults or children, or on whether they are first-, second-, or later-generation citizens. To different degrees and in different ways, all three groups have experienced racism, discrimination, unemployment, and poverty, some in their countries of origin, and most at some time in the United States or other country of destination. Families in all three groups are more likely than European Americans to be church-affiliated or influenced by religious beliefs, though this may be changing

(Wilcox, 2004). One salient dimension in the lives of each group is the importance of family and extended kin networks, with grandparents centrally involved in the rearing of young children together with parents or in parents' absence due to work or other circumstances (Burton & Stack, 1993; Goodman & Silverstein, 2002; Strom et al., 1999).

One cultural influence on family cohesion is centrally important in thinking about psychopathology and family treatment. Especially in Latino and Asian American families in comparison with European American families, there is a high value on connectedness and a lower value on individuation from the nuclear and extended family as adolescents make the transition to adulthood. Current generations of teenagers and young adults struggle with the tension this creates between the two worlds (Falicov, 1996; Hines & Boyd-Franklin, 1996; Matsui, 1996). A second important influence on both the incidence and prevalence of psychopathology and the utilization of mental health services comes in the cultural shaping of beliefs about mental illness. For example, both Latino (Contreras, Fernandez, Malcarne, Ingram, & Vaccarino, 2004) and Asian (Mak & Zane, 2004) beliefs about depression focus more on physical characteristics and less on emotions so that symptom reporting by individuals and family members differs in different cultures. Third, partly on the basis of practices in their country/culture of origin, and partly based on experiences with health and mental health delivery in the United States, all three groups tend to turn elsewhere for help with family members' emotional problems and are often skeptical about whether therapeutic services offered to minority families will meet their need (e.g., Boyd-Franklin, 2003).

Finally, although the content is often different, family members in all ethnic minority groups struggle with issues of (at least) dual identities: Who am I as a Latino, Asian, Black man or woman? Who am I as an American? And how do those identities fit together? In part, this is an issue of acculturation and so may vary with the length of stay in the host country (Tsai, Ying, & Lee, 2000). These issues often place second- and third-generation children and adolescents familiar with European American family practices at odds with their parents and grandparents, and this may lead to behaviors considered problematic or dysfunctional by the families or others in the community (teachers, mental health professionals).

Having focused on similarities among ethnic minority groups in thinking about how culture can affect psychopathology, it is important to acknowledge the obvious differences. The immigration experiences of African Americans are more likely to have occurred in the past, some under

forced conditions of slavery, whereas some Latino and Asian American communities are in a state of fluctuation now due to recent immigration. There are differences in language and literacy, achievement patterns, religious affiliations, marriage and divorce practices, and possibly patterns of emotion regulation in close relationships. It seems reasonable to assume that there are modal differences among ethnic groups in the prevalence of the family risk factors that have been linked with developmental psychopathology in European American families.

Despite the welcome interest in ethnicity and families, a central dilemma remains for the understanding of developmental psychopathology. There is still a dearth of systematic study of how patterns of risk factors may differ from one cultural group to another. The few studies we are aware of that focus on risk-outcome patterns suggest that, despite differences in the prevalence of some very important risk factors such as poverty, family risk models operate similarly across groups. For example, reviews of research by McLoyd and her colleagues (McLoyd, 1990; Mistry, Vandewater, Huston, & McLoyd, 2002) suggest that poverty in African American families has negative effects on children's adaptation because it disrupts family relationships in much the same way that Conger and his colleagues (1994) described for low-income European American farm families. A similar approach to comparisons between Mexican American and European American low-income families (Parke et al., 2004) finds that the same list of family factors (economic stress, parental depression, marital problems, hostile parenting) accounts for variations in children's adaptation or psychopathology, although there are two interesting differences. The primary predictors of children's adjustment problems were marital problems for Mexican American couples and hostile parenting for European American fathers. Acculturation also played a role in the links between family functioning and psychopathology in the Mexican American families: Mothers who were more integrated into the Anglo culture were likely to be less hostile as parents, but more likely to report conflictful marriages.

It is too early, of course, to accept these two studies as proof that there are similarities with variations in risk-outcome patterns among ethnic minority and European American families. It does lead us to expect that among the needed new studies, at least some will find commonalities that may generalize across an even wider range of ethnic groups. For example, new studies of interventions with refugees in African, Asian, and South American countries and in the United States (K. E. Miller & Rasco, 2004) point to the importance of family factors in postimmigration adjustment, especially when the circumstances of migration result in the disruption of family ties. Rasco and Miller (2004) summarize studies of immigrant families using a multidomain risk model that suggests the need for more systemic research on the way political violence and geographic displacement affect individuals, families, and communities, and a cautionary note that these models may show both similarities and differences in different ethnic communities facing different sets of circumstances.

Culturally Sensitive Interventions.   It would be unreasonable to expect family therapists to wait until risk models for each ethnic group have been tested before considering how they can become more sensitive to cultural variations in families. Some edited books present separate chapters with descriptions of different ethnic/racial subgroups (Ancis, 2004; Ho, Rasheed, & Rasheed, 2004; McGoldrick et al., 1996). Other authors avoid a comparative approach by focusing on specific approaches to African American (Boyd-Franklin, 2003), Asian American (Jung, 1998; Ng, 1999), *or* Latino (Falicov, 1998; Flores & Carey, 2000) families.

Each of these works describes the historical, cultural, and political context leading to prejudice, discrimination, and oppression of minorities, the characteristic ways that families within each group are organized, the perceptions of majority cultures and institutions that may make it difficult for the families to utilize existing mental health services, and the special issues and challenges that families within each group may face. The authors, primarily clinicians, tend to focus on issues of language and inability to communicate with the English-speaking majority, loss due to immigration and social disruption, pressures to assimilate rather than adopt a bicultural stance, the obligation of deference to elders in Asian families, and distrust between males and females and the prevalence of single parenthood in African American families. All of this information is designed to provide a contextual definition of what is normal and abnormal from the perspective of a specific ethnic group. One goal of these authors is to make certain that the standards and values involved in the assessment of deviance, which are inevitably involved in the definition of psychopathology, are made more relevant to the culture of the minority. A second goal is to identify therapy practices that are more acceptable and helpful to family members in each group.

We do not yet know whether the attempts to make interventions more relevant to each target population produce benefits for participants, over and above the usefulness of more traditional therapies. Clinicians involved in these pioneering attempts would be correct to argue that it is necessary first to develop new interventions and to rely on in-depth qualitative analyses of their strengths and weaknesses before larger scale clinical trials are designed. This is a necessary first step in any clinical-scientific intervention endeavor. Our aim here is to point out that, especially in a health delivery system context in which validated treatments are more often demanded before program support is given and insurance reimbursements are approved, it is time to embark on more concerted validation efforts of the new approaches that have been created (see Pinsoff & Wynne, 2000).

Nontraditional Families

The research issues concerning family factors in psychopathology in families with gay or lesbian parents are similar to the ones we have discussed for families grouped on the basis of age, income, or ethnicity. We cited research that reveals few differences in adaptation between the children of gay or lesbian parents and those of heterosexual parents. However, questions about similarities and differences in patterns of risk have mostly been left unanswered. An exception is a set of studies showing that the risk models that predict distress in heterosexual couple relationships can be applied equally well to gay and lesbian relationships (J. M. Gottman et al., 2003). We are not aware of research that attempts to link personal distress, couple relationship distress, and parenting style with child outcomes in gay and lesbian parent families, so we do not know whether modifications of existing risk models are required for families with gay and lesbian parents. There have been some recent descriptions of specific issues and therapy approaches to working with gay and lesbian families (Laird, 2003; Laird & Green, 1996; Malley, 2002; Malley & McCann, 2002; Pachankis & Goldfried, 2004; Yarhouse, 2003). Like the writing on family therapy with minority families, this work presents a contextual analysis of special issues faced by gay and lesbian families because of legal, political, and social stigmatization and because most of these families have no examples from prior generations of how families with two same-sex parents function most effectively.

Reading case studies in books and articles in family therapy, we conclude that much of what is currently described as family therapy occurs with a single parent and one or more children. As in many of the other variations we discuss here, there is evidence of higher risk in these families, but no evidence yet to show that the family risk models would differ in different family structures. We have not found any relatively recent books for therapists and only a few articles that go beyond case studies to provide guidelines for treating single parents and their children (Anderson, 2003; Everett & Everett, 2000; Jung, 1996). It is not clear, then, whether new models of family therapy are needed to treat troubled parents or children in this large population.

This survey suggests that there are many sources that family therapists can consult to consider how their practices can meet the challenges of the diversity of contemporary families. Most of these sources refer to the available research on diverse families. However, we are alarmed by the fact that, with the exception of the prevention programs targeting family transitions, none has provided systematic research evidence that (1) the interventions they propose actually work, (2) the modifications they propose function as mechanisms of change, or (3) the therapies provide benefits over and above traditional family therapy approaches.

Family psychopathology researchers and therapists face a dilemma when they attempt to meet the challenges of family diversity. At one extreme, early family systems theories implied that universal system principles, relatively unmodified, could guide the treatment of all families. At the other extreme is the argument that family treatments must be adapted to be appropriate for each demographic group. To follow Tolstoy's (1899, p. 1) dictum to its logical conclusions—"Happy families are all alike; every unhappy family is unhappy in its own way"—therapists could be faced with the task of creating unique therapies for each family. Imagine the complexity of considering even a limited number of variations and trying to develop family therapies specifically targeted to older and younger European American, Asian American, African American, and Latino families in which parents are cohabiting, married, separated, or divorced, native or immigrant, and so on. Even with this specificity, it would be necessary to expand the variations to include other subcultures within the United States and other cultures across the world. Furthermore, it is necessary to remember that individuals and families *within* each category show wide variability in terms of family beliefs, practices, behavior, and adaptation. One cannot simply assume that a particular older Chinese American couple, or an unmarried teen European American couple, or a Latino stepfamily actually display the modal characteristics typical of the group they identify with (Demo et al., 2000).

In the absence of specific risk-outcome models and validated treatment models for specific types of families, what are family therapists to do? In our view, the ideal solution involves a balance of universality and particularity. Clinicians who conduct assessments and therapists who work with family members need to be aware of common principles that can be applied broadly across many different types of families, while staying attuned to the unique features of each family's needs and concerns, some of which may be related to their particular cultural background.

FAMILY RESEARCH AND FAMILY POLICY

Family policy—decisions made by legislative and executive branches of government to regulate and enhance the well-being of families and allocate scarce resources—covers a wide array of topics, including contraception, abortion, marriage and divorce, child support, adoption, family leave, health and mental health, welfare, child labor, the justice systems (adult and juvenile), child care, domestic violence, and child abuse (Sealander, 2003; S. L. Zimmerman, 2001). By designating some families as in need of help, family policy helps to determine what is defined as pathology. At the same time, research on families and psychopathology is often cited in discussions concerning laws, regulations, and service delivery systems.

The links between research-clinical findings and policy are tenuous at best, for three main reasons. First, many policy decisions are made on moral or value grounds, and these grounds are held to provide a sufficient *political* justification for choosing a course of action. Despite the reliance on data by some political advocates and social scientists, research findings are often considered irrelevant to public debate. Second, research conclusions and policy proposals are framed in different languages. Policymakers are trying to find universal rules and solutions to societal problems. They want to know whether their proposed solutions will work for the largest number of citizens. They seek yes-or-no answers to specific questions. By contrast, risk researchers are used to working with probabilities and individual differences. Their answer to a question about whether a plan of action will work is often "It depends; it will for some and not for others." Given these different approaches to the nature of the discourse, it is almost inevitable that policymakers and family researchers and clinicians wind up talking past each other, with neither group benefiting from what the other has to offer. Third, as we have seen, research on hot issues having to do with understanding psychopathology almost always results in disputed interpretations. Researchers are often as divided on family issues as politicians are, and are not immune to the value biases that create controversies in the public or political arena. To illustrate the interplay of family policy and family research on psychopathology, we briefly mention three topics that are currently at issue and likely to be central issues for some time to come.

Father Involvement

Over the past 30 years, societal concern about the negative impact of absent fathers on their children's development stimulated efforts to design interventions that would encourage fathers to take a more active, positive role in their children's daily lives (Mincy & Pouncy, 2002). Research on the definition of father involvement, the consequences of father involvement, and the factors that encourage or discourage father involvement (Tamis-LeMonda & Cabrera, 2002) has led to multidomain risk-outcome models similar to those we have described throughout this chapter. In contrast to political arguments that father involvement is a matter of the motivation and will power of individual fathers (Blankenhorn, 1995), the research suggests that whether or not fathers take an active hands-on role in the daily lives of their children is a complex outcome of a variety of factors, including demographic and psychological characteristics of individual fathers, the quality of their relationship with the mother of their children, intergenerational patterns, and outside-the-family supports for and barriers to men becoming more involved (Tamis-LeMonda & Cabrera, 2002).

Our own summary of the research and intervention literatures (P. A. Cowan & Cowan, 2004) notes a remarkable disconnection between research on father involvement and programs to promote father involvement, just as we see in the family psychopathology field in general. A few program designers draw on risk factor research but rarely provide systematic evaluations of outcomes or mechanisms that would reveal whether targeting the hypothesized risk factors and change mechanisms actually produces the desired change in psychopathology.

We are currently involved as part of a team with Marsha Kline Pruett and Kyle Pruett of Yale University in the Supporting Father Involvement Project, sponsored by the California Office of Child Abuse Prevention. The project evaluates variations of interventions in four California communities with a large proportion of low-income White and Hispanic families. The design of this randomized clinical trail contrasts participation of fathers and their partners in (1) a 16-week fathers group, (2) a 16-week couples group, and (3) a one-time information session about the importance of father involvement (the control condition). The decision to contrast these two styles of ongoing interven-

tion was based in part on research showing that the single best predictor of fathers' involvement with their young children is the quality of their relationship with the child's mother (Bouchard & Lee, 2000; Cohen, 2001; Frosch, Mangelsdorf, & McHale, 2000). Outcome data are in the process of being gathered as this chapter goes to press.

Strengthening Marriage: Strengthening Couple Relationships

Two research studies, one involving the gathering of new data and one involving a survey of the literature, have played important roles in discussions of policy related to low-income unmarried couples. The policy issues are based on a moral concern by some about the high rate of divorce and single parenthood, and a financial concern by others that these families are likely to be poor and their children to have higher rates of problems than children in two-parent families. First, the Fragile Families Study of hospital births in 20 American cities (Carlson & McLanahan, 2002b; McLanahan, 2002; McLanahan et al., 1998) found that around the time of childbirth, more than 80% of the biological fathers were involved in a romantic relationship with the child's mother, and 50% of the couples were living together. Contrary to popular belief, interviews with the couples showed that most of them hope to get married. The "magic moment" around the birth of the baby dissipated somewhat, so that over the next year, 58% of the fathers were still in romantic relationships, mostly those who had been living with the mother when the child was born. Second, an influential book, *The Case for Marriage: Why Married People Are Happier, Healthier, and Better Off Financially* (Waite & Gallagher, 2000), was used to support the argument that if women and children in unmarried families are at risk, then a wise policy alternative is to encourage them to marry. We have discussed elsewhere the frequently ignored fact that correlations do not (should not) prove causal connections and are not adequate to provide support for policy decisions.

In part resulting from a moral concern, and in part using data from these two works as a justification, the U.S. Administration for Children and Families awarded two contracts to research and evaluation agencies for randomized control trials of interventions for unmarried low-income couples making the transition to parenthood (Building Strong Families, administered by Mathematica), and low-income married couples with and without children (Strengthening Healthy Marriages, administered by Manpower Development Research Corporation [MDRC]), to work toward healthy couple relationships and marriages.

Not surprisingly, discussions of these initiatives have generated some public disagreements. Because federal financial support for strengthening couple relationships is novel, the results of these randomized controlled studies of interventions addressed to couples' issues in low-income communities may provide important information about how low-income partners struggle with issues in their lives as couples and whether it is possible to design interventions that make those struggles more manageable.

Welfare Reform

In 1996, President Clinton signed a bill that promised to "end welfare as we know it," in part by requiring women on welfare to work outside the home, and in part by limiting the time they could spend on welfare (see DeParle, 2004, for a fascinating account of the antecedents and consequences of the legislation). Arguments about why this bill would enhance the lives of families were based in part on the assumption that parents' work provides both psychological and financial benefits to the parent and the child. This policy was undertaken without social science research to provide a justification. Evaluation of welfare reform is now in progress; clearly, it has reduced the numbers of families on welfare and the costs associated with welfare programs. Studies of the impact on men, women, and children who move off, or who are forced off, the welfare rolls is still in progress (Chase-Lansdale et al., 2003; Fuller, Kagan, Loeb, Carroll, & Growing Up in Poverty Project, 2002).

These are only three examples of the complex and uneasy intersection of family research and family policy. We are optimistic about the fact that there seems to be a growing tendency at the federal level to encourage, and even fund, systematic evaluations of new policies and programs related to families. We are less optimistic about the tenor of public and academic debate in which research findings are cited in support of one position while ignoring the complexity of drawing conclusions from a welter of conflicting or incomplete evidence. Nevertheless, we believe that attempting to bring systematic evidence from social science into discussions of family policy has the potential for creating more differentiated and nuanced perspectives on the diversity of families for policymakers and social scientists alike.

FUTURE DIRECTIONS

Throughout this chapter, we have attempted to include suggestions about where the field is and should be going. In this final section, we summarize several salient points to highlight what we see as important next steps:

1. *Addressing the diversity of families.* We need investigations of a wider range of risk models for different populations, and evaluations of attempts to modify family therapies to fit the needs of these populations, while preserving generic principles that may work across contexts.

2. *Addressing the diversity of theories.* We have suggested that ideas from family systems and family risk factor approaches are becoming more integrated in clinical work with families. The movement toward the integration of these approaches in research on understanding developmental psychopathology appears to be proceeding more slowly, although there are some indications of movement toward a synthesis of views in this area as well. One indication of the lack of integration in both research and practice is that systematic diagnostic systems for describing the psychopathology of *families* have been slow to develop (Kaslow, 1996). A second arena in which these two approaches remain separate is in family risk researchers' tests of *linear* causal risk models, in which they combine measures of family relationships as independent variables in accounting for variations in the functioning of identified patients—despite family systems' assumptions about bidirectional causality.

In our view, integrations of the multiple perspectives we have outlined here have some way to go. The six-domain family model summarizes the key aspects of family life in which individuals and dyads move toward or away from adaptation. The nine-cell matrix provides a checklist of alternative explanations of stability and change within each of the domains. At some point, family researchers and clinicians must accept the fact that the etiology of both individual and family psychopathology involves combinations of internal, external, and interactive factors that operate at biological, psychological, and social levels of a system.

3. *Explaining risk-outcome linkages.* Perhaps the main difference between research studies cited in this chapter and those in the chapter on family systems and developmental psychopathology in the previous edition of this volume (Wagner & Reiss, 1995) is the vast increase in research on mechanisms to explain *how* risks are connected with developmental psychopathology outcomes. The search for mediators and moderators has become something of an obsession, and despite Baron and Kenny's (1986) often-cited attempt to distinguish between them, there continues to be confusion on this point. Mediators account for existing correlations, for example, when the correlation between maternal depression and children's aggression can be explained by the fact that depressed women are more likely to be in conflictful marriages (N. B. Miller et al., 1993). Moderators are markers of conditions that change the links between risks and outcomes, as, for example, in any finding that shows significantly different patterns for different groups such as boys or girls, or parents with high or low marital conflict.

The identification of both mediators and moderators is essential for family therapists. Learning about modifiable mediators—family process mechanisms linking risks and outcome that can be changed—could help clinicians increase the effectiveness of their interventions. Learning about modifiable moderators—family process mechanisms that increase protective factors or reduce vulnerabilities—could also identify conditions that protect family members from the negative effects of risks that cannot be modified.

4. *Putting the development back in developmental psychopathology.* We know that there are systematic variations in the age of onset of many disorders, such as the risks of externalizing, internalizing, and Schizophrenia that emerge in adolescence. In part restricted by the ubiquity of the *DSM,* developmental psychopathology has not yet become fully developmental. Too many categories like depression and Schizophrenia have the same diagnostic criteria for children and adults, when it is absurd to think that 7-, 17-, and 70-year-old depressed persons have the same underlying disorder. Once a person enters a category, there may be a developmental course of the mental illness and a lawful, systematic change in both its structure and function over time. We believe that these are important lines of inquiry for developmental psychopathologists in the next decade.

5. *More effort directed toward empirically validated treatments.* There has been increased pressure by research funding agencies, service delivery systems, and insurance companies to rely on evidence-based therapies, and decreased support of approaches that have not been validated in systematic studies. The outgoing editor of *Family Process* (Anderson, 2003, p. 323) noted the profound gap between those who create solid research studies and "clinicians [who] tell me that they neither read nor value the research data being produced and that they basically fail to see any relationship it has to the realities of their practice."

There is an important distinction to be made between "empirically validated treatments" and "evidence-based treatments" (Messer, 2004; J. E. Patterson, Miller, Carnes, & Wilson, 2004). Family therapists need to have more in their armamentarium than a list of "valid" therapies, especially when there is such a diversity of families and a dearth of large-scale tests of efficacy and effectiveness of a specific therapy for a specific group. Nevertheless, thera-

pists have two obligations. The first is to read and evaluate the literature to inform their understanding of risk-outcome models of psychopathology and to learn whether certain treatment approaches have received empirical support. The second is to provide systematic information on the course of each treatment in the form of process notes, questionnaires, or audiotaped or videotaped observations that attempt to determine whether families improve after a course of treatment and which characteristics of client, therapist, and their interaction appear to be associated with positive and negative outcomes.

A Final Word

We believe that this is an opportune time for researchers and clinicians eager to grapple with a family systems or family risk factors perspective on developmental psychopathology. The field now has a solid 50-year history in which there has been a remarkable unfolding of creative ideas about how to think about both mental health and mental illness in a family context. An increasing quantity and quality of systematic research studies has provided a solid empirical foundation for models of risk-outcome linkage and therapeutic and preventive intervention. And yet, there is almost endless opportunity to make important contributions to this field—by modifying existing theories to fit the increasing diversity of family life, by testing risk-outcome models in as yet untested diagnostic groups and cultural settings, and by developing new and even more complex models of how family structures and processes are linked with adaptive and maladaptive functioning inside and outside the nuclear family. It is our hope that contemporary family researchers and clinicians will rise to meet the challenge of expanding our understanding of the family context of developmental psychopathology as the field moves into the next 50 years.

REFERENCES

Ablow, J. C. (2005). When parents conflict or disengage: Understanding links between marital distress and children's adaptation to school. In P. A. Cowan, C. P. Cowan, J. Ablow, V. K. Johnson, & J. Measelle (Eds.), *The family context of parenting in children's adaptation to elementary school.* Mahwah, NJ: Erlbaum.

Ackerman, N. W. (1962). Family psychotherapy and psychoanalysis: The implications of a difference. *Family Process, 1*(1), 30–43.

Ackerman, N. W., & Sobel, R. (1950). Family diagnosis: An approach to the pre-school child. *American Journal of Orthopsychiatry, 20,* 744–753.

Ahrons, C. R. (2004). *We're still family: What grown children have to say about their parents' divorce.* New York: HarperCollins.

Ainsworth, M. S., & Wittig, B. A. (1969). Attachment and exploratory behavior of one-year-olds in a Strange Situation. In B. M. Foss (Ed.), *Determinants of infant behavior* (Vol. 4, pp. 113–136). London: Methuen.

Allen, J. P., Hauser, S. T., & Borman-Spurrell, E. (1996). Attachment theory as a framework for understanding sequelae of severe adolescent psychopathology: An 11-year follow-up study. *Journal of Consulting and Clinical Psychology, 64*(2), 254–263.

Allen, K. R., Fine, M. A., & Demo, D. H. (2000). An overview of family diversity: Controversies, questions, and values. In D. H. Demo, K. R. Allen, & M. A. Fine (Eds.), *Handbook of family diversity* (pp. 1–14). New York: Oxford University Press.

Almeida, R. V. (1998). *Transformations of gender and race: Family and developmental perspectives.* New York: Haworth Press.

Amato, P. R. (2000). The consequences of divorce for adults and children. *Journal of Marriage and the Family, 62*(4), 1269–1287.

Amato, P. R. (2001). Children of divorce in the 1990s: An update of the Amato and Keith (1991) meta-analysis. *Journal of Family Psychology, 15*(3), 355–370.

Amato, P. R. (2005). Family change: Decline or resilience? In V. Bengtson, A. C. Acock, K. R. Allen, P. Dilworth-Anderson, & K. Klein (Eds.), *Sourcebook of family theory and research* (pp. 112–114). Thousand Oaks, CA: Sage.

Ancis, J. R. (2004). *Culturally responsive interventions: Innovative approaches to working with diverse populations.* New York: Brunner-Routledge.

Anderson, C. A. (2003). The diversity, strength, and challenges of single-parent households. In F. Walsh (Ed.), *Normal family processes: Growing diversity and complexity* (3rd ed., pp. 121–152). New York: Guilford Press.

Anderson, C. A., Hinshaw, S. P., & Simmel, C. (1994). Mother-child interactions in ADHD and comparison boys: Relationships with overt and covert externalizing behavior. *Journal of Abnormal Child Psychology, 22*(2), 247–265.

Arendell, T. (Ed.). (1997a). *Contemporary parenting: Challenges and issues: Vol. 9. Understanding families.* Thousand Oaks, CA: Sage.

Arendell, T. (1997b). Divorce and remarriage. In T. Arendell (Ed.), *Contemporary parenting: Challenges and issues* (pp. 154–195). Thousand Oaks, CA: Sage.

Bandura, A. (1977). *Social learning theory.* Englewood Cliffs, NJ: Prentice-Hall.

Baron, R. M., & Kenny, D. A. (1986). The moderator-mediator variable distinction in social psychological research: Conceptual, strategic, and statistical considerations. *Journal of Personality and Social Psychology, 51*(6), 1173–1182.

Baucom, D. H., Epstein, N., Rankin, L. A., & Burnett, C. K. (1996). Understanding and treating marital distress from a cognitive-behavioral orientation. In K. S. Dobson & K. D. Craig (Eds.), *Advances in cognitive-behavioral therapy* (Vol. 2, pp. 210–236). Thousand Oaks, CA: Sage.

Baucom, D. H., Shoham, V., Mueser, K. T., Daiuto, A. D., & Stickle, T. R. (1998). Empirically supported couple and family interventions for marital distress and adult mental health problems. *Journal of Consulting and Clinical Psychology, 66*(1), 53–88.

Baumrind, D. (1971). Current patterns of parental authority. *Developmental Psychology Monographs, 4,* 1–103.

Baumrind, D. (1989). Rearing competent children. In W. Damon (Ed.), *Child development today and tomorrow* (pp. 349–378). San Francisco: Jossey-Bass.

Baydar, N., & Brooks-Gunn, J. (1991). Effects of maternal employment and child-care arrangements on preschoolers' cognitive and behavioral outcomes: Evidence from the Children of the National Longitudinal Survey of Youth. *Developmental Psychology, 27*(6), 932–945.

Beavers, W. R., & Hampson, R. B. (1990). *Successful families: Assessment and intervention.* New York: Norton.

Beavers, W. R., & Hampson, R. B. (2003). Measuring family competence: The Beavers systems model. In F. Walsh (Ed.), *Normal family processes: Growing diversity and complexity* (3rd ed., pp. 549–580). New York: Guilford Press.

Bebbington, P., & Kuipers, L. (1994). The predictive utility of expressed emotion in Schizophrenia: An aggregate analysis. *Psychological Medicine, 24*(3), 707–718.

Bell, R. Q. (1968). A reinterpretation of the direction of effects in studies of socialization. *Psychological Review, 75*(2), 81–95.

Bell, R. Q. (1988). Contributions of human infants to care giving and social interaction. In G. Handel (Ed.), *Childhood socialization* (pp. 103–122). Hawthorne, NY: Aldine de Gruyter.

Belsky, J. (1980). Child maltreatment: An ecological integration. *American Psychologist, 35*(4), 320–335.

Belsky, J. (1984). The determinants of parenting: A process model. *Child Development, 55*(1), 83–96.

Belsky, J., & Kelly, J. (1994). *Transition to parenthood.* New York: Delacorte Press.

Belsky, J., & Pensky, E. (1988). Marital change across the transition to parenthood. *Marriage & Family Review, 12*(3/4), 133–156.

Bengtson, V. L. (1996). Continuities and discontinuities in intergenerational relationships over time. In V. L. Bengtson (Ed.), *Adulthood and aging: Research on continuities and discontinuities* (pp. 271–303). New York: Springer.

Bennet, W. J. (1992). *The devaluing of America: The fight for our culture and our children.* New York: Simon & Schuster.

Bertalanffy, L. V. (1973). *General system theory: Foundations, development, applications* (Rev. ed.). New York: G. Braziller.

Bertalanffy, L. V., & Woodger, J. H. (1962). *Modern theories of development: An introduction to theoretical biology.* New York: Harper.

Bierman, K. L., Coie, J. D., Dodge, K. A., Greenberg, M. T., Lochman, J. E., McMahon, R. J., et al. (2002). Using the Fast Track randomized prevention trial to test the early-starter model of the development of serious conduct problems. *Development and Psychopathology, 14*(4), 925–943.

Biller, H. B. (1968). A note on father absence and masculine development in lower-class Negro and White boys. *Child Development, 39*(3), 1003–1006.

Bishop, D. S., Epstein, N. B., Keitner, G. I., Miller, I. W., Zlotnick, C., & Ryan, C. E. (2000). *McMaster Structured Interview of Family Functioning (McSiff).* Providence, RI: Brown University Family Research Program.

Blair, S. L., & Hardesty, C. (1994). Paternal involvement and the well-being of fathers and mothers of young children. *Journal of Men's Studies, 3*(1), 49–68.

Blankenhorn, D. (1995). *Fatherless America: Confronting our most urgent social problem.* New York: Basic Books.

Block, J., Block, J. H., & Gjerde, P. F. (1989). Parental functioning and the home environment in families of divorce: Prospective and concurrent analyses. In S. Chess & M. E. Hertzig (Eds.), *Annual progress in child psychiatry and child development* (pp. 192–207). New York: Brunner/Mazel.

Bograd, M. L. (1991). *Feminist approaches for men in family therapy.* New York: Haworth Press.

Boss, P. (1999). *Ambiguous loss: Learning to live with unresolved grief.* Cambridge, MA: Harvard University Press.

Boss, P., & Mulligan, C. (2003). *Family stress: Classic and contemporary readings.* Thousand Oaks, CA: Sage.

Boszormenyi-Nagy, I., & Framo, J. L. (1965). *Intensive family therapy: Theoretical and practical aspects.* New York: Hoeber Medical Division of Harper & Row.

Bouchard, G., & Lee, C. M. (2000). The marital context for father involvement with their preschool children: The role of partner support. *Journal of Prevention & Intervention in the Community, 20*(1/2), 37–53.

Bowen, M. (1961). The family as the unit of study and treatment: I. Family psychotherapy workshop, 1959. *American Journal of Orthopsychiatry, 31,* 40–60.

Bowen, M. (1978). *Family therapy in clinical practice.* New York: Aronson.

Bowlby, J. (1961). Separation anxiety: A critical review of the literature. *Journal of Child Psychology and Psychiatry, 1,* 251–269.

Bowlby, J. (1982). Attachment and loss: Retrospect and prospect. *American Journal of Orthopsychiatry, 52*(4), 664–678.

Bowlby, J. (1988). *A secure base: Parent-child attachment and healthy human development.* New York: Basic Books.

Bowlby, J. (1989). *The role of attachment in personality development and psychopathology.* Madison, CT: International Universities Press.

Boyd-Franklin, N. (2003). *Black families in therapy: Understanding the African American experience* (2nd ed.). New York: Guilford Press.

Bradbury, T. N., & Karney, B. R. (2004). Understanding and altering the longitudinal course of marriage. *Journal of Marriage and the Family, 66*(4), 862–879.

Braver, S. L., & Griffin, W. A. (2000). Engaging fathers in the post-divorce family. *Marriage & Family Review, 29*(4), 247–267.

Brody, G. H., & Flor, D. L. (1996). Coparenting, family interactions, and competence among African American youths. In J. P. McHale & P. A. Cowan (Eds.), *Understanding how family-level dynamics affect children's development: Studies of two-parent families: Vol. 74. New directions for child development* (pp. 77–91). San Francisco: Jossey-Bass.

Brody, G. H., & Forehand, R. (1985). The efficacy of parent training with maritally distressed and nondistressed mothers: A multimethod assessment. *Behaviour Research and Therapy, 23*(3), 291–296.

Bronfenbrenner, U. (1979). *The ecology of human development: Experiments by nature and design.* Cambridge, MA: Harvard University Press.

Bronstein, P., & Cowan, C. P. (Eds.). (1988). *Fatherhood today: Men's changing role in the family.* New York: Wiley.

Brown, B. V., Kinkukawa, A., Michelsen, E., Moore, A., Moore, K. A., & Sugland, B. W. (1999). *A century of children's health and well-being.* Washington, DC: Child Trends.

Burton, L. M., & Stack, C. B. (1993). Conscripting kin: Reflections on family, generation, and culture. In P. A. Cowan, D. Field, D. A. Hansen, A. Skolnick, & G. E. Swanson (Eds.), *Family, self, and society: Toward a new agenda for family research* (pp. 103–113). Hillsdale, NJ: Erlbaum.

Campbell, S. B., Cohn, J. F., & Meyers, T. (1995). Depression in first-time mothers: Mother-infant interaction and depression chronicity. *Developmental Psychology, 31*(3), 349–357.

Capaldi, D. M., Pears, K. C., Patterson, G. R., & Owen, L. D. (2003). Continuity of parenting practices across generations in an at-risk sample: A prospective comparison of direct and mediated associations. *Journal of Abnormal Child Psychology, 31*(2), 127–142.

Carlson, M., & McLanahan, S. S. (2002a, April). *Characteristics and antecedents of involvement by young, unmarried fathers.* Paper presented at the Society for Research on Adolescence conference, New Orleans, LA.

Carlson, M., & McLanahan, S. S. (2002b). Father involvement, fragile families, and public policy. In C. Tamis-LeMonda & N. Cabrera (Eds.), *Handbook of father involvement: Multidisciplinary perspectives* (pp. 461–488). Mahwah, NJ: Erlbaum.

Carmichael, L. (1954). *Manual of child psychology* (2nd ed.). New York: Wiley.

Carter, E. A., & McGoldrick, M. (2005). *The expanded family life cycle: Individual, family, and social perspectives* (3rd ed.). New York: Pearson Allyn & Bacon.

Caspi, A., & Elder, G. H. J. (1988). Emergent family patterns: The intergenerational construction of problem behaviour and relationships. In R. A. Hinde & J. Stevenson-Hinde (Eds.), *Relationships within families: Mutual influences* (pp. 218–240). Oxford: Clarendon Press.

Caspi, A., McClay, J., Moffitt, T., Mill, J., Martin, J., Craig, I. W., et al. (2002). Role of genotype in the cycle of violence in maltreated children. *Science, 297*(5582), 851–854.

Caspi, A., Moffitt, T. E., Morgan, J., Rutter, M., Taylor, A., Arseneault, L., et al. (2004). Maternal expressed emotion predicts children's antisocial behavior problems: Using monozygotic-twin differences to identify environmental effects on behavioral development. *Developmental Psychology, 40*(2), 149–161.

Charles, S. T., & Carstensen, L. L. (2002). Marriage in old age. In M. Yalom & L. L. Carstensen (Eds.), *Inside the American couple: New thinking/new challenges* (pp. 236–254). Berkeley: University of California Press.

Chase-Lansdale, P. L., Moffitt, R. A., Lohman, B. J., Cherlin, A. J., Coley, R. L., Pittman, L. D., et al. (2003). Mothers' transitions from welfare to work and the well-being of preschoolers and adolescents. *Science, 299*(5612), 1548–1552.

Cherlin, A. J., Chase-Lansdale, P. L., & McRae, C. (1998). Effects of parental divorce on mental health throughout the life course. *American Sociological Review, 63*(2), 239–249.

Cherlin, A. J., Furstenberg, F. F., Chase-Lansdale, P. L., & Kiernan, K. E. (1991). Longitudinal studies of effects of divorce on children in Great Britain and the United States. *Science, 252*(5011), 1386–1389.

Chodorow, N. (1989). *Feminism and psychoanalytic theory.* New Haven, CT: Yale University Press.

Christensen, A., Atkins, D. C., Berns, S., Wheeler, J., Baucom, D. H., & Simpson, L. E. (2004). Traditional versus integrative behavioral couple therapy for significantly and chronically distressed married couples. *Journal of Consulting and Clinical Psychology, 72*(2), 176–191.

Christensen, A., & Jacobson, N. S. (2000). *Reconcilable differences.* New York: Guilford Press.

Christensen, A., Jacobson, N. S., & Babcock, J. C. (1995). Integrative behavioral couple therapy. In N. S. Jacobson & A. S. Gurman (Eds.), *Clinical handbook of couple therapy* (pp. 31–64). New York: Guilford Press.

Cicchetti, D. (2004). An odyssey of discovery: Lessons learned through three decades of research on child maltreatment. *American Psychologist, 59*(8), 731–741.

Cicchetti, D., & Barnett, D. (1991). Attachment organization in maltreated preschoolers [Special issue: Attachment and developmental psychopathology]. *Development and Psychopathology, 3*(4), 397–411.

Cicchetti, D., & Dawson, G. (2002). Multiple levels of analysis [Special issue: Multiple levels of analysis, Editorial]. *Development and Psychopathology, 14*(3), 417–420.

Cicchetti, D., & Hinshaw, S. P. (2002). Prevention and intervention science: Contributions to developmental theory (Editorial). *Development and Psychopathology, 14*(4), 667–671.

Cicchetti, D., & Lynch, M. (1995). Failures in the expectable environment and their impact on individual development: The case of child maltreatment. In D. Cicchetti & D. J. Cohen (Eds.), *Developmental psychopathology: Vol. 2. Risk, disorder, and adaptation* (pp. 32–71). Oxford: Wiley.

Cicchetti, D., & Toth, S. L. (2003). Child maltreatment: Past, present, and future perspectives. In C. B. Kuster, M. U. O'Brien, H. J. Walberg, & R. P. Weissberg (Eds.). (2003). *Long-term trends in the well-being of children and youth: Issues in children's and families lives* (pp. 181–205). Washington, DC: U.S. Child Welfare League of America.

Cicchetti, D., Toth, S. L., & Maughan, A. (2000). An ecological-transactional model of child maltreatment. In A. J. Sameroff, M. Lewis, & S. M. Miller (Eds.), *Handbook of developmental psychopathology* (2nd ed., pp. 689–722). New York: Kluwer Academic/Plenum Press.

Clements, M., & Markman, H. J. (1996). The transition to parenthood: Is having children hazardous to marriage? In N. Vanzetti & S. Duck (Eds.), *A lifetime of relationships* (pp. 290–310). Pacific Grove, CA: Brooks/Cole Publishing.

Clulow, C. F. (1996). *Women, men, and marriage.* Northvale, NJ: Aronson.

Clulow, C. F., & Cudmore, L. (1985). *Marital therapy: An inside view.* Aberdeen, Scotland: Aberdeen University Press.

Cohen, N. A. (2001, April). *Unmarried African American couple relationships and fathers' involvement with their infants.* Paper presented at the Society for Research in Child Development, Minneapolis, MN.

Coie, J. D., Watt, N. F., West, S. G., & Hawkins, J. D. (1993). The science of prevention: A conceptual framework and some directions for a national research program. *American Psychologist, 48*(10), 1013–1022.

Coleman, M., & Ganong, L. H. (2004). *Handbook of contemporary families: Considering the past, contemplating the future.* Thousand Oaks, CA: Sage.

Coley, R. L., & Chase-Lansdale, P. L. (1999). Stability and change in paternal involvement among urban African American fathers. *Journal of Family Psychology, 13*(3), 416–435.

Coll, C. T. G., Meyer, E. C., & Brillon, L. (1995). Ethnic and minority parenting. In M. H. Bornstein (Ed.), *Handbook of parenting: Vol. 2. Biology and ecology of parenting* (pp. 189–209). Hillsdale, NJ: Erlbaum.

Collins, W. A., Maccoby, E. E., Steinberg, L., Hetherington, E. M., & Bornstein, M. H. (2000). Contemporary research on parenting: The case for nature and nurture. *American Psychologist, 55*(2), 218–232.

Conduct Problems Prevention Research Group. (1999a). Initial impact of the Fast Track prevention trial for conduct problems: I. The high-risk sample. *Journal of Consulting and Clinical Psychology, 67*(5), 631–647.

Conduct Problems Prevention Research Group. (1999b). Initial impact of the Fast Track prevention trial for conduct problems: II. Classroom effects. *Journal of Consulting and Clinical Psychology, 67*(5), 648–657.

Conger, R. D., Elder, G. H., Jr., Lorenz, F. O., Simons, R. L., & Whitbeck, L. B. (Eds.). (1994). *Families in troubled times: Adapting to change in rural America.* New York: Aldine de Gruyter.

Conger, R. D., Ge, X., Elder, G. H., & Lorenz, F. O. (1994). Economic stress, coercive family process, and developmental problems of adolescents. *Child Development, 65*(2), 541–561.

Contreras, S., Fernandez, S., Malcarne, V. L., Ingram, R. E., & Vaccarino, V. R. (2004). Reliability and validity of the Beck Depression and Anxiety Inventories in Caucasian Americans and Latinos. *Hispanic Journal of Behavioral Sciences, 26*(4), 446–462.

Cowan, C. P., & Cowan, P. A. (1995). Interventions to ease the transition to parenthood: Why they are needed and what they can do. *Family Relations: Journal of Applied Family and Child Studies, 44*(4), 412–423.

Cowan, C. P., & Cowan, P. A. (2000). *When partners become parents: The big life change for couples.* Mahwah, NJ: Erlbaum.

Cowan, C. P., Cowan, P. A., & Heming, G. (2005). Two variations of a preventive intervention for couples: Effects on parents and children during the transition to elementary school. In P. A. Cowan, C. P. Cowan, J. Ablow, V. K. Johnson, & J. Measelle (Eds.), *The family context of parenting in children's adaptation to elementary school* (pp. 277–312). Mahwah, NJ: Erlbaum.

Cowan, C. P., Cowan, P. A., Heming, G., Garrett, E., Coysh, W. S., Curtis-Boles, H., et al. (1985). Transitions to parenthood: His, hers, and theirs. *Journal of Family Issues, 6,* 451–481.

Cowan, P. A. (1978). *Piaget: With feeling.* New York: Holt, Rinehart and Winston.

Cowan, P. A. (1991). Individual and family life transitions: A proposal for a new definition. In P. A. Cowan & E. M. Hetherington (Eds.), *Family transitions* (pp. 3–30). Hillsdale, NJ: Erlbaum.

Cowan, P. A., Bradburn, I. S., & Cowan, C. P. (2005). Parents' working models of attachment: The intergenerational context of problem behavior in kindergarten. In P. A. Cowan, C. P. Cowan, J. Ablow, V. K. Johnson, & J. Measelle (Eds.), *The family context of parenting in children's adaptation to elementary school* (pp. 209–236). Mahwah, NJ: Erlbaum.

Cowan, P. A., & Cowan, C. P. (2003). Normative family transitions, normal family processes, and healthy child development. In F. Walsh (Ed.), *Normal family processes* (3rd ed., pp. 424–459). New York: Guilford Press.

Cowan, P. A., & Cowan, C. P. (2004). From family relationships to peer rejection to antisocial behavior in middle childhood. In J. B. Kupersmidt & K. A. Dodge (Eds.), *Children's peer relations: From development to intervention (Decade of behavior)* (pp. 159–177). Washington, DC: American Psychological Association.

Cowan, P. A., Cowan, C. P. (2005a). Five-domain models: Putting it all together. In P. A. Cowan, C. P. Cowan, J. Ablow, V. K. Johnson, & J. Measelle (Eds.), *The family context of parenting in children's adaptation to elementary school* (pp. 315–334). Mahwah, NJ: Erlbaum.

Cowan, P. A., & Cowan, C. P. (2005b). *Understanding and encouraging fathers' positive involvement with their children: Toward preventive intervention informed by research.* Unpublished manuscript.

Cowan, P. A., Cowan, C. P., Ablow, J., Johnson, V. K., & Measelle, J. (2005). *The family context of parenting in children's adaptation to elementary school.* Mahwah, NJ: Erlbaum.

Cowan, P. A., Powell, D., & Cowan, C. P. (1998). Parenting interventions: A family systems perspective. In W. Damon (Ed.), *Handbook of child psychology* (5th ed., Vol. 4, pp. 3–72). New York: Wiley.

Cox, M. J., Paley, B., Payne, C. C., & Burchinal, M. (1999). *The transition to parenthood: Marital conflict and withdrawal and parent-infant interactions.* Mahwah, NJ: Erlbaum.

Cummings, E. M., & Davies, P. (1994). *Children and marital conflict: The impact of family dispute and resolution.* New York: Guilford Press.

Cummings, E. M., Davies, P. T., & Campbell, S. B. (2000). *Developmental psychopathology and family process: Theory, research, and clinical implications.* New York: Guilford Press.

Dadds, M. R., Sanders, M. R., Behrens, B. C., & James, J. E. (1987). Marital discord and child behavior problems: A description of family interactions during treatment. *Journal of Clinical Child Psychology, 16*(3), 192–203.

Davies, P. T., Cummings, E. M., & Winter, M. A. (2004). Pathways between profiles of family functioning, child security in the interparental subsystem, and child psychological problems. *Development and Psychopathology, 16*(3), 525–550.

Davison, G. C., & Neale, J. M. (1996). *Abnormal psychology* (6th ed., rev.). New York: Wiley.

Demo, D. H., Allen, K. R., & Fine, M. A. (Eds.). (2000). *Handbook of family diversity.* New York: Oxford University Press.

DeParle, J. (2004). *American dream: Three women, ten kids, and a nation's drive to end welfare.* New York: Viking.

Diamond, G. S., Serrano, A. C., Dickey, M., & Sonis, W. A. (1998). Current status of family-based outcome and process research. In M. E. Hertzig & E. A. Farber (Eds.), *Annual progress in child psy-*

chiatry and child development: 1997 (pp. 379–394). Philadelphia: Brunner/Mazel.

Dicks, H. V. (1967). *Marital tensions; clinical studies towards a psychological theory of interaction.* New York: Basic Books.

Dickstein, S., Seifer, R., Hayden, L. C., Schiller, M., Sameroff, A. J., Keitner, G., et al. (1998). Levels of family assessment: II. Impact of maternal psychopathology on family functioning. *Journal of Family Psychology, 12*(1), 23–40.

Dinkmeyer, D. C., & McKay, G. D. (1982). *The parent's handbook: Systematic Training for Effective Parenting (STEP).* Circle Pines, MN: American Guidance Service.

Dion, M. R., Devaney, B., McConnell, F. M., Hill, H., & Winston, P. (2003). *Helping unwed parents build strong and healthy marriages: A conceptual framework for interventions.* Washington, DC: Mathematica.

Dishion, T. J., & Patterson, G. R. (1997). The timing and severity of antisocial behavior: Three hypotheses within an ecological framework. In D. M. Stoff, J. Breiling, & J. D. Maser (Eds.), *Handbook of antisocial behavior* (pp. 205–217). New York, NY: Wiley.

Dobson, J. C., & Bauer, G. L. (1990). *Children at risk* (2nd ed.). Dallas: Word Publishers.

Dodge, K. A., Pettit, G. S., & Bates, J. E. (1997). How the experience of early physical abuse leads children to become chronically aggressive. In D. Cicchetti & S. L. Toth (Eds.), *Rochester Symposium on Developmental Psychology: Vol. 8. Developmental perspectives on trauma—Theory, research, and intervention* (pp. 263–288). Rochester, NY: University of Rochester Press.

Eberstadt, M. (2004). *Home-alone America: The hidden toll of day care, behavioral drugs, and other parent substitutes.* New York: Sentinel.

Egeland, B., & Carlson, E. A. (2004). Attachment and psychopathology. In L. Atkinson & S. Goldberg (Eds.), *Attachment issues in psychopathology and intervention* (pp. 27–48). Mahwah, NJ: Erlbaum.

Egeland, B., & Sroufe, L. A. (1981). Attachment and early maltreatment. *Child Development, 52*(1), 44–52.

Emery, R. E. (1999). *Marriage, divorce, and children's adjustment* (2nd ed.). Thousand Oaks, CA: Sage.

Engel, G. L. (1980). The clinical application of the biopsychosocial model. *American Journal of Psychiatry, 137,* 535–544.

Epstein, N. B., Baldwin, L. M., & Bishop, D. S. (1983). The McMaster Family Assessment Device. *Journal of Marital and Family Therapy, 9*(2), 171–180.

Epstein, N. B., Ryan, C. E., Bishop, D. S., Miller, I. W., & Keitner, G. I. (2003). The McMaster model: A view of healthy family functioning. In F. Walsh (Ed.), *Normal family processes: Growing diversity and complexity* (3rd ed., pp. 581–607). New York: Guilford Press.

Erikson, E. H. (1980). *Identity and the life cycle.* New York: Norton.

Everett, C. A., & Everett, S. V. (2000). Single-parent families: Dynamics and treatment issues. In W. C. Nichols (Ed.), *Handbook of family development and intervention: Wiley series in couples and family dynamics and treatment* (pp. 323–340). New York: Wiley.

Falicov, C. J. (1996). Mexican families. In M. McGoldrick, J. Giordano, & J. K. Pearce. (Eds.), *Ethnicity and family therapy* (2nd ed., pp. 169–182). New York: Guilford Press.

Falicov, C. J. (1998). *Latino families in therapy: A guide to multicultural practice.* New York: Guilford Press.

Fendrich, M., Warner, V., & Weissman, M. M. (1990). Family risk factors, parental depression, and psychopathology in offspring. *Developmental Psychology, 26*(1), 40–50.

Fiese, B. H. (1992). Dimensions of family rituals across two generations: Relation to adolescent identity. *Family Process, 31*(2), 151–162.

Fincham, F. D., Beach, S. R. H., Harold, G. T., & Osborne, L. N. (1997). Marital satisfaction and depression: Different causal relationships for men and women? *Psychological Science, 8*(5), 351–357.

Fivaz-Depeursinge, E. (2003). L'alliance coparentale et le développement affectif de l'enfant dans le triangle primaire [Coparental alliance and infant affective development in the primary triangle]. *Therapie Familiale, 24*(3), 267–273.

Fivaz-Depeursinge, E., & Corboz-Warnery, A. (1999). *The primary triangle: A developmental systems view of mothers, fathers, and infants.* New York: Basic Books.

Flores, M. T., & Carey, G. (2000). *Family therapy with Hispanics: Toward appreciating diversity.* Boston: Allyn & Bacon.

Fonagy, P., Steele, H., & Steele, M. (1991). Maternal representations of attachment during pregnancy predict the organization of infant-mother attachment at one year of age. *Child Development, 62*(5), 891–905.

Forgatch, M. S., & DeGarmo, D. S. (1999). Parenting through change: An effective prevention program for single mothers. *Journal of Consulting and Clinical Psychology, 67*(5), 711–724.

Fraiberg, S. (1975). Ghosts in the nursery: A psychoanalytic approach to impaired infant-mother relationships. *Journal of the American Academy of Child and Adolescent Psychiatry, 14,* 387–421.

Framo, J. L. (1992). *Family-of-origin therapy: An intergenerational approach.* New York: Brunner/Mazel.

Franklin, C., Streeter, C. L., & Springer, D. W. (2001). Validity of the FACES IV family assessment measure. *Research on Social Work Practice, 11*(5), 576–596.

Frascarolo, F., Favez, N., Carneiro, C., & Fivaz-Depeursinge, E. (2004). Hierarchy of interactive functions in father-mother-baby three-way games. *Infant & Child Development, 13*(4), 301–322.

Freud, A. (1965). *Normality and pathology in childhood.* New York: International Universities Press.

Freud, S. (1905). *Drei Abhandlungen zur Sexualtheorie* [Three Essays on the theory of sexuality]. Leipzig: F. Deuticke.

Freud, S. (1938). *The basic writings of Sigmund Freud* (A. A. Brill, Trans.). New York: Modern Library.

Friedan, B. (1963). *The feminine mystique.* New York: Norton.

Frosch, C. A., Mangelsdorf, S. C., & McHale, J. L. (2000). Marital behavior and the security of preschooler-parent attachment relationships. *Journal of Family Psychology, 14*(1), 144–161.

Fuller, B., Kagan, S. L., Loeb, S., Carroll, J., & Growing Up in Poverty Project. (2002). *New lives for poor families? Mothers and young children move through welfare: The Growing Up in Poverty Project wave 2 findings. California, Connecticut, and Florida* [Technical report]. Berkeley, CA: Growing Up in Poverty Project.

Furstenberg, F. F., & Cherlin, A. J. (1991). *Divided families: What happens to children when parents part?* Cambridge, MA: Harvard University Press.

Furstenberg, F. F., & Kiernan, K. E. (2001). Delayed parental divorce: How much do children benefit? *Journal of Marriage and the Family, 63*(2), 446–457.

Furstenberg, F. F., & Teitler, J. O. (1994). Reconsidering the effects of marital disruption: What happens to children of divorce in early adulthood? *Journal of Family Issues, 15*(2), 173–190.

Gennetian, L. A., Knox, V., & Miller, C. (2000). *Reforming welfare and rewarding work: A summary of the final report on the Minnesota Family Investment Program.* New York: MDRC.

George, C., Kaplan, N., & Main, M. (1985). *The adult attachment interview.* Unpublished manuscript, University of California at Berkeley.

Gesell, A., Ilg, F. L., Learned, J., & Ames, L. B. (1943). *Infant and child in the culture of today: The guidance of development in home and nursery school.* New York: Harper.

Ginott, H. G., Ginott, A., & Goddard, H. W. (2003). *Between parent and child: The best selling classic that revolutionized parent-child communication* (Rev. ed.). New York: Three Rivers Press.

Goldenberg, W. A., & Goldenberg, H. (1996). *Family therapy: An overview* (4th ed.). Pacific Grove, CA: Brooks/Cole.

Golombok, S., & Tasker, F. (1994). Children in lesbian and gay families: Theories and evidence. *Annual Review of Sex Research, 5,* 73–100.

Goodman, C., & Silverstein, M. (2002). Grandmothers raising grandchildren: Family structure and well-being in culturally diverse families. *Gerontologist, 42*(5), 676–689.

Gordon, T. (1980). Parent Effectiveness Training: A preventive program and its effects on families. In M. J. Fine (Ed.), *Handbook on parent education* (pp. 101–121). New York: Academic Press.

Gottesman, I. I. (1991). *Schizophrenia genesis: The origins of madness.* New York: Freeman.

Gottesman, I. I., & Shields, J. (1971). Schizophrenia: Geneticism and environmentalism. *Human Heredity, 21*(6), 517–522.

Gottesman, I. I., Shields, J., & Meehl, P. E. (1972). *Schizophrenia and genetics: A twin study vantage point.* New York: Academic Press.

Gottman, J. (2001). Meta-emotion, children's emotional intelligence, and buffering children from marital conflict. In C. D. Ryff & B. H. Singer (Eds.), *Emotion, social relationships, and health: Series in affective science* (pp. 23–40). London: Oxford University Press.

Gottman, J. M., & Levenson, R. W. (1986). Assessing the role of emotion in marriage. *Behavioral Assessment, 8*(1), 31–48.

Gottman, J. M., Levenson, R. W., Gross, J., Fredrickson, B. L., McCoy, K., Rosenthal, L., et al. (2003). Correlates of gay and lesbian couples' relationship satisfaction and relationship dissolution. *Journal of Homosexuality, 45*(1), 23–43.

Gottman, J. M., Ryan, K. D., Carrere, S., & Erley, A. M. (2002). Toward a scientifically based marital therapy. In H. A. Liddle & D. A. Santisteban (Eds.), *Family psychology: Science-based interventions* (pp. 147–174). Washington, DC: American Psychological Association.

Greenberg, L. S., & Johnson, S. M. (1988). *Emotionally focused therapy for couples.* New York: Guilford Press.

Greer, G. (1980). *The female eunuch.* New York: McGraw-Hill.

Grotevant, H. D., & Carlson, C. I. (1989). *Family assessment: A guide to methods and measures.* New York: Guilford Press.

Grunebaum, H. (1997). Commentary: Why integration may be a misguided goal for family therapy. *Family Process, 36*(1), 19–21.

Grych, J. H., Fincham, F. D., Jouriles, E. N., & McDonald, R. (2000). Interparental conflict and child adjustment: Testing the mediational role of appraisals in the cognitive-contextual framework. *Child Development, 71*(6), 1648–1661.

Gurman, A. S. (2002). Brief integrative marital therapy: A depth-behavioral approach. In A. S. Gurman & N. S. Jacobson (Eds.), *Clinical handbook of couple therapy* (3rd ed., pp. 180–220). New York: Guilford Press.

Gurman, A. S., & Jacobson, N. S. (Eds.). (2002). *Clinical handbook of couple therapy* (3rd ed.). New York: Guilford Press.

Gurman, A. S., & Kniskern, D. P. (1981). *Handbook of family therapy.* New York: Brunner/Mazel.

Gurman, A. S., & Kniskern, D. P. (1991). *Handbook of family therapy* (Vol. 2). New York: Brunner/Mazel.

Guthrie, R. V. (1976). *Even the rat was white: A historical view of psychology.* New York: Harper & Row.

Guzman, L., Lippman, L., Moore, K. A., & O'Hare, W. (2003). *How children are doing: The mismatch between public perception and statistical reality.* Washington, DC: Child Trends.

Haley, J. (1976). *Problem-solving therapy: New strategies for effective family therapy.* San Francisco: Jossey-Bass.

Haley, J. (1990). *Strategies of psychotherapy* (2nd ed.). Rockville, MD: Triangle Press.

Hampson, R. B., & Beavers, W. R. (1996). Family therapy and outcome: Relationships between therapist and family styles. *Contemporary Family Therapy: An International Journal, 18*(3), 345–370.

Hampson, R. B., & Beavers, W. R. (2004). Observational assessment of couples and families. In L. Sperry (Ed.), *Assessment of couples and families: Contemporary and cutting-edge strategies* (pp. 91–115). New York: Brunner-Routledge.

Hampson, R. B., Prince, C. C., & Beavers, W. R. (1999). Marital therapy: Qualities of couples who fare better or worse in treatment. *Journal of Marital and Family Therapy, 25*(4), 411–424.

Hare-Mustin, R. T. (1978). A feminist approach to family therapy. *Family Process, 17*(2), 181–194.

Harvey, E. (1999). Short-term and long-term effects of early parental employment on children of the National Longitudinal Survey of Youth. *Developmental Psychology, 35*(2), 445–459.

Heinicke, C. M. (1984). Impact of prebirth parent personality and marital functioning on family development: A framework and suggestions for further study. *Developmental Psychology, 20*(6), 1044–1053.

Heinicke, C. M. (2002). *The transition to parenting.* Mahwah, NJ: Erlbaum.

Heinicke, C. M., Fineman, N. R., Ruth, G., Recchia, S. L., Guthrie, D., & Rodning, C. (1999). Relationship-based intervention with at-risk mothers: Outcome in the first year of life. *Infant Mental Health Journal, 20*(4), 349–374.

Heinicke, C. M., Rineman, N. R., Ponce, V. A., & Guthrie, D. (2001). Relation-based intervention with at-risk mothers: Outcome in the second year of life. *Infant Mental Health Journal, 22*(4), 431–462.

Henggeler, S. W., & Borduin, C. M. (1990). *Family therapy and beyond: A multisystemic approach to treating the behavior problems of children and adolescents.* Pacific Grove, CA: Brooks/Cole.

Henggeler, S. W., Schoenwald, S. K., & Pickrel, S. G. (1995). Multisystemic therapy: Bridging the gap between university- and community-based treatment. *Journal of Consulting and Clinical Psychology, 63*(5), 709–717.

Hernandez, D. J. (1996). In *Trends in the well-being of America's children and youth, 1996.* Washington, DC: U.S. Bureau of the Census.

Hetherington, E. M. (1966). Effects of paternal absence on sex-typed behaviors in Negro and White preadolescent males. *Journal of Personality and Social Psychology, 4*(1), 87–91.

Hetherington, E. M. (1972). Effects of father absence on personality development in adolescent daughters. *Developmental Psychology, 7,* 313–326.

Hetherington, E. M. (1999). *Coping with divorce, single parenting, and remarriage: A risk and resiliency perspective.* Mahwah, NJ: Erlbaum.

Hetherington, E. M., & Camara, K. A. (1984). Families in transition: The process of dissolution and reconstitution. In R. D. Parke (Ed.), *Review of child development research: The family* (Vol. 7, pp. 184–220). Chicago: University of Chicago Press.

Hetherington, E. M., Cox, M. J., & Cox, R. (1982). Effects of divorce on parents and children. In M. E. Lamb (Ed.), *Nontraditional families* (pp. 233–287). Hillsdale, NJ: Erlbaum.

Hetherington, E. M., & Kelly, J. (2002). *For better or for worse: Divorce reconsidered.* New York: Norton.

Hetherington, E. M., Reiss, D., & Plomin, R. (1994). *Separate social worlds of siblings: The impact of nonshared environment on development.* Hillsdale, NJ: Erlbaum.

Hill, R. (1949). *Families under stress: Adjustment to the crises of war separation and return.* New York: Harper.

Hines, P. M., & Boyd-Franklin, N. (1996). African American families. In M. McGoldrick, J. Giordano, & J. D. Pearce (Eds.), *Ethnicity and family therapy* (2nd ed., pp. 66–84). New York: Guilford Press.

Hinshaw, S. P. (1994). *Attention deficits and hyperactivity in children.* Thousand Oaks, CA: Sage.

Hinshaw, S. P., Zupan, B. A., Simmel, C., Nigg, J. T., & Melnick, S. (1997). Peer status in boys with and without attention-deficit hyperactivity disorder: Predictions from overt and covert antisocial behavior, social isolation, and authoritative parenting beliefs. *Child Development, 68*(5), 880–896.

Ho, M. K., Rasheed, J. M., & Rasheed, M. N. (2004). *Family therapy with ethnic minorities* (2nd ed.). Thousand Oaks, CA: Sage.

Hoffman, L. (1981). *Foundations of family therapy.* New York: Basic Books.

Hooley, J. M. (2004). Do psychiatric patients do better clinically if they live with certain kinds of families? *Current Directions in Psychological Science, 13*(5), 202–205.

Hops, H. (1992). Parental depression and child behavior problems: Implications for behavioural family intervention. *Behaviour Change, 9*(3), 126–138.

Huang, Y.-Y., Cate, S. P., Battistuzzi, C., Oquendo, M. A., Brent, D., & Mann, J. J. (2004). An association between a functional polymorphism in the monoamine oxidase A gene promoter, impulsive traits and early abuse experiences. *Neuropsychopharmacology, 29*(8), 1498–1505.

Huppe, M., & Cyr, M. (1997). Division of household labor and marital satisfaction of dual income couples according to family life cycle. *Canadian Journal of Counselling, 31*(2), 145–162.

Inhelder, B. (1968). *The diagnosis of reasoning in the mentally retarded.* New York: John Day.

Jacobson, N. S., & Gurman, A. S. (1995). *Clinical handbook of couple therapy.* New York: Guilford Press.

Jacobson, N. S., & Margolin, G. (1979). *Marital therapy: Strategies based on social learning and behavior exchange principles.* New York: Brunner/Mazel.

Jacobvitz, D., Hazen, N., Curran, M., & Hitchens, K. (2004). Observations of early triadic family interactions: Boundary disturbances in the family predict symptoms of depression, anxiety, and attention-deficit/hyperactivity disorder in middle childhood. *Development and Psychopathology, 16*(3), 577–592.

Jaffee, S. R., Moffitt, T. E., Caspi, A., Taylor, A., & Arseneault, L. (2002). Influence of adult domestic violence on children's internalizing and externalizing problems: An environmentally informative twin study. *Journal of the American Academy of Child and Adolescent Psychiatry, 41*(9), 1095–1103.

Johnson, S. M. (2004). *The practice of emotionally focused couple therapy: Creating connection* (2nd ed.). New York: Brunner-Routledge.

Johnson, V. K. (2005). Family processes and family structure in children's adaptation to school. In P. A. Cowan, C. P. Cowan, J. Ablow, V. K. Johnson, & J. Measelle (Eds.), *The family context of parenting in children's adaptation to elementary school* (pp. 255–274). Mahwah, NJ: Erlbaum.

Johnson, V. K., Cowan, P. A., & Cowan, C. P. (1999). Children's classroom behavior: The unique contribution of family organization. *Journal of Family Psychology, 13*(3), 355–371.

Johnston, C., & Mash, E. J. (2001). Families of children with attention-deficit/hyperactivity disorder: Review and recommendations for future research. *Clinical Child & Family Psychology Review, 4*(3), 183–207.

Johnston, J. R. (1994). High-conflict divorce. *Future of Children, 4*(1), 165–182.

Jones, E. E., & Korchin, S. J. (1982). Minority mental health: Perspectives. In E. E. Jones & S. J. Korchin (Eds.), *Minority mental health* (pp. 1–25). New York: Praeger.

Jordan, P. L., Stanley, S. M., & Markman, H. (2003). *How to strengthen your marriage as your family grows.* San Francisco: Jossey-Bass.

Jung, M. (1996). Family-centered practice with single-parent families. *Families in Society, 77*(9), 583–590.

Jung, M. (1998). *Chinese American family therapy: A new model for clinicians.* San Francisco: Jossey-Bass.

Kandel, E. R. (2000). Disorders of thought and volition: Schizophrenia. In E. R. Kandel, J. H. Schwartz, & T. M. Jessell (Eds.), *Principles of neural science* (4th ed., pp. 188–1208). New York: McGraw-Hill.

Kaslow, F. W. (Ed.). (1996). *Handbook of relational diagnosis and dysfunctional family patterns.* New York: Wiley.

Katz, L. F., Wilson, B., & Gottman, J. M. (1999). Meta-emotion philosophy and family adjustment: Making an emotional connection. In M. J. Cox & J. Brooks-Gunn (Eds.), *Conflict and cohesion in families: Causes and consequences* (pp. 131–165). Mahwah, NJ: Erlbaum.

Kirby, D. (1999). Reflections on two decades of research on teen sexual behavior and pregnancy. *Journal of School Health, 69,* 89–94.

Klein, M. (1932). *The psycho-analysis of children.* New York: Norton.

Kleinbaum, D. G., Morgenstern, H., & Kupper, L. L. (1982). *Epidemiologic research: Principles and quantitative methods.* Belmont, CA: Lifetime Learning Publications.

Klerman, G. L., & Weissman, M. M. (1986). The interpersonal approach to understanding depression. In T. Millon & L. Gerald (Eds.), *Contemporary directions in psychopathology: Toward the DSM-IV* (pp. 429–456). New York: Guilford Press.

Kohut, H., & Wolf, E. S. (1978). The disorders of the self and their treatment: An outline. *International Journal of Psycho-Analysis, 59*(4), 413–425.

Kouneski, E. (2001). *Circumplex model and FACES: Review of the literature.* Available from http://www.lifeinnovations.com/familyinventoriesdatabase.html.

Laird, J. (2003). Lesbian and gay families. In F. Walsh (Ed.), *Normal family processes: Growing diversity and complexity* (3rd ed., pp. 176–209). New York: Guilford Press.

Laird, J., & Green, R. J. (1996). *Lesbians and gays in couples and families: A handbook for therapists.* San Francisco: Jossey-Bass.

Lamb, M. E. (1999). *Parenting and child development in "nontraditional" families.* Mahwah, NJ: Erlbaum.

Lamb, M. E., Pleck, J. H., Charnov, E. L., & Levine, J. A. (1987). A biosocial perspective on paternal behavior and involvement. In J. B. Lancaster, J. Altmann, A. S. Rossi, & L. R. Sherrod (Eds.), *Parenting across the life span: Biosocial dimensions* (pp. 111–142). Hawthorne, NY: Aldine.

Lazarus, R. S., & Folkman, S. (1984). *Stress, appraisal and coping.* New York: Springer.

Lebow, J. (1997). The integrative revolution in couple and family therapy. *Family Process, 36*(1), 1–17.

Levenson, R. W., Carstensen, L. L., & Gottman, J. M. (1994). Influence of age and gender on affect, physiology, and their interrelations: A study of long-term marriages. *Journal of Personality and Social Psychology, 67*(1), 56–68.

Levenson, R. W., & Gottman, J. M. (1983). Marital interaction: Physiological linkage and affective exchange. *Journal of Personality and Social Psychology, 45*(3), 587–597.

Liddle, H. A. (1995). Conceptual and clinical dimensions of multidimensional, multisystems engagement strategy in family-based adolescent treatment [Special issue: Adolescent treatment: New frontiers and new dimensions]. *Psychotherapy: Theory, Research, Practice, Training, 32*(1), 39–58.

Liddle, H. A., Dakof, G. A., Parker, K., Diamond, G. S., Barrett, K., & Tejeda, M. (2001). Multidimiensional family therapy for adolescent drug abuse: Results of a randomized clinical trial. *American Journal of Drug & Alcohol Abuse, 27*(4), 651–688.

Liddle, H. A., & Hogue, A. (2000). A family-based, developmental-ecological preventive intervention for high-risk adolescents. *Journal of Marital and Family Therapy, 26*(3), 265–279.

Lidz, T., Cornelison, A. R., Fleck, S., & Terry, D. (1957). The intrafamilial environment of schizophrenic patients: II. Marital schism and marital skew. *American Journal of Psychiatry, 114,* 241–248.

Luescher, K., & Pillemer, K. (1998). Intergenerational ambivalence: A new approach to the study of parent-child relations in later life. *Journal of Marriage and the Family, 60*(2), 413–425.

Lyons-Ruth, K., Alpern, L., & Repacholi, B. (1993). Disorganized infant attachment classification and maternal psychosocial problems as predictors of hostile-aggressive behavior in the preschool classroom. *Child Development, 64*(2), 572–585.

Maccoby, E. E., & Martin, J. A. (1983). Socialization in the context of the family: Parent-child interaction. In E. M. Hetherington (Ed.), *Handbook of child psychology: Socialization, personality and social development* (4th ed., Vol. 4, pp. 1–101). New York: Wiley.

Madanes, C. (1984). *Behind the one-way mirror: Advances in the practice of strategic therapy.* San Francisco: Jossey-Bass.

Main, M., Kaplan, N., & Cassidy, J. (1985). Security in infancy, childhood, and adulthood: A move to the level of representation. In *Growing points of attachment theory and research: Monographs of the Society for Research in Child Development, 50,* 66–106.

Mak, W. W. S., & Zane, N. W. S. (2004). The phenomenon of somatization among community Chinese Americans. *Social Psychiatry & Psychiatric Epidemiology, 39*(12), 967–974.

Malley, M. (2002). Systemic therapy with lesbian and gay clients: A truly social approach to psychological practice. *Journal of Community and Applied Social Psychology, 12*(3), 237–241.

Malley, M., & McCann, D. (2002). Family therapy with lesbian and gay clients. In A. Coyle & C. Kitzinger (Eds.), *Lesbian and gay psychology: New perspectives* (pp. 198–218). Malden, MA: Blackwell.

Maslow, A. H. (1962). *Toward a psychology of being.* New York: Van Nostrand.

Matsui, W. T. (1996). Japanese families. In M. McGoldrick, J. Giordano, & J. K. Pearce (Eds.), *Ethnicity and family therapy* (2nd ed., pp. 268–280). New York: Guilford Press.

Mattinson, J., & Sinclair, I. (1979). *Mate and stalemate: Working with marital problems in a social services department.* Oxford: Blackwell.

McCubbin, H. I., & Patterson, J. M. (1983). The family stress process: The double ABCX model of adjustment and adaptation. *Marriage and Family Review, 6*(1/2), 7–37.

McCubbin, H. I., Thompson, E. A., Thompson, A. I., & Futrell, J. A. (Eds.). (1999). *The dynamics of resilient families.* Thousand Oaks, CA: Sage.

McGoldrick, M., Giordano, J., & Pearce, J. K. (1996). *Ethnicity and family therapy* (2nd ed.). New York: Guilford Press.

McHale, J. P., Kazali, C., Rotman, T., Talbot, J., Carleton, M., & Lieberson, R. (2004). The transition to coparenthood: Parents' prebirth expectations and early coparental adjustment at 3 months postpartum. *Development and Psychopathology, 16*(3), 711–733.

McHale, J. P., & Rasmussen, J. L. (1998). Coparental and family group-level dynamics during infancy: Early family precursors of child and family functioning during preschool. *Development and Psychopathology, 10*(1), 39–59.

McHale, S. M., & Huston, T. L. (1985). The effect of the transition to parenthood on the marital relationship. *Journal of Family Issues, 6,* 409–435.

McLanahan, S. S. (2002). *Unwed parents: Myths, realities, and policy making.* Princeton, NJ: Center for Research on Child Wellbeing.

McLanahan, S. S., Garfinkel, I., Brooks-Gunn, J., Zhao, H., Johnson, W., Rich, L., et al. (1998). *Unwed fathers and fragile families.* Princeton, NJ: Center for Research on Child Wellbeing.

McLoyd, V. C. (1990). The impact of economic hardship on Black families and children: Psychological distress, parenting, and socioemotional development. *Child Development, 61*(2), 311–346.

Mednick, S. A., Cudeck, R., Griffith, J. J., Talovic, S. A., & Schulsinger, F. (1984). The Danish High-Risk Project: Recent methods and findings. In N. F. Watt, L. C. Wynne, J. E. Rolf, & E. J. Anthony (Eds.), *Children at risk for Schizophrenia: A longitudinal perspective* (pp. 21–42). New York: Cambridge University Press.

Meehl, P. E. (1962). Schizotaxia, schizotypy, Schizophrenia. *American Psychologist, 17*(12), 827–838.

Messer, S. B. (2004). Evidence-based practice: Beyond empirically supported treatments. *Professional Psychology: Research and Practice, 35*(6), 580–588.

Miklowitz, D. J. (2004). The role of family systems in severe and recurrent psychiatric disorders: A developmental psychopathology view. *Development and Psychopathology, 16*(3), 667–688.

Miller, B. A. (2005). Intergenerational transmission of religiousness and spirituality. In W. R. Miller & H. D. Delaney (Eds.), *Judeo-Christian perspectives on psychology: Human nature, motivation, and change* (pp. 227–244). Washington, DC: American Psychological Association.

Miller, G. E., & Prinz, R. J. (1990). Enhancement of social learning family interventions for childhood conduct disorder. *Psychological Bulletin, 108*(2), 291–307.

Miller, K. E., & Rasco, L. M. (2004). *The mental health of refugees: Ecological approaches to healing and adaptation.* Mahwah, NJ: Erlbaum.

Miller, N. B., Cowan, P. A., Cowan, C. P., Hetherington, E. M., & Clingempeel, G. (1993). Externalizing in preschoolers and early adolescents: A cross-study replication of a family model. *Developmental Psychology, 29*(1), 3–18.

Mincy, R., & Pouncy, H. (2002). The responsible fatherhood field: Evolution and goals. In C. S. Tamis-LeMonda & N. J. Cabrera (Eds.), *Handbook of father involvement: Multidisciplinary perspectives* (pp. 555–598). Mahwah, NJ: Erlbaum.

Minuchin, S. (1974). *Families and family therapy.* Cambridge, MA: Harvard University Press.

Minuchin, S., Montalvo, B. G., Jr., Bosman, B. L., & Schumer, F. (1967). *Families of the slums: An exploration of their structure and treatment.* New York: Basic Books.

Mischel, W. (1961). Father-absence and delay of gratification. *Journal of Abnormal and Social Psychology, 63,* 116–124.

Mistry, R. S., Vandewater, E. A., Huston, A. C., & McLoyd, V. C. (2002). Economic well-being and children's social adjustment: The role of family process in an ethnically diverse low-income sample. *Child Development, 73*(3), 935–951.

Moorehouse, M. J. (1993). Work and family dynamics. In P. A. Cowan, D. Field, D. A. Hansen, A. Skolnick, & G. E. Swanson (Eds.), *Family, self, and society: Toward a new agenda for family research* (pp. 265–286). Hillsdale, NJ: Erlbaum.

Moos, R. H. (1974). *Family Environment Scale.* Palo Alto, CA: Consulting Psychologists Press.

Nash, J. (1965). The father in contemporary culture and current psychological literature. *Child Development, 36*(1), 261–297.

Ng, K. S. (1999). *Counseling Asian families from a systems perspective.* Alexandria, VA: American Counseling Association.

Nolen-Hoeksema, S., Wolfson, A., Mumme, D., & Guskin, K. (1995). Helplessness in children of depressed and nondepressed mothers: Parental depression and distress—Implications for development in infancy, childhood, and adolescence [Special section]. *Developmental Psychology, 31,* 377–387.

Olson, D. H., & Gorall, D. M. (2003). Circumplex model of marital and family systems. In F. Walsh (Ed.), *Normal family processes: Growing diversity and complexity* (3rd ed., pp. 514–548). New York: Guilford Press.

Owen, M. T., & Cox, M. J. (1997). Marital conflict and the development of infant-parent attachment relationships. *Journal of Family Psychology, 11*(2), 152–164.

Owens, E. B., Hinshaw, S. P., Kraemer, H. C., Arnold, L. E., Abikoff, H. B., Cantwell, D. P., et al. (2003). Which treatment for whom for ADHD? Moderators of treatment response in the MTA. *Journal of Consulting and Clinical Psychology, 71*(3), 540–552.

Pachankis, J. E., & Goldfried, M. R. (2004). Clinical issues in working with lesbian, gay, and bisexual clients. *Psychotherapy: Theory, Research, Practice, Training, 41*(3), 227–246.

Parke, R. D., & Buriel, R. (1998). Socialization in the family: Ethnic and ecological perspectives. In N. Eisenberg (Ed.), *Social, emotional, and personality development* (5th ed., Vol. 3, pp. 463–552). New York: Wiley.

Parke, R. D., Coltrane, S., Duffy, S., Buriel, R., Dennis, J., Powers, J., et al. (2004). Economic stress, parenting, and child adjustment in Mexican American and European American families. *Child Development, 75*(6), 1632–1656.

Parker, J. G., & Asher, S. R. (1987). Peer relations and later personal adjustment: Are low-accepted children at risk? *Psychological Bulletin, 102*(3), 357–389.

Patterson, C. J. (2002). Lesbian and gay parenthood. In M. H. Bornstein (Ed.), *Handbook of parenting: Vol. 3. Being and becoming a parent* (2nd ed., pp. 317–338). Mahwah, NJ: Erlbaum.

Patterson, G. R. (1975). *Families: Applications of social learning to family life* (Rev. ed.). Champaign, IL: Research Press.

Patterson, G. R. (1982). *Coercive family process.* Eugene, OR: Castalia.

Patterson, G. R., & Capaldi, D. M. (1991). Antisocial parents: Unskilled and vulnerable. In P. A. Cowan & E. M. Hetherington (Eds.), *Family transitions: Advances in family research* (Vol. 2, pp. 195–218). Hillsdale, NJ: Erlbaum.

Patterson, G. R., Dishion, T. J., & Bank, L. (1984). Family interaction: A process model of deviancy training. *Aggressive Behavior, 10*(3), 253–267.

Patterson, G. R., Reid, J. B., & Dishion, T. J. (1998). Antisocial boys. In J. M. Jenkins, K. Oatley, & N. L. Stein (Eds.), *Human emotions: A reader* (pp. 330–336). Malden, MA: Blackwell.

Patterson, J. E., Miller, R. B., Carnes, S., & Wilson, S. (2004). Evidence-based practice for marriage and family therapists. *Journal of Marital and Family Therapy, 30*(2), 183–195.

Pears, K. C., & Capaldi, D. M. (2001). Intergenerational transmission of abuse: A two-generational prospective study of an at-risk sample. *Child Abuse & Neglect, 25*(11), 1439–1461.

Phares, V. (1992). Where's Poppa? The relative lack of attention to the role of fathers in child and adolescent psychopathology. *American Psychologist, 47*(5), 656–664.

Piaget, J. (1950). *The psychology of intelligence.* New York: Harcourt Brace.

Piaget, J. (1962). *The moral judgment of the child.* New York: Collier Books.

Piaget, J. (1967). *Six psychological studies.* New York: Random House.

Pilling, S., Bebbington, P., Kuipers, E., Garety, P., Geddes, J., Orbach, G., et al. (2002). Psychological treatments in Schizophrenia: I. Meta-analysis of family intervention and cognitive behaviour therapy. *Psychological Medicine, 32*(5), 763–782.

Pinsoff, W. M., & Wynne, L. C. (2000). Toward progress research: Closing the gap between family therapy practice and research. *Journal of Marital and Family Therapy, 26*(1), 1–8.

Plomin, R. (1994). *Genetics and experience: The interplay between nature and nurture.* Thousand Oaks, CA: Sage.

Plomin, R. (2003). *Behavioral genetics in the postgenomic era.* Washington, DC: American Psychological Association.

Popenoe, D. (1993). American family decline, 1960–1990. *Journal of Marriage and the Family*(55), 527–541.

Power, T. G., & Parke, R. D. (1983). Patterns of mother and father play with their 8-month-old infant: A multiple analyses approach. *Infant Behavior & Development, 6*(4), 453–459.

Pratt, M. W., & Fiese, B. H. (2004). *Family stories and the life course: Across time and generations.* Mahwah, NJ: Erlbaum.

Rasco, L. M., & Miller, K. E. (2004). Innovations, challenges, and critical issues in the development of ecological mental health interventions with refugees. In K. E. Miller & L. M. Rasco (Eds.), *The mental health of refugees: Ecological approaches to healing and adaptation* (pp. 375–416). Mahwah, NJ: Erlbaum.

Reid, J. B., Patterson, G. R., & Snyder, J. (2002). *Antisocial behavior in children and adolescents: A developmental analysis and model for intervention.* Washington, DC: American Psychological Association.

Reinecke, M. A., Dattilio, F. M., & Freeman, A. (2003). *Cognitive therapy with children and adolescents: A casebook for clinical practice* (2nd ed.). New York: Guilford Press.

Reiss, D. (1981). *The family's construction of reality.* Cambridge, MA: Harvard University Press.

Reiss, D. (1992). The represented and practicing family: Contrasting visions of family continuity. In A. J. Sameroff & R. Emde (Eds.), *Relationship disturbances in early childhood: A developmental approach* (pp. 191–220). New York: Basic Books.

Reiss, D., Costell, R., Jones, C., & Berkman, H. (1980). The family meets the hospital: A laboratory forecast of the encounter. *Archives of General Psychiatry, 37*(2), 141–154.

Reiss, D., Gonzalez, S., & Kramer, N. (1986). Family process, chronic illness, and death: On the weakness of strong bonds. *Archives of General Psychiatry, 43*(8), 795–804.

Reiss, D., & Klein, D. (1987). Paradigm and pathogenesis: A family-centered approach to problems of etiology and treatment of psychiatric disorders. In T. Jacob (Ed.), *Family interaction and psychopathology: Theories, methods, and findings* (pp. 203–255). New York: Plenum Press.

Reiss, D., & Oliveri, M. E. (1983). The family's construction of social reality and its ties to its kin network: An exploration of causal direction. *Journal of Marriage and the Family, 45*(1), 81–91.

Ringuette, E. L., & Kennedy, T. (1966). An experimental study of the double blind hypothesis. *Journal of Abnormal Psychology, 71*(2), 136–141.

Robbins, M. S., Schwartz, S., & Szapocznik, J. (2004). Structural ecosystems therapy with Hispanic adolescents exhibiting disruptive behavior disorders. In J. R. Ancis (Ed.), *Culturally responsive interventions: Innovative approaches to working with diverse populations* (pp. 71–99). New York: Brunner-Routledge.

Robbins, M. S., Szapocznik, J., Santisteban, D. A., Hervis, O. E., Mitrani, V. B., & Schwartz, S. J. (2003). Brief strategic family therapy for Hispanic youth. In A. E. Kazdin (Ed.), *Evidence-based psychotherapies for children and adolescents* (pp. 407–424). New York: Guilford Press.

Rogers, C. R. (1961). *On becoming a person: A therapist's view of psychotherapy.* Boston: Houghton Mifflin.

Rosenblatt, P. C. (1994). *Metaphors of family systems theory: Toward new constructions.* New York: Guilford Press.

Rosenthal, D. (1967). An historical and methodological review of genetic studies of Schizophrenia. In J. Romano (Ed.), *The origins of Schizophrenia; Proceedings of the first Rochester International Conference on Schizophrenia* (pp. 15–26). Amsterdam: Exerpta Medica Foundation.

Rutter, M. (2002). Nature, nurture, and development: From evangelism through science toward policy and practice. *Child Development, 73*(1), 1–21.

Rutter, M., & Sroufe, L. A. (2000). Developmental psychopathology: Concepts and challenges. *Development and Psychopathology, 12*(3), 265–296.

Ryff, C. D., & Seltzer, M. M. (1996). *The parental experience in midlife.* Chicago: University of Chicago Press.

Sameroff, A. J., Seifer, R., Baldwin, A., & Baldwin, C. (1993). Stability of intelligence from preschool to adolescence: The influence of social and family risk factors. *Child Development, 64*(1), 80–97.

Sameroff, A. J., Seifer, R., & Zax, M. (1982). Early development of children at risk for emotional disorder. *Monographs of the Society for Research in Child Development, 47*(7, Serial No. 199), 82.

Sarason, S. B. (1974). *The psychological sense of community: Prospects for a community psychology.* San Francisco: Jossey-Bass.

Scharff, D. E., & Scharff, J. S. (1991). *Object relations couple therapy.* Northvale, NJ: Aronson.

Scharff, J. S., & Bagnini, C. (2002). Object relations couple therapy. In A. S. Gurman & N. S. Jacobson (Eds.), *Clinical handbook of couple therapy* (3rd ed., pp. 59–85). New York: Guilford Press.

Schmid-Kitsikis, E. (1973). Piagetian theory and its approach to psychopathology. *American Journal of Mental Deficiency, 77*(6), 694–705.

Schultz, S. J. (1984). *Family systems therapy: An integration.* New York: Aronson.

Schulz, M. S., Cowan, C. P., & Cowan, P. A. (in press). Promoting healthy beginnings: Marital quality during the transition to parenthood. *Journal of Clinical and Consulting Psychology.*

Sealander, J. (2003). *The failed century of the child: Governing America's young in the twentieth century.* Cambridge, England: Cambridge University Press.

Selvini Palazzoli, M. (1985). *Self-starvation: From individual to family therapy in the treatment of anorexia nervosa.* New York: Aronson.

Selvini Palazzoli, M., Boscolo, L., Cecchin, G., & Prata, G. (1978). *Paradox and counterparadox.* New York: Aronson.

Serafica, F. C. (1990). *Mental health of ethnic minorities.* New York: Praeger.

Serbin, L. A., & Karp, J. (2004). The intergenerational transfer of psychosocial risk: Mediators of vulnerability and resilience. *Annual Review of Psychology, 55,* 333–363.

Settersten, R. A., Furstenberg, F. F., & Rumbaut, R. G. (Eds.). (2005). *On the frontier of adulthood: Theory, research, and public policy.* Chicago: University of Chicago Press.

Shadish, W. R., Ragsdale, K., Glaser, R. R., & Montgomery, L. M. (1995). The efficacy and effectiveness of marital and family therapy: A perspective from meta-analysis. *Journal of Marital and Family Therapy, 21*(4), 345–360.

Shapiro, A. F., Gottman, J. M., & Carrere, S. (2000). The baby and the marriage: Identifying factors that buffer against decline in marital satisfaction after the first baby arrives. *Journal of Family Psychology, 14*(1), 59–70.

Shaw, D. S., Criss, M. M., Schonberg, M. A., & Beck, J. E. (2004). The development of family hierarchies and their relation to children's conduct problems. *Development and Psychopathology, 16*(3), 483–500.

Silverstein, L. B., & Goodrich, T. J. (2003). *Feminist family therapy: Empowerment in social context.* Washington, DC: American Psychological Association.

Singer, M. T., & Wynne, L. C. (1965a). Thought disorder and family relations of schizophrenics: III. Methodology using projective techniques. *Archives of General Psychiatry, 12*(2), 187–200.

Singer, M. T., & Wynne, L. C. (1965b). Thought disorder and family relations of schizophrenics: IV. Results and implications. *Archives of General Psychiatry, 12*(2), 201–212.

Skinner, H., Steinhauer, P., & Sitarenios, G. (2000). Family assessment measure (FAM) and process model of family functioning [Special issue: Empirical approaches to family assessment]. *Journal of Family Therapy, 22*(2), 190–210.

Skolnick, A. (1991). *Embattled paradise: The American family in an age of uncertainty.* New York: Basic Books.

Smedley, A., & Smedley, B. D. (2005). Race as biology is fiction, racism as a social problem is real: Anthropological and historical perspectives on the social construction of race. *American Psychologist, 60*(1), 16–26.

Spinath, F. M. (2004). The gene illusion: Genetic research in psychiatry and psychology under the microscope. *Intelligence, 32*(4), 425–427.

Sprenkle, D. H. (Ed.). (2002). *Effectiveness research in marriage and family therapy.* Alexandria, VA: American Association of Marriage and Family Therapy.

Sroufe, L. A., Carlson, E. A., Levy, A. K., & Egeland, B. (2003). Implications of attachment theory for developmental psychopathology. In M. E. Hertzig & E. A. Farber (Eds.), *Annual progress in child psychiatry and child development: 2000–2001* (pp. 43–61). New York: Brunner-Routledge.

Sroufe, L. A., Duggal, S., Weinfield, N., & Carlson, E. (2000). Relationships, development, and psychopathology. In A. J. Sameroff, M. Lewis, & S. M. Miller (Eds.), *Handbook of developmental psychopathology* (2nd ed., pp. 75–91). New York: Kluwer Academic/Plenum Press.

Stacey, J. (1996). *In the name of the family: Rethinking family values in the postmodern age.* Boston: Beacon Press.

Stacey, J., & Biblarz, T. J. (2001). (How) does the sexual orientation of parents matter? *American Sociological Review, 66*(2), 159–183.

Steinberg, L. (2001). We know some things: Parent-adolescent relationships in retrospect and prospect. *Journal of Research on Adolescence, 11*(1), 1–19.

Steinhauer, P. D., Santa-Barbara, J., & Skinner, H. (1984). The process model of family functioning. *Canadian Journal of Psychiatry, 29*(2), 77–88.

Strom, R. D., Strom, S. K., Wang, C.-M., Shen, Y.-L., Griswold, D., Chan, H.-S., et al. (1999). Grandparents in the United States and the Republic of China: A comparison of generations and cultures. *International Journal of Aging & Human Development, 49*(4), 279–317.

Szapocznik, J., Feaster, D. J., Mitrani, V. B., Prado, G., Smith, L., Robinson-Batista, C., et al. (2004). Structural ecosystems therapy for HIV-seropositive African American women: Effects on psychological distress, family hassles, and family support. *Journal of Consulting and Clinical Psychology, 72*(2), 288–303.

Tamis-LeMonda, C. S., & Cabrera, N. (Eds.). (2002). *Handbook of father involvement: Multidisciplinary perspectives.* Mahwah, NJ: Erlbaum.

Taylor, S. E., Repetti, R. L., & Seeman, T. (1997). Health psychology: What is an unhealthy environment and how does it get under the skin? *Annual Review of Psychology, 48,* 411–447.

Teichman, Y. (1997). Depression in a marital context. In S. Dreman (Ed.), *The family on the threshold of the 21st century: Trends and implications* (pp. 49–70). Mahwah, NJ: Erlbaum.

Tein, J.-Y., Sandler, I. N., MacKinnon, D. P., & Wolchik, S. A. (2004). How did it work? Who did it work for? Mediation in the context of a moderated prevention effect for children of divorce. *Journal of Consulting and Clinical Psychology, 72*(4), 617–624.

Tienari, P. (1991). Interaction between genetic vulnerability and family environment: The Finnish Adoptive Family Study of Schizophrenia. *Acta Psychiatrica Scandinavica, 84*(5), 460–465.

Tolstoy, L. (1899). *Anna Karenina.* New York: T.Y. Crowell.

Toth, S. L., & Cicchetti, D. (1996). Patterns of relatedness, depressive symptomatology, and perceived competence in maltreated children. *Journal of Consulting and Clinical Psychology, 64*(1), 32–41.

Tsai, J. L., Ying, Y.-W., & Lee, P. A. (2000). The meaning of "being Chinese" and "being American": Variation among Chinese American young adults. *Journal of Cross-Cultural Psychology, 31*(3), 302–332.

Tully, L. A., Arseneault, L., Caspi, A., Moffitt, T. E., & Morgan, J. (2004). Does maternal warmth moderate the effects of birth weight on twins' attention-deficit/hyperactivity disorder (ADHD) symptoms and low IQ? *Journal of Consulting and Clinical Psychology, 72*(2), 218–226.

Turkheimer, E., Haley, A., Waldron, M., D'Onofrio, B., & Gottesman, I. I. (2003). Socioeconomic status modifies heritability of IQ in young children. *Psychological Science, 14*(6), 623–628.

Vandell, D. L., & Ramanan, J. (1992). Effects of early and recent maternal employment on children from low-income families. *Child Development, 63*(4), 938–949.

van Ijzendoorn, M. H. (1992). Intergenerational transmission of parenting: A review of studies in nonclinical populations. *Developmental Review, 12*(1), 76–99.

van Ijzendoorn, M. H., & Bakermans-Kranenburg, M. J. (1997). Intergenerational transmission of attachment: A move to the contextual level. In L. Atkinson & K. J. Zucker (Eds.), *Attachment and psychopathology* (pp. 135–170). New York: Guilford Press.

Vaughn, B. E., Egeland, B. R., Sroufe, L. A., & Waters, E. (1979). Individual differences in infant-mother attachment at twelve and eighteen months: Stability and change in families under stress. *Child Development, 50*(4), 971–975.

Ventura, S. J., Anderson, R. N., Martin, J. A., & Smith, B. L. (1998). Births and deaths: Preliminary data for 1997. *National Vital Statistics Report, 47*(4), 1–32.

Vondra, J. I., Hommerding, K. D., & Shaw, D. S. (1999). Stability and change in infant attachment style in a low-income sample. *Monographs of the Society for Research in Child Development, 64*(3), 119–144.

Von Neumann, J., & Morgenstern, O. (1953). *Theory of games and economic behavior* (3rd ed.). Princeton, NJ: Princeton University Press.

Vygotsky, L. S. (1978). *Mind in society: The development of higher psychological processes.* Cambridge, MA: Harvard University Press.

Wagner, B. M., & Reiss, D. (1995). Family systems and developmental psychopathology: Courtship, marriage, or divorce. In D. Cicchetti & D. J. Cohen (Eds.), *Developmental psychopathology: Vol. 1. Theory and methods* (pp. 696–730). New York: Wiley.

Wahlberg, K.-E., & Wynne, L. C. (2001). Possibilities for prevention of Schizophrenia: Suggestions from research on genotype-environment interaction. *International Journal of Mental Health, 30*(1), 91–103.

Wahlberg, K.-E., Wynne, L. C., Hakko, H., Laksy, K., Moring, J., Miettunen, J., et al. (2004). Interaction of genetic risk and adoptive parent communication deviance: Longitudinal prediction of adoptee psychiatric disorders. *Psychological Medicine, 34*(8), 1531–1541.

Waite, L. J., & Gallagher, M. (2000). *The case for marriage: Why married people are happier, healthier, and better off financially.* New York: Doubleday.

Wallerstein, J. S., & Kelly, J. B. (1980). *Surviving the breakup.* New York: Basic Books.

Walters, M., Carter, B., Papp, P., & Silverstein, O. (1988). *The invisible web: Gender patterns in family relationships.* New York: Guilford Press.

Watson, J. B. (1928). *Psychological care of infant and child.* London: Allen & Unwin.

Webster-Stratton, C. (1984). Randomized trial of two parent-training programs for families with conduct-disordered children. *Journal of Consulting and Clinical Psychology, 52*(4), 666–678.

Webster-Stratton, C. (1994). Advancing videotape parent training: A comparison study. *Journal of Consulting and Clinical Psychology, 62*(3), 583–593.

Webster-Stratton, C., Reid, M. J., & Hammond, M. (2001). Preventing conduct problems, promoting social competence: A parent and teacher training partnership in Head Start. *Journal of Clinical Child & Adolescent Psychology, 30*(3), 283–302.

Weinstein, R. S. (2002). *Reaching higher: The power of expectations in schooling.* Cambridge, MA: Harvard University Press.

Weisz, J. R., Donenberg, G. R., Han, S. S., & Weiss, B. (1995). Bridging the gap between laboratory and clinic in child and adolescent psychotherapy. *Journal of Consulting and Clinical Psychology, 63*(5), 688–701.

Weisz, J. R., Weiss, B., Han, S. S., & Granger, D. A. (1995). Effects of psychotherapy with children and adolescents revisited: A meta-analysis of treatment outcome studies. *Psychological Bulletin, 117*(3), 450–468.

Wenar, C., & Kerig, P. (2000). *Developmental psychopathology: From infancy through adolescence* (4th ed.). Boston: McGraw-Hill.

Whisman, M. A., & Bruce, M. L. (1999). Marital dissatisfaction and incidence of major depressive episode in a community sample. *Journal of Abnormal Psychology, 108*(4), 674–678.

Whisman, M. A., Uebelacker, L. A., & Weinstock, L. M. (2004). Psychopathology and marital satisfaction: The importance of evaluating both partners. *Journal of Consulting and Clinical Psychology, 72*(5), 830–838.

Whitaker, C. A., & Bateson, G. (1958). *Psychotherapy of chronic schizophrenic patients.* Boston: Little, Brown.

Whitbourne, S. K. (2005). *Adult development and aging: Biopsychosocial perspectives* (2nd ed.). Hoboken, NJ: Wiley.

White, L. K., & Booth, A. (1985). The transition to parenthood and marital quality. *Journal of Family Issues, 6*, 435–450.

White, M. (1986). Negative explanation, restraint and double description: A template for family therapy. *Family Process, 25*, 169–184.

White, M., & Epston, D. (1990). *Narrative means to therapeutic ends.* New York: Norton.

Wiener, N. (1961). *Cybernetics or control and communication in the animal and the machine* (2nd ed.). Cambridge, MA: MIT Press.

Wilcox, W. B. (2004). *Soft patriarchs, new men: How Christianity shapes fathers and husbands.* Chicago: University of Chicago Press.

Winnicott, D. W. (1987). *The child, the family, and the outside world.* Reading, MA: Addison-Wesley.

Wolchik, S. A., Sandler, I. N., Millsap, R. E., Plummer, B. A., Greene, S. M., Anderson, E. R., et al. (2002). Six-year follow-up of preventive interventions for children of divorce: A randomized controlled trial. *Journal of the American Medical Association, 288*(15), 1874–1881.

Wolchik, S. A., West, S. G., Westover, S., & Sandler, I. N. (1993). The children of divorce parenting intervention: Outcome evaluation of an empirically based program. *American Journal of Community Psychology, 21*(3), 293–331.

Wood, D., Bruner, J. S., & Ross, G. (1976). The role of tutoring in problem solving. *Journal of Child Psychology and Psychiatry and Allied Disciplines, 17*(2), 89–100.

Wynne, L. C., Ryckoff, I. M., Day, J., & Hirsch, S. I. (1958). Pseudomutuality in the family relations of schizophrenics. *Psychiatry, 21*(2), 205–220.

Yarhouse, M. A. (2003). Working with families affected by HIV/AIDS. *American Journal of Family Therapy, 31*(2), 125–137.

Zetin, M., Stasiek, C., Pangan, E. A. C., & Warren, S. (1988). Toxic psychosis. In J. G. Howells (Ed.), *Modern perspectives in clinical psychiatry* (pp. 231–260). Philadelphia: Brunner/Mazel.

Zimmerman, S. L. (2001). *Family policy: Constructed solutions to family problems.* Thousand Oaks, CA: Sage.

Zimmerman, T. S. (2001). *Integrating gender and culture in family therapy training.* New York: Haworth Press.

CHAPTER 15

Cultural Diversity in the Development of Child Psychopathology

FELICISIMA C. SERAFICA and LUIS A. VARGAS

To more deeply understand the role of culture in the emergence, persistence, and desistance of psychopathology among children and youth, this chapter examines cultural diversity in child and adolescent psychopathology and its development. Based on a selective review of recent comparative studies, we present a synthesis of cross-cultural and ethnic differences that stood out amid the similarities also found. We examine culture's role in child psychopathology and its development through an examination of cultural diversity. Our specific aims are (1) to review and synthesize the findings of recent comparative studies that examined cultural variations in the expression of symptomatology, prevalence, development, and correlates of psychopathology in children and adolescents; (2) to report related findings from ethnic and cultural studies that sampled only one population; (3) to identify conceptual and methodological issues identified in the studies reviewed; and (4) to suggest future directions for research.

A DEVELOPMENTAL-CONTEXTUAL PERSPECTIVE ON PSYCHOPATHOLOGY

The developmental approach to psychopathology, more commonly known as developmental psychopathology, asserts that because there is unity in development, the study of psychopathology or development gone awry in infants, children, and adolescents has to be based on knowledge of normal development and should involve the application of developmental principles. A corollary to this assertion is that research on development gone awry can enhance our understanding of normal development. Therefore, the field of developmental psychopathology focuses on the interplay between normal and abnormal development and on the relationship between deviant and typical forms of a behavior. Like other attempts to describe and explain psychopathology, the developmental approach seeks to understand the etiology, course, and prognosis of a specific disorder. However, its interests extend beyond the identification of predisposing, precipitating, and maintaining factors or risk and protective variables. This approach also seeks to ascertain the internal and external factors that promote competency and resiliency in individuals. Most important, the developmental approach is concerned with describing the developmental sequence of a particular disorder and understanding the processes as well as mechanisms involved. Consistent with a transactional model of the developmental process, the emergence of psychopathology is conceptualized as occurring through a dynamic transaction with intra- and extraorganismic forces (Cicchetti & Cohen, 1995). Acknowledging these forces implies that developmental psychopathology views deviant behavior in context. Thus, it is congruent with a developmental-contextual perspective. Contexts vary; they may be intraorganismic or extraorganismic. An intraorganismic context is organic, involving biologically based characteristics (e.g., genes, brain, central nervous system) and an intrapersonal context involving personal characteristics (e.g., cognitions, emotions, personality). An extraorganismic context subsumes an interpersonal context involving social interactions and relationships (e.g., family, peers) and a superordinate context comprising variables that deal with aggregates of individuals taken as a unit (e.g., ethnic group, social class, culture; Wenar & Kerig, 2000). These different contexts may be considered separately for purposes of analysis, but they are really interrelated (Lerner, 1995). The focus of this chapter is on one type of superordinate context, namely, culture. A cultural perspective to developmental psychopathology necessitates that normal and abnormal development as well as typical and deviant forms of behavior be considered from the standpoint of both dominant mainstream culture and the minority cultures. A developmental-contextual approach is compatible with this perspective.

CULTURE

Culture refers to the designs for living in a specific habitat that have evolved among a particular group of people and are transmitted within and between generations (M. Cole & Cole, 2004). It refers to the entire way of life of a society including its values, beliefs, attitudes, norms, practices, language, religion, and institutions. These designs for living are represented through artifacts, actions, or symbols. North's (1990, p. 37) definition of culture as "a language-based conceptual framework for encoding and interpreting information that the senses are presenting to the brain" emphasizes its symbolic nature. There is shared meaning among those who have the same culture. Their view of the world and its people and how they think and make judgments in general or specific areas of life are filtered through a culturally based information system (Goodenough, 1989).

The term "culture" is usually employed to designate the designs for living among individuals who, frequently but not always, share a common biological ancestry and, initially occupied a particular habitat, namely, an ethnic group. It is in this sense that the term is used in this chapter, though it is acknowledged that the term may also be extended to the values, beliefs, attitudes, norms, and practices common to members of a distinctive group identifiable through a shared characteristic such as gender, social class, sexual orientation, religion, or profession.

Assumptions about Culture

Assumptions about culture have implications for both the research enterprise itself and the applications of research findings.

Culture has an ecological context. The designs for living that constitute an ethnic group's culture are assumed to have evolved because they facilitated adaptation to the group's habitat at a particular time. Thus, the origins of an ethnic group's designs for living and their functions are tied to specific spatial, social, and temporal contexts. This implies that the adaptive value of a specific design for living is relative to context.

At any given time and context, cultural practices are likely to differ in their adaptive value and those that remain prominent in an ethnic group's cultural repertoire may not necessarily be the ones with optimal value for adaptation. It is therefore important to assess the current adaptive value of a cultural belief or practice in its contemporary context. Earlier, social scientists assumed that the cultural values, beliefs, and practices that survive are those that are optimally effective in facilitating adaptation. Contemporary researchers have challenged this assumption. According to Ellen (1982, p. 251), "Cultural adaptations are seldom the best of all possible solutions and never entirely rational." Using recent findings from cognitive science to bolster his contentions, Edgerton (2000) also argued that traditional beliefs and practices may persist not because they are optimally beneficial but because they generally may work well enough without further changes; they are retained in the cultural repertoire because they require the least effort and involve minimal risk. He also cautioned behavioral and social scientists about assuming that any persistent traditional belief or practice in a surviving society must be adaptive. It would be more prudent to assume, he contended, that there is a continuum of adaptive value along which any belief or practice may fall anywhere. A belief or practice may simply be neutral or tolerable, or it may be beneficial to some members of a society while harming others, and sometimes it may even harm everyone.

Culture persists, transmitted from one generation to the next, but the adaptive value of specific cultural variables may change over time. Initially, it was assumed that the deigns for living that make up culture persist because their ecological effectiveness is constant across time and space (Campbell, 1975; Harris, 1960; Kluckhohn & Leighton, 1962). However, contexts change over time and, consequently, the adaptive values of cultural beliefs and practices, even those that were optimally effective at one time, may also shift.

Culture is dynamic rather than static. Previous conceptualizations of culture assumed that it remains static as it is passed on intra- and intergenerationally. However, the nature of individuals and contexts changes over time, and culture becomes modified accordingly. Cultural practices can be altered within a generation, as evidenced by recent changes in American food preferences, or modified across generations. Even when an ethnic group remains in the same geographic context over time, changes can come about through the transactions of the group's members with one another or with members of other ethnic groups and with changes in the physical, social, and technological environments. Changes in the physical environment might necessitate modifications in the means of livelihood and, consequently, in the associated cultural practices. For example, in some areas of the world, polluted waters have made fishing a less lucrative source of income, thus necessitating an occupational change that may, in turn, result in modifications of certain cultural practices that evolved from a fishing economy.

Culture is mediated through social interactions. Initially, this occurs through the parent-child relationship and subsequently through other interpersonal transactions taking place in various ecological systems (Bronfenbrenner, 1977, 1979). Transmission occurs through both verbal and nonverbal modes of communications, directly and indirectly. Children learn cultural values and problem-solving strategies by listening to their mother reading folk tales or to their father and other male adults exchanging stories, but also through observation of adults' attitudes, feelings, and behavioral responses to specific events. Through adult didactic instructions or nonverbal reactions, children learn what is permissible action and emotional expression and what is not, and later infer that there are group norms governing such actions and emotional expressions. From an early age, in addition to these intersubjective experiences, culture is experienced by the child through exposure to various types of media, schooling, and socialization avenues.

Cultural knowledge and practice are not uniformly distributed among members of an ethnic group. Because members of an ethnic group share common values, beliefs, and practices, it used to be assumed that these were uniformly distributed across members. Weisner (2000, p. 141) has disputed this assumption of cultural uniformity, stating that "cultures may have a clear central tendency and normative pattern but they are hardly monolithic and uniform." Within an ethnic group, there are usually subgroups based at least on geography and social class. Within these various subgroups, there may be differential transmission, translation, and implementation of core values and beliefs. Even among members of the same subgroup, there are individual differences in the extent to which they have absorbed cultural values, beliefs, and practices. These individual differences are the result of several factors, including individual characteristics, differential socialization experiences, and differences among their parents' interpretations or implementations of cultural prescriptions. To paraphrase Kluckhohn and Murray (1953), a member of an ethnic group may be like all members of that group, like some members, and like no other members. Cultural uniformity cannot be taken for granted. Cultural knowledge and adherence among members of an ethnic group is characterized by diversity amid unity.

Culture as an Explanatory Variable

Before elucidating the significance of culture for development and psychopathology, a discussion of the controversy regarding culture as an explanatory variable seems warranted. The concept of culture is most often used simply as a descriptive variable, that is, as a category, index, or marker that serves to describe and distinguish values, beliefs, attitudes, and norms of one ethnic group from another. But the concept has also served as a dependent variable and also as an independent variable. It is a dependent variable, for example, in a study of the effects of schooling on women's definitions of gender roles, whereas it has the status of an independent variable in quasi-experimental studies that, for example, examine women's responsiveness to schooling as a function of their ethnic group's gender role definitions. It is culture's research function as an independent or explanatory variable that has encountered resistance (Garcia-Coll, Ackerman, & Cicchetti, 2000) and generated controversy.

Behavioral and social scientists are not always comfortable with the use of culture, however it is operationalized, as a causal explanation. Some would prefer to treat culture only as a descriptive variable or a dependent variable. Others who hold similar views think that, at best, culture may be conceptualized as a "tool kit" from which strategies for action can be selectively drawn for specific purposes (Patterson, 2000). There are several reasons for the unease that is evoked by cultural explanations. First, to those who construe culture as a distinctive product of a particular group of people, culture can be described and interpreted, but it should never be used to explain anything about the people who produced it because such explanations cannot be considered objective (Patterson, 2000). Second, scientists who are willing to consider culture as an explanatory variable are confronted by daunting conceptual and methodological issues. It is difficult to define culture, conceptually and operationally, even when it is disaggregated into its various components. Even when precise definitions are possible, cultural variables operate in a highly complex context, often interacting with a host of other influential variables such that it is difficult to isolate its effects. Furthermore, it is difficult to measure and quantify cultural variables. Psychometrically sound measures for many cultural variables do not yet exist. Moreover, prior attempts to identify cultural bases for behavior or social problems have yielded explanations that too often seem tautological, reductionistic, or static (Patterson, 2000). Third, there are cultural sensitivities to be considered. A search for the cultural bases of maladaptive behaviors can be construed as "blaming the victim" and might preclude changes in social policies and programs that can ameliorate those behaviors. Cultural explanations for maladaptive behavior might also offend ethnic pride. For these and other similar reasons, some scientists think that the safest approach is to describe culture or consider it as a dependent variable.

There is some truth to all of these arguments against treating culture as an explanatory variable. However, the conceptual and methodological problems noted are not unique to the study of culture. Definitional problems are not uncommon in the behavioral and social sciences, especially where relatively few empirical studies on the topic have been conducted. However, as progress is made in disaggregating culture into its various components and isolating it from confounding variables such as economic status, the task of defining and operationalizing cultural variables should become easier. Similarly, measurement and quan-

tification issues have been encountered in other areas and gradually resolved satisfactorily. Furthermore, the issue of complexity is a matter of conceptual clarification and methodological rigor. When there is some understanding of the different causal variables involved, adequate controls can be instituted to permit the isolation of the cultural variable from other variables or to at least examine the extent of its impact on the dependent variable as compared to other contributing factors. Identifying and disentangling the complex explanatory interplay between cultural and noncultural factors can be a stimulating research challenge. Granted that methodological improvements alone may not suffice to gain greater acceptance for the study of culture and its integration into mainstream psychology (Schweder, 1990, as cited in M. Cole, 1996), they are essential if we are to advance significantly in understanding the role of culture in human development and psychopathology.

In answer to those concerned with the possibility that if culture is found to have an effect, it will be concluded, erroneously, that culture determines a particular behavior, Goodenough (1989, p. 218) has made this rejoinder: "Biology helps explain human behavior but does not determine it. Similarly, culture helps explain behavior but it does not determine it either." Finally, cultural sensitivity on the part of researchers can help to overcome an ethnic group's concerns about research on its culture. Concerns about blaming the victim can be allayed by careful interpretation of the results and by using the research findings to advocate for policies and programs directed toward amelioration of any related maladaptive behaviors. A balanced program of research on culturally based values and practices that promote adaptive behaviors as well as maladaptive ones can identify ethnic group strengths that would be a source of ethnic pride.

In sum, the issues surrounding the use of culture as an explanatory variable can be resolved. Culture is so pervasive that not to explore its role as an explanatory variable is to ignore a potentially important source of variance in human behavior.

The Significance of Culture

If culture matters, how does it matter in regard to psychopathology? Culture's relevance to understanding psychopathology derives from two distinguishable but interrelated roles: first, its role in human development, normal or otherwise, and second, its role in shaping societal perspectives on psychopathology and its nature, causes, course, diagnosis, assessment, treatment, and prevention.

Culture and Development

The role of culture in normal development has been discussed at length by developmental scientists (M. Cole, 1996; Garcia-Coll et al., 2000). Even before a child is born, culture defines how the developing fetus is to be treated in utero and at birth, and such treatment has implications for the child's subsequent health and development. Culture designates who will serve as the primary caregiver and how other kin and group members will contribute to the child's care. It also prescribes the appropriate caregiving contexts for infants, children, and adolescents. Most important, culture establishes socialization aims, emphasizing those that are most consistent with cultural values. The child-rearing practices employed to achieve socially desired developmental outcomes are also linked to cultural values, attitudes, beliefs, and norms. These practices may facilitate or inhibit the development of cognitive, emotional, social, and other processes that have implications for the emergence of psychopathology and for the prognosis of a disorder. There is growing evidence that the emergence of specific forms of psychopathology is associated with disruptions in the normal development of certain processes. These disruptions may be largely biologically based in some instances (e.g., Autism); in other cases (e.g., depression), they may be primarily the result of the interaction between biological factors and contextual factors, including specific cultural variables. And in still other cases, culture may be the primary contributing factor. Culture also structures the risk and protective factors that promote or prevent the development of psychopathology.

Culture and Psychopathology

Just as culture defines what is considered normal behavior in a society, so does it specify what is construed as deviant behavior. It categorizes and labels what is considered problem behavior or psychological dysfunction. Through its influence on how the environment is structured, culture helps to determine which behaviors are adaptive and mentally healthy and which are not. Psychopathology may have its intraindividual origins, but how it is experienced, labeled, and expressed is subject to cultural influences. There are even idioms of distress and prototypical behavioral patterns that are unique to societies, cultures, and subcultures. Both culturally distinctive symptoms and culture-specific syndromes have been identified. Culture offers its own culturally congruent explanations for deviant behaviors and psychological disorders. The role of culture and its interaction with biological factors in defining abnormal behavior is evidenced in a case that Greenfield (2002) used to illustrate how culture and biology are mutually adapted for survival. In this case, the daughter of an American couple, social scientists living among the Zinacantec Maya of Nabenchauk in Chiapas, Mexico, began to walk at 9 months, about 5 months earlier than Zinacantec norms. For the Zinacantec, walking at 9 months of age was not only abnormal, it was also dangerous to walk before understanding language. This danger arose from the fact that the Zinacantec houses always have an open fire in the center. Because of this, the Zinacantec assumed that walking at 9 months placed the American child at risk for falling into the fire and her parents now needed to be in a constant state of high alert and close proximity to the child to prevent her from either getting hurt or causing some kind of damage. This case highlights the point that psychopathology has a culturally constituted definition and is referenced usually by the norms of the host culture that frame symptomatology, impairment of functioning, danger to self or others, and so on within the context of the local culture. What is viewed by the Zinacantec as abnormal behavior (making the American girl a *monster* in their eyes) is viewed as normal or even *precocious* in her American parents' eyes. In multicultural contexts, both the host (local) and non-host (foreign) cultures must be considered in defining the nature, causes, course, diagnosis, assessment, treatment, and prevention of *psychopathology*.

Culture's role extends beyond the description and explanation of psychopathology. It influences the course of the disorder and its prognosis because it structures environmental responses to behavioral distress and problematic behavior. Culture specifies the degree of behavioral intensity or problem severity that must be present before an intervention is necessary. Culturally based mental health beliefs and attitudes determine help-seeking responses. Culture designates who may intervene. Last, culture organizes the modes of intervention.

Given the potential significance of culture, a developmental-contextual approach to psychopathology has to address certain questions:

1. Do cultures vary in the expression of psychopathology? Are some patterns of symptomatology or mental disorders more prevalent in certain cultures than in others?

2. What aspects of a given culture are related to high or low prevalence of specific disorders? How do these cultural variables exert their influence? Is the influence direct or indirect? If the latter, what are the mediating variables?

3. What aspects of a given culture moderate the influence of risk or protective factors? How?

4. What is the role of culture in the development of those processes (e.g., emotional self-regulation) that have been implicated in the development of specific disorders (e.g., anxiety or depression)?

5. What are the mental health beliefs and attitudes of a given culture? How do these beliefs and attitudes structure help seeking, diagnosis, treatment, and prevention?

In sum, culture's significance in the study of developmental psychopathology derives from its role in normal development and development gone awry, as well as its role in shaping societal attitudes, beliefs, and practices pertaining to diagnosis, assessment, treatment, and prevention of psychopathology. These two conceptualizations of culture's role bear some resemblance to the two models of cultural influence proposed by Weisz, McCarty, Eastman, Chaiyasit, and Suwanlert (1997), but there are some subtle differences, at least in scope. As currently conceptualized, the two roles may be broader than those of the problem suppression-facilitation model and the adult distress threshold model proposed by Weisz et al.

In the next sections, we examine the available research literature bearing on culture's dual roles, with emphasis on studies of children and adolescents from diverse cultures. It is hoped that this review of development and psychopathology in diverse cultures will broaden our understanding of the role of culture in normal and deviant development. Currently, this understanding is based mostly on theories and research that describe normal and deviant development of European and European American children from middle and lower socioeconomic classes. In these studies, many explanatory variables (e.g., parental beliefs and expectations, child-rearing practices, communication strategies) are actually cultural variables even though they are not identified as such. It is not the case that the study of culture's role in human development and psychopathology has been neglected, but rather that the role of culture has been studied yet not acknowledged.

CULTURAL DIVERSITY IN CHILD AND ADOLESCENT PSYCHOPATHOLOGY

The assumption that culture influences the development, diagnosis, assessment, and treatment of psychopathology is a long-standing one, but to date, the research literature on culture and psychopathology during infancy, childhood, and adolescence is sparse and fragmented. Most of the available data are derived from comparative studies. Al-

though the number of ethnic or cultural studies on adult psychopathology is rapidly increasing, this does not apply to child psychopathology. Developmental-contextual studies that attempt to examine the relationship between culture and psychopathology among children and adolescents are just emerging. Longitudinal studies are even rarer. Our review includes findings from both types of studies.

In the research literature, two terms are used in referring to research involving more than one ethnic group. The term "cross-cultural" is usually used to denote between-group research using samples from two or more countries or nations; the term "ethnic" is applied to between-group research involving different ethnic groups residing within the same country or nation. This seems an artificial distinction, for in both cases, the intent is to discover if there are culturally based differences in the phenomenon under investigation. However, to avoid creating further confusion, we follow this convention for designating research between ethnic groups.

CULTURAL VARIATION IN EXPRESSIONS OF PSYCHOPATHOLOGY

We begin our examination of the relationship between culture and psychopathology by asking the question, Are there cross-cultural or ethnic differences in the expression of distress or psychopathology? Such differences would denote cultural diversity in psychopathology. It is acknowledged that cultural variations in psychopathology may be found in affective, behavioral, or linguistic expressions of distress or in the content of disturbed cognitions and sensory experiences (American Psychiatric Association, 2000), but the study of these variations in children and adolescents and how they change with increasing age has been ignored. Systematic studies directed at identifying, classifying, and validating such variations among children or adolescents are exceedingly rare.

Expressions of Symptomatology

Some interest has been shown in cultural variations in the symptomatology of anxiety. Cross-cultural research has shown that anxiety and disorders of anxiety are universal, or at least evident in all human societies where their presence has been assessed, but there are cultural variations in the phenomenology, meaning, and forms through which distress is expressed and constituted as social reality (Good & Kleinman, 1985). For example, Asians and Latinos may be more likely than European Americans to express anxiety

through somatic and/or physiological complaints. This ethnic difference has been investigated in a number of studies
involving college students or older adults but rarely among
children or adolescents. The hypothesis that Hispanic children and adolescents are more likely than their European
American peers to express anxiety through somatic and
physiological complaints has been confirmed in some studies, albeit with qualifications (Pina & Silverman, 2004;
Varela et al., 2004). The manifestation of ethnic or cultural differences in somatic or physiological expressions of
anxiety was a function of the measure used (Pina & Silverman, 2004). Moreover, although non-Cuban Latino youth
showed greater distress over anxiety-related symptoms
than their European American and Cuban Hispanic peers,
within the non-Cuban Latino group, those whose parents
preferred Spanish as the assessment language evidenced
greater distress over anxiety-related symptoms than their
peers whose parents chose English (Pina & Silverman,
2004).

Linguistic Expressions

The finding that the language in which assessment is conducted is associated with within-ethnic-group differences
in somatic or physiological expression of anxiety and the
amount of distress shown over anxiety-related symptoms
highlights the role of language in the expression of distress.
Besides serving as a means of communication, language
serves as a stimulus in that it evokes cognitions and verbal
and behavioral responses with associated emotions and
other internal states. For bilingual and multilingual individuals, an assessment conducted in the first language may
be more effective at tapping earlier modes of conceptualizing and expressing distress, regardless of acculturation status. Language may facilitate certain modes of symptom
expression and inhibit others, depending on the affect and
experiences that became associated with these modes in
the individual's past. For example, acculturated immigrant
adolescent girls might swear or discuss sexual matters with
ease in English, but may be unable to do so or at least are
more uncomfortable doing so in their native language.
Moreover, there are cultural variations not only in the lexicon of emotion but also in the elaborateness of the language
available for describing certain emotions and emotional experiences (Manson, 1996).

Behavioral Expressions

Few studies of Conduct Disorder or substance use have explored cultural variations in the expression of these problems or the differential cultural bases of apparently similar forms of expression. A couple of sociological studies illustrate such variations and show how the expression of
antisocial tendencies may be patterned after existing cultural practices. In a study of Asian American youth gangs,
Chin (1990a, 1990b, as cited in Chin, Kelly, & Fagan,
1992) identified four types of gang victimization in the
Chinese American community that could be construed as
involving business intimidation: protection, extortion,
forced sales, and "theft" of goods and services. Although
these types of business intimidation may also be used by
gangs in other ethnic groups, an ethnographic study by
Chin et al. (1992) shows how the expression of antisocial
tendencies may be patterned after existing cultural practices. In this study, 603 merchants were interviewed to
identify patterns of extortion and other forms of victimization practiced on Chinese-owned businesses by Asian
adolescent gangs of predominantly Chinese descent operating in three Chinese neighborhoods in New York City.
These interviews yielded data about the prevalence of
these different types of gang victimization, when they occurred, and the behavioral patterns involved. The last is of
particular interest here.

In the Chinese community, protection money, also
known as *po foo fay* (protection fee), *tor ti fay* (territory
fee), or *heung yau chin* (incense oil money), is money paid
by merchants to an individual, gang, or association that
controls the area where the business is conducted. As practiced by Asian American adolescents in New York City,
asking for protection money is patterned after the Chinese
tradition of asking for blessings on a new endeavor. The
custom has been adapted to become a way to obtain the
"blessing" of those (i.e., gangs) who are in a position to
disrupt commercial activities or damage business properties. It is usually initiated at the opening ceremony launch-
ing a business, when some gang members accost the owner
and present their proposal.

Extortion money is also known as *cha chin* (tea money),
hung bao (red envelope), and *lai si* (lucky money, literally
"good for business"). The various names signify several
typical Chinese patterns of gift giving on specific occasions
(e.g., giving a red envelope containing money to family
members, relatives, and even strangers during the Chinese
New Year) that have been subverted into forms of extortion.
The practice of asking for extortion money is a sporadic,
spontaneous act committed by young gang members on an
irregular basis, mostly on major holidays such as the Chinese New Year.

Forced sales or the practice of selling items to business
owners at prices higher than their market value, usually

during Chinese and other holidays, was the most pervasive type of gang exploitation uncovered by Chin et al. (1992). The items sold are typically associated with holidays such as firecrackers or cards or, during the Chinese New Year, mooncakes during the Moon Festival, and Christmas cards or whiskey during the Christmas holidays. To emphasize the "cultural connection," teenage gang members sometimes add embellishments. For example, during one Chinese New Year, a teenage gang presented a merchant with a New Year card and asked him to pay $180, adding that he would prosper during the entire coming year because the first digit denotes "one whole year" and the second digit is pronounced the same as the word "prosperity" in Cantonese.

"Theft" of goods and services involves the practice of gang members refusing to pay for or asking for heavy discounts on goods and services. In the Chinese community, this practice is called *saik pa wong fun* (eating the king's meal) or *tai pa wong hey* (watching the king's movie), with the perpetrator as the king who cannot be refused. This is essentially a power play, with the perpetrator's material gain only secondary to the symbolic meaning it conveys. However, by construing the interaction between the offender and the victim in the traditional Chinese practice of "reciprocal face-giving behavior," the interaction is normalized. The targets of this practice are usually owners of restaurants, bakery shops, barber shops, video rental stores, and other small retail businesses such as groceries and optical stores.

Young gang members who have grown up learning the traditional uses of these Chinese customs are introduced to their new functions in business intimidation by older gang members, including adults who themselves have adopted these practices from Hong Kong and Taiwan. The new applications of these traditional Chinese customs are taught through a combination of didactic instruction and modeling. Adherence is maintained through reinforcement and sanctions. Such socialization contrasts with what Moore and Vigil (1989) have reported about Chicano gangs. These investigators have argued that Chicano gangs do not promote crime but help with normal adolescent concerns around security, respect, and peer approval. In addition, they offer gender role identification and support, frequently providing street-culture role models when none are available at home, and helping the youth in managing identity conflicts (Vigil, 1988). These gang functions might also be true of other Asian American gangs and even of the one studied by Chin et al. (1992) but in the latter, tutoring in the subversion of cultural practices for ends that may be considered criminal also occurs.

Youth gangs from ethnic groups other than Asian American may also engage in the practice of business intimidation and in the specific types of gang victimization found by Chin et al. (1992). However, their modus operandi may differ from that of Asian American youth. The results of the Chin et al. study suggests that an exploration of what lies behind surface similarities in antisocial behavior will reveal culture-specific origins that are of interest to researchers seeking to understand how culture influences the expression of psychopathology. Such cultural variations may not greatly affect diagnosis or prevalence rates based on a particular nosology, but they may have implications for intervention.

CULTURAL DIVERSITY IN PREVALENCE RATES

A review of research on cross-cultural or ethnic differences in psychopathology is an appropriate starting point for examining the role of culture in psychopathology. Although any obtained cross-cultural or ethnic differences may be related to factors other than culture (e.g., socioeconomic status, a country's level of economic development), their presence at least suggests that further investigation might reveal biologically based predispositions associated with race or cultural influences among the etiological factors. Cross-cultural or ethnic differences might be manifest in symptom features or patterns of symptom organization; differences in prevalence rates for specific disorders may be due to culturally related differences in definitions of problem behavior, help-seeking patterns, child-rearing practices, or risk and protective factors. Evidence for both types of manifestation are reviewed next.

Cross-Cultural Differences in Prevalence Rates

Prevalence refers to presence or absence of a symptom or a disorder in a population. Prevalence rate or estimate denotes the proportion of individuals in a population who manifest a particular symptom, symptom cluster, or disorder at a given point in time (Verhulst & Koot, 1992). Differences in prevalence rates of a particular symptom or disorder in two or more population groups may reflect underlying differences between these groups. One of those differences could be an aspect of culture. For example, cross-cultural differences in prevalence rates in a particular symptom or behavior might reflect culturally-based attitudes or modes of responding toward it. The assessment of prevalence rates is a commonly used approach in cross-cultural research on psychopathology. Findings from recent research are reviewed.

Symptomatology

In one of the early cross-cultural studies on psychological problems, M. C. Lambert, Weisz, and Knight (1989) found differences between American and Jamaican reports of children's behaviors reflecting overcontrol versus undercontrol. Problems relating to overcontrol were reported significantly more often for Jamaican youngsters, a finding that was interpreted as consistent with Afro-British Jamaican cultural attitudes and practices that discourage child aggression and other uncontrolled behavior and that foster inhibition and other overcontrolled behavior. The classification of children's behaviors as overcontrolled or undercontrolled has proven to be a useful organizing principle in programmatic cross-cultural research on children's psychological problems for Weisz and his collaborators (M. C. Lambert et al., 1992; Weisz & Sigman, 1993; Weisz et al., 1997).

Achenbach and Edelbrock (1981) also conceptualized children's problems around the issue of behavioral control, specifically as externalizing or internalizing behaviors. The largest number of recent cross-cultural studies on this topic have employed the Child Behavior Checklist (CBCL; Achenbach, 1991a, 1991b) and Youth Self-Report (YSR; Achenbach, 1991c) or translations of these measures. Most studies compared children from two cultures. From a review of published studies, Verhulst and Achenbach (1995) concluded that although some significant differences in problem scores did emerge from studies comparing two cultures, there was a relatively small range of scores derived from administering the CBCL in 11 cultures and its other versions, the Teacher Report Form (TRF; Achenbach & Edelbrock, 1986) in 6 cultures, and the YSR in 3 cultures. Furthermore, there were no significant cross-cultural differences in cross-informant correlations between CBCL, TRF, and YSR scores.

To extend the analyses beyond comparisons of two cultures and achieve a broader, integrated view of children's externalizing and internalizing problems across a greater number of cultures, Crijnen, Achenbach, and Verhulst (1997) conducted an analysis using "omnicultural composites" (Ellis & Kimmel, 1992) derived from CBCL, TRF, and YSR scores collected in the Commonwealth of Puerto Rico and 11 countries (Australia, Belgium, China, Germany, Greece, Israel, Jamaica, the Netherlands, Sweden, Thailand, and the United States). This analysis permitted a test of cross-cultural variations in Total Problem, External-

izing, and Internalizing scores. The results showed significant effects for culture and gender on Total Problem scores from the 12 cultures. Age or interaction effects were not significant. Scores of participants from Puerto Rico, Greece, and China were significantly above the omnicultural mean, whereas those of their peers from Sweden, Israel, Germany, Australia, the Netherlands, and Belgium were significantly below. Boys had higher scores than girls. Culture, but not gender, was also found to have an effect on Total Problem scores of adolescents from 9 cultures. Puerto Rican adolescents had the highest score, and their Swedish counterparts had the lowest. Culture, gender, and age had significant effects on both Externalizing and Internalizing scores, but interactions did not reach significance. For both types of problems, Greek and Puerto Rican participants had scores significantly above the omnicultural mean compared to their Swedish, Dutch, Australian, and Israeli peers, whose scores fell significantly below. Further analyses comparing Externalizing and Internalizing problems revealed small but significant cross-cultural variations, although this finding is qualified because of significant interactions between culture and gender in the analysis of scores from 12 cultures and between culture, gender, and age in the analysis of scores from 9 cultures. Age and gender variations showed cross-cultural consistency. With increasing age, Total Problem and Externalizing scores decreased, whereas Internalizing scores increased; boys had higher Total Problem and Externalizing scores but lower Internalizing scores than girls. Finally, cross-cultural correlations were high among mean item scores. Crijnen et al. are inclined to attribute the cross-cultural variations found to methodological issues, but they do acknowledge that some cultural differences in the relationship between Externalizing and Internalizing scores, as revealed by interactions between culture and age, might possibly reflect differences in how cultures deal with Externalizing problem behavior.

They also note that despite variations among the 12 cultures in the distinctions they make between masculine and feminine roles (Hofstede, 1994), there were consistent gender differences in parent-reported Externalizing and Internalizing problems. Crijnen et al. (1997) hypothesize that this gender difference might represent a "cultural universal" (Berry et al., 1982, cited in Crijnen, 1997).

Cross-cultural comparisons of CBCL factor structure have yielded either similarities (deGroot, Koot, & Verhulst, 1994) or mixed results (Hartman et al., 1999). However, more cross-cultural differences than similarities were found in a study that compared clinic-referred children from two cultures (American and Thai) differing along multiple dimensions and that used parallel measures valid for each culture, the CBCL and Thai Youth Checklist (Weisz et al., 1987). In this study, a few syndromes (e.g., somatic problems) showed concordance across cultures, but more did not. Cross-cultural differences have been reported for both broadband and narrowband syndromes (Weisz, Weiss, Suwanlert, & Chaiyasit, 2003).

Apart from research examining the externalizing-internalizing dimension, recent cross-cultural studies of symptomatology in children and adolescents have focused on symptoms denoting anxiety. Cross-cultural studies of anxiety in children have largely been driven by attempts to establish the cross-cultural validity of certain measures. In general, the results of these studies show that certain developmentally linked fears, such as a fear of loud noises or of being separated from the primary caregiver, occur in children from many cultures and at about the same age. Furthermore, the pattern and content of fears in children from different cultures vary as a function of gender. English or translated versions of the 80-item Fear Survey Schedule for Children-Revised (FSSC-R; Ollendick, 1983a, 1983b) have been administered to children in several countries. These include, besides the United States, Australia, China, Italy, the Netherlands, Northern Ireland, Portugal, Turkey, and the United Kingdom. In a review of these studies, Fonseca, Yule, and Erol (1994) found generally comparable results across countries, except for the score on Total Fear. Scores on Total Fear were lower for the Dutch sample and higher for the Portuguese sample. The observed difference in Total Fear scores between Dutch and Portuguese children has been interpreted as possibly reflecting Nordic and Latin cultural differences in emotional expression and control. Caution about this interpretation is warranted, though, because a gradation of Total Fear scores along the Nordic-Latin dimension was not observed among the various samples. Gender differences were also observed across countries. A content analysis showed both commonality and diversity in children's fears. Among American, Australian, British, Portuguese, and Turkish children, the most frequently endorsed fear was being hit by a car. For children from at least four of those countries, fears of not being able to breathe, a bomb attack or war, fire, a burglar, falling from a height, and death were among the top 10 fears. In at least three countries (Portugal, Turkey, United Kingdom), several items appended to the original 80-item FSSC-R revealed that many children reported fear of a parent's death, with endorsements ranging from 73% to 84%.

There are also ongoing attempts to validate the State Trait Anxiety Inventory for Children (STAIC; Spielberger,

Diaz-Guerrero, & Strelan, 1990). One study (Ahlawat, 1986) yielded similar factor structures between the original STAIC and an Arabic version. Test anxiety has also been examined cross-culturally, using the Test Anxiety Scale for Children (Sarason, Davidson, Lightfall, Waite, & Ruebush, 1960). In a sample comparing children from Chile and the United States, the Chilean students scored higher on test anxiety than the American students (Guida & Ludlow, 1989). Cross-cultural studies of depressive symptomatology in children and adolescents involving countries other than the United States and those in Europe are rare.

Categorical Diagnoses

The *Diagnostic and Statistical Manual of Mental Disorders,* fourth edition, text revision (*DSM-IV-TR;* American Psychiatric Association, 2000), considers the possibility that some mental disorders are culture-bound or specific to certain cultures. Examples of these are *Ataque de Nervios, Susto,* and *Mal Puesto* among Hispanics, *Hwa-Byung* among Koreans, *Taijin Kyofusho* among Japanese, *Koro* among Chinese, and *Voodoo death* among those of African descent. These culture-bound syndromes have been identified in adults. A review of their occurrence in children and adolescents is not possible because relatively little is known of their manifestations in these age groups. Instead, our review concentrates on the prevalence of those disorders for which cross-cultural data from child and/or adolescent samples are available.

A primary goal of many cross-cultural studies that have assessed prevalence rates for different mental disorders is to establish the universality of a disorder or at least to determine if a specific disorder can be identified in two or more countries using the same diagnostic criteria. Cross-cultural research on Autism falls into this category. After reviewing epidemiological studies conducted in several countries, including Canada, England, Iceland, Japan, and Sweden, and brief reports from some countries in Eastern Europe, Klinger, Dawson, and Renner (2003, p. 429) concluded that there is "remarkable consistency in reports of autistic symptomatology, intellectual abilities, and gender differences, and socioeconomic factors associated with autism."

Attention-Deficit/Hyperactivity Disorder (ADHD) is another disorder that has been identified in different countries (Barkley, 2003), albeit with varying prevalence rates. These prevalence rates range from as low as 2% in Japan (Kanbayashi, Nakata, Fujii, Kita, & Wada, 1994) to 20% for boys in Italy (O'Leary, Vivian, & Nisi, 1985), and even as high as 29% for boys in India (Bhata, Nigam, Bohra, & Malik, 1991). These differences in prevalence rates might be a function of differences in diagnostic criteria, sample characteristics, or measures, but such wide variations also raise the question of whether these cross-cultural variations in ADHD prevalence rates reflect differing cultural attitudes and responses toward the behavioral indices of the disorder. Bird (2002) makes the same points in a recent review of epidemiological studies carried out in different cultural settings around the world, including North America (United States, Canada), Great Britain and several other countries in Western Europe, the Asia/Pacific Rim (China, India, Japan, New Zealand), Brazil in South America, and Puerto Rico in the Caribbean. There was remarkable similarity in the pattern of behaviors characteristic of the syndrome, but prevalence rates varied, ranging from as low as 1% to as high as 20%. Bird is more inclined to attribute these variations in rate to differences in the diagnostic system used, methods of ascertainment, and other methodological artifacts rather than culture. He concluded that although ADHD is conceptualized in similar ways in different cultures, differences in rates occur because of an informant effect produced by culturally based differences in the threshold deviance, among both clinicians and other informants. Although Bird does not think so, the differences in the diagnostic system used and the methods of ascertainment may themselves be illustrative of cultural differences.

Anxiety Disorders have also been examined recently in several countries. In community samples, prevalence rates for Obsessive-Compulsive Disorder (OCD) range from 3% for clinical OCD (Valleni-Basile et al., 1994), 4% in community samples of adolescents in Italy (Maggini, Ampollini, Garibaldi, Cella, Peqlizza, & Marchesi, 2001) and older adolescents in Israel (Zohar et al., 1992), and 19% for subclinical OCD (Valleni-Basile et al., 1994). Rates for Simple/Specific Phobia include a lifetime prevalence of 3.5% among adolescents in Germany (Essau, Conradt, & Petermann, 2000) to a 6-month prevalence rate of 9.2% in Dutch adolescents (Verhulst, van der Ende, Ferdinand, & Kasius, 1997). The Dutch sample also yielded a higher rate (6.3%) of Social Phobia than the 1.1% found in a New Zealand sample (McGee, Feehan, Williams, & Partridge, 1990). In addition, a lifetime prevalence rate of 1% for Panic Disorder was found among the Dutch adolescents (Verhulst et al., 1997).

The paucity of cross-cultural research on depressive symptomatology is also true for research on mood disorders in children and adolescents, despite the fact that both have been studied extensively in adults from a cross-cultural perspective. In this respect, cross-cultural research on childhood depression parallels that on childhood Schizophrenia.

Potentially, cross-cultural research has the most to offer for understanding the relationship between culture and psychopathology. The comparative studies reviewed here show that a conceptualization of problem behaviors along the externalizing-internalizing dimension can be employed usefully in different cultures. Furthermore, they reveal that certain mental disorders, notably Autism, ADHD, and Anxiety Disorders can be identified in several cultures, albeit with some variation in prevalence rates. In other words, they provide information about the occurrence and frequency of symptomatology or disorder. They also demonstrate the consistency of a gender difference in pattern and content of symptomatology. Whether this gender difference is culturally based has yet to be determined. Last, they indicate that certain categories of the *DSM* nosology (e.g., Autism) and certain measures developed for American samples (e.g., CBCL, FSSC-R) can be successfully used in other cultures. Beyond these, the findings do not offer much more toward elucidating cultural influences on psychopathology. One reason is that most of these studies were not designed to explore cultural influences but to test the cross-cultural generalizability of a particular conceptualization of psychopathology or to test the usefulness of a specific measure in other cultures. In addition, methodological variations in data collection from several cultures may be confounded with cross-cultural variations, thus making it difficult to arrive at any conclusions regarding cultural influences (e.g., Crijnen et al., 1997). This difficulty can be overcome in future cross-cultural studies through the use of similar sampling techniques and other data collection methods across sites. Another possible reason is that the studies reviewed employed an etic approach, applying concepts and measures derived from one culture to another culture presumably different from the first. The term, *etic,* refers to concepts and methodologies that are universal whereas the term, *emic* applies to those that are group-specific or culture-specific. Berry (1969) distinguished two types of etic: an *imposed etic* when universality is assumed and a *derived etic* when universality has been demonstrated by research. Often, the culturally based rationale for the cross-cultural comparison was not clearly articulated. Furthermore, except for a few studies that added items to the FSSC-R, little was done beyond translations to modify or add measures that might reveal cultural differences. To date, cross-cultural research on psychopathology may be characterized as a search for universals or, at least, for cross-cultural validity of nosology and measures.

Preliminary studies using an emic approach or the combined use of emic and etic approaches might prove more illuminating about the role of culture in psychopathology.

For example, because items on a measure may already represent one level of abstraction from a set of behaviors, different sets of behaviors may underlie an identical response from respondents in different cultures. This implies that direct observations, one-to-one interviews, and focused groups may be needed, along with standardized tests, to detect cultural influences. Moreover, where cross-cultural variations in patterns of symptomatology or prevalence rates did emerge, there were few efforts to examine possible cultural correlates or, at least, the cultural lens through which behavior was viewed that produced differences in rates. Obtained prevalence rates reflect the child's actual behavior and the lens through which it is viewed by others within the same culture (Weisz et al., 2003). In sum, this set of studies accomplished an important first step toward understanding the role of culture in psychopathology. Epidemiological studies and measurement construction are necessary, but not sufficient. Other, more critical steps have yet to be taken.

Ethnic Differences in Prevalence Rates

Empirical studies on ethnic differences in symptomatology and psychiatric disorders among American ethnic minority children and youth have increased in recent years, although still far fewer than the number of studies on European American children or even ethnic minority college students and older adults. The samples used in these studies are also larger in size, no longer limited to convenience samples, and even include probability samples. The available studies have been conducted mainly among the four major ethnic minority groups: African Americans, Asian Americans and Pacific Islanders, Hispanics or Latinos, and Native Americans. Before proceeding with this review of recent empirical studies involving these four ethnic minority groups, it should be mentioned that there are two other important potential sources of scientific data on cultural influences on adaptation, development, and psychopathology. One is the excellent programmatic research on psychopathology among Puerto Ricans residing in Puerto Rico (and therefore not considered an American ethnic minority group) conducted by Bird, Canino, and their colleagues (e.g., Canino et al., 2004). This review will not attempt a thorough coverage of their work but does review those studies that included Island Puerto Ricans in a study of mainland Puerto Ricans and other American ethnic minority groups. The other source is the emerging body of empirical studies on newly arrived immigrant and refugee ethnic groups from Eastern Europe and the former Soviet Union and from several African countries (e.g., Birman, 2005). Relatively

few of the latter have focused on prevalence rates for different kinds of symptomatology or categories of psychiatric disorders, so they will not be reviewed here. In the future, studies of these newly arrived ethnic groups will broaden our scientific database on cultural influences on development and psychopathology.

The preceding review of cross-cultural research on psychiatric symptomatology in children and adolescents suggests that in many cultures, psychological problems can be usefully organized along the externalizing-internalizing dimension, so our review of ethnic differences in psychopathology will be organized likewise. Also, for the sake of coherence, our review is limited to those few disorders that have received the most attention, resulting in a cluster of related studies: Conduct Disorder and substance use/abuse among the externalizing disorders and Anxiety Disorders and depression among the internalizing disorders. For each of these topics, the presentation begins with ethnic differences in symptomatology, followed by ethnic differences in disorders and, if available, data on comorbidity. Then data from noncomparative studies (i.e., studies that looked at only one ethnic minority group) that are consistent or inconsistent with the observed differences are discussed. Within-group differences are examined when pertinent data are available. Finally, the course or development of the disorder is described, again depending on the availability of data. Also for each topic, findings concerning African Americans are presented first, followed by those for American Indians, Asian Americans/Pacific Islanders, and Latinos.

Externalizing Problems and Disorders

Behavior can be conceptualized along a continuous dimension ranging from covert to overt, internal to external, or inhibition to action. Following this view of behavior, problem behaviors can be classified as externalizing or internalizing problems or syndromes. This dimensional approach to the classification of problem behaviors has received strong empirical support, most notably from research conducted by Achenbach and his collaborators (e.g., Achenbach & Edelbrock, 1981; Achenbach, Howell, Quay, & Conners, 1991). Externalizing problems refer to problem behaviors that involved acting out or under-controlled behavior such as aggression, anti-social behaviors, and opposition. Correspondingly, disorders characterized by symptoms that are externalizing problems are considered externalizing disorders. In this section, we chose to review two externalizing problems and disorders for whom prevalence rates from epidemiological studies are available: conduct problems and disorders, as well as substance use and substance-related disorders. Because there are many studies of substance use and substance-related disorders, our review is limited to those that studied American Indians because these topics seem to have been investigated proportionately more than any other mental health-related topic in this population and the number of available studies allowed for a more comprehensive view of the problem and its progression.

Conduct Problems

According to Elliott, Huizinga, and Ageton (1985), minority status is associated with antisocial behavior in the United States, with elevated rates of antisocial behavior in African Americans, Latino Americans, and Native Americans. Conduct problems, particularly antisocial behaviors and substance use, of ethnic minority children and youth have received a great deal of attention from researchers. However, although many of the studies included large numbers of ethnic minority participants (e.g., African Americans), ethnicity was not included as a variable in the data analyses. Among those that were specifically interested in ethnic differences, several early studies employing community or clinical samples of children and/or adolescents have yielded some ethnic differences in symptomatology (e.g., Costello, 1989; Velez, Johnson, & Cohen, 1989). However, studies that controlled for sex, age, socioeconomic status (SES), or referral status, particularly those employing large national samples, revealed few or no ethnic differences in antisocial behavior among European, African, and Latino American children (Achenbach & Edelbrock, 1981; Achenbach, Howell, Quay, & Conners, 1991; Lahey et al., 1995).

Conduct Disorders

Data from the Methods for the Epidemiology of Child and Adolescent Mental Disorders (MECA) study (Lahey et al., 1996; D. Shaffer et al., 1996) were used by Bird et al. (2001) to determine the prevalence of Conduct Disorder (CD), Oppositional Defiant Disorder (ODD), and various levels of antisocial behavior, as well as their correlates, in three ethnic groups: Latinos, subdivided into Island Puerto Ricans and Mainland Latinos, African Americans, and Mainland non-Latino, non-African Americans. All groups were representative samples of four geographically and ethnically diverse communities. The prevalence rate for CD was significantly lower in the Island Puerto Rican sample than in the African American sample. Significant differences in prevalence rates for ODD also emerged: The three ethnic groups on the mainland had higher rates than the Island Puerto Ricans. Bird et al. (2001) also examined the preva-

lence rates for five levels of antisocial behavior representing a hierarchy of seriousness/severity. Again, the three mainland ethnic groups showed higher rates than the Island Puerto Ricans, specifically for level 3 (e.g., lying, disobedience) and level 4 (e.g., damaging property, attacking someone). At first glance, these lower prevalence rates for CD, ODD, and levels of antisocial behaviors seem inconsistent with the Crijnen et al. (1997) finding that among children from 12 cultures, Island Puerto Ricans showed the highest prevalence rate for Externalizing scores. Methodological differences, particularly in sampling, measures, testing procedure, and translation, may largely account for the apparent inconsistency.

Substance Use

Surveys of large samples have yielded reliable information about substance use among American Indians. Plunkett and Mitchell (2000) compared reports on substance use obtained from American Indian high school seniors who participated in the Voices of Indian Teens study (1993, as cited in Plunkett & Mitchell, 2000) with those from non-Indian high school seniors who participated in the Monitoring the Future study (Johnston, O'Malley, & Bachman, 2000, 2001). They found that lifetime substance use among American Indian youth was significantly higher than that of non-American Indian youth for two substances, marijuana and cocaine, whereas non-American Indian youth had significantly higher lifetime use of inhalants and cigarettes. Furthermore, American Indian youth reported significantly higher 30-day use for five (marijuana, cocaine, stimulants, alcohol, and barbiturates) of seven substances assessed than did their non-American Indian peers.

Within-group differences in substance use among American Indians may exist. A study of psychological adjustment among American Indians (Gray & Winterowd, 2002) showed that American Indian students residing in a rural but nonreservation area reported average or below-average levels of health risks, including substance use. However, this study did not include a control group, so it merely suggests a hypothesis that has still to be verified in a study with a better research design. Within-group differences in substance use as a function of region have also been reported for American Indian youth. Plunkett and Mitchell (2000) performed a geographic analysis of their data on substance use from American Indian and non-American Indian teens. This analysis revealed regional variations in patterns of substance use: American Indian youth reported significantly higher rates of more lifetime substance use items in one region; in another region, it was non-American Indian youth who reported significantly higher lifetime substance use. Controlling for region, American Indian youth rates were significantly higher on only three of the seven substances.

A more comprehensive picture of American Indian youth use of substances, with implications for developmental psychopathology, is provided by a study of trends in drug use among American Indian adolescents attending schools on or near Indian reservations in the United States (Beauvais, Jumper-Thurman, Helm, Plested, & Burnside, 2004). Using data from reliable and valid school-administered drug use surveys given every year for 25 years (1975–2000) to representative samples of Indian youth living on reservation and data from non-Indian youth participating in the Monitoring the Future study, Beauvais et al. compared the two groups on lifetime prevalence, use in the past 30 days, and proportions at high risk and at moderate risk and subjected the differences to proportion tests. They found that, in comparison to non-Indian youth, the reservation Indian youth had elevated levels of drug use for most illicit drugs from 1975 to 2000. However, the trends showing increases and decreases over time were similar for the two groups. A comparison of trends among those who engaged in moderate and high use showed that the number of youth in the moderate category varied over time, whereas the number in the high category remained relatively constant.

The sequence of substances used by American Indian adolescents has also been studied. Novins, Beals, and Mitchell (2001) reported that the predominant sequential pattern of use of different classes of substance among a large sample of American Indian adolescents is consistent with a stage theory that was proposed for other ethnic groups. According to this theory, adolescents start with alcohol, then use marijuana, then other illicit drugs, and progress to the use of cocaine. A survey of 1,562 high school students in 1993 (Novins et al., 2001) revealed that 35% of the participants who were using alcohol and marijuana reported using alcohol first, a sequence consistent with stage theory. However, 75% of youth who had used three or more substances reported a sequence of first use that was inconsistent with stage theory. Thus, although overall, a general pattern of using alcohol, marijuana, and/or inhalants prior to the use of cocaine and other illicit drugs emerged, it also appears that alcohol, marijuana, and inhalants are all initiating substances for American Indian youth. Variations in the sequences of first use were a function of gender, age of first substance use, community, and number of classes of substances use. In another study, Novins and Baron (2004) assessed the risk of substance use and progression of substance use in American Indian adolescents ages 14 to 20 years who participated in two or more consecutive waves of a longitudinal study conducted between 1993 and 1996. They found that the risk for initiating use of any substance accelerated in early adolescence and peaked at age 18. The risk for progression from use of alcohol, marijuana, and/or inhalants to the use of other illicit drugs (e.g., cocaine) increased over the first 4.5 years after initiating substance use, then diminished in subsequent years. Adolescents who initiated substance use with marijuana or inhalants were more likely to progress to other illicit drugs than their peers who initiated substance use with alcohol. Novins and Baron also reported that the risk of substance use initiation and progression varied across the four participating communities and by the season of the year.

Substance-Related Disorders

Using the Diagnostic Interview Schedule for Children (DISC) Version 2.1C (Shaffer et al., 1988 as cited in Beals et al., 1997) and following criteria in the *Diagnostic and Statistical Manual,* third edition, revised (*DSM-III-R;* American Psychiatric Association, 1987), Beals et al. (1997) assessed the prevalence of psychiatric disorders among 109 American Indian adolescents, *M* age = 15.6 years, living in a Northern Plains community. Prevalence rates were reported based on the diagnosis-specific impairment criteria. The use of such criteria, they argue, is a step toward cultural validity because it places the symptoms in an environmental context and it more closely approximates the clinical diagnostic process in which the clinician incorporates multiple factors (including degree of impairment and culture) into the assessment. Twenty-nine percent (29.4%) of the sample received a diagnosis of at least one psychiatric disorder, 16.5% qualified for a single diagnosis, and 12.9% met criteria for comorbid disorders. Those diagnosed for substance use disorders made up the largest group (18.3%), followed by those diagnosed for one or more of the disruptive behavior disorders. Alcohol dependence/abuse, marijuana dependence/abuse, and substance dependence/abuse ranked among the five most common specific disorders. Comorbidity was not uncommon: More than half of those with a disruptive behavior disorder also qualified for a substance use disorder, and more than half of those with depressive disorders had a substance use disorder.

Beals et al. (1997) did not include a comparison sample in their study, but they compared their data with those obtained in previous studies (Lewinsohn, Hops, Roberts, Seeley, & Andrews, 1993; Shaffer et al., 1996) whose participants represented other groups, including European Americans. When compared to the adolescents in the

MECA study (D. Shaffer et al., 1996), American Indian adolescents exhibited substance use/dependence disorders. Similarly, when compared to the adolescents studied by Lewinsohn et al., they demonstrated statistically significantly higher 6-month prevalence rates for lifetime prevalence of alcohol abuse/dependence disorder. In addition, the American Indian sample had a significantly higher rate of comorbidity between substance use disorders and disruptive behavior disorders.

Costello, Farmer, Angold, Burns, and Erkanli (1997) examined the 3-month prevalence of *DSM-III-R* psychiatric disorders, the social and family risk factors for these disorders, and met and unmet needs for mental health care in a representative sample of European American and American Indian children ages 9, 11, and 13 years living in southern Appalachia. They found that American Indian children had a slightly lower overall prevalence of psychiatric disorders than the European Americans, an ethnic difference that, according to the investigators, was largely accounted for by different rates of tic disorders in 9-year-old boys. They also reported an ethnic difference in substance use. Although substance use was low in both ethnic groups, at 13 years of age, significantly more American Indian than European American children reported recent use of alcohol. Furthermore, comorbidity of substance use and psychiatric disorder was higher in the American Indian sample. Comorbidity among American Indian youths (ages 13 to 18 years) identified as having a substance abuse disorder has also been reported by Fisckenscher and Novins (2003). They found that 74% of 89 American Indian adolescents receiving treatment for substance abuse also met full *DSM-IV* criteria for Conduct Disorder based on their responses to the Diagnostic Interview Schedule for Children, Youth Version, and the Composite International Diagnostic Interview. Conduct Disorder was common among both boys and girls in this sample of American Indian adolescents, but the specific antisocial behaviors displayed and the relationships to other psychiatric disorders varied by gender.

Despite the use of different methodologies, both the Beals et al. (1997) and the Costello et al. (1997) studies indicate that American Indian adolescents engage in higher rates of substance use and exhibit higher rates of psychiatric comorbidity. This ethnic difference is present at 13 years of age (Costello et al., 1997) and is also manifest in 15-year-olds (Beals et al., 1997). These findings from different samples suggest that once substance-related disorders emerge in early adolescence, they may persist and remain relatively stable in subsequent years. A prospective longitudinal study could verify this or reveal other devel-

opmental trends. Survey data on trends in drug use among American Indian youth show that there is a decrease in late adolescence and young adulthood, but this may not be the case for those whose substance use during early and/or middle adolescence is severe enough to meet the criteria for a *DSM-IV* substance-related disorder.

Internalizing Symptoms and Disorders

Internalizing problems are those problem behaviors that reflect internal distress that is not directly expressed in overt action but indirectly through social withdrawal, anxiety, somatic complaints, or depressed mood. Internalizing disorders are those disorders whose primary symptoms consist of internalizing problem behaviors including the different anxiety disorders, posttraumatic stress disorders, and mood disorders. Most studies of internalizing symptoms or disorders among ethnic minority children and adolescents deal with anxiety symptomatology or disorders and, to a lesser extent, with depressive symptomatology or unipolar depression.

Anxiety Symptoms

As was the case in cross-cultural research, symptoms denoting anxiety in ethnic minority children and youth have received a relatively large share of researchers' attention. Ethnic differences in fear or anxiety have been found in several studies, suggesting that ethnicity or a factor related to ethnic membership is associated with reported levels of fear or anxiety. In a study of a clinical sample, Last and Perrin (1993) found that African American children tended to score higher than their European American peers on the FSSC-R (Ollendick, 1983a, 1983b). Neal, Lilly, and Zakis (1993) also used the FSSC-R to assess the change and stability in the fears of African American children from primarily working-class and low-income families and their European American counterparts. Overall, the children's reported fears were relatively stable over a 2-week period, but African American children's fears were less stable than those of their European American peers. Follow-up assessments (Neal & Knisley, 1995) did not reveal ethnic differences in the rank order that children assigned to their fears; across ethnicity, sex, and grade, the top-ranked fears were those involving possible harm to self or others. Neal and Knisley did not report any ethnic differences in total mean FSSC-R scores across the three assessments. However, they did note that correlational analysis of FSSC-R scores over time showed a significant difference in the stability coefficients of African American and European American children from the original to the 12-month assessment. Over 12 months, African American children's total fear scores showed greater stability than European American children's. The stability of total fear scores also varied as a function of sex and time of reassessment. Boys' total fear scores were more stable than those of girls, but only from the original to the 5-month assessment. For boys, the mean total fear scores decreased after a 5-month interval from the first assessment but increased from the 5-month to the 12-month administration. For girls, the mean total fear scores decreased from the original to the 5-month administration but remained essentially the same from the 5-month to the 12-month assessment. Stability also varied as a function of grade. For younger children, the mean total fear score decreased from the original to the 5-month administration and increased from the 5-month to the 12-month assessment. For older children, mean total fear score decreased from the original to the 5-month assessment but remained relatively the same from the 5- to the 12-month administration.

Data on anxiety sensitivity in African American children come from a study by S. F. Lambert, Cooley, Campbell, Benoit, and Stansbury (2004) that examined the psychometric properties of the Children's Anxiety Sensitivity Index (CASI; Silverman, Fleisig, Rabian, & Peterson, 1991) in a sample of African American children in grades 4 and 5. Because the aim of the study was to assess the psychometric properties of the CASI, there was no comparison group, but results of prior studies provided some basis for comparison. The mean level of anxiety sensitivity among African American children in the S. F. Lambert, Cooley, et al. sample was higher than that found in European American children by Silverman et al. (1991) and among African American adolescents examined by Ginsburg and Drake (2002). However, anxiety level was comparable to that obtained by Rabian, Embry, and McIntyre (1999) in an ethnically diverse community sample (64% African American). Unlike in previous studies of African American adolescents (Ginsburg & Drake, 2002; White & Farrell, 2001), no sex differences were found by S. F. Lambert, Cooley, et al. The lack of sex differences may be due to differences in age, socialization, and/or context.

Some differences in anxiety symptomatology have been found between European American and Asian American children. Shore and Rapport (1998) examined the structure and developmental pattern of fearfulness in an ethnoculturally diverse sample of 385 children, ages 7 to 16 years, living in Hawaii. They reported a significant effect for ethnicity on FSSC-R scores. None of the interactions was significant. Between-group comparisons showed that European American children were less fearful than children from Asian (i.e., of East Asian descent, such as Chinese and Japanese Americans), Filipino, and Hawaiian backgrounds. They had significantly lower FSSC-R Total scores than Asian Americans, Filipino Americans, and Native Hawaiian children. Specific subscale scores also differed significantly among the ethnic groups. European Americans scored lower than Asian Americans, Filipino Americans, and Native Hawaiians on all seven subscales, but only some of these subscale ethnic differences were significant. European Americans' subscale scores on fears of danger, death, and animals differed significantly from those of Native Hawaiians and Asian Americans but not in comparison to those of Filipino Americans. European Americans also did not differ significantly from Native Hawaiians in Anticipatory Social Fears scores. Filipino Americans had significantly higher scores on Anticipatory Social Fears than all the other groups. Consistent with earlier findings, fearfulness, whether indexed by total scores or prevalence scores, was greater in girls than in boys. On both indices, younger children also demonstrated more fearfulness than older ones.

Some ethnic differences between European American children and adolescents and their Latino counterparts have also been reported. Using a Spanish translation of the Revised Children's Manifest Anxiety Scale (RCMAS; Reynolds & Richmond, 1978) deemed culturally sensitive, Varela et al. (2004) examined the reporting of anxiety symptoms among Mexican, Mexican American, and European American children ages 10 to 14 years ($M = 11.1$). As expected, Mexican and Mexican American children reported more physiological anxiety symptoms and more worry symptoms than European children. Mexican and Mexican American children did not differ in physiological symptoms or worry/sensitivity. A subsequent analysis that controlled for scores on the Lie scale, SES, and age of child yielded similar findings. Mexican children endorsed more items on the Lie scale of the RCMAS than did Mexican Americans and European Americans. The two American ethnic groups did not differ from one another on the Lie scale.

In one study, ethnic differences in anxiety symptomatology did not hold up after corrections for experiment wise error were applied. Pina and Silverman (2004) examined the clinical phenomenology, somatic symptoms, and perceptions of anxiety-related somatic/physiological symptoms as distressing among 6- to 17-year-old Latino and European American youth. Latino participants were either of Cuban descent or not. All participants had been administered the Anxiety Disorders Interview Schedule for Children and, based on *DSM-IV* criteria, received a primary diagnosis of Anxiety Disorder. The types of Anxiety Disorder differed; the most common was Separation Anxiety Disorder (SAD), followed by Specific Phobia, Generalized Anxiety Disorder, Social Phobia, and Panic Disorder. Preliminary analyses comparing Latinos and European Americans failed to yield significant differences in scores on the FSSC-R and STAIC but showed a significant ethnic difference in scores on the RCMAS, which disappeared in a subsequent analysis that applied Holm's modified Bonferoni correction. When the Latino sample was further subdivided into Cuban American and non-Cuban American, then compared with European Americans, significant differences in STAIC-T scores emerged, but these, too, did not hold up after Holm's modified Bonferoni correction was applied.

Pina and Silverman (2004) did find ethnic differences in somatic symptoms. These investigators used CBCL somatic T scores and RCMAS Physiological scale scores as indices of somatic symptoms. European Americans and Cuban Americans had significantly lower CBCL somatic T scores than the non-Cuban Americans, a difference that remained even after applying Holm's method. This difference also emerged in a subsequent analysis that included the parents' choice of language (English or Spanish) for the assessment. No significant differences in RCMAS Physiological scale scores were found initially, but when the Latino parents' preferred language for the assessment was included in a subsequent analysis, among the Latino youth whose parents chose English, the non-Cubans had higher RCMAS Physiological scale scores, a difference that disappeared after applying Holm's modified Bonferoni correction. The results of this study suggest that the CBCL may be better than the RCMAS at detecting ethnic differences in somatic symptoms. Pina and Silverman also examined parental reports of somatic symptoms. Parents of European American and Cuban American youths reported their offspring as having fewer somatic symptoms than did parents of non-Cuban American youth.

The degree to which anxiety-related somatic/physiological symptoms are found distressing or aversive by Latino versus European American youths was also investigated by Pina and Silverman (2004). It has been suggested that in addition to expressing distress and worry as somatic/physiological symptoms, Latino youth might at the same time be distressed further by the presence of this symptomatology. For example, a child who is experiencing anxiety-related somatic symptoms might say, "My stomach hurts so much, I worry that I might be very sick." According to Pina and

Silverman, the distress evoked by somatic symptoms is akin to the construct of anxiety sensitivity (Reiss, 1997) in the anxiety research literature. In their study, distress over anxiety-related somatic signs was operationalized as Total scores and Disease Concerns scale scores from the Childhood Anxiety Sensitivity Index (CASI; Silverman et al., 1991). European Americans reported significantly lower CASI Total scores and CASI Disease Concerns scores than non-Cuban American youths. Furthermore, exploratory analyses that included Latino parents' language choice as a variable showed that Cuban American youths whose parents chose to have the assessment administered in English reported significantly less distress associated with anxiety-related somatic/physiological symptoms than non-Cuban American or Latino youth whose parents chose the assessment in English. Among the Latino youth whose parents preferred the assessment in Spanish, Cuban Americans reported significantly more distress than non-Cuban Americans. These findings remained statistically significant even after correction for experiment wise error was applied.

Pina and Silverman's (2004) findings that Latino and European American youths with anxiety disorders differ significantly in terms of somatic/physiological symptoms and distress over these symptoms are consistent with those found in a community sample of adolescents (Weems, Hayward, Killen, & Taylor, 2002) and adults (Novy, Stanley, Averill, & Daza, 2001). Furthermore, they show that among Latino youths, anxiety-related somatic/physiological symptoms and the degree of distress associated with these symptoms vary as a function of ethnocultural group and parents' choice of language for their assessment.

In addition to showing ethnic differences in total and subscale scores on measures of anxiety symptomatology, studies have also revealed some ethnic differences in the structure or patterns of organization of anxiety. Whereas previous research with European American children had shown that the FSSC-R has five factors (e.g., Ollendick, Yule, & Ollier, 1991), an exploratory factor analysis on the data collected by Neal et al. (1993) revealed that a three-factor solution provided the best fit for the data from African American children. The three factors were (1) fear of death, danger, and small animals; (2) fear of the unknown and things that crawl; and (3) medical fears. An ethnic difference in the factor structure of the FSSC-R was also reported by Shore and Rapport (1998). These investigators revised the FSSC-R to make it suitable for children residing in Hawaii, then examined the reliability, validity, and factor structure of the revision, the Fear Survey Schedule for Children-Hawaii (FSSC-HI), and compared it to the FSSC-R and FSSC-II. They found that a seven-factor solution provided the best conceptual fit for the data; six factors were similar to those identified in earlier versions of the FSSC, but the seventh was not. This unique factor reflected children's social conformity fears.

An ethnic difference in the factor structure of the CASI has also been reported. Exploratory analysis of CASI data from African American children has yielded a different factor structure than that obtained from European American children by Silverman et al. (1991). S. F. Lambert, Cooley, et al. (2004) found that for the CASI data from their sample of African Americans, two factors, Physical Concerns and Mental Incapacitation, provided the best fit in a conceptually meaningful way, whereas Silverman et al. reported that a hierarchical structure with three or four first-order factors (Physical Concerns, Mental Incapacitation Concerns, Control, Social Concerns) best fit their CASI data. More recently, Silverman and her colleagues (Silverman, Goodhart, Barrett, & Turner, 2003) reported that a confirmatory analysis of CASI data from across several studies yielded support for a hierarchical model with a single second-order factor and four lower-order factors (Disease Concerns, Unsteady Concerns, Mental Illness Concerns, Social Concerns). These ethnic differences in factor structures suggest that culture influences not only the expression of anxieties, concerns, fears, and worries but also their cognitive patterns of organization.

Anxiety Disorders

Ethnic differences in Anxiety Disorders have also been explored. The evidence on ethnic differences in Anxiety Disorders between African American children or adolescents and their European American peers is mixed. An ethnic difference was found in one study that included relatively large community and clinical samples, but other studies using clinical samples only have found no evidence or limited evidence. In a study that included community ($n = 2,384$) and clinical ($n = 217$) samples, Compton, Nelson, and March (2000) found ethnic differences in the patterning of Anxiety Disorders that were consistent across the two samples despite the large sample size difference. In the community sample, both preadolescent and adolescent African Americans endorsed more symptoms of SAD and fewer symptoms of Social Phobia than their European American peers on the Multidimensional Anxiety Scale for Children. European Americans reported lower Separation Anxiety and higher Social Phobia. Similar results were obtained from the clinical sample.

Last and Perrin (1993) examined *DSM-III-R* Anxiety Disorders in a clinical sample of African and European American children. They did not find any ethnic group dif-

ferences in age, sex, duration of disorder, or lifetime history of Mood Disorder. However, there was a trend for African American children to report a history of Posttraumatic Stress Disorder, whereas European American children showed a trend toward more frequent reports of school refusal and higher diagnostic severity ratings. The investigators raised the possibility that the trend's failure to reach an acceptable level of statistical significance might have been due to the African American sample ($n = 30$) being much smaller than the European American one ($n = 139$). Beidel, Turner, and Morris (1999, 2000) compared African American and European American children with Social Phobia with respect to clinical presentation and treatment outcome. They found only one significant ethnic difference: European American children had higher scores on the Social Phobia and Anxiety Inventory for Children (SPAIC; Beidel, Turner, & Morris, 1995). Ferrell, Beidel, and Turner (2004), however, failed to find ethnic differences in Social Phobia and related symptoms (depression, loneliness, neuroticism, and state-trait anxiety), social skills, or social anxiety in a sample of 39 European American and 19 African American children referred for treatment of Social Phobia. With respect to diagnostic criteria and severity of the disorder, the two ethnic groups presented similar symptoms and degree of functional impairment. Both groups also showed significant improvement on self-report measures, parental reports, and clinician evaluations of Social Phobia and other aspects of psychopathology. Ethnic differences, however, were manifested in treatment outcomes, as indexed by clinical significance and responder status among the 29 children who completed treatment. At the end of treatment, 80% of the African American children but only 63% of their European American counterparts no longer met criteria for Social Phobia, a statistically significant difference. There was also an ethnic difference in treatment responders within the two groups, but in a direction opposite to that found for meeting Social Phobia criteria. Treatment responders were defined a priori as those meeting two criteria: posttreatment scores of less than 18 on the SPAIC and a rating of 8 or 9 on the Children's Global Assessment Scale (C-GAS; D. Shaffer et al., 1983), by an independent evaluator. Fifty-eight percent of European Americans met both criteria, whereas only 30% of African Americans did, a statistically significant difference. Because the two ethnic groups had virtually identical SPAIC scores, the observed ethnic difference was based primarily on C-GAS ratings by a clinician. The investigators suggested that the differential clinician ratings could be interpreted as indicating that the improvements shown by African Americans on the SPAIC were not yet reflected in their behaviors or that there was a difficulty in judging problem severity when the observer and the person being observed came from different ethnic backgrounds.

Few studies have examined Anxiety Disorders among American Indians. Costello et al. (1997) reported that SAD was the most common Anxiety Disorder for both American Indian and European American youths living in Appalachia. Although rates for SAD were slightly higher for American Indians, especially girls, they were really similar for the two groups.

The only data on Anxiety Disorders among Asian American children and adolescents come from studies that used the Revised Child Anxiety and Depression scale (RCADS; Chorpita, Yim, Moffitt, Unemoto, & Francis, 2000), which measures symptoms associated with *DSM-IV* criteria for Anxiety Disorders and depression. Each RCADS subscale comprises empirically derived items. The total scale yields an internally consistent factor structure that corresponds to *DSM-IV* criteria for Social Phobia, separation anxiety, Panic Disorder and Agoraphobia (PDA), OCD, Generalized Anxiety Disorder (GAD), and depression (Chorpita et al., 2000).

Within the framework of the tripartite model of anxiety and depression (Clark & Watson, 1991), Austin and Chorpita (2004) examined temperament, anxiety, and depression in five ethnic groups of children and adolescents residing in Hawaii. In general, the results supported the tripartite model, but significant mean-level differences among ethnic groups were found for several specific anxiety dimensions. Native Hawaiians scored significantly higher on separation anxiety than their Filipino, Japanese, and European American counterparts. Both Native Hawaiians and Filipino Americans scored significantly higher on PDA and OCD than both Japanese Americans and European Americans. In addition, Filipino Americans scored significantly higher on Social Phobia than did European Americans. Last, Chinese Americans scored significantly higher on Social Phobia than Native Hawaiians and Filipino Americans. The investigators also examined the percentage of each ethnic group with clinically elevated scores on each of the six subscales of the RCADS (Chorpita et al., 2000). The percentages of elevated scores on the GAD subscale were fairly similar among the ethnic groups, but they were more variable on the other anxiety subscales. On both PDA and Separation Anxiety, Native Hawaiians and Filipino Americans had significantly higher percentages of clinical elevation than Chinese Americans, Japanese Americans, and European Americans. Significant ethnic differences were not found for percentages of elevated scores on GAD, OCD, and Social Phobia. Austin and Chorpita interpreted these ethnic group differences in Anxiety Disorders as suggesting that factors outside of the tripartite model might explain the observed differences. Cultural norms and expectations might be one of those factors.

Data on Anxiety Disorders in Latino children comes from a study by Ginsburg and Silverman (1996), who compared Latino and European American youth ranging in age from 6 to 17 years. They found that Latino children were more likely to present with a primary diagnosis of SAD. Latino parents also rated their children as more fearful than did European American parents.

Depressive Symptomatology

Early research on ethnic differences in depressive symptomatology and mood disorders produced mixed results. As Roberts, Roberts, and Chen (1997) reported in their review of this literature, some studies reported that minority adolescents showed higher levels of depression and others found lower levels of depression (Doerfler, Felner, Rowling, Raley, & Evans, 1988). Still other studies found no ethnic differences at all (Kandel & Davies, 1982). Furthermore, variability among studies in the ethnicities sampled and the measures employed made it difficult to draw any firm conclusions from the findings.

Few studies have investigated depressive symptomatology in middle childhood among American ethnic minorities. Of those that did, a study of African and European American children in grades 3 to 5 revealed that a significant interaction between ethnicity and sex characterized the frequency of depressive symptoms (Kistner, David, & White, 2003). African American boys reported more depressive symptoms than European American boys, whereas the African American and European American girls had comparable levels. Sex differences in depression varied as a function of ethnicity. Among African Americans, boys were more depressed than girls, but among European Americans, girls were more depressed than boys.

The ethnic difference in depressive symptomatology noted during the third- through fifth-grade years may not necessarily persist in later years. D. A. Cole, Martin, Peeke, Henderson, and Harwell (1998) assessed depression and anxiety symptoms yearly in two cohorts of African Americans and European Americans from grades 3 to 5 and grades 6 to 8. African American children showed more symptoms of depression and anxiety in grades 3, 4, and 5 than did their European American peers. However, ethnic differences obtained from assessments conducted in grades 6, 7, and 8 did not reach a statistically significant level.

This finding raises the possibility that the role of ethnicity in depression may change over the years. Rushton, Forcier, and Schectman (2002) present some evidence suggesting that this may be the case. In an epidemiological study of depressive symptoms among adolescents who participated in the National Longitudinal Study of Adolescent Health, they found that ethnic minority youths (as well as females and older adolescents) were more likely to report depressive symptoms on the Center for Epidemiological Studies Depression Scale (CES-D; Radloff, 1977) than other participants at baseline, but race/ethnicity did not predict the manifestation of depressive symptoms 1 year later.

Perhaps different factors are associated with ethnic differences in depressive symptomatology at different ages. Some support for this hypothesis is provided by a longitudinal study (Gore & Aseltine, 2003) that examined changes in depression in a diverse urban sample over a 2-year period, beginning in the senior year of high school. This study showed that African Americans and Hispanics had higher scores on the CES-D scale than European Americans and Asian Americans. It also revealed that different factors were associated with these ethnic differences. College attendance accounted for the difference in depressive symptomatology between Asian Americans and African Americans or Latinos; the difference between European Americans and African Americans or Latinos was explained by the greater prevalence of problems in relations with peers and parents among the two ethnic minority groups.

Efforts to understand the link between ethnicity and depressive symptomatology include attempts to examine ethnic differences in depressive symptomatology associated with certain developmental transition points. In a study whose main aim was to assess ethnic differences in the association between pubertal status and symptoms of depression in three age groups of African, European, and Latino American adolescents, Hayward, Gotlib, Schraedley, and Litt (1999) found that among the gender/puberty status groups in their sample, African Americans did not show the same increases in depression symptomatology on the Children's Depression Inventory (CDI; Kovacs, 1985) from pre- to postpuberty that prior studies of European Americans had reported, whereas the Caucasian and Hispanic girls in their sample did. Hayward et al. interpreted this finding as suggesting that pubertal status is a better predictor of depressive symptoms than chronological age for European American girls, but not for their African American counterparts. Their findings, however, have to be taken as provisional because they were derived from a cross-sectional rather than a longitudinal sample. Ge et al. (2003) also examined changes in symptoms of depression associated with puberty in a sample of African American children assessed when they were approximately 11 years of age and again at approximately age 13. The results showed that pubertal effects varied as a function of gender and age. Among girls, early maturation was associated with higher levels of depressive symptoms at Time 1 and again at Time 2. Early maturing boys showed higher levels of depression at age 11 but not at age 13 years. Boys who experienced accelerated pubertal growth over time were more likely to have elevated levels of depression. This study provides partial support for the hypothesis that pubertal status is associated with depression in girls, but as there were no other ethnic groups involved, it does not settle the issue of whether pubertal status is better than chronological age at predicting depressive symptomatology in European American girls than in their African American counterparts (Hayward et al., 1999). Moreover, whether or not one finds a relationship between pubertal status and depression in African Americans may be related to other factors, such as depression in childhood. A. Shaffer, Forehand, and Kotchick (2002) conducted a longitudinal study of the correlates of depressive symptomatology in African American children (ages 6 to 11 years); they found that depressive symptoms predicted future adjustment problems.

Depressive symptomatology and mood disorders among American Indian children and youth have received relatively much less attention than have alcohol use, conduct problems, substance use, or smoking. Earlier, it had been reported that depression was the most common diagnosis for adolescent girls seeking help at the Indian Health Service mental health outpatient clinics (Beiser & Attneave, 1982). It has been hypothesized that the high rates of learning problems, Conduct Disorder, substance abuse, and running away among American Indian youth are consequences of depression (Choney, Berryhill-Paapke, & Robbins, 1995). Depression has also been considered a risk factor for suicide in this population. There are, however, conceptual and methodological issues that have yet to be resolved before culturally valid studies of depression can be undertaken. For example, the fact that the term "depression" cannot be directly translated into the Navajo language raises the issue of conceptual equivalence for that group. Also, studies that have examined the structure of depression in Native American samples have yielded findings that differ somewhat from those obtained with European American samples. Dick, Beals, Keane, and Manson (1994) examined the factor structure of the CES-D scale in a sample of American Indian adolescent students at a boarding school. They found that the depressed and somatic factors were highly correlated and suggested that these two factors be collapsed into a single factor. In a more recent attempt to examine the structure of depression among American Indian youth, Rieckmann, Wadsworth, and Deyhle (2004) administered the CDI, two scales (Scale 2 and the Depressive Content Scale) from the Minnesota Multiphasic Personality Inventory, and the *DSM-IV* Questionnaire for Depression, a measure developed specifically for this study, to a random sample of 14- to 20-year-old Navajo youth stratified according to gender and grade (10th, 11th, and 12th). In this sample, the mean CDI total score was 10, slightly less than the cut-off score of 11 for determining depression (Kovacs, 1985). However, 14% of the participants exceeded the CDI cut-off score of 20 suggested by Kovacs (1992) for use with unselected or general samples. The model that best fit the data was a one-factor depression model that included four observed variables from the *DSM-IV* Questionnaire, total CDI score, and the Minnesota Multiphasic Personality Inventory-Adolescent (MMPI-A) Content and Clinical scales. The *DSM-IV* Questionnaire had the highest loading (.84) on the depression factor, followed by the CDI (.73) and MMPI-A Content (.68). The MMPI-A Clinical scale had the lowest (.28) loading. The investigators noted that among American Indian youth, symptoms of depression may also be manifested as stomach aches, other medical ailments, or even spiritual discontent and lack of harmony and balance, which may not be captured in the European American conceptualization of depression.

High rates for suicide or suicide attempts, often considered a correlate of depression, have been reported among American Indian youth. Recently, Freedenthal and Stiffman (2004) explored within-group differences in suicide rates as a function of geographical residence. Interviews of a stratified random sample of urban and reservation American Indian adolescents revealed that although urban and reservation youth reported comparable rates (14% to 18%) of suicide attempts, one-fifth of urban youth reported lifetime suicidal ideation, whereas one-third of reservation youth did. Urban youth had fewer psychosocial problems. Multivariate analyses conducted separately for each group failed to show common correlates of attempted suicide.

Studies of depressive symptomatology among Asian Americans are relatively few.

Using a 16-item scale abbreviation (Lin, 1989) of the CES-D, Greenberger and Chen (1996) assessed depressive symptomatology in a sample of 171 early adolescents and 297 late adolescents from Asian American and European American families. Ethnic differences did not emerge in the early adolescent sample; both ethnic groups reported

having a depressive symptom only once or twice a month. Within-group differences surfaced, however, in the Asian American group. Asian American early adolescents in the first or immigrant generation reported more symptoms than did their peers who were born in the United States. In the late adolescent group, Asian Americans reported significantly more frequent symptoms of depression than did European Americans. Furthermore, among the late adolescent Asian Americans, scores on depressive symptomatology did not differ significantly as a function of generational status. A microanalysis of depressive symptoms revealed significant ethnic differences on 4 of the 16 CES-D items. Asian Americans reported with greater frequency feeling "My life has been a failure." On average, Asian Americans reported feeling this way slightly more than once or twice in the past month, whereas the frequency for European Americans was midway between "never" and "once or twice." Asian Americans also indicated more disabling symptoms ("everything was an effort") and more difficulty in coping with distress ("could not shake off the blues" or "had trouble keeping my mind on things").

Also using the CES-D, Edman et al. (1998) assessed depressive symptomatology in Filipino Americans and European Americans ages 14 to 19 years who were from rural and small towns in Hawaii. No ethnic differences were found. The few Filipino American adolescents who reported having suicidal thoughts had moderately high to very high levels of reported depressive symptoms. Consistent with prior studies, females had higher CES-D scores. Edman et al. (1999) also examined the factor structure of the CES-D among Filipino adolescents. Two factors were found to provide a reasonably good fit to the data: Factor I was a combination of depressed affect, somatic-retardation, and interpersonal items; Factor II was composed of the remaining four items denoting positive affect. The combination of depressed affect and somatic symptoms in Factor I was interpreted as providing support for previous findings regarding an overlap between these two variables among Asian Americans. The loading of interpersonal items on Factor I is more unusual and, according to the investigators, suggests that interpersonal factors were not distinguished from depressed affect in this sample of Filipino adolescents.

As a first step in developing a reliable and culturally valid measure of depression in Korean Americans, Choi, Stafford, Meininger, Roberts, and Smith (2002) administered the *DSM* Scale for Depression (DSD; Choi et al., 2002) to a community sample of Korean Americans, ages 11 to 13 years, and compared their findings to the response patterns of Korean and European Americans who participated in the Teen Life Changes Survey. Overall, Korean Americans had significantly higher depression scores than their European American peers. A correlational analysis of depression scores and scores for related constructs (loneliness, self-esteem, coping, social support, mastery, and somatic symptoms) showed the highest correlation to be between depression and somatic symptoms.

Information on symptoms of depression among Latino children comes from a methodological study and a meta-analytic study. In a study that examined the cross-ethnic equivalence of measures of negative life events and mental health (CDI, Child Hostility Scale, and the Global Self-Worth Scale) among 8- to 14-year-old Latino and European American children, Knight, Virdin, Ocampo, and Roosa (1994) found that the former scored higher on the CDI than the latter. The authors interpreted this ethnic difference to be a function of SES differences between the two ethnic samples, but they did not attempt an analysis that controlled for SES. A meta-analytic study, however, provides stronger evidence that the prevalence of depressive symptomatology may be higher in Latino youngsters than among their African American and European American peers. A meta-analysis performed on 310 samples of children and adolescents (ages 8 to 16; $N = 61,424$) by Twenge and Nolen-Hoeksema (2002) revealed that Latinos had significantly higher CDI scores than African Americans and European Americans. The mean scores of the latter two groups did not differ significantly from one another. The main and interaction effects of SES were not significant. Ethnicity did not have a significant effect on the stability of CDI scores, but gender did. For all three ethnic groups, girls' depression scores stayed steady from age 8 to 11 and then increased between ages 12 and 16. Boys' CDI scores were stable from ages 8 to 16 except for a high CDI mean score at age 12. Girls' scores were slightly lower than boys' during childhood, but girls scored higher beginning at age 13.

More studies of ethnic differences in depressive symptomatology and diagnosis have focused on adolescents. Depression in Mexican adolescents has been the focus of programmatic research by Roberts and his collaborators (Roberts & Chen, 1995; Roberts, Chen, & Solvitz, 1995; Roberts & Sobhan, 1992). Roberts and Sobhan reported that in a national survey of 12- to 17-year-olds, Mexican Americans reported more depressive symptoms on a 12-item version of the CES-D than did their peers of European, African, or other Latino origin. Males of Mexican descent had the highest rate. Their female counterparts

also showed high rates of depressive symptomatology, but to a lesser extent than did the males. Roberts (1994, cited in Roberts et al., 1997) found that middle school students of Mexican descent showed significantly higher rates of depression on the 20-item CES-D and the Weinberg Screening Affective Scale than their counterparts who were of European descent. Further analysis of the same data by Roberts and Chen revealed that adolescents of Mexican origin exhibited significantly more depressive symptomatology and suicidal ideation than the adolescent descendants of Europeans. The highest rates were found among females of Mexican origin. In both ethnic groups, depressive symptomatology and suicidal ideation were strongly related.

Siegel, Aneshensel, Taub, Cantwell, and Driscoll (1998) assessed the effects of race/ethnicity and gender in a multiethnic sample composed using a three-stage area probability sampling frame. Irrespective of socioeconomic status, Latinos reported more symptoms of depression that their European American, African American, and Asian American counterparts. Siegel et al. also investigated whether pubertal development influences depressed mood in a similar manner in gender and race/ethnicity groups. Advancing puberty was associated with depressed mood only among females, but the timing of pubertal changes, relative to one's peers, was related to depressed mood among both males and females and among Latinos.

Depressive symptomatology has been found among rural as well as urban Latino adolescents. In a study of 240 rural Latino adolescents, ages 15 to 20 years, Katragadda and Tidwell (1998) found that 33% of their sample showed moderate to severe levels of depressive symptomatology, and an additional 17% had mild depressive levels on the CES-D scale. Birth order and number of brothers were significantly related to depression. Gender was an important predictor of depressive symptomatology, as was self-esteem. Higher stress scores were also related to higher levels of depression.

Latinos have also been found to differ significantly from their counterparts in other ethnic groups in the prevalence of depression and alcohol use. Guiao and Thompson (2004) assessed the prevalence of depression, alcohol use, and suicidal behaviors in a random sample of 3,310 12- to 19-year-old females of Latino, African, American Indian, Asian, and European ancestry. Measures included the CES-D, number of drinks each time alcohol was consumed in the past year, and a composite measure of suicidal behaviors. Latinos were found to be at significantly higher risk for adolescent depression than the European Americans, and at higher risk for alcohol use than the African Americans and

Asian Americans. There were no significant ethnic differences in risk for suicidal behaviors. Latino middle school students may also be at greater risk for depression and substance use. Kelder et al. (2001) found depressive symptoms and substance use to be associated in a large sample of middle school students who were largely non-White and predominantly (59% to 63%) Latino.

The prevalence of depressive symptomatology in adolescents of Afro-Latino descent has also been explored. Ramos, Jaccard, and Guilamo-Ramos (2003) found that Afro-Latino adolescents in grades 7 through 12 residing in the United States exhibited higher levels of depressive symptoms than their European American, African American, and Latino counterparts. This finding suggests that descent from two ethnic minority groups increases the propensity to depression. Consistent with prior studies, this study also showed that, across ethnic groups, adolescent females had higher levels of depression that males, and older adolescents had higher levels of depressive symptomatology.

More recently, Sen (2004) reported that all minority groups who participated in the 1996 round of Health Behavior in School-Aged Children, a survey of 9,000 6th- to 10th graders constituting a representative sample, were more likely to suffer from depressed mood compared to non-Hispanic Whites, although Blacks were at lower risk for self-injury. Consistent with previous studies, adolescent females were more likely to present a depressed mood than adolescent males.

Depressive Disorders

Few studies have examined ethnic differences in mood disorders among ethnic minority children and youth. Most studies (e.g., Costello et al., 1996) have found few differences in depression between European Americans and African American youths. Roberts, Chen, and Solovitz (1995) investigated ethnocultural factors on the manifestation of *DSM-III-R* symptoms. In their sample of 334 Anglo, African, and Mexican Americans ages 12 to 17 years, 78 were diagnosed with Mood Disorder. There were few "meaningful" ethnic differences through a comparison of prevalence rates of symptoms and criteria for *DSM-III-R,* as well as rank order of criteria.

Among the few studies employing large samples, a study that assessed depression in nine ethnic groupings stands out. Roberts, Roberts, and Chen (1997) assessed depression in 5,423 students representing over 20 ethnicities in grades 6 to 8. For the entire sample, the mean prevalence rate for Major Depressive Episode (MDE) based on *DSM-*

IV criteria was 8.8% without adjusting for impairment and 4.3% with adjustment for impairment. These rates are higher than previously reported in the literature (Fleming & Offord, 1990). Analysis of the scores from the nine largest groups revealed that African Americans and Mexican Americans had significantly higher rates of MDE without impairment than European Americans and all other groups, but only the Mexican American group had significantly higher rates of MDE with impairment, independent of age, gender, and SES. Mexican Americans had the highest prevalence rate adjusted for impairment (6.6%); Chinese Americans had the lowest (1.9%). Consistent with findings from other studies, females overall had higher rates than males. A distinctive contribution of this study is that it examined the interaction between ethnicity and SES in a segment of the sample: European Americans, African Americans, and Mexican Americans. Neither chi-square analysis nor logistic regression analysis yielded a significant interaction effect on prevalence rates with or without adjustment for impairment. Across ethnic groups, prevalences were higher for those reporting lower SES.

Sack, McSharry, Clarke, and Kinney (1994) administered the Diagnostic Instrument for Children and Adolescents and selected sections of the Schedule of Affective Disorders and Schizophrenia for School-age Children-Epidemiologic Version, with the assistance of a Cambodian translator to a nonstratified random sample of 209 13- to 25-year-old Khmer adolescents and young adults; as well, a parent or guardian was interviewed in two Western communities to determine their diagnostic status following their survival of the Pol Pot War in Cambodia in 1975 to 1979. Roughly one-fifth of the adolescents, over half of the mothers, and about one-third of the fathers qualified for a current diagnosis of Posttraumatic Stress Disorder. There was high comorbidity with depression, but other forms of psychopathology were much less evident.

In an ethnically diverse sample of Asian/Pacific Islanders and European Americans, Austin and Chorpita (2004) did not find ethnic differences in depression, indexed through either average scores or percentage with clinically elevated scores, in their study of an ethnically diverse sample from Hawaii. Costello et al. (1997) did not find a significant difference in the rate of depression between Native Americans in Appalachia and their European American counterparts. Beals et al. (1997) reported that the 6-month prevalence rate of depressive disorders found in their sample of Plains Indian youths was essentially equivalent to the lifetime prevalence rate reported by

Lewisohn et al. (1993) for European Americans. It is worth noting that although these recent studies employing *DSM-III-R* have not found ethnic differences in the prevalence of depression among Native American youth, earlier reports suggested that depression is a problem in this population (Beiser & Attneave, 1982; Dinges & Duong-Tran, 1993). More recently, Rieckmann et al. (2004) reported that although the mean CDI score was 10, slightly below the 11 cut-off score for determining depression, 14% of their sample of 332 Navajo adolescents exceeded the CDI cut-off score of 20 suggested for use with general or unselected samples (Kovacs, 1992). It appears that higher rates of depression for Native American youths compared to their counterparts from other population groups emerge from self-report measures but not when *DSM-III-R* criteria for depressive disorders are applied.

In summary, this review found that most studies, including those with large probability samples, revealed some ethnic differences in prevalence rates of symptomatology or disorders among children and adolescents for conduct, substance-related, anxiety, and mood disorders. The presence of an ethnic difference varies as a function of the type of symptomatology or disorder and the ethnic group assessed. This conclusion differs from that presented in the 2001 supplement to the surgeon general's report on mental health that "within the United States, overall rates of mental disorders for most minority groups are largely similar to those of whites" (U.S. Department of Health and Human Services, 2001, p. 42). It is more consistent with the conclusion reached in a more recent review of adult mental disorders that "there is evidence that the various ethnic minority groups may exhibit significant differences in the prevalence of mental disorder" (Sue & Chu, 2003, p. 447). Our literature searches yielded many studies of the four disorders discussed; only the major ones were included in this review. It does not seem to be the case that "the smaller racial and ethnic groups, most notably American Indians, Alaska Natives, Asian Americans and Pacific Islanders are not sufficiently studied" (U.S. Department of Health and Human Services, 2001, p. 42), but rather that epidemiological studies of children and adolescents in this population are rare and community studies, although much greater in number, tend to concentrate on a few disorders or overly focus on a specific disorder when studying one group (e.g., substance-related problems among American Indian adolescents). A wider range of disorders need to be examined, preferably through epidemiological studies using large representative samples with adequate controls for relevant demographic variables.

CULTURAL CORRELATES OF CHILD PSYCHOPATHOLOGY

Some significant associations between psychological variables and symptomatology or disorder have been interpreted as possible reflections of cultural influences (Beals et al., 1997; Bird et al., 2001; Pina & Silverman, 2004). However, few studies have directly investigated the specific linkages between psychological variables (e.g., parental monitoring) and cultural variables (e.g., family closeness as a cultural value) or the role of cultural variables as risk or protective factors. In this section, we present findings on psychological variables associated with ethnic differences in psychopathology and discuss their observed or potential linkages to cultural variables. The role of cultural variables as protective or risk factors is also discussed. Culturally based protective and risk factors are not treated as mutually exclusive. Depending on the presence of other factors or circumstances, a cultural variable may function as a risk or as a protective factor.

Cultural Values

Each society has its own set of values or prized beliefs, concepts, institutions, and so on. These beliefs, concepts, institutions, practices, and so on are not necessarily unique to that society; they may be found in other societies. What is ethnic group- or culture-specific is the emphasis given to a particular belief, concept, or institution, the degree to which it is held dear or valued within a group. Cultural values are considered essential to the well-being of a society and its members. Each society seeks to maintain its values and to instill them in succeeding generations. It has been suggested that certain cultural values are related to development and mental health, either positively or negatively. In this section, we describe three cultural values that have been hypothesized as related to the mental health of ethnic minority youth and examine the evidence.

Family

In most societies, the family is the basic context for human development, including development gone awry. Families characteristics may vary, however, and culture is one source of variation. Cultural differences in family size, composition, structure, and dynamics can influence development. The extent to which they do is sometimes related to the cultural value attached to the family, and this value differs between individualist and collectivist cultures. In the former, individuals and personal goals are given priority over groups and group goals; in the latter, groups such as the ethnic group or the family receive priority, and individual personal goals are subordinated to ethnic group or family goals. The family is considered important in both individualist and collectivist societies, but it receives a stronger emphasis and a higher priority among collectivist cultures, such as those of African Americans, American Indians, Asian Americans, and Latinos. "Familismo" or "familism" are the terms, introduced by Latino researchers, applied to this emphasis on the family, which many consider a mediator variable through which culture influences normal or pathological development.

In regard to conduct problems, one study of academic misconduct in community samples showed that although early adolescent European Americans, Chinese Americans, Taipei Chinese, and Beijing Chinese displayed comparable overall levels and types of self-reported misconduct (academic misconduct, antisocial behaviors, status violations), the relative contributions of family and peers to misconduct differed significantly among the groups (Chen, Greenberger, Leiter, Dong, & Guo, 1998). Family variables were parent-adolescent conflict, parental warmth, and parental monitoring; peer variables were peer approval and peer sanctions for misconduct. Structural equation modeling using only the data from adolescents showed that family relationships and peer sanctions for misconduct accounted for a significant amount of variance in misconduct for all four groups, but the percentage of variance accounted for was much greater for the two American samples than for the two Chinese samples from Asia. The cross-national difference was due mainly to the greater contribution of peer factors to adolescent misconduct among European Americans and Chinese Americans. Structural equation modeling that included data from mothers did not significantly change the proportionate contributions of family and peer factors to adolescent misconduct. Chen et al. suggest that the relatively stronger influence of peers may be due to the fact that American adolescents spend more time with their peers than do their counterparts in Taipei or Beijing.

Family relations and parental monitoring were among the significant predictors of the higher levels (3 = lying, disobedience, 4 = damaging property, attacking someone) of antisocial behavior for three groups of children and adolescents, Island Puerto Ricans and Mainland African Americans and European Americans (non-Hispanic Whites), but not for Mainland Hispanics, possibly due to the small sample size of this group (Bird et al., 2001). Island Puerto Ricans had lower rates for all three levels of

antisocial behavior compared to the three Mainland groups (Hispanics, African Americans, and non-Latino, non-African Americans who were mostly European Americans). Bird et al. also examined the rate of increase (or decrease) in antisocial behavior involved for each of the correlates. Only poor relationships with other members of the family were associated with a substantial increase in antisocial behaviors. Because this variable was significantly lower for Island Puerto Ricans than the three Mainland ethnic groups, Bird et al. concluded that the only finding that stood out as an explanation for the lower rates of antisocial behavior among Island Puerto Rican participants could be accounted for by the association between lower levels of antisocial behavior and better family relations. Although they carefully noted that causality cannot be inferred from a finding obtained in a cross-cultural study, they still asserted that it is, potentially, of cross-cultural importance.

Additional research among Island Puerto Ricans is needed to confirm the role of better family relations as a protective factor against the development of antisocial behavior and to identify other factors that might augment or support its role. Bird et al. (2001) suggest that two such factors might be direct parental control through discipline (Patterson, 1982, cited in Bird et al., 2001) and social control (Hirsch, 1969, cited in Bird et al., 2001). In a collectivist society such as is found in Puerto Rico, strong family attachments are valued and promoted. There are also clear societal and family expectations of what are appropriate behaviors and the sanctions for violations. Direct parental control is exercised through discipline without the coercion that can impair parent-child relationships. At the same time, social control is facilitated by large extended families that, along with parents, monitor and supervise the behavior of children, adolescents, and young adults. In addition, the expectations and sanctions may also be endorsed by other societal institutions such as religious organizations and schools, creating a sense of societal congruence that increases social control. Bird et al. suggest that the levels of direct parental control and social control may have eroded for Mainland Puerto Ricans, who were more like the other Mainland ethnic groups. If erosion has indeed occurred, one contributing factor might be the peer group, as suggested by the Chen et al. (1998) study. Studies are needed to confirm this and also to test the hypothesis that strong family attachments, direct parental control through strict but noncoercive discipline, and social control by extended family members and other socialization agents may prevent the emergence of antisocial behaviors.

Thus far, there is scant evidence for the role of culturally based family variables as correlates of substance use/abuse. Although Costello et al. (1997) reported that some family variables were associated with psychiatric disorders in their sample of American Indians and European American youth living in Appalachia, these do not appear at face value to be culturally based family variables. For both groups, family mental illness appears strongly associated with childhood disorder. Poverty, family deviance, and, to a lesser extent, family adversity were associated with child psychiatric disorder in the European American sample, but not in the American Indian sample. Although Costello et al. did not investigate cultural factors as possible correlates of substance abuse among American Indian youth, other investigators have done so.

Beals et al. (1997) noted that the elevated rates of substance use disorders, specifically alcohol abuse/dependence noted in their sample of American Indian youth, appeared to reflect the elevated rates present among adults in their community and suggested that cultural factors could be among the many reasons for these rates. However, Beals did not specify any culturally based family variables. In the absence of evidence for such variables, the co-occurrence of elevated rates of substance use in both the youth and adult communities might be accounted for in terms of social learning, in some cases building on a biologically based predisposition or "vulnerability to alcoholism" (Ehlers, Garcia-Andrade, & Phillips, 2001; Wall, Garcia-Andrade, Wong, Lau, & Ehlers, 2000). Within their families and communities, youth may observe substance use with few sanctions against it. Acquisition may actually occur within the peer group and be maintained by it. An assessment of the contexts associated with drug use among American Indian adolescents of the Southwest revealed that the most frequent and difficult (i.e., perceived difficulty in resisting use) drug and alcohol situations occurred primarily with cousins or friends at home or after school (Okamoto, LeCroy, Dustman, Hohmann-Marriot, & Kulis, 2004). Last, although it has been hypothesized that how native groups drink has been conditioned by aspects of their respective social organization (families and communities) prior to the advent of Europeans in the New World, Spicer, Novins, Mitchell, and Beals (2003) failed to find evidence for this hypothesis. Their study of four contemporary American Indian groups showed that cultural group differences accounted for a small percentage of the variance in both the quantity and frequency of alcohol use and its negative consequences, but the patterns of alcohol use were not consistent with the hypothesis that they would be related to

aspects of American Indian social organizations prior to European colonialism.

The family as a mediator of culture's influence on internalizing disorders has also been studied by researchers. Ginsburg and Silverman (1996) found support for the hypothesis that separation anxiety would be greater in those ethnic groups that highly value the maintenance of close family relationships and interdependence. The higher rates of SAD among Hispanic children are surprising given a prior suggestion in the attachment literature that children from cultures that have large extended families with multiple caregivers might be less prone to separation anxiety. However, the Latino children studied by Ginsburg and Silverman were more likely to come from families with lower incomes than their European American counterparts. Perhaps they were children from low-income immigrant families who lacked the extended kinship support available in their country of origin while attempting to deal with a new environment. Furthermore, these children might have experienced periods of separation from one or both parents during the process of migration. Because measures of attachment or family closeness were not administered, one cannot conclude that the significant difference in the prevalence of SAD between the two samples can be explained by cultural differences in attachment or family closeness.

Austin and Chorpita (2004) found only partial support for their hypothesis that separation anxiety would be higher in those ethnic groups that place a high value on maintaining close family relationships and interdependence. Although this hypothesis was confirmed for Native Hawaiians based on their mean RCADS score, and for both Native Hawaiians and Filipino Americans based on percentages with clinically elevated RCADS scores, it was not true for the Chinese and Japanese Americans. Because Austin and Chorpita did not actually administer a measure of family closeness and interdependence, it is difficult to explain their findings. Perhaps the assumptions underlying their hypothesis need to be reviewed. Separation anxiety is characterized by developmentally inappropriate anxiety around separation from the home or from one or more attachment figures. It is associated with persistent and excessive worry about losing or being separated from an attachment figure, or about possible harm befalling an attachment figure (American Psychiatric Association, 2000). Implied in these characteristics is a sense of insecurity in the child. Does family closeness necessarily breed insecurity? Or does it actually do the opposite, instill a sense of security that emboldens the child to explore the environment, secure in the knowledge that there is a home base or safe haven to which he or she can return? Perhaps there are varying types of family closeness with different developmental outcomes. Furthermore, strategies for maintaining family closeness and interdependence may have differential developmental outcomes: Some may instill a sense of security, whereas others do not; some may achieve a balance between interdependence and independence that enables the child to feel confident that he or she can function without the constant presence of the attachment figure, whereas other strategies may foster a greater dependence that makes a child feel insecure in the absence of a major attachment figure. The developmental cross-cultural literature on families and attachment (e.g., Harwood, Miller, & Irizarry, 1995) might be helpful in reconceptualizing the relationships among family closeness, interdependence, and separation anxiety.

Depressed mood in late adolescence has been found to be associated with problems in relations with parents, as well as with peers. Based on a 2-year longitudinal study, Gore and Aseltine (2003) reported that 2 years after high school, the difference between European Americans and African Americans or Latinos in depressed mood was accounted for by problems in parental relations and peer relations. In contrast, the difference between Asian Americans and African Americans or Latinos was accounted for by lower college enrollment.

Before leaving this discussion of the family as a possible mediator of the relationship between culture and psychopathology, it should be noted that even when studies find cross-cultural consistency in the relationships between family variables and depressive symptoms among children (Kim, 2000) and adolescents (Dmitrieva, Chen, Greenberger, & Gil-Rivas, 2004), they also reveal cross-cultural differences in the magnitude of associations among variables. This finding underscores the importance of looking beyond surface similarities to distinguish what is culturally specific from what is universal.

Simpatia

Varela et al. (2004) tested the hypothesis that anxiety reporting would be associated positively with the cultural value of *simpatia,* a Spanish construct denoting empathy with others and remaining agreeable even if it entails self-sacrifices (Gabrielidis, Stephan, Ybarra, Pearson, & Villareal, 1997, as cited in Varela et al.; Kagan & Madden, 1970, as cited in Varela et al., 2004). Simpatia is emphasized more in collectivist than in individualist cultures. To ascertain that the participants did indeed have a collectivist orientation, Varela et al. assessed this. As expected, Mexican and Mexican American children endorsed collec-

tivism as a cultural value more than did European Americans. They also exhibited a greater use of strategies reflecting simpatia. In addition, support was found for a direct link between the reporting of physiological anxiety and simpatia.

Interpersonal Relations and Social Conformity

Cultures vary in the value they place on interpersonal relations and adherence to group norms for interpersonal relations. Some support for the hypothesis that there is a relationship between these values and anxiety was obtained by Austin and Chorpita (2004). Based on prior research (Okazaki, 1997) they predicted that Chinese, Japanese, and Filipino American youths whose ethnic groups assign greater negative attributions and shame to violations of norms for interpersonal interaction would have higher mean scores and higher rates of clinical elevation on social anxiety than those with other ethnic affiliations. This prediction turned out to be correct for Chinese Americans and Filipino Americans, but not for Japanese Americans, but only in regard to RCADS mean scores on social anxiety. Although the percentage of Chinese Americans with clinically elevated scores was the highest among all ethnic groups in the diverse sample, the difference was not statistically significant.

Ethnic Socialization

Ethnic socialization is the process whereby parents and other elders in an ethnic group transmit their culture to the younger generation and also prepare them for interacting with other ethnic groups. Thus, it includes enculturation or the task of cultural transmission and what is sometimes referred to as racial socialization. Ethnic socialization for dealing with racial issues has been suggested as a possible correlate of anxiety among African American children. Neal-Barnett (2004) has hypothesized that African American parents who prepare their children to deal with racial stressors may be providing them also with a protection against the development of anxiety and depressive symptoms. Among African Americans, ethnic socialization for racial issues may involve minimizing the gender socialization that is found in other ethnic groups. S. F. Lambert, Cooley, et al. (2004) found that, unlike studies of European American children, their study did not reveal sex differences in anxiety sensitivity among African American children. They interpreted this finding as an indication of a possible lack of gender differentiation in ethnic socialization. According to S. F. Lambert, Cooley, et al., low-income African American families and schools in urban communities characterized by high levels of hostility and violence may minimize gender differences in socialization to provide girls as well as boys with knowledge and skills required for staying safe in these communities that present an "ecological risk" (Prelow, Danoff-Burg, Swenson, & Pulgiano, 2004).

Ethnic socialization has been invoked to account for the observed ethnic differences in anxiety-related somatic and physiological symptoms and distress associated with these symptoms. According to Pina and Silverman (2004), the difference between European American and Hispanic/Latino youth in anxiety-related somatic complaints is attributable to Latino socialization, or more specifically, observational learning and reinforcement. Parental reactions to their own somatic/physiological symptoms (e.g., refraining from daily activities such as going to work) serve as models for coping with such symptoms. Children experiencing distress may then also develop somatic or physiological complaints. Parental reactions to their children's somatic complaints such as allowing them to stay home from school or giving them extra attention, special foods, or get-well gifts reinforce or increase the probability of recurrence of the children's displays of and ideas about the meaning of somatic/physiological symptoms.

Pina and Silverman (2004) did not assess ethnic socialization for expression of anxiety symptomatology. However, observational data on parents' explanations for ambiguous events in family discussions from the Varela et al. (2004) study illustrate how such ethnic socialization might take place. This study yielded support for the hypothesis that Mexican and Mexican American parents would model avoidance of anxious interpretations to potentially threatening situations because these situations could evoke aversive feelings. In talking with their children about solving ambiguous problem situations, Mexican parents generated fewer anxious, nonsomatic interpretations than their European American counterparts. Another hypothesis was also confirmed: Mexican and Mexican American parents did encourage and model somatic, nonanxious interpretations to ambiguous problem situations, probably because expression of emotions in somatic form is more culturally acceptable. In parent-child discussions, Mexican and Mexican American parents generated more somatic, nonanxious (or nonpsychological) interpretations than did European American parents. Additional support for the hypothesized link between culturally based family processes and anxiety reporting in children of Mexican descent was provided by a positive correlation between a parent somatic

interpretation index and children's scores on the Worry scale of the RCMAS. Although ethnic socialization may begin during childhood among those of Mexican descent, a clear preference for somatic explanations of internal ambiguous symptoms or ambiguous social stimuli over anxiety-related interpretations may not be manifested until late adolescence or adulthood, after long-term exposure to cultural mediums (e.g., media, school, peers) that endorse this attribution style (Varela et al., 2004). Thus, parents of Mexican descent would be more likely than their children to show a somatic bias.

Acculturation

The developmental and other outcomes of ethnic socialization can be altered through acculturation, the process of learning about the culture of another ethnic group, when acquired knowledge, attitudes, and behaviors are incorporated into the individual's behavioral repertoire. Pina and Silverman (2004) suggested acculturation as a possible explanation for the differences in reporting of somatic/physiological symptoms of anxiety that they found between subgroups of Cuban American versus non-Cuban Latino Americans and within the non-Cuban group, between those whose parents preferred English as the assessment language and those who chose Spanish. According to these investigators, youth with Hispanic origins whose parents preferred English as the assessment language might have been more acculturated and adopted European American ways of conceptualizing and expressing distress. Hence, their children responded more like European Americans than members of their ethnic group whose parents preferred Spanish. Acculturation was not directly assessed in the Pina and Silverman study, so research is still needed to examine its role as a correlate or predictor of anxiety-related somatic and physiological complaints for Latino youth.

Lacking data on acculturation, Pina and Silverman (2004) suggested that in their study, language choice could have served as a proxy variable for acculturation (Angel & Guarnaccia, 1989). If English as the preferred language is a proxy for acculturation and the choice of Spanish is a proxy for less acculturation, then there should have been no difference between the Cuban Americans and non-Cuban American Latinos in the Spanish language choice group. However, this was not the case. Among those who chose Spanish, Cuban American youth reported somatic/physiological symptoms as significantly more distressing than did non-Cuban American Latino youth. As an alternative explanation, Pina and Silverman proposed that language choice, independent of acculturation level, may still serve as a cultural signifier for reporting psychosocial or psychological distress, including anxiety (Reichman, 1997, as cited in Pina & Silverman, 2004). Research is still needed to examine the role of acculturation in the expression of anxiety and the role of language choice as a proxy for acculturation or as an independent cultural signifier for reporting psychosocial or psychological distress.

At least one study has investigated the relationship between acculturation, childhood depression, and coping. Huang, Leong, and Wagner (1994) assessed the effects of self-esteem and perceived competence on children's perceived stressors, dysphoria, and coping strategies in Chinese American children differing in levels of acculturation. For both acculturation groups, peer stressors were significantly related to feelings of dysphoria. Children's choice of coping strategy differed as a function of acculturation. Consistent with traditional Chinese teaching, low-acculturation children most effectively used suppression in dealing with daily life stressors, whereas high-acculturation children were more likely to use retaliation. Still, retaliation was the least commonly used coping strategy among highly acculturated children. In contrast, low-acculturated children used their most effective strategy—suppression—frequently.

Acculturative stress, that is, perceived stress from the experience of attempting to reconcile cultural differences, has been linked to depressive symptoms. In a study of Mexican American middle school students, Romero and Roberts (2003) found that for both immigrant and native-born Mexican American youths, higher perceived acculturative stress was associated with predepressive symptoms. Immigrant youths reported a higher total number of stressors than did native-born Mexican Americans. The sources of stress also differed between the two groups. Native-born Mexican Americans reported more stress from needing better Spanish-language skills and from the impact of their parents' culture or intergenerational gaps whereas immigrant youths perceived more stress from needing better English proficiency in school.

Ethnic Identification

A study of ethnic pride, biculturalism, and drug use norms of urban American Indian adolescents in seventh grade (age 11 to 15 years) has shown that students who have a more intense sense of ethnic pride adhere more strongly to certain antidrug norms (Kulis, Napoli, & Marsiglia, 2002). In another study, ethnic pride was associated with differential outcomes for different ethnic groups. Marsiglia, Kulis,

and Hech (2001) found that African-American, Mexican-American, and mixed-ethnicity students with a strong sense of ethnic pride reported less drug use and exposure, whereas European-American students who also took great pride in their ethnicity reported more.

Among adults, the strength of identification with an ethnic group is directly associated with fewer depressive symptoms (Mossakowski, 2003). In a sample of African American children ages 10 to 12 years, community ethnic identification was negatively related to depressive symptoms (Simons et al., 2002). There was also evidence that community ethnic identification mediated the relationship between victimization and depressive symptoms.

Ethnic identity is manifested through cultural orientation. In a study involving 9th- and 11th-grade Asian American students ages 14 to 19 years, cultural orientation and interpersonal relationships were significant predictors of depression (Wong, 2001). Subjects with a high orientation toward ethnic culture and a low orientation toward mainstream culture experienced greater depression than those with high orientation toward American culture and low orientation toward ethnic culture. In addition, the presence of more positive parent and peer relationships predicted lower depressive levels. None of the examined demographic variables was a significant predictor of depression, although subjects who immigrated after the age of 12 years were more depressed than U.S.-born adolescents.

Mental Health-Related Beliefs

One of the pathways whereby culture might indirectly influence the emergence and persistence of psychopathology is through an ethnic group's shared beliefs about mental health. The culture of an ethnic group includes beliefs about typical and atypical behaviors, explanations for deviance, and what constitutes significant impairment of functioning. Although a number of studies have assessed ethnic differences among college students and adults in their beliefs about various psychological problems or disorders (e.g., Luk & Bond, 1992), few have done so among children or adolescents and their parents. McKelvey, Baldasar, Sang, and Roberts (1999) found that a large proportion of Vietnamese parents in an Australian community sample attributed a child's mental illness to biological/chemical imbalance, trauma, and metaphysical or spiritual causes. Other studies involving children or adolescents who had been diagnosed and/or were receiving mental health services have yielded inconsistent results. Yeh, Hough, McCabe, Lau, and Garland (2004) asked the parents of 1,338 youths with identified mental health problems about the causes of their children's problems. Beliefs about 11 etiologies fell into three major categories: biopsychosocial, sociological, and spiritual/nature disharmony causes. Parents of African American, Asian/Pacific Islander American, and Latino American children were generally less likely than parents of non-Latino Whites to endorse etiologies consistent with biopsychosocial beliefs about mental illness. These biopsychosocial beliefs included physical causes, personality, relational issues, familial issues, and trauma. Some racial/ethnic differences were evident for sociological causes such as friends, American culture, prejudice, and economic problems. No ethnic differences were found for beliefs in spiritual or nature disharmony etiologies. Analyses controlling for demographic characteristics, child's symptomatology and problem severity, and public service sector affiliation produced fewer significant racial/ethnic differences but a similar pattern of results. These analyses also showed that compared to European American parents, African American parents were less likely to attribute mental illness to relational issues or spiritual issues; Asian/Pacific Islanders were less likely to report physical causes, personality, familial issues, and trauma as causes; and Latinos were less likely to endorse physical causes, personality, relational issues, familial issues, and American culture. Unlike European American parents, African Americans and Asian/Pacific Islanders were more likely to endorse prejudice as a cause and also were more likely to attribute their child's problem to American culture. The authors concluded that racial/ethnic differences in parental beliefs about the causes of their child's problems exist in an at-risk sample.

Another study that employed a sample of children who had been identified as having a disorder was conducted by Bussing, Schoenberg, Rogers, Zima, and Angus (1998). These investigators explored the explanatory models of ADHD held by parents representing two ethnic groups. They reported that whereas European Americans were more likely than their African American counterparts to use medical labels as descriptors for their child with ADHD, the two groups did not differ significantly in their etiological or causal explanations for the disorder. Perhaps the lack of ethnic differences reported by Bussing et al. is a function of their having used two groups of parents whose children essentially had the same disorder. Yeh et al. (2004) found that after controlling for child symptomatology, African American parents did not differ from European American parents in their beliefs about biopsychosocial causes of mental illness, except that they were less likely to attribute mental illness to relational issues.

These findings denoting similar beliefs about a syndrome in parents from different ethnic groups whose children have been diagnosed suggests that cultural beliefs about a syndrome can be altered through exposure to the beliefs of other cultures.

Some support for this suggestion is provided by a British study of beliefs about depression held by two age groups (17 to 28 years and 35 to 42 years) of native-born British and Asian-born immigrants to Britain (Furnham & Malik, 1994). In the middle-aged group, Asian-born participants differed significantly from native-born British in their perceptions of the symptoms and causes of depression. In the younger group of late adolescents and young adults, however, Asian-born immigrants who grew up in Britain did not differ from their native-born British peers. It appears that cultural beliefs about a syndrome are learned during the formative years (Furnham & Malik, 1994). The broader cultural context of concept formation plays an important role; exposure to a different culture during the formative years results in the acquisition of that culture's beliefs about a syndrome even if one's parents hold different cultural beliefs. There is also evidence that cultural beliefs about a syndrome acquired during the formative years are retained in adulthood, even if one immigrates to a country with a different culture (Furnham & Malike, 1994). A new, broader cultural context may not bring about an alteration in cultural beliefs unless accommodation becomes necessary. Change can occur if one's child develops a syndrome that requires direct contact with mental health professionals who hold different cultural beliefs about that syndrome and impart those to the parent (Bussing et al., 1998; Yeh et al., 2004). The nature of how specific alterations occur remains unknown. Is it a case of substitution or integration? Does a change in beliefs about one syndrome result in a change in the pattern of organization among cultural beliefs related to mental health?

Cultural Responses to Deviance and Distress

Cultural beliefs about psychological problems or disorders are important because they set the parameters for threshold tolerance of and responses to atypical or deviant behaviors from the individual and the environment. A longitudinal study of stress-buffering effects for urban male African American adolescent problem behaviors and mental health revealed that although parental support predicted less anxiety and depression longitudinally, the manifestation of psychological symptoms did not predict increased parental support over time. In other words, high parental support may protect African American youth from anxiety and depression, but the appearance of symptoms does not necessarily activate increased levels of support in this ethnic group.

Help Seeking and Preferred Modes of Intervention

Ethnic differences in help seeking have been reported. Based on data from the 1996 round of Health Behavior in School Children, Sen (2004) reported that certain racial groups are at greater risk for not asking for help for depression. In a study of the mental health needs and service utilization of 401 southwestern urban and reservation youth, Stiffman, Striley, Brown, Limb, and Ostmann (2003) found that, regardless of diagnosis, youth meeting criteria for a mental disorder were least likely to use configurations with traditional healers or specialists, and there was little difference in their utilization rates of either. Instead, they were more likely to use service configurations including adults, nonspecialist professionals, and peers before turning to specialists. Sen (2004) found that Black and Asian adolescents were especially prone not to ask for help, with the problem being more acute in the case of males in both groups. The majority of males and females with depressed mood or self-injury risk were not likely to seek help from anyone.

Abe-Kim, Gong, and Takeuchi (2004) examined the influence of religious affiliation, religiosity, and spirituality on help seeking from religious clergy and mental health professionals among 2,285 respondents to the Filipino American Community Epidemiological Survey. After controlling for need (e.g., Symptom Checklist-90 Revised [SCL-90R]; Derogatis & Cleary, 1977; scores, negative life events, and somatic symptoms), demographic variables (e.g., age, gender, marital status, education, county of residence, generational status, and insurance coverage), and cultural variables (e.g., loss of face and language abilities), rates of help seeking from religious clergy (2.5%) were comparable to rates of help seeking from mental health professionals (2.9%). High religiosity was associated with more help seeking from religious clergy but not less help seeking from mental health professionals, whereas high spirituality was associated with less help seeking from mental health professionals.

Experiences with mental health professionals can affect service utilization. Diala et al. (2000) found that, prior to use of services, African Americans had more positive attitudes than European Americans toward seeking such services, though they were less likely to use them. After utilization, however, African American attitudes were found to be less positive than those of European Americans.

Ethnicity, Minority Status, and Perceived Discrimination

Although not a cultural variable, ethnic minority status and its correlates, such as perceived discrimination and low socioeconomic status, with its increased likelihood of exposure to community violence, are often associated with psychological problems and cannot be ignored.

Relationships between these variables and symptomatology or disorder have been found. The ability to perceive racial/ethnic discrimination changes with increasing age. Among Mainland Puerto Ricans, children had a low likelihood of perceiving discrimination, but by adolescence, nearly half of this sample reported perceiving racial/ethnic discrimination (Szalacha et al., 2003). Adolescents were aware of negative stereotypes about Puerto Ricans. Although both groups scored high on multiple indicators of mental health, perceiving discrimination and worrying about discrimination were negatively associated with some dimensions of self-esteem and positively associated with depression and stress. Perceived discrimination and anxiety about discrimination can serve as risk factors for the mental health of Puerto Ricans. Phinney, Madden, and Santos (1998) examined whether perceptions of discrimination may be influenced by one's interpretation of the intentions of others. They studied a sample of Armenian, Mexican American, and Vietnamese adolescents (ages 14 to 19 years) who completed measures of perceived discrimination, self-esteem, mastery, depression/anxiety, intergroup competence, and ethnic identity, as well as demographic variables. A path analysis of the data showed that higher depression/anxiety scores and lower intergroup competence predicted more perceived discrimination. Depression/anxiety and intergroup competence were in turn predicted by self-esteem and mastery, respectively. Birthplace and socioeconomic status had an important effect on perceived discrimination via intergroup competence. Last, Simons et al. (2002) reported that for their sample of African American children (ages 10 to 12 years), at the community level, prevalence of both discrimination and criminal victimization were positively related to depressive symptoms.

CONCEPTUAL AND METHODOLOGICAL ISSUES

Doubts about the conceptual equivalence of certain constructs used in studying internalizing disorders have been raised by several investigators. S. F. Lambert et al. (2004) and Neal-Barnett (2004) have questioned the relevance of the construct anxiety sensitivity for African American children living in high-crime areas. According to these authors, the construct may not have the same meaning and usefulness for this population as it does for other ethnic groups because high anxiety sensitivity may serve as a protective factor and therefore is actually an adaptive strategy in that environment. Given that physical concerns emerged as a robust first factor in the CASI structure for this population, it would seem that the construct of anxiety sensitivity remains meaningful and relevant for African American children and, as shown by S. F. Lambert, McCreary, et al. (2004), for adolescents. However, norms for anxiety sensitivity in this population may be different from those of other ethnic groups or for low-income African-American children living in high-crime areas. This suggests the need to include an assessment of context such as environmental stressors when employing measures such as the FSSC-R and CASI with all children living in poor neighborhoods riddled with crime and other environmental hazards.

Given the overlap of depression with anxiety, somatoform, and dissociative disorders, Kirmayer and Groleau (2001) have raised questions about the universality of the prototype representation for depression in North American psychiatry. They note that culture-specific symptoms may lead to underrecognition or misidentification of syndromes of mania and depression in many ethnocultural groups. Cultural idioms of distress may employ symptoms related to affective disorders to express sentiments and perceptions that do not in themselves indicate psychopathology. A similar concern can be expressed regarding anxiety. Some inconsistent findings on somatic/physiological symptoms of anxiety discussed in this review indicate the need for rethinking the representation of anxiety as well. If increased reporting of anxiety symptoms is the result of cultural influence, as it appears to be at some level, then normative patterns of anxiety reporting in certain populations need to be established and the cultural meaning of such reporting needs to be investigated further.

Much of the extant *cross-cultural* research compares national groups or ethnic groups and implicitly makes the term *culture* equivalent to a label for a sample of subjects (e.g., American versus Chinese). Each person in a given sample is indexed as belonging to a particular national or ethnic group and sharing that group's culture; thus, culture is treated as an index variable (Valsiner, 1997). The problem is that an index variable is a poor substitute for an independent variable that can be manipulated in order to determine its causal relationship to the dependent variable. A persistent methodological problem in studies of cultural diversity in psychopathology is the omission of measures of the assumed cultural basis of the hypothesized ethnic difference. This makes it difficult to reach any definite conclusion about the role of culture. For example, if a collectivist culture is assumed to value family closeness, which, in turn, is hypothesized to serve as protective factor for depression, it would be desirable to include a measure of collectivism in addition to a measure of family closeness. Family closeness may exist for reasons other than that it is culturally valued. The inclusion of data on collectivism strengthens the inference of a cultural basis should the hypothesized association between family closeness and depression be confirmed.

Sampling is another methodological weakness in these studies. Aside from the problem of small sample size in a number of studies, there was ambiguity as to whether the sample was a random sample or the degree to which it was representative of the population being studied. Social class and other relevant characteristics such as generational status were sometimes not reported. Although more studies were careful to use distinct ethnic subgroups (e.g., Cuban Americans) and took this into account in the data analysis, others did not and gave no justification for their use of a heterogeneous ethnic group (e.g., Latinos).

In studies of prevalence rates for disorders whose behavioral indices sometimes overlap with those of other disorders (e.g., somatic symptoms present in both anxiety and depression), comorbidity was not analyzed. Last, many of the measures used are not normed for the population studied. In general, the approach taken in these studies has been an etic rather than an emic approach. Such an approach is not very effective at detecting cultural diversity.

CONCLUSIONS AND FUTURE DIRECTIONS

Cross-cultural studies indicate that certain disorders are identifiable in different countries in various regions of the world, using the same nosology and measures. They also show that gender differences in prevalence rates appear, regardless of that country's view of gender roles and socialization. With rare exceptions, such as the work of Weisz and his collaborators (1997), the cross-cultural studies reviewed in this chapter focused on prevalence rates and measurement validation rather than the cultural correlates of a disorder. Research is needed to investigate culture's role in the development of specific disorders, as well as in their persistence or desistance. This could be incorporated, for example, in the cross-cultural programmatic research on problem behaviors in Dutch children and adolescents by Verhulst and his colleagues (Verhulst & Achenbach, 1995; Verhulst et al., 1997).

Whereas cross-cultural studies did not reveal much evidence of cultural diversity in prevalence rates, comparative ethnic studies did. Ethnic differences in rates of symptoms or *DSM* disorders emerged from epidemiological studies and community and clinical samples. What is notable about these findings is that no one ethnic group showed higher rates across disorders. Rather, one ethnic group may have consistently higher rates than other groups for a particular disorder (e.g., depression among Latinos, substance use/abuse in American Indians) but had rates comparable to those of other groups for other disorders. Furthermore, within-subgroup differences in prevalence rates emerged, indicating the importance of examining ethnic group differences by using ethnic subgroups rather than panethnic groups such as Latinos or Asian Americans, unless prior research has revealed similar findings across subgroups of a panethnic group. Subgroup differences may eventually disappear with succeeding generations also, but until such time as there is solid evidence of similarities across subgroups, findings from a comparison of panethnic groups should be treated with caution. Cross-cultural and cross-ethnic studies that examined the factor structure of specific constructs measured (e.g., fear or anxiety) consistently showed cultural group differences.

Given the paucity of epidemiological studies, the methodological limitations, and, in some cases, inconsistent findings from community and clinical studies, any conclusions about ethnic differences in prevalence rates would be premature. Still, there is sufficient evidence to warrant additional research, preferably involving large representative samples. Prior to undertaking epidemiological studies, more work is needed to ascertain the ways psychopathology is defined in various cultures (Hoagwood & Jensen, 1997), including cultural variations in symptom expression and phenomenology of psychiatric syndromes (Manson, Bechtold, Novins, & Beals, 1997). Despite its acknowledgment of culture's role in psychopathology, the nosological system (i.e., *DSM-IV-TR*) applied currently in cross-cultural research still conceptualizes mental disorder mainly as residing in the individual sans context. Such a nosological system itself emerged from an epistemology that is culturally constituted. The likelihood of finding differences in prevalence rates among other cultural groups may be restricted by the diagnostic criteria and measurement tools employed. To fully understand the relationship

between culture and psychopathology, behaviors that are assumed to be psychopathological (usually culturally defined in Western societies as a *DSM* disorder) have to be explored from other culturally constituted epistemologies. In addition, other culturally constituted expressions of psychopathology have to be explored.

What is initially required is an emic approach. Ethnographic or observational studies to identify and classify cultural variations in the expression of distress or psychopathology can provide data for hypothesis generation, to be followed by more formal, hypothesis-testing research. Other exploratory studies using qualitative, ethnographic, and narrative methods can be used to obtain data for construct definition and identification of culturally appropriate indices as well as correlates that, in turn, can serve as a basis for measurement construction and generation of hypotheses. Quantitative studies using larger, representative samples to establish the psychometric properties of measures and norms would follow. In case the results of exploratory studies suggest that an etic approach would be appropriate in that existing measures might be suitable, the factor structure of relevant constructs (e.g., anxiety) or patterns of organization for symptoms or behavioral indices of a disorder still need to be examined. In addition, it will have to be determined whether the measure fully captures the range of relevant problems or behavior indices of a specific condition in the culture under consideration; if it does not, items will have to be added and the psychometric properties of the revised instrument must be established.

The importance of using reliable, culturally valid measures normed for the specific population cannot be overemphasized. More careful consideration should be given to the following questions: To what degree is what we find the result of measures that are predicated on premises of our dominant, culturally constituted epistemology? If we have developed a measure with samples dominated by majority culture participants and then apply these measures cross-culturally, and find little difference in prevalence and little variability in the expression of, for example, anxiety, what does this finding mean? By defining, via the measurement instruments, what anxiety is in the majority European American culture, there is likely to be a restriction of what we allow ourselves to find, and this will increase the likelihood that the disorder will look the same everywhere. Also, to what degree are our methods of analysis, our statistics, affecting what we find? For example, is our reliance on mean differences very informative? Might mean differences be obfuscating other important information that bears on the issue of the role of culture and, more generally, context in the development of psychopathology? Although approaches that disaggregate the data and look for different patterns of variability are important in examining cultural differences, we need to also explore quantitative methods that are not part of our current statistical repertoire, such as fuzzy logic, which has been used in some cognitive applications. Developmental psychopathology cross-cultural/ethnocultural research can benefit from interdisciplinary collaborations.

Our review of studies on cultural correlates of psychopathology indicated that the same disorder may be associated with different correlates in different ethnic groups or cultures. Furthermore, for a given correlate, the magnitude of associations or the pattern of relationships may differ among different ethnic groups. For the same ethnic group, the magnitude of association between specific symptomatology or disorder and a correlate (e.g., ethnic identity) may vary, depending on how the correlate is operationalized or the age at which the relationship is being assessed.

A developmental-contextual perspective seems lacking in most of the studies reviewed. Culture's role may undergo changes over time, just as in historical time (Bronfenbrenner, 1995) a cultural attribute may change its adaptive function for an individual. Given the lack of sufficient empirical data, it is difficult to predict the direction of the change. It could increase with the individual's increasing age if there is congruence between the individual's ethnicity and that of the surrounding community, or weaken if the dominant culture is different. Changes in the relationship between culture and psychopathology may also depend on the specific cultural and developmental variables involved. Only a few studies have examined age-related changes in culture's role, and longitudinal studies are practically nonexistent. More cross-sectional studies, followed by longitudinal studies, are needed to more precisely elucidate the influence of culture on normal and atypical development and its interaction with other correlates in the course of development.

Culture's role has not been sufficiently explored in the development of any symptomatology or disorder reviewed in this chapter, so there is clearly a need for more research on this issue. However, more thoughtful consideration of the relevant cultural variables and processes ought to precede our choice of cultural variables to study and the disorders that they are hypothesized to influence. It is conceivable that culture may play a less prominent role in the development of those disorders that tend to be reproductive (e.g., Autism) rather than caretaking (e.g., Conduct Disorder) casualties (Sameroff & Chandler, 1975), while continuing to have a strong impact on societal responses to both disorders. Furthermore, the assumptions underlying

our hypotheses need to be based on adequate theoretical or empirical knowledge about both the disorder (e.g., separation anxiety) and the hypothesized cultural correlate (e.g., family closeness). Certain cultural constructs (e.g., family, ethnic identity) require unpacking or further differentiation into their various aspects. The salience of context and time of assessment may have to be taken into consideration. For example, ethnicity may not be found to be salient if assessment is conducted in routine activities at various times of the day; ethnic differences in problem behaviors may not be observed if data are collected at home or in the neighborhood but will appear in school. Perhaps the lack of ethnic differences in prevalence rates for certain symptomatologies or disorders may be due partly to the fact that so many ethnic minority children and youth with these problems do not participate in research because they are disproportionately in foster homes, residential treatment centers, juvenile detention, or jail, or are just simply out on the streets.

As stated in the introduction to this chapter, culture is relevant to an understanding of psychopathology because of its role in development and because it shapes environmental response to distress and atypical behavior. Though culture may not play a prominent role in the development of certain disorders, it may still do so in shaping the environment's response to the emergence of those disorders. There are few studies on the latter role pertaining to the problems of children and adolescents. More work is needed, including studies to determine beliefs about the etiology, prognosis, and treatment of specific clinical syndromes, help-seeking attitudes and preferences, and expectations of treatment held by both the parent and the developing child or adolescent. There is much to be learned in the relationship of context, including culture, to the development of psychopathology, and we are only beginning to get a better appreciation of the importance of this relationship.

REFERENCES

Abe-Kim, J., Gong, F., & Takeuchi, D. (2004). Religiosity, spirituality, and help-seeking among Filipino Americans: Religious clergy or mental health professionals. *Journal of Community Psychology, 32,* 675–689.

Achenbach, T. M. (1991a). *Integrative guide for the 1991 CBCL/4–18, YSR and TSR profiles.* Burlington: University of Vermont, Department of Psychiatry.

Achenbach, T. M. (1991b). *Manual for the Child Behavior Checklist/4–18 and 1991 Profile.* Burlington: University of Vermont, Department of Psychiatry.

Achenbach, T. M. (1991c). *Manual for the Youth Self-Report and 1991 profile.* Burlington: University of Vermont, Department of Psychiatry.

Achenbach, T. M., & Edelbrock, C. (1981). Behavioral problems and competencies reported by parents of normal and disturbed children aged four through sixteen. *Mongraphs of the Society for Research in Child Development, 46*(1, Serial No. 188).

Achenbach, T. M., & Edelbrock, C. S. (1986). *Manual for the teacher version of the Child Behavior Checklist and Child Behavior Profile.* Burlington, VT: Author.

Achenbach, T. M., Howell, C. T., Quay, H. C., & Conners, C. K. (1991). National survey of problems and competencies among four to sixteen-year-olds: Parents' reports for normative and clinical samples. *Monographs of the Society for Research in Child Development, 56*(3, Serial No. 225).

Ahlawat, K. S. (1986). Cross-cultural comparisons of anxiety for Jordanian and United States high school students. In C. D. Spielberger & R. Diaz-Guerrero (Eds.), *Cross-cultural anxiety* (Vol. 3, pp. 93–112). Washington, DC: Hemisphere/Harper & Row.

American Psychiatric Association. (1987). *Diagnostic and statistical manual of mental disorders* (3rd ed., rev.). Washington, DC: Author.

American Psychiatric Association. (2000). *Diagnostic and statistical manual of mental disorders* (4th ed., text rev.). Washington, DC: Author.

Angel, R., & Guarnaccia, P. (1989). Mind, body, and culture: Somatizarion among Hispanics. *Social Science and Medicine, 28,* 1229–1238.

Austin, A. A., & Chorpita, B. F. (2004). Temperament, anxiety, and depression: Comparisons among five ethnic groups of children. *Journal of Clinical Child and Adolescent Psychology, 33,* 216–226.

Barkley, R. A. (2003). Attention deficit/hyperactivity disorder. In E. J. Mash & R. A. Barkley (Eds.), *Child psychopathology* (3rd ed., pp. 75–143). New York: Guilford Press.

Beals, J., Piasecki, J., Nelson, S., Jones, M., Keane, E., Dauphinais, P., et al. (1997). Psychiatric disorder among American Indian adolescents: Prevalence in Northern Plains youth. *Journal of the American Academy of Child and Adolescent Psychiatry, 36,* 1252–1259.

Beauvais, F., Jumper-Thurman, P., Helm, H., Plested, B., & Burnside, M. (2004). Surveillance of drug use among American Indian adolescents: Patterns over 25 years. *Journal of Adolescent Health, 34,* 493–500.

Beidel, D. C., Turner, S. M., & Morris, T. L. (1995). A new inventory to assess childhood social anxiety and phobia: The social phobia and anxiety inventory for children. *Psychological Assessment, 7,* 73–79.

Beidel, D. C., Turner, S. M., & Morris, T. L. (1999). Psychopathology of childhood social phobia. *Journal of the American Academy of Child and Adolescent Psychiatry, 38,* 643–652.

Beidel, D. C., Turner, S. M., & Morris, T. L. (2000). Behavioral treatment of childhood social phobia. *Journal of Consulting and Clinical Psychology, 68,* 1077–1080.

Beiser, M., & Attneave, C. L. (1982). Mental disorders among Native American children: Race and risk periods for entering treatment. *American Journal of Psychiatry, 139,* 193–198.

Berry, J. W. (1969). On cross-cultural comparability. *International Journal of Psychology, 4,* 207–229.

Bhata, M. S., Nigam, V. R., Bohra, N., & Malik, S. C. (1991). Attention deficit disorder with hyperactivity among pediatric outpatients. *Journal of Child Psychology and Psychiatry, 32,* 297–306.

Bird, H. R. (2002). The diagnostic classification, epidemiology, and cross-cultural validity of ADHD. In P. S. Jensen & J. R. Cooper (Eds.), *Attention deficit hyperactivity disorder: State of the science-best practices* (pp. 212–216). Kingston, NJ: Civic Research Institute.

Bird, H. R., Canino, G. J., Davies, M., Zhang, H., Ramirez, R., & Lahey, B. B. (2001). Prevalence and correlates of antisocial behaviors among three ethnic groups. *Journal of Abnormal Child Psychology, 29,* 465–478.

Birman, D. (2005). A tale of two cities: Replication of a study on the acculturation and adaptation of immigrant adolescents from the former Soviet Union in a different community context. *American Journal of Community Psychology, 35,* 83–101.

Bronfenbrenner, U. (1977). Toward an experimental ecology of human development. *American Psychologist, 32,* 513–531.

Bronfenbrenner, U. (1979). *The ecology of human development.* Cambridge, MA: Harvard University Press.

Bronfenbrenner, U. (1995). Developmental ecology through space and time: A future perspective. In P. Moen, G. H. Elder Jr., & K. Luscher (Eds.), *Examining lives in context: Perspectives on the ecology of human development.* Washington, DC: American Psychological Association.

Bussing, R., Schoenberg, N. E., Rogers, K. M., Zima, B. T., & Angus, S. (1998). Explanatory models of ADHD: Do they differ by ethnicity, child gender, treatment status, and sociodemographic status? *Journal of Emotional and Behavioral Disorders, 6,* 233–242.

Campbell, D. T. (1975). On the conflicts between biological and social evolution and between psychology and moral tradition. *American Psychologist, 30,* 1103–1126.

Canino, G., Shrout, P. E., Bird, H. R., Bravo, M., Ramirez, R., Chavez, L., et al. (2004). The DSM-IV rates of child and adolescent disorders in Puerto Rico. *Archives of General Psychiatry, 61,* 85–93.

Chen, C., Greenberger, E., Lester, J., Dong, Q., & Guo, M. (1998). A cross-cultural study of family and peer correlates of adolescent misconduct. *Developmental Psychology, 14,* 770–781.

Chin, K., Kelly, R. J., & Fagan, J. (1992). Patterns of Chinese gang extortion. *Justice Quarterly, 9,* 401–422.

Choi, H., Stafford, L., Meininger, J. C., Roberts, R., & Smith, D. P. (2002). Psychometric properties of the DSM Scale for Depression (DSD) with Korean American youth. *Issues in Mental Health Nursing, 23,* 735–756.

Choney, S. K., Berryhill-Paapke, E., & Robbins, R. R. (1995). The acculturation of American Indians. In J. M. Ponterotto, J. M. Casas, L. A. Suzuki, & C. M. Alexander (Eds.), *Handbook of multicultural counseling* (pp. 75–93). Thousand Oaks, CA: Sage.

Chorpita, B., Yim, L., Moffitt, C., Unemoto, L. A., & Francis, S. E. (2000). Assessment of symptoms of DSM-IV anxiety and depression in children: A revised anxiety and depression scale. *Behavior Research and Therapy, 38,* 835–855.

Cicchetti, D., & Cohen, D. J. (1995). Perspectives on developmental psychopathology. In D. Cicchetti & D. J. Cohen (Eds.), *Developmental psychopathology: Vol. I. Theory and methods* (pp. 3–20). New York: Wiley.

Clark, L. A., & Watson, D. (1991). Tripartite model of anxiety and depression: Psychometric evidence and taxonomic implications. *Journal of Abnormal Psychology, 100,* 316–336.

Cole, D. A., Martin, J. M., Peeke, L., Henderson, A., & Harwell, J. (1998). Validation of depression and anxiety measures in White and Black youths: Multitrait-multimethod analyses. *Psychological Assessment, 10,* 261–271.

Cole, M. (1996). *Cultural psychology: A once and future discipline.* Cambridge, MA: Harvard University Press.

Cole, M., Cole, S. R., & Lightfoot, C. (2004). *The development of children* (5th ed.). New York: Worth.

Compton, S. N., Nelson, A. H., & March, J. S. (2000). Social phobia and separation anxiety symptoms in community and clinical samples of children and adolescents. *Journal of the American Academy of Child and Adolescent Psychiatry, 39,* 1040–1046.

Costello, E. J. (1989). Developments in child psychiatric epidemiology. *Journal of the American Academy of Child and Adolescent Psychiatry, 28,* 836–841.

Costello, E. J., Angold, A., Burns, B. J., Stangl, D. K., Tweed, D. L., Erkanli, A., et al. (1996). The Great Smoky Mountain Study of Youth: Goals, design, methods, and the prevalence of DSM-III-R disorders. *Archives of General Psychiatry, 53,* 1129–1136.

Costello, E. J., Farmer, E. M. Z., Angold, A., Burns, B. J., & Erkanli, A. (1997). Psychiatric disorders among American Indian and White youth in Appalachia: The Great Smoky Mountain Study. *American Journal of Public Health, 87,* 827–832.

Crijnen, A. A. M., Achenbach, T. M., & Verhulst, F. C. (1997). Comparisons of problems reported by parents of children in 12 cultures: Total problems, externalizing, and internalizing. *Journal of the American Academy of Child and Adolescent Psychiatry, 36,* 1269–1277.

Danko, G. P., Miyamoto, R. H., Foster, J. E., Johnson, R. C., Andrade, N. N., Yates, A., et al. (1997). Psychiatric symptoms in offspring of within vs. across racial/ethnic marriages. *Cultural Diversity and Mental Health, 3,* 273–277.

deGroot, A., Koot, H. M., & Verhulst, F. C. (1994). Cross-cultural generalizability of the Child Behavior Checklist cross-informant syndromes. *Psychological Assessment, 6,* 225–230.

Derogatis, L. L., & Cleary, P. A. (1977). Factorial invariance across gender for the primary symptom dimensions of the SCL-90. *British Journal of Social and Clinical Psychology, 10,* 347–356.

Diala, V., Muntaner, C., Walrath, C., Nickerson, K. J., LeVeist, T. A., & Leaf, P. J. (2000). Racial differences in attitudes toward professional mental health care and in the use of services. *American Journal of Orthopsychiatry, 70,* 455–464.

Dick, R. W., Beals, J., Keane, E. M., & Manson, S. M. (1994). Factorial structure of the CES-D among American Indian adolescents. *Journal of Adolescence, 17,* 73–79.

Dinges, N. G., & Duong-Tran, Q. (1993). Stressful life-events and co-occurring depression, substance abuse, and suicidality among American Indian and Alaskan Native adolescents. *Culture, Medicine, and Psychiatry, 16,* 487–502.

Dmitrieva, J., Chen, C., Greenberger, E., & Gil-Rivas, V. (2004). Family relationships and adolescent psychosocial outcomes: Converging findings from Eastern and Western cultures. *Journal of Research on Adolescence, 14,* 425–447.

Doerfler, L. A., Felner, R. A., Rowling, R. T., Raley, P. A., & Evans, E. (1988). Depression in children and adolescents: A comparative analysis of the utility and construct validity of two assessment measures. *Journal of Consulting and Clinical Psychology, 56,* 769–772.

Edgerton, R. B. (2000). Traditional beliefs and practices: Are some better than others. In L. E. Harrison & S. P. Huntington (Eds.), *Culture matters* (pp. 126–140). New York: Basic Books.

Edman, J. L., Andrade, N. N., Glipa, J., Foster, J., Danko, G. P., Yates, A., et al. (1998). Depressive symptoms among Filipino American adolescents. *Cultural Diversity and Ethnic Minority Psychology, 4,* 45–54.

Edman, J. L., Danko, G. P., Andrade, N., McArdle, J. J., Foster, J., & Glipa, J. (1999). Factor structure of the Center for Epidemiological Studies Depression Scale (CES-D) among Filipino-American adolescents. *Social Psychiatry and Epidemiology, 34,* 212–215.

Ehlers, C. L., Garcia-Andrade, C., & Phillips, E. (2001). Effects of age and parental history of alcoholism on EEG findings in mission Indian children and adolescents. *Alcoholism: Clinical and Experimental Research, 25,* 672–679.

Ellen, R. (1982). *Environment, subsistence, and system: The ecology of small-scale social formations.* New York: Cambridge University Press.

Elliott, D. S., Huizinga, D., & Ageton, S. S. (1985). *Explaining delinquency and drug use.* Beverly Hills, CA: Sage.

Ellis, B. B., & Kimmel, H. D. (1992). Identification of unique cultural response patterns by means of item response theory. *Journal of Applied Psychology, 77,* 177–184.

Essau, C. A., Conradt, J., & Petermann, F. (2000). Frequency, comorbidity, and psychosocial impairment of specific phobia in adolescents. *Journal of Clinical Child Psychology, 29,* 221–231.

Ferrell, C. B., Beidel, D. C., & Turner, S. M. (2004). Assessment and treatment of socially phobic children: A cross-cultural comparison. *Journal of Clinical Child and Adolescent Psychology, 33,* 260–268.

Fisckenscher, A., & Novins, D. K. (2001). Gender differences and conduct disorder among American Indian youth in residential substance abuse treatment. *Journal of Psychoactive Drugs, 35,* 79–84.

Fleming, T. E., & Offord, D. R. (1990). Epidemiology of childhood depression disorders: A critical review. *Journal of the Academy of Child and Adolescent Psychiatry, 29,* 571–580.

Fonseca, A. C., Yule, W., & Erol, N. (1994). Cross-cultural issues. In T. H. Ollendick, N. J. King, & W. Yule (Eds.), *International handbook of phobic and anxiety disorders in children and adolescents* (pp. 67–84). New York: Plenum Press.

Freedenthal, S., & Stiffman, A. R. (2004). Suicidal behavior in urban American Indian adolescents: A comparison with reservation youth in a southwestern state. *Suicide and Life Threatening Behavior, 34,* 160–171.

Furnham, A., & Malik, E. (1994). Cross-cultural beliefs "about depression." *International Journal of Social Psychiatry, 40,* 106–123.

Garcia-Coll, C., Ackerman, A., & Cicchetti, D. (2000). Cultural influences on developmental processes and outcomes: Implications for the study of development and psychopathology. *Development and Psychopathology, 12,* 333–356.

Ge, X., Kim, I. J., Brody, G. H., Conger, R., Simone, R. L., Gibbons, F. X., et al. (2003). It's about timing and change: Pubertal transition effects on symptoms of major depression among African American youths. *Developmental Psychology, 39,* 430–429.

Ginsburg, G. S., & Drake, K. (2002). Anxiety sensitivity and panic attack symptomatology among African American adolescents. *Journal of Anxiety Disorders, 16,* 83–96.

Ginsburg, G. S., & Silverman, W. (1996). Phobic and anxiety disorders in Hispanic and Caucasian youth. *Journal of Anxiety Disorders, 14,* 57–67.

Good, B. J., & Kleinman, A. (1985). Epilogue: Culture and depression. In A. Kleinman & B. J. Good (Eds.), *Culture and depression studies in the anthropology and cross-cultural psychiatry of affect and disorder.* Berkeley: University of California Press.

Goodenough, W. (1989). Culture: Concept and phenomenon. In M. Freilich (Ed.), *The relevance of culture* (p. 7). New York: Bergin & Garvey.

Gore, S., & Aseltine, R. (2003). Race and ethnic differences in depressed mood following the transition from high school. *Journal of Health and Social Behavior, 44,* 370–379.

Gray, J. P., & Winterowd, C. L. (2002). Health risks in American Indian adolescents: A descriptive study of a rural, non-reservation sample. *Journal of Pediatric Psychology, 27,* 717–725.

Greenberger, E., & Chen, C. (1996). Perceived family relationships and depressed mood in early and late adolescence: A comparison of European and Asian Americans. *Developmental Psychology, 32,* 707–716.

Greenfield, P. (2002). The mutual definition of culture and biology in development. In H. Keller, Y. H. Poortinga, & A. Scholmerich (Eds.), *Between culture and biology: Perspectives on ontogenetic development* (57–76). Cambridge, England: Cambridge University Press.

Guiao, I., & Thompson, E. A. (2004). Ethnicity and problem behaviors among adolescent females in the United States. *Health Care for Women International, 25,* 296–310.

Guida, F. V., & Ludlow, L. H. (1989). A cross-cultural study of text anxiety. *Journal of Cross-Cultural Psychology, 20,* 178–190.

Harris, M. (1960). Adaptation in biological and cultural science. *Transactions of the New York Academy of Science, 23,* 59–65.

Hartman, C. A., Hox, T., Auerbach, T., Erol, N., Fonseca, A. C., Mellenbergh, G. J., et al. (1999). Syndrome dimensions of the Child Behavior Checklist and the Teacher Report Form: A critical empirical evaluation. *Journal of Child Psychology and Psychiatry, 40,* 1095–1115.

Harwood, R. L., Miller, J. G., & Irizarry, N. L. (1995). *Culture and attachment: Perceptions of the child in context.* New York: Guilford Press.

Hayward, C., Gotlib, I. H., Schraedley, P. K., & Litt, I. F. (1999). Ethnic differences in the association between pubertal status and symptoms of depression in adolescent girls. *Journal of Adolescent Health, 25,* 143–149.

Hoagwood, K., & Jensen, P. (1997). Developmental psychopathology and the notion of culture. *Applied Developmental Science, 1,* 108–112.

Hofstede, G. (1994). *Cultures and organizations.* London: HarperCollins.

Huang, K., Leong, T. L., & Wagner, N. S. (1994). Coping with peer stressors and associated dysphoria: Acculturation differences among Chinese-American children. *Counseling Psychology Quarterly, 7,* 53–68.

Johnston, L., O'Malley, P., & Bachman, J. (2000). *Monitoring the future: National Survey Results on Drug Use, 1975–1999* (NIH Publication No. 00-4802). Bethesda, MD: National Institute on Drug Abuse.

Johnston, L., O'Malley, P., & Bachman, J. (2001). *Monitoring the future: National Results on Adolescent Drug Use—Overview of key findings, 2000* (NIH Publication No. 01-4923). Bethesda, MD: National Institute on Drug Abuse.

Kanbayashi, Y., Nakata, Y., Fujii, K., Kita, M., & Wada, K. (1994). ADHD-related behavior among non-referred children: Parent's ratings of DSM-III-R symptoms. *Child Psychiatry and Human Development, 25,* 13–29.

Kandel, D. B., & Davies, M. (1982). Epidemiology of depressive mood in adolescents. *Archives of General Psychiatry, 39,* 1205–1212.

Katragadda, C. P., & Tidwell, R. (1998). Rural Hispanic adolescents at risk for depressive symptoms. *Journal of Applied Social Psychology, 28,* 1916–1930.

Kelder, S. H., Murray, N. G., Orpinas, P., Prokhorov, A., McReynolds, L., Zhang, Q., et al. (2001). Depression and substance use in minority middle-school students. *American Journal of Public Health, 91,* 761–766.

Kim, S. Y. (2000). Parenting practices and adolescent depressive symptoms in Chinese American families. *Journal of Family Psychology, 14,* 420–435.

Kirmayer, L. J., & Groleau, D. (2001). Affective disorders in cultural context. *Psychiatric Clinics of North America, 24,* 465–478.

Kistner, J. A., David, C. F., & White, B. A. (2003). Ethnic and sex differences in children's depressive symptoms: Mediating effects of perceived and actual competence. *Journal of Clinical Child and Adolescent Psychology, 32,* 341–350.

Klinger, L. G., Dawson, G., & Renner, P. (2003). Autistic disorder. In E. J. Mash & R. A. Barkley (Eds.), *Child psychopathology* (2nd ed., pp. 409–454). New York: Guilford Press.

Kluckhohn, C., & Leighton, D. (1962). *The Navajo* (Rev. ed.). Garden City, NY: Doubleday.

Kluckhohn, C., & Murray, H. A. (1953). Personality formation and its determinants. In C. Kluckhohn & H. A. Murray (Eds.), *Personality, its nature, society, and culture* (2nd ed., pp. 53–67). New York: Alfred Knopf.

Knight, G. P., Virdin, L. M., Ocampo, K. A., & Roosa, M. (1994). An examination of the cross-ethnic equivalence of measures of negative life events and mental health among Hispanic and Anglo-American children. *American Journal of Orthopsychiatry, 22,* 767–783.

Kovacs, M. (1985). Children's Depression Inventory. *Psychopharmacology Bulletin, 21,* 995–998.

Kovacs, M. (1992). *Children's Depression Inventory Manual.* North Tomawanda, NY: Multi-Health Systems.

Kulis, S., Napoli, M., & Marsiglia, F. F. (2002). Ethnic pride, biculturalism, and drug use norms of urban American Indian adolescents. *Social Work Research, 26,* 101–112.

Lahey, B. B., Flagg, E. W., Bird, H. R., Schwab-Stone, M., Canino, G., Dulcan, M. K., et al. (1996). The NIMH Methods for the Epidemiology of Child and Adolescent Mental Disorder (MECA) Study: Background and methodology. *Journal of the American Academy of Child and Adolescent Psychiatry, 35,* 855–864.

Lahey, B. B., Loeber, R., Hart, E. L., Frick, P. J., Applegate, B., Zhang, Q., et al. (1995). Four-year longitudinal study of conduct disorder in boys: Patterns and predictors of persistence. *Journal of Abnormal Psychology, 104,* 83–93.

Lambert, M. C., Weisz, J. R., & Knight, F. (1989). Over- and undercontrolled clinic referral problems in Jamaican clinic-referred children: Teacher reports for ages 6–17. *Journal of Abnormal Child Psychology, 17,* 553–562.

Lambert, M. C., Weisz, J. R., Knight, F., Desrosiers, M., Overly, K., & Thesiger, C. (1992). Jamaican and American adult perspectives on child psychopathology: Further explorations of the threshold model. *Journal of Consulting and Clinical Psychology, 60,* 146–149.

Lambert, S. F., Cooley, M. R., Campbell, K. D. M., Benoit, M. Z., & Stansbury, R. (2004). Assessing anxiety sensitivity in inner-city African American children: Psychometric properties of the childhood anxiety sensitivity index. *Journal of Clinical Child and Adolescent Psychology, 33,* 248–259.

Lambert, S. F., McCreary, B. T., Preston, J. L., Schmidt, N. B., Joiner, T. E., & Ialongo, N. S. (2004). Anxiety sensitivity in African-American adolescents: Evidence of symptom specificity of anxiety sensitivity components. *Journal of the American Academy of Child and Adolescent Psychiatry, 43,* 887–895.

Last, C., & Perrin, S. (1993). Anxiety disorders in African American and White children. *Journal of Abnormal Child Psychology,* 125–138.

Lerner, R. M. (1995). *America's youth in crisis: Challenges and options for programs and policies.* Thousand Oaks, CA: Sage.

Lewinsohn, P. M., Hops, H., Roberts, R. E., Seeley, J. R., & Andrews, J. A. (1993). Adolescent psychopathology: Vol. I. Prevalence and incidence of depression and other DSM-III-R disorders among high school students. *Journal of Abnormal Psychology, 102,* 133–144.

Lin, N. (1989). Measuring depressive symptomatology in China. *Journal of Nervous and Mental Diseases, 177,* 121–131.

Luk, C., & Bond, M. H. (1992). Chinese lay beliefs about the causes and cures of psychological problems. *Journal of Social Clinical Psychology, 11,* 140–157.

Maggini, C., Ampollini, F., Garibaldi, S., Celia, P. I., Peqlizza, I., & Marchesi, C. (2001). The Parma High School Epidemiological Study: Obsessive-compulsive symptoms. *Acta Psychiatrica Scandinavia, 103,* 441–446.

Manson, S. M. (1996). Culture and DSM-IV: Implications for the diagnosis of mood and anxiety disorders. In J. E. Mezzich, A. Kleinman, H. Fabrega Jr., & D. L. Parron (Eds.), *Culture and psychiatric disorders: A DSM-IV perspective* (pp. 99–113). Washington, DC: American Psychiatric Press.

Manson, S. M., Bechtold, D. W., Novins, D. K., & Beals, J. (1997). Assessing psychopathology in American Indian and Alaska Native Children and Adolescents. *Applied Developmental Science, 1,* 135–144.

Marsiglia, F. F., Kulis, S., & Hecht, M. L. (2001). Ethnic labels and ethnic identity as predictors of drug use among middle school students in the Southwest. *Journal of Research on Adolescence, 11,* 21–48.

McGee, R., Feehan, M., Williams, S., & Partridge, F. (1990). DSM-III disorders in a large sample of adolescents. *Journal of the American Academy of Child and Adolescent Psychiatry, 29,* 611–619.

McKelvey, R. S., Baldasar, L. V., Sang, D. L., & Roberts, L. (1999). Vietnamese parental perceptions of child and adolescent mental illness. *Journal of Emotional and Behavioral Disorders, 7,* 72–82.

Moore, J. W., & Vigil, J. D. (1989). Chicano gangs: Group norms and individual factors related to adult criminality. *Atzlan, 18,* 27–44.

Mossakowski, K. (2003). Coping with perceived discrimination: Does ethnic identity protect mental health? *Journal of Health and Social Behavior, 44,* 318–333.

Neal, A. M., & Knisley, H. H. (1995). What are African American children afraid of? Pt. II. A twelve-month follow-up. *Journal of Anxiety Disorders, 9,* 151–161.

Neal, A. M., Lilly, R. S., & Zakis, S. (1993). What are African American children afraid of? A preliminary study. *Journal of Anxiety Disorders, 7,* 129–139.

Neal-Barnett, A. (2004). Orphas no more: A commentary on anxiety and African American youth. *Journal of Clinical Child and Adolescent Psychology, 33,* 276–278.

North, D. C. (1990). *Institutions, institutional change, and economic performance.* Cambridge, MA: Cambridge University Press.

Novins, D. K., & Baron, A. E. (2004). American Indian substance use: The hazards for substance use initiation and progression for adolescents aged 14 to 20 years. *Journal of the American Academy of Child and Adolescent Psychiatry, 43,* 316–324.

Novins, D. K., Beals, J., & Mitchell, C. M. (2001). Sequences of substance use among American Indian adolescents. *Journal of the American Academy of Child and Adolescent Psychiatry, 40,* 1168–1174.

Novy, D. M., Stanley, M. A., Averill, P., & Daza, P. (2001). Psychometric comparability of English- and Spanish-language measures of anxiety and related affective symptoms. *Psychological Assessment, 13,* 347–355.

Okamoto, S. K., LeCroy, C. W., Dustman, P., Hohmann-Marriott, B., & Kulis, S. (2004). An ecological assessment of drug-related problem situations for American Indian adolescents of the Southwest. *Journal of Social Work Practice in the Addictions, 4,* 47–63.

Okazaki, S. (1997). Sources of ethnic differences between Asian American and White American college students on measures of depression and social anxiety. *Journal of Abnormal Psychology, 106,* 52–60.

O'Leary, K. D., Vivian, D., & Nisi, A. (1985). Hyperactivity in Italy. *Journal of Abnormal Child Psychology, 13,* 485–500.

Ollendick, T. H. (1983a). Fear in children and adolescents: Normative data. *Behavior Research and Therapy, 23,* 465–467.

Ollendick, T. H. (1983b). Reliability and validity of the Revised Fear Schedule for Children (FSSC-R). *Behavior Research and Therapy, 21,* 685–692.

Ollendick, T. H., Yule, W., & Ollier, K. (1991). Fears in British children and their relationship to manifest anxiety and depression. *Journal of Child Psychology and Psychiatry, 32,* 321–331.

Patterson, O. (2000). Taking culture seriously: A framework and an Afro-American illustration. In L. E. Harrison & S. P. Huntington (Eds.), *Culture matters.* New York: Basic Books.

Phinney, J. S., Madden, T., & Santos, L. J. (1998). Psychological variables as predictors of perceived ethnic discrimination among minority and immigrant adolescents. *Journal of Applied Social Psychology, 28,* 937–953.

Pina, A. A., & Silverman, W. K. (2004). Clinical phenomenology, somatic symptoms, and distress in Hispanic/Latino and European American youths with anxiety disorders. *Journal of Clinical Child and Adolescent Psychology, 33,* 227–236.

Plunkett, M., & Mitchell, C. (2000). Substance use rates among American Indian adolescents: Regional comparisons with monitoring the future high school seniors. *Journal of Drug Use, 30,* 593–620.

Prelow, H. M., Danoff-Burg, S., Swenson, R. R., & Pulgiano, D. (2004). The impact of ecological risk and perceived discrimination on the psychological adjustment of African American and European American youth. *American Journal of Community Psychology, 32,* 375–389.

Rabian, B., Embry, L., & McIntyre, D. (1999). Behavioral validation of the childhood anxiety sensitivity index in children. *Journal of Clinical Child Psychology, 28,* 105–112.

Radloff, L. S. (1977). The CES-D scale: A new self-report depression scale for research in the general population. *Applied Psychological Measurement, 1,* 345–401.

Ramos, B., Jaccard, J., & Guilamo-Ramos, V. (2003). Dual ethnicity and depressive symptoms: Implications of being Black and Latino in the United States. *Hispanic Journal of Behavioral Sciences, 25,* 147–173.

Reiss, S. (1997). Trait anxiety: It is not what you think it is. *Journal of Anxiety Disorders, 11,* 201–214.

Reynolds, C. R., & Richmond, B. O. (1978). What I think and feel: A revised measure of children's manifest anxiety. *Journal of Abnormal Child Psychology, 6,* 271–280.

Rieckmann, T. R., Wadsworth, M. E., & Deyhle, D. (2004). Cultural identity, explanatory style, and depression in Navajo adolescents. *Cultural Diversity and Ethnic Minority Psychology, 10,* 365–382.

Roberts, R. E., & Chen, Y. C. (1995). Depressive symptoms and suicidal ideation among Mexican origin and Anglo adolescents. *Journal of the American Academy of Child and Adolescent Psychiatry, 34,* 81–90.

Roberts, R. E., Chen, Y. R., & Solovitz, B. L. (1995). Symptoms of DSM-III-R major depression among Anglo, African and Mexican American adolescents. *Journal of Affective Disorders, 36,* 1–9.

Roberts, R. E., Roberts, C. R., & Chen, Y. R. (1997). Ethnocultural differences in prevalence of adolescent depression. *American Journal of Community Psychology, 25,* 95–110.

Roberts, R. E., & Sobhan, M. (1992). Symptoms of depression in adolescence: A comparison of Anglo, African, and Hispanic Americans. *Journal of Youth Adolescence, 21,* 639–651.

Romero, A. J., & Roberts, R. E. (2003). Stress within a bicultural context for adolescents of Mexican descent. *Cultural Diversity and Ethnic Minority Psychology, 9,* 171–184.

Rushton, J. L., Forcier, M., & Schectman, R. M. (2002). Epidemiology of depressive symptoms in the National Longitudinal Study of Adolescent Health. *Journal of the Academy of Child and Adolescent Psychiatry, 41,* 199–205.

Sack, W., McSharry, S., Clarke, G. N., & Kinney, R. (1994). The Khmer adolescent project: Vol. I. Epidemiologic findings in two generations of Cambodian refugees. *Journal of Nervous and Mental Diseases, 182,* 387–395.

Sameroff, A. J., & Chandler, M. J. (1975). Reproductive risk and the continuum of caretaking casualty. In F. D. Horowitz, E. M. Hetherington, S. Scarr-Salapatek, & G. M. Siegel (Eds.), *Review of Child Development Research* (Vol. 4, pp. 187–244). Chicago: University of Chicago Press.

Sarason, S. B., Davidson, K. S., Lightfall, F. F., Waite, R. R., & Ruebush, B. K. (1960). *Anxiety in elementary school children.* New York: Wiley.

Sen, B. (2004). Adolescent propensity for depressed mood and help-seeking. *Journal of Mental Health Policy and Economics, 7,* 133–145.

Shaffer, A., Forehand, R., & Kotchick, B. A. (2002). A longitudinal examination of correlates of depressive symptoms among inner-city African-American children and adolescents. *Journal of Child and Family Studies, 11,* 151–164.

Shaffer, D., Fisher, P., Dulcan, M. K., Davies, M., Piacentini, J., Schwab-Stone, M., et al. (1996). The second version of the NIMH Diagnostic Interview Schedule for Children (DISC-2.3): Vol. 1. Description, acceptability, prevalences and performance in the MECA Study. *Journal of the American Academy of Child and Adolescent Psychiatry, 35,* 865–877.

Shaffer, D., Gould, M. S., Brasic, L., Ambrosini, P., Fisher, P., Bird, H., et al. (1983). A Children's Global Assessment Scale (CGAS). *Archives of General Psychiatry, 40,* 1228–1231.

Shore, G. N., & Rapport, M. D. (1998). The Fear Survey Schedule for Children-Revised (FSSC-HI): Ethnocultural variations in children's fearfulness. *Journal of Anxiety Disorders, 12,* 437–461.

Siegel, J. M., Aneshensel, C. S., Taub, B., Cantwell, D., & Driscoll, A. K. (1998). Adolescent depressed mood in a multiethnic sample. *Journal of Youth and Adolescence, 27,* 413–429.

Silverman, W. K., Fleisig, W., Rabian, B., & Peterson, R. A. (1991). The Childhood Anxiety Sensitivity Index. *Journal of Clinical Child Psychology, 20,* 162–168.

Silverman, W. K., Goodhart, A. W., Barrett, P. M., & Turner, C. (2003). The facets of anxiety sensitivity expressed in the childhood anxiety sensitivity index: Confirmatory analyses of factor models from past studies. *Journal of Abnormal Psychology, 112,* 364–374.

Simons, R. L., Murry, V., McLoyd, V., Lin, K., Cutrona, C., & Conger, R. D. (2002). Discrimination, crime, ethnic identity, and parenting as correlates of depressive symptoms among African-American children: A multilevel analysis. *Development and Psychopathology, 14,* 371–393.

Spicer, P., Novins, D. K., Mitchell, C. M., & Beals, J. (2003). Aboriginal social organization, contemporary experience and American Indian adolescent alcohol use. *Quarterly Journal of Studies on Alcohol, 64,* 450–457.

Spielberger, C. D., Diaz-Guerrero, B., & Strelan, J. (Eds.). (1990). *Cross-cultural anxiety* (Vol. 4). Washington, DC: Hemisphere/Harper & Row.

Stiffman, A., Striley, C., Brown, E., Limb, G., & Ostmann, E. (2003). American Indian youth: Who southwestern urban and reservation youth turn to for help with mental health or addictions. *Journal of Child and Family Studies, 12,* 319–333.

Strauss, C. C., & Last, C. G. (1993). Social and simple phobia in children. *Journal of Anxiety Disorders, 7,* 141–152.

Sue, S., & Chu, J. Y. (2003). The mental health of ethnic minority groups: Challenges posed by the Supplement to the Surgeon General's Report on Mental Health. *Culture, Medicine and Psychiatry, 27,* 447–465.

Szalacha, L., Erkut, S., Garcia-Coll, C., Alarcon, O., Fields, J. P., & Ceder, I. (2003). Discrimination and Puerto Rican children's and adolescent's mental health. *Cultural Diversity and Ethnic Minority Psychology, 9,* 141–155.

Twenge, J. M., & Nolen-Hoeksema, S. (2002). Age, gender, race, socioeconomic status, and birth cohort difference on the children's depression inventory: A meta-analysis. *Journal of Abnormal Psychology, 111,* 578–588.

U.S. Department of Health and Human Services. (2001). *Mental health: Culture, race, and ethnicity—A supplement to mental health: A report of the Surgeon General.* Rockville, MD: U.S. Department of Health and Human Services, Substance Abuse and Mental Health Services Administration, Center for Mental Health Services.

Valleni-Basile, L. A., Garrison, C. Z., Jackson, K. L., Waller, J. L., McKeown, R. E., Addy, C. L., et al. (1994). Frequency of compulsive-obsessive disorder in a community sample of young adolescents. *Journal of the American Academy of Child and Adolescent Psychiatry, 33,* 782–791.

Valsiner, J. (1997). *Culture and the development of children's action: A theory of human development.* New York: Wiley.

Varela, R. E., Vernberg, E. M., Sanchez-Sosa, J. J., Riveros, A., Mitchell, M., & Mashunskashey, J. (2004). Anxiety reporting and culturally associated interpretation biases and cognitive schemas: A comparison of Mexican, Mexican American, and European American families. *Journal of Clinical Child and Adolescent Psychology, 33,* 237–247.

Velez, C. N., Johnson, J., & Cohen, P. (1989). A longitudinal analysis of selected risk factors for childhood psychopathology. *Journal of the American Academy of Child and Adolescent Psychiatry, 28,* 861–864.

Verhulst, F. C., & Achenbach, T. M. (1995). Empirically-based assessment and taxonomy of psychopathology: Cross-cultural applications—A review. *European Child and Adolescent Psychiatry, 4,* 61–76.

Verhulst, F. C., & Koot, H. M. (1992). *Child Psychiatric Epidemiology: Concepts, methods, and findings.* Newbury Park, CA: Sage.

Verhulst, F. C., van der Ende, J., Ferdinand, R. F., & Kasius, M. (1997). The prevalence of DSM-III-R diagnoses in a national sample of Dutch adolescents. *Archives of General Psychiatry, 54,* 129–336.

Vigil, J. D. (1988). Group processes and street identity: Adolescent Chicano gang members. *Ethos, 16,* 421–445.

Wall, T. L., Garcia-Andrade, C., Wong, V., Lau, P., & Ehlers, C. L. (2000). Parental history of alcoholism and problem behaviors in Native American adolescents. *Alcoholism: Clinical and Experimental Research, 24,* 30–34.

Weems, C. F., Hayward, C., Killen, J., & Taylor, C. B. (2002). A longitudinal investigation of anxiety sensitivity in adolescence. *Journal of Abnormal Psychology, 111,* 471–477.

Weisner, T. S. (2000). Culture, childhood, and progress in Sub-Saharan Africa. In L. E. Harrison & S. P. Huntington (Eds.), *Culture matters* (pp. 141–157). New York: Basic Books.

Weisz, J. R., McCarty, C. A., Eastman, K. L., Chaiyasit, W., & Suwanlert, S. (1997). Developmental psychopathology and culture: Ten lessons from Thailand. In S. S. Luthar, J. A. Burack, D. Cicchetti, & J. R. Weiss (Eds.), *Developmental psychopathology* (pp. 568–592). Cambridge: Cambridge University Press.

Weisz, J. R., & Sigman, M. (1993). Parent reports of behavioral and emotional problems among children in Kenya, Thailand, and the United States. *Child Development, 64,* 98–109.

Weisz, J. R., Suwanlert, S., Chaiyasit, W., Weiss, B., Achenbach, T. M., & Walter, B. (1987). Epidemiology of behavioral and emotional problems among Thai and American children: Parent reports for ages 6–11. *Journal of the American Academy of Child and Adolescent Psychiatry, 26,* 890–897.

Weisz, J. R., Weiss, B., Suwanlert, S., & Chaiyasit, W. (2003). Syndromal structure of psychopathology in children of Thailand and the United States. *Journal of Consulting and Clinical Psychology, 71,* 375–385.

Wenar, C., & Kerig, P. (2000). *Developmental psychopathology* (4th ed.). New York: McGraw-Hill.

White, K. S., & Farrell, A. D. (2001). Structure of anxiety sensitivity in urban children: Competing factor models of the Revised Children's Manifest Anxiety Scale. *Journal of Consulting and Clinical Psychology, 69,* 333–337.

Wong, S. (2001). Depression level in inner-city Asian American adolescents: The contributions of cultural orientation and interpersonal relationships. *Journal of Human Behavior in the Social Environment, 3,* 49–64.

Yeh, M., Hough, R. L., McCabe, K., Lau, A., & Garland, A. (2004). Parental beliefs about the causes of child problems: Exploring racial/ethnic patterns. *Journal of the American Academy of Child and Adolescent Psychiatry, 43,* 605–612.

Zohar, A. H., Ratzoni, G., Paula, D. L., Apter, A., Bleich, A., Kron, S., et al. (1992). An epidemiological study of obsessive-compulsive disorder and related disorders in Israeli adolescents. *Journal of the American Academy of Child and Adolescent Psychiatry, 31,* 1057–1061.

CHAPTER 16

Understanding Vulnerability and Resilience from a Normative Developmental Perspective: Implications for Racially and Ethnically Diverse Youth

MARGARET BEALE SPENCER, VINAY HARPALANI, ELAINE CASSIDY, CLEOPATRA Y. JACOBS, SAPANA DONDE, TYHESHA N. GOSS, MICHÈLE MUÑOZ-MILLER, NICOLE CHARLES, and SHAUNQULA WILSON

A multifaceted, context-linked, and systems-oriented human development perspective is essential for a maximized understanding of *resilience* and *vulnerability;* in fact, a carefully nuanced approach is particularly needed when considering broad ethnic enclaves and, more generally, all humans' normative pursuit of stage-specific life

course competencies. The perils that youth face, along with the successful and unsuccessful strategies they employ in coping with these risks, must be understood both in relation to their maturational and identity formation statuses and as linked to the larger social, cultural, and historical contexts of development. Research efforts in developmental psychopathology and applied human development have increasingly focused on risk and resilience. Scholars have begun exploring important conceptual issues that require greater clarity, such as the various definitions of resilience as a construct, and the utility of these in various contexts (e.g., see Luthar, 2003; Luthar & Cicchetti, 2000; Luthar, Cicchetti, & Becker, 2000; Spencer, 2001). A key point to add to this discussion is that risk and resilience cannot be separated from normative developmental processes that occur in multiple contexts. Healthy and normal human development involves *negotiating some level of stage-specific threat* (i.e., given available and honed competencies of salience to the risks confronted) and *demonstrating a degree of resilience* (i.e., successful outcomes) in the face of challenge.

From our perspective, risk is properly conceptualized as the exacerbation of normative challenges encountered in the pursuit of myriad stage-specific competencies and is linked to broad sociopolitical processes (i.e., racism, sexism) and/or lack of resources (e.g., see Gallay & Flanagan, 2000). Protective factors such as social (e.g., cultural capital) and material (e.g., the intergenerational transmission of wealth) resources help individuals to cope with exacerbated normative challenges and, thus, maximize available supports. We define vulnerability as the net experience of risk and protective factors that an individual encounters (see Anthony, 1974). Productive as well as unproductive coping outcomes are possible. Accordingly, as an outcome, resilience involves successful negotiation of exacerbated challenges; however, resilience is not possible without significant challenge being encountered and is associated with heightened risk conditions.

RESILIENT OUTCOMES: LINKAGES WITH CONTEXT, CHARACTER, AND COPING NEEDS

From a service provider perspective, Leon Chestang (1972b) suggests that American culture and social policies are infused with discrepancies concerning what is wanted and expected from citizens of color. He postulates that, on the one hand, *competence, social responsibility, and independence* are desired as life course outcomes. However, independent of the developmental period of concern and efforts made, there remain significant and built-in obstacles to the achievement of those outcomes.

Spencer (2001) describes the consequences of structural racism for minority youth as, at minimum, a twofold blow. First, youth of color frequently live and mature in high-risk contexts characterized by systemic, structural barriers to

individual success. More specifically, these obstacles include conditions in the neighborhood, family, and school contexts, and interactions among these different contexts; additionally, challenges emanate from relationships between these settings and the larger social, economic, and political forces in U.S. society more generally. In fact, Kochman (1992) suggests that there are particular individual-context conditions. In a thorough and broad review, he describes communities where children grow and adults attempt to meet their needs although they are confronted by consistent patterns in the social structural conditions that make goals for competence and productive citizenship virtually impossible. More to the point, Kochman suggests that specifically African American communities are frequently distinguished by crowded conditions, hazardous waste facilities, and other high-risk environmental elements that seldom appear in affluent and suburban communities. Of salience is that these conditions collectively increase stress, decrease one's ability to cope, diminish the sense of community and psychological mutuality, and result in increases in behavior problems that compromise competence. As illustrated by Emmy Werner's (1989; Werner & Smith, 2001) classic studies, many youth manage good outcomes and demonstrate resilience; however, generally speaking and as suggested by standard journal publications and textbooks, when considering mainland youth of color, the mediating processes between risk factors and resilient outcomes are infrequently unpacked when considering ethnic minorities.

From our perspective, a significant contributor to the unpacking of mediating processes evident between risks and resilient outcomes has been Brewster Smith's (1968) classic theorizing about competence formation. deCharms's (1968) ideas aid and complement Smith's, which together enhance our understanding of resilience. Specifically, DeCharms suggests that an *individual's primary motivational propensity is to be effective in producing changes in his or her environment to make a (positive) impact by making a difference.* Although conceptually similar to Smith's and to Robert White's (1959) views concerning competence formation and effectance motivation, DeCharms's theorizing goes a step further. DeCharms describes his construct as one of *personal causation,* which implicitly reinforces the salience of human agency. His perspective suggests that psychosocial processes (i.e., demonstrating personal agency) are fundamental for productive outcomes and stage-specific competencies. The classic ideas put forth by White, DeCharms, and Smith complement each other. Considered together, the conceptual formulations (1) provide accompaniment to James Anthony's

(1974) insightful notions concerning resiliency, (2) afford additional essentials to the race-specific and culturally sensitive contextual perspective of Leon Chestang (1972b), and (3) highlight the person-process context insights made available by Bronfenbrenner (1989). Collectively synthesized, these theorists provide a dynamic and synergistic conceptual formulation that is foundational for Spencer's (2001) suggested second component or outcome that she hypothesizes emanates from structural racism. Specifically, she suggests that the many instances of resilience—success and competence displayed by vulnerable youth in spite of adverse living conditions—often go unrecognized, thus *denying individuals a sense of agency, success, and inferred accomplishment.* Importantly, the oversight forgoes the potential and positive protective factor function of *acknowledged resiliency.* Instead, by ignoring the fact of race and ethnicity linked negative social structural conditions and associations with resiliency, the omission further compromises individual coping and allows the continued interpretational liberties about youth of color that frequently and narrowly label their lives and efforts as suggesting solely deviancy, pathology, deficits, and problems.

Spencer's (2001) synthesis suggests that youths' manifested resiliency should still be associated with future psychological fragility that requires sustained support during subsequent developmental periods and for the critical transitions in between (see Spencer, 2001). To illustrate, a single dose of early intervention against inequitable life course conditions administered during the preschool years *alone*—perhaps as Head Start programming—is inadequate. "The inoculating impact is ineffective given the chronic and multidimensional expressions of structural racism as one moves forward across the life course" (p. 35). As suggested by Anthony (1974), all youth are psychologically vulnerable. However, low-risk environments may offset the manifestation of high vulnerability, whereas chronic high-risk environments may virtually guarantee it. In other words, even in the face of high risk, protective factors may promote generally positive outcomes, stage-specific competencies, and resiliency. The work by Werner and colleagues (Werner, 1989, 2000; Werner & Smith, 2001) with indigenous Hawaiian children quite clearly demonstrates the point.

As described by Cook and Cook (2005), it is heartening to observe children doing well when everything is working for them; however, it is more impressive to see youth doing well when the odds appear insurmountable. Programs of research on resilient children—children who succeed, achieve, or otherwise have positive developmental outcomes despite growing up under negative condi-

tions—have been addressed for youth generally by researchers such as Garmezy (1985), Luthar et al. (2000), and Rutter (1987). However, an identity-focused and context-linked scholarly emphasis on resilience, particularly when considering diverse youth of color, has been a long-term focus of Spencer and colleagues (e.g., see Spencer, 1983, 1984, 1985, 1986, 1987).

Our approach to human development, and thus to vulnerability, risk, and resilience, represents an *identity-focused, cultural-ecological* perspective. We focus on identity statuses that confer either privilege or marginality and consider factors including race and gender. We examine and infer how these factors affect several dimensions of human coping: individuals' perceptions of self and future opportunities; imposed expectations, such as stereotypes that result from inferences about race and gender; and the interaction between these various influences and normative development processes such as physical maturation and identity formation. Furthermore, we emphasize the need to understand these issues as they are impacted by multiple levels of context. This includes both proximal contexts—immediate situational settings such as school, family, and neighborhood—and distal contexts, that is, broad societal influences including political decisions and media messages that are filtered through the more proximal venues. The interactions among these different settings and hierarchical levels of context should also be recognized as they impact human development processes, risk, and resilience.

In this chapter, as an organizational strategy for understanding development in context, we present Spencer's (1995, in press) phenomenological variant of ecological systems theory (PVEST). The identity-focused, cultural-ecological framework of normative human development significantly enhances the examination of resilience and vulnerability among youth. Accordingly, first, we consider major conceptual flaws that have marred research on racially and ethnically diverse youth. We highlight how these conceptual flaws have led to misunderstandings about resilience and vulnerability. Next, we present several theoretical correctives to these flaws in an effort to build toward our comprehensive, racially and culturally sensitive model of human development. We discuss the major theoretical traditions that PVEST builds on, including Erikson's and Marcia's theorizing on identity, racial identity theories, symbolic interactionism, and Bronfenbrenner's ecological systems theory. Subsequently, we lay out the PVEST model and apply it to understand both the unique and patterned challenges—or the absence of major difficulties—faced differentially by racially and ethnically diverse youth. Broader societal factors and historical processes that contribute to the vulnerability of youth are considered; these include structural dimensions of racial inequity, ideological manifestations such as colorism and racial stereotypes, racial/ethnic privilege, and the challenges faced by immigrant youth. We consider how this vulnerability filters through to the everyday lives of youth by discussing experiences of racial stereotypes, attitudes, and negotiation of cultural dissonance, using selected examples to cover these points. Also contemplated are the implications of racial/ethnic experiences for youths' coping strategies, identity formation, and stage-specific outcomes. Finally, we discuss the implications of all of these factors for resilience among racially and ethnically diverse youth. Our conclusion considers, integrates, and addresses these issues and presents additional theoretical themes salient for resilience and vulnerability.

CONCEPTUAL FLAWS IN RESEARCH ON RACIALLY AND ETHNICALLY DIVERSE YOUTH

Historically, several recurring conceptual flaws have characterized research on racially and ethnically diverse youth (Spencer & Harpalani, 2001; Spencer, Noll, Stoltzfus, & Harpalani, 2001; Swanson, Spencer, et al., 2003). First and foremost, in general, discussions about youth of color have often lacked a developmental perspective. African American youth specifically, and male adolescents in particular, are treated as miniature or short adults rather than as progressively complex young people growing and developing in myriad settings given unavoidable maturation processes occurring across domains of human functioning. The frequently static and decontextualized approach applied to youth of color, although compared with outcomes achieved by middle-income and Caucasian youth, further exacerbates interpretational errors and perpetuates stereotyping assumptions applied to both groups. More specifically, pathology assumptions taint the interpretations and assumptions made about the former group (i.e., youth of color), on the one hand, while privileging expectations protect the latter group (i.e., Caucasian youth), on the other. As noted, researchers should not only be cognizant of these assumptions, but should also explicitly address issues of normative development in their research conceptualization and design (Swanson, Spencer, & Petersen, 1998).

Our point is that youth of color are often viewed as nonnormative or pathological. On the other hand, as suggested and given an unquestioned position of privilege, the current majority group in this country, White Americans, is often held as the normative standard by which all other groups are judged. This situation is inferred from most research and implicit in the training of developmental scientists because the issue appears too uncomfortable to either acknowledge as an issue or remedy as a deterrent to inclusive science. In fact, it appears that even when diverse youth are included in programs of research, the perspective taken continues to be deficit dependent at best and pathology focused at worst. Accordingly, for youth of color, particularly African American male youth, normative developmental experiences are not considered or, in general, are misunderstood. The prevailing deficit-oriented perspective focuses on negative outcomes and ignores the resilience demonstrated by many youth of color given the group's consistent encountering of hostile, although generally unacknowledged, contextual experiences (see Chestang, 1972a, 1972b). At the same time, the perspective generally ignores the privileging experiences persistently enjoyed by middle-income and White youths more generally (see McIntosh, 1989). The perspective taken also fails to see the behavior and coping strategies of these youth in light of normative developmental challenges; this is the case whether the given behaviors and coping strategies reactively deployed are adaptive or maladaptive. Deficit-oriented perspectives also overlook the critical function of perceptual processes in normal cognitive maturation and, thus, misinterpret how *youths themselves* make meaning of their own experiences. Such perspectives thus frequently merely substitute assumptions of cultural deficiency (e.g., Fordham & Ogbu, 1986). Racism, manifested through structural and ideological dimensions, is often coupled with economic challenges and other barriers, all of which frequently characterize the environments encountered by minority adolescents (Swanson & Spencer, 1998). The experiences of these youth should be viewed in light of these phenomena—as responses to adverse conditions of stress rather than cultural characteristics. These factors affect adolescent perceptions of self, other, and future life prospects; they therefore require consideration, but without demonizing through stereotyping and pathological inferences imposed about the youth themselves.

It is also important to consider multiple, hierarchical levels of context when examining the experiences of youth. Too often, context is ignored altogether, and even when it is considered, measures of context refer only to immediate, situational influences or settings, such as schools or families, rather than the entire interwoven nexus of historical, political, and societal influences that impact these immediate settings and the interactions among them. A more thorough, theoretically driven view of contextual influences on human development is necessary to understand not only resilience and vulnerability, but the entire realm of experiences and psychosocial attitudes and behaviors of racially and ethnically diverse youth. Such an analysis buttresses the use of resilience as the classification for productive outcomes for some (i.e., those experiencing persistent and significant challenges) versus those whose productive outcomes are due to the consonance (i.e., consistency of experiences) between contextual character (i.e., communicated positive expectations and patterned support) and the sets of stage-specific normative challenges associated with particular developmental periods. That is, we profess the conceptual position that the latter situation and noted stage-specific productive coping outcomes do not necessarily suggest resilience but, instead, indicate *productive coping efforts and outcomes that are the result of significant supports provided in response to normative developmental challenge.*

Finally, a lack of cultural competence is another related flaw in scholarship on youth of color. In a paradoxical way, this is particularly relevant to research on racially and ethnically diverse youth. Ethnic minority status may, on the surface, prompt the researcher to consider issues of culture and context; however, scholarship lacking a comprehensive theoretical framework of normative human development often obscures the most salient issues for particular groups rather than illuminating them (see discussion by Lee, Spencer, & Harpalani, 2003). The behavioral outcomes of youth of color are often analyzed simplistically using culturally deterministic formulations that ignore within-group variation. Conversely, researchers often assume that cultural factors are unnecessary to consider; thus, they are conveniently overlooked in the experiences of White youth. This penchant undermines the field's embrace of culturally competent analyses and encourages a perspective that suggests that culture applies only to youth of color and is associated narrowly with deficit points of view. As suggested, this approach not only neglects salient issues, but also implicitly *pathologizes* the experiences of youth of color by normalizing White youth's developmental experiences (see Spencer, in press). Of particular importance, cultural competence is not merely of clinical and therapeutic relevance: It is a critical factor in the design and interpretation of research. In sum, cultural competence promotes scientific research that is proficient in its incorporation and consideration of culture. As described by Lee et al., adolescents from diverse backgrounds have a variety of understandings of family, school, and neighborhood experiences that cannot be understood with traditionally simplistic, media-hyped, and nonnormative cultural formulations (e.g., Fordham & Ogbu, 1986); such shortsightedness undermines the design, production, and application of good science. Although culturally nuanced perspectives are necessary to understand social and psychological experiences of diverse populations, such an understanding of necessity must also include careful attention to assumptions about normative developmental experiences (Swanson, Spencer, et al., 2003).

MITIGATING CONCEPTUAL SHORTCOMINGS IN RESEARCH: CORRECTIVE STEPS

To address traditional shortcomings in research on racially and ethnically diverse youth, we propose several key steps. All are related and employed to assist in building toward the PVEST.

Normative Human Development Perspective

First, a normative human development perspective should be employed when examining resilience and vulnerability among all youth. As noted earlier, we view risk and resilience as integrally tied to normative developmental processes. The experiences of youth should be viewed in terms of such processes and challenges, including those associated with physical maturation, identity formation, negotiation of relationships with peers and elders, and other situations that require youth to employ problem-solving strategies in response to *normative and nonnormative stage-linked challenges.* For youth of color, these challenges are often exacerbated; for example, for second-generation Asian American youth, navigating peer and family relationships may be compounded by extensive cultural dissonance across family and school settings; for African American youth (males in particular), physical maturation must be negotiated in conjunction with media-propagated negative stereotypes of Black male criminality. The important point is that all of these challenges should be understood as part of normative development in adolescence; although issues such as stereotyping and cultural dissonance may contribute to and exacerbate normative challenges, the experiences of youth of color should not be viewed separately from normative developmental issues. Moreover, we should keep this issue in mind whether we are considering adaptive or maladaptive behaviors by these youth because the behaviors as reactive coping strategies are associated with contextual experiences linked with broad and frequently exacerbating experiences (i.e., for some) as described. Without that admonishment, differences in outcomes accrued both within and between groups are naïvely characterized.

Thorough and Nuanced Integration of Context

Context considerations require careful integration when analyzing the experiences of racially and ethnically diverse youth. Moreover, this should occur not in superficial ways, but in a manner that incorporates all levels of contextual influence. For example, Van Oers (1998) notes that context is often defined improperly in empirical literatures. Often, context is used to refer merely to situational influence, ignoring information processing and meaning making, which translate situational influence into perception-linked interpretation and action. Van Oers argues for a more dynamic approach to the defining of context, one that takes into account these processes and is more accurately described in terms of action (i.e., "contextualizing") rather than static influence. Additionally, Dannefer (1992) describes four components of context: physical setting, social interactions, developing person, and time. Beyond these considerations, it is important to recognize how larger societal biases and historical influences filter through into everyday life and potentially permeate youths' daily experiences. Accordingly, beyond merely placing the experiences of young people in their immediate, situational contexts, there are conceptual benefits to placing these immediate situational settings in their larger social context and, thus, for considering the implications for youth.

Focus on Resilience in Conjunction with Normative Human Development

There should be a focus not only on problem behavior, but also on resilience, the attainment of positive outcomes among high-risk youth who are confronted with significant, persistent, and frequently nonnormative challenges. The notion of resilience, along with the challenges in studying it as a phenomenon, enjoys broad interest. It has been addressed in detail by Suniya Luthar and Dante Cicchetti (Luthar & Cicchetti, 2000; Luthar et al., 2000) and Margaret Beale Spencer (Connell, Spencer, & Aber, 1994; Spencer, 2001; Spencer, Cole, Dupree, Glymph, & Pierce, 1993; Swanson & Spencer, 1991) and their colleagues. Spencer's early work frequently and specifically highlighted African American youth, although more recent research and application include ethnically diverse samples. We build on all of this work to raise several points.

In conjunction with a normative developmental perspective and an emphasis on multiple levels of context, researchers would benefit from analyzing risk and resilience in terms of process, rather than traits. This allows social scientists to consider and integrate perceptual processes that can be employed to help children overcome barriers and access available supports (Spencer, 2001). As youth develop and interact with elders and peers, their perceptions and behaviors change with social and cognitive development. They move from having an egocentric to a more sociocentric view of their world as they develop into more social beings. This conceptually multifaceted approach that simultaneously considers and integrates multiple domains of human development in fact improves our understanding of the manner in which social, cognitive, and maturational development can affect children's perceptions of their immediate and larger worlds. Insights accrued also explain how these developments interact with significant others in different settings that vary as to levels of context and, consequently, their implications for risk, resilience, and vulnerability. Researchers should recognize the developmental plasticity inherent in these phenomena, so as not to assume that particular risks will lead to negative outcomes and that youth cannot employ active strategies to avoid or minimize their exposure to risk. We opine that such thinking is inherently narrow and deterministic and implies that environmental factors are intransigent, unable to be altered by human effort.

The use of certain terminology further suggests a focus on macrosystem influence over individual-level agency. In fact, there have been recommendations for researchers to revise their use of terminology, using the term *resilience* rather than *resiliency* to refer to positive adjustment within challenging contexts, rather than a personal attribute (Masten, 1994). Such a change reflects a move to embrace the transactional nature of resilience. A criticism of using the term resiliency is that it can be associated with a personality trait, and therefore suggests that children are born with (or without) the skills necessary to overcome challenge (Luthar, Cicchetti, & Becker, 2000). It therefore implies that children do not engage in transactions with different elements of their environments and have no independent ability to influence their contextual surroundings to decrease or increase the amount of risk and protection around them. With this in mind, risk and resilience involve dynamic processes, not predetermined traits, and they emerge as a result of constant interactions between children and factors in their environments (Luthar et al., in press; Masten, 1994).

The same argument can be applied to the use of "at risk"; the term has historically been applied to youth who are disproportionately exposed to risk factors at various levels of proximity. Even though children living amid numerous challenges may contend with high amounts of environmental stress, they may simultaneously benefit from having availability and access to numerous supports in their immediate contexts; their availability and accessibility may offset the negative effects of risk and increase children's abilities to exhibit resilience. When the words "at risk" are used to describe youth themselves rather than the high-risk environments in which they live, this suggests, at best, that these children have little autonomy in overcoming challenge and avoiding negative outcomes. Even worse, the association of "at risk" with youth of color has contributed to the perpetuation of negative stereotypes assigned to them, which in turn has led to negative assumptions about their abilities to exhibit success under adverse conditions.

Authentic and Dynamic Consideration of Cultural Influences

Our view is that culture should be understood as a dynamic system and way of living, not as a static entity. Traditionally, culture has been defined as a "complex whole" (e.g., Tylor, 1871/1958, p. 1) or a set of routine practices within a particular socially and historically located group (Cole, 1996). Classical ideas of culture have also been critiqued and expanded on. In analyzing the notion of culture, Gilbert (1989) notes that psychological constructs are often unequipped for describing dynamic processes. In the modern world, rapid social change has become characteristic of all domains in society; thus, the construct of culture is difficult to define. Gilbert proposes a definition as a set of control mechanisms, with individuals acting as self-reflexive agents responding to cultural forces and social change. Segall (1984) has criticized efforts to create a universal definition of culture. He contends that the focus should be on identification of salient ecological, sociological, and cultural variables that influence human behavior. According to Segall, the identification of these variables, rather than a strict, universally applicable definition of culture, is central to theoretical advances in cross-cultural psychology.

Building on these ideas, we propose the analysis of cultural influences in a process-oriented manner—to focus on cultural socialization and the learning of these practices, along with their meaning to the individual (Lee, Spencer,

& Harpalani, 2003). As noted by Ingold (1994, p. 330), "People live culturally rather than . . . live in cultures." Conceptualizing and understanding cultural influences in this way can help mitigate the pitfall of *cultural determinism* and inherently emphasizes the changing nature of cultural practices, at both individual and group levels.

Related to these issues, both etic (general to all cultural groups) and emic (specific to a particular cultural group) perspectives on socialization and human development are important (Garcia Coll, Akerman, & Cicchetti, 2000). One of our major points has been the importance of normative developmental processes and experiences (as understood by the outside observer) as common to all youth. Additionally, we recognize that the meaning attributed to these experiences (and thus the subjective developmental phenomena from the individual's perspective) may vary according to social, historical, and cultural context and be influenced by more proximal factors.

Nuanced Consideration of Race and Ethnicity

Researchers and practitioners should acknowledge the complexity of race and ethnicity and view these phenomena from multiple perspectives: in terms of cultural differences, structural racism, and normative developmental processes such as racial identity formation. Each of these areas is derived from a different disciplinary source—cultural differences from anthropology, structural racism from sociology, and racial identity formation from psychology—and they are seldom integrated into a single body of scholarship. Nevertheless, to properly understand the normative development of racially and ethnically diverse youth, an integrative approach *indicative of a multidisciplinary human development perspective* combining these areas is essential.

With regard to race, our perspective emphasizes the individual's everyday experiences and perceptions; thus, we focus on *how (the salience of) race is lived on a daily basis* and how individuals, including developing youth, make meaning of these experiences. Experiences of race are filtered through larger societal influences, such as manifestations of structural racism (see Bonilla-Silva, 1997), as illustrated by residential and economic segregation, and by encounters of negative stereotypes in the media and in everyday life. It is also necessary to clarify the application of terms such "race" and "ethnicity," which are often used interchangeably. Generally, the former refers to perceptions of observable phenotype, and the later refers to cultural background. At times, it is useful for researchers to focus on ethnicity; for example, the culturally specific family experiences of African Americans and African immigrants may differ. However, of salience is that given the more difficult task of discerning facts of culture, youth from both groups may experience similar racial stereotyping and treatment based on the common denominator of color and identifiability (see Spencer, in press). Depending on the particular circumstances, it may be more useful to focus on one or the other. It is also important to note that many youth and adults perceive their racial and ethnic backgrounds as interchangeable, if not identical, and these are often intricately linked in identity formation. Thus, at times, it may be useful to consider race and ethnicity together, and it is always important to understand how the two interact in shaping the everyday experiences of racially and ethnically diverse youth (for an overview, see Fisher, Jackson, & Villarruel, 1998, pp. 1157–1166; Spencer, in press).

Additionally, it is worth explicitly stating that "racially and ethnically diverse" includes White; if it did not, this would only contribute to the normalization of Whiteness. White youth, like all others, must be studied as one of many diverse groups. Although youth of color are disproportionately represented among the low-economic-resource populations, many White youth are also in this group. The socioeconomic stressors faced by all of these youth may be similar, although low-income Whites typically are not residentially segregated and have greater access to financial resources (through family connections, etc.) than people of color (Conley, 1999; M. L. Sullivan, 1989). Additionally, White youth and youth of color face the same basic developmental challenges; the primary difference between the two is that White youth are considered to be the norm and reap all of the privileges of this status, ranging from greater cultural consonance experienced across school, family, and neighborhood settings to "racial invisibility" (i.e., minimal race-based stereotyping) in everyday encounters. Nonetheless, because the challenges faced by all racially and ethnically diverse youth, generally, and youth of color, more specifically, overlap to an extent, we are nuanced in our use of terminology. We refer differentially to youth of color (designating all non-White youth), low-economic-resource youth (designating those of all race/ethnic backgrounds whose families meet particular socioeconomic criteria such as federal poverty guidelines), marginalized youth (youth from both of the aforementioned categories and others, such as lesbian, gay, bisexual, and transsexual youth, who are accorded lower status on the basis of identity), and all racially and ethnically diverse youth, depending

on the specific developmental issues and challenges being discussed. At times, we also refer to specific racial/ethnic groups, particularly African Americans, to illustrate challenges.

As a function of their net vulnerability and stress levels experienced, *the specific and patterned strategies that youth of color employ to cope with life experiences afford the basis for the formation of identity,* including racial/ethnic identity. As noted, this process occurs both in the larger social context of American society and in the more local contexts of family, school, and neighborhood that youth encounter. Our major point here is that the processes of coping and identity formation are developmentally contingent; they depend on youths' prior experiences and previous coping responses and identities. There is also a need to examine gender identity in interaction with race. Studies of gender identity often yield significant racial and ethnic differences; for example, Parker et al. (1995) note that Black and White adolescent girls think about body image ideals in very different ways. Confounding factors create complex interactions between race/ethnicity and gender.

Phenomenological Perspective on Identity and Self

It is also critical to employ a process-oriented phenomenological perspective in research on youth—to understand how youth understand *their own worlds.* Studies that have overlooked the importance of youth phenomenology have resulted in misinterpretation, as perceptual processes are essential to a full understanding of behavioral outcomes. For example, the interpreters of the program of research by Clark and Clark (1939, 1940) erroneously assumed that children of color needed to respond as Caucasian children did in order to be considered "healthy" and "normal"; thus, scholars and policymakers misinterpreted the self-esteem of African American youth (see Spencer, 1982b, 1984). Such misinterpretation results largely from comparing outcomes among youth of color to Eurocentric expectations. It is important not only to appreciate how youth of color contend with unique risk factors, but also to acknowledge normative developmental responses to these conditions. This can be accomplished only through a phenomenological viewpoint.

As suggested by Bandura's (1978) theorizing, self-system development is reciprocally determined from self/other appraisal processes (Spencer & Dupree, 1996). Self-appraisal processes integrate various aspects of one's life that promote identity formation; these represent social, cognitive, and affective dimensions. As perceptions of the self are gained through interaction with the environment, ethnic and racial identity constitutes integral aspects of youth development. Cultural values afford the information necessary to interpret and proactively respond to environmental experiences and stereotypic messages concerning minority status. Developing a sense of efficacy is crucial during adolescence due to youths' heightened self-consciousness and greater cognitive awareness; however, this self-efficacy is partially determined by the opportunities, limitations, and expectations that society imposes on youth. Successful performance on a particular task increases a sense of personal empowerment (i.e., competence) and the likelihood of future successes in subsequent tasks.

Comprehensive, Developmentally and Contextually Sensitive Theory

The final corrective we propose is a contextually and developmentally sensitive theory that integrates all of these issues. We employ Spencer's (1995) PVEST as an overarching framework to accomplish this end. PVEST builds on multiple theoretical traditions in developmental psychology (e.g., Boykin, 1986; Bronfenbrenner, 1977) and other disciplines (e.g., Chestang, 1972b), including subfields of psychology (e.g., Steele, 1997); all address one or more of the issues noted earlier. As a dynamic and systemic framework, PVEST serves as a tool for examining resilience and vulnerability in conjunction with normative human development, focusing on identity formation while taking into account structural factors, cultural influences, and individual phenomenological experiences and perceptions of these contextualized features. In the next section, we present PVEST as the integration of several developmental traditions, including Erikson's and Marcia's theories of identity formation and symbolic interactionism and Bronfenbrenner's ecological systems theory.

BUILDING TOWARD A PHENOMENOLOGICAL VARIANT OF ECOLOGICAL SYSTEMS THEORY

Spencer's (1995) PVEST builds on a long tradition of theory in the realm of normative human development. The broad scope of this work spans several disciplines, covering ideas about individual developmental processes such as identity formation theories and racial identity theories, traditions such as symbolic interactionism that emphasize

the self in relation to society, particular concerns of applied youth development such as resilience theorizing, and contextually sensitive schools of thought such as the ecological psychology school. Each of these traditions highlights particular salient issues in normative human development. We review the major trends that influenced the model (Spencer, Harpalani, Fegley, Dell'Angelo, & Seaton, 2003) as a strategy to better understand these issues and to gain a more sensitive grasp on PVEST.

Theoretical Underpinnings of Identity Formation Processes

In considering resilience and vulnerability, it is critical to understand the developmental underpinnings of identity and self. In fact, we conceptualize resilience essentially as an identity: an achievement-oriented sense of self attained by the individual to overcome obstacles (risks) by drawing on available resources (protective factors). This process can be best understood within a theoretical framework that seeks to explain how youth effectively meet the demands of developmental tasks in infancy, childhood, and adolescence. Moreover, a child's ability to successfully navigate various life stages emerges in the context of social relationships embedded within the child's unique societal and cultural environment. Knowledge of self, knowledge of the world, and knowledge of how to regulate self in relation to other develop in these contexts. Once we build an understanding of identity and self processes from a normative human development perspective, we can apply this understanding to various contexts of differing levels of vulnerability, thus building toward a normative developmental view of resilience.

Identity in psychological theorizing is viewed as the core character of an individual that provides psychological stability across time and space. More recently, the concept of identity has been expanded to include a wide variety of domains of self; for example, there are growing literatures on racial, ethnic, gender, sexual, and national identity. We cover some of these later in conjunction with our discussion of race and ethnicity. Here, we draw on the classical theoretical frameworks of Erikson and Marcia and limit our discussion to what is commonly referred to as "ego identity."

One of Erikson's (1968) primary contributions was to define stage-specific concepts of development more explicitly. Prior to Erikson, stages of human development between life and death were not clearly formulated or articulated; the individual merely progressed from baby to adult. Of course, there were limited exceptions, for example, Piaget's (1932, 1970) work on cognitive development, but often these involved a limited domain (e.g., cognitive reasoning) or limited stages (e.g., childhood). Stages of life course human development, along with the transitions between them, had not been discussed widely (Zelizer, 1994). In his epigenetic model, Erikson (1968) proposed that development occurred in stages across the life course in a fixed order: childhood, adolescence, adulthood, and old age. He identified eight stage-specific developmental tasks across the life course: trust versus mistrust, autonomy versus shame, industry versus inferiority, identity versus identity confusion, intimacy versus isolation, generativity versus stagnation, and integrity versus despair, and initiative versus guilt. The eight stages represent developmental challenges that must be negotiated and renegotiated throughout the life course.

Erikson's (1959, 1968) model highlights the centrality of identity in human development. In his theorizing, a large component of identity formation occurs during youth and particularly during the period of adolescence—the time marked by the active search for identity. Here, youth must grapple with the challenge, or "crisis," of increased independence, sexual maturation, greater cognitive ability, pressure to conform to social norms, and heightened awareness of others' perceptions of them. Youth rely less on parents for guidance about self, and peer groups begin to play an increasingly important role in this regard. The search for identity is further complicated by the onset of secondary sex characteristics and desire for intimate relationships, all of which play a role in self-definition, particularly with regard to gender identity. In technological, industrialized societies, there are numerous options for managing these newfound capacities and resultant traits of self. The manner in which youth tend to adapt to these circumstances across time and space defines their identity.

Erikson (1968) is also well-known for his concept of identity *crisis*. Crisis refers to a period of emotional and mental stress that can lead to significant alterations in worldview in a limited time. For example, a crisis may lead to changes in group or peer associations, political beliefs, or engagement in risk-taking behaviors. On the surface, crisis may appear to have a negative connotation, but this is not necessarily the case. Erikson's notion of crisis as a state of internalized tension is also an opportunity to cope and grow. When youth are presented with challenges, they have an opportunity to respond to these challenges and to learn in the process—essentially, to display resilience. This is a part of normative human development.

Marcia builds on Erikson's work by elaborating on identity formation and creating a typology for identity development. Like Erikson, Marcia describes adolescence as the time for active engagement in the search for identity, and building on Erikson's notion of crisis, Marcia (1966, 1980) delineates the process of identity development in terms of four different identity statuses: diffusion, foreclosure, moratorium, and achievement. During the first stage, *diffusion,* youth have not encountered significant crisis. The individual is not committed strongly to any particular way of being or perspective on life. *Foreclosure* assumes an early commitment to a conventional standard of behavior. Foreclosed youth do not actively explore different possibilities for identity formation; they tend to follow the traditionally socialized standards of behavior and resultant trajectories. Conversely, *moratorium,* if it occurs, can be a time of exploration, when alternative possibilities are explored. Subsequent to moratorium is identity *achievement,* when the individual has encountered crises and emerged from them with a stronger sense of self or, in Marcia's terminology, "high identity commitment." This is also tantamount to demonstrated resilience. Of course, identity achievement is not universal or final; individuals continue to encounter new crises through the life course—particularly in domains that are not foreclosed or achieved—and thus, given domain-specific challenges encountered, must demonstrate continued resilience in this regard.

Both Erikson's work and Marcia's expansion contribute to and lay the foundation for our general conceptualization of identity development. To examine issues of vulnerability for racially and ethnically diverse youth, it is useful to apply these concepts more specifically in the domains of race and ethnicity and consider racial and ethnic identity theories.

Theories of Racial and Ethnic Identity

Theories of racial and ethnic identity draw on Eriksonian and Marcian theorizing and apply their concepts of identity formation to racial and ethnic awareness. Racial identity development refers to the "process of defining for oneself the personal significance and social meaning of belonging to a particular racial group" (Tatum, 1997, p. 16). William E. Cross is one of the pioneers in the study of racial identity. Cross's original nigrescence model (Cross, 1971; Cross, Parham, & Helms, 1991) delineated four stages of racial identity formation for African Americans. During the *preencounter* status, Black individuals view the world from a White, Eurocentric frame of reference, consciously or unconsciously holding pro-White and anti-

Black attitudes. The second status, the *encounter* phase, involves an event or series of events that cause individuals to recognize that they cannot fully assimilate into White society. These may be tangible experiences of racism, crises in an Eriksonian sense, which facilitate exploration of racial identity. The third phase, *immersion-emersion,* is a consequent reaction to the encounter phase. Here, individuals become more interested in their Black identity and show increased awareness of racism and sensitivity to it. This phase may be characterized by anti-White attitudes. Individuals will also show a superficial immersion in realms associated with Black cultural attributes (e.g., music, speech styles). *Internalization* occurs as individuals become secure with their Black racial identities and move toward a more pluralistic perspective. African Americans then represent the primary reference group, but individuals' attitudes are not anti-White. In contrast to the superficial displays of the immersion-emersion stage, individuals in the internalization stage have more stable, deeply rooted connections to attributes of their Black heritage, and they may also have the ability to connect comfortably with aspects of White society; for example, they may have diverse groups of close friends. Consistent with this train of thought, Edgar Epps's (1985) analysis would suggest youths' adoption of a cultural pluralist perspective: the recognition and valuing of one's own group membership and cultural traditions along with an appreciation of ways of life associated with other groups.

Cross (1991) has modified the nigrescence framework as a more dynamic and flexible model of racial identity development. Individuals may recycle through the different stages at various developmental periods, and depending on parental racial socialization, they may not start in the preencounter stage. Thus, the stages should not always be viewed as a literal progression. Cross also added a fifth stage to the original four; this stage, known as *internalization-commitment,* represents a more consistent internalization phase. He has also described different modes of internalization, some of which include bicultural identities (W. E. Cross, personal communication, November 20, 2000). We would add that the preencounter stage should be further qualified when considered for young children. That is, given cognitive egocentrism manifest in the first 6 or 7 years of life, children's reported outgroup identifications represent a statement of their cultural early *exposure and experience* with particular cultural stereotypes rather than a conscious identification with or preference for Whites (Spencer, 1982a, 1983; Spencer & Markstrom-Adams, 1990). In other words, when considered from a

developmentally sensitive perspective, young children's stated and early identifications have more to do with what they are exposed to (e.g., unchallenged portrayals of racial stereotypes) that an internalized identification or an identity connoting a valuing of Whites and devaluing of Blacks. Unfortunately, for the most part, the absence of development-sensitive analyses continues to plague much of the racial identity literature.

Of course, White racial identity must also be studied to understand how race and ethnicity operate in development. Whiteness is usually not articulated, serving as the implicit norm, but scholars have begun to explore White racial identity. Most notable in this area is the work of Janet Helms (1990). Helms's model of White racial identity development consists of six statuses, organized in two developmental phases. The first phase, abandonment of racism, consists of three stages. *Contact,* the first stage, involves acceptance of the dominant status of White people, although not explicit awareness of this dominance or the subordinate status of people of color. *Disintegration* occurs as White individuals become aware of their dominant status in society and go through a period of dissonance. In *reintegration,* the person acknowledges his or her Whiteness and holds the view that he or she deserves the privileges accorded by this status. The second phase of Helms's model is called defining a nonracist White identity. This initiates with the *pseudo-independent* stage; individuals begin to question the dominant status of White Americans and may become overly involved with trying to help or change people of color. In the *immersion/emersion* stage, individuals begin to focus on changing White people rather than African Americans. With the final stage, *autonomy,* individuals achieve a positive racial identity and also appreciate and seek opportunities to learn from other groups.

Other theorists have built on this work and also examined ethnic identity. For example, Jean Phinney (1992) drew on Cross's (1971, 1991) racial identity theory and Marcia's (1966) work on identity statuses to devise the Multigroup Ethnic Identity Measure, a psychological assessment instrument that can be used across diverse groups. However, even if researchers acknowledge the significance of racial and ethnic identity, conceptual challenges remain. As noted earlier, academics may define race and ethnicity differently and precisely, but these constructs are inextricably linked in people's own meaning-making systems. It is important to be clear about the particular definition of race/ethnicity (or combination of the two) in use, and, of course, this depends on the context and issues that are being examined. For example, Chinese

Americans, Vietnamese Americans, and South Asian Americans may all be classified as Asian American even though there is significant within- and between-group variation in these categories. Their different histories and locations in American society are important to consider in the realm of ethnic identity development. However, at the same time, it is important to note that different groups such as Chinese, Vietnamese, and South Asian Americans may have similar racialized experiences; they may be identified by others as one racial group and thus stereotyped and stigmatized in a similar manner (i.e., the "model minority" myth; see Takaki, 1998). Thus, there may also be a dimension of similarity in their experiences, and depending on the issue and context of investigation, it may be more useful to emphasize the similarity or the difference of various experiences.

In that vein, identity and self should be placed in context to help distinguish salient developmental issues in particular situations. To build toward a PVEST, we must also consider the notion of self in relation to society, as the understanding of self processes is central to our developmental framework.

Self in Society

Identity and self not only develop within larger social contexts; they are also impacted by those contexts. William James (1892/1961) was a pioneer in describing the relational nature of the self. According to James, the self comprises two components: the "I" and the "Me." The "I" includes the self-as-knower, the active observer, the subjective self, the observing ego, and the private self. "I" organizes and interprets the self's experiences and reflects on the "Me." Additionally, "I" is commonly alluded to as the self-conscious, self-reflective element of self.

In contrast, the "Me" is described as the self-as-known, the observed self, the objective self, the empirical self, or the public self. "Me" is the collection of perceptions regarding the self; these include tangible, material aspects of self (body, possessions, family), the social self (others' views of the self, relations, roles, personality), and the spiritual self (inner psychological workings, including thoughts, wishes, desires). "Me" is commonly referred to as the self-concept component of self.

James's (1892/1961) theory has significant implications for identity development. His work emphasized the reciprocal quality of the self, and with the advent of cognitive maturation, adolescents become increasingly aware of the duality of self (Broughton, 1981; Rosenberg, 1979). At this developmental period, youth begin to distinguish be-

tween their own public and private selves, a phenomenon that is central to the identity crisis and exploration associated with adolescence (Erikson, 1968; Marcia, 1966, 1980). As children's social networks also expand at this age, they begin to see themselves in multiple roles, some of which demand very different ways of presenting oneself. Thus, cognitive dissonance is compounded. The central task of adolescence is the quest to integrate the various selves and achieve equilibrium with a stable sense of self (Hart, 1988). Failure to accomplish this can lead to fragmentation and to the impression that one's self is merely an empty shell or façade, malleable to suit every person and situation. This can be problematic in various domains, as future developmental tasks ranging from goal-setting and accomplishment to the development of healthy, stable social relationships all require youth to have a strong sense of who they are.

All of these are normative developmental tasks that all youth must negotiate. But it is important to consider how these issues are compounded for youth of color. Cultural dissonance across school, family, and peer contexts can make the integration of self more difficult. Moreover, racial stereotypes also impact self-concept and may create dissonance about goals and preclude opportunities for exploration. These issues will be explored in greater detail in later sections of the chapter.

The symbolic interactionists, including Charles Horton Cooley and George Herbert Mead, made significant contributions to understanding the social nature of the self. Cooley (1902; Scheibe, 1985) is best known for his metaphor of the "looking-glass" self. According to Cooley, children participate in interpersonal networks, which yield perceptions of reflected appraisals from others. Through this participation and self-appraisal, they develop their own sense of self. It is not others' attitudes that are critical in the formation of self, but rather the individual's perception of other's attitudes (i.e., an individual's personal phenomenology; Rosenberg, 1979).

Mead (1934; Scheibe, 1985; Taylor, 1991) elaborated on Cooley's notion of the looking-glass self. According to Mead, self-aware people see themselves through the eyes of others; consequently, they may act in ways to gain others' approval. Contingent on the situation at hand, individuals may respond to others with varying presentations of self (Goffman, 1959). These presentations of self can elicit varying reactions, all of which have an impact on self-concept and identity formation. For youth of color, these issues are manifested in various ways, from the phenomena of code switching and "double consciousness" (Du Bois, 1903) to the misinterpretations of Fordham and

Ogbu (1986; see Spencer, Cross, Harpalani, & Goss, 2003, for a critique).

Building on the work of Cooley and Mead, Harry Stack Sullivan (1953; Epstein, 1973; Mitchell, 1988), describes how the self system evolves from significant external factors associated with one's cultural, social, and interpersonal experiences. The self system serves as a filter for and organizer of these experiences, influencing how the individual interprets and responds to others. Sullivan posits that the self system develops out of an endless loop of interactions between the individual and others; it is the product of these interpersonal situations and serves as the lens through which self and the social context are perceived and evaluated. Sullivan particularly emphasized the importance of reciprocal relationships between the child's interactions with the parents and significant others; in contrast, Mead focused on relationships with society at large (what he termed the "generalized other"). Of course, all of these levels of context are important in identity formation; they are elaborated in the next section.

Ecological Systems Theory

Bronfenbrenner's (1979, 1989, 1993) ecological systems theory provides an ideal framework to characterize levels of environmental influence that impact human development. These levels of influence are cast in terms of dynamic, interactive systems of person-environment relationships. Ecological systems theory is organized hierarchically, as interactive systems of increasing complexity are nested within the framework of human development. Bronfenbrenner (1979, 1993) starts by transforming Lewin's (1935) formulation that behavior is a function of person and environment; he substitutes development for behavior, stating that development is also a function of person and environment over time. The developmental function is temporally contingent, as each successive developmental period is dependent on all previous stages of development.

Several types of theoretical models characterize research in developmental psychology. According to Bronfenbrenner (1993), theoretical constructs in developmental psychology have usually focused only on characteristics of the individual, ignoring context. Developmental characteristics of individuals make no reference to the environments where they occur; examples of such constructs include standardized psychological measures such as personality and IQ tests. Bronfenbrenner (1989) refers to this type of analysis as the *personal attributes model;* it focuses narrowly on the individual, with the assumption that researchers can generalize conclusions derived from stan-

dardized measures, regardless of context. Bronfenbrenner (1993) questions these assumptions of environmental generalizability; he does note the utility of standardized tests but argues that research must simultaneously incorporate context-oriented measures.

The most common approach in developmental psychology, according to Bronfenbrenner (1989), is the *social address model.* In contrast to the personal attributes model, the social address model examines only general environmental factors, such as social class, family size, and other demographic variables. It tends to neglect specific environmental characteristics, along with activities that occur in particular environments, and the impact of these activities on individuals (Bronfenbrenner & Crouter, 1983). Essentially, the social address model employs the simplistic view of context critiqued by Van Oers (1998), which we noted earlier.

The *person-context model* examines both the individual and the context but neglects the processes involved in development. For example, this might include studies of personality or attitudes that control for specific environmental characteristics, such as parent-child interactions, without specifying how those characteristics are related to the outcome at hand. This person-context model is able to specify ecological niches (Bronfenbrenner, 1989), but it does not delineate the processes by which developmental outcomes are attained. A process-oriented approach is necessary for understanding resilience and vulnerability, which, as noted earlier, should be conceptualized in terms of processes rather than traits.

Conversely, Bronfenbrenner's (1979, 1989, 1993) ecological systems theory is a *process-person-context model;* it underscores the variability within developmental processes as a function of person and environment. Ecological systems theory (Figure 16.1) is organized with four hierarchically nested levels of environmental influence that mediate person-environment interaction: microsystem, mesosystem, exosystem, and macrosystem. The first level of Bronfenbrenner's model, the *microsystem,* involves the interaction of the person with the immediate social and physical environment; examples include home, family, and school settings. All higher levels of environmental influence are filtered through one or more microsystems, where the individual's actual experiences occur. *Proximal processes* are the patterns of person-environment interactions that occur within microsystems, and these change through the development of the person (Bronfenbrenner, 1979, 1989, 1993). Elsewhere, Bronfenbrenner and Ceci (1994) discuss how proximal processes mediate the heritability of traits by allowing individuals to actualize their potentials.

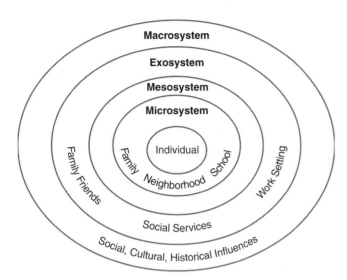

Figure 16.1 Bronfenbrenner's Ecological Systems theory. *Sources:* From *The Ecology of Human Development: Experiments by Nature and Design,* by U. Bronfenbrenner, 1979, Cambridge, MA: Harvard University Press; "Ecological Systems Theory" (pp. 187–248), by U. Bronfenbrenner, in R. Vasta (Ed.), *Annals of Child Development,* 1989, Greenwich, CT: JAI; and "The Ecology of Cognitive Development" (pp. 3–44), by U. Bronfenbrenner, in R. H. Wozniak & K. W. Fischer (Eds.), *Development in Context: Acting and Thinking in Specific Environments,* 1993, Hillsdale, NJ: Erlbaum.

The *mesosystem* is the second level in Bronfenbrenner's (1979, 1989, 1993) ecological systems theory; it describes interactions between the various microsystems in the individual's life. Mesosystems essentially constitute networks of interpersonal relationships that span the various settings. The third level, the *exosystem,* entails more distal influences, such as the structure of the community where the individual resides and settings where the individual is not directly present. For example, interactions at a parent's work setting would constitute exosystemic influences; these do not directly involve the child but may impact his or her development.

The final level, the *macrosystem,* consists of larger societal institutions, such as government, economy, and the media, that lay the broad social and historical context for development (Bronfenbrenner, 1979, 1989, 1993). The impact of macrosystem-level influences may or may not be readily apparent in the lives of individuals, but it is always present in salient ways. The overarching patterns of social practices and relationships found through micro-, meso-, and exosystems often result from macrosystemic factors. Typically, sociologists, political scientists, and economists, rather than developmental psychologists, have studied macrosystems. Nevertheless, developmentalists must also be attuned to the

subtle but explicit ways in which larger societal forces filter through multiple layers of context and influence life trajectories and outcomes. Without attention to this caution, particularly as applied to the experiences of youth of color, the frequent interpretation of "gap outcomes" (e.g., health and achievement disparities) blames performance differences on those experiencing significant risks; further, the risks are often characterized as not representing multiple levels of environmental differences but, instead, are interpreted as deficits and pathologies of the individuals themselves.

Ecological systems theory provides a conceptual foundation for examining the multiple layers of context that influence human development as well as the interactions between these layers. Nevertheless, our aim is to link this comprehensive view of contextual influence with concepts from identity theory and symbolic interactionism, all in an effort to conceptualize how the individual is living in context. Bronfenbrenner's (1989) model provides a means for describing multiple levels of context; Spencer's (1995) PVEST combines a phenomenological perspective with Bronfenbrenner's ecological systems theory, linking context and perception. In contrast to Bronfenbrenner's focus on levels of context (e.g., microsystem, mesosystem) PVEST directly illustrates life course human development *within* context. Additionally, in their provisional role as sources of either risks or protective factors transformed as experiences of challenges or supports, the other levels of the ecological context are also integrated as lives unfold across the life course. A consideration of the combination of influences allows us to describe the components and processes of development. Accordingly, we employ PVEST to analyze the meaning-making processes that underlie identity development and outcomes that transpire as individuals transition across contexts (Spencer, 1995, 1999; Spencer, Dupree, & Hartmann, 1997). In the next section, we synthesize our building blocks to describe Spencer's (1995, in press) PVEST.

PHENOMENOLOGICAL VARIANT OF ECOLOGICAL SYSTEMS THEORY: AN IDENTITY-FOCUSED, CULTURAL-ECOLOGICAL PERSPECTIVE

The PVEST serves as a model to examine normative human development framed through the interaction of identity, culture, and experience as linked with progressively differentiated maturational processes. PVEST utilizes an *identity-focused cultural-ecological* perspective, integrating issues of social, historical, and cultural context with normative developmental processes. The model aims to capture the individual's intersubjectivity and meaning-making processes in light of tangible experiences, which are determined by the proximal and distal contexts of development. PVEST centers on describing individual identity formation unfolding over time. Although both ecological systems theory and PVEST, its phenomenological variant, account for identity formation and context, we believe our focus on direct description of identity formation in a life course framework allows for a more comprehensive explanation of human development. As noted by Cooley (1902), Mead (1934), and Sullivan (1953), the self is mediated by interpersonal relationships, influenced by the phenomenological experience of multilayered, contextual influences and relationships (Spencer et al., 1997). It is the combination of experiencing micro- and macrocontextual influences, normative develop-

mental processes, salient interpersonal relationships, and the cognition-based perceptions and phenomenological experiences that delineate identity formation and eventually yield resilient or adverse outcomes. Determining how we view and comprehend family, peer, and societal expectations, as well as their prospects for competence and success, is central to understanding resilience and devising interventions that promote it (Spencer, Harpalani, Fegley, Dell'Angelo, & Seaton, 2003). Moreover, for youth of color, it is important to understand how broader societal inequities and biases influence these processes.

Considered from this nonstatic perspective, PVEST is a systems theory consisting of five basic components linked with bidirectional processes that form a dynamic developmental framework (see Figure 16.2); it is a cyclic, recursive

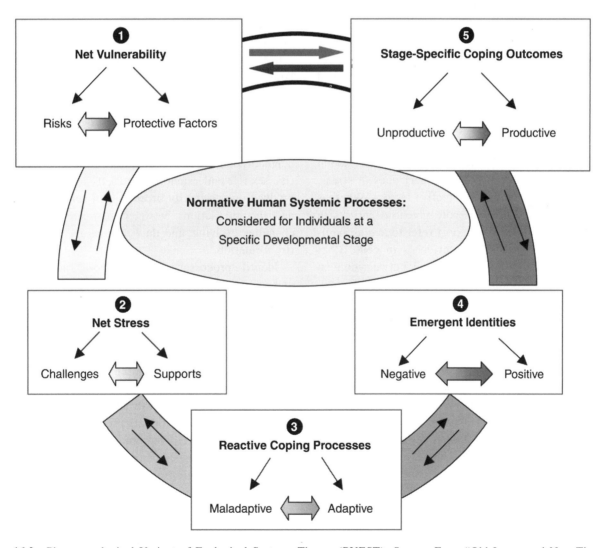

Figure 16.2   Phenomenological Variant of Ecological Systems Theory (PVEST). *Source:* From "Old Issues and New Theorizing about African American Youth: A Phenomenological Variant of Ecological Systems Theory" (pp. 37–70), by M. B. Spencer, in R. L. Taylor (Ed.), *Black Youth: Perspectives on Their Status in the United States, 1995,* Westport, CT: Praeger.

model that describes identity development throughout the life course. Our approach affords a better understanding concerning not just the "what" but, more important, the "how" of development (see Spencer & Harpalani, 2004).

The first component of PVEST, *net vulnerability,* level (1), consists of the contextual and personal characteristics that may potentially pose challenges during an individual's development. Risk contributors are factors that may predispose individuals for adverse outcomes. These may be offset by protective factors, thus defining net vulnerability for a given individual. For marginalized youth, such as youth of color and young people from low-resource families, these include socioeconomic conditions such as living in poverty, imposed expectations such as race and gender stereotypes, and the influences of larger historical processes such as racial subordination and discrimination. Perceptions of the risks one faces and the protective resources available are central to the process of identity formation. Self-appraisal involves constant close scrutiny and evaluation of these risks and resources; the process is particularly salient for identity formation during adolescence, when cognitive and emotional maturation lead to heightened awareness of self and context.

Net stress engagement (2), the second component of PVEST, refers to the actual experience of situations that challenge an individual's well-being. Available social supports can help youth negotiate experiences of stress; thus, supports are actualized protective factors. Whereas risks and protective factors denote potential entities in the environment, stress and support refer to actual manifestations of these entities—experiences in context, as it were. In this way, PVEST forges a link between context and experience. For youth of color, experiences of racism, both subtle and overt, and related dissonance are salient and often chronic stressors; these compound the normative developmental issues encountered by all youth (e.g., puberty, identity exploration, peer relationships). As noted, cognitive maturation results in unavoidable awareness of dissonance, and in adolescence, acute reactions to these experiences are coupled with normative rebellious behavior; thus, this is a period when risk is escalated. Adult role models and other resources in school, family, and community settings can serve as social supports and help youth cope with these experiences.

It is important to note that although stress engagement poses challenges, the construct of stress in PVEST is not entirely negative. It is derived from, and in many ways similar to, Erikson's view of crisis. As we discuss later, stress not only poses challenges but also provides opportunities to develop and hone coping skills.

In response to stressors and in conjunction with supports, *reactive coping methods* (3) are employed to resolve dissonance-producing situations. Reactive coping responses include problem-solving strategies that can lead to either adaptive or maladaptive solutions. Interpreting experiences and determining how to respond to them involves the development of patterns of coping, which are both immediate and long term. All youth must learn to cope with different sources of stress as part of normative human development; but as noted, these issues are compounded for marginalized groups. Additionally, it is important to recognize that a given coping strategy may be adaptive in one context (such as school) and maladaptive in another (e.g., neighborhood; H. C. Stevenson, 1997). Moreover, such dissonance accrued and linked to the deployment of coping strategies is more likely to occur for youth of color (Phelan, Davidson, & Cao, 1991).

Over time, coping processes shape an individual's sense of identity. As youth employ various coping strategies, self-appraisal continues, and individuals replicate those strategies that produce desirable results for the ego. These become stable coping responses that, coupled together, yield *emergent identities* (4). Emergent identities define how individuals view themselves within and between various contexts of development (e.g., family, school, and neighborhood). The combination of cultural/ethnic identity, sex role understanding, and self- and peer appraisal all produce one's identity at any given time; these domains and the interactions between them are also constantly changing, evolving, and thus defining the process of identity formation.

Identity processes afford behavioral stability over time and space; as such, they provide the foundation for future perception, self-appraisal, and behavior. This leads to either adverse or productive *life-stage-specific coping outcomes* (5), the final component of PVEST. Productive outcomes include good health, educational attainment, positive relationships with others, and high self-esteem; on the other hand, adverse outcomes include poor health, incarceration, and self-destructive behaviors. Resilience is the attainment of productive outcomes in spite of adverse conditions (i.e., disproportional to expectations risk level experienced as significant challenge).

PVEST is a cyclic framework that represents dynamic, developmental processes that continue throughout the life span and aids in explaining the "how" of developmental processes. It aids in explaining the frequent diversity obtained for specific life-stage coping outcomes by demonstrating the undergirding mechanisms by which individuals (1) balance new risks against protective factors;

(2) encounter new stressors (i.e., challenges potentially offset by supports); (3) establish new coping strategies (i.e., manifested reactively "in the moment" as either adaptive or maladaptive responsive efforts); and (4) redefine how they view themselves, which also impacts how others view them. PVEST provides a normative human development framework to examine the range of outcomes, including resilience, for all youth. It highlights the importance of development in context, with identity formation at the core. Moreover, it is important to recognize that the five components of PVEST are merely stopping points for analysis; it is the processes that link these components that actually constitute normative human development. PVEST allows us to conceptualize how the normative processes of development are exacerbated for marginalized youth, and how resilience and vulnerability are manifested as part of the context-linked processes of normal human development. Although recent scholarship has thoroughly reviewed literature on youth of color (e.g., Fisher et al., 1998) and provided contextually sensitive models to examine developmental competencies among these youth (Garcia-Coll et al., 1996), it is the direct, process-oriented delineation of developmental trajectories throughout the life span that makes PVEST unique.

VULNERABILITY AMONG RACIALLY AND ETHNICALLY DIVERSE YOUTH: A GENERAL OVERVIEW

Having presented PVEST as a comprehensive, dynamic, normative developmental framework, we now apply this framework to examine vulnerability and resilience among racially and ethnically diverse youth. Although much of our focus here is on the first component of PVEST, net vulnerability level, we consider all five components, along with the developmental processes that link them.

The broad, contextual factors that exacerbate normative developmental challenges for youth of color are vast and numerous; many books have been written about each of these issues. We focus on some illustrative examples highlighting various groups. First, we briefly cover structural and ideological manifestations of racism and then explore one of these, skin color bias and attitudes, in more detail. We then turn our attention to the context of immigration in the United States and explore issues such as cultural dissonance and dual identification that render the task of identity formation more difficult for immigrant youth. These topics are covered as representative of normative undertak-

ings confronted by youth of color, but they are by no means a complete account of these challenges.

Structural and Ideological Legacies of American Racism

Race and racism have been perhaps the most charged political issues in U.S. history. Various historical and political forces brought about the current racial/ethnic composition and demographic trajectory of the United States, and these forces serve as the broader social and historical context for the everyday experiences of all Americans. Traditional definitions of racism view it simply as discrimination based on race; these neglect the innumerable ways the phenomenon of racism impacts lives. Racism is omnipresent, though often subtle; it is channeled through multiple levels of context, as described by Bronfenbrenner (1979). It is inclusive not only of discriminatory behavior, but also of structural power relationships, political ideologies, and institutionalized practices, all of which can be normative, albeit unacknowledged, components of society. There are various and salient ways racism impacts lives, not only by disadvantaging people of color but also by privileging White people.

Omi and Winant's (1994) *racial formation* perspective is among the most widely cited sociological theories of racism, and it presents an ideal framework to describe the formation of racial ideologies, which are also expressed in everyday life through stereotypes, assumptions, and other forms of tangible bias. Omi and Winant define racial formation as "the sociohistorical process by which racial categories are created, inhabited, transformed, and destroyed" (p. 55). Racial formation focuses on the process of racialization and recognizes the multiple levels at which racism occurs, with macrolevel structural manifestations translating into individual everyday experiences at the microlevel. "Racial projects," according to Omi and Winant, are historically situated interpretations and explanations of the racial relationships in a society; these serve to reallocate resources across racial groups and can serve as explanations/justifications for inequities. Other perspectives, such as that of Bonilla-Silva (2001), have built on Omi and Winant's work and emphasized structural and ideological dimensions of racism.

Structural Racism and Economic Inequities

Structural factors center on the social relationships inherent in racial inequity. For example, poverty is a major structural barrier to success for African American youth. Moreover, the racialized nature of poverty goes beyond monetary income; community resources and accumulated wealth also play a critical role. For example, Sampson and Morenoff (1997) reported that in 1980, 85% of poor Black Americans lived in impoverished areas lacking in community resources; only about 30% of poor White Americans lived in such areas. More than 33% of poor African Americans resided in extremely impoverished neighborhoods, as compared to only 7% of poor White Americans. The impoverished communities where poor African Americans often reside are characterized by different family structures, few economic opportunities, few recreational facilities, poor quality of schooling, and lack of available role models.

Similarly, Conley (1999) notes the critical distinction between income and wealth. Even when controlling for income, White Americans tend to have much greater net worth than Black Americans when measuring total assets. This disparity is due partly to differences in home ownership, which have a historical basis in redlining and restrictive covenants, issues that are all the more salient because housing discrimination laws are so weakly enforced. Income has a large impact on many areas, including the ability of Black families to afford higher education. Thus, the history and ecology of poverty and wealth distribution reflect the legacy of structural racism inherent in American society. In the context of these continuing structural barriers, Black youth have limited access to resources and limited opportunities to visualize and comprehend success and attainment. In the absence of resources, successful role models, and social supports, experiences of dissonance and normative developmental challenges can yield negative outcomes such as academic underachievement.

Other sources of vulnerability and potential stress, resulting from poverty and related ecological risks, exacerbate normative developmental challenges when experienced by many African American youth. Growing up in poverty has been related to higher teen pregnancy rates among Black youth (Mayer & Jencks, 1989). More than 50% of African American children are born to unwed teen mothers, with poor nutrition and medical care often characterizing the prenatal period (Spurlock & Norris, 1991). The noted economic conditions are not independent of associated challenges that leave Black men unemployed or underemployed (see M. L. Sullivan, 1989); accordingly, some men may be viewed as less than optimal options for stable marital relationships. The consequences have implications for the character of the surroundings in which children's growth and development take place. Adverse neighborhood conditions, which are not independent of the economic circumstances described, can lead to developmental deficiencies early in

life; for example, anemia, lead poisoning, and ear infections often afflict urban African American and Latino preschool children and, considered long term, have implications for learning and mental health. Of particular importance, they influence the possibility of either high vulnerability or manifested resiliency. Although family and home characteristics vary substantially at all income levels, children growing up in low-economic-resource families and highly impoverished areas are more likely to experience stressors such as an unstable home life, parental neglect, and violence (Tuakli-Williams & Carillo, 1995). Without proper supports, these can lead to impaired cognitive and social development, with consequences such as deficient language acquisition, social withdrawal, and depression. It is the pattern of psychosocial and health-related stressors coupled with low societal expectations that can lead to poor academic achievement and high-risk behavior if proper supports are not provided. For example, appropriately designed and supported interventions can create more stable family structures, effective parenting skills, and conflict-resolution supports.

As indicated, it is also important to note that even in the most adverse circumstances, many families already draw on such resources, and consequently, children are able to attain resilient outcomes in spite of the exacerbated challenges they confront (see Swanson, Spencer, Dell'Angelo, Harpalani, & Spencer, 2002). Vulnerability means that risks are present, but actual experiences of stress can be avoided if adequate protective factors are present or youth can draw on resources to negotiate this stress effectively.

Vulnerability Related to Violence

Violence is another source of vulnerability for urban youth, particularly in terms of victimization. Shakoor and Chalmers (1991) found that approximately 75% of African American youth surveyed in Chicago schools had been "covictimized," witnessing directly the perpetration of serious violence (e.g., shooting, stabbing) against another person. Covictimization may lead to Posttraumatic Stress Disorder, and such exposure to violence has also been linked to the perpetration of violence (DuRant, Cadenheard, & Pendergrast, 1994). Adolescent and young adult Black males have disproportionately high rates of victimization (Donziger, 1996). Moreover, Cunningham (1999) found that Black males are keenly aware of danger, and that cognitive appraisals of risk were significantly strong predictors of hypermasculine coping (i.e., beliefs that violence is manly). May (2001) also found that Black males were significantly more fearful of victimization than their White counterparts and resorted to carrying more lethal defensive weapons. H. C. Stevenson (1997) reports that many Black youth reside in high-risk neighborhoods where displays of anger may be necessary and represent adaptive coping mechanisms to avoid victimization; indeed, display of anger may be a form of competence for social and emotional viability in these contexts. Also, hypermasculine posturing necessary to avoid victimization may also mitigate school adjustment (Spencer, 1999) by means such as reinforcing negative teacher perceptions. Moreover, these kinds of phenomena must be understood in light of the salient, existing negative stereotypes of Black males, which are already rooted in hypermasculine imagery (Ferguson, 2001).

In sum, violence poses a complex series of threats to resilience for Black males. First, violence and victimization are maladaptive, leading to obvious adverse outcomes. Second, African American males are often perceived by society to be especially hostile, and as a consequence, they are treated unjustly by law enforcement and social agencies. Whereas White youth with psychological adjustment problems are often referred to mental health (and often private) services, African Americans are usually placed in the criminal justice system for the same offenses (Spurlock & Norris, 1991). The differences in treatment options available or system type used (i.e., private vs. public), although generally not acknowledged, have implications for the accumulation of statistics in the public domain and their contributions to and reinforcement of negative imagery and stigma. Third, as H. C. Stevenson (1997) describes it, displays of aggression by some Black youth may be adaptive responses in high-risk neighborhoods, where anger displays may be necessary to mitigate victimization. The conundrum, of course, is that such displays, in conjunction with negative stereotypes of African American males, may be misunderstood in school settings, where they constitute maladaptive coping responses. Thus, dissonance across the various settings of development may compound the issue, because violence functions as a complex, multifaceted source of vulnerability for African American youth (Spencer, Dupree, Cunningham, Harpalani, & Munoz-Miller, 2003; Spencer, Fegley, Seaton, & Harpalani, in press).

Racial Stereotyping

A related and significant source of vulnerability for youth of color is racial stereotyping, in all of its manifestations. Awareness of racial stereotypes and group membership status plays a key role in identity formation, particularly in adolescence, as identity and appraisal by self and others become prominent developmental issues. In addition to the negative stereotyping noted earlier with regard to aggres-

sion and violence, racial stereotypes present a barrier to academic achievement and resilience for African American youth. Claude Steele's (1997, 2004; Steele & Aronson, 1995) work on *stereotype threat* highlights these issues. Stereotype threat is essentially the fear of confirming a negative stereotype in circumstances where that stereotype is primed and salient; Steele and colleagues have experimentally demonstrated how stereotypes can negatively impact the academic performance of Black college students. Although their work has emphasized the experiences of college students, we infer that the mechanisms are also relevant for adolescents. Moreover, the phenomenon of stereotype threat is most salient for high-achieving Black youth (i.e., those demonstrating resilience "to date"), who have a great desire and expectation to succeed.

Academic stereotypes can also be a source of vulnerability for Asian American youth, who are often monolithically viewed as high-achieving "model minorities." This can create tremendous pressure to succeed and meet expectations. Even seemingly positive racial stereotypes have a negative side; Asian American youth are often taunted as "geeks" and "nerds," and they are viewed as passive and socially inept. Asian American males are stereotyped as weak and unmasculine, and females are portrayed as submissive. These stereotypes, in conjunction with other factors, can render these youth particularly vulnerable to mental health and social adjustment problems.

Stereotypes can be coupled in ways that complicate their impact and thus require more measured and thoughtful attention. To illustrate, positive and negative stereotypes can be coupled together, as is the case with African American athletes (Harpalani, 2001; Stone, Perry, & Darley, 1997). Here, the idea of African Americans as outstanding athletes, a seemingly positive attribute, is linked to the notion that African Americans are less intelligent and inherently lower achievers, due to genetic (Rushton, 1995) or cultural (Hoberman, 1997) factors. With regard to academic racial stereotyping, another subtle facet of vulnerability is lenient feedback and generally low expectations communicated from teachers; again, this becomes a risk factor as normative human development progresses. Cognitive maturation renders adolescents more sensitive and aware of implicitly communicated attitudes, beliefs, and explicitly conveyed feedback from elders and peers; additionally, they are more perceptive of false or deceptive tactics than younger children, who represent a less sophisticated level of social cognition. Harber (1998) illustrates that Black American college students in late adolescence and young adulthood may be so wary of praise from White Americans that receiving it may, in reality, depress their self-esteem. This is another example of how a seemingly positive action can have negative consequences; intended support, in fact, may not be perceived in ways that are indeed supportive.

Given all of these factors, it is apparent that racial stereotyping is often more complex than stigmatization of mental illness and other devalued statuses. Corrigan and Penn's (1999) distinction between stereotyping (value-neutral cognitive categorization) and stigma ("negative" forms of stereotyping) may obscure salient issues in racial stereotyping. As illustrated, racial stereotypes that appear neutral or positive on the surface can reinforce other, negative stereotypes about respective groups. We've focused on minority youth; however, White adolescents have challenges that emanate from other issues and status concerns.

White Privilege

White privilege is a critical, although often ignored, element of any discussion of race and racism. Whiteness should not be normalized, and the history of White Americans as a racial group in the United States must be understood to explain the current privileges and challenges of White youth. The new field of Whiteness studies is particularly illuminating (e.g., Lipsitz, 1998), although the connections to normative human development have yet to be made in substantive ways. Nevertheless, Haney-Lopez (1996) and Harris (1993) provide compelling legal and historical discussions regarding the centrality of White as a legal category to the very definition of U.S. citizenship. Although formally legalized racial barriers to citizenship have been eliminated, the legacy of White supremacy continues in many ways and filters through multiple levels of context to impact everyday life.

For example, in her widely cited article, "White Privilege: Unpacking the Invisible Knapsack," Peggy McIntosh (1989, p. 10) defines White privilege as a "package of unearned assets which [Whites] can count on cashing in every day . . . an invisible weightless knapsack of special provisions." In this vein, White privilege basically encompasses the advantages that White people secure on the basis of skin color. In many instances, White Americans themselves are not generally aware of these advantages; the lack of consciousness itself may be due to the fact that advantages accrued represent incidents that do not take place, such as not being stopped unjustly by the police, not being followed in a store or suspected as a thief, not being represented in the news media primarily in negative ways (or ignored totally), and not being questioned about one's national loyalty, an even more salient issue in the post-

September 11, 2001, era. Because these are incidents that Caucasians do not generally experience, many fail to acknowledge or do not understand the everyday burdens that people of color encounter, or they tend to minimize the salience of these burdens. White Americans often take their own advantages for granted and attribute them solely to hard work and merit. Through the mechanism of intergenerational transmitted wealth (see Darity & Myers, 1998) and contemporary privileges (see M. L. Sullivan, 1989), White Americans have always had greater access to money, property, social and employment networks, and education than people of color. Moreover, the social and cultural practices of schools and workplaces are defined by White American norms, and cultural expressions by people of color, ranging from hair and clothing styles to language, are either discouraged in these settings, or they are embraced superficially under the rubric of "diversity," without a deep exploration of their meaning and significance. All of these factors contribute to the continuation of White privilege as a salient issue.

Another concept of importance needs to be introduced here: the *downside of privilege*. In the context of Whiteness, privilege is typically viewed as a racially dependent advantage, usually unfair in some broad sense. On the surface, privilege appears to serve as a protective factor, offsetting potential risks that more marginalized individuals may face. However, we can also view a privileged person as one who is not subject to particular experiences of stress engagement, for example, negotiating cultural dissonance or racial stereotyping. Youth of color who must negotiate these challenges have the opportunity to demonstrate resilience: successful coping with the given challenges. In the process, these resilient youth acquire and hone valuable coping skills, whereas privileged youth do not acquire these skills. Employing a PVEST cyclic perspective, youth who do not need to acquire these skills during one developmental cycle may need them at a subsequent time. The lack of requisite coping skills, due to minimal or nonengagement with stress, thus negates or undermines the possibility of resilience. This may lead to adverse outcomes in the future. As indicated, privilege, in fact, precludes the opportunity to hone coping repertoires, which may be necessary for later life challenges. In short, successful resolution of challenges makes youth more resilient, and those who do not encounter those challenges cannot be characterized as resilient because they remain untested outside of the normative encumbrances generally associated with a particular stage of development. Accordingly, being untested and having underdeveloped reactive coping skills enhances their vulnerability. As a consequence, given the function of coping processes both for adequate responses in the moment (i.e., reactive coping strategies) and their patterned character as multiple emergent identities, one should consider the lack of coping skill actualization as the downside of privilege.

Although infrequently described as such, the 1999 student massacre at Columbine High School in Littleton, Colorado, and related incidents, along with the recent White identity theorizing (e.g., Helms, 1990) and general Whiteness discourse, support that there is a downside of privilege. As suggested, due to a lack of coping skill honing and actualization, privileged individuals become more dependent on the built-in and unacknowledged advantages enjoyed rather than developing their own abilities and authentic emergent identities. Much more research is necessary to determine the precise effects of privilege in different contexts. Recent research by Luthar (Luthar & Becker, 2002) and her colleagues provides credibility to this analysis. Of course, privilege is not just limited to race; other statuses such as gender, social class, ethnic/cultural background, skin tone, physical attractiveness, and sexual orientation can also confer privilege. Nonetheless, Kenneth B. Clark (1939, 1940) portended the downside of racial privilege 50 years ago with his expert testimony in *Brown v. Board of Education*. His report included evidence of "racial paranoia" and "unrealistic view of self" that segregation created among White Americans (see Harpalani, 2004). Consistent with the pathological ethos regarding African Americans, the U.S. Supreme Court ignored this evidence in favor of the Clarks' doll studies, which have since been reinterpreted (Spencer, 1982a, 1983, 1984), as will be discussed later.

Multiracial/Biracial Identification

Individuals from biracial and multiracial backgrounds face challenges not only of marginalization as individuals, but also of dissonance of group identification. Historically, terms typically used to classify multiracial persons, such as "mongrel," "half-caste," "half breed," "mulatto," and "hybrid," denote this lack of fit with the dominant realm of American racial categorization. Despite these distinct labels, societal attitudes have also typically asserted that a person with "one drop of [non-White] blood" is by default a member of the non-White group—another historic marker of White privilege.

Theorizing on biracial and multiracial identity development paralleled the deficit-oriented perspectives that char-

acterized previous scholarship on all youth of color. In this case, the dominant view was that biracial individuals face developmental problems because they are caught between two irreconcilable cultural contexts (H. W. Stevenson & Stewart, 1958). Stonequist's (1937) *The Marginal Man* was one of the first proponents of this theory, stating that the biracial individual experiences personally the racial tensions of the society and is therefore alienated from both subcultures. In contrast, Kerwin, Ponterotto, Jackson, and Harris (1993) found that in their study, biracial adolescents did not perceive themselves to be marginalized as such. Much of the current debate still relies heavily on a marginal view of the multiracial individual's development. An important future scholarly endeavor is to determine how the normative challenges of identity formation are exacerbated for biracial and multiracial youth without assuming pathology in the youth themselves. The question of multiracial identification is also highly politicized, with direct implications for U.S. Census categorization and resource allocation (Hernandez, 1998).

W. S. Carlos Poston (1990) and Maria Root (1990) have developed identity development models to address these issues unique to the multiracial population. Specifically, Poston draws on the concepts of personal identity and interpersonal competence with respect to reference group orientation. Similar to those of Cross (1971) and Erikson (1963), Poston's model has a life span focus. His framework consists of five basic stages: personal identity, choice of group categorization, enmeshment/denial, appreciation, and integration. As the biracial individual moves through this process, according to Poston, he or she must examine and reexamine his or her own reference group orientation (again, reminiscent of Cross's recycling process). Particularly in the third stage (enmeshment/denial), the biracial individual feels guilt and self-hatred surrounding his or her own reference group choice. Poston asserts, "When a multiethnic child is unable to identify with both parents, the child has feelings of disloyalty and massive guilt over rejection of one parent" (p. 154). The desired final stage of integration has been reached when the individual has been able to recognize and value all of his or her ethnic identities and feels a sense of wholeness.

Root's (1990) model also acknowledges the guilt and self-hatred noted in Poston's (1990) third stage. However, rather than accepting this stage as a necessary step for biracial development, she suggests an alternative route. According to Root, "For the biracial individual to reject either part of their racial heritage continues an internalized oppression" (p. 193). Also in contrast to Poston's model, Root does not identify a single healthy outcome. Rather, she maintains that there are four distinct possible healthy outcomes for the biracial individual: acceptance of the identity society assigns (similar to Marcia's foreclosure stage), identification with a single racial group (typically the minority group), identification with both racial groups (similar to Poston's integration stage), and, finally, identification as a new racial group. Of course, it is important to understand all of these possibilities in the larger context of racialization, with ever-changing racial categories and ideologies (Omi & Winant, 1994). Additionally, although generally not emphasized, parents' very early cultural socialization efforts (or lack thereof) matter and have important implications for youths' healthy identity resolution and reference group orientation (see Spencer, 1990).

Additional Sources of Vulnerability Due to Racial and Ethnic Marginalization

Numerous other sources of vulnerability are related to racial and ethnic marginalization in the United States. For example, the history of Native Americans in the United States, consisting largely of cultural and physical genocide (Churchill, 1994), has immense consequences for the development of indigenous youth. One of the monumental challenges to resilience of these youth is the need for more culturally sensitive basic research efforts.

Scores of other issues abound; however, owing to limited space and constraints due to expertise, we cannot cover them all. Instead, we supplement our general look at vulnerability among racially and ethnically diverse youth with an in-depth consideration of two issues of particular prominence across racial and ethnic groups: skin color bias and cultural dissonance. Although both of these issues affect the entire spectrum of people of color, we focus largely on African American youth for the former issue and immigrant and second-generation youth for the latter. In the process, we also illustrate in more detail the components of PVEST as unique analytic tools for examining vulnerability within normative human development.

VULNERABILITY AMONG RACIALLY AND ETHNICALLY DIVERSE YOUTH: COLORISM/SKIN COLOR BIAS

To understand how skin color bias can be a risk factor for youth of color (most significantly, Black youth), it is helpful to consider the historical context of race and color stratification. Skin color is probably the most visible and salient phenotypic feature associated with racial categorization and related biases. Colorism, systemic bias, and inequity on the basis of skin color (usually privileging lighter skin tones over darker ones), even predates the notion of race in many societies. John Hope Franklin's (1968) volume *Color and Race* illustrated that colorism has existed in a number of areas around the world, including Japan (Wagatsuma, 1968), Northern Africa (J. S. Brown & Farber, 1968), South Africa (Legum, 1968), and India (Beteille, 1969). In parts of South and Central America, there is a correlation between darker skin tones and socioeconomic and political disadvantages. Issues of color hierarchy are prevalent in countries such as Brazil, where Portuguese invaders established a social system in which lighter-skinned Portuguese were on top, indigenous peoples were in the middle, and Africans were at the bottom (Russell, Wilson, & Hall, 1992). Even as many current Brazilians can claim mixed heritage, skin color still serves as a marker of social status. Other countries, such as Mexico, show similar color hierarchies.

In all of these societies, lighter skin tones are valued over darker skin tones, and color has broad implications for social status. Nevertheless, it is important to note that skin tone has taken on a particular structural significance in the United States. For example, on the surface, the social stratification and organization of the Indian subcontinent, based largely on the caste system, seems similar to the racial subordination inherent in the United States, with the two appearing as parallel hierarchies based on skin tone. However, the caste system of South Asia and the racial stratification of the United States differ in both origin and structure. Although skin color bias is apparent on the Indian subcontinent and perhaps even related to caste, skin color was not a key component in the creation of the caste system. Originally, European translators mistakenly assumed that skin color was the basis for caste divisions; this occurred because the Sanskrit term for caste, *varna,* translates as "color" (Koshy, 1998; Prashad, 2000). As noted by Koshy, there are classical Vedic references to upper-caste individuals with dark skin. Occupational delineation, rather than skin color, was the key component in the formation of the caste system.

In contrast, as Franklin and Moss (1994) note, the identifiably of Africans based on skin color was a key feature in the institution of slavery. Slavery in the Western Hemisphere became a massive economic enterprise. Slaves were systematically captured and bred for profit, creating a system of racial exploitation and segregation. This stood in contrast to previous forms of slavery, where slaves were primarily prisoners of war who were freed after a period of time. Initially, European colonists attempted to enslave Native Americans; however, Africans, because of their lower susceptibility to diseases and easy identification based on skin color, proved to be a more profitable economic commodity (Franklin, 1994). Also, colonial plantation owners served their own interests by elevating their White indentured servants to a higher position than Africans. By providing psychological race-based privileges for marginalized White groups, they largely precluded dissatisfied Black and White workers from revolting together against the landowners (Steinhorn & Diggs-Brown, 1999). This racial division, thwarting a natural coalition of economically marginalized peoples, continues in U.S. politics to this day.

As early as 1622, many of the American colonies passed antimiscegenation laws to preserve these racial boundaries; however, these did not apply or were not enforced with respect to male slave owners and their female slaves. It was not at all unusual for these slave owners, usually aristocratic and propertied White men, to coerce sexual relationships with Black women slaves. The offspring of these coerced relationships further augmented the skin color hierarchy in America, as described by Russell et al. (1992) in *The Color Complex*. Children were classified as "mulatto" (one-half Black), "quadroon" (one-fourth Black), and "octoroon" (one-eighth Black; Izrael, 2001). During the era of slavery, slaves with a White father led a more privileged existence than their counterparts (Frazier, 1957). Lighter-skinned slaves were typically given more prestigious jobs, such as artisan or seamstress, and darker-skinned slaves did more physically demanding, menial work, often as field hands (Blackwell, 1985; Frazier, 1957).

This within-group color hierarchy created friction between many darker- and lighter-skinned slaves and gave rise to colorism in Black communities that has existed since. Skin color privilege continued throughout American society after the abolition of slavery. Educational, economic, and occupational opportunities were more accessible to light-skinned Blacks during the era of *de jure* segregation, often perpetuated by segregated Black institutions. Lighter-skinned African Americans often avoided marriage with darker-skinned individuals and maintained or desired to maintain closer ties with White communities (Hunter, 2004). They also formed social clubs, such as the Bon Ton Society of Washington, DC, and the Blue Vein Society of Nashville, which restricted access based on skin color. These societies adopted formal

and informal barriers to entrance, such as the "brown paper bag" test (skin tone had to be as light or lighter than the color of a paper bag), the "comb test" (a comb had to pass through hair easily), and painted doors (used to judge skin color). The formal traditions have since passed, but the names and legacy (i.e., practiced values) remain (e.g., "Blue vein"). Many major urban cities across the United States have areas that were historically inhabited primarily by light-skinned Black Americans; these were often the most affluent elements of segregated Black communities. For example, one area in Harlem, known as Strivers' Row, housed a number of light-skinned doctors, lawyers, and other professionals. Historically Black colleges and universities also discriminated against applicants based on the color of their skin, using informal barriers such as the aforementioned paper bag test. Even relatively dark-skinned students admitted to institutions have been socially marginalized. All of these biases are driven by the implicit, unacknowledged (and often unintentional today) theme that Whiteness, and anything White-like, is superior, and Blackness, and anything dark, is evil or inferior.

Developmental Significance of Colorism: Skin Color Biases and Attitudes as Risk Contributors

Color consciousness and attitudes begin at an early age. Much of the early literature regarding skin color preference involved preschool populations (e.g., Clark & Clark, 1939). Clark and Clark (1940) found that Black children as young as 3 years old had knowledge of skin color differences and could appropriately self identify. It was posited that the children were not identifying on the basis of race because that concept was too advanced for their development. Instead, young children identified on "the basis of skin color which is to them a concrete reality" (p. 168). In a later experiment, children were given a Black and a White doll and were asked questions, such as which one they would "like to play with" or which one is the "nice doll" (Clark & Clark, 1947). The majority of the participants in that study demonstrated White preferences. The Clarks concluded that the response pattern indicated Black self-hatred, a finding that was cited in the Supreme Court's 1954 landmark decision in *Brown v. Board of Education*. Other studies have found similar results, indicating that Black children display preferences for the color white and White people (Gopaul-McNicol, 1988; J. D. Porter, 1971; Williams & Roberson, 1967). However, the Clarks' (1939, 1940, 1947) and contemporary studies have been criticized as having inaccurate interpretations or methodological flaws (Baldwin,

1979; Brand, Ruiz, & Padilla, 1974; Cross, 1991; Spencer, 1984; Spencer & Markstrom-Adams, 1990). Moreover, their interpretation of children's preference behavior reflected the ethos of Black pathology and deficit-oriented perspectives alluded to earlier.

In contrast to the Black self-hatred theory, other research has shown that despite having a White preference (for dolls, pictures, or other objects), Black children display positive self-esteem and self-concept (Banks, 1976; McAdoo, 1985; Spencer, 1984). In this literature, researchers maintain that Black children's personal self-esteem is independent or separate from racial preference behavior. Most of these studies actually assess self-concept and racial attitudes in the same population, rather than making assumptions, to delineate the relationship of the two constructs. For instance, Spencer sampled 130 Black preschool children between the ages of 4 and 6. She found that 80% of the sample obtained positive self-concept scores, while demonstrating pro-White biased cultural values. She concluded that Black preschool children separated personal identity (i.e., self-concept) from knowledge of racial attitudes. Similarly, Banks found that despite having pro-White attitudes, Black teenagers from predominantly White communities and schools still tended to have positive self-concepts.

As suggested by Spencer's (1982a, 1982b, 1983, 1984; Spencer & Dornbusch, 1990; Spencer & Markstrom-Adams, 1990) program of research, as opposed to those making negative inferences from the Clarks' studies and fomenting "self-hatred" conclusions (e.g., Kardiner & Ovesey, 1951; Pettigrew, 1964), in fact, young Black children may not internalize pro-White/anti-Black messages. The developmentally appropriate explanation credits the "protection" emanating from normal levels of cognitive egocentrism (Piaget, 1932). Spencer (1982a, 1984, 1985) notes that young children are appropriately self-centered and, in general, do not project their preferences inward; in fact, developmentally appropriate cognitive egocentrism serves as a protective factor that prevents the internalization of biased racial attitudes and, thus, generally precludes the acquisition of low self-esteem.

Cross (1991) notes that even in the Clarks' data, it is not clear that Black children systematically preferred White dolls, and in any case, their preference behavior shifted with age; this is not unexpected, given Spencer's (1985) integration of social cognition-dependent developmental processes into the analysis. That is, as children mature and increase their capacity to make inferences about cognitive, social, and affective phenomena, in effect and of necessity they shed what represented "protective ego-

centrism" and become more aware of how society views Blackness. Spencer (1999) describes developmental trends in color/race response patterns from four studies in different geographic regions of the United States. Data indicate that Black preschool children demonstrate Eurocentric attitudes, preferences, and color connotations through early middle childhood (approximately age 9). These attitudes and preferences reflect children's early learning that all things White are more valued in society. However, children do not necessarily internalize potential negative affect due to cognition-linked egocentrism. The onset of concrete operational thought marks a shift in attitudes and preference toward a more Afrocentric orientation. Of particular importance, the end of egocentric thinking can be a source of risk: Once Black children have the veil of protective egocentrism lifted, they begin not only to be aware of and understand societal attitudes and stereotypes of color, but to view themselves in light of them. Data suggest that given the protective character of cultural socialization, many Black children react to potential dissonance by shifting their preference behavior (i.e., becoming more Afrocentric; Spencer, 1983) rather than adopting low self-esteem; nonetheless, this shift itself diverts attention and psychic energy from other developmental tasks, such as academic engagement (see Spencer, 1999).

Nevertheless, the risks associated with race awareness and exposure to biased racial attitudes may be offset by protective factors. Black parents can, and often do, socialize their children to understand the importance and implications of their skin color. Spencer et al. (1997, p. 818) suggest that "minority parent child rearing efforts require, of necessity, providing explicit explanation of the meaning and significance of their youth's [color and] race." Racial socialization can be a protective factor by decreasing the psychological impact of hostilities based on color and race (H. C. Stevenson, 1994). Proactive socialization strategies encourage racial and cultural pride, and protective strategies focus on awareness of racism and related biases such as colorism. Some suggest that this is not just a protective factor but also a necessity for "raising physically and emotionally healthy children who are Black in a society where Black has negative connotations" (Peters, 1985, p. 161).

Color bias also has different implications by gender. For Black females, concerns about skin tone exacerbate the normative challenges of body image and appearance (Fegley, Spencer, Goss, Harpalani, & Charles, in press); these occur because of the greater importance placed on physical attractiveness for females generally. Moreover, the specific developmental period also plays a significant role, given that more general concerns about appearance increase for all youth during adolescence. Thus, risks associated with colorism vary with gender, context, and development. Further, as suggested by Regan Good (2003), in an interview with Randall Kennedy concerning Kennedy's book *Interracial Intimacies,* structural impediments are linked to the persistency of the problem and concerted efforts across significant time will be needed for change.

Colorism and Stress Engagement: Tangible Experiences of Color Bias

For youth of color, experiences related to skin color bias are encounters of stress that must be negotiated in conjunction with normative developmental challenges. These are dissonance- and anxiety-producing experiences generally missing for Caucasian youth. That is, relative to individual context "fit," in general, the experience of consonant conditions is more often the norm. To illustrate, media images, stereotypical labels, and books all communicate skin color bias. Advertising of tanning solutions suggests enhancements and not as a negatively portrayed deficit. Russell et al. (1992) point out that light to medium skin tones (and terms used to describe light skin) are typically linked to intelligence and refinement, whereas dark skin tones suggest toughness, meanness, and physical strength. Historically, slogans and rhymes convey negative attitudes about Black skin tones (K. T. Brown, Ward, Lightbourn, & Jackson, 1998); one such catchphrase is "If you're White you're all right, if you're yellow you're mellow, if you're brown stick around, if you're Black get back."

In a 1972 study by Edwards, darker-skinned participants showed a slightly greater consciousness of racial discrimination than those of lighter complexions. Darker individuals also sensed greater hostility on the part of Whites than those of lighter skin tones. These findings are not surprising considering pro-White messages conveyed in American and other societies. These views are deeply embedded within social structures and serve to perpetuate contemporary beliefs of White supremacy.

By the onset of adolescence, Black youth have well-defined stereotypes about skin color (Parrish, 1946). C. Anderson and Cromwell (1977) focused specifically on positive and negative stereotypical attributes that are associated with skin color. Overall skin color preferences tended toward lighter-brown colors, although darker-skinned teens valued darker skin more highly and lighter-skinned participants valued lighter skin color more highly. Light brown skin was chosen for items that gauged positive characteristics, such as "the nicest, the one best liked to marry" (p. 80). Likewise, for the items that gauged nega-

tive characteristics (e.g., who was the dumbest, the person one would not like to marry), subjects selected dark skin. As noted, such encounters experienced by youth of color suggest an extension and exacerbation of stress related to body image and physical appearance that, in general, all adolescents experience and cope with.

Color biases can also worsen stress in the realm of interpersonal relationships, where skin color may represent a source of acceptance or rejection. The significance begins at birth. As Russell et al. (1992, p. 94) note, "Many Black families can barely disguise their anxious concern about the color and features of a newborn." Given anticipated additional stress, families may pass on their anxieties about structural impediments associated with skin color as specific attitudes. Moreover, cultural socialization efforts that specifically communicate the history of skin color bias to children along the hierarchical system of slavery that produced it vary widely; accordingly, attitudes about skin tone vary (Boyd-Franklin, 1989). Given the dissonance-created character of skin color as a topic, relative to family responses, the relationship is neither simple nor obvious. In some families, light skin color is prized in accordance with societal biases; however, other Black families may develop different preferences, conscious or unconscious, in light of historical influences such as the Black Power movement. In these families, dark-skinned members are preferred and light-skinned members may be viewed and subtly chastised as shameful reminders of slavery and miscegenation.

Albeit sometimes hidden and independent of developmental period, skin tone continues to affect relationships. For example, in a study involving two groups of undergraduates and a group of graduate students at a historically Black university, Marks (1943) discerned that classmates who were lighter than average, but not at the extreme light end of the color spectrum, were perceived as most attractive and charming. Correspondingly, in another experiment, very dark brown and dark brown skin tones were least favored (C. Porter, 1991). Other skin color studies have shown that medium complexions are preferred over the extremes. According to C. Porter, regardless of age or gender, children prefer honey brown tones to darker skin tones. She suggests different gender- and age-related rationales for preferences based on cognitive development, broadening intergroup social experiences, and specific developmental concerns. Children between the ages of 9 and 11 offered reasons related to desire for sameness and desire to be liked by others (e.g., "her friends are that color" and "wants to be like everyone else"). Older children, 12- to 13-year-olds, explained their preference based on physical attractiveness (e.g., "probably thinks she's ugly with that color") and the possibility that people are discriminated against on the basis of skin tone (e.g., "could get more jobs and people would talk to her more"). These findings underscore the significance of normative developmental tasks, such as forming peer relationships, in mediating the impact of skin color biases.

Skin color is, or is perceived to be, a factor in selecting romantic and marital partners (Bond & Cash, 1992; Hughes & Hertel, 1990; Hunter, 1998). In a study with Black undergraduate females attending a southern university, the women were asked about their perceptions of skin color as an influence on mate selection (Bond & Cash, 1992). Regardless of their own skin color, most of the females believed that Black males preferred women with lighter complexions. Not only are light-skinned women preferred as mates, they are more likely to marry higher status husbands (Hunter, 1998). In their study, Hughes and Hertel reported that controlling for age, gender, education, occupational prestige, and parental socioeconomic status, light-skinned women were found to have a spouse with more education and higher occupational status. Obviously, the attainment of resilience (i.e., given the problem of structurally organized and long-term biases) requires specific coping strategies and supports.

Coping and Identity Challenges Related to Colorism

As noted previously, normative cognitive maturation makes awareness of dissonance concerning color bias both unavoidable and potentially acute. Reactive coping responses to experienced dissonance and potential problems lead to the enactment of strategies that may be either adaptive or maladaptive. Spencer (1995) posits that perceptions of self and thoughts about how others perceive you influence behavior. Therefore, internalizing skin color bias can influence psychological equilibrium and require particular coping strategies. Determining how people perceive and interpret the meaning of their skin color is important for understanding coping processes and specific supports required.

On the psychosocial level, studies suggest that skin color is related to perceptions of attractiveness, self-esteem, and satisfaction. Stress related to body image and physical appearance may be among the most palpable manifestations of skin color bias. A basic conclusion drawn in the early research was that lighter skin color was valued more than darker skin color and the valuing of certain skin tones negatively affected self-esteem, especially in children. However, given developmental differences in young

children's cognition, the inferences are not consistent with empirical demonstrations. Specifically, consistent with the doll studies, one should not assume negative outcomes in this domain; stress and coping responses to stress vary significantly within groups given variations in parental socialization strategies and early childhood experiences. Although focused on a very different developmental period, more recently, Coard, Breland, and Raskin (2001) examined the role of skin color as it pertained to self-esteem among 113 Black college students of various skin tones. The authors hypothesized that perceptions of and preferences for darker skin color would be positively related to higher levels of self-esteem, whereas perceptions of and preferences for lighter skin would be positively related to lower levels of self-esteem. In contrast to their hypothesis, they found that the more satisfied darker-skinned males were with their own skin color, the lower was their self-esteem. They suggest two possible explanations for their finding. First, for these dark-skinned males, satisfaction could exist on an intellectual level, but emotional inner conflict may still exist. Second, and more interesting, they suggest that dark-skinned individuals felt satisfied with their skin color, but believe others (Blacks and Whites) perceive their dark skin negatively. Coard et al. contend that given the importance darker-skinned participants attributed to others' ideals, it is understandable that their self-esteem was compromised and reported as lower. However, as cognitively sophisticated young adults who do not deny or reject the fact of their own skin color, the findings might suggest that exposure to and awareness of social stereotypes, when considered together, may result in more dissonant sources of feedback for consideration in normative psychosocial processes.

Similarly, using a young adult sample, Altabe (1998) studied body image and skin color in a racially diverse sample of college students using the Physical Appearance Discrepancy Questionnaire (Altabe, 1996); this measure asks respondents about their own physical appearance, ideal body image, and perception of physical traits believed most valued by their cultural group. Skin color was noted as a salient trait by all racial/ethnic groups in the sample: Black, White, Asian, and Latino. Asians reported valuing light skin the most, followed by African Americans. Conversely, all groups except Black females and Asian males responded that having a darker shade of skin color is on their list of the top five ideal traits. However, in the analysis of cultural values of attractiveness, 23.5% of Asians and 21.2% of Black Americans listed light or lighter skin as a culturally valued trait compared to 10.5% of Latinos and 8% of White Americans, who listed light or lighter skin tone as a trait valued by their culture (10.5% and 8%, respectively). In a study of adolescents, Fegley, Spencer, Goss, Harpalani, and Charles (in press) found that consonance and dissonance (i.e., respectively, satisfaction and dissatisfaction with skin tone) was more significantly related to a variety of measures of psychosocial well-being, including body image, than was skin tone itself. In their multiethnic sample, darker-skinned individuals were more likely to be dissonant than lighter-skinned individuals, although individuals rating their skin tone in the middle showed the greatest amount of satisfaction. Fegley et al. also found Asian/Asian American youth to be the most dissonant with respect to skin tone, and lighter-skinned individuals (of all racial/ethnic groups combined) had lower overall body image and less general positive attitudes. Although not speculated about by the authors, perhaps the latter finding is in fact in keeping with media images of lighter-skinned persons and advertisements that focus on body image perfection, thus again subliminally suggesting a downside of privilege (i.e., sets of subliminally communicated problems associated with possessing stereotypically valued physical attributes).

These findings indicate that the relationships among colorism, coping, and psychological well-being are not independent of cognitive functioning and developmental status and, considered overall, are more complex than one might predict based strictly on societal biases. For immigrant populations, national origin may play a role; for example, Montalvo and Codina (2001) found that relatively dark-skinned Mexican Americans (born in the United States) had lower self-esteem scores than dark-skinned Mexicans born in Mexico. Future work can help link color biases and attitudes along with racial socialization more directly to racial and ethnic identity. Skin color, color biases, and related racial/cultural socialization have evident implications for the different phases of Cross's (1991) nigrescence model, along with other racial/ethnic identity theories (Helms, 1990; Phinney, 1992); however, as suggested, the relationships are significantly more intricate than might be predicted based solely on societal biases.

This research underscores the necessity for a comprehensive, culturally and contextually sensitive framework of human development. As part of the normative developmental processes associated with adolescence, youth negotiate challenges associated with physical appearance and societal standards of attractiveness; without a doubt, color biases exacerbate these challenges for darker-skinned youth of all ethnicities. However, many of these youth are able to

cope successfully and to maintain positive feelings about self, as one might expect from a normative (as opposed to pathological) developmental perspective. Nonetheless, societal biases affect how youth are treated and, as illustrated in the next section, as consistently experienced social impediments, may affect their life chances.

Colorism and Life Outcomes

Empirical studies have illustrated that color bias can have an impact in multiple domains of life outcomes. For example, in the realm of education, studies have historically shown that in general, lighter-skinned Black Americans complete more years of formal schooling than their darker-skinned counterparts. Reuter (1917), for example, noted that 11 out of the first 12 Black men who received doctoral degrees from American universities were of interracial parentage. As noted earlier, predominantly Black universities historically discriminated against applicants based on their skin tone. Schools for light-skinned individuals stressed a liberal arts education, and schools populated by dark-skinned students were mainly oriented toward vocational training (Maddox, 1998). Lighter-skinned African Americans were more likely to engage in scholarly pursuits, and dark-skinned individuals prepared for vocational trades. Thus, lighter-skinned individuals (and often those of interracial background) had greater access to education—already a restricted commodity for all Americans and especially African Americans (Maddox, 1998).

Skin tone disparities in education, although generally unacknowledged, still exist. Studies indicate that lighter skin is positively correlated with education (Hughes & Hertel, 1990). Light-skinned Black Americans complete more years of schooling, on average, than their darker-skinned counterparts even when controlling for gender, age, and parental socioeconomic status. Keith and Herring (1991) report that educational attainment increases as skin color becomes lighter. In their study, they used interviewer assessment of participants' skin color. Each skin color increment, as assessed by the interviewer, corresponded to one-half year of additional education. On average, "very light" respondents attained approximately 2 additional years of education over "very dark" respondents.

Income and occupational attainment is another area where color disparities are still apparent. Hughes and Hertel (1990) note that the effect of skin color on the salaries of lighter versus darker African Americans is as great as the effect of race on the earnings of White Americans and all Black Americans. The family income for those with lighter skin was reportedly 50% more than for those families of darker-skinned Blacks (Keith & Herring, 1991). Additionally, Keith and Herring found that the personal income of light-complexioned African Americans was 65% greater then their darker-skinned counterparts, and light-skinned people were more likely to be employed in professional and technical positions, whereas individuals with dark complexions were more likely to be employed as laborers. These findings suggest that, when considered jointly, colorism and racism are life course-relevant obstacles to the long-term resilience of many racially and ethnically diverse youth. Skin color among offspring even within families remains a genotypic determining outcome; colorism themes in general are sensitive, complex, and, infrequently overtly discussed issues. Accordingly, parents are less likely to consciously and proactively focus on the training of nuanced cultural socialization tactics that would serve as protective factors as youth transition across time and place. However, many parents manage the challenge and, thus, enhance the resilient outcomes of their offspring. In general, when considering vulnerability and resilience, the topic of colorism as linked to cultural socialization across ethnic groups continues to need programmatic, sophisticated, and nuanced research efforts approached from a developmental perspective. Enhanced variability between and within groups due to special situations such as immigration status (and its timing) further complicates the issue and thus contributes to the issues of risk and vulnerability if not offset by equal levels of protective factors experienced as supports.

VULNERABILITY AMONG RACIALLY AND ETHNICALLY DIVERSE YOUTH: CULTURAL DISSONANCE

Based on basic tenets of classic dissonance theory, cultural dissonance refers to the cognitive and emotional stresses resulting from conflicting cultural values or norms confronted by individuals in culturally salient situations; they are hypothesized to be linked with social cognitive processes (see Spencer, 1982a, 1982b, 1984, 1985; Spencer & Markstrom-Adams, 1990). Cultural dissonance can take a variety of forms and be expressed through multiple domains of human development. Cultural practices that vary among groups are potential sources of cultural dissonance. Further, increases in rates of immigration within race may potentially exacerbate complex within-group cultural variation and dissonance as well. Unfortunately, underanalyzed perspectives are prevalent. The

points of view ignore developmental processes, including youths' own perceptions, historical factors, and contextual conditions. The shortsightedness interprets "achievement gaps" as emanating from youths' internal characteristics as opposed to linking them with long-standing issues of *absent privileges* for some and a history of unacknowledged and intergenerationally transmitted broad privileges for others (see critical reviews and critiques by Spencer, 1999, 2001; Spencer, Cross, et al., 2003; and Swanson, Cunningham, & Spencer, 2003).

As illustrated by inferences made by Ogbu (1985) and colleagues, the implications of shortsighted misintrepretations of performance differences both within and between groups further complicate the design and implementation of social supports. Ordinarily overlooked has been the salience of stereotype threat for group performance patterns (see Steele, 1997, 2004; Steele & Aaronson, 1995). Stereotype threat experienced by second-generation youth versus the perceptions and consequent coping of more recent immigrants provides the case in point. We suggest that when considered within ethnic groups, immigrants may perceive and experience differences in apparent sources of risk and psychological and social resource availability, which, considered together, potentially exacerbate overall vulnerability level (see Spencer, Kim, & Marshall, 1987). Accordingly, we consider selected themes to illustrate vulnerability associated with cultural dissonance.

Because the experiences of immigrants vary substantially by generational status, scholars distinguish between *first-generation* immigrants (or Americans), who were born overseas, and *second-generation* Americans, who are born in the United States as children of immigrants. The term *1.5 generation* is sometimes used to describe youth who were born abroad but who arrived in the United States at an early age (usually before adolescence); these youth are technically first-generation Americans but share many of the experiences and challenges of the second generation.

The changing patterns of immigration along with the consistent fact of social cognitive development have rendered cultural dissonance among youth an even more important issue than considered in the past. Immigration accounts for a substantial percentage of U.S. population growth (Camarota, 2001); in particular, immigrant and second-generation children represent the fastest growing segment of the country's total population under the age of 18 years (Portes & Rumbaut, 2001). Previous waves of immigrants to the United States came mainly from European countries; although they faced many challenges, assimilation was more accessible to them because of greater phenotypic similarity to the hosts, greater cultural consonance between European and White American norms, and legal definitions of Whiteness, which dictated eligibility for citizenship (Haney-Lopez, 1996). The passage of the 1965 Immigration Act has led to over 40 years of sustained legal immigration, particularly from Mexico, Central and South America, the Caribbean, and East and South Asia; accordingly, there has been a significant increase in the size of the nation's population of people of color (Portes & MacLeod, 1999).

Of course, the exact nature and experience of cultural dissonance is dependent on the two sets of cultural norms or values that are in conflict; in the United States, this usually involves middle- or upper-middle-class White American values conflicting with some other set, as the former is usually considered the unacknowledged norm for all. This is also an area where it is necessary to distinguish finely between race and ethnicity, as there is tremendous ethnic variation within socially and politically constructed racial groups. Moreover, factors such as immigration history and socioeconomic status also impact the experience of cultural dissonance. In addition to the generational classification noted earlier, John Ogbu (1978, 1985, 1990) presents a controversial historical framework to understand the social and political positions of various racial/ethnic groups in the United States. He classifies American minorities into three groups. *Autonomous minorities* are small numerical groups that self-identify as a minority group in salient ways (e.g., Jews, Mormons). These groups are generally established populations in the United States, but they may continue to face forms of discrimination. *Immigrant minorities* are those who voluntarily come to the United States and have expectations of upward social mobility (e.g., many but not all Asian immigrant groups). As conceptualized by Ogbu (1985), *subordinate* or *caste-like minorities* were involuntarily incorporated by White Americans through slavery or subjugation (e.g., Blacks, Native Americans).

Ogbu's framework specifies the varying historical relationships that different groups have with the United States. These structured relationships influence opportunity and desire for assimilation, along with other factors in the negotiation of cultural dissonance. However, a major critique of Ogbu's conceptual strategy is its penchant to make simplistic, deterministic assumptions about group psychology and cultural behavior from such sociohistorical taxonomies (Ogbu, 1985; Fordham & Ogbu, 1986; for critiques, see Harpalani, 2002; Spencer, Cross, et al., 2003; Spencer et al., 2001). Within-group diversity is a key issue when examining the historical, cultural, and political circumstances of racial/ethnic groups and resultant experiences and coping strategies required for health and psychosocial adjustment.

For example, Latinos would be split across Ogbu's categories of minority groups (see Gonzales, 2000). Many are recent voluntary immigrants and thus would best be described as immigrant minorities (e.g., recent immigrants from Central and South America), and some have the additional challenges associated with refugee status (e.g., Cuban Americans). Others fit better in the category of subordinate minorities (e.g., Puerto Ricans, some Mexican Americans). It is important to understand the historical relationship of particular Latino groups to this country and also to note within-group variation even if historical circumstances are the same; stress engagement associated with cultural dissonance can fluctuate (due to protective factors and their actualization as social supports), and coping strategies can also vary.

Similarly, Asian American groups have diverse immigration histories. Although most (but not all) Asian Americans can be described as immigrant minorities, there are significant differences in their particular immigration histories—even within particular groups (Prashad, 2000; Takaki, 1998). The historical era of immigration is particularly significant. Waves of immigrants from Japan, China, South Asia, and other regions began coming to the United States in the late 1800s. Immigration from these areas was outlawed by the early 1920s, but descendents of these early immigrants remained, and many have retained their particular ethnic identity rather than assimilating completely (Takaki, 1998). When Asian immigration occurred in significant numbers after 1965, the immediate waves of immigrants were largely educated professionals who secured immigration through occupational preferences; this wave laid a large part of the foundation for the "model minority" myth of Asian American academic achievement. However, more recent Asian immigrants have arrived largely on family preferences rather than occupational status; they are often less educated and work in lower status jobs. Of great significance is that stereotypes such as the model minority myth can obscure the challenges faced by this group given significant sources of within-group variability. Attempts to homogenize the group's experiences draw attention away from the larger issues of cultural dissonance faced by many Asian American youth regardless of their educational and socioeconomic backgrounds. Accordingly, attempts to understand and support psychosocial processes are undermined.

Cultural Dissonance as a Risk Contributor: Individualistic versus Collectivist Societies

Societies are characterized by sets of cultural norms that vary and are always evolving. The differences between norms in and across societies can also be described in different ways. One such designation that may be useful to consider is the rubric of individualistic versus collectivist societies (Donde, 2001). *Individualistic* societies, which include the United States, tend to follow an ideology that revolves around personal autonomy, independence, and self-reliance. These societies purport to value individuals who are able to separate themselves from others and from situational contexts. The independent self is constructed to be a fixed entity that supposedly does not change with social situations: "The independent self-system thus seeks to display or assert attributes or features of the self. Others in a social situation are important, but their importance is represented primarily as standards of social comparison or for feedback that can validate the inner attributes of the self" (Markus & Kitayama, 1991, p. 22). Of course, individuals may not always display such individualistic attitudes and behavior, but in an individualistic society, the collective social norms and values center on expectations of such independence.

Collectivist societies, on the other hand, strive to emphasize obedience and conformity. The primary stated goal in these societies, which include many Asian countries, is to shape individuals into *interdependent beings* who are defined by their relationships. The interdependent self is perceived as "fluid" (i.e., able to change when the social environment around one changes). As described by Markus and Kitayama, interdependent individuals are dynamic and defined by roles according to situation and context: "Such an interdependent self is not properly characterized as a bounded whole, because it changes structure with the nature of the particular social context" (in Markus & Kitayama, 1991, p. 23). Again, individuals in a collectivist society may not always model such attitudes and behavior, but this is the stated norm in a collectivist society.

Given the large differences inherent between these two types of societies, it is highly probable that immigrants from collectivist societies who move to the United States may experience cultural dissonance and show difficulties in adjusting to their new surroundings. When individuals choose to immigrate, they may come with practical knowledge of the country to which they are moving, but many will not be learned in the cultural and societal values, beliefs, and attitudes of the foreign country they are adopting as their new home. Even to the extent that they are aware of these, actual experiences of cultural dissonance present new social and psychological challenges for immigrants.

Moreover, these challenges are in some ways compounded for the children of immigrants, the second generation. Immigrants may already have a strong sense of ethnic

identity and self from experiences in their native land; although cultural dissonance poses a challenge, they can draw on their own cultural capital as a resource to promote adaptive coping. The second generation, however, must undergo the challenges of identity formation *at the same time* as they are experiencing cultural dissonance; in fact, the normative challenges of identity formation are exacerbated by cultural dissonance for second-generation youth.

Stress Engagement Related to Cultural Dissonance

On a regular basis, tangible experiences of cultural dissonance create a "clash of cultures" for many immigrant and second-generation children. Mehta (1998, p. 133) addresses these processes specifically for Asian and South Asian American youth: "The second generation has been exposed to distinctly different language, goals, food, rituals, dress, music, landscapes, and values than their parents. There is a strong urge to retain ethnic identity while rapidly acquiring awareness of American values, partially due to financial gains." Because of this disparity between their ethnic identity and their national identity, these children face a salient tension: the collectivist ideologies from valued families constantly coming into conflict with individualistic ideologies from the surrounding environment. While navigating across varied social settings and associated social traditions, immigrant and second-generation children and adolescents must grapple with normative developmental tasks while also confronting the difficult chore of successfully juggling opposing philosophies. There is inadequate developmental research on the specific content of the cultural socialization techniques proven effective for abating the additive and consequent tensions experienced by youth.

Two of the most salient areas where such conflicts come into play are in the choice of career and romantic relationships, as these are two areas that can have long-term effects on the nature of relationships between parents and children. Given the different expectations of male and female children in many societies, gender can pose an additional risk here, exacerbating the tensions created by cultural dissonance. For example, some Asian and South Asian parents may be more protective of female children with regard to dating. Asian American children confront a social environment in the United States, including school, university, peer groups, and the media, that teaches them to exert autonomy and independence and to follow their own aspirations and desires. Youth recognize the availability of many options and are encouraged by American society to choose for themselves among these. However, many Asian American children are also expected to obey their parents and fulfill their obligations to their families. Emphasis on autonomy and self-sufficiency is frequently misinterpreted by immigrant parents as selfishness or lack of caring (Mehta, 1998). As Eng (1999) notes, immigrant parents often feel that they have made many sacrifices for their children; they may employ guilt to compel children to follow their wishes. Many Asian American youth face these struggles; however, particularly for youth of color who are most vulnerable to the experience of cultural dissonance, it is critically important not to make deterministic assumptions about the experiences of immigrant and second-generation youth or their parents. With proper understanding, both parents and peers or significant adults outside the family can serve as sources of support that help youth negotiate the varied sources of cultural dissonance.

It is imperative to note that immigrant parents themselves also continue to undergo a process of identity development; the duality of the role indicates that while being culturally socialized themselves by their children, and while adjusting their views, at the same time parents must engage in the normative parental task of socializing their children. In some families, it is possible for parents to accept and feel comfortable with their children's choices to adapt and conform to their American surroundings. However, new situations and challenges arise throughout youth development that are fairly typical: dilemmas over schoolwork and friends, dating, college and career decisions, and marriage and childbearing. Parents may be more open-minded about some of these areas than others, and children may adopt different cultural values in these various domains.

Coping and Identity Issues Related to Cultural Dissonance

For various reasons, cultural dissonance is unavoidable for many youth. Cultural conflicts between immigrant parents and their children often reflect different belief systems; there are no necessarily right or wrong solutions to these conflicts. Also, as H. C. Stevenson (1997) notes, cultural dissonance is not limited to immigrants and their children. Due to differences in context and the cultural meaning of particular behaviors and sociocultural traditions (e.g., music, dress, dance, and adolescent social relations), as previously noted, many urban African American, Hispanic, and Native American youth may be compelled to employ different coping strategies across school and neighborhood settings. Of salience is that, as typically deployed by adolescent-stage individuals, particular adaptive coping strategies may seek to manage such dissonance rather than resolving it completely.

Phelan et al. (1991) present one framework to help explain issues of cultural dissonance; they define four patterns of interaction with regard to school, family, and peer transitions. In the *congruent worlds/smooth transitions* pattern, social norms, expectations, beliefs about the world, and other factors that shape daily interaction are relatively consistent across school, peer, and family settings. Normative developmental challenges are present, but these are not exacerbated by cultural dissonance, as the larger social and cultural factors are congruent. This congruency pattern may be more common among many White, middle-class youth. Another type of interaction is *different worlds/boundary crossings managed.* In this category, norm and value differences exist across settings, but these are not very great, or they are managed adaptively. One may refer to this particular type as porous as there is more commonality across the settings. In the *different worlds/boundary crossings hazardous* state, youth view their school, family, and peer settings as distinct with regard to cultural norms, suggesting clearly nonporous conditions with significant consequences for transgressions. Language barriers may be salient, and parental values may be significantly different from those encountered in school. These two "different world" profiles are more common among immigrant youth, and the difference between the two may be a matter of available social supports. One should add that the level of cultural awareness, content and sensitivity of professional training, and character of role portrayal clearly play significant roles relative to the adults' contributions as potential sources of support. The too frequent and valid reality is that all labeled supports, when considered from youths' phenomenology, may be actually experienced as neither user-friendly nor reliable sources of support.

In the last of their categories, *borders impenetrable/boundary crossings insurmountable,* Phelan et al. (1991) note that values, beliefs, and expectations across settings are characterized by so much cultural dissonance that interactions across settings are extremely difficult or not possible. The authors note that youth may resist crossing boundaries between settings altogether, leading to negative outcomes such as school failure or rejection by peers. As policies and incentive-linked practices, these situations may require even more social support to allow youth to cope adaptively and for adults to perform more responsibly. In fact, this suggests an exemplar condition that requires both *proximal adult and broad systems recognition* of the condition's problematic character for youth competence. Additionally, the situation suggests the needed introduction, monitoring, and evaluation of culturally sensitive and effective intervention strategies.

Considered proactively, the last two categories (i.e., different worlds/boundary crossings hazardous and borders impenetrable/boundary crossings insurmountable), more often than not, require a full and open discussion of race, social class (i.e., as resource availability), gender, and ethnicity-associated issues. Each introduces significant degrees of uncomfortableness for adults and policymakers. Consequently, the foundational concerns articulated by Phelan et al. (1991) are very seldom directly or indirectly addressed, although "gap" portrayals are prominently discussed in the news media. The systemic outcomes of effects and inferred invisibility of the issues merely contribute to stereotypes and an exacerbation of the troubling border-crossing concerns described. The situation obfuscates youths' opportunities because the undergirding contributors of cultural dissonance are neither adequately understood nor ultimately addressed.

Although cultural dissonance poses a significant source of stress for many youth of color, as suggested, proper (i.e., strategically implemented) resources enhance its successful negotiation. It is important for these youth to develop a strong sense of identity so they can maintain a coherent sense of self across dissonant settings. In addition, we should remember that youth in the first category, congruent worlds/smooth transitions, are also vulnerable; in fact, the aforementioned downside of privilege may be relevant here. In lieu of challenges requiring the negotiation of some cultural dissonance, these youth may not develop the coping skills needed to cross cultural boundaries, and they may not learn to be comfortable when placed in the minority status or other conflict-generating situations (e.g., gender-based changes in the roles available to women). With the growing diversity of the American population, these skills are becoming increasingly important and, when present, potentially serve as protective factors.

Identity challenges relating to cultural dissonance have historically been viewed in light of the "melting pot" ideal, emphasizing assimilation. The straight-line assimilation model was developed in response to European immigrants' process of ethnic identity assimilation. In this model, individuals' identification with mainstream U.S. culture increases with succeeding generations as identification with their native culture decreases. However, theorists believed that the straight-line model of assimilation ignores the assimilation process of immigrants of color (Portes & Böröcz, 1989). A model of segmented assimilation has been proposed to reflect immigrant minorities' process of assimilation; in this model, immigrant and second-generation youth have more options in terms of identity development (Zhou, 1997).

Portes and Rumbaut (2001) investigated the ethnic identity of immigrant and second-generation youth in their Children of Immigrants Longitudinal Study (CILS). The original sample for this study in 1992 included 5,262 eighth- and ninth-graders from Miami/Ft. Lauderdale, Florida, and San Diego, California. A follow-up survey in 1995 included 4,288 of the original participants. The largest immigrant groups represented in the sample were Cubans, Haitians, Nicaraguans, and West Indians in South Florida and Mexicans, Filipinos, Vietnamese, Laotians, and Cambodians in California. The sample was evenly divided with respect to gender, year in school (8th, 9th), and birth status (foreign-born/U.S.-born). Researchers conducted 54% of the interviews in Miami/Ft. Lauderdale and 46% in San Diego.

Portes and colleagues conceptualized immigrant youth ethnic identity in terms of four categories: national identity, hyphenated American, American, and panethnic. A *national identity* (e.g., Chinese) reflects identification with the native country; *hyphenated American* (e.g., Chinese American) reflects a bicultural identity that incorporates features of the homeland and the United States; *American* identity reflects lack of connection with the original homeland and an adoption of "American"[1] values (referring to White American cultural norms); *panethnic* identity (e.g., Asian) refers to a denationalized identification centered on the political context of American racialization (Portes & Rumbaut, 2001; Rumbaut, 1994). These identity categories illustrate the segments of the population that immigrant identity youth can identify with as they assimilate into the United States.

In CILS, adolescents who were nationally identified were more likely to be first-generation or 1.5-generation immigrants (Kasinitz, Battle, & Miyares, 2001; Portes & Rumbaut, 2001; Rumbaut, 1994; Waters, 1994, 1996). Males and youth with two foreign-born parents born in the same country also were more likely to be nationally identified. Living in two-parent families in which both parents are foreign-born is presumed to enhance children's exposure to their native culture and provide a consistent cultural socialization message (Portes & Rumbaut, 2001). Youth living in upper-middle-class families were also more likely to identify nationally because they may have more reason to associate pride and honor with their ethnic identity (Rumbaut, 1994). In addition, parents' economic advantage serves as a protective factor, as they can provide their children with resources to reinforce their ethnic identity, such as trips back to the family's country of origin and involvement in ethnic social organizations. Also, as demonstrated by Cuban immigrants in Miami, economically advantaged families can provide their children with private, bilingual education, which serves to reinforce youth's ethnic identity (Portes & Rumbaut, 2001). Nationally identified immigrant youth report feeling connected to their home country because they had strong family ties there, made frequent trips back, and had plans to return to live as adults (Waters, 1994, 1996).

Portes and Rumbaut (2001) also note the influence of political context on ethnic identity. Specifically, the Mexican-origin students in the California CILS sample showed an increase in choosing to identify as Mexican that coincided with the creation of Proposition 187. Proposition 187 sought to deny undocumented immigrants' access to social and nonemergency health care services and public school education (Portes & Rumbaut, 2001). Mexican-origin participants who identified as Mexican did so largely in reaction to the threat posed by Proposition 187. Their identity choice was also an outgrowth of their increased collective political activity to prevent the passing of Proposition 187.

Youth who chose the hyphenated American identity status were more likely to be female (this finding was specific to the first wave of data collection), born in the United States, and to have one parent born in the United States and the other parent born abroad (Rumbaut, 1994). Females' choice of a hyphenated American identity may be the outgrowth of their greater desire to incorporate all aspects of their experiences into their identity, whereas males, in a quest to simplify their lives, may be more likely to choose one identity over another (Rumbaut, 1994). Classic second-generation youth (children who are born in the United States to immigrant parents) may also choose to adopt a hyphenated American identity as a means to cope with pressure to identify with either their parents' or American culture. Similarly, maintaining a bicultural identity in the presence of one foreign-born and one U.S.-born parent may also constitute a strategy to cope with cultural dissonance (Rumbaut, 1994).

Additionally, those with an American identity reported being more embarrassed when their parents did not know or follow American cultural norms. They also reported a preference for English and chose to solely speak English with their close friends (Rumbaut, 1994). Further, American-identified youth were most commonly found in suburban schools and had a more positive view of the United States in regard to factors such as racism (Portes & Rumbaut, 2001).

Finally, those youth choosing a panethnic identity were more likely to be living in inner-city neighborhoods and to be attending inner-city schools with native U.S.-born minorities (Portes & Rumbaut, 2001; Rumbaut, 1994; Waters, 1994, 1996). It is possible that minorities with an immigrant background chose to identify with native-born minorities to fit in and also because they did not perceive the two groups as being dissimilar (Rumbaut, 1994; Waters, 1994, 1996).

In fact, with regard to race relations, panethnically identified youth, particularly Black and Latino adolescents, expressed greater awareness of society's negative perceptions of visible minorities, along with the categories of racialization in the United States (e.g., Asian American; Portes & Rumbaut, 2001; Rumbaut, 1994; Waters, 1994, 1996).

Consistent with a segmented assimilation model, data from CILS demonstrates that the process of ethnic identity for immigrant youth is not simple and suggests a dense web of context-linked psychosocial processes. From our view, a phenomenological perspective is necessary to understand more fully this process. Youth who are phenotypically similar may choose to identify differently. Developmental trajectories are also important to note; in CILS, 56% of participants reported different identities during both the first and second waves of data collection. National identity had the most overall stability, and participants who reported discrimination were also more likely to have a stable ethnic identity. Having both parents born in the same country and speaking the parental language also increased the likelihood of identity stability across time, and females were more likely to show stability in identity than males (Portes & Rumbaut, 2001).

Of course, much future research is necessary for a more thorough and nuanced understanding of the identity processes of immigrant and second-generation youth. Moreover, a development-sensitive theoretical strategy should inform the process. An integrated sociological delineation of identity with psychological models such as those of Cross (1991), Phinney (1992), and Helms (1990) would benefit segmented assimilation models. In addition, reflecting the various components of PVEST, more developmentally sensitive theorizing will support future research efforts.

Cultural Dissonance and Life Stage Outcomes

Cultural dissonance has implications for developmental outcomes in a variety of domains, including education, health, and psychological well-being. However, its impact is further mediated by structural impediments represented by neighborhood character, family resources, and social policies (e.g., socioeconomic opportunities and immigration status) and by protective factors (e.g., cultural capital, social and economic supports). With respect to depression and self-esteem, Harker (2001) and Rumbaut (1994) reported that first- and 1.5-generation immigrants had more positive outcomes than second-generation youth. One possible explanation for this is that first-generation immigrants reported greater levels of parental supervision and social support. Another possibility is that the two groups have different referent others (Rumbaut, 1994); first- and 1.5-generation youth may compare their circumstances with those of people in their native country, as they were born there and have spent some time living abroad. They may feel that their situation is a significant improvement and, accordingly, not view or experience cultural dissonance in as significant a light. Conversely, second-generation youth are less likely to utilize their parents' home country as a point of reference, and cultural dissonance may be a primary concern. Another explanation may be the role of cultural socialization and pride. In fact, Zhou (1997) examined within-group ethnic identity differences in self-esteem for Vietnamese immigrants and found that Vietnamese adolescents who either identified as Vietnamese or Vietnamese American had higher self-esteem than American and pan ethnically identified students. Zhou attributed this finding to tighter cultural connections and social support among the former groups.

Kao (1995) explores educational achievement among Asian American youth; her findings indicate that achievement for most Asian immigrant groups is largely impacted by socioeconomic status and family characteristics. Kao's findings refute the model minority myth of Asian American academic achievement. A narrow focus on the educational success of Asian American youth in fact detracts attention from the social and cultural dissonance they may experience among peers. This is an area that requires much more research. Moreover, research questions that focus on and explore the experiences of low-income Asian youth, as well as other ethnic groups, who do well academically and enjoy positive peer relations also deserve scholarly attention as resilient young people.

COMPETENCE-PURSUING AND RESILIENCE-DEMONSTRATING OUTCOMES AMONG RACIALLY AND ETHNICALLY DIVERSE YOUTH

Robert White's (1959, 1960) classic theorizing concerning competence and effectance motivation suggests their presence as part of basic human functioning. Consistent with historical reviews (see Cross, 1979, 1991, 2003; Spencer, Cross, et al, 2003), research studies demonstrate that independent of objective social or economic resources available, parents and youth generally value academic success and have high aspirations for future attainments (e.g., Spencer, 1983 1990; Spencer et al., 1993). Additionally, the several reviews presented suggest that for various reasons (e.g., immigration status), racially and ethnically diverse youth may be differentially burdened with adverse experiences given particularly structured social conditions included as impediments for some and unacknowledged privileges for others. Regarding the former (i.e., experienced impediments and systematic challenges), the consequences for some may be associated with feelings of cultural dissonance and perceptions of insurmountable challenge. On the other hand, although generally ignored by media, many others demonstrate marked achievement independent of specific performance domain pursued and character of challenges confronted. As suggested by and consistent with the developmental psychology concept of the *sensitive period,* flexibility and reversibility are possible. The more significant and unfortunate conceptual issue is that the notion of recovery is too infrequently applied to ethnically diverse youngsters who are members of minority groups or, more generally, who grow up in families with few economic resources. Instead, as described and promoted, communicated are long-standing and entrenched sets of a priori assumptions concerning negative outcomes; subsequently, the images themselves may become translated into challenging contexts for self and others.

Specifically, frequently encountered are instances of devaluation perceived as stigma and stereotyping that require the individual's responsive coping. In fact, relative to resilient outcomes, Vander Zander (1985) suggests that recoveries from long-term effects due to short, traumatic episodes are possible. His conclusion stems from a review of classic resiliency findings and includes Werner's (Werner, 1989, 2000; Werner & Smith, 1982, 2001) longitudinal research efforts with Kauai youngsters and Jerome Kagan's (Kagan & Klein, 1973) observations and analysis of his work with Guatemalan children, along with inferences from similar studies by other developmental scientists conducting cross-cultural work.

We bring up the evident point that there continues to be some degree of difficulty or resistance to the introduction of alternative perspectives to account for the experiences of diverse American youth—particularly children of color—and immigrant youngsters. In our introduction of an alternative framework for explaining the "how" of human development for diverse youth (see Spencer, 1995; Spencer & Harpalani, 2003), the intent was to explore human development theorizing that would be sensitive to the unique situations of American minorities specifically, although inclusive of diverse ethnicities more broadly. In fact, the introduction of PVEST was neither intended to foment theoretical controversy nor to create unnecessary complexity. The goal remains to provide a heuristic conceptual device that is inclusive of the broad array of human potential and experiences in diverse cultural contexts. In fact, our perspective is consistent with Alfred North Whitehead's notions concerning the role of new paradigms. He notes: "a clash of doctrines is not a disaster—it is an opportunity" (quoted in Vander Zander, 1985, p. 54).

We take the opportunity and use PVEST as a conceptual tool for broadening our understandings about vulnerability as experienced by diverse groups. The task entails the consideration of human vulnerability that requires the integration of both risks and protective factors; the latter also considers the role of privilege (generally an unacknowledged feature) as a salient protective factor. The inclusion has implications for our thinking about competence and resilience.

Recent theories that emphasize positive youth development, in fact, have infrequently afforded both a competence-exploring view (i.e., that also implicates the fact of privileging opportunities for a select group; see McIntosh, 1989) and a resilience-explaining perspective. Accordingly, PVEST introduces an alternative approach as an overdue option. As a systems theory, the framework provides a context-linked, nondeterministic (i.e., avoids unidirectional and pathologizing points of view), and culturally sensitive human development conceptual strategy. The specific caution for broad sensitivity, we believe, may represent the needs of cultural minorities, including diverse youth from low-resource families and those with a particular history, such as Native American people (Provenzo, 1986). Without doubt, these youth, too, pursue normative development goals of competence formation, albeit under challenging conditions (e.g., see Fuchs & Havighurst, 1972). In fact, as reported by Provenzo, Fuchs and Havighurst describe the failure of American education to adequately meet Native youths' need for competence:

> With minor exceptions the history of Indian Education had been the transmission of white American education, little altered to the Indian children as a one-way process. The institution of the school is one that was imposed and controlled by the non-Indian society, its pedagogy and curriculum little changed for the Indian children, its goals primarily aimed at removing the child from his aboriginal culture and assimilating him into the dominant white culture. Whether coercive or persuasive, this assimilationist goal of schooling has been minimally effective with Indian children, as indicated by their record of absenteeism, retardation, and high dropout rates. (Fuchs & Havighurst, 1972, p. 19 as reported by Provenzo, 1986, pp. 206–207)

According to Wenner (1972), often the value system communicated by the curriculum is at odds with group values and their expression. He suggests that a Hopi child may attempt to manifest the least (personal) effort as a way to diminish the embarrassment experienced by a less talented classmate. It is not that competence supported by effectance motivation does not exist. Conversely, individual-level expression takes second place to Indian customs; in the pursuit of competence outcomes, the latter places group accomplishments over personal achievement (Fuchs, 1986).

Competence Theorizing and Individual Vulnerability

As thoroughly reviewed elsewhere (e.g., Spencer, 1977, 1995), Robert White's (1959) theorizing, first published 50 years ago, suggested that the progression of human development is based on an *intrinsic motivation;* that is, humans possess an essentially biological propensity toward competence and effective interactions with the environment. White did not qualify his analysis based on race, ethnicity, social class, gender, faith group, immigration status, or national origin. As a term, competence suggests a state of "proficiency," "ability," "fitness," "adequacy," "capability," or "answering to all requirements"; he viewed this underlying "human propensity or drive" as the major source of the organism's motivation when interacting in multiple settings. The inference from White's analysis is that the individual wants to be effective; that is, one wishes to make a difference.

In their attempts to understand human motivation, other theorists have provided parallel perspectives. Foote and Cottrell's (1955) views suggest that competence is parallel with ability (i.e., as a satisfactory degree of ability for performing certain implied kinds of tasks). Similarly, deCharms's (1968) notion of personal causation continues the theme that the primary motivational propensity experienced by humans is to be successful in effecting change in their environment. Like White, DeCharms believes that the proclivity to make a difference is an intrinsic biological motivational goal. Considered collectively, their views suggest simultaneous and overlapping inputs from the cognitive and affective domains as individuals socially engage the normative stage-specific tasks of human development (see Havighurst, 1953).

One of the important and positive aspects of S. Anderson and Messick's (1973) contribution to the discussion of competence is that they describe and clarify the broad range of both affective and cognitive dimensions included in the concept of competence. Their explicit detailing of both contributions supports analyses by traditional competence theorists and demonstrates associations between evolving social-cognitive processes and basic social and emotional development. That is, early development of self-other distinctions provides the opportunity for incorporating and understanding context interactions, including important self-inferences that often emanate from such interactions. Consistent with Flavell's (1968) early description of social-cognitive processes as linked to basic social and communication skills along with recent and progressively elegant fine-tuning of these inferential processes by theory of mind researchers such as Frye and More (1991) and Repacholi and Slaughter (2003), several outcomes are evident. Specifically, it is youths' early and progressive social-cognitive development that allows for the cognition-based awareness of others (i.e., their attitudes, beliefs, preferences, biases, and broad perspectives). The gradually unfolding process affords the recursive consideration of "the other" in the construction of the self and the establishment and experience of social-emotional development. Too frequently and unfortunately, theorizing focuses either on cognition or on affect, without relaying their psychological connectedness and unavoidable physiological interdependence. Given the reviews provided, it is evident that specifying these associations is of critical importance; their salience is associated with the varying character of context quality, particularly as linked to group membership and evaluative judgments, and individual differences in sensitivity to their impact.

As individuals transition across settings and produce behavioral products (i.e., coping outcomes as either reactive responses or identifications adopted), variously described by an array of attribution theorists, outcomes are comparatively evaluated. Accordingly, given the recursive character of linkages between levels of the ecosystem and unfolding human development capacities, the individual's unavoidable cognitive and affective processes (experienced both psychologically and physiologically) are associated with the socially constructed character of the context. Consequently, responsive coping will be required and competence or fragility outcomes produced and evaluated. As a recursive system, vulnerability is affected due to changes in either risk level or protective factor level presence—thus continuing the cycle. As illustrated and described by Youngblood and Spencer (2002) regarding educational considerations needed for special needs populations and the goals behind Individuals with Disabilities Education Act (IDEA) legislation, we surmise that independent of assumed need level, supporting the basic intrinsic need for competence should be a core aspect of all inclusive programming. In general, then, when considering the entire life course and stage-specific outcomes from a PVEST systems perspective, a foundationally important and productive coping outcome expected (independent of developmental status, inferred level of support available, or special assistance required) is the acquisition of an array of stage-specific competencies.

Competence generally refers to being robust, healthy, and proficient. As suggested by White's (1959, 1960) earliest essays on the topic, he "urged the relevance to human development of an intrinsic motivation toward competence—toward effective interaction with the environment" (as reported by Fisk & Maddi, 1961, and reviewed by Spencer, 1977). Relatedly, Robert Havighurst's (1953) analysis of human development describes sets of normative tasks that are linked with the several developmental periods and represent the several core domains of human functioning (i.e., social, cognitive, affective, and physical). For each period, mastery of a stage-specific skill set is required for general competence and the successful transition through the current stage and, ultimately, for achieving positive developmental stage-specific outcomes: that is, *demonstrations of competence.*

Competence theorists such as White (1959, 1960) have been insightful in their multidimensional perspectives concerning competence formation. As described earlier, the pursuit of competence is a highly regarded achievement outcome professed by society, lauded by schools, and valued by families. However, literatures indicate that the actual "practiced view" about competence formation is, at best, narrowly applied and monolithic in character. As suggested elsewhere (see Spencer, 1977), when one notes the goals of education and then assesses the outcomes, Edmund Gordon's comments are insightful:

> Although the goals of education tend to be stated in broad terms, when we come to assess education it is always to cognitive development and achievement that we first look for evidence of change. Too often we either stop with these first results or turn with less rigor to look at other areas as a second thought or as a rationalization for failure to find more impressive evidence in the cognitive domain. (quoted in S. Anderson & Messick, 1973, p. 3)

As suggested by Spencer (1977), the outcome of the approach is an inadequate or shortsighted understanding about how individuals come to function as competent members of society. Alternatively, our approach has been to respond to Gordon's long-term admonishment by addressing simultaneously the multiple domains of human development as linked to personal and group demographics along with context features. Spencer's review and synthesis of competence formation theory cites Smith's (1968, p. 272) query, which remains generally unaddressed and, thus, still holds sway today:

> What do we know, and what do we need to know about the conditions under which people come to function as competent members of society? The question arises with urgency as the first generation of crash programs to instill competence in the poor and "culturally deprived" comes under skeptical review, and the path to the millennium remains to be discovered.

We are nearly 40 years past Smith's prescient pronouncement and are 5 years into a new millennium. Unfortunately, there appears to be no closer commitment to broad, multiple domain-relevant analyses of youths' competence formation processes for use in the design and structuring of culture-, context-, and development-sensitive educational systems and intervention/prevention programming strategies and more general practices.

It is important to note that not all efforts expended in pursuit of competence formation are equally rewarded. That is, the environment presents different levels of challenge as well as provides varying levels of supports and privileges. Of special salience, although not frequently acknowledged, is that the hurdles confronted are not independent of individual group members' characteristics (e.g., race, ethnicity, socioeconomic or immigration status, faith group) along with the group's hierarchical placement in American society. Consequently, resilience (i.e., successful effects achieved in the face of challenge) may not always be the outcome. In fact, although originally queried virtually 40 years ago by competence theorists in the mid- to late 1960s, lingering inferred questions remain: How much challenge is motivating for resilient results and stage-specific competencies? On the other hand, how much challenge (given a lack of equivalent, culturally sensitive, customized, and specific support) is undermining of potential competence accrual and resiliency?

CONCLUSIONS AND FUTURE DIRECTIONS

Infrequently explored perspectives provided by this review and synthesis, we believe, afford significant insights for conceptualizing the literature to date. The alternative analyses not only make available helpful conceptual devices but suggest important directions for future research, programming designs, evaluation efforts, and theorizing about intra- and interindividual developmental processes. For example, differential supports are provided and individuals' efforts expended in pursuit of stage-specific competencies as dictated by the normative developmental tasks originally described by Havighurst (1953). That is, although neither formally acknowledged nor openly discussed in the developmental literature, in general, for the diverse groups considered, our review indicates particularly patterned individual-context relationships. They are of relevance for resilience theorizing and suggest the multiple domains of human competence. More to the point, there appears to be specific linkages between the hierarchically organized American social structure and youths' experiences of excessive challenges versus available supports. In fact, the social arrangements translate into at least two patterns. In one case, persistent impediments encountered as one transitions across time and place potentially interfere with the assembly of competent outcomes; on the other hand, and as suggested by McIntosh (1989), particular individuals may experience subtle sets of generally unacknowledged and highly ego-boosting privileges. The differences are important for the allotment of resources and future expectations for human capital investments. That is, they impact current and future planning.

It is important to acknowledge that frequently ignored are the ethnicity-linked mismatches for individual and context associations and, on the other hand, the privileging experiences of particular youth. The long-term and failed appreciation of the dilemma (1) tends to generate significant levels of "social uncomfortableness"; (2) connotes and spawns continuing social inequities; (3) generates, on occasion, heated denials; (4) through stigma and stereotyping spawns experiences of "stereotype threat"; or (5) invokes an "official" policy-relevant response of "motivated forgetfulness." The last is especially perplexing because diverse youth routinely appear on textbook covers, are included in textbook pages, and generate voluminous submissions as research proposals in response to requests for applications, which, too frequently, provide inadequate diversity of ethnic representation in the decision-making ranks of review and oversight teams. Salient for future directions, remaining unaddressed is the reality that differential treatment only further exaggerates the noted lack of fit for some and appearances of broad success for others. Patterns of excessive social impediments are apparent, as experienced particularly by visible and disfavored minority group members (see Chestang, 1972a); on the other hand, also present are demonstrations of conspicuous consonance and supports experienced by others as White privilege (McIntosh, 1989). Laws may be viewed as a source of legal protection for all citizens. Unfortunately, socially structured impediments as social practices are not independent of race, ethnicity, immigration status, gender, religious faith, skin color, and social class; nor are they always easily discernible, although their psychological impact is severe (see Chestang, 1972a, 1972b). The issues of visibility, identifiability, and stigma are important because they represent an individual's recognition of devaluation and difference; the discernment has implications for competence and effectance motivation. A review by Spencer, Kim, and Marshall (1987) describes the experiences of an underperforming outcaste minority of Japan (i.e., Buraka youth) and analyzes the youths' subsequent high-performance experiences in the United States, where they are treated as valued (i.e., "model minority") group members. The cross-national work reviewed by Spencer, Kim, and Marshall suggest the importance of the individual-context match (i.e., consonance) or mismatch (i.e., dissonance producing). Of particular importance, the degree of fit suggests experiences of privilege versus persistent (although generally unacknowledged) inequality.

The burgeoning Whiteness studies engineered by legal scholars (e.g., Bonilla-Silva, 1997, 2001) are insightful in their analyses of the myriad ways through which privilege is bestowed and enjoyed; similarly, the more general exploration of privilege by McIntosh (1989) and Luthar (Luthar & Becker, 2002; Luthar & Latendresse, 2002) has made critically important contributions. Structured impediments that emanate from a hierarchically organized social system are hypothesized as contributing an impact. As obstructions, however, they are experienced by youth as cultural dissonance accrued as a function of a lack of fit between one's cultural distinctiveness and the character of responses from particular contexts (see Spencer, 1999, 2001). Youths' responses to the degree of individual-context fit may result in consequent challenges; adequate counteracting supports are required for offsetting their effects and for limiting overall stress. Their consideration has future implications for resource needs and their planned distribution.

On the other hand, and infrequently addressed, we can infer the need to deploy adaptive coping strategies that are minimally consequential for the individual (e.g., use of an economic privilege such as a "legacy admission" standard as opposed to choosing not to pursue postsecondary education or opting for a less prestigious college). Without supports, maladaptive reactive coping responses adopted, such as declining postsecondary educational options, may have dire consequences for identity processes and long-term stage-specific coping outcomes, such as the maximization of earning potential. Inevitably, although generally overlooked, the frequent and unquestioned use of available privileges may result in the failure to hone adaptive options as reactive coping strategies in response to normative and atypical challenges. Information garnered in the aftermath of the Columbine High School massacre along with other untoward occurrences aids in exploring questions concerning the frequently unacknowledged downside of privilege.

Persistent exposure to atypical levels of patterned obstacles or, on the other hand, to collective experiences of noticeable nonappearance of typical challenges may result in inauthentic self-constructions and difficult affective processes. A general example is inaccurate assessments of self-attributions and personal characteristics that inadequately link inferred effort with coping outcomes. Thus, on the one hand, examples of the former (i.e., atypical levels of patterned obstacles) may suggest inauthentic self-constructions concerning ability or performance potential if one is confronted with too much challenge (e.g., inability inferred given confrontations with unacknowledged negative stereotyping). On the other hand, significant unacknowledged supports and few obstacles might suggest an inauthentic self-construction of ability (i.e., exaggerated intellectual or social prowess, suggesting beliefs of "earned" status).

The former situation (i.e., atypically highly challenging contexts), even if accompanied with significant supports, may result in coping skill development and positive coping products that define and explain resiliency (i.e., positive outcomes in the face of significant challenge). Without adequate supports, on the other hand, we can expect the successful adoption of maladaptive psychological coping skills that provide an identity of short-term salience although accompanied by less than viable long-term identifications and productive coping outcomes.

In the latter situation (i.e., noticeable nonappearance of typical challenge), its accompaniment with unacknowledged and significant levels of support results in specific outcomes: a consequent state of privilege and psychosocial disconnectedness. Associated characteristics include narrowly developed social connectedness; rugged independence; limited, underdeveloped, and narrow sense of interdependence; and inadequate sense of responsibility (i.e., beyond the self). This suggests a failure to acknowledge and internalize social connectedness and sense of responsibility. We hypothesize, as a consequence, a level of personal psychosocial inauthenticity (i.e., overestimation of self), psychological fragility (i.e., lack of honed adaptive coping skill development), and societal inconsistency (i.e., lack of social connectedness or sense of interdependence).

We hypothesize that the perceptual processes involved and reinforced are intergenerationally transmitted and observed both within and between groups (particularly when comparisons are made with White, male, privileged group members). As described, characteristics such as social class, immigration status, English-language proficiency, and skin color may aid the analysis of within- and between-group differences because dissonance is often linked with stereotyping and stigma; the latter, unfortunately, is frequently coupled with membership in a particular identifiable group. The outcomes produced given problematic individual-context matches contribute to additional risks and increased vulnerability; the latter is experienced as challenging conditions that require reactive coping responses by individuals given the developmental tasks confronted at that particular life course placement. Their repeated usage becomes internalized as emergent identities that, without supportive feedback and interventions (for good or bad reasons), may remain manifest across time and place.

For example, Spencer's plan of research in response to Clark and Clark's (1939, 1940) investigations was initiated in the early and middle 1970s and, for the most part, first published in the early 1980s (Spencer, 1982a, 1982b, 1983, 1984; Spencer & Horowitz, 1973). At the time, it was generally assumed that Black children's early Eurocentricity (i.e., White preference responses when queried about racial attitudes, values, preferences, and beliefs suggested high vulnerability—in fact, self-hatred; see Kardiner & Ovesey, 1951; Pettigrew, 1964). Spencer's program of research indicated significant mediating and previously unacknowledged developmental processes: Specifically, the findings were interpreted by Spencer as indicating that children's early and cognition-based egocentrism served to protect ego functioning and from inferring negative stereotypes and internalizing negative affect. Additionally, particularly with middle childhood youths, parents' cultural socialization efforts were found to matter in offsetting the potential negative impact of Eurocentric attitudes and color bias experienced as social stereotypes about racial group membership (see Spencer, 1983, 1990; Spencer & Dornbusch, 1990; Spencer & Markstrom-Adams, 1990); more recent research efforts by H. C. Stevenson (1994, 1997) and colleagues (Arrington, 2002) further validate the assumption. Accordingly, from a future directions perspective, it is evident that new conceptual strategies for thinking about resiliency prediction and broad ego func-

tioning are needed both for youth of color and Whites. When the program of research by Spencer is scrutinized along with recent Whiteness studies (e.g., Haney-Lopez, 1996; Ignatiev, 1995) and McIntosh's analysis of White privilege (see Luthar & Becker, 2002; McIntosh, 1989), the combined perspectives afford broad, innovative, and analytic formulations; of particular importance, the synthesis suggests new criteria for the definition of resilience. As described by Spencer and Swanson (2000), we need frameworks that explain the variations in the character of youths' life course transition (i.e., toward increased vulnerability or the achievement of resilience). Illustrated as a dual-axis formulation of PVEST in Figure 16.3, we infer that significant variations in the experience and prediction of resilience exist. The often patterned variability represents the character of youths' transitions across multiple ecological contexts, as influenced by social structures made manifest through particular experiences in schools, families, peer networks, and neighborhoods.

Anne-Marie Ambert's (1997, p. 41) analysis provides conceptual balance and suggests that "a percentage of adolescents do cause a great deal of problems for parents, society and themselves. They consequently receive media coverage and attention from professionals." The Columbine massacre and many urban homicides are reminiscent of Ambert's analysis. However, as described by Spencer and Swanson (2000), many young people manage to engage in productive coping and to make their way through childhood

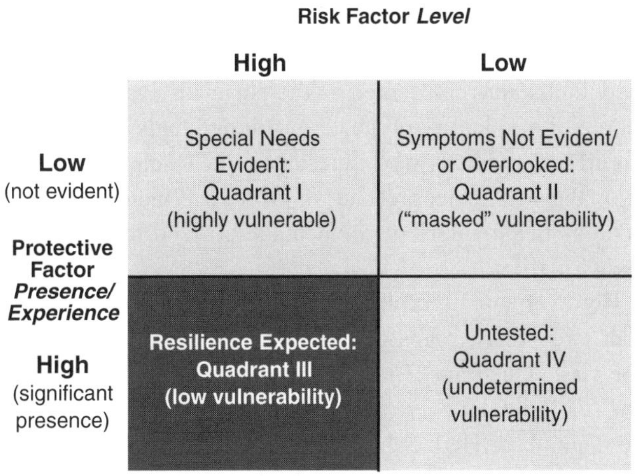

Figure 16.3 *PVEST Dual Axis Coping Formulation.* PVEST-linked Vulnerability Level and Resiliency Dual Axis Model (M. B. Spencer, 2004; in press). Adapted from "Introduction: The Syndrome of the Psychologically Vulnerable Child," by E. J. Anthony, in E. J. Anthony and C. Koupernik (Eds.), *The Child in His Family: Children at Psychiatric Risk,* 1974, New York: John Wiley & Sons, Inc.

and adolescence without much disruption and do not receive much publicity. As resilient young people, such youth grow up with an authentic sense of self and cultural connectedness (i.e., sense of cultural pluralism, defined as the valuing of one's own cultural niche although also respecting the cultural uniqueness of others), social equity, healthy ego functioning, and a sense of social justice.

In fact, the dual-axis formulation of PVEST shown in Figure 16.3 suggests the possibility of determining who is vulnerable or not and describing the conditions and variability of support available to them. Four quadrants of youth are depicted in the PVEST dual-axis coping formulation (typically, only two groups of youngsters are referred to in the literature). Quadrant I represents highly vulnerable young people who have particular and special needs. Considered in the literature that includes diverse youth, Quadrant I individuals have special needs and too frequently are inferred to be either minority, pathological, impoverished, or problem burdened. The reasons for their challenges are generally thought to reside within the individual. They are usually listed in texts as highly vulnerable due to multiple risk factors assumed to be of their own creation (e.g., genetic predisposition, social class, temperament, or a physical or neurological malady).

The second most frequently referred to group, Quadrant IV, comprises everyone else who is doing well and is generally assumed to be White, middle income, and up until the mid-1970s narrowly conceived of as males. These youth are presented as the standard against which everyone else is judged. More specifically, these individuals are generally those demonstrating positive stage-specific outcomes when considered from the cradle to the coffin. Quadrant IV individuals are represented as the norm for evaluating the degree of atypicality of Quadrant I individuals. Stated differently, individuals who experience low levels of risk and enjoy the significant presence of protective factors are heralded as the standard of competence utilized for comparison with all.

However, our literature review suggests that there are at least two other groups of underacknowledged individuals. The first, Quadrant II, are those who have both *low risks and low levels of protective factors* (e.g., demographics of the Columbine High School killers, who enjoyed low risks given affluence and safe neighborhoods but lacked close parental monitoring and social connectedness). These students are seldom carefully scrutinized by socializing adults, given the apparent absence of stereotypic risk factors; in fact, the lack of external scrutiny and lack of supported and positive coping opportunities and history tends to increase their fragility and vulnerability in the face of

acute challenge. The emotional pain associated with acute and often normative challenge, with the lack of honed coping skills and positive adaptive coping strategies, results in the use of maladaptive coping strategies (e.g., mass murders or deviant organization memberships, i.e., Aryan Brotherhood, skinhead societies). Their various behavioral outcomes may not warrant significant attention; they are thus left to their own coping devices and are assumed to be healthy (i.e., their fragility is ignored).

Quadrant III individuals are infrequently the focus of media attention. They are represented by high risks but also have access to and make use of significant protective factors (e.g., high parental monitoring; supportive and available socializing adults; good adaptive coping skill development and use; and salient identifications, i.e., with faith groups, national identities, reference group orientation). We hypothesize that Quadrant III youth are the truly resilient individuals because they habitually demonstrate good and productive outcomes in the face of persistent challenge. For example, work by Spencer and colleagues suggest that parental monitoring matters (e.g., Spencer, Dupree, Swanson, & Cunningham, 1996; Spencer & Swanson, 2000), identity processes are supportive (Spencer, Cunningham, & Swanson, 1995), and neighborhood and family influences make a difference (e.g., Spencer, Cole, Jones, & Swanson, 1997). It is apparent from our dual-axis formulation of PVEST that we know the least about Quadrants II and III. Further, what we assume about Quadrant IV is inadequate because, if considered closely, these youth are untested relative to resiliency presence or absence. If they are actually Quadrant II youth, the mislabeling is important, as opportunities are being missed for providing greater support. For determining their resilience, different research questions will need to be asked because their current positioning suggests inordinately high levels of privilege versus true resiliency. Alternative queries of Quadrant IV should include exploration of identifications that suggest connectedness to others as opposed to a dependence on available supports and an absence of obvious challenge. For Quadrant III, it will be important to understand variability even within this group. That is, as noted previously, given the presence of high risk, how much risk can be handled with traditional supports, and how much risk (and its character) requires equivalent levels of significant supports?

In this chapter, we attempted to detail the myriad challenges experienced by diverse youth and the unique sources of support. We suggest that human vulnerability represents the combination of risk level balanced against protective factors. It is evident that for some youth, there continues to be a significant focus on risks without equivalent analysis of protective factors and their translation into supports that differ for the many groups. For other groups, assumptions of privilege mask our potential understanding of youthful risk as a function of significant support and, for many, unacknowledged privilege. An understanding of all four quadrants of the dual-axis formulation of PVEST is required for designing contexts for maximizing resilient outcomes for all youth. Consistent with theorizing by Robert White, the characterizing of behavioral outcomes as resilient is not possible without a full understanding of challenge, both stage-specific types with normative confrontations and the acute and atypical varieties. The insights have implications for future directions in that they aid the design of supportive programming and policies to assist in obtaining authentic resilient outcomes for youth more generally. This can occur, for some, through providing customized supports for decreasing vulnerability through risk factor reduction. For those who enjoy unacknowledged privilege and infrequent authentic challenge, identity interventions that promote social connectedness and acknowledgment of mutual responsibility may be the type of interventions required.

We submit that the PVEST provides specific implications for future and policy directions needed for diverse communities of children and families. As a process-oriented and systems framework that enhances the interpretation of diverse expressions of human development, including the etiology and character of human vulnerability, it should fine-tune future planning for specific groups' needs. As a context-linked, history-relevant, and culturally sensitive framework, it allows for the customization of strategies and supports for diverse groups, while intended for accomplishing the same outcome for all: resilient outcomes in the pursuit of competence and effectance motivation.

REFERENCES

Altabe, M. (1996). Ethnicity and body image: Quantitative and qualitative analysis. *International Journal of Eating Disorders, 23*(2), 153–159.

Ambert, A. M. (1997). *Parents, children and adolescents: Interactive relationships and development in context.* New York: Haworth Press.

Anderson, C., & Cromwell, R. (1977). "Black is beautiful" and the color preferences of Afro-American youth. *Journal of Negro Education, 46*(1), 76–88.

Anderson, S., & Messick, S. (1973, March). *Social competency in young children* (C Report, OCD Grant # H-2993 A/H). Princeton, NJ: Educational Testing Service.

Anthony, E. J. (1974). Introduction: The syndrome of the psychologically vulnerable child. In E. J. Anthony & C. Koupernik (Eds.), *The child in his family: Children at psychiatric risk* (pp. 103–148). New York: Wiley.

Arrington, E. G. (2002). Negotiating race and racism: Black youth in racially dissonant schools. *Dissertation Abstracts International, 62,* 11B (UMI No. AA13031636).

Baldwin, J. A. (1979). Theory and research concerning the notion of Black self-hatred: A review and reinterpretation. *Journal of Black Psychology, 5,* 51–77.

Bandura, A. (1978). The self system in reciprocal determinism. *American Psychologist, 33,* 344–358.

Banks, W. C. (1976). White preference in Blacks: A paradigm in search of phenomenon. *Psychological Bulletin, 83,* 1179–1186.

Beteille, A. (Ed.). (1965). *Caste, Class and Power: Changing Patterns of Stratification in a Tanjore Village.* Berkeley: University of California Press.

Beteille, A. (Ed.). (1969). *Caste: Old and new.* Bombay: Asia Publishing House.

Beteille, A. (1972). *Inequality and social change.* Delhi: Oxford University Press.

Beteille, A. (1981). *The backward classes and the new social order.* Delhi: Oxford University Press.

Beteille, A. (1983). *The idea of natural inequality and other essays.* Delhi, India: Oxford University Press.

Blackwell, J. E. (1985). *The Black community: Diversity and unity.* New York: Dodd, Mead.

Bond, S., & Cash, T. (1992). Black beauty: Skin color and body images among African American college women. *Journal of Applied Social Psychology, 22*(11), 874–888.

Bonilla-Silva, E. (1997). Rethinking racism: Toward a structural interpretation. *American Sociological Review, 62,* 465–480.

Bonilla-Silva, E. (2001). *White supremacy and racism in the postcivil rights era.* Boulder, CO: Lynne Riener.

Boyd-Franklin, N. (1989). *Black families in therapy: A multisystems approach.* New York: Guilford Press.

Boykin, A. W. (1986). The triple quandary and the schooling of Afro-American children. In U. Neisser (Ed.), *Achievement of minority children* (pp. 57–92). Hillsdale, NJ: Erlbaum.

Brand, E. S., Ruiz, R. A., & Padilla, A. M. (1974). Ethnic identification and preference: A review. *Psychological Bulletin, 81,* 860–890.

Bronfenbrenner, U. (1977). Toward an experimental ecology of human development. *American Psychologist, 32,* 513–530.

Bronfenbrenner, U. (1979). *The ecology of human development: Experiments by nature and design.* Cambridge, MA: Harvard University Press.

Bronfenbrenner, U. (1989). Ecological systems theory. In R. Vasta (Ed.), *Annals of child development* (pp. 187–248). Greenwich, CT: JAI.

Bronfenbrenner, U. (1993). The ecology of cognitive development. In R. H. Wozniak & K. W. Fischer (Eds.), *Development in context: Acting and thinking in specific environments* (pp. 3–44). Hillsdale, NJ: Erlbaum.

Bronfenbrenner, U., & Ceci, S. J. (1994). Nature-nurture reconceptualized in developmental perspective: A bioecological model. *Psychological Review, 101,* 568–586.

Bronfenbrenner, U., & Crouter, A. C. (1983). The evolution of environmental models in developmental research. In P. H. Mussen (Series Ed.) & W. Kessen (Vol. Ed.), *Handbook of child psychology: Vol. 1. History, theory and methods* (pp. 357–414). New York: Wiley.

Broughton, J. (1981). The divided self in adolescence. *Human Development, 24,* 13–32.

Brown, J. S., & Farber, I. E. (1968). Secondary motivational systems. In P. R. Farnsworth (Ed.), *Annual review of psychology* (Vol. 19, pp. 99–134). Palo Alto, CA: Annual Reviews.

Camarota, S. (2001). *Immigrants in the United States—2000*. Retrieved from the Center for Immigration Studies, http//www.cis.org/articles/2001/back101.html.

Chestang, L. W. (1972a). *Character development in a hostile environment* (Occasional Paper No. 3). University of Chicago, School of Social Service Administration.

Chestang, L. W. (1972b), The dilemma of biracial adoptions. *Social Work, 17,* 100–105.

Churchill, W. (1994). *Indians are us? Culture and genocide in native North America.* Monroe, ME: Common Courage Press.

Clark, K. B., & Clark, M. P. (1939). The development of consciousness of self and the emergence of racial identity in Negro preschool children. *Journal of Social Psychology, 10,* 591–599.

Clark, K. B., & Clark, M. P. (1940). Skin color as a factor in racial identification of Negro preschool children. *Journal of Social Psychology, 2,* 159–169.

Clark, K. B., & Clark, M. P. (1947). Racial identification and preferences in Negro children. In T. M. Bewcomb & E. L. Hartley (Eds.), *Readings in social psychology* (pp. 169 –178). New York: Holt.

Coard, S., Breland, A., & Raskin, P. (2001). Perceptions of and preferences for skin color, Black racial identity, and self-esteem among African Americans. *Journal of Applied Social Psychology, 31*(11), 2256–2274.

Cole, M. (1996). *Cultural psychology: A once and future discipline.* Cambridge, MA: Harvard University Press.

Conley, D. (1999). *Being Black, living in the red.* Berkeley: University of California Press.

Connell, J. P., Spencer, M. B., & Aber, J. L. (1994). Educational risk and resilience in African American youth: Context, self, action and outcomes in school. *Child Development, 65,* 493–506.

Cook, J. L., & Cook, G. (2005). *Child development: Principles and perspectives.* Boston: Pearson Education.

Cooley, C. H. (1902). *Human nature and the social order.* New York: Charles Scribner & Sons.

Corrigan, P. W., & Penn, D. L. (1999). Lessons from social psychology on discrediting psychiatric stigma. *American Psychologist, 54,* 765–776.

Cross, W. E., Jr. (1971). Negro-to-Black conversion experience. *Black World, 20,* 13–27.

Cross, W. E., Jr. (1979). Negro to Black conversion experience. *Black World, 20,* 13–27.

Cross, W. E., Jr. (1991). *Shades of black: Diversity in African American identity.* Philadelphia: Temple University Press.

Cross, W. E., Jr. (2003). Tracing the historical origins of youth delinquency and violence: Myths and realities about Black culture. *Journal of Negro Education, 59*(1), 67–82.

Cross, W. E., Jr., Parham, T. A., & J. E. Helms. (1991). Nigrescence revisited: Theory and research. In R. L. Jones (Ed.), *Advances in Black psychology.* Los Angeles: Cobb and Henry.

Cunningham, M. (1999). African American adolescent males' perceptions of their community resources and constraints: A longitudinal analysis. *Journal of Community Psychology, 27,* 569–588.

Dannefer, D. (1992). On the conceptualization of context in developmental discourse. In D. L. Featherman, R. M. Featherman, & M. Perlmutter (Eds.), *Life-span development and behavior* (pp. 83–110). Hillsdale, NJ: Erlbaum.

Darity, W. A., Jr., Myers, S. L. Jr. (1998). *Persistent disparity: Race and economic inequality in the United States since 1945.* Northampton, MA: Edward Elgar.

deCharms, R. (1968). *Personal causation: The internal affective determinant of behavior.* New York: Academy Press.

Donde, S. (2001). *PVEST application to immigrants from collectivist societies living in the U.S.: Special focus on South Asian Americans.* Unpublished manuscript, University of Pennsylvania, Philadelphia.

Donzinger, S. (Ed.). 1996. *The real war on crime.* New York: Harper Perennial.

DuBois, W. E. B. (1903). *Souls of Blackfolk.* Chicago: A.C. McClurg.

DuRant, R. H., Cadenheard, C., & Pendergrast, R. A. (1994). Factors associated with the use of violence among urban Black adolescents. *American Journal of Public Health, 84,* 612–617.

Edwards, O. (1973). Skin color as a variable in racial attitudes of Black urbanites. *Journal of Black Studies, 3*(4), 473–483.

Eng, P. (1999). *Warrior lessons.* New York: Pocket Books.

Epps, E. G. (1985). Preface. In M. B. Spencer, G. K. Brookins, & W. R. Allen (Eds.), *Beginnings: The social and affective development of Black children.* Hillsdale, NJ: Erlbaum.

Epstein, S. (1973). The self-concept revisited, or a theory of a theory. *American Psychologist, 28,* 405–416.

Erikson, E. H. (1959). Identity and the life cycle. *Psychological Issues, 1,* 1–171.

Erikson, E. H. (1963). *Childhood and society.* New York: Norton.

Erikson, E. H. (1968). *Identity: Youth and crisis.* New York: Norton.

Fegley, S. G., Spencer, M. B., Goss, T. N., Harpalani, V., & Charles, N. (in press). Bodily self-awareness: Skin color and psychosocial well-being in adolescence. In W. Overton & U. Mueller (Eds.), *Body in mind, mind in body: Developmental perspectives on embodiment and consciousness.* Mahwah, NJ: LEA.

Ferguson, A. A. (2001). *Bad boys: Public schools and the making of Black masculinity.* Ann Arbor: University of Michigan Press.

Fisher, C. B., Jackson, J. F., & Villarruel, F. A. (1998). The study of African American and Latin American children and youth. In W. Damon & R. M. Lerner (Eds.), *Handbook of child psychology: Vol. 1. Theoretical models of human development* (pp. 1145–1207). Hoboken, NJ: Wiley.

Flavell, J. (1968). *The development of social cognition and communication skills in children.* New York: Wiley.

Foote, N., & Cottrell, L. S. (1955). *Identity and interpersonal competence: A new direction in family research.* Chicago: University of Chicago Press.

Fordham, S., & Ogbu, J. U. (1986). Black students' school success: Coping with the "burden of 'acting White.'" *Urban Review, 18,* 176–206.

Franklin, J. H. (1968). *Color and race.* Boston, MA: Houghton-Miffin.

Franklin, J. H. (1994). *Color line: Legacy for the twenty-first century.* Columbia: University of Missouri Press.

Franklin, J. H., & Moss, A. (1994). *From slavery to freedom: A history of African Americans* (7th ed.). New York: Random House.

Frazier, E. E. (1957). *Black bourgeoisie.* Glencoe, IL: Free Press.

Frye, D., & Moore, C. (1991). *Children's theories of mind: Mental states and social understanding.* Hillsdale, NJ: Erlbaum.

Fuchs, E., & Havighurst, R. J. (1972). *To live on this earth.* Garden City, NY: Doubleday.

Gallay, L., & Flanagan, C. A. (2000). The well-being of children in a changing economy: Time for a new social contract in America. In R. D. Taylor and M. C. Wang (Eds.), *Resilience across contexts: Family, work, culture, and community* (pp. 3–34). Mahwah, NJ: LEA.

Garcia Coll, C., Akerman, A., & Cicchetti, D. (2000). Cultural influences on developmental processes and outcomes: Implications for the study of development and psychopathology. *Development and Psychopathology, 12,* 333–356.

Garcia Coll, C., Lamberty, G., Jenkins, R., McAdoo, H. P., Crnic, K., Wasik, B. H., et al. (1996). An integrative model for the study of developmental competencies in minority children. *Child Development, 67,* 1891–1914.

Garmezy, N. (1985). Stress resistant children: The search for protective factors. In J. E. Stevenson (Ed.), *Recent research in developmental psychopathology* (pp. 213–233). Oxford: Pergamon Press.

Gilbert, A. (1989). Things fall apart? Psychological theory in the context of rapid social change. *South African Journal of Psychology, 19*(2), 91–100.

Goffman, E. (1959). *The presentation of self in everyday life.* Garden City, NY: Doubleday.

Gonzales, J. (2000). *Harvest of empire: A history of Latinos in America.* New York: Viking Press.

Good, R. (2003, February 9). Questions for Randall Kennedy: Color dynamics. *New York Times,* 19.

Gopaul-McNicol, S. (1988). Racial identification and racial preference of Black preschool children in New York and Trinidad. *Journal of Black Psychology, 14,* 65–68.

Haney-Lopez, I. F. (1996). *White by law: The legal construction of race.* New York: New York University Press.

Harber, K. D. (1998). Feedback to minorities: Evidence of a positive bias. *Journal of Personality and Social Psychology, 74*(3), 622–628.

Harker, K. (2001). Immigrant generation, assimilation, and adolescent psychological well-being. *Social Forces, 79,* 969–1004.

Harpalani, V. (2001, April). *Racial stereotyping and Black athletic achievement: Developmental and ethical considerations.* Presented at the biennial meeting of the Society for Research in Child Development (SRCD), Minneapolis, MN.

Harpalani, V. (2002). What does "acting White" really mean? Racial identity formation and academic achievement among Black youth. *Penn GSE Perspectives on Urban Education, 1.* Retrieved December 7, 2002, from http://www.urbanedjournal.org/commentaries/c0001 .html.

Harpalani, V. (2004). Simple justice or complex injustice? American racial dynamics and the ironies of *Brown* and *Grutter. Penn GSE Perspectives on Urban Education, 3*(1). Available from www.urbanedjournal.org.

Harris, C. I. (1993). Whiteness as property. *Harvard Law Review, 106,* 1709–1795.

Hart, D. (1988). A philosophical dilemma approach to adolescent identity. *Merrill-Palmer Quarterly, 34,* 105–114.

Havighurst, R.J. (1953). *Human development and education.* New York: McKay.

Helms, J. E. (Ed.). (1990). *Black and White racial identity: Theory, research, and practice.* New York: Greenwood Press.

Hernandez, D. (1998). *From generation to generation: The health and well-being of children in immigrant families.* Washington, DC: National Academy Press.

Hoberman, J. M. (1997). *Darwin's athletes: How sport has damaged Black America and preserved the myth of race.* Boston: Houghton Mifflin.

Hughes, M., & Hertel, B. R. (1990). The significance of color remains: A study of life chances, mate selection, and ethnic consciousness among African Americans. *Social Forces, 68,* 1105–1120.

Hunter, M. L. (1998). Colorstruck: Skin color stratification in the lives of African American women. *Sociological Inquiry, 58*(4), 517–535.

Hunter, M. L. (2004). Light, bright, and almost White: The advantages and disadvantages of light skin. In C. Herring, V. M. Keith, & H. D. Horton (Eds.), *Skin deep: How race and complexion matter in the "color-blind" era* (pp. 22–44). Chicago: University of Illinois Press.

Ignatiev, N. (1995). *How the Irish became White.* New York: Routledge & Kegan Paul.

Ingold, T. (1994). Introduction to culture. In T. Ingold (Ed.), *Companion encyclopedia of anthropology: Humanity, culture and social life* (pp. 329–349). London: Routledge.

Izrael, J. (2001). *Skin games: Color and skin tone in the Black community.* Available from Africana: Gateway to the Black World, at www .africana.com/articles/daily/index_20010108.asp.

James, W. (1961). *Psychology: The briefer course.* New York: Harper and Brothers. (Original work published 1892)

Kagan, J., & Klein, R. E. (1973). Cross-cultural perspectives on early development. *American Psychologist, 28,* 947–961.

Kao, G. (1995). Asian Americans as model minorities? A look at their academic performance. *American Journal of Education, 103,* 121–159.

Kardiner, A., & Ovesey, L. (1951). *The mark of oppression: Explorations in the personality of the American Nego.* New York: Norton.

Kasinitz, P., Battle, J., & Miyares, I. (2001). Fade to Black? The children of West Indian immigrants in southern Florida. In R. Rumbaut & A. Portes (Eds.), *Ethnicities: Children of immigrants in America* (pp. 267–300). Berkeley: University of California Press.

Keith, V., & Herring, C. (1991). Skin tone and stratification in the Black community. *American Journal of Sociology, 97,* 760–778.

Kerwin, C., Ponterotto, J. G., Jackson, B. L., & Harris, A. (1993). Racial identity in biracial children: A qualitative investigation. *Journal of Counseling Psychology, 40*(2), 221–231.

Kochman, T. J. (1992). *The relationship between environmental characteristics and the psychological functioning of African American youth.* Unpublished honors thesis, Emory University, Atlanta, GA.

Koshy, S. (1998). Category crisis: South Asian Americans and questions of race and ethnicity. *Diaspora, 7*(3), 285–320.

Lee, C., Spencer, M. B., & Harpalani, V. (2003). Every shut eye ain't sleep: Studying how people live culturally. *Educational Researcher Journal, 32*(5), 6–13.

Legum, C. (1968). Color and power in the southern African situation. In J. H. Franklin (Ed.), *Color and race* (pp. 205–217). Boston: Beacon Press.

Lewin, K. (1935). *A dynamic theory of personality.* New York: McGraw-Hill.

Lipsitz, G. (1998). *The possessive investment in Whiteness: How White people profit from identity politics.* Philadelphia: Temple University Press.

Luthar, S. S. (2003). *Resilience and vulnerability: Adaptation in the context of childhood adversities.* Cambridge, MA: Cambridge University Press.

Luthar, S. S., & Becker, B. E. (2002). Privileged but pressured? A study of affluent youth. *Child Development, 73,* 1593–1610.

Luthar, S., & Cicchetti, D. (2000). The construct of resilience: Implications for interventions and social policies. *Development and Psychopathology, 12,* 857–885.

Luthar, S. S., Cicchetti, D., & Becker, B. (2000). The construct of resilience: A critical evaluation and guidelines for future work. *Child Development, 71,* 543–562.

Luthar, S. S., & Latendresse, S. J. (2002). Adolescent risk: The cost of affluence. *New Directions for Youth Development, 95,* 101–121.

Maddox, K. B. (1998). *Cognitive representation of light- versus dark-skinned Blacks: Structure, content, and use of the African American stereotype.* Unpublished doctoral dissertation, University of California, Santa Barbara.

Marcia, J. E. (1966). Development and validation of ego-identity status. *Journal of Personality and Social Psychology, 3,* 551–558.

Marcia, J. E. (1980). Identity in adolescence. In J. Adelson (Ed.), *Handbook of adolescent psychology* (pp. 159–187). New York: Wiley.

Marks, E. S. (1943). Skin color judgments of Negro college students. *Journal of Abnormal and Social Psychology, 38,* 370–376.

Markus, H. R., & Kitayama, S. (1991). Cultural variation in the self-concept. In G. R. Goethals & J. Strauss (Eds.), *Multidisciplinary perspectives on the self* (pp. 18–48). New York: Springer-Verlag.

Masten, A. S. (1994). Resilience in individual development: Successful adaptation despite risk and adversity. In M. C. Wang & E. W. Gordon (Eds.), *Educational resilience in inner-city America: Challenges and prospects* (pp. 3–25). Hillsdale, NJ: Erlbaum.

May, D. (2001). *Adolescent fear of crime, perceptions of risk, and defensive behaviors: An alternative explanation of violent delinquency.* Lewiston, NY: Edwin Mellon Press.

Mayer, S. E., & Jencks, C. (1989). Growing up in poor neighborhoods: How much does it matter? *Science, 243,* 1441–1445.

McAdoo, H. P. (1985). Racial attitude and self-concept of young Black children over time. In H. P. McAdoo & J. L. McAdoo (Eds.), *Black children: Social, educational, and parental environments* (pp. 213–242). Newbury Park, CA: Sage.

McIntosh, P. (1989). White privilege: Unpacking the invisible knapsack. *Peace and Freedom,* 10–12.

McIntosh, P. (1990). White privilege: Unpacking the invisible knapsack. *Independent School, 49*(2). (Excerpted from *White privilege and male privilege: A personal account of coming to see correspondences through work in women's studies,* Working Paper 189, 1988).

Mead, G. H. (1934). *Mind, self, and society.* Chicago: University of Chicago Press.

Mehta, P. (1998). The emergence, conflicts, and integration of the bicultural self. In S. Akhtar & S. Kramer (Eds.), *The colors of childhood* (pp. 129–168). Northvale, NJ: Aronson.

Mitchell, S. A. (1988). *Relational concepts in psychoanalysis: An integration.* Cambridge, MA: Harvard University Press.

Montalvo, F., & Codina, G. E. (2001). Skin color and Latinos in the United States. *Ethnicities, 1*(3), 321–341.

Ogbu, J. U. (1978). *Minority education and caste: The American system in cross-cultural perspective.* New York: Academic Press.

Ogbu, J. U. (1985). A cultural ecology of competence among inner-city Blacks. In M. B. Spencer, G. K. Brookins, & W. R. Allen (Eds.), *Beginnings: The social and affective development of Black children* (pp. 45–66). Hillsdale, NJ: Erlbaum.

Ogbu, J. U. (1990). Minority education in a comparative perspective. *Journal of Negro Education, 59*(1), 45–56.

Omi, M., & Winant, H. (1994). *Racial formation in the United States* (2nd ed.). New York: Routledge.

Parker, S., Nichter, M., Nichter, M., Vuckovic, N., Sims, C., & Ritenbaugh, C. (1995). Body image and weight concerns among African American and White adolescent females: Differences that make a difference. *Human Organization, 54*(2), 103–113.

Parrish, C. H. (1946). Color names and color notions. *Journal of Negro Education, 15,* 13–20.

Peters, M. F. (1985). Racial socialization of young Black children. In H. P. McAdoo & J. L. McAdoo (Eds.), *Black children: Social, educational, and parental environments* (pp. 159–173). Newbury Park, CA: Sage.

Pettigrew, T. F. (1964). *A profile of the Negro American.* Princeton, NJ: Van Nostrand.

Phelan, P., Davidson, A. L., & Cao, H. T. (1991). Students' multiple worlds: Negotiating the boundaries of family, peer, and school cultures. *Anthropology and Education Quarterly, 22,* 224–250.

Phinney, J. (1992). The Multigroup Ethnic Identity Measure: A new scale for use with adolescents and young adults from diverse groups. *Journal of Adolescent Research, 7,* 156–176.

Piaget, J. (1932). *The moral judgment of the child.* London: Routledge & Kegan Paul.

Piaget, J. (1970). *Structuralism.* New York: Basic Books.

Porter, C. (1991). Social reasons for skin tone preferences of Black school-age children. *Journal of the American Orthopsychiatric Association, 61,* 149–154.

Porter, J. D. (1971). *Black child, White child: The development of racial attitudes.* Cambridge, MA: Harvard University Press.

Portes, A., & Böröcz, J. (1989). Contemporary immigration: Theoretical perspectives on its determinants and modes of incorporation. *International Migration Review, 23,* 606–630.

Portes, A., & MacLeod, D. (1999). Educating the second generation: Determinants of academic achievement among children of immigrants in the United States. *Journal of Ethnic and Migration Studies, 25,* 373–396.

Portes, A., & Rumbaut, R. G. (2001). *Legacies: The story of the immigrant second generation.* Los Angeles: University of California Press.

Poston, W. S. C. (1990). The biracial identity development model: A needed addition. *Journal of Counseling and Development, 69*(2), 52–55.

Prashad, V. (2000). *The karma of Brown folk.* Minneapolis: University of Minnesota Press.

Provenzo, E. F. (1986). *An introduction to American education.* Columbus, OH: Charles E. Merrill.

Repacholi, B., & Slaughter, V. (2003). *Individual differences in theory of mind: Implications for typical and atypical development.* [Macquarie monographs in cognitive science.] New York: Psychology Press.

Reuter, E. B. (1917). The superiority of the mulatto. *American Journal of Sociology, 23,* 83–106.

Root, M. P. (1990). Resolving "other" status: Identity development of biracial individuals. *Women and Therapy, 9*(1/2), 185–205.

Rosenberg, M. (1979). *Conceiving the self.* New York: Basic Books.

Rumbaut, R. G. (1994). The crucible within: Ethnic identity, self-esteem, and segmented assimilation among children of immigrants. *International Migration Review, 28,* 748–794.

Rushton, J. P. (1995). *Race, evolution, and behavior: A life-history perspective.* New Brunswick, NJ: Transaction.

Russell, K., Wilson, M., & Hall, R. (1992). *The color complex.* New York: Doubleday.

Rutter, M. (1987). Psychosocial resilience and protective mechanisms. *American Journal of Orthopsychiatry, 57,* 316–331.

Sampson, R. J., & Morenoff, J. D. (1997). Ecological perspectives on the neighborhood context of poverty: Past and present. In J. Brooks-Gunn, G. J. Duncan, & J. L. Abers (Eds.), *Neighborhood poverty: Vol. II. Policy implications in studying neighborhoods* (pp. 1–22). New York: Russell Sage Foundation.

Scheibe, K. E. (1985). Historical perspectives on the presented self. In B. Schlenker (Ed.), *The self and social life* (pp.lnb33–64). New York: McGraw-Hill.

Segall, M. H. (1984). More than we need to know about the culture, but are afraid to ask. *Journal of Cross-Cultural Psychology, 15*(2), 153–162.

Shakoor, B., & Chalmers, D. (1991). Co-victimization of African American children who witness violence: Effects on cognitive, emotional, and behavioral development. *Journal of the National Medical Association, 83,* 233–237.

Smith, M. B. (1968). Competence and socialization. In J. A. Clausen (Ed.), *Socialization and society* (pp. 279–320). Boston: Little, Brown.

Spencer, M. B. (1977, July). The social-cognitive and personality development of the Black preschool child: An exploratory study of developmental process. *Dissertation Abstracts International, 38,* 970.

Spencer, M. B. (1982a). Personal and group identity of Black children: An alternative synthesis. *Genetic Psychology Monographs, 103,* 59–84.

Spencer, M. B. (1982b). Preschool children's social cognition and cultural cognition: A cognitive developmental interpretation of race dissonance findings. *Journal of Psychology, 112,* 275–286.

Spencer, M. B. (1983). Children's cultural values and parental child rearing strategies. *Developmental Review, 3,* 351–370.

Spencer, M. B. (1984). Black children's race awareness, racial attitudes, and self-concept: A reinterpretation. *Journal of Child Psychology and Psychiatry, 25*(3), 433–441.

Spencer, M. B. (1985). Cultural cognition and social cognition as identity factors in Black children's personal-social growth. In M. B. Spencer, G. K. Brookins, & W. R. Allen (Eds.), *Beginnings: The social and affective development of Black children* (pp. 215–230). Hillsdale, NJ: Erlbaum.

Spencer, M. B. (1986). Risk and resilience: How Black children cope with stress. *Social Science, 71*(1), 22–26.

Spencer, M. B. (1987). Black children's ethnic identity formation: Risk and resilience of castelike minorities. In K. S. Phinney & M. J. Rotheram (Eds.), *Children's ethnic socialization* (pp. 103–116). Beverly Hills, CA: Sage.

Spencer, M. B. (1990). Parental values transmission: Implications for the development of African American children. In J. B. Stewart & H. Cheathan (Eds.), *Interdisciplinary perspectives on Black families* (pp. 111–130). Atlanta, GA: Transactions.

Spencer, M. B. (1995). Old issues and new theorizing about African American youth: A phenomenological variant of ecological systems theory. In R. L. Taylor (Ed.), *Black youth: Perspectives on their status in the United States* (pp. 37–70). Westport, CT: Praeger.

Spencer, M. B. (1999). Social and cultural influences on school adjustment: The application of an identity-focused cultural ecological perspective. *Educational Psychologist, 34,* 43–57.

Spencer, M. B. (2001). Identity, achievement, orientation, and race: "Lessons learned" about the normative developmental experiences of African American males. In W. H. Watkins, J. H. Lewis, & V. Chou (Eds.), *Race and education: The roles of history and society in educating African American students* (pp. 100–127). Boston: Allyn & Bacon.

Spencer, M. B. (in press). Phenomenology and ecological systems theory: Development of diverse groups. In W. Damon & R. Lerner (Eds.), Chapter 15. *Handbook of Child Psychology.* New York: Wiley.

Spencer, M. B., Cole, S. P., Dupree, D., Glymph, A., & Pierre, P. (1993). Self-efficacy among urban African American early adolescents: Exploring issues of risk, vulnerability, and resilience. *Development and Psychopathology, 5*(4), 719–739.

Spencer, M. B., Cole, S. P., Jones, S., & Swanson, D. P. (1997). Neighborhood and family influences on young urban adolescents' behavior problems: A multisample multisite analysis. In J. Brooks-Gunn, G. Duncan, & J. Lawrence Aber (Eds.), *Neighborhood poverty: Context and consequences for children* (Vol. 1, pp. 200–218). New York: Russell Sage Foundation Press.

Spencer, M. B., Cross, Jr., W. E., Harpalani, V., & Goss, T. N. (2003). Debunking the "acting White" myth and posing new directions for research. In C. C. Yeakey & R. D. Henderson (Eds.), *Surmounting all odds: Education, opportunity, and society in the new millennium* (pp. 273–304). Greenwich, CT: Information Age Publishing.

Spencer, M. B., Cunningham, M., & Swanson, D. P. (1995). Identity as coping: Adolescent African American males' adaptive responses to high risk environments. In H. W. Harris, H. C. Blue, & E. E. H. Griffith (Eds.), *Racial and ethnic identity: Psychological development and creative expression* (pp. 31–52). New York: Routledge Publishers.

Spencer, M. B., & Dornbusch, S. (1990). Challenges in studying minority youth. In S. Feldman & G. Elliot (Eds.), *At the threshold: The developing adolescent* (pp. 123–146). Cambridge, MA: Harvard University Press.

Spencer, M. B., & Dupree, D. (1996). African American youths' ecocultural challenges and psychosocial opportunities: An alternative analysis of problem behavior outcomes. In D. Cicchetti & S. Toth (Eds.), *Rochester Symposium on Developmental Psychopathology: Vol. 7. Adolescence: Opportunities and Challenges* (pp. 259–282). Rochester, NY: University of Rochester Press.

Spencer, M. B., Dupree, D., Cunningham, M., Harpalani, V., & Munoz-Miller, M. (2003). Vulnerability to violence: A contextually sensitive, developmental perspective on African American adolescents. *Journal of Social Issues, 59,* 33–49.

Spencer, M. B., Dupree, D., & Hartmann, T. (1997). A phenomenological variant of ecological systems theory (PVEST): A self-organization perspective in context. *Development and Psychopathology, 9,* 817–833.

Spencer, M. B., Dupree, D., Swanson, D. P., & Cunningham, M. (1996). Parental monitoring and adolescents' sense of responsibility for their own learning: An examination of sex differences. *Journal of Negro Education, 65*(1), 30–43.

Spencer, M. B., Fegley, S. G., Seaton, G., & Harpalani, V. (in press). Coping in context: A theory-driven analysis of adolescent males' behavioral responses to risk. *Research in Human Development.*

Spencer, M. B., & Harpalani, V. (2001). African American adolescents, research on. In R. M. Lerner & J. V. Lerner (Eds.), *Today's teenager: Adolescents in America* (pp. 30–32). Denver, CO: ABC-CLIO.

Spencer, M. B., & Harpalani, V. (2003). Nature, nurture and the question of "How?": A phenomenological variant of ecological systems theory. In C. Garcia-Coll, K. Kearer, & R. Lerner (Eds.), *Nature and nurture: The complex interplay of genetic development* (pp. 53–77). Mahwah, NJ: Erlbaum.

Spencer, M. B., Harpalani, V., Fegley, S., Dell'Angelo, T., & Seaton, G. (2003). Identity, self, and peers in context: A culturally sensitive, developmental framework for analysis. In R. M. Lerner, F. Jacobs, & D. Wertlieb (Eds.), *Handbook of applied developmental science* (pp. 123–142). Thousand Oaks, CA: Sage.

Spencer, M. B., & Horowitz, F. D. (1973). Racial attitudes and color concept-attitude modification in Black and Caucasian preschool children. *Developmental Psychology, 9,* 246–254.

Spencer, M. B., Kim, S., & Marshall, S. (1987). Double stratification and psychological risk: Adaptational processes and school experiences of Black children. *Journal of Negro Education, 56*(1), 77–86.

Spencer, M. B., & Markstrom-Adams, C. (1990). Identity processes among racial and ethnic minority children in America. *Child Development, 61,* 290–310.

Spencer, M. B., Noll, E., Stoltzfus, J., & Harpalani, V. (2001). Identity and school adjustment: Revisiting the "acting White" hypothesis. *Educational Psychologist, 36*(1), 21–30.

Spencer, M. B., & Swanson, D. P. (2000). Promoting positive outcomes for youth: Resourceful families and communities. In J. Waldfogel and Danzinger (Eds.), *Securing the future* (pp. 182–204). New York: Russell Sage Foundation Press.

Spurlock, J., & Norris, D. M. (1991). The impact of culture and race on the development of African Americans. In A. Tasman & S. M. Goldfinger (Eds.), *American Psychiatric Press review of psychiatry* (pp. 594–607). Washington, DC: American Psychiatric Press.

Steele, C. (1997). A threat in the air: How stereotypes shape intellectual identity and performance. *American Psychologist, 52,* 613–629.

Steele, C. M. (2004, April). *Stereotype threat.* Endowed lectureship sponsored by the University of Michigan, Provost Office.

Steele, C. M., & Aronson, J. (1995). Stereotype threat and the intellectual test performance of African Americans. *Journal of Personality and Social Psychology, 69,* 797–811.

Steinhorn, L., & Diggs-Brown, B. (1999). *By the color of our skin: The illusion of integration and the reality of race.* New York: Dutton Books.

Stevenson, H. C., Jr. (1994). Validation of the Scale of Racial Socialization for Black adolescents: Steps toward multidimensionality. *Journal of Black Psychology, 20*(4), 445–468.

Stevenson, H. C., Jr. (1997). Missed, dissed, and pissed: Making meaning of neighborhood risk, fear and anger management in urban Black youth. *Cultural Diversity and Mental Health, 3,* 37–52.

Stevenson, H. W., & Stewart, E. C. (1958). A developmental study of racial awareness in young children. *Child Development, 29,* 399–409.

Stone, J., Perry, Z. W., & Darley, J. M. (1997). "White men can't jump": Evidence for the perceptual confirmation of racial stereotypes following a basketball game. *Basic and Applied Social Psychology, 19*(3), 291–306.

Stonequist, E. V. (1937). *The marginal man: A study in personality and culture conflict.* New York: Charles Scribner & Sons.

Sullivan, H. S. (1953). *The interpersonal theory of psychiatry.* New York: Norton.

Sullivan, M. L. (1989). *Getting paid: Youth, crime and work in the inner city.* Ithaca, NY: Cornell University Press.

Swanson, D. P., Cunningham, M., & Spencer, M. B. (2003). Black males' structural conditions, achievement patterns, normative needs and opportunities. *Urban Education Journal, 38,* 608–633.

Swanson, D. P., & Spencer, M. B. (1991). Youth policy, poverty, and African Americans: Implications for resilience. *Education and Urban Society, 24*(1), 148–161.

Swanson, D. P., & Spencer, M. B. (1998). Developmental and cultural context considerations for research on African American adolescents. In H. E. Fitzgerald, B. M. Lester, & B. Zuckerman (Eds.), *Children of color: Research, health, and public policy issues* (pp. 53–72). Chicago: University of Chicago Press.

Swanson, D. P., Spencer, M. B., Dell'Angelo, T., Harpalani, V., & Spencer, T. (2002). Identity processes and the positive youth development of African Americans: An exploratory framework. In G. Noam (Series Ed.) & C. Taylor, R. M. Lenner, & A. von Eye (Vol. Eds.), *New Directions for youth development: Vol. 95. Pathways to positive youth development among gang and non-gang youth* (pp. 73–99). San Francisco: Jossey-Bass.

Swanson, D. P., Spencer, M. B., Harpalani, V., Dupree, D., Noll, E., Ginzburg, S., et al. (2003). Psychosocial development in racially and ethnically diverse youth: Conceptual and methodological challenges in the twenty-first century. *Development and Psychopathology, 15,* 743–771.

Swanson, D. P., Spencer, M. B., & Petersen, A. (1998). Identity formation in adolescence. In K. Borman & B. Schneider (Eds.), *The adolescent years: Social influences and educational challenges: Pt. 1. Ninety-seventh yearbook of the National Society for the Study of Education* (pp. 18–41). Chicago: University of Chicago Press.

Takaki, R. (1998). *Strangers from a different shore: A history of Asian Americans.* New York: Little, Brown.

Tatum, B. D. (1997). *Why are all the Black kids sitting together in the cafeteria?* New York: Basic Books.

Taylor, C. (1991). The dialogical self. In D. R. Hiley, J. F. Bohman, & R. Shusterman (Eds.), *The interpretive turn: Philosophy, science, culture* (pp. 304–314). Ithaca, NY: Cornell University Press.

Tuakli-Williams, J., & Carillo, J. (1995). The impact of psychosocial stressors on African American and Latino preschoolers. *Journal of the National Medical Association, 87*(7), 473–478.

Tylor, E. B. (1871/1958). *Primitive culture.* New York: Harper & Row.

Vander Zander, J. W. (1985). *Human development* (3rd ed.). New York: Knopf.

Van Oers, B. (1998). From context to contextualizing. *Learning and Instruction, 8*(6), 473–488.

Wagatsuma, H. (1968). The social perception of skin color in Japan. In J. H. Franklin (Ed.), *Color and race* (pp. 129–165). Boston: Houghton Mifflin.

Waters, M. C. (1994). Ethnic and racial identities of second-generation Black immigrants in New York City. *International Migration Review, 28,*795–820.

Waters, M. C. (1996). The intersection of gender, race, and ethnicity in identity development of Caribbean American teens. In B. J. Ross Leadbeater & N. Way (Eds.), *Urban girls: Resisting stereotypes, creating identities* (pp. 65–81). New York: New York University Press.

Wenner, L. N. (1972). The American Indian and formal education. In W. W. Brichman & S. S. Lehrer (Eds.), *Education and the many faces of the disadvantaged* (pp. 143–152). New York: Wiley.

Werner, E. E. (1989). High risk children in young adulthood: A longitudinal study from birth to 32 years. *American Journal of Orthopsychiatry, 59,* 72–81.

Werner, E. E. (2000). Protective factors and individual resilience. In J. P. Shonkoff & S. J. Meisels (Eds.), *Handbook of early childhood intervention* (2nd ed., pp. 115–132). Cambridge, England: Cambridge University Press.

Werner, E. E., & Smith, R. S. (1982). *Vulnerable but invincible: A longitudinal study of resilient children and youth.* New York: McGraw-Hill.

Werner, E. E., & Smith, R. S. (2001). *Journeys from childhood to midlife: Risk, resilience, and recovery.* Ithaca, NY: Cornell University Press.

White, R. (1959). Motivation reconsidered: The concept of competence. *Psychological Review, 66,* 297–333.

White, R. (1960). Competence and psychosexual development. In M. R. Riley (Ed.), *Nebraska Symposium on Motivation* (pp. 3–32). Lincoln: University of Nebraska Press.

Williams, J. E., & Roberson, J. K. (1967). A method for assessing racial attitudes in preschool children. *Educational and Psychological Measurement, 27,* 671–689.

Youngblood, J., & Spencer, M. B. (2002). Integrating normative identity processes and academic support requirements for special needs adolescents: The application of an identity-focused cultural ecological (ICE) perspective. *Journal of Applied Developmental Science, 6,* 95–108.

Zelizer, V. A. (1994). *Pricing the priceless child: The changing social value of children.* Princeton, NJ: Princeton University Press.

Zhou, M. (1997). Growing up American: The challenge confronting immigrant children and children of immigrants. *Annual Review of Sociology, 23,* 63–95.

Zhou, M., & Bankston, C. L. (1998). *Growing up American: How Vietnamese children adapt to life in the United States.* New York: Russell Sage Foundation.

CHAPTER 17

Probabilistic Epigenesis of Psychopathology

GILBERT GOTTLIEB and MICHAEL T. WILLOUGHBY

The developmental mode of analysis is the only method that can truly explain the structures and functions of maturing and mature organisms. This is an insight that dates back to the resolution of the epigenesis-preformation debate in the 1700s. The crux of the notion of developmental analysis was succinctly stated by Caspar Friedrich Wolff in his great treatise on embryological development of the chick: ". . . each part is first of all an effect of the preceding part, and itself becomes the cause of the following part" (Wolff, 1764, p. 211, cited in Hall, 1999, p. 112). The singularly important role of developmental analysis took a great leap forward in the late 1800s with the establishment of experimental embryology by Wilhelm Roux (reviewed in Gottlieb, 2002c), in which normal development was systematically perturbed to get an understanding of what was called the "mechanics of development" (*Entwicklungsmechanik*). The latter term was used by Roux to describe a new science of causal morphology, that is, an investigation of the development of form, not the mode of action of an already formed mechanism (reviewed in detail by Russell, 1917).

For the present purposes, the results of the various experimental manipulations of the embryo and its developmental

context are of extreme importance. The various manipulations of the early embryo typically caused different outcomes of development, thus giving rise to two significant metatheoretical concepts: *reaction potential* and *interaction*. Reaction potential referred to the heredity of the organism, bits and pieces of which were revealed depending upon the specific interactive influences that were allowed, or made experimentally, to operate during embryonic development. Today in developmental biology, the term *epigenetics* has come to refer to "the control of gene expression by the environments and microenvironments encountered by embryos or parts of embryos . . ." (Hall, 1999, pp. 113–114). So, in developmental biology, the ubiquity of interaction is taken for granted and extends to the activation of genetic activity by nongenic influences, not just the formative influences of cell-cell, tissue-tissue, and organ-organ interactions. It makes good sense to extend this point of view to developmental psychology, and, with some added refinements, that is what the first author has been attempting to do with the metatheoretical model called *probabilistic epigenesis*.

PROBABILISTIC EPIGENESIS

Probabilistic epigenesis is to be contrasted with predetermined epigenesis, the latter holding that genetic activity gives rise to neural (and other) structures that begin to function when they become mature in the unidirectional sense of genetic activity → structure → function. In contrast, in line

The first author's contribution to the preparation of this chapter was supported by National Institutes of Health Grant MH-52429 and National Sciences Foundation Grant BCS-0126475. A portion of the introductory material to probabilistic epigenesis was adapted from an article by the first author that appeared in *Human Development,* volume 46, 2003.

with the evidence now available at all levels of analysis, probabilistic epigenesis holds that there are bidirectional influences within and between levels of analysis so that the appropriate formula for developmental analysis becomes genetic activity ↔ unction. In this view, neural (and other structures) begin to function before they are fully mature, and this activity, whether intrinsically derived ("spontaneous") or extrinsically stimulated (evoked), plays a significant role in the maturation process. This principle of the probabilistic epigenesis of neural development was enunciated by Gottlieb (1971), and its importance is only intermittently recognized in neuroscience. One of the exceptions is the following quotation:

> . . . much current theorizing on the neural basis of sensory, motor, and cognitive development is based on a viewpoint in which the maturation of particular neocortical regions allows or enables new functions to appear. This is clearly based on a predetermined epigenesis viewpoint in which the primary cause of a cognitive change can be attributed to neural maturation. A number of recent reviews of pre- and postnatal brain development have concluded that probabilistic epigenesis is a more appropriate way to view postnatal brain development (e.g., Johnson, 1997; Nelson & Bloom, 1997). Explaining developmental change when there are bi-directional interactions between brain structure and (psychological) function is far more challenging than the maturation view. When adopting a probabilistic-epigenesis viewpoint, the aim remains to unite developmental neuroanatomical observations with functional development. However, a probabilistic-epigenesis approach emphasizes the need for notions of the *partial functioning* of neural pathways. This is because, in order for bi-directional interactions between brain structure and function to work, there needs to be early partial functioning which then shapes subsequent structural developments. The cortical regions are not silent before they abruptly become activated in their mature state. Rather, structural and functional changes in regions of the brain co-develop. (Johnson, Halit, Grice, & Karmiloff-Smith, 2002, pp. 525–526)

Because the coordination of formative functional and structural influences within and between all levels of analysis is not perfect, a probabilistic element is introduced in all developing systems and their outcomes. The fully sketched model, including behavior and extra-organismic environmental influences, is shown in Figure 17.1.

The biggest obstacles in getting the probabilistic-epigenetic model understood and accepted by biologists, neuroscientists, and social scientists concerns (1) its view of the role of genes in the developmental process; (2) implementing the probabilistic-epigenetic framework in ongoing research, including the reciprocity (bidirectionality) of influences

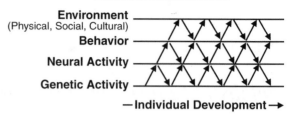

Figure 17. 1   Metatheoretical model of probabilistic epigenesis: Completely bidirectional influences over four levels of analysis (genetic activity, neural activity, behavior, physical, social, cultural aspects of environment). *Source:* From "Emergence of the Developmental Manifold Concept from an Epigenetic Analysis of Instinctive Behavior" (pp. 31–56), by G. Gottlieb, in D. Lewkowicz and R. Lickliter (Eds.), *Conceptions of Development: Lessons from the Laboratory,* 2002a, New York: Psychology Press. Reprinted with permission.

within and between the four levels of analysis (genetic activity, neural activity, behavior, and the physical, social, and cultural influences of the external environment); and (3) a seemingly unorthodox take on the concept of interaction, particularly the ubiquity of gene-environment interaction. There is some necessary overlap in these three issues, but we will discuss them in turn.

Role of Genes in the Developmental Process

The fact that DNA is an inert molecule means that genes can't turn themselves on and off; they require intracellular signals, some of which originate from outside the cell and, indeed, outside the organism. The claim of the central dogma of molecular biology is that proteins are made by the predetermined unidirectional formula DNA → RNA → protein, in which case the genes would be pictured as the unmoved movers of development. (The DNA → RNA relation is called transcription and the RNA → protein relation is called translation.) The truth of the matter is that proteins can and do act on RNA and on DNA, and that in the most dramatic case RNA can transform DNA by a process called reverse transcription. Genes are composed of units called exons (the coding units) and introns (noncoding units). In order for RNA to make protein the introns must be "edited" out by a process called alternative splicing. In alternative splicing there is a reshuffling of the RNA transcription of a gene's nucleotide sequence that generates multiple proteins from the same originating gene. This is accomplished by *spliceosomes,* a specialized group of proteins and ribonucleic acids (RNAs) that not only edits out the introns but can add exons to the transcript! That is how the same gene can be associated with more than one protein. Proteins are what become nerve cells, liver cells, skin cells, muscle cells, and so on, so the development of the structure and function of proteins studied by those involved in *proteomics* is heralded as the next big step in our understanding of genetic activity in the developmental process: "Its [proteome analysis] ability to confirm the existence of gene-products predicted from DNA sequence is a major contribution to genome science" (Humphrey-Smith, Cordwell, & Blackstock, 1977, p. 1217). In terms of attempting to correlate genes with developmental outcomes at the neural and behavioral levels, we need to constantly remind ourselves of the uncertainty involved. Because much of the genetic analysis in humans involves single nucleotide polymorphisms (SNPs), which are merely markers for as yet unidentified genes, RNA editing adds a further complication in trying to specify the involvement of specific genes in neural and behavioral outcomes. One human gene may produce up to five different proteins as a result of alternative splicing (Peters & Boekholdt, 2002).

The search for SNPs has proceeded apace; so far, 3 million of them have been identified and mapped in the human genome, and "these represent only a fraction of the SNPs present in the human genome as a whole" (Venter et al., 2001, p. 1346). Given that there are now considered to be only 26,000 to 38,000 genes in the human genome, the number of SNPs is startling and indicates the arduousness of the task of identifying individual genes or gene complexes, and this complexity comes on top of the problem of alternative splicing. These problems notwithstanding, the scientific program of attempting to correlate genes with neural and behavioral outcomes pushes on using polymorphisms as the stand-in for genes. We have no quarrel with this pursuit, but only wish to alert those readers who may be unfamiliar with the enormity of the problem of actually identifying genes that are involved in the neural and behavioral developmental process of humans. Along with Carolyn T. Halpern, the first author himself is engaged in such a pursuit in collaboration with a geneticist, Trudy Mackay.

We believe it is essential to adopt a probabilistic-epigenetic framework in attempting to correlate genes (and their markers) with neural and behavioral outcomes. The reason this is necessary is that genes are not exempt from influences at other levels of analysis but are, in fact, dependent upon them for initiating and terminating their activity. And when we say "probabilistic-epigenetic framework," we do not mean merely the DNA $\leftrightarrow$ RNA $\leftrightarrow$ protein level of analysis but the other three levels as well. There is considerable evidence that genetic activity is influenced by neu-

ral, behavioral, and external environmental events, and the results of a number of those studies are summarized in Table 17.1.

The failure to replicate genetic studies of psychopathology, as well as genetic $\rightarrow$ neural outcomes, is legion, and we think those numerous failures should be taken as a datum. For example, in reviewing more than 200 studies of the involvement of polymorphisms in dopamine receptors, the latter known to be involved in a number of disorders, Wong, Buckle, and Van Tol (2000, p. 194) came to these conclusions:

> The myriad, conflicting results of association and family linkage studies cannot be easily summarized. There is essentially no clear-cut case in which polymorphisms in any of the dopamine receptor genes are related to neuropsychiatric disorders, or even to a specific phenotype. . . . This uncertain picture is not unique to the pharmacogenetics of dopamine receptors, as a similarly confusing scenario is found in many complex genetic diseases, including some that have been discussed in the review such as Schizophrenia and bipolar disorder.
>
> The fundamental issue may be that dopamine receptors are only one component of the array of neurotransmitter receptor systems that influence behavior in concert with genes that control neurodevelopment, connectivity, neuronal signaling, and synaptic plasticity.

We think this strictly unidirectional, bottom-up approach advocated by the authors in the second paragraph of their quote, though prevalent in this area of study, will not solve the problem: The recognition of the bidirectionality of influences and the involvement of the behavioral and environmental levels of analysis will have to be included in order to successfully link genes and nervous system to developmental-psychopathological outcomes. If this more comprehensive analytic framework is not implemented, we believe there will be continued failures of replication between genotypes and neural and behavioral outcomes, whether psychopathological or otherwise.

Implementing the Probabilistic-Epigenetic Framework

Given the present state of the art and science of the various disciplines involved, implementing the probabilistic-epigenetic framework will necessarily be a piecemeal affair. We have not only the four levels of analysis to deal with but the reciprocity (bidirectionality of influence) among them. We need to be opportunistic in seeking out transdisciplinary collaborations and taking advantage of those that present themselves. We will here document that where it has been

TABLE 17.1 Normally Occurring Environmental and Behavioral Influences on Gene Activity

Species	Environmental Signal or Stimulus	Resulting Alteration
Nematodes	Absence or presence of food	Diminished or enhanced neuronal *daf-7* gene mRNA expression, inhibiting or provoking larval development
Fruit flies	Transient elevated heat stress during larval development	Presence of proteins produced by heat shock and thermotolerance (enhanced thermal regulation)
Fruit flies	Light-dark cycle	Presence of PER and TIM protein expression and circadian rhythms
Various reptiles	Incubation temperature	Sex determination
Songbirds (canaries, zebra finches)	Conspecific song	Increased forebrain mRNA
Hamsters	Light-dark cycle	Increased pituitary hormone mRNA and reproductive behavior
Mice	Acoustic stimulation	Enhanced c-*fos* expression, neuronal activity, and organization of the auditory system
Mice	Light-dark cycle	c-*fos*-induced mRNA expression in hypothalamus, circadian locomotor activity
Rats	Tactile stimulation	Enhanced c-*fos* expression and increased number of somatosensory (sense of touch) cortical neurons
Rats	Learning task involving vestibular (balance) system	Change in nuclear RNA base ratios in vestibular nerve cells
Rats	Visual stimulation	Increased RNA and protein synthesis in visual cortex
Rats	Environmental complexity	Increased brain RNA diversity
Rats	Prenatal nutrition	Increase in cerebral DNA (increased number of brain cells)
Rats	Infantile handling; separation from mother	Increased hypothalamic mRNAs for corticotropin-releasing hormone throughout life
Cats	Visual stimulation	Increased visual cortex RNA complexity (diversity)
Humans	Academic examinations taken by medical students (psychological stress)	Reduced mRNA activity in interleukin 2 receptor (immune system response)

Notes: mRNA = messenger RNA; PER and TIM are proteins arising from *per* (period) and *tim* (timeless) gene activity; activity of c-*fos* genes leads to production of c-FOS protein. References documenting the findings listed can be found in Gottlieb (1998, Table 2).

possible to implement the probabilistic-epigenetic framework, even in a piecemeal fashion, the results have been promising. We will first provide the structure of how we envision the research enterprise that attempts to link genes to neural and behavioral outcomes.

We take it as a given that genes, in and of themselves, cannot produce any neural or behavioral outcome and that gene-environment interaction is a requirement of normal as well as abnormal development. (We critically discuss the thorny issue of the statistical concept of gene-environment interaction in the next section.) Thus, our probabilistic-epigenetic model of developmental outcomes assumes that individuals of the same genotype can have different neural and behavioral outcomes according to the *dissimilarity* of their relevant life experiences, broadly construed. We think this is the basis for the lack of replications among studies that look only at genotypes and attempt to correlate a par-

ticular genotype with a certain neural or behavioral outcome without looking for the presence or absence of intervening life experiences that may be crucial to the presence or absence of the outcome. Take the much-studied inhibitory neurotransmitter serotonin. Low levels of serotonin are associated with depression and alcohol abuse in humans. However, correlates of low serotonin are not behaviorally specific (i.e., low serotonin is involved in a number of psychiatric disorders). In rhesus monkeys, low concentrations of serotonin metabolites (collected from cerebral spinal fluid) are associated with higher levels of impulsive aggression and risk taking (e.g., taking long leaps: Suomi, 2000). Rhesus infants who develop the least secure attachment with their mother are also the most likely to have deficits in their central serotonin metabolism. Because there is a positive correlation between maternal and infant serotonin level, a genetic deficit could be involved, but it is possible that aberrant maternal care may make a necessary contribution to the serotonin deficit. To shed light on the genetic and interactive aspect, Bennett et al. (2002) genotyped the monkeys in Suomi's laboratory for a known polymorphism (long and short allele) in the serotonin transporter gene (5-HTT). The short allele confers low transcriptional efficiency to the 5-HTT gene promoter (relative to the long allele), so low 5-HTT expression may result in lower serotonergic function. However, evidence for this in humans is inconsistent because the necessary life experience correlates have not been examined. In the case of rhesus monkeys, when attempting to correlate the genetic polymorphism to serotonin metabolism, serotonin concentration did not differ as a function of long or short 5-HTT status for mother-reared monkeys, whereas, among peer-reared monkeys, individuals with the short allele had significantly lower serotonin concentrations than those with the long allele (Bennett et al., 2002). Thus, the lowered serotonin metabolism was not simply a consequence of having the short allele but required the life experience of peer rearing in this instance. This result supports our idea that the inconsistencies in the human literature are likely due to unknown but influential differences in the experiential histories of the populations under study.

Thus, the notion that the short allele of the 5-HTT gene is inevitably associated with a central nervous system deficit or defect is not true: The neural outcome depends on the developmental rearing history of the animal, as well as the particular genotype of the animal itself, what has elsewhere been termed "relational causality" (Gottlieb & Halpern, 2002). The present finding most likely also explains why there are inconsistencies in the human literature in finding anxiety-, depression-, and aggression-related personality traits associated with variations in the serotonin transporter gene (inconsistencies are reviewed in Bennett et al., 2002). The association, or lack thereof, reflects not simply genetic causality but developmental-relational causality.

Turning to a similar example concerning the development of psychopathological behavior, a functional polymorphism in the promoter of the monoamine oxidase A (MAOA) gene is or is not associated with Conduct Disorder, violent offenses, disposition toward violence, and Antisocial Personality Disorder, depending on whether or not the adult person was maltreated in childhood (Caspi et al., 2002). Once again, because of the failure to recognize the generality of the necessity of gene-environment interactions in producing outcomes, "Evidence for an association between MAOA and aggressive behavior in the human general population remains inconclusive" (p. 851).

It is thought that the short form of the MAOA polymorphism, resulting in lower production of the MAOA enzyme that metabolizes neurotransmitters such as norepinephrine, serotonin, and dopamine, would make a person more prone to aggressive behavior than possessing the long form of the polymorphism. This inference comes from mouse studies in which the gene encoding MAOA is deleted and aggression is increased, whereas aggression is normalized by restoring MAOA expression.

The results of the Caspi et al. (2002) study support the present model of probabilistic epigenesis in that, when the children with the short form of the MAOA polymorphism are reared under conditions of no maltreatment, probable maltreatment, or severe maltreatment, it is only the latter group in which a substantial number (85%) exhibit some form of the four aggression measures listed above. Alternatively, having the long form of the genotype ("high MAOA activity") significantly reduces the probability of the development of antisocial behavior even under conditions of severe maltreatment.

This study shows very clearly that a knowledge of genotype and the presence or absence of an influential life experience provide indispensable aids to understanding the likelihood of an antisocial outcome in the face of maltreatment in childhood. This is another good example of relational causality, as well as the value of the piecemeal implementation of the probabilistic-epigenetic framework. Much remains to be done, but it is a valuable first step. As the authors themselves say, "Maltreatment studies may benefit from ascertaining genotypes associated with sensitivity to stress, and the known functional properties of MAOA may point toward hypotheses, based on neurotransmitter system development, about how stressful experiences are converted into antisocial behavior toward others in some, but not all, victims of maltreatment" (Caspi et al., 2002, p. 853). The probabilistic aspect is represented by the 85% figure ("some, but not all").

Another important aspect of implementing the probabilistic-epigenetic model is being alert to the reciprocity or bidirectionality of influences within and between the four primary levels of analysis in Figure 17.1. The documentation of bidirectionality is much easier in animal research than in human research because of the possibility of doing the necessary experimental manipulations in animals. Nonetheless, reciprocity has been observed across three levels in some developmental-psychobiological studies of psychopathology.

Let us first take a common environment → behavior example described by Lewis (1990), which begins with the observation that intrusive mothers of 3-month-old infants are likely to have insecurely attached children at 1 year. The bidirectional component is that the mother's overstimulation is related to the child's behavior in children who are not socially oriented at 3 months of age, that is, those who prefer to play with and look at toys rather than people. These children often have mothers who are overstimulating, and the result is an insecurely attached child. In this example, the parent's behavior affects the child's behavior, but the parent's behavior was affected by the child's earlier behavior. Documenting these circular social-developmental patterns, as Lewis calls them, wherein child causes affect the environment and environmental causes affect the child, presents analytic difficulties:

> Such models have intrinsic appeal, but by their nature are difficult to test. Nonlinearity requires a mathematics that still eludes us. Moreover, it is difficult not to treat a child or an environmental characteristic as a "pure" quantity even though we might know better. (Lewis, 1990, p. 25)

Now we turn briefly to some across-level bidirectional examples involving the levels of neural activity, behavior, and environment.

The hypothalamic-pituitary-adrenal (HPA) axis is the most widely studied stress system in animals and humans. Activation of the system in the face of threat, trauma, or other stresses can be determined in humans by measuring the increase (from basal levels) in the neurosecretory hormone cortisol found in saliva. Base levels of cortisol follow a circadian rhythm, being high shortly after awakening in the morning and declining throughout the day. A normative response to stress is a rise in cortisol level that shows up in saliva about 20 minutes after the stressful encounter, followed by a fairly rapid return to baseline. The rise in cortisol helps to focus and coordinate cognitive, emotional, behavioral, and metabolic activity in the face of a stressful psychosocial or physical environmental event, thus constituting a bidirectional relationship across three levels (environment, neural activity, behavior). Whereas brief elevations in cortisol in response to acute stress improves the developing child's ability to manage stressful experiences, chronic hyperactivity of the HPA axis may lead to neuronal loss in the hippocampus, inhibit neurogenesis, delay myelination, create abnormalities in the normative process of synaptic pruning, and thereby contribute to impairments in affective and cognitive functioning (review in Cicchetti & Rogosch, 2001b). On the other hand, in some children, exposure to chronic stress, such as persistent maltreatment, leads to hypocortisolism (reduced adrenocortical secretion), which adversely affects neural development, the development of social and behavioral competence, as well as immunocompetence (cortisol activates the immune system; Cicchetti & Rogosch, 2001a; Granger, Weisz, McCracken, Ikeda, & Douglas, 1996; Gunnar & Davis, 2003; J. Hart, Gunnar, & Cicchetti, 1995). To our knowledge, the developmental psychobiology of the HPA stress reaction has not yet been taken to the genetic level in humans, but that has been accomplished in rodents (Meaney et al., 1996).

So, although Gunnar and Davis (2003) refer to the probabilistic-epigenetic framework as "overwhelmingly complex," they and their colleagues working on the HPA system have managed to implement it quite well across three of the four levels of analysis in human beings.

Ubiquity of Gene-Environment Interaction in Individual Development

The organism-environment interrelationship is at the heart of developmental psychology and psychopathology. Much of what passes for gene-environment interaction is actually organism-environment interaction. As an aside, it is telling that what represents the heart of developmental analysis is rarely found in the population form of behavioral genetics. For sheerly statistical constraints (Wahlsten, 1990), heritability analysis rarely finds gene-environment interaction.

It is ironic that until the advent of high-level statistical tools such as the analysis of variance and the concomitant statistical estimates of heritability, the omnipresence of gene-environment interactions, called the *norm of reaction* in biology, was taken for granted. In 1909, Woltereck introduced the notion of the norm of reaction to operationally and experimentally define Johannsen's (1909) newly coined concepts of gene, genotype, and phenotype. As pointed out by Dunn (1965), Johannsen's synthesis was magnificent and stimulated great progress in experimental genetics because of the analytic clarity of his concepts. However, Woltereck, while acknowledging the general utility of Johannsen's constructs, felt that Johannsen's concept of genotypic influences on phenotypic outcomes under different rearing circumstances was incorrect. Woltereck portrayed Johannsen's understanding of phenotypic development as what Gottesman (1963) introduced into psychology as a reaction range: the preservation of relative phenotypic differences between different genotypes across a number of rearing environments (the more or less parallel lines on the left side of Figure

17.2; Gottesman's depiction is shown in Figure 17.3). The insufficiency (i.e., the lack of generality) of the reaction range concept, in contrast to the norm of reaction, will be discussed later in this chapter.

When Woltereck (1909) experimentally examined the influence of three different quantities of nourishment on the development of head size (helmet height) in three geographic varieties of the freshwater crustacean daphnia

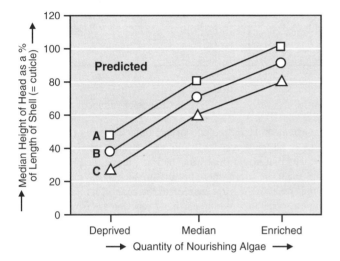

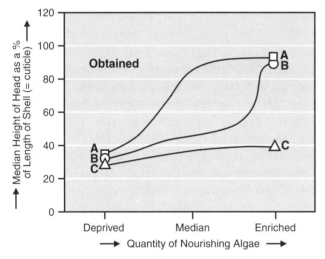

Figure 17.2 Woltereck's interpretation of Johannsen's notion of the genotype's influence on phenotypic expression (predicted) and the actual results (obtained) of rearing three geographic varieties of *Hyalodaphnia cucullata* (females) on different levels of nourishment. Adapted and translated from "Weitere Experimentelle Untersuchungen über Artveränderung, speziell über das Wesen Quantitativer Artunterschiede bei Daphniden" [Further experimental investigations of species modification, particularly the nature of quantitative species differences in daphnia], by R. Woltereck, 1909, *Verhandlungen der Deutschen Zoologischen Gesellschaft, 19,* pp. 138–139, figs. 11 and 12.

(*Hyalodaphnia culcullata*), he obtained three very different curves in moving from the deprived through the normal to the enriched conditions of nutrition, as shown on the right side of Figure 17.2. Woltereck regarded the outcomes of these kinds of developmental experiments—ones designed to empirically determine the phenotypic curves for a range of rearing conditions in closely related but genetically distinct groups—as defining what Johannsen (1909) called the genotype. The generality of Woltereck's concept of the unpredictability of the phenotype of similar genotypes when confronted with novel rearing circumstances has been validated repeatedly in psychology (Erlenmeyer-Kimling, 1972), as well as in biology, down to the present day, and these results conform to the notion that epigenetic outcomes are probabilistic rather than predetermined (Gottlieb, 1970, 1991).

For example, in one of the most ambitious studies of reaction norms, Gupta and Lewontin (1982) examined the number of bristles, viability, and development time in 32 strains from three different natural populations of fruit flies (*Drosophila pseudoobscura*) at two egg densities and three temperatures. They found a considerable number of reversals in relative position in pairwise comparisons between genotypes (e.g., 30% to 45% reversals when temperature was changed). They conclude, "Thus, it is not possible to characterize one genotype as having a higher bristle number or faster development than another, since this can only be relative to a given environment" (p. 947). Their results contradict rather strongly the reaction-range concept, as well as the utility of the breakdown of phenotypic variance into independent hereditary and environmental components as gleaned from heritability estimates.

> As our experiments show, norms of reaction are not parallel, so effects of changing environment and genotype on variance are general. . . . A second consequence of the complex norms of reaction displayed by genotypes in natural populations is that the ordering of different populations in terms of the amounts of the genetic variation they contain may change with environment. . . . A third, and probably most important, consequence of the observed reaction norms is the "myopia" of selection. This is most clearly seen in the viability results . . . genotypes favored by natural selection at 14° C may be quite poor at other temperatures. In fact, there is almost a complete reversal of viabilities in Strawberry Canyon heterozygotes between 14°C and 21°C. (p. 945)

Thus, the limitations implied by the norm of reaction are best viewed as developmental, rather than strictly or solely genetic. The absence of strict predictability is now recognized in many quarters as a defining feature of develop-

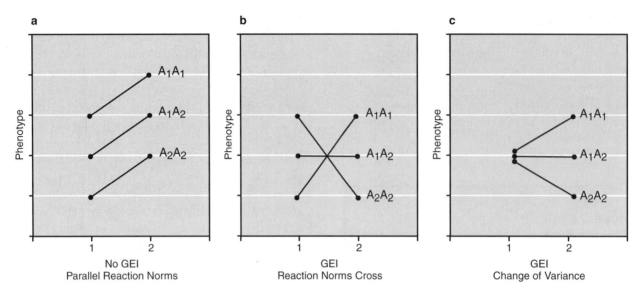

Figure 17.3 (A) Phenotypes are typically sensitive to changes in the environment. Here, the phenotypic value of each of three genotypes is plotted in two different environments (1 and 2). The environments can be the two sexes, social and physical environments (for example, diet, temperature), or alternative genotypes at a second genetic locus that affect the trait. The line joining the phenotypes of the same genotype in different environments is the norm of reaction of the genotype. Here, there are differences in the mean value of the quantitative trait between the two environments, but alternative genotypes react in the same manner to the change in mean. The rank order and absolute magnitude of the difference between the genotypes remains constant, and the norms of reaction are parallel. In this case, there is no statistical genotype-by-environment (GEI) interaction. (B) Genotype-by-environment interactions occur when there is a change of rank order in the two environments. (C) Interactions also occur when there is a change of variance with sex, environment, or genetic background. Adapted from "Quantitative Trait loci in *Drosophila*.," by T. F. C. Mackay, 2001, *Nature Reviews-Genetics, 2,* pp. 11–20. Reproduced with permission of the author and *Nature Reviews-Genetics,* copyright 2001 Macmillan Magazines Ltd.

ment. It is specifically taken into account in such diverse formulations as holistic views of personality (Magnusson & Törestad, 1993), dynamic systems theory (Thelen, 1990), individual-socioecological approaches (Valsiner, 2001, pp. 49ff), and developmental contextualism (Lerner, 2002).

As documented by Wahlsten (1990), the calculation of heritability using the analysis of variance (ANOVA) is often insensitive to the statistical interaction of gene and environment because the detection of such interactions by that statistical procedure requires larger Ns than are usually available in studies using humans.[1] The other weakness (not to say distortion) of relying on ANOVA-like statistics to determine the presence of a gene-environment

---

[1] As the next paragraph makes clear, the statistical concept of an interaction does not have the same meaning as the omnipresent notion of an interaction denoting a primary inseparability or interconnectedness of genes and environment, in the sense that all outcomes are the result of genes operating in a particular developmental milieu and that outcomes are likely to change when the developmental milieu changes. The statistical concept of interaction recognizes only certain changes as qualifying for the term interaction, as described in the next paragraph.

interaction is the peculiar conclusion (for the statistically uninitiated) that obvious empirical interactions do not qualify as statistical interactions, such as the example in the left side of Figure 17.2. To clarify this point further, Figure 17.4 portrays three different forms of norms of reaction for phenotypes that vary quantitatively, such as height, weight, IQ, and amount of extraversion.

This hypothetical figure portrays the phenotypic outcomes of three genotypes studied over two environments. In the left panel, there is said to be no gene-environment interaction because the genotypes have maintained their ranking and the magnitude of the differences among them, resulting in parallel reaction norms. Obviously, this is a very specialized (sheerly statistical) use of the term interaction because the phenotype associated with each of the genotypes has changed from environment 1 to environment 2. The middle and right panels are said to be examples of gene-environment interaction because in the middle panel the reaction norms cross, and in the right panel a phenotypic difference among them is brought out only in environment 2. The term environment is used here in its broadest connotation: "The environments can be the two sexes, physical environments . . . or alternative genotypes

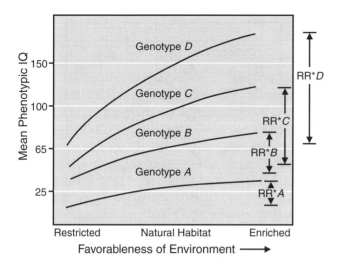

Figure 17.4 Gottesman's schematic illustration of the reaction range concept for four hypothesized genotypes. RR = Reaction range in phenotypic IQ. *Source:* From "Genetic Aspects of Intelligent Behavior" (p. 255), by I. I. Gottesman, in N. R. Ellis (Ed.), *Handbook of mental deficiency: Psychological theory and research,* 1963, New York: McGraw-Hill.

at a second [locus] that affect the trait" (Mackay, 2001, p. 12). Earlier we asserted that gene-environment interaction is the rule; in light of the above, we now adopt the term gene-environment *coaction* to implicate the interconnectedness, if not the statistical interaction, of gene-environment interrelations as far as individual development is concerned.[2]

Norm of Reaction versus Reaction Range

The norm of reaction holds that, if we know the phenotypic outcome of two genotypes under one rearing (environmental) condition, we cannot predict their relative standing when these genotypes (actually, organisms) are reared in a different environment. Gottesman's (1963) reaction range concept, on the other hand, presumes that the genotype imposes a priori limits (a range) on the expression of a

phenotype (Platt & Sanislow, 1988), such that the phenotype has upper and lower bounds that cannot be transcended. In Waddington's (1957, p. 36) terms, the developing phenotype is genetically buffered or genetically canalized (see Figure 17.5). This state of affairs is diagrammed in Figure 17.3. On the right side of the figure, the reaction ranges of the four genotypes are bracketed, as depicted by Gottesman.

It happens that there is an empirical study in the psychological literature that explicitly addresses the reaction norm concept, a study by R. M. Cooper and Zubek (1958). The results very clearly support the reaction norm concept. It is interesting to note that the study was carried out with the idea of a reaction range in mind and that it is cited by Gottesman (1963, p. 273) as supporting the reaction range concept. Cooper and Zubek reared maze-bright and maze-dull rats in either an enriched or a restricted environment and then tested them in a Hebb-Williams maze. Because they had the reaction range concept in mind in performing the experiments, they thought that the learning of both the bright and dull rats would improve relative to each other under the enriched rearing circumstances and would be poorer relative to each other when reared under the restricted (deprived) condition. (This prediction is illustrated on the left side of Figure 17.5.) Instead, as shown on the right side of Figure 17.5, they found equality of performance under both rearing conditions. The dull rats made as few errors as the bright rats after enriched rearing, and the bright rats made as many errors as the dull rats after restricted rearing.

When the so-called bright and dull rats were tested in the Hebb-Williams maze after being reared in their usual way (neither enriched nor deprived), a significant difference between the strains appeared (middle points, right side of Figure 17.5). The reason is that this developmental situation repeats the rearing condition under which the original selective breeding for superior and inferior performance was carried out (Hughes & Zubek, 1956). If the reaction range idea were correct and the genes coded for a range of learning ability (brackets on the right side of Gottesman's Figure 17.3), when these rat strains were reared under enriched or restricted conditions, the relative difference between them would be preserved. Instead, the experiment shows that the genes are part of a developmental system or manifold. The highly specific consequences of rearing under a certain developmental condition were realized by selective breeding under that condition: The animals were selectively bred on the basis of their developmental reaction to that rearing condition. And, as called for by the norm of reaction concept, selective breeding under one developmental regimen does

---

[2] In agreement with our premise, at the conclusion of his critique of the ANOVA and its use in behavioral genetics, Vreek (2000, p. 44) writes, "Behavior geneticists . . . should acknowledge that an analysis of variance is a statistical method that does not fit reality and should be judged against the background of the best material model we have of development, which is one of dynamics and interactions." If the ANOVA is inadequate for getting at the development aspect of behavioral genetics, then it follows that it must not be an appropriate statistical tool for developmental psychology, where it is very widely used. It is clear that we desperately need a more developmentally adequate statistical method to replace the ANOVA.

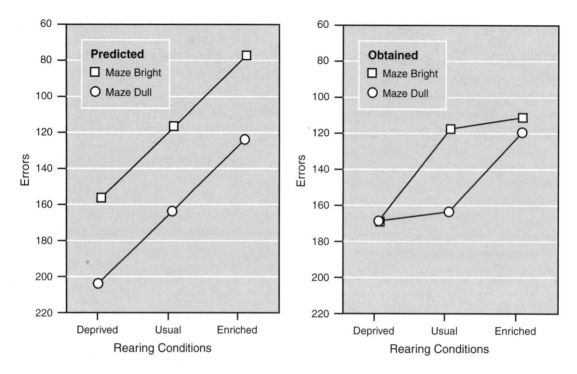

Figure 17.5 Behavioral reaction range (predicted) and norm of reaction (obtained) for maze-bright and maze-dull rats' performance in a Hebb-Williams maze after rearing in three different environments. Obtained deprived and enriched data points are from Cooper and Zubek (1958); obtained usual data points are from Hughes and Zubek (1956). Only the obtained usual data points are significantly different from each other.

not predict outcomes under different rearing conditions. The results of selection depend on the entire developmental manifold, not only on the genes that are involved: To get stable outcomes, the developmental conditions have to remain the same from generation to generation (Gottlieb, 2002a).

A recent study by Kathryn Hood (2005) provides striking support for the developmental manifold idea in the continued dependence of the phenotypic outcome on the specifics of the rearing environment utilized as the basis for selective breeding. Hood and her colleague, Robert B. Cairns, were interested in selectively breeding mice for the expression of high and low levels of aggression. To this end, they placed animals in social isolation after weaning (such rearing enhances aggressive tendencies in some mice) and observed them in aggressive encounters around 4 weeks later. After only several generations of selective breeding based on the animals' response to isolation rearing in each generation, the high and low lines were clearly differentiated. Hood was interested in the question of gene-environment coaction, so after five generations of selective breeding, she raised half of each line in social conditions after weaning and examined their attack frequency in comparison to the other half of the lines reared in social isolation.

As can be seen in Figure 17.6, high-line mice reared under social conditions ("group") were as nonaggressive as the low-line mice, whereas the high-line mice reared in isolation continued to show a high level of aggressive attack behavior. A nice demonstration of gene-environment coaction: the continued dependence of the selectively bred attack response on the rearing environment in which it was selectively bred. What may come as a surprise to some readers is that, after a further 34 generations of selection, the aggressive behavior of the high-line mice is no less dependent on isolation rearing for its manifestation. As shown in Figure 17.7, the attack frequency of the high-line mice drops to slightly below that of the low-line mice when the mice are socially reared in the 39th generation. In Figure 17.7, the 500 line is an unselected line, and their attack frequency is midway between the high and low lines when they are reared in isolation and drops to zero when they are reared socially—yet another example of gene-environment coaction, if we assume a genetic difference between the selected and unselected lines.

Behavioral development is not unique in its continued dependence on gene-environment coaction. Even under strong evolutionary selection pressure, morphological variation is similarly dependent (Griffiths, Owen, & Burke,

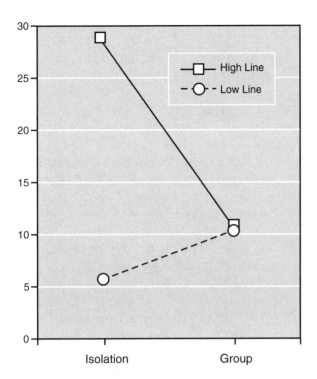

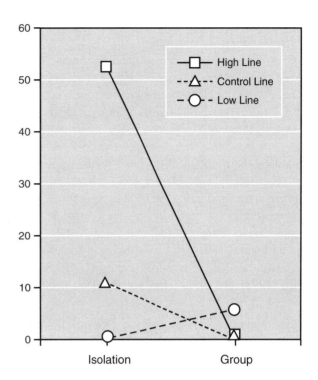

Figure 17.6   After five generations of selective breeding for high and low aggression as a consequence of isolation rearing, Hood (in press) reared the two lines under social conditions ("group") and found no differences in aggressive behavior (i.e., the high line dropping to the level of the low line when socially reared). Modified from K. Hood, 2005.

Figure 17.7   After 39 generations of selective breeding for high and low aggression as a consequence of isolation rearing, Hood (in press) reared the two lines under social conditions ("group") and found no differences in aggressive behavior (i.e., the high line dropping to slightly below the level of the low line when socially reared). The control line is an unselected line. Modified from K. Hood, 2005. Further discussion in text.

1999). Both the behavioral and morphological findings support the idea that understanding development requires a *relational* concept of causality: Development outcomes are a consequence of at least two specific components of coaction from the same or different levels of analysis (Gottlieb & Halpern, 2002). The basic notion here is that the emergent products of development are epigenetic, not just genetic, and this continues to be the case even when we are considering the evolutionary process. A small number of evolutionary biologists are now actively espousing the continued epigenetic basis of morphological evolutionary outcomes, in the sense that the genes correlated to these morphological outcomes may change during the process of evolution while the outcomes are kept stable by epigenetic mechanisms (reviewed in Gottlieb, 2002a, pp. 54–55).

This completes our review of the major contentions of the probabilistic-epigenetic framework. It now remains to give a detailed application of the framework to the development of a specific form of psychopathology: Attention-Deficit/Hyperactivity Disorder. We have chosen to focus on ADHD because we are most conversant with that literature and can thus give a more instructive treatment than would be possi-

ble if we tried to embrace several disorders, or the field in general. Elsewhere, we have dealt with other disorders in an illustrative fashion (Gottlieb & Halpern, 2002).

EXTENDED EXAMPLE

Although often considered a benign right of passage in adolescence, cigarette smoking is the leading cause of preventable death in the United States, responsible for nearly 1 in 5 deaths annually (Brodish, 1998). Cigarette smoking is associated with a variety of diseases, including coronary heart disease and lung cancer. Moreover, experimentation with cigarettes frequently precedes use of illegal substances (Kandel & Yamaguchi, 1993). In addition to disastrous health effects, cigarette smoking represents an enormous financial burden to the country's health care system (Williams & Ziedonis, 2004). In sum, cigarette smoking represents a major public health problem. For the remainder of the chapter, we consider elevated rates of cigarette smoking among youth diagnosed with ADHD. We rely on a probabilistic-epigenetic perspective to better understand why this association exists, as well as to clarify directions for future research.

Over 3 decades ago, Borland and Heckman (1976) reported that childhood hyperactivity was associated with increased risk for cigarette smoking in adulthood. Specifically, in a 25-year follow-up study of individuals who had been designated as hyperactive in childhood, 80% smoked cigarettes as adults. This compared to a 25% rate of smoking among their biological brothers. At the time, the finding was unanticipated and interpreted broadly as a negative outcome associated with childhood hyperactivity.

However, in the past decade, four different research groups have documented that childhood ADHD is associated with an increased risk of smoking in adolescence and early adulthood using both community (Lambert & Hartsough, 1998) and clinic (Barkley, Fischer, Edelbrock, & Smallish, 1990; Milberger, Biederman, Faraone, & Chen, 1997; Molina & Pelham, 2003) samples. Although these studies differed in the definitions of smoking and the age at which participants were assessed, they share a common finding that ADHD is associated with a twofold increase risk for smoking. For example, Lambert and Hartsough reported 46% of ADHD versus 24% of comparison youth smoked on a daily basis at age 18. Barkley et al. reported smoking rates of 48% and 27% for ADHD and comparison youth, respectively, in the adolescent follow-up of their clinic-based sample. Molina and Pelham reported 30% of adolescents with a childhood history of ADHD were daily smokers compared to 12% of the community comparison group. Finally, Milberger et al. reported smoking rates of 19% and 10% for ADHD and comparison youth, respectively, in the follow-up of their clinic-based sample. The lower rate of smoking reported by Milberger and colleagues was likely due to the younger age of the sample at follow-up. Finally, at least one clinic-based study suggested that the twofold increase of smoking associated with ADHD persists into middle adulthood and may even worsen, given that ADHD adults appear to be less successful in quitting smoking than non-ADHD adults (O. F. Pomerleau, Downey, Stelson, & Pomerleau, 1995).

Although it has long been known that childhood ADHD is predictive of adolescent substance (ab)use, many studies have demonstrated that this relationship is an artifact of the overlap between both ADHD and substance (ab)use with conduct problems (Disney, Elkins, McGue, & Iacono, 1999; Fergusson, Lynskey, & Horwood, 1993; Lynskey & Fergusson, 1995; Mannuzza, Klein, Bonagura, et al., 1991). A number of recent studies have questioned this long-standing position, arguing instead that it is the combination (i.e., the interaction) of ADHD and Conduct Disorder that is associated with increased risk for substance use and abuse (Chilcoat & Breslau, 1999; Flory, Milich, Lynam, Leukefeld, & Clayton, 2003; Klein, 2002; Molina, Smith, & Pelham, 1999). Despite these conflicting findings, there is good evidence that ADHD is *uniquely* related to cigarette smoking, even after controlling comorbid conditions, including Conduct Disorder, as well as demographic factors (e.g., ethnicity, familial smoking) that are known risk factors for smoking (Burke, Loeber, & Lahey, 2001; Milberger, Biederman, Faraone, & Chen, 1997; Milberger, Biederman, Faraone, Chen, & Jones, 1997; Molina & Pelham, 2003; Rhode, Kahler, Lewinsohn, & Brown, 2004; Riggs, Mikulich, Whitmore, & Crowley, 1999). Moreover, ADHD is the only psychiatric disorder that consistently precedes the onset of daily smoking (Rhode et al., 2004). Collectively, these studies indicate that the increased rate of smoking observed among ADHD youth is a real phenomenon that merits empirical investigation. For the remainder of this chapter, we rely on a probabilistic-epigenetic perspective to organize the results of previous studies and inform future research.

Multiple Levels of Influence

Figure 17.1 provided a fully sketched model of probabilistic epigenetic. The four general classes of influence that are depicted in Figure 17.1 are intended to serve a heuristic purpose; there are obviously subclasses of influences within each (e.g., environmental influences can range from cultural factors to family processes; neural influences can range from neurotransmitters to brain structure). Figure 17.1 is intended to convey three points. First, there are multiple levels of influence on individual development. Second, it is the coactions within (horizontal) and between (vertical) levels that drive development. Coactions imply bidirectionality between levels and are typically represented by experience. Third, vertical and horizontal coactions occur across time (i.e., development is directional). Next, we consider the environmental, behavioral, neural, and genetic influences that may help to explain elevated rates of cigarette smoking among ADHD youth.

Environmental Influences

There are a variety of environmental factors that have been implicated in the onset and maintenance of cigarette smoking. At a broad level, these include school-level contextual factors that serve to promote or discourage individual smoking behavior (Novak & Clayton, 2001). More immediate factors include the presence of familial and peer smoking (Tercyak, Lerman, & Audrain, 2002). Individuals who have parents and especially peers who smoke are at increased risk of an early onset and stable smoking over time (Chassin, Presson, Pitts, & Sherman, 2000; Fergusson, Lynskey, & Horwood, 1995). In addition, family contextual factors, including lower socioeconomic status (SES) and less supportive family environments, are also risk factors for smoking (Chassin et al., 2000; Fergusson et al., 1995).

Many of these environmental risk factors may be especially salient for ADHD youth. For example, childhood ADHD is predicted by maternal smoking during pregnancy (Milberger, Biederman, Faraone, Chen, & Jones, 1996; Milberger, Biederman, Faraone, Guite, et al., 1997). Moreover, the increased risk of smoking associated with having a sibling who smokes appears to be stronger if that sibling has ADHD (Milberger, Biederman, Faraone, Chen, & Jones, 1997). In addition, the increased risk of smoking that is associated with having peers who smoke (Chassin et al., 2000; Milberger, Biederman, Faraone, Chen, & Jones, 1997; Tercyak, Peshkin, Walker, & Stein, 2002) may be exacerbated among ADHD youth, given that they report spending more time with their peers (versus family) than do non-ADHD youth (Whalen, Jamner, Henker, Delfino, & Lozano, 2002). Finally, the increased risk of adolescent smoking related to low SES (Fergusson et al., 1995; Gilbert & Gilbert, 1995) is noteworthy given that low SES is also predictive of ADHD (Biederman et al., 1995; Scahill & Schwab Stone, 2000).

In sum, a variety of environmental factors are associated with the emergence of smoking. Whereas some of these factors are common to both ADHD and non-ADHD youth (e.g., low SES, school-level influences), others may be particularly salient for ADHD youth (e.g., familial smoking). Any comprehensive explanation of increased rates of smoking among ADHD youth should acknowledge these environmental factors.

Behavioral Influences

The *Diagnostic and Statistical Manual of Mental Disorders (DSM-IV)* distinguishes ADHD youth in terms of their predominant pattern of inattentive and hyperactive-impulsive behaviors. Specifically, youth are differentiated into inattentive, hyperactive-impulsive, and combined subtypes (American Psychiatric Association, 1994; Lahey et al., 1994). Five studies have demonstrated the importance of differentiating dimensions of ADHD as they relate to cigarette smoking. First, using a large community-based sample, Tercyak and colleagues (Tercyak, Lerman, et al., 2002) reported that individuals exhibiting elevated levels of inattentive symptomatology were three times more likely to have ever smoked and to be current smokers relative to in-

dividuals who did not exhibit elevated levels of inattentive symptomatology. In contrast, elevated levels of hyperactive-impulsive symptomatology were not associated with increased risk of smoking. Second, in the context of a smoking cessation program for normal adults, Lerman and colleagues (2001) reported that smoking for stimulation and smoking for withdrawal relief were both uniquely associated with inattentive but not hyperactive-impulsive behaviors, even after accounting for concurrent depressive symptomatology. Third, two well-characterized clinic samples of youth with disruptive behavior disorders demonstrated that inattentive, but not hyperactive-impulsive, behaviors were a significant predictor of adolescent tobacco use even after controlling for Conduct Disorder (Burke et al., 2001; Molina & Pelham, 2003). Fourth, a composite measure of neuropsychological tests that represented attention/executive functioning was predictive of substance use and dependence symptoms over an 8-year period, even after controlling for Conduct Disorder, learning disabilities, demographic factors, and family history of substance use (Tapert, Baratta, Abrantes, & Brown, 2002).

Whereas inattentive behaviors may be directly related to cigarette smoking, hyperactive-impulsive behaviors may play an indirect role in increasing the risk of cigarette smoking among ADHD youth. Hyperactive-impulsive behaviors are conceptually similar to the personality dimension of novelty seeking. Individuals characterized by high levels of novelty seeking are described as exploratory, curious, and impulsive. There is indication that novelty seeking is elevated in both adults who smoke (Gilbert & Gilbert, 1995; Heath, Madden, Slutske, & Martin, 1995) and adults with ADHD (Downey, Pomerleau, & Pomerleau, 1996). Moreover, among both adolescents and adults with ADHD, those who smoke report higher levels of novelty seeking than those who do not smoke (Conners et al., 1996; Downey et al., 1996; O. F. Pomerleau et al., 1995; Tercyak & Audrain-McGovern, 2003). These findings suggest that ADHD youth who exhibit elevated levels of hyperactive-impulsive behaviors may be more likely to experiment with smoking and may do so at earlier ages than non-ADHD youth (Heath et al., 1995).

ADHD subtypes may also be differentially related to smoking due to their overlap with other psychiatric disorders. In general, ADHD youth are known to exhibit high rates of comorbidity with other psychiatric disorders (Angold, Costello, & Erkanli, 1999; Biederman, Newcorn, & Sprich, 1991; Jensen, Martin, & Cantwell, 1997). Whereas inattentive-type youth appear to be at increased risk for exhibiting internalizing disorders, combined-type youth appear to be at increased risk for exhibiting externalizing disorders (Eiraldi, Power, & Nezu, 1997; Nolan, Volpe, Gadow, & Sprafkin, 1999; Willcutt, Pennington, Chhabildas, Friedman, & Alexander, 1999). Both internalizing and externalizing disorders are associated with increased rates of cigarette smoking (Upadhyaya, Deas, Brady, & Kruesi, 2002). Indeed, when multiple psychiatric disorders are considered simultaneously, depression and Conduct Disorder are among the most robust predictors of cigarette smoking (Brown, Lewinsohn, Seeley, & Wagner, 1996; Costello, Erkanli, Federman, & Angold, 1999; Dierker, Avenevoli, Merikangas, Flaherty, & Stolar, 2001; Lerman et al., 2001; Riggs et al., 1999). Thus, although elevated levels of inattentive and hyperactive-impulsive symptoms may serve as risk factors for cigarette smoking, internalizing and externalizing disorders that frequently co-occur with ADHD may represent additional risks for cigarette smoking.

In sum, a variety of personality and behavioral factors are associated with the emergence of smoking. Many of the risk factors for adolescent/adult smoking (e.g., depression, Conduct Disorder, novelty seeking) are also overrepresented among ADHD youth. Any comprehensive explanation of increased rates of smoking among ADHD youth should acknowledge these behavioral factors.

Neural Influences

As noted earlier, the four levels of influence depicted in Figure 17.1 are intended to serve a heuristic function. There are a variety of sublevels of influence within any particular level. For purposes of our example, we focus on neurotransmitters as the primary neural influence related to the association between ADHD and smoking.

It has long been known that altered neurotransmitter systems are implicated in ADHD (Kornetsky, 1970; Wender, 1975). Historically, this association stemmed from the observation that medications that were effective in treating ADHD exerted their effect by influencing areas of the brain rich in catecholamines (i.e., dopamine [DA], norepinephrine [NE]). Over time, it has become clear that DA and NE systems play complementary roles in modulating higher-order processes involving attention and arousal that are relevant to both general neurological functioning (Tucker & Williamson, 1984) and ADHD in particular (Malone, Kershner, & Swanson, 1994; Mercugliano, 1999; Pliszka, McCracken, & Maas, 1996; Solanto, 1998). For example, Malone and colleagues suggested that ADHD is associated with increased levels of NE and decreased levels of DA, and that treatment with psychostimulants (e.g., Ritalin) may ameliorate behavioral and cognitive deficits by reversing these neurotransmitter imbalances.

Cigarette smoking exerts a variety of psychological and physiological effects via the role of nicotine that are directly relevant to ADHD (Rezvani & Levin, 2001). In a series of double-blind placebo controlled studies, Levin and colleagues demonstrated that the administration of nicotine resulted in improved performance on indices of attention that are impaired in ADHD youth/adults. For example, 56% of ADHD adults were rated as exhibiting "much improved" or "very much improved" ADHD symptoms when receiving a nicotine patch by clinicians who were blind to their medication status; this compared to 0% rates of improvement among adults in a placebo condition (Conners et al., 1996; Levin et al., 1996). Nicotine was also associated with faster and less variable reaction times on a continuous performance task among ADHD adults (Conners et al., 1996; Levin, Conners, Silva, Canu, & March, 2001; Levin et al., 1996). A similar pattern of improvements in objective indices of attention associated with nicotine has also been demonstrated among nonsmoking, non-ADHD adults (Ernst, Heishman, Spurgeon, & London, 2001; Levin et al., 1998). These latter studies have helped rule out the possibility that previous reports regarding the beneficial effects of nicotine were due to the relief of nicotine withdrawal among smokers.

The most consistently offered explanation for the beneficial effects of nicotine on ADHD symptoms and associated impairments involves catecholamine changes. Although the specific mechanisms are not clear, it appears that nicotine results in the release of DA and NE, as well as a variety of other neurotransmitters, including acetylcholine (Levin et al., 1998; Rezvani & Levin, 2001). Consistent with this explanation, a recent neuroimaging study demonstrated that nicotine acts in a manner similar to psychostimulants with respect to striatal dopamine transporter binding (Krause et al., 2002).

In addition, as noted earlier, three studies have reported higher levels of novelty seeking among ADHD adults who smoke relative to ADHD adults who do not smoke (Conners et al., 1996; Downey et al., 1996; O. F. Pomerleau et al., 1995). All three of these studies measured novelty seeking using Cloninger's Tridimensional Personality Questionnaire (TPQ) scale. Interestingly, the TPQ was developed to fit into a larger biologically based model of personality (Cloninger, Svrakic, & Przybeck, 1993). The novelty-seeking scale of the TPQ was intended to index the "activation" system that involves the dopaminergic system (Downey et al., 1996). To the extent that the novelty-seeking scale of the TPQ indexes individual differences in dopaminergic functioning, elevated levels of novelty seeking among ADHD adults who smoke provide additional, albeit indirect, support for involvement of the dopaminergic system regarding elevated rates of smoking among ADHD youth/adults.

In sum, the primary neurotransmitter systems that have been implicated in the emergence and maintenance of ADHD are affected by cigarette smoking. For example, whereas ADHD is associated, in part, with low levels of synaptic dopamine, cigarette smoking influences a variety of neurotransmitter systems, including increasing levels of dopamine. Any comprehensive explanation of increased rates of smoking among ADHD youth should acknowledge the role of neurotransmitters.

Genetic Influences

It is well established that ADHD runs in families. For example, biological parents and siblings of children with ADHD are 2 to 7 times more likely to have met diagnostic criteria for ADHD than are parents and siblings of control children (Faraone & Biederman, 1999). The observation that ADHD runs in families provided the impetus for research on genetic influences associated with the disorder. Early efforts included quantitative behavioral genetic studies using twin samples and, to a lesser extent, family and adoption studies (Kuntsi & Stevenson, 2000). More recently, molecular genetic studies of ADHD have been initiated.

The combined success of pharmacological agents that influence the catecholamines in the treatment of ADHD and the existence of models implicating the catecholamines in the etiology of ADHD resulted in dopamine genes being the initial target of molecular genetic studies of ADHD (Swanson et al., 2000). Although in their infancy, molecular genetic studies have indicated that both dopamine transporter (DAT) and dopamine receptor (DRD4) genes are associated with ADHD. Although not universally true, the association between the 10 copy repeat allele of the DAT gene and ADHD has been replicated in multiple studies (Cook, 1999). In addition, there are consistent indications that the 7 repeat allele of the DRD4 gene is associated with ADHD (Faraone, Doyle, Mick, & Biederman, 2001). In both cases, ADHD is associated with specific polymorphisms involving decreased levels of dopamine, due either to enhanced reuptake efficiency (DAT) or suboptimal receptor cells (DRD4).

Tercyak and colleagues (Tercyak, Peshkin, et al., 2002) reviewed the genetic similarities between ADHD and cigarette smoking. For example, like ADHD, cigarette smoking has been described as being intergenerational (i.e., runs in families) and highly heritable. Moreover, the reinforcing properties of cigarette smoking, like other addictive drugs, are attributed to the effect of nicotine on dopamine trans-

mission, as dopamine is involved in reward centers of the brain. Given this association, dopamine genes have also been the early targets of molecular genetic studies of cigarette smoking.

Similar to ADHD, DAT and dopamine receptor (DRD2) genes have been the focus of molecular genetic studies of cigarette smoking (Lerman et al., 1998, 1999; Sabol et al., 1999). Preliminary results have indicated that the 9 repeat allele of the DAT gene predicted less smoking, a later onset of smoking, and longer quit (cessation) periods among active smokers (Lerman et al., 1999). Lerman and colleagues also reported a gene-by-gene interaction. Specifically, the decreased risk of smoking associated with the 9 repeat allele of the DAT gene in their sample was enhanced for individuals with the A2 allele of the DRD2 gene. Lerman and colleagues interpreted this finding as suggesting that "the availability of synaptic dopamine may decease the need for nicotine only if there are sufficient receptors for normal dopamine transmission" (p. 18).

Sabol and colleagues (1999) attempted to replicate the Lerman et al. (1999) findings. Like Lerman and colleagues, they, too, reported that the 9 repeat allele of the DAT gene was associated with less smoking. However, in their study, this was due to greater rates of smoking cessation among individuals with the 9 repeat allele, not reduced rates of smoking initiation. Although there was some indication of an interaction between DAT and DRD2 genes, in contrast to Lerman et al.'s findings, this interaction was not statistically significant.

Sabol and colleagues (1999) also noted that individuals with the 9 repeat allele of the DAT gene reported significantly lower levels of novelty seeking (which was once again measured using Cloninger's TPQ scale) than individuals without the 9 repeat allele. Moreover, current smokers reported significantly higher levels of novelty seeking than did former smokers. These results suggested that the personality dimension of novelty seeking mediated the association between polymorphisms in the DAT gene and elevated rates of smoking. This interpretation is consistent with the idea of gene effects being contingent on life experiences.

In sum, there is an emerging literature on the molecular genetics of both ADHD and cigarette smoking. Although not conclusive, there are early indications that polymorphisms of the dopamine transporter gene that are associated with *decreased* levels of synaptic dopamine are related to *increased* levels of novelty seeking, *increased* risk for ADHD, and *increased* rates of smoking. That said, these relationships are clearly complex and involve moderation both by other dopamine genes (Kirley et al., 2002) and other neurotransmitters (e.g., acetylcholine; Kent et al.,

2001; Todd, Lobos, Sun, & Neuman, 2003) and as yet unidentified life experience (environmental) factors, the necessary participation of which was described in the introductory section of this chapter. Any comprehensive explanation of increased rates of smoking among ADHD youth should acknowledge (atypical) genetic factors.

Self-Influences

Although not explicitly represented in Figure 17.1, the probabilistic-epigenetic perspective emphasizes that individuals contribute to their own development in the sense that they actively seek to structure their experience in ways that are maximally beneficial to them. This idea that individuals actively contribute to their own development is a common feature of systems theories espousing an organismic perspective (Lerner, 2002; Magnusson & Cairns, 1996; Overton & Reese, 1973). In the smoking literature, it is widely acknowledged that there are a variety of reasons people smoke, including management of negative affect, improvement of concentration, and to change arousal states (increase energy or relax). Although many of these common explanations are in need of further empirical scrutiny (Kassel, Stroud, & Paronis, 2003), they are consistent with the idea that individuals use smoking as a means to achieve certain desired states. Building on these beneficial aspects of smoking, one explanation for increased rates of smoking among ADHD youth involves a self-medication hypothesis (Khantzian, 1997; Klein, 2002; Wilens, 2002). The self-medication hypothesis implies that elevated rates of smoking among ADHD youth may be due in part to the ability of cigarette smoking to "treat" ADHD (and related) symptomatology and impairments.

Thus, to the extent that smoking ameliorates difficulties encountered by ADHD youth during the transition to adolescence, it may serve as a form of self-medication. Any comprehensive explanation of increased rates of smoking among ADHD youth should acknowledge efforts on the part of the individual to actively structure his or her experiences in a way that is maximally beneficial (e.g., enhanced mood; improved capacity for academic, occupational, or interpersonal success).

Linking Levels of Influence

A key feature of the probabilistic-epigenetic perspective is that no single level of influence operates independently. Rather, there are bidirectional relationships (i.e., coactions) between and within different levels of influence that, when considered collectively, are responsible for de-velopment. In the sections that follow, we consider coactions that may be implicated in the increased rate of smoking among ADHD youth. We follow this by considering testable predictions that result from these coactions.

Environmental and Behavioral Coactions

Although ADHD youth are twice as likely to smoke as non-ADHD youth, a full half of ADHD youth do not smoke. Thus, despite the increased risk, interindividual differences in smoking behavior are an area of interest. At the behavioral level, it is well-known that inattentive, hyperactive-impulsive, and aggressive behaviors commonly exhibited by ADHD youth interfere with the development of peer relationships, resulting in their rejection by the larger peer group and risk for involvement in delinquent peer groups (Bierman & Wargo, 1995; Hinshaw & Melnick, 1995; Pelham & Bender, 1982; Pope, Bierman, & Mumma, 1991). In turn, their involvement in delinquent peer groups increases the likelihood that they will participate in behaviors and activities that violate societal norms, including early experimentation with illegal substances and cigarette smoking (Fergusson & Horwood, 1996; Fergusson, Woodward, & Horwood, 1999). Indeed, Marshal and colleagues (Marshal, Molina, & Pelham, 2003) recently reported that the association between childhood ADHD symptomatology and the quantity of cigarettes smoked in early adolescence was partially mediated by deviant peer affiliation. Thus, one route by which ADHD youth may come to experiment with cigarette smoking is through vertical coactions between environmental (i.e., delinquent peer group affiliation) and behavioral (i.e., ADHD, conduct problems) influences.

There are clearly other routes by which ADHD youth come to smoke that do not involve affiliation with delinquent peer groups and/or co-occurring conduct problems. As noted earlier, having parents who smoke increases the risk that children will smoke, due probably to a combination of access to cigarettes, modeling, and social reinforcement (Tercyak, Lerman, et al., 2002). Moreover, given that a majority of U.S. high school students report having experimented with cigarettes by age 17 (Tercyak, Peshkin, et al., 2002), most ADHD youth would be exposed to cigarette smoking regardless of the quality or nature of their peer relationships or family involvement in smoking.

Given that there are likely multiple ways in which ADHD youth may be exposed to smoking, future investigation may benefit from considering not only the smoking status of ADHD youth but also the age of onset of their smoking. For example, an *early onset* of smoking may result from affiliation with delinquent peers and be typical for the subset of ADHD youth who score high on dimensions of novelty seeking and/or who have co-occurring conduct problems (i.e., ADHD combined-subtype youth). In contrast, a *later onset* of smoking may represent age-typical exposure via peers and/or family members and be typical of the subset of ADHD youth who do not affiliate with delinquent peers and who do not have co-occurring conduct problems (i.e., ADHD inattentive-subtype youth).

Consistent with this speculation, there is evidence that a history of early-onset conduct problems (i.e., prior to age 15) is associated with an early onset of smoking (i.e., prior to age 14), as well as increased risk for eventual nicotine dependence (Breslau, 1995). Stronger support for this speculation comes from a recent study that indicated that, whereas hyperactive-impulsive and oppositional defiant/conduct symptomatology were associated with an earlier age of cigarette experimentation, inattentive (but not hyperactive-impulsive or oppositional/conduct) symptomatology was associated with the quantity of cigarettes smoked in the past 6 months (Molina & Pelham, 2003).

Behavioral and Neural Coactions

Cigarette smoking increases nicotine in the body and influences a variety of neurotransmitters, including the catecholamines. In turn, changes in these neurotransmitter systems influence mood states and cognitive functioning (Levin et al., 1998). One consequence of the bidirectional relationship between smoking and changes in neurotransmitter systems is that smoking becomes associated with pleasurable mood, improved attention, and greater cognitive control (Coger, Moe, & Serafetinides, 1996; Gilbert & Gilbert, 1995). To the extent that these changes are perceived as beneficial, smoking behavior is reinforced.

Given that both the core behavioral and cognitive deficits (e.g., attention problems), as well as related affective difficulties (e.g., low self-esteem, anxiety, depression) of ADHD are affected by smoking, ADHD youth may perceive greater benefits from smoking compared to non-ADHD youth. Moreover, once they have started smoking, it may be more difficult for ADHD youth to quit smoking given that the psychobiological mechanisms associated with nicotine have ameliorative effects on the core difficulties of ADHD (Coger et al., 1996).

The notion that elevated rates of smoking among ADHD youth may result, in part, from greater perceived benefits of smoking is consistent with a self-medication hypothesis. However, this is not to suggest that ADHD youth actively and consciously smoke to self-medicate. Rather, it is possible that repeated experiences linking the act of smoking to improved mood and enhanced cognitive states increase the

probability of continued smoking among ADHD youth over time. Indeed, individuals who smoke only one pack of cigarettes per week would have more than 1,000 opportunities per year to associate improved cognitive/affective states with smoking. Stated differently, ADHD youth may have more to gain by smoking than their non-ADHD peers, which may contribute to their increased risk for smoking.

Additional support for the idea of cigarette smoking as a form of self-medication among ADHD youth comes from studies that have linked the severity of ADHD symptomatology to the likelihood and timing of smoking. For example, Burke and colleagues (2001) reported that, among ADHD youth, the greater the number of inattentive symptoms exhibited between ages 13 and 15, the greater the number of days of tobacco use during the same period. Using experience sampling methodology, Whalen and colleagues (2002) reported that relative to adolescents with low levels of ADHD behaviors, adolescents with high levels of ADHD behaviors were 10 times more likely to have smoked and 8 times more likely to have experienced the urge to smoke on an hourly basis. Using survival analysis, Lambert (2002) reported that severity of ADHD symptomatology was associated with an earlier onset of smoking. Finally, although nonsmoking and smoking ADHD adults do not differ in terms of their concurrent reports of ADHD symptomatology, they do differ in terms of their retrospective reports of ADHD symptomatology. ADHD adults who smoke retrospectively report higher levels of ADHD symptomatology in childhood relative to nonsmoking ADHD adults (Conners et al., 1996; O. F. Pomerleau et al., 1995).

Neural and Genetic Coactions

Research on coactions between neural and genetic influences related to ADHD and cigarette smoking is limited. However, an increasing number of studies utilizing molecular genetic methods suggest that ADHD is characterized, in part, by a hypodopaminergic system (Kirley et al., 2002). Decreased levels of dopamine appear to result from polymorphisms of specific dopamine genes that result in increased transporter density, subsensitive dopamine receptors, or atypical synthesis of dopamine (Kirley et al., 2002). Many of these same genes have been implicated in cigarette smoking (Lerman et al., 1998, 1999). Nonetheless, in both cases, individual genetic effects are small, and gene-by-gene interactions are anticipated (Faraone et al., 2001; Lerman et al., 1998, 1999).

Although compelling, these studies currently tell only half of the story. That is, these existing molecular genetic studies characterize individual differences in genes as giving rise to individual differences in neurotransmitter functioning (i.e., genetic → neural effects). However, a probabilistic-epigenetic perspective predicts that the reverse is also true. That is, there are likely a variety of experiences (in the broadest sense of the term) that affect gene expression (i.e., neural → genetic effects). Although we are not aware of studies that have examined these issues as they pertain to ADHD and cigarette smoking, we point out this omission in the literature to emphasize that, like all levels of analysis, genetic effects should be considered in the context of the larger developmental systems and do not exist in isolation.

Summary

For purposes of organization, we have considered pairs of influence (i.e., environmental-behavioral, behavioral-neural, and neural-genetic coactions) that may increase rates of smoking among ADHD youth. However, a probabilistic-epigenetic perspective posits that all levels of influence work in concert to drive development. This is not to suggest that every level of influence is equally important for every individual at every point in development. Nonetheless, an essential element of the probabilistic-epigenetic perspective (and of systems models in general) is an emphasis on the *coordination* or *coaction* of influences over time. Environmental, behavioral, neural, and genetic influences are best understood in relation to each other. Moreover, individuals are seen as actively working to bring multiple levels of influence into functional alignment (Cairns, 1986).

Adopting this perspective guards against overly simplistic bottom-up (i.e., genetic) or top-down (i.e., environmental) explanations of greater rates of smoking among ADHD youth that will do little to improve our understanding and eventual targeted treatment of this phenomenon. Although a probabilistic-epigenetic perspective is sometimes criticized for being too complex and claiming that everything is related to everything, it should be evident from the studies reviewed that it does not require dramatically different research than is currently done. However, it does require a different integration of existing research, as well as helping to identify areas in the literature in need of greater attention.

Directions for Future Research

In the sections that follow, we consider a number of predictions that result from utilizing a probabilistic-epigenetic perspective to organize the literature on increased rates of smoking among ADHD youth.

Attention-Deficit/Hyperactivity Disorder Subtype Differences in the Likelihood of and Rationale for Smoking

As noted earlier, the *DSM-IV* (American Psychiatric Association, 1994) differentiates ADHD youth into three subtypes based on their primary behavioral presentation: inattentive, hyperactive-impulsive, and combined subtypes. In addition to differing with respect to inattentive and hyperactive-impulsive behaviors, ADHD subtypes also differ with respect to predominant patterns of comorbidity, types of impairment, the nature of their peer relationships, and demographic factors (Carlson, Shin, & Booth, 1999; Lahey, Schaughency, Strauss, & Frame, 1984; Milich, Balentine, & Lynam, 2001).

Building on our earlier review, we predict that ADHD subtypes will experience differential risk for smoking. Specifically, among ADHD youth, we predict that combined-type youth will be at greatest risk for becoming regular smokers, followed by inattentive-type and then hyperactive-impulsive-type youth. This prediction is based on the idea that elevated levels of both hyperactive-impulsive and inattentive symptoms are differentially associated with increased risk for smoking. Whereas inattentive symptoms have a direct effect on increased rates of smoking, hyperactive-impulsive symptoms have an indirect effect. We predict that the direct effect of inattentive symptoms involves self-medication. That is, cigarette smoking is reinforced because it ameliorates the attention problems and negative affect common to ADHD adolescents and adults. In contrast, we predict that the indirect effect of hyperactive-impulsive symptoms results from increased rates of novelty seeking (including a greater propensity and willingness to experiment with cigarettes), as well as increased rates of conduct problems and association with delinquent peers. Among all subtypes, we further predict that greater rates of comorbidity should result in additional risk for smoking. This is consistent with the results of a recent study that reported a linear relationship between the number of comorbid disorders among ADHD youth and their propensity to smoke, though that study did not consider ADHD subtypes (Milberger, Biederman, Faraone, Chen, & Jones, et al., 1997). A related question is whether ADHD subtype differences in the likelihood of smoking are dependent on the persistence of ADHD symptomatology into adolescence and adulthood. There is limited research addressing this topic, and what does exist is equivocal (Molina & Pelham, 2003; C. S. Pomerleau et al., 2003).

In addition to predictions about differential risk for smoking, we also predict ADHD subtype differences in the developmental timing and rationale for smoking. Specifically, we predict that combined- (and presumably hyperactive-impulsive-) type youth will experiment with smoking at an earlier age than inattentive-type youth. This difference will be mediated by elevated rates of novelty seeking and involvement with delinquent peers. At least initially, the rationale for smoking among these individuals will be due more to perceived peer status and experimentation than self-medication. In contrast, we predict a later initiation of smoking among inattentive-type youth and a rationale for smoking that is less related to peer status and experimentation and due more to self-medication (e.g., improved concentration and enhanced mood).

There are broad parallels between our predictions and a recent motivational model of risky behaviors. Briefly, M. L. Cooper and colleagues (M. L. Cooper, Agocha, & Sheldon, 2000) recently reported that whereas the association between neuroticism (heightened emotional lability, self-doubt, negative rumination) and risky behaviors was partially mediated through aversive motivational processes that were intended to reduce negative emotional states, the association between extraversion and risk behaviors was mediated through appetitive processes that were intended to increase positive affect. Moreover, consistent with their predictions, these associations were moderated by impulsivity. We believe that there are broad similarities between aspects of extraversion and externalizing disorders that typically co-occur with combined-subtype ADHD youth, as well as similarities between aspects of neuroticism and internalizing disorders that typically co-occur with inattentive-subtype ADHD youth. Consideration of personality dimensions (extraversion, neuroticism) that are at least conceptually similar to comorbid diagnoses (Oppositional Defiant Disorder, Conduct Disorder, depression, anxiety) is also appealing given that the former deal more explicitly with emotion and emotion regulation, which is an area that has received limited attention in the ADHD literature (Melnick & Hinshaw, 2000; Peris & Hinshaw, 2003).

Self-Reports of Attention-Deficit/Hyperactivity Disorder Associated with the Onset of Regular Smoking

In childhood, parents and teachers are considered optimal informants of ADHD symptomatology (Loeber, Green, Lahey, & Stouthamer-Loeber, 1989; Power et al., 1998). However, with the transition to adolescence and adulthood, reliance on parent and teacher reports of ADHD symptomatology becomes more difficult. For example, changes in schooling result in individual teachers spending a smaller amount of time with students than was the case in elementary school settings. Moreover, adolescents increasingly spend greater periods alone or with peers than with par-

ents. The result is that parents and teachers have diminished opportunities to observe and interact with youth, making them potentially poorer informants of ADHD symptomatology.

Given these changes, researchers have frequently relied on adolescent and adult self-reports of their own ADHD symptomatology for assessment purposes. Initially, it was hoped that ADHD youth would possess greater levels of self-insight as adolescents and adults and, as a result, become better informants of their own ADHD symptomatology (Conners, 1985). Nonetheless, although the use of adolescent and adult self-reports of ADHD symptomatology has become widespread, they are often only marginally related to other (e.g., parent) reports (Barkley, Fischer, Smallish, & Fletcher, 2002; Mannuzza, Klein, Klein, Bessler, & Shrout, 2002; Smith, Pelham, Gnagy, Molina, & Evans, 2000).

Although discrepancies between self- and other reports of ADHD symptomatology represent a challenge when making diagnoses of ADHD in adolescence/adulthood, this discrepancy may help inform questions about cigarette smoking. Specifically, to the extent that elevated rates of cigarette smoking among ADHD youth relate to a self-medication hypothesis, individuals with high levels of *self-reported* ADHD (particularly inattentive) symptomatology should be more likely to smoke than individuals with high levels of *other-rated* ADHD symptomatology. This stems from an assumption that at least a subset of ADHD youth smoke in an effort to alleviate subjective experiences of distress (e.g., anxiety, depression) and/or the concomitant impairments that result from attention deficits (e.g., poor academic or occupational performance). Consistent with this prediction, Whalen and colleagues (2002) reported that elevated levels of self-reported ADHD symptomatology were more strongly related to both the urge to smoke and to actual smoking than were elevated levels of parent-rated ADHD symptomatology. Moreover, the subset of adolescents with elevated rates of ADHD symptomatology according to both self- and parent report exhibited the highest likelihood of smoking and the urge to smoke (Whalen et al., 2002).

Cigarette Smoking Should Alter the Developmental Course of Inattentive but Not Hyperactive-Impulsive Symptoms Over Time

Although ADHD is currently considered a lifelong chronic disorder, ADHD symptomatology decreases over time for a large number of diagnosed youth, with hyperactive-impulsive behaviors diminishing more rapidly than inattentive behaviors (Biederman, Mick, & Faraone, 2000; E. L. Hart,

Lahey, Loeber, Applegate, & Frick, 1995). Given that cigarette smoking ameliorates inattentive but not hyperactive-impulsive symptoms, we predict that the emergence of regular smoking should alter the rate of change among inattentive, but not hyperactive-impulsive, symptoms over time (see also Conners et al., 1996). Specifically, after controlling for individual differences in the severity of ADHD, we predict that relative to nonsmoking ADHD youth, the initiation of smoking will result in time-specific reductions in inattentive, but not hyperactive-impulsive, symptoms and that emergence of regular smoking will accelerate the rate of decline in inattentive but not hyperactive-impulsive symptoms over time. Given indication that severity of inattentive symptomatology is predictive of future smoking, evaluating this prediction will necessitate matching or controlling for ADHD (primarily inattentive) symptom severity prior to testing whether smoking onset results in greater reductions to inattentive versus hyperactive-impulsive symptoms.

Psychostimulant Treatment Should Buffer against the Onset of Cigarette Smoking

Many of our predictions build on the idea that the adoption of regular smoking (not necessarily early experimentation) among ADHD youth occurs, in part, because it is perceived as beneficial. This assumption could be evaluated by examining the rates of smoking among ADHD youth who are receiving treatment. We predict that individuals who are receiving treatment for ADHD, especially pharmacological treatments that influence the catecholamines, should be less likely to smoke regularly, because their attention deficits should be less salient to them. Similarly, ADHD youth who have comorbid disorders that are associated with subjective feelings of distress (e.g., anxiety, depression) and who are being treated for these disorders should also be less likely to smoke (relative to peers who are not receiving treatment for comorbid conditions).

Previous studies concerning this prediction are equivocal. In support of our prediction, Whalen and colleagues (Whalen, Jamner, Henker, Gehricke, & King, 2003) recently reported that medication treatment among ADHD youth was associated with reduced rates of tobacco use. Specifically, in the context of a community-based longitudinal study, relative to unmedicated ADHD youth, medicated ADHD youth were less likely to have experimented with smoking, to be current smokers, or to have urges to smoke. In addition, over a 2-year window between freshman and sophomore years of high school, levels of salivary cotinine, a biomarker of nicotine intake, increased for un-

medicated ADHD youth but not medicated ADHD youth (Whalen et al., 2003).

Loney and colleagues (Loney, Kramer, & Salisbury, 2002) extended the results of the Whalen study into adulthood. Specifically, in a longitudinal follow-up of clinic-referred ADHD youth who were assigned to psychiatrists with different treatment preferences (medication versus psychosocial), medication treatment in childhood was associated with decreased rates of smoking and other stimulant use in adulthood. In addition to the pseudo-random assignment of children to treatment condition, Loney et al. also controlled for initial levels of ADHD, which reduced the likelihood that their results were confounded by severity levels of ADHD.

Equivocal support for our prediction came from a study by Biederman and colleagues (Biederman, Wilens, Mick, Spencer, & Faraone, 1999). In their study, ADHD youth who were treated with psychostimulants had a decreased likelihood of substance use disorders at follow-up; however, the protective effect associated with psychostimulant treatment did not extend specifically to tobacco use. In contrast to our prediction, Lambert (2002; Lambert & Hartsough, 1998) reported that ADHD youth who were treated with medication were *more* likely to smoke from late adolescence into early adulthood than were ADHD youth who were not treated with medication. Lambert and colleagues' results are interesting in light of an incentive-sensitization theory of addiction (Robinson & Berridge, 2000). Briefly, although based primarily on animal literature, it is conceivable that prolonged pharmacological (psychostimulant) treatment of ADHD in childhood could result in "neuroadaptations in dopamine circuitry" that would increase the probability of regular smoking in adolescence or adulthood (Robinson & Berridge, 2000). Although theoretically compelling, there is no research to directly inform this question.

Resolving discrepancies between these studies is difficult, in that they differ in terms of referral source/recruitment strategy, method of diagnosis, sample size, control of confounding variables, and measures of tobacco use. Moreover, three of the four studies are limited by the use of observational designs. A more rigorous test of whether medication treatment protects against the initiation and maintenance of smoking would involve the random assignment of ADHD youth to treatments that varied with respect to medication use (e.g., placebo/wait list versus psychosocial-only versus medication-only treatment). Randomized treatment studies would eliminate confounds to existing studies (e.g., severity of ADHD symptomatology, psychiatric comorbidity). Given its large sample and random assignment of participants to treatment condition, the National Institute of Mental Health Collaborative Multimodal Treatment Study of Attention-Deficit/Hyperactivety Disorder (MTA) study (Arnold et al., 1997; Richters et al., 1995) would provide an excellent test of whether pharmacological treatment protects against the initiation of regular smoking.

It is noteworthy that cigarette smoking may serve beneficial effects with respect to cognitive deficits and affective distress even in the presence of treatment with psychostimulants. To this end, Levin and colleagues (2001) argued that whereas methylphenidate inhibits the reuptake of monoamines, nicotine potentiates their release. Thus, it is conceivable that cigarette smoking and psychostimulant treatment may play additive roles in the treatment of ADHD. Nonetheless, a small study of 40 nonsmoking ADHD adults who were randomly assigned to treatments involving nicotine, methylphenidate, their combination, or a control condition did not provide support for this alternative hypothesis (Levin et al., 2001).

Genetic Markers as Moderators of Previous Predictions

To this point, our predictions have emphasized the environmental, behavioral, and neural influences that may account for increased rates of smoking among ADHD youth. Throughout this example, we have alluded to the idea of smoking as a form of self-medication for at least a subset of ADHD youth. Implicit in the self-medication argument is the idea that there are individual differences among ADHD youth in both the experience of cognitive deficits and affective distress and in the effectiveness of smoking to alleviate these deficits/distress. One way cigarette smoking may ameliorate difficulties associated with ADHD is through changes in the catecholamines.

Although in their infancy, molecular genetic studies of both ADHD and smoking suggest that polymorphisms associated with dopamine genes are associated with individual differences in synaptic dopamine levels. These individual differences in synaptic dopamine levels may contribute to individual differences in the decision to smoke, the subjective appraisal of the value of smoking, and the likelihood of continuing to smoke. This suggests that many of our previous predictions may be moderated by individual differences in polymorphisms of specific dopamine genes. For example, predictions about increased rates of smoking due to elevated levels of inattentive symptomatology or decreased rates of smoking due to pharmacotherapy may be moderated by individual genotypes/polymorphisms. Incorporating information about individ-

ual differences in polymorphisms for different dopamine genes into studies that examine the increased risk of smoking among ADHD youth may provide a strategy for incorporating molecular genetic studies into the broader literature in a way that is consistent with the organizing principles of a probabilistic-epigenetic perspective (see, e.g., Rohde et al., 2003; Winsberg & Comings, 1999). Just as it is insufficient (incomplete) to rely on solely genetic explanations for increased rates of smoking among ADHD youth, it is equally insufficient to rely exclusively on environmental, behavioral, and neural explanations to account for this association.

Linkages between Probabilistic Epigenesis and Prevention and Resilience

In the previous sections, we considered some of the obstacles that interfere with a greater adoption of probabilistic epigenesis in individual research. We also used probabilistic epigenesis to organize existing research on elevated rates of cigarette smoking among ADHD youth, as well as to identify directions for future research. In this final section, we briefly consider how a probabilistic-epigenetic perspective relates to two major themes in developmental research: prevention science and the study of risk and resilience.

Probabilistic Epigenesis and Prevention

Figure 17.1 provides a concise summary of a probabilistic-epigenetic perspective. Arguably, the most important feature of this perspective is a reliance on the idea of coactions to explain how and why development happens (Gottlieb & Halpern, 2002). Horizontal and vertical coactions refer to the relationship within and between each of the levels of influence depicted in Figure 17.1. The concept most frequently used to designate coactions at the organismic level of functioning is experience, which is used in the broadest sense of the word. Experience includes everything from the "electrical activity of nerve cells" to "neurochemical and hormonal secretion" to "the behavior of the organism" (Gottlieb, Wahlsten, & Lickliter, 1998, p. 242). From a probabilistic-epigenetic perspective, experience is said to play facilitative, inductive, and maintenance functions (Gottlieb, 1976, 1992).

Facilitative experience refers to processes that enhance the likelihood of the outcome, thus influencing the developmental timing or age of onset of a particular outcome. *Inductive* experience refers to changes in an organism that would not normally occur had the organism not had a particular experience. *Maintenance* experience refers to events and processes that serve to sustain an achieved organismic outcome. Figure 17.8 depicts the relationship among facilitative, inductive, and maintenance experiences. Unfortunately, developmental studies often do not specify the different roles that experience plays in development. Next, we suggest how the different roles of experience might relate to three different types of prevention.

Over the past decade, prevention science has flourished (Durlak & Wells, 1997; Koretz & Moscicki, 1997). Prevention trials have been categorized into universal, selective, and indicated programs (Mrazek & Haggerty, 1994). The primary distinction between different models of prevention concerns the targeted population. Whereas universal programs target an entire population, selective preventive interventions target subgroups of the general population that are at higher risk for developing a problem than other members of the broader population, and indicated preventive interventions target individuals who have detectable signs or symptoms of difficulty but not long-standing serious problems or full-blown clinical disorders.

As others have noted, a reciprocal relationship exists between prevention trials and developmental theory. In short, theoretically derived models of the developmental processes implicated in the emergence of dysfunction are necessary before prevention programs can be implemented. In turn, prevention trials address fundamental causal processes and can be used to experimentally test questions about the etiology of dysfunction (Cicchetti & Toth, 1992; Coie et al., 1993). We believe that the combination of the emphasis of probabilistic epigenesis on the three different functions of experience (facilitative, inductive, and maintenance) with the three different types of prevention trials (universal, se-

lected, indicated) provides a means for delineating the *sets of experiences* associated with particular developmental outcomes in ways that have not been fully capitalized on to date.

In keeping with our extended example, we assume that there are facilitative experiences that increase the probability that ADHD youth will smoke, that in some cases these are followed by inductive experiences associated with the start of regular smoking, and that there are maintenance experiences that will serve to keep ADHD youth smoking, once started, on a daily basis. If we define the population of interest as ADHD youth and the developmental outcome of interest as the initiation of daily smoking, direct treatment of ADHD symptomatology may serve as a universal prevention because ADHD symptomatology facilitates smoking. An antismoking program directed to the families whose child is receiving treatment for ADHD may serve as a selective prevention because parental and sibling smoking serve an inductive process, through modeling and the availability of cigarettes. Finally, a coping skills-based program designed to provide ADHD adolescents with appropriate strategies for managing life stress and/or negative affect may serve as an indicated prevention because smoking to cope with interpersonal stress or negative mood serves as a maintenance experience. We could randomly assign ADHD youth to varying levels of prevention (e.g., universal-only, universal+selected, universal+selected+indicated). To the extent that the rates of daily smoking were reduced in the universal+selected and universal+selected+indicated groups relative to the universal-only group, this would provide support for the roles of inductive (familial smoking) and maintenance (smoking to cope with interpersonal stress or negative mood) experiences targeted. Of course, other processes implicated in the emergence of daily smoking could be targeted (e.g., peer group interventions). Our goal is simply to highlight the correspondence between different types of prevention and the different roles that experience plays within the probabilistic-epigenetic framework.

Probabilistic Epigenesis and Resilience

Similar to prevention science, the scientific study of resilience has seen substantial progress over the past 2 decades (Luthar, 2003; Masten, Best, & Garmezy, 1990). Resilience has been defined as a "dynamic process encompassing positive adaptation within the context of significant adversity" that implicitly requires exposure to a threat or adversity and the achievement of positive adaptation (Luthar, Cicchetti, & Becker, 2000, p. 543). Historically, the study of resilience has been primarily restricted to psychosocial/behavioral levels of analysis. However, there is a

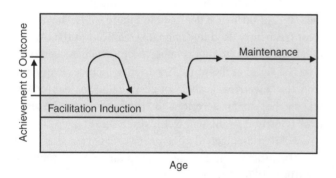

Figure 17.8 Developmental sequence of inductive, facilitative, and maintenance experiences with respect to the etiology of ADHD. If inductive experience is not followed by maintenance experience, the inducted outcome may wane. Facilitative experiences act to accelerate the onset of the outcome of the inducted experience (e.g., if one has friends who smoke that may facilitate the onset of smoking).

growing appreciation that biological processes (genetic and neural levels of influence, in the probabilistic-epigenetic framework) should be integrated into the study of resilience (Curtis & Cicchetti, 2003). This broadening of scope makes the study of resilience more consistent with a probabilistic-epigenetic perspective.

There are two features of the study of resilience that pertain to our extended example. First, resilience is considered a process, not a characteristic of an individual. We strongly believe that process-oriented research is necessary to understand elevated rates of smoking among ADHD youth. Second, the study of resilience orients researchers to think about positive adaptation. Many of the topics developmentalists study are inherently negative (conduct problems, peer rejection, school dropout, etc.). The study of resilience orients researchers to focus not simply on avoidance of negative outcomes, but also on the achievement of positive outcomes. This is consistent with a broader organizing goal of developmental psychopathology, in which the study of normal populations is intended to inform the study of abnormal populations and vice versa (Cicchetti, 1984).

Considering resilience as it pertains to our extended example, an important future goal will be to describe the characteristics and experiences of ADHD youth who do experiment with and/or initiate regular smoking relative to those who do not. For example, it is conceivable that nonsmoking ADHD youth differ from their smoking counterparts in terms of characteristics specifically related to smoking (e.g., concern with physical health) or in terms of more general coping strategies for managing their ADHD symptomatology and its negative sequelae (e.g., academic and occupational problems). In addition, given heterogeneity in the neuropsychological deficits that characterize ADHD youth (Sonuga-Barke, 2002), it will be important to explore whether there are distinct neuropsychological profiles that mediate or moderate smoking outcomes. Once again, our goal is not to make specific recommendations. Rather, it is to suggest that a probabilistic-epigenetic perspective is consistent with the scientific study of resilience in focusing on positive outcomes (adaptation), not simply the avoidance of negative outcomes.

CONCLUSION

Developmental psychopathology is a new discipline. In the 2 decades since its formal inception, there has been a veritable explosion of research on all forms of psychopathology. An ongoing challenge to the field is the integration of research from a variety of disciplines in a way that promotes a cumulative and comprehensive understanding of individual disorders. Probabilistic epigenesis provides a framework for accomplishing this task.

Critics frequently charge that the complexity of probabilistic epigenesis undermines individual efforts to engage in empirical research. This is inaccurate. Although individual researchers who adopt a probabilistic-epigenetic perspective consider their substantive questions from multiple perspectives, there is no expectation that any single researcher will specialize in all levels of analysis. Rather, multidisciplinary collaborations are emphasized. Moreover, individual studies are not expected to measure and/or relate all levels of influence. However, simultaneous consideration of two levels of influence represents an enormous improvement over current research that frequently relies on either environmental or genetic explanations of developmental phenomena.

Throughout this chapter, we have considered some of the obstacles that interfere with a greater adoption of probabilistic epigenesis in individual research. We have also used probabilistic epigenesis to organize existing research on elevated rates of cigarette smoking among ADHD youth, as well as to create testable predictions for future research. Through these efforts, we hope to promote greater reliance on a probabilistic-epigenetic perspective among researchers in their individual research pursuits. We believe that the epistemological superiority of developmental systems thinking has already taken root in multiple disciplines. For examples that have been explicitly informed by the concept of probabilistic epigenesis, see reviews of psychopathology by Cicchetti and Cannon (1999) and Cicchetti and Tucker (1994); neuroscience by Johnson (1999); psycholinguistics by Shanker (2002); and developmental systems theory itself by Molenaar, Huizenga, and Nesselroade (2003). The ongoing challenge is to distill the ideas common to modern developmental metatheory in a way that guides individual research studies.

REFERENCES

American Psychiatric Association. (1994). *Diagnostic and statistical manual of mental disorders* (4th ed.). Washington, DC: Author.

Angold, A., Costello, E. J., & Erkanli, A. (1999). Comorbidity. *Journal of Child Psychology and Psychiatry and Allied Disciplines, 40*(1), 57–87.

Arnold, L. E., Abikoff, H. B., Cantwell, D. P., Conners, C. K., Elliott, G., Greenhill, L. L., et al. (1997). National Institute of Mental Health Collaborative Multimodal Treatment Study of Children with ADHD (the MTA): Design challenges and choices. *Archives of General Psychiatry, 54*(9), 865–870.

Barkley, R. A., Fischer, M., Edelbrock, C. S., & Smallish, L. (1990). The adolescent outcome of hyperactive children diagnosed by research criteria: I. An 8-year prospective follow-up study. *Journal of the American Academy of Child and Adolescent Psychiatry, 29*(4), 546–557.

Barkley, R. A., Fischer, M., Smallish, L., & Fletcher, K. (2002). The persistence of attention-deficit/hyperactivity disorder into young adulthood as a function of reporting source and definition of disorder. *Journal of Abnormal Psychology, 111*(2), 279–289.

Bennett, A. J., Lesch, K. P., Heils, A., Long, J., Lorenz, J., Shoaf, S. E., et al. (2002). Early experience and serotonin transporter gene variation interact to influence primate CNS function. *Molecular Psychiatry, 7,* 118–122.

Biederman, J., Mick, E., & Faraone, S. V. (2000). Age-dependent decline of symptoms of Attention Deficit Hyperactivity Disorder: Impact of remission definition and symptom type. *American Journal of Psychiatry, 157*(5), 816–818.

Biederman, J., Milberger, S., Faraone, S. V., Kiely, K., Guite, J., Mick, E., et al. (1995). Family-environment risk factors for attention-deficit hyperactivity disorder: A test of Rutter's indicators of adversity. *Archives of General Psychiatry, 52*(6), 464–470.

Biederman, J., Newcorn, J., & Sprich, S. (1991). Comorbidity of attention deficit hyperactivity disorder with conduct, depressive, anxiety, and other disorders. *American Journal of Psychiatry, 148*(5), 564–577.

Biederman, J., Wilens, T., Mick, E., Spencer, T., & Faraone, S. V. (1999). Pharmacotherapy of attention-deficit/hyperactivity disorder reduces risk for substance abuse disorder. *Pediatrics (online), 104*(2), 1–5.

Bierman, K. L., & Wargo, J. B. (1995). Predicting the longitudinal course associated with aggressive-rejected, aggressive (nonrejected), and rejected (nonaggressive) status. *Development and Psychopathology, 7*(4), 669–682.

Borland, B. L., & Heckman, H. K. (1976). Hyperactive boys and their brothers. *Archives of General Psychiatry, 33,* 669–675.

Breslau, N. (1995). Psychiatric comorbidity of smoking and nicotine dependence. *Behavior Genetics, 25*(2), 95–101.

Brodish, P. M. (1998). *The irreversible health effects of smoking.* New York: The American Council on Science and Health.

Brown, R. A., Lewinsohn, P. M., Seeley, J. R., & Wagner, E. F. (1996). Cigarette smoking, major depression, and other psychiatric disorders among adolescents. *Journal of the American Academy of Child and Adolescent Psychiatry, 35*(12), 1602–1610.

Burke, J. D., Loeber, R., & Lahey, B. B. (2001). Which aspects of ADHD are associated with tobacco use in early adolescence? *Journal of Child Psychology and Psychiatry and Allied Disciplines, 42*(4), 493–502.

Cairns, R. B. (1986). Phenomena lost. In J. Valsinger (Ed.), *The individual subject and scientific psychology* (pp. 87–111). New York: Plenum Press.

Carlson, C. L., Shin, M., & Booth, J. (1999). The case for DSM-IV subtypes in ADHD. *Mental Retardation and Developmental Disabilities Research Reviews, 5*(3), 199–206.

Caspi, A., McClay, J., Moffitt, T. E., Mill, J., Martin, J., Craig, I. W., et al. (2002, August). Role of genotype in the cycle of violence in maltreated children. *Science, 297*(2), 851–853.

Chassin, L., Presson, C. C., Pitts, S. C., & Sherman, S. J. (2000). The natural history of cigarette smoking from adolescence to adulthood in a midwestern community sample: Multiple trajectories and their psychosocial correlates. *Health Psychology, 19*(3), 223–231.

Chilcoat, H. D., & Breslau, N. (1999). Pathways from ADHD to early drug use. *Journal of the American Academy of Child and Adolescent Psychiatry, 38*(11), 1347–1354.

Cicchetti, D. (1984). The emergence of developmental psychopathology. *Child Development, 55*(1), 1–7.

Cicchetti, D., & Cannon, T. D. (1999). Neurodevelopmental processes in the ontogenesis and epigenesis of psychopathology. *Developmental and Psychopathology, 11,* 375–393.

Cicchetti, D., & Rogosch, F. A. (2001a). Diverse patterns of neuroendocrine activity in maltreated children. *Development and Psychopathology, 13,* 677–693.

Cicchetti, D., & Rogosch, F. A. (2001b). The impact of child maltreatment and psychopathology on neuroendocrine functioning. *Development and Psychopathology, 13,* 783–804.

Cicchetti, D., & Toth, S. L. (1992). The role of developmental theory in prevention and intervention. *Development and Psychopathology, 4*(4), 489–493.

Cicchetti, D., & Tucker, D. (1994). Development and vital self-regulatory structures of the mind. *Development and Psychopathology, 6,* 533–549.

Cloninger, C. R., Svrakic, D. M., & Przybeck, T. R. (1993). A psychobiological model of temperament and character. *Archives of General Psychiatry, 50,* 975–990.

Coger, R. W., Moe, K. L., & Serafetinides, E. A. (1996). Attention deficit disorder in adults and nicotine dependence: Psychobiological factors in resistance to recovery? *Journal of Psychoactive Drugs, 28*(3), 229–240.

Coie, J. D., Watt, N. F., West, S. G., Hawkins, J. D., Asarnow, J. R., Markman, M. J., et al. (1993). The science of prevention: A conceptual framework and some directions for a national research program. *American Psychologist, 48*(10), 1013–1022.

Conners, C. K. (1985). Issues in the study of adolescent ADD-H/hyperactivity. *Psychopharmacology Bulletin, 21*(2), 243–250.

Conners, C. K., Levin, E. D., Sparrow, E., Hinton, S. C., Erhardt, D., Meck, W. H., et al. (1996). Nicotine and attention in adult attention deficit hyperactivity disorder (ADHD). *Psychopharmacology Bulletin, 32*(1), 67–73.

Cook, E. H. (1999). Genetics of attention-deficit hyperactivity disorder. *Mental Retardation and Developmental Disabilities, 5,* 191–198.

Cooper, M. L., Agocha, V. B., & Sheldon, M. S. (2000). A motivational perspective on risky behaviors: The role of personality and affect regulatory processes. *Journal of Personality, 68*(6), 1059–1088.

Cooper, R. M., & Zubek, J. P. (1958). Effects of enriched and restricted early environments on the learning ability of bright and dull rats. *Canadian Journal of Psychology, 12,* 159–164.

Costello, E. J., Erkanli, A., Federman, E., & Angold, A. (1999). Development of psychiatric comorbidity with substance abuse in adolescents: Effects of timing and sex. *Journal of Clinical Child Psychology, 28*(3), 298–311.

Curtis, W. J., & Cicchetti, D. (2003). Moving research on resilience into the twenty-first century: Theoretical and methodological considerations in examining the biological contributions to resilience. *Development and Psychopathology, 15,* 773–810.

Dierker, L. C., Avenevoli, S., Merikangas, K. R., Flaherty, B. P., & Stolar, M. (2001). Association between psychiatric disorders and the progression of tobacco use behaviors. *Journal of the American Academy of Child and Adolescent Psychiatry, 40*(10), 1159–1167.

Disney, E. R., Elkins, I. J., McGue, M., & Iacono, W. G. (1999). Effects of ADHD, conduct disorder, and gender on substance use and abuse in adolescence. *American Journal of Psychiatry, 156*(10), 1515–1521.

Downey, K. K., Pomerleau, C. S., & Pomerleau, O. F. (1996). Personality differences related to smoking and adult attention deficit hyperactivity disorder. *Journal of Substance Abuse, 8*(1), 129–135.

Dunn, L. C. (1965). *A short history of genetics.* New York: McGraw-Hill.

Durlak, J. A., & Wells, A. M. (1997). Primary prevention mental health programs for children and adolescents: A meta-analytic review. *American Journal of Community Psychology, 25*(2), 115–152.

Eiraldi, R. B., Power, T. J., & Nezu, C. M. (1997). Patterns of comorbidity associated with subtypes of attention-deficit hyperactivity disorder among 6- to 12-yr-old children. *Journal of the American Academy of Child and Adolescent Psychiatry, 36*(4), 503–514.

Erlenmeyer-Kimling, L. (1972). Gene-environment interactions and the variability of behavior. In L. Ehrman, G. S. Omenn, & E. Caspari (Eds.), *Genetics, environment, and behavior* (pp. 181–208). New York: Academic Press.

Ernst, M., Heishman, S. J., Spurgeon, L., & London, E. D. (2001). Smoking history and nicotine effects on cognitive performance. *Neuropsychopharmacology, 25*(3), 313–319.

Faraone, S. V., & Biederman, J. (1999). The neurobiology of attention-deficit hyperactivity disorder. In D. S. Charney, E. J. Nestler, & B. S. Bunney (Eds.), *Neurobiology of mental illness* (pp. 788–801). New York: Oxford University Press.

Faraone, S. V., Doyle, A. E., Mick, E., & Biederman, J. (2001). Meta-analysis of the association between the 7-repeat allele of the dopamine D-sub-4 receptor gene and attention deficit hyperactivity disorder. *American Journal of Psychiatry, 158*(7), 1052–1057.

Fergusson, D. M., & Horwood, L. J. (1996). The role of adolescent peer affiliations in the continuity between childhood behavioral adjustment and juvenile offending. *Journal of Abnormal Child Psychology, 24*(2), 205–221.

Fergusson, D. M., Lynskey, M. T., & Horwood, L. J. (1993). Conduct problems and attention deficit behavior in middle childhood and cannabis use by age 15. *Australian and New Zealand Journal of Psychiatry, 27*(4), 673–682.

Fergusson, D. M., Lynskey, M. T., & Horwood, L. J. (1995). The role of peer affiliations, social, family and individual factors in continuities in cigarette smoking between childhood and adolescence. *Addiction, 90*(5), 647–659.

Fergusson, D. M., Woodward, L. J., & Horwood, L. J. (1999). Childhood peer relationship problems and young people's involvement with deviant peers in adolescence. *Journal of Abnormal Child Psychology, 27*(5), 357–369.

Flory, K., Milich, R., Lynam, D. R., Leukefeld, C., & Clayton, R. (2003). Relation between childhood disruptive behavior disorders and substance use and dependence symptoms in young adulthood: Individuals with symptoms of Attention-Deficit/Hyperactivity Disorder and Conduct Disorder are uniquely at risk. *Psychology of Addictive Behaviors, 17*(2), 151–158.

Gilbert, D. G., & Gilbert, B. O. (1995). Personality, psychopathology, and nicotine response as mediators of the genetics of smoking. *Behavior Genetics, 25*(2), 133–147.

Gottesman, I. I. (1963). Genetic aspects of intelligent behavior. In N. R. Ellis (Ed.), *Handbook of mental deficiency: Psychological theory and research* (pp. 253–296). New York: McGraw-Hill.

Gottlieb, G. (1970). Conceptions of prenatal behavior. In L. R. Aronson, E. Tobach, D. S. Lehrman, & L. S. Rosenblatt (Eds.), *Development and evolution of behavior* (pp. 111–137). San Francisco: Freeman.

Gottlieb, G. (1971). Ontogenesis of sensory function in birds and mammals. In E. Tobach, L. R. Aronson, & E. Shaw (Eds.), *The biopsychology of development* (pp. 67–128). New York: Academic Press.

Gottlieb, G. (1976). Conceptions of prenatal development: Behavioral embryology. *Psychological Review, 83*(3), 215–234.

Gottlieb, G. (1991). Experiential canalization of behavioral development: Theory. *Developmental Psychology, 27*, 4–13.

Gottlieb, G. (1992). *Individual development and evolution: The genesis of novel behavior.* New York: Oxford University Press.

Gottlieb, G. (1998). Normally occurring environmental and behavioral influences on gene activity: From central dogma to probabilistic epigenesis. *Psychological Review, 105*, 792–802.

Gottlieb, G. (2002a). Emergence of the developmental manifold concept from an epigenetic analysis of instinctive behavior. In D. Lewkowicz & R. Lickliter (Eds.), *Conceptions of development: Lessons from the laboratory* (pp. 31–56). New York: Psychology Press.

Gottlieb, G. (2002c). Probabilistic epigenesis of development. In J. Valsiner & K. J. Connolly (Eds.), *Handbook of developmental psychology* (pp. 3–17). London: Sage.

Gottlieb, G. (2003). On making behavioral genetics truly developmental. *Human Development, 46*, 337–355.

Gottlieb, G., & Halpern, C. T. (2002). A relational view of causality in normal and abnormal development. *Development and Psychopathology, 14*, 421–435.

Gottlieb, G., Wahlsten, D., & Lickliter, R. (1998). The significance of biology for human development: A developmental psychobiological systems view. In W. Damon (Ed.), *Handbook of child psychology: Theoretical models of human development* (5th ed., Vol. 1, pp. 233–273). New York: Wiley.

Granger, D. A., Weisz, J. R., McCracken, J. T., Ikeda, S. C., & Douglas, P. (1996). Reciprocal influences among adrenocortical activation, psychosocial processes, and the behavioral adjustment of clinic-referred children. *Child Development, 67*, 3250–3262.

Griffiths, S. C., Owens, I. P. F., & Burke, T. (1999). Environmental determination of a sexually selected trait. *Nature, 400*, 358–360.

Gunnar, M. R., & Davis, E. P. (2003). The developmental psychobiology of stress and emotion in early childhood. In R. M. Lerner, M. A. Easterbrooks, & J. Mistry (Eds.), *Comprehensive handbook of psychology: Vol. 6. Developmental psychology* (pp. 113–143). Hoboken, NJ: Wiley.

Gupta, A. P., & Lewontin, R. C. (1982). A study of reaction norms in natural populations of *Drosophila pseudoobscura. Evolution, 36*, 934–948.

Hall, B. K. (1999). *Evolutionary developmental biology* (2nd ed.). Dordrecht, The Netherlands: Klüwer Press.

Hart, E. L., Lahey, B. B., Loeber, R., Applegate, B., & Frick, P. J. (1995). Developmental change in attention-deficit hyperactivity disorder in boys: A four-year longitudinal study. *Journal of Abnormal Child Psychology, 23*(6), 729–749.

Hart, J., Gunnar, M. R., & Cicchetti, D. (1995). Salivary cortisol in maltreated children: Evidence of relations between neuroendocrine activity and social competence. *Development and Psychopathology, 7*, 11–26.

Heath, A. C., Madden, P. A. F., Slutske, W. S., & Martin, N. G. (1995). Personality and the inheritance of smoking behavior: A genetic perspective. *Behavior Genetics, 25*(2), 103–117.

Hinshaw, S. P., & Melnick, S. M. (1995). Peer relationships in boys with attention-deficit hyperactivity disorder with and without comorbid aggression. *Development and Psychopathology, 7*(4), 627–647.

Hood, K. (2005). Development as a dependent variable: Robert B. Cairns on the psychobiology of aggression. In D. M. Stoff & E. J. Susman (Eds.), *Developmental psychobiology of aggression* (pp. 225–251). New York: Cambridge University Press.

Hughes, K. R., & Zubek, J. P. (1956). Effect of glutamic acid on the learning ability of bright and dull rats: I. Administration during infancy. *Canadian Journal of Psychology, 10*, 132–138.

Humphrey-Smith, I., Cordwell, S. J., & Blackstock, W. P. (1997). Proteome research: Complementarity and limitations with respect to the RNA and DNA worlds. *Electrophoresis, 18*, 1217–1242.

Jensen, P. S., Martin, D., & Cantwell, D. P. (1997). Comorbidity in ADHD: Implications for research, practice, and DSM-V. *Journal of the American Academy of Child and Adolescent Psychiatry, 36*(8), 1065–1079.

Johannsen, W. (1909). *Elemente der Exacten Erblichkeitslehre* [Elements of the scientific doctrine of heritability]. Jena, Germany: G. Fischer.

Johnson, M. H. (1997). *Developmental cognitive neuroscience.* Oxford: Basil Blackwell.

Johnson, M. H. (1999). Cortical plasticity in normal and abnormal cognitive development: Evidence and working hypotheses. *Development and Psychopathology, 11,* 419–437.

Johnson, M. H., Halit, H., Grice, S. J., & Karmiloff-Smith, A. (2002). Neuroimaging of typical and atypical development: A perspective from multiple levels of analysis. *Development and Psychopathology, 14,* 521–536.

Kandel, D., & Yamaguchi, K. (1993). From beer to crack: Developmental patterns of drug involvement. *American Journal of Public Health, 83*(6), 851–855.

Kassel, J. D., Stroud, L. R., & Paronis, C. A. (2003). Smoking, stress, and negative affect: Correlation, causation, and context across stages of smoking. *Psychological Bulletin, 129*(2), 270–304.

Kent, L., Middle, F., Hawi, Z., Fitzgerald, M., Gill, M., Feehan, C., et al. (2001). Nicotinic acetylcholine receptor alpha 4 subunit gene polymorphism and attention deficit hyperactivity disorder. *Psychiatric Genetics, 11*(1), 37–40.

Khantzian, E. J. (1997). The self-medication hypothesis of substance use disorders: A reconsideration and recent applications. *Harvard Review of Psychiatry, 4* 231–244.

Kirley, A., Hawi, Z., Daly, G., McCarron, M., Mullins, C., Millar, N., et al. (2002). Dopaminergic system genes in ADHD: Toward a biological hypothesis. *Neuropsychopharmacology, 27*(4), 607–619.

Klein, R. G. (2002). Alcohol, stimulants, nicotine, and other drugs in ADHD. In P. S. Jensen & J. R. Cooper (Eds.), *Attention deficit hyperactivity disorder: State of the science. Best practices* (pp. 16-1–16-17). Livingston, NJ: Civic Research Institute.

Koretz, D. S., & Moscicki, E. K. (1997). An ounce of prevention research: What is it worth? *American Journal of Community Psychology, 25*(2), 189–195.

Kornetsky, C. (1970). Psychoactive drugs in the immature organism. *Psychopharmacologia, 17*(2), 105–136.

Krause, K. H., Dresel, S. H., Krause, J., Kung, H. F., Tatsch, K., & Ackenheil, M. (2002). Stimulant-like action of nicotine on striatal dopamine transporter in the brain of adults with attention deficit hyperactivity disorder. *International Journal of Neuropsychopharmacology, 5*(2), 111–113.

Kuntsi, J., & Stevenson, J. (2000). Hyperactivity in children: A focus on genetic research and psychological theories. *Clinical Child and Family Psychology Review, 3*(1), 1–23.

Lahey, B. B., Applegate, B., McBurnett, K., Biederman, J., Greenhill, L., Hynd, G. W., et al. (1994). DSM-IV field trials for attention deficit hyperactivity disorder in children and adolescents. *American Journal of Psychiatry, 151*(11), 1673–1685.

Lahey, B. B., Schaughency, E. A., Strauss, C. C., & Frame, C. L. (1984). Are attention deficit disorders with and without hyperactivity similar or dissimilar disorders? *Journal of the American Academy of Child Psychiatry, 23*(3), 302–309.

Lambert, N. M. (2002). Stimulant treatment as a risk factor for nicotine use and substance abuse. In P. S. Jensen & J. R. Cooper (Eds.), *Attention deficit hyperactivity disorder: State of the science. Best practices* (pp. 18-11–18-23). Kingston, NJ: Civic Research Institute.

Lambert, N. M., & Hartsough, C. S. (1998). Prospective study of tobacco smoking and substance dependencies among samples of ADHD and non-ADHD participants. *Journal of Learning Disabilities, 31*(6), 533–544.

Lerman, C., Audrain, J., Tercyak, K., Hawk, L. W., Jr., Bush, A., Crystal Mansour, S., et al. (2001). Attention-Deficit Hyperactivity Disorder (ADHD) symptoms and smoking patterns among participants in a smoking-cessation program. *Nicotine and Tobacco Research, 3*(4), 353–359.

Lerman, C., Caporaso, N. E., Audrain, J., Main, D., Bowman, E. D., Lockshin, B., et al. (1999). Evidence suggesting the role of specific genetic factors in cigarette smoking. *Health Psychology, 18*(1), 14–20.

Lerman, C., Caporaso, N. E., Main, D., Audrain, J., Boyd, N. R., Bowman, E. D., et al. (1998). Depression and self-medication with nicotine: The modifying influence of the dopamine D4 receptor gene. *Health Psychology, 17*(1), 56–62.

Lerner, R. M. (2002). *Concepts and theories of human development* (3rd ed.). Mahwah, NJ: Erlbaum.

Levin, E. D., Conners, C. K., Silva, D., Canu, W., & March, J. (2001). Effects of chronic nicotine and methylphenidate in adults with attention deficit/hyperactivity disorder. *Experimental and Clinical Psychopharmacology, 9*(1), 83–90.

Levin, E. D., Conners, C. K., Silva, D., Hinton, S. C., Meck, W. H., March, J., et al. (1998). Transdermal nicotine effects on attention. *Psychopharmacology, 140*(2), 135–141.

Levin, E. D., Conners, C. K., Sparrow, E., Hinton, S. C., Erhardt, D., Meck, W. H., et al. (1996). Nicotine effects on adults with attention-deficit/hyperactivity disorder. *Psychopharmacology, 123*(1), 55–63.

Lewis, M. (1990). Models of developmental psychopathology. In M. Lewis & S. M. Miller (Eds.), *Handbook of developmental psychopathology* (pp. 15–26). New York: Plenum Press.

Loeber, R., Green, S. M., Lahey, B. B., & Stouthamer-Loeber, M. (1989). Optimal informants on childhood disruptive behaviors. *Development and Psychopathology, 1*(4), 317–337.

Loney, J., Kramer, J. R., & Salisbury, H. (2002). Medicated versus unmedicated ADHD children: Adult involvement with legal and illegal drugs. In P. S. Jensen & J. R. Cooper (Eds.), *Attention deficit hyperactivity disorder: State of the science. Best practices* (pp. 17-11–17-15). Kingston, NJ: Civic Research Institute.

Luthar, S. S. (Ed.). (2003). *Resilience and vulnerability: Adaptation in the context of childhood adversities.* Cambridge, England: Cambridge University Press.

Luthar, S. S., Cicchetti, D., & Becker, B. (2000). The construct of resilience: A critical evaluation and guidelines for future work. *Child Development, 71*(3), 543–562.

Lynskey, M. T., & Fergusson, D. M. (1995). Childhood conduct problems, attention deficit behaviors, and adolescent alcohol, tobacco, and illicit drug use. *Journal of Abnormal Child Psychology, 23*(3), 281–302.

Mackay, T. F. C. (2001). Quantitative trait loci in *Drosophila. Nature Reviews-Genetics, 2,* 11–20.

Magnusson, D., & Cairns, R. B. (1996). Developmental science: Toward a unified framework. In R. B. Cairns, G. H. Elder, & E. J. Costello (Eds.), *Developmental science* (pp. 7–30). New York: Cambridge University Press.

Magnusson, D., & Törestad, B. (1993). A holistic view of personality: A model revisited. *Annual Review of Psychology, 44,* 427–452.

Malone, M. A., Kershner, J. R., & Swanson, J. M. (1994). Hemispheric processing and methylphenidate effects in attention-deficit hyperactivity disorder. *Journal of Child Neurology, 9*(2), 181–189.

Mannuzza, S., Klein, R. G., Bonagura, N., Malloy, P., Giampino, T. L., & Addalli, K. A. (1991). Hyperactive boys almost grown up: V. Replication of psychiatric status. *Archives of General Psychiatry, 48*(1), 77–83.

Mannuzza, S., Klein, R. G., Klein, D. F., Bessler, A., & Shrout, P. (2002). Accuracy of adult recall of childhood attention deficit hyperactivity disorder. *American Journal of Psychiatry, 159*(11), 1882–1888.

Marshal, M. P., Molina, B. S. G., & Pelham, W. E. (2003). Childhood ADHD and adolescent substance use: An examination of deviant peer group affiliation as a risk factor. *Psychology of Addictive Behaviors, 17*(4), 293–302.

Masten, A. S., Best, K. M., & Garmezy, N. (1990). Resilience and development: Contributions from the study of children who overcome adversity. *Development and Psychopathology, 2,* 425–444.

Meaney, M. J., Diorio, J., Francis, D., Widdowson, J., LaPlante, P., Caldji, C., et al. (1996). Early environmental regulation of forebrain glucocorticoid receptor gene expression: Implications for adrenocortical responses to stress. *Developmental Neuroscience, 18,* 49–72.

Melnick, S. M., & Hinshaw, S. P. (2000). Emotion regulation and parenting in AD/HD and comparison boys: Linkages with social behaviors and peer preference. *Journal of Abnormal Child Psychology, 28*(1), 73–86.

Mercugliano, M. (1999). Neurotransmitter alterations in Attention-Deficit/Hyperactivity Disorder. *Mental Retardation and Developmental Disabilities, 5,* 220–226.

Milberger, S., Biederman, J., Faraone, S. V., & Chen, L. (1997). ADHD is associated with early initiation of cigarette smoking in children and adolescents. *Journal of the American Academy of Child and Adolescent Psychiatry, 36*(1), 37–44.

Milberger, S., Biederman, J., Faraone, S. V., Chen, L., & Jones, J. (1996). Is maternal smoking during pregnancy a risk factor for attention deficit hyperactivity disorder in children? *American Journal of Psychiatry, 153*(9), 1138–1142.

Milberger, S., Biederman, J., Faraone, S. V., Chen, L., & Jones, J. (1997). Further evidence of an association between attention-deficit/hyperactivity disorder and cigarette smoking: Findings from a high-risk sample of siblings. *American Journal on Addictions, 6*(3), 205–217.

Milberger, S., Biederman, J., Faraone, S. V., Guite, J., & Tsuang, M. T. (1997). Pregnancy, delivery and infancy complications and attention deficit hyperactivity disorder: Issues of gene-environment interaction. *Biological Psychiatry, 41*(1), 65–75.

Milich, R., Balentine, A. C., & Lynam, D. R. (2001). ADHD combined types and ADHD predominately inattentive type are distinct and unrelated disorders. *Clinical Psychology: Science and Practice, 8*(4), 463–488.

Molenaar, P. C. M., Huizenga, H. M., & Nesselroade, J. R. (2003). The relationship between the structure of inter-individual and intra-individual variability: A theoretical and empirical vindication of developmental systems theory. In U. M. Staudinger & U. Lindenberger (Eds.), *Understanding human development* (pp. 339–360). Boston: Klüwer Press.

Molina, B. S. G., & Pelham, W. E. (2003). Childhood predictors of adolescent substance use in a longitudinal study of children with ADHD. *Journal of Abnormal Psychology, 112*(3), 497–507.

Molina, B. S. G., Smith, B. H., & Pelham, W. E. (1999). Interactive effects of attention deficit hyperactivity disorder and conduct disorder on early adolescent substance use. *Psychology of Addictive Behaviors, 13*(4), 348–358.

Mrazek, P., & Haggerty, R. J. (Eds.). (1994). *Reducing risks for mental disorders: Frontiers for preventive intervention research.* Washington, DC: National Academy Press.

Nelson, C. A., & Bloom, F. E. (1997). Child development and neuroscience. *Child Development, 68,* 970–987.

Nolan, E. E., Volpe, R. J., Gadow, K. D., & Sprafkin, J. (1999). Developmental, gender, and comorbidity differences in clinically referred children with ADHD. *Journal of Emotional and Behavioral Disorders, 7*(1), 11–20.

Novak, S. P., & Clayton, R. R. (2001). The influence of school environment and self-regulation on transitions between stages of cigarette smoking: A multilevel analysis. *Health Psychology, 20*(3), 196–207.

Overton, W. F., & Reese, H. W. (1973). Models of development: Methodological implications. In J. R. Nesselroade & H. W. Reese (Eds.), *Life-span developmental psychology* (pp. 65–86). New York: Academic Press.

Pelham, W. E., & Bender, M. E. (1982). Peer relationships in hyperactive children: Description and treatment. *Advances in Learning and Behavioral Disabilities, 1,* 365–436.

Peris, T. S., & Hinshaw, S. P. (2003). Family dynamics and preadolescent girls with ADHD: The relationship between expressed emotion, ADHD symptomatology, and comorbid disruptive behavior. *Journal of Child Psychology and Psychiatry and Allied Disciplines, 44*(8), 1177–1190.

Peters, R. J. G., & Boekholdt, S. M. (2002). Gene polymorphisms and the risk of mycardial infarction: An emerging relation. *New England Journal of Medicine, 347,* 1963–1965.

Platt, S. A., & Sanislow, C. A. (1988). Norm-of-reaction: Definition and misinterpretation of animal research. *Journal of Comparative Psychology, 102,* 254–261.

Pliszka, S. R., McCracken, J. T., & Maas, J. W. (1996). Catecholamines in attention-deficit hyperactivity disorder: Current perspectives. *Journal of the American Academy of Child and Adolescent Psychiatry, 35*(3), 264–272.

Pomerleau, C. S., Downey, K. K., Snedecor, S. M., Mehringer, A. M., Marks, J. L., & Pomerleau, O. F. (2003). Smoking patterns and abstinence effects in smokers with no ADHD, childhood ADHD, and adult ADHD symptomatology. *Addictive Behaviors, 28,* 1149–1157.

Pomerleau, O. F., Downey, K. K., Stelson, F. W., & Pomerleau, C. S. (1995). Cigarette smoking in adult patients diagnosed with attention deficit hyperactivity disorder. *Journal of Substance Abuse, 7*(3), 373–378.

Pope, A. W., Bierman, K. L., & Mumma, G. H. (1991). Aggression, hyperactivity, and inattention-immaturity: Behavior dimensions associated with peer rejection in elementary school boys. *Developmental Psychology, 27*(4), 663–671.

Power, T. J., Andrews, T. J., Eiraldi, R. B., Doherty, B. J., Ikeda, M. J., DuPaul, G. J., et al. (1998). Evaluating attention deficit hyperactivity disorder using multiple informants: The incremental utility of combining teacher with parent reports. *Psychological Assessment, 10*(3), 250–260.

Rezvani, A. H., & Levin, E. D. (2001). Cognitive effects of nicotine. *Biological Psychiatry, 49*(3), 258–267.

Rhode, P., Kahler, C. W., Lewinsohn, P. M., & Brown, R. A. (2004). Psychiatric disorders, family factors, and cigarette smoking: II. Associations with progression to daily smoking. *Nicotine and Tobacco Research, 6*(1), 119–132.

Richters, J. E., Arnold, L. E., Jensen, P. S., Abikoff, H., Conners, C. K., Greenhill, L. L., et al. (1995). NIMH collaborative multisite multimodal treatment study of children with ADHD: I. Background and rationale. *Journal of the American Academy of Child and Adolescent Psychiatry, 34*(8), 987–1000.

Riggs, P. D., Mikulich, S. K., Whitmore, E. A., & Crowley, T. J. (1999). Relationship of ADHD, depression and nontobacco substance use disorders to nicotine dependence in substance-dependent delinquents. *Drug and Alcohol Dependence, 54*(3), 195–205.

Robinson, T. E., & Berridge, K. C. (2000). The psychology and neurobiology of addiction: An incentive-sensitization view. *Addiction, 95*(Suppl. 2), S91–S117.

Rohde, L., Roman, T., Szobot, C., Cunha, R. D., Hutz, M. H., & Biederman, J. (2003). Dopamine transporter gene, response to methylphenidate and cerebral blood flow in attention-deficit/hyperactivity disorder: A pilot study. *Synapse, 48,* 87–89.

Russell, E. S. (1917). *Form and function: A contribution to the history of animal morphology.* New York: Dutton.

Sabol, S. Z., Nelson, M. L., Fisher, C., Gunzerath, L., Brody, C. L., Hu, S., et al. (1999). A genetic association for cigarette smoking behavior. *Health Psychology, 18*(1), 7–13.

Scahill, L., & Schwab Stone, M. (2000). Epidemiology of ADHD in school-age children. *Child and Adolescent Psychiatric Clinics of North America, 9*(3), 541–555.

Shanker, S. (2002). The generativist/interactionist debate over specific language impairment: Psycholinguistics at a crossroads. *American Journal of Psychology, 115,* 415–450.

Smith, B. H., Pelham, W. E., Jr., Gnagy, E., Molina, B., & Evans, S. (2000). The reliability, validity, and unique contributions of self-report by adolescents receiving treatment for attention-deficit/hyperactivity disorder. *Journal of Consulting and Clinical Psychology, 68*(3), 489–499.

Solanto, M. V. (1998). Neuropsychopharmacological mechanisms of stimulant drug action in attention-deficit hyperactivity disorder: A review and integration. *Behavioral Brain Research, 94,* 127–152.

Sonuga-Barke, E. J. (2002). Psychological heterogeneity in AD/HD: A dual pathway model of behavior and cognition. *Behavioral Brain Research, 130,* 29–36.

Suomi, S. J. (2000). A biobehavioral perspective on developmental psychopathology. In A. J. Sameroff, M. Lewis, & S. M. Miller (Eds.), *Handbook of developmental psychopathology* (pp. 237–256). New York: Klüwer Academic/Plenum Press.

Swanson, J. M., Flodman, P., Kennedy, J., Spence, M. A., Moyzis, R., Schuck, S., et al. (2000). Dopamine genes and ADHD. *Neuroscience and Biobehavioral Reviews, 24*(1), 21–25.

Tapert, S. F., Baratta, M. V., Abrantes, A. M., & Brown, S. A. (2002). Attention dysfunction predicts substance involvement in community youths. *Journal of the American Academy of Child and Adolescent Psychiatry, 41*(6), 680–686.

Tercyak, K. P., & Audrain-McGovern, J. (2003). Personality differences associated with smoking experimentation among adolescents with and without comorbid symptoms of ADHD. *Substance Use and Misuse, 38*(14), 1953–1970.

Tercyak, K. P., Lerman, C., & Audrain, J. (2002). Association of attention-deficit/hyperactivity disorder symptoms with levels of cigarette smoking in a community sample of adolescents. *Journal of the American Academy of Child and Adolescent Psychiatry, 41*(7), 799–805.

Tercyak, K. P., Peshkin, B. N., Walker, L. R., & Stein, M. A. (2002). Cigarette smoking among youth with attention-deficit/hyperactivity disorder: Clinical phenomenology, comorbidity, and genetics. *Journal of Clinical Psychology in Medical Settings, 9*(1), 35–50.

Thelen, E. (1990). Dynamical systems and the generation of individual differences. In J. Fagan & J. Colombo (Eds.), *Individual differences in infancy* (pp. 19–43). Hillsdale, NJ: Erlbaum.

Todd, R. D., Lobos, E. A., Sun, L. W., & Neuman, R. J.(2003). Mutational analysis of the nicotinic acetylcholine receptor alpha 4 subunit gene in attention deficit hyperactivity disorder: Evidence for association of an intronic polymorphism with attention problems. *Molecular Psychiatry, 8,* 103–108.

Tucker, D. M., & Williamson, P. A. (1984). Asymmetric neural control systems in human self-regulation. *Psychological Review, 91*(2), 185–215.

Upadhyaya, H. P., Deas, D., Brady, K. T., & Kruesi, M. (2002). Cigarette smoking and psychiatric comorbidity in children and adolescents. *Journal of the American Academy of Child and Adolescent Psychiatry, 41*(11), 1294–1305.

Valsiner, J. (2001). *Comparative study of human cultural development.* Madrid: Fundación Infancia y Aprendizaje.

Venter, J. C., Adams, M. D., Myers, E. W., Li, P. W., Mural, J. R., Sutton, G. G., et al. (2001, February). The sequence of the human genome. *Science, 291,* 1304–1351.

Vreek, G.-J. (2000). Nature, nurture and the future of the analysis of variance. *Human Development, 43,* 32–45.

Waddington, C. H. (1957). *The strategy of the genes.* London: Allen & Unwin.

Wahlsten, D. (1990). Insensitivity of the analysis of variance to heredity-environment interaction. *Behavioral and Brain Sciences, 13,* 109–161.

Wender, P. H. (1975). Speculations concerning a possible biochemical basis of minimal brain dysfunction. *International Journal of Mental Health, 4*(1/2), 11–28.

Whalen, C. K., Jamner, L. D., Henker, B., Delfino, R. J., & Lozano, J. M. (2002). The ADHD spectrum and everyday life: Experience sampling of adolescent moods, activities, smoking, and drinking. *Child Development, 73*(1), 209–227.

Whalen, C. K., Jamner, L. D., Henker, B., Gehricke, J.-G., & King, P. S. (2003). Is there a link between adolescent cigarette smoking and pharmacotherapy for ADHD? *Psychology of Addictive Behaviors, 17*(4), 332–335.

Wilens, T. E. (2002). Attention deficit hyperactivity disorder and substance use disorders: The nature of the relationship, subtypes at risk, and treatment issues. In P. S. Jensen & J. R. Cooper (Eds.), *Attention deficit hyperactivity disorder: State of the science, Best practices* (pp. 19-1–19-17). Livingston, NJ: Civic Research Institute.

Willcutt, E. G., Pennington, B. F., Chhabildas, N. A., Friedman, M. C., & Alexander, J. (1999). Psychiatry comorbidity associated with DSM-IV ADHD in a nonreferred sample of twins. *Journal of the American Academy of Child and Adolescent Psychiatry, 38*(11), 1355–1362.

Williams, J. M., & Ziedonis, D. (2004). Addressing tobacco use among individuals with mental illness or an addiction. *Addictive Behaviors, 29,* 1067–1083.

Winsberg, B. G., & Comings, D. E. (1999). Association of the dopamine transporter gene (DAT1) with poor methylphenidate response. *Journal of the American Academy of Child and Adolescent Psychiatry, 38*(12), 1474–1477.

Wolff, C. F. (1764). *Theorie von der Generation in zwo Abhandlungen.* Berlin: F. W. Birnstiel.

Woltereck, R. (1909). Weitere experimentelle Untersuchungen über Artveränderung, speziell über das Wesen quantitativer Artunterschiede bei Daphniden [Further experimental investigations of species modification, particularly the nature of quantitative species differences in daphnia]. *Verhandlungen der Deutschen Zoologischen Gesellschaft, 19,* 110–173.

Wong, A. H. C., Buckle, C. E., & Van Tol, H. H. M. (2000). Polymorphisms in dopamine receptors: What do they tell us? *European Journal of Pharmacology, 410,* 183–203.

CHAPTER 18

Psychoanalytic Perspectives on Developmental Psychopathology

PETER FONAGY, MARY TARGET, and GEORGE GERGELY

GOALS OF THE CHAPTER

Developmental psychopathology, once the Cinderella of perspectives on mental health even in child psychiatry, has over the past 2 decades become the dominant approach to the study of mental disorder. Emerging findings from longitudinal studies consistently demonstrate that two-thirds to three-fourths of psychological disorders in adulthood are anticipated by childhood psychiatric disturbance (e.g., Kim-Cohen, Caspi, Moffitt, Harrington, & Milne, 2003). This establishes beyond doubt that only a developmental perspective can possibly provide a comprehensive understanding of the nature of mental disorder and offer sufficient information for adequate treatment and prevention.

Psychoanalysis, for better or worse, has exerted considerable influence on developmental psychopathology. Many influential figures in the field of developmental psycho-

pathology received a psychoanalytically orientated clinical training, and others were sympathetic to psychoanalytic ideas. Yet, others were keen to identify crucial differences between the analytic tradition and developmental psychopathology. Psychoanalysis, with its unique if controversial epistemology, continues to have the potential to inform research in developmental psychopathology. The present chapter aims to provide a historical overview of the psychoanalytic approach, taking a dual developmental perspective. We outline the emergence of analytic ideas and the changing assumptions and emphases of the key perspectives between Freud's original discoveries and the present day. In offering this historical overview, we aim to emphasize the contribution that psychoanalytic ideas can make to a developmental understanding of the emergence of psychological disturbance. We critically appraise as well as highlight the contribution of the approaches we consider and evaluate them wherever possible in the context of pertinent empirical evidence. As psychoanalytic formulations were intended to be evaluated in terms of evidence emerging from individual psychotherapeutic treatments rather than systematic empirical studies, often the link to empirical data is suggestive rather than definitive. Nevertheless, we place great emphasis on attempts to make such links in the hope of ensuring that psychodynamic formulations will continue to play a part in theory building and the construction of research questions in the future of this now mature discipline.

THE CENTRAL PLACE OF DEVELOPMENT IN PSYCHOANALYTIC THEORY

Psychoanalysis is all about children. When Sigmund Freud conceived of his "neurotica" he already had a model in mind fundamentally inspired by embryology. When the contemporary analyst addresses unreasonable relational expectations and disturbing preconscious fantasies with her patient, the assumption that she is focusing on childlike modes of thinking runs right through the interaction. The key idea, unchanged since Freud's day, is the notion that pathology is rooted in and in critical respects made up of recapitulated ontogeny. Disorders of the mind are best understood as maladaptive residues of childhood experience, developmentally primitive modes of mental functioning. The developmental point of view is acknowledged by all genuinely psychoanalytic theories to some degree.

For Freud (see S. Freud, 1905/1960, 1914/1957, 1926/1959; S. Freud & Breuer, 1895/1955), the developmental point of view implied that personality types and neurotic symptoms could be linked with specific developmental stages, and that symptoms could be understood in terms of fixations at and regressions to earlier periods of normal development. In Freud's thinking, there was an apparent reversibility between childhood and psychopathology. For example, Freud's theory of narcissism or self-development during infancy was invoked to explain adult psychosis, and conversely, his view of psychic life during infancy was constructed largely on the basis of observations of adult psychopathology. His notion of infantile grandiosity is derived from the grandiosity observed in many instances of psychosis. The presumed confusion, presumed hallucinatory experiences, and lack of reality testing of Freud's infant seem to parallel psychotic experiences.

Alternative clinical foci proposed in accounts of psychological disturbance by contemporary followers of Freud were also based on developmental formulations: Alfred Adler (1916) focused on the child's feelings of inferiority to explain the adult's striving for power and maturity; Ferenczi (1913) wrote of the child's conflicts in developing a

sense of reality as it entailed the simultaneous sacrifice of fantasized omnipotence; Rank (1924) considered the earliest trauma, that of birth, to explain many subsequent human conflicts, defenses, and strivings. More recent psychoanalytic theories continued the developmental motif. Anna Freud (1965) provided a comprehensive model of psychopathology based on the dimensions of normal and abnormal personality development. Melanie Klein (1930, 1935/1984a) offered a radically different perspective both on severe mental disorders and on early child development. Hartmann, Kris, and Loewenstein (1946) focused on the evolution of mental structures necessary for adaptation and elaborated on the common developmental conflicts between mental structures in early childhood. Among the French psychoanalysts, Laplanche (1989) brought a coherent developmental perspective to the emergence of sexuality in infancy. Mahler and her colleagues (Mahler, Pine, & Bergman, 1975) provided a dynamic map of the first 3 years of life and framed a model for the developmental origins of personality disorders. Fairbairn (1952) traced the development of object seeking from immature to mature dependence; E. Jacobson (1964) explored the development of representations of self and other. Kernberg (1975) drew on previous work by M. Klein, Hartmann, and Jacobson to furnish a developmental model of borderline and narcissistic disturbances; Kohut (1971, 1977) constructed a model of narcissistic disturbances based on presumed deficits of early parenting. Relational theorists (e.g., Davies, 1998; S. A. Mitchell, 2000) brought their unique emphasis on active transactional processes to child development, seeing more clearly the parents' unconscious contributions.

Notwithstanding the importance of the developmental perspective for all these theories, the application of knowledge from child development to theorization is centrally flawed by at least two related difficulties. The first concerns unjustified confidence in tracing psychopathology of particular forms to specific phases (an example is the link made between Borderline Personality Disorder and the rapprochement subphase of separation and individuation). The second relates to the overemphasis on early experience, which is frequently found to be at odds with developmental data. Westen et al. (1990a, 1990b) are particularly clear in their evidence that pathological processes of self-representation and object relationships actually characterize developmental phases far later than those that have traditionally concerned psychoanalytic theoreticians. The emphasis on deficits in preverbal periods is a particular problem for psychoanalytic theory because it places so many of the hypotheses beyond any realistic possibility of empirical testing.

Peterfreund (1978) pointed out that there were problems with "adultomorphising infancy," which he felt was a dominant tendency in psychoanalytic developmental theory. This was the tendency to use hypotheses about later states of psychopathology to describe early stages of development. Certainly, if an adult behaved as an infant does, he or she could be described as being in a state of fusion, narcissism, omnipotence, Autism, symbiosis, or as being disoriented and as having hallucinatory experiences and delusions. But logically untenable accounts are produced if an adult-oriented system is used to describe the infant's functioning given his or her limited behavioral possibilities. Some of the regressive manifestations associated with psychosis have no real counterpart in normal development. It has been pointed out that we cannot know what the infant experiences (Stechler & Kaplan, 1980). Thus, it is hard to see how empirical evidence in support of psychoanalytic claims can ever be compiled (A. Green, 2000; Wolff, 1996). Clinically based developmental accounts also tend to mirror the metapsychological commitment of the author to, for example, a drive versus an object relationship-based theory (compare the accounts of Anna Freud and Melanie Klein). Psychoanalytic metapsychology is anyway at best loosely coupled to clinical observations (Gill, 1976; Holt, 1976; G. S. Klein, 1976b; Schafer, 1976), and so it cannot provide an independent test of developmental theory.

Identifying what appear to be childlike modes of mental functioning in individuals with severe disorders, such as Borderline Personality Disorder or Schizophrenia, cannot be taken as evidence for the persistence or regressive recurrence of early pathogenic experiences. Even if putative pathogenic mechanisms such as horizontal splitting (Kohut, 1971) or identity diffusion (Erikson, 1956; Kernberg, 1967) in some way represented early modes of thought, this in no way implies that their reemergence in adult mental functioning is indicative of a developmental timetable. For example, infantile modes of cognition may be evoked in relation to later rather than earlier trauma (Fonagy, 1996). In a review of psychoanalytic theorization about Schizophrenia, Willick (2001) provided a number of current examples from the literature that illustrate that this criticism applies not only to past psychoanalytic theory but also to some work being done today. The general lack of sophistication concerning the process of development in psychoanalysis, the subtle intertwining of phase-specific processes, the qualitative leaps forward as emergent integration brings fresh ways of seeing the world within the grasp of the child, is probably part of a broader epistemic problem that restricts legitimate psychoanalytic theorization to a phenomenon accessible to the analyst through transference and countertransference. There are cogent arguments against the wholesale integration of studies of infant behavior into psychoanalytic theory (A. Green, 2000;

Wolff, 1996). However, by distinguishing between content and mechanism, representation and process (Fonagy, Moran, Edgcumbe, Kennedy, & Target, 1993), we can make excellent use of developmental data to deepen our psychoanalytic understanding of psychological disturbance.

Recent longitudinal, epidemiological birth cohort studies have provided dramatic confirmation that psychoanalysts were on the right track when they emphasized the developmental perspective in their understanding of the clinical problems they faced with their adult patients (Hofstra, van der Ende, & Verhulst, 2002; Kim-Cohen et al., 2003). These studies show that in the vast majority of cases, adult psychopathology is antedated by diagnosable childhood disturbance. Across adult disorders, 75% had a diagnosable childhood problem (Kim-Cohen et al., 2003). It is impossible to conceive of adult problems without considering the development of vulnerabilities, biological and psychosocial, that antedate the disturbance. In fact, there seems to be no other realistic way of thinking of psychopathology other than developmentally (Munir & Beardslee, 1999). However, this only makes the task of examining the status of psychoanalytic theorization from a developmental perspective all the more urgent. In this chapter, we explore the developmental aspects of the major theoretical traditions within psychoanalysis.

FREUD AND THE ESTABLISHMENT OF THE DEVELOPMENTAL PSYCHOANALYTIC TRADITION

Freud's move away from his seduction hypothesis in favor of his second model, which emphasized fantasy determined by the biological drive state, took his attention away from social determinants of development and mental disorder. It led him (S. Freud, 1905/1953) to try to explain all behavior in terms of the failure of the child's mental apparatus to deal adequately with the pressures inherent in a maturationally predetermined sequence of drive states. Adult psychopathology, dreaming, jokes, and slips of the tongue were all seen as the revisiting of unresolved childhood conflicts over sexuality (S. Freud, 1900/1966, 1901/1960, 1905/1960). Freud was the first to give meaning to mental disorder by linking it to childhood experiences (S. Freud & Breuer, 1895/1957) and to the vicissitudes of the developmental process (S. Freud, 1900/1966). One of his greatest contributions was undoubtedly the recognition of infantile sexuality (R. Green, 1985). Freud's discoveries radically altered our perception of the child from one of idealized innocence to that of a person (S. Freud, 1933/1964) struggling to achieve control over his or her biological needs and make them acceptable to society through the microcosm of his or her family (S. Freud, 1930/1961).

S. Freud's (1920/1955, 1922/1961, 1926/1959) third major shift in thinking once again gave a prominent place to the influence of the social environment in analytic theory. This new structural theory long outlasted Freud. In particular, the dual instinct theory provided a compelling fit with clinical observational data (S. Freud, 1920/1955). For example, full recognition was given to the significance for psychopathology of the child's struggle with innate destructive and self-destructive forces (the "death instinct"). S. Freud (1926/1959) also at this time revised his view of anxiety. He now saw it as a psychological state linked to the perception of internal (instinctual or moral) or external danger rather than an epiphenomenal experience associated with inhibited biological drives. The fear of helplessness resulting from loss (loss of the mother, of her esteem, loss of a body part, or loss of self-regard) was specified as the danger situation. This revision recast the theory in more cognitive terms (Schafer, 1983), restoring adaptation to the external world as an essential part of the psychoanalytic account. S. Freud (1926/1959, p. 162) nonetheless retained the concept of a more primitive form of anxiety that would arise in an involuntary, automatic way "whenever a danger situation analogous to birth" occurred. It is this automatic pervasive anxiety and the associated state of overwhelming helplessness that is warded off with the help of "signal anxiety." This prompts the ego to limit the threat of a basic danger situation (see Yorke, Kennedy, & Wiseberg, 1981).

Some developmental evidence supports the central role Freud gave to anxiety in the context of the structural model. Although not a universal finding, the pattern of depression preceded by anxiety occurs sufficiently often to emphasize the fundamental nature of anxiety for psychological disorders. For example, Anxiety Disorder precedes recurrent familial Major Depression in adulthood in most cases (Warner, Weissman, Mufson, & Wickramaratne, 1999). The opposite pattern of depression leading to anxiety has not been seen as a developmental pattern (Zahn-Waxler, Klimes-Dougan, & Slattery, 2000).

This final revision in Freud's thinking resulted in a developmental framework based around the tripartite structural schema of id, ego, and superego (S. Freud, 1922/1961, 1933/1964, 1940/1964). The hypothesis that conflicts within the human mind is chiefly organized around three themes—(1) wish versus moral injunction, (2) wish versus reality, and (3) internal reality versus external reality—has had extraordinary explanatory power. Notably, the ego's capacity to create defenses became the cornerstone of psychoanalytic theorization and clinical work in the United States (Hartmann et al., 1946) and Britain (A. Freud, 1936).

There are many limitations to Freud's developmental model. The many later elaborations of psychoanalytic theories bear testament both to cultural differences in psychological theory and the need of subsequent theorists to make their own contributions. It can be argued that the most important post-Freudian contributions have been in the domains of the cultural and social contexts of development; the significance of early childhood experiences; the developmental significance of the real behavior of the real parents; the role of dependency, attachment, and safety in development alongside the role of instinctual drives; the synthesizing function of the self; and the importance of the nonconflictual aspects of development. Freud's contemporaries pointed out many of these shortcomings, frequently moving away from organized psychoanalysis under a cloud (at least as far as Freud was concerned). Their association with these themes, along with their distancing from psychoanalysis, may have delayed general consideration of their ideas within organized psychoanalysis. For example, Jung's (1912, 1916, 1923) rejection of libido theory led to a neglect of his undoubted advances in the understanding of narcissism and his development of a theory of the self throughout the life cycle.

The picture concerning empirical evidence for Freud's developmental model is not as bleak as many critics think (e.g., Crews, 1996; Webster, 1995). Westen (1998; Westen & Gabbard, 2002a, 2002b) demonstrated that there exists substantial empirical support for Freud's core construct: that human consciousness cannot account for its maladaptive actions. A similar position has been adopted by the outstanding neuroscientist and Freud scholar Mark Solms (1997a, 1997b). There is good evidence for Freud's basic proposition that much of complex mental life is not conscious, that people can think, feel, and experience motivational forces without being aware of them and can therefore also experience psychological problems that they find puzzling. Freud's claim that unconsciously we are in some ways capable of more complex mental operations is supported by literally thousands of research findings, even if the unconscious that such studies point to is composed of processing structures that share little with Freud's original postulate of nonconscious mentation (Kihlstrom, 1987). There is an extensive literature on nonconscious priming, where words are presented briefly, followed by ambiguous stimulus (e.g., the word "bank" when preceded by the word "river" would cause participants to interpret it as a river bank). The interpretation of the ambiguous stimulus could be biased by the prime, even if the participant was not aware of having seen or heard it (Marcel, 1983a, 1983b). Participants in another experiment who were asked to compose a ballad after hearing a series of ballads could follow double the number of rules of ballads in their composition compared to rules they could consciously articulate (Rubin, Wallace, & Houston, 1993).

Much current cognitive science research is focused on how memory can determine behavior implicitly, rather than through remembering a particular episode. Work on procedural, or implicit, memory demonstrates that we act in certain ways because of experience, despite our inability to recall those particular experiences (e.g., Squire & Kandel, 1999). Milner, Squire, and Kandel (1998) describe not one but five memory systems that retain information about experience without conscious knowledge of the experiences that led to the registration of the memories. They are neurologically distinct in location. Thus, whereas explicit memory is underpinned by the hippocampus and related structures, emotional responses are encoded in the neocortex and priming biases in perception are mediated by the sensory neocortex. The separateness of these systems is borne out by lesion studies. Ample evidence is available from research on brain damage that processing relevant to emotional experience can take place outside awareness. An example is an experiment where individuals with hemifield neglect (consistently ignoring one half of the visual field) were presented with two pictures of a house. In one picture, the house was depicted as on fire in the half of the visual field of which they had no awareness (Halligan & Marshall, 1991). The patients could not detect and failed to report a difference between the house that was on fire and the house that was not. Nevertheless, they all said they would prefer to live in the house that was not depicted as being on fire. From a developmental point of view, it is essential that we appreciate that implicit procedural memories are formed from the earliest time, whereas episodic declarative memory processes mature slowly (Nelson, 1993). It follows from this that early childhood experiences are likely to be "remembered" in the sense of implicitly influencing behavior. Yet the experiences that have led to these memories are forever lost. The classical illustration of this process is Claparde's patient who suffered from Korsakoff's syndrome. As is well-known, as part of a demonstration, Claparde shook hands with his patient, pricking her with a pin hidden in his hand. The patient, though having no conscious memory of the experience, declined to shake hands with him the next day. She was aware of her fear of him, but not of the reason why. We can understand this all too well from a neuroscience perspective. The amygdala, unlike the hippocampus, rarely forgets, is implicit, is impressionistic rather than accurate, is nonconscious, and is augmented rather than inhibited by cortisol

(LeDoux, 1996). Thus, although early childhood trauma is unlikely to be remembered because of the immaturity of the memory system, the impact of stress on the functioning of the hippocampus at the time of that experience may affect memory functioning because of the impact of stress hormones on the neural structures underpinning memory. Freud's original observations of the absence of an explicit memory in the presence of emotional remembering may be an artifact of such neuropsychological constellations.

There are many other similarities between Freud's theory of affect and modern ideas such as those of Damasio (1999), LeDoux (1995, 1999), and Panksepp (1998, 2001; for a review of this work, see Westen & Gabbard, 2002a, 2002b). Such "verification" of the psychoanalytic model is in itself fascinating, but knowledge of brain-mind relations are not yet at the point where verification is realistic. Solms and Nersessian (1999, p. 91) themselves admit that "a psychological model only becomes accessible to physical methods of investigation once the neural correlates of the components of the model have been identified." Particularly lacking is detailed knowledge of the developmental changes in neural substrates or psychobehavioral manifestations of specific emotion systems that could enable such direct translations (see Panksepp, 2001). The time will come when Freud's model will be judged against the discoveries of neuroscience. Until then, consistency with experimental and developmental psychological observations is an important and appropriate aim.

THE STRUCTURAL APPROACH

The dominant psychoanalytic model in the United States during much of the second half of the past century was the so-called structural model. The term derives from Freud's emphasis on delineating the three psychic structures of id, ego, and superego, and attempting to explain mental disorder as conflicts between these agencies. Within the structural model, the structure of the ego is emphasized over id and superego and mental disorder is seen partially as a failure of adaptation to internal and external conflict.

The Repositioning of Development in Psychoanalysis

The *ego psychological approach* represents an essential repositioning of psychoanalytic developmental ideas. A dominant tradition of North American psychoanalysis extending over a 60-year period, it is impossible to provide an adequate summary of the many complex ideas to emerge from this school. Our focus is on the key advances of relevance to the developmental perspective and their implications for a model of psychopathology.

Hartmann (1939, p. 25) pointed out that behavior originating at one point in development may serve an entirely different function later on (the concept of the "change of function"). Persistence of dependent behavior in adulthood cannot be treated as if it were a simple repetition of the individual's early relationship with the mother. The same behavior in the adult is likely to be independent of the original drive and may serve quite different functions; in other words, it will have achieved "secondary autonomy" (Hartmann, 1950). The failure to recognize this change has been termed the "genetic fallacy" (Hartmann, 1955, p. 221). The critical adjustments to developmental theory were the twin concepts of primary and secondary autonomy in the ego. Whereas for Freud the ego depended on and only gradually differentiated from the id, for Hartmann and his colleagues (1946) the ego evolved out of an undifferentiated matrix from which the id and superego also emerged, and had autonomous functions that were independent of the id instincts, although these autonomous functions were still thought of as having their own evolutionary design and as being innately based. From the standpoint of aligning psychoanalytic theory with current neuroscience models, this was a critical move in that ego psychologists point to the innate (even modular) design of psychological capacities that involve subsystems of physical and social reality testing. In Hartmann's (Hartmann et al., 1949) model, the ego will remain to some degree linked with the id because it uses energy from the drives. As aggressive impulses are more dangerous than libidinal ones, their neutralization in the course of development is vital. Without it, good object relations are inconceivable and the possibility of defense is forestalled, possibly leading to psychotic illness. Structural developmental theory is psychosocial in that Hartmann and his colleagues conceived of development as relying on an "average expectable environment" that affirms the importance of the actual parent. Development is seen as driven by a maturational pull and fixation in development that is as characteristic of ego as of id development. Individual differences in cognitive function that pervade personality may be understood as the consequence of developmental arrests in specific phases of ego development (Arlow, 1985; Brenner, 1982). Ego regressions, reactivation of developmentally earlier modes of functioning, may be maladaptive but can also serve as adaptive goals, such as artistic or scientific creativity (Blos, 1962; Kris, 1952).

Erik Erikson (1950) was primarily concerned with the interaction of social norms and biological drives in generating self and identity. His well-known description of eight developmental stages, later stages assuming the mastery of earlier ones, was based on biological events that disrupt the equilibrium between drives and social adjustment, cultural and family factors. He conceived of development as covering the entire life cycle. His stress on the basic need for a coherent self-concept only fulfilled in a supportive social milieu anticipated psychoanalytic ideas of the 1960s and 1970s (E. Jacobson, 1964; Kohut, 1971; Stechler & Kaplan, 1980). He extended Freud's problematic erotogenic zone concept to a more subtle idea of "organ modes" (Erikson, 1959). The particular body part involved in a form of drive pleasure and drive expression also defined a mode of functioning. Thus, although the oral drive is initially expressed through the ingestion of milk, the mode of functioning that persists is one of taking in through eyes and ears. The concept of mode of functioning enabled Erikson to stay within the drive model but introduce enduring constructs such as identity, generativity, and basic trust.

Basic trust is defined as the capacity to receive and accept what is given. By emphasizing the interactive, psychosocial aspects of development, Erikson replaced excitement as the organizing construct of psychoanalytic developmental theory with a view that was inherently interpersonal and transactional in nature, organized around the child's development of a sense of self. Westen (1998) considered investigations of Eriksonian concepts of identity (Marcia, 1994), intimacy (Orlofsky, 1993), and generativity (Bradley, 1997) to have been some of the most methodologically sound studies inspired by psychoanalytic theories of development. Erikson (1950) suggested that seemingly insignificant experiences would eventually combine, leading to

> the firm establishment of enduring patterns for the balance of basic trust over basic mistrust. . . . [The] amount of trust derived from earliest infantile experience does not seem to depend on absolute quantities of food or demonstrations of love, but rather on the quality of the maternal relationship. (1959, p. 63)

This remarkable insight foreshadowed what we now understand about the creation of semantic memories (Schachter, 1996) and features in an important way in Bowlby's (1980) concept of internal working models.

Spitz (1959) proposed that major shifts in psychological organization, marked by the emergence of new behaviors and new forms of affective expression (organizers), occur when functions are brought into new relation with one another and are linked into a coherent unit. The way these organizers herald dramatic changes in interpersonal interactions was elaborated by Robert Emde (1980a, 1980b, 1980c). Spitz (1945, 1965) was one of the first to ascribe primary importance to the mother-infant interaction as a force in quickening the development of the child's innate abilities and to describe the role of self-regulatory processes such as the internal regulation of affect protecting the individual from psychological disturbance (Spitz, 1957).

Edith Jacobson (1964) creatively assumed that, because early drive states shifted continuously between the object and the self, a state of primitive fusion existed between early object and self-representations. Jacobson suggested that introjections and identificatory processes replaced the state of primitive fusion and that, through these, traits and actions of objects became internalized parts of self-images. Jacobson applied her developmental perspective to a wide variety of disorders, most particularly to depression, which she recognized as associated with the gap between self-representation and ego ideal.

Hans Loewald was probably the most influential reformist of the North American psychoanalytic tradition. Loewald (1971/1980c, 1973/1980b) proposed a developmental model that has at its center a motive force toward "integrative experience." Organizing activity defines the "basic way of functioning of the psyche." His fundamental assumption was that all mental activity is relational (both interactional and intersubjective; see Loewald, 1971/1980c, 1971/1980d). Internalization (learning) is the basic psychological process that propels development (Loewald, 1973/1980b). Loewald shifted emphasis from structures to processes, de-emphasizing metapsychology. He generated a subtle revision of the classical model that had internalization, understanding, and interpretation at its center (Cooper, 1988).

The Structural Model of Developmental Psychopathology

The structural model locates the origins of neurosis and psychosis at the point when an individual adult's urge to gratify drives reverts to a previously outgrown infantile mode of satisfaction. The symptoms that arise are compromises reflecting the many attempts of the ego to restore equilibrium between the opposing agencies of ego and superego and the unacceptable drive representations. As a result of psychological or organic problems, the ego itself may regress, with resultant pathology. In psychosis, there is a threat of total dissolution of the ego. If the ego resumes functioning characteristic of early childhood, it will come to be dominated by irrational, magical thoughts and uncontrolled impulses. Mental illness thus can be viewed as a

failure of the ego to maintain harmonious interaction between psychic agencies at age-appropriate levels.

A pathogenic sequence for neurotic problems may be delineated as follows: (1) frustration, (2) regression, (3) internal incompatibility, (4) signal anxiety, (5) defense by regression, (6) return of the repressed, and (7) compromise and symptom formation. Characteristic modes of compromise formation and specific developmental fixations result in particular neurotic reactions. The compromise in conversion hysteria reflects an oral or phallic fixation and is dramatically represented in a somatic form. In obsessional neurosis, it is assumed that the ego transforms anal sadistic and aggressive drive derivatives into secondary process thinking such as ruminations and obsessional doubts. The ego is developmentally unable to neutralize these drive derivatives. Aggression and anal concerns will remain apparent and result in massive anxieties (see, e.g., Fenichel, 1945; Glover, 1948). The process of neurotic compromise is seen as located in the thought processes themselves. On the other hand, the fear is externalized in the case of phobias, still possibly reflecting similar unconscious developmental concerns.

One way personality disorders were understood in structural theory was as character neuroses (Alexander, 1930). Here, despite dynamic similarity to neurosis, compromise formations are not split off from the ego and thus the symptoms are not experienced as ego alien or ego dystonic (see Waelder, 1960). The obsessional character neurosis shows better tolerance of the drive derivatives, although it otherwise reflects this compromise between id derivatives, ego, and superego. Another explanation is in terms of ego developmental arrest, deviations, or disharmonies that result in more severe personality disorders, such as Narcissistic Personality Disorder (see A. Freud, 1965). Faulty ego development is seen as at the root in the structural view (see J. Frank, 1956; Gitelson, 1955; Rangell, 1955). Patients may have a semblance of normality as some ego functions maintain their integrity despite impairment of important ego functions, such as reality testing, anxiety tolerance, and stable defenses.

Knight (1953, p. 6) proposed that Borderline Personality Disorder (BPD) resulted from trauma that impaired ego functions such as "integration, concept formation, judgment, realistic planning, and defending against eruption into conscious thinking of id impulses and their fantasy elaborations." In his developmental sequence of identity formation, Erikson (1956, 1959) described the syndrome of identity diffusion (a lack of temporal continuity of self-experience in social contexts). E. Jacobson (1964) described how, at times, individuals with BPD attach their mental and body self to external objects.

Both the problems and the strengths of the structural model are highlighted in psychoanalytic writings concerning Antisocial Personality Disorder (ASPD). The association between social deprivation and ASPD was initially explained as deprivation impeding the renunciation of the pleasure principle (Aichhorn, 1925) and pathological superego function (Fenichel, 1945; W. Reich, 1933). This was further specified as gaps in the superego (superego lacunae) that were believed to occur because of the parent's unconscious wish to act out forbidden impulses (Johnson & Szurek, 1952). Whereas a severe superego with a strong ego ideal was thought to generate depression, a menacing superego and a weak ego ideal led to ASPD. But many of these theoretical suggestions sound very like clinical descriptions. Thus, an absence of guilt concerning antisocial behavior is part of the definition of antisocial personality (Hare & Cox, 1987). Some more recent evidence, however, is in line with these classical works. Supporting Reich's and Fenichel's suggestions, it has been found that the presence of anxiety (autonomic reactivity) in antisocial youth reduces the risk of adult criminal behavior (Raine, Venables, & Williams, 1995). Recent behavior genetics research findings support the observations by Lampl-de-Groot (1949) that depression and antisocial behavior show closeness and opposition. Depressive symptoms and antisocial behavior share common genetic influences and may co-occur because of common genetic roots that increase vulnerability to both these types of problems (O'Connor, McGuire, Reiss, & Hetherington, 1998).

Structural theorists see psychotic symptoms as regressions to normal but very early functioning. Severe ego impairments are seen as being caused by some basic fault in laying down psychic structure during infancy. In Greenacre's (1953, p. 10) view, "The matrix of these severe disturbances lay in the disturbances in that period at the very dawn of the ego, roughly around 6 months and a little later." However, modern developmental observations are inconsistent with the notion of a "normal" confusional state between self and object (Gergely, 1992, 2000). It has been shown that from birth, infants are able to accurately identify their mother and even to imitate facial gestures (Meltzoff & Moore, 1997).

Evaluation of the Structural Model

The structural model, once coterminous with psychoanalysis in the United States, is now all but extinct. Change in the notion of the id undoubtedly foreshadowed its demise. Contemporary structural theorists (see, e.g., Loewald, 1971/ 1980c, 1971/1980d, 1978, 1978/1980a) typically have reinterpreted Freud's concept from a container of all biologically based intense physical desires to an organization related to reality and human figures. The original model was criticized in the 1970s and 1980s for its quasi-physiological character (Compton, 1981; G. S. Klein, 1976a; Rosenblatt & Thickstun, 1977), its homophobic outlook (Schafer, 1974), and the primacy it gave to sexuality in explanations of psychopathology (M. Klein, 1980; Peterfreund, 1978).

The major criticisms of drive theory as being reductionist, biologically naïve, and overinfluenced by the naïve physiology of nineteenth-century Central Europe (Rosenblatt & Thickstun, 1977) have been tempered by more recent reviews of drive theory. Repeated exposure to various drugs of dependence results in sensitization of a specific neural pathway in the brain (the dopaminergic ventral tegmental pathway) that forms the substrate for intense motivations (Berridge & Robinson, 1995). Howard Shevrin (1997) has linked the "wanting system," identified as abnormally sensitized (oversensitive) in drug-dependent individuals, with the ego psychological notion of psychic energy and drives. Further evidence comes from Panksepp's (1998) description of the anatomically linked (Shevrin, 2001) "SEEKING system" (also described as "psychic energisation"; Panksepp, p. 145), which prompts an animal to explore very energetically and self-stimulate endlessly to achieve the state of expectance without needing to fulfill the drive. There is a subjective state of pure anticipation embodied in this system, with no apparent object. A state of wanting exists that later, through processing in more advanced brain systems, acquires an object and mental representation. Finally, the neuropsychological work of Solms (1997a, 2000), linked with recent radiological and pharmacological findings, implies that the brain stem mechanisms that are known to control the REM state can generate dreams only through the mediation of a second, probably dopaminergic, forebrain mechanism. Solms suggests that the dopaminergic ventral tegmental pathways are the initiators of dreaming and that the pathway from the ventral tegmental area connecting the amygdala, septal area, cingulate gyrus, and frontal cortex is the final common path to dreaming. The system that is sensitized in drug addiction is identified by Solms as the neural system forming the substrate for the motivational impetus for dreaming. The neural systems that activate dreaming and that activate craving are thus identical. Each and every dream, however, starts in the neural structure that most closely fits Freud's concept of instinctual drive states: the ventral tegmental area.

SPECIFIC STRUCTURAL DEVELOPMENTAL PERSPECTIVES

Three psychoanalysts, two from the United Kingdom and one from the United States, have made critical contributions to psychoanalytic developmental theory. All three have started from the basis of the structural approach, but all three ended up modifying the structural tradition in various ways.

Anna Freud and Developmental Psychopathology

Anna Freud (1965) was the first psychoanalyst to adopt a coherent developmental perspective on psychopathology. However, her view of development was classically Freudian, in that she saw developmental progress as a child coming to terms with developmentally expectable conflicts, where the child has to find a compromise among diverse wishes, needs, perceptions, physical and social realities, and object relations. Anna Freud took her father's theory forward by identifying ways that the parent contributed to the construction of the child's ego or superego, but she always subordinated this process to the overriding principle of the search for drive satisfaction.

She provided a comprehensive developmental theory using the metaphor of developmental lines to stress the continuity and cumulative character of child development (A. Freud, 1962, 1963). In her initial presentation of this view, six developmental lines were considered, of which the developmental line from dependency to emotional self-reliance and adult relationships was considered the most fundamental. Other lines included the movement from egocentrism to social partnerships, from sucking to rational eating, and from irresponsibility to responsibility in body management. Anna Freud (1974) added other lines in later papers, for example, from animate to inanimate objects and from irresponsibility to guilt.

The lines emphasize observable behavior at the same time as specifying the internal psychic development necessary for the achievement of each step along each line. The lines were not designed to provide a new metapsychology but to reduce the complexity of understanding development through identifying specific sequences of progress (Neubauer, 1984).

Pathology is assessed in terms of large discrepancies among the lines and notable lags with respect to normal progress along each line. Developmental lines have etiological significance, with unevenness of development being regarded as a risk factor for psychiatric disturbance. Arrest or regression in a particular developmental line can be the formulation for a child's problem (A. Freud, 1965). Clinically,

in addressing a child's disturbance, the psychoanalytic clinician should offer "developmental help" to the child, restoring him or her to "the path of normal development" as well as focusing on the determinants of the child's symptoms (Fonagy, Miller, Edgcumbe, Target, & Kennedy, 1993; A. Freud, 1970b, 1983; H. Kennedy & Moran, 1991).

Developmental lines were used to describe a range of pathologies that emerged between neurotic and psychotic states, preneurotic nonconflictual disorders. An analogy may be made between this group of disorders and personality disorder in adults. Anna Freud (1965, pp. 148–154) identified disturbances of narcissism, object relatedness, and the absence of control over aggressive or self-destructive tendencies alongside a range of deficiencies of development. This prescient developmental perspective, however, was never properly reconciled with structural theory.

Anna Freud (1970a) also suggested that there was a developmental aspect to the emergence of anxiety problems in childhood. Both the content and the quality of fears changed with the developmental phase. Earlier fears, with less advanced ego development, were more intense, more likely to be rooted in fear of loss of the object. Later-emerging fears, such as fears of operations, robbers, and ghosts, are more likely to be rooted in Oedipal anxieties. Anxiety can turn into guilt with full development of the superego. There is, however, little evidence to support the notion that affects are more primitive at early stages of development (see also Emde, 1980b, 1980c; Stern, 1985).

A further developmental distinction was made by Anna Freud between "objective anxiety" (such as fear of any aspect of the external world, including the parents' real reactions) and fear of the internal world (impulses, wishes, and feelings; Sandler & Freud, 1985). She noted in the work of the Hampstead war nurseries (A. Freud & Burlingham, 1944) that children and adults showed different reactions to external threat. Children were less likely to be traumatized by being bombed if during this experience they were with their mother and if the mother remained calm. An extremely carefully conducted study of children's reactions to Scud missile attacks in Israel provides more recent support for this finding (Laor et al., 1996). The study showed that if the child's mother showed significant reactive symptoms, the child was far more likely also to show prolonged symptoms of anxiety following the attack.

Anna Freud's concept of ego restriction was substantially elaborated in her later work on developmental deficits. Severe personality disorders were considered as characterized by developmental deviations or disharmonies, such as deficits in reality testing, development of defenses, anxiety tolerance, superego strength, and so on. Inadequate maternal response to an infant's instinctual needs causes dangers and external conflict (Yorke, Wiseberg, & Freeman, 1989). This disharmony between need and environment will be most acute when the developing structure is not yet capable of sustaining the pressures resulting from the consequent internal and external stresses.

Anna Freud should perhaps be described as a modern structural theorist. Her model is fundamentally developmental. The individual is seen as capable of moving back along developmental lines if that is needed to deal with some current, potentially overwhelming challenge. The individual can then move forward again. Here there is no equation of behavior and pathology; a given behavior may not be a true symptom, but a temporary blip. The notions of mobility of function and the meaning of behavior are key assumptions of broader developmental approaches to psychopathology (Cicchetti & Cohen, 1995; Garmezy & Masten, 1994).

Anna Freud and Dorothy Burlingham showed, for psychoanalysts, an unusual commitment to the observational method. Many findings from Anna Freud's observational work during the war in the Hampstead nurseries (1941 to 1945) are consistent with contemporary developmental research. This includes the development of an attachment relationship during the first 6 months of life, the rise in ambivalence to the caregiver between 6 and 12 months, the impact of trauma and its psychic impact (Posttraumatic Stress Disorder), the parent's use of withdrawal of affection to socialize the child, and the early sociability of the infant. She also initiated fascinating research follow-up studies (Bennett & Hellman, 1951; Burlingham, 1952; Burlingham & Barron, 1963; Hellman, 1962; H. E. Kennedy, 1950).

However, Anna Freud's insistence on the literal use of her father's structural model of drives limits the usefulness of her model. She regarded drive fixation, the balance between the three structures of the mind, id, ego, and superego and so on as the most scientific aspects of her father's contribution and was loath to abandon them. But her revision of the structural model is hidden behind her modesty about her innovation. Masten and Curtis (2000) draw attention to the two historically rich traditions of the study of the development of competence and psychopathology, both of which are present in the history of psychiatry and psychoanalysis but are not commonly integrated. Development of competence has remained the domain of developmental psychology, and disturbance and dysfunction have been in the realm of child and adult psychiatry. Perhaps Anna Freud's corpus is a notable exception to this tendency to separate competence from pathology (Masten & Coatsworth, 1995).

Margaret Mahler and the Pathology of Separation-Individuation Processes

Margaret Mahler, with Rene Spitz, was the first thoroughgoing developmentalist of the North American tradition. She elaborated a psychoanalytic model of development based on observations of 6-month to 3-year-old children. Mahler's (Mahler & Furer, 1968, Mahler et al., 1975) developmental model sees object relations and the self as elaborations of instinctual vicissitudes. Her focus is on the move from the unity of "I" and "not-I" to eventual separation and individuation. She holds that the "biological birth of the human infant and the psychological birth of the individual are not coincident in time" (Mahler et al., 1975, p. 3). Separation, in Mahler's model, refers to the child's emergence from a symbiotic fusion with the mother, whereas "individuation consists of those achievements marking the child's assumption of his own individual characteristics" (p. 4).

Mahler's developmental model is as follows:

1. The first weeks of life are considered a stage of "normal Autism." The infant is assumed to be surrounded by an autistic shell that keeps external stimuli out.

2. The symbiotic phase, beginning in the 2nd and 3rd months, is a state of undifferentiated fusion with the mother with a common delusional somatopsychic boundary. This phase is regarded as the basic source of benevolent feelings about the self and toward the object and is the reference for checking back perceptually and emotionally in later phases.

3. Separation-individuation begins with the subphase of differentiation (of the body image; Mahler & Furer, 1968; Mahler et al., 1975).

4. From 9 months to about 15 to 18 months is the second subphase of separation-individuation: practicing. This is thought to be characterized by a sense of omnipotence derived from sharing mother's magical powers, practicing locomotion, and returning for emotional refueling.

5. The rapprochement subphase is dated as the second half of the 2nd year, when the toddler becomes aware of separateness and there is an increased need to be with the mother. Mahler's term for this combination of clinging while pushing or darting away is "ambitendency" (Mahler et al., 1975, p. 95). The mother's handling of this is regarded as crucial.

6. The fourth subphase of separation-individuation is the consolidation of individuality that begins with the 3rd year of life. Its goal is the firm establishment of the cog-

nitive-symbolic inner representation of the object and the achievement of individuality.

Mahler (1974) described her work as enabling clinicians treating adults to make more accurate reconstructions of the preverbal period, thereby making patients more accessible to psychotherapeutic interventions. Her work has been extensively used, particularly by North American clinicians working with personality disordered adults (see Kramer & Akhtar, 1988; Pine, 1985; Settlage, 1977). The clinical conclusions to emerge can be summarized as follows:

1. Narcissistic Personality Disorder may be linked to the inadequate soothing ministrations of the mother during the symbiotic phase and inadequate refueling during separation-individuation. Therefore, the omnipotence of the practicing subphase is never completely renounced. Findings from research on parent-child relationships in Japan and in the United States, however, suggest that prolonging the symbiotic union between mother and infant does not undermine the individual's capacity to achieve autonomy (Rothbaum, Pott, Azuma, Miyake, & Weisz, 2000).

2. Individuals with BPD experience residues of the rapprochement subphase conflicts with persistent longings for and dread of fusion with the other. It is thought to be associated with either aggression or withdrawal on the part of the mother during the rapprochement subphase (Mahler & Kaplan, 1977; Masterson, 1985). Masterson suggests that the object, who is desperate to feel needed, rewards the toddler for demanding and clinging behavior. There is limited evidence available to support the suggestion that BPD is a transgenerational disorder. A positive history of psychopathology is more commonly found in one or both biological parents than would be expected by chance (Paris, 2000; Shachnow et al., 1997). The finding of low parental care combined with high overprotection has been identified in questionnaire-based investigations (Goldberg, Mann, Wise, & Segall, 1985; Torgersen & Alnaes, 1992) and retrospective interview-based studies (Paris & Frank, 1989; Zweig-Frank & Paris, 1991). A recent study of mothers with BPD found that they were more intrusively insensitive toward their 2-month-old infants than were mothers without psychiatric disorder (Crandell, Patrick, & Hobson, 2003).

3. Severe deprivation may prevent the normal psychological birth of the infant from normal Autism and generate a character disorder that resembles schizoid personality, with poverty of affection and relationships (Burland, 1986).

Although Mahler's model has been highly influential, systematic experimental research with infants casts serious doubt on dual notions of normal Autism and self-object merger (Gergely, 2000). Further, the infant does not seem to be a concrete experience of the physical world, as Mahler assumed. Rather, infants are acutely sensitive to abstract, amodal properties and cross-modal invariances. Intensified sucking action translates readily into observed movements of a mobile in the infant's mind (Stern, 1993). However, Mahler's developmental framework may well be appropriate for the truly psychological world of the human infant. The infant is aware of self and object as separate in the physical (bodily) domain but assumes that psychological states extend beyond physical boundaries (Fonagy, Moran, & Target, 1993). The 9-month-old infant conceives of the object as rational behaving in accordance with goals, and initially this early teleological understanding of behavior seems not to be differentially linked to animate rather than inanimate objects (Csibra, Gergely, Brockbank, Biro, & Koos, 1999; Gergely, Nadasdy, Csibra, & Biro, 1995). Thus, a symbiotic intersubjective unity may indeed characterize infancy and even early childhood, but solely at the level of mental representations of mental states.

It is now clear that Mahler's assumptions about severe forms of childhood psychosis, such as infantile Autism and childhood Schizophrenia, poorly fit her developmental model and seem unlikely to be explained by the notion of a developmental fixation in the symbiotic phase. While the most promising explanation for Schizophrenia remains a neurodevelopmental one, with numerous indications of neurological, cognitive, and behavioral dysfunctions long before the onset of the disorder, evidence points to the last months of gestation rather than the first months of life as a critical period for the vulnerability to potential causes of Schizophrenia (Marenco & Weinberger, 2000). Evidence in favor of postnatal pathological processes is meager. Similarly, the early emergence of symptoms characterizing Autism is generally accepted, but the resistance to social interaction is seen as an extreme form of a constitutional bias toward processing information from the physical rather than the interpersonal world (Baron-Cohen, 2000). Thus, although recent research confirms Mahler's theory that these serious disorders are evident from the first months of life, her implication that they are caused by the social events that take place in this period has not been substantiated.

Mahler's original contributions to the understanding of BPD have been most lasting. Her view of these patients as fixated in a rapprochement, wishing to cling but fearing the loss of their fragile sense of self, wishing to be separate but also fearing to move away from the parental figure, has been crucial to both clinical intervention and theoretical understanding. However, her theory is less helpful in understanding the high prevalence of childhood maltreatment in these patients' lives, particularly sexual abuse, for which there is now overwhelming and high-quality evidence (e.g., K. C. Jacobson & Rowe, 1999).

Joseph Sandler and the Bridging of Structural and Object Relations Theory

Joseph Sandler, a student of Anna Freud, was instrumental in the modernization of psychoanalysis, preparing its integration with the developmental sciences. As many of his ideas have been seamlessly integrated into modern core theory, we will only briefly enumerate his central contributions and touch on the relationship with related ideas reviewed elsewhere.

1. Sandler introduced the frame of reference of the representational world, an approach very similar to the schema theory that has come to dominate social and cognitive-behavioral psychology (see Sandler, 1960b; Sandler & Rosenblatt, 1962).

2. Sandler placed feeling states rather than psychic energy at the center of the psychoanalytic theory of motivation (Joffe & Sandler, 1967, p. 64). He introduced the revolutionary concept of background of safety, within which the aim of the ego is to maximize safety or security rather than to avoid anxiety Sandler (1960a). He did not get rid of drives, but he explained their influence on behavior through the impact they had on feelings (Sandler, 1972).

3. Sandler (1976) described how patients tend to create relationships to actualize unconscious fantasies by casting themselves and their therapists in specific relationship patterns, and by extension offered an entirely new theory of internal object representations (Sandler & Sandler, 1978). He showed how wishful fantasies are represented as interactions between self and object, the basic aim being to bring about a good emotional state while distancing a bad one.

4. Sandler differentiated the deeply unconscious hypothetical structures assumed by classical psychoanalysis to develop early in life and that have no chance of directly emerging into consciousness (the past unconscious) from the present unconscious, which also worked as Freud described (irrational, only partly observing the reality principle but principally concerned with current rather than past experience; Sandler & Sandler, 1984). The second system, the present unconscious, consists of here-and-now adaptations to conflicts and anxieties triggered in the first system, which was a genuine continuation of the past into the present (Sandler & Sandler, 1987).

5. It is difficult to overestimate the clinical significance of these and other advances (Fonagy & Cooper, 1999). But Sandler's direct contributions to clinical theory were more limited. In one significant contribution, he linked pleasure in experiencing particular styles of perceptual and cognitive functions with specific forms of pathology (Sandler & Joffe, 1965b). For example, obsessionality, painful though it may be, is also linked to pleasure in childhood. The developmental model of depression that Sandler proposed also made use of the representational world construct (Joffe & Sandler, 1965; Sandler & Joffe, 1965a, 1965b). Loss of the ideal states of young childhood that are omnipotent or unrealistic but failing to adopt new ones that fit with reality generates the depressive response.

6. In further clinical formulations, Sandler (1987) explained the concept of projective identification without making the extravagant assumptions, which many Kleinian authors made (see later discussion). The "other" can come to enact the patient's fantasy because the patient attempts to modify or control the behavior of the other so that it conforms to his or her distorted representation of the other. The patient's representation of the other comes to be distorted through the mechanism of projection, experiencing the other as owning unwanted aspects of the self-representation. This model is helpful in explaining therapeutic phenomena such as countertransference and phenomena identified by emotional developmental research, such as the transgenerational transmission of patterns of mother-infant interaction (Fraiberg, Adelson, & Shapiro, 1975; Sandler, 1994).

Sandler was one of the most creative figures enabling psychoanalysis to be a psychology of feelings, internal representations, and adaptations closely tied to the clinical origins of psychoanalysis. He found common ground between American ego psychology and British object relations theory. His contribution was built on the potential for integration created by the collapse of associationist psychology and the emergence of a cognitive science. A number of individuals commencing their journey from cognitive science research (see, e.g., the outstanding contributions of Bucci, 1997; Erdelyi, 1985; Foulkes, 1978; Stern, 1985; Westen, 1991) attempted to cross this bridge and were at least partially successful in doing so because Sandler created the bridgehead on the other side. Although his theories were, and are, extensively used, those who use his ideas often are unaware of doing so. Thus, there is no psychoanalytic school that bears his name. He advanced thinking by clarifying a range of psychoanalytic concepts but was unable to excite his colleagues with the novelty of his contributions.

A PARADIGM SHIFT TO OBJECT RELATIONS

Many psychoanalysts were dissatisfied with the mechanistic, somewhat reductionist character of structural theory. From Freud's earliest writings relationships had played a key part in his theorization. Most importantly he viewed the relationship between mother and infant as determining expectations about subsequent relationships, although these speculations were mostly translated into the language of drives and cathexes. Increasingly, clinicians confronted with conscious and unconscious concerns about relationships which dominated the narratives of their clients shifted the center of gravity of theorization from concerns about psychic energy and mental structures to attempting to understand the internal representations associated with social relationships, particularly those between the infant and the objects of his affection, the mother and father.

Overview of Object Relations Theory

Object relations theories in psychoanalysis are "concerned with exploring the relationship between real, external people and the internal images and residues of relations with them and the significance of these residues for psychic functioning" (Greenberg & Mitchell, 1983, p. 14). This definition is not satisfactory, as it would include many psychoanalysts who would not consider themselves object relations theorists (e.g., Edith Jacobson, Rene Spitz). It would be more accurate to argue that object relations theories are those psychoanalytic approaches that seek an understanding of psychopathology in terms of mental representations of dyadic self and object relationships that are rooted in past relationships, at first dyadic, later triadic, and still later multiple relationship representations. The increased interest in relationships is part of an underlying refocusing away from psychoanalysis as the study of intrapsychic conflict toward an experientially based perspective emphasizing the individual's experience of being with others and with the therapist during analytic work. This approach, which became dominant during the 1980s, increasingly emphasizes phenomenological constructs such as a person's experience of self, his or her experience of psychic reality

(i.e., subjectivity). As people express themselves mostly in terms of relationships, the move toward a broadly relational psychology may simply be the consequence of clinicians exploring the patient's narrative from the perspective of his or her subjectivity.

Object relations theories assume that the child's mind is shaped by early experiences with the caretaker. Object relations become increasingly complex with development. It is further assumed that early patterns of object relations are repeated. Thus, they are in some sense fixed throughout life. Disturbances in these relations explain pathology, and the patients' reactions to the therapist provide a window for examining healthy and pathological aspects of early relationships. Some theories, but not all, assume an "autonomous relationship drive" that forcibly brings the individual into contact with the caregiver (e.g., attachment theory). Other object relations theories derive relationships from drive theory (e.g., Winnicott), and yet others are able to derive a theory of drives from object relations (e.g., Kernberg). A helpful distinction between these theories was offered by Friedman (1988), who distinguished between hard and soft object relations theories. Hard theories, in which he includes the theories of Melanie Klein, Fairbairn, and Kernberg, see much hate, anger, and destruction and dwell on obstacles, illness, and confrontation, whereas soft object relations theorists (Balint, Winnicott, and Kohut) deal with love, innocence, growth needs, fulfillment, and progressive unfolding.

By the mid-1980s, object relations theory, in one of its many incarnations (see later discussion), was the most widely accepted psychoanalytic model around the world. Home-grown versions of the theory (Kohut, Kernberg) and British imports (Klein, Winnicott) replaced ego psychology in the United States; the British version of the theory came to hegemonize much of Europe, and both North American and British theories in modified forms could be found in the vibrant Latin American psychoanalytic movement (e.g., Etchegoyen, 1991). However, by no means all psychoanalysts have accepted the shift of the basic psychoanalytic model from the classical Freudian structural model to object relations theory. In North America, there are a number of psychoanalysts who remain fully committed to modifications of the structural approach as proposed, for example, by Brenner (1982, 1987, 1994). Other influential writers, such as Harold Blum (1986, 1994), Vann Spruiell (1988), Len Shengold (1989), and the Tysons (Tyson & Tyson, 1990), have managed to retain a broadly ego psychological perspective while selectively adopting certain object relations ideas. None of these writers, however, has wished to advance a psychoanalytic model that may serve as an alternative to object relations theory. Only writers in the interpersonalist tradition have aspired to do this.[1]

The Klein-Bion Model

Melanie Klein and Wilfred Bion are perhaps the two psychoanalysts least concerned with a developmental framework for psychological disorder. Yet their formulations concerning the infant's (or, more realistically, the child's) mental life are important and interesting because they highlight negative aspects of emotional development frequently ignored by nonpsychoanalytic clinicians. Further, as the genetic predisposition to most mental disorders is becoming increasingly well established, psychological models of the mediation of genetic vulnerability are of great interest. M. Klein's (1930, 1935/1984a, 1959/1984d) work combines the structural model with an interpersonal, object relations model of development, with a powerful emphasis on constitutional vulnerability rather than caregiver behavior as the prime determinant of developmental pathways. Klein's papers on the depressive position (1935/1984a, 1940/1984c), her paper on the paranoid-schizoid position (1946), and her book *Envy and Gratitude* (1957/1984b) established her as the leader of an original psychoanalytic tradition. There are several excellent introductions to the work of Klein; these include Segal (1974), Caper (1988), and Hinshelwood (1989).

Fantasies about an Infant's Mental World

The Klein-Bion model of development is highly speculative, all of it retrospectively constructed from observations

---

[1] The sole geographic exception to the domination of object relations theory is the group of French-speaking countries, particularly France and French Canada. Here a specific version of Freudian theory has remained dominant throughout the last decades of the twentieth century. A review of French psychoanalytic ideas would require a separate book of its own (such as the Lebovici & Widlöcher, 1980, volume summarizing postwar French psychoanalytic thinking). One justification for the limited coverage of the French school of psychoanalysis in the present volume is the limited interest of French theoreticians in a developmental perspective (A. Green, 2000), which is the organizing theme of the present chapter. Green regards the developmental frame of reference as part of psychology rather than psychoanalysis. Green's concept of time as nonlinear (polysynchronous) is inconsistent with the fundamental assumptions of developmental psychopathology: the accumulation of risks for development from experience and privileging of early experience as a primary response to later encounters.

of adult patients, children with serious mental disorder, and infants without epistemological restrictions on the attribution of complex internal states to them. Notwithstanding this unpropitious start, the model has been remarkably influential in that it provided a psychological account of puzzling self-destructive and relatively immutable behaviors. Here we summarize key points of this highly complex and elaborate theory.

1. Klein uncritically accepted and built on Freud's speculation of a self-destructive drive (the death instinct; S. Freud, 1920/1955).

2. Klein postulated two modes of mental function, one dominated by the separation of the good and the bad, the idealized and the persecutory (the paranoid-schizoid position), and the other a more mature, simultaneous balanced recognition of the bad in the good and one's role in unrealistically and self-servingly distorting the world into idealized and denigrated components (the depressive position). M. Klein's (1935/1984a) metaphor for these two states of mind was the perception of the mother as separately idealized and persecuting in the paranoid-schizoid state and perceived as a whole person who accounts for both good and bad experiences in the depressive position.

3. It is assumed that discovering one's hostility to a loved object and accepting responsibility for creating an image of her as bad and yet identical with the image of her as perfect is linked to pain and anxiety and is resisted. This is what Klein calls "depressive anxiety," as distinct from the "persecutory anxieties" of the earlier paranoid-schizoid position. Bion (1957) was the first to point out that the depressive position is never permanently achieved. In fact, the very term "position" suggests a permanence that this state of mind rarely has. It is now accepted that the mind cycles between the two (paranoid-schizoid and depressive), as the achievement of depression creates anxiety which can only be handled in the paranoid-schizoid state (by more primitive defenses, such as splitting).

4. The concept of "projective identification" is central to this model (M. Klein, 1946). Whereas in the classical theory of projection, impulses and wishes are experienced as part of the object rather than the self, and identification implies attributing qualities perceived in the object to the self, projective identification involves externalizing "segments of the ego" and attempting to gain control over these unwanted possessions via often highly

manipulative behavior toward the object (i.e., making the other identify with the projections).

5. Projective identification is not a defense, but an interpersonal process where the self gets rid of feelings by evoking the feelings in another self (Bion, 1962a).

6. The origins of this process are to be found in infancy, when the baby projects "unprocessed elements" (beta elements) into another human mind (the container) that can accept them and transform them into meanings (alpha function), which the baby can reinternalize, creating a representation of these experiences (Bion, 1959).

7. Working with children, Klein (1932) was impressed by their ruthless, sadistic fantasies, which she felt were not a reaction to frustration but represented innate aggression. A malign form of this is primitive envy, which is hatred directed at the good but also at times inaccessible object (M. Klein, 1957/1984b). The child resents the inevitable limitations of maternal care, cannot tolerate the mother's control over it, and would prefer to destroy it rather then experience the frustration.

8. While paying lip service to the parent's capacity to mitigate the influence of the child's constitutional tendencies, Klein (1952, 1959/1984d) was convinced that the internal experience of others and self were innate. Post-Kleinian authors argued that although primary destructiveness was constitutional, it could with difficulty be mitigated by or aggravated by environmental influences (e.g., Segal, 1981). It has to be said that recent evidence suggests that physical aggression and destructiveness are indeed particularly marked in the early years in most children and naturally decline in most children over the course of the first decade, with violent children manifesting an absence of this expectable taming rather than an emergence of aggression de novo in response to environmental impingement (Shaw, Gilliom, Ingoldsby, & Nagin, 2002; Tremblay, 2000; Tremblay, Japel, & Perusse, 1999).

The Kleinian Model of Mental Disorder

By and large, the Kleinian model of psychopathology assumes that mental disorder constitutes a persistence of the primitive mental states discussed earlier. Mental disorder indicates the predominance of the paranoid-schizoid position, whereas mental health reflects the relative stability of the depressive framework. The cause of pathology is primarily constitutional (overwhelming envy) and may be aggravated by deficiencies in the mother's capacity for

reverie (Bion, 1967), which is similar to Winnicott's (1962b) concept of primary maternal preoccupation (see later discussion). Persecutory anxiety threatens the ego, and anxiety and experience of fragmentation, annihilation, and a loss of a capacity for integration might be observed—a constellation characteristic of severe personality disorders. In psychotic states, annihilatory/persecutory anxieties are intense, and the object with whom the patient attempts to projectively identify is reintrojected, that is, experienced as entering the ego, creating a delusion of the mind or the body being under external control (M. Klein, 1946).

Neurotic problems are seen as consequences of unresolved, depressive anxiety. For example, depression arises because the experience of loss reminds individuals of the damage they felt they caused to the good object (M. Klein, 1940/1984c). Chronic depression arises when the person cannot escape the fear of injuring the loved object and therefore has to repress all aggressiveness, generating a relentless self-persecution. Narcissistic character structure is considered a defense against envy and dependence. The narcissist's relationship with others is highly destructive. The narcissist makes ruthless use of others and denies his or her need of them (Rosenfeld, 1987). There are two kinds of narcissism: thin-skinned (where the person seeks constant reassurance) and thick-skinned (the hostile, superior, isolationist posture; Rosenfeld, 1971). Character disorders in general, such as narcissism, are thought to be underpinned by relatively stable constructions of impulses, anxieties, and defenses, which allow the individual to create an internal state felt to be protective from the chaos of earlier developmental stages at the cost of developmental progress to more advanced modes of psychic functioning (Steiner, 1993). The system is rigid but unstable. Defenses may shift, but progress is more apparent than real. Bion (1962a) suggests that an early disabling of the psychic processes needed for understanding cognitive and affective aspects of interpersonal relationships is responsible for this.

Evaluating the Klein-Bion Model

Early critics of Kleinian formulations focused on the centrality of really early higher-order cognitive and perceptual capacities (see King & Steiner, 1991, for a definitive account of the "controversial discussions" that took place in the British Psycho-Analytical Society in 1944). These critiques contrasted Kleinian claims with "commonsense" views of what babies can think; that is, Kleinian theory was tested against folk psychology or observation, rather than empirical research (see, e.g., Glover, 1945; Yorke, 1971).[2]

The human infant does indeed have remarkably abstract and complex cognitive capacities (see, e.g., Meltzoff, 1990), but there is no evidence to support Klein's implicit claim that the infant relates to the object as a psychological entity. Melanie Klein consistently held that the baby had awareness of the minds of others, which we now know the child is most unlikely to have until at least the 2nd year (Baron-Cohen, Tager-Flusberg, & Cohen, 2000). Laboratory-based research reveals infants' representations as far less concrete and relatively abstract and amodal (see Bower, 1974), which does not support Kleinian and post-Kleinian assumptions about "infantile part-object" representations such as breasts and penises. Nevertheless, the emergent research-based model of the human mind is increasingly recognizing the importance of innate concepts, wired in and selected by evolution, and in this context (e.g., Buss, 1995), it has to be said that some of Melanie Klein's ideas no longer seem as far-fetched as they did at first. None of this is proof of her ideas, nor is it likely that her fantasies about the infant's mind state will ever be confirmed, but the idea that gene-driven affective reorganization of the brain in infancy influences the later functioning of the brain cannot be dismissed as implausible given the directions in which developmental science is progressing.

Klein's ideas have provoked considerable controversy and ill feeling. There are concerns about attributing adult psychological capacities to infants, considered earlier, but the question also arises as to why Klein dates pathology to such early stages (Bibring, 1947). The answer might be that the mental states of infancy are extremely hard to observe: The postulation of crucial pathogenic processes in infancy is extremely unlikely to be disproven. Psychoanalytic infant observation (Bick, 1964) also permits widely differing interpretations. However, evidence is accumulating that most of the important mental disorders of adulthood are indeed foreshadowed in infancy (e.g., Marenco & Weinberger, 2000). Further, early brain development is increasingly seen as pivotal in the evolution of psychological disturbance (Schore, 2003).

The work of Kleinian writers represents a major advance in clarifying the relationship between emotional de-

velopment and psychological functioning. Many of their ideas have enriched the field of psychoanalytic theory and clinical practice well beyond their own school. Many of these ideas remain to be operationalized for further study, but models such as Bion's (1962a, 1962b) container/contained have lessened the divide between the understanding of cognitive development and that of emotional disorder. This is essential to further advances in the field of developmental psychopathology.

The Independent School of British Psychoanalysis

The appropriately named independent tradition is the work of a number of individual analysts, has no single leader or theorist, and therefore lacks the theoretical coherence of the tighter groups. Fairbairn (1954, 1963) and Guntrip (1961, 1969, 1975, 1978) were the theory builders, with major contributions from Winnicott (1953, 1958), Balint (1959, 1968), Klauber (1966, 1987), Khan (1963, 1974), and Bollas (1987, 1989). They all explicitly refrained from establishing schools of followers. There are some excellent summaries of their work (see, e.g., Hughes, 1989; Kohon, 1986; Rayner, 1991; Sutherland, 1980).

The Developmental Model of the British School

The developmental assumptions of the independent school, with special reference to the work of Donald Winnicott, may be summarized as follows:

1. There is a primary drive for creating object relationships (Fairbairn, 1952), with a less widely held further assumption of a primary human desire to feel loved (Balint, 1968).

2. Insufficient intimacy with the primary object will give rise to a "splitting" in the self, and it is this persistence of incompatible ideas and lack of integration between them rather than intersystemic conflict and repression that is at the root of psychological disorder (Fairbairn, 1952). The intimacy and integration is assured by the holding environment, where the caregiver, in a state of primary maternal preoccupation, holds the infant to give him the illusion that she can accurately respond to his gestures because his wish created her and she is part of him (Winnicott, 1962b, 1965a). Holding is based on comprehension, "a holding in mind of the infant's mental state." Holding protects the infant from unbearable mental experience, overwhelming archaic anxiety, while he or she moves from an unintegrated to an integrated state (Winnicott, 1962a).

---

[2] For example, projection in the paranoid-schizoid position assumes a differentiated sense of self and other, because without this, it would be impossible to displace the source of bad feelings from the self onto another object. It also implies that the baby can blame his or her own feelings on the attributed attitude of the other, that is, make a causal attribution.

3. Holding is communicated by mirroring that is never perfect but is "good enough" and permits repair (Winnicott, 1967). The lack of perfection allows for failure and frustration, which facilitate the break away from infantile omnipotence and give an opportunity to the mother to repair the inevitable hurt by permitting regression to complete fusion.

4. Winnicott (1953) introduced the idea of transitional phenomena in a study of how the infant uses the mother to achieve independent functioning. A corner of blanket may help to soothe the infant as it is grasped when the infant fantasizes about breast-feeding. It is associated with conjuring the mother (and the breast) in her absence. The physical object (blanket) is both the mother (the "not-me" aspect) and the infant (the "me" aspect). Transitional objects are to be found in the space between the self and external reality in which (according to Winnicott) symbolization occurs, meaningful, affectionate, sharing yet separate companionship and love grow, where play and illusion are maintained in the spontaneous, creative activities of healthy people (Winnicott, 1971).

5. The emergence of the self is through an integration of spontaneous, creative interactions with the mother that are nonintrusive and that facilitate the illusion that the object is a product of the baby's creative gestures and therefore controlled and controllable.

6. If the mother cannot comprehend the infant, he or she will be forced into compliance, and a "false (compliant) self" to protect the true self will develop (Winnicott, 1965a).

7. Winnicott distinguishes between privation (never had maternal care) and deprivation (sufficient awareness of care for the self to develop and experience withdrawal of care). Antisocial Personality Disorder is associated with the latter pattern and assumes the presence of a self (Winnicott, 1956).

8. It is the mother's lack of love and lack of recognition of the child's love rather than primary destructiveness that leads the child to believe that his or her hate has destroyed the object (Fairbairn, 1952; Padel, 1972).

British Independent Contributions to Developmental Psychopathology

Fairbairn's (1944) key contribution was the proposition that an early trauma of great severity is stored in memories that are "frozen" or dissociated from a person's central ego or functional self. This is particularly relevant to Narcissistic and Borderline Personality Disorders, but the notion of multiple self-representations is of more general importance. Fairbairn (1952) sees the schizoid reaction of withdrawal from and primitive defense against the trauma of not being intimately known or loved as fundamental to all pathology. Winnicott (1965b) and Fairbairn (1954) associated Schizophrenia with total privation, that is, the complete absence of good enough mothering. It is assumed that the experience of privation makes the infant view his or her love as bad and destructive. This in turn makes the infant withdraw from emotional contact with the outer world and ultimately creates a highly disturbed sense of external reality. Severe personality disorder may be seen as the result of having had a good enough mother who had been lost, and thus feeling forever deprived. Schizoid personality (Fairbairn, 1940, 1952) arises out of the baby's feeling that love for the mother is destructive of her and therefore has to be inhibited along with all intimacy. The ego is split, and neither other nor self is perceived as a whole person. Both hide their love and protect themselves from the love of others. Winnicott (1965a) adds that this includes a falseness in self-presentation which becomes truly maladaptive only when called on to function in the context of an intimate interpersonal relationship. Guntrip (1969) added that the rejection from a hostile object leads to a hunger for objects that are feared. Borderline patients are considered by Winnicott (1960) to share defenses with psychotic patients, which is consistent with many modern epidemiological perspectives (Gunderson, 2001). Winnicott notes that these patients have no sense of others, including the therapist, as having lives of their own and respond with threats of intense anger if their sense of omnipotence is threatened

These observations have been confirmed empirically in studies showing that borderline patients have a specific deficit in mental state awareness in the context of attachment relationships (Fonagy et al., 1996). This phenomenon is explained by Modell (1963, 1968) as individuals with BPD relating to people as if they were transitional objects (inanimate objects from which to obtain comfort in mother's absence). This transitional relatedness makes them use other people as if they were inanimate to serve a self-regulating, soothing function; used, as a toddler uses a teddy bear, in primitive, demanding, and tenacious ways. Searles (1986) and Giovacchini (1987) believe that this shows how patients with BPD may have been treated by their parents—as transitional objects. Narcissistic individuals are thought to have been poorly mirrored; they fall back on a compensatory self-structure to bypass having to rely on inadequate caregivers. This is, however, illusory self-sufficiency and unreal autonomy (Modell, 1975, 1984).

Evaluating the British Independents

The British independents' views have only partially stood the test of time. The general approach to development, the description of infants as biologically prepared to attend to environmental events that respond to them, has been very well supported by infant research (Meltzoff & Moore, 1998; Watson, 2001). It seems highly plausible that there is a biological path to social interaction, in the course of which the infant can be reflected as a mental entity. For example, research on affective interactions between infant and mother support the notion of a dual unit of infant and mother, where the mother and infant mutually create the infant's moods (Jaffe, Beebe, Feldstein, Crown, & Jasnow, 2001; Tronick, 2001). Winnicott's views on the importance of sensitive maternal care are broadly supported by developmental research, although there is general dissatisfaction with the fuzziness of the concept of maternal sensitivity (De Wolff & van IJzendoorn, 1997). Longitudinal research with Romanian infants adopted late strongly supports Fairbairn's and Winnicott's assumptions concerning the long-term impact of privation (Carlson et al., 1995; Chisholm, Carter, Ames, & Morison, 1995; O'Connor, Bredenkamp, Rutter, & the English and Romanian Adoptees Study Team, 1999; O'Connor, Rutter, & Kreppner, 2000). Increasingly, there is evidence of neurophysiological and even neuroanatomical deficit associated with such privation (Chugani et al., 2001; Gunnar, Morison, Chisholm, & Schuder, 2001; Kreppner, O'Connor, & Rutter, 2001).

Research does not, however, support Winnicott's exclusive concern with the infant-mother relationship. Although there is good evidence that low levels of parental warmth and support, as well as parental rejection and hostility and family conflict are associated with a range of psychological problems in children (Ge, Conger, & Simmons, 1996; Sheeber, Hops, Alpert, Davies, & Andrews, 1997), the evidence does not support the privileging of the mother-child relationship (see, e.g., McCauley, Pavidis, & Kendall, 2000, for research on childhood depression). Winnicott's assumption that the relationship between infant and mother provides the basis for all serious mental disorder also flies in the face of accumulating evidence for the importance of genetic factors (Rutter, Silberg, O'Connor, & Simonoff, 1999a, 1999b).

The data from behavior genetics studies should be considered in relation to all psychoanalytic theories (as well as other theories focused on early socialization); we consider these data here because Winnicott's description of the potential toxicities in the infant's psychosocial environment

was highly influential. For example, two large-scale, high-quality, community-based studies, the Virginia Twin Study (Eaves et al., 1997; Hewitt et al., 1997) and the Nonshared Environment and Adolescent Development Project (NEAD; Reiss et al., 1995), have confirmed that most types of childhood psychopathology have quite substantial genetic components. The nonshared environment appears to be the bulk of the environmental component; shared environment, an instance of which would be parental sensitivity, accounts for almost no variance (Plomin, 1994). Modern reviews of the controversy (see particularly Rutter, 2000) offer quite balanced evaluations. For example, it is now clear that claims about the absence of shared environmental effects in behavior genetics studies have been exaggerated because they are estimated simply in terms of how alike or not siblings are. The importance of the influence of factors such as maternal warmth cannot be estimated in this way because the influence impacts different members of the family in different ways: It will appear to be a nonshared environmental influence, whereas it is actually shared. Further, most studies of the influence of early environment on development are based on twin and adoptive studies that sample environments of lower than average risk (Stoolmiller, 1999). There are further technical complications. For example, many studies drawing inferences about causation have conflated nonshared environmental variance with error variance, and other studies have assumed that identical and fraternal twins have "equal environments." It is quite likely that the critics have exaggerated their claims; nevertheless, they have provided a valid challenge to psychosocial researchers (Rutter, 1999).

To summarize, evidence suggests that Winnicott overstated the case for environmental influences on normal and pathological development. Whereas psychoanalysts prior to Winnicott and the British independents have been inclined to environmentalism and preferred nurture to nature explanations of pathology, the Freudian heritage was one of great respect for constitutional factors and the role of genetics, for example, in symptom choice and vulnerability to environmental stress. Although never totally rejecting the role of constitutional factors, in psychosis for example, Winnicott's theory emphasized the exclusive role of the early environment to a degree that has turned out to be clearly incompatible with the behavior genetics data.

The major weakness of Winnicott's theory, which actually runs across the entire British object relations tradition, is what may be called a naïve reconstruction of infancy in the adult mind. Although infant research confirms some speculation and informal observation, the developmental argument of a linear evolution from infancy to adulthood cannot be sustained. Human development is far too complex for infantile experiences to have direct links to adult pathology. In fact, to the extent that such research is available, longitudinal studies of infancy suggest that personality organization is subject to reorganization throughout development based on significant positive and negative influences (e.g., Emde & Spicer, 2000).

Winnicott's view influenced psychoanalysis in a subtle and profound way. For example, Kohut's advances of psychoanalytic theory, which are covered in the next section, are almost entirely anticipated by Winnicott's work, although this is rarely acknowledged. Winnicott's influence has unhappily been epistemological as well as theoretical. His style of writing is highly evocative, and his clinical examples are rich as well as persuasive. His writing is untroubled by considerations of parsimony, the need for unambiguous language or supportive evidence. In Winnicott's hands this approach has been highly creative; in the hands of his followers, evocative language can often disguise convoluted speculation and uninspired content.

The Self Psychological Approach

Self-psychology theory emerged in the late 1960s and early 1970s and became one of the dominant psychoanalytic approaches in the United States, although it never properly penetrated European psychoanalytic thinking (Mollon, 2001). It emerged from the thinking of Heinz Kohut (1971, 1977; Kohut & Wolf, 1978).

Developmental Theory

Kohut was particularly concerned with the difficulties of individuals with Narcissistic Personality Disorder. Self-psychology came to be generalized to other problems of mental disorder and together with a specific therapeutic approach, foregrounding empathy. Although self-psychology is not a coherent theory, Kohut's own thinking having shifted considerably, it is possible to identify a number of key developmental assumptions in this body of work:

1. Kohut's formulation is that narcissistic development proceeds along a path of its own and that parents serve as selfobjects. A selfobject is defined as a person in the environment who performs particular functions for the self; these functions evoke the experience of selfhood (Wolf, 1988a). The mother who treats the child as though the child has a self initiates the process of self

formation. The functions of the selfobject are to integrate the child's affects through differentiating between affects, assisting in tolerating affects, and assisting in thinking about affects (Stolorow, 1997; Stolorow & Atwood, 1991).

2. To begin with, empathic responses from the mirroring selfobject (assumed to be the mother) allow the unfolding of exhibitionism and grandiosity. This aspect of the self emerges as a defense against the awareness of vulnerability and relies on confirmation through an object who mirrors the child's need for admiration and approval. This enables the child to build an idealized image of the parent with whom he or she wishes to merge.

3. Frustration, when phase-appropriate and not too intense, permits a gradual modulation of infantile omnipotence through "a transmuting internalization" of this mirroring function. Transmuting internalization of the selfobject leads gradually to consolidation of the nuclear self (Kohut & Wolf, 1978, pp. 83, 416).

4. The idealization of selfobjects, also through internalization, leads to the development of ideals. The internalizing of the mirroring function and idealized selfobject leads to the emergence of a "bipolar self," with its ambitions and ideals and the natural talents available to it.

5. In Kohut's later writings (1977, 1984), the self was regarded as a superordinate structure incorporating drives and defenses. The main developmental achievement for any individual is the attainment of a cohesive self.

6. It is the "enfeebled self" that turns defensively toward pleasure aims (drives), which are the breakdown products of disappointments to the self, usually involving failures in emotional attunement of the selfobject. Anxiety is primarily the self's experience of a defect or lack of continuity.

The Self Psychological Model of Developmental Psychopathology

The self psychological model of psychopathology is essentially a deficiency theory. A deficiency of facilitating experiences is assumed to lead to a primary psychic deficit: an inadequately developed self. In the self psychological model, fear of losing the sense of who one is underlies all pathology. Secondary conflicts that we observe can occur only because of structural weaknesses in the self. Diagnostic distinctions can be made in terms of the characteristics of the self: (1) Psychosis precludes a cohesive sense of self; (2) personality disordered patients have an enfeebled self vulnerable to temporary fragmentation; and (3) neurotic pathology is thought to be associated with the robustness of self structure. Narcissistic personality is a developmental arrest at the stage of the grandiose exhibitionistic self, which fails to be neutralized by the parent's age-specific mirroring responses. Parental failure causes an arrest in the movement from the grandiose exhibitionistic self to realistic ambition, or the idealization of the parental imago to ego ideal. Repression of the grandiose self is associated with low self-esteem, vague depression, and lack of initiative (Rosenfeld's thin-skinned narcissism). When splitting dominates, the grandiose self manifests as boastfulness, arrogance, and a dismissing attitude out of touch with reality (Rosenfeld's thick-skinned narcissism). Low self-esteem, hypersensitivity to criticism, and the need to continue to be mirrored characterize both.

Neurotic anxieties are also considered a consequence of deficient selfobject function. Thus, agoraphobia may be a consequence of the maternal selfobject's failure that led to a deficit in self-soothing function, that turns anxiety into disintegration anxiety (Kohut, 1984). Violent behavior is triggered by a threat to the self, experienced as a sense of shame, which generates an overwhelming need to inflict injury on the shaming person and repair the narcissistic injury (Gilligan, 1997). Borderline Personality Disorder results from an inability to hold on to selfobjects psychologically who might be soothing to the self. The result is inner emptiness and a failure of self-organization that causes annihilatory panic when relationships are threatened (G. Adler, 1985). Drug addiction is thought to fill a missing gap in the psyche. When the selfobject fails to perform a tension-regulating function and there is traumatic disappointment in the idealized object, the drug is used to fill the gap that the object left behind (Kohut, 1977).

Evaluating Self-Psychology

Because of the fundamental similarities between Kohut's and Winnicott's approaches, much of the evidence bearing on Winnicott's views is also pertinent to self-psychology. Thus, for example, the notion of an innate contingency detection module (Gergely & Watson, 1999) that functions to detect probabilistic relationships between the actions of the infant and environmental events is naturally consistent with both Winnicott's and the self psychological models of development. The hypothesis that at around 3 months of age the infant's orientation shifts from searching for perfect contingencies that help it identify its body to high, but imperfect, degrees of contingency that pinpoint aspects of the social world, links closely to the work of Stolorow and colleagues (Stolorow, Brandschaft, & Atwood, 1987; Watson, 1994) concerning emotional development. Self psycholo-

gists have also felt supported by the identification of so-called mirroring cells in the primate brain (Gallese, 2000, 2001; Gallese & Umilta, in press). These are cells that appear to be activated when the rhesus monkey identifies a movement analogous to its own in the world. (It should be borne in mind that monkeys do not recognize themselves in the mirror; the suggestion here is for a predisposition to identifying environmental events pertaining to the self.) Although prima facie this is consistent with a developmental emphasis on mirroring, it is somewhat far-fetched to consider it a direct confirmation of self psychological ideas. There is evidence that mothers who speak to their infant as if the baby had a self enhance the likelihood of secure attachment (Oppenheim & Koren-Karie, 2002), even when mother-infant interaction is observed at 6 months and attachment at 12 months (Meins, Ferryhough, Fradley, & Tuckey, 2001). There is also a large body of evidence that supports the central role of self-esteem in the generation of psychological disturbance. For example, it is clear that life events that trigger feelings of humiliation and entrapment are particularly powerful in triggering episodes of depression (Brown, Harris, & Hepworth, 1995). Further, individuals with early adverse experiences that are likely to have undermined their self-esteem are most likely to respond with depression to negative life events (Brown, 1998).

There has been appropriate criticism of Kohut's model as parent-blaming. Tyson and Tyson (1990) take issue with his emphasis on pathogenic parents, neglecting the infant's constitution and capacity to modify his or her own environment. At the root of his formulation of narcissistic personality and behavior disorders is the idea that these result from faulty selfobject responses to the narcissistic needs of the growing child between the phase of primary narcissism and the Oedipal phase. This is a naïve environmentalist position, from the perspective of modern developmental psychopathology. Correlations between characteristics of early parenting and later child behavior can be reinterpreted given that any association may be attributable to the 50% of genetic overlap between a parent and a biological child. This has been termed "passive genotype-environment correlation." In a landmark investigation of genetic and environmental influences on adolescent development, Reiss and colleagues (Reiss, Neiderhiser, Hetherington, & Plomin, 2000) found that of 52 statistically significant associations between family relationship (e.g., parental warmth, sibling relationships) and measures of adjustment (e.g., depression and antisocial behavior), 44 showed genetic influences that accounted for more than half of the common variance. In almost half of the 52, little association between family relations and adolescent functioning remained once genetic influence was taken into consideration. Further, there is the so-called child-to-parent effect, where aspects of the family environment are shaped by the child's genetically rooted characteristics (best shown in adoption studies; e.g., Deater-Deckard, Fulker, & Plomin, 1999).

Self-psychology represents a genuinely radical revision of psychoanalytic ideas. It is not surprising, perhaps, that it has been subjected to considerable criticism, particularly from those who see it as having been overextended from an explanation of narcissistic disturbances to all forms of psychological disorder (Schwartz, 1978). Kohut consistently failed to acknowledge the link between his ideas and other theories, including structural theory (Rothstein, 1980), the work of Alexander and French (1946), and the work of Loewald (1960), and there is scant reference to the work of Winnicott. In an apparently helpful clarification, Wolf (1988b) pointed out that selfobject needs are concrete only in infancy; in later development, they can be increasingly abstract, with symbols or ideas serving selfobject functions. Anything that makes a person feel good may be considered to have a selfobject function, and the only way we know if an activity or person has selfobject function is through observing its effects on well-being. Used this broadly, the concept has no explanatory power.

The Structural Object Relations Perspective

Otto Kernberg, who trained as a Kleinian analyst, has mainly worked in the environment of ego psychology and yet achieved a remarkable level of integration between these two, quite possibly epistemologically inconsistent (Greenberg & Mitchell, 1983), developmental frameworks (see Kernberg, 1975, 1980a, 1980b, 1984, 1992). Kernberg does not fully adopt the Kleinian model of development, although he makes good use of Kleinian concepts (such as the model of early object relations and superego formation, aggression, envy, splitting, projective identification) in understanding severe psychopathology. Ultimately, his model is a creative combination of the ideas of the modernizers of structural theory (Jacobson, Sandler, Loewald, Mahler) and the Klein-Bion model. This may account for Kernberg's being the most cited psychoanalyst alive and one of the most influential in the history of the field. In summarizing his views, we focus attention on points of difference between his perspective and those of relational and structural theorists.

The Structural Object Relations Developmental Model

Similarly to Sandler, Kernberg considers affects to be the primary motivational system. The dyadic representation of interaction between self and object, colored by particular affects, constitutes the basic building block of psychic structure (Kernberg, 1982). Drives are hypothetical constructs manifested in mental representations of the self and object linked by some dominant affect state. Self-object-affect triads (object relations units) are stored in affective memory and evolve into drives in the context of the mother-infant relationship, as was originally suggested by Loewald (1971/1980c). Drives remain motivators of behavior and, unlike in the Kleinian or British object relations approaches, are not replaced by object relations structures. The major psychic structures (id, ego, and superego) are integrations of internalizations of object representations in self-object relationships under various emotional states. Thus, a superego may be harsh because of a prevailing affect of anger and criticism.

There are three processes of internalization: (1) introjection, where entire interactions of self and other are internalized in their affective context; (2) identifications that recognize the variety of role dimensions that exist in interaction with others; and (3) ego identity that denotes the overall organization of introjections and identifications (Kernberg, 1976). Kernberg outlines a developmental sequence borrowed from Jacobson and Mahler with a far less specific timetable. In essence, in early stages, good and bad object images are split by the ego to protect good images from the destructive power of bad ones. In the 3rd year of life, the polarized good and bad representations are thought to become gradually more integrated so that total object and self-representations are formed. Ego weakness following the failure to achieve the ego integration associated with integrating good and bad parts of self and object representations creates vulnerability to character pathology, retaining splitting as opposed to repression as the principal mechanism of defense. After age 3, Kernberg's theory follows the structural model of development.

The Structural Object Relations Theory of Psychopathology

Kernberg offers a comprehensive reconsideration of psychological disorders, but his model of neurotic pathology does not differ fundamentally from the structural perspective, although it is influenced by Klein, Fairbairn, and Mahler. Where he differs from these pioneers is in his focus on the current state of the patient's thinking rather than attempting to identify where currently dominant pathogenic conflicts and structural organizations originated. For example, he is not concerned with distinguishing Oedipal from pre-Oedipal pathology but simply asserts that all levels of disturbance are more complex if linked with severe personality disturbance. The treatment literature that shows outcomes from both pharmaco- and psychotherapy of Axis I disorders to be systematically poorer when accompanied by Axis II diagnoses is consistent with this point of view (J. H. Reich & Vasile, 1993; Shea et al., 1990). However, unlike other psychoanalysts, Kernberg is serious in his consideration of psychiatric diagnostic categories as predictors of treatment response. For example, he does not consider severe character problems to be appropriately treated in psychoanalysis. He recommends twice-weekly expressive psychotherapy as the treatment of choice.

We focus on Kernberg's approach to personality disorders (where his contribution is most clearly valued). Even neurotic pathology entails self-object dyadic configurations dating to developmentally earlier stages than the integrated units of self or object and reflecting either a defensive or an impulsive aspect of early psychic conflict. An individual is considered susceptible to anxiety when configurations of self- and object representation are poorly differentiated and highly affectively charged. For example, a representation of the self as weak and vulnerable may be coupled with an object representation of ruthless domination with a violent affective tone (Kernberg, 1984). At mild levels of character pathology, there is some splitting as well as repression. Therefore, inhibitions are considered to be weak and impulsivity is marked. There will be rapid reversals so that self-representation and projected object representations can switch. Patients who believe they are the victims of criticism (from the therapist) can suddenly turn into the vicious unreasonable critic. Note that not only is the ego poorly organized and unstable, but the superego is harsh and sadistic (Kernberg, 1988). At severe levels of character pathology, primitive dissociation or splitting of internalized object relations is marked (Kernberg, 1984). There is a consequent lack of integration of self- and object representations, and integrated representations of object relations are absent. There is no tolerance for ambivalence, which is replaced by a defensive disintegration of self and objects due to libidinally or aggressively invested part-object relations. The individual insists on consistently constructing either idealized or persecutory self and object relations, making relationships with such individuals confused or chaotic (Kernberg, 1984).

Narcissistic personality functioning is rooted in a lack of realistic self-concept and a self-image split into grandiose and devaluing aspects that alternate. The overriding need to gain external support for the grandiose self undermines the capacity for mutual relationships. The admired other stands for qualities that are felt to be lacking in the self and must therefore be constantly controlled, and there is no real empathy. In malignant narcissism, the idealized object images that are normally integrated into the superego are integrated into the grandiose self; such a person may feel empowered to perform severely antisocial acts and take sadistic pleasure in victories over others (Kernberg, 1975). Although narcissistic disorders may sometimes serve to protect an individual against an underlying borderline personality organization, the latter is considered a separate nosological entity characterized by (1) ego weakness (poor affect tolerance, impulse control, and sublimatory capacity), (2) primitive defenses including splitting, (3) identity diffusion, (4) intact reality testing but a propensity to shift toward dreamlike (primary process) thinking, and (5) pathological internalized object relationships. The root cause of borderline states is the intensity of destructive and aggressive impulses and the relative weakness of ego structures available to handle them.

Wisely, Kernberg leaves open the question of whether such excessive aggressiveness is inborn or associated with particularly malevolent early environments. This means that he is far from being embarrassed by emerging evidence concerning the powerful genetic influences that appear to be present in BPD (Livesley, Jang, & Vernon, 1998; Torgersen, 2000; Torgersen et al., 2000). Borderline individuals fail to achieve the main task of stage 3 of development: to be able to blend the good and bad self and object images into a single representation. Projective identification, pervasive in BPD, is seen as the by-product of the absence of self-object differentiation. The use of massive primitive denial ensures that individuals can ignore their good feelings toward the object and that bad ones dominate their consciousness. There is extreme and repetitive oscillation between contradictory self-concepts—as victim or victimizer, dominant or submissive (Kernberg, Selzer, Koenigsberg, Carr, & Appelbaum, 1989). Transient psychotic episodes can occur because of the ready fusion in self- and object representations, but remain transient because reality testing remains adequate. Self-destructiveness, self-mutilation, and suicidal gestures are claimed to coincide with intense attacks of rage against the object (Kernberg, 1987). They can establish control over the environment by evoking guilt feelings. Kernberg points to the infiltration of the self with aggression as one possible cause, but this is not elaborated. Self-mutilation is also seen as protecting from identity diffusion. Kernberg's treatment approach (transference-focused psychotherapy) is almost the only treatment approach that is well grounded in theory, fully operationalized, and subjected to careful process as well as outcome investigation (Clarkin, Kernberg, & Yeomans, 1999; Kernberg, Clarkin, & Yeomans, 2002; Kernberg et al., 1989).

Evaluation of the Structural Object Relations Approach

The elegance of Kernberg's theory lies in its bringing together the metapsychological or structural (experience-distant) and phenomenological (what Kernberg called experience-near) levels of description. Splitting describes how individuals with borderline personality organization tend to manage their relationships. Idealization, devaluation, and denial are at once indicators of the organization of intrapsychic relationship representations and tell-tale signs of the individual's failure to generate more advanced mental mechanisms. Thus, the signs of the disorder relate directly to the underlying metapsychological dysfunction. The dramatic separation of good from bad representations is at once the indicator of a pathogenic process (a shift toward primary process thinking), the cause of the process (the failure to integrate internal representations that would lead to the structuralization of an ego), and the content of the process (pathological internalized object relationships). Kernberg goes beyond traditional ego psychology, as the explanation in terms of ego weakness is no longer circular. Ego weakness is coterminous with an active defensive process that leads to the split ego organizations that cannot withstand close contact with bad object representations.

In line with Kernbrg's speculations, affect theorists suggest that a constitutional affect bias normally becomes consolidated through repetitions of discrete emotions and comes to be organized into rigid patterns. Psychopathology such as depression arises in association with a sadness bias that may arise as a consequence of constitutional characteristics (e.g., stress reactivity and hypothalamic-pituitary-adrenal axis arousal) and socialization experience (Zahn-Waxler et al., 2000). However, an expanded conception of the structure and organization of emotion may be required, compared to Kernberg's formulations to account for the high levels of comorbidity of emotional disorders (Angold, Costello, & Erkanli, 1999).

Many of Kernberg's hypotheses concerning the ego weakness of patients with BPD are receiving support from work at the Personality Disorders Institute. An example is work on effortful control. This is a temperamental ability to inhibit a dominant response in order to perform a subdominant one and is held to consist of three components: (1) inhibitory control (e.g., "I can easily resist talking out of turn, even when I'm excited and want to express an idea"), (2) activation control (e.g., "I can keep performing

a task even when I would rather not do it"), and (3) attentional control (e.g., "It is very hard for me to focus my attention when I am distressed") (Rothbart, Ahadi, & Evans, 2000; Rothbart, Ahadi, & Hershey, 1994). Clarkin and colleagues (2001) explored the capacity of borderline patients to exert effortful control. Patients with BPD, as would be predicted by Kernberg's theory, are particularly high in negative affect (fear, sadness, discomfort, and frustration) and low in effortful control. The findings suggest that the low capacity for effortful control (i.e., ego weakness) may create the risk for negative affect.

Therapeutic as well as theoretical investigations are underway, including a trial contrasting transference-focused psychotherapy with the best available alternative treatment of BPD, dialectical behavior therapy. Initial findings are encouraging. A pilot study of 17 patients with BPD showed substantial improvements over a year of therapy (Clarkin, 2001). This is the most serious attempt so far to demonstrate the effectiveness of a rigorously described and implemented outpatient treatment program for BPD.

Kernberg's work has been extremely influential worldwide. Perhaps even more important than the high level of theoretical integration he has achieved (systematizing psychoanalytic object relations theory into a unitary framework that is consistent with both classical and structural theory and with the work of British object relations theorists, the main elements being Melanie Klein, Wilfred Bion, Edith Jacobson, and Margaret Mahler) was Kernberg's translation of object relations theory into a realistic clinical method, particularly well described for patients he designated as possessing a borderline personality organization. Other object relations theorists, particularly Kohut and the British theorists (Winnicott, Fairbairn), recommend modifications to technique that bring the analyst as a real person into the foreground in the treatment of patients with borderline personality organization; Kernberg retained the neutrality of classical analysis as well as a focus on being expressive rather than supportive, but he was also more pragmatic than other theorists in the various object relations schools.

Kernberg's commitment to drive theory is laudable and may have been politically important in North American psychoanalysis in the 1970s and 1980s. The Kernberg model might lose little of its power to explain pathology, and gain in coherence, if the concept of drive were abandoned. Aggression does not follow the cyclical nature of biological impulses like sex, thirst, and hunger. It is hard to see what the theory gains through the assumption of a mature biological destructive (and self-destructive) force. The distinction between instinctual acts (early) and drives (after 3 or 4 years) forces clinicians to look at the hateful, hostile, destructive acts of individuals with BPD as necessarily developmentally early and primitive. As we have noted, assertiveness, gratification from a sense of agency, is characteristic of the infant from the earliest times (3 months; e.g., Watson, 1995), but there is little evidence to support the notion of vengeful, cruel, and annihilating states of mind characterizing early infancy (Stern, 1990, 1995a; Stern, Hofer, Haft, & Dore, 1985).

Kernberg has been committed to research throughout his career. Consequently, his theories and technical recommendations are testable. His etiological hypotheses inevitably share some of the general weaknesses of psychoanalytic formulations, but his contribution remains a landmark, not just because of his advancement of the psychoanalytic developmental framework for personality disorder but also because it brought about a major shift in the epistemic stance taken by psychoanalysts from a clinical hermeneutic to an empirical perspective.

The Interpersonal Relational Approach

The most rapidly evolving psychoanalytic theoretical orientation in the past decade is the so-called interpersonal relational approach. Its hallmark is the rejection of the classical clinical and epistemic frame for psychoanalysis in favor of conceiving of both development and the therapeutic encounter as co-constructed between two active participants, with the subjectivities of both parent and child, analyst and patient generating the shape and substance of the dialogue. There are many important contributors to this young approach, such as Ogden (1994), McLaughlin (1991), Hoffman (1994), Renik (1993), Benjamin (1998), and Bromberg (1998). Like all new psychoanalytic approaches, this one has powerful historical roots. It is a direct descendent of Harry Stack Sullivan's (1953) interpersonal psychiatry school, linked with British object relations approaches by an influential volume coauthored by the most powerful advocate of this new approach (Greenberg & Mitchell, 1983). There are numerous aspects of this shift: Notions of objective truth are supplemented or replaced with subjectivity, intrapsychic with intersubjective, fantasy (poetics) with pragmatics (descriptions of experience); concepts of truth and distortion are supplemented with perspectivism; and a surge for strong theories is replaced by attempts to avoid theoretical bias.

The Developmental Perspective of the Relational Approach

As the theory is not yet fully formalized, we focus on a small number of key ideas to give a flavor of this important

new orientation. Sullivan (1953), like Fairbairn, was dissatisfied with psychoanalysis ignoring the relationship-seeking aspect of human character. He explicitly rejected Freud's model of libidinal development in general and infantile sexuality in particular as an explanation of behavior. Conflict was not seen as being in the individual, but as produced by conflictual, contradictory signals and values in the environment (Sullivan, 1964). In the interpersonalist tradition, psychopathology results when, in the course of development, the satisfaction of interpersonal needs is disrupted by anxiety, the source of which is interpersonal.

Although many of Sullivan's terms are deliberately changed to underscore the separation from traditional psychoanalytic approaches, the elaboration of the constructs reveals fairly close correlations between the interpersonalist and the psychodynamic domains: "security operations" appear to be the same as defense, and "parataxic distortions" appear analogous to internal object relationships. There are genuine differences, however. The therapist's ideal style is not to impart understanding; it is more active and participatory and does not aim to increase insight into unconscious function, but to explore the nature of and reasons for patterns of behavior. The relational model has the interpersonal model as its starting point, particularly the assumption of the interpersonal nature of subjectivity (S. A. Mitchell, 1988). This is not dissimilar to interpersonalist approaches in self-psychology (Stolorow & Atwood, 1991). The relational model includes individuality, subjectivity, and intersubjectivity, with its philosophical basis in Wittgenstein and Davidson, as clearly formulated by Cavell (1994). This is in distinction to traditional self-psychology, where the nuclear self is conceived as intrapsychic. An individual human mind is a contradiction in terms, as subjectivity is invariably rooted in intersubjectivity (Mitchell, 2000). Mitchell conceives of pathology in terms of conflict arising naturally out of the relational nature of development. The basic units of mind are seen as relational configurations that are intrinsically in conflict. This is unlike the traditional object relations theory view of pathology in terms of developmental arrest. The basic concerns of the psychodynamic approach are the matrices of relational bonds within which personal meanings are embedded.

Whereas classical analytic theory stands or falls on its biological foundations (Sulloway, 1979), the heritage of interpersonal relational theories is qualitatively different, more at home with postmodern deconstructive ideas than with brain-behavior integration. A helpful illustration of the primacy of the relational context is Mitchell's understanding of the role of sexuality. Recognized as a powerful biological and physiological force, it is seen as inevitably emerging in an interpersonal context, which is mutually regulatory, intersubjective, or relational. Its power is not derived from organ pleasure but from its meaning in a relational matrix (Mitchell, 1988). A similar relational argument was advanced by Mitchell (1993) for aggression. The etiological emphasis is on early childhood experience, which teaches the child about "the specific ways in which each of his object relationships will inevitably become painful, disappointing, suffocating, over-sexualised and so on" (Ogden, 1989, pp. 181–182).

There is an emphasis on observable behavior and a reluctance to privilege fantasy over actuality. Reality is not behind the appearance, it is in the appearance (Levenson, 1981). Distortions are produced by interpersonal anxiety in the real world. Fantasy is accepted as formative in the sense that it makes reality relevant (Mitchell, 2000).

The Interpersonal Development Theory of Psychopathology

Mitchell (2000) identified a grouping of four basic modes through which relationality operates to generate psychiatric disorder:

1. Nonreflective, presymbolic behavior is what people actually do with each other that leads to the organization of relational fields around reciprocal influence and mutual regulation. This includes work on the representation of interpersonal interaction into procedural aspects of memory (Crittenden, 1997), whether relegated to this by repression of trauma (Davies & Frawley, 1994) or constraints imposed by cognitive development (Stern, 1994).
2. Affective permeability is the shared experience of intense affect across permeable boundaries where direct resonances emerge in interpersonal dyads (Bromberg, 1998).
3. Experience is organized into self-other configurations, as extensively discussed by Kernberg and other object relations theorists.
4. Intersubjectivity is the mutual recognition of self-reflective agents identified by relationally oriented psychoanalytic feminists such as Chodorow (1989) and Benjamin (1995). The latter explores how any "subject-object discipline" necessarily imposes a dichotomization where only one end of the pole can attain agency. Understanding gender issues in psychological disorder requires a move away from that kind of study. Ultimately, Benjamin argues that fear and defense against a maternal image leads to the ubiquity of masochism in female sexuality.

Relational theory embraces the notion that the absence of a sensitive object causes a child to precociously fulfill a missing parental function, but it is critical of the developmental arrest model (Mitchell, 1988). Childlike needs expressed by adult patients should not be thought of as infantile needs but as adult dependency needs accompanied by intense anxiety. We privilege the earliest periods at the risk of overlooking current relationship needs (Greenberg, 1991). Relational understanding of narcissistic problems represents a compromise between Kohut and Kernberg. The child's need for the narcissistic illusion of grandiosity is accepted but so is Kernberg's recognition of the narcissistic illusion as defensive. Mitchell's suggestion is that the parent must engage in a particular validation through play, a joint pretend that is recognized by both parent and child.

Much of the controversy surrounding the relational approach concerns the declared commitment to a less asymmetrical and more mutual patient-therapist relational structure (Aron, 1996). One focus of this controversy concerns the readiness with which therapists disclose their own feelings (Ehrenberg, 1993). There is a range of views on this, but the mere fact of the controversy signals a willingness to turn away from traditional restrictive conceptions of the social context of offering psychotherapeutic help.

Evaluation of the Interpersonal Relational Approach

The relational approach deviates from most psychotherapeutic approaches in being not primarily developmental in its orientation. The developmental formulations offered lean heavily on other perspectives. As the approach focuses on interpersonal patterns rather than psychiatric categories, evidence for the approach is not readily identified. A review of empirical research in three areas—studies of families and marriages, the role of adult relationships in undoing the adult consequences of destructive childhood experiences, and the relationship of marital variables and the onset and course of depressive disorder—shows that results in all these areas are consistent with the relational assumption that current interpersonal relationships can determine the emergence and course of psychological disturbance. There is substantial developmental evidence that psychopathology is almost inevitably accompanied by relational problems and that good interpersonal relations have a protective influence (e.g., Laub, 1998).

As with all psychosocial approaches, the behavior genetics evidence is a considerable challenge; in the case of interpersonal causes of depression, there are data to support an interaction between life events and genetic vulnerability (e.g., Silberg, Rutter, Neale, & Eaves, 2001). The techniques of interpersonal therapists differ significantly from their other analytic colleagues in being more active, oriented to current relationships, and avoiding identifying a deeper psychic reality beyond the surface. Interpersonal therapists are supposed to be engaged in collaborative investigation, eliciting information, laboriously sorting out the past from the present, the illusory from the real, continually checking the data.

It is important to note that the strongest evidence for the effectiveness of psychodynamic therapy comes from studies in the strictly interpersonalist tradition. The best controlled studies of relatively brief psychotherapy with mood disorders in adults (E. Frank, Kupfer, Wagner, McEachran, & Cornes, 1991; Shapiro et al., 1995; Shea et al., 1992) and adolescents (Mufson & Fairbanks, 1996) with eating disorders (Fairburn, 1994) and with chronic users of health care services (Guthrie et al., 1999) have all shown interpersonal therapy to be at least as effective as other brief therapies. Most studies that have looked at more classically psychoanalytic therapies have been less focused on particular clinical problems and have had less adequate experimental controls (Roth & Fonagy, 1996). Although the model of development and psychopathology may not compare to more mature psychoanalytic approaches, its potential for generating effective, brief clinical interventions may be as good as or better than other theoretical frameworks.

A PARADIGM SHIFT TO EMPIRICAL SCIENCE: PSYCHOANALYTIC SCHEMA THEORIES

The reification and anthropomorphism of psychoanalytic metapsychological formulations and the inevitable logical contradictions they entail led a number of analysts to evolve theories broadly in line with general systems theory (von Bertalanffy, 1968). Systems theory formulations of development are able to address multiple components of a developmental process at several levels of abstraction simultaneously. In a sense, it affords an updating of Freud's nineteenth-century biological metaphor. A number of implementations have attempted a more or less direct translation of structural psychoanalytic theory into a general systems model (e.g., Basch, 1976; Boesky, 1988; Noy, 1977; Peterfreund, 1971; Rosenblatt & Thickstun, 1977; Tyson & Tyson, 1990). Bowlby's attachment theory is a comprehensive implementation of aspects of psychoanalytic theory using general systems theory. There are several other implementations of British object relations theory and cognitive science research in these terms, including person schema

theory (Horowitz, 1992; Horowitz, Eells, Singer, & Salovey, 1995) and cognitive analytic therapy (Ryle, 1995, 1997). Here we review only one approach, which arguably has been the most influential and is the most closely connected to a developmental frame of reference.

The Interpersonal World of the Human Infant

Daniel Stern's (1985) second book was a milestone for psychoanalytic theories of development. It was normative rather than pathomorphic, prospective rather than retrospective, and focused on the developmental organization of subjective perspectives of the self. Unlike other models, it does not come with an immediate set of clinical applications, but it has been widely used, more or less legitimately, in developmental accounts of personality disorder and neurotic problems. The developmental model delineated by Stern has four phases, each linked to a different sense of self: (1) the emerging self from birth to 2 months; (2) the core self, 2 to 6 months: the emergence of a sense of agency and continuity across time; (3) a sense of subjective self emerging between 9 and 18 months, when intentions may be shared and awareness of emotion in the other arises; and (4) the emergence of language in the narrative self, but, in line with the developmental psychopathology perspective, Stern sees prior selves as conditioning later stages of self-development. Damasio (1999) suggested a model of the development of self and consciousness with important features in common:

1. Damasio's "proto-self" (first-order neural maps) links to the emergent self in that it emerges from subcortical structures in the brain.

2. Second-order neural maps (core consciousness) are generated by higher-order circuits and entail the ways the proto-self is changed by its interaction with the world; it compares the proto-self before and after an interaction in a way that is analogous with Stern's description of the core self (Siegel, 2001).

3. Extended consciousness involving third-order neural maps link to Stern's subjective self, as Damasio describes them, as neural representations of the changes in the core self over time.

Stern (1993) describes the subjective integration of all aspects of lived experience as "emergent moments" that derive from a range of schematic representations (event representations, semantic representations, perceptual schemas, sensorimotor representations) in conjunction with a representation of "feeling shapes" (patterns of arousal across time) and "proto-narrative envelopes" that give a proto-plot to an event with an agent, an action, instrumentality, and context (see Bruner, 1990). These are conceptualized in combination as the "schema-of-a-way-of-being-with." It is distortions in this basic schema that lead to vulnerabilities to psychopathology.

Stern (1993) offers a compelling example of a way-of-being with a depressed mother, describing the baby trying repeatedly to recapture and reanimate her. He describes how depressed mothers, monitoring their own failure to stimulate, may make huge efforts to enliven their infant in an unspontaneous way, to which infants respond with what is probably an equally false enlivened interaction. This model maps very closely onto Sandler's model of projection and projective identification, and the two need to be combined to achieve a fully coherent account. The child identifies with the representation of the mother's distorted representation of him, communicated to him by projective identification, and this evolves into an expectation of "a false way-of-being-with" the other.

These schemata come closest to providing a neuropsychologically valid way of depicting a psychoanalytic model of the development of interpersonal experience. Certain features of the model are critical here (see also Stern, 1994, 1995a, 1995b):

1. The schemata are emergent properties of the nervous system.
2. They make use of multiple, simultaneous representations of lived experience.
3. They are based on prototypes and are thus stable in relation to single experiences and naturally aggregate common patterns of lived experience.
4. They can be seen as the simultaneous activation of a set of nodes within a neural network, with each activation automatically strengthening the connections between the nodes (Read, Vanman, & Miller, 1997; Rumelhart & McClelland, 1986).
5. The model allows room for modification from inside as well as outside; reconfiguration is a route by which internally generated activation (fantasy) may strengthen or alter experience.

"Shape" is given to experience through the temporal patterning of arousal. Arousal amalgamates across modalities of experience and, in its purest form, the emotional shape or unfolding across time may be a feature of a prototype experience that is subsequently sought and reen-

acted in interpersonal relationships or in therapy. Arousal systems function by activating the particular modes of cognitive functioning, which, in combination with the experience of arousal, may explain why individuals can persist in repeatedly generating maladaptive interpersonal processes, which nevertheless create desirable configurations or patterns of emotion or cognition.

These moments, or particular ways of experiencing the self with the other, have been exploited by the Boston group in explanations of therapeutic change. It is claimed that change experience in psychotherapy is essentially linked to the rediscovery of these concentrated points of interpersonal experience (Stern et al., 1998). Karlen Lyons-Ruth (1998) points out that classical (problematic) notions of internalization poorly fit the acquisition of procedural knowledge. Both she and Tronick (1998) emphasize the two-person character of such information; awareness of the other is seen as a prerequisite for the articulation, differentiation, and flexible use of these structures. The key assumptions of their model lead the authors inevitably to an interpersonalist psychology. Tronick's dual consciousness model is probably its clearest expression: "I interact, therefore I am." As the authors are well aware, they are contributing to a rich tradition, perhaps beginning with Hegel (1807), reinforced by Mead (1934), Cooley (1902/1964), and more recently by Davidson (1987), and in the psychoanalytic sphere by Cavell (1994). Yet, Stern and his colleagues differ from modern psychoanalytic interpersonalists (see Fiscalini, Mann, & Stern, 1995) in offering a coherent psychological model of intersubjectivity, complete with developmental roots and technical implications.

It is likely that general systems theory will be the favored frame of reference for future psychoanalytic developmental models. Stern's model provides a good fit with developmental data on infancy, but much of its extension to childhood and adult psychopathology is speculative and, on occasion, fanciful. As we have pointed out repeatedly, the adult is not an infant, and continuities from infancy at the level of mental representation are quite unlikely, although they are possible at the procedural implicit level highlighted by Stern and his colleagues. It is in our view more likely that continuity from early childhood will be easier to trace at the level of mental process by identifying those aspects of the psychosocial environment that critically interact with the developmental unfolding of interpersonal mental functions. These interfaces between psychosocial influence and the development of mental structures (mental processes) are most likely to be involved in the psychoanalytic understanding of the developmental psychopathological process.

MENTALIZATION AND THE CHANGING AIMS OF PSYCHOANALYSIS

The influence of attachment theory on psychoanalysis has been constant and relatively strong, notwithstanding the adverse reaction that confronted Bowlby's publication of his first major paper on attachment (Fonagy, 2001a). Few psychoanalytic theorists, however, adopt Bowlby's ideas in their entirety. Within modern psychoanalysis, the mentalization based approach is perhaps the only one that fully integrates attachment theory with psychoanalytic constructs (although see Eagle, 1996; Holmes, 2000; Lieberman & Zeanah, 1999; Lyons-Ruth, Bronfman, & Atwood, 1999; Slade, 1999). Simply put, this model assumes that at the highest level, Bowlby's internal working models assume a shared awareness of mental states between self and other. This is sometimes termed by cognitive psychologists "theory of mind" (Baron-Cohen, 1995). The psychoanalytic adaptation of attachment theory assumes that the capacity to envision mental states in self and others develops and is powerfully influenced by the quality of the attachment relationship between the child and primary caregiver.

A Dialectic Model of the Emergence of the Agentive Self

This psychodynamic model, closely linked to attachment theory, focuses on the developmental emergence of the agentive self, particularly as revealed by the vicissitudes of the unfolding of the capacity to mentalize, to conceive of mental states as explanations of behavior in oneself and in others (Fonagy, Gergely, Jurist, & Target, 2002; Fonagy & Target, 1997a). Our approach is rooted in attachment theory but claims a further evolutionary rationale for the human attachment system that goes beyond Bowlby's (1969) phylogenetic and ontogenetic claims for proximity to the protective caregiver in that we consider the major selective advantage conferred by attachment to humans to be the opportunity that proximity to concerned adults affords for the development of social intelligence and meaning making (Fonagy, 2003). The capacity for "interpretation," which Bogdan (1997) defined as "organisms making sense of each other in contexts where this matters biologically" (p. 10), becomes uniquely human when others are engaged "psychologically in sharing experiences, information and affects" (p. 94). The capacity to interpret human behavior requires the "in-

tentional stance": "treating the object whose behavior you want to predict as a rational agent with beliefs and desires" (Dennett, 1987, p. 15). The biologically based capacity for interpretation in psychological terms, which we have labeled the "interpersonal interpretive function," unfolds within the framework of the complex psychological processes afforded by close proximity in infancy to another human being, the attachment figure. Unlike the internal working model, it does not encode representations of experiences; it is not a repository of personal encounters (see Stern's "schemata-of-ways-of-being-with"). It is a mechanism for processing and interpreting new interpersonal experiences.

A number of emotional processing and control mechanisms probably contribute to interpretative function. So far, we have concerned ourselves with the developmental unfolding of four: (1) the labeling and understanding of affect, (2) arousal regulation, (3) effortful control, and (4) the development of mentalizing or mind-reading capacities proper (what we elsewhere operationalize as reflective function; Fonagy & Target, 2002). Close proximity in infancy to another human being may be an important facilitatory condition for the comprehensive development of these capacities. Thus, we claim that the disruption of early affectional bonds not only sets up possibly lifelong maladaptive attachment patterns (e.g., Hamilton, 2000; Waters, Merrick, Treboux, Crowell, & Albersheim, 2000), but also undermines a range of capabilities vital to the processing of information related to mental states. We claim that the link to attachment (the secure base) is made on the basis of the prediction that individuals secure in their early attachment will do better at tasks that call for these capacities.

Our model of agentive self-development may be summarized briefly as follows. The child normally acquires an understanding of five, increasingly complex, levels of self-agency: physical, social, teleological, intentional, and representational (Fonagy et al., 2002; Gergely, 2001a).

1. Children in the first months begin by understanding that they are a *physically agentive entity* with force that is the source of action and that they are agents whose actions can bring about changes in bodies with which they have immediate physical contact (Leslie, 1994).
2. Developing alongside this is children's understanding of themselves as *social agents*. Interactions with the caregiver (from birth) substantiate babies' experience that their behavior produces effects on their caregiver's behavior and emotions. In other words, babies know that they are social agents, that their communicative displays can produce effects at a distance in the social environment (Neisser, 1988).

Both of these early forms of self-awareness probably evolve through the workings of *an innate contingency-detection mechanism* that enables infants to analyze the probability of causal links between their actions and stimulus events (Watson, 1994, 1995). The discovery of the psychological self (mentalization) probably relies on the same mechanism. At about 3 months, there is a change in contingency preference from infants preferring perfect contingency to preferring nearly, but clearly not, perfect contingencies thereafter (Bahrick & Watson, 1985). The initial preoccupation with perfectly response-contingent stimulation (provided by the proprioceptive sensory feedback that the self's actions always generate) allows infants to differentiate their agentive self as a separate entity in the environment and to construct the primary representation of the bodily self. The switch that takes place in the contingency detection module at about 3 months predisposes infants to turn their attention to *high but imperfect contingencies*—the kind of contingent reactivity that is characteristic of the interactions of infant-attuned caregivers, exemplified by their empathic mirroring reactions to the infant's affective displays. Repeated experience with such affect-reflective caregiver reactions is seen as essential for infants to become sensitized to, and to construct differentiated representations of, their internal self-states, a process we term "social biofeedback" (Gergely & Watson, 1996). It is through providing such a state-reflective scaffolding environment that a congenial and secure attachment relationship can vitally contribute to the emergence of early mentalization capacities, allowing infants to discover or find their psychological self in the social world (Gergely, 2001b).

This approach explicitly rejects the classical Cartesian assumption that emotional and other internal mental states are from the start directly experienced introspectively and will, as a consequence, inevitably give rise to the concept of the emotion in the child's mind, just as the perceptual experience of tables may ultimately generate the concept of "table." In fact, the Cartesian doctrine of the primacy of "first-person" experience has been seriously challenged in current philosophy of mind, cognitive neuroscience, and developmental theory on a number of grounds (Carpendale & Lewis, in press; Damasio, 1994; Dennett, 1991; Gopnik, 1993; Wegner & Wheatley, 1999). In short, we suggest that in the first instance, mental states are discovered through contingent mirroring interactions with the caregiver (Gergely & Watson, 1996, 1999; Target & Fonagy, 1996).

We assume that at first, we are not introspectively aware of our different emotion states. Rather, our representations of these emotions are primarily based on stimuli received from the external world. Babies learn to differentiate the internal patterns of physiological and visceral stimulation that accompany different emotions through observing their caregiver's facial or vocal mirroring responses to these (Legerstee & Varghese, 2001; Meltzoff, 1990; R. W. Mitchell, 1993; Schneider-Rosen & Cicchetti, 1991). Two conditions need to be met for this to take place: reasonable congruency of mirroring, whereby the caregiver accurately matches the infant's mental state, and "markedness" of the mirroring, whereby the caregiver is able to express an affect while indicating that she is not expressing her own feelings (Gergely & Watson, 1996, 1999). Consequently, two impingements can occur. In the case of incongruent mirroring, the infant's representation of internal state will not correspond to a constitutional self state (nothing real), and a predisposition to a narcissistic (false self) structure might be established. In the case of unmarked mirroring, the caregiver's expression may be seen as externalization of the infant's experience, and a predisposition to experience emotion through other people (a borderline personality structure) might be established (Fonagy et al., 2002). This is an instance of the general principle that the child's capacity to create a coherent image of mind is critically dependent on an experience of being perceived as a mind by the attachment figure. Social understanding is an emergent property of the child's experience of referential interactions with the caregiver about an object, which will inevitably generate the discovery that others have differing beliefs about the world from one's own.

The capacity for attentional control, the ability to inhibit a dominant response to perform a subdominant response, is termed "effortful control by attention" by Posner and Rothbart (2000). Early attachment, which allows the child to internalize the mother's ability to divert the child's attention from something immediate to something else (Fonagy, 2001b), serves to equip children with this capacity. Longitudinal studies of self-regulation demonstrate that the capacity for effortful control is strongly related to a child's observed willingness to comply with maternal wishes (committed compliance), that is, the degree to which he or she apparently willingly embraces the maternal agenda (Kochanska, Coy, & Murray, 2001). Withholding an impulsive response is a prerequisite for mentalizing, as this requires the foregrounding of a distal second-order nonvisible stimulus (mental state) in preference to what immediately impinges on the child (physical reality). The successful performance of theory of mind tasks, for example, must involve the inhibition of the child's prepotent responses to directly perceived aspects of current reality in favor of generating a response on the basis of less salient representations of reality attributed to other minds. Alan Leslie (2000, p. 1245), one of the pioneers in the field, has come to consider theory of mind "as a mechanism of selective attention. Mental state concepts simply allow the brain to attend selectively to corresponding mental state properties of agents and thus permit learning about these properties."

Attentional control is also linked to attachment. The major function of attachment is the control of distress, and attentional processes must play a key role if the attachment system is to achieve this objective (Harman, Rothbart, & Posner, 1997). Michael Posner, among others, suggests that the interaction between infant and caregiver is likely to train the infant to control his or her distress through orienting the infant away from the source of distress by soothing and involving him or her in distracting activities. Self-regulation is taught (or, more accurately, modeled) by the caregiver's regulatory activity. It has been suggested that joint-attention with caregiver serves a self-organizing function in early development (Mundy & Neal, 2001). A study of infants who were disorganized in their attachment found that these infants also had difficulties with social attention coordination in interactions with their caregiver (Schölmerich, Lamb, Leyendecker, & Fracasso, 1997). Cocaine-exposed children with disorganized attachment at 12 months showed the greatest dysfunctions of social attention coordination not only with the caregiver but with an experimenter (e.g., they initiated joint attention less often; Claussen, Mundy, Mallik, & Willoughby, 2002). Evidence from late-adopted Romanian orphans with profound disorganizations of attachment suggests that quite severe attention problems are more common in this group than would be expected both in relation to other forms of disturbance and due to epidemiological considerations (Chugani et al., 2001; Kreppner et al., 2001). From the point of view of our model of personality disorder, we argue that an enfeebled attentional control system is a likely consequence of attachment disorganization, perhaps linked with enfeebled affect representation, and serves to undermine the development of mentalization as well as its appropriate functioning in later development. It is probable that trauma further undermines attention regulation and is associated with chronic failures of inhibitory control (Allen, 2001a; Schore, 2003).

The emergence of mentalizing (what we have also called reflective) function follows a well-researched developmental line that identifies "fixation points":

1. During the second half of the first year of life, the child begins to construct causal relations that connect actions to their agents on the one hand and to the world on the other. Around this time, infants begin to differentiate actions from their outcomes and to think about actions as means to an end (Tomasello, 1999). This is the begin-

ning of their understanding of themselves as *teleological agents* who can choose the most efficient way to bring about a goal from a range of alternatives (Csibra & Gergely, 1998). The limitation of this stage of experiencing the agentive self is one of physicality. Actors are expected by infants to behave rationally, given physically apparent goal states and the physical constraints of the situation that are already understood by the infant (Csibra et al., 1999; Gergely & Csibra, 2000, 2003). There is no implication here that infants have an idea about the mental state of the object. They are simply judging rational behavior in terms of the physical constraints that prevail and what is obvious in terms of the physical end state that the object has reached.

We have suggested a connection between the focus on understanding actions in terms of their physical as opposed to mental outcomes (a teleological stance) and the mode of experience of agency that we often see in the self-destructive acts of individuals with BPD (Fonagy, Target, & Gergely, 2000). Thus, slight changes in the physical world can trigger elaborate conclusions concerning states of mind. Patients frequently cannot accept anything other than a modification in the realm of the physical as a true index of the intentions of the other.

2. During the 2nd year, children develop an understanding of agency that is mentalistic: that they and others are *intentional agents* whose actions are caused by prior states of mind such as desires (Wellman & Phillips, 2000) and that their actions can bring about changes in minds as well as bodies (e.g., by pointing; Corkum & Moore, 1995).

2. Around 3 to 4 years of age, understanding of agency in terms of mental causation begins to include the representation of epistemic mind states (beliefs). Young children thus understand themselves as *representational agents*. Their mental states are representational in nature (Wellman, 1990).

4. In the 6th year, we see related advances such as children's ability to relate memories of their intentional activities and experiences into a coherent causal-temporal organization, leading to the establishment of the *temporally extended self* (Povinelli & Eddy, 1995). It is this autobiographical extension of self to ensure coherence across time that is most rapidly and evidently lost in severe personality disorder, in part, we have argued, because of the impact of trauma on the functioning of autobiographical memory (Fonagy & Target, 1997b). Full experience of agency in social interaction can emerge only when actions of the self and other can be

understood as initiated and guided by assumptions concerning the emotions, desires, and beliefs of both.

A Developmental Model of Severe Personality Disorder Based on the Concept of Mentalization

Unlike other models covered in this chapter, our psychodynamic developmental model is restricted to clinical problems associated with dysfunctions of the agentive self, which we consider to be linked to direct or indirect consequences of dysfunctions of the interpersonal interpretive function. They are normally psychiatrically considered to be severe personality disorder or borderline personality organization (Kernberg, 1967). We suggest that the contingent and congruent responding of the attachment figure in infancy is far more than the provision of reassurance about a protective presence. It is the principal means by which we acquire an understanding of our own internal states, which is an intermediate step in the acquisition of an understanding of others as psychological entities. We have elaborated a complex model of the steps involved and identified a significant body of empirical evidence consistent with it (see Allen, 2001b; Allen & Fonagy, 2002; Bateman & Fonagy, 2004; Bleiberg, 2001; Fonagy, Target, Gergely, Allen, & Bateman, 2003). Here only the highlights of the model are presented.

Incongruent unmarked mirroring associated with a nonsecure base generates enfeebled affect representations and attentional control systems. The undermining of these major cognitive mechanisms of attachment results in disorganization of the attachment system. We consider disorganized attachment to be coterminous with a disorganization of the self insofar as incongruent unmarked parenting establishes a part within the self structure that corresponds to the caregiver (as perceived) rather than to the child, but nevertheless exists within the self. We have called this (following Winnicott) the "alien self": Ideas or feelings are experienced as part of the self that do not seem to belong to the self (Fonagy & Target, 1996). The child, unable to find himself or herself as an intentional being, internalizes a representation of the other into the self with distorted agentive characteristics. This disorganization within the self system accounts for the controlling behavior of 5- to 6-year-old children who had been disorganized in their attachment in infancy (Solomon & George, 1999). Their self-representation is incoherent, and they attempt to create a coherent self-representation through externalizing the alien part of the self by controlling, coercive behavior. Trauma, when combined with the sequelae of a deeply insecure early environment, with enfeebled affect represen-

tation and poor affect control systems as well as a disorganized self structure, has profound effects on the development of such vulnerable individuals:

1. It inhibits playfulness, which is essential for the adequate unfolding of the interpersonal interpretive function (Dunn, Davies, O'Connor, & Sturgess, 2000; Emde, Kubicek, & Oppenheim, 1997).
2. It interferes directly with affect regulation and attentional control systems (Arntz, Appels, & Sieswerda, 2000).
3. Most important, in vulnerable individuals, it can bring about a total failure of mentalization. We consider the last to be a consequence of a defensive adaptive maneuver on the part of the child who protects himself or herself from the frankly malevolent and dangerous states of mind of the abuser by affectively decoupling this capacity to conceive of mental states, at least in attachment contexts (Fonagy, 1991).
4. We believe that adult social functioning is impaired by childhood and adolescent adversity to the extent that adversity causes a breakdown of attachment-related mentalization (Fonagy, Stein, Allen, & Fultz, 2003). There is considerable evidence that maltreated children have specific mentalization deficits and that borderline individuals are poor at mentalization following severe experiences of maltreatment (Fonagy et al., 1996).

There is evidence from the work of Toth and her colleagues that maltreated children have specific deficits in social cognition that point to the flawed functioning of the interpersonal interpretive function (described earlier). In a study of 80 maltreated preschoolers, Macfie et al. (1999) showed clear limitations in the representation of social cognition in a story stem completion task where the story stem called for the relief of distress. In a further study (Macfie, Cicchetti, & Toth, 2001), maltreated children, especially physically or sexually abused children, were shown to manifest more dissociation as measured by a coding system for the MacArthur Story Stem Narratives. Maltreated children showed disruptions of identity and incoherence of parental representations, which may be seen as indicators of a failure of mentalizing or metacognitive capacities (Fonagy, 1997). A more detailed report (Toth, Cicchetti, Macfie, Maughan, & Vanmeenen, 2000) points to an important developmental perspective in that the capacity for social cognition, particularly the complexity of the representation of the parent in conflict-imbued settings, decreased with development, while the children's representation of themselves became increasingly simplified and exaggerated. Perhaps the most compelling evidence for maltreatment-related social cognitive deficit rooted in the child-caregiver relationship is provided by the randomized controlled intervention study reported by Toth, Maughan, Manly, Spagnola, and Cicchetti (2002), in which preschooler-parent psychotherapy was offered to 23 maltreating families. This 12-month intervention aimed at elaborating and modifying the relationship between parents and child by linking current maternal conceptualization of relationships to the mother's childhood caregiving response. Social cognitive measures of outcome favored this group over psychoeducational home visitation or treatment as usual in a range of domains, including degree of maladaptiveness of maternal representation and the quality of self and mother-child relationship representation. In all, recent work from the Mount Hope Family Center (Macfie et al. 1999; Macfie, Cicchetti, & Toth, 2001; Toth et al., 2000, 2002) is consistent with the assumption of profound impairment of social cognition associated with maltreatment and the potential for reducing this impairment through a relationship-focused intervention.

The most serious impact of trauma occurs with the defensive identification of the victim with the abuser. The victim offers the dissociated, alien part of himself or herself as a space to be colonized by the traumatic experience. Through this, the alien self will be experienced as torturing from within, and unbearably painful emotional states will be the consequence. Self-esteem is low (e.g., Mullen, Martin, Anderson, Romans, & Herbison, 1996), as the self is now experienced as evil and hateful, and coercive controlling behavior is used to externalize the alien part of the self and sometimes force the other to attack, not from within but from without. This could explain why many who have been abused who are also borderline in personality structure seek out other relationships where they are victimized (e.g., Russell, 1986). Trauma also affects the arousal system. In Arnsten's (1998; Arnsten, Mathew, Ubriani, Taylor, & Li, 1999; Mayes, 2000) dual arousal systems model, prefrontal and posterior cortical and subcortical capacities are maintained by independent arousal systems. As the level of cortical activation increases through the mutually interactive norepinephrine alpha 2 and dopamine D1 systems, prefrontal cortical function improves. With excessive stimulation, norepinephrine alpha 1 and dopamine D1 inhibitory activity increases, prefrontal activity goes offline, and posterior cortical and subcortical functions (e.g., more automatic functions) take over. It has been suggested that the switch-point between the two arousal systems may be shifted by trauma, undoubtedly accounting for some of the inhibitory effects of trauma on mentalization, at least in contexts of relatively high arousal.

The absence of mentalization reveals developmentally earlier modes of representing subjective experience that have been described in developmental studies (e.g., Gopnik, 1993), but we see them reemerging in severe personality disorder. Three modes are particularly prominent:

1. In the *psychic equivalence mode,* mental reality and outer reality are considered equivalent. There is a mind-world correspondence, where internal is conceived as having the power of external, the experience of mind can be terrifying, and there is an intolerance of alternative perspectives.

2. The *pretend mode* is normally used by the prementalizing child to preserve a world that is unrelated to external reality, where ideas are recognized as not real but also as having no implications for the external world. As revealed by the absence of mentalizing following trauma, it yields emptiness, meaninglessness, and dissociation. Therapy sessions consist of endless inconsequential talk of thoughts and feelings.

3. We have already mentioned the teleological stance as an explanation for why patients cannot accept anything other than a modification in the realm of the physical as a true index of the intentions of the other.

Most critically, as mentalization normally hides discontinuities in the self structure in all of us, when it disappears, discontinuities within the self become more evident to the individual, leading to identity diffusion. Individuals feel attacked from within, and creating the persecutory part of the self externally in the other is felt as the only solution. This is why borderline patients require rather than enjoy relationships: Relationships are necessary to stabilize the self-structure but are also the source of greatest vulnerability because in the absence of the other, when the relationships break down, or if the other shows independence, the alien self returns to wreak havoc (persecute from within) and to destabilize the self structure. We suggest that in the absence of a person who may act as a vehicle to externalize the alien part of the self, persons with BPD achieve self-coherence through the externalization of this part of the self into a part of their body. Attempts at self-harm are acts carried out in a mode of psychic equivalence, when a part of the body is considered isomorphic with the alien part of the self, at the same time as creating a respite from intolerable affects. Attempts at self-mutilation are more common when the patient is in isolation or, critically, following the loss of an other who up to that point could fulfill the task of being a vehicle for the alien part of the self (Herpertz, 1995; Kemperman, Russ, & Shearin, 1997).

Suicide is on a continuum of lethality with other types of deliberate self-harm (e.g., Linehan, 1986) consequent on experience of loss of the other. When patients attempt suicide, we consider their subjective experience is likely to be decoupled from reality (in the pretend mode of subjectivity); in a sense, they believe they will survive (or their true self will survive) the attempt, but their alien self will be destroyed forever. Consistent with our view is evidence that suicide attempters with BPD features perceive their suicidal attempts as less lethal, with a greater likelihood of rescue and with less certainty of death (Stanley, Gameroff, Michalsen, & Mann, 2001). Their sensitivity in social interaction is understandable, as their deep, unbearably painful emotional state is readily triggered and is terrifyingly experienced in the mode of psychic equivalence.

The clinical approach to these patients entails presenting a view of the internal world of the patient that is stable and coherent and can be clearly perceived and may be adopted as the reflective part of the self (Bateman & Fonagy, 2004). A randomized controlled trial on 44 patients treated in a partial hospital setting provides tentative evidence for the clinical value of this approach (Bateman & Fonagy, 1999, 2001, 2003).

CONCLUSIONS AND FUTURE DIRECTIONS

Each psychoanalytic model has produced a perspective on development. The reason for this is simple. The general expectation in the psychoanalytic frame of reference is that the explanation of psychopathology lies in development. Thus, to most psychoanalysts, it is axiomatic that the study of development and the study of pathology concern the same psychic processes. We have seen throughout this review that this assumption is sometimes poorly supported by evidence. Even where infantile modes of thought and the adult mind in distress seem to share characteristics, it is unwise to assume that later development would not have altered both the mechanism and function of early structures to a point where similarities are superficial. In many cases, one cannot help concluding that psychoanalytic theoreticians were developmental reductionists, oversimplifying complex developmental processes and omitting to explore comprehensively how an early deficit could be expected to affect subsequent development. Across a number of theories, the review highlighted how theoreticians tended to assume without evidence that the emergent mode of mental functioning somehow could developmentally date the onset and perhaps even the nature of the pathogenic process. Thus, if the problem of individuals with BPD is one of sep-

aration-individuation, the cause of the problem must be maternal behavior in the rapprochement subphase of separation-individuation. Of course, this is a logical fallacy. In syllogistic reasoning, it is the error of affirming the consequent (post hoc, ergo propter hoc). Sadly, all too often the face validity of such reasoning has carried the day, allowing less rhetorically appealing but more detailed and comprehensive models to be rejected in favor of simpler, but potentially simplistic accounts.

There are many other well-known problems with psychodynamic models of developmental psychopathology. In this review, we intend to tackle some head on; others have to be conceded to. Thus, it is untrue that there is no evidence consistent with psychoanalytic theories, but it is true that most clinicians have not tested their conjectures empirically. The status of clinical data in psychology has shifted over the years. For example, the past 15 years have seen a significant drift toward the use of qualitative, small n research, albeit with a deeply phenomenological epistemological standpoint. This is not to say that current psychoanalytic clinical research meets the criteria of this research approach. But it is easier to imagine that with some effort, these new methodologies could be adapted to exploring psychoanalytic developmental constructs.

There have been appropriate criticisms of the absence of specificity in psychoanalytic theoretical speculations. Concepts such as narcissism, borderline personality, and even psychosis are used without care in definition, and consequently related phenomena are poorly understood, for example, the predominance of boys presenting with psychiatric problems in middle childhood. Psychoanalysts frequently show an apparently staggering lack of awareness of the potential impact of broader cultural influences. By the same token, analysts often appear not to recognize the way they may be influenced by their own cultural context. Striking examples of this are the issue of gender in psychoanalysis that was probably only appropriately addressed in the 1970s and 1980s, and the issue of sexual orientation, which is only currently being taken on board by the psychoanalytic community. By contrast, race and racism have never been seriously tackled by psychoanalysts, even though unconscious prejudice on the face of it appears to be a highly appropriate topic for psychoanalytic scrutiny.

It is hardly an intellectual challenge to list epistemological and social concerns about psychoanalysis. It is much harder to justify why serious intellectual energy should still be committed to this area when a strong case could be made that anything of scientific value that had ever existed in the discipline must have surely already been exploited and integrated into current streams of inquiry. Indeed, in some respects, the very success of the psychodynamic approach has undoubtedly contributed to its current crisis. Many of the major insights that psychoanalysis had to offer were taken on board by other orientations, such as cognitive-behavior therapy and folk psychology.

So why should psychoanalytic ideas continue to be taken seriously? First, because psychoanalysis studies human subjectivity at its most complex. It therefore provides an essential counterweight to advances in neuroscience and molecular genetics, which would otherwise potentially obliterate or oversimplify the study of mental disorder. As we hunt for the biological basis of anxiety and depression and the impact of childhood maltreatment, it behooves us to retain our sophistication concerning the nature of the impact of human experience as we attempt to identify its biological corollaries. The interaction between genes and environment can be found only if we retain our grasp of the full complexity of how the human mind grapples with the challenges of adaptation. In this context, it is essential that we do not neglect the nonconscious domain of human experience. Given that folk psychology was able to substantially ignore this facet of human function for most of its existence, we should be wary that our concern with unconscious processes and, most important, unconscious motivation in human behavior does not once again go underground.

Two further points are worthy of mention. First, psychoanalysis has been traditionally concerned with early experience, and modern neuroscience has by and large affirmed the pertinence of the study of this early period. Second, cognitive psychology and cognitive-behavior therapy have increasingly converged with psychoanalytic interest in studying the influence of relationship representation patterns on human conduct. Schema theory, systemic approaches, interpersonal approaches, and attachment theory have converged on this problem since the mid-1980s. It would be a shame if the considerable accumulated experience of 100 years of study of this domain were to be lost through disinterest and neglect.

Psychoanalysis has survived 100 years and continues to produce new ideas and recruit advocates. Some of the greatest minds ever to become interested in psychology and the mental disorders explored or adopted the frame of reference of psychoanalysis. They probably did so because it offered the richest set of ideas as elements for describing mental functioning. What are the strengths of the approach that permit this? The following may be an inadequate attempt to answer the query about the resilience of the psychodynamic approach, which a historian of science 100 years from now might raise:

1. Generativity: Many important psychological theories of psychopathology acknowledge that psychoanalytic ideas have inspired their lines of research (e.g., learned helplessness theory, schema theory, attachment theory, aggression and hostility as causes of psychosomatic conditions, self-serving cognitive distortions based on defense mechanisms).

2. Unifying explanations: Diverse symptoms and behavior can reflect a single hidden problem. For example, why are narcissistic individuals often forgetful of names, prejudiced, inconsiderate of others' time, vulnerable to slights, and unable to remain in love? Psychoanalytic accounts, whether self psychological or based on other object relations views, offer single explanations for such groups of phenomena.

3. A dynamic approach—development as a series of compromise formations: This gives depth, texture, and complexity in line with new knowledge emerging from both neuroscience and developmental psychopathology. Many psychoanalytic accounts provide satisfying functionalist explanations of observed patterns of behavior and the observed characteristics of mental representation.

4. The mind as an instrument: Theory is built from the sensitivity of the therapist in generating models for understanding thoughts, feelings, and behavior beyond the normal range of conscious experience and commonsense psychology. Psychoanalytic listening, regardless of specific model, perhaps equips clinicians to handle and make sense of particularly intense and disturbing interactions. The resulting understanding is more complex and psychologically deeper than other, omnibus theories of human behavior (cognitive-behavioral, humanistic, systemic), even if psychoanalysis is therapeutically no more effective. This contains the appeal of psychoanalytic ideas for many clinicians and others.

The Role of the Internal World in the Expression of the Human Genotype

All agree that development involves a gene-environment interaction. In the case of honeybees, the reproductive and social roles of colony members are fixed by events that occur during the first few days of larval development. Worker or queen bee status is not apparently encoded in the genotype but follows from the differential treatment of larvae by worker bees, resulting in differential gene expression, both up-regulation and down-regulation (Evans & Wheeler, 2000). Some quantitative human behavior genetic studies also strongly suggest interactive processes whereby environmental exposure triggers genetic vulnerability. For example, the classic Finnish adoptive family study of Schizophrenia suggests that children with a schizophrenic biological parent are more likely to develop a range of psychiatric problems if, and only if, they are adopted into dysfunctional families (Tienari, Wynne, Moring, Lahti, & Naarala, 1994). Bohman (1996) reported that criminality appeared to be associated with a genetic risk only if children whose biological parents were criminals were adopted into dysfunctional homes. More recently, studies of single gene-environment interactions are being reported. To give just one example, the promoter region of the serotonin transporter gene (SLC6A4) is involved in re-uptake of serotonin at brain synapses; in the gene-linked polymorphic region, the short (S) allele has a lower transcription efficiency than the long (L) allele. There is inconclusive evidence on direct association with depression (Lerch, 2004). However, an analysis of the Dunedin longitudinal sample has dramatically demonstrated that in the presence of three or more traumatic life events, the likelihood of a diagnosis of Major Depression for those with the S allele increases from 10% to 28% to 32%, whereas in those with the L genotype, the risk of an episode of Major Depression is 10% to 16% regardless of life events (Caspi et al., 2003). Genetic risk may or may not become manifest depending on the quality of the family environment to which a child is exposed. But if this is such a pervasive process, why is the quantitative behavior genetic evidence for gene environment interaction so sparse? Plomin and McGuffin's (2003) systematic review failed to find more than a handful of examples.

We think one aspect of the answer to this complex question is obvious: They failed to find more examples because behavior genetics of developmental psychopathology often studies the *wrong* environment. The environment that triggers the expression of a human gene is not the observable, objective environment. The child's experience of the environment is what counts. The manner in which environment is experienced will act as a filter in the expression of genotype into phenotype. And here we touch on the pivotal role of psychoanalysis for genetic research. The primary concern of psychoanalysis is with the interaction of multiple layers of representations in generating developmental outcomes. Data from genetics call for exactly such sophistication in understanding the way genes may or may not be expressed in particular individuals.

The pathway from genes to phenotypes is a tortuous one, along which genetics and environment constantly interact (Elman et al., 1996). Internal and external stimuli, steps in

the development of the brain, hormones, stress, learning, and social interaction alter the binding of transcription regulators (Kandel, 1998). There is substantial individual variability in response to the risk factors of stress and adversity. Much of this variability is poorly understood (Rutter, 1999, 2005), but it underscores the potential importance of intrapsychic variables. Whether or not specific environmental factors trigger the expression of a gene may depend not only on the nature of those factors, but also on the way the infant or child experiences them, which will be an intrapsychic function, determined by conscious or unconscious meaning attribution to these experiences. The quality of this experiential filter may in turn be a function of either genetic or environmental influences, or their interaction (Kandel, 1998). Thus, intrapsychic representational processes are not just consequences of environmental and genetic effects—they may be critical moderators. An intrapsychic perspective may be helpful in considering, not just what precipitates personality and its disorders, but also which processes influence the course of disorders for better or worse. Five years ago this was theory; now, the collaboration of molecular geneticists and developmental research is making it a reality.

We suggest that psychoanalysis needs to look to the cognitive neurosciences to find its intellectual fulfillment. Current theorization in neuroscience has in the past been sadly devoid of considerations of emotional life and relationality, even around topics such as social development, where the subject matter directly concerns the child's subjectivity. The evidence clearly shows that it is naïve to assume that the child's genotypic destiny is fulfilled in a hermetically sealed brain, somehow isolated from the social environment within which ontogeny occurs and the sound adaptation to which is the organizing purpose of the whole system. Subjectivity, the understanding of the individual response, will be an essential piece in putting together the microbiological puzzle of genetic expression.

Psychoanalysis, with its focus on the representation of subjectivity and how this emerges from early development, might have much to contribute to the understanding of how individual differences in the quality of functioning of basic mental mechanisms arise. Here we suggest that infant attachment functions, in part at least, to facilitate the development of an interpersonal interpretative capacity. We propose that a major selective advantage conferred on humans by early intimate and intense relationships with the primary caregiver was the opportunity it afforded for the development of social intelligence and meaning making. The capacity for "interpretation," which Bogdan (1997) defined as "organisms making sense of each other in contexts where this matters biologically" (p. 10), becomes uniquely human when others are engaged "psychologically in sharing experiences, information and affects" (p. 94). The quality of the early relationship plays a major role in determining the robustness of that capacity, but the nature of such relationships is less relevant to later relationship patterns (Fonagy, 2003). But the interpretive capacity in turn has a key role in the processing of social experience. The level of interpersonal interpretative functioning will be reflected in an individual's ability to function in close interpersonal relationships without needing to have recourse to strategies for amplifying the distinction between self and other representations. The unfolding of disturbance over time is conditioned by the interpretive capacity. We speculate that the expression of pathogenic genotypes is made more likely by the poor functioning of a mechanism designed to differentiate the psychological state of self and other.

This is a function of immense importance, as the laborious move from genotype to phenotype is conditioned this way. A full understanding of the interaction between individual mentalized representations of life experience and the expression of genetic dispositions is the task of psychoanalytic psychopathology of the next decades. Kandel (1999, p. 508) cites Francois Jacob (1998) who wrote in *Of Flies, Mice and Men,* "The century that is ending has been preoccupied with nucleic acids and proteins. The next one will concentrate on memory and desire. Will it be able to answer the questions they pose?"

Neuroscience and Future Clinical Applications of Psychoanalytic Ideas

And what of clinical applications of psychoanalysis? The outcome of psychoanalytic therapy has not been the focus of this chapter. Accumulating evidence is moderately favorable to psychodynamic approaches (Fonagy et al., 2001; Fonagy, Roth, & Higgitt, in press; Leichsenring, Rabung, & Leibing, 2004), as it is to most theory-based structured interventions (Roth & Fonagy, 2005). If psychoanalytic therapy is to continue to be able to make a contribution in the future, it will have to be even more firmly rooted in developmental psychopathology. As we increasingly appreciate that psychiatric disorders of adulthood are rooted in abnormalities already observable in childhood or adolescence, there will be a merging of (developmental) psychopathology and psychotherapy research. It is likely that the elucidation of pathogenic mechanisms—essential for the development of effective and specific psychological interventions (Kazdin, 2003)—will be achieved only through developmental observations. The structured, manualized

psychodynamic psychotherapy techniques of the future will need to be designed to specifically address empirically established developmental dysfunctions. Future psychotherapy trials will be increasingly seen as the only viable experimental tests of rival psychosocial etiological models of personality (e.g., Hudson, Kendall, Coles, Robin, & Webb, 2002; Toth et al., 2002).

One reason for the thin evidence base of psychoanalytic psychotherapy is the non-symptom-oriented nature of the psychodynamic approach to therapy (Gabbard, Gunderson, & Fonagy, 2002). The measures of outcome used in many trials leave room for improvement from a psychodynamic standpoint. Most self-report measures in standard use are oriented toward symptom distress and are of greatest relevance to trials of pharmacological products designed to address specific psychiatric symptoms; they are far more likely to change naturally without intervention than measures of functioning (e.g., Grilo et al., 2004). The virtual absence of user involvement in the devising of these measures has been a flaw in this approach and one that might have selectively disadvantaged long-term psychodynamic therapy, which is often favored by those receiving that kind of help (Seligman, 1995). Most outcome measures are prone to bias and are potentially highly reactive with the mode of intervention (Sechrest, McKnight, & McKnight, 1996). Nonbiased, nonsubjective measures of outcome might provide firmer grounding for evaluating psychoanalytic therapies on a level playing field with cognitive-behavioral approaches, which often are better suited to symptom-focused outcomes measurement. Neuroscience (particularly brain imaging) might deliver nonsubjective measures of outcome sooner rather than later. Psychoneurobiology research is identifying neural correlates of complex subjective states (Adolphs, 2003), for example, the experience of social exclusion (Eisenberger, Lieberman, & Williams, 2003) and concern about the mental states of another person (Frith & Frith, 2003). There are indications that scanning techniques that allow the simultaneous imaging of two individuals interacting (King-Casas et al., in press) will be able to offer unbiased indicators of relationship quality as this changes as a consequence of psychological therapy. When the neurobiology of social cognition is clearer and more accessible, unbiased outcomes of psychotherapy based on brain-behavior interaction might cast psychodynamic interventions in a more favorable light as well as clarifying and assisting with the specification of currently overly complex psychoanalytic ideas.

The greatest contribution of neuroscience to psychodynamic psychotherapy is likely to be through progress in molecular biology. As molecular genetic findings unfold over the next few years, it is likely that biological vulnerability will become increasingly detectable; although single genes and polymorphisms will probably never account for a large proportion of variability, combinations of genes may increasingly identify specific types of environmental vulnerability (Plomin & McGuffin, 2003). Discoveries such as those of Caspi and colleagues (2003) concerning vulnerability for life-event-triggered depression among those with the short allele of the serotonin transported gene, described earlier, may create important opportunities for targeting psychodynamic interventions at those with the S genotype. It is not yet clear what aspects of life events might represent a depressogenic effect to those with the S allele. It might well be that enhancing the capacity of those with the S genotype to cope with adverse life events would reduce the potency of the underlying biological vulnerability to trigger Major Depression. The field of mental illness prevention, although impeccable in its logic, has always had difficulty in appropriately targeting preventive interventions when demographic data were the sole guide to identifying the indicated group. The rationale for enrolling a large number of individuals into prevention programs who are unlikely ever to develop the problem has often led to selective uptakes and prevented a genuine test of the prevention approach (Beardslee, Gladstone, Wright, & Cooper, 2003). Preventive efforts will be enhanced by having powerful biological indicators of environmental vulnerability, so that individuals can appreciate that reducing the impact of specific types of environments will protect them from the disease process.

The true importance of molecular biology in this context, however, is in opening a vista of biologically indicated psychosocial treatments—not just preventions. As we begin to understand the causal path that disease processes follow in the vulnerable brain, the need for specific psychosocial treatments to assist individuals with these vulnerabilities will become acute. Knowing that, in individuals with the S/S genotype, severe maltreatment doubles the probability of Major Depressive Disorder (to over 60% from 30% for those with the genotype) helps us to focus interventions on childhood maltreatment for the first group to a greater extent than for the L/L group. It would be fascinating to know whether severely maltreated individuals with these genotypes give different weights to this experience with respect to their disorder. The psychotherapy would be designed to help these individuals to circumvent and, if possible, reverse the impact of this type of psychosocial event on brain function.

Future psychoanalytic developmental, clinical, and treatment research must entail the removal of the opposition between psychosocial and biological perspectives. As we identify specific brain dysfunctions associated with psychological disorders, the need for psychotherapy will become greater—not less, as some fear and others advocate. Pharmacological interventions specific to the underlying cause of brain dysfunction, particularly etiology-associated brain dysfunctions, will be a long time coming. So far, there is little evidence that genotyping can indicate the choice of psychotropic medication (e.g., Solvason, Ernst, & Roth, 2003). Psychological approaches, in contrast, can be developed and tested rapidly. Psychotherapy can be available to provide a work-around, a set of techniques that the mind can use to overcome a biological deficit. This is not to suggest that psychotherapy could be to the brain as physiotherapy is to the healing of the musculoskeletal system (although this would be nice if true), but rather that the human mind as a system evolved to be able to bypass and overcome dysfunctions in the physical organ on which it depends: the brain. It was to exploit this self-healing capacity that Freud invented psychoanalytic psychotherapy. Increased neuroscientific knowledge will help us to help the brains of our patients to devise and make use of sometimes complex and sometimes simple mental strategies to cope with weaknesses in their brain function, whether these are caused by genetic vulnerability, developmental assault, or a unique combination of the two.

The future of psychoanalysis, if it is to have a future, is in the context of an empirical psychology, abetted by imaging techniques, neuro-anatomical methods, and human genetics. Embedded in the sciences of human cognition, the ideas of psychoanalysis can be tested, and it is here that these ideas can have their greatest impact. (Kandel, 1998, p. 468)

REFERENCES

Adler, A. (1916). *The neurotic constitution.* New York: Moffat Yard.

Adler, G. (1985). *Borderline psychopathology and its treatment.* New York: Aronson.

Adolphs, R. (2003). Cognitive neuroscience of human social behavior. *Nature Reviews, 4,* 165–178.

Aichhorn, A. (1925). *Wayward youth.* New York: Viking.

Alexander, F. (1930). The neurotic character. *International Journal of Psycho-Analysis, 11,* 292–311.

Alexander, F., & French, T. (1946). The principle of corrective emotional experience: The case of Jean Valjean. In F. Alexander & T. French (Eds.), *Psychoanalytic theory, principles and application* (pp. 66–70). New York: Ronald Press.

Allen, J. G. (2001a). *Interpersonal trauma and serious mental disorder.* Chichester, England: Wiley.

Allen, J. G. (2001b). *Traumatic relationships and serious mental disorders.* Chichester, England: Wiley.

Allen, J. G., & Fonagy, P. (2002). *The development of mentalizing and its role in psychopathology and psychotherapy* [Technical Report No. 02-0048]. Topeka, KS: Menninger Clinic, Research Department.

Angold, A., Costello, E. J., & Erkanli, A. (1999). Comorbidity. *Journal of Child Psychology and Psychiatry, 40,* 57–87.

Arlow, J. A. (1985). The structural hypothesis. In A. Rothstein (Ed.), *Models of the mind: Their relationships to clinical work* (pp. 21–34). New York: International Universities Press.

Arnsten, A. F. T. (1998). The biology of being frazzled. *Science, 280,* 1711–1712.

Arnsten, A. F. T., Mathew, R., Ubriani, R., Taylor, J. R., & Li, B.-M. (1999). Alpha-1 noradrenergic receptor stimulation impairs prefrontal cortical cognitive function. *Biological Psychiatry, 45,* 26–31.

Arntz, A., Appels, C., & Sieswerda, S. (2000). Hypervigilance in borderline disorder: A test with the emotional Stroop paradigm. *Journal of Personality Disorders, 14*(4), 366–373.

Aron, L. (1996). *A meeting of minds: Mutuality in psychoanalysis.* New York: International Universities Press.

Bahrick, L. R., & Watson, J. S. (1985). Detection of intermodal proprioceptive-visual contingency as a potential basis of self-perception in infancy. *Developmental Psychology, 21,* 963–973.

Balint, M. (1959). *Thrills and regressions.* London: Hogarth Press.

Balint, M. (1968). *The basic fault.* London: Tavistock.

Baron-Cohen, S. (1995). *Mindblindness: An essay on Autism and theory of mind.* Cambridge, MA: Bradford, MIT Press.

Baron-Cohen, S. (2000). Autism: Deficits in folk psychology exist alongside superiority in folk physics. In S. Baron-Cohen, H. Tager-Flusberg, & D. J. Cohen (Eds.), *Understanding other minds: Perspectives from Autism and developmental cognitive neuroscience* (2nd ed., pp. 59–82). Oxford: Oxford University Press.

Baron-Cohen, S., Tager-Flusberg, H., & Cohen, D. J. (Eds.). (2000). *Understanding other minds: Perspectives from developmental cognitive neuroscience.* Oxford: Oxford University Press.

Basch, M. F. (1976). Psychoanalysis and communication science. *Annals of Psychoanalysis, 4,* 385–421.

Bateman, A. W., & Fonagy, P. (1999). The effectiveness of partial hospitalization in the treatment of borderline personality disorder: A randomised controlled trial. *American Journal of Psychiatry, 156,* 1563–1569.

Bateman, A. W., & Fonagy, P. (2001). Treatment of borderline personality disorder with psychoanalytically oriented partial hospitalization: An 18-month follow-up. *American Journal of Psychiatry, 158*(1), 36–42.

Bateman, A. W., & Fonagy, P. (2003). Health service utilization costs for borderline personality disorder patients treated with psychoanalytically oriented partial hospitalization versus general psychiatric care. *American Journal of Psychiatry, 160*(1), 169–171.

Bateman, A. W., & Fonagy, P. (2004). *Psychotherapy for borderline personality disorder: Mentalization based treatment.* Oxford: Oxford University Press.

Beardslee, W. R., Gladstone, T. R., Wright, E. J., & Cooper, A. B. (2003). A family based approach to the prevention of depressive symptoms in children at risk: Evidence of parental and child change. *Pediatrics, 112*(2), E119–E131.

Benjamin, J. (1995). *Like subjects, love objects.* New Haven, CT: Yale University Press.

Benjamin, J. (1998). *The shadow of the other: Intersubjectivity and gender in psychoanalysis.* New York: Routledge.

Bennett, I., & Hellman, I. (1951). Psychoanalytic material related to observations in early development. *Psychoanalytic Study of the Child, 6,* 307–324.

Berridge, K. C., & Robinson, T. (1995). The mind of an addicted brain: Neural sensitization of wanting versus liking. *Current Directions in Psychological Science, 4,* 71–76.

Bibring, E. (1947). The so-called English school of psychoanalysis. *Psychoanalytic Quarterly, 16,* 69–93.

Bick, E. (1964). Notes on infant observation in psychoanalytic training. *International Journal of Psycho-Analysis, 45,* 558–566.

Bion, W. R. (1957). Differentiation of the psychotic from the nonpsychotic personalities. *International Journal of Psychoanalysis, 38,* 266–275.

Bion, W. R. (1959). Attacks on linking. *International Journal of Psychoanalysis, 40,* 308–315.

Bion, W. R. (1962a). *Learning from experience.* London: Heinemann.

Bion, W. R. (1962b). A theory of thinking. *International Journal of Psychoanalysis, 43,* 306–310.

Bion, W. R. (1967). *Second thoughts.* London: Heinemann.

Bleiberg, E. (2001). *Treating personality disorders in children and adolescents: A relational approach.* New York: Guilford Press.

Blos, P. (1962). *On adolescence: A psychoanalytic interpretation.* New York: Free Press.

Blum, H. (Ed.). (1986). *Defense and resistance: Historical perspectives and current concepts.* New York: International Universities Press.

Blum, H. (1994). *Reconstruction in psychoanalysis.* New York: International Universities Press.

Boesky, D. (1988). The concept of psychic structure. *Journal of the American Psychoanalytic Association, 36*(Suppl.), 113–135.

Bogdan, R. J. (1997). *Interpreting minds.* Cambridge, MA: MIT Press.

Bohman, M. (1996). Predisposition to criminality: Swedish adoption studies in retrospect. In M. Rutter (Ed.), *Genetics of criminal and antisocial behavior* (pp. 99–114). Chichester, England: Wiley.

Bollas, C. (1987). *The shadow of the object: Psychoanalysis of the unthought known.* New York: Columbia University Press.

Bollas, C. (1989). *Forces of destiny: Psychoanalysis and human idiom.* London: Free Association Books.

Bower, T. R. (1974). *Development in infancy.* San Francisco: Freeman.

Bowlby, J. (1969). *Attachment and loss: Vol. 1. Attachment.* London: Hogarth Press.

Bowlby, J. (1980). *Attachment and loss: Vol. 3. Loss, sadness and depression.* London: Hogarth Press.

Bradley, C. (1997). Generativity-stagnation: Development of a status model. *Developmental Review, 17,* 262–290.

Brenner, C. (1982). *The mind in conflict.* New York: International Universities Press.

Brenner, C. (1987). Working through 1914–1984. *Psychoanalytic Quarterly, 56,* 68–108.

Brenner, C. (1994). The mind as conflict and compromise formation. *Journal of Clinical Psychoanalysis, 3,* 473–488.

Bromberg, P. M. (1998). *Standing in the spaces.* Hillsdale, NJ: Analytic Press.

Brown, G. W. (1998). Loss and depressive disorders. In B. P. Dohrenwend (Ed.), *Adversity, stress and psychopathology* (pp, 358–370). New York: Oxford University Press.

Brown, G. W., Harris, T. O., & Hepworth, C. (1995). Loss, humiliation and entrapment among women developing depression: A patient and nonpatient comparison. *Psychological Medicine, 25,* 7–21.

Bruner, J. (1990). *Acts of meaning.* Cambridge, MA: Harvard University Press.

Bucci, W. (1997). Patterns of discourse in "good" and troubled hours: A multiple code theory. *Journal of the American Psychoanalytic Association, 45,* 155–187.

Burland, J. A. (1986). The vicissitudes of maternal deprivation. In S. B. R. F. Lax & J. A. Burland (Eds.), *Self and object constancy: Clinical and theoretical perspectives* (pp. 324–347). New York: Guilford Press.

Burlingham, D. (1952). *Twins: A study of three pairs of identical twins.* New York: International Universities Press.

Burlingham, D., & Barron, A. T. (1963). A study of identical twins: Their analytic material compared with existing observation data of their early childhood. *Psychoanalytic Study of the Child, 18,* 367–423.

Buss, D. M. (1995). Evolutionary psychology: A new paradigm for psychological science. *Psychological Inquiry, 6,* 1–30.

Caper, R. (1988). *Immaterial facts.* Northvale, NJ: Aronson.

Carlson, M., Dragomir, C., Earls, F., Farrell, M., Macovei, O., Nystrom, P., et al. (1995). Effects of social deprivation on cortisol regulation in institutionalized Romanian infants. *Society for Neuroscience Abstracts, 218,* 12.

Carpendale, J. I. M., & Lewis, C. (in press). Constructing an understanding of mind: The development of children's social understanding within social interaction. *Behavioral and Brain Sciences.*

Caspi, A., Sugden, K., Moffitt, T. E., Taylor, A., Craig, I. W., Harrington, H., et al. (2003). Influence of life stress on depression: Moderation by a polymorphism in the 5-HTT gene. *Science, 301*(5631), 386–389.

Cavell, M. (1994). *The psychoanalytic mind.* Cambridge, MA: Harvard University Press.

Chisholm, K., Carter, M. C., Ames, E. W., & Morison, S. J. (1995). Attachment security and indiscriminately friendly behavior in children adopted from Romanian orphanages. *Development and Psychopathology, 7,* 283–294.

Chodorow, N. (1989). *Feminism and psychoanalytic theory.* Cambridge, MA: Polity Press.

Chugani, H. T., Behen, M. E., Muzik, O., Juhasz, C., Nagy, F., & Chugani, D. C. (2001). Local brain functional activity following early deprivation: A study of postinstitutionalized Romanian orphans. *Neuroimage, 14*(6), 1290–1301.

Cicchetti, D., & Cohen, D. J. (1995). Perspectives on developmental psychopathology. In D. Cicchetti & D. J. Cohen (Eds.), *Developmental psychopathology: Vol. 1. Theory and methods* (pp. 3–23). New York: Wiley.

Cicchetti, D., & Toth, S. L. (Eds.). *Rochester Symposium on Developmental Psychopathology: Vol. 8. Developmental perspectives on trauma* (pp. 33–84). Rochester, NY: University of Rochester Press.

Clarkin, J. F. (2001, August). *Borderline personality disorder, mind and brain: A psychoanalytic perspective.* Paper presented at the plenary presentation, 7th IPA Research Training Program, London.

Clarkin, J. F., Foelsch, P. A., Levy, K. N., Hull, J. W., Delaney, J. C., & Kernberg, O. F. (2001). The development of a psychodynamic treatment for patients with borderline personality disorder: A preliminary study of behavioral change. *Journal of Personality Disorders, 15,* 487–495.

Clarkin, J. F., Kernberg, O. F., & Yeomans, F. (1999). *Transference-focused psychotherapy for borderline personality disorder patients.* New York: Guilford Press.

Claussen, A. H., Mundy, P. C., Mallik, S. A., & Willoughby, J. C. (2002). Joint attention and disorganised atachment status in infants at risk. *Development and Psychopathology, 14,* 279–291.

Compton, A. (1981). On the psychoanalytic theory of instinctual drives: Part IV, Instinctual drives and the ego-id-superego model. *Psychoanalytic Quarterly, 50,* 363–392.

Cooley, C. H. (1964). *Human nature and the social order* (Rev. ed.). New York: Shocken Books. (Original work published 1902)

Cooper, A. M. (1988). Our changing views of the therapeutic action of psychoanalysis: Comparing Strachey and Loewald. *Psychoanalytic Quarterly, 57,* 15–27.

Corkum, V., & Moore, C. (1995). Development of joint visual attention in infants. In C. Moore & P. Dunham (Eds.), *Joint attention: Its origins and role in development* (pp. 61–83). New York: Erlbaum.

Crandell, L. E., Patrick, M. P. H., & Hobson, R. P. (2003). "Still-face" interactions between mothers with borderline personality disorder and their 2-month-old infants. *British Journal of Psychiatry, 183,* 239–247.

Crews, F. (1996). The verdict on Freud. *Psychological Science, 7,* 63–67.

Crittenden, P. M. (1997). Toward an integrative theory of trauma: A dynamic-maturation approach. In D. Cicchetti & S. L. Toth (Eds.), *Rochester Symposium on Developmental Psychopathology: Vol. 8. Developmental perspectives on trauma* (pp. 33–84). Rochester, NY: University of Rochester Press.

Csibra, G., & Gergely, G. (1998). The teleological origins of mentalistic action explanations: A developmental hypothesis. *Developmental Science, 1*(2), 255–259.

Csibra, G., Gergely, G., Brockbank, M., Biro, S., & Koos, O. (1999). *Twelve-month-olds can infer a goal for an incomplete action.* Paper presented at the 11th biennial International Conference on Infant Studies (ICIS), Atlanta, GA.

Damasio, A. R. (1994). Descartes' error and the future of human life. *Scientific American, 271*(4), 144.

Damasio, A. R. (1999). *The feeling of what happens: Body and emotion in the making of consciousness.* New York: Harcourt Brace.

Davidson, D. (1987). Knowing one's own mind. *Proceedings and Addresses of the American Philosophical Association, 60,* 441–457.

Davies, J. M. (1998). Between the disclosure and foreclosure of erotic transference-countertransference: Can psychoanalysis find a place for adult sexuality? *Psychoanalytic Dialogues, 8,* 747–766.

Davies, J. M., & Frawley, M. G. (1994). *Treating the adult survivor of childhood sexual abuse: A psychoanalytic perspective.* New York: Basic Books.

Deater-Deckard, K., Fulker, D. W., & Plomin, R. (1999). A genetic study of the family environment in the transition to early adolescence. *Journal of Child Psychology and Psychiatry, 40,* 769–795.

Dennett, D. C. (1987). *The intentional stance.* Cambridge, MA: MIT Press.

Dennett, D. C. (1991). *Consciousness explained.* Boston: Little, Brown.

De Wolff, M. S., & van IJzendoorn, M. H. (1997). Sensitivity and attachment: A meta-analysis on parental antecedents of infant attachment. *Child Development, 68,* 571–591.

Dunn, J., Davies, L. C., O'Connor, T. G., & Sturgess, W. (2000). Parents' and partners' life course and family experiences: Links with parent-child relationships in different family settings. *Journal of Child Psychology and Psychiatry, 41*(8), 955–968.

Eagle, M. (1996). Attachment research and psychoanalytic theory. In J. M. Masling & R. F. Bornstein (Eds.), *Psychoanalytic perspectives on developmental Psychology: Empirical studies of psychoanalytic theories* (Vol. 6, pp. 105–149). Washington DC: American Psychological Association.

Eaves, L. J., Silberg, J. L., Meyer, J. M., Maes, H. H., Simonoff, E., Pickles, A., et al. (1997). Genetics and developmental psychopathology: 2. The main effects of genes and environment on behavioral problems in the Virginia Twin Study of Adolescent Behavioral Development. *Journal of Child Psychology and Psychiatry, 38*(8), 965–980.

Ehrenberg, D. (1993). *The intimate edge.* New York: Norton.

Eisenberger, N. I., Lieberman, M. D., & Williams, K. D. (2003). Does rejection hurt? An fMRI study of social exclusion. *Science, 302*(5643), 290–292.

Elman, J. L., Bates, A. E., Johnson, M. H., Karmiloff-Smith, A., Parisi, D., & Plunkett, K. (1996). *Rethinking innateness: A connectionist perspective on development.* Cambridge, MA: MIT Press.

Emde, R. N. (1980a). Emotional availability: A reciprocal reward system for infants and parents with implications for prevention of psychosocial disorders. In P. M. Taylor & F. Orlando (Eds.), *Parent-infant relationships* (pp. 87–115). New York: Grune & Stratton.

Emde, R. N. (1980b). Toward a psychoanalytic theory of affect: Part I. The organizational model and its propositions. In S. I. Greenspan & G. H. Pollock (Eds.), *The course of life: Infancy and early childhood* (pp. 63–83). Washington, DC: DHSS.

Emde, R. N. (1980c). Toward a psychoanalytic theory of affect: Part II. Emerging models of emotional development in infancy. In S. I. Greenspan & G. H. Pollock (Eds.), *The course of life: Infancy and early childhood* (pp. 85–112). Washington, DC: DHSS.

Emde, R. N., Kubicek, L., & Oppenheim, D. (1997). Imaginative reality observed during early language development. *International Journal of Psycho-Analysis, 78*(1), 115–133.

Emde, R. N., & Spicer, P. (2000). Experience in the midst of variation: New horizons for development and psychopathology. *Development and Psychopathology, 12*(3), 313–332.

Erdelyi, M. H. (1985). *Psychoanalysis: Freud's cognitive psychology.* New York: Freeman.

Erikson, E. H. (1950). *Childhood and society.* New York: Norton.

Erikson, E. H. (1956). The problem of ego identity. In *Identity and the life cycle* (pp. 104–164). New York: International Universities Press.

Erikson, E. H. (1959). *Identity and the life cycle.* New York: International Universities Press.

Etchegoyen, H. (1991). *The fundamentals of psychoanalytic technique.* London: Karnac.

Evans, J. D., & Wheeler, D. E. (2000). Expression profiles during honeybee cast determination. *Genome Biology, 2,* E1–E6.

Fairbairn, W. R. D. (1940). Schizoid factors in the personality. In *An object-relations theory of the personality* (pp. 3–28). New York: Basic Books.

Fairbairn, W. R. D. (1944). Endopsychic structure considered in terms of object-relationships. *International Journal of Psycho-Analysis, 25,* 60–93.

Fairbairn, W. R. D. (1952). *An object-relations theory of the personality.* New York: Basic Books.

Fairbairn, W. R. D. (1954). Observations on the nature of hysterical states. *British Journal of Medical Psychology, 29,* 112–127.

Fairbairn, W. R. D. (1963). Synopsis of an object-relations theory of the personality. *International Journal of Psycho-Analysis, 44,* 224–225.

Fairburn, C. G. (1994). Interpersonal psychotherapy for bulimia nervosa. In G. L. Klerman & M. M. Weissman (Eds.), *New applications of interpersonal psychotherapy* (pp. 353–378). New York: Guilford Press.

Fenichel, O. (1945). *The psychoanalytic theory of neurosis.* New York: Norton.

Ferenczi, S. (1913). Stages in the development of the sense of reality. In *First contributions to psycho-analysis* (pp. 213–244). London: Karnac Books.

Fiscalini, J., Mann, C. H., & Stern, D. B. (1995). *Handbook of interpersonal psychoanalysis.* Hillsdale, NJ: Analytic Press.

Fonagy, P. (1991). Thinking about thinking: Some clinical and theoretical considerations in the treatment of a borderline patient. *International Journal of Psycho-Analysis, 72,* 1–18.

Fonagy, P. (1996). Irrelevance of infant observations. *Journal of the American Psychoanalytic Association, 44,* 404–422.

Fonagy, P. (1997). Multiple voices versus meta-cognition: An attachment theory perspective. *Journal of Psychotherapy Integration, 7,* 181–194.

Fonagy, P. (2001a). Attachment theory and psychoanalysis. New York: Other Press.

Fonagy, P. (2001b, August). *Early intervention and the development of self-regulation.* Paper presented at the keynote address at the meeting of the Australian Association for Infant Mental Health, Perth, Australia.

Fonagy, P. (2003). The development of psychopathology from infancy to adulthood: The mysterious unfolding of disturbance in time. *Infant Mental Health Journal, 24*(3), 212–239.

Fonagy, P., & Cooper, A. (1999). Joseph Sandler's intellectual contributions to theoretical and clinical psychoanalysis. In P. Fonagy, A. Cooper, & R. Wallerstein (Eds.), *Psychoanalysis on the move: The work of Joseph Sandler* (pp. 1–29). London: Routledge.

Fonagy, P., Gergely, G., Jurist, E., & Target, M. (2002). *Affect regulation, mentalization and the development of the self.* New York: Other Press.

Fonagy, P., Kachele, H., Krause, R., Jones, E., Perron, R., Lopez, L., et al. (2001). *An open door review of outcome studies in psychoanalysis* (2nd ed.). London: International Psychoanalytical Association.

Fonagy, P., Leigh, T., Steele, M., Steele, H., Kennedy, R., Mattoon, G., et al. (1996). The relation of attachment status, psychiatric classification, and response to psychotherapy. *Journal of Consulting and Clinical Psychology, 64,* 22–31.

Fonagy, P., Miller, J., Edgcumbe, R., Target, M., & Kennedy, H. (1993). *The Hampstead manual of psychodynamic developmental therapy for children.* Unpublished manuscript, Anna Freud Centre, London.

Fonagy, P., Moran, G. S., Edgcumbe, R., Kennedy, H., & Target, M. (1993). The roles of mental representations and mental processes in therapeutic action. *Psychoanalytic Study of the Child, 48,* 9–48.

Fonagy, P., Moran, G. S., & Target, M. (1993). Aggression and the psychological self. *International Journal of Psycho-Analysis, 74,* 471–485.

Fonagy, P., Roth, A., & Higgitt, A. C. (in press). Psychodynamic psychotherapies: Evidence-based and clinical wisdom. *Bulletin of the Menninger Clinic.*

Fonagy, P., Stein, H., Allen, J., & Fultz, J. (2003, April). *The relationship of mentalization and childhood and adolescent adversity to adult functioning.* Paper presented at the biennial meeting of the Society for Research in Child Development, Tampa, FL.

Fonagy, P., & Target, M. (1996). Playing with reality: I. Theory of mind and the normal development of psychic reality. *International Journal of Psycho-Analysis, 77,* 217–233.

Fonagy, P., & Target, M. (1997a). Attachment and reflective function: Their role in self-organization. *Development and Psychopathology, 9,* 679–700.

Fonagy, P., & Target, M. (1997b). Perspectives on the recovered memories debate. In J. Sandler & P. Fonagy (Eds.), *Recovered memories of abuse: True or false?* (pp. 183–216). London: Karnac Books.

Fonagy, P., & Target, M. (2002). Early intervention and the development of self-regulation. *Psychoanalytic Inquiry, 22*(3), 307–335.

Fonagy, P., Target, M., & Gergely, G. (2000). Attachment and borderline personality disorder: A theory and some evidence. *Psychiatric Clinics of North America, 23,* 103–122.

Fonagy, P., Target, M., Gergely, G., Allen, J. G., & Bateman, A. (2003). The developmental roots of borderline personality disorder in early attachment relationships: A theory and some evidence. *Psychoanalytic Inquiry, 23,* 412–459.

Foulkes, D. (1978). *A grammar of dreams.* New York: Basic Books.

Fraiberg, S. H., Adelson, E., & Shapiro, V. (1975). Ghosts in the nursery: A psychoanalytic approach to the problem of impaired infant-mother relationships. *Journal of the American Academy of Child Psychiatry, 14,* 387–422.

Frank, E., Kupfer, D. J., Wagner, E. F., McEachran, A. B., & Cornes, C. (1991). Efficacy of interpersonal therapy as a maintenance treatment of recurrent depression. *Archives of General Psychiatry, 48,* 1053–1059.

Frank, J. (1956). Contribution to scientific proceedings, reported by L. L. Robbins. *Journal of the American Psychoanalytic Association, 4,* 561–562.

Freud, A. (1936). *The ego and the mechanisms of defense.* New York: International Universities Press.

Freud, A. (1962). Assessment of childhood disturbances. *Psychoanalytic Study of the Child, 17,* 149–158.

Freud, A. (1963). The concept of developmental lines. *Psychoanalytic Study of the Child, 18,* 245–265.

Freud, A. (1965). *Normality and pathology in childhood: Assessments of development.* Madison, CT: International Universities Press.

Freud, A. (1970a). The symptomatology of childhood: A preliminary attempt at classification. In *The Writings of Anna Freud: Vol. 7. Psychoanalytic psychology of normal development 1970–1980* (pp. 157–188). London: Hogarth Press and the Institute of Psychoanalysis.

Freud, A. (1970b). *The writings of Anna Freud: Vol. 8. Psychoanalytic psychology of normal development 1970–1980.* London: Hogarth Press and the Institute of Psychoanalysis.

Freud, A. (1974). A psychoanalytic view of developmental psychopathology. In *The writings of Anna Freud* (Vol. 8, pp. 119–136). New York: International Universities Press.

Freud, A. (1983). Problems of pathogenesis: Introduction to the discussion. *Psychoanalytic Study of the Child, 38,* 383–388.

Freud, A., & Burlingham, D. (1944). *Infants without families: Reports on the Hampstead nurseries—The writings of Anna Freud* (Vol. III). New York: International Universities Press.

Freud, S. (1953). Three essays on the theory of sexuality. In J. Strachey (Ed. & Trans.), *The standard edition of the complete psychological works of Sigmund Freud* (Vol. 7, pp. 130–243). London: Hogarth Press. (Originally published 1905)

Freud, S. (1955). Beyond the pleasure principle. In J. Strachey (Ed.), *The standard edition of the complete psychological works of Sigmund Freud* (Vol. 18, pp. 1–64). London: Hogarth Press. (Original work published 1920)

Freud, S. (1957). On narcissism: An introduction. In J. Strachey (Ed.), *The standard edition of the complete psychological works of Sigmund Freud* (Vol. 14, pp. 67–104). London: Hogarth Press. (Original work published 1914)

Freud, S. (1959). Inhibitions, symptoms and anxiety. In J. Strachey (Ed.), *The standard edition of the complete psychological works of Sigmund Freud* (Vol. 20, pp. 77–172). London: Hogarth Press. (Original work published 1926)

Freud, S. (1960a). Jokes and their relation to the unconscious. In J. Strachey (Ed.), *The standard edition of the complete psychological works of Sigmund Freud* (Vol. 8, pp. 1–236). London: Hogarth Press. (Original work published 1905)

Freud, S. (1960b). The psychopathology of everyday life. In J. Strachey (Ed.), *The standard edition of the complete psychological works of Sigmund Freud* (Vol. 6, pp. 1–190). London: Hogarth Press. (Original work published 1901)

Freud, S. (1961). Civilization and its discontents. In J. Strachey (Ed.), *The standard edition of the complete psychological works of Sigmund Freud* (Vol. 21, pp. 57–146). London: Hogarth Press. (Original work published 1930)

Freud, S. (1961). The ego and the id. In J. Strachey (Ed.), *The standard edition of the complete psychological works of Sigmund Freud* (Vol. 19, pp. 1–59). London: Hogarth Press. (Original work published 1922)

Freud, S. (1964a). New introductory lectures on psychoanalysis. In J. Strachey (Ed.), *The standard edition of the complete psychological works of Sigmund Freud* (Vol. 22, pp. 1–182). London: Hogarth Press. (Original work published 1933)

Freud, S. (1964b). Splitting of the ego in the process of defense. In J. Strachey (Ed.), *The standard edition of the complete psychological works of Sigmund Freud* (Vol. 23, pp. 275–278). London: Hogarth Press. (Original work published 1940)

Freud, S. (1966). The interpretation of dreams. In J. Strachey (Ed.), *The standard edition of the complete psychological works of Sigmund Freud* (Vols. 4 & 5, pp. 1–715). London: Hogarth Press. (Original work published 1900)

Freud, S., & Breuer, J. (1955). Studies on hysteria. In J. Strachey (Ed.), *The standard edition of the complete psychological works of Sigmund Freud* (Vol. 2, pp. 1–305). London: Hogarth Press. (Original work published 1895)

Friedman, L. (1988). The clinical polarity of object relations concepts. *Psychoanalytic Quarterly, 57,* 667–691.

Frith, U., & Frith, C. D. (2003). Development and neurophysiology of mentalizing. *Philosophical Transactions of the Royal Society of London. B., Biological Sciences, 358,* 459–473.

Gabbard, G. O., Gunderson, J. G., & Fonagy, P. (2002). The place of psychoanalytic treatments within psychiatry. *Archives of General Psychiatry, 59,* 505–510.

Gallese, V. (2000). The acting subject: Toward the neural basis of social cognition. In T. Metzinger (Ed.), *Neural correlates of consciousness* (pp. 325–333). Cambridge, MA: MIT Press.

Gallese, V. (2001). The "shared manifold" hypothesis: From mirror neurons to empathy. *Journal of Consciousness Studies, 8,* 33–50.

Gallese, V., & Umilta, M. A. (in press). From self-modeling to the self model: Agency and the representation of the self. *Neuro-Psychoanalysis.*

Garmezy, N., & Masten, A. (1994). Chronic adversities. In M. Rutter, E. Taylor, & L. Hersov (Eds.), *Child and adolescent psychiatry: Modern approaches* (pp. 191–208). Oxford: Blackwell Scientific Publications.

Ge, X., Conger, R. D., & Simmons, R. L. (1996). Parenting behaviors and the occurrence and co-occurrence of adolescent symptoms and conduct problems. *Developmental Psychology, 32,* 717–731.

Gergely, G. (1992). Developmental reconstructions: Infancy from the point of view of psychoanalysis and developmental psychology. *Psychoanalysis and Contemporary Thought, 15,* 3–55.

Gergely, G. (2000). Reapproaching Mahler: New perspectives on normal Autism, normal symbiosis, splitting and libidinal object constancy from cognitive developmental theory. *Journal of the American Psychoanalytic Association, 48*(4), 1197–1228.

Gergely, G. (2001a). The development of understanding of self and agency. In U. Goshwami (Ed.), *Handbook of childhood cognitive development* (pp. 26–46). Oxford: Blackwell.

Gergely, G. (2001b). The obscure object of desire: "Nearly, but clearly not, like me" contingency preference in normal children versus children with Autism. In J. Allen, P. Fonagy, & G. Gergely (Eds.), *Contingency perception and attachment in infancy* [Special issue: Bulletin of the Menninger Clinic]. (pp. 411–426). New York: Guilford Press.

Gergely, G., & Csibra, G. (2000, July). *The teleological origins of naive theory of mind in infancy.* Paper presented at the symposium on Origins of Theory of Mind: Studies with Human Infants and Primates at the 12th biennial International Conference on Infant Studies (ICIS), Brighton, England.

Gergely, G., & Csibra, G. (2003). Teleological reasoning in infancy: The naive theory of rational action. *Trends in Cognitive Sciences, 7,* 287–292.

Gergely, G., Nadasdy, Z., Csibra, G., & Biro, S. (1995). Taking the intentional stance at 12 months of age. *Cognition, 56,* 165–193.

Gergely, G., & Watson, J. (1996). The social biofeedback model of parental affect-mirroring. *International Journal of Psycho-Analysis, 77,* 1181–1212.

Gergely, G., & Watson, J. (1999). Early social-emotional development: Contingency perception and the social biofeedback model. In P. Rochat (Ed.), *Early social cognition: Understanding others in the first months of life* (pp. 101–137). Hillsdale, NJ: Erlbaum.

Gill, M. M. (1976). Metapsychology is not psychology. In M. M. Gill & P. S. Holzman (Eds.), *Psychology versus metapsychology: Essays in memory of George S. Klein.* New York: International Universities Press.

Gilligan, J. (1997). *Violence: Our deadliest epidemic and its causes.* New York: Grosset/Putnam.

Giovacchini, P. (1987). The "unreasonable" patient and the psychotic transference. In J. Grotstein, M. Solomon, & J. Lang (Eds.), *The borderline patient: Emerging concepts in diagnosis, psychodynamics and treatment* (pp. 59–68). Hillsdale, NJ: Analytic Press.

Gitelson, M. (1955). Contribution to scientific proceedings, reported by L Rangell. *Journal of the American Psychoanalytic Association, 3,* 294–295.

Glover, E. (1945). Examination of the Klein system of child psychology. *Psychoanalytic Study of the Child, 1,* 75–118.

Glover, E. (1948). *Psycho-analysis.* London: Staples.

Goldberg, R. L., Mann, L., Wise, T., & Segall, E. A. (1985). Parental qualities as perceived by borderline personality disorders. *Hillside Journal of Clinical Psychiatry, 7,* 134–140.

Gopnik, A. (1993). How we know our minds: The illusion of first-person knowledge of intentionality. *Behavioral and Brain Sciences, 16,* 1–14, 29–113.

Green, A. (2000). Science and science fiction in infant research. In J. Sandler, A.-M. Sandler, & R. Davies (Eds.), *Clinical and observational psychoanalytic research: Roots of a controversy* (pp. 41–73). London: Karnac Books.

Green, R. (1985). Atypical psychosexual development. In M. Rutter & L. Hersov (Eds.), *Child and adolescent psychiatry: Modern approaches* (pp. 638–649). Oxford: Blackwell Scientific Publications.

Greenacre, P. (Ed.). (1953). *Affective disorders.* New York: International Universities Press.

Greenberg, J. R. (1991). *Oedipus and beyond: A clinical theory.* Cambridge, MA: Harvard University Press.

Greenberg, J. R., & Mitchell, S. A. (1983). *Object relations in psychoanalytic theory.* Cambridge, MA: Harvard University Press.

Grilo, C. M., Sanislow, C. A., Gunderson, J. G., Pagano, M. E., Yen, S., Zanarini, M. C., et al. (2004). Two-year stability and change of schizotypal, borderline, avoidant, and obsessive-compulsive personality disorders. *Journal of Consulting and Clinical Psychology, 72*(5), 767–775.

Gunderson, J. G. (2001). *Borderline personality disorder: A clinical guide.* Washington, DC: American Psychiatric Publishing.

Gunnar, M. R., Morison, S. J., Chisholm, K., & Schuder, M. (2001). Long-term effects of institutional rearing on cortisol levels in adopted Romanian children. *Development and Psychopathology, 13*(3), 611–628.

Guntrip, H. (1961). *Personality structure and human interaction.* New York: International University Press.

Guntrip, H. (1969). *Schizoid phenomena, object relations and the self.* New York: International Universities Press.

Guntrip, H. (1975). My experience of analysis with Fairbairn and Winnicott. *International Review of Psychoanalysis, 2,* 145–156.

Guntrip, H. (1978). Psycho-analysis and some scientific and philosophical critics. *British Journal of Medical Psychology, 51,* 207–224.

Guthrie, E., Moorey, J., Margison, F., Barker, H., Palmer, S., McGrath, G., et al. (1999). Cost-effectiveness of brief psychodynamic-interpersonal therapy in high utilizers of psychiatric services. *Archives of General Psychiatry, 56*(6), 519–526.

Halligan, P. W., & Marshall, J. C. (1991). Left neglect for near but not far space in man. *Nature, 350,* 498–500.

Hamilton, C. E. (2000). Continuity and discontinuity of attachment from infancy through adolescence. *Child Development, 71*(3), 690–694.

Hare, R. D., & Cox, D. N. (1987). Clinical and empirical conceptions of psychopathy, and the selection of subjects for research. In R. D. Hare & D. Schalling (Eds.), *Psychopathic behavior: Approaches to research* (pp. 1–21). Toronto, Ontario, Canada: Wiley.

Harman, C., Rothbart, M. K., & Posner, M. I. (1997). Distress and intention interactions in early infancy. *Motivation and Emotion, 21,* 27–43.

Hartmann, H. (1939). *Ego psychology and the problem of adaptation.* New York: International Universities Press.

Hartmann, H. (1950). *Comments on the psychoanalytic theory of the ego.* New York: International Universities Press.

Hartmann, H. (1955). Notes on the theory of sublimation. In *Essays on ego psychology* (pp. 215–240). New York: International Universities Press.

Hartmann, H., Kris, E., & Loewenstein, R. (1946). Comments on the formation of psychic structure. *Psychoanalytic Study of the Child, 2,* 11–38.

Hartmann, H., Kris, H., & Loewenstein, R. (1949). Notes on the theory of aggression. *Psychoanalytic Study of the Child, 3–4,* 9–36.

Hegel, G. (1807). *The phenomenology of spirit.* Oxford: Oxford University Press.

Hellman, I. (1962). Hampstead nursery follow-up studies: I. Sudden separation. *Psychoanalytic Study of the Child, 17,* 159–174.

Herpertz, S. C. (1995). Self-injurious behavior: Psychopathological and nosological characteristics in subtypes of self-injurers. *Acta Psychiatrica Scandinavica, 91,* 57–68.

Hewitt, J. K., Silberg, J. L., Rutter, M., Simonoff, E., Meyer, J. M., Maes, H., et al. (1997). Genetics and developmental psychopathology: 1. Phenotypic assessment in the Virginia Twin Study of Adolescent Behavioral Development. *Journal of Child Psychology and Psychiatry, 38*(8), 943–963.

Hinshelwood, R. (1989). *A dictionary of Kleinian thought.* London: Free Association Books.

Hoffman, I. Z. (1994). Dialectic thinking and therapeutic action in the psychoanalytic process. *Psychoanalytic Quarterly, 63,* 187–218.

Hofstra, M. B., van der Ende, J., & Verhulst, F. C. (2002). Child and adolescent problems predict *DSM-IV* disorders in adulthood: A 14-year follow-up of a Dutch epidemiological sample. *Journal of the American Academy of Child and Adolescent Psychiatry, 41,* 182–189.

Holmes, J. (2000). Attachment theory and psychoanalysis: A rapprochement. *British Journal of Psychotherapy, 17,* 157–180.

Holt, R. R. (1976). *Drive or wish: A reconsideration of the psychoanalytic theory of motivation.* In M. M. Gill & P. S. Holtzman (Eds.), *Psychology vs. metapsychology: Essays in memory of George S. Klen* (pp. 158–197). New York: International Universities Press.

Horowitz, M. J. (1992). *Person schemas and maladaptive interpersonal patterns.* Chicago: University of Chicago Press.

Horowitz, M. J., Eells, T., Singer, J., & Salovey, P. (1995). Role-relationship models for case formulation. *Archives of General Psychiatry, 52,* 625–632.

Hudson, J. L., Kendall, P. C., Coles, M. E., Robin, J. A., & Webb, A. (2002). The other side of the coin: Using intervention research in child anxiety disorders to inform developmental psychopathology. *Developmental Psychopathology, 14*(4), 819–841.

Hughes, J. (1989). *Reshaping the psychoanalytic domain.* Berkeley: University of California Press.

Jacob, F. (1998). *Of flies, mice and men.* Cambridge, MA: Harvard University Press.

Jacobson, E. (1964). *The self and the object world.* New York: International Universities Press.

Jacobson, K. C., & Rowe, D. C. (1999). Genetic and environmental influences on the relationships between family connectedness, school connectedness, and adolescent depressed mood: Sex differences. *Developmental Psychopathology, 35*(4), 926–939.

Jaffe, J., Beebe, B., Feldstein, S., Crown, C. L., & Jasnow, M. D. (2001). Rhythms of dialogue in infancy. *Monographs of the Society for Research in Child Development, 66*(2).

Joffe, W. G., & Sandler, J. (1965). Notes on pain, depression, and individuation. *Psychoanalytic Study of the Child, 20,* 394–424.

Joffe, W. G., & Sandler, J. (1967). Some conceptual problems involved in the consideration of disorders of narcissism. *Journal of Child Psychotherapy, 2,* 56–66.

Johnson, A. M., & Szurek, S. A. (1952). The genesis of antisocial acting out in children and adults. *Psychoanalytic Quarterly, 21,* 323–343.

Jung, C. G. (1912). *Wandlungen und Symbole der Libido.* Leipzig: Deuticke. *The Psychology of the unconscious: A study of the transformations and symbolisms of the libido.* New York: Vail-Ballou Press. (Original work published 1916)

Jung, C. G. (1916). *Psychology of the unconscious.* London: Routledge & Kegan Paul.

Jung, C. G. (1923). *Psychological types.* London: Routledge & Kegan Paul.

Kandel, E. R. (1998). A new intellectual framework for psychiatry. *American Journal of Psychiatry, 155,* 457–469.

Kandel, E. R. (1999). Biology and the future of psychoanalysis: A new intellectual framework for psychiatry revisited. *American Journal of Psychiatry, 156,* 505–524.

Kazdin, A. E. (2003). Psychotherapy for children and adolescents. *Annual Review of Psychology, 54,* 253–276.

Kemperman, I., Russ, M. J., & Shearin, E. (1997). Self-injurious behavior and mood regulation in borderline patients. *Journal of Personality Disorders, 11,* 146–157.

Kennedy, H., & Moran, G. (1991). Reflections on the aims of child psychoanalysis. *Psychoanalytic Study of the Child, 46,* 181–198.

Kennedy, H. E. (1950). Cover memories in formation. *Psychoanalytic Study of the Child, 5,* 275–284.

Kernberg, O. F. (1967). Borderline personality organization. *Journal of the American Psychoanalytic Association, 15,* 641–685.

Kernberg, O. F. (1975). *Borderline conditions and pathological narcissism.* New York: Aronson.

Kernberg, O. F. (1976). *Object relations theory and clinical psychoanalysis.* New York: Aronson.

Kernberg, O. F. (1980a). *Internal world and external reality: Object relations theory applied.* New York: Aronson.

Kernberg, O. F. (1980b). Some implications of object relations theory for psychoanalytic technique. In H. Blum (Ed.), *Psychoanalytic explorations of technique: Discourse on the theory of therapy* (pp. 207–239). New York: International Universities Press.

Kernberg, O. F. (1982). Self, ego, affects and drives. *Journal of the American Psychoanalytic Association, 30,* 893–917.

Kernberg, O. F. (1984). *Severe personality disorders: Psychotherapeutic strategies.* New Haven, CT: Yale University Press.

Kernberg, O. F. (1987). Borderline personality disorder: A psychodynamic approach. *Journal of Personality Disorders, 1,* 344–346.

Kernberg, O. F. (1988). Object relations theory in clinical practice. *Psychoanalytic Quarterly, 57,* 481–504.

Kernberg, O. F. (1992). *Aggression in personality disorders and perversions.* London: Yale University Press.

Kernberg, O. F., Clarkin, J. F., & Yeomans, F. E. (2002). *A primer of transference focused psychotherapy for the borderline patient.* New York: Aronson.

Kernberg, O. F., Selzer, M. A., Koenigsberg, H. W., Carr, A. C., & Appelbaum, A. H. (1989). *Psychodynamic psychotherapy of borderline patients.* New York: Basic Books.

Khan, M. (1963). The concept of cumulative trauma. *Psychoanalytic Study of the Child, 18,* 283–306.

Khan, M. (1974). *The privacy of the self.* London: Hogarth Press.

Kihlstrom, J. (1987). The cognitive unconscious. *Science, 237,* 1445–1452.

Kim-Cohen, J., Caspi, A., Moffitt, T. E., Harrington, H.-L., & Milne, B. J. P. R. (2003). Prior juvenile diagnoses in adults with mental disorder: Developmental follow-back of a prospective longitudinal cohort. *Archives of General Psychiatry, 60,* 709–717.

King, P., & Steiner, R. (1991). *The Freud-Klein controversies: 1941–1945.* London: Routledge.

King-Casas, B., Tomlin, D., Aren, C., Camerer, C. F., Quartz, S. R., & Montague, P. R. (in press). Getting to know you: Reputation and trust in a two-person economic exchange. *Science.*

Klauber, J. (1966). An attempt to differentiate a typical form of transference in neurotic depression. *International Journal of Psycho-Analysis, 47,* 539–545.

Klauber, J. (1987). *Illusion and spontaneity in psycho-analysis.* London: Free Association Books.

Klein, G. S. (1976a). Freud's two theories of sexuality [Monograph]. *Psychological Issues, 36,* 14–70.

Klein, G. S. (1976b). *Psychoanalytic theory: An exploration of essentials.* New York: International Universities Press.

Klein, M. (1930). The psychotherapy of the psychoses. *British Journal of Medical Psychology, 10,* 242–244.

Klein, M. (1932). *The psycho-analysis of children.* London: Hogarth Press.

Klein, M. (1946). Notes on some schizoid mechanisms. In M. Klein, P. Heimann, S. Isaacs, & J. Riviere (Eds.), *Developments in psychoanalysis* (pp. 292–320). London: Hogarth Press.

Klein, M. (1952). The mutual influences in the development of ego and id. *Psychoanalytic Study of the Child, 7,* 51–53.

Klein, M. (1980). On Mahler's autistic and symbiotic phases: An exposition and evolution. *Psychoanalysis and Contemporary Thought, 4,* 69–105.

Klein, M. (1984a). A contribution to the psychogenesis of manic-depressive states. In R. Money-Kyrle (Ed.), *Love, guilt and reparation: The writings of Melanie Klein* (Vol. 1, pp. 236–289). London: Hogarth Press. (Original work published 1935)

Klein, M. (1984b). Envy and gratitude. In R. Money-Kyrle (Ed.), *Love, guilt and reparation: The writings of Melanie Klein* (Vol. 3, pp. 176–235). London: Hogarth Press. (Original work published 1957)

Klein, M. (1984c). Mourning and its relation to manic-depressive states. In R. Money-Kyrle (Ed.), *Love, guilt and reparation: The writings of Melanie Klein* (Vol. 1, pp. 344–369). New York: Macmillan. (Original work published 1940)

Klein, M. (1984d). Our adult world and its roots in infancy. In R. Money-Kyrle (Ed.), *Love, guilt and reparation: The writings of Melanie Klein* (Vol. 3, pp. 247–263). London: Hogarth Press. (Original work published 1959)

Knight, R. (1953). Borderline states. *Bulletin of the Menninger Clinic, 17*, 1–12.

Kochanska, G., Coy, K. C., & Murray, K. T. (2001). The development of self-regulation in the first four years of life. *Child Development, 72*, 1091–1111.

Kohon, G. (1986). *The British school of psycho-analysis: The independent tradition.* London: Free Association Books.

Kohut, H. (1971). *The analysis of the self.* New York: International Universities Press.

Kohut, H. (1977). *The restoration of the self.* New York: International Universities Press.

Kohut, H. (1984). *How does analysis cure?* Chicago: University of Chicago Press.

Kohut, H., & Wolf, E. S. (1978). The disorders of the self and their treatment: An outline. *International Journal of Psycho-Analysis, 59*, 413–426.

Kramer, S., & Akhtar, S. (1988). The developmental context of internalized preoedipal object relations: Clinical applications of Mahler's theory of symbiosis and separation-individuation. *Psychoanalytic Quarterly, 57*, 547–576.

Kreppner, J. M., O'Connor, T. G., & Rutter, M. (2001). Can inattention/overactivity be an institutional deprivation syndrome? *Journal of Abnormal Child Psychology, 29*(6), 513–528.

Kris, E. (1952). *Psychoanalytic explorations in art.* New York: International Universities Press.

Lampl-de-Groot, J. (1949). Neurotics, delinquents and ideal formation. In K. R. Eissler (Ed.), *Searchlights on delinquency* (pp. 225–245). New York: International Universities Press.

Laor, N., Wolmer, L., Mayes, L. C., Golomb, A., Silverberg, D. S., Weizman, I., et al. (1996). Israeli preschoolers under Scud missile attacks: A developmental perspective on risk modifying factors. *Archives of General Psychiatry, 53*, 416–423.

Laplanche, J. (1989). *New foundations for psychoanalysis* (D. Macey, Trans.). Oxford: Blackwell.

Laub, J. H. (1998). The interdependence of school violence with neighbourhood and family conditions. In D. S. Elliot, B. Hamburg, & K. R. Williams (Eds.), *Violence in American schools: A new perspective* (pp. 127–155). New York: Cambridge University Press.

Lebovici, S., & Widlöcher, D. (1980). *Psychoanalysis in France.* New York: International Universities Press.

LeDoux, J. E. (1995). Emotion: Clues from the brain. *Annual Review of Psychology, 46*, 209–235.

LeDoux, J. E. (1996). *The emotional brain: The mysterious underpinnings of emotional life.* New York: Simon & Schuster.

LeDoux, J. E. (1999). Commentary on psychoanalytic theory: Clues from the brain. *Neuro-psychoanalysis, 1*, 44–49.

Legerstee, M., & Varghese, J. (2001). The role of maternal affect mirroring on social expectancies in 2–3 month-old infants. *Child Development, 72*, 1301–1313.

Leichsenring, F., Rabung, S., & Leibing, E. (2004). The efficacy of short-term psychodynamic psychotherapy in specific psychiatric disorders: A meta-analysis. *Archives of General Psychiatry, 61*(12), 1208–1216.

Lerch, K. P. (2004). Gene-enviroment interaction and the genetics of depression. *Journal of Psychiatry and Neuroscience, 29*, 174–184.

Leslie, A. M. (1994). TOMM, ToBy, and agency: Core architecture and domain specificity. In L. Hirschfeld & S. Gelman (Eds.), *Mapping the mind: Domain specificity in cognition and culture* (pp. 119–148). New York: Cambridge University Press.

Leslie, A. M. (2000). "Theory of mind" as a mechanism of selective attention. In M. S. Gazzaniga (Ed.), *The new cognitive neurosciences* (2nd ed., pp. 1235–1247). Cambridge, MA: MIT Press.

Levenson, E. (1981). Facts or fantasies: On the nature of psychoanalytic data. *Contemporary Psychoanalysis, 17*, 486–500.

Lieberman, A. F., & Zeanah, C. H. (1999). Contributions of attachment theory to infant-parent psychotherapy and other interventions with infants and young children. In J. Cassidy & P. R. Shaver (Eds.), *Handbook of attachment: Theory, research and clinical applications* (pp. 555–574). New York: Guilford Press.

Linehan, M. (1986). Suicidal people: One population or two? *Annals of the New York Academy of Sciences, 487*, 16–33.

Livesley, W. J., Jang, K. L., & Vernon, P. A. (1998). Phenotypic and genetic structure of traits delineating personality disorder. *Archives of General Psychiatry, 55*, 941–948.

Loewald, H. W. (1960). On the therapeutic action of psycho-analysis. *International Journal of Psycho-Analysis, 41*, 16–33.

Loewald, H. W. (1978). Instinct theory, object relations and psychic structure formation. *Journal of the American Psychoanalytic Association, 26*, 453–506.

Loewald, H. W. (1980a). Instinct theory, object relations, and psychic structure formation. In *Papers on psychoanalysis* (pp. 384–404). New Haven, CT: Yale University Press. (Original work published 1978)

Loewald, H. W. (1980b). On internalization. In *Papers on psychoanalysis* (pp. 69–86). New Haven, CT: Yale University Press. (Original work published 1973)

Loewald, H. W. (1980c). On motivation and instinct theory. In *Papers on Psychoanalysis* (pp. 102–137). New Haven, CT: Yale University Press. (Original work published 1971)

Loewald, H. W. (1980d). The transference neurosis: Comments on the concept and the phenomenon. In *Papers on Psychoanalysis* (pp. 302–314). New Haven, CT: Yale University Press. (Original work published 1971)

Lyons-Ruth, K. (1998). Implicit relational knowing: Its role in development and psychoanalytic treatment. *Infant Mental Health Journal, 7*, 127–131.

Lyons-Ruth, K., Bronfman, E., & Atwood, G. (1999). A relational diathesis model of hostile-helpless states of mind: Expressions in mother-infant interaction. In J. Solomon & C. George (Eds.), *Attachment disorganization* (pp. 33–70). New York: Guilford Press.

Macfie, J., Cicchetti, D., & Toth, S. L. (2001). The development of dissociation in maltreated preschool-aged children. *Development and Psychopathology, 13*, 233–254.

Macfie, J., Toth, S. L., Rogosch, F. A., Robinson, J., Emde, R. N., & Cicchetti, D. (1999). Effect of maltreatment on preschoolers' narrative representations of responses to relieve distress and of role reversal. *Developmental Psychology, 35*, 460–465.

Mahler, M. S. (1974). Symbiosis and individuation: The psychological birth of the human infant. In *The selected papers of Margaret S. Mahler* (pp. 149–165). New York: Aronson.

Mahler, M. S., & Furer, M. (1968). *On human symbiosis and the vicissitudes of individuation: Vol. 1. Infantile psychosis.* New York: International Universities Press.

Mahler, M. S., & Kaplan, L. (1977). Developmental aspects in the assessment of narcissistic and so-called borderline personalities. In P. Hartocollis (Ed.), *Borderline personality disorders: The concept, the syndrome, the patient* (pp. 71–86). New York: International Universities Press.

Mahler, M. S., Pine, F., & Bergman, A. (1975). *The psychological birth of the human infant: Symbiosis and individuation*. New York: Basic Books.

Marcel, A. J. (1983a). Conscious and unconscious perception: An approach to the relations between phenomenal experience and perceptual processes. *Cognitive Psychology, 15,* 238–300.

Marcel, A. J. (1983b). Conscious and unconscious perception: Experiments on visual masking and word recognition. *Cognitive Psychology, 15,* 197–237.

Marcia, J. E. (1994). The empirical study of ego identity. In H. A. Bosma, T. L. G. Graafsma, H. D. Grotevant, & D. J. de Levita (Eds.), *Identity and development: An interdisciplinary approach* (pp. 67–80). Thousand Oaks, CA: Sage.

Marenco, S., & Weinberger, D. R. (2000). The neurodevelopmental hypothesis of Schizophrenia: Following a trail of evidence from cradle to grave. *Development and Psychopathology, 12*(3), 501–527.

Masten, A. S., & Coatsworth, J. D. (1995). Competence, resilience and psychopathology. In D. Cicchetti & D. J. Cohen (Eds.), *Developmental psychopathology: Vol. 2. Risk, disorder and adaptation* (pp. 715–752). New York: Wiley.

Masten, A. S., & Curtis, W. J. (2000). Integrating competence and psychopathology: Pathways toward a comprehensive science of adaptation and development. *Development and Psychopathology, 12,* 529–550.

Masterson, J. F. (1985). *The real self: A developmental, self, and object relations approach*. New York: Brunner/Mazel.

Mayes, L. C. (2000). A developmental perspective on the regulation of arousal states. *Seminars in Perinatology, 24,* 267–279.

McCauley, E., Pavidis, K., & Kendall, K. (2000). Developmental precursors of depression. In I. Goodyear (Ed.), *The depressed child and adolescent: Developmental and clinical perspectives* (pp. 46—78). New York: Cambridge University Press.

McLaughlin, J. (1991). Clinical and theoretical aspects of enactment. *Journal of the American Psychoanalytic Association, 39,* 595–614.

Mead, G. H. (1934). *Mind, self and society*. Chicago: University of Chicago Press.

Meins, E., Ferryhough, C., Fradley, E., & Tuckey, M. (2001). Rethinking maternal sensitivity: Mothers' comments on infants mental processes predict security of attachment at 12 months. *Journal of Child Psychology and Psychiatry, 42,* 637–648.

Meltzoff, A. N. (1990). Foundations for developing a concept of self: The role of imitation in relating self to other and the value of social mirroring, social modeling and self practice in infancy. In D. Cicchetti & M. Beeghly (Eds.), *The self in transition: Infancy to childhood* (pp. 139–164). Chicago: University of Chicago Press.

Meltzoff, A. N., & Moore, M. K. (1997). Explaining facial imitation: Theoretical model. *Early Development and Parenting, 6,* 179–192.

Meltzoff, A. N., & Moore, M. K. (1998). Infant intersubjectivity: Broadening the dialogue to include imitation, identity and intention. In S. Braten (Ed.), *Intersubjective communication and emotion in early ontogeny* (pp. 47–62). Paris: Cambridge University Press.

Milner, M., Squire, L. R., & Kandel, E. R. (1998). Cognitive neuroscience and the study of memory. *Neuron, 20,* 445–468.

Mitchell, R. W. (1993). Mental models of mirror self-recognition: Two theories. *New Ideas in Psychology, 11,* 295–325.

Mitchell, S. A. (1988). *Relational concepts in psychoanalysis: An integration*. Cambridge, MA: Harvard University Press.

Mitchell, S. A. (1993). Aggression and the endangered self. *Psychoanalytic Quarterly, 62,* 351–382.

Mitchell, S. A. (2000). *Relationality: From attachment to intersubjectivity*. Hillsdale, NJ: Analytic Press.

Modell, A. (1963). Primitive object relations and the predisposition to Schizophrenia. *International Journal of Psycho-Analysis, 44,* 282–292.

Modell, A. (1968). *Object love and reality*. New York: International Universities Press.

Modell, A. (1975). A narcissistic defense against affects and the illusion of self-sufficiency. *International Journal of Psycho-Analysis, 56,* 275–282.

Modell, A. (1984). *Psychoanalysis in a new context*. New York: International Universities Press.

Mollon, P. (2001). *Releasing the self: The healing legacy of Heinz Kohut*. London: Whurr.

Mufson, L., & Fairbanks, J. (1996). Interpersonal psychotherapy for depressed adolescents: A one-year naturalistic follow-up study. *Journal of the American Academy of Child and Adolescent Psychiatry, 35,* 1145–1155.

Mullen, P. E., Martin, J. L., Anderson, J. C., Romans, S. E., & Herbison, G. P. (1996). The long-term impact of the physical, emotional, and sexual abuse of children: A community study. *Child Abuse and Neglect, 20,* 7–21.

Mundy, P., & Neal, R. (2001). Neural plasticity, joint attention, and a transactional social-orienting model of Autism. In L. Masters Glidden (Ed.), *International review of mental retardation: Autism* (Vol. 23, pp. 139–168). San Diego: Academic Press.

Munir, K. M., & Beardslee, W. R. (1999). Developmental psychiatry: Is there any other kind? *Harvard Review of Psychiatry, 6,* 250–262.

Neisser, U. (1988). Five kinds of self-knowledge. *Philosophical Psychology, 1,* 35–59.

Nelson, K. (1993). Explaining the emergence of autobiographical memory in early childhood. In A. Collins, S. E. Gathercole, M. A. Conway, & P. E. Morris (Eds.), *Theories of memory* (pp. 355–385). Hove, England: Erlbaum.

Neubauer, P. B. (1984). Anna Freud's concept of developmental lines. *Psychoanalytic Study of the Child, 39,* 15–27.

Noy, P. (1977). Metapsychology as a multimodel system. *International Review of Psychoanalysis, 4,* 1–12.

O'Connor, T. G., Bredenkamp, D., Rutter, M., & and the English and Romanian Adoptees Study Team. (1999). Attachment disturbances and disorders in children exposed to early severe deprivation. *Infant Mental Health Journal, 20,* 10–29.

O'Connor, T. G., McGuire, S., Reiss, D., & Hetherington, E. M. (1998). Co-occurrence of depressive symptoms and antisocial behavior in adolescence: A common genetic liability. *Journal of Abnormal Psychology, 107,* 27–37.

O'Connor, T. G., Rutter, M., & Kreppner, J. (2000). The effects of global severe privation of cognitive competence: Extension and longitudinal follow-up. *Child Development, 71*(2), 376–390.

Ogden, T. H. (1994). The analytic third: Working with intersubjective clinical facts. *International Journal of Psychoanalysis, 75,* 3–19.

Ogden, T. H. (1989). *The primitive edge of experience*. New York: Aronson.

Oppenheim, D., & Koren-Karie, N. (2002). Mothers' insightfulness regarding their children's internal worlds: The capacity underlying secure child-mother relationships. *Infant Mental Health Journal, 23,* 593–605.

Orlofsky, J. (1993). Intimacy status: Theory and research. In J. E. Marcia, A. S. Waterman, D. R. Matteson, S. L. Archer, & J. L. Orlofsky (Eds.), *Ego identity: A handbook for psychosocial research* (pp. 111–133). New York: Springer-Verlag.

Padel, J. H. (1972). The contribution of W. R. D. Fairbairn. *Bulletin of the European Psycho-Analytical Federation, 2,* 13–26.

Panksepp, J. (1998). *Affective neuroscience: The foundations of human and animal emotions.* Oxford: Oxford University Press.

Panksepp, J. (2001). The long term psychobiological consequences of infant emotions: Prescriptions for the twenty-first century. *Infant Mental Health Journal, 22,* 132–173.

Paris, J. (2000). Childhood precursors of borderline personality disorder. *Psychiatric Clinics of North America, 23*(1), 77–88.

Paris, J., & Frank, H. (1989). Perceptions of parental bonding in borderline patients. *American Journal of Psychiatry, 146,* 1498–1499.

Peterfreund, E. (1971). *Information, systems, and psychoanalysis: An evolutionary biological approach to psychoanalytic theory.* New York: International Universities Press.

Peterfreund, E. (1978). Some critical comments on psychoanalytic conceptualizations of infancy. *International Journal of Psycho-Analysis, 59,* 427–441.

Pine, F. (1985). *Developmental theory and clinical process.* New Haven, CT: Yale University Press.

Plomin, R. (1994). *Genetics and experience: The interplay between nature and nurture.* Thousand Oaks, CA: Sage.

Plomin, R., & McGuffin, P. (2003). Psychopathology in the postgenomic era. *Annual Review of Psychology, 54,* 205–228.

Posner, M. I., & Rothbart, M. K. (2000). Developing mechanisms of self-regulation. *Development and Psychopathology, 12,* 427–441.

Povinelli, D. J., & Eddy, T. J. (1995). The unduplicated self. In P. Rochat (Ed.), *The self in infancy: Theory and research* (pp. 161–192). Amsterdam: Elsevier.

Raine, A., Venables, P. H., & Williams, M. (1995). High autonomic arousal and orienting at age 15 years as protective factors against crime development at age 29 years. *American Journal of Psychiatry, 152,* 1595–1600.

Rangell, L. (1955). The borderline case. *Journal of the American Psychoanalytic Association, 3,* 285–298.

Rank, O. (1924). *The trauma of birth.* New York: Harcourt Brace.

Rayner, E. (1991). *The independent mind in British psychoanalysis.* London: Free Association Books.

Read, S. J., Vanman, E. J., & Miller, L. C. (1997). Connectionism, parallel constraint satisfaction processes, and Gestalt principles: (Re)Introducing cognitive dynamics to social psychology. *Personality and Social Psychology Review, 1,* 26–53.

Reich, J. H., & Vasile, R. G. (1993). Effect of personality disorders on the treatment outcome of Axis I conditions: An update. *Journal of Nervous and Mental Diseases, 181*(8), 475–484.

Reich, W. (1933). *Character analysis* (V. R. Carfagno, Trans., 3rd ed.). New York: Farrar, Strauss and Giroux.

Reiss, D., Hetherington, E. M., Plomin, R., Howe, G. W., Simmens, S. J., Henderson, S. H., et al. (1995). Genetic questions for environmental studies: Differential parenting and psychopathology in adolescence. *Archives of General Psychiatry, 52,* 925–936.

Reiss, D., Neiderhiser, J., Hetherington, E. M., & Plomin, R. (2000). *The relationship code: Deciphering genetic and social patterns in adolescent development.* Cambridge, MA: Harvard University Press.

Renik, O. (1993). Analytic interaction: Conceptualizing technique in the light of the analyst's irreducible subjectivity. *Psychoanalytic Quarterly, 62,* 553–571.

Rosenblatt, A. D., & Thickstun, J. T. (1977). *Modern psychoanalytic concepts in a general psychology: Pt. 1. General concepts and principles. Pt. 2. Motivation.* New York: International Universities Press.

Rosenfeld, H. (1971). A clinical approach to the psychoanalytic theory of the life and death instincts: An investigation into the aggressive aspects of narcissism. *International Journal of Psychoanalysis, 52,* 169–178.

Rosenfeld, H. (1987). *Impasse and interpretation.* London: Tavistock Publications.

Roth, A., & Fonagy, P. (1996). *What works for whom? A critical review of psychotherapy research.* New York: Guilford Press.

Roth, A., & Fonagy, P. (2005). *What works for whom? A critical review of psychotherapy research* (2nd ed.). New York: Guilford Press.

Rothbart, M. K., Ahadi, S. A., & Evans, D. E. (2000). Temperament and personality: Origins and outcomes. *Journal of Personality and Social Psychology, 78,* 122–135.

Rothbart, M. K., Ahadi, S. A., & Hershey, K. L. (1994). Temperament and social behavior in childhood. *Merrill-Palmer Quarterly, 40,* 21–39.

Rothbaum, F., Pott, M., Azuma, H., Miyake, K., & Weisz, J. (2000). The development of close relationships in Japan and the United States: Paths of symbiotic harmony and generative tension. *Child Development, 71,* 1121–1142.

Rothstein, A. (1980). Toward a critique of the psychology of the self. *Psychoanalytic Quarterly, 49,* 423–455.

Rubin, D., Wallace, W., & Houston, B. (1993). The beginnings of expertise for ballads. *Cognitive Science, 17,* 435–462.

Rumelhart, D. E., & McClelland, J. L. (1986). *Parallel distributed processing.* Cambridge, MA: MIT Press.

Russell, D. E. H. (1986). *The secret trauma: Incest in the lives of girls and women.* New York: Basic Books.

Rutter, M. (1999). Psychosocial adversity and child psychopathology. *British Journal of Psychiatry, 174,* 480–493.

Rutter, M. (2000). Psychosocial influences: Critiques, findings and research needs. *Development and Psychopathology, 12,* 375–405.

Rutter, M. (2005). Environmentally mediated risks for psychopathology: Research strategies and findings. *Journal of the American Academy of Child and Adolescent Psychiatry, 44*(1), 3–18.

Rutter, M., Silberg, J., O'Connor, T., & Simonoff, E. (1999a). Genetics and child psychiatry: I. Advances in quantitative and molecular genetics. *Journal of Child Psychology and Psychiatry, 40*(1), 3–18.

Rutter, M., Silberg, J., O'Connor, T., & Simonoff, E. (1999b). Genetics and child psychiatry: II. Empirical research findings. *Journal of Child Psychology and Psychiatry, 40*(1), 19–55.

Ryle, A. (Ed.). (1995). *Cognitive analytic therapy: Developments in theory and practice.* Chichester, England: Wiley.

Ryle, A. (1997). *Cognitive analytic therapy and borderline personality disorder: The model and the method.* Chichester, England: Wiley.

Sandler, J. (1960a). The background of safety. *International Journal of Psycho-Analysis, 41,* 191–198.

Sandler, J. (1960b). On the concept of superego. *Psychoanalytic Study of the Child, 15,* 128–162.

Sandler, J. (1972). The role of affects in psychoanalytic theory. In J. Sandler (Ed.), *From safety to superego: Selected papers of Joseph Sandler* (pp. 285–300). New York: Guilford Press.

Sandler, J. (1976). Countertransference and role-responsiveness. *International Review of Psycho-Analysis, 3,* 43–47.

Sandler, J. (1987). The concept of projective identification. In J. Sandler (Ed.), *Projection, identification, projection identification* (pp. 13–26). Madison, CT: International Universities Press.

Sandler, J. (1994). Fantasy, defense, and the representational world: Fifth World Congress of the World Association for Infant Psychiatry and Allied Disciplines [Special issue]. *Infant Mental Health Journal, 15*(1), 26–35.

Sandler, J., & Freud, A. (1985). *The analysis of defense: The ego and the mechanisnms of defense revisited.* New York: International Universities Press.

Sandler, J., & Joffe, W. G. (1965a). Notes on childhood depression. *International Journal of Psycho-Analysis, 46,* 88–96.

Sandler, J., & Joffe, W. G. (1965b). Notes on obsessional manifestations in children. *Psychoanalytic Study of the Child, 20,* 425–438.

Sandler, J., & Rosenblatt, B. (1962). The concept of the representational world. *Psychoanalytic Study of the Child, 17,* 128–145.

Sandler, J., & Sandler, A.-M. (1978). On the development of object relationships and affects. *International Journal of Psycho-Analysis, 59,* 285–296.

Sandler, J., & Sandler, A.-M. (1984). The past unconscious, the present unconscious, and interpretation of the transference. *Psychoanalytic Inquiry, 4,* 367–399.

Sandler, J., & Sandler, A.-M. (1987). The past unconscious, the present unconscious and the vicissitudes of guilt. *International Journal of Psychoanalysis, 68,* 331–341.

Schachter, D. (1996). *Searching for memory: The brain, the mind, and the past.* New York: Basic Books.

Schafer, R. (1974). Problems in Freud's psychology of women. *Journal of the American Psychoanalytic Association, 22,* 459–485.

Schafer, R. (1976). *A new language for psychoanalysis.* New Haven, CT: Yale University Press.

Schafer, R. (1983). *The analytic attitude.* New York: Basic Books.

Schneider-Rosen, K., & Cicchetti, D. (1991). Early self-knowledge and emotional development: Visual self-recognition and affective reactions to mirror self-image in maltreated and nonmaltreated toddlers. *Developmental Psychology, 27,* 481–488.

Schölmerich, A., Lamb, M. E., Leyendecker, B., & Fracasso, M. P. (1997). Mother-infant teaching interactions and attachment security in Euro-American and Central-American immigrant families. *Infant Behavior and Development, 20,* 165–174.

Schore, A. (2003). *Affect regulation and the repair of the self.* New York: Norton.

Schwartz, L. (1978). Review of "The restoration of the self" by Heinz Kohut. *Psychoanalytic Quarterly, 47,* 436–443.

Searles, H. F. (1986). *My work with borderline patients.* Northvale, NJ: Aronson.

Sechrest, L., McKnight, P., & McKnight, K. (1996). Calibration of measures for psychotherapy outcome studies. *American Psychologist, 51*(10), 1065–1071.

Segal, H. (1974). *An introduction to the work of Melanie Klein* London: Hogarth.

Segal, H. (1981). *The work of Hanna Segal.* New York: Jason Aronson.

Seligman, M. E. P. (1995). The effectiveness of psychotherapy. *American Psychologist, 50,* 965–974.

Settlage, C. F. (1977). The psychoanalytic understanding of narcissistic and borderline personality disorders: Advances in developmental theory. *Journal of the American Psychoanalytic Association, 25,* 805–833.

Shachnow, J., Clarkin, J., DiPalma, C. S., Thurston, F., Hull, J., & Shearin, E. (1997). Biparental psychopathology and borderline personality disorder. *Psychiatry, 60,* 171–181.

Shapiro, D., Rees, A., Barkham, M., Hardy, G., Reynolds, S., & Startup, M. (1995). Effects of treatment duration and severity of depression on the maintenance of gains after cognitive-behavioral and psychodynamic-interpersonal psychotherapy. *Journal of Consulting and Clinical Psychology, 63,* 378–387.

Shaw, D. S., Gilliom, M., Ingoldsby, E. M., & Nagin, D. S. (2002). *Trajectories leading to school age conduct problems.* Unpublished manuscript, University of Pittsburgh, Pittsburgh, PA.

Shea, M. T., Elkin, I., Imber, S. D., Sotsky, S. M., Watkins, J. T., Collins, J. F., et al. (1992). Course of depressive symptoms over follow-up: Findings from the NIMH Treatment of Depression Collaborative Research Program. *Archives of General Psychiatry, 49,* 782–787.

Shea, M. T., Pilkonis, P. A., Beckham, E., Collins, J. F., Elkin, I., Sotsky, S. M., et al. (1990). Personality disorders and treatment outcome in the NIMH Treatment of Depression Collaborative Research Program. *American Journal of Psychiatry, 147,* 711–718.

Sheeber, L., Hops, H., Alpert, A., Davies, B., & Andrews, J. (1997). Family support and conflict: Prospective relations to adolescent depression. *Journal of Abnormal Child Psychology, 25,* 333–344.

Shengold, L. (1989). *Soul murder: The effects of childhood abuse and deprivation.* New York: Ballantine Books.

Shevrin, H. (1997). Psychoanalysis as the patient: High in feeling, low in energy. *Journal of the American Psychoanalytic Association, 45,* 841–864.

Shevrin, H. (2001). Drug dreams: An introduction. *Jounal of the American Psychoanalytic Association, 49,* 69–71.

Siegel, D. J. (2001). Toward an interpersonal neurobiology of the developing mind: Attachment relationships, "mindsight" and neural integration. *Infant Mental Health Journal, 22,* 67–94.

Silberg, J., Rutter, M., Neale, M., & Eaves, L. J. (2001). Genetic moderation of environmental risk for depression and anxiety in adolescent girls. *British Journal of Psychiatry, 179,* 116–121.

Slade, A. (1999). Attachment theory and research: Implications for the theory and practice of individual psychotherapy with adults. In J. Cassidy & P. R. Shaver (Eds.), *Handbook of attachment: Theory, research and clinical applications* (pp. 575–594). New York: Guilford Press.

Solms, M. (1997a). *The neuropsychology of dreams: A clinico-anatomical study.* Mahwah, NJ: Erlbaum.

Solms, M. (1997b). What is consciousness? *Journal of the American Psychoanalytic Association, 45,* 681–703.

Solms, M. (2000). Dreaming and REM sleeping are controlled by different brain mechanisms. *Behavior and Brain Sciences, 23,* 843–850, 904–1121.

Solms, M., & Nersessian, E. (1999). Freud's theory of affect. *Neuro-psychoanalysis, 1,* 5–14.

Solomon, J., & George, C. (1999). *Attachment disorganization.* New York: Guilford Press.

Solvason, H. B., Ernst, H., & Roth, W. (2003). Predictors of response in anxiety disorders. *Psychiatric Clinics of North America, 26*(2), 411–433.

Spitz, R. A. (1945). Hospitalism: An inquiry into the genesis of psychiatric conditions in early childhood. *Psychoanalytic Study of the Child, 1,* 53–73.

Spitz, R. A. (1957). *No and yes: On the genesis of human communication.* New York: International Universities Press.

Spitz, R. A. (1959). *A genetic field theory of ego formation: Its implications for pathology.* New York: International Universities Press.

Spitz, R. A. (1965). *The first year of life.* New York: International Universities Press.

Spruiell, V. (1988). The indivisibility of Freudian object relations and drive theories. *Psychoanalytic Quarterly, 57,* 597–625.

Squire, L. S., & Kandel, E. R. (1999). *Memory: From molecules to memory.* New York: Freeman Press.

Stanley, B., Gameroff, M. J., Michalsen, V., & Mann, J. J. (2001). Are suicide attempters who self-mutilate a unique population? *American Journal of Psychiatry, 158*(3), 427–432.

Stechler, G., & Kaplan, S. (1980). The development of the sense of self: A psychoanalytic perspective. *Psychoanalytic Study of the Child, 35,* 85–105.

Steiner, J. (1993). *Psychic retreats: Pathological organizations in psychotic, neurotic and borderline patients.* London: Routledge.

Stern, D. N. (1985). *The interpersonal world of the infant: A view from psychoanalysis and developmental psychology.* New York: Basic Books.

Stern, D. N. (1990). *Joy and satisfaction in infancy.* New Haven, CT: Yale University Press.

Stern, D. N. (1993). Acting versus remembering and transference love and infantile love. In E. Person, A. Hagelin, & P. Fonagy (Eds.), *On Freud's "Observations and transference-love"* (pp. 172–185). New Haven, CT: Yale University Press.

Stern, D. N. (1994). One way to build a clinically relevant baby. *Infant Mental Health Journal, 15,* 36–54.

Stern, D. N. (1995a). *The motherhood constellation: A unified view of parent-infant psychotherapy.* New York: Basic Books.

Stern, D. N. (1995b). Self/other differentiation in the domain of intimate socioaffective interaction: Some considerations. In P. Rochat (Ed.), *The self in infancy: Theory and research* (pp. 419–429). Amsterdam: Elsevier.

Stern, D. N., Hofer, L., Haft, W., & Dore, J. (1985). Affect attunement: The sharing of feeling states between mother and infant by means of inter-modal fluency. In T. M. Fields & N. A. Fox (Eds.), *Social perception in infants* (pp. 249–268). Norwood, NJ: Ablex Publishing.

Stern, D. N., Sander, L., Nahum, J., Harrison, A., Lyons-Ruth, K., Morgan, A., et al. (1998). Noninterpretive mechanisms in psychoanalytic therapy: The "something more" than interpretation. *International Journal of Psycho-Analysis, 79*(5), 903–921.

Stolorow, R. D. (1997). Review of "A dynamic systems approach to the development of cognition and action." *International Journal of Psycho-Analysis, 78,* 620–623.

Stolorow, R. D., & Atwood, G. (1991). The mind and the body. *Psychoanalytic Dialogues, 1,* 190–202.

Stolorow, R. D., Brandschaft, B., & Atwood, G. (1987). *Psychoanalytic treatment: An intersubjective approach.* Hillsdale, NJ: Analytic Press.

Stoolmiller, M. (1999). Implications of the restricted range of family environments for estimates of heritability and nonshared environment in behavior-genetic adoption studies. *Psychological Bulletin, 125,* 392–409.

Sullivan, H. S. (1953). *The interpersonal theory of psychiatry.* New York: Norton.

Sullivan, H. S. (1964). *The fusion of psychiatry and social science.* New York: Norton.

Sulloway, F. J. (1979). *Freud: Biologist of the mind.* New York: Basic Books.

Sutherland, J. D. (1980). The British object-relations theorists: Balint, Fairbairn, Guntrip. *Journal of the American Psychoanalytic Association, 28,* 829–860.

Target, M., & Fonagy, P. (1996). Playing with reality: II. The development of psychic reality from a theoretical perspective. *International Journal of Psycho-Analysis, 77,* 459–479.

Tienari, P., Wynne, L. C., Moring, J., Lahti, I., & Naarala, M. (1994). The Finnish Adoptive Family Study of Schizophrenia: Implications for family research. *British Journal of Psychiatry, 23*(Suppl. 164), 20–26.

Tomasello, M. (1999). *The cultural origins of human cognition.* Cambridge, MA: Harvard University Press.

Torgersen, S. (2000). Genetics of patients with borderline personality disorder. *Psychiatric Clinics of North America, 23*(1), 1–9.

Torgersen, S., & Alnaes, R. (1992). Differential perception of parental bonding in schizotypal and borderline personality disorder patients. *Comprehensive Psychiatry, 33,* 34–38.

Torgersen, S., Lygren, S., Oien, P. A., Skre, I., Onstad, S., Edvardsen, J., et al. (2000). A twin study of personality disorders. *Comprehensive Psychiatry, 41*(6), 416–425.

Toth, S. L., Cicchetti, D., Macfie, J., Maughan, A., & Vanmeenen, K. (2000). Narrative representations of caregivers and self in maltreated preschoolers. *Attachment and Human Development, 2,* 271–305.

Toth, S. L., Maughan, A., Manly, J. T., Spagnola, M., & Cicchetti, D. (2002). The relative efficacy of two interventions in altering maltreated preschool children's representational models: Implications for attachment theory. *Developmental Psychopathology, 14*(4), 877–908.

Tremblay, R. E. (2000, Autumn). The origins of violence. *ISUMA, 1,* 19–24.

Tremblay, R. E., Japel, C., & Perusse, D. (1999). The search for the age of onset of physical aggression: Rousseau and Bandura revisited. *Criminal Behavior and Mental Health, 9,* 8–23.

Tronick, E. Z. (1998). Dyadically expanded states of consciousness and the process of therapeutic change. *Infant Mental Health Journal, 19,* 290–299.

Tronick, E. Z. (2001). Emotional connection and dyadic consciousness in infant-mother and patient-therapist interactions: Commentary on paper by Frank M. Lachman. *Psychoanalytic Dialogue, 11,* 187–195.

Tyson, P., & Tyson, R. L. (1990). *Psychoanalytic theories of development: An integration.* London: Yale University Press.

von Bertalanffy, L. (1968). *General system theory: Foundations, development, applications.* New York: George Braziller.

Waelder, R. (1960). *Basic theory of psychoanalysis.* New York: International Universities Press.

Warner, V., Weissman, M. M., Mufson, L., & Wickramaratne, P. J. (1999). Grandparents, parents and grandchildren at high risk for depression: A three generation study. *Journal of the American Academy of Child and Adolescent Psychiatry, 38,* 289–296.

Waters, E., Merrick, S. K., Treboux, D., Crowell, J., & Albersheim, L. (2000). Attachment security from infancy to early adulthood: A 20 year longitudinal study. *Child Development, 71*(3), 684–689.

Watson, J. S. (1994). Detection of self: The perfect algorithm. In S. Parker, R. Mitchell, & M. Boccia (Eds.), *Self-awareness in animals and humans: Developmental perspectives* (pp. 131–149): Cambridge, England: Cambridge University Press.

Watson, J. S. (1995). Self-orientation in early infancy: The general role of contingency and the specific case of reaching to the mouth. In P. Rochat (Ed.), *The self in infancy: Theory and research* (pp. 375–393). Amsterdam: Elsevier.

Watson, J. S. (2001). Contingency perception and misperception in infancy: Some potential implications for attachment. *Bulletin of the Menninger Clinic, 65,* 296–320.

Webster, R. (1995). *Why Freud was wrong: Sin, science and psychoanalysis.* London: HarperCollins.

Wegner, D. M., & Wheatley, T. (1999). Apparent mental causation: Sources of the experience of will. *American Psychologist, 54*(7), 480–492.

Wellman, H. M. (1990). *The child's theory of mind.* Cambridge, MA: Bradford Books/MIT Press.

Wellman, H. M., & Phillips, A. T. (2000). Developing intentional understandings. In L. Moses, B. Male, & D. Baldwin (Eds.), *Intentionality: A key to human understanding.* Cambridge, MA: MIT Press.

Westen, D. (1991). Social cognition and object relations. *Psychological Bulletin, 109,* 429–455.

Westen, D. (1998). The scientific legacy of Sigmund Freud: Toward a psychodynamically informed psychological science. *Psychological Bulletin, 124*(3), 333–371.

Westen, D., & Gabbard, G. O. (2002a). Developments in cognitive neuroscience: I. Conflict, compromise, and connectionism. *Journal of the American Psychoanalytic Association, 50*(1), 53–98.

Westen, D., & Gabbard, G. O. (2002b). Developments in cognitive neuroscience: II. Implications for theories of transference. *Journal of the American Psychoanalytic Association, 50*(1), 99–134.

Westen, D., Lohr, N., Silk, K., Gold, L., & Kerber, K. (1990a). Object relations and social cognition in borderlines, major depressives, and normals: A TAT analysis. *Psychological Assessment: A Journal of Consulting and Clinical Psychology, 2,* 355–364.

Westen, D., Ludolph, P., Block, M. J., Wixom, J., & Wiss, C. (1990b). Developmental history and object relations in psychiatrically disturbed adolescent girls. *American Journal of Psychiatry, 147,* 1061–1068.

Willick, M. S. (2001). Psychoanalysis and Schizophrenia: A cautionary tale. *Journal of the American Psychoanalytic Association, 49,* 27–56.

Winnicott, D. W. (1953). Transitional objects and transitional phenomena. *International Journal of Psycho-Analysis, 34,* 1–9.

Winnicott, D. W. (1956). The antisocial tendency. In D. W. Winnicott (Ed.), *Collected papers: Through pediatrics to psycho-analysis.* London: Tavistock, 1958.

Winnicott, D. W. (1958). *Collected papers: Through pediatrics to psychoanalysis.* London: Tavistock.

Winnicott, D. W. (1960). Ego distortion in terms of true and false self. In *The maturational processes and the facilitating environment (1965)* (pp. 140–152). New York: International Universities Press.

Winnicott, D. W. (1962a). Ego integration in child development. In D. W. Winnicott (Ed.), *The maturational processes and the facilitating environment* (pp. 56–63). London: Hogarth Press.

Winnicott, D. W. (1962b). The theory of the parent-infant relationship: Further remarks. *International Journal of Psycho-Analysis, 43,* 238–245.

Winnicott, D. W. (1965a). Ego distortion in terms of true and false self. In *The maturational process and the facilitating environment* (pp. 140–152). New York: International Universities Press.

Winnicott, D. W. (1965b). *The maturational process and the facilitating environment.* London: Hogarth Press.

Winnicott, D. W. (1967). Mirror-role of the mother and family in child development. In P. Lomas (Ed.), *The predicament of the family: A psycho-analytical symposium* (pp. 26–33). London: Hogarth Press.

Winnicott, D. W. (1971). *Playing and reality.* London: Tavistock.

Wolf, E. S. (1988a). Case discussion and position statement. *Psychoanalytic Inquiry, 8,* 546–551.

Wolf, E. S. (1988b). *Treating the self.* New York: Guilford Press.

Wolff, P. H. (1996). The irrelevance of infant observations for psychoanalysis. *Journal of the American Psychoanalytic Association, 44,* 369–392.

Yorke, C. (1971). Some suggestions for a critique of Kleinian psychology. *Psychoanalytic Study of the Child, 26,* 129–155.

Yorke, C., Kennedy, H., & Wiseberg, S. (1981). Some clinical and theoretical aspects of two developmental lines. In *The course of life* (pp. 619–637). Adelphi, MD: U.S. Department of Health.

Yorke, C., Wiseberg, S., & Freeman, T. (1989). *Development and psychopathology: Studies in psychoanalytic psychiatry.* London: Yale University Press.

Zahn-Waxler, C., Klimes-Dougan, B., & Slattery, M. J. (2000). Internalizing problems of childhood and adolescence: Prospects, pitfalls, and progress in understanding the development of anxiety and depression. *Development and Psychopathology, 12,* 443–466.

Zweig-Frank, H., & Paris, J. (1991). Parents' emotional neglect and overprotection according to the recollections of patients with borderline personality disorder. *American Journal of Psychiatry, 148,* 648–651.

CHAPTER 19

Social Cognition, Psychological Symptoms, and Mental Health: The Model, Evidence, and Contribution of Ego Development

GIL G. NOAM, COPELAND H. YOUNG, and JANNA JILNINA

The application of cognitive-developmental paradigms in the study of psychopathology originates from a broader attempt to integrate principles of developmental psychology with those of clinical psychology and psychiatry. One consequence of these efforts has been the emergence of developmental psychopathology as a field of inquiry (Achenbach, 1982; Cicchetti, 1984; Garmezy & Rutter, 1983; Kazdin, 1989; Noam, 1984; Rutter, 1988; Wenar, 1982). The utilization of a cognitive developmental approach in the study of developmental psychopathology was initially alluded to by Rosen (1977) as "cognitive developmental psychopathology." Achenbach (1990) later situated this approach in the context of developmental psychopathology.

Both researchers and clinicians have begun to use this cognitive approach as a basis for exploring and understanding maladaptive behavior (Gordon & Arbuthnot, 1987; Salter, Richardson, & Martin, 1985; Swett, 1985) and psychopathology (e.g., Gondolf, 1987; Hoar, 1983; Ratcliff, 1985; Reinhard, 1990; Strauss & Ryan, 1988; Wilbur, Rounsaville, Sugarman, Casey, & Kleber, 1982), and for use of innovative methods of clinical intervention (Abroms, 1978; Sperry, 1975; Swensen, 1980; Young-Eisendrath, 1982).

Since the cognitive-developmental "revolution" in psychology, a riddle has intrigued many developmental scholars and practitioners. This riddle concerns the nature of the relationship between cognitive complexity and adaptation: Are more complex levels of cognition, social cognition, or personality development also characterized by more successful adjustment patterns? In most developmental traditions, more complex development is also viewed as more adaptive (e.g., Piaget, 1965, 1977, 1978). The stepwise progression from immature thought and impulsivity to complex, self-reflective, and tolerant forms of maturity consists of many components of mental health, yet many people at mature levels of development struggle with mental illness, neurosis, and dysfunctional adaptation to life. How is that possible?

The goal of this review is to assemble the large body of empirical evidence, to shed some light on the nature of this problem, and to add a level of synthesis to this line of developmental psychopathology research. Further questions include: Are there patterns of association between different developmental levels and typical psychological symptoms and psychiatric diagnoses? How has this field of inquiry evolved from simple correlational studies to complex multivariate models?

In this chapter, we review both published and unpublished reports using Loevinger's Washington University Sentence Completion Test in terms of clinical research, assessment, and potential treatment implications. We derive our cognitive developmental approach to developmental psychopathology from a definition of the field set forth by Sroufe and Rutter (1984) as "the study of the origins and course of individual patterns of behavioral maladaptation."

In Loevinger's theory, ego is a cognitive construct, a frame of meaning combining views, approaches, and ideas about one's self—what Loevinger calls "self-theory" (Hauser, 1993; Loevinger, 1976)—and the world around that self. Had Loevinger introduced it later, she would have labeled her work as relating to the development of self; at the time, the word ego seemed to depict the range of processes in which she was interested (Jane Loevinger, personal communication, 1996).

However, today, the term ego sometimes creates confusion as investigators are reminded of the psychoanalytic ego, which is not what Loevinger means (see also Vaillant, 1993). Ego is a frame of reference that enables a person to create new meanings and interpret events and emotions based on personal experience. It includes content (views, memories, isolated ideas) and structure (the complexity of the relationships between those ideas). As pointed out by a number of scholars, this amalgam of content and structure makes Loevinger's theory quasi-structural rather than purely structural in the way Piaget and the cognitive psychologists in his tradition thought of structure (Loevinger, 1991, 1993; Manners & Durkin, 2001; Noam, 1993). Quasi-structural refers to the fact that ego development consists of a mixture of cognitive complexity and content of thought and feeling. Whereas structural psychologists try to differentiate structure and content, Loevinger combines them, having found that people at different developmental levels have typical preoccupations and expected contents of thought that should not be "screened out" but made part of the definition and measurement of what constitutes a level of ego development.

It follows logically from the quasi-structural nature of the ego and its complexity as a "master trait" that no single dimension will be enough to describe the ego in its entirety. Loevinger distinguished four dimensions of the ego: impulse control, cognitive complexity, interpersonal relations, and conscious preoccupations. These dimensions can vary. There are good arguments to be made that all of these dimensions are separate domains of the self and have their own developmental line (e.g., Holt, 1998; Loevinger, 1986; Noam, 1993); there is also good evidence that people attempt to structure the world in some cohesive way that cuts across domains. It is important both to study a person from the perspective of domain specificity and to explore the discrepancy of different domains. The simultaneous importance of looking at the overarching self and its developmental path makes ego development theory and measurement very attractive.

EGO DEVELOPMENT

According to Loevinger, ego develops along a sequence of developmental stages, from the Impulsive stage, where the world is perceived in its dichotomy of black and white (good and bad) and the person is enveloped in his or her own egocentrism; to Self-Protective, where the world is perceived as hostile and threatening; to Conformist, where ideas and behaviors are governed by external rules; to Self-Aware, where self, at last, becomes the focus of its own awareness; to Conscientious, where one's conscience becomes its own judge; to Individualistic, where the value of an individual is fully appreciated; to Autonomous, where the life and the self are perceived in their complexity and interrelatedness. The fuller descriptions of each stage and its characteristics can be found elsewhere (e.g., Hauser, 1976; Loevinger, 1976, 1993; Loevinger & Hy, 1996; Manners & Durkin, 2001; Noam, 1998).

In Loevinger's original theory, only five stages were distinguished (Impulsive, Self-Protective, Conformist, Conscientious, and Integrated); the number was then expanded to seven by making the transitional substages (Conformist/Conscientious and Conscientious/Integrated) separate stages (Loevinger & Hy, 1996), to which Cook-Greuter (2000) added two more: Construct-Aware (E9) and Transcendent (E10). Thus, the most current version of the theory acknowledges the existence of the nine consecutive stages: from E2 (Impulsive) to E10 (Transcendent). The information about stages, summarized in Table 19.1, is based on the descriptions from the latest texts: the Loevinger and Hy manual and Cook-Greuter's paper.

THEORETICAL MODELS OF LINKAGE BETWEEN EGO DEVELOPMENT, PSYCHOPATHOLOGY, AND MENTAL HEALTH

It has become a widely accepted trend in psychology and psychiatry that mental health and psychopathology should be understood, at least in part, in developmental terms (e.g., Cicchetti, 1984, 1990; Noam, 1988), in other words, that developmental dimensions can lend themselves as important lenses for developmental psychopathology.

It is not surprising that a steady number of studies have been conducted using the Loevinger model. We now have sufficient evidence to warrant an in-depth review and to critically reflect on the central dimension of the relationship between ego development and psychopathology.

There are four theoretical perspectives on the nature of the ego development-mental health relationship. On one extreme is the notion that development and mental health are, in fact, one and the same: Individuals at lower stages of development are less "mentally healthy," and those at more mature stages enjoy greater mental health. This is especially the case when people remain in ego development positions beyond their normative age ("age-stage dysynchrony").

Among the evidence in support of this claim is the fact that the stepwise progression from immature thought and impulsivity to complex, self-reflective, and tolerant forms of maturity consists of many components of mental health. Accepting the contradictory nature of the self, relationships, and the world at large is a hallmark of complex development and represents positive adaptation, which clinicians also tend to refer to as mental health. Thus, social-cognitive development from Piaget to Kohlberg and to Loevinger refers not only to evolving structures of meaning, but also to better adaptations between the person and the world. Higher stages promote more stable adaptations to the social world and also indicate more secure mental health. A person who is developmentally immature, for example, has fewer tools at his or her disposal to interpret the actions of others. As a consequence, he or she is more likely to interpret statements of others as hostile and rejecting. This lack of understanding of the inner workings of another person and the multifaceted nature of human communication is a cognitive and developmental vulnerability. As a consequence, the likelihood of distorting ambiguous information and reacting in an aggressive and retaliatory manner is great.

The second view of the association between mental health and development is that the two are conceptually and empirically distinct phenomena. Anyone can be afflicted with any form of psychopathology at any developmental position. The mechanisms underlying psychopathology and ego development are truly orthogonal. The fact that many people at mature levels of development struggle with mental illness, neurosis, and dysfunctional adaptations to life is strong evidence in support of this view. This is also Loevinger's position. She implied in a 1968 chapter entitled "The Relation of Adjustment to Ego Development" that the evolution of the ego and mental health are orthogonal: two distinct constructs that have no conceptual overlap.

A less extreme position than the first two consists of a strong positive relationship between development and mental health such that people at higher stages of development are better adapted or better able to adapt and, therefore, are more apt to be mentally healthy. To put it another way, mental health supports the maturation of the ego. This model is quite common in developmental research; a positive association between development and mental health has been stated or implied by researchers in cognitive development

TABLE 19.1 Ego Development Stages and Features

Level	Code	Features
Impulsive	E2	Impulsivity; dependence on others; world understood in terms of simple dichotomies: good and bad, black and white; prevalence of physical needs
Self-protective	E3	Hostility, seeing interpersonal relationships as exploitative, opportunistic behavior
Conformist	E4	Identification with the group and its authority; preoccupation with appearance, material things, social acceptance, and belonging; stereotypic perception of people
Self-aware	E5	Acute sense of distinction between the self and the group; attention to inner states
Conscientious	E6	Reflectivity; importance of self-evaluated standards; high value of achievement; excessive responsibility for others
Individualistic	E7	A sense of individuality; greater tolerance for individual differences; concern for problems of dependence and independence
Autonomous	E8	Search for self-fulfillment; recognition of other people's need for autonomy; high tolerance of ambiguity and recognition of paradoxes
Construct-aware	E9	Seeing the global world beyond one's culture; rationality; inner conflict around existential paradoxes; fear of losing self
Transcendent	E10	Acceptance and understanding of time-space continuum, of unity concepts; being, noncontrolled conscience, tolerance, full empathy

(Piaget), moral development (Kohlberg), and interpersonal development (Selman) and is one that Loevinger would also subscribe to as an empirical fact. However, this view implies that although people at more mature developmental levels are not necessarily shielded from psychopathology or dysfunctional adaptations, there is greater probability of mental health.

What makes this general view on the relationship between development and mental health more complicated is the multitude of dimensions and factors that underlie psychopathology and maladaptation. Some disorders, such as Schizophrenia, are probably quite unrelated to ego development, whereas antisocial behavior problems could be quite strongly related. As stated before, what makes this empirical relationship more challenging is that ego development definitions have some overlap with typical psychological problem behaviors and protective abilities.

For those disorders that might be connected to ego development, a fourth model can be introduced. This model suggests key vulnerabilities, risks, and symptom combinations that arise at each ego development position. Our model is probabilistic; that is, when we suggest, for instance, an association between the Conformist ego stage and depression, what we mean is the highest risk of depression exists for the people at the Conformist ego development stage, whereas for people further from the Conformist stages, this risk is lower.

There are several claims we are making in this introduction before bringing forth the evidence to support them. First, comparisons of clinical and nonclinical samples suggest that, in general, clinical samples have lower means of ego development than nonclinical samples, thus supporting the third model of linkage. Second, we hypothesized that some disorders are more independent of ego development, such as Schizophrenia and those displaying strong associations, such as delinquency and personality disorders. Third, for several disorders more strongly related to ego development, subgroups within the disorder population have been identified. These groups vary slightly in symptom expression and especially in the meaning-making processes used by patients. The evidence suggests that these groups are also closely tied to ego development difference.

PLAN OF THE REVIEW

Along with the scholarly significance of bringing together evidence that offers support to many points of the theoretical debate on the nature of the relationship between the cognitive-developmental paradigm and clinical research, the practical significance of the topic is also obvious. With a better understanding of which disorders are related to ego development, it becomes possible to make progress in treatment and recovery as a way to support development (especially when there is a developmental delay at hand).

In the next section, we review the literature by diagnosis, using the central way clinical phenomena are divided: the *Diagnostic and Statistical Manual of Mental Disorders (DSM-IV-TR;* American Psychiatric Association, 2000). Many studies were conducted without using this classification system (e.g., using behavior checklists instead), but there is a great deal of overlap between different constructs, and thus it is possible to identify studies that deal with the same symptoms. It is important to recognize that because psychopathology and symptomatology are defined and measured very differently, it is not possible to easily compare studies. Yet we attempt to do that, for the sake of generalization and basing our conclusions on as solid a body of evidence as possible. Thus, while not blurring the lines between, for instance, mood disorders, affective disorders, and depressive symptomatology, we nevertheless consider them in the same subsection.

We begin with a subsection on Conduct Disorder, delinquency, and externalizing behaviors, then move on to personality disorders; following that is a section on mood disorders, internalizing symptoms, and suicidality; then we review studies on anxiety disorders, eating disorders, and alcohol and substance abuse. We conclude with a subsection on defense mechanisms.

In the third section, we concentrate on the relationship between ego development and another end of the mental health spectrum, what many call a positive mental health (e.g., Helson & Srivastava, 2001; Vaillant, 2000). The fourth section covers evidence on the family influences that affect ego development and its relationship to various mental health aspects. The last section are devoted to summary, conclusions, and implications for future research.

EGO DEVELOPMENT AND PSYCHOPATHOLOGY

As a first step we will introduce the measure of ego development and then describe the validity evidence.

Measurement of Ego Development

One of the most prominent features of Loevinger's theory is "the reciprocal relationship between theory and system-

atic data collection" (Hauser, 1993, p. 24). Loevinger and her colleagues did a thorough empirical job making sure that every theoretic idea is grounded in a solid body of evidence and that there is a continual bootstrapping between theory and research.

Washington University Sentence Completion Test (WUSCT) is the instrument used to establish the level of ego development. It is a semiprojective technique that consists of 36 open-ended sentences that the subject has to complete (there are shorter versions, using only 18 or 24 sentences). Two manuals developed by Loevinger and her colleagues (Loevinger & Hy, 1996; Loevinger & Wessler, 1970) serve as help for trained raters scoring WUSCT protocols. Based on hundreds of studies conducted using this instrument since the introduction of the theory, it has been possible to make conclusions concerning reliability and validity of the theory and its measure.

Reliability and Validity

After the first reviews of the 1970s (Hauser, 1976; Loevinger, 1979), hundreds of studies using WUSCT were conducted. Three recent major reviews (Hauser, 1993; Loevinger, 1993; Manners & Durkin, 2001) and numerous less comprehensive papers have brought together evidence in support of the theory and its measure. This section aims at consolidating and integrating evidence from as many sources as possible to draw a comprehensive picture that takes into consideration all the work done in this direction.

Reliability Studies

Test-retest reliability was found to be sufficiently high for total protocol ratings (.72 to .79) and for the item sum scores (.91; Blumentritt, Novy, Gaa, & Liberman, 1996; Loevinger & Wessler, 1970; Redmore & Waldman, 1975) for both normal and clinical populations (Weiss, Zilberg, & Genevro, 1989). Another important reliability aspect, interrater reliability, has been reported as sufficient by virtually every researcher concerned with this problem. Different studies obtained different values of test-retest correlation, yet they were all significantly high, ranging from .70 on individual items to .95 on total protocol ratings (Browning, 1986; Dubow, Huesmann, & Eron, 1987; Hauser et al., 1984; Loevinger & Wessler, 1970; Noam et al., 1984; Novy & Francis, 1992; Snarey & Lydens, 1990; Waugh, 1981; Weiss et al., 1989). As in the case of test-retest reliability, interrater reliability was found to be equally high for psychiatric samples (Weiss et al., 1989).

Split-half reliability was studied by computing correlations between each half and 36-items version and was found significant (Novy & Francis, 1992; Redmore & Waldman, 1975).

Also, internal consistency was reported to be .91 (computed using Cronbach's alpha; Loevinger, 1976; Loevinger & Wessler, 1970); the results were confirmed using psychiatric samples (D. S. Weiss et al., 1989).

Validity Studies

Studies of construct validity of the WUSCT explore the relationship between ego development and related constructs, such as interpersonal behavior, clinical interview data and behaviors, level of defensive functioning, responsibility functioning, and conformity behavior, and were found to be sufficient (Hauser, 1976). External validity was studied extensively, by various means.

Ego level as assessed by WUSCT was found to correlate with the following:

- Ego level as assessed by interviews at about .60 in a rather homogeneous group and .89 in a more variable group (Lucas, 1971; Sutton & Swensen, 1983).
- Other stage tests of personality, for instance, a correlation of about .40 to .60 with Kohlberg's moral judgment test with age partialed out (Lambert, 1972; Sullivan, McCullough, & Stager, 1970).
- Thematic Apperception Test scored for ego development (correlation coefficient of about .80; Sutton & Swensen, 1983).
- Measure of conformity (Hoppe & Loevinger, 1977) and other personality characteristics that, according to Loevinger, were appropriate for certain ego levels (Rozsnafszky, 1981; Westenberg & Block, 1993).
- Competence as measured by the California Personality Inventory (Helson & Wink, 1987).

Sequentiality studies are an important part of evidence in support of the validity of the theory. In numerous studies, both cross-sectional and longitudinal, Loevinger (1976, 1993) demonstrated that ego level steadily increased during the high school and college years, usually up to the Self-Aware stage, the modal stage of the contemporary adult population. Blasi (1976) and Redmore (1976) have shown that there is an asymmetry of comprehension; that is, people could understand ego levels lower than their own, but not those much higher. Another possible use of similar studies would be to measure average normal growth rates for specific age groups. This was done by some researchers (Redmore & Loevinger, 1979; Westenberg & Gjerde, 1999), but

clearly this is an area of the ego development field that needs more research.

Novy (1990) approached the problem of sequentiality from another perspective. In a complex cross-sectional study, Novy (1993) has found that the maturity factor was clearly progressing with ego stages. We have to keep in mind, though, that maturity is not ego development per se, but is considered by some scholars as one ego dimension (Noam, 1998).

Another problem with sequentiality of ego stages is that the opposite tendency—some people regressing rather than progressing in ego development—has also been reported. This phenomenon has been especially pointed out by Manners and Durkin (2001) as it undermines, at least to some extent, the value of sequentiality studies. More research is due in this area so that we know what are "normal" regression proportions for specific ages and specific groups.

Predictive validity of the WUSCT is assessed by Loevinger (1979) herself as probabilistic rather than rigid. Theoretically, ego development is not supposed to directly predict behavior. In this framework, it was found that ego development could be a good probabilistic predictor of helping, responsibility, and conformity (Loevinger, 1979), and even other behaviors, less directly related to the construct of ego, such as consistency of the use of contraceptives by female adolescents (Hart & Hilton, 1988).

Discriminant validity of WUSCT is usually assessed by exploring correlations between ego development scores and several most closely related variables, that is, intelligence as measured by IQ, fluency as measured by the word count in the WUSCT protocol, and various socioeconomic variables.

Most studies report moderate to high significant correlations (.45 to .50) between WUSCT and IQ (Cramer, 1999; Loevinger & Wessler, 1970). Correlations of fluency and ego level were found to be more moderate, at .31 to .35 (Einstein & Lanning, 1998; Loevinger & Wessler, 1970; McCrae & Costa, 1980), and diverse socioeconomic correlates range from .23 to .51. Thus, ego development was found to correlate with, and differ from, IQ, fluency, and diverse socioeconomic variables.

CONDUCT DISORDERS, DELINQUENCY, AND OTHER EXTERNALIZING BEHAVIORS

In this section, we review the research evidence of the relationship between ego development and the family of mental health problems that include Conduct Disorders, delinquency, and externalizing symptoms. Although legally adjudged delinquency and clinically defined Conduct Disorders are not synonymous (Quay, 1965), we maintain that the psychological profiles prompting both sets of behaviors are sufficiently similar to allow for meaningful generalizations from the one to the other (e.g., Smetana, 1990). By the same token, delinquency is usually considered a type of externalizing behavior (along with similar phenomena, such as aggression and running away; Noam, Recklitis, & Paget, 1991). Also, the studies cited show that the patterns of relationships with ego development for Conduct Disorder, delinquency, and externalizing behaviors are quite similar. The main difference lies in the measurement tools used. Studies concerned specifically with Conduct Disorder use clinical tools, usually those that correspond to *DSM-IV-TR* (American Psychiatric Association, 2000) criteria. Externalizing symptoms and delinquency are usually measured either by the Child Behavior Checklist (CBCL; Achenbach & Edelbrock, 1987) or by Achenbach's Youth Self-Report (YSR; Achenbach & Edelbrock, 1991). Both measures produce narrow band factors, which then get combined into broadband factors. The broadband factors are similar: externizing and internalizing symptoms. In the CBCL, internalizing factors include such behaviors and feelings as crying, loneliness, needing to be perfect, and worrying about how others see you. The externalizing factors include arguing, hitting, and destruction of property. In the YSR, the Internalizing scale is a sum of scores for the Withdrawn, Anxious/Depressed, and Somatic Complaints scales. Externalizing is defined as the sum of scores for the Aggressive Behavior and Delinquent scales. Thus, Delinquency can be measured by YSR as one of the narrowband scales. Another way to measure delinquency is with direct behavioral reports, such as case materials for court-directed cases.

We review studies that used those terms separately and then bring the findings together in the summary. We believe this group of mental health problems belongs to the category that has a conceptual and evidential overlap with ego development theory. The characteristics of the lower stages of ego development (particularly egocentrism, poor impulse control, and low empathetic abilities of the Impulsive stage and the hostility of the Self-Protective stage) are also the characteristics of many delinquents.

We start with adolescent studies and then move on to the studies conducted with adult samples. Please note that the tables with details on each study, its sample and measurement, are to be found at the end of the section.

Adolescent Studies

We will now turn to those studies that deal with young people, a populations that is especially vulnerable to delinquency, externalizing, and conduct problems.

Delinquency and Externalizing Behaviors

Frank and Quinlan (1976) studied ego development in delinquent adolescent girls with two comparison groups: girls participating in various recreational programs in an inner-city settlement house and girls who attended regularly a youth development program (YDP). At the time of testing, the delinquents resided in an institution for court-directed cases. Running away, incorrigibility, and sexual delinquency occurred most often among these subjects, whose mean age was 16 years.

Delinquents were split equally between Impulsive and Self-Protective ego stages. As a group, delinquents showed the least mature ego development. The control and YDP subjects did not show significant differences in ego stage, thus bringing the researchers to the conclusion that it is the delinquency factor, not age or social background factors, that primarily accounted for ego development differences.

Hickok (1996) found significant negative correlations (−.32) between ego development level and the level of externalizing symptoms as measured by Achenbach's and Edelbrock's (1983) CBCL in a sample of severely emotionally disturbed adolescents (ages 12 to 18). As discussed earlier, externalizing behavior is a combined score of two subscales in the YSR (delinquent and aggressive behavior) and several subscales in the CBCL (hitting, arguing, destruction of property).

In another correlational study of inpatient adolescents, similar findings were obtained: point-biserial negative correlations between ego development (the sample was divided into Preconformist and Conformist ego development groups) and delinquent, aggressive, and externalizing behaviors as measured by the YSR (Achenbach & Edelbrock, 1991) were at a modest level: .17, .20, and .15, respectively (Schneider, 1996).

Ryf (1996) compared two groups of adolescents: a group of psychiatric patients and a matched control group of high school students. Two aspects of her findings are relevant for this review.

First, the hospital group contained a higher percentage of Preconformist subjects (36% as opposed to 20% in the control group) and a lower percentage of Postconformist subjects (18% as opposed to 46 % in the control group).

Second, delinquent behavior for both groups was found to decrease steadily with ego development (from 67.30 for the Impulsive group to 60.93 for the Conscientious stages group). One seemingly contradictory finding of this study is that aggressive behavior was lowest (56.29) for the Conformist group and higher for both extremes of the sample (60.80 for the Impulsive group and 60.93 for the Conscientious group). Thus, not a linear, but a curvilinear relationship between ego development and aggressiveness was found. This is but one piece of evidence supporting the idea that a curvilinear relationship is possibly in the very nature of ego development.

In another study of a psychiatric adolescent sample, Leong (2000) found delinquent behavior to be equally high for the Impulsive, Self-Protective, and Conformist groups, but much lower for the Postconformist adolescents. The findings on the broadband Externalizing syndrome were completely in line with the other studies presented: Externalizing syndrome was highest for the Impulsive adolescents (65.6), almost as high for the Self-Protective group (63.89), and much lower for the Conformist and Post-conformist groups (59.86 and 59.18, respectively).

Noam et al. (1984) found significant negative correlations between ego development and Externalizing, Internalizing, Aggressive, and Delinquent scales from the CBCL (Achenbach & Edelbrock, 1983) in an adolescent inpatient sample. Yet, in hierarchical multiple regression analyses, after age, gender, and socioeconomic status (SES) were controlled for, only the Externalizing scale kept its significance as a contributor to the variance in ego development. This study, while supporting the strong relationship between ego development and Externalizing behaviors, draws researchers' attention to the importance of using multivariate methods while studying ego development.

To summarize, we note that delinquent behavior was found to have an inverse relationship with ego development by every study (Frank & Quinlan, 1976; Leong, 2000; Noam et al., 1984; Ryf, 1996; Schneider, 1996). A similar pattern was observed for externalizing symptoms and ego development (Hickok, 1996; Noam et al., 1984; Schneider, 1996). This is an important finding, as there are those clinicians who believe that delinquents are often very able to take the perspective of others and are quite evolved but use their significant capacities for devious purposes. The findings on aggressive behavior are somewhat less consistent. The findings presented here suggest that delinquents have not reached levels of development at which they are capable of understanding the world from other people's point of view and that they are developmentally delayed as compared to normative samples.

In order not to be selective and to cite all available, even if contradictory, evidence, we have to mention an unusual study in which a relatively small sample of 42 "normal" African American adolescents participated (Hiraga, 1996). The author explored the relationship between family influences/parenting styles and adolescent ego development. Delinquent and aggressive behaviors were outcome variables, along with ego and moral development. When correlations among outcome variables were obtained, the findings were seemingly in contradiction with the other studies cited: No significant correlations were found between delinquency, aggression, and ego development.

Conduct Disorder and Delinquency: Typologies

Conduct Disorder refers to a variety of maladaptational styles (Hayes & Walker, 1986; Jennings, Kilkenny, & Kohlberg, 1983). The first attempts to distinguish a system of subtypes within this variety were made as early as the 1940s. Many scholars introduced their own typologies, but there are two principles of classification: one based on personality characteristics and another based on age. Even though the research on typology of Conduct Disorder patients and delinquents was not directly related to ego development studies, we show that both classification principles are related to ego development and that the most prominent tendency in delinquency today is to use developmental measurements (particularly WUSCT) to distinguish between the subtypes of delinquents and Conduct Disorder patients.

Early studies on delinquency and personality observed that delinquents were more present oriented and behaved so as to maximize immediate rewards (Barndt & Johnson, 1955; Davids, Kidder, & Reich, 1962). The studies also showed that delinquents had more psychopathic, schizophrenic, and hypomanic tendencies than the average population (Hathaway & Monachesi, 1953, 1961). The next logical step in the same direction was to introduce a classification within delinquent populations that would take personality characteristics into consideration.

The first classification of delinquents was done as early as 1946 by Hewitt and Jenkins, who distinguished three types: unsocialized aggressive, socialized aggressive, and overinhibited delinquents. A series of studies conducted by Quay and colleagues (Quay, 1965; Quay & Blumen, 1963) also arrived at three types, with slight variations. The unsocialized type was called a solitary aggressive, to emphasize this person's acting alone and the aggressiveness of his or her acts; the socialized type was called subcultural delinquent (this was usually a gang member; thus, the typology stressed the presence of gang subculture with its own norms and role models). The overinhibited type was called neurotic delinquent; this was the least numerous category. There are a few readily available parallels with ego development theory even in the very descriptions of these types. Aggressiveness, hostility, and poor impulse control are by definition characteristics of the Preconformist ego development stages. Group membership and importance of group norms and role modeling are the most prominent characteristics of the Conformist stage of ego development. Thus, we would expect solitary aggressive delinquents to be more delayed in ego development than subcultural delinquents. We show how, in the studies cited later, these parallels were supported by the evidence.

Another classification of the Conduct Disorder and delinquent individuals is based on age. It is also the classification used in *DSM-IV-TR*, where there are two main types: childhood-onset type and adolescent-onset type (with a third category, unspecified onset). By definition, the childhood-onset type starts earlier, before 10 years of age, and is likely to be more persistent and more severe than the adolescent-onset type; also, the disorder that started in childhood is more likely to persist into older age and develop into adult Antisocial Personality Disorder (*DSM-IV-TR*).

Moffitt (1993) developed a similar taxonomy and researched the two types of behaviors, showing the logic and features of the adolescence-limited and life-course-persistent antisocial behaviors.

If we look at these classifications from the viewpoint of ego development theory, we should assume that earlier onset of disorder will be associated with a more severe ego development impairment, so we would expect individuals with childhood-onset (life-course-persistent) disorder to remain at the lower, Preconformist stages of ego development. This dysynchrony, as we know, is related to a variety of maladaptations.

The research on ego development and delinquency supports these conceptual parallels.

Next, we review studies that either used directly the typology of delinquent and Conduct Disorder patients based on the personality characteristics, or whose results imply these theoretically defined parallels.

Solitary Aggressive Type

After Quay's (1965) classification, many diverse attempts to categorize the same diagnostic profiles have been used, including the "psychopathic syndrome" (McCord & McCord, 1956), psychopathic personality (Cleckley,

1964), psychopathic delinquency (Quay, 1965), sociopathic personality (Robins, 1966), undersocialized aggressive (*DSM-III;* American Psychiatric Association, 1980), the sadomasochistic violent juvenile offender (Taylor, 1983), psychopathy (Hare, 1985), and developmental psychopathy (Speicker, 1988). Solitary aggressive type Conduct Disorder is distinguished from other Conduct Disorders by an earlier onset at latency. Consequently, these individuals present with the earliest stages of ego development (Taylor, 1983). Robins reported that children presenting with this type of conduct problem frequently follow a trajectory that leads to Antisocial Personality Disorders in adulthood. A concomitant feature of this outcome is retarded ego development, which likely finds its origins in ego developmental delays starting in early childhood.

Hezel (1968) and Imperio (1975) reported a strong inverse association between ego development and psychopathic factor (Quay, 1965). Even though Hezel's sample included younger subjects, 12- to 16-year-old delinquents as opposed to 14- to 15-year-olds of Imperio's sample, both samples brought the researchers to the same conclusions: that Impulsive ego stage was the modal stage for the participants.

A study by Noam, Paget, Valiant, Borst, and Bartok (1994) aimed at comparing Conduct Disorder, Affective Disorder, and mixed Conduct-Affective Disorder groups on ego development level. In line with the earlier findings, the study found significant group differences, with the Conduct Disorder group consisting almost exclusively of the Preconformist subjects (93% Preconformist and 7% Conformist), whereas the Affective Disorder group had more Conformist subjects (25% Conformist and 76% Preconformist). Mixed disorder groups fell between the two, being closer to the Conduct Disorder group (89% Preconformist, 11% Conformist). Besides ego development, another variable to best predict disorder group membership was IQ.

In Borst, Noam, and Bartok (1991), two groups of hospitalized psychiatric adolescents were compared: those classified as suicide attempters and nonsuicidal patients. The group of suicidal adolescents had three times more Conformist subjects and four times fewer Conduct Disorder cases than the group of nonsuicidal adolescents, which implies a strong negative relationship between Conduct Disorder diagnosis and Preconformist ego development levels. Thus, both studies found a strong association between Preconformist levels of ego development and Conduct Disorder in adolescent psychiatric patients.

In Noam et al. (1991), which was devoted to the exploration of two different pathways of adolescent psychiatric patients—those who did progress by at least half an ego level after 9 months of treatment and those who did not progress—statistical analyses revealed significant results relevant to the point of this section. In the progressors group, the percentage of patients diagnosed with Conduct Disorder was 1.5 times less than in the nonprogressors group. Even though the relationship between Conduct Disorder and ego level was not among the research questions of this study, this fact allows us to hypothesize that the Conduct Disorder diagnosis makes it harder for a person to move beyond Preconformist (Impulsive and Self-Protective) stages of ego development. Although Quay's typology was not used in this study, the prevalence of Preconformist functioning among those adolescents points to the solitary aggressive type.

Group Type

Adolescents displaying this disorder have been referred to in the literature under a number of different diagnostic entities, most prominently as subcultural delinquency (Quay, 1965). Although generally presenting with Presocial stages and lower than matched controls, these individuals tend to display greater ego maturity than those with solitary aggressive Conduct Disorders.

The group type Conduct Disorder closely parallels the profile of the lifestyle of a violent juvenile offender defined in Loevingerian terms by Taylor (1983). Disengaged from "normative culture," these offenders join a delinquent peer group or street gang. Adult criminal behavior serves as a source of positive role modeling which is further reinforced through peer support, while finding self-expression through violent behavior. Struggling with both strong dependency needs, in the form of being cared for by others, and inner insecurities, these individuals derive much gratification from delinquent peer group relations. In terms of ego development, Taylor situates these offenders between the Self-Protective and Conformist stages. Imperio (1975) reported that subcultural delinquents (Quay & Parsons, 1971), averaging 15 years of age, display the highest level of ego development of the three Quay delinquency classification types. Clustering between Self-Protective and Conformist stages, some of these adolescents scored as high as the Conscientious ego stage. These findings make perfect sense in the light of Loevinger's theory, as compliance with the group norms is the most prominent characteristic of the Conformist stages of ego development.

Undifferentiated Type

Subjects falling within this category also have been identified as neurotic delinquents (Quay, 1965; *DSM-III-R*, American Psychiatric Association, 1987) and often present with anxiety-related features. Stemming from underlying conflicts, depressed development with the domain of moral competency may reflect a particularly moral component to their anxiety. Another source of the undifferentiated nature of this type of Conduct Disorder may derive from delinquent behavior, which carries a tendency to act neither exclusively in isolation nor within a peer context. Unfortunately, no specific findings on the individuals diagnosed with this subtype of Conduct Disorder were reported.

The summary of the samples and findings of this section on adolescent ego development and Conduct Disorder and delinquency are represented in Table 19.2.

Adult Studies

Even though ego development represents a scale different from a chronological age scale, there is abundant evidence that ego development does correlate with age, at least through the young adulthood years. The delay in ego development is called *age-stage dysynchrony* and is viewed as a source of additional tension and maladaptation (Noam, 1988). It follows that for adults arrested at the Preconformist stages of ego development, psychological problems characteristic of these stages, such as aggressiveness and poor impulse control, will be even more severe than for adolescents at the same ego level. Yet, probably because adolescents at these levels are more numerous than adults, there are fewer adult studies than adolescent studies. Many of the studies conducted are in institutional settings.

England (1997) compared a group of adult incest offenders with a control group of matched nonoffenders. Incest offenders were significantly lower on ego development than the control group. Specifically, the incest group had three times more individuals at the Impulsive ego stage and two times more individuals at the Self-Protective ego stage than the control group.

In a similar study, Hanson (1999) compared a group of men abusing their spouse/partner with a matched control group of nonabusers. The total violence score dropped significantly with the increase in ego development stage. For the Impulsive ego stage, it was found to be as high as 57.0, but for the Self-Protective, only 18.72; it approximated 3.0 for both Conformist and Self-Aware stages, and went down as low as .722 for the Conscientious stage. This is strong evidence showing the drastic drop in violence as age-stage dysynchrony decreases.

Magee (1984) studied ego development in a small sample of 13 men diagnosed with Antisocial Personality Disorder residing in a forensic evaluation center and charged with serious crimes. The obtained distribution was compared to

TABLE 19.2   Conduct Disorders, Delinquency, and Externalizing Behaviors

Study	N	Gender	Age	Disorder	Results
Frank & Quinlan (1976)	66	F	Mean 16	Delinquency	Delayed ED, modal stage, Impulsive
Hickok (1996)	60	Mixed	12–18	Externalizing	Negative correlation with ED
Schneider (1996)	219	Mixed	13–17	Externalizing	Negative correlation with ED
Ryf (1996)	320	Mixed	15–18	Delinquency	Negative correlation with ED
Leong (2000)	188	Mixed	13–18, mean 15.4	Delinquency, externalizing	Negative correlation with ED
Noam et al. (1984)	114	Mixed	Mean 14.3	Externalizing	Negative correlation with ED
Hiraga (1996)	42	F	Mean 15.9	Delinquency, aggressive	No relationship
Hezel (1968)	N/A	Mixed	12–16	Psychopathic factor	Modal stage, Impulsive; inverse association between ED and psychopathic factor
Imperio (1975)	N/A	Mixed	14–15	Psychopathic factor	Modal stage, impulsive; inverse association between ED and psychopathic factor
Noam, Paget, Valiant, Borst, & Bartok (1994)	269	Mixed	11–17, mean 13.9	Conduct	An association between Preconformist ED and Conduct Disorder
Borst, Noam, & Bartok (1991)	219	Mixed	12–16, mean 14	Conduct	An association between Preconformist ED and Conduct Disorder
Noam, Recklitis, & Paget (1991)'	37	Mixed	Mean 13.4	Conduct	An association between Preconformist ED and Conduct Disorder

Note: ED = Ego development.

Loevinger's (1970) normative adult sample. A significantly higher proportion of men scored at the Preconformist ego level than was in Loevinger's sample. While no significant differences were found on the proportions of participants falling into the Conformist and Self-Aware stage, a significantly lower proportion scored at the Conscientious level and higher. We can conclude that although the patients with Antisocial Personality Disorder do score at the Conformist and Self-Aware stages, the tendency for impediment in ego growth is also obvious.

In a similar study of 41 adult male inmates, Angelopoulos (1991) found the Self-Protective ego development stage to be the modal stage for the participants diagnosed with Antisocial Personality Disorder.

Browning (1986) studied problematic ward behavior of inpatient adolescents and young adults (the study is included in this section because of the young adult group who participated in the research) and found a significant inverse relationship (−.35 increment in R squared in a hierarchical multiple regression model) between the total number of behavioral incidents and patients' level of ego development. Even though she used a mixed sample (13 to 28 years old) and mixed incidents (e.g., a suicide attempt and a violent act were both counted as incidents), yet the former is found to be more common at the Conformist and higher ego stages, whereas the latter is frequently observed at the two lower stages of ego development, as has been shown elsewhere in this section), this is one more piece of evidence supporting the strong inverse relationship between ego development and problematic, action-oriented behaviors.

Wright and Reise (1997) explored the relationship between ego development, personality, and sociosexuality, which is defined as unrestricted sexual behavior, or a tendency to engage in casual, noncommittal sexual relationships. Although not exactly an aspect of mental health, sociosexuality is viewed as a risk factor. Two opposing tendencies were expected: On the one hand, openness to new things and an exploratory attitude characteristic of people at higher levels of ego development might lead to an increase in sociosexuality; on the other hand, better impulse control might lead to a decrease in sociosexuality. These authors believe (and show through their results) that these two tendencies are related to the two aspects of ego development expressed through personality factors: agreeableness and openness to new experiences. Both correlate with ego development: Agreeableness correlates negatively with sociosexuality, and openness correlates positively with sociosexuality.

This study, while supporting the idea of curvilinearity, points out another potential source of it: a multidimensionality of the construct of ego. If different dimensions of ego have different relationships with the same variable (in the earlier example, sociosexuality), this might lead to curvilinearity (or no significant linear relationship) between this construct and ego development. This study stresses the need to further explore the multidimensional nature of the ego.

Summary and Implications

The evidence presented in this section supports our theory-driven assumption that there is a strong association between Preconformist stages of ego development and the delinquency/Conduct Disorders/externalizing behavior cluster of problems. This is a finding supported by nearly every study conducted.

The studies that had both clinical and normal samples of adolescents found that, uniformly, clinical samples were lower on ego development and higher on delinquency, aggression, and externalizing behaviors. The adults delayed in ego development were found to have a tendency to display poor control over their impulses and behaviors (see also Fisher, 1991; Recklitis, 1993), engaging in various offensive acts, whether incest or unrestricted sexual behavior. In addition to these overarching tendencies, several aspects of the delinquency-mental health relationship revealed are worth further exploration.

First, very few studies used Quay's typology within the Conduct Disorder diagnostic category, distinguishing among the solitary aggressive, subcultural, and neurotic types. Because clinical instruments are better able to capture this distinction, it appears that their use is preferable in the adolescent research. Another important point that has to be made is that ego development is not a simple upward progression: The stages are qualitatively different from one another, which often makes the relationship between ego development and other relevant variables curvilinear. Thus, the use of curvilinear and multivariate methods seems preferable in ego development and mental health research.

Our last conclusion derived from this section is that ego development might be a more complex construct than is now theorized. As we can see from Wright and Reise (1997), the different aspects of the ego can have different relationships with the same variable, thus, stressing the need to focus on different dimensions of the ego.

PERSONALITY DISORDERS

Evidence has been accumulated on personality disorders and ego development, yet only a few studies have covered all personality disorders in their relationship to ego development scale (see also Vincent & Vincent, 1979). This is understandable; considering the number of personality dis-

orders, to have a representative subgroup of each of them, the sample size should be quite substantial.

Vincent and Castillo (1984) conducted an extensive study with a sample of 400 psychiatric patients who were diagnosed either with one of *DSM-IV* Axis II personality disorders or no personality disorder. The distribution of participants across ego levels is important to this section, thus, we cite the results of the study in full.

No participant scored lower that Self-Protective ego development level or higher than Self-Aware level. The results are organized in Table 19.3, with the personality disorder having the lowest ego mean score beginning the table and the personality disorder with the highest ego mean score ending it.

The lowest ego development was observed in the group diagnosed with Borderline Personality Disorder, and the highest ego development was observed in the group diagnosed with Compulsive Personality Disorder. The authors conclude that, in the personality disorder group, "the majority of individuals below the conformity level were apt to cluster in the personality category of Dramatic, Emotional, or Erratic personality disorder as defined by *DSM-IV*" (Vincent & Castillo, 1984, p. 402).

These findings can be analyzed in several other ways. First, as we can see, most subsamples (excluding the narcissistic subsample that consisted of only one person and thus cannot be analyzed) contain people at all the three ego developmental levels: Self-Protective, Conformist, and Self-Aware. Yet, a few personality disorder groups are restricted to only two ego development levels: The Borderline, Schizoid, and Paranoid Personality Disorder groups consist only of people at Self-Protective and Conformist ego levels, with no one at the Self-Aware ego level. This is

TABLE 19.3   Personality Disorder by Ego Stage

	N	Self-Protective (%)	Conformist (5)	Self-Aware (%)
Borderline	24	67	33	—
Histrionic	75	34	65	1
Schizoid	11	27	73	—
Passive-Aggressive	83	14	83	3
Paranoid	9	11	89	—
Schizotypical	20	15	75	10
Narcissistic	1	—	100	—
Antisocial	7	14	72	14
Dependent	25	8	84	8
Avoidant	41	2	93	5
Compulsive	18	—	89	11

Adapted from "Ego Development and DSM-III Axis II: Personality Disorders," by K. Vincent and I. Castillo, 1984, *Journal of Clinical Psychology, 40*(2), pp. 400–402.

much lower than the normal adult populations (for whom Self-Aware is the modal stage) and even for clinical samples, most of which include at least several subjects scoring beyond the Conformist stage. Thus, we can conclude that Borderline, Schizoid, and Paranoid Personality Disorders are related to a serious impairment in ego development.

On the other hand, the Compulsive Personality Disorder group does not have any subjects who would score below Conformist ego development level. This is not characteristic of adult samples, even of normal adult samples. It seems that the Conformist is the modal stage for the Compulsive Personality Disorder group.

Second, we can compare the personality disorder subsample as a whole to the nondisordered patients in the same study and also to the normative adult and clinical samples (see Table 19.4).

We can conclude that, as a group, people diagnosed with personality disorder scored lower than normal samples and clinical samples. We have to note, though, that "lower" here means not the higher proportion of people at the Preconformist ego levels, as it is, for example, in the delinquency studies, but the lower proportion of people at the ego levels above Conformity. For example, a personality disorder group may be different from the no-disorder group in that it has a similar proportion of individuals at the Preconformist ego level, a higher proportion of the individuals at the Conformist level, and a much lower proportion at the Self-Aware level and beyond. The Conformist ego development level seems to be the modal level for personality disorder patients as a group.

Another study that used the entire range of personality disorder diagnostic categories was conducted not with a clinical sample, but with normal adults: undergraduate students at an urban university. McLauchlin (1997) explored the relationship between the level of ego development and personality pathology measured by the Millon Clinical Multiaxial Inventory III (MCMI-III; Millon, 1983, 1994). Her findings are comparable to those of Vincent and Castillo (1984).

Using a relatively large sample ($N = 249$), McLauchlin (1997) found that some personality types had only one or a few participants. Thus, for the more sound statistical analy-

TABLE 19.4 Distributions for Personality Disorder and Comparative Samples

	Preconformist (%)	Conformist (%)	Aware (%)
Personality disorder group ($N = 314$)	20	76	4
No personality disorder ($N = 74$)	8	85	7
Loevinger's normal adults sample	12	33	25
Accumulative normal adults sample	14	16	41
Accumulative clinical adult sample	23	38	25

TABLE 19.5 Mean Ego Levels for Three Personality Types

	Vincent & Castillo (1984)	McLauchlin (1997)
Borderline cluster	3.85	4.54
Preneurotic cluster	4.00	5.02
Neurotic cluster	3.75 (Compulsive only 4.11)	5.07

ses, and also to make a comparison between more severe and less severe personality disorders, McLauchlin divided her personality types into three clusters: the most severe, Borderline cluster (including Borderline, Schizoid, Schizotypical, Avoidant, Aggressive-Sadistic, Antisocial, and Paranoid); a Preneurotic cluster (mild severity disorders, including depressive, self-defeating, and Narcissistic); and the least severe cluster, Neurotic (including Histrionic and Compulsive Personality Disorders).

To make the results of the two studies comparable, we calculated the mean ego level scores for the three personality type clusters for both studies. The results are represented in Table 19.5.

As we can see, the results of the two studies generally coincide, with two major differences. First, the overall mean ego development level of Vincent and Castillo's sample is lower than the overall ego development level of the McLauchlin sample, which is explained by the fact that, whereas Vincent and Castillo used a clinical sample of psychiatric patients, participants in McLauchlin's study were undergraduate students, some of whom had the personality type as a trait and a few as a disorder. Second, there is a difference in the low mean ego level for the neurotic cluster in the clinical study. We will not try to explain why the patients diagnosed with Histrionic Personality Disorder in clinical study had such a low mean ego level (3.67), but if we consider this a random finding and take the Histrionic group out of the analysis, the results of the two studies are practically identical.

Generally, it seems that the overall conclusion of this section—that the more severe personality pathology is associated with lower ego development levels—is well supported by the evidence. Genden (1995) studied ego development in a sample of 37 patients at a community mental health agency. He found ego development to predict more severe personality pathology and membership in the "odd personality disorder" cluster, whereas less severe personality pathologies were not found to interact with ego development in that study.

Fineman, Beckwith, and Espinosa (1997) studied ego development in a sample of drug-addicted women with children. Their goal was to establish factors affecting maternal sensitivity in these women. On the whole, the sample consisted of poorly functioning, drug-using women, mostly from lower socioeconomic background; however, their ego development was found to positively correlate with maternal sensitivity. The women also were given a clinical interview, and some of them were diagnosed with MCMI-Axis II personality disorder. Although the relationship between ego development and personality disorder diagnosis was not explored in this study, all personality disorders were found to correlate negatively (the significance wasn't high enough, except for Paranoid Personality Disorder) with maternal sensitivity, which correlated positively (and significantly) with ego development. This suggests a negative association between personality disorder diagnosis and ego development found in the previously cited studies. (This study in also reviewed in the substance abuse section of this chapter.)

Borderline Personality Disorder

Among personality disorders, the borderline personality is the one most frequently studied in relationship to ego development. This interest is natural, if we take into consideration the research on the nature of Borderline Personality Disorder (BPD; e.g, West, Keller, Links, & Patrick, 1993).

Most researchers agree that BPD is primarily a disorder of impulse control (Gunderson & Phillips, 1991; Van Reekum, 1993). Thus, it has a conceptual overlap with ego development theory, with the impulse control dimension being one of the main ego dimensions, and with the prevalence of impulse control problems at the Preconformist ego development level. Also, a relationship between brain dysfunction and brain injuries and BPD was found. Brain injury causes disorders of impulse control, affective disintegration, and cognitive disability (Van Reekum, 1993). Two of these factors—impulse control and cognitive functioning—are closely related to ego development.

Still other studies have found a link, probably of biological origin, between BPD and aggressiveness (Korzekwa, Links, & Steiner, 1993), which is also a prevalent characteristic of individuals at the Preconformist levels of ego development, as many studies cited in this review indicate. In light of these findings, the BPD group being the lowest on ego development among the personality disorder groups (Vincent & Castillo, 1984) is not surprising.

These results were challenged by another study, in which ego development of BPD patients and psychiatric outpatients was compared (Marziali, Field, Classen, & Oleniuk, 1993). In this study, the modal stage for BPD was not Self-Protective, but Self-Aware, which is the modal stage for normal adult samples. Yet, no participant in the study scored above Conscientious ego level, a substantial proportion (10%) scored below Conformist level, and the mean ego de-

velopment score for the group was lower than the mean ego level for the D. S. Weiss et al. (1989) results for psychiatric patients. Thus, although different from the Vincent and Castillo (1984) study, this study confirmed the impairment on ego development for the BPD patients, even in comparison with other clinical samples.

Noam and Houlihan (1990) compared distribution between Preconformist and Conformist ego development stages for a sample of psychiatric adolescents in several diagnostic groups. To clarify the comparison, we use the proportion of participants at the Preconformist ego levels as a simple ego development index. The psychotic group had the lowest ego score (100% at the Preconformist ego levels). The next group was the personality disorder group, diagnosed with either atypical or mixed personality disorder, or BPD (86% of the participants at the Preconformist ego levels, only 14% at the Conformist ego level). All other diagnostic categories (Adjustment Disorder, Anxiety Disorder, Conduct Disorder, Affective Disorder) were found to have lower proportions of participants at the Preconformist ego levels and higher proportions of participants at the Conformist ego level. This finding confirms the conclusion arrived at by other researchers: that personality disorder patients, especially BPD patients, typically score lower on ego development even than other psychiatric patients, and lower than normal controls.

Haimes and Katz (1988) compared ego development findings among a sample of adult outpatients presenting with BPD with those of individuals with eating disorders. Findings suggested that subjects divided evenly between those attaining Impulsive through Conformist stages (53%) and those attaining Self-Aware and Conscientious stages (47%). Borderline subjects scored quite significantly lower.

Horton (2001) studied ego development in three groups of patients: those diagnosed with both BPD and Bulimia Nervosa, the group of bulimics only, and a control group of non-eating disorder, non-personality disorder patients. Not surprisingly, the comorbidity group scored the lowest on ego development, and the control group scored the highest, with the bulimics-only group falling in between. Although partial correlations were not obtained in this study, we see that borderline symptomatology contributed significantly to the low ego development score of borderline/bulimics group. This leads to the conclusion that borderline symptomatology is responsible for the lower ego level score, which is in line with other findings cited in this review.

Summary and Conclusions

Generally, the accumulated evidence so far is rather consistent in suggesting that personality disorders represent an impairment for the individual's ego development level. This fact is very important for treatment, as one should assume that increasing cognitive-developmental capacities, and in particular ego development, should help patients to overcome their disease.

On the other hand, it seems that different personality disorders have different relationships with ego development. The severity of the disorder is certainly a factor negatively associated with ego development. Thus, the personality disorders in the most severe cluster result in a more pronounced detrimental effect on ego development. Yet, each personality disorder has a unique profile, which must result in a unique relational pathway between those disorders and ego development. This area, potentially fruitful and useful for clinical practice, has not been thoroughly researched yet. The only exception to this is Borderline Personality Disorder, whose conceptual overlaps with the ego development theory have inspired more than a few studies in this area. With a certain degree of confidence, we can conclude that Borderline Personality Disorder usually results in significantly lower ego development levels in both adolescent and adult populations.

MOOD DISORDERS, INTERNALIZING SYMPTOMS, SUICIDALITY

In this section, we review the literature that explores the relationship between ego development and the family of psychological problems that include depression, suicidality, and internalizing symptoms. The rationale for considering those problems in the same section is evident: Basic internalizing and depressive symptoms are various ways of classifying related problems. They are also very different, but there is enough connection that it is possible to review them in one section. Depressive symptoms such as "negative feelings toward self," "loss of emotional attachments (involvement)," "loss of mirth response," "low self-evaluation," "self-blame and self-criticism," "distortion of body image," "increased dependency," "delusions of worthlessness," and "delusions of crime and punishment" (Beck, 1967) each point toward the same deferential tendency. However, although we consider these phenomena in the same subsection, we do not intend to blur the lines dividing them. These are different constructs; moreover, as will be pointed out, even the same construct, such as depression or suicidality, may have different subtypes, and those subtypes would display different relational patterns when considered in their association with ego development.

The relationship between this family of symptoms and ego development is not conceptually clear. On the one hand, because more advanced ego development provides a person with better tools for coping, it is logical to hypothesize that symptoms in general will subside as the person advances along the ego development continuum.

On the other hand, the many features and ideas that make depression possible (such as a clear differentiation between the self and the other, the idea of a standard to measure up to, understanding how other people view one, an ability to experience intellectually defined shame and guilt) are simply lacking at the lower levels of ego development. Thus, another hypothesis here is that the increase in ego development level will actually increase vulnerability to depressive and suicidal thoughts.

Still another view can take into consideration conceptual features of Loevinger's stages and hypothesize a curvilinear relationship between depressive symptomatology and ego development. The expectation is that depressive symptoms will be low at the Preconformist levels when the person lacks the self-differentiation and the self-consciousness necessary for depressive thought, and then will peak at the Conformist level where the other's opinion of one is crucial and painfully important, and then will go down again for the Postconformist people who realize the value of each person's (and their own) uniqueness and thus feel more free and less judgmental toward others and toward themselves.

Last, we cannot totally disregard the studies that found no relationship between ego development and depressive symptomatology. We bring together evidence in support of those positions, and then, through careful analysis of the differences between those groups of evidence, we try to find a solution, even a tentative one, that will need to be tested in future research.

Inverse Relationship between Symptomatology and Ego Development

In support of this position, we cite studies that found a linear decrease in depressive symptomatology, suicidality, or internalizing symptoms for the more advanced ego levels.

Depression

Noam and Houlihan (1990) studied ego development in a sample of early adolescent psychiatric inpatients presenting with various diagnoses. Preconformists constituted a majority of every group: Adjustment, Anxiety, Conduct, Personality, Affective, and Psychotic Disorders. The general inference was that the severity of symptomatology was much higher for the Preconformist ego group. The Affective Disorder group displayed the same trend pattern.

Rierdan and Koff (1993) studied ego development and menarcheal timing in female 6th graders. They found that, in one-way comparison, the Preconformist girls scored higher on depression. Yet, for the group of postmenarcheal girls (early menarche), there was a significant group difference for those girls who already had and those who had not yet attained Conformist ego levels. For the latter group, the depression levels were lower. Thus, although early menarche is considered a stressor that might cause depression in girls, the Conformist ego level serves as a protecting factor.

In Ryf's (1996) study, a mixed sample of 160 psychiatric and 160 nonpsychiatric adolescents participated. Two aspects of her findings are relevant for the present discussion. First, when two subsamples were compared, the proportion of Preconformist adolescents was much higher in the psychiatric subsample than in the high school subsample. Second, when the entire sample of 320 was considered, both the narrowband Anxious/Depressed scale means and the broadband Internalizing symptoms means were lower for the Conformist group than for the Preconformist group, thus supporting the inverse relationship between internalizing symptomatology, depression, and ego development.

Griffin (1989) found a significant difference in ego development level for the two groups of high school students: the group that scored at the lower extreme of the Beck Depression Inventory and the group that scored at the higher extreme. The depressed group was found to have significantly lower ego scores. Griffin interpreted her finding as an indicator that severe depression might inhibit ego growth.

Somewhat similar findings were obtained in Snodgrass's 1993 study. She compared three groups: psychiatric patients diagnosed with Major Depressive Disorder, nondepressed psychiatric patients, and a control group of normal adolescents. The control group displayed significantly higher ego development scores than both the depressed and nondepressed psychiatric patients, who did not differ from each other. This study points out that the difference between psychiatric and nonpsychiatric subjects on ego development might be more prominent than the difference between depressed and nondepressed groups within the same subsample.

Those were studies conducted with adolescent samples.

In an adult study, Luthar, Doyle, Suchman, and Mayers (2001) studied parenting experience in a representative sample of women from different socioeconomic backgrounds, including substance abusers, low-SES women who were receiving state assistance, and well-functioning women working as staff members in an urban university. They found a linear negative correlation between levels of ego development and parental distress. Although not a clinically defined depression, this is clearly a related construct; it was found to have a strong negative relationship with ego development in both bivariate and multiple regression analyses.

Internalizing Symptoms

Borst and Noam (1993) found significant group differences for Preconformist and Conformist adolescents on the Internalizing scale of the YSR. In this clinical sample, the mean Internalizing score was lower for the Conformist group.

In the Noam et al. (1991) study, two groups of hospitalized adolescents were studied: those who progressed at least one-half of an ego development stage and those who did not progress. Both groups showed a decrease in the internalizing symptoms score as measured by Achenbach's YSR broadband scale as a result of the treatment. The significant difference lies in the fact that the mean decrease for the progressors group was about three times as much as the decrease for the nonprogressors group (from 61.87 to 47.40 for the progressors group; 59.50 to 54.27 for the nonprogressors group). The logical interpretation of these findings is that for the psychiatric adolescents, growth in the ego development stage is usually accompanied by a decrease in the internalizing symptoms. It is important to note, however, that treatment played an important role in these results.

In Hickok's (1996) study, a significant negative correlation between ego development and internalizing symptomatology was found for a group of 60 severely emotionally disturbed adolescents.

Suicide

As mentioned, Browning (1986) found that psychiatric ward behaviors correlated significantly with the level of ego development. She found that the total number of suicide attempts went down with the increase in patients' ego level. Thus, her findings indicate a negative relationship between ego level and suicide attempts. This finding should be interpreted with caution, though, as the suicide attempts were not separated from other problematic behaviors, such as accidents and aggressive acts, that are more characteristic of Preconformist levels of ego development.

Linear Increase in Symptomatology with Increase in Ego Development Level

This model of linkage between ego development and symptomatology receives only partial support. Nevertheless, its rationale is quite strong. With a more complex understanding of oneself and others, the flaws of both are more evident. Such topics, for example, as a keen feeling of responsibility and the main issues of the Conformist persons, such as being tied into the views of others on oneself, the low self-esteem in the face of loss (all potentially present at all levels of development but especially strong at the Conformist levels), a despair at failing to fulfill all these responsibilities, perfectionism, and an existential despair (Noam, 1998)—all found at higher stages of ego development—are nonexistent at the early stages. Yet, as is obvious, these feelings might lead to an increase of self-hate and feelings of one's inadequacy that is closely related to both depression and suicide.

In support of this position, we cite only studies with representative samples that cover the full range of ego development stages, as the linear increase in depressive symptoms for the low end of the ego development continuum—from the Preconformist to Conformist levels—might be an indicator of the curvilinear relationship between depression and ego development.

In a representative sample of creative young musicians and matched controls, Colvin (1994) found that the group of musicians displayed significantly higher ego development levels and also higher incidence of Bipolar Mood Disorder.

Luthar and Quinlan (1993) added a cross-cultural aspect to this discussion. They explored the relationship between ego development and three subscales of the Depressive Experience Questionnaire (Blatt, D'Afflitti, & Quinlan, 1979) in a sample of Indian and American female college students. A positive correlation between the Self-criticism subscale of Depressive Experiences and ego development level was found for Indian women, which nevertheless did not reach a sufficient significance level.

Curvilinear Relationship between Depressive/Internalizing Symptomatology and Ego Development

Many theories point out that a certain level of complexity of thinking is needed for a person to conceive of depressive thought, guilt, and so on. Gibson (1967, p. 100) defines the "prerequisites" for depression:

> In depressive ego states the following developmental level has been reached: (a) Perception and memory have developed sufficiently so that "ideal states" experienced in the past are recorded in the psyche and recalled in their absence, (b) hope and longing for a return of the ideal states are present, and (c) some sense of self has developed—This is obviously necessary if one accepts diminished self-esteem as an essential component of depression.

Einstein and Lanning (1998) found a curvilinear relationship between shame (a construct clearly related to depression) and ego development. The feeling of shame was low at the Preconformist and Postconformist levels, and highest at the Conformist level.

In the light of these findings, it is expected that the depressive and internalizing symptoms will peak at the Conformist ego stage, as this is the stage when the group standards are seen as the strongest, and one's failure to meet them the most catastrophic. The next logical assumption is that with more advanced ego development, starting at the Self-Aware stage when one's own view and ideas acquire importance and one has better means of assessing one's life and oneself, the symptomatology might become less severe. We do not mean, of course, that these problems do not exist before and after the Conformist level, but that it is at this level when these issues of standards and failures are the most severe. In support of this view, we cite studies that have found either a curvilinear relationship between depression and ego development for a representative sample, or a linear relationship for the part of the population: a positive correlation between depressive symptoms and ego development for the low-end samples (mostly adolescent samples) or a negative correlation between depressive symptoms and ego development for the high-end samples.

Depression

Borst and Noam (1993) provided multiple findings that are relevant for this subsection. They explored the relationship between suicidality, diagnostic category (Affective Disorder, Conduct Disorder, mixed Conduct-Affective Disorder), and ego development. As a general tendency, a higher proportion of both Affective Disorder patients and suicide attempters were found to function at the Conformist ego level. This supports a linear increase or, because it was a low-end ego development sample, possibly a curvilinear relationship between ego development and depressive symptomatology.

Moreover, after a careful analysis of each subject's responses, the researchers came to the conclusion that suicide attempters were not a homogeneous group. The suicide attempters who still functioned at the Preconformist ego level were classified as "angry-defiant" type, who direct their aggression toward others as well as toward self. Suicide attempters who have already reached the Conformist ego level were classified as "self-blaming" types. These adolescents were more likely to be diagnosed with Affective Disorder. This study refines our views on both depression and suicide in adolescents and points out the importance of drawing a line more clearly between those two phenomena.

Noam et al. (1994) found statistically significant prevalence of Affective Disorder patients (as opposed to Conduct Disorder and mixed Conduct-Affective Disorders) in the group of inpatient adolescents who have reached the Conformist ego level.

Wilbur et al. (1982) found a positive correlation (controlling for educational level and IQ) between ego development and the sum score for the Beck Depression Inventory for a group of 97 opiate addicts. Because that was a low-end sample, the findings might be interpreted as supporting a curvilinear relationship between depression and ego development.

Gold (1980) explored the relationship between the 10 clinical scales of the MMPI and ego development in normal 14- to 15-year-olds representing a wide range of ego development stages, from Impulsive to Individualistic. The group of Conformist adolescents scored highest on the depression scale, with both Pre- and Postconformist subjects yielding lower depression scores.

Hilmo (1978) reported a small sample of inpatients presenting with unipolar and bipolar depression. These subjects, ranging from 30 to 46 years, ranged from the Self-Protective to the Conscientious stages, with most at the Self-Aware stage. We interpret this finding as support, although a weaker one, for depression being more prevalent among Conformist stages of ego development (Self-Aware stage is classified as Postconformist by some researchers, and as Conformist by others).

Suicidality

Until recently, age was the major developmental dimension considered in the studies of child and adolescent suicidality. It is widely known that children under the age of 12 rarely attempt suicide, yet it constitutes one of the major causes of death among young adults (Hawton, 1986; Shaffer & Fisher, 1981). From the field of developmental psychopathology came a conclusion that young children lack cognitive complexity that makes it less likely to develop full-blown suicide ideation. Yet another step in this line of thinking was to suggest that it is not only cognitive complexity, but, more broadly, aspects of psychological maturity, such as detachment from self, self-hate, and feelings of shame, guilt, and despair that are all signs of a more complex personality organization than that of young children and are hallmarks of a suicidal person. Thus, it was hypothesized that suicide ideation and action will increase with the ego development level (Borst et al., 1991).

In a study of 219 adolescent psychiatric inpatients, significant differences in ego development level were found between the two groups: suicide attempters and nonsuicidal adolescents (Borst & Noam, 1993). Of the Preconformist adolescents, 68% were in the nonsuicidal group, and 32% in the suicidal group. Of the Conformist adolescents, 38% were in the nonsuicidal group, and 62% in the suicidal group. These findings indicate clearly the prevalence of adolescents who have reached Conformist ego development level among suicide attempters. Yet, it indicates that suicide is also possible at earlier developmental levels.

In another study of inpatient adolescents, three diagnostic groups were compared: a Conduct Disorder group, an Affective Disorder group, and a mixed Conduct-Affective Disorder group (Noam et al., 1984). For the Affective Disorder group, the mean ego level was significantly higher than for the other two groups; it was also found to have a significantly higher proportion of suicide attempters (41% of suicide attempters in the Affective Disorder group, only 14% in the Conduct Disorder group; Noam et al., 1994). This finding confirms the association between both Conformist ego levels and suicide, and the suicide and Affective Disorder diagnosis.

No Relationship

Yet another theoretical model of linkage—the one claiming that ego development and mental health are two orthogonal constructs—is supported by studies that found no relationship between ego development and depressive/internalizing symptoms. These are usually studies that hypothesized that the level of depression will be lower for the subjects with higher ego development, yet that failed to support their hypotheses. Dichter (1996) found no significant trend in the relationship between ego development and depression in a large sample of 564 adolescents who attended a public high school in Westchester County, New York, suggesting that "there are no differential patterns of adolescent ego development for level of depression" (Dichter, 1996). In a sample of male and female college students, Wheeler (1994) found "no overall differences according to ego level on the depression or anxiety measures."

Two important factors need to be taken into consideration while examining this evidence. First, these studies are few relative to the ones that have found evidence in support of the position that the relationship between ego development and depressive/internalizing symptomatology does exist. Second, "no relationship" results might be obtained if the data displaying a curvilinear trend are analyzed with linear tools.

Summary and Conclusions

Depression and Affective Disorders

The findings in this area are most contradictory. All three major views on the linkage between ego development and depression have found some empirical support. The findings are summarized in Table 19.6.

Although the findings in this section are contradictory, a few trends are nevertheless evident. First, depression in clinical and normal populations differs in the degree of severity. Thus, when mixed samples (with both clinical and nonclinical participants) were used, the depression rates for the clinical group were so much higher than for the normal group that it overpowered any differences based on ego development levels.

Second, for homogeneous clinical populations, we conclude that the model of linkage between ego development and a mental health status most in tune with the evidence is a curvilinear relationship: The depressive symptoms are highest for the Conformist ego level. This does, indeed, also make the most theoretical sense if one looks at the features of the Conformist ego development, where anger expression is viewed in negative terms and where fears of loss are great, guilt is significant, and there is so much focus on how others view the self and how one can hurt others (see also Schuessler, 2000; Youngren, 1993). But obviously, no one will argue that there is not depression and internalizing disorders at other points of life. At least one explanation for the increase in depression in the adolescent population, one that has been typically overlooked, is the normative move to the Conformist stage, adding to the risk factors of hormonal changes, family reorganization, peer culture, and so on.

Internalizing Symptoms

Although the Depressive scale is one of the narrowband scales that belong to the broad Internalizing symptoms scale in the Achenbach system, the conclusions concerning the relationship between Internalizing scale scores and ego development are much clearer than those for the depression subsection. All four studies cited in this review found the inverse relationship, or a linear decrease in Internalizing symptomatology as measured by Achenbach's YSR as people reach Conformist ego development level. The results are summarized in Table 19.7.

The fact that this pattern of relationship between Internalizing scale score and ego development is so different from the relationship between depression (i.e., supposedly, one subscale of the same broadband scale) and ego development poses another problem as to how to interpret this difference. One possible interpretation is that, being a sum of several scores, broadband scales tap into a wider range of internalizing problems, where depression is only one part rather than one particular psychological tendency. The fact that the severity of symptomatology (be it depression or personality disorder) has an inverse relationship with ego development is supported by virtually every study cited in this review.

ANXIETY DISORDERS

Not many studies have been focused on the relationship between ego development and anxiety, in part because anxiety exists from childhood, and it has been harder for researchers to conceptualize it as a developmental set of processes. Yet, more than a few studies have been conducted in this area, and the complexity of the relationship between anxiety and ego development is such that all major models of linkage described in other sections of this chapter have found some evidentiary support.

We bring together evidence on the relationship between ego development and a family of mental health problems

TABLE 19.6   Ego Development and Depression

Study	N	Disorder	Tool	Sample	Ego Continuum	Linkage
Borst & Noam (1993)	139	Affective	Clinical-diagnostic	Clinical	Low end	Curvilinear
Noam et al. (1994)	269	Affective	Clinical-diagnostic	Clinical	Low end	Curvilinear
Wilber, Rounsaville, Sugarman, Casey, & Kleber (1982)	97	Depression	BDI	Clinical	Low end	Curvilinear
Gold (1980)	150	Depression	Clinical-diagnostic	Normal	Wide range	Curvilinear
Noam & Houlihan (1990)	22	Affective	Clinical-diagnostic	Clinical	Low end	Inverse
Colvin (1994)	80	Mood	Clinical-diagnostic	Mixed	Wide range	Increase
Rierdan & Koff (1993)	336	Depression	BDI	Normal	Low end	Inverse
Ryf (1996)	320	Depression	YSR	Mixed	Middle range	Inverse
Griffin (1988)	40	Depression	BDI	Normal	Middle range	Inverse
Snodgrass (1993)	N/a	Depression	Clinical-diagnostic	Mixed	Middle range	Inverse
Dichter (1996)	564	Depression	Clinical-diagnostic	Normal	Middle range	No trend
Wheeler (1995)	N/a	Depression	BDI	Normal	Middle range	No trend
Luthar & Quinlan (1993)	103	Depression	Quinlan's DQ	Normal	Middle range	No trend
Luthar, Doyle, Suchman, & Mayers (2001)	91	Distress	Parenting Stress Index	Mixed	Wide range	Inverse

Notes: BDI: Beck Depression Inventory; Parenting Stress Index; Quinlan's DQ: Depression Questionnaire; YSR: Youth Self-Report.

TABLE 19.7   Ego Development and Internalizing Disorders

Study	N	Tool	Sample	Ego Development Range	Linkage
Borst & Noam (1993)	139	YSR	Clinical	Low	Inverse
Noam, Recklitis, & Paget (1991)	37	YSR	Clinical	Low	Inverse
Hickok (1996)	60	YSR	Clinical	Low	Inverse
Ryf (1996)	320	YSR	Mixed	Middle range	Inverse

Note: YSR = Youth Self-Report.

broadly defined as anxiety. These include clinically diagnosed anxieties and phobias of childhood, adolescence, and adulthood, anxiety as measure by Anxious/Obsessed and Anxious/Depressed scales of Achenbach and Edelbrock's (1983, 1987) CBCL and YSR, and a specific type of adulthood anxiety, death anxiety, as measured by the Death Anxiety Scale (Templer, 1969).

Inverse Relationship

The first hypothesis concerning the relationship between anxiety and ego development assumes an inverse relationship between the two, in which anxiety symptoms subside with ego development growth, particularly in the transition between the two Preconformist and the Conformist ego development levels.

There are at least two studies that show an inverse relationship between anxiety and ego development. Both used clinical adolescent samples, and the decrease in anxiety with ego development they observed happened in transition from Preconformist to Conformist stages of ego development.

In a Noam et al. (1984) study (which was part of a larger study of adolescent psychopathology conducted at McLean Hospital), for a subsample of 49 hospitalized adolescent girls, an inverse relationship was found between the level of ego development and an Anxious/Obsessed scale score from the CBCL. When the background variables (age, gender, and SES) were entered into the equation, the increment of the anxiety scale as one of the predictors for the ego development level was still significant, even though the significance was lower than that found in the bivariate model (Noam et al., 1984).

Ryf (1996) also found a decrease on the Anxious/Depressed scale of the YSR associated with higher, Conformist and Postconformist stages of ego development for the mixed sample of normal and hospitalized adolescents.

Nicolson (1996) administered the WUSCT and the State-Trait Anxiety Index (Spielberger, 1983) to nontraditional graduate students (all older than 35) who attended liberal arts and professional graduate schools in the New York metropolitan area. He found that all students with lower ego development reported higher rates of state anxiety. This is the only study in this group that used an older sample. It is also important to note that this study did not treat anxiety as a disorder.

Linear Increase

Researchers who expect an increase in anxiety at higher ego development levels base their hypothesis on the assumption that higher ego development also means higher expectations, either on the part of others (for the people on the Conformist ego levels) or on the part of oneself (for the people on the Postconformist ego levels), that can become sources of additional tension and anxiety-inducing stimuli. Especially separation anxiety is very pronounced; also, because anxiety and depression are often associated, one would expect anxiety to increase as depression increases with ego development level in at-risk populations.

At least several studies support this hypothesis, most of them concentrated on a specific type of anxiety: death anxiety.

Barrett (1991) found an increase in two factors of death anxiety in a sample of normal subjects, who were people involved in death education and care of the dying.

Similar findings were obtained in Gutierrez's study (1993). He found that the death anxiety correlated positively with the level of ego development in a sample of 100 community volunteers whose average age was 73 years.

One more finding that constitutes the same trend was found in Geurkink's (1981) study, conducted with a normal sample of college students. She found death anxiety positively related to the level of ego development.

An increase in death anxiety for higher ego development levels found in several studies might seem surprising as, generally, higher ego development levels are thought of as the stages of higher maturity and wisdom that presuppose calm acceptance of reality, including death. The studies just cited seem to suggest that this is not true. Thus, these studies once more draw our attention to the new vulnerabilities that come into existence only at higher ego development levels.

What is missing from this picture are studies that explore the relationship between ego development and anxieties (other than death anxiety) that are specific of higher ego development levels, which implies a line of inquiry for future research.

The only study that found a linear increase in anxiety (other than death anxiety) is Wilber, Rounsaville, Sugarman, Casey, and Kleber's (1982). The researchers found a significant positive, though not very strong, correlation (.20) between clinically measured phobic anxiety and ego development in a sample of opiate addicts. We might consider this a singular finding, yet, if we take into consideration his sample, a population that, as found by numerous studies, usually score at lower ego development levels, Wilber's finding can be interpreted in the framework of the next approach that we are going to delineate, one that assumes a curvilinear relationship between anxiety and ego development.

Curvilinear Relationship

This approach shares a rationale with similar research on depression and ego development. The reasoning is essentially as follows: Anxiety develops along internalizing pathways, and the pressure to live up to a standard, defined by others but experienced in the self, one of the most anxiety-inducing factors, is highest at the Conformist ego development level.

There are at least several studies supporting this position.

Geurkink (1981) found both state and trait anxiety as measured by the State-Trait Anxiety Inventory to be the highest at the Self-Aware stage of ego development, being lower at both the lower and the higher ends of the ego development continuum.

An indirect support to this hypothesis comes from De Loach (1976), who studied ego development in "neurotic outpatients," resembling what we would currently refer to as General Anxiety Disorder. The subjects ranged in age from 20 to 44 years. The modal stage for these subjects was the Conscientious ego stage, which is higher than the Self-Aware stage, the modal stage for normal adult samples.

These studies coincide in that all of them (including Wilber et al., 1982 study) found evidence in support of the curvilinear relationship between anxiety and ego development. On the other hand, they have important differences. In Wilber's study, the stage of the highest anxiety level was the Conformist stage; for Geurkink (1981) it was the Self-Aware stage; and for De Loach

(1976), the Conscientious stage. The only way to resolve these contradictions is to conduct more studies with normal adult samples with Self-Aware or higher modal ego stages.

No Trend

There are several studies that failed to find any significant association between anxiety and ego development. No significant ego development differences between two groups of women: those who became addicted to sedatives while trying to fight their anxiety and matched controls whose anxiety levels were much lower were found. Waugh and McCaulley (1981) found no significant ego development differences when comparing a sample of clinical patients (among them neurotics, diagnostically linked to Anxiety Disorder) and samples of normal subjects similar to those used in Loevinger and Wessler's (1970) studies establishing the reliability of the WUSCT. Harwell (1987) found no significant correlations between ego development and state and trait anxiety in a volunteer sample of 66 community college women. Farrell (1990) found no relationship between ego development level and trait anxiety in a large (504 participants) sample of women.

These findings might indicate that the relationship between anxiety and ego development is weak, or they might imply that the linear relationship between anxiety and ego development is weak, and thus suggest the use of curvilinear, instead of linear, methods in future research.

Qualitative Differences in Anxiety Disorder Type as Related to Ego Level

One very important trend, emerging in nearly every area of inquiry in the mental health/ego development relationship, is to distinguish subgroups within the population of interest and explore ego development differences among those subgroups. This approach has also been used in anxiety research.

Westenberg (Westenberg, Siebelink, Warmenhoven, & Treffers, 1999) hypothesized the existence of qualitative rather than quantitative differences in anxiety disorder as related to ego level. In a study of 118 children and adolescents (ages 8–18), it was found that two disorder subtypes are related significantly to the ego level group differences. Separation Anxiety Disorder was found to be prevalent at the Preconformist ego levels, and Overanxious Disorder was found much more often at the Conformist ego level.

The authors state:

The clinical features of Separation Anxiety Disorder fit the general description of the Impulsive level. The Impulsive person is characterized by a combination of impulsivity, vulnerability, and dependency. Impulsive persons are preoccupied with aggression in others and self, and they depend on others for protection, care, and guidance generally. The frustration of dependency needs arouses strong negative emotions and is met with help-seeking. Similarly, the worst fear of the SAD patient is to lose the care and protection provided by the major attachment figures. . . . The clinical feature of the Overanxious disorder fit the general description of the Conformist level. The Conformist person follows socially desirable standards for appearance, behavior, and achievements. Conformist individuals live up to expectations, and they blame themselves if they fail to do so. In the same way, persons with OAD are worried about the appropriateness of their own behavior and the adequacy of their own achievements. (p. 1002)

These lines of conceptual reasoning were supported by the evidence. M. Moore (1984) arrived at a similar conclusion when studying attitudes toward death and the relationship between death anxiety and ego development level. She concludes that, conceptually and empirically, "ego development appears to have considerable utility in clarifying attitudinal patterns with respect to death and dying." Yet, she proceeds to suggest that the relationship between death anxiety and ego development is not the one best thought of in quantitative terms. Rather, different meaning patterns of thinking about death (e.g., death as personal failure, natural end, courage, pain, and loneliness) were found in people at different ego developmental levels.

Summary and Conclusions

Generally, anxiety does not belong to the mental health disorders that have conceptual overlaps with any of the dimensions or characteristics that define specific stages of ego development. Thus, there are fewer researchers who hypothesized the relationship between anxiety and ego development to be a fruitful area of exploration. The confirmation of this hypothesis is a much higher percentage of the reviewed studies that found no significant relationship between anxiety and ego development level (5 out of 14 studies, as compared to only 2 out of 23 studies on depression, suicide, and internalizing symptoms).

The studies that were able to record a trend yielded contradictory findings. Of the four studies that found an inverse relationship between anxiety and ego development, three used samples of hospitalized adolescents. Thus, for this specific population, the tendency for anxiety to subside with an increase in ego development seems to be strong.

The most strongly supported model for adult samples seems to be a curvilinear relationship between anxiety and ego development level. The explanation for and the mechanisms of this tendency can only be hypothesized. It seems plausible that although the adults at the lower ego development levels lack the cognitive complexity necessary for construction of anxiety-inducing problems, the adults at higher ego development levels might be better equipped for coping with anxiety.

One surprising (and noncontradictory) finding was that death anxiety increases with levels of ego development (Barrett, 1991; Geurkink, 1981; Gutierrez, 1993); that was found to be true for the samples of older people, as well as for the people working with dying patients, even after controlling for age (Barrett, 1991). This area needs more research, because conceptually, one would expect death anxiety to be lower for the highest ego development stages, where wisdom and wider views on the dialectical nature of life and death become more prominent. One possible explanation for this is that those studies did not involve subjects scored at the highest, Postconformist levels of ego development. Such research is definitely needed to resolve this problem.

EATING DISORDERS

Although eating disorders might have a conceptual overlap with ego development, the research in this area remains scarce. This is unfortunate because, in line with what the evidence in the other areas of mental health suggests, we can expect substantial differences in symptom expression for the bulimic and anorexic patients at different ego development levels. Here, we summarize the existing evidence.

Until recently, Anorexia Nervosa has been most prevalent among educated, middle- and upper-class White women (Bruch, 1973). A similar profile has been found for individuals with Bulimia Nervosa (L. Weiss, Katzman, & Wolchik, 1985).

Common to both disorders are salient concerns about interpersonal relationships, meeting others' expectations and retaining others' approval. The critical importance of personal appearance both before others and oneself emerges as a further preoccupation among those with eating disorders. Also of import is the growing differentiation and awareness of the self as an object of self-examination and as discrete from others in interpersonal relationships. Finally, as differentiation of self from others becomes more fully integrated with a larger social perspective, the conflict between dependence and independence grows in significance. Many of these psychological foci are tied to the Conformist and Self-Aware ego development stages. According to the expectations, the modal stage for both anorexics and bulimics is the Self-Aware stage, a finding that is yet to be acknowledged and used in the eating disorders field.

Anorexia Nervosa

Among anorexics, the issue of self-differentiation from others is especially acute. Along these lines, Bruch (1973, p. 102) has observed that anorexics "experienced their bodies as not being truly their own, as being under the influence of others. They felt that they had no control over their bodies and its functions."

A central issue among anorexics relates to social isolation due to extreme feelings of awkwardness and anxiety in interpersonal situations. Corresponding to this issue is a "self-consciousness" and "discomfort" noted in social situations by individuals at the Self-Aware stage.

According to these considerations, we should expect Anorexia Nervosa to be most prominent among individuals at the Self-Aware ego development stage. Yet, as is true about other mental health areas, the prevalence of a disorder at a certain ego stage (e.g., the relationship between depression and Conformist ego stage) does not mean the exclusive occurrence of a given disorder at a given ego stage. Rather, we are referring to the highest probability of its occurrence at this stage, while the probability of it at the consecutive (higher and lower) stages is less. The findings of several studies seem to support this assumption.

Swift, Camp, Bushnell, and Bargman (1984) found that the majority (55.2%) of their subjects (anorexic patients) attained the Self-Aware stage. Yet, this does not lead us to the conclusion that there is a special association between the disorder and the Self-Aware ego stage, as this is also the modal stage for normal adult populations.

To clarify this issue, we compared those percentages from Loevinger and Wessler's (1970) normative sample, which showed 25% of the subjects scored at the Self-Aware stage, and 23% at the Conscientious stage. The percentage of anorexic subjects who scored at the Self-Aware stage is noticeably higher than Loevinger and Wessler's (1970) normative sample of adults, whereas the percentage of subjects who scored at the Conscientious ego development level are quite similar to those from Loevinger and Wessler's (1970) normative sample. This suggests that perhaps the Self-Aware stage may be most common among anorexic individuals, and that further study can prove valuable.

In the same line are Luce's (1983) findings. On a sample of female adult hospitalized inpatients, she has shown that the three groups (anorexics, bulimics, and bulimic anorexics) did not differ from each other on the mean level of ego development, yet scored higher even than the Self-Aware stage, which, as is shown elsewhere, is the modal stage for normal adult populations.

Haimes and Katz (1988) examined sexual and social maturity and ego development (as a measure of social conformity) in restricting anorexics, bulimics, and women with Borderline Personality Disorder. Restrictor anorexics averaged 26 years of age, with an average age of onset at 18 years. Findings again pointed predominantly to the Self-Aware and Conscientious stages.

To fully confirm this finding while taking into consideration other factors, we would need more research in this area of exploration.

Bulimia Nervosa

Teusch (1988) studied ego development in bulimic outpatients age 18 to 39 years. Displaying a pattern similar to the anorexia studies, the majority of participants in this study attained Self-Aware (52.5%) and Conscientious (35%) stages.

We compared these percentages with those from Loevinger and Wessler's (1970) normative sample which reported 25% a the Self-Aware stage and 23% at the Conscientious stage as shown in Table 19.8. This comparison not only illustrates the prevalence of bulimia at the

TABLE 19.8   Comparison of Bulimic Outpatients to Normative Sample

Study	Self-Aware (%)	Conscientious (%)
Teusch (1988)	52.5	35
Loevinger & Wessler (1970) ($N = 1,640$)	25.0	23.0
Normal adult accumulative sample ($N= 1,700$)	41.5	19.6
Clinical adult accumulative sample ($N = 1,224$)	25.1	9.7

Self-Aware stage of ego development but also suggests a noteworthy association between bulimia and the Conscientious ego stage.

As the association between the Self-Aware stage of ego development and eating disorders seems both empirically and theoretically solid, some researchers went further to explore the causative factors that might have led to the disorder (e.g., Billing, 1987; Kutcher, 1989).

Various studies showed that "women with unhealthy eating attitudes tended to overeat following exposure to particular types of threat" (Waller & Meyer, 1997, p. 299). Among these threats were the loss of a relationship (Pyle, Mitchell, & Eckert, 1981), victimization (Root & Fallon, 1989), fear of abandonment (Patton, 1992), and negative evaluation of self (Heatherton & Baumeister, 1991). These preoccupations can be characteristic of several ego stages, especially Conformist and Self-Aware. The parallel is evident, yet, more research is needed to clarify this issue, including controlled intervention studies that simultaneously treat the eating disorder and support ego development.

Qualitative Differences within the Eating Disordered Population

As we pointed out in other sections, a prominent line of contemporary research in the area concentrates not only on correlations between ego development and specific disorder scales, but on the qualitative differences within the patients with the disorder as related to the ego development level.

Horton (2001) hypothesized that there would be differences within the bulimic population based on the Borderline Personality Disorder diagnosis. The hypothesis that individuals with Bulimia Nervosa and BPD functioned at lower ego development levels than the individuals with the eating disorder alone or than those in the control group was based on Smith, Burkey, Nawn, and Reif's (1991) findings.

To make the distinction clearer, Horton (2001, p. 42) refers to Favazza, DeRosear, and Conterio (1989), who suggested that "self-mutilation and eating pathology might be a part of a pathological impulse disorder, which they call 'deliberate self-harm syndrome.'" Thus, she suggests a distinction between the more impulsive groups of bulimics (who function at lower ego developmental levels) and more rational ones.

To support this hypothesis, Horton (2001) divided her 71 women-participants into three groups: group 1 ($n = 27$),

Bulimia Nervosa without BPD, group 2 ($n = 19$), Bulimia Nervosa and BPD, and group 3 ($n = 25$), the non-eating disorder, non-personality disorder group. All three groups were significantly different on the ego development level. The lowest ego level (mean 3.78) was found among the bulimic and BPD group. We can say that the members of this group were divided mostly between the Self-Protective (E3) and Conformist (E4) ego stages. The bulimic-only group had a mean of 4.48. We assume that the members of this group divided approximately equally between Self-Aware and Conformist ego levels. This finding both supports and undermines the idea that the modal stage for bulimics is the Self-Aware stage. It suggests that there are many bulimics functioning at this stage, but even for the more rational, nonimpulsive bulimics, this is the highest among the two modal stages. Impulsive bulimics are found to function at the lower ego stages. To further explain this difference, Horton points out the negative correlation between ego development and the Self-Harm Function score, a score that is highest for the comorbidity (Bulimia and BPS) group.

There are at least two aspects in which this study is important. First, it distinguishes between the two qualitatively different groups within the diagnostic category, the groups that differ mostly based on the subjects' ego development scores. Second, it employs multivariate methods, introducing variables that clarify the relationship between ego development and eating disorder.

Farrell (1990) showed that in a representative sample of 540 women, ego development was inversely related to binge eating. Thus, binge eating as an impulsive aspect of an eating disorder was more prevalent among lower ego developmental levels. We can conclude that binge eating is a more prevalent aspect of eating pathology in the impulsive deliberate self-harm type.

Kennedy (1994) attempted to take a broader perspective on the relationship between eating disorders and ego development. She compared two age cohorts, middle-aged mothers and their college-age daughters, and hypothesized that the changed role of women in contemporary society (in other words, an increase in pressure as much as in freedom) might be responsible for the recent increase in eating pathology. For the mothers, she found that eating disorders were negatively related to ego development level. In other words, among the middle-aged women, those who failed to achieve higher ego development levels were more likely to exhibit eating pathologies, thus, suggesting the deliberate impulsive self-harm type of eating behaviors. For the daughters, contemporary young women, this pattern did not hold, suggesting that the daughters fell more into the more rational type who are higher on ego development. This study further emphasizes the within-diagnosis differences among eating disordered women according to ego level group and introduces broader societal factors that might be related to this dichotomy.

Summary and Conclusions

This evidence, though scarce, points out several tendencies that call for further exploration.

Generally, eating disorder patients are mostly White middle-class women with a high SES and higher ego development levels. The modal stage for both bulimics and anorexics is the Self-Aware ego development stage. There is also a solid proportion of eating disorder subjects who attain the Conscientious ego stage.

On the other hand, if an eating disorder is severe, and especially if it is combined with another pathology (such as BPD or depression), it might inhibit the person's ego growth. Thus, a proportion of ego development subjects do score at lower ego development levels. These subjects seem to be more often bulimics than anorexics, and they have a destructive self-harm tendency that is an expression of impulsivity that thus makes them gravitate to the lower ego development levels. We might hypothesize that the two tendencies—a perfectionistic striving for self-improvement common for the Self-Aware and Conscientious ego levels, and the impulsivity of Preconformist ego levels—might cause the ego dichotomy, a tendency that has not been fully explored yet and is currently a point of conceptual debate (Holt, 1998; Noam, 1993, 1998).

ALCOHOL AND SUBSTANCE ABUSE

The relationship between alcohol/drug abuse and ego development is a potentially rich topic that also has not received enough attention from the research community. There are numerous reasons for this. The conceptual parallels between this problem area and ego development are too complex to generate clear, testable hypotheses. On the one hand, we should except ego development to have a strong association with such an aspect of substance abuse as poor self-control, which, we know, is lowest at the Preconformist stages of ego development. On the other hand, alcohol and substance abuse is often a reaction to one's failure to meet one's own and societal expectations, which become

explicit topics only at the Conformist stages of ego development. Also, the view of alcohol and drug use that might affect a person's consumption and behavior are very different for different social groups. For instance, whereas in the traditionally oriented middle-class circles drug and alcohol use are at least frowned upon, in the younger groups, and in such specific communities as hippies (discussed later), the use of some drugs, especially marijuana, is not necessarily a deviation from the norm. Clearly, drug and alcohol use is not unitary and the causes are many. Thus, the relationship with ego development should not be expected to be a simple one. However, it is hard to imagine that the meaning system people use to interpret themselves and others would not have a potential relationship with the use of drugs and alcohol, the situations that trigger desires for these substances, and the supports that would be especially efficacious.

We would also expect that the patterns of relationships with ego development will be different not only for different social groups, but for different drug types. So far, as will be evident in our discussion, the only drug type that revived special research attention is opioid drugs.

Opioid Abuse and Dependence

Opiate users have been found to struggle with underlying depression, alcoholism, and/or sociopathy (Rounsaville, Weissman, Kleber, & Wilber, 1982). Kurland, Turek, Brown, and Wagman (1976) have suggested that opiate addicts suffer from fundamental feelings of alienation from others and perhaps also struggle with the formation of "adult identity." They use the drug as a "replacement for mature interpersonal relationships and adult sexuality, as a defense against experiences of intense anxiety, depression, and aggression, or as a way of avoiding intolerable somatic and psychic pain" (Blatt, Berman, et al., 1984, p. 156), as relief from inward rage, self-reproach, and despair, and as a means of restoration of self-confidence (Khantzian, 1974; Rado, 1957).

Blatt, Berman, et al. (1984) studied ego development in a relatively homogeneous (young, male, single, White, high school-educated or less, and from lower socioeconomic levels) sample of 99 opiate addicts seeking treatment at a drug dependence unit. Twenty-nine CETA (Comprehensive Employment and Training Act program) applicants, all chronically unemployed and impoverished yet without a history of drug use, were matched with opiate addicts for gender, race, educational level, and social class, constituted a control group. The researchers also used two other control samples, of 100 noncollege males and an equal number of noncollege females. Modal stage for opiate addicts was Ritual-Transitional (Delta-3), a transitional stage between Self-Protective and Conformist and, in the new classification, usually merged with the Self-Protective stage. It is lower than the modal stage for CETA applicants (Conformist) or the modal stage of both normal samples (Self-Aware). Also, the mean ego level is lower for the opiate addicts as a sample than for the three other samples. Not surprisingly, the percentage of opiate addicts at the higher ego stages (26% at each Conformist and Self-Aware stages) implies that it is possible to be an opiate addict and yet function at higher ego development levels.

Another intriguing aspect of the same problem is a strong association between opiate addiction and depressive tendencies. This view is supported by numerous studies and research reports (see Blatt, Rounsaville, Eyre, & Wilber, 1984, for a review) suggesting that depression (and dysfunctional attempts to fight Affective Disorders) may be a central issue in opiate addiction (Blatt, Rounsaville, et al., 1984). This creates a contradiction. On the one hand, the Self-Protective stage seems to be the modal stage for opiate addicts. On the other hand, the association between opiate addiction and depression would lead us to expect that the modal stage for depression—Conformist ego stage—is also the modal stage for opiate addicts. A possible solution to this problem would be to expect that there might be qualitative differences within the opiate user population: Those at the Preconformist ego development levels might be different from those who score at the Conformist ego level (this subpopulation might also have the highest depression scores) and Postconformist ego development levels.

This is the hypothesis that has been tested in another study by Blatt and Berman (1990).

A sample of 53 opiate addicts were given a series of measurements, including the WUSCT, Wechsler Adult Intelligence Test, Bellak Ego Functions Interview, and the Rorschach. Cluster analysis was used with the goal to test the homogeneity of the opiate addicts sample. Three subgroups of opiate addicts were found, all significantly different on many of the 11 variables entered into analysis.

The first cluster, characterized by impaired ego functioning and thought disorders, contained 30% of the sample and was lowest on ego development. The second cluster, a little higher on ego development, contained 42% of the sample and was characterized by impaired interpersonal relationship and affective lability. The third subgroup contained 28% of the sample and was characterized by lower levels of activity (a lower number of responses on the Rorschach) yet better reality testing, indication of better interpersonal relationships and more effective defenses. This subsample also had the highest ego development level.

This study, though following the most promising paradigm of dividing populations in question into different subgroups, nevertheless did not include a depression measure in the set of the variables studied.

Wilber et al. (1982) used the same sample of opiate addicts and CETA applicants to explore the relationship between ego development, substance abuse, and clinical assessment results (the Beck Depression Inventory; Beck & Beck, 1972). While opiate addicts were lower than CETA applicants on ego development level (as indicated in Blatt et al.'s 1984 paper), in opiate addicts ego development was found to correlate negatively with the severity of drug use and positively with several clinical diagnoses: somatization, phobic anxiety, psychoticism, depression, and neuroticism. This study, while exploring the relationship between depression and opiate addiction, did not distinguish among the subgroups within the opiate addict population.

The next step in this line of investigation was to explore the relationship between the three groups of factors—ego development, drug addiction, and depression levels—in their interaction with each other. This was done in another study, yet it did not concentrate only on opiate addiction.

Other Substance Abuse Studies

Luthar et al. (2001) studied ego development and parental experiences in a diverse sample of drug-abusing women. The participants were from different socioeconomic backgrounds. Opiate addicts, women with low SES, and minorities were represented in the sample. The results indicated that the level of ego development correlated significantly (and negatively) with the severity of substance abuse and positively with parental satisfaction. This was the only study that explored the relationship between ego development, distress (not depression, yet a related construct), and substance abuse. For both low and high ego development groups, the distress and substance abuse were inversely related; that is, the people in distress had a much higher chance to be substance abusers, or substance abusers had much higher distress levels. This clearly confirms the other findings cited (Blatt & Berman, 1990; Wilber et al., 1984). The researchers went one step further and explored the interaction between the three groups of factors. They found that the association between distress and severity of abuse was stronger for the high ego level group. The low ego level group experienced a relatively high level of distress independently of whether they were or were not substance abusers. The high ego development group experienced a low level of distress if they did not abuse drugs and a high level of distress if they did. Thus, the high ego development, non-drug-abusing group had the lowest distress and drug abuse put even mature ego development women at the risk of high distress.

In Fineman et al. (1997), a group of drug-abusing women from poor socioeconomic backgrounds was found to have a very large proportion of subjects at the Preconformist levels of ego development (41%) and an unusually low proportion for adult populations of subjects at the Postconformist (E6 and up) levels of ego development (4%). These women, we have to conclude, were significantly delayed in ego development.

Even though opioids are relatively strong drugs, and the severity of abuse has been found to correlate inversely with ego development in every study that has asked this research question, it is not surprising that the modal stage among opiate addicts is the Self-Protective ego stage. Yet, even in the opiate abuser samples, there were substantial proportions of subjects who scored at higher ego development levels. Several other studies have obtained similar results.

Haan, Stroud, and Holstein (1973) studied moral and ego processes in a relatively small ($N = 58$) sample of hippies between age 17 and 35. This was a nontraditional sample consisting of people of higher than average intelligence who chose "a socially dissident, morally uncertain, and personally hazardous" (p. 609) way of living. Drug use was substantial in that community, with marijuana and psychedelic drugs used by almost everybody, along with heavy use of amphetamines. Yet, we should note, there are no data as to whether those people were real drug addicts needing help. The ego scores distribution for this sample is compared with the Loevinger normative data. The study found a lower percentage of people at both the Preconformist and Conformist ego stages combined (12%), however, the vast majority presented with higher ego stages.

Another consideration that the researchers studying ego development in drug users might find useful is that for different drug types, different relationships with ego development might be found.

Hawley (1995) studied ego development and substance abuse in a small sample of 30 volunteers recruited from the patients of the counseling office in a major urban university. The researcher made a clear distinction between those participants who used traditional drugs (with no distinction among the drugs; all participants using them were labeled substance users) and the users of psychotropic medication, a less traditional type of drug. No substance abuser scored

higher than the Conformist ego development level, with the Self-Protective being the modal stage for substance abusers. Yet, no ego development differences were found among psychotropic medication users. Among six of them, two were at the Self-Protective stage, one at the Conformist, one at the Self-Aware, one at the Conscientious, and one at the Individualistic stage of ego development.

Santina (1998) set a goal to find the most powerful predictors for severe substance abuse. The participants in her study were 50 residents (46 males and 4 females) of a most-restricted-order drug rehabilitation program who were polysubstance-addicted and represented the most severe levels of substance addiction. Among the independent variables were object relations (with subscales of alienation, egocentricity, insecure attachment, and social incompetence), ego development, experienced level of childhood trauma, psychopathology, and difficulty discerning and labeling emotions.

Using discriminant analysis, it was found that the best predictor for substance abuse was insecure attachment. Less powerful predictors were alienation, difficulty discerning and labeling emotions, level of childhood trauma, social incompetence, and, finally, psychopathology. Egocentricity and ego development failed to enter into the equation, indicating that scores on these variables did not account for any unique variance among the groups that were not already explained by the variance noted earlier.

The most logical interpretation of these results is that low ego development alone does not lead to substance abuse (see also Guerra, 1991; Pingalore, 1982); rather, both ego development and substance abuse might be influenced by early experiences, in this case, insecurity of attachment. Several researchers studied ego development in relationship to rehabilitational treatment results. The hypothesis was that ego development, while not preventing individuals from substance abuse, provides a better coping response repertoire and thus makes rehabilitation treatment results more likely to be positive. A study was conducted with the residents of a drug abuse rehabilitation program who were administered the WUSCT at the entrance and exit points of the treatment (Loiacono, 1995). The exit group had a significantly higher ego development mean, which supports the hypothesis.

Colan (1988) explored the reaction to treatment in a sample of adult substance abusers undergoing an 18- to 28-day impatient treatment program. The sample contained all three groups of ego development levels: Preconformists, Conformists, and Postconformists. It was hypothesized that the Postconformist patients would benefit more from the treatment and show greater improvement than Preconformist and Conformist patients. The hypothesis was partially confirmed: The Postconformist group showed significantly greater improvement in the two areas of self-concept: self-deprecation and self-confidence. There were no significant differences in the other areas.

Thus, the hypothesis that higher ego development stages provide individuals with better coping strategies has been tentatively confirmed, yet more studies are needed in this area (see also Furstenberg, 1984). And we have to admit that several studies failed to obtain significant group differences on ego development level for drug users and matched controls. Flesher (1986) compared alcohol and drug abusers, day laborers, business and banking analysts, entrepreneurs, and university professors. No significant between-group differences were found, yet the mean ego level for this heterogeneous sample was lower than the normative data in the field indicate is average for normal adult populations.

Menicucci (1983) failed to find significant group differences on ego development when comparing a small sample of treatment facility patients and matched controls. No significant differences on ego development level between a group of sedative-abusing women and matched controls were found. However, the drug-abusing group was found to have a higher frequency of anxiety and neuroticism reports. No attempts were made to build a complex model that would explore three factors simultaneously.

Alcohol Abuse

The onset and course of alcohol-related disorders is gender-dependent. Onset among men occurs in late adolescence or early 20s and begins later among women (*DSM-III-R*). With chronicity, underlying feelings of guilt, shame, anxiety, worthlessness, remorse, and depression become more evident. Incidents of amnesia, for example, evoke fears of having harmed or misconducted oneself while intoxicated (Woodruff, Goodwin, & Guze, 1974). This concern for others reflects underlying structures of social reciprocity and psychological mindedness (see also Moore, 1983). Johnson (1983) and Scott (1980) describe one motive for alcohol consumption as a form of self-esteem regulation. Johnson further describes alcoholics' tendency toward "harsh, punishing, self-directed guilt" following fits of impotent rage.

Rozsnafszky (1981) explored the relationship between the levels of ego development and Q-sort personality ratings in two groups: a group of 65 alcoholics and a control group of 26 medical patients. The modal ego stage for both alcoholics and controls was the Self-Aware ego stage, yet a much higher percentage of alcoholics scored at the Preconformist ego development levels (32% as compared with only 12% of the medical patients), and a lower percentage of alcoholics attained Postconformist developmental levels (15%) than the controls (23%). These findings are similar to the opiate addict findings and leave some space for interpretations. On the one hand, it is evident that alcoholics have a higher chance of scoring at the Preconformist stages of ego development, which is hardly surprising as impulsivity and poor self-control are characteristics of both alcoholic populations and the lower levels of ego development. On the other hand, a rather substantive percentage of alcoholics who scored at the Conformist stage and higher makes us wonder what are the differences between those two groups of alcoholics: Whether the severity of the addiction, or alcohol consumption, patterns are different for Postconformist than they are for the Preconformist, impulsive alcoholics is a question that has not been addressed in this study. Unfortunately, much less evidence is available in this area of exploration, which also leaves an open space for future research. Particularly, a study that would address the subgroups within alcoholic populations based on ego development and (possibly) in relationship to psychopathology would shed light on the developmental differences within adult alcoholic populations and perhaps offer some treatment insights.

Adolescent Studies

The studies that address ego development in adolescent substance and alcohol abusers have to take into consideration the fact that the Self-Protective stage of ego development, the modal stage for adult heavy substance abusers, is also the modal stage for both clinical and normal adolescent samples. So the ego development impairment for adolescent substance abusers will probably be harder to test, at least for younger adolescents.

Geiger (1990) studied ego development in a sample of 50 hospitalized chemically dependent adolescents. The modal ego development stage for them was Self-Protective, yet, as was noted earlier, this finding in itself does not prove that alcohol and substance abuse in adolescents is associated with ego development impairment. To test impairment in other than ego development areas, the researchers used additional variables and found problems in reality testing, poorly managed affect, low self-esteem, and maladaptive interpersonal relationships.

To test the hypothesis that substance abuse in adolescents is related to the delay in ego development, researchers would need to compare proportions of Preconformist adolescents who are substance abusers with those in a non-abusing group. This was done in Noam et al. (1994). These researchers found prevalence of alcohol use and dependence and cannabis use and dependence in the group of Conduct Disorder psychiatric adolescents who were predominantly at the Preconformist ego development levels. The proportion of Preconformist adolescents and substance abuse score was significantly lower for the Affective Disorder group.

Du Mont (1998) studied the "detrimental" influence of early menarche on educational and personality development of adolescent girls. In her complex study, level of ego development, empathy, family warmth, interparental conflict, and depression were used as independent variables hypothesized to influence youths' risk behaviors, such as cigarettes, alcohol and drug use, early coital debut, and low educational attainment. Early pubertal development was found to be a risk factor that promoted risk behaviors, including alcohol and drug use, and higher depression levels. It was also positively associated with the level of ego development. Ego development was found to be associated negatively with depression and risk behaviors. Thus, a complex model emerged. In this model, two positively associated factors—early puberty and ego development—had conflicting influences (e.g., ego development positive, and puberty negative) on the adolescents' levels of depression and risk behaviors. This study, while confirming a negative association between ego development and adolescent substance abuse, also supports the use of multivariate methods as preferable in ego development research.

Summary and Conclusions

The main conclusion of this subsection of the review is that there are many more problematic areas in the field of ego development and alcohol and drug use than there are studies that cover them. From the evidence cited, only a few conclusions can be drawn.

First, the Self-Protective might be the modal stage for heavy adult drug and alcohol users, yet people at all ego development stages abuse drugs. Some studies indicate the Self-Aware as the modal stage, with the percentage of subjects on it higher than in normative adult samples.

Second, the evidence suggests a need to make a distinction between specific drug-using groups. As was shown, the difference between the hippies who scored higher than normative adult samples and opiate addicts, mostly at the Self-Protective ego development stage, is substantial. Another distinction that needs to be made (and this is in line

with the research in every other area of the mental health–ego development relationship) is the differences between subgroups within problematic populations, which, in this particular area, was done in only one study that involved an opiate addict sample.

Another prominent line of research seems to be a relationship between drug use, depression, and inability to be in intimate relationships that possibly can be traced to childhood and attachment mode. Those factors need to be built into research models when studying drug use and ego development. Last, the only noncontradictory finding that has been obtained by every researcher who is concerned with this problem set is that ego development always correlates negatively with the severity of abuse.

Defense Mechanisms

In the Loevingerian framework, it is logical to assume that the way of coping with negative emotions will be different for different ego development stages. It is not surprising, therefore, that the findings on the relationship between the level of ego development and the use of defense mechanisms strongly suggest the relationship between the two.

Most of the studies conducted in this area used the Defense Mechanisms Inventory (DMI; Gleser & Ihilevich, 1969; Ihilevich & Gleser, 1971, 1986). Among the major defenses, turning-against-object (TAO), turning-against-self (TAS), and projection are considered less mature defense mechanisms as they presuppose aggression and an immature distortion of reality. Principalization and reversal, on the other hand, are more intellectual and less aggressive defenses and are considered more mature.

Thus, we should expect the use of TAO, TAS, and projection to decrease with ego development, especially in transition from Preconformist to Conformist ego levels, whereas the use of principalization and reversal should increase. This hypothesis was supported by nearly every study conducted in this area.

In a time-series study of 37 psychiatric adolescent patients, those subjects who displayed progress in ego development over a period of 9 months also demonstrated significant changes in their use of defense mechanisms. With the transition from Preconformist to the Conformist stages of ego development, the use of TAO, TAS, and projection defenses were significantly lowered, and the use of principalization and reversal increased (Noam et al., 1991).

This confirms the earlier findings by Levit (1989), who used a normal sample and found that the use of TAO is inversely related to ego development. Hickok (1996) found significant negative correlations between ego development and TAO and projection; a significant positive correlation was found between ego development level and principalization.

In a study of adolescent girls who were patients at a residential treatment center, Borst and Noam (1993) explored the relationship between ego development, several scales of the YSR, clinical diagnoses, suicidality measurement, and defense mechanisms as measured by DMI (Gleser & Ihilevich, 1969; Ihilevich & Gleser, 1986). The results they obtained were quite in line with the other findings. They found TAO to be higher at the Preconformist ego levels and lower at the Conformist ego level (significance at $p < .01$), even more for the suicidal group than for the nonsuicidal group ($F = 6.99$ for the nonsuicidal group, as compared to $F = 10.81$ for the suicidal group; in both cases, $p < .01$). Projection displayed the same pattern, only the difference between the Pre- and Postconformist groups (and thus the significance of the results) was slightly lower here than for the TAO, and there were no significant group differences between the suicidal and nonsuicidal Conformists in the use of this defense. The use of principalization displayed the reverse tendency: It was found to be higher for the Conformist than for the Preconformist girls. In the use of the TAS defense, the differences between the suicidal and nonsuicidal groups were more significant than the differences between the Pre- and Postconformist (being highest for the suicidal groups), but for the nonsuicidal groups it was higher for the Conformist girls than for the Preconformists. Last, the use of reversal was higher for the Conformist nonsuicidal girls, but not the Conformist suicidal girls, for whom it was almost as low as for the Preconformist nonsuicidal girls.

This study, while pointing at other factors (suicide ideation, in this case) that might influence defense use, nevertheless confirmed the other findings that reported the significance of differences in defense use as a function of ego development level (particularly in transition from Preconformist to Conformist ego development stages). As in the Noam et al. (1991) study, the use of principalization and reversal was higher for the Conformist than for the Preconformist adolescents, and the use of TAO and projection was higher for the Preconformist than for the Conformist adolescents. Amato (1991) explored the relationship between the level of ego development, defense mechanisms, and psychological separation during adolescence in a sample of normal 11th and 12th graders in a suburban Connecticut town. As in other

studies, the use of principalization was positively related to ego development (this association was stronger for males), and the use of TAO was negatively related to ego development.

In Noam's (1984) study, ego development was examined in relation to 14 defenses (classified in four defense factors based on Valliant's (1971, 1993) hierarchy of defenses, from the least to most mature). The results show that the action-oriented and projective defenses are negatively correlated with ego and moral development, and the more delaying and cognitively complex defenses, such as suppression, altruism, and intellectualization, increase as ego development increases.

All these studies were conducted with adolescent populations. A complex study that drew our attention to several problems in this area is Cramer's (1999) that used a sample of 98 young adults. She used a completely different defense mechanism system that only distinguished among three defenses (denial, projection, and identification), and thus her findings cannot be generalized with those cited earlier. However, she makes several points that appear to be extremely important. First, her sample was singularly representative and included subjects at every ego development stage, from Impulsive to Autonomous. All three defense mechanisms in the study were found to have curvilinear relationships with ego development. This fits the similar pattern of the relationship between ego development and other mental health measurements, implying that curvilinearity in ego development is related to mental health.

Another important characteristic of this study is that it considered IQ measurement and age as covariates of ego development and employed multivariate statistical tools. Particularly, IQ seemed to play a mediating role in the use of defense mechanisms (p. 756).

Summary and Conclusions

Every study that explored the relationship between ego development and the use of defense mechanisms employing the DMI found that the incidence of TAS and projection is much higher at the lower, Preconformist stages of ego development than it is at the Conformist stage. The same tendency, only slightly weaker, was found for the TAS defense mechanism. This strong finding does not seem surprising if we take into consideration the nature of those defenses. All of them presuppose not a transformation, but a rerouting of aggressive tendencies, either "through attaching an external object . . . or directing aggressive thoughts and behaviors toward oneself . . . or attributing negative qualities to an object as a justification of expression of aggression" (Noam et al., 1991, p. 318).

Principalization and reversal, on the other hand, were found to be used more at the Conformist ego development stages. These are intellectualizing defenses that deal with negative emotions with a kind of transformation that changes one's view of conflict, either by "splitting of emotions and affect from the content of the conflict . . . or by responding neutrally or positively toward a frustrating object" (Noam et al., 1991, p. 318).

Thus, the findings on relationship between ego development and defense mechanisms are consistent with each other and the conceptual predictions that could be expected in the framework of Loevinger's theory. On the other hand, most of the studies cited used adolescent samples (see Chiesa, 1980) and explored the use of defense in the transition from the Preconformist to the Conformist ego development levels. The higher levels of ego development were left out of the picture. This is a problem that needs to be explored.

Our overall conclusion is that defense mechanisms, or more generally coping and adaptational scales, might be very important bridging constructs between ego development and symptomatology because they share with ego development an aspect of frame of reality/meaning. They also capture distortions and misconceptions, which have been viewed by many clinical traditions (e.g., psychoanalysis, cognitive-behavior psychology) as tied to psychopathology and symptomatology.

POSITIVE MENTAL HEALTH

In this section, we look at another end of the mental health spectrum and present evidence that suggests an answer to the question: Are people with high ego development more likely to have better positive mental health? We present research evidence on this topic, organized in accordance with the views the authors hold on the nature of positive mental health.

Positive Mental Health as a Single Variable, Similar to the Sense of Subjective Well-Being or Life Satisfaction

The hypothesis that people with higher levels of ego development are more satisfied with their lives was proposed as early as 1978 by Alker and Gawin. Using a large heterogeneous sample of religiously active adults ages 18 to 80, they conducted a correlational analysis of two variables: psy-

chological well-being and religious maturity based on Maslow's theoretical model and measured by the Religious Orientation Scale (Allport & Ross, 1967). They found not only that more mature people were happier, but that they understood the very meaning of happiness differently from less mature individuals.

The research evidence obtained using Loevinger's measurement of ego development as maturity does not support this claim. Young (1998) considered positive mental health as synonymous with maturity and measured it with two instruments: the Index of Adult Adjustment (Picano, 1984) and the Psychological Well-Being Scale (Ryf, 1996). A distinct characteristic of the sample was that the participants of her study were White middle-class women who scored higher than the general population on ego development; the Self-Aware stage, the modal stage for the general population, was the lowest stage observed in the sample. The researcher found no significant relationship between ego development and maturity. Among significant findings is that women who are high on both maturity and ego development were found more likely to have raised children than women low on both, or high on ego development but low on maturity. Thus, maturity was found to be a more salient factor for predicting successful completion of life's essential tasks. A similar pattern was observed with income: Women high on both ego development and maturity were found to have higher incomes than women low on both or high on ego development only. The conclusion that one can draw from this study is that for middle-aged, middle-class women, reaching high, Postconformist stages of ego development does not mean having better adjustment or life satisfaction.

McCrae and Costa (1980) failed to find any association between the level of ego development and positive affect from the Affect Balance Scales (Bradburn, 1969) for a sample of 240 men from the Normative Aging Project. A secondary confirmation of the finding that there is no relationship between ego development and the feeling of life satisfaction comes from Diamond's (1996) study. Her main goal was to explore the construct of integrative complexity (IC; Suedfeld & Tetlock, 1977) in its relationship with other variables, including ego development. In Diamond's model, IC is a variable tapping into "structural complexity with which a person narrates and interprets significant autobiographical events" (Diamond, 1997, p. 1). This study explores the relationship between integrative complexity, ego development, and the feeling of life satisfaction as measured by the Satisfaction with Life Survey (Diener, Emmons, Larsen, & Griffin, 1985) and Overall Happiness with Life Scale (Fordyce, 1977). Only the correlations between integrative complexity and life satisfaction, and integrative complexity and ego development were obtained. Both associations were positive and significant, which confirmed the findings obtained by other researchers (Pratt, Diessner, Hunsberger, & Panser, 1991; Slugoski, Marcia, & Koopman, 1984). This is also intuitively understandable, as by definition, integrative complexity and ego development are clearly related constructs, both referring to the complexity of the person's understanding of self and the world around one. Diamond found no significant relationship between integrative complexity and either of the two life satisfaction measurements.

Positive Mental Health as a Compound Construct

Another approach to positive mental health is to consider it as a sum of two aspects: satisfaction with life and satisfaction with oneself. This view goes back to Erikson's (1968, p. 165) writings about identity, which, in its optimal form, should be equal to "a sense of psychological well-being, . . . of being at home in one's body."

King, Scollon, Ramsey, and Williams (2000) explored the relationship between ego development and subjective well-being in parents of children with Down syndrome. Multiple measurements, including WUSCT, the Satisfaction with Life Scale (Diener et al., 1985), the Rosenberg Self-Esteem Scale (Rosenberg, 1979), and narrative account assignments were administered over two time points with an interval of 2 years. Forty-two out of 87 participated in the follow-up study. In line with the other studies, the researchers found no relationship between ego development and life satisfaction on either time point. What did display a significant positive correlation with ego development was the self-esteem measurement. Also, when the narrative accounts were analyzed by content, the variable called "accommodation" (a feeling of being changed, accommodated to life as a result of traumatic events) positively and significantly correlated with ego development.

Several conclusions can be drawn from this study. First, it is likely that ego development does not display an interaction with a person's subjective feeling of satisfaction with life. On the other hand, ego development was found to correlate positively with self-esteem, which the authors took as a component of adjustment. Thus, if successful life adjustment presupposes two components, satisfaction with life and satisfaction with oneself, the former component is independent of ego development (in other words, people at lower levels have equally high chances to be as happy as people at higher levels of ego development), and the latter correlates posi-

tively with ego development (people at higher ego development levels are more satisfied with themselves).

A positive relationship between ego development and self-esteem was found in a number of other studies (e.g., Raygan, 1991; Rogers, 1980; Schaffer, 1983; Schoeberlein, 1997). However, we do not know as of yet the directionality of these relationships: Is it higher self-esteem that supports ego development, or is it ego development that increases the likelihood of high self-esteem?

A similar model of positive mental health as a composite of two or more dimensions was employed in Helson and Srivastava's (2001) study. It was based on Ryff's (1989) model of positive mental health. Ryff proposed two components of positive mental health: personal growth and environmental mastery. Just as in the earlier model, Ryff distinguishes between the component that taps into the person's relationship with the world and the person's relationship with self. Based on the two dimensions, Ryff proposed a positive mental health typology. She divided the population into the following:

- Achievers, high on both environmental mastery and personal growth.
- Seekers, high on personal growth only.
- Conservers, high on environmental mastery only.
- Depleted, low on both: people with a lack of positive mental health.

Helson and Srivastava (2001) employed Ryff's model and, after dividing the sample of 111 women into the four positive mental health types, explored the relationship between positive mental health and a list of related variables, including generativity, social competence, wisdom, ego development, and life satisfaction. The results they obtained are similar to the results of the other studies cited in this review, with several additions.

The Seekers group (high on personal growth) were highest on ego development. This group was also highest on wisdom, thus supporting the relationship between these two constructs. According to Ryff's classification, this is the group concerned with personal growth, but not environmental mastery. This explains and supports the relationship between ego development and self-esteem. People who are concerned about their personal growth and who, most probably, channel their lives so that they can hone their personal growth, are more satisfied with themselves. The same people were relatively low on life satisfaction and conventional social adjustment measured by the Index of Adult Adjustment (Picano, 1984), which, again, is in line with the other findings. (Another approach to adjustment emerges from treatment results or mental health outcomes after counseling.) This topic is dealt with, for example, in Dill and Noam (1990), Loevinger (1980), Shainbart (1995), and Van Ormer (2001).

Ross (2001) arrived at results similar to these, with one important difference. She found that for the people who experienced the death of a parent as adolescents, the ego development levels were higher than for matched controls. Also, the personal congruence was higher (the discrepancy between the real and the ideal self, which is closely related to self-esteem), and the depression levels were no different than for the control group. The model that emerges here is causal: It follows that traumatic events, pain, or conflict (which, of course, would lead to lower levels of happiness or life satisfaction) might in fact be the source of personal growth resulting in high ego development and high personal congruence (self-esteem).

This line of reasoning can be traced back to Piaget, who proposed disequilibrium as a source of development. Far from being conclusive (e.g., other studies show a lack of relationship between happiness and ego development, not a negative correlation), this model nevertheless appeals to investigators. The most suitable research design here seems to be a longitudinal study that would explore the relationship between life events, levels of happiness (life satisfaction), and ego development with the goal of finding their causal path of interdependence over time.

Positive Mental Health as Different for Ego Level Groups

Yet another approach, probably the most advanced one, assumes that there is no point in attempts to measure the association between the feeling of life satisfaction and ego development, because for people at varying ego development levels, the very experience and understanding of happiness will be quite different.

Labouvie-Vief, Hakim-Larson, deVoe, and Schoeberlein (1989) distinguished four levels of emotional understanding: presystemic, intrasystemic, intersystemic, and integrated.

At the lowest (presystemic) level, emotions were described in terms of egocentric standards and impulsive thoughts and actions, and the feeling of life satisfaction was equal to personal comfort. At the next (intrasystemic) level, emotions were described in conventional terms, and the feeling of happiness was a projection of what might be experienced as a positive emotional situation by the people of one's group. At the intersystemic level, inner sensations were recognized; it was only at this level that the true personal feeling of satisfaction appeared and was experienced and acknowledged. At the integrated level, the dual nature

of emotions as bodily and mental phenomena was recognized; thus, happiness could be experienced as harmony with the environment and other people's feelings.

The results of this study showed clearly "a developmental trend in these levels as a function of age" (Labouvie-Vief et al., 1989, p. 279). The emotional level scale correlated at .70 with ego development and with verbal ability for the subsample of 28 adults of different ages. Thus, the researchers showed that for people at different emotional (and thus ego) levels, the experience, understanding, and control of emotions were qualitatively different.

Summary and Conclusions

Even though the evidence of the relationship of ego development and positive mental health is not abundant, a few tendencies can be distinguished, and some conclusions seem well supported.

First, if we consider mental health as a unidimensional construct equal to the feeling of personal well-being and life satisfaction, most studies show no significant relationship between it and ego development. If we distinguish between two aspects of positive mental health, one tapping into a person's relationship with self and another focusing on one's relationship with the environment, a different schema emerges. One's feeling of satisfaction with the environment seems quite unrelated to one's level of ego development, yet one's satisfaction with oneself is definitely higher for people at the higher ego development stages. Thus, at least one component of positive mental health seems to correlate positively and significantly with ego development. This is the finding obtained in the majority of studies concerned with the question.

Another position holds the view that the very meaning and experience of happiness and satisfaction is so different for people at higher ego development levels that it seem meaningless to measure those different sensations with the same instrument, be it a measurement of emotional well-being or of life satisfaction. Definitely, more research in this area would shed more light on the problem, which might offer some answers to the age-old human questions about the meaning and ultimate importance of happiness.

FAMILY CONTEXTS IN RELATIONSHIP TO ADOLESCENT EGO DEVELOPMENT AND MENTAL HEALTH

One area where the topic of mental health in its relationship with ego development becomes extremely important from the theoretical, methodological, and practical points of view is the area of family contexts of adolescent development. The issues of family, attachment, and the interplay of personal and contextual factors in this crucial period of human development are directly connected to psychosocial risks, symptoms, and dysfunction. Also, many studies conducted on the topic are more complex than those that involve only ego development and one particular disorder. Thus, the complex models emerging in this area are representative of the next stage of research, where more complex theoretical and empirical models are being tested.

Another contemporary trend that emerges in most advanced research is a view that a person as much shapes his or her contexts as the context influences the person. In application to the adolescent development field, we take it for granted that adolescents shape their parents and the family atmosphere as much as the family shapes them (Grotevant, 1998; Hauser, 1991). Thus, even though it is customary to use such words as "family influence" and "adolescent outcomes," we will be talking about associations between variables, such as parenting style and adolescent decision-making strategies, in terms of associations, without implying causality, in every instance except for one longitudinal study.

To make sense of the abundant literature on the topic, we find it useful to classify the constructs being studied into three categories. First, we explore the research that studies parenting styles, family warmth, parents' ego development levels, and family history scales in their relationship to ego development (see Guerra, 1991, for parental alcoholism on ego development in offspring). Second, we review studies that focus on characteristics of the adolescents, those that can usually be divided into positive attributes, such as self-esteem, educational attainment, productive decision making, and ego resiliency, and negative dimensions, such as risk behaviors and aggressiveness. In the third class we put four constructs: ego development, mental health status, attachment, and gender. The integrated model that the evidence seems to be implying is that ego development, attachment, and mental health serve as mediators between the family variables and adolescent variables, and gender might be moderating the associations. Thus, even though these complex, integrated models are employed in only some studies and not in others, they are beacons for future research in this area, the next step that is being taken by an increasing number of researchers.

Relationships between Adolescent Variables, Ego Development, and Mental Health

Win (2001) studied the relationship between attachment (as measured by the Inventory of Parent and Peer Attachment; Armsden & Greenberg, 1987), ego development, and utilization of social support for unusually young college students (15 to 17 years). The results show that the ability of those adolescents to utilize social support available for them on campus, such as peers and counselors (which, in turn, translated into the overall college adjustment), was significantly related to both attachment (in that system, not an attachment typology, but a total attachment score is used, with the lowest score representing the weakest and the highest score the strongest attachment) and ego development level. Particularly, student satisfaction with companionship, satisfaction with emotional support, and overall satisfaction with support were higher for those with a higher overall attachment score. Level of ego development was also found to be associated with satisfaction with companionship, with the Postconformist group being more satisfied than the Conformist group and the Preconformist group being the least satisfied of all. Gender was not significantly related to the social support variables.

The relationship between attachment and ego development was tested using the Duncan test of group means and found significantly different (significance at $p < .05$) for the three ego level groups: the lowest for the Preconformists, average for the Conformists, and the highest for the Postconformist adolescents.

One methodological note is due before we proceed any further with this review. As attachment and ego development were found to be related (in Win's 2001 study, as in other studies to be cited), then to achieve accuracy in the conclusions, the partial correlations between the adolescent variables, ego development, and attachment need to be calculated. In doing so, several schemas need to be tested. Ego development and attachment might be considered joint predictors for the outcome variables, or they can mediate each other's influences. Statistically, a variable is a joint predictor if it adds to the proportion of the explained variance, and a mediator if it lessens an increment of an independent variable whose influence it mediates (Baron & Kenny, 1986). The best suggestion is to test all four schemas (each of the variables as a joint predictor and as a mediator) in any research concerning ego development and adolescent outcomes.

In Win's (2001) study, attachment score remained a significant predictor of the satisfaction with social support even when controlling for the level of ego development.

Laird (2000) found ego development to be related to the decision-making patterns in pregnant adolescent girls age 15 to 19. In that study, "the naturalistic patterns of decision-making employed by the young women during their interaction in group sessions and through their conversations about pregnancy resolution decisions were examined"

(p. xiii). These qualitative data were then compared with the six subjects' ego development levels. No other variables were used in this study.

Schoeberlein (1997) found a significant positive association between ego development and self-esteem in a mixed sample of 99 homeless and 99 housed adolescents age 12 to 17. Ego development was tested as a predictor for self-esteem as an outcome variable. In the multiple regression analysis, age and IQ were tested as covariates used to test the unique increment in adolescent self-esteem, explained by ego development only. It was still high: r .20 in bivariate regression, .19 controlling for age, and .22 controlling for both age and IQ (all significances at $p < .01$ level). Although gender was found to be related to ego development in the manner found elsewhere (females having on average higher ego development than males), the moderating role of gender on the ego development-self-esteem relationship was not obtained.

Relationships between Family Variables and Ego Development/Mental Health/Attachment

Allen and colleagues (Allen, Hauser, Bell, & O'Connor, 1994) examined adolescents' level of ego and autonomy-relatedness in their relationships with fathers and mothers as measured by the Autonomy and Relatedness Coding System (Allen, Hauser, Bornam, & Worrell, 1991). In this study, ego development was considered a dependent variable. Not surprisingly, behaviors exhibiting autonomy/relatedness were positively related to ego development. Behaviors exhibiting only autonomy but not relatedness or only relatedness but not autonomy were negatively related to adolescents' ego development. When mental health status (hospitalization history) was taken into account, the relationship between autonomy/relatedness and ego development remained significant. No interaction effects were found for gender. The importance of this study lies in stressing the significance of the balance between two dimensions of family interactions—autonomy and relatedness—and in using gender and mental health history as moderating variables, even though the effect of gender was not found to be significant.

Hiraga (1996) studied family processes and ego development in a sample of 42 adolescent girls. Ego development was predicted by maternal warmth, behavioral control, psychological control, and cognitive enabling. Neither the role of father nor other mediating variables such as attachment were taken into consideration in this study. Thus, for adolescent girls, a combination of maternal warmth and con-

trol was found to be the best predictor for the daughters' ego development.

The importance of Hiraga's (1996) study lies in the fact that she concentrated on the minority family processes; Luthar and Quinlan (1993) added cross-cultural aspects to the topic of family processes. They explored the relationships between parental characteristics (Care and Protect scales from the Parental Bonding Instrument; Parker, Tupling, & Brown, 1979), ego development, depressive tendencies as measured by the Depressive Experience Questionnaire (Blatt, D'Afflitti, & Quinlan, 1976) for the two samples: female college students in the United States and their counterparts in India (these were older adolescents; the mean age was 19.6 for the Indian students and 21.0 for the American students). The results were slightly different for the two cultures. For the Indian students, ego development was found to be associated with both parents' Protection score (though the sufficient significance level has not been achieved); for American students, ego development was positively associated with the paternal Care score.

This study draws our attention to one more methodological consideration related to the problem of family and ego development. As the evidence cited in this review suggests, many mental health problems are related to ego development, and severity of disorder is always inversely related to it. Thus, when exploring the relationship between family variables and ego development, mental health variables should be taken into consideration. Mental health variables and ego development may be tested as joint predictors or as mediators.

In Luthar and Quinlan's (1993) study, only bivariate correlations among parenting variables, ego development, and depression subscales were obtained. Richards, Gitelson, Peterson, and Hurtig (1991) studied effects of a diverse group of parental variables (such as warmth, active involvement, rejection, hostile control) on the levels of ego development of 139 high school students ages 17 to 18. The researchers found that although ego development was associated with more encouraging, warmer mothering for boys, it related weakly to mothering for girls. The fathers' role was not found to be significant for their children's ego development, which contradicts the other studies cited.

Von der Lippe (2000) explored relationships between family interactions and daughters' level of ego development in a sample of 39 families led by fathers and mothers with adolescent daughters ages 16 to 19. The new and important feature of this study is that parents' level of ego development (for both mothers and fathers) was also included in the list of variables. The daughters' ego level was associated significantly with their father's but not their mother's ego level, which confirms the importance of the opposite-sex parent for the adolescent's development. When daughters' age, parental SES, and parental ego development were controlled for in the hierarchical regression analysis, fathers' cognitive and affective enabling and mothers' affective enabling were significant contributors to the daughters' ego development. Another interesting finding of this study is that mothers' challenging behaviors and parental autonomy from responding in kind to their daughters' communications also predicted adolescents' level of ego development, thus supporting the idea proposed in other Von der Lippe works: that family conflict combined with a supportive atmosphere enhance adolescent levels of ego development, in spite of a commonsense view that a good family is a family without problems.

The issue of family conflict was further explored in another Von der Lippe study (Von der Lippe & Moller, 2000). In this study, adolescent level of ego development was used as a predictor for family characteristics of family communication and patterns of conflict negotiation. Thirty-nine late-adolescent females, age 16 to 19 (mean age 17.5), and their parents were studied. It was hypothesized that "the ego development of adolescent females would be positively related to the quality of the conflict negotiation in their families as it reflects the individuation of the [family] system" (p. 60). The hypothesis was confirmed. The results show that when the daughters achieve higher developmental levels, the family as a whole negotiate conflict in more productive ways, the ways that presuppose a balance of "autonomy and relatedness" (Allen et al., 1994) or, in Stierlin (1974), "individuated relationships."

In a similar study by Hauser, DiPlacido, Jacobson, Willett, and Cole (1993), several family coping strategies were found to be related to adolescents' level of ego development in 79 families with adolescent diabetic patients. Among these strategies were cognitive flexibility/perspective taking, experience of mastery, seeking information, direct expression of feelings, and awareness of helplessness. All these strategies were linked with more advanced levels of adaptation to the stress that adolescents' illness represented for the families. The coping strategy avoidance, expected to be linked to lower levels of adaptation, was inversely correlated with adolescents' level of ego development.

In another study by Hauser and colleagues (1984), relationships between family interactions measured by the Constraining and Enabling Coding System, newly developed by the same researchers and later used by many others interested in family and adolescent research, and

parental and adolescents' ego development levels and adolescent mental health, were explored. As in the earlier studies, adolescent ego development was treated as an independent variable and family interactions as dependent variables. After controlling for adolescents' age and mental health status, adolescents' ego development level was found to be positively associated with adolescent enabling behaviors (problem solving, empathy) and negatively correlated with constraining behaviors (devaluing, withholding). Parental behaviors were associated with both parents' and adolescents' ego levels, with enabling behaviors related to higher ego levels and constraining behaviors related to lower ego levels.

Relationships among Ego Development, Mental Health, Attachment, and Gender

There are several studies that explore interrelationships among the four variables that the emerging model implies are the mediators between family and adolescent variables. These studies are extremely important as they provide evidence that the four mediating variables are interrelated and, thus, for the accuracy of conclusions, should be taken into consideration together.

McLauchlin (1997) explored the relationship among three variables: mental health (severity of personality pathology, measured by the MCMI-III), ego development, and attachment status (secure vs. insecure, measured by the Adult Attachment Questionnaire; Feeney, Noller, & Hanrahan, 1994) in a large sample ($N = 249$) of older adolescents—undergraduate students in an urban university. For this sample, where the distribution of the participants across ego development stages was similar to those characteristic of normal adult populations (the majority scoring at the Self-Aware ego stage, with a substantial proportion at the Conscientious stage, and only about 5% scoring below the Conformist stage), ego development was found to be positively associated with secure attachment chi-square of 5.42, significance $p < .02$ for two attachment groups (securely vs. insecurely attached) and two ego development groups (a small fraction of Preconformists plus Conformists in one group and Postconformists in another group). Ego development was inversely associated with severity of personality pathology (Pearson correlation of $-.14$, $p < .05$) and a total personality score for each participant who demonstrated a clearly defined high point and correlation of $-.19$ ($p < .01$) between ego development and the sum of all 14 personality scores. The relationship between attachment style and personality pathology was found to be more complex.

Summed personality scores were computed for each attachment category. Securely attached individuals had the lowest score (and thus the lowest pathology) and preoccupied individuals had the highest score, with dismissing and fearful types falling in between. When particular personality types were considered, dismissing individuals were more likely to have schizoid, avoidant, narcissistic, or compulsive personalities. Participants classified in the preoccupied attachment category were more likely to have borderline, depressive, self-defeating, and histrionic personalities. Participants classified in the fearful attachment category were more likely to have paranoid, antisocial, and aggressive-sadistic personalities. Securely attached individuals were most often classified in the "moving toward others" personality cluster (e.g., depressive, self-defeating, and histrionic, excluding borderline).

England's (1997) study provides more evidence in support of the relationship between attachment category and ego development level. In her study, two groups were compared on both attachment styles measured by Hazan and Shaver's (1987) Measure of Attachment Styles and level of ego development: a group of 99 adult incest offenders and a matched control group. The incest group was significantly lower on ego development and also included more insecurely attached participants than the control group, which implies a positive association between lower levels of ego development and insecure attachment. Yet, because the participants in the study were adults, not adolescents, it is only of secondary significance to the topic of this section.

Studies That Consider Ego Development and Attachment as Mediating Variables between Adolescent and Family Variables

In the following studies, the variables from all three clusters (family, adolescent, and mediating) were explored in their relationship with one another. In many instances, the mediating roles of ego development, mental health, attachment category, and gender were acknowledged and taken into consideration in the statistical analyses.

Du Mont (1998) studied the effects of early pubertal development, family warmth, and ego development on risk behaviors (early coital debut, cigarette smoking, and drug use) in adolescent girls. She used two adolescent variables (early pubertal development and risk behaviors, the former as independent variable and the latter as dependent variable), family variable, and ego development as mediating variable. As predicted, family warmth reduced the risk behaviors, not directly, but through ego development and through pubertal development (family warmth was nega-

tively related to pubertal development, which was positively associated with risk behaviors). Moreover, two adolescent variables—early pubertal development and risk behaviors—were related both directly and through ego development as mediating influences of early pubertal development on risk behaviors. Thus, ego development was found to be able to negate a part of the negative influence of the early pubertal development on risk behaviors (early pubertal development related positively to both risk behaviors and ego development, and ego development reduced the probability of risk behaviors).

In the following two studies, the model we described in the beginning of this section (e.g., ego development, gender, and mental health as mediating relationships between family variables and adolescent variables) was employed. Isberg et al. (1989) explored the influence of family interactions as measured by the Constraining and Enabling Coding System (Hauser et al., 1984, 1987) on adolescents' self-esteem as measured by the Coopersmith Self-Esteem Inventory (Coopersmith, 1967). Mental health status (psychiatric patients, diabetic patients, and healthy high school students were subsamples), gender, and ego development were mediating variables. Among these, health status was the strongest mediator; the significance of age, gender, and parental SES was somewhat lower. Together, the effects of parental accepting or devaluing behaviors were strongest for psychiatrically ill boys. After the health factors were controlled for, all parental influences were still significant for boys, but not for girls, for whom only fathers' acceptance correlated positively with school self-esteem. The importance of this study lies in the fact that moderating effects of ego development were studied here: Parental behaviors correlated significantly with self-esteem in Preconformist but not in Conformist and Postconformist adolescents. This leads us to the conclusion that family processes and their relationship with various adolescent variables depend on adolescents' ego development levels and are different for Preconformist and Conformist adolescents.

Best and Hauser's (1997) study employed a longitudinal design with two time points 11 years apart. Parenting behaviors measured by the Constraining and Enabling Coding System (Hauser et al., 1992) and the Autonomy and Relatedness Coding System (Allen, Hauser, Borman, & Worell, 1991) were tested as predictors of the children's educational attainment and ego resiliency 11 years later. Adolescent ego development and mental health status were used as mediating variables. Even when controlling variables were accounted for, parental encouragement of adolescent autonomy and relatedness was related positively to the young adults' educational attainment. Addition of the ego development significantly improved prediction of the educational attainment 11 years later, accounting for an additional 11% of the variance. Together, ego development and parenting behaviors accounted for 27% of the variance in the young adults' educational attainment. Also, ego development was found to mediate the relationship between parental behaviors and both educational attainment and ego strength in young adults.

This study is also important in that it draws researchers' attention to the statistical difference between using ego development as a joint predictor with a significant increment in multiple regression analyses and using ego development as a mediating variable. In this section, we talk about ego development as a mediator between family and adolescent variables for several reasons. First, it has been confirmed by Best and Hauser's (1997) study. Second, it is theoretically sound to expect the mediating effect if ego development correlates with both parenting and adolescent variables, and several studies cited in this review uniformly confirm that it does. Yet, only some, but not all, studies use ego development as a mediator; many only explore its additional contribution to the magnitude of prediction (see also Chilton, 2001). As the joint evidence brought together here suggests, ego development most probably plays both roles.

Summary

This subsection had a twofold goal: first, to describe the integrated theoretical model that emerges in the recent studies of the mutual influences of adolescents and their families (including the methodological nuances pertinent to the model), and second, to summarize the tentative conclusions that the cited studies seem to suggest.

In the model, four interrelated factors were found to be related to both family and adolescent characteristics and to mediate their mutual influences: mental health status, ego development, attachment, and gender. Thus, we stressed the importance of using these factors in family/adolescent studies, both as mediators and as joint contributors to the predicted variances.

Taken together, the studies we cited suggest that family warmth and relatedness (see also Bartholomew & Horowitz, 1991, for relationships to attachment styles) are as important to adolescent development as challenging and autonomy-encouraging behaviors in parents, but only when they occur in a warm, supportive context. The role of adolescent ego development was found to be important for nearly every aspect of adaptational family functioning, from productive coping strategies and productive ways of

conflict negotiation, to being able to negate destructive influences of risk variables, such as early pubertal development in girls.

SUMMARY AND FUTURE DIRECTIONS

The importance of using the cognitive-developmental personality paradigm in clinical research and practice has become evident as increasing numbers of studies have been conducted at the intersection between Loevinger's theory of ego development and mental health.

In an attempt to generalize the multitude of findings brought together in this review, we need to make a distinction between general conclusions on the nature of the relationship between ego development and psychopathology and more specific findings concerning relationships between ego development and various disorder groups.

Generally, the majority of clinical samples reflect moderate to significant delays in ego development. Another general conclusion supported by the evidence is that for most disorders, symptom expression is different at different ego development stages.

Among specific disorders, personality disorders (especially Borderline Personality Disorder, Conduct Disorder, and delinquency) and substance-related disorders were found to display the strongest relationships with ego development. The former is not surprising, as Loevinger's theory of ego development is a cognitive-developmental personality theory, and thus it is only natural to expect that a delay in personality development would be related to personality disorders. The latter should be expected based on Loevinger's description of one domain of ego, impulse control, an aspect of substance abuse disorders. One specific finding in this area, a possible relationship of substance abuse, ego development, relational deficiency, and depressive tendencies, is a prominent line of research that needs more exploration.

Another emerging tendency that needs further exploration is a nonlinear relationship between ego development and some disorders (such as mood disorders, anxiety, and such mental health-related emotions as guilt and shame). In particular, it has been found that Conformist stages of ego development might be where the social pressure to fit in and measure up to group norms is the highest and the risk of depressive and anxious problems is great. The use of curvilinear statistical tools seems advisable in the ego development research.

Another strong methodological tendency in this area is a movement to more complex models and multivariate methods that account for mutual influences of many variables that allow one to build models. At the other end of the mental health spectrum, positive mental health in its relationship with ego development has not yet become a prominent area of research, yet, we chose to review the studies that have been conducted in this direction as concentration of research efforts on maladaptation alone cannot yield a comprehensive explanation of how ego development interacts with adjustment processes during the course of life. Among the life course periods, adolescence seems to be the time when the developmental stage rather than age or phase is extremely important. Too often in developmental psychopathology research there is a singular focus on chronological age rather than developmental complexity and maturity. Future research will have to systematically take this relationship between chronological age, developmental stage, and psychopathology into consideration.

Methodologically, the use of more complex multivariate models and curvilinear tools is becoming more prevalent and will need to accelerate in this active area of study. Also, more studies with specific psychopathologies, such as personality disorders, anxiety disorders, and eating disorders, are clearly needed to complete the picture of this line of developmental psychopathology research. An intriguing and practically important topic of treatment implication and long-term outcomes in psychopathology has not received sufficient attention. Also, along the line of building more complex models, an integration of other developmental measures into the research on ego development and psychopathology might enrich our understanding of the developmental processes and be useful in assessment and clinical practice.

Taken together, the studies reviewed in this chapter show important patterns that will be significant in shaping a field of study and in developing lines of research that can make an important contribution to how we think about disorders from a developmental point of view. These findings also provide a direction for how we can begin to tailor interventions to augment existing ways of treating mental illness and mental health problems.

REFERENCES

Abroms, G. M. (1978). The place of values in psychotherapy. *Journal of Marriage and Family Counseling, 4,* 3–17.

Achenbach, T. M. (1982). *Developmental psychopathology.* New York: Wiley.

Achenbach, T. M. (1990). What is "developmental" about developmental psychopathology? In J. Rolf, A. S. Masten, D. Cicchetti, K. H. Nuechterlein, & S. Weintraub (Eds.), *Risk and protective factors in the development of psychopathology* (pp. 29–48). New York: Cambridge University Press.

Achenbach, T. M., & Edelbrock, C. (1983). *Manual for the Child Behavior Checklist and revised Child Behavior Profile.* Burlington: University of Vermont, Department of Psychiatry.

Achenbach, T. M., & Edelbrock, C. (1987). *Manual for the Youth Self-Report and profile.* Burlington: University of Vermont, Department of Psychiatry.

Achenbach, T. M., & Edelbrock, C. (1991). *Manual for the Youth Self-Report and profile.* Burlington: University of Vermont.

Alker, H., & Gawin, F. (1978). On the intrapsychic specificity of hippies. *Journal of Personality, 46,* 311–322.

Allen, J. P., Hauser, S. T., Bell, K. L., & O'Connor, T. (1994). Longitudinal assessment of autonomy and relatedness in adolescent-family interactions as predictors of adolescent ego development and self-esteem. *Child Development, 65,* 179–194.

Allen, J. P., Hauser, S. T., Borman, E., & Worrell, C. M. (1991). *The autonomy and relatedness coding system: A scoring manual.* Unpublished manuscript. University of Virginia, Charlottesville.

Allport, G. W., & Ross, J. M. (1967). Personal religious orientation and prejudices. *Journal of Personality and Social Psychology, 5,* 432–433.

Amato, J. (1991). *The relations among ego development, adolescent psychological separation, and defensive style.* Unpublished doctoral dissertation, New York University, New York.

American Psychiatric Association. (2000). *Diagnostic and statistical manual of mental disorders* (4th ed., text rev.). Washington, DC: Author.

American Psychiatric Association. Task Force on Nomenclature and Statistics. (1980). *Diagnostic and statistical manual of mental disorders* (3rd ed.). Washington, DC: Author.

American Psychiatric Association. Task Force on Nomenclature and Statistics. (1987). *Diagnostic and statistical manual of mental disorders* (3rd ed., revised). Washington, DC: Author.

Angelopoulos, J. (1991). *A study of some relationships between locus-of-control and the level of ego and moral development across incarcerated males with a diagnosis of antisocial personality disorder.* Unpublished doctoral dissertation, Vanderbilt University, Nashville, TN.

Armsden, G. C., & Greenberg, M. T. (1987). The Inventory of Parent and Peer Attachment: Individual differences and their relationship to psychological well-being in adolescence. *Journal of Youth and Adolescence, 16*(5), 427–454.

Barndt, R. J., & Johnson, D. M. (1955). Time orientation in delinquents. *Journal of Abnormal and Social Psychology, 51,* 343–345.

Baron, R. M., & Kenny, D. A. (1986). The moderator-mediator variable distinction in social psychological research: Conceptual, strategic, and statistical considerations. *Journal of Personality and Social Psychology, 51,* 1173–1182.

Barrett, D. (1991). *The relationships among ego development, intuition, and death anxiety in a sample of death educators and health care providers working with the dying and their families.* Unpublished doctoral dissertation, University of Minnesota, Minneapolis, MN.

Bartholomew, K., & Horowitz, L. (1991). Attachment styles among young adults: A test of a four-category model. *Journal of Personality and Social Psychology, 61*(2), 226–244.

Beck, A. T. (1967). *Depression: Causes and treatment.* Philadelphia: University of Pennsylvania Press.

Beck, A. T., & Beck, R. V. (1972). Screening depressed patients in family practice: A rapid technique. *Post Graduate Medicine, 52,* 1181–1185.

Best, K., & Hauser, S. (1997). Predicting young adult competencies: Adolescent era parent and individual influences. *Journal of Adolescent Research, 12*(19), 90–103.

Billing, S. (1987). *The relationship between level of ego development and depression, locus-of-control, assertiveness, and severity of disorder within a bulimic population.* Unpublished doctoral dissertation, California School of Professional Psychology, Fresno, CA.

Blasi, A. (1976). Personal responsibility and ego development. In R. Declares (Ed.), *Enhancing motivation: Change in the classroom* (pp. 177–199). New York: Irvington.

Blatt, S., & Berman, W. (1990). Differentiation of personality types among opiate addicts. *Journal of Personality Assessment, 54*(1/2), 87–104.

Blatt, S. J., Berman, W., Boloom-Feshbach, S., Sugarman, A., Wilber, C., & Kleber, H. (1984). Psychological assessment of psychopathology in opiate addicts. *Journal of Nervous and Mental Disease, 172*(3), 156–165.

Blatt, S. J., Rounsaville, B., Eyre, S., & Wilber, C. (1984). The psychodynamics of opiate addiction. *Journal of Nervous and Mental Disease, 172*(6), 342–352.

Blumentritt, T., Novy, D., Gaa, J., & Liberman, D. (1996). Effects of maximum performance instructions on the sentence completion test of ego development. *Journal of Personality Assessment, 67*(1), 79–89.

Borst, S., & Noam, G. (1993). Developmental psychopathology in suicidal and nonsuicidal adolescent girls. *Journal of the American Academy of Child and Adolescent Psychiatry, 32*(3), 501–508.

Borst, S., Noam, G., & Bartok, J. (1991). Adolescent suicidality: A clinical-developmental approach. *Journal of the American Academy of Child and Adolescent Psychiatry, 30*(5), 796–803.

Bradburn, N. M. (1969). *The structure of psychological well-being.* Chicago: Aldine.

Browning, D. (1986). Psychiatric ward behavior and length of stay in adolescent and young adult inpatients: A developmental approach to prediction. *Journal of Consulting and Clinical Psychology, 54*(2), 227–230.

Bruch, H. (1973). *Eating disorders: Obesity, anorexia nervosa and the person within.* New York: Basic Books.

Chiesa, M. (1980). *Ego development and conceptual development systems and their relationship to coping and defense processes in women.* Unpublished doctoral dissertation, Foreham University, Bronx, NY.

Chilton, T. (2001). *The relations among insecure attachment, ego development, and hardiness.* Unpublished doctoral dissertation, Indiana University.

Cicchetti, D. (1984). The emergence of developmental psychopathology. *Child Development, 55*(1), 1–7.

Cicchetti, D. (1990). A historical perspective on the discipline of developmental psychology. In J. Rolf, A. S. Masten, D. Cicchetti, K. H. Nuechterlein, & S. Weintraub (Eds.), *Risk and protective factors in the development of psychopathology* (pp. 29–48). New York: Cambridge University Press.

Cleckley, H. M. (1964). *The mask of sanity.* St. Louis, MO: Mosby.

Colan, N. B. (1988). *Ego development and substance abuse: A study of hospitalized adults.* Unpublished doctoral dissertation, Boston University, Boston, MA.

Colvin, K. (1994). *Mood disorders and symbolic function: An investigation of object relations and ego development in classical musicians.* Unpublished doctoral dissertation. California School of Professional Psychology, San Diego.

Cook-Greuter, S. R. (2000). *Postautonomous ego development: A study of its nature and measurement.* Unpublished doctoral dissertation, Harvard University, Cambridge, MA.

Coopersmith, S. (1967). *The antecedents of self-esteem.* San Francisco: Freeman.

Cramer, P. (1999). Ego functions and ego development: Defense mechanisms and intelligence as predictors of ego level. *Journal of Personality, 67*(5), 735–759.

Davids, A., Kidder, C., & Reich, M. (1962). Time orientation in male and female juvenile delinquents. *Journal of Abnormal and Social Psychology, 64,* 239–240.

De Loach, S. S. (1976). *Level of ego development, degree of psychopathology, and continuation or termination of outpatient psychotherapy involvement.* Unpublished doctoral dissertation, Georgia State University, Atlanta, GA.

Diamond, A. (1997). *Portraits and complexity and simplicity: A study of the integrative complexity of life narratives.* Unpublished doctoral dissertation, Northwestern University, Evanston, IL.

Dichter, J. (1996). *The association between parental marital status, ego development, and level of depression in adolescents.* Unpublished doctoral dissertation, Pace University. New York, NY.

Diener, E., Emmons, R., Larsen, R., & Griffin, S. (1985). The Satisfaction with Life Scale. *Journal of Personality Assessment, 49,* 71–75.

Dill, D., & Noam, G. (1990). Ego development and treatment requests. *Psychiatry, 53,* 85–91.

Dubow, E. F., Huesmann, L. R., & Eron, L. D. (1987). Childhood correlates of adult ego development. *Child Development, 58,* 859–869.

Du Mont, P. (1998). *The effects of early menarche on health risk behaviors.* Unpublished doctoral dissertation, University of Tennessee, Knoxville.

Einstein, D., & Lanning, K. (1998). Shame, guilt, ego development, and the five-factor model of personality. *Journal of Personality, 66*(4), 555–582.

England, R. (1997). *Incest as adult love experience: The role of ego development and attachment.* Unpublished doctoral dissertation, Simon Fraser University, Burnaby, British Columbia, Canada.

Erikson, E. (1968). *Identity, youth, and crisis.* New York: Norton.

Farrell, P. (1990). *Relationship of binge eating, ego development level and anxiety in women age 30 and older.* Unpublished doctoral dissertation, New York University, New York.

Favazza, A. R., DeRosear, L., & Conterio, K. (1989). Self-mutilation and eating disorders. *Suicide and Life-Threatening Behavior, 19,* 352–361.

Feeney, J. A., Noller, P., & Hanrahan, M. (1994). Assessing adult attachment: Developments in the conceptualization of security and insecurity. In M. B. Sperling & W. H. Berman (Eds.), *Attachment in adults: Theory, lifespan developmental and treatment issues.* New York: Guilford.

Fineman, N., Beckwith, L., & Espinosa, M. (1997). Maternal ego development and mother-infant interaction in drug-abusing women. *Journal of Substance Abuse Treatment, 14*(4), 307–317.

Fisher, K. (1991). *Manic episodes, antisocial behavior, and ego development.* Unpublished doctoral dissertation, Pacific Graduate School of Psychology, Palo Alto, CA.

Flesher, S. (1986). *The relationship of ego development to locus-of-control.* Unpublished doctoral dissertation, University of Pittsburgh.

Fordyce, M. (1977). *The happiness measures: A sixty-second index of emotional well-being and mental health.* Manuscript submitted for publication.

Frank, S., & Quinlan, D. (1976). Ego development and female delinquency: A cognitive-developmental approach. *Journal of Abnormal Psychology, 85*(5), 505–510.

Furstenberg, M. (1984). *The meaning of adolscent drug use: A developmental perspective.* Unpublished doctoral dissertation, Harvard University School of Education.

Garmezy, N., & Rutter, M. (1983). *Stress, coping, and development in children.* Stanford: Center for Advanced Study in the Behavioral Sciences.

Genden, S. (1995). Maturity and personality: A study of relationship between developmental maturity, ego defenses, and personality disorders. *Dissertation Abstracts International, 56*(2-B), 1106.

Geurkink, L. (1981). *Manifestations of anxiety at several stages of ego development.* Unpublished doctoral dissertation, University of Maryland, College Park.

Gibson, R. (1967). On the psychology of depression. *Psychiatric Quarterly Supplement, 41*(1), 99–109.

Gleser, G. C., & Ihilevich, D. (1969). An objective instrument for measuring defense mechanisms. *Journal of Consulting and Clinical Psychology, 33,* 51–60.

Gold, S. (1980). Relations between level of ego development and adjustment patterns in adolescents. *Journal of Personality Assessment, 44*(6), 630–638.

Gondolf, E. W. (1987). Changing men who batter: A developmental modal for integrated interventions. *Journal of Family Violence, 2*(4), 335–349.

Gordon, D. A., & Arbuthnot, J. (1987). Individual, group, and family interventions. In H. C. Quay (Ed.), *Handbook of juvenile delinquency* (pp. 290–324). New York: Wiley.

Griffin, M. (1989). *Depression in adolescents: Some cognitive developmental considerations.* Unpublished doctoral dissertation, University of Pittsburgh.

Grotevant, H. (1998). Adolescent development in family contexts. In W. Damon (Editor-in-Chief) & N. Eisenberg (Vol. Ed.), *Handbook of child psychology: Social, emotional, and personality development* (5th ed., Vol. 3, pp. 1097–1149). New York: Wiley.

Guerra, L. (1991). *The impact of parental alcoholism on ego development and affective disorders in offspring.* Unpublished doctoral dissertation, Temple University, Philadelphia, PA.

Gunderson, J. G., & Phillips, K. A. (1991). A current view of the interface between borderline personality disorder and depression. *American Journal of Psychiatry, 148*(8), 967–975.

Gutierrez, C. (1993). *Existential theory, ego development, purpose in life, and death anxiety among older adults.* Unpublished doctoral dissertation, Michigan State University, East Lansing, MI.

Haan, N., Stroud, J., & Holstein, C. (1973). Moral and ego stages in relationship to ego process: A study of "hippies." *Journal of Personality, 41,* 596–612.

Haimes, A. L., & Katz, J. L. (1988). Sexual and social maturity versus social conformity in restricting anorectic, bulimic, and borderline women. *International Journal of Eating Disorders, 7*(3), 331–341.

Hanson, D. (1999). *Stages of ego development and men who physically abuse female spouse/partners.* Unpublished doctoral dissertation, Adler School of Professional Psychology, Vancouver, British Columbia, Canada.

Hare, R. D. (1985). Comparison of procedures for the assessment of psychopathy. *Journal of Consulting and Clinical Psychology, 53*(1), 7–16.

Hart, B., & Hilton, I. (1988). Dimension of personality organization as predictors of the teenage pregnancy risk. *Journal of Personality Assessment, 52,* 116–132.

Harwell, S. (1987). *Ego development, self-concept, anxiety, and role-conflict coping preference styles in reentry and traditional age women students.* Unpublished doctoral dissertation, Vanderbilt University, Nashville, TN.

Hathaway, S. R., & Monachesi, E. D. (1953). *Analyzing and predicting juvenile delinquency with MMPI.* Minneapolis: University of Minnesota Press.

Hathaway, S. R., & Monachesi, E. D. (1961). *An atlas of juvenile MMPI profiles.* Minneapolis: University of Minnesota Press.

Hauser, S. (1976). Loevinger's model and measure of ego development: A critical review. *Psychological Bulletin, 83*(5), 928–955.

Hauser, S. (1991). *Adolescents and their families: Paths of ego development.* New York: Free Press.

Hauser, S. (1993). Loevinger's model and measure of ego development: A critical review II. *Psychological Inquiry, 4*(1), 23–30.

Hauser, S., DiPlacido, J., Jacobson, A., Willett, J., & Cole, C. (1993). Family coping with an adolescent's chronic illness: An approach and three studies. *Journal of Adolescence, 16,* 305–329.

Hauser, S., Houlihan, J., Powers, S. I., Jacobson, A. M., Noam, G., Weiss-Perry, B., et al. (1987). Interaction sequences in families of psychiatrlcally hospitalized and non-patient adolescents. *Psychiatry, 50,* 308–319.

Hauser, S. T., Jacobson, A. M., Milley, J., Wertlieb, D., Hershowitz, R., Wolfsdorf, J., et al. (1992). Ego trajectories and adjustment to diabetes: Longitudinal studies of diabetic and acutely ill patients. In L. Feagens, W. Ray, & E. Susman (Eds.), *Emotion and cognition in child and adolescent health and development.* Hillsdale, NJ: Erlbaum.

Hauser, S., Powers, S., Noam, G., Jacobson, A., Weiss, B., & Follansbee, D. (1984). Familial contexts of adolescent ego development. *Child Development, 55,* 195–213.

Hawley, J. (1995). *Clinical assessment of the developing relational self.* Unpublished doctoral dissertation, Adler School of Professional Psychology, Vancouver, British Columbia, Canada.

Hawton, K. (1986). *Suicide and attempted suicide among children and adolescents.* Beverly Hills, CA: Sage Publications.

Hayes, S. C., & Walker, W. L. (1986). Intellectual and moral development in offenders: A review. *Australian and New Zealand Journal of Criminology, 19,* 53–64.

Hazan, C., & Shaver, P. R. (1987). Romantic love conceptualized as an attachment process. *Journal of Personality and Social Psychology, 52,* 511–524.

Heatherton, T. F., & Baumeister, R. F. (1991). Binge eating as escape from self-awareness. *Psychological Bulletin, 110,* 86–108.

Helson, R., & Srivastava, S. (2001). Three paths of adult development: Conservers, seekers, and achievers. *Journal of Personality and Social Psychology, 80*(6), 995–1010.

Helson, R., & Wink, P. (1987). Two conceptions of maturity examined in the findings of a longitudinal study. *Journal of Personality and Social Psychology, 39,* 909–920.

Hewitt, L. E., & Jenkins, R. L. (1946). *Fundamental patterns of maladjustment; the dynamics of their origin: A statistical analysis based upon five hundred case records of children examined at the Michigan Child Guidance Institute.* Springfield, IL.

Hezel, J. D. (1968). *Some personality correlates of dimensions of delinquency.* Unpublished doctoral dissertation, St. Louis University, St. Louis, MO.

Hickok, L. (1996). *Sex-differences in adolescent psychopathology: The mediating role of anxiety and defense.* Unpublished doctoral dissertation, George Washington University, Washington, DC.

Hilmo, J. A. (1978). *Level of ego development and preference for two different therapy orientations.* Unpublished doctoral dissertation, Purdue University, West Lafayette, IN.

Hiraga, Y. (1996). *Parent-adolescent interactions and ego and moral development within African American families.* Unpublished doctoral dissertation, University of Washington, Seattle, WA.

Hoar, C. H. (1983). Women alcoholics: Are they different from other women? *International Journal of the Addictions, 18*(2), 251–270.

Holt, R. R. (1989). *Freud reappraised: A frest look at psychoanalytic theory.* New York: Guilford Press.

Holt, R. R. (1998). Loevinger's conception of ego development and general systems theory. In P. M. Westenberg, A. Blasi, & L. D. Cohn (Eds.), *Personality development: Theoretical, empirical, and clinical investigations of Loevinger's conception of ego development* (pp. 71–86). Mahwah, NJ: Lawrence Erlbaum.

Hoppe, C. F., & Loevinger, J. (1977). Ego development and conformity: A construct validity study of the Washington University Sentence Completion Test. *Journal of Personality Assessment, 41,* 497–504.

Horton, H. (2001). *The role of ego development in bulimia nervosa and borderline personality disorder.* Unpublished doctoral dissertation, Kent State University, Kent, OH.

Ihilevich, D., & Gleser, G. C. (1971). Relationship of defense mechanism to field-dependence-independence. *Journal of Abnormal Psychology, 77,* 296–302.

Ihilevich, D., & Gleser, G. C. (1986). *Defense mechanisms: their classification, correlates, and measurement with the defense mechanisms inventory.* Owosso, MI: DMI Associates.

Imperio, A. M. (1975). *Ego development, father status, and perception of parents in psychopathic, neurotic, and subcultural delinquents.* Unpublished doctoral dissertation, Fordham University, Bronx, New York, NY.

Isberg, R., Hauser, S., Jacobson, A., Powers, S., Noam, G., Weiss-Perry, B., et al. (1989). Parental contexts of adolescent self-esteem: A developmental perspective. *Journal of Youth and Adolescence, 18*(1), 1–22.

Jennings, W. S., Kilkenny, R., & Kohlberg, L. (1983). Moral-development theory and practice for youthful and adult offenders. In W. S. Laufer (Ed.), *Personality, theory, moral education* (pp. 281–355). Lexington, MA: Lexington Books.

Johnson, R. A. (1983). Ego deficits in the personality of the alcoholic. *Psychiatric Hospital, 15*(1), 37–40.

Kazdin, A. (1989). Developmental psychopathology. *American Psychologist, 44*(2), 180–187.

Kennedy, D. (1994). *Ego development, gender identity development, and eating disorder symptomatology in two matched cohorts: College-aged daughters and their middle-aged mothers.* Unpublished doctoral dissertation, Simmons College, Boston, MA.

Khantzian, E. J. (1974). Opiate addiction: A critique of theory and some implications for treatment. *American Journal of Psychotherapy, 28,* 59–70.

King, L., Scollon, C., Ramsey, C., & Williams, T. (2000). Stories of life transition: Subjective well-being and ego development in parents of children with Down Syndrome. *Journal of Research in Personality, 34*(4), 509–536.

Korzekwa, M., & Links, P., Steiner, M. (1993). Biological markers in borderline personality disorder: New perspectives. *Canadian Journal of Psychiatry, 38*(Suppl. 1), S11–S15.

Kurland, A., Turek, I., Brown, C., & Wagman, A. (1976). Electroconvulsive therapy and EEG correlates in depressive disorders. *Comprehensive Psychiatry, 17*(5), 581–589.

Kutcher, J. (1989). *Incest survivors, incest survivors with eating disorder, and other individuals with eating disorder: The ability to cope with, adapt to, and influence their adult lives.* Unpublished doctoral dissertation, Peabody College for Teachers of Vanderbilt University, Nashville, TN.

Labouvie-Vief, G., Hakim-Larson, J., deVoe, M., & Schoeberlein, S. (1989). Emotions and self-regulation: A life-span view. *Human Development, 32,* 279–299.

Laird, H. (2000). *Ego development and decision-making in pregnant adolescents.* Unpublished doctoral dissertation, University of Houston, TX.

Lambert, H. V. (1972). *A comparison of Jane Loevinger's theory of ego development and Lawrence Kohlberg's theory of moral development.* Unpublished doctoral dissertation, University of Houston, TX.

Leong, H. (2000). *Loevinger's conceptualization of ego development in relation to psychopathology and personality characteristics in an adolescent clinical population.* Unpublished doctoral dissertation, Pace University, Philadelphia, PA.

Levit, D. (1989). *A developmental study of ego defenses in adolescence.* Boston: Boston University Press.

Loevinger, J. (1968). The relation of adjustment to ego development. In S. B. Sells (Ed.), *The definition and measurement of mental health* (pp. 162–180). U.S. Department of Health, Education, and Welfare Public Health Service.

Loevinger, J. (1976). *Ego development.* San Francisco: Jossey-Bass.

Loevinger, J. (1979). *Scientific ways in the study of ego development.* Worcester, MA: Clark University Press.

Loevinger, J. (1980). Some thoughts on ego development and counseling. *Personnel and Guidance Journal [Special Issue: Counseling and the Behavioral Sciences], 58*(5), 389–390.

Loevinger, J. (1986). On Kohlberg's contributions to ego development. In S. Modgil & C. Modgil (Eds.), *Lawrence Kohlberg: Consensus and controversy* (pp. 163–181). London: Falmer Press.

Loevinger, J. (1991). Personality structure and the trait-situation controversy: On the uses of low correlations. In W. M. Grove & D. Cicchetti (Eds.), *Thinking clearly about psychology: Personality and psychopathology* (pp. 36–53). Minneapolis: University of Minnesota Press.

Loevinger, J. (1993). Measurement of personality: True or false. *Psychological Inquiry, 4*(1), 1–16.

Loevinger, J., & Hy, L. H. (1996). *Measuring ego development.* Mahwah, NJ; Lawrence Erlbaum.

Loevinger, J., & Wessler, R. (1970). *Measuring ego development.* San Francisco: Jossey-Bass.

Loiacono, J. (1995). *The relationship between level of ego development and substance abuse and the impact of rehabilitation.* Unpublished doctoral dissertation. Pace University, New York, NY.

Lucas, R. H. (1971). *Validation of the test of ego development by means of standardized interview.* Unpublished doctoral dissertation, Washington University, St. Louis, MO.

Luce, C. (1983). *Ego development, identity status, and locus-of-control among women with eating disorders.* Unpublished doctoral dissertation, University of Pittsburgh.

Luthar, S., Doyle, K., Suchman, N., & Mayers, L. (2001). Developmental themes in women's emotional experience of motherhood. *Development and Psychopathology, 13,* 165–182.

Luthar, S., & Quinlan, D. (1993). Parental images in two cultures: A study of women in India and America. *Journal of Cross-Cultural Psychology, 24*(2), 186–202.

Magee, H. (1984). *The relation of level of ego development to DSM-III diagnosis of antisocial personality disorder.* Unpublished doctoral dissertation, Vanderbilt University, Nashville, TN.

Manners, J., & Durkin, K. (2001). A critical review of the validity of ego development theory and its measurement. *Journal of Personality Assessment, 77*(3), 541–567.

Marziali, E., Field, N., Classen, C., & Oleniuk, J. (1993). The assessment of ego development in borderline personality disorders. *Canadian Journal of Psychiatry, 38*(Suppl. 1), S23–S27.

McCord, W., & McCord, J. (1956). *Psychopathy and delinquency.* New York: Grune & Stratton.

McCrae, R. R., & Costa, P. T. (1980). Openness to experience and ego development level in Loevinger's sentence completion test: Dispositional contributions to the developmental model of personality. *Journal of Personality and Social Psychology, 39,* 1179–1190.

McLauchlin, C. (1997). *Toward an integrated model of internalized representations of self and other: An examination of personality type, adult attachment category, and level of ego development.* Unpublished doctoral dissertation, Georgia State University, Atlanta, GA.

Menicucci, L. (1983). *Family characteristics of drug abusers.* Unpublished doctoral dissertation, California School of Professional Psychology, Berkeley/Alameda.

Millon, T. (1983). *The Millon Clinical Multiaxial Inventory manual* (3rd ed.). Minneapolis, MN: National Computer Systems.

Millon, T. (1994). *Manual for the MCMI-III* (3rd ed.). Minneapolis, MN: National Computer Systems.

Moffitt, T. (1993). Adolescence-limited and life-course-persistent antisocial behavior: A developmental taxonomy. *Psychological Review, 100*(4), 647–701.

Moore, M. (1984). *Death perspectives, death anxiety, and death acceptance as a function of ego development in mid-life women.* Unpublished doctoral dissertation, California School of Professional Psychology, Los Angeles.

Noam, G. (1984). *Self, morality, and biography: Studies in clinical developmental psychopathology.* Unpublished doctoral dissertation, Harvard University, School of Education.

Noam, G. (1988). A constructivist approach to developmental psychopathology. In E. Nannis & P. Cowan (Eds.), *Developmental psychopathology and its treatment* (pp. 91–121). San Francisco: Jossey Bass.

Noam, G. (1993). Ego development: True or false? *Psychological Inquiry, 4*(1), 43–49.

Noam, G. (1998). Solving ego development: Mental health riddle. In P. M. Westenberg, A. Blasi, & L. D. Cohn (Eds.), *Personality development: Theoretical, empirical, and clinical investigations of Loevinger's conception of ego development* (pp. 271–295). Mahwah, NJ: Lawrence Erlbaum.

Noam, G., Hauser, S., Santostefano, S., Garrison, W., Jacobson, A., Powers, S., et al. (1984). Ego development and psychopathology: A study of hospitalized adolescents. *Child Development, 55,* 184–194.

Noam, G., & Houlihan, J. (1990). Developmental dimensions of DSM-III diagnoses in adolescent psychiatric patients. *American Journal of Orthopsychiatry, 60*(3), 371–378.

Noam, G., Paget, K., Valiant, G., Borst, S., & Bartok, J. (1994). Conduct and affective disorders in developmental perspective: A systematic study of adolescent psychopathology. *Development and Psychopathology, 6,* 519–532.

Noam, G., Recklitis, C., & Paget, K. (1991). Pathways of ego development: Contributions to maladaptation and adjustment. *Development and Psychopathology, 3,* 311–328.

Novy, D. M. (1990). *An investigation of the validity of Loevinger's model and measure of ego development.* Unpublished doctoral dissertation, University of Houston, Houston, TX.

Novy, D. M. (1993). An investigation of the progressive sequence of ego development levels. *Journal of Clinical Psychology, 49,* 332–338.

Novy, D. M., & Francis, D. J. (1992). Psychometric properties of the Washington sentence completion test. *Educational and Psychological Measurement, 52,* 1029–1039.

Parker, G., Tupling, H., & Brown, L. B. (1979). A Parental Bonding Instrument. *British Journal of Medical Psychology, 52,* 1–10.

Patton, C. J. (1992). Fear of abandonment and binge eating: A subliminal psychodynamic activation investigation. *Journal of Nervous and Mental Disease, 180,* 484–490.

Piaget, J. (1965). *The moral judgment of the child.* New York: Free Press.

Piaget, J. (1977). *The essential Piaget.* New York: Basic Books.

Piaget, J. (1978). *Success and understanding.* Cambridge, MA: Harvard University Press.

Picano, J. J. (1984). *Ego development and adaptation in middle aged women (Maturity, Coping, Adjustment).* Unpublished doctoral dissertation. California School of Professional Psychology, Berkeley/Alameda.

Pingalore, M. (1982). *The relationship between the preferred drug of abuse and the ego development of the abuser.* Unpublished doctoral dissertation, Boston College.

Pratt, M. W., Diessner, R., Hunsberger, B., & Panser, S. A. (1991). Four pathways in the analysis of adult development and aging: Comparing analyses and reasoning about personal life dilemmas. *Psychology and Aging, 6*(4), 666–675.

Pyle, R. L., Mitchell, J. E., & Eckert, E. D. (1981). Bulimia: A report of 34 cases. *Journal of Clinical Psychiatry, 42,* 60–64.

Quay, H. (Ed.). (1965). *Juvenile delinquency: Research and theory.* Princeton, NJ: Van Nostrand.

Quay, H., & Blumen, L. (1963). Dimensions of delinquent behavior. *Journal of Social Psychology, 61,* 273–277.

Quay, H., & Parsons, L. B. (1971). *The differential behavioral classification of the juvenile offender* (2nd ed.). Washington, DC: Bureau of Prisons, U.S. Department of Justice.

Rado, S. (1957). Narcotic bondage: A general theory of the dependence on narcotic drugs. *American Journal of Psychiatry, 114,* 165–171.

Ratcliff, D. E. (1985). Ministering to the retarded. *Christian Educational Journal, 6,* 24–30.

Raygan, L. (1991). *Social anxiety as a function of gender, ego development, and sociability.* Unpublished doctoral dissertation, Auburn University, Auburn, AL.

Recklitis, C. (1993). *Aggressive behavior in the adolescent psychiatric patient as a function of ego development and ego defenses.* Unpublished doctoral dissertation, Boston University.

Redmore, C. (1976). Susceptibility to faking of a sentence completion test of ego development. *Journal of Personality Assessment, 40,* 607–616.

Redmore, C., & Loevinger, J. (1979). Ego development in adolescence: Longitudinal studies. *Journal of Youth and Adolescence, 8,* 1–20.

Redmore, C., & Waldman, K. (1975). Reliability of sentence completion measure of ego development. *Journal of Personality Assessment, 39,* 236–242.

Reinhard, H. G. (1990). Décalage in moral judgment as a measure of denaturalization weakness of schizophrenic adolescents. *Acta Paedopsychiatrica, 53,* 38–145.

Richards, M. H., Gitelson, I. B., Peterson, A. C., & Hurtig, A. L. (1991). Adolescent personality in girls and boys: The role of mothers and fathers. *Psychology of Women Quarterly, 15,* 65–81.

Rierdan, J., & Koff, E. (1993). Developmental variables in relation to depressive symptoms in adolescent girls. *Development and Psychopathology, 5,* 485–496.

Robins, L. N. (1966). *Deviant children grown up*. Baltimore: Williams & Wilkins.

Rogers, C. P. (1980). *An examination of the relationship between ego development and self-esteem*. University of Minnesota, Minneapolis, MN.

Root, M. P., & Fallon, P. (1989). Treating the victimized bulimic. *Journal of Interpersonal Violence, 4*, 90–100.

Rosen, H. (1977). *Pathway to Piaget: A guide for clinicians, educators, and developmentalists*. Cherry Hill, NJ: Postgraduate International.

Rosenberg, M. (1979). *Conceiving of the self*. New York: Basic Books.

Ross, M. (2001). *Annealed by death: Ego strength and self-congruency following adolescent loss of a parent*. Unpublished doctoral dissertation, Simon Fraser University, Burnaby, British Columbia, Canada.

Rounsaville, B. J., Weissman, M. M., Kleber, H. D., & Wilber, C. H. (1982). Heterogeneity of psychiatric disorders in treated opiate addicts. *Archives of General Psychiatry, 39*, 161–166.

Rozsnafszky, J. (1981). The relationship of level of ego development to Q-sort personality ratings. *Journal of Personality and Social Psychology, 41*(1), 99–120.

Rutter, M. (1988). Epidemiological approaches to developmental psychopathology. *Archives of General Psychiatry, 45*, 486–495.

Ryf, S. (1996). *The association between adolescent ego development and self-reported psychological symptoms and behaviors*. Unpublished doctoral dissertation, Pace University, New York, NY.

Ryff, C. D. (1989). Happiness is everything, or is it? Exploration on the meaning of psychological well-being. *Journal of Personality and Social Psychology, 57*, 1069–1081.

Salter, A. C., Richardson, C. M., & Martin, P. A. (1985). Treating abusive parents. *Child Welfare, 64*(4), 327–341.

Santina, M. (1998). *Object relations, ego development, and affect regulation in severely addicted substance abusers*. Unpublished doctoral dissertation, Columbia University, New York, NY.

Schaffer, S. L. (1983). *The relationship between ego development, self-esteem, and sex-role identity in college-age men*. Unpublished doctoral dissertation, Florida Institute of Technology, Melbourne, FL.

Schneider, P. (1996). *The immaturity scale of MMPI-A: An empirical study of its relationship to Loevinger's model of ego development, clinical utility, and correlation with external variables*. Unpublished doctoral dissertation, Pace University, New York, NY.

Schoeberlein, S. (1997). *Ego development and psychological variables among a matched sample of homeless and housed adolescents*. Unpublished doctoral dissertation, Wayne State University, Detroit, MI.

Schuessler, D. (2000). *Love and work in young adult men and women: The relationship among intimacy, mutuality, occupational choice, depression, and ego development*. Unpublished doctoral dissertation, Columbia University, New York, NY.

Scott, E. M. (1980). Narcissism and alcoholism: Theoretical opinions and some clinical examples. *Psychotherapy: Theory, Research and Practice, 20*(1), 17, 110–113.

Shaffer, D., & Fisher, P. (1981). The epidemiology of suicide in children and adolescents. *Journal of the American Academy of Child and Adolescent Psychiatry, 20*, 545–565.

Shainbart, S. (1995). *Ego development and treatments in residential facility for emotionally disturbed adolescents*. Unpublished doctoral dissertation, Fordham University, Bronx, New York, NY.

Slugoski, B., Marcia, J., & Koopman, R. (1984). Cognitive and social interactional characteristics of ego identity statuses in college males. *Journal of Personality & Social Psychology, 47*(3), 646–661.

Smetana, J. G. (1990). Morality and conduct disorders. In M. Lewis & S. M. Miller (Eds.), *Handbook of developmental psychopathology* (pp. 157–179). New York: Plenum Press.

Smith, T. E., Burkey, N. A., Nawn, J., & Reif, M. C. (1991). A comparison of demographic, behavioral, and ego function data in borderline and eating disorder patients. *Psychiatric Quarterly, 62*, 19–33.

Snarey, J., & Lydens, L. (1990). Worker quality and adult development: The kibbutz as a developmental model. *Psychology and Aging, 5*, 86–93.

Snodgrass, K. (1993). *The relationship of ego development, defense style, and moral maturity to depression in adolescents*. Unpublished doctoral dissertation, University of Texas Southwestern Medical Center, Dallas.

Speicker, B. (1988). Psychopathy: The incapacity to have moral emotions. *Journal of Moral Education, 17*(2), 98–104.

Sperry, L. (1975, January). A hierarchy for clinical interpretation. *The Individual Psychologist, 13* 19–24.

Spielberger C. D. (1983). *Manual for the State-Trait Anxiety Inventory (STAI)*. Palo Alto, CA: Consulting Psychologists Press.

Sroufe, L. A., & Rutter, M. (1984). The domain of developmental psychopathology. *Child Development, 55*, 17–29.

Stierlin, H. (1974). *Separating parents and adolescents. A perspective on running away, Schizophrenia and waywardness*. New York: Quadrangle.

Strauss, J., & Ryan, R. M. (1988). Cognitive dysfunction in eating disorders. *International Journal of Eating Disorders, 7*(1), 19–27.

Suedfeld, P., & Tetlock, P. E. (1977). Integrative complexity of communications in international crises. *Journal of Conflict Resolution, 21*(1), 169–184.

Sullivan, E. V., McCullough, G., & Stager, M. (1970). A developmental study of the relationship between conceptual, ego, and moral development. *Child Development, 41*, 399–411.

Sutton, P. M., & Swensen, C. H. (1983). The reliability and concurrent validity of alternative methods of assessing ego development. *Journal of Personality Assessment, 47*, 468–475.

Swensen, C. H. (1980). Ego development and a general model for counseling and psychotherapy [Special issue: Counseling and the Behavioral Sciences]. *Personnel and Guidance Journal, 58*(5), 382–388.

Swett, C., Jr. (1985). Antecedents of locked seclusion-state and trait variables in relation to violent acts. *McLean Hospital Journal, 10*(2), 59–67.

Swift, W. J., Camp, B. W., Bushnell, N. J., & Bargman, G. J. (1984). Ego development in anorexia inpatients. *International Journal of Eating Disorders, 3*(3), 73–80.

Taylor, L. S. (1983). Aspects of ego development in the serious juvenile offender: Diagnostic considerations and treatment implications. *Corrective and Social Psychiatry and Journal of Behavior Technology Methods, 29*(2), 44–55.

Templer, D. (1969). Death Anxiety Scale. *Proceedings of the Annual Convention of the American Psychological Association, 4*(2), 737–738.

Teusch, R. (1988). Level of ego development and bulimics' conceptualizations of their disorder. *International Journal of Eating Disorders, 7*(5), 607–615.

Vaillant, G. E. (1971). Theoretical hierarchy of adaptive ego mechanisms: A 30-year follow-up of 30 men selected for psychological health. *Archives of General Psychiatry, 24*, 107–118.

Vaillant, G. E. (1993). *The wisdom of the ego*. Cambridge, MA: Harvard University Press.

Vaillant, G. E. (2000). Adaptive mental mechanisms: Their role in a positive psychology. *American Psychologist, 55*(19), 89–98.

Van Ormer, E. (2001). *Developmental status as a predictor of outcomes in a vocational rehabilitation program*. Unpublished doctoral dissertation, Boston College.

Van Reekum, R. (1993). Acquired and developmental brain dysfunction in borderline personality disorder. *Canadian Journal of Psychiatry, 38*(Suppl. 1), S4–S10.

Vincent, K., & Castillo, I. (1984). Ego development and DSM-III Axis II: Personality disorders. *Journal of Clinical Psychology, 40*(2), 400–402.

Vincent, L., & Vincent, K. (1979). Ego development and psychopathology. *Psychological Reports, 44,* 408–410.

Von der Lippe, A. (2000). Family factors in the ego development of adolescent girls. *Journal of Youth and Adolescence, 29*(3), 373–393.

Von der Lippe, A., & Moller, I. (2000). Negotiation of conflict, communication patterns, and ego development in the family of adolescent daughters. *International Journal of Behavioral Development, 24*(1), 59–67.

Waller, G., & Meyer, C. (1997). Cognitive avoidance of threat cues: Association with Eating Disorder Inventory scores among a non-eating-disordered population. *International Journal of Eating Disorders, 22,* 299–308.

Waugh, M. (1981). Reliability of the sentence completion test of ego development in a clinical population. *Journal of Personality Assessment, 45,* 485–487.

Waugh, M., & McCaulley, M. (1981). Relation of level of ego development to type and severity of psychopathology. *Journal of Consulting and Clinical Psychology, 49*(2), 295–296.

Weiss, D. S., Zilberg, W. J., & Genevro, J. L. (1989). Psychometric properties of Loevinger's sentence completion test in an adult psychiatric outpatient sample. *Journal of Personality Assessment, 53*(3), 478–486.

Weiss, L., Katzman, M., & Wolchik, S. (1985). *Treating bulimia: A psychoeducational approach.* New York: Pergamon.

Wenar, C. (1982). Developmental psychology: Its nature and models. *Journal of Clinical Child Psychology, 11*(3), 192–201.

West, M., Keller, A., Links, P., & Patrick, J. (1993). Borderline disorder and attachment pathology. *Canadian Journal of Psychiatry, 38*(Suppl. 1), S16–S22.

Westenberg, P. M., & Block, J. (1993). Ego development and individual differences in personality. *Journal of Personality and Social Psychology, 65,* 792–800.

Westenberg, P. M., & Gjerde, P. F. (1999). Ego development during the transition from adolescence to young adulthood: A 9-year longitudinal study. *Journal of Research in Personality, 33,* 233–252.

Westenberg, P. M., Siebelink, B. M., Warmenhoven, N., & Treffers, P. (1999). Separation anxiety and overanxious disorders: Relations to age and level of psychosocial maturity. *Journal of American Academy of Child and Adolescent Psychiatry, 38*(8), 1000–1007.

Wheeler, R. (1994). *Ego development, self-discrepancy, and vulnerability to emotional distress.* Unpublished doctoral dissertation. University of Wisconsin at Madison.

Wilber, C. H., Rounsaville, B. J., Sugarman, A., Casey, J. B., & Kleber, H. D. (1982). Ego development in opiate addicts. *Journal of Nervous and Mental Disease, 170*(4), 202–208.

Win, J. (2001). *Factors that contribute to the utilization of social support in adolescence.* Unpublished doctoral dissertation, Fielding Institute, Santa Barbara, CA.

Woodruff, R. A., Jr., Goodwin, D. W., & Guze, S. B. (1974). *Psychiatric diagnosis.* New York: Oxford University Press.

Wright, T., & Reise, S. (1997). Personality and unrestricted sexual behavior: Correlations of sociosexuality in Caucasian and Asian college students. *Journal of Research in Personality, 31,* 166–192.

Young, A. (1998). *Psychological maturity in women during later adulthood: Ego development and adjustment.* Unpublished doctoral dissertation, University of Michigan, Ann Arbor, MI.

Young-Eisendrath, P. (1982). Ego development: Inferring the client's frame of reference. *Social Casework, 63*(6), 323–332.

Youngren, V. (1993). Ego development, aggressiveness, and self-destructiveness after abuse: A two-year follow-up study of hospitalized adolescents. Unpublished doctoral dissertation, Boston College.

CHAPTER 20

The Significance of Autonomy and Autonomy Support in Psychological Development and Psychopathology

RICHARD M. RYAN, EDWARD L. DECI, WENDY S. GROLNICK, and JENNIFER G. LA GUARDIA

Concepts related to autonomy figure prominently in organismic and dynamic theories of development and psychopathology. Classical developmental theories, for example, have considered the movement toward greater autonomy and self-initiation to be a hallmark of healthy development (e.g., Hartmann, 1947/1964; Jahoda, 1958; Loevinger, 1976; Piaget, 1981; Werner, 1948). An important theme in the literature on parenting and social development also concerns the promotion of autonomy and self-regulation, as well as the negative impact of controlling parenting environments that thwart autonomy (e.g., Baumrind, 1971; Grusec & Goodnow, 1994). In a similar vein, the literature on psychopathology includes frequent mention of autonomy disturbances (e.g., Bruch, 1973; Shapiro, 1965; Winnicott,

1960/1965), and the obstruction of children's autonomy has been implicated in the onset of many psychopathologies (e.g., McCullough & Maltsberger, 1995; A. Miller, 1981).

At the same time, the concept of autonomy is one of the most controversial theoretical constructs in the literatures of development, socialization, and well-being (Deci & Ryan, 2000; Ryan & Deci, 2003). Some theorists define autonomy as freedom from all environmental influences, a nonsensical concept (Bandura, 1989), whereas others view it as a critically important developmental issue (Zimmer-Gembeck & Collins, 2003). Some view autonomy in terms of breaking emotional bonds with caregivers and becoming "individuated" (e.g., Blos, 1979; L. Steinberg & Silverberg, 1986); they are opposed by theorists who see autonomy and connectedness with significant others not only as compatible but as inherently interdependent (Ryan & Lynch, 1989). Some writers view autonomy as a Western concept, pertinent only to societies that place a high value on individualism and self-direction (Markus, Kitayama, & Heiman, 1996; Oishi, 2000), and others postulate that autonomy is a deeply evolved (Waller, 1998) and therefore universally significant human capacity (Chirkov, Ryan, Kim, & Kaplan, 2003; Kagitçibasi, 1996). Still others have construed autonomy as a masculine attribute that does not address the significance of relatedness and connectedness that is central to women's development (e.g., Gilligan, 1982; Jordon, 1991), but they are opposed by a growing number of feminist and relational perspectives (e.g., Friedman, 2003; Lerner, 1988; Mackenzie & Stoljar, 2000) and by empirical evidence (Deci, La Guardia, Moller, Scheiner, & Ryan, 2004; Ryan & Deci, 2003) supporting the importance of autonomy for women as well as for men.

What such controversies point to is not only the potential significance of autonomy as a psychological construct, but also the need for conceptual clarifications that can address these debates as well as connect with the empirical evidence. Only through such means do semantically based clashes become resolved, conflicting hypotheses highlighted, and practical theory advanced. Thus, although the concept of autonomy is invoked in many theories, relatively few writers have explicated its specific meaning, its developmental, experiential, motivational, and cultural facets, its role in psychopathology and mental health, and the influences of social contexts on which it is dependent.

In this chapter, in keeping with the spirit of the field of developmental psychopathology, our interest is in examining both the developmental underpinnings of healthy autonomy and the processes involved in its disruption and manifestation as pathology (Cicchetti & Tucker, 1994). It is in critically examining this interface between normal and impaired development that the nature of autonomy is most fully revealed. We set forth a definition of autonomy that is informed by both philosophical and clinical analyses and that differentiates autonomy from closely related constructs such as free will, independence, individualism, and detachment. We then explore how autonomy is intertwined with the developmental processes of intrinsic motivation, internalization, attachment, and emotional integration, paying particular attention to how conditions in the social context either support the motivational and emotional bases of normal development or, alternatively, undermine these bases, leading to psychopathology. Fi-

nally, we discuss the experience and dynamics of autonomy with regard to varied psychological disorders, which we view as both outcomes of nonoptimal developmental antecedents and risk factors for continuing difficulties in self-regulation.

AUTONOMY: WHAT IT IS

Etymologically, the term autonomy refers to "self-rule," and indeed we apply the term to actions that are initiated and regulated by the *self*. Autonomous behaviors are those that a person willingly endorses. The opposite of autonomy as we employ the term is heteronomy, which is rule by forces that are experienced as alien to the self. When persons act autonomously, they feel "wholehearted," "together," and "ownership of their actions," all common expressions that convey the characteristic sense of integrity and volition essential to autonomy. Moreover, autonomous behaviors are experienced as fully self-endorsed because they are informed by and reflective of abiding needs and values, and they fit the actual circumstances to the best of the person's knowledge. In this regard, autonomy is therefore often thought of as behavioral regulation that is reflective (Dworkin, 1988; Frankfurt, 1971), mindful (Brown & Ryan, 2003), and integrative (Friedman, 2003; Ryan, 1993; Shapiro, 1981).

Although this definition of autonomy is fundamentally phenomenological, it is also clear that autonomous regulation has a functional side: When acting autonomously, the organism is undivided and fully functioning in the direction of its endorsed aims or goals. As we shall see, this functional quality is manifest in differential outcomes obtained when people act from autonomy versus from compliance, controlling rewards, or coercion. When autonomous people act more persistently toward their aims, they also have a more positive experience and an enhanced sense of self in the process.

The concept of autonomy relates to the distinctions between self-regulation and self-control and between volition and intention. It is clear that whereas all organized actions entail intention, not all intentional behaviors are autonomous. Moreover, although autonomous behavior is directed, it has a quality of openness and flexibility, rather than the rigid doggedness of self-control. Finally, although some theorists have equated autonomy with independence, persons can often be volitionally dependent and/or autonomously connected with others in their aims. Thus, autonomy concerns less whether or not one relies on or cares for others, and more on whether reliance or caring is self-endorsed (Ryan, La Guardia, Solky-Butzel, Chirkov, & Kim, 2005).

Although the concept of autonomy refers, therefore, to regulation by the self, it should be clear that autonomy is always a relative concept in that actions can be more or less characterized by autonomy. Moreover, because both the self and the social demands and tasks that beset it develop, autonomy has to be understood in a developmental perspective. This includes considering not only the changing capacities and experiences of individuals over the life course, but also the actions that they are called on to regulate in social contexts (Ryan, Deci, & Grolnick, 1995).

Autonomy is defined here in terms of its phenomenology; later, we discuss in more detail its functional attributes and correlates. However, it is basic to our view that autonomy is a quality of regulation, characterized by an open processing of possibilities and a matching of these with sensibilities, needs, and known constraints. Obviously, this high quality and depth of processing depends on quite complex neurocircuitry, whose topography differs from that of more controlled motivational processes (Ryan, Kuhl, & Deci, 1997). In general terms, autonomy depends on coordination between prefrontal cortical regions and subcortical striatal-thalamic areas that promote or inhibit motivation, as well as inputs from the hippocampus and amygdala that can provide contextual and affective information (e.g., Bradley, 2000; Chambers, Taylor, & Potenza, 2003). In psychological terms, executive functions must be both selective and fully "informed" by affective and memory-related processes to support autonomy. Interference or damage in the development or functioning of prefrontal areas and connections with limbic structures produces strong vulnerabilities to autonomy disturbances, especially insofar as these entail affective processing (e.g., Bechara, Tranel, Damasio, & Damasio, 1996).

Although the neuropsychology of autonomy is not a central focus of this chapter or of self-determination theory as a motivational theory, there are several points to highlight. First, as we understand more and more about the brain's activity during motivated action, we believe that the differentiations we make on functional grounds between different types of motivation will be manifest in distinct patterns of activation in neurocircuitries. Second, it is clear that just as the integrity of the brain impacts the quality of psychological and behavioral regulation, reciprocally, the social contextual experiences with which we mainly concern ourselves herein shape and often entrain that underlying phys-

iology, a tenet central to developmental psychopathology (Cicchetti & Tucker, 1994; Panksepp, 1998). Finally, autonomy, which is often naïvely dismissed as a "ghost in the machine," is anything but. It is instead a distinct way of regulating activity and experience. At the same time, we believe that even as we connect neurology with psychology, this does not in any way threaten to reduce psychology to biology. Instead, we will continue to find that the regnant causes of behavior remain largely at the cultural, social, and psychological levels of analysis, where much of the "casual" determination of human behavior will always lie (Ryan & Deci, 2004).

Having provided a preliminary definition of autonomy as we employ it, it is important to remember that not all authors who use the term are referring to the same thing (Hmel & Pincus, 2002; Ryan, 1993). In the following sections, we discuss various interpretations of the concept of autonomy that are compatible with our current usage. Then, to further clarify our definition, we contrast it with interpretations of the concept that are not compatible with ours.

Autonomy as Internal Perceived Locus of Causality

Numerous psychological theories, largely in philosophical (Mackenzie & Stoljar, 2000), psychodynamic (Shapiro, 1981), and humanistic (W. R. Miller & Rollnick, 2002) traditions, consider the concept of autonomy to be highly important, whether treated in terms of agency, congruence, self-regulation, authenticity, will, or operating from one's "true self." Different theories have used varied terminologies and have addressed somewhat different issues, yet a shared idea, which we term autonomy, is woven through these various conceptions. Because these theories have been based primarily on clinical practice and experiential discoveries and because the concept reflects a quality of regulation rather than a specific set of behaviors, the concept of autonomy has been slow in making inroads into empirical psychology.

Our own conceptualization of autonomy, which is one aspect of a more general theory of human motivation, basic needs, and development that we refer to as self-determination theory (SDT; see Deci & Ryan, 2000; Grolnick, 2002; Ryan & Deci, 2000c; Ryan & La Guardia, 1999), is itself empirically based. Although we draw from dynamic and humanistic conceptions, the empirical emphasis and approach of SDT has its foundations in the "commonsense language" of attributions proposed by Heider (1958) and extended by deCharms (1968). We use their formulations as a starting point for investigations that have shed new light on issues judged important by many theorists—issues such as authenticity, internalization, volition, and the true self—and that relate such issues to normal versus psychopathological development and to clinical interventions.

Heider (1958) began this tradition with his work *The Psychology of Interpersonal Relations*. The book grew out of his early interests in the fields of phenomenology and Gestalt psychology (e.g., Spiegelberg, 1972). Heider's focus was on the "naïve" psychology that informs our social behavior: the sensibilities and attributions that determine our reactions. Among the concerns that he argued were most central to social experience is making sense of whether behaviors or the outcomes resulting from them are caused by intentional, purposive actions of self and others, or are products of impersonal causes. Specifically, actions and their effects were said by Heider to be *personally caused* to the extent that they were intended—as evidenced by signs of effort, goal directedness, and ability. In contrast, some behaviors or events are not intended, as these result from forces beyond an agent's control; these were said to be *impersonally caused.*

Subsequently, deCharms (1968) suggested that even some intentional behaviors (actions that involve effort and organization) may not embody a true sense of personal causation. He pointed out that many intentional behaviors might be enacted because the person wants to do them or enjoys them, and these certainly appear to represent personal causation. Yet, other goal-directed behaviors may be enacted only because of external pressures or rewards. These represent a more complex case with respect to the personal/impersonal distinction, because although intentional, they are experienced as compelled or heteronomously driven. To handle this issue, deCharms proposed a further distinction within the category of personal causation, namely, that between an *internal* versus an *external perceived locus of causality.* With internal perceived locus of causality, one feels oneself to be an "origin" of action, whereas with an external perceived locus of causality, one experiences oneself as a "pawn" of outside forces. Although both types of action fall within the category of personally caused (or intended) behaviors, only actions with a perceived internal locus of causality represent what we herein describe as autonomy.

Deci and Ryan (1980a, 1985b) elaborated and refined deCharms's distinction, applying theirs to an understanding of intrinsically and extrinsically motivated behaviors. Intrinsically motivated behaviors, which are done for their inherent satisfactions, invariantly have an internal perceived locus of causality. Such actions are experienced as a spontaneous self-expression and are wholly volitional. In contrast, Deci and Ryan argued that extrinsically motivated (i.e., instrumental) behaviors can vary considerably in their relative autonomy. Some extrinsically motivated actions are clearly pressured or compelled by outside forces and thus have an external perceived locus of causality. Other extrinsically motivated actions, however, can have an internal perceived locus of causality, specifically when the individual sees the behavior as reflecting a personally endorsed and well-integrated goal. Indeed, the relative autonomy of extrinsically motivated action directly corresponds to the degree to which the regulation of such action has been internalized and integrated, a point that will receive considerable elaboration as we proceed.

Ryan and Connell (1989) pointed out that this conceptualization of perceived locus of causality shifts the boundary between internal and external from the *person* to the *self.* It is one's phenomenal core, here referred to as self, that is the most appropriate referent for distinguishing between an internal and an external perceived locus of causality. In other words, a behavior would be said to have an internal perceived locus of causality to the extent that one experiences it as expressive of one's true self, when one feels both authentic in and responsible for one's actions.

There is an important implication to the use of the self as the boundary referent, namely, that the proximal cause of an action could be a force within the person that is not integral to the self and thus would have an external perceived locus of causality. This is the case in introjection, for example, in which a person feels compelled to do something to avoid feelings of guilt or to gain a sense of esteem (e.g., Ryan, 1982; Ryan & Connell, 1989). Extending this, we suggest that some extrinsically motivated behaviors are controlled by *external regulations* (e.g., someone else controls you with rewards and punishments); some are controlled by *introjects* within the person but external to the self (e.g., feeling you have to do something to avoid guilt); and some are initiated by processes that have been *identified* with and/or *integrated* into the self (e.g., doing something because of a personally endorsed and well-assimilated value). Although these varied types of extrinsic regulation all involve intentionality and instrumentality, they differ substantially in the degree to which they involve autonomy, each falling at a different place along a gradient of perceived causality (Ryan & Connell, 1989).

Just as internally prompted actions may not be autonomous, events initiated from outside the individual do not necessarily engender heteronomy (Ryan, 1993; Ryan &

Deci, 2004). An authority, for example, may tell you to do something. Insofar as you agree with the order or personally endorse the legitimacy of the authority, your behavior of following the command may be quite volitional and would thus have an internal perceived locus of causality. Yet, when authorities make their power the salient reason for acting, or exercise that power arbitrarily or capriciously, this is likely to undermine feelings of autonomy. As we shall see, the manner in which adults exercise their guidance over children has a great deal of impact on both the children's sense of volition and their likelihood of internalizing the adults' values or guidance. Later, we look more closely at the developmental antecedents and dynamic character of these varied regulatory processes.

DeCharms (1968) portrayed *intrinsically motivated* behaviors as the prototype of an internal perceived locus of causality, and some of the experiential qualities associated with intrinsic motivation do represent a kind of template against which other forms of regulation can be compared. And, as we pointed out, well-integrated extrinsic motivations can be equally highly volitional and self-endorsed and thus approximate intrinsic motivation in terms of the internality of their perceived locus of causality. In either case, assessing a person's experience of an internal versus external locus of causality provides an empirical marker for the extent to which an action is autonomous. It will also relate empirically and theoretically to such constructs as authenticity, true versus false self, and volitional self-regulation.

Whether people are intrinsically or extrinsically motivated, they are engaged in intentional behavior. By contrast, the absence of intentionality represents an amotivational state. Thus, a person is motivated (and actions are personally caused) only to the extent that the person intends an action and follows the intention with an expenditure of effort. *Amotivation,* in contrast, most often refers to a relative lack of action, for example, when one feels hopeless and gives up behaving (Deci, 1980; Deci & Ryan, 1985b). The term amotivation also describes behavioral events the person emits without intention. A spasm, for example—although an action emanating from a body—is not mediated by intention and thus is amotivated and has an impersonal locus of causality. More interesting, however, from both phenomenological and clinical viewpoints, are behaviors such as a reflexive emotional "outburst" in which regulatory processes are overpowered by a sudden surge of energy. In Heider's terminology, these impulsive behaviors have an impersonal perceived locus of causality. In such a case, a person might, for example, say, "I don't know what came over me" or "I lost it," conveying the sense of an impersonal cause and ab-

sence of control in regulating behaviors. Such behaviors are, of course, motivated in the sense of being energized and explicable. Nonetheless, we refer to them as amotivated to convey the extent to which they are experienced by the actor as nonintentional and outside of personal control.

Most empirically based theories of motivation and self-regulation contrast motivation with amotivation but treat the former as a unitary concept (e.g., Bandura, 1989; Seligman, 1991). Yet, a consideration of autonomy requires differentiating the concept of motivation. Specifically, we focus on the extent to which one's motivated actions are *autonomous* (i.e., have an internal perceived locus of causality and emanate from the self) versus *controlled* (i.e., have an external perceived locus of causality and are coerced or regulated by some inter- or intrapersonal force external to the self).

Despite the unfortunate similarity in terminology, an internal versus external perceived locus of causality is quite different from an internal versus external locus of control (Rotter, 1966). An *internal locus of control,* and the closely related concepts of perceived control (E. Skinner & Edge, 2002) and self-efficacy (Bandura, 1989), refer to the belief that one can attain desired outcomes through intentional actions. *External locus of control* refers to believing that one cannot control outcomes, instead believing either that there is no contingency between behavior and outcomes or that one lacks competence to enact the requisite behaviors successfully. Accordingly, one would expect to find intentional (i.e., motivated) behavior in cases of an internal locus of control, and a lack of intentionality (i.e., amotivation) in cases of an external locus of control. Indeed, the concept of an internal versus external locus of control parallels Heider's (1958) distinction between personal and impersonal causation.

An internal locus of control need not imply autonomy or an internal perceived locus of causality. For instance, a girl who learns to successfully hide her feelings and to outwardly comply with demands to avoid arousing her father's abuse might have both an internal locus of control (Rotter, 1966) and self-efficacy (Bandura, 1989) with respect to avoiding abuse. Yet, even though she has the competence to control this outcome, she would likely experience an external perceived locus of causality because she is forced to act in the specified ways. Indeed, someone with an internal locus of control or self-efficacy can as easily be a pawn as an origin (deCharms, 1981; Deci & Ryan, 1985b).

Because of the extent to which these various motivational terminologies overlap in both substance and source, we present a classification table for clarity (Table 20.1). As

TABLE 20.1   Various Theoretical Concepts as They Relate to Autonomous Regulation, Controlling Regulation, and Nonregulation

Types of Regulation	Locus of Control (Rotter, 1966)	Efficacy Theory (Bandura, 1977)	Helplessness Theory (Seligman, 1975)	Attribution Theory (Heider, 1958)	Personal Causation (deCharms, 1968)	Self-Determination Theory (Deci & Ryan, 1985b)
Autonomous regulation	[a]	[a]	[a]	Personal causation	Intrinsic motivation; "origin"; internal PLOC	Intrinsic motivation; integrated extrinsic motivation; internal PLOC[b]
Controlled regulation	Internal locus of control	Self-efficacy	Perceived controllability	Personal causation	Extrinsic motivation; "pawn"; external PLOC	External and introjected extrinsic motivation; external PLOC
Nonregulation	External locus of control	Ineffectance	Helplessness	Impersonal causation	Impersonal causality	Amotivation; impersonal PLOC

[a] The autonomy-control differentiation (or a comparable one) is not made in these theories. All intentional actions would nonetheless be said to involve an internal locus of control, self-efficacy, and perceived controllability.
[b] PLOC = Perceived locus of causality.

can be seen from this table, self-determination theory differentiates not only between motivated and amotivated acts, but also between motivated acts characterized by autonomy and those characterized by being controlled (i.e., by being a pawn to forces outside the self).

As stated earlier, the importance of this phenomenological and attributional approach to autonomy rests primarily on the fact that by applying the perceived locus of causality construct, we have been able to address issues concerning the development and experience of autonomy versus heteronomy with empirical strategies. Factors that affect the perceived locus of causality are, in fact, those that affect autonomy and self-regulation and thus are important to issues of self-development, as research to be reviewed will illustrate. However, before turning to that literature, we first connect the concepts of autonomy and perceived locus of causality with related clinical concepts.

Autonomy as True Self

Autonomous actions, when viewed phenomenologically, emanate from the *self*. Accordingly, not all actions, even intentional ones, that come from the person are characterized by autonomy. Rather, autonomy refers only to those actions that are either experienced as one's own or are well assimilated and self-endorsed. In clinical settings, it is clear that much of what people do is not experienced by them as self-endorsed, but instead is all too often experienced as false, alienated, compulsive, impulsive, or even dissociated. Our concept of autonomy, then, relates rather closely to what some writers have referred to as one's "real" (Horney, 1950) or "true" (Winnicott, 1960/1965) self.

The idea of true self conveys that individuals sometimes behave in ways that reveal their core spirit and convey a sense of integrity and personal endorsement, and at other times they behave in ways that do not express that inner core but instead are more superficial and less integrated. Unintegrated regulatory processes typically develop as an adaptation to being contingently valued and/or controlled and thus serve both to manipulate others and to defend or preserve oneself (A. Miller, 1981).

Winnicott (1960/1965) specifically distinguished between true self and false self by suggesting that when acting from the true self, people feel real and "in touch" with their core needs and emotions. True self embodies their creative nature, their ability to freely initiate, to be vital, to enjoy existence. It is also the basis of informed, "wholehearted" behavior. In contrast, when acting from false self, people display "as-if" personalities that formed while they were attempting to gain approval in a nonaccepting social context (A. Miller, 1981). False self involves taking in aspects of the social context without truly accepting them as one's own. It conveys a splitting between one's outer presentation and one's deeper feelings and needs, a feature of many clinical presentations.

Whereas true self is the source of spontaneous perceptions, needs, and behaviors, false self reflects habitual perceiving and responding that a child adopts instrumentally, in accord with narcissistic needs. According to Winnicott (1949/1958), false self employs cognitive functions to know what is required of it—that is, to know what the situation demands—and in so doing, cognitive processes can gradually become separated from their affective and somatic grounding. In fact, Winnicott argued that living a false self requires ongoing and excessive cognitive activity, to the neglect of feeling and open perception. We see here how the idea of autonomy as activity regulated by one's true self also has implications for the idea of psychological integration as coordination or synchrony among aspects of one's personality. To the extent that one acts from other than the true self, some fractionation and splitting of functioning will result.

Other writers in the psychoanalytic tradition have also discussed the concept of true or real self. Horney (1950) defined the real self in terms of an intrinsic potentiality, a tendency toward personal growth and fulfillment. She tied neurosis to alienation from the real self, which results in the loss of the vital energy that is available to the real self. Jung (1951/1959) described the self as an organismic endowment representing the "center" of personality and possessing the tendency toward integration. Although in Jung's theory, the self is largely unconscious and is manifest through dreams and symbols, the concept still conveys the sense of one's having a vital core that is related to integration in personality.

In self-determination theory (e.g., Deci & Ryan, 1995), an individual's internal processes, structures, and urges can also be described in terms of the extent to which they represent true versus false self. More precisely, we speak of self, or *integrated self,* as that set of coherently organized processes, structures, and energies that are the developmental outcome of organismic integration. All aspects of one's psychological makeup can thus be understood in terms of the degree to which they are integrated. Those that are more integrated are akin to what Winnicott and others called true self.

Autonomy as Authenticity

The term "authentic" typically applies to something that actually proceeds from its reputed "author" (Wild, 1965). Authentic actions are thus ones with which the person identifies and for which he or she accepts responsibility. Accordingly, authenticity can be represented as a continuum describing the extent to which an action is a true expression of one's self (and thus autonomous) versus an expression of pressures or causes external to the self (and thus controlled or amotivated; Ryan, 1993; Ryan & Deci, 2004).

The concept of authenticity has appeared primarily in the writings of existentially oriented philosophers (e.g., Kierkegaard, 1849/1968) and therapists (e.g., Yalom, 1980). The concept is highly apt for describing the phenomenological experience of acting from one's sense of self (Ryan, 1993). When an action is fully endorsed by its au-

thor, the experience is that of integrity or authenticity. As Laing (1969, p. 127) put it, "To be authentic is to be true to oneself." Authenticity is thus acting from the self; it is self-determination. When viewed in this way, authenticity becomes a quality of behavior rather than just an abstract philosophical concept.

Although literatures emphasizing authenticity tend to focus on the behaviors and experiences of adults, the term authenticity can be applied even to very young children. Observation of toddlers in the context of controlling or maltreating families will reveal the sense of surface compliance, as-if affects, and false consciousness as early as the 2nd year of life (e.g., Crittenden, 1988). As Crockenberg and Litman (1990) argued, there is an important difference between a toddler's doing something compliantly, out of fear or force, and doing it autonomously, with a full sense of willingness. Similarly, Kochanska (1997) differentiated situational compliance from committed compliance. In situational compliance, the child is cooperative but lacks a sincere commitment to the behavior; for the behavior to be sustained, the child needs reminders and prompts. By contrast, in committed compliance, the child appears to accept and endorse the behavior as his or her own; he or she maintains the behavior without prompts or reminders. Committed compliance increases with age and is associated with later indices of internalization such as doing required activities in the absence of adults and resisting enticements to cheat (Kochanska & Aksan, 1995). Clearly, such relatively autonomous (rather than merely compliant) performance of uninteresting, though important activities is a significant goal of socialization.

Of course, with further development, the issue of authenticity takes on even greater salience. With the advent of self-consciousness and adolescent egocentrism (Ryan & Kuczkowski, 1994) the potential for presenting an inauthentic self to others and for either hiding or losing touch with one's real or authentic feelings and beliefs is magnified.

The more controlling the social context, the less authentic people are likely to feel, and along with that, the less self-expressive and emotionally integrated they appear to be. That is, authenticity typically depends on a context that supports autonomy. For instance, M. L. Lynch et al. (2004) measured the extent to which individuals in three diverse cultures felt authentic in their relationships to specific significant others, such as mother, father, best friend, romantic partner, and roommates. Results showed that authenticity varied systematically across relationships with the perceived autonomy supportiveness of the other person. Moreover, relationship satisfaction, emotional expressiveness, and self-congruency in trait behaviors were robustly associated with the experience that partners supported one's autonomy.

Autonomy as Will

Autonomy has also been equated with will by some authors (e.g., Deci, 1980; Easterbrook, 1978), although the concept of will has not been widely employed in the psychological literature. In part, this stems from confusion between the concepts of "will" and "free will," and the crux of the issue has to do with whether behaviors that are willed are free from causation. The philosophical debate between free will and "determinism" concerned whether all behaviors are lawful and thus predictable: Free will was interpreted as meaning freedom from causation, whereas determinism was interpreted as meaning that behavior is lawfully caused.

Although in philosophical literatures this issue is largely passé, the free will versus determinism debate seems to resurface periodically in psychology. Wegner (2002) supplies a good recent example. He defined will as behavior whose original impetus is a conscious thought. He then argued, and in some cases demonstrated, that people are mistaken in attributing actions to will, because even thoughts are caused. Wegner concludes that the whole issue of will may be illusory.

As Ryan and Deci (2004) pointed out, however, the concept of will (as autonomy) does not mean freedom from causation; rather, it refers to the regulation of action that is self-directed and concordant with one's values and beliefs. Behaviors that are willed can certainly be said to be caused or determined, in the senses both that historical forces shape the values and sensibilities with which such behaviors concur and that proximal influences set in motion the specific actions that reflect concordance or integration. Understood in this way, it is entirely possible for a person to experience a sense of will (or autonomy) while engaging in actions that can also be described in terms of their material and efficient causal underpinnings.

The concept of will has long been a part of phenomenological analyses. Thus, Pfander (1908/1967) used a phenomenological approach in distinguishing actions that reflect one's will from other forms of motivated behaving. He argued that acts can be described as willed to the extent that they are experienced as being caused by oneself as agent or emanate from one's "ego-center." In contrast, other forms of action are experienced as caused by forces "outside one's ego-center." Interpreted in this way, only willed acts would be considered autonomous, for only they emanate from one's phenomenal sense of self.

Parenthetically, it is worth noting that the term "will power" is sometimes used to describe the process of countering one's urges or organismic nature through force (e.g., Deci, 1980). May (1969) suggested that will power involves self-deceit, and Shapiro (1981) stated that the use of will power is central to rigid character disorders such as obsessive-compulsive personality. Behavior that is regulated through will power, when the term is used in that sense, would not typically be considered autonomous, as that frequently refers to one part of personality dominating another. Highly introjected people may appear "strong willed," even though they may in fact be pressured, rigid, and overcontrolled in their behavioral regulation.

We believe this nonautonomous regulation represented by will power is what underlies or explains what Baumeister, Muraven, and Tice (2000) described as the *ego depletion phenomenon*. They argued that the exercise of self-regulation is draining, and they reviewed a number of creative experiments demonstrating how the exercise of will depletes energy and the capacity for effort. But the conception of self-regulation they employ is undifferentiated and most closely approximates self-control or what we call introjected regulation. In fact, we propose that autonomous self-regulation is not depleting at all, but instead can be vitalizing, whereas nonautonomous regulation, or self-control, is depleting as they suggest. This effect has also been shown in experimental studies (e.g., Nix, Ryan, Manly, & Deci, 1999). This literature on depletion versus vitality again bespeaks the importance of discerning the degree of autonomy underlying behavior.

Autonomy as Agency

To be autonomous means to act agentically and to experience a sense of choice and willingness in those actions. Agency thus connotes something different from merely deciding to act, for one can "decide" to do what one feels compelled or coerced to do. To convey fully the meaning of autonomy as agency thus requires that we again distinguish between the concepts of intentionality and autonomy.

Intentionality refers to purposefulness, to pursuing a desired outcome. Autonomy, however, is a more restrictive term, for it necessitates the experience of feeling that intended actions are an expression of one's values, abiding sensibilities, and interests. An action would thus be considered intentional, but not autonomous, when one feels one "has to" do it, or when one feels pressured by one's craving for the praise it is expected to yield. When one acts compulsively, for example, whether in aligning the magazines on the coffee table or washing one's hands yet again, the behavior is intentional, but it is surely not autonomous, for it lacks the sense of freedom and flexibility that are the phenomenological accompaniments of autonomy.

It is worth noting that some theorists do equate agency with intentionality and thus use it in a way that is not consistent with our definition of the term. For example, Bandura (1989) described all self-efficacious or intentional actions as agentic. In other words, from his perspective, to be motivated is to be agentic, whereas for us, a person is truly agentic only to the extent that he or she is autonomously motivated.

It is precisely because humans have the capacity to act other than from their core—that is, to act from fractionated regulatory processes or divided consciousness—that the concept of human agency takes on its import. A person who is a pawn to forces external to the self with which they do not concur, no matter how intentional, is neither autonomous nor really agentic (Shapiro, 1981). Moreover, as R. N. Williams (1992) put it, agency means engaging the world truthfully, free from self-deceit. How little intentional behavior in everyday life fits that description is something each of us can ponder.

An additional use of the term agency, distinct from our usage, portrays agency as self-interest, which is contrasted with communality, in which one puts others before oneself. This usage stems from Bakan's (1966) distinctions for these terms, later applied by Helgeson (1994) and others. Our view would simply be that autonomy is orthogonal to this distinction, as one can be autonomously agentic or autonomously communal, and similarly one can be heteronomously agentic or communal. Moreover, we suspect that what has been called "unmitigated communality" by Helgeson, and that has been linked to depression and "self-silencing," is largely heteronomous communality. It typically reflects an internalization of various forms of oppression.

Human Autonomy: A Reprise

Phenomenologically, autonomy relates to the experience of agency and authenticity, to the experience of an internal perceived locus of causality. Intrinsically motivated activities are autonomous and are typically accompanied by the experience of spontaneous interest and vitality, whereas extrinsic actions characterized by autonomy are more typically represented as enactments of fully integrated values and goals.

Starting with the concept of autonomy as a phenomenological issue has been important in empirical pursuits, insofar as perceived autonomy—that is, an internal perceived

locus of causality—can be employed to help differentiate among different types of motivational processes. As will be seen in the subsequent review of our empirical work, this approach has been validated in two important ways. First, people's perceptions of autonomy are greater in social contexts that support autonomy rather than control behavior (Deci & Ryan, 1987, 2000). Second, people's experience of autonomy has consequences for the quality of behavior, such as persistence, flexibility, and creativity, and for both psychological and physical health (e.g., Amabile, 1983; Grolnick, Gurland, DeCourcey, & Jacob, 2002; Koestner, Bernieri, & Zuckerman, 1992).

The concept of human autonomy applies directly to developmental psychopathology in that failures in self-regulation, manifest as controlling or amotivational processes, represent impairments in the development of self. Although all people display some nonautonomous regulation, excessive and chronic instances of being controlled or amotivated are quite broadly implicated in many specific disorders. Moreover, the pervasive experience of being controlled during early development sets the stage for later difficulties and deficits in the regulation of both action and experience.

WHAT AUTONOMY IS NOT

Having provided a theoretical and definitional overview of autonomy as being based in the organizational tendencies at the heart of development and the corresponding experience of authenticity and volition, we turn to the question of what autonomy is not. We specifically address a variety of related ideas that are often used to either argue against the importance of autonomy or that are inconsistent with our use of the term.

Autonomy as Independence from Environments?

In his social cognitive theory of human agency, Bandura (1989, p. 1175) defined autonomy as action that is "entirely independent" of the environment. If the environment has an influence on behavior, there can be no autonomy, and thus Bandura claims the construct of autonomy to be without merit. The issue of whether there is or is not acceptance, consent, or volition with respect to environmental influences, despite the myriad empirical consequences of acceptance or consent, was simply not addressed in Bandura's argument.

Such a stance is uninformed in terms of the work of many philosophical thinkers (e.g., Dworkin, 1988; Friedman, 2003) who have articulated that autonomy does not concern the source of the impetus to action, but rather an action's backing by the self—its concordance and its reflective endorsement. Further, Bandura appears to be arguing with a straw man, as we know of no psychologists who consider it necessary for autonomous behavior to emerge independently of supports, prompts, or initiating events.

As noted, by writing off the concept of autonomy, Bandura reduced agency to self-efficacy, without distinguishing those efficacious behaviors that are freely chosen and authentic from those that are pressured and/or not well-anchored within the self. Simply stated, the belief that one can behave so as to successfully control an outcome does not address whether or not one wants to do it or values it—issues that are at the very crux of people's salient concerns about autonomy and agency.

Autonomy as a Denial of Implicit Motives?

Although many clinicians have long recognized that the regulation of some behaviors is nonconscious, there is now growing empirical evidence that actions may be initiated by factors of which people are unaware even when they think they know the causes (Wilson, 2002). Bargh and Ferguson (2000), for example, cited several studies in which people were implicitly or nonconsciously primed to enact intentional behaviors and then attribute their actions to will or self-initiation. Such experiments have been used to suggest that *all* actions may be nonconsciously determined and to question whether the idea of being self-motivated has any veracity.

In our conceptualization, however, the issue of implicit and explicit motivation is largely orthogonal to the issue of autonomous versus heteronomous motivation (Deci & Ryan, 1980b; Ryan & Deci, 2004). Implicit events or cues may prompt either autonomous or controlled behaviors. Further, we suggest that behaviors that are *automatic* (i.e., not consciously experienced or reflected on) may be regulated by either autonomous or controlled processes. A driver who automatically shifts her car into second gear when the cue of engine noise nonconsciously prompts it may be acting fully autonomously. Were she to reflectively consider it, she would wholly endorse her behavior. Conversely, nonconscious or implicit motives can drive heteronomous behavior. A smoker who has made a personal commitment to quit for the sake of his health but, after subliminal exposure to a cigarette ad, finds himself mindlessly pulling out a smoke would be controlled in this action. Were he to reflectively consider this act, he would agree that the behavior was inconsistent with his self-endorsed goals.

Just as nonconscious motives can organize either autonomous or heteronomous actions, conscious or explicit motives can also organize either autonomous or heteronomous behavior. In short, the issues of automaticity versus deliberateness and implicit versus explicit motives does not inform us that well concerning the relative autonomy of actions. Some habits and reactions are ones we would experience as autonomous; others seem alien, imposed, or compulsive, and this consideration is critical in understanding the individual experiences associated with varied psychopathologies.

It is true, however, that people can be more or less mindful or reflective concerning what they have been prompted to do, and this is clearly an aid to ongoing autonomous regulation. This formulation is quite consistent with the experimental findings of Libet (1999), who showed not only that volitional action can be preceded by a readiness potential in the brain before any awareness of intention, but also that consciousness can function to approve (or veto) the commission of the act. Similarly, Levesque and Brown (2003) examined whether mindfulness, or the tendency to be aware of what is occurring in the moment (Brown & Ryan, 2003), would moderate the power of implicit motives. They found that indeed it did: Implicit motivation was a more potent predictor of behavior when mindfulness was low.

Autonomy as Entailing a Disembodied Self?

Often mixed in with the arguments about our ignorance of the actual causes of our behavior is the argument by some that, as we understand more about how the brain is involved in actions, concepts such as will and autonomy become obsolete. Consider this telling passage from Pinker (2002, p. 43), a popular neuroscience author:

> Each of us feels that there is a single "I" in control. But that is an illusion that the brain works hard to produce. . . . The brain does have supervisory systems in the prefrontal lobes and anterior cingulate cortex, which can push the buttons of behavior and override habits and urges. But these systems are gadgets with specific quirks and limitations; they are not implementations of the rational free agent traditionally identified with the soul or the self.

Herein Pinker declares the "I" an "illusion," but linguistically replaces it with a new intentional subject, "the brain," which pushes buttons, controls urges, and works hard on creating illusions. For Pinker, the sense of self is just a postbehavior "spin," whereas the brain, reified as if it were an intentional subject, does the governing and gadget pulling. Such interpretations are pervasive in popular neuroscience but are fraught with philosophical confounds.

The logic is that because the brain is always involved in behavior, there can be no "free rational agent" (a construct that itself is something of a straw man). No matter that the brain itself may be stimulated into action by social events, or that the brain's "quirky gadgets" are mediated by people's psychological interpretations and meaning construction, or that active reflection can alter those meanings.

More generally, it is our view that all events in the universe can be described in material-efficient or causal terms, and this applies to all behaviors as well. Whether a behavior is autonomous or controlled, it requires a brain. However, even at the level of the brain, we believe the dynamics of autonomous regulation differ from those of controlled regulation (Ryan et al., 1997), and increasingly, neuropsychological evidence supports this view. Indeed, it is pretty clear that autonomy typically requires the involvement of executive systems in the right prefrontal cortex, as well as afferent and efferent connections with a variety of emotional centers, and moreover that damage to specific cites can disrupt capacities for volition and valuation of intentions (Ryan, in press). This does not reduce the issue of autonomy to merely a neurological event, but it does suggest the importance of coordinating our understanding of behavioral regulation with brain research (e.g., Walton, Delvin, & Rushworth, 2004). This coordination will, however, require an acknowledgment of bidirectional causation and a sophisticated understanding of the multiple levels of causal analysis that are required to explain social behavior (see Cicchetti & Dawson, 2002; Ryan & Deci, 2004).

Autonomy as Independence from Others?

Perhaps the most common alternative usage of the word autonomy equates it with "independence." Although autonomy and independence do overlap in their secondary dictionary definitions, they can refer to quite distinct attributes. *Independence* typically refers to not relying on others. Its opposite, dependence, correspondingly means being provided or cared for by others (Memmi, 1984). In contrast, autonomy as we use it describes being self-initiating and feeling a sense of freedom or volition. Its opposite, heteronomy or control, conveys that actions stem from forces external to the self, as when one is pressured or coerced.

Once these distinct definitions are clarified it is easy to see how it is possible for various configurations to arise: One could feel heteronomously independent, heteronomously dependent, autonomously dependent, or both autonomous and independent. The first category applies when one feels forced to give up reliance on another. The second pertains to one's feeling compelled to rely on an-

other. The third is possible when one volitionally and willingly enters into or accepts dependence or interdependence. And the fourth is conceivable when one desires and initiates self-reliance, or freedom from reliance on others.

When dependence (versus independence) is viewed in terms of relying on (versus not relying on) others, dependencies of varied sorts can be construed as potentially autonomous at all stages of development. Newborns are highly dependent, and as they grow older, they become gradually less dependent in many respects, but there are significant areas of dependence that remain and are appropriate throughout youth. Moreover, there is no point in the life span in which persons are not at least interdependent. The important issue, therefore, is whether a person's dependence, whatever its level and at whatever stage of development, is experienced as autonomous or controlled. It is possible for someone to be provided for—that is, to be dependent—with a full sense of willingness and volition, just as it is possible to feel pressured or coerced in one's dependence. This does not detract form the recognition, however, that the issues of dependence and autonomy can dynamically interact, as when caregivers use their resources as instruments of control, or when people are taught that dependency is "bad." Similarly, being independent does not ensure autonomy, for one can be pressured into independence, as when a child is forced to "do for oneself" by parents with immoderately high expectations, as often happens, for example, in the development of paranoid personality disorders (Sperry, 2003).

The conceptual demarcation between independence and autonomy is a crucial one not only for developmental thinking, but also for theories of gender and cultural differences. Numerous writers have denigrated the importance of autonomy, suggesting that too much self-reliance is unnatural and unhealthy. For example, the masculine (Gilligan, 1982; Jordon, 1991) and Western (Markus et al., 1996) casts toward noninterdependence and individualism have often been criticized under the rubric of autonomy. As critiques of extreme independence, these arguments may have considerable merit, but they are not meaningful critiques of autonomy. To construe autonomy as an exclusively male and/or Western cultural value and preoccupation is to inappropriately equate autonomy with nonreliance. This unfortunate confusion runs the risk of denying the importance of volition and authenticity to women and non-Western persons, which, of course, constitutes a regressive and potentially disempowering political (see Friedman, 2003) and clinical (see Lerner, 1988; Ryan, 1991) stance. It also precludes an ideal of many relational theories that recognize mutuality of autonomy and volitional interdependencies as optimal forms of interpersonal engagement (see Deci et al., 2004). Finally, it ignores the growing evidence that across cultures, the extent to which people internalize and integrate cultural practices, and therefore embrace them autonomously, matters greatly for mental health and cultural fit (e.g., Chirkov et al., 2003).

Autonomy as Detachment or Separation?

Human beings, out of their innate need for relatedness, are oriented toward attachments with caregivers (Bowlby, 1969), just as they begin immediately to express and strive for greater autonomy. As we argue in SDT, both relatedness and autonomy are fundamental needs. Still, some theorists have cast the development of autonomy in terms of relinquishing attachments, especially during adolescence (e.g., Blos, 1962; Freud, 1958; L. Steinberg & Silverberg, 1986). In doing this, they are construing autonomy in terms of detachment and separation rather than volition and self-regulation. In addition to the conceptual confusion this creates, there is the empirical fact that detachment (especially from parents) is typically counterproductive with regard to the development of autonomy and self-regulation.

Ryan and Lynch (1989) applied this formulation in their reconsideration of research by L. Steinberg and Silverberg (1986) on what the latter authors termed *emotional autonomy* in adolescence. Steinberg and Silverberg drew on Blos's (1962) theory of adolescence, defining emotional autonomy as the relinquishing of dependence on parents, and they developed a measure to assess this construct. Ryan and Lynch, while acknowledging the significance of reliance issues in adolescent development, criticized the labeling of such nonreliance as autonomy. They regarded the so-called emotionally autonomous youths as those who, for a variety of reasons, indicate less willingness to turn to their parents for support, guidance, or help. Rather than indicating volition and agency, such attributes could be better interpreted as emotional *detachment.*

Ryan and Lynch (1989) further suggested that under most circumstances, teenagers who detach from and thus do not utilize or rely on their parents for emotional support would tend to show more negative developmental consequences, whereas autonomy (i.e., volition) has been shown to have positive consequences. Supporting their view, Ryan and Lynch showed in varied adolescent samples that a high degree of what was labeled emotional autonomy by L. Steinberg and Silverberg (1986) was negatively correlated with indices of adjustment such as self-esteem, perceived competence, and lovability. Autonomy, in contrast, has frequently been found to be positively correlated with those

same indices (Deci & Ryan, 2000). Further, Ryan and Lynch provided evidence that the familial contexts associated with high degrees of adolescent emotional autonomy were those lacking in cohesion and support and characterized by insecure attachments. Such evidence points toward both the positive confluence of attachment and autonomy and the importance of differentiating the idea of autonomy from that of detachment and independence. Specifically, a good deal of emotional attachment to caregivers is, according to Ryan and Lynch, conducive rather than antithetical to autonomy and healthy development.

Subsequently, Lamborn and Steinberg (1993) altered their position to suggest a moderation effect. They argued that emotional autonomy as they defined it is beneficial for adolescents who have very high levels of parental support but not for those with less optimal parental supports. Yet, the data they presented nonetheless showed a robust main effect in which emotional autonomy predicts negative well-being, compared to a weak moderation effect. Moreover, these results were subsequently contradicted by Fuhrman and Holmbeck (1995), who showed the same main effect, but an opposite pattern of moderation: Emotional autonomy was more beneficial to teens whose parents were low in support. That is, it appeared better to detach from unsupportive or unreliable parents.

We agree that, under the adverse circumstances of nonnurturant parents, detachment may have some value, and we even agree that, in the presence of very high support, emotional autonomy may represent a type of healthy independence. However, such arguments miss the point of Ryan and Lynch's (1989) original argument that emotional detachment (1) is not the same as emotional or behavioral autonomy and (2) is a nonoptimal developmental course. Indeed, several studies have shown that emotional autonomy is higher when parents are nonnurturing and in families that lack cohesion. In addition, children high in emotional autonomy are more likely to conform to peers, engage in risky behaviors, and achieve less well in school (e.g., McBride-Chang & Chang, 1998; Turner, Irwin, Tschann, & Millstein, 1993). All of this makes sense if emotional autonomy is detachment, but not if it is autonomy.

To be clear then, we do not just argue that L. Steinberg and Silverberg (1986) have mislabeled their construct. We disagree with the original formulation by Freud (1958), Blos (1979), and others who have advocated that detachment or emotional disengagement from parents is in any way a necessary or positive trend in normal development. No doubt, teenagers do become more independent, and sensitive parents can support the development of these competencies. But insofar as parents support the child's autonomy, no emotional detachment need occur. Moreover, our view is that autonomy coexists with dependence and interdependence throughout the life span. In short, a differentiated approach to autonomy need not pit it against attachment or dependence.

Autonomy as Just a Stage?

The development of autonomy, when viewed as an increasing capacity for volition resulting from the integration of regulatory processes, is ongoing throughout life. The form and content of autonomous regulation vary at different developmental stages, but the issue is ever pertinent with respect to mental health. Various writers, however, have portrayed the struggle for autonomy as being primarily evident at, or restricted to, particular developmental stages. We turn to a consideration of some stage models.

Erikson

Perhaps the best known of such theories is Erikson's (1950) theory of psychosocial development. Erikson identified the 2nd and 3rd years of children's lives as a critical period for the development of autonomy. At this time, having achieved a primitive sense of self as a separate entity, children begin to assert themselves, generally in accord with their biological urges, but at times, as all parents know, apparently just to be oppositional, to oppose the word or will of others. Erikson argued that, if allowed to respond to their urges and inner cues, children will develop a sense of autonomy and pride. By contrast, if they face rigid dominance and are not allowed to act on their drives and desires, they will instead develop a sense of shame and doubt. In such cases, they may find it necessary to block awareness of their own inner cues and develop a more passive stance toward the initiation of behavior.

We agree that this period in children's lives, when their sense of self is still quite rudimentary, is crucial for their long-term sense of autonomy, and the responsiveness of the social context is critically important for that development. However, the struggle for autonomy is ongoing across the life span, and although Erikson's theory acknowledges the importance of integration throughout one's life, his relegating the concept of autonomy development to this brief stage diminishes greatly the meaning of autonomy. The dynamic in which people attempt to be self-regulating—to assert their autonomy—and are responded to in either an autonomy-supportive or a controlling manner is played out at all stages of life with regard to varied issues and in varied domains. Our research has consistently shown that the social context's being autonomy-supportive versus control-

ling of people at various ages affects not only their immediate motivation but also their ongoing tendencies to be autonomous.

Piaget

Piaget (1967) suggested that will (which is closely related to autonomy) is a regulatory capacity that comes into existence during middle childhood (7 to 12 years of age) in relation to moral issues. For a child of that age, morality is gradually shifting from being based wholly on authority to being determined more by mutuality and consent. The shift away from exclusive reliance on authority necessitates the development of internal regulatory processes that, as Piaget conceived it, allow a morally superior principle to win out over a morally inferior drive. In our view, this process of developing internal regulatory processes to manage one's drives and emotions is merely an example of developing one's more general sense of will or autonomy and is one that begins before and continues long after middle childhood.

Anna Freud

Anna Freud (1958) is among the earliest thinkers to conceive of autonomy as a "developmental line." Yet, she also focused on adolescence as the important period for the development of autonomy. As noted, adolescence is a period of individuation in which teenagers develop both greater independence and greater autonomy. However, it is the rebellion of a child struggling to free himself or herself from parental control that is often said to reflect autonomous regulation. Rebellion, which typically means insistently doing the opposite of what was demanded of one, does not, however, constitute autonomy. Instead, rebellion is merely the defiant rather than compliant form of being controlled and is not accompanied by the experience of choice, volition, and coherence. The period of adolescence is surely important for the development of autonomy for, as teenagers gradually individuate from parental authority, they are faced with the challenge of developing the type of internal regulatory processes that constitute autonomous rather than controlled regulation. However, as with the struggles in early and middle childhood, this represents one aspect and form of the striving for autonomy that is central to development across the life span.

Loevinger

Finally, Loevinger (1976) used the term autonomy to describe a stage of adulthood that most individuals never attain. This stage is characterized by the ability to accept responsibility for one's actions and emotions and to act out of well-synthesized or integrated social prescriptions. Her description of autonomy thus bespeaks the concepts of integration and awareness that indeed are the hallmarks of mature self-determination. Still, these characteristics can be found to varying degrees in behavior at all ages, not only in some people during adulthood.

These various theories all emphasize the importance of people's striving for autonomy, but they localize the struggle to specific, though different, developmental epochs, ranging from infancy to adulthood. When taken together, however, the theories highlight how significant the dynamics of autonomy are across all stages of development. In infancy, autonomy concerns the consolidation of self and the development of initiative. Progressively, as the child gets older, autonomy relates to assimilating socially important behaviors and ideals while preserving one's initiative, to individuating and forming new attachments while preserving the old, and to fully accepting oneself and respecting the initiative of others. In all cases, the issues concern reaching an accommodation to the social world in a way that allows an internal perceived locus of causality and the experience of agency and volition.

THE SUPPORT OF AUTONOMY AND THE FACILITATION OF DEVELOPMENT

Having conveyed what is (and is not) meant by autonomy, we turn now to an elaboration of the role of autonomy in development and to the factors in social contexts that facilitate or undermine it. To do so, we focus on four developmental processes in which autonomy figures heavily: intrinsic motivation, internalization, attachment, and emotional integration.

Intrinsic Motivation

Intrinsic motivation is an attribute with which humans are liberally endowed and which plays an extremely important role in psychological development. Intrinsic motivational tendencies are evident in the active exploration, manipulation, curiosity, and exercise of skills that foster the growth of competencies, as numerous developmental theorists have argued (e.g., Bruner, 1962; Flavell, 1977; Harter, 1993; White, 1963). Also known as mastery motivation (e.g., Ryan & Connell, 1988), this motivational propensity is evident well before a child's first birthday (Ainsworth, Blehar, Waters, & Wall, 1978; Yarrow, Rubenstein, & Pedersen, 1975) and differentiates into more specific interests as the child grows older (Deci &

Ryan, 2000). These innate or natural tendencies are intrinsically motivated in the sense that they require no incentives or pressures but instead occur spontaneously when the social context does not forestall them (Deci & Ryan, 1985b). Intrinsically motivated activities provide their own rewards in the form of the excitement, interest, and enjoyment that accompanies them. They are in this sense autotelic (Csikszentmihalyi, 1975) rather than being instrumental for some separable consequence.

The concept of intrinsic motivation emerged from the experimental literature during the 1950s and 1960s in opposition to the dominant behavioral theories of that period, namely operant theory and drive theory, both of which viewed all behavior as controlled by contingencies of reinforcement. In drive theory behaviors were said to be motivated through reinforcements associated with drive reduction (Hull, 1943). Operant theory (B. F. Skinner, 1953) similarly proposed that all operant behavior is under the control of contingencies of reinforcement in the environment; in other words, all nonreflexive behaviors are maintained by extrinsic consequences. Proponents of intrinsic motivation (e.g., Harlow, 1953; White, 1959), in contrast, held that there are many behaviors, such as play and exploration, that are "rewarding in their own right," or done out of interest and do not require separable extrinsic rewards or reinforcements (Deci & Ryan, 1980a). This conceptualization of an innate and natural source of activity oriented toward the exercise and growth of capacities has ever since been an important coordinate for the study of developmental and learning processes (Elliot, McGregor, & Thrash, 2002; Koestner & McClelland, 1990; White, 1959).

In our research on intrinsic motivation, we work with the general thesis that intrinsic motivation represents an autonomous organismic striving and is accompanied by people's experiencing their actions as emanating from themselves, as having an internal perceived locus of causality (Ryan & Deci, 2000b). We also reason that, although intrinsic motivation is "natural," it is highly dependent on social conditions that help to support and preserve it. Thus, intrinsic motivation—and the curiosity, assimilative tendency, and joy that attend it—have been predicted to be undermined in conditions that are overly controlling or inconsistent, leading to nonoptimal development and, in extreme cases, the onset of stagnation and psychopathology.

Numerous studies, using widely varied methods, have linked intrinsic motivation to effectively negotiating one's surroundings. For example, children's intrinsic motivation has been positively related to creativity (e.g., Amabile, 1983; Koestner, Ryan, Bernieri, & Holt, 1984), and both elementary school and college students' intrinsic motivation has been positively associated with fuller processing of information and greater conceptual understanding (Benware & Deci, 1984; Grolnick & Ryan, 1987). For example, in a recent experiment, Grolnick et al. (2002) observed mothers and their third-grade children working on poems. Following the interaction, children were asked to complete similar tasks on their own. Children whose mothers interacted with them in a more controlling manner performed just as well as other children when they were with their mothers, but, when completing tasks on their own, the children of more controlling mothers were less accurate in solving the problems and wrote less creative poems. Such studies indicate that undermined intrinsic motivation can have negative consequences for learning, persistence, and performance across a person's first 2 decades.

Even more important, perhaps, individuals' intrinsic motivation has been positively related to mental health. For example, children's intrinsic motivation in a classroom setting has been positively associated with feelings of self-worth (e.g., Deci, Schwartz, Sheinman, & Ryan, 1981; Ryan & Grolnick, 1986). Lower levels of intrinsic motivation have been linked to more aggressive projections (Ryan & Grolnick, 1986), more maladaptive coping (Ryan & Connell, 1989; E. Skinner & Edge, 2002), more tension and anxiety (e.g., Ryan, Mims, & Koestner, 1983), and more negative emotional tone (Garbarino, 1975). These and related studies suggest that when intrinsic motivation is undermined, some adverse consequences for wellness can follow. Because of these effects on both growth and well-being, it seems important to explicate the social-contextual conditions that enhance versus undermine intrinsic motivation.

The Social Context and Intrinsic Motivation

A substantial amount of research has explored the effects of various social contexts on intrinsic motivation, which has been described in a specific minitheory of SDT, cognitive evaluation theory (CET; Deci & Ryan, 1980a). In brief, CET argues that intrinsic motivation is dependent on experiences of both autonomy and competence in action, and thus environmental controls and/or nonoptimal challenges will undermine intrinsic motivation. Studies based on CET have been done with participants ranging from toddlers to adults, allowing us to draw inferences about fundamental, cross-age, aspects of intrinsic motivation.

One type of evidence comes from experimental studies. In the typical paradigm, there are groups of participants working on the same activity under different conditions (usually varied in terms of factors affecting perceived au-

tonomy, perceived competence, or both). Subsequently, intrinsic motivation is assessed by placing participants in a free-choice situation where the target activity is available, as are alternative activities. The amount of time participants spend spontaneously engaging in the target activity is recorded and used as the free-choice or free-play measure of intrinsic motivation. Ratings of how interesting and enjoyable participants found the task are used as a secondary measure of intrinsic motivation. When these two measures are significantly correlated, we are most confident that the free-choice behavior is a true reflection of intrinsic motivation (Ryan, Koestner, & Deci, 1991).

In the earliest studies, Deci (1971, 1972) found that participants who received monetary rewards for solving interesting puzzles subsequently displayed significantly less intrinsic motivation than those who had solved the puzzles for no rewards. Deci (1971) postulated that rewarded participants were more likely to see the impetus or "cause" of their activity as stemming from external, as opposed to internal, sources, thus prompting a shift in their perceived locus of causality. This proposal was provocative precisely because so many psychologists had emphasized that rewards are the primary impetus behind individual behavior. Here, not only was that not the case, but rewards were shown to have a detrimental effect on spontaneous challenge-seeking behaviors.

A study by Lepper, Greene, and Nisbett (1973), in which preschool children were given good-player awards for drawing with magic markers, found results complementary to those of Deci (1971, 1972). Lepper et al. not only showed the generalizability of the undermining of intrinsic motivation by rewards to young children, they also showed that the negative effects persisted across a considerable delay period. A plethora of studies soon converged on this point, documenting that the allure of attractive extrinsic rewards can have a negative effect on people's autonomy. People gradually become "pawns" to the rewards (deCharms, 1968), and their intrinsic motivation is undermined.

The undermining effect of rewards on intrinsic motivation has been, for some behaviors, a flash point for debate. In the early 1980s, there were numerous studies attempting to account for the effect in behavioral terms, most of which failed to provide a convincing counterargument (see Deci & Ryan, 1985b, for a review). The message of a voluminous literature was clear, as meta-analyses began to show. However, the debate was resparked by an *American Psychologist* article about reward effects on intrinsic motivation in which Eisenberger and Cameron (1996) claimed that rewards, regardless of whether they are controlling or informational as cognitive evaluation theory classifies them, do not have negative effects and need not be a source of concern. Despite prior meta-analyses finding support for CET's position, Eisenberger and Cameron claimed that their new analyses showed there was no compelling evidence for an undermining effect by rewards in spite of the accepted view. Detecting a problem, Deci, Koestner, and Ryan (1999) reanalyzed the experimental data, encompassing the studies used by Eisenberger and Cameron, and presented some startling findings. Results detailed how Eisenberger and Cameron's analyses were plagued by miscalculations, inappropriate collapsing of conditions across moderators, incorrect reporting of effect sizes, misclassifications of conditions, and employment of the wrong control groups. The errors were extensive, but when corrected, a quite different picture emerged than that claimed by Eisenberger and Cameron. The results showed an overall significant undermining of intrinsic motivation by rewards, but even more important, the matrix of reward effects on intrinsic motivation was perfectly fitting with the differentiated predictions of CET concerning when rewards should and should not undermine intrinsic motivation. Eisenberger, Pierce, and Cameron's (1999) invited response did not dispute Deci et al.'s primary findings.

What makes this controversy odd, however, is that, from the SDT perspective, we have never doubted the power of external rewards and reinforcements to control behavior. It is rather that, because of their power to control, rewards can lead children away from their intrinsic inclinations, away from behaving authentically in accord with abiding values and interests. Arbitrary rewards, if compelling enough, can get people to do almost anything. Indeed, no one who looks at the reality of today's reward-based economies should doubt that powerful extrinsic rewards can lead people to forgo autonomy, forget their values and needs, and neglect their attachments. That is precisely what unhealthy regulation and alienation is all about (Ryan & Deci, 2000a).

Not only can controlling rewards undermine intrinsic motivation, but so can coercive motivational tactics, such as manipulative praise (Ryan, 1982) and threatened punishments (Deci & Cascio, 1972). Further, surveillance (Lepper & Greene, 1975; Pittman, Davey, Alafat, Wetherill, & Kramer, 1980; Plant & Ryan, 1985), evaluations (Smith, 1974), and controlling language (Ryan, 1982) have also been found to decrease intrinsic motivation. In these studies, the external events employed (e.g., reward, surveillance, threat, controlling language) are those that are frequently used as methods of controlling behavior. The common element in these events is their psychological meaning, or *functional significance,* of being controlling, which in turn tends to negatively affect people's sense of autonomy.

Although material rewards are not widely used during the early years of a child's development, the use of controlling interpersonal rewards is very prevalent. Parents, for example, often use controlling directive language and "withdrawal of love" to shape their children's attitudes and behavior (Grolnick, 2002). The general point of this literature is that, to the extent that adults use these salient prods, prompts, or pressures to induce performance of an interesting activity, they are likely to disrupt intrinsic motivation and autonomous functioning, which may in turn result in a variety of nonoptimal outcomes (Assor, Roth, & Deci, 2004).

The significance of this idea for development cannot be overstated. Children's exploration, challenge seeking, and curiosity with respect to the physical and social worlds, from which specific competencies derive, appear to be curtailed in an impinging, contingency-managed environment. Intrinsic motivational tendencies supporting growth can, it appears, be stifled by well-meaning caretakers who attempt to elicit development through reinforcement or control. Thus, even though, as Piaget (1952), Bruner (1962), and many others have emphasized, the tendency toward assimilation is a basic fact of psychic life, such findings suggest that even this basic fact requires circumstances supportive of autonomy and competence to remain vital and active.

A classic study illustrating this principle was performed by Danner and Lonky (1981). They preclassified children with regard to their current level of cognitive development using Piagetian tasks. They then had children work on these tasks either for or without rewards. Subsequently, they allowed the children to choose activities freely during a play opportunity. When free to choose activities at any level of complexity, unrewarded children gravitated to tasks that were optimally challenging—to those just exceeding their cognitive capacities. However, children who were extrinsically rewarded for problem solving tended to avoid challenges, even during free-choice play. Such results illustrate how attempts to "enhance" development through rewards can clearly backfire (see also Grolnick, 2002; Kruglanski, Stein, & Riter, 1977; Pittman, Emery, & Boggiano, 1982). These studies underscore the idea that developmentally relevant activity has its own fuel and requires conditions supportive of autonomy, rather than external controls, to be sustained.

It is particularly troubling, therefore, that the use of controlling strategies is so pervasive in our modern world because it seems to bring about a general shift away from people's active, autonomous engagement with their surroundings toward a more passive and rigid orientation (e.g.,

Deci et al., 1981; McGraw & McCullers, 1979). By attempting to move children to develop through rewards, trophies, competition, and self-esteem pressures, rather than through support of inherent developmental resources, we all too often run the risk of interfering with what we hope to promote (Kohn, 1996).

Some studies have considered whether any external events will enhance rather than undermine the sense of autonomy essential to intrinsic motivation and related psychological processes. For example, Zuckerman, Porac, Lathin, Smith, and Deci (1978) had college student participants work on interesting puzzles. Half were allowed to make task choices, and, using a yoking procedure, half were assigned the tasks selected by those in the choice condition. Results indicated that participants who had been afforded choice were significantly more intrinsically motivated than those who had not. Swann and Pittman (1977) found similar results with children.

A second external event that has had positive effects on intrinsic motivation is acknowledging the individual's feelings. For example, Koestner et al. (1984) found that when setting limits for early elementary school children, their intrinsic motivation remained high for the activity if their feelings of not wanting to observe the limits were acknowledged, whereas their intrinsic motivation was significantly lowered when their feelings were not acknowledged. A study by Deci, Eghrari, Patrick, and Leone (1994) found that acknowledging college-age participants' conflicting feelings also led to more autonomy and a more positive emotional tone than not acknowledging their feelings. Taken together, such studies indicate that providing choice and acknowledging feelings enhances intrinsic motivation and positive affect because these events leave participants feeling less pressured and more autonomous.

In sum, numerous experiments suggest that contextual conditions that are experienced as *controlling* (i.e., as pressure to think, feel, or behave in specific ways) undermine autonomy, resulting in less self-initiation and greater psychological rigidity. In contrast, contextual conditions that are *autonomy-supportive* (i.e., that take the target individual's frame of reference, providing choice and encouraging self-initiation) have positive effects on intrinsic motivation. Extrapolating from this, it is easy to predict that contexts that are overly controlling rather than autonomy-supportive represent one identifiable input to nonoptimal developmental outcomes.

Although it is not the central focus of this chapter, it is worth noting that numerous studies have shown that persistent feedback indicating incompetence at a task or in an activity domain undermines both intrinsic and extrinsic motivation (e.g., Deci, Cascio, & Krusell, 1973; Hiroto & Seligman, 1975; Koestner & McClelland, 1990). We refer to contexts that continually signify incompetence, potentially resulting in helplessness and depression, as *amotivating*. Indeed, pervasively critical caregivers can lead to the internalization of a sense of self that is incompetent (e.g., Strauss & Ryan, 1987), resulting in a variety of psychological disturbances.

Field Studies

Numerous field studies of parents and teachers have investigated the effects of controlling versus autonomy-supportive social structures on intrinsic motivation. We review some exemplary ones that illustrate effects at different ages.

Grolnick, Bridges, and Frodi (1984) in a study of infants found that those whose mother was more controlling evidenced less mastery motivation and persistence in independent problem solving than did those whose mother tended to support and encourage their initiations and autonomous play.

Deci, Driver, Hotchkiss, Robbins, and Wilson (1993) found similar results in a sample of 5- to 7-year-old children. They reported that mothers who, during an interactive-play period, were rated as being relatively controlling had children whose subsequent intrinsic motivation was lower than those whose vocalizations were rated as more autonomy-supportive.

Deci et al. (1981) found comparable results for late elementary school teachers and their students using teacher self-reports about motivational strategies. When teachers were oriented toward supporting autonomy, the students displayed higher levels of intrinsic motivation, perceived cognitive competence, and self-esteem, whereas when the teachers were oriented toward controlling behavior, the opposite results were obtained. Ryan and Grolnick (1986) reported similar results using children's perceptions of teachers, as did Flink, Boggiano, and Barrett (1990), who also found that when teachers were more controlling students performed less well.

The results of such field studies cohere on several points. When people in positions of responsibility or authority—for example, parents and teachers—support the autonomy of those with whom they interact, the latter individuals tend to display enhanced autonomy, intrinsic motivation, and self-regard. Overcontrol, conversely, is typically associated with diminished motivation and self-esteem. It is noteworthy that the results of these field studies parallel the results of laboratory experiments in which autonomy-supportive versus controlling interpersonal climates were created.

Internalization

When intrinsically motivated, children do what interests them, whether it be exploring a novel space, building a model, or playing with a doll. Although a source of delight for caretakers, it is also a challenge. Often, caregivers think it important to redirect the children's attention and energy away from what interests them to other activities that promote family harmony, improve school performance, or are socially sanctioned. There are many activities, in fact, that children may not find intrinsically interesting but that parents, school systems, and society believe are in the children's best interest. It is thus the task of parents and teachers, as primary socializing agents, to encourage children not only to perform such nonintrinsically motivated activities, but also to aid them in developing internal motivation and willingness to do so.

The shift from an external impetus and sustenance of behaviors to an internal one is characterized herein as the process of *internalization* (Ryan, Connell, & Deci, 1985). Internalization is the means through which someone can become more autonomous in performing an activity that was initially externally prompted. It is an active process of taking in regulatory processes and transforming them into personal values or motivational propensities (Meissner, 1988; Ryan, Connell, et al., 1985; Schafer, 1968).

Internalization is an instance of organismic integration. It is the means through which people, by integrating experiences and the regulatory processes implicit in them, can become more autonomous while at the same time more homonomous, or integrated into one's social world (Angyal, 1965). Through internalization, people acquire values and behaviors that allow them to be effective, to relate to others in a community, and to experience a true sense of willingness in doing so. In other words, internalization functions primarily in the service of people's needs for competence, autonomy, and relatedness, and through effective internalization people become both more homonomous and more autonomous. Conversely, failures of internalization typically imply less effective functioning and vulnerability to alienation and psychopathology.

Because internalization operates in the service of these three basic psychological needs, we can readily predict that aspects of the social context that support autonomy, are adequately structured to support competence, and provide caring interpersonal involvement supporting relatedness will facilitate internalization. When the context allows satisfaction of these needs, and particularly when they are not in any way pitted against each other, there will be optimal socializing circumstances for children to naturally acquire social values subserving nonintrinsically motivated activity.

Conceptualized in this way, one can see that both intrinsic motivation and internalization are related to the construct of autonomy. Intrinsic motivation is the prototype of autonomous regulation, and internalization and integration represent the means by which activities that are not intrinsically interesting can become more autonomous. By integrating values and regulatory processes into one's self, those values and processes become the basis for self-determination of extrinsically motivated (i.e., instrumental) activities. And, although behaviors for which the regulatory processes have been fully integrated do not necessarily become intrinsically motivated (because they retain their instrumental rather than autotelic nature), the more closely the qualities of one's extrinsically motivated behaviors match those of intrinsically motivated behavior, the more likely it is that the extrinsic regulation has been integrated.

In developmental terms, infants express their autonomy through intrinsically motivated engagement and mastery. Gradually, as they develop into toddlerhood, childhood, and adulthood, their autonomous activity is expanded by the integration of regulatory processes that originally had an external impetus or source. It may well be that adults express less intrinsically motivated behavior than children, and instead more frequently display their autonomy in the form of integrated regulation.

When functioning optimally, the internalization process results in values and regulations that are fully integrated with the self. We hypothesize that supports for autonomy and relatedness are necessary for such optimal internalization. Unfortunately, these ideal contextual conditions are not widely prevalent, and full integration of regulations is not often attained. Instead, when socializing agents are too controlling or uninvolved, the internalization process operates nonoptimally, resulting in values and regulations that are only introjected or that remain externally regulated (Ryan, 1993).

Introjection is only partial assimilation in which the internal regulatory process retains essentially the same form it had when it was still external. Perls (1973), for example, vividly described introjection as a process in which some aspect of the environment is "swallowed whole" and never "digested." Metaphorically, it is as if the regulator and regulatee were still separate, even though they are the same person; the regulatory process has *not* been integrated with the self and is thus a source of tension and inner conflict. When a regulation has been introjected (rather than integrated), it tends to be rigid and controlling. Indeed, introjection supplies the developmental basis for *internally controlling* regulation, such as that evidenced in ego involvement (Ryan, 1982). Several studies have now demonstrated that introjection is related to anxiety, self-derogation, and other maladaptive patterns, whereas fuller integration is associated with more positive adaptation (e.g., Ryan & Connell, 1989; Ryan, Rigby, & King, 1993). This suggests, of course, that to the extent that values and regulatory processes are stuck in the form of introjects, a child is at risk for psychopathology.

The importance of distinguishing types of internalization is crucial for developmental theories concerned with the nature and quality of behavioral and psychological functioning. Even in early life it is clear that infants and young children can be either self-regulating or merely compliant. As Crockenberg and Litman (1990) detail, there is a significant difference between a toddler's behaving compliantly, out of fear or force, and behaving autonomously, with a sense of willingness. It is the autonomous performance of uninteresting, though important, activities that should be a goal of socialization. Kochanska's (1995) differentiation of situational compliance from committed compliance reflects a similar perspective.

To provide a framework for making distinctions among various types of internalization, we have specified four regulatory styles that are pertinent to extrinsically motivated behavior (Deci & Ryan, 1985b). *External* regulation describes extrinsically motivated behavior that is initiated and maintained by external rewards and/or punishment avoidance. A girl who does her chores to avoid parental wrath would be externally regulated, as would a child who does them to get rewarded. When an external regulation

has been internalized but not accepted as one's own, it is said to be *introjected*. A boy who cleans up his room because he thinks he should—because that is what "good boys" do—would have introjected the regulation. Gradually, as a child identifies with a value or regulatory process, the child begins to accept it as his or her own. In such cases, the behavior is governed by what we call *identified* regulation, which can be viewed as transitional between introjected and integrated regulation. A girl who studies arithmetic because she believes it is important for her self-selected goal of becoming an architect would be considered identified in terms of this regulation. Finally, *integrated* regulation is the most advanced form of internalized regulation and indicates that a value and its accompanying regulatory process have been reciprocally assimilated with all other aspects of one's self. The internalization process will have been completed, representing further development of one's self. A young man who identifies with working hard at his studies and also identifies with being a good soccer player, and who has organized these differing values within a relatively harmonious regulatory network, can be said to have integrated these regulations.

These varied forms of behavioral regulation are schematically depicted in Figure 20.1. As seen, the four styles of extrinsic motivation can be placed along a continuum of relative autonomy, where external regulation is the least autonomous and integrated regulation is the most autonomous form of extrinsically motivated behavior.

Ryan and Connell (1989) assessed children's external, introjected, and identified regulatory styles for doing schoolwork, as well as their intrinsic motivation. Data confirmed that the external, introjected, identified, and intrin-

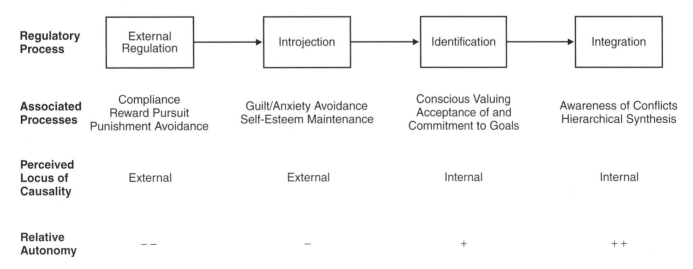

Figure 20.1   The self-determination theory model of internalization.

sic subscales formed a simplex-like pattern, indicating that these four regulatory styles can be ordered along a single dimension of autonomy. The more autonomous styles (identified and intrinsic) were positively correlated with positive affect and proactive coping, whereas the less autonomous styles (i.e., external and introjected) were correlated with negative affect and maladaptive coping. Introjection, in particular, was highly correlated with anxiety and with anxiety amplification following failure, thus highlighting the inner stress and vulnerability caused by these controlling prescriptions.

Ryan and Connell (1989) also found that more autonomous regulation in the prosocial domain was associated with greater empathy, more mature moral reasoning, and more positive relatedness to others, thus signifying the importance of autonomous self-regulation for healthy adaptation in the prosocial as well as the academic domain.

Ryan, Rigby, et al. (1993) examined the degree of internalization of religious values in late adolescents and adults. Results indicated that introjected regulation of religious behaviors was positively associated with symptoms of depression and anxiety and with low self-esteem, whereas identified regulation was negatively associated with these indicators.

Blais, Sabourin, Boucher, and Vallerand (1990) assessed adults' reasons for maintaining their primary relationship, using six types of reasons that vary in their degree of autonomy: amotivational, external, introjected, identified, integrated, and intrinsic. They reported, from a sample of 63 heterosexual couples, that the three regulatory styles constituting non-self-determination (i.e., amotivational, external, and introjected) all correlated significantly negatively with dyadic adjustment and general marital satisfaction. In contrast, the three regulatory styles constituting greater autonomy (i.e., identified, integrated, and intrinsic) all correlated significantly positively with those variables.

Work on self-regulation using the constructs outlined earlier is continuing in the domains of religion (O'Connor & Vallerand, 1990), health care (Ryan, Plant, & O'Malley, 1993; G. C. Williams, Grow, Ryan, Friedman, & Deci, 1996), aging (V. G. Kasser & Ryan, 1999; Vallerand & O'Connor, 1989), education (Grolnick, Ryan, & Deci, 1991; Vallerand & Bissonnette, 1992), and relationships (Deci et al., 2004), among several other areas. Across multiple domains, the findings have indicated consistently that the less integral and autonomous one's motivations, the less positive one's adjustment and well-being.

Introjection results in internally controlling regulation, which is not considered part of one's true or integrated self, but instead can be thought of as akin to a false self. Of course, if the organismic integration process continues to function with respect to an introjected value or process (as, for example, in psychotherapy), that value or regulatory process may, in time, be integrated, but insofar as the integrative process is stalled, introjected regulations remain alien to the self.

Internalization and the Social Context

Although internalization and integration are natural processes, they, like intrinsic motivation and all other such processes in the organismic dialectic, require nutriments and supports from the social context. We saw in the discussion of intrinsic motivation that this natural activity was organized strongly in terms of the fundamental psychological needs for autonomy and competence. According to self-determination theory, people need to feel competent and autonomous, and when they experience these feelings while engaging in an interesting activity, their intrinsic motivation is maintained or enhanced. However, when they engage social contextual conditions that thwart their efforts toward autonomy and competence, their intrinsic motivation is undermined and they tend to become controlled or amotivated in relation to that activity.

Internalization, which involves accepting attitudes, values, and behaviors endorsed by one's social world, is also theorized to function effectively when people experience autonomy and competence, but there is also a third basic psychological need that, according to SDT, is critical for internalization and integration to operate optimally. Specifically, people have a basic need for relatedness or connectedness with others, and this plays a crucial role in internalization and, as we will see, in healthy development and the prevention of psychopathology. Out of the innate desire to be part of a social matrix, to feel connected to significant others, people tend to internalize the beliefs and behaviors of those others. To the degree that the internalization occurs in the context of autonomy support, the internalized values and behavioral regulations are more likely to become integrated.

Based on the proposition that people have these universal psychological needs, Grolnick and Ryan (1989) proposed that there are three parenting dimensions that are important for facilitating children's basic need satisfaction and thus both their intrinsic motivation and the internalization and eventual integration of extrinsic motivations. These critical contextual (i.e., parenting) dimensions are involvement, structure, and autonomy support.

Parents' being involved with their children, relating to them and providing a moderate amount of consistent, clear structure, facilitates internalization of values and regulatory processes, but for those internalized processes to be integrated, the parents must also provide autonomy support. If, instead, parents are excessively controlling, it is likely that any internalized processes will merely be introjected, not integrated.

Being autonomy-supportive for a child implies that one attempts to grasp and acknowledge the child's perspective, use minimal controls to foster behavior, and provide choice when possible. When that occurs, the child will understand the reasons for self-regulating and will feel understood. Further, the behaviors that are encouraged will be performed with a relatively more internal perceived locus of causality. In contrast, being controlling involves parents' pressuring the child to do what they want, emphasizing obedience and compliance.

Most theories of parenting employ a variable that is anchored on one end by a concept essentially equivalent to being controlling. For example, Becker (1964) spoke of restrictive parenting, Schaefer (1959) described controlling parenting, and Baldwin (1955) discussed an autocratic style of parenting. These terms apply to parents who place paramount value on compliance. Children of parents high on these attributes have been found to be hostile (Hoffman, 1960), dysphoric and disaffiliated (Baumrind, 1967), and obedient, low in social interaction, and dominated by peers (Baldwin, 1955).

Although there is general agreement about the controlling end of a parent dimension, there is less agreement about the other end. Whereas some researchers have contrasted control with permissiveness (e.g., Becker, 1964), others have contrasted it with democracy (Baldwin, 1949). We emphasize that autonomy support does not imply permissiveness, neglect, or the absence of action on the part of the parent, but instead conveys an active support of the child's capacity to be self-initiating and autonomous. Of the various concepts that have previously been used in contrast to control, Baldwin's concept of democratic parenting comes closest to autonomy support.

Baumrind (1971) empirically examined the effects of parental styles on internalization. She contrasted authoritative and authoritarian parental styles. The *authoritative* parent communicates openly with the child and encourages independence and individuality, while at the same time holding expectations and standards for mature behavior. The *authoritarian* parent, in contrast, values obedience and compliance and attempts to shape the child according to an absolute standard. Baumrind (1977) found that nursery school girls from authoritarian homes were withdrawn and dependent and boys were aggressive. From our perspective, these two seemingly contrasting behavior patterns are two

sides of a coin, for they are both manifestations of being controlled by authoritarian parents. In one, the child relies excessively on others to control behavior; in the other, the child rebels against the controls and aggresses with little provocation. In contrast, children from authoritative homes were more adaptive in their behavior, displaying assertive, independent, and friendly actions.

Grolnick and Ryan (1989) extended the work of Baumrind and others by proposing a set of three parenting dimensions from which the parenting styles could be derived. The dimensions are autonomy-supportive (versus controlling), structured (versus unstructured), and involved (versus uninvolved). Their dimensionalization recognizes that parental autonomy support can co-occur with parental structure (i.e., consistent and clear expectations, rules, and consequences) or without such structure. Further, any of these parenting styles can be embedded in relationships characterized by various levels of involvement.

Using this three-dimensional model, Grolnick and Ryan (1989) interviewed separately, in their homes, the mothers and fathers of late elementary school students to determine how they deal with their children concerning doing homework and chores. In addition, the children, in their classrooms, completed a self-regulation questionnaire developed by Ryan and Connell (1989), as well as a measure of their understanding of control over school outcomes (Connell, 1985). Teachers rated the children's classroom adjustment and motivation, and school records were accessed to examine objective competence outcomes. Results indicated that parental controllingness predicted children's failure to internalize regulations, as well as poor adjustment and low achievement. Lack of involvement predicted children's not understanding how to control outcomes and contributed to poor adjustment and achievement. Parental inconsistency predicted children's lack of control understanding. Thus, the data indicated that parental autonomy support, structure, and involvement contribute to children's abilities to self-regulate and function effectively in their social contexts. Parents' failure to provide these necessary nutriments leads to poor adjustment and achievement and may set the stage for more profound disturbances.

Grolnick et al. (1991) tested the idea that the effects of the parental environment on children's outcomes are mediated by the children's self-relevant motivations and perceptions. Results indicated that children who perceived their mother and father as less involved and autonomy-supportive also reported poorer self-regulation, perceived competence, and control understanding relative to those who perceived more involvement and autonomy support. These self-relevant motivation variables, in turn, predicted the children's school performance, thus serving as mediators between the home context and children's performance. Elmen, Mounts, and Steinberg (1989) found comparable results using Baumrind's conceptualization.

Deci et al. (1994) performed a laboratory experiment to explore social contextual influences on internalization and integration. They manipulated three contextual factors that were thought to constitute autonomy support and involvement: a meaningful *rationale* so the individual would understand the personal importance of the requested activity; an *acknowledgment* of the individual's feelings so that he or she would feel understood; and an interpersonal style that emphasizes *choice* and minimizes control. Results revealed that the absence of these three facilitating factors impaired internalization, thus complementing the findings from the Grolnick and Ryan (1989) field study. Further, Deci et al. showed that the internalization that occurred in the conditions not supportive of self-determination (viz., those with at most one of the facilitating factors) was introjected, as reflected by negative relations between subsequent behavior and participants' self-reports of perceived choice, importance of the activity, and enjoyment, whereas the internalization that occurred in the conditions supporting self-determination (viz., those with at least two facilitating factors) was better integrated, as reflected by coherence between subsequent behavior and these affective variables.

The critical difference between introjected and identified motivation, which represent two types of internal motivation, was recently confirmed in an experimental study in preadolescent overweight children (Simons, Vansteenkiste, Braet, & Deci, 2005). Half of the overweight children were encouraged in an autonomy-supportive fashion to follow the guidelines of the four-leaf clover, a simplified version of the food pyramid, by providing them opportunities for choice and self-initiative. In a second condition, children were pressured in a subtle and implicit way to follow the guidelines of the four-leaf clover. The subtle controlling manipulation involved practices of guilt induction ("You might feel guilty for not doing so") and self-esteem contingency ("You might feel better about yourself if you would do so").The controlling counseling approach no doubt elicited introjects readily available in individuals, while the autonomy-supportive approach was intended to promote identified regulation. Although any effort to follow the guidelines of the four-leaf clover would be initiated by the person in both cases (and not by external forces), the type of internal motivation guiding children's behavior change was of a considerably different sort. Results showed that children in both conditions adopted a more healthy lifestyle during the week following the experimental manipulation. Yet, after 3 weeks, these gains were maintained only in the condition where an identified regulation was promoted. Children's attendance and weight loss started to decline after two sessions when an introjected regulation was produced, whereas children continued to show up for the diet sessions and lost further weight when an identified regulation was produced.

Similarly, a number of studies speak to the relation between parental autonomy support and internalization. Notably, the model holds up well not only in Western, individualistic cultures where autonomy is a salient value, but also in nations where authority and tradition have predominated. For example, Chirkov and Ryan (2001), in a study of Russian and U.S. high school students' self-reports, found that perceived autonomy support from parents and teachers predicted both more internalized academic motivation and better mental health.

It appears, then, that if the context fails to support self-initiation and choice—that is, if significant others are controlling and uninvolved—people are less likely to internalize values, attitudes, and behaviors than if the significant others are autonomy-supportive and involved. Furthermore, when the context fails to provide the necessary nutriments, internalization that does occur is likely to have the quality of introjection, thus being rigid, conflicted, and marked by negative emotionality.

Weiss and Grolnick (1991) studied the relationship of parental involvement and autonomy support to adolescents' internalizing and externalizing symptoms (Achenbach & Edelbrock, 1987). Adolescents rated their mother and father on dimensions of involvement and autonomy support, and they completed the self-report profile of symptoms. Analyses indicated that parents who were perceived to be *both* highly involved and autonomy-supportive had children who reported very low levels of either internalizing or externalizing symptoms. However, there were significant interactions between perceived parental involvement and autonomy support on both types of symptoms, indicating that the combination of high involvement and low autonomy support yielded a high level of symptoms. It thus appears that feeling close to very controlling parents can be detrimental to a developing child's well-being. This relates as well to the results of Fuhrman and Holmbeck (1995) reported earlier, who showed that emotional autonomy (which we have interpreted as emotional detachment) was more beneficial to teens whose parents were low in support. Having to give up one's autonomy to satisfy the need for relatedness to parents can be quite costly, as can the converse: having to detach to maintain a sense of self.

From these and related studies, we conclude that parental involvement, structure, and autonomy support are necessary for optimal internalization of social values and regulations and, in turn, for adjustment. It is particularly important to note that parental involvement and structure are not enough, for without autonomy support, whatever internalization occurs is likely to be introjected rather than integrated, and the accompanying tension and inner conflict are likely to be associated with greater symptomatology.

Attachment, Intimacy, and Relatedness across the Life Span: The Role of Autonomy

The connection between autonomy and relatedness has been a hotly debated topic among psychological theorists over the past 2 decades. Some authors (e.g., Gilligan, 1982; Iyengar & Lepper, 1999) see autonomy and relatedness as largely independent if not antithetical, and others (e.g., Bakan, 1966) see them as dialectically related to one another (again implying an original opposition that precedes synthesis). Our view differs from these because we do not view autonomy and relatedness as being in opposition. Indeed, we see them as integral to one another.

When we first began to explore the dynamics of autonomy and relatedness, we assumed that the strength and quality of one's connection to others in a given context could be examined separately from one's sense of autonomy. Accordingly, in a variety of studies, using varied age samples and contexts, we attempted to do independent assessments of participants' feeling related to others and feeling that their autonomy was supported by others. For example, we asked children to rate their parents with regard to both the sense of warmth and connectedness (indices of relatedness) and the sense of their parents' taking their perspective, offering choices, and using minimal controls (indices of autonomy support). Separable factors did not emerge, but instead warmth and connectedness ratings invariantly loaded with those representing autonomy support. Similar difficulties in obtaining independent factors for affection/warmth and autonomy support have occurred for other dyads such as teacher-child and physician-patient. Thus, for example, in studies of classroom climate, it is typically difficult to separate perceived teachers' warmth and caring from their autonomy support. This series of psychometric mishaps strongly conveyed how closely connected one's feelings of attachment and relatedness are to the sense that the other acknowledges and supports one. This has led us to explore these seemingly inextricable constructs more deeply.

With more clarity about the meaning of relatedness, we realized that, phenomenologically, one typically feels authentically related to another person only to the extent that one feels free to be oneself with him or her (Ryan, 1989, 1991). In other words, one feels warmly related to and secure in one's connection with others only to the extent that there is receptivity to and acceptance of one's real self. Conversely, insofar as there is a felt absence of autonomy support, the quality of relatedness suffers: One's connection is more superficial, insecure, and contingent.

How deep does this connection between autonomy and relatedness run? We suggest that from the very beginning of life, the strength and security of attachment is in part a function of the autonomy support afforded by caregivers. We therefore begin our analysis of these intertwined needs during infancy, and then we proceed to examine this dynamic across the life span.

Autonomy and Relatedness in Infancy

It is particularly difficult to separate the development of autonomy and relatedness in the child's 1st year of life. During this period, according to Stern (1985), establishing a core self is a primary agenda for the infant. Although the self that is consolidated within the first 6 months does not take the form of a conscious representation, it is manifest as coherence and volition. Because infants are highly dependent on caregivers not only for biological necessities such as food and temperature regulation but also for interpersonal necessities such as love, contact, and comfort, these earliest experiences of the self as "initiator" of action occur in the context of very close parent-child relationships in which responsiveness to rising needs and signals of them strengthens the sense of agency and its connections with action.

The interrelated development of autonomy and relatedness is described, albeit using different terms, in attachment theory. According to Bowlby (1969) and later theorists who have elaborated his framework (e.g., Bretherton, 1987), infants are innately prepared to engage in social relations from birth. The nature of these early social relations with primary caregivers shapes the security of attachment and the corresponding working models of self and others that function to organize future social relations.

Perhaps the most emphasized feature in attachment theory that contributes to security of attachment is the caregiver's responsiveness or *sensitivity* (Ainsworth et al., 1978; Brody & Axelrad, 1978). Sensitivity is defined as the provision of contingent, appropriate, and consistent responses to the child's signals and needs (Lamb & Easterbrooks, 1981). Sensitivity is thus a broad concept conveying that caregivers are responsive to the child's initiations in ways that are empathic and appropriate to the child's needs.

We have suggested that one can unpack the broad concept of sensitivity into its component parts and that these parts will correspond to the dimensions of autonomy support, involvement, and structure. Autonomy support is clearly a component of sensitivity in that what one is being sensitive to are the child's initiations, strivings, needs, and developing self. Indeed, Bretherton's (1987, p. 1075) description of sensitivity in terms of "maternal respect for the child's autonomy" captures the essence of such contingent responsiveness. The sensitive caretaker responds to the initiations, cues, concerns, and needs that emerge from the child, and this contingent responsiveness gradually strengthens the child's inner sense of agency and coherence, and thus the meaningfulness of the child's self-initiated action and expression. When responded to, the child experiences a sense of safety and interconnection that is lacking for one whose biddings and expressions have fallen on deaf ears.

Autonomy support is thus a critical component of early relationships, for it facilitates not only the solidity of attachment but also self-development more generally. Numerous studies have supported this perspective by linking sensitivity and/or autonomy support to more curiosity, effectance, and ego resiliency (Arend, Gove, & Sroufe, 1979; Grolnick et al., 1984; Waters, Wippman, & Sroufe, 1979), greater self-initiation (Stevenson & Lamb, 1981; Watson, 1966), improved learning (Lewis & Coates, 1980; Yarrow et al., 1975), and in general more resourcefulness and better adjustment (Brody, 1956).

This interrelationship among autonomy support, attachment, and self-development is also considered in Bowlby's (1969) speculations concerning infant exploration and mastery motivation. He postulated the existence of two innate systems that guide the child's behavior and development. The *attachment system* has as its goal the attainment and maintenance of close proximity to and contact with the caregiver; the goal of the *exploratory system* is to discover and master the world around one. These two systems are mutually dependent, however, and the satisfactory attainment of one will occur only in concert with the other. According to Bowlby, to the extent that a child experiences security (i.e., a sense that the caregiver will be accessible and responsive in times of need), the child will feel enabled to venture forth to explore with interest. However, to the extent that attachment is insecure, the child will stay close and monitor the parent's status and thus will not display healthy attempts at mastery and autonomous initiation.

This brief analysis of the role of autonomy and relatedness in infancy suggests the following: Autonomy support is a critical component of caregiving in infancy that shapes both the experienced quality of relatedness (as reflected in the security of attachment) and the consolidation and vitality of the self (as reflected in both well-being and mastery motivation). Relatedness that is low in autonomy support, by contrast, will set the stage for attachment disturbances and impoverished agency.

Although we have emphasized the centrality of autonomy support to the construct of sensitivity and to formation of secure attachments, it is not the only component variable contributing to these. The sensitive environment also provides involvement and structure. The involved parent dedicates resources to the child in the form of availability, effort, attention, and concrete nurturance. The sensitive caregiver also contributes to security by providing structure in the form of an optimal environment that modulates stimulation in accord with the infant's capacities and state. These contributions to well-being help to provide a sense of safety and comfort that are the backdrops of secure relations and the development of competencies. However, the patterning of additional contributions must grow out of a reading of the child's actual needs and emotional states to facilitate the emerging self. That is, the optimal environment is one that provides resources and introduces structure in a context of autonomy support.

Autonomy and Relatedness during Childhood

As a result of their experiences with early caretakers, children develop a set of models and expectancies regarding interpersonal interaction that are often referred to as object representations (Behrends & Blatt, 1985) or working models (Bretherton, 1991). These internal representations and models are *hypothetical* rather than inductively derived variables, which are used to explain how experiences in relationships with caregivers foster characteristic patterns of interpersonal perceptions and behaviors that an individual exhibits. Because of their hypothetical status, such representations have been assessed and described in many different ways. Indeed, the methodological and content focus of representational assessments is as varied as the theoretical models that have been brought to bear on early childhood relatedness.

Given the emphasis in self-determination theory on the connections between relatedness and autonomy throughout development, one particularly intriguing conceptualization of object representations is that based on the *mutuality of autonomy* construct. Derived from object relational (Winnicott, 1960/1965) and self psychological (Kohut, 1971) theories, this construct assesses one's internalized schemata of relationships along a dimension ranging from those characterized by reciprocal dialogue and autonomy to those characterized by unifocal power and overwhelming control. Thus, the construct inherently assumes that the quality of one's relatedness is to a great degree a function of the autonomy supportiveness that characterizes it.

In a study of urban preadolescents, Ryan, Avery, and Grolnick (1985) employed a projective measure of mutuality of autonomy developed by Urist (1977). Based on the idea that experiences of relatedness that lack autonomy would be associated with less integrated functioning, these investigators hypothesized and found that poorer mutuality of autonomy predicted lower perceived control, poorer school grades, and, most important, worse interpersonal and classroom adjustment as rated by teachers. Tuber (1992) recently reviewed a number of studies with clinical samples that further document how various forms of psychopathology in childhood and adolescence are typically accompanied by lower levels of mutuality of autonomy.

Avery and Ryan (1988), also working with urban children in middle childhood, utilized a different projective assessment of object representations developed by Blatt, Chevron, Quinlan, and Wein (1981) to examine the parental antecedents of the quality of children's object representations. Avery and Ryan found that two variables derived from self-determination theory, perceived parental autonomy support and involvement, predicted the overall nurturant quality of parental representations. Further, a wide array of functional outcomes, including peer sociometric ratings, general adjustment ratings, and perceived social and cognitive competence, were facilitated by parental autonomy support and involvement. As in infant attachment, these results bespeak the critical components of autonomy support and involvement underlying secure relatedness.

There is evidence that parents' involvement and autonomy support facilitate children's adjustment at key transition points. The transition from elementary school to junior high is a time of vulnerability, with many children experiencing declines in perceptions of competence and control and school grades. Grolnick, Kurowski, Dunlap, and Hevey (2000) examined levels of involvement and autonomy support in parents of children making this transition both before and after the move to junior high. These authors showed that high levels of involvement during sixth grade buffered children from experiencing declines in perceived competence and grades over the transition. Children of parents who displayed high levels of autonomy in sixth grade and those of parents who increased or maintained their levels of autonomy support and involvement over the transition did not display the same increases in acting-out and learning problems as those of parents who were low in autonomy support or decreased their provision of resources

across the transition. The idea that involvement is no longer necessary when children reach preadolescence is inconsistent with these data, which illustrate the ongoing importance of involved, autonomy-supportive parenting.

Autonomy and Relatedness in Middle and Late Adolescence

Adolescence, as we already discussed, is a critical period of life in which the teenager is rapidly developing capacities for independence, while still needing considerable support and nurturance and, we argue, a secure base of attachment. Considerable evidence suggests, however, that the security of attachment in this age is quite dependent on caregiver's support for autonomy.

First, several studies support our view of adolescents' continued need to feel secure relatedness to parents. For example, Ryan, Stiller, and Lynch (1994) investigated the contributions of relatedness to parents, teachers, and friends to the prediction of motivation, adjustment, and self-esteem of early adolescents. They found that the quality of relatedness to parents and teachers, assessed in terms of felt security, as well as utilization and emulation of these target figures, predicted adjustment, again attesting to the facilitating effect of relatedness on one's integration and well-being. Further, they found evidence that the quality of relatedness to parents predicted the quality of relatedness to both teachers and peers and appeared to have priority among working models. Similarly, Bober and Grolnick (1995) assessed adolescents' felt security with and emulation of parents and peers. Adolescents who displayed internalizing symptomatology reported low levels of felt security with parents and peers yet emulated these groups. Adolescents who displayed externalizing symptomatology reported low levels of both felt security and emulation of parents.

Ryan and Kuczkowski (1994) also examined the effects of felt security on the development of autonomy in adolescence. In a cross-sectional design, they assessed adolescents' experience of private audiences (Elkind, 1967), arguing that the private audience phenomenon, a precipitate of cognitive development in early adolescence, typically represents a heteronomous influence on adolescent behavior (Elkind, 1967; Piaget, 1965). This phenomenon is essentially akin to public self-consciousness and can be the basis of internally controlling regulation, particularly if it persists past early adolescence. Ryan and Kuczkowski supported this reasoning by showing that the salience of private audiences to adolescents was negatively related to public individuation. Further, based on theorizing by Lapsley and Rice (1988), Ryan and Kuczkowski predicted and found that whereas security of relatedness to parents was unrelated to the strength of private audiences in early adolescence (when it is an emerging and normative aspect of ego development), it was more strongly related in later adolescence. Those adolescents experiencing emotional insecurity with parents tended to remain more preoccupied with private audiences and were less capable of public individuation, in opposition to normative trends. This shows one specific way in which the growth of autonomy is dependent on one's embeddedness in secure relationships.

Ryan and Lynch (1989), in a study reviewed earlier in this chapter, examined both theoretically and empirically the issues of autonomy and attachment in early, middle, and late adolescent samples. They cited several theorists and researchers who have viewed adolescents' development of autonomy in terms of an increasing independence and nonreliance on parents. Ryan and Lynch, in contrast, argued that autonomy is more typically *facilitated* by attachment and dependence on parents rather than by detachment. Indeed, they suggested that among the primary reasons that adolescents detach from and refuse to rely on parents is that parents have been overly controlling and/or underinvolved. According to Ryan and Lynch, adolescents whose parents provide a more optimal caretaking environment in which there is both involvement and autonomy support do not need to relinquish their attachment in order to become more autonomous and self-regulated. Rather than having to trade off relatedness for autonomy, such adolescents can maintain both, precisely because in an autonomy-supportive context the parent-adolescent relationship itself changes in accord with developing adolescent capacities and needs. In support of their perspective, Ryan and Lynch showed that adolescents with stronger positive ties to parents were, in fact, better adjusted and self-regulated than were those whose connectedness with parents was poorer. This fits with a number of other extant perspectives and findings (e.g., Behrends & Blatt, 1985; Hill & Holmbeck, 1986; Kandel & Lesser, 1969).

T. Kasser, Ryan, Zax, and Sameroff (1995) investigated a racially and economically diverse sample of teenagers and their mothers in a study of the developmental antecedents of extrinsic aspirations for wealth, relative to intrinsic aspirations such as growth, relatedness, and community. The adolescents' perceptions of the degree to which their mother was democratic, noncontrolling, and warm were collected, as were the mothers' self-reports on these same variables. In addition, clinical interviewers made their own ratings of maternal nurturance based on a previously recorded maternal narrative. Low scores on these dimensions, of course, represent the types of social environments that thwart satisfaction of the children's basic psychological needs for autonomy and relatedness. Kasser et al. found that when mothers were low on democracy, noncontrollingness, and warmth, as indexed by any of the three rating sources, the adolescents placed significantly higher relative importance on the extrinsic aspiration for wealth. The results thus suggest that parenting environments that thwart children's need satisfaction facilitate the development of extrinsic aspirations such as wealth that are visible indicators of "worth" and may represent substitutes for basic need satisfaction. Kasser et al. also examined archival data from the mothers of these teenagers that had been collected several years earlier. A variable labeled risk, derived from ratings by trained observers, represented mothers' coldness in interactions with their children and controllingness in parenting beliefs. This risk index significantly predicted higher relative extrinsic aspirations in the teenagers. Moreover, analyses of well-being indicators showed that teens holding extrinsic values were less well adjusted and were less constructively involved in their community. These analyses provide initial support for our developmental speculations that psychological need deprivation can foster "need substitutes" or compensatory motives such as overly strong extrinsic aspirations.

One ramification of the development of strong compensatory motives such as extrinsic aspirations that result from lack of support for autonomy and relatedness is that they tend to perpetuate the lack of need satisfaction. Extrinsic goals keep people focused on the need substitutes and thereby exacerbate the negative consequences for well-being by leading them away from a focus on relationships and growth (see T. Kasser, 2002, for a more extensive discussion of this issue).

Autonomy and Relatedness in Young Adulthood

According to Reis and Shaver (1988), intimate relationships in adulthood not only depend on strong ties, but they also entail an acceptance and encouragement of the true self of one's partner. This affordance of autonomy support breeds a sense of trust and confidence, as well as facilitating self-expression and actualization. Several studies support this critical point concerning wellness and full functioning in adulthood.

Dresner and Grolnick (1992) examined how the autonomy and interpersonal relatedness of college women was influenced by their parental object representations. The women's current relationships were classified as being caring, respectful, and intimate, or alternatively, as being either superficial or enmeshed (Levitz-Jones & Orlofsky, 1985; Orlofsky, Marcia, & Lesser, 1973). Results indicated that whereas women whose relationships were caring and intimate had parental representations that were accepting and autonomy-supportive, the women with more superficial relationships had object representations that were nonaccepting and overcontrolling, and the women with enmeshed relationships had representations that were nonaccepting but idealized. Further, women who were high in autonomy orientation (Deci & Ryan, 1985a) had parental representations that were autonomy-supportive, whereas those who did not display high autonomy had representations that were saliently controlling.

La Guardia, Ryan, Couchman, and Deci (2000) studied patterns of secure and insecure attachment in multiple social partners of college student participants, most of whom were young adults. The focus was especially on within-person variations in security of attachment. La Guardia et al. acknowledged that individual differences in security of attachment (also referred to as between-person security of attachment) are likely to be a significant predictor of security of attachment in later life with other individuals, such as best friends and romantic partners. However, they suggested that there is likely to be a significant amount of variance in a person's security of attachment with each partner, which is a function of what goes on in that particular relationship. More specifically, just as primary caregivers' supporting the autonomy, competence, and relatedness of children affect their children's attachment security with them (and their children's working models), the support for adults' autonomy, competence, and relatedness provided by relational partners will affect the person's security of attachment with that partner. Thus, security of attachment was hypothesized by La Guardia et al. to be a function both of between-person factors (i.e., individual differences) and of within-person factors (i.e., the need satisfaction provided by the particular partner). In three studies, these researchers examined the security of attachment that college students have with their mother, father, romantic partner, and best friend, as well as the level of satisfaction of the needs for autonomy, competence, and relatedness they experience in each of those relationships. Further, they assessed several mental health indices. Using multilevel modeling, the results showed that there was a significant amount of variance in attachment security at the between-person level, thus confirming that attachment security is to some extent an individual difference. However, considerably more than half the variance in attachment security was

at the within-person level, indicating that people's security of attachment differed substantially from partner to partner. Then the researchers examined whether the within-person variability in attachment security could be systematically explained by need satisfaction. In each study, they found that need satisfaction with a relational partner did in fact account for significant variance in attachment security with that partner. Subsequently, they examined satisfaction of each need separately, and they found that feeling autonomous in a relationship was an important predictor of attachment security for that relationship; similarly, feeling competent in a relationship was a weaker though still meaningful predictor of felt attachment. In other words, the degree to which a person experienced satisfaction of each of the three basic psychological needs with an attachment partner affected the degree to which the person was securely attached to that partner. Finally, at the between-person level, both need satisfaction and attachment security predicted psychological health, and, at the within-person level, both need satisfaction and attachment security predicted relationship satisfaction and willingness to rely on the relational partner.

To summarize, the La Guardia et al. (2000) study indicated that satisfaction needs for autonomy, competence, and relatedness in adult attachment relationships predicted security of attachment, relationship quality, and emotional reliance in that relationship. Not only is need satisfaction important for attachment security and relationship satisfaction of children with their parents, but it is similarly important for attachment security and relationship satisfaction within adult relationships.

A study by Deci et al. (2004) examined mutuality of autonomy support in college-age close friends as it predicted satisfaction of the basic psychological needs, security of attachment, emotional reliance on the friend, and indicators of well-being. They assessed the degree to which each relational partner received autonomy support from the friend and the degree to which he or she gave autonomy support to the friend. Results suggested that both receiving and giving autonomy support were related to relationship quality and well-being, and that this was so for female-female pairs as well as male-male pairs. In other words, this study provided another set of data indicating that autonomy is important for females just as it is for males. When a person's receiving and giving autonomy support competed for variance in the relationship quality, both receiving and giving autonomy support contributed independent prediction. Further, when they competed for variance in well-being, giving autonomy support to one's partner was even more important than receiving it. In other words, in peer relationships such as close friendships, mutuality of autonomy support—giving it as well as getting it—was shown to be important for people's psychological well-being.

Old Age: The Continuing Need for Autonomy in Relationships

Increasingly, the issue of autonomy has been understood as equally important in older persons as it is among younger ones (e.g., Langer & Rodin, 1976; O'Connor & Vallerand, 1994). From a developmental perspective, old age brings with it some degree of increasing dependency on others (Baltes & Silverberg, 1994), and thus it catalyzes dynamic interactions in which the needed supports must be willingly accepted, while not controllingly imposed, for optimal adjustment (Ryan & La Guardia, 2000). In this context, the issue of autonomy support plays a central role in determining the quality of one's relationships.

In one such study, V. G. Kasser and Ryan (1999) examined this dynamic picture in the context of a care facility for the elderly where the issue of dependency was salient. They found that the health and vitality of persons under care were significantly related to both the perceived quality, rather than amount, of relationship support and moreover, that autonomy support from others played a critical role. Satisfaction of the need for autonomy was associated with lower depression, higher vitality, more life satisfaction, and higher levels of positive well-being.

In another study, Langer and Rodin (1976) did an intervention among institutional elderly participants in which some were given greater choice and personal responsibility about aspects of their life in the institution, while others were taken care of by staff members who made decisions for them. Those residents who were encouraged to take greater initiative and make choices displayed better psychological and physical health than those who were cared for well but not encouraged to be self-initiating.

Summation

The most general point to be derived from all these studies, which span the period from infancy to old age, is that relatedness and autonomy, rather than being opposing or antithetical variables, function in a complementary, synergistic manner with respect to personality integration. People who are provided with an atmosphere of autonomy support and involvement (i.e., dedication of resources) are likely to experience both greater security of attachment and a greater sense of personal autonomy. In the context of autonomy-supportive relationships, one has the circumstances conducive of agency and mental health. It is worth noting,

however, that social contexts can, of course, turn satisfaction of the fundamental needs for relatedness and autonomy against each other. In other words, although satisfaction of the two needs is inherently synergistic, they can be made antagonistic toward each other by the social context. For example, when parents make love for their children contingent on the children's doing what the parents insist that they do, the parents are essentially requiring the children to give up autonomy to receive relatedness. As expected, research has shown that when parents use this type of conditional regard as a socializing strategy, children pay substantial intrapsychic and interpersonal costs (Assor et al., 2004). Indeed, these findings provide further evidence of the importance of experiencing satisfaction of both the need for autonomy and the need for relatedness.

EMOTIONAL REGULATION

Central to the definition of well-being is the capacity to regulate and integrate emotional experiences (La Guardia & Ryff, 2003; Ryan & Deci, 2001). Equally clear, deficits in the regulation of emotion and the inability to use emotions to appropriately guide behavior are cardinal features of most forms of mental illness. Accordingly, along with examining the developmental processes of intrinsic motivation, internalization, and social relatedness, we turn now to the critical topic of emotional regulation, a topic that is deeply intertwined with the issue of autonomy and its support in social contexts.

In any discussion of autonomy in relation to emotional regulation and integration, we must begin with an acknowledgment of the complexity of emotions and the multiple dimensions that impact their regulation and expression (see Cacioppo, Bernston, Sheridan, & McClintock, 2000). In particular, there are salient individual differences in people's tendencies to experience emotions (e.g., Gable, Reis, & Elliot, 2000) based on both genetic factors and their interactions with early environmental events. Individual difference factors make the problem of emotional regulation and integration much more formidable for some persons, whose sensitivity or deficits in sensitivity make the challenges of accessing, modulating, expressing, and using emotions highly challenging. This is much of what clinicians like ourselves deal with on a daily basis, and it is an issue that interventions from the psychotherapeutic to the pharmacological attempt to address.

This section is not intended to detail the nature of these individual differences in genetics and their expressions in phenotypes. Nonetheless, we believe that any reasonable summary of that complex literature makes clear that, regardless of genetic inputs, there is a significant, albeit interactive, role played by social environments in fostering healthy or unhealthy regulatory styles. This is our particular focus, as our interest throughout this chapter is in understanding the ways social, cultural, and psychological factors affect development and foster wellness versus pathology.

To more concretely understand what it is about social environments that constructively foster versus debilitate a growing person's capacities for emotional awareness and regulation, it is important to have a clear conception of what healthy emotion regulation is and to specify what features of social contexts can facilitate it. We thus begin with a theoretically based conceptualization of healthy emotional regulation based on a eudaemonic rather than hedonic view of wellness (Ryan & Deci, 2001). Specifically, in our view, the state of wellness is not, as some would hold, the presence of positive emotions and the absence of negative ones (see Kahneman, Diener, & Schwartz, 1999, for such a hedonic view). Indeed, our position differs strongly from this. Instead, our model suggests that emotions are *informational* inputs essential to guiding action and growth (Deci & Ryan, 1985b). There are not good or bad emotions because all emotions provide organismically valuable guidance (Deci & Ryan, 2000; Parrott, 1993). A similar view is expressed by Levenson (1999), who suggested that emotions provide organisms with a built-in feedback system—a cascade of cognitive, motivational, and physiological activities—that signals us to evaluate our environment and act in accord with that evaluation. Instead of the hedonic view, then, we view wellness in terms of a person's being fully functioning—being able to exercise potentials, connect with others, find meaning, and experience vitality. A eudaemonic view of wellness suggests rich access to positive and negative feelings, a capacity to express them, and the ability to use them to inform one's behaviors and goals toward the satisfaction of basic psychological needs. This in turn supports personal growth, self-acceptance, and abilities to intimately connect with others. We label such eudaemonically oriented regulation of affect emotional integration.

Emotional Integration: A Theoretical View

Whereas emotional regulation per se refers to the capacity to modulate or manage one's emotions and impulses, *emotional integration* refers to the most autonomous form of emotional regulation. Specifically, emotional integration involves a differentiated awareness of one's emotional states and the capacity to use this sensitivity and awareness

in the volitional regulation of action. In our view, then, autonomous functioning is dependent on emotional integration, because emotions, when they are mindfully perceived, supply essential information that guides one toward the fulfillment of psychological needs and toward the regulation of behavior in the direction of growth and wellness.

From our perspective, healthy emotional integration is characterized by an allowing of and interest in inner experience, rather than the control or stifling of emotion. In contrast to integrated regulation, internally controlling regulation, which involves blocking or suppressing emotions, not only is nonoptimal but, as we will see, is implicated in various forms of psychopathology and ill-being. Of course, emotional integration presupposes regulatory capacities in that being able to choicefully use emotional experiences requires that an individual not be overwhelmed by the experiences, which would result in dysregulation and impulsivity.

In the developmental and child clinical literatures, there has been a great deal written under the broad rubric of emotion regulation, referring to the management or control of affect (e.g., Garber & Dodge, 1991). Much extant work implicitly embraces reduction in negative emotions as the criterion for effective regulation, although there is increasing recognition that the capacity to initiate, increase, and maintain positive emotions is also important (Fredrickson, 2001; Gross & John, 2002). We argue, however, that there is more to optimal regulation than downward modulation of the negative and upward modulation of the positive in the experience and expression of emotions.

At the same time, emotions can be experienced as more than just signals or informational inputs. Indeed, emotions can feel controlling, as when they overwhelm autonomous self-regulation or automatically drive action. Even the etymology of the term emotion conveys this idea of a force that propels motion. Alternatively, emotions can be overcontrolled, so that one loses access to them, and in such cases they can fail to move us when they should. A woman who chronically suppresses her anger at others and distorts it into self-disparagement is therefore disabled in terms of managing the sources of distress in her life, even as she appears to be controlling her anger. Accordingly, any conception of healthy or integrated emotional regulation is based neither on emotions controlling people nor on people controlling their emotions. Between being controlled by emotional presses and controlling them is a third term, namely, the self. When the self can access feelings without being controlled by them, the opportunity for autonomous self-regulation is maximized. This, of course, is something that develops over time.

Developing Emotional Regulation

The development of capacities to regulate and integrate emotions in more flexible and autonomous ways was explored in studies of 12- to 32-month-old children by Grolnick, Bridges, and Connell (1996). This team of investigators observed toddlers in two sets of mildly stressful situations: waiting to play with an attractive toy (or to eat a food) and a brief separation from mother. The child's emotionality (i.e., level of upset) and strategies to regulate this upset were then coded. Results supported an autonomy continuum in that the more autonomous (i.e., proactive) strategies were associated with the least upset, whereas the least autonomous (i.e., the more controlled or passive) strategies were associated with the most upset. Further, there were increases with age in the use of more active strategies, indicating development of emotion regulation through the toddler years. Finally, relations between use of particular strategies and emotions became more consistent with age, as did use of the same strategies across situations, indicating a more coherent emotion regulation system over development.

This evidence is consistent with the idea that, as children move beyond the 1st year, they must increasingly acquire the capacity to voluntarily control impulses and emotional expressions. Vaughn, Kopp, and Krakow (1984), for example, found a linear increase in children's ability to control urges and delay gratification over the period from 18 to 30 months. The failure to develop this and related regulatory capacities, of course, is likely to result in maladaptive behaviors and thoughts, such as aggressive acting out (Dodge, 1991) and having more depressive ideation and self-deprecating expectancies (Garber, Braafladt, & Zeman, 1991).

As noted, the regulation of emotions and impulses is not just a matter of controlling oneself. Some children in a negatively arousing situation, such as being asked to delay gratification, will exert great effort, forcing themselves to push emotions out of their minds. But controlling themselves in this way requires attention and energy and can diminish the capacity for adaptive engagement with the environment. When used as a chronic way to deal with distress, it leads children to experience being controlled by their own harsh thoughts and to display nonadaptive engagement. In contrast, other children in the same stressful settings may be more flexible (i.e., less rigid and pressured) in dealing with the situation, for example by doing alternative activities or talking about their disappointment, signifying that they have developed more adaptive capacities for self-regulation of emotion.

Adaptive modes of self-regulating emotions thus entail gradual movement from reliance on mediation by others for modulation of one's inner forces to reliance on one's own inner resources (Cicchetti, Ganiban, & Barnett, 1991). But increasing self-reliance in coping with emotions does not ensure true emotional self-regulation, for the latter requires being able to flexibly use inner experiences to adaptively interact with the environment.

Block and Block (1980) characterized ego resiliency in terms of a balance between overcontrol and undercontrol, thus conveying that neither dysregulation nor being rigidly regulated is an optimal outcome in developing self-regulation of emotions. Kopp (1982) made a similar distinction between self-control, which is the ability to inhibit behavior in the face of external demands, and self-regulation, which involves a greater capacity for adapting to new situations. From Kopp's viewpoint, self-control and self-regulation are sequential stages of early childhood development, whereas we propose that the rigid versus flexible forms of regulation represent markers on a developmental continuum of autonomous regulation that is relevant throughout life. This movement toward autonomous regulation of emotions and impulses, as noted, is considered a natural aspect of the development of self (Deci & Ryan, 2000; Ryan, 1993).

Deci and Ryan (1985b) drew from Greenspan (1979) in referring to the development of regulatory processes for autonomously managing one's emotions as "integration at the internal boundary" (i.e., the boundary between the self and other aspects of the person). This was contrasted with the development of regulatory processes for engaging in activities deemed important by the social world as "integration at the external boundary" (i.e., the boundary between oneself and the world). Although these two developmental functions, referred to, respectively, as the development of emotion regulation and internalization, are somewhat different, they are similar in many respects. Both involve gaining the capacities to regulate oneself with respect to behavior that is not intrinsically motivated, and both entail a developmental progression in which the child gradually relies less on cues and structures from the social context and more on internal cues and structures. The development of emotional self-regulation can thus be conceptualized as movement from reliance on outside sources to identify, modulate, and regulate affect, toward a growing capacity for autonomous, flexible, and adaptive regulation (Grolnick Weiss, McKenzie, & Wrightman, 1996).

Yet, this developing capacity for emotional regulation is not just a function of time and maturation. In fact, in our view, it is very much an *interpersonal* process. It is in the interpersonal realm that we originally experience emotions as being regulated by caregivers, more or less responsively and effectively. These originally interpersonal regulations then become internalized as regulatory styles. Thus, critical to our position is the interplay between an autonomy-supportive social context that affords access to and expression of emotional experience, and a supportive guidance of that process toward behavioral regulation (Grolnick, Bridges, et al., 1996; Gross, 1999). In other words, responses of significant others are critical to avoiding either the Scylla of dysregulation or the Charybdis of overcontrol.

Mature Emotional Integration

The process of increasingly integrating one's emotions and regulatory capacities is merely a continuation of the work a child does in gaining regulatory capacities with respect to emotions, but it represents a mature version of that process. Whereas emotional regulation is concerned with the modulation of emotional experience and expression, emotional integration is concerned specifically with the degree of flexibility and choice one feels in the regulation of emotions and emotion-related actions. To the extent that one's emotions and regulatory capacities are integrated aspects of the self, one is able to take interest in them and experience them as inputs to autonomous actions. In contrast, if regulatory capacities are merely introjected and thus in conflict with the emotions, a person is likely to suppress the feelings and ignore their personal meaning.

We have suggested that a healthy emotional life requires awareness of feelings—regardless of their valence—and support within the environment to promote fullness of experience and emotional expression. Simply put, when people can authentically engage their emotional life in the context of supportive relationships, they can manage the excitements and challenges offered and engage their emotional world more fully. It is in this interpersonal/social space that people will flourish, at both the psychological and physical level, and will be able to more effectively combat life's stresses at either of these levels.

Emotional integration as herein viewed concerns the degree to which emotions can be assimilated and utilized by the self. It is important to contrast this view of integration with the conception of integration as the synchrony among affective, behavioral, and cognitive systems (Greenberg, Kusche, & Speltz, 1991). In part, synchrony has been equated with integration based on the fact that quite often, synchrony represents the congruence among action, feelings, and consciousness and thus can be a *sign* that emotions have been fully acknowledged and freely expressed and that the behaviors associated with them are integrated and endorsed. But coordination among behaviors, affects, and cognitions (i.e., the fact of synchrony) does not guarantee integration of these processes into the self. Emotional expression and actions related to it can often be characterized by highly correlated systems, yet still can have an external perceived locus of causality. Conversely, one can have affects that one is fully aware of but that one meaningfully chooses not to express behaviorally in a certain context. Such apparent disynchrony can represent a high degree of integration in our current use of that term. Integration to the self and synchrony are thus not the same thing, the crucial issue being the degree to which emotions and regulatory processes have come into harmonious relations with other aspects of the integrated self.

Koestner et al. (1992) explored the relation of autonomy to the integration and synchrony of emotions, cognitions, and behavior. They separated participants into an autonomy-oriented group and a control-oriented group based on a measure developed by Deci and Ryan (1985a) and then explored the consistency of behavior, attitudes, and traits between these two groups. Their general hypothesis was that autonomous participants, because they are more integrated, would evidence greater consistency across these aspects of personality than would controlled participants, who are theorized to be more rigid and fractionated. In the first two experiments presented, the researchers found very high correlations between the behavioral and self-report measures of intrinsic motivation in the autonomous groups, but no correlations in the controlled groups. The autonomy-oriented participants displayed greater congruence between behaviors and feelings than did controlled participants. In another study, Koestner et al. had participants complete a trait measure of conscientiousness, and then they gave them an opportunity to behave conscientiously in the succeeding days. Participants' conscientiousness scores and their conscientious behavior were significantly more highly correlated in the autonomous group than in the controlled group. Finally, a friend of each participant rated him or her on various traits, including conscientiousness, and the self-ratings and peer ratings were also more highly correlated for the autonomy-oriented participants than for the control-oriented participants. Taken together, this set of studies provides support for the theoretical proposition that autonomy is associated with greater congruence among traits, behaviors, and feelings, which we interpret as a reflection of greater integration in personality.

Facilitating or Undermining Emotional Integration: The Role of Autonomy Support

Having articulated the characteristics that define emotional integration, our second interest is in how social environments can enhance or undermine capacities for both regulation and integration of emotional experiences. The importance of the social/interpersonal context is apparent in infancy and childhood (particularly in regard to relationships with caregivers) and continues in relationships throughout life (Reis & Shaver, 1988). Our focus on autonomy support thus homes in on what we believe to be a critical social contextual resource in emotional development.

Emotional Regulation and Caregiving in Early Development

Many theorists view the development of self-regulation of inner impulses and affects as beginning at birth and involving homeostasis as a neurologically based function. Greenspan (1979), for example, described infants during the early weeks of life as being centrally concerned with inner equilibrium. The signals a child sends when experiencing disequilibrium alert caregivers to respond in ways intended to allow the child's return to equilibrium. As Emde (1983) suggested, this initial regulation through caregiver mediation is the basis on which the child gradually learns to monitor and manage his or her own equilibrium.

For this learning to occur, caregivers need to be emotionally responsive and to have effective strategies for initiating, maintaining, and modulating their emotionality (Grolnick & Bridges, 1992). Before addressing that issue, however, it is important to emphasize that the creation of effective regulatory strategies is not solely a function of the caretaking environment, for the child's temperamental qualities may intensify particular emotional states and influence the sequential flow of those states (Lewis & Michalson, 1983). Temperamental factors, which are relatively stable tendencies with biological underpinnings (Goldsmith et al., 1987), may include soothability and irritability (Brazelton, 1973), sociability, adaptability, and difficulty (Thomas, Chess, & Birch, 1968), and reactivity and self-regulation (Rothbart & Derryberry, 1981). Such factors play a significant role in the development of emotional self-regulation, although we view these individual differences in temperament as aspects of the child's "starting point" that interact with the caretaking environment as he or she develops emotional self-regulation. Temperament thus influences how formidable a task the development of emotional self-regulation will be for a child, and as with all developmental processes, the magnitude of the challenge faced by different children can be quite different.

The challenge faced by children with difficult temperaments can also be exacerbated because their temperament and emotional expressiveness affect the socializing environments, which in turn further affect the children. Children who are irritable and not very soothable may influence their caretakers in ways that make them less nurturing and supportive. As Dix (1991) pointed out, children's behavior can stimulate emotions in parents that undermine their effectiveness and responsiveness, thus making it even more difficult for the children to develop personal autonomy and interpersonal relatedness.

Holding Environments as Autonomy-Supportive

Winnicott (1960/1965) described the "holding environment" as one in which the infant's impulses, affects, and frustrations are satisfied by the parent before they become overwhelming, and in which the parent is sensitive to the cues and initiations of the infant. For Winnicott, a responsive holding environment facilitates the infant's developing sense of agency and vitality, although the dynamics of such responsiveness are complex and subtle. For example, when impulses and affects are experienced in the presence of a caregiver who is sensitive to what the child can tolerate, the caregiver will hold and soothe the child when that limit has been reached, and the borders of the child's self experience will be broadened. The child will learn more about his or her own inner world and its relation to the social context; the child will experience both the force of the urges and the nature of gratification. In contrast, to the extent that the child is left alone with strong, unsatisfied urges, the child may either suppress them because they are so threatening or be overwhelmed by them, ending up disoriented. The experience of being responded to and thus, in a sense, regulated by an empathic other is therefore crucial to the child's developing the capacities for regulating himself or herself.

Brazelton, Koslowski, and Main (1974) similarly emphasized the importance of the parents' ability to attend to infants' cues and to appreciate their need to withdraw from stimulation following periods of intense interaction. Sensitive parents recognize their infants' attempts to elicit interaction, but equally important, they respect the infants' need to be without stimulation. Such parents adjust their own rhythm and behavior to that of their infants.

Greenspan's (1981) notion of a growth-promoting early environment emphasizes the capacity of the environment to balance the infant's need to engage the world and to experience self-regulation or homeostasis with respect to inner states. In a growth-promoting environment, the parent is available, providing soothing and comforting to supplement the child's emerging capacities to modulate inner states. The parent also provides stimulation and opportunities to engage the environment at times when the child is alert and ready. In the growth-inhibiting environment, the parent may be unavailable to provide comfort and regulatory help such that the child does not experience comfort and harmony. Without self-regulatory help, the child will need to shut out external stimulation, and engagement of the environment will be undermined.

In a study of normal mother-infant interactions, Field (1987) found that the mother adjusts her behavior to her infant's to provide adequate stimulation and arousal modulation. In an optimal interaction, the mother's and infant's attention and affective behavior are synchronized. If, however, the mother is emotionally unavailable or unresponsive, as in the case of depressed mothers (Tronick & Gianino, 1986), the relationship will be asynchronous and the child will be likely to experience disorganization and to manifest disturbed state regulation. Field, Healy, Goldstein, and Guthertz (1990) in fact found more negative affect and greater asynchrony between mood states in depressed mother-child dyads than in normals. The experiences of regulation and dysregulation in the mother-child dyad thus affect the child's developing the capacity for self-regulation.

In a study of emotional regulation (Shields, Cicchetti, & Ryan, 1994), maltreated children and comparison children were observed on the playground interacting with other children. Behaviors were coded for appropriate and inappropriate instances of positive and negative affect. Maltreated children displayed poorer emotional regulation than matched controls. Presumably, experiences in the family rendered the maltreated children deficient in the processes necessary to deal adaptively with stressful experiences. These children, who were less effective at emotion regulation, also displayed less social competence, emphasizing the adaptive importance of self-regulatory capacities.

This research and theory is consistent with the model of optimal caregiving presented by Grolnick and Ryan (1989) in which involvement, autonomy support, and structure are considered essential for children to self-regulate emotion. Parental involvement helps child maintain a tolerable level of distress so they are not overwhelmed by and can learn to manage the inner forces of emotion. Parents' autonomy support helps the children to build confidence in their abilities to autonomously initiate and maintain regulatory strategies by allowing the children to struggle with distressing situations while letting them know that the parents are available if needed. And parents providing structure in the form of consistency, developmentally appropriate challenges, and limit setting allows the child to trust and take interest in the environment and in his or her affective relation to it.

In support of this framework, there is evidence that children display more adaptive regulatory strategies when their parents are available and involved (Bronson, 2000). However, beyond the importance of availability is the necessity of opportunities for the children to be autonomous. The concept of autonomy support is a complex one (Grolnick, 2002; Reeve, 2002). It entails accepting and nurturing children and relating to them from their perspective. When parents are accepting of the children, understanding what is going on from the children's perspective, it sets the stage for the children's self-acceptance, and this is particularly true with regard to emotions. Further, being accepting of and responsive to the children's emotional initiations, as with any type of initiation, supports and strengthens the children's sense of agency and autonomy and their definition of self as an initiating being. In contrast, when parents fail to respond to their children's emotional expressions or when they react negatively to the emotions, it is likely that the children will internalize those responses, which will become the basis of the children's failing to accept the emotions in themselves.

Calkins (1997) and Calkins and Johnson (1998) found that mothers' use of positive guidance (akin to autonomy support) was associated with greater use of distraction and constructive coping in emotion-inducing situations. On the other hand, children of mothers who used high levels of negative control during free play spent more time orienting to a desired but forbidden stimulus. They used less self-distraction and were less physiologically regulated during a waiting situation relative to children of mothers who used less negative control.

Grolnick, Kurowski, McMenamy, Rivkin, and Bridges (1998) also examined the strategies mothers use to help their young children regulate distress. Children of mothers who maintained their active assistance beyond what the children needed were less able to regulate their distress when on their own. Thus, although responsiveness to distress is important, parents who took responsibility for regulating children's distress and did not allow the children opportunities to self-regulate appeared to undermine children's self-regulatory capacities. Because the capacity to effectively modulate distress is so integral to mental health and the prevention of psychopathology, an environment supporting this capacity is of crucial importance.

Allowing and encouraging the adaptive use of emotions and responding to and supporting them is certainly important, but parents also need to set appropriate limits on behavior while allowing adequate expression of feelings (see Koestner et al., 1984). This facilitates the child's attunement to the social world and acceptance of self in the process of adapting to it. Children can thus learn to be respectful of others—or, as Angyal (1965) put it, to assume a homonomous attitude—while seeking their own gratification and expression. Developing the capacities for respecting others and delaying gratification represents a central agenda for the person from toddlerhood through adulthood; it involves learning when and how it is reasonable and appropriate to express one's feelings and being able to use that information in a way that enhances the autonomous regulation of behavior. Thus, emotional regulation entails internalizing values and regulatory structures provided by caregivers, a process that functions much like the internalization of any other behavioral regulation.

AUTONOMY DISTURBANCES

As the development of self proceeds optimally in social contexts where children experience ongoing supports for their autonomy, competence, and relatedness, they display increasing amounts of self-determination appropriate to their developmental stage. Behaviors are undertaken with a sense of choice, for they emanate from the self in a harmonious fashion.

When development does not proceed optimally, however, because of biological vulnerabilities or because the social context does not provide autonomy support, competence, and involvement, the organismic integration process will be impaired, resulting in psychopathology characterized by disturbances of autonomy. This may involve blocking awareness of urges and developing rigid regulatory processes, or alternatively, displaying inadequate regulatory capacities and being governed by one's urges. Stated differently, when organismic integration is impaired, people become either overcontrolled or undercontrolled, neither of which is adaptive, for both lack the experience of autonomy. In the case of overcontrol, the development of self is undermined as people regulate action through introjected values and controls, whereas in the case of undercontrol, internalization is forestalled, preventing the development of a well-anchored value system to organize and guide behavior.

In cases of either overcontrol or undercontrol, the perceived locus of causality for behavior lies outside the self, and as such there are compromised or distorted volitional processes (Shapiro, 1981). Such circumstances are especially likely to predominate when caregivers have not provided the interpersonal involvement and consistent responsiveness necessary for forming attachments that support the development of self-regulation in all its forms, including intrinsic motivation, internalization, and emotional integration.

Given the generality of this description, it is perhaps more clear why we stated at the outset of this chapter that, although varied in its form and etiology, psychopathology typically entails *impairments of autonomy* (Angyal, 1965), representing failures in organismic integration and the development of self. From the perspective of SDT, explicating the autonomy disturbances that result from failed integration involves a consideration of the dialectical interplay between the psychological needs for autonomy, competence, and relatedness that subserve organismic integration and the social contexts that either nurture or thwart the individual with respect to these psychological needs.

The workings of this dialectical relationship were discussed in the review of research on intrinsic motivation, internalization, attachment, and emotional integration—or, more to the point, on the impairments of those processes. Some of that research was conducted with nonclinical samples and some with clinical populations. However, in what follows we focus on specific disorders, both in terms of a theoretical account of autonomy impairment and a review of relevant research. We argue that the processes that hinder intrinsic motivation, internalization, attachment, and emotional integration are frequently the same processes underlying the disturbed autonomy evident in various forms of psychopathology.

Focusing on these processes, we discuss three general types of autonomy disturbances. First, we consider those in which rigidly introjected controls dominate one's psychic reality. Although there are a variety of internalizing disorders in which introjects play a critical role, we discuss a select few for illustrative purposes. To do that, we begin with a review of Shapiro's (1965, 1981) conception of rigid character as a dimension in psychopathology and then turn to specific diagnostic categories, including Obsessive-Compulsive Disorders, in which internalized but unintegrated pressures and mandates exert periodic regulatory influence over behavior and thought; paranoid personality, in which introjected punitive controls are projected onto the environment; and both self-critical depression and eating disorders (i.e., anorexia and bulimia), in which unreasonable and unattainable introjected standards dominate one's experience and lead invariably to harsh self-evaluations and self-disparagement.

To illustrate autonomy disturbances based in failures to internalize significant values and regulatory processes, we focus on selected externalizing disorders. In these cases, the structures and processes to manage one's urges or to regulate intentional actions are often transient, and there is an emphasis in personality on need substitutes and goals that function to support an impoverished core sense of self. To illustrate these types of autonomy disturbance, we first discuss problems of impulsivity and then focus on motivational dynamics in Conduct and Antisocial Personality Disorders and in Dissociative Identity Disorders.

Finally, we address autonomy disturbance in the context of personality disorders by addressing borderline syndromes. Here our focus is on the integrative difficulties posed by controlling and inconsistent environments that produce the self-pathology associated with these personality styles.

In discussing each of these types of autonomy disturbance our approach is twofold. First, we illustrate how autonomy issues are integral to the disorders, in the sense that phenomenological and regulatory issues related to autonomy and perceived locus of causality are characteristically skewed. Second, we discuss factors relating to the social context of development that contribute to the etiology of these disorders. Although it is the case that any factor that disrupts the organizational tendency, whether biological, interpersonal, or cultural in nature, can potentiate disturbances of autonomy, in many cases the sources of disrupted autonomy can be directly traced to deficiencies in the social environment—that is, to its failure to provide appropriate autonomy support, structure, or involvement.

Internalizing Disorders and Autonomy

The process of introjection is central to a substantial amount of psychopathology. When values, regulations, and standards are taken in but not integrated, they exist as forces dissonant with one's true self that pressure one to act. Thus, many instances of maladjustment involve introjection, particularly those often described as internalizing disorders.

Rigid Character

One class of psychopathology for which introjection is a defining feature is what Shapiro (1981) labeled "rigid character disorders." Rigid character involves an ongoing struggle with authority that begins as a conflict between the strict demands of a socializing agent and the person's own organismic urges and desires. Over time, the person moves the conflict inside by introjecting the demands in the form of rigid, internally controlling structures that hold the urges in check.

Rigid introjects, though products of socialization, regulate action in part through blocking awareness of the person's organismic needs and urges (Rogers, 1951). This victory of the introjects is a peculiarly distorted one, for the person will align with the internalized authority by relinquishing aspects of his or her own organismic nature. Indeed, the process of introjecting rigid structures often results in the type of self-deception in which the person thinks he or she wants what the authority originally prescribed. This is an instance of what Winnicott (1960/1965) referred to as false self, in which cognitive functions gradually lose their grounding in organismic processes. Resolution of the authority conflict by introjecting the authority is therefore accomplished at the expense of a person's need for autonomy.

Intentionality in rigid character disorders is characterized by its heteronomy and inflexibility. Heteronomy is manifest in the pressured experience, backed by threat of anxiety, that drives much of the person's action, and inflexibility is evident in the absence of openness to novel ways of doing things or consideration of alternative values. Rigid character, with its internally controlling regulation, has a clear parallel with what we have observed in research on ego involvement where self-esteem is hinged on particular outcomes so the person is pressured to perform (Ryan, 1982).

The internally controlling regulation of rigid character can, in some instances, be highly stable and self-sustaining, in part because it can yield ongoing external approval and derivative internal gratifications. Among these gratifications are what Deci (1980) referred to as need substitutes. In the case of rigid character, for example, the person will have developed a strong motive (or pseudo-need) to be in control as a substitute for the innate, though unsatisfied, need for autonomy. The substitute need for control is reflected in the exercise of will power (Shapiro, 1965), which Deci described as internally controlling regulations countering one's drives and emotions. Similarly, Lewin (1951) suggested that will power involves concealing the motives that run counter to the controls, and May (1969) asserted that will power involves rationalization and self-deceit. These various views converge to emphasize that rigid internal controls function to block conflicting aspects of the person from awareness, thus allowing the person to disown them. This self-deception is both a result of and a contributor to forestalled organismic integration, and thus represents impaired autonomy even though it involves clear intentionality and mental determination. In this vein, Shapiro (1981) described such displays of will power as "pseudo-autonomy." As an example of rigid character, we turn first to a discussion of obsessive-compulsive disturbances.

The Obsessive-Compulsive Disorders

Two separable diagnoses carry the rubric of obsession and compulsion: Obsessive-Compulsive Disorder (OCD) and obsessive-compulsive personality (OCP). These two distinct entities share some common features in the dynamics of behavior regulation, but they also differ in meaningful ways. OCD, an Axis I disorder, is characterized by the experience of intrusive thoughts and demands that typically can be alleviated only by engaging in some ritualistic, rigid behavior. The thoughts are often ego-dystonic, in that they are unwelcome and anxiety-provoking, and thus are experienced as having an origin outside the self. Indeed, these thoughts often are inconsistent with the person's conscious values and ideals. An example is a woman who was diagnosed with OCD and who reported continuing intrusive thoughts concerning hurting her baby whenever she was near certain objects. These intrusive thoughts raised considerable anxiety precisely because they ran against her seemingly strongly held desire to keep her child safe. To alleviate this anxiety she was compelled to check continuously for dangerous objects in her vicinity. Indeed, OCD is classified as an anxiety disorder precisely because obsessions and rituals often have the function of regulating anxiety, albeit usually only temporarily.

An important feature of the dissonant thoughts often found in OCD is that they are persistent, unwanted, and difficult to control. From the perspective of the individual, the unwanted thoughts have an impersonal locus of causality, in that they "befall" him or her. The person then feels coerced into ritualistic behaviors; he or she must do them or face dreadful anxiety. The ritualistic actions that alleviate obsessional thoughts therefore have an external perceived locus of causality. As an aspect of this external causality, compulsive behavior patterns typically are performed under strict constraints; there is an inner demand to engage in actions in rigidly prescribed ways. These orders are experienced as heteronomous forces, albeit ones within the person. The cost of failure is guilt, anxiety, and self-disparagement, and in more extreme cases a sense of panic and fragmentation of the self. The regulatory process of compulsive acts is thus accompanied by a sense of inner pressure that we would describe as internally controlling. For instance, as Swedo and Rapoport (1990) reported, children with OCD often hide their symptoms in public and re-

port feeling that it takes tremendous energy to stave off compulsive enactments. They then feel compelled to release the pressure of resistance at home, leading parents to attribute willfulness and control to a child who feels little of either with respect to these symptoms.

Unlike OCD, there appears to be little evidence for a biological basis to OCP, though temperament has been implicated as an etiologic vulnerability (Sperry, 2003). Supporting the differential role of biology, Jenike (1991) reported responsiveness among OCD patients to pharmacological interventions, but not those with OCP. Also in contrast to OCD, OCP is more a lifestyle than a symptom, and in many ways OCP can be viewed as a continuum, from a somewhat rigidly focused set of attitudes to a disorder that interferes with ongoing functioning. Accordingly, many features of this controlled lifestyle are ego-syntonic rather than disturbing. For example, patients with OCP might exhibit a stereotyped and rigid manner of organizing their possessions and become distraught whenever things appear to have been moved or misplaced. Such individuals might come to treatment not because they view the orderliness as problematic, but because their pattern of living is causing interpersonal or vocational difficulties. In addition, as reported by Othmer and Othmer (2002), persons with OCP often display their characteristic drivenness, compulsiveness, and inflexibility when events involving authority, intimacy, or lack of structure trigger them. Nonetheless, the surface structure of these behaviors bear similarities with the ritualistic behaviors so often manifest in OCD.

It is particularly clear with OCP that the pathology of obsessive-compulsive actions is not defined by the behavior itself, for the behavior can be productive and beneficial. Rather, it is the rigid regulatory processes underlying compulsive behavior that are pathological. Still, the more severe the disorder, the more one's behaviors become separated from adaptive consequences, and the resulting ritualistic behaviors that serve to bind anxiety themselves become dysfunctional.

Persons with OCP, while not typically afflicted with intrusive or bizarre thoughts, are often inordinately concerned with carrying out the actual or presumed demands of authority. For example, a person with this personality style can be quite industrious and fastidious in complying with the introjected demands, and this may yield high productivity. This industriousness is quite different from the vitality of an autonomous individual, however. A. Miller (1981) described vitality as the freedom to be spontaneous and to experience one's inner feelings, and Ryan and Frederick (1997) argued that vitality concerns the free energy a person has at his or her disposal. The determination of the internally controlled individual with OCP involves neither freedom nor spontaneity and is often experienced as energy draining, in much the manner described by Baumeister, Muraven, and Tice's (2000) ego-depletion model. As Sperry (2003, p. 178) noted, the demeanor of someone with OCP is often "grim and cheerless." Moreover, resistance to inner dictates, when possible, may require a gargantuan effort.

There is an interesting point about OCP that highlights an important aspect of disturbed autonomy. Although obsessive-compulsive individuals often act with determination in carrying out introjected dictates, they sometimes display confusion and indecision. The problem especially arises when there is no dictate, no established course to follow. At such times, the person may be rocked with indecisiveness and ambivalence, and decisions that appear trivial can be the source of painful ruminations. This illustrates clearly how dependence on unintegrated controls leaves one without self-direction, without a clear sense of what one wants for oneself. Once a person has blocked access to his or her affective underpinnings and needs, there is no basis for making decisions when a control or rule is not evident. The anxiety of indecision highlights how the determination of the obsessive-compulsive is not autonomous.

Although the obsessive-compulsive disorders represent clear instances of psychopathology with disturbed autonomy, it is not clear, nor theoretically necessary, that they are exclusively *outcomes* of parental control. In fact, evidence has been quite compelling for a biologic contribution to OCD. To date, research on social factors contributing to obsessive-compulsive behavioral patterns has been sparse compared to studies attempting to document the biologic and genetic contributors. There is some evidence, however, that OCD can be related to rigidity and controllingness in one's family of origin. For example, Rasmussen and Tsuang (1986) examined the backgrounds of adult OCD patients and found evidence of strict, orderly, and inflexible religious styles. Hoover and Insel (1984) reported family entrapment as common among adolescents with OCD, but also emphasized the reciprocal nature of adult-child interactions that might produce such patterns.

In contrast, case literatures concerning OCP have more frequently pointed to controlling, often intrusive parenting (Millon, Davis, Millon, Escovar, & Meagher, 2000). For instance, Benjamin (2003) argued that persons with OCP often come from demanding, even coercive parenting environments. Moreover, she suggested that the controlling emphasis is more often on punishment for failures than on acknowledgment of success. However, here, too, systematic

investigation of the social context of development of OCP individuals is not extensive. It does appear, however, that the controlling regulatory styles of those with OCP are more likely to be linked with excessive parental contollingness than is the case for OCD.

Paranoid Personality

According to Shapiro (1981), even more extreme along the dimension of rigid personality formations is Paranoid Personality Disorder, a long recognized diagnosis. However, in his view, whereas the person with OCP struggles with internal dictates and rules, the person with paranoid propensities perceives the struggle to be with external authorities and forces. It is agents outside the person whose control, influence, and intrusions must be resisted. Thus, the experience of heteronomy is projected to the external arena, whereas the struggle in OCP has its locus more in the realm of internal admonitions and rules. Paranoid personality is characterized by scrutiny, suspiciousness, and a strong rigidity of thought. However, because the issues are projected as external, symptoms such as these may be experienced as ego-syntonic. Meissner (1995) argued that underneath the paranoid person's external preoccupations with authority and control is very low self-esteem and a good deal of fearful and depressive ideation. Avoiding such feelings helps explain these patients' strong need to maintain a sense of control. As Gabbard (2000) pointed out, support for the patient's autonomy is especially critical in the treatment of this disorder.

Benjamin (2003) argued that these preoccupations with control stem from family backgrounds often characterized by parents who could be critical, humiliating, and even sadistic. Often, parents themselves were victims of abuse. Because of the harsh treatment they received, persons afflicted with paranoia are on the lookout for danger. These patients do not own up easily to mistakes or errors, as past instances of mistakes and errors may have catalyzed harsh treatment. As well, people with paranoia hide any vulnerability or weakness. Sperry (2003, p. 207) similarly summarized the parental controllingness that confronts patients with Paranoid Personality Disorder with the injunction "You are different. Don't make mistakes."

Here again we see the results of the deprivation of autonomy and exposure to excessive controls in a form of harsh self-controlling regulation of behavior, and in this case, suspiciousness and alienation from others. Here the problems with autonomy preclude relatedness and intimacy, as these require both trust and vulnerability. Accordingly, basic needs for relatedness and autonomy remain frustrated.

Introjection and Self-Disparagement

At the core of many rigid character pathologies are introjected demands that organize intentional behavior. Although this type of autonomy disturbance involves conflict and tension, individuals with rigid character are often able to behave intentionally and satisfy their introjects. There are other types of introjected demands, however, that individuals cannot easily attain, and these invariably result in experienced failure and self-disparagement. These forms of disturbed autonomy, like those of rigid character, begin with individuals' introjecting the demands of authorities and basing their self-worth on living up to those demands. But here, the pathology and experience are quite different, for these individuals' predominant experience is failure and worthlessness. Thus, not only is their autonomy undermined by the introjects and the social conditions that promoted them, but they also feel incompetent and unloved by significant others in their social world. Two such pathologies of introjection are self-critical depression and eating disorders.

Self-Critical Depression.   Research on depression and its etiology has increasingly pointed to two distinct pathways to the disorder, each of which can build on biological vulnerabilities. The first is concerned primarily with internalization of excessive demands for achievement and is characterized by harsh self-criticism and guilt (Blatt & Homann, 1992; Nietzel & Harris, 1990); the second is concerned more with the loss of relatedness, love, or attachment. Although both of these vulnerabilities involve self-esteem dynamics, and issues of autonomy and relatedness are intertwined in both, the former, self-critical form of depression is particularly relevant to our discussion of autonomy disturbances and internalization. We thus focus on the self-critical depression syndrome, which has been labeled variously as a disorder of achievement-autonomy (Nietzel & Harris, 1990), introjection (Blatt, 1974), self-worth (Swallow & Kuiper, 1988), and autonomy (Beck, 1983).

By whatever label, this syndrome involves a type of disturbed autonomy in which one experiences dysphoric affect and lethargy resulting from the belief that one is a failure. In this disorder there are rigid standards or ideals that have been introjected, along with the belief that failure to attain them means one is unlovable and unworthy. Thus, the punitive introjects, with their ties to contingent self-worth, leave the person vulnerable to ongoing self-scrutiny, and because with such introjects there is little the person can do that is good enough, he or she will invariably feel worth-

less. In other words, self-disparagement tends to be ubiquitous. Individuals with such introjects are harsher in their self-judgments than in their judgments of others, and these self-judgments often form the precursors to depressive episodes (Beck, 1983).

The phenomenological set underlying self-critical depression is particularly relevant to the understanding of depression as involving disturbed autonomy. With respect to significant self-goals, the individual sees the self as responsible and yet as incapable. Thus, the absence of felt competence to attain internalized goals results in a sense of amotivation (Deci & Ryan, 1985b) or helplessness (Abramson, Seligman, & Teasdale, 1978). At the same time, many of the specific demands on the self to achieve or succeed have the character of "have to" and "must," revealing their phenomenological character as having an external perceived locus of causality (i.e., as being heteronomous with respect to the self). This, of course, is the case with all introjects, as they are both internal to the person yet external to the self.

Although the etiology and course of depression are complex, involving both biological and social/environmental factors, the evidence that parental style can contribute to depressive problems is relatively clear. Factors such as loss of parents (and thus of attachment supports), depression in parents (and thus low involvement and/or autonomy support), and excessive parental controllingness have all been implicated in the development of childhood depression (see S. M. Miller, Birnbaum, & Durbin, 1990). For example, in a study done with adolescents 12 to 18 years old, Noom, Dekovic, and Meeus (1999) found that higher levels of autonomy were associated with lower levels of depressed mood and higher self-esteem.

There has been recent interest in the development of perfectionism, a characteristic highly related to self-critical depression. Individuals with high levels of maladaptive perfectionism (including concern over mistakes and doubts about actions) report having experienced harsh (Frost, Novara, & Rheaume, 2002) and authoritarian (Flett, Hewitt, & Singer, 1995; Kawamura, Frost, & Harmatz, 2002) parenting. Further, Enns, Cox, and Clara (2002) found support for a model in which harsh parenting led to maladaptive perfectionism, which in turn was associated with an increased proneness to depression. These studies suggest perfectionism as a pathway through which controlling environments might increase depressive symptoms.

More direct investigations of the parenting environments of self-critical depressives have been increasingly frequent. In one illustrative investigation, McCranie and Bass (1984) found that women high in self-critical depression had parents who maintained strict control, demanded high achievement, and were inconsistent and contingent in their conveyance of love. Similar results concerning self-critical depression in both males and females were reported by Whiffen and Sassville (1991). Finally, Soenens, Vansteenkiste, Luyten, Duriez, and Goossens (in press) recently showed that parental controllingness predicted not only maladaptive perfectionism, but also the severity of associated depression and self-esteem deficits. Such results are consistent with our speculations more generally concerning the social context leading to introjection and internally controlling states. In this sense, one can view self-critical depression as a chronic and pervasive state of ego involvement in which one continuously fails to live up to the demands and is thus punished.

Anorexia and Bulimia.   Bruch (1973), in her classic work on the topic, described eating disorders as pathologies of autonomy. She argued that these eating pathologies typically involve a struggle for control that takes the form of obsession with eating and body image, dynamically staving off a pervasive sense of ineffectiveness. They thus illustrate how bodily states and desires can be manipulated by introjects to preserve the illusion of self-sufficiency and to feel a sense of control with respect to oneself and others. In restrictive anorexia, the introjects around eating and weight are more stable and effective in keeping one's eating behavior in abeyance, whereas in bulimia, there is a more open conflict between rigid controls and akratic eating. Bulimics engage in binge eating—in expressive, uncontrolled consumption—only to be overcome by guilt and self-derogation leading to vomiting or abuse of diuretics.

The psychodynamics highlighted by Bruch (1973) were empirically described in a study by Strauss and Ryan (1987). They found greater self-oppression and self-rejection in both anorexic and bulimic participants than in a matched control group, whereas control-group participants displayed more flexible self-management and self-acceptance than did eating-disordered participants. Furthermore, Strauss and Ryan documented a particularly heightened impersonal causality orientation (Deci & Ryan, 1985a) among restrictive anorexics, which is indicative of an impoverished sense of personal effectiveness.

Internally controlling forms of regulation are readily apparent in the dynamics of eating disorders. Whether anorexic or bulimic, these patients display inordinate concern with how others view them and hypertrophied public self-consciousness. As Plant and Ryan (1985) argued, such consciousness potentiates an external perceived locus of causality in which one has to conform to the projected views of others. Although a focus on weight is often paramount, eating-disordered patients are typically self-conscious, demanding, and self-critical with regard to many aspects of appearance and behavior, which is experienced as a straitjacket to the self. And although restrictive anorexics in particular appear to display a high degree of personal control, the regulatory basis of this control is dictatorial and built on a tenuous foundation of ineffectance.

In a recent article focused on an SDT-based account of motivation in anorexia, Vansteenkiste, Soenens, and Vandereycken (in press) described these dynamics in detail. In their view, these patients' focus on thinness is an attempt to gain a sense of security and worth, yet the thinness never seems to supply the self-confidence and emotional benefits they expect. They are never thin enough, yet they continually believe that positive feelings are just a few pounds away. The paradox, however, is that achieving their extrinsic goal is satisfying to some degree, so it further anchors them in this pattern of behavior. These patients often strongly assert that they do feel better when they lose weight, and thus that the pursuit of weight loss cannot be the source of their distress. Indeed, their own experiences seem to confirm that efforts at weight loss are part of the solution. The transitory nature of relief thus creates an addictive quality to the internally controlling drive for thinness.

Whereas the restrictive anorexic can display a high degree of control with respect to eating, bulimic patients often find their control overwhelmed by an impulse to binge eat. Binges typically occur at times of high stress or anxiety, thus showing how their introjected regulatory structures are not sufficiently stable to keep the impulse in check. The binge impulse is often a reaction to the rise of unacceptable feelings or to being controlled or criticized, so it represents an attempt to escape from the painful sense of self that carries the burdensome, introjected standards (Baumeister, 1991). It is interesting to note that, as the psychic threat increases for someone with the bulimic disorder, the person's regulatory capacity becomes weakened, whereas in someone with obsessive-compulsive personality, the regulatory capacity often becomes even more rigid and dominant. The lack of stability of the regulatory introjects in the bulimic thus allows for the akratic action, but the self-evaluative introjects invariably result in self-disparagement and feelings of depression for having lost control. It is interesting to note in this regard that the long-term course for many restrictive anorexics is a shift to bulimic patterns of coping.

Although again there are multiple contributors to the development of bulimia and related eating disorders, the role of familial factors in setting up the dynamics of introjection and internal control are quite salient. Bruch (1973, 1979) has vividly depicted the role of parents in catalyzing anorexi by depriving their daughter of autonomy and the "right to live her own life" (1979, p. 38). Minuchin, Rosman, and Baker (1978) similarly reported high levels of enmeshment and intrusive control in families of eating-disordered patients. Convergent empirical findings are also extant. Strober and Humphrey (1987) reported that both anorexics and bulimics experience their parents as blaming, rejecting, and critical compared to normals. Strauss and Ryan (1988) found evidence for less mutuality of autonomy in the object representations of both bulimic and anorexic participants compared with normals, and lower reported expressiveness in their families.

Each of the disorders we have considered thus far begins with rigid, demanding, critical introjects that are pervasive in one's psychic makeup. These rigid structures take varied forms and are more or less stable and effective in controlling the person's actions. In some cases, most notably the obsessive-compulsive personality and anorexia nervosa, the disordered individuals can feel a strong sense of personal control and self-efficacy; the OCP can keep his or her personal affairs quite orderly, for example, and the anorexic can keep his or her body image under control. But these, like the other disorders involving salient introjects, constitute disturbed autonomy and can terrorize the person with contingent self-esteem. They thus emphasize the important difference between personal control and autonomy. That is, being self-controlled can yield desired outcomes, but these actions are not experienced as autonomous or volitional.

We turn now to disorders characterized not by the prevalence of introjects, but rather by their absence. These forms of psychopathology involve the lack of adequate regulatory structures that link one effectively to the socializing context.

Failures of Internalization and the Externalizing Disorders

As we argued earlier, the process of internalization is dependent on certain affordances in the caregiving environment—namely, autonomy support, structure, and involvement—which together facilitate both attachment to caregivers and a readiness to assimilate the values they model. Some caretaking environments, particularly those characterized either by coldness and hostility or by neg-lect, are conducive of poor quality of attachments and lessened internalization (Weiss & Grolnick, 1991).

Conduct Disorders and Antisocial Personality

The diagnosis of Antisocial Personality Disorder (APD) applies to persons who lie, steal, manifest an impoverished sense of responsibility, are aggressive and manipulative toward others, and show evidence that these patterns are continuations of behavior disorders earlier in life. Children diagnosed with Conduct Disorders, a frequent antecedent of APD, display control problems, lability, a lack of ability to give and receive affection, and delayed or impaired development of conscience. Often, they show an unusual interest in violence and sensational phenomena such as fire or gore (Magid & McKelvey, 1988). Further, self-aggrandizement and egocentrism typically characterize their behavior, and their lying about accomplishments highlights their excessive need to be shored up or esteemed by other people in an immediate way. Like adults with ADP, these children tend to display a lack of conscience. There is no deep concern with what is good or right, no stable sense of "I should."

Etiologic theories of APD have been varied and include both biologic or genetic factors (such as poor autonomic reactivity) and familial or cultural inputs (see Richters & Cicchetti, 1993). Our contention is that APD is a psychopathology of *failed internalization,* and although internalization may have been made more difficult by biological factors, we maintain that the failure can be robustly linked to deficits during one's early development in the social contextual factors that are essential for internalization to occur. In short, we suggest that people with APD will have failed to internalize societal norms and moral principles, whether in the form of introjected prescriptions or integrated values.

An internalization conceptualization looks to the family environment for the sources of internalized values of a prosocial nature that seem to be lacking in APD. Although there has been little research or theory directly connecting issues of autonomy support, involvement, or structure to the failure of internalization that characterizes APD, considerable evidence points to their importance. First, there is the general literature on prosocial value development, which locates the sources of such positive values in socialization patterns in the family (Kilby, 1993). Most theorists in this area have taken as their point of departure the idea that value transmission is accomplished through a process of *identification,* in which children emulate or model the values and attitudes of their caretakers. Such theoretical models, of course, implicitly assume that prosocial values must be "put in" to the psyche rather than nurtured. One might alternatively assume that human nature is already prosocial (Deci & Ryan, 2000) and simply requires conditions of nurturance to express that tendency. In any case, the empirical evidence supports either view insofar as prosocial values are most likely to be acquired (or expressed) when caregiving is characterized by warmth (Maccoby, 1980), low power-assertive discipline (Hoffman, 1960), and autonomy support (Ryan, 1993).

The experience of growing up in a nurturant, caring, responsive familial environment undoubtedly facilitates prosocial values. As Kohn (1990) argued, a person who grows up in such an environment has many needs met and is freed from being self-preoccupied, so perhaps he or she is more able to turn toward homonomous strivings and to focus on others. Furthermore, the person will have been exposed to models of caring and concern about others from figures whom they are likely to emulate. Support for this description comes from many quarters. For example, Ryan and Connell (1989) reported that children who experience a high quality of relatedness to parents were more autonomously motivated in the prosocial domain. Similarly, Waters et al. (1979) demonstrated a connection between security of attachment as measured with the Strange Situation paradigm and prosocial orientations.

Conversely, a variety of clinical and empirical perspectives have suggested that antisocial personality, oriented toward self-serving, manipulative, and hedonically gratifying acts, has its roots, in part, in a cold, inconsistent, and controlling family environment (e.g., Benjamin, 2003; Greenberg, Speltz, & DeKlyen, 1993; McCord & McCord, 1964). A plethora of studies has also shown that the common backdrop to APD and Conduct Disorders of childhood includes such factors as maternal depression, loss, high family conflict, other parental pathology, and impoverished conditions of life that fragment the family (Coie & Jacobs, 1993; Loeber & Stouthamer-Loeber, 1986). All of these factors potentiate a situation ultimately lacking in the basic nutriments on which internalization depends—namely, autonomy support, adequate structure and guidance, and concerted, caring involvement.

One limitation of these models of value acquisition, and their implications with regard to the development of externalizing disorders such as APD, is that they do not focus on how or why children might develop values of a nonprosocial or nonmoral nature, except as a converse or absence of moral internalization. For example, there are probably very few parents who strive to teach their children to be manipulative, materialistic, or Machiavellian, but there are many children who develop such an orientation. Absence of iden-

tification does not explain why one proactively seeks to act in these ways. Thus, a fuller model of APD requires both explaining why internalization fails and why hedonic, aggressive, self-gratifying values predominate instead.

Ryan, Sheldon, Kasser, and Deci (1996) and T. Kasser (2002) have argued that, to the extent that individuals lack the necessary nutriments of autonomy support and caring involvement (and therefore are deficient in the development of self), they often turn to extrinsic, narcissistically oriented values to gain and sustain some minimal sense of power, importance, and worth. Thus, people place more value on issues of material wealth and other exteriorized qualities to the extent that they have not consolidated a secure sense of an inner self. Put differently, to the extent that one is not anchored in a true self, behavior becomes increasingly organized by narcissistically oriented, false-self values. In line with this theorizing, T. Kasser and Ryan (1993, 1996) found in late adolescent samples that excessive emphasis on materialistic values was associated with greater maladjustment, including narcissism and Conduct Disorders.

T. Kasser et al. (1995) examined the developmental antecedents of this greater emphasis on materialism relative to prosocial values and found that adolescents who were more materialistic came from homes where both they and their mother reported that there was less autonomy support, warmth, and security. The researchers also found that more impoverished, high-crime neighborhoods, in confluence with these more controlling and hostile parenting environments, were likely to promote children's placing strong importance on these extrinsic values, a finding consistent with Coie and Jacob's (1993) analysis of Conduct Disorders. Finally, T. Kasser et al.'s analysis of clinical interviews with participants in an at-risk population (defined in terms of maternal psychopathology and low socioeconomic status) revealed that those with greater centrality of materialistic values were more likely to be clinically diagnosed as conduct disordered. In a conceptual replication with a college population, participants who perceived their parents to be controlling (versus autonomy-supportive) and cold (versus warm) were found to evidence a relatively higher centrality of materialism in their value orientation. Finally, a study by G. C. Williams, Cox, Hedberg, and Deci (2000) found that lack of parental autonomy support not only led high school students to hold strong extrinsic values for wealth, fame, and image, but also led to the high-risk behaviors of alcohol and tobacco use, early sexual intercourse, and excessive television watching.

One important aspect of this work is its clarification that environments that fail to support true-self development promote an emphasis on alienated or substitute needs rather than authentic ones and on the visible trappings of worth. These, in turn, motivate the so-called antisocial personality. The research also highlights the continuity of motivational dynamics between nonclinical and clinical populations.

From the perspective of SDT, the development of Conduct Disorders and an asocial, self-focused goal orientation stem directly from inadequate attachment and failed internalization resulting from an externally controlling, inconsistent, and affection-impoverished social context. To the extent that social values (and the economic conditions that structure them) disable, distract, or fragment the caretaking environment, children will be more oriented to narcissistic goals to gain a temporary sense of worth and importance. Not only is this model applicable to conduct-disordered children, but increasingly to American culture more generally (T. Kasser, 2002). Put succinctly, the more we create conditions that disrupt the quality and stability of familial relationships, the more narcissistically oriented (Lasch, 1978) and antisocial our culture as a whole may become.

Dissociative Identity and the Fragmentation of Self

We have argued that essential to the formation of integrated experience and behavioral regulation is support for autonomy and relatedness. Dissociative Identity Disorders (DID) represent, in most cases, a person whose life experiences were characterized by deprivation of both. People who should have been loving were hurtful, and aspects of the person's life and body over which he or she should have had control were intruded on or violated. Indeed, M. Steinberg and Schnall (2001) reported extremely high rates of early physical and sexual abuse among patients with DID.

DID is highly pertinent to autonomy disturbances because autonomy is closely related to integration, and the violation of self, especially by caregivers, can shatter the integrity that is so essential to autonomy. The splitting of personality has the function of defensively shielding the core self from pain, but the shifts in identity that characterize DID are typically not experienced as within personal control. Indeed, they have an impersonal perceived locus of causality. Depersonalization, another symptom associated with DID, also exemplifies this sense of impersonal causality, as if one's body were acting independently of one's will. As autonomy, or self-rule, depends on a sense of self and an internal perceived locus of causality for behavior, it is clear that autonomy is seriously disturbed in DID.

The perceived lack of personal causation is often part of the despondency these patients report. For example, one patient who came to treatment for depression began to manifest symptoms of DID. She subsequently revealed repeated sexual abuse by her father, which she had "forgotten." As it unfolded, it was clear that she had been threatened with her life if she ever told anyone, a command she had internalized. Only with a high degree of patient, autonomy-supportive empathy was the history told.

Borderline Disorders: Lack of a Stable Self

Personality disorders have become a predominant concern in clinical settings because of their increasing incidence and thus the personal resources demanded in their treatment. Borderline disorders highlight many issues in character pathology generally, and they represent a prototypic example of structural damage to the self that has been associated with failures in autonomy support and involvement of early caregivers.

The core of borderline disorders is the lack of a cohesive and stable sense of self. Among the central features that are associated with this lack of a consistent and organized self are emotional, interpersonal, and self-esteem lability. Borderline individuals show the externalizing attributes of impulsivity, along with some of the features of internalizing disorders such as susceptibility to depression, anxiety, and fragmentation in the face of self-esteem-related losses. A cardinal dynamic of borderline lability concerns anger, both self- and other-directed, which can result in destructive actions and magnify relationship instability and internal feelings of being overwhelmed and disintegrated. More generally, patients with borderline disorders have difficulty differentiating internal needs from external reality, and they are tremendously dependent on concrete supplies from others to maintain a sense of self. They lack the internal controls to modulate anxiety, which can escalate to panic proportions, particularly when no one is available to contain and comfort them.

Another central feature of borderline disorder is a lack of stable identity and commitment, either to a line of action such as a career choice or to a relationship (Meissner, 1988). Patients with this disorder may, however, latch on to something or someone in an effort to derive a temporary feeling of cohesion, but these choices are often inappropriate or destructive. Commitments are difficult because the borderline individual lacks a stable and cohesive self that can form the basis for sharing in committed relationships or endeavors. Closely related to this is the borderline individual's lack of reflective awareness (Bleiberg, 2004; Fonagy & Target, 1997; Ryan, in press).

Phenomenologically, patients with borderline disorders frequently report being both controlled and helpless with respect to their behavior. They often feel like a victim of circumstances without a sense of personal initiative or responsibility for the direction of their own fate. One late adolescent patient, for example, reported that prior to self-mutilation he entered into a "lost" state, where the overwhelming impulse to cut "came upon" him (conveying an impersonal perceived locus of causality), while at the same time he felt he could only obtain relief and release from dysphoric self-hate by engaging in such acts (suggesting external causality). In no sense did he feel autonomous and volitional in these acts, but rather driven, desperate, and helpless. Interestingly, these self-destructive acts typically followed events in which he experienced a sense of rejection or abandonment from a sometimes clinging and sometimes harshly critical parent.

Connected with the lack of feeling of autonomy and identity, patients with borderline disorder may feel empty and isolated (Westen, 1991). Clearly, there is a diminution of the true self whereby the individual loses connection to his or her interests and feelings. Patients with this disorder often report feelings of boredom and may engage in impulsive acts, such as substance abuse, careless spending, and binge eating, to counteract such feelings.

Although there is some evidence of genetic contributions to borderline disorder, in that many borderlines appear to have exhibited a "difficult child" temperamental profile, much of the evidence focuses on the early environment of the child. The formation of a stable and cohesive sense of self depends on the integration of positive identifications and thus it is not surprising that theories and research point to the importance of early family relations. Two sets of characteristics have emerged from these literatures: severely impoverished caregiving during the early years, and the parents' (particularly the mother's) difficulty allowing the child to move toward self-sufficiency and autonomy (Sperry, 2003). In both cases, the parents are thought to fail to bolster the child's autonomous self that sets the stage for self functions such as identity and affect modulation. Having been exposed to caregivers who did not provide autonomy support, who were unable to take the children's perspective, the children failed to develop the sense of reflective awareness that allowed them to be in touch with their own internal states or the internal states of others.

Early caregivers of individuals with borderline disorder have been described as unavailable, inconsistent, and neglectful (Masterson, 1985), with reports of sexual, emotional, and physical abuse (Herman, Perry, & van der Kolk, 1989; Westen, Lodolph, Misle, Ruffins, & Block, 1990; Zanarini, 1997). In one study, 80% of borderline patients were reported to be physically or sexually abused or to have witnessed serious domestic violence (Herman et al., 1989).

Explicating more specifically the affect and behavior regulation difficulties of these patients, Linehan (1993) suggested that patients with borderline disorder come from families that invalidate the affective experience of their children. There is no tolerance for fears or anxieties in the children, and they do not experience soothing or comforting from the parent. Without such care, these children do not internalize the capacity to soothe themselves, resulting in difficulty regulating emotions and tolerating feelings of distress and grief that could help to guide their actions.

According to object relations theorists (Kernberg, 1967; Masterson, 1985), the disorder has its roots in the mother-child relationship, particularly during the phase of separation-individuation when the child is striving to experience himself or herself as separate from the mother. Part of the phase involves a pushing away from the mother. In families of borderline individuals, the mother is not able to tolerate movement toward self-sufficiency as it brings up her own fears of abandonment. Consequently, the mother threatens to withdraw nurturance from the child if he or she moves to act as a separate autonomous individual. In SDT's terms, the child must therefore decide between autonomy and relatedness to the mother and, because of his or her helpless position in relation to the mother, the child gives up autonomy and the trajectory of true self. The connection to mother, however, is not experienced as true relatedness because it is conflicted and fraught with hostility. Given this level of conflict, there is no "good" object that can support the psychological needs underlying a cohesive sense of self.

The problems of the borderline patient thus illustrate how lack of empathy and consistent involvement and autonomy support undermines intrinsic interests and tendencies, as well as self-regulatory functions—all aspects of the autonomous self (Ryan, in press).

SELF-DETERMINATION THEORY AND THE STUDY OF NORMAL DEVELOPMENT AND PSYCHOPATHOLOGY

Among the central aims of SDT is the explication of the social-contextual conditions that promote optimal development of self. Thus, we have focused considerable attention on specifying the conditions that undermine optimal development—namely, ones that are controlling, rejecting, cold, and chaotic, or in other words, ones that thwart satisfaction of the basic psychological needs for competence, autonomy, and relatedness. In studying normal populations, we have observed the undermining of intrinsic motivation, the introjection of rigid demands and punitive contingencies, and the failures of internalization resulting in poor modulation of urges and emotions and inadequate self-regulation.

It is our contention that many of the processes that are integral to nonoptimal functioning in normal populations are also central to various psychopathologies. Indeed, we see continuity in the basic psychological needs for autonomy, competence, and relatedness across types of people, developmental epochs, and cultures, suggesting that thwarting of these basic needs, especially when the thwarting is severe, is a critical component of psychopathology as well as more "normal" or transitory maladjustment.

At the same time, in our focus on psychological and social dynamics, we do not discount the role of biological influences but consider them interactive with these interpersonal, familial influences. Thus, someone with biological factors contributing to psychopathology will be more vulnerable to minor deficits in the parenting environment, and furthermore, the biological-based vulnerabilities may lead the child to behave in ways that make it harder for the caretaker to be supportive of the child's autonomy and relatedness needs.

Grolnick (2002) provided an extensive discussion of such dynamics in her work on parenting environments. She explained how so often parental control is a function of both pressures and ego involvements of the parents, as well as a "pull" to control created by children with difficult temperaments or behavioral tendencies. Unfortunately, such dynamics often create a deepening cycle of difficulties, which, if unhindered, leads to well-anchored disorders in later development. That is, to the extent that caretakers respond by restricting their provision of the critical nutriments for optimal development—namely, autonomy support, structure, and involvement—a negative synergism occurs.

In the studies we have done with abnormal populations, we have found support for our view that disturbed autonomy exists in various pathologies. Further, the work of numerous investigators has confirmed that the caregiving environments of individuals with various disorders were lacking in critical nutriments. We thus see the study of normal and abnormal populations as wholly complementary for explicating the psychological factors involved in psychopathology and for detailing the social-contextual factors that contribute to diminished development and the onset of psychopathology.

The developmental antecedents of disturbed autonomy are multiple, with genetic, biological, interpersonal, and sociocultural factors all being relevant (Cicchetti & Dawson, 2002). Genetic and other biological factors enter

transactionally into interpersonal relationships, facilitating or forestalling the quality of these social contextual inputs, and cultural factors both shape and are emergent from patterns of social and familial functioning. Our focus has been on the social and familial factors, although our aim was not to provide a complete account of the development of autonomy disturbances. Rather, we have attempted to describe the phenomenological significance of autonomy in normal and pathological development and to show empirically and theoretically how interpersonal factors contribute to the etiology of pathologically disturbed autonomy.

Within this approach, we have viewed the development of autonomy as proceeding most effectively in familial and social contexts that provide autonomy support, optimal structure, and interpersonal involvement. In the absence of these necessary social nutrients—in contexts that thwart satisfaction of the needs for autonomy, competence, and relatedness—disturbed self-development is expected, resulting in the emergence of psychopathology. Psychopathology is thus the result of disorganizing influences, of contexts that thwart or forestall personality integration.

We have reviewed a large number of studies indicating that the development of autonomy—the maintenance of intrinsic motivation, the internalization of values and regulatory processes, and the integration of emotions—is facilitated by the contextual nutriments of caregiver attention and interest and of encouragement for exploration and self-initiation. Contexts where interpersonal involvement and autonomy support are absent have been found reliably to diminish autonomous regulation and impair the development of self. The two contextual elements that have consistently been found in our studies to impair autonomy and development—namely, controllingness and lack of interpersonal involvement—have also been emphasized in the clinical literature on the antecedents of disorders that involve either heteronomous introjects or failures of internalization. Thus, there appear to be clear parallels between the results of the empirical explorations of autonomy dynamics in normative development and the conclusions from clinical studies of psychopathology.

CONCLUSIONS AND FUTURE DIRECTIONS

The exciting thing about the convergence between our research results on both normal populations and those experiencing psychopathology is that it sets the stage for further empirical investigations in which autonomy concepts figure heavily. For example, the constructs concerning intrinsic motivation, internalization, and autonomy-supportive relationships all bear on clinical phenomena, and they help us see the continuity of human needs in diverse populations. For example, whereas theories of internalization have been widely discussed in developmental and clinical literatures by such seminal writers as Freud, Mahler, Erikson, Kelman, Perry, Piaget, and Kohlberg, to name a few, there has been a paucity of empirically based studies of the process and little specific theory about factors that facilitate versus undermine internalization. SDT strives to ameliorate this by providing testable hypotheses, amenable to both experimental and field methods, concerning both how to measure internalization and what predicts it.

At the same time, the specificity of dynamics that lead children down different developmental and adjustment pathways is still largely underexplored. Needed research could begin by comparing diagnostic groups to matched control groups, much as Strauss and Ryan (1988) and Grolnick and Ryan (1990) have done with eating-disordered patients and learning disabled students, respectively. Such strategies help to establish that autonomy disturbances do exist within various clinical problems and to specify the nature of the disturbed autonomy. For example, in disorders involving rigid introjects, it would be important to clarify the strength and centrality of introjects, whether the disordered individuals generally live up to or fall short of the introjected demands, and the nature of the intrapsychic punishment that follows inadequate performance. Additionally, in disorders involving inadequate internalization, research should clarify the nature of the impulses that prevail, the conditions within which regulation is more versus less effective, and so on.

More detailed work on the antecedents of specific autonomy disturbances within the various disorders will also be important. It is clear, for example, that the lack of autonomy support and genuine relatedness by caregivers is antecedent to the development of a wide range of pathologies (see, e.g., Ryan, in press). Yet, why an individual develops anorexia nervosa rather than pervasive self-punitive depression in familial contexts that are demanding and critical is an example of the kinds of questions that are important to tackle empirically. That autonomy disturbances are involved in a wide range of disorders and that familial and other interpersonal contexts play a role in their development seems certain, and of course bespeaks SDT's claim of the generalized nature of autonomy-related needs for psychological development. Nonetheless, the more specific processes through which autonomy is derailed and how these processes are linked to specific disorders or symptoms remain to be further clarified. Failures of autonomy support appear to supply a generalized stressor to integrated development, but how this

differentially impacts and interacts with varied diatheses is an area for rich empirical inquiry. The challenge this provides is at once formidable and intrinsically interesting.

The theoretical framework of SDT specifically distinguishes autonomy from independence, and this distinction is one we see as particularly critical to the field of developmental psychopathology, as well as to theories of parenting, attachment, and development more generally. Noting that both independence and dependence can be either heteronomous or autonomous can help future researchers disentangle what heretofore has been a very mixed and confused literature on dependency across the life span (La Guardia & Ryan, 2002). In our view, dependence should be considered not only as a potential problem, but also as a positive capacity. The willingness to rely on and receive support from others is a basic human propensity that is fostered when autonomy is supported (Ryan et al., 2005). Future research can thus build on this distinction, examining more clearly the pros and cons of dependencies in different developmental epochs and interpersonal contexts. It can also inform the growing literature on psychopathology as it relates to gender and culture, where issues of autonomy and independence have too often been melded and confused (see Chirkov et al., 2003).

More generally, we have pointed in this chapter to the connections between the development and integration of personality and the phenomenological experience of autonomy in the regulation of behavior. In our view, the issue of autonomy is a critical one for organizational perspectives on developmental psychopathology because it supplies a deeper meaning to the concepts of organization and integration than mere synchrony or coordination between systems. That is, the experience of autonomy in action is a defining feature of organization, whereas disturbances of autonomy correspond to fragmentation and disorganization in psychological development. We have further pointed to environmental conditions that either thwart or nurture needs for self-determination, competence, and relatedness as determinative factors in development either away from or toward greater organization and integrity, respectively. The differentiated study of how these psychological needs, in interaction with the biological and social conditions of development, result in relative integration and, thus, experiences of integrity and autonomy in action supplies a broad and important agenda for future clinical research.

Implications for Prevention and Treatment

An interesting question for future research concerns the relationship between *etiological factors* such as lack of autonomy and impoverished relatedness and *ameliorative factors* proposed by various treatment approaches. It seems clear that the absence of need-supportive inputs from caregivers can create a cascade of negative developmental processes, both behavioral and biological, that can eventuate in disordered functioning. Prevention efforts thus must focus on attempting to create need-supportive environments for the developing child through, for example, parent education or school reform. On the other hand, ameliorating or treating existing disorders (i.e., tertiary approaches) may entail addressing need deficits both directly (by providing a need-supportive therapeutic context) and/or indirectly (e.g., by providing people with skills or opportunities to better satisfy needs in their natural environment or better cope with maladaptive patterns due to deficits).

Implications of this work for a preventive viewpoint are clear. Indeed, insofar as SDT represents a social psychology of personality development, it offers very specific ideas concerning optimal parenting and teaching. It details, for example, how adults can set appropriate limits (Koestner et al., 1984); how to use praise and rewards effectively (Deci et al., 1999); what familial conditions foster positive value internalization (Grolnick, Deci, & Ryan, 1997); and what a need-supportive classroom environment that fosters learning and self-esteem development entails (Deci & Ryan, 1985b). Moreover, SDT suggests that different cultural practices and social values can differentially affect psychological development (T. Kasser, Ryan, Couchman, & Sheldon, 2003; Ryan et al., 1996). Thus, a body of practical knowledge is emerging form these decades of work on autonomy that concerns how environments can nurture psychological integrity and wellness, one with considerable cross-cultural generality (Ryan & Deci, 2003). However, these understandings have yet to be systematically applied in empirically supported prevention work.

An exception to the paucity of prevention efforts is the Child Development Project (CDP; Solomon, Watson, Battistich, Schaps, & Delucchi, 1996), a school-based reform initiative that focuses on students' needs for autonomy, belongingness, and competence experiences in the context of schools. The CDP specifically emphasizes cooperative learning, the importance of democratic values, student autonomy and self-direction, and a child-centered approach to classroom management in its efforts to meet the psychological needs of students and thereby foster greater school engagement and personal development. Recent evidence suggests that in schools where the CDP approach has been adequately implemented, students show gains in personal adjustment, positive social and ethnic attitudes, internalization of values, and greater self-motivation (Solomon,

Battistich, Watson, Schaps, & Lewis, 2000). Similarly, First Things First (Connell, 1996), a school reform initiative that draws on SDT concepts, has shown empirically verified success in increasing student motivation, engagement, and performance in impoverished urban school districts. The fact that school-based programs focused on supporting psychological needs can effectively alter the course of development suggests the promise of prevention efforts for ameliorating some of the deficits that stem from earlier caregiving deficiencies.

Indeed, the possibilities for prevention are manifold, and the fact that they can succeed raises an important question concerning the relations between prevention efforts and *resilience*. The concept of resilience suggests that there can be protective strengths, either in the individual or the environment, that can ameliorate or forestall the deleterious impact of otherwise toxic environments. Evidence from SDT-based studies of within-person variability over partners, contexts, and time strongly suggests that there is considerable plasticity within persons, such that when individuals find themselves in contexts where psychological needs are supported, they function more optimally, regardless of vulnerabilities or general tendencies. Even an insecurely attached person is more secure in need-supportive contexts (La Guardia et al., 2000); even a detached person may be more likely to reach out when another is empathic and noncontrolling (Ryan et al., 2005). Thus, the presence of even one significant figure who can provide support for basic psychological needs may foster a greater resilience, even amid a social backdrop characterized by negative events and risk factors. This within-person plasticity, so evident in our recent studies (see Brown & Ryan, in press), thus has many implications for the literature on resilience and the design and focus of interventions. Future research should capitalize on within-person methodologies to look at the protective influences that contextual and person-specific sources of support can provide.

Although primary prevention using SDT principles has not been widely attempted, the past few years have seen an increasing interest in applying SDT's formulations in tertiary treatment settings. In particular, promising advances are being made in SDT-informed treatment for addictions, including alcohol, opiate, and tobacco dependencies (Foote et al., 1999; Ryan, Plant, & O'Malley, 1993; G. C. Williams, Deci, & Ryan, 1998; Zeldman, Ryan, & Fiscella, 2004). These studies particularly point to the critical role of patients' volition in successful treatments and how clinicians' autonomy support can foster and sustain that volition. There have also been several articles connecting SDT with the effectiveness of treatments congruent with that theory. For example, W. R. Miller and Rollnick's (2002) motivational interviewing approach has been directly linked to SDT principles in terms of its effective ingredients (e.g., Markland, Ryan, Tobin, & Rollnick, in press; Vansteenkiste & Sheldon, in press). In addition, treatments such as Linehan's (1993) dialectical behavior therapy for borderline and other personality disorders focus on providing autonomy and relatedness supports, a focus for which SDT supplies theoretical justification (Ryan, in press). Sheldon, Williams, and Joiner (2003) have also detailed clinical applications of SDT in health care and counseling settings. These and other papers are increasingly showing the applied value of a basic human needs approach in the clinic.

Additionally, new research is showing how those who treat children with severe psychopathology can themselves suffer stress, which affects the quality of their care and their degree of controllingness (e.g., M. F. Lynch, Plant, & Ryan, in press). That is, psychiatric workers who are stressed and themselves feel more threatened or unsupported tend to have more controlling styles of intervention. At the same time, the data also show that children in such psychiatric care are more likely to positively engage their treatment when the climate supports their autonomy. Such research suggests that an important element in settings concerned with educating, housing, or intervening is an institutional support for the autonomy of the adults involved, which can provide these adults with the psychological resources that allow them, in turn, to nurture and support the children in their care.

Summary

The postulate that there is a core set of basic psychological needs across development and cultures has yielded many testable hypotheses and generative directions for research, a prospect that is both exciting and daunting. It seems clear that experimental and field studies using SDT can contribute descriptively and prescriptively to the field of developmental psychopathology, while at the same time the study of psychological disorders also sheds light on the specific ways in which need thwarting impacts healthy developmental processes. Moreover, SDT's emphasis on need support has much to say about the design of social contexts and the priorities to be stressed in our families, schools, and treatment facilities. Of course, it is the enhancement of autonomy, relatedness, and competence of individuals that supplies an intrinsically valued rationale for the continuance of this work.

REFERENCES

Abramson, L. Y., Seligman, M. E. P., & Teasdale, J. D. (1978). Learned helplessness in humans: Critique and reformulation. *Journal of Abnormal Psychology, 87,* 49–74.

Achenbach, T., & Edelbrock, C. (1987). *Manual for the Youth Self Report.* Unpublished manuscript, University of Vermont at Burlington.

Ainsworth, M. D. S., Blehar, M. C., Waters, E., & Wall, S. (1978). *Patterns of attachment.* Hillsdale, NJ: Erlbaum.

Amabile, T. M. (1983). *The social psychology of creativity.* New York: Springer-Verlag.

Angyal, A. (1965). *Neurosis and treatment: A holistic theory.* New York: Wiley.

Arend, R., Gove, E., & Sroufe, L. A. (1979). Continuity of adaptation from infancy to kindergarten: A predictive study of ego-resiliency and curiosity in preschoolers. *Child Development, 50,* 950–959.

Assor, A., Roth, G., & Deci, E. L. (2004). The emotional costs of parents' conditional regard: A self-determination theory analysis. *Journal of Personality, 72,* 47–88.

Avery, R. R., & Ryan, R. M. (1988). Object relations and ego development: Comparison and correlates in middle childhood. *Journal of Personality, 56,* 547–569.

Bakan, D. (1966). *The duality of human existence.* Boston: Beacon Press.

Baldwin, A. L. (1949). The effect of home environment on nursery school behavior. *Child Development, 20,* 49–62.

Baldwin, A. L. (1955). *Behavior and development in childhood.* New York: Dryden.

Baltes, M. M., & Silverberg, S. B. (1994). The dynamics between dependency and autonomy: Illustrations across the life span. In D. L. Featherman, R. M. Lerner, & M. Perlmutter (Eds.), *Life-span development and behavior* (Vol. 12, pp. 41–90). Hillsdale, NJ: Erlbaum.

Bandura, A. (1989). Human agency in social cognitive theory. *American Psychologist, 44,* 1175–1184.

Bargh, J. A., & Ferguson, M. J. (2000). Beyond behaviorism: On the automaticity of higher mental processes. *Psychological Bulletin, 126,* 925–945.

Baumeister, R. F. (1991). *Escaping the self.* New York: Basic Books.

Baumeister, R. F., Muraven, M., & Tice, D. M. (2000). Ego Depletion: A resource model of volition, self-regulation, and controlled processing. *Social Cognition, 18*(2), 130–150.

Baumrind, D. (1967). Child care practices anteceding three patterns of preschool behavior. *Genetic Psychology Monographs, 75,* 43–88.

Baumrind, D. (1971). Current patterns of parental authority. *Developmental Psychology Monographs, 4,* 1–102.

Baumrind, D. (1977, March). *Socialization determinants of personal agency.* Paper presented at the biennial meeting of the Society for Research in Child Development, New Orleans, LA.

Bechara, A., Tranel, D., Damasio, H., & Damasio, A. R. (1996). Failure to respond autonomically to anticipated future outcomes following damage to prefrontal cortex. *Cerebral Cortex, 6,* 215–225.

Beck, A. T. (1983). Cognitive treatment of depression: New perspectives. In P. J. Clayton & J. E. Barrett (Eds.), *Treatment of depression: Old controversies and new approaches* (pp. 265–290). New York: Raven Press.

Becker, W. C. (1964). Consequences of different kinds of parental discipline. In M. L. Hoffman & L. W. Hoffman (Eds.), *Review of child development research* (Vol. I, pp. 169–208). New York: Russell Sage Foundation.

Behrends, R. S., & Blatt, S. J. (1985). Internalization and psychological development throughout the life cycle. *Psychoanalytic Study of the Child, 40,* 11–39.

Benjamin, L. S. (2003). *Interpersonal diagnosis and treatment of personality disorders* (2nd ed.). New York: Guilford Press.

Benware, C., & Deci, E. L. (1984). Quality of learning with an active versus passive motivational set. *American Educational Research Journal, 21,* 755–765.

Blais, M. R., Sabourin, S., Boucher, C., & Vallerand, R. J. (1990). Toward a motivational model of couple happiness. *Journal of Personality and Social Psychology, 59,* 1021–1031.

Blatt, S. J. (1974). Levels of object representation in anaclitic and introjective depression. *Psychoanalytic Study of the Child, 29,* 107–157.

Blatt, S. J., Chevron, E. S., Quinlan, D. M., & Wein, S. (1981). *The assessment of qualitative and structural dimensions of object representation.* Unpublished manuscript, Yale University, New Haven, CT.

Blatt, S. J., & Homann, E. (1992). Parent-child interaction in the etiology of dependent and self-critical depression. *Clinical Psychology Review, 12,* 47–91.

Bleiberg, E. (2004). *Treating personality disorders in children and adolescents: A relational approach.* New York: Guilford Press.

Block, J. H., & Block, J. (1980). The role of ego-control and ego-resiliency in the organization of behavior. In W. A. Collins (Ed.), *Minnesota Symposia on Child Psychology: Vol. 13. Development of cognitive affect and social relations* (pp. 39–101). Hillsdale, NJ: Erlbaum.

Blos, P. (1962). *On adolescence: A psychoanalytic interpretation.* Glencoe, IL: Free Press.

Blos, P. (1979). *The adolescent passage.* New York: International Universities Press.

Bober, S., & Grolnick, W. S. (1995). Motivational factors related to differences in self-schemas. *Motivation and Emotion, 19,* 307–327.

Bowlby, J. (1969). *Attachment and loss: Vol. 1. Attachment.* New York: Basic Books.

Bradley, S. J. (2000). *Affect regulation and the development of psychopathology.* New York: Guilford Press.

Brazelton, T. B. (1973). *Neonatal Behavioral Assessment Scale.* Philadelphia: Lippincott.

Brazelton, T. B., Koslowski, B., & Main, M. (1974). The origins of mother-infant interaction. In M. Lewis & L. A. Rosenblum (Eds.), *The effect of the infant on its caregiver* (pp. 49–76). New York: Wiley.

Bretherton, I. (1987). New perspectives on attachment relations: Security, communication and internal working models. In J. Osofsky (Ed.), *Handbook of infant development* (pp. 1061–1100). New York: Wiley.

Bretherton, I. (1991). Pouring new wine into old bottles: The social self as internal working model. In M. R. Gunnar & L. A. Sroufe (Eds.), *Minnesota Symposia on Child Development: Vol. 23. Self processes and development* (pp. 1–41). Hillsdale, NJ: Erlbaum.

Brody, D. S. (1956). *Patterns of mothering.* New York: International Universities Press.

Brody, D. S., & Axelrad, S. (1978). *Mother, fathers, and children.* New York: International Universities Press.

Bronson, M. B. (2000). *Self-regulation in early childhood.* New York: Guilford Press.

Brown, K. W., & Ryan, R. M. (2003). The benefits of being present: Mindfulness and its role in psychological well-being. *Journal of Personality and Social Psychology, 84,* 822–848.

Brown, K. W., & Ryan, R. M. (in press). Multilevel modeling of motivation: A self-determination theory analysis of basic psychological needs. In A. D. Ong & M. van Dulmen (Eds.), *Handbook of methods in positive psychology.* New York: Oxford University Press.

Bruch, H. (1973). *Eating disorders.* New York: Basic Books.

Bruch, H. (1979). *The golden cage: The enigma of anorexia nervosa.* New York: Vintage Books.

Bruner, J. (1962). *On knowing: Essays for the left hand.* Cambridge, MA: Harvard University Press.

Cacioppo, J. T., Bernston, G. G., Sheridan, J. F., & McClintock, M. K. (2000). Multilevel integrative analyses of human behavior: Social neuroscience and the complementing nature of social and biological approaches. *Psychological Bulletin, 126,* 829–843.

Calkins, S. D. (1997). Cardiac vagal tone indices of temperamental reactivity and behavioral regulation in young children. *Developmental Psychobiology, 31,* 125–135.

Calkins, S. D., & Johnson, M. C. (1998). Toddler regulation of distress to frustrating events: Temperamental and maternal correlates. *Infant Behavior and Development, 21,* 379–395.

Chambers, R. A., Taylor, J. R., & Potenza, M. N. (2003). Developmental neurocircuitry of motivation in adolescence: A critical period of addiction vulnerability. *American Journal of Psychiatry, 160,* 1041–1052.

Chirkov, V., & Ryan, R. M. (2001). Parent and teacher autonomy-support in Russian and U.S. adolescents: Common effects on well-being and academic motivation. *Journal of Cross-Cultural Psychology, 32,* 618–635.

Chirkov, V., Ryan, R. M., Kim, Y., & Kaplan, U. (2003). Differentiating autonomy from individualism and independence: A self-determination theory perspective on internalization of cultural orientations and well-being. *Journal of Personality and Social Psychology, 84,* 97–110.

Cicchetti, D., & Dawson, G. (2002). Editorial: Multiple levels of analysis. *Development and Psychopathology, 14,* 417–420.

Cicchetti, D., Ganiban, J., & Barnett, D. (1991). Contributions from the study of high-risk populations to understanding the development of emotion regulation. In J. Garber & K. A. Dodge (Eds.), *The development of emotion regulation and dysregulation* (pp. 15–48). New York: Cambridge University Press.

Cicchetti, D., & Tucker, D. (1994). Development and self-regulatory structures of the mind. *Development and Psychopathology, 6,* 533–549.

Coie, J. D., & Jacobs, M. R. (1993). The role of social context in the prevention of conduct disorder. *Development and Psychopathology, 5,* 263–275.

Connell, J. P. (1985). A new multidimensional measure of children's perceptions of control. *Child Development, 56,* 1018–1041.

Connell, J. P. (1996). *First things first: A framework for successful school-site reform.* Rochester, NY: Institute for Research and Reform in Education.

Crittenden, P. (1988). Relationships at risk. In J. Belsky & T. Nezworski (Eds.), *Clinical implications of attachment theory* (pp. 136–174). Hillsdale, NJ: Erlbaum.

Crockenberg, S., & Litman, C. (1990). Autonomy as competence in 2-year-olds: Maternal correlates of child defiance, compliance, and self-assertion. *Developmental Psychology, 26,* 961–971.

Csikszentmihalyi, M. (1975). *Beyond boredom and anxiety.* San Francisco: Jossey-Bass.

Danner, E. W., & Lonky, E. (1981). A cognitive-developmental approach to the effects of rewards on intrinsic motivation. *Child Development, 52,* 1043–1052.

deCharms, R. (1968). *Personal causation: The internal affective determinants of behavior.* New York: Academic Press.

deCharms, R. (1981). Personal causation and locus of control: Two different traditions and two uncorrelated measures. In H. M. Lefcourt

(Ed.), *Research with the locus of control construct: Vol. 1. Assessment methods* (pp. 337–358). New York: Academic Press.

Deci, E. L. (1971). Effects of externally mediated rewards on intrinsic motivation. *Journal of Personality and Social Psychology, 18,* 105–115.

Deci, E. L. (1972). Intrinsic motivation, extrinsic reinforcement, and inequity. *Journal of Personality and Social Psychology, 22,* 113–120.

Deci, E. L. (1980). *The psychology of self-determination.* Lexington, MA: Lexington Books.

Deci, E. L., & Cascio, W. E. (1972, April). *Changes in intrinsic motivation as a function of negative feedback and threats.* Paper presented at the meeting of the Eastern Psychological Association, Boston.

Deci, E. L., Cascio, W. E., & Krusell, J. (1973, May). *Sex differences, verbal reinforcement, and intrinsic motivation.* Paper presented at the meeting of the Eastern Psychological Association, Washington, DC.

Deci, E. L., Driver, R. E., Hotchkiss, L., Robbins, R. J., & Wilson, I. M. (1993). The relation of mothers' controlling vocalizations to children's intrinsic motivation. *Journal of Experimental Child Psychology, 55,* 151–162.

Deci, E. L., Eghrari, H., Patrick, B. C., & Leone, D. R. (1994). Facilitating internalization: The self-determination theory perspective. *Journal of Personality, 62,* 119–142.

Deci, E. L., Koestner, R., & Ryan, R. M. (1999). A meta-analytic review of experiments examining the effects of extrinsic rewards on intrinsic motivation. *Psychological Bulletin, 125,* 627–668.

Deci, E. L., La Guardia, J. G., Moller, A. C., Scheiner, M., & Ryan, R. M. (2004). *On the benefits of giving as well as receiving autonomy support: Mutuality in close friendships.* Unpublished manuscript, University of Rochester, Rochester, NY.

Deci, E. L., & Ryan, R. M. (1980a). The empirical exploration of intrinsic motivational processes. In L. Berkowitz (Ed.), *Advances in experimental social psychology* (Vol. 13, pp. 39–80). New York: Academic Press.

Deci, E. L., & Ryan, R. M. (1980b). Self-determination theory: When mind mediates behavior. *Journal of Mind and Behavior, 1,* 33–43.

Deci, E. L., & Ryan, R. M. (1985a). The General Causality Orientations Scale: Self-determination in personality. *Journal of Research in Personality, 19,* 109–134.

Deci, E. L., & Ryan, R. M. (1985b). *Intrinsic motivation and self-determination in human behavior.* New York: Plenum Press.

Deci, E. L., & Ryan, R. M. (1987). The support of autonomy and the control of behavior. *Journal of Personality and Social Psychology, 53,* 1024–1037.

Deci, E. L., & Ryan, R. M. (1995). Human autonomy: The basis for true self-esteem. In M. H. Kernis (Ed.), *Efficacy, agency, and self-esteem* (pp. 31–49). New York: Plenum Press.

Deci, E. L., & Ryan, R. M. (2000). The "what" and "why" of goal pursuits: Human needs and the self-determination of behavior. *Psychological Inquiry, 11,* 227–268.

Deci, E. L., Schwartz, A. J., Sheinman, L., & Ryan, R. M. (1981). An instrument to assess adults' orientations toward control versus autonomy with children: Reflections on intrinsic motivation and perceived competence. *Journal of Educational Psychology, 73,* 642–650.

Dix, T. (1991). The affective organization of parenting: Adaptive and maladaptive processes. *Psychological Bulletin, 110,* 3–25.

Dodge, K. A. (1991). Emotion and social information processing. In J. Garber & K. A. Dodge (Eds.), *The development of emotion regulation and dysregulation* (pp. 159–181). New York: Cambridge University Press.

Dresner, R., & Grolnick, W. S. (1992). *Constructions of early parenting, intimacy, and autonomy in young women.* Unpublished manuscript, Clark University, Worcester, MA.

Dworkin, G. (1988). *The theory and practice of autonomy.* New York: Cambridge University Press.

Easterbrook, J. A. (1978). *The determinants of free will.* New York: Academic Press.

Eisenberger, R., & Cameron, J. (1996). Detrimental effects of reward: Reality or myth? *American Psychologist, 51,* 1153–1166.

Eisenberger, R., Pierce, W. D., & Cameron, J. (1999). Effects of reward on intrinsic motivation: Negative, neutral, and positive: Comment on Deci, Koestner, and Ryan (1999). *Psychological Bulletin, 125,* 677–691.

Elkind, D. (1967). Egocentrism in adolescence. *Child Development, 38,* 1025–1034.

Elliot, A. J., McGregor, H. A., & Thrash, T. M. (2002). The need for competence. In E. L. Deci & R. M. Ryan (Eds.), *Handbook of self-determination research* (pp. 361–387). Rochester, NY: University of Rochester Press.

Elmen, J., Mounts, N., & Steinberg, L. (1989). Authoritative parenting, psychosocial maturity and academic success among adolescents. *Child Development, 60,* 1424–1436.

Emde, R. (1983). The prerepresentational self and its affective core. *Psychoanalytic Study of the Child, 38,* 165–192.

Enns, M. W., Cox, B. J., & Clara, I. (2002). Adaptive and maladaptive perfectionism: Developmental origins and association with depression proneness. *Personality and Individual Differences, 33,* 921–935.

Erikson, E. H. (1950). *Childhood and society.* New York: Norton.

Field, T. (1987). Interaction and attachment in normal and atypical infants. *Journal of Consulting and Clinical Psychology, 55,* 853–859.

Field, T., Healy, B., Goldstein, S., & Guthertz, M. (1990). Behavior-state matching and synchrony in mother-infant interactions of nondepressed versus depressed dyads. *Developmental Psychology, 26,* 7–14.

Flavell, J. (1977). *Cognitive development.* Englewood Cliffs, NJ: Prentice-Hall.

Flett, G. L., Hewitt, P. L., & Singer, A. (1995). Perfectionism and parental authority styles: Individual psychology. *Journal of Adlerian Theory, Research and Practice, 51,* 50–60.

Flink, C., Boggiano, A. K., & Barrett, M. (1990). Controlling teaching strategies: Undermining children's self-determination and performance. *Journal of Personality and Social Psychology, 59,* 916–924.

Fonagy, P., & Target, M. (1997). Attachment and reflective function: Their role in self-organization. *Development and Psychopathology, 9,* 679–700.

Foote, J., DeLuca, A., Magura, S., Warner, A., Grand, A., Rosenblum, A., et al. (1999). A group motivational treatment for chemical dependency. *Journal of Substance Abuse Treatment, 17,* 181–192.

Frankfurt, H. (1971). Freedom of the will and the concept of person. *Journal of Philosophy, 68,* 5–20.

Fredrickson, B. L. (2001). The role of positive emotions in positive psychology: The broaden-and-build theory of positive emotions. *American Psychologist, 56,* 218–226.

Freud, A. (1958). Adolescence. In R. S. Eissler, A. Freud, H. Hartmann, & M. Kris (Eds.), *Psychoanalytic study of the child* (Vol. 13, pp. 255–278). New York: International Universities Press.

Friedman, M. (2003). *Autonomy, gender, politics.* New York: Oxford University Press.

Frost, R. O., Novara, C., & Rhéaume, J. (2002). Perfectionism in obsessive compulsive disorder. In R. O. Frost & G. Steketee (Eds.), *Cognitive approaches to obsessions and compulsions: Theory, assessment, and treatment* (pp. 91–105). Amsterdam: Pergamon Elsevier Science.

Fuhrman, T., & Holmbeck, G. N. (1995). A contextual-moderator analysis of emotional autonomy and adjustment in adolescence. *Child Development, 66,* 793–811.

Gabbard, G. O. (2000). *Psychodynamic psychiatry in clinical practice* (3rd ed.). Washington, DC: American Psychiatric Press.

Gable, S. L., Reis, H. T., & Elliot, A. J. (2000). Behavioral activation and inhibition in everyday life. *Journal of Personality and Social Psychology, 78,* 1135–1149.

Garbarino, J. (1975). The impact of anticipated reward upon cross-aged tutoring. *Journal of Personality and Social Psychology, 32,* 421–428.

Garber, J., Braafladt, N., & Zeman, J. (1991). The regulation of sad affect: An information processing perspective. In J. Garber & K. A. Dodge (Eds.), *The development of emotion regulation and dysregulation* (pp. 208–242). New York: Cambridge University Press.

Garber, J., & Dodge, K. A. (Eds.). (1991). *The development of emotion regulation and dysregulation.* New York: Cambridge University Press.

Gilligan, C. (1982). *In a different voice.* Cambridge, MA: Harvard University Press.

Goldsmith, H. H., Buss, A. H., Plomin, R., Rothbart, M. K., Thomas, A., Chess, S., et al. (1987). Roundtable: What is temperament? Four approaches. *Child Development, 58,* 505–529.

Greenberg, M. T., Kusche, C. A., & Speltz, M. (1991). Emotional regulation, self-control, and psychopathology: The role of relationships in early childhood. In D. Cicchetti & S. L. Toth (Eds.), *Internalizing and externalizing expressions of dysfunction* (pp. 21–56). Hillsdale, NJ: Erlbaum.

Greenberg, M. T., Speltz, M. L., & DeKlyen, M. (1993). The role of attachment in the early development of disruptive behavior problems. *Development and Psychopathology, 5,* 191–213.

Greenspan, S. I. (1979). *Intelligence and adaptation.* New York: International Universities Press.

Greenspan, S. I. (1981). *Psychopathology and adaptation in infancy and early childhood: Principles of clinical diagnosis and early intervention.* New York: International Universities Press.

Grolnick, W. S. (2002). The psychology of parental control: How well-meant parenting backfires. *Adolescence, 37,* 858–859.

Grolnick, W. S., & Bridges, L. (1992, May). *Emotional self-regulatory strategies, emotionality, and parent-infant interaction in the second year of life.* Paper presented at the International Conference on Infant Studies, Miami, FL.

Grolnick, W. S., Bridges, L. J., & Connell, J. P. (1996). Emotional self-regulation in two-year-olds: Strategies and emotional expression in four contexts. *Child Development, 67,* 928–941.

Grolnick, W. S., Bridges, L., & Frodi, A. (1984). Maternal control style and the mastery motivation of one-year-olds. *Infant Mental Health Journal, 5,* 72–82.

Grolnick, W. S., Deci, E. L., & Ryan, R. M. (1997). Internalization within the family: The self-determination theory perspective. In J. E. Grusec & L. Kuczynski (Eds.), *Parenting and children's internalization of values: A handbook of contemporary theory* (pp. 135–161). New York: Wiley.

Grolnick, W. S., Gurland, S. T., DeCourcey, W., & Jacob, K. (2002). Antecedents and consequences of mothers' autonomy support: An experimental investigation. *Developmental Psychology, 38,* 143–155.

Grolnick, W. S., Kurowski, C. O., Dunlap, K. G., & Hevey, C. (2000). Parental resources and the transition to junior high. *Journal of Research on Adolescence, 10,* 465–488.

Grolnick, W. S., Kurowski, C. O., McMenamy, J. M., Rivkin, I., & Bridges, L. J. (1998). Mothers' strategies for regulating their toddlers' distress. *Infant Behavior and Development, 21,* 437–450.

Grolnick, W. S., & Ryan, R. M. (1987). Autonomy in children's learning: An experimental and individual difference investigation. *Journal of Personality and Social Psychology, 52,* 890–898.

Grolnick, W. S., & Ryan, R. M. (1989). Parent styles associated with children's self-regulation and competence in school. *Journal of Educational Psychology, 81,* 143–154.

Grolnick, W. S., & Ryan, R. M. (1990). Self-perceptions, motivation, and adjustment in children with learning disabilities: A multiple group comparison study. *Journal of Learning Disabilities, 23,* 177–184.

Grolnick, W. S., Ryan, R. M., & Deci, E. L. (1991). The inner resources for school achievement: Motivational mediators of children's perceptions of their parents. *Journal of Educational Psychology, 83,* 508–517.

Grolnick, W. S., Weiss, L., McKenzie, L., & Wrightman, J. (1996). Contextual, cognitive, and adolescent factors associated with parenting in adolescence. *Journal of Youth and Adolescence, 25,* 33–54.

Gross, J. J. (1999). Emotion and emotion regulation. In L. A. Pervin & O. P. John (Eds.), *Handbook of personality: Theory and research* (2nd ed., pp. 525–552). New York: Guilford Press.

Gross, J. J., & John, O. P. (2002). Wise emotion regulation. In L. F. Barrett & P. Salovey (Eds.), *The wisdom in feeling: Psychological processes in emotional intelligence: Emotions and social behavior* (pp. 297–319). New York: Guilford Press.

Grusec, J. E., & Goodnow, J. J. (1994). Impact of parental discipline methods on the child's internalization of values: A reconceptualization of current points of view. *Developmental Psychology, 30,* 4–19.

Harlow, H. F. (1953). Motivation as a factor in the acquisition of new responses. In *Current theory and research on motivation* (pp. 24–49). Lincoln: University of Nebraska Press.

Harter, S. (1993). Visions of self: Beyond the me in the mirror. In J. E. Jacobs (Ed.), *Nebraska Symposium on Motivation: Developmental perspectives on motivation* (Vol. 40, pp. 99–144). Lincoln: University of Nebraska Press.

Hartmann, H. (1964). On rational and irrational action. In *Essays on ego psychology* (pp. 37–68). New York: International Universities Press. (Original work published 1947)

Heider, F. (1958). *The psychology of interpersonal relations.* New York: Wiley.

Helgeson, V. S. (1994). Relation of agency and communion to well-being: Evidence and potential explanations. *Psychological Bulletin, 116,* 412–428.

Herman, J., Perry, J. C., & van der Kolk, B. A. (1989). Childhood trauma in borderline personality disorder. *American Journal of Psychiatry, 146,* 490–495.

Hill, J. P., & Holmbeck, G. (1986). Attachment and autonomy during adolescence. In G. Whitehurst (Ed.), *Annals of child development* (Vol. 3, pp. 145–189). Greenwich, CT: JAI Press.

Hiroto, D. S., & Seligman, M. E. P. (1975). Generality of learned helplessness in man. *Journal of Personality and Social Psychology, 31,* 311–327.

Hmel, B. A., & Pincus, A. L. (2002). The meaning of autonomy: On and beyond the interpersonal circumplex. *Journal of Personality, 70,* 277–310.

Hoffman, M. L. (1960). Power assertion by the parent and its impact on the child. *Child Development, 31,* 129–143.

Hoover, C. E., & Insel, T. R. (1984). Families of origin in obsessive-compulsive disorder. *Journal of Nervous and Mental Disorders, 172,* 207–215.

Horney, K. (1950). *Neurosis and human growth.* New York: Norton.

Hull, C. L. (1943). *Principles of behavior: An introduction to behavior theory.* New York: Appleton-Century-Crofts.

Iyengar, S. S., & Lepper, M. R. (1999). Rethinking the value of choice: A cultural perspective on intrinsic motivation. *Journal of Personality and Social Psychology, 76,* 349–366.

Jahoda, M. (1958). *Current concepts of positive mental health.* New York: Basic Books.

Jenike, M. A. (1991). Obsessive-compulsive disorder. In B. D. Beitman & G. L. Klerman (Eds.), *Integrating pharmacotherapy and psychotherapy* (pp. 183–210). Washington, DC: American Psychiatric Association.

Jordon, J. V. (1991). The relational self: A new perspective for understanding women's development. In J. Strauss & G. R. Goethals (Eds.), *The self: Interdisciplinary approaches* (pp. 36–149). New York: Springer-Verlag.

Jung, C. G. (1959). Aion. In W. McGuire (Executive Editor) & H. Read, M. Fordham, & G. Adler (Vol. Eds.), *Collected works* (Vol. 9). New York: Pantheon Books. (Original work published 1951)

Kagitçibasi, Ç. (1996). The autonomous-relational self: A new synthesis. *European Psychologist, 1,* 180–186.

Kahneman, D., Diener, E., & Schwartz, N. (1999). *Well-being: The foundations of hedonic psychology.* New York: Russell Sage Foundation.

Kandel, D., & Lesser, G. S. (1969). Parent-adolescent relationships and adolescent independence in the United States and Denmark. *Journal of Marriage and the Family, 31,* 348–359.

Kasser, T. (2002). *The high price of materialism.* Cambridge, MA: MIT Press.

Kasser, T., & Ryan, R. M. (1993). A dark side of the American dream: Correlates of financial success as a central life aspiration. *Journal of Personality and Social Psychology, 65,* 410–422.

Kasser, T., & Ryan, R. M. (1996). Further examining the American dream: Differential correlates of intrinsic and extrinsic goals. *Personality and Social Psychology Bulletin, 22,* 80–87.

Kasser, T., Ryan, R. M., Couchman, C., & Sheldon, K. M. (2003) Materialistic values: Their causes and consequences. In T. Kasser & A. D. Kanner (Eds.), *Psychology and the culture of consumption* (pp. 11–28). Washington, DC: American Psychological Association.

Kasser, T., Ryan, R. M., Zax, M., & Sameroff, A. J. (1995). The relations of maternal and social environments to late adolescents' materialistic and prosocial values. *Developmental Psychology, 31,* 907–971.

Kasser, V. G., & Ryan, R. M. (1999). The relation of psychological needs for autonomy and relatedness to vitality, well-being, and mortality in a nursing home. *Journal of Applied Social Psychology, 29,* 935–954.

Kawamura, K. Y., Frost, R. O., & Harmatz, M. G. (2002). The relationship of perceived parenting styles to perfectionism. *Personality and Individual Differences, 32,* 317–327.

Kernberg, O. F. (1967). Borderline personality organization. *Journal of the American Psychoanalytic Association, 15,* 641–685.

Kierkegaard, S. (1968). *The sickness unto death.* Princeton, NJ: Princeton University Press. (Original work published 1849)

Kilby, R. W. (1993). *The study of human values.* Lanham, MD: University Press of America.

Kochanska, G. (1995). Children's temperament, mother's discipline, and security of attachment: Multiple pathways to emerging internalization. *Child Development, 66,* 597–615.

Kochanska, G. (1997). Mutually responsive orientation between mothers and their young children: Implications for early socialization. *Child Development, 68,* 94–112.

Kochanska, G., & Aksan, N. (1995). Mother-child mutually positive affect, the quality of child compliance to requests and prohibitions, and maternal control as correlates of early internalization. *Child Development, 66,* 236–254.

Koestner, R., Bernieri, E., & Zuckerman, M. (1992). Self-regulation and consistency between attitudes, traits, and behaviors. *Personality and Social Psychology Bulletin, 18,* 52–59.

Koestner, R., & McClelland, D. C. (1990). Perspectives on competence motivation. In L. A. Pervin (Ed.), *Handbook of personality: Theory and research* (pp. 527–548). New York: Guilford Press.

Koestner, R., Ryan, R. M., Bernieri, E., & Holt, K. (1984). Setting limits on children's behavior: The differential effects of controlling versus informational styles on intrinsic motivation and creativity. *Journal of Personality, 52,* 233–248.

Kohn, A. (1990). *The brighter side of human nature: Altruism and empathy in everyday life.* New York: Basic Books.

Kohn, A. (1996). By all available means: Cameron and Pierce's defense of extrinsic motivators. *Review of Educational Research, 66,* 1–4.

Kohut, H. (1971). *The analysis of self.* New York: International Universities Press.

Kopp, C. B. (1982). Antecedents of self-regulation: A developmental perspective. *Developmental Psychology, 18,* 199–214.

Kruglanski, A. W., Stein, C., & Riter, A. (1977). Contingencies of exogenous reward and task performance: On the "minimax" strategy in instrumental behavior. *Journal of Applied Social Psychology, 7,* 141–148.

La Guardia, J. G., & Ryan, R. M. (2002). What adolescents need: A self-determination theory perspective on development within families, school and society. In F. Pajares & T. Urdan (Eds.), *Academic motivation of adolescents.* Greenwich CT: IAP.

La Guardia, J. G., Ryan, R. M., Couchman, C. E., & Deci, E. L. (2000). Within-person variation in security of attachment: A self-determination theory perspective on attachment, need fulfillment, and well-being. *Journal of Personality and Social Psychology, 79,* 367–384.

La Guardia, J. G., & Ryff, C. (2003). Self-esteem challenges. *Psychological Inquiry, 14,* 48–51.

Laing, R. D. (1969). *Self and others* (2nd ed.). London: Tavistock.

Lamb, M. E., & Easterbrooks, M. A. (1981). Individual differences in parental sensitivity: Origins, components, and consequences. In M. E. Lamb & L. R. Sherrod (Eds.), *Infant social cognition: Empirical and theoretical considerations* (pp. 127–154). Hillsdale, NJ: Erlbaum.

Lamborn, S. D., & Steinberg, L. (1993). Emotional autonomy redux: Revisiting Ryan and Lynch. *Child Development, 64,* 483–499.

Langer, E. J., & Rodin, J. (1976). The effects of choice and enhanced personal responsibility for the aged: A field experiment in an institutional setting. *Journal of Personality and Social Psychology, 34,* 191–198.

Lapsley, D. K., & Rice, K. (1988). The "new look" at the imaginary audience and personal fable: Toward a general model of adolescent ego development. In D. K. Lapsley & E C. Power (Eds.), *Self, ego and identity: Integrative approaches* (pp. 109–129). New York: Springer-Verlag.

Lasch, C. (1978). *The culture of narcissism: American life in an age of diminishing expectations.* New York: Norton.

Lepper, M. R., & Greene, D. (1975). Turning play into work: Effects of adult surveillance and extrinsic rewards on children's intrinsic motivation. *Journal of Personality and Social Psychology, 31,* 479–486.

Lepper, M. R., Greene, D., & Nisbett, R. E. (1973). Undermining children's intrinsic interest with extrinsic rewards: A test of the "overjustification" hypothesis. *Journal of Personality and Social Psychology, 28,* 129–137.

Lerner, H. G. (1988). *Women in therapy.* New York: Harper & Row.

Levenson, R. W. (1999). The intrapersonal functions of emotion. *Cognition and Emotion, 13,* 481–504.

Levesque, C. S., & Brown, K. W. (). *Overriding motivational automaticity: Mindfulness as a moderator of the influence of implicit motivation on day-to-day behavior.* Manuscript submitted for publication.

Levitz-Jones, E. M., & Orlofsky, J. L. (1985). Separation-individuation and intimacy capacity in college women. *Journal of Personality and Social Psychology, 49,* 156–169.

Lewin, K. (1951). Intention, will, and need. In D. Rapaport (Ed.), *Organization and pathology of thought* (pp. 95–153). New York: Columbia University Press.

Lewis, M., & Coates, D. (1980). Mother-infant interaction and infant cognitive performance. *Infant Behavior and Development, 3,* 95–105.

Lewis, M., & Michalson, L. (1983). *Children's emotions and moods.* New York: Plenum Press.

Libet, B. (1999). How does conscious experience arise? The neural time factor. *Brain Research Bulletin, 50,* 339–340.

Linehan, M. (1993). *Cognitive-behavioral treatment of borderline personality disorder.* New York: Guilford Press.

Loeber, R., & Stouthamer-Loeber, M. (1986). Family factors as correlates and predictors of juvenile conduct disorders. In M. Tonry & N. Morris (Eds.), *Crime and justice* (Vol. 7, pp. 29–149). Chicago: University of Chicago Press.

Loevinger, J. (1976). *Ego development.* San Francisco: Jossey-Bass.

Lynch, M. F., Plant, R., & Ryan, R. M. (in press). Psychological needs and threat to safety: Implications for staff and patients in a psychiatric hospital for youth. *Professional Psychology.*

Lynch, M. L., Ryan, R. M., La Guardia, J. G., Haiyan, L., Yan, R., & Strabakhina, T. N. (2004). *Variability of self-concept across personal relationships: The role of culture, autonomy-support and authenticity.* Unpublished manuscript, University of Rochester, Rochester, NY.

Maccoby, E. E. (1980). *Social development: Psychological growth and the parent-child relationship.* New York: Harcourt Brace Jovanovich.

Mackenzie, C., & Stoljar, N. (2000). Autonomy refigured: Feminist perspectives on autonomy, agency, and the social self. In C. Mackenzie & N. Stoljar (Eds.), *Relational autonomy* (pp. 3–31). New York: Oxford University Press.

Magid, K., & McKelvey, C. A. (1988). *High risk: Children without a conscience.* New York: Bantam Books.

Markland, D., Ryan, R. M., Tobin, V., & Rollnick, S. (in press). Motivational interviewing and self-determination theory. *Journal of Social and Clinical Psychology.*

Markus, H. R., Kitayama, S., & Heiman, R. J. (1996). Culture and "basic" psychological principles. In E. T. Higgins & A. W. Kruglanski (Eds.), *Social psychology: Handbook of basic principles* (pp. 857–913). New York: Guilford Press.

Masterson, J. F. (1985). *Treatment of the borderline adolescent: A developmental approach.* New York: Brunner/Mazel.

May, R. (1969). *Love and will.* New York: Norton.

McBride-Chang, C., & Chang, L. (1998). Adolescent-parent relations in Hong Kong: Parenting styles, emotional autonomy, and school achievement. *Journal of Genetic Psychology, 159,* 421–436.

McCord, W., & McCord, J. (1964). *The psychopath: An essay on the criminal mind.* Princeton, NJ: Van Nostrand.

McCranie, E. W., & Bass, J. D. (1984). Childhood family antecedents of dependency and self-criticism: Implications for depression. *Journal of Abnormal Psychology, 93,* 3–8.

McCullough, P. K., & Maltsberger, J. T. (1995). Obsessive-compulsive personality disorder. In G. Gabbard (Ed.), *Treatments of psychiatric disorders* (pp. 2367–2376). Washington, DC: American Psychiatric Press.

McGraw, K. O., & McCullers, J. C. (1979). Evidence of a detrimental effect of extrinsic incentives on breaking a mental set. *Journal of Experimental Social Psychology, 1*(5), 285–294.

Meissner, W. W. (1988). *Treatment of patients in the borderline spectrum.* Northvale, NJ: Aronson.

Meissner, W. W. (1995). Paranoid personality disorder. In G. O. Gabbard (Ed.), *Treatment of psychiatric disorders for DSM-IV* (2nd ed., Vol. 2, pp. 2249–2259). Washington, DC: American Psychiatric Press.

Memmi, A. (1984). *Dependence.* Boston: Beacon Press.

Miller, A. (1981). *The drama of the gifted child: The search for the true self* (R. Ward, Trans.). New York: Basic Books.

Miller, S. M., Birnbaum, A., & Durbin, D. (1990). Etiologic perspectives on depression in childhood. In M. Lewis & S. Miller (Eds.), *Handbook of developmental psychopathology* (pp. 311–325). New York: Plenum Press.

Miller, W. R., & Rollnick, S. (2002). *Motivational interviewing: Preparing people for change.* New York: Guilford Press.

Millon, T., Davis, R., Millon, C., Escovar, L., & Meagher, S. (2000). *Personality disorders in modern life.* New York: Wiley.

Minuchin, S., Rosman, B., & Baker, L. (1978). *Psychosomatic families.* Cambridge, MA: Harvard University Press.

Nietzel, M. T., & Harris, M. J. (1990). Relationship of dependency and achievement/autonomy to depression. *Clinical Psychology Review, 10,* 279–298.

Nix, G. A., Ryan, R. M., Manly, J. B., & Deci, E. L. (1999). Revitalization through self-regulation: The effects of autonomous and controlled motivation on happiness and vitality. *Journal of Experimental Social Psychology, 35,* 266–284.

Noom, M. J., Dekovic, M., & Meeus, W. H. J. (1999). Autonomy, attachment and psychosocial adjustment during adolescence: A double-edged sword? *Journal of Adolescence, 22,* 771–783.

O'Connor, B. P., & Vallerand, R. J. (1990). Religious motivation in the elderly: A French-Canadian replication and an extension. *Journal of Social Psychology, 130*(1), 53–59.

O'Connor, B. P., & Vallerand, R. J. (1994). The relative effects of actual and experienced autonomy on motivation in nursing home residents. *Canadian Journal on Aging, 13,* 528–538.

Oishi, S. (2000). Goals as cornerstones of subjective well-being: Linking individuals and cultures. In E. Diener & E. M. Suh (Eds.), *Culture and subjective well-being* (pp. 87–112). Cambridge, MA: Bradford.

Orlofsky, J. L., Marcia, J. E., & Lesser, I. (1973). Ego identity status and the intimacy versus isolation crisis of young adulthood. *Journal of Personality and Social Psychology, 27,* 211–219.

Othmer, E., & Othmer, S. C. (2002). *The clinical interview using DSM-IV-TR* (Vols. 1 & 2). Washington, DC: American Psychiatric Publishing.

Panksepp, J. (1998). Attention deficit hyperactivity disorders, psychostimulants and intolerance of childhood playfulness: A tragedy in the making? *Current Directions in Psychological Science, 7,* 91–98.

Parrott, W. G. (1993). Beyond hedonism: Motives for inhibiting good moods and for maintaining bad moods. In D. M. Wegner & J. W. Pennebaker (Eds.), *Handbook of mental control: Century psychology series* (pp. 278–305). Upper Saddle River, NJ: Prentice-Hall.

Perls, F. S. (1973). *The Gestalt approach and eyewitness to therapy.* Ben Lomond, CA: Science and Behavior Books.

Pfander, A. (1967). *Phenomenology of willing and motivation* (H. Spiegelberg, Trans.). Evanston, IL: Northwestern University Press. (Original work published 1908)

Piaget, J. (1952). *The origins of intelligence in children.* New York: International Universities Press.

Piaget, J. (1965). *Moral judgment of the child.* Glencoe, IL: Free Press.

Piaget, J. (1967). *Six psychological studies* (D. Elkind, Ed.). New York: Vintage.

Piaget, J. (1981). *Intelligence and affectivity: Their relationship during child development.* Palo Alto, CA: Annual Reviews.

Pinker, S. (2002). *The blank slate: The modern denial of human nature.* New York: Viking.

Pittman, T. S., Davey, M. E., Alafat, K. A., Wetherill, K. V., & Kramer, N. A. (1980). Informational versus controlling verbal rewards. *Personality and Social Psychology Bulletin, 6,* 228–233.

Pittman, T. S., Emery, J., & Boggiano, A. K. (1982). Intrinsic and extrinsic motivational orientations: Reward-induced changes in preference for complexity. *Journal of Personality and Social Psychology, 42,* 789–797.

Plant, R., & Ryan, R. M. (1985). Intrinsic motivation and the effects of self-consciousness, self-awareness, and ego-involvement: An investigation of internally controlling styles. *Journal of Personality, 53,* 435–449.

Rasmussen, S., & Tsuang, M. (1986). Clinical characteristics and family history in DSM-III obsessive-compulsive disorder. *American Journal of Psychiatry, 143,* 317–322.

Reeve, J. (2002). Self-determination theory applied to educational settings. In E. L. Deci & R. M. Ryan (Eds.), *Handbook of self-determination research* (pp. 183–203). Rochester, NY: University of Rochester Press.

Reis, H. T., & Shaver, P. (1988). Intimacy as an interpersonal process. In S. Duck (Ed.), *Handbook of personal relationships* (pp. 367–389). Chichester, England: Wiley.

Richters, J. E., & Cicchetti, D. (Eds.). (1993). Toward a developmental perspective on conduct disorders [Special issue]. *Development and Psychopathology, 5,* 1–344.

Rogers, C. (1951). *Client centered therapy.* Boston: Houghton-Mifflin.

Rothbart, M. K., & Derryberry, D. (1981). Development of individual differences in temperament. In M. E. Lamb & A. L. Brown (Eds.), *Advances in developmental psychology* (Vol. I, pp. 37–86). Hillsdale, NJ: Erlbaum.

Rotter, J. B. (1966). Generalized expectancies for internal versus external control of reinforcement. *Psychological Monographs, 80*(1), 1–28.

Ryan, R. M. (1982). Control and information in the intrapersonal sphere: An extension of cognitive evaluation theory. *Journal of Personality and Social Psychology, 43,* 450–461.

Ryan, R. M. (1989). The relevance of social ontology to psychological theory. *New Ideas in Psychology, 7,* 115–124.

Ryan, R. M. (1991). The nature of the self in autonomy and relatedness. In J. Strauss & G. R. Goethals (Eds.), *The self: Interdisciplinary approaches* (pp. 208–238). New York: Springer-Verlag.

Ryan, R. M. (1993). Agency and organization: Intrinsic motivation, autonomy and the self in psychological development. In J. Jacobs (Ed.), *Nebraska Symposium on Motivation: Vol. 40. Developmental perspectives on motivation* (pp. 1–56). Lincoln: University of Nebraska Press.

Ryan, R. M. (in press). The developmental line of autonomy in the etiology, dynamics, and treatment of borderline personality disorders. *Development and Psychopathology.*

Ryan, R. M., Avery, R. R., & Grolnick, W. S. (1985). A Rorschach assessment of children's mutuality of autonomy. *Journal of Personality Assessment, 49*(1), 6–12.

Ryan, R. M., & Connell, J. P. (1988). Mastery motivation. In T. Husen & T. N. Postlethwaite (Eds.), *International encyclopedia of education.* New York: Pergamon Press.

Ryan, R. M., & Connell, J. P. (1989). Perceived locus of causality and internalization: Examining reasons for acting in two domains. *Journal of Personality and Social Psychology, 57,* 749–761.

Ryan, R. M., Connell, J. P., & Deci, E. L. (1985). A motivational analysis of self-determination and self-regulation in education. In C. Ames & R. E. Ames (Eds.), *Research on motivation in education: The classroom milieu* (pp. 13–51). New York: Academic Press.

Ryan, R. M., & Deci, E. L. (2000a). The darker and brighter sides of human existence: Basic psychological needs as a unifying concept. *Psychological Inquiry, 11,* 319–338.

Ryan, R. M., & Deci, E. L. (2000b). Intrinsic and extrinsic motivations: Classic definitions and new directions. *Contemporary Educational Psychology, 5,* 54–67.

Ryan, R. M., & Deci, E. L. (2000c). Self-determination theory and the facilitation of intrinsic motivation, social development, and well-being. *American Psychologist, 55,* 68–78.

Ryan, R. M., & Deci, E. L. (2001). On happiness and human potentials: A review of research on hedonic and eudaimonic well-being. *Annual Review of Psychology, 52,* 141–166.

Ryan, R. M., & Deci, E. L. (2003). On assimilating identities to the self: A self-determination theory perspective on internalization and integrity within cultures. In M. R. Leary & J. P. Tangney (Eds.), *Handbook of self and identity* (pp. 253–272). New York: Guilford Press.

Ryan, R. M., & Deci, E. L. (2004). Autonomy is no illusion: Self-determination theory and the empirical study of authenticity, awareness, and will. In J. Greenberg, S. L. Koole, & T. Pyszczynski (Eds.), *Handbook of experimental existential psychology* (pp. 449–479). New York: Guilford Press.

Ryan, R. M., Deci, E. L., & Grolnick, W. S. (1995). Autonomy, relatedness, and the self: Their relation to development and psychopathology. In D. Cicchetti & D. J. Cohen (Eds.), *Developmental psychopathology: Vol. 1. Theory and methods* (pp. 618–655). New York: Wiley.

Ryan, R. M., & Frederick, C. M. (1997). On energy, personality, and health: Subjective vitality as a dynamic reflection of well-being. *Journal of Personality, 65,* 529–565.

Ryan, R. M., & Grolnick, W. S. (1986). Origins and pawns in the classroom: Self-report and projective assessments of individual differences in children's perceptions. *Journal of Personality and Social Psychology, 50,* 550–558.

Ryan, R. M., Koestner, R., & Deci, E. L. (1991). Varied forms of persistence: When free-choice behavior is not intrinsically motivated. *Motivation and Emotion, 15,* 185–205.

Ryan, R. M., & Kuczkowski, R. (1994). Egocentrism and heteronomy: A study of imaginary audience, self-consciousness, and public individuation in adolescence. *Journal of Personality, 62,* 219–238.

Ryan, R. M., Kuhl, J., & Deci, E. L. (1997). Nature and autonomy: Organizational view of social and neurobiological aspects of self-regulation in behavior and development. *Development and Psychopathology, 9,* 701–728.

Ryan, R. M., & La Guardia, J. G. (1999). Achievement motivation within a pressured society: Intrinsic and extrinsic motivations to learn and the politics of school reform. In T. Urdan (Ed.). *Advances in motivation and achievement* (Vol. 11, pp. 45–85). Greenwich, CT: JAI Press.

Ryan, R. M., & La Guardia, J. G. (2000). What is being optimized? Self-determination theory and basic psychological needs. In S. H. Qualls & N. Abeles (Eds.), *Psychology and the aging revolution* (pp. 145–172). Washington, DC: American Psychological Association.

Ryan, R. M., La Guardia, J. G., Solky-Butzel, J., Chirkov, V., & Kim, Y. (2005). On the interpersonal regulation of emotions: Emotional reliance across gender, relationships, and cultures. *Personal Relationships, 12,* 145–163.

Ryan, R. M., & Lynch, J. H. (1989). Emotional autonomy versus detachment: Revisiting the vicissitudes of adolescence and young adulthood. *Child Development, 60,* 340–356.

Ryan, R. M., Mims, V., & Koestner, R. (1983). Relation of reward contingency and interpersonal context to intrinsic motivation: A review and test using cognitive evaluation theory. *Journal of Personality and Social Psychology, 45,* 736–750.

Ryan, R. M., Plant, R. W., & O'Malley, S. (1993). Initial motivations for alcohol treatment: Relations with patient characteristics, treatment involvement and dropout. *Addictive Behaviors, 20,* 279–297.

Ryan, R. M., Rigby, S., & King, K. (1993). Two types of religious internalization and their relations to religious orientations and mental health. *Journal of Personality and Social Psychology, 65,* 586–596.

Ryan, R. M., Sheldon, K. M., Kasser, T., & Deci, E. L. (1996). All goals are not created equal: An organismic perspective on the nature of goals and their regulation. In P. M. Gollwitzer & J. A. Bargh (Eds.), *The psychology of action: Linking cognition and motivation to behavior* (pp. 7–26). New York: Guilford Press.

Ryan, R. M., Stiller, J. D., & Lynch, J. H. (1994). Representations of relationships to teachers, parents, and friends as predictors of academic motivation and self-esteem. *Journal of Early Adolescence, 14,* 226–249.

Schaefer, E. S. (1959). A circumplex model for maternal behavior. *Journal of Abnormal and Social Psychology, 59,* 226–235.

Schafer, R. (1968). *Aspects of internalization.* New York: International Universities Press.

Seligman, M. E. P. (1991). *Learned optimism.* New York: Knopf.

Shapiro, D. (1965). *Neurotic styles.* New York: Basic Books.

Shapiro, D. (1981). *Autonomy and rigid character.* New York: Basic Books.

Sheldon, K. M., Williams, G. C., & Joiner, T. (2003). *Self-determination theory in the clinic: Motivating physical and mental health.* New Haven, CT: Yale University Press.

Shields, A., Cicchetti, D., & Ryan, R. M. (1994). The development of emotional and behavioral self-regulation and social competence among maltreated school-age children. *Development and Psychopathology, 6,* 57–75.

Simons, J., Vansteenkiste, M., Braet, C., & Deci, E. L. (2005). *Promoting maintained weight loss through healthy lifestyle changes among obese children: An experimental test of self-determination theory.* Unpublished manuscript, University of Leuven, Belgium.

Skinner, B. F. (1953). *Science and human behavior.* New York: Macmillan.

Skinner, E., & Edge, K. (2002). Self-determination, coping, and development. In E. L. Deci & R. M. Ryan (Eds.), *Handbook of self-determination research* (pp. 297–338). Rochester, NY: University of Rochester Press.

Smith, W. E. (1974). *The effects of social and monetary rewards on intrinsic motivation.* Unpublished doctoral dissertation, Cornell University, Ithaca, NY.

Soenens, B., Vansteenkiste, M., Luyten, P., Duriez, B., & Goossens, L. (in press). Maladaptive perfectionistic self-representations: The mediational link between psychological control and adjustment. *Personality and Individual Differences.*

Solomon, D., Battistich, V., Watson, M., Schaps, E., & Lewis, C. (2000). A six-district study of educational change: Direct and mediated effects of the Child Development Project. *Social Psychology of Education, 4*(1), 3–51.

Solomon, D., Watson, M. S., Battistich, V., Schaps, E., & Delucchi, K. (1996). Creating classrooms that students experience as communities. *American Journal of Community Psychology, 24*(6), 719–748.

Sperry, L. (2003). *Handbook of diagnosis and treatment of DSM-IV-TR personality disorders.* New York: Brunner-Routledge.

Spiegelberg, H. (1972). *Phenomenology in psychology and psychiatry: An historical introduction.* Oxford: Northwestern University Press.

Steinberg, L., & Silverberg, S. (1986). The vicissitudes of autonomy in adolescence. *Child Development, 57,* 841–851.

Steinberg, M., & Schnall, M. (2001). *The stranger in the mirror.* New York: Cliff Street Books.

Stern, D. N. (1985). *The interpersonal world of the infant.* New York: Basic Books.

Stevenson, M. B., & Lamb, M. E. (1981). The effects of social experience and social style on cognitive competence and performance. In M. E. Lamb & L. R. Sherrod (Eds.), *Infant social cognition* (pp. 375–394). Hillsdale, NJ: Erlbaum.

Strauss, J., & Ryan, R. M. (1987). Autonomy disturbances in subtypes of anorexia nervosa. *Journal of Abnormal Psychology, 96,* 254–258.

Strauss, J., & Ryan, R. M. (1988). Cognitive dysfunction in anorexia nervosa. *International Journal of Eating Disorders, 7,* 19–27.

Strober, M., & Humphrey, L. L. (1987). Familial contributions to the etiology and course of anorexia nervosa and bulimia. *Journal of Consulting and Clinical Psychology, 55,* 654–659.

Swallow, S. R., & Kuiper, N. A. (1988). Social comparison and negative self-evaluations: An application to depression. *Clinical Psychology Review, 8,* 55–76.

Swann, W. B., & Pittman, T. S. (1977). Initiating play activity of children: The moderating influence of verbal cues on intrinsic motivation. *Child Development, 48,* 1128–1132.

Swedo, S. E., & Rapoport, J. L. (1990). Obsessive compulsive disorder in childhood. In M. Hersen & C. G. Last (Eds.), *Handbook of child and adult psychopathology: A longitudinal perspective: Pergamon general psychology series* (Vol. 161, pp. 211–219). Elmsford, NY: Pergamon Press.

Thomas, A., Chess, S., & Birch, H. G. (1968). *Temperament and behavioral disorders in children.* New York: New York University Press.

Tronick, E. Z., & Gianino, A. F. (1986). The transmission of maternal disturbance to the infant. In E. Z. Tronick & T. Field (Eds.), *Maternal depression and infant disturbance* (pp. 5–12). San Francisco: Jossey-Bass.

Tuber, S. (1992). Empirical and clinical assessments of children's object relations and object representations. *Journal of Personality Assessment, 58,* 179–197.

Turner, R. A., Irwin, C. E., Jr., Tschann, J. M., & Millstein, S. G. (1993). Autonomy, relatedness, and the initiation of health-risk behaviors in early adolescence. *Health Psychology, 12*(3), 200–208.

Urist, J. (1977). The Rorschach test and the assessment of object relations. *Journal of Personality Assessment, 41*(1), 3–9.

Vallerand, R. J., & Bissonnette, R. (1992). Intrinsic, extrinsic, and amotivational styles as predictors of behavior: A prospective study. *Journal of Personality, 60,* 599–620.

Vallerand, R. J., & O'Conner, B. P. (1989). Motivation in the elderly: A theoretical framework and some promising findings. *Canadian Psychology, 30,* 538–550.

Vansteenkiste, M., & Sheldon, K. M. (in press). "There is nothing more practical than a good theory": Integrating motivational interviewing and self-determination theory. *British Journal of Clinical Psychology.*

Vansteenkiste, M., Soenens, B., & Vandereycken, W. (in press). Motivation to change in eating disorder patients: A conceptual clarification on the basis of self-determination theory. *International Journal of Eating Disorders.*

Vaughn, B. E., Kopp, C. B., & Krakow, J. B. (1984). The emergence and consolidation of self-control from eighteen to thirty months of age: Normative trends and individual differences. *Child Development, 55,* 990–1004.

Waller, B. N. (1998). *The natural selection of autonomy.* Albany: State University of New York Press.

Walton, M. E., Delvin, J. T., & Rushworth, M. F. S. (2004). Interactions between decision making and performance monitoring within prefrontal cortex. *Nature Neuroscience, 7,* 1259–1265.

Waters, E., Wippman, J., & Sroufe, L. A. (1979). Attachment, positive affect, and competence in the peer group: Two studies in construct validation. *Child Development, 50,* 821–829.

Watson, J. S. (1966). The development and generalization of contingency awareness in early infancy: Some hypotheses. *Merrill-Palmer Quarterly, 12,* 123–135.

Wegner, D. (2002). *The illusion of conscious will.* Cambridge, MA: MIT Press.

Weiss, L. A., & Grolnick, W. S. (1991, April). *The roles of parental involvement and support for autonomy in adolescent symptomatology.* Paper presented at the biennial meeting of the Society for Research in Child Development, Seattle, WA.

Werner, H. (1948). *Comparative psychology of mental development.* New York: International Universities Press.

Westen, D. (1991). Cognitive-behavioral interventions in the psychoanalytic psychotherapy of borderline personality disorders. *Clinical Psychology Review, 11,* 211–230.

Westen, D., Lodolph, P., Misle, B., Ruffins, S., & Block, J. (1990). Physical and sexual abuse of adolescent girls with borderline personality disorder. *American Journal of Orthopsychiatry, 60,* 55–66.

Whiffin, V. E., & Sassville, T. M. (1991). Dependency, self-criticism, and recollections of parenting: Sex differences and the role of depressive affect. *Journal of Social and Clinical Psychology, 10,* 121–133.

White, R. W. (1959). Motivation reconsidered: The concept of competence. *Psychological Review, 66,* 297–333.

White, R. W. (1963). *Ego and reality in psychoanalytic theory.* New York: International Universities Press.

Wild, J. (1965). Authentic existence: A new approach to "value theory." In J. M. Edie (Ed.), *An invitation to phenomenology: Studies in the philosophy of experience* (pp. 59–78). Chicago: Quadrangle.

Williams, G. C., Cox, E. M., Hedberg, V., & Deci, E. L. (2000). Extrinsic life goals and health risk behaviors in adolescents. *Journal of Applied Social Psychology, 30,* 1756–1771.

Williams, G. C., Deci, E. L., & Ryan, R. M. (1998). Building health-care partnerships by supporting autonomy: Promoting maintained behavior change and positive health outcomes. In P. Hinton-Walker, A. L. Suchman, & R. Botelho (Eds.), *Partnerships, power and process: Transforming health care delivery* (pp. 68–87). Rochester, NY: University of Rochester Press.

Williams, G. C., Grow, V. M., Ryan, R. M., Friedman, Z., & Deci, E. L. (1996). Motivational predictors of weight loss and weight-loss maintenance. *Journal of Personality and Social Psychology, 70,* 115–126.

Williams, R. N. (1992). The human context of agency. *American Psychologist, 47,* 752–760.

Wilson, T. D. (2002). *Strangers to ourselves.* Cambridge, MA: Belknap Press.

Winnicott, D. W. (1958). Birth memories, birth trauma, and anxiety. In *Collected papers: Through pediatrics to psychoanalysis.* London: Hogarth Press. (Original work published 1949)

Winnicott, D. W. (1965). *The maturational process and the facilitating environment.* New York: International Universities Press. (Original work published 1960)

Yalom, I. D. (1980). *Existential psychotherapy.* New York: Basic Books.

Yarrow, L. J., Rubenstein, J. C., & Pedersen, F. A. (1975). *Infant and environment: Early cognitive and motivational development.* Washington, DC: Wiley.

Zanarini, M. C. (Ed.). (1997). *Role of sexual abuse in the etiology of borderline personality disorder.* Washington, DC: American Psychiatric Association.

Zeldman, A., Ryan, R. M., & Fiscella, K. (2004). Client motivation, autonomy support and entity beliefs: Their role in methadone maintenance treatment. *Journal of Social and Clinical Psychology, 23,* 675–696.

Zimmer-Gembeck, M. J., & Collins, W. A. (2003). Autonomy development during adolescence. In G. R. Adams & M. D. Berzonsky (Eds.), *Blackwell handbook of adolescence* (pp. 175–204). Malden, MA: Blackwell.

Zuckerman, M., Porac, J., Lathin, D., Smith, R., & Deci, E. L. (1978). On the importance of self-determination for intrinsically motivated behavior. *Personality and Social Psychology Bulletin, 4,* 443–444.

CHAPTER 21

Person-Oriented Research Strategies in Developmental Psychopathology

LARS R. BERGMAN, ALEXANDER VON EYE, and DAVID MAGNUSSON

In this chapter, person-oriented research strategies in developmental psychopathology are reviewed. By person-oriented, we mean research strategies where the focus is on the individual and not on the variable. The information about each individual is regarded, as far as possible, as an indivisible unit, both conceptually and in the empirical analyses. The term usually implies that individuals are studied on the basis of their pattern of information in relevant variables at the appropriate level. This approach is in contrast to the standard variable-oriented approach, where the variable is the main conceptual and methodological unit. In the person-oriented approach, most commonly the variable alone has no importance. Only in combination with other variables in an information pattern does it achieve meaning. These fundamental conceptual and theoretical issues are discussed in the next section.

In this context, it is important to make a distinction between the person-oriented approach as a *theoretical* perspective or framework, as characterized earlier, and its

consequences as a set of pattern-based methods of analysis, which are usually applied to carry out a person-oriented approach.

It is customary in this type of review to draw heavily on earlier work by the current authors as well as others, and this chapter is no exception. This will be clear from the references. Specifically, in some sections material is borrowed from an article that appeared in *Development and Psychopathology* (Bergman & Magnusson, 1997).

After providing the theoretical background to the person-oriented approach, it is our aim to review major types of person-oriented methods that we believe can be useful in research on developmental psychopathology. To make this review more concrete, we also present empirical examples that illustrate some of the methods. We do not claim to cover every method or approach that can be of use to carry out person-oriented research; the methods presented are our selection and they may reflect our own biases. The empirical examples are drawn from our own work, and the methods we have been involved in developing have in some cases been given more extensive attention than other methods. This should not be regarded as indicating that we consider the methods we have worked with as more worthy of focus than other methods. Finally, we discuss issues in implementing a person-oriented research strategy and perspectives for future research.

THE HOLISTIC-INTERACTIONISTIC RESEARCH PARADIGM AND THE PERSON-ORIENTED APPROACH

During the past decades, the concept "person approach" has become increasingly used in developmental research. It is a powerful concept that is important for meaningful scientific communication of theoretical ideas and for correct interpretation of empirical studies to clarify its contents. In this section, as a frame of reference for the further discussion of research strategies and methodological tools in research in developmental psychopathology, we emphasize the distinction between the person approach as a theoretical, paradigmatic concept of the individual as an integrated human being, that is, the holistic-interactionistic perspective, and the appropriate measurement model and its research strategy consequences (see Magnusson, 2003).

The Holistic-Interactionistic Perspective

As a theoretical concept, the person approach means making the individual—as an integrated psychological, biological, and social organism—the organizing principle for scientific inquiry. In developmental research, including research in developmental psychopathology, this proposition entails a holistic perspective. With reference to a holistic-interactionistic view on individual functioning and development, the role of the person approach has been analyzed by Magnusson (1985, 1999a; Magnusson & Allen, 1983), and its methodological and research strategy implications have been discussed by Bergman (2001), Bergman, Magnusson, and El-Khouri (2003), and Magnusson (1998a). Their applications in research on developmental psychopathology have been underlined in Bergman and Magnusson (1997) and Stattin and Magnusson (1996).

From a theoretical perspective, the person approach rests on two fundamental characteristics of developmental processes: (1) They are indivisible, that is, holistic in nature; and (2) a key principle in the functioning and development of the integrated individual is *functional interaction*.

The Holistic View

At a general level, a holistic view has ancient roots. From the beginning of the twentieth century, from H. William Stern (1917) onward, the holistic perspective was emphasized by researchers, particularly in developmental and personality research (see, e.g., Magnusson, 1999b, pp. 223–224). For a long time, however, the holistic view had little, if any, impact on empirical psychological research in general, including developmental research. The reasons for this state of affairs were numerous. Clark Hull (1943) argued that the lack of relevant knowledge of internal psychological and biological processes had the effect that psychological research had to be restricted to "molar behavior." For decades, this view was reflected in classical interactionism, concerned with person-by-situation (environment) interaction, expressed in the well-known Lewin (1936) formula $B = f(P, E)$. In empirical applications, classical interactionism did not include internal working components in the analyses of individual functioning and development.

An increasing number of voices, however, proposed models that help to overcome the limitations of the empty holistic model (see, e.g., Baltes, Lindenberger, & Staudinger, 1997; Cairns, 1979; Cairns & Valsiner, 1984; Emde, 1994; Magnusson, 1985; Wapner & Demick, 1998). Four sources have contributed to overcome this restriction for empirical research and to form the theoretical basis for a modern holistic-interactionistic approach to research on individual functioning and ontogeny (Magnusson, 1998b, pp. 497–498):

1. Research on mental components of individual functioning (information processing, learning, memory, emotions, and values). Research in these areas has gained much from cross-disciplinary approaches in neuroscience.

2. Cross-disciplinary psychobiological research on the interaction of mental, biological, and behavioral components of integrated processes. Progress in research on this issue has been important for understanding developmental processes in general. For psychopathology in particular, the psychobiological research has played an essential role in the understanding of the developmental background of antisocial behaviors.

3. The formulation of models for dynamic, complex processes, including general systems theory and chaos theory. Particular interest is the emphasis in these models of the holistic character of such processes. Among other things, this implies that dynamic, complex processes cannot be understood and explained by the

combination of results from studies of isolated components of the process, independent of other simultaneously working components. This proposition has decisive implications for the methodologies and research strategies that are appropriate in a person approach. However, the correct application of these models is not easy. It presupposes awareness of the fact that human functioning and ontogeny are guided by insight, intentions, emotions, and values. This makes the application of dynamic models that take this into account a very demanding task.

4. Well-planned longitudinal studies that have contributed basic knowledge about individual development. These have strongly demonstrated that it is the integrated human being that keeps its identity and develops over the life span, not single variables.

These contributions have allowed the formulation of a modern holistic-interactionistic theoretical perspective as a frame of reference for the design, implementation, and interpretation of studies of specific aspects of developmental processes (see, e.g., Magnusson, 1990; Magnusson & Stattin, 1998; Magnusson & Törestad, 1993). An individual functions as a totality at each stage of development. Each component of the structures and processes that are operating at a certain level takes on meaning from the role it plays in the subsystems, in order to maintain the organism's integrity in current functioning and in developmental change, within the limits set by its potentials and restrictions. This implies, among other things, that the individual *as a whole* must be considered as the framework for planning, implementing, and interpreting empirical research on specific aspects of individual functioning in a current and a developmental perspective. The application of such a general perspective is a necessary condition for the synthesis of knowledge about why individuals think, feel, act, and react as integrated human beings, both in a current and a developmental perspective.

A basic concept in discussions of individual development is that of *change* of involved structures, which can concern both progressive and regressive change in a life span perspective. From a holistic perspective, individual developmental change is analyzed and discussed in terms of integrated, dynamic, and complex processes. The holistic nature of these is a characteristic of human processes at all levels, from the cellular level to the individual's interaction with his or her environment. Within subsystems, for example, the immune system, the coronary system, psychobiological subsystems, and cognitive subsystems, the operating components work in an integrated way to satisfy

the whole organism's need for stability and integrity in the process of developmental change. In the integrative process, each level has properties that are not the summary of processes at a lower level; new properties emerge from level to level. Accordingly, the integrated individual has properties beyond what belongs to the parts. The consequence is that empirical analysis must always be performed with data from a certain level of individual functioning. Mixing data from different levels inevitably leads to erroneous results.

Functional Interaction

It was emphasized earlier that the integrated nature of developmental processes means that they cannot be understood and explained as the summary of mental, biological, behavioral, and social elements; together they are simultaneously involved in holistic, synchronized processes at all levels of the whole organism. A fundamental principle in these processes is then the *functional interaction* among involved components. Functional interaction is a central concept in biological models for living organisms (Mayr, 1997). Individual developmental change processes get their characteristic features and properties from the functional interaction among the operating elements involved, not by the effect of each part separately on the totality.

There has been a tendency among psychologists to dismiss the role of interaction in psychobiological processes as too vague. In contrast, in theoretical and empirical biological research, functional interaction is a basic concept, and this principle is equally applicable to psychological research on the functioning and development of the human being. Acceptance and application of this proposition is, in our minds, a requirement for further progress in line with what happens in other life sciences.

Developmental Crystallization

The holistic-interactionistic perspective implies, among other things, that a process of *developmental crystallization* occurs (Magnusson & Mahoney, 2002, p. 234). According to this proposition, the developmental processes of individuals whose system organization differs at a certain point in time (as a result of different constitutional factors, maturation, and experiences) will take partly different directions in the next step. In that process, each step confines future developmental alternatives, and eventually more stable "types" than those at the beginning will emerge. This should show up in a clearer homogenization in categories of individuals and a more clear differentiation among categories of individuals across time. The issue of interindividually different life paths was discussed by Moffitt (1993) on theoretical grounds and by Magnusson (1996) with reference to results of empirical, longitudinal studies on antisocial behaviors.

The crystallization hypothesis was supported in an empirical study on what was designated "problem gravitation" by Bergman and Magnusson (1997). This study is briefly reviewed in a later section in this chapter. In a similar way, Loeber, Keenan, and Zhang (1997) found different trajectories for a sample of boys with problem behaviors (see also, e.g., Robins, John, Caspi, Moffit, & Stouthamer-Loeber, 1996).

Comment

The holistic-interactionistic perspective has fundamental methodological and research strategy consequences for empirical research on human ontogeny; they are discussed later in this chapter. However, it is interesting to note how little these have been observed and taken into account in developmental research. This state of the art is an illustration to Rom Harré's (2000, p. 1303) essay in *Science,* in which he made the following observation:

> It is a remarkable feature of mainstream academic psychology that, alone among the sciences, it should be almost wholly immune to critical appraisal as an enterprise. Methods that have long shown to be ineffective or worse are still used on a routine basis by hundreds, perhaps thousands of people. Conceptual muddles long exposed to view are evident in almost every issue of standard psychological journals. This is a curious state of affairs. New pathways and more realistic paradigms of research have been proposed, demonstrated, and ignored.

The frequent mismatch in psychology between the scientific problem and the method chosen to analyze it has also been pointed out by Richters (1997).

To accept and apply the holistic, interactionistic perspective in empirical research on human ontogeny follows the development in other life sciences, particularly biology. As early as 1945, the biologist Novikoff, in an article in *Science,* analyzed the main elements of a holistic perspective for research on living organisms. The role of a holistic or, as the biologists prefer to call it, an organismic model for research on living organisms has been eloquently discussed by Mayr (1997) with reference to its history and its present application. In a lecture at the Swedish Academy of Sciences in April 2003, Thomas Rooswall, the director of the International Council of Scientific Unions, summarized what he regarded as the two main common demands for progress in empirical sciences: holistic and cross-disciplinary approaches.

If psychology aims to be a constructive member of the scientific society, then it is high time we adopt the basic frame of reference for true scientific work in other life sciences and take the methodological and research strategy consequences of this frame of reference seriously.

The Person-Oriented Approach, Its Assumptions, and Conditions for Its Viability

The close alliance of the person-oriented approach to the holistic-interactionistic paradigm should now be obvious. To increase our understanding of the approach, it is informative to take a closer look at the assumptions behind the person-oriented approach and conditions for its viability. Individual development can be conceptualized as a process, characterized at a given time point by its state in multidimensional space, and with state change taking place in continuous time. (By "state," we mean the specific configuration of values of the process model in the variables characterizing the system under study at a given point in time.) Bergman and Magnusson (1997) made the following five assumptions about the basic properties of this process:

1. The process is partly specific to an individual.
2. The process is complex and contains many interacting factors at different levels. They may have complicated relations to each other.
3. There is coherence and structure (a) in individual growth and (b) in different individuals' process characteristics. The lawfulness of the processes in functionally organized structures is found in the development and functioning of the systems at different levels. Assumptions (a) and (b) are similar to those made by Magnusson (1988) when he characterized an interactionistic approach in psychological research.
4. Structures are organized and function as *patterns* of operating factors, where each factor derives its meaning from its relations to the others.
5. At a system level, a limited number of more frequently observed patterns ("common types") will often be found. This assumption is made intraindividually (across development for the same person) and interindividually (across individuals at the same time or over time).

According to Bergman and Magnusson (1997), the assumption of emerging types receives support mainly from two sources:

1. Analogies to system theoretic thinking. Normally only a small number of system constructions and states are in some sense optimal and lead to a stable functioning of

the system. Psychobiological systems have the capability of self-organization. This is a characteristic of open systems and means that new structures and patterns can "spontaneously" emerge, even from chaos (Barton, 1994; Thelen, 1989). Self-organization is a guiding principle in ontogeny, where the operating factors organize themselves to maximize the functioning of each subsystem in relation to the whole system. Such an arrangement has survival value and therefore it persists. Many human biological systems have such characteristics, for instance, the brain and the coronary system. These principles can also be applied to the development of the sensory and cognitive systems (Carlson, Earls, & Todd, 1988; Cicchetti & Tucker, 1994).

2. Support for the assumption of emerging types is also suggested by many examples of biological systems for which distinct types are found (e.g., of species, ecotypes; see Colinvaux, 1980). When studying developmental personality types, Block (1971, p. 110), talked about "'system designs' with more enduring properties" and Gangestad and Snyder (1985), when discussing the motivation for a typological approach, talked about distinct types, with each sharing a common source of influence. Summarizing their own position, Bergman and Magnusson (1997, p. 294) stated, "Viewing individuals in terms of complex dynamic systems we would expect certain states to be more frequent than others, corresponding to optimal patterns and it seems natural to explain and investigate such systems using a pattern-oriented approach."

So what are the conditions when a person-oriented approach is viable? Obviously, it is in situations when it is believed that interactions and nonlinearities operate during development and emerging types can be expected, with each type being characterized in terms of data by a characteristic pattern of values in the relevant variables measuring the system under study. In such situations, a person-oriented approach is natural. Many types of methodological realizations of this approach thrive on interactions and are built for handling them.

Limitations of a Standard Variable-Oriented Perspective

Another way of achieving an increased understanding of the circumstances when a person-oriented approach is useful is to examine the limitations of a standard variable-oriented approach from the perspective provided by the holistic-interactionistic theoretical framework. Without denying that a

variable-oriented approach, focusing on relations between variables, can be useful in studying complex systems in a developmental perspective, it is clear that this approach neglects the crucial importance of the fact that the parts together form a totality. Almost always, the variable-oriented approach is also based on the study of linear relationships, studied across individuals, relationships that in the linear models most often are assumed to be equal for every subject in the sample. It should be clear that such an approach is not well aligned to the assumptions of the holistic-interactionistic paradigm. This state of affairs is illustrated by the fact that in many variable-oriented analyses using, for instance, structural equation modeling (SEM), the correlation matrix or the variance-covariance matrix often becomes the raw data to be analyzed and explained. In this way, all patterns in the data that are not captured by this matrix are disregarded. This is a simplification that disregards higher-order interactions, which can produce misleading results (see, e.g., Bergman, 1988a, for illustrations).

Relations to the Typological Perspective

As discussed by Bergman (2000), few concepts have caused so much debate and even resentment in psychology as *type* and *typology*. When reviewing the concept of type, Cattell (1957) indicated no fewer than 45 different meanings of this concept. It is also used in different ways in other sciences, such as biology and anthropology. For an overview of the typological field from a methodological perspective, the reader should refer to Blashfield (1980).

The meaning of a type is that the subjects that belong to it have in common a number of characteristics. It is this combination or pattern of characteristics that is the essence of the type. The properties of a type are often indicated by a profile of values in the studied variables defining the type. For instance, the cluster centroids (the profiles of the cluster means for the variables) for a set of natural clusters would be one way of presenting the types.

With a typological perspective, we mean an approach in which the focus is on a set of class descriptions or types. All typologies have in common that they contain or refer to a number of classes. For instance, the classes could be the result of an empirical classification analysis where cluster analysis was used to produce the clusters. Or they could be ideal types, theoretically derived, with each type being defined by a distinctive description (Bailey, 1994). If these classes fulfill certain criteria for generalizability and so on, then each class can be called a type and the whole collection of classes, for instance the whole cluster solution, can be called a typology. It should be noted that it is not the clusters and their members per se in the studied sample that constitute the typology, but rather the generic properties of these clusters. A type is sometimes referred to as a *natural cluster*. A number of thoughtful distinctions with regard to type and typology are given by Meehl (1992). He preferred the use of the terms *taxon* for, roughly speaking, a meaningful type and *taxometrics* as a generic name for (his) procedures for searching for taxa. The Meehl approach is discussed in a later section.

When discussing an empirical classification in relation to a typology it is helpful to distinguish between two perspectives of an empirical classification: (1) the description of the properties of the classes in terms of their characteristics (e.g., the cluster centroids are given) and (2) the allocation of subjects to the different classes or clusters. The first aspect is most directly related to the issue of typology and type. An empirical classification analysis is often better at identifying "true" class descriptions in the presence of sampling error and errors of measurement than the analysis is at allocating subjects to the "right" class.

It should be emphasized that a typology, as the term is used here, does not represent anything unchangeable or innate in difference to the classical typologies. This label is often given a typology by its critics but it does not apply to the modern typological approach and the related person-oriented approach. Of course, some degree of stability and generality is implied in a developmental typology, but changing typologies during development and changing types to which an individual may belong during his or her development are of primary interest here. Thus, in a developmental context, we want to study longitudinal typologies and developmental individual differences in membership in different types of these typologies. According to Bergman (2000), a longitudinal typology might be (1) a typology of developmental types arrived at theoretically, (2) an empirically based typology arrived at by analyzing longitudinal data, or (3) a number of cross-sectional typologies from different ages for which the developmental connections are indicated.

In later sections, methods are presented that fall under the heading of (2) or (3). Further discussions of typological issues as well as empirical examples are given by, for instance, Asendorpf (2000) and Robins, John, and Caspi (1998).

MEASUREMENT

In this section, we compare the measurement models for the variable- and the person-oriented approaches to studying development.

Two Measurement Models

Progress in scientific empirical work presupposes, among other things, the application of appropriate methodological tools. That is, the statistics must match the character of the phenomena being investigated. In later sections of this chapter, methods are presented that are suitable for use within a holistic, interactionistic theoretical framework.

It is probably fair to say that in developmental psychopathology, inappropriate measurement models are frequently used: measurement models that do not take into account the holistic-interactionistic nature of the phenomena under study (see, e.g., Granic & Hollenstein, 2003; Richters, 1997). This can be regarded as one aspect of what Harré (2000) meant by the persistence of bad practices in psychology in spite of clear evidence that the approach should be changed. One reason for this situation is the common neglect of the role of measurement models in the research strategy process (Magnusson, 2003). Real progress in developmental research rests on the application of statistical tools using a measurement model that satisfies the assumptions made about the character of the phenomena being investigated.

Developmental crystallization (discussed earlier) has decisive implications for the choice and application of measurement models in developmental research. Here two main measurement models are briefly presented, each with its specific demands and assumptions. The distinction between the two models represents the basic difference between the variable-oriented approach and the person-oriented approach in psychological research, including developmental research. The basic difference between the two measurement models is in the way the psychological significance of a single datum—representing a response to a stimulus, a response to a test or questionnaire item, a rating, and so on— is derived (Magnusson, 1998a, 2003). The two models are shown in Figure 21.1.

According to measurement model 1 (MM1) in Figure 21.1, a single datum for individual A on a latent dimension k derives its psychological significance from its position on that dimension in relation to positions for other individuals, B, C, D, and so on (see Figure 21.1a). MM1 is the measurement model for the variable-oriented approach to psychological research. Empirical developmental research is dominated by the application of MM1. The focus of interest is on a single variable, or a combination of variables, their interrelations (R-R and S-R relations), and their relation to a specific criterion. The problems are formulated in terms of variables, and the results are

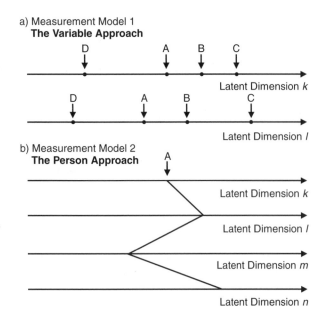

Figure 21.1 Measurement models. *Source:* "The Person Approach: Concepts, Measurement Models, and Research Strategy," by D. Magnusson, 2003, *New Directions for Child and Adolescent Development, 101,* pp. 3–23.

interpreted and generalizations made in such terms. Statistical models include comparisons between means and other location parameters, correlation and regression analyses, factor analysis, structural equation modeling, and contingency tables. A broad range of statistical tools is available and applied in these analyses. The assumption that should be met in the application of MM1 in research on developmental issues has previously been summarized by Magnusson (1998a).

According to measurement model 2 (MM2) in Figure 21.1, a single datum for individual A on a latent dimension k derives its psychological significance from its position in a configuration of data for the same individual, representing his or her positions on the latent dimensions *k, l, m, n,* and so on. These latent dimensions are assumed to represent *simultaneously* working components in the system under investigation (see Figure 21.1b). The application of MM2 is the logical consequence of the analysis of many characteristics of individual developmental processes from a holistic-interactionistic perspective. That is, it fits the character of the individual holistic-interactionistic developmental processes. This is the measurement model that is the basis for most empirical realizations of the person-oriented approach. An implication of MM2 is that statistics applying to this measurement model yield information about the individual, and generalizations refer to individuals.

MM2 is applied for two main purposes (Magnusson, 2003, p. 16):

1. To identify groups of individuals who function in a similar way at the organism level under investigation. In terms of data, individuals are categorized on the basis of profile similarity. A number of statistical tools are available for pattern analysis both cross-sectionally and longitudinally. They are discussed in later sections of this chapter.

2. To analyze short-term and long-term developmental processes in terms of patterns evolving in continuous time. Here, models for dynamic, complex processes, derived from the natural sciences, can contribute to the development and application of methods and models with consideration for the specific character of individual processes.

It should be emphasized that both models are relevant and important in developmental research: They are complementary, not contradictory. Each of the models meets specific assumptions about individual functioning and development, and the results of studies applying one or the other of these models will yield answers to different questions (Bergman et al., 2003; Magnusson, 1998a, 2003). Each of them also has implications for the kind of data to be used and the kind of statistical tools that are relevant in a certain study.

Measurement Tailored to a Person-Oriented Approach

Most commonly, the different variables used in a study are not on "naturally" comparable scales. They are often transformed to comparable scales by some kind of standardization of the variables or methods are used, the results of which do not depend on the means and standard deviations of the variables used in the analyses (e.g., Pearson correlations are computed). The results are then invariant to linear transformations of the involved variables. This is frequently the case in variable-oriented settings. Also, in a person-oriented research context, it is often the case that naturally comparable scales are lacking. Normally, then, the variables are standardized before the analysis to ensure that they obtain comparable weights. The reason for this is that the results of many pattern-based analyses are *not* invariant under linear transformations of the involved variables (Bergman et al., 2003).

However, there are situations when we want to undertake a multivariate scaling of all the variables that constitute the pattern so that the values compared between variables and times of measurement contain more information than is given by standardized scores, computed separately for each variable and measurement occasion. To give an example, if we are concerned with studying adjustment problems indicating possible psychopathology and if standardized variables are used, then one has to assume that it is of no importance for the study that different adjustment problems have a varying prevalence in the sample and/or that the same adjustment problem is more common at one age than at another age (because these differences are washed out by the standardization). The limitations of this approach are discussed in Bergman and Magnusson (1997).

Bergman and Magnusson (1991) discussed the issue of multivariate scaling with regard to the measurement and classification of profiles of adjustment problems. They indicated a *quasi-absolute scaling procedure* that is applied to all variables at all measurement occasions. Without claiming that the scaling produced absolute prevalences of the involved adjustment problems (hence "quasi"), the goal was to obtain profiles of adjustment problems that retained information about prevalences and variability of specific problems, as measured by a comparable tally for all variables. Raw information about each adjustment problem (often from more than one data source) was transformed into a 4-step scale characterized by the following approximate meaning of each scale value: 0 = No problem, 1 = Tendency to problem, 2 = Presence of problem, and 3 = Pronounced problem. The quasi-absolute scaling started by applying a subjective procedure in which independent raters were asked to give each type of raw information its weight. Then a mechanical, objective set of rules, based on these weights, was applied for computing the quasi-absolute scores.

When a person-oriented approach is applied, one often must compute some coefficient of profile (dis)similarity, as a basis for the analysis, to compare the (dis)similarity of the value profiles. This is done for each pair of individuals (e.g., to perform a cluster analysis). For a discussion of methods for measuring (dis)similarities between profiles, the reader can refer to Cronbach and Gleser (1953) and Budescu (1980). Two commonly used coefficients of profile (dis)similarity are the average squared Euclidean distance, which takes both profile form and level into account, and the correlation coefficient (with the pair of persons as the two variables and the variables as the cases), which takes only profile form into account. In line with what was said earlier, it is important to point out that neither of these two coefficients is invariant to linear transformations of

the variables in the profile. Such transformations can change the ordering of the size of the (dis)similarity coefficients and, hence, change the results of, for instance, a cluster analysis.

In a person-oriented analysis, the variables included in a pattern are simultaneously analyzed. Often, a proportion of the sample has missing data in one or several variables. However, the standard classification analysis demands complete data in all variables, and subjects with a missing value in one or more variables have to be deleted from the analysis. If a large number of subjects have one or a few missing values, then the deletion of these subjects might not be desirable. Demanding complete data then implies losing many subjects with almost complete data and possibly creating a dropout bias. The solution might be to "guess" missing values for subjects with almost complete data, that is, to perform imputation. To accomplish such a solution, a number of methods are available, which usually are based on linear models (for an overview, see Pierzchala, 1990). However, from a person-oriented perspective, it might be useful to use a twin approach for imputation (so-called hot deck imputation). The imputation procedure is then consistent with the pattern-oriented perspective. In this method, a missing value for a subject is replaced by the corresponding value for the subject with complete data that is most similar to the subject with the missing datum (El-Khouri & Bergman, 1992). It should be pointed out that imputation, of course, produces a temporary file for a certain analysis. The *data* are what they were from the beginning.

MAJOR TYPES OF PERSON-ORIENTED METHODS

In this section, major types of person-oriented methods are introduced.

Methods for Studying the Single Individual

At the heart of understanding individual development lies the intensive study of the single individual. In the field of psychopathology this is, of course, well-known, and this approach is often applied in a qualitative sense, doing, for instance, case studies. However, there are also quantitative methods developed for that purpose that can be useful. John Nesselroade and his coworkers have carried out many developments in this area. For instance, Jones and Nesselroade (1990) advocate a multivariate, replicated, single-subject, repeated measures design that can use P-technique factor analysis to carry out the analyses. This type of factor analysis has been developed by, for instance, Molenaar (1985). An example of a study of the short-term development of the single individual in the field of psychopathology is presented in Nesselroade and Featherman's (1991) study of intraindividual variability in older adults' depression scores. The subjects were studied on 23 successive occasions, usually 1 week apart. The purpose was to gain information about the stability and magnitude of short-term intraindividual variability. They found evidence for coherent short-term changes, and their results point both to the importance of studying the single individual—and in doing so discriminating between state change and trait level—and to the importance of studying stable interindividual differences in intraindividual variability.

Another set of analytical techniques that can be useful for studying the short-term development of the single individual is time-series analysis, especially if "seasonal" components are believed to be involved in the developmental process. This approach is exemplified by the work of Schmitz (Schmitz & Skinner, 1993). Of course, in this approach, as in the one discussed earlier, one has the problem of how to generalize from a single subject to a population of subjects (see Molenaar, Huizenga, & Nesselroade, 2003, for a discussion of this critical issue). On the other hand, as pointed out by Molenaar and colleagues, this problem does not go away when one carries out a standard interindividual approach of the type discussed later; it just takes another form and can be more severe because the results of such an approach can be claimed to apply to single individuals only under special assumptions. To give just one example: Biological maturation occurs at a different pace for different individuals, and if this is not taken into account in a study, it can contaminate the relationships between the variables that are studied if they are related to biological maturation (Magnusson, 1985).

It is probably no exaggeration to say that most researchers in the field of developmental psychopathology in principle subscribe to a metatheoretical holistic-interactionistic view of the type discussed. Against this background, the quantitative study of the single individual using a dynamic systems approach is potentially attractive, as many evolving phenomena have been shown to be well described by a nonlinear dynamic systems (NOLIDS) approach. In NOLIDS, a mathematical model with differential or difference equations is set up that explains the changes that occur in the observed states of the system under study. Not only can the model handle interactions and nonlinearities, but it also may account for attractor states such as the resistance of a psychopathological condition to change despite efforts to change it and despite its nonoptimality. A spectacular property of certain NOLIDS models is their capacity to model even very complex behavior such as chaos, with its extreme sensitivity to initial conditions. This raises the hope of being able to explain a seemingly complex phenomenon with a powerful, simple NOLIDS model. For general overviews of NOLIDS, the reader can refer to Gleick (1987) and Jackson (1989), and for discussions of the usefulness of NOLIDS in psychology, the reader can refer to Abraham and Gilgen (1995), Barton (1994), and Smith and Thelen (1993).

However, there are many complications with the NOLIDS approach that are not yet fully solved with regard to the delineation of the system to study and in the estimation of the parameters. Bergman (2001) concluded that useful NOLIDS models in psychology are rare and that often the application of the approach stops at the metaphoric-conceptual level. Exceptions can be found in some more molecular areas that lend themselves to precise inquiry and controlled experiments. A good example is given by Kelso (1995) and his colleagues' work on the dynamics of motor coordination. Extending the study of NOLIDS models beyond the study of the single individual and to take an example of an application of NOLIDS that is closer to developmental psychopathology, Boker and Graham (1998) carried out an interesting NOLIDS study of adolescent substance use. Boker and Nesselroade (2002) also presented a method for fitting differential equations to panel data that appears to be able to recover the parameters of the model based on only three waves of data for a sample of 100 subjects. This is important because standard methods demand many more measurement occasions for that purpose.

Classification-Based Methods

As discussed by Bergman and Magnusson (1997), a typological approach has roots far back in time in psychopathology and abnormal psychology. Such typologies are but a few examples of a basic tendency in human beings to create order in the phenomena around them (for a historic overview, see Misiak & Sexton, 1966; for a review of cluster analysis in psychiatry, see Skinner & Blashfield, 1982). Classification has always had a stronger standing in psychiatry than in psychology, probably because diagnostic classification is basic in medicine. During the previous century, the classification of individuals as a research method became less prominent in psychology. The expansion of sophisticated methods for variable-oriented analysis and hypothesis testing has contributed to this change.

However, as previously pointed out, the person-oriented approach has led to an interest in methods for data treatment focusing on individual value patterns or structures rather than focusing on variables. Classification analysis can be used for this purpose, but a number of methodological alternatives exist for studying interindividual differences in pattern development.

A crude distinction can be made between model-based and mainly descriptive methods (i.e., methods that describe the data without the use of a coherent model). Log-linear analysis (Bishop, Fienberg, & Holland, 1975) is an example of a model-based method without latent variables. In this method, a statistical model is created for explaining the cell frequencies (or rather, the logarithms of the cell frequencies) in a higher-order contingency table. So, in the sense that the multivariate outcome pattern is the dependent variable rather than variables considered singly, it is a person-oriented method. This type of approach has also been tailored to the study of change (Clogg, Eliason, & Grego, 1990). One class of model-based methods with latent variables is based on latent class analysis, for instance, latent transition analysis. This method is presented after the descriptive methods have been overviewed. We start by discussing cluster analysis-based methods for studying the development of psychopathology. Before this, however, it is helpful to give a short overview of some principles of cluster analysis.

Cluster Analysis

The basic idea in cluster analysis is that subjects are sorted into mutually exclusive clusters (classes) according to their similarity. Hence, subjects that are alike are assigned to the same cluster. There are also methods that allow overlap between clusters. Although such methods have attractive properties, they are not further discussed here as they seem often to lead to interpretational problems (Wiener-Ehrlich, 1981).

A wide variety of methods for cluster analysis exist. Most of them use the (dis)similarity matrix between all pairs of subjects' value profiles as the basic data for analysis. The elements in this matrix are usually calculated by applying some formula for computing a (dis)similarity coefficient, based on quantitative information in a number of variables, constituting the value profile. Other methods for obtaining (dis)similarities are, of course, possible (e.g., raters could be used to directly obtain the [dis]similarities).

Two major types of cluster analysis are hierarchical methods (agglomerative or divisive) and partitioning methods. In each type, many methods and algorithms exist, and there is no method that is generally considered superior to the other ones. The sensitivity of different clustering algorithms to error perturbation and the method's ability to recover a known structure depend on a number of conditions. Ward's (1963) hierarchical minimum variance method, average linkage (sometimes called group average; UPGMA) and k-means relocation, based on a sound start classification, have often been reported to be useful methods (Milligan, 1980, 1981; Morey, Blashfield, & Skinner, 1983). Promising methods based on so-called beta-flexible clustering have also been suggested (Belbin, Faith, & Milligan, 1992).

It is well-known that outliers can distort the results of many statistical analyses (e.g., of a correlational analysis). Similarly, multivariate outliers can distort the results of a cluster analysis. Based on this reason, it has been suggested for some situations that not everybody should be classified and that outliers should be removed before the classification analysis is carried out (Edelbrock, 1979; Milligan, 1980). Bergman (1988b) also emphasized that a small number of truly "unique" individuals may exist and that they should not be forced into a classification. They should instead be brought to a set of nonclassified subjects, called a "residue." In the LICUR method for classification analysis, presented later, a procedure for accomplishing this is indicated. Of course, residue subjects can be highly interesting, but they should be analyzed separately, perhaps using qualitative methods.

Longitudinal Cluster Analysis

A direct way to study individual development in terms of patterns is by exposing the subjects' complete observed longitudinal patterns to a cluster analysis. In this way, the clusters are formed in one analytical step and, it is hoped, a full account is taken of each subject's developmental pattern in forming the clusters. A related approach is to use an ordination strategy to first reduce the number of dimensions (e.g., using principal components analysis) and then perform a cluster analysis of the factor scores (e.g., Mumford & Owens, 1984). Although potentially attractive, this genuinely longitudinal approach can be problematic; for instance, it often results in heterogeneous clusters that are less useful. When only profile form is a focus, a direct longitudinal classification approach may be more useful, because less information has to then be summarized by the cluster membership variable than when both profile form and level are to be accounted for by the method. Therefore, taking into account only profile form increases the chances of obtaining homogeneous clusters in that sense. Block (1971) presented a good example of the potential of a longitudinal classification strategy in his study of longitudinal personality types.

Cross-Sectional Pattern Analysis Followed by Linking over Time

A natural way of studying development using a classificatory approach is to first perform a cross-sectional cluster analysis at each point in time separately and then link the results; this is most frequently accomplished by cross-tabulating results between adjacent time points. For this purpose, different methods can be used; the choice of method should, of course, be tailored to the specific case.

There is also value in a standard method that is reasonably robust, can be applied in a variety of situations, and can serve as a reference method. For this purpose, Bergman (1998) developed a cluster analysis-based procedure, LICUR (Linking of Clusters after removal of Residue), for cross-sectional classification, after removal of a residue, followed by the linking of results between measurement occasions. It is suitable for interval-scaled data in situations when both the form and level of the profile are of relevance, and when an important goal is to obtain homogeneous clusters. The key aspects of LICUR are as follows:

- First, at each measurement occasion separately, a residue of subjects (outliers) is identified according to criteria defined beforehand. They should not be classified together with the others and are removed as a residue for separate analysis (often 1% to 3% of the sample are categorized in this way). The size of the residue can be a valuable indicator of the "classificability" of the sample, with a large residue perhaps indicating that there is no clear classification structure to be found.

- Then, on each measurement occasion separately, a cluster analysis is performed using Ward's hierarchical cluster analysis method as the standard option, and the cluster solution with the optimal number of clusters is chosen. Four different criteria are used to guide this decision.

- If the hierarchical property of the cluster solution is vital, each cross-sectional analysis stops here. When there is a very strong focus on obtaining as homogeneous clusters as possible, the Ward cluster solution is used as a start solution in a k-means relocation cluster analysis. In this procedure, the objects are relocated to maximize the explained error sum of squares and, hence, cluster homogeneity.

- In the last step, the results of the cluster analyses carried out at each age separately are linked by cross-tabulating adjacent classifications and tested for significant types and antitypes of cluster membership combinations, using exact cell-wise tests (Bergman & El-Khouri, 1987). In this way, we can identify developmental trajectories, defined at each measurement occasion as a typical pattern, that occur more frequently or less frequently than expected by chance.

By comparing the cluster solutions at the different ages, we can study *structural stability and change*. By studying the cross-tabulations across age, we can study *individual stability* (which is shown if it is a significant type to belong to approximately the same cluster at both ages) and *individual change* (which is shown if it is a significant type to move from one cluster to another).

In our opinion, LICUR is a robust and basic method that is applicable in a large number of settings. For instance, it can also be used when different variables are measured at the different measurement occasions and during periods of dramatic developmental shifts. For a more full description of LICUR, the reader is referred to Bergman (1998) or Bergman et al. (2003).

An Empirical Example of a Person-Oriented Classification Approach

In the following, an empirical example is given of a person-oriented approach for studying the development of boys' externalizing problems. It builds mainly on findings reported in Bergman and Magnusson (1991, 1997), and the example illustrates mainly the use of the LICUR procedure. For a description of the background to these studies and for technical details, the reader can refer to these sources.

The data were taken from the longitudinal research program Individual Development and Adaptation (IDA; Magnusson, 1988). Depending on the analysis, the sample size varied between $n = 517$ and $n = 540$. At age 10 and age 13, the same six variables were measured: Aggression, Motor Restlessness, Lack of Concentration, Low School Motivation, Poor Peer Relations, and Low School Achievement. All variables were scaled on a quasi-absolute scale, with 0 = absence of a problem, 1 = tendency to a problem, 2 = presence of a problem, and 3 = pronounced problem. Each boy's profile of values in these six variables constituted the basic unit of analysis. For instance, the profile "000000" at age 10 would indicate a boy with no problems at that age, and the profile "022202" would indicate a boy with a low school motivation syndrome. At adult age, information from official records was used. The presence or absence in official records for psychiatric care was noted. In addition, the presence more than once, the presence once, or the absence in official records for criminality and alcohol abuse was noted.

First, a cross-sectional analysis was carried out at age 10. The first step in this analysis was to identify a preliminary residue of nine boys with unique value profiles. They were removed before further analyses were undertaken. The second step was to use Ward's hierarchical method to obtain a nine-clusters solution according to the LICUR criteria. This solution was used as a start classification in a relocation analysis that was undertaken to further improve cluster homogeneity (the final explained error sum of squares was 72%). Three subjects that did not fit any cluster were removed in this step, increasing the size of the residue to 12 subjects. At age 13, the same analytic procedure was used, resulting in an eight-clusters solution with an explained error sum of squares of 71% and with eight subjects being identified as residue subjects. In Figure 21.2, we give the means in the variables in the profile for each cluster at age 10, with the cluster means for the best matching cluster at age 13 drawn in the same picture. Please note that the matching is a forced, pairwise matching; therefore, it is possible that a cluster at age 10 must be paired with the next best matching cluster at age 13, if the best matching cluster is better matched to another age 10 cluster and, hence, already "occupied."

From Figure 21.2, we can see that six of the age 10 clusters showed structural stability and an additional two clusters showed partial stability. Cluster 2 at age 10 had no matching cluster at age 13 but is rather similar to Cluster 4 at that age. The picture is one of considerable structural stability across these two ages. To summarize, the following stable typical patterns were found: a pattern showing a complete lack of any adjustment problems, one characterized by only a tendency to Motor Restlessness and no other problems, one characterized by Poor Peer Relations and no other problems, one characterized by Low School Achievement and no other problems, a low school motivation syndrome, and a syndrome characterized by severe generalized conduct problems. The conclusion is that most typical patterns of externalizing problems that appeared at age 10 also emerged at age 13.

The next question is, of course, whether the structurally stable typical patterns also exhibited individual stability. Do boys tend to stay in the same type of cluster at both ages? Are there also significant movements from one cluster to another across ages? Following the LICUR paradigm, a cross-tabulation of cluster membership between age 10 and age 13 was carried out and translated into a summarizing LICUR figure. Bergman and Magnusson (1991) report this LICUR figure. The essence of those results is that all the structurally stable typical patterns listed earlier also showed significant individual stability.

For the problem clusters it was, depending on the cluster, 2.2 to 7.6 times more likely than expected by chance that they would end up in the same type of cluster 3 years later. (For a review of these results, the reader is referred to Bergman and Magnusson, 1991.) To comment on just one typical pattern at age 10: Belonging to the most severe problem cluster (Cluster 9) entailed a very high risk for later severe problems at age 13. There were significant streams both to Cluster 8 at age 13, that is, the most severe multiproblem cluster at that age, and to Cluster 6 at age 13, that is, the low school motivation syndrome. No boy completely lost his adjustment problems and moved from Cluster 9 at age 10 to Cluster 1 at age 13. This raises the question of whether this very high risk also operates over a longer time period into adulthood. The results presented next shed some light on the matter.

Now we address the analysis of the adulthood data. For the purpose of this study, we had information for three variables at adult age: Criminality (trichotomized), Psychiatric Care (dichotomized), and Alcohol Abuse (trichotomized). These variables were analyzed using the CFA technique, described in a later section, and the results are reported in Bergman and Magnusson (1997). We have three possible values in each of Criminality and Alcohol Abuse and two in Psychiatric Care. That renders a total of $3 \times 3 \times 2 = 18$ configurations to study. Five significant types were found. They were either characterized by both Criminality and Alcohol Abuse but not Psychiatric Care (three types) or by all three problems occurring together (two types). The last two types were extremely clear, with observed frequencies almost 20 times larger than expected. It is apparent that such problems strongly come together at adult age. For a further discussion, the reader can refer to Magnusson (1988). Based on this information, Bergman and Magnusson (1997) constructed a classification of adult adjustment problems into five categories: (A) No problems, (B) Criminality only, (C) Psychiatric Care only, (D) Criminality and Alcohol Abuse, and (E) a mixed group (those that did not fit into the other categories).

It is of interest to study how childhood adjustment problems are related to problems in adulthood at a pattern level. This can be done using the LICUR procedure and are reported by Bergman and Magnusson (1997). The basic LICUR rationale was followed so that the eight typical patterns at age 13 were related to the five categories of adult problem combinations. This was done in an 8×5 cross-tabulation that is summarized in Figure 21.3 on page 863.

As shown in Figure 21.3, four strong types occurred: (1) It was more frequent than expected by chance to

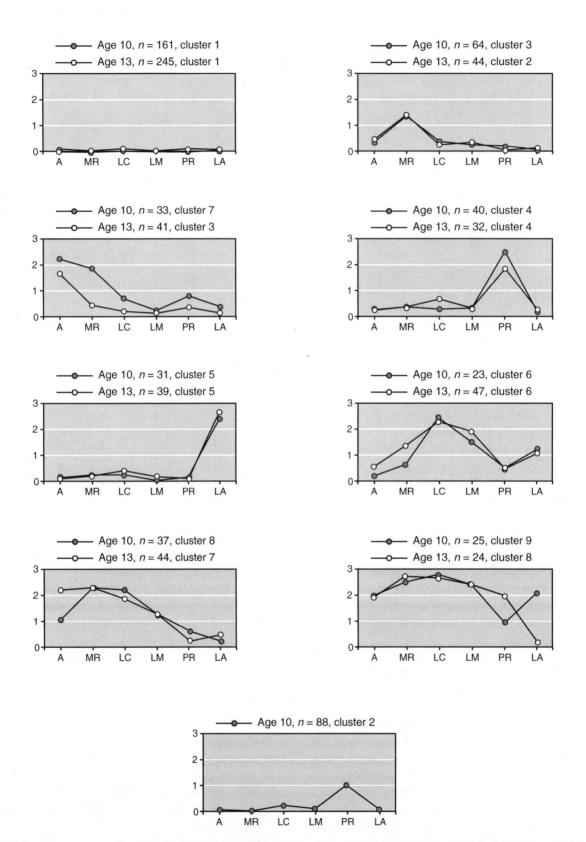

Figure 21.2 Cluster means for the cluster solutions at age 10 and age 13. *Notes:* A = Aggression; MR = Moror restlessness; LC = Lack of concentration; LM = Low school motivation; PR = Poor peer relations; and LA = Low school achievement.

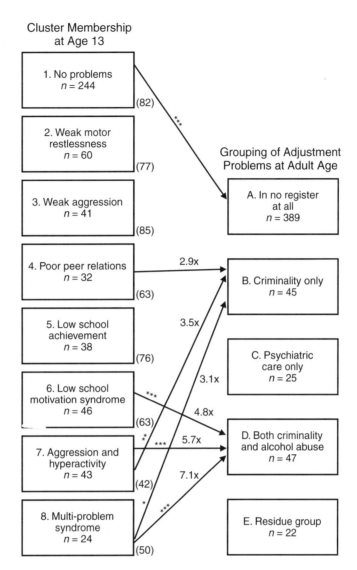

Figure 21.3 Significant longitudinal streams between age 13 and adult age. Figures on arrows indicate how many times more frequent the pattern combination is from what is expected from the development of the No Problems cluster. Figures within parentheses indicate the percent of the cluster that are found in the normal group of adult age. Only significant streams are presented and an exact one-tailed hypergeometric test was used. *Notes: * $p < .05$, $p < .01$, $p < .001$. Reprinted with permission from "A Person Oriented Approach in Research on Developmental Psychopathology," by R. L. Bergman and D. Magnusson, 1997, *Development and Psychopathology, 9,* 291–319.

belong to the "well-adjusted" group at both ages, and (2) belonging to any of the three multiproblem clusters at age 13 was strongly related to showing both Criminality and Alcohol Abuse at adult age. This risk was 5 to 7 times higher than expected by an independence model and highest for Cluster 8, that is, for the most severe multiproblem syndrome at age 13. There were also marginally significant longitudinal streams involving mainly the two most severe multiproblem clusters and Category B, characterized by Criminality only. It is also of interest to observe the *absence* of significant longitudinal streams between,

on the one hand, Cluster 2 and Cluster 3 at age 13 (weak Motor Restlessness and Aggression, respectively) and, on the other hand, any of the adult adjustment problem groups. Not even a tendency was found in this direction.

Based on these and other results, Bergman and Magnusson (1997, p. 309) write:

Seen in perspective, an overall picture emerges: At each age severe problems tend to occur together. Boys with multiple childhood problems have a much higher risk than other boys of exhibiting both criminal behavior and alcohol problems as adults, perhaps also psychiatric problems. Single adjustment problems in childhood do not usually have strong manifestations and are not related to adult problems. Alcohol problems in adulthood rarely occur alone, while psychiatric problems occurring alone are not related to patterns of childhood externalizing problems. The conclusion is inescapable: Problems tend to occur together in syndromes. It is the severe problem syndromes in late childhood and adulthood that link up; the rest is secondary. Hence, attention should be focused on such syndromes characterizing individuals rather than on variables viewed separately.

Next, we briefly indicate a few more examples of research findings that are based on the use of person-oriented methods for analyzing the IDA data set introduced previously. This is done in order for the reader to obtain some idea of the variance of problems and methods that can be used in a person-oriented perspective. Of course, other problems could have been tackled and many other methods could have been used, some of which are discussed in this chapter. However, we must draw the line somewhere, and we chose the three following simple examples:

1. Bergman and Magnusson (1997, p. 303) proposed a hypothesis of *problem gravitation* that deals with how patterns of externalizing adjustment problems evolve: "With age there is a tendency for externalizing problem patterns characterized by just a single problem or a few mild problems to become less frequent in relation to the well-adjusted patterns and the more severe multiproblem patterns. Either the child outgrows mild problems or these become worse. New problems for initially well-adjusted children emerge less frequently at a higher age than at lower ages." One way this hypothesis was tested was by comparing the multiproblem to single problem ratio between age 10 and age 13. This ratio increased from 0.75 to 1.28. Based on this and other evidence, Bergman and Magnusson concluded that the hypothesis was supported. They also pointed out that the concept of problem gravitation is natural to study in a person-oriented perspective, but it is largely overlooked in variable-oriented research (it is *not* identical to the concept of increased comorbidity with age). As an empirical phenomenon, problem gravitation may lie hidden in many data sets, not shown by standard variable-oriented analyses and perhaps obscured by variable standardization, and so on. Once the concept is on the table it can, of course, be studied using suitable variable-oriented methods. Problem gravitation was also discussed by Stattin and Magnusson (1996) from the standpoint of the development of antisocial behavior.

2. What is the importance of a childhood variable versus the pattern it is a part of? This is an interesting question to ask when you want to understand the roots of adult adjustment problems. Magnusson and Bergman (1988) noted two things when analyzing the predictive power of boys' late childhood aggression for adult criminality and alcohol abuse: that aggression predicted adult problems, and that aggression often appeared in a value pattern of many externalizing problems; it exhibited comorbidity with, especially, other conduct problems. This is nothing new. They then posed the question of whether it is the multiproblem pattern that is behind the relationship aggression showed with adult adjustment problems. That is, aggression in itself is perhaps of no importance for predicting criminality. It is only because it is a rather good indicator of a multiproblem pattern that the relationship appeared. This was tested by removing those that belonged to a multiproblem pattern and then recalculating the relationship between aggression and criminality/alcohol abuse. The relationship then vanished, supporting the conclusion that aggression in itself was of no importance. This issue has been analyzed in more depth by Bergman and Magnusson (1997) and Stattin and Magnusson (1996).

3. It is probably fair to say that in developmental research, the focus is on finding things that go together and explaining the common developmental paths. However, when discussing Lienert's concept of antitype, Lienert and zur Oeveste (1985) pointed out that what does *not* occur can also be informative. Why do certain configurations occur less frequently than expected by chance? When Bergman (1988b) discussed the residue concept, he pointed out that unique cases tell us about what occurs rarely, and that this knowledge may be of theoretical relevance. You can formulate hypotheses of value patterns that should not occur according to your theory and test them using his Residue Analysis (RESIDAN) approach. This line of thinking was also developed by Bergman and Magnusson (1997), who coined the term "white spots." They reported results indicating that certain important adjustment problems rarely occurred alone (e.g., lack of concentration and being repeatedly registered for alcohol abuse), and they also discussed questions about causal mechanisms. The concept of white spots is further elaborated in the discussion part of this chapter.

Studying Development through an Age-Invariant Classificatory Grid

Considering individuals as dynamic systems studied in an interactional paradigm, Bergman and El-Khouri (1999) stressed the usefulness of the concept of *i-state* from their classificatory perspective. They defined i-state as a specific subject's profile of scores at a specific point in time. In other words, they drew a parallel between the standard person-oriented basic unit of observation and the corresponding concept in dynamic systems terminology, that is, the state of the system at a given time. A dynamic systems perspective suggested that it might be interesting to identify the typical i-states for a sample of subjects across time. These would, in a way, correspond to attractors in a dynamic system. The first task is then to identify the typical i-states that exist *irrespective of the time points they refer to*. This is done in i-states-as-objects analysis (ISOA) by considering each i-state as a "subindividual" and then carrying out a classification analysis for all i-states. Hence, the number of objects in this analysis is the number of time points × the sample size. To carry out ISOA, you must have longitudinal data with the same variables measured at the different points in time so that the value profiles are comparable across age. The result of the first step of the ISOA analysis is a set of typical i-states (= classes of value profiles) that occur in the sample, disregarding the age at which they occur. The relative frequencies of the different typical i-states are then compared between ages to study structural stability and change.

In a second step of ISOA, it is noted, for each subject, what typical i-state he or she belongs to on each measurement occasion. In this way, each subject's sequence of i-states is established. These sequences are further analyzed to study individual stability and change.

In certain situations, ISOA can extract more information from the data than conventional methods can, especially when there are many measurement occasions. However, the applicability of ISOA is normally restricted to rather short periods of development as it must be assumed that, in principle, the same typical i-states occur at all measurement occasions, although with varying frequencies.

Partial Classification in a Developmental Setting

Earlier, we pointed out that we cannot always expect that every subject belongs to one of a small number of mutually exclusive classes or clusters, and we argued for the usefulness of removing multivariate outliers before the classification analysis is carried out. These normally constitute just 1% to 3% of the sample. However, for some data sets, one might not want to assume that anything like a complete classification structure exists. On the other hand, it might be reasonable to believe that a proportion of the sample belongs to one of a small number of typical patterns, with the rest of the sample exhibiting no clear classification structure and being best regarded as "noise." This line of reasoning is suggested by an analogy to results from studying complex dynamic systems, where one often finds a number of attractor states but also other states, some of which can be the result of a chaos-generating mechanism.

Against this background, Bergman and El-Khouri (2001) indicated a method, types-at-focus (TYFO), in which they attempted to find dense points in a longitudinal data space. When applying TYFO, it is assumed that a profile of interval-scaled variables is the basic unit of analysis and that a classification of (almost) all subjects' profiles is unrealistic. On the other hand, it is assumed that a partial classification of "core subjects" is possible, with each of the core subjects belonging to one of a small number of homogeneous groups on each measurement occasion. The aim of the analysis is to find and replicate these dense points and then to provide information on the core subjects' stability and change across time with regard to belonging to these dense points.

Classifying Sequences of States

I-state sequence analysis (ISSA; Bergman, 1995) is a truly longitudinal classification method for studying the development of individual patterns. It is based on a person-oriented framework and uses concepts and ideas taken from the study of nonlinear dynamic systems. As in ISOA, a basic concept in ISSA is the i-state, that is, an individual's configuration of values in the relevant variables at a specific point in time. Intraindividual i-state sequence development is first described, and every subject is classified as being characterized by belonging to one of the following five general classes of i-state evolvement: fixed i-states, semistable i-states, directed i-states, transient i-states, or irregular i-states. Then the typical states in each class that exist in the sample are searched for, and, finally, interindividual development is studied by analyzing the sequences of typical i-state classes the subjects belong to.

Both a general procedure, which can be tailored by the researcher according to his or her needs, and a standardized procedure exist. The empirical results that have been obtained for a test data set and a replication data set are encouraging. In some situations, ISSA is a viable alternative to other types of descriptive longitudinal classification methods, and it may provide a more robust classification than these methods do. However, ISSA appears to be optimal for situations when development is studied over limited time periods without dramatic shifts in basic characteristics of the studied system.

Latent Transition Analysis

Collins and Wugalter (1992) presented a rationale and a program called latent transition analysis (LTA) for the developmental classification of discrete latent variables. LTA builds on latent class analysis (LCA), where a discrete latent variable is inferred from manifest discrete variables. The cases are described by the values in a number of categorical variables and the covariations among these variables are studied. A nonobserved latent categorical variable is then searched for, the values of which will decompose the original data set into classes in such a way that all systematic relationships between the variables vanish (the assumption of local independence). If such a variable is found, it is said to "explain" the relationships.

Latent class probabilities and conditional probabilities are two types of probabilities in LCA. The relative sizes and the number of latent classes reflect the latent class probabilities. With regard to conditional probabilities, it should be kept in mind that the classes are not deterministically characterized in the same sense that clusters are in cluster analysis. Rather, a case is regarded as belonging to a class if its conditional probability of belonging to that class is high, depending on the subject's response pattern.

In LTA, a model can be constructed with an array of latent classes representing latent status at a given time. The latent statuses are used to construct what Collins and Wugalter (1992) call stage-sequential dynamic latent variables. Transition probabilities for the latent statuses between adjacent time points are estimated in the model. Using LTA, different models about pattern development can be tested and the model can handle certain types of measurement errors. After reviewing LTA, Bergman et al. (2003) suggested that the power of LTA to reject a "bad" model might be low for small to medium sized samples unless a "strong" model can be tested (i.e., a model with almost all parameters fixed). Nevertheless, the LTA approach can be highly relevant and has several attractive features, two prominent ones being that it allows for model testing and that its model parameters can in some situations nicely mirror a theoretical person-oriented model.

Meehl's Taxometric Approach

An important classificatory approach is given by Meehl's taxometric procedures. The reading of his work is educative for anyone interested in searching for natural categorical entities (see also Gangestad & Snyder, 1985). Meehl (1992) makes the distinction between what he calls a taxon (a "natural class") and an arbitrary class, and he discusses different procedures for finding and verifying a taxonomic

structure. Meehl is skeptical of the use of cluster analysis for taxometric purposes: "The cluster methods are at best viewed as 'plausible' numerifications of the intuitive notion of clumping in the phenotypic descriptor hyperspace" (p. 130). The essence of his argument is that certain other types of classification approaches than cluster analysis have larger chances of finding and validating a "natural" classification structure.

The contrast of his thinking to the principles presented in earlier sections is not as large as it may at first seem. From our perspective, we see the complete procedure of finding a sound classification system as containing two steps. The first is to establish a trustworthy classification in the sense that it is reliable and nonarbitrary. This is similar to Meehl's emphasis that the communalities and differences in classification results should be studied using different procedures. The second step is to study the usefulness and validity of the obtained trustworthy classification, and in doing that, the results will either prove or disprove that the classification has produced what Meehl calls taxa. This similarity will become more obvious from the brief description of his procedures.

Meehl especially advocates the use of his own latent class procedure where he applies a system of "coherent cut kinetics" (Meehl & Yonce, 1992; see also Waller & Meehl, 1998) to establish taxonicity, estimate parameters of the latent model, and assign subjects to the appropriate class. For instance, Meehl (1992) mentions two procedures for accomplishing this: maximum covariance (MAXCOV) and mean above minus below a cut (MAMBAC). However, the power of these procedures to establish taxonicity is unclear (see Maraun, Slaney, & Goddyn, 2003).

The term coherent cut kinetics refers to a procedure where one creates value intervals for an input variable and then examines the behavior of other variables in the different intervals. This behavior, among other things, gives important information about the taxonicity of the data set under study. Meehl (1992, p. 136) summarizes his procedures as follows:

> We hypothesize a certain latent structure underlying our data (i.e., that there is a taxon group and a complement group) and we know that if we are correct certain quantitative relations in the data are entailed by others. We examine these several relations to see if they obtain, as they will if our conjecture about the latent structure is correct.

In connection with presenting his procedures, Meehl (1992) pays attention to the issue of how we decide whether we should trust the results produced by a taxometric procedure. This issue is complex. First, different procedures or operations on the data set under study should be used to show that there is a convergence of evidence. He indicated a number of ingenious procedures for evaluating the validity and general usefulness of a classification method. A point raised by Meehl is the importance of discriminating between two purposes one might have with a classification: to show the existence of types (taxa, in Meehl's terminology) and to assign subjects to the appropriate class. Quite frequently, these two purposes are not kept apart, and it is not always realized that a classification can be successful with regard to the first purpose but not with regard to the second one.

A Person-Centered Strategy for Linking Life Histories to Outcomes

There is a tension between, on one hand, the need to account for individual life trajectories in a case-wise manner, where the richness of the individual life is retained, and, on the other hand, the frequent need to study fairly large samples and compare results across individuals. An innovative way of tackling this problem is an approach developed by Singer and coworkers (Singer, Ryff, Carr, & Magee, 1998). The basic principle of this approach is that information available in a longitudinal study (including quantitative variable-oriented information) is used to create detailed descriptions of individual lives, and from these descriptions generalizable characteristics are found and compared between outcome groups. They present principles for the organization and interpretation of life history information. In their empirical example, Singer et al. used data from the Wisconsin Longitudinal Study and analyzed life histories of what they call "resilient" women (having a history of depression but at the time of follow-up reporting a high level of well-being). In a step-wise fashion, first narratives of life histories were written, and then they were reviewed for communalities and transformed into more generic descriptions. Finally, the distinguishability in them between the resilient and three other mental health groups was tested.

Hongxin, Brooks-Gunn, McLanahan, and Singer (2000) suggested an extension and exemplification of this approach in the context of child development. They discussed the issue of bringing back the person into developmental studies, using the phrase "studying the real child rather than the ideal child" (p. 393). In this discussion, they gave good arguments for the usefulness of the narrative approach, of which they provided an empirical example. In the example, they used longitudinal survey data from the Child Supplement to the National Longitudinal Survey of Youth. Their aim was to study the multiple pathways that subgroups of children follow to arrive at either an outcome indicating resiliency to adversity (adversity defined as having a teenage mother) or an outcome indicating vulnerability to adversity. The analytic strategy included five steps:

1. The construction of narrative stories for a subsample of cases from each of the two outcome groups.
2. Identifying similar and distinct pathways within each group.
3. Response vectors that mirror the developmental process according to the organizing principles.
4. Summary representations of developmental experiences.
5. Tests of distinguishability to study whether the developmental pathways differ between the two groups.

Distinct differences in the pathways were found between the resilient and the vulnerable group, and the results provided a wealth of interesting information that contributes to the understanding of the development of persons "as wholes" in a way that cannot be accomplished by an ordinary variable-oriented approach.

Configural Frequency Analysis

Configural frequency analysis (CFA; Lienert & Krauth, 1975; von Eye, 2002) allows one to identify *patterns of variable categories,* also called *configurations,* that are observed more often (types) or less often (antitypes) than expected based on some chance model. If these discrepancies are significant, then configurations reflect local associations, that is, associations that exist only in particular sectors of the variable space (Havránek & Lienert, 1984).

Cross-classifications can be analyzed from both variable-oriented and person-oriented perspectives. Variable-oriented analysis of cross-classifications focuses on three kinds of research questions (Goodman, 1991):

- What is the joint frequency distribution in the table?
- What is the association structure of the variables that span the cross-classification?
- What is the dependency structure of the variables that spans the cross-classification?

Each of these questions can be answered using log-linear modeling and related methods, for example, logistic regression.

In contrast, under a person orientation, researchers would ask such questions as:

- Can the *c* configurations in the table—these configurations are defined by the *c* cells of the table—be classified in $g < c$ groups such that within-group similarity is maximized while between-group dissimilarity is also maximized?

- Do individual cells or groups of cells contain fewer or more cases than expected based on some *chance model* (also called *base model;* von Eye, 2002)?

The first of these questions can, of course, also be answered using methods of clustering or latent class analysis. The method of choice for the second question is CFA. This second question comes in many different forms. The following are four sample questions (cf. von Eye, 2002):

1. *How do the observed frequencies compare with the expected frequencies?* As will be explained below, the first step of a CFA application involves selecting a chance model, also called a *base model.* This model specifies the expectations under which we inspect the observed frequencies. For example, one can create a base model that posits that no variable interactions of whatever order exist. If a configuration violates this assumption, then an interaction must exist, at least locally. Other base models posit that first-order associations (parallel to zero-order correlations) exist. Violations of this assumption point to the existence of second- or higher-order associations, also at least locally. Selecting a base model is of utmost importance in CFA because decisions as to whether or not particular configurations were observed more or less often than expected depend on the base model. It is a frequent result of CFA that configurations are identified as types under one base model, but remain inconspicuous or even constitute antitypes under some different base model.

2. *Do two or more existing groups differ in their multivariate frequency distributions?* Here again, several base models are conceivable. In each case, however, the main question is whether group-specific associations or dependency structures exist. If such a structure is group-specific, then at least one of the groups under study will show more (or fewer) cases in a particular configuration than expected based on the assumption of, for instance, independence of groups, and these types should differ between groups.

3. *What are the characteristics of changes in interaction patterns over time?* To answer this question, a base model proposes, for instance, that the interaction pattern remains unchanged over time. In addition, one can ask whether changes are group-specific, thus combining group comparisons with longitudinal CFA.

4. *Can predictor-criterion relationships be identified at the level of configurations?* Here, we ask whether particular predictor-criterion patterns occur more or less often than expected. If such a pattern is observed more often than expected, then one can conclude that the predictor configuration allows one to predict the criterion configuration. If there are fewer cases than expected, then one can conclude that this predictor configuration allows one to predict that the companion criterion configuration will not be observed (or will be observed less often than expected). Depending on the nature of the data under study, this latter situation may open the doors for the conclusion that a particular predictor pattern prevents the companion criterion pattern from occurring, a result that can be of importance in intervention research.

Configural Frequency Analysis Requires Five Steps

When performing CFA, five steps are required, with their corresponding decisions. In the following paragraphs, these five steps are introduced (for more detail, see, e.g., von Eye, 2002; von Eye & Niedermeier, 1999).

Step 1: The Selection of a Base Model. This is most important because the base model is the background in front of which CFA types and antitypes are interpreted. The base model reflects the theoretical assumptions that carry an analysis. If the base model does not correspond to these assumptions, then types and antitypes cannot be interpreted without problems. Changing the base model can have the effect that new types and antitypes emerge or existing types and antitypes disappear. Most CFA base models can be expressed as log-linear models. The comparison of the estimated values computed from this model with the corresponding observed frequencies leads to the decision of whether a configuration constitutes a type or an antitype or conforms to the prediction made by the base model.

The original model of CFA (Lienert, 1969) used the model of variable independence as its base model. This model reflects the assumption that the variables that span the cross-classification under study are unrelated to each other. They can show only main effects. If types and antitypes emerge, then associations must exist. Another well-known example of a CFA base model is that of *Prediction CFA.* The base model for this CFA variant proposes that:

- Predictors are related to each other as in a saturated model. That is, all possible associations among predictors are part of the base model.

- Criteria are related to each other as in a saturated model.

- Predictors and criteria are independent of each other.

This model can be contradicted only if predictor-criterion relationships exist. These relationships indicate that, for the configurations that stand out as types or antitypes, predictive relationships such as the ones indicated exist. If the number of types and antitypes is small, then predictive relationships exist only in parts of the multivariate data space (as opposed to the entire space, as is often assumed in the analysis of continuous variables).

Two or multigroup CFA is a special case of Prediction CFA. This model of CFA proposes that (1) the variables that are used to predict group membership are related to each other as in a saturated model, and (2) these variables are unrelated to the variable that denotes group membership.

A few CFA base models exist that are not log-linear (von Eye, 2002). For example, in certain contexts, events and configurations can come with a priori determined probabilities. Examples of such cases include the a priori probabilities of patterns of change in categorical variables. Other non-log-linear base models include those that take into account a priori probabilities taken from population statistics.

In either case, the selection of a base model can have major implications for the interpretability of CFA results. Therefore, researchers typically take great care in the specification of base models and often reanalyze their data using different base models to determine the effects of different choices of base models. The specification of base models follows the three rules proposed by von Eye and Schuster (1998):

1. CFA base models are parsimonious. Thus, they contain as few terms as possible, and these terms are of the lowest possible order.

2. CFA base models take sampling schemes into account. This rule implies that the margins of variables that are observed under a product-multinomial sampling scheme must be reproduced by the base model.

3. The most important of the three rules is the third: CFA base models must be specified such that only one reason for deviations between observed and expected cell frequencies can exist. For example, the CFA base model that takes only main effects into account can be contradicted only if associations exist. The base model for Prediction CFA can be contradicted only if predictor-criterion relationships exist, and so on.

Step 2: The Concept of Independence. Most base models of CFA incorporate some concept of independence. There are two aspects of independence in CFA. The first of

these is that many base models posit some type of independence among variables or variable groups. This applies even if associations of first or higher order are part of the base model. In these cases, independence refers to higher-order associations.

The second aspect, and this is the one at issue when a concept of deviation from independence is selected, concerns the type of deviation from independence. Typically, deviations from independence are cast in terms of deviance residuals, that is, the difference of estimated expected cell frequencies from observed cell frequencies, or standardized versions of this discrepancy measure. In addition, the marginal frequencies are typically taken into account when the discrepancies between the estimated expected cell frequencies and their observed counterparts are evaluated. The measures that depict the relative magnitude of the discrepancies between the estimated expected and the observed cell frequencies are thus termed *marginal-dependent* (Goodman, 1991; von Eye & Mun, 2003). Sample measures include the well-known Pearson χ^{-2}-component and the standardized residual, a *z*-measure. However, there exist measures of deviation from independence that do not take the marginal frequencies into account. These measures are termed *marginal-free*. Examples of such measures include the log-odds ratio. Von Eye, Spiel, and Rovine (1995) proposed using marginal-free measures for two-sample CFA. The authors showed that type and antitype patterns depend on whether marginal-free or marginal-dependent measures are used. When the marginal frequencies differ dramatically and associations are strong, marginal-free measures may be more appropriate (see also von Eye & Mun, 2003) because they are sensitive to interactions without taking main effects into account. This is of importance in particular for two-sample CFA and Prediction CFA.

Step 3: The Selection of Significance Tests. This issue has been widely discussed in the development of CFA methods. This discussion has addressed issues of statistical power, the α- and the ß-errors, the relative frequencies of types and antitypes, the distribution of the various measures, the assumptions that need to be made when using a measure, the small sample performance of measures, the sensitivity of measures to different sampling schemes, the performance of measures under various marginal distributions, and the performance of measures in tables of varying sizes (von Eye, 2002, 2003; von Eye, Lautsch, & von Weber, 2004; von Eye & Mun, 2003). In the following sections, we present a selection of three measures that (1) perform well under many conditions, (2) display a number of other desirable characteristics, and (3) differ in the assumptions they require users to make. Let m_i be the estimated expected frequency of Cell i and f_i the corresponding observed frequency.

The first test that was proposed for use in CFA is the Pearson χ^2-test:

$$X^2 = \frac{(f_i - m_i)^2}{m_i}$$

This statistic has the following characteristics:

- It is nonparametric.
- It is marginal-dependent.
- It is powerful, in particular when samples are large.
- It is, for large samples, asymptotically distributed as the χ^2 with $df = 1$.
- It requires large samples to keep α and χ low.
- It needs large samples to reach a power of $p = .8$.
- It tends to detect more types than antitypes when samples are small.
- It tends to detect more antitypes than types when samples are large.

In addition, it is easy to calculate.

The second measure is Lehmacher's (1981) asymptotic hypergeometric test. The formula for it is rather complicated and is omitted here. The test has the following characteristics:

- It requires sampling to be product-multinomial.
- It is marginal-dependent.
- It is most powerful, regardless of sample size.
- It approximates the normal distribution only for very large sample sizes; for smaller sample sizes, the statistic can suggest nonconservative decisions.
- It requires large samples to keep α and χ low.
- It needs only small samples to reach a power of $p = .8$.
- It detects equal numbers of types and antitypes for 2×2 tables and approximately equal numbers of types and antitypes for large samples in tables of different sizes than 2×2.
- It can be applied only in first-order CFA.

The third test to be discussed here is the binomial test. Let the estimated probability for Cell i be $p = m_i/N$ and $q = 1 - p$. Then, the exact tail probability for the frequency found for Cell i is

$$B(if) = \sum_{i=f_i}^{N} \binom{N}{i} p^i q^{N-i}$$

where N indicates the sample size. This test has the following characteristics:

- It is nonparametric.
- It is exact.
- Although this test is exact, it can be conservative. Typically, the probability p is estimated from the data. Therefore, it can be closer to the data under analysis than if it were known from the population. If p is closer to the data than should be, discrepancies will be perceived as smaller, and statistical decisions will be conservative.

There exist many more tests that are suitable for CFA. These tests allow the researcher to take into account a large number of assumptions and data characteristics. Unfortunately, recent simulations have shown that many of the tests, in particular the asymptotic tests, perform poorly under CFA conditions, that is, when the cell probability p is small (von Eye, 2003). Therefore, the binomial test is typically recommended. The asymptotic tests perform well mostly for very large samples.

Step 4: The Identification of Types and Antitypes in CFA. This involves two steps. The first is the application of a significance test. The second concerns the protection of the a priori selected significance threshold α. As is well-known, the significance threshold is guaranteed only for the first of a series of tests on the same data. CFA almost always involves inspecting several or even all configurations to determine whether they constitute types or antitypes. CFA is thus a method that involves *multiple testing*. If multiple tests are performed at some level α, then the risk of committing an α-error (Type I error) is not equal to α. Rather, if one takes a risk of size α multiple times, the overall risk can be much greater. This applies even if the tests are independent of each other. Taking the risk of rejecting one or more true null hypotheses is known as *capitalizing on chance*.

This risk is exacerbated when tests are dependent. In CFA, tests are dependent because they are performed on cells of the same contingency table. Von Weber, von Eye, and Lautsch (2004) showed that the magnitude of this risk depends on the size of the table. In 2×2 tables, already the result of the second type/antitype decision is completely determined by the result of the first decision. In larger tables, this dependency is smaller, but it is always present.

Two methods of protecting the a priori determined significance level have been developed. The first method (Bonferroni correction) keeps the protected, also called the *adjusted* significance level, α*, constant for each test performed. The second method allows one to take into account (1) the number of tests already performed, (2) the total number of tests, (3) dependency patterns, and (4) whether the tests that were already performed led to rejections of null hypotheses. As one can imagine, the method that keeps the adjusted α-level constant suggests more conservative decisions, often already for the first test. The methods are reviewed in von Eye (2002).

In CFA applications, protection of the significance level is routine. One implication of this procedure is that only extreme configurations, that is, configurations that show large discrepancies from expectancy, emerge as types or antitypes. A second implication is that the sample sizes one needs for types and antitypes to emerge are often large. This applies in particular when the cross-classification under study contains many cells.

This second implication may seem prohibitive. However, considering that many test statistics that are popular in CFA applications also require large samples to approximate their respective sampling distributions, one would only reluctantly trust type and antitype claims that are based on small samples and approximate tests. Therefore, large samples are preferred for protection of the nominal α-level and performance of trustworthy significance tests. Only if both conditions are fulfilled can types and antitypes be trusted.

Step 5: The Interpretation of Types and Antitypes. This interpretation is mainly fueled by the base model used to run a configural analysis. The base model contains all variable relations that are not of interest for possibly resulting types and antitypes. Therefore, types and antitypes indicate which configurations contradict the base model. To give examples of type/antitype interpretation, consider the sample base models discussed later. Table 21.1 lists these (and one other) models and the assumptions made by them and indicates the interpretation of types and antitypes that result for these models.

As can be seen from Table 21.1, types and antitypes in CFA have conceptually different interpretations, depending on the base model selected for analysis. It is also clear that different base models can result in different patterns of types and antitypes, because they make different assumptions. These assumptions result in different design matrices for the estimation of the expected cell frequencies, and thus in different distributions of the measures used to establish types and antitypes.

TABLE 21.1 Sample Base Models of CFA, Their Assumptions, and the Interpretation of Their Types and Antitypes

Base Model	Sample Assumptions	Type/Antitype Interpretation
Zero order	No effects present in table	Types and antitypes indicate that, locally, main effects and interactions exist
First order	Only main effects exist; variables are independent	Types and antitypes indicate that, locally, variable interactions exist
Second order	Main effects and pairwise interactions exist	Types and antitypes indicate that, locally, interactions of second or higher order exist
k-sample CFA	Variables used to compare the groups can be associated at any level Variable that indicates group membership and variables used for comparisons are independent of each other	Patterns of variables that are used for group comparison discriminate among groups
Prediction CFA	Predictor variables can be associated at any level Criterion variables can be associated at any level	Patterns of predictor variables go hand in hand with patterns of criterion variables (types); patterns of predictor variables do not combine with patterns of criterion variables (antitypes)
Longitudinal CFA of differences	Mean differences from one observation point to the next can have main effects, but are independent of each other	Types indicate the patterns of change that are more likely than chance; antitypes indicate unlikely patterns of change

Data Example

With the following example, we show that different base models can result in different harvests of types and antitypes. The data are taken from a project on the development of aggression in adolescence (Finkelstein, von Eye, & Preece, 1994). In a sample of 114 adolescents (38 boys and 76 girls), among others, the self-rated variable physical aggression against peers (PAAP) was observed three times, in the years 1983, 1985, and 1987. In the CFA analyses, low aggression is coded 1 and high aggression is coded 2. In the following paragraphs, we subject these data, along with the variable gender, to two configural analyses. In the first, we perform a 2-sample gender comparison. In the second, we run a first-order CFA.

The 2-sample CFA of the variables PAAP83, PAAP85, PAAP87, and Gender proceeds under the following base model:

- The variables PAAP83, PAAP85, and PAAP87 can show main effects and interactions of any order; thus, the model is saturated in these, the discrimination variables; types and antitypes cannot emerge because of differential autocorrelation patterns.
- The variable Gender can show a main effect; that is, the fact is taken into account that more girls than boys participated in this study.
- Gender and the discrimination variables are independent.

From this base model, types and antitypes can emerge only if the discrimination variables interact with Gender. If this is the case, discrimination types indicate Gender differences such that particular patterns of the discrimination variables are observed more often in one of the gender groups than expected based on the assumption of independence of discrimination variables and Gender. To identify possible discrimination types in this 2-sample CFA, we use the χ^2-test and the Bonferroni-adjusted $\alpha^* = 0.05/8 = 0.00625$. Table 21.2 displays the results of this 2-sample CFA.

The first column in Table 21.2 indicates the configurations that are compared in pairs. For example, the first comparison pair is Configuration 1111 and 1112. These are the

TABLE 21.2   2-Sample CFA of the Variables PAAP83, PAAP85, PAAP87, and Gender

Configuration	f	χ^2	p	Type?
1111	13			
1112	14	3.494	.061582	
1121	4			
1122	7	0.050	.822527	
1211	3			
1212	6	0.000	1.000000	
1221	6			
1222	6	1.676	.195394	
2111	2			
2112	5	0.076	.782652	
2121	4			
2122	4	1.075	.299713	
2211	1			
2212	11	3.772	.052115	
2221	5			
2222	23	4.000	.045489	

boys (Gender = 1) and girls (Gender = 2) who show physical aggression levels below the sample medians across all three observation points. The second column shows the observed cell frequencies. For example, the 13 cases in Cell 1111 indicate that 13 out of 38 boys showed consistent below-the-median aggression levels. The number 14 in Cell 1112 indicates that 14 out of 76 girls also showed consistent below-the-median aggression levels. This proportion difference of .34 for the boys to .18 for the girls comes with a χ^2-value of 3.494 and a tail probability of 0.06. This value is greater than the Bonferroni-adjusted $\alpha^* = 0.00625$. Thus, we cannot reject the null hypothesis of equal proportions. The same applies to all gender comparisons in this analysis.

We thus conclude that, based on the present results from 2-sample CFA, there are, across three observation periods during adolescence, no significant gender differences in physical aggression against peers. We now ask whether first-order CFA presents a different picture.

As was indicated in Table 21.2, *first-order CFA* assumes that the variables that span a cross-classification are independent of each other. Types and antitypes thus reflect local associations. In the present example, we ask with first-order CFA whether local associations exist and where they are located. Tests are performed at the level of individual cells. The resulting types and antitypes therefore describe individual cells instead of pairs in cells, as in 2-sample CFA. In contrast, 2-sample CFA, as performed in the previous paragraph, performs tests at the level of comparing two cells with each other.

Table 21.3 displays the results of first-order CFA. We used the χ^2-test again, under the Bonferroni-adjusted significance level $\alpha^* = 0.05/16 = 0.003125$. We see that, because tests are performed at the level of individual cells, the number of tests in first-order CFA is twice that in a 2-sample CFA. Consequently, the adjusted α^* is more extreme in first-order CFA than in 2-sample CFA.

Table 21.3 contains in its first column the cell indices configurations. The second column contains the observed cell frequencies. These are the same as in Table 21.2. Column 3 presents the expected cell frequencies, estimated using the base model of variable independence. The fourth column contains the χ^2-statistics, the fifth column shows the one-sided tail probabilities, and the last column indicates the significant types/antitypes after Bonferroni correction.

The χ^2-values for two configurations are so large that their configurations constitute types. There are no antitypes. The first type is constituted for Configuration 1111. These are the 13 boys that show below-median physical aggression against peers throughout the observation phase. Only slightly over 4 boys had been expected to show this

TABLE 21.3   First-Order CFA of the Variables PAAP83, PAAP85, PAAP87, and Gender

Value Combination*	f	m	χ^2	p	Type?
1111	13	4.411	16.723	.0000	Type
1112	14	8.822	3.038	.0813	
1121	4	4.732	0.113	.7365	
1122	7	9.464	0.642	.4231	
1211	3	5.077	0.850	.3566	
1212	6	10.154	1.699	.1924	
1221	6	5.446	0.056	.8125	
1222	6	10.893	2.198	.1382	
2111	2	4.112	1.085	.2976	
2112	5	8.224	1.264	.2609	
2121	4	4.411	0.038	.8448	
2122	4	8.822	2.636	.1045	
2211	1	4.733	2.944	.0862	
2212	11	9.466	0.249	.6180	
2221	5	5.077	0.001	.9727	
2222	23	10.154	16.251	.0001	Type

* "Value combination" indicates the value pattern for PAAP83, PAAP85, PAAP87, and Gender.

pattern. It is interesting to note that pattern 1112 almost formed a type of girls with below-median aggression. However, the discrepancy from expectancy is less extreme for the girls than for the boys. Therefore, the type is constituted for the boys but not for the girls.

The second type is constituted by Configuration 2222. These are the 23 girls (10.15 had been expected) who indicated consistent above-median physical aggression against peers. For boys with the corresponding pattern, we see that the observed frequency is very similar to the expected one. Still, the 2-sample CFA presented in Table 21.2 suggests that the gender discrepancy is not significant. Nevertheless, the results from first-order CFA suggest that only the girls deviate significantly from expectancy for the consistent high-aggression pattern.

From the comparison of the results in Tables 21.2 and 21.3 we conclude that indeed, types and antitypes can emerge or disappear when different base models are used. In the present example, we find that gender-specific types can exist although the gender comparison does not indicate it. An explanation of such a phenomenon, which at first sight may seem implausible, can be given using Configurations 1111 and 1112. The first of these two configurations constitutes a type. More boys showed this pattern than expected. The second of these two configurations fails to show a type. However, the comparison of the observed with the estimated expected cell frequency shows that there were also more girls with the aggression pattern 111 than expected. This difference, however, was not significant. We see that, although in both gender groups, pattern 111 occurs more often than expected, this discrepancy is signifi-

cant only for boys. The gender difference is not significant because both discrepancies go in the same direction.

When looking at Configurations 2221 and 2222, we see that the differences between observed and expected cell frequencies do go in opposite directions. However, the discrepancy is still not large enough to constitute a discrimination type (the odds ratio for this comparison is 0.435, which indicates that more girls than boys show this pattern; the tail probability for this ratio is 0.025, a value near the one shown in Table 21.2; however, this value is larger than the adjusted α^*). So, again, we note that whereas a gender-specific type emerges, the gender difference is not large enough to be significant.

From these results, we see that a CFA analysis from a person-oriented perspective can yield results that go beyond what routine application of statistical methods can give us. Using a repeated measures ANOVA, we find that, overall, the amount of aggression is different for the two gender groups ($F(1, 112) = 26.41$; $p < .01$), with boys being more aggressive than girls, and we find that there is a linear trend ($F(1, 112) = 49.43$; $p < .01$) but no quadratic trend ($F(1, 112) = 0.30$). Furthermore, there is a Gender × Linear Trend interaction ($F(1, 112) = 9.10$; $p < .01$) such that the decrease is steeper in boys than in girls. These are important results. However, this ANOVA cannot tell us that there are more boys than expected from chance who show consistent below-average physical aggression against peers, and more girls than expected who show consistent above-average physical aggression against peers. We thus conclude that data analysis can fruitfully be undertaken from both the variable orientation and the person orientation. In many instances, the two approaches yield complementary results.

One may wonder how this result may be interpreted. We found that boys are more aggressive, yet the pattern that was found more often than expected was that of consistent low aggression. For girls, who are less aggressive, the type pattern was that of consistent high aggression. This seemingly contradictory result can be explained as follows. ANOVA is sensitive to mean differences and found the expected gender difference. In contrast, repeated-measures CFA, as performed for Table 21.3, is sensitive to particular patterns of autocorrelation. Thus, although boys are more aggressive than girls, there are more boys than expected who show consistent low levels of aggression.

Accordingly, although girls are, in general, less aggressive than boys, there are more girls than expected who show consistent high levels of aggression. Both of these groups would have remained undetected by routine application of ANOVA. We thus conclude that person-oriented research can yield results that are hard to find from a variable-oriented perspective.

Studying Individual Trajectories

When information is available for a variable from many points in time, we talk about each individual having a trajectory of values. The study of individual trajectories can be a focus of interest. During the past decades, a variety of methods has been advanced for the purpose of studying both average trajectories and individual variation in trajectories. Two classes of methods within this framework are latent growth curve analysis (McArdle & Epstein, 1987; Muthén, 1989) and hierarchical modeling (Bryk & Raudenbush, 1992). Such methods can be highly useful but, from a more strict person-oriented perspective, focusing on typical patterns or natural classes, they are not the first choice because in their basic formulations they assume continuous variation. Nagin (1999) presented an interesting approach for studying trajectories that considers the possibility of distinct groups of individuals with different trajectories. The approach can handle three types of data—count, binary, and psychometric scale data—and for each type of data, probability distributions are proposed. The method can identify and test for a distinctive number of typical trajectories, estimate the proportion of the population that belongs to each trajectory group, and relate group membership probabilities to individual characteristics.

Nagin and Tremblay (2001) have extended the group trajectory method to handle the simultaneous study of developmental trajectories for related series of measurement in two variables. The authors point out that this approach can be useful for the study of comorbidity and heterotypic continuity. They give two empirical examples. First, the comorbidity of hyperactivity and physical aggression is studied; second, the heterotypic continuity between opposition and property offending is investigated. Based on their models, they show that the interpretation of marginal, conditional, and joint probabilities of membership in a trajectory group can be highly informative.

The extension to handling two different but related variables is useful because it enables the researcher to link the developmental trajectory of two different characteristics in a person-oriented framework where typical trajectories are a focus. Nagin and Tremblay (2001) point out that they regard the groups as an approximation of an underlying continuous process. The method allows for fuzziness in group membership by giving it a probabilistic framework. This approach does not build on the latent variable concept as it

is commonly interpreted, and it does not explicitly handle errors of measurement. Of course, from our person-oriented perspective, it is a limitation that the method cannot handle multivariate developmental trajectories; that is, developmental trajectories of patterns of more than two variables cannot be studied. It is hoped that an extension of the methodology to this more general situation will follow in the future.

STRUCTURAL EQUATIONS MODELING AS A METHOD FOR PERSON-ORIENTED ANALYSIS

We start this section with a review of the concept of *dimensional identity*. This is a concept that has been elaborated by von Eye and is defined as follows: "A set of variables can be defined as displaying dimensional identity if the interrelations among the variables in this set remain unchanged across the levels or categories of other variables" (von Eye & Bergman, 2003, p. 554). This identity can be specified at different levels, for instance, with regard to mean structures and correlation structures. Only if there is dimensional identity can variable-oriented methods studying the whole population be justified (see also Schmitz, 2000, on conditions when the aggregation of individual processes is warranted). Otherwise, person-oriented methods are appropriate. From this perspective, one way of handling the situation where there is not dimensional identity, in addition to the previously mentioned approaches, is to tailor a variable-oriented method to take into account group differences in model parameters. This meets the person-oriented requirement of individualizing the relationships (although normally not the requirement of taking patterns of operating factors into account). For that purpose, extensions of structural equations modeling (SEM; Bentler, 1985; Jöreskog & Sörbom, 1993; Pugesek, Tomer, & von Eye, 2003) can be a natural choice.

SEM is a broadly applicable statistical method that allows one to combine features of regression analysis and factor analysis. McArdle and Bell (2000) describe SEM as a method that provides the mathematical and statistical tools for the specification and testing of theoretical propositions. The first proposition concerns the *measurement model,* which specifies which *manifest variable (observed)* loads on which *latent variable (factor).*

Measurement models are needed to establish the loading structure of variables, both on the dependent and on the independent variables sides. If a variable fails to load on its factor, that is, if a variable shows low or nonsignificant loadings, then researchers tend to eliminate this variable. Often, one attempts to specify measurement models such that each manifest variable loads on only one latent variable. Unless an orthogonal factor structure is hypothesized, factors are typically allowed to correlate. Second- and higher-order factors can be considered.

If one includes a regression component in the model, that is, if one links the measurement model for the independent variables with the measurement model for the dependent variables (or if one includes regression hypotheses for the factors on the dependent side of the model), then one extends measurement models into *structural models*. That is, the structural model part is the one that contains regression hypotheses in which factors are regressed onto each other.

A large number of variations of models has been proposed in the domain of SEM. For example, one can test models with only manifest variables (these are the well-known *path models*); one can test models with no variables or factors regarded as independent; one can test *longitudinal models* (e.g., von Eye, Spiel, & Wagner, 2003); one can test group-comparative models (*multigroup models*); and, recently, it has been shown that SEM can be the platform for building hierarchical linear models (for an overview, see Bauer, 2003).

Although SEM was designed with variable-oriented applications in mind, this methodological approach can be applied for some types of person-oriented analysis. From the perspective of person-oriented data analysis, multigroup models and random coefficient models are most interesting. Using such methods, the models become more individualized or person-oriented in that they take into account that the studied population is not homogeneous in the model that describes it. By such methods the issue of dimensional identity can be studied. To identify exactly where in the model groups differ, multigroup models are often performed by estimating a hierarchy of models. This hierarchy contains four hierarchically related sets of models:

1. The strictest models posit that factor loadings, factor covariances, and the regression coefficients in the structural part of the model, as well as the properties of residuals, are identical across groups. Specific groups make their own contribution to the overall goodness-of-fit χ^2. It is conceivable that a model describes a number of groups well, but one group shows significant deviations.

2. If the strictest model fails to fit (which is likely to be the case), one can allow residuals to vary across groups while positing that all other parameters are equal across groups.

3. At the third hierarchical level, one can allow factor loadings or factor covariances to vary across groups in addition to the residuals, while the remaining parameters are posited to be invariant across groups. Often, researchers allow all estimated parameters to vary across groups. The only constraint that remains is that the same parameters are estimated in each group. Here again, groups may respond differently to this set of relaxed hypotheses.

4. If the attempts at the third level of the hierarchy fail, that is, do not lead to models that describe the data satisfactorily, one can introduce group-specific model modifications. One can, for example, allow that a selection of residual covariances be estimated for one group but not for others.

Multigroup models can be specified for practically any model in SEM. This includes models with means and longitudinal models. This option is of great importance for person-oriented research because it allows one to specify precisely where in the variable or dependency structure groups differ. For example, groups can differ in the magnitude of factor loadings. In extreme cases, factor loadings can differ to the extent that a manifest variable does load on a particular factor in one group but not the other. Structural regression coefficients can differ also. It is conceivable that a factor on the dependent variable side is predictable from a particular factor on the independent variable side in one group but not the other.

Data Example

The following data example stems from a study published by Ohannessian, Lerner, Lerner, and von Eye (1994). The authors studied perception of family functioning in families with adolescent children. Family functioning was measured as perceived family adjustment (Spanier, 1976), family adaptability (Olson, Portner, & Lavee, 1985), and family cohesion (Olson et al., 1985). In each of the 74 families, both parents and the male or the female adolescent responded to the questionnaires. One score each was created from the instruments for perceived family adjustment, cohesion, and adaptability. The instruments were administered repeatedly as part of a larger adolescent transition study (Lerner, Lerner, & von Eye, 1988). Here, we use the data from the fall and spring of the adolescents' 2nd year in middle school.

We approach these data with two questions. First, we ask whether family functioning is viewed differently in families with boys than in families with girls. Second, we ask whether the comparison of families with girls and families with boys results in the same conclusions at both points in time. To answer these questions, we perform one two-group analysis for each data set. Because of the small number of variables, we perform the analyses at the level of manifest variables.

More specifically, the first question is answered by comparing the correlation matrices for families with girls to the correlation matrices for families with boys. The correlation matrices for the first observation point appear in Table 21.4. These correlations may be unstable, considering the small sample size. Replication studies may have to show whether the results presented here and in previous studies need to be reformulated.

The information in Table 21.4 is structured as follows. Two correlation matrices are given. The correlations above the diagonal are for families with girls. The correlations below the diagonal are for families with boys. As mentioned, the first block contains the correlations for family adjustment, the second contains the correlations for family cohesion, and the third contains the correlations for family adaptability. The first correlation in block 1 is equal to 1. It describes the correlation of the adolescents' ratings with themselves. The second correlation relates the adolescents' ratings to the mothers' ratings, and the third correlation relates the adolescents' ratings to the fathers' ratings. For example, the correlation of 0.09 in the first line relates the girls' ratings of family adjustment to their mother's ratings. The corresponding correlation in the boys' sample is 0.01.

The next series of three correlations relates the family adjustment ratings to the family cohesion ratings; following that, the series of three correlations relates the family adjustment ratings to the family adaptability ratings. This scheme is followed accordingly in the second and third blocks of the table. In each block, the first line presents correlations with adolescents' ratings, the second line presents correlations with mothers' ratings, and the third line presents correlations with fathers' ratings.

Each of these triangular correlation (or covariance) matrices can be approached from a number of perspectives. For example, one can apply methods from *multitrait-multimethod* analysis (Campbell & Fiske, 1959) and ask questions concerning the convergent and discriminant validity of a set of tests that vary in the way they measure phenomena. In the present example, the three respondents in each family would create this variation. Estimates could then be derived concerning the effect of traits and methods on the observed scores (for examples, see Kline, 2004). For present purposes, however, we compare the correlation pattern found for families with girls to the pattern found for families with boys.

Let the correlation matrix of the rating variables be labeled M. The correlation matrix of the families with girls is M_g, and the correlation matrix of the families with boys is M_b. Now, if we propose that the structures of the reported perceptions of adolescent children and their parents are identical, we posit that $M_g = M_b$. The proper null hypothesis for this proposition is $M = M_g = M_b$, where M indicates the population correlation matrix that, under the null hypothesis, both M_g and M_b were drawn from. The residuals for this two-group model are $M - M_b$ and $M - M_g$.

According to the hierarchical steps listed earlier, the strictest model is the one that proposes that all estimated parameters as well as the residuals are identical. Specifically, this model proposes that $M = M_g = M_b$ and that $M - M_b = M - M_g$. This model poorly represents the present data. We obtain a goodness-of-fit (GFI) score of 0.88 for the girl sample, the overall χ^2 is 65.93 ($df = 45$; $p = .023$), and the overall root mean square error of approximation (RMSEA) is 0.31. None of these values is in support of the strict model. In particular, the RMSEA score is far from the desired 0.05. In favor of the model is only the overall GFI = 0.92. Still, there is ample reason to reject this model.

To see which modifications are necessary to obtain a satisfactory model fit, we retracted the *invariant* option for four residuals, and we relaxed the invariant option also for four correlations, all in the boys group. Specifically, we freed the following four correlations: son-father correlation of adjustment ratings, son-father correlation of family adjustment and adaptability ratings, the correlation of fathers' perceptions of adaptability and cohesion ratings, and the correlation of mothers' perceptions of cohesion and adjustment. This model contains elements of hierarchical levels 2, 3, and 4. It describes the data very well. We obtain a GFI for girls of 0.96. The overall χ^2 is 29.33 ($df = 37$; $p = .81$). The overall RMSEA is 0.067 (indicating an

TABLE 21.4 Correlation Matrices for Family Functioning Variables at Time 1

Block 1: Family Adjustment

1	.09	.49	.47	.02	.07	.50	.26	.00
.01	1	.59	.06	.63	.48	.04	.20	−.07
.12	.29	1	.15	.57	.54	.08	.30	.08

Block 2: Family Cohesion

.61	.05	.24	1	.03	.21	.53	.14	.04
.03	.64	.18	−.09	1	.64	.01	.25	.07
−.05	.57	.18	.12	.47	1	.08	.20	.02

Block 3: Family Adaptability

.17	−.02	.01	.51	−.10	.16	1	.03	−.07
.12	.48	.29	.16	.56	.47	.01	1	.64
.15	.12	−.12	.26	.18	.40	.15	.43	1

acceptable fit), and the overall GFI is 0.95. The improvement from the strictest to this more relaxed model is significant ($\chi^2 = 36.60$; or $df = 8$; $p < .01$). We thus retain the modified model.

This result can be interpreted as follows. In general, at Time 1, the degree of similarity of adolescents' and their parents' rating of family functioning is no higher than moderate. In addition, there are clear gender differences in the following four structural elements:

1. The father-son correlation of perceptions of family adjustment is lower than the father-daughter correlation.
2. The correlation between the girls' perceptions of family adjustment and adaptability is higher than for the boys' perceptions.
3. In the girls' group, the correlation between fathers' perceptions of adaptability and cohesion is lower than in the boys group.
4. The correlation between mothers' perceptions of cohesion and adjustment is lower in the girls' than in the boys' families.

Interestingly, and this result was reported already by Ohannessian et al. (1994), it also seems that the correlations in the boys' families are, on average, lower than in the girls' families. This result makes one wonder whether the instruments used to rate family functioning are equally valid for girls and boys in this age group of 11- to 12-year-olds.

Both sets of results, the structural differences and the differences in the magnitude of the correlations, are of importance from the perspective of person-oriented analysis. It is not just the case that mean ratings differ (Ohannessian et al., 1994). It is also the case that the structure of rating elements differs across boy and girl families. One thus can doubt that dimensional identity exists. That is, one can doubt that the ratings in the two family groups have the same dimensional structure.

If indeed there is no correspondence between the dimensional structures of the ratings, mean comparisons are hardly valid. We thus have to conclude that the earlier results reported by Ohannessian et al. (1994) for this age bracket have to be interpreted with caution. The instruments used to assess the parental and adolescent perceptions of family functioning may be differentially valid for boy and girl families. Specifically, it seems that whereas the correlations of the girls' ratings and the correlations of the parental ratings are about equal in magnitude, the corresponding correlations for boy families are lower. We thus suspect that boys in particular harbor different concepts of

family functioning than girls and parents. Considering the implications of discord (see later discussion), this result needs further study because discord can be observed at the level of magnitude of ratings but also at the structural level.

It may very well be that this lack of structural identity has a developmental aspect to it in that boys may grow to use the same structure of family functioning as girls and parents. If this is the case, the comparison of the correlation matrices at the second point in time will show fewer discrepancies. Table 21.5 displays the same correlation matrices as Table 21.4, based on the data from Time 2.

In comparison with the correlations at Time 1 (Table 21.4), the correlations at Time 2 are generally higher in both groups. In addition, they are of about equal magnitude in both groups. This is most important from a differential validity perspective. When the correlations are equal in magnitude, one can assume that the validity of the instruments used in this study is, at Time 2, no longer gender-specific.

We now ask whether the correlation matrices for girl families are, at Time 2, also structurally more similar to the correlation matrices for boy families. As in the analysis of the correlations in Table 21.4, we begin with the strict model that requires all parameters to be equal. That is, we begin with the model that hypothesizes that $M_g = M_b$ and $M - M_g = M - M_b$. This model fits poorly. We obtain GFI = 0.86 for girls, an overall $\chi^2 = 116.33$ ($df = 45$; $p < .01$), an overall RMSEA = 0.13, and overall GFI = 0.89. These results are about as bad as for the correlations in Table 21.4. However, only half the number of modifications was needed to obtain a model that describes the data well. Only one correlation in the boy families needed to be allowed to differ from the corresponding correlation in the girl families (the correlation between mothers' and their boys' perceptions of family cohesion), and one residual

TABLE 21.5 Correlation Matrices for Family Functioning Variables at Time 2

Block 1: Family Adjustment

1	.26	.07	.58	.03	−.05	.29	−.31	−.02
.30	1	.32	.24	.35	.17	.06	.13	.02
.20	.41	1	.09	.12	.51	.03	.12	.49

Block 2: Family Cohesion

.63	.14	.21	1	.26	.21	.60	−.09	.00
.38	.72	.29	.07	1	.33	.29	.22	.33
.03	.40	.60	.19	.52	1	.05	.20	.36

Block 3: Family Adaptability

.40	.02	−.03	.56	.02	.06	1	.09	.12
.40	.26	.14	.27	.55	.25	.25	1	.49
.35	.03	.11	.32	.08	.13	.37	.52	1

covariance in the boys' group and two in the girls' group needed to be freed. With these modifications, we arrived at a well-fitting model. We obtained GFI = 0.95 for girls, the overall χ^{-2} = 45.58 (df = 41; p = .29), the overall RMSEA = 0.015 (indicating exact fit), and the overall GFI = 0.93.

From these results, we conclude that, at Time 2, the structural differences between ratings in girl families and ratings in boy families are minimal. In addition, they are reduced as compared to the first observation point. Regardless of whether this change in structural comparability reflects development, differential responses to repeated administration of the same instruments, or both, these small differences do not prevent one to directly compare the correlations and means. The mean comparisons performed by Ohannessian et al. (1994; Ohannessian, Lerner, Lerner, & von Eye, 2000) can thus be defended. Ohannessian et al. had reported that mean differences exist. Both boys and girls reported lower levels of family cohesion than did their parents. Girls also perceived lower levels of family adjustment than did both parents. Discrepancies in perceptions of family functioning were also related to adolescents' reported increased levels of depression and anxiety, in particular for girls.

In general, we see that level of ratings and structure of ratings are independent of each other. Even if the structure is perceived in the same way, there can be mean differences. If construct validity is established using correlation patterns, then there is a hierarchy in analytic procedures. If there are substantial differences between correlation or covariance structures, then mean differences may be hard to interpret, because differences in covariance structures may indicate different interpretations of items in questionnaires or tests. Therefore, structural equivalence or identity needs to be established before hypotheses concerning mean comparisons are meaningfully entertained.

From the perspective of person-oriented research, we note that groups of individuals can differ in any parameter. These include means, standard deviations, higher-order moments, covariances, covariance structures, factorial structures, factor loadings, and factor loading patterns. Each of these needs to be tested for equivalence across groups before dimensional identity can be considered fully established.

SOME COMPUTER PROGRAMS FOR CARRYING OUT PERSON-ORIENTED ANALYSES

Many of the analyses discussed in this chapter can be accomplished with a sophisticated use of the standard statis-

tical packages such as SPSS and SAS. The most extensive package for cluster analysis is the CLUSTAN package (Wishart, 1987). All LICUR-type analyses, as well as ISOA and TYFO, can be performed using the SLEIPNER package, which was developed especially for person-oriented analyses (Bergman & El-Khouri, 1998; Bergman et al., 2003). SLEIPNER also contains modules for the exact analysis of single cells in contingency tables. Packages especially designed for CFA have been developed by von Eye (2001) and Krauth (1993). Waller and Meehl (1998) indicate programs for performing taxometric analyses, and Collins and Wugalter (1992) have created a program for carrying out LTA.

DISCUSSION

In this concluding section we discuss person-oriented approach from a number of different perspectives and point to future paths.

The Need for Person-Oriented Strategies in Developmental Psychopathology

By now, the reader is familiar with a variety of person-oriented strategies that can be used to carry out research in the field of developmental psychopathology. What they have in common is that the focus of analysis is not on the variable, studied across individuals, but rather on the individual as an integrated organism, as captured by the available information. In an interindividual context, this usually means that, in one way or another, information is searched for categories of subjects where each category is homogeneous in a number of variables considered simultaneously and across time.

It has been said repeatedly that we need to move away from studying associations between variables and instead study mechanisms if we want to increase our understanding of developmental phenomena (see, e.g., Magnusson, 1988; Rutter, 2004). It is our belief that this is especially true in the field of developmental psychopathology. We have learned a great deal about basic relationships by studying simple developmental associations, but to further advance our knowledge about the processes and to formulate theories that explain them we need to use approaches that are *theoretically informative*. By this we mean that the results are interpretable in such a way that estimated parameter values, result structures, and so on have an affinity to the theoretical concepts believed to hold (see Richters, 1997).

For instance, if it is believed that continuous functional interactions operate and crystallize in typical syndromes of psychopathology, a methodological approach should be used that reflects this. We believe a person-oriented strategy, appropriately carried out, in many situations can produce theoretically informative results for understanding developmental mechanisms.

A person-oriented research strategy has been criticized from mainly two perspectives. The first line of criticism has its starting point in an acceptance of the variable-oriented research paradigm and a belief that the standard methods used in this paradigm are (almost always) valid and useful and provide a rather complete toolbox. To give just one example: It is believed by some that a structural equation approach, studying linear relations over time, would, if competently executed on good data, give in-depth information about the process in which psychopathology is formed. Different models could be tested and the results would provide valuable information for advancing theories in the field. According to this extreme variable-oriented perspective, there is no real need for other types of approaches. We believe such a rejection of person-oriented research strategies out of complacency is misplaced and dangerous. In this chapter, we have strongly argued that, from a holistic-interactionistic paradigm, it is quite problematic to carry out research on the developmental processes of psychopathology at the group level that rely on linear models and on the study of relations between pairs of variables. Then one has to make strong assumptions about the process under study, assumptions that, in many situations, are hard to defend. We do not live in a linear world; linear models are used mainly for reasons of mathematical convenience and not because they correspond to the dynamics believed to hold for the processes we are interested in (cf. Brown, 1995).

The second line of criticism against using a person-oriented research strategy focuses on problems with the methodological implementation of this approach. Thus, the criticism is not against the strategy as such but against the means of carrying it out. This type of skepticism must be taken seriously. Undoubtedly, there are difficult issues that must be handled satisfactorily to carry out a successful person-oriented analysis. In the following, a number of such issues are discussed.

Establishing the Trustworthiness of the Results from a Classification Analysis

In this section, we discuss how to establish the trustworthiness of a classification obtained in a developmental set-

ting. We do this from the starting point that a cluster analysis-based method has been used to produce the basic classifications, but much of the reasoning also holds when other types of classification methods have been used. The presentation is largely a summary of work by Bergman et al. (2003). Admittedly, this overview is restricted to the present authors' perspectives; for a broader overview, the reader should refer to Blashfield (1980), El-Khouri (2001), Meehl (1992), and Milligan (1980, 1981, 1996).

Let us start with the examination of the results of a single cluster analysis, which is the basic building block in most types of developmental classifications. A number of procedures can be carried out to establish the trustworthiness of this cluster solution:

- The homogeneity of the clusters is studied (i.e., to what extent the cluster means in the variables represent the individual profiles belonging to each cluster). Two ways of studying the homogeneity are:
  a. To compute the averaged squared Euclidean distances between all members in a cluster. For the whole sample and standardized variables (i.e., the one-cluster solution), this coefficient is 2.00. A value below 1.00 for a cluster is sometimes regarded as a minimum requirement and a value below 0.50 is often regarded as desirable.
  b. To compute the percentage of the total error sum of squares that is explained by the cluster solution (EESS). Bergman (1998) suggested that a value of at least 67% is often desirable. Of course, there are other indices that measure the "quality" of a cluster solution or a whole classification tree. For instance, the point biseral correlation and the gamma coefficient could be used for that purpose (see the sources mentioned earlier for details).

- Whether a model of no relationships can be rejected is investigated. It can be studied if the cluster solution shows evidence of being a "real structure." A cluster analysis will find some structure even in random data, and we may want to dismiss the possibility that the reported cluster solution is compatible with such a trivial null hypothesis. For this purpose, a significance test procedure of EESS (or some other measure of cluster homogeneity) can be used that is based on data simulation. Artificial data are produced that are of the same type as the real data but where all relationships between the variables have been wiped out. It is then tested if the EESS is higher for the real data set than for the artificial data sets. This testing is, in principle, slightly similar to the significance testing of a correlation coefficient; it is described in Bergman et al. (2003).

- The stability of a cluster solution can be studied when the method for cluster analysis and the sample are varied. With regard to sample size, as can be expected, the detailed results from a cluster analysis are not very stable to sampling variation if the sample is small (Milligan, 1980). Therefore, a split-half analysis demands a certain initial sample size, say 400 to 500 subjects. For smaller samples, one might have to accept a less satisfactory sampling variation study and, for instance, rerun the results on a random three-fourths of the original sample. To also study the effects on the results of method variation, another method can be chosen. For instance, beta-flexible cluster analysis could be used with the parameter set to, say, −0.15. The results of the original cluster analysis are then compared to the results obtained after the method variation was implemented. In principle, two types of comparisons can be made: The centroids of the two cluster solutions are compared, using multidimensional scaling or some other method to see if the same typical profiles are obtained or if the focus is on the quality of the assignment of subjects to clusters, for instance, the Rand index is used to compare the classifications (see El-Khouri, 2001, for overviews of different coefficients for comparing cluster solutions). It is also possible to use the classification rules generated by the use of a cluster analysis of one sample to classify another equivalent sample and then compare these results to those obtained by directly cluster analyzing the equivalent sample.

- We can obtain some idea of the power of the cluster solution to account for the linear correlations between the variables that constitute the value profile that was studied in the cluster analysis. Lazarsfeld (Lazarsfeld & Henry, 1968) has suggested that one criterion for a "real" latent class is that, within a class, all the correlations between the variables should vanish (local independence). Following his line of reasoning, one can study if the correlations among the variables in the profile are strongly reduced or disappear when the correlation analysis is done *within* each cluster. This would indicate that the cluster solution can "explain" the correlations between the variables.

- Differences between the clusters can be studied in validation variables. If the reported classification structure is informative, we should find differences between the clusters in the theoretically expected direction for important validation variables.

If the longitudinal classification is done in one step, then these procedures are directly applicable. If the classification is first done separately at each point in time and then the classifications are linked, as in LICUR, then the establishment of the trustworthiness of the final classification structure is more complex. A first step could be that these procedures are applied to each cross-sectional classification separately. The whole LICUR sequence of analyses could also be rerun after varying the sample and method.

However helpful these procedures are for establishing the trustworthiness of a classification, they do not directly answer the question of whether, in some sense, a true or "natural" classification has been obtained. This difficult issue was briefly discussed in a preceding section when Meehl's procedures for taxometric analysis were introduced. Our own position is rather pragmatic. If a classification has been shown to be trustworthy and if it leads to theoretically meaningful predictions, then it is useful and deserves to be taken seriously. As Meehl (1992) pointed out, it is difficult—and may not even be necessary—to define what is a natural cluster or taxon, and we might have to be satisfied with some provisional definition.

Combining a Variable-Oriented and a Person-Oriented Approach

Many experienced researchers would probably agree with us that the choice between a variable-oriented and a person-oriented research strategy cannot be made without reference to the specific problem under study, as discussed in various places in this chapter. We would add that, in some situations, it might be useful to combine these two research strategies in the same study for a number of reasons:

- In this way, a binocular view may be obtained. The results and theories related to a variable-oriented and a person-oriented approach often refer to quite different perspectives on reality. However, in some cases, they can relate to the same scientific problem, and if the results of these two different methodological approaches then support each other, it increases the confidence that the findings are not method-bound. For instance, the claim for having found an important externalizing personality dimension obtains additional general value if it is found not only by a factor analysis, showing high loadings in the relevant variables, but if a personality type is also found, characterized by a profile that is high (or low) in all the relevant variables.

- As mentioned earlier, an initial variable-oriented study of the relationships in data can be of use for identifying relevant variables and obtaining a preliminary picture of how the variables to be studied are related. This information can be helpful in identifying the relevant variable profile to be studied in a person-oriented analysis.

- Interactions and nonlinearities can sometimes to a certain extent be handled by a variable-oriented approach, for instance, by applying nonlinear regression analysis— if one knows beforehand what interactions to specify. If one does not know that, then one might carry out a preliminary person-oriented pattern analysis to obtain information about likely interactions in the data set and use that information to define the interaction terms.

Classes and Continua

Physics advanced when the categorical approach of the scholastics was replaced with a dimensional approach, based on measurement and mathematics. Making the jump to psychiatry and, especially, to psychology, the use of objective measurement techniques and of statistics, based on the analysis of variables, has advanced these sciences beyond what would have been possible if research had relied on a categorical, typological approach (see Ekman, 1951, for a critique of the old typological approaches). However, these facts should not be overinterpreted, as pointed out by, for instance, Bergman (1998) and Meehl (1992). In defense of the judicious use of a modern classificatory approach, the following can be said:

- In contrast to what is the case for the old typological approaches, the input in a modern typological analysis is usually the same dimensional data that are used for standard analyses. This means that the classification can be done objectively and that the results can be checked against those obtained using other methods.
- All data analysis implies some sort of simplification or summary; some "model" is always produced to represent the data. Therefore, a typological representation should not be compared to the original data set and found deficient if it does not cover all aspects of these data. Rather, the comparison should be between the typological representation and an alternative standard model of the data, for instance, a regression model or a structural equation model, and with regard to which representation best reflects the essential characteristics of the data.
- A modern classificatory approach should, in many situations, be regarded as a method for obtaining information about the effects on the studied system of higher-order interactions and nonlinear relationships, information that cannot be obtained by standard variable-oriented methods. This does not mean that the classificatory ap-

proach should be regarded as the end point. Rather, in our opinion, in the future it will become possible in many situations to apply nonlinear dynamic systems models that will be superior in certain respects: superior in that they can provide a powerful mathematical model of the process of psychopathology development that takes continuous interactions into account and that provides a model of the change process—in contrast to most statistical models that primarily provide a static model of data referring to discrete time points (Bergman, 2002).

We believe we can learn from the history of science with regard to the categorical or classificatory approach versus the variable-oriented dimensional approach that the severe limitations of the early types of the first approach naturally led to a major shift in focus to the other type of approach. Now, as our knowledge base has advanced and we have become more interested in sophisticated questions involving interactions and so on, the limitations of standard variable-oriented approaches become obvious. For certain classes of problems, it is then natural to move on to a modern typological approach. No doubt, more advanced dimensional and typological approaches will emerge, and both classes of approaches will be needed.

It must be pointed out that when we reviewed classificatory approaches we focused on methods that provide mutually exclusive clusters. In, for instance, latent class analysis, the allocation of subjects to classes is probabilistic and there also are other types of methods that allow for overlapping clusters: A subject can be regarded as belonging to more than one cluster. However, allowing for overlap can give complex results that are difficult to interpret. If a weight is given for each subject, indicating his or her degree of closeness to each cluster, then we are, in a way, back at a variable-oriented representation but of a rather strange kind, with a multidimensional density, called a cluster, being treated as a unidimensional variable.

Observation versus Theory Testing

Most researchers would probably agree that in the initial stages of a new field, careful open-minded observation is of crucial importance. Help from theories in what to look for is, of course, important but, as formulated by Bergman and Magnusson (1997, p. 315), "Theories prematurely transformed into statistical models of data can become blinkers. If the model window opens at the wrong place, the interesting things may be missed." This is by no means a new point. It has been made many times before by, for instance, Cronbach (1975), Greenwald, Pratkanis, Lieppe, and Baumgardner (1986), and Magnusson (1992). We would argue that one is usually at this initial stage when applying a person-oriented approach to understand a developmental process in the psychopathology field. Therefore, the use of methods that are descriptively oriented—in the sense that they do not attempt to construct a comprehensive model of the data—should be regarded as natural in many cases and often more appropriate than premature model-based approaches at this stage. Besides, also with so-called descriptive classification approaches, procedures exist for testing theoretical predictions of, for instance, developmental streams.

In a person-oriented framework, the following sequence of analyses often seems to be natural: (1) preliminary variable-based analyses to identify operating factors, create measurement models, and aid in the formulation of relevant patterns; (2) predominantly descriptive pattern-based analyses, including testing that the results are consistent with theoretical expectations; and (3) predominantly model-based pattern analyses for formulating and testing models of person-oriented theories.

Prediction and the Person-Oriented Approach

We believe that it is dangerous and misleading to set up predictive power as the main criterion for a successful theory or method. This point was made by Magnusson (1985) and Bergman and Magnusson (1997). They discussed the issue in relation to the empirical examples they gave in their article that dealt with the study of patterns of adjustment problems from childhood to adulthood and pointed out that the following very simple argument is often used against a pattern approach: The prediction of an adult maladjustment variable can be (almost) maximized by using a linear model, and the prediction is usually not improved by considering more elaborated models. Therefore, the connection of typical patterns of childhood problems to typical patterns of adult problems is not likely to lead to more precise predictions of an outcome variable, and until that has been shown, it is to be regarded an unnecessarily complex approach.

To this argument it can be added that because linear models are optimized to maximize prediction, they are likely to do better than other approaches that are not optimized for this purpose. However, this is true only with modification. The success of the prediction can be measured in different ways, and usually the square of the correlation between the actual value and the predicted value is used for that purpose. This is a definition that largely

has arisen out of mathematical convenience, and it happens to be the one that the linear prediction equation is built to maximize.

The relevancy of the prediction argument, of course, stands and falls with the assumption that prediction is the goal. As underlined by Magnusson (1985), this is a simplistic perspective. To be able to predict a phenomenon is neither sufficient nor necessary for understanding it. Meteorologists understand fairly well what factors regulate the weather and its dynamics, and yet, long-term prediction of the weather on a specific day is inherently unreliable due to the principle of infinite sensitivity to the initial conditions leading eventually to chaos. In spite of this, few would, for that reason, call meteorology a primitive science. We can also show that it is possible to have powerful relations across time for patterns and yet to have all pairwise correlations be zero (see, e.g., Bergman, 1988a, 1998). Are these interactions irrelevant just because no *linear* prediction can be made? Bergman and Magnusson (1997, p. 316) summed up their arguments against prediction as the main goal in the following way: "We have pointed in this article to typical patterns of adjustment problems in childhood that are connected to typical patterns of problems in adulthood. The value of such results cannot be measured by some prediction coefficient pertaining to a linear model alien to a pattern approach."

The Boundaries of Development

It is an interesting thought that, as much as we want to study what happens through development and that these findings can tell us important things about the process of developmental psychopathology, we can also learn about this process by finding out what does *not* happen in development. Together, these two complementary perspectives teach us about the boundaries of development. The issue was touched on in the empirical example about studying white spots given in an earlier section.

Of course, this idea is by no means new. For instance, Lewin (1933, p. 598) discussed boundary conditions in terms of "region of freedom of movement," and Valsiner (1984) pointed out that a person's observed behavioral variability is only a fraction of its possible range of variability. An early advocate of the importance of this perspective was Lienert (Krauth & Lienert, 1982), who, within the framework of CFA, introduced the term antitype for an observed value combination that occurred more rarely than one should expect by chance. Bergman and Magnusson (1997, p. 309) introduced the term white spots for patterns that rarely occurred (but were not necessarily antitypes). These white spots could be searched for using different methods. Some ways of doing this cross-sectionally are presented in the methods section (searching for antitypes, identification of a residue, etc.). It can also be made developmentally, looking for pathways of pattern development that for some reason are closed, using, for instance, the LICUR procedure.

This reasoning may be of special relevance for the study of psychopathology as it is at the boundaries of what can occur when "normal" development has gone off track.

CONCLUSION AND FUTURE PERSPECTIVE

What is psychopathology from a person-oriented perspective? Does this perspective lead to a radically different view on the important phenomena collected under that heading? We would argue that this may not be the case as the theoretical framework that we have put forward in this chapter is rather akin to the theoretical thinking of most researchers who study developmental psychopathology. (It is another matter that the approach put forward here is at variance with most common *methodological* approaches that are used in the developmental psychopathology field, as these are variable-oriented and tend not to correspond to the interactionistic notions about the psychopathology process that most researchers have.) In this context and from the vantage point of the person-oriented perspective, Bergman and Magnusson (1997) made the following observations.

Psychopathology is a set of states of the dynamic systems describing the development of psychiatric health, states that usually are not common in the general population and that are in certain ways maladaptive. Many such states tend to be "recognized" by the individual's dynamic system as being nonoptimal. Hence, they often should be expected to be transient and not stable. We therefore often expect fluctuating symptomatology through development, even through short time spans, and these changes merit investigation. They should be contrasted to more stable psychopathological states, characterized by symptoms that often occur in typical syndromes of maladaptive behavior, feelings, and so on. Such states, indicating a specific typical pattern of psychopathology that exhibits individual stability across time, must have powerful factors that keep throwing the individuals off track in such a consistent way. It is a surmise that there are probably only a very limited number of constellations of operating factors that can accomplish this for a certain syndrome, and only a very limited number of syndromes that show long-term stability. To

identify these, as we discussed, studying both typical patterns (e.g., using classification analysis, analyzing dense points) and white spots seems to be a promising avenue of research in the field of developmental psychopathology. The importance of studying different types of variables in psychopathology, as advocated by Cicchetti (1993), supports this focus on patterns of operating factors.

In spite of possible technical imperfections and so on, the person-oriented strategy has a reasonable correspondence to many researchers' theoretical conceptualizations of how the phenomena operate. We claim that, in many situations, this is not the case with standard variable-oriented methods, and that this correspondence—the match between problem and method—should be the single most decisive factor when selecting a methodological approach (Magnusson, Bergman, Rudinger, & Törestad, 1991). Richters (1997) has eloquently argued for the existence of what he calls the developmentalist's dilemma, by which he means the contrast between the open systems theoretical concepts in developmental psychopathology and the closed systems approach usually applied, taken from mainstream developmental psychology. Although he means something more and different from the mere application of a person-oriented research strategy, we claim that this approach to a certain extent answers his call for a research paradigm that is more aligned to the complexity of the developmental phenomena we are interested in.

Already today there exists a large toolbox of useful person-oriented methods to carry out research on developmental psychopathology, both model-based and more exploratory. The infusion of ideas, models, and technical solutions from the field of nonlinear dynamics will also give a powerful impetus to a more sophisticated study of psychopathological processes. In doing this, it is possible that we will rediscover the primary importance of studying the singe individual, not only as case studies in clinical work but also in rigorous research aiming at revealing mechanisms involved in the emergence of psychopathological conditions. In fact, we feel uneasy about the present overreliance on the study of interindividual differences as the road to understanding influences that operate at the level of the single individual. As we discussed earlier, for this to be a valid approach, you have to make a number of assumptions. A challenge for the next generation of methodologists will be to find new ways of combining the study of several single individuals with a sound strategy for how to generalize the findings.

An aspect of the person-oriented approach that partly overlaps what has been presented in this chapter has to do with the different perspective taken with regard to making inferences to individuals from group data, as compared to what is typically the case in the variable-oriented approach. The latter approach proceeds under the assumption that samples are typically drawn from one large parent population. This population is typically normally distributed. Samples are considered representatives of the population, and sample statistics are sufficient, efficient, and unbiased estimates of population parameters. In contrast, the assumptions that need to be made for person-oriented research include multiple populations, nonnormal distributions, and often nonlinear variable relationships (Bergman, 1998). Research may qualify as at least partly person-oriented if researchers focus on the establishment and comparison of homogeneous groups of individuals that differ in function and development even if no explicit study is made of patterns of operating characteristics. These groups are either defined as a priori, for example, the women in violent relationships versus women in nonviolent relationships, or need to be found in larger samples, for example, the trajectories of recovery in alcoholics. In this context, in a discussion with Molenaar (2004), von Eye (2004) noted an important implication of the wider adoption of person-oriented scholarship. It implies an increase in the number of models at the data level that are needed for valid description of human functioning and development. If one model is insufficient to describe the whole population, more than one model is needed. Some of these models will differ fundamentally, for instance, in the number of factors needed to describe a phenomenon or in the structural elements of a path model. The means of statistics can be used to decide whether a different model needs to be specified for a subgroup of individuals, or whether a model needs to be updated because of the developments in a population over the course of historical time.

With regard to future methodological developments, von Eye and Schuster (2000) identified six general trends for the future:

1. There will be an increase in the number of available statistical methods, as new statistical methods are being developed at a very rapid pace.
2. Substantive thinking triggers the development of new methods of data analysis.
3. Statistical methods become increasingly flexible.
4. Computers do the thinking. Expert systems and built-in checks of whether the conditions for proper application of statistical methods are fulfilled will make the selection of methods of analysis easier, if not foolproof.

5. There will be new research paradigms, such as the person-oriented approach. These new paradigms will lead to statements that are more valid and describe a larger portion of the population. However, these statements will also be more complex, and they require more effort.
6. Statistical methods will be custom-tailored to substantive questions.

These six trends indicate that the emergence and development of new paradigms and research questions in the context of person-oriented scholarship has a transactional, reciprocal relationship with ongoing efforts to develop more useful methods of data analysis. Thus, there will be cross-fertilization to the benefit of both the fields of statistics and substantive research. The person orientation as a research paradigm is also constantly being developed itself. For instance, von Eye and Bogat (in press) discussed the relationship of person-oriented scholarship to differential psychology. The authors note that differential psychology is based on the assumption that all individuals can be placed on different locations of the same scales. In contrast, person-oriented concepts go a step further in that the idea that the same scales are applicable to everybody is challenged.

Perhaps the most important vehicle for promoting the person-oriented approach is a good training of young researchers in it. This training must comprise three parts: (1) introduction to the theory behind the approach and the motivation for it, (2) presentation of selected methods and training in how to use them, and (3) the provision of good empirical examples of the use of the person-oriented approach. Today it is a problem that few universities have methodologists who are experts in this approach. While waiting for this situation to change, it is an important duty for those of us who have this expertise to arrange such courses, preferably as internationally open workshops. Then we cannot underline enough the importance of (1) when such a course is planned. Often, students want to go straight to learning and applying an exciting new methodological tool, but if the theory that motivates its use is not understood, the chances are slim that good research will come out of it.

REFERENCES

Abraham, F. D., & Gilgen, A. R. (Eds.). (1995). *Chaos theory in psychology*. London: Praeger.

Asendorpf, J. B. (2000). A person-centered approach to personality and social relationships: Findings from the Berlin Relationship Study. In L. R. Bergman, R. B. Cairns, L.-G. Nilsson, & L. Nystedt (Eds.), *De-*

velopmental science and the holistic approach (pp. 281–298). Mahwah, NJ: Erlbaum.

Bailey, K. D. (1994). *Typologies and taxonomies.* New York: Sage.

Baltes, P. B., Lindenberger, U., & Staudinger, U. M. (1997). Life-span theory in developmental psychology. In W. Damon (Series Ed.) & R. M. Lerner (Vol. Ed.), *Handbook of child psychology: Theoretical models of human development* (Vol. 1, pp. 1029–1143). New York: Wiley.

Barton, S. (1994). Chaos, self-organization, and psychology. *American Psychologist, 49,* 5–15.

Bauer, D. J. (2003). Estimating multilevel linear models as structural equation models. *Journal of Educational and Behavioral Statistics, 28,* 135–167.

Belbin, L., Faith, D. P., & Milligan, G. W. (1992). A comparison of two approaches to beta-flexible clustering. *Multivariate Behavioral Research, 27,* 417–433.

Bentler, P. (1985). *EQS: Structural Equations Program manual.* Encino, CA: Multivariate Software.

Bergman, L. R. (1988a). Modeling reality: Some comments. In M. Rutter (Ed.), *Studies of psychosocial risk* (pp. 354–366). Cambridge, England: Cambridge University Press.

Bergman, L. R. (1988b). You can't classify all of the people all of the time. *Multivariate Behavioral Research, 23,* 425–441.

Bergman, L. R. (1995). *Describing individual development using i-state sequence analysis (ISSA)* (Report No. 805). Department of Psychology, Stockholm University, Sweden.

Bergman, L. R. (1998). A pattern-oriented approach to studying individual development: Snapshots and processes. In R. B. Cairns, L. R. Bergman, & J. Kagan (Eds.), *Methods and models for studying the individual* (pp. 83–121). Thousand Oaks, CA: Sage.

Bergman, L. R. (1999). Studying individual patterns of development using i-states as objects analysis (ISOA). *Biometrical Journal, 41,* 753–770.

Bergman, L. R. (2000). The application of a person-oriented approach: Types and clusters. In L. R. Bergman, R. B. Cairns, L.-G. Nilsson, & L. Nystedt (Eds.), *Developmental science and the holistic approach* (pp. 137–154). Mahwah, NJ: Erlbaum.

Bergman, L. R. (2001). A person approach in research on adolescence: Some methodological challenges. *Journal of Adolescent Research, 16*(1), 28–53.

Bergman, L. R. (2002). Studying processes: Some methodological considerations. In L. Pulkkinen & A. Caspi (Eds.), *Paths to successful development: Personality in the life course* (pp. 177–199). Cambridge, MA: Cambridge University Press.

Bergman, L. R., & El-Khouri, B. M. (1987). EXACON: A Fortran 77 program for the exact analysis of single cells in a contingency table. *Educational and Psychological Measurement, 47,* 155–161.

Bergman, L. R., & El-Khouri, B. M. (1998). *SLEIPNER: A statistical package for pattern-oriented analyses—Version II* [Manual]. Stockholm, Sweden: Stockholm University, Department of Psychology.

Bergman, L. R., & El-Khouri, B. M. (1999). Studying individual patterns of development using i-states as objects analysis (ISOA). *Biometrical Journal, 41,* 753–770.

Bergman, L. R., & El-Khouri, B. M. (2001). Developmental processes and the modern typological perspective. *European Psychologist, 6,* 177–186.

Bergman, L. R., & Magnusson, D. (1991). Stability and change in patterns of extrinsic adjustment problems. In D. Magnusson, L. R. Bergman, G. Rudinger, & B. Törestad (Eds.), *Problems and methods in longitudinal research: Stability and change* (pp. 323–346). Cambridge, England: Cambridge University Press.

Bergman, L. R., & Magnusson, D. (1997). A person-oriented approach in research on developmental psychopathology. *Development and Psychopathology, 9,* 291–319.

Bergman, L. R., Magnusson, D., & El-Khouri, B. M. (2003). Studying individual development in interindividual context: A person-oriented approach. In D. Magnusson (Series Ed.), *Paths through life* (Vol. 4). Mahwah, NJ: Erlbaum.

Bishop, Y. M. M., Fienberg, S. E., & Holland, P. W. (1975). *Discrete multivariate analysis: Theory and practice.* Cambridge, MA: MIT Press.

Blashfield, R. K. (1980). The growth of cluster analysis: Tryon, Ward and Johnson. *Multivariate Behavioral Research, 15,* 439–458.

Block, J. (1971). *Lives through time.* Berkeley, CA: Bancroft Books.

Boker, S. M., & Graham, J. (1998). A dynamic systems analysis of adolescent substance use. *Multivariate Behavioral Research, 33,* 479–507.

Boker, S. M., & Nesselroade, J. R. (2002). A method for modeling the intrinsic dynamics of intraindividual variability: Recovering the parameters of simulated oscillators in multiwave data. *Multivariate Behavioral Research, 37,* 127–160.

Brown, C. (1995). Chaos and catastrophe theories. *Quantitative applications in the social sciences* (Vol. 107). Thousand Oaks, CA: Sage.

Bryk, A. S., & Raudenbush, S. W. (1992). *Hierachical linear models for social and behavioral research: Application and data analysis methods.* Newbury Park, CA: Sage.

Budescu, D. V. (1980). Some new measures of profile dissimilarity. *Applied Psychological Measurement, 4,* 261–272.

Cairns, R. B. (1979). *Social development: The origins and plasticity of interchanges.* San Francisco: Freeman.

Cairns, R. B., & Valsiner, J. (1984). Child psychology. *Annual Review of Psychology, 35,* 553–577.

Campbell, D. T., & Fiske, D. W. (1959). Convergent and discriminant validation by the multitrait-multimethod matrix. *Psychological Bulletin, 56,* 81–105.

Carlson, M., Earls, F., & Todd, R. D. (1988). The importance of regressive changes in the development of the nervous system: Toward a neurobiological theory of child development. *Psychiatric Developments, 1,* 1–22.

Cattell, R. B. (1957). *Personality and motivation structure and measurement.* New York: World Books.

Cicchetti, D. (1993). Developmental psychopathology: Reactions, reflections, projections. *Developmental Review, 13,* 471–502.

Cicchetti, D., & Tucker, D. (1994). Development and self-regulatory structures of the mind. *Development and Psychopathology, 6,* 533–549.

Clogg, C. C., Eliason, S. R., & Grego, J. M. (1990). Models for the analysis of change in discrete variables. In A. von Eye (Ed.), *Statistical methods in longitudinal research: Vol. II. Time series and categorical longitudinal data* (pp. 409–441). New York: Academic Press.

Colinvaux, P. (1980). *Why big fierce animals are rare.* London: Pelican Books.

Collins, L. M., & Wugalter, S. E. (1992). Latent class models for stage-sequential dynamic latent variables. *Multivariate Behavioral Research, 27,* 131–157.

Cronbach, L. J. (1975). Beyond the two disciplines of scientific psychology. *American Psychologist, 30,* 116–127.

Cronbach, L. J., & Gleser, G. C. (1953). Assessing similarity between profiles. *Psychological Bulletin, 50,* 456–473.

Edelbrock, C. (1979). Mixture model tests of hierarchical clustering algorithms: The problem of classifying everybody. *Multivariate Behavioral Research, 14,* 367–384.

Ekman, G. (1951). On typological and dimensional systems of reference in describing personality. *Acta Psychologica, 8,* 1–24.

El-Khouri, B. (2001). *Classification in a person-oriented context.* Doctoral thesis, Stockholm University, Department of Psychology, Stockholm, Sweden.

El-Khouri, B., & Bergman, L. R. (1992). *M-PREP: A Fortran 77 program for the preparatory analysis of multivariate data* (Report No. 751). Department of Psychology, Stockholm University, Sweden.

Emde, R. N. (1994). Individuality, context, and the search for meaning. *Child Development, 65,* 719–737.

Finkelstein, J. W., von Eye, A., & Preece, M. A. (1994). The relationship between aggressive behavior and puberty in normal adolescents: A longitudinal study. *Journal of Adolescent Health, 15,* 319–326.

Gangestad, S., & Snyder, M. (1985). To carve nature at its joints: On the existence of discrete classes in personality. *Psychological Review, 92,* 317–349.

Gleick, J. (1987). *Chaos: Making a new science.* New York: Penguin Books.

Goodman, L. A. (1984), *The analysis of cross-classified data having ordered categories.* Cambridge, MA: Harvard University Press.

Goodman, L. A. (1991). Measures, models, and graphical displays in the analysis of cross-classified data. *Journal of the American Statistical Association, 86,* 1085–1111.

Granic, I., & Hollenstein, T. (2003). Dynamic systems methods for models of developmental psychopathology. *Development and Psychopathology, 15,* 641–669.

Greenwald, A. G., Pratkanis, A. R., Lieppe, M. R., & Baumgardner, M. H. (1986). Under what conditions does theory obstruct research progress? *Psychological Review, 93,* 216–299.

Harré, R. (2000). Acts of living. *Science, 289,* 1303–1304.

Havránek, T., & Lienert, G. A. (1984). Local and regional versus global contingency testing. *Biometrical Journal, 26,* 483–494.

Hongxin, Z., Brooks-Gunn, J., McLanahan, S., & Singer, B. (2000). Studying the real person in developmental studies. In L. R. Bergman, R. B. Cairns, L.-G. Nilsson, & L. Nystedt (Eds.), *Developmental science and the holistic approach* (pp. 393–420). Mahwah, NJ: Erlbaum.

Hull, C. L. (1943). The problem of intervening variables in molar behavior theory. *Psychological Review, 50,* 273–291.

Jackson, A. E. (1989). *Perspectives on nonlinear dynamics* (Vol. 1). Cambridge, MA: Cambridge University Press.

Jones, C. J., & Nesselroade, J. R. (1990). Multivariate, replicated, single-subject designs and P-technique factor analysis: A selective review of the literature. *Experimental Aging Research, 16,* 171–183.

Jöreskog, K., & Sörbom, D. (1993). *LISREL 9: User's reference guide.* Chicago: Scientific Software International.

Kelso, J. A. S. (1995). *Dynamic patterns: The self-organization of brain and behavior.* Cambridge, MA: MIT Press.

Kline, R. B. (2004). *Principles and practice of structural equation modeling* (2nd ed.). New York: Guilford Press.

Krauth, J. (1993). *Einführung in die Konfigurationsfrequenzanalyse (KFA)* [Introduction to configural frequency analysis (CFA)]. Weinheim, Basel, Switzerland: Beltz, Psychologie-Verl.-Union.

Krauth, J., & Lienert, G. A. (1982). Fundamentals and modifications of configural frequency analysis (CFA). *Interdisciplinaria, 3*(1), 1–14.

Lazarsfeld, P. F., & Henry, N. W. (1968). *Latent structure analysis.* New York: Houghton Mifflin.

Lehmacher, W. (1981). A more powerful simultaneous test procedure in configural frequency analysis. *Biometrical Journal, 23,* 429–436.

Lerner, R. M., Lerner, J. V., & von Eye, A. (1988). *Early adolescent school achievement: Organismic bases* [NICHD Grant No. HD 23 229]. Washington, DC: National Institute of Child Health and Human Development.

Lewin, K. (1933). Environmental forces. In C. Murchison (Ed.), *A handbook of child psychology* (2nd ed., pp. 590–625). Worcester, MA: Clark University Press.

Lewin, K. (1936). *Principles of topological psychology* (F. Heider & G. M. Heider, Trans.). New York: McGraw-Hill.

Lienert, G. A. (1969). Die Konfigurationsfrequenzanalyse als Klassifikationsmittel in der klinischen psychologie [Configural frequency analysis or a classification method in clinical psychology]. In M. Irle (Ed.), *Bericht über den 26. Kongreß der Deutschen Gesellschaft für Psychologie 1968 in Tübingen [Proceedings of the 26th Congress of the Gesellschaft Psychological Auxiliary, 1968, in Tübingen]* (pp. 244–255). Göttingen, Germany: Hogrefe.

Lienert, G. A., & Krauth, J. (1975). Configural frequency analysis as a statistical tool for defining types. *Educational and Psychological Measurement, 35,* 231–238.

Lienert, G. A., & zur Oeveste, H. (1985). CFA as a statistical tool for developmental research. *Educational and Psychological Measurement, 45,* 301–307.

Loeber, R., Keenan, K., & Zhang, Q. (1997). Boys' experimentation and persistence in developmental pathways toward serious delinquency. *Journal of Child and Family Studies, 6,* 321–357.

Magnusson, D. (1985). Implications of an interactional paradigm for research on human development. *International Journal of Behavioral Development, 8,* 115–137.

Magnusson, D. (1988). Individual development from an interactional perspective. In D. Magnusson (Series Ed.), *Paths through life* (Vol. 1). Hillsdale, NJ: Erlbaum.

Magnusson, D. (1990). Personality development from an interactional perspective. In L. Pervin (Ed.), *Handbook of personality* (pp. 193–222). New York: Guilford Press.

Magnusson, D. (1992). Back to the phenomena: Theory, methods and statistics in psychological research. *European Journal of Personality, 6,* 1–14.

Magnusson, D. (Ed.). (1996). *The life-span development of individuals: Behavioral, neurobiological and psychosocial perspectives. A synthesis.* Cambridge, England: Cambridge University Press.

Magnusson, D. (1998a). The logic and implications of a person approach. In R. B. Cairns, L. R. Bergman, & J. Kagan (Eds.), *Methods and models for studying the individual* (pp. 33–63). Thousand Oaks, CA: Sage.

Magnusson, D. (1998b). The person in developmental research. In J. G Adair, D. Bélanger, & K. L. Dion (Eds.), *Advances in psychological sciences* (Vol. 1, pp. 495–511). Hove, England: Psychology Press.

Magnusson, D. (1999a). Holistic interactionism: A perspective for research on personality development. In L. A. Pervin & O. P. John (Eds.), *Handbook of personality: Theory and research* (2nd ed., pp. 219–247). New York: Guilford Press.

Magnusson, D. (1999b). On the individual: A person oriented approach to developmental research. *European Psychologist, 4*(4), 205–218.

Magnusson, D. (2003). The person approach: Concepts, measurement models, and research strategy. *New Directions for Child and Adolescent Development, 101,* 3–23.

Magnusson, D., & Allen, V. L. (1983). Implications and applications of an interactional perspective for human development. In D. Magnusson & V. L. Allen (Eds.), *Human development: An interactional perspective* (pp. 369–387). New York: Academic Press.

Magnusson, D., & Bergman, L. R. (1988). Individual and variable-based approaches to longitudinal research on early risk factors. In M. Rutter (Ed.), *Studies of psychosocial risk* (pp. 45–61). Cambridge, England: Cambridge University Press.

Magnusson, D., Bergman, L. R., Rudinger, G., & Törestad, B. (Eds.). (1991). *Problems and methods in longitudinal research: Stability and change.* Cambridge, England: Cambridge University Press.

Magnusson, D., & Mahoney, J. L. (2002). A holistic person approach for research on positive development. In L. G. Aspenwill & U. M.

Staudinger (Eds.), *Human strengths* (pp. 227–243). Washington, DC: American Psychological Association.

Magnusson, D., & Stattin, H. (1998). Person-context interaction theories. In W. Damon (Series Ed.) & R. M. Lerner (Vol. Ed.), *Handbook of child psychology: Theoretical models of human development* (Vol. 1, pp. 685–759). New York: Wiley.

Magnusson, D., & Törestad, B. (1993). A holistic view of personality: A model revisited. *Annual Review of Psychology, 44,* 427–452.

Maraun, M. D., Slaney, K., & Goddyn, L. (2003). An analysis of Meehl's MAXCOV-HITMAX procedure for the case of dichotomous indicators. *Multivariate Behavioral Research, 38*(1), 81–112.

Mayr, E. (1997). *This is biology.* Cambridge, MA: Belknap Press of Harvard University Press.

McArdle, J. J., & Bell, R. Q. (2000). An introduction to latent growth models for developmental data analysis. In T. D. Little, K. U. Schnabel, & J. Baumert (Eds.), *Modeling longitudinal and multilevel data: Practical issues, applied approaches, and specific examples* (pp. 69–107). Mahwah, NJ: Erlbaum.

McArdle, J. J., & Epstein, D. B. (1987). Latent growth curves within developmental structural equation models. *Child Development, 58,* 110–133.

Meehl, P. E. (1992). Factors and taxa, traits and types, differences of degree and differences in kind. *Journal of Personality, 60,* 117–174.

Meehl, P. E., & Yonce, L. J. (1992). *Taxometric analysis by the method of coherent cut kinetics* [Tech. Rep.]. Minneapolis: University of Minnesota Psychology Department.

Milligan, G. W. (1980). An examination of the effect of six types of error perturbation on fifteen clustering algorithms. *Psychometrika, 45,* 325–342.

Milligan, G. W. (1981). A Monte Carlo study of thirty internal criterion measures for cluster analyses. *Psykometrika, 46,* 187–199.

Milligan, G. W. (1996). Clustering validation: Results and implications for applied analyses. In P. Arabie, L. Hubert, & G. De Soete (Eds.), *Clustering and classification* (pp. 341–375). River Edge, NJ: World Scientific Press.

Misiak, H., & Sexton, V. (1966). *History of psychology.* New York: Grune & Stratton.

Moffitt, T. E. (1993). Adolescence-limited and life-course persistent antisocial behavior: A developmental taxonomy. *Psychological Review, 100,* 674–701.

Molenaar, P. C. M. (1985). A dynamic factor model for the analysis of multivariate time series. *Psychometrika, 50,* 181–202.

Molenaar, P. C. M. (2004). A manifesto on psychology as an idiographic science: Bringing the person back into scientific psychology: This time forever. *Measurement: Interdisciplinary Research and Perspectives, 2,* 201–218.

Molenaar, P. C. M., Huizenga, H. M., & Nesselroade, J. R. (2003). The relationship between the structure of inter-individual and intra-individual variability: A theoretical and empirical vindication of developmental systems theory. In U. M. Staudinger & U. Lindenberger (Eds.), *Understanding human development* (pp. 339–360). London: Kluwer Academic.

Morey, L. C., Blashfield, R. K., & Skinner, H. A. (1983). A comparison of cluster analysis techniques within a sequential validation framework. *Multivariate Behavioral Research, 18,* 309–329.

Mumford, M. D., & Owens, W. A. (1984). Individuality in a developmental context: Some empirical and theoretical considerations. *Human Development, 27,* 84–108.

Muthén, B. O. (1989). Latent variable modeling in heterogeneous populations. *Psychometrika, 54*(4), 557–585.

Nagin, D. S. (1999). Analyzing developmental trajectories: A semiparametric, group-based approach. *Psychological Methods, 4,* 139–157.

Nagin, D. S., & Tremblay, R. E. (2001). Analyzing developmental trajectories of distinct but related behaviors: A group-based method. *Psychological Methods, 6*(1), 18–34.

Nesselroade, J. R., & Featherman, D. L. (1991). Intraindividual variability in older adults' depression scores: Some implications for developmental theory and longitudinal research. In D. Magnusson, L. Bergman, G. Rudinger, & B. Torestad (Eds.), *Problems and methods in longitudinal research: Stability and change: Methods and models for data treatment* (pp. 47–66). Cambridge, England: Cambridge University Press.

Novikoff, A. B. (1945). The concept of integrative levels and biology. *Science, 101,* 209–215.

Ohannessian, C. M., Lerner, R. M., Lerner, J. V., & von Eye, A. (1994). A longitudinal study of perceived family adjustment and emotional adjustment in early adolescence. *Journal of Early Adolescence, 14,* 371–390.

Ohannessian, C. M., Lerner, R. M., Lerner, J. V., & von Eye, A. (2000). Adolescent-parent discrepancies in perceptions of family functioning and early adolescent self-competence. *International Journal of Behavioral Development, 24,* 362–372.

Olson, D. H., Portner, J., & Lavee, Y. (1985). *FACES III.* Unpublished manuscript, University of Minneapolis Minnesota, Family Social Science.

Pierzchala, M. (1990). A review of the state of the art in automated data editing and imputation. *Journal of Official Statistics, 6*(1) 463–475.

Pugesek, B., Tomer, A., & von Eye, A. (Eds.). (2003). *Structural equation modeling: Applications in ecological and evolutionary biology.* Cambridge, England: Cambridge University Press.

Richters, J. E. (1997). The Hubble hypothesis and the developmentalist's dilemma. *Development and Psychopathology, 9,* 193–229.

Robins, R. W., John, O. P., & Caspi, A. (1998). The typological approach to studying personality. In R. B. Cairns, L. R. Bergman, & J. Kagan (Eds.), *Methods and models for studying the individual* (pp. 135–157). New York: Sage.

Robins, R. W., John, O. P., Caspi, A., Moffit, T. E., & Stouthamer-Loeber, M. (1996). Resilient, overcontrolled, and undercontrolled boys: Three replicable personality types. *Journal of Personality and Social Psychology, 70,* 157–171.

Rooswall, T. (2003, April). Lecture at the Swedish Academy of Sciences. Stockholm, Sweden.

Rutter, M. (2004). Crucial paths from risk indicators to causal mechanism. In B. B. Lahey, T. Moffit, & A. Caspi (Eds.), *Causes of conduct disorders and juvenile delinquency.* London: Guilford Press.

Schmitz, B. (2000). Auf der Suche nach dem verlorenen Individuum: Vier Theoreme zur Aggregation von Prozessen [Researching the lost individual]. *Psychologische Rundschau, 51,* 83–92.

Schmitz, B., & Skinner, E. (1993). Perceived control, effort, and academic performance: Interindividual, intraindividual, and multivariate time-series analyses. *Journal of Personality and Social Psychology, 64*(6), 1010–1028.

Singer, B., Ryff, C., Carr, D., & Magee, W. (1998). Linking life histories and mental health: A person-centered strategy. *Sociological Methodology, 28,* 1–51.

Skinner, H. A., & Blashfield, R. K. (1982). Increasing the impact of cluster analysis research: The case of psychiatric classification. *Journal of Consulting and Clinical Psychology, 50,* 727–735.

Smith, L. B., & Thelen, E. (1993). *A dynamic systems approach to development applications.* Cambridge, MA: MIT Press.

Spanier, G. B. (1976). Measuring dyadic adjustment: New scales for assessing the quality of marriage and similar dyads. *Journal of Marriage and the Family, 38,* 15–28.

Stattin, H., & Magnusson, D. (1996). Antisocial behavior: A holistic perspective. *Development and Psychopathology, 8,* 617–645.

Stern, H. W. (1917). *Die Psychologie und der Personalismus* [Psychology and the focus on personality]. Leipzig, Germany: Barth.

Thelen, E. (1989). Self organization in developmental processes: Can systems approaches work? In M. R. Gunnar & E. Thelen (Eds.), *Systems and development* (pp. 77–117). Hillsdale, NJ: Erlbaum.

Valsiner, J. (1984). Two alternative epistemological frameworks in psychology: The typological and variational modes of thinking. *Journal of Mind and Behavior, 5,* 449–470.

von Eye, A. (2001). Configural frequency analysis: Version, 2000, program for 32 bit operating systems. *Methods of Psychological Research: Online, 6,* 129–139.

von Eye, A. (2002). *Configural frequency analysis: Methods, models, and applications.* Mahwah, NJ: Erlbaum.

von Eye, A. (2003). A comparison of residual measures under configural frequency analysis conditions. In A. González Fragoso, R. Perera Salazar, & K. Anaya Izquierdo (Eds.), *Memorias del XVII Foro Nacional de Estadística* [Proceedings of the 17th meetings of the Mexican Statistical Association] (pp. 143–150). Aguascalientes, Mexico: Instituto Nacional de Estadística, Geografía e Informática References.

von Eye, A. (2004). The treasures of Pandora's box. *Measurement: Interdisciplinary Research and Perspectives, 2,* 244–247.

von Eye, A., & Bergman, L. R. (2003). Research strategies in developmental psychopathology: Dimensional identity and the person-oriented approach. *Development and Psychopathology, 15,* 553–580.

von Eye, A., & Bogat, G. A. (in press). Person orientation: Concepts, results, and development. *Merrill Palmer Quarterly.*

von Eye, A., & Lautsch, E., & von Weber, S. (2004). The Type II error of measures for the analysis of 2 x 2 tables. *Understanding Statistics, 3,* 259–282.

von Eye, A., & Mun, E.-Y. (2003). Characteristics of measures for 2 x 2 tables. *Understanding Statistics, 2,* 243–266.

von Eye, A., & Niedermeier, K. E. (1999). *Statistical analysis of longitudinal categorical data: An introduction with computer illustrations.* Mahwah, NJ: Erlbaum.

von Eye, A., & Schuster, C. (1998). On the specification of models for configural frequency analysis: Sampling schemes in prediction CFA. *Methods of Psychological Research—Online, 3,* 55–73.

von Eye, A., & Schuster, C. (2000). The road to freedom: Developmental methodology in the third millennium. *International Journal of Behavioral Development, 24,* 35–43.

von Eye, A., Spiel, C., & Rovine, M. J. (1995). Concepts of nonindependence in configural frequency analysis. *Journal of Mathematical Sociology, 20,* 41–45.

von Eye, A., Spiel, C., & Wagner, P. (2003). Structural equations modeling in developmental research: Concepts and applications. *Methods of Psychological Research—Online, 8,* 75–112.

Von Weber, S., von Eye, A., & Lautsch, E. (2004). The Type II error of measures for the analysis of 2 × 2 tables. *Understanding Statistics, 3*(4), 259–282.

Waller, N. G., & Meehl, P. E. (1998). *Multivariate taxometric procedures: Distinguishing types from continua.* Thousand Oaks, CA: Sage.

Wapner, S., & Demick, J. (1998). Developmental analysis: A holistic, developmental, systems-oriented perspective. In W. Damon (Series Ed.) & R. M. Lerner (Vol. Ed.), *Handbook of child psychology: Theoretical models of human development* (Vol. 1, pp. 761–805). New York: Wiley.

Ward, J. H. (1963). Hierarchical grouping to optimize an objective function. *Journal of the American Statistical Association, 58,* 236–244.

Wiener-Ehrlich, W. K. (1981). Hierachical versus generally overlapping models in psychiatric classification. *Multivariate Behavioral Research, 16,* 455–482.

Wishart, D. (1987). *Clustan user manual* (4th ed.). Edinburgh, Scotland: University of St. Andrews.

CHAPTER 22

A Survey of Dynamic Systems Methods for Developmental Psychopathology

ISABELA GRANIC and TOM HOLLENSTEIN

Decades ago, Lewin (1931) criticized psychology for its overreliance on methodologies that were originally designed for studying closed, physical systems. These methods, he warned, were inappropriate for the study of complex, developmental processes. Over 70 years later, the same criticisms continue to be raised, and with increasing urgency. Specifically, leading theorists (Cicchetti & Cohen, 1995b; Ford & Lerner, 1992; Hinde, 1992; Kagan, 1992; Keating, 1990; Overton & Horowitz, 1991; Richters, 1997) suggest that there is a fundamental incompatibility between developmentalists' organismic, open systems models and the mechanistic research methods with which these models are tested.

Developmental psychopathologists have been particularly concerned with their inherited mechanistic paradigm. Many of them have developed heuristically rich, complex models based on open systems concepts, but little headway has been made in finding alternative analytic tools appropriate for testing these models—a predicament Richters dubbed "the developmentalist's dilemma."

In this chapter, we suggest that methods derived from dynamic systems (DS) theory may be useful for addressing this dilemma. We have three main objectives: (1) to outline key dynamic systems principles and highlight their commensurability with developmental psychopathologists' core conceptual concerns; (2) to provide a survey of research designs, methodological techniques, and measurement strategies currently being used and refined by developmental DS researchers; and (3) to elaborate on one specific DS method, state space grid analysis, and provide several empirical examples using this method. The state space grid approach (Lewis, Lamey, & Douglas, 1999) was developed as a middle road between DS methods that

An earlier, less detailed version of this chapter appeared in *Development and Psychopathology, 15* (2003). We gratefully acknowledge the financial support of Grant 1 R21 MH 67357 from the National Institute of Mental Health (to D. Pepler and I. Granic) as well as Grant 410-2003-1335 from the Social Sciences and Humanities Research Council of Canada (to the first author).

are mathematically demanding (and, thus, often inaccessible or inappropriate for developmental psychopathology) and those that are purely descriptive. We have included most DS methods currently available for developmentalists. The methodological techniques and specific examples we have selected were chosen because they seemed most appropriate for addressing the types of research questions developmental psychopathologists tend to pursue. In the end, however, our main purpose is to provide a clear enough picture of various DS methods to inspire developmental psychopathologists to expand their analytic repertoire and, thus, test their systems-based models more directly.

THE DEVELOPMENTALIST'S DILEMMA

Before proceeding to discuss DS theory and its methodological bag of tricks, we briefly review the strong rationale for developing new methods for the field of developmental psychopathology (also see Cicchetti & Cohen, 1995b). Developmental psychopathologists have adopted an organismic, holistic, transactional framework for conceptualizing individual differences in normal and atypical development (e.g., Cicchetti, 1993; Cicchetti & Cohen, 1995a, 1995b; Cummings, Davies, & Campbell, 2000; Garmezy & Rutter, 1983; Sameroff, 1983, 1995; Sroufe & Rutter, 1984). These scholars often frame their models in terms of organizational principles and systems language. The systems theories that inform these models include General Systems Theory (Sameroff, 1983, 1995; von Bertalanffy, 1968), Developmental Systems Theory (Ford & Lerner, 1992), the ecological framework (Bronfenbrenner, 1979), contextualism (Dixon & Lerner, 1988), the transactional perspective (Dumas, LaFreniere, & Serketich, 1995), the organizational approach (Cicchetti & Schneider-Rosen, 1986; Erickson, Egeland, & Pianta, 1989; Garmezy, 1974; Sroufe, 1979, 1986; Sroufe & Rutter, 1984), the holistic-interactionistic view (Bergman & Magnusson, 1997), and the epigenetic view (Gottlieb, 1991, 1992). As a class of models, these approaches focus on process-level accounts of human behavior and on the context dependence and heterogeneity of developmental phenomena. They are concerned with the equi- and multifinality of development, the hierarchically embedded nature of intrapersonal (e.g., neurochemical activity, cognitive and emotional processes), interpersonal (e.g., parent-child relationships; peer networks), and higher-order social (e.g., communities, cultures) systems. They are also

fundamentally concerned with the mechanisms that underlie change and novelty (as well as stability) in normal and clinically significant trajectories.

As a result of inadequate measurement techniques, however, the complex developmental models informed by the language of systems thinking remain largely untested (Richters, 1997). For example, in the field of childhood aggression, a number of leading scholars have become concerned with highlighting the heterogeneity of aggressive youth and advocating the development of causal models that recognize the equifinality of aggression (e.g., Cicchetti & Richters, 1993; Hinshaw & Zupan, 1997; Moffitt, 1993). But it remains difficult to test these models because most of our current research methods and analytic techniques (e.g., regression analysis, t-tests, path analysis) rely on strategies that aggregate overtly similar subjects into one group or another (e.g., aggressive and nonaggressive children) to conduct group-level statistical analyses. Thus, although we may know that aggressive children show the same behavioral pattern for very different reasons (e.g., abuse, permissive parenting, marital conflict, birth of a new sibling), this variability cannot be systematically addressed because multivariate analytic strategies carry an a priori assumption of within-group homogeneity. This is not just a niggling statistical detail. Several leading methodologists have argued that, in most cases, these assumptions are completely unfounded and have likely led to serious misinterpretations of data (e.g., Hinshaw, 1999; Lykken, 1991; Meehl, 1978; Richters, 1997).

How did this gap between methods and models come about? Numerous critics (e.g., Hinde, 1992; Meehl, 1978; Lykken, 1991; Overton & Horowitz, 1991; Richters, 1997) have pointed to psychology's original sin for an explanation: In an effort to gain credibility and align itself with the hard sciences, psychology appropriated the methods and analytic techniques of mechanistic, nineteenth-century physical sciences. This paradigm is inappropriate for the study of self-organizing, active, reactive, interactive, and adaptive organisms (i.e., the stuff of psychology). The irony is that psychology's embrace of this mechanistic paradigm came at the same time as the physical and biological sciences were advancing a radically new one—one based on open systems concepts (Overton & Horowitz, 1991; Richters, 1997).

For some domains of psychology, adopting techniques from statistical mechanics may not be as paralyzing as it has become for developmental psychology (Thelen & Smith, 1994, 1998; Thelen & Ulrich, 1991; van Geert, 1998b, 1998c). At the heart of developmental questions, however, is how things *change*. By what process do novel structures (e.g., formal operational thought) or skills (e.g., emotion regulation, walking, language) emerge? The pioneers of developmental science (Piaget, Vygotsky, Werner) concerned themselves with the pursuit of abstract laws or properties that govern development: the structural explanation of how development unfolds (Cicchetti, 1990; van Geert, 1998b, 1998c). As van Geert (1998b) has argued, however, change and the emergence of novelty may no longer be the focus of contemporary developmental psychology. This state of affairs can be traced to the "adoption of a statistics that was designed for different purposes, namely distinguishing populations characterized by some special feature . . . and estimating the linear association between the variance of some independent variable on the one hand and a dependent variable on the other" (p. 146). The adoption of such statistics seems to have missed the point of the original questions laid out by the founding scholars of developmental science (Thelen & Smith, 1994; van Geert, 1998b).

Developmental psychopathology, having grown in part from this tradition, inherited the same schism. But developmental psychopathology also grew from several other disciplines that were less hampered by this statistical baggage. Embryology (e.g., Kuo, 1967; Spemann, 1938) was one of these disciplines (for a review, see Cicchetti, 1990). In the pursuit of understanding normal embryological functioning, "early embryologists derived the principles of a dynamically active organism and of a hierarchically integrated system that were later used in investigations of the processes of abnormal development within the neurosciences, embryology, and experimental psychopathology" (Cicchetti, 1990, p. 4). These insights formed the basis for the organizational approach in developmental psychopathology. Another avenue of influence comes from the discipline of ethology, which views the organism as a comprehensive whole and advocates a "multidomain, multidiscipline approach to psychopathology" (p. 19), an approach that is at the heart of developmental psychopathology (see also Hinde, 1983).

Interestingly, developmental psychopathology also shares its roots with the founders of child psychoanalysis (e.g., A. Freud, Klein, Winnicott, Bowlby, Erikson) who, like Piaget and Vygotsky, formalized theories based on detailed observations of children in their natural environments (Cicchetti, 1990; Cicchetti & Cohen, 1995b). These original, individual-based, ethnographic methods, however, are rarely applied in contemporary research (but see Cicchetti & Aber, 1998, for an exception). Yet it seems clear to us that these

organismic, systems-oriented roots lend themselves well to DS principles and the methods they suggest.

As it stands now, the field of developmental psychopathology seems to be at an impasse. On the one hand, some scholars have suggested that systems approaches to studying development have provided an interesting metaphor, but offer little more (Cox & Paley, 1997; Reis, Collins, & Bersheid, 2000; Vetere & Gale, 1987). Thus, one option is to give up the search for the grail, abandon this well-intentioned enterprise, and build simpler, more linear models that can be tested with established statistical rigor. Another option is offered by Richters (1997, p. 226): "Resolving the developmentalist's dilemma will require more than a recognition of the inadequacies of the existing paradigm. It will require intensive efforts to develop indigenous research strategies, methods, and standards with fidelity to the complexity of developmental phenomena." At the close of his essay, Richters offered some general instructions for how this new generation of studies should proceed:

1. There should be intense focus placed on understanding *individuals* and the causal structures that underpin specific individuals' development, with particular attention to "well-characterized exemplars" (i.e., nonextreme) cases.
2. No single method should be held as superior or inferior (e.g., case-based, variable-based, cross-sectional, longitudinal, historical, ethnographic); instead, methodological pluralism should be encouraged and may vary in degree depending on the phenomena investigated.
3. "Ritualized" hypothesis-testing should be generally abandoned for more exploratory, creative approaches that emphasize the discovery process.
4. A narrow focus on "explained variance" and prediction should take a secondary role to explanatory power.

These directions provide the springboard from which to consider the potential contributions that DS methods can make to addressing systems-inspired models.

PRINCIPLES OF DYNAMIC SYSTEMS

Developmental psychopathologists will be familiar with most of the concepts in DS theory because of their long-standing familiarity with systems concepts in general. Nevertheless, for the sake of clarity and precision, we believe it is important to delineate this framework from the systems approaches mentioned previously (Lewis & Granic, 2000).

Formally, a *dynamical system* is a set of mathematical equations that specify how a system changes over time. The various patterns and processes that emerge from this set of equations rely on a technical language originally developed in the fields of mathematics and physics. The concepts derived from this mathematical framework constitute the principles of dynamic systems approaches. The terms that are most commonly associated with this framework are attractors, repellors, state space, perturbations, bifurcations, catastrophe, chaos, hysteresis, complexity, nonlinearity, and far from equilibrium. Thus, what we refer to as dynamic systems theory or dynamic systems principles is a *metatheoretical* framework that encompasses a set of abstract principles that have been applied in different disciplines (e.g., physics, chemistry, biology, psychology) and to various phenomena (e.g., lasers, ant colonies, brain dynamics) at vastly different scales of analysis (from cells to economic trends and from milliseconds to millennia).

Consistent with developmental DS theorists (e.g., Fogel, 1993; Lewis, 2000; Thelen & Smith, 1994, 1998), we use the term dynamic systems to refer to the systems themselves (not the equations) that change over time. DS principles provide a framework for describing how novel forms emerge and stabilize through a system's own internal feedback processes (Prigogine & Stengers, 1984). This process is known as *self-organization* and refers to the spontaneously generated (i.e., emergent) order in complex, adaptive systems. In fields as various as physics (e.g., Haken, 1977), chemistry (e.g., Prigogine & Stengers, 1984), biology (e.g., Kauffman, 1993), and neuroscience (Freeman, 1995), DS principles have proven essential for providing process-level accounts of the structure and organization of system behavior and changes in that structure over time (Lewis & Granic, 2000).

DS principles resonate with most systems concepts in general. DS approaches to development emphasize the multiple reciprocal interactions among system elements that are hierarchically nested and mutually influential. The context or ecology in which the system is embedded is critical for understanding a dynamic system's behavior. Also consistent with various systems perspectives, development is conceptualized as movement toward greater levels of complexity through the interplay between positive and negative feedback cycles (Lewis & Granic, 1999b).

As will become clear from our selection of methods, we are most strongly influenced by the pioneering work of Esther Thelen, Linda Smith, Alan Fogel, Marc Lewis, and Paul van Geert, developmental psychologists who brought DS principles to the attention of the field at large. Because our focus is on methods specifically, a thorough theoretical discussion of DS concepts and their relevance to developmental science is precluded; the reader is strongly encouraged to supplement the current theoretical introduction with reviews by Thelen and Smith (1994, 1998), Fogel (1993), and Lewis (2000). In the following discussion, we highlight some key principles and then move on to their methodological implications.

State Space, Attractors, and Dynamic Stability

Dynamic, self-organizing systems share several key properties, some of which have already been mentioned. One key feature of open systems is that, although theoretically they have the potential to exhibit an enormous number of behavioral patterns, they tend to stabilize in a limited range of these possibilities. Stable patterns emerge through feedback among many lower-order (more basic) system elements; these emergent patterns are referred to as *attractors* in DS terminology. In real time, attractors may be understood as absorbing states that "pull" the system from other potential states. Behavior moves in a trajectory across the state space toward these attractors. Over developmental time, attractors represent recurrent patterns that have stabilized and are increasingly predictable. As noted by Thelen and Smith (1994), all developmental acquisitions can be described as attractor patterns that emerge over weeks, months, or years.

As recurring stable forms, attractors are often represented topographically as valleys on a dynamic landscape (see Figure 22.1). The deeper and wider the attractor, the more likely it is that behavior falls into it and remains there, and the more resistant it is to small changes in the environment. *Repellors,* or states that the system tends to avoid or be repelled from, are represented as hills on this landscape—states in which the system cannot rest. As the system develops, a unique *state space,* defined as a model of all possible states a system can attain, is configured by several attractors and repellors. Critically, living systems are characterized by *multistability* (Kelso, 1995); that is, their state space (i.e., behavioral repertoire) includes several coexisting attractors. Contextual constraints probabilistically guide behavior toward a particular attractor at any given moment in time.

As we will see later, the concepts of state space, attractors, and multistability have informed several research designs and methodologies in recent years. The operationalization of these principles, either graphically, math-

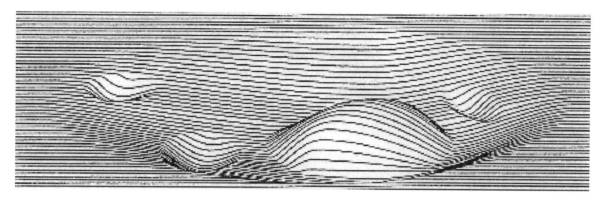

Figure 22.1   A state space with three attractors (the wells) and one repellor (the hill).

ematically, or heuristically, have helped DS researchers uncover previously undetected behavioral variability, as well as the processes by which this variability stabilizes into unpredicted, but nevertheless stable, attractor patterns.

Interrelations between Time Scales

DS researchers are fundamentally concerned with the interplay between different time scales. From a DS perspective, the same principles of change and stability can be applied at the moment-to-moment scale (real time) and to developmental time (weeks, months, years). The interplay between nested time scales is constant and reciprocal (Thelen & Smith, 1994, 1998). Self-organization at the real-time scale constrains self-organization at the developmental scale, which, in turn, constrains real-time behavior (Port & van Gelder, 1995). Thelen and Smith (1998, p. 593) elaborate:

> Each behavioral act occurs *over time* ... but every act changes the overall system and builds a history of acts over time. . . . Habituation, memory, learning, adaptation, and development form one seamless web built on processes over time—activities in the real world.

Research designs based on DS principles almost always measure behavior on at least two time scales. The manner and extent to which the two or more levels of analysis are related to each other are subsequently examined. Thus, DS-informed studies often involve collecting real-time, observational data over repeated sessions in a longitudinal design such that moment-to-moment behavioral patterns, and changes in those patterns, can be traced along a longitudinal trajectory (Lee & Karmiloff-Smith, 2002).

Hierarchically Embedded Levels of Organization

Dynamic systems are not only nested processes in time, they are also coupled hierarchically. Mechanisms in development may be defined at different levels of organization (e.g., physiological, emotional, behavioral, social), and these levels are thought to be embedded, linked by feedback processes, and mutually constraining. Especially important, DS theorists insist that no level of organization is any more "basic" or "primary" in terms of causality. Thus, for example, from a DS perspective, neural processes are accorded no higher causal privilege than psychological or social processes. Instead, "descriptions of change of many components are needed so that multilevel processes and their mutual interactions can be fully integrated. . . . Moreover, explanations at every level must be consistent and ultimately reconcilable" (Thelen & Smith, 1998, p. 596–597). This view of causality contrasts with most approaches in psychology (but see Cicchetti & Dawson, 2002b).

Rather than simple linear relationships, DS researchers often understand relations among multiple levels in terms of *circular causality* (Hakens, 1977). Circular causality suggests that interactions among lower-order elements provide the means by which higher-order patterns emerge, and these emergent attractors exert top-down influences to maintain the entrainment of lower-level components. Developmental psychopathologists, particularly those in the neurosciences, have recently become interested in understanding how different levels of analysis can shed light on typical and atypical development (Calkins & Fox, 2002; Cicchetti & Dawson, 2002a; Nelson et al., 2002). The DS metatheoretical framework, with concepts such as circular causality, may help researchers organize their findings and parsimoniously integrate the various theories about different levels into one coherent model. Indeed, it is likely that common dynamic principles of self-organization govern different levels of organization (e.g., neural, cardiac, emotional, behavioral, societal); if this is so, then synergistic DS methods that can be applied similarly at different levels of analysis will provide a powerful means by which integrative models can be developed and empirically supported. The extent to which real-time and developmental time scales are interrelated and hierarchical levels of organization are embedded is further clarified when considering perturbations and their relation to phase transitions.

Perturbations, Phase Transitions, and Nonlinear Change

Through the amplification properties of positive feedback, nonlinear changes in the organizational structure of a dynamic system can be observed. As shown in Figure 22.2, these abrupt changes are referred to as *phase transitions;* they occur at *points of bifurcation,* or junctures in the system's development. At these thresholds, small fluctuations have the potential to disproportionately affect the interactions of other elements, leading to the emergence of new forms. Novelty does not have to originate from outside the system; it can emerge spontaneously through feedback within the system. During a phase transition, systems are extremely sensitive to *perturbations.* Between these points, however, self-organizing systems tend toward coherence and stability.

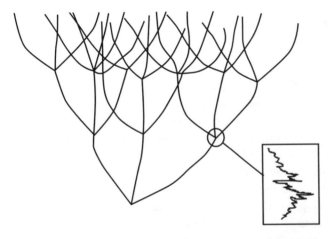

Figure 22.2 Alternative developmental trajectories. Phase transitions occur at regular junctures in development. Increased variability at phase transitions is shown in magnified segment. *Source:* From "A Dynamic Systems Approach to Cognition-Emotion Interactions in Development" (pp. 159–188), by M. D. Lewis and L. Douglas, in *What Develops in Emotional Development?* M. F. Mascolo & S. Griffins (Eds.), 1998, New York: Plenum Press.

Phase transitions are characterized by interrelated changes in real and developmental time. In developmental time, periods of stability and relative predictability are followed by a period of disequilibrium in which established patterns are destabilized. After this period of flux, developmental systems restabilize and settle into new habits of interactions. Corresponding to this developmental profile, real-time behavior during a phase transition is more variable, flexible, and sensitive to perturbations; behavior may change from one state to another frequently and is less likely to settle in any one state for very long (Thelen & Ulrich, 1991). However, before and after the phase transition, real-time behavior is far less variable; only a small number of behavioral states are available to the system, and once the system settles into one of these stable patterns, it tends to remain there for an extended time period (e.g., Thelen & Smith, 1994; van der Maas & Molenaar, 1992; van Geert, 1998a).

DS researchers have used the concept of perturbations on a real-time scale as an empirical design innovation to test the relative stability of observed behavioral patterns. Perturbations have the potential to abruptly "push" the system from one stable pattern to another (Fogel, 1993; Thelen & Smith, 1994). But this is only a potential—whether and how a system becomes reorganized is determined by its underlying structure. A perturbation can be considered a focal aspect of environmental context, and sensitivity to perturbations (which typifies phase transitions) is a special case of the more general sensitivity of dynamic systems to their contexts—a sensitivity that changes with system development gradually or more suddenly. Thus, context sensitivity for DS researchers is not just "a form of jargon for anything environmental, as if invoking the term suggests compliance with current scientific and conceptual canons" (Boyce et al., 1998, p. 145). DS researchers systematically observe changes in behavior, as it varies with contextual forces, to infer the underlying structure of the system (e.g., Fogel, 1993; Granic & Lamey, 2002; Lewis & Granic, 1999b, 2000; Thelen & Smith, 1994; Thelen & Ulrich, 1991).

On a developmental scale, principles of nonlinear change, phase transitions, and perturbations have been most often used for the explicit purpose of studying the structural profile of developmental transitions (e.g., Fogel & Thelen, 1987; Granic, Hollenstein, Dishion, & Patterson, 2003; Lewis, 2000; Lewis & Granic, 2000; Thelen & Ulrich, 1991; van Geert, 1991, 1994). Neo-Piagetian scholars such as van der Maas and Molenaar (e.g., 1992) have used a particular type of dynamic model, the cusp-catastrophe model, to represent the nonlinear nature of stage transitions. Borrowing from Gilmore (1981), they suggest a number of criteria or "flags" that can be used to operationalize a transition. Among the transition flags are a sudden jump from one parameter value to another, evidence of hysteresis (i.e., when the same conditions elicit different behaviors, depending on the immediate prior history of the system), anomalous variance, and an increased sensitivity to perturbations. Transitions in motor, cognitive, linguistic, and socioemotional development have been successfully modeled by the application of variants of these flags (Case et al., 1996; Lewis et al., 1999; Lewis, Zimmerman, Hollenstein, & Lamey, 2004; van der Maas & Molenaar, 1992; van Geert, 1991, 1994). Structural changes in parent-adolescent interactions at the early adolescent stage transition have also been shown to exhibit the properties of a phase transition (Granic, Dishion, & Hollenstein, 2003; Granic, Hollenstein, et al., 2003).

Many of the DS concepts described here are clearly resonant with other systems views. But as a point of distinction, we suggest that there are four principles that are central to the DS framework which are either neglected or less emphasized in other approaches and which hold great promise for new empirical directions in developmental psychopathology. First, DS theory is primarily concerned with the emergence of novelty through the process of self-organization, whereas, with some notable exceptions (Ford & Lerner, 1992), most of the emphasis in more general systems views is on mechanisms of stability (i.e., negative feedback processes; for examples, see cybernetic models; Granic, 2000; Lewis & Granic, 1999a). Second, although systems views may acknowledge the nonlinear nature of change in developmental systems, this is the hallmark principle of DS approaches to development, and it has led to the exploration of radical new strategies such as catastrophe theory (e.g., van der Maas & Molenaar, 1992), developmental growth curve modeling (van Geert, 1991, 1994), and the study of phase transitions (e.g., Thelen & Smith, 1994; Thelen & Ulrich, 1991). Third, variability represents critical information in DS research. Conventionally, variability in developmental data has been seen as the result of measurement error and, thus, a source of noise that should be minimized. DS theorists make a radical departure from this approach: Variability is considered a rich source of information, indexing impending change and "the essential ground for exploration and selection" (van Geert & van Dijk, 2002, p. 345). Methods that tap changes in variability are a mainstay of DS researchers (e.g., Thelen & Ulrich, 1991; van Geert & van Dijk, 2002). Finally, DS theorists are fundamentally concerned with the interrelations between time scales of development and put a great deal of

emphasis on understanding the unfolding patterns of real-time behavior (Thelen & Smith, 1998). This final principle is critical in terms of its methodological implications, and it is most often ignored in other systems frameworks.

In the following sections, we describe a number of dynamic systems approaches to research designs and measurement strategies. To limit the scope of our review, we do not discuss the exciting work emerging in the neurosciences (a field that has long embraced the principles of self-organization). This work is clearly relevant to developmental psychopathologists, and the reader is referred to the neuroimaging methods detailed in the second volume of *Developmental Psychopathology* (2nd edition). We also spend less time proportionally on the mathematical modeling techniques than the graphical, descriptive, and statistical ones because we believe that the latter group of methodologies are generally more accessible and may ultimately prove more appropriate for the types of research questions put forward by developmental psychopathologists.

We first review some general DS-informed research design concepts and strategies put forth by Thelen and her colleagues (e.g., Thelen & Smith, 1994; Thelen & Ulrich, 1991). Next, we discuss the types of data most suitable for DS analyses. We then provide a list of graphical techniques and quantitative strategies appropriate for the analysis of real-time and developmental data; these descriptions are supplemented with actual or hypothetical examples relevant to developmental psychopathologists. We also highlight the limitations inherent in some of the techniques and argue that a newly developed DS methodology, state space grid analysis, may help address a number of these weaknesses. The last part of this chapter provides a detailed description of the state space grid technique, which combines graphical methods with statistical analysis in a way that maintains fidelity to DS concepts. We provide several examples of programs of research and individual studies that have used variations of this approach.

RESEARCH DESIGN STRATEGIES INFORMED BY DS PRINCIPLES

Thelen and her colleagues have explicitly laid out a methodological strategy for developmental psychologists interested in dynamic analyses (Thelen & Smith, 1994, 1998; Thelen & Ulrich, 1991). Their strategy involves the following six steps.

Identify the Collective Variable of Interest

A collective variable must be an observable phenomenon (not a construct or latent variable) that captures the coordination of the elements of a multidimensional system. Because Thelen and Ulrich (1991) were interested in motor development, they chose the phasing of alternating steps as the collective variable that condensed the many aspects of interlimb coordination. Changes in this collective variable can then be tracked over developmental time. This is the first challenging step; unlike in physical systems, it is difficult to identify a collective variable in psychological systems. Extensive developmental observations and experiments are recommended as a first step toward this goal. An example relevant to developmental psychopathologists might be the observed intensity of a child's oppositional behavior—a collective variable that may capture the coordination of mood states, arousal level, appraisal processes, and so on (these processes themselves would need to be assessed in multiple contexts).

Describe the Attractors for That System

This step involves mapping the real-time trajectory of the collective variable in various contexts across different developmental periods and identifying its relative stability. Thus, the contexts in which a child's oppositional behavior is most stable can be identified (e.g., with a parent), as well as the contexts in which such behavior is less stable (i.e., more easily changed), is never observed, or is rarely observed. High stability indicates an attractor state.

Attractor states may be tested by examining the variability of the collective variable given particular contexts (e.g., How often does the child become oppositional in response to a request to clean up at home versus at school?). Additional features can help identify attractors as well. First, an attractor may be present if behavior takes a relatively short time to return back to the state once it has left it (latency to return to the attractor is short). Second, behavior tends to stay in an attractor for longer durations than other states. Third, it should take a much larger perturbation to move behavior out of a strong attractor state relative to weaker attractors or other regions of the state space.

This last point is also a reminder that living systems exhibit multistability. The implication is that researchers should attempt to identify all or many of the attractors that are available to a particular system. Then the critical question becomes: What are the conditions under which behavior will gravitate toward one attractor versus an-

other? Returning to the oppositional child, most conventional approaches focus on describing and predicting the child's negative, destructive behavior. But a DS approach would map out not only the negative behavior attractors, but also the interested/engaged states, the joyful, and the neutral states and, especially important, the pathways to and from these attractors. Although these latter states may be weaker attractors, the goal would be to track the contextual conditions under which the child moves from more positive to more negative attractors and vice versa in order to get a better picture of the underlying dynamics of this child's behavioral landscape.

Map the Individual Developmental Trajectories of the Collective Variable

This step requires collecting observations at many time points in a longitudinal design (also see Fogel, 1993). The density of time samples depends on the developmental period in question (i.e., in infancy, weekly observations may be needed, whereas in late childhood, data collected monthly might suffice; Fogel, 1993). Then developmental profiles can be graphed on a case-by-case basis and the similarities and differences among profiles can be described. Stable (i.e., fixed or cycling) segments of the time series denote an attractor. At this stage, the multifinality and equifinality of developmental trajectories can be discovered. Some developmental profiles may start out looking similar, and then, from very small differences that become amplified, trajectories may diverge. Other developmental profiles may show the opposite pattern, of different initial conditions being pulled toward a particular attractor. The key at this stage is to create *individual* profiles rather than aggregate across subjects; otherwise, the variability inherent in developmental processes will be obscured.

As described in more detail later, an alternative to averaging developmental profiles is to cluster individual trajectories into groups that share profile characteristics (Hollenstein, Granic, Stoolmiller, & Snyder, 2004). In developmental psychopathology, a similar point has been emphasized by researchers doing case-based, or person-oriented, analysis (e.g., Bergman & Magnusson, 1997).

Identify Phase Transitions in Development

As described earlier, transitions in development are characterized by increased variability, a breakdown of stable patterns, and the emergence of new forms. The various catastrophe flags described earlier can help researchers identify points of transition. Transition periods are critical to mark because they allow researchers to access and manipulate mechanisms underlying change. This point is particularly relevant for developmental psychopathologists interested in clinical interventions. For instance, there may be normative stage transitions in children's development during which, as a result of normal maturational processes, the coordination among system elements begins to break down, previous attractors are destabilized, and there is an increased potential for new patterns to emerge (e.g., Granic, Hollenstein, et al., 2003; Lewis & Granic, 1999b; Lewis et al., 1999; Lewis et al., 2004). Clinical interventions may have their greatest impact if they are targeted at these sensitive periods.

The idea of fluctuations at phase transitions is not new to developmental psychopathology, although it has rarely been pursued empirically. One fascinating example comes from a study conducted by Inhelder (1976), who found that some mentally retarded children's skill performance oscillated between various stage levels prior to reaching a new stage. Interpreting these findings, Cicchetti (1990) suggested two possibilities: The processes accounting for these children's development may simply be different from those of normal children, or, more intriguingly, "their oscillations are universal phenomena that become visible only in retarded children because of the slower nature of their development" (p. 16; see also Cicchetti & Sroufe, 1976).

Bertenthal (1999) further emphasizes the importance of variability at phase transitions. He suggests that variability is not just an index of change, but actually helps *drive* change. According to Bertenthal, "Variability offers flexibility, which drives development following Darwinian principles. Principles of variation and selection cause successful behaviors to be stored and repeated more frequently than the less successful" (also see van Geert & van Dijk, 2002, p. 343; cf. Thelen & Smith, 1994). The theoretical implications for understanding intervention effects are compelling. Successful interventions may *induce* a phase transition during which behavioral, cognitive, and affective variability increases, providing the fertile ground from which more positive, or less distressing, patterns can be selected, repeated, and potentially stabilized. This possibility can be empirically verified by using simple descriptive statistics (e.g., looking for an increase in standard deviations and variance and a breakdown of correlations; additional measures of variance are described later) or more formal techniques (described in the section on state space grids).

Identify Control Parameters

In DS language, control parameters are the "agents of change." The purpose of tracking the collective variable across different contexts and developmental transition points is to ultimately identify the mechanisms underlying processes of change. Control parameters are not simply independent variables (although they can be considered a special type of these). Usually, independent variables are static measures that are assumed to have a linear effect on outcomes. Control parameters are better understood as mediators with special properties; continuous and small changes in the values of these parameters can result in abrupt threshold effects on a collective variable. Moreover, these nonlinear changes occur at different values depending on whether the control parameter is increasing or decreasing. For example, through fine-grained longitudinal observations, Thelen and Ulrich (1991) were able to identify overall changes in muscle mass as the control parameter that was related to improvements in infants' treadmill stepping. In many areas of developmental psychopathology, however, this step is the most difficult, because psychological systems are incredibly complex, and the problem of identifying and manipulating one or very few causal mechanisms is often insoluble. Moreover, a control parameter may not always be something that *can* be manipulated (e.g., temperament, parental depression). Nevertheless, DS researchers urge us to at least keep the concept in mind.

Manipulate Control Parameters to Experimentally Generate Phase Transitions

Despite its difficulty, this suggestion is a familiar one to many developmental psychopathologists. Simply put, once a causal factor has been inferred from careful descriptive analysis, it should be experimentally manipulated to examine whether it does indeed trigger the expected shift in behavior. In this respect, intervention studies are an exceptional avenue for testing the role of specific control parameters in developmental psychopathology (see Dishion, Bullock, & Granic, 2002; Dishion & Patterson, 1999; Eddy & Chamberlain, 2000; Forgatch & DeGarmo, 1999).

One of the best examples of following this proposed strategy comes from the work on the etiology and treatment of aggressive behavior. For instance, based on decades of microsocial observational studies with families, coercion has been identified as a mediating causal mechanism underlying the etiology of childhood aggression (e.g., Patterson, 1982; Patterson, Reid, & Dishion, 1992). To confirm this supposition experimentally, Forgatch and DeGarmo

(1999) investigated the impact of a randomized control intervention that aimed to decrease the rate at which parents engaged in coercive interchanges. Results confirmed that, indeed, changes in coercion resulted in decreases in children's aggressive behavior. From a DS perspective, parental discipline strategies, for example, could have been the control parameter that was adjusted through the intervention (i.e., coercion decreased).

Despite the advantages of Thelen and colleagues' approach, many researchers are likely to experience some problems with implementing their general strategy. First, it requires collecting continuous time-series data (e.g., physiological data, behavioral observations coded in real time); this type of data is time-consuming and expensive to collect. More important, time-series data may not capture the type of information pertinent to many developmental psychopathologists. Second, and related, unlike motor or cognitive development, in which some skill or task performance increases or decreases quantitatively over time, psychopathology may not involve such graded changes (cf. Lewis & Granic, 1999b; Lewis et al., 2004). Instead, the development of psychopathology may be better characterized as emergent patterns of interconnected changes in different domains (e.g., biological, cognitive, emotional) that are nonlinearly related to one another and change qualitatively as well as quantitatively (i.e., it is often categorical or ordinal). We address this issue at greater length when we discuss state space grid analysis and the limitations it addresses in this regard.

SUITABLE DATA FOR DS ANALYSES

There are several types of data that developmental psychopathologists collect that are appropriate for DS analyses. Because a DS perspective is fundamentally about changes in time, the most important data characteristic is multiple measurements over time. Thus, questionnaire data collected at one time point would be inappropriate for tapping dynamic processes (e.g., Cummings et al., 2000). Next, we list the four types of data that lend themselves most easily to DS analyses and name some examples of analytic techniques that can be conducted. These techniques are then explained in more detail in the following section. Table 22.1 lists the techniques and the appropriate data types for each and provides some (nonexhaustive) examples of empirical papers that have applied the various DS methods.

Observational data—continuous: Includes data obtained in time units less than 1 second; these data often comprise physiological measures. The density of data points

allows for the more sophisticated techniques adopted from the natural sciences, where this type of data is most common. These techniques are often based on time-series analysis and include the domain of elaborate mathematical models based on coupled equations and dynamical catastrophe models. Quantitative measures of chaos—Lyupanov exponents, entropy, correlational dimensions, and so on—can also be derived from such continuous data. Furthermore, all of the methods available to the other data types are available with this kind of data, either as time-series or summaries of time-series.

Observational data—discrete: Includes live and taped observational data that are converted to codes along time units as small as 1 second. These codes can represent the sequence of behavior for one or more subjects and are typically inappropriate for time-series techniques unless they have a sufficiently large number of data points. By applying DS graphical techniques such as state space grids, Karnaugh maps, and phase plots, the temporal patterns embedded in the temporal sequence can be uncovered. These data can be used to identify attractors, perturbations, phase transitions, and other DS patterns.

Longitudinal data—short: Includes, for example, hourly/daily/weekly self-report measures (e.g., diary or beeper studies), repeated phone interviews, or repeated observational sessions (e.g., therapy sessions). The time points may be frequent enough to allow the use of some of the real-time techniques available to the first type of data or may be analyzed using techniques applicable to developmental-time data (Type 4).

Longitudinal data—long: Includes any combination of the previous data types collected at different time points that may span weeks, months, or years. The main distinction from data type 3 is the time span between first and last measurements. Data collected in three or more waves is often used to depict change, growth, or intervention effects, and a variety of DS methods including state space grid analysis, dynamic growth modeling, developmental profile analysis, and catastrophe modeling can be applied. Developmental phase transitions are detectable through the application of these techniques.

DS METHODS

In the following two sections, real-time and developmental methods are discussed. A number of these techniques have been developed specifically for testing DS-based hypotheses. Other methods were not designed specifically to ad-

TABLE 22.1 Summary of Dynamic Systems Techniques and Concepts and Examples of Studies That Have Applied These Techniques

Techniques	DS Concept	Examples
Real Time		
Case studies	Self-organization	Fogel (1990, 1993)
Time series	Attractors	Bakeman & Gottman (1997)
		Granic & Dishion (2003)
Phase plots	Phase space	Sabelli, Carlson-Sabelli, Patel, Levy, & Diez-Martin (1995)
	Attractors	
Event history analysis	Attractors	Snyder, Stoolmiller, Wilson, & Yamamoto (in press)
Fourier analysis	Attractors	Newtson (1994, 1998)
		Schroeck (1994)
Karnaugh maps	Phase transition	Dumas, Lemay, & Dauwalder (2001)
	State space	
Coupled equations	Attractors	Gottman, Guralnick, Wilson, Swanson, & Murray (1997)
	Feedback	Gottman, Murray, Swanson, Tyson, & Swanson (2002)
		Nowak & Vallacher (1998)
		Ryan, Gottman, Murray, Carrere, & Swanson (2000)
Nonlinear dynamics	Entropy	Dishion, Nelson, Bullock, & Winter (in press)
	Attractors Phase space	Guastello (1995)
	Feedback	Heath (2000)
	Chaos and determinism	Newell & Molenaar (1998)
		Pincas (2001)
SSG	State space	Granic & Lamey (2002)
	Attractors	Hollenstein, Granic, Stoolmiller, & Snyder (2004)
	Variability	Lewis, Lamey, & Douglas (1999)
	Perturbation	
	Phase transitions	
Developmental		
Descriptive developmental profile	Phase space	Thelen & Smith (1994)
	Self-organization	Thelen & Ulrich (1991)
	Attractors	van Geert & van Dijk (2002)
	Phase transition	
Latent class analysis	Attractors	van der Maas (1998)
	Self-organization	
	Phase transition	
Dynamic growth modeling	Phase space	Ruhland & van Geert (1998)
	Self-organization	Steenbeek & van Geert (in press)
	Feedback	Thelen, Schoner, Scheier, & Smith (2001)
	Phase transition	van Geert (1994, 1998a, 1998b)
	Attractors	
Connectionist modeling	Attractors	Johnson & Morton (1991)
	Bifurcations	McClelland (1979)
	Phase transition	Rumelhart & McClelland (1986)
	Chaos	Smith (1993, 1995)
		Smith & Thelen (in press)
		Thelen et al. (2001)
Catastrophe modeling	Phase transition	Hartleman, van der Maas, & Molenaar (1998)
	Hysteresis	van der Maas & Molenaar (1992)
SSG	State space	Granic, Dishion, & Hollenstein (2003)
	Phase transition	Granic, Hollenstein, Dishion, & Patterson (2003)
		Lewis, Lamey, & Douglas (1999)
		Lewis, Zimmerman, Hollenstein, & Lamey (in press)

dress DS questions; however, they may be quite fruitful in this regard. Moreover, perhaps the greatest advantages of conducting DS research is in combining methods at different scales of analysis in one study.

Real-Time Measures

As most teachers of research methods and statistics in general insist, eyeballing your data is an important part of the analytic procedure. For DS researchers, graphical techniques provide the core of their analytic armament. Perhaps because dynamic systems theory is a descriptive framework and because it aims to describe phenomena in geometric terms (recall our discussion of behavioral trajectories on a state space), plotting data is the mainstay of DS researchers (Norton, 1995). As described later, a number of these real-time and developmental time graphical methods can be complemented with various quantitative tools. We have grouped the following methods under the rubric of real-time methods because that is how they have tended to be applied. But it is important to note that because the same principles of self-organization apply at different time scales, many of these techniques can be adapted easily to study phenomena in developmental time.

Case Studies

Perhaps the one common recommendation DS researchers offer is to start with fine-grained, real-time observations of the phenomenon of interest and follow this behavior across a significant developmental period. One of the most basic first steps toward this end is the careful description of case studies. Fogel's (e.g., 1990, 1993) research on mother-infant relationship processes is exemplary in this respect. His "microgenetic" research relies heavily on detailed descriptions of videotaped interactions as they proceed in real time. He uses these case histories as a "means to seek patterns in sequences of action in a context, in both real and developmental time scales" (1990, p. 343). Metaphors based on DS principles serve as guides for identifying dynamically stable dyadic patterns ("frames") and changes in those patterns across development.

Although these narrative descriptions are rich in detail and provide ample fodder for generating hypotheses, they are intentionally not quantified at this stage. As such, this method does not address developmental psychopathologists' search for quantitative techniques to test their conceptual models. To quantify impressions from case studies and statistically test hypotheses, Fogel and his colleagues have used a number of techniques (for a review, see Lavelli, Pantoja, Hsu, Messinger, & Fogel, in press), including sim-

ple descriptive statistics, individual growth curve modeling (Fogel, 1995; Hsu & Fogel, 2001), and event history analysis (Hsu & Fogel, 2001) to measure the emergence, strength, and dissipation of parent-infant attractors. These methods are discussed in later sections of this chapter.

Time-Series Analysis

The group of methods that fall under time-series analysis offer some useful approaches to characterizing the real-time behavior of dynamic systems. The methods include visual representations as well as simple statistics that can be used to examine the qualities and predictive power of hypothesized attractor patterns. To illustrate the utility of this approach, we summarize the rationale, time-series procedures, and results from a study we have recently completed using data from antisocial and normal friendship interactions.

Past research suggested that antisocial adolescents can be distinguished from their prosocial counterparts by the extent to which they engage in reciprocal deviant talk (e.g., talk about stealing, lying; Dishion, Capaldi, Spracklen, & Li, 1995; Dishion, Spracklen, Andrews, & Patterson, 1996; Dishion, Eddy, Haas, Li, & Spracklen, 1997). Observational studies showed that antisocial peers had a higher mean duration of deviant talk (or "rule-break" talk) than prosocial peers. Central tendency measures, however, do not speak directly to the processes underlying these interactions. Moreover, they obscure potentially critical temporal patterns. To come closer to a process-level explanation, we began by conceptualizing deviant talk as an attractor for antisocial, but not prosocial, peers (Granic & Dishion, 2003). Our interest was not in examining whether one group showed more deviant talk than another, but whether, over the course of an interaction, antisocial adolescents became stuck in an antisocial talk attractor. That is, did they become increasingly engrossed in topics organized around deviancy? One way to explore this hypothesis was to examine whether, as the interaction unfolded and antisocial dyads repeatedly returned to talking about deviant topics, they also spent increasingly more time in that deviant pattern. Time-series procedures were well-suited for our purposes.

Deviant (or rule-break talk) and normative talk were coded continuously from videotaped interactions between best friends. Time-series plots were derived for each dyad, with the duration of each deviant talk bout on the y axis and each successive bout represented along the x axis (Figures 22.3 and 22.4). The slope of that time series (i.e., the standardized beta) was then calculated using simple regression analysis. Slope is one parameter that can be identified from a time series; others include cyclicity (number of cycles in a series, length of cycles) and autocorrelation.

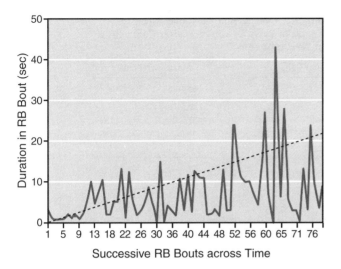

Figure 22.3 Example of a time-series for an antisocial youth with a positive rule-break bout slope.

We used the slope measure in a somewhat unique way to highlight a key DS principle. If deviant talk indeed functioned as an attractor for antisocial youth, then we expected to see a time series that showed a positive slope, as exemplified in Figure 22.3. If it was not an attractor for a dyad, then we expected to see a time series with either a flat or a negative slope, as shown in Figure 22.4. Thus, each participant was assigned a deviant-talk slope value, and these values were then used in regression analyses to predict antisocial outcomes 3 years later.

The results are summarized in Table 22.2 As hypothesized, the attractor index (the slope of deviant talk bouts)

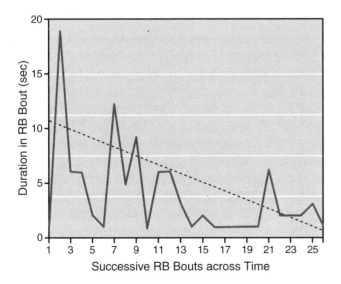

Figure 22.4 Example of a time-series for a normal adolescent with a negative rule-break bout slope.

predicted serious authority conflict (e.g., number of arrests, school expulsion) and drug abuse 3 years later. These results were particularly strong because they remained statistically significant even after controlling for arguably the three most predictive risk factors in childhood: prior deviant behavior, family coercion, and deviant peer associations in childhood. We also showed that the mean duration of deviant talk bouts was not sufficient to predict these outcomes. Thus, these findings showed that reconceptualizing deviant talk as an attractor is not simply an exercise in relabeling; there are specific hypotheses that are engendered by applying this approach. From a DS perspective, although the frequency and amount of time spent talking about deviant topics is important, even more critical is the process by which dyadic behavior continues to be drawn toward, and held, in this deviant pattern. Both antisocial and prosocial peers discussed deviant acts and breaking rules. *It was the dynamic (time-based) characteristics of these conversations, as revealed by a simple time-series analysis, that differentiated antisocial and normal friendships.*

A similar analytic approach was used by Bakeman and Gottman (1997). They analyzed data from marital couples' interactions using this time-series technique, except they plotted the interevent interval between successive displays of negative affect (i.e., the time between one negative affect and the next, across the interaction). They showed that, for distressed dyads, the time between each negative affect display became shorter and shorter over the course of the conversation (i.e., return time to the attractor became shorter over the interaction). Thus, negative affect was an absorbing state for distressed, but not happily married, couples.

Phase Plots

Phase portraits generally are state spaces filled with behavioral trajectories. More often, these plots are called phase plots when the variables being plotted are continuous, such as velocity and displacement of a pendulum. With the continuous data sometimes used by developmental psychopathologists, it is possible, for example, to create plots that depict the magnitude of change against the rate of that change (e.g., with galvanic skin response or heart rate data).

For the more common types of discrete, turn-taking (e.g., conversational turns) observational data that developmental psychopathologists collect, phase space can be "reconstructed" by plotting behavior at time *t* against behavior at time *t* + 1 (sometimes called a lag-1 plot). These types of plots can alert researchers to different types of attractor states (i.e., cyclical, fixed point, oscillating) and, thus, uncover process-level information not otherwise

TABLE 22.2   Regression Results Predicting Adolescent Authority Conflict and Substance Abuse in Midadolescence from the Strength of the Deviant Talk Attractor in Early Adolescence, after Controlling for Previous Child Deviancy, Family Coercion, and Deviant Peer Affiliation

	Antisocial Behavior		Substance Abuse	
Steps in Regression	R^2 Change	Total R^2	R^2 Change	Total R^2
1. Child deviancy	.28[a]		.16[b]	
2. Child family coercion	.02	.30	.02	.18
3. Child deviant peer affiliation	.07[b]	.36	.06[c]	.24
4. Attractor strength (slope of deviant talk)	.05[b]	.41	.06[c]	.30

[a] $p < .001$
[b] $p < .01$
[c] $p < .05.$

accessible. For example, in the study previously described, Granic and Dishion (2003) initially used phase plots to explore the dynamic patterns underlying adolescent friendship interactions. From the time series previously described, a "floating window" was used to plot each value of the time series such that the duration of the deviant talk bout at time t was represented on the x axis and the duration value at time $t + 1$ was plotted on the y axis.

The plots look much like scatter plots of first-order autocorrelations except that a trajectory connects successive points; thus, the temporal integrity of the interaction is maintained. Figure 22.5 is an example of an antisocial dyad's phase plot. Much like the time-series plots indicated, the phase plot shows that this dyad began with very short durations in the deviant talk pattern (points 1 to 3), but, over time, they spent more and more time in this state (points 49 to 52). The plot suggests that for this antisocial dyad, antisocial talk was an attractor state, the strength of which held the dyad in the pattern for longer and longer time periods. Eventually, this dyadic system may move to-

ward continuous deviant talk. There are several other possible patterns that phase plots can exhibit. For example, a large proportion of prosocial dyads showed a relatively "random" phase plot similar to the example presented in Figure 22.6, suggesting that deviant talk was not an attractor for these peers.

Event History Analysis

As can be seen from the previous examples, and others to follow, it is not always necessary to invent new methods to explore DS-inspired hypotheses. Another method that can help researchers explore the different characteristics of attractor processes is event history analysis. A variant of survival analysis and Cox regression models, event history analysis calculates transition rates (also called hazard rate or latency to recurrence) of state changes in categorical time series (Allison, 1984; Blossfeld & Rohwer, 2002). The rate of transition in and out of a behavioral state (e.g., tantrum, laugh) can be interpreted as an index of attractor strength. Several other measures, including the frequency,

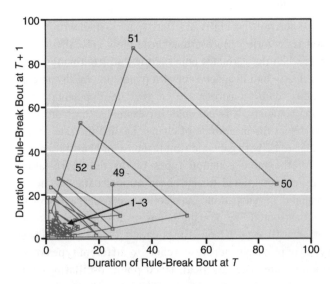

Figure 22.5   Phase plot for an antisocial dyad.

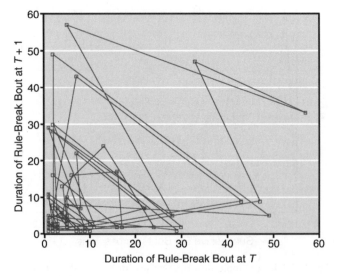

Figure 22.6   Phase plot of a prosocial dyad.

DS Methods 903

duration, total time, and the time since the last occurrence of the behavior, can be included in these models to determine the absorbing quality of a hypothesized attractor. Furthermore, time-invariant (e.g., gender) and time-varying (e.g., changes in context) covariates can be added to these models as predictors of the transition rate.

Figure 22.7 shows a schematic diagram of an interactive sequence. The bottom plot line represents the time line of events being modeled. In this case, there are only two states possible: in the "proposed" attractor or out of that state. This example illustrates a dichotomous response set, but it is not necessary for event streams to be binary for event history analyses; multiple states can be modeled as competing risks. The three episodes in this example correspond to the start and end times of the behavior of interest. The first episode lasts 14 seconds, the second episode lasts 18 seconds, and the third is 14 seconds long. With just this information it is possible to model the probability of transitions into the attractor as one instantaneous rate, and the duration since the last episode can be added into the model as a predictor.

Presumably, whatever behavior is being researched does not occur in a vacuum. There is the nature of the task at hand, the influence of other people, and even factors unique to each individual that must be considered. Thus, as shown by the time-varying covariates (upper two lines) in Figure 22.7, more elaborate models can tease apart the relative contributions of various covariates to the recurrence of a particular behavior. For example, Snyder, Stoolmiller, Wilson, and Yamamoto (in press) used event history models in a study of emotion regulation in early childhood. The events of interest were children's anger episodes while interacting with a parent over the course of an hour in a variety of tasks on two separate occasions. They ran two

models. The first analyzed the time it took until the first display of anger, and the second modeled the time between repeated displays of the child's anger. For these models, Snyder et al. included time-invariant effects of the child's gender, ratings of child antisocial behavior, and parental discipline (as well as which of several observers coded the session). Time-varying covariates included the activity or task in which the dyad was involved, the parent's "negative process" behavior, the cumulative frequency of the parent's negative process events, and the session time.

In the first multivariate model (time to first anger display), only the parent's negative process and the cumulative frequency of parent negative process were significant. The child's anger was 4 times more likely to occur when the parent was in a negative process state. In the second multivariate model (repeated anger displays), because the power increased substantially due to the greater number of data points, all predictors were significant. There was one very interesting interaction effect wherein the accumulation of the parent's negative process throughout the session increased the probability that subsequent parent negative process behaviors would elicit child anger. Thus, these results may be an indication of a dyadic, rather than an individual, attractor that exists for anger displays. A follow-up to this study could include collapsing the parent and child behaviors into one categorical stream and using an event history model to explore the possible effects on mutual anger displays.

The primary advantage of event history analysis is the versatility of the modeling procedures. These models can be run on individuals or pooled across an entire sample. It is not only the potential of identifying predictors of attractor strength that is the appeal for DS researchers but the fact that *time* itself can be used as a predictor. Probably the most difficult process of event history analysis is restructuring data into the appropriate format. Despite this difficulty, we expect that event history analysis will be used with increasing frequency as a method to model attractor dynamics.

Fourier analysis or spectral decomposition can be used for finding periodicities (i.e., cyclic patterns) in time-series data such as those used in phase plots. In general, this procedure treats a time series as a conglomerate wave form, breaks it down into a collection of pure waves (each of uniform frequency), and identifies the most prominent waves (Schroeck, 1994). Newtson (1994, 1998) has used this method to analyze the coupled dynamics of dyadic interactions. The relative amplitudes and temporal synchrony of these "behavior waves" were associated with the degree of mutuality or competition in interpersonal relationships. In other applications, different types of attractors,

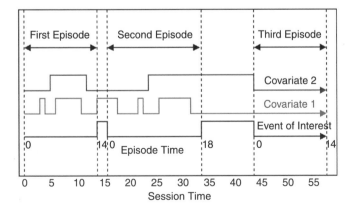

Figure 22.7 Schematic diagram of a behavioral interaction with some of the components that can be analyzed through event history analysis.

including oscillating and periodic attractors, can be identified. For behavioral scientists, however, this method has its limitations. Like all time-series procedures, it requires the researcher to collapse meaningful categorically coded observational data into one or very few continuous dimensions (e.g., Bakeman & Gottman, 1997). For example, most observational coding schemes used in developmental psychopathology (e.g., FPC: Dishion, Gardner, Patterson, Reid, & Thibodeaux, 1983; SPAFF: Gottman, McCoy, Coan, & Collier, 1996; MAX: Izard, 1979) code discrete behaviors such as "contempt," "argue," "belligerence," and "whining." To conduct Fourier analysis, these codes would have to fall along a single dimension (i.e., intensity of negativity). This type of collapsing is often either conceptually unfeasible or it is unappealing because of its oversimplification.

Karnaugh Maps

Inspired by synergetics, a type of dynamics developed by Haken (1977), Dumas, Lemay, and Dauwalder (2001) adapted this technique from Boolean algebra to study parent-child interactions. Karnaugh maps depict all possible combinations of up to four binary variables in one table or grid. A simple two-variable Karnaugh map is basically a 4-cell cross-tabulation of event frequencies with one dichotomous variable to each axis. Three- and four-variable maps are somewhat more complicated. Figure 22.8 shows a schematic 4-variable Karnaugh map. Each variable (*A, B, C,* and *D*) can have a value of 0 or 1, and each is displayed on one side of the square table (bottom, left, top, and right). Each cell in the map can be represented as a unique combination of the binary values of the four variables. Thus, a Karnaugh map is a state space of all possible states of the system and represents the relative frequencies in each state. Dumas and colleagues extended the application of these maps by plotting the transitions between states to depict temporal patterns across the space.

In their study, Dumas et al. (2001) plotted every minute of 6-hour home observations according to four parent and child dichotomous variables that included control, compliance, and aversive and positive behavior. Each behavior was plotted according to the 4-variable configuration, and successive behaviors were connected by a trajectory. They were primarily interested in comparing the maps of clinically referred dyads with randomly selected controls. They analyzed the "recurring transactions" (i.e., attractors) that were found most frequently in each group and aggregated these findings graphically on one summary Karnaugh map. Their results showed differences in transactional patterns between the groups, mostly involving positive interactions

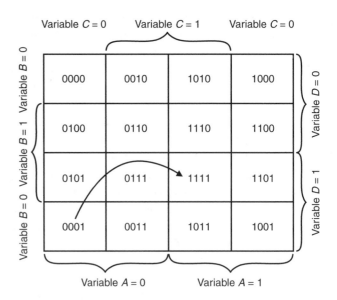

Figure 22.8   Schematic of a four-variable Karnaugh map. Each cell is a unique combination of four binary variables. The arrow shows a sample transition from one state, where only variable *D* is present (i.e., only *D* = 1), to the next state in time, where all four variables are present (i.e., all = 1).

and cycles of maternal control and child compliance. In addition to the graphical depiction of interaction sequences, the authors computed a "complexity index" that was designed to quantify each map on a continuum from completely deterministic to completely random. They found that all maps, regardless of group assignment, were neither random nor deterministic but somewhere in between.

Although this approach was unique and interesting (particularly from a methodological standpoint), from a DS perspective there is no reason to think that social behavior, especially in dyads with a rich history, is ever random or ever completely determined. Nevertheless, the complexity measure has a great deal of potential. For example, it might be used to determine whether stable coercive parent-child interaction patterns become less determined (i.e., the old attractor patterns break down) during developmental transitions such as puberty.

Karnaugh maps hold considerable promise for several reasons. First, because this method allows for the representation of behavior in up to four dimensions (five if you count time), a great deal of the complexity in interactional behavior can be nicely captured. The temporal quality of dyadic behavior is also maintained and can be tracked easily through visual inspection. Moreover, the systemic properties of dyadic interactions are kept intact, in contrast to conventional methods that often require analyzing each dyad member separately.

This methodology as applied to behavioral science, however, is very much in its infancy; thus, there are some limitations that may need to be addressed before Karnaugh maps can be applied to a broad range of behavioral data. One problem is that the adaptation of these maps to behavioral research requires data that can be collected or converted into dichotomous variables that occur concurrently. Developmental psychopathologists are often interested in data that cannot be meaningfully transformed into dichotomous values; continuous or categorical data cannot be adequately captured with these maps. Also, this method does not provide quantifiable tests of the strength of dyadic patterns, nor opportunities for comparing patterns. In this respect, the new developments in state space grid analysis may provide some promising avenues. Although the two approaches are not entirely similar, some of the quantitative measures that may be derived from state space grids may also be applicable to Karnaugh maps.

Coupled Equations

Most generally, this method refers to the use of paired equations derived from two synchronized time series that produce parameters that describe the underlying dynamics of a system. The use of coupled equations may involve mathematically demanding procedures and often requires fine-grained time-series data or simulated data. One particularly successful application in the field has been the work by John Gottman and colleagues, who have used coupled differential equations to model the dynamics of marital couples and to predict from those dynamics couples who will remain married or end by divorcing (Gottman, Coan, Carrere, & Swanson, 1998; Ryan, Gottman, Murray, Carrere, & Swanson, 2000). They have also used this method to study how peer interactions influence the behavior of developmentally delayed versus normal children (Gottman, Guralnick, Wilson, Swanson, & Murray, 1997) and parent-infant interaction (Gottman, Murray, Swanson, Tyson, & Swanson, 2002).

Gottman and colleagues' modeling procedures, based on mathematical biology, are an attempt to mathematically formalize theoretical assertions made by general systems theorists such as von Bertalanffy (1968). Their model itself represents a theory about the mechanisms and dynamics of marriage. Their approach is to model marital interactions using the mathematics of difference and differential equations. These equations express hypothesized mechanisms of change over time. Gottman and colleagues offer their model of marital interactions as a first attempt to create an explanatory theory of marriage; they recognize the value of cycling from theory development, to modeling, to

experiments, and back to theory development. As the authors comment, "The theory may be dead wrong, but it is precise" (Gottman et al., 2002).

The modeling process is guided by posing two questions: What are the steady states? and Which of these states are stable (i.e., the attractors) and which are unstable (i.e., repellors)? The first step is to set up the phase space such that each axis represents a variable corresponding to each participant. (This procedure is not the same as the one we described earlier in lag-1 phase plots.) The next step was to identify the steady states by graphing the "null clines," curves in phase space for which variables stay constant. These curves help to determine the steady states by partitioning the phase space into regions where changes in each variable are increasing or decreasing.

Gottman's technique uses a time series of coded observational data to create an equation for each person in the interaction. For this method, Gottman uses variables that are codes or categories of codes that fall along a single continuous dimension from very negative to very positive, with neutral in the middle. Equations are created to reflect the theoretical presumption that one person's behavior at time t is a function of his or her own behavior at time $t - 1$ as well as the other participant's behavior at time $t - 1$. Thus, there is an "uninfluenced" and an "influenced" factor in each equation that determines the behavior at each time t. The uninfluenced component is what each person brings to the interaction independent of the other. The uninfluenced set point can be thought of as a temperamental factor, which is assumed to be the attractor a person, left on his or her own, will eventually approach. Mathematically, this is denoted by a parameter that represents the rate of change toward the uninfluenced set point, also called "emotional inertia," plus a constant that is specific to the person. The influenced component is a mathematical function representing the other person's previous behavior. These functions can be used to plot curves that describe the degree of influence based on one assumption: Positive behavior influences positively and negative behavior influences negatively. Thus, the equations for a husband (H) and wife (W) are:

$$W_{t+1} = r_1 W_t + a + I(H_t)$$
$$H_{t+1} = r_2 H_t + b + I(W_t)$$

where r is the emotional inertia, a and b are constants specific to the individual, and I is the influence function. These equations are then manipulated to estimate the parameters and to determine the uninfluenced and influenced set points. Plotting both of the null clines (the curves for which the values of the variables remain constant) in phase space allows for the identification of stable steady states: the points where the two curves intersect.

Consider the example in Figure 22.9a, which shows bilinear null clines for a husband and wife. There is one positive and one negative stable state, or attractor, for this couple (the circles at the intersection of the two null clines). Over the course of the interaction, their behavior is drawn to one or the other of these attractors. One of the interesting uses of this modeling technique is its depiction of how a system exhibits sensitivity to initial conditions and how marriages can change over time. For example, situations at work may lead the husband to feel a lot of stress, and he may begin to express this stress in his interactions with his wife. This would be reflected in a change in the parameter b in the model that corresponds to the husband's uninfluenced state, or what he brings to the interaction. A change in this constant shifts his influence function to the left (Figure 22.9b), to the point where the positive attractor no longer exists. Thus, this type of modeling can distinguish between superficial change (i.e., a move to a different stable state) and deeper change (i.e., a fundamental change in the influence function that eliminates or adds a stable state to the marital couple's behavioral repertoire).

Gottman and his colleagues (2002) have used this basic model and more elaborated versions to identify mechanisms related to specific types of marriages. Some couples have only one stable steady state; if it is positive the marriage is "happy," if it is negative the marriage is "unhappy." Typically, the situation is more complex. Happy couples also tend to have both positive and negative attractors. In fact, high influence and high inertia couples tend to have multiple steady states and thus will most likely have at least one negative attractor. It may be the relative strengths of these attractors that best distinguish distressed and nondistressed couples.

Gottman and colleagues' (2002) approach to mathematical modeling seems to hold exciting potential for developmental psychopathologists who are interested in understanding social processes of various kinds. For example, their model can be easily adjusted to simulate interactions that have different types of power imbalances: parent-child interactions, therapist-client sessions, sibling interactions, bully-victim relations, and so on. Developmental psychopathologists have constructed detailed theoretical models that hypothesize specific influence functions among social partners (e.g., coercion processes in families with aggressive children, authoritative parenting and anxiety-disordered children). Gottman's approach challenges scholars in the field to translate these theories into mathematically specified mechanisms. This approach

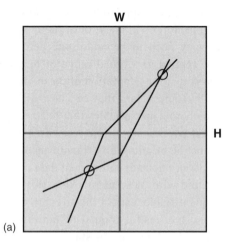

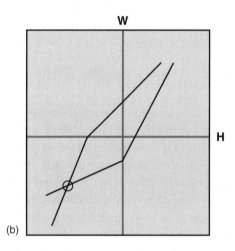

Figure 22.9 Null clines and the stability of steady states. Steady states are circled and represented by the point at which the null clines intersect.

may be particularly rewarding if developmental principles can be formalized and included in these endeavors.

Nonlinear Dynamics

These methods are derived from mathematical procedures in physics and other sciences that aim to measure and model nonlinear phenomena (Abraham, Abraham, & Shaw, 1990; Heath, 2000; Norton, 1995). The simplest of these is nonlinear regression, wherein the parameters are exponential functions or the predictive combinations are not simply additive. Other applications from this area are those related to chaos theory (Newell & Molenaar, 1998). One can use nonlinear dynamic techniques to find the embedding dimension, entropy, determinism, recurrence, or fractal dimension of any time series of sufficient length and sufficient precision. This class of techniques is typically applied to continuous time-series data (type 1), often physiological. For those developmental psychopathologists who are increasingly collecting this sort of data (e.g., heart rate, skin conductance, neural activity), this class of methods holds a great deal of promise, particularly if there are reasons to hypothesize nonlinearities. Moreover, there are many software packages available for free or at minimal cost that can calculate these measures for any appropriate time series. The challenge, therefore, lies not in the calculation but in the psychological interpretation of these measures.

There are a number of diverse applications of this class of techniques. One of the main reasons for using these methods is to determine the degree of orderliness, complexity, or predictability in the behavior of a given system. One recent example in developmental psychopathology comes from the work of Dishion, Nelson, Bullock, and Winter (in press). They applied a technique that calculated the degree of complexity of peer interactions, in the hopes of characterizing and differentiating prosocial versus antisocial peer interactions. The authors drew on information theory and applied Shannon's entropy measure (Shannon & Weaver, 1949) as an index of the degree of disorganization, uncertainty, or information in a dyadic interaction. In information theory, uncertainty and information are related because "information about an unknown event is more useful as one knows less about the event" (Wickens, 1989, p. 231). For example, if 100% of a set of communications is of one type (e.g., deviant talk), there is total certainty and no information is conveyed from one communication to another. This is a case of low entropy. Conversely, if there are a variety of types of communications and all are equally probable, then there is total uncertainty and a maximal amount of information is gained by finding out which event occurred. This is an example of maximum entropy.

Shannon's entropy measure is typically used with contingency tables where the values in each cell represent the probability of a different two-event sequence. A simple way to think of entropy is the average number of dichotomous decisions (yes/no) that need to be made to classify an event in that table (Wickens, 1989). Thus, in the previous example, the situation where only one event is observed would have a minimal entropy value of 1 because only one dichotomous decision is necessary to classify any event. Shannon's entropy is calculated as follows:

$$Entropy = H = \Sigma p_{ij}\left(\log_2\left(\frac{1}{p_{ij}}\right)\right)$$

where p_{ij} is the conditional probability in the cell that is in row i and column j of a contingency table.

Dishion et al. (in press) used turn-taking observational data of boys interacting with their closest friend to calculate entropy. Their conversational turns were coded into five categories: negative engagement, directive, converse, positive engagement, and other. Thus, there was a 5 × 5 matrix of two-event sequences for each peer dyad. The frequencies in each cell of the matrix were used to calculate the conditional probabilities necessary for the entropy calculation. The findings from this study showed that all of the friendship dyads' interactions (regardless of whether or not they were antisocial) became more ordered (less entropic) over three time points: at 14, 16, and 18 years old. This finding in itself is compelling. It supports the DS view that development is characterized by increasing orderliness—a crystallization of interaction patterns. As relationships of all kinds develop, they stabilize and, thus, become more predictable over time. When the authors compared early-onset antisocial boys with prosocial boys, they found that antisocial boys' interactions corresponded to higher entropy scores, suggesting a more disorganized pattern, and were characterized by more deviant talk than interactions of the typically developing boys. These results may suggest that antisocial boys are less skilled than prosocial boys at carrying on a fluid, appropriately contingent conversation.

Some other potentially useful applications of this approach are found in clinical therapy research (e.g., Badalamenti & Langs, 1992; Burlingame, Fuhriman, & Barnum, 1995; Butz, Chamberlain, & McCown, 1997; Lichtenberg & Heck, 1986; Pincas, 2001; Tschacher, Scheier, & Grawe, 1998). Lichtenberg and Heck examined the "Gloria" psychotherapy tapes and compared the results of Shannon's entropy measure, Markov chain analysis, and sequential analysis. Each of these approaches showed some merit and each had associated limitations. In terms of therapeutic process and outcome, two therapy studies have applied Shannon's entropy measure with somewhat contradictory results; one found that, over the course of intervention, verbal utterances became increasingly complex (Badalamenti & Langs, 1992), and the other found that client and therapist measures of therapy sessions became increasingly coherent (i.e., less complex, according to the entropy measure) and that this tendency was related to treatment success (Tschacher et al., 1998).

Finally, a study conducted by Pincas (2001) recently set out to demonstrate that when treatment works, therapy sessions become both more complex and more coherent. This preliminary study may be particularly relevant to developmental psychopathologists because it was based on assumptions from family systems theory (Minuchin, 1974). Pincas was interested in empirically testing one of the basic assumptions of family systems therapy: that families maintain a state of equilibrium through negative feedback processes that dampen deviations. These deviations (e.g., depressive withdrawal, angry outbursts) manifest as symptoms for a particular family member but also serve to maintain homeostasis in the family (e.g., Minuchin, 1974; Minuchin & Fishman, 1974). For example, a child may become oppositional in order to (consciously or unconsciously) distract the family from the "real" problem: intense marital discord. When the child acts out, the parents join forces and attend to the disruptive behavior, which precludes escalation of the marital conflict (dampening process); thus, the family maintains a state of equilibrium, however dysfunctional it may be. The goal of family therapy is twofold: "to disrupt or block these negative feedback processes, promoting family disequilibrium and reorganization" and to "capitalize on natural deviation-amplifying processes within family systems in order to bring about systemic change" (positive feedback; Pincas, 2001, p. 145). In short, the goal of therapy is to induce a phase transition in the family system.

As a first step toward validating these assumptions, Pincas conducted a pilot study in which he analyzed the conversations of one family undergoing therapy. He used an analytic technique called *orbital decomposition* (OD; Guastello, Hyde, & Odak, 1998), which combines Shannon's entropy measure and measures of Lyapunov dimensionality, as well as others, to identify hierarchical patterns, the extent of randomness in a time series, and the optimal level of analysis for any particular series (i.e., the number of units in a string that best captures the information for a time series). The results confirmed that, indeed, the family exhibited evidence of both coherence and complexity across treatment sessions. Because this was a pilot study, we are hesitant to make too much of these findings. But OD may hold particular promise for developmental psychopathologists because it was developed for analyzing *categorical* time-series data, instead of the usual continuous series. As such, it addresses a major limitation that has been repeatedly raised with the other time-series techniques reviewed here.

The use of the entropy measure has only begun to be explored in clinical research. Some of the kinds of questions that can be explored with this measure include the following: Do families at the beginning of a particular intervention exhibit interactions that are highly stable and predictable (i.e., low entropy)? Does the entropy index change over the course

of treatment as old rigid patterns of interaction disintegrate and new ones get the chance to emerge? Does successful treatment necessarily show this kind of rise in unpredictability profile across sessions? Do families restabilize in new patterns at the end of treatment, as indicated by a fallback to a relatively low entropy score? In other words, can effective treatment be characterized by a developmental phase transition?

The methods for analyzing nonlinear dynamics described in this section have been applied to single-time series. These are appropriate for some biological measures with high temporal resolution (e.g., heart rate), but another form of continuous data, electrical activity in the brain, presents a more complex challenge. There are increasingly more developmental psychopathologists who are integrating brain activity measures in their research programs (e.g., Calkins & Fox, 2002; Cicchetti & Dawson, 2002b; Nelson et al., 2002). Although there is clearly not enough space to discuss the various brain imaging methods in the current review, a word on these techniques is warranted. Ongoing electrical activity in the brain, measured by electroencephalogram (EEG), can involve as many as 256 separate time series, one per electrode. Methods that analyze these kinds of complex data are designed to find relations and patterns among and across these various time series. For example, developmental neuroscientists interested in the self-organization of brain dynamics have found real-time synchronization across distal cortical areas to be correlated with attentional states or focused perception (Lewis, 2005). Transient, organized activity in different regions oscillating in phase ("phase synchrony") and cortical "coherence" (a similar measure that incorporates both amplitude and phase) are detected through various temporal correlation methods and have been found to correspond with attentional (e.g., Engel, Fries, & Singer, 2001) and emotional (Paré & Collins, 2000) events.

We close this section with a cautionary note that applies to any dynamical mathematical technique. Because these techniques are derived from other fields, often it may be easier to input numbers into the equations than to sensibly interpret the results of the computations. A number of DS researchers have been criticized for interpreting their mathematical functions too literally; either the data inserted into the equations do not conform to the mathematical assumptions or, perhaps more serious, the data are potentially arbitrary in terms of their psychological meaning. These methods hold a great deal of promise, but there also remains a great deal of theoretical and empirical work before the psychological meaning of nonlinear dynamic techniques is clearly understood.

Developmental Time Measures

In the following section, methods appropriate for the study of developmental phenomena are described. Like the real-time techniques, some of these methodologies have been specifically designed to test DS-based hypotheses, while others seem to us particularly commensurate with this aim.

Descriptive Developmental Profile Analysis

The empirical work by Thelen and colleagues (e.g., Thelen & Smith, 1994; Thelen & Ulrich, 1991) has been characterized as descriptive in that it is nonparametric, uses descriptive statistics, and often relies heavily on displaying individual developmental profiles graphically. These researchers most often collect continuous time-series data (e.g., in toddlers learning to walk, the number of alternating steps, degree of displacement of foot, proportion of stepping cycle) over repeated occasions across a significant developmental period. They create developmental profiles on a case-by-case basis and describe the similarities and differences among these profiles. A core concern in this type of analysis is to identify periods of transition during which variability dramatically increases and old behavioral habits dissolve, giving rise to new ones (e.g., from crawling to walking).

The most straightforward way to graph developmental growth profiles is to simply plot scores for the collective variable (e.g., alternate stepping) on the *y* axis across several developmental time points on the *x* axis, and to do so for each case individually. Van Geert and van Dijk (2002) offer a number of additional methods for visualizing and describing intraindividual time-series data over repeated observations. These methods were specifically created for measuring changes in variability across developmental time, and they are well-suited for one-dimensional continuous longitudinal data. In addition, with any individual developmental profile plot, several trajectories can be grouped into clusters that show similar profiles by using variations of a cluster analytic procedure (e.g., Hollenstein et al., 2004).

One simple but elegant plotting technique is referred to as the *moving min-max graph* (van Geert & van Dijk, 2002). This graph represents the developmental trend line, but also the variability around this trend line in a bandwidth of observed scores. A moving window is used; that is, a time frame that is selected by the researcher (e.g., 2 weeks, 3 months) is moved over one position all the way across the time series such that each window partly overlaps with the previous window. There is no absolute window length that is required, but van Geert and van Dijk suggest that the window size should be about one-tenth the

size of the entire data set and no less than five data points. The maximum and minimum score at each time window is plotted, and then the bandwidth of these scores can be examined in terms of its stability and change. In addition, a moving average that corresponds to the moving min-max window can be computed and displayed along the middle of the bandwidth. Figure 22.10 shows a graph taken from van Geert and van Dijk's study in which they showed the developmental trend for one child's acquisition of spatial prepositions. They used a time window of 18 days across a 10-month period. The graph shows that there is a moderate size bandwidth in the beginning of the trajectory and then, after a couple of oscillations, a large increase in the bandwidth, which is maintained until the end of the observation period. The authors interpreted this plot as suggesting a developmental transition (one that showed the characteristics of a phase transition) in the use of spatial prepositions. For a more detailed examination of the values in the bandwidth, the authors also propose using an "altitude line graph," which simply depicts intermediate values as well (e.g., the second highest and second lowest values, percentiles), with a line connecting these values. The result is a plot that resembles the contour lines in a geographical relief map. A number of other variations of these variability charts can be found in van Geert and van Dijk.

To explore developmental trends in individual or group data, developmentalists commonly plot idealized or "processed" estimations of a data series (e.g., regression models, smoothing techniques) that obscure information on

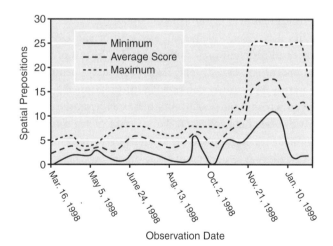

Figure 22.10 Moving min-max graph representing one child's acquisition of spatial prepositions (time window of 18 days; last window = 15 days). *Source:* From "Focus on Variability: New Tools to Study Intra-Individual Variability in Developmental Data," by P. van Geert and M. van Dijk, 2002, *Infant Behavior and Development, 25,* pp. 340–370.

variability (this is what they are designed to do: smooth out fluctuations). In general, developmentalists constrain themselves to a very small repertoire of smoothing techniques and, thus, lose potentially critical information about the characteristics of transitions and the idiosyncratic nature of development (van Geert & van Dijk, 2002). Van Geert and van Dijk argue for the application of more sophisticated smoothing models "which follow the actual rise and fall of the data as faithfully as one wishes" (p. 351). They provide alternatives, many of which are options available in commonly used statistical packages, including SPSS. Some of these techniques include spline models and local polynomial regression models, or loess smoothers, which allow researchers to detect fluctuations and nonlinear trends in their data sets (Simonoff, 1996; van Geert & van Dijk, 2002).

To complement the impressions gained from the graphical developmental profiles, DS researchers may use simple statistics such as within-subject measures of variance (e.g., standard deviations) and correlations to track increases in variability across developmental transition points. The well-known standard deviation (SD) measure is sometimes problematic, however, because of its sensitivity to the mean (i.e., if distributions are censored at a low score, the SD tends to increase when the mean increases), making SDs difficult to compare across individual subjects or samples. To address this limitation, another, less common measure of variability can be used: the coefficient of variation (CV; van Geert & van Dijk, 2002). The CV is simply the SD divided by the mean and, although it too has limitations, it can be used as an alternative to the SD.

Skewness is another easily calculated measure that provides a great deal of information about the pattern of variability in a given trajectory (van Geert & van Dijk, 2002). A skewed distribution is one potential indicator of bimodality, one of the catastrophe flags previously mentioned. In DS terms, bimodality can provide information about the extent to which a particular skill has been acquired or a pattern has been consolidated. For example, in the context of acquiring theory of mind (ToM), a 3½-year-old child who is just beginning to understand that others may hold false beliefs about the child will likely show very few correct responses to ToM tests over several weeks of repeated testing; these will show up as positive outliers. In general, the child will still be responding "incorrectly," as if he or she has no false belief understanding; thus, the distribution will be positively skewed. At the age of 4, however, this child will likely show a negatively skewed distribution of responses; the child's ToM skills will have consolidated and now only very rarely will the child respond as if he or she did not understand that others can hold false beliefs.

A similar example might be used for thinking about children in treatment. For instance, at first, a child undergoing cognitive-behavioral therapy for problems with anxiety may respond to frightening or challenging situations with predominantly avoidant strategies and very few proactive, assertive behaviors (i.e., the distribution will be positively skewed, with most behaviors falling toward the avoidant end of the continuum and a few outliers falling toward the assertive end). But if treatment is successful, this child may end therapy showing a pattern of responses that is negatively skewed. The point at which the distribution shifts from being positively to negatively skewed may provide key information about the timing and profile of change across treatment. From a DS perspective, it is likely that this child's distribution of avoidant-assertive scores from pre- to posttreatment will shift from positively skewed to bimodal to negatively skewed; that is, at no point will the child exhibit responses that show a normal distribution. This pattern would suggest an abrupt shift (a phase transition) in response styles that may be related to treatment success. The main point here is that instead of trying to "normalize" distributions at any stage, information about skewness and variability can provide insights about the nature of transitions and developmental change.

Standard statistical packages (e.g., SPSS, SAS) provide tests for assessing skewness. A Kolmogorow-Smirnov test provides a statistic for sample sizes (or number of observations) greater than 50, and the Shapiro-Wild test for sample sizes less than 50 (van Geert & van Dijk, 2002). In addition, van Geert and van Dijk describe bootstrapping methods that provide researchers a "random sample" with which to compare statistically significant differences in skewness values across a given developmental trajectory.

Finally, individual growth curve modeling procedures can be applied to examine different profiles of change on both the individual and group level. This method is familiar to many developmentalists; it has been applied to examine different trajectories of antisocial behavior (e.g., Nagin & Tremblay, 1999), infant vocal development (Hsu & Fogel, 2001), and infant-mother interactions (van den Boom & Hoeksma, 1994), as well as many other domains. Several easily accessible computer programs are available to run these modeling procedures, including multilevel analysis and hierarchical linear modeling.

Latent Class Analysis

Descriptive developmental profile analyses, as we have described them, are generally restricted to continuous one-dimensional data. Categorical and nominal data are difficult to use with these approaches (without somehow transforming them into continuous data). In this regard, combining different types of developmental profile analyses with methods that can capture content-specific changes in categorical or ordinal variables may be important. Another elegant option for investigating the bimodal properties of a distribution is offered by van der Maas (1998): latent class analysis (LCA). This technique is appropriate for analyzing categorical data. A number of developmental psychopathologists familiar with modeling procedures such as structural equation modeling (SEM) and hierarchical linear modeling (HLM) may also be aware of this method. LCA is conceptually similar to cluster analytic procedures in that it identifies subgroups or types. But it has additional power because it also provides a maximum likelihood estimation and is adaptable to different data structures with no a priori assumptions about the distributions.

As a cognitive developmentalist, van der Maas (1998) is particularly interested in this method for modeling the bimodal response distributions identified on various cognitive tasks at developmental transition points or across various contexts. He argues that cognitive strategies can be best understood as attractors that are more or less available at different ages and in different contexts. In his approach, response patterns to multiple tasks are analyzed in terms of a cusp-catastrophe model, and multistable states (bimodality) are identified through LCA procedures. By presenting several examples of the application of rule and strategy detection in multiple domains, van der Maas showed that LCA may be one of the more promising psychometric models for identifying attractors and multistable states with categorical data.

Dynamic Growth Modeling

A group of scholars from the Netherlands can be credited for having pioneered the use of dynamic growth models in the study of cognitive developmental transitions (e.g., van der Maas, 1998; van der Maas & Molenaar, 1992; van Geert, 1994, 1995, 1997a). The class of techniques advocated by these researchers is often grouped under the heading *nonlinear dynamics,* in reference to the modeling techniques and equations that are associated with this branch of mathematics. Although the techniques have often been applied to real-time data, these scholars explore various applications to developmental modeling instead.

Dynamic growth modeling was developed to simulate change over time (or growth) using logistic difference equations. Van Geert (1994) has used this procedure to model the processes underlying stage-like transitions in the growth of syntactic forms. The basic DS premise of van Geert's technique is that development of cognitive capacities is much like the self-organized proliferation of multiple species over the course of evolution. Van Geert models cognitive "growers" that constitute a complex system of intraindividual and environmental relations. Like the real-time coupled equations described earlier in reference to Gottman's work, the modeling procedure is realized with iterative equations in which behavioral states are updated by the amplifying and dampening forces inherent in the system's (i.e., the child's) experiential history combined with current external (contextual) resources and limitations. The growth models depict the kinds of nonlinear developmental profiles predicted by stage theorists (e.g., Piaget and Vygotsky). They also emphasize the use of graphical procedures to plot empirical data from longitudinal studies of children's cognitive skill acquisition to match these empirical profiles to the data from simulations derived from the equations. The mathematical formulations used in these models are common in other disciplines; what makes these models unique is the application of both psychological and DS concepts to identify the mechanisms of growth in observed developmental profiles. Another critical strength of this approach is that the process of developing simulations forces the researcher to specify the null hypothesis explicitly. The conventional a priori comparison between the hypothesized result and a lack of any effect is replaced by a specific null hypothesis of an alternative pattern of results.

Recently, van Geert and his colleagues (Steenbeek & van Geert, in press) have broadened their cognitive developmental focus and have become interested in modeling children's peer play interactions. This new modeling endeavor may be more relevant to developmental psychopathologists because of its content (i.e., peer interactions), but more important, it may prove more generalizable to a large body of social interaction problems that developmental psychopathologists are interested in tackling.

Similar to previous endeavors, the procedure begins with a theoretical model. In this case, Steenbeek and van Geert (in press) developed a theoretical model that stipulated that differences in peer interactions with rejected versus popular children can be understood as a function of the following reciprocally interacting factors: each child's goals (autonomy and involvement), the drive that results from the extent to which these goals are met, the emotional appraisal at each given moment, and the resulting emotional expression and behavior. These theoretical factors are then formalized into a mathematical model that stipulates the mechanism differentiating rejected and popular children's dyadic interactions. Because this is a DS-based model, the mathematical formulation necessarily includes reciprocal, iterative processes and feedback cycles within and across occasions, as well as sensitivity to random or chance variations and the potential for nonlinear results. Next, the simulation is run repeatedly, and the results of the simulation are compared to theoretical expectations. Finally, the results of the simulation are compared to empirical data from real dyadic interactions.

The model includes a number of input parameters that can be set at the outset. These values can be start values for a particular variable or the strength of the connection between two variables. Rejected and popular children, for example, are assigned different preference values according to the original theoretical model. Figure 22.11 is a representation of the simulation model with all of the reciprocal and iterative processes depicted by arrows. Table 22.3 shows the different parameters and what values can be manipulated at the outset. The table also shows the parameter profiles for each type of dyad (the various combinations with rejected, popular, and average children). The model is run, for example, 1,000 times with the particular inputs specified in Table 22.3 for children with different sociometric status.

One of the unexpected results that emerged from running the simulations was that, contrary to what previous literature suggested, the data representing rejected children playing with normal-status children showed more positive emotional expressions than that for popular children with normal-status children (Steenbeek & van Geert, in press). When these simulation results were compared to actual empirical data, the results matched (statistical tests described by the authors in detail were run to compare the simulated and empirical results). The authors concluded that, because rejected children seldom had a chance to play with other children in general, the new experience of playing with someone else led to the expression of more happy emotions than expected. The popular children, on the other hand, were not as pleased with the experience because they were not playing with their regular friends and had plenty of opportunities to play with other children.

The authors suggest that the modeling results are consistent with contextualist, functionalist, and dynamic systems perspectives. Indeed, their models remain true to fundamental DS assumptions. Broadly, the simulation technique demonstrated that emotions and behavior

> [are not a function of] personality characteristics that are relatively independent of the contexts and of the local and temporal realization of the concerns. . . . [Instead, the findings] emphasize the importance of iterative and interacting processes that take place in real time. It overthrows the classical distinction between independent and dependent variables in favor of a process of mutually interacting and simultaneous processes. (Steenbeek & van Geert, in press)

Van Geert (1998c) emphasizes the critical role mathematical modeling plays in developmental research: "In order to find out the implications of theories, they have to be transformed into mathematical models that capture the

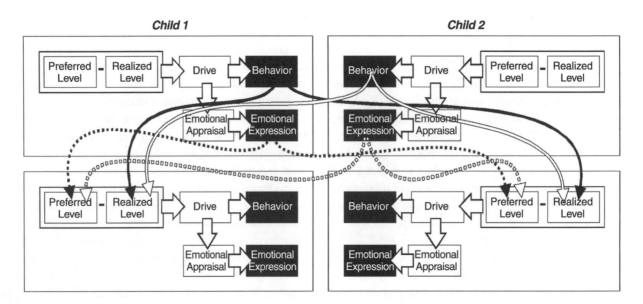

Figure 22.11   Steenbeek and van Geert's (in press) peer interaction simulation model. The first row of boxes represents the first moment in time, *t;* the second row represents the second moment, *t* + 1. Thin arrows represent the iterative feedback components (the output of one iteration is the input for the next).

TABLE 22.3   Parameter Profiles for Various Types of Dyads

Start Values Input Parameters	Average Status Partner: Average	**Average Status** Partner: Popular	Average Status Partner: Rejected	Popular Status Partner: Average	**Rejected Status** Partner: Average
Concerns	I stronger than A −Stronger than	I stronger than A −**Much** stronger than	I stronger than A −**Little bit** stronger than	I stronger than A −Stronger than	I stronger than A −**Much** stronger than
Contribution B → RC	I: average A: average	I: average A: **high**	I: average A: average	I: average A: average	I: average A: **high**
EA and EE	Pos: moderate Neg: moderate	Pos: moderate Neg: **difficult**	Pos: moderate Neg: moderate	Pos: moderate Neg: moderate	Pos: moderate Neg: **difficult**
Contribution EE → PC	Pos: average Neg: average	Pos: **big** Neg: **big**	Pos: average Neg: average	Pos: average Neg: average	Pos: **big** Neg: **big**
Basic principles	C: average S: average	C: average S: **big**	C: average S: average	C: average S: average	C: average S: **big**

Source: From "A Dynamic Systems Model of Dyadic Child-Peer Play Interactions," by H. Steenbeck and P. Geert, in press, *European Journal of Developmental Psychology.*

major dynamic principles of such models and that can be used to explore the range of developmental trajectories under all possible or likely parameter conditions" (p. 155; also see Newtson, 1994; van Geert, 1994). But despite van Geert's concerted efforts to make his approach accessible, its impact on developmental psychology and developmental psychopathology may be limited because of its use of mathematical procedures that are daunting to most psychologists. More important, a great deal of the developmental phenomena that researchers are interested in examining are not conducive to this sort of modeling because they are not easily quantified as continuous variables. Also, regardless of the domain in which this method is applied, and as with all simulation techniques, the correspondence of the parameters in the model with genuine psychological mechanisms is often difficult to evaluate and runs the risk of seeming "arbitrary." Nevertheless, this modeling technique and others may prove useful for developmental psychopathologists who have very precise hypotheses that can be faithfully translated into mathematical functions that specify mechanisms of change, influence, and interaction.

Connectionist Modeling

Connectionist and dynamic systems theories have separate histories but share a great many commonalities (Spencer & Thelen, in press). Although it is not quite accurate to characterize connectionism as a dynamic systems methodology, we would be missing an important contribution if we were not to include this modeling approach. Many (but not all) connectionist models are indeed dynamic systems, and researchers working with these models often turn to concepts such as attractors, bifurcations, and chaos to understand their properties (Smith & Samuelson, in press).

Connectionism is often characterized as a framework for simulating idealized brain-like, or "neural network," processing. This is because connectionist modeling starts with the propagation of activation across a network of abstract units that can be hypothetically likened to networks of neurons that fire or do not, depending on the context. Knowledge, representation, or meaning is understood as being "stored" not in one or two units, but in connection weights between processing units. Learning and development is evidenced by changes in connections between these units. These changes result from statistical regularities in the input to the network, and these regularities are governed by the Hebbian learning principle: Units that fire together, wire together. Thus, "the connection weights between layers [of units]—the response of the network to a specific input—depend on the statistical regularities in the network's *history* of experiences" (Thelen & Smith, 1998, p. 580). Through their own real-time activity, without any additional intervention, connectionist networks change their own connections and, thus, "teach" themselves. One of the best-known examples of a connectionist model is Rumelhart and McClelland's (1986) demonstration of a network that acquired irregular and regular forms of past tense and overgeneralized (as real children were thought to do) the irregular forms. Their breakthrough was to show that a network could behave as if it was governed by higher-order rules with no such rules having been prespecified.

In most connectionist models, activation among units is a continuous temporal process. Differential equations are used to simulate this continuous activation process such that weighted connections link the rate of change in one variable to the inputs received from the other units (e.g., Munakata & McClelland, in press). In many recent models, the activation process is assumed to be nonlinear. A simple example is provided by a nonlinear adjustment to McClelland's (1979) cascade model:

$$\frac{dneta_i}{dt} = k_j \left(\Sigma \, a_j w_{ij} - a_i \right)$$

$$a_i = f \left(net_i \right)$$

where a represents the activation of receiving unit i, a_j is the activation of sending unit j, w_{ij} represents the connection weight from unit j to unit i, and k is a time constant that sets the rate of change. $Neta_i$ refers to the net input to unit i, and f is a nonlinear function (Munakata & McClelland, in press).

In terms of development, connectionist simulations based on variations of the nonlinear differential equation have been developed to understand category and word learning (Plunkett, 1993; Smith, 1993, 1995), children's knowledge of dimension words and their selective attention to each dimension (Gasser & Smith, 1996; Smith, 1993), the development of face recognition (Johnson & Morton, 1991), and the "A-not-B error" (Munakata, 1998), among others. In terms of the A-not-B error, Thelen and colleagues (Smith & Thelen, in press; Thelen, Schoener, Scheier, & Smith, 2001) extended past connectionist models by applying the dynamic systems principles of multicausality and nested time scales and developed a "dynamic field" model. They incorporated the idea that instabilities in network activities (i.e., variability) index qualitative changes in systemic behavior. Spencer and Schoener (in press) summarize this dynamic connectionist model: "Instabilities disrupt the one-to-one input-output mapping and make dynamic fields nonstandard neural networks."

Connectionist modeling, like other dynamical modeling techniques we have described, requires either a great deal of technical expertise or collaboration among researchers with various talents (e.g., computer programming, mathematics, developmental theory). We are aware of very few efforts in developmental psychopathology to apply this type of simulation procedure, but there may be a number of phenomena in the field that could benefit from such an approach. For example, different types of friendship formations on the playground may be modeled through connectionist procedures. Children seem to self-organize into coalitions or cliques very quickly at the beginning of a school year. These emergent groupings may be modeled as networks of units that become strengthened over time. Different types of coalitions (e.g., bullies and victims versus supportive friendship relationships) may exhibit unique

properties (e.g., bullies/victims may be less stable, more perturbable, and less likely to include new members than other types of friendships). These unique properties may suggest adjustments to existing theoretical models of friendship formation and even have the potential to suggest change mechanisms that may be targeted through intervention.

Readers interested in applying connectionist modeling are directed to *Rethinking Innateness: A Connectionist Perspective on Development* (Elman et al., 1996) and the companion book *Exercises in Rethinking Innateness: A Handbook for Connectionist Simulations* (Plunkett & Elman, 1997). These volumes provide a thorough primer in connectionist modeling and give novices an opportunity for hands-on practice. The authors make important distinctions between mechanisms of change and development and the content of those changes. Of special concern is the attempt to understand emergence and nested interactions at multiple time scales. The exercise book is a practical step-by-step manual that includes computer software and several example simulations that model, for example, stagewise development and how children learn the past tense.

Catastrophe Modeling

This is a mathematical procedure wherein several control parameters can be used to account for discontinuous change in one of seven topological forms (catastrophe models; Thom, 1975; cf. Guastello, 1995). As such, it has some appeal for developmental psychopathologists interested in incorporating insights from developmental stage theories or modeling nonlinear changes in behavior due to treatment or trauma. These models show how each of the possible combinations of control parameters results in different values of a dependent variable. The potential values of the dependent variable are represented on a plane, much like a state space. Nonlinear shifts can be depicted as a fold or curl in the plane, showing where behavior changes suddenly rather than continuously.

The simplest and most commonly used catastrophe model is a cusp catastrophe, as depicted in Figure 22.12. The top surface of this three-dimensional figure is the behavior plane, which is made up of all the possible values of the response variable (i.e., collective variable). The location of a point in the behavior plane is predicted by the values of the control parameter and the splitting factor (the axes on the bottom plane, called the control plane), which are equivalent to independent variables in these models. The top left position on the behavior plane (point A), for instance, is a combination of a low value of the control pa-

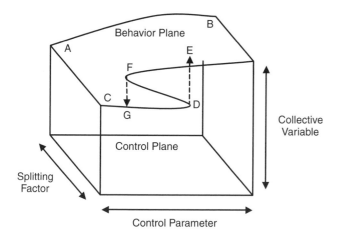

Figure 22.12 Basic cusp-catastrophe model.

rameter and a low value of the splitting factor. Keeping the splitting factor constant for the moment, follow the movement from point A to point B. Here we see that there is a linear response in behavior as the control parameter increases continuously. However, when the values of the splitting factor are high, there are some values of the control parameter that result in two possible locations on the behavior plane (points D and E or F and G). This cusp fold in the behavior plane is the region that describes the nonlinear response dynamics of the system. As the control parameter increases from the lowest value at point C, the behavior increases through points G and D. However, at point D, the collective variable value suddenly "jumps" to point E on the plane. When the control parameter decreases from its maximum value, behavior passes through point E to point F in a linear response. Now at point F, behavior suddenly "jumps" down to point G, a much lower value for the collective variable. This difference in response, depending on whether the control parameter is increasing or decreasing, is one of the unique features represented by cusp models and exemplifies the process of hysteresis.

For example, consider the relationship between frustration and anger. The first step in catastrophe modeling is to identify that a catastrophe exists. The catastrophe flags mentioned earlier are used for this purpose. Presence of hysteresis, divergence from linear response, sudden jumps, bimodality, anomalous variance, and critical slowing down can all serve as flags. For the current example, suppose that through experimentation a researcher discovers a bimodality in the distribution of anger responses to frustration. In cases where frustration is moderate, anger is either high or low but never in between. This would be an indication that a cusp catastrophe could be an appropriate model. Moreover, suppose that this bimodality occurs only in high-reward

contexts, and that frustration and anger have a positive linear relationship in low-reward contexts. Thus, for this example, anger is the collective variable of interest, frustration is the control parameter, and amount of reward in the context is the splitting factor (Figure 22.13). In a low-reward task (e.g., no motivational incentive other than following instructions), as frustration increases, the anger response would increase gradually (path A to B in Figure 22.13). In a high-reward task (e.g., in a gambling context), as frustration increases, the anger response would break from linearity at point D. Anger would suddenly jump to a higher level at point E. If frustration continues to increase, there would again be a linear increase in anger. However, frustration would have to subside well below the levels at which the previous jump occurred (point F) before anger decreased nonlinearly to its former level.

The next step of the modeling procedure is to fit the model to empirical data, much like linear regressions are fit to data. Catastrophe models have been used to model diverse developmental transitions such as conservation of liquid (van der Maas & Molenaar, 1992), acquisition of syntax (Ruhland & van Geert, 1998), infant reaching with grasping (Wimmers, Savelsbergh, van der Kamp, & Hartelman, 1998), dating (Tesser & Achee, 1994), blame responses of victims of assault (Lanza, 1999), adolescent smoking (Byrne, Mazanov, & Gregson, 2001), alcohol use (Clair, 1998), and anxiety in preuniversity students (Haslett, Smyrnios, & Osbourne, 1998). These and other examples indicate that, despite the difficulty in specifying or measuring control parameters, as discussed earlier, important insights about the profiles and mechanisms of change can be gained. Catastrophe theory and models will likely become more applicable as more researchers address

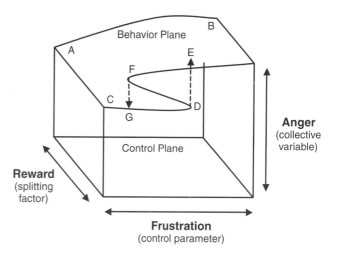

Figure 22.13 Cusp catastrophe model representing the relationship between anger and frustration in different contexts.

the nonlinearities in their data and work to measure hypothesized control parameters.

STATE SPACE GRID ANALYSIS: A GRAPHICAL AND STATISTICAL MIDDLE ROAD

The various DS techniques introduced thus far have considerable potential for addressing some of the analytic challenges faced by developmental psychopathologists. However, we have also pointed out some obstacles for implementing these techniques. In general, most techniques require continuous data, whereas ordinal and categorical variables are more common in developmental psychopathology, especially in observational studies. In addition, many of the techniques are either solely descriptive, preventing researchers from testing the strength and reliability of their findings, or they require complex mathematical procedures that may be inaccessible or irrelevant to most developmental psychopathologists. Recently, a middle ground of hybrid strategies has been developed that combines graphical techniques that capture the descriptive richness of DS concepts with simple statistical procedures that stay true to systems assumptions (Granic, Hollenstein, et al., 2003; Granic & Lamey, 2002; Lewis et al., 1999).

In this section of our review, we introduce this new method, state space grid (SSG) analysis. This technique was developed by Lewis and his colleagues to address some of the limitations in previous DS methods. It is a graphical and statistical strategy that links the analysis of real-time and developmental time patterns and allows for the identification of individual and group differences. Thus, the flexibility of this methodology may prove to be valuable for developmental psychopathologists. We begin by describing the graphical technique and then move on to the various measures that can be derived from these graphs for statistical analysis. Examples of studies in developmental psychology and developmental psychopathology are provided throughout.

State Space Grids

Recall that DS theorists use the concept of a *state space* to represent the range of behavioral habits, or attractors, for a given system. In real time, behavior is conceptualized as moving along a trajectory on this hypothetical landscape, being pulled toward certain attractors and freed from others (see Figure 22.1). Based on these abstract formalizations, Lewis et al. (1999) developed a graphical approach that utilizes observational data and quantifies these data according to two ordinal variables that define the state space for any particular system. Lewis and his colleagues (e.g., Lewis

et al., 1999; Lewis et al., 2004) have primarily studied intraindividual attractor patterns that emerge and change in the early years of life. The grids they originally developed utilized two ordinal variables (e.g., degree of engagement and intensity of distress) that tapped individual infants' socioemotional habits across several developmental epochs.

State space grids (SSGs) have also been developed to represent dyadic behavior (e.g., parent-child interactions, peer relations; Granic & Lamey, 2002; Granic, Hollenstein, et al., 2003). The dyad's trajectory (i.e., the sequence of behavioral states) is plotted as it proceeds in real time on a grid representing all possible behavioral combinations. Much like a scatter plot, one dyad member's (e.g., parent) coded behavior is plotted on the x axis and the other member's (e.g., child) behavior is plotted on the y axis. What is different, however, is that each x-y coordinate represents a moment (e.g., second, event, bin) in time, rather than a case in a group of cases. Two behavior streams are segmented into time points or events, and simultaneous values are plotted. Thus, in dyadic grids, each point on the grid represents a two-event sequence or a simultaneously coded parent-child event (i.e., a dyadic state). A trajectory is drawn through the successive dyadic points in the temporal sequence as they were observed. When the behavior changes, a line is drawn connecting the new point and the previous point. For example, a hypothetical trajectory representing 10 seconds of coded behavior is presented in Figure 22.14. The sequence depicted begins with 2 seconds in negative engagement/negative engagement,[1] 2 seconds in negative engagement/neutral, 3 seconds in neutral/neutral, 1 second in neutral/negative engagement, and 2 seconds in negative engagement/negative engagement. Note that the points are also plotted in sequence along a diagonal such that the first state is plotted in the lower left of the first cell and the final state is plotted in the upper right of the final cell. Plotting the points along the diagonal allows researchers to identify when in the session a behavioral event occurred.

The SSG methodology can tap both the content of interactions (e.g., mutual hostility, permissive parenting) and the structure of these interactions. When we refer to structure, we mean the patterning of behavior, regardless of content, such as the relative flexibility versus rigidity of interaction patterns. With SSGs, we are able to examine whether behavior clusters in very few or many states (i.e., cells) or regions (i.e., a subset of cells) of the state space. We can also track how long the trajectory remains in some cells but not others, and how quickly it returns to particular

---

[1] Note that the labeling of cells follows the x/y convention such that the first half of the label is the parent's category and the second half of the label is the child's category.

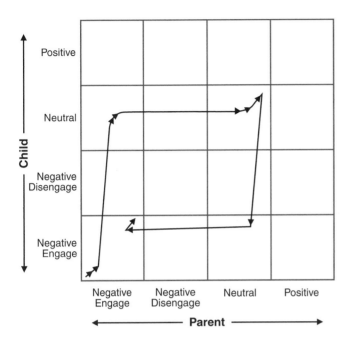

Figure 22.14 Example of a state space grid with a hypothetical trajectory representing 10 seconds of coded behavior, one arrowhead per second. Plotting begins in the lower left part of the cell and moves in a diagonal as each second is plotted, ending in the upper right.

cells. If a dyadic trajectory remains in a small number of cells and makes very few transitions between cells, this system may be thought of as rigid, inflexible, or stuck. In contrast, a trajectory that moves around to many cells in the state space grid and makes frequent changes between these cells may indicate a highly flexible, or variable, system. We can identify attractors as those cells to which behavior is drawn repeatedly, in which it rests over extended periods, and/or to which it returns quickly. Moreover, as discussed in the following sections, a range of variables that capture the relative stability of particular attractors may be derived from SSGs, and these values can be tested statistically for changes in real and developmental time.

A major advantage of SSGs is that they provide an intuitively appealing way to view complex, interactional behavior; thus, they are first and foremost a useful tool for exploratory analysis. A recent study in which we examined the heterogeneity of family interactions with aggressive children may help illustrate this point (Granic & Lamey, 2002). SSGs were used to explore differences in the parent-child interactions of "pure" externalizing children (EXT) and children comorbid (MIXED) for externalizing and internalizing problems. This study is useful not only for demonstrating how the grids work, but also for demonstrating design innovations based on DS principles that are useful with or without SSGs, in this case, a systematic perturbation.

Parents and clinically referred children discussed a problem for 4 minutes and then tried to "wrap up and end on a good note" in response to a signal (the perturbation) within the next 2 minutes. The perturbation was intended to increase the emotional pressure on the dyad, triggering a reorganization of their behavioral system. We hypothesized that, as a function of differences in the underlying structure of their relationships, EXT and MIXED dyads would be differentially sensitive to the perturbation and would reorganize to different parts of the state space. Prior to the perturbation, however, we expected dyads' interactions to look relatively similar. Separate grids were constructed for the pre- and postperturbation interaction sessions. For this study, the lines (trajectories) are less important to notice than the points that show clustering in particular cells. Figure 22.15 shows an example of an interaction between a pure EXT child and his parent, pre- and post perturbation. As exemplified in these grids, EXT dyads tended to go to the permissive region (child hostile-parent neutral/positive) of the state space grid, as well as other regions (i.e., mutual neutrality and negativity), before the perturbation. After the perturbation, EXT dyads tended to remain and stabilize in the permissive region. Figure 22.16 represents the interaction of a MIXED dyad. Similar to EXT dyads, the MIXED dyads occupied the permissive region, as well as other areas, before the perturbation. But in contrast with the EXT group, MIXED dyads tended to move toward the mutual hostility, or mutual negativity, region of the state space grid after the perturbation. Granic and Lamey (2002) concluded that the perturbation was a critical design innovation that provided the means by which clinical subtypes could be differentiated.

Another contribution of this study was a more general one: The use of SSGs, with their rich case-by-case temporal narratives, provided a technique to further parse interaction processes that have been previously assumed to represent one coherent pattern. In this case, the coercive process (Patterson, 1982; Patterson et al., 1992; Snyder, Edwards, McGraw, Kilgore, & Holton, 1994) was shown to constitute two separate microsocial patterns—two separate attractors on a state space (Granic & Patterson, 2001). Moreover, the conditions under which dyads would be drawn toward one region or the other were found to differ for subtypes. The use of SSGs to uncover heterogeneous processes may be relevant to a variety of phenomena in developmental psychopathology, including variability in the real-time unfolding of attachment patterns (cf. Coleman & Watson, 2000), in bullying interactions on the playground (cf. Pepler, Craig, & O'Connell, 1999), and in parent-adolescent interactions during puberty (Granic, Dishion, et al., 2003; Granic, Hollenstein, et al., 2003).

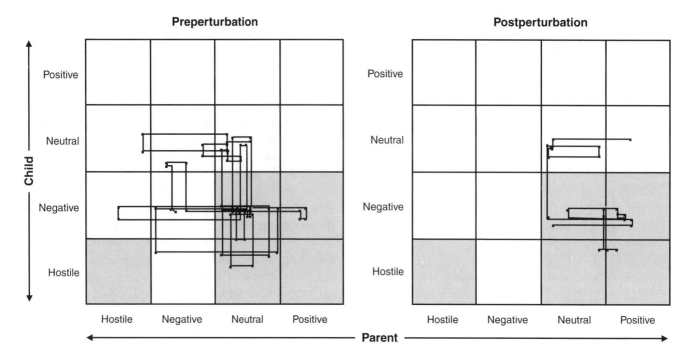

Figure 22.15   Pre- and postperturbation state space grids for an EXT dyad.

State Space Grid Analysis: Real-Time Measures

SSG patterns can be quantified and used as variables for statistical analyses. Variables that capture the temporal and spatial patterning of behavior have been developed for time-based (e.g., second-by-second coding) as well as event-based (e.g., conversational turns) data (Lewis et al., 1999). The same variables may be used regardless of whether the researcher is using the grids to map individual or dyadic behavioral trajectories. We have provided a list of some of these variables but, depending on the research question, additional ones may be created. Once these parameters have been computed, different types of attractors may be identified and the relative stability of these dynamic states can be

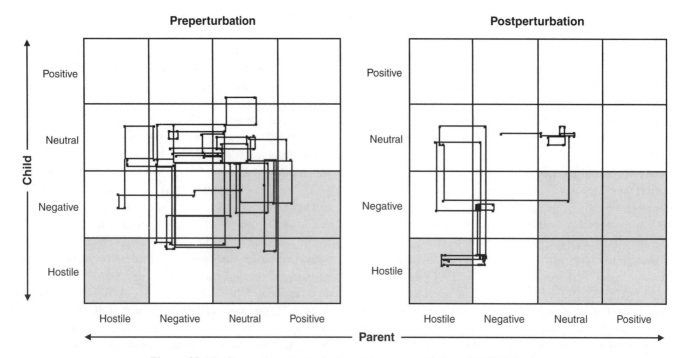

Figure 22.16   Pre- and postperturbation state space grids for a MIXED dyad.

measured and subsequently compared in a variety of ways (Lewis et al., 1999, 2004).

In general, long durations and/or frequent recurrences of behavior in a particular cell or region suggest an attractor on the state space, and these hypothetical attractors can be compared and tested within individuals across development as well as between individuals. Moreover, parameters describing the stability or variability of behavior across the state space can be calculated for each grid, allowing global, structural comparisons over time, populations, or individuals. As we list the parameters that can be derived from the grids, we refer to Figure 22.17 for examples. These grids were taken from a study conducted by Lewis and colleagues (1999) that examined the socioemotional coping patterns of infants and changes in those patterns over a hypothesized stage transition. Originally, these grids were representations of intraindividual behavior plotted according to two ordinal variables, but we have left out the axes labels because they can just as easily represent dyadic behavior, and our intention is to provide a generic description that can be adapted to a variety of observational data. It should also be noted that unlike the grids in the Granic and Lamey study, which used event-based data (conversational turns as observational units), time-based data are plotted in Figure 22.17; larger dots in these plots represent longer durations.

The following are parameters that may be computed for each cell in the grid: (1) raw density: cumulative duration (or number of hits) per cell; (2) proportional density: density divided by total episode duration or total number of events; (3) perseverance 1: mean duration (or mean number of consecutive hits) per cell; (4) perseverance 2: longest duration (or longest series of consecutive hits) per cell; (5) return time: latency to return to a cell following an event in that cell. This can be measured in units of time, number of events, or number of unique cells visited en route. For ex-

ample, in Figure 22.17, grid B shows a high raw density in cells 2/2 (again, cell labels follow the x/y convention) and 2/3 and a very low raw density in cell 1/3. In grid C, cell 3/1 shows a high value for perseverance 1 (each time behavior goes to that cell, and it tends to stay there for some time), whereas cell 1/1 in that same grid shows a low perseverance value. Finally, grid B shows a very low return time for cell 2/2 (every time behavior leaves that cell, and it returns in approximately one turn) but a high return time for grid A, cell 1/0.

There are also several parameters and summary values that can be computed for the entire grid (rather than cell by cell): (1) dispersion: total number of cells visited (with or without controlling for total time or total number of events); (2) fluctuation: number of transitions between cells (with or without controlling for total time or events); note that fluctuation may be high even though dispersion is low, providing an additional useful parameter (see grid B); (3) stability 1: average of either mean or maximum cell duration values (or events per cell) across all cells; note that high values indicate overall stability or stickiness of behavioral states; (4) stability 2: mean return time (in time or event units) across all cells; note that low values indicate overall stability or resilience of behavioral states; (5) peak stability: maximum single duration (in time or event units) out of all the cells occupied. Returning to Figure 22.17, grids A and C show high dispersion, compared to grid B, and grid A shows a low stability 1 value, compared to grid B.

Researchers may choose to calculate one or a few of these whole-grid parameters, depending on what makes most sense in any particular study. Another option is to combine two or more of the whole-grid parameters into one summary construct score or latent variable that represents "flexibility/rigidity" of interaction patterns (e.g., Granic, 2003; Hollenstein et al., 2004). For example, to

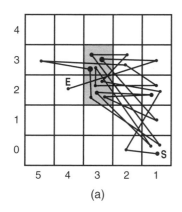 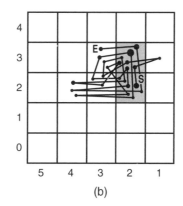 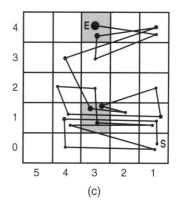

(a)   (b)   (c)

Figure 22.17   Examples of three state space grids. *Source:* From "A New Dynamic Systems Method for the Analysis of Early Socioemotional Development," by M. D. Lewis, A. V. Lamey, and L. Douglas, 1999, *Developmental Science, 2,* pp. 457–475.

create a flexibility/rigidity construct, the SSG parameters of interest are transferred into z-scores and a reliability analysis is conducted to ensure that the chosen parameters are sufficiently correlated and reliably hang together (measured by Cronbach's standardized alphas and Pearson correlations). Any parameters that do not meet appropriate criteria can be dropped, and the z-scores from the remaining reliable parameters can be averaged into one flexibility/rigidity construct score. This potentially more robust score can then be used in any kind of appropriate statistical analysis (e.g., growth curve analyses, SEM, regression analyses, ANOVAs).

In addition to examining the patterns across the entire grid, developmental psychopathologists are often interested in the relative stability of one or just a few behavioral patterns or attractors (e.g., depressed mother-infant mutual gaze, coercive interactions). Lewis and colleagues (1999, in press) have developed a number of quantitative strategies for identifying attractors on a state space grid. Using the measures previously listed (density, perseverance, return time), attractors can be defined as the cell or group of cells highest in these values. Once attractor cells are identified, the computed parameters for those cells serve to characterize the strength, endurance, and stability of the attractor for comparison purposes. These comparisons are particularly powerful when they are conducted across developmental time.

State Space Grid Analysis: Developmental Measures

After computing the parameters that are most relevant for a particular research question, statistical techniques (most of which are quite familiar to developmental psychopathologists) may be applied. We recommend using these statistical procedures in a way that maintains the integrity of the individual (or dyadic) case (e.g., curve estimation procedures, cluster analysis). However, multivariate analyses, including ANOVAs, regressions, and SEM, can just as easily be run on the grid variables.

One example of a developmental state space grid analysis comes from a recently completed study by Lewis et al. (2004). These researchers were examining a developmental transition in late infancy that was hypothesized to exhibit the properties of a phase transition (i.e., increased variability in real-time patterns, a breakdown of old attractors and the emergence of new ones over developmental time). The general hypothesis that guided this study and similar DS-inspired studies that focus on phase transitions is presented in Figure 22.18. Infants were videotaped in frustrating situations on 12 monthly visits before, during, and after a hypothesized transition point at 18 to 20 months. SSGs were

constructed for each episode and grid-to-grid differences were compared over age. As predicted, grid-to-grid differences were greater during the transitional period than before or after, indicating a developmental reorganization of behavioral responses to negative emotion. Also, new attractors appeared more frequently during the period of transition than at other ages.

Lewis and colleagues provide two techniques to measure *within-subject* differences among SSGs. The first is called *intergrid distance* score (IDS) and is computed in the following steps. Grid-to-grid Euclidian distance scores yield a global metric of the difference in behavioral landscapes from month to month, based on the sum of squared differences across all cells. For each grid cell, the difference in duration values over two consecutive months is calculated, then squared, and then these values are summed for all cells. Next, the square root of this sum is taken as the distance score between the two grids.

A second developmental analysis they explored was a cluster analysis technique to look at changes over time. The first step is to categorize the grids by entering all grids for all months for every child into a k-means cluster analysis. The most parsimonious cluster solution is chosen (based on preset criteria). The cluster score for each grid is then recorded. Visual inspection of the grids is recommended at this point to ensure that the same cluster scores look alike topographically, having similar duration values for many of the same cells. Developmental continuity would thus be indicated by a sequence of months (2 or more) with the same cluster score, and developmental variability would be indicated by month-to-month change in cluster membership.

Another method of analyzing changes in SSG patterns over developmental time comes from a recent study that examined changes in the structure of family interactions during the early adolescent transition period (Granic, Dishion, et al., 2003; Granic, Hollenstein, et al., 2003). Following Lewis and colleagues' stage transition hypothesis, we examined whether early adolescence (i.e., around puberty; age 13 to 14 for boys) constitutes a phase transition (a period of reorganization) marked by a peak in the variability of family interactions; before and after this period, interactions were expected to be stable (refer to Figure 22.18 for schematic representation of hypothesis). Longitudinal observational data were collected in five waves prior to, during, and after the transition period. We observed 149 parents and boys problem-solving at 9 to 10 years old, and every 2 years thereafter until they were 17 to 18 years old. Based on this data, state space grids were constructed for all families across all waves. An example of a parent-child dyad across five longitudinal waves is shown in Figure

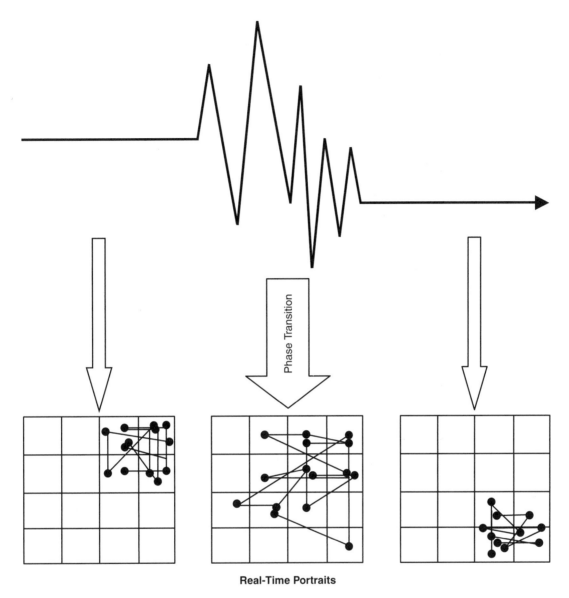

Real-Time Portraits

Figure 22.18   Model of a developmental phase transition; developmental phase transitions are periods of fluctuation in developmental time and increased variability in real time.

22.19. Consistent with our hypothesis, this was a characteristic pattern for the sample: The sequence of state space grids showed that behavior became more variable (i.e., occupied more cells and moved around the grid more frequently) at the third wave, when the boys were in early adolescence (age 13 to 14 years old). Before and after this period, dyadic behavior looked more stable and less flexible; fewer cells were occupied and there were fewer changes between cells. Two parameters indexing the variability of

the interactions (fluctuation and stability) were derived from these grids. Repeated measures ANOVAs on these variables revealed a significant quadratic effect. To ensure that these results were not just significant on the group level, but also characterized the majority of families in the sample (and, thus, to be more faithful to systems-oriented, case-based assumptions), the wave at which flexibility peaked (when fluctuation was highest) was recorded. Results revealed that the majority of families showed a

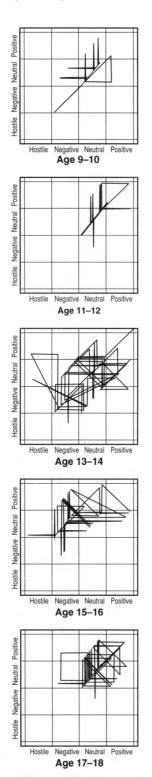

Figure 22.19 Sample state space grids for one dyad across five longitudinal waves. *Source:* "Longitudinal Analysis of Flexibility and Reorganization in Early Adolescence: A Dynamic Systems Study of Family Interactions," by I. Granic, T. Hollenstein, T. J. Dishion, and G. R. Patterson, 2003, *Developmental Psychology, 39,* pp. 606–617.

significant peak in variability in the middle wave—and hardly any families peaked in the first or last wave.

From these examples, it should be clear that any statistical tool that has been developed to measure growth or change over time can be combined with SSG analysis. The important difference in these variables (compared to questionnaire data, for instance) is that they capture temporal patterns as they unfold over time. The importance of tapping these dynamic processes in terms of explanatory power cannot be overstated, but developmental psychopathologists are also interested in predicting outcomes. Although some systems scholars have argued that prediction should not be a goal for developmental scientists (much as prediction is not a goal for biologists), others in the field still consider it critical.

We recently completed a study in which one of our objectives was to predict antisocial behavior from dynamic systems measures of parent-child interactions. The study combined descriptive developmental profiles, SSG analysis, and more traditional multivariate statistical procedures (Hollenstein et al., 2004). The main goal of this study was to examine the connection between rigidity in parent-child interactions and the early development of antisocial behavior. We began the study by conceptualizing psychopathology as "diminished flexibility and constrictions in the affective, cognitive, and behavioral correlates of adaptational patterns" (Overton & Horowitz, 1991, p. 3). Clinical researchers have long viewed psychopathology as overlearned, automatized cognitive, affective, and behavioral patterns that are impervious to changes in the environment and interfere with an individual's ability to function socially (e.g., Cicchetti & Cohen, 1995b; Mahoney, 1991). This view of psychopathology as rigidified patterns of interaction has been theoretically extended to the family system (Minuchin, 1974) and coercive family processes specifically (Patterson, 1982), but empirical studies have not explicitly focused on rigid parent-child interactions and the emergence of child psychopathology.

In this study (Hollenstein et al., 2004), high-risk children in kindergarten ($n = 275$) and their parents were observed for 2 hours engaging in a variety of tasks (e.g., playing a game, problem-solving) that were expected to elicit a range of affect for most families. SSGs were constructed from the coded observational data, and several whole-grid measures of rigidity were derived from the grids. A rigidity construct was created, using methods previously described. As hypothesized, results showed that parent- and teacher-reported antisocial behavior, measured concurrently and 18 months later, were positively correlated with rigidity scores. Children rated high on antisocial behavior were significantly more likely to exhibit more rigid parent-child interaction patterns than their non-antisocial counterparts. Regression analyses also indicated that rigidity scores in the fall of kindergarten predicted growth over 18 months in parent-reported antisocial behavior after controlling for concurrent levels.

We recently extended these results by examining the developmental growth profiles in both externalizing and internalizing behavior for this same sample (Hollenstein et al., 2004). As shown in Figure 22.20, children's growth profiles in externalizing behavior across four waves of data collection (over 24 months) showed four distinct types of trajectories: growers, desistors, stable high, and stable low. Figure 22.21 shows the means on the rigidity construct for the four growth trajectory groups. Results indicated that the growers and stable-high groups scored significantly higher on parent-child rigidity scores than the stable-low and desistors groups. This was an exciting finding for us because of the potential diagnostic implications. Returning to Figure 22.20, the growers and desistors began approximately at the same level of antisocial behavior. What distinguished the group of children who became increasingly more antisocial over time from those children who became less so over time was how rigid the parent-child interactions were at the first wave.

Although the SSG method is clearly still in its early stages of development, we are encouraged by its potential. One of the important advantages to this technique is its inherent flexibility. At the very least, it is a visual, exploratory tool to develop and refine hypotheses. At best, this methodology provides a source from which novel, temporal-based, process-level predictors may be tapped and used to strengthen current models of normal and atypical development. Researchers are not limited to using continuous time series, as is the case with many other DS methods. Categorical and ordinal data are also appropriate for this type of analysis. Also, the grids are malleable in that they can represent systemic behavior on the individual as well as dyadic level. In addition to the examples mentioned, changes in peer, romantic couple, and sibling interactions, for example, can easily be tracked using SSGs. In fact, apart from the difficulties in visually representing the data, the variables derived from the grids can be extended past the two dimensions on which we have focused. For instance, triadic family interactions or family interactions with siblings as well as parents can be measured for attractor strengths, fluctuations, and so on. Along similar lines, peer interactions with three or more children on the playground can be analyzed with this strategy.

Another benefit of this approach is the extent to which it remains user-friendly and does not require expertise in mathematical modeling. In addition, we have developed a graphics-based, point-and-click, SSG software program that will output grids, compute all the grid parameters mentioned previously, and conduct statistical analyses on these parameters (real-time and developmental analyses). The SSG program is available from the current authors.

FUTURE DIRECTIONS: IMPLICATIONS FOR CLINICAL RESEARCH

There are no limits to the diverse topics and varied problems that can potentially be addressed with the application of DS methods; listing all of them here would be impossible. In this final section, we have chosen to limit our discussion to the implications for clinical research, an area in which many developmental psychopathologists share an interest. Because DS methods are specifically designed to capture change processes, and because the study of psychopathology often breaks down into the study of individual patterning, one of the most exciting potential applications of SSGs, as well as other DS tools, may be in treatment research.

SSGs may be particularly well-suited for the study of heterogeneous change processes that may underlie treatment progress and outcome. For example, a great deal of research has shown that family-based treatments targeting coercive interactions can decrease levels of aggression in children, but there remains a great deal of variability in treatment outcome and almost no understanding about the mechanisms of change (Kazdin, 2000, 2001, 2002). The state space grid methodology should be able to provide a microsocial, process-level account of how family and peer relationships change over the course of treatment and follow-up. In addition to identifying content-specific changes (e.g., less hostility and more mutual positivity in parent-child interactions), this method has the potential to tap structural changes associated with treatment success. For instance, as a result of treatment, do parent-child dyads move more quickly from a hostile, conflictual interaction into a reparative one? Do they develop several alternative problem-solving strategies that they can maneuver through more flexibly? These same sorts of questions can be applied to treatments with children with anxiety disorders, depression, and so on.

Recently, we have begun a new program of research focusing on clinical questions in the area of childhood

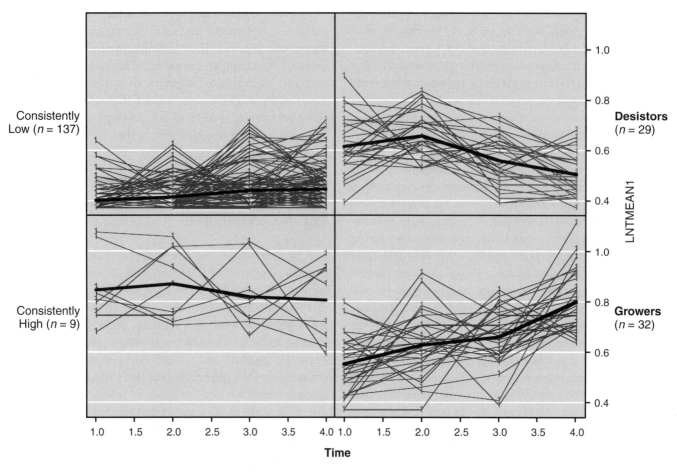

Figure 22.20   Clusters of antisocial trajectories.

aggression using DS principles and methods. We briefly summarize this program of research, including our design and some of our hypotheses, to illustrate how this novel methodological lens may address previously untenable questions. Our hope is that this research framework may be equally applicable to a range of child psychopathologies and treatment modalities.

The two main objectives of our research are to (1) describe and explain the fine-grained changes in parent-child interactions over the course of intervention and (2) study differences in processes of change and stability according to clinical subtypes. To examine how change unfolds over the course of treatment—and to pinpoint the real-time processes underlying such change—a fine-grained, longitudinal design is required, with repeated assessment points between baseline and termination phases of the intervention. Our focus is on real-time interpersonal processes in family interactions. Direct observations of parent-child problem-solving interactions—with an emotional perturbation introduced partway through the interaction—are collected every other week during the intervention period. These observations are

videotaped and coded for affect and problem-solving content. SSG analysis will be applied to uncover content-specific changes in parent-child interactions, content-free changes in the structure of these interactions, and changes in dyads' sensitivity to the perturbation, all in relation to suc-

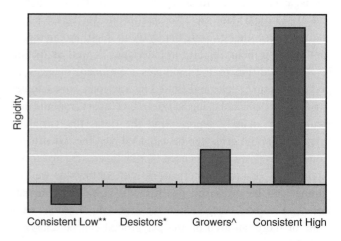

Figure 22.21   Means scores on rigidity construct by antisocial trajectory cluster.

cessful treatment outcomes (as measured by standardized clinical instruments). These trajectories will also be compared by gender and clinical subtype to identify distinct change processes associated with these groupings.

Two of the questions and hypotheses that are being examined are the following:

1. When treatment is successful, what changes can be observed in parent-child problem-solving interactions from pre- to posttreatment? In terms of content-specific hypotheses, we go beyond just hypothesizing that dyads will become less negative and more positive. With the help of the grids, more complex, process-level hypotheses can be put forward. For example, we expect that dyads will spend less time in the mutually hostile/coercive region of the state space, but even with duration in that cell held constant, we expect that when exiting this region, dyads will show longer return times to that cell (i.e., coercion will become less "absorbing"). We do expect that they will be more positive and supportive, but this may happen over the course of an interaction (i.e., dyads will end up in that region, even if they start in the more negative region). Thus, the temporally based, multistable nature of family interactions will be assessed. In addition, the structural properties of the dyad are important to measure. In terms of the behavioral repertoire in general, we expect that those youth who benefit from treatment will develop a less rigid, more flexible interaction style. That is, from pre- to posttreatment, dyads with successful outcomes will visit more behavioral states and fluctuate from one state to another more frequently.

2. Is there a characteristic profile of change in parent-child interactions over the course of successful intervention? Based on DS principles, we expect that when treatment is successful, the biweekly longitudinal profile of change will exhibit the properties of a phase transition. That is, parent-child interactions are expected to be initially stable (i.e., similar from week to week) and mutually hostile, to fluctuate markedly some time after treatment begins (i.e., differ considerably from week to week), and then to restabilize, but in more positive patterns of interactions (and still more flexible than at baseline).

With the application of SSGs, and the parameters derived from the grids, it is possible to test our process-specific hypotheses. As mentioned, we expect that those youth who benefit from treatment will not abandon negative behavioral habits but will soften them through the development of a less rigid, more flexible behavioral repertoire.

This approach can specify at what point in the interaction dyads become hostile, how long they maintain hostile exchanges, the ease with which they escape them, the range of alternative patterns available to them, and the tendency to return to hostility. Dispersion, stability, and fluctuation measures can be computed, and changes in any of these parameters can then be tracked over the course of treatment and follow-up to assess the hypothesis of increased behavioral flexibility in relation to successful interventions. Instead of relying on central tendency measures (e.g., means and correlations), this technique maintains the temporal integrity of real-time interactions and, thus, can better capture some of the microsocial processes hypothesized to be most important.

Our two general research questions are applicable to a range of disorders and treatment programs. Also, different domains of behavior and functioning can be tracked. Changes in peer interactions and sibling interactions, group behavior in the playground, and individual behavior in a variety of contexts can be examined in terms of similar types of process-level questions. The main point is that DS techniques can bring us closer to understanding the change process itself, in whatever domain, and this is a critical new direction in clinical research that we have been repeatedly urged to take. As Kazdin (2000) and others have argued, we have more than sufficient evidence about which treatments work; it is time to shift our resources and develop theories about *how* they work and *for whom*. Such theories may be best informed by DS principles and appropriately tested with some of the diverse set of methods we have reviewed in this chapter.

CONCLUSION

From the beginning of its establishment as a discipline, one of the core priorities in developmental psychopathology has been methodological diversity (e.g., Cicchetti & Cohen, 1995b; Cummings et al., 2000; Richters, 1997). One reason for encouraging this analytic pluralism is the recognition of the disparity between systems-based models of developmental psychopathology and the inadequate methodological tools that are available to test them (Richters, 1997). We have argued that DS approaches to development offer research methods that show greater fidelity to the complex, heterogeneous, temporal nature of developmental phenomena. Clearly, no set of analytic methods can address the mismatch of methods and models entirely; thus, we are not arguing for the complete abandonment of well-established techniques. Instead, our purpose in providing a survey of

DS methods is to encourage developmental psychopathologists to begin examining empirically questions that may have previously seemed out of analytic reach.

REFERENCES

Abraham, F. D., Abraham, R. H., & Shaw, C. D. (1990). *A visual introduction to dynamical systems theory for psychology*. Santa Cruz, CA: Aerial Press.

Allison, P. D. (1984). *Event history analysis: Regression for longitudinal event data*. Beverly Hills, CA: Sage.

Badalamenti, A. F., & Langs, R. J. (1992). The thermodynamics of psychotherapeutic communication. *Behavioral Science, 37*, 152–180.

Bakeman, R., & Gottman, J. M. (1997). *Observing interaction: An introduction to sequential analysis* (2nd ed.). Cambridge, England: Cambridge University Press.

Bergman, L. R., & Magnusson, D. (1997). A person oriented approach in research on developmental psychopathology. *Development and Psychopathology, 9*, 291–319.

Bertenthal, B. (1999). Variation and selection in the development of perception and action. In G. Savelsbergh, H. van der Maas, & P. van Geert (Eds.), *Nonlinear developmental processes* (Vol. 175, pp. 105–121). Amsterdam, The Netherlands: Royal Netherlands Academy of Arts and Sciences.

Blossfeld, H., & Rohwer, G. (2002). *Techniques of event history modeling: New approaches to causal analysis* (2nd ed.). Mahwah, NJ: Erlbaum.

Boyce, W. T., Frank, E., Jensen, P. S., Kessler, R. C., Nelson, C. A., & Steinberg, L. (1998). Social context in developmental psychopathology: Recommendations for future research from the MacArthur Network on Psychopathology and Development. *Development and Psychopathology, 10*, 143–164.

Bronfenbrenner, U. (1979). *The ecology of human development: Experiments by nature and design*. Cambridge, MA: Harvard University Press.

Burlingame, G. M., Fuhriman, A., & Barnum, K. R. (1995). Group therapy as a nonlinear dynamical system: Analysis of therapeutic communication for chaotic patterns. In F. D. Abraham & A. R. Gilgen (Eds.), *Chaos theory in psychology* (pp. 87–105). Westport, CT: Greenwood Press.

Butz, M. R., Chamberlain, L. L., & McCown, W. G. (1997). *Strange attractors: Chaos, complexity, and the art of family therapy*. New York: Wiley.

Byrne, D. G., Mazanov, J., Gregson, R. A. M. (2001). A cusp catastrophe analysis of changes to adolescent smoking behavior in response to smoking prevention programs. *Nonlinear Dynamics, Psychology, and Life Sciences, 5*, 115–137.

Calkins, S. D., & Fox, N. A. (2002). Self-regulatory processes in early personality development: A multilevel approach to the study of childhood social withdrawal and aggression. *Development and Psychopathology, 14*, 477–498.

Case, R., Okamoto, Y., Griffin, S., McKeough, A., Bleiker, C., Henderson, B., et al. (1996). The role of central conceptual structures in the development of children's thought. *Monographs of the Society for Research in Child Development, 246*, 61.

Cicchetti, D. (1990). A historical perspective on the discipline of developmental psychopathology. In J. E. Rolf, A. S. Masten, D. Cicchetti, & K. H. Nuechterlein (Eds.), *Risk and protective factors in the development of psychopathology* (pp. 2–28). New York: Cambridge University Press.

Cicchetti, D. (1993). Developmental psychopathology: Reactions, reflections, projections. [Special issue: Setting a path for the coming decade: Some goals and challenges] *Developmental Review, 13*, 471–502.

Cicchetti, D., & Aber, J. L. (1998). Contextualism and developmental psychopathology. *Development and Psychopathology, 10*, 137–141.

Cicchetti, D., & Cohen, D. J. (Eds.). (1995a). *Developmental psychopathology: Vol. 1. Theory and methods*. New York: Wiley.

Cicchetti, D., & Cohen, D. J. (1995b). Perspectives on developmental psychopathology. In D. Cicchetti & Cohen, D. J. (Eds.), *Developmental psychopathology: Vol. 1. Theory and methods* (pp. 3–20). New York: Wiley.

Cicchetti, D., & Dawson, G. (2002a). Editorial: Multiple levels of analysis. *Development and Psychopathology, 14*, 417–420.

Cicchetti, D., & Dawson, G. (2002b). *Special issue: Multiple levels of analysis, development and psychopathology* (Vol. 14). New York: Cambridge University Press.

Cicchetti, D., & Richters, J. E. (1993). Developmental considerations in the investigation of conduct disorder. *Development and Psychopathology, 5*, 331–334.

Cicchetti, D., & Schneider-Rosen, K. (1986). Theoretical and empirical considerations in the investigation of the relationship between affect and cognition in atypical populations of infants. In C. E. Izard, J. Kagan, & R. B. Zajonc (Eds.), *Emotions, cognition, and behavior* (pp. 366–406). New York: Cambridge University Press.

Cicchetti, D., & Sroufe, L. A. (1976). The relationship between affective and cognitive development in Down's syndrome infants. *Child Development, 47*, 920–929.

Clair, S. (1998). A cusp catastrophe model for adolescent alcohol use: An empirical test. *Nonlinear Dynamics, Psychology, and Life Sciences, 2*, 217–241.

Coleman, P., & Watson, A. (2000). Infant attachment as a dynamic system. *Human Development, 43*, 295–313.

Cox, M. J., & Paley, B. (1997). Families as systems. *Annual Review of Psychology, 48*, 243–267.

Cummings, E. M., Davies, P. T., & Campbell, S. B. (2000). *Developmental psychopathology and family process: Theory, research, and clinical implications*. New York: Guilford Press.

Dishion, T. J., Bullock, B. M., & Granic, I. (2002). Pragmatism in modeling peer influence: Dynamics, outcomes, and change processes: How prevention intervention studies in the field of developmental psychopathology can inform developmental theories and models. [Special issue] *Development and Psychopathology, 14*, 969–981.

Dishion, T. J., Capaldi, D. M., Spracklen, K. M., & Li, F. (1995). Peer ecology of male adolescent drug use. *Development and Psychopathology, 7*, 803–824.

Dishion, T. J., Eddy, J. M., Haas, E., Li, F., & Spracklen, K. (1997). Friendships and violent behavior during adolescence. *Social Development, 6*, 207–223.

Dishion, T. J., Gardner, K., Patterson, G. R., Reid, J. B., & Thibodeaux, S. (1983). *The family process code: A multidimensional system for observing family interactions*. Unpublished technical manual, Oregon Social Learning Center, Eugene, OR.

Dishion, T. J., Nelson, S. E., Bullock, B. M., & Winter, C. E. (in press). Adolescent friendship as a dynamic system: Entropy and deviance in the etiology and course of male antisocial behavior. *Journal of Abnormal Child Psychology*.

Dishion, T. J., & Patterson, G. R. (1999). Model building in developmental psychopathology: A pragmatic approach to understanding and intervention. *Journal of Clinical Child Psychology, 28*, 502–512.

Dishion, T. J., Spracklen, K. M., Andrews, D. W., & Patterson, G. R. (1996). Deviancy training in male adolescent friendships. *Behavior Therapy, 27*, 373–390.

Dixon, R. A., & Lerner, R. M. (1988). A history of systems in developmental psychology. In M. H. Bornstein & M. E. Lamb (Eds.), *Developmental psychology: An advanced textbook* (2nd ed., pp. 3–50). Hillsdale, NJ: Erlbaum.

Dumas, J. E., LaFreniere, P. J., & Serketich, W. J. (1995). "Balance of power": A transactional analysis of control in mother-child dyads involving socially competent, aggressive, and anxious children. *Journal of Abnormal Psychology, 104*, 104–113.

Dumas, J. E., Lemay, P., & Dauwalder, J. P. (2001). Dynamic analyses of mother-child interactions in functional and dysfunctional dyads: A synergetic approach. *Journal of Abnormal Child Psychology, 29*, 317–329.

Eddy, J. M., & Chamberlain, P. (2000). Family management and deviant peer association as mediators of the impact of treatment condition on youth antisocial behavior. *Journal of Consulting and Clinical Psychology, 68*, 857–863.

Elman, J. L., Bates, E. A., Johnson, M. H., Karmiloff-Smith, A., Parisi, D., & Plunkett, K. (1996). *Rethinking innateness: A connectionist perspective on development.* Cambridge, MA: MIT Press.

Engel, A. K., Fries, P., & Singer, W. (2001). Dynamic predictions, oscillations and synchrony in top-down processing. *Nature Reviews Neuroscience, 2*, 704–716.

Erickson, M. F., Egeland, B., & Pianta, R. (1989). The effects of maltreatment on the development of young children. In D. Cicchetti & V. Carlson (Eds.), *Child maltreatment: Theory and research on the causes and consequences of child abuse and neglect* (pp. 647–684). New York: Cambridge University Press.

Fogel, A. (1990). The process of developmental change in infant communicative action: Using dynamic systems theory to study individual ontogenies. In J. Colombo & J. Fagen (Eds.), *Individual differences in infancy: Reliability, stability, prediction* (pp. 341–358). Hillsdale, NJ: Erlbaum.

Fogel, A. (1993). *Developing through relationships: Origins of communication, self and culture.* Chicago: University of Chicago Press.

Fogel, A. (1995). Development and relationships: A dynamic model of communication. *Advances in the Study of Behavior, 24*, 259–290.

Fogel, A., & Thelen, E. (1987). The development of early expressive and communicative action: Re-interpreting the evidence from a dynamic systems perspective. *Developmental Psychology, 23*, 747–761.

Ford, D. H., & Lerner, R. M. (1992). *Developmental systems theory: An integrative approach.* Newbury Park, CA: Sage.

Forgatch, M. S., & DeGarmo, D. S. (1999). Parenting through change: An effective prevention program for single mothers. *Journal of Consulting and Clinical Psychology, 67*, 711–724.

Freeman, W. (1995). *Societies of brains: A study in the neuroscience of love and hate.* Hillsdale, NJ: Erlbaum.

Garmezy, N. (1974). The study of competence in children at risk for severe psychopathology. In E. J. Anthony & C. Koupernik (Eds.), *The child in his family: Children at psychiatric risk* (pp. 77–97). Oxford: Wiley.

Garmezy, N., & Rutter, M. (Eds.). (1983). *Stress, coping, and development in children.* Baltimore: Johns Hopkins University Press.

Gasser, M., & Smith, L. B. (1998). Learning nouns and adjective meanings: A connectionist account. *Language and Cognitive Processes, 13*, 269–306.

Gilmore, R. (1981). *Catastrophe theory for scientists and engineers.* New York: Wiley.

Gottlieb, G. (1991). Epigenetic systems view of human development. *Developmental Psychology, 27*, 33–34.

Gottlieb, G. (1992). *Individual development and evolution: The genesis of novel behavior.* London: Oxford University Press.

Gottman, J. M., Coan, J., Carrere, S., & Swanson, C. (1998). Predicting marital happiness and stability from newlywed interactions. *Journal of Marriage and the Family, 60*, 5–22.

Gottman, J. M., Guralnick, M. J., Wilson, B., Swanson, C. C., & Murray, J. D. (1997). What should be the focus of emotion regulation in children? A nonlinear dynamic mathematical model of children's peer interaction in groups. *Development and Psychopathology, 9*, 421–452.

Gottman, J. M., McCoy, K., Coan, J., & Collier, H. (1996). *The specific affect coding system (SPAFF) for observing emotional communication in marital and family interaction.* Mahwah, NJ: Erlbaum.

Gottman, J. M., Murray, J. D., Swanson, C. C., Tyson, R., & Swanson, K. R. (2002). *The mathematics of marriage: Dynamic nonlinear models.* London: MIT Press.

Granic, I. (2000). The self-organization of parent-child relations: Beyond bi-directional models. In M. D. Lewis & I. Granic (Eds.), *Emotion, development and self-organization: Dynamic systems approaches to emotional development* (pp. 267–297). New York: Cambridge University Press.

Granic, I. (2003, April). *Dynamic systems methods tap previously undetected socialization processes associated with antisocial outcomes.* Paper presented at the biennial meeting of the Society for Research in Child Development, Tampa, FL.

Granic, I., & Dishion, T. (2003). Deviant talk in adolescent friendships: A step toward measuring a pathogenic attractor process. *Social Development, 12*, 314–334.

Granic, I., Dishion, T. J., & Hollenstein, T. (2003). The family ecology of adolescence: A dynamic systems perspective on normative development. In G. Adams & M. Berzonsky (Eds.), *Blackwell handbook of adolescence* (pp. 60–91). New York: Blackwell.

Granic, I., Hollenstein, T., Dishion, T. J., & Patterson, G. R. (2003). Longitudinal analysis of flexibility and reorganization in early adolescence: A dynamic systems study of family interactions. *Developmental Psychology, 39*, 606–617.

Granic, I., & Lamey, A. V. (2002). Combining dynamic-systems and multivariate analyses to compare the mother-child interactions of externalizing subtypes. *Journal of Abnormal Child Psychology, 30*, 265–283.

Granic, I., & Patterson, G. R. (2001, July). *Innovations in the study of coercive microsocial processes in middle childhood: New methods and models based on dynamic systems principles.* Paper presented at the meeting of the International Society for Research in Child and Adolescent Psychopathology, Vancouver, British Columbia, Canada.

Guastello, S. J. (1995). *Chaos, catastrophe, and human affairs: Applications of nonlinear dynamics to work, organizations, and social evolution.* Mahwah, NJ: Erlbaum.

Guastello, S. J., Hyde, T., & Odak, M. (1998). Symbolic dynamic patterns of verbal exchange in a creative problem solving group. *Nonlinear Dynamics, Psychology, and Life Sciences, 2*, 35–58.

Hakens, H. (1977). *Synergetics: An introduction: Nonequilibrium phase transitions and self-organization in physics, chemistry and biology.* Berlin, Germany: Springer-Verlag.

Haslett, T., Smyrnios, K. X., & Osbourne, C. (1998). A cusp catastrophe analysis of anxiety levels in preuniversity students. *Journal of Psychology, 132*, 5–24.

Heath, R. A. (2000). *Nonlinear dynamics: Techniques and applications in psychology.* Mahwah, NJ: Erlbaum.

Hinde, R. A. (1983). Ethology and child development. In M. Haith & J. Campos (Eds.), *Carmichael's manual of child psychology* (Vol. 2, pp. 27–94). New York: Wiley.

Hinde, R. A. (1992). Some complexities in aggressive behavior. In A. Fraczek & H. Zumkley (Eds.), *Socialization and aggression* (pp. 3–10). New York: Springer-Verlag.

Hinshaw, S. P. (1999, June). *Risk-factor research in developmental psychopathology.* Paper presented at symposium conducted at the biennial meeting of the International Society for Research in Child and Adolescent Psychopathology, Barcelona, Spain.

Hinshaw, S. P., & Zupan, B. A. (1997). Assessment of antisocial behavior in children and adolescents. In D. M. Stoff, J. Breiling, & J. D. Maser (Eds.), *Handbook of antisocial behavior* (pp. 36–50). New York: Wiley.

Hollenstein, T., Granic, I., Stoolmiller, M., & Snyder, J. (2004). Rigidity in parent-child interactions and the development of externalizing and internalizing behavior in early childhood. *Journal of Abnormal Child Psychology, 32,* 595–607.

Hsu, H., & Fogel, A. (2001). Infant vocal development in a dynamic mother-infant communication system. *Infancy, 2,* 87–109.

Inhelder, B. (1976). Some pathologic phenomena analyzed in the perspective of developmental psychology. In B. Inhelder & H. Chipman (Eds.), *Piaget and his school* (pp. 221–227). New York: Springer.

Izard, C. E. (1979). *The maximally discriminative facial movement coding system (MAX).* Newark, NJ: University of Delaware Press.

Johnson, M. H., & Morton, J. (1991). *Biology and cognitive development: The case of face recognition.* Oxford: Blackwell.

Kagan, J. (1992). Yesterday's premises, tomorrow's promises. *Developmental Psychology, 28,* 990–997.

Kauffman, S. A. (1993). *The origins of order: Self-organization and selection in evolution.* New York: Oxford University Press.

Kazdin, A. E. (2000). *Psychotherapy for children and adolescents: Directions for research and practice.* New York: Oxford University Press.

Kazdin, A. E. (2001). Progression of therapy research and clinical application of treatment require better understanding of the change process. *Clinical Psychology, 8,* 143–151.

Kazdin, A. E. (2002). Psychosocial treatments for conduct disorder in children and adolescents. In P. E. Nathan & J. M. Gorman (Eds.), *A guide to treatments that work* (2nd ed., pp. 57–85). London: Oxford University Press.

Keating, D. P. (1990). Developmental processes in the socialization of cognitive structures. In *Development and learning: Proceedings of a symposium in honour of Wolfgang Edelstein on his 60th birthday* (pp. 37–72). Berlin, Germany: Max Planck Institute.

Kelso, J. A. S. (1995). *Dynamic patterns: The self-organization of brain and behavior.* Cambridge, MA: Bradford/MIT Press.

Kuo, Z. Y. (1967). *The dynamics of behavior development.* New York: Random House.

Lanza, M. L. (1999). Catastrophe theory: Application of nonlinear dynamics to assault victim responses. *Journal of the American Psychiatric Nurses Association, 5,* 117–121.

Lavelli, M., Pantoja, A. P. F., Hsu, H., Messinger, D., & Fogel, A. (in press). Using microgenetic designs to study change processes. In D. G. Teti (Ed.), *Handbook of research methods in developmental psychology.* London: Blackwell.

Lee, K., & Karmiloff-Smith, A. (2002). Macro- and microdevelopmental research: Assumptions, research strategies, constraints, and utilities. In N. Granott & J. Parziale (Eds.), *Microdevelopment: Transition processes in development and learning: Cambridge studies in cognitive perceptual development* (pp. 243–292). New York: Cambridge University Press.

Lewin, K. (1931). The conflict between Aristotelian and Galilean models of thought in contemporary psychology. *Journal of General Psychology, 5,* 147–177.

Lewis, M. D. (2000). The promise of dynamic systems approaches for an integrated account of human development. *Child Development, 71,* 36–43.

Lewis, M. D. (2005). Bridging theory and neurobiology through dynamic systems modeling. *Behavioral and Brain Sciences, 28,* 105–131.

Lewis, M. D., & Douglas, L. (1998). A dynamic systems approach to cognition-emotion interactions in development. In M. F. Mascolo & S. Griffins (Eds.), *What develops in emotional development?* (pp. 159–188). New York: Plenum Press.

Lewis, M. D., & Granic, I. (1999a). Self-organization of cognition-emotion interactions. In T. Dalgleish & M. Power (Eds.), *The handbook of cognition and emotion* (pp. 683–701). Chichester, England: Wiley. Lewis, M. D., & Granic, I. (1999b). Who put the self in self-organization? A clarification of terms and concepts for developmental psychopathology. *Development and Psychopathology, 11,* 365–374.

Lewis, M. D., & Granic, I. (Eds.). (2000). *Emotion, development and self-organization: Dynamic systems approaches to emotional development.* New York: Cambridge University Press.

Lewis, M. D., Lamey, A. V., & Douglas, L. (1999). A new dynamic systems method for the analysis of early socioemotional development. *Developmental Science, 2,* 457–475.

Lewis, M. D., Zimmerman, S., Hollenstein, T., & Lamey, A. V. (2004). Reorganization of coping behavior at 1½ years: Dynamic systems and normative change. *Developmental Science, 7,* 56–73.

Lichtenberg, J. W., & Heck, E. J. (1986). Analysis of sequence and pattern in process research. *Journal of Counseling Psychology, 33,* 170–180.

Lykken, D. T. (1991). What's wrong with psychology anyway. In D. Cicchetti & W. M. Grove (Eds.), *Thinking clearly about psychology* (Vol. 1, pp. 3–39). Minneapolis: University of Minnesota Press.

Mahoney, M. J. (1991). *Human change processes: The scientific foundations of psychotherapy.* New York: Basic Books.

McClelland, J. L. (1979). On the time relations of mental processes: An examination of systems of processes in cascade. *Psychological Review, 86,* 287–330.

Meehl, P. E. (1978). Theoretical risks and tabular asterisks: Sir Karl, Sir Ronald, and the slow progress of soft psychology. *Journal of Consulting and Clinical Psychology, 46,* 1–42.

Minuchin, S. (1974). *Families and family therapy.* Cambridge, MA: Harvard University Press.

Minuchin, S., & Fishman, C. H. (1974). *Family therapy techniques.* Cambridge, MA: Harvard University Press.

Moffitt, T. E. (1993). "Adolescence-limited" and "life-course persistent" antisocial behavior: A developmental taxonomy. *Psychological Review, 100,* 674–701.

Munakata, Y. (1998). Infant perseveration and implications for object permanence theories: A PDP model of the AB task. *Developmental Science, 1,* 161–184.

Munakata, Y., & McClelland, J. L. (in press). Connectionist models of development: Connectionism and dynamic systems theory: Are these really different approaches to development? [Special issue] *Developmental Science.*

Nagin, D. S., & Tremblay, R. E. (1999). Trajectories of boys' aggression, opposition, and hyperactivity on the path to physically violent and nonviolent juvenile delinquency. *Child Development, 70,* 1181–1196.

Nelson, C. A., Bloom, F. E., Cameron, J. L., Amaral, D., Dahl, R. E., & Pine, D. (2002). An integrative, multidisciplinary approach to the study of brain-behavior relations in the context of typical and atypical development. *Development and Psychopathology, 14,* 499–520.

Newell, K. M., & Molenaar, P. (1998). *Applications of nonlinear dynamics to developmental process modeling.* Mahwah, NJ: Erlbaum.

Newtson, D. (1994). The perception and coupling of behavior waves. In R. R. Vallacher & A. Nowak (Eds.), *Dynamical systems in social psychology* (pp. 139–166). San Diego: Academic Press.

Newtson, D. (1998). Dynamical systems and the structure of behavior. In K. M. Newell & P. C. Molenaar (Eds.), *Applications of nonlinear dynamics to developmental process modeling* (pp. 129–160). Mahwah, NJ: Erlbaum.

Norton, A. (1995). Dynamics: An introduction. In R. F. Port & T. van Gelder (Eds.), *Mind as motion: Explorations in the dynamics of cognition* (pp. 45–68). Cambridge, MA: MIT Press.

Overton, W. F., & Horowitz, H. A. (1991). Developmental psychopathology: Integrations and differentiations. In D. Cicchetti & S. L. Toth (Eds.), *Rochester Symposium on Developmental Psychopathology: Vol. 3. Models and integrations* (pp. 1–42). Rochester, NY: University of Rochester Press.

Paré, D., & Collins, D. R. (2000). Neuronal correlates of fear in the lateral amygdala: Multiple extracellular recordings in conscious cats. *Journal of Neuroscience, 20,* 2701–2710.

Patterson, G. R. (1982). *Coercive family processes.* Eugene, OR: Castalia.

Patterson, G. R., Reid, J. B., & Dishion, T. (1992). *Antisocial boys.* Eugene, OR: Castalia.

Pepler, D., Craig, W., & O'Connell, P. (1999). Understanding bullying from a dynamic systems perspective. In A. Slater & D. Muir (Eds.), *The Blackwell reader in developmental psychology* (pp. 440–451). Malden, MA: Blackwell.

Pincas, D. (2001). A framework and methodology for the study of nonlinear, self-organizing family dynamics. *Nonlinear Dynamics, Psychology, and Life Sciences, 5,* 139–173.

Plunkett, K. (1993). Lexical segmentation and vocabulary growth in early language acquisition. *Journal of Child Language, 20,* 43–60.

Plunkett, K., & Elman, J. L. (1997). *Exercises in rethinking innateness: A handbook for connectionist simulations.* Cambridge, MA: MIT Press.

Port, R. F., & van Gelder, T. (1995). *Mind as motion: Explorations in the dynamics of cognition.* Cambridge, MA: MIT Press.

Prigogine, I., & Stengers, I. (1984). *Order out of chaos.* New York: Bantam.

Reis, H. T., Collins, W. A., & Bersheid, E. (2000). The relationship context of human behavior and development. [Special issue: Psychology in the twenty-first century] *Psychological Bulletin, 126,* 844–872.

Richters, J. E. (1997). The Hubble hypothesis and the developmentalist's dilemma. *Development and Psychopathology, 9,* 193–229.

Ruhland, R., & van Geert, P. (1998). Jumping into syntax: Transitions in the development of closed class words. *British Journal of Developmental Psychology, 16,* 65–95.

Rumelhart, D. E., & McClelland, J. L. (Eds.). (1986). *Parallel distributed processing: Explorations in the microstructure of cognition: Vol. 1. Foundations.* Cambridge, MA: Bradford Books/MIT Press.

Ryan, K. D., Gottman, J. M., Murray, J. D., Carrere, S., & Swanson, C. (2000). Theoretical and mathematical modeling of marriage. In M. D. Lewis & I. Granic (Eds.), *Emotion, development and self-organization: Dynamic systems approaches to emotional development* (pp. 349–372). New York: Cambridge University Press.

Sabelli, H. C., Carlson-Sabelli, L., Patel, M., Levy, A., & Diez-Martin, J. (1995). Anger, fear, depression, and crime: Physiological and psycho-logical studies using the process method. In R. Robertson & A. Combs (Eds.), *Chaos theory in psychology and the life sciences* (pp. 65–88). Mahwah, NJ: Erlbaum.

Sameroff, A. J. (1983). Developmental systems: Contexts and evolution. In W. Kessen (Ed.), *History, theory, and methods* (4th ed., Vol. 1, pp. 237–294). New York: Wiley.

Sameroff, A. J. (1995). General systems theories and developmental psychopathology. In D. Cicchetti & D. J. Cohen (Eds.), *Developmental psychopathology: Vol. 1. Theory and methods* (pp. 659–695). New York: Wiley.

Schroeck, F. E. (1994). New mathematical techniques for pattern recognition. In R. R. Vallacher & A. Nowak (Eds.), *Dynamical systems in social psychology* (pp. 139–166). San Diego: Academic Press.

Shannon, C. E., & Weaver, W. (1949). *The mathematical theory of communication.* Urbana: University of Illinois Press.

Simonoff, J. S. (1996). *Smoothing methods in statistics.* New York: Springer-Verlag.

Smith, L. B. (1993). The concept of same. *Advances in Child Development and Behavior, 24,* 216–253.

Smith, L. B. (1995). Self-organizing processes in learning to learn words: Development is not induction. In *Minnesota Symposia on Child Psychology: Vol. 28. Basic and applied perspectives on learning, cognition, and development* (pp. 1–32). Mahwah, NJ: Erlbaum.

Smith, L. B., & Samuelson, L. K. (in press). Different is good: Connectionism and dynamic systems theory are complementary emergentist approaches to development. [Special issue: Connectionism and dynamic systems theory: Are these really different approaches to development?] *Developmental Science.*

Smith, L. B., & Thelen, E. (in press). Development as a dynamic system. *Trends in Cognitive Science.*

Snyder, J., Edwards, P., McGraw, K., Kilgore, K., & Holton, A. (1994). Escalation and reinforcement in mother-child conflict: Social processes associated with the development of physical aggression. *Development and Psychopathology, 6,* 305–321.

Snyder, J., Stoolmiller, M., Wilson, M., & Yamamoto, M. (in press). Child emotion regulation, parent emotion coaching, and early child antisocial behavior. *Social Development.*

Spemann, H. (1938). *Embryonic development and induction.* New Haven, CT: Yale University Press.

Spencer, J. P., & Schoner, G. (in press). Bridging the representational gap in the dynamic systems approach to development. [Special issue: Connectionism and dynamic systems theory: Are these really different approaches to development?] *Developmental Science.*

Spencer, J. P., & Thelen, E. (Eds.). (in press). Connectionism and dynamic systems theory: Are these really different approaches to development? [Special issue] *Developmental Science.*

Sroufe, L. A. (1979). The coherence of individual development: Early care, attachment, and subsequent developmental issues. *American Psychologist, 34,* 834–841.

Sroufe, L. A. (1986). Appraisal: Bowlby's contribution to psychoanalytic theory and developmental psychology: Attachment, separation, loss. [Special issue: 30th anniversary of the Association for Child Psychology and Psychiatry and Allied Disciplines] *Journal of Child Psychology and Psychiatry and Allied Disciplines, 27,* 841–849.

Sroufe, L. A., & Rutter, M. (1984). The domain of developmental psychopathology. *Child Development, 55,* 17–29.

Steenbeek, H., & van Geert, P. (in press). A dynamic systems model of dyadic child-peer play interactions. *European Journal of Developmental Psychology.*

Tesser, A., & Achee, J. (1994). Aggression, love, conformity, and other social psychological catastrophes. In R. R. Vallacher & A. Nowak

(Eds.), *Dynamical systems in social psychology* (pp. 95–109). San Diego: Academic Press.

Thelen, E., Schoener, G., Scheier, C., & Smith, L. B. (2001). The dynamics of embodiment: A field theory of infant perseverative reaching. *Behavioral and Brain Sciences, 24,* 1–34.

Thelen, E., & Smith, L. B. (1994). *A dynamic systems approach to the development of cognition and action.* Cambridge, MA: Bradford/MIT Press.

Thelen, E., & Smith, L. B. (1998). Dynamic systems theories. In W. Damon (Ed.), *Handbook of child psychology: Vol. 1. Theoretical models of human development* (5th ed., pp. 563–633). New York: Wiley.

Thelen, E., & Ulrich, B. D. (1991). Hidden skills: A dynamic systems analysis of treadmill stepping during the first year. *Monographs of the Society for Research in Child Development, 56*(1, Serial No. 223).

Thom, R. (1975). *Structural stability and morphogenesis.* New York: Benjamin-Addison-Wesley.

van den Boom, D. C., & Hoeksma, J. B. (1994). The effect of infant irritability on mother-infant interation: A growth curve analysis. *Developmental Psychology, 30,* 581–590.

van der Maas, H. (1998). The dynamical and statistical properties of cognitive strategies: Relations between strategies, attractors, and latent classes. In K. M. Newell & P. C. M. Molenaar (Eds.), *Applications of nonlinear dynamics to developmental process modeling* (pp. 161–176). Mahwah, NJ: Erlbaum.

van der Maas, H., & Molenaar, P. (1992). Stagewise cognitive development: An application of catastrophe theory. *Psychological Review, 99,* 395–417.

van Geert, P. (1991). A dynamic systems model of cognitive and language growth. *Psychological Review, 98,* 3–53.

van Geert, P. (1994). *Dynamic systems of development: Change between complexity and chaos.* New York: Prentice-Hall/Harvester Wheatsheaf.

van Geert, P. (1997a). Nonlinear dynamics and the explanation of mental and behavioral development. *Journal of Mind and Behavior, 18,* 269–290.

van Geert, P. (1997b). Que sera sera: Determinism and nonlinear dynamic model building in development. In A. Fogel, M. C. D. P. Lyra, & J. Valsiner (Eds.), *Dynamics and indeterminism in developmental and social processes* (pp. 13–38). Hillsdale, NJ: Erlbaum.

van Geert, P. (1998a). Dynamic modeling of cognitive and language development: From growth processes to sudden jumps and multimodality. In K. M. Newell & P. C. Molenaar (Eds.), *Applications of nonlinear dynamics to developmental process modeling* (pp. 129–160). Mahwah, NJ: Erlbaum.

van Geert, P. (1998b). A dynamic systems model of basic developmental mechanisms: Piaget, Vygotsky, and beyond. *Psychological Review, 105,* 634–677.

van Geert, P. (1998c). We almost had a great future behind us: The contribution of nonlinear dynamics to developmental-science-in-the-making. *Developmental Science, 1,* 143–159.

van Geert, P., & van Dijk, M. (2002). Focus on variability: New tools to study intra-individual variability in developmental data. *Infant Behavior and Development, 25,* 340–370.

Vetere, A., & Gale, A. (1987). The family: A failure in psychological theory and research. In A. Vetere, A. Gale, S. Lewis, C. Jolly, & S. Reynolds (Eds.), *Ecological studies of family life* (pp. 1–17). Chichester, England: Wiley.

von Bertalanffy, L. (1968). *General systems theory.* New York: Braziller.

Wickens, T. D. (1989). *Multiway contingency table analysis for the social sciences.* Hillsdale, NJ: Erlbaum.

Wimmers, R. H., Savelsbergh, G. J. P., van der Kamp, J., & Hartelman, P. (1998). A developmental transition in prehension modeled as a cusp catastrophe. *Developmental Psychobiology, 32,* 23–35.

CHAPTER 23

Taxometric Methods: Enhancing Early Detection and Prevention of Psychopathology by Identifying Latent Vulnerability Traits

THEODORE P. BEAUCHAINE and PENNY MARSH

It has been 20 years since Sroufe and Rutter's (1984) seminal paper formalized the boundaries of developmental psychopathology. Although roots of the developmental psychopathology perspective extend to at least a decade earlier (Achenbach, 1974), Sroufe and Rutter identified several fundamental themes that defined the burgeoning field and continue to shape our scientific agenda today. Foremost in their exposition was a call for improved prediction of psychopathological outcomes through "the study of the origins and course of individual patterns of behavioral maladapta-

tion" (p. 18). As they noted more recently (Rutter & Sroufe, 2000), this emphasis on prediction of individual differences emerged in large part out of concern that traditional diagnostic classes, although in many cases reliable, were often reified despite limited evidence of construct validity (see also Kendell, 1989). In becoming so reified, descriptive psychiatric syndromes were being mistaken for and used as explanatory constructs, without acknowledgment of how little was known about the etiological substrates of most disorders. By focusing on causal processes implicated in the emergence of individual differences in behavioral adaptation and maladaptation, it was hoped that the complexities of psychopathological development would become more appreciated and further explored.

Developmental psychopathology's focus on individual differences in the emergence of behavioral maladaptation followed from recognition that almost all psychiatric categories reflect etiologically heterogeneous groups. For example, the impulsive behaviors characteristic of

Work on this chapter was supported by Grant R01 MH63699 to Theodore P. Beauchaine from the National Institute of Mental Health and by Graduate Research Fellowship DGE0203031 to Penny Marsh from the National Science Foundation. We express our gratitude to Sheila Crowell for her helpful comments on an earlier draft. Address correspondence to Theodore P. Beauchaine, Department of Psychology, University of Washington, Box 351525, Seattle, WA 98195-1525. E-mail: tbeaucha@u.washington.edu.

Attention-Deficit/Hyperactivity Disorder (ADHD) can result from numerous causal pathways, including genetically influenced central dopamine dysfunction (e.g., Swanson & Castellanos, 2002), structural insults to the central nervous system (e.g., Gerring et al., 2000), and in utero exposure to alcohol and other drugs of abuse (e.g., Niccols, 1994). Moreover, each of these vulnerabilities may interact somewhat differently with environmental risk in producing psychopathological outcomes. The term *equifinality* has been reserved by developmental psychopathologists to refer to instances in which multiple etiological pathways lead to an apparently single behavioral syndrome. Reliance on the behavioral symptoms of ADHD as an explanatory construct obscures this etiological heterogeneity and is likely to hamper our efforts to predict the longitudinal course of individuals afflicted with the disorder. As Sroufe and Rutter (1984) astutely noted, prediction and control are the objectives of all scientific disciplines, and improving our ability to predict longitudinal outcomes is essential for more accurate diagnosis, more effective treatment, and ultimately the prevention of debilitating psychiatric conditions (see also Cicchetti & Rogosch, 2002).

The value of considering individual differences in the development of psychopathology toward improving both diagnosis and treatment is probably best exemplified in the literature addressing childhood externalizing disorders. Moffitt's (1993) reformulation of Conduct Disorder (CD) as either adolescent-limited or life-course-persistent revealed that externalizing children and adolescents with topographically similar cross-sectional behavior patterns can be distinguished from one another based on differences in the longitudinal course of their symptoms. Moreover, these distinct symptom trajectories mark differences in genetic liability, treatment response, and long-term prognosis (e.g., Myers, Brown, & Mott, 1995; Taylor, Iacono, & McGue, 2000; Werry, 1997). Revisions to the *Diagnostic and Statistical Manual of Mental Disorders* (*DSM;* American Psychiatric Association, 1994) specifying early- and late-onset subtypes of CD therefore reflect an improved understanding of the etiological substrates of the disorder. Indeed, etiology-based diagnosis usually marks progression in the evolution of our nosologic system because it results from increased basic knowledge of the ontology of disordered behavior (Beauchaine & Gartner, 2003; Kendell, 1989).

Even when not developmentally focused, efforts to characterize heterogeneous subgroups of externalizing children have led to advances in intervention research, where several moderating effects of individual differences on treatment response have recently been identified. In the Multimodal Treatment of ADHD study, children with ADHD and both comorbid anxiety and conduct problems fared best when behavioral management was included with medication management in their treatment. In comparison, no benefit of including behavioral management was observed for children with ADHD who did not suffer from comorbid psychopathology (Jensen et al., 2001). Intervention research on child conduct problems has uncovered similar individual difference moderators of treatment outcome. For example, children treated for early-onset conduct problems improve more when their interventions include teacher training in behavioral management practices if they suffer from comorbid ADHD. In contrast, CD children without comorbid ADHD improve at the same rate whether or not teacher training is included in their intervention (Beauchaine, Webster-Stratton, & Reid, in press). Taken together, these findings illustrate how delineating heterogeneous subgroups of children within current psychiatric classes can improve diagnostic accuracy and increase treatment efficacy. Identifying individual differences that predict treatment response among children with behavior disorders has therefore become an explicit priority of child psychopathology researchers (see Brestan & Eyberg, 1998; Owens et al., 2003).

Yet, from a developmental psychopathology perspective, defining heterogeneities among children already diagnosed with psychiatric disorders is not enough. Rather, efforts to design more effective prevention and intervention programs will be maximized only by identifying children at risk for heterogeneous patterns of morbidity *before* they meet criteria for a psychiatric disorder. As we demonstrate in later sections of this chapter, it is already possible to prospectively identify children at considerable risk for a number of severely debilitating conditions, and to reduce such risk with targeted prevention programs. Nevertheless, considerable barriers must be surmounted before the full potential of the developmental psychopathology perspective is realized. First, methodological techniques that can accommodate and identify individual symptom patterns and trajectories must be further developed and put to use by developmental psychopathologists. Conventional data analytic approaches born from the Fisherian statistical tradition are not well suited for characterizing individual patterns of behavior (see Richters, 1997). Rather, such approaches, including the *t*-test, analysis of variance (ANOVA), and many linear regression applications, assess the significance of group differences on outcome variables of interest. Although questions regarding group differences will always be important in psychopathology research, alternative statistical approaches that are often referred to as *person-centered* techniques must become part of researchers' data analytic armament to fully elucidate the etiological heterogeneity of psychopathological states and outcomes (see also Beauchaine, 2003b; Cicchetti & Rogosch, 1999). Since its inception, developmental psychopathology has been an integrative discipline concerned with unique combinations of biological, psychological, and environmental risk. Unfortunately, our theoretical models have outstripped the availability and use of appropriate data analytic strategies for characterizing the etiological heterogeneity that such integrative theories imply and predict. Our primary objective in writing this chapter is to describe the strengths and limitations of one class of person-centered techniques, often referred to collectively as *taxometrics*.

A second barrier that must be overcome for the full potential of the developmental psychopathology perspective to be realized is the precedence placed on overt behavioral symptoms in defining and validating diagnostic classes. At present, all diagnostic categories in the *DSM-IV-TR* (American Psychiatric Association, 2000) are composed entirely of behavioral markers of latent psychopathology traits. Because these traits cannot be observed directly, psychopathologists have come to rely exclusively on behavioral indicators to infer unobservable compromises in biological and psychological functioning. As we discuss in greater detail later, this is necessary in the early stages of delineating a psychiatric syndrome, yet it actively inhibits specification of the diverse causes of psychopathology in later stages of diagnostic validation. Here again, the problem results from a failure to delineate etiological heterogeneity within psychiatric groups. This problem is best illustrated by difficulties faced among behavior geneticists in identifying candidate genes for major psychiatric disorders. In behavior genetics research on ADHD, for example, groups of probands are typically selected based on *phenotypic* markers, including hyperactive, impulsive, and inattentive behaviors. Searches for candidate genes are then conducted by comparing allelic frequencies among probands with either siblings, parents, or controls, depending on the design of the study. As we noted, however, symptoms of ADHD have been linked to numerous equifinal pathways, including central dopamine dysfunction, in utero exposure to stimulants and alcohol, and insults to the central nervous system. These pathways do not share a common genetic etiology, which necessarily attenuates estimates of genetic association and may preclude the identification of the genetic substrates of certain subtypes of ADHD. Although more recent behavior genetics studies have attempted to purify the ADHD phenotype by screening out children with head injuries and perinatal insults, etiological heterogene-

ity may nevertheless explain why findings from genetics studies have often been conflicting, with primarily small risk ratios observed (Swanson & Castellanos, 2002). As Castellanos and Tannock (2002, p. 619) recently noted, "Nearly two decades of unsuccessful efforts in psychiatric genetics have led to the conclusion that symptom-based diagnostic classification systems do not facilitate (and can actively obstruct) mapping between susceptibility genes and behavioral outcomes."

To deal with this problem, several authors have suggested that psychopathologists avoid an exclusive reliance on phenotypic indicators, or readily observable signs and symptoms, when assessing psychopathology and defining psychiatric classes. Rather, more progress toward characterizing etiological heterogeneities within behavioral syndromes is likely to be made by using both phenotypic and *endophenotypic* markers in future research. Gottesman and Gould (2003, p. 636) define endophenotypes as "*measurable components unseen by the unaided eye along the pathway between disease and distal genotype.*" In other words, endophenotypes are biological and behavioral markers of latent vulnerabilities for psychopathology that cannot be observed without careful measurement. Endophenotypic markers fall along the causal chain between genotype and phenotype and therefore lie closer to the genetic substrates of psychiatric disorders than does behavior (Lenzenweger, 2004). Figure 23.1 depicts two levels of endophenotypes falling between the genetic substrates of Schizophrenia and the behavioral expression of the disorder. On the far left are candidate genes associated with

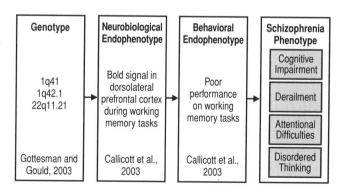

Figure 23.1 Relations among genotypes, endophenotypes, and phenotypes for the example of Schizophrenia. Note that endophenotypes can be identified at multiple levels of analysis including neurobiological and behavioral, and that many additional genetic, endophenotypic, and phenotypic indicators of Schizophrenia have been specified that are not depicted here. *Source:* From "The Endophenotype Concept in Psychiatry: Etymology and Strategic Intentions," by I. I. Gottesman, and T. D. Gould, 2003, *American Journal of Psychiatry, 160,* pp. 636–645.

working memory deficiencies in patients with Schizophrenia. These genes are expressed at multiple endophenotypic levels, including neurobiological and behavioral. At the neurobiological level, both patients with Schizophrenia and their nonaffected siblings exhibit increased blood oxygenation in the right dorsolateral prefrontal cortex during working memory tasks compared with controls (Callicott et al., 2003; Manoach et al., 1999). Thus, both probands and their siblings recruit a broader prefrontal neural network to accomplish such tasks. Notably, however, siblings without the disorder do not exhibit the behavioral endophenotype, poor performance on working memory tasks, nor do they exhibit the phenotypic indicators of Schizophrenia.

This example illustrates several important points about the potential value of endophenotypes in developmental psychopathology research. First, endophenotypic markers that are more proximal to the genetic substrates of Schizophrenia are also more sensitive to shared genetic vulnerabilities than more distant behavioral endophenotypes and phenotypes. Second, carefully chosen endophenotypes often identify latent genetic vulnerabilities *before* full-blown expression of psychiatric disorders, which has major implications for prevention (see also Castellanos & Tannock, 2002; Cornblatt & Malhotra, 2001). Finally, specification of the mechanisms of etiologically heterogeneous psychopathological outcomes will require a focus on latent vulnerability *traits* rather than strictly behavioral syndromes, a view expressed recently by a number of authors (e.g., Krueger et al., 2002; Skuse, 2001) and a point we return to in later sections.

With this discussion in mind, a second objective of writing this chapter is to emphasize the importance of using endophenotypic markers when conducting both psychopathology and developmental psychopathology research. As we will demonstrate, carefully chosen endophenotypes are particularly advantageous when conducting taxometrics studies, both because they are located more proximally to the etiological substrates of psychopathology and because their psychometric properties offer significant advantages over those of strictly behavioral measures (see also Meehl, 1995a, 2001a, 2001b).

In the sections to follow, we first describe the prevailing approach to construct validation in psychiatric research and the problems posed by that approach for identifying etiologically homogeneous diagnostic groups. Next, we outline the potential role that well-designed taxometrics studies could play in improving the construct validation process and the advantages of using taxometric methods compared with other person-centered techniques. Although these sections do not speak to developmental psychopathology specifically,

they are necessary to lay the foundations for the remainder of the chapter. We then provide an overview of commonly used taxometric methods, including recommendations for researchers seeking to perform such analyses. Although other sources of similar descriptions exist (e.g., Beauchaine & Beauchaine, 2002; Lenzenweger, 2004; J. Ruscio & Ruscio, 2004a, 2004b; Schmidt, Kotov, & Joiner, 2004; Waller & Meehl, 1998), our emphasis is on addressing questions of particular concern to developmental psychopathologists, who have been slower to adopt taxometric methods than adult psychopathology researchers (Beauchaine, 2003b). Following this overview, we discuss the implications of using endophenotypes in taxometrics studies for (1) identifying premorbid latent vulnerabilities for psychopathology among at-risk children and (2) targeting children with such vulnerabilities for prevention. Finally, we discuss several additional questions that developmental psychopathologists can address in future taxometrics studies.

CONSTRUCT VALIDATION IN PSYCHIATRIC RESEARCH

As most readers are undoubtedly aware, authors both within and outside the field of developmental psychopathology have criticized the *DSM* on a number of grounds (see, e.g., Hinshaw & Park, 1999; Jensen & Hoagwood, 1997; Richters & Cicchetti, 1993; Winokur, Zimmerman, & Cadoret, 1988). These criticisms include allegations that the *DSM* framework places the locus of disorder within the individual, ignoring contextual information about environmental influences on behavior; assumes biological bases for psychiatric disorders despite claims of being atheoretical and descriptive; lacks developmental guidelines for assessment and diagnosis; fails to capture cultural differences in the manifestations of behavioral maladaptation; is of limited clinical utility because of symptom heterogeneity within diagnostic classes and homogeneity across diagnostic classes; assumes that psychiatric diagnoses are etiologically discrete and categorical; and reduces reliability and statistical power by dichotomizing continuous symptom profiles into categorical diagnoses (Cantwell, 1996; Clark, Watson, & Reynolds, 1995; Cummings, Davies, & Campbell, 2000; Hinshaw, Lahey, & Hart, 1993; Hinshaw & Park, 1999; Jensen & Hoagwood, 1997; MacCallum, Zhang, Preacher, & Rucker, 2002; Sonuga-Barke, 1998; Sroufe, 1997).

Although it is not our objective to review these criticisms in detail, it is noteworthy that to one extent or another, many of them address the inability of *DSM* syndromes to capture heterogeneities in psychopathological processes and outcomes, raising questions about the *construct validity* of many current diagnostic classes. In psychiatric research, construct validity refers to the extent to which symptoms of a diagnosis mark an objective, nonarbitrary latent entity or attribute, and in doing so discriminate the diagnosis from alternative syndromes. Construct validity must be evaluated whenever the latent cause of a putative trait or disorder cannot be observed directly (Cronbach & Meehl, 1955). Consider the difference between a medical syndrome such as pancreatic cancer, and a common psychiatric condition such as Major Depressive Disorder. In the case of pancreatic cancer, a patient presents at her physician's office with a cluster of symptoms, including nausea, jaundice, abdominal pain, dark urine, and weight loss. This cluster of symptoms enables the treating physician to generate a hypothesis about the etiological substrate of the symptom profile. Of particular importance, this hypothesis is either confirmed or disconfirmed through a biopsy. If the biopsy is negative, a new hypothesis is generated and tested until the pathogen that is responsible for the overt symptoms is identified.

The depressed individual also presents with a cluster of symptoms, including anhedonia, depressed mood, fatigue, weight loss, and insomnia. In contrast to the case of pancreatic cancer, however, there are no pathognomic signs of depression, either biological or behavioral. This leads to somewhat tautological definitions of mental disorders. In the case at hand, the patient is depressed because she presents with a cluster of symptoms, and she presents with a cluster of symptoms because she is depressed; there are no litmus tests to confirm or disconfirm the diagnosis. As Meehl (1995a) noted, behavioral scientists are usually forced to infer latent psychopathological traits using fallible indicators and no gold standard of disease state.

Although often ignored, the difficulties posed for construct validation of psychiatric disorders by the absence of pathognomic signs are quite formidable (Meehl, 1973a, 2004). These difficulties are reflected in the history of the *DSM,* first published by the American Psychiatric Association in 1952. Both the *DSM-I* (American Psychiatric Association, 1952) and the *DSM-II* (American Psychiatric Association, 1968) included symptom lists for major psychiatric disorders that were compiled based on the expert opinions of a small number of primarily psychoanalytically oriented academic psychiatrists. As a result, the diagnostic classes represented in these documents were theoretically rather than empirically based and suffered from poor reliability and validity (see, e.g., Malik & Beutler, 2002). Diagnostic agreement tended to be poor across different clinical and research sites, particularly those representing alternative theoretical orientations. Moreover, almost no evidence

was provided for the validity of most diagnostic categories (Kendell, 1989).

In an effort to address the validity of psychiatric diagnosis, Robins and Guze (1970) published a brief yet influential paper in which they advanced a five-step process toward establishing an objective behavioral syndrome. An extension of Cronbach and Meehl's (1955) construct validation procedure, this five-step approach included clinical description, laboratory studies, delimitation from other disorders, follow-up studies, and family studies. Thus, diagnostic validity is established when a clinical syndrome is characterized by (1) a cluster of covarying symptoms and etiological precursors; (2) reliable physiological, biological, and/or psychological markers; (3) readily definable exclusionary criteria; (4) a predictable course; and (5) increased rates of the same disorder among first-degree relatives. These criteria were applied in the first classification system of mental disorders that emphasized empirically derived diagnostic classes (Feighner et al., 1972). This system, now referred to as the *Feighner criteria,* was adopted by the American Psychiatric Association and has impacted all subsequent versions of the *DSM* (see Cloninger, 1989).

When the Feighner et al. (1972) criteria are met, much greater confidence in the construct validity of a diagnostic class is warranted because more is known about the etiological mechanisms responsible for psychopathology. The rationale behind this conclusion is illustrated in the diagnostic hierarchy presented in Figure 23.2 (Preskorn & Baker, 2002). At the bottom of the hierarchy is *symptomatic* diagnosis, which is purely descriptive. This may include the simple observation that a person appears unhappy, despondent, and hopeless. At the next level is *syn-*

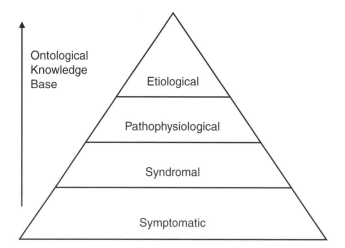

Figure 23.2   Levels of diagnosis. Each move up the hierarchy reflects an increment in knowledge about the causes of a particular diagnostic class. Most psychiatric disorders are specified at the syndromal level.

dromal diagnosis, which follows from the observation that a subgroup of people present with a similar cluster of co-varying symptoms. Here a clinician or group of clinicians may note, for example, that anhedonia, fatigue, irritability, sleep problems, and changes in appetite have been observed across a number of individuals. As noted earlier, all diagnostic classes represented in the *DSM-IV-TR* (American Psychiatric Association, 2000) are syndromal. At the next level of the hierarchy is *pathophysiological* diagnosis. This is possible when the pathophysiology that gives rise to the behavioral syndrome is identified. If appropriate laboratory tests reveal, for example, that the depressive behavioral syndrome is due to hypothyroidism, a pathophysiological diagnosis can be rendered. It is at this level that we begin to understand the process or processes through which the observed symptom profile emerged. *Etiological* diagnosis is at the highest level of the hierarchy. Here, the specific mechanism underlying the symptom pattern is identified. For instance, if antibodies are found that reveal Hashimoto thyroiditis, an autoimmune disease among several pathogenic processes that cause hypothyroidism, then the specific etiology of the depressive syndrome is understood. In general, the development of effective treatments improves as we move up the diagnostic hierarchy because etiological mechanisms can be targeted directly. In the specific case of depression at hand, a strictly syndromal diagnosis would most likely lead to a trial of either cognitive-behavioral therapy or an antidepressant, both of which would be of limited effectiveness because neither targets the etiological substrate of the behavioral syndrome, Hashimoto thyroiditis. The Feighner criteria were published in an effort to move psychiatry away from purely syndromal diagnoses to pathophysiological and etiological diagnoses.[1]

---

[1] In this example, the etiology is clearly biological. It is not our intent, however, to suggest that all etiological agents are disease based. In the case of Posttraumatic Stress Disorder, for example, knowledge of the precipitating traumatic event is essential for a full understanding of any individual case and for effective treatment. Nevertheless, both genetic vulnerabilities and pathophysiological mechanisms are important in the development of the disorder (see Metzger et al., 2004; Orr et al., 2003; Stein, Jang, Taylor, Vernon, & Livesley, 2002). As will become evident in later sections of this chapter, we assume that most psychiatric disorders follow a diathesis-stress model in which biological vulnerabilities are either amplified or attenuated by environmental risk or protection, respectively. Consistent with the Sroufe and Rutter (1984) thesis, the more complex the interplay between biological vulnerability and environmental risk, the more symptom-only-based diagnosis is likely to obscure etiology.

In response to the Robins and Guze (1970) and Feighner et al. (1972) papers, significant effort was expended beginning with the *DSM-III* (American Psychiatric Association, 1980) toward specifying associated features, explicit inclusion and exclusion criteria, the projected course, and the familial pattern of many psychiatric disorders. Nevertheless, nearly 20 years later, most diagnostic categories had not been validated adequately (Kendell, 1989). Although this situation has improved somewhat since the arrival of the *DSM-IV* (American Psychiatric Association, 1994) and *DSM-IV-TR* (American Psychiatric Association, 2000), considerable validation work remains for many if not most psychiatric disorders. Moreover, a number of critics have noted that the expansive proliferation of diagnostic categories in each subsequent version of the *DSM,* from 106 in 1952 (*DSM-I*) to 365 in 1994 (*DSM-IV*), far outstrips observed advances in scientific understanding of both the construct validities and etiological substrates of the additional disorders (Houts, 2002).

An Overreliance on Symptoms

Adoption of the Feigner et al. (1972) criteria as a prototype for construct validation of diagnostic classes is viewed by many as a watershed event in psychiatry that precipitated the rejection of subjectively defined behavioral syndromes in favor of an empirically based, scientifically rigorous nosology of mental disorders (e.g., Spitzer, 1997). How, then, are we in the position just outlined, in which evidence for the validity of most diagnostic classes remains somewhat limited? As we will demonstrate, an overreliance on behavioral symptoms as gold standards in psychiatric diagnosis has impeded specification of heterogeneities in the etiological underpinnings of most disorders. Furthermore, even when endophenotypic markers with the potential to identify etiologically homogeneous groups are identified, they are often eschewed for diagnostic purposes in favor of strictly behavioral criteria. This practice can have serious consequences for our ability to predict the longitudinal course of individuals afflicted with psychiatric disorders, and therefore has significant implications for developmental psychopathologists. Nowhere is this more apparent than in the case of Major Depression.

As we have noted elsewhere (Beauchaine, 2003b), some cases of depression appear to be influenced more by environmental risk, whereas others appear to be influenced more by biological risk (see also Cicchetti & Rogosch, 2002; Harrington, Rutter, & Fombonne, 1996). Although these depression subtypes cannot be readily differentiated based on the behavioral criteria outlined in the *DSM-IV-TR,* evidence suggests that the dexamethasone suppression test (DST), an indicator of hypothalamic-pituitary-adrenal (HPA) axis reactivity, can identify a subgroup of depressed patients who are at particularly high biological risk for mood disturbance and who are especially prone to later suicide. The DST involves administration of dexamethasone, a synthetic corticosteroid, which normally suppresses cortisol production by the HPA axis. In cases of HPA axis hyperactivity, however, cortisol production is not suppressed. In a long-term follow-up study of 78 depressed patients who were administered the DST, Coryell and Schlesser (2001) found that suppressors had a 15-year suicide risk of 2.9%, whereas nonsuppressors had a 15-year suicide risk of 26.8%. Thus, DST nonsuppression offered an *order of magnitude* improvement in the prediction of an extremely important clinical outcome. Moreover, no behavioral indicator performed better than chance in predicting eventual suicide. Yet, by combining behavioral (mood disorder) and biological (DST) criteria, an approach long advocated by some (e.g., Akiskal, 1978; van Praag, 1990), and a suicide risk of greater than 1 in 4 was identified. Furthermore, recent evidence suggests that disturbances in cortisol reactivity may mark liability for melancholic depression among children as young as ages 3 to 5, providing for very early identification of risk (Luby et al., 2003; Luby, Mrakotsky, Heffelfinger, Brown, & Spitznagel, 2004). Given these findings, it is instructive to consider that in the early 1980s, the DST was hailed by many as a promising biological marker of endogenous depression but was abandoned because it did not correspond well enough with the behavioral syndrome. For example, after reporting a sensitivity rate of 55.5% and a specificity rate of 74.5% for the DST in predicting Major Depression, Casat and Powell (1988) concluded that clinical symptoms were more useful than the DST, a conclusion also reached by other authors (e.g., Lu, Ho, Huang, & Lin, 1988). Thus, a heterogeneous behavioral syndrome was used as the gold standard against which the validity of the DST was judged, and an opportunity to refine our diagnostic system in a manner that would allow for better longitudinal prediction of outcome was lost. We now know from family and twin studies that HPA axis activity is roughly 60% heritable (Bartels, de Geus, Kirschbaum, Sluyter, & Boomsma, 2004; Bartels, Van den Berg, Sluyter, Boomsma, & de Geus, 2003) and that polymorphisms in the glucocorticoid receptor gene are associated with some cases of DST nonsuppression (Ruiz et al., 2001). Glucocorticoid receptor gene polymorphisms may therefore mark a homogeneous subgroup within the depressive phenotype who have an especially virulent form of the disorder (see Figure 23.3), a conjecture that will be confirmed or disconfirmed by future research. This is but one

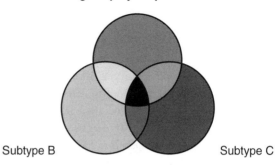

Figure 23.3 Venn diagram depicting heterogeneity (i.e., equifinality) in the depressive phenotype. All three subtypes are captured by the behavioral criteria for depression, but endophenotypic markers are required to subdivide the group into homogeneous subsets.

example of the advantages of conducting assessments at multiple levels of analysis, including both behavioral and biological, toward improving our ability to specify the longitudinal course of psychopathology (see also Cicchetti & Dawson, 2002) and identify premorbid risk.

THE IMPORTANCE OF IDENTIFYING DISCRETE LATENT CLASSES

To this point in this chapter, we have emphasized the significance of using endophenotypes to identify homogeneous diagnostic groups and the implications of doing so for construct validation and for developmental psychopathology models of adjustment. We now turn our attention to approaches identifying discrete latent classes of individuals who are either at risk for developing psychopathology or are already afflicted by psychopathology.

Although most psychopathological vulnerability traits probably are dimensional in nature (D. N. Klein & Riso, 1993), identifying those that are discrete is important because it allows us to draw objective diagnostic boundaries, to identify more homogeneous diagnostic subgroups, and to more accurately predict the long-term course of those afflicted with psychopathology (Beauchaine, 2003b; Beauchaine & Waters, 2003; Meehl, 1995a). For these reasons and others to be outlined, strong evidence for the construct validity of a disorder is provided when members of the diagnostic group comprise a discrete class (Meehl, 1995a). Moreover, when evidence of discrete latent structure is obtained using both endophenotypic markers and psychological symptoms, the first three of the Feighner et al. (1972) criteria are largely met (Beauchaine & Beauchaine, 2002).

Searching for Boundaries

Despite the advantages of identifying discretely distributed traits, it can be exceedingly difficult to determine whether a distribution of scores on a measured attribute marks a single continuous dimension or an admixture of two or more discrete groups (see Beauchaine & Beauchaine, 2002; Meehl, 1995a; J. Ruscio & Ruscio, 2004a). This is because discrete distributions, when present, are likely to overlap substantially due to both within-group variability and measurement error, rendering most statistical approaches ineffective in detecting multimodal latent structure (Beauchaine, 2003b). Nevertheless, a number of largely ineffective strategies for identifying discrete traits continue to appear in the psychology and psychiatry literatures. We consider several of these in turn.

Bimodality

Perhaps the oldest and least powerful means of identifying discrete subgroups of individuals is to plot the univariate distributions of measured traits or symptoms and inspect those distributions for bimodality. If a bimodal distribution is consistently found across samples, a diagnostic boundary can be inferred at the point of rarity between the two modes (Kendell, 1989). Unfortunately, two discrete distributions usually appear to be unimodal when mixed, even at quite large effect sizes (Grayson, 1987; Murphy, 1964; Waller & Meehl, 1998). The top panel of Figure 23.4 illustrates this for distributions of equal size that are separated by 2.0 within-group standard deviation units. Recall that Cohen (1988) defined 0.8 standard deviation units of separation between group means as a large effect in psychological research. Although the effect size illustrated in the top panel of Figure 23.4 is 2½ times the size of Cohen's definition of a large effect, no evidence of bimodality appears in the admixed distribution. This state of affairs is exacerbated when the mixed distributions are unequal in size, which is usually the case in psychopathology research. The bottom panel of Figure 23.4 depicts two discrete distributions that are mixed, the larger of which comprises 95% of the combined distribution, and the smaller of which comprises 5%. Although the two distributions are separated by 3.0 within-group standard deviations, there is still no evidence of bimodality in the mixed distribution, which appears to be continuous yet skewed. In fact, the combined distribution is almost identical to a distribution of Social Responsiveness

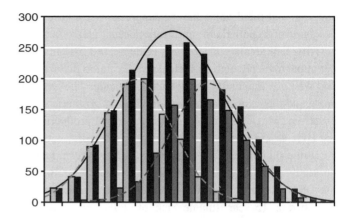

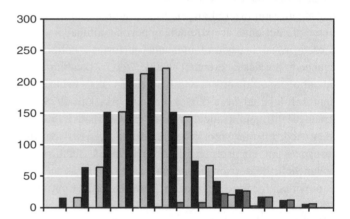

Figure 23.4 Top panel: Mixture of two normally distributed discrete groups $n = 1000$, each indicated by gray bars and dashed lines. Although the distributions are separated by 2.0 standard deviations, there is no evidence of bimodality in the combined sample, indicated by solid lines and black bars (adapted from Beauchaine, 2003). Bottom panel: Mixture of two normally distributed groups of $n = 950$ (left distribution) and $n = 50$ (right distribution). Although these distributions are separated by 3.0 standard deviations, there is still no evidence of bimodality in the combined sample, which appears to be continuous yet skewed, as indicated by the black bars.

Scale (Constantino, 2002) scores that Constantino and Todd (2003) recently reported in a large twin study of autistic traits. Based on this distribution, the authors concluded that autistic traits are distributed continuously, and that any diagnostic cutoff is therefore arbitrary. As Figure 23.4 indicates, however, such a conclusion is probably unwarranted until more sophisticated data analytic techniques are applied to the question.[2] Indeed, bimodality provides a very weak test for inferring discrete latent structure.

Figure 23.4 also illustrates why discretely distributed traits and disorders are rarely marked by distinct bound-

---

[2] Further recommendations for resolving the latent structure of Autism are presented in later sections.

aries (see also Lilienfeld & Marino, 1995; Meehl, 1995a; Sonuga-Barke, 1998). Here it is useful to consider the difference between latent constructs and manifest indicators. As we noted earlier, the mechanisms responsible for placing individuals into discretely distributed high-risk groups are almost always latent (unobservable) constructs, which are assessed by imperfect manifest (observable) indicators. As we have discussed elsewhere (Beauchaine, 2003b), even single gene disorders are manifested differently across individuals (see also Meehl, 1995a, 2001a). For example, Huntington's chorea, a progressive degenerative disorder of the nervous system that produces emotional instability, mood lability, and motor control difficulties, and is transmitted by an allelic variant of a single dominant gene, has a variable course across individuals. Age of onset, for example, varies considerably from person to person (Brooks, Murphy, Janota, & Lishman, 1987). Thus, despite having a latent genetic etiology that is discrete, manifest indicators of the illness are variable. Additionally, almost all behavioral indicators of psychopathology are measured with imperfect precision and reliability. Because of this, measurement error contributes to distributional overlap even when the latent structure of a trait or disorder is truly discrete. Because measurement precision plays an important role in the efficiency and power of all statistical approaches, we return to it in later sections.

Cluster Analysis

Given the limitations of bimodality for identifying discretely distributed traits, a number of alternative methods have been developed. To date, by far the most popular of these in the psychology and psychiatry literatures is the set of algorithms collectively referred to as *cluster analysis* (Blashfield & Aldenderfer, 1988). In general, these methods divide data sets into multiple partitions, either by maximizing between-group variance or by minimizing within-group variance. Although over 300 such algorithms exist, they can be broadly divided into two overarching categories, each of which we describe briefly (for comprehensive reviews, see Aldenderfer & Blashfield, 1984; Blashfield & Aldenderfer, 1988; Everitt, 1993; Milligan & Cooper, 1987).

Hierarchical agglomerative methods start with each data point representing a unique cluster. Points close to one another in *n* dimensional space as assessed by correlational, Euclidean, or other distance metrics are combined into progressively larger clusters, a process that is repeated until all data points are included in a single group. When performing a hierarchical agglomerative analysis, the researcher must decide when to stop the process, retaining a specific number of clusters that presumably best captures homogeneities within subgroups and heterogeneities across subgroups. In psychopathology research, these differences and similarities are typically measured by behavioral symptoms. Hierarchical agglomerative methods are frequently used for exploratory purposes, when the true number of clusters, if any, is unknown.

In contrast to hierarchical agglomerative methods, iterative partitioning, or *k*-means procedures, begin with a user-specified number of clusters. Individuals are then allocated into clusters and reallocated on successive passes through the data until the within-cluster sums of squares are minimized (Hartigan, 1975). Thus, the researcher determines the preferred number of clusters a priori, and the clustering algorithm creates groups that are as homogeneous as possible.

Clustering algorithms provide two significant advantages for psychopathology research. First, they are multivariate and can therefore accommodate large numbers of variables into a single analysis. Thus, rather than examining one symptom or marker at a time for evidence of discrete latent structure, all relevant symptoms can be analyzed together. Second, they can accommodate models containing any number of homogeneous groups. In contrast, and as described in later sections, taxometric techniques are restricted to instances in which only two groups are hypothesized.[3] Despite these strengths, however, clustering algorithms suffer from one very important limitation that has reduced their popularity among psychopathology researchers. Because clustering algorithms are *structure imposing* rather than *structure seeking,* they nearly always identify subgroups within a data set, whether or not those subgroups are truly homogeneous or discrete (Blashfield & Aldenderfer, 1988). For example, when IQ scores from representative samples are cluster analyzed, a two-cluster solution will almost invariably divide the distribution into high- and low-IQ groups, despite the fact that intelligence is continuously distributed in the population (Aldenderfer & Blashfield, 1984). Moreover, consistently effective methods of cluster validation have yet to be identified. Inferring validity by testing for group differences

---

[3] In two of his later papers, Meehl (1999, 2001a) described a newly developed technique called TAXSCAN, which does enable researchers to identify multiple discrete traits within a population given sufficiently valid indicators. To date, however, no empirical instantiations of TAXSCAN have appeared in the literature, nor have any large-scale Monte Carlo evaluations of the technique been conducted. For these reasons, we do not consider TAXSCAN in the present chapter.

based on cluster membership, for example, once a common practice among psychopathology researchers, is circular because these differences have been systematically maximized by the clustering algorithm (Aldenderfer & Blashfield, 1984; Blashfield & Aldenderfer, 1988). Similarly, replication does not ensure that clusters are discrete. Clustering algorithms can divide any sample of IQ scores into high and low groups who will differ from one another on numerous external correlates. This does not imply that the groups are discrete. Furthermore, analyses of data sets of known structure indicate that hierarchical agglomerative techniques often fail to identify the correct number of clusters (Krieger & Green, 1999).

These difficulties have led to several efforts to develop both stopping rules for determining the correct number of clusters in a data set and numerical indices of cluster integrity or validity (Milligan, 1981; Milligan & Cooper, 1985). Unfortunately, such methods have been developed using largely nonoverlapping distributions (Blashfield & Aldenderfer, 1988; Waller, Kaiser, Illian, & Manry, 1998), which are rarely observed in psychopathology research. Furthermore, despite clear improvements in recent years, the accuracy of cluster recovery still degrades rather quickly when cluster overlap is increased, and stopping rules remain limited in their ability to determine the presence versus absence of genuinely discrete groups (Atlas & Overall, 1994; Edelbrock, 1979; Grove, 1991; Tonidandel & Overall, 2004). Thus, cutoffs for group membership that are derived from cluster analyses are just as likely to be arbitrarily located along a continuous dimension as they are to distinguish between discretely distributed subgroups. Clustering algorithms therefore provide very weak tests of discrete latent structure (Meehl, 1979). Nevertheless, iterative partitioning methods can be quite accurate in sorting participants into the proper discrete latent class when the existence of that class has been verified beforehand by taxometric methods, which are structure seeking rather than structure imposing (Beauchaine & Beauchaine, 2002).

Mixture Modeling

Mixture modeling refers to a number of related methods that search for homogeneous groups within assumed mixed samples (McLachlan & Basford, 1988). These include *latent class analysis* (e.g., Lazarsfeld & Henry, 1968), which was designed specifically for use with dichotomous and/or Likert data; *latent profile analysis* and *finite mixture analysis* (Gibson, 1959; Lazarsfeld & Henry, 1968; McLachlan & Peel, 2000), which identify latent classes within continuous data; and *growth mixture modeling* (Muthén, 2001; Muthén & Shedden, 1999; Nagin, 1999; Nagin & Tremblay,

2001), which identifies groups from latent growth trajectories in symptoms or other variables of interest over time. Given the capacity to handle longitudinal data, growth mixture modeling approaches have enjoyed rapidly increasing popularity in the developmental psychopathology literature in recent years (e.g., Nagin & Tremblay, 1999; Shaw, Gilliom, Ingoldsby, & Nagin, 2003). Although space constraints preclude us from reviewing the extensive technical bases of these methods, each suffers from the same primary limitation as cluster analysis: They are structure-imposing techniques. Thus, when latent subgroups are identified, it cannot be determined whether or not they are truly discrete. This is true of both traditional approaches to mixture analysis (D. N. Klein & Riso, 1993; McLachlan & Peel, 2000) and newer growth mixture modeling techniques (Bauer & Curran, 2003, 2004). As Bauer and Curran have demonstrated, growth mixture models are prone to identifying spurious latent classes when only one group is represented in a population. Although this does not necessarily undermine the heuristic utility of mixture modeling (Cudeck & Henly, 2003), it clearly limits conclusions that might be drawn about diagnostic boundaries based on results from the techniques.

COHERENT CUT KINETICS

In an effort to address the inherent difficulties faced in identifying discrete psychopathological traits and drawing appropriate diagnostic boundaries, P. E. Meehl and his colleagues invented a set of algorithms collectively referred to as *coherent cut kinetics* (CCKs; Grove & Meehl, 1993; Meehl, 1973b, 1995a; Meehl & Yonce, 1994, 1996; Waller & Meehl, 1998). These methods were designed with the explicit objective of identifying discrete groups when they exist in a larger population, without the false-positive problem that characterizes most alternative approaches. The term CCK is intended to capture common attributes of the algorithms (Meehl & Yonce, 1994, 1996; Waller & Meehl, 1998). Each includes analysis of the statistical behavior of one or more variables in successive regions (cuts) of an input variable. These cuts are moved (kinetics) across the entire range of the input variable, and numerical values of latent parameters are estimated. If a discrete subgroup or *taxon* is present and the variables chosen are valid indicators of that taxon, estimates of these parameters are consistent (coherent) across analyses. In total, Meehl and colleagues specified 13 such taxometric procedures.

The impetus for developing taxometric methods was to test Meehl's (1962) diathesis-stress model of Schizophrenia.

Meehl hypothesized that a genetic vulnerability, which he called *schizotaxia,* was transmitted through a single dominant gene that was not fully penetrant. In other words, the schizotaxic genotype was thought to be a necessary but insufficient cause of Schizophrenia, resulting in the disorder for only a subset of genetically susceptible people. He also believed that a carefully selected group of observable phenotypic markers, expressed as *schizotypy,* could be used to identify the genetic vulnerability, whether or not a person developed Schizophrenia. After observing hundreds of patients and their family members in clinical contexts, Meehl (1962) outlined four putative schizotypic phenotypes as markers of the schizotaxic genotype: *interpersonal aversiveness,* or social fear, distrust, and anticipation of rejection; *ambivalence,* or concurrent motivation toward interpersonal approach and withdrawal; *cognitive slippage,* or loose control of associations; and *anhedonia,* or a limited capacity to experience pleasure.[4] Of note, in the intervening years since Meehl proposed his theory, a number of promising endophenotypic markers of genetic vulnerability for Schizophrenia have also been specified. As outlined in the introduction to this chapter, increased blood oxygenation in the right dorsolateral prefrontal cortex during working memory tasks has been identified in nonaffected siblings of patients with Schizophrenia (Callicott et al., 2003; Manoach et al., 1999). Similarly, smooth pursuit and saccade eye tracking abnormalities are observed in both patients with Schizophrenia and their first-degree relatives (Avila, McMahon, Elliott, & Thaker, 2002; Curtis, Calkins, Grove, Feil, & Iacono, 2001; Levy, Holzman, Matthysse, & Mendell, 1993).

Meehl understood that phenotypes are measured with considerable error, and that the distribution of schizotypic traits among genetic positives would therefore overlap substantially with the distribution of similar traits in the population. Given this, new methods aimed at disentangling such mixed distributions would need to be developed. The taxometric procedures we describe are the result of an over-30-year effort by Meehl and his colleagues to address this problem. Although it is now recognized that Schizophrenia is a polygenically determined disorder, schizotypy has been shown in numerous studies using CCK procedures to be distributed as a discrete latent class among genetically vulner-

able individuals (Blanchard, Gangestad, Brown, & Horan, 2000; Erlenmeyer-Kimling, Golden, & Cornblatt, 1989; Golden & Meehl, 1979; Horan, Blanchard, Gangestad, & Kwapil, 2004; Korfine & Lenzenweger, 1995; Lenzenweger, 1999; Lenzenweger & Korfine, 1992, 1995; Tyrka, Cannon, et al., 1995; Tyrka, Haslam, & Cannon, 1995).

In the next section, we describe four of Meehl's taxometric algorithms. We begin with MAXimum SLOPE (MAXSLOPE), a less popular taxometric procedure that is nevertheless informative pedagogically. We then describe three commonly used taxometric procedures including MAXimum COVariance (MAXCOV), MAXimum EIGenvalue (MAXEIG), and Mean Above Minus Below A sliding Cut (MAMBAC). Because comprehensive descriptions of these procedures are readily available, our presentations are purposefully brief.

MAXSLOPE

In the MAXSLOPE procedure (Grove & Meehl, 1993), putative indicators of taxon group membership are plotted against one another, and a smoothed regression function is fitted to the scatter plot. The regression slope (dy/dx) is then calculated in successive intervals of the input (x) variable. An example appears in Figure 23.5, where a hypothetical plot of ambivalence and eye-tracking abnormality is presented. When a taxon group is present and an adequate

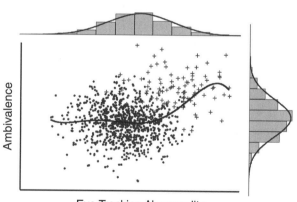

Figure 23.5 Illustration of the MAXSLOPE procedure using a fictitious bivariate distribution of ambivalence and eye tracking abnormality. The slope of the regression function is maximized at the point that best discriminates schizotypes ($n = 100$), indicated by solid dots, from controls ($n = 900$), indicated by crosses. This point on x is referred to as the hitmax cut. When no taxon group is present, the regression line is flat. Note that despite an effect size (d) of 2.0, the marginal univariate distributions are near normal, with no evidence of bimodality.

effect size is observed, then a discontinuity appears in the regression function, which is maximized at the level of variable x (eye-tracking abnormality) that best discriminates the taxon group from the *complement class* (nontaxon group). Put another way, the correlation between eye-tracking abnormality (x) and ambivalence (y), represented by the regression slope, is highest at the value of x that maximizes diagnostic accuracy. This is referred to as the *hitmax* cut.

There are a number of points to be made about this example that generalize to more complex CCK procedures described later. First, both the inflection in the regression slope and the observed correlation, or standardized covariance between eye-tracking abnormality and ambivalence ($r = .2$), are caused entirely by mixing two discrete groups. In either group, the covariance between variables is zero. Covariation between variables that is produced by mixing of a taxon group and its complement class is described in the general covariance mixture theorem (Meehl, 1995a, p. 271; Meehl & Yonce, 1996, p. 1097):

$$\text{cov}(xy) = {}^{P}\text{cov}_c(xy) + pq(x_t - x_c)(y_t - y_c) \qquad (1)$$

where $\text{cov}_t(xy)$ represents the covariance of variables x and y in the taxon group, $\text{cov}_c(xy)$ represents the covariance of variables x and y in the complement class, p and q represent the proportions of taxon group and complement class members, respectively, in the bivariate sample, and and represent the means of variable x and y in group i. Typically, the simplifying assumption is made that within-group correlations are zero (conditional independence), and the first two terms are dropped.[5] Along with some auxiliary formulae, this theorem provides the mathematical basis for estimating latent parameters, including the taxon base rate and both the taxon and complement class means.

It is worth noting that even when a taxon is detected, assigning individuals to groups remains probabilistic.

---

[5] The assumption of zero nuisance correlation is referred to as conditional independence in the latent class analysis literature. In practice, within-class correlations are likely to be nonzero. However, Monte Carlo studies have revealed that under most conditions, CCKs are robust when such *nuisance correlations* approach and in some cases exceed .30 (Beauchaine & Beauchaine, 2002; Cleland & Haslam, 1996; Haslam & Cleland, 1996; Meehl, 1995b).

As noted by Bauer and Curran (2004), a multivariate generalization of the general covariance mixture theorem underlies latent profile analysis models, which also make the assumption that all observed covariances among k variables are the result of admixing discrete groups.

Thus, it is not possible to be perfectly accurate in assigning individuals to groups, as long as those groups overlap. Nevertheless, the hitmax cut provides an objective boundary that optimizes diagnostic accuracy. The location of this boundary is determined by the base rate of the taxon group in the population. When the base rate is 50, for example, the hitmax cut appears near the grand mean on variable x. When the base rate is lower, such as .10 in the present example, the hitmax cut shifts toward the right.

MAXCOV

Conceptually related to MAXSLOPE, MAXCOV (Meehl, 1973b; Meehl & Yonce, 1996; Waller & Meehl, 1998) is the most thoroughly evaluated and most commonly used taxometric procedure (Haslam & Kim, 2002). It assesses the covariance of two putative indicators of taxon group membership across successive intervals of a third indicator, with a smoothed regression function fitted through the resulting covariance values. For example, suppose that a third schizotypy indicator, such as anhedonia, is available for analysis. We can now examine the covariance of eye-tracking abnormality (x) and ambivalence (y) within successive intervals of anhedonia (z). The previously presented scatter plot of ambivalence and eye-tracking abnormality is reproduced in the top left panel of Figure 23.6, with the covariance of both variables across intervals of anhedonia appearing below. If a taxon is present and the effect size is adequate, then a clear peak is observed in the covariance of variables x (eye-tracking abnormality) and y (ambivalence), which is maximized at the level of variable z (anhedonia) that best discriminates between groups. This is demonstrated in the bottom left panel of Figure 23.6. As with the MAXSLOPE example, this value is referred to as the hitmax interval because group assignment of individuals is optimized at this boundary. The MAXCOV peak shifts toward the left at higher taxon base rates. When no taxon is present, the covariance function of variables x and y across intervals of z is relatively flat, as shown in the bottom right panel of Figure 23.6.

For each three-way combination of indicators, MAXCOV produces estimates of several latent distributional parameters, including the hitmax value, the taxon base rate, the sample sizes of the taxon group and complement class, and the false-positive and false-negative rates of group membership assignments. Furthermore, MAXCOV can be used to assign individuals to the taxon group and complement class using Bayes's theorem (see Beauchaine

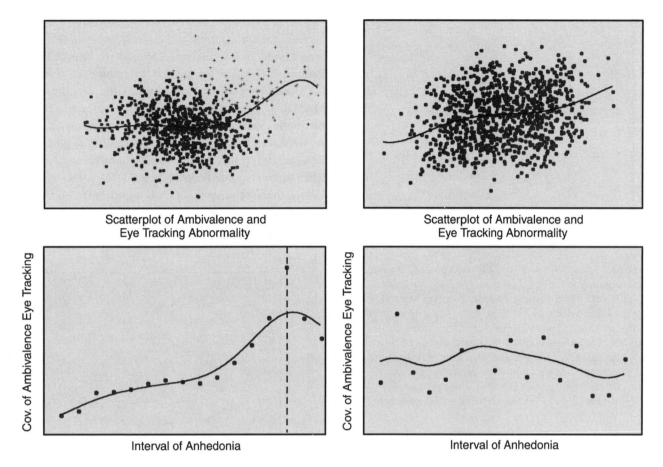

Figure 23.6   Illustration of the MAXCOV procedure using fictitious distributions of ambivalence and eye tracking abnormality across successive intervals of anhedonia. For comparison purposes, the top panels represent scatterplots of taxonic data (left) and continuous data (right), with MAXSLOPE functions fitted to each. MAXCOV functions are presented in the bottom panels. Note that in the taxonic case (left) the covariance between ambivalence and eye tracking abnormality is maximized within the interval of anhedonia that best discriminates between schizotypes ($n = 100$), indicated by solid dots, from controls ($n = 900$), indicated by open squares. This is referred to as the hitmax interval, as indicated by the dashed line. In the continuous case (right) there is no clear peak in the covariance function. Note the agreement between MAXSLOPE and MAXCOV in identifying the hitmax value. The bivariate correlation (r) is .20 in both samples.

& Beauchaine, 2002; Meehl & Yonce, 1996; Waller & Meehl, 1998).

MAXEIG

Although MAXEIG (Waller & Meehl, 1998) has been used less frequently than MAXCOV (Haslam & Kim, 2002), it has recently gained in popularity, with some authors advocating that it become the CCK of choice in taxometrics research (e.g., J. Ruscio & Ruscio, 2004a). For reasons stated in later sections, we do not share this opinion. Nevertheless, MAXEIG can be a useful complement to other CCK procedures.

MAXEIG operates on any number of putative taxon indicators greater than or equal to three. One variable serves as the "input" indicator, and the remaining variables serve

as "output" indicators. The input variable is divided into a series of overlapping windows, and the variance-covariance matrix of the output variables is computed within each. The diagonal elements (variances) of the variance-covariance matrix are replaced with zeros, and the first eigenvalue from a principal components analysis is extracted. These eigenvalues are then plotted across the entire range of the input variable. Similar to the case of MAXCOV, a peak is observed in the MAXEIG function if a taxon is present in the multivariate data set. This is because larger eigenvalues indicate greater intercorrelations among the output variables. When such intercorrelations are driven by the admixture of two discrete groups, the eigenvalues are largest in the hitmax window, which again indicates the point along the input variable that best discriminates between taxon group and complement class

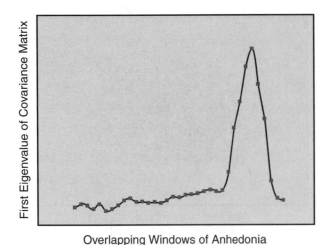

Figure 23.7 Illustration of the MAXEIG procedure using fictitious distributions of ambivalence, eye tracking abnormality, anhedonia, and social anxiety. Anhedonia serves as the input (x) variable, along which eigenvalues from the ambivalence/eye tracking abnormality/working memory impairment covariance matrix are plotted in successive windows. The eigenvalue function is maximized in the window of x that best discriminates between schizotypes ($n = 100$) and controls ($n = 900$). In the continuous case (not pictured), eigenvalues in successive overlapping windows tend to fluctuate around a single number.

members. A sample MAXEIG plot is presented in Figure 23.7, which was derived from the schizotypy example used in earlier sections.

MAMBAC

To date, MAMBAC (Meehl, 1995a; Meehl & Yonce, 1994) is the second most frequently used taxometric algorithm (Haslam & Kim, 2002). When using MAMBAC, indicators are analyzed in variable pairs. One variable is first sorted, which also sorts the other if both are valid markers of the analyzed trait. To continue with the example of schizotypy, sorting on anhedonia (x) also sorts on eye-tracking abnormality (y). Next, a sliding cut is moved across all values of anhedonia, and the mean of eye-tracking abnormality is calculated both above and below this cut. At each point, the mean above the cut is subtracted from the mean below the cut, and the resulting values are plotted. If a taxon group is present and the effect size is sufficient, then a peak is produced in the MAMBAC function at the value of anhedonia (x) that best discriminates between those in the taxon group and those in the complement class. In contrast, continuously distributed data produce U-shaped MAMBAC functions.

Figure 23.8 depicts all pairwise combinations of six indicators for both taxonic and dimensional data sets from a recent experiment conducted in our lab (Beauchaine & Waters, 2003). For the present discussion, details about the experiment are unimportant. Rather, we present the MAMBAC plots to illustrate the clear difference between functions derived from discrete versus dimensional data. As we shall see in later sections, the ability to plot MAMBAC curves in this fashion offers significant advantages when screening candidate indicators for additional taxometric analyses using other CCK algorithms. We now turn our attention to recommendations for conducting taxometrics research.

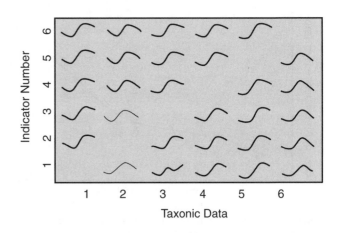

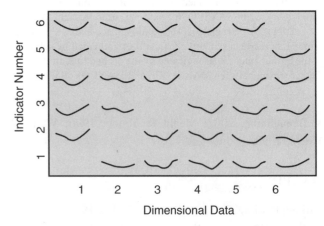

Figure 23.8 Illustration of the MAMBAC procedure. The top panel represents all pairwise MAMBAC plots from taxonic data (total $n = 1125$) with a baserate of .34. Note the consistency of the location of peaks across MAMBAC runs. The bottom panel represents all pairwise MAMBAC plots from dimensional data (total $n = 1125$). In contrast to the plots derived from taxonic data, all MAMBAC functions from dimensional data are dish-shaped. *Source:* "Pseudotaxonicity in MAMBAC and MAXCOV Analyses of Rating Scale Data: Turning Continua into Classes by Manipulating Observer's Expectations," by T. P. Beauchaine, and E. Waters, 2003, *Psychological Methods, 8,* pp. 3–15.

TESTING TAXONIC CONJECTURES

Although taxometric methods have been used infrequently by developmental psychopathologists (Beauchaine, 2003b), they now commonly appear in the adult psychopathology literature. As a reflection of their growing popularity, recent special sections devoted to taxometrics have appeared in both the *Journal of Abnormal Psychology* (Cole & Baker, 2004) and *Clinical Psychology Science and Practice* (Barlow, 2001). In a comprehensive review of empirical taxometrics investigations, Haslam and Kim (2002) identified 66 separate studies that have used at least one CCK procedure. Moreover, a PsychINFO database search conducted on July 27, 2004, using the keywords MAMBAC, MAXCOV, MAXEIG, and taxometric yielded 127 hits. Thus, it is clear that CCKs are increasing in popularity. Although only a handful of these studies have included child or adolescent samples or addressed developmental questions, there is much to be learned from the adult psychopathology literature about conducting taxometrics research.

In the following sections, we discuss both the planning and implementation of taxometric analyses. To date, most taxometrics studies have been conducted using large data sets of convenience, with primarily self-report and informant-report measures of symptoms derived from *DSM-IV* criterion lists. In light of our discussion in the introduction to this chapter, this general approach poses a number of problems for identifying latent vulnerability traits that predispose individuals to psychopathology. Indeed, we argue that the greatest potential of taxometric methods lies in identifying such vulnerability traits *before* psychopathological outcomes emerge.

Selecting Candidate Indicators

Given the advantages of identifying latent vulnerability traits premorbidly, perhaps the most important step in conducting taxometrics research is selecting viable candidate indicators that are sensitive to genotypic susceptibility. In doing so, several important issues must be considered. We discuss these in turn.

From Behavioral Syndromes to Latent Vulnerabilities

As we noted earlier in this chapter, developmental psychopathologists have long emphasized the importance of identifying traits that place individuals at risk for psychopathology, recognizing that diagnostic syndromes are often insufficient for capturing life course trajectories in behavioral functioning. This is instantiated in the notion of *heterotypic continuity,* which refers to cases in which a single etiologic vulnerability gives rise to seemingly different disorders across subsequent developmental periods. Seriously delinquent adult males, for example, are likely to have followed a developmental progression that began with incipient hyperactive/impulsive behaviors in toddlerhood, followed by Oppositional Defiant Disorder emerging in preschool, early-onset CD emerging in elementary school, and both substance abuse and Antisocial Personality Disorder (ASPD) emerging in adolescence and adulthood (see Loeber & Hay, 1997; Loeber & Keenan, 1994; Lynam, 1996, 1998). Given that substance use disorders are diagnosed separately for each drug, a delinquent male on such a trajectory could qualify for five or more diagnoses by the time he reaches early adulthood. In previous sections, we discussed how an overreliance on behavioral syndromes obscures etiological heterogeneity within groups of people afflicted with psychiatric disorders. This example demonstrates that focusing on behavioral syndromes can also obscure developmental heterogeneity in the expression of psychopathological vulnerability traits within individuals. Indeed, full appreciation of heterotypic continuity among externalizing disorders followed nearly a century of systematic efforts to study delinquency, in part because most researchers specialize in single behavioral syndromes.

Recently, however, Krueger and colleagues (2002) demonstrated that comorbidity among disinhibition, conduct problems, antisocial behavior, alcohol dependence, and drug dependence is accounted for almost entirely by a single underlying latent genetic vulnerability. Figure 23.9 depicts the common pathway model of externalizing disorders among the large sample of twins in the Krueger et al. study. Note that additive genetic effects accounted for 81% of the variance in the latent vulnerability for externalizing disorders. At the behavioral syndrome level, however, shared and nonshared environmental contributions were larger than genetic effects. This suggests that the overt expression of the latent vulnerability trait depends on environmental opportunities and that the study of behavioral syndromes such as drug dependence and ASPD fails to capture the ontology of externalizing psychopathology. As Skuse (2001, p. 395) recently noted, "A focus on traits, rather than syndromes, is appropriate and could in due course contribute to the redefinition of traditional psychiatric syndromes."

This discussion suggests that researchers who are interested in uncovering the latent structure of vulnerability

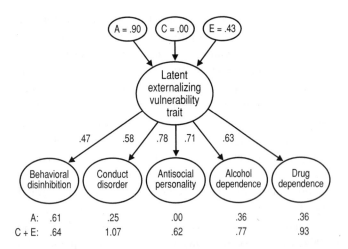

Figure 23.9 Genetic and environmental effects on five externalizing behavioral syndromes, and their loadings on a common latent vulnerability. A = Additive genetic effects; C = Shared environmental effects; E = Nonshared environmental effects. Adapted from "Etiologic Connections among Substance Dependence, Antisocial Behavior, and Personality: Modeling the Externalizing Spectrum," by R. F. Krueger et al., 2002, *Journal of Abnormal Psychology, 111,* pp. 411–424.

for externalizing disorders should include indicators that cut across traditional psychiatric boundaries. To date, several studies have addressed the question of whether antisocial behavior is distributed discretely, yet each has included rating scales of particular behavioral syndromes rather than broader vulnerability traits. Harris, Rice, and Quinsey (1994) found a discrete latent class of psychopaths among institutionalized offenders using items from the Psychopathy Checklist (Hare et al., 1990), a finding that was later replicated using both psychopathic features and *DSM-IV* ASPD criteria (Skilling, Harris, Rice, & Quinsey, 2001). Moreover, Skilling, Quinsey, and Craig (2001) reported evidence for an antisocial behavior taxon in a large community sample of fourth- through eighth-grade boys, as did Ayers, Haslam, Bernstein, Tryon, and Handelsman (1999) in a large sample of adults. Interestingly, items that were most useful in identifying the latent taxon from the Psychopathy Checklist were those representing chronic, childhood-onset delinquent behavior (Haslam, 2003), suggesting that the group identified were those on the life-course-persistent trajectory described earlier. Although there are problems with using strictly rating scale data in taxometrics research (Beauchaine & Waters, 2003), these findings suggest that additional studies should be conducted to explore the la-

tent structure of vulnerability to externalizing disorders. Ideally, these research efforts will include endophenotypic markers with potential to capture the latent genetic vulnerability to externalizing syndromes described by Krueger et al. (2002), with greater precision than behavioral rating scales provide (see later discussion).

From Phenotype to Endophenotype

As we argued earlier, and as recently emphasized by a number of authors (Castellanos & Tannock, 2002; Gottesman & Gould, 2003; Skuse, 2001), identifying latent vulnerabilities for psychopathology will almost certainly be facilitated by including endophenotypic markers of risk in future research. Continuing with the example of externalizing disorders, Patrick et al. (2005) recently demonstrated that reduced amplitude of the P300 event-related brain potential marks vulnerability across the entire externalizing spectrum among adolescent males. Although reduced P300 amplitude has long been associated with genetic vulnerability for alcoholism (Begleiter, Porjesz, Bihari, & Kissin, 1984; Porjesz, Begleiter, & Garozzo, 1980), it had not previously been explored as a broader marker of risk. In our own lab, we have consistently found attenuated sympathetic nervous system-linked cardiac reactivity to monetary incentives among adolescents with early-onset CD and among children as young as age 4 who are at risk for conduct problems (Beauchaine, 2003a, 2004; Beauchaine, Katkin, Strassberg, & Snarr, 2001; Beauchaine, Gatzke-Kopp & Mead, in press; Crowell, Beauchaine, Gatzke-Kopp, Sylvers, & Mead, in press). Moreover, numerous studies have demonstrated low levels of electrodermal responding among impulsive, aggressive, and delinquent males, both at baseline and in response to mild punishment (see Beauchaine, 2001). Variables such as these are ideal candidates for future taxometrics research designed to determine whether the antisocial taxon can be identified before psychopathic and antisocial behavior patterns are established. It is well-known that empirically supported interventions for conduct problems are more effective with younger as opposed to older children (e.g., Dishion & Patterson, 1992; Ruma, Burke, & Thompson, 1996). Premorbid identification of latent genetic vulnerability may therefore provide for more effective prevention and intervention programs. In later sections, we outline how identification of latent genetic risk for Schizophrenia can already contribute to enhanced prevention of first-episode psychosis.

Indicator Validity

The term validity has multiple meanings in the behavioral sciences, some of which were discussed in earlier sections. In the context of taxometrics research, validity refers to the degree to which a variable distinguishes between a taxon group and its complement class (Cole, 2004; Meehl, 1995a). For example, consistent with Meehl's (1962) original thesis, taxometric studies of schizotypy have repeatedly demonstrated that anhedonia, social withdrawal, and perceptual aberration mark a discretely distributed group of individuals who are at heightened risk for developing Schizophrenia (Blanchard et al., 2000; Erlenmeyer-Kimling et al., 1989; Golden & Meehl, 1979; Korfine & Lenzenweger, 1995; Lenzenweger, 1999; Lenzenweger & Korfine, 1992; Tyrka, Cannon, et al., 1995). Thus, each of these indicators is of established validity. It is important to remember, however, that performing a taxometric analysis is a bootstrapping endeavor, so one cannot know the validity of a marker a priori. Given this, candidate indicators should be selected based on strong theoretical considerations (Beauchaine & Waters, 2003; Lenzenweger, 2004; Meehl, 1999; Waters & Beauchaine, 2003). Otherwise, failure to detect a taxon could be the result of using invalid indicators.

In recent years, it has become common for researchers to perform taxometric analyses on large data sets that were collected for other purposes. Often, these data sets contain rating scales assessing all symptoms in a diagnostic class, which are subjected to one or more CCK procedures. Among several problems with this approach is the lack of attention paid to indicator validity. When a taxon exists, some markers are more valid than others and are therefore more effective in distinguishing group members from complement class members. When invalid indicators are used, taxa simply go undetected.

One example of the importance of carefully selecting indicators comes from taxometric research on depression, where several studies have yielded evidence of a discretely distributed depressive taxon group in both adolescent and adult samples (Ambrosini, Bennett, Cleland, & Haslam, 2002; Beach & Amir, 2003; Grove et al., 1987; Haslam & Beck, 1994). In each of these studies, identification of the depressive taxon was contingent on the use of melancholic or vegetative symptoms including psychomotor retardation, agitation, anhedonia, sleep disturbance, loss of weight, loss of appetite, and diminished libido. Such somatic symptoms have been proposed to mark disturbances in homeostatic regulation characteristic of endogenous depression.

In taxometric analyses conducted that have not distinguished melancholic symptoms from symptoms of distress, no taxon has been found (Beach & Amir, 2003; Haslam & Beck, 1994; J. Ruscio & Ruscio, 2000).[6] Thus, when both valid (melancholic) and invalid (distress) markers of endogenous depression are included in the same analysis, the taxon goes undetected. This is because CCKs require that each and every indicator be of high validity. We illustrate this in Figure 23.10, where all three-way combinations of MAXCOV plots are presented for two artificially created multivariate data sets, each with three indicators. The left panels depict plots in which all three indicators (x, y, and z) mark a .10 base rate latent taxon with high validity, as indexed by 2.0 standard deviations of separation (Cohen's d) between the taxon group and complement class means. In contrast, the right panels depict MAXCOV plots in which one indicator (x) was replaced with a fourth indicator (w) of low validity ($d = .50$). Note that there is no evidence of a latent taxon in the right three panels despite two out of three variables being high in validity. Moreover, estimates of the taxon base rate are widely divergent and inaccurate. This suggests that great care should be taken in the selection of putative indicators for taxometric analyses and that atheoretical investigations that include all available markers are likely to be ineffective in identifying existing taxa (see also Lenzenweger, 2004).

---

[6] Recently, J. Ruscio et al. (2004) have challenged the existence of an endogenous depression taxon, arguing that indicator skew is likely responsible for false-positive identifications of discrete latent structure in each of the studies cited. This claim is based on analyses using a technique advanced by A. Ruscio and Ruscio (2002; J. Ruscio & Ruscio, 2004a) in which both latent dimensional and latent taxonic data sets are simulated to match observed data parameters. Taxometric analyses are then conducted on all three data sets (observed, simulated dimensional, simulated taxonic), and inferences are drawn regarding latent structure based on whether results obtained from the observed data are more similar to results obtained from the simulated dimensional or simulated taxonic data. However, when J. Ruscio et al. reported their results refuting the endogenous depressive taxon, no studies had been published describing the operating characteristics of the simulated comparison technique. Since that time, a large-scale Monte Carlo analysis (Beach, Amir, & Bau, in press) has revealed that the method is prone to false negatives when the taxon base rate is low and skew is high—precisely the conditions for endogenous depression and for most other psychiatric taxa. For these reasons, J. Ruscio et al. may have been mistaken in refuting the endogenous depression taxon, and their technique will not be considered further in this chapter.

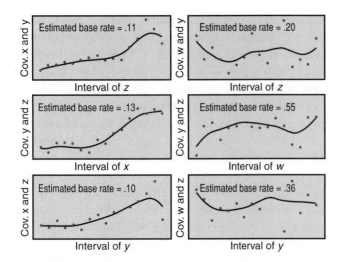

Figure 23.10   Effects on MAXCOV analyses of adding one invalid indicator. The left three panels depict all MAXCOV plots for three indicators (*x*, *y*, *z*) of high validity (Cohen's $d = 2.0$). The right three panels depict all MAXCOV plots with variable *x* replaced with an indicator (*w*) of low validity ($d = .50$). In both cases the overall sample size is 1000 with a taxon baserate of .10. Note the effect on MAXCOV-derived base rate estimates of including just one indicator of low validity.

Measurement Precision

To date, most researchers have also paid little attention to measurement precision when selecting candidate indicators for taxometric analyses. This is unfortunate because precision has a profound effect on indicator validity. Precision refers to our ability to measure a construct without error. Here it is useful to recall the distinctions among nominal, ordinal, interval, and ratio scales of measurement offered by Stevens (1951). *Nominal* scales are strictly categorical and do not allow for statements of inequality. For example, it makes little sense to suggest that one zip code is more or less than another zip code; they simply refer to different geographic locations. In contrast, *ordinal* measurement scales do imply quantitative differences between measured attributes, yet they do not allow the magnitude of those differences to be specified in absolute terms. Likert scales in which respondents rate a statement as "strongly agree," "agree," "neutral," "disagree," or "strongly disagree" represent an ordinal level of measurement. Although it may be appropriate to state that "strongly agree" > "agree" and that "disagree" > "strongly disagree," the distance between anchors cannot be assumed to be equal, nor can we necessarily assume that "agree" = "agree" from one question to another. For these reasons, we should be wary about performing complex mathematical and/or statistical operations on ordinal scales. *Interval* and *ratio* scales do provide equal intervals between anchors and therefore allow for

strong statements about equality and inequality and for much more sophisticated mathematical and statistical transformations and operations.

Of particular importance, all data collected via rating scales carry at best ordinal-level measurement precision. Moreover, Likert ratings on attributes such as personality and psychopathology traits, which require significant inference on the part of raters, contain up to 50% error variance, reducing precision substantially (Hoyt & Kerns, 1999). The relation between measurement error and precision is depicted in Figure 23.11, where two pairs of distributions appear. In the left pair, an effect size (*d*) of .5 separates the group means, resulting in 67% overlap. In contrast, in the right pair, an effect size of 2.0 separates the group means, resulting in only 19% overlap. Note that the distance between means is identical in both cases. What is different is that the right distributions contain considerably less measurement error, as indicated by narrower dispersion along the *x* axis. This illustrates the importance of seeking precise measures for taxometric analyses, where large effect sizes are *essential* for CCKs to be effective. Extensive Monte Carlo simulations have revealed that MAXCOV, the most commonly used algorithm, is effective in detecting latent taxa only at effect sizes (*d*) of 1.2 or larger (Beauchaine & Beauchaine, 2002; Meehl, 1995a). Recall that a typical effect size in psychological research is around .6, or half this size (Cohen, 1988). Thus, existing taxa cannot be detected if the taxon group and complement class means are separated by anything less than a very large effect.

One strategy for increasing measurement precision is to combine items into scales, either by aggregating based on conceptual considerations (J. Ruscio & Ruscio, 2004b) or

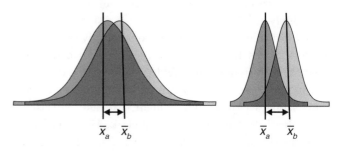

Figure 23.11   Relationship between measurement precision and effect size. The left pair of distributions are separated by .5 standard deviations, a typical effect size in psychology, and overlap 67%. The right distributions are separated by 2.0 standard deviations, and overlap only 19%. Although the distance between means is equal in both cases, a larger effect size is obtained when measurement error, indicated by distributional dispersion, is reduced.

by factor analyzing individual items into common components, which reduces measurement error by isolating shared variance (see Nunnally & Bernstein, 1994). Using factor scores as indicators can therefore enhance the sensitivity of CCKs to underlying taxa. It should be noted, however, that using all extracted factors from a large pool of items is a poor strategy for taxometrics research because each factor is likely to capture a different facet of behavior among a given sample. For example, although the Child Behavior Checklist (CBCL; Achenbach, 1991) was constructed using factor analysis, one would not include factor scores from conceptually unrelated scales (e.g., withdrawn, aggressive) in a single taxometric analysis, because each indicator should be conceptually related to the putative latent taxon. However, it would be perfectly reasonable to use factor scores on related but different scales from measures such as the CBCL and the Eyberg Child Behavior Inventory (Robinson, Eyberg, & Ross, 1980). Unfortunately, many taxometrics investigations conducted to date have used individual scale items. Although this strategy increases the number of indicators available for analysis, it is likely to result in underpowered tests for latent taxonic structure due to low measurement precision.

A second strategy for reducing measurement error, although one that has not been used to date in taxometrics research, is to assess growth in the same construct over time. It is well-known that each additional assessment point included in a growth parameter increases measurement precision (Rogosa, Brandt, & Zimowski, 1982). This is why sex differences in the growth trajectories of depressive symptoms emerge *before* mean differences can be detected (Cole et al., 2002). Longitudinal growth trajectories may therefore be useful in future taxometrics investigations. Thus far, only one longitudinal taxometric study has been conducted, and growth trajectories were not used as indicators (Tyrka, Haslam, et al., 1995). However, a number of large longitudinal data sets, such as the Pittsburgh Youth Study (see Loeber, Farrington, Stouthamer-Loeber, & Van Kammen, 1998), exist that might be used to address questions concerning the development of discretely distributed psychopathological traits.

However potentially useful, none of these ad hoc strategies can replace deliberate and careful selection of precise measures. For this reason, a consensus has begun to emerge among taxometrics researchers regarding the advantages of using indicators that are both continuous and objective (Beauchaine, 2003b; Lenzenweger, 2004; Meehl, 1995a; Waters & Beauchaine, 2003). Such measures are inherently more precise than Likert scales obtained from either self-report or observer report. Note that this provides yet another

reason to search for endophenotypic markers of risk for use in taxometrics studies of psychopathology, as most biological measures carry ratio-level precision and yield continuous scores. Nevertheless, other potential data sources that carry interval or ratio scale properties, such as objective behavior observations, might also be used. We want to emphasize that we are not advocating that psychometric data be eliminated from taxometrics research entirely. Rather, we are suggesting that as many data sources as possible be included.

Number of Indicators

Using the methods described in this chapter, taxometric inferences can be investigated with as few as two indicators (with the MAXSLOPE procedure). However, we are aware of no published studies in which so few indicators were used, and we do not recommend conducting taxometrics research with fewer than five to six indicators (or more if possible). Monte Carlo studies with MAXCOV in particular suggest that both taxon identification and classification accuracy increase markedly with more available indicators, with an asymptote around seven to eight (Beauchaine & Beauchaine, 2002). Although few studies have used this many indicators (for exceptions, see Harris et al., 1994; Korfine & Lenzenweger, 1995; Waller, Putnam, & Carlson, 1996; Waller & Ross, 1997), it is clear that power to detect latent taxa is optimized in this range. Given that some potential indicators are almost surely to be dropped from most taxometric analyses (see later discussion), our advice is to include as many items as possible in the planning stages of a study. This raises the question of whether item redundancy is appropriate. In psychometric theory, *redundant* variables are those that mark the same latent construct. In this sense, multiple redundant indicators are preferred because they allow us to increase measurement precision, as described earlier. Thus, redundancy is welcome in taxometrics research, provided that variables from alternative levels of analysis (e.g., biological, psychological, behavior observation) are represented in the item pool. Although some authors have argued against item redundancy in taxometrics research (J. Ruscio & Ruscio, 2004b), our reading suggests that they are equating redundancy with item independence. In contrast, we use the term redundancy in the strict psychometric sense.

Sample Size

Monte Carlo studies have established clear guidelines for the minimum sample size required when using the MAMBAC and MAXCOV algorithms, suggesting a lower bound for reliable taxon detection of about $n = 200$ with highly valid indicators (e.g., Beauchaine & Beauchaine, 2002;

Meehl, 1995a; Meehl & Yonce, 1994). However, given that indicator validity is likely to vary considerably in any given study, sample sizes of 300 or more are preferred. Thus, many data sets are unsuitable for taxometric analyses, aside from those derived from epidemiological samples. Yet, if variables are chosen carefully across studies and equivalent sampling procedures are used, data sets may be combined to pursue taxonic questions. Additionally, evidence presented by Waller and Meehl (1998) provides preliminary support for using smaller samples with the MAXEIG algorithm. To date, however, the operating characteristics of MAXEIG remain largely unexplored compared with MAMBAC and MAXCOV, both of which have been evaluated in considerable detail (Beauchaine & Beauchaine, 2002; Cleland & Haslam, 1996; Cleland, Rothschild, & Haslam, 2000; Haslam & Cleland, 1996, 2002; Meehl, 1995b; Meehl & Yonce, 1994, 1996).

Winnowing the Item Pool and Evaluating Consistency Tests

As we noted earlier, even when a latent construct is distributed discretely, some markers are more precise than others and are therefore more efficient in differentiating taxon group members from nontaxon group members. This is true regardless of how carefully one chooses among candidate indicators. Given the likelihood of missing underlying taxa when inefficient indicators are used, systematic screening of each candidate variable is required to ensure that failure to find a taxon is not a false negative outcome. Accordingly, we have advocated that a two-step process initially proposed by Meehl (1995a, 2001a; see also Waller et al., 1996) be conducted to winnow an initial set of potential indicators. This includes preliminary screening of all candidates using MAMBAC. If these MAMBAC analyses suggest the possibility of discrete latent structure among a subset of indicators, only that subset is subjected to further analyses using MAXCOV and/or MAXEIG (Beauchaine, 2003b). This procedure filters the initial set of candidate indicators into a smaller number that are more efficient at differentiating between groups. Our recommendation is to plot all pairwise combinations of MAMBAC functions in a similar fashion to that appearing in Figure 23.8. This matrix can then be scanned for indications of taxonic structure. If nearly all of the MAMBAC functions are dish-shaped, then no further analyses are indicated, as there is no evidence of taxonic structure. If a taxon is present, the most likely scenario is that some MAMBAC plots will be hill-shaped, whereas others will be dish-shaped. The advantage of arranging all pairwise MAMBAC functions as in Figure 23.8 is that specific

variables that do not mark the latent taxon can be identified rather easily because most of the MAMBAC plots in the rows and columns representing such variables will be dish-shaped. These variables can then be eliminated from the indictor pool.

Next, remaining indicators are subjected to further analyses using MAXCOV or MAXEIG, which are used as *consistency tests* for judging the veracity of taxonic hypotheses. The term consistency test refers to comparisons of several parameters describing the latent distribution of a taxon and its complement. For example, if 10 potential indicators of melancholic depression are winnowed down to 6 through initial MAMBAC analyses, the first consistency test is to examine all base rate estimates from the MAMBAC runs. Six indicators produce

$$2\binom{k}{2}$$

, or 30 combinations of variables for analysis (see Figure 23.8). If there is a latent taxon present, then valid indicators should produce consistent estimates of the taxon base rate across variable pairings. If most base rate estimates fall within a small range, then the taxonic hypothesis is conditionally supported and the indicators are subjected to MAXCOV and/or MAXEIG analyses. With 6 indicators, there are

$$i \times \frac{(i-1)!}{(i-3)!2!}$$

or 60 three-way combinations of variables available for MAXCOV analysis, each of which produces estimates of the base rate, the taxon and complement class means, and the hitmax value, among other latent parameters. Again, only when the preponderance of within-parameter estimates converge on single values is the taxonic hypothesis supported. Evidence also suggests that a goodness-of-fit index (Jöreskog & Sörbom, 2001) above .90 indicates taxonic structure (Waller & Meehl, 1998).

Type I and Type II Errors

As with any statistical approach, taxometric analyses can yield (a) spurious positive findings, thereby identifying taxa that do not exist (Type I errors) or (b) false negative findings, or failures to identify taxa that do exist (Type II errors). To date, more emphasis has been placed on avoiding the former than on avoiding the latter. As we have noted elsewhere, however, Type II errors may be more common that Type I errors in taxometrics research given the requirements of high measurement precision and indicator validity outlined earlier. We now outline considerations for avoiding both types of error.

Pseudotaxonicity

The winnowing of candidate indicators into subsets that are more efficient at identifying a putative latent taxon has been criticized by some authors as a means of stacking the deck in favor of confirming taxonic hypotheses (Widiger, 2001), or of committing Type I errors. Part of this concern arises from the observation that attitudes and beliefs are particularly susceptible to dichotomous thought processes, a notion with considerable support in the literature on decision making (e.g., Simon, Pham, Le, & Holyoak, 2001). Thus, taxometric analyses of such variables could be reflecting the cognitive sets of raters rather than an objective underlying taxon. In an experimental paradigm in which we manipulated raters' implicit beliefs about a construct as dimensional versus dichotomous, we recently demonstrated that taxonic distributions can be readily imparted in Likert-type ratings (Beauchaine & Waters, 2003). Given that most taxometric studies have used such data exclusively, Widiger's concern may be justified. Indeed, rating scales reliably elicit positive and negative response biases (e.g., Macmillan & Creelman, 1990; Rajendar, 1996) and halo effects (e.g., Saal, Downey, & Lahey, 1980), both of which might result in artifactual taxonic structure, sometimes referred to as *pseudotaxonicity* (Beauchaine & Waters, 2003; Brown, 2001; Meehl, 1996). It is also well-known that human beings have natural tendencies to categorize continua (see Malt, 1993; Rosch & Lloyd, 1978; Smith, 1995) and to classify based on preexisting beliefs (see Cantor & Genero, 1986; Cantor & Mischel, 1979; Flanagan & Blashfield, 2002; Semin & Rosch, 1981).

All of these findings suggest due caution in interpreting latent taxonic structure that emerges from strictly rating scale data. However, when appropriate indicators are used that represent multiple levels of analysis including carefully chosen endophenotypes, and when multiple consistency tests converge on similar latent parameter estimates across CCK procedures (Meehl, 1995a; Waller & Meehl, 1998), the Type I error rate is exceedingly low. In fact, the prior probability of multiple objective indicators drawn from several levels of analysis converging on consistent base rate, hitmax, taxon group mean, and complement class mean estimates across 30 MAMBAC and 60 MAXCOV

runs approaches zero if there is no latent taxon present in a multivariate data set.

Sampling

A second potential source of artifactual taxonic structure and resulting Type I error comes from inappropriate sampling procedures. For example, if a clinical sample of individuals is recruited and their psychiatric impairment scores on a construct of interest are admixed with those of participants from a normative control group, then confirmation of a taxonic hypothesis is tautological. In fact, it would be surprising indeed if no taxon was detected among participants recruited with a bimodal distribution of symptoms. Unfortunately, evidence for taxonic structure among eating disorders derives directly from such sampling practices. Two separate studies have now appeared in which taxometric analyses were conducted on eating disorder symptoms among women diagnosed with anorexia, bulimia, or binge eating disorder. In both cases, these psychiatric groups were combined with nonclinical control groups, and MAMBAC and MAXCOV analyses were performed on symptoms in the admixed sample (Gleaves, Lowe, Green, Cororve, & Williams, 2000; Williamson et al., 2002). Not surprisingly, evidence for discrete latent structure among eating disorders was found. The proper sampling procedure for testing taxonic hypotheses is to recruit across a wide range of symptoms for a given disorder, with a *representative* proportion of participants at each symptom level. In a recent study in which representative sampling procedures were followed, no evidence for latent taxonic structure among eating disorders emerged (Tylka & Subich, 2003). Although some authors have suggested that the usefulness of taxometric methods depends on their ability to differentiate true taxa from pseudotaxa (Waldman & Lilienfeld, 2001), no statistical procedure is immune to sampling biases, and holding taxometric methods to a higher standard than other inferential statistics is almost certainly unjustified (Meehl, 1995a).

Proving the Null

Although a number of researchers have issued warnings about the potential for committing Type I errors in taxometrics research (Beauchaine & Waters, 2003; M. B. Miller, 1996; A. Ruscio & Ruscio, 2002; J. Ruscio & Ruscio, 2004a, 2004b; Widiger, 2001), few have addressed the possibility of committing Type II errors, or concluding that constructs are dimensionally distributed when they are in fact taxonic. We consider this to be a serious omission from the discourse on taxometric methods and propose that Type II errors may in fact be more likely than Type I errors. This is because many researchers equate negative findings from taxometric analyses with proof of continuous latent structure. However, because taxometric procedures are structure seeking, the effective null hypothesis is that the analyzed trait or disorder is distributed continuously, and the alternative hypothesis is that it is distributed categorically. Thus, CCKs do not identify continua; they identify taxa. This maps directly onto both null hypothesis significance testing and signal detection theory. When there is inadequate separation of the null or noise distribution (complement class) from the alternative or signal distribution (taxon), no effect will be found even if one exists. Moreover, in the two-group case using null hypothesis significance testing, the null hypothesis is that both sets of scores derive from one distribution. The alternative hypothesis is that they derive from two discrete distributions. This is completely analogous to the multivariate case addressed by CCKs. Concluding that a negative result from a taxometric procedure suggests a continuous distribution is therefore tantamount to proving the null and should be avoided. Consider the case of a latent taxon group and complement class with a mean separation of $d = .80$ on all indicators. Despite the fact that this represents a large effect size in psychological research, CCKs cannot resolve the groups. Yet, if one concluded based on the results of a taxometric analysis that the latent distribution was continuous, one would be wrong. This is particularly important when we consider that the data sources commonly subjected to taxometric analyses are imprecise (see earlier discussion). Many taxometrics studies are therefore underpowered due to both low measurement precision and the large effect sizes required for a taxon to be detected. It is always possible that more precise measures could yield a latent taxon in future investigations.

Interpreting null outcomes as evidence of continua is particularly problematic when insufficient attention is paid to indicator validity. For example, in their otherwise impressive assessment of the latent structure of attachment, Fraley and Spieker (2003) used all potential indicators that correlated .20 or higher with a given attachment security subtype in their taxometric analyses, assuming implicitly that all such indicators were equally valid markers of any existing latent taxon. In analyses of the avoidant subtype, 12 indicators met this criterion, which were subjected to all possible combinations of MAXCOV analyses ($n = 660$). Based on their results, Fraley and Spieker concluded that avoidant attachment is distributed continuously. Although this may be the correct conclusion, the taxonic hypothesis was probably not put to a

strong test because it is a priori unlikely that all 12 indicators could mark a group of avoidant children with sufficient precision for MAXCOV to detect a discrete latent distribution (see earlier discussion). For these reasons, we recommend that researchers exercise prudence in interpreting null findings.

IMPLICATIONS FOR DEVELOPMENTAL PSYCHOPATHOLOGY

In describing taxometric methods, we have thus far outlined several examples in which CCKs have been applied to questions about the latent structure of psychopathology. Among these examples, we have presented evidence of discrete latent structure for schizotypy, endogenous depression, and extreme antisocial behavior. Each of these traits has been demonstrated as taxonic in multiple studies by different research labs. This provides some degree of confidence that the findings reported are not spurious. In contrast, evidence for an eating disorder taxon appears to be an artifact of inappropriate sampling procedures.

Although we do not intend to review all taxometrics studies conducted to date, it is instructive to provide a partial list of additional traits and disorders for which evidence of discrete latent structure has been published (for reviews, see Haslam, 2003; Haslam & Kim, 2002). This serves the dual functions of communicating the scope of the current literature and providing insights into traits that might also be examined (or further examined) in developmental samples, whether child, adolescent, or adult. In addition to the traits mentioned previously, evidence of latent taxonic structure has been reported for dementia (Golden, 1982), dissociative experiences (Waller et al., 1996; Waller & Ross, 1997), infant behavioral reactivity (Woodward, Lenzenweger, Kagan, Snidman, & Arcus, 2000), hypnotic susceptibility (Oakman & Woody, 1996), self-monitoring (Gangestad & Snyder, 1985), sexual orientation (Gangestad, Bailey, & Martin, 2000), vulnerability to depression (Strong, Brown, Kahler, Lloyd-Richardson, & Niaura, 2004), and Type A behavior patterns (Strube, 1989). Among these findings, only the dissociative experiences taxon has been replicated in independent samples, and only the infant behavioral reactivity taxon was derived using objective, continuous indicators. Thus, even though the use of CCKs has become increasingly popular, imprecise measures continue to predominate in taxometric analyses, despite the caveats outlined earlier.

We now turn our attention to questions of specific concern to developmental psychopathologists that CCKs are well suited to address. We begin with a detailed account of the role that taxometric methods have already played in the identification of genetic vulnerability for Schizophrenia among children and adolescents. These findings have significant implications for development of the next generation of prevention programs. Moreover, research on the latent structure of schizotypy provides an exemplar for those seeking to conduct taxometrics studies in other areas. This is because Schizophrenia researchers have long recognized the importance of using precise endophenotypes to identify individuals at risk for the disorder. As we outline, this has led to remarkable advances in early detection of vulnerability to Schizophrenia spectrum disorders.

Identifying Children at Risk for Schizophrenia

Almost 40 years ago, long before the emergence of developmental psychopathology as a distinct discipline, Dawes and Meehl (1966) suggested that premorbid identification of individuals at risk for psychiatric disorders should be an urgent concern among psychopathology researchers because it is a necessary antecedent to prevention. It is therefore fitting that the most widely replicated finding in the taxometrics literature confirms Meehl's (1962) hypothesis that schizotypy is distributed as a discrete latent class that can be identified premorbidly. Through taxometric analyses of sustained visual attention, neuromotor performance, and intelligence measures, Erlenmeyer-Kimling et al. (1989) identified a schizotypy taxon group among the 7- to 12-year-old offspring of parents with Schizophrenia. Although the base rate of schizotypy is about 5% in the general population (Blanchard et al., 2000; Golden & Meehl, 1979; Korfine & Lenzenweger, 1995; Lenzenweger, 1999; Lenzenweger & Korfine, 1992), 47% of children with an afflicted parent were members of the schizotypy taxon group, compared with the expected 4% of controls. Moreover, 43% of the schizotypy taxon group were either hospitalized or had received significant treatment by age 22 to 29. Similar findings were reported by Tyrka, Cannon, et al. (1995), who used behavioral data derived from school reports and psychiatric interviews to identify a schizotypy taxon group among the 10- to 19-year-old offspring of mothers with Schizophrenia. The base rate of the taxon (48%) was almost identical to that found by Erlenmeyer-Kimling et al. Furthermore, 40% of those in the taxon group were diagnosed with a Schizophrenia spectrum disorder 24 to 27 years later. Thus, taxometric analyses of selected behavioral and endophenotypic markers can provide significantly improved prediction of clinical outcomes across considerable periods of time.

The implications of these findings for prevention can hardly be overstated. Targeting all children of parents with Schizophrenia for prevention is woefully inefficient because only 10% to 15% will go on to develop a Schizophrenia spectrum disorder (see Cornblatt, Obuchowski, Roberts, Pollack, & Erlenmeyer-Kimling, 1999). In the studies just reported, however, taxon group members were at 3 to 4 times this level of risk. More reliable identification of risk makes prevention programs much more plausible (Cornblatt, 2001). Furthermore, recent developments in the identification of precise endophenotypes in at-risk children, including impaired attention (Cornblatt & Malhotra, 2001), saccadic intrusions in smooth pursuit eye tracking (Ross, 2003), and spatial working memory deficits (Glahn et al., 2003), may allow for premorbid identification of vulnerability at even younger ages. In theory, the earlier an environmentally focused intervention is implemented, the more likely it is to alter the trajectory toward Schizophrenia because accumulated environmental risk contributes to the expression of genetic vulnerability (see Goldsmith, Gottesman, & Lemery, 1997; Gottesman & Gould, 2003; Rutter et al., 1997). Indeed, Raine, Mellingen, Liu, Venables, and Mednick (2003) reported that a very nonspecific environmental enrichment intervention for 3- to 5-year-olds reduced rates of schizotypal personality at age 23. This finding is especially impressive given that they did not target children specifically at risk for Schizophrenia, nor was their intervention tailored for reducing Schizophrenia risk. Rather, it was a blanket intervention including nutritional enhancement, child social skills training, and teacher instruction in behavioral management.

Evidence suggests that more focused interventions targeting children at particularly high risk could improve outcome and course, and perhaps even delay and in some cases prevent the onset of Schizophrenia (see Cornblatt, 2001; Cornblatt et al., 1999). Such prevention programs might include psychosocial components aimed at reducing expressed emotion, which is observed at high levels in families of at-risk children and exerts strong influences on both course and prognosis (Falloon et al., 1985; Hamilton, Asarnow, & Tompson, 1999; Hogarty et al., 1991). Although not without ethical complications (Cornblatt, Lencz, & Kane, 2001), prevention programs might also include a pharmacological component in extremely high-risk cases. McGorry et al. (2002) recently demonstrated that a low dose of risperidone (1 to 2 mg/day) substantially reduced the emergence of first-episode psychosis in high-risk patients who had a positive family history and incipient but subthreshold symptoms. Survival analyses revealed that patients who took risperidone and participated in cognitive behavioral therapy were 95% psychosis free 3 years later, compared with 30% of patients who received a typical needs-based intervention, and 40% of patients who did not adhere to the risperidone treatment. These findings are especially important given evidence that early and successful treatment of psychosis is associated with a better long-term prognosis (see Cornblatt et al., 2001).

Early Identification of Other High-Risk Traits

A second high-risk trait that has been identified as taxonic in very young children is behavioral reactivity. In a taxometric study of the responses of 599 4-month-old infant to a series of visual, auditory, and olfactory stimuli, Woodward et al. (2000) identified an extremely reactive taxon group who engaged in more arching, crying, hyperextension, and leg movements during stimulus presentations than other infants. Moreover, the 10% of infants who belonged to the taxon group scored high on measures of behavioral inhibition at age 4½, suggesting a potential vulnerability to later anxiety and depressive disorders (Kagan, 1994). Although these findings followed from a well-articulated theory, and although continuous and objective indicators were used in taxometric analyses with a large sample, future replications will be important in establishing the validity of the behaviorally reactive taxon group, as will follow-up studies specifying long-term outcomes for group members. Interestingly, the 10% base rate obtained by Woodward et al. is very close to the base rate observed among young adults by Beach and Amir (2003) in their taxometric study of involuntary defeat syndrome, a construct similar to endogenous depression. Given the high degree of overlap between depression and anxiety, and given findings that behavioral inhibition and anxiety both precede and predict later depression (Caspi, Moffitt, Newman, & Silva, 1996; Cole, Peeke, Martin, Truglio, & Seroczynski, 1998), the question arises as to whether behaviorally reactive taxon group members are at particularly high risk for later mood disorders. The value of identifying the behavioral reactivity taxon will be determined when more is known about its predictive potential.

Finally, as we reviewed in previous sections, Skilling, Quinsey, et al. (2001) reported evidence for an antisocial behavior taxon in a large community sample of fourth-through eighth-grade boys. This followed three studies identifying potentially similar taxon groups among substance abusing and incarcerated adult males (Ayers et al., 1999; Harris et al., 1994; Skilling, Harris, et al., 2001; Skilling, Quinsey, et al., 2001). Unfortunately, because sampling procedures differed across studies, base rate estimates cannot be compared. Nevertheless, the 8% base rate in the community sample is a plausible figure for those at risk for continued delinquency into adolescence and adulthood.

As we also noted earlier, although each of the studies used primarily rating scale indicators, taxometric analyses of a number of potential endophenotypes may allow for more precise specification of a high-risk taxon group at younger ages. These markers include the P300 event-related brain potential (Patrick et al., 2005), sympathetic nervous system-linked cardiac insensitivity to reward (e.g., Beauchaine et al., 2001), attenuated electrodermal responding (e.g., Fowles, 2000), and reduced central nervous system striatal activation during response inhibition tasks (e.g., Durston et al., 2003; Vaidya et al., 1998).[7] Candidate behavioral markers include manipulativeness, callousness, and lack of empathy, each of which has been tied to severe conduct problems and psychopathy (e.g., Barry et al., 2000; Frick, Cornell, Barry, Bodin, & Dane, 2003). As in the case of schizotypy, early identification of risk can facilitate targeted interventions with young at-risk children, who are known to respond better to prevention and intervention programs for conduct problems than older children and adolescents with established patterns of delinquent behavior (see Dishion & Patterson, 1992; Ruma et al., 1996; Webster-Stratton & Hammond, 1997; Webster-Stratton, Reid, & Hammond, 2002). Recent findings suggest that very early intervention may even alter endophenotypic markers of impulsivity and aggression that were once thought to reflect stable traits. Raine et al. (2001) reported that a prevention program for 3- to 5-year-old children including child social skills training, behavioral management instruction for teachers, and weekly counseling sessions for parents resulted in a 61% increase in electrodermal activity in participant children 6 to 8 years later, compared with controls who received no treat-

---

[7] Although both the Durston et al. (2003) and Vaidya et al. (1998) studies were framed as comparisons of ADHD participants with controls, those with Oppositional Defiant Disorder and CD were not excluded. Given both theoretical and empirical evidence linking delinquency to deficient central nervous system reward processing (see Beauchaine, 2001; Beauchaine et al., 2001), and given the high degree of overlap between conduct problems and ADHD in clinical samples (R. G. Klein et al., 1997; Lynam, 1996, 1998), striatal dysfunction may in part give rise to the latent vulnerability underlying both behavioral syndromes. It should therefore be considered a potential endophenotype.

ment. Thus, long-term changes in a marker that has repeatedly been associated with impulsive aggression resulted from a straightforward preschool intervention. These findings are particularly encouraging because they suggest a potential mechanism through which early intervention may exert its effects.

Drawing Boundaries between Subtypes of Disorders

Although not necessarily developmental in nature, taxometrics can also contribute to defining boundaries between subtypes of psychiatric disorders. In previous sections, we outlined the role that taxometric studies have already played in differentiating between subtypes of depression. These studies have identified a discretely distributed melancholic subgroup in both adolescent and adult samples (Ambrosini et al., 2002; Beach & Amir, 2003; Grove et al., 1987; Haslam & Beck, 1994). It has been known for some time that melancholic symptoms are associated with nonsuppression of cortisol in response to dexamethasone challenge (Rush & Weissenburger, 1994). In turn, cortisol nonsuppression was recently shown to mark a 10-fold increase in suicide risk at 15-year follow-up among depressed patients (Coryell & Schlesser, 2001). Although no taxometric studies of depression have used biological markers, these findings suggest that the dexamethasone suppression test may be a promising endophenotype for prospective identification of risk. Other possible endophenotypes include measures of sleep disturbance such as REM latency, which has also discriminated between melancholic and nonmelancholic depression subgroups (e.g., Rush, Giles, Schlesser, & Orsulak, 1997). In addition to the potential advantages of using endophenotypes such as HPA axis reactivity to identify vulnerability in younger children (Luby et al., 2003, 2004), replication of taxonic findings using such markers might resolve the controversy surrounding the latent structure of depression described in footnote 6.

Taxometrics research might also elucidate boundaries between subtypes of ADHD, where debate continues over the distinctiveness of the *combined* type (ADHD/C), characterized by hyperactivity/impulsivity and inattention, and the *inattentive* type (ADHD/I), characterized primarily by inattention. Some authors have argued that the disorders are probably discrete (e.g., Milich, Balentine, & Lynam, 2001), whereas others have suggested that current data are inconclusive (Barkley, 2001; Hinshaw, 2001; Lahey, 2001). Evidence for discrete subtypes is derived from factor analyses that differentiate among symptoms and from cluster analyses that differentiate among chil-

dren based on disparities in symptoms. As described earlier in this chapter, these methods are not well suited for evaluating the latent structure of psychopathology. Moreover, results have been somewhat inconsistent (Milich et al., 2001), and few studies have included markers that correlate specifically with ADHD/I. Among viable candidates is the construct *sluggish cognitive tempo* (SCT), which includes symptoms of lethargy, daydreaming, drowsiness, and hypoactivity (Carlson & Mann, 2002; Lahey, Carlson, & Frick, 1997). Although SCT items correlated specifically with ADHD/I in the *DSM-IV* field trials, they were dropped from the final criterion list because the workgroup sought a single set of inattentive items for both ADHD subtypes (Carlson & Mann, 2002; Frick et al., 1994). Yet, children with ADHD/I score higher on measures of SCT than other children with ADHD (McBurnett, Pfiffner, & Frick, 2001; Milich et al., 2001). Indices of SCT might therefore be useful in taxometric investigations that directly address the distinctiveness of ADHD/I and ADHD/C.

Additional symptoms that may differentiate between ADHD/I and ADHD/C include lower levels of externalizing behaviors and higher levels of anxiety, depression, and social withdrawal (Carlson & Mann, 2002). Such internalizing symptoms were more strongly associated with inattention than with impulsivity in the Multimodal Treatment of ADHD trial (Newcorn et al., 2001). Two final behavioral markers that might differentiate between ADHD subtypes are age of onset and age of referral, both of which occur earlier in ADHD/C than in ADHD/I (e.g., Faraone, Biederman, Weber, & Russell, 1998; Frick et al., 1994).

Research on the nuerobiology of ADHD also suggests some potential endophenotypes for taxometric analyses. For example, several studies have revealed reduced urinary MHPG, a norepinephrine metabolite, among children with ADHD (e.g., Shekim, Dekirmenjian, Chapel, & Davis, 1982; Shekim et al., 1987). These MHPG deficiencies have been linked specifically with the biobehavioral substrates of impulsivity (see Beauchaine, 2001) and are therefore more likely to be associated with ADHD/C than ADHD/I. Consistent with this prediction, Kagan, Reznick, and Snidman (1987) found increased urinary MHPG in anxious children. Given the higher rates of anxiety among children with ADHD/I and SCT (Carlson & Mann, 2002; Hinshaw, 2002a), urinary MHPG may be a promising endophenotype for taxometric analyses assessing the latent structure of ADHD subtypes.

Yet another diagnostic conundrum that might be addressed with taxometric methods is whether Autistic

Disorder and Asperger's Disorder reflect discrete behavioral syndromes or fall along a continuum of severity. This question has received substantial attention in both the child psychopathology and developmental psychopathology literatures since Asperger's Disorder was added to the *DSM-IV,* but it has yet to be resolved (Volkmar, Klin, Schultz, Rubin, & Bronen, 2000). Criteria shared by both disorders include impaired social interaction, stereotyped behaviors, and restricted interests and activities. Autism includes additional delays in verbal communication and/or cognitive development, whereas Asperger's Disorder does not.

Some authors have concluded that Autistic Disorder and Asperger's Disorder are likely to be discrete (see Klin, 1994; Ozonoff, Rogers, & Pennington, 1991). This argument is based on different patterns of comorbidity across diagnostic groups (Ghaziuddin, Weidmer-Mikhail, & Ghaziuddin, 1998), differences in verbal and nonverbal communication skills (e.g., Klin, Volkmar, Sparrow, Cicchetti, & Roarke, 1995; Volkmar et al., 1994), and different concordance rates across disorders in the first-degree relatives of affected patients (Volkmar, Klin, & Pauls, 1998). However, each of these characteristics could be observed in groups that differ in severity due to an arbitrary dichotomization on a continuous dimension.

Proponents of a continuous Autism spectrum model point to similarities in clinical features (e.g., Eisenmajer et al., 1996), neuropsychological test performance (J. N. Miller & Ozonoff, 2000), and brain stem abnormities (Bauman, 1996). However, none of these necessarily precludes latent discontinuities on other criteria. Additionally, Constantino and Todd (2003) recently advocated for a continuum model of severity based on the absence of bimodality in a distribution of Social Responsiveness Scale (Constantino, 2002) scores collected from a large sample. Yet, as we outlined earlier, this is probably the least powerful method for resolving discrete latent structure.

As stressed repeatedly by Meehl (e.g., 1995a, 2004), ontological questions such as these cannot be addressed without subjecting phenotypic and endophenotypic markers to taxometric analyses. Although many disorders lack indicators of sufficient validity to perform such analyses, this is not the case for Autism spectrum disorders, where a number of precise markers have been specified at several levels of analysis (see Akshoomoff, Pierce, & Courchesne, 2002; Dawson, Webb, et al., 2002; Klin, Jones, Schultz, Volkmar, & Cohen, 2002). In the social domain, infants with Autism direct their gaze toward others less frequently and orient to their names less often than controls, and adults attend less to the eyes of others when observing social interactions (Klin et al., 2002; Osterling, Dawson, & Munson, 2002). At the psychophysiological level, children with Autism spectrum disorders exhibit attenuated event-related brain potentials when presented with familiar faces (Dawson, Carver, et al., 2002). Finally, children with Autism exhibit a number of brain chemical alterations (Friedman et al., 2003) and experience accelerated trajectories in brain growth between the ages of 2 and 4 (Courchesne et al., 2001); as outlined earlier, growth trajectories typically provide increased measurement precision over cross-sectional measures and may therefore be useful in taxometrics research. These are but a few examples of potential phenotypes and endophenotypes for Autism (see Dawson, Webb, et al., 2002). If taxometric studies suggest that subsets of these markers identify a discrete latent class, studies aimed at elucidating the differential etiological mechanisms of Autism and Asperger's Disorder will need to be pursued.

Specifying Equifinal and Multifinal Pathways to Psychopathology

As outlined earlier, equifinality refers to the processes through which multiple etiological pathways lead to an apparently single behavioral syndrome. Using our previous example, findings suggesting that ADHD can result from genetically mediated central dopamine dysfunction, structural insults to the central nervous system, and in utero exposure to drugs of abuse represent an example of equifinality. In contrast, multifinality refers to processes through which children who are at similar risk levels diverge toward disparate behavioral outcomes, only some of which are disordered (Cicchetti & Rogosch, 1996). For example, accumulating evidence suggests that children who are temperamentally impulsive fare poorly in terms of delinquency outcomes when raised in high-risk neighborhoods compared with similar children raised in low-risk neighborhoods (e.g., Lynam et al., 2000). Equifinality and multifinality imply that a full appreciation for heterogeneity in individual outcomes can be attained only through longitudinal assessment of interactions between child-specific variables (e.g., temperament) and environmental experiences (e.g., neighborhood context). Thus, specifying mechanisms of equifinality and multifinality requires that homogeneous subgroups of children who are at differential risk for psychopathology be followed throughout the natural course of development (Hinshaw, 2002b; Richters & Cicchetti, 1993).

For vulnerability traits that are discrete, taxometric methods provide a means of characterizing homogeneous subgroups for such follow-up studies. As described previously, for example, Woodward et al. (2000) identified a discrete behavioral reactivity taxon comprising 10% of 4-month-old infants in a large sample. Four years later, members of this extremely reactive group scored high on measures of behavioral inhibition. These findings provide a unique opportunity to explore developmental outcomes among qualitatively distinct subgroups of children who are at differential risk for later internalizing disorders (see Kagan, 1997). Longitudinal follow-ups will provide for identification of environmental experiences in the home, school, and neighborhood that both mitigate and attenuate vulnerability to psychopathology. In addition to evaluating mechanisms for such multifinal outcomes, longitudinal follow-ups will also provide the opportunity to determine what sets of differential experiences result in similar outcomes for taxon and complement class members, thereby addressing questions of equifinality as well. For discrete vulnerability traits, well-designed taxometric analyses ensure that subgroups of children in such studies are not specified arbitrarily.

Specifying Etiologically Homogeneous Subgroups for Behavior Genetics Research

As we noted in the introduction to this chapter, most proponents of the search for endophenotypes in psychopathology research have expressed particular concern about the etiological heterogeneity of groups defined strictly by behavioral syndromes, due to the attenuating effect this has on estimates of genetic linkages and associations (Castellanos & Tannock, 2002; Cornblatt & Malhotra, 2001; Gottesman & Gould, 2003; Skuse, 2001). For example, although behavior genetics studies have repeatedly demonstrated heritability coefficients of about .80 for impulsive behavior (Cadoret, Leve, & Devor, 1997; Hinshaw, 2002a), both population- and family-based studies of two promising candidate genes, DAT1 and DRD4, suggest relatively low-risk values (e.g., LaHoste et al., 1996; Smalley et al., 1998). Although additional genes are clearly implicated in ADHD (Castellanos & Tannock, 2002; Swanson & Castellanos, 2002), part of the reason for low genetic associations is that the ADHD phenotype identifies an etiologically heterogeneous group whose symptoms arise from multiple equifinal causes, only some of which involve central dopamine dysfunction (see earlier discussion). To the extent that taxometric analyses performed on precise endophenotypes can identify more etiologically homogeneous subgroups for behavior genetics studies, advances in our understanding of gene-behavior relations will almost certainly be realized. This in turn will provide for early identification of genetic risk, earlier delivery of services, and longitudinal follow-ups of high-risk individuals. Thus, rather than focusing on fully developed dis-

orders in childhood, premorbid identification of risk will allow us to take full advantage of the strengths offered by a developmental psychopathology framework.

Identifying Person-Specific Moderators of Treatment Outcome

In intervention research, taxometric studies can also help to identify person-specific moderators of treatment outcome. A moderator is any variable present at baseline that discriminates between those who respond differentially to treatment (e.g., Hinshaw et al., 2000; Kraemer, Stice, Kazdin, Offord, & Kupfer, 2001; Kraemer, Wilson, Fairburn, & Agras, 2002). For discretely distributed traits, taxometrics can identify nonarbitrary groups for whom differential treatment response may be assessed. When moderating variables are found, they facilitate identification of processes that enhance or diminish the impact of an intervention in different groups (see Hinshaw, 2002b). For example, if a group of endogenous depressives, as identified through taxometric analyses of appropriate phenotypic and endophenotypic markers, responds less favorably to cognitive-behavioral therapy than their exogenous depressive counterparts, then we know more about the treatment of depression than we would have known had we not identified the person-specific moderator (endogenous depression). Moreover, we may be in a position to offer an alternative treatment that provides a comparative advantage.

In treatment-outcome research on conduct problems, a number of authors have called for identification of person-specific treatment moderators (Beauchaine et al., in press; Brestan & Eyberg, 1998; Nock, 2003). These calls have followed from recognition that fully one-third of children do not benefit from the most successful interventions (Webster-Stratton & Hammond, 1997; Webster-Stratton et al., 2002), yet we currently know very little about child-specific predictors of treatment response. In future research, it will be of interest to see whether the severe antisocial/psychopathy taxon can be detected in young children, and if so, whether children in the taxon group respond differentially to treatment. Such a finding would enable treatment providers to identify children who are less likely to be treatment responders before initiating an intervention. This information could be invaluable for formulating more targeted interventions for specific subgroups of children who are not benefiting from current approaches.

Informing Research on Comorbidity

Before offering specific recommendations for future research, we would also like to comment on the utility of taxometrics for comorbidity research. Several authors have recently expressed enthusiasm for the potential role that taxometric methods might play in disentangling different sources of comorbidity (Meehl, 2001a; J. Ruscio & Ruscio, 2004a; Waldman & Lilienfeld, 2001). For example, suppose, for the sake of argument, that I subscribe to the theory that both the schizotypy taxon and the dissociative experiences taxon are identifying the same latent class using different indicators. In other words, dissociative experiences are simply a marker of schizotypy. Given approximate population base rates of around 5% for each taxon, and given some conceptual overlap in criteria, such an argument might be plausible. This hypothesis suggests that any apparent comorbidity is artifactual (D. N. Klein & Riso, 1993), because the two traits are actually identifying the same group. If this is the case, error-free taxometric analyses of both sets of indicators would yield perfect agreement in a 2 × 2 contingency table, classifying 5% of individuals into the taxon group and 95% of individuals into the complement class (J. Ruscio & Ruscio, 2004a). In contrast, suppose my colleague believes that the taxa are independent, in which case, the number of individuals assigned to the taxon by analyses of both sets of indicators should equal the product of the base rates (.05 × .05 = .0025). Again, this assumes error-free classification.

Unfortunately, Bayes's theorem dictates that considerable error will be observed in the classification of any low base rate phenomenon (Baldessarini, Finklestein, & Arana, 1983), regardless of the approach to classification that is used. Accordingly, Monte Carlo simulations of the MAXCOV procedure in particular suggest that under low base rate conditions that are likely to face psychopathology researchers, the procedure is quite effective at detecting latent taxa but yields significant false-positive rates when classifying individuals into groups (Beauchaine & Beauchaine, 2002). For example, at a base rate of 5% using five indicators, a sample size of 300, an effect size of 1.25, and within-group correlations of .30, MAXCOV correctly classifies about 65% of individuals, with a false-positive rate of about 30% and a false-negative rate of about 10%. Thus, even if my colleague is correct in suggesting that schizotypy and dissociative experiences are independent, taxometric analyses with different sets of indicators will place roughly 10% (.30 × .30 = .09) of individuals into the same taxon. Note that this is actually double the 5% base rate observed in both populations. This would lead to the erroneous conclusion that the two disorders are etiologically related (see J. Ruscio & Ruscio, 2004a), an incorrect interpretation that neither of us

hypothesized! Although other potential inferential errors could be described, this example alone tempers our enthusiasm for the utility of taxometrics in clarifying questions of comorbidity. In samples where base rates are higher, classification errors are far less common, and these limitations do not apply.

FUTURE DIRECTIONS

To date, CCKs have been used quite sparingly by developmental psychopathologists, yet their popularity continues to increase in other areas of psychopathology research. Although longitudinal taxometric studies remain exceedingly rare (for an exception, see Tyrka, Haslam, et al., 1995), several authors have begun to consider the developmental sequelae of members of high-risk taxon groups (Erlenmeyer-Kimling et al., 1989; Tyrka, Cannon, et al., 1995; Woodward et al., 2000). Taxometric analyses of antisocial traits have also been conducted in separate samples spanning middle school through adulthood (Ayers et al., 1999; Harris et al., 1994; Skilling, Harris, et al., 2001; Skilling, Quinsey, et al., 2001). Similarly, taxometric analyses of melancholic depression have now been conducted among adolescents as well as adults (Ambrosini et al., 2002; Beach & Amir, 2003; Grove et al., 1987; Haslam & Beck, 1994). These research efforts are encouraging given the advantages of person-centered techniques to identify heterogeneous longitudinal trajectories in behavioral maladaptation. Further efforts to specify the developmental sequelae of individuals afflicted with discretely distributed psychopathological traits will almost certainly identify specific mechanisms of equifinality and multifinality that produce diverse adjustment outcomes.

Consistent with these objectives, the most important future application of taxometric methods lies in identifying latent vulnerability traits that place children at significant risk for later psychopathology. Using the example of schizotypy, we described how taxometric analyses of carefully chosen endophenotypes have provided a three- to fourfold increase in our ability to predict later Schizophrenia among children with an affected parent. Early identification can in turn lead to targeted prevention programs designed to mitigate environmental risk before overt expression of the disorder. Although the research is in early stages, premorbid identification of vulnerability for both severe antisocial behavior and anxiety/depressive disorders may also be possible. If this potential is to be realized, researchers must continue to search for promising endophenotypes that mark latent vulnerabilities with greater precision than rating scale measures.

Furthermore, future research must be conducted with more careful attention to indicator validity. In other words, variables must be chosen for analysis based on strong theory regarding the latent trait they are assumed to mark (Beauchaine & Waters, 2003; Lenzenweger, 2004; Meehl, 1999; Waters & Beauchaine, 2003). The most common approach to taxometrics currently used is to extract all symptoms of a psychiatric disorder from a large data set of convenience and subject the entire set to multiple CCK algorithms. Often, this means that the only variables used are Likert-type ratings of psychopathology, with little or no attention to core versus peripheral symptoms of the underlying vulnerability trait. This shotgun approach is unlikely to be fruitful in future research for several reasons. First, most if not all current criterion lists of disorders in the *DSM-IV-TR* do not map onto a single vulnerability trait. For example, criteria for ADHD include inattentiveness, hyperactivity, and impulsivity items. Although there is currently no evidence of latent taxa for any of these traits, subjecting all ADHD symptoms to taxometric analyses would almost surely obscure any such taxon if it existed given that inattention and impulsivity are separable behavioral traits (Milich et al., 2001). For this reason, *DSM-IV-TR* criterion lists cannot be assumed to offer a proper starting point for taxonic searches.

Consider the case of schizotypy. As outlined earlier, Meehl (1962) offered an elaborate theory of Schizophrenia vulnerability well before he invented most of his taxometric algorithms. This theory included a set of core symptoms that Meehl believed were markers of a single latent vulnerability to Schizophrenia. These symptoms, including interpersonal aversiveness, ambivalence, cognitive slippage, and anhedonia, did not map directly onto the criteria of Schizophrenia of the day, nor do they map directly onto current criteria for the disorder. Given this, subjecting all symptoms of Schizophrenia to a taxometric analysis would almost certainly result in a false negative outcome when searching for discrete latent structure, even though schizotypy is the most well-replicated taxonic psychopathology trait yet identified (Blanchard et al., 2000; Erlenmeyer-Kimling et al., 1989; Golden & Meehl, 1979; Horan et al., 2004; Korfine & Lenzenweger, 1995; Lenzenweger, 1999; Lenzenweger & Korfine, 1992, 1995; Tyrka, Cannon, et al., 1995; Tyrka, Haslam, et al., 1995). A similar argument can be advanced for dissociation, a trait that is also distributed discretely (Waller et al., 1996; Waller & Ross, 1997) but does not map onto any specific psychiatric disorder.

These examples illustrate the importance of theoretically guided taxometrics research, where candidate indicators are identified before data collection and are measured with as much precision as possible, preferably with at least some laboratory measures. When only psychometric data are used in taxometrics research, it is difficult to surmise the extent to which rater biases, halo effects, response biases, and/or low measurement precision are impacting one's results (see Beauchaine & Waters, 2003; Lenzenweger, 2004). Because most laboratory markers are both more precise than psychometric measures and are indexed on ratio scales, they are particularly well suited for taxometric analyses when chosen carefully.

To date, the predominant approach to dealing with measurement imprecision has been to develop ad hoc and ancillary techniques aimed at resolving discrete latent structure with suboptimal data. These include special procedures for accommodating dichotomous indicators (Golden, 1982, 1991), simulation techniques for resolving discrete latent structure with skewed indicators, and similar methods aimed at establishing the suitability of data for taxometric analyses (J. Ruscio & Ruscio, 2004a, 2004b). Although many of these methods are ingenious, they are almost never ideal solutions to the problems they address (see, e.g., Footnote 6). In future studies, developmental psychopathologists and other researchers will benefit from careful selection of highly precise indicators. There are probably no putative taxa for which dichotomous measures cannot be avoided. Moreover, unpublished data from our lab suggest that skewed indicators are far less likely to produce spurious taxonic outcomes if they are continuous rather than discretely anchored.

These issues are not trivial. Ongoing arguments and inconsistencies in the adult psychopathology literature over the latent structure of both endogenous depression and psychopathy derive in part from issues of measurement imprecision and skew (Beach & Amir, 2003; Harris et al., 1994; Marcus, John, & Edens, 2004; J. Ruscio, Ruscio, & Keane, 2004). These controversies will probably never be resolved definitively without including more precise indicators of putative taxonic constructs, preferably from psychophysiological cognitive, neurologic, and other levels of analysis, as originally advocated by Meehl (1995a, 2001b).

Developmental psychopathologists have long recognized the importance of addressing individual patterns of adaptation and maladaptation from multiple levels of analysis, including behavioral, physiological, and genetic, among others (Cicchetti & Dawson, 2002). Many developmental psychopathologists also reject the reification of diagnostic classes, preferring instead to focus on interactions between vulnerability traits and environmental experiences in shaping behavior and psychological adjustment. We are therefore perplexed by the omission of taxometrics from the armamentarium of methodological techniques used by researchers in the field. Yet, we are optimistic that this will soon change. The potential of taxometrics to identify individuals at especially high risk for future psychopathology is simply too consistent with developmental psychopathology objectives for the techniques to remain unused. Furthermore, developmental psychopathologists are well positioned to make significant contributions to taxometrics research given the strong role of theory in their conceptualizations of mental disorders and behavioral adjustment. These emphases make it likely that developmental psychopathologists will conduct theoretically informed taxometric analyses toward identifying young children at particular risk for behavioral maladaptation.

As we continue to conduct taxometric research with younger samples, it will be particularly important to follow the same individuals over extended periods of time. As the schizotypy literature demonstrates, the greatest value of identifying latent vulnerabilities lies in prediction of future outcomes for group members. Specifying and predicting trajectories in behavioral adaptation and maladaptation have been the objectives of developmental psychopathology since its inception, and they remain so today (Rutter & Sroufe, 2000; Sroufe & Rutter, 1984). The taxometric methods of Meehl and his colleagues offer an as yet underutilized tool to aid in achieving these goals.

REFERENCES

Achenbach, T. (1974). *Developmental psychopathology.* New York: Ronald.

Achenbach, T. (1991). *Manual for the Child Behavior Checklist/4–18 and 1991 profile.* Burlington: University of Vermont, Department of Psychiatry.

Akiskal, H. S. (1978). The joint use of clinical and biological criteria for psychiatric diagnosis: I. A historical and methodological review. In H. S. Akiskal & W. L. Webb (Eds.), *Psychiatric diagnosis: Exploration of biological predictors* (pp. 103–132). New York: Medical and Scientific Books.

Akshoomoff, N., Pierce, K., & Courchesne, E. (2002). The neurobiological basis of Autism from a developmental perspective. *Development and Psychopathology, 14,* 613–634.

Aldenderfer, M. S., & Blashfield, R. K. (1984). *Cluster analysis.* Newbury Park, CA: Sage.

Ambrosini, P. J., Bennett, D. S., Cleland, C. M., & Haslam, N. (2002). Taxonicity of adolescent melancholia: A categorical or dimensional construct? *Journal of Psychiatric Research, 36,* 247–256.

American Psychiatric Association. (1952). *Diagnostic and statistical manual of mental disorders.* Washington, DC: Author.

American Psychiatric Association. (1968). *Diagnostic and statistical manual of mental disorders* (2nd ed.). Washington, DC: Author.

American Psychiatric Association. (1980). *Diagnostic and statistical manual of mental disorders* (3rd ed.). Washington, DC: Author.

American Psychiatric Association. (1994). *Diagnostic and statistical manual of mental disorders* (4th ed.). Washington, DC: Author.

American Psychiatric Association. (2000). *Diagnostic and statistical manual of mental disorders* (4th ed., text rev.). Washington, DC: Author.

Atlas, R. S., & Overall, J. E. (1994). Comparative evaluation of two superior stopping rules for hierarchical cluster analysis. *Psychometrika, 59,* 581–591.

Avila, M. T., McMahon, R. P., Elliott, A. R., & Thaker, G. K. (2002). Neuropsychological markers of vulnerability to Schizophrenia: Sensitivity and specificity of specific quantitative eye movement measures. *Journal of Abnormal Psychology, 111,* 259–267.

Ayers, W., Haslam, N., Bernstein, D., Tryon, W. T., & Handelsman, L. (1999). *Categorical versus dimensional models of personality disorder in substance abusers: A taxometric analysis.* Poster presented at the annual meeting of the American Psychiatric Association.

Baldessarini, R. J., Finklestein, S., & Arana, G. W. (1983). The predictive power of diagnostic tests and the effect of prevalence of illness. *Archives of General Psychiatry, 40,* 569–573.

Barkley, R. A. (2001). The inattentive type of ADHD as a distinct disorder: What remains to be done. *Clinical Psychology Science and Practice, 8,* 489–493.

Barlow, D. H. (Ed.). (2001). *Clinical Psychology Science and Practice, 8,* 507–541.

Barry, C. T., Frick, P. J., DeShazo, T. M., McCoy, M. Ellis, M., & Loney, B. R. (2000). The importance of callous-unemotional traits for extending the concept of psychopathy to children. *Journal of Abnormal Psychology, 109,* 335–340.

Bartels, M., de Geus, E. J. C., Kirschbaum, C., Sluyter, F., & Boomsma, D. I. (2004). Heritability of daytime cortisol levels in children. *Behavior Genetics, 33,* 421–433.

Bartels, M., Van den Berg, M., Sluyter, F., Boomsma, D. I., & de Geus, E. J. C. (2003). Heritability of cortisol levels: Review and simultaneous analysis of twin studies. *Psychoneuroendocrinology, 28,* 121–137.

Bauer, D. J., & Curran, P. J. (2003). Distributional assumptions of growth mixture models: Implications for overextraction of latent trajectory classes. *Psychological Methods, 8,* 338–363.

Bauer, D. J., & Curran, P. J. (2004). The integration of continuous and discrete latent variable models: Potential problems and promising opportunities. *Psychological Methods, 9,* 3–29.

Bauman, M. L. (1996). Neuroanatomic observations of the brain in pervasive developmental disorders. *Journal of Autism and Developmental Disorders, 26,* 199–203.

Beach, S. R. H., & Amir, N. (2003). Is depression taxonic, dimensional, or both? *Journal of Abnormal Psychology, 112,* 228–236.

Beach, S. R. H., Amir, N., & Bau, J. (in press). Can sample specific simulations help detect low base rate taxonicity? *Psychological Assessment.*

Beauchaine, T. P. (2001). Vagal tone, development, and Gray's motivational theory: Toward an integrated model of autonomic nervous system functioning in psychopathology. *Development and Psychopathology, 13,* 183–214.

Beauchaine, T. P. (2003a). Autonomic substrates of heart rate reactivity in adolescent males with conduct disorder and/or attention-deficit/hyperactivity disorder. In T. A. Prester (Ed.), *Psychology of adolescents* (pp. 133–145). New York: Nova Science.

Beauchaine, T. P. (2003b). Taxometrics and developmental psychopathology. *Development and Psychopathology, 15,* 501–527.

Beauchaine, T. P. (2004). *BAS motivation, affect regulation, and externalizing psychopathology: Three studies spanning preschool to late adolescence.* Paper presented at the annual meeting of the Society for Psychophysiological Research, Albuquerque, NM.

Beauchaine, T. P., & Beauchaine, R. J. III. (2002). A comparison of maximum covariance and *k*-means cluster analysis in classifying cases into known taxon groups. *Psychological Methods, 7,* 245–261.

Beauchaine, T. P., & Gartner, J. (2003). A linear growth curve analysis of inpatient treatment response by conduct-disordered, ADHD, and comorbid preadolescents. *Aggressive Behavior, 29,* 440–456.

Beauchaine, T. P., Katkin, E. S., Strassberg, Z., & Snarr, J. (2001). Disinhibitory psychopathology in male adolescents: Discriminating conduct disorder from attention-deficit/hyperactivity disorder through concurrent assessment of multiple autonomic states. *Journal of Abnormal Psychology, 110,* 610–624.

Beauchaine, T. P., Gatzke-Kopp, L., & Mead, H. K. (in press). Polyvagal theory and developmental psychopathology: Emotion dysregulation and conduct problems from preschool to adolescence. *Biological Psychology.*

Beauchaine, T. P., & Waters, E. (2003). Pseudotaxonicity in MAMBAC and MAXCOV analyses of rating scale data: Turning continua into classes by manipulating observer's expectations. *Psychological Methods, 8,* 3–15.

Beauchaine, T. P., Webster-Stratton, C., & Reid, J. (in press). One-year outcomes of children treated for early onset conduct problems: A latent growth curve analysis. *Journal of Consulting and Clinical Psychology.*

Begleiter, H., Porjesz, B., Bihari, B., & Kissin, B. (1984). Event-related brain potentials in boys at risk for alcoholism. *Science, 225,* 1493–1496.

Blanchard, J. J., Gangestad, S. W., Brown, S. A., & Horan, W. P. (2000). Hedonic capacity and schizotypy revisited: A taxometric analysis of social anhedonia. *Journal of Abnormal Psychology, 109,* 87–95.

Blashfield, R. K., & Aldenderfer, M. S. (1988). The methods and problems of cluster analysis. In J. Nesselroade & R. B. Cattell (Eds.), *Handbook of multivariate experimental psychology* (2nd ed., pp. 447–474). New York: Plenum Press.

Brestan, E. V., & Eyberg, S. M. (1998). Effective psychosocial treatments of conduct-disordered children and adolescents: 29 years, 82 studies, and 5,272 kids. *Journal of Clinical Child Psychology, 27,* 180–189.

Brooks, D. S., Murphy, D., Janota, I., & Lishman, W. A. (1987). Early-onset Huntington's chorea. *British Journal of Psychiatry, 151,* 850–852.

Brown, T. A. (2001). Taxometric methods and the classification and comorbidity of mental disorders: Methodological and conceptual considerations. *Clinical Psychology Science and Practice, 8,* 534–541.

Cadoret, R. J., Leve, L. D., & Devor, E. (1997). Genetics of aggressive and violent behavior. *Psychiatric Clinics of North America, 20,* 301–322.

Callicott, J. H., Egan, M. F., Mattay, V. S., Bertolino, A., Bone, A. D., Verchinksi, B., et al. (2003). Abnormal fMRI response of the dorsolateral prefrontal cortex in cognitively intact siblings of patients with Schizophrenia. *American Journal of Psychiatry, 160,* 709–719.

Cantor, N., & Genero, N. (1986). Psychiatric diagnosis and natural categorization: A close analogy. In T. Milton & G. Klerman (Eds.), *Contemporary directions in psychopathology: Toward the DSM-IV* (pp. 233–256). New York: Guilford Press.

Cantor, N., & Mischel, W. (1979). Prototypes in person perception. In L. Berkowitz (Ed.), *Advances in experimental social psychology* (Vol. 12, pp. 3–52). Orlando, FL: Academic Press.

Cantwell, D. P. (1996). Classification of child and adolescent psychopathology. *Journal of Child Psychology and Psychiatry, 37,* 3–12.

Carlson, C. L., & Mann, M. (2002). Sluggish cognitive tempo predicts a different pattern of impairment in the attention deficit hyperactivity disorder, predominantly inattentive type. *Journal of Clinical Child and Adolescent Psychology, 31,* 123–129.

Casat, C. D., & Powell, K. (1988). The dexamethasone suppression test in children and adolescents with major depressive disorder: A review. *Journal of Clinical Psychiatry, 10,* 390–393.

Caspi, A., Moffitt, T. E., Newman, D. L., & Silva, P. A. (1996). Behavioral observations at age 3 years predict adult psychiatric disorders. *Archives of General Psychiatry, 53,* 1033–1039.

Castellanos, F. X., & Tannock, R. (2002). Neuroscience of attention-deficit/hyperactivity disorder: The search for endophenotypes. *Nature Reviews Neuroscience, 3,* 617–628.

Cicchetti, D., & Dawson, G. (Eds.). (2002). Multiple levels of analysis [Special issue]. *Development and Psychopathology, 14,* 417–666.

Cicchetti, D., & Rogosch, F. A. (1996). Equifinality and multifinality in developmental psychopathology. *Development and Psychopathology, 8,* 597–600.

Cicchetti, D., & Rogosch, F. A. (1999). Conceptual and methodological issues in developmental psychopathology research. In P. C. Kendall, J. N. Butcher, & G. N. Holmbeck (Eds.), *Handbook of research methods in clinical psychology* (2nd ed., pp. 433–465). New York: Wiley.

Cicchetti, D., & Rogosch, F. A. (2002). A developmental psychopathology perspective on adolescence. *Journal of Consulting and Clinical Psychology, 70,* 6–20.

Clark, L. A., Watson, D., & Reynolds, S. (1995). Diagnosis and classification in psychopathology: Challenges to the current system and future directions. *Annual Review of Psychology, 46,* 121–153.

Cleland, C., & Haslam, N. (1996). Robustness of taxometric analyses with skewed indicators: I. A Monte Carlo study of the MAMBAC procedure. *Psychological Reports, 79,* 243–248.

Cleland, C., Rothschild, L., & Haslam, N. (2000). Detacting latent taxa: Comparison of taxometric, mixture model, and clustering procedures. *Psychological Reports, 87,* 37–47.

Cloninger, C. R. (1989). Establishment of diagnostic validity in psychiatric illness: Robins and Guze's method revisited. In L. N. Robins & J. E. Barrett (Eds.), *The validity of psychiatric diagnosis* (pp. 9–18). New York: Raven.

Cohen, J. (1988). *Statistical power analysis for the behavioral sciences* (2nd ed.). New York: Academic Press.

Cole, D. A. (2004). Taxometrics in psychopathology research: An introduction to some of the procedures and related methodological issues. *Journal of Abnormal Psychology, 113,* 3–9.

Cole, D. A., & Baker, T. B. (Eds.). (2004). Taxometrics in psychopathology research [Special section]. *Journal of Abnormal Psychology, 113,* 3–43.

Cole, D. A., Peeke, L. G., Martin, J. M., Truglio, R., & Seroczynski, A. D. (1998). A longitudinal look at the relation between depression and anxiety in children and adolescents. *Journal of Consulting and Clinical Psychology, 66,* 451–460.

Cole, D. A., Tram, J. M., Martin, J. M., Hoffman, K. B., Ruiz, M. D., Jacquez, F. M., et al. (2002). Individual differences in the emergence of depressive symptoms in children and adolescents: A longitudinal investigation of parent and child reports. *Journal of Abnormal Psychology, 111,* 156–165.

Constantino, J. N. (2002). *The Social Responsive Scale.* Los Angeles: Western Psychological Services.

Constantino, J. N., & Todd, R. D. (2003). Autistic traits in the general population. *Archives of General Psychiatry, 60,* 524–530.

Cornblatt, B. A. (2001). Predictors of Schizophrenia and preventive intervention. In A. Breier & P. Tran (Eds.), *Current issues in the psychopharmacology of Schizophrenia* (pp. 389–406). Philadelphia: Lippincott, Williams, & Wilkins.

Cornblatt, B. A., Lencz, T., & Kane, J. M. (2001). Treating the Schizophrenia prodrome: Is it presently ethical? *Schizophrenia Research, 51,* 31–38.

Cornblatt, B. A., & Malhotra, A. K. (2001). Impaired attention as an endophenotype for molecular genetics studies of Schizophrenia. *American Journal of Medical Genetics, 105,* 11–15.

Cornblatt, B. A., Obuchowski, M., Roberts, S., Pollack, S., & Erlenmeyer-Kimling, L. (1999). Cognitive and behavioral precursors of Schizophrenia. *Developmental Psychopathology, 11,* 487–508.

Coryell, W., & Schlesser, M. (2001). The dexamethasone suppression test and suicide prediction. *American Journal of Psychiatry, 158,* 748–753.

Courchesne, E., Karns, C., Davis, H. R., Ziccardi, R., Carper, R., Tigue, Z., et al. (2001). Unusual brain growth patterns in early life in patients with autistic disorder. *Neurology, 57,* 245–254.

Cronbach, L. J., & Meehl, P. E. (1955). Construct validity in psychological tests. *Psychological Bulletin, 52,* 281–302.

Crowell, S., Beauchaine, T. P., Gatzke-Kopp, L., Sylvers, P., & Mead, H. (in press). Autonomic correlates of attention-deficit/hyperactivity disorder and oppositional defiant disorder in preschool children. *Journal of Abnormal Psychology.*

Cudeck, R., & Henly, S. J. (2003). A realistic perspective on pattern representation in growth data: Comment on Bauer and Curran (2003). *Psychological Methods, 8,* 378–383.

Cummings, E. M., Davies, P. T., & Campbell, S. B. (2000). *Developmental psychopathology and family process.* New York: Guilford Press.

Curtis, C. E., Calkins, M. E., Grove, W. M., Feil, K. J., & Iacono, W. G. (2001). Saccadic disinhibition in patients with acute and remitted Schizophrenia and their first-degree biological relatives. *American Journal of Psychiatry, 158,* 100–106.

Dawes, R. M., & Meehl, P. E. (1966). Mixed group validation: A method for determining the validity of diagnostic signs without using criterion groups. *Psychological Bulletin, 66,* 63–67.

Dawson, G., Carver, L., Meltzoff, A. N., Panagiotides, H., McPartland, J., & Webb, S. J. (2002). Neural correlates of face and object recognition in young children with Autism spectrum disorder, developmental delay, and typical development. *Child Development, 73,* 700–717.

Dawson, G., Webb, S., Schellenberg, G. D., Dager, S., Friedman, S., Aylward, E., et al. (2002). Defining the broader phenotype of Autism: Genetic, brain, and behavioral perspectives. *Development and Psychopathology, 14,* 581–611.

Dishion, T. J., & Patterson, G. R. (1992). Age effects in parent training outcome. *Behavior Therapy, 23,* 719–729.

Durston, S., Tottenham, N. T., Thomas, K. M., Davidson, M. C., Eigsti, I. M., Yang, Y., et al. (2003). Differential patterns of striatal activation in young children with and without ADHD. *Biological Psychiatry, 53,* 871–878.

Edelbrock, C. (1979). Mixture model tests of hierarchical clustering algorithms: The problem of classifying everybody. *Multivariate Behavioral Research, 14,* 367–384.

Eisenmajer, R., Prior, M., Leekam, S., Wing, L., Gould, J., Welham, M., et al. (1996). Comparison of clinical symptoms in Autism and Asperger's disorder. *Journal of the American Academy of Child and Adolescent Psychiatry, 35,* 1523–1531.

Erlenmeyer-Kimling, L., Golden, R. R., & Cornblatt, B. A. (1989). A taxometric analysis of cognitive and neuromotor variables in children at risk for Schizophrenia. *Journal of Abnormal Psychology, 98,* 203–208.

Everitt, B. S. (1993). *Cluster analysis* (3rd ed.). London: Edward Arnold.

Falloon, I. R. H., Boyd, J. L., McGill, C. W., Williamson, M., Razani, J., Moss, H. B., et al. (1985). Family management in the prevention of morbidity in Schizophrenia. *Archives of General Psychiatry, 42,* 887–896.

Faraone, S. V., Biederman, J., Weber, W., & Russell, R. L. (1998). Psychiatric, neuropsychological, and psychosocial features of DSM-IV subtypes of attention-deficit/hyperactivity disorder: Results from a clinically referred sample. *Journal of the American Academy of Child and Adolescent Psychiatry, 37,* 185–193.

Feighner, J. P., Robins, E., Guze, S. B., Woodruff, R. A., Winokur, G., & Munoz, R. (1972). Diagnostic criteria for use in psychiatric research. *Archives of General Psychiatry, 26,* 57–63.

Flanagan, E. H., & Blashfield, R. K. (2002). Psychiatric classification through the lens of ethnobiology. In L. E. Beutler & M. L. Malik (Eds.), *Rethinking the DSM* (pp. 121–145). Washington, DC: American Psychological Association.

Fowles, D. C. (2000). Electrodermal hyporeactivity and antisocial behavior: Does anxiety mediate the relationship? *Journal of Affective Disorders, 61,* 177–189.

Fraley, R. C., & Spieker, S. J. (2003). Are infant attachment patterns continuously or categorically distributed? A taxometric analysis of Strange Situation behavior. *Developmental Psychology, 39,* 387–404.

Frick, P. J., Cornell, A. H., Barry, C. T., Bodin, S. D., & Dane, H. E. (2003). Callous-unemotional traits and conduct problems in the prediction of conduct problem severity, aggression, and self-report of delinquency. *Journal of Abnormal Child Psychology, 31,* 457–470.

Frick, P. J., Lahey, B. B., Applegate, B., Kerdyck, L., Ollendick, T., Hynd, G. W., et al. (1994). *DSM-IV* field trials for the disruptive behavior disorders: Symptom utility estimates. *Journal of the American Academy of Child and Adolescent Psychiatry, 33,* 529–539.

Friedman, S. D., Shaw, D. W. W., Artru, A. A., Gardner, J., Richards, T. L., Posse, S., et al. (2003). Regional brain chemical alterations in young children with Autism spectrum disorder. *Neurology, 60,* 100–107.

Gangestad, S. W., Bailey, J. M., & Martin, N. G. (2000). Taxometric analyses of sexual orientation and gender identity. *Journal of Personality and Social Psychology, 78,* 1109–1121.

Gangestad, S. W., & Snyder, M. (1985). "To carve nature at its joints": On the existence of discrete classes in personality. *Psychological Review, 92,* 317–349.

Gerring, J., Brandy, K., Chen, A., Quinn, C., Herskovits, E., Bandeen-Roche, K., et al. (2000). Neuroimaging variables related to development of secondary attention deficit hyperactivity disorder after closed head injury in children and adolescents. *Brain Injury, 14,* 205–218.

Ghaziuddin, M., Weidmer-Mikhail, E., & Ghaziuddin, N. (1998). Comorbidity of Asperger syndrome: A preliminary report. *Journal of Intellectual Disabilities Research, 42,* 279–283.

Gibson, W. A. (1959). Three multivariate models: Factor analysis, latent structure analysis, and latent profile analysis. *Psychometrika, 24,* 229–252.

Glahn, D. C., Therman, S., Manninen, M., Huttunen, M., Kapiro, J., Lönnqvist, J., et al. (2003). Spatial working memory as an endophenotype for Schizophrenia. *Biological Psychiatry, 53,* 624–626.

Gleaves, D. H., Lowe, M. R., Green, B. A., Cororve, M. B., & Williams, T. L. (2000). Do anorexia and bulimia nervosa occur on a continuum? A taxometric analysis. *Behavior Therapy, 31,* 195–219.

Golden, R. R. (1982). A taxometric model for the detection of a conjectured latent taxon. *Multivariate Behavioral Research, 17,* 389–416.

Golden, R. R. (1991). Bootstrapping taxometrics: On the development of a method for detection of a single major gene. In D. Cicchetti & W. M. Grove (Eds.), *Thinking clearly about psychology* (Vol. 2, pp. 259–294). Minneapolis: University of Minnesota Press.

Golden, R. R., & Meehl, P. E. (1979). Detection of the schizoid taxon with MMPI indicators. *Journal of Abnormal Psychology, 88,* 212–233.

Goldsmith, H. H., Gottesman, I. I., & Lemery, K. S. (1997). Epigenetic approaches to developmental psychopathology. *Development and Psychopathology, 9,* 365–387.

Gottesman, I. I., & Gould, T. D. (2003). The endophenotype concept in psychiatry: Etymology and strategic intentions. *American Journal of Psychiatry, 160,* 636–645.

Grayson, D. A. (1987). Can categorical and dimensional views of psychiatric illness be distinguished? *British Journal of Psychiatry, 151,* 355–361.

Grove, W. M. (1991). Validity of taxonic inferences based on cluster analysis stopping rules. In D. Cicchetti & W. M. Grove (Eds.), *Thinking clearly about psychology* (Vol. 2, pp. 313–329). Minneapolis: University of Minnesota Press.

Grove, W. M., Andreasen, N. C., Young, M., Endicott, J., Keller, M. B., Hirschfeld, R. M. A., et al. (1987). Isolation and characterization of a nuclear depressive syndrome. *Psychological Medicine, 17,* 471–484.

Grove, W. M., & Meehl, P. E. (1993). Simple regression-based procedures for taxometric investigation. *Psychological Reports, 73,* 707–737.

Hamilton, E. B., Asarnow, J. R., & Tompson, M. C. (1999). Family interaction styles of children with depressive disorders, Schizophrenia-spectrum disorders, and normal controls. *Family Process, 38,* 463–476.

Hare, R. D., Harpur, T. J., Hakstian, A. R., Forth, A. E., Hart, S. D., & Newman, J. P. (1990). The revised Psychopathy Checklist: Reliability and factor structure. *Psychological Assessment, 2,* 338–341.

Harrington, R., Rutter, M., & Fombonne, E. (1996). Developmental pathways in depression: Multiple meanings, antecedents, and endpoints. *Development and Psychopathology, 8,* 601–616.

Harris, G. T., Rice, M. E., & Quinsey, V. L. (1994). Psychopathy as a taxon: Evidence that psychopaths are a discrete class. *Journal of Consulting and Clinical Psychology, 62,* 387–397.

Hartigan, J. A. (1975). *Clustering algorithms.* New York: Wiley.

Haslam, N. (2003). The dimensional view of personality disorders: A review of the taxometric evidence. *Clinical Psychology Review, 23,* 75–93.

Haslam, N., & Beck, A. T. (1994). Subtyping major depression: A taxometric analysis. *Journal of Abnormal Psychology, 103,* 686–692.

Haslam, N., & Cleland, C. (1996). Robustness of taxometric analysis with skewed indicators: II. A Monte Carlo study of the MAXCOV procedure. *Psychological Reports, 79,* 1035–1039.

Haslam, N., & Cleland, C. (2002). Taxometric analysis of fuzzy categories: A Monte Carlo study. *Psychological Reports, 90,* 401–404.

Haslam, N., & Kim, H. C. (2002). Categories and continua: A review of taxometric research. *Genetic, Social, and General Psychology Monographs, 128,* 271–320.

Hinshaw, S. P. (2001). Is the inattentive subtype of ADHD a separate disorder? *Clinical Psychology Science and Practice, 8,* 498–501.

Hinshaw, S. P. (2002a). Is ADHD an impairing condition in childhood and adolescence? In P. S. Jensen & J. R. Cooper (Eds.), *Attention deficit hyperactivity disorder* (pp. 5.1–5.21). Kingston, NJ: Civic Research Institute.

Hinshaw, S. P. (2002b). Prevention/intervention trials and developmental theory: Commentary on the Fast Track special section. *Journal of Abnormal Child Psychology, 30,* 53–59.

Hinshaw, S. P., Lahey, B. B., & Hart, E. L. (1993). Issues of taxonomy and comorbidity in the development of conduct disorder. *Development and Psychopathology, 5,* 31–49.

Hinshaw, S. P., Owens, E. B., Wells, K. C., Kraemer, H. C., Abikoff, H. B., Arnold, L. E., et al. (2000). Family processes and treatment outcome in the MTA: Negative/ineffective parenting practices in relation to multimodal treatment. *Journal of Abnormal Child Psychology, 28,* 555–568.

Hinshaw, S. P., & Park, T. (1999). Research problems and issues: Toward a more definitive science of disruptive behavior disorders. In H. C. Quay & A. E. Hogan (Eds.), *Handbook of disruptive behavior disorders* (pp. 593–620). New York: Plenum Press.

Hogarty, G. E., Anderson, C. M., Teiss, D. J., Kornblith, S. J., Greenwald, D. P., Ulrich, R. F., et al. (1991). Family psychoeducation, social skills training, and maintenance chemotherapy in the aftercare treatment of Schizophrenia. *Archives of General Psychiatry, 48,* 340–347.

Horan, W. P., Blanchard, J. J., Gangestad, S. W., & Kwapil, T. R. (2004). The psychometric detection of schizotypy: Do putative schizotypy indicators identify the same latent class? *Journal of Abnormal Psychology, 113,* 339–357.

Houts, A. C. (2002). Discovery, invention, and the expansion of the modern Diagnostic and statistical manual of mental disorders. In L. E. Beutler & M. L. Malik (Eds.), *Rethinking the DSM* (pp. 17–65). Washington, DC: American Psychological Association.

Hoyt, W. T., & Kerns, M. D. (1999). Magnitude and moderators of bias in observer ratings: A meta-analysis. *Psychological Methods, 4,* 403–424.

Jensen, P. S., Hinshaw, S. P., Kraemer, H. C., Lenora, N., Newcorn, J. H., Abikoff, H. B., et al. (2001). ADHD comorbidity findings from the MTA study: Comparing comorbid subgroups. *Journal of the American Academy of Child and Adolescent Psychiatry, 40,* 147–158.

Jensen, P. S., & Hoagwood, K. (1997). The book of names: DSM-IV in context. *Development and Psychopathology, 9,* 231–249.

Jöreskog, K. G., & Sörbom, D. (2001). *LISREL 8: User's reference guide.* Lincolnwood, IL: Scientific Software International.

Kagan, J. (1994). *Galen's prophecy.* New York: Basic Books.

Kagan, J. (1997). Conceptualizing psychopathology: The importance of developmental profiles. *Development and Psychopathology, 9,* 321–334.

Kagan, J., Reznick, J. S., & Snidman, N. (1987). The physiology and psychology of behavioral inhibition in children. *Child Development, 58,* 1459–1473.

Kendell, R. E. (1989). Clinical validity. *Psychological Medicine, 19,* 45–55.

Klein, D. N., & Riso, L. P. (1993). Psychiatric disorders: Problems of boundaries and comorbidity. In C. G. Costello (Ed.), *Basic issues in psychopathology* (pp. 19–66). New York: Guilford Press.

Klein, R. G., Abikoff, H., Klass, E., Ganeles, D., Seese, L. M., & Pollack, S. (1997). Clinical efficacy of methylphenidate in conduct disorder with and without attention deficit hyperactivity disorder. *Archives of General Psychiatry, 54,* 1073–1080.

Klin, A. (1994). Asperger syndrome. *Psychiatric Clinics of North America, 3,* 131–148.

Klin, A., Jones, W., Schultz, R., Volkmar, F., & Cohen, D. (2002). Defining and quantifying the social phenotype of Autism. *American Journal of Psychiatry, 159,* 895–908.

Klin, A., Volkmar, F. R., Sparrow, S. S., Cicchetti, D. V., & Roarke, B. P. (1995). Validity and neuropsychological characterization of Asperger syndrome: Convergence with nonverbal learning disabilities syndrome. *Journal of Child Psychology and Psychiatry, 36,* 1127–1140.

Korfine, L., & Lenzenweger, M. F. (1995). The taxonicity of schizotypy: A replication. *Journal of Abnormal Psychology, 104,* 26–31.

Kraemer, H. C., Stice, E., Kazdin, A., Offord, D., & Kupfer, D. (2001). How do risk factors work together? Mediators, moderators, and independent, overlapping, and proxy risk factors. *American Journal of Psychiatry, 158,* 848–856.

Kraemer, H. C., Wilson, G. T., Fairburn, C. G., & Agras, W. S. (2002). Mediators and moderators of treatment effects in randomized clinical trials. *Archives of General Psychiatry, 59,* 877–883.

Krieger, A. M., & Green, P. E. (1999). A cautionary note on using internal cross validation to select the number of clusters. *Psychometrika, 64,* 341–353.

Krueger, R. F., Hicks, B. M., Patrick, C. J., Carlson, S. R., Iacono, W. G., & McGue, M. (2002). Etiologic connections among substance dependence, antisocial behavior, and personality: Modeling the externalizing spectrum. *Journal of Abnormal Psychology, 111,* 411–424.

Lahey, B. B. (2001). Should the combined and predominantly inattentive types of ADHD be considered distinct and unrelated disorders? Not now, at least. *Clinical Psychology Science and Practice, 8,* 494–497.

Lahey, B. B., Carlson, C. L., & Frick, P. J. (1997). Attention-deficit disorder without hyperactivity. In T. A. Widiger, A. J. Frances, H. A. Pincus, R. Ross, M. B. First, & W. Davis (Eds.), *DSM-IV sourcebook* (Vol. 3, pp. 163–188). Washington, DC: American Psychiatric Association.

LaHoste, G. J., Swanson, J. M., Wigal, S. B., Glabe, C., Wigal, T., King, N., et al. (1996). Dopamine D4 receptor polymorphism is associated with attention deficit hyperactivity disorder. *Molecular Psychiatry, 1,* 121–124.

Lazarsfeld, P. F., & Henry, N. W. (1968). *Latent structure analysis.* Boston: Houghton Mifflin.

Lenzenweger, M. F. (1999). Deeper into the schizotypy taxon: On the robust nature of maximum covariance analysis. *Journal of Abnormal Psychology, 108,* 182–187.

Lenzenweger, M. F. (2004). Consideration of the challenges, complications, and pitfalls of taxometric analysis. *Journal of Abnormal Psychology, 113,* 10–23.

Lenzenweger, M. F., & Korfine, L. (1992). Confirming the latent structure and base rate of schizotypy: A taxometric analysis. *Journal of Abnormal Psychology, 101,* 567–571.

Lenzenweger, M. F., & Korfine, L. (1995). Tracking the taxon: On the latent structure and base rate of schizotypy. In A. Raine, T. Lencz, & S. A. Mednick (Eds.), *Schizotypal personality disorder* (pp. 135–167). New York: Cambridge University Press.

Levy, D. L., Holzman, P. S., Matthysse, S., & Mendell, N. R. (1993). Eye tracking dysfunction and Schizophrenia. *Schizophrenia Bulletin, 19,* 461–536.

Lilienfeld, S. O., & Marino, L. (1995). Mental disorder as a Roschian concept: A critique of Wakefield's "harmful dysfunction" analysis. *Journal of Abnormal Psychology, 104,* 411–420.

Loeber, R., Farrington, D. P., Stouthamer-Loeber, M., & Van Kammen, W. B. (1998). *Antisocial behavior and mental health problems: Explanatory factors in childhood and adolescence.* Mahwah, NJ: Erlbaum.

Loeber, R., & Hay, D. (1997). Key issues in the development of aggression and violence from childhood to early adulthood. *Annual Review of Psychology, 48,* 371–410.

Loeber, R., & Keenan, K. (1994). Interaction between conduct disorder and its comorbid conditions: Effects of age and gender. *Clinical Psychology Review, 14,* 497–523.

Lu, R., Ho, S., Huang, H., & Lin, Y. (1988). The specificity of the dexamethasone suppression test in endogenous depressive patients. *Neuropsychopharmacology, 1,* 157–162.

Luby, J. L., Heffelfinger, A., Mrakotsky, C., Brown, K., Hessler, M., & Spitznagel, E. (2003). Alterations in stress cortisol reactivity in depressed preschoolers relative to psychiatric and no-disorder comparison groups. *Archives of General Psychiatry, 60,* 1248–1255.

Luby, J. L., Mrakotsky, C., Heffelfinger, A., Brown, K., & Spitznagel, E. (2004). Characteristics of depressed preschoolers with and without anhedonia: Evidence for a melancholic depressive subtype in young children. *American Journal of Psychiatry, 161,* 1998–2004.

Lynam, D. R. (1996). The early identification of chronic offenders: Who is the fledgling psychopath? *Psychological Bulletin, 120,* 209–234.

Lynam, D. R. (1998). Early identification of the fledgling psychopath: Locating the psychopathic child in the current nomenclature. *Journal of Abnormal Psychology, 107,* 566–575.

Lynam, D. R., Caspi, A., Moffitt, T. E., Wikström, P. H., Loeber, R., & Novak, S. (2000). The interaction between impulsivity and neighborhood context on offending: The effects of impulsivity are stronger in poorer neighborhoods. *Journal of Abnormal Psychology, 109,* 563–574.

MacCallum, R. C., Zhang, S., Preacher, K. J., & Rucker, D. D. (2002). On the practice of dichotomization of quantitative variables. *Psychological Methods, 7,* 19–40.

Macmillan, N. A., & Creelman, C. D. (1990). Response bias: Characteristics of detection theory, threshold theory and "nonparametric" indices. *Psychological Bulletin, 107,* 401–413.

Malik, M. L., & Beutler, L. E. (2002). The emergence of dissatisfaction with the DSM. In L. E. Beutler & M. L. Malik (Eds.), *Rethinking the DSM* (pp. 3–15). Washington, DC: American Psychological Association.

Malt, B. (1993). Concept structure and category boundaries. In G. V. Nakamura, D. L. Medin, & R. Taraban (Eds.), *Categorization by humans and machines: The psychology of learning and motivation: Advances in research and theory* (Vol. 29, pp. 363–390). San Diego, CA: Academic Press.

Manoach, D. S., Press, D. Z., Thangaraj, V., Searl, M. M., Goff, D. C., Halpern, E., et al. (1999). Schizophrenic subjects activate dorsolateral prefrontal cortex during a working memory task, as measured by fMRI. *Biological Psychiatry, 45,* 1128–1137.

Marcus, D. K., John, S. L., & Edens, J. F. (2004). A taxometric analysis of psychopathic personality. *Journal of Abnormal Psychology, 113,* 626–635.

McBurnett, K., Pfiffner, L. J., & Frick, P. J. (2001). Symptom properties as a function of ADHD type: An argument for continued study of sluggish cognitive tempo. *Journal of Abnormal Child Psychology, 29,* 207–213.

McGorry, P. D., Yung, A. R., Phillips, L. J., Yuen, H. P., Francey, S., Cosgrave, E. M., et al. (2002). Randomized controlled trial of interventions designed to reduce the risk of progression to first episode psychosis in a clinical sample with subthreshold symptoms. *Archives of General Psychiatry, 59,* 921–928.

McLachlan, G. J., & Basford, K. E. (1988). *Mixture models.* New York: Marcel Dekker.

McLachlan, G. J., & Peel, D. (2000). Finite mixture models. In D. L. Medin & R. Taraban (Eds.), *Categorization by humans and machines: The psychology of learning and motivation: Advances in research and theory* (Vol. 29, pp. 363–390). San Diego: Academic Press.

Meehl, P. E. (1962). Schizotaxia, schizotypy, Schizophrenia. *American Psychologist, 17,* 827–838.

Meehl, P. E. (1973a). Why I do not attend case conferences. In *Psychodiagnosis: Selected papers* (pp. 225–302). Minneapolis: University of Minnesota Press.

Meehl, P. E. (1973b). MAXCOV-HITMAX: A taxonomic search method for loose genetic syndromes. In *Psychodiagnosis: Selected papers* (pp. 200–224). Minneapolis: University of Minnesota Press.

Meehl, P. E. (1975). Hedonic capacity: Some conjectures. *Bulletin of the Menninger Clinic, 39,* 295–307.

Meehl, P. E. (1979). A funny thing happened to us on the way to the latent entities. *Journal of Personality Assessment, 43,* 563–581.

Meehl, P. E. (1989). Schizotaxia revisited. *Archives of General Psychiatry, 46,* 935–944.

Meehl, P. E. (1990). Toward an integrated theory of schizotaxia, schizotypy, and Schizophrenia. *Journal of Personality Disorders, 4,* 1–99.

Meehl, P. E. (1995a). Bootstraps taxometrics: Solving the classification problem in psychopathology. *American Psychologist, 50,* 266–275.

Meehl, P. E. (1995b). Extention of the MAXCOV-HITMAX taxometric procedure to situations of sizable nuisance covariance. In D. Lubinski & R. V. Dawis (Eds.), *Assessing individual differences in human behavior: New concepts, methods, and findings* (pp. 81–92). Palo Alto, CA: Davies-Black.

Meehl, P. E. (1996). MOXCOV pseudotaxonicity. *American Psychologist, 51,* 1184–1186.

Meehl, P. E. (1999). Clarifications about taxometric method. *Applied and Preventive Psychology, 8,* 165–174.

Meehl, P. E. (2001a). Comorbidity and taxometrics. *Clinical Psychology Science and Practice, 8,* 507–519.

Meehl, P. E. (2001b). Primary and secondary hypohedonia. *Journal of Abnormal Psychology, 110,* 188–193.

Meehl, P. E. (2004). What's in a taxon. *Journal of Abnormal Psychology, 113,* 39–43.

Meehl, P. E., & Yonce, L. J. (1994). Taxometric analysis: I. Detecting taxonicity with two quantitative indicators using means above and below a sliding cut (MAMBAC procedure). *Psychological Reports, 74,* 1059–1274.

Meehl, P. E., & Yonce, L. J. (1996). Taxometric analyses: II. Detecting taxonicity using covariance of two quantitative indicators in successive intervals of a third indicator. *Psychological Reports, 78,* 1091–1227.

Metzger, L. J., Paige, S. R., Carson, M. A., Lasko, N. B., Paulus, L. A., Pitman, R. K., et al. (2004). PTSD arousal and depression symptoms associated with increased right-sided parietal EEG asymmetry. *Journal of Abnormal Psychology, 113,* 324–329.

Milich, R., Balentine, A. C., & Lynam, D. R. (2001). ADHD combined type and ADHD predominantly inattentive type are distinct and unrelated disorders. *Clinical Psychology Science and Practice, 8,* 463–488.

Miller, J. N., & Ozonoff, S. (2000). The external validity of Asperger disorder: Lack of evidence from the domain of neuropsychology. *Journal of Abnormal Psychology, 109,* 227–238.

Miller, M. B. (1996). Limitations of Meehl's MAXCOV-HITMAX procedure. *American Psychologist, 51,* 554–556.

Milligan, G. W. (1981). A Monte Carlo study of thirty internal criterion measures for cluster analysis. *Psychometrika, 46,* 187–199.

Milligan, G. W., & Cooper, M. C. (1985). An examination of procedures for determining the number of clusters in a data set. *Psychometrika, 50,* 159–179.

Milligan, G. W., & Cooper, M. C. (1987). Methodology review: Clustering methods. *Applied Psychological Measurement, 11,* 329–354.

Moffitt, T. E. (1993). Adolescent-limited and life-course-persistent antisocial behavior: A developmental taxonomy. *Psychological Review, 100,* 674–701.

Murphy, E. A. (1964). One cause? Many causes? The argument from the bimodal distribution. *Journal of Chronic Disease, 17,* 301–324.

Muthén, B. O. (2001). Second-generation structural equation modeling with a combination of categorical and continuous latent variables: New opportunities for latent class/latent growth modeling. In A. Sayer & L. Collins (Eds.), *New methods for analysis of change* (pp. 291–322). Washington, DC: American Psychological Association.

Muthén, B. O., & Shedden, K. (1999). Finite mixture modeling with mixture outcomes using the EM algorithm. *Biometrics, 55,* 463–469.

Myers, M. G., Brown, S. A., & Mott, M. A. (1995). Preadolescent conduct disorder behaviors predict relapse and progression of addiction for adolescent alcohol and drug abusers. *Alcoholism: Clinical and Experimental Research, 19,* 1525–1536.

Nagin, D. S. (1999). Analyzing developmental trajectories: A semiparametric, group-based approach. *Psychological Methods, 4,* 139–157.

Nagin, D. S., & Tremblay, R. E. (1999). Trajectories of boys' physical aggression, opposition, and hyperactivity on the path to physical violent and nonviolent juvenile delinquency. *Child Development, 70,* 1181–1196.

Nagin, D. S., & Tremblay, R. E. (2001). Analyzing developmental trajectories of distinct but related behaviors: A group-based method. *Psychological Methods, 6,* 18–34.

Newcorn, J. H., Halperin, J. M., Jensen, P. S., Abikoff, H. B., Arnold, L. E., Cantwell, D. P., et al. (2001). Symptom profiles in children with ADHD: Effects of comorbidity and gender. *Journal of the American Academy of Child and Adolescent Psychiatry, 40,* 137–146.

Niccols, G. A. (1994). Fetal alcohol syndrome: Implications for psychologists. *Clinical Psychology Review, 14,* 91–111.

Nock, M. K. (2003). Progress review of the psychosocial treatment of child conduct problems. *Clinical Psychology Science and Practice, 10,* 1–28.

Nunnally, J. C., & Bernstein, I. H. (1994). *Psychometric theory* (3rd ed.). New York: McGraw-Hill.

Oakman, J. M., & Woody, E. Z. (1996). A taxometric analysis of hypnotic susceptibility. *Journal of Personality and Social Psychology, 71,* 980–991.

Orr, S. P., Metzger, L. J., Lasko, N. B., Macklin, M. L., Hu, F. B., Shalev, A. Y., et al. (2003). Physiologic responses to sudden, loud tones in monozygotic twins discordant for combat exposure: Association with posttraumatic stress disorder. *Archives of General Psychiatry, 60,* 283–288.

Osterling, J. A., Dawson, G., & Munson, J. A. (2002). Early recognition of 1-year-old infants with Autism spectrum disorders versus mental retardation. *Development and Psychopathology, 14,* 239–251.

Owens, E. B., Hinshaw, S. P., Kraemer, H. C., Arnold, L. E., Abikoff, H. B., Cantwell, D. P., et al. (2003). Which treatment for whom for ADHD? Moderators of treatment response in the MTA. *Journal of Consulting and Clinical Psychology, 71,* 540–552.

Ozonoff, S., Rogers, S. J., & Pennington, B. F. (1991). Asperger's syndrome: Evidence of an empirical distinction from high-functioning Autism. *Journal of Child Psychology and Psychiatry, 32,* 1107–1122.

Patrick, C. J., Bernat, E. M., Malone, S. M., Iacono, W. G., Krueger, R. F., & McGue, M. (2005). *P300 amplitude as an indicator of vulnerability to externalizing psychopathology in adolescent males.* Manuscript submitted for publication.

Porjesz, B., Begleiter, H., & Garozzo, R. (1980). Visual evoked potential correlates of information processing deficits in chronic alcoholics. In H. Begleiter (Ed.), *Biological effects of alcohol* (pp. 603–623). New York: Plenum Press.

Preskorn, S. H., & Baker, B. (2002). The overlap of DSM-IV syndromes: Potential implications for the practice of polypsychopharmacology, psychiatric drug development, and the human genome project. *Journal of Psychiatric Practice, 8,* 170–177.

Raine, A., Mellingen, K., Liu, J., Venebles, P., & Mednick, S. A. (2003). Effects of environmental enrichment at ages 3–5 years on schizotypal personality and antisocial behavior at ages 17 and 23 years. *American Journal of Psychiatry, 160,* 1627–1635.

Raine, A., Venables, P. H., Dalais, C., Mellingen, K., Reynolds, C., & Mednick, S. A. (2001). Early educational and health enrichment at age 3–5 years is associated with increased autonomic and central nervous system arousal and orienting at age 11 years: Evidence from the Mauritius Child Health Project. *Psychophysiology, 38,* 254–266.

Rajendar, G. K. (1996). The influence of positive and negative wording and issue involvement on responses to Likert scales in marketing research. *Journal of the Market Research Society, 38,* 235–246.

Richters, J. E. (1997). The Hubble hypothesis and the developmentalist's dilemma. *Development and Psychopathology, 9,* 193–229.

Richters, J. E., & Cicchetti, D. (1993). Mark Twain meets *DSM-III-R:* Conduct disorder, development, and the concept of harmful dysfunction. *Development and Psychopathology, 5,* 5–29.

Robins, E., & Guze, S. B. (1970). Establishment of diagnostic validity in psychiatric illness: Its application to Schizophrenia. *American Journal of Psychiatry, 126,* 983–987.

Robinson, E. A., Eyberg, S. M., & Ross, A. W. (1980). The standardization of an inventory of child conduct problem behaviors. *Journal of Clinical Child Psychology, 9,* 22–28.

Rogosa, D., Brandt, D., & Zimowski, M. (1982). A growth curve approach to the measurement of change. *Psychological Bulletin, 92,* 726–748.

Rosch, E., & Lloyd, B. (1978). *Cognition and categorization.* New York: Wiley.

Ross, R. G. (2003). Early expression of a pathophysiological feature of Schizophrenia: Saccadic intrusions into smooth-pursuit eye movements in school-age children vulnerable to Schizophrenia. *Journal of the American Academy of Child and Adolescent Psychiatry, 42,* 468–476.

Ruiz, M., Lind, U., Gåfvels, M., Eggertsen, G., Carlstedt-Duke, J., Nilsson, L., et al. (2001). Characterization of two novel mutations in the glucocorticoid receptor gene in patients with primary cortisol resistance. *Clinical Endocrinology, 55,* 363–371.

Ruma, P. R., Burke, R. V., & Thompson, R. W. (1996). Group parent training: Is it effective for children of all ages? *Behavior Therapy, 27,* 159–169.

Ruscio, A., & Ruscio, J. (2002). The latent structure of analogue depression: Should the Beck Depression Inventory be used to classify groups? *Psychological Assessment, 14,* 135–145.

Ruscio, J., & Ruscio, A. (2000). Informing the continuity controversy: A taxometric analysis of depression. *Journal of Abnormal Psychology, 109,* 473–487.

Ruscio, J., & Ruscio, A. M. (2004a). Clarifying boundary issues in psychopathology: The role of taxometrics in a comprehensive program of structural research. *Journal of Abnormal Psychology, 113,* 24–38.

Ruscio, J., & Ruscio, A. M. (2004b). A conceptual and methodological checklist for conducting a taxometric investigation. *Behavior Therapy, 35,* 403–447.

Ruscio, J., Ruscio, A. M., & Keane, T. M. (2004). Using taxometric analysis to distinguish a small latent taxon from a latent dimension with positively skewed indicators: The case of involuntary defeat syndrome. *Journal of Abnormal Psychology, 113,* 145–154.

Rush, A. J., Giles, D. E., Schlesser, M. A., & Orsulak, P. J. (1997). Dexamethasone response, thyrotropin-releasing hormone stimulation, rapid eye movement latency and subtypes of depression. *Biological Psychiatry, 41,* 915–928.

Rush, A. J., & Weissenburger, J. E. (1994). Melancholic symptom features and DSM-IV. *American Journal of Psychiatry, 151,* 489–498.

Rutter, M., Dunn, J., Plomin, R., Simonoff, E., Pickles, A., Maughan, B., et al. (1997). Integrating nature and nurture: Implications of person-environment correlations and interactions for developmental psychopathology. *Development and Psychopathology, 9,* 335–364.

Rutter, M., & Sroufe, L. A. (2000). Developmental psychopathology: Concepts and challenges. *Development and Psychopathology, 12,* 265–296.

Saal, F. E., Downey, R. G., & Lahey, M. A. (1980). Rating the ratings: Assessing the psychometric quality of rating data. *Psychological Bulletin, 88,* 413–428.

Schmidt, N. B., Kotov, R., & Joiner, T. E. (2004). *Taxometrics.* Washington, DC: American Psychological Association.

Semin, G. R., & Rosch, E. (1981). Activation of bipolar prototypes in attribute inferences. *Journal of Experimental Social Psychology, 17,* 472–484.

Shaw, D. S., Gilliom, M., Ingoldsby, E. M., & Nagin, D. S. (2003). Trajectories leading to school-age conduct problems. *Developmental Psychology, 39,* 189–200.

Shekim, W. O., Dekirmenjian, H., Chapel, J. L., & Davis, J. M. (1982). Effects of d-amphetamine on urinary metabolites of dopamine and norepinephrine in hyperactive boys. *American Journal of Psychiatry, 139,* 485–488.

Shekim, W. O., Sinclair, E., Glaser, R., Horwitz, E., Javaid, J., & Bylund, D. B. (1987). Norepinephrine and dopamine metabolites and educational variables in boys with attention deficit disorder and hyperactivity. *Journal of Child Neurology, 2,* 50–56.

Simon, D., Pham, L. B., Le, Q. A., & Holyoak, K. J. (2001). The emergence of coherence over the course of decision making. *Journal of Experimental Psychology: Learning, Memory, and Cognition, 27,* 1250–1260.

Skilling, T. A., Harris, G. T., Rice, M. T., & Quinsey, V. L. (2001). Identifying persistently antisocial offenders using the Hare Psychopathy Checklist and the DSM-IV antisocial personality disorder criteria. *Psychological Assessment, 14,* 27–38.

Skilling, T. A., Quinsey, V. L., & Craig, W. M. (2001). Evidence of a taxon underlying serious antisocial behavior in boys. *Criminal Justice and Behavior, 28,* 450–470.

Skuse, D. H. (2001). Endophenotypes in child psychiatry. *British Journal of Psychiatry, 178,* 395–396.

Smalley, S. L., Bailey, J. N., Palmer, C. G., Cantwell, D. P., McGough, J. J., Del-Homme, M. A., et al. (1998). Evidence that the dopamine D4 receptor is a susceptibility gene in attention deficit hyperactivity disorder. *Molecular Psychiatry, 3,* 427–430.

Smith, E. E. (1995). Concepts and categorization. In E. Smith & D. Osherson (Eds.), *Thinking: An invitation to cognitive science* (2nd ed., Vol. 3, pp. 3–33). Cambridge, MA: MIT Press.

Sonuga-Barke, E. J. S. (1998). Categorical models of childhood disorder: A conceptual and empirical analysis. *Journal of Child Psychology and Psychiatry, 39,* 115–133.

Spitzer, R. L. (1997). From Feighner to RDC, *DSM-III, DSM-III-R, DSM-IV,* and ICD-10. In *The Feighner criteria: Their role in psychiatric progress* (pp. 11–13). Secaucus, NJ: Churchill Communications.

Sroufe, L. A. (1997). Psychopathology as an outcome of development. *Development and Psychopathology, 9,* 251–268.

Sroufe, L. A., & Rutter, M. (1984). The domain of developmental psychopathology. *Child Development, 55,* 17–29.

Stein, M. B., Jang, K. L., Taylor, S., Vernon, P. A., & Livesley, W. J. (2002). Genetic and environmental influences on trauma exposure and posttraumatic stress disorder symptoms: A twin study. *American Journal of Psychiatry, 159,* 1675–1681.

Stevens, S. S. (1951). *Handbook of experimental psychology*. New York: Wiley.

Strong, D. R., Brown, R. A., Kahler, C. W., Lloyd-Richardson, E. E., & Niaura, R. (2004). Depression proneness in treatment-seeking smokers: A taxometric analysis. *Personality and Individual Differences, 36,* 1155–1170.

Strube, M. J. (1989). Evidence for the Type in Type A behavior: A taxometric analysis. *Journal of Personality and Social Psychology, 56,* 972–987.

Swanson, J. M., & Castellanos, F. X. (2002). Biological bases of ADHD: Neuroanatomy, genetics, and pathophysiology. In P. S. Jensen & J. R. Cooper (Eds.), *Attention deficit hyperactivity disorder* (pp. 7-1 to 7-20). Kingston, NJ: Civic Research Institute.

Taylor, J., Iacono, W. G., & McGue, M. (2000). Evidence for a genetic etiology for early onset delinquency. *Journal of Abnormal Psychology, 109,* 634–643.

Tonidandel, S., & Overall, J. E. (2004). Determining the number of clusters by sampling with replacement. *Psychological Methods, 9,* 238–249.

Tylka, T. L., & Subich, L. M. (2003). Revisiting the latent structure of eating disorders: Taxometric analyses with nonbehavioral indicators. *Journal of Counseling Psychology, 50,* 276–286.

Tyrka, A. R., Cannon, T. D., Haslam, N., Mednick, S. A., Schulsinger, F., Schulsinger, H., et al. (1995). The latent structure of schizotypy: I. Premorbid indicators of a taxon in individuals at risk for Schizophrenia-spectrum disorders. *Journal of Abnormal Psychology, 104,* 173–183.

Tyrka, A. R., Haslam, N., & Cannon, T. D. (1995). Detection of a longitudinally stable taxon of individuals at risk for Schizophrenia spectrum disorders. In A. Raine, T. Lencz, & S. A. Mednick (Eds.), *Schizotypal personality disorder* (pp. 168–191). New York: Cambridge University Press.

Vaidya, C. J., Austin, G., Kirkorian, G., Ridlehuber, H. W., Desmond, J. E., Glover, G. H., et al. (1998). Selective effects of methylphenidate in attention deficit hyperactivity disorder: A functional magnetic resonance study. *Proceedings of the National Academy of Sciences, 95,* 14494–14499.

van Praag, H. M. (1990). Two-tier diagnosis in psychiatry. *Psychiatry Research, 34,* 1–11.

Volkmar, F. R., Klin, A., & Pauls, D. (1998). Nosological and genetic aspects of Asperger syndrome. *Journal of Autism and Developmental Disorders, 28,* 457–463.

Volkmar, F. R., Klin, A., Schultz, R. T., Rubin, E., & Bronen, R. (2000). Asperger's disorder. *American Journal of Psychiatry, 157,* 262–267.

Volkmar, F. R., Klin, A., Siegel, B., Szatmari, P., Lord, C., Campbell, M., et al. (1994). Field trial for autistic disorder in DSM-IV. *American Journal of Psychiatry, 151,* 1361–1367.

Waldman, I. D., & Lilienfeld, S. O. (2001). Applications of taxometric methods to problems of comorbidity: Perspectives and challenges. *Clinical Psychology Science and Practice, 8,* 520–527.

Waller, N. G., Kaiser, H. A., Illian, J. B., & Manry, M. (1998). A comparison of the classification capabilities of the 1-dimensional Kohonen neural network with two partitioning and three hierarchical cluster analysis algorithms. *Psychometrika, 63,* 5–22.

Waller, N. G., & Meehl, P. E. (1998). *Multivariate taxometric procedures: Distinguishing types from continua*. Newbury Park, CA: Sage.

Waller, N. G., Putnam, F. W., & Carlson, E. B. (1996). Types of dissociation and dissociative types: A taxometric analysis of dissociative experiences. *Psychological Methods, 1,* 300–321.

Waller, N. G., & Ross, C. A. (1997). The prevalence and biometric structure of pathological dissociation in the general population: Taxometric and behavior genetic findings. *Journal of Abnormal Psychology, 106,* 499–510.

Waters, E., & Beauchaine, T. P. (2003). Are there really patterns of attachment? Comment on Fraley and Spieker (2003). *Developmental Psychology, 39,* 417–422.

Webster-Stratton, C., & Hammond, M. (1997). Treating children with early onset conduct problems: A comparison of child and parent training interventions. *Journal of Consulting and Clinical Psychology, 65,* 93–109.

Webster-Stratton, C., Reid, M. J., & Hammond, M. (2002). Social skills and problem solving training for children with early onset conduct problems: Who benefits? *Journal of Child Psychology and Psychiatry, 42,* 943–952.

Werry, J. S. (1997). Severe conduct disorder: Some key issues. *Canadian Journal of Psychiatry, 42,* 577–583.

Widiger, T. A. (2001). What can be learned from taxometric analyses? *Clinical Psychology Science and Practice, 8,* 528–533.

Williamson, D. A., Womble, L. G., Smeets, M. A. M., Netemeyer, R. G., Thaw, J. M., Kutlesic, V., et al. (2002). Latent structure of eating disorders symptoms: A factor analytic and taxometric investigation. *American Journal of Psychiatry, 159,* 412–418.

Winokur, G., Zimmerman, M., & Cadoret, R. (1988). Cause the Bible tells me so. *Archives of General Psychiatry, 45,* 683–684.

Woodward, S. A., Lenzenweger, M. F., Kagan, J., Snidman, N., & Arcus, D. (2000). Taxonic structure of infant reactivity: Evidence from a taxometric perspective. *Psychological Science, 11,* 296–301.

CHAPTER 24

A Developmental Psychopathology Approach to the Prevention of Mental Health Disorders

NICHOLAS S. IALONGO, FRED A. ROGOSCH, DANTE CICCHETTI, SHEREE L. TOTH,
JACQUELYN BUCKLEY, HANNO PETRAS, and JENAE NEIDERHISER

INTRODUCTION

According to the World Health Organization (2003), there are 450 million people worldwide affected by mental or behavioral problems at any one time. In the United States alone, the National Institutes of Mental Health (2001) estimate that 22.1% of Americans ages 18 and older suffer from a diagnosable mental disorder in a given year, which translates into approximately 44.3 million people. The consequences of having a mental disorder can be severe. For example, persons with mental disorders are often subjected to social isolation and have a poor quality of life. Furthermore, mental disorders account for 4 of the top 10 causes of disability, and persons with mental disorders have an increased risk for health problems and increased rates of mortality.

The numbers are staggering, and most people would agree that it is better to prevent the emergence of mental disorders and prevent suffering rather than waiting for a disorder to develop and then offer treatment. The prevention of mental and substance abuse disorders is not an easy task, however, and requires a complex understanding of both typical and atypical development, a strong underlying theory guiding preventive efforts, and a solid understanding of the sequential steps required to develop effective prevention programs.

The overarching goal of this chapter is to elaborate a developmental psychopathology approach to prevention science. In the first part of the chapter, we review basic research on normal and abnormal development and developmental psychopathology and articulate its integral relation to preventive interventions. As theory informs practice, practice also informs theory. Accordingly, we go on to describe how results from preventive intervention trials are uniquely able to serve as tests of developmental theory. "Prevention" is a widely, and often misused, term. We offer a brief history of the terminology associated with prevention and describe the prevention research cycle that takes into account the planned, sequential steps necessary to develop strong prevention programs that have the opportunity to promote the best outcomes as well as provide a wealth of information for developmental theory. We also discuss the interface of developmental psychopathology, epidemiology, and public health as it relates to prevention. Numerous prevention programs and outcomes examples are offered from

Preparation of this chapter was supported by grants from National Institutes of Mental Health and Drug Abuse to Drs. Ialongo and Cicchetti (Ialongo, MH066247, MH57005, DA11796; Cicchetti, MH 450\27, MH54643, DA12903).

large-scale prevention trials in Baltimore, Maryland, as well as prevention programs targeted for the prevention of the negative sequelae of child maltreatment and maternal depressive disorder. The chapter concludes with directions for future research in preventive interventions.

THE IMPORTANCE OF UTILIZING AND TRANSLATING BASIC RESEARCH KNOWLEDGE ON NORMAL AND ABNORMAL DEVELOPMENT INTO PREVENTIVE INTERVENTIONS

The overarching and pragmatic goal of prevention science is to intervene in the course of development to reduce or eliminate the emergence of maladaptation and psychopathology. As such, a complex understanding of the course of normal development is essential to conceptualize how deviations in normal ontogenesis give rise to psychopathology. The discipline of developmental psychopathology, with its keen interest in the dialectic between normal and abnormal development, is thus uniquely poised to provide the theoretical foundations for prevention science.

An organizational perspective on development is central to developmental psychopathology (Cicchetti, 1993; Cicchetti & Schneider-Rosen, 1986; Cicchetti & Sroufe, 1978; Sroufe & Rutter, 1984). From this vantage point, development is conceptualized as a series of qualitative reorganizations within and among multiple domains of biological and psychological functioning. The individual successively advances from a state of diffuse undifferentiation to levels of increasingly differentiated and hierarchically organized biological and behavioral complexity (Werner & Kaplan, 1963). Across development, qualitative reorganizations among biological and psychological systems occur as the developing individual progressively is challenged with a series of stage-salient developmental tasks (e.g., physiological homeostasis, differentiation and regulation of affects, development of a secure attachment relationship, emergence of a positive and autonomous self, representational capacities, development of effective peer relationships, adaptation to school). How the individual strives to adapt to these developmental challenges influences the competence of functioning and the preparedness of the individual to successfully negotiate subsequent developmental tasks. Through progressive differentiation and hierarchic integration, the quality of adaptation at successive stages of development is incorporated into the reorganization of developmental systems. In this way, coherence of the individual is maintained over time (Sroufe, 1979). Nevertheless, there is both continuity and discontinuity in the course of development. Competent adaptation at one period of development increases the likelihood of later competence, whereas incompetent adaptation promotes the probability of later incompetence. However, based on experience and the degree of success in meeting new developmental challenges, change in the quality of adaptation may occur (Cicchetti & Tucker, 1994).

From this perspective, maladaptation and psychopathology evolve from progressive liabilities in the developmental organization of biological and psychological systems, resulting in the undermining of the individual's efforts to adapt to experience effectively. The organizational developmental conceptualization appreciates that psychopathology can be differentiated both as a maladaptive extreme on a continuum of functioning and as a qualitatively distinct disorder discontinuous from normal functioning (Rutter & Garmezy, 1983; Rutter & Sroufe, 2000).

This theoretical perspective directs prevention science to focus on the progressive organization of developmental competencies and incompetencies in the developmental course in order to structure preventive efforts. To effect change in the course of development and avert psychopathological outcomes, preventive interventions should be guided by an emphasis on promoting competence and reducing ineffective resolution of the stage-salient developmental tasks at different periods of development. In so doing, deflection of adaptation onto more adaptive developmental pathways may be achieved, thereby enhancing the individual's capacity for a greater likelihood of subsequent successful adaptation. Thus, attending to developmental competencies and liabilities rather than a sole focus on symptom reduction is crucial. Inherent in this developmental perspective is the value of early intervention, before developmental liabilities may become more consolidated. For those individuals at a particular developmental period who already are more vulnerable due to a compromised developmental organization, more intensive preventive efforts may be needed to promote accessing of more competent development pathways.

From the organizational perspective, it is clear that diverse pathways of development may unfold, as each developmental period presents new opportunities and challenges. Accordingly, the principles of multifinality and equifinality in developmental pathways are central to a developmental psychopathology conceptualization (Cicchetti & Rogosch, 1996). Multifinality implies that diverse and varied outcomes will occur in development despite a common early liability or risk condition. In turn, equifinality specifies that a common pathological outcome will eventuate from various origins and developmental routes. Prevention scientists thus realize that there are multiple pathways to disorder and dysfunction and that varied causal processes likely operate for

different individuals. Moreover, early vulnerability does not doom the individual to later disturbance, but rather, subsequent experience may promote the overcoming of early liabilities. Understanding pathways of resilient adaptation among individuals exposed to extreme risks and early adversity presents an important opportunity for prevention researchers (Luthar & Cicchetti, 2000). Identification of processes contributing to self-righting in the course of development for these individuals may be particularly valuable to incorporate into the design of preventive interventions (Cicchetti & Rogosch, 1997; Luthar & Cicchetti, 2000). Longitudinal research in developmental psychopathology is vital for delineating the varied developmental pathways that ensue for individuals experiencing high-risk conditions and for tracking the emergence of psychopathology. Such research is invaluable for delineating the mechanisms that translate risk and vulnerability into dysfunction (Rutter & Sroufe, 2000), forming a foundation on which to base preventive efforts.

A cornerstone of research in developmental psychopathology has been focused on risk and protective factors and their role in understanding psychopathological development. The dynamic interplay of risk and protective factors influences the developmental course by affecting the quality of the organization of biological and psychological systems as the individual develops. With the expansion of attention to risk factors, developmental psychopathology research has incorporated probabilistic, rather than deterministic, models of dysfunction. Moreover, consideration of individual risk factors in isolation is often insufficient to explain developmental variation. Rather, different risk factors frequently tend to co-occur, and the cumulative effects of multiple risk factors have been found to be particularly detrimental to competent development, thereby promoting the development of psychopathology (Deater-Deckard, Dodge, Bates, & Pettit, 1998; Rutter, 1979; Sameroff, Seifer, Barocas, Zax, & Greenspan, 1987). Thus, models elucidating the co-action of multiple risk factors are important, and risk factors at multiple levels of biological and psychological organization need to be considered (Cicchetti & Blender, 2004; Cicchetti & Dawson, 2002). In this regard, understanding the interplay between environmental and genetic risks is crucial, and models of gene-environment correlation and gene-environment interaction illustrate the complexity of risk mechanisms that operate to engender psychopathology. Additionally, research has demonstrated that specific risk factors may have greater salience in influencing the quality of developmental adaptation at different periods of the life course than at others (Kazdin, Kraemer, Kessler, Kupfer, & Offord, 1997). Moreover, different risk factors may contribute probabilistically to the emergence of dysfunction, whereas other risk factors may be more influential in the maintenance of dysfunction or in subsequent relapse (Post, 1992).

In addition to risk factors, the other side of the equation involves a full appreciation of the protective factors that individuals experience across development. Protective factors may promote competence in their own right. Alternatively, some protective factors may be influential in safeguarding competent functioning, particularly in the context of specific risks. Research on protective factors is vitally important for identifying processes that contribute to resilient adaptation in the face of risk (Luthar, 2003; Luthar, Cicchetti, & Becker, 2000; Masten, 2001; Masten et al., 2004). Understanding the dynamic interplay of risk and protective factors is central to building models of prevention. Broadly speaking, prevention efforts are largely based on the goals of reducing the impact of identified risk factors as well as enhancing the complementary ameliorative effects of identified protective factors. Through increasing the relative balance of protective processes over risk factors, the potential for righting the developmental course, attaining adaptive developmental pathways, and reducing the emergence of psychopathology may be achieved (Cicchetti & Lynch, 1993; Cicchetti & Rizley, 1981).

PREVENTIVE INTERVENTION TRIALS AS TESTS OF DEVELOPMENTAL THEORY

The practical application of prevention science is clear. Effective prevention programs have the potential to significantly impact the developmental pathways for individuals and improve subsequent adjustment or reduce the emergence of future problems (Durlak, 1997). Although the quintessential goal of prevention science is to right the developmental course and prevent the emergence of psychopathology, the results of prevention trials also have important implications for developmental theory by providing a wealth of information about the developmental processes of typical and atypical development (Cicchetti & Hinshaw, 2002; Cicchetti & Toth, 1991, 1992; Hinshaw, 2002; Kellam & Rebok, 1992). Developmental theory forms the foundation for the practice of prevention, and the practice of prevention needs to form a circular link back to theory to advance both the theory and resulting practice. Because prevention scientists are often, and understandably, most interested in the practical outcomes of a prevention program, the research design and implementation of the program are often not optimal for informing developmental theory. The following section describes

a conceptual and practical framework for designing prevention programs that are maximally informative to developmental theory.

A CONCEPTUAL FRAMEWORK FOR DEFINING RISK IN THE CONTEXT OF DESIGNING PREVENTIVE INTERVENTIONS

Prevention scientists attempt to reduce the impact of identified risk factors, but the term "risk factor" has not always been consistently applied in research and policy (Kraemer et al., 1997). A risk factor has been defined as a measurable characteristic of each subject in a specified population that precedes the outcome of interest and divides the population into two groups: a high- and low-risk group (Kazdin et al., 1997; Kraemer et al., 1997). According to Kraemer et al., the subject does not necessarily have to be an individual person, but could be a family, school, community, or other unit of interest. Furthermore, the characteristic may be on the individual level (e.g., gender, size of school) or contextual level (e.g., family context, location of school). Overall, the probability of the outcome must be higher in the high-risk group than in the low-risk group (Kraemer et al., 1997) for a characteristic to be considered a potential risk factor. However, once this significant association is established between the risk factor and the outcome, researchers need to consider the clinical significance of the risk factor. According to Jacobi, Hayward, de Zwaan, Kraemer, and Agras (2004), clinical significance can be determined by understanding the magnitude or potency of the risk factor. Potency has been defined as the ability of the risk factor to achieve maximal discrepancy for dichotomizing the population into high- and low-risk groups (Kraemer et al., 1997). Potency can be expressed by a variety of summary measures including odds ratios, risk ratios, relative risk, and attributable risk.

The population and outcome of interest must be well defined before evaluation of risk factors and before the typology of risk factors can be defined. Jacobi et al. (2004) clearly depict risk factor typology and the corresponding study designs necessary for identification of risk factors. Most important, a risk must occur *before* the observed outcome. That is, a characteristic can be categorized as a risk factor only if a subject's risk status precedes the outcome of interest. If a characteristic meets all requirements for definition of a risk factor but fails to precede the outcome of interest (e.g., occurs concomitantly with the outcome), then it is considered merely a correlate of the outcome. A correlate is simply a statistical association between the factor and the outcome. A risk factor can therefore be considered a special type of correlate that occurs before the outcome (Jacobi et al., 2004; Kraemer et al., 1997). An additional typology of risk factors includes a *fixed marker,* which is a risk factor that cannot be changed (e.g., race); a *variable risk factor,* a factor that can be changed or changes spontaneously (e.g., age); a *variable marker,* a variable risk factor where manipulation of the marker does not change the risk of the outcome; and a *causal risk factor,* which is a variable risk factor that changes the risk of the outcome as a result of experimental manipulation (Jacobi et al., 2004).

Determining whether a characteristic is a correlate can be discerned from cross-sectional, epidemiological, case-control, or family history study designs. Because of the precedence requirement, longitudinal studies are the best designs to determine whether a given characteristic meets the requirements for a risk factor. Cross-sectional and longitudinal research designs are both well equipped to discern fixed markers, and longitudinal studies are well suited for discovering variable risk factors. Knowledge gained from these types of studies is limited, however, to inferences about risk factors as causal mechanisms. Although the precedence criterion for risk factors can be met through these studies, it is only through experimental manipulation that causality can be determined. Just because a risk factor consistently precedes an outcome such as a mental disorder, this does not necessarily mean that the risk factor *causes* the disorder. Causality is important for prevention scientists to be maximally effective in preventing the onset or diminishing the effects of mental disorders. A randomized clinical trial, whether preventive or therapeutic in nature, is the only design that will allow researchers to discern whether a variable risk factor is a variable marker or a causal risk factor. Although various research designs provide important information for prevention researchers, from exploratory longitudinal studies to identify definitive risk factors to randomized clinical trials to test the causal status of risk factors that precede the onset of a disorder (Jacobi et al., 2004), it is only the randomized clinical trial design that will allow researchers to make definitive statements about malleability and causality of risk factors.

DISTINGUISHING BETWEEN MEDIATORS AND MODERATORS IN PREVENTION RESEARCH

As Kraemer, Wilson, Fairburn, and Agras (2002) point out, the distinction between mediators and moderators of intervention effects is important for prevention researchers not just conceptually, but also for understanding the importance of each for prevention program evaluation, which in turn informs developmental theory. Simply stated, treatment moderators determine what treatment works for whom and under what conditions (Baron & Kenny, 1986; Kraemer et al., 2002). Moderators are third variables that affect the direction or strength of the relationship between predictor and outcome variables, and can be qualitative (e.g., gender) or quantitative (e.g., level of reinforcement) in nature (Baron & Kenny, 1986). Ideally, moderating variables are uncorrelated with either the predictor or the outcome variable, but will have an interactive effect with treatment or intervention on the outcome (Baron & Kenny, 1986; Kraemer et al., 2002). Presence of an interaction between moderators and outcomes does not explain the overall effect of treatment, but will help researchers understand individual differences in the effect of treatment. For example, if gender is a moderating variable, it will indicate for whom the intervention will have the most significant effect (e.g., females; Kraemer et al., 2002), but this does not suggest that gender is the causal factor for the observed improved outcomes for females. Even powerful programs will not prevent the targeted disorder for some people; understanding moderators and therefore understanding who is most likely to benefit from the prevention program will help researchers to clarify inclusionary and exclusionary criteria for their program to maximize power in randomized trials (Kraemer et al., 2002).

Although moderators are important for understanding who will be the most responsive to a prevention program, it is treatment mediators that will identify mechanisms of change, or causal links between the prevention program and program outcomes (Kraemer et al., 2002). Identifying mediators will help researchers to understand why program effects occur and identify the mechanism through which the prevention program achieves its positive outcomes, or lack of positive outcomes (Baron & Kenny, 1986; Kraemer et al., 2002). In a prevention trial, determining whether a variable functions as a mediator depends on the extent to which the variable accounts for the relationship between the predictor variables and the outcome of interest (Baron & Kenny, 1986). In other words, a mediator "represents the generative mechanism through which the focal independent variable is able to influence the dependent variable of interest" (Baron & Kenny, 1986, p. 1173); these mechanisms are causal links (Kraemer et al., 2002). Mediators should be strongly related to both the predictor variable and the outcome in a prevention trial so that the intervention condition should predict a change in the mediator, which will in turn be significantly associated with a change in the outcome (Baron & Kenny, 1986; Kraemer et al., 2002).

Tests of mediation in mental health and substance abuse research are severely lacking (Hinshaw, 2002) but are necessary for understanding mechanisms of change in prevention trials and the underlying theory guiding the prevention trial. If a change in a hypothesized mediator is not associated with a change in outcome, or if a change in outcome is observed in the absence of a change in the mediator variable, there may be a problem with the prevention theory (Coie et al., 1993). Furthermore, tests of mediation can allow researchers to elucidate intervention components that are most important to elicit change in the mediating variable, and therefore most important for achieving the desired outcomes (Kraemer et al., 2002).

Prevention scientists need to be cognizant of developmental variables (e.g., age) when examining mediators and moderators of prevention program outcomes. A program to prevent depression, for example, may or may not achieve the same outcomes for middle school students as high school students. If the program achieves similar positive outcomes across the age groups, then developmental variations among participants may not be important to achieving program outcomes. If it is found that age is in fact a moderator, then critical periods in the developmental process of depression can be revealed, including the most effective time to implement a program to prevent depression to achieve the best outcomes (Rutter, 1988).

Identifying mediators and moderators is essential for prevention researchers who want to help the largest number of people with a judicious use of resources. Knowing for whom the treatment works and understanding mechanisms of change in prevention programs will allow prevention scientists to develop the most effective programs for the largest number of people across all levels of risk. Identification of the key ingredients of programs is also possible; programs can then be streamlined so that ineffective program components are modified or eliminated.

RANDOMIZED PREVENTION TRIALS

As noted previously, randomized clinical trials are optimal for determining malleability and causality and whether a prevention program works. The purpose of this section is to discuss why randomized trials are considered the gold standard in prevention research and to describe what could be considered the essential elements of prevention trials that allow prevention research to fully inform developmental theory. The theoretical and methodological guidelines presented here are drawn primarily from Howe, Reiss, and Yuh (2002), who focus on methodological issues associated with randomized prevention trials, and Coie et al. (1993), who present a conceptual framework for studying the prevention of human disorders.

First and foremost, as stressed previously, is the need for prevention researchers to utilize randomized clinical trial designs. Howe et al. (2002) argue for a hybrid design, called *randomized prevention trials* (RPTs), which combines elements of experimental clinical designs with longitudinal designs. RPTs are uniquely able to test whether the course of psychopathology can be altered through experimental manipulation. The challenge for prevention trials is to provide evidence that the resulting change in the later course of psychopathology is due to the trial itself and not confounding factors. RPTs are better able to do this by utilizing a control or comparison group, with random assignment of participants to intervention or control group conditions. Successful randomization greatly reduces the likelihood that group assignment will be correlated with any other third variable, as well as being better able to control for other possible confounding variables. Results from methodologically sound RPTs will increase confidence in the conclusion that it was the prevention program that led to the changes in outcomes, not a host of other variables that could also be associated with the change in outcome.

The hybrid design espoused by Howe et al. (2002) also includes elements of longitudinal designs, such as repeated measurement of risk and protective factors over the duration of the study. Repeated measurement can test whether change in risk or protective factors is related to change in likelihood of psychopathology. These repeated measures should occur not only with the prevention group, but also with the control group to understand naturally occurring developmental trajectories. Additional information about randomized trails can be found elsewhere (e.g., Friedman, Furberg, & DeMets, 1998; Meinert & Tonascia, 1986). The purpose of this section is not to provide detailed descriptions of randomized trials, but rather to discuss how to set up randomized prevention trials that will bear the most fruit for theoretical implications.

Even in the context of an RPT, prevention programs will have an effect only if the *targeted risk factors associated with the outcome are malleable.* The ability to actually change a risk factor is an essential precondition for using prevention trials to test theory (Howe et al., 2002). Some factors may change naturally, but it is through a prevention trial that the malleability, or *our* ability to change risk or protective factors, can be determined.

The *intervention components must also be linked conceptually to risk or maintaining factors* for certain forms of psychopathology (Hinshaw, 2002). The focus of the prevention trial is to alter risk factors or mediating processes in such a way as to reduce emergence of a disorder; therefore, components that will address those factors or processes need to be included in the intervention design.

An RPT design also allows researchers to test whether a change in risk and protective factors is related to a change in the likelihood of developing psychopathology. Because of the inclusion of a control group and because, by definition, the prevention program is implemented before the emergence of the disorder, it can also be determined whether the change in risk and protective factors preceded the onset of psychopathology, or conversely, whether the emergence of psychopathology shaped the risk and protective factors (Howe et al., 2002). Furthermore, it can lend support for the conclusion that the targeted risk and protective factors were true causal agents and that the change was not due to any other extraneous variables (Howe et al., 2002; Kraemer et al., 1997). Developmental psychopathology theory is supported if the specific risk factors targeted by the intervention have been reduced, and it was the changes in the risk factors that accounted for the improvement in the maladaptive behavior (Baron & Kenny, 1986; Coie et al., 1993).

In a longitudinal design, Howe et al. (2002) argue, RPTs can also serve as *tests of developmental phase and progression*. Expression of psychopathology can show developmental progression over years or decades; expression of psychopathology during different periods in this progression may reflect the effects of different risk and protective mechanisms. RPTs can test this as well as whether the preventive intervention was able to stop progression to later phases by altering risk and protective mechanisms in the current phase. The longitudinal aspects of the design also allow for the detection of possible negative chains of events that may intensify the course of disorder over time.

In addition, well-planned prevention trials can lead to an increased *understanding of causal pathways to dysfunction*. Prevention research is based on theoretical models of how risk conditions are related to adverse outcomes, positing processes that link the risk condition to the negative outcome (Mrazek & Haggerty, 1994; Munoz, Mrazek, & Haggerty, 1996; Reiss & Price, 1996), and theories of prevention should specify developmental processes that alter trajectories toward the onset or maintenance of dysfunction. If the developmental course is changed due to a prevention program and the risk of the disorder or negative outcome is reduced, then the research results will contribute to our understanding of the developmental processes (Cicchetti & Rogosch, 1999; Coie et al., 1993). If the reduction of a targeted risk factor does *not* appear to have changed the pathogenic process, then that risk factor

would not be viewed as a causal agent but may be a marker of atypical development (Cicchetti & Hinshaw, 2002).

Common Design Flaws

Despite adhering to these key theoretical components, Howe et al. (2002) warn against the following common design flaws that limit the informative impact prevention trials can have on theory.

Failure to Measure Important Risk and Protective Factors

Once the arduous task of creating a prevention program is complete, researchers will not realize the full impact of their program unless every factor that is explicitly targeted by an intervention component is measured, especially when multiple component programs are being tested. It is important, however, to consider and measure risk and protective factors that might be influenced by the program, even if they are not direct targets of the intervention. Furthermore, the relevant risk and protective factors need to be tested before and immediately after intervention to demonstrate change as a result of the intervention program, as well as measured more than once across the course of follow-up. This will allow for understanding the role of the targeted risk and protective factors in the etiology of the disorder as well as the mechanisms through which the factors operate (Howe et al., 2002).

Failure to Change Important Risk or Protective Mechanisms

A prevention trial must be able to bring about enough change in the targeted factors to have a long-term effect on later psychopathology. If the targeted risk factors have a low association with the outcome, even though the results may show a reduction in risk, then the program's ability to effect change profoundly will be much lower than if the targeted risk factors were highly associated with the outcome. To combat this problem, researchers can include multiple program components that target a much broader range of risk and protective factors. Alternatively, program components can be added that might not be specifically designed to alter targeted risk factors but are believed to boost the impact and effects of the other program components (Howe et al., 2002).

Breakdown of Randomization

Many researchers will argue that random assignment of participants to conditions is often impractical or simply too burdensome, and they will employ quasi-experimental designs such as matched controls (Howe et al., 2002). These designs may not be able to eliminate all potential confounds, but with careful attention to the procedures used, they still provide a better avenue than other designs (e.g., simple correlation designs) to test developmental psychopathological theory. Furthermore, randomization does not mean equality of groups, especially because attrition or noncompliance will occur (Howe et al., 2002).

Mediational Confounds

The theoretical impact of RPTs can suffer when mediational confounds (e.g., expectancy effects) are introduced. Although randomization minimizes the impact of potential confounds, a mediational confound can occur when an unintended change in risk or protective factors results from the prevention program. This could happen when, for example, a therapist implements the prevention, and the change occurs due to the therapeutic relationship that develops between therapist and client rather than the prevention program itself. To address this, RPTs can utilize commonly employed procedures in clinical trials such as double-blind placebo controls (Howe et al., 2002).

Moderated Mediation

There will be significant threats to external validity if moderated mediation exists, where a set of targeted risk factors operate differently based on group membership. For example, risk and protective factors may operate differently for boys and girls. When those risk factors are targeted, the prevention program will have different effects on psychopathology for boys and girls. RPTs should test for moderated mediation (Howe et al., 2002).

Lack of Long-Term Follow-Up

As a minimum evaluation requirement, prevention research designs should include long-term follow-up of samples to provide critical information on developmental processes and to track changes in both process and outcome variables into the next developmental stage. RPTs should therefore incorporate an initial assessment of prior history of psychopathology, as well as continued measurement of putative risk and protective factors and psychological functioning (Howe et al., 2002).

Randomized prevention trials that incorporate aspects of randomized clinical trials with longitudinal designs have great potential for improving our understanding of the etiology of disorders and informing the next generation of prevention efforts.

TYPES OF PREVENTION: CURRENT DEFINITIONS OF PREVENTION AND NOMENCLATURE

Thus far we have discussed aspects of prevention science that relate to all prevention efforts, regardless of targeted population or outcome. A solid theoretical foundation for a program tested through an RPT is essential for all prevention work. The term "prevention," however, is applicable to a wide variety of programs that fall under the umbrella of prevention efforts and often get confused with programs that are actually "treatment." It seems simple enough to define prevention as "stopping an event from occurring," but there has been considerable discussion over recent decades of how to define prevention. Because different frameworks have been used to describe prevention, the nomenclature used in the prevention field has changed over time (Durlak, 1997). The original classification system developed in 1957 by the Commission on Chronic Illness was designed as a public health classification system of disease prevention (Mrazek & Haggerty, 1994). The three original types of prevention were primary, secondary, and tertiary (Durlak, 1997; Mrazek & Haggerty, 1994). Primary prevention was an intervention delivered to "normal" populations, or those without disease, to decrease the incidence (new cases) of disorder or illness. The intentions of secondary prevention programs were to decrease the prevalence, or lower the rate, of established cases of disorder or disease. The target populations for secondary programs are those at higher risk for early signs of disease or disorder. Tertiary prevention programs were directed at reducing or eliminating the duration or consequences (e.g., amount of disability) of a disorder (Durlak, 1997; Mrazek & Haggerty, 1994). In this original classification system, however, there was no explicit depiction of the relationship between the mechanisms linking the cause of disease and the outcomes or occurrence of disease. There was little understanding of cause and effect; if an implemented program changed the disease outcome, then it was successful. Early research did not recognize the complex association between risk factors and disease outcomes, including the impact of intervening mechanisms (Mrazek & Haggerty, 1994). Furthermore, because tertiary prevention has been directed at persons with existing disease, it has often been confused with treatment, therapy, or rehabilitation.

With time came a more sophisticated understanding of the complexity involved in the relationship between risk and protective factors and health outcomes, variation in developmental pathways, and empirical ways to test these relationships. A classification system based on these empirical relationships and a risk-benefit point of view was developed by Gordon in 1987 (Mrazek & Haggerty, 1994). He believed that need and benefits of prevention programs can be examined by comparing an individual's risk of developing a disorder with the cost, risk, or potential side effects of the preventive intervention. Those are usually positively correlated: The higher the risk of developing the disorder, the higher the costs and risk associated with the prevention program. The three categories of prevention Gordon proposed, based on a public health framework, were universal, selective, and indicated preventive programs. His classification stressed the differentiation of prevention from treatment.

The Institute of Medicine (IOM) report (Mrazek & Haggerty, 1994) endorsed a universal, selective, indicated system to differentiate prevention from treatment, drawing primarily on Gordon's (1983, 1987) work. Neither the original (primary, secondary, tertiary) or Gordon's work was designed for mental and substance abuse disorders, so the application to mental health or substance abuse was not straightforward. For example, it is complicated to identify a "case" for mental disorders, and young children may just have cognitive or psychosocial development difficulties rather than an identified mental health disorder (Mrazek & Haggerty, 1994). To address the needs of the mental health and substance abuse fields, the IOM reserves the term prevention to apply to interventions that occur prior to the onset of a disorder (Mrazek & Haggerty, 1994). The IOM endorsed a three-tiered system for prevention:

Universal prevention is applied to everyone in a defined population; participants are not chosen on the basis of any risk factor. Universal programs can often be applied for relatively low cost and risk and typically do not require specially trained professionals to implement. Examples of universal prevention programs include prenatal care and immunization, school-based violence prevention/competency enhancement programs, and behavioral techniques for classroom management (Mrazek & Haggerty, 1994).

Selective prevention is applied to individuals or a subgroup of the population who are at an above-average risk for developing a mental disorder. Examples are home visitation for high-risk infants and preschool programs for children from low-socioeconomic neighborhoods. The risk and cost are justified by the increased risk of illness or disorder, especially if the interventions are moderate in cost with minimal negative side effects (Mrazek & Haggerty, 1994).

Indicated prevention would apply to individuals with early symptoms of mental disorders, or when biological markers indicating predisposition for a disorder but do not meet *Diagnostic and Statistical Manual of Mental Disorders (DSM-IV)* criteria. An example of an indicated prevention program is parent-child interaction training for students with behavioral problems. With indicated prevention, the cost may be somewhat high and participation in the program may involve some risk; however, the costs and risk are justified because the needs of the individual are great (Mrazek & Haggarty, 1994).

The two classifications—the original primary, secondary, and tertiary prevention and universal, selective, and indicated prevention—appear to have many similarities, but they have distinct differences. "At times, there even are attempts to use the three-tiered systems interchangeably. This sort of erroneous integration of terms has slipped into the prevention research field and added to the confusion regarding definitions" (Mrazek & Haggerty, 1994, p. 21). Primary and universal prevention are largely comparable, but there are differences that suggest that selective and secondary prevention cannot be used interchangeably. Most important, tertiary prevention or treatment of a disease should not be confused with indicated prevention. Indicated interventions are based on probabilities of a disorder developing rather than the treatment of an existing condition (Mrazek & Haggerty, 1994).

The IOM report (Mrazek & Haggerty, 1994) posits prevention as just one part of the whole spectrum of interventions for mental disorders. Treatment would be applied to individuals who are in immediate need for therapeutic interventions (e.g., psychotherapy) for *DSM-IV* disorders (or those who closely meet *DSM-IV* criteria). Maintenance programs are for those with *DSM-IV* disorders who require ongoing care (Mrazek & Haggerty, 1994).

The general prevention strategies are often integrated within an overall public health plan. For example, a universal intervention can be applied to a population where the benefits for the general public far outweigh the risk. Selective programs can be implemented to target those individuals with significant risk factors that warrant the use of a higher-cost, higher-risk program. Indicated programs can be designed for those individuals showing early signs of a disorder, with the intent to prevent more serious dysfunction and the onset of the full-blown disorder (Mrazek & Haggerty, 1994). Despite our best efforts, there will still be individuals for whom the prevention programs were not effective, and those persons will need access to treatment programs to address their needs.

Building on the definitions and nomenclature offered in the IOM report on prevention, Kellam and colleagues (Ialongo, Kellam, & Poduska, 2000; Kellam & Rebok, 1992) offer a schema for organizing preventive intervention efforts in K–12 school settings that involves multiple levels of interventions nested in a public health/human services system. At the first level, *universal interventions* (Mrazek & Haggerty, 1994) are applied to the population as a whole. At the second level, *selective interventions* are targeted at children at risk for disorder based on some known risk factor such as parental divorce. *Indicated interventions* are at the third level and back up the first and second levels. At the fourth and final level are treatment services for those individuals who fail to benefit from the universal, selective, and indicated interventions. The first, or universal, level addresses the socialization structure and processes by which public institutions such as schools foster social, cognitive, emotional, and behavioral development. The second and third levels are typically more specialized and may feature a more remedial focus rather than strengthening the socialization structures in institutions such as Head Start, grade school, and/or the family. The fourth level, treatment services, typically involves the provision of highly specialized habilitative or rehabilitative care within traditional mental health or substance abuse treatment settings.

Kellam and colleagues (Ialongo et al., 2000; Kellam & Rebok, 1992) make the case that the costs and benefits of selective and indicated preventive interventions and treatment services are likely to be optimized if nested in a universal intervention. First, an individual's response to a universal intervention, as opposed to crudely measured risk factors at a single point in development, could be used to more accurately determine the need for more intensive intervention in the form of indicated or treatment interventions. Second, if the universal intervention proves effective, then the number of individuals in need of an indicated or treatment intervention is reduced. For those who require additional interventions beyond the universal intervention, the impact of the selective, indicated, and treatment interventions may be enhanced if the key figures in the social contexts the individual operates within are partners in the intervention. For instance, in the case of a child receiving a treatment intervention for conduct problems based on social learning principles, the clinician is quite likely to involve the teacher in any behavior change program. If the teacher has some background in social learning theory and its therapeutic applications, the task of involving the teacher should be much easier for the clinician.

The Johns Hopkins University Preventive Intervention Research Center's (JHU PIRC) ongoing intervention development efforts in the Baltimore City Public Schools embody this nested approach to preventive and mental health and substance abuse services. The JHU PIRC has developed and is now evaluating a universal parenting and classroom behavior management preventive intervention. In addition, the JHU PIRC is developing a system for assessment and identification of mental health and substance abuse service needs and linkage to mental health and substance abuse services for the participating children and families. This system of identification and linkages builds on the integration of a school-based mental health specialist into a school-level interdisciplinary team. This team is responsible for seeing that the mental health needs of the children are met along with their social and physical health needs. Through the school-based mental health specialist and the school-based interdisciplinary team, the JHU PIRC is developing a network of linkages to mental health and substance abuse treatment providers in Baltimore. The JHU PIRC also is developing a set of first-stage, or screening, assessment tools that will be used by teachers and parents to identify children and families who may be in need of mental health and/or substance abuse services. Those children and families identified to be in need based on these first-stage measures are then referred to the school-based mental health specialist and interdisciplinary team for a more comprehensive assessment and the development of a treatment plan. In the event the plan calls for linkage to mental health and substance abuse treatment service providers in the community, the mental health specialist serves as the family's advocate and liaison to those agencies and remains in a case manager role throughout the process.

In addition to assessment and linkage to services, the role of the mental health specialist includes (1) training and supervising teachers in identification of children and families in need of mental health services; (2) consulting with and training teachers on the use of effective classroom behavior management strategies; (3) training and supervising the paraprofessionals who lead the universal parenting intervention; (4) providing on-site, time-limited mental health services to families and children; (5) developing and maintaining a computer databank of available mental health and substance abuse services in the community; and (6) establishing contractual agreements with the local mental and substance abuse treatments providers for on-site services whose costs are covered through third-party billing.

THE PREVENTION INTERVENTION RESEARCH CYCLE

The implementation of prevention programs, is not something that can be done quickly or haphazardly. A series of carefully planned sequential steps are required to achieve maximum benefit for program outcomes as well as future prevention efforts (Mrazek & Haggerty, 1994).

Step 1 in the research cycle is to identify the problem or disorder that is to be the target of the intervention and to gather appropriate knowledge of the disorder (e.g., incidence and prevalence) to first determine whether a preventive intervention is warranted. Information important to consider when deciding whether the intervention is warranted is the potential personal, economic, and social cost of the disorder to communities. It is at this point in the cycle when partnerships between researchers and community members should be forged. Partnering early with community members is essential to make sure the problem or disorder is actually an important issue for the community and to determine community responsiveness and the feasibility of implementing programs in that community (Mrazek & Haggerty, 1994).

Once a specific disorder or problem is identified as the target for a preventive intervention, *Step 2* in the cycle is to review risk and protective factors from the knowledge base gathered in Step 1. Knowing the critical risk factors associated with onset of the disorder is critical for decisions about the nature of and targets for a prevention strategy. A variety of research disciplines can be examined for this information, including molecular biology, behavioral and molecular genetics, gene-environment interactions, developmental, experimental, and social psychology, behavior analysis, developmental psychopathology, and epidemiology, among others (Mrazek & Haggerty, 1994).

Step 3 begins the process of designing, conducting, and analyzing the research program. Once the pertinent information is collected, the researcher is ready to begin an exploratory or pilot study and confirmatory and replication studies to determine the efficacy of the program (i.e., that the program produces a beneficial result under ideal conditions). It is during this stage that many decisions are made about the prevention program, such as intervention techniques, implementation sites, and participant recruitment. It is important at this stage to integrate knowledge from Steps 1 and 2 and design the prevention program based on your chosen theoretical model. The choice of a theoretical model comes not only from information about risk and protective factors, but also from analysis of inter-

vention research. According to the IOM report (Mrazek & Haggerty, 1994), the most current evidence supports the risk-reduction model as a strong theoretical basis for preventive interventions. That is, the most productive strategy for researchers when choosing a theory and designing the resulting prevention programs is to focus on the reduction of risk and/or the enhancement of protective factors.

Step 4, conducting large scale field trials, offers an opportunity to expand Stage 3 work for programs that were found to be efficacious. Replicating the program in large-scale trials in the community allows for a more realistic assessment of benefits and costs of the program as well as generalizability of the program in naturalistic settings with regard to different personnel, participants, settings, cultures, and conditions. Although researchers may theoretically be in charge, they will quickly lose control of the program unless a great deal of attention is given to the limplementation and data collection procedures. If community members have been involved with program development from the beginning, this stage may flow more smoothly. Regardless of how well designed a program is, a single randomized field trial is not enough evidence to support large-scale community implementation of the program. Multiple generations of trials and multiple sites may be necessary before the core elements of a prevention program can truly be determined. After multiple field trials have determined the key ingredients of an efficacious program, a final field trial will be necessary to determine the program's effectiveness (e.g., Does the program do what it is intended to do?). For this trial, although the research protocol stays in place, much of the implementation of the program is handed over to the organization that hopes to run the program (Mrazek & Haggerty, 1994).

The last stage of the cycle, *Step 5,* is facilitation of large-scale community implementation and ongoing evaluation of the program. For this stage, the researcher should provide a manual to community members to guide program implementation. At this point, after repeated field trials in Stage 4, it will also be known which components of the program are core ingredients and which components may be modified to suit the needs of the community. Providing a manual to the community implementers will help them in making decisions about if and how to modify the program. Also, the researcher can continue to be involved with the community by facilitating decisions regarding ongoing community-based evaluation of the program, though control over implementation at this stage is the primary responsibility of the community organization.

ISSUES IN THE USE OF INDICES OF RISK FOR IDENTIFYING AND SELECTING INDIVIDUALS FOR PREVENTIVE AND TREATMENT INTERVENTIONS

Step 2 in the prevention intervention research cycle requires the careful identification and selection of individuals for the prevention program, and this becomes especially important when implementing a multiple-tiered prevention model to clearly define the criteria for qualification for more intensive intervention if necessary. However, as Kraemer et al. (1999) point out, the identification and selection process involves a series of difficult choices that cannot be based on statistical significance alone. Kraemer et al. provide a comprehensive compilation of measures of association that have been employed in research on risk and protective factors. They point out that no one measure of association is superior to the others when it comes to identifying individuals at risk for untoward outcome and in need of intervention. Implicit in Kraemer et al.'s thesis is that perfect prediction or diagnostic accuracy is the exception rather than the rule in the domains of health and behavior.

Kraemer et al. (1999) go on to argue that when engaging in social policy or clinical decision making based on the assessment of risk and protective factors, decision makers need to consider a number of issues: (1) the cost of the intervention and the screening and identification process, (2) any iatrogenic effects associated with the intervention to be employed and the screening and identification process, (3) the population base rate of the targeted disorder, and (4) the effectiveness of the intervention in reducing the population base rate of the targeted disorder. Kraemer et al. offer three decision-making scenarios that may arise. The first is where the intervention and screening and identification processes are relatively cheap and there are minimal or no iatrogenic effects associated with either. However, the population base rate of the disorder is either modest and/or the intervention only moderately effective in reducing the population base rate. In such a case, decision makers may want to choose a cutoff on their index of risk that minimizes false negatives (i.e., incorrectly concluding that an individual will not develop the targeted disorder), while largely ignoring the rate of false positives (i.e., incorrectly concluding that an individual will develop the targeted disorder). In this scenario, by employing a cutoff that minimizes false negatives and ignores false positives, one is likely to achieve a greater reduction in the population base rate of the disorder given that a large proportion of the population at risk for the disorder will be exposed to the intervention. The fact that the intervention is inexpensive and without major iatrogenic effects should serve to assuage concerns about the potential for a high rate of false positives.

A second scenario that Kraemer et al. (1999) offer for consideration is when the intervention may be costly and/or feature the potential for serious iatrogenic or side effects. Moreover, the population base rate of the targeted disorder and the effectiveness of the intervention are relatively high. In such a case, one might want to choose a cutoff on the index of risk that minimizes false positives while largely ignoring false negatives. Given that both the population base rate and intervention effectiveness are high, one can afford a high false-negative rate and still potentially make a substantial reduction in the population base rate of the identified disorder.

Kraemer et al. (1999) offer a third scenario that appears much more realistic when it comes to preventing mental disorders. In this scenario, the intervention and assessment and identification process is likely to be expensive, but both the population base rate and the effectiveness of the intervention will be modest. Consequently, the decision maker will want to place equal emphasis on reducing both false negatives and false positives. Petras, Kellam, Brown, Poduska, and Ialongo (2003) provide an empirical example of the use of Kraemer and colleagues' framework in the context of a study of the diagnostic utility of teacher ratings in identifying elementary school children at risk for committing a violent act in adolescence. Petras et al. employ a software program developed by Kraemer to carry out analyses that allow one to compare and contrast variations on the scenarios described earlier in predicting outcomes of interest. Ultimately, as Kraemer et al. point out, the choice of a cut point will not be based on statistics, but on what the social policy and clinical decision makers judge to be acceptable in terms of the consequences of emphasizing one form of misclassification versus the other, or attempting to achieve a balance between the two.

A DEVELOPMENTAL EPIDEMIOLOGIC FRAMEWORK FOR PREVENTION

Although this chapter argues for a developmental psychopathology approach to prevention, it does not imply that other theories or approaches are not important to prevention work, or that a developmental psychopathology approach cannot be incorporated into other approaches to prevention. For example, Kellam and Rebok (1992) and Ialongo et al. (2000) propose a developmental epidemiologic framework for preventive intervention research that draws on concepts and principles from developmental psychopathology as well as life course development, community epidemiology, and public health perspectives. The interdisciplinary perspective reflected in Kellam and colleagues' (Kellam & Rebok, 1992) *life course/social fields* framework for prevention is consistent with recent advances in mental health and substance abuse research that have caused investigators to question to whom their research findings pertain and the role of context in shaping human development. Indeed, current sampling procedures often leave uncertain the populations of individuals or families to whom the research findings can be generalized. That is, the sample is not representative of a defined population. Serving to highlight the need for defining the population under study is the fact that the frequency and distribution of the causal processes that put children and their families at increased risk may vary across social contexts such as neighborhoods or communities. In Kellam and colleagues' view of prevention and mental health and substance abuse services research, the need for defining the population under study is particularly important because the causal model provides the specific targets for our preventive and mental health and substance abuse services interventions. For example, a preventive intervention aimed at reducing the risk of antisocial behavior is likely to be of little value to a community if the prevalence of the targeted risk factors (e.g., exposure to deviant peers) or processes (e.g., inept parenting practices) in that community is quite low. An alternative causal model and preventive intervention may be a better fit for that community. Finally, Kellam and colleagues' adoption of an interdisciplinary perspective stems from the fact that the causal models of psychopathological development are frequently limited by the absence of attention to relevant aspects of the environmental context.

Life Course Development

As indicated earlier, the developmental epidemiologic framework offered by Kellam and colleagues reflects a life course development orientation. Life course development focuses on the mapping of developmental paths, including antecedents, mediators, and moderators of developmental processes and consequences (Kellam, Branch, Agrawal, & Ensminger, 1975; Kellam & Ensminger, 1980; Kellam & Rebok, 1992). Research on developmental paths that includes searching for antecedents and elements that enhance or inhibit developmentally appropriate outcomes is viewed in the context of variation in

individuals within defined populations. The purpose of carrying out research on developmental paths is to uncover aspects of developmental models that may be important in the developmental and etiological outcomes *and that are amenable to intervention trials.*

Central to Kellam and colleagues' (Kellam & Rebok, 1992) life course/social fields framework is the concept that individuals face specific social task demands in various social fields across the major *periods* of the life span (Kellam & Rebok, 1992). The social task demands that the individual confronts are defined by individuals in each social field, referred to as *natural raters.* The natural rater not only defines the tasks but also rates the individual's performance in that social field. Parents function as natural raters in the family, peers in the peer group, and teachers in the classroom (Kellam, 1990; Kellam et al., 1975; Kellam & Ensminger, 1980). This interactive process of demand and response is termed *social adaptation,* and the judgments of the individual's performance by the natural raters is referred to as *social adaptational status* (SAS; Kellam et al., 1975).

In contrast to SAS, *psychological well-being* (PWB) in Kellam and colleagues' (Kellam & Rebok, 1992) framework refers to the individual's internal state, as reflected in anxious and depressive symptoms and mood disorders. They hypothesize that PWB and SAS are intimately related, such that PWB is in large part determined by the degree to which the individual is successful in meeting the demands of his or her natural raters. Kellam and colleagues' conceptualization of the link between SAS and PWB is grounded in the basic principles of social learning theories of depression (Bandura, 1978). The more successful individuals are in meeting the demands of their natural raters, the more likely they will be reinforced for their successes. Alternatively, failure to meet the demands of the natural raters will be associated with reductions in reinforcement and increased punishment, which may then lead to decrements in PWB. In terms of the influence of PWB on SAS, the concentration problems that often accompany depressed mood may serve to disrupt the mastering of new, or complex, social task demands (Kovacs & Goldston, 1991), leading to social adaptational failure. Moreover, the feelings of hopelessness, helplessness, and low self-efficacy frequently associated with depressed mood may also reduce the likelihood that the individual will succeed in meeting social task demands that require sustained concentration and effort (Kovacs & Goldston, 1991).

In line with the organizational approach to development (Cicchetti & Schneider-Rosen, 1984), Kellam and colleagues (Kellam & Rebok, 1992) view normal development as marked by the integration of earlier competencies into later modes of function, with the earlier competencies remaining accessible, ready to be activated and utilized during times of stress, crisis, novelty, and creativity. It follows, then, that early successful SAS in the face of prominent developmental challenges tends to promote later adaptation as the individual traverses the life course and encounters new and different social task demands across the main social fields (Cicchetti & Schneider-Rosen, 1984). This key developmental principle, along with a growing empirical literature, forms the basis for Kellam and colleagues' focus on early adaptation to social task demands as a means of improving SAS and PWB over the life course and preventing mental disorders and substance use (Ialongo et al., 2000; Kellam & Rebok, 1992).

Community Epidemiology

The community epidemiologic perspective also is represented in Kellam and colleagues' (Kellam & Rebok, 1992) developmental epidemiologic framework for prevention. Community epidemiology is concerned with the nonrandom distribution of a health problem or related factor in a fairly small population in the context of its environment, such as a neighborhood, school, or classroom. Community epidemiology provides a means of identifying variation in developmental paths, including the roles of antecedents, mediators, and moderators, as they vary in frequency and function within and across different subgroups and contexts of a defined population. Traditionally, the phrase "host/agent/environment" is part of the epidemiological lexicon (Morris, 1975). It refers to a way of conceptualizing cause or etiology as involving vulnerability in the person (the host), conditions in the environment as producing illness, and a causal process of interaction (the agent) between the individual and environmental risk conditions. Thus, the integration of life course development with community epidemiology allows the study of variation in developmental antecedents and paths in a defined population in defined ecological contexts.

Defining the Ecological Context

From a community epidemiologic perspective, a neighborhood can be defined in terms of its geographic boundaries and its sociodemographic characteristics—particularly those social indicators that may be relevant to mental health and substance abuse research. The Health Demographic Profile (Goldsmith et al., 1984) developed by the National Institute of Mental Health's biometry and epi-

demiology branch, using census data, provides a means of rapidly characterizing neighborhoods with respect to small area social indicators that have been found to be related to the incidence and prevalence of mental disorder. In fact, the original Health Demographic Profile was developed to determine the need for community mental health centers in neighborhoods and communities across the country based on small area social indicators. That is, the small area social indicators were used to predict the rate of mental disorder in the community and to estimate the need for mental health services based on that rate.

The Advantages of Defining the Ecological Context

With the use of samples of convenience or clinic samples, participants tend to be viewed in isolation from their socioenvironmental characteristics. For example, the characteristics of a child's classroom, peer group, family, or neighborhood cannot be included as precisely as needed to understand variation in intervention impact or variation in the developmental course. The community epidemiologic perspective is in keeping with Bronfenbrenner's (1979) admonition to consider the determinants of human development arising from the broader environment in which children and families are embedded.

Effects of the Classroom Social Ecology

In terms of evidence that supports the need for a community epidemiologic perspective in designing and evaluating preventive intervention trials, Kellam, Mayer, Rebok, and Hawkins (1998) found that the level and duration of response to school-based preventive interventions may vary as a function of the characteristics of the child's classmates and of the classroom and school. More specifically, they found that the risk of being rated highly aggressive in middle school for boys varied as a function of the level of aggression in the first-grade classroom, after controlling for the youth's level of aggression in first grade. That is, controlling for boys' level of aggression in first grade, boys in first-grade classrooms rated highly aggressive were at 4 times greater risk of being rated as aggressive in sixth grade than boys who were in low-aggressive first-grade classrooms.

As another example of the potential impact of classroom/school characteristics on intervention outcomes, large class sizes may serve to reduce teachers' capacity to adequately and consistently monitor and discipline each of their students. Moreover, either of the above—high rates of disruptive behavior and/or large class sizes—may result in teachers spending less time on rehabilitative work with students who are falling behind academically and/or who are aggressive.

Effects of the Neighborhood Social Ecology

A community epidemiologic perspective leads prevention scientists to study factors operating at the level of the neighborhood that may influence the risk for a mental disorder or the effects of preventive or services interventions (Brook, Nomura, & Cohen, 1989). In the case of the former, the risk of depression for African American adults in the NIMH Epidemiologic Catchment Area studies varied as a function of the racial composition of the neighborhood they lived in (Goldsmith et al., 1984). If one were African American and lived in a majority African American neighborhood, one was at lower risk for depression than if one were in a majority White neighborhood. Without careful definition of the population and its social context, such phenomena may not have been discovered.

As to neighborhood influences on the effects of preventive interventions, consider an intervention aimed at preventing substance use. Whether such an intervention is successful may vary with the availability of substances in the neighborhood: The greater the availability, the greater likelihood of use. Consequently, one may see poorer intervention response in neighborhoods with high availability (Johnston, O'Malley, & Bachman, 1995; Office of Applied Studies, Substance Abuse and Mental Health Services Administration, 1995). In addition, the individual youth's attitudes and beliefs about substance use may be shaped by the prevailing attitudes and beliefs at the level of the neighborhood. In a neighborhood where the prevailing attitudes are accepting of substance use, the individual's attitudes may become more accepting as well. Johnston et al. found that as disapproval and perceptions of harm of marijuana use have decreased since 1992, use of marijuana has increased. Relatedly, Crum, Lillie-Blanton, and Anthony (1996) report that Baltimore youths living in neighborhoods in the highest tertile of crime and drug use were 3.8 times more likely to have been offered cocaine than youths in the lowest tertile.

In terms of neighborhood influences on preventive interventions aimed at educational outcomes, children in neighborhoods characterized by high levels of unemployment may perceive that regardless of their academic efforts and successes, high-paying jobs may be unattainable once they enter the workforce. Consequently, they may be less likely to demonstrate sustained academic effort and more likely to drop out of school. An additional factor operating at the level of the neighborhood that may influence intervention

response is the availability of formal support systems, such as affordable, quality child care services and well-supervised afterschool programs that provide children with opportunities to engage in appropriate educational, recreational, and social activities. Finally, the availability of child and family mental health and substance abuse services may serve to influence intervention response through direct facilitation of adaptation to normative developmental demands and/or by facilitating children's coping with failure to meet task demands, either through psychosocial or pharmacologic means.

The Community Epidemiologic Approach versus the Use of Weighted National Samples

Community epidemiology (as distinguished from the use of weighted national samples) is well suited for analytic and explanatory goals of preventive and mental health and substances abuse services research. More specifically, utilizing community epidemiologic principles and methods, one can hold constant the macro characteristics of a population, for example, an urban neighborhood. One can then examine diverging developmental paths in the context of variation in small social fields such as family, classroom, and classmate/peer group within that neighborhood. In contrast to the community epidemiologic approach, the use of weighted national probability samples leaves one with too few cases in any one ecological context to study the effects of that context on development.

Community Epidemiology and Sampling

The community epidemiologic perspective offers a number of advantages, particularly with respect to sampling. Volunteer samples, or samples drawn from clinics, come from unknown total populations. Such samples typically entail selection bias because those families who volunteer or who seek help may be different in important aspects from families with similar problems who do not (Greenley & Mechanic, 1976; Greenley, Mechanic, & Cleary, 1987; Kellam, Branch, Brown, & Russell, 1981). Those who seek help from the church may be quite different from those who seek help from the clinic. Subjects in volunteer or clinic samples differ from the general population by the very fact that they seek help (Kellam et al., 1981). Relying on volunteer participants in prevention or services intervention trials sought through newspaper or poster advertising has similar problems. Those who respond may not be representative of those who do not. Of note, the work of Leaf, Alegria, and Cohen (1996) and others (Offord, Boyle, & Szatmari, 1987; Zaner, Pawelkiewicz, De-

Francesco, & Adnopoz, 1992) suggest that fewer than 25% of children and adolescents in need of mental health services receive such services. Thus, the children who do come to mental health specialty clinics represent only a fraction of the population with mental health problems.

Among the most critical of the potential biases associated with the use of clinic samples is the tendency for only the most socially impaired children to be referred to and seen in clinics (Berkson, 1946; Caron & Rutter, 1991). Indeed, Caron and Rutter demonstrate that the prevalence of psychiatric disorders and their comorbidity are vastly overestimated when clinic-based samples are used. In avoiding this bias, epidemiologically defined community samples ensure that generalizations to known populations can be drawn and the degree of social and cognitive impairment associated with psychiatric symptoms, syndromes, or disorders, along with their incidence, prevalence rates, and comorbidity, can be validly inferred (Kellam, 1990). In the absence of such data, informed decisions with regard to the allocation of the limited treatment and preventive intervention services available are difficult to make (Kellam, 1990; National Institute of Mental Health, 1991). Thus, mental health service needs may go unmet.

An Understanding of Who Participates and Who Does Not

An additional advantage of the community epidemiologic perspective is that few samples are likely to be complete in the sense of all members of the targeted population being constantly and continuously available. Prevention or treatment research with children is particularly difficult given the mobility of families. Here, a community epidemiological orientation providing information about the total population offers an understanding of who participates compared to those who do not.

Community Epidemiology and the Efficiency of Multistage Sampling

Research on developmental antecedents, paths, and outcomes from a *life course* perspective requires population-based measurement designs that control for selection bias in ways that samples derived from clinics or voluntary samples cannot. In turn, developmental epidemiologically based research requires ecologically valid and economical measures, which provide important information about the characteristics of the individuals in the population and the antecedents, mediators, and moderators of developmental processes and consequences. These measures should also inform us of the extent to which developmental outcomes and their putative mediators and moderators vary in fre-

quency and function within and across different subgroups of a defined population in the context of a community.

An important strategy for maximizing efficiency in epidemiologic research is the multistage sampling strategy (Anthony, 1990). It conserves resources by using efficient assessments of large population-based, probabilistic samples and more expensive and burdensome assessments on subsamples selected by reason of supposed high risk (Anthony, 1990). Through multistage, representative sampling, the data from our first-stage, or population-based, measures can be used to draw smaller samples for studies requiring more frequent and comprehensive measurement and close laboratory control. Population estimates for the more intensive measures can be made through use of sample selection weights (Anthony, 1990).

First-stage, or population-based, measures can serve at least three key functions in preventive intervention field trials. First, they can be relied on to provide measures of intervention effects and outcomes. Consequently, they need to be reliable and sensitive measures of change that can be briefly and economically administered to the entire population of interest. Second, they can be used to identify individuals from the population in need of selected or indicated preventive interventions or treatment. As noted earlier, Kellam and Rebok (1992) and Ialongo et al. (2000) advocate a nested approach to preventive and mental health and substance abuse services interventions, with universal preventive interventions serving as routing mechanisms to selective and/or indicated interventions. That is, first-stage measures are used to measure response to the universal interventions and, as such, serve to identify individuals in need of more intensive mental health and substance abuse services.

Thirdly, first-stage measures can provide the needed bridge for linking developmental epidemiology to studies based on more frequent or precise observations on smaller samples. That is, research on total cohorts within specified populations can be related through multistage representative sampling to microanalytic studies on selected smaller populations requiring more frequent measurement and close laboratory control. For example, a smaller, stratified probability sample was drawn from the first cohort of elementary school children who participated in the JHU PIRC trials (Mirsky et al., 1991). This subsample was drawn to study attention/concentration processes in young children. The sample was selected using relevant first-stage measures that were administered to the entire cohort briefly and economically. This second-stage sample was drawn to represent the stratum from which it was derived as well as the total population. The first-stage measures revealed an intimate relation between teacher-rated concentration problems and aggressive as well as shy behaviors, classroom achievement, and depression. The representative smaller sample studied periodically with more precise measures of attention confirmed the associations and specified the kinds of attention deficits involved (Mirsky et al., 1991). These results then led to the inclusion of attention deficits in our analyses of impact of the JHU PIRC's preventive trials and to the development of new trials for children at risk for attention disorders.

As Kellam (1990) has noted, this same approach could be used to identify cases of interest for research on etiology. For instance, Ialongo, Reider, and Kellam (2005) were interested in studying the prognostic power of young children's self-reports of depressive and anxious symptoms. Detailed psychiatric assessments were carried out in the context of a multistage sampling design. At the first stage, a relatively economical yet sensitive screening instrument was used to identify cases for more precise and comprehensive assessment at a second stage. A random stratified sampling procedure was then employed at the second stage to select representative samples of children from the entire distribution of scores on the first-stage measure of depressive symptoms. Bird, Gould, Yager, Staghezza, and Canino (1989) and others (e.g., Offord, Boyle, & Racine, 1989) provide examples of the use of multistage designs to estimate the prevalence of psychiatric disorders in children and adolescents. Bird et al. and Offord et al. used the Child Behavior Checklist (CBCL; Achenbach, 1991) at the first-stage or population level, which is likely one of the most well researched and psychometrically sound first-stage or screening measures of child and adolescent psychopathology. The administration of the CBCL was followed by clinical interviews at the second stage for those children identified as cases by the CBCL and a random-stratified sample of controls (Bird et al., 1989; Offord et al., 1989).

Anthony (1990) describes how a multistage sampling strategy can be incorporated into a longitudinal, prospective design. At each longitudinal assessment, new cases are identified through the use of the first-stage measure(s) administered at the population level. For each new case, matched controls are drawn from the remaining noncase population for more intensive study, along with the previously identified cases and their second-stage controls. This link between population-based epidemiological research and the smaller samples required for microanalytic study shows great promise for future prevention research.

Each of these designs are variants of the case-control design, which provides an efficient means of studying rela-

tively rare disorders or phenomena (Lilienfeld & Stolley, 1994; Schlesselman, 1982). In the case-control design, a suitable number of matched controls are drawn for each case. The controls may be drawn from the same classroom or school or neighborhood, depending on the investigator's hypotheses with respect to the level of the ecological context that will contribute the most to understanding the phenomena of interest. Snow's (1849) work on the outbreak of cholera in nineteenth-century London aptly illustrates the advantage of a case-control design. While comparing cases of cholera to cholera-free, matched controls, Snow discovered that the discriminating factor was the use of a particular public well. The cases used it, and the controls did not. Subsequently, this public well was established as the source of the cholera.

In summary, these uses represent some of the most important reasons Kellam and colleagues (Ialongo et al., 2000; Kellam & Rebok, 1992) argue for drawing on community epidemiologic principles and concepts in designing and evaluating preventive intervention field trials. Community epidemiology provides the methodology for obtaining population rates and distributions of antecedents and outcomes, and tools and concepts for integrating disciplines into a broader, more ecological perspective for preventive intervention research.

The Public Health Perspective

In addition to life course development and community epidemiology, the developmental epidemiologic framework that Kellam and colleagues (Ialongo et al., 2000; Kellam & Rebok, 1992) offer for preventive intervention research features a public health perspective. An important advantage of the public health perspective is that the diffusion of effective programs is facilitated by partnerships fostered with the major institutions charged with the public's health, education, and welfare. Preventive intervention efforts are developed in conjunction with personnel from the institutions expected to implement them and are integrated into the ongoing activities of those institutions. This serves to better ensure that once the research funds are no longer available, the institution retains a trained cadre of interveners with the materials and protocols necessary to sustain effective programs. In line with the public health perspective, one way prevention scientists can ensure the dissemination and acceptability of interventions is to enter into a partnership with the existing public institutions mandated by the city, county, or state to meet the needs of the populations they serve. By way of example, Kellam and colleagues describe a partnership with the Baltimore City

Public School System (BCPSS), which was the basis for two generations of preventive intervention trials that are described in more detail later in the chapter. Kellam and colleagues' partnership with the BCPSS evolved to the point that members of their research team were integrated into the BCPSS's curriculum, parent involvement, special education, and mental health and substance abuse services planning committees. Consequently, the preventive interventions represented not only what the BCPSS thought was affordable and feasible, but also the directions in which the BCPSS was going in terms of new initiatives in the areas of curriculum, parent involvement efforts, and mental health and substance abuse services. Each element of the interventions reflected the thinking of the BCPSS superintendent, administrators, principals, and teachers. In addition, each element of the interventions was piloted with feedback solicited not only from principals, teachers, and school social workers/psychologists, but also from parents and children. Moreover, rather than importing experts to provide preventive services, existing school staff—principals, teachers, school psychologists and social workers—collaborated on the development, implementation, and evaluation of the preventive intervention trials. Thus, this public health approach allows Kellam and colleagues to confirm the applicability of findings from laboratory and microanalytic studies to population settings and to ensure that the public benefits of large-scale interventions outweigh public costs (Kellam, Rebok, Ialongo, & Mayer, 1994; Kellam, Rebok, Mayer, Ialongo, & Kalodner, 1994). Strong collaborative partnerships are also necessary for population-based intervention trials requiring random assignment of teachers, children, and families to intervention and control conditions.

Pentz (1993) and others (Perry et al., 1996; Wagenaar, Murray, Wolfson, Forster, & Finnegan, 1994) offer examples of large-scale community preventive intervention efforts involving strong collaborative partnerships with local, county, and statewide institutions. Minkler (1990) provides a theoretical model for developing collaborative relationships with the institutions integral to the public's mental health, along with the pragmatics of achieving a successful collaboration. Jason (1982) has described similar partnership strategies for developing community and institutional support. Such partnerships require considerable time to build, along with a mutual sense of trust and shared interests (Kellam et al., 1975). Kellam and colleagues' initial intervention efforts in the Baltimore public schools required a 30-month development period. Such prolonged start-up times may serve to deter most prevention researchers. But once such collaborations are developed, they

prove productive to the institutions involved, reducing start-up times for future research efforts.

ILLUSTRATIVE EXAMPLES OF UNIVERSAL PREVENTIVE INTERVENTIONS: THE JOHNS HOPKINS PREVENTIVE INTERVENTION RESEARCH CENTER (JHU PIRC) FIRST AND SECOND GENERATION TRIALS

In this next section, we provide illustrative examples of developmentally oriented universal intervention trials. Besides providing an overview of the underlying conceptual framework for the interventions and the design of the trials, findings are presented that illustrate the use of prevention intervention trials to test developmental theory.

Overview of the Rationale and Design of the Johns Hopkins Preventive Intervention Research Center Trials: The First-Generation Trial

In response to the relative dearth of well-controlled, longitudinal evaluations of preventive interventions targeting the early antecedents of substance abuse, depression, and antisocial behavior, the JHU PIRC mounted two first-grade, universal, preventive intervention trials in collaboration with the Baltimore City Department of Education. In the initial, or first-generation, JHU PIRC intervention trial, two theory-based preventive interventions were evaluated in two consecutive cohorts of approximately 1,000 first-graders in the 1985 to 1986 and 1986 to 1987 school years in 19 Baltimore city schools. One intervention, the Good Behavior Game (GBG; Barrish, Saunders, & Wolfe, 1969), was aimed at aggressive disruptive behavior, whereas the other intervention, Mastery Learning (ML; Guskey, 1985), targeted poor academic performance. The two universal classroom-based interventions were implemented over first and second grades for each of two cohorts.

Five different urban areas within one large elementary school district in eastern Baltimore were selected with the involvement of the Baltimore City Planning Department. Each of these five urban areas varied in terms of socioeconomic and ethnic characteristics. In each urban area, three or four schools were selected that were well matched with regard to census tract, school level, and first- and second-grade data. Within these clusters of schools, by a random process, one school received the ML intervention, one the GBG intervention, and one served as a control school (to provide protection against within-school contamination). In each intervention school, children were randomly assigned to classrooms. Classrooms not receiving any interventions were included as internal controls, thus holding constant school, family, and/or community differences such as the effect of the principal on school environment. Teachers also were randomly assigned to intervention conditions. Both interventions were applied at the classroom level by the teacher after intensive training. Baseline assessments were carried out before initiation of the intervention. Intervention and control teachers received equal attention and incentives. The training sessions continued throughout the intervention period (grades 1 and 2 for both cohorts) for approximately 40 hours for each intervention. Control teachers were involved in meetings, workshops, and seminars not related to intervention targets.

The GBG, which was directed at improving classroom aggressive behavior, involved the systematic use of behavior modification for classroom management. The GBG was selected because of its earlier demonstrated efficacy and acceptability to the schools and the community. ML is a teaching strategy with demonstrated effectiveness in improving achievement. The theory and research on which ML is based specifies that under appropriate instructional conditions, virtually all students will learn most of what they are taught (Block & Burns, 1976; Bloom, 1976, 1982; Dolan, 1986; Guskey, 1985).

The immediate results of this initial JHU PIRC trial yielded evidence that the proximal targets of poor academic performance and aggressive disruptive behavior were malleable (Dolan et al., 1993; Kellam, Rebok, Ialongo et al., 1994; Kellam, Rebok, Mayer, et al., 1994). More specifically, ML resulted in significant improvement in academic performance by the end of first grade, whereas the GBG resulted in significant reductions relative to controls in aggressive and disruptive behaviors based on teacher ratings and peer nominations in first grade.

Overview of the Rationale and Design of the Johns Hopkins Preventive Intervention Research Center Trials: The Second-Generation Trial

Although promising, the immediate results of the first-generation trial raised a number of questions; thus the reason for the second-generation trial. In this second-generation field trial, the two classroom-based interventions used in the first-generation JHU PIRC trial were revised to enhance their effectiveness. The revised intervention protocol included a specific focus on reducing off-task behavior and improving academic performance. The revised protocol also featured a focus on both aggressive disruptive behavior and academic performance. The decision to focus on both academic performance and aggressive disruptive behavior was driven by the evidence from the 1985 to 1986 trial that whereas ML had a beneficial impact on early academic performance, it had only a modest to moderate crossover, or indirect, effect on aggressive disruptive behavior. Similarly, the GBG had a beneficial impact on aggressive and shy behavior, but not on academic performance. Each intervention thus appeared to be specific to its proximal target. Consequently, to reduce the later risk for substance abuse, depression, and antisocial behavior, both early aggressive disruptive behavior and academic performance needed to be targeted.

In addition to combining the two classroom interventions for this second-generation intervention trial, a universal, family-school partnership (FSP) intervention was developed and fielded to contrast with the combined classroom intervention. Like the classroom-centered intervention, the proximal targets of the FSP intervention were poor academic performance and aggressive disruptive behavior. The FSP intervention sought to reduce these early risk behaviors by enhancing family-school communication and parenting practices associated with learning and behavior. The decision to develop a family-based intervention component was consistent with existing theory and the considerable empirical evidence of the important influences that families exert on their children's academic success (Gallagher, 1987; Rutter, 1985; Scott-Jones, 1984; Sines, 1987) and social development (Kazdin, 1985; Patterson, Reid, & Dishion, 1992) and the benefits of strong parent-teacher partnerships and parent involvement (Henderson, 1987; Sattes, 1985) on children's behavior and achievement. The addition of a family-based component also was consistent with the pioneering work of Hawkins and his colleagues (1992) in Seattle and Reid, Eddy, and Fetrow (1999) at the Oregon Social Learning Center; in both sites, the feasibility and effectiveness of a universal family component, along with classroom-based preventive efforts, were demonstrated in elementary school children.

The final design of this second-generation JHU PIRC trial thus involved the evaluation of two theory-based, first-grade, universal preventive interventions. One sought to reduce the early risk behaviors of poor academic performance and aggressive disruptive behavior through the enhancement of classroom curricula and teacher instructional and behavior management practices. The second sought to reduce these early risk behaviors by improving parent-teacher collaboration and by enhancing parents' teaching and behavior management skills.

A randomized block design was employed, with schools serving as the blocking factor. Three first-grade classrooms in each of nine urban elementary schools were randomly assigned to one of the two intervention conditions or to a control condition. As with the first-generation trial, teachers and children were randomly assigned to intervention conditions. A total of 678 children and their parents were available for the fall of first-grade pretest measures. The immediate impacts of the interventions are described in Ialongo, Werthamer, Brown, Kellam, and Wang (1999); the middle school outcomes are reported in a series of reports (Furr-Holden, Ialongo, Anthony, Petras, & Kellam, 2004; Ialongo, Poduska, Werthamer, & Kellam, 2001; Storr, Ialongo, Anthony, & Kellam, 2002).

The Conceptual Framework Guiding the Johns Hopkins Preventive Intervention Research Center First- and Second-Generation Trials

The JHU PIRC's conceptualizations of normal and pathologic development and, in turn, the choice of its preventive interventions and their proximal and distal targets have been guided by the *life course/social field* framework (Kellam & Rebok, 1992), as described earlier. This framework focuses on the measurement within epidemiologically defined populations of early maladaptive responses to social task demands that increase the risk of poor psychological well-being and mental and substance abuse disorders over the life course.

The integration of our life course/social fields framework and Patterson, Reid, et al.'s (1992) model of the development of antisocial behavior provides the theoretical basis for the JHU PIRC's understanding of normal and pathogenic development and the impact of the intervention components targeting the early antecedent risk behaviors of aggressive disruptive behavior and their distal correlates. According to Patterson and colleagues, there are at least two major pathways to substance use, antisocial behavior, and depression in adolescence. One—the *early starter* model—begins in the toddler years, when parents' success in teaching their child to interact within a normal range of compliance and aversive behavior is a prerequisite for the child's development of social survival skills. Alternatively, the parents' failure to effectively punish coercive behavior during these formative years and to teach reasonable levels of compliance constitutes the first step in a process that serves to train the child to become progressively more coercive and antisocial. In the classroom setting, such children prove difficult for teachers or peers to teach appropriate forms of social interaction and problem solving. Moreover, their coercive style may be further reinforced in the presence of inconsistent and coercive teacher

disciplinary practices. Ultimately, parents, teachers, and well-adjusted peers reject the coercive child, which results in the child's failure to develop academic, social, and occupational survival skills. That is, the opportunities to learn these skills through interaction with teachers, parents, and peers are greatly reduced due to the rejection.

Patterson, Reid, et al. (1992) argue that the lack of adequate monitoring by parents in early adolescence and rejection by teachers and mainstream peers precipitates "drift" into a deviant peer group, wherein a wide array of antisocial and delinquent behavior, including alcohol and drug use, may be reinforced, along with rejection of mainstream norms and mores (Brook et al., 1989; Hirschi, 1969; Jessor, 1978; Patterson, Reid, et al., 1992). The rejection of such norms and mores appears also to be associated with a higher likelihood of premarital sex and teenage pregnancy, child bearing, and parenthood (Capaldi, Crosby, & Stoolmiller, 1996). Concomitant with the drift into a deviant peer group, the opportunities for obtaining positive reinforcement from mainstream natural raters—such as, parents, teachers, and well-adjusted peers—are significantly reduced. In turn, the coercive youth will be more likely to use substances as a means of obtaining reinforcement and negating the reductions in reinforcement dispensed by mainstream natural raters. Relatedly, the lack of positive reinforcement received from mainstream natural raters may lead to decrements in psychological well-being (Capaldi, 1991, 1992), which the youth seeks to alleviate through substance use (Chen, Anthony, & Crum, 1999). In turn, the youth's substance use may lead to further failure in meeting the demands of the school, peer group, family, work, and intimate relationship social fields. In an escalating, cyclic fashion, these failures may lead to further decrements in psychological well-being and increased substance use, abuse, and dependence.

One potential mechanism by which substance use may undermine social adaptation is via attention/concentration problems and impulsivity, which may, in turn, undermine success in the classroom social field by reducing on-task time and disrupting the encoding of task-relevant information into memory (Rebok, Hawkins, Krener, Mayer, & Kellam, 1996). The attention/concentration problems and impulsivity associated with substance use may also contribute to increased aggressive behavior by disrupting the process of encoding social cues essential to social problem solving and conflict resolution with adults and peers (Crick & Dodge, 1994; Dodge, 1986).

Patterson, Reid, et al. (1992) offer a second model of the development of antisocial behavior, which seeks to explain the relatively high prevalence of late-onset (i.e., in the pre-

or early adolescent years) antisocial behavior and substance use. Patterson, Reid, et al. argue that the *late starters* typically exhibit marginal levels of social adaptation in the elementary school years in terms of aggressive disruptive behavior and the development of social survival skills. Moreover, their caregivers' discipline and monitoring skills may be marginal at best. Consequently, these children are quite vulnerable to perturbations in parental monitoring and supervision, which may lead to rapid escalation of behavior and/or academic achievement problems. More specifically, Patterson, Reid, et al. hypothesize that the escalation in antisocial behavior seen in these late starters in early adolescence is the product of disruptions in parental monitoring and supervision, brought on by serious family adversities that first surface in the middle school years and tend to be chronic in nature. The disruptors include divorce, serious financial distress associated with the loss of a job, and the late onset of parental psychiatric distress or substance use, abuse, or dependence. Like the early starters, these late-onset children are then rejected by their mainstream natural raters as a result of their coercive and antisocial behavior. Their limited social survival skills and the rejection by their mainstream natural raters then precipitate drift into a deviant peer group, where antisocial behavior, substance use, and rejection of mainstream social values, mores, and institutions are reinforced.

In keeping with the JHU PIRC's life course/social fields framework and its integration with Patterson, Reid, et al.'s (1992) early starter model, the JHU PIRC's interventions were hypothesized to reduce the early aggressive disruptive behavior and its distal correlates in the following manner:

1. The interventions should improve teachers' and parents' disciplinary practices, which should then result in a reduction of early aggressive and coercive behavior at the level of the youth and the classroom.

2. As a result of the reduction in aggressive behavior at the level of the classroom, there should be fewer opportunities for the youth to learn inappropriate behavior through modeling of classmates' aggressive behavior.

3. The youth should then be at decreased risk of being rejected by parents/caregivers, teachers, and peers.

4. Parents should be more likely to monitor and supervise their child and engage in jointly reinforcing activities with him or her.

5. The youth should be less likely to drift into a deviant peer group, where substance use and antisocial behavior may be reinforced and mainstream norms and mores

rejected, including those around pre-marital sex and teenage pregnancy, child bearing, and parenting (Brook et al., 1989; Hirschi, 1969; Jessor, 1978).

6. Ultimately, the youth should be less likely to fail in the classroom, in family, peer, and intimate relations, and in the work social fields in adolescence and early adulthood.

7. The youth should be at reduced risk for decrements in psychological well-being.

8. The youth should be at reduced risk for early and sustained substance use, given the high level of psychological well-being and the ample opportunities for positive reinforcement from mainstream natural raters.

9. The lower the risk of substance use, the more likely the youth will successfully meet the demands of the school, peer group, family, work, and intimate/romantic relationship social fields.

10. Consequently, psychological well-being should be high.

As noted earlier, Patterson, Reid, et al. (1992) posit a second, or late starter, pathway to substance use and antisocial behavior, which begins in the pre- to early adolescent years. Their late starter model centers on disruptions in parental supervision and discipline during the late childhood and early adolescent years among parents with marginal parenting skills. The disruptions may be brought on by events such as a divorce, parental illness, unemployment, or spousal conflict. With respect to the late starter model and mechanisms of intervention impact, it was hypothesized that the family-school partnership intervention would enhance the parenting skills of those parents with marginal as well as those with poor parenting skills in first grade. Thus, the parenting skills of those parents in the FSP intervention would be less likely to be disrupted in the later childhood and early adolescent years by adverse life events. In turn, relative to standard-setting youth, FSP youth would be less likely to develop antisocial behavior and drift into a deviant peer group, where antisocial behavior, substance use, and rejection of mainstream social values, mores, and institutions are reinforced. These FSP youth would also have higher levels of psychological well-being given that they would be less likely to be rejected by parents, teachers, and mainstream peers and more likely to be reinforced for success in the academic/school, peer group, and family social fields.

In terms of the classroom-based interventions and the late starter model, youth with marginal skills in the academic, conduct/behavioral, and peer relations domains prior to the intervention would have higher levels of social adaptation in these domains over the childhood and adolescent years relative to their standard-setting counterparts. Consequently, the youth who participated in the classroom-based interventions would maintain higher levels of social adaptation in the face of disruptions in parent supervision, discipline, and reinforcement in the pre- to early adolescent years than their standard-setting counterparts. As a result, these youth would be less likely to drift into a deviant peer group and engage in serious antisocial behavior and heavy substance use and abuse. Moreover, due to their success in the academic/school, peer group, and family social fields, these youth would have higher levels of psychological well-being than their standard-setting counterparts.

The JHU PIRC interventions were hypothesized to reduce the early antecedent risk behavior of poor achievement, its distal correlates, and the corresponding need for and use of youth mental health and special education services in the following manner:

1. The interventions should improve teachers' and parents' instructional practices and parent support and involvement for children's academic achievement.

2. Youth achievement should then improve, along with the classroom's overall level of achievement.

3. As a result of the overall improvement in classroom academic achievement, there will be a greater number of academically successful youth in the classroom for their classmates to model, which may result in increased academic effort and achievement.

4. Success in the achievement domain over the elementary school years should result in greater perceptions of personal control and increased perceived competence in the scholastic domain during the middle and high school years.

5. These successes should set the stage for improved psychological well-being and success in meeting the demands of the postsecondary education and work social fields.

6. Relatedly, youth who succeed academically should be less likely to engage in disruptive and off-task behavior, which should then reduce the risk of their being rejected by teachers, parents, and peers.

7. Consequently, these youth may be more likely to develop the social survival skills necessary for success in the school, peer group, family, and work social fields.

8. Thus, they would be at reduced risk for decrements in psychological well-being.

9. These youth would also be at reduced risk for early and sustained substance use, given their high level of psychological well-being and the ample opportunities for positive reinforcement from their mainstream natural raters.

10. The lower the risk of substance use, the more likely these youth will be successful in meeting the demands of the school, peer group, family, work, and intimate relationship social fields.

11. They also will be less likely to drift into a deviant peer group, where substance use and antisocial behavior may be reinforced and mainstream norms may be rejected (Brook et al., 1989; Hirschi, 1969; Jessor, 1978; Patterson, Reid, et al., 1992).

ILLUSTRATIVE EXAMPLES OF UNIVERSAL PREVENTIVE INTERVENTION TRIALS AS TESTS OF DEVELOPMENTAL THEORY

Theoretical models of the development of antisocial behavior have proposed distinct pathways leading to criminal activity. Petras et al. (2003) used general growth mixture modeling (GGMM) to find empirical evidence for these pathways in the first-generation JHU PIRC participants. Petras et al. also examined the relationship between these pathways and later outcomes, including Conduct Disorder, Antisocial Personality Disorder, juvenile arrest, and adult incarceration. We offer the findings from Petras et al. as an example of a test of the link between early and later adaptation, consistent with a major tenet of the life course/social fields framework and the organizational theory of development.

Data for Petras et al. (2003) were gathered in the fall and spring of first and second grades, the spring of third through seventh grades, and at an age 19 to 20 follow-up assessment. The data gathered in the first through seventh grade assessments included teacher reports of child aggressive disruptive behavior and free lunch eligibility. At the age 19 to 20 follow-up, a structured clinical interview was used to ascertain whether the participant met criteria for Antisocial Personality Disorder (ASPD).

The statistical methods used in Petras et al. (2003) were consistent with a person-centered approach to data analysis, which emphasizes individual differences in development (Bergman & Magnusson, 1997). GGMM (Muthén & Muthén, 2000), as implemented in the Mplus Version 2 statistical software package (Muthén & Muthén, 1998), was used to identify distinct patterns of growth in aggressive disruptive behavior over time. Like traditional growth modeling techniques, GGMM estimates latent variables based on multiple indicators. The multiple indicators of latent growth parameters correspond to repeated univariate outcomes at different time points. However, rather than assuming that the population is constructed of a single continuous distribution, GGMM tests whether the population is constructed of two or more discrete classes (pathways) of individuals, with the goal of determining optimal class membership for each individual. Evidence for these different pathways in aggressive disruptive behavior exists when models involving two or more latent classes of growth provide a better fit than a traditional single-class growth model.

GGMM is similar to the semiparametric group-based (SPGB) modeling approach described by Nagin (1999) in that classes define different trends over time in repeated measures (Muthén, 2000). However, unlike SPGB, GGMM allows for the modeling of class-specific levels of variation. For models in which all parameters are the same, GGMM and SPGM provide identical results. GGMM was selected to allow for the possibility of heterogeneity within classes as it did not seem reasonable to assume that all youth within a given class would have identical patterns of aggressive behavior. Allowing for heterogeneity also tends to improve overall model fit and classification accuracy (Muthén, 2000). The observed time variant indicators consisted of teacher-rated classroom aggressive disruptive behavior measured at 9 time points: fall and spring of first grade, fall and spring of second grade, and spring of third through seventh grades.

The GGMM analyses in Petras et al. (2003) revealed three distinct high-risk trajectories for males (see Figure 24.1): start high and remain high, start low and increase in aggressive disruptive behavior over elementary school, and start low and stay low in aggressive disruptive behavior. These growth trajectories were largely consistent with Paterson, Reid, et al.'s (1992) early and later starter models of antisocial behavior. Males in the start high and remain high and increasing trajectories were at increased risk for

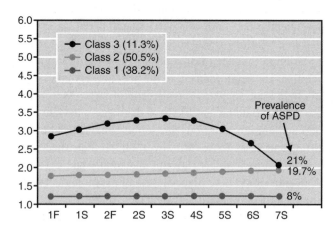

Figure 24.2 General growth mixture model for females based on teacher rated aggressive disruptive behavior from grades 1 to 7 and an antisocial personality diagnosis at age 19–20.

ASPD in young adulthood (see Figure 24.1). Of importance, Pertras et al. found a similar set of early aggressive disruptive behavior pathways among girls in the first-generation JHU PIRC data. As with the boys, these early pathways were highly predictive of later ASPD in young adulthood (see Figure 24.2).

These findings provide strong support for the posited link between early and later social adaptation consistent with the life course/social fields framework and the organizational theory of development. However, Petras et al. (2003) also carried out an experimental test of the hypothesized causal relationship between early and later social adaptation, utilizing the GBG intervention and control group participants. In a first step in their analysis, Petras et al. assessed the impact of the GBG intervention on growth of aggressive disruptive behavior within each class or aggressive disruptive behavior trajectory class. More specifically, Petras et al. examined the effect of the GBG intervention on the slope parameter within each of the trajectory classes. The slope represents the shape of the growth process within each trajectory class. The comparison or standard setting (control) classrooms for this analysis were those standard setting classrooms in schools that included GBG classrooms. For males, Petras et al. found a significant impact of the GBG intervention on the slope of aggressive disruptive behavior in the start and remain high aggressive disruptive behavior trajectory. In contrast to GBG control males, the slope for GBG intervention males showed a significantly greater decline in the rate of growth of aggressive disruptive behavior. In addition, the GBG intervention males in this start high and remain high aggressive disruptive behavior trajectory class had a significantly lower rate of ASPD at the age 19 to 20 follow-up interview.

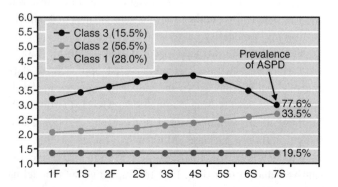

Figure 24.1 General growth mixture model for males based on teacher rated aggressive disruptive behavior from grades 1 to 7 and an antisocial personality diagnosis at age 19–20.

One of the questions that remained was whether the impact of the GBG on ASPD at age 20 to 21 was mediated via the GBG's impact on the early growth of aggressive disruptive behavior. Consistent with Baron and Kenny (1986), to demonstrate mediation one must first establish that the independent variable is statistically associated with the mediator and the outcome and that the mediator is significantly associated with the outcome. One must then show that after controlling for the effect of the intervention on the mediator, the direct effect of the independent variable on the outcome should no longer be significant and that the change in the size of the estimate of the direct effect should be statistically significant. However, a straightforward test for mediation in the GGMM framework is not presently possible. The distal outcome in growth mixture modeling is regressed on the categorical variable representing class membership and not the within-class growth parameters (intercept and slope). Moreover, the goal in growth mixture modeling is to derive classes with limited within-class variance in terms of the growth parameters (intercept and slope). Consequently, if one wished to test for mediation using the within-class slope as a mediator, intervention condition as the independent variable, and ASPD as the outcome, it is likely that slope variance would be too small to provide an adequately powered test of mediation.

In the absence of an established method to test for mediation consistent with Baron and Kenny (1986), Petras et al. (2003) employed what can be best described as an approximation of the Baron and Kenny method. Their approximation involved the use of the likelihood ratio test to compare competing models. More specifically, Petras et al. constrained the path from the GBG intervention condition to the slope within the start and remain high aggressive disruptive behavior class to zero. Petras et al. then compared the log likelihoods between the latter model and one where the path from the GBG intervention condition to the slope was freely estimated. The difference was not significant, suggesting that the impact of the GBG intervention on ASPD in males was not mediated through its impact on the slope of aggressive disruptive behavior in the start high and remain high growth trajectory. However, as pointed out earlier, this is at best an approximation of the test for mediation offered by Baron and Kenny, given that one cannot truly test for mediation in the growth mixture modeling framework. Nevertheless, although an approximation, the model fit worsened when the path between the intervention condition and the slope of aggressive disruptive behavior within the start high and remain high aggressive behavior growth trajectory was constrained to zero. The worsening in fit was consistent with the expectation that the impact of

the GBG on the distal outcome of ASPD was via its impact on the growth of aggressive behavior in elementary school.

One explanation for failure to find a significant difference between model fits may simply be that the sample size was too small to detect a difference. As MacKinnon, Lockwood, Hoffman, West, and Sheets (2002) point out, tests of mediation in the social sciences are often underpowered, not only due to sample size, but as a result of the joint distributions of the independent, mediator, and outcome variables. In the case of growth mixture modeling, this issue is amplified due to the fact that the object of growth mixture modeling is to account for the variance in the growth of the mediator via the assignment of individuals into trajectory classes based on similarities in their growth parameters: intercept and slope.

Petras et al. (2003) also examined the effect of the GBG on the increasing and stable low aggressive disruptive behavior growth trajectories among males (Figure 24.1). No effect was found for the GBG on the slope of aggressive disruptive behavior in the increasing class or in the stable low class. The absence of an effect on the slope of the low class was not surprising as it was close to zero; consequently, there was virtually no room for improvement. With regard to the increasing or late starter class, the hypothesis that the GBG would protect youth from the effects of disruptions in parenting in the late childhood and early adolescent years via improvement in social adaptation in the early elementary school years was not supported. Of note, the growth of aggressive disruptive behavior showed a precipitous rise after the completion of the intervention in aggressive disruptive behavior at the end of second grade and the beginning of second grade. Thus, it may be that the intervention suppressed the growth of aggressive disruptive behavior during the period that the intervention was in place, but once the systematic classroom behavior management practices associated with the GBG were no longer in place, those individual, family, classroom, and/or peer group factors hypothesized by Patterson, Reid, et al. (1992) to play a role in their late starter model may have overcome any benefits of the GBG.

Finally, Petras et al. (2003) studied the effects of the GBG on females (Figure 24.2). In general, the pattern of results was consistent with the effects of the GBG on males, such that the most beneficial effects were seen in the high aggressive behavior trajectory. However, unlike the males, the effects of the intervention did not prove statistically significant, either in terms of the impact of the GBG on the growth of aggressive disruptive behavior in the high aggressive disruptive behavior growth trajectory class or on the distal outcome. The most likely explanation for the lack of significant intervention effects for females relative to males was that the number of females in the high aggressive

disruptive behavior trajectory was substantially lower—
about 50%—than among males. Consequently, the statistical power to detect significant effects was likely lower.

To summarize, Petras et al. (2003) found evidence to support a major premise of the life course/social fields framework and organizational theory of development: Success or
failure at later stages of development may be a function in
part of success or failure at early stages of development.
More specifically, Petras et al. found that children who exhibited either a high or increasing course of aggressive disruptive behavior over the elementary school years were at
significantly higher risk of antisocial outcomes in early
adulthood, in contrast to those who exhibited a stable low
level of aggressive behavior. This finding held for both
males and females. In addition, Petras et al. demonstrated a
significant and beneficial impact of the GBG intervention
on both the growth of aggressive disruptive behavior among
boys in the start high and remain high trajectory class and
the distal outcome of ASPD. This suggests that early aggressive behavior may be malleable and, in turn, that a reduction
in the growth of aggressive disruptive behavior among boys
in the start high and remain high growth trajectory may
translate into later reductions in antisocial behavior in young
adulthood. In the absence of a formal test of mediation in
the growth mixture modeling framework, Petras et al. could
not conclude, however, that the GBG effect was mediated
through its impact on the early growth of aggressive disruptive behavior. A formal test of mediation in the growth mixture framework awaits further development. The absence of
an effect of the GBG on growth of aggressive disruptive behavior among females in Petras et al.'s study was likely due
to insufficient statistical power and not a differential impact
of the GBG, given that the pattern of intervention effects
were similar to those seen in boys. The fact that there were
fewer females than males in the start high and remain high
growth trajectory may account for the failure to find a statistically significant intervention impact for females. In general, the data from Petras et al. suggest the need for much
larger samples when evaluating the impact of universal preventive interventions such as the GBG, given that the benefits of such universal interventions are likely to be seen only
in those individuals evidencing some elevation in risk.

A Test of the Link between the Initiation of
Substance Use and Early and Later Adaptation to
the Developmental Demands of the Classroom

As described, Petras et al. (2003) illustrated the use of
GGMM to test Patterson, Reid, et al.'s (1992) theory of
early and late starter growth trajectories of aggressive disruptive behavior and the development of ASPD among males

and females. Using data from the second-generation JHU
PIRC trial, we present an example where we replicate and
extend Petras et al.'s study to include the influence of
class membership—with respect to the growth of aggressive
disruptive behavior over grades 1 to 3—on survival to first
use of marijuana. The focus on survival to first use is consistent with evidence that early use may predict later use
(Brunswick, Messeri, & Titus, 1992; Kandel & Davies,
1992), particularly heavy use. In this example, we also employed parallel and sequential growth mixture modeling to
test the moderating influence of peer rejection on the growth
of aggressive disruptive behavior in grades 1 to 3 and their
joint influence on the growth trajectories of conduct problems in grades 6 to 9. This is in keeping with Patterson, Reid,
et al.'s theory that high levels of aggressive disruptive behavior and peer rejection in the elementary school years would
be associated with high levels of conduct problems in the
adolescent years and the early onset of drug use.

The goal of this example is to illustrate how one can use
parallel and sequential process GGMM to understand the
moderating influences of child, family, peer group, school,
and neighborhood/community variables on the classes of
growth of early and later aggressive disruptive behavior and
survival to substance use. Of course, the number of constructs one can examine within these parallel and sequential
process models is limited by sample size and, relatedly, the
statistical power to detect differences between classes with
respect to the distal outcomes of interest. As such, we examine here a small subset of moderators within the GGMM
framework, beginning with the subset with the strongest
theoretical and empirical evidence of their importance.

The first step in this parallel and sequential process
GGMM analysis involved carrying out a separate GGMM
analysis for both teacher-rated aggressive disruptive behavior and peer rejection in grades 1 to 3, and for teacher-
rated conduct problems in grades 6 to 9. We confine this
analysis to males given the relatively low frequency of
marijuana use in girls by grade 9 and the resulting reduction in statistical power. The separate GGMM analyses
yielded three classes, or growth trajectories (high, increasing, and low), for aggressive disruptive behavior in
grades 1 to 3, two classes (high and low) for peer rejection
in grades 1 to 3, and three classes for conduct problems in
grades 6 to 9 (high, increasing, and low).

In the second step, we created 18 classes, or growth trajectories, for the parallel and sequential process component
of the analysis (based on the total number of possible
unique combinations of aggressive disruptive behavior, peer
rejection, and conduct problem classes established in Step
1). The growth parameters used in the modeling of these 18
classes were drawn from the separate GGMM analyses in

the first step. For example, the growth parameters for the class representing those participants who were high on aggressive disruptive behavior, peer rejection, and conduct problems were drawn from the high classes found in the separate GGMM analyses carried out in Step 1. The 18 class parallel and sequential process GGMM model failed to converge, owing to the number of classes with too few participants to estimate the necessary model parameters. This was an expected finding from a substantive standpoint. For example, given theory and empirical evidence, we thought it unlikely that we would see a class that featured participants who were high on aggressive disruptive behavior and low on peer rejection in grades 1 to 3—which proved to be the case. Ultimately, a model featuring six classes converged and yielded acceptable model fit indices.

In the third and final step, survival to first use of marijuana was incorporated into the model in accord with Muthén and Masyn (2005). This model allowed us to examine whether survival to first use of marijuana varied across the six classes found in the sequential and parallel process GGMM analysis. Although preliminary, the results suggested that the key to survival to first use of marijuana—at least through entrance to high school—was the growth of conduct problems in grades 6 to 9. Specifically, those classes containing participants demonstrating an increasing or a steadily high trajectory of conduct problems in grades 6 to 9 demonstrated the lowest rates of survival to first use of marijuana, and the highest survival rates were found in the classes with low levels of conduct problems in grades 6 to 9. This is not to suggest that high levels of aggressive disruptive behavior and peer rejection are not of importance to survival to first onset of marijuana use, but rather that increasing or high levels of conduct problems in grades 6 to 9 must be present as well, which is consistent with Patterson, Reid, et al.'s (1992) model. Indeed, it is important to note that the odds of being in the high class of conduct problems in grades 6 to 9 was significantly higher for those participants in the high class of aggressive disruptive behavior in grades 1 to 3 relative to their counterparts in the low class.

ILLUSTRATIVE EXAMPLES OF SELECTIVE/INDICATED PREVENTIVE INTERVENTION TRIALS AS TESTS OF DEVELOPMENTAL THEORY: MOUNT HOPE FAMILY CENTER, UNIVERSITY OF ROCHESTER

Although many risk factors for the development of maladaptation and psychopathology have been identified, longitudinal correlational research has demonstrated some specific risk conditions that carry substantial burden for the developing individual. These risk factors present unique challenges to children and families and are not likely to be sufficiently altered by broad-based universal interventions. For example, parental divorce or loss of a parent through death results in major disruptions in family life, parental distress, high potential for conflictual parent-child relationships, and additional stressors, such as income loss. To address the negative consequences of these atypical life events, preventive interventions tailored to the unique experiences of such families are necessary (Sandler et al., 2003; Wolchik et al., 2002).

Other risk factors involve family contexts with negative effects that are more pervasive and pernicious. For example, child maltreatment involves extreme family dysfunction, posing severe impediments to competent child development. Extensive, deleterious sequelae of child maltreatment on psychological and biological functioning have been enumerated, and the maltreated child is at high risk for the emergence of diverse forms of psychopathology. Parental mental illness, such as depression, Schizophrenia, and alcohol and substance abuse, confers risk on children through compromised parenting, difficulties in parent-child relationships, and marital discord, as well as potential genetic vulnerabilities. The risk processes involved in child maltreatment and parental mental illness may extend from the prenatal period onward. Thus, preventive interventions occurring early in the life course are indicated, given the early signs of nonoptimal development that may begin to unfold. In this section, we focus our discussion of targeted preventive interventions on two potent risk factors, child abuse and neglect and maternal depression, with illustrations provided by preventive trials conducted at Mt. Hope Family Center, University of Rochester.

The organizational perspective on development, as discussed earlier, forms the foundation for formulating early interventions to address these risk conditions. At each stage of development, the individual is confronted with central age- and stage-relevant challenges or tasks. Competent resolution of each of these developmental tasks promotes better preparedness to adapt to subsequent developmental challenges, whereas incompetent resolution may engender compromised capacities to adapt successfully. As each stage-salient issue emerges, it remains important to adaptation henceforth, and the quality of the developmental task resolution is consolidated and integrated across biological and psychological systems. Through progressive reorganization as the individual develops, different pathways unfold, varying in degree of developmental competence versus maladaptation. Continuity in development is preserved through the ongoing processes of differentiation and hierarchic integration. However, based on new experience, developmental divergence and discontinuity also are possible. From this perspective, psychopathology evolves as a result of an integration of incompetent developmental structures across biological and psychological systems, or as a lack of integration across systems.

From this perspective, child abuse and neglect and maternal depression occurring early in the life course confront the developing child with a family and relational environment that does not support the successful resolution of stage-salient developmental tasks. Accordingly, over the early years of development, these risk factors set in motion a progression of compromised developmental attainments that generate vulnerabilities in the organization of developmental systems. As a result, children reared under these conditions are liable to develop diverse forms of psychopathology. To combat this progression, the preventive strategy involves early interventions to instill competence on stage-salient developmental tasks to direct children onto adaptive developmental trajectories.

Effects of Child Maltreatment during Infancy

Extensive evidence exists documenting the deleterious effects of child maltreatment on developmental systems across the life course (Cicchetti, 2002; Cicchetti & Lynch, 1995; Cicchetti & Toth, 2000; DeBellis, 2001; Trickett & McBride-Chang, 1995). In focusing on the early years of life, we briefly highlight findings related to difficulties in affect regulation, attachment, and self-development.

In terms of early affect differentiation, maltreated infants have been observed to display four atypical patterns: developmentally and affectively retarded, depressed, ambivalent/affectively labile, and angry (Gaensbauer, Mrazek, & Harmon, 1981). Physically abused infants were more likely to exhibit restricted positive affect and high negative affect, including fear, anger, and sadness, whereas neglected infants appeared affectively blunted. Beyond infancy, maltreated children have been found to have a selective bias and sensitivity toward the detection of anger (Camras et al., 1990; Pollak, Cicchetti, Hornung, & Reed, 2000) and are hypervigilant to aggressive stimuli (Rieder & Cicchetti, 1989). Psychophysiological studies have further demonstrated via event-related potentials (ERPs) that maltreated children evince a differential processing of emotion stimuli that is specific to anger (Pollak, Cicchetti, Klorman, & Brumaghim, 1997; Pollak, Klorman, Thatcher, & Cicchetti, 2001; Pollak & Tolley-Schell, 2003). Patterns of emotion dysregulation in response to interadult anger have been found among preschool-age maltreated children

(Maughan & Cicchetti, 2002), and school-age maltreated children evince attenuated emotion regulation in the form of emotional lability/negativity and inappropriate affect in interactions with their peers (Shields & Cicchetti, 2001).

The development of an attachment relationship with the primary caregiver allows the infant to maintain internal security while beginning to explore the environment. Sensitive and responsive maternal care is associated with secure attachment relationship formation, whereas inconsistent, intrusive, and rejecting care contributes to varied forms of insecure attachments. Among maltreated infants, high rates of insecure attachment (i.e., two-thirds avoidant or resistant) have been observed (Egeland & Sroufe, 1981; Schneider-Rosen, Braunwald, Carlson, & Cicchetti, 1985). Moreover, in studying maltreated infants, considerable difficulty in classification routinely occurred because of the frequency of many atypical and unusual attachment behaviors. As a result of this observation, patterns of disorganized/disoriented attachment were identified (Main & Solomon, 1986, 1990). Another atypical pattern detected involved infants exhibiting both avoidant and resistant attachment behaviors (Crittenden, 1988). When the attachment behavior of maltreated infants was reevaluated with the inclusion of the disorganized and avoidant-resistant patterns, insecure attachment classifications were found for as many as 90% of maltreated infants, with 80% showing the atypical, disorganized patterns (Barnett, Ganiban, & Cicchetti, 1999; Carlson, Cicchetti, Barnett, & Braunwald, 1989; Lyons-Ruth, Repacholi, McLeod, & Silva, 1991). As development proceeds, children form representational models of attachment figures, the self, and the self in relation to others (Bowlby, 1969, 1982; Bretherton, 1985; Crittenden, 1990). These representational models organize affect, cognitions, and behavior and serve as guides for later interpersonal behavior in subsequent relationships (Sroufe & Fleeson, 1986, 1988). Thus, for maltreated infants, highly insecure representational models are likely to evolve, boding poorly for later relationship experiences.

Because insecure and disorganized attachment relationships are almost universally observed among maltreated infants, the development of an autonomous self during the toddler period is likely to be impaired. Although the cognitive capacity for visual self-recognition emerging during this period is not delayed among maltreated children, they do differ in the affect they exhibit when regarding the self, with more frequent negative or neutral affect, rather than the positive affect more commonly shown by nonmaltreated youngsters (Schneider-Rosen & Cicchetti, 1984, 1991). Other early self-system deficits also have been discovered, including a restricted ability to talk about themselves and their internal states (Beeghly & Cicchetti, 1994; Coster & Cicchetti, 1993). Allesandri and Lewis (1996) have shown that maltreated children show atypical patterns of self-conscious emotion expression, with maltreated girls showing heightened shame and low levels of pride and maltreated boys exhibiting limited self-conscious emotions generally. Toth and colleagues have shown that maltreated preschool-age children, particularly those who were physically abused, had more negative self-representations (Toth, Cicchetti, Macfie, & Emde, 1997), and longitudinally, increases in grandiose self-representations were observed (Toth, Cicchetti, Macfie, Maughan, & VanMeenan, 2000). Evidence for the development of a "false self" (Koenig, Cicchetti, & Rogosch, 2000) and delays in theory of mind development (Cicchetti, Rogosch, Maughan, Toth, & Bruce, 2003) further attest to early difficulties that maltreated children have in the development of an adaptive self-system.

This sampling of research indicates that children maltreated early in life already exhibit signs of compromised developmental competencies on early stage-salient tasks. Consequently, these liabilities contribute to the emergence of developmental pathways that are likely to be progressively maladaptive and conducive to the development of varied forms of psychopathology. Preventive intervention thus must alter these trajectories through reducing ongoing risks and promoting protective processes. When maltreatment has already occurred, efforts to prevent further maltreatment are crucial, and intervening to reduce sources of dysfunctional parenting and parent-child relationships is central to this goal.

Many parents in maltreating families experienced child maltreatment in their own family of origin; as a result, the risk for intergenerational transmission of maltreatment with one's own children is heightened, yet not inevitable (Kaufman & Zigler, 1989). For parents who endured maltreatment as children, understanding and relating to children sensitively and responsively may be difficult, given the lack of experience in benign parent-child relationships. Research with maltreating parents has identified affective, cognitive, and behavioral deficits and atypicalities that conspire to undermine appropriate caregiving and responsiveness to children's evolving emotional and physical needs (Azar, 2002; Rogosch, Cicchetti, Shields, & Toth, 1995). Such parents lack effective parenting skills and general knowledge of child development, have difficulty relating affectively to their children, and misread and misinterpret their children's behavior and emotional expression. Furthermore, as a result of maltreatment during childhood and other problematic parent-child relationship experiences, many maltreating parents have insecure internal representational models of self and of

attachment relationships (Crittenden & Ainsworth, 1989), and these models intrude on their ability to relate to their children and provide "good enough care" (Winnicott, 1958). Insecure representational models also contribute to conflict and instability in adult relationships. Coupled with poverty, single parenthood, and myriad associated stressors, maltreatment may occur as multiple risk factors overwhelm limited protective resources (Cicchetti & Lynch, 1995).

Randomized Prevention Trials for Child Maltreatment

Two models of preventive intervention, psychoeducational home visitation (PHV) and infant-parent psychotherapy (IPP), were evaluated in a randomized prevention trial to determine whether they would be efficacious in reducing the risk for further maltreatment, improving parenting, and fostering adaptive parent-child relationships, and as a result altering the developmental trajectories of 1-year-old maltreated infants. Given the centrality of attachment during this developmental period, establishing a secure attachment relationship was the targeted intervention outcome.

An agreement for a recruitment liaison was established with the local Department of Human and Health Services (DHHS). Because the liaison was an employee of DHHS, she was able to access DHHS and Child Protective Service (CPS) records to identify all infants in families where maltreatment had occurred. The liaison approached potential participants meeting inclusion criteria and explained the study; if interested, families signed a consent authorizing their names to be released to the project. Families were assessed at baseline when infants were 12 months of age, and follow-up postintervention assessments were conducted at age 26 months.

In addition to the two active interventions, a community standard (CS) group also was included in the study design. The CS group received standard care available in the community. This typically involved monitoring by CPS but may have included referral to other community programs. Mothers in the PHV and IPP groups also were able to receive any standard community services. Following completion of the baseline assessments, mother-infant dyads were randomly assigned to the PHV, IPP, and CS groups. In addition to the three maltreatment groups, the DHHS liaison also recruited a nonmaltreated comparison (NC) group from the population of families receiving Temporary Assistance to Needy Families but with no history of child maltreatment. This strategy allowed for the inclusion of a normative comparison group that was comparable in terms of socioeconomic characteristics to the maltreating families.

Psychoeducational Home Visitation

This model of preventive intervention is derived from the work of Olds (Olds et al., 1997, 1998; Olds & Kitzman, 1990), involving visitation by nurses to the homes of low-income, teenage mothers of newborns over a 2-year period. The nurses provided a home-based education program on infant physical and psychological development and parenting, encouraged mothers to seek further education and employment, and enhanced informal social support. The home visitation program was effective in reducing the emergence of child maltreatment and fostered improved health and mental health outcomes for mothers and children. Although very promising, it is not known whether this approach is effective when maltreatment already had occurred during infancy. Accordingly, the PHV intervention was supplemented by a variety of cognitive and behavioral techniques to address parenting skill deficits and social-ecological factors, such as limited personal resources, poor social support, and stresses in the home, associated with maltreatment. Master's level therapists experienced in working with multiproblem families conducted home visits scheduled weekly over a 12-month period. The PHV model was psychoeducationally based, striving to address current concerns, provide parental education and parenting skill training, reduce maternal stress, foster social support, and increase life satisfaction. The approach is didactic in nature, providing mothers with specific information and knowledge regarding child development. Training in parenting techniques, problem solving, and relaxation was utilized. Within a core agenda of topics on parenting and social skills to be addressed with all mothers, flexibility and latitude on the amount of time spent on each area were stressed to tailor the intervention to each mother's primary needs.

Infant-Parent Psychotherapy

This model of intervention is derived from the work of Fraiberg (Fraiberg, Adelson, & Shapiro, 1975) and has been shown to be efficacious in fostering secure attachment in high-risk, low-income, immigrant families (Lieberman, 1991, 1992; Lieberman & Pawl, 1988). A guiding assumption of IPP is that difficulties in the parent-infant relationship do not result from deficits in parenting knowledge and skill alone. Rather, the problems that maltreating mothers have in relating sensitively and responsively to their infants stem from insecure internal representational models that evolved in response to the mother's own experiences in childhood. The infant evokes affects and memories associated with the mother's childhood relationship experiences, and in the process, the mother's unresolved and conflictual feelings can be projected onto the infant, resulting in distorted perceptions of the infant, a lack of attunement, and insensitive care.

In IPP, the patient is not the mother or the infant; rather, it is the relationship between the mother and her baby. Master's level therapists met weekly with mothers and their 12-month-old infants during sessions conducted in the home over the course of 1 year. The approach is supportive, nondirective, and nondidactic and includes developmental guidance based on the mother's concerns. During the sessions, the therapist and the mother engage in joint observation of the infant. The therapist's empathic responsiveness to the mother and the baby allows for expansion of parental understanding and exploration of maternal misperceptions of the infant. Therapists strive to allow distorted emotional reactions and perceptions of the infant as they are enacted during mother-infant interaction to be associated with memories and affects from the mother's prior childhood experiences. Through respect, empathic concern, and unfailing positive regard, the therapeutic relationship provides the mother with a corrective emotional experience, through which the mother is able to differentiate current from past relationships and form positive internal representations of herself and of herself in relationship to others, particularly her infant. As a result of this process, mothers are able to expand their responsiveness, sensitivity, and attunement to the infant, fostering security in the mother-child relationship and promoting emerging autonomy in the child.

Both the IPP and PHV interventions were manualized, with central components and core principles of each approach specified. Therapists participated in individual and group supervision on a weekly basis, and checks on the fidelity of the intervention implementation for each approach were conducted throughout the course of intervention.

Program Outcomes

Consistent with prior research, mothers in the maltreatment groups compared to those in the nonmaltreatment group were found to differ substantially on important constructs expected to confer vulnerability on the mother's capacity to form a secure attachment relationship with her infant. In terms of the mother's own childhood history and her representation of her relationship with her own mother, maltreatment group mothers reported significantly more adverse childhood experiences than nonmaltreating mothers. Emotional and physical abuse and neglect as well as sexual abuse during childhood were reported more frequently among mothers in the maltreatment group. Furthermore, maternal representations of the quality of their relationship in childhood with their own mother were marked by feelings of being unloved and highly rejected. In terms of current adult perspectives, maltreating mothers also derogated the importance of attachment and mother-child relationships and harbored considerable current anger toward their mother. The experiential and representational vulnerabilities forecast difficulties in the maltreatment group mothers in forming a sensitive and responsive relationship with their own infants.

In keeping with early relationship difficulties and current anger and resentment, mothers in the maltreatment group also reported less availability of social support from family members. Thus, the ability of these mothers to rely on family in times of need appears compromised. Maltreatment group mothers also reported significantly higher current stress. This stress was related to feeling more demands and struggles in relation to their child, as well as feeling less competent as a parent. Depression and health concerns also were more prominent stressors for these mothers. Contrary to expectations, the mothers in the maltreatment group did not convey deficits in their understanding of appropriate parenting attitudes and behavior, relative to nonmaltreating mothers. However, based on extensive observation, home observers who were unaware of group status rated mothers in the maltreatment group as substantially lower in maternal sensitivity to their infants than nonmaltreating mothers. Thus, histories of abuse and neglect in childhood, insecure relationship representations, limited family social support, stressors in multiple domains, and insensitive maternal patterns of relating to her infant likely conspire to impair secure attachment relationship formation.

During the baseline assessment at age 12 months, infant attachment organization was measured using the standard Strange Situation observation procedures. Videotapes were subsequently coded utilizing Ainsworth's (1969) criteria for the A, B, and C classifications; D classifications were based on the Main and Solomon (1990) criteria. The baseline attachment classifications indicated that the maltreated infants exhibited an extremely high rate of insecure attachment. In fact, only one infant in the maltreatment group (less than 1%) was classified as secure. The rate of secure attachment was substantially higher in the nonmaltreatment group (31.7%), yet below the rates observed in middle-class, nondisadvantaged samples. In terms of the specific insecure attachment organizations observed, not only were the maltreated infants rated as insecure, but nearly 90% were rated as disorganized, contrasting with 42.3% of the nonmaltreated infants. Thus, disorganized attachment was almost ubiquitous among the maltreated infants. No differences in rate of insecure or disorganized attachment were observed among the three maltreatment groups.

Following the intervention, attachment organization was again assessed with the Strange Situation at age 26 months. Dramatic changes in attachment classification were observed. At follow-up, the rate of secure attachment had increased markedly in the two intervention groups to 60.7% and 54.5% for the IPP and PHV groups, respectively. In contrast, the rate of secure attachment in the CS group remained virtually nonexistent (1.9%). Moreover, the rate of secure attachment in the IPP and the PHV groups even surpassed the rate of security in the nonmaltreated group (38.6%). Thus, marked gains were achieved in establishing secure attachment organizations in both of the intervention groups. Change from insecure to secure attachment was significantly more likely in the IPP and PHV groups than in the CS and nonmaltreated control groups.

In contrast to the reorganization in attachment that had occurred in the intervention groups, stability of insecure attachment was almost universal in the CS group (98.1%). Similarly, stability of attachment also was more common in the nonmaltreated group, with 70.4% of the insecure nonmaltreated children remaining insecure at follow-up, and 53.9% of those who were secure remaining secure. Overall, stability of secure/insecure attachment was 63.7% in the nonmaltreated group. Thus, continuity of attachment organization was more characteristic of the groups not participating in the active preventive interventions.

Given the extremely high rate of disorganized attachment in the maltreated infants at age 12 months, it is remarkable that the two preventive interventions were efficacious in reducing this atypical attachment pattern. Stable disorganized attachment was observed among 74.1% of the CS children, whereas stable disorganized attachment occurred at much lower rates in the two intervention groups, 28.6% and 36.4% for the IPP and PHV groups, respectively, comparable to the rate observed in the nonmaltreated group, 27.3%. Thus, infants who have been maltreated are highly likely to maintain disorganized/disoriented attachments in the absence of intensive efforts to improve the mother-child relationship and parenting.

The results of the intervention provide strong support for the benefits of the preventive interventions in altering the developmental trajectories of maltreated infants. Through targeting a central developmental task of the infancy/toddler period, the interventions were successful in transforming the attachment organization of a substantial percentage of maltreated infants. Not only were marked reductions achieved in the rate of insecure attachment, but disorganized attachments were shown to be modifiable and secure attachments were attained. These results are noteworthy for demonstrating the malleability and plasticity of the attachment system through focusing on changing aspects of the early mother-child relationship. The establishment of secure attachment relationships in the maltreated youngsters through the preventive interventions holds promise for achieving more competent resolutions of subsequent developmental tasks. In the context of a secure attachment relationship, the secure maltreated children are more likely to develop positive self-representations. Secure representational models of the self and self in relation to others will further promote competent striving to adapt to subsequent developmental challenges as these children begin forming relationships with other adults and peers. By intervening to promote more competent developmental trajectories through instilling a secure attachment organization, it is anticipated that maladjustment and the development of psychopathology will more likely be averted as these children develop.

Preventive Intervention for Maltreated Preschoolers: Preschooler-Parent Psychotherapy

The preschool years are a critical time for symbolic and representational development; therefore, this period provides an opportunity to help children with histories of child maltreatment avert difficulties with respect to their perceptions of self and their expectations about relationships with others. Because a considerable body of research has documented the deleterious effects of maltreatment on the representational development of abused and neglected children (Cicchetti & Toth, 2005), this population emerges as one that could benefit from targeted preventions.

Drawing from the extant literature, we implemented two interventions that shared the goal of improving attachment insecurity but that differed in the strategies utilized to attain this goal. These interventions were comparable to those utilized in the study of maltreated infants. Given the older age of the children, however, the IPP model of intervention was renamed preschooler-parent psychotherapy (PPP). In view of the importance of representational development, we assessed children's representations of self and of self in relation to others both prior to and following the provision of our preventive interventions.

At baseline and at postintervention, 11 narrative story stems, selected from the MacArthur Story-Stem Battery (Bretherton, Oppenheim, Buchsbaum, Emde, & the MacArthur Narrative Group, 1990) and from the Attachment Story Completion Test (Bretherton, Ridgeway, & Cassidy, 1990), were individually administered to child

participants. The narratives depicted moral dilemmas and emotionally charged events in the context of parent-child and family relationships. Narrative story stems included vignettes designed to elicit children's perceptions of the parent-child relationship, of self, and of maternal behavior in response to child transgressions, intrafamilial conflicts, and child accidents.

Children's narratives were videotaped and maternal and self-representations were subsequently coded according to the MacArthur *Narrative Coding Manual,* Rochester revision (Robinson, Mantz-Simmons, Macfie, & the MacArthur Narrative Working Group, 1992). A modified version of Bickham and Fiese's (1999) child narrative code book was utilized to assess expectations of the mother-child relationship (for details of these coding systems, see Toth, Maughan, Manly, Spagnola, & Cicchetti, 2002).

Children in the PPP intervention evidenced a greater decline in maladaptive maternal representations over time than did children in the PHV and CS interventions. Moreover, children who took part in the PPP intervention displayed a greater decrease in negative self-representations than did children in the CS, PHV, and NC groups. Additionally, the mother-child relationship expectations of PPP children became more positive over the course of the intervention as compared with children in the PHV and NC groups. These results suggest that a model of intervention informed by attachment theory (PPP) is more effective at improving representations of self and of caregivers than is a didactic model of intervention (PHV) directed at parenting skills. The results contradict predictions that would emanate from the meta-analysis of interventions targeting maternal sensitivity and child attachment (Bakersman-Kranenburg, van Izendoorn, & Juffer, 2003). Because the intervention focused on changing representational models utilizing a narrative story stem measure, outcomes that might be expected to improve more dramatically in the PHV model (e.g., parenting skills, knowledge of child development) could not be addressed.

Because this intervention and the intervention for maltreated infants are the first to demonstrate that representations can be modified through the provision of an intervention informed by attachment-theory, it is important to consider factors that may have contributed to the efficacy of these approaches. We believe that the utilization of skilled and well-trained therapists, adherence to manualized treatment models, and monitoring of the fidelity of the provision of the interventions contributed to the efficacious findings. Moreover, given prior research that has found that the type of maternal attachment insecurity that is present may affect maternal responsivity to various intervention strategies (Bakermans-Kranenburg, Juffer, & van Ijzendoorn, 1998), it will be important to assess baseline attachment organization of mothers in relation to intervention outcome.

Preventive Intervention for Toddlers of Mothers with Major Depressive Disorder: Toddler-Parent Psychotherapy

Interest in the risk imposed on offspring by parental psychopathology was spearheaded by research on children of parents with Schizophrenia. Downey and Coyne (1990) noted that in this research, comparison groups were composed of children of parents with depression, with the anticipation that the difficulties would be substantially stronger in the children of parents with Schizophrenia. However, the findings indicated that the children of depressed parents exhibited the same range of disturbances. Relative to Schizophrenia, depressive disorders are far more prevalent. In the National Comorbidity Study, nearly 16% of the participants met lifetime diagnostic criteria for Major Depressive Disorder (MDD; Kessler, Davies, & Kender, 1997; Kessler, McGonagle, Zhao, & Nelson, 1994), and of those with a history of a depressive episode, 80% or more experience recurrent episodes. Consequently, offspring of depressed parents constitute a sizable population of children at high risk.

Mothers with MDD often struggle with the responsive care essential for infants and young children. Aspects of the disorder, including anhedonia, difficulty regulating negative affect, sleep disturbances, feelings of worthlessness, hopelessness, and helplessness, and difficulties in role functioning, are likely to challenge the early relational environment. Ensuing difficulties in parenting, sensitivity, responsivity, and affective attunement to the child may intrude on the development of the mother-child relationship, with adverse effects on child adaptation and functioning (Cicchetti, Rogosch, & Toth, 1998; Goodman & Gotlib, 2002). Moreover, for many of these mothers, depressive disorders have evolved with contributions from unresolved problems stemming from the mother's own attachment relationships in childhood (Arieti & Bemporad, 1978; Bowlby, 1980). Consequently, issues stemming from the mother's childhood attachment experiences may intrude on the quality of the attachment relationship formed with her own child via maternal internal representational models.

From the organizational perspective on development, precursors to later depressive disorders likely have origins in the quality of developmental competencies emerging across the early years of life. In particular, difficulties in affect regulation, attachment, and self-development correspond to symptoms expressed in depressive disorders, including high levels of negative affect, interpersonal difficulties, and such diverse self-processes as low self-esteem, negative attributions, and feelings of helplessness and hopelessness. Evidence for atypicalities in biological systems of children of mothers with depressive disorders also have been documented. For example, infants of depressed mothers during the first 6 months of life have been found to have greater right-frontal brain activation as a result of lower left-frontal activation than comparison infants (Field, Fox, Pickens, & Nawrocki, 1995; Jones, Field, Fox, Lundy, & Davalos, 1997). This pattern of hemispheric asymmetry is associated with greater sensitivity and distraction to environmental change resulting in higher levels of distress. These early brain activation differences may suggest a diathesis for later depression and constitute a vulnerability that may be elaborated by subsequent parent-child relationship experiences. Other biological systems also are likely involved. For example, variation in the limbic-hypothalamic-pituitary-adrenal axis, which mediates the stress response, has been found in offspring of depressed mothers. In particular, 7-year-olds with high internalizing symptoms evinced high levels of baseline cortisol, and the best predictor of the elevated cortisol was maternal depression during the first 2 years (Ashman, Dawson, Panagiotides, Yamada, & Wilkinson, 2002).

A number of investigations of attachment in young children of depressed mothers have been conducted, and the results have been varied, based on differences in the demographic characteristics of the samples and variations in maternal depressive symptomatology and chronicity. Martins and Gaffan (2000) conducted a meta-analysis of studies in this area and concluded that there was evidence for increased rates of avoidant and disorganized attachment among these young offspring. The emergence of insecure attachment is a crucial concern because insecure attachment in infancy portends the development of insecure internal representational models of self and of self in relation to others. Evolving social, emotional, and cognitive competencies may be compromised and contribute to the development of a depressotypic developmental organization of psychological and biological systems (Cicchetti, Rogosch, & Toth, 1997; Cicchetti & Toth, 1998). Affect associated with the early development of the self has been shown to be more negative and less positive in toddlers of mothers with MDD, and insecure attachment in these offspring was related to affective instability and delayed self-emergence (Cicchetti et al., 1997). Depressed mothers are more likely to express criticism regarding their toddler-age children, and these youngsters exist in a relational context dominated by interspousal criticism, negative affect, and marital conflict (Cicchetti et al., 1998; Downey & Coyne, 1990; Rogosch, Cicchetti, & Toth, 2004). Radke-Yarrow, Belmont, Nottelmann, and Bottomly (1990) found that mothers with mood disorders were more likely to make negative attributions about their toddlers and the child's emotions, and there was correspondence between the negativity of attributions and statements about the self. Thus, insecure attachment and early negative self-development may portend the development of negative self-structure and self-understanding, self-cognitions and attributions, and self-schemata that constitute precursors to depressive disorder (Cicchetti & Schneider-Rosen, 1986; Cicchetti & Toth, 1995, 1998).

Intervention Design

To prevent the early development of a depressotypic developmental organization in young children of mothers with MDD, our strategy was to target the mother-child relationship to promote the development of secure mother-child attachment relationships and positive self-development. A number of interventions informed by attachment theory have been developed (Bakermans-Kranenburg et al., 2003; van Ijzendoorn, Juffer, & Duyvesteyn, 1995). However, the diversity in the multiproblem populations investigated, variation in the approaches taken, and multiple intervention components utilized (e.g., Egeland & Erickson, 1990; Erickson, Korfmacher, & Egeland, 1992; Lieberman, Weston, & Pawl, 1991; Lyons-Ruth, Connell, Grunebaum, & Botein, 1990) have made understanding the central processes contributing to effectiveness uncertain. Two interventions have been targeted specifically for altering attachment security in young children of depressed mothers (Cooper & Murray, 1997; Gelfand, Teti, Seiner, & Jameson, 1996). Although these studies demonstrated positive intervention effects, fostering the development of secure attachments was not accomplished. Further efforts in this area are thus needed.

When women have a depressive disorder, the focus of treatment, whether psychotherapeutic or pharmacologic, centers on the individual as an adult. Attention to the woman's role as mother and the implications for the depressive disorder on her children are not priority concerns. An implicit assumption is that if maternal depression abates, then any adverse effects on the child will be minimal. However, difficulties in the mother-child relationship may not easily dissipate, and the likelihood of future depressive episodes indicates that the child continues to be at risk. Thus, strengthening the mother-child relationship, promoting child competence, and averting the emergence of a depressotypic developmental organization are important considerations, in addition to the mother's depressive disorder.

The approach utilized herein was toddler-paren psychotherapy (TPP), an extension of infant-parent psychotherapy discussed earlier (Lieberman, 1992). Toddlerhood was targeted because of the central stage-salient task of the period, that is, the development of an autonomous self. Accordingly, we sought to foster increased security in the mother-child attachment relationship and thereby promote the positive development of self and corresponding positive internal representational models of self and other. Young children during the toddler period are growing in verbal skills and comprehension. As a result, the content of conversations between therapist and mother during the dyadic sessions of TPP and children's reactions must be given greater attention. Furthermore, as mothers and their toddlers increasingly are able to communicate verbally, both verbal as well as nonverbal communications offer opportunities for understanding the mother-child relationship. During this period, toddlers are increasingly asserting their autonomy, and attempts to negotiate differing maternal and child goals become more common during sessions. As the attachment relationship transforms, a goal-directed partnership between the mother and child represents an important achievement. As in IPP, TPP strives to expand maternal awareness and insight regarding influences on the mother's capacity to relate affectively and sensitively to the toddler and establish more positive maternal internal representational models of herself, her relationships, and her child.

Depressed mothers with a child approximately 18 months of age were recruited for a randomized preventive trial to evaluate the efficacy of TPP in improving the mother-child relationship and fostering competent development in the child, particularly secure attachment, with the intent of preventing a depressotypic developmental organization. Depressed mothers were recruited via referral from mental health professionals and through notices placed in newspapers, physicians' offices, and community libraries. To focus the RPT specifically on maternal depression rather than multiple co-occurring risk factors associated with poverty, the socioeconomic status of the participants was restricted to middle-class or higher. All depressed mothers met criteria for MDD with a major depressive episode occurring at some time since the child's birth; most mothers were currently depressed. In addition to the depressed mothers and their toddlers, a sample of toddlers and their mothers ($n = 66$) who had no history of current or prior major psychopathology were recruited to serve as a normative comparison (NC) group. The children in the depressed and nondepressed samples were on average 20 months of age when baseline assessments were conducted; mothers averaged 31.6 years of age. Following baseline assessments, the depressed mothers and the toddlers ($n = 102$) were randomly assigned to the depressed intervention (DI) or the depressed control (DC) group.

The TPP was conducted with mothers from the time of completion of baseline assessments until children were 3 years old. Because of the middle-class socioeconomic status of the sample, sessions were conducted in an office setting rather than in the home, as with traditional IPP (Fraiberg et al., 1975). This was preferable to the middle-class mothers, who would have experienced sessions in the home as intrusive. Intervention sessions were typically scheduled on a weekly basis. The intervention lasted on average 57 weeks, and the mean number of sessions conducted was 45. Therapists received weekly group and individual supervision, and over the course of the implementation of the TPP intervention, fidelity was monitored by reviewing videotapes of the sessions.

Effects of Toddler-Parent Psychotherapy on Attachment

Prior to the intervention, substantial differences in Strange Situation attachment classification were found among the DI, DC, and NC groups. Consistent with expectations for greater insecurity in the depressed groups, significantly fewer children were classified as secure in the DI group (16.7%) and in the DC group (21.9%), as compared to the NC group (55.9%). Thus, approximately 80% of the toddlers of depressed mothers were found to have insecure attachment organizations. Although resistant and avoidant attachments were observed, the major differences in insecure attachment types between groups involved disorganized attachment. Whereas the rate of disorganized attachment in the NC group was relatively low (19.1%), significantly higher rates of disorganized attachment were found in the two depressed groups, 37.9% and 40.6% for the DI and DC groups, respectively.

At age 3, following completion of the TPP intervention, attachment organization was reassessed, and significant group differences in the distribution of attachment classifications were again observed. However, the pattern of group differences had changed markedly. Specifically, the rate of secure attachment had increased substantially in the DI group, to 67.4%, whereas no improvement in the rate of secure attachment was found in the DC group (16.7%). Moreover, the DI group no longer differed significantly from the NC group (47.6%) in the rate of secure attachment, but the rate of secure attachment in the NC group far exceeded the rate in the DC group. The pattern of secure versus insecure classification at postintervention had shifted in accord with the predicted effects of the preventive intervention, with substantial increases in attachment security among children who had been in the preventive interventions; in contrast, insecure attachment characterized over 80% of the children of depressed mothers not receiving TPP.

The pattern of stability and change in attachment from pre- to postintervention indicated that change for insecure to secure was most commonly observed in the DI group (54.3%), whereas the most stable pattern in the DC group was stable insecure attachment (72.2%). Among children classified as avoidant at baseline, 63.2% of those in the DI group changed to secure at follow-up, contrasting with only 7.1% of the DC group. Dramatic change in disorganized attachment also was observed: 58.8% of children classified as disorganized in the DI group changed to secure, whereas only 8.0% of DC children who were disorganized changed to secure. Stable disorganized attachment was more common in the DC group (56.0%) than in the DI group (11.8%). Thus, the TPP preventive intervention was effective in promoting reorganization of different forms of insecure attachment into secure attachment, and in the absence of the intervention, youngsters of depressed mothers continued along a vulnerable trajectory of insecure attachment over time.

Effects of Toddler-Parent Psychotherapy on Cognitive Development

In addition to the important influence of TPP on promoting secure attachment organization, evidence for other intervention effects was examined. In particular, because of the goal of promoting self-development and autonomy and improvements in mother-child communication as a result of the intervention, the effects of TPP on cognitive development were investigated. At baseline, the Bayley Scales of Infant Development were administered, and the three study groups were found to be equivalent on the Mental Development Index. After the completion of the preventive intervention, all children at age 3 were administered the Wechsler Preschool and Primary Scale of Intelligence-Revised (WPPSI-R; Wechsler, 1989), and significant group differences emerged. The DI and NC groups continued to be equivalent in terms of Full-Scale IQ scores. However, the DC group attained lower mean scores than the DI and NC groups. Additionally, Verbal IQ scores, but not Performance IQ scores, showed the same pattern of group differences. Thus, in the absence of the preventive intervention, children of depressed mothers did not appear to make the same cognitive advances as did children of nondepressed mothers. Moreover, the TPP preventive intervention appeared to safeguard the children of depressed mothers in the DI group, promoting competent cognitive development, consistent with that of the NC group.

Although the primary goals of TPP were to promote improved mother-child relationships and more competent child developmental attainments, it was anticipated that the strong therapeutic relationship and the corrective emotional experience afforded by TPP would contribute to reducing maternal depression. However, diagnostic and questionnaire assessments with the mothers following the intervention did not provide support for these changes. In fact, 30% of the mothers in the two depressed groups had major depressive episodes during the period from baseline to follow-up assessments. Consequently, whether subsequent depressive episodes influenced the intervention effects on cognitive development was examined for the DI and DC groups. Overall, whether mothers had a subsequent depressive episode did not influence child cognitive development. However, interaction effects of the DI group and subsequent depressive episode were found for Full-Scale IQ and Verbal IQ. For children in the DI group, cognitive scores were equivalent whether or not mothers had further depression. In contrast, for the DC group, children whose mothers had further depressive episodes attained lower cognitive scores than those whose mothers did not have a subsequent episode. These findings indicate that maternal depression poses ongoing risk to competent developmental attainments in children in the absence of intervention. Nevertheless, even though some mothers in the DI group continued to struggle with Major Depression, TPP appeared to protect these children's cognitive development.

Translation of the Preventive Intervention for Low-Income Mothers and Infants

Given the positive results of the RPT in demonstrating the efficacy of the preventive intervention for fostering positive developmental outcomes among toddlers of depressed mothers from a middle-class sample, a current RPT is under way to evaluate the efficacy of the intervention in a low-income sample. The difference in socioeconomic status and the high levels of social adversity faced by low-income families necessitated additional considerations in designing and implementing the intervention. Based on the implementation of IPP with the low-income maltreating sample, it was clear that attention to the poverty, limited resources, frequent single parentage, and dangerous neigh-

borhoods was crucial to reach this population. Accordingly, therapists experienced in working with low-income mothers implement the current preventive intervention. Because transportation difficulties, particularly with an infant, are frequent, the intervention is conducted in the home rather than being center-based. The home-based sessions reduce the demands on depressed women with young infants and instill trust between therapist and mother, as the therapist engages the mother in her home environment.

Another important reality faced by low-income women is the limitation in available and accessible mental health care. Accordingly, despite major depression, few low-income mothers are likely to seek or continue mental health treatment. Thus, an active intervention to treat maternal depression, interpersonal psychotherapy (IPT), was incorporated into the preventive intervention. IPT was chosen because its focus on interpersonal stresses and processes is consistent with relational issues addressed in IPP. Furthermore, because IPT is structured and time-limited, future implementation in the community is likely to be more feasible.

IPT also has been shown to be effective in treating maternal depression (O'Hara, Stuart, Gorman, & Wenzel, 2000; Stuart & O'Hara, 1995) and for treatment of depression in low-income populations (Spinelli, 1997). In the current RPT, depressed mothers and their infants are randomly assigned to one of three intervention groups: One group receives IPT, the second group receives IPT followed by 8 months of IPP, and the third group receives group informational meetings and referral to other mental health services in the community. A fourth demographically comparable group comprises mothers with no history of major psychiatric disorder and their infants. The evaluation study will determine whether IPP is effective in fostering positive child developmental outcomes in the low-income sample. Additionally, contrasting the IPT-only and the combined IPT/IPP intervention will address whether treating maternal depression alone is sufficient to alter child outcomes, or whether additional intervention focused on the mother-child relationship is crucial for promoting positive child developmental attainments.

FUTURE DIRECTIONS FOR PREVENTION TRIALS

Although much progress has been made in research on the prevention of mental health disorders, there are many important next steps that the field needs to address. In this section, we comment on the need for (1) continued refinement of the design and analysis of preventive intervention trials, (2) greater attention to effectiveness and efficacy trials, and (3) a better understanding of the implications advances in behavior and molecular genetics has for prevention science.

Design and Analysis of Preventive Intervention Trials

Although an exhaustive review of the mental health preventive intervention literature was not an objective of this chapter, recent reviews suggest that randomized control trials with long-term follow-up are the exception rather than the rule. Equally rare are prevention trials where the putative mechanisms of intervention change are rigorously assessed and tested. Even rarer are trials where the costs of the intervention are enumerated and the ultimate value of the intervention determined based on a cost-benefit or cost-effectiveness analysis (see Haddix, Teutsch, Shaffer, & Dunet, 1996, for a comprehensive treatment of cost-benefit analysis in the context of preventive intervention trials). Thus, in terms of future directions, there is a clear need to remedy each of these shortcomings.

An equally important set of issues that must be addressed revolves around the analysis of the data from preventive and treatment intervention trials. In most randomized trials of preventive and treatment interventions, the estimation of intervention effects is complicated by variation in the degree to which an intervention is provided to and/or taken by the targeted population as designed. Barnard, Du, Hill, and Rubin (1998) use the term "broken randomized experiments" to refer to intervention trials where such variation in the receipt and/or provision of the intervention is present. Broken randomized experiments stem from the obvious fact that intervention researchers cannot ethically require the intervention recipients or providers to actually take or implement the intervention as designed. Rather, as Frangakis and Rubin (1999, 2002) point out, they can only randomize "encouragement" to participation. Accordingly, Frangakis and Rubin refer to randomized preventive and treatment and intervention trials as "encouragement studies," where the focus is not only on the effect of encouragement itself (assignment to the intervention condition), but also on the effect of the intervention being encouraged.

A common practice among intervention researchers is to ignore in their evaluation of intervention effects the presence of variation in the degree to which an intervention is provided to and/or received by the targeted population as designed. This is typically referred to as an intent-to-treat analysis (ITT), where one simply estimates the difference in mean outcomes between those assigned to the interven-

tion group and those assigned to the control group. The ITT analysis thus yields the causal effect of intervention assignment and not the treatment received (Little & Yau, 1998). Although the ITT estimate of the effect of intervention assignment is protected from bias by randomized treatment allocation, it is distorted by the fact that variation in the receipt and/or provision of the intervention is ignored. As an alternative to the ITT analysis, intervention researchers often resort to an "as-treated analysis," wherein only those who completed and/or provided the intervention as designed are considered in the comparison with the control group. As Little and Yau point out, the problem with this approach is that randomization is violated.

In recent years there has been substantial progress in the analysis of encouragement designs based on building bridges between statistical and econometric approaches to causal inference. In particular, the widely accepted approach in statistics to formulating causal questions is in terms of "potential outcomes." Although this approach has roots dating back to Neyman and Rubin in the context of perfect randomized experiments (Neyman, 1923; Rubin, 1990), it is generally referred to as Rubin's causal model (Holland, 1986) for work extending the framework to observational studies (Rubin, 1974, 1977) and including modes of inference other than randomization-based—in particular, Bayesian methods (Rubin, 1978, 1990). In economics, the technique of instrumental variables (Haavelmo, 1943; Tinbergen, 1930) has been a main tool of causal inference in the type of nonrandomized studies prevalent in that field. Angrist, Imbens, and Rubin (1996) showed how these approaches can be viewed as completely compatible, thereby clarifying and strengthening each approach. The result was an interpretation of the instrumental variables technology as a way to approach a randomized experiment that suffers from variation in the degree to which an intervention is provided to and/or taken by the targeted population as designed, such as a randomized encouragement design.

In encouragement designs with compliance as the only partially uncontrolled factor, and where there are full outcome data, Imbens and Rubin (1997) extended Rubin's (1978) Bayesian approach to causal inference to handle simple randomized experiments with noncompliance. Imbens and Rubin focused on estimating the average intervention effect for compliers, which they termed the complier average causal effect (CACE). More specifically, CACE is the effect of the randomized encouragement on all subjects who would comply with their treatment assignment, no matter which assignment they would be given.

As an alternative to the Bayesian approach to CACE analysis, Jo and Muthén (2001, 2002) describe the use of the random coefficient growth mixture modeling framework for estimating CACE in intervention trials featuring single and repeated assessments of intervention outcomes. Jo and Muthén (2002) also explore an approach for dealing with the complication that compliance is rarely measured in intervention trials such as ours on a binary scale (yes or no). Rather, it is typically measured on an ordinal, interval, or continuous scale. Jo (2002b) studied the estimation of intervention effects with noncompliance under alternative model specifications; Jo (2002a) focused on model misspecification sensitivity analysis in estimating causal effects of interventions with noncompliance. In another work (Jo, 2002c), the issues of statistical power and estimating it in randomized intervention trials with noncompliance were addressed.

Despite the considerable advances made in the analysis of randomized encouragement designs, a number of complications often encountered in trials where randomization occurs at the level of the group (schools, classrooms, clinics, etc.) rather than at the level of the individual remain to be dealt with if valid estimates of intervention effects are to be obtained in the presence of variation in the level of intervention implementation fidelity. First, besides the fact that compliance or fidelity is typically measured on an ordinal, interval, or continuous scale, methodologically rigorous intervention trials typically assess the compliance behaviors of those providing it as well as of the participants assigned to receive it. Moreover, multiple indices of the compliance behaviors of the recipients and providers are typically gathered. The second complication involves the modeling of treatment-baseline interactions. More specifically, from a developmental perspective, one assumes that children or adults do not proceed in lockstep fashion in terms of their social and behavioral development. This raises the question of whether the effects of an intervention designed to target social and behavioral development will vary as a function of the variation across the participants in their developmental course prior to the intervention (see, e.g., Shirk, 1999; Toth & Cicchetti, 1999). To study such a treatment-baseline interaction (or treatment-trajectory interaction), one must switch from a pretest-posttest analysis framework (essentially an ANCOVA-type analysis) to the growth mixture modeling framework as described in Muthén et al. (2002). A third complication centers on trials where randomization to intervention condition is done at the group level (e.g., children are clustered within classrooms and schools). Here, the data are multilevel, which must be taken into account in estimating intervention effects.

Another important methodological challenge that prevention researchers face is the fact that they often collect information from multiple informants and/or via multiple methods. Yet up until now, there appeared to be little guidance in the literature as to methodologically and conceptually sound ways to integrate data from multiple informants and methods. Kraemer and colleagues (2003) offer a framework for accomplishing this task that makes sense from both a conceptual and a statistical standpoint. In their model:

> The choice of informants is based on conceptualizing the contexts and perspectives that influence expression of the characteristic of interest and then identifying informants who represent those contexts and perspectives in such a way as to have the weaknesses of one informant canceled by the strengths of another. (p. 1566)

Kraemer and colleagues go on to elaborate a sequence of steps and procedures to integrate data from multiple informants:

1. A reliable and reasonably valid informant's report (I) comprises information on the trait or characteristic in question (T), some contribution from the context in which that informant is likely to observe the subject (C), a contribution from the perspective from which that informant views the subject (P), and random error (E). Each of these pieces of information, or sources of variance, can be defined as orthogonal latent variables.

2. For this three-dimensional model, we need at least three informants, each carefully selected to report reliable information about the specific characteristic, knowing that no one informant has all the pertinent information.

3. In selecting our informants, we would not choose informants likely to give collinear (highly correlated) reports because they would simply reproduce the same incomplete information.

4. Rather, we would try to select informants likely to give orthogonal (valid, but not redundant) reports, in such a way as to have the flaws (i.e., variability in the data that is not linked to the target characteristic) in one informant's data "corrected" by other informants.

5. Instead of asking, "How many informants do we need, and how do we combine their reports?" we suggest that the question should rather be, "How do we select informants in such a way that the imperfections in one informant's reports are corrected by another's reports?"

6. To reduce the influence of perspective (P) and context (C), one triangulates the data by using a mix-and-match strategy, in which specific selected contexts are viewed from the same perspective and selected perspectives are viewed in the same context. By choosing informants to implement this mix-and-match strategy, one structures the data from multiple informants in such a way that principal-component analysis will yield a gold standard measure as the first principal component, T^*, and measures of the

contrasts in context and perspectives as the second and third principal components (C* and P*).

7. If the theory and implementation are correct, T* will be a reliable and valid measure of T. C* and P* are both reliable measures, but they are invalid for T. Thus, the model removes from T* the sources of error about T that are represented by C and P in the individual informants' reports. (pp. 1575–1576)

These seven steps that Kraemer and colleagues (2003) elaborate provide an excellent roadmap for the design and analysis of future prevention trials. Adherence to these steps should serve to provide a more efficient and valid approach to assessing and reporting on the impact of preventive intervention trials when multiple informants and methods are employed.

These are some of the key design and analysis issues that will need to be addressed in future preventive intervention trials. This overview was not meant to be an exhaustive treatment of the topic. Shadish (2002) identifies a number of additional methodological and analysis issues that will need to be addressed in future preventive intervention field trials.

The Need for Effectiveness and Efficacy Trials

Although there is a continuing need for more randomized control trials of preventive interventions with long-term follow-up, recent research reviews and reports on efficacy studies document the growing number of preventive and other interventions that either reduce the onset of common mental and substance disorders or decrease the duration and disability of initial episodes of these disorders (Burns, Compton, Egger, Farmer, & Robertson, 2002; Burns, Hoagwood, & Mrazek, 1999; Catalano, Berglund, Ryan, Lonczak, & Hawkins, 1998; Coie et al., 1993; Greenberg, Domitrovich, & Bumbarger, 1999, 2001; Kazdin, 2000; National Institute of Mental Health, 1998; Olds, Robinson, Song, Little, & Hill, 1999). As described by Nathan, Stuart, and Dolan (2000, pp. 964–965):

> Effectiveness research aims to determine whether treatments are feasible and have measurable beneficial effects across broad populations and in real-world settings, whereas the focus of the efficacy trial is on the performance of the intervention given the controls employed by the investigator.

Despite the growing number of efficacy studies demonstrating that common mental disorders can be prevented or their consequences greatly reduced when treated early, few

research studies examine (1) the extent that efficacious programs exhibit equally positive outcomes when implemented in natural service/treatment settings, (2) how dosage and quality of implementation affect outcomes, (3) how different program models and training strategies affect outcomes, and (4) the conditions necessary for successful program outcomes in natural settings with local ownership of the intervention process (Mrazek & Haggerty, 1994). These four issues constitute the key differences between efficacy and effectiveness research.

Earlier we discussed the prevention research cycle contained in the IOM report on the prevention of mental disorders (Mrazek & Haggerty, 1994). A critical juncture in the cycle centers on the progression from efficacy to effectiveness trials. We argue that the focus on feasibility in the prevention research cycle should not be restricted to the effectiveness stage. Rather, prevention scientists should consider in the efficacy stage the capacity of the existing public health structures and institutions to deploy their intervention if it is found to be efficacious. Here we are talking about not only the affordability of the intervention, but whether the relevant public health agencies have an efficient and effective means of gaining access to the population of interest. Preventive interventions based in public school settings have the advantage that by law children in the United States have to attend school from age 5 to age 16. But few social or public health institutions offer the access that the public schools do. Prevention scientists must also consider whether the public health institution that will likely be charged with the deployment of their preventive intervention has the personnel with the necessary expertise and motivation to implement it.

Along these lines, Schoenwald and Hoagwood (2001) integrated the findings from the operations research, industrial organizational psychology, community psychology, and educational sociology literatures. They then derived a conceptual model that identifies the key principles and relevant issues with respect to successful dissemination, adoption, implementation, and sustainability of innovation. These key principles are largely consistent with those elaborated by Rogers (1995) in his model of the diffusion of innovation and include (1) perceived relevance of the innovation to the system and extra organizational systems1 (2) the credibility of the innovation to these systems, (3) the clarity of the innovation, (4) whether the innovations contrast sharply with prevailing practices, and (5) the extent to which the prevailing practices are supported by fiscal, organizational, and values structures.

In terms of conceptual models and empirical research specific to the influence of organizational context on the delivery of children's mental health services, Glisson and colleagues (Glisson, 2002; Glisson & Hemmelgarn, 1998; Glisson & James, 2002) have done groundbreaking work. Their work has largely centered on the organizational context of community-based child welfare agencies and has focused on three key constructs: (1) organizational climate (i.e., the way persons perceive their work environment); (2) organizational culture (the ways things are routinely done in an organizational unit that are reflective of the norms and shared expectations of an organizational unit); and (3) organizational structure (the formal aspects of an organization, including elements such as the centralization of power and formalization of roles in an organization). Glisson and Hemmelgarn provided evidence of the impact of the organizational climate on psychosocial outcomes of children being seen in the child welfare system in Tennessee; Glisson and James report that service quality was associated with organizational culture.

McDougal, Clonan, and Martens (2000) offer a model involving the role of organizational change in the delivery of high-quality mental health services in schools that is likely applicable to most preventive intervention trials. Organizational readiness (e.g., support and active participation with administration and staff about the goals of the project), implementation support (support for training, supervision, and monitoring), and support for expansion of the model and its diffusion were identified as keys to successful implementation, diffusion, and maintenance.

In addition to McDougal et al. (2000), Hoagwood and Johnson (2003) and Ringeisen, Henderson, and Hoagwood (2003) identify organizational issues unique to school settings that may influence the delivery of evidence-based child mental health interventions. As with McDougal et al.'s model, many of the elements of their framework are relevant to preventive interventions in general. The issues they identify are largely consistent with those described by McDougal et al.: (1) whether the individuals chosen to implement the evidence-based interventions have roles associated with mental health and have played a role in either intervention development or implementation planning; (2) whether professional training and ongoing infrastructure are in place to support the providers in the implementation of the interventions; (3) whether current intervention programs and their allotted resources add to or detract from the implementation of the evidence-based mental health interventions; (4) whether such evidence-based interventions replace and improve on existing programs (maximizing available resources) or take valued resources from existing programs; (5) whether the school resources necessary to support an evidence-based intervention exist or have to be created, supported, and sustained; and (6) whether the primary outcomes of the evidence-based interventions are seen as consistent or conflicting with a school's response to state and federal academic accountability concerns.

To summarize, there is a need for effectiveness as well as efficacy research in prevention. Although Nathan et al. (2000, p. 977) note that there is currently an "absence of agreement on the essential components of either efficacy or effectiveness trials," Kraemer (2000) has sought to reconcile these conflicting views. She suggests that efficacy and effectiveness be seen as representing the anchor points on a single continuum, as opposed to separate and distinct entities. Consistent with Kraemer, Hoagwood, Burns, and Weisz (2002) offer a phased, or incremental, approach to effectiveness research that is consistent with the prevention research cycle described in the IOM report (Mrazek & Haggerty, 1994). Hoagwood et al. contend that this incremental approach represents a "profitable conjunction" of science to service in mental health research.

Implications of Advances in Behavior and Molecular Genetics for Prevention

Developmental research has focused on understanding how the family and relationships within the family impact child and adolescent adjustment. In general, studies examining the impact of family relationships on adjustment have found that warm and supportive relationships within the family are associated with positive child and adolescent outcomes, whereas coercive and conflictual relationships are associated with the development of problems (e.g., Cummings, Goeke-Morey, & Dukewich, 2001; Maccoby, 2002; Markman & Jones-Leonard, 1985; Patterson, Crosby, & Vuchinich, 1992). Because the majority of research in this area has not used genetically sensitive designs and in most cases has not examined more than one child per family, it has not been possible to distinguish environmental from genetic contributions to these associations. The need to consider genetic influences on family relationships is clear based on the rapidly accumulating number of studies that have found evidence for genetic influences on measures of family environment, ranging from parent-child relationships (e.g., Neiderhiser et al., 2004; Plomin, 1994; Towers, Spotts, & Neiderhiser, 2001) to sibling relationships (Bussell et al., 1999) to marital relationships (Spotts et al., 2004).

There has been a recent flurry of research examining genotype-environment interaction, many of these studies examining nonclinical samples of twins or siblings (e.g., Koeppen-Schomerus, Eley, Wolke, Gringas, & Plomin,

2000; Wichers et al., 2002). In addition, there are at least two studies that have found evidence for the interaction between a specific gene and a particular environment (Caspi et al., 2002, 2003). These findings of interactions between genes and the environment have inspired many researchers to take a second look at the importance of genes and genotype, especially in the context of a well-characterized environment. In part, this is because the field has long suspected that the interplay between genes and environment was interactional and not simply additive. In fact, some had proposed that disentangling the effects of genes from the effects of the environment was a nearly hopeless endeavor (Gottlieb, 1999). The recent findings of clear and significant interactions between genes and the environment indicate that this is not the case. The challenge remains, however, of how to translate such findings into prevention. Some have suggested that pharmacological intervention strategies may be appropriate (Caspi et al., 2002), although behavioral strategies focused on changing the environmental aspects of the interaction are also likely to be fruitful. In many cases, the information needed to target a pharmacological intervention will not be available, so somewhat broader behavioral interventions may be the only feasible approach, at least in the near future. One message that is clear from findings of genotype × environment interaction and genotype-environment correlation is that targeted interventions are much more likely to be effective as they are more likely to incorporate a response to an individual's genotype.

Practical Implications and Limitations of Genetic Research for Informing Prevention

The most useful and immediate implication of findings from genetic research for prevention is in increasing our understanding of the etiology and processes involved. Through studies that have clarified genotype-environment correlation and interaction, it is clear that environmental factors do not operate independently of an individual and that at least part of the individual influence is through genetic factors. Both quantitative behavioral genetics and association-based molecular genetic designs are population-based and provide little information about *individual* risk. In other words, although knowing an individual's genotype may provide some information about the sorts of environments he or she may be particularly sensitive to—such as high levels of stress for those with the homozygous short form of the 5-HTTLPR polymorphism—the amount of total variance accounted for in predicting outcome is modest. Nonetheless, there are few studies of specific nongenetic risk factors that account for large portions of variance. In both cases, it is the accumula-

tion of risk factors or the interaction among different risk factors that provides the best description of risk.

Based on the current state of the fields of quantitative and molecular genetics, there are three primary messages for prevention:

1. Individual characteristics have an important and substantial impact on environment, often for genetic reasons, at least in part.
2. Because most genetic designs are population-based, changing the environment will result in a change in outcome. In other words, heritability does not imply immutability.
3. Genetic factors may be protective. Although it is common to emphasize interactions in terms of a specific risk gene or genotype interacting with a specific high-risk environment, the flip side is that individuals with a different genotype or gene are protected even in high-risk environments. This is news and is consistent with much of the literature on resilience. We already knew that a low-risk environment was associated with fewer problems, but understanding that genes and genetic factors can operate in a similar way is also important and underscores the role of a wide range of resiliency factors that may not be considered.

It also is important to consider the extent to which preventive interventions may alter gene expression. Among genetically vulnerable individuals, for example, offspring of parents with major mental disorders, environmental stress and adversity are likely involved in activating genes that are influential in the manifestation of different forms of psychopathology. Through preventive interventions, the individual may be instilled with increased capacities for coping with stress and improved physiological and neurobiological self-regulation. As a result, the expression of genes associated with psychopathology may be reduced. As sophistication in the understanding of genetic process in vulnerability to psychopathology increases, it will be important to examine how preventive interventions may operate in the moderation of the expression of genes contributing to mental disorders.

To summarize, advances in behavior and molecular genetics may ultimately allow for the tailoring of selective and indicated preventive interventions to reflect an individual's genetic makeup, which, in turn, should facilitate the appropriate matching of individuals to efficacious interventions. Besides leading to improved intervention outcomes, such matching should ensure that the finite mental health resources available from the standpoints of cost and the number of well-trained and qualified providers are more efficiently allocated. In addition, the individual receiving the tailored intervention would be spared the discourage-ment and delay in symptom relief associated with a failed in-tervention experience. The fact that universal preventive interventions target the population as a whole likely pre-cludes the matching of an intervention to an individual's genotype. Nevertheless, variation in response to the univer-sal preventive intervention could serve to identify those who would benefit from genetic screening and the tailoring of an indicated or selective preventive intervention to their ge-netic makeup.

Despite the great promise of behavior and molecular genetics to inform the next generation of preventive inter-ventions, a number of challenges must be met before that promise can be fully realized. We identify just a few of those challenges here. First, in terms of infrastructure, what agency, institution, or organization will be responsible for collecting, analyzing, storing, safeguarding, and report-ing on and interpreting an individual's genetic information? Where will the funds come from to cover the costs of such genetic screening? Second, new interventions, or variants of existing ones, will need to be developed for those individu-als whose genotype is associated with a failed or poor inter-vention response to the currently available interventions. This will require a more precise understanding of the mech-anisms by which genes and existing interventions have their effect on an individual. Such knowledge would likely be necessary before existing interventions could be refined or new interventions developed to accommodate the nonre-sponders. The importance of having interventions available to address the needs of the various subgroups within the larger population is that individuals may be denied inter-vention resources owing to evidence that their genetic makeup was associated with a poor response to existing in-terventions. Third, given that intervention response is typi-cally measured with error (e.g., participant self-reports, clinical observations), we will be faced with the same con-cerns raised by Kraemer et al. (1999); that is, the choice of a cut point cannot be based on statistics alone, but on what the social policy and clinical decision makers judge to be acceptable in terms of the consequences of emphasizing one form of misclassification versus the other.

Integrating Biological and Psychological Processes in Preventive Intervention Evaluations

The recent biological and genetic research has implications not only for informing prevention (i.e., determining targets for intervention, inclusion criteria) but also has significant implications for evaluation of preventive interventions. The conceptualization of most preventive interventions and the design of measurement batteries for preventive trial evalua-tions are currently dominated by assessments of processes at the psychological and behavioral level. Prevention trials are evaluated for the degree to which they are successful in re-ducing behavioral symptoms and rates of clinical disorder and improving developmental competencies; measures of changes in psychological and environmental processes hy-pothesized to account for the intervention effects also are central. However, attention to neurobiological and physio-logical systems in prevention research has been limited. From the integrative perspective of developmental psycho-pathology, prevention scientists should strive to integrate bi-ological assessments into the evaluation of preventive trials to derive a more comprehensive understanding of interven-tion effects. Accordingly, we advocate a multiple-levels-of-analysis approach (Cicchetti & Blender, 2004; Cicchetti & Dawson, 2002) in the design of prevention research.

The dearth of attention to biological processes in pre-vention evaluation may stem in part from beliefs that bio-logical processes are not malleable or are less amenable to positive change as a result of experience. Evidence for neu-robiological change in response to changes in the environ-ment may be less apparent in normative populations where there is likely greater stability in supportive milieus. Al-though adversity and trauma are known to be detrimental to biological systems, how preventive interventions may con-tribute to recovery or repair of biological sequelae is little understood. A dynamics systems view posits bidirectional transactions between different levels of organismic organi-zation, and in so doing it must be recognized that experi-ence influences biology. While biological factors influence psychological processes, psychological experience also ex-erts action on the brain by feeding back on it to modify gene expression and brain function, structure, and organi-zation (Cicchetti & Tucker, 1994; Eisenberg, 1995; Kandel, 1998). Thus, it is important to consider how changes in ex-perience and behavioral functioning resulting from preven-tive interventions may alter biological processes.

The concept of neural plasticity offers a valuable heuris-tic for conceptualizing how preventive interventions may affect brain structure and function, contributing to re-silience among individuals confronted with adversity (Cur-tis & Cicchetti, 2003). Analogous to recovery from physical injury to the brain, neural plasticity also may involve recov-ery from the damaging effects of trauma and extreme stress. Adverse environmental experience can induce phys-iological changes in the brain; conversely, experiences to ameliorate and safeguard against severe adversity may sim-ilarly produce physiological changes that are advantageous to the CNS (Cicchetti & Tucker, 1994; Nelson, 1999). Greenough and colleagues (Black, Jones, Nelson, & Greenough, 1998; Greenough & Black, 1992; Greenough, Black, & Wallace, 1987) identify two forms of neural plasticity in mammalian brains: experience-expectant and experience-dependent plasticity. Most notably in early development, the brain "expects" to receive particular forms of information from the environment, and based on input, an early overabundance of neurons is pruned and new neuronal connections are formed as brain development proceeds. Appropriate timing and quality are important for optimal brain development, whereas deprivation and atypical experience may lead to detrimental consequences for brain neurobiological development (Cicchetti & Cannon, 1999). Given the rapid rate of growth and organization occurring during the early years of life, early interventions that alter adverse and stressful environments may influence the type of brain that emerges during this important period of neurobiological epigenesis. In contrast to experience-expectant plasticity, experience-dependent plasticity occurs in later periods of development as the established yet evolving brain responds to new experience through the formation of new neural connections. Thus, for high-risk individuals who are confronted with multiple environmental stresses, the positive effects of preventive interventions may occur in part through alterations that are set in motion in the structure and functioning of neurobiological systems.

In broad terms, many preventive interventions strive to reduce stress experienced by children exposed to social adversity and multiple risk factors. Accordingly, inclusion of physiological stress measurements in preventive trial measurement batteries would greatly augment knowledge regarding physiological responses to preventive interventions, in tandem with changes in psychological functioning. In recent years, research on rodents, nonhuman primates, and humans has focused on the effects of stress and social adversity on the neuroendocrine system (Gunnar, 1998; Ladd et al., 2000; Meaney, 2001; Sanchez, Ladd, & Plotsky, 2001; Sapolsky, 1992, 1996). The activation of the hypothalamic-pituitary-adrenal (HPA) axis in response to stress is an adaptive mechanism serving a protective function for the organism (McEwen, 1998). However, extreme and prolonged stress may dysregulate neuroendocrine functioning, resulting in damaging effects to neurons. Measuring the stress hormone cortisol through saliva sampling has provided an easily accessible window into neuroendocrine regulation in biobehavioral studies. In preventive intervention trials, measurement of average basal cortisol levels and cortisol reactivity in response to stress could readily be incorporated into pre- and postintervention and follow-up assessment batteries. In so doing, improvements in neuroendocrine functioning and concomitant relations to behavioral change could be articulated for a more complete appraisal of the range of impact of the prevention trial and processes through which its effects are achieved.

Investigations of emotion processing and emotion regulation constitute another area in which behavioral and neurobiological changes resulting from preventive interventions could be examined in tandem. Research on brain hemispheric asymmetry in electroencephalogram (EEG) activation indicates generally that positive emotions are processed by greater activation of the left hemisphere, whereas negative emotions are associated with greater right hemisphere activation (Davidson, Ekman, Saron, Senulis, & Friesen, 1990; Fox, 1991). Evidence exists that adults diagnosed with depression exhibit reduced left prefrontal cortex activation (Henriques & Davidson, 1991), and reduced left frontal EEG activation has been observed among infants and toddlers of mothers with depression (Dawson, Grofer Klinger, Panagiotides, Spieker, & Frey, 1992). Consequently, it would be interesting to incorporate longitudinal EEG measurements of hemispheric asymmetry as a component of, for example, preventive interventions designed to reduce the risk for depression. Altering patterns of hemispheric activation could accompany reduction in the risk for depressive symptomatology resulting from the intervention, and the dynamic interrelations between brain and behavioral systems would be clarified, particularly in terms of the multiple levels at which intervention effects may occur.

Other technologies utilized in investigations of brain structure and function also could be applied to understanding preventive intervention effects. For example, psychophysiological studies of neurological processing of discrete stimuli using EEG recordings of ERPs allow for monitoring of neural activity as it occurs. As previously discussed, ERP differences in response to anger stimuli have been observed in abused children (Pollak et al., 1997, 2001). As a preventive trial measurement, the extent to which there is a normalization of ERP waveform profiles as a result of intervention could be investigated. Similarly, atypicalities in the startle reflex have been observed in adults with Posttraumatic Stress Disorder (PTSD), including combat veterans and women who were sexually assaulted (Morgan, Grillon, Lubin, & Southwick, 1997; Orr, Lasko, Shalev, & Pitman, 1995), as well as children with PTSD (Ornitz & Pynoos, 1989) and maltreated children (Klorman, Cicchetti, Thatcher, & Ison, 2003). By including assessments of the startle reflex, preventive interventions designed to reduce the risk for anxiety disorders due to trauma could determine whether the effects of the intervention also occurred at the physiological level. Additionally, the inclusion of measures of neuropsychological abilities and executive functions could identify improvements in, for example, attention, inhibition, memory, and logical planning resulting from a preventive intervention. The Cambridge Neuropsychological Testing Automated Battery (Sahakian & Owen, 1992) is a computer-administered neuropsychological assessment that could be readily included in an evaluation battery, thereby allowing for an examination of how potential change in executive functions was associated with reduced risk for the development of psychopathology.

Thus, the incorporation of a neurobiological framework into the conceptualization of preventive interventions holds considerable promise for expansion of knowledge regarding the complexity of the developmental process. By basing preventive trials on more comprehensive, integrative developmental theories of psychopathology, prevention research offers the opportunity to conduct developmental experiments that alter environment and experience in efforts to promote resilience among individuals faced with adversity. Determining the multiple levels at which change is engendered through preventive trials will provide more insights into the mechanisms of change, the extent to which neural plasticity may be promoted, and the interrelations between biological and psychological processes in risk, resilience, and psychopathology (Curtis & Cicchetti, 2003).

SUMMARY

In this chapter, we have elaborated a perspective on prevention that is informed by developmental psychopathology theory and complemented with theories and perspectives from epidemiology and public health. The prevention of mental and substance abuse disorders requires a solid understanding of the interplay among risk and protective factors and typical and atypical developmental processes. Results of preventive intervention programs will most certainly inform practice, but this chapter supports the position that it is also vital for prevention scientists to design prevention trials in such as way (i.e., randomized prevention trials) that allows the results to increase our understanding of development as well. Furthermore, following the carefully planned steps in the research cycle discussed, prevention programs with the most empirical support can be implemented in community or real-world settings to reach the broadest number of people and prevent, or alleviate, suffering from mental and substance abuse disorders.

Examples provided from the Johns Hopkins Prevention Intervention Research Center and the Mt. Hope Family Center, University of Rochester, illustrated the cyclical information-sharing process between theory and practice. These exemplars also highlight the successful partnership between academia and community organizations required to effectively implement and research large-scale preventive interventions. We end the chapter discussing future research efforts. We believe a rich area of future prevention research is in the transactional relationship between biology and the development of mental health disorders.

As much as was written in this chapter about prevention research, the field of prevention is broader still, even that part focused on mental and substance abuse disorders. There are many established and promising programs of research that could not be covered in the confines of this chapter. Prevention also ranges across the life span, and programs for older adults, such as prevention of dementia in older age, are extremely valuable lines of research and practice.

REFERENCES

Achenbach, T. M. (1991). *Manual for the Child Behavior Checklist/4–18 and 1991 profile*. Burlington: University of Vermont, Department of Psychiatry.

Alessandri, S. M., & Lewis, M. (1996). Differences in pride and shame in maltreated and non-maltreated preschoolers. *Child Development, 67,* 1857–1869.

Ainsworth, M. D. S. (1969). Object relations, dependency and attachment: A theoretical review of the infant-mother relationship. *Child Development, 40,* 969–1025.

Angrist, J. D., Imbens, G. W., & Rubin, D. B. (1996). Identification of causal effects using instrumental variables (with discussion). *Journal of the American Statistical Association, 91,* 444–472.

Anthony, J. C. (1990). Prevention research in the context of epidemiology, with a discussion of public health models. In P. Muehrer (Ed.), *Conceptual research models for preventing mental disorders* (pp. 1–32, DHHS Publication No. ADM 90-1713). Washington, DC: U.S. Government Printing Office.

Arieti, S., & Bemporad, J. (1978). *Severe and mild depression.* New York: Basic Books.

Ashman, S. B., Dawson, G., Panagiotides, H., Yamada, E., & Wilkinson, C. W. (2002). Stress hormone levels of children of depressed mothers. *Development and Psychopathology, 14,* 333–350.

Azar, S. T. (2002). Parenting and child maltreatment. In M. H. Bornstein (Ed.), *Handbook of parenting: Vol. 4. Social conditions and applied parenting* (2nd ed., pp. 361–388). Mahwah, NJ: Erlbaum.

Bakermans-Kranenburg, M. J., Juffer, F., & van Ijzendoorn, M. H. (1998). Interventions with video feedback and attachment discussions: Does type of maternal insecurity make a difference? *Infant Mental Health Journal, 19,* 202–219.

Bakermans-Kranenburg, M. J., van Ijzendoorn, M. H., & Juffer, F. (2003). Less is more: Meta-analysis of sensitivity and attachment interventions in early childhood. *Psychological Bulletin, 129,* 195–215.

Bandura, A. (1978). The self system in reciprocal determinism. *American Psychologist, 33,* 344–358.

Barnard, J., Du, J., Hill, J. L., & Rubin, D. B. (1998). A broader template for analyzing broken randomized experiments. *Sociological Methods and Research, 27,* 285–317.

Barnett, D., Ganiban, J., & Cicchetti, D. (1999). Maltreatment, negative expressivity, and the development of Type D attachments from 12- to 24-months of age. *Society for Research in Child Development Monograph, 64,* 97–118.

Baron, R. M., & Kenny, D. A. (1986). The moderator-mediator variable distinction in social psychological research: Conceptual, strategic and statistical considerations. *Journal of Personality and Social Psychology, 51,* 1173–1182.

Barrish, H. H., Saunders, M., & Wolfe, M. D. (1969). Good behavior game: Effects of individual contingencies for group consequences and disruptive behavior in a classroom. *Journal of Applied Behavior Analysis, 2,* 119–124.

Beeghly, M., & Cicchetti, D. (1994). Child maltreatment, attachment, and the self system: Emergence of an internal state lexicon in toddlers at high social risk. *Development and Psychopathology, 6,* 5–30.

Bergman, L. R., & Magnusson, D. (1997). A person-oriented approach in research on developmental psychopathology. *Development and Psychopathology, 9,* 291–319.

Berkson, J. (1946). Limitations of the application of the fourfold contingency table. *Biometrics Bulletin, 2,* 47–53.

Bickham, N., & Friese, B. (1999). *Child narrative coding system.* Syracuse, NY: Syracuse University.

Bird, H., Gould, M., Yager, T., Staghezza, B., & Canino, G. (1989). Risk factors for maladjustment in Puerto Rican children. *Journal of the American Academy of Child and Adolescent Psychiatry, 28,* 847–850.

Black, J., Jones, T. A., Nelson, C. A., & Greenough, W. T. (1998). Neuronal plasticity and the developing brain. In N. E. Alessi, J. T. Coyle, S. I. Harrison, & S. Eth (Eds.), *Handbook of child and adolescent psychiatry* (pp. 31–53). New York: Wiley.

Block, J., & Burns, R. (1976). Mastery learning. In L. Shulman (Ed.), *Review of research in education* (Vol. 4, pp. 3–49). Itasca, IL: Peacock Press.

Bloom, B. S. (1976). *Human characteristics and school learning.* New York: McGraw-Hill.

Bloom, B. S. (1982). *All our children learning.* New York: McGraw-Hill.

Bowlby, J. (1969). *Attachment and loss: Vol. I. Attachment.* New York: Basic Books.

Bowlby, J. (1980). *Attachment and loss: Vol. III. Loss, sadness, and depression.* New York: Basic Books.

Bowlby, J. (1982). *Attachment and loss: Vol. I. Attachment* (2nd ed.). New York: Basic Books.

Bretherton, I. (1985). Attachment theory: Retrospect and prospect. *Monographs for the Society for Research in Child Development, 50,* 3–35.

Bretherton, I., Oppenheim, D., Buchsbaum, H., Emde, R. N., & the MacArthur Narrative Group. (1990). *MacArthur Story Stem Battery.* Unpublished manuscript.

Bretherton, I., Ridgeway, D., & Cassidy, J. (1990). Assessing internal working models of the attachment relationship: An attachment story completion task for 3-year-olds. In M. Greenberg, D. Cicchetti, & E. M. Cummings (Eds.), *Attachment in the preschool years* (pp. 273–308). Chicago: University of Chicago Press.

Bronfenbrenner, U. (1979). *The ecology of human development.* Cambridge, MA: Harvard University Press.

Brook, J. S., Nomura, C., & Cohen, P. (1989). A network of influence on adolescent drug involvement: Neighborhood, school, peer, and family. *Genetic, Social, & General Psychology Monographs, 115,* 125–145.

Brunswick, A., Messeri, P., & Titus, S. (1992). Predictive factors in adult substance use: A prospective study of African-American adolescents. In M. D. Glantz & R. W. Pickens (Eds.), *Vulnerability to drug abuse* (pp. 419–472). Washington, DC: American Psychological Association.

Burns, B. J., Compton, S., Egger, H., Farmer, E., & Robertson, E. (2002). An annotated bibliography of evidence for diagnostic-specific psychosocial and psychopharmacological interventions. In B. J. Burns & K. Hoagwood (Eds.), *Community treatment for youth* (pp. 212–276). New York: Oxford University Press.

Burns, B. J., Hoagwood, K., & Mrazek, P. (1999). Effective treatment for mental disorders in children and adolescents. *Clinical Child and Family Psychology Review, 2,* 199–254.

Bussell, D. A., Neiderhiser, J. M., Pike, A., Plomin, R., Simmens, S., Howe, G. W., et al. (1999). Adolescents' relationships to siblings and mothers: A multivariate genetic analysis. *Developmental Psychology, 35*(5), 1248–1259.

Camras, L. A., Ribordy, S., Hill, J., Martino, S., Sachs, V., Spaccarelli, S., et al. (1990). Maternal facial behavior and the recognition and production of emotional expressions by maltreated and nonmaltreated children. *Developmental Psychology, 26,* 304–312.

Capaldi, D. M. (1991). Co-occurrence of conduct problems and depressive symptoms in early adolescent boys: I. Familial factors and general adjustment at grade 6. *Development and Psychopathology, 3,* 277–300.

Capaldi, D. M. (1992). Co-occurrence of conduct problems and depressive symptoms in early adolescent boys: II. A two-year follow-up at grade 8. *Development and Psychopathology, 4,* 125–144.

Capaldi, D. M., Crosby, L., & Stoolmiller, M. (1996). Predicting the timing of first sexual intercourse for at-risk adolescent males. *Child Development, 67,* 344–359.

Carlson, V., Cicchetti, D., Barnett, D., & Braunwald, K. (1989). Disorganized/disoriented attachment relationships in maltreated infants. *Developmental Psychology, 25,* 525–531.

Caron, C., & Rutter, M. (1991). Comorbidity in child psychopathology: Concepts, issues, and research strategies. *Journal of Child Psychology and Psychiatry, 32,* 1063–1080.

Caspi, A., McClay, J., Moffitt, T., Mill, J., Martin, J., Craig, I. W., et al. (2002). Role of genotype in the cycle of violence in maltreated children. *Science, 297,* 851–854.

Caspi, A., Sugden, K., Moffitt, T. E., Taylor, A., Craig, W., Harrington, H. L., et al. (2003). Influence of life stress on depression: Moderation by a polymorphism in the 5-HTT gene. *Science, 301,* 386–389.

Catalano, R. F., Berglund, M. L., Ryan, J. A. M., Lonczak, H. C., & Hawkins, J. D. (1998). *Positive youth development in the United States: Research findings on evaluations of positive youth development programs* (NICHD Publication). Washington, DC: U.S. Department of Health and Human Services.

Chen, L. S., Anthony, J. C., & Crum, R. M. (1999). Perceived cognitive competence, depressive symptoms and the incidence of alcohol-related problems in urban school children. *Journal of Child and Adolescent Substance Abuse, 8,* 37–53.

Cicchetti, D. (1993). Developmental psychopathology: Reactions, reflections, projections. *Developmental Review, 13,* 471–502.

Cicchetti, D. (2002). How a child builds a brain: Insights from normality and psychopathology. In W. W. Hartup & R. A. Weinberg (Eds.), *Minnesota Symposia on Child Psychology: Child psychology in retrospect and prospect* (Vol. 32, pp. 23–71). Mawah, NJ: Erlbaum.

Cicchetti, D., & Blender, J. A. (2004). A multiple-levels-of-analysis approach to the study of developmental processes in maltreated children. *Proceedings of the National Academy of Sciences, 101*(50), 17325–17326.

Cicchetti, D., & Cannon, T. D. (1999). Neurodevelopmental processes in the ontogenesis and epigenesis of psychopathology. *Development and Psychopathology, 11,* 375–393.

Cicchetti, D., & Dawson, G. (Eds.). (2002). Multiple levels of analysis [Special issue]. *Development and Psychopathology, 14,* 417–666.

Cicchetti, D., & Hinshaw, S. (2002). Prevention and intervention science: Contributions to developmental theory. *Development and Psychopathology, 14,* 667–671.

Cicchetti, D., & Lynch, M. (1993). Toward an ecological/transactional model of community violence and child maltreatment: Consequences for children's development. *Psychiatry, 56,* 96–118.

Cicchetti, D., & Lynch, M. (1995). Failures in the expectable environment and their impact on individual development: The case of child maltreatment. In D. Cicchetti & D. J. Cohen (Eds.), *Developmental psychology: Vol. 2. Risk, disorder, and adaptation* (pp. 32–71). New York: Wiley.

Cicchetti, D., & Rizley, R. (1981). Developmental perspectives on the etiology, intergenerational transmission, and sequelae of child maltreatment. *New Directions for Child Development, 11,* 32–59.

Cicchetti, D., & Rogosch, F. A. (1996). Equifinality and multifinality in developmental psychopathology. *Development and Psychopathology, 8,* 597–600.

Cicchetti, D., & Rogosch, F. A. (1997). The role of self-organization in the promotion of resilience in maltreated children. *Development and Psychopathology, 9,* 797–815.

Cicchetti, D., & Rogosch, F. A. (1999). Psychopathology as risk for adolescent substance use disorders: A developmental psychopathology perspective. *Journal of Clinical Child Psychology, 28,* 355–365.

Cicchetti, D., Rogosch, F. A., Maughan, A., Toth, S. L., & Bruce, J. (2003). False belief understanding in maltreated children. *Development and Psychopathology, 15,* 1067–1091.

Cicchetti, D., Rogosch, F. A., & Toth, S. L. (1997). Ontogenesis, depressotypic organization, and the depressive spectrum. In S. S. Luthar, J. A. Burack, D. Cicchetti, & J. R. Weisz (Eds.), *Developmental psychopathology: Perspectives on adjustment, risk, and disorder* (pp. 273–313). New York: Cambridge University Press.

Cicchetti, D., Rogosch, F. A., & Toth, S. L. (1998). Maternal depressive disorder and contextual risk: Contributions to the development of attachment insecurity and behavior problems in toddlerhood. *Development and Psychopathology, 10,* 283–300.

Cicchetti, D., & Schneider-Rosen, K. (1984). Toward a transactional model of childhood depression. *New Directions for Child Development, 26,* 5–27.

Cicchetti, D., & Schneider-Rosen, K. (1986). An organizational approach to childhood depression. In M. Rutter, C. Izard, & P. Read (Eds.), *Depression in young people: Clinical and developmental perspectives* (pp. 71–134). New York: Guilford Press.

Cicchetti, D., & Sroufe, L. A. (1978). An organizational view of affect: Illustration from the study of Down's syndrome infants. In M. Lewis & L. Rosenblum (Eds.), *The development of affect* (pp. 309–350). New York: Plenum Press.

Cicchetti, D., & Toth, S. L. (1991). The making of a developmental psychopathologist. In J. Cantor, C. Spiker, & L. Lipsitt (Eds.), *Child behavior and development: Training for diversity* (pp. 34–72). Norwood, NJ: Ablex.

Cicchetti, D., & Toth, S. L. (1992). The role of developmental theory in prevention and intervention. *Development and Psychopathology, 4,* 489–493.

Cicchetti, D., & Toth, S. L. (1995). Developmental psychopathology and disorders of affect. In D. Cicchetti & D. J. Cohen (Eds.), *Developmental psychopathology: Vol. 2. Risk, disorder, and adaptation* (pp. 369–420). New York: Wiley.

Cicchetti, D., & Toth, S. L. (1998). The development of depression in children and adolescents. *American Psychologist, 53,* 221–241.

Cicchetti, D., & Toth, S. L. (2000). Developmental processes in maltreated children. In D. Hansen (Ed.), *Nebraska Symposium on Motivation* (Vol. 46, pp. 85–116). Lincoln: University of Nebraska Press.

Cicchetti, D., & Toth, S. L. (2005). Child maltreatment. *Annual Review of Clinical Psychology, 1,* 409–438.

Cicchetti, D., & Tucker, D. (1994). Development and self-regulatory structures of the mind. *Development and Psychopathology, 6,* 533–549.

Coie, J. D., Watt, N. F., West, S. G., Hawkins, J. D., Asarnow, J. R., Markman, H. J., et al. (1993). The science of prevention: A conceptual framework and some directions for a national research program. *American Psychologist, 48,* 1013–1022.

Cooper, P., & Murray, L. (1997). The impact of psychological treatment of postpartum depression on maternal mood and infant development. In L. Murray & P. Cooper (Eds.), *Postpartum depression and child development* (pp. 201–220). New York: Guilford Press.

Coster, W., & Cicchetti, D. (1993). Research on the communicative development of maltreated children: Clinical implications. *Topics in Language Disorders, 13,* 25–38.

Crick, N. R., & Dodge, K. A. (1994). A review and reformulation of social information-processing mechanisms in children's social adjustment. *Psychological Bulletin, 115,* 74–101.

Crittenden, P. M. (1988). Relationships at risk. In J. Belsky & T. Nezworski (Eds.), *Clinical implications of attachment theory* (pp. 136–174). Hillsdale, NJ: Erlbaum.

Crittenden, P. M. (1990). Internal representational models of attachment relationships. *Infant Mental Health Journal, 11,* 259–277.

Crittenden, P. M., & Ainsworth, M. D. S. (1989). Child maltreatment and attachment theory. In D. Cicchetti & V. Carlson (Eds.), *Child maltreatment: Theory and research on the causes and consequences of child abuse and neglect* (pp. 432–463). New York: Cambridge University Press.

Crum, R. L., Lillie-Blanton, M., & Anthony, J. C. (1996). Neighborhood environment and opportunity to use cocaine and other drugs in late childhood and early adolescence. *Drug and Alcohol Dependence, 43,* 155–161.

Cummings, E., Goeke-Morey, M. C., & Dukewich, T. L. (2001). The study of relations between marital conflict and child adjustment: Challenges and new directions for methodology. In J. H. Grych & F. D. Fincham (Eds.), *Interparental conflict and child development: Theory, research, and applications* (pp. 39–63). New York: Cambridge University Press.

Curtis, W. J., & Cicchetti, D. (2003). Moving research on resilience into the 21st century: Theoretical and methodological considerations in examining the biological contributors to resilience. *Development and Psychopathology, 15,* 773–810.

Davidson, R. J., Ekman, P., Saron, C., Senulis, J. A., & Friesen, W. V. (1990). Approach-withdrawal and cerebral asymmetry: Emotional expression and brain physiology, I. *Journal of Personality and Social Psychology, 58,* 330–341.

Dawson, G., Grofer Klinger, L., Panagiotides, H., Spieker, S., & Frey, K. (1992). Infants of mothers with depressive symptoms: Electroencephalographic and behavioral findings related to attachment status. *Development and Psychopathology, 4,* 67–80.

Deater-Deckard, K., Dodge, K. A., Bates, J. E., & Pettit, G. S. (1998). Multiple risk factors in the development of externalizing behavior problems: Group and individual differences. *Development and Psychopathology, 10,* 469–493.

DeBellis, M. D. (2001). Developmental traumatology: The psychobiological development of maltreated children and its implications for research, treatment, and policy. *Development and Psychopathology, 13,* 539–564.

Dodge, K. A. (1986). A social information processing model of social competence in children. In M. Perlmutter (Ed.), *Minnesota Symposia on Child Psychology* (Vol. 18, pp. 77–125). Hillsdale, NJ: Erlbaum.

Dolan, L. J. (1986). Mastery learning as a preventive strategy. *Outcomes, 5,* 20–27.

Dolan, L. J., Kellam, S. G., Brown, C. H., Werthamer-Larsson, L., Rebok, G. W., Mayer, L. S., et al. (1993). The short-term impact of two classroom-based preventive interventions on aggressive and shy behaviors and poor achievement. *Journal of Applied Developmental Psychology, 14,* 317–345.

Downey, G., & Coyne, J. C. (1990). Children of depressed parents: An integrative review. *Psychological Bulletin, 108,* 50–76.

Durlak, J. A. (1997). *School-based prevention programs for children and adolescents.* Thousand Oaks, CA: Sage.

Egeland, B., & Erickson, M. F. (1990). Rising above the past: Strategies for helping new mothers break the cycle of abuse and neglect. *Zero to Three, 11,* 29–35.

Egeland, B., & Sroufe, L. A. (1981). Developmental sequelae of maltreatment in infancy. *New Directions for Child Development, 11,* 77–92.

Eisenberg, L. (1995). The social construction of the human brain. *American Journal of Psychiatry, 152,* 1563–1575.

Erickson, M. F., Korfmacher, J., & Egeland, B. (1992). Attachments past and present: Implications for therapeutic intervention with mother-infant dyads. *Development and Psychopathology, 4,* 495–507.

Field, T. M., Fox, N., Pickens, J., & Nawrocki, T. (1995). Relative right frontal EEG activation in 3- to 6-month old infants of "depressed" mothers. *Developmental Psychology, 31,* 358–363.

Fox, N. A. (1991). If it's not left, it's right: Electroencephalograph asymmetry and the development of emotion. *American Psychologist, 46,* 863–872.

Fraiberg, S., Adelson, E., & Shapiro, V. (1975). Ghosts in the nursery: A psychoanalytic approach to impaired infant-mother relationships. *Journal of the American Academy of Child Psychiatry, 14,* 387–421.

Frangakis, C. E., & Rubin, D. B. (1999). Addressing complications of intention-to-treat analysis in the combined presence of all-or-none treatment-noncompliance and subsequent missing outcomes. *Biometrika, 86,* 365–379.

Frangakis, C. E., & Rubin, D. B. (2002). Principal stratification in causal inference. *Biometrics, 58,* 20–29.

Friedman, L. M., Furberg, C. D., & DeMets, D. L. (1998). *Fundamentals of clinical trials.* New York: Springer-Verlag.

Furr-Holden, D., Ialongo, N., Anthony, J., Petras, H., & Kellam, S. (2004). Developmentally inspired drug prevention: Middle school outcomes in a school-based randomized prevention trial. *Drug and Alcohol Dependence, 73,* 149–158.

Gaensbauer, T., Mrazek, D., & Harmon, R. (1981). Emotional expression in abused and/or neglected infants. In N. Frude (Ed.), *Psychological approaches to child abuse* (pp. 120–135). Totowa, NJ: Rowman and Littlefield.

Gallagher, J. J. (1987). Public policy and the malleability of children. In J. J. Gallagher & C. T. Ramey (Eds.), *The malleability of children* (pp. 199–208). Baltimore: Paul H. Brookes.

Gelfand, D. M., Teti, D. M., Seiner, S. A., & Jameson, P. B. (1996). Helping mothers fight depression: Evaluation of a home-based intervention program for depressed mothers and their infants. *Journal of Clinical Child Psychology, 25,* 406–422.

Glisson, C. (2002). The organizational context of children's mental health services. *Clinical Child and Family Psychology Review, 5,* 233–254.

Glisson, C., & Hemmelgarn, A. (1998). The effects of organizational climate and interorganizational coordination on the quality and outcomes of children's service system. *Child Abuse and Neglect, 25,* 401–421.

Glisson, C., & James, L. R. (2002). The cross-level effects of culture and climate in human service teams. *Journal of Organizational Behavior, 23,* 767–794.

Goldsmith, H., Jackson, D., Doenhoefer, S., Johnson, W., Tweed, D., Stiles, D., et al. (1984). *The health demographic profile systems inventory of small area social indicators* (NIMH Series BN-No. 4, DHHS Pub. ADM84-1354). Washington, DC: U.S. Government Printing Office.

Goodman, S., & Gotlib, I. H. (Eds.). (2002). *Children of depressed parents: Mechanisms of risk and implications for treatment.* Washington, DC: American Psychological Association.

Gordon, R. (1983). An operational classification of disease prevention. *Public Health Reports, 98,* 107–109.

Gordon, R. (1987). An operational classification of disease prevention. In J. A. Steinberg & M. M. Silverman (Eds.), *Preventing mental disorders* (pp. 20–26). Rockville, MD: Department of Health and Human Services.

Gottlieb, G. (1999). *Probabilistic epigenesis and evolution.* Worcester, MA: Clark University Press.

Greenberg, M. T., Domitrovich, C., & Bumbarger, B. (1999). *Preventing mental disorder in school-aged children: A review of the effectiveness of prevention programs.* Report submitted to the Center for Mental Health Services (SAMHSA), Prevention Research Center, Pennsylvania State University. Available from http://www.psu.edu/dept/prevention.

Greenberg, M. T., Domitrovich, C., & Bumbarger, B. (2001). The prevention of mental disorders in school-aged children: Current state of the field. *Prevention and Treatment, 4,* NP.

Greenley, J. R., & Mechanic, D. (1976). Social selection in seeking help for psychological problems. *Health and Social Behavior, 17,* 249–262.

Greenley, J. R., Mechanic, D., & Cleary, P. (1987). Seeking help for psychologic problems: A replication and extension. *Medical Care, 25,* 1113–1128.

Greenough, W., & Black, J. (1992). Induction of brain structure by experience: Substrates for cognitive development. In M. Gunnar & C. A. Nelson (Eds.), *Minnesota Symposia on Child Psychology: Vol. 24. Developmental behavioral neuroscience* (pp. 155–200). Hillsdale, NJ: Erlbaum.

Greenough, W., Black, J., & Wallace, C. (1987). Experience and brain development. *Child Development, 58,* 539–559.

Gunnar, M. R. (1998). Quality of early care and buffering of neuroendocrine stress reactions: Potential effects on the developing human brain. *Preventive Medicine, 27,* 208–211.

Guskey, T. (1985). *Implementing mastery learning.* Belmont, CA: Wadsworth.

Haavelmo, T. (1943). The statistical implications of a system of simultaneous equations. *Econometrica, 11,* 1–12.

Haddix, A. C., Teutsch, S. M., Shaffer, P. A., & Dunet, D. O. (1996). *Prevention effectiveness: A guide to decision analysis and economic evaluation.* New York: Oxford University Press.

Hawkins, J. D., Catalano, R., Morrison, D., O'Donnell, J., Abbott, R. D., & Day, L. E. (1992). The Seattle Social Development Project: Effects of the first four years on protective factors and problem behaviors. In J. McCord & R. E. Tremblay (Eds.), *Preventing antisocial behavior: Interventions from birth through adolescence* (pp. 139–161). New York: Guilford Press.

Henderson, A. (1987). *The evidence continues to grow: Parent involvement improves student achievement.* Columbia, MD: National Committee for Citizens in Education.

Henriques, J. B., & Davidson, R. J. (1991). Left frontal hypoactivation in depression. *Journal of Abnormal Psychology, 100,* 535–545.

Hinshaw, S. P. (2002). Prevention/intervention trials and developmental theory: Commentary on the Fast Track special section. *Journal of Abnormal Psychology, 30,* 53–59.

Hirschi, T. (1969). *Causes of delinquency.* Berkley: University of California Press.

Hoagwood, K., Burns, B. J., & Weisz, J. R. (2002). A profitable conjunction: From science to service in children's mental health. In B. J. Burns & K. Hoagwood (Eds.), *Community treatment for youth: Evidence-based interventions for serious emotional and behavioral disorders* (pp. 1079–1089). New York: Oxford University Press.

Hoagwood, K., & Johnson, J. (2003). School psychology: A public health framework: Pt. I. From evidence-based practices to evidence-based policies. *Journal of School Psychology, 41,* 3–21.

Holland, P. (1986). Statistics and causal inference. *Journal of the American Statistical Association, 81,* 945–970.

Howe, G. W., Reiss, D., & Yuh, J. (2002). Can prevention trials test theories of etiology? *Development and Psychopathology, 14,* 673–694.

Ialongo, N., Kellam, S., & Poduska, J. (2000). A developmental epidemiologic framework for clinical and pediatric psychology research. In D. Drotar (Ed.), *Handbook on pediatric and clinical psychology* (pp. 1–25). New York: Kluwer Academic/Plenum Press.

Ialongo, N., Poduska, J., Werthamer, L., & Kellam, S. (2001). The distal impact of two first grade preventive interventions on conduct problems and disorder in early adolescence. *Journal of Emotional and Behavioral Disorders, 9,* 146–160.

Ialongo, N., Reider, E., & Kellam, S. (2005). *Depressive symptoms and disorders in young children.* Manuscript in preparation. Johns Hopkins Bloomberg School of Public Health.

Ialongo, N., Werthamer, L., Brown, H. B., Kellam, S., & Wang, S. B. (1999). The proximal impact of two first grade preventive interventions on the early risk behaviors for later substance abuse, depression and antisocial behavior. *American Journal of Community Psychology, 27,* 599–642.

Imbens, G. W., & Rubin, D. B. (1997). Bayesian inference for causal effects in randomized experiments with noncompliance. *Annals of Statistics, 25,* 305–327.

Jacobi, C., Hayward, C., de Zwaan, M., Kraemer, H. C., & Agras, W. S. (2004). Coming to terms with risk factors for eating disorders: Application of risk terminology and suggestions for a general taxonomy. *Psychological Bulletin, 130,* 14–65.

Jason, L. A. (1982). Community-based approaches in preventing adolescent problems. *School Psychology Review, 11,* 417–424.

Jessor, R. (1978). Psychosocial factors in the patterning of drinking behavior. In J. Fishman (Ed.), *The bases of addiction* (pp. 67–80). Berlin, Federal Republic of Germany: Dahlem Konferenzen.

Jo, B. (2002a). Estimation of intervention effects with noncompliance: Alternative model specifications. *Journal of Educational and Behavioral Statistics, 27,* 385–409.

Jo, B. (2002b). Model misspecification sensitivity analysis in estimating causal effects of interventions with noncompliance. *Statistics in Medicine, 21,* 3161–3181.

Jo, B. (2002c). Statistical power in randomized intervention studies with noncompliance. *Psychological Methods, 7,* 178–193.

Jo, B., & Muthén, B. O. (2001). Modeling of intervention effects with noncompliance: A latent variable modeling approach for randomized trials. In G. A. Marcoulides & R. E. Schumacker (Eds.), *Advanced structural equation modeling: New developments and techniques* (pp. 57–87). Hillsdale, NJ: Erlbaum.

Jo, B., & Muthén, B. O. (2002). Longitudinal studies with intervention and noncompliance: Estimation of causal effects in growth mixture modeling. In N. Duan & S. Reise (Eds.), *Multilevel modeling: Methodological advances, issues, and applications: Multivariate applications book series* (pp. 112–139). Mahwah, NJ: Erlbaum.

Johnston, L. D., O'Malley, P., & Bachman, J. G. (1995). *National survey results on drug use from the Monitoring the Future study, 1975–1994: Vol. 1. Secondary school students* (Pub. No. 95-4026). Washington, DC: U.S. Department of Health and Human Services, Public Health Service, National Institutes of Health.

Jones, N. A., Field, T., Fox, N. A., Lundy, B., & Davalos, M. (1997). EEG activation in 1-month-old infants of depressed mothers. *Development and Psychopathology, 9,* 491–505.

Kandel, D., & Davies, M. (1992). Progression to regular marijuana involvement: Phenomenology and risk factors for near daily use. In M. D. Glantz & R. W. Pickens (Eds.), *Vulnerability to drug abuse* (pp. 211–253). Washington, DC: American Psychological Association.

Kandel, E. R. (1998). A new intellectual framework for psychiatry. *American Journal of Psychiatry, 156,* 505–524.

Kaufman, J., & Zigler, E. F. (1989). The intergenerational transmission of child abuse. In D. Cicchetti & V. Carlson (Eds.), *Child maltreatment: Theory and research on the causes and consequences of child abuse and neglect* (pp. 129–150). New York: Cambridge University Press.

Kazdin, A. E. (1985). *Treatment of antisocial behavior in children and adolescents.* Homewood, IL: Dorsey Press.

Kazdin, A. E. (2000). Treatments for aggressive and antisocial children. *Child and Adolescent Psychiatric Clinics of North America, 9,* 841–858.

Kazdin, A. E., Kraemer, H., Kessler, R., Kupfer, D., & Offord, D. (1997). Contributions of risk-factor research to developmental psychopathology. *Clinical Psychology Review, 17,* 375–406.

Kellam, S. G. (1990). Developmental epidemiologic framework for family research on depression and aggression. In G. R. Patterson (Ed.), *Depression and aggression in family interaction* (pp. 11–48). Hillsdale, NJ: Erlbaum.

Kellam, S. G., Branch, J. D., Agrawal, K. C., & Ensminger, M. E. (1975). *Mental health and going to school: The Woodlawn program of assessment, early intervention, and evaluation.* Chicago: University of Chicago Press.

Kellam, S. G., Branch, J. D., Brown, C. H., & Russell, G. (1981). Why teenagers come for treatment: A ten year prospective epidemiological study in Woodlawn. *Journal of the American Academy of Child Psychiatry, 20,* 477–495.

Kellam, S. G., & Ensminger, M. E. (1980). Theory and method in child psychiatric epidemiology. In F. Earls (Ed.), *International monograph series in psychosocial epidemiology: Studying children epidemiologically* (Vol. 1, pp. 145–180). New York: Neale Watson Academic.

Kellam, S. G., Mayer, L. S., Rebok, G. W., & Hawkins, W. E. (1998). The effects of improving achievement on aggressive behavior and of improving aggressive behavior on achievement through two prevention interventions: An investigation of etiological roles. In B. Dohrenwend (Ed.), *Adversity, stress and psychopathology* (Vol. 27, pp. 486–505). New York: Oxford University Press.

Kellam, S. G., & Rebok, G. W. (1992). Building developmental and etiological theory through epidemiologically based preventive intervention trials. In J. McCord & R. E. Tremblay (Eds.), *Preventing antisocial behavior: Interventions from birth through adolescence* (pp. 162–195). New York: Guilford Press.

Kellam, S. G., Rebok, G. W., Ialongo, N., & Mayer, L. S. (1994). The course and malleability of aggressive behavior from early first grade into middle school: Results of a developmental epidemiologically-based preventive trial. *Journal of Child Psychology and Psychiatry and Allied Disciplines, 3,* 259–281.

Kellam, S. G., Rebok, G. W., Mayer, L. S., Ialongo, N., & Kalodner, C. R. (1994). Depressive symptoms over first grade and their response to a developmental epidemiologically based preventive trial aimed at improving achievement. *Development and Psychopathology, 6,* 463–481.

Kessler, R. C., Davies, C. G., & Kender, K. S. (1997). Childhood adversity and adult psychiatric disorder in the U.S. National Comorbidity Study. *Psychological Medicine, 27,* 1079–1089.

Kessler, R. C., McGonagle, K. A., Zhao, S., & Nelson, C. B. (1994). Lifetime and 12-month prevalence of DSM-III-R psychiatric disorders in the United States: Results from the National Comorbidity Study. *Archives of General Psychiatry, 51,* 8–19.

Klorman, R., Cicchetti, D., Thatcher, J. E., & Ison, J. R. (2003). Acoustic startle in maltreated children. *Journal of Abnormal Child Psychology, 31,* 359–370.

Koenig, A. L., Cicchetti, D., & Rogosch, F. A. (2000). Child compliance/noncompliance and maternal contributors to internalization in maltreating and nonmaltreating dyads. *Child Development, 71,* 1018–1032.

Koeppen-Schomerus, G., Eley, T. C., Wolke, D., Gringas, P., & Plomin, R. (2000). The interaction of prematurity with genetic and environmental influences on cognitive development in twins. *Journal of Pediatrics, 4,* 527–533.

Kovacs, M., & Goldston, D. (1991). Cognitive and social cognitive development of depressed children and adolescents. *Journal of the American Academy of Child and Adolescent Psychiatry, 30,* 388–392.

Kraemer, H. C. (2000). Pitfalls of multisite randomized clinical trials of efficacy and effectiveness. *Schizophrenia Bulletin, 26,* 533–541.

Kraemer, H. C., Kazdin, A. E., Offord, D. R., Kessler, R. C., Jensen, P. S., & Kupfer, D. J. (1997). Coming to terms with the terms of risk. *Archives of General Psychiatry, 54,* 337–343.

Kraemer, H. C., Kazdin, A. E., Offord, D. R., Kessler, R. C., Jensen, P. S., & Kupfer, D. J. (1999). Measuring the potency of risk factors for clinical or policy significance. *Psychological Methods, 4,* 257–271.

Kraemer, H. C., Measelle, J. R., Ablow, J. C., Essex, M. J., Boyce, W. T., & Kupfer, D. J. (2003). A new approach to integrating data from multiple informants in psychiatric assessment and research: Mixing and matching contexts and perspectives. *American Journal of Psychiatry, 160,* 1566–1577.

Kraemer, H. C., Wilson, G. T., Fairburn, C. G., & Agras, W. S. (2002). Mediators and moderators of treatment effects in randomized clinical trials. *Archives of General Psychiatry, 59,* 877–884.

Ladd, C. O., Huot, R. L., Thrivikraman, K. V., Nemeroff, C. B., Meaney, M. J., & Plotsky, P. M. (2000). Long-term behavioral and neuroendocrine adaptation to adverse early experience. *Progress in Brain Research, 122,* 81–103.

Leaf, P., Alegria, M., & Cohen, P. (1996). Mental health service use in the community: Results from the four community MECA study. *Journal of the American Academy of Child and Adolescent Psychiatry, 35,* 889–897.

Lieberman, A. F. (1991). Attachment theory and infant-parent psychotherapy: Some conceptual, clinical, and research considerations. In D. Cicchetti & S. L. Toth (Eds.), *Rochester Symposium on Developmental Psychopathology: Vol. 3. Models and integrations* (pp. 261–287). Rochester, NY: University of Rochester Press.

Lieberman, A. F. (1992). Infant-parent psychotherapy with toddlers. *Development and Psychopathology, 4,* 559–574.

Lieberman, A. F., & Pawl, J. H. (1988). Clinical applications of attachment theory. In J. Belsky & T. Nezworski (Eds.), *Clinical implications of attachment* (pp. 325–351). Hillsdale, NJ: Erlbaum.

Lieberman, A. F., Weston, D., & Pawl, J. H. (1991). Preventive intervention and outcome with anxiously attached dyads. *Child Development, 62,* 199–209.

Lilienfeld, D. E., & Stolley, P. D. (1994). *Foundations of epidemiology* (3rd ed.). New York: Oxford University Press.

Little, R. J., & Yau, L. (1998). Statistical techniques for analyzing data from prevention trials: Treatment of no-shows using Rubin's causal model. *Psychological Methods, 3,* 147–159.

Luthar, S. S. (Ed.). (2003). *Resilience and vulnerability: Adaptation in the context of childhood adversities.* New York: Cambridge University Press.

Luthar, S. S., & Cicchetti, D. (2000). The construct of resilience: Implications for intervention and social policy. *Development and Psychopathology, 12,* 857–885.

Luthar, S. S., Cicchetti, D., & Becker, B. (2000). The construct of resilience: A critical evaluation and guidelines for future work. *Child Development, 71,* 543–562.

Lyons-Ruth, K., Connell, D., Grunebaum, H., & Botein, S. (1990). Infants at social risk: Maternal depression and family support services as mediators of infant development and security of attachment. *Child Development, 61,* 85–98.

Lyons-Ruth, K., Repacholi, B., McLeod, S., & Silva, E. (1991). Disorganized attachment behavior in infancy: Short-term stability, maternal and infant correlates, and risk-related subtypes. *Development and Psychopathology, 3,* 377–396.

Maccoby, E. E. (2002). Parenting effects: Issues and controversies. In J. G. Borkowski, S. L. Ramey, & M. Bristol-Power (Eds.), *Parenting and the child's world: Influences on academic, intellectual, and social-emotional development* (pp. 35–46). Mahwah, NJ: Erlbaum.

MacKinnon, D. P., Lockwood, C. M., Hoffman, J. M., West, S. G., & Sheets, V. (2002). A comparison of methods to test mediation and other intervening variable effects. *Psychological Methods, 7,* 83–104.

Main, M., & Solomon, J. (1986). Discovery of a disorganized/disoriented attachment pattern. In T. B. Brazelton & M. W. Yogman (Eds.), *Affective development in infancy* (pp. 95–124). Norwood, NJ: Ablex.

Main, M., & Solomon, J. (1990). Procedures for identifying infants as disorganized/disoriented during the Ainsworth Strange Situation. In M. Greenberg, D. Cicchetti, & E. M. Cummings (Eds.), *Attachment in the preschool years* (pp. 121–160). Chicago: University of Chicago Press.

Markman, H. J., & Jones-Leonard, D. (1985). Marital discord and children at risk: Implications for research and prevention. In W. Frankenberg & R. Emde (Eds.), *Early identification of children at risk* (pp. 59–77). New York: Plenum Press.

Martins, C., & Gaffan, E. A. (2000). Effects of early maternal depression on patterns of infant-mother attachment: A meta-analytic investigation. *Journal of Child Psychology and Psychiatry, 41,* 737–746.

Masten, A. S. (2001). Ordinary magic: Resilience processes in development. *American Psychologist, 56,* 227–238.

Masten, A. S., Burt, K. B., Roisman, G. I., Obradovic, J., Long, J. D., & Tellegen, A. (2004). Resources and resilience in the transition to adulthood: Continuity and change. *Development and Psychopathology, 16*(4), 1071–1096.

Maughan, A., & Cicchetti, D. (2002). The impact of child maltreatment and interadult violence on children's emotion regulation abilities. *Child Development, 73,* 1525–1542.

McDougal, J. L., Clonan, S. M., & Martens, B. K. (2000). Using organizational change procedures to promote the acceptability of pre-referral intervention services: The school-based intervention team project. *School Psychology Quarterly, 15,* 149–171.

McEwen, B. S. (1998). Protective and damaging effects of stress mediators. *Seminars in Medicine of Beth Israel Deaconess Medical Center, 338,* 171–179.

Meaney, M. J. (2001). Maternal care, gene expression, and the transmission of individual differences in stress reactivity across generations. *Annual Review of Neuroscience, 24,* 1161–1192.

Meinert, C. L., & Tonascia, S. (1986). *Clinical trials: Design, conduct, and analysis.* New York: New York University Press.

Minkler, M. (1990). Improving health through community organization. In K. Glanz, F. M. Lewis, & B. Rimer (Eds.), *Health behavior and health education: Theory research and practice* (pp. 257–287). San Francisco: Jossey-Bass.

Mirsky, A. F., Anthony, B. J., Duncan, C. C., Brouwers, P., Ahearn, M. B., & Kellam, S. G. (1991). Analyses of the elements of attention: A neuropsychological approach. *Neuropsychology Review, 2,* 109–145.

Morgan, C. A., Grillon, C., Lubin, H., & Southwick, S. M. (1997). Startle abnormalities in women with sexual assault related PTSD. *American Journal of Psychiatry, 154,* 1076–1080.

Morris, J. N. (1975). *Uses of epidemiology* (3rd ed.). New York: Churchill Livingstone.

Mrazek, P. G., & Haggerty, R. J. (Eds.). (1994). *Reducing risks for mental disorders: Frontiers for preventive intervention research.* Washington, DC: National Academy Press.

Munoz, R. F., Mrazek, P. J., & Haggerty, R. J. (1996). Institute of Medicine report on prevention of mental disorders: Summary and commentary. *American Psychologist, 51,* 1116–1122.

Muthén, B. O. (2000). Methodological issues in random coefficient growth modeling using a latent variable framework. In J. Rose, L. Chassin, C. Presson, & J. Sherman (Eds.), *Multivariate applications in substance use research* (pp. 113–140). Hillsdale, NJ: Erlbaum.

Muthén, B. O., Brown, C. H., Masyn, K., Jo, B., Khoo, S. T., Yang, C. C., et al. (2002). General growth mixture modeling for randomized preventive interventions. *Biostatistics, 3,* 459–475.

Muthén, B. O., & Masyn, K. (2005). Discrete-time survival mixture analysis. *Journal of Educational and Behavioral Statistics, 30,* 27–58.

Muthén, B. O., & Muthén, L. (1998). *Mplus user's guide.* Los Angeles: Author.

Muthén, B. O., & Muthén, L. (2000). Integrating person-centered and variable-centered analysis: Growth mixture modeling with latent trajectory classes. *Alcoholism: Clinical and Experimental Research, 24,* 882–891.

Nagin, D. S. (1999). Analyzing developmental trajectories: A semiparametric, group-based approach. *Psychological Methods, 4,* 139–157.

Nathan, P. E., Stuart, S. P., & Dolan, S. L. (2000). Research on psychotherapy efficacy and effectiveness: Between Scylla and Charybdis? *Psychological Bulletin, 126,* 964–981.

National Institute of Mental Health. (1991). *Implementation of the national plan for research on child and adolescent mental disorders* (Program Announcement PA-91-46). Washington, DC: U.S. Government Printing Office.

National Institute of Mental Health. (1998). *Priorities for prevention research* (NIH Publication No. 98-4321). Washington, DC: U.S. Government Printing Office.

National Institute of Mental Health. (2001). *The numbers count: Mental disorders in America.* Retrieved May 5, 2005, from http://www.nimh.nih.gov/publicat/numbers.cfm.

Neiderhiser, J. M., Reiss, D., Pedersen, N., Lichtenstein, P., Spotts, E. L., Hansson, K., et al. (2004). Genetic and environmental influences on mothering of adolescents: A comparison of two samples. *Developmental Psychology, 40*(3), 335–351.

Nelson, C. A. (1999). Neural plasticity and human development. *Current Directions in Psychological Science, 8,* 42–45.

Neyman, J. (1923). On the application of probability theory to agricultural experiments. Essay on principles. Section 9. *Statistical Science, 5,* 465–472.

Office of Applied Studies, Substance Abuse and Mental Health Services Administration. (1995). *National household survey on drug abuse: Population estimates 1994* (DHHS Publication No. SMA 95-3063). Rockville, MD: Author.

Offord, D. R., Boyle, M. H., & Racine, Y. A. (1989). Ontario Child Health Study: Correlates of disorder. *Journal of the American Academy of Child and Adolescent Psychiatry, 28,* 856–860.

Offord, D. R., Boyle, M., & Szatmari, P. (1987). Ontario Child Health Study: Pt. II. Six month prevalence of disorder and rates of service utilization. *Archives of General Psychiatry, 44,* 832–836.

O'Hara, M. W., Stuart, S., Gorman, L., & Wenzel, A. (2000). Efficacy of interpersonal psychotherapy for postpartum depression. *Archives of General Psychiatry, 57,* 1039–1045.

Olds, D. L., Eckenrode, J., Henderson, C., Kitzman, H., Powers, J., Cole, R., et al. (1997). Long-term effects of home visitation on maternal life course and child abuse and neglect: Fifteen-year follow-up of a randomized trial. *Journal of the American Medical Association, 278,* 637–643.

Olds, D. L., Henderson, C., Kitzman, H., Eckenrode, J., Cole, R., & Tatelbaum, R. (1998). The promise of home visitation: Results of two randomized trials. *Journal of Community Psychology, 26,* 5–21.

Olds, D. L., & Kitzman, H. (1990). Can home visitation improve the health of women and children at environmental risk? *Pediatrics, 86,* 108–116.

Olds, D. L., Robinson, J., Song, N., Little, C., & Hill, P. (1999). *Reducing the risks for mental disorders during the first five years of life: A review of preventive interventions.* Report submitted to the Center for Mental Health Services, Prevention Research Center for Family and Child Health, University of Colorado Health Sciences Center.

Ornitz, E. M., & Pynoos, R. S. (1989). Startle modulation in children with posttraumatic stress disorder. *American Journal of Psychiatry, 146,* 866–870.

Orr, S. P., Lasko, N. B., Shalev, A. Y., & Pitman, R. K. (1995). Physiologic responses to loud tones in Vietnam veterans with posttraumatic stress disorder. *Journal of Abnormal Psychology, 104,* 75–82.

Patterson, G. R., Crosby, L., & Vuchinich, S. (1992). Predicting risk for early police arrest. *Journal of Quantitative Criminology, 8,* 333–355.

Patterson, G. R., Reid J., & Dishion, T. (1992). *A social learning approach: IV. Antisocial boys.* Eugene, OR: Castalia.

Pentz, M. A. (1993). Directions in future research in drug abuse prevention. *Preventive Medicine, 23,* 646–652.

Perry, C., Williams, C., Veblen-Mortenson, S., Toomey, T., Komro, K., Anstine, P., et al. (1996). Project Northland: Outcomes of a community-wide alcohol use prevention program during early adolescence. *American Journal of Public Health, 86,* 956–965.

Petras, H., Kellam, S., Brown, C. H., Poduska, J., & Ialongo, N. (2003, May). *Effects of a universal first grade classroom based preventive intervention on the developmental paths and prevention of anti-social personality disorder in young adulthood.* Paper presented at the annual meeting of the Society for Prevention Research, Washington, DC.

Plomin, R. (1994). *Genetics and experience: The interplay between nature and nurture* (Vol. 6). Thousand Oaks, CA: Sage.

Pollak, S. D., Cicchetti, D., Hornung, K., & Reed, A. (2000). Recognizing emotion in faces: Developmental effects of child abuse and neglect. *Developmental Psychology, 36,* 679–688.

Pollak, S. D., Cicchetti, D., Klorman, R., & Brumaghim, J. T. (1997). Cognitive brain event-related potentials and emotion processing in maltreated children. *Child Development, 68,* 773–787.

Pollak, S. D., Klorman, R., Thatcher, J. E., & Cicchetti, D. (2001). P3b reflects maltreated children's reactions to facial displays of emotion. *Psychophysiology, 38,* 267–274.

Pollak, S. D., & Tolley-Schell, S. A. (2003). Selective attention to facial emotion in physically abused children. *Journal of Abnormal Psychology, 112*(3), 323–338.

Post, R. (1992). Transduction of psychosocial stress into neurobiology of recurrent affective disorder. *American Journal of Psychiatry, 149,* 999–1010.

Radke-Yarrow, M., Belmont, B., Nottelmann, E., & Bottomly, L. (1990). Young children's self-conceptions: Origins in the natural discourse of depressed and normal mothers and their children. In D. Cicchetti & M. Beeghly (Eds.), *The self in transition* (pp. 345–361). Chicago: University of Chicago Press.

Rebok, G. W., Hawkins, W. E., Krener, P., Mayer, L. S., & Kellam, S. G. (1996). The effect of concentration problems on the malleability of aggressive and shy behaviors in an epidemiologically-based preventive trial. *Journal of the American Academy of Child and Adolescent Psychiatry, 35,* 193–203.

Reid, J., Eddy, M., & Fetrow, R. (1999). Description and immediate impacts of a preventive intervention for conduct problems. *American Journal of Community Psychology, 27,* 483–517.

Reiss, D., & Price, R. H. (1996). National research agenda for prevention research: The National Institute of Mental Health report. *American Psychologist, 51,* 1109–1115.

Rieder, C., & Cicchetti, D. (1989). Organizational perspective on cognitive control functioning and cognitive-affective balance in maltreated children. *Developmental Psychology, 25,* 382–393.

Ringeisen, H., Henderson, K., & Hoagwood, K. (2003). Context matters: Schools and the "research to practice gap" in children's mental health. *School Psychology Review, 32,* 153–168.

Robinson, J., Mantz-Simmons, L., Macfie, J., & the MacArthur Narrative Working Group. (1992). *The narrative coding manual.* Unpublished manuscript.

Rogers, E. M. (1995). *Diffusion of innovations* (4th ed.). New York: Free Press.

Rogosch, F. A., Cicchetti, D., Shields, A., & Toth, S. L. (1995). Parenting dysfunction in child maltreatment. In M. H. Bornstein (Ed.), *Handbook of parenting: Vol. 4. Applied and practical parenting* (pp. 127–159). Hillsdale, NJ: Erlbaum.

Rogosch, F. A., Cicchetti, D., & Toth, S. L. (2004). Expressed emotion in multiple subsystems of the families of toddlers with depressed mothers. *Development and Psychopathology, 16,* 689–706.

Rubin, D. B. (1974). Estimating causal effects of treatments in randomized and nonrandomized studies. *Journal of Educational Psychology, 66,* 688–701.

Rubin, D. B. (1977). Assignment to a treatment group on the basis of a covariate. *Journal of Educational Statistics, 2,* 1–26.

Rubin, D. B. (1978). Bayesian inference for causal effects. *Annals of Statistics, 6,* 34–58.

Rubin, D. B. (1990). Comment: Neyman (1923) and causal inference in experiments and observational studies. *Statistical Science, 5,* 472–480.

Rutter, M. (1979). Protective factors in children's responses to stress and disadvantage. In M. W. Kent & J. E. Rolf (Eds.), *Primary prevention in psychopathology: Vol. 8. Social competence in children* (pp. 49–74). Hanover, NH: University Press of New England.

Rutter, M. (1985). Family and school influences on cognitive development. *Journal of Child Psychology and Psychiatry and Allied Disciplines, 26,* 683–704.

Rutter, M. (1988). Epidemiological approaches to developmental psychopathology. *Archives of General Psychiatry, 45,* 486–495.

Rutter, M., & Garmezy, N. (1983). Developmental psychopathology. In E. M. Hetherington (Ed.), *Handbook of child psychology* (4th ed., Vol. 4, pp. 774–911). New York: Wiley.

Rutter, M., & Sroufe, L. A. (2000). Developmental psychopathology: Concepts and challenges. *Development and Psychopathology, 12,* 265–296.

Sahakian, B. J., & Owen, A. M. (1992). Computerized assessment in neuropsychiatry using CANTAB. *Journal of the Royal Society of Medicine, 85,* 399–402.

Sameroff, A. J., Seifer, R., Barocas, R., Zax, M., & Greenspan, S. (1987). Intelligence quotient scores of 4-year-old children: Social-environmental risk factors. *Pediatrics, 79,* 343–350.

Sanchez, M. M., Ladd, C. O., & Plotsky, P. M. (2001). Early adverse experience as a developmental risk factor for later psychopathology: Evidence from rodent and primate models. *Development and Psychopathology, 13,* 419–450.

Sandler, I. N., Ayers, T. S., Wolchik, S. A., Tein, Y., Kwok, O., Haine, R., et al. (2003). The Family Bereavement Program: Efficacy evaluation of a theory-based prevention program for parentally bereaved children and adolescents. *Journal of Consulting and Clinical Psychology, 71,* 587–600.

Sapolsky, R. M. (1992). *Stress, the aging brain and the mechanisms of neuron death.* Cambridge, MA: MIT Press.

Sapolsky, R. M. (1996). Stress, glucocorticoids, and damage to the NS: The current state of confusion. *Stress, 1,* 1–19.

Sattes, B. D. (1985). *Parent involvement: A review of the literature* (Occasional Paper Series). Charleston, WV: Appalachia Educational Laboratory.

Schlesselman, J. (1982). *Case-control studies: Design, conduct, analysis.* New York: Oxford University Press.

Schneider-Rosen, K., Braunwald, K., Carlson, V., & Cicchetti, D. (1985). Current perspectives in attachment theory: Illustrations from the study of maltreated infants. *Monographs of the Society for Research in Child Development, 50,* 194–210.

Schneider-Rosen, K., & Cicchetti, D. (1984). The relationship between affect and cognition in maltreated infants: Quality of attachment and the development of visual self-recognition. *Child Development, 55,* 648–658.

Schneider-Rosen, K., & Cicchetti, D. (1991). Early self-knowledge and emotional development: Visual self-recognition and affective reactions to mirror self-image in maltreated and nonmaltreated toddlers. *Developmental Psychology, 27,* 481–488.

Schoenwald, S. K., & Hoagwood, K. (2001). Effectiveness, transportability, and dissemination of interventions: What matters when? *Psychiatric Services, 52,* 1190–1197.

Scott-Jones, D. (1984). Family influences on cognitive development and school achievement. In R. Berliner (Ed.), *Review of research in education* (Vol. 11, pp. 259–304). Itasca, IL: F.E. Peacock Publishers.

Shadish, W. (2002). Revisiting field experimentation: Field notes for the future. *Psychological Methods, 7,* 3–18.

Shields, A., & Cicchetti, D. (2001). Parental maltreatment and emotion dysregulation as risk factors for bullying and victimization in middle childhood. *Journal of Clinical Child Psychology, 30,* 349–363.

Shirk, S. R. (1999). Integrated child psychotherapy: Treatment ingredients in search of a recipe. In S. W. Russ & T. H. Ollendick (Eds.), *Handbook of psychotherapies with children and families: Issues in clinical child psychology* (pp. 369–384). Dordrecht, Netherlands: Kluwer Academic.

Sines, J. (1987). Influence of the home and family environment on childhood dysfunction. In B. Lahey & A. Kazdin (Eds.), *Advances in clinical child psychology* (Vol. 10, pp. 1–54). New York: Plenum Press.

Snow, J. (1849). On the pathology and mode of communication of cholera. *London Medical Gazette, 44,* 745–752.

Spinelli, M. G. (1997). Interpersonal psychotherapy for depressed antepartum women: A pilot study. *American Journal of Psychiatry, 154,* 1028–1030.

Spotts, E. L., Neiderhiser, J. M., Towers, H., Hansson, K., Lichtenstein, P., Cederblad, M., et al. (2004). Genetic and environmental influences on marital relationships. *Journal of Family Psychology, 18*(1), 107–119.

Sroufe, L. A. (1979). The coherence of individual development: Early care, attachment, and subsequent developmental issues. *American Psychologist, 34,* 834–841.

Sroufe, L. A., & Fleeson, J. (1986). Attachment and the construction of relationships. In W. Hartup & Z. Rubin (Eds.), *Relationships and development* (pp. 51–76). Hillsdale, NJ: Erlbaum.

Sroufe, L. A., & Fleeson, J. (1988). The coherence of family relationships. In R. A. Hinde & J. Stevenson-Hinde (Eds.), *Relationships within families: Mutual influences* (pp. 27–47). Oxford: Oxford University Press.

Sroufe, L. A., & Rutter, M. (1984). The domain of developmental psychopathology. *Child Development, 55,* 17–29.

Storr, C., Ialongo, N., Anthony, J., & Kellam, S. G. (2002). A randomized prevention trial of early onset tobacco use by school and family-based interventions implemented in primary school. *Drug and Alcohol Dependence, 66,* 51–60.

Stuart, S., & O'Hara, M. (1995). Interpersonal psychotherapy for postpartum depression: A treatment program. *Journal of Psychotherapy Practice and Research, 4,* 18–29.

Tinbergen, J. (1930). Determination and interpretation of supply curves: An example. In D. Hendry & M. Morgan (Eds.), *The foundations of econometric analysis* (pp. 233–248). Cambridge, England: Cambridge University Press.

Toth, S. L., & Cicchetti, D. (1999). Developmental psychopathology and child psychotherapy. In S. Russ & T. Ollendick (Eds.), *Handbook of psychotherapies with children and families* (pp. 15–44). New York: Plenum Press.

Toth, S. L., Cicchetti, D., Macfie, J., & Emde, R. N. (1997). Representations of self and other in the narratives of neglected, physically abused, and sexually abused preschoolers. *Development and Psychopathology, 9,* 781–796.

Toth, S. L., Cicchetti, D., Macfie, J., Maughan, A., & VanMeenan, K. (2000). Narrative representations of caregivers and self in maltreated preschoolers. *Attachment and Human Development, 2,* 271–305.

Toth, S. L., Maughan, A., Manly, J. T., Spagnola, M., & Cicchetti, D. (2002). The relative efficacy of two interventions in altering maltreated preschool children's representational models: Implications for attachment theory. *Development and Psychopathology, 14,* 777–808.

Towers, H., Spotts, E. L., & Neiderhiser, J. M. (2001). Genetic and environmental influences on parenting and marital relationships: Current findings and future directions. *Marriage and Family Review, 33*(1), 11–29.

Trickett, P. K., & McBride-Chang, C. (1995). The developmental impact of different types of child abuse and neglect. *Developmental Review, 15,* 311–337.

van Ijzendoorn, M. H., Juffer, F., & Duyvesteyn, M. G. C. (1995). Breaking the intergenerational cycle of insecure attachment: A review of the effects of attachment-based interventions on maternal sensitivity and infant security. *Journal of Child Psychology and Psychiatry, 36,* 225–248.

Wagenaar, A., Murray, D., Wolfson, M., Forster, J., & Finnegan, J. R. (1994). Communities mobilizing for change on alcohol: Design of a randomized community trial [Special issue: CSAP]. *Journal of Community Psychology,* 79–101.

Weschler, D. (1989). *Wechsler Preschool and Primary Scale of Intelligence (WPPSI)* (Rev. ed.). New York: Psychological Corporation.

Werner, H., & Kaplan, B. (1963). *Symbol formation.* New York: Wiley.

Wichers, M. C., Purcell, S., Danckaerts, M., Derom, C., Derom, R., Vlietinck, R., et al. (2002). Prenatal life and post-natal psychopathology: Evidence for negative gene-birth weight interaction. *Psychological Medicine, 32,* 1165–1174.

Winnicott, D. W. (1958). *Through pediatrics to psycho-analysis: Collected papers.* New York: Basic Books.

Wolchik, S. A., Sandler, I. N., Millsap, R. E., Plummer, B. A., Greene, S. M., Anderson, E. R., et al. (2002). Six-year follow-up of preventive interventions for children of divorce: A randomized controlled trial. *Journal of the American Medical Association, 288,* 1874–1881.

World Health Organization. (2003). *Investing in Mental health.* Retrieved May 5, 2005, from http://www.who.int/mental_health/en.

Zaner, G., Pawelkiewicz, W., DeFrancesco, J., & Adnopoz, J. (1992). Children's mental health service needs and utilization patterns in an urban community: An epidemiological assessment. *Journal of the American Academy of Child and Adolescent Psychiatry, 31,* 951–960.

Author Index

Baldwin, D. A., 257, 293, 294, 299, 300, 305
Baldwin, J. A., 649
Baldwin, L. M., 550
Balentine, A. C., 690, 955, 959
Balge, K. A., 258
Balint, M., 716
Balla, D. A., 191, 203, 210
Baltaxa, C. A. M., 273
Baltes, M. M., 822
Baltes, P. B., 5, 154, 851
Balthazor, M., 453
Ban, T., 321
Bandeen-Roche, K., 932
Bandura, A., 141, 382, 439, 513, 562, 634, 795, 799, 800, 803, 980
Bank, L., 97, 563
Banks, W. C., 650
Bankston, C. L., 67
Baratta, M. V., 685
Barbarin, O., 497, 501, 502, 515
Barbee, A. P., 440
Barber, B., 429, 432
Bard, K., 313
Bardenstein, K. K., 115
Bardone-Cone, A. M., 115
Bargh, J. A., 385, 804
Bargman, G. J., 772
Barker, D. J., 66
Barker, E. T., 161
Barker, H., 726
Barker, J. L., 84
Barkham, M., 726
Barkley, R. A., 29, 95, 96, 153, 451, 597, 684, 691, 955
Barlow, D. H., 246, 253, 264, 265, 269, 270, 271, 452, 945
Barnard, J., 1003
Barndt, R. J., 757
Barnett, D., 339, 355, 379, 562, 824, 994
Barnhill, G. P., 452
Barnum, K. R., 907
Barocas, R., 5, 9, 34, 459, 970
Baron, A. E., 601
Baron, R. M., 231, 576, 783, 784, 972, 974, 991
Baron-Cohen, S., 6, 12, 90, 94, 117, 248, 273, 276, 277, 278, 295, 302, 310, 311, 323, 711, 716, 728
Barratt, S., 306
Barrera, M., 102, 103, 106
Barrett, D., 769, 771
Barrett, K., 108, 111, 245, 564
Barrett, L. F., 263
Barrett, M., 811
Barrett, P. M., 605
Barrish, H. H., 985
Barron, A. T., 710
Barrow, M. V., 262
Barrowclough, C., 257
Barry, C. T., 269, 270, 954
Barry, D., 454
Barry, R. J., 96
Bartels, A., 84

Bartels, M., 937
Barth, J. M., 253
Bartholomew, K., 787
Bartko, J. J., 33
Bartok, J., 758, 760, 767, 768, 778
Barton, M., 323
Barton, S., 854, 858
Basch, M. F., 726
Basford, K. E., 940
Bass, J. D., 832
Bastiani, A., 253
Bateman, A., 731, 733
Bates, A. E., 735
Bates, E., 294, 297, 298, 301, 377, 914
Bates, J., 50, 67, 70, 99, 220, 294, 296, 341, 342, 343, 426, 439, 451, 456, 459, 464, 465, 560
Bateson, G., 544
Battacchi, M. W., 275
Battaglia, A., 184, 185
Battistich, V., 500, 504, 508, 514, 519, 840
Battistuzzi, C., 560
Battle, J., 658
Bau, J., 947, 954
Baucom, D. H., 547, 549, 557
Bauer, C. R., 304, 339, 344, 348, 357
Bauer, D. J., 875, 940, 942
Bauer, G. L., 566
Baugher, M., 28
Bauman, K., 432, 516
Bauman, M. L., 956
Baumeister, R. F., 245, 253, 269, 271, 397, 426, 428, 773, 802, 831, 833
Baumgardner, M. H., 882
Bauminger, N., 272, 276, 281, 452
Baumrind, D., 538, 541, 795, 815
Bax, M., 196
Baxter, L., 320, 321
Baydar, N., 567
Bayley, N., 142
Beach, S. R. H., 560, 947, 954, 955, 958, 959
Beals, J., 601, 602, 607, 610, 611, 613, 620
Bear, G. G., 247, 269
Beardsall, L., 380
Beardslee, W. R., 105, 106, 703, 737
Bearman, P. S., 516
Bearman, S., 105, 113, 114
Beauchaine, R. J., III, 937, 938, 940, 942, 948, 949, 950, 958
Beauchaine, T. P., 260, 932, 933, 934, 936, 937, 938, 939, 940, 941, 942, 944, 946, 947, 948, 949, 950, 951, 954, 955, 957, 958, 959
Beauducel, A., 259
Beauvais, F., 601
Beavers, W. R., 550, 551
Bebbington, P., 44, 226, 236, 556, 557
Bechara, A., 247, 250, 251, 259, 797
Bechtold, D. W., 620
Beck, A. T., 253, 264, 764, 775, 832, 947, 955, 958
Beck, J. E., 255, 271, 272, 556

Beck, R. V., 775
Beck, S. J., 201
Becker, B., 8, 9, 14, 15, 628, 629, 647, 664, 665, 694, 971
Becker, W. C., 815
Beckett, C., 222
Beckham, E., 722
Beckwith, L., 762, 776
Beebe, B., 718
Beeghly, M., 106, 248, 374, 379, 995
Beeghly-Smith, M., 249
Beery, S. H., 109, 453, 470
Begleiter, H., 946
Behen, M. E., 718, 730
Behrends, R. S., 818, 820
Behrens, B. C., 548
Beidel, D. C., 452, 470, 605
Beierle, I., 86
Beiser, M., 607, 611
Beitchman, J., 148, 196, 294, 305
Belansky, E., 504, 509, 521
Belbin, L., 859
Bell, D. J., 78, 87
Bell, K., 445, 784, 785
Bell, R., 154, 300, 542, 874
Bell, S., 296
Bellack, A. S., 184
Bell-Dolan, D. J., 464
Belle, D., 441
Bellinger, D., 42, 60
Bellissimo, A., 107
Bellmore, A. D., 474
Belmont, B., 1000
Belouad, F., 89, 111
Belsky, J., 44, 60, 105, 193, 336, 338, 340, 341, 343, 351, 354, 356, 359, 363, 445, 447, 520, 552, 561
Bem, S. L., 90
Bemporad, J., 999
Benasich, A. A., 196
Ben-Avie, M., 513, 514
Bender, M. E., 688
Benenson, J. F., 425, 428, 429, 447, 473, 474, 476
Bengtson, V. L., 562
Benigni, L., 297, 298, 301
Benjamin, J., 724, 725
Benjamin, L. S., 831, 835
Bennet, W. J., 566
Bennett, A. J., 677
Bennett, C., 425
Bennett, D. S., 947, 955, 958
Bennett, I., 710
Bennett, K. J., 24
Benoit, D., 352, 359
Benoit, M. Z., 603, 605, 614, 619
Bensadoun, J., 502, 507
Ben-Shlomo, Y., 65, 66
Benson, K., 48
Benson, R. M., 148
Bentin, S., 317
Bentler, P., 874
Benware, C., 809
Berg, C. Z., 109

Bookheimer, S. Y., 278
Boomsma, D. I., 171, 937
Booth, A., 82, 111, 554
Booth, C., 355, 428, 445, 453, 455, 470
Booth, J., 690
Booth-LaForce, C., 420, 449, 455, 464, 466, 469, 474
Borden, M. G., 456
Borduin, C. M., 100, 564
Borges, G., 102
Borland, B. L., 684
Borman, E., 784, 787
Borman-Spurrell, E., 345, 350, 562
Born, L., 82
Bornstein, M. H., 548
Böröcz, J., 658
Borowiecki, J., 115
Borst, S., 758, 760, 765, 766, 767, 768, 769, 778, 779
Boruch, R., 355
Bosch, J. D., 464, 465, 466
Boscolo, L., 545
Bosman, B. L., 536
Boss, P., 555
Bost, K. K., 424
Bosworth, K., 429, 452
Boszormenyi-Nagy, I., 545
Botein, S., 1000
Bottomly, L., 1000
Botvin, G. J., 99
Bouchard, G., 575
Boucher, C., 814
Bouchey, H., 362, 391, 392, 401, 402, 408, 445, 475
Boulton, M. J., 421, 426, 443, 453, 454, 455
Boundy, C. A. P., 55
Bourdais, C., 306
Bourdon, K. H., 68
Bourne, E. J., 30
Bowden, C., 171, 262
Bowen, F., 464
Bowen, M., 535, 571
Bower, G., 112
Bower, T. R., 716
Bowker, A., 464, 472
Bowlby, J., 249, 253, 333, 334, 335, 336, 337, 338, 339, 340, 351, 353, 364, 377, 379, 380, 435, 444, 445, 538, 542, 547, 562, 571, 706, 728, 806, 817, 818, 994, 999
Bowman, E. D., 687, 689
Boyce, W. T., 4, 11, 31, 35, 111, 182, 183, 206, 500, 501, 502, 504, 507, 509, 510, 511, 512, 894, 1004, 1005
Boyd, J. L., 953
Boyd, N. R., 687, 689
Boyd-Franklin, N., 572, 573, 664
Boyd-Zacharias, J., 513
Boykin, A. W., 635
Boykin McElhaney, K., 339, 345, 350, 352, 360
Boyle, M., 24, 60, 106, 502, 982, 984

Braaten, E., 96
Bradburn, I. S., 563
Bradburn, N. M., 780
Bradbury, T. N., 552
Bradley, C., 706
Bradley, M. M., 256
Bradley, R., 509, 511, 513, 515
Bradley, S. J., 81, 263, 266, 797
Brady, K. T., 686
Braet, C., 816
Braham, E., 321
Brame, B., 50, 426
Brammer, M., 248, 277, 321
Branch, J. D., 980, 982, 985
Brand, A. E., 119
Brand, E. S., 650
Brand, S., 502, 504, 508, 510, 511, 518, 521
Brandschaft, B., 720
Brandt, D., 160, 949
Brandy, K., 932
Brasic, L., 605
Braunwald, K., 379, 994
Braver, S. L., 554
Bravo, M., 30, 599
Brawnman-Mintzer, O., 122
Brazelton, T. B., 826
Bredekamp, S., 520
Bredenkamp, D., 718
Bredy, T., 237
Breland, A., 652
Bremmer, J., 83
Brendgen, M., 420, 439, 449, 453, 455, 464, 507, 508
Brenner, C., 706, 713
Brenner, J., 423
Brent, D., 28, 45, 105, 560
Breslau, N., 109, 112, 684, 689
Breslow, N. E., 58, 59
Bresnick, S., 391, 392, 401, 402, 408
Brestan, E. V., 932, 957
Bretherton, I., 249, 295, 297, 298, 301, 306, 310, 337, 374, 376, 379, 380, 389, 395, 435, 444, 817, 818, 994, 998
Breton, J. J., 142, 164, 165
Breuer, J., 702, 703
Brewer, D. J., 513
Bridger, R., 514
Bridges, L., 811, 818, 824, 825, 826, 827
Briere, J., 379, 383, 389, 390
Briggs-Gowan, M., 108, 190, 199, 201, 205, 305, 313
Brillon, L., 571
Brinales, J., 68
Brink, J., 272
Britner, P. A., 353
Broafladt, N., 824
Brockbank, M., 711, 730
Brocke, B., 259
Brodish, P. M., 683
Brody, C. L., 687
Brody, D. S., 817, 818

Brody, G., 60, 358, 500, 502, 548, 571, 607
Brody, L. M., 426
Brody, L. R., 88, 92
Broidy, L., 50
Bromberg, P. M., 724, 725
Bromley, L. J., 443
Brondino, M. J., 67
Bronen, R., 218, 956
Bronfenbrenner, U., 10, 184, 192, 421, 502, 506, 519, 569, 590, 621, 629, 635, 639, 640, 643, 890, 981
Bronfman, E., 352, 354, 359, 728
Bronson, M. B., 827
Bronstein, P., 546
Brook, J., 50, 62, 106, 109, 111, 115, 982, 987, 988, 989
Brooke, E., 46
Brooker, M., 429
Brooks, D. S., 939
Brooks, R., 311, 313
Brooks-Gunn, J., 10, 104, 105, 110, 113, 114, 193, 205, 221, 357, 372, 495, 500, 507, 567, 575, 867
Brophy, J. E., 508, 514
Brosschot, J. F., 346
Brothers, L., 277
Brough, S., 265
Broughton, J., 400, 638
Brouwers, P., 983, 984
Brown, A. C., 500, 502
Brown, B., 519
Brown, B. B., 408, 428, 431, 432, 433, 434
Brown, B. V., 568
Brown, C., 68, 502, 507, 509, 518, 774, 879, 979, 982, 986, 989, 990, 991, 992, 1004
Brown, E., 314, 316, 618
Brown, G. W., 60, 218, 226, 236, 720
Brown, H. B., 987
Brown, J., 380
Brown, J. L., 514, 515
Brown, J. S., 648
Brown, K., 796, 804, 840, 937, 955
Brown, L. B., 784
Brown, L. S., 345
Brown, P. J., 454
Brown, R. A., 63, 684, 686, 952
Brown, S., 24, 165, 685, 932, 941, 947, 953, 959
Brown, T. A., 264, 951
Brown, V., 321
Browne, W., 509, 513
Brownell, C. A., 255, 503, 505, 511, 514, 515, 518
Brownell, K. D., 101, 102
Browning, D., 754, 760, 765
Bruce, J., 12, 324, 995
Bruce, M. L., 103, 560
Bruch, H., 771, 772, 795, 833, 834
Bruer, J., 14
Brumaghim, J. T., 248, 994, 1009
Brumback, B., 48, 223, 231

Subject Index